HISTORY
of the
WORLD

HISTORY
of the
WORLD

Earliest Times to the Present Day

JOHN WHITNEY HALL, GENERAL EDITOR

JOHN GRAYSON KIRK, EDITOR

JG
PRESS

World Publications Group, Inc.
455 Somerset Avenue
North Dighton, MA 02764

ISBN: 1-57215-316-4

Library of Congress Cataloging in Publication data available on request.

Color separations by <insert sep house>
Printed and bound in China by Leefung-Asco Printers LTD

Printed in China

1 2 3 4 5   06 05 04 03 02

Executive Editor: Adrian Gilbert
Picture Research: Maria Constantino, Melanie Earnshaw, Mandy Little
Design: David Eldred

The Authors

Michael D. Coe Professor of Anthropology, Yale University (Early Civilization, America)
Kevin Grant Assistant Professor of History, Hamilton College (Post-Cold War)
Erich S. Gruen Professor of History, University of California at Berkeley (Greece, Rome to AD 337)
John Whitney Hall A. Whitney Griswold Professor Emeritus of History, Yale University (Byzantium, Central Asia, Japan)
William W. Hallo William M. Laffan Professor of Assyriology and Babylonian Literature, Yale University (Ancient Near East)
Gavin R. G. Hambly Professor of History, University of Texas at Dallas (Iran, India, Islam)
Firuz Kazemzadeh Professor of History, Yale University (Russia)
John G. Kirk Editor
Harry A. Miskimin Chairman, Department of History, Yale University (Europe)
David Pilbeam Professor of Anthropology, Harvard University (Emergence of Man)
Jonathan D. Spence George B. Adams Professor of History, Yale University (Medieval China)
Leonard M. Thomson Charles J. Stille Professor Emeritus of History, Yale University (Africa)
Arthur F. Wright formerly Charles Seymour Professor of History, Yale University (Ancient and Medieval China)

Publisher's Note

The genesis of *History of the World* goes back to the late 1960s, when Professor John Whitney Hall, the leading scholar in Japanese history of his generation, and some of his colleagues on the faculty of Yale University conceived the idea of writing a large world history composed of contributions by specialist scholars. In addition to Professor Hall, other historians and anthropologists who agreed to contribute to the project included such well-known names as Harry Benda, Michael Coe, Erich Gruen, William Hallo, Gavin Hambly, Firuz Kazemzadeh, Howard Lamar, Wolfgang Leonhard, Harry Miskimin, Richard Morse, David Pilbeam, Jonathan Spence, Leonard Thompson, and Arthur Wright.

The project soon found a publisher and work on the lengthy manuscript began in earnest. By the early 1970s, however, the publishers found themselves unable to complete the project and it was effectively abandoned. Fortunately, this considerable body of scholarly work was not permanently lost to potential readers. In the late 1980s, the Bison Group acquired rights to publish the manuscript on condition that new text be commissioned to fill in the lacunae. In order that the original contributions be as up to date as possible, they were extensively revised and updated by the publisher to include both the latest findings from historical research and the most recent of contemporary events. In all, sixteen new chapters were added, not counting updates. It should be noted that had the original group of authors written their contributions today instead of the 1970s, some might well have chosen to approach their subjects in other ways or to put different emphasis on certain facts or interpretations. This of course in no way reflects on the validity of their original contributions: it merely acknowledges that historians, like anyone else, are free to modify their views over time. Also it should be borne in mind that all post-1971 updatings of original contributions are the work of the publisher, who takes sole responsibility for the accuracy of their content.

More recently, World Publications Group acquired rights to the project. World commissioned a respected historian to bring the book up to date once again. The result is this new volume of *History of the World*.

Page 2: An Ancient Roman statue of Atlas supporting the world. According to mythology, Atlas challenged Zeus and was sentenced to hold the weight of the world on his shoulders as punishment.

Contents

PART I
Earliest Times to the Renaissance

Introduction

In the organization and content of this work, certain ideas which the authors share about the history of man will soon become apparent to the reader. We have been, above all else, impressed by the overwhelming variety of the human condition and the multiplicity of responses which man has made to his environment, and our object has been to convey a sense of the great movements of peoples, of their confluences into societies and cultures, of their restless surges of creative energy, and of their many styles of life and systems of religion and thought.

We begin with the origins of human culture, when man was still confined to limited locales by uncomplicatged technologies of hunting and fishing, hand agriculture or nomadic herding. Human communities then were still small and isolated from their neighbors, and the relationship between each group and with the natural environment was the dominant concern. Religion evolved as a way of explaining and glorifying man's position in nature and of dealing with the uncertainties of life and death. From these early origins human society added to its repertory of technical skills and organizational institutions. Metal work, pottery, ships, the horse and camel and the plow added a range to the human community and greater capacity to the processes of agriculture and animal husbandry. Writing and counting systems were developed to handle more elaborate systems of government and economy. And in time some of these early cultures evolved in size and complexity to a point where we give them the name of civilizations.

It is well to bear in mind that the concept of civilization is a construct, a way of giving manageable coherency to much more complex and diffuse phenomena: we simply draw boundaries around particular clusters of communities on the basis of certain shared political and cultural features. The earliest civilizations were confined to limited geographical locations: those of Sumer and Babylon to the valleys of the Tigris and Euphrates; of Egypt to the valley of the Nile; of India along the banks of the Indus; of China to the Yellow River; and those of the New World to the temperate highlands of Meroamerica and the Andes. In the main these civilized communities were isolated from one another; each was a world to itself, organized around localized religions and led by priest-kings.

In most places today the continuity between the early civilizations and the present-day inhabitants of the area has been broken. To whatever remote antiquity the people of the present look back, it is not to the cultural content of the earliest civilization, but rather to what we call the 'classical civilizations,' or the 'classical traditions' of the past. For the Western world, Greece has provided a permanent legacy of philosophical ideas, political institutions, laws and artistic genres. China today still bears the marks of the classical tradition created by Confucius and the first unifying emperors of the third centuries BC. Classical Iranian culture was differentiated from the more limited Mesopotamian base in the sixth century BC with the rise of the Achaemenid Empire. In India it was with the era of the Vedas and Upanishads that the social customs and beliefs that have persisted to modern times were given their initial form.

The lines of continuity between the origins of civilization and the later classical developments are not always neatly divisible, but in each of the major areas where early civilizations reached a certain level of development, there came into being systems of thought and social and political institutions that were to have an extremely long-lasting influence. There was a tendency toward generalization in thought and rationalism in human organization, toward the development of philosophies that transcended locale and individual community, toward the working out of systematic laws of government and social control and toward the development of technologies of travel and communication that made possible the integration of large regions.

It was only when the political vitality of the classical civilizations began to wane that in several parts of Eurasia the great religious movements appeared. Some historians have considered the origins of the great universal religions sufficiently close in time to consider their appearance as part of a worldwide phenomenon, a watershed in world history. Karl Jaspers, for example, considered the period beginning in the sixth century BC with the formulation of the first universal religions, Buddhism and Zoroastrianism, and concluding with the founding of Christianity and Islam, to be what he called an Axial Age, one that forever transformed the direction of human history and man's values.

Although some details of Jasper's theory may raise problems – for example, nearly a millenium separated Buddha from Muhammad, and many centuries elapsed between the founding of the great religions and their spread into influential movements – it is certainly true that at about the time of the growth of the new religions whole clusters of ideological, organizational and technological changes were at work transforming the classical civilizations. Beyond the many localized changes that we can see in the areas formerly dominated by the classical civilizations after the middle of the first millenium AD, there is one very obvious general change that stands out, namely a heightened tempo of interaction between the civilized centers of Eurasia that eventually led to the formation of ever larger 'world communities' such as the European community of feudal states, the vast Islamic world and the east-Asian Confucian-Buddhist world which stretched from Japan through China, Tibet and Indo-China. These multi-state conglomerations were held together by new developments in trade, communications, political organization and military capacity, but they derived their sense of cohesiveness and individuality from shared religious beliefs that made it possible for Christian English and French, for example, to unite against Muslim Arab and Turk. In a very loose way, then, it does become possible to think of the period from roughly AD 500 to AD 1500, at least on the Eurasian landmass, as being characterized by vast multi-state communities whose borders touched, but whose cultures were held separate by styles of life and thought largely derived from different universal religions.

This view must be held loosely because there are some exceptions. The Indian subcontinent, increasingly dominated by Islamic rulers, nevertheless remained basically Hindu in its religious belief and social practices. Nor do the African and New World civilizations share the same pattern. Yet the great world communities were real enough, and their contribution to the history of the world is accordingly emphasized.

In the chapters that follow we have sought to present in as full a measure as possible the great variety of cultures and civilizations that have existed in the past and have left their marks upon the present. If there is any 'approach' that could be said to unite us in our effort, it is that we have attempted to bring to the description of each historical community both a sense of immediacy and a desire to treat each in terms of its own internal dynanmics and cultural coherence. For ours is the age of world history, and as citizens of the world we must transcend the barriers of national bias and parochial attitude to adopt a wider, fuller view not only of the world but of ourselves.

Above: A female figurine discovered near the Austrian town of Willendorf. Such figures, notable for the accentuation of their sexual characteristics, are generically termed 'venuses' and were obvious fertility symbols.
The Willendorf Venus dates back to around 30,000 BC.

Above right: The humped bull seal is an early example of Mohenjodaro art from the period 2500-2000 BC. The civilizations of the Indus Valley rank alongside those of Egypt and Mesopotamia in age and importance.

Right: King Tutankhamun engages in battle against a Nubian enemy. This Egyptian wall painting was made during the late XVIII Dynasty, 1378-1362 BC.

Left: The great Ziggurat at Ur, one of the most imposing remains of ancient Mesopotamian culture.

The Emergence of Man

We now know that modern man, *Homo sapiens*, has existed in his present form for at least the last 40,000 or 50,000 years and that the present disparate populations of mankind form a single species. All modern human beings are fully compatible genetically, and the superficial physical features by which we delineate 'races' or 'subspecies' almost certainly evolved as selective responses to local environmental pressures. Historians, sociologists and cultural anthropologists tend to concentrate on contrasts between groups of people, but the student of human evolution emphasizes similarities, for whatever behavioral differences may differentiate populations today they are cultural not genetic.

Homo sapiens is classified in the order primates, along with apes, monkeys and such lesser primates as lorises, lemurs and tarsiers. The order first differentiated from other mammals some 70 million years ago. One of the dominant mammalian orders during the first 20 or 30 million years of their existence, the early primates evolved as arboreal animals, living for the most part in relatively complex social groups consisting of permanent aggregations of adults and young of both sexes. Compared with other mammalian orders the primates had relatively large brains, a

fact that tended to exaggerate the basic mammalian tendency to supplement genetically controlled behavior with learned behavior. Primates evolved a variety of means for communicating information of social importance, particularly in their social groups. Vocalizations, postures, gestures and various types of contact between individuals, such as mutual grooming, touching and clasping, evolved as responses to the need to keep groups together and to maintain, as far as possible, amicable relations within the groups.

Beginning some 40 million years ago a new level of primate organization emerged. The selective pressures responsible for this adaptive shift are still elusive. The result was the establishment, in Southern America and Africa, of two stocks of higher primates, the ancestors of the living monkeys, apes and man. These forms had still larger brains than their ancestors, lived in yet more complex social groups and their behavior was more flexible, manipulative and agile. In the Old World they had evolved, by some 20 million years ago, into the forerunners of modern chimpanzees and gorillas.

Sometime between 15 million and five million years ago the line of human ancestry diverged from those leading to the other modern primates.

The divergent creatures are placed, together with modern man, in the primate family Hominidae. Thus man and his ancestors are known as 'hominids': the living and extinct apes, or Pongidae, are termed colloquially 'pongids.'

The rise of the hominid

The major features of human physical evolution are now fairly well understood. There are still many gaps in the fossil record and many problems remain to be settled. And yet, at the anatomical level the evolutionary sequence leading to *Homo sapiens* can now be traced with reasonable certainty. By contrast, the principal features of human behaviorial evolution are less well known and, for obvious reasons, are likely to remain so: behavior cannot be preserved in fossil form.

The earliest hominoids, the forms ancestral to both pongids and hominids, evolved in Africa around 40 million years ago during the Eocene or Oligocene epochs of the Cenozoic era. By the beginning of the Miocene era pongids ancestral to (or close to the ancestry of) both the African apes and the hominids were living in Africa and are known from sites in Kenya and Uganda during the early Miocene period, between 20 and 18 million years ago. The sites indicate that at the

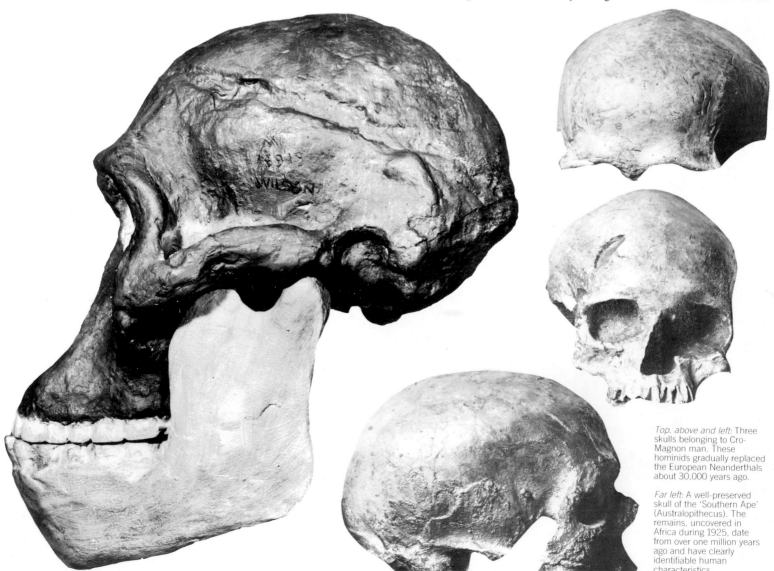

Top, above and left: Three skulls belonging to Cro-Magnon man. These hominids gradually replaced the European Neanderthals about 30,000 years ago.

Far left: A well-preserved skull of the 'Southern Ape' (Australopithecus). The remains, uncovered in Africa during 1925, date from over one million years ago and have clearly identifiable human characteristics.

time of deposition the area was generally forested. The middle Miocene (18 to 12 million years ago) is an almost total blank in the record of both pongids and hominids in Africa. However, one site in Kenya, Fort Ternen, which has been dated to between 14 and 12.5 million years, has yielded the jaws and teeth of an animal that may well prove to be the oldest known hominid. Originally described as *Kenyapithecus wickeri*, it is now generally termed *Ramapithecus wickeri*. Unlike the pongid-bearing sites of the early Miocene, the Fort Ternen site appears to indicate a relatively open habitat of grassland and woodland, rather than forest.

Commencing around 18 million years ago, the African continent, which had been drifting north during the middle Cenozoic, came into contact with Eurasia, and species of mammals, including primates, crossed the land bridge. After 18 million years ago, the area encompassing East and North Africa, South West Asia and the Indian peninsula can be regarded as one broad continental and faunal zone, not to be segmented again until the relatively recent era. Within this zone (rather than in Africa alone) the earliest hominids are thought to have evolved.

It is easier to describe how early hominids looked than how they lived. As we have said, one of the earliest known hominids is *Rampithecus wickeri*, who, about 14 million years ago, lived in the area around Fort Ternen in Kenya. Although similar in some ways to the chimpanzee, the jaws and teeth of *R wickeri* indicate a shift away from a diet of nuts, fruit and other vegetable material to one composed of tougher, smaller items (grains,

for example), such as might be found in more open country. It is also possible that *Ramapithecus* might have eaten meat.

There is no evidence as yet to support the claim made by some scholars that *Ramapithecus* was a tool-maker. The fact that its canine teeth were apparently already reduced need not necessarily point to tool-making. On the other hand, since the chimpanzee frequently uses and even modifies natural objects in the wild, it is likely that earliest hominids did too.

The next evolutionary development was the arrival of a small African hominid, known as *Australopithecus*. The oldest known specimen of *Australopithecus* is a jawbone which comes from Lothagam in Kenya, a site dated at around 5.5 million years. This jaw is referred to as *A africanus*. (The classification of *Australopithecus* has always been controversial, but never more so than now.) *A africanus* is known from other sites in East Africa (Omo in Ethiopia, for example) and also from South Africa (Taung, Sterkfontein, and Makapansgat). It appears to have evolved, around two million years ago, into a form known variously as *Homo habilis*, *Australopithecus habilis* or *A africanus habilis*. At present, it seems best to refer this form simply as *A habilis*. The only obvious differences between *A africanus* and *A habilis* are the larger brain and somewhat smaller cheek teeth of *A habilis*; otherwise, they are similar. Still a third hominid lineage is known during this period (actually from approximately four million to some 1.5 million years), also classified within *Australopithecus*. It contained creatures larger and more heavily built than the *A africa-*

Above. Charles Robert Darwin (1809-92), the celebrated naturalist responsible for the revolutionary Theory of Evolution.

Left: Detailed engravings on these bones found in a French cave indicate a high degree of cultural development. They date from the Paleolithic period.

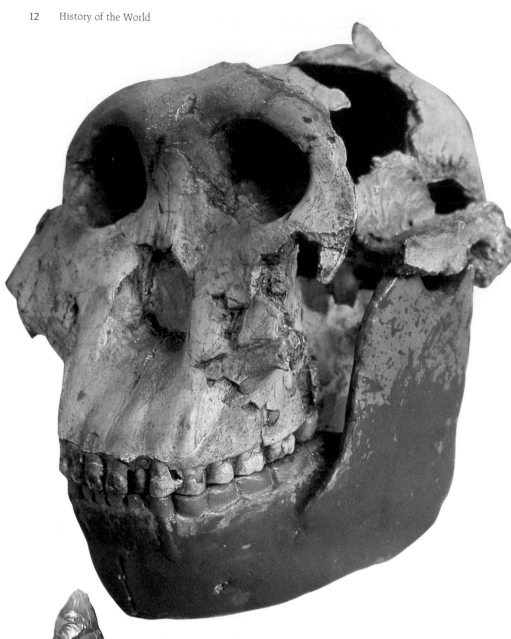

nus-A *habilis* lineage, with massive jaws and cheek teeth. It is believed that these so-called 'robust' *Australopithecus* became extinct, whereas the smaller 'gracile' forms were, at least broadly, ancestral to the genus *Homo*.

The gracile australopithecines were small, standing only about four-and-a-half feet tall and weighing probably no more than 50 to 80lbs. Thus they were approximately the same body size as the extant pygmy chimpanzee. They were bipedal, although less perfectly so than the species of *Homo*; apparently they would have had some difficulty in balancing and rotating the trunk on the hindlimbs, in particular during walking. Their shoulder girdles were more like those of extant apes than those of man, perhaps because selection had not yet favored the ability to throw overarm accurately or because these early hominids still retained the ability to climb trees. Their hands were capable of powerful grasping and were morphologically intermediate between the living apes and modern man. The fact that the gracile *Australopithecus* species retained massive jaws and teeth relative to their body size is a sure indication that they or their ancestors were primarily herbivores, eating tough vegetable foods. But they also sometimes ate meat.

The development of tool makers

The stone tools associated with *Australopithecus* are known as Oldowan tools, and consist of at least a half dozen different categories, each well defined as to form and function. From Olduvai Gorge in Tanzania, dated at just under two million years ago, comes evidence of the oldest undoubted hominid living site. The area contains stone tools, debris from tool making and the remains of animals killed and eaten by the hominids. From comparisons with campsites of living hunters it can be inferred that the size of the band using the site was around 30 individuals. Circular piles of stones suggest that the hominids had constructed a windbreak at the site, and this, together with the amount of stone and bone re-

Top: Skull from Olduvai Gorge, Tanzania. Other debris found at the site indicates that these hominids were skilled hunters.

Above: A flint hand-axe from the Paleolithic period, found in southern England.

Right: An example of cave painting from the Paleolithic period.

covered, indicates that by this time hominids were no longer completely nomadic (shifting sleeping areas from night to night) like the apes. Also, the associated remains of large mammals proves that these hominids were capable hunters, and this, in turn, implies division of labor, cooperation and reciprocity, the economic foundations upon which was built the hominid success story.

One final point, perhaps the most important one, which can be made about *A africanus* – and, by inference, *A habilis* – is based upon recent studies of maturation rates. If X-rays are taken of *Australopithecus africanus* jaws, we find that these primitive hominids had, surprisingly, tooth-maturation patterns identical to those of modern man. The inference therefore would be that their period of social maturation was similarly extended. That so long a learning period would have been necessary, or even possible, without the existence of language is hard to believe.

The phase of human evolution after *A habilis* began some 1.5 million years ago and lasted approximately one million years. The Old-World hominids of this period are known as *Homo erectus* and have been recovered from Indonesia, China and Europe, as well as Africa. *Homo erectus* was a larger creature than *A habilis*, and, judging from post-cranial remains, was fully adapted to habitual erect bipedalism. Brain size had also increased.

Material cultures of *H erectus* populations were advanced over those of earlier hominids: their stone tools were more diversified, and the workmanship was more standardized. However, from the beginnings of the Oldowan culture, through the succeeding Acheulian (hand-axe) cultures found throughout much of the western Old World between 1.5 million and 100,000 years ago, there was only very slow change in tool design, diversity and standardization. Nor did change occur in a steady fashion, but rather in bursts. It seems likely that the slow rate of change reflects the fact that technology was still linked intimately to biologically determined capabilities.

Above right: A reconstructed skull of Homo erectus. Analysis of remains indicates a creature fully adapted to erect bipedalism with a larger brain than its predecessors.

Right: Although cave painting indicates a measure of cultural development, its gradual decline was not the product of social collapse but rather ecological change as the climate got colder.

lithic' tools). Using this new technique a workman could produce ten times as many cutting edges as he could using older methods, clearly a major advance. Second, hunting patterns changed away from generalized big game hunting to the hunting of large migratory herd animals (for example, wild cattle, *Bos primigenius*, the bulls of which stood six feet tall at the shoulder).

Third, there were shifts in burial styles, suggesting that social roles within groups were becoming more clearly differentiated and that temporary social aggregations were becoming very large. A single grave might contain hundreds of mammoth shoulder blades or thousands of shells, suggesting very considerable intergroup contacts. Increased hunting group size is also indicated by some Upper Paleolithic campsites.

Fourth, there were probably some significant advances in the use of language. Neanderthal skulls show evidence of pharynxs – vocal organs of great importance in articulate speech – that were markedly less developed than those in modern men. If the earlier forms of *H sapiens* were simply anatomically less well able to talk than their successors, we may have a clue to at least one of the reasons for the relatively low rate of cultural change in the Pliocene and Pleistocene.

Finally, there was the fact of modern man's extraordinary mobility. The migration to the New World – over the Bering land bridge that then connected Siberia and Alaska – began about 20,000 years ago, and by about 9000 BC men had reached the southern tip of South America. In due course, human groups established themselves on every part of the globe save Antarctica.

both cognitive and manipulative, and that these capacities changed only slowly in the hominids of the Pliocene and Pleistocene up to a few hundred thousand years ago.

Homo erectus populations seem to have been more efficient hunters than their predecessors, hunting large quantities of big game. Perhaps this points to cooperative associations between bands, although it appears that individual bands still numbered only 30 or 40 individuals. Northern populations, at least, had discovered fire by about 700,000 years ago, and presumably used it for protection, cooking, stampeding game and to extend the length of the working day. And perhaps for something else, as well. Many tribal peoples living today cook meat partly in order to transform it and make it 'clean,' to emphasize the separateness of man from the rest of the animate world. If this was true of *H erectus*, then we should have to say that the advent of fire marked an important stage in the evolution of human self-consciousness.

Modern man

A date for the emergence of *Homo sapiens* would be impossible to come by; it is difficult to find even moderately unambiguous criteria for separating *H erectus* and early *H sapiens*. Perhaps the best is brain size and skull shape: by at least 250,000 years ago human groups had brain sizes close to modern values, and the larger brain was surrounded by a less angulated skull than that typical of *H erectus*.

Stone tool cultures continued to increase in complexity, indicating that hominids were increasing their impact on the environment (though for a long time men were still tied to rivers and lakes, not having invented containers for carrying with them precious water). Clothing had certainly been invented by this stage, if not before, and hominid bands were living in dwellings that were, although temporary, nevertheless quite large.

The best known populations of archaic *Homo sapiens* are the Neanderthals, a group found in Europe (including European Russia), North Africa and Southwest Asia between 100,000 and 40,000 years ago. The Neanderthals had made at least two sets of advances over earlier hominids. First, their material culture was more complex. At this time (100,000 to 50,000 years ago) hominid material cultures seem to show the beginnings of regional differentiation, suggesting the development of culturally homogeneous (and perhaps linguistically distinct) regions separated by areas of minimal contact. Second, the Neanderthals buried their dead, complete with personal ornaments, wreaths and, in some cases, grave goods. Thus another major cultural development was achieved, the belief in an after-life. Within the perspective of 14 million years of hominid evolution, the Neanderthals – separated from us by a few tens of thousands of years – were almost fully human. Certainly they were far from being ape-like and brutish (if that is not insulting to the apes), as some have portrayed them.

Men with modern skulls first appeared in Africa some 90,000 years ago, although in very small numbers. However, beginning about 50,000 years ago, they became much more plentiful, and by some 40,000 years ago had completely replaced archaic *H sapiens* populations. In some areas the replacement probably involved pushing older inhabitants out; in most regions, more modern groups probably hybridized with the earlier ones; and some archaic populations actually evolved into modern types.

The transition to modern man, and his spread, has yet to be fully explained; but recent work suggests that quite profound behavioral changes occurred at or before the time he became dominant. First, there was a marked technological shift, at least in Southwest Asia, North Africa and Europe, to the manufacturing of blades (narrow flakes) by punch striking (so-called 'Upper Paleo-

Man as artist

All groups of modern men continued to live as hunters and gatherers for at least 20,000 years. While social organization remained static, tool kits diversified at ever increasing rates, as workmanship became refined. Tools were made in bone for the first time. The dog made his appearance as a domesticated extension of man's olfactory system in the vital search for game. The men in the Upper Paleolithic were also artists, painting on rocks and in caves, mostly for ritual and magical purposes. The rapid pace of cultural change, together with the other evidence, points to the presence of men very much like ourselves, in which biological and cultural change no longer went hand in hand. Rather, the advent of modern man saw the final evolution of a central nervous system capable of generating behaviors so flexible that all subsequent major behavioral changes were to be cultural.

With the retreat of the glaciers in Europe some 10,000 years ago, the ecological setting of human groups began to change, and the groups themselves had also to change, to accommodate or become extinct. In Western Europe, plains teeming with game gave way to forests in which hunting was more difficult. At this time cave painting disappears in Europe. The disappearance was once thought to reflect cultural degeneration, but this seems implausible. It may well be, however, that cave painting – in many cases used ritually to aid hunting success – was abandoned because it had failed to stem the encroaching forest. The environment was making different demands upon human society.

Meanwhile in other parts of the world, notably in Southwest Asia, man stood on the threshold of another technological change that was to modify the entire basis of his livelihood. This was the mastery of techniques of plant and animal domestication, techniques that would make it possible for him to maintain sedentary populations in villages or pastoral camps and, for the first time, to produce levels of food surplus sufficient for him to create what we now know as civilization.

Above: A fertility symbol dating from 4000 BC.

Right: Found in France, this sculpture of a mammoth carved from reindeer antler dates from 17,000 to 11,000 BC.

Left: This clay female statuette with its enlarged sexual characteristics was probably used as a fertility symbol.

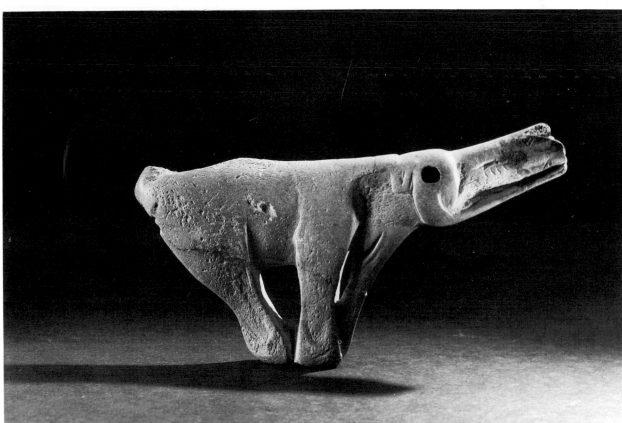

Civilization

What archaeologists and historians call 'civilization' is a very recent phenomenon in man's immensely long cultural development, appearing only in the last four-hundredth part of his known history. Yet in this brief moment mankind has managed to dominate all other living matter and has transformed the earth.

Of the many cultural preconditions for the emergence of civilization none was more fundamental than the so-called agricultural revolution. The domestication of plants and animals, we now know, came about gradually and was carried forward in a variety of ways by human groups living in several different places. At least 12,000 years ago, for example, in upland areas between the Nile and the Tigris and Euphrates, men began to harvest wild wheat and other grasses. It then became easier for populations to rise, because a storable food surplus could be accumulated. Animals were no doubt attracted to the grain-rich fields, to be either killed off or tamed. Loose settlements sprang up, and over a period of several millenia a whole series of plants and animals were domesticated (wheat, barley, sheep, goats, pigs). By 8000 years ago villages made their

appearance. New techniques and tools were invented – hoes, plows, irrigation – and each resulted in increased productivity.

One way in which the technical or economic efficiency of a system can be evaluated is by calculating the ratio of caloric output to input (in the form of work). In the case of Bushmen this index has a value of just under 10. A present day West African rudimentary hoe-based agriculture, lacking irrigation techniques, yields a value of a little over 11, hardly more efficient than the hunting and gathering economy. With slash and burn agriculture, as practiced in parts of New Guinea, for instance, the ratio rises to 18. Irrigation agriculture with intensive cultivation, as found in China, for example, raises the ratio to around 50. The ratio for mechanical cultivation as practiced in the United States is over 200.

With every improvement of this ratio man has always had two choices: to reduce input in terms of work done or to raise population size and density, thereby allowing him to increase the number of non-productive dependents. The choice has always been population increase.

Historically, with larger populations came

social differentiation and the appearance of classes and categories – peasants, priests, soldiers, artisans, aristocrats. And with stratification came ownership and exploitation – of land and of men – and at the same time, warfare. Thus agriculture produced the base, and much of the incentive for the development, of civilization. The same, only to a lesser degree, was true of the emergence of a pastoral economy.

Although at one time historians supposed that agricultural technology originated in the Near East and was diffused to other parts of the world, this was disproven some years ago by the discovery of evidence of the independent origin of plant cultivation in Central America. There, plant domestication, beginning with pumpkin and bottle gourd, can be traced back to perhaps 7000 BC. The cultivation of maize appeared somewhat later, perhaps 5000 BC. It now appears likely that a number of other independent 'origins' of plant domestication will be found. In Southeast Asia the local fishing communities may have domesticated such items as bamboo and gourds for use as containers before they began to cultivate food crops such as yams. In north China by at

Below left: Early civilization in action – an Assyrian ship on the Euphrates.

Right: The development of agriculture was the essential precondition for the emergence of civilization. Relics of a very ancient agricultural settlement have been found at Jericho in Palestine: the bones of wild and domesticated (top right) goats; grains of cultivated barley alongside the less bountiful wild variety; a simple grindstone for grinding corn; and a flint sickle for cutting ears of corn.

least 4000 BC millet and soybeans were being cultivated, and it is possible that the fusion of this northern cereal economy with that of the southern region gave rise to the technology of growing rice in irrigated paddies. As archaeologists investigate other environments where plant domestication may have evolved out of the dominant hunting culture – in southwest Africa, Ethiopia and central India, for example – the likelihood of a greatly extended and diverse threshold between Paleolithic and Neolithic societies has begun to take shape.

Clearly the transition to the sedentary agricultural way of life did not occur alone or take place as a single revolutionary step. Agriculture in all areas had to compete with the earlier hunting and gathering economy, and it was only gradually that the superiority of agriculture proved itself. In many areas men continued to live by hunting and fishing and were to do so down to the present, as, for instance, in portions of Australia, East Africa, Southeast Asia, the remoter regions of South America and the northern sub-Arctic stretches of Eurasia and North America.

From its early origins in regions favorable to plant and animal domestication, however, the agricultural and pastoral economies spread to become the primary support for human existence down to the time of the industrial revolution. Thus at the fundamental level of food production, the basic elements of man's relationship to his natural environment were established as these two types of economy took root. And with the spread of agriculture and pastoralism pre-modern man's adjustment to environmental conditions took on the pattern historically familiar to us. It is only in the twentieth century that man has transcended his geographic limitations, and even then in only the most highly industrialized areas of the world. For most of man's civilized history geography – far more than any other single factor – has provided the primary variation upon which human civilization has had to make its regional adjustments.

The triumph of agriculture

With the spread of the technologies of food production the geographic contours of human history begin to take shape and the primary zones of human historical activity begin to emerge. We see, as well, the beginnings of great variations in styles of life, for agriculture was not a uniform technology. In certain areas where land was extensive and hilly or partially forested, for example, the technique of 'slash and burn' proved effective. This was a method whereby areas were cleared of trees and underbrush by burning. The cleared land, made fertile as a result of the ash from the fires, produced rich crops for a limited period of time. But once the soil was exhausted, generally after two seasons of staple cropping, the fields would be abandoned, and the farmers would move on to fresh land that would be prepared by burning. This technique was relatively wasteful of land and did not permit the support of a dense sedentary population, yet it persisted, and continues to be used today in parts of Southeast Asia, Africa and South America.

Sedentary agriculture can vary according to crops – whether maize, rice or roots for instance – or method of applying moisture and method of replenishing the soil. Large areas of Asia came to depend upon irrigation, either as in the relatively dry areas of the Middle East and India, for the production of barley and wheat, or in the moist monsoon areas of east and southern Asia, for the production of rice. Elaborate irrigation systems fed the fertile oases fields from wells or distant mountain streams in the plateau lands of Iran or served to keep water at constant levels in the rice paddies of China and Japan. Often such irrigated fields proved so fertile as to permit double cropping for generation after generation, since the water brought in minerals and other plant foods necessary to renew the soil. Irrigated agriculture produced the highest yields per unit of land and thus made possible the greatest density of population. It also required the greatest intensity of labor.

Dry agriculture, which depended on natural rainfall, developed in portions of the Near East, northern China and Europe and was relatively less labor-demanding than irrigation farming. It was also less productive, since the replenishment of the soil was achieved chiefly by leaving fields fallow for several seasons. It was characteristic of European agriculture that the demands of land clearing and the variegated topography encouraged the combination of animal husbandry with farming and the use of animal power – the ox or horse to the cultivation of fields. The expansion of agricultural technology into the forests of Europe was relatively late and depended on the prior appearance of certain technical inventions: the iron axe and the traction plow. And it is probable that the continuing problems of maintaining a productive base in Europe put a premium on the use of non-human sources of energy in agriculture.

Pastoral nomadism as a way of life was a fairly late development, depending on the domestication of the horse and camel for the conveyance of herders, over and beyond the simple domestication of food-producing animals such as cattle, pigs, sheep and goats. Beginning about 1500 BC, however, the techniques of pastoralism were perfected, and the vast semi-arid stretches of central Eurasia and the hinterlands of North Africa and Arabia were occupied by tribes of nomadic herders. Pastoral nomadism could support only the thinnest human population in the relatively inhospitable stretches of interior Eurasia, and hence did not give support to great indigenous civilizations and urban centers. Yet the nomadic peoples, from the moment of their establishment, were to exert powerful and continuous political influences on the agrarian civilizations of Eurasia.

The ultimate spread of the agricultural-pastoral way of life was not dependent on the emergence of the great civilizations. These had begun to emerge well before the new food-producing cultures had reached the limits of their expansion across the globe. Yet with the appearance of the centers of civilized life, the attention of historians has generally been deflected to these more dramatic areas of historical activity. But it must be remembered that farmers and herders, until the age of the machine, have made up 80 to 90 percent of the population of any civilization. Their ways of life changed very slowly – as they were forced to accommodate to commercial demands and the spread of urban life – and improved only gradually as new technologies were passed down to them. The life of the simple farmer and herder has remained the context of existence for the vast majority of men and women over the last ten thousand years. This vast substratum of human society has provided the foundation upon which civilizations have been built or destroyed, the persistent 'little tradition' as described by the anthropologists, upon which the civilized 'great traditions' have rested.

How the little and great traditions have interacted historically is not well known and is still poorly studied. How much of the religious beliefs and social norms of 'higher societies' have been drawn from the folk beliefs and family organizations of peasant culture can only be guessed at. But until the modern machine cut civilization off from its dependence on the land and the workers of the soil, the relationship between the two traditions was intimate.

Civilization from surplus

The prime importance of agriculture to the growth of civilization was its capacity to produce a sufficient surplus so that others, not agriculturalists themselves, could live off the surplus, carrying on ways of life different from that of the peasants. Yet the term 'civilization' is not easy to define, nor are the origins of civilization easily accounted for. The word is ultimately derived from the Latin *civitas*, the community, which gave the townsman the polish and refinement lacking in his barbarous contemporaries. The idea of the city has always clung to the term. But, as we shall see, there were some ancient civilizations that never had cities as we think of them. By the mid-nineteenth century AD, archaeologists and anthropologists had become familiar with the ancient and literate civilizations of the Near East, and writing became the criterion by which they distinguished 'higher' from 'lower' cultures, separating the disciplines of *pre-history* – the study of preliterate cultures – and history. Again, this criterion is not entirely satisfactory. One important civilization, the Inca, had no writing whatsoever.

Thus, rather than on technology or even literacy, we might better place our emphasis on features of social, and ultimately political, organization. It is no accident that the earliest known 'high' cultures in both hemispheres arose in exactly those areas in which food production had first taken place: Mesopotamia, the Yellow River Valley of China, Mesoamerica (Mexico and Central America) and the Andes of South America. For advanced social and political organization was the only means by which these cultures could cope with the problems raised by their own spiralling populations.

Foundation of the state

In general, there are two kinds of environments in which population pressures are felt. The first is what can be called an 'open' environment, such as the Amazon basin and parts of sub-Saharan Africa. In such a situation there is so much land open for the taking that surplus persons in a hamlet or village that has grown too large for its own subsistence economy can simply migrate to new

lands. In such settings, with perpetually expanding frontiers, the only known socio-political organizations are tribal.

But this is not the case in a 'closed' environment, one limited geographically, say, by large bodies of water or by mountains or hemmed in by rival peoples. Here there is no exit for landless younger sons and their families, and an entirely different organization of society is necessary, one that allows for different kinds of distribution of goods, that identifies people's self-interest with a fixed territory and that prompts them to think in terms of war as a means of defending or expanding that territory. This new mode of organization is the state.

All the so-called 'primitive' peoples of the world are organized primarily on the basis of blood ties or kinship. Families, lineages and clans are the channels through which all power in these societies flows. A kinless man is a dead man without access to food, shelter, or protection. In a state, on the other hand, a person's rights and obligations are primarily based upon the fact of his having been born in such-and-such a territory, regardless of his kinship affiliations. Over this territory the state authorities enforce their rule through police powers, and the distinction between the governors and the governed thus becomes intensified.

This is not to say that the move from blood-ties to territoriality has anywhere been absolute. The kinship principle has often been used as a kind of building block in the construction of state bureaucracies. In recent Africa, as well as in the earliest kingdoms revealed by archaeology, the royal house is merely the leading lineage among many contenders; and administrative departments and even the priestly hierarchy are staffed through nepotic practices. In the past, entire cities, such as the Aztec capital of Tenochtitlan, were organized as though they consisted of locally-based tribes, and the ancient kingdom of Israel was similarly organized. Ancient state religions, such as those of Mesopotamia and China,

look very much like projections of the social set-up within the royal household, often providing divine justification for the obvious inequalities between the rulers and the ruled.

In all early civilizations we know of there was always a social class that has had greater access to the necessities of life than others. We can see, for example, in most of these cultures the great storehouses, often attached either to the royal place, or, in the case of Mesopotamia, to the temples. The god-king was the great provider, redistributing grain and other goods to the people as wages for labor and providing sustenance to the non-agricultural specialists. Taxes were sometimes indistinguishable from tribute, as among the Aztec, who had an intricate and far-reaching system of exploiting the lower classes to support the royal household, nobility and army. And the concept of nobility itself, very early in the history of civilization, became identified with the supreme landowning class, for it is an important trait of most civilizations that the tiller of the land be alienated from the land itself. Among so-called primitive tribes, such as the semi-nomadic American Indians of the western plains, it was almost inconceivable that the land actually *belonged* to somebody. The principle of communality and usufruct privileges did not entirely die out, for in the New World civilizations and even in Europe there were always lands held in common which the freemen of the society could work for their own needs.

Hydraulic communities

Not only did social inequalities take on great importance in the civilized world, but the land itself began to vary greatly in value. Since most early civilizations were to be found in closed environments, demographic pressures resulted in the intensification of agricultural practices. This was particularly the case in the more arid areas of the world, where rainfall farming could hardly have satisfied an ever-increasing number of hungry

Left: A tomb painting from the Valley of the Kings at Thebes shows some of the agricultural acitivities of ancient Egypt. Olives are being pressed for their oil, and on the right is a vineyard.

Right: These Assyrian hunters have bagged a hare and some birds. Although agriculture replaced the life of the hunter-gatherer, hunting still remained both an important source of food and a favorite sport.

Below: A magical Aztec calendar. The accurate calculation of the time of year was essential to agriculture, leading early civilizations to take a great interest in astronomy.

mouths. Irrigation came to play an immensely important role in these areas. We can see the evolution of water-control systems in the valleys of coastal Peru, which are barren deserts traversed by watercourses, starting with simple irrigation ditches about the time of Christ, and ending, by the Spanish conquest, with tremendous canals linking together many valleys into one complex hydraulic system. Irrigation systems were similarly well advanced in Mesopotamia, Egypt, north China, probably the Indus and perhaps also in the central Mexican highlands of Mesoamerica.

Even in the wetter regions irrigation was important, particularly with the adoption of wet-rice agriculture in Southeast Asia, and south China. And where excess water was a problem, drainage and reclamation acted as the counterpart to irrigation. The *chinampas* of central Mexico, mistakenly called 'floating gardens' in the tourist literature, are actually a land drainage system on the edge of the great lake that once filled the basin surrounding Mexico City, and they are at least as old as the first urban civilization in that area.

Fields reclaimed from irrigated deserts and by draining swamplands often have yields vastly higher than other fields. So also do levee lands along watercourses in humid environments. And the elite class saw to it that land of such elevated value passed into its hands. But water control systems bring their own problems. Canals must not only be built (often a task involving thousands of laborers), but they must be constantly maintained to avoid damage from erosion and floods. They must also be protected from the

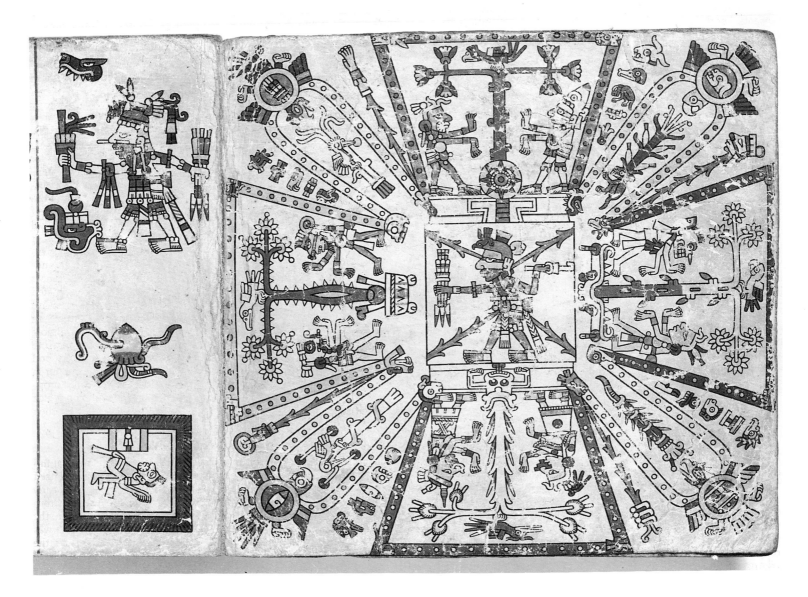

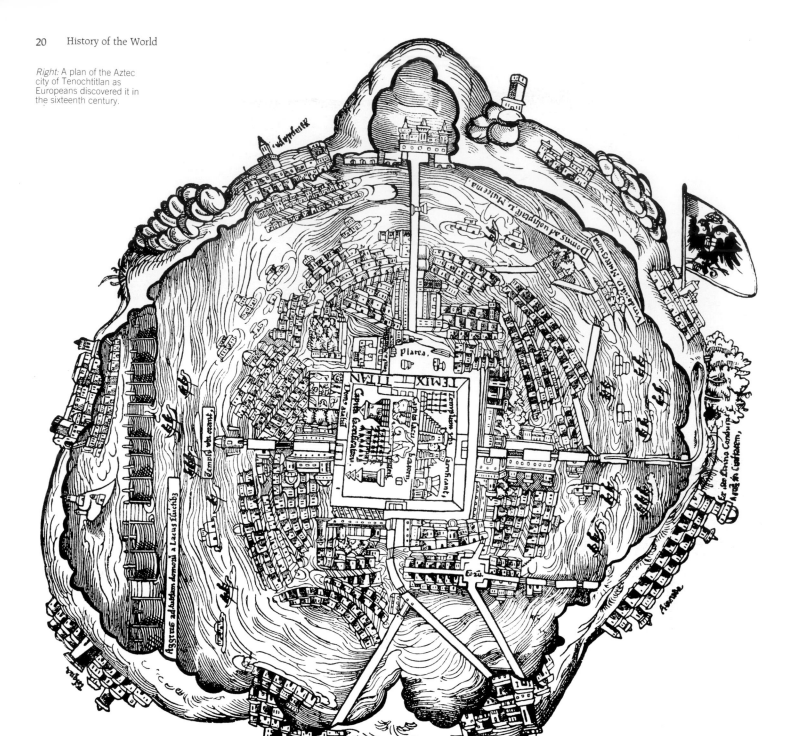

threat of enemies. In the Andes, for instance, the first move of the expanding Inca against the coastal valley kingdoms was to destroy the dams impounding the water for their canals.

The conflicts that are inherent in all human groups become greatly exacerbated by disputes over water rights. This truth led one historian of ancient China, Karl Wittfogel, to maintain (in opposition to Marxist theory) that it was the need for water-control systems, rather than class conflict, that led to the rise of the state. He argued that wherever early civilizations arose in the world they were demonstrably predicated upon hydraulic systems and that only a state-like organization was capable of creating, maintaining and defending such systems.

Unfortunately, there is a good deal of archaeological and ethnological evidence that does not really fit this 'waterworks' theory. Some very extensive and advanced water-control systems were created by cultures that never advanced beyond a tribal polity, a few examples being the complex canals of the Hohokam culture in southern Arizona, the incredible rice terraces of north-

ern Luzon and the thousands of square miles of drained fields in lowland South America. On the other hand, in the best known of early civilizations, Mesopotamia, the state bureaucracy was already in existence *before* irrigation canals played much of a role in the economy.

War and progress

Another hallmark of settled life and civilization was war. Warfare on a large scale is a luxury few tribal peoples can afford. War conducted by primitive peoples is often merely token and ceremonial, carried out for prestige as much as anything else. In contrast, real war seems to have been endemic to all settled societies from the earliest farming peoples to this day. Men of the royal line and of the noble class were by definition warriors, with elaborate codes of ferocity and chivalry. In many societies there was a dual rulership, consisting of an *internal* leader, whose functions were mainly concerned with peacetime administration and with the rituals and ceremonies of the group itself, and of an *external* warlord – perhaps reflecting the division by halves, or moieties, that

is such a striking feature of the tribal level of organization. Thus Mycenaean Greek society was headed by a man called the *wanax*, or king, and another known as the *lawagetas*, or war leader.

Another variant of early state organization was that of the so called 'conquest state.' Of this, we have a number of documented examples from East Africa, where typically a society of agriculturalists was overcome by a group of bellicose pastoralists, both previously on the tribal level of organization. Such recent states as that of the Watutsi surely arose by such a process, the herdsmen dominating the tillers of the soil by right of conquest, and the state apparatus being entirely in the hands of the conquerors, who continue to live and believe as though they were yet wandering across the savannahs with their cattle. Probably many early states and civilizations came about in this way. It is surely significant that a great many ancient dynasties stoutly maintained in their 'official histories' that they themselves had originated in some distant homeland and migrated to their present territory, after overcoming the original inhabitants. While such legends

Right: Sumerian warriors advance into battle. From the earliest times, warfare has been a prominent feature of all civilizations.

Below: A gold death-mask from Peru.

as the Israelite conquest of Palestine may have only a small grain of truth in them, the ideology which they illustrate is a reality: the right of an elite class to exact tribute/taxes and labor from a putative native group who were bested in fair combat. At times, as in post-Norman England or in Africa, the legend is based in demonstrable fact; at other times, as in Mesoamerica, it appears to have been a social fiction.

So far, we have considered some of the circumstances which may have led to the origin of the state and civilization: early and successful subsistence agriculture; the presence of a 'closed environment' and spiralling population; the move from kin-based to territorial organization; the differential access to scarce goods by emerging social classes; the increasing differentiation in land values with intensified agriculture and the concentration of the most valued land in the hands of the elite; and a vastly expanded interest in warfare and conquest.

The urban dimensions

The emergence of cities is certainly typical of the onset of civilization, yet even this phenomenon is not universal. According to Egyptologists, there were no cities in the Nile Valley until the Eighteenth Dynasty. Cities are likewise not to be discerned in the Mycenaean and Minoan states of the ancient Mediterranean; sites like Knossos and Mycenae itself are nothing more than palace-administrative centers. Neither the extremely early Olmec of Mesoamerica nor their descendants, the Maya, had true cities (although these are known for the central highlands of Mexico). It is probably more correct to call these non-urban capitals 'elite centers,' for in them lived only the royal house, some of the nobility engaged in administration and the administrative and priestly hierarchy, plus servants, who maintained the functions of the state.

In such non-urban states the bulk of the population – farmers, naturally – seem to have been dispersed in small hamlets and villages across the landscape, arranged only with regard to topography and access to good land and water. Their participation in affairs of state was confined to seasonal corvée labor and to attendance at calendrical festivals in the capitals.

In contrast, the earliest great cities seem vir-

Above: The distinctive geometric carvings of the Mitla tombs in Oaxaca Province, Mexico.

Left: The Pyramid of the Sun at Teotihuacán, Mexico. Probably built about the time of the birth of Christ, Teotihuacán was the first great city to appear in the New World.

Above right: An ancient Egyptian sepulchral barge – the vessel that carried a dead man and his retinue to the other world.

tually to have drained the immediate countryside of its populace. During the Teotihuacán civilization (c AD1-600), when the great city of central Mexico may have contained over 150,000 souls, there was, according to the archaeological evidence, almost nothing save some scattered farming going on in the countryside for a radius of 100 miles. Perhaps most of these cities started out as elite centers. Then, with the rapid growth of trade (most are found in environments of high diversity in which interregional exchange was a necessity), large groups of artisans and merchants began to cluster together in sufficient numbers so that, added to the state hierarchy, a true city can be said to have existed.

Probably few ancient cities conformed to our idea of what a metropolis should look like. Grid plan streets appeared in Greece and China relatively late in the pre-Christian era and in Teotihuacán by about the time of Christ. Most ancient cities resembled the chaotic, crowded towns of the Near East today, with low, one-storey houses arranged around courtyards and surrounded by high walls. Streets were winding and deep in filth. At the center was the administrative heart of the state, if this was indeed the capital, consisting of palaces, temples, and other state structures. In the Mesopotamian city-state, the focus was the temple of the tutelary god, who had his own treasury and storehouses. Many early cities were surrounded by high walls pierced by gates, and were often divided into quarters oriented north, east, south and west. Certain quarters typically were occupied by artisans and other specialists or by designated foreigners, a feature found from China to ancient Mexico. Some civilizations were so thoroughly urbanized that, as in much of modern Sicily, the farmers lived within its walls by night, and ventured to distant fields in the dim light of dawn.

Like war, disease must have been a new and sinister element accompanying cultural development. Peoples who had formerly lived in camps or in tiny villages were now crowded cheek-by-jowl into increasingly insanitary urban dwellings. (The Indus civilization prior to 1500 BC had something resembling plumbing, but that was an exception.) Dysentery, cholera, typhoid and other diseases caused by fecal contamination of drinking water

must have taken a fearful toll, especially among children. Rats and fleas, both urban pests, acted as plague carriers. Eventually, some degree or resistance to native viruses and bacillae must have built up, but this may have taken millennia.

Environmental transformation

Another consequence of urban civilization was the unwitting destruction of the physical environment, usually gradual but sometimes rapid. In Mesopotamia, a result of the greatly stepped-up canal irrigation necessary to support its urban centers was the accumulation of salts in fields, eventually causing their abandonment; this also happened in Peru and probably in the Indus Valley. The construction of the cities usually required the cutting of great tracts of forest, if such still existed. As rice terraces spread in southern China and Southeast Asia, so did the forests retreat. By the time Egypt had become a trading power, in the Eighteenth Dynasty, the proliferating wooden fleets of the Mediterranean were also hastening the deforestation process. Perhaps the final blow was the introduction of sheep and goats from the ancient Near East into the Mediterranean, for these animals relentlessly destroyed shrubs and grasses and so caused much of the erosion that has dessicated these once verdant lands.

With the rise of state bureaucracies came an urgent requirement for some form of permanent record-keeping, since many territories supported up to several hundred thousand persons on whom tabs had to be kept for purposes of taxation, corvée labor, military conscription and other services to the state. Inventories of what was kept in the royal or temple storehouses likewise were essential. Even the illiterate Inca kept records on *quipus*, knotted strings on which numbers of men or things were kept in an intricate system based upon decimal numeration.

The world's oldest known written texts, incised clay tablets from southern Mesopotamia dating from a few centuries before 3000 BC, deal exclusively with inventories and transactions in agricultural products. It has been shown that the Mycenaean Greek tablets written in the Linear B script are mundane inventories of goods contained in the royal storehouses. But in other early scripts three other kinds of subject matter are pre-

sent: celebrations of royal events such as marriages and military conquests; decrees of the state (such as the laws known as the Code of Hammurabi) and rituals and other transactions involving men and their gods.

Probably at first, most people were 'literate' to the extent that they could both encode and decode elementary written messages. This is because most, perhaps all, writing systems began as pictograms, pictures of the events set forth in the message. Such were the highly pictorial 'winter counts' of the Plains Indians, or the marvelous polychrome paintings of Lascaux cave. Eventually, however, as scripts advanced beyond mere pictures of things (the early inventories were little more than a drawing of the object with a number attached), concepts difficult to draw had to be put into the message. But since most languages contain many homonyms, especially the more monosyllabic ones like Chinese, rebus writing could be employed, in which a somewhat abstract concept would be written by its more easily pictured homonym. Children's puzzles of the 'I saw Aunt Rose' type still employ the rebus principle.

Attempts to extend the scope of messages and to eliminate ambiguities in them resulted in two separate lines of development in the evolution of writing. One was in the semantic direction, employing larger numbers of pictures and their derivatives (often unrecognizable) to express ideographic units of meaning. The other was in the phonetic direction, deriving signs on the rebus principle that can stand for sound units. The Chinese writing system as of about 1700 BC was highly pictographic. In the next five centuries, however, its signs became what may be rightfully called 'logograms,' each standing for a complete word, usually of only one syllable. The meaning of the logogram was expressed by its main sign, a stylized pictogram, while its sound was given by a phonetic rebus component. Most ancient writing systems, including Mesopotamian cuneiform, Egyptian, and Maya, are of this mixed nature. Eventually, the move toward a completely phonetic script was taken, but this came relatively late in the development of most civilizations. The Japanese evolved a phonetic syllabary from Chinese logograms and the Maya are known to have had a fairly complete syllabary at the time of the Spanish conquest. But the most significant steps were taken in the ancient Levant, in which cuneiform writing evolved into an alphabet that is ancestral to the one we use today.

A transport revolution

With the growth of the trading city transportation improved rapidly. The Old World was far ahead of the New in this respect, since a wide range of animals had been domesticated almost at the beginning of the agricultural revolution. In Egypt, Mesopotamia, the Indus and China, draft animals were extensively used for both commercial and royal-military purposes. Onagers and oxen were employed as cart-pullers in Mesopotamia, and clay models of ox-carts have been discovered in the remains of the Indus civilization. The horse was more often employed in pulling war chariots than ridden.

In the Andes, two camelids, the llama and the alpaca, had been domesticated, but the alpaca was raised only for its wool and meat, while the llama acted as a pack animal. Thus, wheeled vehicles were unknown in the civilizations of the western hemisphere, since there were no beasts suitable for hauling them.

Road construction on any large scale is generally thought to have been initiated by the Romans, but early road-building was probably widespread. Even in South America, where carts and wagons were absent, the Inca had several thousand miles of first-class roads traversing the Andean highlands and coastal deserts exclusively used by foot traffic. Royal couriers carrying important messages ran in relays along the Inca highways, and there were rest houses along the route for merchants and other travelers. Communications networks of this sort were an essential element in the survival of territorially large states; for many a dynasty has fallen, in China and elsewhere, from revolts started on remote frontiers.

Everywhere in antiquity we find extensive evidence of long-range trade. Much of this must have been by sea, for dangerous as they were, maritime routes were far safer than roads, trails and passes beset by brigands or free-wheeling warlords. This was an important element in diffusing artifacts and ideas from one civilization to another. Unfortunately, archaeological evidence relating to the hull construction and rigging of the earliest sailing ships is very sparse. Almost all of the wrecked or intentionally buried ships that have been discovered belong to the Classical Age in the Mediterranean or later.

Certainly sailing craft were plying the Mediterranean and other bodies of water by the Bronze Age, for the faint remains of a ship wrecked at that period with a cargo of copper ingots has been recovered off the Turkish coast. Ancient sea trade must have been largely coastal, since the scientific knowledge necessary for open-sea navigation was not yet in hand. Yet some of the maritime interchange in ancient times that has been revealed by archeology is fascinating. For instance, the extent of contact (if any) between the Sumerians of lower Mesopotamia and the Indus civilization of the Indian sub-continent has often been debated. The distinctive Indus stone seals, carved with their yet-unread writing and with figures of gods and fantastic animals, have been found at several Sumerian cities. Another kind of seal, not of the Indus type, has been recovered not only at ancient Ur in Mesopotamia, but also at Lothal, probably the major port of the Indus civilization. These latter seals are now known to have been manufactured in Bahrein on the Persian Gulf, an island which might well be the 'Dilmun' mentioned as a trading entrepôt in the Mesopotamian records. Evidence of this sort makes one wonder what other kinds of cultural traits might have been interchanged along with these imperishable artifacts, mute testimonials to the reality of contact between two civilizations.

Trans-oceanic diffusion

This brings us to the vexed problem of diffusion. There is general agreement that there were essentially six civilizations that can be called 'pristine' because they were the first to develop in their respective areas. These were, in chronological order, the civilizations of Mesopotamia, Egypt, Indus, China, Mesoamerica, and the Andes. All the other complex cultures of the world, including our own, obviously draw upon the experiences and innovations of those ancient peoples. But were they *really* independent of each other? Does each constitute a separate case? Late Proto-historic and Early Dynastic Egypt can, for example, be shown to have artistic and perhaps even religious traits that go back to Mesopotamian prototypes. It has been claimed by diffusionists that the Indus civil-

ization and even that of Shang China are derivative from Mesopotamia, and hyper-diffusionists have even gone so far to propose that New World high cultures are a reflection of Indo-Chinese civilization of the late Bronze Age.

Many of these assertions cannot be finally refuted, as evidence is lacking. On examination, however, it is usually found that the native element in an ancient culture is far more important than what is said to be imported, or else that the case for importation is weak. Such is the case for Shang China, which is supposed to have received from the Near East (albeit by stimulus diffusion rather than direct importation) the traits of bronze-making, writing, the horse-drawn chariot and domesticated wheat. In fact, some of these items may actually have originated in an area intermediate to both civilizations.

The most controversial subject, and one that has attracted the greatest number of eccentrics, is that of trans-Pacific or trans-Atlantic diffusion. A

Left: The development of writing was of vital importance to the growth of civilization. This is an ancient Semitic script.

Below left: An Assyrian relief, showing the high level of skill in the depiction of men and animals achieved by early civilizations.

Right: Norwegian explorer Thor Heyerdahl set out to prove that the ancient Egyptians could have sailed to Central America by performing the feat himself in his papyrus boat, *Ra II*. Despite the success of Heyerdahl's voyage, however, most experts still believe that American civilization developed independently, rather than by 'diffusion' from the Old World.

good case can be made that all of the high cultures of the Old World form part of a great and complex diffusion network. But are the New World civilizations indigenous? Against the thesis of transoceanic diffusion is the uncontrovertible fact that before the Spanish Conquest not one Old World domesticated plant was found in the New, nor one domesticated animal other than the dog. By the same token, no New World domesticates ever came to the other side of the Atlantic until the Spanish ships returned to their home ports.

Most anthropologists believe that the high cultures of the New World were developed by the American Indians independently from those of the Old. The similarities between the civilizations of both hemispheres can probably be best explained by parallel cultural evolution: that all complex societies will make similar cultural responses to similar circumstances and problems.

Yet a few puzzles remain. One very careful study has powerfully argued that the manufacture of bark paper, on which ritual books were made in Mesoamerica, must have been derived about 1500 BC from a single point of origin in the Celebes and Moluccas islands of Southeast Asia. Another scholar has presented convincing evidence that the Mesoamerican ritual calendar of 20 specifically named days is a reduction of a lunar calendar widely spread in the Old World, including Southeast Asia. So the possibility that purposeful voyages *were* made across the Pacific, or even the Atlantic, in ancient times is not absolutely closed.

The Ancient Near East

It is easy to understand why it was in the Near East that man first acquired the attributes of civilization. No other part of the globe contains, within a span of comparable size, as varied a topography and as diverse a conjunction of human types and life styles as the area bounded by the eastern Mediterranean, the Caspian Sea and the Persian Gulf. Since neolithic times this has been the crossroads of the world, the meeting ground of the peoples of Africa, Europe and Asia. Contained within it are innumerable different environments – the fertile alluvial plains of Mesopotamia and Egypt, the sandy deserts of Arabia and inner Iran, the coastal seaboards of the Levant and the Persian Gulf, the plateau lands of Anatolia and Iran, the grasslands of Syria and the fringes of the Arabian Desert and many others. Moreover, these contrasting ecological environments are often in close proximity. From the lush banks of the Nile an Egyptian farmer can see

desert on both sides of the river. Along the eastern edge of the Mediterranean, hilly uplands are seldom far from the ports and coastal fishing villages. The green valleys of Isfahan or Shiraz are fringed by the arid lands of pastoral nomads.

The geographic core zone of the Near East is so complex that we can describe it here only in generalities. The region that served as the physical setting for ancient history consists of the territory between the Iranian Plateau in the east to the Sahara Desert beyond Egypt to the west, and from the Aegean Sea in the northwest to the First Cataract of the Nile and the end of the Persian Gulf on the south. Within this region historically there have been two major arcs of dense habitation: one, the well known 'Fertile Crescent,' stretched along the courses of the Tigris and Euphrates Rivers across Syria and into Palestine; the other, the arc of the Mediterranean coast, extends northward from Egypt to Greece.

Cradle of civilization

Since Mesopotamia and Egypt were the sites of the earliest and most rapid cultural development, they call for more detailed attention. Both are basically floodwater river valleys, yet with some quite different geographical features. The Tigris and Euphrates flow out of open upland areas made up of numerous tributary valleys and surrounded by belts of steppe and mountainous land. The upper fringes of the Tigris and Euphrates valleys thus divide into a large number of separate agricultural regions, each surrounded by lands suitable only for pastoral economy, while the desert lies farther beyond. Such variety of environment is almost totally lacking in Egypt. From Aswan, at the point of the First Cataract, the Nile flows for 550 miles (720 miles if one counts the meanderings of the river itself) through desert on both sides, watering a strip of land never more than 13 miles in width. Above the First Cataract,

Left: The Nile and its valley played a key role in early Egyptian society. Annual flooding and uniform topography ensured that Egypt remained a predominantly rural, agrarian society.

Right: A pot dating from Ancient Egypt's Nagada period, adorned with crocodiles.

Far right: A model skull recovered from the remains of Jericho. Note the shells used as eyes.

the once heavily forested region of Nubia long remained African in population and culture and was penetrated by the Egyptians only cautiously and gradually.

The contrasting physical environments of Mesopotamia and Egypt affected the political styles of the two areas as well as their economic and technological institutions. Territorial unity was strong in the Nile valley, and hence political unity tended to prevail in Egypt. Only two divisions within the Nile valley were historically significant. A characteristic of the Nile valley civilization was that it gave rise to few large cities and no city states like those of Mesopotamia or Greece. The Egyptians, relying on the predictable annual flooding of the Nile River, were not obliged to create elaborate irrigation networks as in Mesopotamia, and this, plus the unified topography and the easy navigability of the Nile, may help to account for the reason that Egyptian culture remained more rooted in agrarian than in urban life. Such capital cities as did appear tended to grow up around the residences of the reigning kings.

Lower Mesopotamia, the region of the flood plain, was divisible into a southern section, historically dominated by the Sumerian cities of Uridu and Ur along the then shore of the Persian Gulf, and a northern section centering on Kish and Babylon. Upper Mesopotamia was divided between the valley of the upper Tigris in the east and that of the upper Euphrates in the west. The former provided the basis of the historic Assyrian states, and the latter produced in ancient times (fifteenth century BC) the Hurrian kingdom of Mitanni. Both the variegated terrain and the prevalence of semi-arid soil that could be cultivated only through the use of elaborate irrigation systems made Mesopotamia a region of city states in which high urban concentrations of the population subsisted on hinterlands of irrigated agricultural lands. Regional political influence beyond any individual city state required the exercise of political and military dominance over other similar, and often rival, city states. Meanwhile, in all parts of Mesopotamia the sedentary population was never far removed from various pastoral or semi-pastoral groups, often of differing ethnic origin.

The chronological scaffolding on which the history of the Near East rests is built both on the archaeological evidence and on written record. From the origin of civilization in Mesopotamia to roughly 1200 BC when iron began to be extensively used, the basic medium of tools and weapons was bronze, an alloy typically composed of seven parts of copper and one part of a harder substance, usually tin. Products made of this tin-

bronze are eminently durable, and have been excavated at numerous sites in the Near East. They have thus been used by archeologists to date all the other items typically found with them. The entire historical interval from the introduction of bronze to its replacement by iron is therefore conveniently referred to as the Bronze Age, and the succeeding seven hundred years as the Iron Age.

Important as the record of artifacts is for the historian, it is overshadowed in all the Bronze Age by the written evidence. Like bronze, writing was a key component of civilization at its first emergence, but unlike bronze, it has continued to play a key role ever since. In a very real sense history in the Near East begins when and where writing begins. At present the invention of writing can be traced to that focal part of the Near East where the Tigris and Euphrates rivers empty into the Persian Gulf, the land whose first known name was Sumer.

Antediluvian traditions and the Urban Revolution

The Old Stone Age came to an end throughout the Near East about 10,000 BC. It was succeeded (except possibly in Egypt) by a brief mesolithic interval, when the older types of stone tools became much more refined and elaborate. A more

decisive change took place around the eighth millennium, justifying the term 'neolithic (or agricultural) revolution.' After a first or pre-pottery neolithic phase, the invention of handmade and subsequently of wheel-made pottery provides an abundant ceramic index by which to date successive strata of occupation at individual archeological sites, and to connect contemporaneous strata at diverse sites. Where the connections are impressive enough to suggest a common culture, archeologists apply the name of the first site at which it was identified, or of a typical site (type-site) at which it is best represented, to that culture. Thus the name Ubaid, based on the Arabic village of that name near Ur in southern Iraq not only identifies the ruin-mound excavated there but also describes similar cultures found at widely scattered sites from the late neolithic Near East. What may be the earliest examples of the pottery and other wares associated with this culture have turned up on the Persian Gulf coast of Arabia; by the sixth millennium BC, they are attested throughout southern Mesopotamia, and before the end of the fifth, also in northern Mesopotamia. For want of a known native name, we call the producers of this culture Ubaidians; they constitute the substrate population of western Asia at the dawn of civilization, and important and iden-

tifiable traces of their achievements as well as of their language survived into the historic period.

Civilization began in southern Mesopotamia toward the end of the fourth millennium BC, a time when the original, or substrate culture, was amalgamated with as many as four new waves of immigration into the area. If later written traditions may be relied on, it would seem that these migrations took place in quick succession and from all four points of the compass. From the north came the Subarians; from the south, apparently via the Persian Gulf, the Sumerians; from the Arabian and Syrian deserts in the west came Amorites; and from the Iranian highlands to the east the Elamites. All four groups spoke totally unrelated languages, and three of them continued to retain linguistic and other indices of their cultural identity. Only the Sumerians appear to have made a permanent break with their still unidentified homeland. They amalgamated with the substrate population but emerged as the dominant element in the amalgam, in the process creating the first civilization. Sumer became the name of the land at the head of the Persian Gulf, and Sumerian its language.

In their later mythological traditions, the Sumerians claimed for themselves, or rather for their gods, the invention of most of the essential components of civilization. As they interpreted their origins, the arts and institutions of civilized society were introduced into Sumer by semidivine intermediaries from somewhere in the Persian Gulf. Stripped of their theological formulations, these traditions may contain a measure of truth.

While there is some evidence that writing was a pre-Sumerian invention, it certainly reached its full development when it was adapted to Sumerian. The same may be the case with the full exploitation of bronze metallurgy. Two other innovations of fundamental importance were the first accumulations of capital and the beginnings of monumental architecture. These combined to create the first cities and, together with a number of secondary innovations, added up to what is commonly designated the 'urban revolution.'

Sumerian traditions are particularly insistent on laying claim to the first cities. In the later schematizations of both mythology and historiography, the very first city was Eridu, a tradition that survived (albeit garbled and unrecognized) in Genesis 4:17-18: 'And Cain knew his wife and she conceived and bore Enoch who became the (first) builder of a city and Enoch called the name of the city after the name of his son, for to Enoch was born *Irad*.' The antiquity of Eridu is well documented in excavations; it is indeed the oldest site

attested in southern Mesopotamia, its pre-urban levels reaching back into the sixth millennium. Situated as it was on the ancient coastline of the Persian Gulf (which has since then receded southward) it would have formed a logical point of entry for seaborne immigrants.

Four other cities enjoy almost equal antiquity in the Sumerian view of history: Bad-tibira, Larak, Sippar and Shuruppak. Each was supposedly

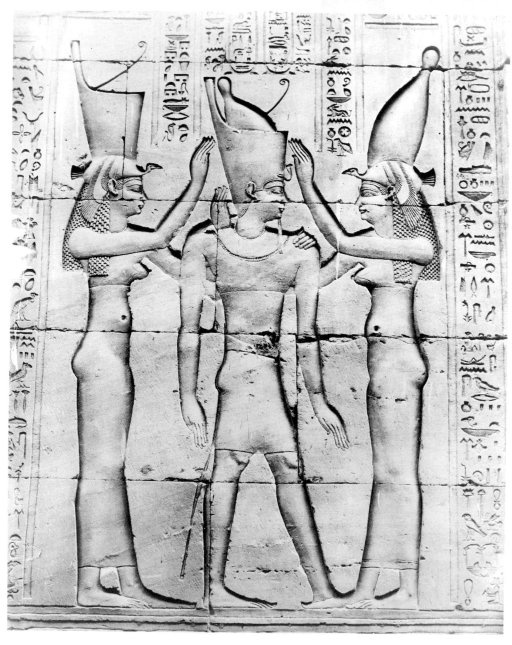

Far left: A Sumerian seal, dating from 1900 to 1700 BC, shows a goddess (center) engaged in fanning a deity who is drinking from a vessel placed on a stand.

Left: The stele of Hammurabi. Dating from 1800 BC, the 282 laws inscribed on the black basalt pillar have provided scholars with essential information of life in Mesopotamia during this period.

Below left: Seti I being crowned by the Goddess of the north, Buto, and the Goddess of the south, Nekhebet.

Right: The Valley of the Kings, burial place of some of Egypt's rulers.

ruled by one or more incredibly long-lived kings before a calamitous deluge swept all before it; only Ziusudra, the king of Shuruppak, saved himself for immortality and mankind from destruction by taking flight on a huge boat. In this Sumerian version of the familiar Noah-legend, the antediluvian period has an even longer span than in Genesis. In reality the interval between the culmination of the Sumerian urban revolution and whatever cataclysm inspired the original Flood narratives was probably no more than two centuries (*c* 3100-2900 BC). In Mesopotamian archeology, this interval of extraordinary creativity is known as the Jemdet Nasr period. It is also the time of the First Dynasty in Egypt, to which we now turn.

Like Western Asia, Egypt in the outgoing Stone Age had a substrate population which already boasted a flourishing culture ready to make the transition to civilization. In Egypt's case, both physical and cultural links point to the substrate population's having originated in Africa, and the general progress of culture seems to have been downstream along the Nile, from south to north or in some cases from west to east along the coastal or desert trade routes. Thus the earliest ceramic cultures of neolithic Egypt have been identified in southern Egypt. These are the so-called Badarian and Amratian, or Nagada I, cultures. Apart from some disputed finds west of the Nile and in the Delta, the first datable settlements in central Egypt are of Gerzean type, also known as Nagada II because of the correlation with later developments in the South.

As in Mesopotamia, in Egypt the transformation to urbanism and the other elements of civilization seems to have originated under the stimulus of an immigrant element interacting with the substrate population. Indeed, there are so many striking similarities between the specific products of the incipient Bronze Age in Egypt and Sumer that one cannot rule out the possibility of some direct Sumerian influence. According to one theory, such influence reached Egypt by sea, since much of the evidence comes from sites along the Wadi Hammamat in Upper Egypt, the point where the Nile comes closest to the Red Sea. The evidence includes the conception of writing; the use of certain motifs in art, such as the symmetrical ('heraldic') disposition of antithetical figures around a central axis; the recessed niche pattern in monumental architecture; and the employment of the characteristically Mesopotamian cylinder seal.

But the foreign stimulus, even if conceded, was no more than a catalyst. Almost immediately, the innovations mentioned, and many others, were radically transformed and developed along lines that clearly and permanently distinguished Egyptian civilization from Mesopotamian. Egyptian history can be said to begin as early as Sumerian, about 3100 BC, with a First Dynasty of eight kings which, like the antediluvians of the Mesopotamian (and Biblical) traditions, must have spanned a period of some two centuries. The great achievement of this First Dynasty was the unification of the two great halves into which Egypt has always been divided by geography. Upper Egypt is the long, narrow strip of cultivated lowland that the Nile River has carved out between the mountains and deserts lying to either side. It reaches from the Nubian border at the First Cataract in the south to what is now Cairo in the north. Lower Egypt is essentially the region of the Delta. All the evidence suggests that Upper Egypt was already ruled by kings of some stature in pre-dynastic times, and that unification involved their conquest of Lower Egypt and their consequent assumption of a double crown. The Egyptians continued to call their country 'The Two Lands' in conscious recognition of the many disparities between its two parts.

Like the contemporary Jemdet Nasr period in Mesopotamia, the time of the First Dynasty in Egypt was one of astonishing creativity. The most impressive monuments of the dynasty are the tombs of the kings and their favored retainers, especially at Abydos in the south and Sakkara in the north. They introduce us to an abiding characteristic of ancient Egyptian civilization, its real or apparent emphasis on burial and proper provision for the afterlife. This emphasis is real enough in absolute terms, as attested by an undeniably vast investment of art, architecture and literature devoted to the dead. But it may be more apparent than real in relative terms. The barren rocks on either side of the Nile Valley which serve as tombs probably provide a disproportionate share of evidence, for the valley itself has been continually occupied, and most traces of the life of the living Egyptians has vanished in the wake of uninterrupted occupation and cultivation. A similar disproportion applies to the evidence from Lower Egypt, for the moist conditions in the Delta are far more destructive of organic antiquities, notably papyrus texts, than the dry soil of Upper Egypt. These limitations need to be remembered whenever we try to reconstruct what life was really like in Ancient Egypt. And while it is highly likely that an urban revolution took place in Egypt at this time, the archeological evidence for it is less conclusive than in Mesopotamia.

The Golden Era (*c* 2900-2700 BC)

The second phase of the Early Bronze Age is still very little illuminated by contemporaneous written documents, and its outlines must be reconstructed from artifacts on the one hand, and from the imperfect memory of later mythology and historiography on the other. In the Biblical version, the Deluge was followed by the building of Babylon and its tower, and this led directly to the confusion of tongues (Genesis 11). In the Sumerian conception, the confusion of tongues follows, and terminates, a Golden Age in which the whole known world lived in peace and harmony. During this era of tranquility the Sumerian portion of the world was always under the rule of a single city, whose kingship derived from Heaven, and whose hegemony was freely acknowledged by all the other Sumerian cities so long as divine favor continued to rest on it. When it incurred divine wrath or displeasure, however, the assembly of the gods would then confer hegemony on another city and its king. This doctrine finds its clearest expression in the Sumerian King List, the most important document for reconstructing a relative framework of Mesopotamian chronology throughout the third millennium. Composed (or at any rate completed) in 1794 BC, this list attempted to catalogue all the different cities that had at one time or another enjoyed the supreme rule of Sumer from the time of the Flood to the accession of Hammurabi in 1793 BC. There were 11 such cities, some of only ephemeral importance, while others succeeded in attaining a hegemony as many as five or even six times. Together they accounted for 134 kings whose total combined reign was inflated to five figures.

The first, and for the period in question, the only city to which, in the King List's formulation, kingship descended from Heaven after the Flood, was Kish. Kish lay well upstream from all the antediluvian cities except Sippar, and thus a relatively localized flood – such as is attested archeologically at Kish about this time – would have receded here before the older cities to the southeast had again become habitable. In any event, Kish continued throughout Early Dynastic times to be the center of a northern concentration of cities that constituted an effective counterweight to the cities of the south. At the end of the early dynastic times it spawned the dynasty of Akkad, after which, in contrast to the Sumerian south, the entire northern group of cities was collectively designated the land of Akkad. This area was the center of Semitic (Akkadian) speech, as the south was of Sumerian.

These realities seem to be reflected in the King List's 23 different rulers, many of them bearing

Left: The famous Narmer palette, which depicts an Egyptian king of the Protodynastic Period exercising his regal authority over a hapless victim.

Above right: An intricately carved marble paving slab from Babylon.

Below left: A Sumerian bas relief of 2800 BC. A king carries a basket filled with bricks for building a new temple. The scene below shows the same ruler seated on his throne while an attendant refills his goblet.

Semitic names, who constituted the first dynasty of Kish, and in associated traditions that claimed for Kish the undisputed leadership over both Sumer and what later came to be called Akkad during the Golden Age. Twenty of the actual royal names are unknown from any other source, and probably represent no more than about eight generations or two centuries, instead of the various legendary and wholly fantastic figures supplied by the different manuscripts of the King List.

In its most complete form, the Sumerian King List began with the antediluvian kings and ended with the end of the First Dynasty of Isin in 1794 BC. The Babylonian King List carried on where the Sumerian King List left off. Beginning with the ancestors and predecessors of Hammurabi of Babylon, who succeeded to the throne in 1793 BC, its cataloged the ten dynasties that ruled Babylonia till the Persian conquest. Other king lists continued the record into Greek times. All these traditions were collected early in the third century BC by a Babylonian priest named Benossos in a Greek work entitled *Babylonaeca*, which was intended to impress both his royal Seleucid patron and the Hellenistic world in general with the antiquity of Mesopotamian civilization. It is preserved for us only in excerpts quoted by later Hellenistic historians, notably Josephus.

In Egypt, the identical object was pursued by another priest, Manetho, a contemporary of

Benossos. He structured all of Egyptian history before the Greek conquest by dynasties, but he identified these dynasties by number rather than by name. His scheme serves as a chronological framework for ancient Egyptian history to this day, for, with modifications, we still follow his outline of 30 dynasties. But it should be remembered that the continuity of Manetho's numbering implies no greater continuity, or lesser diversity of the ethnic affiliation, capital cities or other distinguishing characteristics, of the royal houses which actually ruled Egypt than was the case in Mesopotamia.

The available evidence suggests that no event of the magnitude of the Babylonian flood separated Manetho's first two dynasties. Both ruled, or at least derived, from This in the area of Abydos. They are thus sometimes jointly referred to as the Thinite dynasties, and approximately the four centuries (c 3100-2700) of their 18 kings as the Protodynastic, or Early Dynastic, Period. Unlike their Mesopotamian contemporaries, these early kings have left a number of inscriptions, but these are far from sufficient to write a connected history of the period. For the Second Dynasty, the single most important event that can be reconstructed from later evidence is the introduction of the calendar. The regular recurrence of the season has, of course, led to an approximation of the solar year among many peoples, but in Egypt such approximations were very early refined by the observation of the annual rise of the Nile. The Nile, swollen by the melting snows of the equatorial mountains of East Africa, each year floods its banks, depositing a rich topsoil on which Egyptian agriculture subsists for the ensuing year. It was further observed that this event regularly coincided with the heliacal rising of the Dogstar, Sirius (in Egyptian, Sothis), that is, with the day when this star, the brightest in the Egyptian sky, first emerges from the sun's rays and becomes visible just before sunrise. The interval between the occurrences was established as 365 days and gave rise to a calendar year just short of the true solar year. It takes 1460 solar years to restore the discrepancy, and since such convergences of the Egyptian year and the solar year were recorded for AD 140 and 1320 BC, it is assumed that the calendar originated at a previous convergence. (By this calculation, the year 4241 BC was once regarded as the earliest date in human history, but this day has since had to be lowered by one Sothic cycle to

about 2776 BC.) The introduction of the Egyptian calendar, ancestral to the Julian calendar and thus ultimately to our own, may then be dated hypothetically to the time of the Second Dynasty.

The Heroic Era (c 2700-2500 BC)

The Golden Age of national unity under the First Dynasty of Kish in Mesopotamia and the Thinite dynasties in Egypt contained within themselves the seeds of very divergent developments. In both cases, the nature and conception of kingship was a crucial factor in these developments. In Egypt, the king was regarded and worshiped as a god, and as such he served as the warrant for maintaining the newly achieved unity. In Sumer, on the other hand, national unity was only an ideal, with real power vested in competing city states whose rulers ranked, not as gods, but only as deputies appointed by the gods. In theory, they were nominated by the god of their city and confirmed by the assembly of all the great gods, with one city-ruler at any given time being accorded the rank of first among equals by the divine assembly. In practice, these mythological descriptions (preserved from a later period) may reflect an elective leadership on the levels both of the individual city-states and of the larger grouping of all the Sumerian cities. It is theorized that a Sumer-league (or Kengir-league, to use the Sumerians' own word for their country) was formed as an instrument of a kind of primitive democracy. It deliberated at Nippur, if we may argue from the analogy of the divine assembly of the myths, and since Nippur was sacred to the god Enlil, it reflected at the same time a shift in religious loyalties away from Enki of Eridu, the original city.

Nippur was not itself the seat of a significant city-state, but it was strategically situated between the two principal urban clusters of lower Mesopotamia: Sumer in the south(east) and in the north(west) Akkad (to anticipate somewhat anachronistically the name conferred on the area after the founding of the city of Akkad about 2300 BC). In both areas, urbanization involved a significant expansion of monumental architecture, specifically the building of temples and the fortification of the urban settlements that grew up around the temples. The whole river valley was presently organized in such a way that the entire population could, if the need arose, find shelter behind the walls of a city. In the process, each city

not only assumed the protection but also aspired to the control of the open countryside surrounding it. The rivalry that inevitably ensued between neighboring cities led to increasing militarization and to the concentration of political leadership in the hands of warrior-princes.

The art of the period reflected the tastes of the new heroic age, particularly in the seal cylinders which by this time had become the most characteristic Mesopotamian art form. Typically, they illustrate contests between warriors, animals or both. And though there is no contemporary literature, later literature dwelt by preference on the real or supposed exploits of these warrior-princes. Some stories tell of struggles between Kish, the chief northern city, and Uruk, the bulwark of the south. Others recall embassies, single combats and sieges involving Uruk with the city-state of Aratta far to the east, perhaps in what is now Afghanistan. (This city was the source of lapis lazuli and other materials needed in Mesopotamia, and a whole cycle of epics climaxes in the successful establishment of trade relations between Uruk and Aratta.)

Of the many names attested in later literary sources, enough recur on contemporary inscriptions to inspire some confidence in their overall reality, and a rough historical framework may thus be attempted for the period, even though a continuous history in the proper sense is not yet possible. Mebaragesi of Kish was best remembered later for first building the Tummal, one of the great sanctuaries at Nippur. He and his son Agga fought against Gilgamesh, who became the most famous ruler of Uruk by virtue of the Sumerian epics about him and their later Akkadian adaptations. Uruk shared the hegemony of the south with Ur, whose first rulers were buried, in some cases with their living retinue, in the magnificent Royal Cemetery excavated by Sir Leonard Woolley at Ur. The brilliantly executed gold vessels and cylinder seals interred with them preserve their names, while their successors are known variously from contemporary building inscriptions and from allusions in the King List, in the Tummal inscription (which records the successive kings whose benefactions to Nippur followed Mebaragesi's example) and in proverbs.

The wealth of the royal grave deposits, the penchant for temple building, the vigor of the representational art, the indelible impress which the principal rulers left on later literature – all these mark this so-called Early Dynastic II period as the Heroic Age of Mesopotamian tradition, eventually assuming a place not unlike that of the Homeric heroes in Greek tradition.

In Egypt the same period witnessed the beginning of the Old Kingdom under the third and fourth dynasties. It was the first fully historic period for that country, and a time of major cultural and political innovations destined to mark out the country's subsequent course for millennia. The many and diverse achievements of the period still arouse admiration, but none so much as the pyramids. Growing organically out of the more modest royal graves of the Thinite period, the first Third Dynasty tombs are essentially elaborations of the squat *mastabas* that continued to serve the needs of the courtiers. By adding successive layers on top of the larger base, the king expressed his superiority over the courtiers to be buried around him. The result was at first a simple step-pyramid, such as those of Djoser and Sekhemkhet at Sakkara. But the aggrandizement of political and economic power by the king combined with the genius of semi-legendary architects such as Imhotep soon led to the construction of the true pyramid, a massive structure designed to support (like

Right: The gateway to the enclosure at Sakkara, Egypt, with the pyramid of Djoser in the background.

Left: The Great Sphinx at Giza was built around 2500 BC.

Below: A terracotta head of a woman dating from 3000 to 2000 BC discovered in Mesopotamia.

the more modest tombs and obelisks) a small pyramidion, or apex, at the very top, while guarding the royal burial chamber in its innermost recesses. By the Fourth Dynasty each king provided for an entire pyramid complex for himself, his queen and his court, and some, like Snefru, even built more than one, perhaps to foil would-be despoilers. To the later Greeks the great pyramids thus erected at Giza, along with the famous Sphinx, were among the seven wonders of the world, and to this day, they symbolize the might of the Old Kingdom and the total deification of its monarchs.

But the pyramids of the Old Kingdom were only the most visible outward symptom of Egypt's break with whatever cultural stimuli it may have owed to or shared with the earliest Mesopotamian civilization. A more fundamental distinction was the consolidation of Egypt's provincial structure in the form of the traditional nomes. The nomes, originally clans united by ties of kinship, shared a common totem and divided the productive agricultural land of Upper and Lower Egypt among them; but they did so without resorting to the kind of urbanization that produced the city-states characteristic of Mesopotamia. Thus they readily formed the basic units of a monarchic structure, constituting provinces under strong kings and only asserting their independence under weak central administrations. At the same time, urbanization took a different form in Egypt. Although new towns were founded with as many as 10,000 inhabitants, they lacked monumental architecture and the fortifications necessary for

independence. These features were concentrated in only a few capital cities, or even a single one, in any given period. For the Old Kingdom, Memphis first emerged in this role. Located at the border of Upper and Lower Egypt, its function paralleled in some measure that of Nippur. But in the absence of rival centers, its emergence did not immediately involve the displacement of any earlier theology, as when Enlil of Nippur displaced Enki and the theology of Eridu. Instead, the chief deity of Memphis, Ptah, figured as the universal creator and protagonist in a work known as the 'Theology of Memphis,' and this in turn served as the theoretical justification for the new political reality. Though attested only in much later copies, this text, which probably originated at this time, marks the beginning of Egyptian literature. Other arts also began to flourish under royal patronage, notably sculpture. Some of the finest portraiture dates from this period, as for example the bust of Ankhaef, architect of the pyramid of Orefren at Gizeh. In the economic realm, too, the new state proved its initiative; and it is probable that the mines of Sinai were exploited for turquoise and metals as early as the Third Dynasty.

The Dynastic Age (*c* 2500-2300 BC)

In Mesopotamia the elective principle of kingship soon proved unequal to the twin demands of military and economic leadership. The pace of conflict quickened between competing city-states; cities needed to be fortified; huge temples were considered a necessity to appease a growing pantheon of gods; and irrigation demanded large inputs of collective labor. Under these pressures elective leadership gradually gave way to a more institutionalized and permanent system of succession based on the hereditary principle. More often than before, brother was succeeded by brother, or father by son, and the dynastic era opened. A theology of kingship emerged to justify the new structure. The ruling king ensured the choice of his successor by invoking the sanction of divine right, a claim that rested on his 'sacred marriage' with the goddess (or her priestly stand-in), and that was strengthened at every turn by an alliance with a newly emerging and expanding priesthood.

The new political and religious pattern brought grave social and economic consequences in its train. A continuous process of royal, priestly and noble purchases of productive agricultural land ensued, and the previously free citizenry was inexorably reduced to the status of a client population, dependent on palace, temple or noble

estates for subsistence rations. These rations, carefully inventoried in the first sizeable corpus of intelligible cuneiform texts, proved henceforth to consist typically of cereals, oil, fish, milk, wool and garments. An attempt to reverse this trend is recorded as early as *c* 2300, when Urukagina of Lagash sought to 'restore the ancient mores' by an alliance with the newly dispossessed classes at the expense of the more powerful ones, including his own royal family. The attempt failed, but it was subsequently emulated and institutionalized in periodic royal proclamations relating to release from debt slavery, price stabilization and promulgation of legal precedents. A basic pattern had been set: Palace and temple were to remain the principal foci of economic activity throughout Mesopotamian history. A private sector still remained, but thenceforth it would be an ever less significant factor.

The fusion of the dynastic principle with the earlier concept of the city-state was not confined to the traditional core of Sumerian cities clustered around the head of the Persian Gulf. We find evidence of it as far away as Mari on the middle Euphrates and at Awan and Hamazi in Elam (western Iran). In addition to the traditional centers of power at Kish, Uruk and Ur, new places such as Akshak, Adab, Lagash and Umma also began to assert themselves. All shared the Sumerian language and worshiped the same pantheon, though each city was sacred to a deity or divine couple of its own. At the end of the period, a certain Lugal-zagesi emerged from his modest base at Umma as a conqueror, first of neighboring Lagash and successively of all the principal Sumerian city-states, thus laying the basis for the first Mesopotamian imperium.

In Egypt, the same two centuries were roughly coeval with the Fifth Dynasty, a time marked by the rising power of the priesthood. Where the Sumerians venerated different gods in each of their many city-states, the political centralization of Egypt's Old Kingdom was reflected in the supremacy of a single god, specifically Re, the sun-god. Great temple complexes were dedicated to Re by the first six of the nine kings of the Fifth Dynasty on the testimony of the inscriptions, and two of these complexes have been identified and excavated. Whereas in Sumer the temple complex occupied the most prominent place within each city, in Egypt, where there were no comparable cities, these sun-temples were built in the necropoles ('cities of the dead') in the western desert. They seem in fact to have played a part in the cult of the deceased king, and thus to have helped to compensate for the more modest size of the Fifth Dynasty pyramids.

In addition to Re, another deity prominently worshiped at this time was Hathor, the 'Mistress of Dendera.' Dendera was one of the more strategically located nomes of Upper Egypt during the Old Kingdom, and the worship of its principal goddess spread to the court at Memphis and to a number of other nomes. On many sun-temples, priests served both Re and Hathor. Like many lesser deities, Hathor was conceived of in animal form, in her case in the form of the cow, but this conceptualization took a number of forms, from metaphoric attribution of certain bovine characteristics grafted onto a human torso (either in the art or in the orthography) to an outright identification of goddess and animal. In the last case, the result was frequently the actual worship of living animals as manifestations of the deity.

In Egypt, as in Sumer, the second half of the third millennium marked the first significant archives of economic texts. Though written on papyrus, and thus less durable than cuneiform records on clay, they survive in sufficient numbers – either in the safety of tombs high above the annual innundation, or in copies on stelae – to illuminate the many facets of an expanding economy. Together with the rich representational art, notably in the wall-paintings and wooden carvings which decorated graves, they provide priceless insights into daily life of both nobleman and commoner.

The Imperial Era (2300-2150 BC)

It was at the court of Ur-Zababa of Kish that Sargon began his career, as a royal cupbearer. He was destined to displace the last dynasty of Kish and to forge the first Mesopotamian empire. For most of the 55 or 56 years of rule credited to Sargon, he was more likely a contemporary of Ur-Zababa's successors, who ruled another 50 years at least. It was presumably during these same 50 years, beginning around 2236 BC, that Sargon constructed, not far from Kish, a new city and palace at Agade (Biblical Akkad) somewhere on the Euphrates, and waged the numerous campaigns to distant lands. If all the sources are to be given equal credence, these campaigns took him up the Euphrates into the Syrian desert and the Anatolian highlands; across the Tigris into Assyria and Elam; and down the Persian Gulf as far as Dilmun and beyond. These conquests brought large areas of the Asiatic Near East for the first time into the orbit of recorded history and under the influences of Mesopotamian civilization. But as yet they did not touch the urban centers of Sumer and Akkad themselves. It was only in his old age that Sargon, responding to their challenge, defeated Lugalzagesi of Uruk, together with the petty kings of all the separate city-states. And it was, perhaps, for no more than his last five or six years that the entire country was united under the usurper-king.

Nevertheless, Sargon's achievement is worthy of the fame it won him in later memory. He successfully united two previously discrete constitutional principles – the tradition of a pre-eminent kingship of Kish, and the dynastic principle – to forge the first real imperial structure in history. The core of his empire consisted of Sumer and Akkad, two areas in their way as distinct as Lower and Upper Egypt. He ruled as king of Kish and Akkad, but he also assumed the traditional royal titles of Uruk and Ur, the principal southern centers, thus becoming 'king of the (Sumerian) nation.' His far-reaching reforms in the religious sphere were intended to cement the unification achieved initially by military means, while his political innovations served to centralize administration under his aegis and to offset the deep-seated traditions of fragmentation into petty city-states.

His family, including his numerous progeny, figured prominently in these plans. His daughter, Enheduanna, became the first high-priestess of the Moon-god at Ur, a post filled by imperial princesses henceforth. Like her father, she seems also to have held office at Uruk, the city sacred to the Heaven-god, An, and henceforth to the female deity, Inanna, as well. This traditional Sumerian goddess of love and fertility was now equated with the warlike Semitic Ishtar and exalted to equal rank with An as his consort. A cycle of poems celebrates both the military victories which the Sargonic kings ascribed to Ishtar and her exaltation to the acme of the Sumerian pantheon. The composition of these poems, together with another cycle of poems apostrophizing all the great sanctuaries of Sumer and Akkad, is attributed to Enheduanna, who thus emerges as possibly the first identifiable author in world literature. Equally high priestly and civil offices throughout the empire were filled by other sons and daughters of the king or, failing that, by officials who owed their appointments, and thus their primary allegiance, to him rather than to the populations entrusted to their care. In some cases, he even felt strong enough to re-confirm the native dynasts in their old posts.

Two of Sargon's sons succeeded him as kings of Kish and Akkad, and fought hard to maintain the Akkadian supremacy in Sumer and further afield. After reigns totaling 22 or 24 years, however, both met violent deaths in palace revolts, and it was left for Sargon's grandson to consolidate his

conquests and to raise the Akkadian empire to its greatest height. Naram-Sin was destined to reign for 56 years, to hold sway throughout the valley of the Tigris and Euphrates and to carry Akkadian arms beyond the valley to Anatolia in the northwest, to the Iranian highlands in the east and to the shores and islands of the Persian Gulf in the southeast. Palaces, fortresses, temples and votive objects proclaimed his name and achievements at home and abroad. Steles and rock reliefs pictured him as the conquering hero. Growing archives of letters and contracts attested to the expansion of economic activity and prosperity set in motion by his reign. Outside of Sumer proper many of the archival documents were now inscribed in Akkadian, which thus emerged as a vehicle of written communication to challenge, though not as yet to

Above: A bronze bust of King Sargon of Akkad. Under his leadership the Semites occupied the whole plain of Shinar and created the greatest Mesopotamian empire.

Left: An Egyptian stele dedicated to Horus, Osiris and Isis.

Far left: A reconstruction of Sumerian headdress and jewelry from Ur (2500 BC).

Left and below: Details of the 'Standard of Ur' from Sumeria.

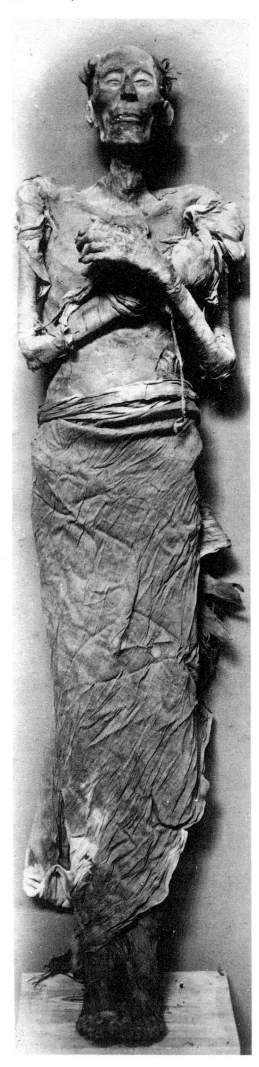

displace, the traditional Sumerian. Though Akkadian remained indebted to Sumerian for its system of writing and for many of its legal formulations and literary conventions, the foundation was thus laid for a discrete Semitic legal and literary tradition that was destined to have a profound influence throughout the subsequent Near East.

To match earthly achievements, Naram-Sin allowed himself to be addressed and worshiped as a god in the latter part of his reign. This conception of kingship, more at home in Egypt than in Mesopotamia, was honored also by his son and successor, Shar-kali-sharri, and sporadically by other Mesopotamian kings for the next four centuries. A more enduring institution was the consolidation of the dating system introduced by Sargon and necessitated by the growth of the economy. In place of purely local dating systems based on regnal years of local rulers or on the names of local officials, the king now decreed that each year should be named throughout the realm after some significant event – political, military, religious or otherwise – of the preceding year. This system, combined with lists of such year names circulated for contemporary consultation, serves the modern historian as an invaluable record of the events and accomplishments of successive Mesopotamian dynasties until it was again replaced, in Babylonia by the regnal year system beginning in Kassite times, and in Assyria by the eponym system.

The Sixth Dynasty of Egypt made far less of a break with its predecessor than had the Sargonic Dynasty in Mesopotamia, nor were its achievements nearly so memorable. Rather, it marked the continuation and conclusion of the Old Kingdom, whose principal innovations were perpetuated and institutionalized. The outstanding rulers of the dynasty, if only by sheer length of reign, were Pepi I (40 or 49 years) and his son Pepi II (94 years), but they were not otherwise the equals of Sargon and Naram-Sin. Pepi II, having ascended the throne at the age of six, died in his 100th, the longest reign in the history of Egypt, and perhaps of recorded history generally. During Pepi II's minority, and again in his old age, co-regencies were instituted to help assure the succession, and effective power was in the hands of the vizier. In fact, throughout the Sixth Dynasty, the vizierate grew in importance, and other royal prerogatives were dissipated in the direction of the provincial nomarchs (rulers of nomes) and temples. Soon the nomarchs began to carve their tombs out of the cliffs overlooking their respective provinces from the Western Desert, in preference to being buried in the mastabas that surrounded the earlier Old Kingdom pyramids.

The practice of building pyramids continued at this time; indeed, each of the Sixth Dynasty kings contrived to have an entire pyramid complex built in his honor, with the smaller ones intended for the several queens and other members of the court. But whereas the earlier Old Kingdom pyramids were scattered along the Western Desert from Zawyet el Aryan, just north of Memphis, to Dahshur and even Medum, south of Memphis, the Sixth Dynasty pyramids were concentrated at Saqqara, in the immediate vicinity of the capital. Other funerary practices also thrived, with mummification (first attested in the Second Dynasty) becoming a fine art. Funerary inscriptions assumed a canonical form, and most of the great collection known as the Pyramid Texts date from this period. These texts were essentially collections of spells designed to assure the deceased king of safe passage, nourishment and other necessities of the after-life, but they also incorporated and preserved many of the mythological and theological conceptions of earlier periods. They were inscribed on the walls of the funerary chamber and adjoining portions of the pyramid, and were subsequently copied as well for the benefit of lesser mortals.

The Fall of Akkad, the Gutians, the First Intermediate Period (c 2150-2100 BC)

The long reigns of Naram-Sin of Akkad and Pepi II both came to an end about 2180 BC, and the great empires that they ruled survived them by but a few years. By about 2150 a collapse ensued in both areas that was as dramatic as it is enigmatic. Ancient historians sought to account for it in religious terms, as a mark of divine retribution for human deliction, particularly for royal transgressions against the gods. Modern explanations tend to run to natural causes, such as climatological changes with consequent protracted famine. But no one really knows.

In Mesopotamia the immediate origin of the collapse was the assassination of the Shar-kali-sharri, son and successor of Naram-Sin, after an apparently successful rule of 25 years. In the three-year anarchy that followed, four obscure pretenders contended for the throne, a situation expressed tellingly both in the omen literature and in the King List by the phrase 'Who was king, who was not king?' The city of Akkad fell into ruins so completely that it was never reoccupied and alone among the great capitals of ancient Mesopotamia remains unidentified and unlocated to this day. Its once proud empire was reduced to a narrow strip of land straddling the Tigris at its confluence with the Diyala River. The ancient city-states of the Sumerian south reasserted their independence, while the more distant conquests submitted to the various barbarian or semi-nomadic tribes whom the Sargonic kings had kept at bay. On the long northeastern frontiers, these tribes included Hurrians, Lullubaean mountaineers and Elamites; on the west, the principal pressure came from the Amorites. According to the 'Curse of Akkad' and other literary accounts in which these events were later memorialized, the chief agents of the collapse were the Gutians, a warlike and uncivilized horde of obscure origins. The interregnum which they inaugurated is therefore sometimes alluded to as the Gutian period, both in the ancient sources and in modern treatments. But this period lasted a bare 40 years, and the Gutian role in it is elusive at best. Gutians are mentioned in texts from Umma, where their kings may have claimed sovereignty, and Gutian royal names, or names that sound like them, are found scattered through northern Mesopotamia. But the real significance of their role was to release the Sumerians from their submission to Akkad, thus freeing them for a new Sumerian renaissance. Uruk resumed its traditional hegemony, succeeding Akkad in the King List and, by implication, in the possession of Nippur, while Ur maintained its importance as the center of the moon-cult. But it was Lagash that took most immediate advantage of the situation. Freed not only from Akkad but from the traditional rivalry of neighboring Umma, it enjoyed a new period of flourishing artistic, literary, religious and commercial activity under independent governors such as Ur-Bau and his son-in-law, Gudea. Their magnificent statues represent the high point of Sumerian sculpture, while the two Cylinders of Gudea preserve, in their poetic description of the building of the temple to the chief deity of Lagash, one of the finest examples of Sumerian literature. Thus the groundwork was laid for a new flowering of Sumerian culture in the ashes of the Akkadian empire.

Left: The embalmed remains of Ramses II. His great achievements included the excavation of the rock temples at Abu Simbel and the completion of the great hall of Karnak. However, a long war against the Hittites left Egypt much impoverished.

Right: A relief from the Middle Kingdom tomb of Hounenou.

Below: Statue of Gudea, priest-king of Lagash. The representation of Gudea marks a high point in the history of Sumerian sculpture.

the worst in better years. Such individuals have left telling memorials to their role in their tomb inscriptions, and it is from them that the reconstruction of both Egyptian society and monarchy would have to come.

The Etatist Era (2100-2000 BC)

The half millennium from 2100 to 1600 BC is generally regarded by archeologists as the Middle Bronze Age of Palestine, Syria and Anatolia, and the term can usefully be extended to cover most of the civilized Near East of the time, for it marked a definable mid-point – indeed a high-point – of Bronze Age civilization. Mesopotamia entered its classical phase during the neo-Sumerian and Old Babylonian periods, and Egypt rose to new heights under the Middle Kingdom. In the Aegean world, the age is roughly coterminous with the Middle Minoan period of Crete, the Middle Cycladic period of the lesser islands and the Middle Helladic period of the mainland, as all these areas began to reflect the stimulus of contact with the older centers of culture. Throughout the Near East, there was a perceptible regeneration of urban life as the high civilizations recouped from the disasters that marked the end of the Early Bronze Age.

In Mesopotamia the revival began in the extreme south, when Utu-hegal, the short-lived and sole ruler of the fifth dynasty of Uruk, expelled the Gutians. But it was the city of Ur that was destined to restore a Mesopotamian empire almost to its Sargonic borders. At first Ur was administered as a province of Uruk by a governor who may have been Utuhegal's son. But presently the governor of Ur, Ur-Nammu, asserted the city's independence. Still honoring his cultic and dynastic ties to Uruk, he launched a massive program of building in and around Ur that assured that city's primacy as a religious and commercial capital. The ziggurat or stepped tower, to the moon-god Nanna soon dominated the city's sacred precinct and served as a model wherever Sumerian religious architecture spread subsequently. It may have inspired the Biblical account of the Tower of Babel (Gen. 11) and continues to impress modern visitors. The harbor of Ur was reopened for trade via the Persian Gulf, and the agricultural self sufficiency of the area was promoted by the dredging of old canals, the digging of new ones and the completion of extensive irrigation projects. At the traditional religious capital of Nippur, Ur-Nammu rebuilt the ancient temples of Enlil and Ninlil and won the title of King of Sumer and Akkad and the allegiance of all the ancient city-states. A new code of laws was promulgated, and it proved a model for all subsequent precedent-law in the Ancient Near East. In it a variety of cases from the law of persons and things, as well as procedures, were phrased in the conditional form that was to become characteristic of later Babylonian, Assyrian, Hittite and Hebrew case law (hence also called conditional legislation). It codified extreme situations, rather than typical or marginal ones, and was designed less for practical application in the courts than for proclaiming the king's wisdom and his concern for his subjects. His peaceful reign was, in fact, marred only by his defeat of Lagash, whose last independent governor he killed, and by his own death in battle, an event that was appropriately memorialized in the closing chapter of his hymnic biography.

The succession passed smoothly to his son Shulgi and for the first half of his long 48-year rule, the consolidation of the neo-Sumerian empire continued in its peaceful path. But the second half of the reign of this, the greatest of the Ur III kings, was spent in almost continuous war-

The collapse of the Old Kingdom was equally precipitate. The last, obscure members of the Sixth Dynasty (including the Queen Nit-oqrety or Nitocris) were contemporary with the numerous ephemeral pretenders of the Seventh and Eighth Dynasties. There were at least 18 of these in 30 years, if Manetho is to be believed. One novel hypothesis accounts for these traditions by positing the institution of the murder or suicide of the king for his failure to harness the natural cosmic order for the benefit of his people. Certainly extreme conditions of famine over an extended period of time could have shaken the Egyptians' traditional faith in the powers of this king, whom they worshiped as the embodiment of the annual inundation by the Nile, the prerequisite of a successful agricultural year. That Pepi II's successors were unable to stem the economic and agricultural disaster that overtook Egypt is graphically depicted in 'The Admonitions of Ipuwer,' an Egyptian sage whose eyewitness accounts almost certainly reflect conditions of this First Intermediate Period. As he describes it, law and order broke down, the peasant abandoned his plot in despair, the birth rate declined and the death rate increased. Corpses were abandoned to the Nile, yet its waters, thus polluted, were drunk for want of better. The sand dunes advanced over the arable land; foreign commerce came to a halt; royal tombs were plundered; all Egypt was laid open to invasion; even cannibalism appeared.

In these circumstances, the position of the king became indeed untenable. Men could at best look to local governors who, with greater foresight or luck than their fellow monarchs, had prepared for

fare. On the testimony of the date formulas, the consistent target of his attacks was the northeastern frontier, whose warlike mountain tribes had proved the undoing of Akkad. By his victories here, especially over Tappan-darah of Simurrum, Shulgi not only secured his most vulnerable border, but apparently reopened the overland trade routes leading to the sources of tin (essential for the bronze industry), lapis lazuli and other metals and stones lacking in Mesopotamia itself. A startling economic revival followed these military triumphs, and trade and industry flourished. Both were under state control, either directly or through the agency of the great temples, and a growing bureaucracy developed. Its meticulous bookkeeping is preserved for us in tens of thousands of cuneiform accounts from the archives of half a dozen different cities. No other single century of Mesopotamian history is so amply documented, and it is possible to reconstruct the components of international trade, the prices of commodities, the processes of manufacture in the areas of metallurgy, textiles, leather and other industries at this time. Numerous court records reveal the workings of a sophisticated judicial system; letter-orders include drafts on the royal storage-centers that anticipate modern banking techniques; and the balanced accounts of Drehem disclose a great stockyard supplied every month by a designated city of the Sumerian Commonwealth so that the temples of nearby Nippur would be well supplied with meat – both for the gods (in the guise of statues) and for their priestly retinues.

Although the capital city of Ur was the principal beneficiary of the royal largesse, votive art and religious architecture were spread liberally and extensively throughout the empire. The neo-Sumerian renaissance thus reached as far as Assur, Susa and other outposts of the fallen empire of Akkad, thereby nurturing the Mesopotamian seed planted there in Sargonic times.

The reunification of Egypt, and its emergence from the chaos of the First Intermediate Period, lagged by only a few decades behind that of Mesopotamia. Its impetus came from the south, specifically from the fifth nome of Upper Egypt, whose nomarchs had begun to distinguish themselves even before the end of the Tenth Dynasty. They founded a new dynasty at Thebes about 2130 BC and raised that city to a commanding position it was to retain through most of the second millennium. Three pharaohs of the Eleventh Dynasty bore the dynastic (or personal) name In-yotef and three or four that of Montu-hotpe. Of these, it was Montu-hotpe II (c 2060-2010 BC) who most deserves attention. A worthy counterpart and near contemporary of Shulgi, he succeeded in asserting himself over his fellow nomarchs. Although these retained a greater measure of autonomy than their counterparts in contemporary Sumer, they did not dispute Montu-hotpe's assumption of the double crown of Upper and Lower Egypt about 2050 or 2040 BC. In later tradition, he was regarded as the equal of Menes and Ahmose, the founders of the Old Kingdom and New Kingdom respectively. In short, he may be credited with establishing the Middle Kingdom.

The new king's building program was worthy of these pretensions. Though concentrating on mortuary architecture, he broke entirely with the specific forms this had taken in the pyramid age. The single small pyramid that he erected contained no burial chamber, and the royal tomb instead formed part of an elaborate complex of buildings overlooking Thebes from the western bank of the Nile at Deir el Bahri. Only slightly less monumental structures provided for his deceased

queens and the officials and ladies of his court. A colonnaded mortuary temple dominated the whole complex, which is therefore sometimes known in its entirety by the king's throne name as the Temple of Neb-hepet-Re. It attests the continuing vitality of the Egyptian concept of divine kingship: even though the ravages of the First Intermediate Period had shaken the faith in the absolute and automatic divinity of the pharaoh, it was still possible for outstanding kings (and even lesser mortals) to command divine honors during and sometimes long after their lifetime.

That the Egyptian economy enjoyed good health in the later Eleventh Dynasty is shown by a small group of letters and accounts from Thebes dating c 2000 BC. They belong to a typical farmer-priest of moderate means who amassed a small fortune in rentals of land and commodities without, however, appearing interested in expanding his land holdings as such. Perhaps he was saving his money and other liquid assets toward a decent burial, for the funerary practices of private persons in the Middle Kingdom were proportionately as costly as those of wealthier nobility. In any case, such examples of economic texts from the outgoing third millennium, rare as they are by comparison to the overflowing archives of contemporary Sumer, suggest that agricultural wealth had filtered downward in the Eleventh Dynasty, a process that probably originated in the First Intermediate Period as a concomitant to political decentralization.

The Emergence of the Amorites/the Twelfth Dynasty (c 2000-1800 BC)

Amurru (or Amaru) was, in its earliest cuneiform attestations, simply a geographical name for the west, or for the deserts bordering the right bank of the Euphrates. This area, which stretched without apparent limit into the Syrian and Arabian Deserts, was traditionally the home of nomadic tribes of Semitic speech who were drawn to the

civilized river valley as if by a magnet and invaded or infiltrated it whenever opportunity beckoned. In the process they increasingly began to adopt the ways and outlook of the river-valley civilization, first as semi-nomads who spent part of the year as settled agriculturalists in an uneasy symbiosis with the urban society of the irrigation civilizations, and ultimately as fully integrated members of that society, retaining at most the linguistic traces of their origins. It was thus, perhaps as early as c 2900 BC, the first major wave of westerners had entered the Mesopotamian amalgam and, under the kings of Kish and Akkad, had become full partners in the Sumero-Akkadian civilization. When, however, the Akkadian sources themselves spoke of Amorites, as they did beginning with Shar-kali-sharri about 2150 BC, they were alluding to a new wave of invaders from the desert, not yet acclimated to Mesopotamian ways. Such references multiply in the neo-Sumerian texts of the twenty-first century and correlate with growing linguistic evidence based chiefly on the recorded personal names of persons identified as Amorites, which shows that the new group spoke a variety of Semitic ancestral to later Hebrew, Aramaic and Phoenician.

Amorite influence was not, however, confined to linguistics. Many cultural innovations of the second millennium can be traced to the new immigration, notably in literature and law. And since the migrations moved in the direction of Syria-Palestine as well as toward Mesopotamia, it is not surprising that numerous common traditions – linguistic, legal, literary – subsequently crop up at both ends of the Asiatic Near East. Among these common traditions, those of the semi-nomadic wanderings preserved in the patriarchal narratives in Genesis and elsewhere in the Hebrew Bible deserve special notice. Their glimpses of tribal organization, methods of bestowing personal names, kinship patterns, rules of inheritance and land tenure, genealogical schemes and other vestiges of nomadic life are too close to the more limited evidence of the cuneiform records to be dismissed out of hand as later fabrications.

Only when the natural arenas of centralized political power in Mesopotamia and Egypt were in eclipse, did the intervening area, destined by geography for division into petty states, enjoy an opportunity to make its influence felt. The simultaneous collapse of the Sargonic Empire of Akkad and the Old Kingdom in Egypt provided this opportunity, and Shulgi of Ur had to construct a defensive wall, presumably at the point where Tigris and Euphrates flow closest together, to deflect unwanted barbarians from the cities that lay to the south. Shulgi was succeeded by two of his many sons, Amar-Sin and Shu-Sin, each of whom reigned for nine years. Like him, they conducted most of their military campaigns in the east, across the Tigris, but Shu-Sin also greatly strengthened the wall, calling it 'the one which keeps Didanum at bay,' a direct reference to the Amorite threat. He managed thereby to postpone the final reckoning, and even enjoyed divine honors in his lifetime beyond those of his predecessors. His son Ibbi-Sin was less fortunate. Unable to withstand the simultaneous onslaughts of Elamites and Subarians from the east and Amorites from the west, he appealed for help to Ishbi-Irra of Mari, only to end up with Ishbi-Irra extorting ever more powers for himself until he was able to found a dynasty of his own at Isin, and subsequently allowing the capital city of Ur to be sacked and Ibbi-Sin to be carried off to exile and ultimate death and burial in Elam.

The fall of Ur about 2000 BC did not mark so

Left: Found in foundations dating back to the III Dynasty of Ur in south Babylon, this bronze figure bears an inscription of Warad-Sin, King of Lassa.

Right: Wooden model of oxen pulling a plough from the Middle Kingdom (2000 BC).

Below: A detail of a wall painting from the tomb of Nakht, Thebes, from the XVIII Dynasty.

clear a break in the historical continuum as has sometimes been assumed. Ishbi-Irra paid homage to the Sumero-Akkadian traditions of the Ur III dynasty, reigning as king of Ur and perpetuating such time-honored practices as the cult of the deified king, the patronage of the priesthood and scribal schools of Nippur, the installation of royal princes and priestesses at the principal national shrines and of making loyal officials governors of the principal provinces. But whether with his consent or not, these governors were now increasingly of Amorite stock, and wherever possible aspired to royal status for themselves and to independence for their cities. This was particularly true at Assur, Eshnunna, Der and Susa beyond the Tigris, as well as upstream on the Euphrates and its tributaries. From Assur and northern Mesopotamia, a lively trade soon carried Amorite and Akkadian influence even further afield, into Cappadocia in modern Turkey.

Closer to home, the traditional central control was at first maintained, but even here the loyalty of the provinces was short-lived. For most of the twentieth century, Ishbi-Irra's descendants at Isin were unchallenged as the successors of the kings of Ur, but before the century was over the Amorite governors of the southeast, probably based at the ancient city of Lagash, asserted their independence in order to protect the dwindling water resources of their region. Under Gungunum they established a rival kingdom at Larsa, which soon wrested Ur from Isin. In short succession other Amorite chieftains established independent dynasties at Uruk, Babylon, Kish and nearly all the former provinces of the united kingom, until Isin effectively controlled little more than its own city and Nippur. With the more distant marches long since under Amorite rule, the nineteenth century was thus characterized by political fragmentation, with outbursts of warfare that embroiled all the separate petty states at one time or another.

The staging-area for the Amorite expansion

was probably the Jebel Bishri (Mount Basar), which divides the Euphrates River and the Syrian Desert. From here it was a comparatively short and easy march down the river to Babylonia or across the river to Assyria. The way to Egypt was not only longer but led through more hilly and difficult land. This may be one reason that the Amorite wave was longer in reaching the Egyptian border. When it did, it confronted just such a wall as Shu-Sin (c 2036-2028 BC) had built 'to keep Didanum at bay.' This wall is attributed by the 'Prophecy of Nefer-rohu (or Neferti)' to Amon-em-het I (c 1991-1961 BC), whose accession marked the beginning of the Twelfth Dynasty. But more than the wall, it was the extraordinary revitalization of the Egyptian monarchy by this Dynasty that was the real reason the Amorite wave broke harmlessly at the Egyptian border, and the characteristic petty-statism that it brought in its train was deferred for another two centuries.

The successive Amon-em-het's and Sen-Usert's (Sesostris) who made up the Twelfth Dynasty enjoyed long reigns and smooth patrilinear successions. They consciously adopted policies calculated to reestablish the political authority of the king, if not his divine status, as it had existed in the Old Kingdom. The Eleventh Dynasty had tolerated a large measure of local autonomy on the part of the separate nomarchs, but the new dynasty changed this. While continuing to endow Thebes lavishly with public buildings and confirming the nomarchs in their hereditary offices, the new kings moved the political capital back to the Memphis region, specifically to the new town of It-towy somewhere on the way to the Fayyum, an area which was now opened for development. They erected their tomb complexes, including more modest pyramids, nearby at Lisht and other sites south of Memphis favored in the Pyramid Age. They redrew the provincial boundaries and curbed the powers of the nomarchs by appointing court officials to supervise them and insure that tax quotas were properly met. The office of the vizier was reduced in importance, and the practice of co-regency was institutionalized, with the designated crown prince joining his father in the kingship at an early enough date to ensure a smooth succession.

An important literary source from this time is the story of Sinuhe, an autobiographical narrative describing a courtier's self-imposed exile to Asia at the time of the assassination of Amon-em-het I,

and his ultimate reprieve and return to Egypt. In the course of the story it becomes clear that the Egypt of the Twelfth Dynasty was successful in restoring not only royal prestige but also a healthy economy and successful military and foreign policies, whereby the borders of the state were successfully defended on the east against the Asiatics and on the west against the Lybians, while the Egyptians aggressively expanded southward into Nubia. The gold of Nubia and the turquoise of Sinai flowed into royal and private hands as a result and are only two examples of the prosperity that ensued. The material remains of the Twelfth Dynasty, chiefly recovered from tomb deposits, are eloquent testimony to the high standard of living in these two centuries.

Assyria and Babylon/the Thirteenth Dynasty (c 1800-1650 BC)

The small northern kingdom of Assur was one of the beneficiaries of the anarchy that afflicted Mesopotamia after the Amorite incursions and the fall of Ur. From the early-to-middle nineteenth century Assyrian merchants ranged far afield, exporting tin and textiles in return for copper and silver and establishing trade colonies in such distant places as Kanesh in modern Turkey.

About the early Assyrian kings we know almost nothing. Only with the 31st monarchy on the traditional Assyrian King List do we begin to find corroborative royal inscriptions, and these tell us little enough. Typical of this obscurity is the fact that the 37th king bore the same name, Naram-sin, as that of a ruler of Eshnunna. But whether they were the same, and, if so, which kingdom ruled which, is unknown.

Matters became clearer after the 38th king was deposed by a western Semite conqueror named Shamshi-Adad in about 1820 BC. Shamshi-Adad, who seems to have originated in Terqa, and may, in his youth, have sojourned in Babylon, had already conquered the middle-Euphrates kingdom of Mari, and when he seized power in Assur, he made it, for a time, the capital of his new realm, installing his son, Yashmak-Adad, as viceroy in Mari. Shamshi-Adad built temples in Assur, but he subsequently constructed a new capital called Shubat-Enlil, whose site has tentatively been identified as that of Tell Chagar Bazar in the Khabur region.

The inland kingdom over which Shamsi-Adad wielded his highly personal authority was prob-

ably reasonably extensive and fairly wealthy, but it would be quite misleading to style it, as some have done, the first Assyrian Empire. In addition to the fact that it was not really based on Assur, its dimensions both fluctuated and were, at best, hardly overwhelming. In any case, it was destined to collapse almost immediately after Shamshi-Adad's death.

A much more important center of power was rising in the south. The way had been paved by the kingdoms of Warium and Larsa. Warium, with its capital at Eshnunna in the valley of the Diyala River, included the ancient center of the Akkadian empire, while Larsa controlled the ancient Sumerian cities. These two Amorite kingdoms had succeeded in subjecting most of the independent city-states of Sumer and Akkad, and thus reversed the tide of particularism that had followed the collapse of the Ur III empire. They directed their expansionist policies into separate spheres of influence: Eshnunna north and west towards Assyria and upper Mesopotamia, Larsa eastward toward Elam. That they avoided an open clash was due largely to the existence, between the two, of a relatively small state that nonetheless maintained its independence from both and was destined shortly to succeed and surpass them as well as the kingdom of Shamshi-Adad.

The city of Babylon was a relative newcomer among the members of the old Sumero-Akkadian collection of city-states, though later it claimed a fictitious antiquity reaching back to antediluvian times. It was strategically located near the narrow waist of the Tigris-Euphrates valley, where the two rivers come closest together and whence the capital of successive Mesopotamian empires have ruled the civilized world from Kish and Akkad down to Ctesiphon and Baghdad. Throughout the nineteenth century it was the seat of an independent dynasty that claimed a common ancestry with Shamshi-Adad, and whose rulers enjoyed long reigns and an unbroken succession passing smoothly from father to son. In 1793 BC, the succession of this First Dynasty of Babylon (also known simply as the Amorite Dynasty), passed to Hammurabi (1792-1750 BC). In him we meet one of the great rulers of history, a man of personal genius and vision who left his indelible impress on all his heirs.

At first Hammurabi's prospects seemed anything but favorable. A celebrated Mari letter phrased his situation thus: 'There is no king who

Left: Egyptian model from 1850 BC.

Above right: Part of the stele of Hammurabi setting out the laws of Babylon. The code is one of the earliest known legal systems.

Right: Detail from an Assyrian depiction of a royal hunt.

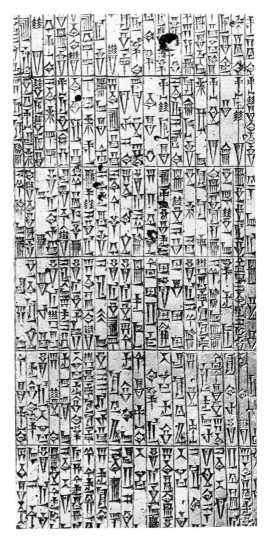

laws of Hammurapi, recognized as classic, were copied and studied for over a thousand years more. Framed by a hymnic prologue that cataloged his conquests and by an epilogue that stressed his concern for justice, the laws are less a detailed code than an expression of legal principles. As such they remain the starting point for the understanding not only of Babylonian but all Near Eastern legal ideals.

It is important, in spite of all this, to see Hammurabi's achievement in its proper perspective. His reunification of Mesopotamia, completed at the end of his reign, survived him by only a few years. His son and successor had to surrender much of the new empire before he had ruled more than a decade. The extreme south was lost to a new dynasty sometimes called the First Sealand Dynasty. Across the Tigris, Emutbal and Elam regained their independence. And the middle Euphrates was soon occupied by Hanaean nomads from the desert and by Kassites. The enduring legacy of Hammurapi lies rather in the legal, literary and artistic realms, where his reign marked both the preservation and canonization of what was best in the received traditions and a flowering of creative innovations.

Contemporary Egypt produced no comparable kings. Though the Thirteenth Dynasty (c 1786-1633 BC) attempted to govern along the lines laid down by the strong kings of the Twelfth, the royal power was diluted in many ways. The most obvious was the sheer number of kings attested – from 50 to 60 – which implies a fratrilinear succession and must have prevented the development of long-term policies by royal initiative. The patrilinear principle was, instead, reserved for the vizierate, a post that now grew proportionately in influence. Moreover, a rival dynasty, the Fourteenth, came into being and ruled in the western Delta, and others followed to begin the dismemberment of the pharaonic kingdom. The Amorite threat, which had been kept at bay under the Twelfth Dynasty, became more insistent. The Execration Texts, directed against the princelings of Syria and Palestine among others, suggest the growing inability of Egypt to keep them at arm's length, while Amorite names in lists of domestic slaves (chiefly women) from this period indicate one of the ways in which Egypt itself was increasingly infiltrated and the stage set for the 'Rulers of Foreign Lands' to take over much of the country.

The fall of Babylon/the Hyksos
(c 1650-1550 BC)

As the fall of Akkad ushered in the end of the Early Bronze Age, so the end of the Middle Bronze Age was marked by the capture of Babylon and Memphis. The two great capitals fell to different captors, but a common source may have set in motion the train of events that culminated in their defeat. To the north of both centers of high civilization an entirely new ethnic element now made its entry onto the stage of history: the Hittites. These first bearers of Indo-European names played a minor role in the nineteenth and early eighteenth centuries, when Hattic princes ruled Anatolia and Assyrian traders criss-crossed the highlands. But the last known Assyrian caravan set out about 1770 (under Zimri-Lim of Mari); the centers of trade were destroyed, and by about 1740, the Hittites were able to forge a united kingdom out of the remains of the Hattic principalities. The Hittite king Hattushili I (c 1650-1620 BC) felt strong enough to rebuild the city of Hattusha (from which he took his throne-name) in spite of the curse laid on it a century earlier by its Hattic conqueror, and to rule a growing Anatolian kingdom from this relatively remote base.

is all-powerful by himself: ten or 15 kings follow in the train of Hammurabi of Babylon, as many follow Rim-Sin of Larsa, as many follow Ibal-pi-El of Eshnunna, as many follow Amut-pi-el of Iatna, and 20 kings follow in the train of Yarim-Lim of Yamhad.' A lesser personality would have fallen victim to the struggles between these and other major powers of the time. But by an adroit alternation of warfare and diplomacy, Hammurabi succeeded where others had failed. He maintained the friendship of Larsa's Rim-Sin until his 30th year, when, in defeating him, he became heir to all that Larsa had conquered. He avoided challenging Shamshi-Adad, his older contemporary, but defeated his successor two years after disposing of Rim-Sin. Three years later, he conquered Mari, where Zimri-Lim had reestablished a native dynasty after the Assyrian defeat. Eshnunna and the lesser states across the Tigris fell to Hammurabi's armies before the end of his reign, and only the powerful kingdoms beyond the Euphrates – notably Yamhad and Qatna – escaped his clutches.

He was a zealous administrator, and his concern for every detail of domestic policy is well documented in his surviving correspondence. He is most famous for his collection of laws, which, in the manner initiated by Ur-Nammu of Ur and elaborated in the interval at Isin and Eshnunna, collected instructive legal precedents as a monument to 'the King of Justice.' That was the name he gave to the steles inscribed with the laws that were erected in Babylon and, no doubt, in other cities of his kingdom. Fragments of several were carried off centuries later as booty to Susa, where they were rediscovered in modern times. Some of the missing portions can be restored from later copies prepared in the scribal schools, where the

Soon his ambitions extended beyond the Anatolian highlands to the fertile southern plains that beckoned from across the Taurus Mountains. Cilicia fell into his power first, and the Cilician gates opened the way through the Amanus Mountains, the last natural barrier on the way south. But the Mediterranean coastal route was barred by the Amorite kingdom of Yamhad, centered on Halat (Aleppo) and still retaining some of its vigor. After neutralizing this threat, Hattushili, and more particularly his adopted son, Murshili I, therefore directed their principal efforts against the Hurrian kingdom of Carchemish, which controlled the Euphrates. After a long siege of the Hurrian stronghold at Urshu, the Hittites found that they could march unopposed down the rest of the Euphrates all the way to Babylon itself. Here they put an end to the rule of Samsu-ditana, last of the descendants of Hammurabi. The great city was sacked, and its humiliation was completed when the statues of its god, Marduk, and his consort, Sarpanitum, were carried into captivity.

The Hittites could not press their advantage farther, for they were now 750 miles from their home city of Hattusha, and Murshili had overextended himself. He returned home, only to meet his death at the hands of a palace conspiracy that plunged the Hittite kingdom into several generations of turmoil and weakness. The immediate beneficiaries of the sack of Babylon were, rather, the rulers of the Sealand who moved north from their independent stronghold in the old Sumerian south and, in the wake of the withdrawing Hittites, seized Babylon for themselves and thus qualified for inclusion in the Babylonian King List as the Second Dynasty of Babylon.

But their occupation, too, was destined to be transitory: within a couple of years the city was occupied by the Kassites, who had moved downstream from their foothold in the Kingdom of Hana on the middle Euphrates. With their arrival in Babylonia proper, a curtain of silence descended over the documentation from the area. For the first time since the invention of writing there is a nearly total eclipse of cuneiform textual evidence, and for the rest of the sixteenth century the Asiatic Near East was plunged into a dark age.

In the meantime the Amorite kingdoms of the Mediterranean littoral also reacted to the stirrings set in motion by the Hittites. Cut off from their kinsmen in the east, they looked in the opposite direction, toward Egypt, for new lands to conquer. Their peaceful penetration of Lower Egypt had begun together with the Thirteenth Dynasty, and before the end of that Dynasty they had succeeded in setting themselves up as rulers of the eastern Delta (c 1720 BC). By about 1675, they had acquired sufficient prestige and had assimilated enough Egyptian patterns of government to be recognized as an Egyptian dynasty in their own right, probably the Fifteenth. At first, these shared power with the legitimate pharaohs at Memphis, as well as with the other contemporary dynasties that had assumed power in the western Delta (the Fourteenth Dynasty) and in Upper Egypt (the Seventeenth Dynasty). They were known in the native sources as Hyksos, or 'Rulers of Foreign Lands,' and their ethnic identification has been much debated. Probably they included a mixture of stocks, but many of them, including most of their kings, were evidently Amorites. By 1600 they had captured Memphis, supplanted the Thirteenth Dynasty, and reunited all of Lower Egypt, while reducing Upper Egypt to vassal status. But their rule was felt as an alien one, and has left few monuments. A dark age settled over Egypt as it had over the Asian Near East.

The Feudal Era (c 1550-1400 BC)

The first century of the Late Bronze Age (c 1600-1500 BC) in Western Asia is virtually devoid of textual testimony, and we have to rely instead on archaeological evidence. This reveals the introduction of new technologies that had far-reaching repercussions particularly in warfare. The large-scale use of the horse-drawn light chariot increased the mobility and effective range of armies and the consolidation of far-flung empires. At the same time, defensive tactics improved as fortifications grew ever more impregnable and great fortresses arose to defy all but the most protracted sieges. Partly as a result of such developments, the map of the Near East presented a very different appearance in 1500 BC than it had 300 years earlier. In place of numerous small and medium-sized Amorite states, a few large non-Semitic royal houses now ruled the Fertile Crescent, assisted by a nobility based on the ability to maintain horses, equipment and retainers. The indigenous Semitic population was, at least for the time being, reduced either to the status of a semi-free peasantry or to that of roving mercenaries.

Just as geography had favored Shamshi-Adad at the beginning of the eighteenth century, so now it served to favor a kingdom similarly centered in the triangle formed by the tributaries of the Habur River in Upper Mesopotamia. Somewhere in this Habur Triangle, at a site still not rediscovered, lay the city of Washukanni, capital of an empire that stretched clear across northern Mesopotamia, to the Mediterranean in the west to beyond the Tigris in the east. The empire, called Mitanni, was headed by a small aristocratic ruling class whose names identify them as Indo-Aryans, a part of the western branch of a migration that was at the same time overflowing India. They invoked Indian deities and perfected horse-raising and horse-racing, employing in part an Indo-Aryan terminology for the purpose. Yet the kingdom they ruled was nevertheless a Hurrian state, for it was the Hurrian stratum of the population that made up the bulk of its chariot-nobility.

The Hurrians had begun to settle, and even rule, on the northern and eastern frontiers of Mesopotamia even before the end of the Akkadian empire (to whose fall they may have contributed). They had begun to enter Mesopotamia proper in increasing numbers in the neo-Sumerian and Old Babylonian periods. They had ruled such minor localities as Shushara (Shashrum) under Shamshi-Adad and had left their mark at Mari in the form of Hurrian incantations. But it was only now, with the creation of the Mitanni state, that they took advantage of their strategic location to assume a commanding position. The center of their power in the Habur region was known as Hanigalbat. To the east they claimed

Left: Statue of Teti-Sheri, the grandmother of Ahmose and Kamose (c 1550 BC).

Above right: A depiction of crop gathering in Ancient Egypt.

Right: A relief showing a well-armed Hittite warrior.

sovereignty over the client kingdoms of Assyria and Arrapkha, and to the west over those of Mukish and Yamhad. Most of the documentation comes from these client states rather than from the center of the empire, and it throws valuable light on the newly emerging institutions of a society thought by some scholars to have had a direct impact on the institutions of pre-monarchic Israel.

A separate Hurrian state grew up at the same time northwest of Mitanni. In the fertile plain later known as Cilicia, the kingdom of Kizzuwatna united the areas lying between Mitanni and the Hittite lands of Anatolia. It served both as a buffer between them in political and military terms and as a bridge in cultural terms. It was at least in part by this road that Hurrian literary and religious influences reached Asia Minor, where they were soon to play a major role. The Hurrians, however, were important beyond that, since they were transmitters of the older traditions of Babylonia, many of which reached the West – that is, the Hittites and Phoenicians, and via them, ultimately also the Greeks and Hebrews.

Although Babylonian culture retained its prestige, Babylonian power was in decline. The country was now securely in the hands of the Kassites, who had already controlled the middle Euphrates for over a century (c 1735-1595 BC) before they seized Babylon, and who went on to rule

Babylonia proper (which they gave the name of Karduniash) for over four centuries thereafter (c 1595-1157 BC) – longer than any other dynasty. They also conquered the Sealand in the south at about the beginning of the fifteenth century. Under Kurigalzu I they built a great new administrative capital named Fortress of Kurigalzu (Dur-Kurigalzu) in the strategic narrow waist of the valley. (Its traditional stepped tower, or ziggurat, is the best preserved example of its kind in Mesopotamia.) They adjusted their northern frontiers with varying fortunes in occasional battles with the emerging Assyrians, and one of their fifteenth century kings even met on friendly terms with Pharoah Tuthmosis III on the Euphrates. They evolved an essentially feudal society which both secured and diluted the royal power through grants of land and remission of taxes to favored retainers. But by and large they were content to depend on their inherited Babylonian prestige in order to seek a place for themselves in the shifting kaleidoscope of Late Bronze Age international relations.

This prestige had, in some sense, never been higher. Throughout the Near East the cuneiform script was being put to use in one form or another, and Akkadian was becoming the language of international diplomacy. In order to master the 'script and language of the Chaldeans,' as it was later known (cf Daniel 1:4), scribal schools arose as far away as Anatolia and Egypt, and their curriculum followed the Babylonian model. Many of the great scribal families of later Babylonia traced their ancestry to Kassite times, and it was probably then that the major works of cuneiform literature were put into their canonical form. Thus it was through the patronage of Kassite overlords and the mediating role of the Hurrians that traditional Sumero-Akkadian literature and learning spread far from its ancestral home.

In the west military and political hegemony was also passing out of the hands of Semitic-speaking peoples. A new dynasty of Theban rulers, the Eighteenth, had succeeded by the middle of the sixteenth century in driving the Hyksos from Egypt and reuniting the country. Its first king, Ahmose, previously a vassal ruler of

Left: An XVIII Dynasty papyrus showing Hathor, the cow-goddess licking the arm of a dead man as he enters the 'other world.'

Right: The coffin of King Tutankhamun, Egyptian boy-king of the XVIII Dynasty.

Below right: Relief showing Osiris flanked by the goddess of the 'other world' taken from the time of Amon-hotep III (1375 BC).

Thebes, is thus regarded as the founder of the New Kingdom, which his successors would transform into a true empire when they crossed the frontier into Asia and brought all of Palestine and Syria under Egyptian control. First, however, the southern frontier had to be secured. The first four pharaohs of the new dynasty (1558-1490 BC), while they conducted punitive raids into Asia, concentrated their greatest efforts against Nubia and the Sudan, where they created a virtual African empire. Queen Hatshepsut, who, as widow of Tuthmosis II, ruled Egypt for 20 years, first as regent and then in her own right (1490-1469 BC), even sent a commercial expedition down the Red Sea as far as Punt (the Somali coast) to bring back its exotic products. The record of this celebrated voyage decorated the magnificent mortuary temple that she erected for herself at Deir-el-Bahri, opposite Thebes, in the Valley of the Kings.

But it was left for her successor to forge a real Egyptian empire in Asia. Tuthmosis III (1490-1436 BC) had been pharaoh in name only during Hatshepsut's lifetime, but immediately after her death he launched a succession of campaigns into Retenu, as the Egyptians called Palestine and southern Syria. Seventeen campaigns in 20 years carried Egyptian arms as far as the Euphrates and reduced all the intervening city-states to vassalage. His greatest victory was won on the very first campaign, when he defeated the armies that had been combined, if not exactly united, under the prince of Kadesh at the great battle of Megiddo. Megiddo itself fell after a siege of seven months. This first 'Armageddon' (the Greek form of Har-Megiddo, 'hill of Megiddo') was duly commemorated in loving detail on the walls of the great temple at Karnak, a part of Thebes that was

now wholly given over to the worship of the sun god Amon-Re, patron deity of the New Kingdom.

With Retenu firmly in his grasp, Tuthmosis III even challenged the armies of Mitanni and eventually extracted a treaty that recognized a common frontier running between Hama and Qatna (*c* 1448 BC). His successors Amon-hotep II and Tuthmosis IV continued to maintain the Asiatic empire by repeated incursions into Palestine and Syria to receive the submission of loyal vassal-princes and compel that of the recalcitrant ones.

Thus the subjection of the indigenous Amorites was completed before the end of the fifteenth century throughout the Near East. There was, however, one exception to this rule. Since the emergence of the Amorites, cuneiform texts from very diverse regions had begun to make mention of a group of people called Habiru with ever increasing frequency until, by the fifteenth century, they appear in texts from all over the Near East. On philological grounds, these Habiru can be conclusively equated with the Apiru of Egyptian texts and with the Hebrews of the Bible. The word originally seems to have been used in a slightly derogatory sense, having such connotations as 'robbers,' 'dusty ones' or 'migrants.' These Habiru were not an ethnic, but a social entity. Though largely of Amorite stock, they constituted that portion of the population unwilling to submit to Amorite rule or, subsequently and more particularly, to that of their non-Semitic conquerors. Instead they chose to serve as roving mercenaries under successive masters or, alternatively, to band together in order to impose their own rule in areas beyond the reach of the various imperial armies. The latter was particularly true of the wooded hill country of Syria and Palestine.

There they maintained a tenacious and much maligned independence while the great powers were dividing up the cleared lowlands.

The Amarna Era (*c* 1400-1300 BC)

The Near East of the fourteenth century witnessed the convergence of so many of the factors that we have already isolated – ethnic, economic, ecologic, military, technical and so on – that its history can hardly be written in other than international terms. Because the records found at El-Amarna in Egypt, and similar texts from Asia, are characteristic of the period, and because the revolutionary events at Amarna itself were among the most dramatic of the time, it is appropriate to designate the entire period as the Amarna Age.

The immediate source of the new cosmopolitanism were royal courts. In each of the major states the capital city featured a courtly society where arts and learning blossomed under royal patronage, where foreign princes were educated while serving as hostages and where foreign princesses graced the royal harem. The last was perhaps most characteristic of the age, for although there had been individual queens of considerable personal stature earlier, the practice of dynastic marriage was now elevated to a high principle of statecraft. The new internationalism thus implied a much elevated status for women, and even a commoner of character and energy could rise to the rank of princess and first wife of a pharaoh such as Amon-hotep III.

The leading proponents of dynastic marriage (as of the education of foreign hostage-princes) appear to have been the pharaohs of the Eighteenth Dynasty of Egypt. This dynasty derived its original legitimacy from an ancestress (Tani) related by descent to the Seventeenth (Theban)

Dynasty and perhaps to the Nubians, and by marriage possibly to the Hyksos (Fifteenth and Sixteenth Dynasties). It displayed a strong matriarchal tendency in its early phase, climaxed by Queen Hatshepsut. When her step-son, Tuthmosis III, finally assumed sole reign after her death (1468 BC), he may have already been married to three queens thought to have been Syrian princesses, thus inaugurating the practice of dynastic marriages. The practice became official policy under Tuthmosis IV (1412-1402 BC), who recognized the importance of an alliance with Mitanni to counter the growing strength of the Hittites. After four rounds of negotiations, a daughter of Artatama of Mitanni finally entered his harem to seal the agreement. His son, Amon-hotep III (1402-1363 BC), pursued the policy most consistently. Although he made the Egyptian Tiy his principal wife, his marriage to Gilu-hepa, daughter of Shuttarna of Mitanni, was celebrated on an elaborate scarab, and he sought the hand of a second Mitanni princess. In addition, he succeeded in acquiring two Kassite princesses and one from Arzawa in southwestern Anatolia for his harem. His son, Amon-hotep IV (1363-1347 BC), succeeded to some of these queens by right of inheritance, but is most famous for his marriage to the beautiful Nefertiti, and for the lavish attention he bestowed on her and her daughters after abandoning the traditional cult of Amon at Thebes for that of the sun-disc (Aten) at the new capital that he constructed at Akhetaten (Amarna) and where he ruled under the new name of Akhenaten. The many novel artistic, literary and theological concepts spawned in these surroundings are among the most impressive in Egyptian history.

After Akhetaten's death the succession eventually passed, through one of his daughters, to her husband Tutankhaten, but now the Amun priesthood reasserted itself, the new capital was abandoned again, and the king changed his name, significantly, to Tutankhamun. His tomb near Thebes, miraculously escaping ancient pillage, has preserved for modern excavators the most elaborate burial deposits of any pharaoh. But he was himself a minor ruler of a declining power, for the Amarna interlude had exacted a high price in terms of Egypt's military posture and international prestige. It had been firm Egyptian policy, while accepting foreign princesses for the royal harem, to refuse to send Egyptian princesses abroad. But now the widow of the pharaoh

appealed to the Hittite king Shuppiluliuma (c 1375-1335 BC), who had by this time displaced the Mitanni king as the greatest monarch of his time, to give her a son of his own as her consrt. This remarkable request was fraught with consequences. When the Hittite king finally granted the request, the prince dispatched for the purpose was slain on the way to Egypt. The Eighteenth Dynasty came to an end in the hands of Ay (1337-1333 BC) and Horemheb (1333-1303 BC), two generals of non-royal lineage. Shuppiluliuma, for his part, revenged himself for the death of his son by declaring war on Egypt and taking captives from the populations under Egyptian protection. Although the Egyptians were powerless to oppose him, both of these actions constituted breaches of the treaties which by now bound Egypt and the Hittites. According to the 'Confessions' of Shuppiluliuma's surviving son and successor, Murshili II (c 1334-1306 BC), these treaty violations triggered their own penalty, for the captives brought a

plague with them which devastated the Hittite country and counted Shuppiluliuma himself among its victims.

The decline of the Mitannian power in the middle of the fourteenth century under the combined impact of Hittite pressure and the progressive disengagement from Asiatic affairs by the Amarna pharaohs set the stage for the emergence of Assyria as a major Near Eastern power. The ancient city of Assur on the Tigris, sacred to the god of the same name, had been ruled by an almost uninterrupted succession of foreign masters for a thousand years, but the accession of Assur-uballit (c 1365-1330 BC) marked a distinct change. The new ruler saw his chance and threw off the Hurrian overlordship of Mitanni. Disdaining that of Kassite Babylonia, which claimed to have inherited it, he began to negotiate on a footing of equality with all the great powers of his time, as well as to show the Assyrian mettle in battle, chiefly against the Kassites. The fortunes of Assyria and Babylonia were henceforth closely linked: dynastic intermarriages and treaties alternated with breaches of peace and adjustments of the common border in favor of the victor. The Kassites began to abandon their earlier, persistent efforts to shore up their sagging prestige by marriage alliances with Egypt and the Hittites, and at last recognized the Assyrians as their political equals and military superiors. But a deep-seated respect for the older religions and culture of Babylonia, which they regarded as ancestral to their own, constrained the Assyrians from following up their advantage – for the time being.

The Era of Migrations and the end of the Bronze Age (1300-1200 BC)

The delicate balance of power constructed on the novel ideas of international negotiations and accommodation in the fourteenth century survived even the ambitions of particularly strong rulers such as the Hittite Shuppiluliuma. But it was not equal to the threat from below; in the end it succumbed to the tidal waves of diverse new ethnic groups which flooded the Near East and destroyed the last vestiges of the age of diplomacy. At the outset of the thirteenth century, however, these momentous developments could hardly have been foreseen by contemporaries. Instead, war and peace revolved as before around the major powers. In the east, Adad-nirari I (1307-1275 BC) of Assyria fought with Nazi-maruttash (1323-1298 BC) at Kar-Ishtar at the turn of the century and, at least in his historical and epic versions of the event, won the day. In the west, the Nineteenth Dynasty ruled Egypt throughout the century; it is also known as the First Ramesside Dynasty, after its most illustrious member, the long-lived Ramses II (c 1290-1224 BC), who is sometimes regarded as the unnamed pharaoh of the Biblical book of Exodus. There is actually little to recommend this identification beyond the tenuous equation of the 'storage-city' called Ramses in Exodus 1:11 with Per-Ramses, 'the House of Ramses,' which was the name given by Ramses II to Tanis (elsewhere in the Bible called Zo'an), a city in the Eastern Delta which his dynasty, true to its lower Egyptian origins, used as its capital. What is beyond dispute, however, is that this reign, whose length was exceeded only by that of Pepi II at the end of the Old Kingdom, left its monuments all over Egypt and inspired a cult of the ruler that survived his reign by many centuries. Most of the inscriptions and reliefs commemorate the pharaoh's great encounter with the Hittites at the Battle of Kadesh on the Orontes River. Here, in his fifth year (c 1285 BC), Ramses encountered Muwatalli, son of Murshili II, and a worthy successor to his father and his grandfather, Shuppiluliuma. The battle of Kadesh, one of the best-documented in antiquity, ended in something of a stalemate, and left the Hittites in firm possession of northern Syria. Some 15 years later, however, it led Ramses and Hattushili III, a brother and successor of Muwatalli, to conclude an elaborate treaty of peace which is one of the more remarkable examples of its genre. Alone among the treaties of its time it is preserved in two versions, one in Egyptian and one in Hittite, and it was observed scrupulously, for both countries now faced a common danger, the immigration of the so-called Sea Peoples.

If there was any one event that may be said to have unleashed the migrations, it may conceivably have been the sack of Troy about 1250 BC, and the subsequent fall of the Mycenaean cities of the Greek mainland. The survivors of these catastrophes fled by sea (hence the collective name Sea Peoples) along the coasts. They sought new lands

to conquer and settle wherever the established powers were too weak to withstand them, and left their names scattered across the Mediterranean littorals and islands to this day, from Cilicia and Philistia (Palestine) in the east to Sicily, Etruria (Tuscany) and Sardinia in the west. The populations displaced by their arrival fled elsewhere to spread the process in a chain-reaction, until confronted by corresponding migrations from an opposite direction. Thus the Hurrians of Cilicia fled northeast into Hittite Anatolia, putting an end to the Hittite empire there; the Hittite refugees in turn moved southeast into the former Mitanni area of northern Syria. Here they encountered and joined forces with the Aramaeans, a new wave of Semitic-speaking semi-nomads moving north out of the Syrian desert. The Hurrians of Mitanni, in turn, fled northeast toward the area of Lake Van, where they coalesced with the ancestors of the Urartians. Further south, the

Amorite and other peoples of Canaan were squeezed between the Philistines occupying the coast and the Israelites moving into the land from the south and east. In an inscription of Pharaoh Merneptah (c 1224-1214 BC), the collective name of Israel first appears in an extra-Biblical source. Merneptah himself managed to hold off the Sea Peoples, and about 1190 BC they were decisively defeated in the Delta in a great land and sea battle that sent many of them westward across the Mediterranean.

This victory belongs to Ramses III and the Twentieth (or Second Ramesside) Dynasty. The Nineteenth Dynasty had come to an undistinguished end by 1200. Egypt fell briefly under the domination of a foreign usurper called Irsu (who may be identical with the Cushan-Rishataim of Judges 3:8,10) and the many Ramses' who restored Egyptian authority at home in the twelfth century were unable to save her Asiatic empire or

Left: The back panel of the throne of Tutankhamun. The Queen is shown annointing the King's collar with oil from the cup in her hand.

Right: Detail of the stone statue of Ramses II at Luxor.

Below: The Egyptian Empire in 1275 BC.

Below right: The great hall temple at Luxor. The pillars are separated by statues of Ramses II.

to stave off for long the end of the New Kingdom.

In Mesopotamia, meanwhile, the Assyrians had been more successful than the Babylonians in withstanding the new pressures and now pressed their advantage. Tukulti-Ninurta I (*c* 1244-1208 BC), one of the few intriguing personalities in the long line of Assyrian kings, dropped the restraint that had marked his predecessors' policy toward Babylonia. So far from respecting the sanctity of Babylon, he took its defeated king into captivity, together with the statue of Marduk, its god, razed the walls of the city, and assumed the rule of all of Babylonia in his own person. At home, he claimed almost divine honors and, not content with an extensive building program at Assur, he moved across the Tigris to found a whole new capital, which he named after himself.

But in all this he aroused increasing enmity, both for the sacrilege against Babylon and for the heavy exactions of his military and building programs. A reaction set in and, led by the king's own son and successor, the more conservative party imprisoned the king in his new capital and set fire to it. The fame of Tukulti-Ninurta was such that garbled features of his reign are thought to be preserved in both Biblical and Greek literature. Thus he is supposed to have suggested the figure of

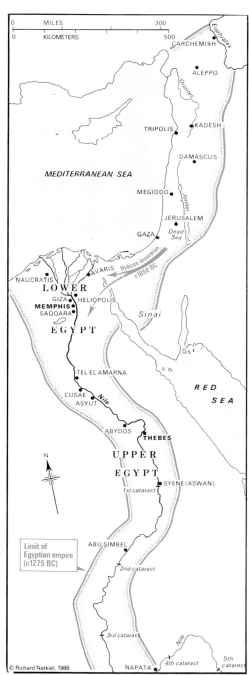

Limit of
Egyptian empire
(c1275 BC)

© Richard Natkiel, 1988

Nimrod, the conqueror and hunter, of Genesis 10; the King Ninos who built the city of Ninos according to Greek legend; and the Sardanapalos who died a fiery death in his own city according to another. Separating fact from legend, it is clear that his death ushered in a temporary eclipse of the newly emergent Assyrian power that was destined to last for almost a century. Thus the end of the Bronze Age was marked by the demise of all the great nation-states of the time, and new protagonists were to rule the Near East in the Iron Age that ensued.

Mesopotamia in the Iron Age

Meteoric iron was known and sporadically used at least as early as the Bronze Age, but terrestrial iron was virtually unknown outside of Asia Minor, where it is already mentioned in the Old Assyrian commercial documents. The Hittites were the first to develop a substantial iron metallurgy, which involved the fusing of molten iron with the help of bellows. With the collapse of the Hittite Empire about 1200 BC, their iron monopoly

was broken, and the superiority of the new medium for tools and weapons was quickly and widely recognized. The Bible recalls the advantage that it gave to the Philistines over the Israelites in the eleventh century (I Samuel 13:19-22). Archaeologists thus are generally agreed on about 1200 BC as the start of the Iron Age, though they differ on its end, which is variously equated with the beginning of the neo-Babylonian, Persian or Greek periods – or even of the Atomic Age.

The new age dawned on a radically transformed Near East. In Egypt, Ramses III was succeeded by eight more Pharaohs of the same name (1198-1085 BC) but these late Ramesside reigns, though exceptionally well documented, were undistinguished and led inexorably into the partitions and foreign domination of the Third Intermediate Period. In Palestine, Philistines and Israelites contended with each other and with the surviving Canaanites for the possession of the 'promised land,' the outcome in doubt until Saul, David and Solomon forged the United Monarchy out of the disparate tribes with their jealously guarded tribal heritages. In Syria and northern Mesopotamia a similar struggle ensued between the neo-Hittite and Aramaean newcomers to the area. A number of city-states, however, successfully fused these two elements into a hybrid Aramaeo-Hittite or Syro-Hittite culture. They probably were increasingly Aramaic in daily speech but favored a Hittite dialect and the so-called 'Hittite hieroglyphic' script for their monuments, which themselves were often provincial hybrids of many different artistic styles. In this way such city-states as Carchemish, Guzana, Kuhulua and Til Barsib were able to maintain an independent course until they were at last incorporated either into the expanding Assyrian empire in the East or the Aramaic nation-state that eventually emerged around Damascus in the West.

In Babylonia the waning dynasty of the weary Kassites, and the various dynasties that succeeded them, had only indifferent success in coping with the influx of Aramaeans and other newcomers. For several centuries the political history of both Babylonia and Assyria had little noticeable impact beyond the borders of Mesopotamia, and they cannot therefore claim the attention of historians in the same measure as in earlier periods. Occasional royal figures stand out for specific achievements; their names, in consequence, were copied by later kings and thus in some cases survived in Biblical or modern guise. Merodach-baladan I (1173-1161 BC), for example, was the last Kassite king who still exercised effective control over Babylonia; a considerable number of boundary stones (kudurru's) attest to the vitality of the system of land grants that characterized this dynasty's relations to its feudal retainers. Nebukadnezar I (1124-1103 BC) was the outstanding ruler of the Second Dynasty of Isin, which succeeded the Kassites in Babylonia. He is generally thought to have retrieved the statue of Marduk from captivity, elevated Marduk to his role as undisputed head of the Babylonian pantheon and commissioned the so-called Epic of Creation (enuma elish), a hymnic exaltation of Marduk often cited for its parallels to the Biblical versions of creation, though in fact it is more nearly relevant for the exaltation of the God of Israel in the Song of the Sea (Exodus 15). His younger Assyrian contemporary, Tiglath-pileser I (c 1115-1077 BC), was a worthy adversary who reestablished Assyria's military reputation and, while respecting the common frontier with Babylonia in the south and holding off the warlike mountaineers on Assyria's eastern and northern

borders, laid the foundations for her expansion to the west. An Assyrian campaign down the Tigris to the Babylonian frontier and then up the Euphrates and Habur rivers to rejoin the Tigris north of Assur had become an annual event by the time of Tukulti-Ninurta II (890-884 BC), and the petty chieftains of the Aramaeo-Hittite lands west of Assyria learned to expect swift retribution if they did not pay the tribute exacted on these expeditions. The 'calculated frightfulness' of Assurnasirpal II (883-859 BC) was graphically impressed on his visiting vassals by the reliefs he carved on the walls of his new palace at Kalhu ('Nimrud).

Under Shalmaneser III (858-824 BC), the Assyrian policy took on all the hallmarks of a grand design. The repeated hammer blows of his armies were directed with an almost single-minded dedication and persistence against Assyria's western neighbors and brought about the first direct contact between Assyria and Israel. The battle of Qarqar in 853 BC pitted Shalmaneser against a grand coalition of western states, including Israelites, Aramaeans, Cilicians, Egyptians, Arabians, Ammonites and Phoenicians. King Ahab of Israel contributed significantly to the infantry and more especially the chariotry on the allied side, which held the Assyrians to a draw if it did not actually defeat them. Ahab died within the year, but the coalition survived with minor changes, and met Shalmaneser four more times (849, 848, 845 and 841 BC). Only after the last of these encounters could the Assyrian king truthfully claim the submission of the western states, and the triumphal march across the now prostrate westland by 'Shalman' was recalled more than a century later in the first explicit Biblical reference to an Assyrian king (Hosea 10:14). The prompt submission of Jehu, who usurped the throne of Israel at this time, and other kings is graphically depicted on Shalmaneser's Black Obelisk, which may preserve the only contemporary pictorial representation of an Israelite figure known from the Bible.

Shalmaneser's reign nevertheless ended in disaster. His last six years (827-822 BC) were marked by revolts at home and the loss of all his western conquests abroad, and not until 805 BC did Assyria reassert itself there. It was Adad-nirari III (810-783 BC) who, by relieving the Aramaean pressure, was regarded as a veritable deliverer in Israel (2 Kings 13:5), and his stela from Tell al Rimeh records the grateful tribute of Jehoash of Israel (797-782 BC), among others. But Assyria was not yet strong enough to reclaim its western conquests. Urartu (the Biblical Ararat), a state based around Lake Van in what is now Armenia, rallied the remnants of the Hurrian populations who had fled upper Mesopotamia in the wake of the mass migrations at the end of the Bronze Age and now sought to restore its influence in northern Syria. Throughout the first half of the eighth century, Assyrians, Aramaeans and Urartians thus fought each other to a standstill in Syria while the Divided Monarchy briefly regained the economic strength and territorial extent of the Solomonic kingdom. Israelite tradition reflected the memory of these four decades of her resurgence and Assyrian weakness by attaching the legend of the near-collapse of Ninevah to Jonah, a prophetic contemporary of Jeroboam II (793-753 BC) or, conversely, by assigning the Jonah of legend to the reign of Jeroboam (II Kings 14:25).

But the Mesopotamian eclipse was far from final. Both Assyria and Babylonia were destined to reassert themselves once more and, indeed, to scale the heights of world fame and influence. The accession of Nabunasir (Nabonassar) in Babylonia in 747 BC seems to have been regarded by the

Below left: An Assyrian stone carving reporting the privileges granted to Ritti-Marduk by Nebukadnezar I.

Right: The Assyrian King Shalmaneser's army in battle.

Below: A marble slab depicting an Assyrian deity holding a pine cone and a sacred basket. To his front stands a court official.

native sources themselves as ushering in the Mesopotamian revival. Among other things, the scribes of Babylon inaugurated a reform of the calendar which systematized the intercalation of a thirteenth month, seven times in every nineteen years, according to the so-called Metonic cycle. Taken over later by the Jews, it continues as the basis of the Jewish luni-solar calendar to this day.

Babylonia was by now divided largely between urbanized Chaldaeans and still mainly rural Aramaeans, and since the Chaldaeans soon became the principal experts of Babylonic astronomy, the very word Chaldaean came to be equated with 'astronomer' or 'sage' in Hebrew, Aramaic and Greek. These astronomers now began to keep monthly diaries listing celestial observations together with fluctuations in such matters as commodity prices, river levels and the weather, as well as occasional political events. Perhaps on the basis of the last, they also created a valuable new historiographic record, the 'Babylonian Chronicle,' into which they entered the outstanding events of each year. In the Ptolemaic Canon, the 'Nabonassar Era' was recognized as a turning point in the history of science by Hellenistic astronomy.

Nonetheless, Nabonassar himself was but a minor figure. When he enlisted the help of his greater Assyrian contemporary Tiglath-pileser III (744-727 BC) in his struggles against both Chaldaeans and Aramaeans, the step proved fateful. Tiglath-pileser was a usurper, the beneficiary of still another palace revolt that had unseated his weak predecessor. He and his first two successors changed the whole balance of power in the Near East, destroying Israel, among many other states, and reducing the rest, including Judah, to vassalage. They found Assyria in a difficult, even desperate, military and economic situation, but during the next 40 years they revived it and consolidated its control of all its old territories, reestablishing Assyria's major power status.

Tiglath-pileser's first great campaign against the west (743-738 BC) involved organizing the nearer Syrian provinces under Assyrian adminis-

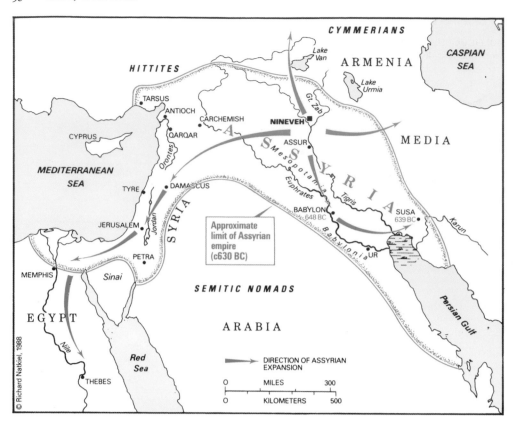

tration, regulating the succession to the king's liking in a middle tier of states and waging war against the more distant ones. The semi-autonomous Assyrian proconsulships were broken up into smaller, more tightly controlled administrative units. The Urartians were conclusively driven out of northern Syria, and the northern and eastern frontiers were pacified (737-735 BC). The second great campaign to the west (734-732 BC) was in response to Judah's call for help, according to 2 Kings 16:7, and reduced Israel to a fraction of its former size as more and more of the coastal and Transjordanian lands were either incorporated in the growing empire or reduced to vassalage. If Israel was allowed to remain a vassal for now, it was only because the Assyrian king's attention was briefly diverted by the rebellion of Nabu-mukin-zeri in Babylonia (731-729 BC). When this was crushed, Tiglath-pileser himself 'seized the hands of Bel,' that is, he led the statue of Bel (Marduk) in procession in the gesture of legitimation and ostensible submission to the Marduk priesthood that was traditionally demanded of Babylonian kings. The first Assyrian king who had ventured to take this step since the ill-fated Tukulti-Ninurta I, he was duly enrolled in the Babylonian King List under his nickname of Pulu, a name that passed, more or less intact, into the later Biblical and Greek accounts of his reign.

His short-lived successor, Shalmaneser V

Above left: Map showing the main directions of Assyrian expansion and the farthest extent of the empire by 630 BC.

Left: The gates of Ishtar, Babylon.

(726-722 BC), followed this example, reigning in Babylon as Ululaia, but left few records of his reign in Assyria. His greatest achievement was the capture of Samaria in 722 BC and the final incorporation of the Kingdom of Israel in the Assyrian empire, but the event is better attested in the Babylonian Chronicle and the Bible than in the Assyrian annals. Here he is thoroughly overshadowed by his successor.

Sargon II of Assyria (721-705 BC) took the name of the great founder of the Akkadian empire and lived up to it. He founded the last royal house of Assyria, called Sargonid after him. Perhaps the most militant of all the Iron Age Assyrian kings, he conducted a major campaign every single year of his reign (or had his annals edited to this effect); he frequently led the army in person and commissioned elaborate reports of his exploits en route in the form of open letters to the god Assur. He even died in battle on his last campaign, a fate unknown for Mesopotamian kings since Ur-Nammu of Ur. His major opponents were Merodach-baladan II, the Chaldaean who tenaciously fought for Babylonian independence; the Elamites, allied with Babylon at the great battle of Der before the Iranian foothills (720 BC); the inhabitants of the supposedly impregnable island-fortress of Tyre, who he finally reduced to submission; and the Egyptians, who for the first time were defeated by an Assyrian army and forced to pay tribute. The rump kingdom of Judah was no match against a figure of this stature, and Ahaz wisely heeded Isaiah's counsels of caution. When the accession of Hezekiah (715-687 BC) restored the anti-Assyrian party in Judah, retribution was not slow in coming. In 712 BC, Sargon dispatched his commander-in-chief, or *turtānu* (the 'tartan' of Isaiah 20:1), against Ashdod, a city allied with Judah, which was captured. The recent discovery of steles of Sargon at Ashdod on the one hand, and in western Iran (Godin Tepe) on the other, typify the monarch's far-flung exploits, as does his death on the northern frontier fighting a campaign far from his capital.

The accession of Sennaherib (704-681 BC) marked a new phase in Assyrian imperialism. No longer did the Assyrian army march annually toward new conquests. Only eight campaigns occupied the 24 years of the new monarch, plus two conducted by his generals. Assyrian power was approaching the natural limits of which it was capable. Although the warlike ideals of their forebears continued to color the records of the later Sargonid kings, the impression of sustained militarism that they create is an exaggerated one.

The new *Pax Assyriaca* was, of course, not unbroken. Sennaherib's unsuccessful siege of Jerusalem in 701 BC is well known from both the Assyrian and Biblical accounts (II Kings 18:13-19:37; Isaiah 36-37). His generals campaigned against Cilicia and Anatolia (696-695 BC), while his successor, Esarhaddon (680-669 BC), is perhaps most famous for his conquest of Egypt. Esarhaddon had succeeded to the throne in the troubled times following his father's assassination (II Kings 19:37; Isaiah 37:38), and was determined to secure a smoother succession for his own sons. The vassals of the empire were therefore forced to swear to abide by his arrangements, and the treaties to this effect, excavated at Kalah, have proved a new key to the understanding of Deuteronomy. The king's planning at first bore fruit, and for 17 years his designated successors ruled the empire side by side, Assurbanipal from Nineveh and Shamash-shum-ukin from Babylon. But in 652 BC, civil war broke out between the two brothers. After four years of bloody warfare, Assurbanipal emerged victorious, but at a heavy

price. The *Pax Assyriaca* had been irreparably broken, and the period of Assyrian greatness was over. The last 40 years of Assyrian history were marked by constant warfare, in which Assyria, in spite of occasional successes, was on the defensive. At the same time the basis for a Babylonian resurgence was being laid.

Assurbanipal had installed a certain Kandalanu as loyal ruler in Babylon, after crushing his brother's rebellion. When this regent died in 627 BC, Babylonia was without any recognized ruler for a year. Then the throne was seized by Nabopolassar (625-605 BC), who established a new dynasty, generally known as the neo-Babylonian, or Chaldaean, Dynasty. Although the Assyrian military machine continued to be a highly effective instrument for almost 20 years, Nabopolassar successfully defended Babylonia's newly won independence and, with the help of the Medes and of Josiah of Judah (639-609 BC), finally eliminated Assyria itself. The annihilation of the Assyrian capitals – Nineveh, Kalah, Assur, Dur-Sharrukin – between 615 and 612 BC is attested in part by the Babylonian Chronicle and even more tellingly in the archaeological evidence from these sites. Its impact on the contemporaneous world can still be measured in the prophecies of Nahum, and possibly of Zephaniah. Only Egypt remained loyal to Assyria, and Pharaoh Neko's efforts to aid the last remnants of Assyrian power at Harran under Assur-uballit II (611-609 BC) were seriously impaired by Josiah at Megiddo in 609 BC. The last Assyrian king fled Harran in the same year, and Assyrian history came to a sudden end.

Four years later, the Battle of Carchemish (605 BC) consolidated the Babylonian success with a defeat of the Egyptians by the crown-prince, who presently succeeded to the throne as Nebukadnezar II (604-562 BC). Under him, the Chaldaean empire fell heir to most of Assyria's conquests and briefly regained for Babylonia the position of leading power in the ancient world. Nebukadnezar's conquest of Jerusalem and Judah, with the exile of the Judean aristocracy to Babylonia, is the most famous of his many triumphs, but his own inscriptions prefer to stress his more peaceful achievements. These certainly matched his foreign conquests. He reconstructed Babylon in its entirety, filling it with magnificent temples and palaces and turning the city into one of the wonders of the ancient world. Its fame traveled far and wide with those who had seen it, and even after its destruction by Xerxes in 478 BC its ruins fired the imagination of later ages. Nebukadnezar's contemporaries were so moved by his achievements that they cataloged the topography of the restored capital in all its details, thus providing an unrivaled description of an ancient city. Among its more noteworthy sights were the ziggurat, the famous hanging gardens and the museum attached to Nebukadnezar's new palace. Here the king and his successors brought together statues, stelae, and other inscribed relics of the then already long antiquity of Mesopotamia. This interest in the monuments of the past thus complemented those neo-Assyrian efforts to collect the literary heritage of Babylonia that climaxed in the creation of the library of Assurbanipal.

The same antiquarian interest characterized the rule of Nabonidus (555-539 BC), who succeeded to the throne of Babylon after the three brief reigns of Nebukadnezar's son, son-in-law and grandson. He was not related to the royal Chaldaean house, although he was the namesake of a son of Nebukadnezar, whom he had served as a high diplomatic official. The biography of his mother, Adad-guppi, is preserved on inscriptions from Harran, from which we learn that she lived

for 104 years. Her long devotion to Harran and its deity may help to explain her son's similar, but more fateful, preoccupation. Virtually alone among the former Assyrian strongholds, Harran recovered some of its old glory under the neo-Babylonians and survived for many centuries thereafter as the center of successive forms of the worship of the moon god, Sin. According to Adad-guppi's biography, Harran lay desolate (that is, in the possession of the Medes) for 54 years until, at the very beginning of the reign of Nabonidus (555-539 BC), a vision informed him, in words strangely reminiscent of Isaiah 44:28-45:1, that Marduk would raise up 'his young servant' Cyrus to scatter the Medes. In obedience to the divine injunction, Nabonidus presently rebuilt the great temple of Harran and reconsecrated it to Sin. At the same time he singled out the other centers of moon worship, at Ur in Babylonia and at the oasis of Teima in Arabia, for special attention. The latter move, which carried Babylonian arms for the first time all the way to Yatrib (modern Medina), was particularly fateful. Though it may have been inspired by reasonable strategic or even commercial considerations, it was regarded as an act of outright madness by the Babylonians, and as a self-imposed exile of the king by later legend. The Book of Daniel associates this sojourn of seven years (or, in the cuneiform sources, ten years) in the desert with Nabonidus' more famous predecessor, Nebukadnezar, but new finds from Qumran show that other Jewish traditions linked it with the correct king. In any case, his sojourn in Arabia was resented by the population of Babylon, and the veneration of Sin there and at Harran and Ur was regarded as a veritable betrayal of Marduk, the national deity. Led by the Marduk priesthood, Babylon turned against Belshazzar, the son whom Nabonidus had left behind at the capital, and delivered the city into the waiting hands of Cyrus the Persian. In a bloodless conquest (539 BC), he assumed control of all of Babylonia and brought down the curtain on the last native Akkadian state.

The world beyond the near east

This survey of the history of the ancient Near East ends with the year 539 BC, the time of the Persian conquest of Babylon. (Egypt did not succumb to Persian armies until 523 BC.) The formation of the great Persian empire marks the beginning of a new epoch in Near Eastern history, signaling the end of the line of direct cultural continuity from the original civilizations of Mesopotamia and Egypt. Thereafter the prime growing points of civilization in the Old World were to shift to other localities: to Greece and Rome, Iran, India, and China. And all of this was indicative of the extent to which civilization characterized an increasing number of human societies around the globe.

Between the start of the third millennium BC, when we began our story with the origin of civilization in Mesopotamia and Egypt, down to the middle of the fifth century BC, the civilized mode of life had spread extensively – by diffusion from the early centers in the Near East into Iran and India to the east, and into the Aegean Islands and Greece to the west. Elsewhere around the world independent centers of civilization came into being: notably in north China and in the New World. Our coverage of the ancient world could well have taken up these other early beginnings along with those we have just surveyed. Their descriptions, however, will be left to subsequent chapters largely for reasons of symmetry, since the origins of Greco-Roman, Indian, Chinese and Mesoamerican civilization can be more satisfactorily told in conjunction with their later histories.

The Classical Civilizations

The idea of classicism as a historical concept originated in the European Renaissance, but the idea that in antiquity one's ancestors had fashioned a model state of existence worthy of contemporary emulation is common to most societies. Among the classical traditions that remain influential today some, like the Greek, Iranian, Chinese and Indian, can be accepted without question as being of major importance to the world at large. Others are influential on a smaller scale but are nevertheless of great importance to the peoples whom they directly affect.

Is it possible to identify any particular attributes that might account for the staying power of these civilizations? If we are careful not to assume too exact a uniformity among the various civilized traditions, some common patterns emerge. During the earliest pre-classical stages of civilization the fundamental inventions of intensive agriculture, metal working, writing, cities, kingship and state religious beliefs were perfected. The city states of Mesopotamia and China, or the temple-cultured states of Olmec Mexico and Egypt were essentially similar in terms of available technology and political organization. Each was confined to a narrow, well-defined locale. Each was focused on the ruler's palace or the temple of the local deity. Rulers were either conceived of as living gods or as the agents of the gods, but in either case their authority rested on divine right. And the rulers controlled, through a priesthood, the rituals by which the gods were worshipped and their powers were drawn to the protection of human society.

By contrast, all the classical civilizations were much more open. Part of this was due to technological improvements – better-designed plows, iron weapons and agricultural tools, coinage, less cumbersome methods of writing, horseback riding and the like – all of which strengthened the economic base of society and extended the geographic range of the centers of civilization, bringing entire regions into a single dominant cultural pattern.

At the same time, societies developed the political and ideological institutions necessary to cope with their enlarged and more varied populations. The change is visible in the shift from 'god kings' to philosophers and religious leaders. The classical age in nearly every civilized tradition is remembered as a time when philosophy first began to embrace systematic conceptions of the relationship between the individual and the government, to propound fundamental laws, and to devise ethical systems.

Above all, the classical civilizations succeeded in creating a body of written or artistic works that could be transmitted to later ages as the essence of a continuing ideological and linguistic tradition. In Greece the writings of Plato and Aristotle, in China the works of Confucius and Mencius, in India the Vedic hymns and Upanishads – each are looked upon as classical inheritances of undying value. To be sure, there were also bodies of legend that dated from pre-classical times – the Hebrew *Old Testament*, for example, or the *Homeric Odes*, or the Chinese *Book of History* – but almost all of these were given their transmittable shape during the classical ages.

A final aspect of the classical civilizations of the Old World, though not of the New, was the element of ethnic diversity. Historians have probably overused the concept of periodic barbarian invasions to explain turning points in Eurasian history. Yet it is undeniable that each of the major Eurasian classical civilizations was the work of the new ethnic groups who either overran the older centers or carried the elements of civilization to their own homelands. Classical Greece emerged only after the Dorian invasion of the Mycenaean homelands. Rome emerged in the contested area between the Etruscan cities and the Greek colonies of southern Italy. In Mesopotamia the Persians transmuted the civilization of Babylon and Assyria into the more durable Iranian tradition. Classical India was the work of the Indo-European invasions of the second millenium BC Confucian China derived from an earlier conquest of the Yellow River plain by the founders of the Chou dynasty. Perhaps invasion was not necessary for civilizations to move to the classical stage, but some form of innovative influence probably was. For, above all, what we have called the classical states rested on a broadening of the conception of human society. Government and ethical practice rested on general rules rather than upon practices tied to specific local customs, rules that could embrace a variety of peoples or races under a single government or philosophy of community.

In the chapters that follow, we shall look at the great classical civilizations, but the first of these will be the Iranian, for it, along with the Indian, is the most direct successor to the Ancient civilizations of the Near East.

Far left: A particularly fine bronze head of the Greek god Hermes, excavated near the famous battle site of Marathon. The quality of Greek sculpture remained unsurpassed until Renaissance times.

Left: An example of Attic red figure ware from the mid-sixth century BC. The painting depicts Dionysus sailing in a typical Greek ship of the time.

Right: The east face of the Arch of Titus in the Roman forum. The arch was erected to commemorate Titus's conquest of Judea and the fall of the city of Jerusalem in AD 79.

Iranian Civilization

Neither ancient Mesopotamia nor ancient Egypt produced lasting cultural traditions. In both areas the continuity of early civilization was broken by invasion and foreign influence. The valleys of the Tigris-Euphrates and the Nile did not cease to remain centers of wealth and learning. But just as first Ctesiphon and then Baghdad replaced Babylon, and as Cairo replaced Memphis, the old lands were occupied by new rulers with different origins and objectives. In fact both areas were subject to a bewildering sequence of foreign conquerors, beginning with the Persians in the sixth century BC, the Greeks under Alexander during the fourth century BC, the Romans and Parthians of the first century BC, the Arabs of the seventh century AD, the Mongols of the thirteenth century, and the Ottoman Turks of the sixteenth century to name only the major groups whose leaders appear as conquerors of the Near East. Thus it was the fate of both the river valley areas that had nurtured the earliest civilizations to be succeeded by 'classical civilizations' that would be the handiwork of other peoples.

For Mesopotamia, the successor civilization was that of Iran, the creation of a people of completely foreign ethnic origin, language and cultural background. From the time of Cyrus the Great in the middle of the sixth century BC to the comming of the Arabs in the middle of the seventh century AD – a period of some 1200 years – the plateau country of Iran became the homeland of the dominant military and cultural force in the eastern Near East.

The Persians seem to have had a powerful sense of cultural identity for a very long time, well before the advent of classical Iranian civilization, and that sense of being Persian, even when Iran was under foreign domination and Iranian civilization was deeply embedded in a medieval Islamic *ekumene* (world community), endured to re-emerge relatively unscathed in response to the pressures of nineteenth century European imperialism. This sense of identity has largely been maintained by a linguistic continuity: the Persian language of today differs little from that of the tenth century, which, in turn, derived from the Middle Persian of the Sasanid period, and ultimately from the Old Persian of the Achaemenid period. Iranian identity has been maintained, as well, in both literature and art in the form of a recurring disposition to use established forms and motifs, a preoccupation with the writing of history and, most obviously, a desire to seek escape from the ills of the present in the evocation of an imagined Golden Age in the remote past.

A somewhat different kind of continuity was provided by the priestly and bureaucratic elites – in Muslim times, the *ahl-i qalam*, or People of the Pen – which both promoted the cultural self-awareness of the Iranians and preserved traditional political and social values while serving foreign, and often barbarous, conquerors. These conquerors, in fact, were often slowly conditioned into accepting Iranian values, as, for example, the characteristically Iranian concept of Divine-right monarchy in place of the tribal Arab or Turkish concepts of authority.

Another approach to Iranian civilization is in terms of its geographical spread, rather like ripples in a pond that diminish in strength the further they go from the center. The Iranian plateau – more specifically, the area stretching northeast from the Zagros Mountains to the Amu-Darya, the heartland of Iranian culture – was the center of the pond, with the ripples spreading out west and south-west into Anatolia and Mesopotamia, north and north-east towards the Caucasus and across the Amu-Darya, and east through Afghanistan and the Punjab to Delhi and beyond. The cultural influence of Iran is the more striking because it was rarely the product of political or military aggression by the Iranians themselves. One may ponder the appeal of such a tradition to peoples who were, at least initially, so often its foes and its plunderers. The preservation of an Achaemenid pile-carpet of the fourth century BC in the frozen grave of a Scythian chieftain in the Altai, the Persepolitan element in the art of Mauryan India (or the Sasanid in pre-Turkish Central Asia), the adoption of Iranian concepts of kingship among both the Turkish Sultans of thirteenth century Delhi and contemporary Mongol rulers in Qipchaq, Mawarannahr and Iran itself, the contribution of Persian prototypes in shaping the development of Ottoman poetry, the Iranian element in the architecture, painting and life-style of the Indian Mughuls – these are but random examples of the pervasiveness of a cultural tradition rarely reinforced by military or political dominance.

The geographical dimension

The Iranian plateau, with an average altitude of between 1000 and 4000 feet, with little rain and great extremes of heat and cold, does not at first appear a likely setting for a dynamic and enduring civilization. Indeed, it has been said that much of the center of Iran has a climate and living conditions not very different from those prevailing in the interior of Australia where agriculture has been considered impractical on any considerable scale. Certainly the central desert region of Iran, the Dasht-i Lut and the Dasht-i Kavir, is forbidding in the extreme, and settlement on its fringes or penetration far into it has only been made possible by the exercise of maximum ingenuity in the quest for water.

Far left: A Median nobleman (left), carrying a bow in its case, and a Persian armed with a heavy dagger. The Achaemenid Persians under Cyrus the Great overthrew the Medes in the sixth century BC.

Left: This gold plaque, originally part of a belt buckle, was made by the Sarmatians around the time of the birth of Christ. The Persian stylistic influence is clearly visible.

Above right: Further remarkable evidence of the far-flung influence of Persian culture – an Achaemenid pile-carpet found in the grave of a Scythian chief at Dazyryk Altai.

To be sure, not all of Iran presents so uninviting a prospect for settlement. Around the rim of the plateau – in Azarbaijan, in the Caspian provinces, in the valleys of the Atrek and Gurgan rivers or on the upper reaches of the Hari Rud and the Murghab (now in Afghanistan) – regular rainfall or the volume of the mountain streams provide adequate water to ensure productive cultivation and, in parts, even a lush countryside. Elsewhere, however, water has to be brought to the surface and distributed sparingly, and there was never any question of constructing an irrigation-system comparable to that in Iraq.

Since surface water was inadequate, the Iranians hit upon a technical solution that ultimately spread as far as Libya, in the west, and Sind, in the east. This was the *qanat* or *kariz*, a device whereby water is carried through a series of underground channels from the base of a mountain or suitably high ground to a point where the water is drawn off into open channels to supply a particular village and its fields. The tunnels have a gentle gradient, and, being beneath the surface, evaporation is minimal.

Although their lengths vary, some *qanats* can be as long as 10 miles and can have shafts between 50 and 300 feet deep. The construction of a *qanat* is therefore a difficult and costly undertaking, as is the recurring need to keep the underground channels clear of debris and in good repair. Construction and maintenance together necessitate considerable capital outlay and usually only a landowner of considerable wealth will be able to bear the cost. Irrigation by means of *qanats* has thus played no small part in determining class relationships and accounting for the ubiquitous presence of the Iranian landlord at almost all periods of the country's history.

Peasants and townsmen account for only part of the Iranian population. Much of Iran is ideally suited for nomadic pastoralism. In much of Azarbaijan, Kurdistan, Luristan, Fars, Gurgan and Khurasan the tented tribesman with his moveable dwelling, his flocks of sheep and goats, his horses and his hunting falcons has always been an important part of the Iranian scene. It was as nomads – horse and cattle breeders – that the Aryan Iranians had moved onto the plateau in

successive, although perhaps numerically not very significant waves throughout the first half of the first millennium BC, and it is from their arrival that the beginnings of a distinct Iranian civilization may be dated.

Villages, towns and cities

For the cultivator the proximity of warlike nomads always represented a threat to life, livestock and property. The cultivators' response was to build fortified villages which, at their most simple, consisted of an open central area into which the animals were driven at night or in times of danger, surrounded by dwellings facing onto it and enclosed on the outside by a high windowless wall pierced by a single gateway. Such villages can still be seen within a few miles of Tehran. The Iranian town was, in part at least, an outgrowth of this prototype. Little research has been done as yet on the history of urban settlement in Iran, but what is clear is that virtually all early towns, whether they were comparatively modest focal points for the distribution of local goods and services or thriving entrepots on a major trade

Left: The ruins of the royal palace in the city of Persepolis, founded during the reign of Darius the Great (521-486 BC).

Above right: A carved relief at Persepolis shows tribute being brought to the King of Kings.

Below right: Darius the Great (seated) and his successor Xerxes I. Much of Darius's achievement was dissipated under later, less energetic kings.

route, depended for survival upon the two prerequisites of a regular supply of water and adequate defences against nomadic raiders. Except when sited within an oasis (as in the case of Isfahan), the normal location for an Iranian city was on a gentle slope at the base of rising ground, allowing *qanats* to feed the narrow open channels that provided the town with its water supply, while the massive mud-brick or rubble-filled walls, easily constructed from local materials, could resist all but the most persistent and resourceful attackers.

Most larger Iranian cities grew up around a citadel (*qaleh*), often sited on an outcrop of rock or a natural mound which gave it some elevation over the surrounding country-side. Under its protecting walls temporary stalls, and eventually more permanent *sarais* and warehouses, would be established, and gradually a town (*shahristan*) with markets, bazaars, places of worship and residential quarters would grow up between the citadel and the outer ramparts. Outside the walls was a belt of intense cultivation providing the town with most of its perishable food supply. In what was often a harsh, arid and antagonistic countryside the inhabitants of the town, or of the oasis of which it was the center, were naturally parochial in outlook, intellectually isolated and intensely suspicious of the world beyond their walls.

Tribe and clan, town and guild, and above all, family – these were the transcending loyalties, rather than state, nation or even dynasty. Tribe fought with tribe when not preying on the nearby settled communities; cities and even townships sought to divert a rival's commerce or water supply. In the larger cities each quarter was divided from its neighbor by walls and gateways which were closed at night. The homes of all but the poorest consisted of variants of a central courtyard surrounded by rooms facing inwards, usually on one level, enclosed within windowless walls which excluded prying eyes and ensured maximum privacy. This arrangement, with appropriate elaboration, applied also to the palace of the ruler.

The foregoing has stressed some of the constant factors at work in early Iranian society over many centuries, but the record of history is of course one of change, and it is to that eventful record that we now turn.

The early Achaemenid era

The founding of the Achaemenid Empire dates from the years immediately preceding 550 BC when Cyrus the Great, a tribal leader of genius with an established power-base in the mountainous country of Parsa (modern Fars) and the rich lowlands of Anshan (modern Khuzistan), embarked upon his remarkable career of conquest. He began by toppling his Median overlord, Astyages, whose kingdom extended over much of northern and northwestern Iran, with his capital at Ecbatana (modern Hamadan). Cyrus's predecessors are shadowy figures, including an eponymous ancestor, Hakamanish, whose name in Old Persian was rendered into Greek as Achaemenes, just as the Old Persian name of Karush became the Greek Cyrus. The various tribes and clans which composed his following were known as 'Parsua,' or 'Persians,' and during the first half of the first millennium BC there are Assyrian references to them moving slowly down the Zagros in the general direction of the Persian Gulf. Prior to the time of Cyrus, however, they were far less important than the more powerful Madai, or Medes, a people closely related to them in race and speech and occupying the mountainous country of what is now Kurdistan.

Not much is known about the composition of the tribal confederacy with which Cyrus, allied to the Babylonian usurper Nabonidus, replaced Median domination with that of his own Persians, but Herodotus, in an interesting passage in which he gives the Greek form of names for the most part unidentifiable in Old Persian, explains – with a fair degree of accuracy – how the Achaemenid royal clan stood in relation to the other tribes and clans collectively termed Persians:

Now the Persian nation is made up of many tribes. Those which Cyrus assembled and persuaded to revolt from the Medes, were the principal ones on which all the others are dependent. These are the Pasargadae, the Maraphians, and the Maspians, of whom the Pasargadae are the noblest. The Achaemenidae, from which spring all the Perseid kings, is one of their clans. The rest of the Persian tribes are the following: the Panthialaeans, the Derusiaeans, the Germanians, who are engaged in husbandry; the Daans, the Mardians, the Dropicans, and the Sagartians, who are Nomads.

The overthrow of Median hegemony by Cyrus and his Persians should be seen not so much as the replacement of one ruling elite by another as the re-structuring of a partnership between two peoples, ethnically closely related, in pursuit of a greater *imperium* from which both were to benefit. With the new confederacy an established fact, Cyrus set out upon a course of empire-building. In 547 BC he overthrew Croesus of Lydia, the ruler of an extensive kingdom in Asia Minor, with its capital at Sardis, and brought Persian arms to within striking distance of the Aegean. In 539 BC he captured Babylon, and at the time of his death in 530 BC his possessions stretched from the Syr-Darya and the Hindu Kush in the east, across Iran and Mesopotamia, deep into Asia Minor and the southwestern extension of the Fertile Crescent. He was killed fighting the Massagetae, nomadic Aryan tribesmen beyond the Syr-Darya.

His son, Cambyses (529-522 BC), conquered Egypt, but it was Darius I (521-486 BC) who extended the frontiers of the empire from the Danube to the Indus and from the southern shores of the Aral Sea to the Libyan desert, and to beyond the first cataract of the Nile. His attempt to invade mainland Greece was, however, foiled by the Athenian army at Marathon in 490 BC.

He did more than conquer, for he then established a broad administrative framework that for the next century and a half would impose upon those diverse and far-flung possessions a modicum of order and good government, a *Pax Persica* under which subject peoples could develop, with relatively little coercion from the center, their economic potentials and their cultural identities. In a rock-inscription carved at Behistun, near Kirmanshah in the heart of Media, Darius listed the 23 provinces or satrapies into which he had divided his empire.

Persian Satrapy/Greek or modern equivalent

1. Parsa/Fars
2. Uvja/Elam
3. Babirush/Babylonia, Syria, Palestine, Cyprus
4. Athura/Assyria
5. Arabaya Northern Arabia
6. Mudraya/Egypt
7. Tyaiy Drayahya/'The lands beside the sea', the Black Sea coast of Asia Minor
8. Sparda/Lydia
9. Yauna/Ionia
10. Mada/Media
11. Armina/Armenia
12. Katpatuka/Cappadocia
13. Parthava/Parthia
14. Zraka/Drangiana: Sistan
15. Haraiva/Aria: the country around Herat
16. Uvarazmish/Chorasmia: Khwarazm on the lower Amu-Darya
17. Bakhtrish/Bactria: the country north of the Hindu Kush
18. Suguda/Sogdiana: the country around the Samarqand region
19. Gadara/Gandhara: the country around Peshawar and on the upper Indus
20. Saka/The steppe country beyond Suguda on the Syr-Darya inhabited by nomadic Saca (Scythian) tribes
21. Thatagush/Sattagydia: the country around Kabul south of Bakhtrish and east of Haraiva, later known as Kapisa
22. Harauvatish/Arachosia: the country around Kandahar
23. Maka/Gedrosia: Baluchistan and the Makran coast

To this list, dating from the early part of a reign of 35 years, were added in later inscriptions Putaya (Libya), Kushiya (Ethiopia), Hindush (Sind), Skudra (Thrace), and Karka (Caria), but Persian rule over the first three cannot have been more than nominal. The same is true of the three different groups of Saca tribes listed in the Naqsh-i Rustam inscription: the Saka HaumaVarga, or Amyrgian Scythians beyond Sogdiana; the Saka Tigrakhauda, or 'pointed-cap' Scythians north of the Aral Sea; and the Saka Tyaiya Paradraya, or 'the Scythians who are across the Sea,' north-east of the Danube on the South Russian steppes. But even allowing for some inflation of claims, the extent of the Achaemenid Empire (an empire confirmed by hostile but impressed Greek observers) was very great indeed.

Decline after Darius

With the death of Darius I, not inappropriately styled The Great, there was a marked decline in the caliber of the ruling house, which did not produce a figure of comparable stature until, near the end of the line, Artaxerxes III ascended the throne in 359 BC. The effectiveness of the Achaemenid administrative system rested ultimately upon the Great King paying unremitting attention to the day-to-day business of governing the empire, but for the most part Darius's successors lacked the will or the ability to work the system effectively. If the Greek historians can be trusted, the enervating effect of a luxurious court, the interference of the eunuchs and women of the royal harem in the

conduct of public affairs, and disputes over the succession to the throne sapped the Empire at its center long before the rise of Macedonia confronted it with the only really formidable threat it was ever to know. On the other hand, a major factor contributing toward stability was the length of the reigns of the majority of Achaemenid rulers: Cyrus, 30 years; Darius I, 35 years; Xerxes I, 21 years; Artaxerxes I, 40 years; Darius II, 19 years; Artaxerxes II, 46 years; and Artaxerxes III, 21 years.

Darius I's immediate successor, Xerxes I (486-465 BC), barely retained his father's conquests intact, again failed to conquer mainland Greece in 480-79 BC and bequeathed to his successor, Artaxerxes I (465-425 BC), a weakened empire, with Egypt in revolt and a Greek counterattack threatening. A moderately competent ruler, Artaxerxes I, discovered a simple formula that had eluded both his father and grandfather: that the Greeks were easier to control by diplomacy and a policy of *divide et impera* than by naked force, a line pursued also during the reigns of Darius II (424-405 BC) and Artaxerxes II (405-359 BC). A last flash of greatness returned with Artaxerxes III (359-338 BC), a ruler of stupendous energy and military talent, but he appeared too late to save an empire in the final stages of

Left: The winged deity Ahuramazda dominates a panel above the tomb of Artaxerxes. In the Zoroastrian religion, Ahuramazda was worshipped as the spirit of Light, at constant war with Ahriman, the spirit of Darkness.

Right: Greek foot soldiers in combat with Persian cavalry.

Far right: A lion hunt provides the decoration for a gold scabbard of the Achaemenid period.

Below right: Two Persian seals, showing Ahuramazda supported by four-winged sphinxes, and a nomadic horseman firing backwards from the saddle in the famous 'Parthian shot.'

decay, threatened now by the dynamic eastward thrust of Alexander the Great's young Macedonian state and its unbeatable phalanx. In three great battles – the Granicus (334 BC), Issus (333 BC) and Gaugamela (331 BC) – Alexander defeated the last Achaemenid, Darius III (336-330 BC), who fled eastwards, only to be murdered by the ambitious satrap of Bactria.

The Achaemenid Empire was now at an end, yet the Achaemenids were to enjoy a posthumous revenge. Alexander and his Macedonians, even more his Seleucid successors, were seduced by the opulent splendor of the Achaemenid court and tamed by Persian ways and women (Alexander married two Iranian princesses: Roxana, daughter of a Bactrian chieftain, and Statira, daughter of Darius III). Alexander, perhaps influenced by the Achaemenid concept of a universalist state, ruled an empire that owed at least as much to its immediate Achaemenid predecessor as to more remote Macedonian antecedents. In the folklore of Asia, Alexander himself, far from being seen as an alien intruder, became 'Iskandar of the Two Horns,' not only a mighty conqueror but a wizard and a seer and most significant of all, the long-lost half-brother of Darius III!

Government under the Achaemenids

Wherein lay the Achaemenid achievement, or, to put it another way, how justified is the twentieth century Iranian national glorification of this remote period? Prior to the rise of Rome, the empire of Darius I was the most extensive political and administrative unit known to ancient man. Other empires there had been, but none that posed such problems of communication over such vast distances or of physical control over such diverse peoples. Yet the Great King's writ ran from the Nile to the Syr-Darya and from the Danube to the Indus. Predictably, though both the style and methods of government were intensely personal and authoritarian, in practice, distance necessitated a very considerable *de facto* delegation of authority to the satraps, or provincial governors, recruited mainly from the ranks of the Persian

nobility. Their responsibilities were immense and varied. At one extreme, they might have to face the complexities of handling the turbulent Ionian cities or of coping with the serpentine intrigues that lay beneath the impassive surface of Egyptian conservatism; at the other, they might have to serve as distant wardens of the marches, watching the movements of the unpredictable and always dangerous nomads. They kept the king's peace, collected revenue and tribute and led the contingents from their satrapies on the battlefield. Because of their physical remoteness from the seat of government they naturally possessed a considerable degree of initiative, but this immunity from close control was curbed by the maintenance of a system of post-roads, unique in the fifth century BC, along which the messengers of the Great King rode back and forth, bearing the royal commands and returning with information regarding the state of satrapies.

At the center, fiscal and chancellery methods followed Babylonian and Elamite predecents, for the Achaemenids were quick to adopt the practices of their more experienced neighbors and to use foreign ideas or techniques to meet their needs. Such was especially the case in the development of monarchical institutions. The influence of pre-Islamic Iranian monarchy was rooted in two distinct traditions – the concept of divine kingship, with its roots in Mesopotamian culture, and a no less pervasive concept of the ruler as the leader of a war-band, with its origin in the period of the Iranian migrations. The title 'King of Kings' was probably adopted by the Achaemenids from the conquered Medes and almost certainly exemplified the kind of loose allegiance exacted by both Median and Persian rulers from subordinate chieftains. It was a relationship with distinctly feudal and chivalric overtones, a striking contrast to the Mesopotamian tradition of the God-King. The result was an ambiguity in Achaemenid kingship that was to be a recurring theme in Iranian history. Among the subject peoples of the Near East the king was absolute lord by right of conquest; among the

Iranians he was first and foremost a tribal and clan leader, although on the grandest scale imaginable.

What does seem to have been characteristic of Achaemenid rule was the enunciation of a lofty and novel intent to govern in accordance with the moral precepts of Mazdaism. And this went a tolerance towards alien faiths and cultures that was one of the most striking aspects of Achaemenid rule. 'Of all men,' noted Herodotus, 'the Persians most welcome foreign customs.' The Achaemenids, when they imposed their rule over conquered peoples, demanded obedience and the regular payment of tribute, but little more. Indeed, there was for the most part a prudent spirit of conciliation in the way they dealt with their subjects. Cyrus restored the temples of Babylon and permitted the Jews to return to Jerusalem, while both Cambyses and Darius I were careful to establish in the minds of the Egyptians a belief that their rule constituted no break in the continuity of the dynastic past.

The religion of the Achaemenids, centered upon the worship of Ahuramazda, with its emphasis upon Light and Truth in conflict with Darkness and 'the Lie,' laid great stress upon personal responsibility for good conduct. Although the precise relationship between the Achaemenids and Zoroaster, probably an older contemporary of Darius I, remains obscure, it seems likely that both the cult of Ahuramazda, which flourished in the west, and the Zoroastrianism of the Gatha hymns, originating in the northeast, derived from common spiritual roots. In any case, the precepts of these cults appear to have had a powerful influence on the governing style of the Achaemenids, and their effects did not vanish with the murder of Darius III or the burning of Persepolis. Alexander's unfulfilled dream of an imperial partnership between his Macedonian and Persian subjects, the universalism and syncretism that flourished so luxuriantly in the Hellenistic east and, above all, the governing framework of the Mauryan Empire in India all show traces of the Achaemenid heritage.

The nomadic challenge

Whether in practice Achaemenid rule was less harsh or more responsive to the needs of the subject population than that of preceding or contemporary conquerors is, however, an open question. Persian rule seems to have compared favorably enough with that of the Assyrians or the Romans, but it is certainly true that with some of their subject peoples the Persians proved unable to achieve any kind of lasting modus vivendi, particularly where the indigenous traditions were wholly alien to those of Iran. In Egypt revolt followed revolt in monotonous succession. And with the nomadic peoples of the Eurasian steppe the Achaemenids experienced even less success. Cyrus was killed in battle with the Massagetae. Darius I's elaborate expedition against the Scythian tribes north of the Black Sea ended in disaster. And even Alexander (in the role of successor to the Achaemenid Great King) encountered his most formidable opponents among the nomad warriors beyond the Hindu Kush and the Amu-Darya. Even then, the pastoral nomadic peoples of Central Asia already enjoyed a military superiority over their sedentary neighbors, and this was to last until the advent of firearms on the steppes. As mounted warriors they possessed a mobility unknown to armies recruited largely from peasant cultivators fighting on foot, and those tribes which specialized in horse-breeding enjoyed something like a monopoly of these precious beasts. Also, the fact that the wealth of the nomads lay in their flocks and that their dependents participated with them in a life of migration from old pastures to new rendered them virtually invulnerable to punitive raiding by the forces available to their sedentary neighbors. Finally, in the compound bow, habitually shot from the saddle and skillfully handled even at the gallup, the nomads possessed a weapon against which their opponents could offer no resistance other than to shelter behind protective walls – a lesson dearly learned by the Romans in their wars with the Parthians. For the mounted archer was, in a sense, born and not made. Only a way of life that required from the earliest childhood expert horsemanship and lifelong practice in handling the bow could make him what he was. These were not skills that village-bound cultivators or city-bred artisans, recruited in an emergency for short-term service, could ever be expected to acquire.

It would, however, be wrong to suppose that unceasing enmity governed the relations between the Achaemenids and the nomads beyond the imperial frontier. Some of the nearer tribes were incorporated, at least nominally, within the satrapal framework, a delegation of 'pointed-cap' Sacas marched in the procession of tribute-bearers at Persepolis and a contingent accompanied Xerxes I into Greece. Then, as always, there was a degree of economic interdependence between the cultivated lands and the steppe. Nomads, however self-sufficient in most respects, looked to their sedentary neighbors to obtain metal utensils, weapons, small quantities of cereals and luxury commodities of various kinds for their ruling elites. In return, the nomads traded livestock, hides, leather, slaves, gold from the Urals and the products of the far north – amber and, at a later date, mammoth-ivory. This pattern of exchange would endure for centuries.

Life in Iran

The sources for early Iranian history, with their emphasis upon warfare and the activities of the ruler, provide little material for reconstructing the way of life of the ordinary inhabitants of the Iranian plateau. The extent of the population and its distribution and the relative prosperity of different satrapies remain for the most part matters for conjecture, although there is some ground for assuming that the western and central part of Iran was more prosperous and more densely populated than the east or northeast. The majority of Iranians were sedentary cultivators of farming land which, in theory, belonged to the king, who distributed much of it to his nobles as fiefs in return for military and administrative services. With the noble upon whose estate he worked, the cultivator probably maintained a quasi-feudal relationship, mitigated by the fact that he was also a military retainer and was perhaps often bound to his lord by ties of tribe or clan. Like every other able-bodied Persian, he was liable for military service. On the royal estates much of the

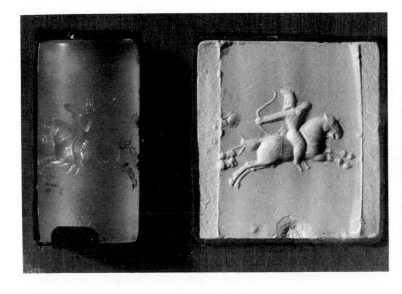

labor was performed by slaves, presumably prisoners of war, but surviving evidence from Persepolis shows them to have been better paid than free labor, not surprisingly perhaps, since they were government property. The Achaemenids also established military colonies in the conquered territories, and since these appear to have been settled with Persians, it is possible that this implies population-pressure in the Achaemenid homeland of Fars.

Irrigation by means of *qanats* was already widely practised, and it was perhaps under the *Pax Persica* that *qanat*-irrigation spread as far afield as Libya, Sind and Chinese Turkestan, while the so-called 'Persian Wheel' for raising water to the surface and, in the east, the vertical windmill, were also in general use. The principal crops were wheat, barley and alfalfa clover, the last grown mainly in Media as fodder for the powerful Nesaean horses which so aroused the admiration of the Greeks. The staple food of the entire population was wheat; rice, today so important a part of the Iranian diet, was virtually unknown in Achaemenid times.

A wide range of temperate fruits and vegetables were also consumed, but notwithstanding the Greek association of peaches and apricots with Iran, these fruits were first cultivated by the Chinese and did not reach Iran before the second century BC, whence they quickly passed into Europe. The grape-vine was extensively cultivated and much wine was drunk, Strabo noting at a somewhat later date the peculiar excellence of the wines of Margiana and Aria, the country around Marv and Herat. On the other hand, the watermelon, so long a basic item in the diet of all classes in the Muslim east, was still unknown and did not reach Iran (perhaps from India) before the Sasanid period.

Though only a minority of the total population were pastoralists, they were a growing minority, and there was a slow but steady shift in the use of land from cultivation to grazing. Stock-rearing was becoming a major activity, especially horse-breeding, since heavy cavalry was so much a part of the military effectiveness of the Achaemenids and, to a far greater extent, of the Arsacids and Sasanids. Unlike the short, squat horse native to the steppe, the horse of the Iranian uplands, with its powerful neck and chest and its well-formed feet, was an ideal cavalry mount, the 'blood-sweating' celestial horses of Farghana so much desired by the T'ang Emperors.

Apparently all classes of the population ate meat whenever they could and, in addition, their livestock – cattle, horses, camels, sheep and goats – provided valuable by-products such as leather, wool and hides. Indigenous textiles were mainly of wool, while most other fabrics were imported – cotton from Sind, for example, and linen from Egypt. For the garments of the wealthy gold and silver thread was much favored, as was silk, which probably entered the country only irregularly and in limited quantities. Herodotus noted that upper-class Persian delighted in sumptuous costumes, which were worn even on the battlefield.

Only a small proportion of the total population lived in the larger towns or cities, and of these many would have been foreign slaves or artisans. Textiles apart, probably most urban craftsmen were employed in metallurgy) of some kind. Few of the towns can have been very large by modern standards, and this would have been true of even the seat of government in most satrapies. Artacoana, for example, the headquarters of the satrap of Haraiva (Aria) in the vicinity of Herat, was probably little more than a market center for local produce from the Hari Rud valley. The only city in Iran to compare in size or importance with Babylon or Lydian Sardis was the capital, Susa, the old Elamite metropolis close to the Karkheh river in Khuzistan. The former Median capital of Ecbatana (modern Hamadan) also had some importance, due partly to its central location on the main trade-route from the Tigris up to the plateau, and partly because it was the summer-residence of the court. Pasargadae, deep in the mountains of Fars, was probably built by Cyrus as a royal retreat and a stronghold for storing treasure. The same was true, although on a far vaster scale, of Persepolis itself, located on a site no less remote, but significantly close to the Achaemenid royal tombs at Naqsh-i Rustam. Persepolis seems to have been conceived of by Darius I, its original builder, as a purely ceremonial residence, the setting for the elaborate solemnities with which the Great King received the annual tribute of his far-flung empire, and where he celebrated in splendor the Nuruz, the Iranian New Year festivities. The permanent population of Persepolis was probably never very great and the enormous platform upon which the palace was built seems not to have been surrounded by a large residential area. Before the time of Alexander no Greek is known to have visited or even made mention of this extraordinary monument, and it was perhaps its peculiar function as a kind of dynastic palladium of the empire that accounts for Alexander's uncharacteristic order for its destruction.

Of the Persians themselves there emerge from the pages of the Greek historians a striking series of vignettes in which the code of behavior is clearly feudal, emphasising ideals of courage, loyalty and service to the king. Hunting, horsemanship and wrestling were the chief pastimes of the elite, and it is interesting to note that Darius I had heard of the famous wrestler Milon of Croton, whose daughter married his runaway physician Democedes. Although the Greeks noted a certain formality in the conduct of the Persians towards each other, as well as an ingrained habit of deference in the presence of superior rank, the prevailing impression was of a pleasure-loving people, much given to feasting and wine-drinking, with polygamy and the keeping of concubines widely practised among the wealthy. In Athenian eyes the Great King and his soldiers were, of course, architypes of 'Oriental Despotism,' but there was also a grudging respect for their Persian foes, a respect echoed in the Hebraic memory of the unswerving 'law of the Medes and Persians, which altereth not.'

The Macedonian interlude and the Seleucids

Alexander died too soon after his conquest of the Achaemenid Empire to attempt any major restructuring of its institutions, but his establishment of military colonies, already a feature of Achaemenid rule, and his founding of cities in the relatively unpacified east were to have considerable significance in the future. In choosing the sites of the latter he displayed an unerring eye for a strategic location, exemplified by the continuing importance century after century of Alexandria-in-Ariana (Herat) and Alexandria-in-Arachosia (Kandahar). His death left the situation in Iran fluid and uncertain, but when his former general, Seleucus, entered Babylon in 312 BC, and when the eastern provinces submitted, it was obvious to all that there was still a Persian Empire spanning the Middle East from the Orontes to the Indus, albeit

Left: The palace of Darius at Persepolis.

Right: Camels formed part of the livestock of the peoples of the Achaemenid Empire.

Far right: The craftsmen of ancient Persia were skilled in metalwork, as this gold jug with its lion-headed handle testifies.

Below: Darius the Great is the seated figure at the center of this Greek depiction of the luxurious Achaemenid court.

now with an admixture of Hellenistic traditions overlaying those of Achaemenid Persia.

Seleucus I (312-280 BC) followed Alexander's example in founding military colonies and cities in which the population was predominantly Greek or Macedonian. The most important of these was his capital Seleucia, built close to Babylon, which it superseded as a metropolis. He also founded no less than five cities which he named in honor of his Iranian wife, Apama, the daughter of the Sogdian chieftain, Spitamenes, Alexander's most formidable opponent. Their half-Iranian son, Antiochus I (280-261 BC), proved himself to be a vigorous warden of the northeastern marches during his father's lifetime, repelling Saca invasions and strengthening the defenses of the Achaemenid settlement at Marv, which he renamed Antiochia. But when he eventually succeeded his father he became embroiled in affairs in the west, and the eastern provinces were in consequence left to go their own way.

In retrospect, it is clear that the besetting weakness of the Seleucid Empire was its rulers' preoccupation with Syria and Asia Minor at the expense of the dangerous northeastern frontier. As early as 304 BC Seleucus I had felt compelled to cede the satrapies east of Sistan (but probably excluding Aria) to the Mauryan ruler of northern India, Chandragupta (died *c* 297 BC), in exchange for a matrimonial alliance and 300 war-elephants. By the middle years of the third century BC Parthia, east of the Caspian Sea, and Hyrcania, due south of it, were in the hands of invading nomads, the Parni. Bactria sheltered a vigorous Greek principality founded by Diodotus I (*c* 247-235 BC) and consolidated by his son, Diodotus II (*c* 235-225 BC). This line was shortly afterwards superseded by a certain Euthydemus of Magnesia, whose son, Demetrius I (*c* 189-167 BC), perhaps threatened by Saca pressure from across the Amu-Darya, took advantage of the decay of Mauryan power to cross the Hindu Kush and advance first into Kapisa, due

Above: Head of a Sasanid king.

Left: Ctesiphon, originally founded by the Parthian Mithradates I in the second century BC, was later adopted by the Sasanids as the capital of their powerful empire.

Below right: Persian noblemen of around the second century AD; a typical feature is the costume of tunic and baggy trousers.

north of Kabul, and then into Arachosia. (The fortunes of this Graeco-Bactrian kingdom and of Greek rule in the Punjab will be treated later in the account of the early history of the Indian subcontinent.) In Iran, Seleucid rule lasted for little more than half a century, and its legacy was accordingly slight. It favored the growth of urban life, with an accompanying increase in the Greek and Macedonian element in the population, and it spread a fairly thin veneer of Hellenistic culture, mainly in the towns and cities, which the new rulers of the country, the Parthians, at first absorbed with considerable enthusiasm.

The Arsacid era

During the reign of Seleucus II (246-226 BC) the Seleucid Empire was first threatened by the appearance of two agressive neighbors on its northern marches, the Graeco-Bactrian kingdom of Diodotus I and the confederacy of the Parni, or Parthians. The Parni were an Iranian people, perhaps distant kin of the Saca tribes to their north, and their original homeland was probably on the lower Amu-Darya south of the Aral Sea, where they were nomadic horse and cattle-breeders. Around the middle years of the third century BC they were hovering in the vicinity of the lower Hari Rud, whence they were expelled by Diodotus I, who drove them into the Seleucid satrapy of Parthia, due east of the Caspian. There they rapidly established a reputation as formidable mounted-archers governed by a fierce warrior code. Their chieftains were two brothers, Arsaces and Tiridates, and although Arsaces fell in battle around 248 BC, Tiridates consolidated his hold over what is today Gurgan and Mazandaran, establishing his headquarters at the former Greek settlement of Hecatompylos (perhaps Shahr-i Qumis, near Damghan). Control of the Elburz region provided an excellent base from which to embark upon the conquest of the plateau, and under the leadership of Mithradates I (c 171-138 BC) the whole region from the Helmand and the Hari Rud, in the east, to the Euphrates, in the

west, was brought under Arsacid control. On the Tigris, close to the commercial entrepot of Seleucia, Mithradates constructed a great fortified camp at Ctesiphon, where he established his headquarters. The site was well chosen for the capital of a growing empire. It lay at the crossroads of the Middle East, a pledge and a proof of imperial ambitions, and centuries later the Sasanid supplanters of the Arsacids would likewise make it the seat of their government.

At this stage the Arsacid dynasty possessed no true imperial ideology, although it was perhaps no more than natural that in taking over from the Seleucids they adopted some of their imperial pretensions and also demonstrated a token appreciation of Hellenistic civilization. But Arsacid control over the vast territories they had conquered was still fragile. Two rulers in rapid succession were killed during the course of fighting the Saca nomads on the northeastern marches, and province after province threw off its allegiance. Thus the work of empire-building had to begin all over again, this time by Mithradates II (c 123-87 BC).

Mithradates' most pressing task was to restore Parthian authority in his western provinces, but once this was done he turned eastward to deal with the Saca menace, compelling those tribes already established in Sistan and in Aria to recognize his suzerainty, while driving the remnant of the invaders north of the Paropamisus back across the Amu-Darya. During this time, too, diplomatic and commercial exchanges with China were beginning to reveal the central role of the Parthian Empire in the trans-continental caravan trade and, in particular, in the transit of Chinese silk to the Mediterranean world, an important source of revenue for an Iranian state by no means favored with natural resources.

The Roman threat

The death of Mithradates II was followed, as was so often to be the case in Arsacid history, by a period of weakness that coincided with the beginning of Roman probing in the west. On balance,

the evidence suggests that Parthia constituted in those early years no conceivable threat to Rome's Mediterranean hegemony and that it was Rome's failure to comprehend the real strength of her mysterious eastern neighbor that initiated the protracted conflict which ensued. What is certain is that in the recurring cycles of debilitation and recovery characteristic of the five centuries of Arsacid rule, Roman intervention, whether military or diplomatic, played a consistently disruptive role.

The second half of the first century BC, spanning the reigns of Orodes II (c 57-37 BC) and Phraates IV (c 38-02 BC), was one of the phases of recovery. It had been ushered in by a victory over the Romans at Carrhae in 53 BC, the result of the co-ordinated tactics of the Parthian heavy cavalry, with its laminated armor and long lances, and light mounted archers, whose mobility and skill in use of the compound bow were thereafter to give the Romans a healthy respect for the 'Parthian shot.' Carrhae, a personal triumph for the young chieftain of the Suren clan, was followed by the Persian invasion of Syria in 51 BC and again in 40-38 BC Orodes II was murdered by his son, Phraates IV, but under the new ruler the Parthians continued to retain the advantage over their Roman opponents, and it was Phraates who drove back the invading army of Mark Antony in 36 BC, a feat that no doubt contributed to the more prudent policy of military disengagement and regularized intercourse between the two empires that was later initiated by Augustus.

The first stage of the struggle with Rome seems both to have aroused Arsacid imperial aspirations and to have intensified their awareness of their Iranian – as opposed to Hellenistic – heritage, and it was from this period that the Arsacid dynasty began to claim Achaemenid descent. This search for legitimization deriving from the Iranian past was intensified during the first half of the first century AD, when aggressive Roman diplomacy in the internal affairs of Parthia seriously weakened a state in which one ineffectual ruler after another succeeded to an unstable throne by usurpation and assassination. This period of rule of royal puppets subservient to a domineering and truculent nobility, divided against itself by Roman intrigues, produced a predictable, if long-delayed, reaction. As early as AD 12 the line of Mithradates I had been replaced by a cadet line descended from Arsaces, but it was not until the accession of Vologeses I (51-80) that Parthia again had a ruler who was master in his own house and strong enough to set the regime on a new course. During his reign the title of 'King of Kings' came to be used more extensively than by former Arsacid rulers. On the obverse of the coinage letters in Pahlavi, the Arsacid script appeared for the first time, and the reverse showed a Zoroastrian fire-altar with an officiating priest. There was also a tendency to substitute indigenous for Greek names – eg, Marv for Antiochia-in-Margiana. And the founding of Vologasia, near Ctesiphon, as a rival emporium to Seleucia may have been intended to undermine the supremacy of that turbulent and very Greek city. It was to this period, too, that the compilation of the Avesta was later ascribed.

The century and a half that separated the death of Vologeses I AD 80 from that of the last Arsacid ruler, Artabanus V, in 224, continued to witness an indecisive contest between Parthia and Rome in which neither side could retain any lasting advantage. The Romans twice entered Ctesiphon – under Trajan in 115 and under Septimius Severus in 198 – but on each occasion the Parthians, as soon as they had recovered, vigorously counter-attacked, first under Vologeses III (148-192) and then under Artabanus V (213-224).

The duel with Rome had debarred the Arsacids from playing an active role in the east after the death of Mithradates II in 87 BC. Earlier, during the second half of the second century BC, Saca nomads had penetrated Bactria and had brought that remote Greek kingdom to an end around 125 BC. Thereafter, while some Saca elements must have made their way southeast into the Kabul valley and Gandhara (perhaps as mercenaries of the Greek rulers south of the Hindu Kush), the main thrust had been in a southwesterly direction across the Paropamisus into Aria, Drangiana and Arachosia. Here they were temporarily brought under control by Mithradates II, but with his

death all semblance of Parthian suzerainty disappeared, and the Sacas themselves expanded east out of Arachosia across the Indus, bypassing the remaining Greek principalities in the Kabul valley and Gandhara, and penetrating deep into India. Our knowledge of the Saca rulers of Arachosia derives mainly from their coinage. Especially voluminous is that of Azes I, from whose assumption of paramountcy over extensive tracts on both sides of the Indus in 57 BC is dated the beginning of the Saca calendar, 'the Era of Azes'. By the opening of the Christian Era, however, Saca fortunes in the west were in decline as a result of an advance into Sistan and Arachosia by a local Parthian dynasty whose relationship with the imperial Arsacids is still obscure, but which was certainly free of any restraint from Ctesiphon. The greatest of the line, Gondophares (c AD 20-46), ruled an extensive kingdom stretching from Sistan to the Punjab.

This Indo-Parthian kingdom eventually expired under pressure from fresh invaders from inner Asia, the Kushans, who are now widely assumed to have been the ruling clans of the nomad confederacy known to the Chinese as the Yueh-chih, and called by western sources the Tochari. Kushan chronology remains a matter of scholarly controversy but it must have been early in the first century AD, under Kujula Kadphises, that the Kushans occupied all the country between the Syr-Darya and the Amu-Darya, as well as Marv and Bactria, before crossing the Hindu Kush to annex the Kabul valley and the country eastwards to the Indus. One of Kujula's successors, Vima Kadphises, entered the Punjab, gained control of the whole Indus valley and seized Arachosia and Sistan from the house of Gondophares. As a powerful neighboring state, the Kushan Empire posed a real threat to the Arsacids because it was in a position to strangle Iranian caravan-trade with the Far East. The Kushans, if they had wished, could have forced the trade to bypass Iran altogether by diverting the caravans either across the steppes north of the Caspian Sea or down the Indus towards the ports of Sind. But fortunately for the Arsacids this threat never materialized. Preoccupied with the Indian subcontinent and its wealth, the Kushan emperors from the outset seem to have eschewed aggres-

sive designs against Iran proper, and the presumption of economic rivalry between the two regimes is largely conjectural, despite some historians' claims to the contrary.

But even before the appearance of the Kushans the Arsacid Empire had come to adopt a mainly defensive posture toward its neighbors, only occasionally belied by random outbursts of aggressive energy. The reasons for Parthian decline are still obscure, but there can be little doubt that it was related to the increasingly unfavorable position of the monarchy vis-a-vis the nobility. No doubt there had always been, a somewhat precarious balance of power between the ruler and his closest supporters, but now this relationship had deteriorated into open conflict, and in the end this conflict proved fatal to the Arsacids.

Rise of the Sasanids

Arsacid rule ended in AD 224 with the successful revolt of a local sub-king in Fars, Ardashir. It was from Ardashir's grandfather, Sasan, that the new dynasty took its name. The Sasanid Empire, which was to endure for more than four centuries until its extinction by the Arabs in 651, was perhaps the most resilient and powerful regime ever to be established by people of Iranian stock, and its cultural impact was to be immense, spreading Iranian civilization far beyond the boundaries of the empire itself. To a far greater extent than either the Achaemenid or the Arsacid Empires, the Sasanid Empire was aggressive and belligerent, a stance no doubt justified by the fact that it was encircled by extremely dangerous foes - the Romans, and later the Byzantines, to the west; the Kushans, and later the Hephthalite Huns, to the east; and by various Hunnish confederacies to the north. Unlike their Arsacid predecessors, the Sasanids were able from the beginning to assert their authority over the nobility and to create what was, by the standards of that age, a highly centralized bureaucratic structure of government. Their success in both endeavors was, in turn, the outcome of their considerable military achievements.

It took Ardashir 10 years of constant warfare following the death of Artabanus V in 224 to break a hostile coalition composed of the Arsacid

king of Armenia, the Romans, the Sacas and the Kushans, but by the end of that time he was undisputed master of the entire plateau, as well as a large part of the former Kushan lands in the east. He then turned west to restore the Mesopotamian frontiers to what they had been under the early Arsacids and soon took from the Romans the two great fortresses of Nisibis and Carrhae between the upper Euphrates and Tigris on the southern frontier of modern Turkey. During these years he shared the throne with his son, Shapur, who as crown-prince had directed campaigns against the Kushan Empire and had emerged from the conflict with a vast appanage that stretched from the upper Syr-Darya near Tashkent to the upper Indus and included the Kabul valley, Bactria and Sogdiana. We do not know exactly when Ardashir died, but not long after Shapur I's accession around 240 the new king found himself threatened by the advance of a Roman army under Gordian III down the Euphrates. Shapur met the invaders at al-Anbar and routed them, Gordian himself being killed in battle, and the new Roman emperor hastily chosen by the survivors, Philip the Arab, agreeing to pay an enormous indemnity. Between 256 and 260 war broke out again, this time over Armenia, and Shapur marched through Cappadocia and Syria, taking 37 cities, including Antioch. When the main Roman army under Valerian came to grips with the Persians near Edessa, it met with total defeat, and Valerian himself was captured – possibly a personal feat of arms of Shapur himself.

Military successes on this scale go far to explaining the ease with which these two rulers were able to create a strong centralized monarchy. The basis on which their power rested was, of course, the army, and here the early Sasanids, warned by the Arsacid failure to curb the military power of the nobility, were careful to concentrate authority in the hands of a commander-in-chief who was invariably a member of the royal family. Unlike the Arsacids, who had relied solely upon cavalry, the Sasanids also employed both infantry and war-elephants, but for offensive warfare they continued to rely upon heavy cavalry, with its long iron lances and with laminated armor protecting both man and mount. Despite the fact that

the riders rode without stirrups, the sheer wreght of a Sasanid cavalry charge was almost impossible to withstand. There were also light cavalry units armed with powerful compound bows fired from the saddle, as well as auxiliary cavalry recruited from among frontier peoples such as Armenians, Kushans and Hephthalites.

Sasanid administration was the preserve of a carefully graded bureaucracy organized in secretariats – of finance, war, justice and soon – under the supervision of a *vazir* or prime minister, while a separate hierarchy of officials managed the royal household, a pattern that was to imprint itself upon later Muslim administrative practice. Fiscal administration was probably especially important, since in addition to the spoils of war the Sasanid state derived its income from a wide range of sources: from a proportion of the value of the produce of cultivated land, from the income derived from crown lands, from state-owned mines and from dues levied on commerce. According to Shapur's Naqsh-i Rustam inscription, the empire was divided into 27 provinces governed not by local chieftains but either by members of the royal family or officials appointed by the king and directly answerable to him. The great northeastern viceroyalty of Kushanshahr was usually reserved for the heir-apparent, with the right to mint coinage in his own name and bear the lofty title of *Kushanshah*. The Sasanids did not favor client-kingdoms and steadily reduced their number.

Powerful religious forces

The Sasanids were much concerned with establishing in the minds of their subjects both the legitimacy of the house of Sasan and a feeling of continuity with the past. Like the Arsacids, whose memory they did everything possible to eradicate, they claimed to be descended from the Achaemenids and invented eponymous dynastic legends relating to the origin of their family fortunes. Both their patronage of the arts and of Zoroastrianism had a consciously archaic ring about it, and they set about the transformation of Zoroastrianism, hitherto a fairly amorphous cult, into a state-church, Erastian and aggressive. In consequence, there rapidly developed a church hierarchy with a

passion for orthodoxy and ritual and a capacity for occasional ferocious outbursts of persecution against heretics and the worshipers of other faiths.

The vigor with which the Zoroastrian religion adapted itself to this new role may reflect the extent to which it felt the challenge of rival religious communities, Jewish and Nestorian Christian, but a far more formidable potential rival than either of these was Manichaeanism, a new faith embodying a dynamic quest for salvation. Its charismatic founder, Mani, was born in 216, his father reputedly coming from Hamadan and his mother claiming distant kinship with the Arsacid royal house. During his childhood Mani experienced some kind of spiritual revelation which, as he grew older, took the form of a conviction that he had a prophetic mission and that he was the last in a sequence of prophets sent to redeem mankind. His message was universal, an amalgam of elements in Christianity, Gnosticism, Mazdaism and even Buddhism, but its essence was dualism, the unending struggle between the forces of light and darkness, good and evil. Matter, including the human body, was evil; the spirit, good. The object of human existence was to emancipate the spirit from the body by following the strict ethical precepts of the new faith. Believers were organized into two categories: the Elect, a celibate and vegetarian priesthood, and the Hearers, who lived and worked in the world and enjoyed a normal family life and supported the Elect with alms.

The new faith was spread by a vigorous missionary movement, the first of these missions being undertaken by Mani himself when he sailed down the Persian Gulf to the Makran coast and Sind. He returned to Iran about the time of Shapur's accession around 240 and then proceeded through Fars, Khuzistan, Babylonia and Media, expounding his beliefs. The reception he met was mixed, but he managed to win a royal convert in a brother of Shapur, who apparently arranged for him to be received in audience by the king. Mani is said to have had three audiences with Shapur at Ctesiphon, and at the last one, probably around 241, he was given leave to continue his proselytizing throughout the empire. Thereafter, he appears to have alternately passed his time in attendance at court and in increasing the number of his followers. Missions were sent as far afield as northern Mesopotamia, Egypt, Margiana and Bactria, and there can be little doubt that by the time of Shapur's death the new faith had spread throughout the Sasanid Empire and had become a serious challenge to the Zoroastrian church. After Shapur's death Mani continued his work under Shapur's two sons, Hormizd I (272-273) and Bahram I (273-276), but he was no doubt well aware of the lack of interest of the one and the hostility of the other. He was finally summoned to Bahram's presence at Jundai Shapur and imprisoned at the instigation of the Zoroastrian priesthood, dying or being murdered after a captivity of 26 days.

Neither Mani's death nor the subsequent savage proscription of his followers prevented the spread of the new faith far beyond the frontiers of Iran, westward into Asia Minor and Roman North Africa, and eastward across the Amu-Darya in Mawarannahr, where it found sanctuary among the local Sogdian population, and whence it spread into Chinese Turkestan (Xinjiang) in the wake of itinerant Sogdian merchants. It was well-established there by the time of the conquest of the region by the Turkish Uighurs in the middle of the eighth century, and in consequence of the conversion of the third Uighur Kaghan in 763 it

became the dominant faith of that interesting people until their overthrow at the hands of the Kirghiz of the upper Yenisei in 840. In and around the Turfan basin, however, Manichaeanism probably survived down to the early thirteenth century.

Following the death of Shapur I there was some loss of momentum in the Sasanid monarchy, and for nearly four decades it seemed to survive mainly upon the reflected glory of its two founders. During the long reign of Shapur II (309-379), however, there was a forceful reassertion of royal primacy and renewed aggression against Rome, only temporarily suspended between 353 and 358 while the northeastern frontier was secured from the Huns.

The coming of the Huns

The role of the Huns in the history of the Eurasian steppe zone extends for a little more than 200 years, from the middle of the fourth to the middle of the sixth century. Their presence in Europe lasted for an even shorter period, *c* 370- *c* 455. They remain for historians what they were for their contemporaries, a mysterious people of unknown speech and of uncertain origin, although it is now thought that they were probably the northern section of a confederacy known to the Chinese as the Hsiung-nu.

Left: A triumphant moment in Sasanid military history – King Shapur I captures the Emperor Valerian after the defeat of the Roman army at the battle of Edessa in AD 260.

Above: Manichean priests in ritual costume. The Manichean faith posed a serious threat to the official state religion, Zoroastrianism, under the Sasanids.

Above right: The prophet Mani, founder of Manicheanism, who was probably murdered at the instigation of the Zoroastrian priesthood in around AD 276.

Right: Religion gave legitimacy to Sasanid rule. Here Ardashir II is invested with royal authority by the influential gods Ahuramazda and Mithras.

Although some scholars consider these invaders to be a single people, they will be treated here as three distinct groups: the Chionites, the Kidarites and the Hephthalites, or White Huns. It was against the first of these groups, the Chionites, that Shapur II fought so successfully, eventually drawing them into subsidiary alliance. During the last quarter of the fourth century the Chionite power in Sogdiana and Bactria seems to have been overwhelmed by a new group of Huns under a chieftain (or a succession of chieftains) named Kidara. But the Kidarites were soon to be driven south into the Punjab, probably sometime during the first quarter of the fifth century, by a third and more formidable confederacy, that of the Hephthalites. Of this people, later to be so terrible a scourge in northern India, the Byzantine historian Procopius left a strangely favorable account. He wrote: 'They are the only ones among the Huns who have white bodies and countenances which are not ugly. It is also true that their manner of life is unlike that of their kinsmen, nor do they live a savage life as they do; but they are ruled by one king, and since they possess a lawful constitution, they observe right and justice in their dealings both with one another and with their neighbors, in no degree less than the Romans and the Persians.'

Against these new invaders the Sasanid warrior-king, Bahram V (420-438), scored some notable triumphs, but for over a century after his death the Sasanid Empire was in some sense a client kingdom of the Hephthalites until Khusru I, in alliance with the western Turks, brought about their destruction around 557. Dependence upon the Hephthalites continued during the reigns of both Firuz (457-484) and his son, Kavadh or Qubad (488-496 and 498-531). Firuz only managed to wrest the throne from his elder brother as a result of Hephthalite support, but in due course he turned against his benefactors, was defeated by them and was taken prisoner. To secure his own release he was compelled to leave Kavadh, the heir-apparent, as a hostage, and when he rashly returned to the attack a second time, the Hephthalites overwhelmed and killed him. Like his father, Kavadh only secured the throne through the intervention of the Hephthalites and when, eight years later, he was expelled from Iran by his subjects, it was the Hephthalites who brought him back a second time.

Kavadh's reign constitutes one of the more interesting phases in the history of the Sasanid Empire. The administrative framework created by Ardashir and Shapur I, and the social structure that sustained it, had become increasingly rigid and impervious to changing conditions. A caste-like division of society had developed along occupational lines and there had been a disproportionate growth in the power of the nobility at the expense of the cultivators and artisans. During the last decades of the fifth century, when the buildup of social tensions had become severe the oppressed sections of the population found a champion in a shadowy figure called Mazdak, who professed a dualistic ideology that was an offshoot of Manichaeanism. Little is known about the tenets of the Mazdakite faith except what was reported of it by hostile commentators, who accused it of antisocial practices such as holding land and women in common. In any event, the movement rapidly gathered momentum, resulting in widespread disturbances that challenged the existing social order. Kavadh himself appears to have been to some extent a follower of Mazdak and initiated a series of reforms intended to alleviate popular distress, but there was a predictable reaction among the nobility and the Zoroastrian

clergy. The king was deposed, and he fled to the Hephthalites. On regaining his throne two years later as a Hephthalite protegé he judged it expedient to abandon the Mazdakite cause and sought diversion in a renewed struggle with Byzantium. At the same time he brought the heir-apparent, Khusru, into the government of the empire, and the latter, a strict Zoroastrian, embarked upon the systematic extirpation of the Mazdakites. So successful was he that not a single fragment of Mazdakite literature has survived.

Triumphs and disasters

The reign of Khusru I Anushirvan (531-579) marked a dramatic revival of Sasanid fortunes, and in later Islamic tradition the justice of Anushirvan and the wisdom of his *vazir*, Buzurgmihr, were to become proverbial. During the preceding 100 years the survival of the empire had been imperiled by the external threat of the Hephthalites, coupled with internal unrest resulting from the ossification of the social structure. The problem of the Hephthalites Khusru solved with the assistance of the western Turks beyond the Syr-Darya, and in a short-lived alliance with their Khan, Silzibul or Sinjibu, he finally crushed the confederacy in c 557 and reoccupied the long-abandoned Kushan territory in Bactria. This was far from being an isolated triumph. As early as 540 he had invaded Syria and captured Antioch, and after the destruction of the Hephthalites he again advanced westward to contain a threatening Byzantine-Turkish alliance. He also sent an expedition to expel the Ethiopians from Yemen, which thereafter became a Sasanid dependency.

His campaigns, spectacular in themselves, were in the long run less significant than the measures taken to improve the administration of the empire and to repair the ravages inflicted upon the exhausted countryside, and there is some suggestion that credit for their initiation is due to Kavadh as much as to his son. In any event, it appears that while in former times the land revenue was assessed on the basis of crop-sharing at the time of the harvest, Khusru (or Kavadh) instituted fixed assessments based on the estimated yield, the new system requiring both careful surveying and the maintenance of registers. This was to be the basis of the Muslim system of taxation under the Abbasid Caliphs.

Khusru's successor, Hormizd IV (579-590), was deposed by a usurping general, who, in turn, was soon replaced by Hormizd's son, Khusru II Parviz (590-628). Khusru II acquired legendary fame for the splendor of his court, for the notable victories he won and for the subsequent dramatic reversal of his fortunes. Campaigning against the Byzan-

tines, his armies reached the shores of the Bosphorus in 610, Antioch in 611, Damascus in 613, Jerusalem in 614 and Alexandria in 616. These unprecedented triumphs were followed by hardly less spectacular disasters. In 622 the Byzantine Emperor Heraclius took the field against the Persians. In 624 he invaded Azarbaijan, and in 627 he won the great victory of Arbela, near Niniveh on the Tigris. Khusru fled to Ctesiphon, where he was murdered in the following year in the first of a sequence of palace revolutions that placed one nonentity after another upon the throne. The troops of the last of the line, Yazdgird III (632-651), melted away after their final defeat at the hands of the Muslim Arab invaders at Nihavand in 642, and the fugitive Shah was murdered near Marv in 651.

The Sasanid achievement

The wealth of Iran in Sasanid times was due in large measure to the expansion of urban life. To take an example from one reign only, to Shapur I is attributed the founding of Nishapur in Khurasan, a city on the site of modern Qazvin; Fushanj, near Herat; Jundai Shapur, near Dizful; and Bishapur, near Kazerun.

Comparatively little Pahlavi literature has survived from the Sasanid period, but Shapur I is known to have initiated the translation into Pahlavi of Greek, Syriac and Sanskrit works covering a wide range of subjects including mathematics, astronomy and medicine. He also established at Jundai Shapur a celebrated medical school. Regular communication with India by the sea-route permitted fruitful exchanges between two civilizations at their prime. From India came the celebrated collection of fables, *Kalila va Dimna*, and the game of chess was said to have been introduced into Iran on the initiative of Buzurgmihr, the *vazir* of Khusru Anushirvan. The Sasanids skill in metalwork, gem engraving and textile weaving has never been surpassed in its ability to convey the impression of a truly imperial art of sumptuous magnificence. The same is true of the monumental bas-reliefs carved at Naqsh-i Rustam, Naqsh-i Rajab, Firuzabad, Taq-i Bustan and elsewhere.

The Sasanid Empire was the culminating phase of the 12 centuries during which the lands stretching from the Euphrates to the Syr-Darya and the Tarim merged into a single Iranian culture-zone. It would have been surprising, therefore, if the Muslim Arab conquest, for all its violence, had depleted to any great extent this deep-rooted Iranian heritage, and indeed it did not. The year that saw the death of Yazdgird III may be a convenient point in time from which to look back upon this Iranian world about to be integrated into an even larger Islamic *ekumene*. In fact, much less happened in and around 651 than might be supposed. Although the Sasanid dynasty and court, as well as the Zoroastrian hierarchy, had been swept aside, the greater nobility for the most part survived without undue erosion of the economic basis of its power. So too did the *dihqans* upon whom the new Arab rulers, like the Sasanid administration before them, depended for the effective taxation of the countryside. Although the status of many *dihqans* was depressed, compelling them to acquiesce in a client relationship with larger landowners and local chieftains, they remained the guardians of a distinctly Iranian way of life and of old values and ideals such as those enshrined long afterwards in the *Shahnameh* of Firdausi. Nor did Islam spread very rapidly outside the towns or the areas of Arab colonization. In the more remote regions such as Tabaristan, sheltered behind the Elburz mountains, or Badghis and Ghur, beyond Herat, Zoroastrian and even Mazdakite communities survived long after the rest of the plateau had converted to Islam, and local revolts triggered by economic or social grievances had a way of assuming a Zoroastrian or Mazdakite complexion. Islamic sectarian movements likewise tended to acquire the stamp of Iranian particularism. Across the Amu-Darya in Sogdiana, the cultural syncretism of the period of the early Arab occupation was peculiarly complex, featuring Zoroastrian, Manichaean, Nestorian, Jewish, Buddhist and Turkish Shamanist influences.

But apart from Arab inability (if indeed there was a will) to eradicate the Iranian past, the new rulers found that they were compelled to draw upon that past to govern effectively. A small but telling indication of this is the fact that in the Iranian East silver *dirhams*, fashioned in the style of the Sasanid *drahm*, circulated for nearly two centuries after the Arab conquest, bearing legends in Pahlavi as well as in Arabic, and having on their obverse the crowned head of a Sasanid ruler – generally Khusru II – and on their reverse a Zoroastrian fire-altar. Arab-Sasanid coins were still being minted in Tabaristan and Bukhara during the first quarter of the ninth century.

In the former Sasanid provinces Pahlavi continued to be used, side by side with Arabic, as the language of administration for nearly half a century after the conquest, and in Khurasan for at least another 45 years. More important, the Arabs adapted the administrative system and bureaucratic traditions of the Sasanid Empire to meet their own, rather different, needs, and the *kuttab*, the men who staffed the secretariats of Abbasid Baghdad, with the *vazir* at their head, were a living link with the pre-Islamic past. At the same time, the concept of the Iranian 'King of Kings' as the fount of all earthly authority proved increasingly attractive as Islam drew further away from its roots in tribal Arabia. The precedent of Sasanid absolutism came to haunt both the theory and practice of Muslim statecraft, transfiguring the figure of the Abbasid Caliph – strictly speaking, the earthly representative of the Prophet, and his successor as leader of the Muslim community –

into a quasi-sacred personage, 'the Shadow of God on Earth' (*zilullah*). For all who ruled or who aspired to rule in the Muslim east the memory of pre-Islamic Iran and its hero-kings, whether historical or purely legendary, was as pervasive as it was appealing and persisted through centuries of Turkish or Turko-Mongol rule. Thus when the Ottoman Turkish Sultan, Mehmet II, rode through the streets of ravaged Constantinople in 1453, it was lines from Firdausi which came most naturally to his lips: 'The spider weaves her web in the palace of the Caesars and the owl keeps her vigil in the watch-tower of Afrasiab.'

More than anything else, it is the sheer persistence of the traditions of pre-Islamic civilization that warrants our calling that civilization 'classical.' When, from the ninth century onwards, the universalist state of the Abbasids began to disintegrate and Iranian particularism revived under local leaders, mainly from the eastern provinces where the *dihqans* had preserved the Iranian epic tradition inviolate, it was natural that every dynasty with pretensions to independence should want a stake in that inspiring past. Thus the Samanids claimed descent from Bahram Chubin, the Buyids from Bahram V and the Ghurids from the tyrant Dahak. Apart from the obvious local appeal that such genealogies, however spurious, possessed, they were the Iranian answer to Arab pride of descent from the family of the Prophet or from his tribe, the Quraish. But the full history of how the ancient traditions of Iran survived the vicissitudes of history will be related farther on.

Above far left: A Sasanian silver-gilt dish depicting King Ardashir III engaged in the traditional royal pursuit of hunting wild animals.

Above left: The moment of truth – a Persian monarch fires his arrow into the lion, while a further victim lies prostrate below.

Right: A detail of a silk cloth with lions and palm trees, a sixth-century textile artifact featuring traditional objects of Persian design.

Indian Civilization

Indian civilization, like that of Iran, began with the coming of the Aryans, probably in the latter part of the second millennium BC. Centuries later, northwestern India was to experience a succession of invasions and occupations by Greeks, Sacas, Kushans and Huns, peoples all known to the Iranians, mainly as predators. The Arabs also made their way to India, although unlike their invasion of Iran, their penetration into Sind was to be short-lived and for the most part the Arab presence in India meant Arab traders and seamen in the ports of Gujarat and of the Malabar coast. From the eleventh to the eighteenth century much of northern and central India was ruled by Turkish and Turko-Mongol Muslim military elites such as also ruled Iran in the same period, bringing into India in their train a diverse following of fellow-Muslims, principally Iranians and Afghans. Only in the eighteenth century did the patterns diverge, for while thereafter Iran suffered European pressures of various kinds, including loss of territory in the northwest to Czarist Russia, India experienced the full weight of European colonialism.

Indian civilization was seldom expansionist in any politico-military sense. Unlike Iran, India is no corridor for the passage of peoples and no crossroads for transmission of cultures. Rather it is a goal and a point of no return to which invaders – and ideas – arrive at the end of their journey and where they are compelled to yield themselves, in part at least, to the overwhelming pressures of the Indian environment. And since India, unlike Iran, offers no very favorable conditions for the preservation of a pastoral nomadic life, even the fiercest of warrior herdsmen become, in a few generations, settled cultivators living the ordered life of village India.

If India today is overpopulated, and if too much of her agriculture remains at subsistence level, it does not follow that such has always been the case. The subcontinent today, including Pakistan, sustains a population of upwards of 740 million. It has been estimated that the India of Akbar (AD 1556-1605) may have had a population of 100 million. These figures, however approximate, tell their own story – of a vast area of the globe where until very recently the need was for people and not for land, where cultivation provided a surplus of grain for internal distribution or for hoarding against hard times and where there was still an internal frontier of jungle and scrub to be cleared and cultivated. When the provinces of the Achaemenid Empire sent their annual tribute to Persepolis, all paid in silver talents except Hindush (Sind), which paid in gold dust. To contemporaries this must have seemed peculiarly appropriate, for Sind was a part of what was then and for long afterward held to be the wealthiest region known to man.

Geographical textures

The variety of the Indian landscape goes far to explaining the diversity and complexity of the country's history. India is enclosed, but not wholly, by the great chain of mountain ranges that skirt the northern plains and make contact with China, Central Asia and the Middle East arduous. On the east the barrier is effectively reinforced by the dense jungles and hills of Assam and Manipur, while the main central stretch of the chain, approached through foothills and valleys of remarkable beauty and fertility, faces the bleak plateau of Tibet. To the west, however, the picture is different, for here the ranges are lower and less forbidding, bisected by passes such as the Khyber and the Bolan that give access to Afghanistan and the Iranian highlands and, in former times, to the network of caravan routes of Inner Asia. Through these passes came the invaders who, for good or ill, left an abiding impact upon Indian society and culture, and through those passes too Buddhism made its way on to the steppes and so to China.

But the low, rugged mountains of the west, inhabited by fierce Pathan and Baluch tribesmen, are hardly characteristic of the Indian landscape. Nor, for that matter, are the softer foothills to the north of the Gangetic plain which run from Swat and Kashmir, through Chamba and the Simla hill-states, into Nepal. More typical of the north are the great plains – the Punjab, in the west, watered by its five rivers which flow southwestward to join the Indus on its way to the Arabian Sea, and in the east, the great Gangetic plain, through which the Ganges flows for some 1500 miles southeast to the Bay of Bengal.

The Punjab and much of the Gangetic plain are rich wheatlands, easily able to sustain two harvests a year. But southeast of the Punjab is a

region of arid hills and rocky outcrops, Rajasthan, home of the warrior Rajputs, which extends southward into the bleak wastes of the Thar Desert and ultimately to the salt flats of the Great Rann of Cutch. And south of the Ganges the ground begins to rise and form a broken tableland that gradually ascends to the Vindhya range, falls steeply away to the valley of the Narbada and then beyond it again ascends to the Satpura range.

At this point northern India gives way to peninsular India, and here begins the Deccan, the great central plateau that extends south for nearly 500 miles although less fertile and wellwatered than some other regions of the subcontinent the Deccan enjoys considerable mineral wealth and a mild climate. The Deccan ends at the line of the Kistna River, and to the south lie the narrow tropical coastal belt of the Malabar Coast below the Western Ghats, the temperate plateau of Mysore and, between the Eastern Ghats and the Coromandel Coast, the rich plains of the Carnatic.

On both west and east the Deccan is flanked by two ranges that form a barrier separating the interior from the coastal lands. Of these ranges, the Western Ghats are steep and difficult to ascend, and from the vicinity of Bombay they sweep southward so close to the ocean as to leave only a narrow strip at sea level. The Eastern Ghats are less steep and descend gradually to the broad plains of the Carnatic, which extend for some 300 miles from the delta of the Kistna south to that of the Kaveri, the ricebowl of Tamiland.

In all, the Indian subcontinent covers an area almost as large as Europe (exclusive of Russia), and the spectrum of its racial types and linguistic patterns is more diverse than anything to be found in Europe. Excluding tribal languages spoken by relatively small groups of people and numerous dialectical variants, 20 major languages are spoken in modern India. Among the more important are Eastern and Western Hindi, Bengali, Bihari, Tamil, Telugu, Marathi and the *lingua franca* of the Muslims, Urdu. Under Muslim rule, and especially during the period of the Mughul Empire, Persian was also widely spoken, not only by the ruling elite but also by all those (whether Hindu or Muslim) who had dealings with the elite or who sought government employment.

The phases of Hinduism

Geography, language and race have all contributed to giving the Indian subcontinent a bewildering human and historical diversity, yet there have been other factors that have made for an

Left: Suttee, one of the less attractive Hindu customs — a widow is burnt to death on her husband's funeral pyre.

Right: This bronze statue of a dancing girl from the pre-Aryan Indus Valley civilization is dated at around 2500 BC.

Above right: Benares, on the Ganges, a center of Hindu religion and philosophy for over 3000 years.

Below right: Shiva, Lord of the Cosmic Dance.

Indian cultural identity. Of these, none has been more important than Classical Hinduism.

Historically, Hinduism has passed through four main periods: the Vedic phase, which dated from the arrival of the Aryans in India around 1500 BC; a second phase, beginning around 600 BC, characterized by pantheistic monism; a third phase, dating from around the beginning of the Christian era, which introduced the worship of the great gods of later Hinduism, many of whom were of non-Aryan origin; and finally, a fourth phase dating from the ninth century, in which there developed popular and, in essence, monotheistic cults characterized by fervent personal devotion to a particular deity.

The Vedic phase is known mainly from the surviving hymns of the *Rig-veda* composed in Vedic by the Aryan invaders who made their way into India sometime around the middle of the second millennium BC, displacing its original Dravidian inhabitants, who were driven steadily southward. The Indo-Aryans, like the pre-Achaemenid Iranians, believed in deities who were primarily personifications of natural phenomena such as wind, water, fire and thunder. These and others they worshiped with complicated rituals and blood-sacrifices in which an intoxicating beverage known in Sanskrit as *soma*, and in the Iranian Avesta as *hauma*, played an important part.

There is no evidence that the Aryans knew anything of the doctrine that was to become the most characteristic tenet of later Hinduism, the belief in the transmigration of the soul through an unceasing chain of reincarnations. This concept may have originated with some now unidentifiable pre-Aryan indigenous group, but in any case it seems to have spread exceedingly rapidly, and it was certainly well established by the second half of the first millennium BC. It was accompanied by the emergence of the concept of *karma*, the law of cause and effect by means of which the righteous (those who observe *dharma*, the moral duty imposed by their caste and circumstances) are reborn into a higher condition than before, while evildoers descend to a lower and more degrading one, perhaps even to that of a beast. The goal of existence is *moksha*, release from the chain of rebirth.

The period that saw the formulation of the concepts of *karma*, *dharma* and *moksha*, roughly between 600 BC and AD 300 also saw the appearance of the Sanskrit treatises known as the *Upanishads*, which invested both the gods and the rituals with which they were worshiped with symbolic qualities, an approach that was probably too remote and intellectual for most ordinary worshipers. At the same time there occurred an unprecedented elevation in status of the brah-

mins, who now emerged for the first time as an exclusive and dominant caste and as the exploiters of the masses beneath them.

This second phase also saw a falling-off in the worship of the older Vedic deities and a growing distaste for ritual sacrifices. There was a steadily growing concern with *dharma*, embodied in elaborate texts on correct social and personal conduct, the *dharma-sutras* and the *dharma-shastras*, as well as in the great Sanskrit epics, the *Ramayana* and the *Mahabharata*, which were full of concern for *dharma*.

The third phase in the development of Hinduism was marked by the assertion of brahminical pretension on a scale hitherto unknown and by the emergence of cow-worship, which by the fourth century AD had reached a point where the killing of a cow was regarded as heinous an offence as killing a Brahmin. But most important in this phase was the rise to prominence and to an assured place within the framework of the Hindu pantheon of numerous deities, often pre-Aryan in origin and very local in character, who tended to replace or become substitutes for the older Aryan gods. By the beginning of the Christian era ceremonial worship of these deities was beginning to assume forms which would be maintained for the next 2000 years. The gods themselves were represented in the form of idols carved in stone or other suitable material, and they were housed in temples which ranged from constructions of mud and palm branches to stone structures of enormous size and complexity, Brahmins performing all the required rites.

Mounds, rivers, groves of trees and even cities became sacred to individual deities, and certain locations, such as Badrinath and Kedarnath on the snowline above Rishikesh, and temples, such as that of Jagannatha at Puri, acquired reputations for sanctity and became centers of pilgrimage. In certain places, too, periodic religious fairs were held, and these also attracted enormous numbers of pilgrims and a great diversity of cults, leading to a steady diffusion of beliefs which might otherwise have remained extremely localized.

Vishnu and Shiva

Of all the gods worshipped in the Hindu pantheon, two – Vishnu and Shiva – stand out above the rest. Although the worship of Vishnu can be traced back to Rig-vedic times, it is from the period of the great epics that Vishnu came to occupy a central oposition in the Hindu pantheon as protector, preserver and eventual redeemer of the world. Vishnu was believed to have assumed 10 divine incarnations *(avatārs)*, favorite themes of Hindu painters and sculptors, and these include not only such familiar subjects as the boar Varaha and the man-lion Narasimha, but also the hero Rama, the chief protagonist of the *Ramayana*; Krishna, the greatest of all *avatars*; and Kalki, the last *avatar* who will appear at the end of the present *Kali-yuga* or Age of Darkness.

Vaishnavism, the cult of Vishnu, stimulated the rise of numerous sects and philosophical schools, in addition to the highly personalized devotional movement known as *Bhakti*. Personalized worship of certain individual gods probably dates back as far as the ninth century AD, but it reached its most intense and creative phase between the twelfth and eighteenth centuries, stimulated no doubt to some extent by the influence of Islamic

Above left: A seal showing a zebu (humped bull), found at Mohenjodaro, one of the main sites of the Indus Valley civilization.

Left: The Hindu god Vishnu, sustainer and redeemer of the world.

Right: Shiva in one of his most peaceful manifestations. The same god was often seen as 'the destroyer' and 'the terrible one.'

fearsome are certain aspects of his Shakti, although as the beautiful and devoted Parvati she ranks as one of the most attractive and revered of Hindu goddesses. But as Durga the destroyer, as Kali, goddess of death, disease and unreasoning terror, or as Bhavani, whom the Thugs worshiped, she is a drinker of blood

The caste system

The doctrine of reincarnation, the quest for escape from the chain of rebirth, the fulfillment of *dharma*, the worship of the gods and the observation of the rites prescribed by the Sanskrit Great Tradition – these are the main elements of Hinduism, common ground upon which a very substantial number of those who call themselves Hindus would feel able to agree. For the non-Hindu, however, the most striking feature of Hinduism is that peculiar form of social organization known as caste.

According to Hindu tradition, in the first age of mankind all men were virtuous and of one caste, the *brahmins*. In the second age there was some diminution of righteousness, and the residue of that age where the *kshattriyas* In the third age came the first signs of misery and misfortune, and the survivors of that age were the *vaishyas*. Finally came the fourth and present age, a period of unspeakable degradation and calamity which saw the appearance of the *shudras* and even lower forms of human life.

Already, by the last half of the first millennium BC the four main castes were differentiated according to their respective functions in society. The *brahmins*, at the pinnacle of the social hierarchy, constituted the priestly order. Below them, in order of rank, came the *kshattriyas* or warriors, the *vaishyas* or traders, and the *shudras* or cultivators. At first sight this kind of division of society along occupational lines does not seem very different from that prevailing in Sasanid Iran or even in medieval Europe. What has made the Indian institution of caste unique has been the interlocking relationship between the concept of society as a rigidly stratified hierarchy, the belief that human existence consists of an unending chain of reincarnations, and preoccupation with avoidance of ritual pollution, which for the orthodox Hindu inhibits social intercourse by debarring him from physical contact with those in a higher or lower caste than his own. The three highest castes – *brahmins*, *kshattriyas* and *vaishyas* – are known as the 'twice-born' because they experience a spiritual rebirth during the initiation ceremonies which accompany their donning of the sacred thread, ceremonies forbidden to *shudras*, as well as to the even more wretched *panchamas* (outcastes).

Color, race, a desire to keep rulers and subjects apart and a natural tendency to divide society into compartments according to function probably all played a part in constructing the complex and bizarre institution of caste, but the outcome was, in practice, something very different from that classic division into *brahmins*, *kshattriyas*, *vaishyas* and *shudras*, with the *panchamas* beyond the pale. Instead, there emerged during the course of 2000 years a whole multiplicity of castes, some 3000, and over 2500 sub-castes, of which some consist of hardly more than a few hundred people. While for the orthodox Hindu there is no such thing as social mobility in the sense of transferring from one caste to another, there is another form of mobility in which an entire caste may rise or decline in relation to other castes, a process that in former times could be legitimized by the state, even when the rulers were 'unclean' Mughuls or Englishmen.

---

monotheism and by mystical Persian Sufism. Very alien in spirit to both the ancient Rig-vedic religion and to later Brahminism, *Bhakti* was at heart instinctively monotheistic, enjoining self-effacing devotion to a single deity, usually Krishna, and showing a remarkable indifference to matters of caste. In this ardent devotional phase of Hinduism the relationship between the worshiper and the object of worship was sometimes explicitly erotic. Another, rather different strand in the *Bhakti* tradition has its roots in the *Bhagavadgita*, the Song of the Lord, consisting of a philosophical discussion between Arjuna, one of the heroes of the *Mahabharata*, and Krishna before the battle of Kurukshetra. Although commentators on the text have disagreed fundamentally regarding its meaning there can be no doubt as to the extraordinary influence which it has exercised at all periods down to the present day.

The *Bhakti* movement is closely identified with the worship of Vishnu in the form of his principal *avatar*, Krishna, but perhaps even more deeply embedded in the heart of Hinduism is the figure of the most awe-inspiring and ambivalent of all the gods – Shiva, personification of terror, death

and annihilation, of unbridled sexuality and of the creative forces of nature, the eternal destroyer of the cosmos whose act of destruction precedes his act of recreation. Often he is conceived as the supreme ascetic, lord of *yogis* and *sannyasis*, haunting the burning-grounds with his tiger skin and with his hair matted with serpents and with the skulls of the dead laced into a necklace around his shoulders. Equally often he figures as the supreme erotic deity, worshipped with his *Shakti*, or female-counterpart, in cults in which his *linga* (phallus) and her *yoni* (vulva) are the principal objects of worship. But above all he is Nataraja, or Natesvara, Lord of the Cosmic Dance, the manifestation of the principle of eternal energy, dancing the Tandava upon the body of the demon Muyalaka in the Golden Hall of Tillai.

Yet another manifestation of this great god, the personification of the daemonic energy which is as much an element of Hindu culture as the renunciatory and meditative, is that of Bhairava, 'the terrible one,' or Bhutesvara, 'the demon-lord,' and in this form, 10 armed, smeared with the ashes of corpses, he dances a horrific Tandava in the company of ghosts and evil spirits. Even more

Caste interests, caste factionalism and ultimately caste opportunism have traditionally worked against the emergence of a wider sense of Indian community. This explains in large measure the relative ease with which, throughout Indian history, small bands of invaders secured control over extensive parts of the country, maintained themselves in power without undue effort and regularly extracted tribute from the indigenous population, even when concerted effort on the part of the subject masses might easily have dislodged or contained them.

The beginnings of Indian civilization

For the historian, if not for the archeologist, the story of the Indian people begins with the so-called Indus Valley civilization, which flourished between about 2500 and 1500 BC over much of the northwest. The sites excavated so far – Mohenjodaro and Kot Diji in Sind, Harappa and Rupar in the Punjab, Kalibangan in Rajasthan, and Lothal in Kathiawar – have revealed a comparatively

advanced urban culture centered on large carefully planned cities constructed of brick, with wide streets and remarkable drainage systems. The absence of elaborate fortifications suggests that their original builders felt little need to protect themselves from external attack, while the fact that archeologists have failed to uncover anything resembling a palace complex implies that there was no court or royal bureaucracy. How these cities were ruled remains a mystery, but it is possible that they were governed by some kind of theocratic regime similar to those to be found in the contemporary Sumerian city-states. The religion of the inhabitants of Mohenjodaro and Harappa also remains a mystery, although the cult figures that have been discovered include a phallic deity who may be a prototype of Shiva.

In relation to the surrounding countryside these urban complexes were clearly parasitic and exploitive, maintaining their food supply of grains and cereals by siphoning off the agricultural surplus produced by the rural population and storing it in large granaries. The Indus Valley cities also maintained an active commerce, and probably close cultural contacts, with Sumeria and the Persian Gulf region. Knowledge of iron they altogether lacked, but the metals they did possess – copper and bronze – they wrought with considerable skill, exemplified by the famous bronze statuette of a dancing-girl recovered from Mohenjodaro.

Elsewhere in India the picture during the first two millennia BC remains shadowy. In the Gangetic plain there were settlements of a people who made a crude ochre-colored pottery and perhaps combined hunting with primitive agriculture. In the Deccan the evidence points to a culture where flint tools were in use side by side with artifacts of bronze and copper. In the far south there was a more complex megalithic culture that may conceivably have had links with Mediterranean megalithic culture. The racial composition of peninsular India was by this time already extremely diverse, and although it has now become an accepted convention to refer to the inhabitants of the south as Dravidians, the term is, strictly speaking, a linguistic one and should properly be applied only to speakers of the four main Dravidian tongues of the south – Tamil, Telugu, Malayalam and Kannada.

Sometime after 1500 BC the subcontinent was entered from the northwest by a formidable wave of invaders whose conquest and colonization of the north and of the Deccan imposed upon the country patterns of social organization, culture and belief which, although greatly modified by the passage of time, have survived to the present. As in the case of the term Dravidian, long-established convention has styled these invaders Aryans, again a linguistic rather than a racial designation. But the usage is now so hallowed that it would be pedantic to attempt to substitute an alternative. The Aryans who entered India were a part of the same great migration of pastoralists out of Central Asia that also led to the occupation of the Iranian plateau in the course of the first two millennia BC. And, like the latter, these newcomers to India were both iron-workers and horse-breeders. They also shared with their Iranian kinsfolk a common spiritual and linguistic heritage.

The Aryans brought with them into India the Vedic gods they had worshipped on the steppes. In addition to the sacrificial rites they performed, they brought, as well, a surprisingly speculative turn of mind that was later to be manifested in the literature of the *Upanishads*. They were also, it would seem, the founders of the caste system.

No less important, as soon as they made themselves masters of the Gangetic plain, gradually abandoning their pastoral lifestyle, they began to clear the forests and to establish village communities based exclusively upon agriculture. In the course of time these communities began to yield what must have been a substantial surplus of agricultural produce, for without that surplus neither the elaborate bureaucratic framework of the ancient Indian polity nor its vigorous and ingenious cultural life would have been possible. The agricultural revolution of Vedic India was indispensable foundation upon which all the subsequent empires were built.

Kingdoms of the plains

The process by which the Aryans' older forms of social and political organization were forgotten or abandoned did not occur everywhere at the same pace, and while in the central area of the Gangetic plain powerful chieftains staked out their claims to independent kingdoms, there survived in the Punjab and in the direction of the foothills oligarchical 'republics' founded by single tribes or by groups of inter-related tribes in places where it was still possible to cling to the old ways. These republics may also have served as centers of resistance to the rapid spread of brahminical power that was characteristic of the kingdoms of the plains, and this may explain why the areas controlled by these republics were later to play so important a part in the diffusion of Buddhism.

The future, however, lay with the kingdoms of the plains. Here, rulers wielding great coercive authority and enjoying extensive economic resources derived from an expanding agricultural base promoted an ideology of government that emphasized brahminical domination of society. While many communities in this region remained little more than overgrown villages, some were to become great metropolitan centers, such as Taxila, between the Indus and the Jhelum in the Punjab, Pataliputra and Benares on the Ganges, Ayodhya on the Ghaghra in Oudh, and Ujjain on the Sipra in Malwa.

Of the various kingdoms established in the Gangetic plain the most important was Magadha, with its capital at Rajagriha in southern Bihar. From the middle of the sixth century BC down to the second half of the fourth century BC successive dynasties in control of this region maintained a formidable military establishment based upon an expanding revenue from agriculture, monopoly of the river trade and the effective coercion of their subjects through the agency of a powerful bureaucracy. The last of the dynasties of Magadha, the Nandas, managed to keep a very large army on a permanent war footing and developed an elaborate system of land revenue assessment and collection. They were thus in a position to carve out for themselves what would have been the first empire in northern India and would surely have done so had they not been overthrown by Chandragupta Maurya, who in 322 BC toppled the Nanda kingdom and built upon its ruins the short-lived Mauryan Empire, the first and only indigenous Indian regime to control a substantial part of the subcontinent.

The Mauryan Empire

There is a legend that, as a young fugitive, the future founder of the Mauryan Empire sought refuge in the camp of Alexander the Great, who briefly invaded the Punjab as far as the river Beas in 326 BC. Whatever the truth of the story, the fact remains that India's first great adventure in imperial rule followed close upon the Macedonian irruption into the Punjab. But if the far eastern

Left: Little is known of the religion of the Indus Valley civilization, but this terracotta figurine is believed to represent a mother-goddess.

Right: A Buddhist stupa built on the site of ancient Mohenjodaro, striking evidence of the cultural continuity of India.

Below: The conception of the Buddha – his mother dreams that he enters into her womb in the form of a small white elephant.

conquests of Alexander held any fascination for the young Chandragupta, it was probably less the military aspects of Alexander's campaigns than what lay behind them – the example of the mighty empire of the Achaemenids, of which first Alexander and then Seleucus I (312-280 BC) were the heirs.

The foreign element in Mauryan imperialism has long been a matter of scholarly controversy, but the Mauryans' debt to Achaemenid Iran seems clear. The elaborate organization of the Mauryan bureaucracy, the provincial structure modeled on the Achaemenid satrapies, the system of espionage recommended in the *Arthashastra* (a political manual attributed to Chandragupta's minister, Kautilya), the construction of a highway across northern India like that which ran from Susa to Sardis and even the very concept of empire, all reflect Persian influence. The Kharoshthi script used in the Ashokan edicts found in north western India was itself an offshoot of Aramaic, the *lingua franca* of the Achaemenid Empire, while the use of rock inscriptions as vehicles for propaganda was surely derived

from Achaemenid practice, as was – consciously or unconsciously – the style of their phrasing. Similarly, Mauryan art betrays unmistakable Persian elements.

In religious matters the Mauryans appear to have been distinctly eclectic. Chandragupta Maurya, having carved out for himself a north Indian empire stretching from Bengal to the former Achaemenid satrapy of Arachosia (the Kandahar region), and extending as far south as the Narbada, is said to have renounced his throne, to have become a Jain monk and to have starved himself to death around 297 BC. His son, Bindusare (297-272 BC), who was apparently something of a philhellenist (he asked Antiochus I to send him a Sophist) and who pushed the frontiers of the empire southward as far as Mysore and the Carnatic, reputedly patronized the sect of ascetics known as Ajivikas.

The third Mauryan Emperor, Ashoka (c 272-232 BC), who rounded off his father's and grandfather's conquests with the annexation of Kalinga (Orissa), was allegedly so sickened by the carnage that accompanied it that he resolved to abandon aggressive warfare against his neighbors, to practice non-violence and to become a Buddhist. Such, at least, is the tradition. Probably Ashoka's conversion was neither so sudden nor so straightforward a decision, but Buddhism was undoubtedly the most dynamic spiritual force of the age, and it is doubtful whether, in some form or another, any ruler in northern India during the third century BC could have avoided coming to terms with it.

The influence of Buddhism

Siddhartha the Buddha was born around 566 BC, the son of a *kshattriya* ruler of the Gautama clan of the Sakya tribe, whose capital, Kapilavastu, was situated north of Benares within the frontiers of modern Nepal. At the age of 29 he abandoned his home, including a wife and new-born son, for the life of a wandering ascetic, and after experimenting for a period of six years with various auster-

ities and penances which failed to bring him the enlightenment he sought so ardently, he turned to meditation. For seven weeks he meditated beneath a fig tree at a place now known as Budh Gaya in the Gay District of Bihar, and there he attained enlightenment – knowledge that the suffering in the world was rooted in human desire, which in turn resulted from ignorance. He was now 35 years old, and for the remaining 45 years of his life he wandered through northern India as an itinerant sage and was honored as the Buddha, or the Enlightened One. The essence of his teachings was the belief that *karma*, the doctrine of rebirth so deeply embedded at the heart of Hinduism, was a burden that could only be discarded by the attainment of *Nirvana*, or annihilation, which meant release from the wheel of rebirth. Salvation was possible by following a Noble Eightfold Path consisting of right views, right aspirations, right speech, right conduct, right livelihood, right effort, right mindfulness and right meditation.

Even during his own lifetime (he died around 483 BC) the Buddha's impact was felt far and wide. He himself established orders of monks, and while at first these lived as wandering mendicants, spreading his teaching from village to village, they were later brought together in permanent monastic communities. Even more revolutionary, orders of nuns were established. The monastic framework imposed a kind of discipline upon the new sect and provided dedicated agents for the propagation of its tenets. It also favored the development of formalized religious teaching, and in course of time there would emerge great centers of Buddhist learning – in effect, India's oldest universities – at Nalanda in Bihar and at Taxila in the Punjab.

Among other things, Buddhism was a movement of protest against the tightening grip of brahminical orthodoxy. Both the caste system in its original form and the subsequent ascendancy of the *brahmins* over other castes were phenomena of the pre-urban phase of Indian history,

Left: Prince Siddhartha, the Buddha, decides to abandon his home and family to seek the meaning of existence.

Below: The south gate of the Buddhist stupa at Sanchi, dating from the middle of the second century BC.

Right: A reliquary from the period of Kanishka's rule over the Kushan empire in northern India, early second century AD.

Below right: Most of these ruins outside Delhi are Islamic, but the imposing iron pillar was erected by Chandragupta II, the greatest of the Gupta rulers.

but with the appearance of towns and cities and with the growing importance of commerce, passive acquiescence of their relatively depressed status became increasingly irksome to the lower castes, especially to the *vaishyas* engaged in trade and manufacturing. For these urban folk, merchants and artisans alike, as well as for the *shudras* and *panchamas*, Buddhism proved extremely appealing. Indeed, it was these same groups that, centuries later, would be drawn to the *Bhakti* cults and to Sufi Islam.

Doctrinal schism

By Ashoka's time the first signs of doctrinal schism had already began to appear within the Buddhist community. There were differences of opinion over what should be included in the sacred writings, the *Tripitaka*, over the rules of religious training and above all over the true meaning of Buddha's teachings. The schism gradually widened until, during the first century BC the Buddhist world was split into two divisions, one adhering to the *Mahayana* (or Great Vehicle) doctrine, the other to the *Theravada* doctrine (also referred to as Hinayana or Lesser Vehicle by Mahayana partisans.) Theravada adherents eventually became predominant in the south and east, penetrating all of southern India, Ceylon, and Indochina. Mahayana Buddhism spread predominantly to the west and north into Afghanistan, China, Korea and eventually, by the sixth century, to Japan. The early Buddhist influence in Indonesia was also of Mahayana pursuasion. In Tibet yet another distinct form of Buddhism came into being through fusion with the indigenous Bon beliefs. Sectarian development was particularly rich in China and Japan, when imported ideas were fused with indigenous beliefs to create sects such as Zen and Jodo (pure hand), which were different from the Indian-based sects.

Yet for all Buddhism's success in areas outside of its country of origin, Brahminical Hinduism remained the religion of the majority of the inhabitants of the Mauryan Empire, and remained so in the centuries that followed. That Buddhism survived in India for so many centuries after the fall of the Mauryan Empire must be attributed in part to the fact that it appealed so strongly to the various invaders who were shortly to begin successive penetrations of the Punjab from the hills beyond the Indus.

The Shungas, Satavahanas and Bactrian Greeks

With Ashoka's death in 232 BC the outlying provinces of the empire soon detached themselves. The Gangetic plain, however, remained under the control of his successors for a further half century before passing into the hands of the Shunga dynasty of Magadha (183-73 BC).

The founder of this line, Pushyamitra Shunga (183-151 BC), commander in chief of the last Mauryan emperor, whom he murdered, was very probably of Iranian stock but he and his descendants were apparently accepted as *brahmins*, and the Shungas, as the instruments of a resurgent brahminism, savagely persecuted the Buddhists and destroyed their monasteries.

Meanwhile, in the Deccan a Telugu-speaking people, the Andhras, from the region now called Andhra Pradesh (the former Hyderabad State) began to build up a powerful and long-lived kingdom that extended over a vast area in central India. The greatest dynasty of the Andhras, the Satavahana, ruled from 28 BC to AD 250. Like the Shungas, the Satavahanas assumed the status of *brahmins*, although the founder of the line, Simuka, may well have been, like Pushyamitra, of Iranian stock. Unlike the Shungas, however, the early Satavahanas, far from persecuting the Buddhists, actively supported them and patronized their religious establishments. Thus to the Satavahanas, who repaired and reconstructed the original Mauryan shrines at Sanchi near Bhopal and at Amaravati in Guntur District, is probably due to the survival of some of the finest examples of Buddhist art.

A third, non-indigenous, and on the whole rather mysterious, people who affected Indian history were the Greek colonists who inhabited Bactria, northwest of the Hindu Kush, and who began to move into India during the second century BC. The first Greek ruler of Bactria to penetrate south of the Kabul Valley was Demetrius I (c 189-167 BC), whose father, Euthydemus of Magnesia, had superseded the line of Diodotus. Demetrius almost certainly did not penetrate into India proper, but he advanced into Arachosia (the Kandahar region) and perhaps Sind, in consequence of which he assumed the elephant-scalp helmet of Alexander on his coinage. Probably around the same time other Greeks began to make their way across the Indus, at first as raiders (and perhaps also as mercenaries), but later as colonizers intent upon permanent occupation. The newcomers appear to have maintained their hold over the country from fortified urban bases, and probably their impact upon the cultivating communities of the region was minimal. The centers of their power were Pushkalavati (the modern Charsada, near Peshawar), Taxila, between the Indus and the Jhelum, and Sakala, an unknown site in the eastern Punjab, probably in Jammu. Wherever they went they founded settlements that conformed to their established notions of what constituted a civilized urban environment, and excavation has shown that at Taxila the earlier Achaemenid city was replaced by a new settlement (Sircap) laid out with Hellenistic grid-planning. An important stage on the caravan route between India and Central Asia, Taxila was a populous and wealthy emporium that sheltered within its walls a vigorous, if highly syncretistic, cultural and religious life. It was the revenue drawn from the commerce of such cities, rather than the yield from agriculture, that accounted for the prosperity of the Indo-Greek communities in the Punjab.

No records exist of the foundation of the Indo-Greek kingdom, but two factors that may have accelerated its establishment were the overthrow of Demetrius I by Eucratides I and the steady pressure of Saca raiders from the north, which together may have led the successors of Demetrius I to probe deeper into the subcontinent. This would have been largely the work of Apollodotus I (c 167-160 BC) and his immediate successors – Menander (c 155-154 BC), Antialcidas (c 145-135 BC), and Strato I (c 135-25 BC). Menander's sumptuous capital, Sakala, is described admiringly by the author of the *Milindapanha*, a Buddhist treatise in a form resembling a Platonic dialogue, in which King Milinda (Menander) interrogates a Buddhist missionary regarding the nature of his beliefs. Whether Menander actually embraced Buddhism is unknown, but the tradition that he did convert underscores the fact that the Indo-Greeks, like the Sacas and Kushans who followed them, soon came to terms with what must have been the most dynamic religious movement they had encountered during their advance eastward. Although the first half of the first century BC saw Indo-Greek rule in the Punjab collapse under the weight of Saca incursions from beyond the Indus, the 'valiant Yavanas' found a permanent place in Sanskrit literature as a result of Greek traders and adventurers having penetrated far beyond the limits of Menander's kingdom, even reaching dis-

tant Tamilnad (in present day southern India), where the rulers of Madurai employed a body-guard of Yavanas to keep their own subjects in check.

The Saca conquests

The Indo-Greeks had originally been expelled from Bactria by Saca tribesmen advancing from beyond the Amu-Darya, and those same nomads now made their way southward into Kapisa, Gandhara and Arachosia before turning east across the Indus to establish regimes which inter-mittently would dominate much of northern India for the next 400 years – not only in the Pun-jab, Sind, Rajasthan and Gujarat, but also as far east as Mathura on the Jumna and Ujjain in Malwa, and as far south as Nasik in the Deccan.

The Sacas had been deflected by the Parthians under Mithridates II (c 123-87 BC) from occupying the Iranian plateau. As a result, they turned toward India as the only alternative to westward expansion. The chronology of their conquests is confusing, but it appears that the first Saca ruler of whom there is numismatic evidence, Maues (97-c 77 BC), who perhaps began his career as a mercenary commander in the service of the Indo-Greek kings, established his headquarters at Taxila, and by the time of his death he had pene-trated as far east as Mathura. Maues was suc-ceeded by a line of chieftains all of whom seem to have struck an abundant coinage. Then, around the beginning of the Christian Era, this Saca dynasty in Arachosia and northwestern India (if indeed it was a single dynasty) was replaced by a line of Parthian rulers originating from Sistan and perhaps distantly related to the Arsacid royal house. Like the Sacas the Indo-Parthian rulers seem to have established themselves in the former centers of Indo-Greek rule, and they too made Taxila their capital. The best-known of the line, Gondophares (c 20-46 AD), received the Apostle St Thomas who, according to an early Syriac tradition, converted him to Christianity. The Indo-Parthian kings were undoubtedly powerful rulers, but from the point of view of their Indian subjects their rule was perhaps not very different from that of the Greeks and the Saca chieftains. In course of time the Indo-Par-thian royal house and its personal retainers must have become inextricably mingled by marriage alliances with the Saca tribal nobility, and all were eventually absorbed into the indigenous popu-lation of northwestern India as *kshattriyas*. Liter-ary references in Sanskrit to the 'Pahlavas,' as in the case of the 'Yavanas,' long survived their dis-appearance from the political scene.

Invasion by the Kushans

The Indo-Parthian kingdom succumbed to the Kushans, invaders who had already established themselves as dangerous neighbors of the Arsa-cids on the northeastern marches of Iran. The original homeland of the Kushans, as well as their race and language, have long baffled historians. Whether they were Indo-Europeans, Turks, Mon-gols or even Tibetans (as some have improbably argued), it is certain that by the time they entered India, probably in the middle decades of the first century AD, prior familiarity with the Iranian borderlands and with the Saca tribes whom they had subjugated had resulted in their paartial Iran-icization. Like the Parthians they wore baggy trousers, long shirts and loose cloaks, and by choice they fought on horseback, wearing laminated armor like the Parthians and the Sacas, and favoring 3-foot swords in addition to lances and bows.

Toward the middle of the first century AD the

Kushan chieftain Kujula Kadphises, who had carved out a large realm north of the Hindu Kush, rounded off his earlier conquests by occupying the Kabul Valley and advancing toward the Indus. These eastern campaigns were essentially probing operations, and the true bent of his interests, which was toward the west, was reflected in the style of his coinage, which was an imitation of the Roman *denarius*. It was his successor, Vima Kad-phises, who staked out a north Indian empire for himself when he advanced into the Punjab, brought to an end the rule of the Indo-Parthian line of Gondophares and drove the defeated rem-nants of the Sacas southeastward into Malwa and Gujarat. Of the five Saca satrapies known to have existed, three fell to the Kushans. The remaining two, however, survived the coming of the Kushans under two virtually independent dynas-ties – the Kshaharata and the Kardamaka (AD 77-398), a long-lived dynasty that in due course swallowed up the Kshaharatas and that, at its most flourishing, controlled much of western India. Under the most powerful Kardamaka ruler, Rudradaman (130-158), Ujjain, his capital, became an unrivalled center of Sanskrit learning and literature.

Vima Kadphises extended the Kushan con-quests eastward down the Ganges as far as Benares, but although the center of his power rested in the Gandhara country, midway between the northwestern and southeastern frontiers of his far-flung realm, it is clear that by the time of his death the fulcrum of the Kushan Empire rested in India. The date of the accession of his successor, the celebrated Kanishka, has been variously calculated between AD 78 and 144, with perhaps the earlier date being closer to the mark. Under Kanishka the Kushan Empire reached its greatest extent: its Indian territories stretched eastward into Bihar and southward at least as far as the vicinity of Sanchi in Madhya Pradesh and perhaps even as far as the Konkan; the Central Asian territories included the Kabul Valley, Bac-

Left: A decapitated statue of the Kushan emperor Kanishka, a ruler who positively encouraged the spread of Buddhism.

Below: This sculpture of the Buddha, like many others from the early centuries AD, reveals an unmistakable Greek influence.

Right: One of two giant Buddhas carved out of the rock face at Bamiyan, in central Afghanistan.

tria north of the Hindu Kush, the area between the Amu-Darya and the Syr-Darya, Kashmir and part of what is now Sinkiang.

Methods of government

Inevitably Kushan rule, like that of all early Indian empires, involved a considerable degree of admi-nistrative decentralization. Yet notwithstanding a certain looseness in their control of their outlying possessions, the Kushan rulers, contemporaries of the Roman Antonines, were well aware of the scale of their empire and hence assumed appro-priate titles such as *Maharajatiraja*, equivalent to the Iranian 'King of Kings' and *Daivaputra*, equiva-lent to the Chinese 'Son of Heaven.'

The wealth of the Kushans was founded on their control of the transcontinental caravan

Kushan artistic achievements

The imperial art of the Kushans, which included both the Hellenized style of Gandhara and the more obviously indigenous style of the Mathura region, reflected that syncretistic spirit which was so vital an element in the social, institutional and cultural patterns that emerged in northern India, after the fall of the Mauryas, under a succession of alien conquerors. The significance of that art, both for future developments within the subcontinent and for the growth of a continental Buddhist inconography can hardly be exaggerated.

The confusion surrounding the chronology of both the Gandhara School and the dynasty that was its most lavish patron renders it almost impossible to date the course of early Buddhist iconography. It seems probable, however, that by the time that the figure of the Buddha appeared on the Bimaran casket (assigned to the second half of the first century AD) representation of the figure of the Buddha had become accepted practice, at least in the northwest. What is significant, however, is that from the outset the techniques employed, as well as the features and dress of the figures, bore the unmistakable stamp of Hellenistic influence. Whether the actual sculptors of Gandhara were Greeks by descent or Indian apprentices of former Greek masters, the figures that emerged from their workshops betrayed a western ancestry. The Buddha himself was rendered as a contemplative Apollo, serene and handsome, dressed in richly draped robes, with an elaborate *chignon* and with elongated earlobes. Similarly, the Bodhisattvas and other figures in the growing Buddhist pantheon were generally represented as noble Central Asian chieftains, with Saca or Kushan features.

Meanwhile, from the second century AD onwards, there began to be carved in Mathura and elsewhere statues of the Buddha which, if they lacked the spiritual abstraction of the Buddha images of Gupta times, nevertheless seemed to express a more intense awareness of the Buddha's inner spirituality than did the aristocratic Buddhas of Gandhara. Thus there emerged in the Kushan period two more or less independent traditions of Buddhist iconography, the one looking northwest and the other south and east. It was, however, the Gandhara style, linked as it was to Kushan missionary activity in Central Asia, that was to play the dominant role in the shaping of the Buddhist iconographic tradition.

The Gandhara style, like the religion it served, followed the caravan trails trodden by Buddhist monks, pausing here and there to establish a permanent community at some suitable location, as happened at Bamiyan, or to found *viharas* or monastaries built around a central *stupa*, such as can still be seen in Afghanistan beside ancient highways like the one formerly linking Gardiz and Kabul. The spread of the style must have been remarkably rapid, for it is probable that the frescoes uncovered by Sir Aurel Stein at Miran in the Tarim basin in Xinjiang date from the lifetime of Kanishka.

The causes of the fall of the Kushan Empire are shrouded in obscurity. It is possible that the decay of Kushan rule was connected with changing patterns of commerce, upon which the wealth of the empire was based. On the other hand, the large numbers of figures of Hariti, goddess of smallpox, that have survived from Kushan times may indicate the prevalance of devastating epidemics. In the near term, however, the downfall of the Kushans followed directly from the foundation of the Sasanid Empire in Iran by Ardashir I (*c* 224-*c* 239). According to Iranian sources, the Kushans were defeated in battle by Ardashir or his son,

trade by means of which Rome and Parthia acquired the silks of China and the Chinese obtained, among other luxury goods, Indian ivories and Alexandrian glassware. The Kushans adapted and modified to suit their own needs both the surviving administrative framework of the remote Mauryan past and, perhaps more important, the surviving administrative techniques of the Achaemenids and of the Bactrian Greeks. Thus the empire was divided into satrapies, each of which was ruled by a *kshatrapa*. The Greek titles of *meridarch* (governor) and *strategos* (general) were also retained.

The Kushan emperors, and in particular Kanishka, gave positive encouragement to the dissemination of Buddhism. Under Kanishka's patronage the Fourth Buddhist Council was convened in Kashmir and was attended by 500 monks from throughout the subcontinent. At Purushapura he commissioned the construction of an enormous *stups* (a solid dome of masonry containing a relic such as a hair or a tooth of the Buddha), seemingly the work of a Greek architect, Agesilaus. In it, excavations in 1908 uncovered a copper-gilt reliquary that, together with the Bimaran gold-casket, exemplifies Gandhara metal-work at its best. Kanishka's reign saw the rapid spread of Buddhism into Central Asia and along the Silk Road through Khotan into China, and it is perhaps to this period that the earliest of the two colossal figures of the Buddha carved in the cliff-face at Bamiyan, a secluded valley between the Hindu Kush and the Koh-i Baba in Central Afghanistan, should be assigned.

The period of the Gupta empire, from about AD 320 to 530, is generally regarded as a Golden Age in Indian history. The Ajanta caves (left), near Aurangabad in the Deccan, contain perhaps the finest relics of Gupta civilization. They include Buddhist statues and shrines (below) and a magnificent series of wall-paintings (right), showing exceptional refinement of taste and realism of detail.

point where they may actually have been regarded as outside the caste system altogether.

It was Chandragupta's son and successor, Samudragupta (330-79), who laid the real foundations of the empire by conquering Bengal to the east, the region of the upper Ganges and the Jumna to the west and extensive tracts in central India, although he refrained from advancing into the Panjab and from challenging the once-formidable Sacas who had for so long ruled Malwa and Gujarat. That conquest was to be the achievement of his son, Chandragupta II Vikramaditya (380-413), the greatest ruler of the line, who broke the Saca power, annexed Malwa, Gujarat and Kathiawar, and bequeathed to his son, Kumaragupta I (415-55), an empire extending from the Bay of Bengal to the Arabian Sea and from the Himalayas to the Narbada. He may even have extended his frontiers south of the Narbada into the Deccan, where perhaps he exercised a nominal overlordship, but at all events his prestige was sufficiently great to justify his performing a great *ashvamedha*, or horse-sacrifice.

Historians of the subcontinent are almost unanimous in regarding the Gupta period as a sort of Golden Age. Despite the aggressive policy of the Gupta emperors towards their neighbors and ceaseless frontier warfare, it appears that the heartlands of the empire enjoyed a remarkable degree of peace and security. Gupta rule pressed comparatively lightly upon the cultivator, and the administrative system was less harsh than that of Mauryan times or during the post-Gupta period. The land revenue tax was fixed at as little as one-sixth of the gross produce of the soil, whereas it was one-quarter under the Mauryans and one-third under the Mughul Emperor Akbar in the second half of the sixteenth century. Probably a substantial part of the revenue of the state was derived from plunder acquired during the successful campaigns of such tireless warriors as Samudragupta and Chandragupta II.

For the wealthy, life in Gupta India must have been very good indeed, a full and leisured existence in which secular pastimes and pleasures played at least as important a part as the fulfillment of *dharma* or the performance of the prescribed rituals. Certainly much of the surviving literature of the age is imbued with a vibrant, life-affirming humanism such as is rarely associated in the European mind with the Hindu 'Great Tradition.' Thus in the celebrated treatise on erotics, the *Kamasutra* of Vatsyayana, who may have lived during the reign of Kumaragupta I or his son Skandagupta, the ideal qualities with which the poet endowed model lovers reflect the prevailing values of the day, or at least those of the ruling elite:

Men of high birth, learned, with a good knowledge of the world, and doing the proper things at the proper times; poets, good storytellers, eloquent men, energetic men skilled in various arts, farseeing into the future, possessed of great minds, full of perseverance, of a firm devotion, free from anger, liberal, affectionate to their parents, and with a liking for all social gatherings, skilled in completing verses begun by others and in various other sports, free from all disease, possessed of a perfect body, strong, and not addicted to drinking, powerful in sexual enjoyment, sociable, showing love toward women and attracting their hearts to himself but not entirely devoted to them, possessed of independent means of livelihood, free from envy and, last of all, free from suspicion.

The list is one that would have been wholly acceptable in Periclean Athens.

The religious policy adopted by the Guptas was one of toleration, and although the dynasty itself

---

Shapur I, and their territories west of the Indus passed under Sasanid control, perhaps in the last year of the reign of Vasudeva. Kushan rule continued in an emasculated state east of the Indus, where a branch of the imperial line survived at Mathura for nearly a century, but it is known almost solely from its coinage. By the beginning of the fourth century the Kushans had virtually disappeared from the Indian scene.

The golden age of the Guptas

The rule of the Guptas extended from the first quarter of the fourth century AD until the second half of the fifth century, when it was shattered by the invasions of the Hephthalite Huns. (A cadet line, however, survived in Magadha down to the eighth century.) In certain respects the Gupta Empire in northern India complimented the contemporary Sasanid Empire in Iran. Like the Sasanids, the Guptas were of indigenous stock, and so their rise, after centuries of rule by alien Central Asian warlords, is interpreted by Indian historians as something of a national revival, in the same way that Iranian historians interpret the rise of the Sasanids. Like the Sasanids, too, the Guptas were aggressive rulers who waged bloody wars upon their neighbors, reckless of the cost in human suffering. There has grown up in the twentieth century, largely due to the charismatic personality of Mahatma Gandhi, a misconception

that India possessed a long-standing tradition of non-violence, but, disregarding the fact that his concept is of Buddhist rather than of Hindu derivation, the historian of the subcontinent is bound to record that there is little evidence to suggest that the history of India has been any less violent than that of Europe or the Middle East. Medieval Indian society was intensely militaristic, and Indian literature as a whole tended to glorify the warrior's creed and only rarely condemn warfare as such.

Although its antecedents are uncertain, there seems to be no reason to doubt the tradition that the Gupta dynasty itself was of low caste, and there is surely some significance in the fact that several Gupta rulers formed marriage alliances with non-Aryan and even foreign women. Chandragupta I (320-28), who began his career by seizing Magadha, where the Kushans had never ruled, allied himself with a Lichchhavi princess, presumably in order to enlist military support from that warlike tribe. The Lichchhavis were probably of Mongoloid stock, perhaps with an Aryan layer superimposed at the top, and occupied the territory north and east of Magadha as far as present-day Nepal and southern Tibet. Centuries before, their caste status had been comparatively illustrious, and the family of the Buddha's mother had been of Lichchhavi descent, but by the third and fourth centuries AD their status had fallen to a

Left, right and below right:
Carved Buddhas at the Ajanta caves. Although themselves Hindus, the Guptas actively patronised Buddhist religion and art.

was Hindu, Buddhism continued to flourish, even enjoying the active patronage of members of the ruling house. In literature and in intellectual life, in education, in the arts and architecture, there was an upsurge the like of which India has probably never experienced with such intensity before

Two of the best known examples are the paintings in the famous Buddhist caves at Ajanta, near Aurangabad in the Deccan (in fact, beyond the frontiers of the Gupta Empire and within the bounds of the Chalukya kingdom), and the writings of the Sanskrit poet Kalidasa, Meghaduta, or Cloud Messenger.

Fall of the Empire

The glory of the Guptas could not last. During the second half of the fifth century the empire was assaulted and felled by the most destructive invaders India ever experienced – the Hephthalites, or White Huns, known in Sanskrit literature as 'Hunas.' These were part of that great Hephthalite confederacy that established its headquarters in the Bamiyan Valley in central Afghanistan and that, from early in the fifth century until the middle of the sixth, was so formidable a scourge on the northeastern borderlands of Sasanid Iran. It must have been a branch of the ruling sept in Babiyan that turned southeastward to cross the Indus and penetrate the rich and prosperous territories of the Guptas, notwithstanding the strenuous efforts of Skandagupta (455-567), the son of Kumaragupta, to repel them. For a while he met with some success, so that at first his reign seemed to witness a partial revival of those scenes of imperial splendor over which his father and

grandfather had presided, but during his last years the coinage was debased, unmistakable evidence that all was not well with the state, and after his death there began once more the familiar pattern of declining authority at the center, flouted by ambitious satraps bent upon establishing *de facto* autonomy in their respective regions.

Then, in the last years of the century, the Hunnish pressure began again, this time directed by a powerful chieftain, Toramana, who brought a vast area of northwestern India including Kashmir, Rajasthan, Gujarat and Malwa under the yoke of the Huns and who established his capital at Sakala in the eastern Panjab. He was succeeded by his son, Mihirakula (died *c* 542), but the latter's rule was so oppressive that it provoked militant countermeasures by a confederacy of local chieftains drawn from a wide area and led by Yasodharma, a Saca ruler of Mandasor in Malwa. Mihirakula withdrew into Kashmir, where the *Rajatarangini* of Kalhana preserves two somewhat disparate traditions concerning his rule. In the first, his insane cruelties led the author to compare him with the God of Death himself. But Kalhana also described Mihirakula as a devotee of Shiva, a builder of temples and a pious benefactor of *brahmins* who finally immolates himself upon a funerary pyre in order to attain salvation. The Chinese traveler Hsüan Tsang, writing in the seventh century, stigmatised Mihirakula as a savage foe of the Buddhists, and it is possible to interpret both his persecution of Buddhism and his patronage of *brahmins* as evidence of a mounting upsurge of Brahminical Hinduism,

largely held in check under the rule of the tolerant Guptas.

Both in the Indian and the Central Asian lands conquered by the Huns, Buddhism suffered greatly at the hands of these barbarians, but classical Hindu civilization, as it had evolved under the Guptas, was hardly less of a casualty. By the middle decades of the sixth century, however, Hunnish domination was little more than an evil memory, for the Huns had disappeared within the infinitely capacious caste system, like the Sacas and Kushans who had preceded them. In all probability the racial components of the Gurjara confederacy of the ninth and tenth centuries included a Hunnish element descended from the rank and file of the original invaders, while the chieftains and ruling clans among the Huns were given *kshattriya* status, to be included among the ancestors of the later Rajputs. Nevertheless, the careers of Toramana and Mihirakula had contributed substantially to the ending of one of the most brilliant phases in the history of Indian civilization.

Yet the social and cultural patterns established in the Gupta period outlasted the passing of the empire itself, albeit in attenuated forms, preserved by regional dynasties with mainly regional interests. Even Buddhism survived relatively unscathed in distant Magadha and Bengal, where such centers of learning as Nalanda and Vikramashila, a Tantric university supported by the Pala kings of Bengal (760-1142), continued to attract students and scholars as well as send missionaries into Tibet to effect the conversion of that country.

Greek Civilization

The agricultural revolution of the neolithic had come to the eastern Mediterranean lands by 6000 BC, and the art of pottery was known soon thereafter. By 3000 BC Greece, Ionia and the Levant formed a distinctive cultural zone, in which sea trade was beginning both to diffuse Mesopotamian and Egyptian cultural influences throughout the region and to lay the foundations for local accumulations of wealth. By 2300 BC various trading cities, such as Troy on the Anatolian side of the Hellespont, were rich and thriving, but by far the most important center of Aegean civilization developed on Crete.

Crete was fortunate in several respects. It was large and fertile enough to be able to generate substantial agricultural surpluses. It was ideally situated to conduct sea trade simultaneously with Greece, the Cyclades, Anatolia, the Levant and Egypt. And, as an island, it was relatively immune from any but the most determined outside attack. In these circumstances Bronze-Age Crete flourished, and by 2000 BC it had become the dominant commercial force in the Aegean.

Because scholars have so far been unable to translate either the Cretans' phonic script, the so-called Linear A, or a hieroglyphic script they also used, what we know of their history has to be gleaned from foreign and/or later written sources and from what inferences we can draw from their surviving artifacts. The latter are nothing if not impressive. Cretan pottery, ceramic statuary, jewelry and metalwork are all of the highest order of sophistication and beauty, and from the vivid frescoes with which the Cretans loved to adorn their palace walls we can catch glimpses of other remarkably advanced technologies in textile manufacture, ship design and the like.

Perhaps most impressive of all are the palaces themselves. As in many other early civilizations, as Cretan wealth accumulated, politico-religious

power became more concentrated and eventually began to manifest itself in the erection of great stone palaces in such quasi-urban centers as Knossos, Mallia and Phaestos. These sprawling, richly decorated palaces were very large and so complicated in layout that they have given us the word 'labyrinth' (from the *labrys*, or double axe, a common decorative motif in the palace chambers). Functionally, the palaces were at once the residences of kings, temples dedicated to the mother goddess, warehouses and administrative

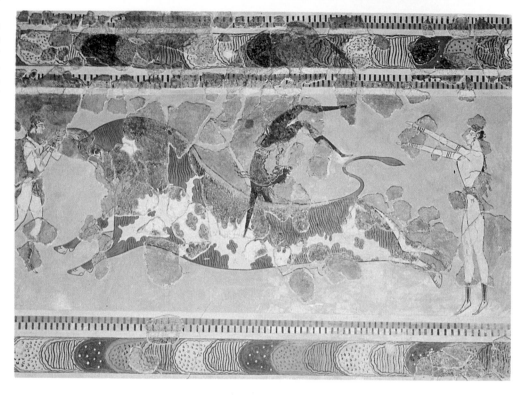

headquarters. The legendary King Minos is said to have governed from the greatest of these palaces, the one at Knossos, and it is from his name that we have coined the adjective meant to denote Cretan civilization at its most powerful and opulent – Minoan.

The Minoan period lasted roughly from 2000 to 1400 BC, the high point being the so-called New Palace Period between 1700 and 1450. It is thought that during this time Crete established a kind of Aegean commercial empire consisting of

Above: Youths engage in the daring sport of bull leaping, in this Minoan wall-painting from the palace at Knossos. A wild bull would be captured and herded into a palace courtyard, to be tormented by the leapers until its ritual slaughter. This may be the truth behind the mythical Minotaur, the body of a man with the head of a bull killed by the Athenian hero Theseus in the labyrinth.

Left: One of the important features of the Minoan palaces was their extensive storerooms. The palaces seem to have served as storage centers for the products of the farms and villages surrounding them.

many far-flung colonies – or, at any rate, subject trading centers – but few details of this polity are known. What *is* obvious is that Cretan cultural influence throughout the Aegean area was immense, and it was nowhere more important than for the mainland tribes who inhabited the Peloponnese of Greece.

The rise of Mycenae

We know little about the origins of these people. Apparently around 2000 BC they arrived in southern Greece as barbarous migrants and established small kingdoms in various locales such as Pylos, Tiryns, Orchomenos and especially Mycenae. Under Minoan influence they rapidly became civilized and developed a distinctive culture that we have named after their pre-eminent kingdom at Mycenae. Interestingly, the Mycenaeans did not use the Cretan Linear A script, and when their own Linear B script was finally deciphered in 1952, it proved to be an extremely primitive form of Greek. It is thus now widely supposed that they were the first Greek-speaking people to live on the mainland.

Mycenaean culture seems to have been based on a curious blend of war and commerce. Semi-divine soldier-kings ruled martial, rigidly stratified societies that also included many skilled artisans – especially metallurgists, architects and

Above: The view from the Lion Gate at Mycenae. In the foreground is Grave Circle A, the site of six burials rich in golden goods. The Mycenean society they represent was the first genuinely Greek society in history, in the sense that they spoke a language recognizable as Greek.

Left: 'I have looked upon the face of Agamemnon,' wrote an excited Heinrich Schliemann when he discovered this golden burial mask in one of the tombs of Mycenae. Schliemann, who had already excavated Troy, was obsessed by the Homeric epics, and uncovered the wonders of Bronze Age Greece in his ultimately futile quest for the burial places of the great heroes of mythology.

Right: A tablet inscribed with the Linear B script, the earliest alphabet known for the Greek language. The symbols remained undeciphered from its rediscovery in the early 1900s until 1953, when Michael Ventris and John Chadwick cracked the mystery of this long-forgotten writing.

Below: The entrance to the 'Treasury of Atreus' – a Mycenean tomb of the Beehive variety. An artificial mound was constructed over a stone chamber vault reached through a long passageway. The doorway of this particular tomb is 19 feet high.

Thera, but this is yet to be proven, and recent evidence suggests that this explosion may have occurred as early as the seventeenth century.) In any event Crete now passed under Mycenaean rule, the Mycenaeans became the dominant commercial power in the Aegean and Mycenaean civilization reached its zenith. Exactly how the new Mycenaean 'empire' was organized or how far it extended we do not know. Probably it was a federation of states loosely centered on Mycenae. This, at any rate, is the impression given by Homer's *Iliad*, a work composed many centuries later and that may or may not accurately represent the facts. As for extent, this empire or ekumene reached at least as far north on the mainland as Boeotia, as well as to Rhodes, Cyprus and doubtless many islands in the Cyclades. And possibly it was much larger, since Mycenaean artifacts have been found as far afield as southern Italy, coastal Syria and Anatolia. The Hittite word *Ahchiyawa* may have been a form of *Achaean*, a word the Greeks would later use to describe themselves. And certainly the tradition of the Mycenaean siege of Troy seems rooted in fact, although scholars dispute the date of the event, some putting it at the beginning of Mycenaean age of dominance and others at the end.

Beginning around 1200 BC the Mycenaeans' Golden Age came to an end under pressure of a new wave of barbarian migrations from the north. At this time the entire eastern part of the Mediterranean was in turmoil. The newcomers, to whom we give the collective name of Dorians, were warlike Greek-speaking peoples who had been living in the Danube valley. For unknown reasons they erupted first into Macedonia and Thessaly and then fanned out southeast and southwest across peninsular Greece and into the Peloponnese. As the Mycenaean kingdoms one by one collapsed under the Dorian onslaught. Greece became a chaos of uprooted peoples moving about in search of sanctuary and stability.

By 1100 BC the Mycenaean ekumene was in ruins, and by 900 BC the whole Greek world was in the depths of a Dark Age that was, if something better than outright barbarism, nevertheless a pale shadow of the civilization that preceded it. Yet out of this night, phoenix-like and almost inexplicably, there would arise the most extraordinary and influential of all the many classical civilizations.

gem-makers – and that were heavily involved in overseas trade. Terracotta vases, textiles, beads, wine and olive oil were among the items the Mycenaeans exported, sometimes over great distances, in return for such necessities as metal and grain.

Unlike the undefended palaces of Crete, Mycenaean palaces took the form of somewhat cheerless stone fortresses built on strategically located hilltops. Kings were sometimes buried in shaft graves inside these citadels and at other times in separate beehive tombs. At the height of Myce-

naean power – roughly 1400 to 1200 BC – both the palace-forts and the tombs grew to massive proportions. The tomb known as The Treasury of Atreus at Mycenae is one of the largest domed structures known to have been built anywhere in the ancient world.

Some time in the fifteenth century BC Minoan power collapsed, and Crete was invaded by Mycenaeans, though whether the invasion caused or followed the collapse is unclear. (Some theorists insist that the Minoan collapse was due to a cataclysmic volcanic explosion on the nearby island of

The songs of Homer materialize like a flash of lightning suddenly illuminating the contours of Greek history some time in the eighth or early seventh century BC. Before them, all – or almost all – is darkness. The great Mycenaean kingdoms had collapsed about four centuries earlier, together with the Hittite empire in Asia Minor and the states of northern Syria. A curtain descends thereafter. Between the time of the legendary Mycenaean King Agamemnon and the Homeric epics there extends a lengthy stretch of Dark Age. It was doubly dark. Dark in the sense that Mycenaean civilization had vanished, the art of writing had been lost and the accoutrements of culture were gone. And dark, too, in the fact that our knowledge of the era is negligible. Later Greek tradition speaks of a Dorian invasion, evidently from the north, just as Egyptian records preserve traces of incursions by mysterious 'sea-peoples.' Perhaps these movements were not so sudden as tradition reports, but the cataclysmic effects cannot be gainsaid: destruction of the palaces in Greece and Crete, dissolution of the royal bureaucracies, impoverishment of the upper classes, virtual collapse of Mediterranean trade, evaporation of bronze-working and luxury crafts, the onset of the Iron Age. Invasions produced devastation, reduction of the populace to the subsistence level and scattering of many inhabitants of Greece to the Aegean islands and the western littoral of Asia Minor.

When the curtain rose again, around 750 BC, a new society had emerged. Greeks now extended across the Aegean to the borders of Near Eastern kingdoms. Literacy had reappeared, learned from Phoenician sailors and traders who transmitted the Semitic alphabet. The effects of fragmentation were still there. That much is demonstrated by a variety of Greek dialects, primarily Aeolic, Ionic and Doric, running in bands, north to south, in Asia Minor and the islands, and distributed in more scattered fashion on the mainland. But the written language built the Aegean into a community. Artisans were also at work. A new style of pottery is evident: 'geometric pottery' scholars have dubbed it. The potters' ware exhibits a developed sense of form and line, reflecting in part the logic and structure of the world about them, a feeling of confidence in its stability. To be sure, the process of change had been in some ways gradual. Continuity was nowhere totally shattered in the Dark Age. Geometric ware grew out of earlier styles which prefigured it, just as Homer's epics depended on a lengthy oral tradition preserved through the era when literacy was lost. But nevertheless, the age that dawned in Greece in the eighth century was genuinely new.

The *Iliad* and *Odyssey* were created in Ionia, a symptom of the maturing Greek culture of Asia Minor. Tradition ascribed both poems to Homer, reputedly a blind bard from Chios. Many modern scholars now incline to see two poets, separated by a generation or more, one in the eighth, one perhaps as late as the early seventh century. Be that as it may, the two poems stand as monuments of the creative mind. A long-standing oral tradition was there to be drawn upon, but out of it were fashioned and consolidated sweeping narratives of epic grandeur and compelling power. For the Greeks, Homer was their nearest approximation to Holy Writ. The epics were endlessly recited and committed to memory by generations of Greek schoolboys. Homeric heroes and themes from the poems reappear again and again in all succeeding eras of Greek literature and art. As such they formed a common heritage for the Hellenes – perhaps the single most important element in their sense of cultural identity.

Not the least of the poems' value lies in their reflection of the new society. To be sure, they look back to a distant past, an idealized golden era of heroes and men who were larger than life, the era of Mycenae and Agamemnon, of the Trojan War, and the wanderings of Odysseus, before darkness enveloped the Bronze Age. But remembrance of things past was not perfect. The poet filled in by describing a social structure more closely akin to that of his own day, and in the process providing a rare insight into Greek life.

Societies ruled by nobles

Greek society of the eighth century BC was essentially an aristocratic society. The Homeric heroes are called kings, *basileis*, but the appellation is misleading. Their kingdoms are minor principalities or petty baronies. There is no trace of the elaborate royal prerogatives or intricate bureaucracies disclosed by the Linear B tablets of Mycenaean Greece. And the terms are different. The Mycenaean monarch was a *wanax*, a king in the larger sense. To Homer, rulers are princelings, *basilois*. Agamemnon, king of Mycenae, captained the expedition to Troy. But his position, as described by Homer, was no more than a first among equals, his power subject to challenge by proud and independent leaders of contingents from elsewhere in Greece. Nor was the king's authority absolute at home. Odysseus returned to find his realm an object of contention among several nobles; Agamemnon's homecoming was followed by assassination and a palace revolt. The predominant impression is that of a weakening of monarchy and a division of power among the principal noble clans. Again the process must have been slow rather than sudden. But by Homer's day the aristocratic character of Greek societies was a fact.

The term 'societies' rather than 'states' is here crucial. It will not do to imagine sophisticated political organization. There was no formal constitutional order, no elaborate legal system or bureaucratic machinery, no hierarchy of governmental officials. These were yet to come. The lines

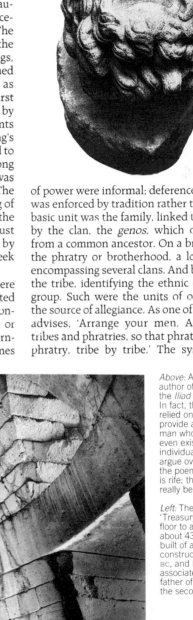

of power were informal; deference due the nobles was enforced by tradition rather than by law. The basic unit was the family, linked to other families by the clan, the *genos*, which claimed descent from a common ancestor. On a broader level was the phratry or brotherhood, a loose association encompassing several clans. And beyond that was the tribe, identifying the ethnic connection of a group. Such were the units of organization and the source of allegiance. As one of Homer's figures advises, 'Arrange your men, Agamemnon, by tribes and phratries, so that phratry may stand by phratry, tribe by tribe.' The system depended

Above: A bust of Homer, author of the great epics, the *Iliad* and the *Odyssey*. In fact, the sculptor has relied on his imagination to provide an idealization of a man who may not have even existed as a single individual. Scholars still argue over the authorship of the poems and speculation is rife; the truth will never really be known.

Left: The interior of the 'Treasury of Atreus.' From floor to apex, the vault is about 43 feet in height, and built of ashlar blocks. It was constructed around 1250 BC, and has been associated with Atreus, father of Agamemnon, since the second century AD.

upon familial ties and associational bonds, not political institutions. One may speak of membership in a tribe; but citizenship in a state would be an anachronism. Nobles wielded power as leading families within the clans. Originally perhaps their positions were gained by military success; lesser folk gathered under their protection as clients or retainers. Later the aristocrat might provide economic assistance in return for services and obeisance from his followers. Wealth, solidarity and a rigid code of behavior united the ruling class. And wealth consisted in ownership of land. The stage of society was still pre-urban, though communal centers might exist in villages or small towns. The bulk of arable land was in the hands of a small group. Control of the community's resources was theirs. And without written statutes or constitutions, theirs too was the administration of justice, the supervision of religion, the spoils of war. The gap between nobles and commons was wide.

The world of the eighth century affords us a first real glimpse into Greek culture and society, and the cultural revival is evident. The regaining of literacy spurred consolidation and transformation of a rich oral tradition. And the best of geometric pottery reveals a high level of artistic sophistication. But social structure remained simple. It was a pre-political and pre-urban society. A ruling class maintained dominance through institutions of kinship and local associations and a tradition of deference. The gulf between rich and poor was large – and the institutions to cope with it had yet to be developed. It was the Greek genius that broke this socio-political pattern in a way that was to have unexpected consequences.

A real revolution – social, political and cultural – occurred over the next two centuries to transform Greece. Again one can fasten on no specific point on which all turned, no single explosion that changed Greek society at a stroke. The crucial time span was between 750 and 550 BC. By its conclusion the simplistic structure based on informal tribal bonds had dissolved. The Greek city-state, the *polis*, had emerged – a genuine urbanization and politicization of the rudimentary communal system.

Overseas expansion

The first step – and a critical one – was the expansion of Greece itself, and, as a consequence, an enrichment of the content of Greek culture. We begin with an Aegean community which embraced both sides of the Aegean Sea: the Greek peninsula, the islands, as well as Ionia on the Asia Minor coast. Overseas settlements and colonies spread everywhere in the Mediterranean – to Sicily, southern Italy and as far away as Marseilles in the west, to the north coast of the Aegean, the Propontis and the Black Sea, to North Africa and to the Levant.

The motives for expansion were many and varied. Land-hunger was a prime factor. The hardships which faced the small farmer, cursed with poor soil and dependent upon the benefactions of his patron, induced some to look elsewhere. Traditional fear of the sea was alleviated by invention of the *pentekonter*, the long galley that could be sailed or rowed by two groups of 50 men, which was to convoy the colonizing contingents. Areas that took the lead in much of the expansion were those where land was at a premium and the soil not very productive: areas such as Corinth, Megara and Euboea. And, most notably, Achaea, a narrow and cramped stretch of territory in the northern Peloponnese that sent colonists to snatch some of the most fertile sites in the instep of the Italian boot.

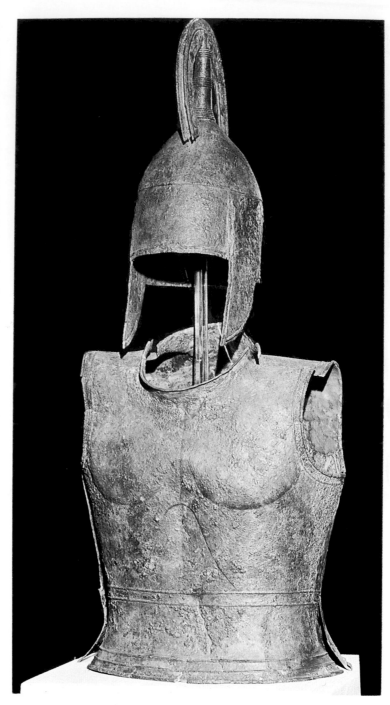

Left: The earliest example yet found of hoplite-style armor. It dates from the eighth century BC and was found in a tomb at Argos. The rise of the hoplite – in its own time an exclusively military development – has come to sybolize the waning power of the old aristocracy.

Below: The funeral of an aristocrat, painted in the geometric style by the Hirschfeld painter in the middle of the eighth century BC.

Right: The myths of the Greeks, developed from the oral literature of the Dark Age period, fired the imaginations of later artists. Here Achilles slays the Amazon Queen Penthesilea – the work of the famous Black Figure painter Exekias, from around 530 BC.

Far right: The growth of Greek contacts with other cultures of the eastern Mediterranean exerted a great influence on the decorative arts. This marble sculpture of a horseman, found on the Acropolis, has evident similarities with the statuary of Syria and Egypt, particularly in the carving of the face.

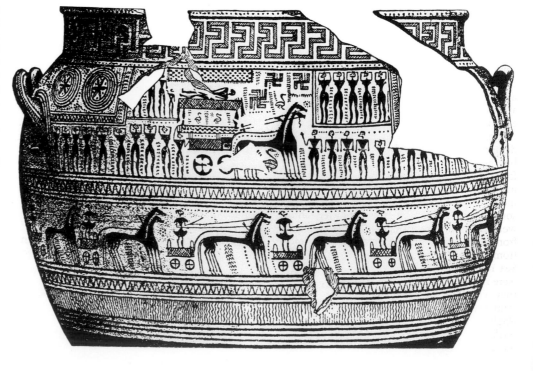

But it was not the poor alone who benefited. The planting of a colony required mobilization of resources on a large scale: ships, arms, tools, supplies. There must have been support, encouragement and financing from the wealthy. The interests of the upper classes were well served: transplantation of restive elements provided a safety-valve for the social hierarchy at home. Internal dissension also provided recruits for overseas foundations. The Greeks who settled Tarentum in Italy were said to be bastard sons of Spartan women, born when the husbands were off at war. When the island of Thera set out to colonize Cyrene it conscripted, upon pain of death, one son from every family of some size. Evidently, social problems and economic pressure at this time contributed mightily to the burst of expansionism.

It has been fashionable in recent scholarship to denigrate the commercial motive in colonization, but the pendulum of fashion may have swung too far. Of course, Achaean settlers in Italy were looking for agricultural land, not business investments. Yet exchange of goods surely induced some overseas expansion: the metal trade in the western Mediterranean, luxury manufactures from the Levant, mining products and timber from the north Aegean and grain from the Black Sea regions. The Greeks who planted colonies were not groping in the dark. They knew where they were going. By tradition, the earliest Greek foundation in the west was Cumae on the bay of Naples, and a glance at the map will show that no settlers sailing from Greece could have stumbled on that distant site by mistake. Cumae's attraction

was its place in the orbit of Etruscan metal trade. Thus Corinth founded Corcyra as a way-station to Italy and the west, and Euboeans occupied both sides of the Straits of Messina – the fabled Scylla and Charybdis – because it was on the route to Italian trade. Similarly, Al Mina in northern Syria and Naucratis in the Nile Delta were less colonies than trading posts. The shores of the Black Sea were also soon to be dotted with Greek settlements obviously designed to profit from commercial traffic. No other motives can explain the occupation of an area where, as someone put it, 'there were eight months of winter and four months of foul weather.'

The consequences of expansion

Overseas expansion had significant repercussions on the economy. A quickening of trade with east and west must have produced a more complex and more highly diversified economic structure and a more cosmopolitan outlook. Merchants increased in numbers, and, with them, shipbuilders, dock-workers, craftsmen, small manufacturers. The landless or land-poor might turn to other occupations or settle across the now less forbidding seas. The agricultural basis of Greek society remained unshaken, but increase in economic mobility and diversification opened new dimensions – the indispensable prerequisite for a genuine urbanization. Effects may be seen also in the cultural sphere. Importation of metals from Etruria and the north inspired new handicrafts in Greece, and luxury trade from the east also had its impact on Greek art. The change may be observed in the pottery, especially from

Corinth, a leader among colonizing cities and a commercial center. The stark and disciplined motifs of geometric ware gave way to curvilinear decoration and floral patterns. There was room for rich and imaginative creations on the vases: the ferocious and fabled griffins, sphinxes, two-headed animals, even humans and battle scenes. The bursting of former restraints made possible by overseas expansion is exemplified in the joy and energy of the art.

Expansionism had profound political and social consequences as well. Men engaged in trade, manufacture and commercial labor were shaking loose from old ties with dependency upon a landed aristocracy. Contact with other civilizations permitted them to gain a glimpse of different political and social systems. A greater awareness of the outside world, combined with increased independence among the lower classes, made serious inroads in traditional patterns. Among the ruling orders themselves there were the beginnings of a transformation. Power resided in wealth, but men successful in overseas ventures or business investments demonstrated new means of acquiring income. To be sure, in many instances the leaders in these new operations may have been aristocrats of inherited property who adapted to changing times; and certainly ownership of land remained the prime mark of status and prestige. But social mobility was increased. The structure became more fluid and dynamic. Birth alone was no longer sufficient for a lofty station. The breakdown of the old aristocratic order was underway.

Expansion was accompanied by signs of a

growing panhellenic consciousness. The shrine of Apollo at Delphi began no doubt as a local cult, situated in dramatic austerity under the sheer cliffs of Mt Parnassus, which looked out upon a deep and rugged glen. In the eighth century, however, the age of colonization allowed Delphi to become an international center. Time and again, prospective colonists approached the Oracle to obtain advice and religious sanction for their new ventures. On a less exalted plane, men came to Delphi for information; the incessant passing-through of pilgrims, worshippers and political leaders made her a clearing-house for data on the whole Greek world. The Delphic priests rapidly rose in popular estimation, and not only in Greece. Foreign princes honored the Oracle by seeking its advice and presenting it gifts. The same period witnessed the creation of the Olympic Games. The list of Olympic victors dates from 776 BC. The quadrennial festival held at Olympia brought together Greeks from throughout the Hellenic area. Such centers could only stimulate panhellenic sentiment and a sense of common values.

The other side of the coin, however, was equally telling. The scramble for colonies, land and commercial gain produced intensive rivalries among Greek states. Some colonies were joint foundations, but co-operation was the exception rather than the rule. The heady successes of over-seas colonies brought pride and glory to the mother-cities – and keen competition among them. Loyalty to the mother-city did not always linger among the settlers. If a colony thrived and prospered it might become a powerful entity in its own right. So Corcyra, originally a Corinthian settlement, eventually became a fierce foe of Corinth. The era of colonization thus stoked those twin fires that burned throughout Greek history: a pride in cultural distinctiveness of the whole, and a particularism and fragmentization in the component parts.

Overseas expansion laid the groundwork and engendered some of the attitudes that produced what may be termed a political revolution. But another aspect instrumental in this process warrants note: a change in military system and organization. Fighting dominates the Homeric *Iliad.* But the fighters are all individuals – nominally heads of contingents, in fact bearing the brunt of combat themselves. An aristocratic society relied for victory upon its champions and leaders. They alone could afford battle equipment and were trained for war. They fought on horseback or from chariots. When on foot, they used their spears as missiles and protected themselves with long shields fastened loosely by straps around the shoulders. Individual heroism and courage carried the day. Living up to the warrior's code of honor, not military organization or effi-

Far left: The grave-marker of Aristion, an Athenian who died around 510 BC. He is depicted wearing some of his hoplite equipment, which indicates that he had reached middle age; a younger man would probably have been carved as an athlete.

Left: This example of early Greek amphora decoration gave the original purchaser a generous variety of images and motifs. Women dancers are shown in the top panel, while lions prowl in the center one. The main illustration is of chariot and horse riders in procession. The rest is covered in geometric designs, a characteristic of this period, the seventh century BC.

Above right: The ruins of Apollo's temple at Delphi, one of the most sacred places in Greece. It was the site of a famous oracle, whose pronouncements were consulted before colonists were sent out, wars waged, or law codes approved. Delphi was also the site of the Pythian games, one of the great athletic festivals that served as a potent reminder to Greeks throughout the Mediterranean of their shared heritage.

ciency, was paramount. The mass of troops, light-armed if at all, engaged only marginally and often were little more than spectators. Warfare was a matter of individual duels by expert warriors.

That chivalric style did not endure, and its disappearance betokens a significant change in the social order. Economic opportunities and advances in the eighth century brought wealth, or at least moderate wealth, to a larger portion of the Greek population. More men could afford armor and equipment, as well as the time to train under arms. Materials were also more readily available: the thriving metal trade had seen to that. A new army emerged in the late eighth century: the army of the hoplite soldier, designed not to showcase its individual heroes but to fight as a unit. The hoplite carried a thrusting spear, rather than the old hurling javelin. Encased in heavy corselet and greaves, he carried a shield no longer strapped to his body but gripped firmly in one hand. Each man's left side was protected by the shield; his right depended on cover from the hoplite next to him. Hence the force fought as a mass, a phalanx. It depended on solidity, unity and weight. This new army carried a sense of common purpose and relied on teamwork; there was little room for the solo virtuoso or the superstar. All this was symptomatic of the passing of the old aristocracy, but we must beware of imagining a social revolution or an arming of the commons. The hoplite still had to supply his own equipment, and only a man of means could do that. But he was also an aristocrat in neither the Homeric nor Assyrian sense.

The ranks now consisted of middling farmers of some substance, or men who had earned a reasonable income through other means, and thus the monopoly of economic and social privilege owned by a hereditary class evaporated.

Hoplite warfare demanded a disciplined and ordered structure, a more self-conscious and articulated sense of community. It was not to be long before those characteristics spilled over into the political system to produce a radically new form of government. The first step was the creation of a legal system to protect against the arbitrary rule of a hereditary power.

The aristocratic society depicted by the Homeric epics had no need for written constitutions or legal enactments. The *aristoi* handled all matters of common concern; they were princes, generals, judges and priests rolled into one. Birth and breeding guaranteed that they would operate under their own unwritten code of morality. The lesser orders of society did not usually begrudge them their monopoly. Clients and dependents of the *aristoi*, they nestled under their protection and trusted in their judgment. But the economic and military changes wrought in the course of the eighth century gradually made the old system obsolete. A sense of independence fostered by the expansionist era and a new confidence in their role engendered by service in the phalanx brought forth greater pressures from classes outside the hereditary nobility. The social and political effects of these pressures began to become manifest in the following century.

A new legal order

In the middle of the seventh century we have the first reports of written constitutions and codes of law. That step, sometimes slighted by historians, is, in fact, of telling significance. The articulation of rules and procedures sounded the death-knell for that informal, deferential society in which all control was left, by tacit common consent, in the hands of a pedigreed aristocracy. Tradition records that the earliest laws published on stone came in 660 from Locri, a Greek colony in southern Italy. It is significant that the initial steps should have been taken in the colonies rather than in the homeland. Custom had not yet solidified in the new foundations. The hardier and more vigorous men who had ventured across the seas were not eager to slip back into the system they had left at home.

Once begun, the constitutional idea quickly spread. Probably some time in the seventh century Sparta acquired a constitution, fashioned by the respected leader Lycurgus. Toward the end of the century Draco gave Athens her first code of laws, elaborated a generation later by Solon's reforms. Many other communities followed suit. A new order had now come into being, but we should not imagine that it entailed anything like what we consider democracy. The Spartan system enshrined a clear hierarchy, as did the laws of Gortyn in Crete. Draco's code was brutal and severe, 'written in blood,' so it was said. But the writing down of fixed principles and regulations was nevertheless an act of momentous propor-

Left: The Cretan city-state of Gortyn's law code was written on the wall of a public building for all citizens to see. Strictly codified laws, together with organized law-courts, protected ordinary people from the arbitrary justice of the old military aristocracy, and helped the development of a more democratic system of government.

Right: While there was great progress toward a fairer society in the seventh and sixth centuries BC, these advances were totally confined to the rights of men. For most women, daily life was little better than that of a slave's. There were exceptions, however: this statuette of a Spartan girl-athlete underlines how paradoxically the most regimented society allowed greater freedom to its women than other Greek states.

Below right: Another relief from a grave-marker, of an athlete attended by a boy slave. The athlete holds his strigil, which cleaned the body of oil, sweat and dirt after training or a contest. The ancient Greeks developed a cult of the young male body from their devotion to sport and athletics that was of almost religious dimensions.

tions. Law was now public knowledge, and its administration would have to be in accord with established enactments. Arbitrary judgments claiming divine inspiration or rooted in hereditary right were replaced by a legal system. The community had become the *polis*. In contrast with the governments of Iran or India this was indeed a major innovation.

In cities where the old aristocracy remained recalcitrant or incapable of adapting to new circumstances, the change manifested itself in different fashion: the rise of tyrannies. Tyrants were a familiar, almost a general, phenomenon in seventh-century Greece, but again we must avoid misconceptions. The word 'tyrant' conjures up images of rapacious despots grinding down their subjects. Not so in Greece – or not necessarily so. In many cities tyrannies represented a movement *against* an exclusivist aristocratic corporation. In other words, tyrants were not kings, but rather rulers who often served at the will of the *polis*.

Of Theagenes' tyranny in Megara only a single item is known, but it is a revealing one: he slaughtered the flocks of the wealthy. When Periander, Cypselus' successor in Corinth, sought advice from a fellow-tyrant, Thrasybulus of Miletus, he was told to 'lop off the tallest ears of corn.' That, of course, can only be reference to the realm's most powerful nobles.

Thus tyranny both succeeded in opening up the ruling circles to wider elements of the upper and middle classes and performed a necessary task of modernization in the cities. The tyrants nurtured trade and industry and increased communications among the Greek states. Pheidon is credited with instituting the first 'weights and measures.' While that should not be taken as the introduc-

tion of coinage, the first appearance of which in Greece comes only at the end of the seventh century, it exemplifies that same drive toward rationalization and systematization that we have seen in the new law codes of other states. Tyrannic dynasties did not normally endure beyond three generations. But by their conclusion, old-fashioned aristocratic rule was dead. The *polis* had developed a more sophisticated economy, had broadened the basis of its political structure and had articulated a set of principles accessible not just to the privileged but also to the whole community.

Poetic sentiments

This freer society released its energies in varied forms. Not the least of them was a brilliant blossoming of lyric poetry. The breathless erotic verses of the Lesbian poetess Sappho are justly celebrated. But other artists, too, even more pointedly reflect the changing circumstances and attitudes of the seventh and early sixth centuries. Archilochus, from the Aegean isle of Paros, was born an aristocrat, but hardly of the traditional sort. No epic poetry for Archilochus, no celebration of heroic figures. He wrote intensely personal lyrics – of his own hates, loves and griefs, of his cynicism and his mockery. Archilochus knew battle, but he was not ashamed to sing of his own flight: 'A Thracian now displays my trusty shield. I left it behind but saved my life. So what is a shield? I'll get another.' Homer would have groaned in his grave. But this was a new age; the chivalric code was no longer paramount. The individual was now supreme, and it had become acceptable to ask the question of the individual's relationship to political authority.

The stirring lines with which the Spartan Tyrtaeus encouraged his city's soldiers – 'Nothing counts in war but this: courage and steadfastness amidst bloody carnage, boldness in the face of battle' – sound like a Homeric call to aristocratic fighters. There is, however, a major difference. Tyrtaeus is not addressing epic heroes, but hoplite soldiers. No individual stars, but a joint effort by a community of fighters. Sparta's new constitution gave principles, structure and unity to the state – what Tyrtaeus called *eunomia*, good order, and to which he dedicated a major poem.

The grip on affairs of state by a hereditary nobility was decisively loosened. Observe the striking sentiments of the sixth-century poet Phocylides from Miletus: 'What profit is noble birth in one whose counsel is useless and words graceless? Best are things of moderate degree; the middle status is sufficient for me.' And at Athens, the law-giver Solon himself propagandized for his program through verses that criticized aristocratic injustice and pled for a communal spirit under rule of law: 'Our rulers conceive only injustice, bent on the rewards of violence . . . But good laws give us right, stability and strength, and imprison vice and evil.'

A greater human self-awareness, if one may employ such an abstraction, seems characteristic of the Greek world in the seventh and sixth centuries. It was this quality, in fact, that was to mark Greek civilization off from its Asian contemporaries. Increased share in the political and social process brought a sense of individual dignity and a confidence in the rational structure of things. These traits may be variously illustrated. The personal character and celebration of the individual in Greek lyric poetry has already been men-

was a religious as well as a political community, but the religious element was kept under control: the priesthood remained subservient to the political power of the *polis*.

Philosophical inquiry

Perhaps the most prodigious achievement of this 'archaic age' was the birth of philosophy in Ionian Miletus. Numerous influences were at work in inspiring speculative enterprises: the proximity to eastern learning, the new prosperity that afforded leisure time, the burst of economic activity that asked for scientific investigation to solve problems of navigation, geography and engineering. But more basic, perhaps, was a confidence that the world possessed a rational structure and was subject to logical analysis. Since human affairs had now been ordered in a systematic fashion, surely nature herself operated by discernible and comprehensible laws. The Milesian philosophers of the sixth century, Thales, Anaximander and Anaximenes, speculated on the first principles of the universe and the nature of matter. In the west two refugees from Ionia further advanced learning: Pythagoras developed mathematics and ethics, and Xenophanes pierced through myth to find a rational basis for religion, becoming, in the process, the first Greek monotheist. At the end of the century Parmenides of Elea insisted upon an exacting logic to resolve the paradoxes of sense perception, and Heracleitus, generally cited for his notorious statement, 'one cannot step into the same river twice,' nonetheless affirmed faith in *logos*, that is reason, as a governing principle of the universe.

Cosmological speculation, astronomy and mathematics were not, of course, Greek inventions. But whereas Near Eastern thinkers were concerned primarily with problem-solving, the Greeks raised their investigations to the level of generalization and theory. The Egyptians had long known how to work with geometrical problems, but it took Pythagoras to conceive his famed theorem on the square of the hypotenuse. Thales, the paradigm of the absent-minded professor, was said to have fallen in a well while contemplating the heavens; and Pythagoras, a believer in the transmigration of souls, once professed to hear in the yelps of a puppy the voice of a departed friend. But these men had not withdrawn from the world. Thales employed calculation to forecast fruitful harvests and advised the Ionians on creating a federal union. Anaximander gathered geographical data to construct a map of the world and introduced the sundial to Greece. The Pythagorean society became actively engaged in the politics of Croton in southern Italy. And Heracleitus recognized, better than anyone, the connection between the order of the universe and the laws of man. As he once remarked, 'All human laws are nourished by a single law that is divine . . . The people should fight for their laws as for their walls.' The statement sums up the spirit of the new *polis*.

The Spartan way

A general pattern of change is discernible in Greek states from about 750 to 500 BC. But the pattern, like most patterns, is most useful for understanding only so long as it is not applied too strictly. The two greatest cities of Greece do not readily fall into it. For later writers Sparta and Athens represented opposite poles, competing systems of value: Athens, the cultural, intellectual and artistic leader of the Hellenes; Sparta, emblematic not only of military prowess and power, but morality, stability, law and order. The competition became confrontation in the fifth century, a struggle that

tioned. But we should note also the appearance of sculpture on a large scale in the early seventh century. The gods were depicted in human shape. And not only the gods. There was a fascination with man himself. The standing nude male and seated clothed female were produced in ever greater quantities. Military training and the attendant athletic exercise put a premium on physical development. In the gymnasium the male body was given near religious reverence. Human figures appear regularly on vase-paintings, a decisive break with the stylized pottery of earlier eras. Experimentation in color, line and figure-drawing, especially in Attic ware, exhibits a freer spirit and increased interest in the world and man. It is no coincidence that around 600 BC individual pieces of art, both statuary and ceramic ware, were being signed by individual artists, announcing their own personalities and styles.

Religion remained a potent feature of Greek life. But abstract divinities and the generalized Olympian gods came to be more and more associated with particular city-states. Each *polis* adopted its own god or goddess as patron deity – Athena at Athens or Demeter at Eleusis. And matters were brought more closely down to earth. Cities or ethnic groups developed cults of heroes, demigods and partly mythical figures to dramatize local traditions, heroes such as Heracles in Dorian states and Theseus at Athens. The *polis*

Far left: A statuette of Athena in her guise of a war-goddess. According to myth Athena sprang from the forehead of her father Zeus, fully armed and bellowing her war cry.

Left: A bronze of Athena from the Acropolis Museum at Athens. She was also the goddess of arts and crafts, and gave her name to the Greek city most associated with excellence in these fields.

Below right: A scene of a successful hunter with his dogs returning from the fields. It is painted on the inside of a drinking cup's bowl in the Black Figure style, popular in the middle of the sixth century BC. Athenian skills in pottery gave the city an important export industry and laid the foundation for its becoming the leading urban center of the Greek world.

engaged much of the Greek world and would generate profound transformations in both the principal antagonists. It is to these two states that we must now turn our attention.

Two major cultivable plains lay in the southern Peloponnese: Laconia and Messenia. The city of Sparta was situated on the Eurotas River at the head of the Laconian plain. There was no convenient access to the sea, but the land was rich, and Sparta was in a position to dominate Laconia. When economic problems and overpopulation beset Greece in the eighth century, most states turned to overseas colonization. Sparta turned inward, and by the end of that century Messenia, as well as Laconia, was under her sway. Trade, imports, foreign connections were of small consequence. Sparta did not need them. She possessed fertile fields and a vigorous agricultural populace.

The southern Peloponnese comprised an enormous territory for one city to dominate. The point was brought home by a major revolt of the Messenians in the mid-seventh century, and it was put down only with great difficulty. To maintain control of so extensive a subject population required extraordinary effort, and Sparta accepted the challenge. Internal crises and social pressures had created tyrannies elsewhere in Greece, but not in Sparta. Instead there was a serious overhauling of the structure and the development of a new mentality, under which training and education would be directed primarily toward the cultivation of martial virtues and a strictly ordered polity.

To contemporaries and later observers alike Sparta was a fascinating state, a unique combination of the most austere communalism and the most exclusive oligarchical principles. Only a tiny minority of the population ran the state. But they

were, to all intents and purposes, the state. The Spartiates, full-blooded Spartans, formed the ruling class, a hoplite aristocracy *par excellence*. Two kings headed the government, but Sparta was in no real sense a monarchy. The dual kingship was itself cumbersome and hemmed about by a council of 30 elders, not to mention five annual magistrates, the *ephors*, elected by the assembly of the people (ie the Spartiates). A 'mixed constitution' later admirers termed it. But it did not pretend to represent the whole populace. Other towns in the southern Peloponnese which owed allegiance to Sparta had no share in the central government, and the remaining population of Laconia and Messenia had been reduced to a status of serfdom. The serfs, or *helots*, belonged, however, not to individual owners but to the state. That was the Spartan way. Land was tilled by the helots to allow their rulers to defend the nation.

Spartan citizenry, therefore, was essentially a collection of absentee landowners. The fact explains much. The greatest of Greek *poleis* by the late sixth century, Sparta nonetheless never developed the flavor of an urban metropolis. As the historian Thucydides acutely observed, 'If Sparta were to be deserted, with nothing left but temples and building foundations, later ages would never believe that her power equalled her reputation . . . for Spartans live in villages in the old Greek fashion.'

The Spartan ruling class was released from all economic worries and activities. Agriculture could be left to the helots, trade and industry to the inhabitants of subject towns. The Spartiates were a warrior order. They conducted domestic and foreign affairs, protected the community, perpetuated and spread Spartan ideals. It was not a

nobility of leisure. They imposed upon themselves the most rigid principles and endured the most gruelling and disciplined training. The Laconian concept of education was one of a lengthy and incessant ordeal, featuring such items as common meals with unvarying fare, frequent floggings for disciplinary purposes and violent athletic contests, either individual or *en masse*, which ended only when the losers were reduced to insensibility. The sparse common table that Spartiates kept all their lives, with its proverbial black bread and broth, was almost enough in itself to mold character. A foreigner invited to the public mess once remarked, 'Now I understand why Spartans do not fear death.'

Sparta had hardened herself into a military barracks, a state dominated by a tight military caste in a permanent condition of mobilization. Property, at least in principle, was divided equally among Spartans. There was to be no rivalry for wealth or superfluous distinctions. Foreigners and foreign customs were excluded as subversive. Lacedaemon would be an island of excellence unto itself. Conversation was confined to crisp, pointed statements – 'Laconic speech.' Spartan songs were framed to instill patriotic spirit. All was geared to skill in war and devotion to country. Austerity, ordered discipline, a Puritanical morality – those were Spartan trademarks.

Changes in Athenian society

A wholly different set of ideals were represented by Athens. The collapse of Mycenaean civilization and the devastations of the Dorians had left Athens relatively unscarred. Her citadel had resisted Dorian incursions, and, so far as can be surmised from the pottery, there was little break in her continuous development through the Dark

Ages. The district of Attica, some 1000 square miles, was reasonably fertile as Greek land goes. Not so rich as Laconia or Messenia, but there was also a long coastline and productive silver mines to bolster the economy. During the course of the Dark Ages the territory had been unified under Athenian control, a feat ascribed by the tradition to a legendary hero Theseus. The process is obscured by time, but the result is clear. Attic unity was of a sort very different from that of Laconia. There were no subject populations, no oppressed helots. All dwellers in Attica were equally members of the Athenian common-wealth.

Relative prosperity meant that Athens did not feel the pinch of economic depression and over-population common in eighth-century Greece. She took no part in the colonization of that era, nor even in the kind of internal expansion that Sparta effected in the Peloponnese. The social pressures upon aristocracies elsewhere in Greece came late to Athens. Her ruling class of noble families, the Eupatrids ('well born'), remained without serious challenge until well into the seventh century. Like most aristocracies, they were wealthy landowners who controlled the magistracies (*archonships*), and sat on the governing council of the Areopagus, an assemblage of ex-magistrates and senior statesmen.

But Athens could not escape change forever. The conflicts that had beset other states a generation or two earlier began to trouble Athens in the latter part of the seventh century. Prosperous men outside the ruling circles began to lay claim to a share in political power. An attempt to install a tyranny is recorded about 630. It proved abortive. But the demand for a defined set of laws had to be met. That demand produced the codification ascribed to Draco in the 620s. The new set of statutes removed arbitrary judgments by aristocrats and served as foundation for a legal system. But their harshness was unpopular with the commons, and they did little to satisfy the political aspirations of those men who sought to break the Eupatrid monopoly.

Rumbling came from below at the beginning of the sixth century. Debt-slavery had become a problem, and there were cries once more for a tyranny to shatter the control of the Eupatrids. A revolution seemed in the offing, but Athens side-stepped extremist solutions. A reformer from the aristocracy, Solon, was appointed to alleviate the crisis. His measures cancelled debts, public and private, freed those enslaved for debt and banned all loans on personal security. The bonded peasant could now recover his property. For the moment, at least, the crisis was resolved.

Solon was no revolutionary. His poems lambasted the rich for their injustice and greed, yet he claimed also to have given the *demos* only the privileges that were due them, and no more. His program, he later asserted, had saved the rich and powerful from what might otherwise have been revolutionary upheaval. Solon is perhaps best regarded as a representative of the well-to-do men who had been frozen out of political power by the Eupatrids, men who sought to take advantage of the social turmoil but who had no interest in revolution. Not the mercantile classes, for Solon shows little sympathy for them, but farmers of substance, successful cultivators of the vine and olive who did not belong to the old grain-growing aristocracy. It is noteworthy, for example, that one of the Solonian measures prohibited all export, except for that of olive oil. More important, he altered the traditional system of eligibility for office. Henceforth it would be based on wealth, not birth; and a man's wealth was determined by the productivity of his land, reckoned in both 'dry and wet measures,' ie both grain *and* wine and oil.

Solon's achievement was dramatic, but it should not be misjudged. He converted an oligarchic into a timocratic system. By basing distinctions upon wealth rather than blood, he opened up the aristocracy and allowed for social mobility, but not very far down the social ladder. The lower classes had benefited both from abolition of debts and from a more rational and sympathetic law code. But the ban on export of grain hurt the small farmer as well as the large, since it depressed grain prices on the domestic market. Unsuccessful rural peasants, no longer permitted to contract personal loans, began to drift into the city. Thus a burgeoning city populace was created without ties to the Eupatrids. Athens now possessed a more liberated citizenry, but also a more rootless one.

Hopes had been raised, discontents not altogether satisfied, and the result was further strife. The Eupatrids did not yield their exclusivist privileges easily; the new men quarreled among themselves; and there were stirrings in the city, troubled now by overpopulation and by the rapidity of economic change which had caused dislocation and instability. A generation of political strife finally resulted in the tyranny of Peisistratus, and the dynasty of Peisistratus and his sons, from 546 to 510 BC, proved to be a pivotal period in Athenian history.

Toward a centralized state

Again we must divest ourselves of customary notions about tyrants. Peisistratus was no absolute monarch. His rule was a beneficent one – and an intelligent one. Economic progress was marked and consciously encouraged. To relieve overcrowdedness in the city and to bring new land into cultivation, Peisistratus advanced state loans for individuals to purchase farms. Overseas commerce blossomed, for the tyrant made full use of his many foreign connections. The mid-sixth century was the high-water mark of Athens' beautiful black-figure pottery and the beginnings of her famed red-figure ware. Attic vases were now to be found everywhere in the Mediterranean and the Black Sea, having driven Corinthian ware almost entirely off the market. The fact attests not only the explosive acceleration of trade, but to the prosperity of Athenian craftsmen and industry in the city.

An extensive building program provided employment and profit for an urban populace, but the program involved more than mere pump-priming. The building of Athena's temple on the Acropolis and the design of an even more majestic structure for Zeus had larger purposes in mind: the encouragement of national cults centered in Athens to break down the power of local rulers. Peisistratean policy was thorough and consistent in this regard. The quadrennial Panathenaic festival dramatized Attic unity and proclaimed the city's greatness. The Dionysiac festival became an annual event, at which the old agrarian ritual drama was converted into genuine art forms – the origins of Greek tragedy and comedy. At the same time the Aegean world witnessed the vast circulation of new Attic coins, with Athena's head on one side and her symbol, the owl, on the other. It was the first self-consciously national issue. And Peisistratus' ostentatious purification of the island of Delos emphasized Athenian primacy among Ionian peoples. Patronage of culture on a large scale was everywhere evident: the ceramic ware, architecture, sculpture, coinage, drama and the poets who flocked to the tyrant's court. Local

clans and phratries dominated by old aristocratic families now yielded primacy to a central government and to national pride. Ties of the commons to their traditional patrons were loosened. A genuine concept of citizenship had now been created. It was the decisive step in laying the ground for democracy.

The Peisistratid dynasty ended with the expulsion of Peisistratus' son, Hippias, in 510. But Athens' course had been set. The reformer Cleisthenes secured prominence after the tyrants' fall. But his program was, in fundamentals, an expansion on their own. Aristocratic clans traditionally rested their power on control of the four Attic tribes and the phratries, a system built up, as we have seen, on a conglomerate of families. Cleisthenes' regulations made that system obsolete. He created 10 new tribes, each containing elements of the population from three different areas of Attica – the city, the coast and inland. By combining mixed geographical areas within each political unit, Cleisthenes short-circuited the control that noble families had exercised over their local constituencies. As basic building-blocks of this new organization Cleisthenes used the *demes*, individual villages and boroughs in the countryside and districts of the city. Henceforth a man's citizenship rested solely on membership of a deme, a geographical entity, rather than on membership of a phratry. A secular, political system had replaced a religious, familial one. It was through these units that citizens elected *archons* and representatives to a new annual council of 500. The state itself, not the local aristocrat, could now become the focus of loyalty. It would be rash to regard Cleisthenes as an ideological democrat. The term *democratia* (power of the people) had not yet been invented. Eligibility for the archonship still required wealth and

influence, the Areopagus retained its prestige, and only the hoplite classes or better could afford the time to serve on the new council. Cleisthenes' term for his new system was not democracy, but *isonomia* – equality under the law, an equal share in citizenship and political rights. But that in itself placed Athens well ahead of most of her contemporaries.

Alliance against the Persians

Direct relationship between Sparta and Athens was minimal before the end of the sixth century. Sparta's insularity kept her attention largely riveted on the Peloponnese. Internal problems had occupied most Athenian energies. But Sparta had developed a reputation, exaggerated but real, for putting down tyrannies in Greece. She was now the avowed champion of constitutional government – or, more realistically, of oligarchic rule. By the late sixth century, Spartan policy was guided by the aggressive and erratic King Cleomenes. It was Cleomenes, with Lacedaemonian troops, who effected the expulsion of Hippias from Athens in 510. He attempted further intervention in Athenian affairs during subsequent years, but without success. The friction was shortlived, however, for there was a more compelling reason for cooperation – the menace of Persia.

Already in the mid-sixth century Sparta had issued a boastful message to the Persian court: she would not permit Greeks to become Persian subjects. In 525 an expedition to Samos expressed Sparta's displeasure at Samian collaboration with Persia. And the expulsion of Hippias may have been motivated in part by his marriage alliance with a pro-Persian tyrant. As for Athens, a revolt of Ionian cities against their Persian conquerors brought Athenian sympathy and assistance – and

brought the wrath of Cyrus the Great of Persia on Athens. By 491 Sparta and Athens were united in an anti-Persian policy.

Both states could call on substantial military resources. Sparta's martial repute was unchallenged. The Cleisthenic reforms in Athens had brought a rejuvenated spirit of patriotism, and military regiments based on the new tribal units had proven their mettle in successful wars against the Boeotians and Chalcidians. And after the initial Persian invasion of 490, Athens used the revenues from her silver mines to construct a major fleet of 200 triremes.

Details of the Persian Wars will not concern us here. Athens demonstrated her skill and courage in fighting off a Persian attack at the plain of Marathon on the east coast of Attica in 490. The Spartans, delayed by a religious festival (or so they claimed), failed to appear until the battle was won. The outnumbered Athenian troops, under their general Miltiades, had earned the victory alone. But when Persia mounted a far more formidable invasion a decade later, headed by King Xerxes himself, both of Greece's leading states were conjoined in resistance. Sparta's warriors earned undying fame after their spectacular holding action at Thermopylae, where all 300 Spartiates perished to a man against overwhelming odds. But the key victory was gained at sea, at Salamis in 480, by the Athenian fleet headed by Themistocles. In the following year Spartan hoplites, outnumbered five to one, routed Xerxes' troops at Plataea, and a combined Greek force finished the job by destroying the Persian navy at Mycale on the east coast of the Aegean. The triumph was decisive: a high-water mark of Greek pride and nationalism.

The impact upon notions of Hellenic excellence was far-reaching. The stirring victory over Persian 'barbarians' confirmed at a stroke all that the Greeks had led themselves to believe. And it resulted in a flood of literary and artistic productions which at once proclaimed the superiority of Hellenic culture and institutions.

The first, and perhaps greatest, of Athens' leading dramatists, Aeschylus, had served on the battlefield at Marathon. Thirty-five years later, after a lifetime of brilliant artistic success, Aeschylus had one item only inscribed on his epitaph: his presence at Marathon. He also created the one extant Greek tragedy on an historical theme, *The Persians*, commemorating the victory of the Hellenes. Much has been written about the play as exemplifying divine vengeance upon Xerxes for his overweening arrogance, his *hubris*. But more than that, it is a testament to the nobility of Greek ideals when juxtaposed to the ways of the barbarian. The Greeks 'bow to no man and are no man's slaves,' Aeschylus asserted. Their triumph was that of free citizens in defense of their civilization over men driven to war by the lash of a despot.

Similar themes appear in the lyric poetry of Simonides, from the tiny island of Keos in the Aegean. Simonides' verses celebrated heroic deeds in battle and constructed epitaphs for the fallen warriors. For him, Greek fighters 'defeated the barbarian hordes and secured liberty.' Like sentiments may be found even in the works of the greatest composer of choral odes, Pindar. Not normally a glorifier of war, after the war Pindar, too, could acknowledge its significance: 'the sons of Athens laid the bright foundations of freedom.'

More telling still was a work published in the following generation. Herodotus, from Halicarnassus in Asia Minor, became the historian of the Persian Wars, in fact, the first expositor of historical prose in Greek literature. Herodotus also saw the clash between Greek and Persian as an epic

Right: The Athenian naval victories at Salamis and Mycale were achieved through the seamanship of the ordinary citizens who manned the oars of the fleet's triremes. This rock carving depicts the outrigger arrangement of the three rowing banks.

Below left: The disciplined ranks of the Greek hoplites overcame the might of the Persian empire at the battles of Marathon and Platea.

Below: When the Persians occupied Athens in 480 BC they destroyed the temples of the city's Acropolis. After the final Greek victory the Acropolis was rebuilt, and became more magnificent than before. This is a marble copy of the highlight of the new work, the great sculptor Phidias' statue of Athena.

Below right: Themistocles, one of the tragic figures of Greek political history. He broadened the powers of the poor in the Athenian political system, and fought off a number of conservative attempts to exile him. In 480 BC he was responsible for the strategy that earned Athens the victory of Salamis. His political fortunes waned in the 470s BC, and the conservatives were finally able to send him into exile.

panorama, pitting the forces of freedom and law against despotism and slavery. The words he places in the mouth of the Spartan Demaratus, speaking to Xerxes, are exemplary: 'Spartans are free, to be sure – but not altogether free; their master is Law, a master to whom they are bound in a respect far stronger than the fear which binds your subjects to you.' The panhellenic consciousness generated by the common effort is also dramatically conveyed by Herodotus. An Athenian in his story explains the reason for refusal to treat with the Persians: 'There is our common brotherhood with the Greeks, our common language, the altars and sacrifices of which we all partake, the common character which we share.'

End of the alliance

The common purpose, called forth by struggle against the Persian invader, represented the acme of Greek cooperation. The euphoria did not last. The Hellenic alliance headed by Sparta and Athens endured in name but crumbled in fact. When Ionian cities in Asia Minor appealed to the alliance for assistance in their effort to break the Persian yoke once and for all, Sparta advised them to abandon their homes and settle elsewhere in the Greek world. The Athenians took exactly the opposite course, brought the Ionians into the alliance and went on to besiege Persian outposts in the Hellespont. The division was symptomatic. Sparta was soon to abandon interest in extra-

Peloponnesian affairs, whereas Athens seized the opportunity to expand her contacts and her power. In 478 she inaugurated a new alliance, the so-called Delian League, consisting principally of Greek states in the Aegean and on the coast of Asia Minor. Initially an offensive and defensive alliance to harass Persia and ravage the Great King's land, it was eventually to become an instrument of Athenian imperialism.

The profound differences in attitude and institutions that divided Sparta and Athens became more marked in the fifth century. After abortive efforts by the Spartan King Leotychidas and the regent Pausanias to meddle abroad, Sparta abandoned overseas ventures. When a Lacedaemonian

Left: One of the new temples that arose on the Athenian Acropolis during the 430s BC – the temple of Athena *Nike* (Athena the Victorious).

Right: A bust of Pericles, the Athenian statesman who played an important role in eliminating the last vestiges of aristocratic power in Athenian political life. For 40 years Pericles was the most powerful man in Athens, and guided a democratic empire through its golden age.

Far right: The Parthenon, chief temple of the Acropolis at Athens. Pericles was commissioner for its construction, and it was elaborately decorated with sculptures and reliefs.

Below right: Athens based its power on its fleets, both merchant and military. This drinking-cup is decorated with a painting of two racing merchantmen.

commander was rejected by the allies in 477, Sparta shrugged her shoulders and was content to leave the naval war to Athens. When Themistocles urged Athenians to rebuild their walls and those of the port at Piraeus, Sparta registered a protest, but did not intervene. Sparta was induced to send armies into central Greece on three occasions in the 450s and 440s to check Athenian ambitions, but those ventures were half-hearted. Under an agreement of 446, Athens gave up claims to a continental empire, but, more significant, Sparta gave official recognition to Athens' overseas holdings. Lacedaemonian forces returned to the Peloponnese and to isolationism. For Sparta the half century after the Persian Wars brought greater conservatism and a firmer hardening of her institutions. Foreign contacts and influences were discouraged. Cultural and artistic developments passed her by.

The memorable achievements of the age almost all belonged to Athens. Brimming with self-confidence after the Persian Wars, she was anxious to flex new-found muscles and to find outlets for restless energies. The Cleisthenic institutions received further development in a decidedly democratic direction. Selection of archons was made subject to lot – for Athenians the ultimate in democratic procedure. In the 460s the Areopagus was shorn of much of its power: decisions rested now with the council of 500, the popular assembly and the popular courts. These were changes on paper. Of greater substance was the introduction of pay for members of the council and for service on the juries, for that opened the door for genuine participation in the governmental process for members of all classes.

A number of elements bolstered the spirit of the new democracy. Not least of them was military success. It was the Attic navy that had sunk Persian hopes at Salamis. And it was the Attic navy that earned Athens a host of allies in the

Aegean and dominated the Delian League. It required capital and social standing to be a hoplite, but not to be a sailor. Oarsmen and other crew members came from lesser social backgrounds: laborers, peasants, the urban and rural poor. Exhilaration from success on the waters was translated into political power at home. Men of the lowest census class, the *thetes*, voted in the assembly, sat on the courts and, in some instances, served on the council.

The great dramas of Aeschylus expounded on the democratic spirit. His *Suppliants*, though set in ancient Argos, was, in fact, a depiction of Athenian democratic principles: the power of the people founded on divine protection and the

maintenance of divine law. The *Eumenides*, closing play of the majestic *Oresteia* trilogy, dramatizes the administration of justice, again guided by the divine, but now in the hands of men. The Athenian courts are Aeschylus' model.

More striking still is an anonymous treatise written by an Athenian who, though out of sympathy with the democracy, nonetheless pays it grudging admiration. As the so-called 'Old Oligarch' writes, 'Any wretch who wants to can just stand up and say whatever he thinks, and can sit on the council. This may be bad government, but it is the very basis of the people's power and liberty ... The masses give strength to the city.'

Access to the council, assembly and courts was

open to all. But real executive power rested in a board of 10 *strategoi*, generals or admirals, elected annually and eligible for re-election. The people were sovereign, but they preferred experts at the helm. Not that the generals were professional military men. Athens abhorred that very concept so beloved by Sparta. The men elected to the generalship were political leaders, respected figures in the community and usually aristocrats. The office was a political platform as well as the source of military authority.

The age of Pericles

It was from that position that the most dominant politician of the era exercised his sway: Pericles, son of Xanthippus. Pericles was elected repeatedly to the *strategeia*. His powers of persuasion and reputation for incorruptibility left him without a peer in the affections of the people. As the historian Thucydides acutely remarked, 'Athens was in name a democracy, in fact ruled by her first citizen.'

The Age of Pericles is no misnomer. To Pericles is ascribed the initiation of pay for public services, the key step in effecting genuine participation by the *demos*. Under Pericles, in the mid-fifth century, came the greatest expanse of Athenian international power and prestige. Athens' navy patrolled the Aegean, unmatched anywhere in Greece; colonies were dispatched abroad; the Athenian port, Piraeus, was the major emporium of the Greek world; Athenian allies and connections stretched from the Black Sea to Sicily. All citizens shared in the benefits: land distribution in the colonies, employment in the fleet, paid service on the juries and public offices. And in Pericles Athens found her greatest patron of the arts. Vast sums were expended on buildings, both secular and religious, on festivals and cults dramatizing the glory of Athens for all to observe and admire. The crowning achievement, of course, was the Parthenon, atop Athens' citadel, the Acropolis. The temple was dedicated to Athena, the city's patron goddess and symbol of man's reasoning powers. Enhancing the Parthenon's stunning beauty were pediments and friezes sculptured under the direction of Athens' greatest artist, Phidias, a personal friend of Pericles.

There is another side to the story. Full involvement in the city's affairs was available for all citizens. But citizenship did not include women or resident foreigners or slaves. To be sure, the oft-repeated assertion that Athens' culture rested upon the bowed back of her slaves is misguided. The majority of slaves were domestic servants. Few if any worked in the fields, and in industry slaves and free men labored side by side. In general, Athenian slaves were not mistreated and were allotted liberties which induced a scornful Spartan to remark that one could not tell a citizen from a slave in Athens. Nonetheless it is salutary to bear in mind that Greece's most advanced democracy never questioned the propriety of slavery as an institution.

More significant, but equally disturbing, is the fact that Athens' cultural flowering was possible only because of her empire. The Delian League was organized initially to punish the Persians. The Persian menace soon vanished, but Athens had no intention of resigning her hegemony. Allies who wished to secede were swiftly coerced. Athens drew her reins tighter. The treasury was transferred from Delos to the Acropolis in the 450s. The mistress city imposed Athenian coinage, weights and measures on all allied states and, wherever possible, installed democratic governments loyal to herself. Tribute collected from subject-states was once earmarked for mutual defense; by mid-century it found its way into Athenian coffers. It was the tribute that financed those temples and architectural monuments in which Athens took such pride; and it was the tribute that permitted pay for public offices, the cornerstone of Attic democracy. The subject-allies

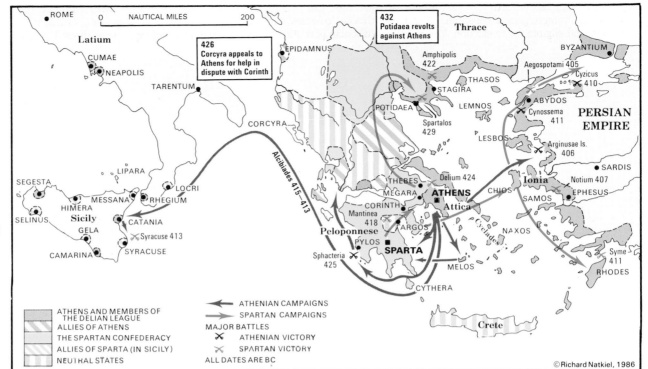

432
Potidaea revolts
against Athens

426
Corcyra appeals to
Athens for help in
dispute with Corinth

Below left: A view of the Parthenon from the west. The building was completed in 438 BC, but the decorative sculptures were not finished until 432 BC.

Below: A detail of the Parthenon's frieze, which ran around the top of the second row of columns, on the inside. The scene was of the annual Panathenaic procession, when the goddess Athena was presented with a new embroidered *peplos*, a kind of Greek dress.

Right: The Peloponnesian Wars were a catastrophe for the Greek city-states. They lasted for nearly 30 years, and drained away the wealth of the two main contestants, Sparta and Athens.

might grumble and complain – some tried revolt – but from the power of Athens' fleet, bolstered and augmented by tribute payments, there was no appeal.

Yet for all that, there is no denying the attractiveness of the spirit of Periclean Athens: the restless energy, the exuberance and enthusiasm, the tremendous pride in her institutions and culture. Athenian educational theory exemplifies the attitude. It was developed in the fifth century by sophists, itinerant teachers. The Spartan notion of excellence, *arete*, rested in selfless service to the state; an intellectual culture in the broadest sense was the Athenian notion. Everything was grist to

their mill. Protagoras, greatest of the sophists and another friend of Pericles, provided the rationale for what is today termed 'liberal education.' His teachings, so he claimed, would not transform students into better human beings. Spartans were specialists. The basis of Athenian education was antipathy to specialization, its aim the cultivation of all of man's faculties.

Probably the most renowned Athenian document is Pericles' own funeral oration, as reconstructed by the historian Thucydides. Pericles denounces the truncated aims of Lacedaemon which convert men into machines for the sake of military prowess; Athenians are equally skillful in

war, but without sacrificing the pursuits which make life more meaningful than mere survival. Their courage is informed by knowledge, not molded by routine: 'Our love of the beautiful does not lead to extravagance; our love of the things of the mind does not make us soft.' The city is both the hub and the model of Hellas. 'Future generations will marvel at us, as the present generation marvels at us now. For our adventurous spirit has brought us access into every sea and every land . . . Our system of government is rather a model to others than an imitation of anyone else . . . Our city is the school of Hellas.'

Polarization of the Greek world

The two major powers of Hellas came into confrontation and bitter conflict in 432. Temptation is great to see their drift into war as fated and inexorable, and though there is some truth in that judgment, it is best to eschew notions of inevitability. A *modus vivendi* had in fact been reached in 446, and neither Sparta nor Athens then seemed bent on a showdown. Athenian expansion was directed to the sea, to the north and east, areas of small concern to Sparta. The latter could not easily be drawn into international conflict when her domestic interests were secure.

Major powers, however, sometimes lose control of events. Issues of prestige and 'face' can take precedence over rational calculation. Although Athens posed no direct menace to Sparta, her expansionism became of concern to some of Sparta's allies, most notably to Corinth. It was Corinth and, to a lesser extent, Megara and Aegina, who in 432 urged the Spartans into war. They railed against Spartan sluggishness, stressed the grasping and insatiable character of Athenian imperialism and harped upon the diminishing stature of Sparta in the eyes of the world. Sparta could not forever turn a deaf ear to the complaints of allies, lest there be a dissolution of the Peloponnesian League itself. The result engulfed Greece in total war for 27 years, from 431 to 404.

Once again the events of the military struggle, the Peloponnesian War, will not be our concern. Of greater interest is its effect on the character of the two cities, the painful and irreversible internal changes which both underwent. In the strictly military sense, Sparta emerged the victor; in a more fundamental way, both were losers. Under the pressure of prolonged external crisis, traditional Spartan principles, the submerging of the individual in the community, began to erode. Under this same pressure, the Athenian democracy began to degenerate into jealous bickering, inconsistency, a lack of trust in the institutions and a more heavy-handed regimen. War, so stated Thucydides, is a harsh task-master. It was never truer than in the struggle between Athens and Sparta.

Let us look first at Sparta. As usual, evidence is slighter there. Ever xenophobic and insular, Sparta discouraged reporters and inquirers. In particular, we are ill-informed on the personalities of men responsible for making and executing decisions. That, to be sure, is itself somewhat revealing. The Spartan system did not readily promote strong personalities. Individuals were supposed to be consumed in the common effort. Sparta's King Archidamus was representative: colorless, bound by traditional ways of warfare, a man of limited imagination and little spark, but with a sober sense of the possible. He had counseled against rushing into war at the outset, with a typically Laconian slap at Athenians: 'We are not led astray by the pleasure of hearing ourselves praised when people are urging us towards dangers that seem unnecessary . . . We trained to avoid being too clever in matters that are of no use, such as producing armchair analyses of one's military enemies, and then failing in practice to cope with them.'

When war came, Archidamus conducted Spartan campaigns in the conventional way. There were annual invasions of the Attic countryside in the hopes that the Athenians might come out and fight or, even better, come to terms when they witnessed the approach of Spartan soldiers. It was not to be. The ravaging of land and burning of crops damaged Athenian morale but did not draw her citizens into reckless acts. They were secure within the walls and thoroughly supplied by sea. Sparta's lack of imagination and distrust of innovation were working against her. Worse still, her exclusive reliance upon that tight circle of Spartiates proved to be most precarious. When Spartiates fell into Athenian hands at Pylos in 425, the war was almost over at a stroke.

A bolder spirit appeared in the Spartan general Brasidas. No fruitless marches into empty Attic fields for him. Brasidas proposed to encourage defections among Athenian allies. In 424 he took forces through neutral Thessaly and detached a number of key sites in Thrace from Athens' alliance. Skillful as a soldier, he was even more skillful as a diplomat. Brasidas presented the Spartan case as that of the liberator of people crushed by the imperialist city. 'He was not at all a bad speaker – for a Spartan,' so Thucydides remarked, one of the few times we may detect his tongue in cheek.

But Sparta still remained sluggish. Brasidas received little support from home. He had to employ helots as a fighting force and swelled his troops by use of mercenaries – a most un-Laconian procedure. And when Brasidas perished in battle in 421, Sparta was willing to come to terms, with the Athenian enemy, despite the gains she had made in the north.

It took an Athenian to snap Sparta out of her lethargy. The dashing but unscrupulous Alcibiades had been deposed from command by his own countrymen during Athens' ill-fated Sicilian expedition in 415. He next turned up in Sparta, and it was on his advice that the Lacedaemonians dispatched assistance to Sicily and set up a permanent garrison in Attica, robbing Athens of an over-

land route and encouraging desertion among her slaves and disaffected. The tide of war began to flow in Sparta's direction. Alcibiades' advice was sound; Lacedaemon was for the first time taking a decisive initiative. But the change in policy also betokened a change in character. Sparta had not in the past welcomed foreigners, much less defectors. That she had to be lectured on elemental strategy and goaded into activity by an Athenian shows she was not the Sparta of old.

In fact the change in Sparta's character went far deeper than that. When the Athenian venture in Sicily ended in disaster Sparta had smelled victory. She needed only to assemble a fleet to wipe out Athens' empire in the Aegean. For that purpose cash was required. Persia was prepared to supply it, and, incredibly, Sparta was ready to accept it. More than two decades of warfare had so eroded old principles that Sparta did not scruple to cooperate with the ancient enemy of Greece itself. A new Lacedaemonian leader reflects the attitude. Lysander was arrogant, unscrupulous and brutal, but also charismatic. He won the favor of Persia's young prince Cyrus, and gold poured into the Spartan war chest. Persia exacted her own price; control of the Greek cities in Asia Minor, and the Spartans did not balk at the request. Athens did not succumb easily. The city showed remarkable resilience and continued to maintain her position at sea until 405, but then

her fleet was wiped out at Aegospotami in the Hellespont, and having lost her most vital resource she was forced to capitulate.

The war had occupied more than a quarter-century. The self-sufficient, insular Spartans of the outset of the conflict were no longer recognizable at its conclusion. Those other city-states which had welcomed Athens' defeat as the beginning of freedom were swiftly disillusioned. Sparta stepped immediately into Athens' shoes. Lysander deposed governments throughout Greece, setting new regimes in power manned by his own friends and flatterers. His enemies were butchered, his associates given free rein. Worse still, the corruptive powers of money had insinuated themselves. Lacedaemon had long banned gold and silver from the state, but Lysander's victories and the subjugation of tribute-paying states filled the coffers. Within a decade after the war there were signs of social dislocation in Sparta – the emergence of inequality among Spartiates themselves, and insurrection of helots and neighboring towns. Sparta's victory had come at a high price. Pride in tradition and honor had yielded to a grasping for wealth and power. She had gained an empire but lost the respect of most of the Hellenes. As Aristotle later put it, 'the Spartans prevailed in war but were destroyed by empire, for they did not know how to use the leisure they had won.'

Athens in decline

Athens had come off no better. Pericles' authority had stood high at the war's beginning. Periclean strategy had dictated playing to his city's strengths. Let the Spartans wear themselves out in pointless expeditions. Athens' navy secured her food supply and her income, and periodic naval raids on Peloponnesian territory would reduce Sparta's confidence. Cash reserves and continued tribute guaranteed that Athens could endure a lengthy war. Such was the plan.

But a war of attrition did not always sit well with an energetic populace. When Athenian fields were ravaged, Pericles' policy came under fire and many pressed for more offensive action. Then, in 429, after two years of invasions, aggravated by a grievous plague, Pericles again suffered criticism, this time from Athenians who were yielding to despair. Internal divisions were already threatening Attic unity and morale.

A plague ended Pericles' life in the third year of the war. There was no successor of his caliber available. Leadership fell into the hands of jin-goist demagogues such as Cleon, one of Pericles' harshest critics, who whipped up popular enthusiasm and played to the moods of the crowd. Cleon, reportedly a tanner, may be taken as representative of the emergence of new families in Athenian politics. He was a brilliant financier, and, in the field, he was instrumental in the capture of Spartiates at Pylos. But he brought an element of ruthlessness, violence and even anti-intellectualism into Athenian policy. In 427, when Athens debated punishment of Mytilene, one of her allied cities that had unsuccessfully revolted, Cleon advocated wholesale execution. The Athenians did not take Cleon's advice on this occasion. But the vote was narrow. And the sparing of Mytilene was for reasons of state, not out of humanity.

Meanwhile, in certain Athenian circles, anti-war sentiment was growing. Many artists and intellectuals engaged in protest activities. The attitude may be seen in the plays of the brilliant young comic dramatist Aristophanes, especially *The Archanians* and *The Knights*, produced in the 420s. Aristophanes takes Pericles to task as the initiator of the war, but reserves his most biting barbs for Cleon, portrayed as a shameless demagogue and war-monger, a man of no breeding who fawns upon the mob. The poet's pacifism is hammered home again in later plays written while war was raging, *Peace* and *Lysistrata*. Equally telling and more poignant were the tragedies of Euripides. Unlike his older contemporary Sophocles, Euripides did not exalt divine law; he was uncompromisingly secular. The common laws of humanity were Euripides' concern – and their violation by the ravages of war. He held no brief for Sparta. The hard-headed historian Thucydides did not engage in flights of rhetoric. But his relentless tale leaves no doubt as to his vision of the effects of war upon individuals and states. His account of a revolution in Corcyra is the most graphic picture ever drawn of the abandonment of humanity and the dissolution of principle in war-time.

Military setbacks and mob rule

Athens blundered badly in the massive expedition to Sicily in 415. But the venture, as Thucydides remarks, was an error in execution, not in conception. The ambitious and gifted aristocrat Alcibiades had urged the expedition and was appointed one of its commanders. But once Alcibiades left, political wrangling and backbiting began at home. The same Athenian populace that had elected him as leader now removed him from his post, thereby depriving themselves of the one man who might have pulled off the venture. The remaining commander, Nicias, was hamstrung by his own timidity and misgivings. Fearful of the vengeance of the assembly lest he make a false step, Nicias' excessive caution ruined the Athenian position in Sicily. The fickle demos had deposed one general and intimidated another. When Alcibiades defected to Sparta, he branded democracy as 'acknowledged folly.' None had a better right to the statement.

The Sicilian debacle was more than a military disaster. It exposed the fragility of the democracy. An oligarchic coup in 411 seized the reins of government, attaching severe restrictions on the franchise and abolishing pay for public office, a

Above left: Aristotle was one of the great philosophers of history. A considerable part of his written work has survived, partly because of his popularity with medieval theologians, philosophers and intellectuals. His thought is characterized by a dedication to common sense as opposed to logical extremes, and an emphasis on orderly classification of thoughts, things and deeds.

Above: A frieze from the Piraeus, Athens' port, shows actors making an offering to their patron deity, Dionysus.

Right: The theater at Epidaurus, in the Peloponnese. Plays were a significant part of Greek culture, both as artistic expressions and religious rituals. Only a very small number of Greek plays have survived, but they are regarded as masterpieces of the art form.

desperate attempt to turn back the clock. Democracy was restored in 410, but it was a pale shadow of the confident, enthusiastic pre-war Athens. Political contests had degenerated into revolutionary strife which cost the lives of many prominent individuals. Legal traditions were scrapped: the 'will of the people' became identified with the capricious mood of the mob. The process is graphically illustrated by the trial of eight generals in 406 for failure to rescue survivors after a naval battle. Mass hysteria ran roughshod over procedural regulations. The assembled people shouted that no laws could restrain the popular will. A kangaroo court pronounced all defendants guilty, and those who were in Athens were promptly executed. It was a grotesque distortion of democratic principles.

The most persistent and most maddening critic of the mob mentality was the self-styled 'gadfly' Socrates. Not that he advocated either oligarchy or anarchy. Socrates fought in the war when called upon and served on the council. But he spoke his mind at all times. In 406 he was the sole voice of reason in the council, resisting summary trial and execution of the generals. He developed no formal philosophic system. His way was conversation and inquiring dialogue. He developed a devoted following of pupils who spent endless hours of discussion on matters of logic, ethics and the cultivation of virtue. The cultivation of critical minds was his goal. In the end it proved to be his undoing.

After the war Athens' material sufferings were swiftly repaired; not so her moral failings. Lysander installed a pro-Spartan oligarchy that proved both ruthless and short-lived. Athens had her democracy back in 403, but not her self-confidence. It was the democracy that executed Socrates in 399. The charges were atheism and corrupting the young. But the unspoken indictment was that he was perceived as somehow being a danger to the fragile, fearful state. He had spoken out before, as in 406, against the excesses of democracy. And among his pupils had been men sympathetic to oligarchy and disruptive figures such as Alcibiades. The nervousness of the older generation that had gone through the war was bound to find Socrates' questioning uncongenial. The Athenian system had been built on the principles of an open society which encouraged free expression. But prolonged war and constitutional upheaval had shaken faith in those principles. That was the cause of Socrates' martyrdom. The funeral oration of Pericles had conjured up an image of Athens that still remains dominant. But one may bear in mind that it was Athens, too, to whom Socrates could address these words: 'No man who conscientiously opposes you or any other established democracy, and openly criticizes the injustices and illegalities of the state to which he belongs, can possibly escape alive.'

It is customary to designate the year 404 as the turning point in Greek history. The fall of Athens marks the termination of the Golden Age. Thereafter, Hellas, so it is usually asserted, went into a tailspin. The *polis*, once vigorous, became flabby and obsolete, and citizens lost their attachment to the state. Greece was ripe for the plucking. And in 338 she crumbled before the armies of Macedon. On the surface that gloomy portrait seems accurate. Yet there was a vitality in Hellas that is not always given its due. The city-states wore themselves out militarily, but the concept of the *polis* and the loyalty it commanded by no means vanished. At the same time, the panhellenic concept received new and more decisive content. The fourth century produced no Aeschylus, no Aristophanes, no Thucydides. But it was the era of Plato, of Aristotle, of Demosthenes. Intellectual endeavor ran in different channels, but the contributions were no less significant for that. And it was Hellenic culture that infused the crusades of the Macedonian monarchs themselves.

Limits of space forbid a detailed account of political history in the fourth century. The story, on the whole, is not an edifying one. A dizzying cycle of wars engulfed Greece between 404 and 338 as various states vied for supremacy, expending manpower and resources in vain attempts at pre-eminence. Alliances among cities were forged and reforged at a rate almost impossible to follow. And those alliances were not inspired by a spirit of cooperation or mutual affection. A depressing pattern settled over events. If any state gained temporary military advantage, it was customarily confronted with a hostile coalition which restored the balance until another power emerged, reshuffling the alignments and starting the cycle anew.

Slide into weakness and disunity

At the conclusion of the Peloponnesian War, Sparta possessed an ideal opportunity to weld Greece into a unity behind competent and stable leadership. But the opportunity was fumbled away. The lure of empire whetted ambitions and caused increasing resentment. In order to defeat Athens, Sparta had bargained away Asiatic Greeks for Persian gold, thus belying her claim to be liberator of Hellas. After the war her position became even more embarrassing. Sparta's options were limited by the double requirement that control over an empire could not be secured by denuding Laconia of Spartiates and that Spartan commanders were needed abroad. This led naturally to the hated system of garrisons headed by Spartan generals (*harmosts*) and manned, at least for the most part, by enfranchised helots. The widespread imposition of tribute and installation of pro-Spartan oligarchies created further hostility. The Spartan at home and the Spartan abroad were two very different men, so the Greeks were fond of saying. The remark was thoroughly substantiated in the fourth century.

A vigorous and ambitious King Agesilaus hoped to save some Spartan face by breaking relations with Persia and invaded Asia in the 390s. It did not help matters at home. Athens had already removed her Sparta-installed oligarchy in 403 and restored the democracy. In the 390s a coalition of disparate states – Thebes, Corinth, Argos and Athens – united by nothing but hostility for Sparta, roused a major war against her. Lysander perished in the conflict, and a defeat at sea in 394 wiped out Sparta's naval hegemony. She succeeded in obtaining a stalemate only by reviving cooperation with Persia. That unscrupulous shift cost her further credit in Greece.

Sparta had learned no lessons. Her policy under Agesilaus after the 'King's Peace' of 386 was a revival of ruthlessness and incessant interference with the internal affairs of other states. At the same time Sparta cracked down more vigorously

Below left: At the time of Pericles' political dominance, the Athenian artistic scene blossomed. A steady stream of masterpieces in sculpture, architecture and murals emerged. The older art of vase-painting declined, although some fine artists continued to work in pottery's less lucrative field. This sensitive work, of a mistress and her maid, done in the White Ground technique, is by the Achilles Painter, who specialized in domestic scenes using this medium.

Right: In its own time the art of Greece was a colorful spectacle. The plain marble works, such as this Parthenon frieze, were originally painted.

on her old allies in the Peloponnese, soon abandoning altogether the facade of League meetings and joint decisions. Her position could not be maintained indefinitely in the face of widespread resentment and the erosion of old Spartan institutions. Worse yet was her manpower problem. A decline in the number of full-blooded Spartiates can be traced from the mid-fifth century. The proceeds of empire had caused glaring inequities in the distribution of wealth and undermined the concept of common ownership of land, which had been the basis of the Spartan phalanx. The results became gradually more evident. Nor did Sparta make any change in her military system to adjust to new conditions. The heavy-armed citizen infantry fighting on level plains might have served her well in the past, but the rest of the Greek world was passing Sparta by. Athenians and others were making good use of mercenary soldiers and of light-armed troops capable of fighting on rugged terrain. The legend of Sparta's military invincibility was shattered once for all on the battlefield of Leuctra in 371, when Theban hoplites, massing a line of 50 deep, crushed the Spartan force. The Peloponnesian League crumbled at a stroke. The whole of Arcadia broke away and formed a new confederacy, and Messenia itself, after 300 years of subjection, became an independent state again.

Athens' recovery after the Peloponnesian War was remarkable. Loss of her empire had not entailed loss of her commerce. Economic rejuvenation was swift, and relatively even distribution of wealth enabled Athens to avoid the class wars suffered in other states. Democracy was restored and extended. In addition to pay for public offices and service on the juries, attendance at the assembly now received remuneration. Participation in decision-making could encompass larger segments of the population, and the state's commitment to its lower classes is illustrated by a policy of distributing cash to the poor for the purpose of attending the theater. (Pride in Attic culture remained high: the drama was the possession of all Athenian citizens.)

Democratic leaders were still jittery in the aftermath of the war – witness the trial of Socrates – but the insecurity passed. There were no further efforts at oligarchic coups. The grim memories of Sparta's oligarchic henchmen of 404 and 403 made certain of that. In the military sphere, too, there was recovery. Sparta's defeat at sea in 394 signalled renewed vitality for the Athenian navy and permitted rebuilding of the long walls which linked Athens to Piraeus and the sea. New bonds of alliance were gradually forged with states in the Aegean, in Thrace and on the Asian coast.

In 377 Athens converted these piecemeal efforts into a renewal of the fifth-century confederacy. Profiting from past errors, she hoped for a more secure system this time. Athens promised not to acquire property in the territory of any member state, and the policy of the alliance was to be decided by agreement between the Athenian state and the Council of Allies. On paper it was an equitable arrangement and a purely defensive alliance. But the facts, as usual, proved to be different. Athens again succumbed to ambitions for aggrandizement. Forays into the west overstrained her resources. Soon there was new political intervention in the affairs of allied states, and Athens became almost incessantly involved in international warfare.

Other states, too, had emerged as major powers in the fourth century – notably Thebes and Thessaly – but with only temporary success. Thebes, in Boeotia, an uneasy ally of Sparta in the Peloponnesian War, broke with her partner decisively in the aftermath. Led by the brilliant tactician Pelopidas and the taciturn but exceptionally able statesman Epaminondas, Thebes moved into the first rank of Greek powers. It was the Theban army that crippled Sparta at Leuctra in 371 and disassembled the Peloponnesian League. In Thessaly, long fragmented and on the fringes of Greek politics, new energy emerged with the tyrant Jason of Pherae. Jason succeeded in welding disparate Thessalian cities into a unity during the 370s, but the aspirations of these states, as of so

many other ambitious cities, rested on fragile foundations. Jason was assassinated in 370, his successors were incompetent and the schemes of Thessalian hegemony vanished. Epaminondas perished on the battlefield of Mantinea in 362. Despite their victory there, Theban troops were demoralized, and the city was drained of energy. Thebes sank back into the role of a second-class power.

The Macedonian triumph

The seemingly endless struggles and chaotic disunity weakened Hellas irretrievably. Into the vacuum stepped Philip of Macedon. The Macedonians were of Greek stock but were outside the mainstream and regarded as semi-barbarians by the Hellenes. The weakness of her government and general backwardness and divisions among her people had prevented Macedon from being a major force. But Philip, who had spent valuable time as a hostage in Thebes, where he had absorbed the techniques of Pelopidas and Epaminondas, changed all that. In the 350s he subdued Macedon's barbaric neighbors and consolidated the realm as never before. Adoption of Greek silver and gold coinage enabled Macedon to trade freely in the Hellenic world. Conquered territory was absorbed into the Macedonian dominion and new citizens were created by granting holdings to natives or Greeks who dwelled therein. Philip's object was clearly the establishment of a real national state, something that had escaped the genius of the Greeks. And the fashioning of a professional army with a national spirit permitted him to eclipse all rivals.

Macedonian expansion need not be recounted in detail here. Philip achieved it as much by bribery and diplomacy as by force of arms. As he once boasted, no fortress was so strong that it could resist an assload of gold. Thessaly fell under Macedonian sway, as did much of the Thracian coast. In the 340s Philip's influence extended to central Greece, and he now took his place as president of the Pythian games at Delphi, the most sacred precinct of Hellas. There was desperate resistance at the last moment, too little and too late. At Chaeronea in 338 Philip crushed a coalition of Athens, Thebes and lesser states. The exhaustion of Greece through more than a half-century of inter-state struggles left her no match for the Macedonian invader.

After his victory at Chaeronea, Philip instituted a new Hellenic confederacy that was to encompass all of Greece. The aim was to arrest that cycle of inter-state rivalries and internal revolution that wracked Hellas throughout the fourth century. Philip also announced his intention to lead the Hellenes against Persia, to liberate the Greeks of Asia and to punish the barbarian once for all.

Lingering appeal of the city-state

Chaeronea, it is often asserted, sounded the death-knell for the *polis* system. Perhaps so, if by that is meant that it lost some of the vitality and self-assurance that had been characteristic of earlier eras, but the concept died hard. Greek particularism and jealous independence could not be wiped out at a moment. Philip himself recognized the fact. While assuring his military superiority with garrisons at key sites in Greece, he paid due homage to Greek sensitivities. The constitution of his new Hellenic League was hedged about with clauses assuring autonomy for all cities, forbidding interference in the internal affairs of any member state.

Philip's most formidable opponent and the most eloquent spokesman for the *polis* was the Athenian orator and statesman Demosthenes. The fire of his rhetoric had roused Athens against Philip and steeled her resolve for the death struggle at Chaeronea. His commitment to the *polis* was absolute, his uncompromising speeches a monument to the noblest ambitions of Athens and of the city-state generally. Chaeronea ruined his hopes but did not dampen his passion. In 330, when forced to defend his policy in retrospect, Demosthenes delivered his greatest speech, *On the Crown*, and maintained his position with unflagging ardor: 'Will anyone say that it was fitting for this man [Philip] brought up in Pella – an insignificant little hole of a place at the time – to entertain a desire for hegemony over Greece, while you Athenians, who witness daily the mon-

uments of your ancestors' greatness in every word you hear and in everything you see, should have been so perverse as to make a present of your freedom to Philip?' Demosthenes carried the fight well beyond Chaeronea. Against Philip's successor, Alexander, and even after Alexander's death, he fought on for Athenian liberty and for the *polis*, eventually perishing in the attempt.

More striking still are the works of political theory. Plato lived through that turbulent period when Greek cities tore each other apart in debilitating warfare. And no finer mind was ever produced in Hellas. Yet he advocated no supranational state, no federal system of government. Plato's vision was limited to the *polis*. His blueprint for an ideal city, as outlined in the *Republic*, would contain no more than 5000 citizens. His pupil Aristotle formulated much of his political constructs after Chaeronea and even dwelled for a time at the court of Philip himself. But Aristotle too could conceive of no governmental entity more suitable than the city-state. In a properly constituted *polis*, he argued, citizens should all know one another by sight. Attachment to the *polis* concept and to Greek particularism stayed firm long after international conditions had cancelled its practical force.

Signs of cultural vitality

The vitality that marks Demosthenes' speeches even in Athens' darkest days is significant. Failures in political institutions and international relations were not translated into a decline of Hellenic culture. Tragic drama is sometimes cited as an instance of a decline in creativity. Yet the keen interest in tragedy did not fade, new plays were created each year for production at the Dionysiac festival in Athens and there were revivals too of the masters, Aeschylus, Sophocles and Euripides. Nor was Athens the only city where tragedies were produced and performed. If the grandeur of fifth-century drama did not have counterparts in the succeeding era, there were nevertheless plenty of exciting stories, appeals to the emotions, theatrical effects, melodrama – characteristics foreshadowed already in the later plays of Euripides. Above all, there was keen interest in personality: the characters were not to be types

shouldering the burdens of humanity, but individuals with their own quirks and personality traits that appealed to audience sympathy or antipathy. A similar change seems to have taken place in comedy. In the fourth century it was not so much a vehicle for political criticism (though that was present too) as a burlesque of private and domestic life.

Nor does one need the plays to discern the dramatic quality of fourth-century literature. Plato is the acknowledged master of Attic prose and a philosophic genius. And his philosophic dialogues, especially the early ones, are themselves dramatic pieces of high quality. Thus Socrates is made known to us through Plato not only as a philosopher but as a human being of warmth, humor, courage and, let us not forget, physical ugliness. The same interest in literary portraiture appears in the historian Xenophon, who picked up the story of Greece where Thucydides left off. Xenophon did not possess the intellectual power and penetrating acumen of his predecessor, but his characters come to life as Thucydides' often do not.

The plastic arts moved in parallel directions. Sculptured portraits dwell on realistic features, as in the famed depiction of Socrates – replete with snub-nose, bald head and protruding belly. The frontal direction of grave reliefs permitted similar details for their subjects. The austere serenity and idealism of fifth-century art gave way to more direct appeals to the viewers' emotions, exemplified by ecstatic Dionysiac scenes on fourth-century vases or the passionate movement in the sculpture of the Parian artist Scopas.

Nor should one overlook in this connection the great philosopher Aristotle. A prolific writer of perhaps 400 works, his scope is unmatched, encompassing treatises on biology, physics, metaphysics, logic, ethics and politics, among others. Aristotle is generally classified as the practical and scientific philosopher, in contrast with the idealism and imaginative flights of Plato. But we must remember that Aristotle was also a writer of dialogues, though these have unfortunately perished, and an assiduous student of literature. Aristotle's *Rhetoric* is a shrewd analysis of the art of persuasion, and his *Poetics* became antiquity's most influential work of literary criticism.

The empire of Alexander the Great

Philip of Macedon was assassinated in 336. It was an occasion of jubilant rejoicing in Greece, or at least in certain parts of Greece. But the enthusiasm was premature. Philip's 20-year-old son, Alexander, had taken the reins and grasped them firmly. Revolt in Greece was soon crushed, and Alexander succeeded fully to the position of his father as hegemon of the Hellenic League. The remarkable career and talents of that young man have long inspired awe in all scholars and students of the era. Alexander the Great went on to conquer the Persian kingdom and well beyond, even in to India. His 11 years of campaigning in Asia covered over 20,000 miles and subdued all before him. Alexander's conquests widened the boundaries of the classical world far beyond the most fantastic dreams of his predecessors.

It was the end of the old Greek system, so we are usually told. Alexander had burst the traditional confines of the *polis*, opening the way to vast empire and a world order. The contrast between what came before and what after is apparent, yet it will not do to neglect the continuities. Alexander was a Greek and, to his own mind, at least, not a destroyer but a purveyor of Hellenic culture.

The Greeks themselves, or a significant portion

of them, continued to chafe at the Macedonian bit. For many the Macedonian remained a barbarian. City-states with proud traditions like Athens, Thebes and Sparta regarded the invader from the north as the chief threat to Greek freedom. There was an incipient revolt in Athens that fizzled when the monarch swooped down into central Greece in 336. Thebes flared into insurrection the following year. Alexander's fury was unbounded, and Thebes was crushed, 6000 men were slaughtered and the city was totally destroyed. After Alexander's departure for Persia, Sparta rose in revolt, vainly attempting to recapture former glories. In 323 the report came back to Greece that Alexander had perished. An Athenian orator refused it credit, asserting that 'the whole world would have reeked of his corpse.' It was a signal for widespread uprisings in Greece, during which Demosthenes, among others, lost his life in the unsuccessful struggle.

But Alexander showed another side. Like his father, who planned but did not live to execute the scheme, Alexander invaded Persia to liberate the Asian Greeks and punish the barbarian. This was to be the supreme panhellenic enterprise. Not that the Greeks welcomed the Macedonian as their champion and avenger. Indeed many of them were willing to take Persian gold to effect his overthrow. But Alexander's own feelings for Hellenic culture were genuine. Aristotle had been his tutor, and Aristotle, it is reported, advised him that the proper relationship between Greek and barbarian was that of master to slave. When Alexander razed Thebes to the ground, he ordered one house alone to be spared – that of the great Theban poet Pindar. The Macedonian monarch was a devoted reader of Homer and prided himself upon descent from Achilles. At Troy he sacrificed in the temple of Athena and crowned the tomb of Achilles. Hercules and Dionysius were his guiding spirits. Alexander was bearing Greek traditions into the heart of Asia. He dispatched back to Athens statuary that had been captured by Xerxes a century and a half before and ostentatiously set alight the royal place at Persepolis in retaliation for Xerxes' burning of the Athenian Acropolis.

The territory subdued by Alexander was vast. Persian forces were no match for the cavalry of

Far left: Demosthenes was a brilliant orator and Athenian nationalist. He was a vehement opponent of Philip of Macedon's plans for imposing unity on the fractious Greek city-states.

Left: Plato first studied philosophy under Socrates, and succeeded his renowned teacher as Greece's leading man of ideas.

Above: Alexander the Great was the ancient world's most admired individual. His military success led to the spread of Greek culture into the Middle East and India.

Right: The sarcophagus of Alexander. After his death his body was hi-jacked by one of his generals, Ptolemy, and carried off to Alexandria.

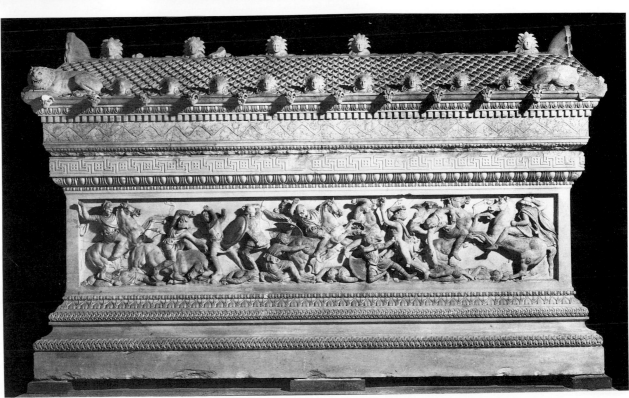

Alexander and the Macedonian phalanx. At Issus, in 333, Alexander routed the enemy decisively and put the Persian King Darius to flight. Two years later at Gaugamela he destroyed their army; the Persian Empire lay at his feet. The realm was enormous, stretching from the Mediterranean to the Indus. Alexander proposed to rule it all, and much more.

But the construction of a massive empire was not tantamount to the passing of the *polis*. Quite the contrary. When the Greek city-states of Asia Minor were liberated from the Persian they were to be treated like European *poleis* and to join in the common panhellenic crusade. After the Great King's treasures fell into Alexander's hands the Greek cities no longer needed even to provide financial contributions. They were brought into the common Hellenic League, but they otherwise retained their own institutions and even autonomy – that is, so long as they were loyal to Alexander. That condition, of course, was crucial, and Alexander had the means to enforce it. He had his own governors or satraps to maintain order and unity. But the fact is that the *poleis* did not lose identity and were not absorbed into a larger entity. Alexander thus conceived of empire in terms of an assemblage of city-states. He created, so we are told, 70 new cities in Asia, many of the larger ones no doubt with the full panoply of Greek institutions. Of particular note is the foundation of Alexandria in Egypt, whose ground plan the king himself traced out. It was to become the greatest of Greek cities in subsequent years.

Alexander had a genius that transcended that of his contemporaries. Having conquered the 'barbarians' in the name of Greece he did not proceed to enslave or humiliate them. He adopted many Persian customs himself. He was to be the successor of Darius as ruler of Persia and the heir of the Pharaohs in Egypt. He married a Persian princess and had many of his officers and men intermarry with the Persians as well. At a famed banquet he toasted the humanity and fellowship of Macedonians and Orientals. But he was no advocate of cultural fusion or the unity of mankind. Alexander saw himself as the bearer of Hellenic civilization. Greek was to be taught to the family of Darius, and the children of mixed marriages were to be brought up in the Greek and Macedonian tradition. Hence, the man who had created a world empire was also the most important agent in the spread of city-states. And the man most intimately associated with a cosmopolitan outlook was also the greatest instrument in the spread of Greek culture and institutions. Alexander sought to surmount the barriers between Hellenes and barbarians, but primarily in order to make of the barbarian a Hellene.

The Hellenistic age

The conquests of Alexander were swift but not sure. Perhaps even his genius could not have held that heterogeneous realm together for long. In any case, he never got the opportunity. Premature death claimed him in 323, at the age of 33. No unchallenged successor was in sight. The generals and marshals of Alexander, fired with personal ambitions, quarreled over supreme power. Forty years of warfare and chaos ensued. The Macedonian throne changed hands eight or nine times as rival claimants fought to the death. The empire fell into fragments. It was only around 275 that the dust settled somewhat, and the pieces fell into place. The realization had at last dawned that there were limits on the amount of territory that one man could control. A rough boundary had been agreed on between Macedon and Greece on the one hand, and Thrace and Asia on the other. Three major kingdoms had been carved out of Alexander's empire. The Antigonid dynasty ruled in Macedon and controlled much of Greece; the Seleucids, based in Syria, dominated the bulk of what had been the Persian empire in Asia; and the Ptolemies formed the reigning house of Egypt. All their dynasties were named and descended from ex-generals of Alexander. Not that peace and tranquillity prevailed thereafter. Rivalries persisted and intermittent warfare in Greece, the Aegean, Asia Minor and Syria. The Ptolemies clashed frequently with the Syrian monarchy and also stirred up trouble in Greece against the Antigonids. However, after 275 it is possible to speak of three definable realms – the Hellenistic monarchies.

The Hellenistic era is the appellation normally assigned to the centuries between Alexander's death and the establishment of Roman suzerainty over the Greeks. Civilization was no longer Hellenic but Hellenistic; that is, no longer Greek, but 'of a Greek sort.' Whether this new civilization was decadent, as many hold, is moot: too much depends on the viewer's vantage point. In the artistic sphere, it can be argued, creativity gave way to imitativeness, innovation to scholarship. To a certain extent, the Hellenistic age was parasitic on earlier eras. But that common generalization misleads. For strides of significant proportions came in science, philosophy and in political experimentation. Greek civilization now possessed a geographic expanse unparalleled in its history. Greek itself for a brief period became a *lingua franca* for most of the known world from southern Italy to India. Hellenic institutions were transmitted into distant areas by a Greek ruling class conscious of its common traditions and of its hegemony over native elements.

Social and political diversion

The three principal monarchies themselves were separate and very different entities. In Macedon the kings carefully respected national traditions. That was a matter of prudence; they were claimants to the throne of Alexander, not conquerors. The monarch eschewed elaborate courts and ceremonials; there would be no aura of divinity, as in Oriental kingdoms. His power rested constitutionally on election by the citizenry – that is, by the army. Whatever the realities of the situation, that constitutional principle was jealously guarded. Under the careful and competent Antigonus Gonatas, *c* 280-240, the realm was consolidated and made secure, resting on that citizen soldiery that Philip and Alexander had made the supreme fighting force in the Greek world. Gonatas avoided overreaching himself. On the whole he maintained a detente with the Syrian monarchy and developed a sphere of influence in the Aegean. Fortifications at a few key sites allowed him to exercise ascendancy in Greece, but did not involve obtrusive Macedonian officials who might stir Greek resentment. Subsequent monarchs like Antigonus Doson and Philip V had greater ambitions and more aggressive policies. But most of Hellas was not in a state of subjection. And the Macedonians maintained the principle that their kingship grew out of the people.

In Egypt and Syria matters were quite different. Here the Greek monarchs were usurpers and conquerors. Their control depended in part upon accepting and utilizing native traditions for their own purposes. One of Alexander's shrewdest generals, Ptolemy I, recognized the wealth, powerful position and advantages of Egypt, and ensconced himself there. A strong fleet, cash and a compact kingdom made it the most swiftly unified of the realms. The Ptolemies, unlike their counterparts in Macedon, claimed divinity. In the land of the Pharaohs that was natural and expected: anything less would have been adjudged a sign of weakness, not humility. Information on Egypt is plentiful but lopsided. The dry Egyptian countryside has yielded a host of papyri; but none for Alexandria, the seat of the monarchy. Hence our evidence dwells on administrative details: tax-rolls, clerical lists, bureaucratic matters. It is clear that Ptolemaic Egypt was organized – abundantly so. A multitude of officials were employed, and the country was divided and subdivided into administrative districts, with ponderous bureaucratic machinery. Those are not characteristics normally associated with the Greek spirit, but Egypt was a peculiar country. If it did not exhibit 'Hellenic spirit,' it did exemplify Hellenic ingenuity. All administrative lines ran to the center. Control of the land appropriately termed 'the gift of the Nile' could allow for no divisiveness. The king was the state. He possessed all Egyptian land by divine right, and almost all businesses were organized as royal monopolies. And the economy prospered. The Ptolemies introduced silver coinage to what had largely been a barter economy, resulting in a brisker production and exchange of commodities all over the land of the Nile. Wealth flowed into the coffers of the crown and the Greco-Macedonian ruling class, though the native peasants benefited little from it. Until dynastic rivalries wracked the throne from the late third century, the Ptolemies were largely free from serious opposition. A tightly organized realm secured their power.

Different still was the Seleucid kingdom. The rulers there did not have the advantages of either Egypt or Macedon. There was no compact area, as in Egypt, nor were there subjects with common traditions, as in Macedon. The empire comprised a bewildering variety of peoples and cultures: Iranian and pre-Iranian tribes which had been the heart of the Persian Empire, the oasis states of Turkistan and Afghanistan, the ancient cultures of Babylon and Mesopotamia, peoples as different as Phoenician merchants and the Jews of Palestine, as well as the complex of native dynasts and Greek city-states in Asia Minor. It goes without saying that suzerainty over this heterogeneous area was often very loose. The situation was fluid; much of the territory was held only shakily or intermittently, Greek institutions penetrated very little into the political and social subsoil. The monarchy itself, based in Syrian Antioch, had to be the focus of loyalty, assisted through the institution of a divine cult of the king. But the Seleucids were careful not to encroach on native religions and cults. The sanctity of temple lands was recognized. The foundation of numerous cities in Asia and the planting of military colonies helped secure the realm, insofar as it could be secured. Much depended on the quality of the man on the throne. With weak monarchs or divided counsels, the empire tended to break apart. But a vigorous ruler, such as Antiochus III in the late third century, could prove successful in recovering territory and also in restoring loyalty to the throne.

The three great monarchies do not exhaust the complicated Hellenistic picture. There was much political experimentation in Greece in the aftermath of Alexander among states not directly subject to any of the major kingdoms, experiments like *sympoliteia*, the gathering of several villages or towns into a single entity, and *isopoliteia*, the exchange of citizenships between *poleis*. More important was the expansion of federal leagues with representative systems. This took place notably in Achaea, where the cities combined internal autonomy with a common federal citizenship, and in Aetolia, not a league of states but an

Above left: A Roman copy of a Greek wall-painting that showed Alexander and the Persian emperor Darius at the Battle of Issus. Darius is fleeing the field in terror at the approach of Alexander and his cavalry.

Above: Another detail from the mosaic shows the triumphant Alexander, as usual in the thick of the fighting.

Right: Alexander's conquests were extensive, but did not long survive his death. Many of his generals had the same vision of a unified empire, but each saw himself at its head.

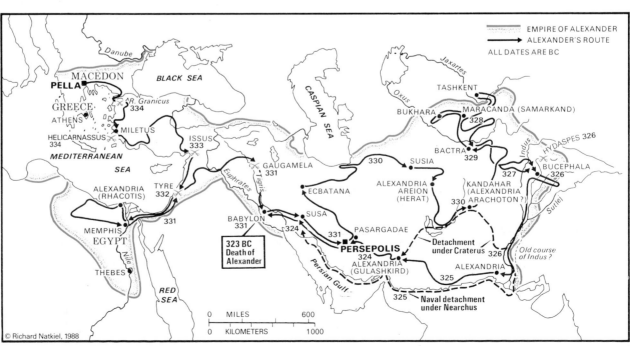

of Greek culture enabled Pergamum to control most of Asia Minor north of the Taurus and west of Bithynia by the latter part of the third century. An analogous case was that of the island of Rhodes, first and foremost a commercial community, and one which cherished its independence. Clashes at sea between Antigonid and Ptolemaic forces were to the detriment of both states and to the advantage of Rhodes. A center of international banking and exchange, as well as of Greek learning, Rhodes efficiently policed the seas and stood out as the principal power in the Aegean.

Bonds of unity

Monarchies, leagues, federations and minor empires divided the political landscape of the Hellenistic world. Through it all, however, the traditions of the *polis* endured. At Alexandria in Egypt, the greatest of Hellenistic cities, the Greeks were organized in a *polis*, juridically and politically separate from the Jewish and Egyptian components of the city. In Asia the Seleucids founded new *poleis* by the score. Some did not outgrow their origins as military colonies, but others became full-fledged city-states with organized corporate life and self-government. The fact is attested by the numbers of cities designated Seleucia, Antioch, Laodicea or Apamea, all named from the dynastic house of the Seleucids.

Throughout the Hellenistic world Greeks and Macedonians retained their sense of identity and of superiority over native elements. They formed the ruling class everywhere. Men who at home were of small significance began to flock to the east to serve in the Ptolemaic bureaucracy or in the officialdom of the Seleucid empire. The eastern areas also attracted artisans, merchants and intellectuals. Social mobility was considerably enhanced. Enterprising young Greeks could rise high and fast in Asia and Egypt. Land-ownership was not a prerequisite for aristocratic pretensions as in Greece itself. Bureaucratic competence counted for more; energy and enterprise distinguished the new ruling orders.

The vastness and complexity of the Hellenistic world made this an era of specialization and pro-

fessionalism. Bankers, merchants and shippers plied their trade with greater expertise, contributing to the era's economic prosperity. Vigorous exploratory activities were encouraged, and with them came a dramatic expansion of commerce. The Seleucids opened up the Persian Gulf and Arabian trade, as well as the overland caravan route to India. Ptolemaic exploration of the Red Sea and Africa brought Greek trade into those areas. The traffic was heavy in metals, corn, textiles, spices and luxury items. Great ports like Alexandria and Seleucia on the Orontes blossomed. The ancient world was open as it had never been before. Fruits of the prosperity naturally went into the pockets of the Greco-Macedonian ruling class in Asia and Egypt. Natives shared little in the benefits. As so often, when the economy prospered there were great discrepancies in wealth. Large quantities of silver and gold were placed in circulation, loosed from the great treasuries of the Persian empire. The swift rise in prices that followed was a boon to the business classes and the rulers, but not to the commons. Conditions for the lower classes were sometimes less than tolerable. The consequences are discernible in Egypt where we possess evidence of workmen's strikes, riots and even abandonment of land. In Greece itself there was social unrest too: movements for debt-abolition, redistribution of land and, at times, even liberation of slaves. Uprisings occurred in Aetolia, Thessaly, Boeotia, the islands and, most importantly, in Sparta, where the kings themselves led movements aimed at a form of social revolution. Discontents from below indirectly assisted Macedonian domination, for upper class elements throughout Greece looked to Macedon, as later to Rome, for suppression of social unrest. In a world so vast and so prosperous there were concomitant miseries. Society was mobile and fluid – and also insecure.

Advances in learning and literature

The same professionalism, specialization and cosmopolitanism were evident in other areas of life as well. The gifted and versatile artist was in short supply, but the era saw a proliferation of

outgrowth of ethnic and tribal groups. Intermittently cooperating with Macedon and subsidized by the Ptolemies, the Achaean confederacy was the most powerful force in the Peloponnese by the end of the third century. The Aetolian league obtained great prestige through its control of Delphi and the chief religious organization of Greece, and it also rose to a position of considerable authority in the mid-third century. Other Greek states also went their own ways. Pergamum in Asia Minor, initially a hill fortress during the wars of Alexander's successors, adopted the forms of a *polis* with a superimposed monarchy. Under shrewd and enterprising rulers Pergamum carved out a minor empire for herself in Asia Minor. A policy of neutrality with the major powers, generous gifts to neighbors, aggressive actions against native 'barbarians' and an ostentatious patronage

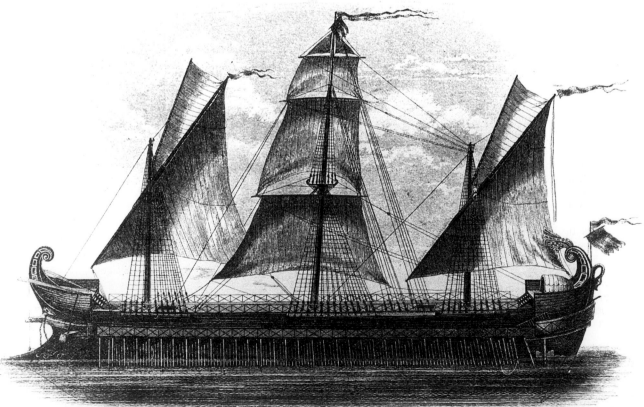

Above: Ancient Greece produced many excellent mathematicians, but the greatest was Archimedes, a native of Syracuse on the island of Sicily.

Left: Greek naval engineers produced larger and larger ships in the fourth and third centuries BC, such as the quinquereme, imaginatively recreated in this sketch. Many of the techniques of Greek naval design are unknown, and the exact construction of ships larger than a trireme remains a mystery.

Above right: A Black Figure vase-painting of Patroclus's funeral games, from Homer's *Iliad*. Greek culture laid the foundation of western civilization. Its myths and legends, as recreated in its literature, painting or sculpture, have been a great inspiration to writers and artists down to the present day.

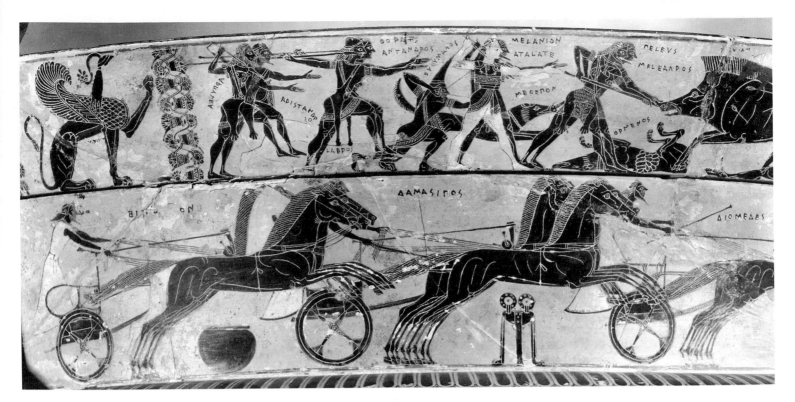

specialized scholars, with the accompanying paraphernalia. The notion of public collections of books was a Hellenistic invention. Monarchs established state libraries at key cities such as Antioch and Pergamum, and the most famed one at Alexandria, which eventually housed a collection of 700,000 volumes – that is, papyrus rolls. Scholars were soon at work on commentaries and critical editions of literary works, and they were responsible for creating systematic disciplines such as philology, lexicography and grammatical studies. Their achievement is not to be gainsaid, for it marks the emergence of a critical and rational approach to literature which stands behind the whole tradition of subsequent scholarship in the West.

The development of what may be termed the precursors of academic disciplines produced advances of real magnitude. The mathematician Euclid's careful researches brought up to date the sum of geometric knowledge in a treatise that is still the basis of today's texts. Scrupulous empirical investigation produced the first systematic works on botany by Aristotle's student Theophrastus, incorporating the information gathered in Alexander's eastern conquests. Similar application brought advances in medical science, especially in anatomy and physiology such as the discovery of the nervous system and the use of drugs for medicinal purposes. Long before Ptolemy (c AD 150) elaborated his geocentric theory, which took 1500 years to undo, Hellenistic astronomers had contrived the view that the earth turned on its axis and the planets revolved about the sun.

Skilled engineers and architects turned out works requiring extraordinary patience and craftsmanship. One need think only of the great lighthouse in Alexandria, a 400-foot tower with three diminishing stories, built by Sostratus; or of the massive statue of the sun known as the Colossus of Rhodes and admired as one of the wonders of the world; or, on a more practical level, of the enormous galleys, sometimes accommodating as many as 20 or 30 men to an oar, with which Hellenistic monarchs fought naval battles. Dozens of minor inventions, too, came out of this period, such as the water-clock, the water-mill, even a water-organ.

Fertile imaginations were required for these items – but more than that. The wealth accumulated by the monarchs and the centralization of power made it possible. Subsidization permitted organized research, collaborative activity. The great academies and seats of learning, especially at Alexandria, made possible scientific progress on a scale unthinkable in classical Greece. The celebrated Eratosthenes of Cyrene is credited with a calculation of the earth's circumference that missed the correct figure by just a small fraction. And the era's greatest genius was undoubtedly Archimedes of Syracuse, a mathematical theorist of the highest order, who formulated, among other things, a value for *pi*, created the science of hydrostatics and constructed a system for calculation of the infinite.

Nor was creativity in the arts lacking. The massive altar of Zeus at Pergamum depicting the battle of the gods and Titans reflects some of the monumental contests of the age. Restraint and idealism were no longer prime qualities. Theatricality and emotionalism were more common. Sculptured figures were uncompromisingly realistic – also akin to the temper of the times – and rarely in a state of repose. But there were creations of remarkable beauty and power, such as the famed Dying Gaul from Pergamum, the Venus of Milo and the Winged Victory of Samothrace. Like scientists and scholars, the artists benefited from the patronage of the mighty and the wealth of Hellenistic society. The volume alone of Hellenistic art, the buildings commissioned by monarchs and rulers, far eclipsed all preceding eras.

Literary figures flourished too. The so-called 'New Comedy' of manners dealt with bourgeois society, its foibles and follies, yet with a sympathetic treatment of individuals which eschewed excessive caricature. Its greatest representative, Menander of Athens, inspired a tradition whose impact was felt by the Roman comic dramatists Plautus and Terence, and endures in the comedies of Molière and Shakespeare.

There was epic poetry too, such as Apollonius' lengthy and learned *Argonautica*, the story of the quest for the Golden Fleece, which spurred a host of ancient imitators and commentators. The simultaneous presence in Alexandria of such gifted and different poets as Apollonius, Callimachus and Theocritus attests the status of that city, with its great Library and Museum, as the new cultural capital of the Greek world.

Hellenistic contributions to historiography were also outstanding. By far its most notable exponent was Polybius of Megalopolis, a prominent politician in the Achaean League and Greece's greatest historian since Thucydides. Polybius wrote his massive history of Greece and Rome while an honored and patronized hostage in Rome in the mid-second century.

The central paradox in the Hellenistic world remains, however, its peculiar combination of cosmopolitanism and fragmentation. Its horizons were broad. It professed to encompass a universal Greek culture. But its divisions were as sharp as ever. The internal struggles were incessant. The *polis* concept remained dominant in theory, but *poleis*, more often than not, were overshadowed by larger combinations and frustrated by major powers. Objects of loyalty were now more remote, fragile and shifting. The philosophic teachings of Plato's Academy and of the Aristotelian school seemed progressively more irrelevant. In their place, the third century witnessed the emergence of two new philosophies that pointedly illustrate the attitudes of the Hellenistic era. Stoicism, inaugurated by the thin and ascetic Phoenician Zeno, answered certain needs. Accepting the cosmopolitan aspirations of the day, it sought to make man's place more secure within that vast compass. By postulating a rational, divine plan that embraced all events, Stoicism softened the impact of an impersonal universe and the ever-fluctuating institutions of man. A rather different approach was taken by the gentle Epicurus, who created a philosophical school from discussions with friends in his garden. Epicureanism recognized the futility of attachment to ephemeral institutions and warring states. It preached rather a self-reliant individualism, a form of escapism in which a rigorous reduction of material wants would offer the sole route to happiness. Resignation and faith in a universal order marked the Stoics, imperturbability and inner confidence the Epicureans. The circumstances of the Hellenistic world produced these philosophic attitudes, and they, in turn, provide the most penetrating criticism of the world that Rome was soon to inherit.

Roman Civilization

In the sphere of high culture, Romans acknowledged the superiority of the Greeks. Roman genius lay elsewhere: in the arts of government, law, organization and administration. The bickerings and unhappy divisions which tormented Greek history were transcended by the Romans, who fashioned an enduring empire. 'Law and order' is a suspect phrase nowadays, and we may be sure that it brought little comfort to many of the subject peoples exploited by Rome's imperial ambitions. As the historian Tacitus sneered, 'the Romans create a wasteland and call it peace.' Nonetheless, the achievement was prodigious, inspiring awe among contemporaries and successors alike. Rome succeeded where others had failed in welding the entire Mediterranean area into a viable unity. She can justly claim responsibility for preserving the legacy of Greece and spreading it throughout the area that is now western Europe.

None could have predicted it from the beginning. The small town on the Tiber was a slow starter and took a long time in emerging to prominence. Rome was not located in an especially fertile area, nor on a powerful eminence, nor even on the sea. But there were other advantages. Italy's central position in the Mediterranean, jutting out like a long pier, made it the obvious focus of contact between east and west. The country is mountainous, but unlike the mountains of Greece, the Apennines do not chop up the land into small segments. A temperate climate and a general, if not overwhelming, fertility help to explain the heavy population which provided manpower for Roman expansion. And the city of Rome itself proved to have geographic endowments. Its site was far enough from the sea to protect inhabitants from piracy, yet it sat astride the Tiber which flowed down to the sea. Rome was also situated on the most convenient crossing point of the Tiber, thereby being in a position to

control the main line of communications along the western side of Italy. Excellent building materials, easily quarried, could be found in the vicinity. And Rome's location in the very heart of Italy made her the natural starting point for the great roads that eventually would stretch through all parts of the peninsula.

Speculation on the origins of Italic peoples have been many and varied. The general Mediterranean dislocations which occurred toward the end of the second millennium BC may have produced migratory movements that brought settlers to Italy and established Indo-European tongues there. Did the 'true Italians' come from across the Alps, from the Balkans, from the east, or were they indigenous? In the absence of written

records, we cannot really know what constitutes the coming of a new culture and people. Changes in burial rites, language or material remains like pottery do not necessarily entail racial change. Near the beginning of the Italian Bronze Age, about 1700 BC, there appears in the Po Valley a people traditionally referred to as the Terremare. They not only possessed a knowledge of how to make bronze implements but also practiced cremation rather than the burial that had been characteristic of prior inhabitants of the area. More strikingly, they built their homes on piles, as if to protect from the flooding of lakes. Hence, it has been concluded, the Terremare came from the Alpine lakes and kept on building their homes in the old way out of force of habit. But how much

Above: Romulus and Remus, the legendary founders of Rome, suckling at the teats of the she-wolf who saved them from drowning.

Left: An Etruscan ivory panel, carved to depict two diners conversing on a banqueting couch. The Etruscan peoples of Tuscany built a rich culture in the sixth and fifth centuries BC. Many Roman customs were adapted from Etruscan ones.

Right: A Roman altar from Ostia shows Romulus and Remus about to be discovered by the shepherd who would raise them to manhood.

Above right: Terracotta sarcophagi were a traditional Etruscan art form with no counterpart in Greek culture.

can be made of that? In fact, the Po Valley in the Bronze Age was a melting pot in which a variety of cultures, indigenous and immigrant, mingled. It is fruitless to try to isolate the strands.

The same ambiguities exist with the coming of the Iron Age, around 1000 BC, allegedly dominated by a people called the Villanovans, so named from a small site in Bologna. Because they cremated their dead, some see them as descendants of the Terremare; others argue that they came from across the Alps; still others that they originated in the east where the techniques of forging iron were developed. But the various theories dissolve into sheer speculation.

Light does not begin to dawn until the eighth century BC. Here for the first time we can speak with some assurance about the influence of external peoples upon the formation of the Roman experience: namely, the Greeks and Etruscans. Evidence is no longer restricted to material implements and traces of buildings; we are in the presence of full-fledged civilizations which produced painting, sculpture, religion, mythology and literature, all of which passed into the culture of Rome.

The Greeks, it will be recalled, embarked on large-scale colonization in the eighth century, and among their primary targets were much of southern Italy and Sicily. By the mid-sixth century Greeks were installed all over the lower end of the Italian boot in towns such as Naples, Syracuse and

Tarentum. It was Greek colonization, with its concomitant urban institutions, commercial contacts, artistic and intellectual currents, that brought the south of Italy and Sicily out of the Iron Age and into the full flush of civilization.

A similar service was performed for northern Italy by the Etruscans. That mysterious people has left a rich institutional and cultural heritage, and even a written language, which is, as yet, undeciphered. Etruscan origins are obscure. Evidence points to an eastern provenance. But whoever the settlers were, they mingled with an indigenous populace and were changed in the process. Etruscan civilization was not imported wholesale. Literary traditions depict the Etruscans as great seafarers with a widespread dominion. Archeological remains support this, since there is an abundance of Etruscan ware, especially black-glazed pottery, all along the shores of Italy, Sardinia, Corsica, North Africa, Greece, southern France and Spain. The Etruscans had much to offer. The only great iron, copper, silver and lead mines in the central Mediterranean are those in Etruria and in the island of Elba just off the Etruscan coast, a feature that first attracted the Greeks themselves into the Etruscan commercial orbit. More than that, Etruscans penetrated far inland and controlled a large continental empire which included the whole of the Po Valley to the north and much of Latium and Campania to the south. It was only at the end of the sixth century that those holdings began to crumble. Etruscans faced the same problem that plagued the Greeks: lack of a solid political entity. Etruscan history was really the history of a number of powerful, independent cities like Caere, Volsinii and Tarquinii. The contrast between Etruria's glorious age and her decline can be seen in tomb paintings. Earlier ones portray lavish scenes of banquets, sport, leisure and dances, the mark of an affluent society. Later, when the empire was lost, Etruscan portraiture took on a dark aspect, absorbed with the dead, with figures of grimness and horror. For three centuries, however, from about 800 to 500, Etruria was the center of Italian history.

Rome was the ultimate beneficiary. Located

directly between the Etruscan and Greek spheres of influence, she was in an ideal position to profit from both. The Greek influence came later and was perhaps more telling in the long run, but Etruscan influence was more direct and more potent in Rome's early formation. From Etruria came the alphabet – at second hand, to be sure, but it was the Latin version of the written Etruscan that the Western world employs today. The ceremony of the triumph and the *fasces,* which symbolized Rome's chief magistracy, as well as religious practices such as the art of divining, were Etruscan survivals. So also are the arch and the vault, the origin of Rome's monumental architecture. Many other items could be mentioned, but of primary importance is the fact that the Etruscans made of Rome a city. Through their influence Romans adopted the pattern of systematic urban design with long, straight streets, regular blocks of houses and a checkerboard effect. Thus the Etruscans were responsible for converting what had been a conglomeration of shepherd villages into a genuine urban community.

Romulus and Remus

Legend reports that Rome was founded in 753 BC by Romulus, who killed his twin brother Remus and became Rome's first king. The story itself is typical of Indo-European myths involving the slaying of one brother by another who becomes the progenitor of a great race. One needs think only of Cain and Abel or Jacob and Esau. But the date may not be far off the mark. Excavations show the earliest settlements to have been on the Palatine Hill, fitting nicely with the tradition that Romulus' home was located there. Habitation gradually spread to the other hills; in the seventh century the forum lost its character as a burial ground and became a place for dwellings. Tradition refers to an era when the various hill villages were separate entities. The ceremony of the Septimontium, festival of the seven hills, commemorated a union or federation of those communities which had once been independent.

Rome's transition into a city came in the sixth century. Again tradition is a useful guide. It records that Rome's last kings were Etruscans. They are supposed to have been only individual immigrants, but the stories conceal a larger Etruscan domination. Metalwork and pottery from Etruria appear in ever larger quantities. Around 575 came the first real pebble pavement in the forum, which began to take on the characteristics of a public square. Also dating from this time are the earliest remains on the Capitoline Hill, soon to become the citadel of historic Rome. The creation of a central market place superseding the scattered huts marks a real turning point. A similar process can be traced in many other towns of Latium and Campania where the Etruscans converted rural sites into urban centers, and for the expansion of Etruscan influence Rome provided a particularly convenient and desirable locus of operations.

Thus it was under Etruscan rule that Rome suddenly developed a discernible industry and trade: contacts with the Greek world are disclosed by the presence of Attic black and red figure ware, and a treaty records commercial contact with the thriving Phoenician merchants at Carthage. The construction of public buildings and temples, such as the great house of Jupiter on the Capitol, marks the new affluence. When Roman traditions, therefore, speak of great conquests by the city under the last kings, they preserve important truths – though not for the right reasons. Those conquests were Etruscan conquests, with Rome employed as one of the strongholds of the Etrus-

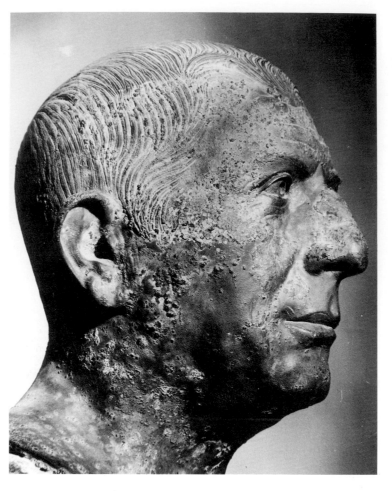

Left: A bust of Lucius Caecilius Jucundus, a banker of Pompeii. Rome pursued a clever policy of extending its citizenship to the wealthy inhabitants of other towns. As a result, in time the whole of the Italian peninsula came under Roman rule.

Below right: A bronze plate decorated with a scene showing the plowing of fields. Throughout its history Romans remained very conscious of the importance of farming to their way of life. Their national poet, Virgil, commemorated this relationship in his poem *Georgics.*

can empire. But when Etruscan kings were eventually expelled near the end of the sixth century, Rome had developed the institutions and self-confidence that enabled her to become a power in her own right. The city had benefited profoundly from foreign rule and had applied the lessons for her own purposes.

The Roman conquest of Italy, like the history of the monarchy, is shrouded in legend. Expansion was probably slow and plodding, marked by setbacks as well as triumphs. Moreover, the eventual domination of Italy seems to have been achieved as much by diplomacy as by force of arms. It was in the course of this expansion that Roman soldiers and statesmen developed the skill, patience and trust in institutions that marked the city's character. The slowness of the process deserves emphasis because the Romans, for all their faults, were supreme in one category: they learned from experience. That quality explains their peculiar combination of flexibility and conservatism.

The expulsion of the Etruscan kings in 509 (if that is the correct date) did not mean the evaporation of Etruscan influence. In the following quarter-century Rome was caught up in larger conflicts with Etruscan cities, Latin towns and the Greeks of Campania. The pages of Livy recount these years as a stirring series of Roman triumphs over the hill tribes of the Aequi and Volsci, in the east and south respectively. But there were Roman defeats as well. One report of heavy losses at the hands of the Volsci could not be papered over by historians. Thus was created the legend of Coriolanus, allegedly a Roman warrior who defected to the Volsci and led assaults against his homeland. Since Roman losses were undeniable, the best way to salvage the city's military reputation was to make a Roman himself responsible for them. Other folk-tales grew up about these wars, including the famed story of Cincinnatus, the soldier-farmer who saved his country and went

back to his plow – the idealized image of the yeoman warrior. Stories of this sort formed the staple diet of young Roman schoolboys in the late Republic. If they are not genuine history, they are genuine representations of Roman ideals. In reality, the conflicts with Sabines, Aequi and Volsci were little more than annual raids and counter-raids on one another's crops. Rome's emergence as a power of real significance did not come before the end of the fifth century, but it was in these petty battles that Rome learned the art of war and developed the martial discipline that was to prove indispensable.

The Latin League

The same period saw the formation of treaties and interstate negotiations that began to school Rome in diplomacy. The collapse of Etruscan power brought independence and renewed vigor to the cities of Latium, formed in a federation of towns called the Latin League. Relations with Rome had been rocky, but the common menace of invasions from Aequi and Volsci produced a formal treaty of alliance in the 490s. At the same time, Rome concluded a lesser known but equally important treaty with people called the Hernici in the Trerus valley. Alliance with the Hernici provided a corridor between the Aequi and Volsci, an early example of 'divide and conquer.' More important, it was a formal link to a non-Latin people. Though Rome was allied by then to the Latin League and the Hernici, those two had no official ties with one another. It was through Rome alone that the partners could come into formal contact. As a consequence, when the wars against common foes dragged on, leadership naturally fell more and more to Rome. That rudimentary set of alliances became the foundation for her eventual hegemony.

Subsequent stages of expansion need not be traced step by step. It was Roman doggedness rather than a string of easy victories that eventually won continental Italy. One serious interruption in the process came when marauding bands of Celts, whom the Romans called Gauls, swept into the Po Valley and central Italy, destroying a Roman army and sacking the city itself about 390. It took more than a generation for Rome to recover. But in the long run the Gallic invasion proved to be a boon, for the Gauls had effected the final disintegration of Etruscan power. From the mid-fourth century Rome gradually moved into those areas where Etruscans had once held sway, including Etruria itself to the north and Campania in the south.

The Latin League made one dying gasp in 340, a final attempt to get out from under the tightening Roman vise. But the so-called Great Latin War ended in two years, and the League was dissolved, each city now to be tied directly to Rome. Only one major Italian power stood in the way thereafter: the Samnites, rugged mountain dwellers of the Apennines. The clashes between Roman and Samnite were long and bloody, leaving bitter memories, but patience and manpower proved telling in the end. The Latin towns, now humbled, supplied additional soldiers; the Appian Way was under construction and Rome was soon to have a pathway through Campania. The Samnites eventually succumbed in the 290s. Rome's hegemony in the peninsula below the Po Valley was unchallenged.

The means which Rome employed to organize her relations with Italian states were many and varied. Arrangements came through a gradual process of trial and error, ultimately producing a patchwork system. The development was foreshadowed, however, in the early pact with the Latin League, an agreement which provided for mutually inter-changeable citizenships. Any Latin who moved to Rome would automatically attain full Roman citizenship, and vice-versa. In practice, most of the movement went in one direction, with a concomitant swelling of the Roman citizen-body. The concept of mutual citizenships was occasionally toyed with, but only intermittently implemented in Greece. The Romans made it work, and this gave Rome a manpower base far superior to anything the Greek cities could manage.

Conscription of Latin troops for what were essentially Rome's wars led to the Latin revolt of 340-338. Rome again learned a valuable lesson. After conclusion of the conflict, the Latin League was disbanded forever. Individual Latin towns were henceforth to have relations with Rome but none with one another. The nearest towns were incorporated into the Roman body-politic and eliminated as independent political entities. Other Latin cities concluded individual treaties with Rome. Rome began to establish formal relationships with towns outside Latium that had come under her influence. One of the formulas adopted was the *civitas sine suffragio*, granted to Volscian and Campanian communities. Residents of a *civitas sine suffragio* became Roman citizens, but without the privileges of voting or holding office in Rome. They could be called on for military service and paid Roman taxes, but retained their own local governments. Spread of citizenship was effected in other ways as well: through the planting of military colonies in strategic spots, some of them small enclaves of Roman citizens, others large self-governing communities called Latin colonies, placed on territory confiscated from defeated foes. Colonial foundations and eventual elevation of *civitates sine suffragio* extended the citizen population into remote areas of Italy.

An analogous development, equally illustrative of Roman character, may be traced in the city's internal evolution. Tradition records an overthrow of the Etruscan dynasty, the Tarquins, in 509, and the creation of the Republic, a milestone in Rome's constitutional history. In fact, many Etruscan institutions endured, as well as other items that date from the monarchical period. Romans did not readily discard institutions. The monarchy itself was abolished, replaced by two annual magistrates, the consuls, as heads of government. But the consuls themselves retained some of the accoutrements of monarchy – not only such symbols of authority, as the *fasces*, but the *imperium* itself, the absolute executive authority, at home and in the field. The Roman senate, which was the balance-wheel of Republican government, grew directly out of the advisory body of elders consulted by the kings. The personnel of that body doubtless altered very little with the inception of the Republic.

In addition, there was a more fundamental social structure, continuous from monarchy to republic. A sharp distinction divided patricians and plebeians. Origins of the difference remain obscure: perhaps a racial difference, the plebeians being descendants of what had once been a conquered people; or else an economic origin, the class of plebeians being formed of farmers who had lost their property and urban dwellers, humble tradesmen and craftsmen. Their relationship at the end of the monarchy and in the early Republic is, in any case, clear. The aristocratic structure resembles closely that of Greece in the archaic period. Patricians were organized in clans, *gentes*, headed by powerful noble families whose authority rested on ownership of land. Inter-marriage and class solidarity perpetuated patrician ascendancy. Plebeians were tied to their noble patrons as clients, dependent upon them for legal protection, economic assistance and military leadership. Both patricians and plebeians had full citizen rights, but only patricians could attain high office, sit in the senate or hold religious posts. Most important, knowledge of the law, still unwritten, was carefully preserved in the patrician order. All citizens, however, were eligible to vote for the consulship – and ex-consuls comprised the leadership of the senate. But the voters were grouped in 'centuries,' originally military divisions, where individual ballots were subsumed in larger voting units determined by the wealth of the participants. This centuriate assembly was heavily weighted toward men of property who could supply their own arms. Thus it is easy to see why patricians maintained control of political institutions.

Struggle of the orders

Our sources on the first two centuries of the Republic tell of a persistent, though intermittent, contest between the patricians and plebeians, 'the struggle of the orders.' What were the issues at stake? Economic grievances loom large in the tradition. The plebeians are frequently depicted as desirous of land distribution and oppressed by heavy debts. Such matters are appropriate to the late Republic, with its problems of overpopulation, unemployment, military upheavals and ruin of the countryside, but hardly to the fifth century. The subsoil of Latium is relatively rich and more than capable of supporting a moderate population. When the citizen-body

increased and population became denser in the fifth century, the surplus was still manageable through the growth of Roman territory and the creation of colonies and settlements all over Italy. The real grievances of the *plebs* lay elsewhere: in the basic need for protection and for some genuine representation.

These conclusions may be substantiated from the concessions actually won by the plebeians. They had little to do with economics. The *plebs* in 494 created their own annual representative, the tribune, empowered with right of *auxilium*, ie the authority to come to the aid of any plebeian threatened or coerced by a magistrate. Somewhat later came the institution of another popular assembly, this one organized geographically by tribes, rather than in accordance with wealth as in the older centuriate assembly. But the centuriate assembly continued to operate alongside the tribal assembly, the former responsible for electing consuls and for matters of peace and war, the latter for electing tribunes and other plebeian officers.

The combination of concession with conservatism is evident also in another sphere: the agitation for equality under the law. So long as patricians guarded the secrets of legal lore, the *plebs* were at their mercy. A growing self-consciousness on the part of the commons, however, produced the first codification and publication of Roman law in the mid-fifth century, the Twelve Tables. Patricians could no longer invent regulations in their own interests, but the laws contained in the Twelve Tables offered little comfort to the *plebs*: they were harsh and rigid, incorporated a scrupulous enforcement of debt regulations and perpetuated patrician exclusiveness by forbidding intermarriage between patricians and plebeians. They served to solidify informal arrangements rather than to liberalize relations – in much the same spirit as Draco's code in Athens.

But the plebs continued to make gains. Such, for example, was the acquisition of *provocatio*, the right of any citizen to appeal the decision of a magistrate to the people. Eventually the plebeians won certification that measures passed by the plebeian assembly would have the full force of law. And when normal constitutional channels were closed to the plebeians they resorted to *secessio* – a form of general strike combined with a refusal to accept conscription in the army. In its extreme form, this meant seceding from the body politic, setting up their own magistrates, assemblies and

constitutional structure. The tactics frequently worked, but at no time do they seem to have threatened a disintegration of the social fabric.

The 'struggle of the orders' is often seen as an effort by plebeians to gain access to patrician magistracies. That battle seems to have been won by the plebeians in 367, for thereafter plebeians regularly held one of the two annual consulships. But it is important to understand the nature of that victory. It was not a triumph of the have-nots over the haves. Rather, it meant the emergence of a relatively small group of plebeian aristocrats who had now gained equal status with patricians, and it was not long before there emerged a new and equally exclusive patricio-plebeian nobility.

The circumstances of an increasingly complex society explain the development. With growing burdens at home and abroad, the ruling class had added responsibilities not readily discharged by a small group. The number of magistracies was increased, with a more definite division of responsibilities. In addition to the consuls, Rome instituted praetors to discharge judicial functions, quaestors to handle financial matters, aediles to supervise municipal business, and a host of minor

officials. It is in this context that the 'rise of the plebeians' must be understood. Patrician families did not have the manpower to monopolize either the civil administration or the military leadership of an ever more complicated and sophisticated society, but social and economic inequalities remained. The ruling class had maintained its hold by compromise and concession, by expanding and diluting its membership. Thus the 'struggle of the orders' ended by avoiding revolutionary upheaval, by establishing equality under the law and by creating a new, if broadened, aristocracy. All in all, it was a typically Roman exercise.

The age of expansion

By the early third century patience and adaptability had earned Rome the hegemony of Italy – and given her citizens confidence in a flexible but firmly anchored constitutional structure. She was now on the brink of overseas expansion. The beginnings were slow. Rome was not then a maritime power and had only an embryonic fleet. She did not appear to have discernible imperialist ambitions, but her large network of treaties and alliances brought contact with maritime states

Left: Inhabitants of a Roman province pay their taxes. Taxation was either on the basis of the value of one's property, or took the form of a poll tax; income was never taxed in the ancient world.

Right: A small boat is pulled upstream along a river. The barrels probably contain wine. The lack of an effective horse harness meant that men, in all likelihood slaves, had to do the pulling.

and gradually drew her into a web of interlocking relationships that looked beyond Italy. A series of treaties were concluded with Carthage, the greatest mercantile power in the western Mediterranean. And when Rome moved into Campania and then southern Italy, she secured alliances with important Greek trading centers such as Naples.

With the Hellenistic world in process of formation, one of Alexander's would-be successors, Pyrrhus of Epirus, sought by military means to win a foothold in the Greek zone of Italy. Rome was called to assist the city of Thurii. Pyrrhus was no mean foe. A skilled general whose massive elephants threw the Italians into confusion, he earned his triumphs, but they were costly ones – the origin of the term 'Pyrrhic victory.' As he allegedly exclaimed at the conclusion of one battle, 'One more such victory and I am lost!' Roman manpower and the strength of her alliance system eventually wore Pyrrhus down, and in 275 he was expelled from Italy.

From Pyrrhus, as from most of her foes, Rome learned through experience. She streamlined her legions, developed a more mobile formation and picked up the technique of utilizing fortified camps. And of greater long-run significance, Rome now extended her suzerainty to the Greek harbor towns of Tarentum and Rhegium, thus bringing her into direct contact with the commercial routes to Hellenistic Greece. That matrix of associations was soon to involve confrontation with Carthage.

Left: A scene of a shoemaker at work, taken from a marble sarcophagus found at Ostia, the port of Rome. The sarcophagus belonged to a Greek who had settled in Ostia.

Above right: A Roman shipwright at work. He is preparing a rib for insertion into the finished hull of a merchant ship. The relief is taken from the funeral monument of a shipwright named Longidienus.

Right: A butcher at work in his shop in Rome. As Rome's population increased so food supplies became a major problem, and in time the city became dependent upon imports from sources far beyond the Italian peninsula.

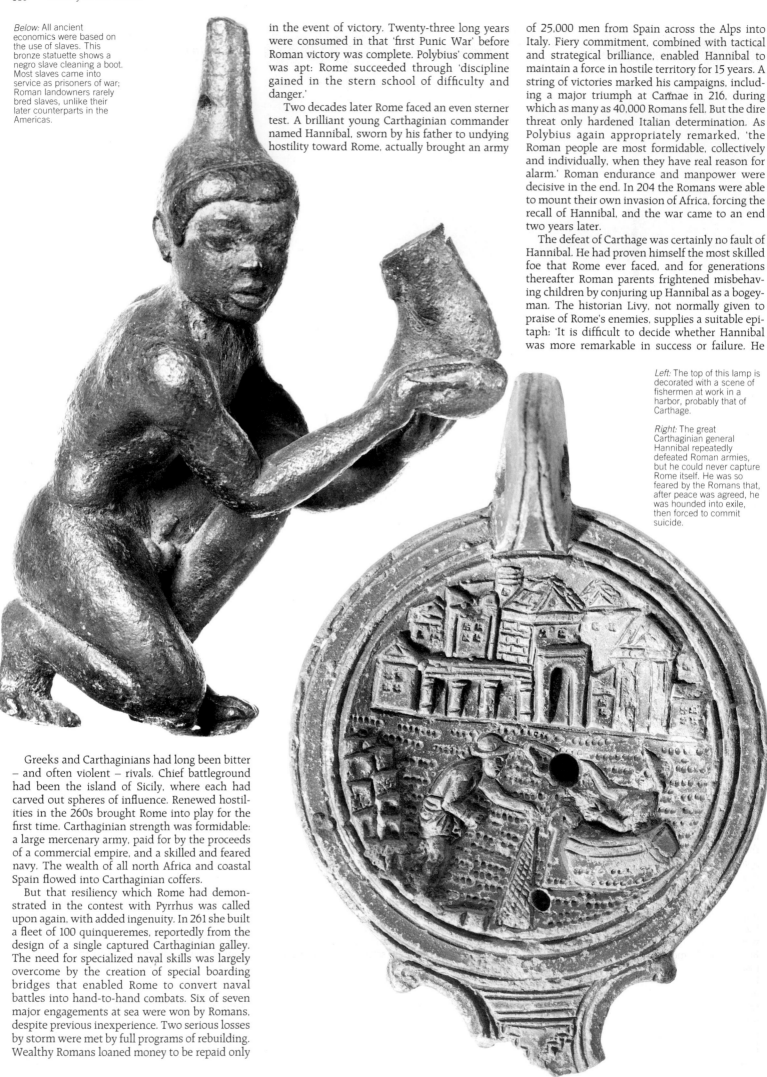

Below: All ancient economics were based on the use of slaves. This bronze statuette shows a negro slave cleaning a boot. Most slaves came into service as prisoners of war; Roman landowners rarely bred slaves, unlike their later counterparts in the Americas.

Left: The top of this lamp is decorated with a scene of fishermen at work in a harbor, probably that of Carthage.

Right: The great Carthaginian general Hannibal repeatedly defeated Roman armies, but he could never capture Rome itself. He was so feared by the Romans that, after peace was agreed, he was hounded into exile, then forced to commit suicide.

in the event of victory. Twenty-three long years were consumed in that 'first Punic War' before Roman victory was complete. Polybius' comment was apt: Rome succeeded through 'discipline gained in the stern school of difficulty and danger.'

Two decades later Rome faced an even sterner test. A brilliant young Carthaginian commander named Hannibal, sworn by his father to undying hostility toward Rome, actually brought an army of 25,000 men from Spain across the Alps into Italy. Fiery commitment, combined with tactical and strategical brilliance, enabled Hannibal to maintain a force in hostile territory for 15 years. A string of victories marked his campaigns, including a major triumph at Cannae in 216, during which as many as 40,000 Romans fell. But the dire threat only hardened Italian determination. As Polybius again appropriately remarked, 'the Roman people are most formidable, collectively and individually, when they have real reason for alarm.' Roman endurance and manpower were decisive in the end. In 204 the Romans were able to mount their own invasion of Africa, forcing the recall of Hannibal, and the war came to an end two years later.

The defeat of Carthage was certainly no fault of Hannibal. He had proven himself the most skilled foe that Rome ever faced, and for generations thereafter Roman parents frightened misbehaving children by conjuring up Hannibal as a bogeyman. The historian Livy, not normally given to praise of Rome's enemies, supplies a suitable epitaph: 'It is difficult to decide whether Hannibal was more remarkable in success or failure. He

Greeks and Carthaginians had long been bitter – and often violent – rivals. Chief battleground had been the island of Sicily, where each had carved out spheres of influence. Renewed hostilities in the 260s brought Rome into play for the first time. Carthaginian strength was formidable: a large mercenary army, paid for by the proceeds of a commercial empire, and a skilled and feared navy. The wealth of all north Africa and coastal Spain flowed into Carthaginian coffers.

But that resiliency which Rome had demonstrated in the contest with Pyrrhus was called upon again, with added ingenuity. In 261 she built a fleet of 100 quinqueremes, reportedly from the design of a single captured Carthaginian galley. The need for specialized naval skills was largely overcome by the creation of special boarding bridges that enabled Rome to convert naval battles into hand-to-hand combats. Six of seven major engagements at sea were won by Romans, despite previous inexperience. Two serious losses by storm were met by full programs of rebuilding. Wealthy Romans loaned money to be repaid only

engaged in military action in Illyria in order to protect Italian shipping from piracy in the Adriatic. Her military power made short work of the Illyrians, but more important were the diplomatic contacts inaugurated. While much of the Illyrian coast became a Roman protectorate, there were also informal pacts of *amicitia* (friendship) established with certain Greek towns and tribes. The *amicitia* relationship admirably suited both sides. Minor Greek states, long accustomed to the suzerainty of large Hellenistic powers, welcomed Roman protection, especially since Rome's yoke was light, with no demand for money or troops. Without formal treaties, Rome was not obliged to intervene, and obviously preferred it that way.

Involvement in Illyria brought Rome to the fringes of the Macedonian kingdom now being expanded under the aggressive monarch Philip V. While Hannibal roamed in Italy, Philip concluded an alliance with him and invaded the Roman protectorate in Illyria. This provoked a storm of protest among Philip's Greek rivals, who hastened to Rome's aid in checking Philip's advance. The event produced a whole new set of treaties and *amicitiae* with Hellenistic states. By the end of the third century Roman connections extended to the Aetolian League, Corcyra and Athens in central and western Greece, to Sparta and Messenia in the Peloponnese and to Pergamum, Rhodes and even Egypt in the Aegean world.

This background is indispensable to an understanding of the full-fledged war that Rome undertook against Macedon immediately upon conclusion of the Hannibalic conflict. We need not postulate philhellenic sympathies or, alternatively, a policy of territorial and commercial expansionism. The fact is that Rome had already, by varied stages, been drawn into the vortex of Hellenistic diplomacy. Flattered and benefited by attentions paid her by Greek states, Rome heeded the appeals of Rhodes, Pergamum and Athens to engage against Philip.

In the next half-century the Hellenistic powers which had dominated the eastern Mediterranean crumbled one by one before the Roman military machine. Macedon succumbed by 196 BC, as the more mobile Roman legions crushed the vaunted Macedonian phalanx. Not long thereafter came a confrontation with Antiochus III, greatest of the Seleucid kings, who sought to reclaim possessions in Asia Minor and Thrace. Scipio Africanus resumed charge of Roman forces, and by 188 Antiochus had lost all of Asia Minor. A revival of Macedonian power under Philip's son, Perseus, stirred up the Greek world again, including some wavering allies of Rome, from 171 to 167, but Roman armies emerged triumphant once more, the climactic battle coming at Pydna in 168. This time there were harsher crackdowns on former friends and foes alike. The Macedonian monarchy was abolished, and the country itself was divided into four separate republics. A final flareup occurred in Greece in 149, provoking sharp reaction: the city of Corinth was ruthlessly sacked, the Achaean League was disbanded and a Roman governor was installed in Macedon to control all of mainland Greece.

The conquest of Spain

Roman power advanced also in the west during the second century. Here the problems were very different, as were the solutions. In Spain there were no sophisticated Greek diplomats, no subtle webs of interstate relationships to baffle embassies and negotiators. Spain was largely uncivilized. An immense number of independent tribes operated there, men with a fierce sense of personal loyalty to their leaders, but not to

waged war far from his home, in enemy territory, for 15 years of varied fortunes, at the head of an army not from his own country, but a mixed force from peoples differing in law, customs and language . . . yet he bound them as with a chain so that, though money and supplies were often lacking, there was never any division or mutiny against their leader.'

The second Punic War abounded in Roman heroes as well. There was the canny Fabius Cunctator ('the delayer'), who devised a strategy of attrition, avoiding pitched battles, dogging Hannibal's heels and driving him to frustration. There was the impetuous and forceful Marcellus, 'Rome's sword, as Fabius was her shield,' who conducted the critical siege of Syracuse, overcoming the catapults of Archimedes. And there was the dashing youth Scipio Africanus, who captured Spain, adopted Hannibal's own techniques and headed the invasion of Africa that brought Carthage to her knees. The leadership, skill and experience of the Roman aristocracy was of central importance. Military tactics learned from Pyrrhus, the Carthaginian navy and from Hannibal himself were appropriated and used in Roman interests. But the single most telling factor was persistent loyalty from the heart of Rome's alliance in Italy: Latium, Samnium and Etruria. No single Latin or Roman colony defected. And the Greek towns themselves, except when overawed militarily, remained faithful to Rome. It is eloquent testimony to the solidity and intelligence of that Italian coalition.

Rome had not entered the Punic Wars with plans of territorial expansion. But the Carthaginian collapse added enormous areas which now looked to Rome as suzerain. Sicily fell to her charge after the first Punic War, Sardinia and Corsica between the wars and the coast of Spain and north Africa after the second Punic War. Still there was no conscious policy of imperialism. In Sicily, Rome introduced the same kind of patchwork system that had been operative in Italy. With some cities, such as Syracuse and Messana, she formed alliances; others were left autonomous; and in much of the island she simply adapted Carthaginian practice and collected tithes in the form of grain. Only in 227 did Rome organize Sicily into the first of her overseas provinces, governed by a praetor and a staff dispatched from the capital. The step, once taken, was easy to repeat. Sardinia and Corsica were snatched from Carthage and similarly organized. But there was still no standard system applied everywhere. After Hannibal's defeat, Carthaginian territory in Spain came into Roman hands, yet Rome sent out no regular magistrates for several years, and tribute was collected in the Carthaginian manner. With certain large towns, especially Phoenician and Greek settlements, Rome concluded separate treaties. North Africa itself was not reduced to provincial status. Carthage retained her autonomy and secured alliance with Rome, though it was clear that her situation was essentially that of a client-state.

This spreading net of foreign entanglements brought Rome into the world of the Hellenistic powers. Between the Punic Wars she became

abstract entities such as states and governments. Nor were Roman legions readily equipped to deal with guerrilla warfare. The result was more than a half-century of brutality, cruelty and treachery, perhaps the darkest chapter of Roman history. The rich mineral resources of the land provoked Roman greed and drove her leaders to a policy of conquest without the niceties of *amicitia* or a consistent respect for treaty obligations. It was not until Scipio Aemilianus, grandson of Hannibal's conqueror, subdued the Spaniards at Numantia in 134 that these bloody contests came to a conclusion. Two new provinces were carved out of Spanish territory, providing enormous wealth for Rome's treasury and recruits for her auxiliary forces.

Rome displayed an equal lack of compunction in her dealings in North Africa. Concern about Carthage took hold again in mid-century. The fears were groundless, but the stentorian tones of Cato the Elder fired the senate with irrational determination: 'Carthage must be destroyed!' In this third Punic War the ancient foe was deceived, then defeated and brutally destroyed. In Africa, as in the Greek east, the concept of balance of power had broken down.

By 133 Rome had created six wholly dependent provinces: Sicily, Sardinia, the two Spains, Macedon and Africa. The establishment of dominion throughout the Mediterranean, accomplished within a century and a half, was a feat of remarkable proportions. And it was the work of a society that had itself become remarkable.

Rome's involvement with the Greek world had meant exposure to Hellenic culture and ideas. Spoils of war included private art collections and even libraries. Greek slaves were brought to Rome, many of them to become tutors of children of the Roman aristocracy. Hostages and exiles included intellectuals such as Polybius. Rome became a magnet for cultured Hellenic diplomats, for philosophers and professors of rhetoric. Even Cato taught himself Greek and was responsible for bringing the poet Ennius to Rome at the end of the third century. It became a source of pride for Roman nobles such as Scipio Aemilianus to sponsor and patronize Greek intellectuals.

The formation of a Latin culture owed much to the Greeks, but the impact was not altogether one-sided. Hellenic elements were woven into a Roman fabric and then molded by Roman needs. This Greek political theory was adopted and

adapted. A long tradition stemming from Plato and Aristotle tended to see governments rising and falling in a cyclical pattern, from monarchy to tyranny, aristocracy to oligarchy, democracy to mob rule – and then a repetition of the pattern. The cycle could only be broken with a 'mixed constitution,' combining monarchic, aristocratic and democratic elements and incorporating a system of checks and balances. In the intellectual circle of Scipio Aemilianus, Greek thinkers such as Panaetius and Polybius were persuaded that Rome's constitution approximated to the ideal. The consuls represented the monarchical element, the senate the aristocratic, the assemblies the democratic, and it was all a perfectly balanced, self-adjusting mechanism. Such was the analysis, schematic and myopic. Rome's institutions, in fact, were based on no such blueprint. Whatever the apparent mixture, the structure was geared to promote aristocratic rule. But realities notwithstanding, the theories were flattering to Roman thinkers, and by the late Republic they had been adopted as canonical descriptions of Rome's constitutional process.

Literary developments, too, show the influence of Greece and the molding by Rome. Greek legends and literature were introduced through contacts with the towns of southern Italy in the third century. A Greek slave from Tarentum, Livius Andronicus, captured after the Pyrrhic War, fashioned the first Latin translation of the *Odyssey*. Odysseus soon became a popular hero, largely because he was emblematic of virtues celebrated by Rome: piety, courage, endurance and patience. Even more popular were legends surrounding the Trojan War. Here Roman mythmakers shamelessly appropriated the story for their own antique past: the Trojan hero Aeneas became grandfather of Romulus and ancestor of Rome's initial ruling dynasty. Roman pride received even more potent expression in the stirring verses of Ennius. An assiduous student of Homer, Ennius, born in Calabria and brought to Rome by Cato, produced a poetic chronicle of the city's history in Homeric hexameters, but in the Latin language. The Greek form was consciously adapted to express those martial qualities the Romans saw as so important.

Hellenic dominance was more difficult to shake off in the theater. Roman tragedians in the second century drew heavily on Attic models, especially the dramas of Euripides, and their themes were predominantly those of Greek mythology. Similarly in comic drama. The raucous comedies of Plautus and the more refined and polished plays of Terence were confessed adaptations of Greek New Comedy. Even here, however, Romans introduced their own features. In Plautus' plays, for example, there are numerous contemporary references and unmistakable Italic types.

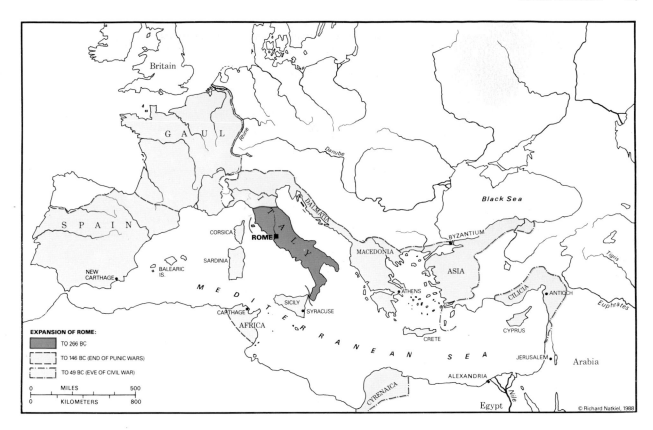

Far left: Cato the Younger, who was the last champion of the Roman Republic. He was the great-grandson of the politician who sought Carthage's destruction.

Below left: Virgil's poem the *Aeneid* was written in emulation of the great Homeric epics to give Rome a similar cultural heritage. This wall-painting depicts a scene from the story. Aeneas leans on his young son Ascanius while a doctor operates on an arrow wound. His protectress, the goddess Venus, looks on.

Right: Roman expansion was no sudden event. It was a gradual process, the product of many generations' work.

Below: The prevalence of Greek myths in Roman life can be seen in this mosaic, from Lullingstone in Kent, England, depicting Zeus (in the form of a bull) carrying off Europa.

Roman intellectuals were sensitive to the debt to Greece. To many Greek *litterati*, Rome was still the 'rude barbarian.' Hence the Roman use of Greek forms and style even when the spirit was Roman; hence also the need for fashioning a mythology that was tacked on to the Trojan cycle. And when serious history began to be written in the late third century by Roman senators such as Fabius Pictor and Cincius Alimentus, it was written in Greek, primarily for Greek audiences.

But this convention passed as Roman self-confidence increased. The reaction had set in already with the gruff but cultured Cato. When a certain Roman historian apologized for his lack of elegance in the Greek tongue, Cato upbraided him for using Greek in the first place. Cato produced the first Latin history, perhaps indeed the first significant work of prose in Latin, the *Origines*. By the latter part of the second century, the biting satirist Lucilius was firing barbs at the Hellenic affectations of his literary predecessors. Satire was a Latin specialty.

By the late second century Latin had come of age as a literary and intellectual tongue. Apologies or nods to Greece were no longer required. In the cultural sphere, as in the political, the military and the diplomatic, the patient absorption and conversion of lessons had characterized Rome's maturation.

A republican empire

The year 146 BC is generally cited as a watershed for the Roman Republic. The brutal destruction of Carthage and Corinth marked the apogee of Roman power and ruthlessness. None could challenge her supremacy in the Mediterranean world. But had she, like Sparta in 404, won an empire only to lose her soul?

A social, economic and political crisis faced Rome in the late second century. Her great burst of expansion was over. Booty and war indemnities stocked the public treasury and also filled the pockets of generals and their staffs. The rich silver mines of Spain, as well as tribute from Macedon and the east, appreciably added to Roman wealth. The knitting together of the Mediterranean world stimulated commerce in foodstuffs, textiles, metals, slaves and luxury items, to the profit especially of Italian traders and capitalists. Provinces and provincial populations were exploited. Spain called forth Roman brutality; the east stimulated Roman avarice, and Roman moralists began complaining that such developments had corrupted their countrymen's characters. What had once been a nation of conquerors was now a nation of consumers. As Cato lamented, 'it is the surest sign of deterioration when jars of caviar cost more than fields, and pretty boys more than farmers.' But moral degeneration, a conventional topic among ancient writers, is a slippery abstraction. More concrete effects of Roman expansion produced the crisis.

The simple agricultural society of Rome's antique past had vanished. Small manufacture began to flourish, particularly the arms industry. There was a building boom in the second century. Commercial transactions had produced a whole new class of financiers, merchants and businessmen who maintained offices in Rome but indulged their speculations in the provinces. Agriculture itself had undergone the most telling changes. Small farms devoted to cereal crops had once dotted almost the entire Italian peninsula, but no longer. Deforestation and overpasturage had made much of the land, especially in southern Italy, unsuitable to cereal cultivation. The pressure of growing population and the need for timber had meant a gradual denuding of the hillsides, with inevitable subsequent erosion. More cultivators turned to pasturage and ranching. Elsewhere, viticulture and olive orchards began to dominate.

In none of these pursuits could the small farmer compete, for extensive capital was required to finance olive groves, vineyards or large ranches. Wars in the second century drew many small cultivators into military service for long periods of time. Some never returned, and their wives or widows could not always resist the temptation to sell out to prosperous purchasers. The availability of rural employment for the freeman was limited. Slave labor had become increasingly common on the land, supplied through the highly organized slave trade of the second century. To the plantation owner servile workers possessed many advantages. There were no stoppages, no movements to other jobs and, most important, no drafting into the army. For grazing operations gangs of slaves were ideal. Cultivation of vine and olive also went hand in hand with the increase in agricultural slave labor; they were year-round crops, furnishing a maximum continuity of employment, and the process of cultivation was simple, easy to standardize and reduce to a routine. The free population on the land had dwindled to insignificance.

The rural problem also had repercussions in the city. Influx into Rome from Latin towns quickened as small farmers who had lost their property drifted into the city. Soldiers who had seen service in the lavish capitals of the east were not always anxious to return to rural settings. Money flowed in after the destruction of Corinth and Carthage, stimulating a building program, providing ephemeral employment opportunities and adding to the swelling urban population. A depression hit in the 130s. Wars in Spain, Macedon and a slave rebellion in Sicily reduced government spending on domestic projects. Unemployment began to pose a serious threat to economic stability.

Depopulation of the countryside affected the military as well. The foreign wars of the second century had drained Roman manpower. Rome cherished the principle that conscription into the army was limited to men of some property; those with a stake in the country should bear the brunt of her defense. But as former land-holders lost property and moved into the city, the pool of eligible military recruits shrank. For dangerous and unprofitable assignments like Spain, even eligible conscripts were not easily persuaded. On more than one occasion Draft calls were resisted through appeals to tribunes.

The Roman ruling class also found itself embat-

tled. The patricio-plebeian oligarchy had long operated like an exclusivist club, secure in control of its clients, self-perpetuating through intermarriage, and dominant in the councils of state. The nobility took great pride in their ancestral heritage. But the collective unity of the nobles began to crack in the late Republic. Imperial expansion created men of substance and wealth outside the traditional ruling circles. The business classes were by no means natural enemies of the aristocracy, but they had their own interests to protect, especially in the provinces. Fierce political battles ensued on occasion over control of the courts which heard cases against provincial magistrates. Magnates from Italian municipalities gradually became more sensitive to their exclusion from Roman seats of authority, thus producing additional friction. Meanwhile, the influx of men into the city from the countryside upset previous political patterns. Nobles accustomed to controlling elections and legislation through hereditary clients found a growing mass of new voters without ancestral ties to aristocratic houses. Some politicians were more sensitive to the needs of groups outside the senatorial order; others hoped to capitalize upon them for their own political purposes. There followed embittered factional struggles and fiercer senatorial infighting.

The volatile atmosphere engendered a series of upheavals. In 133 the reformist tribune Tiberius Gracchus sponsored legislation to restrict the amount of public land held by private owners and to redistribute the surplus in small plots for the poor. Resistance in the senate was considerable, but popular enthusiasm backed Tiberius' efforts. A decade later, Tiberius' brother Gaius Gracchus instituted an even broader program. A fiery orator and shrewd politician, Gaius attacked social abuses on several fronts. His corn law authorized the state to purchase grain in bulk and sell it at a rate not subject to market fluctuations, thereby easing the plight of the city proletariat. Citizen colonies were planned as an outlet for surplus population. Gaius also solicited the support of the *equites*, wealthy businessmen and landowners outside the senatorial order. To them was accorded the privilege of collecting taxes from the new province of Asia and of sitting in judgment

Left: A Roman farmer goes to market. Most of the load is slung over the bull's back, but he carries a basket of fruit and an animal trussed up on a stick.

Below left: Transport by water was much more economical than transport overland. This riverboat, a merchant's funerary monument, is carrying barrels of wine.

Right: The shops of Roman times, like this pharmacy, are much like those that can be found in present-day Italy: a long, narrow room with the goods displayed on the streetfront. At the back soap is being made.

on any senatorial governor who might interfere with their interests abroad. In addition, Gaius proposed the extension of full Roman franchise or Latin status to Italian allies desirous of those prerogatives. Enactment of all the bills would have constituted a long stride toward alleviating social grievances and broadening the Roman political base. But there was strong opposition in the aristocracy, either from fear of excessive popular participation or from concern for the growing power of the Gracchi brothers and their political faction. Each of the brothers in turn was branded as a would-be tyrant. Tiberius Gracchus and numerous followers were slain in a riot in 133. Gaius' coalition lasted longer, but he too was eventually assassinated, on the grounds that he was undermining the state.

Violence perpetrated in the name of public order had effected the demise of the Gracchi, but it could not undo their achievements. The Gracchi, for the first time, had brought a measure of self-consciousness and class identity to extra-senatorial groups. The aristocracy could no longer take for granted the allegiance of the lower orders. Conflicts among political leaders grew more heated in subsequent decades.

The reforms of Marius

Foreign wars, too, especially the guerrilla warfare in Africa against the Numidian prince Jugurtha, aggravated matters at the end of the second century. A 'new man' Gaius Marius, from the Italian municipality of Arpinum, salvaged Roman honor by effecting the conquest of Jugurtha and later saving Rome from an invasion by Germanic barbarians. But it was not generalship alone that made those achievements possible. He had found

a new way to swell the size of his army. Marius instituted an ominous reform, abolition of the property requirement for military service, thus creating a volunteer, essentially mercenary, army. The move had telling social as well as military consequences. Marius arranged landed rewards for his veterans. The impoverished rural masses of Italy were now eligible for the service.

Marius, like the Gracchi before him, was outmaneuvered by senatorial foes and thrust into the shade, but the social and political forces that he and they had helped to unleash were not readily stilled. Italian veterans, men from outside Rome, expected the same benefits as their Roman compatriots but possessed less leverage at Rome. Similarly, Italian leaders, both municipal aristocrats and businessmen, felt more keenly their inferiority to Roman counterparts. When the tribune Livius Drusus was assassinated in 91 BC after sponsoring an abortive measure to extend the franchise beyond Rome, the Italians lost patience. The result was a massive and brutal conflict between Rome and her *socii* (allies), the 'Social War.' That breakdown of trust held fateful consequences. Since Romans were called upon to wage war upon their own former comrades, soldiers' loyalties tended to focus more and more upon their own commanders than upon the state itself. The war ended in 88 BC with the extension of citizenship throughout the peninsula. But the deeper wounds did not heal easily. When political conflict erupted again in the same year, the Roman consul L Cornelius Sulla called upon his forces to march on Rome herself and put his rivals to rout – the first such occasion in the Republic's history. With the state (to all appearances) tottering, security seemed to lie only in obeying the dic-

tates of military leaders. Civil war flared again in the late 80s, convulsing Italy and issuing in the dictatorship of Sulla. Republican procedures were suspended, the dictator's enemies were ruthlessly hunted down, their property was confiscated and their children were disfranchised.

Sulla's post-war settlement was conservative, however. Once in command of the city he disbanded his army and restored control to the Senate. Sulla, in fact, resigned and retired by 78 BC. His legislation was predicated on the continuation of senatorial ascendancy. But he was not blind to the changes that had occurred in recent decades. A Sullan measure expanded the Roman senate to twice its size, now to accommodate many *equites* and leaders from the Italian municipalities. Politicians now proved willing to espouse popular causes in their own interests. For many in the *plebs*, military service could be a source of livelihood or a promise of landed property in the future. Ambitious businessmen and Italian aristocrats now had access to the ruling circles in Rome. Distinctions of citizenship had been abolished in Italy. The broadened political base was a fact, and with it came increased political instability.

It is a commonplace in modern interpretations to remark that Sulla's ruthless rise to power inspired emulation, that the subsequent generation – the Republic's last – produced a new series of military men with semi-professional armies who undermined or trampled institutional precedents. The analysis, however, is misguided – or at least overdrawn. Traditional respect for institutions remained a persistent element, not least among the so-called 'military men' themselves. Roman society was more complicated and change more rapid than in earlier eras. But traditionalist attitudes continued to shape the process of change.

Towering personalities march through the pages of late Republican history: Pompey, Cicero, Caesar, Crassus, Lucullus, the younger Cato. Fascinating and complex, they became the subjects of biographies and the central focus of historical reconstructions, thereby fostering the impression that institutions became swallowed up in the actions of individuals. But context and circumstances cannot be ignored; nor can late Republican history be reduced to a record of the titans.

Military reforms stemming from Marius created larger armies, drawn partly from the urban poor, but principally from the rural masses. Victorious commanders earned splendid triumphs, lavished benefits upon their troops and hoped to employ them as loyal adherents in the political realm. Pompey had leaped into prominence as a brilliant young lieutenant of Sulla in the civil wars. And in the following decade, his campaigns against Mediterranean pirates and against the rebellious prince Mithridates of Pontus established Pompey as a commander without peer. His victories cleared the seas for Rome and established a whole new organization for Roman control over the eastern provinces. Lucullus won similar plaudits for his bold campaigns in Asia Minor in the 70s, marching his troops even into Armenia, where no Roman forces had trod before. Crassus, a shrewd speculator, who earned a fortune during the Sullan proscriptions, added military laurels by crushing a slave rebellion in the 70s and then led a Roman army against Parthia in the 50s. The era's most renowned achievement was Julius Caesar's conquest of Gaul, nine years of rugged campaigning against Gallic tribes, which extended Rome's empire to the Rhine and to the Atlantic.

Huge armies followed these men abroad, and great political power followed them home. When Crassus, Caesar and Pompey formed political alliance in the early 50s against conservative factions such as those of Lucullus and Cato, senatorial struggles took on heightened tensions, with new levels of violence.

Civil war and chaos

Turmoil and disruption in varied forms jarred the late Republic. The embers of civil war had not been altogether stamped out by Sulla. In the 70s they were fanned into flame again by Lepidus in Italy and Sertorius in Spain, and were quenched only with difficulty by government forces under Pompey. Then a desperate revolt by slaves and gladiators organized by Sertorius racked the Italian countryside at the end of that decade. Frequent outbursts of violence plagued the city. Acute grain shortages provoked food riots, and mob violence often erupted in connection with legislation, elections and political trials. Genuine reformers or unscrupulous agitators made good use of proletariate passions. The shrewd and tempestuous patrician Clodius even organized urban followers into disciplined bands which occasionally terrorized the streets in the 50s. A more serious threat was a conspiracy to overthrow the government, engineered by the disgruntled aristocrat Catiline in 63. But the plot fizzled when it was discovered and made public by the consul Cicero.

The catalogue is grim. But it is insufficient to assess the Republic's last generation as a relentless march toward self-destruction. A larger perspective is necessary. Rome's leading figures did

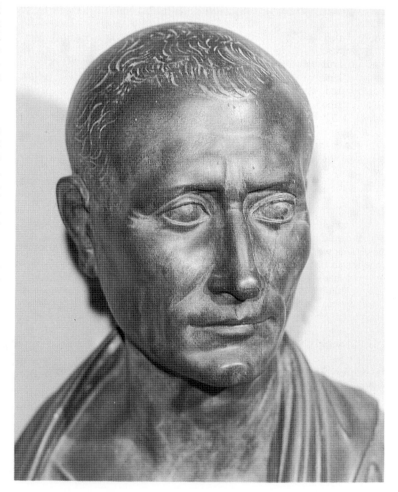

Above: The Roman forum was the center of political life under the Republic. The great politicians could be heard in the lawcourts, or seen walking about, surrounded by their clients and allies. Temples and other public buildings were built around the open space.

Left: Julius Caesar was a brilliantly successful general and popular political leader. A fear that he would declare himself king led to his assassination.

Far right: A sarcophagus decorated with a scene of battle between Romans and Gauls. Above, prisoners await their fate – to be sold into slavery. The addition of Gaul to the empire was largely due to the ambition of Julius Caesar, who sought military glory there and political influence in Rome.

not regard themselves as destroyers of the Republic. It never occurred to Lucullus to march his troops on the capital and institute a military despotism. Pompey controlled enormous armies in the east during the 60s, and autocratic authority was his for the asking, but Pompey discharged his forces immediately upon return to Italy. Julius Caesar, too, proceeded steadily through elective offices. It was not his purpose to tear down Republican institutions. Pompey's eastern wars, Caesar's Gallic conquest, Crassus' invasion of Parthia were not private adventures, but fully sanctioned by the state. The coalition of Pompey, Caesar and Crassus was a potent political force in the 50s, but it stood within the constitutional structure. Like most factions, it sought positions of leadership for the principal organizers, offices for their supporters and legislation in their interests. That was traditional operating procedure.

Nor was the ruling class of the late Republic blind to changing circumstances. Increased participation in the governing process is evident for men of municipal families or equestrian backgrounds. Few could reach as far as the consulship, and Cicero was an exception. An *eques* from Arpinum, he had extraordinary talents and had gathered powerful political support. But his rise to the top is only the most dramatic example of accelerated social mobility at the upper levels. More and more Italians and 'new men' were securing election to office, taking seats in the senate and filling the ranks of junior officers in the army. A more representative ruling class was also more responsive to grievances that needed attention. A massive bulk of legislation is on record: electoral reform, judicial procedure, criminal laws and administrative regulations, all to correct abuses and to provide a more rational system. And there was significant legislation in the social and economic realms. Increased government involvement secured the city's food supply. A number of grain bills were sponsored, culminating in Clodius' measure in 58 which provided for free distribution to needy citizens. There were agrarian measures also, allocating land to veterans and to the urban proletariate. The laws were carefully drafted to avoid confiscation or rural dislocation. Property titles were respected; land was to be purchased by the state and distributed to deserving applicants. One need not ascribe altruistic motives to the Roman ruling class. They shrank from any drastic change that might alter with the social structure. The aim, rather, was to institute prudent reform and forestall social disruption. The approach was as characteristic of the late Republic as of earlier periods. For all its difficulties, the Roman state remained vital.

Nowhere is late Republican vitality more evident than in its literature. Roman writers had gained the self-confidence that could dispense with apology or defensiveness. This was the age of Cicero. There was a change too in the literary public. In the second century it had been restricted largely to a cultured, aristocratic class. But the audience now was much wider. Many orators reserved their better speeches for the populace, not the senate, and the practice of publishing speeches became widespread. Sophisticated comedy and tragedy declined, replaced by the growth of popular short sketches and farces. A greater interest materialized in contemporary history rather than antiquarian pursuits. Publishing houses began to flourish. An expanded public and a greater number of artists in every phase of cultural activity marked the era.

Hellenistic philosophy also flourished in Rome, both Epicureanism and Stoicism. The former, preaching withdrawal and self-sufficiency, may have appealed to many in an era of strife, unrest and instability. It appealed certainly to Lucretius, whose exposition of Epicurean doctrine in *On the Nature of Things* raised it to a new level of beauty and power. Stoicism, as preached by the Greeks, could be doctrinaire and dogmatic, but Cicero leavened Stoic rigidity with a healthy skepticism and humanitarianism. Nothing is more Roman than his assertion that 'my theories are for us everyday people who can observe and live up to moral ideals only as far as is in our power.' He was, more than anyone else, responsible for creating a philosophic literature in Latin. And until only a little more than a hundred years ago his works continued to form the backbone of most European higher education.

Greek political theory was also refashioned to make it relevant for Rome. Cicero's *Republic* and *Laws* received inspiration from similarly titled treatises by Plato. But unlike Plato, the Roman's work was pervaded with a sense of history. The Ciceronian tracts looked to an earlier age, but their aim was to preserve the Republic's integrity under the rule of law and the guidance of an enlightened governing class. The Roman tendency to celebrate the past in order to instruct the present is evident throughout.

Such an attitude certainly pervades the works of the historian Sallust. Having lived through the grim civil war of the 40s, Sallust sought its roots in history of the recent past, stressing factional contests and civil dissension in his monographs on the Jugurthine War, the aftermath of Sulla and the Catilinarian conspiracy. Most other contemporary Roman historians also looked to the past to provide practical lessons for the present. We should remember, as well, that historical writing was still an art form, produced for publication and circulation, to entertain as well as to inform, and sometimes to persuade. Caesar's commentaries on the Gallic Wars are the finest example. The style possesses a disarming simplicity, all the more artful for its apparent artlessness. The format was one of objectivity and detachment. Ostensibly, the facts are allowed to speak for themselves. But the cumulative effect is to show a flattering self-portrait of a powerful commander, thoroughly in control, manipulating officers and enemies, dictating events to conform to his own plans. Caesar's commentaries are a literary *tour de force*.

In many ways the most characteristic and most highly developed art form of the era was oratory. Its master was Cicero, author not only of influential rhetorical treatises, but a spell-binding speaker. He had no peer in conveying praise or blame. The characters of men like Verres, Clodius, Catiline and Marc Antony are blackened beyond recall; Pompey and others received praise far beyond their deserts. But Cicero could also use the courts or the speaker's rostrum for loftier purposes. His defense of his old teacher Archias became a noble plea for the value and dignity of literature; his speech for Sestius is a ringing call for constitutional government and the rule of law.

Julius Caeser

This vital Republic did not collapse of its own weight. Political contests produced the disaster, not revolutions from below or from the provinces. Factional leaders in the Ciceronian period could call on much wider and more diversified support than ever before. The far-flung conquests of Pompey and Caesar permitted them to build personal followings on a grand scale, not only in Italy but in Gaul, Africa, Spain and the East. Hence, when those two proud politicians broke in 50, the result was conflagration on a massive level. Civil war raged for four years, devastating Italy, and engaging provincial populations, client-states and foreign rulers such as Caesar's ally and mistress, Cleopatra of Egypt. Caesar emerged victorious, but at great cost in terms of Roman lives and in terms of faith in a shattered system.

Whether the Republic could have been reconstituted after these four years of dreadful turmoil is moot. In the event, Caesar undertook another kind of reconstruction, as dictator, in 45, filling up the empty benches of the senate with new members, sparing enemies and passing intelligent legislation on debt, land allocation and grain distribution. His approach, despite hyperbolic statements by moderns, was restrained and moderate. In time, Caesar might have emulated Sulla and retired from his position. But he was not given the opportunity. Disgruntled aristocrats and faithless

friends plotted his assassination. The Ides of March in 44 put an end to his plans.

Whatever chance the Republic had of survival vanished in the aftermath of that assassination. Caesar had warned his enemies in advance: 'to murder me will only bring renewed civil war.' He was right, of course. The contest over Caesar's mantle came swiftly thereafter. The 'liberators,' Brutus and Cassius, claimed to be carrying the Republican torch. But so did all aspirants to power. The key, as everyone knew, lay not in pious platitudes but in control of Caesar's veteran legionaries. Chief contenders were Caesar's forceful, hard-drinking and ambitious lieutenant, Marc Antony, and the dictator's grand-nephew, Octavian. The latter was a sickly and unheralded youth of 19 – 'that boy,' Cicero scornfully termed him. But the dictator's will gave him the name Caesar and hereditary claims on Caesar's massive clientage. When Antony and Octavian coalesced in 43, the Republican forces of Brutus and Cassius were wiped out, Cicero was brutally slain and a new round of proscriptions and confiscations ensued. An uneasy truce prevailed between Antony and Octavian in subsequent years, punctuated by friction and quarrels, but it could not endure. Renewed civil war engulfed the Mediterranean world again until Octavian routed the eastern forces of Antony and his consort Cleopatra in 31. The naval battle at Actium in that year was a minor skirmish militarily, but it was one of history's most decisive battles. When it was over, Octavian was undisputed ruler of the Mediterranean world.

The New Order

Reconstruction on a grand and dramatic scale was required after nearly two decades of bloodletting. A return to the old system was now unthinkable. Octavian, or Augustus, as he was termed after 27 BC, assumed extraordinary powers. Yet the watchword of his regime was *res publica restituta*, 'the Republic restored.' Was Augustus an absolute monarch, the creator of a new order, or was he sincere in claiming that he had reinstituted the *res publica*? The debate is superfluous. Augustus was both, and the combination was indispensable.

Augustus eschewed obnoxious titles. He would not be *dictator*, much less *rex*. He preferred *princeps*, 'first citizen' – not an official designation, but a mark of esteem. The positions Augustus held were Republican positions. He was consul, an elective office, and Augustus stood for election annually. In addition, he was awarded provincial command by the senate in AD 27 over Gaul, Spain and Syria. Those provinces contained the bulk of Rome's military forces, and with the armies under

his control, he could have no serious rival. The granting of provincial commissions by the senate was standard Republican procedure, and the formality itself was significant. Further authority was voted the *princeps* in subsequent years. Though as a patrician he could not hold the tribunate, Augustus received 'tribunician power.' The gesture was meaningful primarily as a symbol: Augustus now assumed the role of champion and patron of the Roman *plebs*. He was also given superior authority even in provinces over which he was not formally governor. A few years later

Augustus, no longer holding consular office, was voted the powers of a consul, thereby to assure his supremacy in the city. That his position was, in effect, monarchical, is clear. The offices and positions he held were all Republican, but the accumulation of those positions in one man was the important fact. And even more telling was his possession of powers not tied to office. There is no clearer sign of autocracy.

The senate retained little of the independent authority it had exercised in the Republic, but Augustus knew better than to treat it with disdain. The numbers of that body, grossly inflated by Caesar, were reduced to their former size by Augustus, another example of his return to pre-civil war practices. And this new senate was even more broadly representative. Personnel of the old ruling class had been drastically decimated during the years of anarchy, and the Augustan senate consequently contained a heavy proportion of municipal Italians, former *equites*, military lieutenants, 'new men' and even some provincials. It became the principal vehicle for Augustus' patronage.

Pulling together an empire torn by civil strife and chaos required not just firm leadership, but administrative reform. Important changes occurred under Augustus. The public role of the *equites* appreciably increased. In the Republic, provincial tax collection had been farmed out by the government to private companies, the *publicani*. Augustus, at least in Syria and Asia,

Above far left: The badge of a slave. It authorizes his arrest if he has run away. The sophisticated Roman legal system had numerous rules governing the ownership of human beings.

Above left: This coin of Augustus shows a German surrendering a standard. In reality, however, it was Augustus's army that lost four legionary standards in the Battle of the Teutoburg forest in AD 9.

Left: A statue of Julius Caesar. His unprecedented deification after his death helped to pave the way for the establishment of the Augustan system of imperial autocracy.

Above right: A cameo bearing the head of Augustus. The nephew of Caesar, he used his position as his uncle's heir to create a new Roman order based on the rule of an emperor and his army.

Right: This Roman temple at Nimes in France is the only one surviving intact. They were essentially similar to Greek structures, the main difference being a temple floor raised above the level of the topmost step.

employed procurators, personal agents from the equestrian class, to collect provincial revenues. This was indeed a move toward centralization and standardization.

The equestrian class was itself reorganized by Augustus. Property qualification for membership was reduced, and the *princeps* exercised the prerogative of enrolling people into the order. As a result, many young men who might be useful in public service now possessed the opportunity. Recruitment into the *ordo equester* was made from Italian families, senior centurions in the army and men of good business sense generally, even in some cases ex-slaves.

Many of the most important administrative posts created by Augustus were open to *equites* only. Such, for example, was the prefect of the praetorian guard, commander of the nine cohorts in Rome and Italy, the elite corps of the Roman army, responsible directly to the *princeps*. Seven cohorts of *vigiles*, headed also by an equestrian prefect, formed the first regular fire department in the city. Another *eques* had charge of the corn supply, thereby placing that operation on a systematized basis and advertising Augustus' role as benefactor of the *plebs*. Augustus' policy of reserving several chief posts for *equites*, rather than senators, and of opening the equestrian class to capable and interested individuals was a key step toward a trained civil service.

Opening the way for new talent was, of course, not the same thing as democratization. The empire was to be controlled by the Roman and Italian upper classes. The spread of citizenship in the provinces, accelerated by Caesar, was halted or slowed by Augustus. Service in the legions was restricted to Roman citizens; foreigners could serve only in the auxiliary forces. Augustus claimed to be benefactor of the *plebs*, but his generosity was limited. A famous boast announces that he 'found a city of brick and left it a city of marble.' That may have been true of public buildings and temples, but not of tenement houses. The number of free grain recipients probably did not go beyond one quarter of the citizen population.

The *princeps* saw himself as the champion of antique Roman morality. He sponsored strict legislation against adultery, while encouraging marriage and large families. Other measures restricted the freeing of slaves and limited freedmen to Latin status rather than full citizenship. The purpose clearly was to reduce the influence of foreign elements in Rome and to hold the line against racial mixture. It was a policy of 'Italy for the Italians.'

Religion and literature

In religious affairs foreign cults were suppressed, while Augustus reached back into Republican history to restore old shrines and rebuild temples. Obsolete or obsolescent religious rites and priesthoods were revived. The deification of the ruler's person was, to be sure, an innovation, but the initiative came from the subject populace, not from the *princeps*. And Augustus knew how far he could go. Where the imperial cult was popular and expected – in the East and less developed areas of the West – Augustus was encouraging. Where it was unacceptable – in Italy and the Romanized provinces – he did not push matters.

The literature of the Augustan era echoed his ideals. Peace and prosperity and the cessation of internal bloodletting called forth literary fervor of the highest order. The Mantuan poet Virgil had lived through the grisly years of war and rural dislocation. His pastoral *Eclogues* longed for serenity and expressed the insecurity of the era. With the establishment of the Augustan regime, Virgil moved into court circles, and his poetry reflected the new order. His *Georgics* celebrated the glories of Italian agriculture, the revival of the yeoman farmer. Augustus was overtly praised. Virgil's masterpiece, the *Aeneid*, was the poetic epic of Rome's origins and her destiny. The greatness of Rome, for Virgil, was part of a divine plan, deter-

mined from the beginning. Aeneas, the favorite of the gods, stood at the beginning and from him the line of heroes and champions proceeded to culminate in Augustus. Augustus Caesar, said Virgil, was the founder of golden centuries *once more* in the land of Latium. Rome could leave to others art, science, philosophy. It was her destiny 'to govern, to humble the haughty, protect the weak and bring peace to the universe.'

The historian Livy was also made welcome at the court, for his inclinations, like those of Virgil, suited the temper of the times. His massive work – in 142 volumes – traced Rome's history from the origins to his own day. He gloried in the ancient virtues of the early Romans: simplicity, fortitude in war, selfless patriotism, chastity, religious orthodoxy.

Above: Nero, adopted son of Claudius and the last of the Julio-Claudian dynasty.

Left: The ruins of the temple of Vesta, Roman goddess of the hearth.

Below: The Colosseum is a magnificent structure, built for the combats and displays that entertained the people of Rome. It could hold around 50,000 spectators, five percent of the city's population at the time of its construction.

Below right: A statue of Tiberius, successor to Augustus. He is remembered even today as a keen collector of pornography.

Below far right: An extremely flattering sculpture of the crippled emperor Claudius, here presented as Jupiter, king of the gods.

For the poet Horace, as for Livy and Virgil, Republican principles and ideals were inborn. Horace, in fact, had fought in the ranks of Brutus and Cassius, and he knew the sufferings of civil war. The Horatian odes expressed the relief of a generation which had survived civil war. Augustus was portrayed as the conveyer of universal peace, the vigilant protector and defender of the empire, the agent of Jupiter, destined to rule the world for the benefit of mankind. To a man like Horace, who asked only for the simple life and rustic joys, the Augustan revival of antique simplicity was most congenial.

Augustus lived to be 77, dying in his bed in AD 14. By sheer survival he provided the continuity necessary to solidify a stable order. His shrewd use of the past in the service of the future produced a system which was to give two centuries of productive prosperity to the Mediterranean world. The era is symbolized by the superbly sculptured *Ara Pacis*, 'Altar of Peace,' representing Augustus as the heir of Roman traditions and the architect of a peaceful universe.

Problems of succession

An awkward moment ensued upon Augustus' death. The principate was not an office and hence, technically, was not transferable. Nor would the 'restorer of the Republic' overtly espouse a hereditary monarchy. But Augustus had made his calculations. He had arranged to share certain prerogatives with his step-son Tiberius – the proconsular authority and the tribunician power. Those prerogatives therefore did not perish with Augus-tus. Tiberius' control, in fact, went unchallenged. The principate had spawned a dynasty. Members of Augustus' family by heredity, adoption or marriage controlled what was now a throne for the next half-century. This 'Julio-Claudian' dynasty ended with the death of Nero in AD 68, but only because the blood-line had perished. The event threw the empire into brief turmoil until Vespasian, a victor in civil war, installed his own family on the throne. The dynastic principle was now fixed, whatever the theoretical formulations of the principate. In the second century a series of rulers, none blessed with male heirs, designated their successors by adopting them as sons. Conferral of powers by the senate continued to be standard practice. Like so much else, it was an institution demanded by tradition. But the monarchy was a fact.

Ancient writers dwell endlessly on the personalities, foibles and wickedness of the rulers. It was an obsession in imperial historiography. Even the greatest of Roman historians, Tacitus, writing in the early second century, focused almost exclusively on court intrigues and political machinations within the royal family, and struggles for power in ruling circles. Tacitus has left unforgettable, if somewhat one-sided, portraits of the emperors: the dour, hypocritical and misanthropic Tiberius (14-37); the psychopath Caligula (37-41); the hen-pecked and physically repugnant Claudius (41-54); the fanatical esthete and cruel egotist Nero (54-68).

Resentment and opposition to the Caesars was keen among many aristocrats and intellectuals who harkened back to a freer past. The Stoic philosopher and dramatist Seneca suffered exile under Claudius but came back to serve as Nero's tutor, hoping to school him in virtue and benevolence. A vicious lampoon on the funeral and deification of Claudius is ascribed to Seneca, describing the intellectuals' abhorrence of that emperor. But Seneca's influence over Nero also faded. His fiery young nephew Lucan produced an epic poem dealing with the fall of the Republic, praising past heroes and damning the monarchy by comparison. Such independence could not endure. Both Seneca and Lucan were executed on Nero's orders in AD 65, together with the genial satirist Petronius, author of the brilliant comic novel and mock-epic *Satyricon*.

As rulers, the Roman emperors have not left an image of great strength. Dynasties rose and fell. The Julio-Claudians dissolved in military revolt after Nero's death in 68. The Flavian dynasty founded by Vespasian endured until the despotic activities of Domitian provoked its overthrow in 96. There followed a succession of 'good emperors,' which means no more than that they receive praise in the literary tradition. It was an artificial dynasty, secured by a series of adoptions, stretching from the military hero Trajan to the Stoic philosopher Marcus Aurelius, who perished in 180. But more fundamental developments were at work below the uneven surface of individual reigns: a growing centralization and bureaucratization, a tightened regimen, a more structured imperial organization and a drawing together of the Mediterranean world.

The Flavian dynasty

Vicissitudes in imperial dynasties did not prevent the consolidation of the principate. Under Augustus, it was a bundle of powers rather than a formal office. There was no theoretical basis for a successor. But Tiberius rounded that awkward corner. Augustus saw to it in advance by having the senate confer upon Tiberius the *imperium*, authority over the empire's military forces. Upon Augustus' death, the senate formally acknowledged Tiberius' assumption of his power. The practice was followed in the future. Each emperor, by sharing honors, distinctions or functions, was able, in effect, to designate a successor, though the formality of senatorial approval persisted.

Vespasian, the first Flavian emperor, attained the throne through civil war when the Julio-Claudian line perished. He felt the need of clear authorization to justify the installation of a new dynasty, and he got it. A fragmentary inscription records a law of the people, based on a senatorial decree, that formally conferred prerogatives on the new emperor. The principate, to all intents and purposes, was now acknowledged as an office, not just a conglomerate of powers.

Roman emperors were more than just possessors of supreme power; they also acquired close connections with the divine. Julius Caesar was deified after his death, thereby setting a precedent. Decision on deification of deceased rulers was a senatorial prerogative, a process not very different from the canonization of a saint. Worship of a deified emperor after his death was easily acceptable. It meant only the addition of a new god to the already established list of deities, and Rome was always tolerant of new gods. Worship of the emperor while still alive was a rather more delicate matter. On the whole, it was not official policy in the early Empire. But even when emperors did not systematically encourage it, subjects and provincials might identify them with gods. Among Egyptians, for example, it would

have been unthinkable not to worship the man who was king of Egypt, as the Roman emperor now was. The practice spread, at first with tacit, later with open support by the emperor. The institution provided a common base of loyalty for subjects who were otherwise diverse in race, religion and tradition. It could promote not only the constitutional dignity of the monarch but the unity of the empire.

Administrative changes in the first two centuries of the Empire produced a marked growth in the bureaucracy. Bureaucratic tasks were generally frowned on by snobbish members of the senatorial order. Hence the tasks tended to devolve upon two main classes: the *equites*, and the freedmen brought into the imperial service from a variety of servile classes. Neither was encumbered by weighty senatorial traditions which forbade the sordid exercise of financial duties and administrative matters. The old private tax-farming companies saw their top men drained off to serve the government. The growing responsibilities of the emperor and the expansion of his office into all spheres of public activity meant that what had been household servants became, in fact, imperial officials, highly trained bureaucrats in the service of the emperor.

An incipient bureaucracy can begin to be traced in the reign of Claudius (41-54): the first indications of a ladder of offices for *equites*. Posts such as military tribunes and prefects of the fleet were now open to *equites*, and men who served in those capacities might go on to become imperial procurators (provincial tax superintendents) or even to govern small provinces. From the ranks of these men were recruited the top equestrian officials, such as the prefect of the praetorian guard and the prefect of Egypt. Other duties, primarily secretarial or ministerial, were handled by freedmen under Claudius and Nero. In subsequent years equestrian and freedmen tasks tended more and more to overlap and divisions of functions

became unclear. It took the bureaucratic mind of the emperor Hadrian (AD 117-138) to tidy up matters. A twofold policy is discernible: the replacement of freedmen by *equites* in many imperial posts and the creation of new posts open only to *equites*, in order to provide the stages for systematic advancement. Bureaucratization proceeded apace. Under Augustus there were about 25 different equestrian posts; under Claudius it had risen to 39; with Hadrian the numbers reached 107; and by the end of the second century they were up to 174.

The requirements of empire entailed a gradual professionalization of the army as well. Augustus disbanded the bulk of his forces after the civil wars. But the demobilization was not complete, for 28 legions were retained under arms in the provinces – the minimum needed for security. The bulk of the forces were posted on the dangerous frontiers: in Egypt and Syria, and along the Rhine and Danube. Exact demarcation of frontiers and the establishment of permanent forts were chiefly the attainment of the Flavian emperors. Legions then approximated genuine garrison troops, rather than the more mobile units of the Julio-Claudians. An equally important change came in the nature of military rewards. Individual commanders no longer possessed the prerogative of dispensing benefits to veterans. Augustus established a military treasury for the purpose, the first attempt to treat the question of discharge as a real business proposition. Similar motives guided policy toward junior officers such as military tribunes. That post became a key stepping stone in the early career of men hoping to reach top civil magistracies and to enter the elite group of appointed governors of imperial provinces. Hence, Augustus and his successors had, on the one hand, created a true professional army and had, on the other, prevented what might have been the dangerous growth of a professional officer class.

Far left: A bust of the Emperor Hadrian, who ruled from 117 to 138. The English historian Gibbon, narrator of the empire's decline, referred to Hadrian's reign as 'a happy period,' and regarded it as the pinnacle of Roman success.

Left: A bust of an unknown Roman lady. The development of a sculptor's drill made it possible to recreate in marble the mountainous curls of hair fashionable at the beginning of the second century AD.

Right: The emperor Caracalla formulated an astute public relations trick that also broadened the empire's tax base: he extended Roman citizenship to all the free inhabitants of cities within the empire. For many, this 'gift' was of dubious value.

The empire and its subjects

The annexation of Egypt under Augustus had completed Rome's domination of the Mediterranean. Four new Danubian provinces erected a definitive barrier between the northern shores of the Mediterranean and the barbarian tribes of central Europe. The Flavians linked the Upper Rhine and the sources of the Danube. Apart from the acquisition of Britain under Claudius and the conquest of Dacia by Trajan, there was no significant expansion of the boundaries. The Roman Empire could now be looked upon as a relatively fixed area.

Corresponding to this development was a basic change in attitude: the empire should be a well-knit unity, not a group of provinces loosely strung together. Augustus and his successors gradually built up an efficient body of salaried professional administrators; and the expansion of road systems in the provinces, the creation of an imperial postal service and the general improvement of communications made it easier for the *princeps* to control his officials. Strict and detailed legislation cracked down on misbehavior by imperial appointees abroad, and councils of provincials were organized to facilitate the airing of grievances to the emperor. To be sure, certain subject peoples, like the Jews of Alexandria, were not allowed to petition against a governor without his own consent. One can imagine how often it was given.

With systematization of the provincial order came the spread of Roman citizenship abroad. The settlement of Roman veterans in provincial areas, plus the practice of granting citizenship to discharged foreign veterans, produced new towns with a certain degree of Romanization. These communities soon achieved Latin status and eventually full franchise. Under Vespasian, 350 towns in Spain received municipal charters and incorporation. At the same time, the use of Roman law and institutions led to a greater uniformity. In the late second century, the status of Roman municipality was conferred on urbanized Greek and eastern sites even without prior stages such as Latin rights. And by 212 the emperor Caracalla would bestow the citizenship automatically upon all inhabitants of the empire.

Spread of Roman law in the provinces produced an enduring legacy for western Europe. In the beginning the law had been varied and confusing. It was not until the reign of Hadrian that real order was introduced into the chaos, and the new legal code became a permanent part of a centrally established judicial administration. Further development came under Septimius Severus (193-211). Codification and consolidation did not necessarily mean equal justice for all. The fact is often forgotten in modern tributes to the Roman legal system. The code provided differing penalties and procedures for *honestiores* and *humiliores*, the upper and lower classes as recognized by law. But the bringing of system and order into the legal structure was an achievement of lasting value.

Under Augustus the total of Roman citizens was perhaps 10 million. The numbers unquestionably increased through the next century and a half. The Augustan peace ushered in an era of prosperity. With the political situation secure, money could be invested in land once more, and Italian agriculture revived quickly. Prosperity was not limited to Italy. The vineyards and olive orchards of Gaul, Spain and Africa soon equaled and eclipsed Italian agriculture.

Peace was also a great spur to industry and commerce. Pottery and glass industries were especially notable. The famed Arretine pottery was produced mainly in Etruria, but branch factories existed in Gaul, in Spain, even in Britain and on the Danube. In an era of vast construction projects, there was a boom in industries producing building and plumbing materials. Commerce, too, profited from an empire more tightly bound together. And there was extensive trade outside the empire – with Germans, tribes across the Danube, in the North Sea, in East Africa and even in India.

The common notion that economic prosperity rested chiefly on slave labor is unsupportable. In fact, as foreign wars and expansion virtually ceased, the supply of slaves soon dried up. The emergence of the tenant-farmer suggests a decrease in the number of slaves active on the land. It is true that slave labor was employed on a large scale in the pottery industry, but it is noteworthy that when factories were sold, slaves continued in their jobs and did not depart with their former owners. In this respect, they were hardly any different from free laborers. Little servile labor was used in the provinces, especially in the west.

In general, the Roman economy rested on a balance of free enterprise and state management. Agriculture, industry and commerce were almost entirely in private hands. But the emperors maintained a controled and standardized currency, took responsibility for the grain supply and fostered the extension of road networks. They also promoted the steady increase of urbanization, even in remote and backward provinces. In this they were so successful that the numbers of new municipalities increased while the dispatching of Roman colonies abroad decreased.

The Age of the Antonines, from Trajan to Marcus Aurelius, has traditionally received much praise. Its people had no further need for Republican nostalgia. The emperors were temperate, intelligent and benevolent – or so they were portrayed. The standard line is expressed in the *Panegyricus* to Trajan, composed by the cultured intellectual, philanthropist and orator Pliny the Younger. For Pliny, Trajan represented the ideal constitutional monarch who obeyed the laws, cooperated with the senate and served as shepherd of his people. 'You have subjected yourself to the laws, Caesar, laws which no one ever meant for an emperor. But you want no more rights for yourself than we enjoy; consequently we seek all the more for you.'

Inscriptions from all over the empire, set up by provincials, also attest Rome's benefits. The empire had never been so 'civilized' as it was under the Antonines. There was scientific drainage, well-paved streets, abundant water-supply and all those embellishments that made urban life appealing and attractive: gymnasia, baths, amphitheaters, splendid temples, large and imposing public buildings.

The rosy portrait dominates, but is it the whole story? The upper classes produced the panegyrics and paid for the inscriptions. Peasants and tenant farmers remain largely voiceless. But there are some hints. Egyptian papyri reveal frequent expressions of discontent and uprisings by villagers and workers who refused to pay steep taxes or perform compulsory labor. An insurrection of native peasants in Dacia and Dalmatia occurred in the latter second century. War raged in the reign of Aurelius – against Germanic invaders on the Danubian frontier – and a plague aggravated the situation. It was the peasants who suffered devastation of the land and conscription into the service. Spokesmen for the higher orders like Aelius Aristides have largely drowned out dissenting voices. Only scraps remain now of underground literature showing discontent with Roman rule. But such messages may be the more authentic expressions of provincial opinion.

This is not to say that the greatest of the Antonines, Marcus Aurelius, was over-praised. He was a man born for a better age – or perhaps for a different role. Marcus was an intellectual and a Stoic philosopher. His *Meditations* were composed in

Far left: Mithras slays the bull. The cult of this oriental god spread through the empire in the first and second centuries AD. It was popular with soldiers and businessmen.

Left: The Emperor Trajan pushed the frontiers of the empire to their furthest extent. The Roman world, in his time, ran from Scotland to Mesopotamia, into eastern Europe and the Sahara.

Below left: The family of Septimius Severus, emperor between 193 and 211. He is shown with his wife and two sons. The face of Geta, his younger son, has been obliterated, probably after his murder by his elder brother, Caracalla.

the later, grim years of his reign, spent in almost incessant warfare on the Danube. None can deny the heroic tenacity expressed, the ascetic dedication to duty whatever the consequences. But his thoughts do not represent affirmation so much as resignation. The dominant note of the *Meditations* is one of melancholy. Marcus Aurelius never confused his era with a golden age.

The Antonine age was a period of desperate religious searching. The staid and remote worship of the Olympian gods remained the official religion, but it had lost much of its attraction for the masses. The religions that appealed came from the east, many of them orgiastic, emotional, secretive and sensationalistic. The cult of the Great Mother, with its eunuch priests from Phrygia, drew enthusiastic adherents. Even more popular was the religion of Isis from Egypt, offering the promise of an ecstasy of divine communion. Mithraism, a form of sun worship, came out of Persia with an elaborate set of rites, a full-blown theological system and a complex clerical organization. Many of its devotees were drawn from Roman legions in the field, especially the lonely soldiers on the frontiers. In addition, an infinity of lesser cults and minor deities appealed to men of every persuasion. It was an age of extraordinary credulity and superstition. Astrologers, Chaldean seers, sorcerers and practitioners of black magic made their way all over the empire, attracting faithful followers. No era was so ripe for charlatans and con-men. As one ancient skeptic sneered, 'there was an oracle under every rock and tree prepared to say whatever was wanted – so long as it was paid for in advance.' The emperor Hadrian was drawn to things supernatural. So indeed was Marcus Aurelius: rational philosopher and Stoic though he was. It would not be excessive to term the era of the Antonines an age of anxiety.

Among the religions to which the subjects of the empire turned was Christianity. The creed of Jesus and his followers already had had considerable impact by the second century. Indeed, its tenets were not entirely unfamiliar. The doctrines of other Eastern religions had much in common with Christianity: they too spoke of sin and guilt, of expiation and rebirth, of salvation, immortality and union with divinity. Monotheism was also familiar to the Romans. The Stoics themselves were close to it, and the scattering of Jews all over the eastern part of the empire exposed numerous Romans to the whole concept of monotheistic doctrine.

Christianity emerged in the land of the Hebrews and out of the religion of the Hebrews. Jesus himself was a Jew, as were all his initial followers. The Messianic tradition was strong in Judaism, as the Dead Sea scrolls reaffirm once again, but the preaching of Messianic doctrine made the established Jewish hierarchy uncomfortable. They might have accepted the coming of the Messiah in principle, but they did not want him to arrive while they were around. Nor was the Roman governor of Judaea, Pontius Pilate, anxious to countenance friction which might disturb the peace of his administration. Jesus was executed in the reign of Tiberius, under Roman law and evidently on a charge of treason against the state.

The event can hardly have caused a ripple at the time. The Christian community was then still

limited to Jerusalem and still limited to Jews. It required the brilliant Hellenized Jew from Tarsus, Paul, to break Christianity out of its Judaic shell. Paul's preaching to the Gentiles was a turning point: the idea that the Church was independent of the Synagogue was never again seriously questioned. The Pauline Epistles, preceding by several years the writing of the Gospels, were the foundation of Christian theology. Paul's tireless missionary activity, the voluminous messages stemming from a powerful intellect trained in both Rabbinic law and Greek learning, made him far and away the towering figure in the history of the early Church.

Paul was executed, so tradition records, in the reign of Nero, together with Peter and other disciples of Christ. The blood of martyrs became indeed the seed of the Church. For a time Christianity remained largely an urban religion, attracting its devotees primarily from the metropolitan areas of the Near East. The earliest converts were drawn from the middle and lower strata of society – artisans, merchants, slaves and especially women. But the process snowballed. By the early second-century Pliny could speak of numerous Christians of all ages and conditions in Asia Minor. In Syria, Antioch was the center of dissemination for pagan converts all over the Near East. The Church in Egyptian Alexandria was flourishing by the mid-second century. North Africa was probably evangelized before the end of the first century. There were large congregations in Gaul during the reign of Marcus Aurelius.

What held the Christians together and made their multiplication possible? Two factors bolstered the sect in its early years: a Holy Book, the Hebrew Scriptures, which they took as prophesying the coming of Christ, and a firm belief in a Second Coming, which they regarded as imminent. While Christians waited in vain for the Last Judgment, the faith became increasingly intellec-

tualized. The Second Coming took on allegorical import, and was no less meaningful for that. The canon of scriptures was also expanded, the New Testament gradually acquiring the character of authority and holy writ in the second century. At the same time, Church organization developed a sophisticated form that enabled it to perpetuate and expand the creed. Missionary activity was originally in the hands of the Apostles, but the hierarchy later spread, as the Apostles appointed from their earlier converts men who were designated to act as bishops and deacons for future believers. By the late first century bishops emerged as the real heads of local congregations, with an officialdom of priests and deacons under them. The bonds of a tight morality and an organized hierarchical structure kept the religion alive in its early years and provided a basis for expansion.

It is a common misconception that Christians were incessantly being hurled to the lions to satisfy the grisly pleasures of emperors and the mob. In fact, Roman polytheism was a loose and tolerant creed. The emperor Hadrian, it is said, offered to enroll Jesus Christ among the pantheon of official deities. The offer was unacceptable to Christians, but it was symptomatic of Roman attitudes. A policy of absorption and accommodation had deep roots in Roman history. Administrators did not normally worry about some new Oriental religion – they already had plenty of them – unless it threatened to provoke some civil disturbance. To be sure, ugly rumors were spread about Christians, damaging their reputation. Their scorn of the state religion roused suspicions of atheism, and their Eucharistic banquets were misinterpreted by some Romans as cannibalistic.

Left: Like Mithraism, the Christian faith was an oriental religion that spread west through the empire. Evangelists such as St Paul, shown here in his escape from Damascus, used the strength of faith and the power of argument to deliver the Christian message.

Below: A detail from the Arch of Constantine, the first of the Christian emperors.

truth. Plato, after all, had taught that God was transcendent, immutable and incorporeal. And the Stoic doctrine that all rational beings share in a universal Reason was readily adaptable to Christianity: Christian theologians identified divine Reason or *Logos* with Christ.

Not all pagan intellectuals were willing to be drawn into the Christian orbit. Neoplatonism, developed in the third century by powerful minds like Plotinus and Porphyry, viewed itself as the prime intellectual opponent of Christianity. The debate endured for over a century. That debate, however, was more often a matter of scholarly pedantry than fundamental difference. A striking fact emerges from the confrontation: while Christianity was becoming more philosophical, Neoplatonism was becoming more of a religion, its followers occupied like their Christian counterparts in expounding and reconciling sacred texts. In the very age when discussion was most bitter, an unconscious fusion was taking place. The process of assimilation that had been the hallmark of Roman flexibility became a feature of Christianity itself, and the most significant harbinger of the future.

Collapse and recovery

The insecurities felt in the latter second century proved to be justified. The size and extent of the Roman empire turned out to be a liability. In the third century there was collapse – not permanent but devastating. The half-century between 235 and 285 produced a kind of prolonged panic and terror. Roman emperors were now ephemeral creatures, a depressing series of incompetent or helpless rulers. For every new monarch there were often two or three pretenders to the throne. In a period of half a century no fewer than 60 men were proclaimed emperor by some collection of individuals, usually soldiers, at some time or other. Many of them, we may imagine, did not actively seek the crown. But when troops elevated their generals to the purple, the reluctant appointees had little choice but to abide by their will. One minor commander who was hailed *imperator* by his men expressed the pathetic condition: 'Fellow-soldiers, you have lost a good general and made a bad emperor.'

The rulers now came no longer from Italy and the west. Most hailed from the rugged frontier areas of Illyria and Pannonia – hardy military types who could appeal to the troops and to provincials desperate for protection. Struggles among Romans, weakness and confusion opened the gates to the barbarian tribes which ringed the frontiers, and invasions were virtually constant during that half-century. Some pressure came from the free Dacian peoples, outside the province of Dacia, tribes that eventually forced the evacuation of that province. Other pressures came from the Goths, who had made their way from the Baltic to the north shore of the Black Sea, and who in the mid-third century, crossed the Danube into Roman territory and also ravaged Asia Minor and Greece. West German tribes such as the Franks carried out raids into Gaul and even Italy. Coin hoards, carefully salted away, reveal the constant sense of insecurity that spread along the Rhine. Matters were no better in the east, where the Sassanid dynasty of Persia revived the old glories of the Persian Empire and even captured a Roman emperor.

Clearly the size of the empire had gotten out of hand. It had become impossible for imperial officials alone to administer it, and greater reliance had to be placed upon local magistrates and provincial leaders. During periods of peace the situation was acceptable. But the pressures of war and

And there was a general feeling that Christians were all misanthropic. What else could be surmised from their insistence that their 'kingdom was not of this world?' Nonetheless, there is very little evidence for official persecutions in the first two centuries after Christ. Christian-baiting allegedly began with Nero, who sought to blame them for the great fire. But no contemporary author substantiates the report. The Christian theologian Origen in the third century admitted that the number of martyrs down to his own day was not large. Pliny, in one of his letters to Trajan, spoke of Christianity as an odious and depraved superstition. But Trajan's reply was moderate and restrained: he also disapproved of the sect, but specifically renounced any inquisitorial procedures on the part of Rome. That, we may take it, remained official state policy through most of the second century.

The anxieties of the second century stimulated an increase in Christian converts. Success of the religion rested in its firm maintenance of the faith combined with adaptation of classical philosophy and learning itself. Christian writers from the mid-second century were no longer concerned just to shepherd the flock and to strengthen the faith of the faltering, but to raise the level of argument to philosophic discussion. They were now appealing to a world of cultivated and educated pagans. Much has been made of a ringing phrase by the African churchman and pamphleteer Tertullian: *credo quia absurdum* ('I believe precisely because it is absurd'). The stress was on uncompromising faith. But Tertullian himself was a highly educated man, well versed in Greek and Latin literature, trained in philosophy and law. His aim was to maintain the distinctiveness of the faith, not to remove its intellectual content.

Christian thinkers from the east, under the direct impact of Hellenic traditions, took a more subtle line. Justin Martyr in the mid-second century and his successors, Clement of Alexandria and Origen, in the third century developed theological systems that both assimilated and eclipsed pagan philosophy. It was their purpose to demonstrate that the message of the gospels and the lessons of both Plato and the Stoics were slightly different ways of apprehending the same

Top far left: This silver casket has both pagan and Christian elements in its decoration. The religions of the Roman empire mingled in the second and third centuries as its population discovered a need for a deeper meaning to life than could be found in traditional Hellenistic culture.

Below far left: A funerary mosaic from a city in the province of Africa. The church in Africa was badly affected by doctrinal disputes that gave rise to the Donatists, a heresy whose followers physically attacked any opponents.

Above: The key to Roman frontier defense was the use of fortified walls, or chains of individual forts. Hadrian's wall is the most famous example of these structures, and parts of it are very well preserved.

Right: Trajan's column commemorates his campaign against the Dacians, a people who lived in the area of modern Rumania. The narrative of his victory is told in the relief that spirals around the outside of the column.

foreign invasions brought the latent decentralization sharply to the surface. Rome's ability to neutralize and adopt alien elements into her system had been the foundation of her success. But those absorptive powers had been stretched to the utmost. The third century crisis exposed the fragility of the structure.

Rome's fighting forces had been drawn increasingly from the frontier provinces. Nor was this true of the army only. The Roman senate itself, from the mid-second century, was recruited in large part from men of wealth and standing in the provinces. These were individuals whose first concern was with their estates in local areas and who often did not bother to take trips to Rome for senatorial meetings. The provincial populaces no longer had the luxury of looking to Rome in a crisis. Their loyalties shifted swiftly to the nearest strong man who could offer protection and a promise of security. Hence the bewildering maze of pretenders and would-be emperors.

The process of decentralization also affected the economy. As the center declined in agricultural importance, the periphery prospered. Money began to flow abroad from Italy. Entrepreneurs with surplus funds invested them in large estates in Gaul, Spain, the east and even in the Danubian areas. As the military situation worsened and more troops were drawn to the frontiers on a more permanent basis, economic demands naturally increased on the outskirts. While local needs grew, so did local means to satisfy those

needs. The economic fragmentation could no longer be arrested.

Invasions and internal chaos during the third century placed a heavy strain on the monetary resources of the empire. Taxable resources shrank rapidly. Progressive devaluation of the imperial coinage resulted in an unchecked increase in prices. The instability of finances wreaked havoc and ruin upon the monied classes.

Incessant invasions by plundering tribes and warfare between rival emperors must have brought business activity to a virtual standstill in many locations. Productivity naturally decreased, large tracts of land went to waste, irrigation and drainage works were neglected, population declined sharply, exchange of goods became irregular and hazardous, individuals and communities had to depend almost wholly upon themselves. Economic collapse meant that the communities were consistently unable to pay their bills; local officials were expected to make up the deficit, and they could not evade the responsibility. So municipal office was no longer sought, and the state had to resort to compulsion. An Egyptian papyrus records the pathetic lament of one individual: 'Is my property to be confiscated? Is it to be sold by auction? Am I to become a beggar? Shall I take to flight? Am I going to be chosen for the municipal council?' That last alternative was evidently the grimmest prospect of all.

Amid chaos, deprivation and depopulation, the most remarkable fact is that the empire survived at all. Credit is customarily given to the reforms of the emperors Diocletian and Constantine, but

administrative changes from the top could have had little effect in themselves. There were more fundamental changes occurring throughout the third century – in a word, the ancient Roman capacity for adaptation and modification. This time the emphasis was on location, decentralization and privatization.

The lower ranks of the army were recruited primarily from the artisans and workers of the cities. Such men did not abandon their trades and skills upon joining the service. As warfare became endemic and soldiers became accustomed to almost permanent service, the army camps themselves were gradually transformed into something like cities in their own right. At the outset they must have resembled nothing so much as the frontier towns of the early American West. As time passed, however, these settlements lost the character of military posts: they attracted merchants, traders and discharged veterans who stayed on as permanent dwellers. Large facilities were built, the accoutrements of civilization: amphitheaters, baths, aqueducts, temples. Barracks life increasingly overlapped with domestic life. Military men or ex-military men became civil administrators and even municipal magistrates. As the older cities took on an ever more military aspect, military forts were becoming permanent towns. The two-way process, the merging of roles, produced a new kind of urban life: the fortified community, civilized and self-sufficient, created out of necessity and fashioned for survival.

Analogous transformation and adaptation occurred on the land. Already under Marcus Aure-

lius some of the Germanic population had been settled inside Roman boundaries. Payments to German tribes to assure quiescence gradually evolved into a regular system and produced a new half-breed warrior caste, a mingling of the races. In the economic crisis of the third century, with fields devastated or going out of cultivation, the settling of barbarians, often enroled as foreign auxiliary troops, became a deliberate process designed both to repopulate and defend the countryside. Just as the soldier-administrators recreated urban life, so these soldier-farmers brought lands back into cultivation. The Roman empire was resilient. In the economic decentralization, the fortified communities and the gradual fusion of a Romano-German populace there can be discerned the seeds of medieval Europe.

Developments of this sort – not of his own doing – enabled the emperor Diocletian (284-305) to reconstitute a tattered empire. A wily and resourceful Illyrian, Diocletian reestablished order by drawing appropriate conclusions from his predecessors' failures and by making necessary adjustments. Constant struggles to defend the boundaries of the realm had shifted the locus of power away from Rome and toward the frontiers. Diocletian's Tetrarchy was an answer to the problem. The empire was divided into two spheres, east and west. There were to be two co-equal emperors, (two Augusti), one responsible for the east and one for the west, and with them two Caesars, junior partners, shouldering some of the burden and themselves in training to become Augusti. Little time was spent in Rome. The four rulers established centers of authority in militarized zones: Treves, Milan, Byzantium and Sirmium. Rome was taking a back seat. The formal division of responsibility was a useful instrument, but it was the moral dominance of Diocletian that kept the system in hand. The third-century anarchy had been punctuated by recurrent assassinations of emperors by their own intimates, subordinates and soldiers. Diocletian consequently fostered a more august and detached aura about the person of the ruler. Court ritual became more elaborate, lavish attire and jewelry marked the emperor's appearance, the custom of bowing at his feet became established practice. The sovereign's seclusion entailed greater difficulty of access: public appearances were rarer and attended with more splendid ceremony. The holder of the crown became unapproachable, almost divine.

The decentralization of the empire was a fact, and Diocletian had turned it to his own advantage. Roman provinces were divided and subdivided: the empire was now restructured into approximately 100 administrative districts, each with its own military and civil governors – all drawn from the equestrian order. For every official there was a virtual army of subordinates, clerks and assistants.

An analogous restructuring occurred in the military. The number of legions, reported as 33 in the early third century, was augmented to about 60 under Diocletian. The emperor effected it in part by vigorous recruitment, but, more importantly, by combining small units into full legionary complements – the same passion for system and order that marked the civil reorganization.

An expanded bureaucracy and a larger army placed a serious strain on the treasury. The wherewithal now had to originate from the municipalities and rural areas of the provinces. Diocletian hardened a process of hereditary office holding and encouraged the process of privatization of land holding. Municipal aristocracies were responsible for collecting the taxes; business cor-

Top left: The largest standing Roman monument in northern Europe is the Porta Nigra at Trier. It dates from the fourth century, part of a complex of walls that surrounded the largest city of the western provinces.

Left: The Arch of Constantine at Rome was erected in honor of the emperor who instituted Christianity as Rome's official religion. It is an unusual combination of reliefs stolen from other monuments, and newly carved ones.

Right: This huddled group (whether they clasp each other out of friendship or fear for the future is uncertain) represents the Tetrarchy, Diocletian's answer to the government of the large Roman empire. It was a successful solution only in that it postponed for a time the collapse of the empire in the west.

porations and labor groups were saddled with fixed assessments. None could evade his responsibilities. Each man was tied by law to his profession and position, whether urban noble or rural peasant. And to insure permanence the positions were made hereditary.

Particularly in the west this was the time of great estates. The rich could acquire lands while engaged in military affairs or while in office. The small landholder, crushed by taxes, increasingly sought refuge under the protection of the rich. Peasants became serfs and petty landowners clients. When the great proprietors acquired criminal jurisdiction over their estates, a new kind of private dependence came into being. Here too were the seeds of medieval Europe.

The triumph of Christianity

The imperial structure, thus modified, survived the third-century chaos. So did the Christian Church. Its darkest days too came in the third century. Matters had taken a turn for the worse already in the reign of Marcus Aurelius. That noble emperor showed little sympathy for minority groups. His stern Stoic philosophy permitted him to confront death and disaster with equanimity, but he could not understand Christian martyrs who provoked their own doom or courted their own disasters. Persecutions came with stepped-up intensity during the chaos of the third century, though with unpredictable irregularity. Christians were convenient scapegoats for insecure rulers and vengeful subjects.

Misinformation concerning Christian morals was compounded by misunderstanding concerning Christian politics. Adherents of the sect did not seem to behave like loyal citizens. They would not, of course, indulge in emperor worship. Moreover, many – though by no means all – Christians were pacifists, and it was difficult to recruit them into the service. In addition, there was the persistent notion that every natural calamity testified to divine wrath – and the gods were especially offended by atheists. Christians bore the brunt of the blame. As Tertullian lamented, 'If the Tiber floods the town or the Nile fails to water the fields, if the sky stands still or the earth moves, the first reaction is "Christians to the lions!"'

The situation was bad enough in the mid-third

century. Worse was to come under Diocletian, whose elaborate imperial system could not easily endure a rival Church organization that cut across its hierarchical arrangements. In 303 an edict of the emperor outlawed Christianity, ordered all copies of the Scriptures to be burned, churches to be demolished and Christian meetings to be banned. There followed the most brutal and devastating persecutions in the Church's history, engineered not so much by Diocletian himself as by his Caesar, the violent religious fanatic Galerius. The triumph – at least in a formal sense – came with the emperor Constantine (306-337). In the course of his reign Christianity became the official religion of the empire – within a generation of its most grievous persecution. That remarkable phenomenon does not easily lend itself to explanation. Christian writers ascribed it to a sudden conversion of Constantine to the faith. A dream or a vision effected the conversion, according to Constantine's own assertion later. The event occurred in 312 at the battle of the Milvian Bridge. Diocletian's tetrarchical arrangement had crumbled shortly after his retirement. Constantine eventually emerged as the sole inheritor of imperial power, but not without a fight. Constantine's victory over Maxentius at the Milvian Bridge was one of the more decisive contests in that struggle for it gave the victor mastery of Rome and the empire in the west. Before the battle Constantine is said to have had Christian symbols engraved on his soldiers' shields, and it was to this that he attributed his victory.

The nature of Constantine's 'conversion' has been endlessly debated. Long-range psychoanalysis of the man bears little fruit. The change, like all other significant changes in Roman history, did not come overnight. A long background exists to the events of 312. Religious attitudes had increasingly pervaded the empire during the third century. Constantine's father was a deeply religious man and subscribed to a vague sort of monotheism. The official coinage of Constantine himself, even before 312, shows a prominent role played by devotion to Sol Invictus, a single deity. And in his entourage was Hosius, the Christian bishop of Cordova. Whatever happened in 312, it is demonstrable that Constantine's sympathetic attitude toward Christianity became more pronounced thereafter. Christians were soon granted

full equality in law and state and generously indemnified for lost property. The emperor overtly subsidized Christian communities, exempted the clergy from heavy tax burdens and brought Christians into the higher administrative posts of the empire. Constantine was no theologian and had little taste for or understanding of theological controversies. Nor was he attracted to Christianity for its moral teachings. A hard, often cruel, military man, he lived up to few of those teachings. Power was a compelling factor for Constantine. It is revealing that in references to Christ throughout his later life, the emperor rarely speaks of him as a savior or as loving and compassionate, but in terms such as 'the Mighty One,' 'the Lord of all' or 'God Almighty.'

The senatorial aristocracy was still exclusively pagan, as were almost all leading administrators and, more important, the army itself, both officers and men. But the Christian god had been good to Constantine – and the emperor did not withhold his favor. His contest against Licinius, co-emperor in the east who had undertaken vexatious measures against the Church, was openly advertised as a religious crusade. Once more Constantine's victory was complete. By 324 Licinius had been executed and Constantine was unchallenged ruler of the realm. The Christians and their god were the beneficiaries. Constantine issued an edict of toleration – only this time it was the pagans, not the Christians, who were being tolerated. Rome's empire was now officially a Christian empire.

Constantine felt obliged even to intervene in doctrinal disputes. The power of the imperial office was to be used to enforce unity in the Church. The orthodox might welcome such interference; but not those who were pronounced heretics, like the Donatists in Africa, who incurred the wrath of the emperor. On the theological wrangle over the relationship of Christ to God the Father, Constantine convened a general council of the Church at Nicaea in 325, presided over the proceedings and introduced the key resolution. He then took it upon himself to enforce that Nicene creed against heretics. The Church had acquired a protector, but also a master. Con-

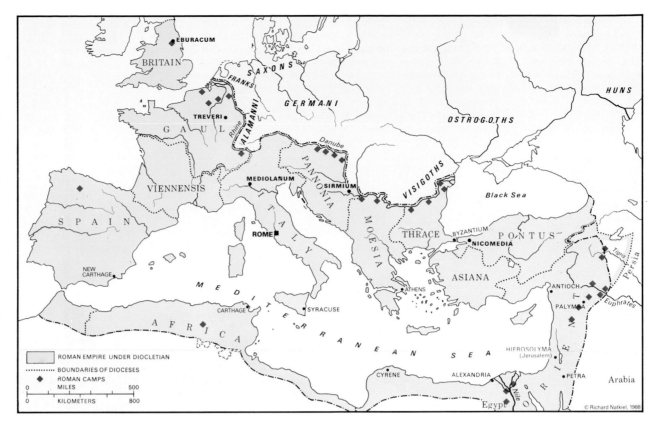

© Richard Natkiel, 1988

Left: The head of a now-broken colossal statue of Constantine the Great. When Diocletian's system temporarily broke down in a series of civil wars, Constantine emerged the victor and, briefly, sole emperor. He moved the imperial center east, to the new capital Constantinople (Constantine's city – he was not a modest man).

Below left: Constantine's deathbed baptism was frequently commemorated in later Christian art. It marked the final triumph of Christianity over Hellenism, despite the efforts of Julian the Apostate (emperor, 361-3) to reverse the trend.

Below: This silver bowl, found in Huntingdonshire, England, is marked with the Christian Chi-Rho symbol.

Right: The empire entered the third century having undergone nearly 50 years of war, civil strife and economic collapse. But the worst trials – the barbarian invasions – were yet to come.

stantine himself had moved a long way, from tolerance of Christianity among other creeds to direct involvement of the imperial power within the religious structure of the Church.

Problems of unity and stability

The year 325 provides a convenient terminus for this part of the discussion of the ancient Roman world. Imperial coercion in order to maintain unity and stability in the secular world had been legitimized by Diocletian. Through the Council of Nicaea Constantine claimed similar rights in the religious realm. The premises for Caesaro-Papism had been laid. In the same year Constantine began to rebuild and transform the ancient city of Byzantium, now to be renamed Constantinople. The shift away from Rome as the center of empire had been going on for some time, as we have seen. Diocletian chose Nicomedia as his official residence; other emperors of the Tetrarchy spent their time in major cities near the centers of fighting – at Sirmium, Treves and Milan. But Constantine carried the process to fruition. He had a special reason for transferring the administrative capital away from Rome. For Rome, with its traditions, its aristocracy, its rituals and its memories, was irrevocably identified with paganism and with the glories of an ancient past. That was something that not even Constantine could erad-

icate. But he could and did create a new Rome, a new city, a Christian city, unencumbered by pagan memories, the center of a new Christian empire.

The 'decline and fall of the Roman Empire' is largely a creation of the eighteenth century. The intelligentsia of that era prided themselves upon their classical learning. Scorning predecessors in previous ages, whom they regarded as mired in superstition and ignorance, they looked back to the ancients as the repositors of learning and wisdom, the only proper model for their own Age of Reason. Such intellectual snobbery is responsible for the term 'middle ages,' the badly abused notion of a dark chronological valley between the gleaming peaks of antiquity and the modern enlightenment. A natural corollary of the view has been the postulating of Rome's fall, after which ancient culture was buried by medieval Christendom. That hoary concept ought to be laid to rest. 'Decline and fall' is a phrase best eschewed.

Roman institutions, albeit dramatically transformed, adapted and altered, survived. The medieval social and economic structure of the entire region from Byzantium to Britain was a direct descendant of the Roman system. The process of decentralization, of self-sufficient and fortified landed estates, of men tied to the soil, of professions, guilds and corporations, had already begun in the late second century. Roman engineering achievements, the roads, aqueducts, fortifications, drainage constructions, endured – not as museum pieces but as functioning entities. Latin remained unchallenged as the linguistic bond of western Europe for a millennium. Roman law and legal institutions afforded a permanent legacy that underlies the codes and jurisprudence of European peoples to this day. The organization of the universal Church was modeled largely on that of the Roman empire itself. Constantine's gleaming Christian capital at Constantinople became the center of Byzantine civilization, which preserved the literary, philosophical and intellectual traditions of the classical world. The 'barbarian invasions' were more often than not gradual settlement of tribes within Roman boundaries. The practice was continuous with Rome's ancient

tradition of assimilating outside peoples into her own culture and system. It was not without justification that Charlemagne in AD 800 could regard himself as in the direct and unbroken line of Roman emperors dating straight back to Augustus himself.

Roman twilight

For all the reasons detailed in the preceding pages the great period of both traditional Roman civilization and of the Roman Empire may be said to have come to a close by the time of Constantine's death in 337. The major forces tending toward economic and social fragmentation and political decentralization were then not only well advanced but probably irreversible. Christianity had triumphed over the old religion, Rome's enemies were gathering on her frontiers and the decision to create a new, eastern seat of empire in Byzantium had already been formally taken. This new Eastern Empire would survive for another thousand years, but for the western Empire and for Rome herself the future held nothing but protracted decay. To many commentators of the time, the outlook was poor.

How long did it take for the western Empire to collapse? Traditionally it is said that the Roman twilight lasted for another 139 years, until AD 476, when the last western emperor was finally deposed. Some scholars prefer earlier dates – 378, for example, when the Visigoths defeated the Roman legions at Adrianople, or 410, when Rome was first sacked by the Goths, or 454, when Aetius, Rome's last capable military commander, was murdered by his emperor. Others argue that none of these dates is truly significant and that the whole period is best understood simply as part of a longer and deeper historical transition from what had once been a viable empire to what would become early medieval Europe.

In the summary that follows we shall accept the traditionalist scheme and briefly trace the course of events in the West to 476 – not so much because these events have much more to tell us about the nature of Rome's empire, but because of what they imply about the new order that was in the process of succeeding it. As to the burgeoning new Eastern Empire, that is properly a subject for another chapter.

Constantine's provisions for succession were ill-conceived, and for 13 years after his death his sons and nephews engaged in a lethal power struggle that ended only when his third son, Constantius II, who had been reigning in the East, finally seized control of the whole empire. Constantius both consolidated most of his father's reforms and reaffirmed official recognition of Christianity as the state religion. But his eastern-oriented military and foreign policies were primarily concerned with checking the rising power of Persia's aggressive Sassanid emperor, Shapur II. The task of dealing with the potentially more serious threat of a barbarian invasion from the west he left to a rather obscure 24-year-old nephew named Julian.

Exactly why barbarian pressure on the western frontiers should suddenly have begun to mount at this time is not clear. Possibly migrations of Goths along the Danubian frontier had had a billiard-ball effect on other more westerly tribes, but even why the Goths were moving is something of a mystery. In any case, in 353 the Alemanni, a German tribe that had been living peacefully on their assigned territory north and east of the Rhine, between the Swiss Alps and Alsace, abruptly crossed the river. Within three years they controled both banks of the Rhine from Mainz to Lake Constance and were posing a serious threat to Rome's freedom of access to Gaul. Young Julian, having been created Caesar by his uncle in 355, hastened to this sagging portion of the frontier, and by 357 he had assembled an army of sufficient strength to defeat the Alemanni in a major battle at Argentoratum, near modern Strasbourg. He continued his campaign against the Alemans steadily and successfully for the next six years, but in the meantime, on Constantinian's death in 361, he had been proclaimed Emperor of Rome.

Julian's three-year reign was, and still is, controversial. A pagan, he reversed the policy of his forebears and decreed liberty of conscience in religious matters, thus demoting Christianity from the status of state religion and winning the enmity of future Christian historians, who would refer to him as Julian the Apostate. (In fact, his religious policy was not particularly popular in his own time, and Christianity was reinstated almost immediately after his death.) His economic policies were fairly enlightened: He sharply reduced taxation in an effort to restore the health of the associated towns that had been the strength of the empire under the Flavians, and he was partially successful in cutting back the outflow of precious metals, one of the factors contributing to Rome's long-standing inflation. But his foreign/military policy, so successful in the West, led to a major disaster in the East.

Determined to put an end once and for all to Shapur II's continuing harassment of the Roman Empire's Middle Eastern frontiers, Julian decided on a large-scale invasion of the Persian Empire. At a minimum he intended to break Sassanid power in Mesopotamia, and if all went well he was probably prepared to push on into the Iranian Plateau itself. For this enterprise Julian assembled a very large army of some 65,000 men, recruited largely from the elite units of the 'mobile forces,' the Italy-based strategic reserve that had been created to provide rapid reinforcement to frontier troops whenever they came under serious attack anywhere along the Empire's periphery.

Julian's strategy was to stab southeast toward the Persian capital of Ctesiphon, on the Tigris, thus forcing Shapur to commit himself to a major battle and probable destruction. But Shapur refused to cooperate and defend the city. Instead, he retreated, harassing, scorching the earth, stretching Roman supply lines to the breaking point and causing great affliction to the Roman troops. When, in 363, the main armies at last came to grips at Maranga, the Romans had been so weakened that they could not force a decision. Three days later Julian was killed in a small action near Samarra, and the Roman campaign disintegrated. Julian's successor, a general named Jovian, was forced to conclude a humiliating peace with the Persians, by which Rome lost a considerable part of her former holdings in northern Mesopotamia. The effect on Roman prestige had been bad enough, but the extent to which the Roman army had been eroded in this, its first major defeat, was truly ominous.

Jovian's reign lasted only eight months. He was replaced by another general, Valantinian I (364-75), an unlettered former peasant from Slavia whom most historians now regard as the last militarily competent Roman emperor. Julian's withdrawal of a large part of the mobile force from Italy, capped by his disaster in Mesopotamia, had provoked a new wave of militant barbarian pressures on Rome's western frontiers, and Valantinian perceived the stabilization of these frontiers as his first priority. Accordingly, he named his brother, Valens (364-78), as co-emperor to handle eastern affairs. The energetic Valantinian was surprisingly successful both in his defense of the frontiers and in his efforts to revive the Roman army, but his tenure was not long enough to achieve decisive effects in either endeavor. It was left to the far less competent Valens to preside over the next great Roman disaster.

Barbarian pressure

In 375 the Goths, under severe pressure from westward-advancing Huns, had asked permission to cross the Danube and seek sanctuary within the borders of the Empire. Valantinian, probably wisely, had opposed the idea, but after Valantinian's death Valens wavered, first permitting some Goths to cross (and allowing provincial officials to exploit them mercilessly) and then refusing permission to others. The inevitable result was conflict, and by 378 Gothic armies were besieging the Thracian provincial capital of Adrianople. Valens responded by rushing an army to the scene, not even pausing to join forces with another army that had been dispatched by the new Western Emperor, Gratian (378-83). On 9 August Valens' army met the Goths outside Adrianople in a straightforward infantry encounter. (It was *not*, as one tradition has it, primarily a cavalry v infantry duel.) The result was the worst defeat any Roman army had suffered in battle since Hannibal's victory at Cannae in 216 BC. About 60 percent of the Roman troops were killed or captured, and among the dead was Valens.

Valens' successor in the East was Theodosius I (378-95). In the first few years of his reign he attempted to renew the campaign against the Goths, but the enfeebled post-Adrianople Roman army was now incapable of expelling the intruders. Both Theodosius and Gratian realized that nothing significant could be accomplished until the army was rebuilt, and for this they needed to buy time. Accordingly, in 382 Theodosius signed a treaty with the Visigoths (ie the western Goths) whereby they were given exten-

Below far left: Germanic barbarians were not the only threat to the empire. In the east an aggressive Persian dynasty, the Sassanids, came to power around AD 225 with dreams of restoring the glory of the old Achaemenid period.

Below left: The Roman empire had been built by the fighting skills of the legionaries: highly trained heavy infantrymen. During the third century, however, there was an increase in the numbers of cavalrymen; by the middle of the fourth century, heavy cavalry was the most important arm of Rome's forces.

Right: A scene from the column of Antoninus, a monument similar to that of Trajan's but of a slightly later date. German nobles are having their heads cut off by Roman soldiers. Although the Roman army was able to block the marauding Germanic tribes for two and a half centuries after Augustus, the frontier began to give way in the third century.

sive lands south of the Danube in northern Thrace in exchange for their promise to lay down their arms and serve as Rome's allies (*foederati*) in defending the Empire. Gratian followed suit, making somewhat similar arrangements with the Ostrogoths, Franks and Scots. Many observers in both Constantinople and Rome saw these moves as ill-omened, for in effect the barbarians had succeeded in breaching the frontiers by force of arms and in setting up virtually independent kingdoms inside the Empire.

Even as Theodosius set about trying to rebuild his army, the West fell victim to yet another spasm of lethal political in-fighting. Gratian was murdered in 383, and his successor, the boy-Emperor Valantinian II, was at once challenged by a would-be usurper, Miximus, Count of Britain. At length Theodosius felt himself obliged to intervene, and in 388 he invaded Italy, bested Maximus' army and killed the pretender. Theodosius remained in Italy for the next three years, but almost as soon as he had returned to Constantinople Valantinian was murdered by one of his barbarian field marshals, Arbogast, who put forward a certain Eugenius as the Western Augustus. Once again Theodosius led his weary army west, this time considerably supplemented by his Visigothic *foederati.* In a hard-fought and costly battle at the Frigidus River (394) he finally prevailed, and both Arbogast and Eugenius were killed.

Theodosius now found himself sole emperor of the Roman Empire, but he had no intention of perpetuating the principle of unified rule. He immediately announced that upon his death his younger son, Honorius, would rule in the West, and his elder son, Arcadius, would rule in the East. In the event, Theodosius died so soon thereafter (395) that neither boy was old enough or sufficiently prepared to rule competently, but the division was a fact, and never again would the Empire be ruled by one man.

Would the Empire have fared better in the years to come under unified rule? It is attractive to think that a consolidated military force serving a single, coherent policy might have made a difference. And certainly there would be many occasions in the future when the East would fail to give desperately needed assistance to the beleagured West. But the old Roman army – in the East or West – was a thing of the past. Julian's disastrous Near Eastern campaign, Adrianople and the frightful losses suffered by both (Roman) sides in the internecine wars that culminated in the Battle of the Frigidus had gutted the army. To be sure, it had for many years been becoming ever more dependent on its barbarian recruits and allies, but now it was nearly hostage to them.

The new Western Emperor, Honorius, was still a boy, and the office of regent was assumed by a shrewd, thoroughly Romanized Vandal named Stilicho. He soon had much to do, for in 396 Rome's *foederati,* the Visigoths, suddenly burst out of their lands in northern Thrace and began rampaging through Thessaly and the Peloponnese. The Eastern Emperor either would not or could not cope with the crisis, so Stilicho rushed troops into Greece and succeeded in arresting the Visigoths' onrush, although he by no means broke their power. Indeed, he had broken their power so little that in 401, while Stilicho's attention was diverted in combating some barbarian tribes in the Alps, the Visigothic leader, Alaric, led his army into Italy itself.

With some difficulty Stilicho was able to drive Alaric off, and for the next few years he was generally successful in holding the various barbarian tribes that ringed the Western Empire at bay. But in 407 a large body of Vandals, Alans and Suevi, fleeing before westward-advancing Huns, crossed the frozen Rhine and stormed into northern Gaul. In short order this whole sector of the frontier was in a state of collapse. Stilicho, who was unable to cope with a crisis of this magnitude, was soon denounced by his enemies in the court (by now removed to Ravenna) and eventually, on Honorius' orders, was executed.

The sack of Rome

The growing chaos in the West presented a temptation too great for Alaric to resist. In 408 he led his Visigoths back into Italy, demanding money and new lands for his people. When these demands were refused he besieged Rome itself. In the year 410 he succeeded in breaking into the city and pillaged it.

The sack of Rome sent psychological shock waves gusting across both empires. Not for 800 years had any foreign invader violated Rome's sanctity. Yet disastrous though the event was, it was not the end. Alaric remained in Rome only three days and then headed south, with the intention of crossing over into the rich lands of North Africa. He died before that goal was achieved, and his successor then led the Visigoths into southern

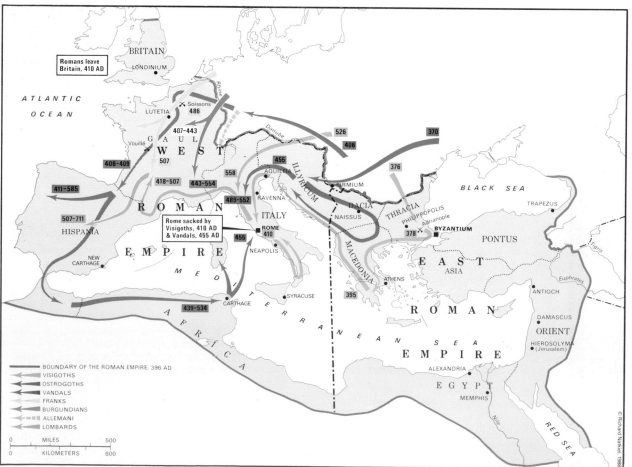

BOUNDARY OF THE ROMAN EMPIRE, 396 AD
VISIGOTHS
OSTROGOTHS
VANDALS
FRANKS
BURGUNDIANS
ALLEMANI
LOMBARDS

0   MILES   500
0   KILOMETERS   800

Above: Roman soldiers battle fiercely with their German opponents in the decorative relief on this sarcophagus. In the fourth century AD the Roman army suffered a number of defeats at the hands of the barbarians, most notably at Adrianople in 378. In 407 the Rhine frontier gave way after it had been stripped of troops to fight off an invasion elsewhere – it was the final catastrophe.

Left: The collapse of the Western Empire was a rapid event. Between 400 and 450 the old order collapsed under the burdens of barbarian attack and administrative incompetence. The last emperor of the west was deposed in 476, but for 25 years before emperors ruled little more than a shadow realm.

Right: A Hunnic sacrificial pot. The Huns were the key barbarian group in the destruction of the empire. They pushed the German tribes over the border, and then followed in their wake to ravage in turn. They were fine horsemen, and good at metalworking – but these were small compensations for what they destroyed.

Gaul, settled there and asked to be placed in Roman service. Honorius accepted, and, indeed, within a few years the Visigoths were ably assisting Roman troops in subduing the Vandals in Spain.

This whole strange episode is significant not only as a demonstration of how far Roman power had decayed, but equally as an indication of the Visigoths' mentality, and, by extension, that of several other barbarian tribes. That Alaric was prepared to overthrow Honorius was nothing new in Roman politics; emperors were constantly being overthrown. But there is no evidence that Alaric ever imagined that *he* might wear the diadem, and still less that he meant to be the destroyer of the Empire. On the contrary, he seems to have considered himself a *citizen* of the Empire, who was claiming his rights under Roman law and justice. The subsequent behavior of the Visigoths in Gaul bears out the impression that they saw themselves not as Rome's foreign invaders but as her sons. The distinction, whether or not it seemed meaningful to the hapless Romans in 410, would nevertheless be of considerable importance in the dark days to come, when the fate of Roman culture would depend on the barbarians' readiness to preserve and transmit it.

The Empire's amazing resiliency is attested by the fact that within about 10 years of the sack of Rome the situation in the West had been returned to a reasonable level of stability. This was in part due to the helpful role played by the Visigoths in subduing other barbarian tribes in Gaul and Spain – for which, in 418, the Visigoths were given Aquitaine as a homeland, a region they would inhabit for the next century. But it was also due to the fact that Honorius had the good luck to find a new and remarkably competent general in the person of an Illyrian named Constantius. By the time of Honorius' death in 423, though most of Britain had been lost and Roman control over northern Gaul and Spain was somewhat more tenuous than

before, all serious military threats to Italy had – at least for the time being – been removed.

The stability of this diminished Empire did not last long. In 429 the king of the Vandals in southern Spain, Gaiseric, seized a fleet of ships and, with 80,000 followers, crossed the Strait of Gibraltar and invaded North Africa. After 10 years of systematic, bloody conquest Gaiseric had gotten as far east as Carthage and was preparing to attack Sicily. This looming military threat was forestalled, thanks largely to the intervention of the Eastern Empire's fleet, and Gaiseric signed a peace treaty with Rome in 442. But the loss of her African provinces was nonetheless a bitter blow to the Western Empire. Italy, especially, had become heavily dependent on the grain supply from Africa, and control of the African ports had been crucial to Rome's naval dominion over the western Mediterranean. Worst of all, Rome now had a potentially formidable enemy on her heretofore secure southern flank.

The loss of Africa took place during the reign of Rome's last effective emperor, Valentinian III (425-55), and such power as Valentinian wielded was due largely to the military and diplomatic skills of his best general, Aetius, who spent much of his career serving in Gaul. Aetius had enjoyed fairly good relations with the Huns, and from time to time had made use of their services as allies in fighting fractious German tribes. But in the mid 430s the Huns came under the rule of a new and aggressive khan, Attila, and Aetius' influence over these fierce Asiatic tribesmen began to wane. In the spring of 451 Attila led an army of 70,000 over the Rhine and swept down through northern Gaul. Aetius hastily patched together a confederacy of Romans, Visigoths, Franks and Burgundians, confronted Attila near Châlons, on the Loire, and carried the day, thus saving Gaul and probably Italy and destroying the Huns' fearsome reputation of invincibility.

The Huns had been beaten but not destroyed, and the following year they descended into northern Italy. Their greatly weakened forces caused considerable devastation in Aquileia, but Pope Leo I managed by negotiation to halt their advance on Rome, and after a time, for reasons not altogether clear, they withdrew from Italy. After Attila's death in 453 the Hunnish 'empire' collapsed, and the disorganized tribesmen slowly drifted back toward the East.

If Aetius could have been said to have saved Rome from the Huns, his reward was to be murdered by his jealous emperor's own hand. As one shocked courtier remarked to Valentinian, 'You have cut off your right hand with your left.' So it proved. Within a year, in 455, Valentinian was himself murdered by some of Aetius' friends, and profiting from the ensuing confusion, Gaiseric's Vandals launched a brief seaborne raid on Italy that resulted in the second sacking of Rome.

The power of the emperors who succeeded Valentinian steadily dwindled into insignificance. By 461 an ambitious barbarian (half Visigoth, half Suevian) named Ricimer was ruling what little was left of the Western Empire through imperial puppets. Ricimer died in 472 and four years later a Herul chieftain named Odovacer almost casually deposed the last Western Emperor, Romulus Augustulus, and proclaimed himself King of Italy. In theory he still acknowledged the authority of the Eastern Emperor, Zeno, but both men understood this to be a polite fiction, and after Odovacer was murdered and replaced by the Ostrogothic chieftain Theodoric in 492, even the fiction fell into desuetude.

With the deposition of Romulus Augustulus in

476 the last great symbol of the old Roman Empire had vanished, but of course its political substance had withered away long before that. At precisely what point Rome ceased to deserve to be called an empire is a subject scholars still love to debate, either in spite or because of the fact that it is an argument that can never be settled. The same is true of the question of Roman 'civilization.' That in the succeeding centuries Rome's cultural legacy became attenuated – sometimes severely – in the West is hardly arguable; but equally unarguable is the fact that it was never obliterated and that, either directly or in transmuted forms, it has always profoundly affected the character of Western civilization, even down to our own times.

A new empire?

Our story of the collapse of the Western Empire properly ends in the late fifth century, but perhaps a cursory glance at the salient events that followed in its aftermath will help to put into context certain allusions that will appear in later chapters on Byzantium, Islam and medieval Europe. Doubtless the most important development in the West following the deposition of the last emperor was the conquest and unification of Gaul by the energetic Frankish king, Clovis (481-511). Even though the kingdom was subsequently subdivided among Clovis' four sons and thereafter, for nearly three centuries, saw only brief periods of completely unified rule, this *Regnum Frankorum* remained an entity and the single greatest power in western Europe. An important aspect of this power was the fact that the Frankish kings, from Clovis on, were Christians and maintained generally good relations with the papacy. In 751 Pope Stephen II personally crowned Pepin, first of the Carolingian dynasty, the sole Frankish king, thus signalizing an alliance that, in the hands of Pepin's son, Charlemagne, would have profound consequences for the course of European history.

The Frankish conquest of Gaul had driven the Visigoths south into Spain, where they set up a kingdom that survived until the Islamic conquest early in the eighth century. The Vandal kingdom in North Africa, on the other hand, survived only into the first half of the sixth century, being overwhelmed in the 530s by the forces of Byzantium's greatest emperor, Justinian. The Byzantines thereafter ruled the region – never very firmly, to be sure – until it, too, fell to Islam.

The history of Italy was more complex. The Ostrogothic kingdom founded by Theodoric in 492 had, by 563, been crushed by Justinian's invading forces, and all Italy then became a province of the Eastern Empire. But within a few years Byzantine control in Italy began to slacken under pressure from a new wave of barbarous Germanic invaders, the Lombards. By the early part of the seventh century the Lombards had established a firmly entrenched kingdom in the north-west and Tuscany, as well as semi-independent duchies in the south-central part of the peninsula. Byzantium's authority over the remainder of Italy and Sicily was further eroded during the following 150 years by the growing spiritual and political influence of the Rome-based papacy, which, though nominally subservient to Byzantium, was steadily growing more independent. And when the Franks and the papacy cemented their formidable alliance in the second half of the eighth century the days both of Byzantine control in Italy and of the independent survival of the Lombard kingdom were plainly numbered. From the dead ashes of the old Roman Empire a new Holy Roman Empire was to arise.

Chinese Civilization

From the western end of the Eurasian continent we now turn to the extreme eastern end and to the classical civilization of China. Modern China occupies an area of sub-continental dimensions. It is approximately 20 percent larger than the United States in land area. North to south it stretches from the latitude of Maine to that of Cuba; from east to west it equals the distance from New York to Oregon. How, from small beginnings, did a tiny group of Paleolithic hunters in the North China plain evolve into 'the Chinese,' with their distinctive way and view of life, and how did their descendants spread their evolving culture across this huge and varied area and make of it what we know as 'China?' That is the subject of this chapter, and it is one of the great success stories of human history.

China's history has been heavily influenced by her geography. China is like a huge oasis, surrounded on all sides by physical barriers. To the east and south lies the Pacific, to the west the Tibetan plateau, to the north 1000 miles of desert. There are routes of access, of course, but relatively speaking, China's geography imposes a remarkable degree of self-sufficiency and isolation from outside influences. By contrast, the civilization of Western Europe was centered on the Mediterranean and Aegean, which offered easy intercourse among the Europeans and with the countries of North Africa and the Near East. Similarly, India was open by land and sea to influences from the Middle East, the West and even Africa.

Proceeding from the northeast, the Liao River Plain has the highlands of Manchuria and Korea on the east and the mountains, steppe-lands and deserts of Mongolia to the west. This plain and its contiguous areas have become part of China proper only within the last hundred years. Though the growing season is short, it is very productive; the principal crops are corn, wheat, millet and a grain sorghum called kao-liang. The hills east of the plain are richly forested.

Advancing from the lower Liao River Plain in a southwesterly direction, arid hills and steppe-lands rise just beyond a narrow coastal plain, while on the east is the Gulf of Bohai, a part of the Yellow Sea. This coastal plain leads into the northern part of the North China Plain. Here is Peking, and here the Great Wall completes its 1500-mile zigzag course along the northern frontier of China proper and reaches the sea. The North China Plain, interrupted only by the mountains of Shantung, is flat and fertile farmland, alluvial soil mixed with the rich silt spread by repeated flooding of the Yellow River.

The North China Plain shades imperceptibly into the Yangtse delta plain. On a map it may look like a continuation of the same sort of terrain, but just south of the 35th parallel, along what geographers and historians call the Huai River line, there are important climatic, soil and crop boundaries. North of this line rainfall is scant, and wheat and millet are the principal crops. Below it are the green and humid ricelands of the south, enormously productive and densely populated. The majestic Yangtse, which forms this plain, rises in the Tibetan plateau, emerging from its gorges a thousand miles from the sea. It is fed by countless tributaries as it flows through its rich plains, and at the summer flood stage it carries

twice the volume of water as the Mississippi at its record peak. South of the central course of the Yangtse the land is rich and productive, but the river valleys are narrow, and one is seldom out of sight of hills and mountains. The hills have been terraced into rice paddies where ever possible. In the more remote mountain districts aboriginal people still live.

East of this area lie the provinces which border China's southeastern and southern coasts from Hangchow Bay to Indo-China. Here the mountains rise steeply behind a narrow coastal plain which opens out at only four locations where steep and largely unnavigable rivers empty into the sea. The southernmost of these delta plains, and by far the largest, is that of the Pearl River, where Canton is located. It should be noted that the southeast coast, though far from hospitable, has supported significant fishing and shipbuilding industries ever since it was settled.

To deal with inland and highland China we must return again to the north and work southward. When one looks westward from Peking, one sees the 'Western Hills.' This is typical of the

whole geography of China, for whenever one moves west from the great river valleys and their rich plains, one is in the highlands – hills, mountains or plateux. The T'ai-hang mountains, running roughly north to south, form the western boundary of the North China Plain. The province just west of them is Shansi, which means 'west of the mountains.' This province in modern times reaches from the borders of the Mongolian steppe to the great bend of the Yellow River; it is virtually all a plateau, and its capital is at an altitude of more than 3000 feet. It is bisected by the Fen River, which flows into the Yellow River above its great bend. North of the province's capital are the Wu-t'ai mountains, in the past considered holy.

Shansi is separated from Shensi, its neighbor to the west, by the north-south course of the Yellow River. Shansi, Shensi and the westernmost province of Kansu (whose long neck stretches out to the borders of Chinese Turkestan) are grouped by the geographers as the 'loess highlands,' because much of the area is covered, often to great depths, by the fine wind-blown dust known as loess. This soil has great moisture-holding qualities, and

Left: The remains of a commander's chariot dating from the Yangshao (Neolithic) period.

Above right: A decorative pot of the Neolithic period. Artifacts from this culture suggest a culture with a highly developed sense of design.

Right: A Neolithic burial site consisting of ranks of stone coffins, uncovered in the Dayi Mountains.

despite low annual rainfall, it is relatively productive. Terracing and irrigation works have, in historic time, added to this productivity.

In the southern part of the loess highlands is a broad basin known in Chinese history as Kuan-chung, 'the area within the passes.' It is bisected by the Wei River flowing from west to east and is watered by that river and its tributaries. Historically Kuan-chung was valued for its great productivity, much diminished in modern times, and for its natural defenses: mountains to the south and east, hill country to the north and west.

The southern boundary of the Kuan-chung plain is marked by the east-west mountains which divide China into its two great climatic zones: the relatively dry north and the heavily watered south. These mountains, which are a continuation of a Tibetan range, reach, in the area south of the plain, to altitudes of 10,000 feet, and

in the past the whole belt formed one of the most formidable natural barriers in China.

The official road south from the Kuan-chung plain, built in the early imperial period, was 430 miles long, much of it built on trestles propped against mountain walls or along stream beds. The southern terminus of this road was a second fertile area, the so called Red Basin, the heart of the modern province of Szechwan. This is one of the most fertile and populous parts of China, and generations of effort have terraced all the usable hillsides. Rice is the principal crop, but a great variety of other crops are grown, and many farmers in the area are able to grow three crops a year.

In the southern part of the Szechwan basin, the Yangtse ends its steep descent from the remote Tibetan highlands and becomes navigable; this point is 1630 miles from the Pacific. When the river leaves the Szechwan plain, it shortly enters the Yangtse gorges and some of the most spectacular scenery in the world. There are sheer cliffs on either side rising one to two thousand feet, and at places narrowing the river to 150 yards. When it emerges from the gorges it becomes the main artery of the southern provinces described earlier in this section.

South of Szechwan are two large provinces that are topographically highlands and mountains, extensions of the Tibetan massif. They have little level or fertile land, and what there is is intensively cultivated. Further south and slightly to the east is the province of Kwangsi, which borders Vietnam, and the province of Kwangtung. This province, like Kwangtung to its east, has a tropical climate, but its western portion is made up of less fertile highlands.

So much for the setting. Now let us see how a great civilization developed within it.

Ancient settlements

Archeologists call China's early stage of Neolithic culture Yang-shao. The sites are scattered in a west-east band at the southernmost part of what we have called the 'loess highlands,' with some spill-over into the region beyond the great bend of the Yellow River. The settlements were concentrated for the most part in the river valleys which flowed through the loess lands. The highly porous, moisture-retentive soil was easily worked by the most primitive implements, and the principal crop was a species of millet. The early settlers may have moved their villages frequently to take advantage of fresh land. Stone arrowheads, fish-hooks and the remains of edible weeds testify to hunting, fishing and gathering as ways of supplementing the planted crops. There is evidence that these people had hemp, silk and other fabrics, and pottery vessels of all kinds, painted or decorated with cord, mat or basketry impressions abound and testify to a well developed sense of design. Their most important domesticated animals were pigs and dogs.

One excavated site provides a most detailed picture of a Yang-shao village. It was oval in shape and sited on a shelf of land safely above the river bed. In the center was the area of houses (46 have been excavated), animal pens and storage pits, surrounded by a ditch about 20 feet deep and wide. North of this area lay the pottery kilns and the village cemetery. At a later stage of occupation a kind of plaza at the center of the village was occupied by a long house, with small family houses opening into the plaza. Many of the houses were semi-subterranean with wattle-and-daub foundations and (in all probability) a thatched roof supported by posts and lintels.

The next stage in the early settlement of China

is that called Lung-shan, after the location of the first excavation that typified it. If we follow the hypothesis put forward by K C Chang and others, this second stage witnesses two momentous developments. First was the expansion of Neolithic culture across much of the alluvial plain of North China and, more thinly, into the Yangtse valley and down the southeast coast. Second was the appearance at all these sites of elements of a markedly more advanced Neolithic material culture, including both sophisticated pottery-making technique and a greater variety of vessels (called 'black pottery'); polished stone agricultural implements of considerable variety, suggesting both advanced stoneworking and more complex agriculture; rice cultivation; village walls made of pounded earth applied in layers within a wooden form – a technique that has come down to our own times; the domestication of cattle and sheep in addition to the dogs and pigs of Yang-shao culture; and concentrations of jade artifacts and differentiated burials at the same site, suggesting the beginnings of status differentiation among the people. It now seems clear that the Lung-shan culture of the late Neolithic formed the basis of the first historic civilization in North China, that of the Shang.

The bronze age and the Shang order

The term Shang denotes, first, a loose but increasingly complex political order that lasted, according to traditional dating, from 1766 to 1122 BC; and second, a cultural style that spread beyond the reach of the Shang political order and ultimately survived it. The earliest urban centers identifiable as Shang lie in the Lo basin, a fertile area watered by tributaries of the Yellow River at the eastern extremity of the loess area. Here the bronze artifacts testify to a high technological level, while the pottery, in form and decoration, shows close connections with the earlier Lung-shan culture. The earliest Shang city to be excavated is at Cheng-chow, a short distance east of the sites just mentioned. It is clearly a long-occupied site, with many strata reaching back in time, but for us its chief interest is that it was probably an early capital of the Shang (from about 1650 BC) and that it begins to reveal the character of Shang culture.

Above far left: An ornate four-legged vessel dating from China's Shang Dynasty (1766-1122 BC).

Above and left: Ritual vessels of the Shang Dynasty. Essentially an agricultural society, the Shang people believed in the ability of nature to interact with men's affairs.

Right: A jade pi-disc. These objects have been found in burial chambers, placed on or around the dead body; their function remains uncertain, however.

Rectangular in shape, the city was surrounded by a pounded earth wall 23,600 feet in circumference, 33 feet high and about 65 feet thick at the base. It has been estimated that the labor used in its construction was equal to 10,000 workers working 330 days a year for 18 years. Such a city clearly could dominate and draw upon the materials and labor of a wide area.

The city itself probably contained the center of government, the residences of the king and his nobles, ceremonial buildings, and possibly the graves of upper-class citizens. Beyond the walls there is a pottery quarter, with the remains of kilns, storage pits and the residences of the potters; a bone workshop, where large quantities of arrowheads and hairpins have been found, together with grinding stones used in their manufacture; and impressive bronze workshops, indicating advanced methods of metalworking and the relatively high social status of bronzesmiths. The fields which the farmers tilled for their own sustenance and for the support of the city lay beyond the suburbs.

Though we know little about it, the size and complexity of this ancient city reflects a relatively advanced stage of the division of labor and the articulation of classes. We may suppose that greater complexity developed as the Shang culture and political power spread over the North China Plain.

The Shang had seven capitals in succession, and the one we have just described may well have been the second, whose ancient name was Ao. Yin, the last capital of the Shang, has been the subject of major excavations carried on almost continuously in northern Honan province since 1928. Yin was the capital from 1384 BC to the fall of the Shang, traditionally said to be 1122 BC The remains of Yin not only sketch a vivid picture of life at the Shang capital but also make it possible to reconstruct much of the social and political order, and even something of the values and the world view of the Shang elite. Although no city wall has yet been found, the city of Yin and associated sites are much larger than the city at Chengchow. Yin was probably divided into three areas: one for dwellings, one for the royal palaces and one for temples and ceremonial purposes. The main structures were all of wattle-and-daub construction on pounded earth foundations, and the more important had carved marble pediments for the wooden pillars, which in turn held up the roof structure. The ceremonial altar and the temples were massive, and their construction was accompanied by many human sacrifices.

In addition to a wealth of artifacts, the chief evidence for a reconstruction of Shang society, state, and its world view are the oracle bones and shells

found at the city of Yin. By no means have all the archaic characters been deciphered, but a great deal can be learned. The question to be asked of the Unseen Powers was inscribed on the bone or shell, which was then heated. The cracks which appeared were then interpreted, and the answer inscribed and often signed with the name of the professional diviners. The system of writing is highly sophisticated, and it is clearly the forerunner of the written language of later times.

The king was very much the center of Shang life, and his activities were multifarious. His ritual calendar refers to 360 sacrifices per year. He and his nobles were inveterate hunters, in the style common to most of Asia: A wild area was chosen and surrounded with beaters who drove animals great and small into a limited space where the nobles killed them with bows and arrows or battle axes. The hunt was more than a sport, for it yielded meat, hides, fur and bones.

Throwing back the barbarians

The Shang king also made stately journeys into the hinterland to display his might and his wealth and to awe or coerce farmers along his routes into providing tribute in goods or slaves. The itineraries of several of these expeditions have been reconstructed; the most serious were military campaigns. The rich North China Plain contained clusters of people who were not yet Shang in culture, and similar people inhabited the whole periphery of the plain. Probably they were tribal hunters, gatherers and herders who looted Shang agricultural settlements whenever they could. Against these barbarians the Shang hurled their superior military forces. As time went on the area of Shang control expanded, and Shang culture spread across the plain. But the struggle was prolonged. The very last ruler of the Shang was campaigning against barbarians east and south of his capital when hostile forces from the west took the city of Yin and brought the Shang to an end.

As to the social structure of the Shang, the mass base was the tiller of the soil – whether free or bound to a specific plot of land we do not know. The tillers lived in clusters of dwellings and walked out to their fields for their endless round of toil. Villages close in to the capital possibly paid a regular proportion of their harvest to representatives of the king. Those further away may have been subject to less regular levies, or perhaps in time came under the sway of regional centers of Shang power. All the tillers were subject to labor and military service, though no details of the system are known.

Above the tillers were the artisans – the specialized makers of leather armor, chariots, the implements of war, textiles, the great ritual bronzes, bronze weapons, pottery and sumptuous sculpture in jade or stone. These were the people who made possible the elaborate life of the Shang capital. It is consistent with what we know of later times that the ateliers would be either familial or pseudo-familial in organization, with a master-craftsman passing on the shop's techniques to younger apprentices. Again, whether the artisans were bound or free we do not know, but their status and living conditions were obviously better than those of the peasants.

Far above either of these groups were the nobles. The highest ranking of the nobles were the close relatives of the king, but the nobility also included lords appointed by the king to control one or another outlying settlement and, at least late in the Shang, lords who held de facto power in distant regions and who perhaps paid tribute but were outside the reach of Shang military or political power.

Assisting the king and the nobles were diviners, genealogists, specialists in the calendar and no doubt other technical specialists about whom nothing is known. One hesitates to call this a priestly class (though the diviners and genealogists had priestly functions) because the king himself performed all the most solemn sacrifices, and the role of the specialists was to organize and prepare for the rites and to act as assistants in his performance.

The Shang king was apparently a derivative of the chieftain-priests who presided over settlements in Neolithic times. The absence of a priestly caste or class was to be typical of Chinese civilization and provides a marked contrast with what happened in India.

From the oracle bones one can infer something of the Shang view of themselves, the world, and the forces at work in it. The oracle bones contain many specific names for various barbarian tribes, suggesting that the Shang had a lively sense of their own identity and of the superiority of their culture over those of their neighbors. Secondly, there is evidence of a very strong concern with genealogy and with ancestors, particularly of the royal house. Ancestors, the living and the yet unborn form a continuum, a single blood line, and ancestors, particularly the ultimate ancestor of the royal house, had potency in the affairs of men. They had to be placated or invoked with sacrifices and prayers.

Beyond ancestor powers, the Shang people seem to have sensed a generalized potency in nature that was constantly interacting with men's affairs. Occasions when this potency favored proposed actions – hunts, wars, weddings, banquets, journeys, locating a tomb, etc. – were 'auspicious,' while others were 'inauspicious.' This notion contains the basic elements of an organic view of the universe: the heavens, all the features of earth, all the doings of man, all the unseen spirits comprise a huge and delicate organism. This concept, well developed in Shang times, is a constant and important feature of the later Chinese world view.

In the course of time Shang culture made its way across the North China Plain and into the loess highlands to the west, and artifacts of Shang type have been found scattered in more distant places. But the area of effective political control was more restricted. There is some evidence in the oracle bones of giving titles of nobility to those who were, in all probability, regional satraps. One of these titles, that of 'Lord of the West' was given to the chief of people who had established themselves in the fertile Kuan-chung area in the southern part of the modern Shensi province: the Chou.

Archeology confirms that the Chou were indebted to the Shang for all the elements of higher culture: writing, bronze-casting, architecture. But despite significant finds at the sites of two of their capitals, the record of the Chou as nominal tributaries of the Shang is sparse. But as so often happens in history, the Chou, as lords of frontier lands, developed formidable military skills which they eventually turned against the Shang. They came down from the highlands through the passes and moved against the Shang capital in the plain. The conquering army undoubtedly contained units which were recently or still 'barbarians' from the periphery of the Chou domain in the west. The Shang armies were away from the capital fighting barbarians to the east and south of it, and the Chou easily triumphed. Though it would be many years before the triumph was consolidated, this conquest heralded the coming of an entirely and different order.

The Chou kings

The Chou victory over the Shang occurred about 1100 BC, but the Shang and their barbarian allies briefly rallied, and it was a decade before firm Chou control was established. The center of Chou power remained in their ancient capital in the west, but they built a second capital at Loyang, on the eastern plain. This was done with the labor of Shang captives, and to this center the Chou moved large numbers of former Shang subjects, probably for the dual purpose of keeping a close watch on potential dissidents and adding to their skilled labor force. Loyang had further uses: as a base for operations against the barbarians of the east and south, whom the Shang had by no means eliminated, and as a center for controlling their own lords, to whom the Chou now parceled out regional power. This system, at its inception, was a new method for the control of land and populations, and, in the eye of the historian, it is also a new base line from which to follow the successive stages of evolution of the Chinese political and social order.

Authentic documents of the early Chou are few: a scattering of authentic texts, inscriptions on bronzes and the results of archeological digs. But the early Chou became idealized in the writings of generation after generation of later thinkers, and this idealization was important in the history of Chinese thought. Whether the realities of Chou rule warrented such idealization is another matter.

The Chou kings, who adopted the Shang kingly title of 'wang,' ruled directly the 'royal domain,' which included both the ancient seat of Chou in the Kuan-chung basin and a substantial area east of the mountains including the eastern capital at Loyang. But although the early Chou kings drew economic sustenance and manpower from the royal domain, they also called upon the lords, the holders of regional power, to furnish them with levies and, in the words of a contemporary inscription, to be 'a protecting fence to the royal throne.'

Beyond the royal domain those who were related to the Chou king, and perhaps some others who had participated in the conquest, were given allotments of lands and their populations. The estates given initially to the Chou lords varied in size according to the lords' degree of kinship with the kingly line and to the role they had played in the conquest. Some were large and located in long-settled and productive areas; others were small and in less-favored locations; still others were around the periphery, where war with the barbarians was endemic and there was a chance of either being over-run or, with luck, enlarging the estate through conquest. In some respects these estates resembled the feudal domains of medieval Europe, though by no means all the features of European feudalism were present. The lords controlled their populations, were ready to contribute levies to the king when he called for them and may well have sent ceremonial gifts or tribute to the king on set occasions. In the early years after their victory, the lords met to-

gether in the king's capital for a celebration commemorating that victory; such celebrations were marked by a great hunt, an archery contest, and much drinking and feasting.

The lords lived in the capitals of their estates – in some cases earthen walled cities, in others probably no more than stockaded towns. They extracted tribute in grain, cloth and other necessities from the peasants, and labor service as well. In the richer estates, the lords, their families and their functionaries (ministers) probably lived in considerable comfort, even splendor while, in the poorer estates, especially along the frontiers, life was probably fairly spartan.

Lower in social status than the lords were the families of functionaries who assisted the Chou king or his lords in matters of ritual and practical administration. For their services these families were rewarded with smaller grants of land and of the peasants attached to the land. They would then collect a proportion of the agricultural yield for their own use. This was the standard way of paying one's functionaries at a time when money was used little, if at all, when valuable goods were scarce and land abundant.

The functionaries, who served both kings and lords, though small in numbers, were all-important for the development of the civilized arts. They were masters of the ritual operations by which were managed the delicate relations among the parts of the organic universe and ancestral spirits were placated. The functionaries also kept records of genealogy and of the crop yields of the lordly domains; they served as envoys to ceremonies

being held in other estates; they divined by the tortoise and the scapula to take the auspices for their lords; they advised on diplomatic and military matters. In short they were indispensable to the exercise of power by the king in his royal domain and the lords in their domains.

At the bottom, making up the overwhelming majority of the population, were the peasants. They were bound to agricultural villages where they worked with primitive stone and wooden tools to raise the crops that kept them alive and provided something for the lord or functionary who happened to control them. They had, in addition, an annual period of labor service and were liable to recruitment as beaters for the hunt or as infantrymen for a campaign. Above the peasants were the artisans, still commoners and no doubt illiterate, but living in the capitals of the domains (certain crafts were concentrated in designated sectors of these cities). These were the people who in their workshops produced the many objects of ceremonial and daily use: great ritual bronzes, pottery, jewelry, and all the inventory of things needed for warfare and the hunt. They also designed buildings, laid out towns and supervised construction.

Chou metaphysics were at first similar to those of the Shang, stressing ancestor worship and an organic concept of creation, but in time they also made some important innovations. The Chou introduced a new supreme potency, Heaven (t'ien), which assimilated to itself the Shang high god, Shang-ti and, like Shang-ti, was the locus of the power of royal ancestors. But it seems to have

Above: A well-preserved example of Chinese bronze 'knife' money dating from 500 BC.

Left: Dating from the Chou Dynasty (1122-255 BC), this jade symbol of the Earth indicates the culture's belief that the world was square.

Far right: Part of the *Chan Kuo Tse, The Record of the Warring States.* This collection of speeches by members of the ruling elite of the Han Dynasty was uncovered in central China.

become a supreme deity as well. Its potency was more generally invoked later, but in the early Chou, the Chou kings had exclusive access to it, in special rituals. The Chou kings were referred to as Son of Heaven (*T'ein-tzu*), and this expressed the special relation they had to the supreme deity. More generally there was the potency of earth, and this was invoked, especially for fertility, in the royal capital, in the lords' domains and very probably in the villages at a shrine, generally called the earth mound. This complex of inter-related potencies was to be controlled by appropriate prayers and sacrifices, and the proper balancing of all these operations was the responsibility of the Chou king and his lords, assisted by skilled functionaries. The proper oracles, leading to ritually perfect performances on exactly the right occasions were believed to lead to that cosmic balance of forces which was the highest good. Here is the lament of a king of the ninth century BC whose measures against a drought brought no relief:

Bright was that milky way,
Shining and revolving in the heavens.
The king said, 'Oh!
What crime are we charged with now,
That Heaven sends down death and disorder?
Famine comes again and again . . .
I have not ceased offering pure sacrifices;
From the suburban altars to Heaven and Earth
I have gone to the ancestral temple.
To the powers above and below I have made my
offerings . . .
There is no spirit I have not honored.
But the Millet God has not delivered us
And Shang-ti has not come to us . . .

Because the political ideology of the early Chou became permanently embedded in the Chinese idea of monarchy, it has an importance that transcends the Chou period itself. The Chou king, as we have seen, was a cosmic pivot – the human who had the most power to keep all the unseen forces in the universe working in harmony. How had he acquired such awesome responsibilities accompanied by power over the lands and peoples of North China? What, indeed, had justified his forcible replacement of the ancient Shang ruling house? Through the elaborate rhetoric of the archaic texts which survive we are able to see the answers the Chou conquerors gave to these questions. Because, they said, the Shang had declined, because their rulers were lechers and drunkards, because they neglected their people when they were not oppressing them, all the human factors in the great cosmic harmony became grossly out of balance. So Heaven, through the divinations, sent the message to the Chou leaders that they were to take over. They were to receive Heaven's appointment, the Mandate of Heaven (*t'ien-ming*). This established the Chou's right to rule, but it also introduced into Chinese political thought the idea that one could rule only so long as he dealt justly with his lords and equitably with his subjects.

Another element of political ideology which appears at this time is the idea of the 'Central Kingdom.' A text which may date from the early Chou reads: 'Great Heaven, having given this *central kingdom*, with its people and territory, to the former kings, do you, our present sovereign employ your virtue, effecting a gentle harmony among the deluded people . . .' This idea of the Central Kingdom, located at the epicenter of the world – with the nearer and more distant barbarians stretching away in the four directions, and with its ruler radiating the power to civilize and transform – this is still a fundamental image of the Chinese world view, and has remained so over the millenia.

Transformation of the Chou order

The early or Western Chou system lasted until 771 BC, when the Chou king was defeated by nomadic tribes in the west and driven from the ancient seat of his ancestors in the Kuan-chung basin. The royal domain was greatly reduced in size, and the one remaining capital at Loyang became little more than a ceremonial center, a locus of legitimacy. No longer was it a base for control of the lords of the eastern plain or of the peoples of the Yangtse valley. Who then exercised the political and military power which had once been the Chou king's? This devolved upon the most important lords of the great domains, who had, in fact, been slowly accumulating it for a century or two before. These lords destroyed all but the strongest of the 40 or so estates that had been set up in the wake of the Chou conquest and engrossed their land and populations. In so doing they became militarily strong enough as defenders of the frontiers to push back or assimilate the barbarians, thus expanding the territory of their own domains even more. Finally, they legitimized the autonomy of their new domains – states, really – by fabricating genealogies linking their rulers to the Chou kingly house. The most striking example of this last is the state of Ch'u, which spread over the whole central southern part of the great plain and reached well beyond the Yangtse.

The net effect was of course a vastly altered map of China. The frontiers had been pushed out in all directions, mainly at the expense of the barbarians of the periphery. The domains had been greatly reduced in number and expanded in land area. And the royal domain had been as shrunken in size as it was in political power.

Political change on such a scale – and it was to continue for the next four centuries – was accompanied by the most sweeping social and cultural changes. The power of the remaining hereditary ruling houses gradually ebbed away, and from about 650 BC on, the families of high functionaries pushed their way into *de facto* control of many of the great estates. Then, from the beginning of the fifth century, as war and competition among the great estates sharpened, people of even lower social status – people from minor functionary families or upstart military leaders – replaced the older ministerial families. In the largest and strongest of these petty states government became more impersonal and bureaucratized. The dues in kind which a subject might once have taken to a lord's capital were replaced by regular taxes and land rents. A much larger bureaucratic class grew up to administer this system. And, as one would expect, the capitals of the states had to be rebuilt and expanded to accommodate this elaborated style of government.

Cities also became centers of trade and citadels for defense against the aggression of a neighbor. Between 722 and 480 BC there are records of the building of 78 new towns. This is probably only a fraction of what was built in reality, and the pace of building probably increased after the year 480. Cities also grew in size, and there is evidence from archeology of functional zoning within the pounded earth walls: an area for ceremonial uses and aristocratic residence, an area for artisans, an area for shops and commerce and in some cases an area of fields for intensive farming within the outer wall.

There is evidence of active inter-state and inter-city trade, and communication routes, both by land and by water were gradually established, but equally important was the steady proliferation of inter-state war. This was frequent from about 700 BC onward, and almost incessant in the period the

Chinese refer to as that of the 'Warring States,' from about 450 to 221 BC

It is against this background of sweeping change, growth and endemic violence that China's first true philosophers appeared. They were for the most part people personally affected by the drastic changes going on around them, men perhaps deprived of hereditary privileges or men who were highly trained but unemployed. They were all versed in one or more traditions of their culture: in legend and folklore, oral and written history and literature; in complex ritual procedures; in astronomy-astrology; in statecraft; or in the art of war. And all of them were concerned with trying to understand what had gone wrong with their society and finding ways to set things right.

They took their diagnoses and prescriptions to the courts of the various states and there propounded them, if they were fortunate enough to get a hearing, before the ruler. The rulers, being mostly illiterate, often enjoyed listening to these itinerant talkers, with their pithy anecdotes and illustrative tales, as a change from their usual dancing troupes, performing dwarfs and musicians. Occasionally, they even listened with care, but seldom were the power-holders willing to adopt any set of prescriptions in their totality or to give their advocate what he almost invariably wanted – a ministerial position.

Between 400 and 350 BC there was a host of such thinkers wandering from state to state, often accompanied by disciples. They ranged from propounders of theories of agricultural management to word-players, people who, with the newly discovered resources of language, could turn propositions inside out or make nonsense of the most commonsensical assertions. We cannot deal with all these thinkers, with all the groups that made this the age of the 'hundred schools.' But three of these schools had such a profound influence on all subsequent Chinese civilization that we must pause to consider them, however briefly. These are the school of Confucius, the school of Tao and the school of Law (fa).

Confucius, who lived from about 551 to 479 BC was easily one of the most influential teachers in human history, yet we know little about the man. He was a native of the state of Lu, very near the center of the earliest Chinese civilization. He seems to have been, like many other early thinkers, educated, but without a position of any consequence and without a regular income. After seeking official employment in neighboring states he returned to Lu and opened a school for the sons of the noble and well-to-do. There, according to tradition, he taught the 'winter curriculum' which consisted of music, the reading and memorization of the ancient books and the rules of proper deportment, ie manners for court and social intercourse as well as ceremonial occasions. During his wanderings from court to court, and later in his school, he developed his principal ideas. He looked about him at the society in which he lived, with its militarists, charlatans and upstarts of all kinds pushing aside the older elite, and he felt a profound revulsion. Looking for a model of the way things *should* be, he found it in

a greatly idealized picture of the Chou in the years just after the conquest. That society, as he saw it across five centuries, had been an ideal hierarchy, with the king and his faithful minister, the Duke of Chou at the top, with the lords and functionaries performing their ritual and practical duties to perfection and the common people contented and productive.

How could such an ideal state of things be revived? Here he propounds no system but, in the sayings that have come down to us, he recommends certain values and courses of action over others, for he deeply believed in the power of cultivated men to affect for the better the whole social climate in which, they live. 'When gentlemen deal generously with their own kin, the

common people are incited to Goodness. When old dependents are not discarded, the common people will not be fickle.' For him the power for reconstituting society lies in the perfected man. Such men are not born good, though he assumes that all men have inherent proclivities toward the good. Rather, they must strive to attain perfection through the study of the oral and written traditions which had come down from the past. His sayings are full of admonitions on self-discipline, on the rejection of anything morally compromising, on maintaining self-respect in adversity, on the proper observance of ritual prescriptions – in short on all the ways in which a man is to overcome his appetites and become wise, good and effective.

All such struggle is directed toward public service, toward finding office under a just prince. Yet Confucius' prescription, with its emphasis on moral perfection and the moral transformation of society, had little appeal for the fearful or callous rulers of his day. It was the work of two successors to develop and defend Confucius' ideas and keep Confucianism in active competition with the other schools through the fifth and fourth centuries BC.

Mencius was born about a century after Confucius. He, like his master before him, was born in the state of Lu, and like his master, traveled vainly through various states in search of official employment. He did, however, spend considerable time at the court of the great state of Ch'i, to the north of Lu, which attracted itinerant thinkers and talkers of all schools. There he laid his interpretations of the principles of Confucius before a sophisticated ruler. Mencius shows in these dialogues that he believes the restoration of peace and the return of order should begin with moral reconstruction, that if the rulers reform themselves and appoint ministers who are themselves exemplars of the virtues, then the people will be moved to reform and the state will prosper and will have nothing to fear from its predatory neighbors. The King of Ch'i, who reveled in the pleasures of his exalted position and who was deeply enmeshed in the system of alliances and counteralliances which maintained a precarious balance of power in the land, was unconvinced. Mencius is best regarded as a political moralist, as one who elaborated the principles of public and private morality that had been implicit in Confucius' teaching. In doing this he became a resourceful polemicist. In theoretical terms he does not differ greatly from Confucius, except, perhaps, that he lays greater stress on innate human goodness, and even this deviation may have been less a matter of theory than a device for scoring debaters' points.

Hsün-tzu was born about 320, when the struggle among the various states was growing in intensity. By the time of his maturity, the number of remaining states was reduced to seven, and in 256, the last remnant of the shrunken Chou royal domain was eliminated. At the same time, the great states of the north, west and south had expanded outward, taking in the cultures of a wide variety of barbarians. Hsün-tzu traveled widely through the contending states, and is said to have had brief and unsatisfactory official employment in several of them. No doubt the tough and somber tone of his writings reflects his observations of contemporary life. His view of man's innate nature is different from Mencius; he holds that man is a bundle of desires, passions and aversions and that these must be controlled. The sages of antiquity invented standards of morality and delimited social classes to provide this. Thus the way to harmonious order is for a ruler to instill morality in his people, teach them the norms (li), the fabric of moral standards. This should be done by education, and whenever necessary by the use of rewards and punishments. The advice he gives to rulers is toughminded: advance the worthy; kill the incorrigible; realize that inequality among subjects is essential to the functioning of the state and prevents disorder; always have up-to-date and detailed statistical knowledge of your state; and so on. His harsh and practical tone, and especially his suggestion that the Confucian in office should bend to the wind of circumstances, show Hsün-tzu to have staked out a new position for the Confucians: that of realistic, hard-headed manipulators of political actualities.

The group of thinkers we call Taoists presented a diagnosis and a set of prescriptions for the ills of mankind quite different from those of Confucians. What was wrong was not the falling away from ideal standards prescribed by the sage kings of long ago. The root of men's ills was the existence of standards themselves, and, in the eyes of the Taoists, the 'sages' were to blame for them. What the Taoists would have man do was to strip away the impedimenta of civilization and let the natural organic harmony of the universe reassert itself. They called the all-pervading force making for such harmony the Tao, and its modes of operating yin and yang. In the poetic phrases of the two great books of this school, the Chuang-tzu and the Lao-tzu, (also called the Tao-te ching) the writers make fun of all laws and conventions, ridicule the solemn Confucians, parody the wordmongers, denounce as totally misleading all verbal statements. What they prescribe is the natural life, free of all convention and constraint, a gentle regimen – including breath control – designed to bring one into consonance with the Tao. One who follows this may become a hsien, a genie, and wander beyond space and time. If all follow it society will become a frictionless anarchy, and frenetic activity and competition will be replaced by quiet passivity. This was, of course, another response to a time of troubles – a response that is mystical, aesthetic and individualistic, that recommends withdrawal. It could hardly have swayed the war-hardened rulers of the day, but it expressed then, and continued to express in the millennia which followed, a view of life and time with immense appeal for all manner of men.

Almost inevitably there emerged toward the end of this troubled time a school of thought that advocated the use of coercion and draconian methods of social control. The members of this school are called the 'Realists' or 'Legalists.' One of their leaders had studied with Hsün-tzu but had chosen to follow out to its logical end Hsün-tzu's

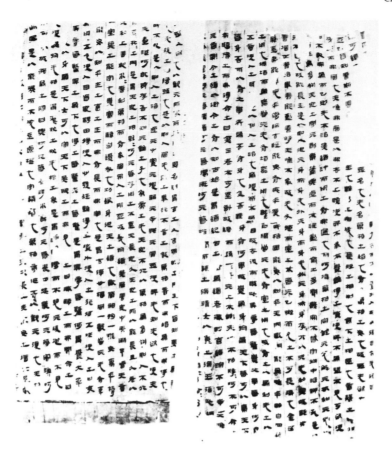

Left: An extract from the book Laotzu, one of the two great works of the Taoist school of thought.

Below: A bronze mirror from the Han Dynasty (206 BC-AD 220). Decoration comprises a green dragon, white tiger, scarlet bird and tortoise – symbols of the four seasons and the four quadrants of the sky and earth.

view of the nature of man and the role of authority. The Realists cut through the conflicting opinions of the thinkers of all schools and came to drastic simplifications: The days of the sages are long past; the principles they taught are now irrelevant and inapplicable; men should devise new measures to suit their times. The key problem of this time was the survival of the state, and the Realists developed detailed policies which, they maintained, would assure the state's survival and prosperity. First of all it was necessary to get rid of what they called the 10 evils: ritual, music, the Book of Poetry, the Book of History (beloved of the Confucians), virtue, moral culture, filial piety, brotherly duty, integrity and sophistry. Then they said, 'If the state eliminates these 10 things and the ruler can make his people fight, he will prosper and attain supremacy.' To eliminate those evils – which amount to all the bases of private or individual standards, as well as most of the heritage of Chinese civilization to that date – called for severe measures. The books which contained this heritage were to be declared subversive and those found in possession of them executed. The people who passed these things on orally were all to be liquidated. The population of the state would thus be reduced to a mindless mass, infinitely malleable to the king's will, knowing nothing but agriculture and war.

The machinery they recommended to accomplish this cultural and social revolution was first of all the centralized bureaucratic state and secondly the 'law.' The law the Realists propounded bears few resemblances to Western law as it has evolved from Roman times. Basically it was not a collection of rights, contractual formulas and the like, but an instrument to promote the strength of the state and uniformity and conformity among the governed. It was totalitarian in intent, ie, it prescribed for everything in life for all the people under any and all circumstances. The ratio of reward to punishment was to be one to 10: 10 units for a demerit; one unit for a comparable merit. He who denounced a violator of the law was to get the same reward as he who takes an

enemy's head in battle. He who failed to denounce an infractor was to be cut in two at the waist. And so on.

This ruthless and self-consistent scheme for controlling the people and building the power of the state might well have become one of the curiosities of the history of thought, save for the fact that it was adopted by one of the most aggressive states and was then used by that state to establish China's first unified empire. But before turning to these momentous events, let us pause to recapitulate some of the dimensions of change in the years from around 750 to 250 BC.

The area of 'Chinese' order had expanded southward into the Yangtse valley and beyond, northeasterly into the valley of the Liao River and southwest to begin the settlement of Szechwan. Agriculture was improved in countless ways: mules, donkeys, and camels were introduced, as well as the ox-drawn plow, and improved cultivation over ever-widening areas spurred a significant population growth. Technology advanced

rapidly, as iron implements replaced costlier bronze. Large public works were undertaken in many of the states: canals for irrigation and communication, roads, massive walls along the borders of the northern and western states, new walled cities referred to earlier. Horse archers armed with the crossbow came into use about the year 300 and quickly replaced the chariots used in earlier warfare. Archeological finds testify to the wealth and the rich material culture of the major cities, to the increasing sophistication of artisan skills.

Thus a period that saw the breakdown of old institutions, the destruction of ancient states, incessant warfare and massive human suffering at the same time witnessed an explosion of technology, a great expansion of populated land area and a vast increase in knowledge and speculative thought. For reasons both negative and positive, the stage was set for the coming of a new order.

The conquest of the Ch'in

In 361 BC a Realist attained what all the itinerant thinkers had dreamed of: the post of chief minister under a prince well-disposed to his ideas. The man who persuaded his way into this situation was Shang Yang, and his master was the ruler of the western state of Ch'in. The center of Ch'in was in the rich Kuan-chung basin where the Chou had had their capitals down to 771 BC. The cultural level here was relatively low compared to the civilized states in the great plain. Constant warfare against hostile neighbors – including the steppe peoples to the west and north – had bred a strong military tradition, and the ruling princes tended to be men of action and to be unencumbered by learning, traditions and moral scruples. Thus Shang Yang, who came from the east, found it relatively easy to implement the ruthless policies prescribed by the law. Indeed, he did his work so well that even after his death (he was accused of plotting rebellion and torn apart by four chariots) Realists continued to dominate the Ch'in court.

As the people were shaped according to Realist principles, the productivity of the land steadily increased, and a formidable war machine also

gradually developed. As occasion offered, it was thrown against one or another state in the east, and in the 20 years preceding 222 BC Ch'in attacked without mercy and almost without surcease. The states of the plain formed a north-south alliance, but to no avail. The first of China's great historians describes the end of this process:

... the north-south alliance collapsed, its treaties came to naught, and the various states hastened to present Ch'in with parts of their territories as bribes for peace. With its superior strength Ch'in pressed the crumbling forces of its rivals, pursued those who had fled in defeat, and overwhelmed and slaughtered the army of a million until their shields floated upon a river of blood. Following up the advantages of its victory, Ch'in gained mastery over the empire and divided up its mountains and rivers.

The prince who had won this bloody and unprecedented victory immediately had a decision to make: he could divide the conquered lands among his relatives and top generals, or he could attempt to impose on the whole land the centralization that had been tried with such success in Ch'in. Under the influence of the last of the great Realist statesmen, Li Ssu, he chose the second course, and that choice was to have incalculable effects on the subsequent history of China. Thereafter the norm to which the Chinese always sought to return was political and cultural unity. The kind of regional fragmentation characteristic of most of Indian and European history became the exception, not the rule.

A new title had to be chosen for the first ruler of a unified empire, and the Prince of Ch'in, in 221 BC became Ch'in Shih-huang-ti, 'First Sovereign Emperor of the line of Ch'in.' In calling himself 'First' he stated in an edict that he envisioned his descendants calling themselves 'second,' third' and 'so unto a thousand and ten thousand generations.' His prime minister began to develop a new ideology and mystique of supreme emperorship but we shall delay discussion of this until the next section. The measures the Ch'in took to consolidate their victory and establish the new system are of staggering sweep and ruthless boldness. To get rid of the Chou order and the remains

of the old multi-state system was the first objective. Princely families were simply liquidated, though the new emperor took care to have their ancestral halls reconstructed at his own capital so that the ghosts could be placated. Old families which had served in the various states and commanded prestige and influence were uprooted and moved – 120,000 of them – to the imperial capital of Hsienyang in the Kuan-chung basin: the explicit object was 'to strengthen the trunk and weaken the branches.' The old state boundaries were obliterated, and the land was divided into rational administrative units: 36 commanderies, each subdivided into counties. The walls of towns which made them potentially useful as strongpoints in a counter-revolution were ordered destroyed. The farm-lands within the administrative districts were distributed to the cultivators; under the Ch'in system these new holders had no dues or obligations of the old kind, but simply paid a tax in kind – usually grain – to the representative of the emperor. To assure an increased farming population the state offered bounties to large families.

The break with the past, so essential to the Realist formula, was reinforced by other measures: the destruction and banning of ancient books and harsh measures to prevent Confucian scholars from earning a living by teaching. Going along with this was a group of measures to level the population *down* so that they would be docile subjects of the monarch. The numerous armies of the various states presented a problem; if left together in their home areas they might form into rebel or restorationist forces. So the emperor broke them up, and the former soldiers were assigned to building projects all over the empire: building roads, palaces and canals, constructing at the northern end of the North China Plain the Great Wall, an assignment from which many did not return.

All these measures were made effective by a corps of bureaucrats recruited according to merit and serving at the emperor's pleasure. Above them, and pervading all parts of life in the whole realm, was the law, applied without mercy and re-

Left: The Great Wall of China was originally built before the third century BC although it was extended and repaired by the king of the Ch'in in 221 BC.

Right: Bamboo slips recording the laws of the Ch'in Dynasty. The lefthand slip records a system of weights and measures and lists punishments for offenders who broke the code.

Far right: One of the terracotta warriors unearthed near the tomb of Ch'in Shih-huang-ti.

inforced by the system of mutual surveillance (*pao-chia*) notable for its cheapness, effectiveness and utter inhumanity. Briefly, it divided all the population into groups of 10 families. Then if one member of one family committed a crime, the group was obliged to report it. If they did not, and it was detected, every member of all 10 families would be subject to severe punishment.

The new unified empire required uniform communications and standards for its efficient functioning. During the preceding period a great diversity of writing styles, weights, measures, coinage and so on had developed within the various states. The Ch'in, with its formidable apparatus of law and officialdom, simply decreed new empire-wide standards and appropriate punishments for those who perversely held to the old. Thus, there were uniform standards in everything from writing to the length of cart axles.

The arrogance and power of the Ch'in, and particularly of the First Emperor, Ch'in Shih-huang-ti (221-210 BC), is probably best expressed by the scale of their physical monuments. *Cyclopean* is a word that springs to mind. The 1864-mile-long Great Wall, begun under the supervision of General Meng T'ien around 214 BC to keep out Hunnish invaders from the north, is only the most famous of these relics. Almost as celebrated is the incredible underground mausoleum that Ch'in Shih-huang-ti constructed at Mount Li, 25 miles east of present-day Sian, capital of Shensi province. Discovered in 1974, the Mount Li site, with its approximately 7000 exquisitely carved lifesize terracotta statues of fully armed warriors and their horses, has been called the 'most spectacular excavation of modern archaeology,' and to this day it continues to reveal a cornucopia of unexpected details about Ch'in civilization. And there was much more: large-scale water conser-

vancy projects, a grandiose network of imperial trunk roads, the great complex of new palaces and temples at Hsienyang, the gigantic palace at A-fang. The numbers of laborers that must have been required for these works, all completed in a comparatively brief period, is staggering. A Han historian, Ssu-ma Ch'ien (145-*c* 90 BC), says that 700,000 workers were used for the Mount Li and A-fang projects alone. Some modern estimates of the labor force dedicated to all of Ch'in Shih-huang-ti's various constructions run as high as three million, or 15 percent of the total population.

The Ch'in system, as it was imposed across the

land, naturally generated resentments of all kinds among all those who had benefited in any way from the old order – among the noble families, who were now transported to the Ch'in capital, and among their former retainers, who were now forced into labor gangs far from home; among quite ordinary people who preferred local and customary ways of handling the frictions of life to the impersonal laws murderously enforced by bureaucrats from the capital. In the end, it was the severity of fixed punishments that provoked the first armed revolt. A poor farmer was ordered to report, with 900 other conscripts, for garrison duty at a distant town. Along the way the rain was

Above: Some of the rows of terracotta warriors, dating from the Ch'in period, discovered in 1974 in Xian.

Left: An impressed brick dating from the Han Dynasty, uncovered from a tomb.

Right: Detail of a Han Dynasty brick relief showing a chariot at speed.

heavy, and the party made poor progress through the mud. So the farmer appealed to his fellows:

Because of the rain . . . we cannot reach our rendezvous on time. And anyone who misses a rendezvous has his head cut off! Even if you should somehow escape with your heads, six or seven out of every 10 of you are bound to die in the course of garrison duty. Now, my brave fellows, if you are unwilling to die, we have nothing more to say. But if you would risk death, then let us risk it for the sake of fame and glory!

This was simply the spark that set off a series of revolts all over the country. Some rebels rallied for a time around local leaders. Soon regional strong men pulled together the rebel bands into armies. The heirs of the old ruling houses and their followers also rose against the Ch'in. Less than 15 years after the proclamation of universal empire, the Ch'in was destroyed, and the land was plunged into another period of destructive civil war. The fortunes of war ebbed and flowed; at times it seemed that the champions of the old decentralized aristocratic order might triumph, but finally – after a terrible struggle – a tough commoner, or man who had been a local constable and part-time farmer under the Ch'in, won the day, and on 28 February, 202 BC assumed the title of Sovereign Emperor and proclaimed the dynasty of Han.

The Han empire

It is often said that the Ch'in Dynasty, brief as it was, prepared the way for the Han and for its success. It is true that the Ch'in, in its rise to power and in its brief tenure, performed the drastic surgery needed to eliminate old ways and old norms, thus making possible a new social and political order. More than this, it left a legacy of institutions which became part of the Han imperial order and thereafter part of the imperial system that lasted, through many vicissitudes, until 1912.

In beginning to describe the Han order, the first thing to be specified is what it took over from the Ch'in. First, and most important, was the concept of a unified empire. Notions of unity and also uni-formity in the Chinese cultural area had been discussed by several of the thinkers of the late Chou, but the Ch'in, by the most drastic and ruthless measures, had actually brought such a unified empire into being. This empire, in its conception, was something very different from many more recent empires, such as the Byzantine, Spanish or the Austro-Hungarian. It was not based on a metropolitan center, with semi-autonomous subject peoples around the periphery or at the other end of the sea-lanes from the capital. It was conceived as co-terminous with the civilized world, and it was referred to as T'ien-hsia, 'under heaven.' It was far more than a political arrangement. The emperor had an extensive network of divine relations with the land, as space, with its mountains and rivers, and with the stars and, indeed, the whole cosmos. Thus the complex of ritual responsibilities for the harmony of the world that had begun to accumulate around the Shang kings a millennium earlier was now incorporated into the concept of a single Chinese empire and of its single imperial ruler.

We have noted that the First Sovereign Emperor of the short-lived Ch'in was in name and in fact a new kind of ruler – all-powerful, the center of networks of controls which were designed to regulate every level of activity in the empire. The title 'huang-ti,' which we translate as 'emperor,' is made up of two words of great antiquity and accumulated potency. One interpretation is that it evokes the potency of the legendary rulers and culture heroes of misty antiquity, namely the three 'Huang' and the five 'Ti.' But it is more likely that the term 'huang,' which had the meaning of majestic or awesome, was combined with 'ti,' which under the Shang had had a religious meaning but had been gradually secularized during the Chou. The Han founder was persuaded to take this awesome title, despite its recent use by the hated Ch'in rulers, in 202 BC, and for the next 21 centuries it was used to refer to all the emperors of China. Each of its components has supernatural and cosmic overtones to underline the cosmic responsibilities of the emperor.

The central bureaucracy that carried out the Han emperor's orders was, initially, very much a continuation of the Ch'in system. The nine ranking ministers divided among their offices similar governmental functions under the Ch'in and Han, and five out of nine had the same titles under the two dynasties. Some of the ministers with well defined functions reflected in their titles were the Commandant of Palace Guards, the Minister of Justice, the Minister of Agriculture and the Treasurer of the Imperial Household. One of the most powerful was the Minister of Ceremonies, who had many responsibilities beyond the ceremonial; for example, his office screened the candidates for public office sent up from the commanderies and supervised the Imperial Academy that had been set up in the capital for their training.

The administrative system of 36 commanderies (chün), each divided into counties (hsien), that the Ch'in had devised was taken over by the Han, who continued to staff the local units with central government appointees. But there were complications, for the Han founder had been obliged to parcel out a measure of regional power to his relatives and companions-in-arms as rewards for their contributions to the Han victory. The country was thus divided into local units of administration *and* into princedoms, with the imperially appointed governors of the commanderies meant to keep watch on the princes and to warn of any signs of subversion or separatism.

There was a cultural difference between the capital area in the west and the princedoms of the eastern plain; the plain was, after all, the ancient center of Chinese civilized life, and the princes there attracted men of talent and learning to their courts. The jealousies and rivalry between the two areas are reflected in contemporary texts, for example, a recommendation for a teacher at the Imperial University in the capital read: 'He has had no record of communicating with the princes nor accepting their gifts,' and an old regulation that no subject of any principality could take office at the capital no matter how great his ability. Nevertheless, in the reign of Emperor Wu (140-87 BC), the principalities were finally eliminated, their locally prominent supporters were uprooted and moved to the capital area and support for regional or separatist movements was dispersed. The Ch'in system of local government exclusively by appointees from the capital had finally prevailed. It thus became the norm to which all strong dynasties always returned.

In the early Han many Ch'in laws remained in effect, even that which banned Confucian books. But the Han, during the four centuries of its life, developed its own elaborate code of laws. Toward the end of the second century AD the published commentaries on the law numbered 26,272 paragraphs. Yet the law under the Han, as it had been under the Ch'in, remained principally an instrument by which the state controlled, coerced and punished the emperor's subjects. The harshness of the laws was scarcely less than those of the Ch'in, and this is reflected in the punishments laid down in the portions of the Han code which survive, for example, beheading, cutting in two at the waist, extermination of relatives of the criminal, boiling alive, castration and so on.

There was another aspect of the law that is equally important. The law provided the basis for an *impersonal* government, whereby the ruler treated all people of the same classes, or those guilty of similar crimes, according to common rules which his officials enforced. And this in turn meant that officials could not, under such a system, be local worthies who knew their neighbors and local conditions. On the contrary, they

structure of relatively heavy and centralized government was greatly modified by a cluster of other elements that served as social and cultural counterweights. Above the voiceless mass of the peasantry were literate and landed families, living in the varied regions of the empire but most heavily concentrated in the North China Plain. They had been able to accumulate land and wealth and to educate their sons, and they commanded respect in their localities. In the early part of the Han dynasty some members of these families took service at the courts of the regional princes. Later, a family might occasionally secure a recommendation for a promising young member to enter the imperial academy in the capital, and if he succeeded at the academy and in a succession of offices, he would bring fame and wealth to his family and thus add to its local prestige. Yet the Han emperors, like the Ch'in before them and others after them, were often fearful of these local elites as potential threats to the central government. The strong centralizing Emperor Wu of the Han (140-87 BC) promulgated a series of drastic measures to curb their power, including the transplanting of groups of such families to the west to be hereditary guardians of the precincts of imperial tombs. Yet to exterminate the whole class was unthinkable, even if it had been possible, and the Han state needed literate men both at the local level, to keep records, collect taxes and adjudicate disputes, and at the state level, to guide the emperor's varied decisions and to provide the specialized learning he needed in the performance of his duties. By the same token, the families needed a powerful state to defend them against the evils of attack from without and rebellion from within, the two catastrophes most likely to destroy their accumulated wealth and their privileged position. For them to live with that power was always tense and difficult; to live without it was impossible.

The second counterweight to the centralized power of the state was cultural – specifically, the complex of knowledge, lore and traditions which was to be found mainly in the ancient writings, in books written on bamboo slips, wooden plaques or on rolls of silk. These were the writings of the Chou period which had survived the two decades of murderous warfare that led to the Ch'in triumph and had then survived both the Ch'in destruction of ancient books and the violent civil war which followed the Ch'in's downfall. Much was lost, but some families had hidden the banned books, and after the Han triumph, still others joined in the collection of surviving fragments. One leader in this was the Prince of Ho-chien (d. 132 BC), who presided over one of the princedoms in the North China Plain and was on excellent terms with the local elite.

Restoring a cultural heritage

What was thus salvaged, combined with traditionally approved ways of doing things, comprised the cultural heritage of the local elites. Among the fragmentary texts were sections of the ancient *Books of Odes*, in part transcriptions of folk songs of the middle Chou or before. Even more important was the *Book of History*, a miscellaneous collection of official edicts, speeches and the like; the sayings of the great moral and political thinkers; parts of the canonical rituals of some of the states; and the dry annals *(ch'un-ch'iu)* of the state of Lu, which Confucius was alleged to have edited. Also surviving, or pieced together from fragments, were less formal works: stories, handbooks of strategy and such like. From parts of it the literate elite taught their sons to read and write; from other parts (and no doubt

were intended to be the emperor's servants carrying out the laws and regulations wherever they might be with strict impartiality and, in theory, with total disregard for local and individual variations. Thus the idea of the strict and responsible official is closely tied in with law and with the impersonal government that the law implied. But how were such officials to be recruited, trained and supervised? Here we find another institution which, in idea and practice, the Han inherited from the Ch'in.

The roots of an impersonal system of recruiting officials go back to the increasingly complex states of the late Chou, where centralized government was already well advanced. We know the bare outlines of the Ch'in system of recruitment, but few details. The Han founder, in 196 BC, issued an order to the governors of the commanderies which read in part:

If any of the governors has among his people men with an excellent reputation and manifest virtue, such people are to be persuaded to come to the imperial capital. They are to be provided with a chariot and sent to the offices of the State Chancellor where their accomplishments, their appearance and their age shall be made a matter of record. If an official fails to recommend such people and this becomes known, he shall be dismissed . . .

It will be noted that in this first order there was no mention of mastery of texts, which were later to become an important criterion, nor for any other of the specific virtues advocated by the Confucians. It was simply an urgent request for people qualified to become bureaucrats, and as such might have been issued by the Ch'in. Yet it was obviously necessary to have training schools where talent arriving from the commanderies might be instructed in their administrative tasks. Such schools were gradually established in the capital, and, as we shall see, in time became centers of a renaiscent Confucianism.

Once the idea of using well-endowed, trained and responsible officials developed, there inevitably arose the problem of how to make sure they did their duty honestly and well. Officials in the capital administration were under the direct supervision of their superiors, and malfeasance was punished, perhaps not as drastically as it had been under the Ch'in, but severely. Inspectors to check on the administrators in the various commanderies had been begun by the Ch'in, and the institution was continued and elaborated by the Han. A fragment of a Han document that survived in the arid lands of the west reads: 'in the . . . month inspections are held, and the good marks for the various classes of administrators are fixed . . . This procedure is well known to the Governors of Commanderies and to the officials of the princedoms. Not to obey imperial edicts relating to this is to be sentenced . . . ' Out of these various supervisory measures there developed the elaborate Censorate – a standard and much-feared fixture of every subsequent imperial government.

It was a basic principle of the Realist statesmen of the Ch'in empire that the government should have up-to-date figures on all things that affected the state's welfare: the number of people, the amount of land under cultivation, the number of draft animals, the amount of stored grain. The Han and later empires adopted this, and the first Han census – used primarily for the assessment of taxes and labor service quotas – was carried out in AD 2. In the first two centuries of Han rule the government had to make do with less systematic surveys, but the idea of statistical control – yet another part of the legacy of Ch'in – was built into the Han imperial system.

I have stressed the Ch'in heritage not merely because it was important for the Han but because it deeply influenced all later dynasties. Yet this

eminent for its unspoiled naturalness. The *Book of Rites* regulates social distinctions and therefore is pre-eminent for order and refinement. The *Classic of Music* intones virtue and therefore is pre-eminent in its influencing power. The *Book of History* records achievements and is therefore pre-eminent concerning events. The *Book of Changes* takes Heaven and Earth as its bases and therefore is best for calculating probabilities. The *Ch'un-ch'iu* of the State of Lu rectifies right and wrong and therefore stands pre-eminent in ruling men.

The *Classic of Music*, if it ever existed, has disappeared, but the Chinese, like the ancient Greeks, regarded music as morally uplifting. The *Book of Changes* was originally a handbook for taking auguries by throwing milfoil stalks, and it is doubtful if Confucius knew it or esteemed it. The *Book of Rites*, put together in Han times is an authoritarian and rigorous set of prescriptions: one suspects Confucius would have found it profoundly antipathetic. Yet such texts became the core of what, by a process of accretion, eventually became the Thirteen Classics.

Tung Chung-shu and his successors continually pressed the claims of their learning. They got 'chairs' for the various texts established in the Imperial Academy, and before long they had it made the basis for examination for public office. And they wanted it to be the *sole* way of thought. Here is Tung Chung-shu addressing his sovereign:

Your unworthy servant considers that all which is not encompassed by the Six Disciplines and the arts of Confucius should be suppressed and not allowed to continue further, and evil and vain theories stamped out. Only then will unity be achieved, the laws be made clear, and the people know what to follow.

But the victory of this kind of imperial orthodoxy was never as complete as Tung Chung-shu wanted it to be. Other traditions and a variety of independent thinkers continued to thrive in Han China. And several strong emperors in the Han, and throughout Chinese history, were impatient with the archaism and the moralism of the Confucians. A Han emperor's response to his son's and heir's recommendation that he appoint more Confucians typifies this attitude:

The Han dynasty has its own institutions, based on a mixture of the practices of the Confucians' ideal kings and of the Lords Protectors (the tough practitioners of Real-politik who flourished towards the end of the Chou). Why should I put my faith only in moral instruction (as the Confucians urge) . . . Moreover the vulgar Confucians do not understand what is appropriate to our times; they love to approve the ancient and disapprove the present, making the people confused . . . Why on earth should they be entrusted with responsibility? (Dubs II.301)

So much for the theoretical and intellectual bases of Han rule. Physically, the Han Empire was, at its greatest extent (around the beginning of the Christian era), immense. The capital, Ch'ang-an, in the plain 'within the passes,' was a dusty, untidy, ever-growing city where the symmetry which, it was thought, should govern the activities of the Son of Heaven was conspicuously absent, though his heavy ceremonial duties were not. Aborigines to the south and east had constantly to be driven back to make way for Han colonization. In the far south, in the region of the modern Hanoi, the Han established a major port where products and embassies from Southeast Asia and beyond could be received. In the far northeast the Han established a colony in what is now North Korea where the territory was divided into regular prefectures and counties; archeology attests to the high level of material culture in the colony's principal settlement.

By far the most serious threat was from the

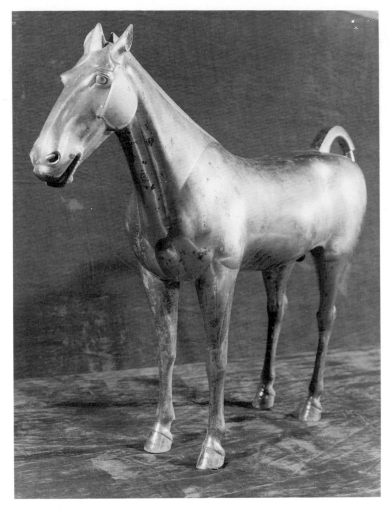

Left: A bronze container decorated with a spinning and weaving scene from the Western Han Dynasty (206 BC to AD 24). These vessels were used to hold cowrie shells which served as money during the period.

Right: A gilded bronze horse dating from the time of the Western Han Dynasty. The overlay is of gold leaf.

from custom as well) they drew together a working code of moral behavior and of etiquette toward superiors and inferiors. From still others they drew models for the writing of prose and poetry. And from the whole, in the course of time, they constructed a set of values, a view of the cosmos and of the place of people like themselves in such a cosmos.

It must not be imagined that all the adults among the local elites devoted themselves to restoring or developing their literary heritage. Most were busy with the supervision of the land, with the settlement of disputes and, in some regions, with aborigine problems and a hundred other practical activities. But in many elite families there was at least one *Ju*, classicist, who devoted himself to learning. Such people would travel to study with a master of a certain text, exchange views with one another and, most important, serve as teachers of the young.

How did all this become a counterweight to imperial power? First, it ensured to the local elites a virtual monopoly of literacy – literacy that was essential to all the transactions and record keeping of a bureaucratic state. Second, because of their literacy they came in time to have a monopoly on access to public office. Third, the ritual forms, the ideas, the precedents they knew about were the emperor's only recourse once the Han moved from military conquest to the consolidation of power.

During the early part of the Han period the Classicists' stronghold was the Great Plain, with its princedoms and its literate local elites, but gradually the Classicists began to benefit from the local selection system, to take positions in the training colleges in the capital and occasionally to rise to high office in the central government. As the Han emperors became personally more knowledgeable and more favorable to the civil arts and

to a prudent and peaceful domestic policy, the position of the Classicists became far less precarious.

The next step was the creation of a Han imperial ideology that was to blend many strains from the pre-Ch'in period with strong authoritarian elements from the Ch'in. The formation of this ideology was gradual, and there was at first no certainty that it would be Confucian. But the Classicists increasingly pulled the diverse elements of the pre-Ch'in heritage together around the central figure of Confucius, whom they apotheosized into the 'peerless sage of ten thousand generations.' While in life he had been a disappointed office seeker and a humble teacher, he now became an 'uncrowned king' *(su-wang)* – a man with great plans which, if adopted, would have made his native state of Lu, and not hated Ch'in, the power that unified China.

While it is true that the real Confucius had recommended to his pupils that they read the old books and learn from them rhetoric and the lessons of history, and that they study the ritual traditions current in their time, he would have been amazed to find his name associated with many of the books that in Han times became the 'Confucian Classics.' Yet they now became a kind of canon, an all-encompassing body of holy writ which, it was claimed, covered all that man needed to know. Here is Tung Chung-shu, one of the systematizers, arguing the supreme value of this Canon. Notice that its various parts are held to be as relevant for the ruler as for the ruled:

The Prince knows that he who is in power cannot by evil methods (i.e. force, law) make men submit to him. Therefore he chooses the six disciplines [embodied in the Six Classics] through which to develop the people . . . These six disciplines are all great and at the same time each has that in which it is pre-eminent. The *Book of Odes* describes the human will and therefore is pre-

nomadic Hsiung-nu people along China's northern and western frontiers. From an initial policy of 'appeasement,' the Han, as it consolidated power within China, moved to the attack. The intricacies of successive alliances and counter-alliances need not detain us, but the effort to deal with the Hsiung-nu led to a steady expansion of the northern and western borders, and this, in turn, led to the development of flourishing trade and Chinese domination of the trade routes which led across Central Asia, a process begun during the reign of the great Han Wu-ti (140-87 BC). Via various middlemen, Chinese goods found their way to Europe, and by the time of the reign of Roman Emperor Tiberius (AD 14-37) laws had to be passed against the extravagant dresses of Chinese silk worn by the ladies of Rome.

This combination of expanding military-diplomatic relations, exploration and trade led to greatly increased Chinese knowledge of the 'western regions' (hsi-yü). In their struggles against the Hsiung-nu the Chinese also began to develop the arsenal of techniques and strategies for dealing with nomadic and semi-nomadic neighbors, an arsenal that was to become in time the most sophisticated ever assembled by any agricultural people that faced repeated threats from the steppe lands. Almost from the outset such strategies as the following were used: seeking steppe allies against the principal threat, using agents provocateurs to fan the latent divisiveness in tribal politics, giving munificent gifts and high-sounding titles to tribal satraps and offering to such leaders Chinese 'princesses' as wives. By the end of the first half of the Han dynasty, the empire had, in effect, become a world power and, indeed, was, probably the richest and most populous state on earth at that time. There was reason for the 'Men of Han,' as Chinese called themselves then and thereafter, to be proud of their collective accomplishments.

The break-up of the first imperial order

The second or Later Han began, in AD 25, after the failure of a challenger called Wang Mang to found a new dynasty. The founder of this second Han was a relative of the original Han ruling house, but he had to fight and compromise his way to the throne against formidable opposition. The result was that the second Han was never as strong a central government as the first, and its emperors were under constant pressure from regional and other groupings of local elite families. The capital, now moved east to Loyang, received less tax in kind from areas now dominated by local elites, and the central government had to rely heavily on state monopolies – salt, iron and liquor – for income. To add to these difficulties, bureaus proliferated, and the size of the bureaucracy grew to enormous proportions. In the second century BC, for example, the Bureau of the Eastern Gate, which was in charge of the paperwork on the nomination, placing and promotion of officials, had been staffed by nine bureaucrats; by AD 117 the number had risen to 362. The use of public office for private gain became endemic. And all the while, the Han imperial line was becoming increasingly feeble. As in most hereditary autocracies the princes of the imperial line were increasingly isolated from normal life, brought up in the intrigue-laden atmosphere of the palace and waited on by obsequious servants. As time passed they became increasingly self-indulgent, and when they took power, they were often grossly unprepared and fell prey to self-interested individuals or cliques.

As more of the emperors tended to be helpless infants manipulated by eunuchs or women, it

became increasingly difficult for Confucian scholars to accept the emperor's role of cosmic pivot, or to believe in the efficacy of the rituals performed by him. One of the most articulate critics was a scholar called Wang Ch'ung (27-c 97), who attacked many of the myths and shibboleths of the time – some of which were indeed the building blocks of the imperial ideology.

Among the groups who struggled to manipulate a diminished but still considerable power were two which appeared throughout Chinese history in periods of dynastic weakness. These were the families of empresses (what the Chinese call the wai-ch'i, or outside clans) and the palace eunuchs. Toward the end of the Han, empresses' families contributed considerably to the further weakening of imperial power. For example, the notorious Liang clan dominated the court for 20 years, enthroned two puppet emperors, placed all their family members in lucrative posts, enthroned three Liang women as empresses and placed six as imperial concubines. They accumulated vast riches and built a pleasure park in Loyang that rivaled that of the emperors. The head of the clan for all these years was very much like a political boss. Only he could get a young man an office, and he would do so only for the promise of a kickback and loyalty to Liang family interests. Only he could get a merchant the lucrative business of supplying the imperial palace, and for such help the merchant paid well.

The second group, the eunuchs, were often men of plebeian origin, generally with only the rudiments of literacy and without moral training to inhibit their actions. They, like the empresses' families, could not count on a long period of influence, and when a group of them took control of the inner palace and the emperor's person, their rapacity knew no bounds. They, too, made lucrative deals with merchants, sold their influence at a high price and accumulated vast fortunes.

Directly opposed to both these groups were the Confucian Classicists, drawn from local elite families and, in the Han's prime, the holders of great power and makers of imperial policy. The great families, those who had, for generations, enjoyed almost automatic access to high office, were by now pleasure-loving, corrupt and lazy. But members of the lesser families were articulate and bitter critics of the corruption at the capital. They denounced particularly the empresses' families and the eunuchs, who had intruded themselves into that special relation between monarch and

minister which the Confucians of the earlier Han had designed as their particular monopoly. In 166 and 167 the eunuchs had imperial edicts issued which debarred their critics from public office. The following year the Confucians attempted a massacre of the eunuchs, and when this failed it brought fierce reprisals.

With Han government undermined by decay and riven by dissension, the oppression of the ordinary peasant at the hands of landlords and greedy tax collectors can well be imagined. Uprooted, oppressed beyond endurance, the peasantry took the first steps toward massive armed rebellion. The Yellow Turban movement began as a religious cult – secret communities with their own organizations, rituals, catechisms (they worshipped Lao-tzu and regarded the Lao-tzu book as a sacred text), faith-healing practices, modes of mutual aid and of maintaining internal discipline. The movement found many adherents among peasants driven from their land by the exactions of landlords and corrupt tax collectors, among the poor and the desperate generally. As its units grew in number and spread across the land, it even began to take over some of the functions once performed by the Han government. For example, Yellow Turban units kept order, repaired roads and bridges and along the roads built rest-houses open to all except Han officials!

The movement had two geographical centers, one in the east, centering in what is now Kiangsu Province, and one in the west, centered in Szechwan. With control over people, land and communications growing, the next step – seizure of power – was seemingly inevitable. Religious communities were turned into military units, a hierarchy of commands was established, and the Yellow Turbans began indoctrinating their followers with the idea that the time of the Han had run out, that the Chinese year corresponding to AD 184 would begin the new millennium of the 'Great Peace' (T'ai-p'ing). At that time they rose in armed rebellion. Whole clusters of prefectures were forcibly seized, and the bickering factions at the Han court first panicked and then managed to unite in the face of catastrophe. Armies were raised against the rebels, and, in a bitter civil war, succeeded in crushing them. But with bitter feuding at the center and local administration in shambles, the fate of the Han was nevertheless sealed.

The armies that had crushed the Yellow Turbans now became the breeding ground for mili-

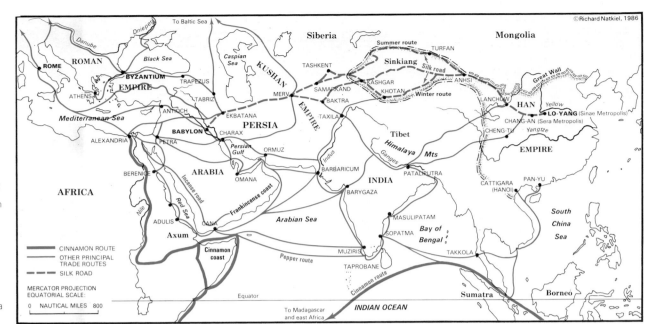

Left: A brick impressed with a design of a mounted archer, the key fighting man of the steppe regions to the north of China proper.

Right: A map showing Han Dynasty China and the major trade routes with Rome and Persia.

Below: A mountain scene depicting wild animals and a derrick – possibly part of a salt mine – from the Han period.

forms which accompanied them. But politically, the spreading anarchy led to a collapse in which invading steppe peoples wrested control first of part and then of all the ancient Chinese culture area from the enfeebled regimes which succeeded the Han. And finally, in these same years, China was penetrated and deeply influenced by the Indian religion of Buddhism. These similarities and differences provide the main themes by which we can understand this complex period.

Ts'ao Ts'ao had seized power in 196 as a military adventurer, a warlord. The Chinese regimes that succeeded the Wei did so invariably by coup d'état. Each coup was engineered by a coalition of powerful clans which had become impatient with this or that policy or were simply tired of being among the 'outs,' and once they had seized power they tended to dissolve into feuding groups, from which yet another combination would in time set up yet another ruling house. From Ts'ao Ts'ao's Wei to reunification in 589, there were seven Chinese dynasties – the first two with their capitals at Loyang or Ch'ang-an in the north, the last five with their capitals at Nanking on the lower Yangtse. The power of these governments, particularly the last five, was distinctly limited, and powerful clans with great estates dominated the countryside and turned the formerly tax-paying peasants into their serfs. One estimate is that between 156 and 280, two-thirds of the peasant population were taken off the imperial tax rolls. For appointment of local officials in the prefectures and counties there slowly evolved a system of selection of candidates by recommendation. The recommendations were to some extent made on the basis of the candidate's character and local repute, but more decisively they were based on his documented genealogy on both his father's and his mother's side. The people who weighed these qualifications were called 'Recommending Legates' (*Chung-cheng*). They were from powerful clans and their offices soon became hereditary. Confucian learning, indeed literacy, were not prerequisites for public office. A contemporary estimate during the period 240-49 is that of the 400 top officials of the central government, there were not 10 who could wield a writing brush. Nor did these courts place a high value on men whose characters had been shaped by Confucian morality. Ts'ao Ts'ao, in a famous edict summoning people to serve at his court, stated that he did not want men who allowed moral scruples to impede their effectiveness.

tary adventurers, men who drew their followers from the impoverished local elites, from landless peasants, from refugees and bandits. These adventurers roamed about with their bands, pillaging one province, then another, seizing a walled town and holding it until dislodged by a rival band. In short the whole social order was violently disrupted, millions of people were dead, the rest torn from their roots, wandering across the land without hope or recourse. It was one of these military adventurers, Ts'ao Ts'ao, who in 196, finally took over the shreds of imperial power from the dying Han. The Chinese historian's judgment of him is: 'A vile bandit in times of peace, a heroic leader in a world of turmoil.'

Ts'ao Ts'ao set up the dynasty of Wei, and this competed with rival dynasties in the lower Yangtse area and in Szechwan. Eventually the Wei and its successor, the Chin, having a stronger economic base and more plentiful manpower in the North China Plain, triumphed over their rivals.

But this forcible reunification did not lead to the reconstruction of Han institutions, or to anything like the revival of a strong centralized empire. Many historians see the period from 196 to 581 as a sort of a re-enactment of the Warring States period at the end of the Chou (403-221 BC), and there are resemblances. For example, in place of a centralized empire, power was shared among privileged clans, and the 'imperial' clan of the moment was only *primus inter pares*. The access to power was again given on the basis of heredity, not talent selected by examinations based on the Confucian Classics. Further, there was a similar questioning, among segments of an alienated elite, of received values, and along with this came a new flowering of creative thought.

But the differences between this and the earlier period are still more striking than the similarities. Land settlement had produced and continued to produce a vastly expanded land area subject both to Chinese agricultural methods and the social

Liu Ling was an inveterate drinker and heedlessly indulged himself. Sometimes he stripped off his clothes and would be in his room stark naked. Some men coming by saw him and rebuked him. Liu Ling said, I consider Heaven and Earth as my dwelling and my house as my trousers. How dare you come into my trousers?

The Neo-Taoists at their best taught a high-minded spiritual anarchism; at their worst they behaved like animals. But there was no practical viable way of life for them in the society of their time, nor did their thinking lead to ideas which would reconstruct a liveable society. So, in the end, some were executed, some made a cynical peace with the authorities (one took a post because it had a wine cellar), and some lived out their lives in drunkenness, or bitterness or both. Their ideas became the playthings of idle aristocrats; their exalted dialogues degenerated into salon repartee. Yet the range of their speculations – philosophical and psychological – prepared the ground for the successful penetration of Buddhism into Chinese thought and society.

But before turning to the Buddhists' impact, we should pause to review the series of disasters that reduced the enfeebled state almost to impotence, rent the remaining social fabric and so prepared the way for the coming of the new faith. During the last years of the third century a series of natural disasters struck the main northern provinces. The modern provinces of Shensi and Kansu were hit by drought, accompanied by famine, every year from 281 to 290. Terrible famines and plagues followed in 294 and 297. Locusts devastated most of the North China Plain in 310, and floods struck the northernmost area in 298 and again in 302. These areas were both the most populous and the principal food-producing areas of China. In some areas, according to contemporary reports of officials, only 20 percent of the population remained, and these mostly the aged and the weak. The rest were dead or were in flight in a series of chain migrations from one marginal subsistence region to another. The decayed central government could neither provide relief nor even maintain order.

Worse was to follow. Since Han times it had been Chinese policy to allow non-Chinese populations which, through their leaders, made the proper gestures of submission, to settle in areas inside the Great Wall. It was believed that the superior ways of China would shortly transform the character of these settlers and turn them into hard-working, tax and rent-paying subjects. This

The trauma of the Han's disintegration and the emergence of successor regimes that were tyrannical, corrupt and ineffectual produced both a profound alienation of the remaining educated elite and a renewed interest in speculation about the causes of the plight of man and society. The first speculative wave was an attempt to analyze these matters in purely Confucian terms. The argument went that the present intolerable situation had arisen because the precepts of the ancient sages beloved of the Confucians were no longer followed. The world could only be set right if the traditional pattern of social relations was restored and everyone returned to his proper place in the social hierarchy. The key values to be revived were *li*, the codified conventions which gave order to social relations and *i*, often translated as 'righteousness' but meaning also impartiality, equitable dealings between people of superior rank and devotion to duty on the part of inferiors. But this formula was not in vogue for long. Since the Han imperial ideology had been an eclectic Confucianism, Confucianism now tended to be discredited along with the order it had supported. In any case, there was now no center of power that could effect a return to the old and desirable ways, even if this were desired.

The second body of theory was frankly Realist. It postulated that the long years of peace and prosperity under the Han had produced a self-indulgent and irresponsible elite. Moreover, the study of the classics and the preoccupation with antiquity had made the elite too bookish, resistant to change and unable to see the real problems of their time. What was needed was the re-establishment of harsh laws, uniformly and strictly applied. Although none of the weak dynasties of the period explicitly accepted this Realist analysis, the codification of laws and ordinances, as under

the Ch'in and Han, continued unabated and eventually grew to absurd proportions.

By far the most interesting group of thinkers – and certainly in the long run the most influential – were those we call the Neo-Taoists. They turned back to the classics of Taoism, which dated from the last part of the Chou: the *Lao-tzu* and the *Chuang-tzu*. Another source of their ideas was the *I-ching*, and they paid particular attention to the metaphysical sections that had been added to the original peasant core. While they expressed their ideas in essays and in commentaries on their favorite books, their characteristic way of communicating was a dialogue form called *ch'ing-t'an* ('pure talk'). These dialogues at their best were full of wit, irony, word-play, and allusions to passages in the Neo-Taoist classics. Yet the Neo-Taoists were, for all their seeming frivolity, sharp critics of the contemporary scene. They blamed Confucian morality and Confucian conventions for the Han debacle. For the Confucian ideal man they had the most withering scorn, for the classics only contempt. They attacked both the laws in which the Realists believed and the established mores or ways of doing things in which the Confucians believed as equally harmful to the basic instinctual nature of man. Naturalness was for them an absolute good, a synonym for Tao, the critical measure of all things human. To act in accord with naturalness was to enter into an egoless state of harmony with one's fellow creatures. For some Neo-Taoists it seemed that the natural life, meditation, breath control exercises and other steps could only be taken in a retreat, and the most famous group of recluses was the Seven Sages of the Bamboo Grove. But the doctrine of naturalness, for less exalted spirits, led to endless drinking bouts and truly grotesque behavior. Here is an anecdote about one of them:

was all very well in times of dynastic strength, but the emperor who came to the throne in 265 was a usurper with very shaky control over the empire as a whole. Nevertheless, he allowed mass settlement throughout the Shansi-Kansu area. An official who investigated the area in about 300 estimated that the population was then half non-Chinese, and he predicted that if bad times came, these people would prove to be more enduring than the Chinese themselves. So it was that the empire, on top of all its other troubles, introduced within its borders a Trojan horse in the form of a semi-barbarian, imperfectly Sinicized minority. The price to be paid for this misbegotten policy was immense. In 311 a mixed group of immigrants with a Hsiung-nu leader captured and sacked the imperial capital of Loyang – perhaps the greatest city in Asia at that time. The Son of Heaven was taken prisoner and later forced to wait on table in the barbarians' camp. A contemporary letter by a Sogdian merchant to his home office in Samarkand has been found in a ruined watch tower on the western frontiers of China. The letter expresses astonishment that 'those Huns who yesterday were the Emperor's vassals' should have now overthrown the empire. 'And Sir,' the letter continues, 'the last Emperor – so they say – fled from Saragh (ie Loyang) because of the famine, and his palace and walled city were set on fire . . .

So Saragh is no more! . . . ' The destruction of Loyang can be compared to the sack of Rome by the Visigoths in 410. In both cases a great city, the functioning center of a once-great empire and the symbol of a great civilization was overrun by alien invaders from lands long kept subjugated. Yet Rome was built of stone, and much of it survived, while Loyang, like all Chinese capitals, was built of wood, mud bricks and tile, and it was totally destroyed. Some of the ruling house and their aristocratic officials held out for a while in the west in the then secondary capital of Ch'ang-an. But the passes were breached, and in 316 the city fell. Not only the two great capital sites – hallowed by 15 centuries of history – fell to the barbarians, the whole of the great plain, the whole length of the Great Wall, the tomb of Confucius, the sacred mountains, all the land from which a distinct Chinese civilization had sprung were lost as well. All of China down to the Huai River line was for the first time under alien control. This was a major cataclysm that had long-lasting effects in Chinese history. One such effect was that it greatly effected the spread of Buddhism in China.

Buddhism, the great world religion that began in India and drew upon its spiritual heritage, only gradually became a missionary faith. But it had developed deities and saints, philosophical texts and catechisms, homely moral tales, art forms and

iconography that gave it a vast richness and variety and made it able to adapt itself to all the diverse cultures it encountered. Perhaps its key driving force was the Bodhisattva ideal, the pledge Buddhist monks made not to break free of earthly bonds until salvation had been brought to all living creatures. This is what drove the missionary monks across the fearsome Hindu Kush and the Pamirs and steadied them in their long efforts to establish Buddhism in the oasis kingdoms of Central Asia. It was along the caravan routes from this area that Buddhism penetrated the Chinese empire.

In complexity, in geographical scale, in regional variation, the Buddhist penetration of China may be compared with the Christianization of Europe. Its spread can perhaps best be understood in terms of the ways it affected the various social classes in post-Han China. To begin at the bottom of the social scale, the peasantry everywhere lived in depressed conditions. Many were attached as semi-servile workers on great estates, living and dying at the very margin of subsistence. Some were obliged to serve in the private armies of their landlords, while others lived out their lives as household slaves. After the experience that many had had with popular communal religion, and then the abortive rebellion of the Yellow Turbans, they were especially open to the appeals of the

Left: A bronze mirror depicting Taoist gods from the third century AD.

Below left: An ornately carved stone stele from the Wei Dynasty, the successor to the Han period.

Right: Statue of Buddha. Buddhism grew out of India; its missionaries able to penetrate China along well-established trade routes.

new religion. Initially Buddhism was seen in peasant communities as a variation on the popular Taoism that had been at the heart of the Yellow Turban religion. Its spells and incantations were novel and seemed potentially powerful. The divinities it invoked, who gradually assumed Chinese forms, promised help and solace. But beyond all, the appeal of Buddhism at the mass level was its promise of some compensation in another life for the sufferings of this world. At the same time it promised that the evil and the unjust would be punished in the lives to come.

As the Buddhist missionaries and Chinese pioneer adherents found converts, the ways of penetrating the peasant world multiplied. For example, certain seasonal feasts in honor of folk deities were taken over and turned into Buddhist feasts. The holy places of the Chinese landscape where some divine power had long been worshipped, were slowly appropriated by the Buddhists and became places of Buddhist worship and pilgrimage. The numerous pantheon of Buddhist saints (Bodhisattvas) was so varied that one after another fused with and absorbed the native folk divinities. Buddhists introduced (probably echoing some Yellow Turban practices) a variety of humble associations which the peasant could join for mutual aid, to collect funds for funerals or to engage collectively in other projects, such as the making of a holy image or the building of a local temple or reliquary, which would add to the peasants' store of good karma for the future. Finally, what were called 'country monks,' without particular learning or discipline, took over functions in the villages which had been performed since the dawn of time by local shamans: driving out demons, purification rituals, healing rituals, funerals and burial rites. All of this, so briefly summarized, took many centuries to develop fully, but these were the principal modes by which Buddhism penetrated peasant society.

Among Chinese landed families, and particularly to their educated members, Buddhism offered different appeals and gradually won them over by quite different means. But when we recall the doubt and disillusionment of the intellectuals of the third and fourth centuries and the weaknesses of neo-Taoism as an alternative to the discredited Confucian way, it helps us to understand Buddhist strategies and Buddhist successes. The early Buddhist missionaries coming in along the Central Asian trade routes and settling somewhere along the routes of internal trade in China were for the most part men of the oasis kingdoms, speaking and writing in one of the Central Asian languages. It was exceedingly difficult for them to get their message across to the Chinese, and particularly difficult to do so in writing. The first efforts at written translations of the Buddhist scriptures were stumbling and imperfect. Understandably so. The Chinese written language had developed independently, and it was now a rich literary medium, but almost everything it referred to was indigenous, part of the Chinese landscape and of Chinese history. While the Indian languages, the sacred languages of Buddhism, were inflected languages, Chinese was not. The Indians (including the Buddhists) had made grammar a formalized system of great complexity, but the Chinese had nothing in any way comparable. Herculean efforts over many centuries were needed before anything like full communication was attained, but the interim strategies of the first centuries of Buddhism are what concern us here.

The Buddhists used the most universal of missionary strategies and presented their unfamiliar ideas in familiar terms. Thus they appropriated the neo-Taoist vocabulary that had so long been

Left: A painting, entitled *Lady Historian,* by the painter Ku K'ai-chih (AD 345-406).

Below right: Admonitions of the Instructress to the Court Ladies by Ku K'ai-chih.

current in upper class circles. For example, the most central word in the neo-Taoist vocabulary, *tao,* was used initially to translate *dharma,* 'the teaching' and sometimes *bodhi,* 'enlightenment.' The Taoist term for perfected men, *chen-jen,* was used to translate the Buddhist *arhat,* 'the fully enlightened one.' And *wu-wei,* 'non-action,' a concept of enormous importance for neo-Taoism, was used for the Buddhist concept of ultimate release, *nirvana.* An early Buddhist preacher was taken to task for just such verbal strategy. He replied to his critic:

I knew you were familiar with the ideas of the Chinese Classics, and for this reason I quoted from them. If I had spoken in the words of the Buddhist scriptures . . . it would have been like speaking of the five colors to a blind man or playing the five sounds to one who is deaf.

But apart from presentation, what did the great body of Buddhist teachings offer the educated Chinese?

First of all, the educated, like the peasants, were impressed with the idea of a law of reward for good and punishment for evil spread over an infinite succession of past and future incarnations. There was nothing analogous to this in Chinese tradition, nothing to explain why, for example, in the society around them the good perished miserably, while the evil flourished. Second, Buddhism seemed to offer alternative ways to live, as a monk or nun or as a layman living according to the Buddhist vows. The contemplative life, particularly, had an ethical justification, for one's religious observances, prayers and meditations were believed to contribute to the ultimate salvation of all living creatures. Third, for those of more active and worldly disposition, Buddhism promised that a life dedicated to good works – feeding the poor, building temples or free dispensaries, for example – would redound to one's spiritual credit in the lives to

come. Fourth, for those of scholarly or bookish inclinations, Buddhism came in time to offer rich possibilities: one could become a doctrinal specialist in one of the branches of Buddhist learning, a book collector or a bibliographer, a historian of Buddhism or a biographer of the monks. And, again, all such activities accumulated good karma for oneself and others.

When we turn to the matter of the appeals of Buddhism for the rulers of China in this period of division, we should keep in mind the difference between the south and the north. In the south a Chinese elite did their best to perpetuate, in many fields, traditional ways which were the legacy of the Han. In the north a series of rulers from the steppe-land dominated a population of subject Chinese, who followed as best they could the ways of their ancestors. In the north the non-Chinese rulers insisted on the control of Buddhist clergy and establishments by government officials and on the submission by Buddhist clerics to the ruling house. Since this sort of submission to secular power went against the vows the monks took, they eventually resolved the difficulty by proclaiming that the reigning emperor *was* a Bodhisattva. In the south relations were differently handled. Buddhism enjoyed the patronage of one or more of the aristocratic factions which in turn dominated the southern courts. Hence no emperor dared bring the Buddhists to full submission, lest he be challenged (and possibly overthrown) by an aristocratic faction favorable to Buddhism. Yet despite these basic differences in policy, both northern and southern rulers sought to use Buddhism to add luster and legitimacy to their regimes. Both sought in it spiritual solace and performed Buddhist acts of atonement for their crimes. Both used Buddhist rituals and the chanting of certain scriptures to obtain important results: to bring rain, to stop a plague, to protect the state against its enemies. For both northern and southern rulers, then, Buddhism was regarded as a new potency to be drawn upon for their own or their state's benefit.

But a tolerance for Buddhism was one of the few things north and south had in common. The division of China in 316 into two hostile sectors had far reaching effects in all the spheres of life. The south continued the weakly centralized governments that had emerged after the fall of Han. They perpetuated the pomp and symbolism of the Han, but the capital at Nanking was a battleground of aristocratic factions, and strong inherited claims to control were asserted at the regional and local levels. This meant that the southern dynasties could not find the military manpower or the resources, or indeed the unity or purpose, needed to reconquer the great plain and the highland areas to the west of it. Expeditions were talked about, and those led by Huan Wen between 347 and 368 were partial successes. He did regain the rich western area of Szechwan for the southern court, but after early victories, he was defeated in the northern plain, and the southern court, with minor exceptions, remained on the defensive behind the Yangtse defense line.

The governments in North China had been initially the camp governments of a succession of non-Chinese warlords unstable, transient and cruel. But with the slow growth of the power of the Wei Dynasty, founded in 386 by Hsien-pei Tartars, a somewhat more stable government took form. The dominant minority, in fighting off fresh invaders from outside and in periodic moves

to conquer the south, had built a formidable war machine. Like its transient predecessors, the Wei was autocratic in the extreme, and it reserved most of the power and sources of wealth for ranking Hsien-pei clans, especially those related to the ruling house. The Hsien-pei language was spoken at court, but records, as North China was gradually restored to productivity, had to be kept in Chinese. In time, some Chinese landed families gradually won back a measure of regional power and slowly, thanks to their superior literate skills and to some well-calculated intermarriages with the conquerors, won positions of influence at court. When, in 494 the Wei capital was moved from the northern highlands to the ancient Chinese capital site of Loyang, the process of Sinicization became still more accelerated.

The cultural contrasts between north and south cover a wide spectrum. The Chinese refugees from the north, when they fled to the Yangtse valley, entered the second of China's distinctive ecological zones. At first they missed the milk products, the millet and wheat dumplings and other foods characteristic of the north. But gradually they found southern substitutes which they eventually came to prefer. At first they tried to maintain as a court and literary language in Nanking the dialect of their lost capital in the north, Loyang. But this was viewed with scorn by the locals. When the famous painter Ku K'ai-chih (c 345–c 406) was asked why he did not recite poems in the Loyang dialect, replied: 'Why should I make noises like an old serving maid?' Soon the

speech of the southern upper class began to show a heavy admixture, in the west, of the old Ch'u dialect, and of the dialects of Wu and Yueh in the east.

Customs in the north and south came to diverge in a myriad ways. For example, the Chinese in the south took concubines and kept their women at home. In the monogamous north women rode horseback, intervened in political and economic life and bustled about on family business. The south, as more and more land was brought under cultivation, prospered. The southern aristocrats lived in a leisured and cultivated way, perpetuating Han traditions in literature and music. Many among them were specialists in court ritual and the complex imperial ceremonies that were continued by the weak dynasties at Nanking. The northern upper class, both Chinese and non-Chinese, had a far different and considerably less cultivated style of life. For men the hunt and falconry were major avocations. Near the end of this period a young northern prince said that he would rather go three days without eating than a day without hunting.

In brief, as a result of conquest from the outside, China was divided along its natural ecological boundary into two contrasting and increasingly divergent cultures. Northern dynasts dreamed of reuniting the two cultures, and indeed several attempted it. But the task was not accomplished until a final successful effort was made by the Sui Dynasty and was consolidated by the T'ang.

The Middle Ages

The millennium from AD 500 to 1500 was not a period of rapid progress for humanity. Although changes in political power were sometimes devastatingly swift, changes in technology and in the texture of everyday life were extremely slow. The emphasis of civilization rested not on innovation, but on the preservation and transmission of knowledge and culture, threatened by the pressure of repeated barbarian invasion and the forces of internal disintegration. The related monotheistic religions of Christianity and Islam triumphed over much of Eurasia and North Africa, but the legacy of the Greco-Roman world remained a dominant source of inspiration.

The collapse of the western half of the Roman Empire in the fifth century AD was not repeated in the east. At Constantinople, emperors continued to rule for another thousand years, although often almost unrecognizable as successors of Augustus. This Byzantine Empire was Greek in culture and language, and Christian Orthodox in religion. By the eleventh century it had evolved so far from the Latin and Catholic Christianity of western Europe that Rome and Constantinople confronted one another as centers of essentially alien cultures. The civilization of Byzantium was for many centuries a glittering achievement, far outshining western Christendom in prosperity, the organization of government, and the art and sciences. And yet for most of its existence it was a civilization on the defensive, one which finally succumbed to repeated blows from its enemies to the east and the west.

Byzantium was responsible for preserving much of the legacy of classical civilization for the modern world, but this was also a role performed by the new dynamic force of Islam. From its roots in the Arabian peninsula, this last of the great world religions inspired an astonishing series of Arab conquests in the seventh and eighth centuries that spread Muslim power across a vast area from central Asia to the south of France. Although this dominion could not for long be ruled as a unified empire, it laid the foundations for a magnificent civilization, which both absorbed much of Greek learning and improved upon it, especially in science and mathematics. The great cities of Islam – Baghdad, Cairo, Cordoba – surpassed any in Christendom for size and magnificence, save possibly Constantinople itself.

Arab predominance lasted only a few centuries but, like Christianity in Europe, Islam proved able to ensure a continuity of culture. Political power passed to other peoples – Berbers, Kurds, Turks – but the civilization survived. Even the Mongol hordes, who laid waste much of the Islamic world in the thirteenth century, later became Muslim rulers. The Turks, another central Asian people, were the eventual inheritors of the caliphate, the acknowledged leadership of Islamic civilization. Only Christianity, Islam's religious cousin, could actually press back the boundaries of the Muslim world, recovering Spain by the end of the fifteenth century. But Islam remained dynamic and expansive, both as a proselytizing creed and as a military force.

In contrast to the advanced and prosperous lands of Byzantium and Islam, western Europe remained for long a backwater. In the aftermath of the fall of the Roman Empire in the West, war-

Above: A brass of the thirteenth century knight Sir John D'Aubernoun. The concept of chivalry, as exemplified by knights like Sir John, was one of the main driving forces in Europe in the Middle Ages.

Left: An interesting synthesis of Christian and Muslim religions depicted in an Islamic history of AD 1307, in which Jesus (on donkey) rides alongside the prophet Muhammad. Islam recognised the reality and importance of Jesus, but only as one of many holy men who preceded Muhammad.

Right: The church of San Apollinare Nuovo in the Italian city of Ravenna demonstrates the influence of Byzantine art in the Middle Ages. A distinctive Byzantine feature is the series of mosaics that adorn the church's interior.

rior kings held sway over a thinly-spread population barely sustained by subsistence agriculture. Every aspect of civilization – knowledge, literacy, technological skills, trade, political organization – fell catastrophically from the high levels achieved under the rule of Rome. The Empire was never forgotten, and its ghost haunted barbarian Europe. Yet disintegration had gone too far for a revival of imperial unity. The Christian Church inherited what was left of Roman authority and organization, but the early Popes had limited power and abilities. The Frankish ruler Charlemagne made the last serious attempt to revive the empire in Europe. His imperial coronation by the Pope in 800 did establish something durable, a tradition that became the Holy Roman Empire. But this was not a revival of Ancient Rome; the Empire was merely another one among the warring powers of Europe.

Yet although the civilization that emerged in western Europe was primitive and crude compared with its contemporaries in the Near East and Muslim Spain, it had a genuine vigor and at least a semblance of unity through the universal adoption of Christianity. In the eleventh century the Normans first inflicted defeats on Byzantine and Islamic forces in the Mediterranean, and at the end of that century the First Crusade took western Christian knights into the heart of the Near East, to Jerusalem. The flow of culture was all the other way – learning, along with other luxury goods, came to the west from Byzantium and Islam – but the dynamic aggression of Europe revealed in the Crusades was a portent of the future.

Slowly western Europe evolved a more sophisticated economy, culture and political order. There were grave setbacks in the fourteenth century, when famine, plague and war cut a swathe through populations. But the general trend was upward. In Italy a renaissance of art and learning flourished in cities like Venice and Florence, grown rich on trade and banking. The monarchies of England and France upheld central authority against the local powers of feudal barons, establishing strong, unified kingdoms with a new sense of national identity. Toward the end of the fifteenth century they were joined by Spain, at last a fully Christian land. These kingdoms of the Atlantic seaboard, voyaging in the wake of the Portuguese, were ready to back maritime exploration westward to the Americas and southward around Africa, exploiting the bold aggression of the European temper and the open-minded investigative spirit of the Renaissance. In more ways than one, by 1500 they stood on the threshold of a new world.

Meanwhile, to the east an unlikely inheritor of the Roman imperial tradition had emerged. Russia had evolved as a strange hybrid, owing allegiance to central Asian Tatars for centuries, yet in religion an offshoot of the Orthodox Christian church of Byzantium. After the fall of the Byzantine Empire in 1453, the Russian Church encouraged the country's rulers to adopt the title of Czar – Caesar – as the legitimate successor to the emperors of Constantinople, now that Russia remained as the last bastion – and a beleaguered one at that – of the Orthodox faith. It was a strange fate for the imperial idea to be embodied in such a backward outpost of civilization as the modern era began.

The Byzantine Empire

From the establishment of Constantine's supremacy over the Roman Empire and the doctrinal division of the Christian Church in AD 325, the once vast Roman community began pulling apart into two separate spheres, east and west. Furthermore, with the construction of the great metropolis of New Rome, it was clear that it was in the east that the major successes in the preservation of the Roman heritage would be achieved. Byzantium, the Eastern Empire, which survived until 1453, has been somewhat pushed aside in

the historiography of Europe – assigned an anomalous place in the history of the line of political and cultural succession from Rome. The main reason for this is that the two spheres into which the Roman Empire had divided had grown so far apart, despite their equal claim of adherence to the Christian faith, that when they met in the thirteenth century, at the time of the Fourth Crusade, they hardly recognized each other. Institutions of government and law, relations between state and church and general style of life had gone

in such different directions that Crusaders from the west could look upon Byzantium as almost a different world, somehow closer to Asia than to Christendom, certainly more Greek than Latin.

Yet in the larger context of world history, Byzantium played a significant role, not so much as a link in the preservation of the Roman tradition for a yet-unrealized European civilization, but in its own right, as a significant Christian part of the world community during a period when Western Europe was still torn by barbarian inva-

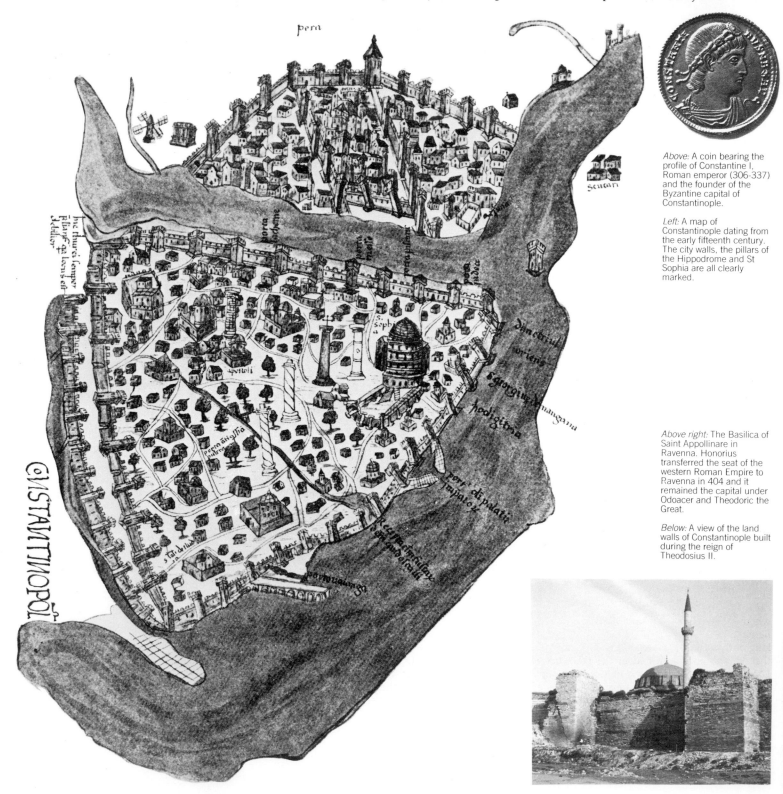

Above: A coin bearing the profile of Constantine I, Roman emperor (306-337) and the founder of the Byzantine capital of Constantinople.

Left: A map of Constantinople dating from the early fifteenth century. The city walls, the pillars of the Hippodrome and St Sophia are all clearly marked.

Above right: The Basilica of Saint Appollinare in Ravenna. Honorius transferred the seat of the western Roman Empire to Ravenna in 404 and it remained the capital under Odoacer and Theodoric the Great.

Below: A view of the land walls of Constantinople built during the reign of Theodosius II.

sions and when Eurasia was dominated by the influences of Islam and Buddhism. For Asia, during the thousand years after the fall of Rome, Byzantium *was* the Christian world. This is not to say that Byzantium did not serve as an important conserver of the Roman tradition, salvaging an intellectual and artistic heritage, preserving and systematizing Roman law, assembling and annotating collections of Hellenistic literature and philosophy. But the most direct recipients of Byzantine influence were, first of all, the Arabic and Turkish peoples of Asia Minor and the eastern Mediterranean and, secondly, the Slavic peoples of eastern Europe and Russia. It is doubtless this eastward thrust of Byzantium's world influence that has led so many European historians to undervalue its role. But for the world historian the story of Byzantium, as bridge between Asia and Europe, must occupy an important place.

To the inhabitants of Constantinople in its heyday – let us say in the reign of Basil II (976-1025) – the city was unquestionably the center of the civilized Christian world. There the standard of living, the style and excellence of the arts and letters, the grandeur of the imperial court and the potency of its military organization was far beyond anything that contemporary Rome could show. Above all, Constantinople had proven its capacity to hold off the enemies of Christendom, whether Bulgar or Arab, and to retain intact a heritage of Greco-Roman institutions that had long been dissipated in the west. The strength that Byzantium manifested in the years before 1204, when the Latin sack of Constantinople during the Fourth Crusade irreparably weakened the empire, was to be found in the strategic location of the city of Constantinople itself. Situated on a hilly promontory that juts out from the European side of the Bosporous straits, Constantinople occupied a position that commanded all traffic between the Black Sea and the Aegean, and at the same time controlled the natural bridge be-

tween Asia and Europe. The city itself possessed a magnificent harbor, and on its landward side it was protected by the Balkan Mountains. This natural line of defense was supplemented by a series of massive walls, one a double wall, and an extensive moat 20 feet wide, which made attack from the land side of the city virtually impossible under existing seige technology. When Constantinople did finally fall to the Ottomans in 1453, it was only after the city had been reduced by internal troubles to a shadow of its former defensive capacity.

Establishment of the Byzantine Empire

During the 1128 years between the founding of Constantinople and its eventual fall, the Byzantine empire passed through a number of distinct phases of expansion and contraction, and it is on this basis that the main periods of Byzantine history are generally defined. The history begins, of course, with Byzantium still very much a part of an empire centered on Rome. Constantine and his successors shared their rule with co-emperors in the West, and often the two were related by blood or marriage. Rome was still the city of the Pope, the recognized head of the Church, and the two poles of the Empire continued to work together in their common defense against the Hunnish and Germanic tribes who steadily infiltrated the northern frontiers. When, in 476, Romulus Augustulus was deposed in the West, the eastern emperors consequently regard themselves as heirs to the entire Empire. Though Gaul, Britain, Spain and North Africa were lost, Constantinople continued to stand at the center of a territory which stretched from northern Italy to Armenia and contained all of Greece, Macedonia, Egypt, the Levant, Syria and the intervening Mediterranean islands.

Justinian I, emperor in the East from 527 to 565, sought to recover the boundaries of the 'Universal Christian Roman Empire.' His armies recon-

quered Italy from the Ostrogoths, North Africa (Carthage) from the Vandals and southern Spain from the Visigoths. But undue attention to the west weakened the eastern frontier between Byzantium and the Sasanid Persians, who captured and sacked Antioch in 540. In retrospect, Justinian's efforts at recovery of the empire proved unwise, for Byzantium itself was weakened economically and militarily. Following the emperor's death the Lombards were soon in control of all but the southern and northeastern portions of Italy. Meanwhile, the Avars and Slavs were penetrating the Danube frontier and infiltrating the Balkans. By 619 the Persians had occupied Syria, Palestine and Egypt, and Byzantine influence in the Balkans was close to non-existant.

Thus the Emperor Heraclius (610-41) found the Empire in a precarious state, threatened by the Slavs to the north and the Persians in Asia Minor. An able organizer and general, he successfully mobilized the resources of Byzantium to ward off both threats. In 627 he decisively defeated the Persians at Nineveh, then marched to Ctesiphon and extracted a peace settlement that returned all Persian conquests in Asia Minor. The Slav menace was handled by diplomacy, the several Slavic groups being assigned spheres of settlement along the northern frontiers, from the head of the Adriatic to the mouth of the Danube, in return for their recognition of Byzantine sovereignty.

But Heraclius's successes were short-lived. Within a decade of his victory over the Persians, the entire Near East had been transformed by the sudden expansion of the Muslim Arabs. By 636 Arabic forces had overrun Syria. Palestine fell in 637; Alexandria, the last outpost of Hellenistic civilization in Egypt, in 643. The Arabs, having quickly assembled a war fleet, occupied Cyprus in 650. By 673 the Arab fleet had blockaded Constantinople by sea, while their land forces had reached the walls of the city in 716.

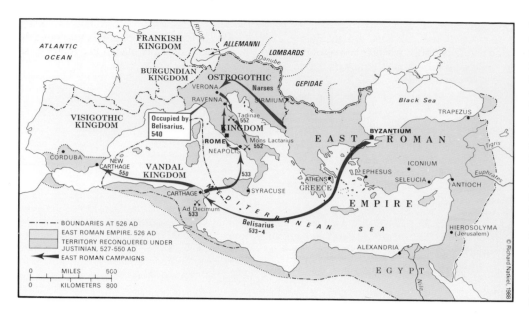

the emperor, taking the title *Basileus* (the Greek equivalent of the Persian term 'King of Kings'), shared religious powers with, and claimed administrative authority over, the patriarch. The emperor was recognized as Christ's agent on earth, the 'equal of the Apostles.' Thus he took the throne as one 'crowned by God,' and not by a separate authority vested in the church. Increasingly, the line between secular and religious authority was to become blurred. Imperial interference in religious matters had had its origin in the actions of Constantine I. On the Greek side of the Empire final authority in doctrinal matters rested in the Church Council, and the Council was called by the emperor. In Rome such authority was presumably vested in the Pope, the successor to Peter. Hence the frequent convening of councils in the East. Constantine had set the example of imperial interference in the deliberations of the Council of Nicaea, and thereafter Byzantine emperors frequently exercised decisive authority in religious matters, influencing the choice of

Again Byzantium managed to avert disaster under the leadership of an able general from Anatolia. Having distinguished himself in the defense of Constantinople against the Arabs, he took the throne as Leo III (717-741) Leo managed to secure the Empire's frontiers, but over territory greatly reduced in size. Except for a narrow hold on the extreme south of the Italian boot, the Byzantine Empire consisted of the Balkan Peninsula south of the Danube and Anatolia to the Tarsus Mountains. Yet reduction in size meant greater compactness and homogenity. A period of consolidation and restrengthening followed. By the 750s, an accommodation had been reached with the Arabs which laid the basis for a coexistence which lasted for around three hundred years.

Preoccupation with problems in the east had drawn Constantinople farther and farther away from Rome. When, in 800, the western Pope legitimized Charlemagne as Holy Roman Emperor, the Eastern Empire refused recognition. By 812 that recognition had been given although a clear division of the former Empire was acknowledged. Now, both in terms of ecclesiastical organization and culture (the Greek language prevailed in the East and Latin in the West) the two halves of the old Empire had consciously broken with each other. Byzantium was now a self-contained entity.

State and Church under the Macedonian Empire

Between the ninth and eleventh centuries the Byzantine Empire reached its highest and most secure development under the rule of the Macedonian dynasty begun by Basil I (867-86). Stable, powerful and wealthy, not distracted by futile efforts to regain distant territories, the Empire exemplified the particular institutions that were to distinguish Byzantium as a civilization in its own right. The third ruler of the dynasty, Constantine VII (944-59), left a remarkably candid and detailed book, *On the Administration of the Empire*, written for the enlightenment of his heir to the throne. In it we catch a glimpse of the rationale which stood behind the Empire's political, religious and economic institutions.

By now the Byzantine emperor had assumed a status, particularly with regard to the Church, that was quite different from that of the historic Roman emperors and one that was increasingly at variance with the practices prevailing in the West. Whereas in Rome the division between church and state was exemplified by the practice of Papal legitimation of the emperor, in Constantinople

Above left: The Byzantine Empire under Justinian I. His policy of reconquest of former possessions in Africa, Spain and Italy did much to restore the empire to its former glory.

Left: A contemporary depiction of Constantine VII being crowned by Christ. More of a scholar than a ruler, he allowed others to control and run the empire.

Right: An ornate gold reliquary. The Eastern Orthodox Church considered that every religious relic or image contained the essence of God.

Far right: A Byzantine enamel of St. Paul, the great founding father of the Christian Church, dating from the late tenth or eleventh century.

Patriarch, deciding matters of dogma, posing as defenders of the faith. The Patriarch of Constantinople received his installation 'by the will of God and Emperor.' Conversely the emperor absorbed increasing supernatural connotation in his style of life. Part secular ruler, part priest, the emperor could preach in church and take the communion cup with his own hands.

Historians have debated whether this Byzantine tendency to fuse church and state was influenced by the example of Asian societies, in which secular rule was generally legitimized as a manifestation of divine power exercised through a deified ruler. The trend toward deification of the ruler was noticeable even in the late Roman Empire, and Constantine, himself a product of the West, had already taken several steps toward the practice of deification. But it may well be that the Byzantine emperors, in their continuous struggle against the Persians and Arabs, were influenced to adopt some of the traits of the Near Eastern rulers. At any rate, for whatever reason, Byzantine practice did move increasingly toward the Oriental pattern of theocracy.

More than in the West, therefore, the church played a fundamental and powerful role within Byzantine politics and society. Church organization in many ways paralleled civil administration, the priesthood commanding a network of clerical offices which rose in hierarchal fashion from the local parish priest to the regional bishop and finally to the Patriarch at the capital. The priestly hierarchy, unified and disciplined, formed a powerful organization within the state. The Church became immensely wealthy through the collection of dues and the exploitation of lands immune from imperial taxation, which were lavished upon it by the emperors and the nobility. Bishops lived in the style of princes. That the Patriarch in the East lacked the kind of political power acquired by the Popes in Italy is the other side of the coin, the inevitable result of the Byzantine emperor's special caesaropapist status.

But it was not simply differences in the powers of the supreme *pontifex* which distinguished the Roman from the Orthodox branches of the Christian Church. Matters of doctrinal interpretation increasingly separated the two branches. These

began in the age of Constantine, with the so called Arian controversy. At issue was the question of the nature of Christ, whether he was of the same or different substance from that of God. The Nicaean Council, called by Constantine, decided against Arius and in favor of the Roman party, which claimed that God and Christ were of the same substance. Constantine and his successors moved increasingly in favor of the opposite interpretation, in other words, that Christ was *both* human and divine. The controversy raged in a variety of forms to the time of Justinian, when the so called 'monophysites' were supressed in Byzantium and a single orthodoxy was imposed.

While matters of doctrine provided the excuse for ecclesiastical controversies, rivalries between jurisdictions within the Christian Empire, compounded by ethnic and cultural difference, were at the root of most of the conflict. The Council of Chalcedon in 451 had established five patriarchal sees: Alexandria (Egypt and Cyrenaica), Jerusalem (Palestine), Antioch (Syria), Constantinople (Thrace, Greece, Asia Minor), and Rome (the West). But this was no guarantee of unity, since Rome and Alexandria continued to resent the way the Byzantine emperor influenced the Church's stands on doctrinal issues.

During the eighth century another controversy over the permissibility of the worship of religious images (the iconoclastic controversy) split the Christian community in Byzantium itself. Again the emperors took strong stands in the controversy, most often on the side of iconoclasm (though religious paintings were permitted). If the decision in 812 to recognize Charlemagne had marked the political separation between East and West, the date 867 marks an equally important separation within the Church. At the Council of Constantinople, the Patriarch Photius accused the Roman papacy of doctrinal aberrations and rejected the idea of the primacy of Rome. Thereafter the Eastern Orthodox Church went increasingly its own way, leading to the final 'Greek Schism' of 1054, brought on by the Roman Pope's support of the Norman conquest of Byzantine lands in southern Italy.

While its doctrinal distinctions are difficult for us to comprehend now, the external features of

Orthodox worship, particularly the emphasis on ritual and outer forms, is clearly understandable. Byzantine Christianity offered two routes to salvation, one through monastic life, the other through the sacraments. Monasteries received much greater attention in the East than in the West, and by the tenth century they constituted a real problem for the state because of the amount of land and manpower they withdrew from state control. The use of sacraments was also taken to an extreme. Rome had limited the sacraments to seven. In Byzantium every religious act, every image or relic was considered sacred; that is, was believed to contain the essence of God himself. Increasingly the emphasis was placed on the mystery, even the magic, inherent in ritual performance. Thus both in doctrine and practice, in the relationship of the priesthood to state and to the parish, East and West came to differ immensely. And these differences were widened by a deepening sense of bitterness and mistrust. The final stage in this antagonism came during the twelfth and thirteenth centuries as the West, becoming increasingly more potent militarily, thrust a series of Crusades against the Near East for the recovery of Palestine. Each Crusade added to the misunderstanding between the Empire and the West, and ultimately led to the occupation of Byzantium by the Crusaders.

A centralized state

In Byzantium's heyday the dominant position of the emperor in both religious and political affairs was matched by a remarkable effectiveness in the governance of the Eastern Empire. The kind of bureaucratically administered and centrally taxed state that had exemplified the early Roman Empire remained more characteristic of Byzantium and for a longer space of time than in medieval Europe, where feudal decentralization and privatization became so common. In the East the emperor was able to act the *autocrator*, governing the empire directly through a personal bureaucracy until at least the thirteenth century. To accomplish this the primacy of Constantinple was carefully maintained. The Empire, as territory, was divided into provinces. These, in response to the needs of military defense, had by the seventh

century been reorganized into military districts (*themes*), over which military governors (*strategoi*) were placed by imperial command. The military governors combined both military and civil functions: mobilized local population for defense, collected taxes, adjusted land rights and the like.

Throughout the history of Byzantium, the struggle between imperial power and local separatism remained strong, as elsewhere, but the Byzantine emperors staved off localism much longer than in the West, most obviously because their territory was not overrun by Germanic tribes. But there were institutionalized safeguards as well. Every effort was made to protect the free small farmer, the backbone of armed service. Governors of *themes* were forbidden to own lands within their jurisdiction or to marry into local families. Imperial laws attempted to prevent the purchase of land by wealthy land owners. It was not until the twelfth century that central control was seriously diluted. Then a militarized nobility in control of estates worked by serfs became largely independent of the imperial command, and when localism forced the emperor to rely increasingly on mercenary troops paid out of the imperial treasury for his own needs.

The economic strength of the Byzantine empire rested, first, upon the maintenance of a free peasantry who worked imperial lands in return for military service. But the income from trade and manufacture gave the imperial government an economic independence found in few other states of the time. Constantinople was a natural commercial entrepôt. Through it passed silk and porcelain from China, spices and gems from India, furs from beyond the Black Sea, papyrus from Egypt. Byzantine artisans produced goods of the highest quality, and a complex guild system regulated production and presumably maintained standards of quality. All of this worked to the benefit of the imperial treasury. The government taxed all trade which moved through Constantinople, and state customs offices were established throughout the empire. State monopolies brought in further income. During the reign of Justinian knowledge of silk production was surreptitiously acquired from China, leading to the state silk textile monopoly. Gold coins manufactured in Byzantium became standard currency throughout much of the trading world of the time.

No aspect of Byzantium's life better illustrates the wealth of the Empire than the public architecture of the city of Constantinople. The great church of St Sophia, erected by Justinian between 532 and 537, remains a world landmark. The massive construction of walls, ports, public baths, churches, palaces, roads and bridges made Constantinople the marvel of the Christian world, eliciting from one of its visitors the exclamation, 'We know not whether we are in heaven or on earth.' Today the remnants of Byzantine material culture give some indication of the opulence which must once have elicited such words. Westerners have found Byzantine art, especially the sumptuous but rigidly stylized murals and mosaics lacking in naturalism, particularly by comparison with the work of the classical Greeks or the Renaissance Europeans. Only in comparatively recent times has a renewed interest in symbolic art made it possible for large numbers of westerners to recapture the full meaning and vitality of the Byzantine artistic achievement and accord it the high esteem it so richly deserves.

In the field of laws and letters Byzantine writers have been looked upon chiefly as the preservers (and sometimes distorters) of a Roman classical tradition. True, the Code of Justinian (AD 529) was chiefly an act of compilation. And it is through this compilation that Roman Law was transmitted to later generations both in the East and the West. But Justinian also published his own studies of earlier laws and a series of new legislation. The practice of recompilation and revision continued thereafter, and manuals of customary law were added to the central *codex*, the most famous being Leo III's *Ecologa* of 726.

All these developments point to the continuous encouragement of scholarship by the state and the Church in Byzantium. The Imperial College of Constantinople, which probably dated from the time of Constantine, trained students in philosophy, astronomy, mathematics, law and medicine and was used to train aspirants to the civil bureaucracy. The School of the Patriarch provided instruction in theology and other sacred subjects. In both, the classics, going back to the Greeks, was the common base of study. To a large extent it was the work of Byzantine scholars that kept alive the tradition of Greek classical scholarship and saved for posterity knowledge of the work of such writers as Plato, Aristotle and Ptolemy.

Decline of the Byzantine Empire

With the passing of the Macedonian dynasty in 1056, the Byzantine Empire started on a period of general decline. The reasons were both internal and external. Externally, the environment around Byzantium had changed considerably by the eleventh century. To the west, Europe was beginning to recover its economic and military strength. New cities such as Venice were beginning to extend their trading influence around the eastern Mediterranean and were soon to intrude on the trading sphere of Constantinople. The First Crusade, in 1097, exemplified the newly stirring energy of the feudal states of Europe. On the eastern side of the Empire, the Muslim world was newly activated by the Seljuk Turks, who, having captured Baghdad in 1055, had revitalized the Islamic world from the borders of Egypt to the frontiers of India. The year 1071 proved a double disaster for Byzantium, for in that year the Normans destroyed the remaining Byzantine outpost in southern Italy and the Seljuks won a decisive victory over the Byzantine emperor at Manzikert, on the extreme eastern frontier. Thereafter, Turks began to infiltrate Anatolia and commenced the process that was to convert Asia Minor into a homeland of Turkish people.

It was at this dark moment that the Empire was saved through the leadership of Alexius Commenus, a military figure who seized Constantinople and set himself up as emperor in 1081. He himself ruled until 1118, and his dynasty lasted until the sack of 1204. Alexius fought against the Normans in Italy, won the support of the Venetians and beat back the Seljuks from Anatolia, but his achievements were made possible by a drastic and destructive change in the structure of power in Byzantine society. Alexius was a representative of the locally powerful military aristocracy that had recently begun to appear within the empire. His seizure of power marked the domination over the state by the new aristocracy and led to the gradual eclipse of the imperial bureaucracy and of the civil and military institutions by which the Macedonian emperors had exerted centralized control. Under Alexius and his successors, the accumulation of lands and serfs, and the formation of private armies by local men of influence, went unchecked. With the weakening of central control and the growth of local magnates, a society that in structure resembled the feudalism of Europe and Japan arose.

The trend toward privatization of land and military predominance had begun under the previous dynasty, when the emperor had given out immense lands to local magnates in exchange for military support. These grants, known as *pronoia*, were at first not supposed to be hereditary possessions, but in time they became so and took on a nature similar to the fief in western European feudalism. In time, as the central bureaucracy lost power and the local *pronoiars* became more powerful, small land-holders and peasants began the practice of commending their land to them for protection, thus increasing the size of the immune estates. Increasingly the emperor had to depend upon the support of local magnates and their private military forces, or upon foreign mercenaries. The imperial jurisdiction rapidly shrank, and political decentralization made unified action difficult. Economic organization was also decentralized and localized, and Constantinople began

to lose its primacy over trade in the eastern Mediterranean. No longer able to dominate trade and manufacture through their own officials, the later Byzantine emperors looked to Venetian merchants for assistance. The economic concessions and privileges won by the Venetians from hard-pressed emperors eventually gave them a stranglehold over Byzantine trade.

Byzantium was already in disarray when the Fourth Crusade turned from its original objective of saving Palestine to attack Constantinople. The sack was carried out by a force of French, Germans, Flemings and Venetians, and when it was over, the leaders of the Crusade divided Byzantium among themselves and set up small feudal states over the expropriated territory. The states were ill-conceived and failed to establish a viable relationship between conquering rulers and local population. Yet in the wake of the Crusader a flood of European invaders moved into Greece

and Macedonia. The entire region was cut up into petty principalities and baronies. A French Dukedom of Athens was established, the Peloponnesus became the Principality of Achaia, Thessalonica became the capital of a new kingdom and various islands were converted into private lordships. European feudalism was now thoroughly implanted in the east.

By 1261 Constantinople was recaptured by the Greeks, but it would be hard to say that the Empire was restored. Byzantium consisted in the main of two cities, Constantinople and Thessalonica, and their environs. This fragile entity was ringed by hostile groups. There were Serbians and Bulgars to the north, Latin ex-Crusaders still held much of Greece and the intervening islands, Italian cities dominated trade in the Aegean and in Asia Minor the Ottoman Turks began to press for full control of Anatolia. During the fourteenth century Turks penetrated most of Byzantium's territory as settlers, often having been invited by the Byzantines themselves in the course of their own factional struggles. In 1356 the Turks established themselves in Adrianople, north of Constantinople, as a headquarters, and soon they were occupying territory well into the Balkans. When they eventually took Constantinople in 1453, the whole of the now-diminished Byzantine Empire fell to the Turks within a decade.

The legacy

The capture of Constantinople by the Turks put the heart of historic Byzantium and the eastern capital of the Roman empire, into the hands of people of Asian origin, cultural style and religion. Although Greece and the northern regions of the Balkan Peninsula were gradually to slip out of Turkish control in the centuries after the Turks' failure to take Vienna in 1683, Constantinople and Anatolia has remained to this day under Muslim Turkish rule. In the history of the world there

have been numerous similar examples of societies caught between more powerful neighboring civilizations and/or religions. The several states that appeared in the region between the Iranian Plateau, India and Central Asia come to mind as examples. Continuously subject to new groups of invaders of different cultural background and religious persuasion, these states appear in the writings of historians as preservers, transformers, conveyers or assimilators of the cultural traditions to which they were subjected. Byzantium, despite her considerable power and extraordinary longevity, in the end proved to be such a society, one in which peoples and cultures tended to meet and fuse, consolidate and dissipate in endless succession. Byzantium was both successor to the Rome of Augustus and a new 'Oriental' Christian state, both the end of the line in a Hellenic succession and the initial impetus in the spread of Christian civilization to the Slavs. If, for example, from the point of view of later Europeans, Byzantium was the terminal and distorted phase of the Roman tradition, for the Russians it was the beginning of a new spiritual life.

Above all, Byzantium illustrates the interchangeability of life in the great zones of civilization that divided Eurasia in the middle ages. The common picture of sectarian intolerance and religious warfare, when Christian Crusader fought Saracen infidel, when Muslim fanatics relentlessly pressed their holy wars in Africa and India, may suggest too rigid a conception of a world divided by religious conviction. Indeed there was plenty of religious violence, but mainly when religion was linked to political objective and economic ambition. In the absence of such linkage, accommodation and coexistence could and did take place, and nowhere more obviously than in Byzantium. Perhaps more than anything else, it was a monument to the malleability and resiliency of the human spirit.

Above: A wall mosaic from St Sophia in Constantinople. Its centerpiece features Mary and the infant Jesus.

Left: A fragment of a woven wall-hanging decorated with an ornate pattern of lions.

Right: The cathedral of St Sophia. Built by Constantine, it was extensively altered by both Theodosius and Justinian. After the fall of Constantinople in 1453 it was adapted for use as a mosque.

The Islamic World

Aside from the dramatic conquests of the Central Asian nomadic peoples, the most significant development in Eurasia during the period from AD 500 to 1500 was the expansion of the Arabic people and the consequent spread of the Muslim faith over fully two-thirds of the then known world. To a world traveler in the fifteenth century Islam would have seemed almost overwhelming, providing the common spiritual bond that bound together a vast spread of societies stretching from North Africa to Southeast Asia and penetrating even into western China and eastern Europe. In terms of scale there was nothing that approached the grandeur of life in Muslim Baghdad or Delhi; in terms of total wealth and resources Muslim princes and merchants far exceeded their European or East Asian competitors. Learned academies and monasteries from Cordoba in Spain to Herat in Afghanistan kept abreast of scientific and philosophical knowledge from around the world.

It would have been hard to imagine that the future of the world was not contained in the realm over which the Islamic sun rose and fell.

Some European writers on Islam have dwelt upon the close relationship between the three monotheistic religions of Semitic origin – Judaism, Christianity and Islam – stressing the elements they all share and the strong continuity of the Abrahamic tradition. Indeed, some writers, unconsciously echoing the Christian theologians of the early Middle Ages, who supposed Islam to be a Christian heresy, have stressed the derivative nature of Islam. But this approach tends to be both distorting and self-defeating, for notwithstanding obvious similarities and a common heritage, the central fact of Islam is the uniqueness of its message.

The uniqueness of Islam begins with the function of its Prophet. There had been, in the Muslim view, a succession of prophets before Muhammad – Abraham, Moses, and Jesus among them – each of whom had conveyed to their contemporaries a divine message in accordance with which they should frame their lives. But Muhammad was the last and greatest of the line. He was selected to carry out the final mission of making known to men the most complete revelation of God's will and purpose, and hence he is called in Arabic *Hakam al-Ambiyar*, the Seal of the Prophets, since there will never be another. Muhammad's function was to make known to his people the will of God and this he did by means of the *Qur'an* (Koran). A comparison between the *Qur'an* and the Bible is not really applicable, since, in the Muslim view, the *Qur'an* is not a 'scripture' put together by human skill, but is the Word of God made known through the historic personality of Muhammad. Any attempt to question or qualify this central tenet of the Muslim faith is to lapse straightaway into unbelief. Human frailty may result in disputed interpretations of the meaning of obscure passages in the *Qur'an*, but there can be no gradation of truth. It is a case of all or nothing.

The Muslim faith requires belief in the One God and unswerving obedience to His Will, in the unique prophetic function of Muhammad and in the perfection of the *Qur'an*. This core of belief is reinforced by a simple, if exacting, framework of religious observance: prayer five times a day in a carefully prescribed manner *(Salat)*; the setting aside of a portion of one's income for charitable purposes *(Zakat)*; fasting *(Sawm)* during the daylight hours of the month of Ramadan, the first month of the Muslim year; and the pilgrimage to Mecca *(Hajj)*.

Muhammad was born, around 570, in the city of Mecca in the western Hijaz, where his tribe, the Quraysh, monopolized much of the commerce of what was a busy and expanding emporium for the caravans coming up from southern Arabia and the Red Sea ports on their way to the Mediterranean. Although the bedouin tribes controlled the desert

Below far left: Religious observance at the Sultan Ahmet Mosque, Istanbul.

Below left: An ornately scripted page from an eleventh-century *Qur'an (Koran)*, the holy book at the heart of Muslim faith.

Right: Muhammad the Prophet replaces the sacred black stone in the Ka'ba at Mecca, after this place of pilgrimage had been cleared of pagan idols and consecrated to Islam.

Below: A caravanserai at Damascus, the capital of the Umayyad dynasty.

itself, exacting tolls on the trade which passed through their territory, the Hijaz supported both urban communities such as Mecca and nearby Medina, and also some sedentary agricultural settlements. The milieu in which Muhammad grew up was not, therefore, bounded by the outlook of the bedouin encampment, but was both self-consciously mercantile and moderately cosmopolitan. Although he had a lonely and deprived childhood, he was born into a ruling elite, an elite that at this period appears to have been undergoing a phase of irresponsible factionalism and greedy indifference to the sufferings of poorer kinsmen and dependants. Among the Quraysh, the young Muhammad appears to have been a relatively insignificant figure, but his status

among the Meccans improved when he was about 25 as a result of his marriage to an elderly widow. Nevertheless, when he had already turned forty and began to exhort his fellow citizens to accept his prophetic vocation his reception was anything but encouraging. Threats and violence forced him to flee to Medina, where he and a small band of followers found sanctuary.

In 622 he had made Medina the base for his operations against his opponents in Mecca, and in 630, after eight years of negotiation and desultory fighting, he at last obtained possession of the latter city, where he destroyed the pagan idols and converted the site of the *Ka'ba* into a Muslim sanctuary. Otherwise he treated the inhabitants with leniency and even liberality. By the time of

his death two years later, in 632, his followers had demonstrated their ascendancy over virtually all the major tribal groups of the Arabian peninsula, and the broad framework of Arabo-Muslim social and political relationships had been worked out, including those with non-Muslims, among whom the Christians and the Jews acquired the status of *dhimmis*, or protected communities, while idolators were regarded as beyond the pale. From this time there grew up the idea of a world divided into two – the *Dar al-Islam* consisting of the lands where Muslims could live secure in the practice of their religion and governed by their own Law, and the *Dar al-Harb*, the lands inhabited by infidels who one day, God willing, would be brought into the community of Islam.

Succession and conquest

Muhammad's death provoked consternation in the Muslim community, since while it was obvious that as the last and greatest of the line of prophets sent by God he could have no successor who fulfilled any prophetic function, it was nevertheless certain that the struggling community required firm leadership, especially in its dealings with neighboring states beyond the frontiers of the peninsula. Had Muhammad chosen to assert the principle of hereditary succession to the leadership of the community (the title of *Khalif*, rendered into English as Caliph, means 'Deputy of the Apostle of God'), his heir would have been his son-in-law and cousin, 'Ali, who had married his daughter, Fatima (Muhammad himself had no sons), and their sons, Hasan and Husayn – as indeed the Shi'is (from *Shi'at 'Ali*, the Party of 'Ali) always maintained. According to the orthodox Sunnis, however, no provision was made for a successor, and on the advice of 'Umar, a close personal friend and trusted adviser of Muhammad, the former 'Companions' of the Prophet selected Abu-Bakr, father of Muhammad's young widow 'A'isha, as the first Caliph. Abu-Bakr ruled for only a brief period (632-34) and was succeeded by 'Umar, who was to prove one of the greatest Muslim rulers and was the first to assume the title of *Amir al-Mu'minin* (Commander of the Faithful). During his reign of 10 years (634-44) the Arab conquests, begun in the reign of Abu-Bakr, were

given fresh impetus and inspired direction by the new Caliph and in the recently acquired territories a viable and efficient administration was set up. In 633 the Arabs invaded southern Palestine; in 634 Jerusalem was taken and in 635, Damascus. The Byzantine surrender of Edessa in 636 rounded off the conquest of northern Syria. The invasion of Egypt took place in 639 and was completed by the capture of Alexandria in 642. Meanwhile, the Mesopotamian territories of the Sasanids, including their capital at Ctesiphon, were occupied in 636, and in 642 an Arab army penetrated the Iranian plateau and at Nihavand, near Hamadan, defeated the last Sasanid ruler, Yazdgird III.

The relative ease with which these vast territories were acquired was not due solely to the fighting elan or religious zeal of the Arabs. More significant was the military exhaustion of the Byzantine and Sasanid empires as a result of the long and costly wars recently waged between Heraclius and Khusru II. Also, in the Byzantine provinces there had been a growing hostility among certain local Christian communities – the Copts in Egypt and the Jacobites in Syria – towards Byzantine Orthodoxy. Initially, therefore, in both Syria and Egypt the Arabs found themselves regarded in some sense as liberators, especially by the ecclesiastical hierarchies of those Christian sects regarded with disfavor by the Byzantine State. Moreover, the Arabs lacked the requisite knowledge and skills to govern their

new conquests without an intermediary elite to maintain continuity of administration and to collect taxes. Contrary to the assumption made by many European historians they were by no means dedicated to effecting the conversion of the subject peoples. Only in the Arabian peninsula were religions other than Islam forbidden. Elsewhere Christian, Jewish and Sabaean communities were left undisturbed so long as they paid the *kharaj*, or land tax, and the *jizyeh*, or poll tax. The Arabs, in theory at least, were not permitted to settle in the new lands occupied by the subject races, to colonize cultivable wastelands or to establish themselves in the Christian cities of Syria or Mesopotamia. (In any case, few of them would have wanted to do so in the early years immediately following the conquests since most of the troops were of bedouin stock and averse to agricultural labor.) Instead, they were concentrated in military camps where they lived apart from the subject population as a professional warrior-caste maintained by means of booty and pensions paid by the State. These camps eventually evolved into permanent settlements, and some, like Dasra, Wasit in Iraq and Fustat (Old Cairo) in Egypt, became major urban centers.

'Umar was succeeded by 'Uthman (644-56), a former Companion of the Prophet and from the same tribe, the Quraysh. He in turn was succeeded by the Prophet's son-in-law, 'Ali (656-61). 'Uthman was a pious and respected figure who enjoyed the support of the Arab aristocracy, but during his reign the administration deteriorated markedly. With 'Ali matters became worse. As the nearest male relative of the Prophet his claims to the Caliphate were obvious, and he had acquired a reputation for being brave as a lion in battle, as well as magnanimous and generous to his foes. But unfortunately for him and his descendants, he lacked the astuteness prerequisite in a ruler. Once he had become Caliph he shifted his headquarters from Medina, the capital of the three previous rulers, to southern Iraq, where he faced the rebellion of some former Companions of the Prophet, led by his widow 'A'isha. Even more serious was the challenge of the brilliant soldier-politician, Mu'awiya, a kinsman of the former Caliph 'Uthman, whose murder he (wrongly) attributed to 'Ali. Mu'awiya had behind him the considerable resources of the province of Syria. 'Ali was easily outmaneuvered by Mu'awiya, whose ambitions were essentially political, but to offset this humiliation he gained a striking victory over the Kharijites, adherents of a radical fundamentalist sect which believed that only a uniquely pious person could hold the office of Caliph and that neither birth into the 'magic circle' of the Meccan aristocracy nor the support of the consensus of the community weighed against this essential requirement. In 658 'Ali defeated the Kharijites in battle at Nahrawan, but they remained a formidable threat to the established order, and in 661 a Kharijite fanatic murdered 'Ali at Kufah. With his death ended the rule of the four 'rightly guided' Caliphs, so called to distinguish them from the sybaritic and worldly Umayyads.

The Caliphate now passed into the hands of Mu'awiya (661-80), founder of the Umayyad dynasty, who set himself the task of reorganizing the empire of which he had become the master, and in North Africa and Khurasan the frontiers continued to move steadily outward. The family of Mu'awiya and the Umayyad ruling elite in general made little attempt to disguise the fact that they were, for the most part, members of a highly sophisticated and hedonistic aristocracy that was far removed from either the pious sup

porters of Abu-Bakr and 'Umar or the fanatical Kharijites. But the regime faced no very serious enemies: 'Ali's eldest son, Hasan, had allegedly waived any claims he might have possessed to succeed his father and lived out the rest of his days as a private citizen in Medina. His brother, Husayn, led an abortive uprising in 680 at the accession of the second Umayyad Caliph, Yazid I (680-83), but was soon defeated and killed.

The frontiers of Islam continued to expand. In Anatolia the struggle with the Byzantine Empire continued in sporadic fashion, but in 717 and 718 Arab forces were actually besieging Constantinople. In Mawarannahr Muslim rule was extended as far as the Syr-Darya – largely due to the brilliant campaigning of Qutayba b Muslim – in the face of concerted opposition on the part of the Sogdian princes and their Turkish allies. In 711 Muhammad b Qasim conquered Sind, and in the same year Tariq b Ziyad (from whose name is derived Gibraltar, *Jabal Tariq* or Tariq's Mountain) crossed over from Africa into Spain, where the Visigothic kingdom was in an advanced state of decay. The Arabs swiftly mastered all of the peninsula, except for the far north, and by 732 they had penetrated into France as far as the country around Poitiers, where they were repulsed in an engagement with the Frankish troops of Charles Martel.

Some of the later Umayyads were men of outstanding capacity, but in its last years the dynasty produced a succession of pleasure-loving incompetents, and long before the end came the Umayyads had already acquired among God-fearing Muslims that reputation for worldliness and impiety which writers in 'Abbasid times would record so meticulously.

The 'Abbasid universal state

In 750 the Umayyads were swept aside in a revolutionary upheaval that placed the Caliphate in the hands of the 'Abbasids, the descendants of the Prophet's uncle, 'Abbas, around whom had been sedulously woven a reputation of legitimacy and piety by their underground adherents. The movement which destroyed the Umayyads (reputedly,

only a single member of the family survived the holocaust to flee to Spain and found the Amirate of Cordoba) originated in Khurasan and centered on the mysterious personality of Abu Muslim, secret emissary, master propagandist and (once the movement emerged into the light of day) supreme architect of the 'Abbasid victory. Not unnaturally, therefore, the second 'Abbasid Caliph, al-Mansur, prudently took the first available opportunity, which came in 754, to put to death this all too ingenious servant.

The 'Abbasid revolution succeeded primarily because the Umayyads had so utterly lost the support of their subjects. In Medina and elsewhere the Shi'is were irreconcilably opposed to the regime. So, too, were the Arab tribes quartered in Iraq and Khurasan. More important still, the newly converted *mawalis* (clients), especially the Iranians, were seething with discontent against a state in which they were clearly second-class citizens and which, in the final analysis, was rooted in the racial exclusiveness of a relatively small number of pure-bred Arabs. It was the *mawalis*, in particular, who provided the mass support for Abu Muslim's movement in Khurasan.

The new order established by the 'Abbasids took account of all these factors. The discontent of the Shi'is was, at least for the time being, neutralized. Iraq was made the center of the new Caliphate, and although at first Kufah served as the capital, in 762 al-Mansur laid out the city of Baghdad, thereafter to remain the capital of the Caliphate, with only temporary breaks, until the Mongol conquest of 1258. Finally, the Iranians were drawn in to share the glory and rewards of empire and to make a significant contribution to the civilization of 'Abbasid Baghdad, which, unlike that of Umayyad Damascus, must be regarded as 'Islamic' rather than specifically 'Arab.' There was an increasingly Iranian character to the Caliphate, which now began to acquire many of the trappings of the old Sasanid kingship – unfettered autocracy, elaborate court ceremony and protocol, government by bureaucratic traditions alien to both Damascus and Medina and even the gradual assumption by the *Amir al-Mu'minin* of a quasi-sacred personality. Yet despite the appearance of dangerous sectarian movements and no less formidable rebellions in the years to come, the 'Abbasid Caliphate, founded by al-Saffah (749-54) and given shape by his brother, al-Mansur (754-75), met the needs of the Muslim community in a way no previous regime had done. Their rule enjoyed at nearly all times broad support from a majority of their subjects. Their Caliphate survived more or less intact for 500 years and then fell not to a usurping line of fellow Muslims but to the Mongols.

The 'Abbasid Caliph was an absolute ruler, but his authority could only be transformed into executive action through an elaborate bureaucracy possessing a markedly Iranian character. At the head of this bureaucracy stood the *vazir* (vizier), holding an office of almost unlimited power, provided the incumbent enjoyed the confidence of his master. There was a tendency for the *vizarat* to become semi-hereditary. The origin of the *vizarat* has been a subject of some controversy, but while serious doubts have been raised regarding the theory that it was an office directly descended from the Sasanid office of *vuzurg framadar*, its ultimate derivation from Iran can hardly be doubted. Under the *vazir* were *diwans* (departments) responsible for finance, the army, postal communications and the provincial administration. The organization of the finances, in particular, was highly sophisticated and only at a later

Above left: The elephants on this tenth-century Persian carpet are depicted in the style of the pre-Islamic Sasanid dynasty, 300 years after its defeat by the Arab invaders. When the Abbasid dynasty moved its capital to Baghdad, Persian cultural influence soon came to predominate in the Islamic empire.

Right: The huge minaret of the ninth-century Great Mosque of Samarra, north of Baghdad. The city of Samarra was probably the most splendid ever built by the Abbasids, yet only two of its buildings have survived.

date did the elaborate system of taxation give way to the disastrous practice of tax-farming. The postal system was especially important in view of the enormous distances involved in controlling so vast an empire, and its antecedents undoubtedly extended back to Achaemenid times. Its staff also served as intelligence agents, highly trained individuals who acted as the local eyes and ears of the *vazir* and his master.

The 'Abbasids had inherited from the Umayyads an empire stretching from the Maghrib to the Syr-Darya, and with a fluctuating but generally expanding frontier in Anatolia, the Caucasus and Mawarannahr. Spain, however, was lost to them when, in 755, a surviving Umayyad prince of unusual resourcefulness, 'Abd at-Rahman I (756-88), established the Amirate of Cordoba, soon to become the setting for some of the most spectacular achievements in the intellectual and cultural history of Islam. Elsewhere, however, direct confrontations with the regime were of an extremely local character.

The outward appearance of the 'Abbasid Caliphate in the first century of its history was one of impressive achievement – in its effective control over vast and diverse regions, in the widespread peace and prosperity which existed for Muslims and non-Muslims alike under its aegis and in the civilized affluence enjoyed by its ruling elite. Some credit for all this must go to the personalities of the early Caliphs: al-Mansur, who died in 775, was an outstanding ruler, but so were al-Mahdi (775-85), Harun al-Rashid (786-809) and in particular al-Ma'mun (813-33). The popular tradition that linked the tales of *The Thousand and One Nights* with Harun al-Rashid (in this context a composite figure of folklore) did no more than justice to an epoch of unusual splendor, reflected in the following account of a feast held by al-Mutawakkil (847-61):

After the great commanders and nobles had finished eating, al-Mutawakkil sat down, and he caused to be set down in front of himself jewel-encrusted golden stands on which were heaped pieces of ambergris, amber and musk molded into shapes and figures, and these stands were placed stretched out in a row. The great commanders, courtiers and holders of high official positions were gathered round. There were placed before them large trays of gold set with all kinds of jewels on both surfaces. Between the two rows was a space. The attendants brought in palm-leaf baskets covered over with leather sheets and filled with dirhams and dinars in equal proportions. These were now poured into the space until they became piled high above the level of the trays. Those present were told to drink, and then those who had drunk were each to draw out three handfuls, with their fists gripping as much as they could, from the coins poured from the baskets. Whenever one place

became empty, more coins were poured out of the baskets to refill it just as it was before. Slave boys stood at the end of the assembled gathering, crying out. 'The Commander of the Faithful bids all of you to take as much as you like!' So everyone there stretched forth his hands and took some of the money. They became weighted down with all that they had taken, so would go out and pass the money over to their slave boys and then return to their places. When the entertainment came to an end, 1000 robes of honor were distributed among those present. They were given 1000 mounts to depart on, each with gold and silver trappings, and 1000 slaves were freed.

What was the economic base that supported such wealth? So far as the evidence permits a definitive answer, it seems that it rested solidly upon the profit derived from a far-flung and com-

plex network of intercontinental commerce, in which the lands of the 'Abbasid Caliphate and, in particular, of the Fertile Crescent were at the center of almost all the major trade routes of the known world. Commercial activity on such a scale and the ceaseless demand for consumer goods also greatly stimulated manufacturing. The commercial prosperity of the early 'Abbasid period owed much to the political unity imposed by the Caliph's government over so much of the Middle East and of the Mediterranean world. It also owed much to the social esteem in which the merchant was traditionally held by the entire Muslim community. Above all, it was made possible by the existence of a sound agricultural foundation, with the central and provincial governments assuming responsibility for the initiation of irrigation projects and with perhaps less land taken over by pastoralists, at least in the eastern provinces, than would be the case three or four centuries later.

Neither in agriculture nor in manufacturing processes is there any evidence of major technological innovation in this period. The glory of 'Abbasid Baghdad rested most emphatically upon manpower and the skill of the human hand. Slaves were everywhere, but there is no way of estimating what proportion of the population had

the servile status clearly defined in Muslim Law. Slaves were to be found in a wide spectrum of occupations, and they included virtually every infidel race with whom the Muslims had contact, either in commerce or war. They ranged from the East African Negroes (zanj) employed on the salt flats near Basra to the heterogeneous crews of the Mediterranean galleys and, at a later date, to the predominantly Turkish slave armies recruited from beyond the Syr-Darya. Most, however, were domestics of one kind or another, including concubines and the occupants of royal and aristocratic harems.

The Muslim world: trade and the city

The importance of trade in 'Abbasid times can be observed with the emergence of the long-distance merchant, with his headquarters in, say, Baghdad or Basra, and with his agents handling his goods in bazaars and caravanserais as far away as Morocco, India or China. It is no coincidence that the 'Abbasid period left behind it a rich legacy of works on geography and travel. Cartography, too, was very much in vogue. Sinbad the Sailor passing down the Persian Gulf from Basra into the Indian Ocean, his dhow laden with precious cargo, is an archetypal figure of the period, and current excavations at the port of Siraf on the coast of Fars confirm the wealth and size of the ports frequented by generations of such adventurers.

One striking feature of the 'Abbasid period was the expansion of urban life, especially in the great commercial and manufacturing emporiums. Islam is in many ways an urban phenomenon, and in order to be a good Muslim – to participate in public prayer with one's fellow believers, to carry out the prescribed ablutions (which presupposes access to a public bath-house) and to live in a godly community govered by Muslim law, the Shari'at – it is desirable to live in an urban community. The coming of Islam had led to the founding of numerous new cities, often the garrison towns of conquering Arab armies, but in addition, many Hellenistic and Sasanid cities continued to thrive and prosper under Muslim rule. The Muslim city was a place where believers met

non-believers and acquired such knowledge of alien or earlier civilizations as they deemed worth knowing. It was in the cities of Mesopotamia that they gained access to the Hellenistic heritage through contacts with Syriac Christians, and it was in the cities of Iran that they acquired their enthusiasm for the remnants of Sasanid culture. Except for merchants and those who organized the caravan trade, or for itinerant academics and craftsmen, most city-dwellers rarely left the places of their birth unless driven by fear or need. Significantly, once they left their native town or city they carried it with them as an appelation all their lives – al-Baghdadi, al-Tusi, for example. The Muslim city was also the repository of what may be styled the Islamic 'Great Tradition,' enshrining the theologian's vision of an orthodox world order and the social and political values of the partly Iranicized bureaucracy. Without the Muslim city, classical Islamic civilization would have been unthinkable.

A unifying force

Outwardly, at least, those who inhabited the 'Abbasid state felt themselves to be living in a single entity, the Dar al-Islam, in which a Muslim from, say, Spain could feel at home in Egypt or Iraq. In some respects, however, this feeling served as a screen concealing pronounced ethnic and regional idiosyncracies, tensions and rivalries – as between Arab and Iranian, for example, or between Arab and Berber. Yet the cultural homogeneity of classical Islamic civilization was nevertheless a reality, made possible not so much as a result of the Caliph's authority (on the wane in the late ninth century) as of more subtle and enduring elements. These included the unifying role of the Arabic language, even in the Persian-speaking lands beyond the Tigris, a standard pattern of belief and worship, a legal system of universal applicability and the doctrinal orthodoxy imposed by members of the ulama (whether jurists, theologians or teachers) trained in an educational system that inculcated into its students a common body of knowledge.

Notwithstanding the orthodoxy of the ulama

Above: A silver coin minted by the Umayyad caliphs in the seventh century AD.

Above left: The Dome of the Rock in Jerusalem was built in AD 691 on the site from which Muhammad is believed to have ascended into heaven.

Left: The courtyard of the ninth-century Great Mosque at Kairouan, Tunisia. Kairouan is one of the holiest places of Islam, along with Mecca and Jerusalem.

Right: The Arab conquests in the century after the death of Muhammad took the desert people east through Persia to central Asia and west through north Africa into Spain and France. Even when this initial impetus was spent, the Islamic world continued to expand.

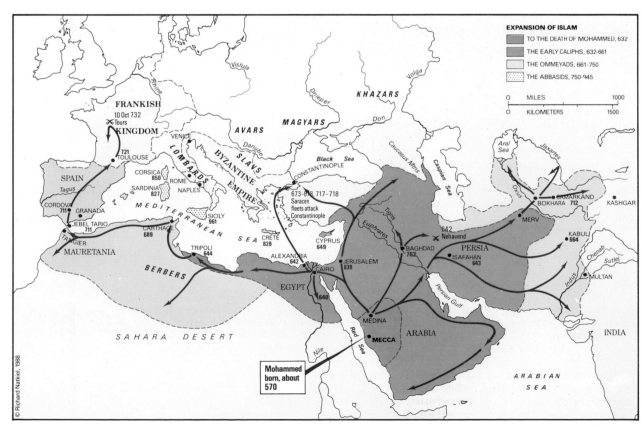

© Richard Natkiel, 1988

EXPANSION OF ISLAM

▓	TO THE DEATH OF MOHAMMED, 632
▓	THE EARLY CALIPHS, 632-661
░	THE OMMEYADS, 661-750
▒	THE ABBASIDS, 750-945

Mohammed born, about 570

and the theocratic element in 'Abbasid government, the intellectual life of the early 'Abbasid period was both complex and many-sided, deriving its inspiration from diverse sources – from Hellenistic and Christian Syriac traditions, from Byzantium and Sasanid Iran and even from India. As a result, the spirit of intellectual inquiry, especially in the fields of philosophy, metaphysics and the natural sciences, far outstripped the narrow horizons of the theologians, and in consequence heterodoxy and heresy were rife, resulting in sporadic outbursts of witch-hunting and the coercion of intellectuals who challenged conventional assumptions without first securing a powerful protector.

The 'Abbasid government had some justification for regarding heterodox movements with apprehension. Both the Kharijite and Shi'i sects had long threatened the existing political order, and their leaders repeatedly showed unerring judgment in linking Messianic and millennial preaching with movements of social discontent, as in the case of the Shi'i leader of the uprising of East African slaves (zanj) in southern Iraq, which lasted from 869 to 883. Shi'ism, in particular, flourished underground in the early 'Abbasid period, and while the objectives of its leaders were frequently political, its followers were drawn by the emotional appeal of a Messianic faith that appealed to the oppressed and the discontented in a way which Sunni Islam could hardly expect to. The central tenet of Shi'ism, today largely restricted to Iran and certain communities in Iraq, Lebanon and India, is belief in the divine office and perfectibility of the Twelve Imams: the Caliph 'Ali and his descendants, of whom the twelfth, the Hidden Imam, disappeared in Samarra in 873 and is believed to be living in concealment, to return on the Day of Judgment as the Sahib-i Zaman (the Lord of the Age). Shi'ism has shown a constant tendency to proliferate sects, thereby weakening its capacity to challenge the Sunni Establishment, but the 'Abbasids, usurpers themselves, rightly regarded any form of Shi'ism as a potential threat.

The decline and disintegration of the 'Abbasid state

During the ninth and tenth centuries the 'Abbasid Caliphate descended to such a level of impotence and degradation that it must have seemed impossible for it to recover. In tracing this decline the historian has constantly to distinguish between cause and symptom. The diminished personal authority of the ninth century Caliphs who succeeded al-Ma'mum (d 833) was undoubtedly a contributing factor, but the problem is to decide whether this was the result of personal failures or the consequence of more profound weaknesses in the overall structure of the regime. Much the same may be said of the trend for provincial governors to establish their de facto independence while nevertheless maintaining an outward show of respect for the Caliph's office. Such was the case with al-Ma'mun's Iranian governor of Khurasan, Tahir, who reigned in Nishapur as virtually his own master. When he died al-Ma'mun confirmed his son, Talha, in his father's stead, and the Tahirids continued to rule Khurasan until 873. Much the same occurred in Egypt. There an assertive deputy governor, Ahmad b Tulun, the son of a Turkish slave, retained power from 868 to 884 and declined to obey the Caliph's summons to relinquish his post. He remained an independent ruler, as did his successors, and Egypt remained severed from Baghdad until 905, when an 'Abbasid army reconquered it. Later another dynasty of Turkish governors, the Ikhshidids (935-69), fol-

lowed the Tulunid precedent. The powerlessness of the Caliphs to control these ambitious satraps was primarily a military problem. The first 'Abbasids, like the Umayyads, had relied upon Arab tribal levies that were turbulent, factious and, with the passing years, increasingly unreliable. In consequence the later Caliphs sought to escape from too great a dependence upon their Arab troops by enlisting non-Arab mercenaries or by maintaining armies of slave soldiers. The former were generally Turks or (also predominantly Turkic) the tough tribesmen from Daylam, the mountainous region just south of the Caspian in Iran. With the arrival of Turkish warriors in large numbers in the metropolitan provinces of the Caliphate there began a slow process that was to convert the Muslim world, apart from Spain and North Africa, into the preserve of Turkish military elites. Contemporary writers concurred in the belief that Turkish troops, whether slaves or mercenaries, displayed qualities which made them militarily superior to all other groups. They revelled in war for its own sake, fought like lions, were reckoned tolerably obedient and produced resourceful and skillful leaders. But they were also ambitious and grasping, and whether bond or free they displayed a cohesive strength and a sense of racial pride that, added to their other formidable qualities, made them potentially dangerous to their masters.

The 'Abbasid Caliphs soon found themselves the captive paymasters of their restless Praetorians, and although one Caliph, al-Mutawakkil (847-61), transferred his capital from Baghdad to Samarra in the hope of escaping the proximity of his Turkish troops, it was to no avail. The Caliphs then turned to their Daylami troops to balance the Turks. In consequence, by the middle of the tenth century a dynasty from Daylam, the Buyids, had conquered all the western and southern part of the Iranian plateau. In 945 they took Baghdad itself, where Mu'izz al-Dawla Ahmad became 'Mayor of the Palace' to the helpless Caliph, the paradox being that while theoretically the 'Abbasid Caliph was spiritual leader of the Sunni world, Mu'izz al-Dawla Ahmad was a Shi'i who looked upon the Caliph as a usurper. Under Mu'izz al-Dawla Ahmad and his brothers, as well as later under the greatest Buyid ruler, Adud al-Dawla Fana-Khusru (978-83), Iran and Mesopotamia were part of a proselytizing Shi'i state, and during this period both religious dissent and regional loyalties on the Iranian plateau found free play for their development. The Buyids, it is interesting to note, claimed a Sasanid pedigree and were the first Muslim rulers in Iran to revive the pre-Islamic title of Shahanshah ('King of Kings').

The period of Buyid dominance (932-1062) marked an important phase in Iran's political and cultural revival, but the center of the so-called 'New Iranian Renaissance' lay further east, in Mawarannahr, in the territories of the Samanid dynasty. Samanid rule (819-1005) represented in a different way from that of the Buyids a challenge to the universalist state of the 'Abbasid Caliphs, though the dynasty always maintained a suitably deferential attitude toward the Caliphate. The Samanids were originally dihqans (petty landowners) from the Balkh region and claimed descent from the Sasanid general, Bahram Chubin. Emerging first as officials in the service of the Tahirids, and then of the 'Abbasids in Khurasan and Mawarannahr, their rise to de facto independence coincided with the decline of the Tahirids. It was confirmed in 875 when Nasr I b Ahmad was appointed amir of Mawarannahr by the Caliph, al-Mu'tamid. The 'Abbasids were perfectly content to recognize the existence of a Samanid imperium

in imperio within the framework of Caliphal suzerainty, not least because the Samanids served the interests of Baghdad by containing the Saffarids within Sistan and by acting as a counterweight to the Buyids in the west. The fact that the Samanids, unlike the Buyids, were orthodox Sunnis also enhanced their prestige with Baghdad.

The Samanid territories consciously preserved both the pre-Islamic social system of the eastern Iranian lands and the cultural traditions of the old Iranian landowning class. With their capital at Bukhara, a brilliant center of Irano-Islamic culture, and with their power based in Mawarannahr, facing the Turkish world beyond the Syr-Darya, they served as a focal point for a revival of Iranian feelings of cultural identity. An important aspect of this was a flowering of the Persian language, which at this time was being shaped by such master poets as Daqiqi, Rudaki and Firdausi. Samanid culture proved to have a magnetic appeal for those neighboring Turkish peoples now being drawn for the first time into the orbit of Islamic civilization. At the height of their power the Samanid amirs – especially Nasr I b Ahmad (864-92), Isma'il I b Ahmad (892-907) and al-Amir as-Sa'id Nasr II (914-43) – enjoyed a reputation throughout the Muslim world as rulers of a king-

Right: The Mu'adham Mosque, near Baghdad in modern-day Iraq, is used by the faithful of the majority Sunni branch of Islam. Many of Iraq's Muslim population owe allegiance to Shi'ism, however, which has survived since the earliest centuries of Islam as a powerful alternative to Sunni othodoxy.

dom that was rich, peaceful and prosperous, and their court boasted among its attendant figures the *vazir* and historian Bal'ami, the *vazir* and geographer al-Jayhani and the polymath Ibn Sina (Avicenna), whose writings dealt with philosophy, medicine, natural history, mathematics, physics, chemistry, astronomy and music, and who was perhaps the outstanding example of the range and depth of the medieval Muslim mind at its best.

The Samanid legacy

The importance of the Samanid period for later developments lay in the regime's conscious promotion of Iranian traditions and attitudes which, as in the case of Firdausi's *Shahnameh*, presented essentially non-Muslim values in a way too appealing for Muslims to discard. It was not the Iranians alone who were the heirs of this Samanid legacy, since through complex processes of acculturation it came to be shared by both the Eastern and Western Turks, and even by the Mongols. The Samanid regime, despite its orthodoxy, infused into the Muslim East cultural values which were in many respects alien to Islam, but which nevertheless enriched Islamic civilization beyond measure.

On a different scale a somewhat similar function was performed by the wholly Turkish Qarakhanid dynasty, which gradually superseded the Saminids in Mawarannahr during the second half of the tenth century until, in 992, the Qarakhanid ruler Harun Bughra Khan temporarily seized Bukhara, the Samanid capital, an occupation made permanent in 999. The Qarakhanids were no barbarians, but the heirs to Turkish traditions of culture and state-craft going back to the Orkhon Turks and the Uighurs. Later, like other Turkish dynasties of Central Asian origin, they would claim descent from the mythical Afrasiab, King of Turan, the unrelenting foe of the Iranians in Firdausi's *Shahnameh*.

Little is known of either the political history or the governing institutions of the Qarakhanids, but it appears that in characteristic Turko-Mongol fashion they recognized the sovereignty of a ruling house rather than of a single individual and that their realm was divided into separate appanages for the senior princes of the line. The head of this loosely knit tribal confederacy carried the title of *Ilek*, and his administration seems to have followed the usual pattern in the Muslim East. Thus there was a threefold division, no doubt frequently blurred in practice, into the bureaucracy, the army and the royal household. The bureaucracy was headed by a *vazir (ulugh hajib)*, a principal secretary (*bikitchi*), who was also responsible for the administration of justice and foreign relations, and a treasurer (*aghiji*). The commander of the army (*subashi*) headed a separate hierarchy. The officers of the royal household included such posts as chamberlain, cup-bearer, standard-bearer, chief falconer and master of the horse. The level of culture of the ruling elite was, by the eleventh century, probably in no way inferior to that of the Samanids. Here, for example, is a Qarakhanid description of an ideal envoy:

A successful ambassador must know how to read and write. He should be able to read and recite poetry. He must have a beautiful handwriting and be able to read all types of script . . . He must be skilled in astronomy . . . medicine . . . accounting . . . surveying and geometry . . . and in the science of interpreting dreams . . . He must be skilled in games like cards, chess, polo, jereed [javelin-throwing], archery and hunting, for these are a means of winning friends . . . He must be an orator and fluent in many languages, for ambassadors perform their duties by means of words.

Source material relating to the Qarakhanid period is scant, but two important sources have survived, written within a decade of each other.

Left: The thirteenth-century citadel at Aleppo, Syria, a stronghold of the Ayyubid dynasty founded by the famous warrior Salah al-Din (Saladin).

Below: A gold coin minted by the mysterious sect of the Assassins.

Below right: One of the Assassins' most formidable fortresses, Masyaf Castle. It was from such strongholds that the sect's Grand Masters organized their now infamous political assassinations. Despite its reputation for violence the sect was also a center of intellectual life.

The first is a dictionary of Khaqani, the Turkish language spoken by the Qarakhanids, entitled the *Diwan lughat al-Turk* and written by Mahmud Kashghari, a learned Turk who completed his work in Baghdad between 1072 and 1074. The other is a didactic epic known as the *Qutadghu bilig,* written in Kashgar by Yusuf Khass Hajib in 1069-70, which throws some tangential light upon the spread of Islam among the Qarluq. As has often been the case in the history of both Christianity and Islam, legend has compressed what must certainly have been a gradual process into a single incident by providing a royal convert to lead his subjects into the fold, in this case Satuq Dughra Khan, who took the Muslim name of 'Abd al-Karim and who died in 955. It is frequently asserted that on conversion to Islam the Turks usually demonstrated their fervor by ferocious persecution of the adherents of other religions. In the case of the Qarakhanids this does not appear to have been the case. Shamanist practices undoubtedly survived, to give a distinctly syncretic character to Islam on the steppes, and there is no evidence of persecution of the Nestorian Christian communities of Central Asia at this time. The *Qutadghu bilig* does, however, imply hostility to Buddhism, perhaps less for its own sake than because it was patronized by the rival Uighur Qaghanate east of Kashgaria.

Turkish slave armies

The Samanids and, in time, the Qarakhanids followed 'Abbasid precedent in their reliance upon armies composed of Turkish slaves. So too did the Ghaznavid dynasty (977-1186), which seized the possessions of the Samanids south of the Amu Darya, harried the Buyid principalities in the west and eventually dominated the greater part of the Iranian world between the Tigris and the Indus. The founder of this dynasty was a Turkish slave commander of the Samanids, Sebüktigin, but it was his son Yamin al-Dawla Mahmud (998-1030) who was the real architect of the vast Ghaznavid empire, as well as the sword-arm of the 'Abbasid

Caliph in his disputes with the heretical Buyids and the leader of numerous plundering expeditions into northwestern India. Mahmud's court at Ghazni, in eastern Afghanistan, extended the Irano-Islamic synthesis farther east and south than it had ever reached before. The Sultan himself, a figure in Muslim folklore no less famous than Harun al-Rashid, collected scholarly celebrities in much the same way as a modern millionaire buys pictures. When persuasion failed, he was not above resorting to threats and even kidnapping. Ibn Sina withdrew into the Elburz mountains, and then to distant Hamadan, to avoid his attentions, while Firdausi, disgusted at the Sultan's ingratitude, penned a savage satire and fled. The great al-Biruni, insatiable student of geography, the natural sciences and the human condition, seems on the other hand to have felt no qualms about his life at Ghazni, where he wrote a remarkable account of Hindu beliefs and customs that was not to be bettered until the nineteenth century.

Mahmud of Ghazni was a type of Turkish warlord and empire-builder who would emerge again and again in the Muslim East. His success, like that of most of those who came after him down to the Mongol eruption of the thirteenth century, rested upon an institution that was one of the strangest, as well as one of the most effective, military innovations of medieval times. The slave army, composed of slave troops led by slave commanders, had been an innovation of the 'Abbasids. It was used extensively by the Buyids, the Samanids and the Ghaznavids. It was taken into India by the Ghurids and was introduced into Anatolia by the Seljuqs, where it provided a model for the Ottoman Janissaries. The Egyptian Mamluks between the thirteenth and the sixteenth centuries maintained a regime where power was monopolized exclusively by an elite of military slaves. Even in the far west the Umayyad Amirate of Cordoba recruited Frankish slaves for its armies. The attraction of the slave soldier (*mamluk, ghulam*) rested upon the assumption of his

unswerving loyalty to his master. Other kinds of troops, tribal levies or men recruited to fight for pay, were held to be unreliable or treacherous, for in a crisis a tribesman's loyalty toward a fellow tribesman usually transcended his loyalty to his ruler. Kinsmen were even more unreliable, and the Seljuq *vazir,* Nizam al-Mulk (1018-92), observed:

One obedient slave is better than three hundred sons. For the latter desire their father's death: the former long life for his master.

A slave soldier was a professional, and the farther he had been brought from the land of his birth the better. He was better trained and disciplined than most other soldiers, for he had been taught over many years to perfect his handling of his horse and his skill with the bow and other weapons. Generally he was a pagan Turk from Central Asia, though other races were also recruited. In some respects his servile status was ambiguous, since although he was a slave in Muslim law, purchased by a master who could sell him at any time and to whom his property theoretically escheated at his death, some slave commanders accumulated vast possessions, transferred themselves at their master's death to some other commander at will and often married their masters' daughters. The most able were employed as administrators, and some were made high officers of state or provincial governors. Three of the greatest thirteenth-century Sultans of Delhi were slave commanders who reached the throne apparently without bothering to seek formal manumission. There was little or no opprobrium attached to their servile status, and the sources suggest that successful slave commanders encouraged members of their own tribes to join their slave establishments. These slave armies and slave administrations became closed corporations, jealously resentful of free-born intruders and especially of non-Turks. In thirteenth-century India the Turkish slave nobles ruthlessly intrigued to exclude the free-born Turkish nobles from office, but both groups would band together against Indian-born converts. Until the coming of the Mongols of Chingiz (Genghis) Khan the Turkish slave armies were widely thought to be nearly unbeatable.

The political power of the 'Abbasid Caliphate foundered upon many rocks: the transfer of Arab military supremacy to the Turks, the growth of *de facto* independent viceroyalties, protracted social upheavals such as the *zanj* rebellion of East African slaves in lower Iraq during the ninth century and the growing ineffectiveness of the Baghdad government. Yet dispite all this the Caliph was still Caliph, the Commander of the Faithful, the nominal leader of all the Muslim community except for the heretical sects and the subjects of the Umayyad Amirate of Cordoba. The regime might experience temporary setbacks and embarrassments, a Praetorian mutiny in Baghdad, for example, the insubordination of Ahmad b Tulun in Egypt or the pretensions of the distant Samanids, but it seemed that nothing could shake what was seen as a divinely ordained world order.

Yet there was one event that struck deeply at the concept of the 'Abbasid universalist state, and it struck the more deeply because of its theological implications. This was the rise of the Fatimids (909-1171). Hitherto the history of political Shi'ism had been one of almost total failure. Ruthless suppression, first by the Umayyads and then by the 'Abbasids, had brought every bid for power to nothing, but the Shi'ite community, battered and tormented, nevertheless retained an unswerving loyalty to the memory of 'Ali and a conviction that the Prophet's spiritual descendants enjoyed a special favor in the eyes of God. Shi'ism is so often associated with Iran that it is easy to overlook the fact that Shi'ism had been at first an almost exclusively Arab phenomenon and that the most spectacular triumph ever achieved by political Shi'ism was a combined Arab-Berber movement originating in the Maghrib.

The Fatimids

Like other Shi'ite movements, that of the Fatimids (who claimed descent from Muhammad's daughter, Fatima) possessed a pronounced Messianic character. This was first personified in the mysterious figure of 'Ubaydallah al-Mahdi (909-34), who arrived in North Africa from Syria and proceeded to enlist the support of Berber tribesmen, hitherto Kharijite, in the establishment of a new world order in place of that of the 'usurping' 'Abbasids. His military success was spectacular, and although by the time of his death Egypt was still unconquered, as was Umayyad Spain, he had seized the Aghlabid possessions in Ifriqiyya (now Tunisia), subdued the Shi'i Idrisids in Fez, occupied Sicily and had at his disposal the entire resources of the Maghrib. From the first, however, he had looked eastward toward Egypt and the Fertile Crescent, rather than westward toward Spain, and since his quarrel with the 'Abbasids was primarily ideological, he took the momentous step of proclaiming himself Caliph. Not long afterwards, the greatest of the Umayyad Amirs of Cordoba, 'Abd al-Rahman III (912-61), did the same. The demoralizing effect of the assumption of these titles upon the Muslim commuity may be compared in medieval Europe to the scandal of two or (prior to the Council of Constance) three rival Popes.

It was the fourth Fatimid Caliph, al-Mu'izz (953-75), who enjoyed the long deferred conquest of Egypt, and it was he who laid out a new capital near Fustat or Old Cairo, perhaps consciously emulating al-Mansur's foundation of Baghdad. Contemporary accounts indicate that under the Fatimids al-Qahira (New Cairo) was a city of quite remarkable affluence and distinction. Here, soon after the conquest, the Fatimids founded the college of al-Az'har (today a center of Sunni orthodoxy) as a seminary for the training of Shi'i *da'is* (missionaries) and for the dissemination of Shi'i beliefs.

Propaganda war

At their zenith under the Caliph al-Mustansir (1036-94) the Fatimids controlled a vast area that extended into the Fertile Crescent as far as Mosul, on the upper Tigris. They well understood, however, that the challenge they presented to the 'Abbasid regime was not one to be fought out upon the battlefield, but in the minds of men. It was in propaganda, in the secret dissemination of esoteric doctrine, in political subversion by means of what today would be described as underground cells in enemy territory, that the Fatimids advanced their cause in the Muslim East. It was their agents and *da'is*, not their armies, that the 'Abbasid Caliphate and their orthodox Sunni protectors, the Turkish Seljuqs, most feared. The Fatimid *da'is* spread slowly throughout the 'Abbasid Caliphate, and wherever they went they established cells among those who were disillusioned with the 'Abbasid Establishment – in the cities, the poorer craftsmen and artisans; in the mountains of Syria and northern Iran, the inhabitants of half-forgotten valleys which had long served as sanctuaries for heretical and deviationist sects. The message was compelling and infectious, the more so when the movement produced a leader of genius, Hasan-i Sabbah (1090-1124).

The career and personality of this mysterious figure, the founder of the Nizari Isma'ili sect, known in Europe as the Assassins, is veiled in legend and uncertainty. The architect of a community located in the Elburz mountains, where he ruled from his citadel of Alamut, this Old Man of the Mountain was probably not the monster his enemies depicted, even if there was something in him of the bandit chieftain. What is clear is that he was a man with a mission, an eloquent harvester of souls, an organizer who could mold a dedicated community out of the most unpromising material. If he and his successors preferred to make their will felt by means of the assassin's dagger rather than by more conventional, if equally bloodthirsty, methods, it was, at least initially, the weapon of the weak rather than the strong. In any case, virtually everything known about them has been preserved in the literature of their most bitter foes.

What, other than the charismatic leadership of Hasan-i Sabbah, drew men to serve the community of Alamut? Partly it must have been the nature of Nizari Isma'ili beliefs, and especially, under the Grand Master Hasan II (1162-66), the intoxicating concept of *qiyama*, the presence of the Imam incarnate on earth. In addition there were the appeals of apartness, intense community participation, obedience to the will of an inspiring leader and, later, persecution. But historians have always had difficulty in trying to explain a movement that embraced so diverse a range of converts, from the fanatics allegedly drugged with hashish who were employed to assassinate the political foes of the Grand Masters to scholars like Nasir-i Khusru (1003-c1060) and Nasir al-Din Tusi (1201-74) perhaps the most original thinker of the thirteenth century. One frequently expressed view is that the Isma'ili movement was a political manifestation of Iranian cultural identity reacting against the orthodoxy of an 'Abbasid universalist state buttressed by the harsh and alien regime of the

Seljuq Turks. Other historians have sought for explanations in terms of discontent among the urban poor or of a last resurgence of the dying class of *dihqans* in their remote hill forts, protesting against ever-increasing urban domination. Yet it was surely the esoteric beliefs of the Nizari Isma'ilis as much as anything which accounted for the strength of a movement which even the Seljuq Sultans at the height of their power were unable to overcome. It was not until 1256 that the Mongols of Hülegü succeeded in penetrating to Alamut, where they destroyed the Isma'ili fortresses, executed the last Grand Master, Rukn an-Din Khurshah, and massacred his followers so completely that, in the words of the historian Juwayni, they 'became but a tale on men's lips and a tradition in the world.' Yet again Mongol power proved overwhelming.

Long before then, however, the Fatimid Caliphate had passed away, ousted by the Kurdish Ayyubids (1169-1252), an unambiguously Sunni dynasty founded by the famous conqueror Salah al-Din (1169-93), whose exploits against the Crusaders has made the name of 'Saladin' better known in the West than perhaps that of any other Muslim. The strictly orthodox character of the Ayyubid regimes of the twelfth and thirteenth centuries, whether based on Cairo, Damascus or Aleppo, was merely one facet of a broader reaction in favor of Sunni orthodoxy which had been gaining ground since the eleventh century and which manifested itself not only in Egypt and the Fertile Crescent but also in the Maghrib and in the heartlands of the 'Abbasid Caliphate. The Caliph's office now enjoyed a striking revival in power and prestige. The revival of the 'Abbasid Caliphate itself resulted directly from the alliance of the Caliphs with the new masters of the Iranian plateau, the Seljuq Turks, who, as relatively recent arrivals in the *Dar al-Islam*, displayed all the traditional zeal of the newly converted.

Seljuqs, Almoravids and Almohads

The Seljuqs were originally clan chieftains in the confederacy of the Oghuz Turks on the steppes north of the Caspian and the Aral Sea. They gradually infiltrated into Khwarazm and Mawarannahr in the first decades of the eleventh century. In 1038 Toghril, their leader, proclaimed himself Sultan in Nishapur, thereby giving notice that Ghaznavid hegemony in eastern Iran was at an end, and in 1055 his title was recognized by the 'Abbasid Caliph, following Toghril's triumphal entry into Baghdad. Under Toghril (1038-63), Alp-Arslan (1063-72) and Malik-Shah (1072-92) the Seljuq Sultanate became the most powerful state in the Muslim East, with frontiers extending at one period from Kashgar to the Mediterranean. During part of this time a cadet line of the reigning house ruled an independent Sultanate of Rum (1077-1307) in central Anatolia. The Seljuqs buttressed the spiritual authority of the Caliph partly out of genuine concern to uphold the office of the *Amir al Mu'minin*, whose sword-arm was now the Seljuq Sultan, and partly because Caliph and Sultan were alike threatened by the spread of heterodoxy in the form of the Nizari Isma'ili movement. For while the pretensions of the Grand Masters of Alamut struck at the roots of the Caliph's spiritual authority, their plots and assassinations also aimed to weaken Seljuq political control of the Iranian plateau.

Nizari Isma'ili propaganda in the eleventh century was widespread and pervasive, and there was no obvious military solution to a problem which lay primarily in the minds of men. Thus the great Seljuq *vazir*, Nizam al-Mulk, whose career exemplified the way in which the traditional Iranian *Ahl-i qalam* (literally, Men of the Pen, or bureaucracy) came to terms with their 'barbarian' conquerors, established a number of colleges throughout the Seljuq domains to train theologians and officials in the orthodox Islamic

sciences and thus combat the spread of heresy. The theological position maintained by teachers at these *Nizamiyyehs* (so called in honor of their founder), of which the two most famous were located at Baghdad and Nishapur, was to provide an intellectual framework for orthodox theology by applying to it the dialectical methods of the Mu'tazilites. The *Nizamiyyehs* attracted some of the most distinguished intellectuals of the period, as either teachers or students, and among the former was al-Ghazali (1058-1111), perhaps the last truly original thinker to be thrown up by the theological controversies which had continued unabated down to that time. The contribution of al-Ghazali to the orthodox reaction that began to make itself felt from the eleventh century onward was threefold: he mounted a rigorous defense of

Above and left: The Umayyad Mosque in Cordoba, one of the world's most beautiful buildings. Founded in 785, and both enlarged and enriched in succeeding centuries, the mosque typifies the high level of cultural achievement in Umayyad Spain.

Right: Fez, one of the chief cities of the Berbers in Morocco. The Berber Almoravids and Almohads crossed into Muslim Spain after the fall of the Umayyad Caliphate in the eleventh century, making it a virtual dependency of North Africa.

the theological position of the Ash'arites; he subjected the whole spectrum of Shi'i belief, and especially that of the Nizari Isma'ilis, to relentless attack, and he endeavored to reconcile the goal of the Sufi with that of the orthodox believer, seeking to integrate the intuitive approach of the mystic within the framework of the Sunni 'Great Tradition.'

The Seljuqs' restless ambition, religous zeal and willingness to absorb the cultural and imperial traditions of the old Islamic heartland found some parallels in North Africa and Spain in the form of the Almoravid and Almohad movements. The Umayyad Caliphate of Cordoba had been at its zenith during the reigns of 'Abd al-Rahman III (912-61) and al-Hakam II (961-76) while even under the feeble Hisham II (976-1009 and 1010-13) the military victories of the *hajib*, al-Mansur, against the Christian states of the north obscured the extent to which the regime had already entered into a decline. After the death of al-Mansur, and under circumstances still far from clear, the Caliphate disintegrated (1031) and was replaced by a number of mutually hostile dynasties known as the *Muluk al Tawa'if* or *Reyes de Taifas* ('the Party Kings'), of which the most important ruled at Cordoba, Seville, Malaga, Badajoz, Toledo, Valencia and Saragossa. Factious and quarrelsome, they none the less provided the setting for a Hispano-Islamic culture of extraordinary brilliance and refinement exemplified by patrons such as Muhammad II al-Mu'tamid, the poet-ruler of Seville (1069-91), and by scholars such as Ibn Hazm of Cordoba (994-1064).

But the divisions among the *Muluk al Tawa'if* threatened the very foundations of Muslim rule in Spain when the Christian north, in the person of Alfonso VI of Leon and Castile (1065-1109), began to press southward and in 1085 actually captured Toledo. Led by al-Mu'tamid of Seville, the Muslim rulers of Spain appealed for aid to the Berber conqueror of the Maghrib, Yusuf b Tashfin, the Almoravid (1061-1106). In 1086 Yusuf landed at Algeciras and administered a devastating blow against the Castilians at Malaga. He returned again in 1090, once more at the invitation of the *Muluk al Tawa'if,* but this time, disgusted by the Party Kings' ceaseless squabbles in the face of their Christian enemies, and by what he regarded as their impiety, he annexed their kingdoms and added them to his own extensive possessions in Africa. In this way Muslim Spain, its northern frontier following an uncertain line from just south of Coimbra in the west to just south of Tortosa in the east, but excluding Toledo, became part of the Almoravid Empire.

The Almoravid movement of the eleventh century exemplified the way in which a hitherto submerged and discontented group could express its political aspirations in the language and style of sectarian fervor. The movement was, in essence, puritanical, reformist and fundamentalist. It had its theological roots in the rigorous Malikite school of jurisprudence favored in the Maghrib, but it derived its popular appeal as well as its organizational strength from the institution of the *ribat,* a kind of fortified hermitage or monastery on the fringes of the Muslim world inhabited by ascetic warriors dedicated to the propagation of Islam. These men were known as *al-Murabitun,* later to be rendered into Spanish as *Almoravides.* The dynamic role of the Almoravid movement in the history of Islam in the Maghrib lay in the fascination it exercised over the Berber mind, as yet only very imperfectly Islamicized but highly responsive to fiery preaching. The Almoravid missionaries offered them the exalted role of serving as the spearhead of a movement for the purification of Muslim society which would be directed primarily against the Arab ruling elite and the Arab cities of the Maghrib, with their promise of inexhaustible plunder.

Among the Berbers the earliest and the most devoted supporters of the *Murabitun* were the tribes of the Sanhaja confederacy, whose grazing grounds extended from the Atlas mountains to the Senegal river. Pastoral nomads, with a penchant for making raids that took them from central Morocco to as far as the vicinity of Timbuktu, they also kept open the caravan routes across the western Sudan, whence they derived revenues which gave them a margin of affluence over their neighbors. Thus, like those Turko-Mongol tribes in Central Asia which grazed their flocks close to the transcontinental caravan routes, the Sanhaja participated in economic activities which far transcended the usual limitations imposed by a pastoral nomadic way of life and which also exposed them to more extensive contacts with the outside world than would otherwise have been the case.

Around 1039 some notables of the Sanhaja, returning from the *Hajj,* brought back with them a learned Moroccan, 'Abdallah b Yasin, whose mission was to restore what he conceived to have been the faith of the first Muslims, stripped of later worldly accretions. He and some of his new disciples withdrew to a *ribat* on an island in the Senegal river on the fringes of the *Dar al-Islam,* where they endeavored to disseminate the faith among the pagan peoples to the south. Here he slowly built up an armed following, with whose support he began to coerce those tribes of the Sanhaja whom he regarded as unfriendly, calling for a *jihad,* or Holy War, against those who rejected his teaching. After various setbacks he succeeded in making his name feared throughout the entire Western Sudan, and by the time of his death in 1057 there had come into existence a powerful tribal confederacy only too eager to embark upon extended conquests.

After the death of 'Abdellah b Yasin, leadership of the Almoravids passed in rapid succession to

three Sanhaja chieftains, of whom the last, Yusuf b Tashfin, was to prove one of the most remarkable figures in the history of the Maghrib. Yusuf b Tashfin was the product of a wholly Berber environment upon which the fierce winds of Malikite revivalism had beaten to a point where Yusuf had become a man with a single-minded mission to transform and purify the whole social ethos of the Muslim West. He was also an outstanding military leader. With these assets, and at the head of a Berber tribal confederacy dominated by the Sanhaja, he embarked upon the conquest of central and northern Morocco, founding Marrakesh as his capital in 1062. Fez was taken in 1070, Tangier in 1078 and by 1082 Yusuf b Tashfin's conquests extended eastward to include the greater part of Algeria. By 1090 he was undisputed master of Muslim Spain, and at his death in 1106 he bequeathed to his son, 'Ali b Yusuf (1106-43), the greatest empire yet seen in the Muslim West. He himself remained to the end a model of the puritan virtues he had preached so relentlessly, but during the reign of 'Ali b Yusuf there began that mating of refined Hispano-Islamic culture with rough Berber ways which was so soon to result in a rapid loss of both religious zeal and barbarian vigor.

Yet the Almoravids hardly survived as an imperial power for more than three-quarters of a century. There were several reasons for this. First, it appears that in the tribal confederacy that secured these far-flung conquests the Sanhaja chose to exclude other important Berber groups, in particular the Masmuda of the High Atlas, from the fruits of victory, thereby exacerbating traditional inter-tribal rivalries. Second, toward their new Spanish subjects, and especially toward the former Arabo-Andalusian ruling elite, the Almoravids behaved less as fellow Muslims than as savage oppressors, hardly less dreaded than the Christians to the north. Third, the Almoravids eventually succumbed to the higher civilization of

Muslim Spain. Their fanaticism, it is true, wrought havoc for a time upon the intellectual life of the country, and among those who fled the peninsula as a consequence were the ancestors of the historian Ibn Khaldun (1332-1406), who settled in Tunis. When al-Ghazali's *Revival of the Sciences of Religion* reached Spain it was publicly burned, and prospective readers were threatened with capital punishment. Yet despite the anti-intellectual climate of the times the Almoravid court and the ruling elite during the reign of 'Ali b Yusuf proved incapable of resisting either the blandishments of Hispano-Islamic culture or the fleshpots of the Spanish cities. The example was set by the ruler himself, no Berber warrior like his father but a docile, pious prince, during whose long reign the dynamic quality of the Almoravid movement was entirely dissipated.

The Almohad movement which overthrew the empire founded by Yusuf b Tashfin bore certain resemblences to the Almoravid movement. Like the latter it was a puritanical fundamentalist movement, the followers of which were convinced that the Muslims of the Maghrib and of Spain had grievously departed from what they held to be the true path of Islam. Like the Almoravid movement, the Almohad movement also became identified with the grievances and ambitions of a major Berber tribal confederacy, the Masmuda. And like the Almoravid movement it was set in motion by an inspiring religious leader, in this case a Berber reformer named Ibn Tumart (d 1130).

By assuming the title of *al-Mahdi*, Ibn Tumart gave the movement both a Messianic style and a mass appeal with which to challenge the ruling Almoravid establishment. His uncompromising assertion of the absolute Unity of God *(taw'hid)* resulted in his followers becoming known as *al-Muwahhidun*, 'those who affirm the unity of God' (Spanish: *Almohades*). By selecting as his Caliph or deputy a brilliant commander, 'Abd al-Mu'min,

he ensured that his mission should be translated into political reality after his death.

With infinite caution and patience 'Abd al Mu'min consolidated his hold over central Morocco. His objective was assisted by the death of the last Almoravid ruler in 1145, the year in which an Almohad army was sent into Spain to compel the former Almoravid provinces there to acknowledge his overlordship. In 1147 he seized Marrakesh, which he made his capital. By 1151 his conquests extended into eastern Algeria, and during 1159-60 his troops advanced along the North African seaboard as far as Tunis and Tripoli. 'Abd al Mu'min's successors, Abu Ya'qub Yusuf I (1163-84) and Abu Yusuf Ya'qub al-Mansur (1184-99), continued the momentum of expansion, and under their rule much of Spain and the Maghrib enjoyed a high degree of prosperity. Despite their unpromising beginnings the Almohads were outstanding patrons of the arts and sciences: the philosopher Ibn Tufayl (c 1105-85) was court physician to Abu Ya'qub Yusuf, and Ibn Rushd (1126-98), greatest of the Arab Aristotelians and known to the Christian Schoolmen as Averroes, served both Abu Ya'qub Yusuf and Abu Yusuf Ya'qub in the same capacity.

By the beginning of the thirteenth century, however, the Almohads were clearly past their prime. The reasons for this are far from clear but there seems to have been a growing lack of popular support, especially in Spain. Meanwhile, the Christian kingdoms of Castile and Leon were mounting a strenuous assault from the north. Earlier, in 1195, Abu Yusuf Ya'qub had defeated Alfonso VIII of Castile in a notable engagement at Alarcos, but the memory of that victory had been erased by the far more dramatic defeat of the Almohads in 1212 at Las Navas de Tolosa at the hands of a coalition consisting of the kings of Castile, Leon, Aragon and Navarre. The *reconquista* now proceeded in earnest, especially after the union of the thrones of Castile and Leon in

Far left: The 144-foot Hassan Tower, all that remains of the famous mosque in the present-day Moroccan capital of Rabat, destroyed by an earthquake in 1755.

Left and right: The Alhambra Palace, Granada, stands as the most splendid relic of the Narids, a ruling dynasty who brought a last flowering of high culture to Muslim Spain before its final eradication at the hands of the Christians in 1492.

1230. In 1236 Cordoba fell to the Christians, and in 1248 Seville. Only the Nasrid kingdom of Granada was to hold out until 1492.

The Christian *reconquista* in Spain was the most successful and enduring part of the militant European response to the Islamic presence on its southern and eastern flanks. This response had begun in the eleventh century with the Norman conquest of Sicily in 1060 and of Malta in 1091. It reached a far more threatening stage with the arrival of Godfrey of Bouillon and his Crusaders in Jerusalem in 1099, after their brilliant and victorious march across Seljuq Anatolia.

In fact, the pressure of the Crusaders in Syria was only one factor in the collapse of the Seljuq empire. After the death of Malik Shah in 1092 the dynasty was torn by dissensions and rivalries which even the last great ruler of the line, Mu'izz al-Din Sanjor (1118-57), was unable to heal. Notwithstanding their highly efficient slave armies and their application of the Irano-Islamic bureaucratic tradition to the consolidation and administration of their conquests, they failed to emancipate themselves sufficiently from their tribal Central Asian past, especially in the matter of patrimonial concepts regarding the succession and the sovereign claims of the various princes of the royal house. Thus, in addition to the Seljuqs of Rum (1077-1307), quasi-independent Seljuq principalities had emerged in Syria, Iraq, western Iran and Kirman, all of which maintained what was at best an ambiguous relationship with the senior line in Khurasan. At the same time the Seljuq hold over Iraq, the heartland of Islamic civilization, was much reduced by a revival of the political influence of the 'Abbasids in the twelfth century, especially during the reigns of two unusually resourceful Caliphs, al-Muqtafi (1136-60) and al-Nasir (1180-1225).

It had been Seljuq practice to confer the nominal charge of important provinces upon princes of the royal house, including minors, to whom were attached *Atabegs* (guardians), Turkish slave commanders already possessing extensive military and administrative experience. While the central government had wrestled with the problem of dynastic disputes, with invading Ghuzz and Qarakhitan tribesmen from the east and with their own unassimilated Turkoman followers, the more enterprising of these *Atabegs* had established independent dynasties of considerable resilience. Greatest of all these was that of the Khwarazmshahs (c 1077-1231) in Khwarazm (Khiva), of which the last effective ruler, 'Ala-al-Din Muhammad b Takash (1200-20), made a striking bid to resuscitate the empire of the Great Seljuqs before going down before the Mongols of Chingiz Khan.

The Mongol invasions

The eruption of Chingiz Khan and his Mongols into the *Dar al-Islam* may be regarded as a turning-point in the history of Islam. The devastation the Mongols wrought set off a chain-reaction that extended far beyond the lands they ravaged, dispersing refugees from Mawarannahr, Iran and Iraq into northern India, Anatolia and Egypt. Yet there was also a diffusion of ideas, of styles and of knowledge of the world along the ancient caravan routes where commerce flourished anew under the *Pax Mongolica*. This new mobility was illustrated by the ease with which Ibn Battuta, that redoubtable Moroccan globe-trotter of the early fourteenth century, made himself at home wherever he found a Muslim court to welcome him.

But for those regions of the Muslim world that absorbed the initial blows, the Mongol conquests meant incalculable human suffering, not only in terms of massacres and transfers of population but also in terms of the epidemics, famines and the dislocation of everyday economic life that followed in the wake of the invaders. Even where the Mongols did not deliberately destroy irrigation systems, the decline in local manpower spelled their decay, since barrages, watercourses and *qanats* require constant maintenance. There was also an incalculable loss of livestock. We can only speculate about how low various native populations fell, but the assumption is that in certain areas the drop was drastic. Some cities sacked by the Mongols – including Marv, Balkh, Tus, Nishapur and Ray – never fully recovered. There was also probably a tendency for cultivation to give way to pastoralism over large areas.

The impact is less easy to calculate in terms of its effect on the intellectual life of Islam. The liquidation of scholars during the course of the holocaust must be reckoned, together with the destruction of libraries, as a factor contributing to the retarded condition of the intellectual life of Islam in the late medieval period. Against this, however, must be set the effect of the dispersal of scholars fleeing to safer localities such as Cairo, Konya or Delhi, and the fact that, following their partial adoption of an Irano-Islamic life-style, the Mongols themselves became lavish patrons of certain kinds of intellectual activity – medicine, mathematics, astronomy and history.

But for the Muslim world as a whole the Mongol invasions also induced a deep psychological malaise. For a devout Muslim the invasions of the thirteenth century, reaching their climax with the sack of Baghdad in 1258 and the murder of the last Abbasid Caliph, al-Musta'sim, must have been events of unique horror. Hitherto he had believed not only that he was a member of a community of believers assured of absolute salvation in the after-life but also that on this earth the future lay with his community. Wherever the Muslim faith had been propagated it had prospered, and with it the material welfare of all true believers. Neither the Crusades of the twelfth century and the beginnings of the Spanish *reconquista* nor the slowness of the advance of Islam in northern India and the steppe region had raised serious doubts about these assumptions. But the Mongol invasions did, since the sheer extent of the misery, the degradation and the destruction were such that it was hardly possible to reconcile them with the belief that the Muslims alone were the chosen of God. What inscrutable purpose had He in mind when He willed that in holy Bukhara, the city that men called the *Qutb al-Islam* (the Pillar of Islam), the unclean, carrion-eating savage, Chingiz Khan, should proclaim himself a scourge divinely appointed to punish the people of Bukhara for their sins. To a member of his congregation the Imam of the *Masjid-i Jomeh* confessed his bewilderment: 'It is the wind of God's omnipotence that bloweth, and we have no power to speak.' The implications of those harrowing middle decades of the thirteenth century seem to have caused the Muslim community to turn in upon itself in doubt and despair, seeking in intensified mysticism, whether individual or communal, the only meaningful response to such horrors. In so doing it unconsciously rejected the intellectual heritage of the past. The long slumber of Islam had begun.

It was in 1220-21 that the Muslim world first acquired knowledge of the vast Eurasian empire of the Mongols. Several years before, Muslim merchants had encountered the Mongols on the eastern stretches of the network of caravan routes that crossed Central Asia. At first they may to some extent have regarded Chingiz Khan as a protector, but in 1220-21 he launched his brilliant campaign against 'Ala' al-Din Muhammad b Takash, the Khwarazmshah, in the course of which the ancient centers of Irano-Islamic civilization in Mawarannahr and Khurasan – Samarqand, Bukhara, Balkh, Merv, Herat, Nishapur, etc – were taken and sacked, and their inhabitants massacred. While Chingiz Khan himself advanced southward as far as the Indus, two of his lieutenants led a force through Azerbayjan and the Caucasus and launched themselves upon the Muslim Turkish tribes on the Dasht-i Qipchaq, north of the Black Sea.

For the next three decades the Mongols continued to probe deep into Iran, keeping north of the Dasht-i Kavir and learning much about the unconquered lands to the west of them. About the same time (*c* 1238) a grandson of Chingiz, Batu, began the systematic pacification of the Dasht-i Qipchaq and the Russian principalities to the north, establishing his headquarters some 50 miles up from the mouth of the Volga at an *ordu* known as Saray-Batu. Then, in 1256, another grandson of Chingiz, Hülegü, acting in the name of his elder brother, Möngke, the supreme Khaqan, embarked upon the conquest of the entire Iranian plateau, liquidating the remnants of the Nizari Isma'ili state in the Elburz and capturing Baghdad in 1258. His troops penetrated as far south as the vicinity of Jerusalem before being defeated by the Egyptian Mamluks at 'Ayn Jalut in 1260, but despite this reverse his successors, the Il-Khans, continued to expand their frontiers into Syria, the Caucasus and Anatolia, where the Seljuq Sultans of Rum had become their clients as early as 1243.

As a result of Chingiz Khan's division of his empire prior to his death in 1227, and of the reallocation of fiefs on the accession of his grandson, Möngke, in 1251, the Muslim territories of the Mongol Empire were divided into three mutually hostile appanages. First there was Batu's *ulus*, known in Russian history as the Golden Horde and comprising the Dasht-i Qipchaq, north of the Caspian and the Black Sea, as well as most of European Russia, western Siberia and Khwarazm. Hülegü's *ulus*, known as the Il-Khanate, since its rulers took the title of Il-Khan, included

Iran, Iraq, eastern Anatolia and parts of Afghanistan. The third *ulus*, known as the Chaghatai Khanate (from Chaghatai, Chingiz Khan's second son), consisted of Mawarannahr, Kashgaria east of the Pamirs and the grasslands of the Yeti Su (Semirechie), north of the Tien Shan. In all these vast territories the initial conquest and subjugation was necessarily followed by a return to regular government. Revenue had to be collected, cultivation restored and the caravan trade got moving again. In all three Khanates the majority of the population was Muslim, and hence, notwithstanding the strength of traditional Mongol feeling and the veneration felt for Chingiz Khan's memory, the conquerors were slowly drawn into the Muslim fold, renewing old ways, working through the old bureaucracies. Moreover, obvious considerations of expediency prompted Mongol rulers in lands where they were themselves only a minority, even among their own Turkish or Turko-Mongol troops, to adopt the faith of the Turkish or Turkoman tribes already established in their new possessions. There was also, as a more personal motive for conversion, the appeal of the Irano-Islamic way of life, which was gradually adopted by the Mongol ruling elite, especially in Iran and Mawarannahr.

Assimilation and opposition

The process of conversion to Islam, and with it the assimilation of the Mongols into the *Dar al-Islam*, took place over many decades, and it often incurred strenuous opposition from Mongol traditionalists, particularly in the Chaghatai Khanate, where conditions most closely resembled those prevailing in Mongolia. There the process of acculturation was never complete, and even in Mawarannahr it had begun to take effect only by the middle of the fourteenth century. In Qipchaq, despite the early conversion of Batu's brother, Berke (1257-67), who surrounded himself with a bodyguard of 30,000 Muslim tribesmen who carried prayer-rugs beneath their saddles and had foresworn alcohol, it was not until the reign of Ghiyas al-Din Muhammad Özbeg (1312-41), one of the greatest rulers of the line, that the Khanate became a Muslim state. In the Il-Khanate, despite the abortive conversion of Ahmad Tegüdar (1282-84), the conversion of the Mongol elite as a whole did not fully get under way until the reigns of Ghazan (1295-1304) and his brother Öljeytü (1304-17).

Ghazan exemplified better than any other Chingizkhanid the extent of Mongol assimilation of Islamic and Iranian values, becoming almost a model Muslim ruler. In addition to exercising the traditional functions of administering justice, maintaining order and defending the frontiers of his kingdom, he reformed the system of land tenure and the fiscal structure with the assistance of his *vazir*, Rashid al-Din Fazlullah, the first known writer to have attempted to put together a genuine world-history. He also standardized the weights and measures and took steps to protect merchants both from bandits and from the rapacity of his own officials.

Under rulers such as Ghazan, and ministers like Rashid al-Din, some regions devastated by the Mongols began to recover. This was especially true of cities such as the old Seljuq town of Maragheh, near Lake Rizaiyeh, which Hülegü made the seat of his government, of Veramin, near Tehran, and Tabriz, which by the late thirteenth century had become one of the largest cities in the world outside China. Ghazan and his *vazir* both constructed new suburbs outside Tabriz, while Öljeytü began a new capital at Sultaniyeh, due west of Qazvin, and another residence

near Kirmanshah. Some cities, such as Shiraz, had altogether escaped the original Mongol onslaught, but even in ravaged Khurasan and Iraq urban recovery could be surprisingly swift, reflecting the resilience characteristic of the Muslim cities located on or close to important trade routes. Eighty years after the original invasion, even Baghdad and Mosul in Iraq were once again great manufacturing centers. Traveling across the Qipchaq Khanate, Ibn Battuta was astounded by the wealth and size of its scattered cities, especially Saray-Berke on the Volga and Urganj in Khwarazm.

The revival of urban life under the later Mongols contributed to the artistic and intellectual vigor that manifested itself during this period, a vigor that owed something to the curiosity of the Mongol rulers themselves and something to the new cosmopolitanism that the conquests had engendered. Building was undertaken upon a more ambitious scale than perhaps at any time since the Sasanid period, although this may be no more than an indication of the extent of the original destruction. The same was true in the field of ceramics and book illustration, and here Far Eastern influences were especially important. Libraries and *madrasehs* had been among the worst casualties of the initial invasions, but the new regime endeavored to make amends of a kind.

When Hülegü's troops entered the fortress of

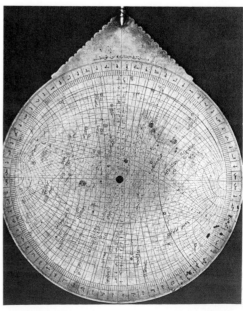

Right: A sixteenth-century Indian miniature depicts the Mongol cavalry of Chingiz Khan scattering its enemies. The civilized rulers of Islam could not resist the onslaught of these fierce Central Asian warriors

Left: Two astrolabes, one from Muslim Spain (top) and the other from Syria (bottom). The development of such advanced navigational instruments was a striking example of the mathematical and scientific skills bred in the medieval Islamic world.

Alamut they found there the greatest scholar of the age, Nasir al-Din Tusi, theologian, philosopher and mathematician (*d* 1273), who thereafter became the Il-Khan's trusted adviser. The Mongol service seems to have attracted such men, and in addition to Rashid al-Din Fazlullah historians such as 'Ata' Malik Juwagni and Hamdullah Mustaufi served in the Mongol bureaucracy. The Mongols had a taste for history, a reflection of their interest in the extraordinary events that had made them masters of so much of the known world and of the expanding intellectual horizons of the times. Lavish patrons, they were also keenly interested in mathematics, astronomy and medicine, although their interests in all sciences were strictly practical. Hülegü established an observatory at Maragheh, where he assembled a cosmopolitan team of scholars that included a Chinese astronomer and the Syriac polymath, Barhebraeus. Hülegü's grandson, Arghun, brought together an equally diverse team of physicians to assist him in his search for the Elixir of Life, a quest that ended in the premature death of this otherwise able ruler through mercury poisoning. Persian literature also thrived in the Mongol period. Sa'di (*d* 1291) and Hafiz (*d* 1389), the two most celebrated poets of Iran, spent most of their lives in Shiraz under vassal-rulers of the distant Il-Khans in Tabriz, while the poet and mystic Jalal al-Din Rumi (*d* 1273) lived at Konya in the Seljuq kingdom of Rum, just out of the reach of the Mongol warbands.

The Mongol regimes established in the middle of the century were not remarkably long-lived, and in every case they came to grief as a result of a succession of incompetent rulers or minors. The governments of the Khanates also suffered from weak institutional foundations. The Il-Khanate disintegrated in 1335, following the death of Abu Sa'id, the last able ruler of the line. In Qipchaq the death of Jani Beg (1341-57) led to a disputed succession, rivalry among the clan leaders and signs of truculent insubordination on the part of some of the Russian princes, a Muscovite force in 1380 actually defeating the army of a would-be kingmaker, Mamay, at Kulikovo Polye. In the Chaghatai Khanate the tribal leaders and their followers in Mawarannahr were drawn more and more into the world of Irano-Islamic culture, while the tribes to the northeast of the Syr-Darya, in the Semirechie, continued to cling more or less successfully to the old Mongol ways.

Acute instability

The characteristic of the second and third quarters of the fourteenth century, at least in the Islamic heartlands of Iraq and Iran, was one of acute instability. In Baghdad and Azerbayjan a local Mongol regime, that of the Jalayarids (1336-1432), demonstrated considerable staying-power and a taste for enlightened patronage, but its resources were too limited to permit it to expand its territory. In Anatolia the old possessions of the Seljuqs of Rum, dragged down in the

fall of their Mongol overlords, were being fought over by rival Turkoman dynasties, among which the Ottomans were already showing an unusual capacity to survive. By the close of the fourteenth century Bayazid I Yildirim, 'the Thunderbolt' (1389-1402), had overcome the Qaramanids of the Taurus region, had conquered Bulgaria and had defeated a great crusading army at Nicopolis in 1396. Southern and central Iran had fallen to a native dynasty, the Muzaffarids (1314-93), whose limited resources, slighter even than those of the Jalayarids, were incapable of effective deployment beyond the Shiraz-Isfahan-Kirman triangle, while the Herat region was firmly held by the Kart dynasty, erstwhile vassals of the Il-Khans.

In regions which escaped the ravages of the Mongols the pattern was somewhat different. In Egypt and Syria the Mamluks, Turkish slaves from the Qipchaq region who had successfully fought off the Crusaders, recovering Acre in 1261, had taken the full weight of Il-Khanid aggression in the north. Yet they still survived, with a century and a half of life ahead of them. In India two vigorous and expansionist dynasties had emerged in Delhi, the Khaljis (1290-1320) and the Tughluqids (1320-1414), under whom the exclusive composition of the ruling elite of the old Turkish 'Slave Dynasty' of Shams al-Din Iltutmish and Ghiyas al-Din Balban was broadened to include a growing Indian Muslim element. The Khaljis successfully survived the last thrusts of the Mongols across the Indus, and under 'Ala' al-Din Muhammad Shah (1296-1316), perhaps the greatest pre-Moghul ruler of Muslim India, expanded into the Deccan, a precedent followed by the Tughluqid Sultan, Ghiyas al-Din Muhammad Shah (1325-51), a few decades later. These raids, and the very unsteady local administrations set up to consolidate them, did nothing to strengthen the Delhi Sultanate in the north, but they did result in the gradual spread of Islam southward, although such was not their prime purpose. Those Muslims who remained in the south as officials and soldiers tended to put down local roots, and their presence encouraged missionary activity by the Sufi orders that had been so successful in the north a century or so earlier. In Delhi the fourteenth-century Sultanate displayed much of that ambivalence which was to be found in all Muslim regimes in India. In its administrative and military structure it swayed uneasily between a Turkish regime based upon a professional slave army characteristic of the previous century and the more 'Indian' style of 'Ala' al-Din Muhammad Shah Khalji. Under the last of the major Tughluqid Sultans, Firuz Shah (1351-88), a similar kind of tension existed between the Sultan's old-fashioned orthodoxy and the willingness of members of the royal entourage to come to terms with their Hindu environment.

Toqtamish and Timur

The Indian subcontinent, Egypt and, above all, Africa were only indirectly affected by the coming of the Mongols. But in the Islamic heartlands their conquests had left a political as well as an intellectual vacuum. The 'Abbasid Caliphate had been swept aside, and with it the old Classical Islamic civilization. At the end of the fourteenth century two serious attempts were made to resuscitate the Chingiz great achievement. Both failed, and, given the circumstances, the failures were perhaps doomed from the beginning. The first originated on the Qipchaq steppes with a descendant of Batu's elder brother, Orda, Khan of the White Horde north of the Aral Sea. Supported by the tribes of the White Horde, an incipient empire-builder, Ghiyas al-Din Toqtamish

and Fars, then against the Jalayarids in Baghdad, the Mamluks in Damascus and, finally, the Ottomans in Anatolia. He defeated each in turn, crowning his conquest by capturing the Ottoman Sultan, Bayazid I, at the Battle of Ankara in 1402. Meanwhile, he had attacked Toqtamïsh from across the Caucasus and also across the steppes from Khwarazm, penetrating far into Russia and reducing the cities of the Qipchaq Khanate to a shambles. Presumably this was part of a deliberate policy of ensuring the permanent diversion of the transcontinental caravan trade that ran north of the Black Sea and the Caspian to the southern route that ran through Iran and Mawarannahr. In 1398-99 he entered the Punjab, defeated the Tughluqid army near Delhi and systematically sacked that city, carrying off thousands of slaves (mainly women and skilled craftsmen) to his capital at Samarqand and virtually bringing to an end the Delhi Sultanate. At the time of his death, at Otrar, on the Syr-Darya, in 1405, he was in the process of leading an immense expeditionary force against Ming China.

In the folklore of Central Asia Timur ranks with Alexander (Iskandar) and Chingiz Khan as a supreme master of the art of warfare, and certainly his career of appalling destruction displayed all the signs of a commander of genius. There was, however, a curious impermanence about it all. Timur may well have been a supreme warlord, but he was totally without any of the attributes of an empire-builder. He could win victories, but he could not use them, and this absence of statecraft partly explains his failure to reconstruct the former *Pax Mongolica*.

Timur's position from the beginning had been an ambiguous one, since although he was the quintessence of nomadic savagery to the townsfolk and cultivators of the heartlands of the *Dar al-Islam*, he was also, from his base in Mawarannahr, a warden of the marches of Islam, a *ghazi* who sought the approval of famous dervishes and *shaykhs* to justify his actions. To the Muslims he was yet another Scourge of God, but to the tribes beyond the Syr-Darya he was the sword-arm of Islam.

Almost nothing good can be said about Timur's career. He destroyed what remained of the Qipchaq Khanate and of the Delhi Sultanate, he did irreparable damage to urban life everywhere he went, he contributed to the further weakening of Mamluk power and he almost extinguished the rising Ottoman State. Paradoxically, his defeat of Sultan Bayazid delayed the Ottoman conquest of Constantinople for half a century, a fact not without significance in the history of the European Renaissance. In crushing Toqtamïsh he shattered the one power that might have kept the Russian princes in subordination, with incalculable consequences for Islam on the Volga and the steppes.

Timurid succession

The Timurid Empire was too inchoate and flaccid at the time of Timur's death to pass intact to any of his descendants. Hence it was the core of his conquests – Mawarannahr and the Iranian plateau, together with a large measure of prestige thrown in – that made up the inheritance of his son and successor, Shah Rukh (1405-47), who reigned at Herat. Ulugh Beg, son of Shah Rukh, ruled on his father's behalf in Samarqand, preoccupied with mathematical and astronomical interests. As the decades passed the area under Timurid control steadily contracted. Ulugh Beg, when at last he succeeded his father in 1447, inherited a much-reduced kingdom; a great-grandson of Timur, Abu Sa'id (1451-69), ruled even less; and the last Timurid ruler of any importance in

(1376-95), first welded together the fragmented Qipchaq Khanate and then embarked upon the conquest of Central Asia. At the outset he possessed much the same advantages as his Mongol ancestors had once possessed – the support of a powerful tribal confederacy providing numerous, well-mounted followers (Qipchaq in the thirteenth century had exported horses even to distant India) and unrivaled mobility when pitted against non-pastrol opponents. What his forces lacked was both the discipline of the Mongol armies of Batu and Berke and their leadership, failings that became manifest as soon as he showed his hand against the Chaghatai Khanate.

More or less simultaneously with the rise of Toqtamïsh, there emerged a rival empire-builder, but in this instance one who was richly endowed with the capacity for providing the old-style Mongol leadership and discipline. Timur (Tamerlane), a Turko-Mongol chieftain of the Barlas clan

from Shahrisafz in Mawarannahr, shared Toqtamïsh's dreams of boundless empire, but once having embarked upon a course of expansion each got in the way of the other. Timur's campaigns, at least initially, observed the same geographical logic as Chingiz Khan's, first consolidating his hold over the southwestern region of the Chaghatai Khanate (Mawarannahr), although always in the name of a puppet Chaghatai Khan, since, unlike Toqtamïsh, he lacked the patent of Chingizkhanid ancestry. Even at the height of his power he never assumed a higher title than that of Amir and Gurkhan, the latter meaning 'son-in-law' (of the Chaghatai Khan whose daughter he had married). From his base in Mawarannahr he set out first to conquer Iran, the former realm of the Il-Khans, and he did so with a savagery that may even have exceeded the atrocities committed by the Chingizkhanids. His westward advance brought him against the Muzaffarids in Kirman

it was that the Uzbeks came to occupy all the lands between the Amu-Darya and the Syr-Darya, while the Kazakh Hordes, consolidated into a powerful nomadic confederacy under Burunduk Khan (1488-1506), remained north of the Syr-Darya, dominating the steppe region from the Ural river to the slopes of the Altai.

While the Kazakhs and the Uzbeks were acquiring the territories they have continued to occupy ever since, the Ottoman Turks were recovering from their defeat at the hands of Timur, and by the reign of Mehmet II Fatih, 'the Conqueror' (1444-81), the European frontier of the empire had reached the lower Danube. Symptomatic of Ottoman preoccupation with Balkan affairs was the fact that since 1366 their capital had been at Edirne (Adrianople) in Thrace. Finally, in 1453 Constantinople (Istanbul) was taken with comparatively little effort and the Ottoman Empire became the heir to Byzantium.

Across the Black Sea the Khanate of Qipchaq was in an advanced state of disintegration throughout the fifteenth century. Following the final defeat of Toqtamish by Timur in 1395 there had been a temporary revival of Tatar fortunes under the leadership of an able Noghay Tatar, Idiku or Edigü, who unfortunately lacked the prerequisite for sovereignty – Chingizkhanid descent – and was therefore compelled to exercise authority in the name of *fainéant* Khans. In 1405-06 he actually led his forces to within striking distance of Bukhara, and in 1408 he punished Moscow for withholding tribute. But his death in 1419 opened a phase of permanent fragmentation, and amid suicidal rivalries among the clan chieftains and interference from Lithuania and Moscow, the Khanate dissolved into four principal successor states – the Khanate of Tiumen in western Siberia, the Khanates of Kazan and Astrakhan on the Volga and the Khanate of the Crimea – while major tribes such as the Noghay Tatars on the lower reaches of the Ural river remained, as they had long been, virtually independent. The history of these Khanates was for the most part short and inglorious: Kazan fell to the troops of Ivan IV in 1552 and Astrakhan in 1554, while Tiumen, after protracted resistance, submitted to Boris Godunov, the line surviving at Kazimov until 1681.

The Khanate of the Crimea (1426-1792), separated from Moscow by the Ukraine steppe zone,

Left: Timur, known in the West as Tamburlaine or Tamerlane, was a conqueror of legendary ferocity. Here, having taken a city, he had ordered that the walls be razed and a tower built with the heads of the slain defenders.

Right: Timur inspects his army and receives the homage of his followers.

Below right: Timurid horsemen and infantry assault a walled city defended by archers.

Central Asia, Husayn Bayqara (1470-1506) exercised authority only over Khurasan, Sistan and Gurgan. At the same time, the numbers of Timur's descendants multiplied swiftly, and all these Timurid princelings had pretensions to ruling a fief, however small. By the second half of the fifteenth century Mawarannahr and Khurasan, in particular, saw the rapid proliferation of a number of petty principalities, quarrelsome and ill-governed.

The Timurids were soon threatened from the west and from the north by formidable foes. In the west they had to face the rise in rapid succession of two vigorous Turkoman confederacies, that of the Qara Qoyunlu (1380-1468), from the region around Lake Van and Lake Rizaiyeh, and that of the Aq Qoyunlu (1378-1508), from Diyarbakir. The Aq Qoyunlu were the obvious successors of the Timurids in western Iran, and might well have established a powerful regime based on Tabriz, their capital, but further west they had to face the emerging power of the Ottomans and of the Safavid *shaykhs* of Ardabil. Their function, therefore, seems to have been to weaken the Timurid position west of the Dasht-i Kavir and to prepare the ground for the more complex tribal confederacy which the Safavids would eventually bring into being.

To the north, across the Syr-Darya, the Timurids were threatened by a far more dangerous foe, the Uzbeks. These people were descendents of the tribes of Batu's youngest brother, Shibaqan (Arab-

icized to Shayban), whose *ulus* had been east of the Urals in the vicinity of the Tobol river. Probably they became Muslims in the first half of the fourteenth century, when they took the name of the ruler of the Qipchaq Khanate, Ghiyas al-Din Muhammad Özbeg. In the first half of the fifteenth century, for reasons unknown, they shifted their grazing-grounds southeastward, and under the leadership of Abu-l-Khayr (1429-68), a descendant of Shibaqan, reached the lower course of the Syr-Darya, where the scattered towns on the north side of the river soon passed into their hands. Abu-l-Khayr intervened in the family squabbles of the Timurids in Mawarannahr and would doubtless have made a permanent crossing into that tempting region but for an unlooked-for defection of a part of his own Horde. Led by two kinsmen, Jani Beg and Giray, certain clans rebelled against his authority and withdrew their tents to the Jeti Su, submitting to the nominal overlordship of the Chaghatai Khan, who still ruled north of the Tien Shan and becoming the ancestors of the Kazakh Hordes of the sixteenth and seventeenth centuries.

Abu-l-Khayr was killed in battle in 1468, and about 30 years later it was his grandson, Muhammad Shaybani, who led the Uzbeks into Mawarannahr and hunted down the remaining Timurids. He seized Samarqand in 1500, Herat in 1506, and thereafter penetrated deep into Iran until he was defeated and killed at Marv in 1510 by Shah Isma'il I, the founder of the Safavid dynasty. Thus

would survive far longer, but as a nominal vassal of the Ottoman Sultan. This relationship between the Khans at Baghche Saray and the Istanbul government, in addition to turning the Black Sea into an Ottoman lake, would offer the Sultans such obvious advantages as contingents of Tatar irregulars to accompany the Ottoman army on its European campaigns and a steady supply of horses, cattle and slaves. In return, the Khanate had to be defended from the north – a task for which the Ottoman government had rather less relish. In fact, for a century after the well-timed submission of Mengli Giray I (1466-1514) to Mehmet II the Khanate remained a formidable power to reckon with, and under Dawlat Giray I (1551-77) was strong enough to burn Moscow (1571) when tribute was withheld. Meanwhile, as the level of Tatar culture on the Volga declined with the passing of the Khanates of Kazan and Astrakhan, the Crimean Tatar capital at Baghche Saray became, as it was to be once again in the late nineteenth century, the main center of Tatar civilization.

The Mamluks of Egypt

Even in the great days of the 'Abbasids Egypt had shown a tendency to go its own way – first, under independently minded 'Abbasid governors such as the Tulunids (868-905) and the Ikhshidids (935-69), and then under the Fatimid Caliphs (909-1171) and the Kurdish Ayyubids (1169-1252). This trend continued under the long-surviving Mamluk regime (1250-1517), which also perpetuated an even older political tradition, the con-

junction under one rule of both the Nile Valley and the western half of the arc of the Fertile Crescent.

The Mamluks were originally Turkish slave soldiers recruited from the Dasht-i Qipchaq. Their commanders, former slaves themselves, eventually established a regime that drew its power from this alien military elite. Like the slave armies of the Samanids, of the Ghaznavids and of thirteenth-century Delhi, the Mamluks had all the attributes of a closed fraternity bound together by self-interest, intense racial pride in their Turkish ancestry and an accompanying contempt for their non-Turkish subjects. Their government, although heavy-handed, was undoubtedly effective, and they were content to allow Arabs, Jews and Christian Copts to be employed as subordinate officials in posts which had little attraction for men devoted to the military life. Over a period of two-and-a-half centuries the system produced an unusually high proportion of able rulers. For a little less than half that time (1259-1390) the Mamluk Sultans were Qipchaq slaves, known as Bahris from the location of their barracks in Cairo. Thereafter, the Sultanate passed into the hands of the Burjis (1382-1517), who were mainly Circassians. Under the Burji Sultans hereditary succession, rare enough under the Bahri Sultans, was unknown, and their rule was apparently more rapacious.

Commanding great financial resources, the Mamluks were lavish builders, and in addition to maintaining the vital hydraulic works which controlled and distributed the Nile's precious annual

flood they adorned their cities with splendid mosques, colleges and mausoleums, as well as such military landmarks as barracks, walls, fortified gateways and the like. Although perhaps the majority of the Mamluk rank-and-file were life-long illiterates who spoke a Turkish dialect known as Mamluk-Qipchaq (of which the surviving literature consists mainly of translations from Arabic and Persian), the Mamluk Sultans themselves were generous patrons of traditional Islamic learning. Throughout this period Cairo enjoyed the reputation of being a bastion of Islamic values, with Mamluk Damascus coming only a short way behind.

Both the political independence and the wealth of Egypt during this period call for some explanation. Notwithstanding a succession of palace revolutions which substituted one Sultan for another, the fact remains that so far as the economic life and the day-to-day administration of the country were concerned, the Mamluk regime was remarkably stable. This stability rested upon the security provided by the Mamluk army, whose discipline, skill and courage enabled Rukn al-Din Baybars I (1260-77) to wipe out the remaining Crusader enclaves, and a succession of Sultans to withstand the hitherto invincible forces of the Mongol Il-Khans. Subsequently, it enabled them to hold at bay even the great Timur, although Mamluk contempt for firearms (a counterpart of the attitude of the military aristocracy of contemporary Europe) resulted in their ignominious defeat at the hands of the Ottoman Janissaries at Marj Dabiq in 1516.

Left: The mosque of Sultan Hassan, Cairo, built by Egypt's Mamluk rulers in the fourteenth century.

Above right: Husayn Bayqara (1470-1506) ruled the remnants of the Timurid Empire from Herat, site of a flourishing school of miniature painting.

Below right: An example of a Turkoman miniature – the scene depicted is Bahram Gur hunting.

Far right: A Berber village in Libya. For all its cultural sophistication, Islam has never forgotten its roots in the harsh simplicities of desert life.

The bulk and the value of the commerce flowing through Mamluk Egypt underscores Egypt's role during this period as an entrepot for both overland and maritime trade, an entrepot where the products of the Black Sea littoral and the Mediterranean were exchanged for goods brought from the countries bordering the Red Sea and the Indian Ocean, as well as from sub-Saharan Africa. It was, for example, through Egypt's Red Sea ports that Western Europe obtained virtually all its spices prior to Vasco da Gama's circumnavigation of Africa in 1498. Furthermore, although the Il-Khans in Iran sought to channel as much East-West trade as possible through Tabriz or Baghdad, Mongol destructiveness and Crusading frontier warfare had taken their toll. The maritime route via Egypt was generally regarded as a safer artery of trade than the overland routes across Iran, and it remained so during both the period when Timur was carving out an empire for himself and during the century of fragmentation that followed his death.

Although Egypt was spared the devastation so much of the Middle East experienced at Mongol hands during the thirteenth century, and although the Mamluk Sultanate stood forth as a resolute bastion of Islam against all infidels, the fact remains that the Mamluk state was profoundly influenced by Mongol example. If successive Mamluk Sultans succeeded in beating back the armies of the Il-Khans, they did so using much the same sort of manpower, arms and tactics as the Il-Khans themselves used.

Only in the far west, in the Maghrib, were there to be found Muslim states wholly free of Mongol influence. During the period of the Chingizkhanid conquests the Almohad regime had been sinking into torpor, enfeebled by recurrent tribal strife and by the negative character of its last rulers. Spain had been more or less lost to the Almohads following the great Christian victory at Las Navas de Tolosa in 1212. Cordoba fell to the Christians in 1236 and Seville in 1248, though Granada survived until 1492. In Morocco the Banu-Marin slowly extended their hold over the country, and in 1269 they finally captured the Almohad capital of Marrakesh.

The new rulers of the Maghrib were Zenata Berbers, but unlike the Berber Almoravids and Almohads, the Marinids neither rose to power on

a great wave of religious revivalism nor aspired very actively to far-flung conquests. Strictly orthodox in matters of faith, they ruled Morocco for more than two centuries (1196-1465), with only occasional sallies in the direction of Spain or Tunisia, the latter ruled by the long-lived line of the Hafsids (1228-1574). Unlike the Almohads, the Marinids did little to foster intellectual life, but under their rule Fez, their capital, which they adorned with splendid colleges and mosques, became one of the most celebrated cities of the Muslim world. It also played host for a time to the historian and philosopher Ibn Khaldun.

Born in Tunis in 1332 into a family that had fled from Spain in Almoravid times, Ibn Khaldun lived a varied and full life as a jurist, civil servant and scholar, serving the Hafsids of Tunis, the Marinids of Fez and the Nasrids of Granada. In 1384 he emigrated to Cairo, where he was warmly received by the Mamluk Sultan, Sayf al-Din Barquq (1382-99), and where he served on and off as Malikite *qazi* until his death in 1406. In the course of an unusually full life he wrote a *History of the World* distinguished both for its breadth of scholarship and for its profound understanding of

the factors which mold the human condition. In its prologue *(muqaddimah)* he attempted to explain the workings of history not in terms of the rise and fall of dynasties but as the complex outcome of interacting forces, geographical and environmental, social and psychological. The forgotten father of the social sciences, his masterpiece has been described by Arnold Toynbee as 'the greatest work of its kind that has ever yet been created by any mind in any time or place.'

India after Timur

Developments in India in the fifteenth century were only tenuously related to events in the West. Timur had virtually destroyed the Delhi Sultanate during his raid of 1398-99, and what survived thereafter was a minor affair, first under the Sayyids (1414-51), who began their rule as Timurid deputies, and then under the Lodi Afghans (1451-1526). Elsewhere in northern India, independent Sultanates arose at Lakhnawati (Gaur) in Bengal, Jaunpur near Benares, Mandu in Malwa, Ahmadabad in Gujarat and Burhanpur in Khandesh. All these states were more or less equally matched and, having only limited resources, they were compelled to be conciliatory towards their Hindu subjects to an extent to which the former Delhi Sultanate never was. They tended to come to terms with Hindu culture, patronize the Hindu vernaculars and build in the regional style, as exemplified by the architecture of Gaur or Ahmadabad. The Muslim half of the Indian equation of the fifteenth century was a Sufism which spoke the same pantheistic language as did the Hindu *bhakti* saints.

The parochial character of Indian Islam in the fifteenth century had its parallels elsewhere, for this was not an age of burning issues or striking gestures. Coming after the strife and desolation of the thirteenth and fourteenth centuries, it was an age which did not seem to know its way, which had no clear course to chart but which perhaps did not mind getting lost down its own backwaters. The ineffectuality and triviality of so much of the political life of the period only enhances the distinction of the cultural achievement: the intellectual breadth of Ibn Khaldun, the Sufi poetry of Jami and Mir 'Ali Shir, the miniatures of the Timurid School of Herat or the Turkoman Schools farther west, the sumptuously decorated buildings of Samarqand, Herat and Tabriz, the colleges of Fez or the stonework of Ahmadabad, Mandu or Jaunpur. And under the surface the ground swell was mounting for the great events that would lead to an Islamic revival in the sixteenth century.

Europe in the Middle Ages

The reasons for the failure of the Roman Empire were many and had existed for centuries before its eventual end, but the strengths and contributions of the empire to the future development of the West must not be neglected through excess consideration of the symptoms of decay. The Roman administrative system endured, though in greatly altered form, long after the empire itself had ceased to exist. The most important administrative subdivision, the *civitas* – broadly, a city and the area surrounding it – fell into decay as a unit of imperial government, but it remained a major factor in the organization of the church. As the empire waned, the church grew strong, and the pagan *civitas* became the episcopal see throughout western Europe. Indeed, when neither economic nor imperial requirements sufficed to preserve the cities, they survived as centers of ecclesiastical administration, although greatly reduced in size and population.

This merger of ecclesiastical and administrative units was one of the great legacies of the later Roman Empire, and one with major consequences for the subsequent history of the West. In an empire without other rationale for its existence, the Emperor Diocletian (284-305) introduced Mithraism, an eastern religion, as a state creed in an effort to integrate the empire through the infusion of a religious bond. Christians were for a time persecuted as a divisive element, but Constantine, Diocletian's successor, soon abandoned this policy and removed all sanctions against the Christians in the year AD 312. By the end of the fourth century, Christianity had become the official state religion, and thus it was only logical that the ecclesiastical administration should follow the structure already extant for the governance of the empire.

Even more significant for the future than the preservation and transmutation of the Roman administrative structure was the Roman concept of law. True, some of the emperors governed despotically, arbitrarily, and, despite their touted divinity, with total absence of moral restraint. Theoretically, however, the emperor drew his authority from the consent of the people and was expected to govern within limits set by a higher law, not subject to imperial mutation. The precise meaning of the consent of the governed must be considered with some care, as it could, and ultimately did, lead to several quite distinct forms of government. In Rome it never implied democracy or a state where each individual had a voice in governance. Rather, it entailed a transfer of sovereignty from the people to the ruler – a transfer that was quite compatible with absolute rule. Later interpretations would associate the doctrine of consent with popular sovereignty, but even in this case, the 'people' were usually a theoretical construct, distinct from the actual citizens of the territory being governed.

As in the case of consent, the abstract ideal of a law existing beyond man and not subject to imperial whim was more honored in the breach than in observance by the later emperors. Still, intellectual developments in the empire left a residue for the subsequent enlightenment of the West. While Greek philosophy was a major intellectual stimulus throughout the history of the medieval West, as it was slowly recovered and worked into the fabric of medieval thought, one of its most important early influences was upon and through the Roman stoics. Roman stoicism taught that the world was essentially rational and that all men, since they shared the ability to comprehend this rationality, were in some sense kindred spirits without regard to station. From these roots grew the concept of natural law, a law above the written positive law and applicable to all men, both protectively and proscriptively. Doctrines of natural law are always in some sense egalitarian, since all men stand in the same relationship to a law beyond the power of men. Stoicism consequently implied that justice was at least theoretically available to all men and thus that certain, if vague, limits were established upon the behavior of those who governed. The implantation of this notion in the corpus of Roman law was an extremely important event for the future of jurisprudence and survived, along with the major elements of written Roman law, to help shape the medieval concept of justice.

Summing up then, among the most significant legacies of Rome, and excluding those which appear only during the Renaissance, were the Christian religion firmly established within the old imperial administrative structure, a concept of natural law that elevated justice to a place beyond the control of men, and a doctrine that implied limits upon the excesses of the powerful. In addition, of course, from Rome Europe inherited Latin, the language of law, scholarship and lay and ecclesiastical administration for the millennium following the decline of the empire. From spoken Latin grew the chief Romantic vernacular tongues of continental Europe: French, Spanish and Italian.

The barbarian challenge

Who were the northern barbarians who were to be the heirs to the Roman tradition? Did they come merely as empty-handed destroyers, or did they, too, make a contribution to the development of the West? From the first, barbarian was a relative term. The tribes scattered along the outer

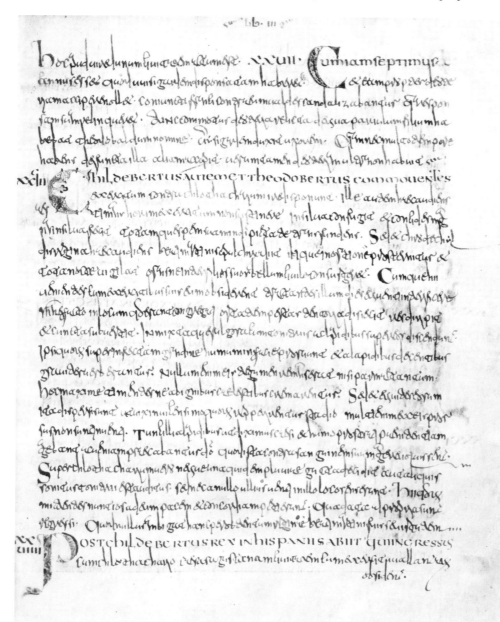

Above: A coin depicting Alaric the Goth, modelled on the coinage of the Roman emperors. Despite being responsible for the sack of Rome in AD 410, Alaric saw himself as being part of the great Roman tradition.

Right: As the Roman Empire collapsed in the face of barbarian invasions, Roman craftsmen could still produce exquisite carvings like this Apotheosis of Antoninus Pius, looking back to Rome's golden age.

Below left: A page from an early eighth-century manuscript of Gregory of Tours' *History of the Franks*, written in the semi-barbarous Latin of the Merovingian period. Throughout the Middle Ages the influence of Rome remained strong at the literary and cultural level.

This richly decorated Frankish helmet was buried with a barbarian warrior when he died. Although the Franks had mastered skills like metal-working, they were far inferior to their Roman predecessors in both technology and artistic achievement.

edges of the empire had been in contact with Rome for some centuries before such contact grew to an intensity of friction that justified the term invasions. Minor hostilities along the borders alternated with periods of military co-operation, and thus some of the tribes, particularly the Visigoths, gradually came to admire Roman civilization. Indeed through the efforts of Ulfilas, a Christian missionary of Gothic descent, a Gothic alphabet was invented, and after the Bible had been translated, the Visigoths adopted Christianity, albeit in the Arian form that denied the equality of the Father and the Son within the Trinity. Since the Germanic tribes were descended from a common racial and linguistic stock, Christianity radiated out from its Visigothic base, increasing the affinities between Romans and barbarians.

Historians are often tempted to speculate on the alternatives of the past. Had the slow process of Romanization been allowed to continue, it is possible that the German tribes might slowly have been integrated into the empire and have provided the manpower and energy necessary for its survival. As it was, the semi-Romanized tribes were thrust against the limits of the empire by totally uncivilized hordes from the east. Emerging from the central plains of Asia, the Huns swept westward, destroying all before them. The Ostrogoths, the easternmost Gothic tribe, were vanquished and scattered before them, but the Visigoths sought the protection of Rome and in 376 were granted permission to enter the empire. The opportunity for peaceful integration was lost

through the greed and venality of the Roman administrators who treated the Visigoths not as guests but as victims, subjecting them to plunder and rapine. Left without hope or choice, the Visigoths organized to fight back and marched against the imperial forces, sweeping through Greece and the Balkans. Finally, in 410, under Alaric, they sacked Rome itself but did not in fact seek to destroy either the city or the empire. Indeed, the Visigoths later fought on the side of Rome and aided in the defeat of Attila's Huns in 451, in northern France, in the crucial battle of Châlons that helped to spare most of Italy from the fiercest of the barbarians.

During the same period, the Huns drove the Ostrogoths, who had re-grouped and fled into the vacuum left by the Visigoths, along the northern edges of the empire, until they too found themselves with no further escape path, crossed the borders, and marched directly on Rome herself. It was this tribe, under the leadership of Theodoric, who deposed the Visigoth, Odovacar, and made Italy a separate kingdom. Yet even then the idea of the empire endured. Theodoric's kingship in Italy ended the need for a western emperor, but the Ostrogoth chieftain accepted the eastern emperor as his superior. Distance and the continued external threat from the eastern hordes precluded the possibility that the emperor might actually rule. Costly, and even moderately successful, efforts at recovery were made, but after the fifth century the Roman Empire remained a creature of the eastern Mediterranean – in the form of the Byzantine Empire, based on Constantinople.

Kingdom of the Franks

Despite the eastern emperors' attempts to preserve the fiction of unity by asserting that the barbarian kings governed with imperial sanction, the history of the West after the fifth century is largely the history of the Germanic kingdoms. The most important of these was that of the Franks, who emigrated from the shores of the North Sea and established a kingdom in the north of France. Little is known of their early history save that they were more remote from the empire than many tribes and consequently were not yet Christianized by the end of the fifth century. Legend, preserved through the *History of the Franks* written by Gregory of Tours in the sixth century, links the conversion of the Franks to that of their king, Clovis (481-511). Clovis, whose primary calling was warrior – he had driven the last Roman governor from France – had a Christian wife, Clothilda. Gregory's version records that during a battle against the Allamanni, another barbarian tribe, Clovis observed that the odds were favoring the enemy and called upon his wife's god for aid. In return for victory, Clovis superstitiously offered the conversion of the Franks; then victory came, the tribe was baptized into the Catholic faith.

The decline and confusion of the empire coincided with the increasing strength and confidence of the Roman church. Concomitantly, the early popes grew ever more careful to preserve the integrity of the true faith. By the sixth century, the church was everywhere attempting to purify itself and to eradicate heresy. The Arian form of Christianity, common among the Gothic peoples, was declared heretical and strongly opposed. The Franks, whether through good fortune in the timing and miraculous nature of their conversion or through crafty policy, became orthodox Christians, subscribing in name, if not altogether in spirit, to the correct doctrine newly defined by the Roman church. Thus, the Franks gained powerful allies among the Catholic bishops and in time became the natural defenders of the church. Equally, under the pretext of fighting heresy, they could justify and gain allies for their endeavors against the other Germanic tribes.

The two principal enemies of the Franks within Gaul were the Burgundians, a small and consequently weak tribe located in the southwest of France, and the powerful Visigoths, whose territory stretched from southeastern France throughout most of the Iberian Peninsula. By 500, four years after his conversion, Clovis had undertaken a campaign against the Burgundians and had so reduced their power to resist that he was able to consider more ambitious projects and even to enlist his former victims as allies. Urged on by the eastern Roman emperor, who, despite the impotence of the empire, still followed the feeble defensive policy of pitting one tribe against the other, and supported by the Burgundians and the Catholic bishops of southern France, Clovis attacked the Visigothic kingdom. After a short campaign (507-08), the Visigoths were driven across the Pyrenees, and the Franks gained control over most of the territory that is now modern France, in addition to their previous conquests east of the Rhine.

By the time of his death in 511, Clovis had founded the Merovingian dynasty, named after his grandfather, Merovech, and had assembled a formidable land base. He had not, however, founded a nation nor even a viable state. Under Germanic custom, the conquered territory was treated as a private estate. Thus when Clovis died, the kingdom was divided among his four sons. A period of vicious and intense fratricidal war followed, but miraculously, instead of disintegrating, the Frankish territories actually expanded over the course of the next half-century.

This success was primarily the result of good luck, rather than political or military skill. Theodoric, whose Ostrogothic kingdom spread over Italy, the Po Valley and Yugoslavia, died in 526; his successors lacked his political skill, and conse-

quently the Ostrogothic kingdom began to disintegrate. Justinian, the great eastern emperor, who collected and codified Roman law, directed the remaining resources of the eastern empire toward the reconquest of Italy and briefly succeeded in bringing the peninsula back within the imperial borders. The effort and expense were too great, however, and the prime result of the destruction of the Ostrogothic state was the creation of a political vacuum. The Franks capitalized on this weakness in 536, invading northern Italy and adding Provence to their subject territories. The Italian conquests were destined to be temporary; the migrations continued throughout the sixth century and the eastward movement, forcing new peoples into Italy, remained undiminished. Driven westward by the Avars, the Lombards, who had settled in the Hungarian plains by the mid-sixth century, entered Italy in 568, only slightly later than the Franks. They quickly justified their reputation for ferocity and military prowess by sweeping through the peninsula and seizing all but the offshore islands of Corsica, Sardinia and Sicily, a small portion of the extreme south and an equally small area in the north at the head of the Adriatic. These territories remained under the control of the Byzantine Empire.

Rule based on wealth

The Merovingian Franks had been able to expand at the expense of the Ostrogoths, but they had acquired a more troublesome and dangerous neighbor in the Lombards. Their conquests held together mainly because no stronger or more organized force opposed them, but success in war was not equivalent to the creation of a viable state. We have already seen that the Merovingian idea of kingship was little more than the possession of vast lands. It is no great distortion to say that the king was simply the richest man in the kingdom. Extending this farther and converting it to a theoretical proposition, wealth was the only enduring justification of the right to govern. Wealth was, of course, transmitted from a father to his sons, so the basis for hereditary monarchy is subsumed within the notion that wealth or possession of land entails the right to rule.

Since kingship and ownership were one and the same, it follows that the Merovingian idea of kingship did not imply any obligation on the part of the monarch to serve his people or to provide

for the public welfare. Thus, the function of royal officials was essentially to collect, rather than to render services. As a result, Merovingian government was extremely simple, borrowing titles and functions from the remnants of the imperial administration and blending them with those derived from the Germanic military structure.

For each *civitas*, the Roman administrative division that had been incorporated into the ecclesiastical structure as well, the king appointed a count who acted, with full powers, in all matters on behalf of the king. The counts were initially entirely under the control of the king and served only at his pleasure. Dukes were created to lead royal armies and, as in the case of the counts, to exercise full royal powers while remaining totally subject to the king himself. Since the prime purpose of government was to gather wealth for the king, the kingdom was subdivided into fiscal districts, and each was placed under the charge of a steward called a *domesticus*. At the head of all the stewards was the chief steward, a court official, with the title *major palatii*, or mayor of the palace. Other minor officials, essentially the personal retinue of the king, holding either German or Roman titles, existed, but the most notable government personages were the counts, the dukes, and the mayors of the palace, whose importance steadily increased.

In view of the fact that western society was everywhere breaking up, becoming more localized and forming into small, almost self-sufficient economic units, there is reason to doubt that a more complex government *could* have endured. Attempts were made to preserve the Roman tax system, but the necessary administrators could neither be found nor trained. The coinage was maintained at the Roman standard, and continued to be struck against the Roman pound, but as bullion became more scarce and as trade declined, the volume of coinage decreased sharply. In the absence of adequate administrative personnel and of sufficient specie, the direct taxation inherited from Rome collapsed. In its stead, logically following the pattern of the rest of the economy, indirect local taxes assumed much greater importance. Tolls, market dues and fines derived from the administration of justice became the main source of regular revenue for the Merovingian monarchy. Government officials were expected to live at the expense of their locality; con-

sequently, the greater portion of the revenues that actually reached the king were net income. In addition to the regular revenues were the extraordinary revenues which came from plunder or, in a slightly more permanent form, from tribute. This source of funds was perhaps the most crucial of all for the monarchy.

Since the Merovingian monarchy lacked any abstract justification beyond wealth for its claim to the right to rule, loyalty was at best only personal, and given to a specific king rather than to his line. Subdivision of the kingdom, through the Frankish custom of multiple inheritance, strained what loyalty there was for the dynasty, but the succession of incompetent and quarrelsome heirs of Clovis diluted it even further. Localism, and the independence from central government that grew out of the practice of making counts and dukes self-sufficient within their districts, inevitably rendered these officials jealous of their private hegemonies and competitive with the king. Obedience could be obtained, public order restored and services bought from these increasingly independent officials only by means of outright bribes. Bribes in turn required funds, which were adequate only when the normal revenues were supplemented with booty won through conquest. The inherent weakness of such a system is obvious. The more successful the king was in his systematic bribery, the more affluent and powerful did the recipients become. If the

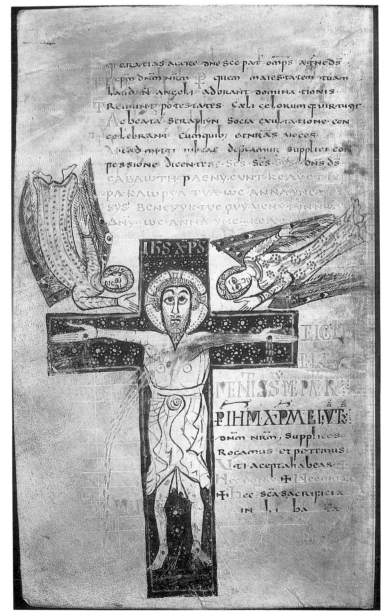

Above right: The first Benedictine monastery was established at Monte Cassino in 529. The Benedictines became a spearhead of Christian missionary work, in pagan England and Germany.

Right: A Merovingian illuminated manuscript depicting the crucifixion, evidence both of the immense influence of Christianity in post-Roman Europe, and of the decline in artistic standards from Roman times.

Below left: A casket carved out of whalebone by an Anglo-Saxon artist in the eighth century. It shows, on the right, the Magi bringing their gifts to the infant Jesus – a new theme for a people only recently converted to Christianity.

king gave away enough, there was a danger that he would no longer be the richest man in the kingdom.

Signs that such a trend was underway were already apparent by 614. The nobles, both ecclesiastical and lay, banded together against King Chlotar II and forced him to grant a number of concessions. The church gained additional independence, the nobles were guaranteed their lands and taxes were further reduced. Yet the nobles had not really gained the upper hand. Fragmentation of the governmental processes made the king weak, but it also assured that no one else could be truly strong. The nobles had found their natural leader in the mayor of the palace, but even so, the custom of dividing the kingdom among the heirs of the king had resulted in the creation of three great mayoralties. Neustria, in the northeast of France, Austrasia, in the northwest of France and across the Rhine, and Burgundy, in the southwest, – each had a mayor of the palace. The power struggle among the kinglets was thus replicated among the mayors, and indeed at every level down to the most local.

The search for security

In such a situation of constant war and personal hazard, it is little wonder that men sought every means, no matter how desperate, to protect themselves. One path was to find a more powerful man who would provide defense. This practice, formally known as commendation, became increasingly common during the seventh century, though it probably developed from much older roots in German military custom. Here, in return for protection, one man commended or placed himself in the service of another through a reciprocal agreement. Such commendations were binding, in their early form, during the consent of both parties, but subsequently they extended for life. Property itself could be transferred by means of the benefice, or *precarium*, a device similar in intent to commendation, whereby property would be given, often to a church, and in return the donor would be allowed to remain on the property, even though it had legally passed into stronger hands. The defensive intention of the transaction is apparent.

Another institution, though a collective one, ideally suited for the turbulent conditions prevailing during the early Middle Ages, was the monastery. First, of course, they provided spiritual peace in a time when the world was full of trouble, but equally they offered some degree of collective security for the monks within. In addition, they were economic units appropriate to the declining economy and to the trend toward self-sufficient estates. St Benedict, who founded the famous monastery at Monte Cassino in Italy around 525, in writing the Benedictine Rule that regulated the behavior of the monks, seems to have comprehended well the problems of his time. Regular prayers and services catered to the spiritual needs of man and the worship of God, but these were balanced by manual labor, both in the fields and, for the more skilled, in the crafts. The ideal monastery thus was economically independent, as well as remote and far from potential enemies. An abbot, who ruled with absolute authority after his election, was instituted to maintain morality and uphold the rule, but his presence also assured that the monastery would cohere and gain in political strength. Monasteries also provided social services by feeding the poor, aiding the traveler and, most important for the survival of western culture, by preserving some of the learning and more of the books of antiquity from which scholarship could again begin. Indeed, the leading scholars of the early medieval period were Irish monks who traveled throughout western Europe, missionaries of both Catholicism and knowledge.

From the institutions and customs created in response to the crises of the period 400-700 would develop the more stable society of the high Middle Ages, but in themselves these efforts were insufficient to order the chaos of the earlier period. From commendation would come the more orderly feudal structure. From the monastic movement would come the energy and personnel required to reform the church – indeed, Gregory I (590-604), the first great medieval pope, began as a monk. Yet nothing could prevent the history of the Merovingian dynasty from being one of continuous failure until its dismal end in the eighth century.

After the reign of Dagobert (629-39) the monarchy disintegrated before the forces of localism and petty feuds. The tripartite division of the kingdom into Austrasia, Neustria and Burgundy became ever more rigid and permanent. Further external conquest failed, and, as a result, the extra funds needed to sustain the monarchy were no longer available. Inevitably the mayors of the palace gained greater prominence and governed, at first on behalf of, but then merely in the name of, a series of shadow kings. Despite the disadvantages inherent in such a fictitious monarchy and in the squabbling among the mayors, competence and talent eventually emerged from within the mayoralty of Austrasia in the person of Pepin of Heristal. This remarkable figure was able to conquer Neustria (687), thus reuniting the greater portion of the Frankish hegemony and at the same time winning a truly dominant position within the kingdom as a result of the financial resources captured in the process. Pepin died in 714, leaving no legitimate adult heirs, but fortunately for the future he had not devoted himself solely to the business of government. His bastard son, Charles, was to be the founder of a new dynasty.

Pepin's death threatened to return the Frankish kingdom to anarchy. His widow, Plectrude, attempted to control the three mayoralities, but, as had so often been the case before, the death of a king or mayor was a signal for revolt. In this instance, the dangers of anarchy were magnified by the presence of a major new political force in the Mediterranean. The death of Pepin coincided almost exactly with the Arabs' arrival at the pinnacle of their military and political power. Less than a century after the death of Muhammad, Saracen forces had swept through North Africa and established an empire that stretched from the Caspian Sea and the Persian Gulf to the Atlantic. In 711 the Visigoths were defeated and Spain fell under the control of the Umayyad Caliphate. Possessed of wealth, committed soldiers and an organizing idea, and representing a much more sophisticated culture than that of the West in the eighth century, the Arabs appeared invincible in their march against Europe. No western leader seemed to have the strength to resist their onslaught.

In 716, however, Charles Martel escaped from the prison where he had been incarcerated by Plectrude in her vain endeavor to preserve the inheritance due to her infant children. In a series of brilliant campaigns between 716 and 730 Charles successfully reduced Neustria, Aquitaine in southwestern France, and the armies of Plectrude. Once in control of Gaul he was able to defeat the Frisians and Saxons in the north and the Bavarians and Alamanni to the east. His most significant battle, however, was fought against the Arab armies advancing upward through southern France. In 732 near Tours the Frankish soldiers, employing some cavalry but mainly on foot, met the more lightly armed Saracen horsemen and defeated them. The battle did not end Arab power in western Europe – indeed Arab forces remained in southern France for more than 200 years thereafter – but it did underscore the battlefield potential of heavy cavalry. The age of chivalry, of the mounted knight, began in the eighth century.

Charles Martel had reassembled the Merovingian territories, but he continued to rule under the fictional role of mayor of the palace, despite the fact that he did not bother to create a king from 727 until his death in 741. He followed the Frankish custom and divided his lands between his two sons, Carloman, who inherited Austrasia and the land across the Rhine, and Pepin, who obtained Burgundy and Neustria. In 747 Carloman entered a monastery and Pepin alone remained to become the last mayor of the palace and the first Carolingian monarch.

A new era in Europe

The ascent of Pepin was not accomplished without further struggle and revolt. Indeed, so serious was the reaction after Charles Martel's death in 743 that his sons were forced to create a new Merovingian king, Childeric III, and to pretend to rule through him. After enough stability had been restored so that it was possible for Carloman to follow his pious instincts and enter a monastery, this most shadowy and unfortunate of all the Merovingian kings clearly became little more than a useless encumbrance to Pepin, but one not disposed of easily. A principle of authority was required to give a change in the succession some semblance of legality; the church seemed able to provide such authority.

The Franks had long been allies of the pope. Since Clovis' conversion, they had been true, not Arian, Christians, and the sword of Charles Martel had carried the word of St Boniface throughout Germany, making it possible to convert large numbers there. Only fear of further Arab advances had prevented Charles from answering Pope Gregory III's call for aid against the Lombards in 739, and the church's problems with the Lombards had worsened in the years between 739 and 751. The pope consequently needed a military force capable of containing the Lombards, who had held most of Italy since the collapse of the last vestiges of the eastern emperors' real power within the peninsula. Pepin, on the other hand, needed to find legal and moral justification for dispensing with the last of the Merovingian line. Thus the pope needed Pepin, and Pepin needed the pope.

Carefully briefed ambassadors, the abbot of St Denis and a German bishop, were sent to ask the pope whether it were better 'to call him king who has the royal power than him who has not.' Pope Zacharius responded that it was better to call him king who had the power, and as a result of this papal sanction, Childeric III was forthwith tonsured and hurried into monastic retirement in 751. Pepin was shrewdly concerned with the details of his coronation. First he had himself acclaimed king by an assembly of nobles at Soisson, following the Frankish tradition. Then he was annointed with holy oil by St Boniface in the presence of an assembly of bishops. Three years later, he was again consecrated and annointed with holy oil by Pope Stephen II himself, who declared that the throne should never pass to any but a direct heir of Pepin.

The remarkable attention given to the coronation was clearly designed to bring stability to the realm and to protect the dynasty, but it did much more. The whole theory of kingship had changed. No longer was the right to rule based only on ownership and force, though both were still required. The king was now the Lord's annointed, and ruled as the chosen of God. Revolt against the king became, if not revolt against God, an act with moral as well as political implications. On his part, the king now would have duties and obligations as the regent of God, and not merely benefits. Further, since the coronation of a king was now much more explicitly a religious ceremony within the church, the definition of the respective roles of king and pope became a crucial problem, and one that has endured into modern times. The many ramifications that would follow could not, of course, have been foreseen in 751, but the consecration of the first Carolingian was also the consecration of a new era in Europe.

In return for its approval, Pepin was expected to protect the church from the Lombards; he did not delay in this task. In two campaigns, closely following his final consecration by the pope, Pepin attacked the Lombards and triumphed over them. Then, led simultaneously by his own piety and by forged precedent, he placed the keys to several liberated cities upon the tomb of St Peter, an act which became known as the 'Donation of Pepin.' Pepin's act was in imitation of the more famous Donation of Constantine, whereby that emperor allegedly (the document was a forgery) gave the pope what amounted to territorial and secular power over the western half of the empire. The document recording the Donation of Pepin has never emerged from the papal archives. Nevertheless, both documents were to have a long history and to form the basis for future papal claims to more than spiritual power over western Europe.

Victory was as distinct from security in the early Middle Ages as now. Despite Pepin's success, the kingdom continued to exist only through the force and energy of its king. Indeed, many of the battles won by Pepin had been won earlier by his father and would have to be fought again by his son. Yet the accomplishment of the reign was substantial. The legacy of the Merovingians was held and in fact enlarged; new blood and energy had been infused into the monarchy;

and the conception of kingship had been expanded and could develop into a viable means of governance. The alliance with the pope had given moral sanction as well as moral obligation to the monarchy, and thus the lines of allegiance upon which the monarchy depended could be strengthened through a sense of Christian mission and purpose. All depended upon Pepin's successors.

The Age of Charlemagne

Pepin died in 768, and the kingdom was divided between two sons, Charles and Carloman. Fortunately for the future, the latter died within three years, and the kingdom was reunited under Charles, or, including the soubriquet, Charlemagne. A giant of a man, with a taste for hunting, war and women, he was ideally suited to lead the rough Franks, to win the respect of his nobles and to withstand the many years of military expeditions that were required of him. He was not merely a warrior, however, but also a man of considerable intelligence, although unpolished by schooling. He was also apparently a faithful, though certainly not monkish, Christian. He forced the Saxons to convert, under penalty of death for any violation of Christianity, yet he kept at least four semi-permanent mistresses and took and repudiated wives by Frankish rather than Christian customs.

The Saxons, who inhabited northern Germany, had long troubled the Franks, but Charlemagne finally subdued them and added their territory to his own. Other conquests expanded the kingdom southeast into modern Austria, and also to the south, incorporating a small portion of Spain beyond the Pyrenees, a campaign that later provided the inspiration for the *Song of Roland*, an epic poem celebrating the Arabs' destruction of the heroic rearguard of Charlemagne's army. Less inspiring to poets, perhaps, but more significant territorially and politically, was Charlemagne's success against the Lombards. After first attempting an alliance with them through the marriage of his daughter to the son of their king, Desiderius, and his own marriage to that king's daughter, Charlemagne became exasperated by the continued growth of Lombard power in Italy and set his armies afield, after thrice warning Desiderius. The campaign was successful and in 774 Charle-

Above right: The kings of the Carolingian dynasty pay homage to Christ. On the top left is the dynasty's founder, Pepin, and opposite him stands the greatest of the line, Charlemagne

Right: The kingdom of the Franks was already a large area in the eighth century, but Charlemagne expanded it into the biggest realm in Europe since the Romans.

KINGDOM OF THE FRANKS, 768
EXTENT OF CHARLEMAGNE'S EMPIRE

0   MILES   400
0   KILOMETERS   600

© Richard Natkiel, 1988

FRIESLAND   SAXONY   Elbe
SORBS
COLOGNE   AUSTRIA   BOHEMIA
  MAINZ
ROUEN   TRIER   MORAVIA
REIMS   SLOVAKIA
BRITTANY   NEUSTRIA   BAVARIA
  TOURS   ALAMANNIA   SALZBURG   Danube
BRETON   Loire   AWAREN
MARCH   CARINTHIA   Drava
  BURGUNDY   FRIULI   AQUILEIA   Save
AQUITAINE   LYONS   MILAN
BORDEAUX   Garonne   Po
KINGDOM   PATRIMONY
OF ITALY   OF PETER
SPANISH MARCH   SPOLETO
SARAGOSSA   CORSICA   ROME
EMIRATE   BARCELONA   BENEVENTO
OF CORDOVA   SARDINIA

magne became king of the Lombards as well as of the Franks. The Frankish Empire had now grown to include most of northern Italy. The Donation of Pepin was confirmed, and the papal lands were increased, but Charlemagne delayed before turning over much more land to the church. Rome remained within the expanded Frankish kingdom and under its control; once more, after a lapse of centuries, the center of the church lay within a single kingdom, grown vast enough to compare with the ancient Roman empire.

The pope's security depended more than ever on support from the king of the Franks. When Pope Leo III (795-816) barely escaped with his life after a Roman mob assaulted him in the spring of 799, Charlemagne came to his aid and reinstated the pope. In 800 he sat in judgment of the pope. In a formal ceremony, Leo was compelled to clear himself by oath of the varied criminal charges that the Romans had leveled against him. Reluctantly the pope did so, and thus a Frankish king was able to impose moral authority over the spiritual leader of the Catholic church and of Christendom itself. The dangers inherent in such a precedent were not lost upon the pope and his advisers, but protest was useless in the face of necessity.

Two days after Leo had established his innocence, Charlemagne celebrated Christmas in St Peter's, and while he knelt in prayer, the pope placed the imperial crown upon his head, and the assembled crowd hailed him Emperor. Historians have given various interpretations of this event. It has been called by some an incident of crucial importance for the West, a rebirth of Rome, and by others a symbolic but not very significant occurrence whose importance, if any, was but dimly comprehended by the participants. Charles' biographer, Einhard, without explaining the cause, reports that Charles was angered by the proceedings, but this seems unlikely, since the king must have been aware of the preparations for the event, and since the pope could not really afford to offend him. On the other hand, the imperial title did not actually give Charles a great deal more power than he had held before his elevation. And in some ways it was awkward. He was now, as emperor, entitled to rule Rome and, by long custom, to exercise control of papal elections, but he was after all in Rome through military force and had just sat in judgment over the pope.

There was some question concerning the legal-

This small bronze statue of Charlemagne is thought to be a contemporary portrait of the man who became the first Holy Roman Emperor, a ruler of territories comparable in size to the old Roman Empire in the west.

ity of his coronation, since the true seat of the empire was in the east, at Constantinople. Thus Charles' elevation could from that quarter only be viewed as usurpation. While he gained an enemy there, Charlemagne also established a dangerous precedent in that he had implicitly allowed the pope to assume the power to create an emperor. Yet this precedent was already inherent in the ceremonies surrounding the coronation of Pepin and the inception of the Carolingian line. Whatever significance the elevation of the king of the Franks to emperor of the Romans had for the future, it must have been obscure to contemporaries and participants, for by 806 Charlemagne was planning the division of his kingdom among his three sons, in total disregard for the integrity of the imperial idea. The influence of the new empire and of the imperial idea developed only slowly; its preservation was due solely to the historical accident of the death of two of Charlemagne's three sons.

If the papal re-creation of the empire in 800 did not result in any marked change in the institutions or practices of the government or in the degree of loyalty to Frankish customs, the energy which Charlemagne infused into the existing institutions ended by making the empire a reality. The curse of the Merovingian era – localism and the loss of central authority – was countered with traditional but skillfully employed tools. The counts continued to be the major local authorities, ruling over carefully defined areas in the name of the emperor and drawing their incomes from the localities they governed; they remained, theoretically at least, subject to replacement at the emperor's pleasure. Under Charlemagne, the effort to control the counts was forcefully conducted, and officials known as *missi dominici* traversed the empire as his direct representatives, gathering information and inspecting the activities of the counts. *Missi dominici* had existed earlier, but their jurisdiction and authority were now greatly enhanced. The frequency of their visits and the fact that their displeasure produced real and immediate consequences served simultaneously to demonstrate the power of the central administration and to increase it.

Parallel in geographical jurisdiction to the counts were the bishops, whose dioceses usually corresponded with the secular counties. They too were subject to inspection by the *missi dominici*, and were controlled by the emperor, at least at the time of their installation, since imperial nomination was equivalent to appointment. In upholding the faith and spreading Christianity, the bishops exerted a strong force for unification and centralism. If the Merovingians lacked a rationale for the organic integration of their conquests, the Carolingians almost found one in the church. On the one hand, the sacerdotal nature of the coronation closely associated the ruler with the spiritual unity and belief implicit in Christendom, a force whose earthly presence was symbolized by the congruence of the ecclesiastical and secular structures of governance. On the other hand, upon reaching the age of 12 every male in the empire was compelled to take an oath of loyalty to the emperor before God. Inevitably, as the forces of God grew, both through religious conversion and through expansion of the physical power of the church, the significance of the oath as a binding force was also enhanced.

Despite all efforts to bring order from localism and chaos, the empire still suffered from innate weaknesses. The strength of the system lay in its simplicity. Counts governed their localities using their own revenues. The army was raised through the sworn obligation of each man to fight for the emperor, and served at its own expense. The church was sustained through its own lands, although its revenues were supplemented by the tithe, a legal obligation to pay a tenth of all income to the church. The judicial system was self-supporting and even produced revenue for the emperor through his share of the fines levied against malfeasants. Finally, the emperor himself lived on the income of his own domain lands. Such strengths were also potential weaknesses, however. Controlled by Charlemagne, the system was a satisfactory vehicle for the imposition of central authority, but there was no inherent tendency toward centralization. Indeed, precisely because of the simplicity of government, the empire could be divided into any number of segments without disrupting its efficiency.

The one institution within the empire that did have a coherent internal structure implicitly leading toward central control was the church. Economically, it could withstand fragmentation of the empire, since its revenues came from local sources; ultimately the hierarchical structure of the church had become more durable than that of the empire. By the ninth century, the pope was clearly the head of the church, and the church was unquestionably an indivisible institution. Tradition, doctrine, control of the sacraments and the location of the Holy See in Rome all assured that the unity of the church would endure. It was inevitable that the power of the church would increase, despite some dangerous false steps that served only to prove the innate strength resident in the institution. It was equally inevitable that the empire would succumb to its own essential fragility.

The legacies of Charlemagne's empire must include a greatly strengthened church and, as a corollary, a much more coherent culture. The potent combination of religious conversion and the relatively brief period of effective central control did much to weaken and erode old tribal loyalties and to create a more homogeneous culture among the diverse peoples of Europe. Henceforward, while men still murdered and fought among themselves, they did so less as tribes than as brigands, a small but not unimportant step forward for mankind. Charles' attempts to bring about a revival of learning must also be counted among the imperial legacies, although the term 'Carolingian Renaissance' is perhaps excessive. The court school, supported by the king, sought scholars from all corners of the world and provided a focus for intellectual discourse. Alcuin, an Englishman, and perhaps the most learned man of his time, reformed the script used for copying manuscripts, and the new handwriting, Carolingian minuscule, survived for centuries to influence modern printing. The script was not merely admired for its beauty, but was used extensively for copying the texts of Latin authors, and while our debt to the Caroline scholars for their originality may be small, it is great when measured in terms of the number of classical works that have survived only in ninth-century manuscripts. Other, more minor accomplishments of the reign, such as coinage reform and the standardization of weights and measures, also survived for a term, but perhaps the lasting residue of the empire lay in placing the center of a new civilization firmly in the north of Europe, and away from the Mediterranean. Little is known of economic development in the eighth and ninth centuries, but there are signs that new agricultural techniques, suitable for the fertile European plains, were urged upon the managers of the imperial estates and were thus diffused throughout the empire. Ultimately, they would make northwestern Europe a rich and populous region and free at least some men to create the monuments of the high Middle Ages.

A divided succession

The benefits that were to come from the accomplishments of Charlemagne lay mainly in the future. By eliminating two of the emperor's three sons, the high mortality rate of the period temporarily forestalled the division of the empire when Charlemagne died in 814, but the successor, although certainly more gentle, was not as capable as his father. Louis the Pious richly deserved his sobriquet for he was a religious and moral man whose work was more often in the service of the church than of the empire. Louis' earliest acts were devoted to purifying the court. The women who had, if not graced, at least enlivened Charlemagne's court were hustled off to nunneries and officials were named to eradicate turpitude from the environs of the court. Such endeavors must have dismayed the rough warriors who had served under the more lenient Charlemagne, and perhaps may have called into question their

loyalty to the new moralist. Other imperial policies were also altered. In 817 Louis granted to the papacy much that his father had withheld: the papal lands were formally enumerated, and the emperor engaged himself never to attempt to exercise power within them except at the express invitation of the pope. Papal elections were to be free from imperial control, and an extradition agreement was made to allow the pope to recover fugitives who escaped to imperial territory. Substantial steps toward papal independence were made in this act, and it established precedents for subsequent actions that ultimately would cause dramatic conflict between pope and emperor. For the moment, however, events led Louis to reconsider, and in 824, drawn to Rome by the execution of two high church officials who favored the emperor, Louis reasserted imperial control over the papal state and required an oath of loyalty from each newly elected pope before he could be consecrated.

If Louis revealed indecision in his treatment of the papacy, he outdid himself with regard to the succession. Some sympathy must be accorded to his desire to remedy the long-standing problem of the succession, as indeed one can applaud his wish to create an independent papacy, but the result of his actions was worse than the pre-existing Frankish custom. An initial division of the kingdom, anticipating Louis' death by many years, was made in 817. The eldest son, Lothair, was to be emperor and sole heir. Two younger sons, Pepin and Louis, each received separate kingships, but were to remain subservient to Lothair. The following year the emperor remarried and shortly afterwards his wife gave birth to a son, Charles, in the same year that Lothair was crowned co-emperor by the pope. The problem of the succession was now more difficult because of Charles' birth, but Louis bravely made a new attempt to settle the question in 831 by redividing the kingdom and giving equal shares to Charles, Louis and Pepin. Lothair was to have Italy, but the emperorship was not mentioned. In 838 Pepin died, and Louis the Pious was again compelled to take up the issue. This time, since Louis, the son, was in revolt against his father, the division was an equal one between Charles, who got the west, and Lothair who kept the east of the kingdom, while the rebellious Louis received a greatly reduced share.

In 840 Louis the Pious died, and it would be hard to imagine a more hopelessly muddled legacy than the one he left his heirs. Each surviving son had a vested interest in preserving the terms of one of the three settlements, but there was no other common ground among them. Civil war had already erupted prior to the death of Louis the Pious; inevitably it worsened in 840 as each son sought to enforce the settlement that favored him most. For a time it seemed that cooperation was only possible when one of the sons gained the upper hand and thus forced the other two to ally against him, but exhaustion finally brought about what reason could not accomplish. In 843 the Treaty of Verdun divided the kingdom once more: Louis gained the eastern portion of the German territories; Charles received the west, whch included most of France; and Lothair retained a thin strip between the holdings of the other two, along with Italy and the imperial title. When Lothair died a dozen years later, his portion was shared among three sons: Lothair II kept the territory north of the Alps, while Louis got the imperial title and Italy; Charles, an infant, recived the rest.

The struggles, jealousies and intrigues generated by these tangled political settlements greatly

enhanced the stature of the papacy, which remained unified while the empire crumbled. It was now strong enough to intervene directly in the problem of the succession. Lothair II had married a noblewoman, Theutberga, who turned out to be barren, but he had also found a more appealing female companion named Waldrada, who granted him the satisfactions of fatherhood. Frankish custom and the precedents set by Charlemagne in dispensing with unwanted wives would have permitted Lothair II simply to renounce Theutberga and marry Waldrada, thus making his children legitimate and capable of inheriting the kingdom. The church had by now, however, acquired greater confidence and moral authority, and as a result Pope Nicholas I refused to allow Lothair II to abrogate the marriage, under threat of excommunication and the consequent loss of access to the sacraments. Despite considerable opposition the pope was able to make his judgment stand. Lothair was thus without legitimate heir when he died in 869. By the Treaty of Mersen his portion was divided between Charles and Louis, the sons of Louis the Pious, while Louis II, the son of Lothair I, retained the kingdom of Italy.

We have reviewed this settlement and the events that led up to it in detail because they were rich with portent. The Treaty of Mersen effectively divided Europe into its modern linguistic partitions and gave formal recognition to the emergence of the vernacular languages. Further, it was largely the result of the pope's imposition of his moral authority, although this was supplemented by political skill. Both Charlemagne and Louis the Pious had been able to sit in judgment of the papacy and to hold the popes under their tutelage, but now the papacy had, in effect, sat in judgment over the Frankish monarchy and had demonstrated effective political power. Excommunication and control of the sacraments had become a forceful weapon; the conversion of the Franks had become a reality. The unity and prestige of the church had held, but even in that quarter, events revealed the need for the reform of the episcopacy. Early in the controversy the German bishops were under Lothair's control, and at his request they had declared the marriage to Theutberga void. The danger that the bishops would develop into mere tools of the emperor was already manifest in the middle of the ninth century. For the church to survive, it was necessary that the pope increase his political independence and preserve his moral prestige. Such was not yet to be the case, however, for after the death of Nicholas I the papacy itself fell to a level of debasement that remained unduplicated even during the worst outrages of the Renaissance.

While the descendants of Charlemagne were consuming the empire in fratricidal warfare, a new wave of invasions began. Effective resistance would have required the full force of the united empire, but this was not forthcoming. The Arabs continued to menace the south. Corsica, Sardinia and Sicily were seized during the course of the ninth century, and from 840 to 870 the Muslims established a substantial land base in southern Italy. Saracen raids from permanent land bases continued to terrorize southern France and to drain away church funds in ransom payments for captured Christians.

An even greater danger appeared in the north. Viking raids that had begun at the end of the eighth century now became a regular spring occurrence and grew in audacity, scope and terror as the empire deteriorated. Annually the long ships carried men from the Scandinavian peninsula both to harass the Atlantic frontier of the empire and, when the Vikings followed the rivers

inland, even to drive into the heartlands, sometimes as far as Paris itself. The squabbling monarchs of Christendom were helpless against these invaders who plundered the churches and carried away the wealth of the land.

Out of the east, after the middle of the ninth century, came the Hungarians who, as so many pagan tribes had done 400 years earlier, pushed across the imperial borders to spread annual havoc among the peoples of Germany. Europe was thus under attack from three sides and, given the added confusion of perpetual civil war and petty domestic power struggles at every level of society, it is little wonder that the flickering light of Carolingian learning was extinguished, that economic and demographic growth halted and that weak men were again compelled to seek the aid of the strong as civil society collapsed.

The feudal system

As the strength of the public power waned, government fell into private hands and became essentially a personal possession of a favored few. The earlier practice of commendation developed into vassalage, whereby one individual became the 'man' of another through a double ceremony that first required the vassal to place his clasped hands between those of his lord (homage) and then to take an oath to serve the lord faithfully for life (fealty). The oath, a Carolingian addition, brought the church firmly into this most basic of feudal institutions, both lending clerical sanction to a personal and political arrangement and greatly increasing the effectiveness of excommunication, since excommunication of the lord freed the vassal from his oath. Sometimes the ceremony was concluded by the reciprocal exchange of a kiss to indicate that the relationship was one of honor rather than servitude, for vassalage was reserved to those of high social status.

From a blending of the *precarium* or *beneficium*, which were originally temporary grants of land from a patron to his man and of the outright gifts made by barbarian chiefs to their faithful supporters, grew the institution of the 'fief,' a grant of land by a lord to his vassal, tenable during the lives of the two parties, and theoretically terminated by the death of either. Very shortly, however, the feudal system rigidified. The notion of reciprocity was retained – service was still demanded in return for the fief – but by the end of the ninth century fiefs had become, in fact if not in theory, heritable. Homage continued to be required at the death of either contracting party, but normally, at the death of a vassal, his son would perform homage and fealty and take over the fief. As the strength of the central authority failed, fiefdoms took on an increasingly independent character, and the functions of government were performed almost solely on a local basis.

The evolution of feudalism was not only a response to political and social disintegration, it also reflected increased specialization among the Franks. In their nomadic stage the German tribes had exacted military service from every man, but by the ninth century technological change had altered the terms of war. After Charles Martel's victory at Tours in 732 the mounted horseman became increasingly important. The introduction of the horseshoe and the stirrup, probably in the eighth or ninth centuries, improved the performance of the horse over rough terrain, allowed the warrior to wear heavier armor and, because of the support given by the stirrup, permitted the rider to wield a heavier sword. As the cost of military equipment increased and more specialized training became necessary, the warrior required both more revenue and more free time to pursue his vocation. Consequently, while the stronger and more fortunate became highly skilled profession-

als, the rest tended to lose their military function altogether. The weakest and least fortunate of those who had commended themselves to a lord tended to sink into servitude, and it was not long before many men had become serfs, tied to the land and their lords not simply for the term of their own lives, but binding their descendants as well.

Even though the so-called feudal system was born out of disintegration and chaos, it is perhaps still necessary to insert a word of caution at this point. It is much more difficult to give specific meaning to the term 'feudalism' than to 'vassalage,' 'homage' or 'fief.' Often ill-defined, the term has been much abused. It manifested itself historically in many variant forms and degrees. In some areas ties of vassalage remained less than comprehensive, and some members of society avoided them altogether. In others vassalage overlapped, and men, even great men, found that they owed service to more than one lord, or that they had conflicting claims to the same territories. At the bottom of the social scale, outside the feudal system strictly defined, the lower classes did not all become serfs: Some retained their independence on their own land, while others managed to find occupations that allowed them to remain unattached. There were geographical disparities as well: Norman feudalism was a much more complete and developed system than its Italian counterpart, where the existence of greater towns and a more durable commerical sector provided alternatives. Uniformity could hardly have been expected to arise from a makeshift response to multiple invasions and from political disorganization.

The feudal system may have preserved some small semblance of social order during a period of anarchy, but the true reconstruction of civil society first required an end to the invasions.

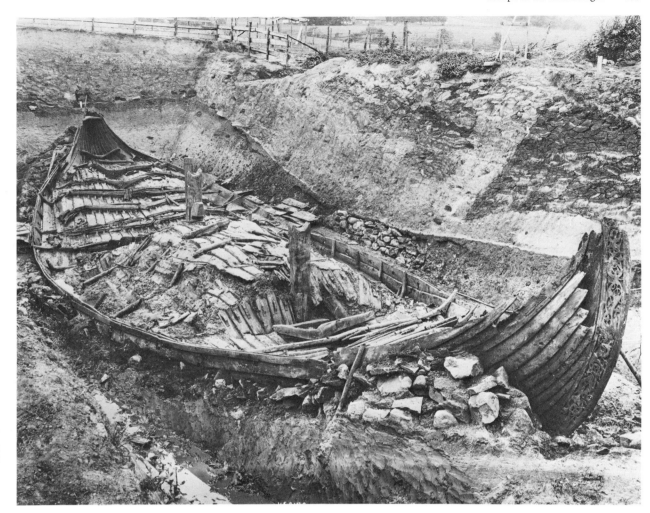

Far left: One of the earliest pictures of horsemen using stirrups; a band of Frankish warriors riding out to war. The stirrup allowed the mounted armored knight to dominate the battlefield – with far-reaching consequences for the organization of society.

Left: Frankish ruler Charles the Bald is presented with a Bible. The painstaking copying of religious and classical texts was the Carolingians' greatest contribution to Western civilization.

This page: A Viking longship unearthed at Oseberg, Norway, in 1904 (right), now restored in an Oslo museum (below). The Vikings performed extraordinary feats of navigation in these vessels, and terrorized Christian Europe.

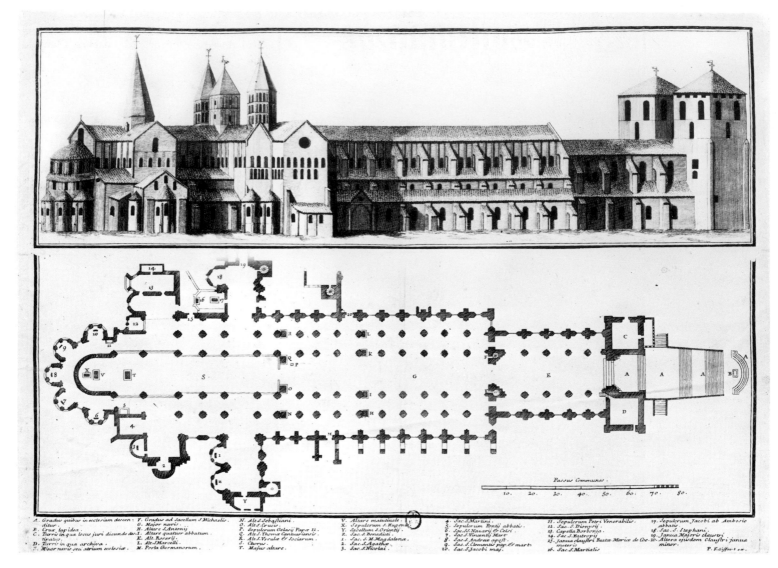

A. Gradus quibus in ecclesiam descen- | F. Gradus ad Sacellum S Michaelis. | N. Alt. S. Sebastiani. | V. Altare matutinale. | 4. Sac. S. Martini. | 11. Sepulcrum Petri Venerabilis. | 17. Sepulcrum Jacobi ab Ambosio
ditur. | G. Major navis. | O. Alt. S. Crucis. | X. Sepulcrum S. Hugonis. | 5. Sepulcrum Pontij abbati. | 12. Sac. S. Dionysij. | abbatis.
B. Crux lapidea. | H. Altare S. Antonij. | P. Sepulcrum Gelasij Papæ II. | Y. Sacellum S. Orientij. | 6. Sac. St Nauarij & Celsi. | 13. Capella Borbonia. | 18. Sac. S. Stephani.
C. Turris in qua locus juri dicundo des- | I. Altare quatuor abbatum. | Q. Alt. S. Thomæ Cantuariensi. | Z. Sac. S. Benedicti. | 7. Sac. S. Vincentij Mart. | 14. Sac S. Eutropij. | 19. Janua Majoris claustri.
tinatio. | K. Alt. Rosarij. | R. Alt. S. Thomæ & Sociarum. | 1. Sac. S. M. Magdalenæ. | 8. Sac. S. Andreæ apost. | 15. Janua clausttri Beatæ Mariæ de Gr- | 20. Altera ejusdem claustri janua
D. Turris in qua archiva. | L. Alt. S. Marcelli. | S. Chorus. | 2. Sac. S. Agathæ. | 9. Sac. S. Clementis pap. & martu. | materio. | minor.
E. Minor navis seu atrium ecclesiæ. | M. Porta Germanorum. | T. Majus altare. | 3. Sac. S. Nicolai. | 10. Sac. S. Jacobi maj. | 16. Sac. S. Martialis. | P. Giffart ex.

During the tenth century a series of remarkable kings appeared in Germany, the greatest of whom, Otto I (936-73), dominated the century and very nearly succeeded in converting feudalism into a viable system of government. Recognizing that the independence of the nobles was the greatest block to the reimposition of central authority, Otto I turned the German episcopate into an arm of secular government. Since bishops could not legally marry (although some did, and others kept concubines), they could not pass lands on to their heirs. To this extent the bishops could be more easily controlled than the secular nobles, whose independence grew over the generations. Under Otto the bishops received enormous grants of land, and consequently became his vassals, as well as men of the church. As vassals they owed military service on their fiefs, and they ultimately supplied as many as three-quarters of the soldiers required by the king in some years toward the end of the tenth century.

Once Otto I consolidated his control over Germany he could direct his attention to wider issues. The Hungarians had lessened their attacks somewhat after the first quarter of the century, yet the menace remained. But in 955, at the battle of Lechfeld, Otto defeated them so soundly that they were never again tempted to return. As so many tribes before them had done, they settled down, found land to farm, and in time became Christians and part of the European community.

The victory greatly enhanced Otto's stature, raising him above the petty lords and kings of his time. The pope acknowledged this by calling upon him for aid in handling the turbulent politics of Rome. In 961 Otto traveled to Italy, where he was acclaimed king. In 962, when the imperial title had lain unclaimed for almost 40 years, he was crowned emperor. The new empire was but a pale shadow of that ruled by Charlemagne, but even though it included only Germany and a portion of Italy, it was more lasting and in some ways more important. The renovation of the empire and, more important, of the imperial idea provided a focal point for the continuing struggle to define the relationship between church and state, as well as a political counterbalance to the strength of the papacy. The interplay between pope and emperor would affect all aspects of medieval life – not merely the theological, but the political, economic and social frameworks as well.

Authority under attack

While Germany had found strong kings during the tenth century, France suffered from a series of weak and incompetent monarchs who had allowed their power to erode to such an extent that they were scarcely distinguishable from other feudal lords. Indeed, they were often weaker and less well endowed with land, the basic source of strength in feudal society. None of these French kings could hope to muster the support and unity required to provide a real defense of the kingdom. Yet despite political weakness, certain factors came to favor the French monarchy simply through the passage of time. In the first place there was an obvious limit to the number of profitable raids that the Vikings could make against any country. Sooner or later the impoverished countryside would cease to yield enough booty to make it a worthy target for attack. Second, since the raids were regularly conducted over great distances, the raiders' ties to the homeland were always in danger of eroding. Some of the raiders would inevitably remain in the territories they had pillaged, either to strike further inland in search of richer victims or to build advanced bases for those who would follow. Both of these influences were working upon the Vikings by the beginning of the tenth century. As Normandy began to yield less booty, the Norsemen had formed semi-permanent camps there as bases for inland attacks.

As a result, Charles the Simple, the French king, succeeded in implementing an idea that, though not altogether new, provided a solution to the problem of the invasions. In 912, in a ceremony that left the king little dignity if the chronicle version is accurate, Charles acceded to political necessity and named Rollo, a Viking chief, duke of Normandy. Abject as the action was, it proved to be a successful maneuver. The fearsome northmen soon turned to agriculture and began to farm the rolling fertile plains of Normandy. More important from the French viewpoint, they acted as a buffer state, insulating central France from further depredations and consequently allowing the slow process of civil reconstruction to occur. When Hugh Capet was elected king of France in 987, initiating the illustrious Capetian line, his political position was as weak as that of his predecessors with regard to his own nobles – they had elected him, after all – but the region around Paris and the Ile-de-France was no longer threatened by invasion. The climate was right for the rebirth of civil authority and political order.

In southern France the Saracens had lost their capacity to mount what might properly be called

Left: The abbey of Cluny, founded in 910, became the center of a powerful reform movement in the church; its abbot was one of the most important men in Europe.

Right: The heavy wheeled plow, drawn by oxen, made a crucial contribution to the process of clearing forests and extending arable land.

Below: Although medieval agricultural techniques appear primitive to our eyes, for the most part they generated a sufficient surplus to feed the growing if still small urban population.

who was, in turn, under the direct tutelage of the abbot of Cluny. An effective chain of command had thus been introduced, enabling Cluny to resist the moral decay that set in so rapidly as a result of the isolation of branch houses in other orders. Further, the existence of a great number of houses, widely diffused throughout Europe, increased the political independence of the order of Cluny, since no petty feudatory could dominate all of the broadly dispersed houses. The example set by Cluny of moral conviction in a period of general turpitude throughout the church generated considerable respect and, subsequently, a movement for broad reform of the entire ecclesiastical structure. The latter came to fruition during the eleventh century. For the moment, however, let us note just one important political side-effect that stemmed indirectly from the great reputation Cluny had won during the tenth century.

In 972 the highly respected abbot of Cluny was carried off by the Saracen brigands who remained lodged in southern France. The scandalized count of Provence pursued the Arabs and recaptured the good abbot, but the count was not satisfied to stop there. Assembling more men as he marched, he attacked the Saracen stronghold at Freinet, near the modern town of St Tropez, and captured it. At a stroke Arab threat in France had been ended, and, more important, a new thrust had been initiated that would shortly drive the Arabs from the northern Mediterranean, clear the Italian islands and open the commercial and political horizons of Christendom for rapid expansion.

Progress in agriculture

With the cessation of the invasions and the gradual return of political security, prosperity came to western Europe. The farmer sowing his seed could expect with increasing confidence that he would live to harvest his crop. The merchant setting out on a trading venture could reasonably anticipate a safe return and the enjoyment of the fruits of his labors. Risk and danger still abounded, but the eleventh century witnessed the attainment of a critical balance between hazard and security that kept profits high without making the personal costs of seeking them so great as to discourage enterprise. Land was available and people were few. Conditions were right for demographic expansion, agrarian improvement and the extension of the arable terrain. The basic conditions of human life, at all levels could improve substantially for the first time in many centuries.

Roman-style agriculture was practiced along the borders of the Mediterranean, where the weather was dry, particularly during the summers, and the soil was light and sandy. Beyond the Alps and the Pyrenees, in the centers of the new Frankish kingdoms, agricultural conditions were different. Extending from southern England and northern France all the way to the Urals was the great European plain. Unlike the land of the south, the soil here was relatively flat and composed of heavy clay. The prevailing southwest wind blowing over the Atlantic made the northern summers moist and mitigated the severity of winter. Yet because the land was relatively level, the greater rainfall did not wash from the soil the rich minerals that had been deposited there by glacial run-off in the past. The cultivation of these lands required different tools and techniques from those used near the Mediterranean, but as the soil was rich and the climate capable of sustaining a more intensive exploitation, the rewards were greater.

Initially, northern agriculture employed a

an invasion, but they remained dangerous, preying on travelers and impeding commerce. Their final expulsion from France, and indeed from the Mediterranean itself, was as much a result of the reform of the church as of the reconstruction of civil society. In the dark days following the death of Pope Nicholas I, the church had suffered deep moral and spiritual degradation. In Germany, as we have seen, bishops had become secular officials and tools of the monarchy. Similarly, the monasteries had become royal, rather than ecclesiastical, foundations. Freed from all secular control save the king's, and only vaguely dependent on a distant and corrupt pope, many monasteries

allowed the rule of Benedict to fall into desuetude while the monks sought worldly pleasures.

In France a new monastery was founded in 910 by William, Duke of Aquitaine, who hoped to provide institutional safeguards that would protect the new order and preserve its moral and religious purpose. Cluny was freed from all secular authority, including the duke's, and was placed under the direct control of the pope. The central house was under the leadership of an abbot, but as expansion took place and new houses were formed, they remained under the supervision of the main house. Each new house and each older monastery that joined Cluny was ruled by a prior

heavy wheeled plow, drawn by oxen, to cut the hard soil and turn it so as to return minerals to the surface, break up clods and destroy weeds during fallow years. This plow seems to have been a barbarian innovation, introduced perhaps during the sixth century, although there are earlier references to what may have been a similar device. With the aid of this plow, new lands could be opened to cultivation and the slow process of clearing the woodlands and expanding the arable was carried on. At first, crop rotation followed the Mediterranean practice, allowing half the land to lie fallow each year, but after the eighth century there is evidence of a new three-field rotation, not yet widely diffused but available for use on recently cleared lands where inertia, past practice and long custom did not hinder its deployment. Under the three-field system the land was divided into thirds, and each field was farmed on a three-year cycle of spring wheat, winter wheat and fallow. Thus only a third of the land was in fallow under the new system, compared to one-half under the old. Further plowing time was reduced, since the fallow, which was plowed twice to reduce weeds, was smaller. With the new rotation the same amount of labor could yield 50 percent more food on 12 percent more land. In an economy where the yield/seed ratio was very low – four or five to one – any advance of this nature could have profound effects. Despite the great potential increase, however, institutional rigidities and custom rendered the diffusion of the new technology painfully slow on old estates.

Nevertheless the combination of land clearance, better technology and greater political security increased the food supply after the year 1000, and population began to rise. With demographic growth came greater efforts at land clearing, and a colonization movement developed within Europe. As early as the beginning of the eleventh century the count of Flanders was encouraging the reclamation of land from the sea. Louis VI (1108-37) and Louis VII (1137-80), Kings of France, took an active interest in founding new villages and supporting the extension of the acreage under cultivation. In the twelfth and thirteenth centuries the colonization movement overran territorial boundaries and marched eastward, sending Flemish, German and Dutch farmers across the Elbe and into Silesia, Poland and Austria. Economic growth had finally come to reverse the direction of the invasions.

Not only had the existence of an agricultural surplus allowed population to grow, it permitted changes in population density and distribution. Towns which had survived since Roman times primarily as a consequence of their utility as administrative centers for the church or, less frequently for the counts, began to expand. More men moved close to the old centers for security and for commercial opportunity. In time the clusters of new residents outside the old walls came to dominate the towns, and the suburbs eventually swallowed up the old centers. All over Europe towns grew and walls were extended to include new residents. In Italy the physical expansion of towns seems to have reached its peak late in the twelfth century; in northern Europe, always somewhat behind Italy during this period, the greatest rate of growth in new construction appears to have occurred in the first half of the thirteenth century. As urbanization progressed so did the number of local fairs and markets devoted to the provisionment of the towns. The regularity of economic exchange was forwarded by the creation of permanent markets. And with permanent and regular commercial opportunities, more economic specialization could develop.

Urban expansion

The curse of the late Roman and early medieval world had been the tendency toward economic autarchy on large estates. The growth of towns exorcized that curse. Local autarchy was now not only no longer necessary, it was demonstrably less efficient. As the twelfth and thirteenth centuries passed, towns increasingly provided markets for surplus agricultural goods and in turn sent manufactured goods and equipment back to the land. Productivity grew as artisans improved their skills, providing peasants with better tools containing more iron and less wood. The large estate, or manor, became more closely bound to the urban market, and in response to market forces the manorial economy gradually shifted its character and became more commercial. From the mid-thirteenth century on serfs began increasingly to be freed from the old labor services that were owed to the lord and to make money payments instead. The continuous rise in prices from 1100 to 1300 reduced the real cost of these fixed rents and thus improved the lot of those peasants who were more or less self-sufficient and capable of growing their own food. The existence of the towns also provided an escape route for the enterprising peasant since, if he could leave the land and remain in a town for a year and a day, he often became free of all servile obligations. The peasants' conditions of life could equally be enhanced if they joined the colonization movement and migrated to new lands. Efforts to attract settlers in new areas were often undertaken by lords and monasteries through the grant of land on more favorable terms than those prevalent on older estates: rents were cheaper and services lighter. Comparatively, the twelfth and thirteenth centuries were good times.

As population rose and towns grew, long distance commerce developed as well. In the north, particularly in the region around Flanders, some degree of political security had been attained by the end of the tenth century, and an active coastal trade emerged. The Flemish towns of Ypres, Ghent, Douai and Bruges became cloth manufacturing centers – Chalemagne had sent their cloth as a present to the Arab caliph, Harun al-Rashid – and their product was widely traded. Liège supplied copper and brass; Cologne specialized in linen, thread and some metals; England offered lead, tin and wool. The trade connections within the northern region expanded constantly. Lübeck was rebuilt in 1143 and supplied furs, honey, naval stores and grain to the populous Flemish towns. Salt from France and Spain was used to preserve the fish of the north, and Gascon wines graced the tables of German merchants. By the twelfth century the northern trading community stretched from Spain to Novgorod.

In the south, although Italy had suffered dreadfully during the Lombard invasions, the potential for commerce was never entirely destroyed. Throughout the period of disasters endured by the West, the eastern empire had retained its commercial, if not its political strength, and such cities as Bari and Amalfi had kept up active trade connections with Constantinople from the ninth century. In the northern Adriatic, protected by her location from barbarian invaders and by her ships from the wrath of the Saracens, Venice flourished, eventually to supplant Byzantium as the major commercial hub of the eastern Mediterranean.

The commercial sophistication of the southern merchants, long accustomed to diversifying their risks through partnerships and *commenda* contracts – a device for sending venture capital abroad with another merchant – and to trading on credit through bills of exchange, now came into contact with the less subtle commercial practice of the north. The southerners retained the commercial advantage, since northerners were slow to adopt the more advanced techniques, but fairs evolved into international clearing houses for credit instruments. Since the fair cycle was regular, debts contracted at one fair could be

could not be permitted to become independent of him. As landholders they controlled vast territories in Germany – so vast that if episcopal allegiance were directed solely to the pope, the emperor would have been virtually powerless. The imperial claim to the right of appointing bishops was thus based on economic and political necessity as well as on long-established custom.

From the viewpoint of the pope, the only way to maintain the spiritual integrity of the church was to render it independent of secular authority. The investiture or appointment of bishops would thus, of necessity, fall under the control of the pope. The power struggle could not be avoided. Between 1045 and 1049 there were six popes, all of whom were either appointed or deposed by Emperor Henry III. One pope, who was subsequently deposed, had so little regard for the papacy that he sold the office to his successor. By the time Henry III finally appointed Leo IX as pope in 1049, the Christian world was outraged at the debasement of the office, at the unprecedented dramatization of imperial control and at the scandal that simony – the sale of ecclesiastical office – had reached the papacy itself. Demands for the reform of the church became stronger and were boldly articulated by the monks of Cluny, at once powerful in their own right and distrustful of the bishops of Germany, who had made a practice of seizing land from the monasteries. Now, with Leo IX, a former Cluniac, as pope, the reform movement found a significant voice. A synod held at Rheims in 1049 reasserted the independence of papal elections from imperial control; simony was denounced; and French bishops, whose allegiance to the king had prevented them from attending the synod, were excommunicated. In 1059 the college of cardinals was created to maintain the independence of papal elections.

Much of this early reform was accomplished as a result of favorable circumstance; Henry III died in 1056 and was succeeded by Henry IV, a six-year-old boy who did not reach even formal majority until 1065. In 1073 Hildebrand, a former monk who had long been involved in the reform movement, became Pope Gregory VII. In the meantime Henry IV had experienced considerable difficulty in establishing his authority. The German bishops had used the minority to seize land from the imperial monasteries, while the Saxon nobles had been in revolt for several years prior to Gregory's accession. The towns of Italy were

Right: The medieval town was above all a center of trade, a meeting place, opening out the closed self-sufficient rural economy to a wider commercial world.

Below left and right: The city of Venice, depicted in the mid-fourteenth century (left) and the late fifteenth century (right). Venice achieved extraordinary wealth and power through its control of the trade in luxury goods from the East.

settled at another, and consequently multilateral clearing reduced the need for hard cash. Further the counts were careful to preserve the integrity of their coinage, and as a result many international contracts specified payment in the money of Provins, one of the fair towns. The existence of a stable currency outside of Italy aided the southerners in avoiding the church's ban on interest payments and usury; by making a loan in one currency and specifying repayment in another, interest could be concealed in the exchange rate.

Economic growth was well under way by the beginning of the eleventh century and so it continued unabated until the first decades of the fourteenth century. Upward social mobility was possible for any man who had the drive, courage and ambition to risk the struggle. Even a peasant might make his way to town and improve his social condition by entering the evolving world of manufacture and commerce. An oarsman on a Venetian galley might reasonably aspire to become a merchant in his own right. Economic growth, however, does not occur in a vacuum; it both affects and is affected by political developments. We have already noted that the end of the invasions contributed much to economic recovery, but let us now consider the interaction of this growth with other segments of society. Political recovery and the re-establishment of domestic security was at times aided and at other times hindered by the rise of commerce and towns. Regional variations make it necessary to consider the emergence of secular monarchy country by country.

Church-state rivalry

In the empire the political fortunes of both the state and the church were delicately counterbalanced. At the end of the fifth century Pope Gelasius I had enunciated the Doctrine of the Two

Swords, which declared that the world was ruled by two powers, the sacred authority of the pontiffs and the royal power. The authority of each came from on high and each had a defined area of action in which he was supreme. The moral authority was of greater weight, but only in spiritual matters. If each followed the rules of divine law, there should be no conflict. By the eleventh century the two swords doctrine was broadly accepted, but even though both pope and emperor concurred in the abstract, in practice conflict was virtually inevitable. The imperial custom of using the bishops as an arm of secular government placed the church firmly in the middle of the secular sphere. As feudal lords the bishops owed service to the emperor and thus

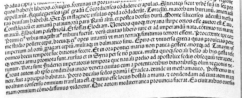

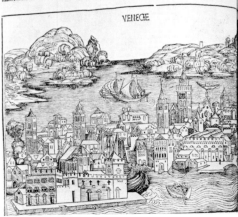

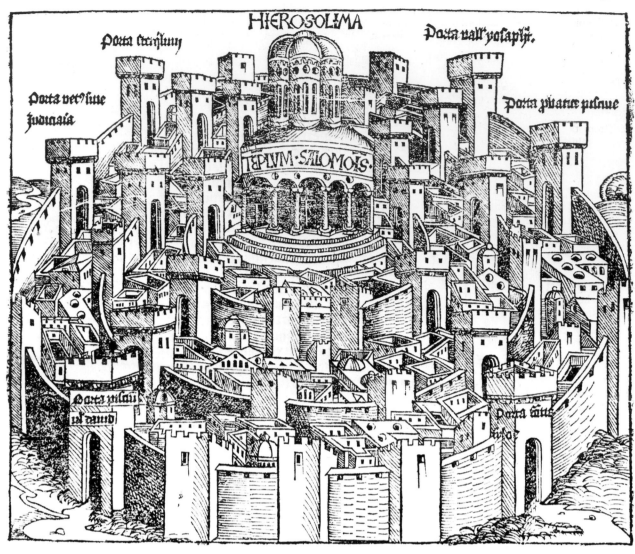

HIEROSOLIMA

Porta ccclium   Porta uall'pofaph.

Porta ver?fue juomaia

TEPLVM·SALOMOIS·

Porta pbacce picue

Porta milau ul danid

Porta vins ticia

Left: A woodcut view of medieval Jerusalem, a holy city to both Christians and Muslims, and thus an important symbolic objective in religious warfare. Taken by the crusader knights in 1099, it was lost again in 1187 to the Muslim army of Saladin.

Below right: Leo IX, pope from 1049 to 1056. A former Cluniac, he set in motion the reform of the church and helped restore the dignity and authority of the papacy.

broadening and deepening their economic power and increasingly sought to pursue their own interests both totally outside of feudal control and in ways that lay beyond feudal comprehension. The players were all on hand, and within a few years one of the most dramatic scenes of medieval history would unfold. The question of investiture would be directly confronted, if not actually settled, but the power balance within Europe would be forever altered.

The excommunication crisis

In 1075 Gregory determined that the time had come to end the lay investiture of bishops, and decreed the penalty of excommunication for the offense. Henry IV had just routed the rebellious Saxons at the battle of Langensalza and felt himself to be in firm control of his German territories. He too felt that the moment was propitious for the final assertion of his authority over the German bishops at Worms, and compelled them to renounce Pope Gregory for moral corruption as well as for having been elected irregularly. The latter charge was technically true, although the appropriate procedure had been followed shortly after Gregory became pope. Gregory countered Henry's move by excommunicating him, and the German magnates used this as a signal for general revolt. In October they met and agreed to depose the emperor unless he were pardoned by the pope within 12 months. Henry escaped and fled Germany, making his way with incredible difficulty to the castle of Canossa, where the pope was in residence. There Henry presented himself as a penitent, barefoot and in wretched clothing, and forced the pope to grant him the absolution that

had been declared open to all, no matter what the crime, by the church fathers of the third and fourth centuries.

As yet the outcome was unclear. The pope had literally brought the emperor to his knees, but the emperor had won back his kingdom and gained the diplomatic victory. The struggle was not yet over. The German nobles elected one of their number, Rudolf, king and sought papal support, which the pope gave by again excommunicating Henry. This time, however, the weight of moral authority was no longer so clearly with Gregory, whose concerns now appeared political rather than spiritual, and his allies faded away. Henry was able to defeat the anti-king in battle, and in turn, through the agency of the German bishops, to install Clement III as an anti-pope. Gregory VII died an exile. Three decades later, in 1111, the victory still seemed to belong to the empire. A compromise, whereby the church would relinquish its secular fiefs in return for the crown's abandonment of its claims to investiture, was accepted by Pope Pascal II but subsequently renounced by the church. Henry V imprisoned the unfortunate pope and so pressured him that he gave in on all points, but the struggle continued for another decade, until 1122, when compromise was again reached, this time at the Concordat of Worms. Investiture was divided into two parts. The emperor was to grant the fiefs and the secular authority, but the pope would invest the bishops with their title and their spiritual authority. The emperor thus retained some control over the election of bishops within Germany, but his power over the church and his control of ecclesiastical resources was greatly reduced. The papacy, on the

other hand, had made major gains in prestige and power. It was firmly in control of papal lands in Italy, was free of Roman politics and had broadly established its independence.

Further, the papacy had discovered that it had powerful allies. German efforts to rule Italy were resisted by the growing commercial towns, particularly Milan, which had taken the papal side early in the investiture conflict. When imperial control threatened to become a reality in Italy, the towns, out of self-interest, could usually be counted on to support the pope. Equally important, the attempt to govern by deepening and extending the feudal lines of allegiance combined with the spread of Christianity to increase the political impact of excommunication, since the oath of fealty was abrogated by the pronouncement of the anathema. Beyond this, in a world where the communications network was virtually nonexistent, the papal ban was perhaps the only clear signal for political action that could be successfully and quickly transmitted to large numbers of people. Through the pulpit, the church controlled the media.

Reform of the church led logically to the investiture conflict, but it led as well to an intensification of the efforts to spread the faith. Early sallies against the Saracens had been undertaken by the pope in the Italian peninsula, and the reformist abbot of Cluny had been, albeit somewhat against his will, the motivating force behind the expulsion of the Arabs from the south of France. The strengthening of the faith that came with reform had increased both the interest in, and the number of, pilgrimages to the holy places of the East, and as the numbers of the pilgrims rose their safety became a greater concern of the church. Requisite manpower to protect the pilgrims was at hand in the numerous feudatories who were continually at war with each other despite the efforts of the church to impose the 'Peace of God' and the 'Truce of God,' two only moderately successful attempts to preserve civil order.

The Crusades

In 1095 Pope Urban received from the eastern emperor a request for military aid against the infidel, and despite the fact that the eastern church had recently broken from the Roman church, the pope decided to send the aid. In a superb speech delivered at Clermont, in southern France, Urban pulled all the threads together, blending the ideas of pilgrimage, restoration of domestic peace, remission of sin, self-interest through conquest and the recovery of the Holy Land into one flashing conception: crusade. The response was immediate, and the enthusiasm was so great that restraint and organization became more crucial than further preaching, although the evangelical message was carried with great success throughout Germany by Peter the Hermit, an itinerant preacher who traveled from town to town.

Late in the year 1096, armies began to travel overland and by ship to the Byzantine Empire. Their passage was turbulent, since the propensity of the crusaders to take supplies from the countryside through which they passed without paying for them evoked hostility from those who might otherwise have been allies. When they arrived at Constantinople the crusaders received a mixed reception. The emperor feared both their numbers and their reputation as fighting men – the Normans had but recently taken southern Italy from the empire – but he agreed to help them on condition that they turn over all recaptured territories to him. Nicea was the first city taken, and it was duly given to the emperor, but Edessa fell shortly thereafter, and one of the crusaders kept it for his own kingdom. Dissension and greed grew among the other leaders, and the ever-present distrust of the emperor worsened after he failed to relieve the crusaders besieged at Antioch. Even so, the crusade was successful and Jerusalem was at last recovered in the summer of 1099. Having served the Lord and accomplished their original mission many of the crusaders departed, leaving a relatively small garrison of defenders to hold a vastly overextended and therefore vulnerable Kingdom of Jerusalem.

The crusading kingdoms were far removed from sources of supply in Europe and would surely have fallen sooner, or perhaps never have been succesfully conquered, without the naval power of the Italian city states. Both Genoa and Pisa aided in the conquests, and each was rewarded by the crusaders. Genoa gained several dozen houses and a bazaar in Antioch, while Pisa received an entire quarter of the port city of Jaffa, far to the south. Venice sensed the political wind a bit later, but she sent several hundred ships to the east in 1100 and in return obtained trading privileges in all the towns of the new kingdom of Jerusalem. As a result, trade became much more active and the Tyrhennian towns of Italy were drawn more deeply into trade with the eastern Mediterranean and the empire. The crusaders observed the luxuries of the East and coveted them. Indeed, close contact, both personal and commercial, soon developed between the soldiers of the Lord and the servants of Allah, and considerable cultural exchange inevitably took place. Crusaders assumed the more practical attire of the enemy, and finding that their own money was not acceptable, paid their enemies the ultimate compliment

of counterfeiting their currency, complete with an inscription in praise of the infidels' god. Much was learned by the crusaders, and eastern tastes were quickly assimilated. At the same time that they had opened a source of supply for eastern goods, the crusaders created a market for them as they returned home.

The Italian cities of Pisa, Genoa and Venice gained most materially from the crusades, but as we shall observe later, the subsequent cultural exchange was a major stimulus to the intellectual development of the West. Equally important, the increasing economic strength of the towns of northern Italy that resulted from the opening of new markets made it ever more difficult to govern the western empire. How could a commercial town, whose wealth depended on sea power, be absorbed into a feudal state where land alone was the ultimate source of power and wealth?

The crusading states, even when served by the growing Italian navies, were inherently indefensible. The crusaders' distrust of each other and the absence of any long-range planning or organization weakened them from within, while the infidels found stronger leaders and greater unity as the twelfth century progressed. In 1144 the kingdom of Edessa fell, and three years later the abortive Second Crusade was organized to attempt to shore up the defenses of the distant kingdom of Jerusalem. Conrad III, the German emperor, and Louis VII, the king of France, led armies to the Holy Land and sought to capture the city of Damascus. When they failed they returned to Europe, leaving the original defenders to their own devices. Although little was accomplished in the East, the Second Crusade had greater political significance in the West. In the first place, it was led by kings rather than great nobles, a fact that at once reflected and promoted the development of royal power. Second, abject failure cooled the ardor of the crusaders for a time and allowed the monarchs to turn their attention to domestic problems. Finally, the personal lives of the participants in the crusade affected the balance of power between France and England for centuries to come. But in order to comprehend these deeper ramifications, it is necessary to return to the eleventh century and to trace the evolution of the English and French monarchies.

The monarchy in England

During the tenth century England was perhaps the most politically sophisticated country in Europe. King Alfred had contained the Danish invaders, reconquered most of the kingdom and instituted a viable system of central control through the sheriffs, who supervised the shires, collected taxes and represented royal justice throughout the land. Despite these achievements the system still depended on the presence of a strong king. In the eleventh century such a figure was lacking, and the governmental structure began to disintegrate. Canute, a Dane, was acknowledged king in 1016 and the legitimate English heirs were driven to exile in Normandy. When Edward the Confessor was restored after the death of Canute in 1035, the line was resumed, but Edward died without children. Edward had initially bestowed the succession upon William, Duke of Normandy, but subsequently he promised it to Harold, scion of one of the great families of England, who was accepted as king. William raised an army in Normandy but before he could land, Harald Hardrada, King of Norway, invaded England and claimed the throne as heir of Canute. Harold of England overwhelmed Harald of Norway, who died in the battle of Stamford Bridge, but in the meantime William had been able to land, and in October 1066 he defeated and killed the English king at the battle of Hastings. On Christmas Day 1066 William the Conqueror was consecrated king of England.

William ruled England both by right of conquest and by legitimate succession as Edward's first chosen heir. Further, he had been consecrated by the church and accepted by the England council or *witan*. As a result he was able to capitalize on his two-fold source of authority to preserve the best of the Anglo-Saxon institutions, while at the same time supplementing them with forms borrowed from Norman feudalism. The ancient division of the country into shires was maintained, and the sheriffs remained to uphold the authority of the crown throughout the land. The land itself was treated as forfeit through rebellion and was redistributed to the Norman barons in fiefs. Normally these were rather small ones, so that great lords often held many fiefs but no central power base. Strict obedience and service

S· LEO IX· PONTIFEX CLIV·
ANNO DOMINI MXLIX.

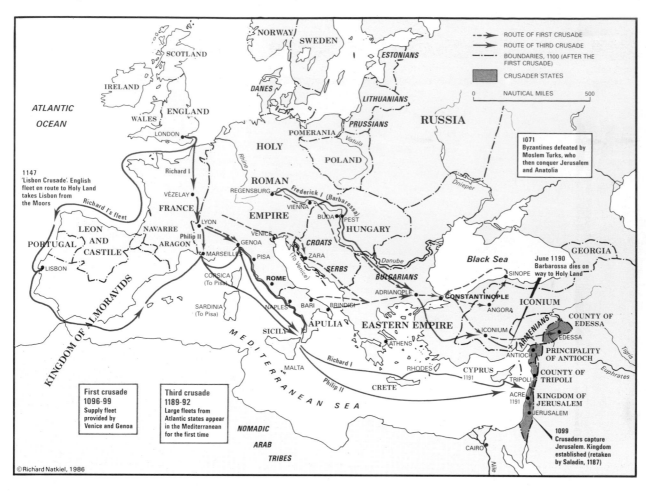

ROUTE OF FIRST CRUSADE
ROUTE OF THIRD CRUSADE
BOUNDARIES, 1100 (AFTER THE FIRST CRUSADE)
CRUSADER STATES

0   NAUTICAL MILES   500

1071 Byzantines defeated by Moslem Turks, who then conquer Jerusalem and Anatolia

1147 'Lisbon Crusade'. English fleet en route to Holy Land takes Lisbon from the Moors

June 1190 Barbarossa dies on way to Holy Land

First crusade 1096-99 Supply fleet provided by Venice and Genoa

Third crusade 1189-92 Large fleets from Atlantic states appear in the Mediterranean for the first time

1099 Crusaders capture Jerusalem. Kingdom established (retaken by Saladin, 1187)

©Richard Natkiel, 1986

Left: The routes followed by the two most important crusades. Although led by Richard the Lionheart, Philip Augustus of France and Frederick Barbarossa, the Third Crusade failed to win back Jerusalem, originally seized by the knights of the First Crusade 90 years earlier.

Below: Crusaders encounter an alien civilization.

Right: Henry II of England clashes with ecclesiastical authority in the person of the Archbishop of Canterbury, Thomas à Becket. The quarrel over clerical privilege led eventually to the assassination of the Archbishop.

Below right: Frederick Barbarossa's empire included northern Italy, but the Italians soon rose up against imperial authority.

was required from the royal vassals, and a considerable amount of central control was achieved. All the powerful men of England now owed direct allegiance to the king; thus feudalism progressed rapidly from the anarchy that it had been in France and Germany to a highly successful means of government. It still, however, depended greatly on the personality of the monarch, a system of government fraught with danger.

The Norman sucession

When William died in 1807 he left three sons. The first, Robert, was duke of Normandy by primogeniture, but the second son, William Rufus, William's favorite, became king of England, while the third received only a cash settlement, although he too was later to become king of England. Normandy had been separated from England upon the death of the Conqueror and it remained so until 1106 when, 40 years to the day after William I landed in England, his son, Henry I (1100-35), conquered Normandy. The English monarchy now held a substantial portion of France, and even though the English king was technically still a vassal in that land, the English presence was bound to conflict with the political aims of the Capetian monarchy. At the time, however, possession of Normandy may have given the English more trouble than profit. Endless revolts in Normandy required the king's attention, and when he gave it the result was often rebellion at home. Despite this cycle of unrest Henry I made significant gains in the establishment of a centralized monarchy. The court was expanded, and the exchequer, or treasury, was professionalized, assuring the king greater financial power and a body of loyal officials independent of the great barons. A similar tendency toward centralized power was apparent in the development of royal justice and in the substitution of lesser lords for the greater and more dangerous ones who had originally served as sheriffs.

Yet Henry I failed to establish central authority fully, and the terrible dispute over the succession at his death in 1135 destroyed much of what he had achieved. Under Stephen, England endured a period of anarchy as every feudal lord again pressed his claims to independence. At the accession of Henry II in 1154 much of the work remained to be redone, but the dual precedents of good rule under Henry I and of its collapse under Stephen won many allies for the cause of strong monarchy.

Consolidation in France

In France the monarchy faced a considerably more difficult task, since feudal disintegration was untempered by the unifying effects of a general conquest. The kings of France derived such strength as they had from the relatively small district around Paris and the Isle de France. To their credit they usually recognized this fact. Even though they were surrounded by great feudatories, often more powerful then they, the French kings possessed certain advantages which

they used well. First, the Capetian claim to the throne was widely recognized as legitimate, and everything possible was done to enhance this legitimacy. Direct descent from Charlemagne through the female line was asserted, as was the sacerdotal character of kingship itself. Miraculous legends concerning the heavenly replenishment of the holy oil used for royal anointment traced the line back to the conversion of Clovis, and the supernatural power of French kings that supposedly enabled them to cure scrofula by touch was fully exploited. Also, the Capetians were fortunate both in their longevity and in the succession. Between 987 and 1328 the length of the average reign was 29 years, and there was always a male heir. Succession became hereditary as each monarch associated his son with him on the throne prior to his death, a practice maintained for the first 200 years of Capetian rule.

Cautiously and slowly the Capetians worked to secure control of their own domain before attempting to challenge the great feudatories. Economic growth in the towns was tolerated, if

not encouraged, while new villages were founded by Louis VI (1108-37) and Louis VII (1137-80). The new economic forces strengthened the king. While only slight territorial gain or loss was accomplished or suffered during the first 200 years of the monarchy there is little doubt that by 1180 the kings of France had firm command over their own domain lands and that they had established the nucleus of an administration that would be able to undertake greater and more challenging projects. The presence of Louis VII on the Second Crusade is perhaps a measure of this ability, since the kingdom was well governed in his absence.

Louis had married Eleanor of Aquitaine in 1137, when she was a beautiful and enticing girl of 16 and he a young prince. Louis loved Eleanor deeply, indeed the clergy thought overmuch, and initially the marriage appeared to be a brilliant success, both romantically and politically. Eleanor was one of the great heiresses of France, and if a male child had been born the duchy of Aquitaine, which represented approximately one-quarter of modern France, would have been added to the royal domain. Unfortunately time tempered the passions of Eleanor, and tempted perhaps by the romantic tales prevalent in the brilliant traditions of southern France, she sought the delights of love beyond her marriage. During the Second Crusade she shamed Louis at Antioch in a scandal involving her uncle, and though Louis was persuaded by the pope and Suger, the abbot of St Denis not to renounce her, he remained suspicious and angry. Suger, who had acted as regent while Louis was on crusade and had brought peace and order to the kingdom in that period, died in 1151. By then Eleanor had entered into a flirtation with Henry of Anjou, whose father had forcefully seized the duchy of Normandy, and this was more than Louis would tolerate in the absence of Suger's counsel: he divorced Eleanor on grounds of consanguinity. Within two months Eleanor married Henry of Anjou, who became king of England in 1154.

Historians have long criticized Louis VII for his impetuous behavior and for allowing so vast a portion of France to fall from his grasp, and beyond doubt, it is true that he created a major problem fraught with danger for his successors. On the other hand, after 15 years of marriage, Eleanor had produced only two daughters, and the succession remained in doubt. The political consequences of the divorce must also include the fact that Louis' third wife, Adela of Champagne, gave birth in 1165 to one of the great kings of France, Philip Augustus (1180-1223).

The Third Crusade

The Second Crusade had failed in its mission to the Holy Land, but England had indirectly benefited by becoming the greatest feudatory in France. In 1187 Jerusalem was captured by Salah al-Din, the legendary leader of the Saracens, and a Third Crusade was organized. This time it was led by the three most powerful rulers of the west, Frederick Barbarossa of Germany, Richard I of England and Philip Augustus of France, and consequently it may serve as a touchstone for events in western Europe, in addition to measuring western involvement in the near east. Richard (1189-99) was absent from England during most of his 10-year reign, yet despite high taxes to support the crusade, the country was relatively peaceful and the government stable. Richard's father, Henry II, had done his work well: royal justice had been greatly extended, and both barons and bishops had suffered substantial reductions in the jurisdiction of their courts. Royal justice and its concomitants, royal power and centralized authority, had grown proportionately, so that even in the absence of the ruler the government continued to function.

Frederick Barbarossa (1152-90), the German emperor, began his reign auspiciously but shortly encountered serious difficulties when he endeavored to extend and intensify his authority in Germany. Initially he had followed a policy similar to that of the Capetians, unifying his German domains and building up a firm system of central control, but the process was slow, and inevitably,

as he rationalized his own rights through exchange with neighboring feudatories, he also made their control more certain and increased their strength. In order perhaps to gain wealth for his struggle in Germany, or possibly because he recognized them as a threat to strong imperial rule in Italy, Frederick sought to suppress the Italian city-states. Under pressure the towns of northern Italy, led by Milan, formed a league to resist the emperor, but they were crushed and Milan was leveled in 1162.

In the meantime, however, a schism had developed in the church with the simultaneous election of two popes, Alexander III, who had the support of the majority of the cardinals and of public opinion generally, and Victor, who was endorsed by the emperor. The assertion of imperial authority in Italy in general, and over the papacy in particular, drove the towns of Lombardy and the pope into coalition. Formed in 1167 the Lombard League of northern towns was supported by Pope Alexander. Milan was rebuilt and quickly reassumed its dominant position among the towns. Nine years later, in 1176, the league was able to crush Frederick's forces and to end his attempt to impose centralized feudalism upon Italy. New and more successful efforts would be made by Frederick's successor, Henry VI, but fortunately for the papacy, Henry was short-lived, dying in 1197 at the age of 32. Although Frederick failed in Italy he enjoyed some success in Germany, and once the Italian dream was forsaken Germany was secure enough to permit the emperor to join the Third Crusade. There he died in 1190.

Richard's spiritual commitment to the crusade was sincere, but he alienated virtually every other ruler in Christendom through his arrogantly high-handed behavior and his ill-concealed contempt for his fellow rulers and allies. Philip Augustus' zeal was markedly less manifest, and he quickly seized the opportunity offered him by a quarrel

THE HOLY ROMAN EMPIRE AT THE ACCESSION OF FREDERICK BARBAROSSA, 1152

© Richard Natkiel, 1988

bie que a   Trop grande repletion

with Richard to abandon the crusade in order to return to France and to pursue his European political interests. The capture of Acre, where incidentally the Teutonic Order of Knights was founded, allowed the French king to depart without loss of face. Alone, Richard was able only to negotiate a truce with Saladin; pilgrims were permitted to visit Jerusalem, but the earlier kingdom was not restored.

Philip benefited from Richard's absence – indeed when the returning Richard was held for ransom by Emperor Henry VI, Philip offered large sums to extend the period of captivity – as well as from the divided succession after Richard's death in 1199, which enabled Philip to reduce the great English fiefs in France. In 1204 Normandy was recovered as a result of the disputed claims of Richard's brother, John, and his nephew, Arthur. Fortune smiled on Philip. By marriage he was able to claim the Vermandois, the region around Amiens, in 1186, and in 1214 French suzerainty was established over Flanders by conquest. Then, when Pope Innocent III declared Raymond VI, Count of Toulouse, a heretic and preached a crusade against him, under the banner of the Albigensian crusade Philip and his son Louis VIII were able to extend royal government over the southwest of France. Slowly and legally, the strength of the French crown grew in that area until finally, in 1270, failure in the succession gave Toulouse to the king of France.

A stable Europe

By about the year 1200 the basic territorial divisions of Europe were established in the form that they were to retain for several centuries. Small additions and subtractions would be made, the Arabs would be driven from Spain and in time the Iberian Peninsula would be united under one rule. New states would be formed in northern Italy as the empire receded, and everywhere the internal problems of reducing the power of the great lords would continue to plague western rulers, but by 1200 a political balance had been attained and the future map of Europe was more or less settled.

Expansionist political pretensions were not abandoned by western rulers, but countervailing forces held them in check. Though Richard I spent much of his life warring against Philip Augustus in France, victory eluded him and ultimately English power in France waned. Louis VIII, Philip's son, might invade England with the con-

sent of the English barons in 1216, yet he could not conquer and was fortunate to be able to withdraw safely the following year. Emperor Henry VI (1190-97), despite his intelligence, power and dominant personality, could not validate his claims to universal rule in the face of universal opposition from other kings and the Pope. Such limited success as he had was frustrated and eroded by his early death and the subsequent disputed succession and a minority rule. Even the strength of the Papacy, though at its zenith in this period, depended on the manipulation of political forces within Europe, and while the close balance of power gave the pope considerable political leverage, it also meant that subtle and mercurial realignments could totally recast the balance. Even the powerful Innocent III (1179-81) was unable to force the English to accept papal revocation of Magna Carta.

Equal matching of political forces within Europe created an era of relative stability, though not one free from internal tension, that proved favorable for the rapid development and fruition of medieval culture. Disparate cultural influences coalesced, cross-pollinated and germinated into new and magnificent hybrids. Newly recovered learning from antiquity supplemented and sometimes challenged medieval custom and traditional wisdom, but in any event memories of the ancient world stimulated historical scholarship, synthesis and the creative process – all this long before the 'Renaissance.'

The crusades had led western scholars to the resources of Syria and Constantinople, while at the other end of the Mediterranean the slow reconquest of Spain, continuing from the eleventh to the fifteenth century, made available both Arab science and mathematics and Arabic and Hebrew translations of the ancients. Slowly at first, and then with increasing intensity during the late twelfth and early thirteenth centuries, the work of Aristotle, but dimly known to the early Middle Ages through the writings of the late Roman philosopher Boethius, was recovered and it served to stimulate an intellectual revolution broadly diffused throughout all fields of human endeavor.

The philosophy of Thomas Aquinas

The recovery of Aristotle's *Politics* in the mid-thirteenth century virtually forced the emergence of a more highly refined political theory. For Aristotle the state was worthy in itself and was not simply the necessary consequence of the fallen state of man, the conception of earlier medieval and clerical authors. In addition, natural law enjoyed a prime role in his philosophy, as did the conception of an ordered hierarchy whereby each being had its place in the political order, the higher governing the lower. Working with elements borrowed from Aristotle, but supplementing them with the metaphysics of Platonism and Christianity, Thomas Aquinas (*d* 1274) created the most original and powerful philosophical system

Above left: A medieval medical practitioner bleeding a patient. European medicine remained a primitive business and had much to learn from the Arabs and the Greeks.

Below left: The Magna Carta, extorted from King John of England by a baronial revolt, set legal limits to the power of the monarch over his subjects.

Right: The great philospher of the Christian Middle Ages, Thomas Aquinas, pictured at the center of the diverse influences that he reconciled in his work – the Biblical authorities, the Greek thinkers Plato and Aristotle, and the twelfth-century Islamic philosopher Ibn Rushd (Averroes).

of the Middle Ages. Where Aristotle's ordered natural world rose to a pinnacle but vaguely defined, Aquinas unhesitatingly placed on it the Christian God. This not only converted a pagan philosophy into a Christian one, but it ended the medieval dichotomy between faith and reason as well. Natural law, built into the Aristotelian system, implied the value of human reason as a guide to morality, ethics and the highest purposes of man. The Thomistic system retained this notion, but modified it: human reason could lead to knowledge of God, but for fuller knowledge, faith and revelation must supplement human reason.

The Thomistic system must be seen in the context of the earlier recovery of Roman law if its full significance is to be comprehended. From the beginning of the twelfth century, perhaps first at the law school of Bologna, the study of Roman law had been revived, and legal studies based on the *Corpus Juris* became a legitimate competitor to theology in the intellectual endeavors of the high Middle Ages. The *Corpus Juris*, however, reflected the legislation of an absolutist and pagan government where the will of the prince was almost equivalent to law. This bias, and the obvious personal advantage that could be gained from it, was not lost upon the rulers of the twelfth century who were, much like their modern counterparts, ever willing to support doctrines that served to increase their power. Consequently, from the start of its rediscovery, Roman law enjoyed strong political support and concerted governmental efforts to extend the area of its jurisdiction. Frederick Barbarossa, for example, found it a useful device for legitimizing his assertion of imperial authority over the rapidly developing commercial towns of northern Italy. That he failed was due

not to the superior legal position of the towns, but rather to their political and economic strength. Most legal judgments based on Roman law favored his position.

The extension of Roman law clearly threatened the balance between church and state set forth by Gelasius; it tended as well to remove from the state any kind of moral constraint. To be sure, one could argue that the prince was expected to rule by law and that he derived his power from the people. Such arguments were indeed made, but they were of a weak order. Constraints based upon the will of the people, in the absence of any institutional vehicle for the expression of that will, had little real force, while the explicit sanction to rule within the law was surely a light burden to a prince whose will was virtually equivalent to that law.

Seen in this context the accomplishment of Aquinas was no small achievement. The revival of Roman law created a vital interest in law and legal studies, but it neither controlled the state nor defined its purpose. Aquinas postulated a hierarchy of laws: eternal law, divine law, natural law and human law. The first closely approximated the will or wisdom of God, while the second was essentially divine revelation, known to man only through faith. Natural law was common to all men and could be discovered through reason, since it had been implanted in the human mind by divine will at the time of creation and thus, though a lower order of law, corresponded to the higher forms: it was less complete, but it could not contradict divine or eternal law. The fourth, human law, was specifically that law made by civil governments. It must accord with natural law, upon which it is based, and served to adjust the

prescriptions of that law to varying human circumstances. Thus, for example, while all property ultimately belonged to God without provision for private holdings under natural law, in human law, division of property was made formal for the sake of convenience. to avoid squabbling and to provide better care of goods and property. Such an arrangement did not conflict with natural law but rather supplemented it in the real world. In the final analysis, possession belonged to God, and consequently the resources of the earth must be used for the benefit of all men.

Within the Thomistic system the hierarchy of laws provided a direct and precise succession of links, stretching from the will of God to the least significant human law. The state was thus contained within a much larger and moral whole. Its purpose was defined as the public good, and not simply the will or pleasure of the ruler. While no notion of democracy or popular sovereignty was present, the role of the individual was protected. Since God had made man the supreme earthly being by endowing him with a soul, there were implicit limits to the power of the state over the individual. Civil society was organized to aid that individual in his aspirations towards self-perfection. Thus the state had a moral purpose. In addition, the very nature of the social hierarchy of men tended to insulate and preserve the individual. Though the ordinary man was not expected to rise within the social hierarchy he was, by the same token, not expected to fall. The implicit stability of the system generated a kind of philosophical bias toward insuring continuity of status for every member of society.

Strengthening the rule of law

Political philosophy as conceived by saints is rarely congruent with political reality, and consequently Aquinas failed to make as great an impact on his time as his subsequent reputation might suggest. Yet the very balance of political forces during the thirteenth century did create an ethos in which Thomism could be more than mere idealism. Louis IX (1226-70), the French king who died on crusade and later, in 1297, attained canonization, was in fact a ruler with a deep and sincere belief in the values of Christianity. Although St Louis' crusading zeal accomplished little, and indeed for a time threatened to cause him to neglect his duties of France, his belief in fair play and rule by law led him to assert his rights without alienating his people. Despite his efforts to unseat Blanche of Castile, Louis' regent during his minority, and his continuous conflict with the English throughout the reign, Louis' policies contributed markedly to the development of the institutions of royal government and to stabilization and strengthening of central authority. The *curia regis* was subdivided into specialized administrative branches, while the systematic control of local government through *baillis* and *seneschals*, royal territorial governors developed by Philip Augustus, was tightened and extended. In fact as in theory, the functions of church and state were more carefully distinguished, royal and baronial rights were separated and respected, and while the power of royal government was greatly enhanced, it was contained within the law and did not yield to excess.

In England, too, where royal government and centralized institutions were temporally in advance of the French, and where itinerant justices had preceded their continental counterparts, the *baillis*, by a century, rule by law was established and powers carefully counterbalanced. The disastrous foreign policy pursued by John (1199-1215) resulted in increasingly onerous taxa-

tion that served only to support equally spectacular defeat. From the initial loss of Normandy in 1204 to the rout and the battle of Bouvines in 1214, John directed all England's resources to the reconquest of French territories.

His ultimate failure and stubborn refusal to acknowledge defeat led to baronial revolt. Yet instead of repeating the abortive attempt at regicide that occurred a few years before, in the wars against Stephen, the English barons in effect collected complaints and evidence of royal abuses of power and sought to remedy them by forcing the king to forswear such excesses for all time. The resulting document, Magna Carta, preserved the power of the king, but constrained him to rule within law. The sixty-first clause of Magna Carta assigns the role of enforcing the whole to 'five and twenty' barons and specifically grants them the right to conduct civil war against the king in the event of his failure to comply with the sanctions of Magna Carta. So long as the king ruled within the law – and even if he had strayed from the true path, as soon as he mended his ways – the king had the right to rule with full power and to exercise all royal prerogatives. Individual, ecclesiastical, urban and property rights were protected, but the authority of the king was preserved. Once again, government for the public good within the rule of law, as envisioned by Aquinas, was demonstrably not remote from the thirteenth-century reality of England.

The sense of ordered hierarchy, of progression from the greatest to the smallest, of the 'unity of truth' visible in legal thought and jurisprudence, appears to be as close to an accepted premise in the thirteenth century as any such philosophical system can be within a given social fabric. One scholar has even asserted the existence of a direct parallel between the scholastic *summa*, the form of written discourse that reached perfection in the hands of Thomas Aquinas, and high Gothic architecture of the period. The *summa* form,

Above left: The fan-vaulted ceiling of the Henry VII Chapel in Westminster Abbey, a masterpiece of late Gothic.

Above: Durham Cathedral, a Romanesque building with added Gothic features.

Left: Masons building a city wall – they were far more than inspired artisans, rather skilled and highly respected professionals.

Right: An alchemist applies his secret formulae in the search for the 'philosopher's stone' – one of the major intellectual pursuits of the Middle Ages.

proceeding hierarchically from the major statement to its parts and the further subdivisions thereof, sought to be comprehensive, to include all, but not to blur the distinction among parts. Within this stately format it was possible, so the argument runs, to predict or experience the whole from close inspection of the separate articles.

The new gothic architecture

It is not uncommon for the architecture of a period simultaneously to reflect and derive from its values, and it is certain that high Gothic and high scholasticism flourished together in the affluent years of the thirteenth century. Resources for building were increasingly available as towns grew and more land was turned to cultivation under improved technology. The moment was right for the glory of the Lord in his heavens to find expression in the stone of the earth. A common iconographical metaphor for the creation, after all, shows God with the tools of the masterbuilder. The basic techniques and innovations – the rib-vault and the pointed arch – were long known and had probably been borrowed from the East by the crusaders. Their extensive use in combination, however, so altered the nature of ecclesiastical construction that a marked stylistic break occurred as the new 'Gothic' replaced the earlier 'Romanesque.' St Denis, the first truly Gothic building, was constructed prior to 1140 under the careful supervision of the Abbot Suger, Louis VII's brilliant adviser who, while he lived, was able to save Eleanor, and thus Aquitaine, for France. Although earlier examples of such features as the Gothic rib-vault appear in Durham Cathedral, begun 30 years before St Denis, the overall quality of that great English church remained Romanesque.

Once the elements of the Gothic style were introduced into Europe their development and articulation proceeded swiftly. Everywhere, as new buildings were commissioned, the heavy stone facades of Romanesque yielded to the increasingly airy tracery of the new mode. Weightless strength, gained from the flying buttress and the ribbed groin-vault, enabled architects to remove or cut away stone formerly required for external support. Stone became plastic, ethereal and marvelously fluid as it was carved into the intricate designs incorporated in rose windows and the delicate tracery that replaced walls. Where before there had been inanimate stone, glass was substituted, and the interiors of cathedrals were suffused with the rich, warm light that passed through the deep reds and blues of windows stained in patterns reflecting both sacred and secular themes. Within the churches, spaces grew ever larger and heights increased. At once imitating and competing, architects strove to enhance the delicacy of the interior vaulting almost in defiance of gravity, until finally, in the early-sixteenth-century chapel at Westminster Abbey in England, the pendant ceiling has the quality more of a lacelike veil than of a stone structure. It was as if the Lord had granted his earthly architects exemption from physical laws.

Intellectual development

The architects and masons who created the vast Gothic monuments of the Middle Ages were professionals with considerable social status, and not as was once thought merely inspired artisans acting under divine guidance. A few sketchbooks and plans have survived, and they reveal both the careful planning and minute attention to detail obviously necessary to carry through so extended and grand a construction project as a cathedral. The internal regulations of late medieval masons'

guilds further document the skilled and professional character of the craft by stressing the importance of Euclidean geometry. Indeed, without a working knowledge of practical geometry it is inconceivable that the great churches could have been brought to completion.

The recovery of Euclid was part of the scientific and intellectual resurgence that occurred in the beginning of the twelfth century and which, not surprisingly, was simultaneous with the inception of Gothic architecture. Mathematics developed swiftly as a result of new translation from the Arabic; this was apparently the route by which Euclid was recovered. Equally important were Adelard of Bath's translation of al-Khwarizmi's trigonometrical tables, a subsequent version of his *Algebra* that appeared in 1145 and the introduction, through the same source, both of the concept of zero and the arabic numerals that replaced the far less readily manipulated Roman system. This combined cultural infusion raised western mathematics to a level not surpassed until seventeenth-century thinkers developed the calculus.

Three centers of intellectual contact between East and West played a major role in dispersing both ancient and Arabic culture. In Constantinople, Sicily and Spain translators labored to recover long-neglected learning. A flood of Arabic

literature concerned both with astrology and astronomy was loosed upon Europe through the tireless efforts of the translators. Under pressure of the need to calculate precisely the dates of Christian movable feasts such as Easter, this material was quickly absorbed into western culture. Even so great a figure of modern astronomy as Copernicus saw fit to quote the work of two tenth-century Arab astronomers, of whom one, al-Zarqali, through his estimate of the length of the Mediterranean in degrees, had apparently arrived at a virtually correct measure of the circumference of the earth. Alchemy and its modern descendant, chemistry, also advanced sharply and many of our present English chemical terms reflect their Arabic etymologies. One may cite, for example, alcohol, alkali and alchemy.

The cosmopolitan kingdom of Sicily became a center for the study of medicine. There Greek learning blended with Arab practice to produce the highest state of the art in the West. At Salerno the earliest medical school in Europe first assimilated the work of the ancient writers, Hippocrates and Galen, and then, based on eastern medical experience and direct observation, began to create a medical literature that was new. Arabic medicine was generally more simple, more commonsensical and certainly less superstitious than current western practice. The Arab doctors depended

heavily on such precautionary measures as diet and hygiene, although theories of infectious contagion were articulated in the fourteenth century in the Spanish school at Granada. Some major contributions and suggestions for the future were also derived from Arab surgeons. One, al-Zahrawi, in the beginning of the eleventh century, was recommending the cauterization of wounds and, perhaps more significantly, stressing the need for vivisection and dissection. Such empirical procedures would ultimately set medicine on its modern scientific path, but the time was not yet right for major breakthroughs. Scholasticism valued logic more than empiricism.

The reign of Frederick II

In the kingdom of Sicily, Frederick II (1218-50) presided over a court where real learning and sophisticated research were actively pursued. That ruler, however, was in almost every way an exception to his times. When his father, the remarkable Henry VI, died in 1197, Frederick was only three; the death of his mother the following year made him king of the south Italian kingdom of Sicily. His early years were extremely troubled, since there was no formal regency to protect him from becoming a pawn in the convoluted politics of the melting-pot of ideas, men and races that Sicily was in the early thirteenth century. As a result Frederick became suspicious, distrustful, sceptical and deceitful, characteristics that would serve him well in his political career but would deprive him of the opportunity to build his kingdom on the strength of faithful advisers. From the beginning it was clear that he would rule alone, placing confidence only in himself, and as absolutely as possible.

In Germany, where perhaps because of his extreme youth Frederick had been passed over for the imperial succession, one faction of nobles elected Philip of Swabia to the emperorship, while another faction supported Otto of Brunswick. The pope, hoping to extract the greatest possible security for the papal estates in Italy, refused to recognize either pretender until 1201, when he declared for the weaker Otto. Neither contender was capable of enforcing his claim, and consequently a period of turbulent civil war ensued.

When Otto, apparently beaten and defeated, fled in 1207, Philip briefly wore the imperial robes, but he was murdered the following year and Otto returned triumphantly to be crowned by the pope in 1209. Innocent III soon had cause to regret his actions, for the emperor did not hesitate to resume his assault on papal independence in northern Italy. His excommunication followed in 1210 and dissident German nobles, casting about for a legitimate counterweight to support their rebellion, elected Frederick II to the imperial throne with the support of the pope. Further conflict was inevitable, but fortunately for Frederick, Otto supported John of England at the battle of Bouvines in 1214 and consequently lost both his army and his effectiveness in imperial politics. Otto's death in 1218 left Frederick II the unchallenged claimant for the emperorship.

Frederick was too clever to imitate the mistakes of his predecessors by involving himself in the German morass without first developing an adequate economic and political base of operations. After a few years of desultory maneuvering to establish a semblance of order north of the Alps, he devoted himself wholeheartedly to the consolidation of his power in Sicily. This was a policy in direct conflict with papal interests, and one whose every success rekindled and inflamed papal fears of imperial encirclement. The papacy had two weapons that could be directed against Frederick's ambitions. Innocent III had extracted from that ruler a solemn oath that if he were ever named emperor he would renounce his claim to Sicily in favor of his son. In addition, though somewhat earlier, Frederick had taken the crusader's vow and was under the obligation to fulfill that duty.

Throughout Europe crusading zeal had waned with successive failures. The disastrous Fourth Crusade, ill-financed and ill-planned, had been turned to the service of Italian commerical interests rather than against the infidel. Incapable of paying for supplies and passage, the crusaders, at the request of Venice, had first sacked the Christian city of Zara, a commercial port on the eastern shore of the Adriatic, and then in 1204 had turned their wrath against Constantinople. The sacred image of crusade was badly sullied by this

performance, while at the same time it was becoming increasingly clear that the unity of purpose and energy required for effective military and political action in the East was impossible to attain.

Although Frederick had apparently made his vow in good faith, despite the dismal history of the Fourth Crusade, pressing events in Germany and his continuing concern for the affairs of Sicily caused him to delay as long as possible, casting about for any excuse. At last, under threat of excommunication by Pope Gregory, Frederick was compelled to make the crusade. He set forth with great ceremony in 1227, only to return a few days later, pleading that the sickness of his army made the journey impossible. The pope swiftly excommunicated him for failing in his vow, and when he set sail again a few months later, the pontiff again pronounced the anathema, this time for undertaking a crusade while excommunicate. The emperor, undeterred, made peace with the infidels, and while still under the ban had himself crowned king of Jerusalem. Relations between emperor and pope deteriorated still further when a papal army invaded the Sicilian kingdom, where it met with disastrous defeat. Frederick was finally able to turn himself to the business of governing his Sicilian kingdom so as to gain the strength to command all Italy, and not just the southern part of the peninsula.

An absolute law-maker

In 1231 through a code known as the *Lex Augustalis*, Frederick introduced a new and comprehensive system of government that, with its subsequent revisions, replaced customary and feudal law and limited the jurisdiction of ecclesiastical courts to adultery cases. Largely inspired by Roman law, the new code supported in every particular Frederick's natural propensities toward absolutism, and at the same time imposed extremely severe penalties for any breach. Power rested entirely in the hands of the ruler. Absolutism, however, is not necessarily equivalent to tyranny, and the kingdom prospered under Frederick's guidance. As a rancher cares for his cattle, Frederick looked after the wealth and activity of his people and, it must be admitted, with virtually the same end in view. Affluent subjects could pay high taxes, so policies were adjusted to allow the populace to gain as much as possible, in order to pay as much as would not harm their continued ability to create wealth. Internal customs were abolished to encourage trade. Agriculture was fostered, and seizures of agricultural equipment for debt were prohibited. New crops were introduced, and internal colonization, both urban and rural, was aided. For a time Sicily became one of the most advanced areas in the West and served as the breadbasket of Europe, in addition to continuing her role in providing financial support for Frederick's seemingly endless campaigns in northern Italy.

Learning was not neglected by this brilliant emperor, who spoke six languages and wrote poetry. The new university founded at Naples attracted scholars from all over the world. Grants were offered to scholars, while deserving students were subsidized on the basis of merit without regard to family background. The resources of Frederick's government were partially directed toward research, but more significantly for his time, to research of an empirical nature. Animals were collected from around the world, and direct observation considerably advanced the budding science of zoology. Frederick himself produced a remarkable treatise on falconry which was in fact a sophisticated text of ornithology. Tales relating the emperor's brutal experiments – disemboweling live subjects to study the digestive system – are probably apocryphal, but they accurately reflected the Sicilian court's precocious interest in experimental science.

Frederick's triumphs in Sicily were bought at the expense of the empire in Germany. During his entire reign, the emperor spent barely eight years north of the Alps, where he found the climate forbidding and the people alien. As a result he readily granted concessions to both church and nobles in order to have peace and freedom to pursue his Italian ambitions. Consequently, by the time of Frederick's death in 1250 the empire had virtually ceased to exist as a major political force. The brief rule of Frederick's son, Conrad IV (1250-54) was adequate, if not dynamic, but upon that ruler's death factionalism prevented the election of another emperor, agreed upon by all, until 1273. The papacy had finally triumphed, for the empire never again regained sufficient authority to challenge or threaten the church. Even in the kingdom of Sicily, success was fleeting; each advance accomplished by Frederick increased the number of his enemies. World opinion, and its more dangerous manifestation, military force, were marshaled against the emperor, whose outlandish pronouncements and worse behavior – he sank a Genoese fleet carrying bishops from all over the West to a conference called to endorse his excommunication in 1239 – alienated forces that might otherwise, in common fear of the papacy, have allied in mutual self-interest. The Sicilian economy faltered, taxes rose, war, particularly naval war, intensified and when Frederick died, the strength and vigor of the kingdom quickly dissipated.

Above left: Dante Alighieri, the poet whose *Divine Comedy* assigned many contemporary secular rulers and princes of the church to the circles of Hell.

Right: Edward I of England asks the clergy to make a financial contribution to the cost of his wars with Wales and Scotland. After a trial of strength between church and state, the pope was forced to allow the taxation of ecclesiastical revenue.

The challenge to the political balance of Europe was temporarily ended, but in politics, as in so many areas, the mercurial Frederick was half a century ahead of his time. Soon national monarchies would attack that balance, new tensions would arise and the methods of Frederick would serve durable new states to whom the precariously balanced system of Aquinas would be an irrelevant anachronism.

Strong national monarchies

Dante Alighieri, the greatest poet of the European Middle Ages, spent the latter part of his life, the period from 1302 to 1321, in exile as a result of the internecine conflicts endemic to the Italy of his day. The *Divine Comedy*, his masterpiece of 100 cantos describing the poet's symbolic journey through Hell, Purgatory and finally Paradise, is unique among the many allegorical poems of the Middle Ages in that its characters – kings, popes, bishops and lesser men – are drawn from contemporary history. It is also unique in being written in the vernacular Tuscan dialect of Dante's native Florence, a fact that at once established that dialect as a proper vehicle for high literature and modern literary Italian. Here, and perhaps also in the disregard for ecclesiastical doctrine implicit in the freedom with which he condemns major contemporary churchmen to the tortures of the Inferno, Dante appears as an innovator. Yet when, undoubtedly motivated by his own despair and suffering in the turbulence of his time, he sets forth his ideal vision of politics and the state in his *De Monarchia*, Dante is a voice of the past, recalling what never was completed and what could never be built again.

Dante recognized that papal politics were largely at the root of Italian unrest, and he sought the remedy in universal monarchy, in the restoration of the empire as in Roman times, but Christianized. Arguing from a position predicated on Roman law, Dante refutes those papal claims to secular authority that derive from the spurious 'Donation of Constantine,' since that early emperor could not legally have divested himself of secular control of the empire. While Dante assigned full and total authority in the secular sphere to the emperor, he did not challenge or reject papal authority over moral and spiritual matters. Indeed the church was expected to continue its efforts in forwarding the spiritual perfection of mankind, and thus in equipping men to live in peace and harmony within the secular empire. Dante differed from Aquinas in his reversal of the relative positions of pope and emperor, but the basic assumptions were fundamentally the same. For each the state had a moral purpose, and for each the image and model for the temporal ruler was the King of Heaven.

By 1300, however, universal monarchy was an impossible dream. Papal success in reducing the empire had been all but complete, and national monarchies, long devoted to the consolidation of their power, had begun to grow strong and independent. With the assertion and expansion of royal authority came the concomitant needs for new sources of revenue and a wider tax base – needs that inevitably led to conflict between the monarchies and the papacy.

War and the economy

At the end of the thirteenth century France and England were at war, and military costs rose sharply as the scale and scope of war increased. Philip IV of France (1285-1314), for example, in 1295 spent more than 1.5 million livres tournois on the navy alone, a sum far in excess of the ordinary annual revenues of France, yet only a fraction of the budget required for that year. Pressed by the persistent shortage of money, both Philip IV and Edward I of England (1272-1307) exploited every available source. Forced loans recurred with the seasons in France. The Jews were periodically expelled, as they had been from England in 1290, and their assets seized. Italian merchants were subjected to heavy fines. Inevitably the wealth of the church came under attack. In 1295 the monarchs of both France and England demanded clerical subsidies to finance the war. Pope Boniface VIII resisted the levies, and in the following year promulgated the bull *Clericis Laicos*, decreeing excommunication to any who taxed the church or who paid such taxes.

The same ecclesiastical wealth that had attracted Philip's attention provided him with a weapon to counter the papal anathema. By prohibiting all exports of gold and silver from France he deprived the church of a major source of funds at the precise moment that its Italian political involvements heightened the need. In addition Philip instituted a policy of currency debasement and thus was able to reduce the real value of money rents collected by all great landholders, including the church. For this crime Dante, despite his admiration for universal monarchy, placed Philip in the Inferno as a counterfeiter. In England the king denied royal justice to the clergy, an action that classed them with common criminals and put them at the mercy of the citizenry at large. Faced with the concerted opposition of the two most powerful monarchs of the west, Boniface was forced to retreat, seeking to placate the kings by permitting taxation of the clergy 'in times of great stress' and, incidentally, by canonizing King Louis IX in 1297.

Boniface made a strategic withdrawal, but he

had not comprehended the new forces afield in the fourteenth century. In a series of bulls issued in 1302 the pope reasserted ecclesiastical independence from taxation. Then, after it appeared from his disastrous defeat at the battle of Courtrai in 1302, where angry Flemish townsmen slew thousands of French nobles, that Philip's power was ebbing, Boniface issued the bull *Unam Sanctam*. Here the pope declared that it was necessary for 'the temporal authority to be subject to the spiritual authority' and that 'every human being to be saved must be subject to the Roman Pontiff.' The claim was ambiguous. If it meant 'subject' in spiritual matters it was not new, but if it were taken literally it was the strongest assertion of papal power ever articulated in the Middle Ages. Philip IV saw to it that the latter interpretation received great currency and made every effort to inflame public opinion. In September 1303 Philip's minister, Nogaret, seized Boniface in his summer palace at Anagni. Although he was subsequently rescued by indignant townspeople, the 85-year-old pontiff died shortly after his release, a victim of shock at the outrage committed against him, and possibly of physical abuse as well.

Boniface's successor lasted but a few months, enough time for him judiciously to agree to demands for clerical subsidies, and was in turn succeeded by Clement V, a Frenchman. Clement moved the papal curia from its traditional and historically prestigious seat at Rome and relocated it in Avignon. There it remained from 1309 to 1379, a 70-year period that came to be known as the 'Babylonian Captivity.'

Papal authority in decline

The initial blow to church prestige was severe, but the suspicions regarding the 'captivity' of the French pope were swiftly reinforced by Clement's complicity in, or at least consent to, Philip's successful attack on the Knights of the Temple. The Templars had originally been a crusading order,

but after the fall of Acre in 1291 their role shifted to that of bankers and financial agents for the French and other governments. Internal improvement within the French administrative system and the development of a separate financial body, the *Chambres des Comptes*, freed Philip from dependence on the Temple. The Templars ceased to provide a vital service to the monarchy and were thus metamorphosed into a simple source of riches. In 1307 the king ordered the arrest of all the Templars in France and charged them with acts against God and sordid sexual abuses. Imprisonment, torture and the execution of several score of their number at the stake elicited confessions from the survivors. The papal investigatory commission was apparently satisfied with the confessions, and in 1312 Pope Clement abolished the order and turned its lands over to the Knights of the Hospital. Philip gained a large cash payment, five years of the order's revenues and the cancellation of his debts to the Temple.

The charges against the Temple were suspect from the start, and the evidence was indeed flimsy. Early in the proceedings, when they thought themselves free from Philip's tortures and safely in the hands of a papal investigatory commission, many members of the order had recanted their forced confessions. Further, in other countries, where there was less duress, the Templars neither pleaded nor were found to be guilty of the charges brought against the order in France. Whatever the facts of the case, the trial of the Templars, in conjunction with the transferral of the papal court from Rome to Avignon, served to undercut the moral credibility of the papacy, and did so immediately after Boniface had demanded greater subjection to papal authority than had been claimed by any previous pontiff.

Reassessment of papal authority was inevitable under the circumstances, and a lively literature of claims and counter claims proliferated in the early fourteenth century. Marsiglio of Padua stated the

anti-papal, imperial argument in unique and prescient terms in his *Defensor Pacis* of 1324. Marsiglio had taught at the University of Paris and was familiar with the work of the great English philosopher, William of Ockham, and the nominalist school that questioned the reality of universals and doubted the value of human reason in attaining Christian truth. Such knowledge was considered to be available only through revelation, and consequently to be dependent entirely on the will of God.

Marsiglio inverted the claims of Pope Boniface and maintained that the state should dominate the church. The prince was not to be a despot, but rather was to govern within the rule of law and with moderation. Once, however, universals were called into question, the very meaning of law was thrown into doubt. The hierarchical progression of laws as set forth by Aquinas depended simultaneously on the reality of universals and on their availability through human reason. Marsiglio solved the dilemma of the origin of law by defining law as the initial creation of the *legislator humanus*, a body that was equivalent to the will of the community. This conception was not popular sovereignty, however, since the *legislator humanus* was comprised only of 'the weightier part' of the citizens, a qualitative distinction that precluded democracy and left open the problem of the precise determination of that weightier part.

For Marsiglio, then, law, so far as the civil state was concerned, was entirely a human creation. This consequence was, in part, a corollary of his proposition that law, to have political reality, required an enforcing agent, and that agent was the secular prince. Since the *legislator humanus* was not a legally constituted body, such as Parliament or the Congress, and since its very composition was uncertain, due to the difficulties inherent in defining 'the weightier part,' it is apparent that the prince held extremely broad powers. Not only

Far left: The tomb of Marsiglio of Padua, eloquent advocate of the supremacy of the state over the church.

Left: Grape-picking illustrated in *The Grete Herball.* More people could afford to drink wine as food prices fell after the mid-fourteenth century.

Right: A mass burial of victims of bubonic plague at Tournai in 1349 – a scene repeated all over Europe. In many areas the Black Death killed more than a third of the population.

must he enforce the law, but over a considerable area he must define it. Further, since there was no universal model, a great deal was left to his unchecked and independent judgment. It is of course true that the *legislator humanus* could rise up and reconvene to eject the prince, but the process through which such action could occur is cloudy. Inconceivable to Aquinas, the powers here relegated to the prince would have alarmed even Dante, despite his advocacy of universal monarchy. The outcome of Marsiglio's theories was more likely to be absolutism than popular sovereignty.

Ravages of famine

Simultaneously with the development of a clear and logical literature in support of increased secular authority, economic and social forces began at once to weaken the political opposition to strong monarchy in Europe, and to force kings to concern themselves with matters that were formerly ignored or left to private hands. The economic achievements of the thirteenth century had not been accomplished without cost, and by the beginning of the fourteenth century that cost was becoming increasingly apparent. Demographic growth had been continuous for several centuries, and more and more land had been pressed into cultivation to sustain the increase. Ultimately, as demanded by population pressure, marginal lands such as fens, swamps and poor or nearly sterile soils were brought under the plow and often subjected to the newer, more intensive three-field system. With increased demand for food grains, less land was allowed to lie fallow, and the amount of pasture was reduced. Now there was less likelihood that natural forces or grazing herds would restore the fertility of the soil. Low yields per acre simultaneously necessitated the exploitation of vast land areas to support even the limited population of medieval Europe.

In 1315-17 disaster finally occurred. Crops failed throughout Europe, and multitudes starved. In some Flemish cities the mortality rate approached 10 percent. The Great European Famine was a catastrophe made spectacular by its duration and severity, but it was only one highly dramatic manifestation of the more basic problem of imbalance between the population and the food supply. The first half of the fourteenth century was to witness numerous other famines and scarcities, both locally and over wide regions, and throughout several decades Europe's population was afflicted by food shortage and the consequent lowering of general nutritional standards.

The Black Death

The famine that stalked Europe in the first half of the fourteenth century was abruptly eased by an even grimmer specter. Moving from the East across the Mediterranean, the Black Death, or bubonic plague, swept over the West in 1348-49, carrying off millions of inhabitants. In many regions the mortality rate exceeded 30 percent. Demographic calamities and periods of sharp depopulation are normally followed by rapid recovery, as the young find it economically feasible to marry earlier and the pace of family formation quickens. But in the fourteenth century the plague recurred in major waves almost precisely at 10-year intervals, while local outbreaks remained a perpetual terror in nearly all regions. As a result the population of Europe was prevented from recovering its pre-plague levels until at least 1500, although there was marked improvement and a consistent upward trend after the mid-fifteenth century.

Falling population initially alleviated the food shortage by reducing demand. Grain prices fell, and it is probable that the average man's diet improved. Low grain prices freed consumers to supplement their diets with more meat, butter, fish, beer and even wine, but they also led to mas-

sive dislocation in traditional grain-producing areas. As agricultural rents and profits followed grain prices in a downward spiral, farming became unprofitable in many regions. Where they could, landlords converted to the production of meat, dyestuffs, barley for beer, dairy products and other semi-luxuries in an attempt to preserve profits. Success was elusive, however, save in a few economically specialized areas such as northern Italy, where the presence of cities so large that they could not be supplied from the neighboring countryside alone assured a continuing market for foodstuffs. Elsewhere, marginal land was abandoned and fields reverted to waste or pasture. In Germany land became so redundant that it was allowed to return to forest for the sake of swineherding.

Overproduction was not a problem in the towns, since the effects of plague in reducing the number of highly skilled artisans could not easily or quickly be overcome. Consequently, prices of manufactured goods rose sharply, a phenomenon that was harmful to the agricultural sector. As the price of goods produced fell, and that of goods purchased rose, the farming class found that it suffered an adverse balance of payments with regard to the towns. Money accumulated in urban centers, and it was not returned to the countryside in the ordinary course of economic transactions. In addition to this economic advantage, townsmen benefited from inheritance effects resultant upon the greatly increased death rates. Rising mortality tended to concentrate wealth in the hands of the survivors, and thus in the immediate wake of the Black Death there was a marked, though temporary, increment in urban affluence at almost all social levels.

While plague brought wealth to some, it brought terror to all. The responses and reactions varied with the individual. Some, dismayed and frightened by this world, prepared for the next and sought solace in religion and faith. Some

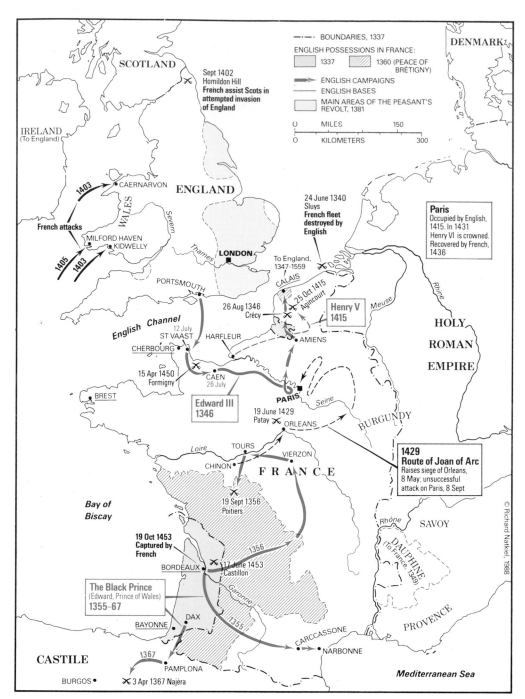

Intractable economic problems

The economic crises of the early Renaissance were insoluble at a local level, and consequently were beyond the competence of feudal powers. Such powers could be, and were, hurt by the dislocations. Labor scarcity increased labor mobility and raised wages at the same time as grain prices were falling, so landlords were ensnared in a profit squeeze. With landlords' consent, and often at their request, monarchs attempted to meet the problem at the national level through restrictive legislation, forcing the able-bodied to work at pre-plague wage rates and creating legal impediments to the geographical mobility of laborers. Through such legislation as the Statute of Laborers of 1351 in England and similar laws elsewhere, the monarchies assumed responsibility for direct control of wages and labor services, and thus, in response to economic crisis, then greatly extended the scope of royal jurisdiction.

The complex and intractable problem of the adverse balance of payments reinforced the tendency of monarchies to expand their activities in the economic sphere. In the first place, the direct connection between excess consumption of imported luxury goods and the sharp outflow of funds was noted by contemporary specialists and economic advisers. Merchants and tradesmen, desperately in need of cash for their commercial transactions, observed that the requisite specie was draining away to foreign ports and that it was not being replaced by domestic mining output, for northwestern mines had reached the limits of productivity within the context of fourteenth-century technology. Commercial pressures developed for the national central government to provide remedies, and, again with substantial public support, kings were drawn further into new areas of legislation in the international money market. Sumptuary laws, directly restricting personal consumption of food, drink, clothing and jewelry, proliferated, as did stringent limitations on the export of money. Attempts were even made to force the flow of commerce into patterns that would favor individual countries. England, for example, required that a portion of the foreign sales price of English wool be brought home in cash.

The adverse commercial balance and excess personal consumption were not the only causes of specie export. The church had benefited from the

exaggerated this course, and new sects, often radically heretical, sprang up. Bands of flagellants, seeking to expiate the sins of man, traversed Europe. Others, convinced that their lives were to be short, sought at least to live them lustily, and they turned to the pleasures of the earth, consuming as much as they could afford and adorning their persons to a degree far in excess of their social rank. Demand for luxuries grew, but the supply was limited; the reduced population of artisans could not provide adequate quantities of fine goods to satisfy the swollen demand. As a result, consumers clamored for exotic goods imported from the East, while at the same time high domestic demand limited the amount of exportable goods.

Throughout most of northwestern Europe the balance of payments turned unfavorable, and bullion was exported through Italy to the Levant and further east, as well as to the northeast and the Baltic, the source of luxury furs, wax and amber. As the drain continued the momentary affluence of the northern towns waned, and during the fifteenth century the prices of manufactured goods fell back toward their old relative position with respect to agricultural prices.

Left: The shifting course of the Hundred Years' War, 1337 to 1453.

Below left: The burghers of Calais petition the English King Edward III for mercy, following the fall of the town in 1347 after a prolonged siege.

Right: These thirteenth-century illustrations give a graphic image of battle between medieval knights on horseback. By the time of the Hundred Years' War, however, armored knights were vulnerable both to pikemen and archers.

increased death rate through legacies and, to a lesser extent, through contributions from the living and fearful pious. Despite the losses suffered through falling rents the church had, as a result of these enhanced sources of funds, gained substantial sums in liquid form, and it was actively withdrawing them from countries already afflicted by monetary famine and bullion shortage. This might perhaps have been tolerable had the papacy retained its old prestige and moral integrity, but relocation in Avignon and widespread scepticism concerning papal independence from the French monarchy had already seriously undermined the pontiff's status in the eyes of the world.

The Papacy in retreat

Even more unfortunate events followed the initial return of the papacy to Rome in 1378. In that year the cardinals met to elect a new pope, hoping to leave Rome as soon as possible for Avignon and be freed from the riotous Roman populace who were clamoring for a native pope. The candidate elected as Urban VI – Italian but not Roman – turned out to be a severe taskmaster and a stern reformer who quickly alienated the startled cardinals by reducing their incomes and refusing to leave the Holy City. After enduring as much as they could, the cardinals found their limited patience exhausted, fled to Anagni and elected a new pope, Clement VII. Urban, however, refused to acknowledge his deposition and remained in Rome as pope.

Precedent was not lacking for the simultaneous existence of two or more popes, but it had always been reasonably clear that one held a superior moral claim. In this instance, however, each of the claimants had been duly elected by the college of cardinals, and there was no extant precedent for the cardinals' reversal of their own decision. Verification of the legitimate pope fell by default to the secular authorities, and the decisions followed political allegiance. Charles V of France (1364-80) declared for Clement, along with the Spanish kingdoms, Scotland and Portugal. England and Germany supported Urban. Agreement could not be reached, so as each of the schismatic popes died, he was replaced by one faction or the other of the cardinals, and the Great Schism continued until 1415-17, when it was finally resolved at the council of Constance with the deposition of three popes and the election of Martin V.

This disgraceful situation and the resultant public confusion that arose with regard to the validity of sacraments administered by an apostate pope and his adherents lowered even further the moral prestige of the church and encouraged men to reconsider the social and economic costs of this seemingly corrupt institution. Papal transfers of specie from bullion-short countries, tainted by the charge that they were being used for political rather than spiritual purposes, were enormously unpopular with the economically sophisticated and powerful few. In England demands were made that the papal collector be an Englishman and that ecclesiastical revenues be exported only in the form of native commodities. In 1366 Edward III (1327-77) prohibited the collection of Peter's Pence, originally a penny from every Christian in the kingdom. Such legislation was repeated in 1376, 1384, 1399, 1409 and 1443. Similar laws were enacted in France, where, for the 20 years following 1378, papal exports of gold amounted to one-third of the known total coinage of that metal. In 1438 under Charles VII (1422-61), the Pragmatic Sanction freed the French church from papal taxation and gave the king broad powers over the French church. Twenty-three years later the Paris Parlement still gave its adamant support to the Pragmatic Sanction, on the grounds that its abrogation would lead to huge losses of bullion.

A combination of forces thus altered the relative balance between the papacy and the secular monarchies, reducing the strength of the former and enhancing that of the latter. The decline in moral prestige weakened the church, and the weakness was exacerbated on the economic front by the decline in agricultural revenues. At the same time the church's role in the crisis of international payments generated a new host of urban critics, who turned the power of the towns to the support of the monarchy.

Nobility in decline

Similar factors lessened the strength of the nobility, a formidable impediment to the growth of royal power, although in Germany and the east of Europe, where royal power was weak to start with, the nobility met the new economic strains by seizing more authority and creating political anarchy. In the west the economic position of the nobles was undermined by the scarcity of labor, high wage rates and the falling grain prices that resulted from massive depopulation in the fourteenth century.

Equally significant, perhaps, the prestige of the noble class also fell, though not for the same reasons as that of the church. Superbly trained as equestrian fighting men, the nobles had in the past been able to justify their privilege by their skill as warriors, providing defense for the weak. Unfortunately for them the techniques of war changed sharply in the fourteenth century, and the heavily-armored knight became increasingly obsolete. Every effort was made, but no amount of skill could render plate armor impermeable in an age of projectile warfare. Weight increased, mobility fell and costs rose. In 1302 at Courtrai the

townsmen of Flanders gave dramatic proof of the altered nature of war by toppling the French knights from their horses with long pikes and slaughtering the unfortunate nobles on the ground where they lay immobilized, defeated by the weight of their own armor. The experience was repeated with distressing regularity in the great battles of the Hundred Years' War as English archers, armed with longbows that gave them rapid firepower and a range of nearly 400 yards, destroyed French chivalry at Crecy in 1346, Poitiers in 1356 and Agincourt in 1415. Such military failure literally forced kings to adjust their tactics. Mercenary soldiers, with new skills, were at once more efficient and more dependable; no feudal custom limited their time or place of service. Command of mercenary troops increased royal power and reduced that of the nobility.

The Hundred Years' War

Fought between 1337 and 1453, the Hundred Years War greatly expanded the royal participants' dependence on mercenary forces. In 1328 the last direct male descendant in the Capetian line died, and the succession passed to the Valois. Edward III of England (1327-77), only a minor at the time, was too enmeshed in his domestic political difficulties to attempt to exercise his own tenuous claim to the throne of France, based on descent through the female line from Philip IV. Conflict concerning the English possessions in France, however, had been endemic for centuries, and when a decade later, under pressure of an English embargo on wool exports, the suffering clothworkers of Flanders offered to recognize Edward as king of France, he accepted. Although the fighting was not continuous, the Anglo-French war that followed lasted for more than a century and destroyed, over vast regions, what little French prosperity had been spared by famine, plague and the related economic crises.

The English were spectacularly successful at first, winning a major sea battle at Sluys in 1340, and then marching forward to defeat the French forces at Crecy in 1346. Calais was captured several years later. Control of the Channel was theirs, and the first English gold coin, struck in 1344, commemorated British domination of the seas. Further victories followed, and in 1356, at Poitiers in central France, English forces captured the unfortunate King John the Good (1350-64) and compelled the French to sue for peace. In 1360 the Treaty of Brétigny gave Edward full sovereignty over a vast area in southwestern France

that amounted to nearly a third of the kingdom. He set the ransom for King John at the enormous sum of 3 million écus of gold. While the ransom was never fully paid, the tax measures established to raise the money outlived the captive king and became, in the long run, one of the primary resources of the French crown and a source of independence from political controls comparable to those extant in England. There, Parliament grew in strength as it established, through precedent, its control over national funds, while subsidizing the highly successful Edward in his French adventures.

Briefly during the reign of Charles V (1364-80) the French enjoyed success in the field. Bertrand DuGuesclin, a brilliant Gascon general, terminated the heroic but disastrous strategy of the chivalric cavalry charge and instead played a waiting game, retreating into walled cities, waiting for the advantage and allowing the forces of nature and starvation to decimate the enemy. This policy was so effective that by the time of Charles' death most of Aquitaine had been recovered and the English had been driven back to a small region around Bordeaux in the south and to Calais and Ponthieu in the north. Charles tried to protect his heir by dividing the regency among several great nobles in order to limit their power, and by making them forswear further foreign wars, but this was to no avail. Louis of Anjou seized the treasury almost immediately after the king's death and attempted to conquer the kingdom of Naples, leaving Charles VI with financial resources no greater than his intellectual ones. The young king attained his majority in 1388, only four years before he went mad.

Political jousting among the nobles precluded concerted military action in France, but in England, the deposition of Richard II in 1399 brought the Lancastrian line to the throne in the person of Henry IV (1399-1413). His son Henry V (1413-22) was young, spirited and warlike, and since he had inherited the throne legitimately – unlike his father who had seized it with the aid of the barons – he was more free to make his own decisions. He reasserted the English claim to the throne of France, crossed the Channel in 1415 and destroyed the army of Charles VI at Agincourt, leaving Normandy open for systematic conquest. By the time of his premature death in 1422, Brittany and almost all of France north of the Loire were under English control, as was a substantial area in the regions surrounding Bordeaux.

The pathetic inheritance of Charles VII

(1422-61) was so reduced that he was sarcastically entitled the 'king of Bourges,' the modest southern town where he held court. Introspective, lethargic, cowardly and given to self-doubt concerning his own legitimacy, Charles took little initiative toward improving his position. In 1428 the future seemed darker than ever. The English had consolidated their conquests in Normandy and the north of France and were preparing a campaign in the south. The prerequisite step in that course was the capture of Orleans, the city that controlled access to Charles' little kingdom.

The king did little to relieve the besieged city, but a peasant girl in her late teens, Jeanne d'Arc, heard voices from God calling upon her to save France. She set out from her native Domrémy, a small peasant village, equipped only with her extraordinary faith and her equally remarkable gift of charismatic leadership. Incredibly, she was able to persuade the French court to grant her a small detachment of troops. She set out to relieve Orleans, and indeed was miraculously successful. Having accomplished this feat she convinced Charles to risk the journey to Rheims in order to hold coronation ceremonies in the cathedral there, according to the custom of the kings of France before him. Jeanne again triumphed. In the eyes of the people the 'king of Bourges' became the king of France and regained legitimacy and the loyalty of Frenchmen everywhere as a consequence of the traditional ceremonies that gave him divine sanction to rule.

Charles, however, irresolute and hesitant, delayed and missed the moment for riding the psychological crest and driving the English from his land. Instead of acting he waited, and Jeanne was captured in 1430, to be tried for witchcraft before a pro-English ecclesiastical tribunal the following year. The king, who owed his kingdom to her, did nothing to save the maid, and in effect permitted her to be burned at the stake by the English in Rouen in 1431. Years passed before Charles could muster the courage to acknowledge the girl's sacrifice in any way. Finally, in 1456, a quarter of a century after her death, a second tribunal, endorsed and supported by the king, vindicated Jeanne and attested to her complete orthodoxy.

What Jeanne had inspired could not be destroyed at the stake. The spirit of France was at last reborn, and events turned in favor of Charles. Burgundy, the rich and powerful dukedom on the eastern border of France – so vast indeed that there was a real danger of a resurrection of the old ninth-century kingdom of Lotharingia – had long been allied with the English. In 1435, however, at Arras, Philip the Good, Duke of Burgundy, made peace with Charles VII, and from that moment the English cause was lost. Slowly over the next 18 years Charles was able to reconquer and to assert authority over his kingdom, until finally in 1453 the Hundred Years' War came to a close.

The long war had increased the need for armor, for warships and mercenaries, and at the same time had multiplied the diplomatic expenses of the northern powers. While the northern countries were bled and exhausted by the intermittant combat, some southern cities prospered. Milan profited by supplying the finest armor in Europe, while Genoa and other maritime city-states in Italy provided mercenary troops and navies. As a result of these sources of foreign earnings and of their more peaceful incomes as suppliers of luxury goods, many of the towns of northern Italy temporarily avoided the worst aspects of the economic recession that followed the Black Death. Old industries, which served mass markets or their medieval equivalent, faltered and some collapsed – the Florentine woolen cloth industry contracted sharply – but luxury industries such as silk, fine armor and fine gold work prospered, as did trade in precious stones, coral and exotic spices. Unemployment might rise and income distribution might become even more unequal, but the rich remained rich and they continued to derive funds from the northwest portion of Europe. The intensity of the struggle to earn more and the incentive to strike out anew, however, may possibly have diminished.

Above left: In the Renaissance, artists not only developed new styles of painting, but also chose new subject-matter, moving away from exclusively religious scenes. This work is based on a story by Boccaccio.

Above: Francesco Petrarch, one of the most influential figures of the early Renaissance, both as lyric poet and as classical scholar.

Right: An illuminated manuscript of the Wife of Bath's Tale from Chaucer's *Canterbury Tales.*

The Renaissance

During the fourteenth century many men found the life of business tedious or simply unprofitable and turned their attention to cultural matters, although interest in political intrigue, endemic to Italy, never waned. Francesco Petrarch (1304-74), for example, whose father had suffered exile from Florence at the same time as Dante, was given legal training in the hope that he might recoup the family fortune, but he soon found such studies dull and turned instead to Roman antiquity and the Latin classics. Here he found his true calling, and while he was not the first of the early humanists he quickly became the most influential.

An idealized conception of ancient Rome came to dominate his life, both politically and intellectually. In the former sphere he supported the hopeless cause of actually restoring the old empire, first through a revolution in Rome that failed disastrously, and then, with only slightly more practicality, through appealing to the ambitions of the emperor, Charles IV. In intellectual matters, triumphal restoration was attainable. Petrarch perfected his Latin style, removing the encrustations of a millennium of linguistic change and development so as to reconstruct literary Latin as it was at the time of Cicero. The endeavor to purify style required a more careful study of history, entailing deeper involvement with the ancient authors on a broad scale, and it ultimately resulted in enduring contributions to historical scholarship and method. From the tradition of Petrarch came Lorenzo Valla (1407-57), who used the methodology of history and philology to prove that the Donation of Constantine was a forgery, and thereby added one more dimension to the general attack on the prestige of the church.

In its early stages, however, Italian humanism remained the product of deeply religious men. Petrarch died, perhaps as he had wished, while reading of St Augustine. Even Boccaccio (1313-75), whose modern fame rests largely upon the earthy tales assembled in the *Decameron*, a cycle of 100 fables narrated by a group of 10 men and women who had retreated to the country to avoid the plague then raging in Florence, was a sincere Christian, though he had no formal position in the ecclesiastical hierarchy. In his later years he renounced the *Decameron* and even attempted to recall it, and his subsequent work was more serious, often in Latin and reflecting the new learning of the humanists. Yet without the *Decameron* it is unlikely that Boccaccio would be so well known, and it is through his secular works that his greatest influence was transmitted. Like his English contemporary, Geoffrey Chaucer, whose late-fourteenth-century *Canterbury Tales* is similarly a cycle of stories, in this instance told by pilgrims traveling to Canterbury Cathedral, Boccaccio proved himself to be a fertile source of inspiration, even to the modern theater. He has often been imitated, even plagiarized, but remains unequalled in wit and style.

The humanist recovery of classical learning, particularly Latin letters, but also and increasingly Greek as well, was begun in the fourteenth century, but humanism flourished most strongly in the fifteenth. Antiquity became almost a fetish, and classical studies attracted even the most powerful as devotees, practitioners and patrons. Julius II, pope from 1503 to 1513, traveled extensively to recover the relics of the Roman past and devoted immense sums to the visual and plastic arts. The Medici, the most prominent Florentine family in fifteenth-century banking and politics, spent their fortune supporting the new intellectual movement. Indicative of the economy of the time, their fortune was in large part derived from their highly profitable operation in Rome, where they acted as bankers for the papacy, and thus benefited from northern Europe's imbalance of payments.

Latin letters were predominant in the first phase of the Renaissance. They generated more than a clear view of the distant past: they created a whole new life style. Man's complete personality and person became an art form. If one cultivated and refined Latin prose, so too should one cultivate and refine his manner of living. Castiligione (1478-1529), in his *Book of the Courtier*, provides a handbook for the polite and cultured human. Ideally a man was expected to have a taste for the arts, for literature, to be widely read, to know foreign languages and to be highly capable in physical activities, both sport and war. This ubiquitous sense of personal style was no new development in the fifteenth century, for even Petrarch lived as though he were watching his own performance on the stage of life. Yet conjoined with the very broad and intense interest in scholarship there was in the Renaissance a somewhat less attractive quality, a kind of pettiness and conceit, as well as a sense of personal destiny so inflated that it produced provincialism with regard to the immediate past, and even to some of the most important events of the period itself.

The humanist tradition

In the arts, however, the effects of humanism were profound. Concern for the individual, distinct and natural form restored sculpture as a representational art similar to that of the classical period. This mode triumphed over the symbolic and spiritual sculpture of the Middle Ages, whose distortions from nature the cultivated men of the Renaissance considered to be incompetent and barbarous. This movement was already under way in the late thirteenth century, fertilized to some extent by the artistic eclecticism of the court of Frederick II, but the zenith of sculpture was struck during the 15th and early 16th centuries.

In 1401 the city of Florence held a contest among artists to choose the sculptor for the doors of the Baptistery of San Giovanni. Lorenzo Ghiberti (1378-1455) won the contract. The doors themselves, bas-relief panels depicting the life of Christ, are masterpieces of technical skill in both casting and composition, but more important, they show true genius in the control of linear perspective, for the depths of the fields of vision far exceed the actual depth of the relief itself. The individual figures, in their fine detail and their close imitation of nature, established the standard for the future, a standard that was rapidly met, exceeded, and perfected by the many sculptors of the two subsequent centuries. From Ghiberti through Donatello (1386-1466) to Michelangelo (1475-1564), Italian sculpture transcended the classical models, defined a style that was truly its own, and demonstrated creative genius that has not since been equaled.

Classical themes more than classical relics influenced painting, and perhaps for this reason, painting is the art form where the genius and originality of the Renaissance is most prominent. Here too, however, the roots of the new movement lie in the thirteenth century. Cimabue (1240-1302) had modified and developed the Byzantine tradition of mosaic portraiture, a highly conventionalized style, by giving expression to his own interest in individual and natural detail. His student Giotto (1276-1336) surpassed the master and thus became to painting what Petrarch was to humanism. Concern for verisimilitude led painters to study the anatomy of the human body and to attempt to portray with great accuracy not

only the surface image but also the structural truth that underlay that image. Perspective, through shading, rounding, and the careful positioning of background detail, was consciously explored and meticulously refined.

Painting in the fifteenth and sixteenth centuries, as in sculpture, witnessed the perfection of the new techniques. Following a somewhat lean period just prior to 1400, perhaps the result of the high mortality rates of the late fourteenth century, painting attained a golden age. Massaccio (1401-28) died prematurely, but he carried his art to a high state of technical perfection. Subsequent artists – Fra Lippo Lippi (1406-69), Botticelli (1447-1510), Raphael (1448-1520) and Michelangelo – brought the painter's skill to such a high level of genius that the difficulty of surpassing it continues to haunt painters to this day. Leonardo da Vinci (1452-1519), whose *Mona Lisa* and *Last Supper* are universally familiar, was perhaps the most versatile and profound artist of his time. His work attains realism not only at the two levels of surface image and of the physical reality beneath, but goes further and plumbs the inner, more elusive, depths of the human soul.

If the fifteenth century was truly a period when genius flourished in Italy, it was also a period of political turmoil and deepening economic dislocation. Early in the century Italian prosperity derived in large part from access to the East and the ports of the Levant, yet for many decades a new force had been emerging to threaten Italian commercial interests in these regions. Gradually the Ottoman Turks extended their domination over the area, taking the south shore of the Dardanelles by 1326, both shores by 1354, the Balkan Peninsula in 1393 and finally, in 1453, simultaneously with the close of the Hundred Years' War, capturing Constantinople herself. The Turks soon became a major sea-power in the eastern Mediterranean, simultaneously forcing the Italian city-states to expend vast sums on naval defense and reducing their access to strategic supplies of increasingly scarce naval timber, while making its

availability more crucial for survival. The Venetian naval arsenal grew eight-fold between 1313 and 1473. Shipping costs consequently rose rapidly, while at the same time both the Turks and the Egyptians, through prohibitive tariff rates on exports, elevated the basic costs of trade. Commercial activity in the traditional eastern ports became increasingly difficult, and uncertain.

To make matters worse, the end of the Hundred Years' War freed northern countries, particularly France, from impediments to productive activity and enhanced the power of monarchs to indulge in proto-mercantilist restrictions on international trade flows; this was invariably directed against the hated Italians. As the northern European population slowly recovered, domestic food prices rose, and the mechanism that had worked to assure large bullion exports operated less efficiently. Especially in banking, but also in other sectors of the economy, the late fifteenth century in Italy was a period of sharp recession.

Expansion of royal power

Elsewhere in Europe, signs of recovery were appearing, and with economic recovery came a resurgence of the power of the monarchies. In France the wily Louis XI (1461-83) capitalized on the many concessions that had been made to royal authority during the troubled decades of the fourteenth and fifteenth centuries. The 'Spider King,' a sobriquet richly deserved, was able to draw together all the threads left by his predecessors and to create a powerful new monarchy. Towns that had revolted lost their legal independence. Guilds, formed through royal charter under pressure of recession, found themselves tools of the king, working to gather his revenues. The church was brought under royal control, tax revenues rose three-fold, the army was professionalized, and by the end of the reign the duke of Burgundy was destroyed and the dukedom so reduced that it could no longer threaten France.

In England, despite the so-called Wars of the

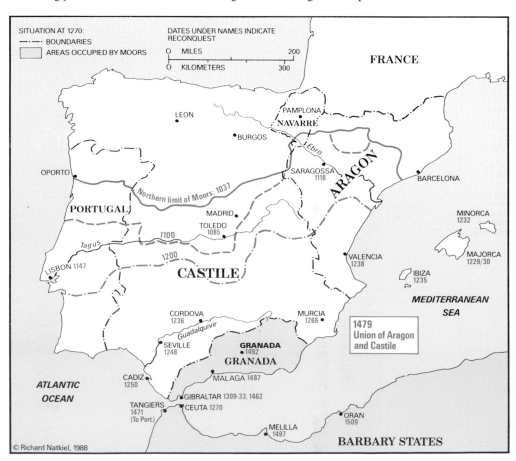

SITUATION AT 1270:
-·-·- BOUNDARIES
▒ AREAS OCCUPIED BY MOORS

DATES UNDER NAMES INDICATE RECONQUEST

0   MILES   200
0   KILOMETERS   300

FRANCE

LEON

PAMPLONA
NAVARRE

• BURGOS

OPORTO

Ebro

SARAGOSSA 1118

ARAGON

BARCELONA

Northern limit of Moors: 1037

PORTUGAL

MADRID

TOLEDO 1085

MINORCA 1232

1100

Tagus

1200

LISBON 1147

CASTILE

VALENCIA 1238

MAJORCA 1229/30

IBIZA 1235

MEDITERRANEAN SEA

CORDOVA 1236

Guadalquivir

MURCIA 1266

1479
Union of Aragon and Castile

SEVILLE 1248

GRANADA •1492

GRANADA

ATLANTIC OCEAN

CADIZ 1250

MALAGA 1487

GIBRALTAR 1309-33, 1462

TANGIERS 1471 (To Port.)

CEUTA 1270

ORAN 1509

MELILLA 1497

BARBARY STATES

© Richard Natkiel, 1988

Roses (1455-87) – a struggle for the monarchy between the houses of Lancaster and York – the monarchy itself did not suffer loss of its potential power. When Henry Tudor defeated and killed Richard III (1483-85) at Bosworth Field and became Henry VII (1485-1509), the monarchy quickly regained its strength. Although the Tudors never dared to attempt to rule without Parliament, and although they were always subject to its constraints, it is yet possible to speak of 'Tudor absolutism.' There was no doubt about their power.

The expansion of royal power, visible everywhere in western Europe, was not absent from Spain. The reconquest of the Iberian Peninsula after the Arab occupation had progressed slowly from the tenth century. By the fifteenth century the Moorish domains had been reduced to a small area around Granada, but Spain was not yet united into one kingdom. With the land divided into the separate domains of Aragon, Castile, Navarre, Portugal and the Moorish kingdom of Granada, the various rulers of Spain could only look with envy at the powerful and absolutist monarchy that Louis XI was building in France and which he was determined to prevent an imitation of across the Pyrenees. Despite Louis' efforts, however, Ferdinand, heir of Aragon and king of Sicily, married Isabella, heiress of Castile, in a clandestine ceremony kept secret to evade the dark intrigues of the Spider King. In 1474 Isabella received her inheritance, and when Ferdinand acceded to his throne five years later, in 1479, the kingdoms of Aragon and Castile were united. The conquest of Navarre in 1485, its incorporation into the joint kingdom in 1512 and the capture of Granada in 1492 completed the unification of Spain and established her modern borders. Despite a period of war from 1474-79, however, Portugal preserved her independence until 1580.

Spanish unification gave political dominance to Castile, a fact that was ruinous for the active commercial interests of Aragon, and gave impetus to the extension of absolutist rule throughout the country. The trend was reinforced by the voyage of Christopher Columbus in 1492, the same year that Granada fell. Atlantic exploration had been proceeding at a regular pace during the fifteenth century, though its beginnings lie even earlier. (The Canary Islands were claimed by Castile in the mid-fourteenth century, and it is probable that the Madeiras and the Azores were known by then as well.) Spurred on by the European bullion shortage and by the Turkish threat in the eastern Mediterranean, the Portuguese advanced slowly but persistently down the west coast of Africa, where they established several trading posts, found some gold and more pepper, and opened up the slave trade to provide labor for the offshore islands, where sugar and wine were becoming major cash crops.

The discovery of the New World, and the massive wealth that it yielded to Spanish plunderers in the sixteenth century, however, simultaneously transmuted the very conception of the world, thus further eroding the conservative medieval order, and provided the Spanish monarchy with seemingly limitless resources for the sustenance of royal authority. The vastly increased scale and scope of trade combined with distance and expense to render commerce the concern of nations rather than of individuals, and consequently to accelerate the growth of state control and absolutist measures.

The emergence at the end of the fifteenth century of the works of Machiavelli (1469-1527), the greatest Italian political thinker, hardly appears accidental. Everywhere the states of Europe provided his raw material. When Machiavelli theorized in *The Prince* (1513) that the chief purpose of government was to preserve itself, thus completely divorcing politics from morality, he was but reflecting the nature of his contemporary world. If he admired rulers, who through strength and craft, became virtually absolute, it was because, despite reliance upon despotic methods, France and Spain were better governed than Italy at the beginning of the sixteenth century. The vision that had been put forth by Aquinas, of balanced rule, proceeding according to, and limited by, immutable divine, moral and natural laws, had been irreparably destroyed during the last two centuries of the Middle Ages. No realist could continue to assert the morality of politics; even the standard by which morality was measured seemed flexible and uncertain.

Above: Christopher Columbus, whose voyage to the New World in 1492 has often been taken as marking the end of the medieval era and the beginning of modern times.

Left: The reconquest of Iberia by the Christians progressed steadily in the two centuries up to 1270 although Granada remained in Muslim hands until 1492 – coincidentally, the date of Columbus's famous voyage.

Right: Boccaccio, author of the immensely influential story-cycle The Decameron.

Far right: A guild warden watches as a mason and a carpenter attempt to prove their skills. The guild system was an important element in the expansion of urban society during the course of the Middle Ages.

The Emergence of Russia

In the seventh century, or even earlier, the valley of the Dnieper and the plain to the north of the Black Sea began to be settled by eastern Slavs. The Slavs had been known for centuries to the Romans, who referred to them as Venedi and Antes. They were mentioned by Tacitus. The Emperor Trajan unsuccessfully attempted to extend Roman dominion over them. The Slavs entered into close relations with the Scytho-Sarmatians and the Greeks, fought the Goths and the Huns and absorbed much of the cultures of their neighbors.

The origin of the first recognizable Slav state in the plain north of the Black Sea and the provenance of the word 'Rus' (from which is derived the name Russia) have long been matters of controversy. The *Primary Chronicle*, a source dating back to 1377 and based on a text written in the eleventh century, says that in AD 862 the Slavs, who perpetually quarreled among themselves, went to the Varangian Russes (Scandinavians) and invited them to 'reign and rule' over the Slavs. According to tradition, the Varangian (Viking) Riurik accepted the invitation and became the first prince of Novgorod, a commercial republic in northern Russia. Other Vikings established themselves elsewhere. When Riurik's son, Igor, became the ruler of Kiev in 882, the Riurik dynasty was launched and with it the Russian state.

Though this story bears the marks of legend, it undoubtedly contains elements of truth. In the eighteenth century the newly awakened Russian national consciousness made it difficult for some

historians to accept the notion that their state had been founded by foreign invaders; the theory came under attack, giving rise to long and largely fruitless disputes. The whole story of the role of the Vikings in the formation of the Kievan Russian state will probably never be known. The sources are insufficient and the arguments must remain inconclusive. It is reasonable to suppose, however, that the Vikings who did penetrate Russia in the ninth century, just as they penetrated much of the rest of Europe, played a part in the development of Kievan society and state.

Whatever its origin, Kiev grew and prospered. The Dnieper became an important trade route between Scandinavia and Constantinople. Russian merchants ventured as far afield as Khwarazm, Baghdad and Alexandria. At home, agriculture and commerce provided the economic base for the growth of towns, some of which reached considerable proportions. When Prince Vladimir (980-1015) imposed Christianity upon his people, Kievan Rus was exposed to strong Byzantine influence. Orthodox priests introduced not only an especially devised alphabet (Cyrillic), but also the Bible, some works of Church fathers, lives of saints, bits of Byzantine law and much art. Kievans were quick to learn. Monasteries began to produce chronicles, sermons and lives of saints. A collection of laws, *Russkaia Pravda*, was compiled. Churches were built and richly decorated with mosaics which show the predominance of Byzantine influence that radiated from Constantinople.

Kievan Rus reached its peak in the reign of

Yaroslav The Wise (1019-54). The state was relatively strong. The Prince had connections with a dozen reigning houses of Europe. Married to a Scandinavian princess, he gave his daughters in marriage to the kings of France, Hungary and Norway. The borders were well protected, and a crushing defeat was inflicted on the nomadic Pechenegs who threatened Rus from the East. Yaroslav bequeathed the country to his sons, each of whom was to rule a principality. The provisions for succession were confused and unrealistic. Yaroslav's progeny quarreled among themselves and eventually plunged Rus into the state of chronic civil war. Central authority disintegrated, while virtually independent principalities sprang up in the north and the west. Trade declined. Frequent incursions of wild steppe nomads, among whom the Polovtsy were the fiercest, scattered the population of the Dnieper valley, sending a stream of emigrants to the shelter of northern forests. Agriculture declined. Towns lost inhabitants. Kiev itself was sacked in 1169 by Andrei Bogoliubskii, himself a grandson of a Kievan prince.

The Mongol terror

Russia, along with much of the rest of Eurasia, was drastically affected by the thirteenth-century eruption of the Mongols out of Central Asia. In 1215 the Mongols had seized Peking. Three years later from the banks of the Irtysh they launched their campaign against the Turko-Iranian states of Central Asia. Samarqand, Bukhara, Marv, Khwarazm and other cities fell before the seemingly irresistible force of the nomads. In 1220 a detachment of Chingiz (Genghis) Khan's army led by

In medieval Russia, religion, alphabet and artistic styles were all influenced by the Christian culture of Byzantium, although the Russians imposed their own stamp on such borrowings. For example, whereas Byzantine church art was exclusively religious in character, the Cathedral of St Sophia at Kiev has frescoes of scenes drawn from everyday life – including its musicians (left) and jesters (below left).

Below: Mongol cavalry in action on the banks of the River Don. The Mongols began their conquest of Russia in 1236 and by 1240 had subjugated most of it to establish the western outpost of their Eurasian domain.

Right: An engraving showing Novgorod, the major city of northern Russia in the medieval period.

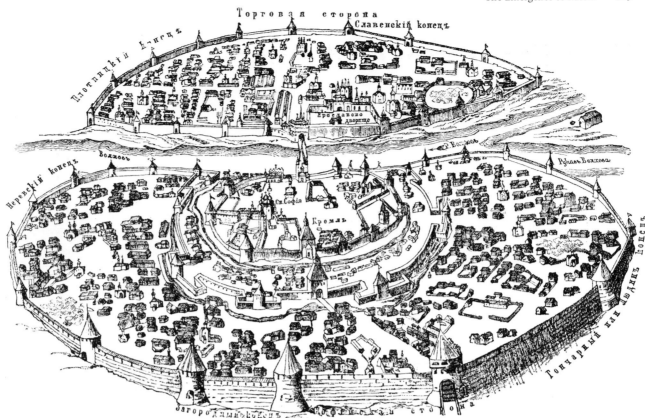

the veteran commander Subutay invaded northern Iran and penetrated the Caucasus. In 1223, on the river Kalka in southern Russia, Subutay defeated a combined force of Russian princes. However, the Mongols then withdrew as rapidly as they had come and did not return until 1237.

While the Russian campaign of 1223 had been a deep reconnaissance raid, that of 1236-40 was a major invasion. The horde led by Batu Khan, grandson of Chingiz, was composed of many ethnic elements, the most prominent of whom, the Tatars, gave their name not only to the invasion but to the entire subsequent period of Russian history. Well disciplined, commanded by experienced generals, including Subutay, the Tataro-Mongols rapidly conquered virtually all of Russia. Riazan fell in December 1237 after a six-day siege. Kolomna and Moscow fell in January 1238; Vladimir, the seat of the Grand Prince, in February, Suzdal in March. In 1240 Kiev, already ruined by internecine struggles of Russian princes, was almost totally destroyed. The Tataro-Mongols went on to invade Hungary and Poland and reached the Adriatic Sea in 1241. The death of the Khaghan, Ogetei, and Batu's desire to influence the election of the next khaghan prompted him to return to Asia.

Defeated and shattered by the invasion, Russia became part of an alien empire ruled by distant masters who were principally interested in recruiting men for their armies and collecting taxes. The Tatars tolerated the Orthodox Church, exempted it from taxation, and otherwise protected its interests. They did not interfere with the customs and the way of life of the masses. However, in the early years of their dominion they exercised strict control over the government of the subjugated territories.

Those princes of the house of Riurik who had not died fighting the Tatars sought the khan's favor, prostrating themselves at his feet to obtain a *yarlik* (patent) that would confirm them in possession of their principalities. Upon the death of a prince, his heir had to be invested by the khan. Russian princes frequently traveled to Sarai, capital of the Golden Horde, to plead their cases with the khan. The more realistic among them realized that all resistance was foolish and loyally co-operated with the conquerors. Alexander Nevskii, who eventually was canonized by the Church and became a national hero, bowed to the Tatars and worked closely with them. The princes of Moscow were in many instances the principal agents of the Tatars in Russia.

The need of a *yarlik* and of Tatar support made the power of the princes independent of old institutions such as the *veche* (popular assemblies), which survived only in the merchant republics of Novgorod and Pskov. The authority of the khan also provided an autocratic model for the princes of Moscow. Though N Karamzin, a great nineteenth-century historian, exaggerated when he claimed that Russia owed her greatness to the khans, his view contained a grain of truth. During the thirteenth and fourteenth centuries governing institutions inherited from Kiev were radically and permanently transformed.

To maintain their authority in Russia the Tatars created special military units, recruited partly from the local population but commanded by Tatars. These were at the disposal of the *baskaks*, political and fiscal representatives of the khan. In 1257 the Tatars conducted Russia's first census. Later they gave up direct tax collecting, preferring to entrust this unpleasant task to faithful Russian princes, who were anxious to assume the burden since it permitted them to fleece their people in the name of the Tatars.

Pressure from the West

Much as the Russians hated their Tatar overlords, they preferred them to the Swedes, the Germans, the Poles and other European Catholics who took advantage of Russia's prostration to attack from the West. The rule of the Khans was heavy, but the Tatars at least did not threaten the religion and the spiritual identity of the Russians, whereas the West was determined to convert the Orthodox to the 'one true faith.' In 1240, the year of the fall of Kiev, when most of Russia had already been occupied by the Tatars, the Swedes struck from the northwest. They were defeated on the Neva by the Novgorodian troops under Prince Alexander, who therefore became known as Nevskii.

No sooner had the Swedes been repelled than a new foe appeared in the west. Late in the twelfth century there came to the Baltic German knights who had been left unemployed by the failure of the crusades. Several orders had been formed, and the blessings of Rome had been secured for the conquest and conversion of the Lithuanians, Letts, Estonians, Prussians and other pagan peoples of the north. Fighting the small pagan tribes of the Baltic proved easier than fighting Muslims in the East, and conquest promised wealth and power in addition to remission of sins and papal favor. The Teutonic and Livonian knights marched through Latvian and Estonian villages, looting, burning, raping and killing.

Left: An icon picturing St George, from the crypt of Alexander Nevskii. Nevskii was canonized by the Russian Orthodox Church in the sixteenth century.

Below left: The Mongols of the Golden Horde were the supreme rulers of medieval Russia for almost 200 years. No Russian prince could hold his position of power unless the khans of Saray, the Tatar capital, gave their approval.

Right: A seventeenth-century wallpainting of Alexander Nevskii. Although he was hailed as a national hero, in fact he collaborated with the Mongol suzerains of Russia. His reputation rests on victories over western opponents, the Teutonic Order and the Swedes.

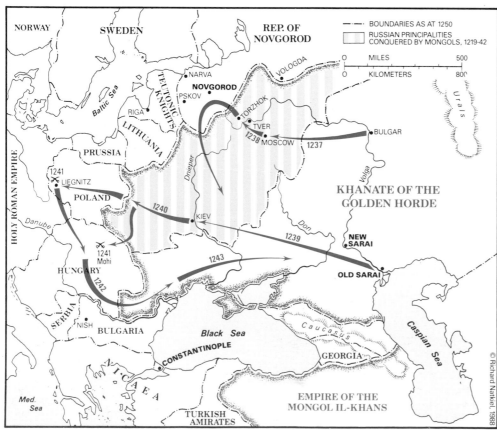

(Bishop Albrecht, sometimes called the founder of the Livonian state and the 'armed apostle,' rode into battle with his sword in one hand and his crucifix in the other.)

In 1240 Livonian knights took Izborsk and Pskov, and early in 1241 they tried to establish themselves on the banks of the Neva and in Karelia. Once again Prince Alexander Nevskii led the Russian defense. On 5 April 1242, on the ice of Lake Chud (Peipus), the Germans suffered defeat. For his part in saving Russia from Catholicism Prince Alexander was canonized by the Russian Church, and he remains a national hero to this day.

The Tatar conquest and the bitter conflict with her western neighbors isolated Russia. Frequent Tatar raids, the breakdown of order, large-scale banditry, civil strife and the never-ending power struggle among the princes produced chaos and suffering of unimagined proportions. The economy was shattered. Much of the cultivated land south of the Oka River was abandoned, becoming *dikoe pole*, wild prairie. Escaping Tatar raids, the population of southern regions fled to the forests of the northeast, settling the area between the Oka and the Volga and spreading farther north. Gradually, out of a mixture of old Novgorodian settlers, the inhabitants of the principalities of Vladimir, Suzdal and Rostov, the immigrants from the devastated south and some Finnish forest tribes, the Great Russian nation came into being. The term Great Rus was first

people in the fourteenth century, and in the fifteenth the word Russia came into being. The territory it occupied, the language it spoke, the form of government it developed and the way it lived marked it as a new people, related to Kievan Rus as Italians or Spaniards are related to ancient Rome. It is worth noting, however, that the Kievan dynasty continued uninterrupted and supplied the princes who ruled in Vladimir, Tver, Riazan, Moscow and other states of central, northern and eastern Russia.

The rise of Moscow

Among Russian principalities there were several contenders for leadership of the land. Novgorod was the center of a veritable empire in the north and could have claimed primacy. Vladimir was the seat of the Grand Prince, and thus the acknowledged successor of Kiev as capital of Rus. Tver and Riazan could have played the role of unifier. But it was a relative latecomer, Moscow, that succeeded in 'gathering the Russian land' and making its name synonymous with Russia.

Left: This engraving shows stunned mourners viewing the death and destruction visited upon Vladimir by Batu Khan's Mongols in 1238. The city's ruler, Yaroslav, who was the senior prince of Russia at the time, lay among the slain.

Historians have advanced many theories to explain Moscow's rise to supremacy. These can be reduced to two categories, geographical and political. Situated relatively far from the main routes of foreign incursions, protected by thick forests, the village on the banks of a muddy tributary of a tributary of the Volga was first mentioned in the chronicles under the year 1147. Ninety years later, while still a small and insignificant town, Moscow was sacked by the Turko-Mongols. In spite of this it became the refuge for multitudes escaping the greater devastation wrought by the enemy in the south and in the east.

The rivers and the forests provided fish, game and wild honey. In the clearings peasants planted rye, barley, oats and, to a lesser extent, wheat, millet and buckwheat. Though agricultural techniques remained primitive, enough food was raised to feed the growing population. Also, Moscow was located near the head-waters of several great river systems and occupied an exceptionally favorable position in regard to commerce, transportation and communications, not to mention the strategic advantages of its central position. Though the iron, leather and other products of Moscow craftsmen were sold in Novgorod and along the Volga, and the beaver and sable pelts gathered by Moscow hunters were in demand all over the east, the total volume of trade was not significant. Indeed, the economic development of Russia in general in the fourteenth and fifteenth centuries was painfully slow.

Perhaps the most important reason for the elevation of Moscow had to do with the policies of the Moscovite princes, descendants of Alexander Nevskii through his son Daniel. No one was more determined than they to build their family fortunes at the expense of others or more assiduous in courting the Khans of the Golden Horde. Close political and family ties with Sarai assured them the assistance of the Tatars in domestic conflicts. The rivalry between the princes was bitter and cruel. The achievement of supremacy was the end that justified all means. The losers fled or were exiled from their domains. Many were locked up in monasteries or blinded or murdered.

One such prince was Ivan I, surnamed *Kalita* (1325-40), the money bag, a scheming, frugal, farsighted and utterly amoral politician. He not only collected taxes for the Tatars but in 1327 led a Tatar force against Tver to punish the city for the murder of a Tatar official and, incidentally, to avenge his own brother and predecessor, Yurii, who had been killed by the Prince of Tver. But

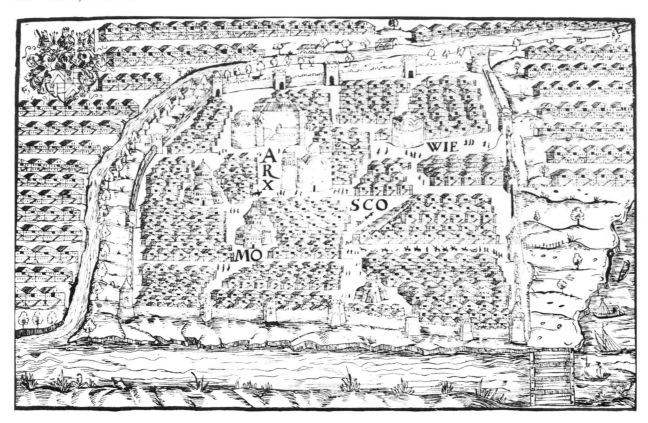

Left: The city of Moscow emerged as the most powerful of the Russian principalities during the fourteenth century. It was located at the center of a network of rivers and trade routes which gave it a strategic advantage over its rivals, but it perhaps owed its rise mainly to the ruthlessness of its ruling princes.

Below: A fifteenth-century illustration of the brewing of *Kvass,* a homemade beer renowned for its potency.

Right: The monastery at Tikhvin. Built like fortresses Russian monasteries functioned as refuges when Tatar raids struck.

Below right: The Tatar influence in Russian life was examplified in the literal person of Boris Godunov – the first czar of Russia to be of Tatar descent.

Ivan also allied himself with the Russian Church, offering protection to its Metropolitan, Peter, who transferred his see to Moscow, where he soon died. Ivan procured his canonization, giving Moscow her own saint and establishing her claim to being the religious center of the country.

Ivan's grandson, Dmitrii, felt strong enough to defy the Mongols, who were undergoing a period of internal strife and turmoil. In 1380, at Kulikovo field on the Don, he defeated a Mongol punitive expedition, inflicting upon the Tatars their first major defeat in Russia. Dmitrii did not harvest the fruits of his daring, for two years later the Tatars returned, under the formidable Toqtamïsh, defeated the Russians and sacked Moscow. The attempt at liberation had been premature. Yet the victory of 1380, for which Dmitrii was surnamed Donskoi, added to the prestige of Moscow, giving her princes the aura of defenders of the land and champions of the faith.

For the next hundred years the princes of Moscow continued to consolidate their power and influence, adding fresh territories to their already considerable domain. As the power of the Grand Prince grew, his opponents sensed the danger and made every attempt to resist. Ever since the reign of Ivan I the Grand Prince had left a major portion of his territories to the son who succeeded him on the throne of Moscow, other sons receiving much smaller allotments. Thus in each subsequent generation the Grand Prince waxed greater at the expense of brother, cousins and uncles. The last major attempt to reverse the trend was made in the fifteenth century by Vasilii II's uncle, Yurii, and Yurii's sons, and Russia was plunged into a prolonged civil war of unexampled ferocity. Moscow was seized more than once by rebellious princes. Vasilii (1425-62) was captured, blinded and imprisoned for a time. Once at liberty, he continued to struggle with the faithful help of his son, the future Ivan III (1462-1505).

Vasilii's triumph led to a further strengthening of Muscovite authority. A number of princes had lost their lives. Their territories were more often than not incorporated into the domain of the Grand Prince of Moscow. Other princes were so weakened that Vasilii, and after him Ivan III, was able to curtail their rights and immunities. Moreover, the boyars, or nobles, who served the various princes, began to desert them and to enter the service of the Prince of Moscow. The process of the formation of a centralized Russian nation-state was completed in the reign of Ivan III, who annexed the principalities of Yaroslavl and Rostov, conquered the republic of Novgorod, abolishing its ancient liberties and settling in its territories a considerable number of Muscovites.

The Tatar retreat

Domestic power struggles weakened the authority exerted from Sarai over the extended Khanate. Timur (Tamerlane) had dealt Mongol unity a mortal blow in the 1380s with his relentless campaigns against the Golden Horde. There followed a brief Tatar revival under Idiku, but centrifugal forces could not be contained. Between 1420 and 1480 major portions of the Tatar empire broke away: the Khanate of Sibir, the

ships. Isolation had led to parochialism. The seeds of enlightenment inherited from Kiev had fallen on rocky ground, and from the thirteenth to the fifteenth centuries there was a steady regression. Even princes were no longer educated men. Vasilii II was illiterate, and so was the majority of the clergy. Tatar rule and the murderous strife among the princes led to barbarization and to the spread of superstition. Early in the fifteenth century the Metropolitan Photius preached the coming end of the world: 'This brief age is passing. Night is approaching; the end of our existence.' Even the date was fixed: 1492.

Orthodoxy under attack

Fear and demoralization within the Church led to the appearance of heresies. About 1471 in Novgorod a number of priests began to preach unorthodox doctrines, for which they were given the name of Judaizers. They denied the Trinity and Incarnation, though accepting Jesus as a prophet. They also repudiated the sacraments and the hierarchy of the Church, and denied that the world would end in 1492. Important persons such as the future Metropolitan of Russia and a daughter-in-law of Ivan III either joined or were close to the sect. The reaction of the Church was swift and unequivocal. Gennadii, Bishop of Novgorod, set in motion the machinery of persecution. So intent was he on the task of exterminating the heretics

that in spite of all his Orthodoxy he found words of praise for the Spanish Inquisition.

Joseph Sanin, Abbot of the Volokolamsk monastery, seconded Gennadii, and 'threw himself like a lion to tear the entrails of those horrible heretics who had drunk Jewish poison . . . ' He became the most influential cleric of his day and left a deep mark on the history of the Russian Church. Joseph's approach to religion was formulaic and ritualistic. He saw the Church as the institution possessing a monopoly on truth and salvation. This institution must be closely associated with the state, reinforcing the latter and being protected by it in return.

Such views were disputed by the disciples of Nil Sorskii, one of the most remarkable individuals in the history of Russian Christianity. He was an unusually well-educated monk who had spent several years on Mount Athos, a center of contemplative monasticism in Greece. There he was exposed to Platonism, mysticism and to some Buddhist influences. Upon his return to Russia, Nil settled in solitude on the Sora River to cultivate the spirit, and hope for religious ecstasy and the vision of divine light. His fame spread. Small self-supporting groups of disciples began to arise in the trans-Volga forests.

Unlike Joseph, Abbot of Volokolamsk, Nil Sorskii preached internalized religion. Outward forms and rituals were less important to him than

Khanate of Kazan (c 1438), the Noghay Horde of southern Russia, the Crimea (1443), the Kazakh, the Uzbek and the Astrakhan Khanates, and finally Russia (1480).

The Tatar yoke had been imposed on Russia at the cost of enormous human, cultural and economic losses. Whole provinces were depopulated, towns and villages ceased to exist. The original Mongol invasion was sudden, thunderous and definitive. The liberation of Russia from Tatar domination was rather less dramatic. In 1476 Ivan III quietly stopped paying the customary tribute to the Tatar khan. In 1480 Ahmad Khan marched on Moscow. Ivan met the Tatars on the banks of the little Ugra River, preventing the enemy from making a crossing. Afraid of an attack by the Crimeans to his rear, Ahmad Khan dared not force battle. Ivan, beset by domestic troubles involving two of his own brothers, and fearing Lithuanian intervention, played for time. Neither army made a move until Ahmad Khan lost his nerve and withdrew. Thus, without even a battle, the Tatar yoke was quietly cast off.

On balance Russian historians have tended to minimize the significance of the Tatar period. They have claimed that essentially Russia's economic, political and cultural development was unaffected by almost 250 years of Mongol dominion, except in so far as it may have been retarded and perhaps warped in some minor aspects. Yet it is really not possible to believe that any nation could exist for such a long period of its history under the rule of another and not be significantly altered by the experience. In fact Russian political institutions, Russian law, Russian culture, even Russian family life, were affected by the Tatars. Moreover, Tatar influences increased, rather than diminished, after the liberation of Russia. Thousands of Tatars entered Muscovite service. Many received large estates, were baptized and joined the Russian nobility. It has been estimated that at the opening of the eighteenth century 17 percent of Russia's nobility was of Tatar origin. Russia even had a czar, Boris Godunov, whose ancestors were Tatar.

Cultural life in Russia under the Tatars had been stunted by political and economic hard-

states of the soul. Since the cultivation of the soul was a purely spiritual matter, the Church had no need of wealth and should not own land and serfs. For holding this view Nil's disciples became known as 'non-possessors' or, more correctly, 'non-acquirers.' Another significant idea which permeated Nil's teachings was that of freedom. Without freedom, he believed, there could be no merit in faith. And freedom in turn implied tolerance. The 'non-acquirers' were the only group that pleaded for such tolerance at the Church Council in 1490, when Joseph, and the Russian Church remained essentially Josephian. Yet the Sorskian strain survived in some monastic communities and for centuries to come continued to be an important component of Russian spirituality.

A turning-point in the history of Russian Christianity came in 1439, when the Greek Orthodox Church agreed to a union with Rome. This was widely denounced in Russia as a betrayal of the faith. The Metropolitan of Russia, Isidor, who accepted the union, was deposed and jailed by the Grand Prince. A new Metropolitan was appointed without the consent of the Patriarch of Constantinople, making the Russian Church entirely independent of the Greek Church. The fall of Constantinople in 1453 was then perceived as Divine punishment inflicted upon the Greeks for having abandoned 'true Christianity.'

In the eyes of the Russians, Moscow remained the only Christian kingdom on earth. Centuries of isolation, fear and mistrust of the aggressive Catholic West, hatred for the Islamized Tatars and ignorance about the rest of the world induced a sense of exclusiveness and superiority. The rise of a strong autocratic monarchy toward the end of the fifteenth century required the formulation of a theory that would account for the strange and unsettling experiences of the last hundred years. Such a theory was provided by Filofei, a Pskovian monk.

To Filofei history was the gradual unfolding of

Above left: Theophanes the Greek's icon *The Assumption*, a work completed in 1392 and a major example of the icon painter's *oeuvre*.

Right: Andrei Rublev, Russia's greatest painter of icons, executed *Trinity* for the Holy Trinity Monastery outside Moscow. Even though the once intense colors have faded, the icon remains a masterpiece.

Left: Another icon by Andrei Rublev, this depicting the Ascension of Christ. Most of Rublev's work was done in the cities of Moscow, Vladimir and Zvenigorod.

Right: The characteristic architecture of Russian churches – onion domes and sloping roofs – rendered here in wood, instead of the more familiar stucco-covered brick.

God's plan for mankind. History culminated in three successive world empires. The fall of the third of these would signal the end of the world and the arrival of the day of judgment. The first Rome had perverted the faith and was punished through its fall. The second Rome, Constantinople, had accepted the Roman heresy and had similarly been cast down. Now Russia remained the only Orthodox kingdom on earth, the third and last empire of the world. 'I pray thee,' Filofei addressed Vasilii II, 'listen for the sake of God, how all the Christian kingdoms have come together in your kingdom . . . Two Romes have fallen, the third stands and a fourth there shall not be. The ruler of Russia is the Czar (Caesar), the legitimate Emperor, who carries the double burden as Czar of Russia and keeper of Orthodoxy throughout the world. God-elected, God-crowned, pious and holy, he is a new Noah's ark in which the Church finds refuge from the flood.'

Russia's intellectual poverty under the Tatars, and for centuries after, stood in striking contrast to the vigor and beauty of Russian art. It was precisely in those dark years after the fall of Kiev that Russia found her own artistic language in wooden architecture and in icon painting. Byzantine models were still followed, but new native elements transformed them into something genuinely Russian.

Icon painting reached its summit in the works of Theophanes the Greek and Andrei Rublev. Theophanes (Feofan) came to Russia from Byzantium in the second half of the fourteenth century. Though he continued to work in the late Byzantine idiom, his icons also bore the imprint of his own strong individuality, projecting great spiritual power. But the greatest of all Russian painters, Andrei Rublev (c 1360-1430), was a younger contemporary of Feofan, by whom he was influenced. Yet Rublev's icons are not imitative. His elaborate compositions, full of Christian symbolism, breathe the spirit of quiet contemplation and ineffable joy.

Under Ivan III political fact and theory had fused to create the preconditions for a new type of autocracy in Russia. But it would be Ivan's son, Ivan IV or 'Terrible,' who would make czarism a reality.

The Asian World

The opposition between nomads and settled peoples has been one of the great dramas of human history, played out at many different times and places, but never on a grander scale than in Asia between the fourth and fourteenth centuries AD. Nomadic invasions had an overwhelming effect on the evolution of the major civilizations of Eurasia – in India, China, Iran and the eastern Mediterranean. The whole millennium can be envisaged as an interplay between the settled religions and cultures along the southern edge of the continent and the dynamic warriors propeled outward from the central steppes by some still uncomprehended centrifugal force.

Never numerically strong, the central Asian nomads achieved some astonishing successes. The Huns ravaged cities from deep in the Roman Empire to the Ganges; the Turks established durable regimes throughout western Asia – in Baghdad, Cairo and, eventually, Constantinople; and most remarkable of all, in the thirteenth century the Mongol hordes of Chingiz (Genghis) Khan and his successors ruled an empire that stretched from Peking to Kiev. Militarily, the Mongol warriors were virtually unbeatable. They were superb horsemen and expert bowmen, led into battle by chieftains who often showed great tactical skills. The Mongols successfully exploited massacre as a form of psychological warfare – many rich cities surrendered at their approach rather than suffer the well-publicized fate of those that resisted. But they are not to be remembered merely as fierce and cruel barbarians. They could give many of the 'civilized' rulers lessons in religious and racial tolerance, and at the height of Mongol power an unprecedented peace and security reigned along the trade routes to China.

Yet the nomads could not replace the settled civilizations with anything of their own. If their rule was to endure, it could only be through adopting the culture and religion of the lands they had entered or conquered. Once in power, the nomads employed local officials and inevitably bowed to local customs. If not, their triumph was shortlived. The Mongol Empire, although prosperous and massive in extent, quickly fragmented into the cultures of its component parts, It straddled civilizations, but could not unite them.

By the seventeenth century, the highly civilized rulers of the eastern Mediterranean (the Ottoman Empire), northern India and Iran were all of central Asian nomad stock. Yet they showed few signs of the customs or beliefs of their nomadic ancestors. The nomads had conquered the settled civilizations, but settled civilization had slowly but irrevocably triumphed over nomadism.

The persistence of civilizations in Asia is itself an astonishing phenomenon. In both India and China, basic patterns of belief and social organization established well before the birth of Christ persisted through to modern times. Chinese medieval history is a tale of extraordinary vicissitudes, including submission to Mongol conquest, yet through it all Chinese society retained an unshakeable sense of cultural identity. After each upheaval the idea of a strong centralized bureaucracy, and the cultural ideal of Confucianism, reasserted itself against the forces of disorder. Although reinterpreted to meet new needs, Confucianism remained a consistent basis for government and society until the twentieth century. And although for much of this period the Chinese emperors ruled only part of China, the memory of the full extent of the territory proper to the Chinese Empire was never lost.

Yet the powerful capacity for self-perpetuation in Chinese culture also embodied a conservatism, a resistance to change. There is little doubt that under the rule of the medieval T'ang and Sung Dynasties, China had the most advanced civilization in the world. It excelled in the size and wealth of its cities, the sophistication of its cultural life, and the cultivation of the arts of government. A whole range of inventions was made that would later transform the world. – printing, gunpowder, paper money, navigational devices. But strong forces of conservatism within Chinese society stopped these having their full impact, and it would be Europeans who exploited the new inventions to achieve world domination.

Whereas in China the idea of unity was never lost, in India such an idea was never found. No single empire would rule the subcontinent until the British in the nineteenth century. The north of India was open to invasion from central Asia, and thus by the fourteenth century had come under the dominance of Muslim rulers of nomadic origin. In the south, Hindu kingdoms rose and fell, expanded and contracted according to their own rhythm. The Europeans who arrived in the sixteenth century would be impressed by the wealth and splendor of India compared with their native continent. But India's political weaknesses and divisions were a profound fact of its history.

Japan stood at the opposite extreme, a state remarkable from its earliest days for its sense of unity and resistance to invasion. The site of a rather late flowering of civilization under Chinese influence in around the sixth century AD, Japan developed a unique political system focused on an emperor who was both deified and powerless, a sacred figurehead who guaranteed the unity of Japan through all political conflict and civil war. The succession of emperors remained unbroken as Japan evolved from a Chinese-style centralized bureaucracy to rule by a refined court aristocracy, and then to a form of feudalism under the military rule of the shoguns.

Despite the original influence of China on Japanese culture and the impact of the imported beliefs of Buddhism, the main theme of Japanese history is its isolation from outside influences, its literal and metaphorical insularity. In the thirteenth century Mongol invaders were repulsed; in the seventeenth century, the door was slammed in the face of European traders and missionaries. Yet surprisingly, in this isolation Japan developed a social system and mental attitudes that proved amazingly adaptable and resilient.

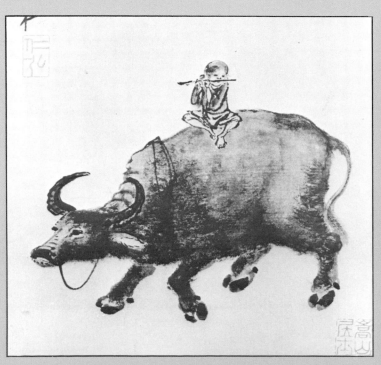

Far left: A Chinese painting of the Sung Dynasty (AD 960-1280), showing a shepherd boy playing the flute while sitting on the back of a water buffalo.

Left: This Indian painting depicts Dhyanibodhisattva Shadaknavi sitting beneath the Buddha. Although disfigured over the course of time this work is typical of Indian religious art, and its florid intensity makes a striking contrast with the delicate lyricism of the Chinese illustration (*far left*).

Right: The Mongol conqueror Ghingiz (Genghis) Khan lectures the survivors of the recently sacked city of Bokhara, warning them that he is the Punishment of God. Some 20,000 people were slaughtered when the Mongols captured the city.

The Nomads of Central Asia

For about 1000 years, from roughly AD 400 to 1400, the theme of recurrent invasion by Central Asian nomads runs like a leitmotif through the histories of all the major centers of civilization in Eurasia. Even in the remote west, where the physical impact of these invasions was never felt, the imaginations of Western Europeans continued for centuries to be haunted by fearsome images of Attila's Huns, Chingiz Khan's Mongols and Timur's Tatars.

In our accounts of pre-Muslim Iran, the later Roman Empire and Byzantium, of China, India and Islam, we have perforce treated the nomads in a somewhat fragmentary way, describing how they affected the particular civilizations or areas under discussion and viewing them, as it were, from the inside looking out. In this brief chapter we shall try to paint a somewhat broader and more coherent picture of the history of the steppe peoples. And because these nomads affected such a large geographical area for such a long period of time, we may, in the process, even gain some useful perspectives on Eurasian history as a whole.

The Eurasian pastoral zones

To appreciate the nomad phenomenon, it is first necessary to have an understanding of the geography of the primary pastoral zones and their physical relationships to the settled regions with which they communicated. The vast stretches of Central Asia may appear devoid of form or detail on the common political maps of Eurasia. But far from constituting a single amorphous mass they have an intricate physical and ecological configuration of their own which bears an intimate relationship to the dispositions of the principal nomadic communities and the pattern of their movements.

Providing the basic bone structure to the region is, first of all, the massive system of mountains which run in an arc through the area from north to south: the Altai of western Mongolia; the Tien Shan, Pamirs and Hindu Kush, which stretch along the border of Sinkiang and into present-day Afghanistan; and the Himalayas, which mark the southern border of Tibet. Cutting horizontally through this arc of mountains is another type of physical barrier, a line of deserts stretching from the Gobi of Mongolia to the Taklamakan of Sinkiang and the Kizil Kum and Kara Kum of Russian Turkestan. These two lines of physical barriers intersect, creating four distinct quadrants: above the desert line, to the east, lie the steppelands of Mongolia, and to the west, the steppelands of Turkestan. Below the line of deserts lie arid plateau zones, Inner Mongolia and Sinkiang in the east and southern Turkestan and northern Afghanistan in the west. While the northern steppelands became the true home of Inner Asian nomads, the plateau regions to the south gave rise to a mixed pastoral and oasis culture in which the nomads played a considerable role.

From ancient times two routes passed through Central Asia, permitting travel and migration between the western and eastern quadrants. To the north the wide steppes of Mongolia and Turkestan offered a passage for migratory tribes. To the south, following a line of isolated oasis communities into the high valleys of the Hindu Kush and over the Pamirs into the Tarim Basin of Sinkiang,

passed the caravan route used by traders and religious adventurers. The first was historically the route of conquest, the second the route of commerce and cultural contact between the distant centers of civilization in Europe, Iran, India and China.

Throughout recorded history the heartland of the Huns, Turks, Mongols and Tungus has been the area in northern Mongolia to the east of the headwaters of the Orkhon River. It is out of this region that major nomadic conquerors and empire-builders were to emerge: the Hsiung-nu of the second century BC, who later appear in the west as Huns; the Hsien-pei of the third century AD; the Juan-juan of the fifth; the T'u-chueh of the sixth; the Uighurs of the eighth; the Khitan of the tenth; the Jurched of the twelfth; and the Mongols of the thirteenth. We do not know for sure whether this sequence of nomadic peoples of different ethnic origin simply represented shifts in leadership from one to another group within an existing heterogeneous steppe society or whether it was indicative of periodic changes in the composition of the nomadic community as a whole, possibly through the infiltration of the steppes by peoples from the even more distant forest lands of Siberia. The first possibility seems a more likely one on the basis of what we know about the Mongols. The total human population of the area in question was remarkably thin, so that changes in dominant leadership could be accomplished by relatively small groups over short periods of time. Mongolia today supports under two persons per square mile and the entire Mongolian People's Republic has a population of under a million per-

sons. The Mongols at the height of their drive for empire during the thirteenth century could hardly have numbered over half a million in all. It was not their numbers or their wealth that gave the pastoral tribes the capacity to become world conquerors, but rather the nature of nomadic life and culture, particularly the military striking power they were capable of assembling. And it was an accompanying axiom that the nomads, because of their limited numbers, remained weak in their staying power. Their dynasties of conquest were shortlived, and they as conquerors were quickly assimilated into the greater mass of the societies they so easily devastated.

Nomadism is a distinct way of life contrasting fundamentally with that of the agricultural villages or the urban concentrations of China, India and Iran. The Central Asian Turks and Mongols lived basically on a sheep and cattle economy supplemented by the breeding of horses or camels for their own transportation and for trade. Herding conditioned the life of the nomad. From his flocks he devised a rough, though relatively self-sufficient, economy. He wore sheepskins or other furs for clothing and lived in movable tents made from wool felt. His basic diet was mutton and cheese, butter and alcoholic *kumis* made from the milk of his flocks. His flocks and herds even provided him with fuel in the form of dried dung. Horses, or in some areas camels, gave him mobility for the management of his flocks, for hunting and for warfare. This pastoral economy had only a minimal dependence upon the products of the settled societies. Some grain was always desirable to supplant an exclusively animal diet, and there was

Below left: The earliest of the central Asian nomad groups to have an impact on history were the Scythians of southern Russia. They first appear in the seventh-century BC as the rulers of the lands between Mesopotamia and the Caucasus Mountains. The graves of their leaders were rich in treasure and artifacts, such as this linen shirt found in a burial place dating from the fifth-century BC.

Above: A detail from a Scythian saddle cloth shows a griffin, a mythical beast closely associated with that people, killing a ram.

Above right: The Scythians were master metalworkers, and often depicted scenes from everyday life on the objects they made. This pectoral chain is decorated with a herdsman milking a goat.

Right: The camp was the focus of the life of the nomad tribes of Asia. This Persian illustration shows Mongols moving camp.

Far right: A view of the pectoral chain shown in close-up above. It dates from the fourth-century BC and was found at a burial place in the Ukraine.

need for manufactured goods such as cloth and metals for tools and weapons. Thus while the nomad developed a way of life which was fundamentally incompatible with that of the populated agricultural lands and commercial centers, he remained connected with the frontiers of the civilized world because of his dependence on its products which he obtained legitimately by trade or forcibly as tribute or by plunder.

In the pastoral economy many of the routine chores of managing the camp and tending flocks and herds were handled by the women. The men could thus devote themselves to the more rugged tasks of rounding up herds, hunting and warfare. Brought up in the saddle, inured to life in the open with minimum shelter, trained to live off the land, the nomad men developed great individual strength and capacity for endurance. Their skills at riding and hunting were easily converted to the needs of warfare. While the peasants of the agricultural villages could not leave their fields during the growing season, the men of the steppe were free to join in hunt or battle at almost any time. As warriors their superior ability as horsemen and their frightening accuracy with the bow made them the most formidable fighters in the world until the advent of modern firearms. All that remained to form the nomads into formidable conquerors was leadership and incentive.

The traditional structure of nomadic society provided the basis for effective military organization and territorial control. At the foundation of this organization was the nomadic camp in which groups of families lived together in a tightly knit kinship or quasi-kinship. Such units, in varying numbers, were further joined into clans and clans into tribes, or, as they were frequently referred to in European literature, 'hordes.' The Mongols applied the term *ulus* to both the tribal confederacy and the territory it occupied. Under the Mongols, at least, nomadic society was strongly differentiated between families of aristocratic lineage and the general mass of common tribesmen and others of servile or slave status. This hierarchic relationship, sometimes characterized as a kind of 'nomadic vassalage,' was not personal but applied to the camp or clan as a whole – the subordinate group providing services for the superior in the form of assistance in setting up tents, tending herds and performing military service. Within the *ulus* superior tribal chieftains could grant or guarantee subordinate chiefs their authority over still more subordinate levels of vassal camps.

Nomad political organization did not stop at the level of the tribal *ulus*. Across the Inner Asian steppes there developed a number of loose, but nonetheless persistent, traditions of regional rulership which permitted powerful chieftains to appear from time to time at the head of tribal confederations capable of unifying major subdivisions of the steppe or even all of Inner Asia. Hordes, in other words, could be united into a steppeland nation. The Hsiung-nu, who dominated Mongolia and menaced the Chinese frontier from the third century BC, acknowledged the authority of a supreme leader, who according

to the Chinese bore the title *shang-yü*. Among the Juan-juan, during the fourth century, the term *Khaghan* came into use to refer to the supreme chieftain of Mongolia. By the time of the Mongols a difference had grown up between the status of *Khaghan*, or supreme ruler, and *khan*, or ruler of a division of the great *Khaghan*'s empire.

Thus from early times it appears that the Turks and Mongols recognized the ideal of a national unity, an empire within the steppe. The horde or *ulus* might generally stand independently under the leadership of its *khan*, but from time to time a leader of sufficient stature would emerge who could forge a steppeland confederation and claim the title of *Khaghan*. Such was Chingiz Khan, the creator of the Mongol Empire. It is from the example of this great domain, and particularly from the evidence of its breakup and dissolution, that we are able to get a sense of the several major geographical divisions acknowledged by the nomadic peoples of Inner Asia. These divisions followed closely the contours of the four topographical and human-geographical quadrants which we identified within the Inner Asian landmass. Mongolia, as the traditional homeland of the Mongol peoples, was prized as the heartland of the nomadic way of life and was retained as the *ulus* of the *Khaghan*, generally serving as the base from which control was exercised over Inner Mongolia and North China. Sinkiang (Chinese Turkestan), the ancient home of the Uighurs, became the main base of the Khanate of Chaghatai. Russian Turkestan, above the desert line, served as the base from which the vast western Khanate of Qipchaq (the Golden Horde) was held.

Turkestan, below the steppe and the western portion of Afghanistan, formed the base from which the Mongols took over Iran, creating the Il-Khanate.

The steppe and cultivated lands

In the long history of the interaction of the steppe and the cultivated lands, the majority of so-called barbarians who menaced the frontiers of civilization were nomadic societies of mixed cultural background, groups which, unlike the Huns and the Mongols, had previously moved into the buffer zones between the pastoral and agricultural societies and had thereby absorbed some aspects of sedentary life and manner of government. By 'buffer zone' we mean such areas as inner Mongolia, just outside the Great Wall of China; the oasis settlements of the Tarim Basin and north of the Hindu Kush in Khurasan and Mawarannahr; the mountainous areas of Afghanistan bordering India; and in Europe the territory just to the east of the Rhine and on either side of the Danube. Standing between the true steppe and the great centers of civilization, these areas played an important role in the relationship between the nomadic and sedentary societies.

During the centuries when the classical civilizations were in their prime, political and military control of the border regions tended to accrue to the sedentary empires, and cultural influence flowed outward into the Asian marches. Thus from the time of Iranian expansion in the sixth century BC the regions between the Iranian plateau and the high ranges of Central Asia were considered integral and necessary parts of the Persian

Below far left: In 221 BC the Chinese emperor Tsin Chi Hwang-t'i built the Great Wall to keep out the nomads inhabiting the steppelands north of China. The system worked reasonably well for over a thousand years, but in 1213 it could not keep out the army of Chingiz (Genghis) Khan.

Below left: Gold pendants that once belonged to one of the queens of Scythia.

Right: This Scythian ornament, made of gold, is of a coiled panther. Inlays of precious stones once filled its eyes, nostrils, ear, claws and tail.

conception of empire. By the time of Cyrus (550–30 BC) the Inner Asian frontiers of the Persian Empire stretched from the Jaxartes (present Syr Darya) to the Indus, and the tradition that subsequent empires should achieve the same boundaries was firmly established. It was largely through Persian initiative that the remarkable irrigation works upon which the stable agrarian base of the interior city communities rested were brought into being. When in the fourth century BC control of these communities passed to the Greeks of Alexander and his successors, they continued to prosper as military colonies and as administrative centers of the far-flung Macedonian conquests. Alexander's empire soon fell apart, but Greek ruling houses continued in such areas as Bactria and Gandhara down to the second century, and with them Greek influence persisted. During the period from roughly the second century BC to the fifth century AD, the eastern marches passed out of Iranian control. The interior regions entered a new phase in their history, during which they were either able to stand alone as independent political entities or were brought under influences emanating from India.

It was during the third century BC that the Huns (known to the Chinese as Hsiung-nu), having formed a powerful coalition of tribes on the northwest frontier of China, came under attack by the military forces of an expanding Chinese Empire. The Hunnish coalition was pushed westward into what is now Jungaria. As a result two groups of pastoral tribes, known to the Chinese as the Sai-wang, the Saca of Bactrian history, and Yüeh-chih, or Tochari in Western sources, were thrust out of Chinese Turkestan. By 125 BC the Saca had taken the region of Khurasan, whence they expanded their control westward around the Hindu Kush to the western part of present-day Afghanistan into the region of Sistan. By the middle of the next century they had penetrated India and could boast an empire that stretched from the Amu Darya to the eastern side of the Indus. Meanwhile the Tochari had moved into the high territory between the upper Syr Darya and Amu Darya. From there they gradually spread out to eliminate the Saca. By the first century AD the Tochari had established the Kushan Empire, a vast Inner Asian state that extended from the Ganges valley in India to the banks of the Syr Darya and from Sistan to the Tarim Basin. The Kushan Empire provided one of the few instances in history when Inner Asia on both sides of the Pamirs was united under an indigenous ruling house.

Yet the Kushan rulers also had their prime orientation toward one of the high civilizations, in this case India. By the reign of Kanishka (perhaps AD 78-96) the primary base of the Kushan Empire was the Punjab in northern India. As a consequence Indian cultural influence and the Buddhist religion permeated the areas under Kushan control. The conversion of the whole zone of populated centers along the trade routes from the frontiers of Iran to China was to prove a significant episode in the history of Inner Asia, if only for the terrible religious persecutions which were to come to the region in the wake of subsequent invasion by Huns, Turks and Muslim Arabs. Whole Buddhist communities were slaughtered by the Hunnish conquerors and thriving monasteries were destroyed and works of art defaced by Turks and Arabs of later centuries. By the middle of the sixth century the area had been forcibly returned to its earlier Iranian orientation, and by the end of the seventh century the region had been thoroughly converted to Islam.

Building the Great Wall

The border zone to the east of the Pamirs (Chinese Turkestan) had a somewhat different history. China was more remote from the Pamirs, so that the Chinese presence in the Tarim Basin tended to be less heavy-handed. Nonetheless the area was very much a part of the Chinese consciousness of empire. Control of the interior border lands was presumed to be a necessary concomitant to a secure dynasty. Or if they could not be controled, at least the maintenance of the Great Wall defenses was necessary as a protective device.

The Great Wall, first created into a unified defensive system by the emperor of the Ch'in Dynasty in 221 BC, and frequently rebuilt, relocated and extended by later dynasties, has remained to this day as remarkable evidence of Chinese concern with the 'barbarian menace' to the north and west. The wall, however, was a passive device, and vigorous Chinese emperors pursued a more positive Inner Asian policy. During the two Han Dynasties (202 BC – AD 220) suppression of the Huns and control of the silk route were major dynastic objectives. Under the Emperor Wu Ti, of the former Han Dynasty, Chinese armies went on the offensive against the Huns and from time to time asserted Chinese suzerainty over the oasis cities of the Tarim Basin. It was this Chinese aggressiveness that began the chain-reaction that started the Saca and Tochari conquests west of the Pamirs. A century and a half later, during the Later Han Dynasty, the Chinese general Pan Ch'ao (32-120) again established Chinese control over Chinese Turkestan. With the collapse of the Han Dynasty in the third century, the Chinese presence in Turkestan faded. Not until four centuries later did the emperors of the T'ang Dynasty again send Chinese troops into Mongolia and the Tarim Basin. But the T'ang thrust led to no lasting Chinese control and evaporated once the dynasty relaxed its military policy.

Geography was clearly against the Chinese presence in the Tarim area, for the region lay both far beyond even the terminus of the Great Wall and across the fearsome Taklamakan desert. Historically, therefore, such cities as Kashgar and Khotan remained more accessible from the west, and the cities themselves were inhabited mainly by people of Iranian or Indian cultural orientation. In the end it took a dynasty of nomadic origin, the Manchus, to bring Chinese Turkestan securely within Chinese administration as the 'New Province' (Sinkiang), and this only in 1757.

Thus until comparatively recent times, between the Great Wall and the Pamirs to the west, Mongolia to the north and Tibet to the south, great open stretches of Inner Asia remained largely the domain of nomadic tribes. To a considerable extent, therefore, China's relationship with the 'barbarians' on its marches was more similar to that which existed on the northern and eastern frontiers of the late Roman Empire. Frontier tribes remained in a state of pastoral existence unless they settled down on the frontier marches, often by invitation from Chinese dynasties who wished to build up a belt of friendly 'barbarians' to defend against still more dangerous groups behind them. Such semi-sinicized groups, rather than giving rise to steppe- or oasis-based empires, tended instead, when the opportunity presented itself, to move into North China to create dynasties of their own in the Chinese image.

By the fourth century the pastoral tribes of Central Asia were in particularly vigorous motion, and the settled communities throughout Eurasia were to be subjected to over a thousand years of periodic disruption by nomadic invaders. While the movement seems to have had its original impetus in the high Mongolian homelands of the Turks and Mongols, it was to affect the frontiers of all the sedentary societies from China and India to Iran and Europe. Furthermore, in the midst of this general acceleration of the activities of the Turko-Mongol pastoral peoples, a powerful explosion from among the nomadic population of Arabia was also literally to remake the Iranian world. What brought on this particular phenomenon of nomadic restlessness and expansion is a matter of controversy among historians. Did it have a climatic origin, the result of a possible desiccation of the steppe which forced the pastoral tribes into more aggressive competition for grazing lands and plunder? Or was it the reverse, the increased accumulation of surpluses of food and manpower within the steppe communities, which made it possible for them to expand their hori-

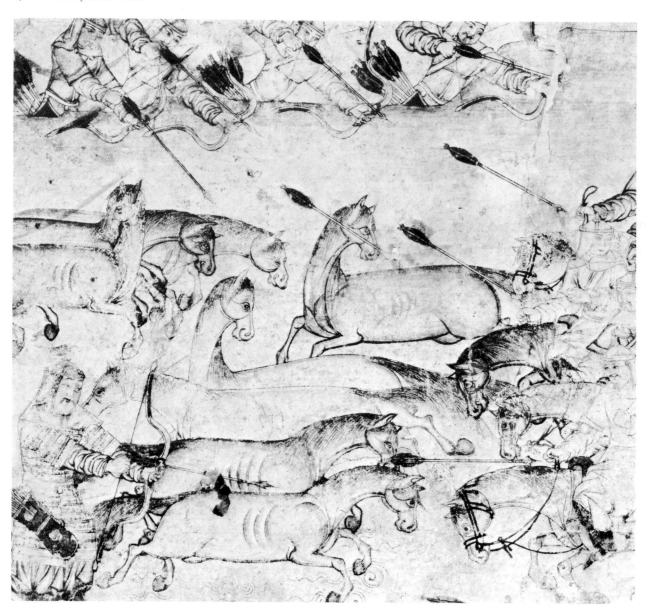

Left: A Persian manuscript illustration showing a fortress under a nomad army's attack. The individual soldiers each had a string of horses to enable the changing of mounts at regular intervals. Here they are used to upset the aim of the archers on the walls.

Right: A Scythian wall-hanging shows a mounted warrior approaching his seated leader. It is thought by scholars that the man on the throne could be a representation of Alexander the Great, who set a fashion for being clean-shaven.

zons? Was it a matter of technology, the development of the iron stirrup by the nomads, so that for a millennium the mounted archer was master of the battlefield? Was it due to a general raising of the cultural and economic level of the Inner Asian peoples by fruitful periods of contact with higher civilizations and their agrarian economies? There is no clear answer, and the steppeland conquerors themselves have left no evidence to assist us in our answer.

Invasion and assimilation

Several points are clear, however. While the image of the Huns and Mongols driving out of high Mongolia toward their terrible missions of plunder and slaughter has stuck in the historical imagination, the more prevalent pattern of barbarian takeover was that of infiltration and assimilation. Indeed, long-established buffer zones played a significant role in facilitating the Mongol conquest, for the Mongol Empire was fashioned only after the prior formation of dynasties of conquest in China by the T'o-pa, Khitan and Jurched and in Iran by the Seljuq Turks. The Mongols, in other words, were not an isolated phenomenon but rather the culmination of a process.

Another point to bear in mind is that the dividing line between barbarism and civilization can be a subjective matter. This was illustrated in a famous exchange between Emperor Ch'ien-lung of China (himself a Manchu) and King George III of Great Britain in 1793 in which Ch'ien-lung rather contemptuously accorded the British sove-

reign the same status of 'barbarian' as those nomadic leaders who had approached the Celestial Empire from across the Great Wall. As modern historians have looked more intently into the conditions of so-called barbarian rule their attention has been attracted more by the evidence of superior qualities of leadership and organization than to the lack of civilizing amenities. It is well to remember the many times in history when barbarian leaders moved from the frontiers to the centers of civilization by invitation, as mercenary fighters or as 'protectors.' Thus Turkish slave armies had long been fighting for the Abbasid Caliphs before the Seljuqs moved in upon the dynasty itself.

The ease with which Turkish tribes on the eastern and northern frontiers of Iran infiltrated Iranian society leads to a final observation about the nomadic phenomenon. A common statement made about the movements of the Mongols and Turks is that they tended to move from east to west along what is called an 'east-west gradient.' The concept is less than helpful for it leads to the view that the Inner Asian environment itself propeled the nomadic people from out of the high Mongolian steppe toward Iran and the Caspian. Although there is no easy answer to why groups like the Huns, Mongols and Turks tended to push westward once they moved out of Mongolia, one important factor is surely the contrasting reception given to such groups by the Chinese people and the Iranians. On the Chinese side of the Mongolian plateau the reception was consistently hos-

tile, and the Great Wall, symbolic of China's separatism and ethnocentricity, had come into being as a barrier against barbarian incursion as early as the third century BC. The nomadic groups emerging from Mongolia in an easterly direction found few transitional way-points on the way to China and met physical barriers of considerable effectiveness. But no wall attempted to prevent the nomads from crossing the Syr Darya or descending the Pamirs into the valleys of Afghanistan, and on the western side the irrigation agriculturalists were far readier to try to coexist, both economically and culturally, with the pastoralists.

China and its nomadic frontiers

To be sure, when we speak of China we must make a distinction between North China and the Chinese heartland in the South. With the disintegration of the Han Empire and the formation of weak successor states, Chinese pressure on the frontier was relaxed, and the way was open for gradual penetration of North China by the peoples of the steppe. During the time of the Three Kingdoms (220-65), for instance, Chinese rulers began the practice of alliance with the Hsiung-nu of the South in much the same manner that the late Roman emperors allied themselves with Gothic and Frankish leaders. As military confederates of the Chinese rulers in North China during the Three Kingdoms period, Hunnish Hsiung-nu leaders were invited inside the Wall, and their followers were permitted to settle in the Ordos region. Thus began the gradual infiltration of

North China by Turkish, Mongol and Tungusic tribesmen and the eventual displacement of Chinese rule north of the Huai River by various mixed regimes established by warlord leaders of nomadic origin.

The similarity between China's period of 'barbarian' conquest and that of Europe after the Germanic takeover of the Roman Empire in the west is striking. The retreat of Chinese civilization south of the Yangtze River is also in some ways analogous to the shift of power to the Eastern Roman Empire when the West was succumbing to barbarian pressure. But in the long run the outcome at the two ends of the Eurasian continent was to be quite different. For while barbarian invaders freely overran North China, they seem to have had less impact on changing the fundamentally agrarian economy and the ethnic composition of the Chinese substructure. The conquest dynasties seem, furthermore, to have accepted the Chinese imperial ideal once they were in power, ruling in the Chinese manner and encouraging Chinese cultural institutions. South China, as a reservoir of the Chinese way of life, remained vigorous and accessible and bulked ever larger in the total balance between North and South. Thus by the sixth century the Chinese empire had recreated itself, and the barbarians had been absorbed into a new and vigorous revival of the Chinese tradition.

One significant feature in the fourth- and fifth-century period of 'barbarian' regimes in North China is that while a succession of nomadic tribal leaders were able to establish themselves within the Great Wall, none ever succeeded, as did the later Mongols and Manchus, in combining control over both the high Mongolian steppe and the North China Plain. On the contrary, as these leaders established themselves within the Wall they tended to become defenders of their sinified regimes against pressures from out of the very steppe they had recently left. The most successful of these regimes, that of the Northern Wei (386-534), has been likened to that of the Franks under Clovis, both for its patronage of a new religion and for its defense of the earlier imperial tradition.

While movement out of Mongolia was blocked in the direction of China by the Wei consolidation, regions to the west were less resistant to nomadic infiltration. The Juan-juan confederacy spread westward north of the Tien Shan range out of Jungaria. And at about the same time several sequences of tribal eruptions thrust nomadic hordes westward and southward. What set these various groups in motion is not known, though Juan-juan pressure may have been one of the reasons. At any rate the Huns brought devastation in the wake of their several waves of conquest. In Europe, having penetrated to the environs of Rome, the Huns faded back to the Russian steppe after Attila's death in 453. In India the Huns began their raids in the early fifth century. The Hephthalites, having conquered a territory roughly equivalent to the second-century Kushan Empire, and having aided in the destruction of the Gupta Dynasty of India, passed from the scene after roughly a century. They are remembered chiefly for the terrible persecution which they visited upon the Buddhist priesthood of the former Kushan territories.

That Iranian civilization succeeded in withstanding these nomadic pressures on its frontier, confining the Hephthalites to the region between the Amu Darya and the Pamirs, may well be, as some historians have suggested, the result of the early development by the Sasanid Dynasty of a superior defensive mechanism, the heavily

armored mounted warrior. The creation of a localized military aristocracy in Iran in which land holding was tied to military service appears to have proven the effective weapon against the lighter nomad cavalry many centuries before the feudal knight made his appearance in Europe.

Following the subsidence of the Hunnish push into central and western Asia and the stabilization of the frontiers by mixed regimes on the Chinese, Central Asian and European borders, the Inner Asian steppelands returned to a condition of internal competition among a number of tribal coalitions of moderate size. No predominant power emerged to join these groups together, nor were the nomadic tribes to exert great pressure upon their outer frontiers for another four or five centuries.

Sedentary ascendancy

Whether the containment of the steppe was due to internal division and lack of energy on the part of the Inner Asian tribes or because of the stiffening defense put up by the major centers of civilization cannot be said for certain. Yet it is a fact that the sedentary societies showed renewed signs of strength at about this time all across Eurasia. In China the T'ang Dynasty rewon the empire inside the Wall, and by the seventh century had matched the exploits of the Han armies in Central Asia. The Kansu corridor was again secured and the Tarim Basin oasis communities accepted Chinese, rather than Turko-Mongolian, suzerainty. T'ang emperors between 626 and 683 sent powerful Chinese armies into Mongolia against the T'u-chüeh, exacerbating the rift between the Eastern and Western Khanates. Meanwhile, from the other side of the Pamirs, Arab conquests in the name of Islam had reinvigorated the Iranian empire under the new Abbasid Caliphate. Arab control over the border lands of Mawarannahr, Khurasan and Afghanistan was achieved between 657 and 751. The historic battle on the River Talas in 751, in which an Arab army defeated a Chinese expeditionary force under Kao Hsien-chih, definitively turned back the Chinese thrust into the region beyond the Tien Shan.

Whether Chinese control of Central Asia could have been retained indefinitely, given the great effort required to maintain the Chinese presence in the area, is doubtful. At any rate loss of Chinese interest in the area after 751 meant that Irano-Muslim influence now flowed unopposed into the high oasis communities which had, since the days of Kushan rule, existed as an extension of the Indo-Buddhist world.

China's loss of initiative in Central Asia served to relax pressure upon the steppes of Outer Mongolia, and again a series of tribal confederacies of considerable magnitude came into being in the lands beyond the Great Wall. During the period from the middle of the eighth century to the middle of the ninth the dominant power was held by the Uighurs, a dynasty of Turkish leaders who had taken over the territories of the eastern T'u-chüeh. The supreme Uighur leader took the title of *Khaghan*, or supreme *khan*, and established a great tent city on the banks of the Orkhon. It was the Uighurs who helped in the reconstitution of the T'ang Dynasty after the An Lu-shan rebellion and as a result the Uighur *Khaghan* remained in close relations with the Chinese court. The cultural advances made by the Uighur aristocracy are illustrated by their conversion to Nestorian Christianity and their subsequent patronage of Nestorian monasteries and religious art in the region of the Tarim oases.

The Uighurs confined themselves exclusively to Central Asia, lingering on into the twelfth century as masters of the Tarim Basin. As they lost ground westward new tribal coalitions appeared in their wake as masters of the Mongolian heartlands. Succeeding first to the Uighur dominance in Mongolia was a group called the Khitan, who established themselves in the region of Inner Mongolia between Manchuria and the Great Wall. There they created a mixed pastoral-agricultural state that stretched from the Orkhon to a belt of prefectures within the Great Wall. Having organized their domain in 947 as the Liao Dynasty, in imitation of the Chinese system of imperial rule, the Khitan provided a classical illustration of what the Chinese called a dynasty of conquest and its dual system of government. To govern the sedentary portions of their empire the Yeh-lu tribe set up a Chinese-style bureaucracy with its own prime minister, central administration and provincial branches. But the Khitan tribesmen made an effort to resist sinification, and the Liao emperor continued the habit of conducting his administration from his tent capital during the hunting months.

Even more fully sinicized than the Liao was the Chinese state that replaced Khitan rule in 1115. Created by the Jürched, the Chin domain was larger than the one it displaced, adding all of Manchuria and of North China below the Yellow River to the banks of the Hwai. Under the Jürched 'barbarian' control of China was strengthened by the practice of settling Jürched tribesmen on Chinese soil as a superior military caste. Distributed on pieces of tax-free land assigned to them by the government, the Jürched tribesmen were expected to use the resources of the land to maintain their military readiness and be available for instant call from their regional commanders.

The Jürched effort to hold a domain on both sides of the Great Wall tended increasingly to orient them toward China and away from the steppe. Once established as a dynasty within the Wall, in fact, the Jürched found themselves on the defensive against more aggressive tribes from farther Mongolia. Thus we find them engaging in a massive extension of the Great Wall defenses, creating a palisade and ditch barrier which stretched from the great bend in the Yellow River far into northern Manchuria as a defense against the threats of Tatar and Mongol tribes of the interior.

Across the Tien Shan and the Pamirs, Turkish and Mongolian tribes tended to coexist with the Iranian farmers along the broad frontier where irrigation agriculture interpenetrated with

Left: The backbone of the Mongol armies was the lightly equipped horseman armed with a bow. They would skirmish with the enemy to tempt him into making rash charges. Once the opponent was exhausted by the Mongol delaying tactics, the nomads would close in to finish him off.

Below: The Mongols built a huge empire extending across the Eurasian land-mass. In 1274 they attempted the conquest of Japan, but were forced to withdraw when their arrow-supply ran low. This is an illustration from a Japanese scroll made to celebrate their victory; it shows Mongols under Japanese fire. A second Mongol attempt in 1281 was defeated by the *kamikaze* storm that destroyed the Mongol fleet.

Far right: Ögetei, second son and a successor to Chingiz Khan.

pastureland. The habit, moreover, from the time of the Abbasid Dynasty, of using slave armies recruited from among frontier tribesmen created a very different relationship between the steppe tribes and the established centers of civilization in Iran. Where strong leaders grew up among the assimilated groups on the frontiers, they were able to take over the centers of Iranian power directly, without the necessity of first establishing separate frontier states. The Abbasid Empire was in fact twice revivified through takeover by Turkish military dynasties that came in by conquest. Both dynasties, the Seljuk and Khwarazm

shahs, quickly identified with the territories over which they had acquired dominion. And as both dynasties were staunchly Muslim, the sense of identification with local tradition was complete.

The gradual Turkish infiltration south of the Aral, Caspian and Black seas actually led to a return of nomadism into areas which had once laboriously been captured from the steppe by industrious Iranian peasants. The spread of Turkish peoples into these regions also served to change the ethnic composition of the zone, which stretched from Anatolia to Turkestan in a way that was never done in China. It was during these

centuries that the ethnic base was laid for the great Ottoman Empire and for the existence of modern Turkey. China below the Wall, on the other hand, remained ethnically unaffected even by the Manchu takeover.

Golden Age of the Mongols

By the end of the twelfth century conditions throughout Eurasia in the arid steppes of Mongolia, in the border regions of mixed economy and in the traditional centers of sedentary civilization, favored the appearance of a strong Inner Asian power. The pastoral tribes of the high steppes were disunited to be sure, but their disunity consisted of rivalries among a number of powerful tribal confederations. Recent absorption of cultural and technological improvements from China and Iran, along with a rise in standards of living through trade, gave to these peoples a new capacity for conquest. On their outer frontiers lay a broad zone of border states under the leadership of semi-pastoral people: the Chin and Hsi Hsia north of China, the Uighurs and Qarakhitan of Turkestan, the Khazar and Qipchaq tribes beyond the Caspian. Beyond the frontier states neither China under the Sung Dynasty nor Iran under the Khwarazmshahs appeared capable of offering particularly vigorous resistance to the military forces of the steppe nomads. It was Chingiz (Genghis) Khan's destiny to provide the catalyst to unify the tribal energies of the steppeland peoples and to channel the military and organizational capacities of these peoples to the task of world conquest.

The future Chingiz Khan was born between 1155 and 1167 as Temujin, of the aristocratic Borjigin clan of Outer Mongolia. Two generations earlier the clan chief, Temujin's grandfather, had laid claim to the title of *Khaghan* over the tribes which nomadized the region between the Orkhon and Kerulen. But the ascendancy of the Borjigin clan had been shortlived, and Temujin passed his youth in hardship, remaining until middle age a vassal of the chief of the Karait tribe. During the 1190s Temujin joined the Karait leader in successful attacks upon the Tatars, a group that was giving trouble to both the Mongols and the Chin state in North China. By 1203 Temujin had gained a sufficient following to attack his superior and to gain the submission of the Karait tribesmen. From this point it took him but three years to unite all the tribes of Mongolia under his suzerainty. At the great *quriltai* of 1206, the periodic general gathering of the Mongol tribes at the headwaters of the Onon, he had himself acclaimed *Khaghan* and took the title Chingiz Khan or 'Universal Ruler.'

It is probable that the caution and calculation he learned in his years of adversity gave him the wisdom to use his new-won power without rashness, so that he was never to leave himself open to possible failure. He gave the most meticulous attention to the organization of his forces, to their equipment and to the acquisition of the prior intelligence necessary before sending troops into unfamiliar territory. And unlike most previous leaders of steppeland empires, when he moved into the settled communities outside the Mongolian heartland, he did so only on the assurance that the heartland remained fully under his control. Thus despite his interest in China and Iran, his attention frequently returned to the Mongolian steppe and to the politics of the inner core of his empire.

Chingiz Khan's success at conquest rested first of all on a military machine which proved to be of irresistible power. This force and its organization was not the invention of Chingiz Khan alone, though he undoubtedly brought to a high point of perfection the various techniques developed by previous generations of steppeland warriors. His fighting forces were organized into an elite corps under the *Khaghan*'s personal command and into regular army units which were grouped into three wings. The personal guard, which eventually numbered some 10,000 men, was composed of young men selected from among the sons of clan leaders, and all were held to an exacting code of loyalty and obedience. The Mongol army, which at the height of its activity may have numbered 250,000 men, was small by comparison with those of China or Iran, but it had superior mobility and striking power. The entire Mongol fighting force was mounted and armed with powerful recurve bows that could kill at 200 yards. Army units of tens, hundreds, thousands and ten thousands were trained to execute difficult attack maneuvers with precision and coordination. They were especially skilled at strategies of surprise and deception, frequently luring much larger armies into positions from which they could easily be cut to pieces by the more mobile Mongol cavalry.

Once the Mongols had begun to move out of their homelands they quickly took advantage of their conquests. Men from recently subjugated populations were forcibly added to the Mongol forces, where they were obliged to take the vanguard in succeeding campaigns. Korean and Chinese sailors and soldiers, for instance, made up the bulk of the amphibious forces sent against Japan in 1274 and 1281. The Mongols were also quick to absorb new techniques of warfare from the areas they occupied. When they first faced the walled cities of North China and Iran they clearly lacked knowledge of siegecraft. Yet they soon rectified this by employing Chinese and Arab engineers and artisans. By the time the Mongols took up the conquest of South China they had mastered both the techniques of firing catapults and of using gunpowder for explosive devices. Far distant army units were supported by a commissariat organization that provided remounts and brought up siege equipment when needed. A rapid messenger service linked Mongol operations in the field to the *Khaghan*'s headquarters. Even the seemingly senseless slaughter of civilian inhabitants of captured cities was often done for planned psychological effect. Terror became a weapon to force the capitulation of still unconquered lands and to induce the docility of subject populations over which the Mongols could place but limited occupation forces.

Pax Mongolica

The campaigns which won the Mongols control of fully two-thirds of the Eurasian land-mass were carried out over some 75 years, first under Chingiz Khan and then his sons and grandsons. Between 1206 and 1209 the *Khaghan* strengthened his position in Central Asia, conquering the Oirot and Kirghiz tribes and receiving the submission of the Uighurs of the Tarim Basin. From the Uighurs the Mongol chief obtained the services of the first important body of specialists skilled in Chinese techniques of government and social theory. He was now prepared to move in upon the frontier states which lay between him and China proper. In 1209 he invaded the Tangut state of Hsi Hsia and forced its ruler to become a Mongol vassal. In 1211 he began the conquest of the Jürched state of Chin. By 1215 he had occupied Peking, gaining vast quantities of booty. Even more important, he obtained the services of sinified Jürched officials who could instruct the Mongols on how to tax and administer sedentary societies. The most important of these was Yeh-lü Ch'u-ts'ai, a Khitan

nobleman, who became Chingiz Khan's most trusted advisor on administrative matters. It is he who supposedly convinced the Mongols of the futility of nomadizing North China.

After the conquest of the Chin, Chingiz prudently refrained from moving south against the Sung Empire and its well-defended cities. Instead he returned to his Mongolian base to tighten his control over the tribal confederacy which remained his ultimate source of strength. Then, having taken care of any remaining resistance to his leadership, he moved toward his western frontier. In 1218 his armies absorbed the remnants of the Qarakhitan state and pushed to the borders of the eastern Iranian state of Khwarazm, roughly the equivalent of the Chin in the east. Between 1219 and 1221, Mongol forces numbering perhaps as many as 150,000 men assaulted one after another of the rich oasis cities of Mawarannahr, Khurasan and Afghanistan. In 1220 Bukkara and Samarkand were captured and their riches plundered. In the following year Balkh, Herat, Marv and Nishapur were taken and sacked. The capture of Bamiyan cost the Mongols the life of Chingiz Khan's favorite grandson, and in retaliation he had the city leveled and every inhabitant massacred. Chingiz himself eventually pushed as far south as the Indus, while two of his commanders probed westward as far as the territory of the Qipchaq tribes north of the Black Sea. These conquests not only added to the wealth of the growing Mongol state but augmented the Mongol military and administrative services by the addition of Turkish tribesmen and Muslim merchants and financiers. But many of the cities of eastern Iran were never to recover from the destruction visited upon them by the Mongols. In too many cases systematic slaughter of entire populations and the destruction of learned and religious communities literally made wastelands out of what had once been flourishing commercial and cultural centers. Chingiz Khan had yet to strike a reasonable balance between the traditional concern of his tribesmen for plunder and the possibility of a more permanent empire based on political control and systematic taxation.

At his death in 1227, Chingiz Khan's conquests were partitioned in the traditional Mongol manner among his descendants. Three khanates were established: that of a son, Chaghatai (roughly equivalent to the old Qarakhitan Empire), of a

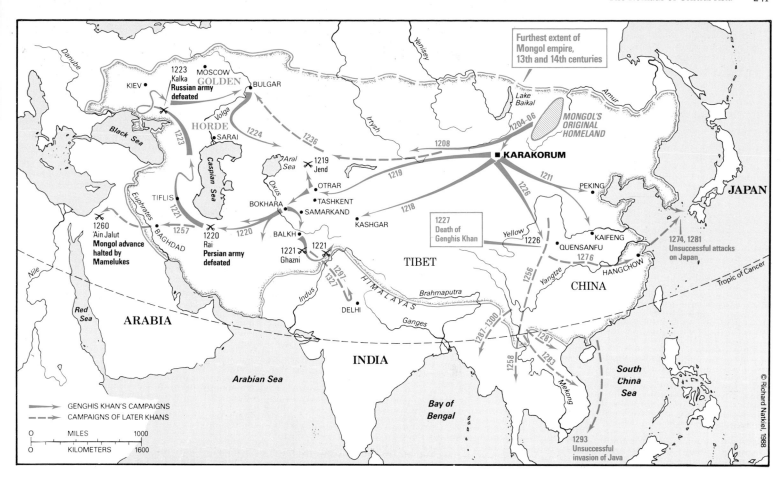

Furthest extent of
Mongol empire,
13th and 14th centuries

GENGHIS KHAN'S CAMPAIGNS
CAMPAIGNS OF LATER KHANS

| MILES | 1000 |
| KILOMETERS | 1600 |

© Richard Natkiel, 1988

grandson, Batu (eventually the Qipchaq *ulus*, which embraced the Mongol conquests west of the River Irtysh), and of another son, Ögetei (the old tribal homelands in Mongolia, Jungaria and North China). The Mongol drive for empire continued strong and remained coordinated. From the foundations laid by Chingiz this drive was to extend in two phases to reach, by 1279, its farthest limits. The first of these, lasting from 1227 to 1259, was marked by expansion westward: the filling out of the Qipchaq *ulus* and the establishment of the Il-Khanate, which brought Mongol rule to Baghdad. The second began in 1264, when Kublai was chosen *Khaghan*, and ended with the final conquest of South China by the Mongols in 1279.

By the time of Kublai's conquest of China it was already evident that the Mongol legacy was beginning to function as quite distinct divisions. The Khanate of Qipchaq (known to the Russians as Golden Horde) stretched from the Irtysh to the Volga. The Il-Khanate included all of Iran from the Euphrates to the Amu Darya. The Central Asian Khanate of Chagatai and the *ulus* of the *Khaghan* combined Mongolia and all of China. The traditional method of keeping such separate divisions bound together had been to rely on clan unity. In other words, the far-flung Mongol conquests were to be held under the overlordship of successive *Khaghan* chosen from among the descendants of Chingiz by popular acclamation. But by the end of the thirteenth century, two generations after the original conquests of Chingiz Khan, the Mongol rulers in the four quarters of Eurasia had

Left: A Persian manuscript's depiction of the enthronement of Temujin as the Chingiz ('Universal') Khan. His achievement in welding a great Mongol empire out of the fractious nomads of Inner Asia and using them to conquer half the world can best be compared – in European history – to the deeds of Alexander the Great.

Above: The Mongol conquests were completed rapidly. In a little more than 15 years Chingiz Khan established the basic outline of the Mongol realm. Mongol expansion only ceased when they reached lands that could not easily support the vast levels of horses required by their armies.

Right: The last great nomad conqueror was Timur the Lame (Tamerlane) who constructed an empire encompassing most of the Middle East. Yet his achievement was an ephemeral one, which fell apart immediately after his death.

Far right: Coins of Timur's empire.

begun to drift apart, finding themselves pre-occupied with the tasks of local administration and undergoing progressive accommodation to the cultural styles of the several occupied regions. By the fourteenth century the history of Mongol rule had become part of the indigenous history of China, Central Asia, Iran and Eastern Europe.

But before this fragmentation took place there was a period when a genuine *Pax Mongolica* really did exist, from roughly 1227 to 1294. At its height the Mongol Empire was a remarkable achievement in which the tent city of the *Khaghan* held together the largest contiguous land-mass ever conquered by sword and bow. Once the initial conquests were over and the new dispensation by which Eurasia was to be governed from the steppes of Central Asia was firmly set, the Mongols were able to construct a remarkably vigorous and coordinated administrative machine for the governance of their empire. In China and Iran they relied on the mixed system that permitted local officials to administer in accustomed ways, under the supervision of Mongol or other foreign occupation officials. For their supervisory officials the Mongols built up an international corps of specialists – Chinese, Khitans, Iranians, Jews, Arabs, even Europeans such as Marco Polo. Physically linking this corps of officials together was the famed Mongol post system. Radiating outward from out of Kharakorum, the Mongolian capital, the Mongols devised an elaborate network of post routes that were supplied with regularly placed relay stations and over which couriers, sometimes traveling at the rate of 200 miles a day, carried official messages. Along the same routes, protected by military guard-posts and serviced by caravanserai, moved traders and travelers of all sorts. At no time before, nor for many centuries after, were the trade routes which joined the ancient Occident to the Orient more open and secure. Aside from the known journeys of historically famous international travelers, countless thousands of private and official travelers made their way in relative security through the formidable stretches of mountains and semi-desert wastes of Central Asia.

To those contemporary Europeans who read Marco Polo's description of his travels the story seemed utterly fantastic and unbelievable. Yet there were other travelers, particularly Turks, Arabs and Chinese, for whom the route across Central Asia or around India was more or less a routine matter. The trade route from Baghdad to China ran both inland between the high oasis cities of Central Asia and by sea from the Persian Gulf, around India and through the Straits of Malacca to ports on the south coast of China. The amount of cultural exchange that went on at this time between the ends of Eurasia was remarkable, even though it was little known to Europeans. These were the years when Muslim communities settled in China's port cities and on the inner frontier areas of Kansu and Yünnan, where they remain to this day. From Iran, China was to acquire new knowledge in the fields of mathematics, astronomy, music and ceramics. In the reverse direction, Chinese technicians, spreading out over the Mongol Empire, took knowledge of gunpowder, paper money, printing, textiles and medicine into the Arab world. In view of such large-scale interregional contact, the fact that Marco Polo was doubted by his European contemporaries simply underscores the degree to which thirteenth-century Europe was shut off from the main axis of Eurasian international exchanges.

Of the four great khanates into which the Mongol Empire eventually evolved, the largest was the *ulus* of the *Khaghan*. Unlike the others, it sharply divided between the high steppe territories, centered on Kharakorum, and China, ruled from the northern capital of Peking. Kublai, who had finally succeeded in conquering the Sung, was to be almost fully occupied with China after 1251. Having established his headquarters at Peking and having manipulated his election as *Khaghan* in 1260, he devoted himself to the task, which took his full energies until 1279. He adopted the guise of a Chinese dynastic founder, proclaiming in 1271 the establishment of a new dynasty, the Yüan. Thus when the Sung Dynasty was finally destroyed, the Mongols took their place as a legitimate, if alien, Chinese imperial house. Kublai's descendants ruled in China until 1367, when the Mongol administrators and occupation forces were driven back into the steppe by the Chinese.

The khanates of Ögetei and Chaghatai, which together occupied the Central Asian portion of the Mongol Empire, frequently acted in concert after the death of Chingiz, and appear eventually to have been fused – at any rate the Ögetei *ulus* lost its separate existence after 1310. The history of this area is confused by constant internal conflicts. Never establishing themselves as rulers of an urban-based state, Chaghatai's successors remained pastoralists whose only interest in the oasis cities under their control was as sources of tribute. In the course of internal power struggles among these leaders, therefore, the wealthy cities of Bukhara, Samarkand, Tirmiz, Balkh and Marv were several times plundered. Even a hundred years later several remained in total ruins. One of the fundamental problems of keeping the Chaghatai Khanate together was geographical. The steppes of Jungaria did not provide an adequate base from which to govern the oasis communities of Kashgaria or Mawarannahr. Thus Kebek Khan, who reigned from 1318 to 1326, shifted his capital to near Bukhara. His successors, however, soon lost their hold over Mawarannahr. Confined to the Inner Asian regions of the Tarim Basin and Jungaria, the Chaghatai Khanate managed to survive into the seventeenth century. But the western territories were destined to pursue a history more closely associated with events in Iran, and the rise of Timur in Mawarannahr after about 1370 completed the separation of the western oasis cities from the territory east of the Pamirs and the Tien Shan.

In the Il-Khanate created by Hülegü in Iran, indigenous cultural and religious traditions tended to remain intact under Mongol dominance, so that the Mongols remained at the top of the political apparatus as precarious military occupiers. But once Hülegü's line became established in Iran, the Il-Khans assimilated Muslim ways and achieved a relatively stable and respon-

Above: A Samanid mausoleum at Bokhara. The rulers of the Turkic states between the Caspian and the Pamirs were the last remnants of the once-mighty nomad empires. The last Khan of Bokhara was a vassal of the Russian Czar, both overthrown in 1917 – an event marking the end of Chingiz Khan's legacy.

Left: A Mongol cavalryman plaits the tail of his horse, a common practice among the steppe nomads.

Right: Batu, the first khan of the Golden Horde. This Mongol grouping dominated Russia for 200 years.

Far right: Hülegü, grandson of Chingiz, who founded the Il-Khan dynasty of Iran in 1256. It was eventually overthrown by Timur in the 1380s.

sible rule until the 1330s. Ironically, almost from the start, the Il-Khans were placed under attack from the Chaghatai Khans. Their defense of the Iranian heartlands indicated their strong commitment to urbanized culture and to the trade economy that centered in Tabriz. But again, after 1375, with the weakening of the line of Hülegü, the khanate was pulled apart by competing clan interests among the Mongol aristocracy. The original *ulus* consequently separated into a number of independent successor dynasties before being swept away by the conquests of Timur.

The fourth division of the Mongol Empire, the Khanate of Qipchaq, was given its ultimate shape by Batu, grandson of Chingiz Khan. Between 1237 and 1242 Batu extended this territory by absorbing the lands of the Qipchaq tribes west of the Volga and the Russians of Kiev. His descendants ruled this vast domain from bases on the lower Volga for two centuries. The ruling Mongols of the Qipchaq Khanate were noteworthy for the manner in which they worked out a balance between their tribal steppe heritage and the sedentary ways of the south Russian plains. Batu's line held court in their tents yet promoted trade and encouraged the growth of thriving commercial cities. The location of these centers, however, tended to direct the interest of the Golden Horde southward, across the Caucasus toward the Muslim communities of Azerbaijan.

Under the rule of Berke (1258-67) the Golden Horde began hostilities against their kinsmen the Il-Khans. Berke himself became a Muslim and began the process whereby the Golden Horde rulers eventually became fully converted to Islam and its legal practices, thus permanently dividing them from the Christianized Russians. Berke also, as a result of his feud with Hülegü, initiated an alliance with the Egyptian Mameluks. This association served increasingly to isolate subsequent Golden Horde rulers from Mongol politics to the east and to draw the Qipchaq Khanate toward the ports of the Black Sea and the culture of the eastern Mediterranean. The vitality of the line of Batu remained strong through the fourteenth century, weathering the devastation of Timur's attacks upon the cities of the lower Volga. Only during the fifteenth century did the Golden Horde succumb to the divisive clan rivalries which had

already affected the other parts of the Mongol Empire. By the middle of the century the great *ulus* of Batu had begun to fragment into separate successor khanates and local separatist movements. Lithuania and Muscovy were soon to throw off the Mongol yoke, while Mongol leadership itself divided into independent khanates at Kazan, Astrakhan and Crimea in the west, and into the White Horde and the Khanate of Sibir to the east. When by the middle of the sixteenth century Ivan the Terrible captured both Kazan and Astrakhan, the Golden Horde had essentially been extinguished.

Mongol decline

The breakup of the Mongol Empire proceeded in several predictable stages. First came the fragmentation into separate khanates, then the internal fragmentation of leadership within the khanates among the Mongol ruling clans, then the reassertion of local rule by indigenous dynasties in the older centers of civilization while Inner Asia returned to a state of tribal rivalry. This general cycle by which the nomadic dominion over the settled communities was weakened or assimilated was subjected to one major effort at reversal under the ruthless sword of Timur. In 30 years of campaigning, from 1370 to 1402, his armies penetrated western Iran, Anatolia, southern Russia and northern India. At his death in 1405 he was preparing for a massive invasion of Ming China. His armies were powerful, and he wrought tremendous havoc, but his capacity to leave behind a political structure for the governance of an empire was even more ineffectual than that of the Chingizkhanid Mongols. His effect upon the civilized world, largely confined to Iran and India, is described more fully elsewhere.

With the death of Timur we can say that a major cycle in the relationship between the steppe and the sower came to an end, that in which a nomadic empire based in the high Inner Asian steppe would rule significant parts of the rest of the Eurasian world. Timur in fact having only briefly held Jungaria was hardly a true successor to Chingiz Khan. With his passing, the relationship between Inner Asia and the traditional spheres of empire was again reversed, as the initiative passed increasingly to dynasties based in

China, India, Iran or Europe. Among the nomadic peoples no single leader was able to provide the unifying force necessary for world conquest, as a succession of tribal groups competed for control of shifting portions of the vast Inner Asian steppe.

While the passing of the Mongols and the spread of firearms brought an end to the cycle of direct nomadic rule of the areas peripheral to Central Asia, we should not forget that the influence of nomadic peoples was still to be felt in the settled societies of the Near East, India and the Far East for many centuries after the collapse of nomad power in the steppes. As will be described in the succeeding chapters, a whole series of Turkish dynasties ruled in the Near East following the breakup of the Mongol khanates and their immediate successors. In the west, with Anatolia as their base, the Ottoman Turks emerged during the fourteenth and fifteenth centuries as masters of the western half of the Muslim world. From the beginning of the sixteenth century into the early years of the eighteenth century the Turkish Safavid dynasty ruled over Iran and Khurasan, while the Shaybanids controled Mawarannahr for most of the sixteenth century. India, from 1526 to 1859, was governed by the Moghuls who claimed descent from Chingiz Khan and Timur. In the Far East, between 1644 and 1910, China was ruled by Manchu emperors who considered themselves successors to the Eastern Khanate conquered by Kublai. Thus the phenomenon of partially assimilated nomadic peoples moving in upon the sedentary states by conquest (as in the case of the Manchus in China) or taking over after having been used as mercenary or slave fighters (as in most of the Near Eastern examples) was to persist well beyond the fading of Turko-Mongol power in the steppe. Europe alone remained unaffected by this last phase of Turko-Mongolian influence. It is of more than passing significance, therefore, that when the last of the great 'barbarian migrations' took the peoples of Europe by ship to the far corners of the earth, they discovered in each of the major areas of Asia alien ruling dynasties of nomadic origin. Doubtless that is why in most of Asia, European colonial rule came to be looked upon by indigenous peoples as hardly more than another episode in a long line of rule by outsiders.

India

From the end of the fifth century, which saw the defeat of the Guptas at the hands of the Huns, until the Turkish conquests of the twelfth century, the history of northern India centered on the fortunes of a succession of regimes, none of which, with the exception of the short-lived kingdom of Harsha of Kanauj, possessed the resources to conquer and hold what the Guptas, Kushans or Mauryans had held. The first half of the sixth century was pre-eminently the age of the Huns. Their disappearance resulted in the emergence of new contenders for power, including the Maitrakas (450-775), former vassals of the Guptas, in Kathiawar and in Gujarat, and the short-lived Maukharis, in the country of the upper Ganges, where their capital, Kanauj (Kanyakubja), was to remain a center of north Indian culture until the Turkish conquest. Allied to the Maukharis was the Pushyabhuti family of Thanesar, north of Delhi, and when the heads of both families were killed in battle, there emerged as heir of both Thanesar and Kanauj the warrior-king Harsha (606-48). Harsha's wars resulted in a virtual reconstruction of the part of the former Gupta Empire stretching from Assam to Gujarat, but like other northern conquerors, he made no headway south of the Narbada, where he was repulsed by Pulakeshin II, the Chalukya ruler of Badami in the Deccan. A vigorous administrator who traveled ceaselessly from one end of his empire to the other, Harsha was a generous patron of Sanskrit learning (he himself wrote three dramas in Sanskrit) and a friend to both *brahmins* and Buddhists. But since he had no heir, his empire fell apart at his death.

From the eighth to the tenth century control of the north was shared uneasily between the Pala Dynasty (760-1142), ruling in Bengal and Bihar, and the Gurjara-Pratihara Dynasty (c 730-1014) of Kanauj, with the Rashtrakuta Dynasty (750-973) of the western Deccan periodically challenging their hegemony. The Palas were active patrons of Tibetan Tantric Buddhism, and during their rule cultural contacts between Bengal and Tibet were to prove very enriching to the latter country. The Gurjara-Pratiharas, under their greatest rulers, Mihira Bhoja (c 836-85) and Mahendrapala (c 885-901), came to dominate virtually all northern India other than those areas controled by the Palas, but shortly afterwards they experienced a marked decline, exemplified by the temporary loss of their capital, Kanauj, in 916 to the invading forces of the Rashtrakutas of the Deccan. Throughout the tenth century their hold over their vassals steadily weakened, and they were thus in no position to withstand successive assaults by the Muslim Turkish armies of Sultan Mahmud (997-1030) of Ghazni, a city in Afghanistan lying midway between Kabul and Kandahar and ideally situated as a base for raiding into northwestern India. Between 1001 and 1027 Mahmud led 17 expeditions across the Indus, spreading untold havoc and acquiring fabulous plunder in the sack of such cities as Thanesar, Mathura and Kanauj and of the great temple of Shiva at Somnath in Kathiawar.

The fall of the Gurjara-Pratiharas did not result in the establishment of a Ghaznavid Empire in its place, although the Ghaznavids brought the Punjab under their formal control and it was from this time that Lahore, the administrative capital of their Indian possessions, began its long history as a major center of Indo-Muslim culture. Elsewhere, independent Hindu regimes sprang up in place of the defunct rule of the Gurjara-Pratiharas. But all these dynasties were preoccupied with short-sighted aggrandisement at the expense of their immediate neighbors and were incapable of any kind of effective combination against the Turkish threat from the northwest.

Rise of the Ghurid state

In 1149 the Ghaznavids, grown feeble, were overthrown by the Ghurids, a family of Iranian origin from the mountains east of Herat but which based its power upon Turkish slave-armies like those which had served the Ghaznavids. The real architect of the Ghurid state, Ghiyas al-Din Muhammad, often referred to as Muhammad of Ghur, had already extended his Indian conquests far beyond the former Ghaznavid possessions in the Punjab. In 1191 the Chauhan Rajput chieftain, Prithviraj III, repulsed the Ghurids at Tarain, near Thanesar, but in the following year they returned and on the same battleground decisively crushed the opposing Rajput forces. Shihab al-Din Muhammad's slave-commander, Qutb al-Din Aibak, then seized the Rajput strongholds of Ajmer and Delhi (where, following the death of his master in 1206, he became the first of the so-called 'Slave Kings' of Delhi), while another Ghurid slave-commander, Muhammad ibn Bakhtiyar, advanced down the Ganges to establish Turkish rule in Bihar and Bengal.

These events resulted in the north of India passing into the hands of successive Central Asian Muslim dynasties whose rule would endure until the coming of the British in the eighteenth century. In the arid and inhospitable terrain of Rajasthan, however, the Rajputs would hold their own with varying degrees of success against both the Sultans of Delhi and the Moghul emperors, while Hindu polities would also survive for lengthy periods in Kashmir and the Himalayan foothills, in Orissa and distant Assam, areas where an unfavorable climate, difficult conditions for campaigning or the absence of obvious wealth discouraged penetration by the newcomers.

The Deccan and the far south

The preceding survey of the various dynasties and peoples who dominated northern India during the millennium and a half prior to AD 1200 underscores at least one recurring feature: the failure of virtually every regime (apart from the short-lived empire of Ashoka) to establish a permanent foot-

Left: A Hindu widow is burned alive following the death of her husband, a bizarre practice known as *sati* or suttee. The Hindu religion had managed to fend off the Buddhist challenge and remain India's leading faith. It would soon come under a new pressure, however, from Muslim invaders pushing their way into the sub-continent from the north.

Above right: A temple at Mamallapuram in southern India. It was built by the Pallava Dynasty, rulers of the area from 350 to 740.

Above far right: The Chalukyah Dynasty of the Deccan built several magnificent Hindu temples in their realm. This one, at Aihole, is dedicated to the god Durga.

Right: Buddhism grew out of a movement to reform the Hindu faith, but soon became a genuine alternative. Some Indian dynasties adopted it, but the religion found more favor farther east in China and Southeast Asia. On Sri Lanka, however, where this colossal statue of the Buddha was carved, it laid solid roots that survived the 100-year annexation of the island by the Hindu Cholas.

hold south of the Narbada. It is this failure which justifies the treatment of north and south as distinct entities in terms of political history – and not only political history, since the inability of the northern empires to expand into the Deccan meant that neither the racial composition of peninsular India nor its basic social and cultural patterns underwent the degree of adulteration that occurred in the north.

The early history of peninsular India revolves around the fortunes of three extensive kingdoms: that of the Pandyas south of the Kaveri, with its capital at Madurai; that of the Cheras centered on Kerala; and that of the Cholas on the Coromandel Coast (from Chola-mandal, Chola territory) and in what was later to become known to Europeans as the Carnatic. Of these, the Chera kingdom was somewhat isolated from the Tamil kingdoms facing the Bay of Bengal and in due course developed a regional Tamil that evolved into an independent language, Malayalam, with a rich literary tradition of its own. Over a period of many centuries this region enjoyed unbroken communication with the countries bordering the Arabian Sea to the north and west. This was the result of its key location in relation to the trade-routes of the Indian Ocean and of the widespread demand for Malabar pepper, celebrated from very early times. Kerala was well known to both Greek and Roman traders, was said to have been visited by St Thomas and provided a haven for a small but prosperous Jewish community which has survived there from the fourth century AD down to the present day. From the eighth century onward the Cheras welcomed Arab seafarers, who established themselves on the coast, intermarried with the local population and became the ancestors of the present Moplahs or Malabar Muslims. Under the Perumal dynasty (400-826), in particular, Kerala enjoyed an exceptionally vigorous cultural life.

The Tamil kingdom that enjoyed the most continuous prosperity was, however, that of the Cholas. It also made the greatest contribution to Tamil learning, literature, music and the arts. As in the case of all other polities in ancient India, the wealth of Chola was based upon a thriving agriculture, with two monsoons annually permitting the intensive cultivation of rice, barley and millet. Everywhere the village, organized along caste lines, was the dominant social unit, but urban life was also well developed, sustained by a sophisticated commerce. Excavations at Arikamedu, near Pondicherry, have revealed the impressive extent of the trade between the Coromandel Coast and the Roman Empire from the first century BC to the beginning of the second century AD.

The first three centuries of the Christian era were a period of extreme confusion in the south, involving, in addition to the rivalries of the three Tamil kingdoms, the movement of peoples into and across the peninsula. By the middle of the fourth century Chola was in the hands of the powerful and long-lived Pallava dynasty, a family of northern origin whom some have sought to identify with the 'Pahlavas' (Parthians) and who spoke no Dravidian language, keeping their records in Sanskrit or Prakrit. At the height of their power under Mahendravarman I (600-30), Narasimhavarman I (630-60) and Narasimhavarman II (695-722), the Pallavas were a power to be feared throughout the south, and in 642 Narasimhavarman I defeated the Chalukya ruler of the Deccan, Pulakeshin II (already referred to as having beaten back the great Harsha of Kanauj) and occupied his capital of Badami. Under the Pallavas Tamilnad was exposed to increased Sanskritic influences from the north, and at this

Left: The Chola empire was a prosperous state, and its material wealth enabled the production of artistic works of the highest quality. This fine bronze statue represents Parvati, consort to the Hindu god Siva.

Right: In northern India Buddhism adapted Hindu gods to its own purposes. This carving, from the inner shrine of a Buddhist monastery at Ajanta, shows the Buddha preaching, flanked – and therefore inspired – by figures of the Hindu god Indra.

Below right: A Tibetan statue of Buddha, cast in bronze. The Pala Dynasty, who established their rule over Bengal and Bihar in the eighth century, favored the spread of Buddhism and forged close links with their co-religionists over the Himalayas.

Below far right: A bronze statue of Siva, god of destruction and renovation, the work of artists of the Chola Empire.

period both Shaivism and Vaishnavism became deeply embedded in Tamil culture. Lavish patrons of the arts, the Pallavas were great builders, and their temples at Kanchipuram (Conjeeveram), their capital, and at Mamallapuram (Mahabalipuram), on the coast south of Madras, are among the finest examples of South Indian sacred architecture.

In 740 the Chalukyas occupied Kanchipuram and not long afterwards the Pallavas were forced to submit to the rising power of the Rashtrakutas of the western Deccan. Finally, around 900, the Cholas, long submerged under the rule of the Pallavas, re-emerged to overthrow their erstwhile masters and establish a great empire that, beginning in the ninth century and reaching its zenith during the tenth and eleventh centuries, survived until the thirteenth century, when it was overthrown by the Pandyas of Madurai and the Hoysala Dynasty of Halebid in Mysore.

Rise and fall of the Chola Empire

The Chola Empire, with its capital at Chidambaram, was perhaps the most impressive Hindu polity to emerge in the south, and it was certainly the best administered, consisting not only of a highly efficient royal bureaucracy at the center, but also of local government by assemblies

(*periyanadu*) dominated by the higher cultivating castes, with jurisdiction over extensive tracts. There was a high level of material prosperity, as confirmed by the surviving examples of Chola art and architecture – the bronzes, which rank among the supreme achievements of the Indian craftsman, and such temples as those at Chidambaram and Tanjore. It was the builder of the great Shiva temple at Tanjore, Rajaraja I (985-1014), who extended the bounds of the Chola Empire to include virtually the whole of south India, Sri Lanka and the Maldive and Laccadive Islands. His son, Rajendra I (1014-42), in addition to defeating the Pala ruler of Bengal, dispatched a naval expedition against the Srivijaya Empire in Sumatra and the Malay Peninsula, which was apparently interfering with Chola trade with China through the Straits of Malacca.

But throughout the twelfth century Chola power steadily declined, and although a series of protracted wars with the Chalukyas ended in victory for the Cholas, their strength was sapped in the long struggle. Moreover, the overthrow of the Chalukyas resulted in the emergence in the western Deccan of vigorous new regimes, one-time Chalukya vassals, of which the Hoysalas were undoubtedly the most formidable. Part of the Chola Empire passed into Hoysala hands in 1216.

thereby loosening the ties that bound many vassal chieftains to the Chola throne. In 1257 the Pandyas invaded from the south, and the next two decades witnessed the death-throes of the dynasty.

Between Tamilnad and the Narbada, the great plateau of the Deccan was the setting for the rise of a succession of dynasties, some of which wielded authority beyond the limits of the Deccan proper. In all the Deccan-based kingdoms, however, the feudal element was especially prominent, and the strong bureaucratic scaffolding characteristic of the Chola Empire in the south, or of the earlier Gupta Empire in the north, was lacking. Instability was, therefore, at all times proportionately greater. To some extent this lack of strong centralized government was due to the rugged terrain of so much of the Deccan, which made it harder to control than either the Gangetic plain or the Carnatic below the Eastern Ghats.

At the time of the fall of the Mauryan Empire there had emerged in the Deccan the Satvahana Dynasty (28 BC – AD 250), the first of a series of Andhra dynasties which lasted down to the beginning of the seventh century, when they were finally disposed of by the Chalukyas. The First or Early Chalukya Dynasty (453-757) controled a large area in central India, and the greatest of their rulers, Pulakeshin II (c 610 – c 642), fought both Harsha of Kanauj and the Pallava king Narasimhavarman I. By this time, however, Pulakeshin's brother had established what became known as the Eastern Chalukya Dynasty (624-1070) in the region between the Godavari and the Kistna, with its capital at Vengi. This line survived until it was annexed by the Chola Empire in 1070.

In 757 the Western Chalukyas were overthrown by the Rashtrakuta Dynasty (750-973), but in 973 the Rashtrakutas went down before a Western Chalukya revival, this Second or Later

Chalukya Dynasty reigning from then until 1189, when it finally disappeared, partly as the result of protracted wars of attrition with the Cholas.

These Deccani dynasties contributed substantially to the history of Indian painting, sculpture and architecture. The later work at Ajanta dates from the Early Chalukya period, and so do the magnificent temples at Aihole, Badami and Pattadakal, where the finest sculpture is in no way inferior to the best Gupta work. The famous temples at Ellora and the Elephanta Caves near Bombay were built by members of the Rashtrakuta Dynasty.

The Deccan divided

The fall of the Chalukyas resulted in the division of the Deccan into three mutually hostile successor-kingdoms, all of which were eventually swept aside or reduced to vassal status by the expansionist Sultan of Delhi, 'Ala' al-Din Muhammad Shah Khalji (1296-1316).

But the Delhi sultanate was no more able than its predecessors to bring the Deccan and the south into permanent subjugation. Attempts were made to hold the Deccan by the distribution of military garrisons and by the imposition of a formal administration, but these arrangements soon broke down, the result of the distance from Delhi and the ambitions of local commanders.

In 1347 'Ala' al-Din Hasan Bahman Shah founded a secessionist regime, the Bahmanid sultanate, that dominated virtually all the Deccan from the Tapti to the Kistna, with its capital first at Gulbarga and subsequently at Bidar. But almost from the start this sultanate found itself engaged in conflict with its Hindu neighbor to the south, the extremely powerful and aggressive empire of Vijayanagar.

The founding of the Vijayanagar Empire dates from 1336, and may in part be regarded as the south's response to the danger now threatening

Above: The famous cave temples at Ellora were built by the Rashtrakuta Dynasty of the Deccan. The rulers of this region were important patrons of Indian painting, sculpture and architecture.

Left: A temple to the god Siva built by the Pallava rulers of south India at Kanchipuram. The ziggurat-like structure has ten tiers decorated with sculptures.

Right: A tiger-hunt by one of the Muslim rulers of Delhi. The power of India's Hindu dynasties steadily waned, while Muslim invaders from central Asia took over large areas of the subcontinent. By the time the Moghul sultanate was established in the sixteenth century the Muslims were India's rulers.

from the north. Contemporary visitors to Vijaya-nagar, such as Portuguese travelers and an Iranian envoy, were overwhelmed by the wealth and splendor they saw there, but they also provide evidence, substantiated elsewhere, that the regime possessed a brutal and rapacious character at variance with the traditions of the south.

In 1527 the Bahmanid Sultanate came to an end as the result of internal dissensions. In its place there sprang up five successor states. Two of these were relatively inconsequential but the other three – the Nizam-Shahi Dynasty of Ahmadnagar (1491-1633), the Adil-Shahi Dynasty of Bijapur (1490-1686) and the Qutb-Shahi Dynasty of Golconda (1512-1687) – dominated the greater part of the peninsula until well into the seventeenth century. Toward these successor-states the Vijayanagar Empire from the outset behaved with such relentless hostility that it provoked an improbable and short-lived alliance among the rival Deccani Sultans. In a great battle on the Kistna in 1565, commonly known as the Battle of Talikota, the allies totally defeated the Vijayana-gar forces and thereafter sacked the imperial capital. The Sultanates of Bijapur and Golconda subsequently annexed the greater part of the Vijayanagar territories, but some former local governors of the Rayas maintained themselves as independent rulers, and it was from one of these, the Naik of Wandewash, that the English East India Company was to obtain the lease of Fort St George, the nucleus around which the later city of Madras would grow up in 1639.

Traditionally, historians have been content to divide the Indian past into three broad periods: Ancient or Hindu India, Medieval or Muslim India and Modern (British and Post-British) India. Our narrative so far has been concerned with the first of these periods, but already we can see some of the problems inherent in the over-simple tradi-tional three-part periodization. Exactly when did Hindu India become Muslim India? Did it begin with the raids of Sultan Mahamud of Ghazni around AD 1000? Or with the Delhi Sultanate of the thirteenth century? Or with the various regional sultanates that succeeded the Delhi Sultanate in the fourteenth century? Perhaps the most that can be said is that, in general, over a period of about 400 years, Hindu political control over various parts of India gradually (though cer-tainly not continuously) waned, and Muslim con-trol expanded. In any case, by the sixteenth century, with the advent of the Moghuls, Muslim dominion had become the major fact of Indian political life.

The transition from Hindu India to Muslim India was not only gradual, it was at all times incomplete. Even at its greatest extent, when the armies of Shah Jahan and Aurangzeb briefly pene-trated the Carnatic in the seventeenth century, the Moghul Empire never controled the whole subcontinent. Thus, as always in the past, India continued to defy political unification – despite the efforts of would-be emperors of India – and remained, as some Indians still describe her today, not a nation, but a congress of nations.

China

There was nothing inevitable about the reunification of China after its longest period of disunion. Yet despite the divergence, both natural and cultural, between the north and the south, the ideal of a united empire was ever-present in men's minds. As the north became more sinicized, the power of the old Han traditions was increasingly felt there. One of the sixth century Hsien-pei rulers in the north mocked at southern pretensions, saying: 'Beyond the Yangtse there is still the aged Hsiao Yen [Emperor Wu of the Liang, ruled 502-49] who concerns himself solely with ritually approved clothes and caps, with rites and liturgical music. Yet the Chinese nobility of the North China Plain regard him with veneration and consider him the incarnation of legitimacy.' He went on to say, half seriously, that if he didn't behave himself, all his upper-class Chinese subjects would rush to adhere to the feeble but legitimate Emperor Wu. Yet the military power to reunify China lay in the north, and finally it was successfully used to that end.

The Sui founder and his associates who seized power in the north in 581 were all of mixed descent and mixed culture, experienced in war and the brutal politics of the time. They knew how to use the powerful war machine built up by all their predecessors since the northern Wei. But did they

also have the imagination, the vision, to build anything more than another regional power, as transient as those which had gone before? Many signs appeared in the very first years that they intended to re-create a politically centralized empire on the model of the Ch'in and Early Han. A vast capital city was planned and thrown up in less than two years near the sites of earlier imperial capitals in the Kuan-chung plain. As soon as the Sui's physical control of the great plain was assured, a series of reform edicts began to appear, and these clearly indicated that a new institutional structure was going to emerge. In 589, after thorough preparations, the campaign against the South began. Huge armies moved by land and water against the enfeebled regime centered in Nanking. The Sui forces made quick work of it, and the last southern ruler and his courtiers, along with the contents of his treasuries, were carried off to the new Sui capital. Sporadic southern resistance continued for some time, and the whole task of cultural and political reunification was to take decades. Yet this was accomplished and the second of China's great centralized empires gradually took shape. Although the Sui lasted less than 40 years, the T'ang took over from it a great legacy of new institutions. It is thus reasonable to consider the two together.

Although both the Sui and the T'ang asserted that the Han was their model, much time had passed since the Han's decay, the area to be ruled was expanded far beyond the Han boundaries, Buddhism had become part of life in North and South alike and a cultural variety unknown in Han times had to be reckoned with. Therefore the Sui and T'ang rulers could not afford to be slavish archaists seeking simply to revive the ghost of the long-dead Han. Rather, they had to sweep away much of the institutional detritus of the years of disunion and to innovate on a grand scale.

Government reforms

Perhaps the most striking innovation was the reform of recruitment for government service. This was not only a political measure but was also designed to alter the character of the elite – of the group of persons who had access to wealth and power. In the period of disunion, heredity had become the principal basis for admission to the elite. The Sui by decree abolished the institutions which embodied this principle and instead set up a system of examinations administered to candidates sent up from the provinces. The system was greatly elaborated in the T'ang, and although family influence still counted in most high appointments, those who came up by the exam-

Right: A detail from a silk scroll dating from the T'ang Dynasty (618-906) depicting scenes from rural life.

Below left: A marble statue of Buddha. Although China was open to several new religions, Buddhism remained dominant.

Below, far left: Tai Tsung, emperor of the T'ang Dynasty from 627 to 650.

ination route had a special prestige. In society at large their presence let it be known that merit and performance could gain recognition.

To make this new impersonal system of elite recruitment work, a great number of other measures were needed and were instituted. For example, the 'rule of avoidance' which prevented an official's being assigned to his own home district was established; it was designed to make sure that officials sent from the capital represented central government interests and not those of the prestigious families of the locality where they were assigned. Triennial transfers of local officials served the same purpose. A triennial audit of official performance was instituted, and appropriate promotions or demotions given. Surveillance of official performance was entrusted to the Censorate, and an unfavorable censors' report could lead to reprimands, demotions or severe punishments. All these measures and many lesser ones were intended to assure centralized government of the type first instituted by the Ch'in in the third century BC.

To make the official system work, a hierarchy of rational units of local administration was established, very similar to that of the Ch'in. The country was divided into prefectures (*chou*) and counties (*hsien*). In the early seventh century there were in the empire 190 prefectures and 1255 counties. These were graded according to their relative size and productivity, and officials of appropriate rank were assigned to them. These local officials were responsible for all the basic functions of government: registration of the population, periodic re-allocation of lands, collection of taxes, maintenance of records of corvée labor service (20 days per year per adult male was the standard), trying and judging legal cases of all kinds. In time they came to be assisted by various specialized officials, but their duties were nonetheless heavy and their hours long.

The Sui and T'ang empires depended on taxes in kind, mainly grain and textile fibers collected at the local level. To get these tax goods into regional storehouses and to the capitals (Ch'ang-an in Kuan-chung, Loyang in the Great Plain) required an elaborate system of transport. The great imperial canals and an extensive system of roads were begun by the Sui and completed by the T'ang. They were designed, of course, to get the tax goods where the government wanted them, but they also had important strategic and political uses. The transport of troops to an area of disturbance or to a frontier base was greatly facilitated, and the show of imperial power – the emperor making a progress across the land with all the opulent display that marked these trips – served to remind local people of the power and grandeur of their supreme ruler. In Sui-T'ang times there was also a particular geo-political purpose in the building of the canal system: the principal capital was in the Kuan-chung plain, far to the west of the main centers of population and wealth.

The Kuan-chung plain had great strategic advantages (not to mention its historical-symbolic importance), but it was a food deficit area and, particularly as the bureaucratic population grew in size, it had to be massively supplied from the east. The Sui began building in the west, with a short canal paralleling the shallow Wei River. They then linked the Yellow River to the productive Huai valley area by two further canals, and from there built two linking canals, first south to the Yangtse and then, further south, to the head of Hangchow Bay. The Sui's final effort was to build a very long canal to the northeast, terminating in the vicinity of modern Peking. It was the forerunner of the later north-south 'Grand Canals' that did for north-south communication what the Sui-T'ang canals did for northwest-southeast.

The hierarchy of government

The central government which managed the affairs of this complex empire was far more elaborate than anything that had gone before, indeed far more sophisticated than any in the world at that time. All those accepted into the bureaucratic class were given an initial rank – one of nine, each of which was further subdivided to make a total of 30 grades. The assignment of rank entailed the payment of a stipend calculated in bushels of grain. Thereafter each office to which the person was assigned had a certain statutory rank, and at the time of each triennial reassignment the Board of Civil Office decided whether the official would advance or be degraded. Dossiers of performance were kept in the files of that board, and routine reports would be supplemented by reports of censors or of special investigatory commissions. The structure of government was pyramidal and symmetrical. At the top was the emperor and his intimate counselors of the moment, a group that changed frequently at the emperor's will. At the next level were three departments: State Affairs, Imperial Chancellery, Imperial Secretariat, all with their assigned number of officials of various ranks. By far the most important was State Affairs, for under it were the six functional offices of the central government: Government Personnel, Finance, Ritual, Army, Punishments (*not* justice) and Public Works. In addition to this rather tidy system there were a host of other offices, eg the History Office, the Bureau of Astronomy, the Court of Imperial Sacrifices, the Supreme Court of Punishment, and so on, again with their complements of officials at various ranks.

The formal system for making policy decisions was the dawn audience held in one of the audience halls of the imperial palace. The officials assembled outside well before sunrise. As the chiming water clock struck the moment of dawn, they filed into the great hall, and each proceeded to his position assigned according to rank and office; each wore the approved robes of his rank and carried in front of him a wooden plaque inscribed with his rank and office. When all were assembled, the emperor entered from a side hall and crossed to the throne. New appointees were presented to him, and then policy matters were discussed, with oral presentations by various officials, the emperor's questioning and argument from other officials. The great audiences were supplemented by smaller less formal 'discussions of state affairs' held almost daily among the emperor and his chief ministers. When these gatherings were dismissed, the officials returned to their offices and directed their staffs in drafting the edicts, decrees and regulations which would implement decisions taken.

Cosmopolitan spirit

This elaborate network of institutions assured for many decades a rising curve of productivity and a consequent rise in the power and splendor of the state. It also made possible the assertion of T'ang authority over nearby peoples and strong influence in more distant lands. Central Asian trade routes were opened and controled by the Chinese. The prosperity of the empire attracted traders of many nations, and these arrived in large numbers by land at Ch'ang-an, or by sea at the thriving port of Canton. The T'ang dynasty, like the Sui before it, was partly non-Chinese in background and style, and as a consequence was hospitable to foreigners and cosmopolitan in spirit. Buddhism continued to be the dominant religion. Islam was imported, and from Iran came Zoroastrianism, Manicheanism and a great variety of influences on art and music, dance and drama, dress and ornament, food and drink. In the West Market at Ch'ang-an could be seen a wide range of exotica such as rugs from Iran; pearls from India; jade, diamonds and other precious stones from half a dozen foreign countries; gold and silver coins and worked objects from all parts of Western Eurasia, including Byzantium. Great families collected rarities in their mansions – parakeets, parrots, performing dwarfs, negrito domestic slaves, as well as gold, precious stones and exquisite textiles. In their sumptuous tombs they placed terra-cotta replicas of many of the things they had cherished in life.

The capital that the Sui had laid out and the T'ang brought to completion was the functioning center of imperial power and of the institutional system, but it was far more. Ch'ang-an was a great cosmopolis from which T'ang influences radiated in all directions. The city's pulse was the pulse of the whole culture of Eastern Asia. It had been laid out as a walled rectangle roughly six by five and a quarter miles. Following ancient tradition, it was oriented to the points of the compass. It was divided into three precincts. The first was the palace city where the emperor lived with his family and intimate servitors and where, in the early part of the dynasty, he held audience, performed innumerable ceremonies and transacted the business of state. The second was the administrative city, with all the offices of government ranged along streets within its walls. The third was the outer city, divided by great avenues into 106 walled wards and two walled markets. Officials and commoners lived in these wards. In them, too, were the many temples of Buddhism and of religious Taoism and ancestral halls of wealthy officials. Some wards were specialized to function – for example the P'ing-k'ang ward, where the brothels were.

The emperor and the officialdom set the tone and the pace of the city's life. The emperor fixed the calendar of ceremonial observances, decreed the times for holidays and seasonal festivals, for religious abstinence, for state mourning. His will was the ultimate arbiter of all things. He could favor certain artists or architects with his patronage. He could honor certain of the great poets of the time and even exchange verses with them. His favor determined which schools of Buddhism prospered and which declined or went underground. In his name were issued the innumerable decrees meant to govern every aspect of life in the capital, provinces and in neighboring lands dutifully subservient to the T'ang. The imperial government was omnipresent in the city; for example it licensed the liquor shops, supervised the markets, had its troops police the city, issued ordination certificates to monks and nuns, settled disputes and punished criminals.

Contrasting fortunes

Officials busied themselves with their duties and with politics, which meant being constantly on the watch for shifts in the direction of imperial favor so that one was with the 'ins' rather than the 'outs.' One needed luck to stay on top, for bad timing and imperial displeasure could mean an ill-paid provincial assignment or exile to the distant South, or still worse, removal of one's name from the official rolls. But if one were energetic and lucky and well-connected, life in Ch'ang-an could be pleasant indeed. Here is a poet's evocation of the high noon of his life in the capital city:

Since I first came to the capital
Bringing only a bundle of books
Thirty years of toilsome work
Have enabled me to own this house . . .
The central hall is lofty and newly built,
And there at the seasonal festivals I offer sacrifices of
    meat and vegetables.
At the front portico I feast the visiting noble kinfolk,
When they have come for a capping or a wedding.
Within the courtyard there is an open space,
And tall trees, eight or nine,
With wistaria vines about them,
Lush with spring flowers or summer shade.
In the eastern hall I sit looking at the mountains,
While the clouds and the wind urge each other on . . .
The mountain birds sing morning and evening,
It is like dwelling in a misty valley.
My principal wife presides over the northern hall,
Providing suitable food and clothing for relatives near
    and far.
She is graced by the title of Lady of Kao-p'ing,
And her sons and grandsons follow when she wears the
    robes of court.
When the door is opened and one asks who is coming to
    call,
It is nearly always a ranking nobleman.
In case one doesn't know whether his office is high or
    low,
Hanging from his jade belt is a golden fish.
[insignia of the third rank and above]

Right: A scene depicting a musical occasion during the T'ang Dynasty. Royal patronage ensured a flowering of the arts during this period.

Below left: A fine example of decorative three-color pottery of the T'ang era showing a group of musicians on the back of a camel.

Such were the satisfactions which came to the fortunate. Life for the commoner resident in the city, however, was gray and constricted, with only a brief time at New Year when he might rest from his labor. He was without rights and subject to abuse and exactions from those in authority, perhaps given a little hope and charity by the Buddhist monks. Here the poet Po Chü-i evokes the contrast between rich and poor:

In the Royal City spring is almost over.
Tinkle, tinkle – the coaches and horsemen pass.
We tell each other, 'This is the peony season':
And follow with the crowd that goes to the Flower
    Market.
'Cheap and dear – no uniform price;
The cost of the plant depends on the number of
    blossoms.
For the fine flower, a hundred pieces of damask:
For the cheap flower, five bits of silk . . .'
Each household thoughtlessly follows the custom,
Man by man, no one realizing
There happened to be an old farm laborer who came by
    chance that way.
He bowed his head and sighed a deep sigh
But his sigh nobody understood.
He was thinking, 'A cluster of deep-red flowers
Would pay the taxes on ten poor houses.'

The T'ang's period of brilliance and success ended in 755 with the insurrection of An Lu-shan, though the dynasty continued for another century and a half and even enjoyed brief periods of prosperity. Subtly and slowly the centralized political order and the society and economy which went with it were transformed. In the long twilight of the T'ang a new order emerged, and to this we now turn.

Decline of the T'ang

Dynastic names do not help us to understand the crucial period from about 755 to the consolidation of Sung power in 979, so we shall concentrate on the dimensions of political and social change which in effect destroyed the T'ang order and gave birth to what many regard as a proto-modern order under the Sung. Superficially, the centrifu-gal movement of political power was similar to what occurred during the decline and fall of Han. The T'ang had initiated a system of military governorships (*chieh-tu shih*) for the defense of the northern frontiers. At first the functions of these governors were purely those of military defense. But gradually they were granted control over civil administration in their areas, and in time this spread to neighboring areas and was accompanied by other controls.

An Lu-shan, a Central Asian of humble birth and mixed ancestry, by luck, ability and guile became military governor of the important frontier army base at Peking. His power grew, and, after finding accomplices in the T'ang capital, he turned his well trained army southward to challenge the reigning dynasty. An Lu-shan died soon thereafter, but not before the T'ang system had been irremediably damaged. His armies had taken and held the two capitals and had driven the reigning emperor into far Szechwan where he was obliged to abdicate. Although the T'ang dynasty was restored to power in 760, thanks to the intercession of its Uighur Turkish allies, it had lost control of most of the Great Plain from which the T'ang had felt itself obliged to set up military governors in strategic areas such as those that guarded the capital and the canal route to southern grain supplies. These governors were now a law unto themselves and pre-empted the revenues of huge areas. The government sought new sources of revenue, one of the principal devices being the Salt Monopoly. (Salt is an absolute necessity for people living mainly on a vegetable and cereal diet.) Salt Commissioners for the various regions became in time far more powerful than regular officials and had great power over the court and the regions where they were assigned. The prestige of the other officials was further undermined by the eunuchs, whose power grew as the T'ang house declined. Eunuchs gained great influence not only over the palace and the private imperial treasury but also over imperial succession, official appointments and the principal armies.

Thus the orderly and rational working of local administration and the symmetrical pyramid of central power were both badly eroded, and the T'ang emperors were on the defensive for the last 150 years of the dynasty. Funds for the central government, despite all expedients, were sadly diminished, and the capital buildings fell into disrepair or, when burned, were not rebuilt. Examinations were held less often, and posts went unfilled for lack of funds.

As the system gradually broke down, those in authority showed a weakening of self-confidence. One expression of this was a growing mood of xenophobia, the end of T'ang cosmopolitanism, that culminated in the suppression of Buddhism and other foreign religions in the years 842-45. Advisers had played upon the reigning emperor's need for funds, and in a virulent decree he ordered the confiscation of Buddhist temples, their wealth and lands, the destruction of the paintings which had graced their walls, the smelting down of their images, the return of their clergy to lay life. Here is a passage from the decree:

From the Han and Wei onward, Buddhism prospered more and more, and in recent times they propagated this foreign way; consequently its contaminating practices grew luxuriantly and became more and more prevalent. Thereby it came to corrupt our national customs; gradually and unnoticed, it deluded men's minds, and the masses were ever more beguiled. It reached to the mountains and plains . . ., to the castelated gates of the two capitals. The monks and their followers daily increased, and the Buddhist temples daily multiplied. They overtaxed people's strength in the work of construction; they despoiled people of their wealth for ornaments of gold and precious stones. Buddhism causes people to abandon prince and parents for their religious masters; it causes the separation of mates by monastic laws. For breaking down the laws and ruining the people, there is nothing to surpass it.

Buddhism remained as an important force in Chinese life, but its great days were past.

In the insurrection of An Lu-shan many once-great families had lost their land-holding, status and wealth. In the even more massive rebellion of

Huang Ch'ao (875-84) and associated disorders, the rest of the T'ang elite was destroyed, along with the great capitals, the prosperous ports of foreign trade and much else. Those who survived as power-holders were mainly local military chiefs – some of them commanders of Huang Ch'ao's armies, some of them commanders of the imperial armies sent against the rebels. As they fastened their hold on provinces and whole regions they inevitably developed groups around them to do their bidding and share their wealth. These were neither the eunuchs, so long favored by the dying T'ang, nor members of the families which had furnished members for the T'ang bureaucracy. Rather, they were a mixed lot of 'new men,' of relatively humble origin, who became part of the apparatus of the regional warlords and whose fortunes rose or fell with theirs. These people survived the period of upheaval accompanying the end of the T'ang and the struggle for succession and they formed one element of the new elite of the Sung dynasty, which was founded by one of the warlords in 960 and consolidated by 979.

Growth of the South under the Sung

The map of Sung China looks very different from the maps of earlier periods. The Sung did not control the Great Wall frontier. A formidable power straddling the wall, but with its center in the Liao

Valley of Manchuria, the Khitan state of Liao exerted continuing pressure on the northern and northeastern frontiers. In 1005 a treaty was signed, under which the Sung paid annual tribute to Liao, and peace was assured for nearly four decades. To the west, the Sung Empire was unable to reassert control of Central Asia and its trade routes, for there the Hsi-Hsia kingdom maintained hegemony and posed regular threats from the west from 1032 to 1227. But the lower part of the map also looked very different. The shift southward of China's center of population, which had begun in T'ang times, now rapidly accelerated, and the lower Yangtse and southeast coastal provinces became ever more productive, populous and rich. A feature of this demographic change was the growth of sprawling port cities, four of which eventually attained populations of at least two million. The southern and eastern areas became more productive than ever after the introduction of early-ripening rice in 1012, and by 1119 over 70 percent of the money and goods reaching the Sung capital of K'ai-feng came from the lower Yangtse area. The canal system linked into the two great river systems was enlarged to an unprecedented capacity, and inter-regional traders as well as government ships made use of it. The capital of the Northern Sung (960-1126) was on the Yellow River plain, not far east of the ancient

fire departments and much more. Though the Confucian schoolmasters still taught that virtue could only be nurtured on a farm, it was hardly surprising that people flocked to the cities. Su Tung-p'o, the great poet, was in office in the port city of Hangchow when he wrote these lines after returning from a night's ramble through the hills behind the West Lake:

Suddenly rubbing my sleepy eyes
I saw the brilliant lights of Hotang.
The milling people were clapping their hands
And frolicking like young deer in the wilds.
I realized then that the simple joys of life
Could be enjoyed only by the simple men . . . .

The fall of the Northern Sung

Yet in this empire of reduced size and uprecedented prosperity there were still problems. For one thing, the new official elite invested continuously in land, and their estates (*chuang-yüan*), worked by tenant farmers, became – especially in the southeast – the prevailing system. It had its advantages, particularly for mobilizing capital and labor to open new land, but the tenants lived miserably, obliged to pay both rent to the landlord and taxes to the government.

Nor was rural poverty in the midst of a booming economy the only problem. The government at K'ai-feng had, as the bureaucracy grew in size and complexity, an increasingly heavy burden of official salaries to pay. It was also obliged annually to pay large amounts of gold and silk to the Khitan in the north and the Hsi-hsia kingdom in the west. This tribute was both the price for peace and a guarantee of a continuing supply of horses, essential for the Sung military establishment. Whatever expedients the Sung Government tried, their natural enemies made them pay dearly for every horse they bought. Thus the Sung military establishment, though poorly organized and badly officered, was nonetheless a great financial drain on the government. (A million men were in the army for the defense of the northern frontier.)

The eleventh century saw one set of plans after another aimed at solving the fiscal crisis by one expedient or another. Other plans were designed to restore social morale by, for example, the abolition of the forced labor system, the redistribution

Right: A student completes his final examinations. In the Sung Dynasty, the ready availability of cheap books and a growing network of academies permitted the development of an educated governing elite.

Left: A silk scroll entitled 'Going up the river at the Spring Festival.' Emperors of the period decreed the timing of religious festivals.

Below left: A golden mask uncovered in a princess's tomb from the Liao Dynasty (907-1125). This tomb formed part of a joint burial site for the princess and her husband, and contained jewelry made from a wide variety of materials including gold, silver, jade, pearl and amber.

Below right: Emperor Jin Sung (c 1022-63)

capital city of Loyang. It was not merely the symbolic center of empire and the seat of government, but also a thriving commercial and industrial city, and may well have been the greatest such city in the world prior to the Industrial Revolution. It was located at a key point in the transportation network, and we can see in accounts of it and in pictures the intense bustle of its commercial life. It was surely indicative of a new order that one Sung emperor thought of expanding his palace (which was indeed cramped) but gave up the idea when he saw that the project would be disruptive of businesses.

The Sung, then, was far more knit into South China than any of the dynasties which preceded it, and beyond the South – out of the ports of the southeast coast – there grew to be a huge volume of Chinese trade carried in new and improved Chinese ships. To give some index of the shift away from a northwestern landward orientation and towards a southern and seaward one, we might note that by 1126, 65 percent of all tribute missions accompanied by traders which reached China came by sea, and only 35 percent by land. Later, the seaborne percentage became even higher.

Far-reaching changes

Such a vastly changed social and economic landscape required a new type of governing elite. The Sung opened the examination system to many times the number of candidates of T'ang times, and those who passed became virtually the whole of the governing class. The old families familiar for more than three centuries in the records of Sui

and T'ang appear no more, and instead there is a high percentage of 'new men' taking the examinations and rising through the official ranks.

The rise of the new men was encouraged by a network of private academies and by the availability of cheap books, which followed the spread of printing in the eleventh and twelfth centuries. While the examinations were based, as before, on study of the classics and of ancient literature, there were long periods under the Sung when the candidates were asked to interpet and apply to questions of public policy the principles they had acquired in their studies. The Sung was the first dynasty to pay their officials generously and regularly, for in earlier times it was assumed that most officials had private wealth.

With the shift in the economic center of empire and changes in economic life (such as the growth of a money economy and the use of credit), and with rapid urbanization, there emerged a popular culture of an unprecedented kind. We can only sample some of its features. Printing has been noted as contributing to the spread of classical learning, but its impact was far wider. Millions, especially in the great port cities, acquired the rudiments of literacy, and writers appeared who wrote in a popular vein to entertain. Both the short story and the novel began to take shape, and the popular theater developed and found its audience. There were story-tellers, jugglers, cheap taverns, puppet-shows and any number of entertainments for ordinary people. The southeastern port cities also had a variety of public social services unknown in earlier cities: parks, free dispensaries, homes for the aged, public graveyards,

of communal lands and the reform of public education. All these schemes had, to use the words of one reformer, the aim of 'enriching the state, making the army strong and the people content.' But the most sweeping plan was that which Wang An-shih first presented to the emperor in 1058. He won the emperor's support, and new laws and regulations issued in a steady stream. They dealt with financial planning for the whole empire; a new system of transporting and distributing tax goods; inexpensive loans to farmers intended to save them from usurers; a graduated tax in lieu of labor service, which was to be abolished; a militia and mutual security system meant to reduce the cost of the standing army; and changes in the examination system designed to de-emphasize poetry and lyrical prose in favor of broad principles and policy judgment.

Wang remained in favor for some seven years, but long before he resigned he had run into strenuous opposition. That opposition hardened into a fully worked-out conservative position which was resorted to again and again in later centuries to block large-scale efforts at reform. The key element in the conservative position was that reform could only proceed by the moral reformation of those in power, beginning with the emperor and proceeding down through the ranks of elite officials, and thence, by example, to the people as a whole. No institutional measure, no 'law,' was any use unless this had first occurred. Such a view was, of course, drawn from the most fundamental tenets of Confucian teaching, as interpreted by Mencius. Against it Wang An-shih threw the hard, more mordant views early stated by Hsun-tzu and embodied in the systematized Confucian classics of Han times. He stressed the need for stern and steadfast authority, the need for rewards and punishments as a supplement to persuasion and the power of example. The conservatives stressed the resolution of conflict by reference to good custom and the mediation of morally educated men, and they opposed the detailed expedients written into Wang's laws and regulations.

The battle lines were thus drawn, and though many on the conservative side had in fact supported one or more of the measures proposed by Wang, they now attacked his program as a whole. Wang's difficult personality, his impatience, arrogance and slovenliness, were also made much of, and his opponents in the bureaucracy were able to frustrate his plans by deliberate inaction. The

Left: 'The Haunt of the Sage' by a member of the Ma yuam school, painted 1190-1225.

Right: The cavalry of Chingiz Khan. By 1279 all of China was controled by the Mongols.

Below right: Pottery actors and dancers from the Yuan Dynasty (1271-1368).

Below: A painting by Li T'ang (*c* 1050-1130) entitled 'Playing the Flute at Ching Chi' – an example of the delicacy and subtlety of Chinese art.

struggle between the reformers and the conservatives continued to the end of Northern Sung. It envenomed political life and thus contributed to the debacle of 1126 when K'ai-feng fell to the northeastern power of the Jürched, who had replaced the Khitan. The Emperor Hui-tsung, the most famous aesthete to occupy the throne of China, was taken off to Manchuria and remnants of the imperial house fled south as their predecessors had done in 317, leaving North China down to the Huai River line again in alien hands.

Rule of Southern Sung

Those of the Sung ruling house who fled south in 1126-27 had had long experience in dealing with pressure from the northern and western frontiers. They had seen tedious diplomacy result in fragile, costly treaties. They had seen sporadic trade interrupted by embargoes and smuggling. They had lived with staggering military costs and the near certainty that their army would collapse if attacked. When the first Sung ruler of the new kingdom in the South was in search of a capital, his first choice was Nanking from which he could

view – if his vision was good enough – the whole of the North China Plain all the way to the Great Wall. Neither he nor those around him had forgotten that this was where the successors of the Han, seven centuries before, had made a base from which they defended Chinese culture behind the broad expanse of the Yangtse. Yet the Sung, on balance, found Nanking vulnerable, and they finally settled on the port of Hangchow, then a great, rich and populous city but never before considered for the site of a Chinese capital. Indeed, it never was referred to as the 'capital,' but only as the 'temporary residence of the emperor' (*hsing-tsai,* Marco Polo's Quinsai). It was set on a lozenge-shaped piece of land, and contrary to all the precedent for capitals, its main gate was at the north, and the palaces and ceremonial buildings had to be placed in the south suburbs. The city fathers and the merchants adapted themselves to the arrival of the Sung remnants, and in time the city was greatly improved and beautified. It was described with awe and enthusiasm by thirteenth-century European visitors. One of them from Italy remarked:

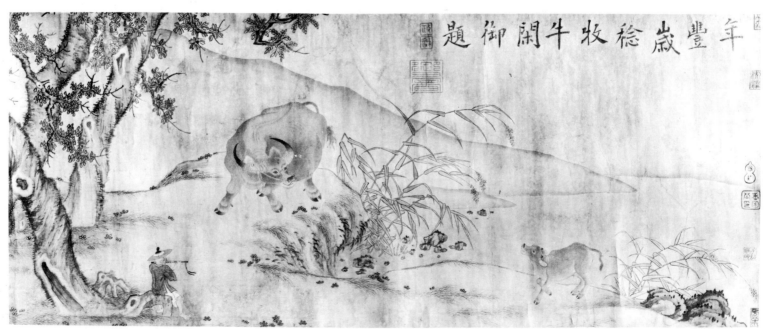

This city is greater than any in the world, and is quite 100 miles round . . . The city has also great suburbs containing more people than the city itself contains. It has 12 principal gates, and at each of these gates . . . are cities larger than Venice or Padua might be.

The Southern Sung (1127-1279) existed in a productive, highly populated but restricted land area. It drew revenues from the land tax, but a large proportion of its income came from taxes on sea trade at the great port cities. It was obliged to take a defensive position *vis à vis* its enemies who occupied North China, but it developed a formidable navy, useable on the waterways of the Yangtse Valley and at sea. Examinations were resumed, and a bureaucracy recruited. The political issues which were argued bitterly at court were mainly echoes of Northern Sung issues because, indeed, the problems were very similar: how to maintain an adequate military force without bankrupting the government; whether to remain on the defensive or attempt a reconquest of the northern provinces; what to do about the engrossment of land; and how to apportion the land tax. The enemy in the North continued to exert serious, if intermittent, pressure. In 1161 they attempted to cross the Yangtse in force, only to have their fleet of 600 ships destroyed by the Sung, who used explosives against them, one of the first such uses in world history.

A further source of friction at court and in the ranks of the elite generally was the heated debate over a new Confucian ideology. We have noted that during the time of the Northern Sung the conservatives had formulated a political position that they attempted to justify by citing selected works from the Confucian Canon. But mere selective quotation was not really adequate to their purposes, and in the end they began trying to reinterpret Confucianism itself. The effort involved trying to borrow sufficiently from Buddhist and Taoist thought to make Confucianism less archaic and fully competitive with its rivals. Until the time of the Southern Sung, this effort had been scattered and uncoordinated, but then a man named Chu Hsi (1130-1200) knitted together the ideas of the Northern Sung thinkers into a single system – not without violence to some of their ideas. He and his followers, both at court and outside, now insisted that theirs was the only true interpretation of the Way of Confucians (*Tao-hsüeh*) and that those who studied or taught differently had to be classified as following false or unorthodox teachings (*Wei-hsüeh*). He lashed out in high polemical style against both Buddhism and Taoism.

Chu Hsi's opponents attacked him unmercifully, accusing him of propagating 'false learnings,' or giving himself the airs of a sage and of being arrogant about his absolute rightness while refusing to lend a hand with the problems which faced the government. Supported by sinecures, he produced a staggering volume of writing: his own commentaries to the Confucian classics, his own record of the founders of the new Confucianism (*Chin-ssu lu*), his own rearrangement of the great Northern Sung historical work, *Tzu-chih T'ung-chien*, to point up the moral lessons of history and, finally, his *Yü-lu* or 'Recorded conversations,' whose title bears a suspicious similarity to the *Lun-yü* or 'discourses' of Confucius. Not long after his death, his new orthodoxy took hold and by 1313, under the Mongol dynasty of Yüan, it had been made the official basis of the examination curriculum. It remained *the* official orthodoxy until the abolition of the examination system in 1906.

Despite its defensive posture, a series of mediocre emperors and divisions over state policies and ideology among the elite, the time of the Southern Sung was in many ways a creative period. In mathematics, medicine and agricultural technology there were striking advances, as there were in shipbuilding and navigation. Southern Sung painters continued the brilliant tradition of amateur painting that had flourished in the North. Poets developed forms which had their origin in popular literature. In the prosperous south-eastern cities, life for the literate elite and the merchant princes was opulent, and the shops and places of entertainment offered everything for their delectation. The common people, if they were fortunate, belonged to one of the guilds which monopolized all the crafts, trades and services of the cities.

The Mongol threat

The Southern Sung was apparently unaware for a long time of the rise in the steppeland of a people more formidable than any which China had dealt with before. These were the Mongols. Chingiz Khan began in the early thirteenth century by putting together a coalition of Mongol tribes in his ancestral homeland. From there he began a career of ferocious and far-flung conquests that were continued by his sucessors and that engrossed most of the civilizations surrounding Central Asia and, but for good luck, might well have included

Western Europe as well. The area of China proved the most resistant to the Mongol campaigners and their allies. The Jürched, who had driven the Sung from the north in 1126, held K'ai-feng until 1234, when they were overwhelmed by Mongol forces.

The Sung at first tried to bargain with the Mongols and then tried to attack them. Neither policy worked. With this terrible force on their doorstep, the Chinese made a final reform effort to improve social morale and raise revenues for the army by severely limiting the great estates accumulated by landlords. This of course alienated some of the most powerful people in the empire, and after the fall of the dynasty, one writer noted, 'When in our days the Sung seized the land of the people, they lost the affection of the people' (for people read landlords). There was bickering and dissension at court, and a growing number of Chinese defected to the Mongols. In 1274 the Mongol general Bayan crossed the Yangtse. When one major city resisted, following uniform Mongol policy, once it was captured Bayan massacred all its inhabitants. The following year Hangchow surrendered and was spared. The emperor became a fugitive and in 1279 the Sung came to an end. All of China, for the first time in its history, was under alien rule.

China under the Mongols

The new emperor of China was Kublai, grandson of the great Chingiz, who had proclaimed himself

Emperor of China and of the great dynasty of Yüan in 1260, 19 years before the Sung was extinguished. Kublai claimed to be Khan of Khans, head of the Mongol world empire, as well as Emperor of China, but by this time the various descendants of Chingiz were in fact dividing the empires they had conquered among themselves. As a result, Kublai spent much of his time on campaigns outside China, seeking the military conquests that alone would establish his prestige in the Mongol world. He held court during the summer at his tent capital of Karakorum in the high steppe country; in winter he held court in his Chinese capital, Ta-tu, on the site of modern Peking, which had been built for him by Chinese artisans according to Chinese traditional capital plans. Thus there was a dualism about his reign, and the Mongols similarly imposed a half-Mongol, half-Chinese order in the administration of conquered China. Probably none of China's conquerors was less influenced by Chinese culture than were the Mongols. Kublai and his successors used Mongol as the only court language. Few of Kublai's successors as emperor were even literate in Chinese, and to the very end of the dynasty there were felt tents in the great walled capital city.

The structure of the imperial government was twofold, with the Mongol part in control. The Mongols and their Central Asian henchmen at the capital ran the inner court, where policy was

made, while the Chinese were relegated to the outer court, where the paperwork of this highly centralized state was carried on. The Chinese designed a symmetrical and highly rational set of institutions, improving on T'ang and Sung practices, yet the man who occupied the summit of this structure was in no way committed to Chinese cultural values and was really only concerned with the preservation of Mongol supremacy over both the steppelands and his Chinese subjects. The great centralization of power which could be seen in Sung institutions after the disappearance of the T'ang aristocratic order was further accentuated by alien rule. In the conquered provinces military control was assigned to a trusted Mongol, and the necessary civilian apparatus – usually Chinese – was attached to the military office. The examination system was reinstituted in 1313 and examinations were held irregularly thereafter, but those who succeeded could not rise to high office; they worked instead at routine work under Mongol military officials or the Central Asians who assisted them. The tax system was in many ways derived from earlier Chinese systems, but the disposition of the proceeds was in alien hands. State monopolies, commercial taxes, economic measures of all kinds (including planned inflation and deflation) were for the benefit of the ruling Mongol minority. The opening of a world market to Chinese trade via land and sea routes brought in vast new wealth which the Mongol overlords taxed heavily.

As was usual in the lands that they had conquered, the Mongols deliberately set about redefining social classes. In China this worked out as a four-part stratification: Mongols; their henchmen, chiefly Central Asians; *Han-jen*, operationally, all the peoples of North China; and *Nan-jen*, southern Chinese, those who held out longest against Mongol attack. Although Mongol measures, especially taxation, made use of this discriminatory system, the natural Chinese elite in both North and South – the perpetuators of Chinese culture – ultimately prevailed. In time, they would absorb the Central Asians, the Mongols would be killed or would return to the steppe, and this natural elite would once more share in the governance of the state and the management of society. Yet the century of subordination, and the brutal political arena in which they had played a role, left deep scars, and these in turn would have long-term effects on the subsequent history of imperial China.

How did the natural elite – the Confucian-educated landholding families – survive this long period of discriminatory treatment, of being barred from high office in which, according to the doctrine, a Confucian finds real fulfillment? Some, the poorer, were caught on the horns of a dilemma of Confucian origin: they despised the ruler and thus should not have served him; yet they were poor, and the moral imperative of filial obedience said that one must support one's parents in their old age. Such people swallowed their pride, took the examinations, gained a subordinate office and lived wretched lives as underlings to some Mongol colonel or his aides. Their lives often ended, after torture, in prison, but they had drawn their stipends and fulfilled their filial obligation. Others, better off, could take one of several roads, none of which included an official career. Some used up their lives and their substance in sensual indulgence. Others followed one or another form of Buddhist or Taoist withdrawal and sought, in the pursuit of other-worldly goods, compensation for life in a world that offered them little satisfaction and no fulfillment. Still others

二物、
之輒前燒十餘步、人亦不敢近、蒙古惟畏此
牛皮皆碎迸無迹、又有飛火槍注藥以火發、
鐵繩懸震天雷順城而下、至掘處火發人與
可容人、則城上不可奈何矣、人有獻策者以
透蒙古又為牛皮洞、直至城下、掘城為龕間、
聞百里外、所爇圍半畝已上、火點著鐵甲皆
用鐵罐盛藥以火點之、砲起火發、其聲如雷、
特有火砲名震天雷者

were made of sterner stuff and led an austere life in society, if not of it. They read the Confucian classics, they wrote commentaries, they ruled their households according to strict Confucian principles and some among them took private pupils or started schools to impart their understandings of the classics. All this was done with the steadfast faith that better government would someday come. Thus was China's great tradition perpetuated in dire adversity.

The pattern of withdrawal from political life fostered a great burst of creativity, though the fact that the Yüan dynasty is one of the great periods of Chinese landscape painting is perhaps less the result of social trends than of the inner dynamic of Chinese painting itself. The Yüan painters recaptured the glories of Northern Sung landscape painting, and they, in turn, were to exert a far-reaching influence on painting during the rest of the imperial era. The development of drama is another striking featue of Yüan cultural life, and the drama, unlike landscape painting, was a product of popular culture, of city life, where the drama found both its themes and its audiences. Perhaps the absence of Confucians in high places to watch over public morals had something to do with the vitality of the drama, and indeed of the novel and popular stories.

Challenges to Mongol rule

As one looks at the record, it is a wonder that the Mongols lasted nearly a century. Only their superior military prowess over the Chinese managed to keep them in their position of power. Their rule was unenlightened; they and their henchmen were a parasitic superstratum on a headless Chinese system that creaked along, interrupted from time to time by rapacious forays from the overlords who needed more funds. The first center of mass dissent was in the very heart of China, the Huai Valley and the adjoining areas to the north and south. The immediate cause was a series of natural disasters: plagues, floods, locusts. The dissidents were led by the Red Turbans, who rose in the late 1340s. Their ranks were swelled by defectors from a forced labor corps of 170,000 that the Mongols had assembled in southwest Shantung to work on a much-resented canal project. To cope with local disorders, the officials appointed some of the bandit chiefs to governorships, acts that merely accelerated the process of political and social disintergration. A contemporary ditty of anonymous origin was said to be circulating all the way from Peking to south of the Yangtse. It went like this:

Splendid this Great Yüan where sycophants and traitors command.
Digging the canal and changing the currency are the roots of the troubles.
Stirred up by Red Turbans, by the thousands and tens of thousands.
Chaotic this government; cruel its punishments, and the people's resentment daily grows.
Humans eat humans while paper is traded for paper [managed inflation]; who has ever seen the likes of it!
Thieves get to be officials and officials behave like thieves.
The good can't be told from the bad! Alas how sad it is!

Out of the myriad discontents at all social levels there arose a number of challengers to the decrepit rule of the Mongol Yüan, and by the 1350s China had become a chaotic battleground on which dozens of rebel armies contended with one another and with the Yüan for various scraps of territory. Out of this anarchy there finally emerged a single victor, a peasant-born Chinese war leader named Chu Yüan-chang, and with his ascendancy came the founding of a new dynasty, the Ming (1368-1644). The story of the Ming and its successor dynasty, the Ch'ing (1644-1911), represented a new phase of Chinese history, especially in its relations with the outside world.

Above: The formula for gunpowder, a Chinese invention that was first used against the Mongols in the twelfth century.

Left: Chingiz Khan, the great ruler of the Mongols who began the conquest of much of Asia after uniting the Mongol tribal groups of the Asian steppelands.

Right: Mongol polo players. This work, dating from the Ming period, was probably painted by the famed Chinese artist Li Lin.

Japan

The island nation of Japan, lying off the northeastern corner of Asia, had from early historic times played an active role in East Asian history within the context of its isolation from the major centers of continental political and cultural activity. It is, of course, the phenomenal rise of Japan as a world force in the nineteenth and twentieth centuries that engages our special interest today. But it would be a mistake to think of Japan as simply a modern phenomenon, a kind of belated and accidental product of a favorable geographical location and a new scientific and industrial technology. The modern Japanese state rests on cultural and institutional foundations of considerable durability and antiquity.

Insularity and isolation were, until modern times, major factors in Japan's relationship to the outside world. The analogy with Britain comes naturally to mind. Both island countries, located at the opposite ends of the Eurasian land-mass, began their histories as territories on the outer limits of civilization. Both existed as culs-de-sac, the terminal points of migration movements and cultural influences from the continent. Neither had until modern times the resources with which to exert major political or civilizing influences upon their neighbors, although they did from time to time engage in continental politics. And, perhaps because of their insularity, both countries were among the first to develop a consciousness of national identity, each taking the lead in its portion of the world in the creation of a modern nation state.

These superficial similarities between the two island nations, however, serve to accentuate differences of considerable historical significance. Japan's isolation was much greater than Britain's. The Straits of Tsushima are 120 miles wide; the Straits of Dover but 20 miles. Moreover, the Tsushima crossing ends in southern Korea, still over a thousand miles from the major centers in China. Such isolation worked two ways. Japan's contact with the continent was limited in volume and frequency, and Japan's capacity to maintain a military presence even in Korea evaporated in the seventh century. On the other hand, Japan was almost completely free from military or political interference from the continent. There were, for instance, no instances of intermarriage between Chinese and Japanese ruling families and no claim by a continentally based Church to religious authority over the Japanese islands. Japan experienced no parallel to Britain's conquest by Rome. And if the Norman conquest could be said to have its analogue in the Mongol invasions of 1274 and 1281, the results were dramatically different. For the Japanese fighters repulsed both invasions, thrusting back with great slaughter the massive second armada with its more than 150,000 Mongol, Chinese and Korean soldiers.

Japan's separation from the continent was more than geographical. The Japanese as a people, though basically of the same Mongoloid stock as the other peoples of East Asia, are physically and linguistically quite distinct from the Chinese. The Japanese language is now assigned by linguists to the Altaic group of languages that predominates in north Asia and includes the Turkic, Tungusic and Mongolian families. But Japanese is sufficiently different from its closest continental paral-

lel, Korean, for its origin as a separate language to appear extremely remote. Polysyllabic and highly inflected, it is clearly a member of a quite different family of languages from Chinese, which is basically monosyllabic and uninflected.

Where the Japanese came from and when they formed into the people they are today, is very much a moot question. They are clearly an admixture of a number of ethnic strains which pushed into the islands from the continent. Most recent archeological evidence indicates that paleolithic life existed on the islands perhaps as early as 200,000 years ago. But the antecedents of the present-day Japanese are identified more clearly with a succession of much later ceramic cultures. The first of these, known as Jōmon from its style of pottery, dates from at least the sixth millennium BC. Studies of the Jōmon people are not sufficiently advanced to determine their origin or in what way if any they are related to other streams of people who were on the move at that time in the lands surrounding the Pacific. At any rate Jōmon culture was submerged, and to some degree assimilated, by another cultural complex that moved into the Japanese islands from Korea as late as the third century BC. This culture, known as Yayoi from the name of an archeological site, was distinguished by its use of irrigated rice cultivation. It is regarded as directly ancestral to historic Japanese culture in terms of political organization, religion, social structure and economy. With the spread of Yayoi culture, the basis was laid for the emergence of the first historic state, sometime in the fourth century AD.

It is common to look upon the Japanese from the time of their appearance in the annals of East Asian history to the time of their encounter with European influence in the nineteenth century as illustrating in their way of life and higher culture simply a variation of the dominant Chinese civilization. To be sure, many elements of Chinese culture – the written language, technology, arts and letters, certain political forms – were adopted by the Japanese. And Buddhism became a common religious belief. But the East Asian zone of civilization was probably never as homogeneously knit together as was the European community of peoples. The Confucian world view that emanated from China had to compete in Japan with the localized religious beliefs of Shinto, while the more universal conceptions of man and his relationship to the unknown provided by Buddhism were equally of alien origin to Japan and to China. Thus despite Japan's emulation of China throughout the many centuries when it represented the epitome of higher civilization in East Asia, the Japanese people retained a certain sense of detachment from the continent, clinging to indigenous religious beliefs and social customs which were to provide the ultimate basis for their alienation from the continent in modern times.

Confucianism, both as ethical theory and social practice, was both advised and questioned by the Japanese. This held true even for the period from the early seventeenth century, which constitutes Japan's primary Confucian age. In the intellectual revival of the seventeenth century, the Japanese ruling class avidly studied and applied Confucian

Above right: Aerial view of the Hall of the Great Buddha, part of the Tōdaiji temple in Nara. The temple was founded in AD 745.

Left: A 'Doggu' figure in terracotta from the Jomon culture of the third or fourth centuries BC.

Right: A European ship fires a broadside. Western traders reached Japan in the sixteenth century.

theories of government, law and ethics to the society of the times. Yet by the nineteenth century a reaction had set in. Japanese writers urged their countrymen to resist their intellectual subordination to China, and heaped scorn on those who would eat Japanese rice yet bow to the superiority of everything Chinese. The Japanese, they argued, should return to a belief in their own unique identity, for theirs was 'a divine land where the sun rises and the primordial energy originates,' and they themselves were completely different from and 'superior to the peoples of China, India, Russia, Holland, Siam and Cambodia.' They revived, in other words, the concept that Japan was 'the Land of the Gods,' and the conviction that the Japanese gods had provided the Japanese people with a superior morality and a superior polity centered on a ruling house descended from the Sun Goddess.

The early Japanese state

The origin of this polity takes us back to the third century AD and the formation of the first unified political order in Japan. It was at this time that

certain of the most fundamental elements of the Japanese ways of life and thought were crystallized. Clearly, by the fourth century, despite the diverse origins of the Japanese people and the uncertain provenance of the cultural influences exerted upon the islands, the Japanese had fused into a homogeneous ethnic and social community, united in language, political organization and style of life. Once the Japanese islands were politically unified, the ruling family that had achieved the unification established a sovereignty that was to endure without displacement to modern times. The political history of Japan was to involve no competing sovereignties, no struggles with a Scotland or Wales, as in the British analogy.

Unity in Japan was from the first a matter of imposing order upon diversity. An early Chinese report that mentions Japan in the third century describes the land of 'Wa' as comprising 'more than a hundred communities' ruled over by a great chieftain who relied on magical powers. In ancient Japan both the geographical base and the system of social organization made for a fragmentation of internal political units. From the time we first know of them members of the ruling class appear to have been organized by lineages into clan-like groupings, known as *uji*, whose members claimed common descent from some deity. Each geographical locality gave rise to a hierarchy of families which recognized the authority of a locally powerful chief. By the time of the establishment of the Yamato hegemony in the fourth century AD, the distribution of local chiefs had stabilized, giving rise to a large number – perhaps as many as 500 – small units. The identification of early political power with local topography is revealed by the fact that in many of these units the ruling family bore the name of the district. These districts were eventually consolidated during the eighth century into the traditional 66 provinces into which Japan was divided until modern times, but the boundaries of the smaller units were to remain as sub-units of the provinces. Political fragmentation under locally based clan leadership thus provided the ground from which Japan's ruling class was to emerge and the foundation upon which the national unity rested.

It is difficult to reconstruct any sort of coherent political history of Japan before the fifth century AD, since until the introduction of Chinese writing around the beginning of the eighth century the Japanese had no good way to keep historical records. The two earliest written chronicles, the *Kojiki* (712) and the *Nihon-Shoki* (720), purport to recount the history of Japan from the earliest times, but in addition to being written long after

the events described, they are heavily infused with myth and slavishly adhere to Chinese literary coventions that consistently exaggerate the importance of rulers and their doings. Nor has archeology so far been much help, since until the end of World War II archeological excavation languished in Japan because it was thought to be a potentially sacrilegious activity.

What we now infer is that the *uji* were probably descendants of tribes that originally entered Japan from Korea. Certainly there is evidence of a long cultural and political interaction with Korea. It was from Korea that iron seems to have been introduced into Japan some time in the third century. And there appears to be little doubt that in the fourth century Japanese soldiers were used by the Korean kingdom of Mimana in the bickerings among the petty states that had sprung up in Korea after that nation ceased to be a Chinese colony (following the collapse of the Wei dynasty). There are references in the annals of the Korean kingdom of Silla to a Japanese invasion in the fourth century, and Chinese records of the fifth century refer to a Japanese 'king''s claims of military supremacy in the peninsula.

These fragmentary allusions are tantalizing. It seems impossible that the Japanese could have mounted such a sustained and effective military presence in fourth-century Korea if Japan's political organization were nothing more than a congeries of autonomous *uji* and if, in the next century, there really was some individual who merited the title of 'king.' Yet we know very little about the process by which Japan's early political unification took place, other than that by the beginning of the fifth century certain chieftains living in the vicinity of present-day Nara and Osaka, in the modern province of Yamato, seem to have established some form of sovereignty over their neighboring clans.

The Yamato hegemony

The great chieftains of the Yamato area, and also lesser chiefs in the more favorable locales of the Inland Sea region and in the Kanto area, have left evidence of a way of life emulating that of the continental aristocracy. Their prime cultural legacies to posterity are great burial mounds (called *kofun* by the Japanese) containing megalithic chambers built with rocks of enormous size. In these chambers have been found burial objects such as armor, iron weapons, bronze mirrors, earthenware artifacts and figurines depicting houses, horses and various human types. These give evidence of a style of life based upon a fusion of the ways of the horse-riding warriors of northeast

Asia with the sedentary ways of rice farmers. Already the Japanese long sword and the compound bow were well known on the continent, while the well-watered valleys of the Japanese islands provided an ample agricultural base for a growing and self-sufficient population.

The Yamato polity, which perhaps had its origin as early as the middle of the fourth century, took the shape of a military-political hegemony exerted over a federation of locally based chiefs. It was put together over the course of perhaps a century by a group of *uji* associated with the powerful clan which claimed the Sun Goddess (Amaterasu) as its *uji-gami*, or divine progenitor. The Sun Line, or Tenson, established themselves first in northern Kyushu, but eventually worked their way to central Japan, subjugating local chiefs along the way. Establishing an ancestral shrine at Ise and a political base in the Yamato Plain, the Tenson chieftains exerted both temporal and spiritual sovereignty over the Japanese islands, assuming the title of *mikoto*. Under the Yamato chieftains a hierarchy of clan chiefs acknowledged the suzerainty of the *mikoto*, maintaining various relationships with the Sun Line as either kin-*uji*, subjugated *uji*, or as subordinate *uji* who functioned as members of the extended household.

What is of greatest historical interest about this early Japanese political organization is that, both in terms of the balance of power and the exercise of authority, the Yamato hegemony became the prototype for later Japanese political regimes. Not only did the Yamato clan-state establish the historical legitimacy of a single ruling house, it also gave shape to a form of political balance of interest that was to endure in Japan so long as power rested on the control of land and the labor required to exploit it. In the Yamato hegemony is foreshadowed the system of feudal localism under a national overlord that was to characterize the Japanese state structure throughout Japan's middle ages.

From the time of the Yamato hegemony onward the government in Japan was aristocratic and, except for one notable period, comprised a military oligarchy. The Japanese ruling class began as a military elite and remained such into the nineteenth century. The Sun Line chieftains, having fought their way to a national suzerainty over a hierarchy of military clans, became the essential keystone in a balance of power. The sovereign's critical role as keeper of the peace and as legitimizer of the oligarchic hierarchy would remain crucial even after he had lost all but symbolic authority. It is here that an important difference appears between the Japanese and

Chinese political systems. For while China was governed by a succession of dynasties which rode to power after periods of civil war and internal turmoil, and whereas the Chinese emperor sought to exercise a full range of imperial powers over a unitary state, the Japanese emperor, having risen to the top of an aristocratic hierarchy, a first among those who had once been his equals, served more as symbol of the unity of a decentralized ruling elite than as absolute monarch.

This role of the *mikoto* helps explain the longevity of the Sun Line house. For once a sovereign was recognized and his hereditary rights established, the remaining elite houses refused to permit any other among themselves to usurp the role of sovereign by intrigue. And as far as achieving usurpation by conquest was concerned, no leader was ever able to fashion a military base of sufficient size and potency to make possible what would have had to be a second conquest of the Japanese islands. As viewed from the continent, Japan appeared throughout most of its history as a land of military aristocrats held together under the authority, though often only the symbolic authority, of a sacerdotal leader. And this leader, by the seventh century, had styled himself as emperor (*tennō*) in the continental fashion.

The early Imperial age

While the fourth and fifth centuries, during which the Yamato hegemony was being consolidated, proved critical for the shaping of certain indigenous political and religious practices, the next few centuries stand out for a quite different reason, namely the heavy absorption of cultural and institutional influences from the continent. By the sixth century, and increasingly in the seventh, Japan, which had been a relatively undeveloped state on the frontier of Chinese civilization, had acquired the political organization and the economic means to enable its ruling class to emulate the advanced civilization of China. Moreover, just at this time, under the leadership of the Siu and T'ang dynasties, a second great classical Chinese Empire was spreading the prestige of Chinese civilization to the far corners of East Asia. Adding impetus to the expansion of Chinese influence was the missionary spirit of the Buddhist priests, in their zeal to spread the benefits of the 'three treasures,' aggressively pushed toward Japan, bringing with them knowledge of Chinese arts and letters.

Knowledge of Buddhism reached Japan in the early sixth century. And while the religion was opposed by some members of the Yamato leadership on the grounds that it would weaken the indigenous system of belief in native deities and in the authority of the great *uji*, the new religion was ultimately accepted and patronized by the *mikoto* and other great families of Yamato. In 645, after a violent factional dispute known as the Taika *coup d'état*, the Yamato leadership undertook a drastic political reorganization on Chinese lines. Over the course of the next half-century they pulled down the Yamato clan federation, creating in its place a centralized system of imperial government housed in a newly built capital city. They created in addition a far-reaching provincial administration and a new and uniform procedure for the public control of agricultural land and for systematic tax collection. In 702 these institutional changes were given form in officially prepared penal and administrative codes (the Taihō Codes), which were to provide the basis of imperial law and administration for the next five centuries. With the completion of the capital city of Heijō in the Yamato Plain in 710, Japan's effort to emulate T'ang China reached its climax. Heijō (more commonly known as Nara) was a brilliant reflection of the great capital cities of China, containing palaces, government offices, residences of the aristocracy, market places and numerous Buddhist temples.

The name Nara is used by historians to cover the period from 710 to 784, during which the Japanese laid the foundation for their aristocratic age. Adapting Chinese conceptions of social organization and state administration to their own needs, the Japanese ruling class completed a dramatic transition from clan-based localism to

Above left: A Tōdaiji scene depicting the great Buddha in the Shigian Engi.

Above right: A model of a warrior found in an early Japanese burial chamber.

Right: Founded in AD 607 by Prince Shotoku, Horyuji Temple is regarded as a fountainhead of Japanese culture. Horyuji is the oldest existing temple in Japan.

bureaucratic centralization in government, and from a loosely organized clan hierarchy to a highly regulated aristocratic society. During the seventh and eighth centuries the leading *uji* migrated toward the Yamato area and into the city of Nara, where they established themselves as a civil aristocracy and as officials in the imperial government. The *uji* elite gave up for the moment their local military authority to become a civil nobility, sustaining themselves through income and privileges received in recompense for their services to the central government. They momentarily subordinated themselves and their lands to the authority of a state system that was in theory embodied in the person of the emperor.

Chinese conceptions of imperial dignity and state authority made important contributions to the Japanese system of government during the Nara period. In Nara the former priest-chief of the Sun Line became in visible reality an emperor, reigning through a centralized machinery of government and claiming uniform authority over the entire country. It was at this time that the *mikoto* enhanced his position by adopting the titles of Son of Heaven (*tenshi*) and Emperor (*tennō*). The *uji* chiefs over whom he had once served as overlord were now regulated into an aristocratic officialdom and assigned titles and ranks according to their relationship to the state. The income from the land (taxes in kind and in labor) was in theory accumulated by the state, and officials were assigned lands and services under state regulation. A central bureaucracy, capped by a high administrative council of state, was organized into separate bureaux or ministries with their special areas of competence: imperial ordinances, taxes, justice, war, state officials, ceremonies and the imperial house. Outside of the capital, the country was divided for administrative purposes into provinces, 66 in number, and governors appointed by the central government from out of the court aristocracy were placed over them. The most remarkable achievement of all was the program of paddy-field rationalization by which agricultural land was brought under uniform regulation. Paddy lands and their workers were placed under government authority, and fields were divided into parcels of uniform size and shape so that they could be assigned to cultivators on a uniform allotment basis. Cultivators were then systematically taxed in kind, household produce, and labor and military service.

The city of Nara embodied the outstanding achievements of Japan's early aristocratic age. Its palaces and temples, some of which remain to this day, displayed the grand continental style in which multicolored tile roofs swept out from lofty wooden pillars coated with crimabar. The emperors who ruled from Nara lived in true imperial grandeur, as attested by the remarkable artifacts which remain in the imperial storehouse (Shosoin). Among the many objects of brocaded silk, gold, lacquer, mother of pearl and glass, most of them the work of Japanese state artisans, are exotic products of Chinese and even Central Asian origin. In Nara the Japanese aristocracy wrote the first histories of their country and the Yamato Dynasty, the *Kojiki* and *Nihon-Shoki*, and recorded their first efforts at poetry in both native and Chinese style. Above all they patronized the building of magnificent temples filled with religious objects of great artistic merit.

Patronage by the imperial family and the nobility gave the Buddhist centers in Nara a status that momentarily seemed to eclipse that enjoyed by the Shinto priesthood. Buddhism was incorporated into the ideology of government. The imperial house poured resources into the great temple of Tōdaiji of Nara. It served both as the emperor's 'family temple' and as headquarters for a national network of provincially based state temples which were looked to for divine protection of the nation. When in 752 the emperor Shōmu dedicated the great 54-foot-high image of Vairocana Buddha at Tōdaiji, he posed both as the 'slave of the Buddha' and exalted sovereign. In worshipping Vairocana, the power of cosmic unity, the emperor was clearly symbolizing his own position as the unifying force within the country.

But although the Buddhist centers were lavishly patronized, heaped with treasure and tax-free lands, the Buddhist priesthood was barred from gaining any ascendancy over the state or the secular society. Significantly, the emperor established in parallel with the central organs of state administration an office of Shinto affairs (*jingi-kan*), and he himself continued to pose as a 'manifest God' in the Shinto manner. The court nobility also continued their belief in their ancestral shrines and the efficacy of Shinto's countless minor divinities, the *kami*. Thus when the Nara priesthood gave indications of becoming too powerful and when one of their members, the priest Dōkyō, expressed imperial aspirations, the emperor and his court simply abandoned Nara in 784 and transferred the capital to a new location 30 miles away. The new capital of Heian (present-day Kyoto) was entered in 794, and from it the Nara priesthood was carefully excluded.

Heian and the flowering of aristocratic culture

The move to Heian marked a turning-point both in Japan's relationship to China and in the continental style adopted in Nara. During the eighth century and into the ninth Japan continued to make an effort to become a part of the Chinese cultural world. Official Japanese embassies traveled to Chinese capitals, Chinese priests made the long journey to Japan to become respected

patriarchs on Japanese soil. The aristocracy modeled its style of life on that of the Chinese upper class. Yet for all their emulation of China, the Japanese clearly remained committed to certain fundamental political and social practices which had distinguished them up to the seventh century. Government remained an aristocratic prerogative, and both the institutions of organized religion (whether Shinto or Buddhist) and of state administration remained subordinated to the hereditary powers of the ruling house and the aristocracy. The clan-like structure of Japanese society and government had never really been abandoned.

During the Nara period the aristocracy had found it profitable to use the concept of an imperial state and its administrative organs to enhance their monopoly of political power and wealth. Once their status was secure, however, a general trend toward privatization in government and economy set in. By the ninth century the aristocracy and the religious institutions had acquired permanent possession of lands and titles, and the state itself was stripped of its superior authority.

Underlying the privatization of government was the growth of the proprietary domain, or *shōen*, sometimes likened to the pre-feudal manor in Europe. *Shōen* came into being as the principle of public regulation of agricultural land was relaxed. As various forms of private tenure became a legal possibility, and, in addition, as tax exemptions were also obtained from the government, large aggregations of tax-free lands were assembled under the legal protection of powerful court families and religious centers. By the tenth century the process of *shōen* formation was accelerated by the practice of commendation, whereby local cultivators and small landholders placed their lands under the protection of court families and religious institutions as a means of acquiring immunity from state regulation and taxation. As the *shōen* spread, therefore, the sources of public revenue diminished. But since the proprietorships paid their dues to the court aristocracy, there was no great diminution in the wealth and services which flowed to the capital. Heian became a city of aristocratics who governed the country through their absentee proprietorships.

Left: The ceremonial hall of the old imperial palace in Kyoto. The hall was used for important functions of state including the enthronement of the emperor and the New Year's audience.

Right: Pilgrims attend a shrine at Tōdaiji, which features the outsize figure of the Buddha visible in this photograph.

With the gradual privatization of land ownership and the establishment of a hereditary nobility subsisting on a secure flow of goods and manpower from provincial proprietorships, a significant change took place not only in the nature of the central government but in the status of the emperor. Shortly after the transfer of the capital to Heian, one of the court families, the Fujiwara, asserted a virtual hegemony over the other noble houses, and in the process reduced the emperor to the status of a ceremonial figurehead. It is significant that the Fujiwara did not attempt to usurp imperial authority. As the primary consort family for the imperial house, they were content to establish themselves first among the emperor's subjects, dominating the imperial family through intermarriage and controling affairs of state by monopolizing the post of imperial regent (*sesshō-kampaku*). From the time of

the establishment of the Fujiwara regency, in 858, the emperor was permanently denied the role of actual ruler. Political leadership in Japan was henceforth exercised by a series of leaders from among the civil or military aristocracy, and their *de facto* hegemony over the government was legitimized by the imperial sanction. The emperor was pushed into a ceremonial role 'above politics' to serve as a symbol of the ultimate cohesion of the Japanese political elite, a reminder that the game of political competition must be played within the context of a single sovereignty. The emperor's loss of actual political power proved fortuitous, for in modern times the Japanese emperor was able to function as a symbol of nationhood in a way which few other Asian heads of state were able to do.

The period when the court aristocracy controled the country from the city of Heian proved,

from the cultural standpoint, to be one of the most distinctively creative in all Japanese history. The Heian court circle, a group of perhaps 5000 aristocrats, was a self-satisfied society, increasingly isolated from the rest of the country and the continent. For them family connections and gradations of courtly rank provided the framework of a genteel existence that placed particular emphasis on polite social accomplishments. The model Heian courtier is exemplified, though in fictionalized form to be sure, in the figure of Prince Genji, the hero of Murasaki Shikibu's eleventh-century novel, *The Tale of Genji*. A man of delicate sensibility and elegant behavior, given to discreet dalliance, skilled in dancing and the writing of poetry, he constantly demonstrated both his sensitivity to the nuances of personal relationships at court and his high breeding and aesthetic taste. *The Tale of Genji* is judged to be one of the world's

Left: An early photograph of the imperial palace at Kyoto. The complex dates from 1855.

Right: An example of the ornate lacquer armor as worn by Japan's warrior class of samurai.

Below right: Tairi no Kiyoari (1118-81), the first ruler of all Japan, futilely attempts to order the sun to stand still.

Below: A tryptich of Tairi no Kiyoari, who surveys his garden filled with the skulls of his opponents, victims of his ruthless rise to power.

earliest and greatest novels, but the age produced numerous other literary products – a variety of intimate diaries, for example, and poetic anthologis – many by women. In these the Japanese showed themselves to be masters of a delicate poetic sense, in which sentiments of love and appreciation of natural beauty predominated. Secular and hedonistic in approach, many of the aristocratic *belles-lettres* of Heian Japan speak to the modern reader with a remarkable freshness and directness.

The court families who successfully dominated Japan for half a millennium ultimately lost control both of the emperor and their proprietorships. Yet no sharp change of dynasty or revolutionary upsurge eliminated them from their ancestral residences in Heian or the exalted social prestige which they climed by virtue of their noble birth. What happened was that the *kuge*, as the civil artistocracy came to be known, were gradually reduced in numbers and stripped of influence after the middle of the twelfth century when a provincially based warrior aristocracy asserted itself and step by step squeezed off domanial revenues. By the beginning of the fifteenth century the *kuge* had been bypassed politically and were reduced to a precarious life of dependence upon the now-dominant military aristocracy. And by the seventeenth century the court aristocracy, then consisting of only about 360 families, had been squeezed into the narrow confines of the Imperial Compound, an enclosure three-quarters of a mile by half a mile in the center of Kyoto. As a group the *kuge* had been converted to a ceremonial institution, providing background for the imperial dignity, serving the ritualism of a legitimacy by which the military hegemons claimed their right to rule the nation. In the faintly Chinese life of the Imperial Compound the Japanese kept alive their remembrance of imperial state structure once borrowed from China.

The rise of the Bushi class

It was during the late twelfth and early thirteenth centuries that the court nobility began to lose its political influence to an emerging provincial military aristocracy. This provincial warrior class would bring with them new practices of political

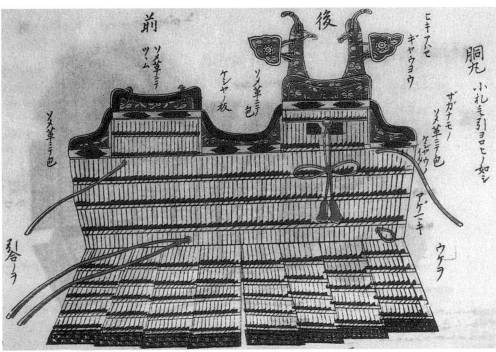

control and social organization, practices which historians have customarily described as feudal. Whether feudalism as a system of government and society can be said to have existed anywhere but in Europe is a point of debate among scholars. Partly, of course, it is a matter of definition. Yet comparative historians have tended to see sufficient similarity between the elements of European feudalism and those of Japanese society from the twelfth through to the middle of the seventeenth centuries to permit the view that feudalism can be considered a phenomenon of more than limited application to Europe, and furthermore that, of the many feudalisms in world history, those of Europe and Japan were undoubtedly the most similar in form and in pattern of historical evolution.

In Japan after the twelfth century the ruling class consisted increasingly of aristocratic fighting men organized into groups held together by personal bonds or agreements in arms and supported by peasants. Authority relationships among the military aristocracy in Japan proved to be remarkably similar to those which characterized the European feudal system. The lord (*tono*) required of his vassals or retainers (*kenin*) service in terms of military duty. The vassals were rewarded by the lord's benefice most frequently in terms of free tenures of land. As the fief developed in Japan it gave rise to localized military rule in which, as in Europe, there was a fusion at all levels between personal and public authority. Thus in both societies social distinction and the capacity to exercise public rights and obligations coincided to a large extent with the private tenures of land.

As in Europe, the privatized landed estate, the *shōen*, served as the economic base for the emergence of feudal government. But whereas in Europe the militarization of local authority was caused by both the breakup of the Roman Empire and the incursions of less civilized tribesmen, in Japan the element of external threat and barbarization was absent. The spread of feudal practices was mainly the result of the slow weakening of the imperial system of local administration and the consequent conversion of the provincial gentry into a military class. The warrior aristocracy in Japan (*bushi* or *samurai*) evolved out of the old provincial aristocracy, which during the Heian period served as local officials under the imperial system or as estate managers in the court-owned *shōen*.

It is probably true that the provincial upper class had never been completely separated from a military orientation in Japan. Although a conscript army was adopted as part of the Taiho institutions, and peasants were conscripted to serve as the government's armed forces, officers were generally drawn from the ranks of the provincial aristocracy. In the eighth century the conscript system was abandoned, and the idea of the elite fighter was revived. With it there came into being a 'technological gap' that marked off the *bushi*,

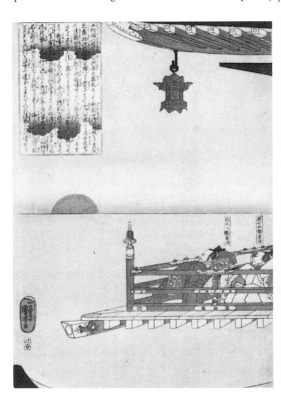

Left: Japanese samurai pose for the camera. Originally members of the provincial gentry, they gradually gained positions of national importance during the twelfth century.

Right: Model of a seated priest from the Kamakura Shogunate, the period that saw the final transition of Japan into a feudal society.

the mounted and armored warrior, from the rest of society. Gradually the private bearing of arms became a general mark of the local gentry, who served as officials of the provincial administrations or as managers of the great proprietary domains. Generations of local unrest tended to convert the various levels of the rural populace into a military order in which all were expected to serve local leaders in time of necessity.

The conversion of the provincial gentry into a military elite did not immediately affect the existing order or the power of the court nobility. The *bushi* remained within the system and dutifully served their noble superiors. But gradually, as the general security in the provinces began to deteriorate and as the court families and central monasteries began to quarrel among themselves, members of the provincial military class were drawn into positions of greater influence and, consequently, independence. The higher levels of the provincial titled class, serving as deputy governors

in the provinces or as heads of military units in the capital attached to the Fujiwara or the imperial house, found themselves playing significant roles in the politics of the twelfth century both at court and in the countryside.

During the eleventh century two provincial families, both scions of the imperial house, gained prominence as leaders of bands of provincial military families. The two factions soon came into conflict, taking opposite sides in certain disputes that had already begun to divide the court aristocracy. Thus members and supporters of the Taira clan became active, both locally and at court, as supporters of the imperial family, while the members of the Minamoto clan began to serve the Fujiwara house in a similar capacity. Eventually these conflicts degenerated into a bloody civil war between the Minamoto and Taira factions.

The rise of the militarized provincial aristocracy to power over the court nobility came in two steps. First, during the twelfth and thirteenth

centuries, the Taira faction, under the leadership of Kiyomori, made the breakthrough to hegemony over the court as a result of a military victory over the Minamoto supporters of the Fujiwara. Having cleared the capital of opposing military leaders Kiyomori found himself in a position of armed ascendancy in Kyoto, and within a short time he was able to gain control over the emperor and assert a powerful dictatorship over the court. His regime was short-lived, however, as he neglected his provincial sources of support, and so himself succumbed to a counter-current of opposition from the countryside led by the Minamoto.

In 1180 remnants of the Minamoto leadership, which had been defeated 20 years earlier, rose in the eastern provinces under the leadership of Yoritomo (1147-99). Yoritomo soon gained control of the eastern provinces and consolidated his position as military hegemon of the Kantō area. Other Minamoto leaders captured the capital

from the Taira and finally, in 1185, defeated the Taira forces in a naval battle off the western tip of Honshu. During the extensive fighting that had taken place in central Japan, Yoritomo had assumed complete military and police authority in the provinces, posing as protector of the court. After establishing his headquarters at Kamakura, in the center of the eastern provinces, he extended the practice of enlisting *bushi* of all types into his vassal band as 'housemen' (*gokenin*). Through his network of vassals, pledged in loyalty to him, Yoritomo was able to breathe new life into the decaying provincial administration. When, in 1192, he received from the emperor the title of Shogun (supreme military commander) he had become *de facto* the most powerful political figure in the country. The Kamakura Shogunate thus initiated the long period of military rule in Japan which lasted until 1868.

The Kamakura Shogunate

The emergence of the *bushi* into positions of political power and the establishment of Shogunal government at Kamakura marked a new era in Japanese history. Yet the transition to a feudal order did not really occur suddenly, nor did it spread uniformly throughout the country. The outstanding feature of the first two centuries after the establishment of the Shogunate was the delicate balance that existed between the influence of the civil and military aristocracies. At first the balance was more or less equal. Kyoto retained its prestige as the residence of the court and the upper nobility, and the court families retained most of their sources of income and their ability to maintain their sophisticated style of life. Their far-flung proprietorships were, if anything, now

managed more firmly because of the controls exercised over the land stewards and other *shōen* managerial staff by the military officials commanded by the Shogun. Yet civil authority was placed increasingly at a disadvantage in the face of the growing power of the military aristocracy, which squeezed off more and more of the income from the land as their price for maintaining law and order. The direction in which things were moving became obvious in 1221 when the retired Emperor Gotoba tried to combat Kamakura leaders by raising an imperial army from nearby estates and Buddhist centers. The Kamakura leaders, still claiming to be subjects of the throne, dispatched their own army, and it easily put down what Kamakura defined as the ex-emperor's 'rebellion.' In the resulting settlement Gotoba and his fellow conspirators were exiled, and the titular emperor was deposed. The Shogunate confiscated large numbers of *shōen* from the implicated court aristocracy for redistribution among its followers. It set up in Kyoto a Deputy Shogun and asserted the right to determine succession to the throne.

Kamakura, as a new political center, represented two new institutions. It was the headquarters of the Minamoto feudal alliance, the group of perhaps 2000 military houses that had been enlisted as Yoritomo's vassals or housemen [*gokenin*]. It was also the headquarters of the Shogun's administration. The Shogun's government, or *bakufu*, as it was called, consisted of simple organs of military and legal administration, dedicated chiefly to the supervision of the vassal band and their lands. As for the post of Shogun itself, it became largely a titular position embodying the legitimacy of the military regime. For after Yoritomo's death, the power of the Mira-

moto family soon gravitated into the hands of Yoritomo's widow's family, the Hōjō, which established, through its control of the office of 'chief (*Shikken*) of the *bakufu*' what was essentially a regency over the post of Shogun. Fortunately for Japan, the Hōjō family produced a series of vigorous and able leaders who not only maintained peace at home but at a critical moment were able to defend Japan from two invasions launched from the continent by the Mongols.

The effectiveness of the power of the Shogunate to keep order in the country rested on its primary military base in the eastern provinces. But what made the Shogunate more than a factional military power was its development of a field administration that extended into the rest of the country. This was achieved through Yoritomo's establishment of two new classes of local officials. The first were the military land stewards (*jito*), with functions similar to those of the provincial tax collectors and *shōen* managers. These officers, all vassals of Yoritomo, were assigned to the provinces, ostensibly to reinforce the existing local administration and to assure the flow of land dues to the rightful authority. Aside from such duties, the military land stewards asserted a variety of administrative and judicial powers and served as representatives of the Shogun's police and military authority in the rural districts.

Above the land stewards, and generally selected from among the more powerful of them, Yoritomo established the post of Provincial Military Governor (*shugo*), with powers of judicial decision, pursuit of criminals and military recruitment. As the principal military authority in each province, the *shugo* held supervisory authority over the Shogun's housemen, recruiting and assigning them to guard duty. The combination of military governorships and stewardships thus provided the Kamakura authorities with a complete system of provincial administration that paralleled the decaying imperial administration, supporting it at first but gradually competing with it. It was this dissemination of the Shogun's vassals into the provincial administrative structure which provided the opening wedge for the gradual takeover of the country by the military aristocracy and their feudal system of government.

As the city of the *bushi*, Kamakura exemplified the ascendancy of a new type of leader in Japan, distinct among the elite types admired by the several cultures of eastern Asia. Unlike the Chinese scholar-officials, the *bushi* regarded military training and service as both noble and important. Though the ruling class, the *bushi* were gentry by origin and outlook, preoccupied with problems of the sword and the land. While they may have envied and emulated the life of the city-dwelling nobility, they tended to scorn the effete qualities of the courtiers. Theirs was the more robust world of military training in horsemanship, archery, swordsmanship and the leadership of men. *Bushi* exalted personal qualities of loyalty, honor, physical toughness and frugal and disciplined living. It was, to be sure, some time before the *bushi* ideal was clearly formulated; in fact it was not until the seventeenth century that the code of the samurai (*bushidō*) was fully spelled out. But there were nevertheless many features of the *bushi*'s value system which were obvious from the start.

Central to the warrior aristocrat's life was his lineage and his status, for the whole system of military obligations and service relationships was tied in with his benefice. The hierarchy of service to the lord was the ladder of achievement, and battle provided the principal opportunity to advance the status of the lineage. The *bushi*, like

the European knight, made a cult of his sword, which he poetically believed to be spiritually endowed. He made a fetish of bravery and the willingness to die, taking as his emblem the cherry blossom, which of all flowers most easily dropped its petals at the slightest touch of wind or rain. 'Bushidō means death,' wrote a samurai of the sixteenth century. 'When the mind is set on death, the way through life will always be straight and simple . . . On the field of battle close your mind to reasoning. Reasoning robs you of that force with which alone you can carve your way to your objective.' The cult of death was carried to its extreme in the practice of ritual suicide, known as *seppuku*. Used as a means of avoiding dishonor to one's family name, *seppuku*, or cutting open the belly, was a particularly grisly method of self-inflicted death. The sixteenth-century European visitors to Japan found the Japanese warrior aristocracy the most fiercely warlike and the most protective of their honor of any people they had seen outside of Europe.

The growth of Buddhist influence

If the Kamakura age brought the *bushi* to the fore as the new rulers of Japan, it also brought into new prominence the Buddhist priesthood and the monastic way of life. As in medieval Europe, the early feudal age was a time of deep religious fervor. Buddhism, in its early years a religion of the aristocracy and carrying the stamp of state patronage, became, for the first time, a force that touched all classes, common folk as well as noble. In an age of political uncertainty, the monastic life offered refuge for those who abhorred violence; in the world of the *bushi*, it was the religious centers which alone afforded a refuge for the arts and letters. During the twelfth and thirteenth centuries there began, as a consequence, a tremendous growth in the Buddhist content of Japanese life, and in the number of Buddhist institutions. This sudden expansion of the role of Buddhism was both the result of the spread of the existing religious orders into the countryside and of the emergence of new and vigorous religious leaders who founded popular sects. The Kamakura 'religious awakening' not only represented a major increase in the assimilation of Buddhism into everyday life, but also gave rise as well to new movements and beliefs which were distinctly Japanese in spirit. The Amida sects of Jōdō (begun by Hōnen, 1133-1212) and Jōdō Shinshū (founded by Shinran, 1173-1262) preached salvation through faith in the 'original vow' of Buddha to save all beings. The Lotus sect (founded by Nichuin, 1226-82) taught a similar, though more militant, path to salvation via faith in the Lotus Sutra. Zen, or meditative Buddhism, which sought enlightenment through life experience and mental discipline, was given sectarian organization by Eisai (1141-1215) and Dōgen (1200-53). These new religious movements not only brought the priesthood out into the countryside, preaching to the common people and establishing temples among the villages, but also brought the priesthood back into the company of political leaders. Zen priests who were given official patronage by the Shogunate regularly assisted the Hōjō regents in their administration. Conversely, it became common practice for retired samurai to become lay priests in their declining years. Thus the priests became active members of feudal Japanese society, though we should bear in mind that the religious establishment continued in a role subservient to political power and never acquired either the degree of independence from secular control or the legitimizing authority of the Church in feudal Europe. Feudal Japan, the most

Left: A painting showing a lord dispensing justice. Provincial military governors were empowered to recruit troops and pursue criminals.

Right: The temple of the Gold Pavilion at Kinakakuji, Kyoto.

Below right: A giant bronze statue of the Buddha. Buddhism began to be influential in Japan from the twelfth century onward.

Below far right: The Gold Pavilion at Kyoto, set in traditional Japanese gardens.

thoroughly converted to Buddhism of any of the East Asian countries, was to remain a primary repository of the Buddhist faith in East Asia. Even in modern times Japan has continued as a major Buddhist nation.

By Kamakura times Japan had begun to emerge from seclusion to engage once again in contact with the continent. The China of the Sung Dynasty became a major cultural attraction, and Zen monasteries in Kamakura and Kyoto entered into regular communication and exchanges with their counterparts on the continent. It was in the context of this growing interest in continental affairs that Japan was faced with the challenge of an external invasion.

The Mongols, long active along the northern frontier of China, had reduced Korea in 1258, and in 1260 they had established the Yüan dynasty, under Kublai, in North China. Although South China still remained to be won, Kublai turned his attention to Japan in 1267. The Hōjō regent, Tokimune, prodded the Kyoto court into rejecting Kublai's overtures for submission and mobilized the Kamakura housemen. A Mongol invasion force carried in Korean ships reached northern Kyushu in 1274, disgorging Mongol warriors, whose long bows, formation tactics and use of explosives overwhelmed the Japanese warriors for a time. A timely storm, however, broke up the invasion fleet, and the surviving Mongols withdrew. Kublai Khan, having won control of South China in 1279, directed a second invasion of Japan in 1281. This time the Japanese were better prepared. All possible *bushi* in western Japan were mobilized, and a defense wall was built to obstruct landing. Although the Mongols reached Japan with an estimated 150,000 men, the Japanese held their ground until another great storm destroyed the invasion fleet.

The Japanese *bushi* had obviously proven themselves, but the ideological guardians of the country, the Shinto priests and the court nobility, also took credit for the power of the 'divine wind' (*Kamikaze*), which they claimed to have evoked. The Mongol crisis thus became a major epic for Japan, in which the native deities had intervened to save Japan from foreign conquest. It occasioned a revival of belief and trust in the native *kami*, and especially in the Sun Goddess, whose shrine at Ise was maintained by the imperial family. Ideas of Japanese nationhood, together with the military mobilization against the attack, led to an upsurge of feeling that was to add to Japan's belief in its own uniqueness as a land apart.

The Ashikaga Shogunate

The Hōjō political grip was noticeably weakened after the Mongol invasions. Defense had been costly in life and treasure, and in the aftermath dangerous breaks had begun to appear in the Kamakura household. Sensing that an opportunity was at hand, the reigning emperor, Godaigo, plotted to overthrow the Hōjō in 1333. Kamakura reacted quickly, but the generals sent against Godaigo defected: Ashikaga Takauji captured Kyoto in the name of the emperor, and Nitta Yoshisada destroyed the Hōjō at Kamakura. Between 1334 and 1336 Godaigo attempted a revival of imperial rule, in what is known as the 'restoration' of the Kemmu Era. The attempt was foredoomed. Godaigo was driven out of the capital by a disgruntled Takauji, who soon set up another emperor. In 1338 Takauji took the title of Shogun.

Takauji established his headquarters in Kyoto (eventually at Muromachi), thereby signaling the final dominance of the military over the civil aristocracy. In Kyoto the Ashikaga family and other high members of the *bushi* aristocracy settled down among the court aristocracy, emulating their manners and absorbing their lands. The parallel administrative systems, military and civil, were now reduced to one.

A *shugo* confederation

The Ashikaga Shoguns ruled Japan with only the most perfunctory reference to the imperial sanction. In the province the system of military governorships and stewardships had absorbed all functions of local government. The *shugo* houses, having aggrandized themselves in the previous century, emerged as the leading figures in the provinces, able to enlist local *bushi* into their own retinues. The Ashikaga hegemony thus took the form of a federation of *shugo* houses which maintained control over the provinces. The balance of power remained precarious, since the Ashikaga never acquired a sufficient preponderance to dominate conclusively their supposed vassals. The next two and a half centuries were marred by constant warfare between the great lords. What little control the Ashikaga house was able to assert over its vassals finally collapsed in 1467. In that year a dispute broke out over Ashikaga succession. The *shugo* divided into two factions and drew up contending armies within the city of Kyoto. The resulting Onin War lasted for 10 years. It devastated Kyoto, weakened the main *shugo* houses and destroyed the remaining influence of the Ashikaga Shogunate. Thereafter Japan gradually disintegrated into a condition of regional decentralization in which local lords asserted their independence from all central control. The end of the fifteenth century consequently brought Japan to its period of high feudalism.

Yet despite its political turbulence the Ashikaga period was a time of overall national growth. The regional lords improved the productivity of their territories by such activities as river control and land reclamation. Demand for special products for use in warfare and in daily life stimulated commercial farming and the growth of market centers. New market towns and port cities came into existence. Trade organizations, known as *za*, extended their activities throughout the country, somewhat on the scale of the European trading guilds. Coins for the first time became economically functional, though they had in the main to be imported from China.

By the fourteenth century Japan was becoming a trading power of some magnitude. Stimulated by the efforts to prepare against the Mongols, the Japanese now produced their own vessels capable of sailing the high seas. Japanese freebooters, called *wakō*, ranged the coasts of Korea and China. Encouraged by the Zen monasteries of Kyoto, the Ashikaga Shoguns began direct trade with China in 1342, entering into negotiations with the Chinese government. Later the Ming emperors pressured the Ashikaga into controling the *wakō* and restricting Japanese trade with China to a licensed 'tally trade' on a tributary basis. In 1402 the third Shogun Yoshimitsu accepted investiture as 'king of Japan' from the Yung-lo emperor and symbolically enlisted Japan as a tributary to the Ming court. But the motivation was mainly economic. Japanese ships sailed to China with gold, raw copper, sulfur and large quantities of swords and folding fans; they returned with Chinese copper coins, silks and objects of artistic and religious significance. This trade continued into the middle of the sixteenth century, when the lawlessness of the Japanese caused the Chinese to withdraw official trade relations. Thereafter the age of freebooters returned, and Japanese ships were soon venturing as far as the Indian Ocean.

Under the Ashikaga Shoguns Kyoto became the center of a remarkable cultural flowering. It resulted from the fortuitous fusion of several traditions: the old court aristocracy, the Zen priesthood, whose wealthy monasteries fringed the outskirts of the city, and the artistic and intellectual stimulus provided by renewed contact with China. The artistic monuments of this period are found first in public architecture. The Shogunal villas of Kinkakuji (the Golden Pavilion, built in 1397) and Ginkakuji (the Silver Pavilion, begun in 1474) and numerous Zen monasteries perfected the style in which buildings were subtly subordinated to their natural settings or were surrounded by spacious gardens combining rocks, water, trees and shrubs into naturally pleasing, yet religiously meaningful, assemblages. Chinese-style monochrome landscape painting was developed to a high point. Japan's unique form of medieval drama, *nō*, took shape as a form of entertainment for the military aristocracy. *Nō* amalgamated existing traditions of dance, mime and Buddhist *sutra*, changing into a style of dance-drama often compared with classical Greek drama. There were also such ancillary arts as the tea ceremony and flower arrangement. Thus the Ashikaga period became the source of a repertory of aesthetic forms and practices that have survived into modern times as the main elements of Japan's particular aesthetic tradition.

The daimyō and the first visitors from Europe

The Onin War (1467-77), which destroyed many of Kyoto's cultural movements, divides the Ashikaga period into two parts. The century following the war is given the name Sengoku, or Warring States Period. Warfare became endemic, and Shogunal authority was at its nadir. In the countryside the families that had served as *shugo* under the Ashikaga were gradually superseded by militarily more potent leaders. These were the locally entrenched feudal lords known as *daimyō*. The *daimyō* domains were smaller than the province-size territories over which the *shugo* had held authority, but they were more compactly organized, and over them the *daimyō* exercised absolute control. Within their territories the *daimyō* attempted to make all lands theirs and all *bushi* their enfeoffed vassals. On their territories they now erected defensive castles to which they could gather their vassals and troops in time of war. By the early sixteenth century Japan had

Left: A dramatic moment in a Japanese *nō* play. The theater has been an integral part of Japanese cultural life.

Above right: Originally built by the Shogun Ashikaga Yoshimitsu, the Gold Pavilion was rebuilt in the 1950s after a fire.

Above far right: Mount Fuji as seen from Nara in Suraga province. The mountain's religious significance is highlighted by the *daimyos'* procession in the foreground of this painting.

probably reached its period of greatest feudal fragmentation as 200 or so *daimyō* struggled among themselves for regional influence.

It was at this time that Japan came in contact with Europe for the first time. The Mongol invasions had briefly brought Japan into the orbit of the Eurasian world. But the contact was brief, and when it was over Europe was left with only a fantastic dream of Japan as a land of gold. 'The natives are white and civilized,' Marco Polo had written, 'the land is rich in natural resources; gold is inexhaustible beyond supposition, and the palace is roofed with pure gold . . . and the paving-stones of the palace are made of gold of the thickness of about two fingers.' When in 1543 Portuguese traders finally reached Japan they found a land not particularly rich in natural resources but inhabited by a tough and energetic people who greatly impressed the Europeans. Francis Xavier, who arrived in Japan in 1549 as the first Jesuit missionary, wrote of the Japanese: 'I would say that the Japanese are the best race yet discovered, and I do not think that you will find their match among the pagan nations. They are very sociable . . . and much concerned with their honor . . . For the most part they are poor, but they do not despise the poverty of nobles and common folk . . . They prize their weapons and place much reliance upon them . . . They will not suffer any affront or contemptuous speech.'

The Europeans arrived at an opportune moment, a time when Japan was divided and there was no authority which might have resisted the visitors. For a hundred years Europeans entered Japan freely, trading at her ports, even

spreading an alien religion. But later, when Japan was politically reunified, free European activity in Japan was gradually turned off. Japan, like China, closed its doors on Western adventurers and Christian missionaries and Christianity was suppressed with great severity. The so-called 'Christian Century' was, in fact, a minor episode in Japanese history.

The story of the first round of European contact with Japan is probably most remarkable as an episode in the history of the expansion of Europe. For Japan was literally at the far end of the world, a tremendous distance to travel for the European traders and missionaries. It is astounding that Xavier should have reached Japan only nine years after participating in the founding of the Society of Jesus, and that by 1582 an estimated 150,000 Japanese Christian converts could be counted as the work of perhaps 75 Jesuit fathers. The Jesuits developed Nagasaki, after 1571, as a port and a Catholic religious center. And it was here that the regular arrival of Portuguese carracks from Macao profitably joined trade and evangelism. The city was to remain Japan's only port for foreign trade during the long period of seclusion that followed the expulsion of the Spanish and Portuguese between 1624 and 1637.

The most far-reaching impact that the Europeans made on Japan came through the introduction of firearms. From their very first exposure to them the Japanese understood clearly the superior capacity of the Portuguese musket and cannon. Weapons were avidly sought by feudal lords, and Japanese artisans began almost immediately to manufacture firearms in large

quantities. By the 1570s warfare among the feudal lords was being revolutionized by the effect of firepower. Castles with large moats and walls became a necessity to protect against enemy cannon, and large masses of musketeers dominated the field. Firearms both hastened the reconsolidation of the political order in Japan and profoundly affected the social order. They did not, as in Europe, bring the feudal order to an end. For the Japanese retained the noble status of the samurai into the nineteenth century, and once the wars of consolidation were over and the doors of the country closed, firearms were de-emphasized.

Thanks to the activities of Westerners in Japan, the expansion of Japanese freebooters into waters increasingly distant from Japan and the warfare among the feudal lords at home, the sixteenth century proved to be one of the dramatic turning-points in Japanese history. By the end of the century a new political hegemony would emerge and Japanese armies would twice cross over into Korea with destructive effect. For the first time, Japan as a feudal military power would become a world phenomenon.

Hideyoshi and the unification of the daimyō

By the turn into the sixteenth century a movement toward military consolidation was under way. A number of *daimyō* had become powerful enough to coerce their neighbors into submission, thereby creating regional hegemonies of some size. By the 1560s such regional coalitions numbered roughly 20, and a struggle for national supremacy was building up among them. Ultimately one of the great regional hegemons managed to put down his military rivals and emerge the dominant power in the land. First to appear on the scene was Oda Nobunaga (1534-82), whose entrance into Kyoto in 1568 is taken as the start of the consolidation movement. Before his early death he had gained control of the *daimyō* of central Japan and had destroyed the power of the great Buddhist monastery of Euryakuji, which menaced the capital. Nobunaga was succeeded by his foremost general, Toyotomi Hideyoshi (1536-98). With armies sometimes numbering as many as 200,000 men, Hideyoshi systematically put down the remaining regional hegemonies. By 1590 all *daimyō* had either been destroyed or had pledged allegiance to Hideyoshi, who stood as full military suzerain over the country.

Hideyoshi did not become Shogun because of his low birth. But he managed to gain adoption into the Fujiwara family, thereby qualifying for high court office. In 1585 he took the title of Imperial Regent (*kampaku*) and subsequently used the imperial presence as a means of legitimizing his claim to supreme military and political authority. Building a military headquarters at Osaka, as well as a fortified residential palace outside of Kyoto at Momoyama, he combined military might with traditional symbols of rulership in a grandiose manner. Hideyoshi's government took the form of a feudal despotism placed over approximately a hundred *daimyō* who held their territories at Hideyoshi's pleasure. These local rulers were given considerable independence and paid no dues to the overlord. They were responsible for the peaceful governance of their territories, they were obliged to join their armies in battle with Hideyoshi's and they were frequently called upon to supply labor and material for public works. They were also bound by pledges of loyalty, which were ensured by giving hostages.

Why, once he acquired national hegemony, did Hideyoshi not carry centralization further by eliminating the *daimyō* and creating a monarchy of his own? The answer is that Hideyoshi was simply not powerful enough. He had achieved his position of hegemon through the military efforts of a coalition army in which he was merely first among equals. Tokugawa Ieyasu, to whom he gave the Kanto after 1590, in fact possessed more territory than did Hideyoshi. As local rulers the *daimyō* were still a necessary part of the system of government in Japan, and indeed they persisted until 1871. As for the emperor, far from having any thought of eliminating him, Hideyoshi relied upon the imperial sanction to bolster his legitimacy in the eyes of his vassal *daimyō*.

Having achieved military supremacy, Hideyoshi developed Osaka into a great stronghold and port city and played the monarch in all but name, minting gold coins, regulating foreign trade and negotiating with foreign countries. His domestic successes and his own private megalomania led him to dream of a vast East Asian empire. China, he believed, should be an easy conquest for Japan's superior military machine, and he boasted of dividing China among his vassals and moving the Japanese imperial court to Peking. In 1592 the combined armies of his vassal *daimyō* overran Korea, but the Japanese supply lines were inadequate. A second expedition in 1597, largely punitive in intent, was hastily withdrawn upon the news of Hideyoshi's death. Within half a century all thought of foreign expansion was abandoned, and the Japanese had adopted a policy of national seclusion which would restrict any of them from going abroad.

Hideyoshi died without having established a stable governmental structure or even an assured

succession. His primary interests had been military, yet he presided over major changes in Japan's social and economic institutions. In 1595 Hideyoshi had begun a systematic survey of agricultural land. Superior land rights were clarified and redefined, so that they rested entirely in the hands of the national overlord and, through infeudation, in those of the *daimyō*, a few court families and to a lesser extent the temples and shrines. After being surveyed, fields were registered in the names of peasant cultivators (*hyakushō*), who were given security as copyholders in their tenures but were made responsible for dues. Cultivator families were grouped into villages (*mura*) which became the basic fiscal and administrative units in the countryside. Fields were graded by quality and assessed according to yield in measures of *koku*, or about five bushels of grain. Taxes were calculated on the basis of these assessment figures and paid in rice.

Rise of the samurai

The social implications of Hideyoshi's survey were enormous, for they led to both the physical and legal separation of the samurai from the farming classes. During the period of wars between the

daimyō there had been a growing tendency for the *bushi* to leave the countryside and to congregate in the castle headquarters of regional lords, for the new style of warfare emphasized garrisoned fortresses and large mobile armies. Increasingly, the lesser ranks of *bushi* left their village fiefs to become stipended retainers in the castle towns of the *daimyō*. With the new land survey this movement was completed by legally severing the farming and non-farming sectors of society. Those listed on the land registry books became by definition *hyakushō*; those recorded in the *daimyō*'s house rolls as fief holders or stipendiaries were *bushi*. In 1588 Hideyoshi ordered the collection of all arms in the possession of non-samurai. This was accompanied by edicts clarifying the several classes and prohibiting movement between them. Thus the basis was laid for the four-class system whereby samurai, farmer, artisan and merchant were given separate legal status and prohibited from intermingling for the next 300 years.

Despite the fact that Japan was divided into small autonomous *daimyō* domains, institutions of political and economic control were made relatively uniform throughout Japan by virtue of Hideyoshi's powers as overlord. Techniques of

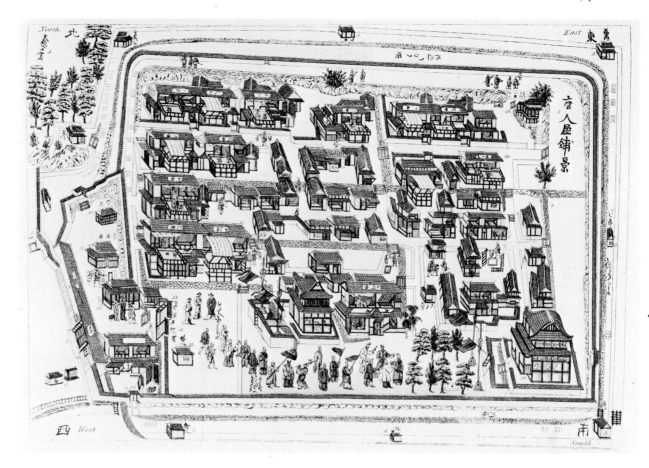

Left: The shogu shrine, dedicated to Ieyasu Tokugawa (1542-1616) – one of Japan's great statesmen and generals. Built in 1636 the shrine is noted for the complexity of its construction and the splendor of its carvings.

Right: The beginnings of Japan's industrial development – a factory in Nagasaki founded in 1688, a consequence of expanding links with the West.

Below left: Osaka Castle, a well-fortified defensive system and the residence of Japan's emperors.

administration and taxation systematized by Hideyoshi provided Japan with the most effective government the country had yet had. The *daimyō* now had full power to mobilize the manpower and economic resources of their territories, and they did so by organizing their retainers into tightly disciplined military and administrative bureaucracies. Laws and procedures were systematized and strictly applied. Thus Japan entered an age in which, down to the level of the village and the town ward, government was in the hands of the military aristocracy. From this time until the abolition of the samurai class in 1871 Japan was to be sternly governed by military officials in positions of civilian authority.

The emergence of regional *daimyō* headquarters, consisting of castles and garrisons combined with new capacities for commerce and manufacture to stimulate a remarkable urban growth during the latter half of the sixteenth century. Kyoto developed into a commercial metropolis of more than 300,000 inhabitants who specialized in art and luxury products. Among the castle cities, Osaka, with a similar population, and Edo, which was to reach a population of one million by 1800, were of particular importance. In fact all of the major *daimyō* encouraged their military and administrative headquarters to grow into flourishing cities by establishing merchant quarters and offering special inducements to traders and artisans. By the early decades of the seventeenth century Japan was rapidly becoming the most heavily urbanized country in East Asia, and a vigorous merchant class was beginning to assert itself. By the end of the seventeenth century, the non-samurai segments in Japan's great cities were adding an entirely new bourgeois element to Japanese culture.

But the commercial class in Japan remained subservient to the samurai, and one reason for this was surely the seclusion policy adopted by Hideyoshi's successors. It is not generally understood that Japan's decision to close its doors to foreign contact came as an act of strength rather

than weakness. The same was true of China under the Manchus. Both countries, having come under strong military regimes, proceeded to restrict the activities of Europeans who presumably threatened the domestic security. Japan entered this period of deliberate seclusion at the time of greatest national potential under the Shogunal administration established by the Tokugawa house. Hideyoshi's death in 1598 had left the balance of power in a precarious state, and soon the *daimyō* were at odds. In two decisive battles, Sekigahara (1600) and Osaka Castle (1615), Tokugawa Ieyasu managed to seize power and inherit the position of Japan's military suzerain. Having taken the title of Shogun in 1603, Tokugawa developed his castle town of Edo (present Tokyo) into the new power center of Japan. By the time of his death in 1616, he had put together a political regime that was to last until 1867.

Tokugawa and the seclusion policy

Tokugawa continued the practice of decentralized rule through *daimyō*. But the balance of power was now significantly in favor of the central authority vested in the Shogun. The Tokugawa house controled about a quarter of Japan's territory, and the Shogun's domain not only included most of central Japan but all of the Kantō and much of the land in between. More important, it included nearly all of the great cities, such as Kyoto, Osaka, Edo and Nagasaki. The *daimyō* now were larger in number – over 260 – and consequently their individual territories were much smaller than those of the Shogun. It is hardly surprising that the Tokugawa system was significantly more stable than that of Hideyoshi.

Why did the Tokugawa regime close its frontiers to foreign adventure and turn its attention so dramatically inward? No doubt Japan in 1600 was economically and culturally self-sufficient enough for the desire for domestic security to prove more attractive than the inducements of overseas expansion. Tokugawa Ieyasu had favored the development of foreign trade in his

early years as Shogun, but fear of subversion by Christianity and by the political activity of the Portuguese and Spanish traders proved a more powerful influence, even though the arrival of the Dutch after 1600 offered the possibility of trade without religion. Tokugawa was also jealous of the possibility of aggrandizement possessed by the *daimyō* of Kyushu, who controled the ports to which the foreign ships came. Thus, step by step, the Tokugawa effort to suppress Christianity and monopolize foreign trade led to a policy of general seclusion. Vigorous persecutions of Christians began in 1614, the first executions of missionaries and believers came in 1622. Soon all Japanese were obliged to register at Buddhist temples in order to prove their rejection of Christianity. In 1637 some 20,000 peasants of a heavily Catholic area near Nagasaki rose up in rebellion against a small local *daimyō*. Ultimately put down in 1638 with Shogunal assistance and with great slaughter, the event brought forth the last drastic steps toward seclusion. In 1635 the Shogunate had issued an edict prohibiting any Japanese nationals from going abroad. The Spanish had been excluded in 1624, the Portuguese in 1637. In 1641 the Dutch and Chinese alone were permitted a restricted trade at the port of Nagasaki which had been placed under Shogunal rule. The Dutch factory, confined to the small island of Deshima in Nagasaki harbor, became a virtual prison for the few representatives of the Dutch East India Company who remained to trade with the Shogun's commercial agents. That the Japanese intended to abide by their new policy was made abundantly clear when in 1640 members of a Portuguese mission from Macao attempted to negotiate for a reversal of the expulsion edict. Their petition was rejected and their leaders were executed. Thus Japan closed its frontiers. For more than two centuries, under the strict administration of the samurai class, the country was to develop in isolation from the rest of the world. And yet Japan would emerge from this period of isolation to face the world with an extraordinary resilience.

Africa and the Americas

In Africa and Central and South America, standard versions of world history have often been viewed as part of the European imperialist enterprise, an intellectual counterpart of military conquest which marginalizes or disparages the cultural traditions and civilized achievements of the original inhabitants. Recently, many historians have reacted by attempting to correct the Eurocentric bias of history writing and re-evaluate the accomplishments of both African and American societies before the Age of Columbus. Early African history in particular has become of great importance to black Africans seeking self-respect after the humiliations of white imperialism. Yet it remains very difficult to investigate successfully the history of areas of the world that have left few, if any, written records. In both America and Africa before 1500, evidence for the historian is very limited and much conjecture enters into all historical accounts.

Apart from this shared obscurity, the early histories of America and Africa have little in common. Whereas American civilizations developed in isolation from the rest of the world, at least some of Africa was always permeable to outside inflences. Indeed, the north of the continent formed an integral part of the Mediterranean world. North Africa generated one major civilization of its own – in Egypt – and its peoples were an integral part of the cultural achievement of the Islamic cities of the Mediterranean coast and its hinterland. From this northern zone, cultural influences spread southward down the Nile or across the formidable barrier of the Sahara desert.

Visitors also came by sea, especially to the east coast of Africa from the Islamic lands to the north.

But Africa south of the Sahara remained very short of developed civilizations. In Ethiopia a state Christianized under the influence of the Egyptian Copts maintained itself for over a thousand years, cut off from the rest of Christendom by the spread of Islam. In West Africa there were kingdoms ruling considerable territorial empires, first Ghana from perhaps the eighth to the thirteenth centuries AD, and then Mali, an Islamic kingdom whose wealth appeared fabulous to fourteenth-century Arab traders who led their camel caravans across the Sahara in search of slaves and gold. A century later in southern Africa the people of Zimbabwe were creating the great stone buildings of their capital, the ruins of which still stand today as a testimony of their existence. But such kingdoms were rare. By 1500, most of Africa south of the Sahara consisted of small societies that had achieved the cultivation of crops and the domestication of animals, but were without literacy, state organizations or more advanced technology.

There is, in truth, nothing very surprising about this tardiness in development. Only in a very few cases have major civilizations emerged spontaneously, and none of the conditions for such spontaneous emergence existed in Africa south of the Sahara. The adverse climate, generally poor soils and the vast land mass with few navigable rivers combined to keep population thinly spread, preventing the concentration of agricultural people in sufficient density to precipitate the shift to a more complex society. Black Africa was just

like northwest Europe in that it invented neither literacy nor the wheel, receiving both by diffusion from other cultures. But Africa was much larger than Europe and far more difficult to penetrate, so the diffusion of skills was slow and limited to only parts of the continent.

If there was any outside influence on the development of civilization in the Americas, then it was so slight that it has remained disputable. As with Africa, much of the continent was inhabited by simple agricultural societies or even hunter-gatherers until the Europeans arrived. But in two main areas, Mesoamerica (centered on modern-day Mexico and Guatemala) and the Andes of South America, by around 1000 BC a tradition of civilization was established that was to last for about 2500 years. The vital agricultural base for these civilizations was provided in Central America by the cultivation of maize, and in the Andes by the potato and the domestication of the llama.

The first civilization was that of the Olmec in Central America, which may have lasted about a thousand years before it faded in around the second century BC. With the Olmec began so many of the customs common to most civilizations of the area – hieroglyphs, monumental religious sites with pyramids, and distinctive gods. The greatest successors of the Olmecs in the region were the Mayas, who built impressive religious sites in the jungle, yet seem to have created no town or cities. By the time the Europeans arrived at the start of the sixteenth century, the Mayas had declined to virtual extinction, and the

Aztecs ruled much of Central America. Theirs was a fierce civilization, based on the exaction of tribute from subject peoples and constant warfare to procure prisoners for use in blood sacrifices to the god of the Sun, whose representative on Earth the Aztec emperor claimed to be.

A similarly aggressive civilization, that of the Incas, ruled a large area of South America centred on the Andes. Starting with the Chavin, contemporaries of the Olmec, local and imperial cultures had alternated in the Andes until the rise of the Incas in the fifteenth century. With neither the wheel nor writing, the Incas nonetheless created an empire notable for its magnificent architecture, its feats of road-building and its sophisticated system of domination. The Inca emperor was sacred, a descendant of the Sun, for whom, as in Ancient Egypt, incestuous marriage was the rule.

It remains a source of astonishment that the Aztec and Inca Empires, both in full vigor, should have collapsed so completely and suddenly when a handfull of Europeans arrived. One reason was undoubtedly their cruelty and oppression, which led their subject peoples to cooperate with the new arrivals. But they must also have been exceptionally brittle cultures, unable to absorb or respond adequately to a sudden irruption from outside their closed world.

It is inevitable that historians who see human history as the story of progress, leading up by stages to the present peak of achievement in the twentieth century, should regard early America and Black Africa as having little to contribute to this triumphant process. At most Africa will be credited with creating an influential tradition of sculpture, music and dance, and American agriculture thanked for the domestication of maize and the potato. Those more sceptical of the achievements of Western civilization, on the other hand, will see more to value in the rich and varied societies that were later crushed beneath the wheels of the European juggernaut.

Right: A stucco head from a funeral chamber inside a Maya pyramid. A notable feature of this figure is the deformation of the skull, a common practice amongst the Maya peoples.

Below left: Africa's highest mountain, Mount Kilimanjaro, dominates the surrounding land, a reminder of the influence of geographical factors in determining the history of the continent. Vast deserts and jungles combined with few navigable rivers have all acted as a brake on human development in Africa.

Below: The great archeological site of Teotihuacan in present-day Mexico. Such sites have provided vital evidence of day-to-day life in pre-Columbian Mesoamerica.

Africa

Forming one-fifth of the earth's land surface, Africa extends from 37 degrees North at Cape Blanco on the Mediterranean Sea to 35 degrees South at Cape Agulhas on the Indian Ocean. At the northern and southern ends of the continent there are narrow strips of land with the climate and vegetation characteristic of the Mediterranean region. Proceeding from their extreme toward the tropics, one enters arid zones that culminate, in the north, in the Sahara, the world's largest desert, and in the south, in the Namib desert. As one moves farther into the interior these arid zones gradually yield to savannas and tropical woodlands with summer rainfall. These, in turn, give way to an equatorial belt of tropical forest in the center of the continent. In eastern and southern Africa this symmetrical pattern is modified by the effects of high altitudes. Desert does not encroach on the well-watered Ethiopian highlands, nor into the plateau of southern Africa, and in the equatorial belt east of the sources of the Congo River there are woodlands and savannas rather than forests.

As we have seen, the woodlands and savannas of tropical eastern Africa were the scene of important phases in the evolution of hominids and, eventually, of *homo sapiens*. Yet the inhabitants of Africa west and south of the lower Nile valley created no 'primary civilization' comparable to those of Mesopotamia, the Indus valley, China, Mesoamerica or Peru. Nor did they produce a 'secondary civilization' such as that of the Europeans.

The reasons for this are essentially ecological. For one thing, after the Sahara became desiccated over 4000 years ago, it formed a formidable barrier which man only began to overcome when the camel was introduced into northern Africa from Arabia in late Roman times. Also the winter-rainfall crops that were domesticated in Mesopotamia some 12,000 years ago were unsuitable for cultivation in the summer-rainfall African savannas or the equatorial forest. Africans did eventually domesticate sorghum and other local grasses in the northern savannas and local yams in the forest, but not before some 3000 years ago. In any case, even in the most favorable areas African soils are relatively poor, and in the African savannas rainfall is extremely unreliable, with the result that people and livestock were periodically reduced by drought and famine. Finally, even where intensive agriculture did promote the build-up of relatively dense populations, as in southern Nigeria, Rwanda and Burundi and southern Uganda, they did not reach the kind of concentrations that led to 'civilization' elsewhere because the terrain in subSaharan Africa is so vast, so 'open,' that it encourages dispersion. Egyptian civilization developed because intensive agriculture promoted dense population growth in a river valley that was flanked by country that was too arid for agriculture. But south of the Sahara populations remained below the critical level necessary for the development of urban civilization because surplus people could always resettle in relatively sparsely populated areas near their original homes. Even today the subcontinent remains comparatively thinly populated, containing only about nine percent of the world's population on 20 percent of its land area.

Thus, except in Egypt and in the middle Nile valley and Ethiopia (which were directly affected by their Egyptian and Arabian neighbors), the inhabitants of Africa developed no mature form of writing and created no large, enduring state systems before the arrival of Arabs and Europeans. Perhaps for this reason, until recently subSaharan Africa remained outside the main steam of Eurasian history. Yet it was never completely isolated from Eurasian influences; its geographic location saw to that. The Isthmus of Suez connected Egypt with Asia; the Red Sea was a short crossing from Arabia; the east coast down to Cape Delgado was accessible from India, thanks to the annual monsoon winds; and North Africa was separated from Europe only by the Mediterranean Sea. Consequently, nearly half the African coastline has frequently been exposed to influences emanating from the Near East, Europe and Southeast Asia. Fire, crops, domestic animals and iron, Christianity and Islam, all spread fairly rapidly from their points of origin in the Near East

to the lower Nile valley and the Ethiopian highlands; Phoenicians, Romans, Vandals, Byzantines and Arabs successively conquered parts of North Africa; and at various times Arabs, Indians, Indonesians and even Chinese made landfalls on the East African coast.

Yet it was never easy to penetrate from the coast to the interior. The Nile is the only great African river that provides access to the hinterland, and even there the first of five great cataracts breaks navigational continuity up the Nile at Aswan (24 degrees North) and the Sudd swamps (around 8 degrees North) are a formidable barrier to communication with Uganda. Except for the Senegal and the Gambia, which are relatively short, the other African rivers have not helped travelers to reach the interior. The Niger delta is a maze of small and tortuous streams, there are tumultuous rapids within a hundred miles of the mouth of the Congo, and the mouths of the Zambezi and Limpopo are almost blocked by sandbars.

Everywhere beyond the lower Nile, therefore,

Left: Bronze figure of a matchlock-armed Portuguese adventurer. The piece originates from Benin, Nigeria, and dates from the seventeenth century.

Right: An example of early European involvement in the affairs of Africa – the second-century forum in the Roman city of Suffetula.

Below: A carved ornamental box in the shape of the Oba palace in Benin. Armed with European weapons, the warriors suggest the growing trade links with European colonial powers.

travelers had to use land routes into the continent, and the Sahara desert has been a formidable impediment to penetration from the north. Yet by the end of the first millennium AD Arab traders were beginning to cross the desert to the northern savannas with camel caravans. In the fifteenth century Europeans began to probe the coastline and a few parts of the interior; but until the middle of the nineteenth century much of central and southern Africa remained isolated from the rest of the world. It was only then that Europeans thoroughly explored what to them was the 'dark continent'; and it was not until the early twentieth century that many of the peoples of sub-Saharan Africa became aware of the existence of the wider world, when the first European missionaries, tax-collectors, traders or settlers reached their villages.

The development of African societies

It would, however, be wrong to regard Africa as a mere receptacle for external forces. People in Africa, as in Europe during the last five or six centuries, not only adapted the technological inventions that came to them to the diverse potentialities of their environments, but made many independent innovations in social and political organization and in the arts. Down to the present day, African societies have varied immensely. If they have been conditioned in part by the ideas and techniques that have been imported from outside and the wide range of climates and resource distribution, they have also been very importantly conditioned by the cumulative effects of local customs and institutions which the historian can trace back – often imperfectly – through time.

Preindustrial African societies formed a spectrum, from the very simple to the relatively complex, and in traditional Africa there were several societies near the 'civilized' end of the spectrum. In Benin, on the western side of the Niger delta, for example, the population was fairly dense; the capital city, with artisans and traders, was considerably more than a mere center for the ruling elite, the political system was complex and there were considerable technical achievements,

Far left: A bronze cockerel from the 1600s, evidence of the standard of artistic development of Benin.

Left: A ritual dance mask from Bakuba in the Congo.

Above right: Two examples of hats worn by the Bushmen of southern Africa. They are made from spider's web, cloth, grass and feathers.

Right: A rock carving from southern Africa, typical of the representational art practiced by many hunter-gatherer societies.

Below: A rock painting of two antelope – the prey of Bushmen.

including the lost-wax process of casting bronze and an embryonic form of writing. Indeed, the 'civilized-uncivilized' dichotomy probably stresses technology and politics to the detriment of other factors. African sculpture, music and dance are among mankind's important aesthetic traditions and they have had profound effects upon the arts of Europe and America during the last century.

Hunters and gatherers

It seems probable that Africa was the scene of crucial stages in the evolution of humanity. We know that some 1,750,000 years ago creatures about 4 feet 6 inches tall, who could run fast upright, throw objects with their arms and make clumsy stone and bone tools with their hands, were living in small lakeside communities, supplementing their basically vegetable diets with game. At sites from Casablanca in Morocco to Taunga in Botswana, archeologists have found their tools, their fossils, or the fossils of their prey. Dr L S B Leakey has found all three in conjunction at the lowest level of 300 feet of ancient lake sediments at Olduvai Gorge in northern Tanzania. These creatures, the Australopithecines, were by far the most ancient hominids yet identified by modern archeologists and physical anthropologists.

The rate of change was accelerated when man learned to control fire – a practice that probably began in Southeast Asia and that had spread to Africa by about 55,000 BC. People in Africa then increased more rapidly in numbers and occupied more and more territory, including the tropical forest. They learned to make better and more specialized tools – for digging, hunting, fishing, skinning animals, making clothing and building shelters. They sought explanations of the universe as they experienced it and, as shown in their burial practices, they believed in a life after death.

They also gave expression to their aesthetic impulses by decorating their bodies, carving objects for ritual purposes, painting and engraving on rocks and dancing.

The earlier human cultures were probably very much alike. But after the introduction of fire, cultures diverged, as man acquired the capacity to make ever more specialized adaptations to different environments. Broadly speaking, two main types of hunting and gathering societies developed in Africa (each with many variations): those in the forests and those in the savannas.

The San Bushmen of the Kalahari desert are survivors of the hunting and collecting peoples who formerly lived throughout the African savannas. Modern scientists who have lived among the San have described their profound knowledge of their environment, their physical endurance especially when hunting, their capacity for relaxed enjoyment in dancing and their psychological stability. They still hunt as their remote ancestors must have done, smearing insect or vegetable poisons on the tips of their tiny arrows, tracking their pray with infinite patience and pursuing a wounded beast for hours. Now they no longer paint or engrave on stone; but their ancestors were responsible for some extremely affecting art. Rock engravings and paintings are to be found

from the Maghrib to southern Africa, where they were still being made into the nineteenth century. As examples of their art show, they are by no means uniform in style or substance. Some are representational, others symbolic; some are crude, others astonishingly delicate. Such a variety of styles is in itself impressive.

The hunting and gathering life imposed severe limitations on early man, as it does on the modern San. If people were not to starve, they could not generally form bands of more than about 50 persons. Each little band was generally obliged to move about frequently from one location to another within the territory it claimed for itself. Nevertheless, by about 6000 BC some communities had managed to transcend these limitations. Thus these were fishing communities settled by rivers, lakes and oceans. A site that has been excavated at Ishango on Lake Albert was occupied by people who fished with barbed harpoons. As they had a plentiful food supply in one location, they did not have to move about. They built permanent homes and lived in villages of up to a thousand people. Thus village life began at favored sites in

Africa, long before their inhabitants had learned to cultivate the soil or domesticate animals. It was in such villages that more complex forms of social organization first developed. And it was such communities that became the first recipients and the disseminators of the most fundamental changes in Africa before the colonial period: the transition from hunting and collecting to crop cultivation and stock farming.

Food-producers and iron-workers

By about 5000 BC cereals (wheat and barley) and domestic animals (sheep, goats and cattle) had been introduced into the lower Nile valley from the Near East, and the Egyptians proceeded to build their impressive civilization upon that economic base. By 3000 BC agriculture had spread westward throughout North Africa and southward into the Sahara, which received a good rainfall at that time and was cultivable in many areas and suitable for stock-farming almost everywhere. After about 2500 BC, however, the Sahara began to dry up, and some of its inhabitants were obliged to move northward toward the Mediter-

ranean coastal plain or southward into the Sudanic savanna country. In the savanna, where wheat and barley do not prosper, people gradually domesticated local grasses – sorghum, millet and rice. They also began to produce crops and herd livestock in the Ethiopian highlands.

Two types of late Stone Age cultures then developed south of the Sahara. One, which Professor Desmond Clark has called the West African complex, extended across the Sudanic savanna from the Senegal valley to western Ethiopia. Here the basis of life was agriculture and people lived in compact villages, building the kind of social systems that had previously been adopted by the fishing communities. The other late Stone Age culture Clark has called the East African complex. This he traces to cattle-keepers who were forced out of the drying Sahara and settled east of the Rift Valley in Ethiopia, Eritrea and Somaliland, and down the East African highlands into northern Tanzania. These people tended to be exclusively pastoral. During the dry season they formed large communities around permanent water; in the wet season they split into small, dispersed groups.

The late Stone Age people eventually acquired one more crucial asset: iron. Iron-working is a complex combination of skills. It involves mining ores, smelting them to extract the iron, and manufacturing tools and weapons. Iron-working reached Egypt soon after it was first invented in Anatolia in about 1500 BC, and from there it spread up the Nile river beyond the frontier of the Egyptian kingdom. During the same period Phoenician and Greek traders brought it to their settlements along the North African coast, and Greek and Persian traders to Ethiopia. By the second century BC iron was also being worked in northern Nigeria and probably elsewhere in the West African savanna; and by the second century AD on the Kenyan coast.

The West African and Congolese forests were an obstacle to the expansion of food production, being inhospitable to livestock and to the savanna food crops. Nevertheless, during the last centuries BC people were beginning to produce food in the forests by domesticating local plants, such as African yams. In the first few centuries AD forest farming was made easier by the introduction of bananas and Asian yams, which spread rapidly in tropical Africa after having been brought to the east coast by Indonesians, who were settling in large numbers in Madagascar at that time. In the same period people began to produce crops and herd livestock on the savanna south of the Congolese forest. In addition iron was being worked at various places in the southern savanna and southeastern Africa by AD 500.

By AD 1500 the material basis of life had been transformed in nearly every part of the continent. People were no longer exclusively dependent on the food they could win by collecting and hunting. They were growing cereals or food plants, or herding sheep, cattle or goats and they had specialists who made metal tools and weapons. At the very least, except for diminishing communities such as the San in southern Africa, they were obtaining grain by exchange with those who produced it.

The processes involved in this transformation were varied and the results most uneven. In some cases large bodies of people migrated *en masse* over long distances and conquered the previous inhabitants of the region where they settled. In other cases food-producing peoples had formed continuously expanding frontiers of settlement, as families and family groups pushed out beyond their native villages to occupy fresh land. In still others, travelers, traders or Islamic or Christian missionaries were the bearers of new techniques to the peoples they visited.

The diffusion of a new technique to an established community required skill in the receiver as well as the donor, because the natural resources to which the skill could be applied differed from region to region. Crops that thrived in one region were useless in another. Often, indeed, the effective diffusion of a new technique involved something like a secondary invention – the domestication of new plants, or the breeding of new strains of livestock – before it became productive in a fresh locality.

People adopted the new techniques in varying degrees. Where game was plentiful, hunting continued to yield a high proportion of the diet; and where iron was scarce, stone and wooden implements continued in general use.

Although archeology enables us to talk with some confidence about the diffusion of technical skills, we are on much less firm ground when we deal with social institutions. Attempts have been made to establish historical connections between societies on evidence that they had similar institutions. But before such evidence can be accepted as proof of a relationship, we need corroborative evidence from other sources. The reason is that the range of institutional arrangements open to man is limited – and the simpler the material culture, the greater the limitations. In similar natural environments, preindustrial man often created remarkably similar institutions in every continent quite independently. Moreover, when institutions, as distinct from technical skills, were diffused, they did not simply replace existing institutions in the receiving society. What happened was that a society adapted specific institutional ideas into its own existing system, and the ideas were necessarily transformed as they became part of a new integrated whole.

African races and languages

In the preceding pages we have refrained from applying racial labels to the peoples of Africa. There are good reasons for this. Western scholars used to classify Africans as Bushmanoid, Negroid or Caucasoid, and modern African populations were believed to be either pure examples of these races or mixtures of them. Each race was said to possess unique, innate and immutable physical characteristics, and some Western scholars also considered that each race had unique, innate and immutable cultures.

These ideas of racial 'purity,' which still linger on in more or less diluted forms to bedevil man's

relations with man in the world today, were simply wrong. The supposed pure Caucasoid, Bushmanoid and Negroid stocks never existed, as, indeed, pure stocks of other races have never existed. In Africa in particular, with its openness to immigration from other continents, notably through Suez and the Red Sea, and its lack of internal barriers to movement, actual populations have rarely been isolated from others for long periods and have been subjected to more or less continuous secretions of new members. In addition, when actual populations have changed their diets, as with the shift from hunting and gathering to food production, their physical characteristics have changed.

And obviously there are no causal relationships between man's physical and cultural qualities. For example, at various times and in various places peoples with marked Negroid physical characteristics have lived by hunting and collecting, by cultivating cereals or food plants and by herding cattle and sheep. Negroid peoples have lived in stateless societies, in small chiefdoms and in large kingdoms. Some have been conservative, others innovative. In fact all African populations have been more or less mixed, open and changing, and their achievements have never been determined by their racial characteristics.

There is great linguistic as well as physical differentiation in Africa. By AD 1500 languages were distributed in the continent approximately, but not precisely, as they are today. Linguists now identify over 600 distinct languages in the continent and consider that most of them belong to four independent language families. Joseph Greenberg calls these Afro-Asiatic, Niger-Congo (or Congo-Kordofanian), Nilo-Saharan and Khoisan.

Afro-Asiatic languages are spoken by most of the inhabitants of North Africa, as well as the neighboring parts of Asia. One of the branches, Berber, was formerly spoken very widely, but by 1500, as a result of the Arab invasions, Arabic, a sub-branch of the Semitic branch of the Afro-Asiatic family, was replacing it, except in parts of Morocco and Algeria, where Berber is spoken to this day. The Chad branch of this family is spoken on the southern side of the Sahara in northern Nigeria and its vicinity, where Hausa has now become one of the most widely spoken languages in Africa. Languages of the Semitic and Cushitic branches of the family are prevalent in Ethiopia and the Horn.

The Niger-Congo family extends over almost all of Africa south of the Sahara, including most of West Africa, the Congo basin and East, Central and South Africa, all the way from Wolof in Senegal to Xhosa in the Cape Province and Zande in the Sudan. Greenberg groups these languages in seven or eight branches, and classifies the Bantu languages as a sub-branch of the central branch of this extensive family. Recently, having decided that languages spoken in Kordofan in the Republic of the Sudan are to be classified with this family, Greenberg has proposed that the family name be changed to Congo-Kordofanian.

The Nilo-Saharan family consists of many languages, generally spoken by small groups of people living between Afro-Asiatic speakers and Niger-Congo speakers, and ranging from Songhai on the Niger bend in the west to Masai in Kenya and Tanzania in the east. Finally, the Khoisan family, sometimes called the Click family because of the presence of click sounds, includes the languages formerly spoken by hunter-gatherers in at least eastern and southern Africa. They survive among the Khoi, the San and the Sandawe.

Left: An indication of the impact of the Arabs on sub-Saharan Africa – the principal mosque at Timbuktu in modern-day Mali.

Above right: Kirina in Mali, one of three Malinke towns that formed the heart of the empire of Sundiata. It was also the site of a decisive battle in 1235 that secured the future of the empire through the defeat of Sundiata's great rival, Sumanguru.

Right: Nomadic hunters and gatherers, the pygmies live in small, close-knit groups with no organized political structure.

Linguists have made vital contributions to historical knowledge by deductions from linguistic comparisons. The great similarity among the Bantu languages shows that they are derived from a single language that began to split in the last two or three millennia; and their similarity to the other languages of the central branch of the Niger-Congo family suggests an original connection with the speakers of those languages, all of which are spoken in eastern Nigeria or Cameroun. However, historical linguistics is a relatively new and very specialized subject, and much more work needs to be done before we can rely on it to provide us with any very grand historical hypotheses.

African culture

Throughout Africa the basic social groupings were descent groups. The primary group was the family, and many of a person's rights and duties were derived from his status in the family. Polygyny was almost universal. It was possible because men married late and girls married at puberty, and a widow became the wife of a relative of her deceased husband. The typical family consisted of a male head, his wife or wives and his unmarried children. Women shared their fathers' or husbands' ranks, though men took the leading roles in most political, legal and religious matters. Thus women's roles were decidedly, and oppressively, subordinate.

People also had loyalties to larger descent groups than the family – to the lineage and the clan. Descent was reckoned through the male line in some societies, through the female in others.

Lineages were usually calculated three to five generations deep, clans deeper.

In most societies there were other types of association that cut across kinship groupings. Age associations were very common, especially in eastern and southern Africa. Secret societies were strong in West Africa and the Congo basin. Where there was pronounced economic specialization, as in much of West Africa, craft and professional associations also existed.

People know their place well in African societies. At about the age of puberty boys were separated from their homes for periods of up to six months and trained by experienced men to become effective adult members of society. The training included social norms, political indoctrination and sexual hygiene, and was accompanied by severe physical ordeals, often including circumcision. In some societies senior women were responsible for giving appropriate training to girls. Thus education was a strong conservative force in Africa, a method of transmitting established beliefs and rules of conduct.

Religious beliefs and rituals were closely associated with the social groupings in society. The primacy of descent groups was accompanied by the belief that the living were associated with the dead in a continuum. People performed rituals to propitiate their ancestors and a pantheon of other supernatural beings who could influence the living generation. Even where Christian and Muslim practices had been introduced, traditional beliefs and rituals were rarely abandoned. Indeed there was a relationship between the success of a newly introduced universal religion and the

extent to which it accommodated older African beliefs and rituals.

Patterns of settlement varied with the environment. In arid regions, as in Somalia, predominantly pastoral societies moved with the seasons. During the dry season they congregated in large clans around water supplies; during the wet season they scattered in small lineages over the pastures. In regions where agriculture was possible, people lived permanently in scattered homesteads or villages. Only in societies where long-distance trade or economic specialization was significant, or where states had developed, did large aggregations of people of different clans live permanently at specific sites, as happened at east-coast ports and at trading and administrative centers in West Africa.

Though descent was always important in determining the roles of men and women, African societies were never closed systems. Strangers who had perhaps been dislodged from their homes by warfare or had come into conflict with their own authorities often attached themselves as clients of established members of societies. This often led to status differentiation. In societies such as the Akan (in what is now Ghana) there were several inferior categories whose status was very precisely defined. Europeans generally regarded such subordinate groups as slaves, but this was often not the case, since African patrons usually treated their clients as members of their own families and gave them privileges seldom granted the slaves owned by Europeans in the Americas. In some other societies, notably those to the west of Lake Victoria,

Far left and left: Two ritual dance masks belonging to the 'ekpo' society of southern Nigeria.

Right: The shrine of the Keita clan whose ancestor is the semi-mythical Sundiata, the founder of Mali.

Below: A carving of an ancestor figure from the Baluba culture of Zaire.

there were caste-like systems, with ruling groups of pastoralists dominating the agricultural communities. But these were unusual in traditional Africa.

Cultural boundaries did not always correspond with political boundaries, and neither were very clearly defined. A person would often be conscious of belonging to a cultural and linguistic community that extended far beyond his political community. For example, the Nguni people of southern Africa, who lived on the coastal side of the mountain escarpment between Delagoa Bay and the Transkei, all spoke mutually intelligible dialects of the same language and observed essentially the same customs; but down to the late eighteenth century they were divided among several hundred small autonomous chiefdoms.

The political systems in traditional Africa have been classified by modern scholars in different ways. In addition to the small bands of the surviving hunting and gathering peoples, we may distinguish kingdoms, chiefdoms and stateless societies. Stateless societies were communities in which there was no ruling political hierarchy, only kinship institutions and associations such as age sects and secret societies. Such societies were widespread in East Africa, but they were also to be found in West Africa, as among the Ibo of Nigeria. Chiefdoms were small political communities comprising people who spoke the same language and had the same customs, and who were ruled more or less directly by chiefs. Kingdoms were larger communities, including peoples of different cultures. The roles of rulers and subjects were more clearly differentiated and there was a relatively complex hierarchy of territorial office-holders, from the king down through various intermediaries to village heads, as well as a central bureaucracy. No single cause was responsible for the rise of kingdoms in different parts of Africa. In each case they arose out of the dynamics of the local situation, which were often related to popu-

lation growth and the expansion of long-distance trade and, sometimes, to migration and conquest. The authority of kings was usually unquestioned in the core area of the state, but then it progressively weakened until it reached a frontier zone where it overlapped with the claims of other political authorities. Chiefdoms and kingdoms alike had recurring periods of weakness when the ruler died, for even though succession was by descent, there were often conflicts among the eligible relatives of the deceased ruler.

The rate of change in traditional African societies was far slower than the rate of change in modern industrial societies. But that is not to say that traditional societies were static. Today the vast majority of the structural changes that took place in pre-Columbian African societies cannot be reconstructed, but in later chapters we shall trace some of the more dramatic changes that have left substantial traces in the historical record.

Was there a traditional African culture, as distinct from a series of more or less related local variations on the kind of early culture in societies on all continents at comparable technological states? The answer offered is a qualified affirmative, though it is difficult to define its qualities in precise terms, because different parts of the continent were exposed in different degrees to external influences. African societies rested not only on descent groupings but also on the polygynous family (which was not universal). Most African societies gave similar sorts of explanations for man's place in the universe and devised similar methods for coping with forces which they could not control by methods we would call rational. For ritual and political purposes most of them produced works of art which unmistakably share a style we can only think of as African. Yet despite these defining characteristics, the history of Africa is a story that cannot be told in terms of cultural and political unity, but only in terms of the most extreme diversity.

The Early Civilizations of America

On a summer day in the year 1502 the tiny fleet of Christopher Columbus lay at anchor off one of the Bay Islands of Honduras. The Admiral had ordered his brother, Bartholomew, to go ashore and reconnoiter the island, which the latter found to be inhabited by natives not very different in culture from the primitive peoples of the Antilles. But while on his mission Bartholomew and his men were astonished to witness the arrival of a great trading canoe, so large that it was paddled by 25 men. Unlike the simple Arawak 'Indians' they had previously known, these foreigners had copper tools and ornaments, and possibly gold, and men and women were fully clothed in finely woven textiles. Their chief indicated that they had come from a land to the west, and the Spaniards had every reason to believe that this country was rich and cultured.

We now know that these traders were Maya, representatives of one of the great early civilizations. What makes that moment so fascinating is that it marks the first contact between the civilizations of the Old World and the New. Until then millennia had passed, during which the peoples of both hemispheres had gone their own separate courses, utterly oblivious to the existence of any others but themselves.

Once the splendors of the New World civilizations had been witnessed – and totally destroyed – in the sixteenth century, their character deeply impressed such European philosophers as Michel de Montaigne and artists such as Albrecht Dürer. The abilities of the Mexicans and Peruvians in architecture, goldwork and the other arts were quickly appreciated, even by the hard-bitten *conquistadores*. But what especially interested the thinkers of Europe was that on those distant shores, in a world whose very existence had never been surmised, there had evolved elaborate cultures with traits very similar to those of their own people and to others, such as the civilizations of antiquity, with which they were acquainted. They were confronted with political states, with kings, palaces, courtiers, priests, temples, roads and money.

Peopling the New World

How had all this come about? Many of the Spanish friars firmly believed that some of the famous Lost Tribes of Israel had reached this side of the water, but one, Father Acosta, reasoned that the ancestors of the American Indians had migrated long ago from Siberia while still in a primitive state, and that their elaborate civilizations had evolved in isolation since that time. Needless to say, modern scholarship has proven that the Acosta thesis was almost certainly the correct one, though the possibility of transoceanic diffusion has continued to haunt a few New World archeologists. If, as seems most likely, these civilizations are largely autochthonous, they constitute an independent case on which to test hypotheses and theories of history developed in the Old World.

The date of the arrival of the ancestral Indians into the hemisphere remains a problem. It is generally believed to have occurred during the last glacial maximum, when sea levels would have been several hundred feet lower than today owing to the quantity of water held in the northern ice

sheets. At that time a thousand-mile-wide land platform would have been exposed between Siberia and Alaska. Across this cold, bleak, tundra-covered bridge small groups of Siberian hunters and their families could have expanded their hunting territories into the unexploited lands on the other side. Radiocarbon dates on very early sites in Mexico indicate that the initial migration must have been before 21,000 years ago, and it could have been as long ago as 40,000 years.

The New World into which the newcomers intruded was a kind of hunter's paradise. Huge herds of great herbivores – mammoth, mastadon, horse, various camelids and giant bison – roamed the grassy plains away from the ice sheets. By about 10,000 BC man had occupied all suitable land from the Bering Straits down to Tierra del Fuego. We probably should not underestimate the complexity of the culture brought into the hemisphere by these Asiatic migrants. Certain religious and cosmological concepts that are nearly universal among American Indian groups have close counterparts in Asia, such as the notion of a universe oriented to world directions that are associated with specific colors, plants and animals, and of a universe that has gone through repeating cycles of creation and destruction. On the material side, the early hunters had a stone tool kit that emphasized spear or dart points, hide

scrapers and crude chopping tools. Remains of this sort have been found in ancient campsites in western North America, in Mexico and over large parts of South America away from the tropical forest.

Following the final retreat of the glacial ice after 8000 BC profound climatic and ecological changes took place throughout the hemisphere. Lush grasslands often turned to desert, and the large game either died off or (as some authorities believe) was annihilated by man. The old hunting patterns had to change drastically for any peoples to survive. More humble quarry, such as rabbits and lizards, became the main goal of inland hunters, while those who dwelled along rivers and seacoasts concentrated upon fish and various kinds of seafood.

Plant domestication

It was in this context that the most important event in the development of the New World cultures took place: the domestication of plants. Vegetable foods were a prime source of energy for post-Pleistocene hunters, and their systematic exploitation must have suggested to more than one group of semi-sedentary Indians that their seeds or roots could be planted and tended.

By 5000 BC an extremely significant event had taken place in the arid highlands of southern

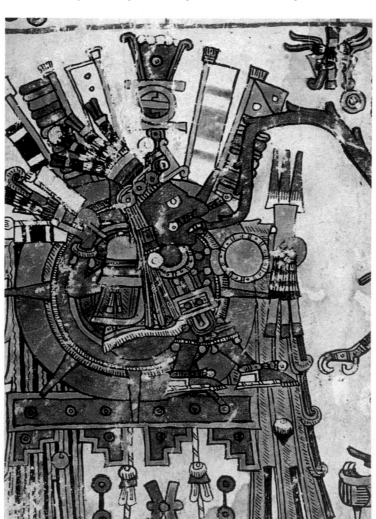

Above right: An example of Mayan hieroglyphics.

Above far right: Dating from the seventh to ninth centuries, these stone figures of Toltec warriors served as columns to support a pyramid temple erected to the deity Quetzalcoatl.

Left: Taken from an old Maya illuminated manuscript, this picture depicts a religious ceremony where human sacrifices are made to the Sun.

Right: The Pyramid of the Sun, a powerful symbol of the all-pervading significance of religion in the Teotihuacan culture (100 BC–AD 600).

Mexico: maize or Indian corn had been domesticated. This plant, at first a very unpromising grass, became the primary source of energy for almost all peoples in the New World areas which were to be civilized. Only the American Indians living in the highest mountain valleys of Peru and Bolivia relied upon another plant (the white potato), for maize does not do well at very high altitudes. Various kinds of squashes and chili pepper have an even greater antiquity in both Mexico and the Andes, and in both areas cotton was brought under human control, perhaps first as a food crop and then for its spinnable lint. The result of this vast reservoir of hitherto untapped energy was the appearance of simple villages. By 2000 BC permanent human settlements dotted the landscape from central Mexico to southern Peru.

So far we have been talking about these widely scattered regions as though they represented a single cultural tradition. In fact they showed as many contrasts as similarities in their development. The New World civilizations extended all the way from the Tropic of Cancer to the Tropic of Capricorn. The part we now call Mesoamerica comprised central and southern Mexico and those parts of neighboring Central America which were dominated by the Maya before the Conquest. To the south the Andean area essentially covered the old Inca Empire: highland and coastal Peru, southern Ecuador, western Bolivia and far northern Chile. For reasons still obscure, the entire intervening region from eastern Honduras to northern Ecuador failed to reach the level of civilization, and must be excluded from our present survey.

Mesoamerica

Mesoamerica, like the Andean area, is a region of extreme geographical diversity. Almost every kind of environment can be found, from tropical jungle to cactus-strewn desert to high altitude tundra. But basically there are two contrasting settings: the highlands, which are relatively dry, but in which soils can be cultivated the year round, and the lowlands, covered with high forest, with high rainfall but much poorer soils, which are farmed by the slash-and-burn method. In slash-and-burn lowland peasants usually select a patch of forest, cut it toward the end of the dry season (which lasts from November to May) and then burn it just before the onslaught of the rains. Corn, beans and other crops are planted in holes poked through the ashes. Competition from weeds and declining fertility force the farmer to abandon his field after anywhere from 3 to 20 years, after which he selects another patch and begins the process again. It thus takes a far greater amount of territory to support a lowland family than a highland one, and this is probably the main reason why lowland settlements were widely scattered and cities had hardly taken hold on the eve of the Spanish Conquest.

Certain features of Mesoamerican culture were unique in the New World, while others were shared with the Andean and other areas. Most distinctive were hieroglyphic writing, recorded in folding-screen books of bark paper or deer hide coated with stucco, and a highly involved calendar. This calendar was based upon a non-corrected solar year of 365 days arranged in 52-year cycles. The Mesoamericans had a considerable knowledge of astronomy, and celestial phenomena played an important role in their various religious systems. All worshiped a rain god, as well as a culture hero known everywhere as the Feathered Serpent. While rubber-ball games were known in Amazonian South America and in the

Antilles, in Mesoamerica they were played in a special court and served an athletic as well as a religious role. The Mesoamerican economy, especially in the highlands, was centered upon markets of great size and complexity which were administered by judges and constabulary. The principal purpose of warfare was not territorial conquest but to glean captives for sacrifice to the Sun God and other sanguinary deities. In fact it is doubtful if any other peoples of the world have ever practiced religious sacrifice on this same scale.

The history of Mesoamerica may be divided into three periods, the Formative Period (1500 BC–AD 200), the Classic Period (AD 200-900) and the Post-Classic Period (AD 900 to the Spanish Conquest). By the advent of the Formative Period various important Mesoamerican traits were already set. Village life based upon maize, beans, squashes and other cultigens was already well established. Pottery was known, and simple clay figurines of nude females were being fashioned. The true loom had appeared, and cotton textiles

of considerable complexity were being woven.

It used to be thought that the Formative Period was a simple counterpart to the Neolithic of the Old World, with nothing more than peasant communities organized on a basically egalitarian basis. But recent discoveries have shown that Mesoamerica's first civilization, the Olmec, was coexistent with these rural farmers. The Olmec civilization has been justifiably called the 'mother culture' of Mesoamerica, since all of the later high cultures – Maya, Teotihuacán, Zapotec, Toltec, Aztec and so forth – are to some extent derived from Olmec. While Olmec-style objects, particularly finely carved jades, are found over much of Mesoamerica, its great, and presumably first, development is found in a relatively restricted zone on the southern Gulf Coast of Mexico. There great rivers meander over the jungle-covered plains, creating natural levees of mud and silt which are still today prized by farmers for their dry-season crops. It seems likely that levee lands such as these provided the economic impetus which eventually gave rise to the precocious Olmec state.

The oldest Olmec site known thus far is at San Lorenzo, lying on a plateau that is at least partly man-made. Shortly after 1200 BC the Olmec of San Lorenzo began to carve the enormous stone monuments for which they are famous, the raw material being basalt brought in from many miles away. Most characteristic are the colossal heads, huge portraits of helmeted rulers which may weigh up to 20 or more tons each. By 900 BC San Lorenzo had been effectively destroyed, perhaps by a combination of invasion and internal revolt, and La Venta, isolated on an island in the midst of a swampy plain, had become dominant. There Olmec mastery of stone sculpture continued, but jade also now made its appearance on the scene. In La Venta offerings have been found: delicately carved jade figurines of strange part-jaguar, part-infant human creatures that were the object of Olmec worship. La Venta in turn was destroyed and its monuments smashed about 400 BC, and the Olmec torch passed to Tres Zapotes, which maintained itself as an epi-Olmec center until the first century BC (by which time Maya civilization was beginning to crystallize).

There is much yet to be learned about the nature of Olmec society and politics. While Olmec centers, with their earth-and-clay pyramids and other public constructions, were probably focal points for religious ceremonies, they were certainly staffed by political groups owing allegiance to mighty rulers who were more than mere chiefs. There is ample reason to believe that each Olmec capital in turn held sway over large areas of Mesoamerica, from central Mexico and Guerrero down as far as El Salvador. This could have been a kind of proto-empire based upon the Olmec need for scarce materials – jade, iron ores for mirrors, serpentine – which the Olmec elite consumed in vast quantities for prestige purposes. In return the Olmec could have exchanged with native rulers finished products fashioned in the likenesses of the prestigious Olmec gods. Their religion, like Christianity in later times, would have become the basis for all later state religions.

Left: A relief from a Maya temple. A high priest (*right*), overlooked by the war god Kukulkan (*left*), prepares to tear out his tongue with a rope entwined with thorns. A feature of Mesoamerican religions was the barbarity of their sacrificial ceremonies.

Right: An example of pre-Columbian art – a massive stone head from the Olmec civilization.

By the latter part of the Formative Period, from about 300 BC to AD 200, a number of regional civilizations were usurping the role previously played by the monolithic Olmec state. Among these was the Zapotec civilization of Monte Albán, a major center lying in the Oaxaca Valley of southern Mexico. Although isolated hieroglyphs are known on only a few Olmec monuments, Late Formative Monte Albán was fully literate. Fixed into the façade of platforms and buildings were slabs depicting the rulers of conquered towns, with these events fixed in the 52-year calendar cycle. In the old Olmec area itself, and in the state of Chiapas, several reliefs dating to the first century BC are known, dated in the Long Count system, which used to be thought a purely Maya invention. Writing and calendrics are found extended from the Gulf Coast down across the Isthmus of Tehuantepec, along the Pacific Coast of Chiapas and Guatemala, and up into the Guatemalan highlands; they are accompanied by an elaborate relief style called Izapan, which seems to be ancestral to the lowland Maya style developed at a later date.

The Classic Period

The 'Golden Age' of Mesoamerica was the Classic Period, when there was a great flowering of art, architecture, commerce and intellectual achievement. It used to be thought that this period was one of tranquility and stability, characterized by peaceable theocracies whose leadership was uninterested in military activities and conquest. This misconception was based upon a misunderstanding of the nature of the Classic Maya civilization, which flourished at this time. In fact it is likely that the Classic Period states were just as warlike as the bellicose polities which succeeded them. Furthermore, it is not only unlikely that Classic governments were under control of the priesthood. In the case of Teotihuacán, we are sure that a military-commercial empire as large as or larger than that of the later Aztec was in existence.

Teotihuacán, founded at some time during the

first centuries of the Christian era, was the most gigantic city of the Pre-Columbian New World. Its ruins dominate a valley on the northeastern side of the Valley of Mexico (the great landlocked basin in which Mexico City is located), and it was a planned urban capital laid out on a grid pattern. Two avenues meet at the center, dividing it into quarters. Along the north-south thoroughfare (the Avenue of the Dead) are the major ceremonial structures of Teotihuacán, including the huge Pyramid of the Sun, which is over 200 feet high and measures some 700 feet long on the sides. At the center of the city is the so-called Citadel, which most probably was the Royal Palace itself.

Teotihuacán buildings were constructed by facing adobe-brick or rubble cores with broken volcanic stones set in clay and covered over with smooth plaster. The dominant motif is called *talud-tablero*: a rectangular panel with inset placed over the sloping outer face, the panel often being elaborately painted with mythological scenes. To the east and west of the Avenue of the Dead were the principal palaces, abodes of the elite who ran the Teotihuacán state. These were square compounds surrounded by high walls; inside them were open courts on to which faced the dwelling quarters. Some of the most spectacular mural paintings have been discovered in these palaces.

At its height, shortly before AD 600, Teotihuacán covered some 11 square miles. As usual, it is not easy to estimate the ancient population, but a recent mapping project suggests that there were at least 125,000 persons living in the city, and possibly over 200,000. What was the basis for this spectacular urban development, unknown in the Formative Period? Certainly many of the residents, perhaps most, were engaged in craft specializations, such as the manufacture of fine ceremonial pottery or the fashioning of obsidian tools. Areas of the city have been found in which foreign traders from places such as the Maya Empire, Veracruz and Oaxaca resided. But more important than any local trade or manufacture is the fact that the Teotihuacán people dominated not only the Valley of Mexico but most of Mesoamerica during the first half of the Classic Period. If the Aztec model can be applied here, then the state and the city itself would have been supported by the forced tribute of millions who had been swept by military conquest into the Teotihuacán empire. At any rate, whatever the nature of the Teotihuacán state, it was destroyed in the seventh century AD, and most of the capital was burned to the ground by hands unknown. Thus the all-pervasive Teotihuacán influence to be seen in the Early Classic Period had completely disappeared by the Late Classic.

The Maya civilization

The other great Classic civilization was that of the Maya, in their homeland in southern Mexico and neighboring Central America. A stronger contrast with the highly urbanized and expansionist culture of Teotihuacán could hardly be imagined. The Maya realm was one of lowland tropical forest, with high rainfall during the summer months. Because of the demanding ecological conditions set by this environment, Maya agriculture was necessarily of the slash-and-burn sort, which can produce a surplus but not support the huge populations and urban concentrations typical of the Mexican highlands. Accordingly, the ancient Maya 'city' seems not to have been a city at all, but rather what has been called a ceremonial center, inhabited by rulers and their retinues, the priesthood, some traders and craftsmen and servants and slaves. The bulk of the populace ap-

Left: The pyramid of Kukulkan, built by the Maya between the tenth and twelfth centuries.

Right: An example of the bat and dot code used by Maya mathematicians.

Below far left: The deity Quetzalcoatl with a symbolic headdress representing a coyote.

Below left: The Sun stone – the basis for the Aztec calendar of the sixteenth century.

parently lived in small rural hamlets much like those of their modern descendants, and were called to the centers for labor or for the celebration of great events.

Nonetheless, many Maya centers are of great size and impressiveness, with their immense pyramid-temples reaching up through the canopy of the rain forest. The principle used in Classic Maya construction was that of the corbel or false arch, in which successive courses of stones were set in overlapping rows up to the vault summit, which was capped with flat stones. Maya temples and 'palaces' thus have very narrow rooms. The abundance of limestone resulted in an architectural style in which rubble-and-lime cores were covered with limestone blocks, and then the whole structure coated with thick layers of stucco.

The Maya temple-pyramids are truly spectacular buildings. At the largest Maya site, Tikal, there are no fewer than six of these, connected to each other by broad causeways. Their function and that of the so-called 'palaces' is still uncertain, but evidence is mounting that originally the pyramids themselves served to house the remains of great lords. In contrast to Teotihuacán, little if any planning is apparent in the Maya centers – a strange fact, since it is now known that Teotihuacán exerted powerful influence (perhaps even political control) in the fifth and sixth centuries AD upon the developing Maya states. Other structures to be found are masonry courts for the rubber-ball game that was played by the Maya nobility, and sweat baths.

Maya art is baroque, elegant and narrative, testifying to its ultimate derivation from the Izapan style of the Late Formative Period. The Maya were master carvers, and embellished their temples and palaces with highly involved limestone and stucco reliefs of men and gods. The walls of rooms were often painted with murals depicting scenes of real life, such as the wonderful paintings of Bonampak showing a tremendous jungle battle followed by the torture of prisoners and victory celebrations. In contradiction to the idea of Maya peacefulness, the theme of war and the mistreatment of captives is extremely common, especially on carved stone stelae set up in rows before temples.

This leads one to wonder about the nature of Classic Maya society and politics. Recent research into the subject matter of the inscriptions on stone has shown that most of these deal not with gods and supposedly deified time periods, but rather with mundane matters concerning the rise of local dynasties, conquests, marriage alliances and the birth of heirs. Unless Teotihuacán filled that role in the early Classic, there was no overall authority in the Maya area, although great sites like Tikal, Naranjo and Yaxchilán must have made their influence felt over wide regions. In this case the Maya would have more closely resembled the feudal states of Europe or China than imperial Teotihuacán.

The Maya were fully literate and intellectually advanced. Basic to Maya thought was a highly involved calendar to which all their ceremonies were geared. In it the Mesoamerican calendar cycle of 52 years merged with the Long Count (almost certainly an Olmec invention). The Long Count itself is a time count of elapsed days based upon the tun, a period of 360 days, which was useful in computations. On some Maya monuments there are Long Count calculations reaching thousands, sometimes even millions, of years into the past and future. In their books, made of bark paper coated with stucco and folded like screens, accurate records and working tables were kept on the motions of heavenly bodies such as the Moon and Venus. The Maya savants had actually worked out a method to predict solar and lunar eclipses and had arrived at a very close approximation of the length of the tropical year.

Maya writing was the most elaborate ever developed in Mesoamerica, and we have records, many of them clearly historical in nature, extending over the entire Classic Period. As it evolved over the centuries until the Spaniards ended its use, this script, which had originally been ideographic, became more and more phonetic. The Soviet epigrapher Yuri Knorosov has been able to show that by the Post-Classic Period the Maya could write almost any word by means of a syllabary. However, there are many details of the system still to be worked out.

One of the most intriguing puzzles in New World archeology is the sudden collapse of the lowland Maya civilization around AD 900. All of the great ceremonial centers fell into ruin, and the central part of the Maya area (focused on northern Guatemala) was almost totally abandoned to the forest. Various ecological explanations have been put forward, none of them very convincing. It is clear that foreigners from further west were then intruding into the central Maya area, and it is possible that the downfall of the western Maya sites triggered a larger-scale collapse elsewhere, perhaps through a series of internal revolts.

Another Classic civilization worthy of note was that of Monte Albán. It will be remembered that this site in Oaxaca, a mountaintop citadel, had a precocious development of writing in the Late Formative Period. The Zapotec peoples probably ruled over much of Oaxaca from Monte Albán in the Classic Period, but there is strong evidence in the stone reliefs commemorating victories, as well as in tomb murals, that Teotihuacán held some sort of hegemony, perhaps only cultural, over the site. To the east, in the lowlands of central Veracruz, there flourished yet another interesting civilization that featured ceremonial objects connected with the ball game. These are carved in a strange, interlaced style that closely recalls decoration on vessels and jades from Bronze Age China.

The Post-Classic Period

After AD 900 with the beginning of the Post-Classic Period, we enter into a well-documented yet maddeningly imprecise kind of history for Mesoamerica. There are rich records written down after the Conquest which pertain to this period – from the early Spanish friars and from native intelligentsia who recorded their past in Spanish letters – but unfortunately these records are difficult to interpret, since in Post-Classic times all events were recorded in the 52-year calendar cycle (and we do not know which 52-year interval was being talked about) or, in the case of the Maya of Yucatán, in similarly recurrent cycles of 256¼ years' duration. The Post-Classic, then, is to be distinguished from the Classic not in terms of its supposedly militaristic bent, but by the more detailed information which we have about it.

The early part of the Post-Classic (900-1200) is marked by the rise of a people called the Toltec, who ruled much of Mexico and most of the Maya area (except the empty central region) from a capital at Tula, a site lying about 50 miles northwest of Mexico City. To all of the later peoples of Mesoamerica, including the Aztec and the Maya-Mexican dynasties, the Toltec were a marvelous people, living in a never-never-land of riches and culture after migrating to their new home from the deserts of northern Mexico. The archeological facts are that the Toltec of Tula inherited the remains of what was left of the old Teotihuacán civilization, which they combined with certain cultural elements contributed by the Late Classic Maya. In the tenth century AD they re-created an empire resembling that of Teotihuacán, and carried their hard, cruel but vigorous art style to such distant places as Yucatán, which they ruled from the great site of Chichén Itzá.

The last great people on the Mesoamerican scene were the Aztec. According to their own records, they migrated into central Mexico in the twelfth century, having originated in western Mexico as a barbarian tribe. After they had established themselves on the shore of the great lake that then filled the Valley of Mexico, the Aztec, inspired by their tribal war god Huitzilopochtli, representative of the life-giving Sun, began a systematic program of subduing their more powerful neighbors.

By the mid thirteenth century the Aztec had founded their capital, Tenochtitlán, on an island in the Great Lake. From there they managed to conquer all of Mesoamerica except the Maya area in the next two centuries. The urban center was surrounded by *chinampas*, drained fields surrounded by canals (which still exist today in the southern part of the lake). This circumstance made Tenochtitlán look like another Venice to the Spaniards who conquered the ancient city in the early fifteenth century.

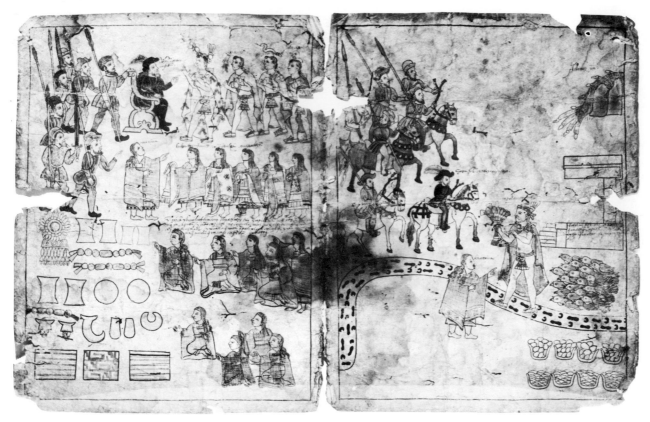

Left: The Spanish adventurer Cortes is met by the lords of Tlaxcala bearing gifts.

Right: An example of weaving from the Nasca in what is now Peru (AD 600-700).

Below right: Two 'stirrup' vases, one with a geometric design and the other with a sacred dog motif, both from the pre-Inca civilizations of Peru.

Below: A greenstone carving of Quetzalcoatl rising from the jaws of a feathered serpent.

Into the city, dominated by its twin pyramids sacred to Huitzilopochtli and to the Rain God, streamed vast quantities of goods exacted as tribute from conquered provinces. The streets were thronged with craftsmen, traders and practitioners of a myriad occupations. Cortes and his companions were enormously struck by the huge size and complexity of the great market, the daily din from which could be heard miles away.

Aztec religion, described in great detail by the Spanish fathers, was extremely complex, and closely meshed with the calendar cycle. Human sacrifice was practiced on a large scale, since the gods, particularly Huitzilopochtli, demanded the hearts and blood of brave captives so that the Sun might move across the sky each day. The Aztec priests were celibate and were under the patronage of the great god Quetzalcóatl, or Feathered Serpent, a deity who was said to have once lived at Tula and who brought learning and religion to the people.

At the head of the state was the emperor, a hereditary ruler who exacted complete homage from his people in his role as war leader and representative of the Sun. Yet it is now known that he shared his rule with a strange figure called 'Snake Woman,' in fact a holy man who held power over the city itself; dual rulership of this kind was widely spread among the American Indians. Most civil offices were in the hands of the nobility. Below them were the freemen, farmers who worked lands belonging to the clans. At the bottom were slaves taken in war and the serfs who labored on the private lands of the rich nobility.

All of this came to a brutal end on 13 August 1521, when the Spaniards and their Indian allies finally were able to wipe out all Aztec resistance, and the once great city capitulated. Mexico City was built upon its ruins.

The Andean area

The peculiar geographic conditions of the Andean area have shaped its cultural destiny. Its cool, moist highlands rise up to 20,000 feet, and its mountain valleys contain some of the world's highest-living – in the literal sense – populations. In these basins root crops such as white potato and seed crops such as quinoas were domesticated. While maize is extensively grown, above 10,000 feet its yields are too low to make it worth while as a crop.

Utterly different from the highlands is the coast, intersected by innumerable small rivers flowing into the Pacific from the east. Basically the coast is a barren desert, a result of the cold Humboldt Current that wells up from the south and makes the air exceptionally moistureless. (There is little or no rainfall, but fogs prevail between June and October, the Andean winter.) Nonetheless, there have always been human settlements in the coastal valleys. For one thing the coastal waters are richly stocked with fish and other seafood. Furthermore, the valleys have excellent soils and have been irrigated for many centuries. Thus one is confronted with a myriad Niles in miniature – green valleys surrounded by rocky, bone-dry desert.

The ecological setting of the Andean area is thus very different from that of Mesoamerica. And there is one additional feature that was peculiar to the Andes: the domestication of large mammals (unknown in Mesoamerica, where the dog, turkey and stingless bee were the only animal domesticates). The llama and the alpaca are closely related camelids that have been bred by Andean Indians for millennia, the former as a pack animal and the latter for its meat and fine wool. As none of the members of the camel family is suitable for traction, wheeled vehicles were quite unknown in the Andes.

The peoples of the Andean area were above all master technicians and engineers. Metallurgy has a far greater time depth here than in Mesoamerica and was put to utilitarian rather than merely ornamental uses. In stone masonry, road-building, canal engineering and other feats they were far more advanced than their contemporaries to the north. Where they were definitely inferior was in intellectual accomplishment and in aestheic achievement; the total absence of writing throughout Andean cultural history is evidence of this. On the other hand, in matters of statecraft and administration the Andean Indians eclipsed all other native peoples of the hemisphere.

By 2500 to 1800 BC many of the basic Andean patterns had been set. There were permanent settlements of fisher-farmers in every coastal valley, relying mainly on seafood but practicing simple flood-water cultivation inland. The first Andean art appeared at this time, in the form of textiles made by the twining method: figures of crabs, mythological serpents, people and perhaps even gods have been detected in fragments from the Huaca Prieta, a coastal site. On the central coast, the site of Chuquitanta seems to have functioned as a kind of ceremonial center, with platforms surmounted by rooms constructed of stones set in mud mortar.

In the highlands the earliest groups had at first been hunters of camelids, and little more than simple camps are known. However, within this time span there existed ceremonial complexes even more impressive than those of Chuquitanta. As an example, the site of Kotosh, on the headwaters of a tributary of the Amazon, already had stone-masonry temples, one of which was embellished with human (or supernatural) figures of clay with crossed hands. Presumably the impetus for most of these developments was the introduction of domestic maize from Mesoamerica, where it has a far greater antiquity.

Around 1800 BC two important technological innovations made their appearance: pottery and the heddle loom. The question of whether these were locally invented or were diffused from some other place, such as eastern or southeastern Asia, is still up in the air. Some archeologists, for instance, make a case for a Japanese neolithic origin for the earliest Ecuadorian pottery, which has been dated to around 2800 BC. At any rate the efforts which Andean weavers subsequently put into their textiles resulted in this manufacture becoming the most important source of wealth. (Inca bureaucrats, for instance, were paid in textiles.) The construction of ceremonial centers also increased significantly during the period between 1800 and 900 BC, in particular in the coastal valleys where platform and temple complexes similar to those of the Olmec have been discovered.

There were three moments or 'horizons' of cultural coalescence in the Andean area, of which the last two were certainly empires. The Early Horizon 900 to 200 BC, marks the rise and spread of the Chavín civilization, which in many respects is the counterpart of the Olmec culture of Mesoamerica. The type site is Chavín de Huantar, an impressive ceremonial complex in the Upper Marañon drainage. Its principal feature is the Castillo, a masonry temple with long interior galleries which probably were the focus for religious worship. The carving style of Chavín is perhaps the greatest art ever produced in Peru. Like that of the Olmec, it centered upon fearsome felines with gnashing tusks and huge claws, often combined with human elements. Harpy eagles and snakes also enter into Chavín iconography, along with monstrous caymans, or alligators. The tropical forest elements in this mix have led some scholars to postulate strong Amazonian influence upon developing Andean civilization at this time.

Whether by missionaries, militarists or both, the Chavín style was carried throughout much of the Andean area, both highland and coastal. It appears on pottery, on painted and woven textiles, on bonework and on fine gold objects

decorated by the *repoussé* method. Possibly Chavín de Huantar was the great shrine center for a pan-Andean ceremonial cult, but it may also have functioned as the capital for a very large conquest state. Archeology still has much to discover.

In the last centuries before the Christian era, the unity that was Chavín civilization had broken down, to be replaced by a number of vigorous regional cultures that flourished in a kind of intermediate period that lasted from 200 BC to AD 600. In the small valleys of the north coast irrigation had appeared for the first time, and the number of villages and towns increased at an impressive rate. The most interesting of these cultures was the Moche civilization, famed for its 'stirrup spout' pots and other ceramics. These were painted and modeled with extremely realistic scenes of daily life among the elite, such as hunting in the desert, warfare and the torture and

mutilation of captives, as well as a wide variety of sexual activities. Some Moche vessels deal with the supernatural world, and here the old Chavín heritage is still evident. Perhaps most significant of all are the portrait vessels, depicting great Moche rulers with features as dignified as those of Venetian Doges. The same portrait will often be found in different valleys, arguing for an overall political unity of some sort among them. Moche architects erected the first great pyramids in the Andean area, using unfired mud bricks. The huge Huaca de Sol is the largest, rising some 130 feet above the surrounding plain.

Another striking culture was the Nazca civilization of the south coast, which featured brightly painted polychrome ceramics and magnificently embroidered textiles. Unlike those of Moche, Nazca potters concerned themselves exclusively with religious themes (again derived from the Chavín), in particular with a cult centering on trophy heads taken from slain enemies. Nazca textiles are some of the largest and most complex known. It is believed that many, perhaps all, were produced to accompany the dead into the next world. This is a remarkable example of conspicuous waste, considering that many must have taken more than a year to weave.

The Tiahuanaco state

The first purely imperial state in the Andean area had its origins in the southern half of the highlands during the Middle Horizon AD 600 to 1000. Lake Titicaca lies in a large basin at an altitude of almost 14,000 feet. At its southern end, on the Bolivian shore, lies the great site of Tiahuanaco, which may have been a city containing up to 20,000 souls. Aerial photographs of the lake shore have disclosed areas of drained and ridged fields closely similar to the *chinampas* of Mexico, and which may have provided the economic base for such a concentration. The ceremonial nucleus of Tiahuanaco consists of temples, platforms and sunken courts built from enormous and beautifully dressed stone blocks. There are monolithic carvings and fine reliefs, such as those on the Gateway of the Sun, in a hard, rather geometrical style that was clearly influenced by the use of copper tools. A common theme is that of winged humans running in toward a weeping god.

Tiahuanaco was founded several centuries before the opening of the Middle Horizon, but after 600 the Tiahuanaco style spread rapidly throughout the Andean area, obliterating all of the regional styles which had once flourished there. It is now apparent that the key site involved in its spread was not Tiahuanaco but Huari, a fully urbanized center in the Mantaro Basin of Peru. Brillantly polychromed ceramics in the hybrid Huari-Tiahuanaco style are found all along the Peruvian coast, and on the south coast graves were stocked with tapestry shirts and other woolen textiles bearing the same motifs as the Gateway of the Sun. Most scholars accept the idea that the spread of Huari-Tiahuanaco culture was carried out by means of imperial expansion of a kind practiced by the later Inca. In any case it certainly unified the Andean area at a time when regionalism threatened to break down the overall Andean cultural tradition.

In its own turn, the Huari-Tiahuanaco state seems to have collapsed around AD 1000, to be replaced by the same regional traditions that were submerged by its spread. The best known of these local cultures was that of the Chimú of the north coast, a people with whom the Inca were familiar. In this case the revived tradition was essentially that of the Moche, but with some significant differences.

The Chimú capital was Chanchan, the ruins of which cover six square miles. Built of unfired adobe bricks, the main structures of Chanchan consist of ten great quadrangles, within which were numerous large and small rooms, courtyards and sunken gardens irrigated by serpentine canals. Recent investigations have shown that these quadrangles were occupied by the Chimú elite and their retinues but that the overall population of the city was not as large as might be imagined from its size.

According to the Inca, the Chimú state was an empire controlling most of the north coast from strategically located fortresses. The imperial court seems to have been elaborately specialized into categories of royal retainers. The royal families and the nobility appear to have been immensely wealthy, with great stocks of gold and silver, much of which was said to have been buried at the Inca conquest. Yet the Chimú's art is much inferior to that of their Moche ancestors, with the pottery mass-produced in molds, and embellishments of walls, wooden objects and textiles being carried out in a highly repetitious style.

The rise of the Inca Empire

The Chimú Empire came to an end in 1476, with the total destruction of Chanchan by the Inca armies. Yet the Inca learned much from this great civilization, particularly statecraft and various technological innovations.

With the Inca we come to the last of the 'horizons,' the Late Horizon, that extended from 1476 to 1534. Like the Aztec of Mexico, the Inca had begun as an insignificant and somewhat barbaric tribe on the margins of civilization. By the beginning of the fifteenth century they were jockeying for power among several similar tribes in the southern Peruvian highlands. After 1438, when they beat their rivals decisively and made Cuzco their capital, the Inca entered upon a systematic program of military conquest under a succession of kings, starting with the general Pachacuti Inca Yupanqui. By the late fifteenth century the Inca armies had reduced all of the Andean area proper, western Ecuador, the northern half of Chile and northwesternmost Argentina, including within their empire a vast realm which may have contained over six million persons, one of the largest states of its day. The Inca language, Quechua, was established as the official tongue of the empire, and there are still more than seven million who speak it.

The Inca Empire has long been known as one of the greatest and most intriguing administrative systems the world has seen. It was headed by the emperor, believed to have been descended from the Sun. Because of his holy lineage, his chief wife was his own sister, a form of royal incest also documented for the Egyptian and Hawaiian dynasties, but there were also secondary wives. Since all Andean peoples were organized into localized, endogamous kin groups called ayllu, it is only natural that the most prestigious ayllu should have been the royal line itself.

Below the emperor was the nobility, who filled all of the higher administrative posts. The empire was divided into four quarters, the north-south and east-west lines which divided them meeting in the center of Cuzco, the capital. Each quarter was composed of provinces, and each province was a grouping of ayllus. In addition to this, the Inca rulers imposed a decimally based system of classification for all heads of families. This was both for tax purposes and appropriate numbers of men could be called at any time for military conscription or for corvée labor on public works. The famous string records called quipu, the Andean area's only approximation of writing, were accounting devices for keeping tabs on the decimal organization.

An empire of several thousand miles' extent would have quickly collapsed if it had not been for an extraordinarily efficient communications system. Two highways, one coastal and the other highland, extended the length of the empire, and messages were carried 150 miles a day by foot runners in relay. Along the routes were resthouses for the communications staffs. Always great technicians, the Inca engineers spanned highland chasms with bridges so well constructed that some still stand.

One of the main Inca problems was the organization of conquered populations. Like the British in nineteenth-century India and Africa, the Inca preferred to rule through native chiefs, and the sons of conquered rulers were sent to Cuzco for education, much as African and Indian princes went to Sandhurst. For especially unruly peoples the mitimaes system was put into effect, entire nations being removed wholesale from their own land and transferred to totally unfamiliar regions where they were surrounded by unfriendly neighbors.

Inca architecture is unsurpassed in the New World. The masonry construction of Inca buildings – palaces, temples and fortresses – was so sophisticated that in the great earthquakes which have taken place in Cuzco during the last few centuries it has been Inca walls which have survived, while flimsy Spanish constructions came tumbling down. The most famous Inca site is Machu Picchu, discovered in 1911 by a Yale expedition led by Hiram Bingham. Located on the headwaters of the Urubamba River on the eastern slopes of the

Andes, this late Inca town was built on a saddle between two mountain peaks. The prospect is breathtaking, with steep mountain walls falling away on all sides. Civic buildings are mixed with domestic houses which originally had steeply pitched roofs covered with thatch. Everywhere the masonry shows signs of having been dressed with the kind of bronze tools that have been found in the debris by archeologists. Below the town are agricultural terraces built on unbelievably steep slopes, on which maize and other crops were sown. Through Machu Picchu's streets walked people leading llama trains bringing in produce and trade goods from nearby towns, connected to Machu Picchu by well-made roads.

There can be no doubt that the Inca yoke, like that of the Aztec, was heavy. But the Spanish conquest, which began in 1532 and was completed by 1538, was no deliverance for the common people. As so often happens in great upheavals, they merely changed one set of rulers for worse. In this case the new conquerors were not merely bad. There, as in Mesoamerica, the Spaniards carried out a material and spiritual oppression which in our day would be called genocide. But civilizations as large and vigorous as those of the Andes and Mesoamerica cannot be wholly exterminated. Whether partially absorbed into a larger but sympathetic society, as in modern Mexico, or isolated and despised by their neighbors, as in the Andean countries, the Indians of Central and South America have managed to keep alive many of the ancient traditions of their once glorious past.

Far left: The Inca city of Machu Picchu was first discovered by US archeologists in the early twentieth century. The site had been untouched by the Spanish conquerors and therefore provided archeologists with good first-hand evidence of life in pre-Columbian America.

Left: Machu Picchu was built on the steep slopes of a saddle of land between two peaks. Its precipitous slopes necessitated the construction of a complex terrace system, still very much extant.

Right: The ruins of the city suggest a well-organized society with a vigorous economic system.

PART II
The Renaissance to World War I

The Dawning of the Modern Age

The year 1500 serves as a convenient date with which to begin the modern history of the world, for it marks in a general way the origin of two powerful historic movements that have in our time transformed the nature of human life around the world. The date, of course is symbolic rather than exact, for the two movements in question – the expansion of Europe and the modernization of society – cannot be said to have originated at a precise moment in history. The first impetus to European maritime exploration is probably best linked to an event that occurred half a century earlier, when the Turkish conquest of Constantinople closed the eastern Mediterranean to the merchants of Italy and forced upon the people of Europe a search for a new route to Asia. The technological and intellectual elements of modern life, on the other hand, while vaguely apparent in sixteenth-century Europe, had not by 1500 become the dominant features of European civilization, and they were not to do so until at least a century later.

If the significance of the year 1500 as origin needs explanation, so also does the term 'modern,' for its meaning, too, is symbolic rather than precise. Each generation throughout history has undoubtedly thought of itself as being more up to date, and hence more modern, than some preceding age. It would seem a mark of arrogance that our own age presumes to call itself modern, and the term, as it was originally applied by self-satisfied Enlightenment thinkers, may well have carried with it a sense of arrogance. But their sense of confidence has been tempered, and the contemporary use of the term carries with it no judgment of whether our present condition is more or less desirable than what was before. But it does recognize that life today is different, that since the Renaissance there was a dramatic change in Western culture.

One of the most obvious features of life after 1500 was the development of urbanization. While the city has played a significant role in civilized society for at least 5000 years – indeed the term civilization is derived from the Greek word for city – it was only by the nineteenth century that the tremendous spread of urban life and of the urban outlook had occurred among the population as a whole. While in premodern societies cities grew up as important points of concentration for a community's rulers, aristocratic families, merchants and artists, cities were few and the total urban population small in comparison with the much larger rural society. The modern city was essentially a function of the agricultural and industrial revolutions that made possible a massive transfer of the population from mere agricultural subsistence to specialized urban occupation.

Another obvious way in which life was changed from that of premodern times is in technology and in the sources of energy upon which technology depended. To many historians and anthropologists, technological change is the key factor which accounts for cultural change. The modern capacity to rely increasingly on nonanimate sources of energy was intimately associated with the development of various complex technological inventions and new systems of economic and political organization. To the economist and sociologist the basic ingredient characterizing modern industrial economy is its capacity for sustained and continuous growth. It was the apparently autonomous nature of this growth that seemed to pull society along with it.

One could go on to describe many other elements of life at the end of the nineteenth century which distinguish it from what went before, but the essential features are evident enough. Urbanization, industrialization, continuous economic growth, social mobility, popular government, mass education, secular scientific knowledge and a psyche capable of living with change – these elements taken together amounted to a new condition of human existence that can only be called modern.

However the modern phenomenon is to be explained, it is a matter of record that it was in Western Europe that the first breakthroughs toward modern conditions took place. And it was in Europe and in the major extensions of European civilization elsewhere in the world that the first highly developed modern societies came into existence. The histories of Britain, Scandinavia, the Low Countries and the United States provide the most visible starting points of the complex process. Both France and Germany also modernized early and rapidly, but they nevertheless belong in a different category of society in which modernization proceeded less rapidly and less smoothly and in which external influences played a significant role.

Britain, the Scandinavian countries and Holland in the sixteenth and seventeenth centuries had highly developed and diversified economies in which commercial agriculture and urban-based commerce had led to the differentiation of numerous social groups and strata among the landed aristocracy, peasantry, merchants and priesthood. The countries were small, and the exercise of central monarchal authority was less absolute than in, say, France. In each the political processes that forced the sharing of monarchal authority with aristocratic and non-aristocratic groups occurred without destroying the continuity of central symbol of national loyalty and without creating deep and lasting social cleavages. Thus Britain would retain a more aristocratic society than France even though its government was to become more responsive to the popular will. The civil wars and the Glorious Revolution in England (1642-89), the Revolt of the Netherlands (1566-1609), the American Revolution (1775-83) were all far less revolutionary and socially disruptive than the French Revolution (1789-99). Moreover, though Britain and the Low Countries probably did no more to initiate the scientific and technical revolution that swept Europe between 1500 and 1800 than did France, Germany, Italy or Spain, because they had developed strong entrepreneurial middle classes they were in a much better position to apply and exploit new technologies on a broad scale.

During much of the eighteenth and nineteenth centuries, revolutionary ideas and the examples of the successful modernizers among the European states influenced the rest of Europe. The 'second phase' of European modernization, however, produced states which were still divided internally between traditional and modern sectors, aristocratic localism and republican nationalism, Church and secular authority. Italy was never thoroughly unified politically, nor was the traditional social structure uniformly revolutionized. In post-revolutionary France technological modernization proceeded in a politically crippling atmosphere of violent antagonism between monarchists and republicans, and only as the French middle class began to assert itself did the nation begin to achieve a degree of social stability. In Spain and Portugal, despite their having been invaded by Napoleon, monarchal rule and aristocratic and religious dominance hung on much longer than in the other West European states.

In Russia under Peter the Great and Catherine the Great, the monarchal interests became con-

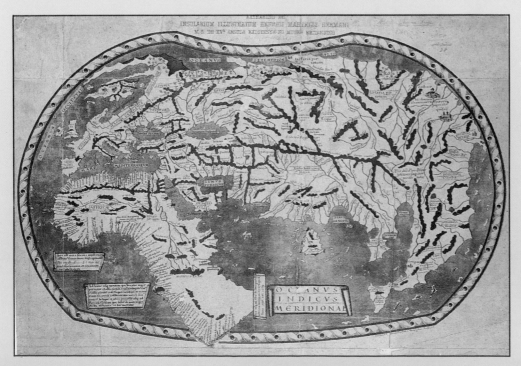

Below left: A map of the world made by the fifteenth-century cartographer Henry Martelli. As the cartographer moves away from Western Europe and the Mediterranean the map becomes increasingly conjectural, reflecting the state of European knowledge of the rest of the world prior to 'Age of Discovery.'

Right: A sixteenth-century painting by the Mexican artist Lienzo de Tlazcala depicting the destruction of the Aztec Empire in Mexico by the Spanish *conquistador* Cortez.

Below right: A factory in the northern industrial region of the United States in the 1880s. By the late nineteenth century the United States was developing into a major economic power.

vinced of the need to modernize the country but attempted to do so 'from the top.' Thus industrialization did not lead to the formation of a middle group powerful enough to demand political participation. Among the German states, particularly Prussia, the pattern of modernization from the top for purposes of national strengthening was somewhat more successful but nonetheless protected the monarchy and the interests of the landed aristocracy and the military against those of any nascent middle class. What the history of modernization in Europe shows above all is that while it is possible to think of the modern condition in the abstract as having certain specifications – industrialization, popular government, mass culture – in fact few societies have fully exemplified the abstract model. The transition from monarchal to popular government, which is the essence of political modernization, has shown extreme variations in the political process are still at work in many of the European countries.

The development of modern Europe forms the basis of the first two sections of this volume: how Europe achieved its dominance, the reasons behind it and the consequences that followed upon Europe's world position.

What would have happened to the rest of the world in the centuries after 1500 if there had been no political, economic and scientific explosion in the West? The answer can only be guessed at, but we should not assume that the world would have stood still or that mankind would have been condemned to live on indefinitely under conditions of human exploitation, ignorance, scarcity and disease. No doubt a truly universal vision of the history of the world since 1500 would reveal a continuing autonomous growth by the non-European cultures and a much greater reciprocity of influence than is generally admitted. But even so, there is no getting away from the fact that the effect that the Europeans, as agents of modernization, had on the rest of the world was nothing short of massive.

The story of the West's relationship to the world begins with an early phase during which European explorers spread out into what was for them the unknown, laying the groundwork for the first maritime empires and early colonial settlements. The age of exploration starts with the exploits of the Portuguese under Prince Henry, beginning as early as 1418 with the first push into the Atlantic southward around Africa. The rounding of the Cape of Good Hope in 1487

quickly opened up the sea route to India, while the discovery of the New World in 1492 opened up a vast new region for European exploitation. By 1522 Magellan had circumnavigated the globe. Already the Spanish had begun the conquest of Central and South America: Mexico was taken between 1519 and 1521, and Peru between 1531 and 1535. The Portuguese, having defeated the Arabs for mastery of the waters off India in 1509, quickly established bases at Goa and Malacca and had reached China by 1513. These remarkable exploits changed the human structure of the earth. The globe had for the first time been unified in the experience of one people and by a single technology of communication. The oceans had been converted from barriers to passageways, so that the peoples of the world would for the next four centuries find their attention drawn increasingly outward beyond their shores.

The two centuries that followed the initial phase of discovery and exploration saw the completion of two further movements which were to lay the basis for the great empires by the nineteenth century. One was the actual emigration of European peoples to virgin territories or lands sparsely occupied by tribal societies: such was the push of the British and French into North America, the Spanish and Portuguese into Central and South America, the Russians into Siberia and the British into Australia and New Zealand. This would eventually lead to the creation of vast new immigrant colonies. The second movement was the establishment of outposts or bases in settled parts of Asia which were strategically important but weakly defended. These were used initially to gain control of the spice and Oriental-goods trades, but they eventually became the beachheads from which colonial rule was asserted over such people as the Indonesians, Indians and Africans.

The first wave of European expansion, while it was devastatingly destructive to the technologically less advanced societies of the Americas, Africa and Northeast Asia, made comparatively little impact on the established states of Southern and Eastern Asia. The Chinese ability to expel the Portuguese from Canton in 1522, and the Japanese capacity to exclude the Spanish and Portuguese traders and Christian missionaries from Nagasaki by 1640, reflected a close balance in military strength, on land at least, between the principal East Asian states and the Europeans. But during the century and a half following the signing of the

Peace of Paris in 1763 the two major types of European expansion entered their second phase of development.

The significance of this date is that it marked the end of the war between Britain and France for possession of India and North America. The British victory settled the shape which European colonial rule would take in the ensuing century or more, assuring for Britain the leading role among the maritime colonial powers. But the date serves symbolically for a more profound qualitative change. The second wave of colonial expansion was conducted by people who had the capacity to penetrate into the heart of the advanced non-European societies, gaining political and economic dominion over peoples whose cultural traditions antedated their own.

The great phenomena of the second phase of colonial expansion which culminated in the nineteenth century were the collapse of the traditional empires of Asia, Africa and India, the formation of the British Empire and the emergence of Russia and the United States as the potential superpowers of the future. By 1914, on the eve of World War I, the peoples of the West had not only infiltrated to the corners of the earth, they had imposed upon the globe their culture and their political and economic institutions. The British Empire encircled the earth, and ancient civilizations in Africa and Asia were brought under British rule. The world was now unified by transport and communications technologies, and English became by far the world's *lingua franca*. Independent of the colonial system itself, the world was being joined together by a universal science and a worldwide economy and financial system. And, on the debit side, for the first time in man's history wars would become truly world wars. The year 1914 marked the high point of Western dominance over the world; a period which had begun around 1500 and reached its zenith four centuries later. The twentieth century would witness the decline of European pre-eminance in the world, and the rise of the superpowers of the USA and the Soviet Union.

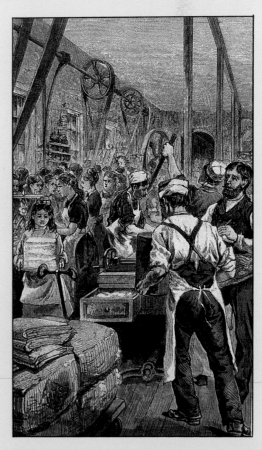

The Renaissance in Europe

To the ordinary observer in Italy in the late fourteenth and fifteenth centuries the idea that historians of the nineteenth and twentieth centuries should refer to his times as 'The Renaissance' would have seemed extraordinary. Amid plague, famine, the ravages of incessant warfare, the advance of the Turks into the eastern Mediterranean and the schism of Western Christianity, many Europeans could imagine that the horrors of the Apocalypse had been unleashed upon the world and that shortly Christ, the Just Judge, would appear in his majesty to call the wicked to account. Many modern historians locate the inception of the Renaissance around the time the Black Death ravaged Europe (1347-49). If we accept this dating then we must also say that the first century and a half of the Renaissance was really a time when agriculture declined, trade dwindled and population decreased.

In the middle of this bleak picture stood isolated individuals who somehow saw beyond such dismal circumstances and affirmed that their age was special. Historians have generally concurred in their judgment by labeling the period from roughly 1350 to the early 1500s as the Age of the Renaissance in Italy, for they have long discerned in these years the rebirth, if not invention, of distinctively new ideas, methods and technologies across a vast range of human pursuits, from art and architecture and the analysis of political institutions to education, the writing of history, navigation, warfare and commerce. But though historians have generally insisted that there was something new in this period, each has tended to look for it in his or her own way.

The term 'Renaissance' is used to signify a 'rebirth' of something. For the great nineteenth-century Swiss historian Jacob Burckhardt and most modern historians it has come to mean especially the ideas and efforts of the men and women of this era who consciously sought to restore to their age the achievements of Roman (and later Greek) civilization that they had come to recognize as lost. Concretely, this meant consciously recapturing the classical forms of art, architecture, literature and moral life, or what Cicero had called 'the art of living well and happily.' But this idea was not something sprung full blown from the heads of the Italians living in the 1300s. The idea developed slowly, and often with great difficulties. As it developed, clear-sighted individuals began to understand its ramifications and often questioned themselves about how best to restore the ancient past. What should be restored? How much really might be better abandoned? The ancient world of the pagans, for example, was inimical to Christianity: should paganism be resurrected? The language of the Latin Vulgate was crude compared with the sublime poetry of Virgil: should it be discarded in favor of a more elegant style? Many quite intelligent people of this era were, in fact, critical of contemporary trends to resurrect the Roman past. The period had many opposing voices, and it was never as homogeneous as some historians – Burckhardt, for one – have implied. Indeed, it continued to bear many traces of the Middle Ages. Still, something new was emerging, and it emerged in Italy.

The geography of Italy conferred many peculiar advantages and disadvantages on the Italian city-states. The unusually large expanse of coastline provided numerous safe harbors for merchant ships and turned many Italians more to the sea than inland to the other city-states of the peninsula. The Italian cities close to the coast became entrepots of the East and the West. Venice, Genoa, Florence, Pisa, Lucca and Naples made available to the rest of Italy and Western Europe the spices, fine textiles, jewelry and other commodities that became increasingly in demand. Travel inland, on the other hand, was always troublesome because of the Apennine mountains that ran down the 'boot' from northern to central Italy. From the mountain peaks and high hills rivers raged swiftly to the sea, often swelling quickly and causing devastating floods. If natural obstacles were not enough, travel was also hindered by the constant presence of bandits, the collections of tolls for bridges and roads, and wars between city-states.

In this natural setting a strong tendency toward isolation developed among the Italian city-states, fostering in each place a particular way of life and often highly distinctive institutions. Each area was relatively small. Venice, Naples, Florence and Milan had populations of no more than 100,000 each. But a city of 20,000 was still considered exceptionally large. The relatively small size of these towns tended to create rather close-knit communities, ones highly conscious of their differences from other communities. City-dwellers tended to know one another well. They often lived close together. They belonged to the same parishes, guilds and confraternities. They

Left: A classical city, spacious and orderly – one of the ideals of the Italian Renaissance as imagined by fifteenth-century artist Piero della Francesca.

Above right: A view of Florence around 1500. Although large by the standards of the time, the main Italian cities were still small enough to have a close-knit community life.

Right: Portrait of a *condottiere* – a mercenary military commander – by Donatello. The Renaissance city-states relied on such men to fight their wars and maintain public order.

celebrated masses together and attended one another's christenings, marriages and funerals. Their lives consisted of many concentric communities – social, economic, political, military, religious – the largest of course being the city itself. Italians referred to this as *campanilismo* from the word 'bell' (*campana*): one belonged to the community within earshot of the bells of his own city (*città*). One was not an Italian but a citizen of Siena, Parma, Mantua, Milan, Capua, Bergamo. To each belonged distinct customs, ways of speech, networks of human relationships. Each viewed his own city as the most beautiful, the most noble, the place where he truly was at home.

Such diversity on the peninsula contributed much to the meteoric rise of the Italians as merchants and purveyors of culture. But the Italians held other advantages that helped explain their extraordinary success. On the eve of the Renaissance, the Italians found themselves far more urbanized than their northern European counterparts, who dwelt mostly in castles and in rural areas and for whom the phenomenon of the city had appeared in only a few places such as Paris and London. In the north, where the nobles lived off their lands and the burghers lived off the profits of commerce, little intermingling between these two groups ever took place, and the distinction between town and country dwellers would take a long time to break down. But on the Italian peninsula life was predominantly urban, in the open, 'on the street' and far less rigid. The Italian aristocracy and the merchant classes in time became often indistinguishable. Rich and poor intermingled, working together in commercial enterprises such as importing and exporting goods, banking and even religious associations. Among the Italians greater opportunity existed for social advancement through education, marriage and entrepreneurship.

The urban phenomenon held other advantages still. Due to the growing belief that profit-making was not necessarily sinful if kept within limits, merchants felt freer to work for their own gain, and in time many accumulated enormous fortunes. With this freedom came the invention of new skills for business, such as double-entry bookkeeping, bills of exchange and of course banking – all of which greatly facilitated trade and increased profits. This wealth resulted not merely in the construction of private *palazzi*, but also was channeled into projects to beautify and give pres-

tige to the city. The splendor of such Italian cities as Florence, Siena, Milan, Venice and, later, Rome was legendary.

If the geography of Italy inhibited inland commerce, it did favor the rise of the city-state. Military domination of large areas of Italy could be achieved only at a very great cost, and many of those who tried to achieve it met with failure and suffered great losses of men and matériel. Throughout the Middle Ages the Holy Roman Emperors had often descended into Italy only to quell revolts, subdue fractious towns and plunder whatever they could. The towns, understandably, developed an increasingly violent and effective antipathy to such outside interferences. The result was that by the mid fourteenth century no grand power such as the papacy, the Holy Roman Emperor or any other outside military force held sway over the Italian city-states. Without external control these political units were completely free to pursue their own interests in commerce and civic life, and conditions were ripe for the rise of a large merchant class.

Before the Renaissance most towns of Italy existed as city-republics, little urban democracies in which the merchants were directly involved in city government. But this urban experience was characteristically one of violence, for the cities were beset with problems of social unrest, warring families, large-scale vendettas. In many cities certain pro-papal (Guelf) and pro-imperial (Ghibelline) factions sought to reinstate one or the other external power's authority, and in doing so often became embroiled in small-scale civil wars. As a remedy, the populace often called upon the services of a *podestà*, a magistrate from outside

the city, to preside over the town for a fixed length of time, usually about six months. Often these magistrates were *condottieri*, leaders of mercenary armies which helped them impose order upon fractious towns. This solution had many successes, but many failures as well. Some *podestà* did impose a temporary, if fragile, order upon communities, but others took the opportunity to seize control of the towns. Whether by a *coup d'état* or by peaceful process, most communes eventually developed a kind of government known as the *Signoria*, in which the important men (*signori*) of the commune formed oligarchies. These in turn developed into a kind of tyranny in which the leading individual struggled to make his position hereditary. With the exception of Venice, by the early fifteenth century most of the city-states had fallen under the control of one or another preponderant family – the Medici in Florence, for example, or the Sforza in Milan. Only a few lesser states such as the republics of Genoa, Lucca and Siena and the duchies of Ferrara and of Mantua managed to retain a semblance of self-government.

In the early years of the Renaissance, Italy looked like a mosaic of small independent cities, but by the mid fifteenth century five major political units had emerged to dominate the political scene: the republics of Florence and Venice, the Duchy of Milan, the Papal States and the Kingdom of Naples. These five major powers tended to stretch out into their surrounding territories and to control the small cities near by, for each realized that to maintain its own standing among the other larger political aggregates it needed the people and resources. Each of the five polities realized its survival depended upon keeping any of the other four from becoming predominant. The result was a bewildering skein of strange, ephemeral political alliances, fluid jockeyings for advantage and protracted internecine warfare

Left: Detail of a fourteenth-century Florentine fresco, *The Triumph of Death* by Andrea Orcagna.

Below left: A villa owned by the Medicis, one of the major Florentine families who dominated the city in the fifteenth century. Their wealth, earned by banking and trade, was poured into art and magnificent buildings.

Right: The great Florentine poet, Dante, painted by his contemporary, Giotto.

among neighbors. The 1400s in Italy was a period of constant wrangling and unprecedented abuses of power: cities fell to the whims of conspirators, mercenary armies roamed the countryside exacting enormous sums for protection and despots rose and fell overnight.

A turning point in this deepening anarchy came with the Peace of Lodi in 1454, which settled the dispute over the right of succession to the Duchy of Milan. The signatories of this treaty – Venice, Florence and Milan – promised not to attack the others and to respect territorial boundaries and spheres of influence. For the next 40 years the Italian peninsula would experience comparative peace, though not without continuing rivalries.

In the phenomenon of intricately calculated, constantly shifting alliance – both before and after 1454 – some historians have seen a new achievement: the first consciously pursued strategy of a 'balance of power.' Whether new or not, the situation undeniably gave rise to a complex art of diplomacy that required skills in speaking, writing, negotiation and collecting intelligence, along with bureaucracies to handle the lengthy correspondence, record documents and review policies. In the management of foreign affairs at least, Italian government was approaching a level of genuine sophistication.

Milan

Unlike her rivals, Milan was centrally located on the Italian peninsula and far from the sea. Holding sway over the large alluvial plain of the River Po at the head of the Italian peninsula, Milan enjoyed an impressive position. Guarded by the Alps to the North, controlling the smaller-city states as far as her borders with the territories of Florence, Venice and Genoa, Milan grew quickly into a formidable power whose threats often caused Florence and the other Italian cities to tremble. After having flirted with forms of demo-

cratic government, the city succumbed to the Visconti in 1277, and this family of mercenaries from the Romagna held power almost uninterrupted until 1447. The most famous of the Visconti, Gian Galeazzo (1378-1402), did away with his uncle Bernabò in 1385 and took full control. After consolidating his rule with a favorable marriage to the daughter of the French king (which later gave the French claim to the Duchy of Milan), he expanded his domination of the surrounding territories, going after Padua, Pisa, Verona and Vicenza, and, but for a premature death, he might have added the Republic of Florence to his list of conquests.

The Visconti hegemony, however, declined at Milan under Gian Galeazzo's weak offspring and was finally extinguished in 1447 with the death of Filippo Maria Visconti. After a brief Milanese experiment with republicanism (1447-50), Francesco Sforza (1450-66), a remarkably competent *condottiere* who had married the illegitimate daughter of Filippo Maria, seized power in Milan and established a peaceful and prosperous Sforza rule that lasted until 1535. In that year the Milanese succumbed to the armies of Charles V, and from that time on the city remained firmly in the grip of Spain.

The Milanese state was one of the better exemplars of Renaissance statecraft, displaying a combination of political cunning, force of arms, convenient marriage and iron control. The despots of Milan had some difficulties in ruling their domain, but in general they were more successful than others. They realized the importance of territorial expansion for controlling men and resources, especially in the event of war yet, like the many cities that had fallen to her own domination, Milan at length succumbed to the still greater power of a nation-state. Indeed, as the power of the nation-states increased during the sixteenth century so the position of the city-states became increasingly vulnerable.

Florence

Of all Italian cities associated with the Italian Renaissance, Florence has always commanded the greatest attention of scholars, for it was here that the first signs of creativity appeared, and for this reason the Florentines have always held a consciousness of their special importance among the peoples of Italy. Florence gave birth to Dante (1265-1321), author of *The Divine Comedy* and other influential works; and in the shadow of the city other men of brilliant literary disposition, such as Petrarch and Boccaccio, produced for Florence a lustre of great literary refinement. To these achievements, Florence added an unequaled reputation in commerce, statecraft, architecture and the plastic arts.

By the late thirteenth century the Florentine republic had already set its course. In the ordinances of 1293 the *commune* stipulated that no one could take part in government without belonging to a guild. This legislation represented an enormous triumph for the guilds over the nobles. It forced them to stay out of politics, or, if they wished to participate in government, they were obliged to become involved in trade. The ordinance further divided society into four major units: the 'great men' (though now politically powerless), the major guilds (*arti maggiori*), the lesser guilds (*arti minori*) and the *ciompi* (those not represented in government). The Florentine political system sought to prevent any one group or individual from holding power too long, and above all to thwart takeover by a single individual. The Florentines therefore established a rotating system of the highest offices (*priors*), which lasted just two months. At each two-month interval nine new priors were elected, and these made up the *Signoria*, the central executive committee of the Florentine republic. In addition to this central group the constitution also provided for a *Balìe* – a committee to control the list of nominees for the priorships – and various representative assemblies of Florentine citizens.

In terms of foreign policy, Florence pursued and achieved three prime objectives. Realizing the need for open access to the sea, the Florentines subdued Pisa, which stood on the Arno River between their town and the Mediterranean. Understanding, too, the strategic importance of their surrounding territories (*contado*), they brought these under their domination as well. And because so much of the commune's wealth came from its role as the Popes' bankers, Florence sought to maintain excellent diplomatic and economic relations with the papacy, and with other European monarchies and polities as well.

The uniqueness of Florence was largely a result of her early amassing of capital and her great successes in banking. But the Florentines took their losses as well. In the early 1320s Florence's armies were humbled by the Lucchese. In 1343, and later in 1344, the great banking houses of the Peruzzi and the Bardi fell, due in large measure to Edward III of England's repudiating his debts. After these costly reversals, citizens recognized the limitations of a government virtually controled by its banking magnates, and they demanded changes. Civil war erupted and was only suppressed when Walter of Brienne, the Duke of Athens, was called in by the citizens. Walter, however, turned out to be an usurper, and when he was finally ousted another revolt broke out in 1345. Famines followed, and matters worsened considerably when, in 1347-48, the Black Death struck at Florence and reduced her population perhaps by as much as 50 percent. This was only the first of many plagues which would return in cycles of 10 to 15 years. Not until the middle of the sixteenth century would the population of Florence return to what it had been in 1300. Yet despite such setbacks Florence retained her position as a cultural and commercial leader. To a large extent, credit for this lies with the Medici.

Among the banking families of Florence, the Medici started out somewhat obscurely around 1200. By the 1340s they had become rivals to the bankers of Bardi and Peruzzi, and in the crucial years between 1340 and 1344 they did not fail, as did their competition. By a stroke of genius or luck the Medici were able to enjoy the continued support of the lesser citizens of Florence, those in the smaller guilds and among the *ciompi*, and from this they leveraged their influence and resources into a position of strength. Giovanni de' Medici (1360-1429), a wool merchant and international banker, amassed the great fortune for the family. Giovanni was particularly blessed with a son, Cosimo (1389-1464), who proved every bit his father's equal. In the 1430s the Medici family faced their stiffest rival in the degli Albizzi, a powerful Florentine family which in 1433 had managed to exile Cosimo and his family. But by 1434 the Albizzi policies in Florence had failed, and Cosimo was invited by the *Signoria* to return to the city. Once returned, Cosimo never again lost control over Florentine political and commercial affairs, though he only rarely allowed himself to be elected to any office. Cosimo, among other things, was highly skilled in international affairs. Knowing that the power of the French monarchy was on the rise and that it still laid claims on Naples, in 1454 Cosimo astutely arranged an alliance among Florence, Milan and Naples to thwart the French menace and to keep Venice in check. This alliance, the Peace of Lodi, maintained the peace for the next 40 years.

Like his own father, Cosimo had the fortune of competent offspring. His son, Piero, who maintained the Medici's power from 1464 to 1469, was succeeded by his other sons – Giuliano, who ruled from 1469 to 1478, and Lorenzo the Magnificent (1478-92). The sons of Piero had the further fortune of a superior education, provided for them by their mother, Lucrezia Tornabuoni. From her the Medici children acquired their great love for intellectual refinement, for the language of Tuscany and for Platonic philosophy. In politics they held to their forebears' course of maintaining peace on the Italian peninsula, safeguarding the fragile relations with the French and keeping up their banking with the papacy and the other powers.

The first assault on the Medici position was the Pazzi conspiracy, called after a rival banking family of Florence. The Riario and the Pazzi families plotted (perhaps with the complicity of Pope Sixtus IV) to assassinate Giuliano and Lorenzo at the cathedral of Florence at Easter Mass in 1478. The attempt was only partially successful: Giuliano was murdered, but Lorenzo escaped with only a wound. Lorenzo's thirst for revenge knew no limits and he so relentlessly persecuted the Pazzi and the Riarii that the Pope excommunicated him. Equally menacing, the papacy had allied itself with Ferrante, the King of Naples, and Lorenzo was still at odds with Venice. To maintain his position Lorenzo made a personal appeal in 1480 to Ferrante of Naples. This was at least temporarily successful, and Lorenzo returned to Florence, where he prevailed upon the people to open up the government to a Council of Seventy, which then ruled Florence under the strong hand of the Medici.

But Lorenzo the Magnificent's control over Florence, her foreign policies and the destiny of

the Medici family encountered still other setbacks. Foreign branches of the Medici bank in London, Lyons and Bruges failed. The Medici had by now lost papal accounts. And the Medici's lavish patronage of the arts had drained the family fortune. The fortunes of Florence ebbed with those of the Medici. The level of taxation became onerous. When Lorenzo debased the Florentine currency he was accused of living off the public wealth of the city. At length a general depression set in.

In 1491 a young Dominican preacher named Girolamo Savonarola (1452-98) was elected prior of the influential Dominican convent of San Marco in Florence. There he drew the attention of

Above: Lorenzo de' Medici, known as 'the Magnificent.' Ruling Florence from 1478 to 1492, he was an outstanding patron of art and learning, and at the same time pursued his political enemies with relentless cruelty.

Left: The execution of the monk Savonarola and his companions in Piazza della Signoria, Florence, 28 May 1498. Savonarola's advocacy of puritanical reform had threatened both the artistic Renaissance and the power of the Medicis.

Above right: A plaque commemorating Savonarola's execution.

Right: Dante depicted on the walls of Florence cathedral, with a view of the city and scenes from his *The Divine Comedy.*

his religious brothers and of many wealthy men and women of Florence. His prophetic message, based upon personal revelations, demanded a moral and spiritual reform of the city and predicted imminent judgment with the coming of a religious and political savior who would wield God's sword 'soon and swiftly.' Besides railing against Church, society, the Pope and his curia, Savonarola attacked Lorenzo for his personal profligacy and domestic and foreign policies. In 1492, on his deathbed, Lorenzo received absolution from Savonarola; but Florence was yet to do its penance.

In the autumn of 1494 the King of France, Charles VIII, marched with his armies into Italy in what has been called a 'leveling of the Alps.' Charles's pretext for invasion was an invitation by the Duke of Milan, Lodovico Sforza, who had usurped power from his nephew. This nephew also happened to be the son-in-law of King Alfonso of Naples, who now threatened to restore power to the rightful claimant. Charles VIII willingly obliged the Duke of Milan, but his objectives were more far-reaching than Lodovico had at first understood, for the king sought to annex Milan to the French monarchy. In 1495, when the states of Italy grasped the import of this French invasion, they allied themselves quickly in a 'Holy League,' comprising Venice, the Papal States, the Kingdom of Naples and even the Duchy of Milan. The French were forced to withdraw, but they returned five years later upon the accession of Louis XII. Although Louis was never able to conquer the Kingdom of Naples, he acquired Milan, and the French presence there, like the Spanish domination of southern Italy, spelled the end of Italy's experiment in balance-of-power politics.

One of the few to gain from Charles VIII's invasion of Italy was Savonarola, who, after the withdrawal of the Medici from Florence and with assistance from the French, seemed providentially destined to lead the city to reform. The preacher's message was to a large extent a call for the restoration of the long-defunct Florentine republic, and the man who was to restore to Florence her ancient liberties was Charles VIII. With this savior's appearance – which Savonarola

had fostered through political bargaining – his credibility among the citizens rose. Savonarola also had prevailed upon the French not to enter the city, an achievement that further endeared him to the populace. From 1494 to 1498 Savonarola pressed his program of reforms; calling upon the people of Florence to repent, burn such vanities as clothes, pictures and jewelry, and demanding the end of oligarchic rule and the implementation of a popular government.

But events did not materialize as clearly as his visions. Savonarola had his enemies in Florence, and they grew increasingly impatient with his puritanical program. They approached Pope Alexander VI (1492-1503), who excommunicated the friar in 1497 for his disobedience and his diatribes against Rome. Savonarola retaliated by denouncing the Pope's act as illegal and called for a general council of the Church to judge his case. In the showdown a certain Franciscan challenged Savonarola to prove his sanctity in a public ordeal by fire. To Savonarola's great misfortune, a storm came up, the ordeal could not take place and Savonarola was arrested and tortured and eventually he confessed (though he subsequently recanted). On 28 May 1498 he was hanged and burned publicly, along with two of his followers, in the public piazza of Florence. However history might judge the man, his own contemporaries held him in great esteem. The Florentine historian Francesco Guicciardini commented that 'those who long observed his life and habits found in them not the slightest trace of avarice or lust or any other sort of greed or weakness.'

After the death of Savonarola, Florence faced other crises whose seriousness was to some extent mitigated by the presence of the French army under Louis XII, who had subdued Milan in 1499 and generally kept peace in northern Italy. Externally, the Florentines' greatest threat was the infamous Cesare Borgia, the Pope's son, who had plans to enlarge the Papal States and establish himself as next-in-line for the papal tiara. Internally, the Florentines faced a constitutional crisis. Leaders understood the necessity for continuity in military and foreign policies and the consequent need for executive officers to hold office

longer than two months. In 1502 the republic elected a permanent *gonfaloniere* of justice, Piero Soderini, who held office until 1512. Under the aegis of the French, Soderini's republic functioned well, although always with an aristocracy reluctant to participate in the Grand Council. It was during this time that the Florentine government won back control over Pisa, and the young statesman Niccolò Machiavelli served his government on 24 missions to France and to the papal court.

But the fate of the Florentine republic was tied to the fortunes of the French, who were not welcome visitors to the Italian peninsula. In 1512 the states of the Holy League joined to oust the French. Under the command of the resourceful Gaston de Foix, the king's nephew, the French armies at first (1512) routed the Holy League at Brescia and again at Ravenna. The immediate outcome of the victory boded well for the Florentines, but de Foix soon died from wounds suffered in combat, and his successors on the battlefield could not match his successes, nor could the French army hold out against the greater numbers and resources of the Italians. In time the Holy League routed the French, who retreated over the Alps. But in short order they returned, this time under the direction of their new king, Francis I, who in 1515 smashed the Italian forces at Marignano and seized Milan. The Italians were learning some painful lessons about the rising power of the new national monarchies.

When the French departed the Medici again returned to Florence, and the republican regime, though keeping a semblance of its forms (except the Great Council), was effectively rendered powerless. Except for one brief two-year interval of republican government from 1527 to 1529, the Medici would control the fortunes of Florence for the next two centuries.

The Papal States

In the years of the Renaissance papacy, roughly between 1450 and 1527, pontiffs lived little differently from their secular counterparts. Access to the spiritual leadership of the Catholic Church and to lifetime rule of the Papal States came about through election by the college of cardinals. Once installed upon the throne of St Peter, the Popes' political ambitions were limited only by their personalities and their resources. They competed openly with princes, dukes and republics for territories, political influence and wealth. Although its military leverage did not always equal that of other Italian states, Rome possessed a potent spiritual authority. In every land of Christendom the Pope held a place of special privilege as the vicar of Christ and the successor of St Peter. His

excommunication and interdict could deprive a king or doge, kingdom or territory, of all spiritual benefits, thus ensuring that at death their souls would not be counted among the blessed. Taking on the Pope in a military engagement meant much more than seeking to best a rival temporal ruler. Even if one did gain the whole world, the loss of spiritual benefits could mean damnation.

In the fourteenth century the Papal States, an ecclesiastical domain in central Italy under the political control of the Pope, posed little threat to the stability of the other towns of Italy. In 1305, the Pope had abandoned his see, and from 1305 until 1378, during the Babylonian Captivity, Popes resided at Avignon in southern France, giving little thought to military expansion or to the political problems of Italy. Even after the Popes returned to Rome, their political position was hardly enviable. Only after the Great Schism (1378-1417), with the election of Pope Martin V (1417-31), when Popes at last gave evidence that they were firm in their resolve to stay at Rome and to build up the city, did the Papal States start to rival the other powers of Italy. Still, Martin V and his successors were never really secure there; their struggle for political and military respectability was arduous, as Rome and the Papal States had always been difficult to govern. The Popes did all they could to strengthen their positions. Nicholas V, for example, presided at the coronation of Frederick III of Habsburg (the last coronation to take place at Rome), which put him on good terms with the imperial party. But in Rome the Pope's position remained shaky. Nicholas faced a serious threat in the Conspiracy of Stefano Porcaro (1453), which sought to oust the Pope.

Outside Rome, the Pope had his hands full with the territories he nominally controled. The Papal States, bordered in the north by the territories of Florence and Venice and in the south by the Kingdom of Naples, were ruled by numerous local strongmen who had long recognized no other temporal authorities. Cities such as Bologna and Perugia, which were in the Papal States, fiercely resisted any attempts to increase papal control. By the reign of Nicholas V (1447-55), the papacy had only begun to consolidate its political and military position. Subsequent Popes, such as Pius II, Aeneas Sylvius Piccolomini (1458-62), made somewhat greater inroads against the entrenched local leaders within their territories. But only with Cesare Borgia (1475-1507), the son of Pope Alexander VI (1492-1503), did the papacy at last gain the upper hand.

Left: The Doge of Venice receives the ring with which this maritime city was symbolically wedded to the sea.

Above right: The son of Pope Alexander VI, Cesare Borgia, whose ruthless career may have made him the model for Machiavelli's *The Prince.* As commander of the papal armies, he strengthened the papacy's hold on central Italy.

Below right: A Renaissanace view of Venice's advantageous geographical situation, virtually invulnerable to attack from the land.

Cesare Borgia's military abilities shone in his conquest of Romagna, to the northeast of the Papal States. Borgia's seizure of these lands gave the papacy great strategic advantage, especially against the Venetians, who also had had designs on this territory. Some scholars claim that Machiavelli used Cesare Borgia as the model for *The Prince*: the man who knew how to gain power and how to hold it. Certainly Borgia's ruthless methods of warfare, deceit, murder and power politics stunned even his bitterest enemies, but his rule was remarkably just and unoppressive.

His downfall was as meteoric as his successes. At the death of his father, Borgia lay ill and unable to participate in the papal conclave which (as he had so schemed it) was to elect him to the papacy. Instead the cardinals chose Pius II, whose reign lasted little more than a few days, and after his death they elected Giuliano della Rovere, an inveterate opponent of the Borgias, who took the name Julius II (1503-13). Cesare Borgia fled Rome. But he had left the papal lands well consolidated, and Julius had enough men and resources to lead his own armies against his enemies in the north and to oust the French from Italy.

By the early 1500s the papacy had at last established a strong, centralized power that could play politics with the other states of Europe. Papal temporal authority after Julius held firm, but its spiritual authority was being called increasingly into question in some parts of Christendom. In the era of the two Medici popes, Leo X (1513-21) and Clement VII (1523-34), dissension mounted. In Germany, protests against certain ecclesiastical practices of piety were being made by a young Augustinian friar, Martin Luther, who was attracting a strong following. After the death of Leo, the cardinals gave heed to the loud calls for the reform of the Church and unanimously selected the Dutchman Adrian Dedel, who took the name Adrian VI (1522). Adrian's program for reform was well understood, though short-lived: to reform the Roman Curia, unite Christian princes, check the advance of the Turks and subdue the heresy of Luther. Adrian died with nothing accomplished, and few seemed willing to advance his program. After his death, the cardinals elected Clement, and in just a few short years they would at last realize how important the matter of reform truly was. In 1527, when this Pope

witnessed his city being sacked and devastated by troops of the emperor, many reform-minded clergymen knew there was no other course but radical change. But the process, which was to last for many decades, would be slow and immensely painful.

Venice

Venice's peculiar position on the lagoons of the northern Adriatic gave her an enviable immunity from the hostilities on the Italian mainland. Though her origins in the fifth and sixth centuries are obscure, by the era of the crusades Venice had become a major center of shipping and trade. After the War of Chioggia (1378-81) with Genoa and a treaty with the Turks (1388), which allowed Venetian ships to trade with the east in relative security, the maritime republic became the dominant mercantile power in the eastern Mediterranean. Venetians of the fifteenth century could look back on their history as one of relative peace and prosperity. They proudly referred to their state as 'the Most Serene Republic' (*La Serenissima*), and were content with their style of life in pursuing peace and wealth and the values of culture amid orderly government. Venice's success lay only partly in her superb geographical location and in the energy of her populace. Human ingenuity accounted for a great deal as well. The Venetians understood the necessity of a civil order based upon sound government, and they combined much wisdom, shrewd calculation and consistent planning in developing a republican constitution to promote commerce and their treasured way of life.

Controled by her merchant aristocracy, Venice's government was very different to those of other cities. There were four principal organs of state. First there was the Grand Council, in which the great families of Venice presided: limited to 200-300 elected members, this group deliberated major decisions of state. Next there was the College, or cabinet, which administered affairs. Then there was the Council of Ten, an inquisitorial committee whose purpose was to investigate and move quickly against subversive elements. Finally there was the Doge and his *Signoria*, which, together with the Council of Ten, made up the Council of Seventeen. The figurehead of the Venetian republic was the Doge, the leader who was

elected for life, and who later became more of a ceremonial functionary.

Though republican in form, participation in the government of Venice in fact was tightly restricted to members of the patrician families of the city. Their places in the Great Council were hereditary and strictly limited. In effect, there was virtually no entry into government without patrician membership. These circumstances generated conservative attitudes among members of the patriciate and made them particularly sensitive to the need to protect their position: hence the value of the Council of Ten as a safeguard against internal threats to the established order. This same concern for control affected the Venetian outlook in general, and helps explain the constant supervision over every aspect of her political and commercial enterprises. The Venetians, for example, were the first to develop the practice of resident ambassadors in those foreign places where the city had commercial interests such as Cyprus, Negroponte, Lemnos, Constantinople, Thessalonica, as well as the larger cities of Italy and northern

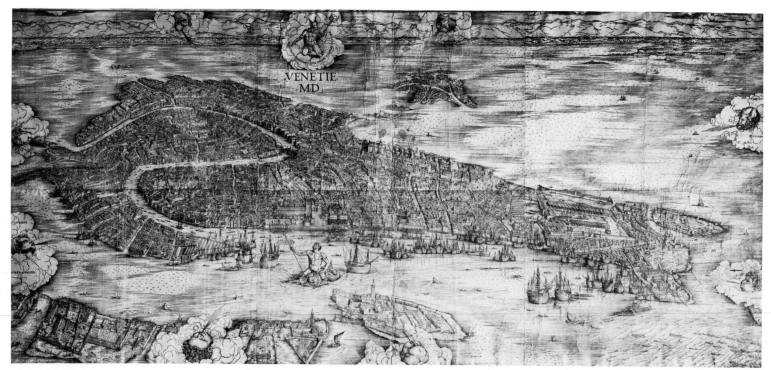

Europe. Regularly these ambassadors wrote reports (*relazioni*) on their hosts' political, social and cultural situations – reports that have proven of inestimable value to later historians.

One advantage of Venice's all-controlling government was that her merchant ships were built to government specification for use, if necessary, as warships. To protect her shipping lanes and foreign outposts, the Venetians frequently went to war, often with the Turks. In the fifteenth century, with the rise of the Ottoman Empire, Venice engaged in three major battles with the Turks, mostly over the islands of the eastern Mediterranean. From 1463 to 1479 Venice fought a protracted war with the Turks that ended in a dismal defeat, and by the Treaty of Constantinople (1479) Venice was required to pay tribute to the Turks for the right to trade in the Black Sea. For almost another 100 years Venice would live in the shadow of this humiliating defeat. Yet Venice continued to prosper: the decline of markets in the eastern Mediterranean was counter-balanced by new opportunities toward the west.

The precariousness of Venice's dependence on the sea impressed upon her citizens the importance of a stable food supply. For this Venice turned her eyes to the *terra firma* of northern Italy. Through conquest and treaty the towns of Padua, Triviso, Belluno, Verona, Vicenza, Brescia, Bergamo, Crema and Rovigo fell under the hegemony of Venice. Her steady expansion into the peninsula alarmed the other powers of Italy, and whenever possible they joined to check Venetian expansion. Finally, in 1508, the most major of the powers of Italy, and some European states, including France, joined in the League of Cambrai and put an end to Venice's unlimited ambitions on the mainland. Venice retained her independence but suffered great loss of territory. In 1511, to regain her former possessions and to expel the French from Milan, the Venetians joined the same league (now, however, without the French) under the leadership of the warrior Pope, Julius II, who yearned to drive Louis XII and all the 'barbarians' for ever from Italy. Venice and the Holy League were successful.

In the sixteenth century Venice's dealings with the powers of Italy proceeded with far greater caution, especially since her merchant ships were encountering formidable difficulties with the Ottoman Turks in the eastern Mediterranean. Venice also had long-standing disputes with Spain. Nevertheless, the social order at Venice remained stable, and the sixteenth century proved to be a sort of golden age for the maritime republic. Its great wealth was used to adorn the many private palaces along the canals, and to erect churches and public monuments. Though the commercial power of Venice was clearly waning, she would leave to posterity a splendor and charm that few other cities have ever equaled.

Naples

Another manifestation of the great diversity of the Italian political picture was that of feudal monarchy known as the Kingdom of Naples and Sicily (or the Two Sicilies). The history of southern Italy evolved to a large extent from the policies of the papacy, which feared a pincer movement from the Holy Roman Emperor, whose power in the thirteenth century in northern and southern Italy threatened to dominate the Papal States. In 1250, the Pope had invited Charles of Anjou, brother to King Louis IX of France, to rule over the Two Sicilies, but the Angevins soon proved to be unpopular. In 1282, in Sicily, after a riot during vespers (the Sicilian Vespers), the Angevins fled and Peter III of Aragon (Spain) took power in Sicily. The Angevins were similarly ousted from Naples in 1435 when Alphonsus I of Aragon, the Magnanimous (1435-58), moved into Naples and made it the eastern pole of the Aragonese power in the Mediterranean. In both cases the French had been forced to leave, and so had never surrendered their rights to the Aragonese usurpers, but despite French claims, for the next two centuries Naples and the rest of southern Italy remained firmly in the hands of the Aragonese. In 1503 Ferdinand of Aragon assumed control of Naples, and thanks to his union with Isabella of Castile, the city now fell under the authority of the new Spanish monarchy. The two Sicilies would remain under Spanish dominion for the next two centuries.

The Italian humanists

The turbulent and confused political history of Italy from the fourteenth to the early sixteenth centuries would probably be of limited interest if it had not served as the background for a cultural explosion that transformed the West and, ultimately, the world. Scholars have debated endlessly about the degree to which certain confluences of political, economic and social forces peculiar to Italy made this explosion inevitable. Certainly Italy's exceptional urbanization, the wealth that its cities accumulated through commerce, the relatively progressive nature of many of its civic governments and the absence of external controls or the constraints of feudal economic and social organization were necessary preconditions for the flowering of Renaissance culture. But this historical background cannot fully explain why Italy's cultural eruption assumed the particular form that it did. To explain this we can only advert to such historically slippery concepts as 'the spirit of time' and to the effects that a few men of exceptional talent seem to have had on their contemporaries.

Italians living in the fourteenth and fifteenth centuries often described themselves as men born into a new age, one emerging from the ignorance and barbarism of the dark ages and destined to restore the culture, especially the great learning, of ancient Rome and Greece. Among the first to speak in these terms was Francesco Petrarch (1304-74), the father of Italian humanism, who towered above his contemporaries as a poet, writer, antiquarian and, above all, as a man of vision. Petrarch and later followers became aware of a gap between themselves and the great poets, writers and statesmen of ancient Rome. 'There was a decline of ancient civilization with the decline of Rome and . . . this led to a period of barbaric darkness.'

The humanists were above all educators who concerned themselves with 'humane studies' (*studia humanitatis*), that is, the five 'humanities': grammar, rhetoric, poetry, history and moral philosophy (ethics). Unlike modern denotations of the word, a humanist was a member of a cultural movement that recognized the primacy of the Latin (and later Greek) classics as models for imitation and repositories of ideas. Though never referring to their movement as Humanism, their educational goals contrasted with, but were not always antithetical to, those pursued in the great universities of the north, Paris or Oxford, where theology, 'the queen of the sciences,' reigned supreme. In Italy, the humanities were geared to life in the towns. They facilitated written and oral communication and were useful for political and commercial pursuits, for they taught one to be persuasive and eloquent and promoted social interaction. They also gave new insights into the ethics of enterprise and profit.

At the core of the humanists' pursuit was the Latin language, which, as Petrarch and others lamented, had fallen into neglect and bore the ignominious imprint of the barbarians in its words and syntax. Realizing how much of classical literature was in jeopardy of being lost for ever, Petrarch and other humanists set about to recover and transcribe all the extant texts of the classical authors. For the next centuries these hunters combed monastic and royal libraries, churches and every other location where precious manuscripts might be found. Among the more famous discoveries was that of the text of Quintilian in the monastery of St Gall, near Constance, made by the itinerant Poggio Bracciolini (1380-1459), bibliophile and later Florentine chancellor. For days he copied out the manuscript and then sent

it to his friends that they might copy it as well. Throughout these years many speeches of Cicero and the works of Latin poets and writers also came to light. Such discoveries made available to humanists a far wider range of classical sources than had ever been known before. Collecting and copying classical manuscripts became the particular occupation of many wealthy patrons, of Popes, dukes and leading magnates. Greek and Latin scholars at Florence, such as Poggio Bracciolini, Leonardo Bruni (1369-1444) and Lorenzo Valla (1405-57), took the lead in reconstituting and emending the entire corpus of classical texts.

In other towns and polities, leaders on fire with the humanist spirit undertook similar projects. Federico da Montefeltre, the Duke of Urbino, spent enormous sums to maintain a cadre of copyists to expand his collection of classical texts. At Rome, Pope Nicholas V assembled distinguished Greek and Latin scholars to translate the vast quantities of texts which he had collected from the Middle East. The Vatican Library in the late fifteenth century became a beehive of scholars such as the Greeks George of Trebizond, Theodore of Gaza, Gregorio of Città Castello and Cardinal Bessarion. By the end of the fifteenth

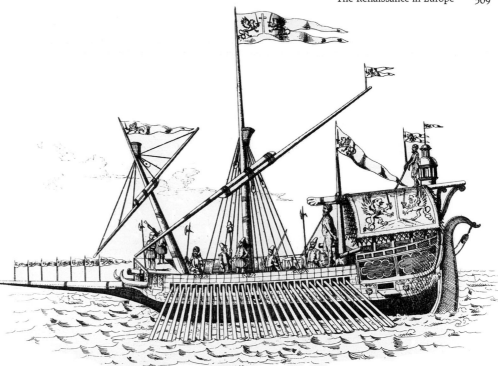

Below left: Pico della Mirandola (left) and Marsiglio Ficino (center) were two of the leading humanist scholars of the fifteenth century. Not surprisingly Mirandola's *Oration on the Dignity of Man* was condemned by the Pope.

Above right: A Venetian galley. With such vessels, the Venetians dominated the eastern Mediterranean until their defeat by the Ottoman Turks.

Right: Beatrice Sforza, a member of the famous Sforza family of Milan. The Sforzas, like most of the great Renaissance families, were great patrons of the arts.

century nearly all the extant texts of antiquity had been recovered, translated, published and annotated. This accomplishment alone was monumental, and it realized Petrarch's dream that Rome's literary achievements could be recovered.

Even more than expanding and correcting the corpus of classical texts, it significantly stimulated new modes of thinking. It was one thing to have collected the corpus of Latin and Greek antiquity, but the greater challenge, as it seemed to the humanists, was to emulate antiquity in speaking, writing and in every other area where it had attained eminence. Inspired by the ancient sources, humanists strove to regain a command of the elegant Latin of earlier times. By using the classical texts, especially those of Cicero, to imitate the ancient Romans' use of words and syntax, the humanists sought to distinguish themselves and their intellectual pursuits from those other traditional speakers and writers of Latin, the theologians and lawyers. Many attained a remarkable degree of linguistic facility and were enormously learned, but all too often they alienated their contemporaries with their pride of accomplishment and contempt for the less pure of speech. Yet nearly all the leading men of their times and of later generations studied under their tutelage. Their prodigious contribution can be understood only when one considers the importance of language in the religious debates and in the great flowering of literature in the sixteenth century.

With the discovery of new texts came a richer understanding of the ancient world, and with this new ideas to apply to the contemporary world. The new researches sometimes led to startling revelations, as well as acrimonious divisions. In 1440 Lorenzo Valla, the brilliant Florentine humanist, discovered that the time-honored 'Donation of Constantine' was a forgery. This document, supposedly the testament of the fourth-century Emperor Constantine, in which he handed over to Pope Silvester I (314-35) and his successors all power in the West, was found to be an early medieval forgery. Valla pursued his new method of historical criticism by comparing the Latin Vulgate edition of the New Testament with the Greek and discovered many errors in translation and interpretation. Valla was followed by other humanists, most notably the Dutch humanist Desiderius Erasmus (1466-1536). The more

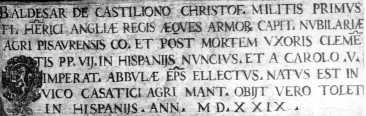

BALDESAR DE CASTILIONO CHRISTOF. MILITIS PRIMVS
FI. HÉRICI ANGLIÆ REGIS ÆQVES ARMOR. CAPIT. NVBILARIÆ
AGRI PISAVRENSIS CO. ET POST MORTEM VXORIS CLEMÉ
TIS PP. VIJ. IN HISPANIJS NVNCIVS. ET A CAROLO .V.
IMPERAT. ABBVLÆ ÉPS ELLECTVS. NATVS EST IN
VICO CASATICI AGRI MANT. OBIJT VERO TOLETI
IN HISPANIJS. ANN. M D. X X I X .

NICOLAVS MACHIAVELLVS.
HISTORIAR SCRIPTOR

they studied the old texts, the more they sharpened their sense of historical perspective and their understanding both of how words had formerly been used in different senses and how ideas and institutions had changed over the centuries. But the recovery of the past introduced complications. How was one supposed to imitate the past? Which ideas and institutions should one favor, and which disregard? Should one keep one's eyes closed to errors of translation and interpretation if these raised questions about doctrines of the faith?

The 'civic humanism' of the Florentines of the early fifteenth century illustrates how the recovery of antiquity could be used for political purposes. Most of the Florentine statesmen of this time had been trained in the *studia humanitatis* and were steeped in the ideas of Cicero, the great champion of the Roman republic against the tyranny of Julius Caesar. They presented Florence as a continuation of the Roman republic and made Cicero's republicanism the model of their own. Some scholars hold that Florence's civic humanism was born in 1402, with the threat of invasion by the Milanese despot Gian Galeazzo Visconti. Others see it as more generally developing as a result of the threats of the Milanese and the Neapolitans between 1380 and 1440. At any rate, in rallying Florentines to a defense of their city and their liberties the chancellors of Florence increasingly appealed to their fellow citizens by using the ideas of Cicero and other expositors of ancient Roman republicanism. They spoke of the need for participatory government and liberty for the growth of the full individual. Should the republic fall, they warned, Florence would go the way of the Roman Empire, and so fall subservient to the capricious will of one man. In stressing this historical analogy they were in effect rewriting their own history to strengthen their republican consciousness.

In the latter part of the fifteenth century, during the reign of the Medici, the Florentine humanists discarded, at least publicly, the cause of republican liberty, trading civic involvement and the active life for the pursuit of wisdom (*vita contemplativa*). In Florence, Rome, Venice, Naples and other princely courts scholars took particular interest in the philosophy of Plato and in other classics of Greek civilization, whose revival had begun both before and after the fall of Constantinople (1453) with the influx of Greek scholars to Florence. In Florence the Platonic Academy, under the patronage of Cosimo and later Lorenzo the Magnificent, consisted of renowned humanists such as Marsiglio Ficino (1433-99), who translated the corpus of Plato and published this in 1483-4. From all parts the academy drew scholars who took up the texts of Plato, wrote poetry and debated questions such as the meaning of true love, virtue, the best kind of life and the end of man. The circle of scholars in Florence included luminaries such as Giovanni Pico, count of Mirandola (1463-94), whose *Oration on the Dignity of Man*, an introduction to his *Nine Hundred Theses* – a grand synthesis of all philosophic and religious traditions – is a classic statement of the Renaissance's optimism about the human will and its limitless capacities.

The Florentine Academy's interest in the texts of the ancients was enkindled by the belief that the knowledge encoded in these works would lead them back to the divine wisdom. Convinced that in the earliest ages of the world God's message was more clearly revealed, academicians turned to the Hebrew scriptures and other writings such as the Cabala, Talmud and the Zohar, in addition to writings of the Greeks, the Chaldaeans and the Arabs. This passion for antiquity also stimulated a greater interest in the texts of early Christian tradition, of such Fathers of the Church as Athanasius, Chrysostom, Basil, Augustine and

Jerome. As philological methods developed, scholars increasingly came to perceive the great gaps between the original texts and the ones customarily used. These developments, unsettling in their own time, were to have an enormous impact on the next generation of scholars in the age of the Reformation.

By the early sixteenth century many Italians were pondering their political situation, scrutinizing their histories to uncover the reasons for their success and failures, especially the failure to repulse the barbarians of the north who now were masters of their peninsula. Among the most astute observers of this age was the Florentine statesman Niccolò Machiavelli (1469-1527), whose many writings explored these questions in depth. Machiavelli's *The Prince* (1514) is the classic Renaissance treatise on political theory and practice. By 1527, the year of his death, his work had become something of a wistful reflection upon a world that had already dissolved, but for centuries to come Europeans everywhere would seek to evaluate their own rulers on the basis of Machiavelli's penetrating observations.

The urgency to answer why things were the way they were gave rise to new approaches to historiography. Finding models in such ancients as Livy, Suetonius and Tacitus, scholars discarded the traditional all-embracing biblical patterns, and studied the dynamics of historical situations and patterns of human causality. Explanations for defeat in war or the success of certain forms of government were sought more in the structure of human decisions and events than in the all-ordaining mind of God.

This is not to say that the Renaissance works were completely modern in our sense, but they do indicate clearly the impact of new perspectives, new ways of thinking and new models for writing history. Typical of this new kind of history are Machiavelli's *History of Florence and of the*

Affairs of Italy (completed in 1527) and Francesco Guicciardini's (1483-1540) *History of Italy*. Machiavelli's work investigates the role of human events and decisions in shaping history and bringing about the tragedies that beset Italy; yet there is much stress, too, on non-human causes, on fate and the hand of God. In the final words of his work, Machiavelli talks of the death of Lorenzo the Magnificent in 1492 and notes that: 'As from his death the greatest devastation would shortly ensue, the heavens gave many evident tokens of its approach; among other signs, the highest pinnacle of the church of Santa Reparata was struck with lightning, and a great part of it thrown down, to the terror and amazement of everyone.'

Among the great works of the closing years of the Italian Renaissance is that of the refined statesman and writer Baldassare Castiglione, whose *Book of the Courtier* (1528) became the handbook of courtly etiquette for the age. Castiglione's work sets out to describe 'what manner of man he must be who deserves the name of perfect Courtier, without defect of any kind.' The work pretends to recall the blissful world of the Court of Urbino, where in the evenings the Duchess, Elisabetta Gonzaga, had the custom of holding lofty discussion with many 'very noble talents.' In this atmosphere of refined taste, elegance, urbanity and wit the world of the streets seems far removed. The hurly-burly of the early Renaissance city-states, with their 'violent tenor of life,' seems to belong to the past. This is the world of the high-Renaissance court, a model for all courts to come.

Indeed, the measure of a court's magnificence now no longer lay solely in its size or military strength. Splendor required talent of all varieties, and in the early sixteenth century such talent congregated in Rome, at first under Pope Julius II and then under his Medici successors, Leo X and Clement VII. During the period from 1503 to 1527 the court of the Popes outshone all others in Europe, with artists and humanists such as Bramante,

Raphael, Michelangelo, Thomas di Vio (Cajetan), Fabio Calvo, Pietro Bembo and Tommaso Inghirami, to name but a few. But the glory of the Renaissance papal courts was short-lived. In 1527 the troops of Charles V, the Holy Roman Emperor, sacked Rome, and after three months of looting and destruction by soldiers of the imperial army the papal court awoke to find that its artists, humanists and almost all other talent had fled. With this ignominious event the Renaissance papacy was brought low, and Rome's Renaissance had ended.

The art of the Italian Renaissance

The first Renaissance historian of art, Giorgio Vasari (1511-74), noted that before 1250 artists had merely reproduced medieval forms. Only in the thirteenth century, 'helped by some subtle influence in the very air of Italy, the new generations started to purge their minds of the grossness of the past.' This revival occurred in Tuscany, and the Renaissance artists came at last 'to imitate

Far left: Baldassare Castiglione, author of the *Book of the Courtier*, an influential volume which expressed the high-Renaissance ideal of a court life refined by good taste, exquisite manners and urbane wit.

Left: Niccolo Machiavelli, the most famous political theorist of the Renaissance period. He viewed political success and failure as largely the result of human decisions, rather than fate or divine intervention.

Right: St Francis abandoning all his worldly goods and taking the vow of poverty, as painted by Giotto. The patrons of art in the Renaissance were wealthy merchants or leading ecclesiastics whose lifestyle had little in common with Christian self-renunciation.

the works of antiquity as skillfully and carefully as they could.' For Vasari, 'it was Giotto [1276-1336] alone who, by God's favor, rescued and restored art.' Giotto's paintings featured strongly modeled forms, dramatic narratives, naturalistic facial expressions and poses and more attention to perspective than had been paid before. His followers followed his lead and by the next century had revolutionized painting. Like their contemporaries, the humanists, they sought to recreate classical forms by introducing into art and architecture harmony, balance and the principles of three-dimensionality. The churches and convents of Florence became repositories of bold and spectacular works of art that evoked highly emotional responses from their viewers.

Though such works caused much controversy, they soon became standards for other artists competing for commissions from religious orders, parishes and wealthy citizens. In a short time Florence became known for its extraordinary wealth of treasures in marble and bronze sculpture, architecture, frescoes, mosaics and medallions. Donatello's *David* (c 1430-32), Lorenzo Ghiberti's (1378-1455) bronze doors for the Baptistry of Florence's cathedral (Duomo), Brunelleschi's dome for the cathedral and the Pazzi Chapel (1430-33) lent Florence a splendor unrivaled anywhere in Europe. Toward the middle and the end of the century, Florence continued to generate painters, sculptors and architects of exceptional talent and delicacy – Fra Filippo Lippi, Piero della Francesca, Paolo Uccello, Andrea del Castagno, Leon Battista Alberti, Andrea Mantegna, Sandro Botticelli, Antonio Rossellino, Antonio del Pollaiuolo, Domenico del Ghirlandaio and many more.

The convergence of such talent in one city created optimal conditions for artists to acquire new techniques and understand better the theory of their arts. Among the leading theorists was Leon Battista Alberti, *l'uomo universale*, whose treatises on painting and architecture put these arts on a more scientific basis. Artists quickly realized that to render nature more exactly they had to learn the principles of perspective, mathematics, geometry and anatomy. Many artists and architects spent long periods in Rome studying the ancient ruins to grasp how the Romans had produced buildings of such grace, elegant lines and proportion. Of particular help was the discovery of classical texts that dealt with these principles, such as Vitruvius's *Ten Books on Architecture*.

After the French invasion of 1494 much of the artistic talent left Florence for other cities. In the subsequent period, generally known as the High Renaissance, six individuals dominated the artistic world: Leonardo da Vinci (1452-1519), Donato Bramante (1444-1514), Michelangelo Buonarotti (1475-1564), Raphael Sanzio (1483-1520), Giorgione (1477-1510) and Titian (1488[?]-1576). Most began working in Tuscany, but then branched out, some to Rome, others to Venice and elsewhere, to seek new commissions from patrons. Among those whose services were in the highest demand was Leonardo. Trained by the Florentine painter Andrea del Verrocchio (1435-88), he worked most of his life in Milan, primarily as a military engineer for the Sforzas, but he also did work for the Florentines, the French and other rulers. Known for his inventiveness and vision, Leonardo's designs for fortifications, submarines, tanks and even flying machines seemed to put

him closer to the twentieth century than to his own. But Leonardo is known today far more as a painter, for works such as the *Mona Lisa*, *The Madonna on the Rocks* and *The Last Supper*.

Beginning with Nicholas V (1447-55), Popes took special interest in urban planning and commissioned works that consciously alluded to Rome's continuities with her ancient Roman and Christian past. Besides securing their own residence with well-designed military fortifications, Popes commissioned artists such as Fra Angelico to fresco the walls of their private chapels. Sixtus IV (1471-84) commissioned the building of the large Sistine Chapel within the walls of the Vatican, and on its walls he had the leading artists pin fresco cycles of Moses and Christ. With the advent of Julius II (1503-13) the artistic commissioning in Rome grew at an unprecedented pace.

Among the first to receive Julius's favor was Donato Bramante, who had worked in Milan for the Sforzas and where he had known Leonardo well. When Milan fell to the French in 1500 Bramante went to Rome, where he accepted a commission from the Catholic Kings of Spain to undertake the Tempietto at San Pietro in Monotrio, the spot on the Janiculum hill where St Peter was supposedly crucified. Bramante's 'little temple' was a breakthrough in the new style of architecture, and no doubt his success with this commission confirmed Julius II in his decision to select him as architect for the new St Peter's in Rome. Although Bramante's design for St Peter's was never executed, the sheer size of the project was no doubt much to the Pope's liking. Yet even more, the drawings show a church whose plans correspond perfectly to Alberti's canon of classical architectural principles for sacred buildings.

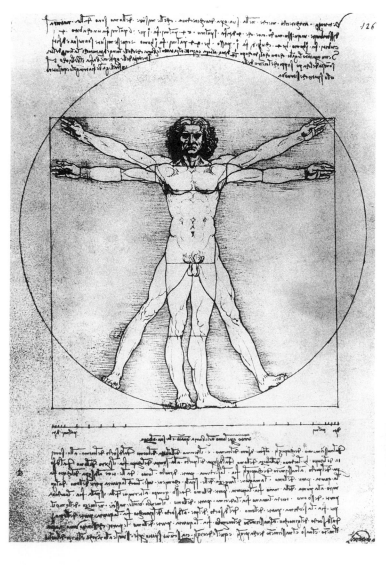

Far left: A study of human proportions by Leonardo da Vinci which now stands as a symbol of the proud Renaissance ideal of mental and physical perfection.

Left: Bramante's Tempietto, or 'little temple,' on the supposed site of St Peter's martyrdom in Rome, was one of the first successful examples of the new classical architecture.

Right: The Storm by the Venetian artist Giorgione. The subject of this work is obscure, but it exists in an atmosphere far removed from the religious serenity and clarity of earlier Renaissance painting.

Michelangelo's lengthy career as sculptor, artist and architect is known for its limitless versatility and range of creations. In his early career in Florence he executed his famous *David*, which graced the central square. But his career was to soar later at Rome, first under Julius and off and on until the reign of Pius IV (1560-66). At Rome Michelangelo was commissioned to design the tomb of Pope Julius; and though the project was never completed, his *Moses*, one of the figures for the tomb, testifies to its masterful conception and massive size. Michelangelo followed with other masterpieces for the papal chapel: the Sistine ceiling frescoes and *The Last Judgment*. By the mid sixteenth century the classical style had triumphed at home in many enduring works, such as Michelangelo's Campidoglio and the Porta Pia. Of singular importance was Michelangelo's plan for St Peter's Basilica, which occupied him in the final years of his life. Although much of the

plan itself was never carried out, the dome of St Peter's still dominates the skyline of Rome as a sublime and impressive testimony of Michelangelo's great genius.

Raphael Sanzio, Michelangelo's younger contemporary, was also commissioned at this time by Julius to fresco the rooms of the papal apartments. In the Stanza della Segnatura are found on opposite walls two of his most famous works: *The School of Athens* and the *Disputà*. These works highlight the love for continuities and contrasts: they depict the continuities of wisdom from the pagan past and the discontinuities with that past by virtue of Christian revelation. The works point to the special significance of Rome, as understood by Julius and his circle: Rome was the recapitulation of human history, the summation of wisdom and divine revelation, and the focal point of all history. After the death of Bramante, Leo X appointed Raphael chief architect of St Peter's

Basilica, a position he occupied until his death. When he died at the young age of 37, he bequeathed to posterity numerous paintings of exquisite delicacy, masterly embodiments of the Renaissance ideal.

The legendary wealth of Venice also produced great cultural monuments, many of which can be viewed today along the Grand Canal, in the Doges' Palace, at the church of St Mark and in St Mark's Square. Venice had long boasted of splendid painters, such as Giovanni Bellini and Carpaccio, and among the masters of Venetian painting in the early sixteenth century stood Giorgione who, following Bellini, brought exquisite Renaissance landscape painting to a city not known for its landscapes. Giorgione's *Adoration of the Shepherds*, *Sleeping Venus* and *The Tempest* rank among the great masterpieces of Venetian art.

Titian (Tiziano Vecellio) was born in northern

Italy and came to Venice around 1500, where he studied with Giorgione. It was his good fortune to find favor with Emperor Charles V (1500-58), the Farnese Pope, Paul III (1534-49), the senate of Venice and many other notables of the century. His style, known for its warmth, richness and luminous quality, gave Titian supremacy among the painters of Venice and a stature rivaling perhaps only that of Michelangelo. His *Gypsy Madonna*, *Assumption of the Virgin*, *Sacred and Profane Love*, and *Portrait of Paul III*, are only some of the masterworks on which his formidable reputation rests.

Among its many achievements, Venice was also a major center for printing. Although humanist scholars and wealthy patrons at first disdained the printed book, such rapid advances were made in printing technology that they eventually commanded universal respect for the new invention. In Venice the printing house of Aldus Manutius (1450-1515) became legendary for the extraordinary quality of its works. There, in the late fifteenth and early sixteenth centuries, humanists such as Erasmus of Rotterdam, along with refugee scholars from Greece, gathered to publish the ancient pagan and Christian authors. From the press of Aldus came standard Greek texts that enabled scholars everywhere to advance their understanding of the past and ponder new ideas. The fact that the Aldine press was located in Venice was particularly fortunate, for probably from no other city could printed books have been more quickly or widely disseminated, not only in Europe, but throughout the whole Mediterranean world.

The spread of humanism in Europe

The exuberance of the new learning and culture of Italy traveled rapidly to Spain and the countries of northern Europe. Unlike the Italians, however, humanists of the north continued the tradition in ways less committed to the revival of Roman antiquity and more to the reform of Church and society. The ancient texts of Christianity, especially those of the Fathers of the Church, seemed to them to offer refreshing alternatives to the rigid dogmas and dubious practices to which the Church was now committed. In Spain the appeal of humanism was somewhat different. There the Spanish Church itself embraced it for the reform of its own clergy, and the impact of this upon Catholic Europe in the sixteenth century would be dramatic.

In 1492 the Queen of Castile, Isabella, appointed the Franciscan Francisco Ximenez de Cisneros as her personal confessor. Ximenez, who had studied theology at Alcala and Salamanca, had also, until 1465, spent a number of years in Rome, where he had come to know many of the humanists laboring for Popes Nicholas V, Pius II (1458-64) and Paul II (1464-71). Ximenez soon found himself giving the queen advice on foreign affairs as well as on ecclesiastical matters. In 1495 he became both Archbishop of Toledo, a position of supreme leadership in the Spanish Church, and High Chancellor of the Kingdom of Castile. In 1500 he personally funded the University of Alcala de Henares, to which he invited humanist scholars from all over Europe. Ximenez's greatest contribution to the humanist movement was the Complutensian Polyglot (1514-17), a four-volume edition of the Bible in Hebrew, Greek and Latin, along with relevant annotations.

The Spanish contribution, like that of the north, lay primarily in putting the tools of humanism to work for traditional Christianity. Yet the movement was not embraced without opposition. The Spanish Inquisition viewed the movement

Left: The title page of *Letters of Obscure Men*. Mostly written by the German humanist Ulrich von Hutten, the book was a satirical defense of academic freedom against the religious authorities, presaging the disputes of the Reformation.

Below: Erasmus, 'Prince of the Humanists.' He encouraged the spread of classical education and argued for a renewal of Christianity through the reform of the clergy and the defeat of superstition.

with much suspicion, and in the wake of the radical protestantism of Luther and Calvin, whose ideas often appeared indistinguishable from the humanism of Erasmus, the Spanish authorities temporarily thwarted humanism's advance, causing many Spanish humanists to emigrate. Juan Luis Vives (1492-1540), the highly gifted son of Jewish converts to Christianity, left Spain for Bruges, in Spanish-held Flanders. There, like his friend Erasmus, he wrote works critical of the dogmatism of the Church's scholastics and of their subservience to the authority of Aristotle. His most influential work, *On Education* (1530), testifies well to the humanists' ideal of using the classics of pagan and Christian antiquity in learning to live well as a Christian.

Spain would eventually reap the fruits of the humanist movement, if belatedly. Its influence would be felt at first in the histories written by two Italian scholars, Lucio Marineo Siculo (1446-1533) and Pietro Martire d'Anghiera (1459-1526) for the king of Spain. With the poetry of Garcilaso de la Vega (d 1536) and Juan Boscán (d 1542), in the literature of Bartolomé de Torres Naharro and the dramas of Lope de Rueda (d 1565), humanism found noble Spanish heirs. And in later writers such as Cervantes, Calderón, Lope de Vega and Gongora, Spain's advance to its cultural *siglo de oro*, century of gold, was well assured.

In the north the Renaissance was not particularly located in any one center. Humanistic studies sprang up in towns close to the printing presses, among wealthy patrons and in various universities and schools. Also, the northern humanists were an itinerant lot. Many moved where they could find employment as tutors, teachers, writers of history or poetry, or merely as ornaments for some prince's court. Erasmus, for example, made visits to Italy, England and Switzerland. Yet no matter where they were, most humanists took seriously the religious probing of the times, and they furthered the cause of a more simplified faith by making available commentaries on scripture and publishing the homilies, commentaries and other texts of the early Church Fathers.

By this time, too, the urban experience in the towns of southern Germany and Flanders more closely approximated the conditions that in Italy had given rise to the Renaissance. For generations Italians and Germans had traveled back and forth from one land to the other, and most of the early German humanists had studied in Italy. But the crucial moment came with the invention of printing in the mid fifteenth century, for this hugely facilitated the dissemination of both the classics and challenging new treatises on education, philology and history. By the second half of the fifteenth century humanism in Germany was well represented by such as Johann Wessel Gansfort (1420-89), Rudolf Agricola (1444-85), Conrad Celtis (1459-1508), Jacob Wimpheling (1450-1528) and Ulrich von Hutten (1488-1523). Though interested in the classics as much as their Italian counterparts, the Germans were all too conscious of the Italians' view of northerners as barbarians, and German humanism began to assume a patriotic quality, as it sought to snatch from the Italians the palm of classical scholarship. Celtis, for example, made a point of publishing the *Germania* of Tacitus as the beginning of a projected history of Germany.

The Germans also injected specific religious concerns into their literary efforts. In von Hutten, whose contributions to *Letters of Obscure Men* (1515) – a savage attack on clerical debauchery, scholastic wrangling and poor ecclesiastical Latin – German humanism entered into the defense of academic freedom. This work was a response to the debate stirred up in 1506 by a Jewish convert to Christianity named Pfefferkorn, who was supported by the Dominican scholastic theologians at Cologne. Pfefferkorn attacked the eminent humanist Johann Reuchlin (1455-1522), an authority on Hebrew, Jewish writings and religious traditions, who had studied in Italy under Pico della Mirandola. Pfefferkorn demanded that the Hebrew books be burned. Von Hutten and the humanists rallied to Reuchlin's side against Pfefferkorn and the Dominicans. Their immediate and enthusiastic stand against Church authorities would presage their later support in 1517 for a young professor of Scripture, Martin Luther. The spread of humanism in Germany would provide the Reformation with strong support and a good reason for its lasting success.

'Prince of the Humanists'

In the Netherlands, also, humanism gained a firm foothold and ultimately produced one of its greatest exemplars. At the close of the fourteenth century a spiritual movement known as the *Devotio Moderna* had spread throughout the Netherlands and into France, Germany and even Italy. This movement, with its emphasis on inwardness, union with Christ, meditation, frequent confession and communion, found wide acceptance. Though its members did include some priests, it was essentially a lay movement, and something of a challenge to the authority of the scholastic theologians, whose philosophical dicta about the good life and salvation were being increasingly perceived as deficient. Out of this background came Desiderius Erasmus, 'Prince of the Humanists,' whose towering influence on the events of the sixteenth century can hardly be overstated. Erasmus espoused an education based upon a rigorous study of classical texts, both pagan and Christian, which promoted 'the philosophy of Christ.' His ideal Christians had been such Fathers of the Church as Jerome and Augustine, who had been thoroughly immersed in classical learning, yet whose works spoke abundantly and deeply of Christ and his work of redemption. Erasmus admired the achievement of the Italian humanists, and indeed continued their work, but mostly by producing editions of the texts of the Greek and Latin Fathers and of Sacred Scripture. In 1516 Erasmus produced an edition of the Greek New Testament that showed the scholarly world how the standard Latin edition, the Vulgate, had in many instances deviated from the original Greek text. By returning to the original sources and making these widely available, Erasmus hoped for a wide-scale reform or renewal of Christianity.

Yet inspiring others was not Erasmus's only approach to reform. With wit and often biting criticism he also goaded both clergy and laity to change their attitudes and review their superstitious practices. Because of its mordant attitude toward the clergy, however, Erasmus's *Handbook of the Militant Christian* (1504), his *In Praise of Folly* (1509) and other writings not only goaded but also infuriated many clergy. But the humanists' words were listened to, not just by the courts or members of society's elite, but by increasing numbers of the educated middle class – the class that would shortly become the vanguard of the Reformation.

In France humanism followed a somewhat less militant path. Although French humanism claimed its origin with Petrarch (who had lived in France), it developed slowly, and always under the shadow of the formidable University of Paris, a bastion of Scholasticism, where theologians were critical of any new movements that tended to infringe upon their domain. The French did produce a few humanist scholars who were interested in religious reform – notably Jacques Lefèvre d'Etaples (1450-1536) and Guillaume Budé (1468-1544) – and their influence was considerable. But by far the greatest impact that humanism had on France was in the field of literature. Marguerite of Navarre's (the sister of Francis I) *Heptameron* (1492-1549), a collection of stories similar to Boccaccio's *Decameron*, and Francois Rabelais's (1494-1553) *Gargantua* and *Pantagruel* expressed a rich, widely popular interest in the classics that would flourish even during the great Wars of Religion. But the outstanding humanist author of the time was Michel Eyquem, Lord of Montaigne (1533-92), one of France's most intriguing and brilliant literary men. Montaigne's *Essays*, written from 1571 to 1590, probe the richness and profundity of human experience – death, suffering, imagination, senses – and testify to the inquisitive nature of one immersed from childhood in the classics. In his words, 'The greatest thing in the world is to know how to belong to oneself.' Yet in spite of his spirited and inquisitive mind and self-possession, Montaigne remained loyal to the Church in the French Wars of Religion. 'Luther left behind him as many schisms and dissensions – yes, more – about the uncertainty of his opinions than he himself raised about Holy Scripture.' On questions of faith and doctrine, he replied, '*Que sais-je?*' ('What do I know?'). His open mind and his fideism were clearly a product of the Renaissance.

Like their continental (Dutch and German) counterparts, the early English humanists aimed for a reform of Church and society. John Colet (1466-1519), dean of St Paul's Cathedral, had studied at the Florentine Academy, though not without first having studied scholastic philosophy at Oxford and at Paris. When Colet returned from Florence in 1497 he lectured on Paul's Epistles. With their Platonic orientation and critical inquiry into the historical sense of the text, his lectures differed greatly from the scholastic approach. Colet advocated a return to the discipline of the primitive Church, to its simplicity of life and fervent piety. Thomas More (1478-1535), lawyer, statesman and a close friend of Colet, Erasmus and other humanists, became the great light of the early English Renaissance. Like his friends, More took a keen interest in reform and in bringing this about through active service to his king. In this More combined harmoniously the civic humanism of the Florentine chancellors and the ethic of the courtier in the service of the prince, as described by Castiglione. But More was also an accomplished writer, one of ingenuity and profound feeling. His *Utopia* (1516) imaginatively and wittily constructs a society in which human values are completely reversed, and thus free of human selfishness and injustice. Historiography also became widely popular among the English humanists. And More himself wrote a history of Richard III that was used by William Shakespeare (1564-1616) for his portrayal of the last Yorkist king. The Tudor court, too, promoted its own cause by employing the Italian historian Polydor Vegil (1470-1555) to write a *History of England*.

Tudor patronage of artists reached its apogee in Shakespeare, arguably the greatest dramatist of all time. His keen knowledge of human psychology, extraordinary skill with language and versatility as a writer of sonnets, tragedies, comedies and historical drama are unique in history. His work is without doubt the single most glorious testimonial to the lasting influence of the Renaissance.

Reformation and Counter-Reformation

On 31 October 1517 Martin Luther (1483-1546), a young Augustinian monk and professor of scripture at the University of Wittenberg, posted his 95 theses to the door of the castle church. Tradition tells us that with this 'blow of the hammer,' the Reformation was born. But Luther himself could never have foreseen the impact of his theses – statements that challenged traditional Catholic beliefs and practices. He was following a standard custom of the time among professors who wished to debate some academic question, and in this case Luther challenged other theologians to defend the Church's practice of granting indulgences (that is, partial or full remission of the punishment to be suffered in Purgatory for one's sins). But in the course of just a few months Germany would take note of Luther's challenge and follow his turbulent career. Soon Luther would answer the Pope's special legate, later the emperor himself, and at length find himself excommunicated from the Catholic Church.

But Luther's ideas, his tenacity and conviction would also rally large numbers of Germans to his side. For the next 150 years Germany – and much of Western Europe – would find itself in a turmoil of social unrest, war and insurrection. The small peak of the indulgence question rested upon a pyramid of Catholic theology and practice whose foundations were centuries old. Yet the mighty edifice of the medieval Church and society would eventually shatter and plunge Western Europe into a period of bitter religious strife and political confusion.

The immediate reason for the challenge was well known to everyone with any interest at all in saving his soul. In the neighboring territory the Pope's preacher, the Dominican John Tetzel, had proclaimed a plenary (or full) indulgence to anyone contributing money to build the new St Peter's Basilica in Rome. With a significant contribution to his pious project the good Christian obtained a certificate of indulgence, guaranteeing the release from Purgatory for himself or anyone else whom he chose. As the jingle went: 'As soon as the coin in the coffer rings The soul from Purgatory springs.' Indeed, one could purchase as many as needed. The opportunity to settle the accounts with God could hardly be missed. Tetzel's sermons reminded the laity of their poor dead mothers, fathers, brothers and sisters, all crying out for relief from the torments of Purgatory. Just one small contribution could bring about their deliverance from torment to heaven.

Martin Luther's objections to the papal appeal for money arose more from his own personal struggle for certainty about his own salvation than from any compulsion for theological correctness. The question of knowing if he were saved had at one time thoroughly wracked Luther. Born into a family of moderate means, the young Martin first intended to become a lawyer. All went well until Martin, aged 21, on his way back from his parents' house to his legal studies at the University of Erfurt, found himself in a severe thunderstorm. He fell from his horse and in panic uttered a vow: 'Saint Anne, help me! I will become a monk.' Two weeks later Martin Luther entered the Order of the Hermits of St Augustine at Erfurt, and in less than two years he was ordained.

Shortly afterwards, Martin grew deeply troubled, developed scruples about his own worthiness and felt himself under God's wrath. In his desperation to cleanse his soul of sin he confessed every thought and movement which he felt might somehow be contrary to God's commandments. But like St Paul, Luther too found himself always in violation of some commandment. What must he do to be saved? Luther's personal quest for certainty about his own salvation eventually achieved a breakthrough, and his insights would become central to Reformation theology.

Luther's persistent struggle with this anxiety was resolved sometime after 1513 in an event which years later he referred to as his 'tower experience,' his insight into the righteousness of God. What exactly occurred in this experience is not clear, but it seems that, after scrutinizing the Greek text of the New Testament, Luther suddenly understood that 'God's justice is that righteousness by which through grace and utter mercy God justifies to us through faith.' It is possible therefore to be 'at one and the same time a just man and a sinner' (*simul justus et peccator*). Man must only believe in the mercy of God. Man was free – free to live a Christian life, free to believe that God was merciful, free from the crushing burden of having to work for God's grace by incessantly hearing masses, going on pilgrimages, taking vows and paying for indulgences. He had only to accept his condition and believe that God's mercy in Christ had freed humankind.

Though Luther never publicly debated Tetzel on indulgences and justification by faith alone, his ideas had a winning effect on Christians throughout Wittenberg, and soon throughout Germany. The Germans saw Luther as their champion against the Pope and other exploiters of the German people, against a clergy using religion to fill their pockets, against the arid theologians who could not speak on matters of the heart. Luther's sudden popularity gave rise for papal concern. In October 1518 the Pope dispatched one of the most eminent theologians of the time, the Dominican Cardinal Thomas di Vio (known as Cajetan), to speak with Luther and dissuade him from his position. Cajetan failed, but in June 1519 Luther engaged in debate with another eminent theologian, Johann Eck (1486-1543), who pushed him to admit positions that had been condemned by the Council of Constance (1414-17). With this his fate was sealed. In June 1520, the Pope issued a bull, *Exsurge Domine*, giving Luther 60 days to recant.

A break with Rome

Between August and November 1520 Luther wrote three short treatises that expressed his new theology and became a challenge to the Church of Rome to reform. In August the presses printed his *Address to the Christian Nobility of the German Nation*, which called upon the princes themselves to reform the churches within their jurisdiction. Luther advocated eliminating the tribute to Rome, abolishing clerical celibacy and giving up religious 'works' such as pilgrimages, masses for the dead,

IN SILENTIO FORTITVDO

ET SPE ERIT VESTRA.

Left: Cranach's portrait of Martin Luther, the German monk whose challenge to the Catholic Church split Christianity into two warring camps.

Above right: Luther unsuccessfully defends his theses in front of the young Emperor Charles V at Worms in April 1521.

Right: The ruler of the Ottoman Empire from 1520 to 1566, Suleiman the Magnificent. His Turkish armies advanced into Europe, distracting Charles V from the defense of the Church against Lutheranism.

monastic vows and so forth. In October he wrote his *Babylonian Captivity of the Church*, in which he explained to the Germans the papacy's tactics of immunity from reform. In this treatise, Luther presented his theory of 'the priesthood of all believers,' proclaimed the primacy of Scripture in the Church, asserted the authority of general councils and argued that the only true sacraments were Baptism and the Eucharist. (And even the Eucharist, he said, did not involve the miracle of Transubstantiation, in which the substance of bread and wine were changed by the priest's words into the body and blood of Christ.) In November Luther wrote *On the Freedom of a Christian*, an open letter addressed to Pope Leo X, in which he explained his theory of faith by justification which frees man from the obligation to perform good works. These three treatises made it clear to papal theologians how far Luther had deviated from traditional doctrine. He had to be punished.

When Luther refused to submit to the Pope's demand to recant he was summoned to appear before the Emperor Charles V (1500-58) at Worms in April 1521. There Luther made his final statement: 'I cannot and will not recant anything, for to go against conscience is neither right nor safe. God help me. Amen.' Promptly the emperor responded: 'Having heard the obstinate defense of Luther, I regret that I have so long delayed in proceeding against him and his false teaching.' Pope Leo X formally excommunicated Luther with his bull *Decet Pontificem Romanum*.

The Reformation might have been cut short at this point but for events which neither Luther nor anyone else expected. Emperor Charles V was only 19 when he first met Luther at Worms. No doubt he fully intended to prosecute Luther, but in arranging for (or purchasing) the title of Holy Roman Emperor the year before, Charles had made concessions to his Electors, among which was the promise to call the diet (or general assembly) of the Empire for consultation before he took any action. When the Edict of Worms was issued Charles was further constrained, for the Electors of Saxony and of the Palatinate had already left the city without signing the document. In 1526, at the Diet of Speyer, Charles gave each territory of Germany a free hand in enforcing the Edict of Worms as it saw fit. In effect, Charles promised his princes that without their consent he would not enter their territories in search of Luther.

Charles, however, had more to worry about than the monk Luther. He needed the help of the Germans in his war against the French king, Francis I (1517-47), a war that had begun in 1521 and would last until 1529. Charles also needed the Germans' help in his long struggle against Selim I (1512-20) and Suleyman the Magnificent (1520-66), whose Ottoman Turks were threatening the eastern Empire. (In 1521 they had captured Belgrad; in 1522, Rhodes; in 1526, Hungary; and by 1529 they were at the gates of Vienna. And in the Mediterranean, Ottoman-ruled Barbary corsairs were marauding shipping even beyond Gibraltar.)

After Luther departed Worms he took refuge at the Wartburg Castle, near Eisenach in Thuringia. For nearly a year he corresponded with like-minded reformers and devoted himself to translating the New Testament into German from Erasmus's Greek edition. In his absence his associate Andreas von Bodenstein, better known as Carlstadt, took over at Wittenberg. There, on Christmas Day in 1521, vested in a simple black robe, he held his 'reformed' version of the Christmas Mass, much of which was said in German. Among his innovations, Carlstadt advocated one practice that would eventually bring about his break with Luther but would nevertheless ally him to many other non-German reformers: he believed churches should rid themselves of 'idols,' such as religious paintings, decorations, music and altars, since these he saw as opposed to the second commandment about graven images. The iconoclast movement and similar radical developments shocked Luther and the other moderate reformers such as Philip Melanchthon (1497-1560). People were using Lutheran theology in ways Luther had never dreamed of – in support of something very like revolution.

In 1525 the German princes appealed to Luther for assistance in quelling the uprising of peasants who were using Luther's words on 'the Freedom of a Christian' to justify their actions. Although sympathizing with the peasants' complaints, Luther could not countenance a revolt in which thousands perished and countless estates, monasteries and castles were plundered and destroyed. In his pamphlet *Against the Rapacious and Murdering Peasants* Luther condemned the rebels and called upon the German princes to 'strike, strangle, stab secretly or publicly, and remember there is nothing more venomous than a rebel.' The revolt, which left nearly 100,000 dead, lost Luther much of his popularity among the peasants, and from this time the tide of the Reformation in Germany would ebb somewhat, only to pick up greater momentum in Switzerland.

Zwingli and the Reformation in Zürich

Even before Luther's excommunication, other reformers, many more radical than Luther himself, had stepped forth to challenge Rome's grip on worship and the channels of grace. Among these was a Swiss clergyman from Zürich, Huldreich Zwingli (1484-1531). Elected People's Preacher at Zürich in December 1518, Zwingli attained widespread popularity and served his community until he died. Having pursued humanistic studies in Greek and Hebrew, he was very much a product of the Humanist tradition and was in fact a great admirer of Erasmus. Between 1519 and 1522

Zwingli began to elaborate his own theology. Taking Luther's fundamental insight on justification by faith alone, he openly called into question the authority of the Church in virtually all aspects of doctrine and discipline. In time his theology came to resemble that of Carlstadt. He rejected the doctrine that the Mass was a sacrifice, and he condemned the worship of images, the veneration of saints and the Blessed Mother, the doctrine of Purgatory, monasticism, fasting and the performance of all religious 'works.' He also denounced the Church of Rome, the hierarchical priesthood and the validity of sacraments as channels of grace.

A crucial test of Zwingli's hold over Zürich came in January 1523, when he drew into debate Johann Faber, the Vicar General of the bishop of Constance. Fortunately for Zwingli, no one in Zürich stepped up to accuse him at this debate; instead the city government upheld his theology on the primacy of Scripture. From this point, Zürich became a town of the Reformation.

Zwingli and the Protestant princes of the German lands knew that the fate of the Reformation might ultimately depend on the degree to which Protestant theological differences could be resolved. There must be consensus in doctrine, above all on the doctrine of Eucharist, the symbol of unity for all Christians. By 1525 Zwingli had formulated a position on the Eucharist which understood it merely as a symbol of the Lord's presence. In 1529 the Landgrave Philip of Hesse (1504-67) brought the Swiss and German princes and their theologians together at the Colloquy at Marburg, where Zwingli tried to reconcile his position with Luther's view. The talks ended in a stalemate, with Luther remarking, 'Your spirit is not our spirit.' Thus no political alliance could be formed

because of the divergent theologies, and it had become all too apparent that these two reformations were set upon different paths. Zwingli's tenets continued to spread throughout the Swiss cantons, soon causing a split in the Swiss Confederation. In 1531 war broke out, and in a skirmish outside the town of Cappel Zwingli was killed. On his death, the leadership at Zürich passed to Heinrich Bullinger (1504-75), who would successfully consolidate Reformation in Switzerland.

In Germany, though Luther continued to represent the path of moderation, radicalism also flourished. No sooner had Luther fled to the Wartburg in 1521 than his adherents got their first look at the Zwickau Prophets, extremists who appeared in Wittenberg and who applied the principle of 'Scripture alone' (*sola scriptura*) with fanatic literalism. Still others appeared who rejected the Bible entirely and would only follow the promptings of the Holy Spirit. These extremists have often been lumped under the general heading of Anabaptists (that is, 'rebaptizers') because of their belief that Scripture does not attest to infant baptism, only an adult baptism of believers. Yet the group was far more diverse than that. The name embraces everything from the violent militants and pacifists to the scriptural literalists and spiritualists. Some fled from the world to establish perfect communities; others gave free rein to their slightest impulses, claiming freedom in the Spirit. Luther and Melanchthon disapproved of almost all of them. It began to seem that in rejecting the hierarchical authority of Rome the Reformation had unleashed an uncontrollable anarchy.

In 1527 Anabaptists in Switzerland even challenged Zwingli's authority at Zürich and issued their own Schleitheim Confession, which laid down a code of religious behavior for their mem-

VENITE AD ME·QVI   LABORATIS·UEGO REFICIÃVOS

HVLDRICVS·ZVINGLIVS·
ANNO ÆTATIS·44·
· B ·

Below far left: Calvin, the most important influence on the Reformation after Luther himself. He saw human nature as totally corrupt, and individuals as predestined to either heaven or hell.

Below left: Emperor Charles V, who despite all his best efforts proved incapable of imposing religious unity on the German states.

Right: Huldreich Zwingli, the influential leader of Protestantism in Zurich.

Below right: John of Leyden, one of the Anabaptist leaders whose attempt to establish a theocracy in Munster alienated both Catholics and Lutherans.

Lutheran princes, the more he was frustrated in mending the unity of the faith. In 1530 he again summoned the princes to a diet, this time at Augsburg. With little hope for compromise, Charles firmly ordered all Lutherans to return to the Catholic faith, but again his mandate met a cold reception. Instead, under the lead of Philip Melanchthon, the Lutherans presented Charles with a summary of their belief, known as the Augsburg Confession. The emperor's theologians refuted this with their own *Confutatio pontificia.* Dialogue had ended, and Charles contemplated military action to bring the Lutherans to submission. Getting wind of the emperor's plans, the Lutheran princes banded together at Schmalkald in 1530, and there they promised mutual cooperation in the event of an imperial attack. For a while the Schmalkaldic League effectively checked Charles, and gave further encouragement to other less committed princes to go over to the Reform.

Charles might yet have broken the League's resistance had it not been once again for his responsibilities on other fronts: against his archrival, Francis I of France, against Turkish pirates in the Mediterranean and at times even against the Pope himself. Still, whether through peace or war, Charles relentlessly pursued his project of unity, only to see his successes, like his stunning victory in 1547 over the Protestant princes at the battle of Muhlberg (Germany), unable to change the well-entrenched course of the Reformation. In 1555 the emperor and the Electors finally agreed to a settlement known as the Peace of Augsburg, whereby each prince could dictate the religion within his own territory. The principle of *cuius regio eius religio* ('whose rule, his religion') recognized only two religions, Lutheranism and Catholicism.

bers – physical separation from non-believers, no taking of oaths, no public offices – that set them widely apart from the congregation. The problem of Anabaptism grew throughout the 1520s, so much so that Catholics, Zwinglians and Lutherans often joined forces to disband and often to kill these nonconformists. The most serious confrontation occurred at Münster between 1534 and 1535, when two Dutch leaders, Jan Mattys (d 1534) and John of Leyden (1510-35), attempted to set up their Kingdom of the Saints by forcing the Lutherans and Catholics of the town either to leave or join the sect. Their theocracy caused such horror that both Catholic and Lutheran armies soon moved in to crush them. After Münster, Anabaptism was noted more for its pacifism, such as was practiced by Menno Simons (1496-1561), organizer of the Mennonites.

The Imperial reaction to the Reformation

It had been of great benefit to Martin Luther that his attack on the Church had begun in the land of the Elector of Saxony, a deeply religious man interested in reform, and one who was favorable to Luther and whose territory was outside the control of the emperor. To regain control over the rebellious princes, Charles V had at first tried to meet them on their own terms. In 1529 he met with the princes at Speyer and legislated that Lutheranism in Catholic territories was no longer to be tolerated. But in April a group of princes and representatives of cities presented to the Archduke Ferdinand a formal protest, in which they advocated the principle of freedom of conscience and religious toleration of minorities. From this was born the term 'Protestant,' which in time came to be applied to all non-Catholic and non-Eastern Orthodox Christians.

The more Charles sought to negotiate with the

John Calvin and the new generation of reformers

The phenomenon of Lutheranism was generally contained within the territories of Germany, though many of its theological ideas found a wider audience. In France, for example, the Most Christian King, Francis I, carefully monitored events in Germany, yet his country, like Spain, was different. Enjoying the prerogatives of a more centralized state, Francis could extinguish smolderings of heresy far more effectively than could Charles in Germany. The faculty of theology at the University of Paris (the Sorbonne), almost infamous for its orthodoxy, brooked no innovation in theological matters. Indeed, they were the first to condemn the Lutheran heresy. France, which prided herself on being the first daughter of the Church, also recognized the danger of her government if the Catholic faith, a major principle of political unity, should ever be compromised. Yet a challenge nevertheless arose.

John Calvin (1509-64) was born (as Jean Cauvin) at Noyon, in Picardy, the son of middle-class parents who intended him to study for the priesthood. When Calvin was 12 his father had arranged a future benefice for the boy, and at 15 young John left for Paris to study theology in preparation for the priesthood. After taking a master's degree in theology, Calvin studied law at Orleans, Bourges and Paris, and during this time he came into contact with a group of Protestants who instructed him in the new ideas. In 1532 Calvin received his doctor of laws degree, and shortly afterwards, it seems, he experienced his conversion to the Reform, which carried with it a mission to reform the Church to its pristine purity. In 1534, shortly after his conversion, Calvin fled Paris because of 'The Affair of the Placards,' an event in which posters decrying the abuses in the Church were posted throughout Paris (one even was found outside the bedchamber of the king). Until then Francis I had been fairly tolerant of the reformers' ideas, but with this he abruptly changed his policy.

On his flight to Strasburg Calvin took a detour through Geneva to avoid a battle between the troops of Charles V and Francis I. This detour for ever changed his life. At that time Guillaume Farel was leader of the reform movement in Geneva. Hearing Calvin was in the city, he pleaded with him to help complete the Reformation there. After much persuading Calvin agreed. Among his first actions was a rewriting of the constitution of Geneva along harsh reformist lines. By 1538 his severe laws had drawn down upon him the ire of the citizens, and both he and Farel were exiled. But in 1541, when Calvin's party at Geneva eventually regained control, he returned and implemented his *Ecclesiastical Ordinances*, Geneva's new constitution. For the rest of his life Calvin remained at Geneva, eventually making it the center of the Reformation for all Europe.

When John Calvin published his *Institutes of the Christian Faith* in March 1536, he dedicated the work to Francis I, his king. This work, which would undergo many revisions until its final form in 1559, was widely disseminated in Europe and was immensely influential. The *Institutes* were the product of a clear intellect and an excellent education in theology, humanistic studies and law. Calvin saw man as totally corrupted by Original Sin, so that every human work was vitiated by sin. Man was therefore no longer free, but was led either by God's grace or his own sinful nature. Yet anyone who truly accepted Christ in faith became certain of his eternal salvation. On this belief Calvin formulated his doctrine of 'absolute predestination,' whereby God had predes-

BEATVS IGNATIVS DE LOYOLA
Auctor et Fundator Societatis Iesu.

Left: Ignatius de Loyola, the founder of the militant Society of Jesus which provided both missionaries and an intellectual basis for the reassertion of Catholicism in the Counter-Reformation.

Right: John Knox transplanted the ideas of the Reformation from Geneva to Scotland, where he established the Presbyterian Church.

Below right: An *auto-da-fé* – the burning to death of heretics condemned by the Spanish Inquisition.

tined all humans, some to heaven and some to hell. This idea stood in total contrast with the Catholic belief that one could sin, and so fall out of God's grace, but could be restored to friendship with God through sacramental confession. Calvin's concept of the Church also departed from the Catholics – and from Luther, who believed in the supremacy of the state – for Calvin believed that the state must be subservient to the Church, an ideal he certainly realized at Geneva.

As Calvin gained a tighter grip on the city, Geneva became an international center where zealous individuals went to study, discuss ideas of the Reformation and experience a reformed city firsthand. Among the many to dwell at Geneva in this time were John Knox (1513-72), who would direct the Reformation in Scotland. While at Geneva in 1558, Knox published his violent denunciation of Mary of Guise, *The First Blast of the Trumpet against the Monstrous Regiment of Women*, in which he asserted that the rule of a woman was contrary to the law of God and nature. Knox eventually returned to Scotland in 1559, there to preach and write for the cause of the Reformation, although only after his death did it succeed there.

Knox was only one of a host of militant reformers who took the ideas of the Reformation from Geneva back to the Netherlands, Italy, France, England and to virtually every other country of Europe. Often clandestinely, they met in small groups to pray, to read the scriptures in their own language, sing psalms and celebrate the communion service. Many kept their new allegiances secret, others preached openly; but in

each country, as the groundswell grew, it became ever more important to be open about one's beliefs. There were indeed issues about which a true believer would not be silent, for it was his divinely appointed duty to purify the community of the trappings of the old religion – the ritual of the Mass, the veneration of saints, images in churches, the priesthood, dependence upon Rome for decisions of doctrine and morals, clerical greed and immorality. When town magistrates did not comply with the zealots' demands crowds often took measures into their own hands. Switzerland, the Netherlands and other places experienced violent outbursts of iconoclasm, in which precious pieces of religious art were smashed and burned. That Catholics would eventually have to react to this spreading tumult was obvious. The question was how.

The Counter-Reformation

Long before Luther first raised the call for reform, many devout Catholics had been concerned about the need to correct abuses such as clerical ignorance, greed and concubinage; superstition; indulgence hawking; bishops' holding of more than one benefice; and simony (the buyng of ecclesiastical offices). Action was taken frequently to correct these ills: councils met, reform measures were drawn up and clerics and laymen undertook charitable works to educate the laity, relieve the poor and establish hospices for the sick and dying. Many excellent bishops implemented reforms in their dioceses; confraternities were started to intensify people's spiritual lives; new religious orders were founded. Luther's own call for reforms, especially in the matter of indulgences, was part of this general concern for reform. But no one had ever imagined starting a new Church. And long after the Reformation was underway, most members of the reform movement still saw themselves as Catholics, doing what had to be done and urging other Catholics to follow.

But by the early 1540s, when Calvin had returned to Geneva for good, Catholic attitudes were everywhere beginning to harden. Many Catholic leaders were at last convinced that the Protestants had inflicted grave damage upon the Church, the seamless garment of Christ. They

concluded that colloquies, debates and discussions had not only borne no fruit but had prolonged the divisions in Christendom. Since the Protestants would not change their doctrines, they were heretics, and had to be treated as such. Yet it was often difficult to determine exactly what constituted heresy. None of the reformist doctrines had yet been explicitly condemned by a Church council or by the Pope. In fact, many Catholic authors used words and ideas in their religious writings that suggested the influence of Luther or Calvin, such as 'justification by faith,' 'reliance upon God's word,' and 'predestination.' Yet these words were also acceptable in a Catholic sense, and it was often difficult to determine where the line was between orthodoxy and heterodoxy.

In 1542 certain champions of orthodoxy in Rome persuaded Pope Paul III (1534-49) to establish a Roman Inquisition, thus giving the papacy direct control over suspect doctrines in Italy. Although many other polities in Italy, especially Venice, resented this bold assertion of papal power, the Roman Inquisition did slow the advance of Protestant ideas considerably. In 1559 Pope Paul IV (1555-59) set up the Congregation of the Index of Forbidden Books, an office commissioned to inspect each printed book and to pass judgment on its orthodoxy. If a book failed the test the author was asked to rewrite whatever was offensive. In the case of public heretics the works were banned and burned. Erasmus of Rotterdam was one of the first to fall to the new Index, and all his writings were indiscriminately forbidden to pious Catholics.

Among the Catholic reformers Ignatius of

Loyola (1493-1556) is especially noteworthy. The son of a minor noble, Inigo (as he was baptized) was born at Azpeizia, in the Basque province of Guipuzcoa. From his earliest days he was destined for a career in the Church. As a young boy, however, he was sent to the royal court to work for its treasurer. There he was exposed to the values of the Spanish courtier: militant Catholicism, ideals of chivalry, the thirst to perform great deeds and win honor. Afterwards, he joined the Spanish forces battling Francis I, and in 1521, while he was defending the walls of Pamplona, his leg was shattered by a cannon ball. During his convalescence he underwent a conversion and decided to devote himself to the service of Christ. Shortly thereafter he wrote his *Spiritual Exercises*, a program for individual reform through meditation, prayer and self-abnegation. He also attracted to himself a small group of younger like-minded individuals searching for spiritual direction. After study at Alcala, Barcelona and Paris, as well as journeys throughout much of Europe, Ignatius and his companions found themselves at Rome. There, in 1540, the Pope officially approved their request to become an order of the Church and to be known as the Society of Jesus. Among many bold innovations, the Jesuits took – in addition to the three vows of poverty, chastity and obedience – a special vow to the Pope 'to go without subterfuge or excuse, as far as in us lies, to whatsoever provinces they may choose to send us – whether they are pleased to send us among the Turks or any other infidels, even those who live in the region called the Indies, or among any heretics whatever, or schismatics, or any of the faithful.' This crusading spirit was to propel the young

order into the first ranks of the Church in its battle with the Protestants.

Understanding reform principally as a matter of individual conversion, the companions of Ignatius undertook preaching, distributing the sacraments, catechetical instruction and above all teaching. Their work aimed at moving sinners to repentance and getting them to turn to the Church and the many graces she offered for salvation. Because of their theological expertise, the Jesuits also attracted the attention of many prelates, including the Pope, who often requested that Jesuits instruct him and preach to his court. In 1544 the Pope removed the original membership limit of 60. By 1556 there were over 1000 members; by 1580 the number had grown to 5000. Their influence far outstripped their numbers. Journeying to embattled regions, Jesuits met with

princes and other nobles to plead the Catholic cause. They set up schools to educate the youth as Catholics; they debated with heretics whenever possible; they wrote vigorous defenses of the Church and her sacraments; they undertook clandestine missionary journeys to heretical regions and distant lands; they gave the *Spiritual Exercises* to those seeking to amend their lives; and they often suffered death for their efforts.

In the early 1540s Paul III convoked a general council to be held at the town of Trent, in northern Italy. This council, which included bishops from the Latin West and all other ecclesiastical authorities in union with Rome, met periodically for the next 18 years (1545-63), thus responding to Luther's original request to be heard by a general council of the Church. Convoking the council was a necessity because one reason why the Reforma-

tion thrived so strongly was that many of the clergy and laity believed that until the Lutheran and Calvinist teachings had been approved or condemned by a general council one might continue believing as one wished.

The work of the Council of Trent was laborious but of lasting significance. Its results reaffirmed the teachings of the Church: that there were seven sacraments, that transubstantiation was the official explanation for the Eucharistic miracle, that both the Bible and tradition were sources of Catholic belief. Both faith and good works were necessary for salvation. Original Sin was removed with baptism. The existence of Purgatory, the communion of saints, indulgences, clerical celibacy, communion under bread alone for the laity were all upheld. The Council thus made very few concessions to the Protestants, but it did sincerely

Above left: The Council of Trent pursued its deliberations for 18 years, producing a comprehensive reaffirmation of traditional Catholic beliefs and laying down a program of action for the Counter-Reformation.

Above: The cruelty of the Turks, as depicted by a Christian propagandist.

Left: The Duke of Alba arrives in Rotterdam in 1567, sent by Philip II of Spain to stamp out heresy in the Netherlands.

Right: The Spanish Armada sails past Cornwall on its way into the English Channel. Harried by lighter English vessels and battered by storms, the galleons failed in their mission to mount an invasion of England.

seek to curb many of the abuses that had crept into the Church. In its disciplinary decrees the Council made strides by legislating the establishment of a seminary in each diocese for the education of the clergy, by insisting upon preaching, by condemning the practice of bishops holding more than one diocese and mandating the residence of bishops in their own diocese.

The decrees of the Council of Trent were an impressive milestone in the work of reform, but the decrees still had to be put into practice – no easy matter. From 1563 onward the Church pursued its program of reform with varying success, and by the end of the seventeenth century it could justly claim to have made substantial progress. But many things would happen in the interim, and to understand the complex evolution of both the Reformation and Counter Reformation in the later sixteenth century we must now turn to a consideration of the events that took place in individual countries.

Spain and Philip II

Philip II (1527-98) succeeded to the Spanish throne in 1556, after his father, Charles V, exhausted by incessant battles and diplomatic frustrations, relinquished power to Philip and his brother Ferdinand. These two zealously Catholic rulers divided the Habsburg Empire. Philip held claim to Spain, the Netherlands, the Duchy of Milan, the Kingdom of Naples, Sicily and all the lands of the Indies. Ferdinand assumed the title of Holy Roman Emperor, inheriting the eastern territories. Both were staunch supporters of the Counter Reformation, although they often clashed with the papacy over questions of temporal power and the limits of papal authority. Yet in three matters both the papacy and the Catholic monarchs were unanimous: the Turkish menace had to be checked, heresy had to be extirpated and all lands lost to the Reformation had to be regained at any cost. Aided by the gold and silver bullion from the New World, Philip was well able to meet such cost. He contributed generously to the papacy's support of the Counter Reformation,

and he also used his monies to outfit a formidable army and navy to check both the spread of heresy and the incursions of the Turks. During most of Philip's reign the Spanish army was the most dreaded in Europe, and his navy was considered invincible.

Having concluded a peace treaty at Cateau-Cambrésis in 1559, both the French and the Spanish monarchs suddenly found themselves free to turn their attention to the nagging problem of the spread of heresy within their dominions. In Philip's case, mainland Spain was never really threatened; due to the unlimited powers given the Spanish Inquisition by the crown, Protestantism never had a chance to germinate. But in the Netherlands Calvinist ideas were widely diffused. Calvinists from Geneva preached publicly, distributed pamphlets against the Roman Church, held prayer meetings and eucharistic fellowships and made many converts to the new religion. In some towns priests were killed or magistrates ousted. Catholics, in turn, were hardly more tolerant of the Protestants. Their enmities often broke out into wide-scale conflicts.

Philip's rule over the Netherlands was essential to the health of his empire. In the 1560s Antwerp, for example, had the highest per capita income in Europe, and its taxes gave Philip a rich revenue. Maintaining peace in the Netherlands should have been a high priority for Spain, yet the Spanish authorities acted unwisely, especially in the matter of religion. By pressing for a stepped-up role for the Inquisition, demanding further taxes and rejecting demands for religious toleration, he alienated his nobility. They in turn found support among the growing Calvinist population, many of whom were Huguenot refugees from France.

In 1567 serious violence erupted when groups of Calvinists went on a rampage in Antwerp. Philip reacted swiftly, calling on the dreaded Duke of Alba (1507-82) and 10,000 Spanish troops to crack down on the heretics. Alba established himself as head of the 'Council of Blood,' which brought suspects to trial and dispatched them

with little fair hearing. In short order the entire population was in arms. In 1568 two of the principal Dutch nobles, William the Silent and his brother, Louis of Nassau, from the House of Orange, brought an army of German troops into the Netherlands, but the towns did not rise up in support, and the two brothers were defeated. Instead of showing gratitude to the townsmen for not participating in the revolt, Alba then turned up the pressure on them by imposing an additional 10 percent tax. The Dutch response to this was violent and the Spanish soon found themselves faced with a revolution of virtually the whole citizenry.

Unlike the 10 provinces of the southern Netherlands (now Belgium) which were more tightly under the control of the Spanish armies, the seven northern provinces, with their open access to the sea, growing fleet of ships and many hiding places, proved difficult to subdue. In 1572, 'the Water Beggars,' sea captains from the northern provinces under William of Orange, badgered Spanish shipping, cut their supply lines and seized control of Brill, Amsterdam and other towns in Holland. When the Spanish approached, the rebels opened the dikes to flood out the invaders. In 1579 the seven provinces of the north joined together in the Union of Utrecht, forming the United Provinces, which declared its independence from Spain. War dragged on, with Spain gaining some territories, but in 1584, when the new Spanish commander, Alexander Farnese, Duke of Parma, captured Antwerp, the English entered the conflict on the side of the rebels.

Now faced with an Anglo-Dutch alliance, Philip decided to deliver a crushing blow with his 'Invincible Armada' of some 130 ships and 30,000 men. The Armada was to meet up with Farnese's troops in Flanders and ferry them across the Channel to invade England. On its way north in July 1588, just off the coast at Plymouth, Philip's galleons were met by an English fleet commanded by Drake, Hawkins and other capable commanders. The bold tactics of the English in their swift, maneuverable ships far outmatched the cumber-

some Spanish galleons. For 10 days the English relentlessly pursued and harassed the Armada as it made its way to the Netherlands, and by the time it had reached Calais its fate was sealed. Once the Armada was harbored in the shallow port, the English sent in fire ships to burn the Spanish fleet. At this point nature allied herself with the English, as gales ravaged what was left of the battered Armada. Although many of Philip's ships returned, he gave up his 'Enterprise of England,' and eventually Spain gave up the Dutch Netherlands as well. In 1609, long after Philip II and William of Orange had died, Spain made a truce with the seven United Provinces in the north. This proved ephemeral, however, for after 1621 war was resumed and continued until 1648, when Spain finally recognized the independence of the Netherlands. The lower 10 provinces of Belgium, on the other hand, remained Catholic and under the Spanish crown.

Despite defeat in the Netherlands, Philip had his moments of glory. Among his most splendid victories was that of the Holy League, which united the naval forces of Spain, the papacy and Venice in 1571. On the morning of 7 October the Catholic forces attacked the vast fleet of Ali Pasha in the bay of Lepanto near the Gulf of Corinth and soundly defeated the Ottoman Turks in what was the last battle of the Christian crusades. At least 30,000 Turks were killed, and over 8000 were captured, with 230 Turkish ships either destroyed or taken as prizes. In addition, the victors set free over 15,000 captured Christian slaves. After centuries of humiliation at the hands of the Turks, the Christians at last had scored a major military victory. The myth of Turkish invulnerability was shattered. Catholic Europe was delirious. Yet in its moment of exultation the Holy League failed to capitalize on its advantage. After the victory at Lepanto it departed, so giving the Turks time to recuperate and once again achieve virtual mastery of the Mediterranean.

Henry VIII and the Reformation in England

In the early years of the Reformation, England stood as a bastion of the faith against the innovations of Luther. England's young king Henry VIII (b 1491, ruled 1509-47), had in fact acquired the title from the Pope as 'Defender of the Faith' for his treatise in defense of the seven sacraments of the Church. Yet, after 18 years of marriage to Cath-

erine of Aragon (1485-1536), the aunt of Charles V, Henry had produced no offspring except one daughter, Mary. In 1527, when Catherine was beyond the age of childbearing, Henry needed a male to succeed him in the Tudor line, and so he petitioned the Medici Pope, Clement VII, for an annulment of this marriage. Fearing to lose England to the Reformation if he refused, but fearing the wrath of Charles V if he agreed, Clement delayed as long as he could. When, in 1531, Henry had lost patience with Rome, he enjoined an assembly of his clergy to have him declared the

supreme head of the English Church. This title was granted to him by Parliament in 1534. In effect this meant that the Pope of Rome held 'no greater jurisdiction in the realm of England than has any other foreign bishop.' Henry thus assumed for himself the right to appoint bishops and dispose of ecclesiastical lands and wealth.

Although extreme, the king's initiatives were not necessarily heretical. Henry regarded his actions as more of a political nature, and not really touching upon Catholic doctrine. In fact, to check the spread of heretical ideas within his kingdom, he issued the Six Articles of 1539, which reasserted Catholic doctrine and discipline. Nevertheless, with the separation from Rome, Protestant ideas grew popular. Calvinism had begun to attract adherents and the English delighted in the new Bible translation of Tyndale and Coverdale. With the ascent of Henry's nine-year-old son, Edward VI (1547-53), Protestantism acquired official recognition. This was largely due to the efforts of the Archbishop of Canterbury, Thomas Cranmer (1489-1556), whose *Book of Common Prayer* helped confirm the reformist character of the English Church. Yet Cranmer's fortunes, as well as those of English Protestants, turned with the death of Edward. When Mary Tudor (1516-58), daughter of Henry VIII and Catherine of Aragon, became queen, Cranmer was burned at the stake at Oxford.

Queen Mary (1553-58), known as 'Bloody Mary,' despite the initial success in restoring Roman Catholicism, provoked tremendous resentment among her subjects. A staunch Catholic, Mary had Parliament formally absolved of schism in 1554 by the papal legate Cardinal Reginald Pole. Promptly she restored the Mass, the sacraments, clerical celibacy and all other

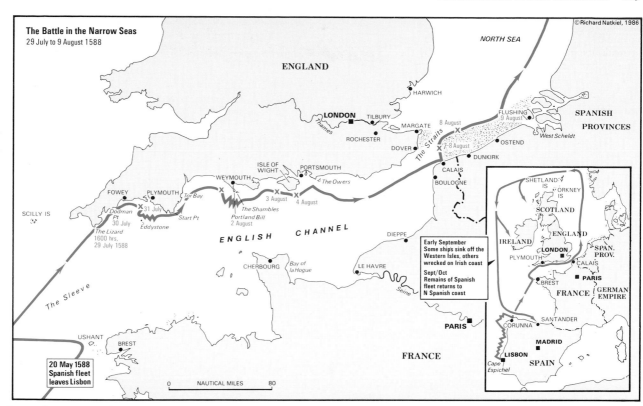

The Battle in the Narrow Seas
29 July to 9 August 1588

© Richard Natkiel, 1986

NORTH SEA

ENGLAND

HARWICH

LONDON

TILBURY

MARGATE

ROCHESTER

8 August

FLUSHING
9 August

SPANISH
PROVINCES

West Scheldt

DOVER

The Straits

7-8 August

OSTEND

DUNKIRK

WEYMOUTH

ISLE OF
WIGHT

PORTSMOUTH

The Owers

CALAIS

BOULOGNE

FOWEY

PLYMOUTH

Tor Bay

3 August

4 August

SHETLAND
IS

ORKNEY
IS

SCILLY IS

Dodman
Pt
30 July

31 July

Start Pt

Eddystone

The Shambles
Portland Bill
2 August

SCOTLAND

IRELAND

ENGLAND

The Lizard
1600 hrs,
29 July 1588

ENGLISH CHANNEL

DIEPPE

Early September
Some ships sink off the
Western Isles, others
wrecked on Irish coast

Sept/Oct
Remains of Spanish
fleet returns to
N Spanish coast

PLYMOUTH

LONDON

SPAN.
PROV.

CALAIS

CHERBOURG

Bay of
la Hogue

LE HAVRE

Seine

BREST

PARIS

FRANCE

GERMAN
EMPIRE

The Sleeve

USHANT

BREST

SANTANDER

PARIS

CORUNNA

MADRID

**20 May 1588
Spanish fleet
leaves Lisbon**

FRANCE

0   NAUTICAL MILES   80

LISBON

Cape
Espichel

SPAIN

Left: England's King Henry VIII uses Pope Clement VII as a footstool. Henry's breach with Rome was a personal and political act, not a deliberate alignment with Protestantism.

Below left: Galley rams galley during the Battle of Lepanto in 1571. The fleet of the Holy League, commanded by Don John of Austria, routed Ali Pasha's Ottoman Turks. Despite the completeness of their victory the forces of the Holy League failed to follow it up and the Turks remained the dominating influence in the eastern Merditerranean.

Right: The course followed by Philip II's 'Invincible Armada.' Encounters with the English fleet are marked with a cross.

Below: A desperate engagement between the Spanish and English fleets. This style of warfare contrasts strongly with the more old-fashioned use of galleys at Lepanto, a Mediterranean battle, where the tactics used were little different from those of naval warfare in classical times.

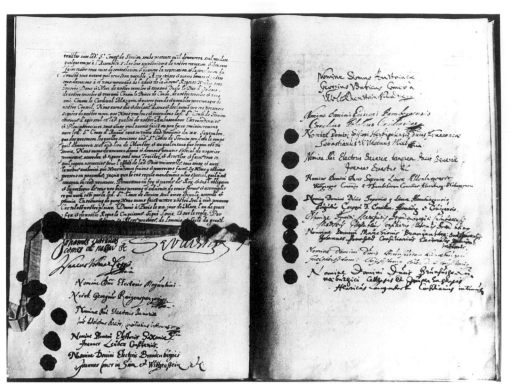

Catholic practices. Mary then took the hand of Philip II in marriage to strengthen her bond to the Catholic cause. This produced for her neither offspring nor goodwill among her subjects. Indeed, Mary's intentions hardly took into account the realities of her time. For some years Catholics had grown accustomed to the Reformation and were hostile to Spain and its connection with papal policies. Nobles had grown wealthy with the confiscated properties of the ecclesiastical lands, and many clergymen felt at home with the practices of the Reform. Despite Mary's execution of Cranmer and other Protestant dissenters, attachment to Protestantism remained strong, and resentment against Mary became increasingly bitter. When Mary was succeeded by her half-sister Elizabeth (1533-1603), daughter of Henry and Anne Boleyn, the new queen, though not of strong personal religious convictions, skillfully steered a moderate, though difficult, course between Catholic and Calvinist extremists.

Upon her accession, Elizabeth abolished Mary's Catholic legislation, and with the Act of Supremacy (1559) had herself declared supreme governor of the Church of England. But Eliza-

beth's battle with the Catholics had yet to be won. Despite the activities of the Jesuits to overthrow her, and Catholic plots to replace her with Mary Stuart, Queen of Scots (whose claim upon the throne was through her mother, the sister of Henry VIII), Elizabeth held her grip tightly. Matters came to a head in 1570, when Pius V excommunicated her and declared her subjects' allegiance to her no longer binding. Elizabeth responded resourcefully. To keep the Spanish threat low, she commissioned freebooter admirals such as Sir Francis Drake and Sir John Hawkins to disrupt Spanish shipping. Often seizing enormous quantities of bullion, they provided the royal treasury with the means to keep Elizabeth solvent. Elizabeth dallied with Philip II, who grew more frustrated by the freebooters and by Elizabeth's evasiveness on his marriage proposals. After the Spanish invasion of England had been thwarted with the disaster of the Armada in 1588, Philip would doggedly pursue a fruitless war with Elizabeth until his death in 1598. When Elizabeth herself died, she had kept both Catholics and Calvinists at bay and had brilliantly consolidated her reign.

France and the Reformation

In France, meanwhile, the Reformation and Counter Reformation took their own course. At his untimely death in a jousting accident in 1559, Henry II (ruled (1546-59) bequeathed to his four sons a highly unsettled religious climate. There had been several earlier efforts to suppress the Calvinists (known in France as Huguenots), such as the Edict of Fontainebleau (1540) and the Edict of Chateaubriand (1551), which empowered the Inquisition to investigate Huguenot suspects and secular courts to take legal action against them; yet the new religious ideas continued to gain wide popularity. Francis II (born 1544, ruled 1559-60), a feeble shadow of his father, came to the throne at the age of 15 under the regency of his mother, Catherine de' Medici (1519-89). He was followed one year later by his brother, Charles IX (1560-74). Because of the youthfulness of the kings and the foreign origins of Catherine, three major families among the French nobility jockeyed for the envied role of adviser and effective ruler of France – the Guise, the Bourbon and Montmorency-Cha-

tillon. The Guise – who boasted two cardinals, the former general of Henry II's army and Mary, Queen of Scots – held the upper hand throughout most of the struggle and stoutly championed the Catholic cause. But the other two families held strong support among the growing Huguenot population, which by 1560 counted over 2000 congregations. Many of the better-educated professionals and at least two-fifths of the nobility had joined the Huguenot ranks and were pressing for radical political changes and religious concessions.

Catherine at first sought to resolve doctrinal differences between Calvinist and Catholic theologies by public debate, and she even permitted public Huguenot worship outside towns and private worship within. But in 1562 this policy was sabotaged when the Duke of Guise massacred a congregation of Huguenots holding services near Vassy, in Champagne. With this act the protracted and ghastly French Wars of Religion began. Horrendous bloodshed and atrocities were committed by both sides. The most notorious was the infamous St Bartholomew's Day Massacre. Catherine, fearing the Protestant ascendancy, had secretly plotted with her son Charles to exterminate the Huguenots with a single stroke, and on 24 August 1572, with no prior warning, the Catholic party in Paris launched an attack that killed over 3000 Huguenots. Within the next few days over 20,000 more were slaughtered throughout France. This Catholic victory was greeted with elation in Rome and Madrid, but in France it only served to intensify the bitterness of the civil war.

Catherine de' Medici's third son, Henry III (1574-89) was childless, and since no males of the Valois line remained, he named the Huguenot Henry Bourbon, King of Navarre, as his successor, provided he renounce his Protestantism and become a Catholic. This Henry did not do, and on the king's death in 1589 the Catholic party opposed Henry's succession with military force. Henry defeated the Catholic armies at Argues and Ivry but was unable to take Paris. Then, in 1593, Henry at last renounced his heretical past and swore his allegiance to the Catholic faith. quipping, 'Paris is worth a Mass.' He entered the city the following year, to begin a remarkably benign and conciliatory reign. In 1598 Henry signed the Edict of Nantes, which granted the Huguenots freedom of religion on their own estates and in certain towns (those controlled by Protestants before 1597), along with equal civil rights under the law and state support for their pastors and garrisons. But France was to remain officially Catholic, and its Huguenot population would have to face further persecution in the century ahead. In 1610 Henry IV was assassinated by a fanatic, but in the years of his peaceful rule his enlightened domestic policies and the financial acumen of his minister, Sully, put France on a path of consolidation which would be expertly continued by his son's minister, Cardinal Richelieu.

The Thirty Years' War

After the gradual subsidence of the religious conflicts of the sixteenth century Europe had some reason to expect a period of peace and prosperity. And the early years of the seventeenth century brought some fulfillment of that promise. Within less than two decades, however, most of Europe found itself again plunged in a protracted war of unprecedented bloodshed, starvation and untold human misery. Internecine religious strife had by no means spent itself, but now the cause of religion would increasingly yield to political motives and an unbridled grabbing for territory.

The resolution of the religious conflict in Germany that was signaled by the Peace of Augsburg (1555) held relatively well until 1618, when an incident occurred in the Kingdom of Bohemia that has since come to be known as the 'defenestration of Prague.' Protestant rebels overran the castle of Prague and threw out the window two officers in the service of the Bohemian king, Ferdinand II. The seriousness of the offense was magnified by the fact that Ferdinand was heir-designate to the Holy Roman Empire, which imperium he assumed in 1619. When the emperor sent forces against the rebels, they declared him deposed and elected a rival emperor, Frederick V. Ferdinand then enlisted help from the Spanish and from the Duke of Bavaria. In 1620 the Catholic forces won a stunning victory at the Battle of White Mountain, and for the next 10 years the fortunes of the Catholic Habsburg emperor were bright. With his armies in the hands of the extremely competent commander, Albrecht von Wallenstein (one of the great profiteers of war and one of Europe's richest men at the time), the emperor pressed his advantage. Wallenstein's successes were so impressive that the emperor at length awarded him the duchy of Mecklenburg on the Baltic Sea. But Wallenstein's proximity to the kingdom of Denmark was seen as a threat by its king, Christian IV, who invaded Germany in 1625, only to be defeated by Wallenstein. Wherever Ferdinand had the opportunity, he imposed Catholicism upon areas that had long been strong centers of Lutheranism. His Edict of Restitution (1629), which gave to Catholics all territories lost since 1552, infuriated Protestant princes, each of whom now saw himself gravely threatened. The emperor also aroused the suspicions of many Catholic princes, who feared Wallenstein's growing power, and eventually they pressured the emperor to dismiss his commander.

This marked the beginning of the Habsburg misfortunes. Without competent leadership the imperial forces began to lose ground, especially after the King of Sweden, Gustavus Adolphus

Left: The Treaty of Munster, part of the Peace of Westphalia which finally ended the Thirty Years' War in 1648.

Below left: Albrecht von Wallenstein, brilliant commander of the Catholic forces in the Thirty Years' War.

Right: Elizabeth I of England, posed in celebration of her victory over the Spanish Armada. England, literally at the top of the world, bathes in sunshine as the Catholic stormclouds flee.

Below: The St Bartholomew's Day Massacre, 24 August 1572. Some 3000 Huguenots were killed by Catholics in Paris and over 20,000 more died in religious slaughter throughout the rest of France.

(1594-1632), a man of grand territorial ambitions, invaded Germany in 1630 and scored some impressive victories. Wallenstein was recalled and met Gustavus at the battle of Lutzen (1632), in which the Swedish king smashed the Catholic armies, though losing his life. Peace was subsequently concluded between the Habsburg emperor and the Protestant princes. Wallenstein was again dismissed and was later murdered (1634) with the complicity of the emperor.

With his passing a new phase of conflict began,

for now France attacked the empire. Ever fearful of the menacing might and political ambitions of the Habsburgs, France hoped to strike a blow against this most bitter enemy. From 1635 to 1659 the two great continental powers attacked and pillaged each other's territories. Eventually the new emperor, Ferdinand III (1637-57), pressed for peace. Negotiations lasted over five years, but in 1648 the Treaties of Osnabruck and Munster, known as the Peace of Westphalia, finally ended the conflict in the German lands. Over one third of

Germany's population had been slaughtered, and economic depression, political fragmentation, plague, famine and massive physical destruction plunged Germany into an abyss from which it would not recover for centuries.

The last of Philip's II's four wives, Anne of Austria, gave birth to a son, who ensured the continuation of the Spanish Habsburgs for the next 100 years. Philip III (1598-1621) succeeded his father, and his son, Philip IV (1621-65), would continue the Spanish monarchy. But the blessing of succes-

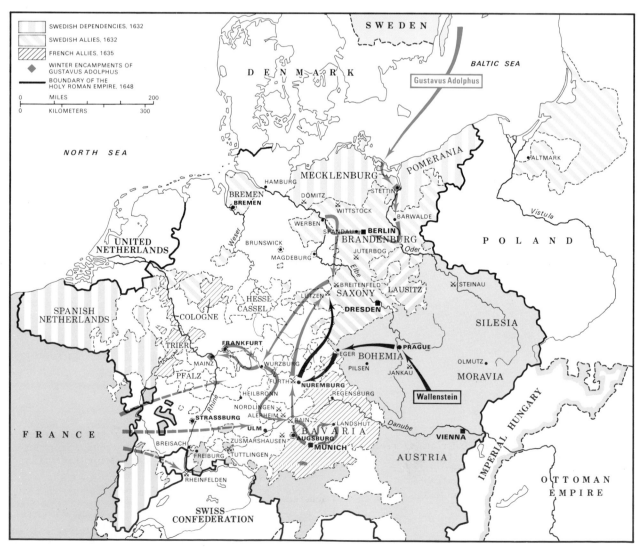

Above left: The first Stuart king of England, James I. His arrogant treatment of Parliament and his *rapprochement* with Spain stirred up political discontent.

Above: Louis XIV of France (seated), the Bourbon 'Sun King' who was to provide his country with a strong centralized authority after many years of internal conflict.

Above right: Seventeenth-century Amsterdam, the hub of European banking and trade.

Left: A map of central Europe during the Thirty Years' War detailing the main campaigns of the great Swedish general, Gustavus Adolphus, and the intervention of France in the later stages of the war.

sion did not carry with it wise governance. Both monarchs pursued the course and tactics of Philip II in an age that called for different, more flexible approaches. Like the heavy Spanish galleons which were no longer a match for the swifter 'fly-boats' of the Dutch Sea Beggars or the more nimble ships of the English, Spanish policy made few accommodations to the new age. Philip IV's selection of the powerful and energetic Count-Duke Olivares as his chief statesman is illustrative. Committed to Spanish world hegemony and autocratic government, Olivares allocated huge resources to upgrade the fleet and provision the army, while relentlessly increasing taxation, abolishing government offices and slashing pensions, all without reference to the Spanish parliament. In the event, none of these measures would prove sufficient for the needs created by his aggressive foreign policy.

In 1621, in the first days of his office, the truce with the United Provinces expired. Possibly Spain could have coped with the renewed fighting in the Netherlands, but Olivares soon found his armies committed on a second front, in Germany, where Spain assisted the Austrian Habsburgs. Soon the war began to bleed Castile, which had always supplied the bulk of the manpower and taxes to keep the Spanish Empire together. Efforts to make other Spanish kingdoms, such as Catalonia, Aragon and Portugal, bear more of the financial burden did more to provoke internal dissension than satisfy Spain's need. Despite the silver from the Indies, Castile continued to slump. Then fighting with France broke out in northern Italy (1628-31), and afterwards tensions between the two countries continued to escalate. More money was required to keep open Spanish access to northern Europe, but finances were dwindling as every new tax only underscored the fundamental impoverishment of Castile.

Other heavy setbacks struck Olivares. Dutch marauders captured Spanish treasure fleets and in 1640 savaged the Spanish-Portuguese armadas. The Dutch armies retook strategic cities in the Netherlands, such as Breda and Breisach. Bullion imports from the Americas dwindled. The French began to menace northern Spain. Olivares's pres-

sures on the Catalans for men and support again fired up fierce resentment against Olivares, and in 1640 Catalonia rebeled. Portugal followed. On 19 May 1643, when French armies won a dramatic victory over the Spanish at Rocroi, it was clear that Spain had lost all hope of ascendancy in Europe. By the time Olivares retired as the king's minister, Philip IV presided over an ageing empire whose once mighty strength had vanished like her gold.

The Dutch Empire

Since the revolt of the United Provinces in 1568 the Spanish monarchy had never surrendered the hope of holding on to its wealthy seven provinces in the north of Holland. But Spain could never subdue the Dutch, and in 1609, when resources had dwindled so gravely that it could no longer prosecute the war, it signed a 12-year truce with the United Provinces. By its expiration in 1621 Spain had prepared itself to regain the former territories. But despite Spain's early military successes, such as the capture of Breda in 1625 (immortalized by Velázquez's painting), the war wore Spain down quickly, while the Dutch held on indefatigably. The Dutch, it seemed, had inexhaustible resources to prolong a war which the Spanish had hoped to end quickly. After years marked by futile military ventures, great financial hardship and growing difficulties in maintaining its overland route from Genoa to Flanders, Spain at length gave formal recognition to the Republic of United Provinces in the Peace of Westphalia (1648).

Among the many strengths of the Dutch was an enviable economy that lent them the financial support so lacking to the Spanish. Long before the war itself the Dutch had built up a formidable navy and merchant fleet. By 1600 they had at least 10,000 vessels of all types and had become Europe's major carrier for seaborne goods. In 1602 they founded the Dutch East India Company and soon supplanted the Portuguese in the Far East. In 1612 they founded New Amsterdam on Manhattan Island, and in 1652 they established a colony on the Cape of Good Hope in South Africa. As the United Provinces gathered strength, Amsterdam supplanted Antwerp as the major

center for international trade and finance. The new Bank of Amsterdam, founded in 1609, drew money from rich merchants and investors all over Europe who were seeking a safe haven for their fortunes in a period of unprecedented social and political upheavals.

Unlike Belgium to the south, dominated by the King of Spain, the United Provinces was a loose-knit republic in which each of the seven provinces enjoyed a great deal of independence. As there was no governor (*stadholder*) for the entire United Provinces, collective action could only take place as the result of decisions made in the representative assembly known as the Estates General, and then only with the consent of all the provinces. Each province had its own form of government and elected its own *stadholder* as executive. Most provinces generally elected the same man, usually some member of the House of Orange, which had enjoyed much favor among the Dutch ever since William the Silent's championing of Dutch liberties against Philip II. Throughout most of the seventeenth century, however, the House of Orange played a relatively minor role in European affairs. Yet that, too, would change in 1688, when, because of his marriage in 1677 to Mary, daughter of James II of England, William of Orange (William III) and his wife would be proclaimed joint rulers of England, thereby ensuring the Protestant succession.

The rise of France

Although not the clear victor in the Thirty Years' War, France nevertheless emerged from the conflict far stronger than Germany, Spain or England. Having eclipsed the political and economic strength of the Italians, France was rivaled only by the United Provinces of the Dutch, whose mercantile empire in the seventeenth century was producing the highest per capita wealth anywhere. Yet France's power clearly was waxing, and much credit was due to the shrewd domestic and foreign policies of one man, Armand Jan du Plessis de Richelieu (1585-1642). This great churchman and statesman in 1624 became President of the Council of Ministers and virtual master of France during the reign of Louis XIII

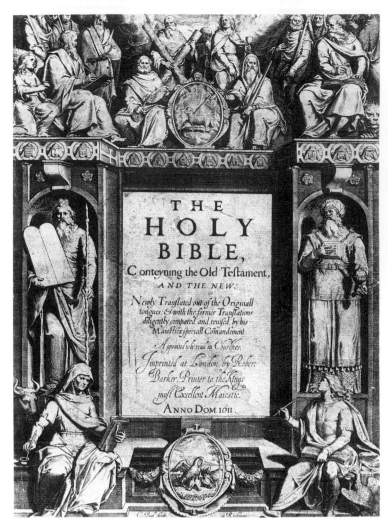

(1610-43). Richelieu was a realist with clear objectives: internally, to create an absolutist, centralized state, and externally, to reduce the power of the Habsburgs in Spain, Belgium and in the German lands. In 1628 the French king's army crushed the Huguenot stronghold at LaRochelle, thus breaking their resistance to the monarchy and abolishing their religious and political privileges. Richelieu relentlessly forced recalcitrant nobles to submit to the power of the crown, and those who resisted were crushed and sometimes executed.

In 1643, Cardinal Mazarin (1602-61) succeeded Richelieu and became regent for the five-year-old Louis XIV (1638-1715). Mazarin continued Richelieu's policies and pressed even further his plans to tighten the grip of the monarchy over the nobility and the towns. Through increased taxation, revocation of towns' rights, substitution of state for local officials and the sale of offices, Mazarin headed for a showdown with all adherents of France's feudal system. In 1649 nobles, bureaucrats and peasants alike revolted in a movement known as the Fronde (from the slingshot used by street urchins) and forced Mazarin to make many concessions, after which he and the young Louis XIV were exiled from Paris. The revolt, which terrified the young king, lasted three years (1649-52), but it eventually foundered as the result of internal wrangling, and as its course became increasingly chaotic many Frenchmen began to yearn for the kind of stability that only a strong king could maintain. Mazarin and Louis were invited to return, and in the young king France would at last find the type of monarchy for which Richelieu and Mazarin had labored so long.

In 1603, James VI of Scotland (the son of Henry Stuart and Mary, Queen of Scots) succeeded Elizabeth, who had died without naming a successor.

The new monarch, now called James I, King of Great Britain (1566-1625), inherited a well-established royal authority, an improving economy, a relatively peaceful religious situation and a very heavy royal debt. Unfortunately, James lacked the subtlety and shrewdness of Elizabeth in negotiating with Parliament and in winning popular support for his programs. Headstrong, opinionated and spendthrift, James believed in an extreme theory of the divine right of kings which many Englishmen found both absurd and offensive. Disdainful of Parliament (which he convoked only four times during his reign), he even lectured the assembly on its duties toward the king. Rather than going there for money, he devised irritating new ways of raising money for his extravagances – new levies, fines, the sale of offices and patents of nobility. James's financial methods and arrogance soon provoked conflict.

In 1604 the first challenge came from the Puritans, a group within the Anglican Church seeking to purify it of the trappings of Roman Catholicism, above all by removing the episcopal system and replacing it with a presbyterian governance similar to those in Geneva and in the Netherlands. James, however, was adamant to retain the episcopacy: 'A Scottish presbytery agreeth as well with monarchy as God and the devil. No bishops, no king.' The Puritans were equally recalcitrant and thereafter refused to conform with the Church of England, many in fact emigrating from England to more tolerant lands, such as the United Provinces and the colonies of New England.

The course of James's reign was one of rapidly deteriorating relations between the crown and the people. Reports of court behavior – the king's public affection for the Duke of Buckingham, his disputes with the authority of the civil courts, the granting of monopolies for a high price, the *rapprochement* with Spain and the favored treatment given Catholics – widened the distance between him and his nobles and subjects. Among the very few achievements of James's reign was a new translation of the Bible, known as the Authorized Version (or the King James Version). Though given credit for this, the text was actually the work of numerous scholars who, between 1604 and 1611, produced the literary masterpiece that was 'appointed to be read in Churches.' When James died in 1625 he left his crown to his son Charles I (1600-49), who soon outstripped even his father in incurring the reproach of the people and Parliament.

Crown versus Commons

The main issue was Charles's insistence on taxing without consent of Parliament. In 1628, when Charles appeared before the Commons to request funds, they handed him their Petition of Right, a charter detailing the limits of royal power, among which was that the king had no power to force loans or collect taxes without consent of Parliament. Charles signed but ignored this Petition. The following year Parliament demanded that the king curb the creeping restoration of the trappings of 'popery,' but Charles became even bolder and in 1633 appointed as Archbishop of Canterbury William Laud (1573-1645), whose heavy-handed imposition of ceremony and conformity enraged many others besides the Puritans.

Charles's policies were rapidly becoming his undoing. Attempts to impose the English liturgy upon the Scottish Church led to a revolt in Scotland which Charles could not suppress for lack of funds. Desperate for new money, Charles summoned Parliament (The Short Parliament) in 1640, but its members refused to grant any money until all grievances were resolved, whereupon Charles dissolved the assembly in disgust. Still unable to bring the Scots to heel, Charles had no choice but to call Parliament again, late in 1640. Because it continued to meet until 1660, this assembly came to be known as 'The Long Parliament.' During this time, the Parliament presented the king with the 'Grand Remonstrance,' a package of over 200 reforms for the churches, for the legal system and for parliamentary rights. Instead of acceding or even negotiating, Charles took police action. In 1642 he invaded Parliament with 400 soldiers to arrest its five leaders. He was too late: forewarned, they had escaped and gone into hiding. To prevent future such incursions upon its freedom, Parliament passed the Militia Ordinance, which withdrew control of the army from the king and gave it to Parliament.

When Charles refused to submit to this, civil war erupted. The king's party, soon to be known as the Royalists, was mostly made up of nobles and their soldiers. On the side of Parliament were the Roundheads (known for their short haircuts), made up of townsmen, Puritans and members of the gentry and nobility at odds with the king's impossible behavior. The major leaders of the Parliamentary cause were Thomas Fairfax (1612-71) and Oliver Cromwell (1599-1658) who managed to organize the disparate collection of forces under their control into an effective army. After an uncertain start the Parliamentarians gained an irrevocable military ascendancy over the Royalists and their 'New Model Army' won brilliant victories at Marston Moor (1644) and at Naseby (1645), where Royalist power was effectively destroyed. Shortly afterwards Charles surrendered to the Scots, who later handed him over to Parliament. Charles was tried by Parliament, was declared guilty and was beheaded on 30 January 1649 at Whitehall. England had now declared itself a revolutionary Commonwealth. Within less than five years it would become a dictatorship.

Europe at a turning point

By the mid seventeenth century the bloody wars over religion and political power had exhausted the resources and manpower of the continent. Except for a few manifestations, such as the witch-hunting craze, Jansenism and the persecution of certain religious movements (discussed in the next chapter), most religious issues were settled and sectarian feuding had ended. Questions of government, however, would take on even more importance. The English civil war, though precipitated by religious wrangling, was essentially a struggle between the crown and Parliament over the question of sovereignty, of who possessed the power to govern and what was the extent of that power, especially in matters of religion and taxation. This was the same struggle the French faced and that resulted in the Fronde. It was the same struggle, too, that brought Catalonia and Portugal and other territories of the Spanish monarchy into revolt just a few years earlier.

As European monarchies extended themselves, they inevitably incurred the wrath of the nobility and the bourgeoisie, both of whom saw their traditional privileges and freedoms eroded by monarchs whose high-handed policies in taxation, religion and legislation rendered them little more than pawns. In 1649 no one could have predicted the strikingly different outcomes of these revolts – that in France the monarchy of Louis XIV should return with nearly absolute power, or that in England a constitutional system would be established to limit the power of kings and give Parliament the sole right to decide questions of religion, fiscal policy, war and peace. These and other developments central to the making of modern Europe will be the subject of succeeding chapters.

Above far left: The frontispiece of the original King James Bible of 1611, a masterpiece of the English language.

Above left: A contemporary illustration of Oliver Cromwell, Lord Protector of the Commonwealth, trampling on Error and Faction, while Fame trumpets his virtues.

Left: Parliament as portrayed in 1651. The English Civil War was in essence a power struggle between monarchic and parliamentary authority.

Right: Matthew Hopkins, the Puritan 'Witchfinder General,' flushes out some witches and their attendant demons. The Commonwealth period saw the last major outbreak of the witch-hunting craze in England.

Matthew Hopkins Witch Finder Generall

My Imps names are

Holt

1 Ilemauzar
2 Byewackett

Jarmara

Sacke & Sugar

3 Pecke in the Crowne
4 Griezzell Greedigutt

Newes

Vinegar tom

The Age of Discovery: 1450-1700

To the eye of most modern observers, the achievements of Western Europe from the fifteenth to the eighteenth centuries in geographical exploration, science and technological invention represented nothing less than a revolution, especially when compared to the accomplishments of earlier centuries. Remarkably, too, this revolution occurred within Western Europe, with few or no borrowings from any other known part of the world; and its beginning happened at a time when Europe itself was beleaguered by an enemy without, and from within by the scourges of war, disease, schism, economic depression, weak political leadership and population shortages. During the mid fifteenth century many of the brightest minds of the day displayed little optimism for Europe's future prospects. Aeneas Sylvius Piccolomini, the future Pope Pius II, wrote in the year 1454: 'I cannot persuade myself that there is anything good in prospect.' And yet, in that very year, the fortunes of Europe were turning decisively, and the results of this, however imperceptible at first, would change for ever the course of the world.

For many years Western Europeans, especially those in coastal areas, had dreamed of reaching the East by means of the sea. At the same time they wished 'to know the land that lay beyond the Isles of Canary and that Cape called Bojador' (off the coast of present-day southern Morocco). Until the fifteenth century, all trade with the East was conducted via overland transport. The silks, cotton cloth and spices (pepper, cinnamon, cloves, sugar, ginger, mace, asafoetida) from the East came westward by camel from India and beyond; these then were transhipped by the Venetians or Genoese from the Levant to Western Europe. Powdered gold from Guinea and other parts of Africa similarly traveled by camel to the Mediterranean, where merchants bartered the precious metal for the goods of Western Europe. In the fifteenth century, with the rise of the Ottoman Turks and their predatory attacks on shipping, trade in the eastern Mediterranean slowed down,

and other routes were sought for supplying Europeans with the silks, spices and gold they had come so long to favor. New opportunities for trade and discovery; embarking on missionary work and pushing back the territories of Islam; the fabled hope of reaching isolated lands of other Christians – all motivated the Portuguese and later the Spanish to push beyond their borders.

By the mid 1400s the Portuguese were well positioned to realize their long-cherished dreams. Until this time ship pilots were unlikely to venture much farther than sight of land, for beyond this one had to rely on crude means of navigation. After 1450, however, a new understanding of ancient geography and astronomy yielded new methods of navigation; and mariners took with them more refined navigational instruments, such as the quadrant and the astrolabe, which had long been used by astronomers on shore. But more than this, sturdier ships, a variety of sails for harnessing the winds, new sailing techniques and shipboard artillery at last gave the Portuguese the freedom to advance beyond their customary borders and the self-imposed limits of their trade routes with Africa.

Prince Henry the Navigator (1394-1460), who likely never went on a voyage himself, embodied much of the crusading spirit of Portuguese discovery in the fifteenth century. A generous supporter of research in cosmography, astronomy, cartography and the techniques of sailing, Henry obtained funds to send out well-planned expeditions almost each year. Using the latest research and sailing methods, the Portuguese made rapid strides in exploring uncharted regions. Portugal's aggressive ventures into discovery and empire-building began as early as 1415 with the conquest of Ceuta in North Africa. With a toehold in Africa, the Portuguese progressed ever further south along the African coast into unknown regions. Between 1418 and 1419 they advanced as far as the Madeira Islands, and between 1427 and 1431 ventured into the Atlantic to explore the Azores. In 1433, Gil Eannes shattered the contemporary

myth of the excessive heat of the south when he sailed beyond Cape Bojador, which lay at a point 25 degrees North.

Further discoveries followed. With each successive venture the spoils of exploration – gold dust and Negro slaves – headed for Portugal. By 1443 the Portuguese had started shipping African slaves to Europe (a practice Prince Henry later forbade), though the market for slaves there was not particularly great. As the Portuguese moved further down the African coast, they established trading posts (and often forts) maintaining the supply of gold, spices and other similarly precious goods. By 1460 the Portuguese had at last reached Guinea, the legendary land of gold, and began to explore the country to find its riches. In 1472 they crossed the equator and continued their explorations further south. The Portuguese ability to deliver greater quantities of goods speedily broke the monopoly of Islamic merchants whose camel caravans could neither transport the same quantity of goods, nor move as quickly, as the sailing vessels plying the direct route up the African coast to Portugal and the other markets of Europe.

A jewel in the crown

Toward the end of the fifteenth century, the Portuguese investment in her fleets paid off when the country made its most significant discoveries. In 1487 Bartolomeu Dias (1450-1500), following the African coast, was propelled by a storm beyond the tip of Africa; sailing then to the east, Dias discovered land, which he named 'Good Hope, for the promise it gave of finding India, so desired and for so many years sought after.' In this same year the Portuguese had also sent Pedro da Covilhã on an overland expedition which passed through Cairo and Aden and eventually reached India. The promise that India could in fact be reached by sea became all the more tantalizing. Ten years later, Vasco da Gama (1460-1524) sailed the 4500-mile course to India and reached Calicut on the Malabar coast on 22 May 1498. A sea route to India had at last been found.

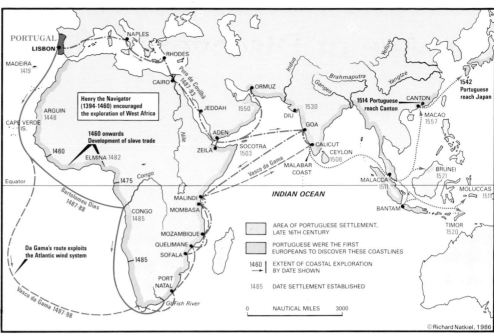

©Richard Natkiel, 1986

Vasco da Gama's expedition had been the fruit of more than 10 years of careful planning, and it yielded a profit over 60 times the original value of the Portuguese merchandise sent to the East. Upon da Gama's return King Manual II grandly proclaimed himself 'Lord of the Conquest, Navigation and Commerce of Arabia, Persia and India.' Da Gama's next expedition made good his king's claim: loaded with arms as well as merchandise his men shattered any resistance of the infidel inhabitants to Portuguese incursions into the spice trade. With the greatest brutality, da Gama ravaged cities to burn and pillage whatever lay within his path; prisoners were mutilated and slaughtered. Da Gama established an unfortunate pattern for European expansion, one that would hardly endear the Europeans to the inhabitants of distant lands. From their base in India, the Portu-

guese pushed on eastward. Between 1509 and 1515 the astute governor, Afonso de Albaquerque, established the capital of the Portuguese territories at Goa. In 1509 they penetrated as far as the Straits of Malacca, then to Amboina and the Spice Islands and from there further expeditions set out for China. In 1513 Jorge Alvarez reached the Chinese port of Canton, and in 1556 the Portuguese founded a trading facility at Macao, not far from Canton.

Navigational skills

Portugal's monopoly in gold and spices from Africa and India swiftly gave the country the edge over Venice, her principal trading rival in the western Mediterranean, and Portugal became widely admired for her new wealth, enterprising ventures and navigational expertise. By the 1440s

Portugal had already minted its first gold coin, the crusado. And as years passed it became evident that Henry the Navigator's vision and support, and the royal investment in exploration, had paid off handsomely. In 1484 a commission called by King John II of Portugal (ruled 1481-95) issued a manual of navigation *Regimento do Astrolabio e do Quadrante*, which made available to sailors the most advanced methods of navigation. Portuguese pilots were acknowledged as the leading navigators of Europe; and as they made ever bolder ventures, they were aided by ever more refined navigational instruments and, significantly, by more exacting methods of measuring latitude at sea by fixing one's position in relation to that of the sun. Fixing latitude was especially useful in allowing mariners to determine their location without reference to land.

Above: Prince Henry the Navigator, founder of the world's first school of navigation at Sagres in the south of Portugal, and an enthusiastic supporter of Portuguese exploration during the fifteenth century.

Above right: Portuguese sailors steadily worked their way down the west coast of Africa until in 1487 Dias rounded the Cape of Good Hope. The way was then open for a series of spectacular voyages to Asia.

Left: Taking a bearing with a rather cumbersome early navigational instrument.

Right: A caravel, the kind of vessel used by most of the Portuguese explorers. They were very small ships by modern standards, normally no more than 70 or 80 feet long.

Dom Vasco da Gama   6.

Within a few decades the science of navigation would overcome still other problems, such as determining the variations between magnetic north and true north at various points of the earth. And in 1569 the Flemish cartographer Gerard de Cremer (1512-94), known as Mercator, devised a method of projecting on a flat piece of paper an accurate picture of the curved earth, so making it possible for navigators to chart a course by drawing straight lines. The study of maps and mapmaking increased, thereby giving sailors greater precision in charting courses and identifying their discoveries. The development of the hourglass also gave sailors greater precision in a ship's speed. By attaching to a log a long rope with equally spaced knots and casting this off the back of a ship, mariners could determine their speed according to nautical 'knots.' Other problems, such as determining longitude, would have to await the eighteenth century and the invention of accurate shipboard timepieces. But the rudiments of long-distance navigation were in place, thus making it possible for adventurous individuals to press beyond the safe and long-respected boundaries of their ancestors.

The Portuguese successes in the East continued for many years, as bases were established for trade and protection, like those at Goa, Aden and Hormuz. The paths blazed by Portuguese explorers and merchants in turn became routes for missionary activity, as one of the avowed principal reasons for exploration lay in determining the whereabouts of peoples in need of conversion to the 'true faith.' With the explorers went forth many missionaries, among whom the most famous was the Jesuit Francis Xavier (1506-52), 'Apostle of the Indies and of Japan,' who in 1541

left Rome for the East at the invitation of King John III of Portugal. Until his death in 1552 Xavier worked among the natives in Goa, Travancore, Malacca, and even traveled as far as Japan. He is said to have baptized nearly 700,000 among the native populations. He died on the island of Chang-Chuen Shan, hoping to carry the Gospel to China.

Spanish competition

Throughout the later years of the fifteenth century the Portuguese faced serious competition from Castile, whose ships frequently crossed course with those of the Portuguese. Interested too in reaching India, the Spanish sought an alternative, shorter route to India; yet the concerns of the crown lay first in establishing royal control over their territories on the Iberian Peninsula. In the exuberant climate of the early 1490s, when the Spanish *reconquista* was on the verge of expelling the Moors from Granada and southern Spain, the advantages of such an adventure made greater sense. The 'Catholic Kings,' Ferdinand and Isabella, at last entertained the proposition of the Genoese Christopher Columbus (1451-1506). Believing like many of his contemporaries that a shorter route to India could be found by sailing directly west, Columbus requested ships for an expedition to cross the Atlantic. Hoping to outflank the Portuguese in the East, the Catholic Kings also saw opportunities for refilling the depleted coffers of the crown, spreading the Catholic faith to new lands and keeping up the offensive against Islam. Striking a bargain with the King that he would be given the title of Grand Admiral and receive a tenth of all profits from the voyage, Columbus departed from Palos on 3

August 1492 with 90 men in three moderate-sized ships. He reached the Bahamas (possibly Watling Island, or more probably now Samana Cay) on 12 October. Columbus named the first island San Salvador and then moved southward to Cuba and to Hispaniola (modern Haiti and the Dominican Republic). Columbus's return to Spain with some gold and a few natives fueled high expectations of wealth and conquest. In total, Columbus made three additional trips to the New World in search of wealth and empire. On his third journey Columbus discovered the mouth of the Orinoco River in present-day Venezuela. Here he believed he had found the Indies and that he was even close to the entrance to the Biblical Garden of Paradise, 'where no one can go but by God's permission.' Until Columbus died in 1506 he continued to hold fast to the conviction that he had indeed reached Asia via the West. Many of his contemporaries, however, knew he was mistaken: Columbus had grossly misjudged the distance of the earth's circumference. But what he had discovered was nothing less than a 'new world.'

Columbus's discoveries, as could be expected, aroused the Portuguese – always fearful of Spanish incursions into their waters – who claimed that they were entitled to whatever discoveries Columbus had made, as these fell under the terms of the Treaty of Alcaçovas (6 March 1480), which gave the Canary Islands to Castile, while granting West Africa, Guinea and the Atlantic islands to Portugal. The Spanish monarchs therefore petitioned the Pope, Alexander VI (1492-1503), also a Spaniard and deeply indebted to Ferdinand and Isabella, to divide the disputed territories between the two countries. On four occasions Alexander VI issued a papal

DANTHES
Aligerius
Florentinus
Poëta, Anno
Sal. M.CCC.
descripsit
IIII. stellas
Antarcticas
cap. pr° purg.

His verbis
ab Americo
Vespuccio
in suis
Epistolis
adductis.

Io mi volsi a man destra, e posimente
A l'altro polo, e vidi quattro stelle
Non viste mai fuer ch'a la prima gente,
Goder pareua il ciel di lor fiammelle;
O Settentrional vedruo sito,
Pri che priuato sei di mirar quelle.

Ego inde versus intuebar æthera,
Poli Nothi adnotaui ibi astra quattuor,
Nisi à priore gente, visa nemini.
Nitet, micatq; flamma quadrupla æthere,
Mihi plaga orbis orba nosse cerneris
Nequis videre quando tanta lumina.

Ioan.Stradanus inuent.   Ioan.Collaert sculp.

Far left: A contemporary woodcut showing the islands discovered by Christopher Columbus.

Left: Vasco da Gama, who commanded the small Portuguese fleet that sailed to India in 1497-8, was not a sailor, but an aristocratic soldier and diplomat.

Right: Amerigo Vespucci, armed with navigational equipment, observes the Southern Cross, linked here to a constellation described in Dante's *Divine Comedy*. Unlike Columbus or da Gama, Vespucci did not lead expeditions, only accompanying them as a geographer and publicist.

Below: Columbus bids farewell to his backers, Spain's rulers Ferdinand and Isabella.

bull, each going further than the previous document, which gave to Spain exclusive rights to the new lands. The third of these bulls, *Inter Caetera Divinae* (4 May 1493), drew an imaginary line of demarcation from north to south one hundred leagues (ie about 300 miles) to the west of the Azores and Cape Verde Islands. Everything beyond this line fell to the Spanish monarchs. The fourth bull, *Dudum siquidem,* was even more generous, as it granted Spain 'all islands and mainlands whatever, found or to be found . . . in sailing or traveling toward the west and south, whether they be in regions occidental or meridional and oriental and of India.' However, when the Portuguese eventually reached India by going eastward around Africa, the provision about India had to be restricted to mean only the Western Hemisphere. In the following year (7 June 1494) the Spanish and the Portuguese signed the Treaty of Tordesillas, which moved the line of demarcation a further 270 degrees to the west, thus entit-

ling Portugal to the land in what is now Brazil.

In Columbus's wake followed numerous expeditions to explore the new lands for God, gold and the glory of Spain. In 1501 the Florentine Amerigo Vespucci (1451-1512), flying the Spanish flag, explored the coast of South America, sailing beyond the Rio de la Plata to the coast of Patagonia, and so becoming the first explorer to grasp the enormous size of the southern continent. In 1504 Vespucci published his *Mundus novus* (The New World), calling attention to the southern land-mass of the Western Hemisphere, which he himself had explored between 1501 and 1502. Soon Vespucci's first name was linked to this new southern world, and eventually to the whole hemisphere – to become 'America.'

By 1508 Columbus's original discovery, Hispaniola, had fallen well under Spanish control and became a base for further exploration of the West Indies. In 1513 Vasco Nuñez de Balboa (1475-1517) crossed the Isthmus of Panama and became the first European to cast eyes on the Pacific Ocean. A few years later Spain established a base on the Pacific side of the Isthmus of Panama. In 1519, just six years later, Ferdinand Magellan (1480-1521) set out to discover a route to Asia by sailing around South America and heading west across the Pacific. Though this expedition encountered misfortunes of every kind – storms, shipwreck, skirmishes, scurvy, starvation – and Magellan himself died in a battle with the natives in the present-day Philippines, the survivors of the voyage (15 out of 280) at length returned to Spain. Any prospect for an easy route to Asia via the west was destroyed. Nonetheless, as the Spanish soon came to realize, the Americas held an extraordinary wealth of their own, and little time was lost in capitalizing on their newly discovered riches.

On the heels of the explorers sprang up Spanish settlements in the New World, first to provide bases for further explorations and settlements and for the exploitation of the resources of these new lands. Among the first of the new

colonies there was Santo Domingo (in the present-day Dominican Republic), which was used as a major base for excursions throughout the Caribbean into Florida, Mexico, Panama, Yucatan, Guatemala and Nicaragua. Other major Spanish settlements at Santiago de Cuba (founded in 1514) and Havana (1519) became important harbors for commerce. In the wake of the first explorers like Columbus also came new kinds of individuals who rank among the greatest risk-takers of all time. These men were the conquerors, or *conquistadores*, Spanish adventurers, many of them minor nobles (*hidalgos*) from Estremadura, the western part of Castile. Because of the law of primogeniture – where the estate went to the eldest son – these men could not share in their family inheritance and so went in search of their own glory and fortune.

Empires in the New World

In 1519 the *conquistador* Hernán Cortés (1485-1547) set sail from the Spanish base in Cuba to subdue Mexico. Though some 600 men strong and well armed, Cortés faced insuperable odds in attempting to overthrow the Aztec Empire of more than one million people. Strangely, however, Cortés was aided by a prophecy held by the Aztecs that a priest named Quetzalcoatl, who had departed centuries before, would return; and this, coincidentally, was to have occurred in the very years of Cortés's appearance. The Aztec leader, Montezuma, at first thought Cortés was this priest-god, and he bestowed upon him gifts and rich offerings. Cortés, however, was not appeased: his intention was to conquer. Skillfully negotiating with tribes subjected to the Aztecs, Cortés in time mustered sufficient strength to attack the Aztec capital of Tenochtitlán (now Mexico City) and to capture Montezuma, who died shortly afterwards. With this victory, Cortés proclaimed his conquered land 'New Spain.'

Cortés's stunning victory was followed 12 years later by an equally amazing conquest engineered by the base-born and ruthless adventurer, Francisco Pizarro (1470-1541), who left Panama in 1530 to subdue the vast empire of the Incas in Peru. Braving rugged mountains, enormous distances and unknown dangers, Pizarro's small army of 180 men swiftly overran the stronghold of the Inca leader Atahualpa at Cajamarca. Shortly afterwards Pizarro was joined by the *conquistador* Diego de Almagro with a force of 200 men. Together they marched on the great capital of the Incas at Cuzco, which they seized in November 1533. Whereupon the Spanish looted its treasures, killed its leaders and claimed the new land for Spain. In 1535 Pizarro established his capital at Lima, and his territories became known as 'New Castile.' Pizarro's exploits were followed by those of other *conquistadores*, always in search of fabulous wealth and glory. Some men continued the conquests into Ecuador and Chile, although in the latter land they met fierce resistance from the Araucan Indians. Hernando de Soto (c 1499-1542) led expeditions into remote areas of Tampa Bay and north toward the Appalachians and westward toward the Mississippi River. Francisco Vásquez Coronado (c 1500-54) explored the lands north of the Rio Grande and Pecos River.

Although often meeting great difficulties in establishing their rule among the Incas and keeping peace among themselves – Pizarro in fact later fell in a civil war among his fellow rulers – the Spanish had asserted their dominance and would not be driven out. Shortly after the victories of Cortés and Pizarro, colonial governments – viceroyalties – were established in Mexico and Peru, which the Spanish monarchy's newly created Council of the Indies controled from Madrid. Two enormous territories had been won for Europe's greatest monarch, Charles V, King of Spain and Holy Roman Emperor. And well into the seventeenth century the wealth of these new lands would keep Spain well positioned as the most formidable military and political power of Europe.

Even before the conquests of Cortés and Pizarro, Spain began to reap rewards from the Americas. Hispaniola was the first to yield up her gold, as the Spanish commandeered the native population to work the local mines. When Columbus originally landed on the island, some one million peace-loving Arawak inhabitants dwelt there. Yet within just three decades the population had been all but wiped out as a result of bloodshed, starvation, the brutal mining conditions imposed upon the natives, and infectious European diseases, especially smallpox and measles, for which the natives had no immunological defenses. To remedy these manpower losses the Spanish imported Negro slaves from Africa who were accustomed to working in tropical conditions. Before long the slaves would become particularly necessary with the development of the larger sugar plantations (similar practises of this type were later continued by the French, Dutch and English).

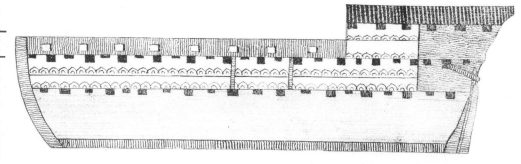

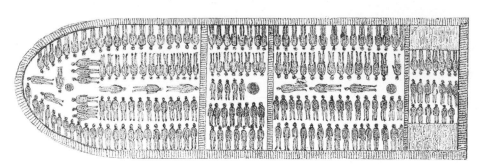

The slave trade develops

As Europe expanded into the Western Hemisphere, the slave trade promised lucrative rewards to merchants who could provide a substitute work force for the all-too-vulnerable native populations of Mexico and the West Indies. In the sixteenth century, scholars have estimated that about 900,000 slaves were imported to the New World; in the seventeenth century the figure was close to 3,000,000. To maximize their profits, slave merchants chained their human cargo beneath the ship's deck in tightly packed inhuman quarters, with little room for them to breathe or to move. It is estimated that in the seventeenth century nearly one-quarter of all slaves died during the voyage, although in the eighteenth century, as the price of slaves went up, the fatalities decreased to 10 percent. From the

Above: How a slave ship was packed with its human cargo. At one time it was normal for one in four slaves to die during the voyage.

Left: Ferdinand Magellan is pictured top left with his ship the *Victoria*, in the company of other explorers. The map shows the route of the voyage round the world that Magellan never lived to complete.

Top right: Hernán Cortés, the first of the *conquistadores*, who destroyed the Aztec Empire with a force of 600 men.

Above right: Spanish gold from the New World, found in a sunken galleon.

Far right: The expansion of Spanish power in the Americas was swift, especially to the south.

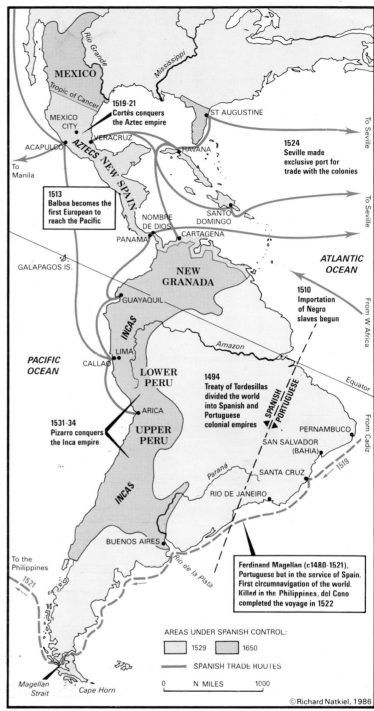

sixteenth to the nineteenth centuries, no one country held a lasting monopoly on the slave trade. The Portuguese and the Spanish were the first to transport slaves; they were followed by the Dutch and British in the seventeenth century. Merchants of other countries – Germans, French, Danes, Swedes – also played their part. But it is now recognized that a large proportion of the first immigrants to the Americas up to 1700 were not European.

As Spanish ships docked at the port of Seville the tangible rewards of mercantilism became evident, and every measure was taken to maximize these. The Spanish monarchy exercised the tightest controls over monopolies, whether silver, gold, slaves or sugar; and the crown insisted on its royalties and fees. Only Spanish merchants might receive licences to trade, and all shipping was to be transacted at the port of Seville on the Guadalquivir River. (Later, however, the more accessible port of Cadiz on the Atlantic was chosen as commercial center.) Although gold was always the most prized commodity, it had been acquired mostly from the accumulated treasures of the

Aztecs and Incas, and some from placer mining. Yet it grew somewhat scarce after the *conquistadores'* initial plunderings. Silver proved to be the more abundant metal, and it was obtained mostly through mining. Famous among the new silver mines in the New World were those at Zacatecas and Guanajuato near Mexico City; but by far the most famous was the Cerro Rico of Potosí in Bolivia (discovered in 1545) which almost overnight became the principal silver producer in the world. Located at nearly three miles above sea level, Potosí boasted a population rivaling that of any of the largest European cities of its day. With the forced labor of the natives and a large contingent of German mining experts, the rich silver veins of Potosí were developed with the latest European ideas on metallurgy and mining, made popular by the German Georg Agricola's (1490-1555) *De re metallica* (published in 1556). With the introduction of the new process of mercury-amalgamation, the silver mountain of Potosí promptly yielded enormous quantities of silver, which rapidly replaced gold as the colonies' major export.

The latter half of the sixteenth century witnessed massive shipments of silver (and some gold) pouring into Spain at the port of Seville. The crest of this tide lay between 1580 and 1620, when approximately 10 thousand tons of new bullion flooded Europe. By 1590 Spain was receiving over 10 million ounces of silver each year. This astonishing increase of new monies into the European currency markets corresponded with a drastic rise in prices – 'the price revolution' – which at first stimulated rapid commercial expansion, but also helped to bring about a severe inflation. With each new arrival of bullion, prices climbed sharply. Of each shipment of bullion the king was entitled to take his 'royal fifth' (*quinto real*). These new monies however did not stay long within the Spanish kingdoms. Because of the short-sighted fiscal policies of the Spanish monarchy, the king's fortune passed almost immediately into the hands of everyone supporting the armies and administration and goals of Spain – in the Netherlands, Germany, the Papal States, Milan, Naples, Sicily, etc. The Spanish monarchy became little more than a conduit for funneling new

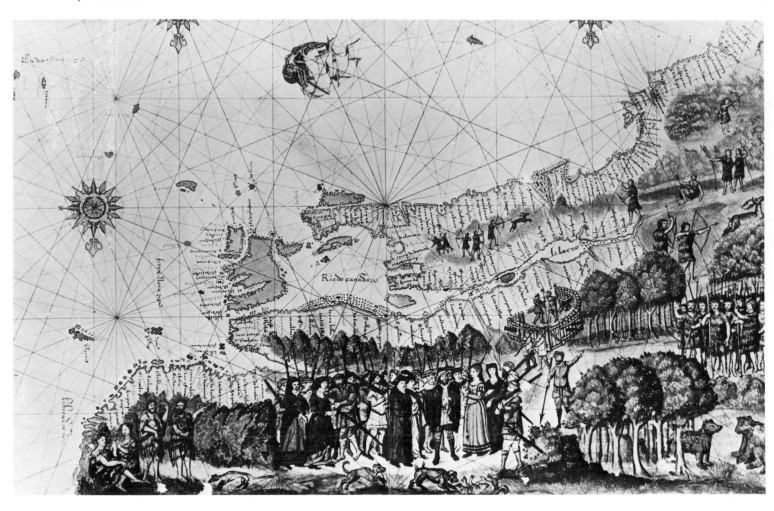

money into the expanding economies of Europe.

Throughout the sixteenth and seventeenth centuries the volume of specie in Europe skyrocketed, not merely from the bullion imports but from the opening of silver mines in Europe as well. By 1650 Europe's supply of silver bullion had trebled, and gold had increased by a fifth. The appearance of the Portuguese crusado, the Spanish gold escudo and silver real, the French louis d'or and the silver pound (livre), English gold guineas (1663-1813) and silver shillings, and new coinage from other European countries facilitated capital formation, investment, and briskly stimulated commerce. Yet the new coinage did not prevent Europe from facing economic problems of other sorts resulting from debased coinage, price rises in staples (such as food), bankruptcies and so forth. It did, however, give rise, if slowly at first, to new ideas about the relation between government policy and foreign trade.

Historians have long looked upon the sixteenth century as a milestone in the development of capitalism (that is, an economy in which the means of production are held by groups or individuals other than those contributing the physical or mental labor to the process of production). Although many forms of primitive capitalism had been functioning for some time, such as the production of wool and silk, joint ventures at sea and shipbuilding, new inventions made possible other types of capitalist ventures as well. Depending upon its sophistication, a printing press, for example, could require substantial financial outlays for its manifold operations before any return occurred. Mining too required large capital expenditures before profits could be realized. While newly available monies encouraged capital investment, other social and political factors contributed to the economic expansion as well; notable were an increase in optimism among Europeans, due likely to a greater overall political stability, an increase in the birth rate, greater market demand for services and goods of all kinds, higher prices and greater opportunities for profit. Europeans from all segments of society were motivated to take greater risks.

Conquest and aggrandizement

With each wave of Europeans to the New World came Old World methods of social and political organization. Spanish colonization in the New World followed predictably the long-familiar patterns of the mother country. But it was also a pattern of enforced compliance in which the conquistadores (and later the viceregents) imposed the Spanish system of government, laws, language, education and culture upon the indigenous population. The Spanish were the first to found universities in the New World: in 1551, they established a university in Lima, Peru; and by 1636, the year the Puritans founded Harvard in Cambridge, Spain had already chartered five universities in its new territories. Despite this evidence of Spain's commitment to cultural institutions, the newcomers understood their role far more as conquerors. They were to acquire new lands for their country, and these were to yield riches for the aggrandizement of Spain. Native populations were considered as conquered peoples, and so were to work for their conquerors in whatever capacities would ensure a return in wealth to Spain, whether in agriculture or mining. Some conquistadores and other settlers became like grandees of Spain with their large parcels of land and feudal rights of tribute, although in the New World the crown retained far greater control over these estates than over those in Spain itself. This imported feudal system, known as the encomienda, allowed the Indians the freedom to hold their own lands, but the lord could demand labor services from them, a maximum of four days a week. It is true that many lords respected the Indians' rights and traditions; they gave them the right to bring cases to their courts and in some instances even allowed them to hold minor administrative offices. But in practice, the facts suggest that life among the conquered peoples was far from idyllic. Frequently the natives were subjected to harsh conditions, and little heed was given to the royal decrees that the natives' rights be respected.

As in the Portuguese Empire, missionaries quickly followed in the wake of the Spanish conquistadores. Many clergymen were highly critical of the ruthless exploitation of the Indians by their countrymen, and they pleaded that they be treated as human beings. The Dominican Antonio de Montesinos was among the first to upbraid the settlers of Hispaniola for their cruelties to the native population. His reproaches were loudly echoed by Bartolomé de las Casas (1474-1566), who even presented accounts of these injustices to the Emperor Charles V (and later Philip II) and was granted powers to correct abuses and ensure that the Indians were granted their rights as subjects of the Spanish crown. Although arousing the ire of his countrymen, Las Casas nonetheless made inroads into the Spanish conscience. In 1530 and again in 1542 royal decrees forbade the enslavement of Indians under any circumstances. After 1560 the use of Indian slaves had all but ended.

Although it is true that the Spanish (and the Portuguese) sorely mistreated the native populations and their imported slaves, their methods in the West Indies differed from those of the British and the French, who never recognized the human beings or the immortal soul in these living chattels. While the Spanish and the Portuguese in Brazil acknowledged the existence of a soul and even had their slaves baptized into the Church, and in some cases even paid them wages, the English and French saw no reason to treat them as

Left: Jacques Cartier lands in Canada in 1542, leading an unsuccessful first attempt to colonize the area for France.

Right: The trading center at Quebec founded in 1608 by Samuel de Champlain, the first governor of Canada.

Below: A lurid illustration from a tract by the Dominican monk Bartolomé de las Casas, denouncing Spanish mistreatment of the native population in the New World.

other than beasts which could be replaced quickly and cheaply if they could no longer work the plantation. The records from Barbados suggest that the death-rate among slaves outpaced the birth rate nearly six to one. No protests against such treatment were ever raised. Unlike most Spanish Catholic clergy, the English Protestant clergymen took little interest in changing the consciences of their flocks. Even the early Quakers who visited the plantations of the Caribbean never registered a protest against these indignities and lamentable conditions.

New rivals for Spain

As with Spain, which turned to explore the sea after the *reconquista* and the consolidation of her territories, so did the quest for wealth by other European countries correspond to their own political position and military successes. After the heyday of Portugal and Spain came that of France, Holland and Britain, with each staking its claim to overseas possessions, and each newly acquired land coming to exist solely for the wealth of the mother country. With each expansion bringing new trading opportunities, so each country also watched jealously the rival European powers which were likely to encroach upon the trading routes, wealth and spheres of influence of every other colonial power.

As the Portuguese and Spanish sought their routes to the East and in the process claimed the huge lands of the Western Hemisphere in the Caribbean and South America, France in turn eventually sent her explorers to North America in search of a northwest passage. In 1524 the Florentine navigator Giovanni da Verrazano (1485-1528) sailed under the flag of France along the coast of North America from Florida to the present-day harbor of New York and the mouth of what would be the Hudson River. Between 1534 and 1541 Jacques Cartier followed up Verrazano's expeditions, reaching Newfoundland, the Bay of Fundy, Labrador and traveling up the St Lawrence River to the La Chine Rapids (at present-day Montreal), which was as far as his ships could navigate. Initial efforts to colonize the area were unsuccessful,

however, and the French gained a stronghold in the region only in the seventeenth century after further explorations by Samuel de Champlain (1567-1635), who founded the trading center at Quebec in 1608, opened up fur-trading routes throughout France's new territories and became the first governor of Canada. Champlain's explorations were followed by the Jesuit missionary Jacques Marquette and his companion Louis Joliet, who in 1673 traveled throughout the Great Lakes and trekked to the Fox and Wisconsin Rivers and then pushed forward into the Mississippi River valley, which they navigated as far south as the mouth of the Arkansas River. In 1682 another explorer, Robert Cavelier, Sieur de La Salle (1643-87), reached the Gulf of Mexico. On the map, at least, France's empire cast an imposing arc extending from the Atlantic Ocean, along the St Lawrence River, through the Great Lakes Region and down the Mississippi to the Gulf of Mexico.

Although chronically hampered by too few settlers, the French experiments in New France were generally successful. In 1642 Montreal was founded, and farming settlements stretching from the mouth of the St Lawrence westward sprang up along the river's fertile banks. The cities of Quebec, Three Rivers and Montreal became major shipping ports, where goods from France were unloaded and abundant furs onloaded for sale in France and for export to other European countries. In 1699 the French established a colony in Louisiana (named after King Louis XIV) and in 1718 founded the city of New Orleans. In general, the French dealt reasonably amicably with the native population of North America. A major difficulty remained, however: the conflicts between the other European powers which were transferred to the new lands. The French, for example, got along well with the Huron and other Indian tribes except the Iroquois, whom the Dutch, and later the British, used to thwart French advances.

As the French concentrated on exploring the lands of the St Lawrence and then the Ohio and Mississippi River valleys, the English made attempts to settle those areas neglected by the Spanish (or taken from them by force) in the Caribbean and along the Atlantic coast of North America (from present-day South Carolina to New Hampshire). The first colony was founded at Jamestown (Virginia) in May 1607 and directed successfully by Captain John Smith (1580-1631), to be followed by other settlements in North America. Yet the colonizing efforts of the English were made initially with little intention of enriching the mother country. Most of the early English settlers came to the New World not to find wealth but to escape religious persecution. In November 1620 Puritan pilgrims sailing on the *Mayflower* under charter from the London Company arrived at Plymouth Rock in Massachusetts. Finding themselves outside the jurisdiction of their charter, they wrote their Mayflower Compact, which incorporated their members into an autonomous political body with legislative powers. And at least until 1684 the colonists of Massachusetts maintained a government separate from the English crown. In the years from 1630 to 1642 numerous groups of settlers, perhaps as many as 16,000, streamed into the Massachusetts Bay Colony in what has become known as the Great Migration.

Like the Portuguese, the English also invested considerably in mastering the seas. In 1597 Gresham College was founded in London to promote the study of navigation, astronomy, geometry and mathematics. The professors of Gresham College collaborated with officials of the English navy, merchant sea-captains and shipbuilders. During the mid and late seventeenth century,

governments of Oliver Cromwell and later Charles II began to take an interest in the vast commercial possibilities open to England in the New World. In 1651 and again in 1660 the English government issued Navigation Acts which directed that all traffic to and from the colonies be carried out only in English ships and only through English ports. These directives formed the basis of the economic system known as mercantilism. The colonies were now almost wholly dependent upon the mother country. For a considerable sum English merchants could purchase from the monarch patents or monopolies on delivering English goods to the colonists. For the English merchants and monarch the new technologies, legislation and sale of commercial rights reaped rich rewards in the colonies of the New World: furs from New England, tobacco from Virginia and sugar from the West Indies poured into England, so transforming these once rare commodities into almost standard items of high demand, and bringing new wealth to the mother country. As colonies expanded along with their markets, so did the need arise to control shipping lanes and the colonies themselves. Central to this enterprise was the Royal Navy, which by the eighteenth century surpassed that of any other European power.

Dutch enterprise

Alongside the English, who were at first slow to exploit their overseas possessions, the Dutch moved with great speed and single-mindedness. Interestingly, too, Dutch enterprises were undertaken by private individuals working in joint-stock companies with little governmental interference. In 1602 the Dutch formed the East India Company, a joint-stock company comprising hundreds of stockholders who pooled an initial 6,500,000 florins to begin their ventures. Only members of this company could hold trading rights. The East India Company quickly amassed huge profits as Dutch explorers and merchants sailed to Ceylon, to Java (Indonesia) and to Dutch Guiana (Surinam). In 1652 the Dutch East India Company established the Cape Colony in South Africa, to be used principally as a base for ships sailing to the Spice Islands. Using slaves imported from Asia and West Africa for farming purposes,

the base provided food and wine for passing ships; and in time the need for fresh meat and other commodities brought about a broad expansion by the Dutch into the territory of southern Africa.

The Dutch set their sights to the west as well. In 1608 the Englishman Henry Hudson, sailing for the Dutch, plied the coast of North America in the *Half Moon* in search of the elusive northwest passage to the East. But Hudson, realizing the futility of the project, abandoned the search and instead put in at Sandy Hook (in present-day New Jersey); he then sailed up the river that now bears his name. In 1621 the Dutch formed the West India Company to handle the North American traffic in furs and later slaves. In 1626 Peter Minuit purchased the island of Manhattan from the natives, and there and at Albany the Dutch established small colonies for protection and trade along the Hudson River. Under the capable leadership of Peter Stuyvesant (1592-1672), the Dutch remained in the New Netherlands (ie New York) area until 1664, when they surrendered to the English. New Amsterdam now became New York.

Of all the colonial powers Britain would prove to be the most capable, both in sustaining and in augmenting her overseas possessions. Britain, in fact, wrested from Spain many overseas ports, whenever they lay across her military and commercial interests; and with her superior navy, Britain had little difficulty in acquiring further territories and trading monopolies. The Peace of Utrecht in 1713 gave Britain the *asiento*, a monopoly on the slave trade; with this Britain virtually supplanted the Spanish and Dutch. The growing maritime strength of the British soon rendered Spain ineffective as a supplier of those goods needed by her own colonies. British pirates and warships preyed incessantly on Spanish shipping, at times strangling Spain's source of bullion, and so rendering the monarchy often economically unstable. By cutting off goods from reaching Spain's colonies, the growing hordes of British freebooters made smuggling and other kinds of profiteering increasingly attractive.

In each new colony systems of administration and social organizations were established that closely reflected those of the mother country. Spain created two new viceroyalties in the New

World, thus raising to nine the number of such administrative territories throughout the kingdom. Each new unit replicated the offices, imposed many of the same demands, administered the same justice, fostered the same religion and in general promoted the same culture as was found throughout Spain. Similarly, the French in New France set up at Quebec a local governor, while the Dutch in the New Netherlands and the British in the American colonies imposed their own political and social structures upon the new colonies, thus closely reproducing the model of their own political, economic and social organization. But it was one thing to govern the settlers from the Old World and another to impose the European mores upon the native populations. In most instances the first colonists gave little consideration to the treatment of the indigenous populations. Wherever possible, as in New Spain and New Castile, the Spanish used the natives as an abundant supply of cheap labor to work the silver mines; and only the missionaries' cry of outrage prevented further brutalities. In North America the British Puritans did little to evangelize the Indians, perhaps in the belief that there was small hope in such a venture. Instead, they co-existed with them, trading when expedient, but as the settlers' need for land escalated they pushed them further from their birthright.

French missionaries in North America took a more benign view of the native population, however, and in fact sought to convert the Indians, and often to educate them. Like Spain, France too had retained its allegiance to the Roman Catholic faith in the era of the Reformation. In 1622 the papacy established the Congregation for the Propagation of the Faith which had made conversion a priority. Franciscan and Dominican missionaries journeyed to the lands of Spain, and Jesuit missionaries traveled to India, China and the New World. One such missionary, Jacques Marquette, spoke clearly of this as the purpose for his explorations: 'to seek toward the South Sea new nations that are unknown to us, to teach them to know our great God, of whom hitherto they have been ignorant.' In India, the Philippines and China, missions, churches, schools and seminaries sprang up to carry on the work of converting the native populations. The Ursuline sisters

Above right: An 'equatorial armillary,' invented by the brilliant and eccentric Danish astronomer Tycho Brahe to measure longitude and latitude. A ferment of scientific ideas was the background to the age of discovery.

Above far right: A Dutch ship arrives at New Amsterdam. In 1664 the town was seized by the British and later renamed New York.

Right: The routes of early voyages to North America, and Drake's round-the-world journey of 1577-80.

Left: The Dutch governor's palace at Batavia (now Jakarta) in the East Indies. The Europeans transported their own styles of architecture to exotic locations.

established in Quebec the first school for girls in North America, and in this accepted both French and Indian students.

The commercial successes of these colonial ventures made a strong impression upon the leaders of the European nations. Controling the sea and foreign markets, reducing imports, expanding exports, capturing monopolies at other nations' expense – all made the advantages of mercantilism particularly obvious. By the mid seventeenth century the struggle for empire was on, not merely in Europe but throughout the world. European wars were carried to the New

World: nations struck at one another's overseas possessions, seeing in this an effective tactic to inflict economic punishment by cutting off a rival's lifeline. The victor in these wars was ultimately the nation who could rule the seas, but upon this much depended. Besides adopting a committed foreign policy, the successful colonizing power had to make use of the latest techniques in navigation, warfare and even agriculture. It became increasingly obvious that imperial success required a concerted effort on many fronts, and that the prize would fall to those nations willing to take sizeable risks and make

firm monetary commitments both to their navies and to those branches of science and technology that would render these navies effective instruments of foreign policy.

The scientific revolution

The European nations' drive for possessions world-wide could hardly have occurred without the scientific and technological breakthroughs of the late fifteenth, sixteenth and seventeenth centuries. In this period the expansion in learning, and the development of new methods of mining, shipping, warfare, medicine and communications, provided Europeans with a powerful stimulus to explore beyond the world they knew. Nevertheless, this revolution in science and technology had many deep roots in antiquity with the Greeks and the Romans. The Middle Ages, too, made its contributions with scientist-clergymen such as Robert Grosseteste (1168-1253), Albertus Magnus (1200-80), Roger Bacon (c 1214-92), Nicolas Oresme (c 1320-82), and Nicholas of Cusa (1401-64). And the Renaissance's rediscovery of antiquity prompted thinkers to translate and to study afresh the scientific works of the ancients. The placement of science on a mathematical basis in the early modern period – which is associated with the names of Copernicus, Kepler, Galileo and Newton – was therefore not altogether original with them, but their dedication to this procedure and the impressive results it yielded pointed to the direction of modern science.

Among the most significant scientific breakthroughs of the sixteenth century was that of Nicholas Copernicus (1473-1543), a Polish physician, canon lawyer, mathematician and astro-

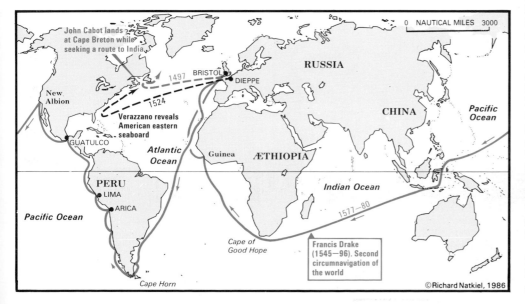

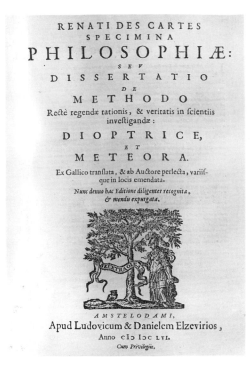

RENATI DES CARTES
SPECIMINA

PHILOSOPHIÆ:

SEV

DISSERTATIO

DE

METHODO

Rectè regendæ rationis, & veritatis in scientiis
investigandæ:

DIOPTRICE,

ET

METEORA.

Ex Gallico tranflata, & ab Auctore perlecta, variif-
que in locis emendata.

Nunc denuo hac Editione diligenter recognita,
& mendis expurgata.

AMSTELODAMI,

Apud Ludovicum & Danielem Elzevirios,

Anno cIƆ IƆc LVI.

Cum Privilegiis.

nomer who questioned the ancient Ptolemaic cosmology which had dominated scientific thinking since the second century AD. Arguing that the sun was far too large a body to revolve about the smaller earth, he proposed instead the Pythagorean system at the center of which stood the sun, around which the earth and the other planets revolved in concentric circles. In the year of his death (1543), Copernicus published his 'revolutionary' theory, *On the Revolutions of the Celestial Spheres*, which – although a dissenting account – aroused no major criticism from Roman Catholic authorities. In fact, even the Pope, Clement VII, had been impressed when he heard a lecture on the new theory. Nonetheless, in going against centuries of accepted practice and 'common' sense, Copernicus found no wide and immediate acceptance of his ideas, and many of his own contemporaries such as Martin Luther and

Philipp Melanchthon were skeptical, if not contemptuous.

The storm broke later with the affair of Galileo, when the religious implications of this theory became an issue, for Copernicus's heliocentric system no longer positioned man and his earth at the center of God's cosmos, and in places it seemed to contradict texts from the Scriptures. And even in the field of astronomy itself, Copernicus had his opponents. The Danish astronomer Tycho Brahe (1546-1601), an accurate observer of the heavens, proposed a highly complex theory of his own, one in which all the planets revolved about the sun, but the sun and the planets revolved about the earth.

Johannes Kepler (1571-1630), court astronomer to the Holy Roman Emperor Rudolph II, while accepting the basic Copernican model had his own objections to the assumption that the planets traveled in circular orbits. Kepler's thesis proposed elliptical paths for the planets and he put forward three laws to account for their movement. Kepler's theories represented a milestone in astronomy and significantly they gave a mighty shove in unseating Aristotle as the incontestable authority on all scientific matters.

Galileo Galilei (1564-1642) made the next great contribution to the development of astronomy as a science. His refinement of the telescope in 1609 and 1610 allowed Galileo to peer into the heavens to observe more closely than any man before the movement of the heavenly bodies. The publication of his *Siderius Nuntius* (Starry Messenger) in 1611 brought Galileo immediate fame, and its findings were discussed everywhere in Europe. Galileo had become the first to discern the rings of Saturn, to see the four moons of Jupiter, to observe mountains upon the moon and the spots on the sun, and to appreciate the distinction between our solar system and the Milky Way. It was however Galileo's great misfortune to have provoked the ire of certain clerics, especially those of the Dominican Order, the traditional champions of Aristotle and of the teachings of St Thomas Aquinas (1225-74), who was himself a Dominican. In 1616, after an investigation by theologians of

the Holy Office of the Roman Inquisition, Galileo was told that the 'doctrine of Copernicus . . . cannot be defended or held.' Galileo, however, was free to teach Copernicanism as an hypothesis. Nevertheless, as years passed more enemies joined in against him.

In 1632 Galileo published his *Dialogue Concerning the Two Chief World Systems*, which he intended as 'a most ample confirmation' of Copernicus's theory; in this work, however, he also unfortunately upbraided the followers of Aristotelian doctrine, the 'Peripatetics' who 'philosophize not with due circumspection but merely from having memorized a few ill-understood principles.' Immediately after its appearance Galileo's work incurred both the wrath of Pope Urban VIII (1623-44) and of the Roman Inquisition which had its publication terminated and called Galileo to Rome. After an investigation Galileo was forced to recant his position. Released from prison after a few months, he returned to his villa at Arcetri near Florence where he lived under house arrest until his death on 8 January 1642. In his final years Galileo wrote his *Discourse Concerning Two New Sciences* (1636), another highly significant contribution to the development of modern science. In spite of Galileo's retraction, he is reported to have uttered the famous words *'Eppur si muove'* ('And still it does move'); that is, the earth does in fact move. Whether or not the saying was properly Galileo's, it reflected Galileo's scientific understanding which was based upon the critical observation of phenomena, experimentation, the induction of ideas from these phenomena, deducing from these ideas, and verifying these ideas through further experiment.

A new scientific methodology

Galileo's insistence upon empirical evidence and the new scientific method was not unique, however. Two other leading thinkers, Sir Francis Bacon (1561-1626) and René Descartes (1596-1650), similarly advocated rejecting the authority of tradition and changing the scientific method, although each took a somewhat different course. Bacon's treatise *Novum Organum* (1620) represented a radical rejection of the scholastic approach and a wholly new approach to scientific procedures. Bacon argued for the inductive method which 'derives axioms from . . . particulars, rising by a gradual and unbroken ascent, so that it arrives at the most general axioms last of all.' Descartes' *Discourse on Method* (1637) optimistically viewed the material world as fully intelligible and ruled by mathematical laws, all of which could be deduced from each other to form a comprehensive system. Descartes would accept only 'clear and distinct' ideas. His starting point was the famous *'Cogito ergo sum'* ('I think, therefore I am'), and upon this solid foundation he proceeded to build his new physics and metaphysics.

Galileo's astronomical observations were complemented, if not surpassed, by his impressive investigations into the laws of dynamics, which he did by direct observation of falling bodies. Arguing that every phenomenon in nature could be displayed in 'mathematical language,' and thus rejecting Aristotelian explanations, Galileo encouraged his contemporaries to explore the universe through the language and symbols of mathematics. He contended that all bodies fell to the earth at the same speed, which increases with the square of the time involved in the fall, and that in a vacuum all bodies would fall at the same rate.

Galileo's advances in understanding the laws of motion were given solid confirmation and pushed

Left: The title page of French philosopher René Descartes' *Discourse on Method.* He believed in logical deduction, rather than induction from experimental evidence.

Below left: Sir Isaac Newton, the seventeenth-century English scientist who explained the movement of heavenly bodies by the force of gravity.

Right: Tycho Brahe in his observatory at Uraniburg on the island of Hveen.

Below right: Galileo Galilei, the great Italian astronomer who was forced by the Inquisition to recant his theories.

much further by the brilliant English mathematician Sir Isaac Newton (1642-1727). Newton's contribution to astronomy lay chiefly in his explanation of the regular movement of the heavenly bodies. Why was it these moved with such orderly precision? In 1687 Newton published his *The Mathematical Principles of Natural Philosophy (Principia Mathematica)* in which he argued that gravity, or a mutual attraction, explained the movement of bodies in relation to each other. From Newton's day onward mathematics – emphasizing a quantitative approach, and not the qualitative approach of traditional philosophy – became the norm. Mathematics uncovered the laws of nature. Experimentation, empirical evidence, observation, hypothesis – all replaced the previous ways of working that relied on authority and deduction, and felt little need for experiment. Sir Isaac Newton's mathematical genius won him immediate renown in England. He was showered with honors, appointed the Royal Treasurer, and upon his death was given a state burial in St Paul's Cathedral in London. Alexander Pope's intended epitaph for Sir Isaac Newton summarizes the popular admiration for him:

Nature and Nature's laws lay hid in night:
God said, Let Newton be! and all was light.

Newton's successful life stands in strong contrast to that of Galileo.

New technologies

Of the new technological discoveries, that of the printing press by Johann Gutenberg (*d* 1468) of Mainz some time around 1450 ranks as one of the greatest in the Western World. Aiding Gutenberg were advances in the production of paper. Up to this time, documents were made from the hides

of animals; parchment from sheep and vellum from calves. As each animal yielded at the most four suitable folios, the production of a Bible, for example, would require the slaughter of large numbers of costly animals. Paper however could be produced for roughly one sixth the cost of animal skins; and printing itself greatly reduced the cost by producing many identical copies without the tedious, time-consuming chore of copying out each book by hand. Gutenberg's invention, in effect, meant that the cost of learning to read and write declined, and with this began a time of growing literacy, which in turn further fueled the need for books and the establishment of printing presses throughout the towns of Europe.

Although many wealthy Europeans, especially among the Italians, were at first reluctant to accept the new printed books, the sheer availability of new writings and of previously scarce works – pamphlets, classical literature, religious reading, handbooks – and the ideas these contained made them highly desirable. The invention of the printing press began nothing less than a revolution in communication. Ideas from Wittenberg, Germany, for example, could be transmitted rapidly to Switzerland or Paris in a matter of days. Martin Luther's success as a reformer owes a particular debt to the press. His pamphlets were avidly snapped up by readers, and the growing numbers of printers willingly accommodated his many adherents. In no time presses were at work in Italy, France and Spain; by 1544 the Spanish had even brought the printing press to Mexico.

Advances in technology increasingly made a strong impact on the way of life, patterns of thought and emotional responses of Europeans. The development of mechanical clocks fostered a sense of chronology and made men and women

conscious of time's passing. Clocks became ever more elaborate, striking the hours, displaying the waxing and waning of the moon, the course of the sun and the position of the planets. As clock-making became more refined, smaller passages of time could be measured accurately. In 1657 the brilliant Dutch astronomer Christian Huygens (1629-95) invented the pendulum clock, which made possible the measurement of seconds – another major step toward greater accuracy in scientific experiments. The attention to correct time also made it particularly necessary to overhaul the Julian calendar, which had been in use since the early Roman Empire. By the sixteenth century the Julian calendar had moved farther away from its usual occurrence in March. To correct this Pope Gregory XIII (1572-85) assembled a group of mathematicians and astronomers who adjusted the calendar. This group first eliminated the 10 extra calendar days. It then calculated that by eliminating the extra leap-year day in February every century year (eg 1900), except in each century with multiples of four (eg the year 2000), the calendar once again would measure accurately the course of the solar year. By the 1700s most countries, except Russia, had accepted the Gregorian calendar, and it is a testimony to the technological advance of Europe at this time that the calendar in use today nearly everywhere in the world is that established in Europe during its scientific revolution.

New to the laboratories of the seventeenth century were advanced instruments for the quantitative measure of nature. Around 1608 the Dutch lensmaker Hans Lippershey invented the telescope, which Galileo refined, thus opening up a view of the heavens that no one before had ever seen or imagined. One of Galileo's students, Evangelista Torricelli (1608-47), invented the barometer which made it possible to measure changes in air pressure. Other inventions, too, furthered the progress of experimental science, such as the thermometer and the air pump. The multi-lens microscope gave ever greater exactness in observation, and, like the telescope, confirmed or refuted what investigators of nature had previously been merely able to hypothesize.

Among the many influences of the Renaissance

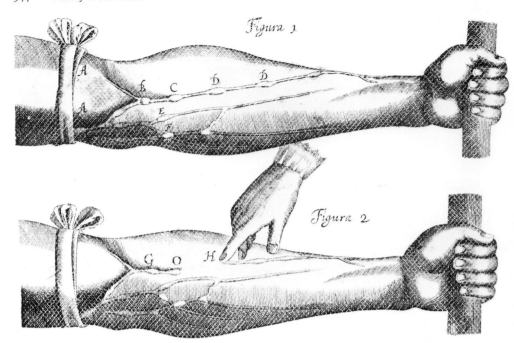

and of Humanism was the rediscovery of antiquity, which while at first uncritically admiring of the Greeks' and Romans' accomplishments later called into question their theories and methods. Traditional medicine was among the first subjects to come under fire. In the sixteenth century, one of the first to break with the authority of Hippocrates (460?-377? BC), Celsus (*fl* AD 14-27) and Galen (AD 130-200) was Philippus von Hohenheim (1493-1541), an arrogant Swiss-German, born near Zürich, who called himself Theophrastus Paracelsus, 'Prince of Philosophy and of Medicine ... chosen by God to extinguish and blot out all the phantasies of elaborate and false works' (namely, Aristotle, Galen, Avicenna, etc.), and who insisted on his own originality based upon 'experiment and reason.' Although soon driven from his position at Basel, and too extreme an iconoclast to be accepted anywhere else, he wandered from place to place expounding his novel ideas that rejected Galen's idea of disease as an imbalance of the four humors. He taught instead that diseases settled in different organs, and that each disease had its own peculiarities. Paracelsus also advocated the use of homeopathic medicine, unlike Galen who believed that opposite remedies were effective in curing diseases (that is, that a cold remedy, for example, would cure a disease caused by an overheating of the humors). Paracelsus further opposed Galen's herbal remedies for diseases, insisting instead on chemical compounds for treatment.

The Renaissance discovery of antiquity also produced an important effect upon the world of the physicians as well as the artists. With the discovery of linear perspective based upon geometry and with the impulse for greater exactness in delineating the human form, artists such as Leonardo da Vinci strove to attain an ever more precise knowledge of human anatomy by dissecting cadavers. Leonardo and other artists' insistence on careful observation and correctness in the study of human anatomy no doubt had its impact on physicians. Andreas Vesalius of Brussels (1514-64), a member of the faculty at the University of Padua, owed as much to Leonardo as he did to Galen, whose recently discovered work *On Anatomical Procedures* advised readers to involve themselves experimentally (rather than theoretically, as was the case in medieval medicine). While lecturing, Vesalius would dissect the bodies himself, rather than leaving this task to an assistant. Vesalius's great work, *On the Structure*

ANDREAE VESALII BRVXELLENSIS, SCHOLAE medicorum Patauinæ professoris, de Humani corporis fabrica Libri septem.

CVM CAESAREAE Maiess. Galliarum Regis, ac Senatus Veneti gratia & priuilegio, ut in diplomatis eorundem continetur.

Far left: An illustration of the work of English physician William Harvey, demonstrating the circulation of the blood – one of the great advances in the development of a truly scientific approach to medicine.

Left: King Gustavus Adolphus of Sweden, a military innovator who mastered the tactical use of lightweight cannon.

Below left: The title page of the seventh book of Vesalius's masterpiece *On the Structure of the Human Body.*

Right: The capture of the Inca ruler Atahualpa by Pizarro's *conquistadores* in Peru. The use of horses, cannon and other firearms helped intimidate the Indians and bring about the amazing success of the Spanish *conquistadores.*

Below: Paracelsus, the Swiss physician and alchemist, made the first significant break with classical medicine in the sixteenth century.

of the Human Body (1543), which included finely illustrated examples, was itself based upon careful experimentation. Vesalius proved that many of Galen's assertions on human anatomy (which were based really more on the dissection of animals) were incorrect.

Vesalius, however, still accepted much of Galen, as for example the idea of the ebb and flow of the blood (like the tides). This theory was finally shattered by the Englishman William Harvey (1578-1657), physician to kings James I and Charles I, whose work *On the Motion of the Heart and Blood* (1628) revolutionized the study of anatomy, as it finally explained how the blood circulated through the arteries and the veins, starting from the heart and not the liver. Despite the significance of this discovery, few practical effects followed in the area of applied medicine. Physicians continued to bleed patients in the belief that this restored the balance of the humors. However, it would be some time before Harvey's discoveries made an impact on physicians' methods and the practical medicine of the ancients finally fell out of favor.

A transformation of warfare

The European discoveries and conquests of the New World could hardly have advanced far without wide-scale developments in the techniques of sailing. The invention of new types of sail, for example, made maneuvering more easy. But these new aids might still not have counted for much had Europeans not been able to establish bases on their newly discovered lands or devised ways to secure their shipping routes. To the new technologies in sailing, Europeans also added new instruments of dread for all who opposed them, above all firearms. The Portuguese conquest of the Indian coast and their superiority over Arab fleets resulted from their superior firepower. Mounting, at first, a simple cannon on the forecastle of a ship's deck led quickly to adopting ways of placing more and heavier pieces of artillery on board ship. Between 1500 and 1588, the year of the Spanish Armada's defeat, the number of guns on a ship grew dramatically. Cortés's and Pizarro's conquests in the Americas were greatly aided by the cannons and muskets taken along for battles with the Aztecs and Incas.

While *conquistadores* were at work reducing native civilizations to the dominion of Spain, military tacticians in Europe were busy changing the art of warfare, and with this indirectly bringing about major political and social changes as well. The wide-scale production of gunpowder gave an impetus for perfecting larger – and more costly – pieces of artillery. And huge cannons and advanced weapons were expensive; kings and emperors might afford them for their own armies, but hardly the lesser nobles who had traditionally retained sizeable armies of their own. To the expense of new artillery pieces must be added the extraordinary costs of outfitting, billeting and paying ever larger numbers of soldiers who were wont to revolt whenever they were not paid. In a short time armies became, by necessity, a royal monopoly. The appearance of towns changed, too. Towns that had fortified themselves with high walls and steep battlements were again rendered vulnerable by the battering of cannon balls. The fortification of towns in this era generally acquired pentagonal forms both to give defensive artillery pieces multiple angles for firing and to reduce the effects of ballistic impact upon the walls. Towns also made extensive use of trenches to halt advancing horses and foot soldiers. The introduction of more accurate and larger pieces of artillery thus gave rise to military science that addressed questions of fortification, defense, gunnery, siege warfare and offensive tactics.

By the early seventeenth century military tactics had changed as well. In the early sixteenth century, the Spanish infantry had been innovative in its strategies and tactics. Spain's armies then consisted of huge square masses of men called *tercios,* usually some 3000 to 4000 troops, who carried guns, crossbows and pikes – highly effective weapons against the cavalry charge of well-armored knights. Each army might have 10 to 12 such squares which could be positioned for maximum effect. By the early seventeenth century, however, the weaknesses in these tactics had been exposed. In their revolt against Spain, the Dutch used new tactics on the heavy Spanish armies. Sacrificing cumbersome strength for flexibility and speed, they learned to throw their musclebound opponents off guard and inflict devastating casualties. In the Thirty Years' War, King Gustavus Adolphus of Sweden refined this system further and built up the most formidable army in Europe. As part of these tactics the Swedish king introduced a new lightweight cannon which could be moved from station to station on a battlefield. The effect of new military strategies was also seen on the seas in 1588 during the naval encounter between the Spanish Armada and the faster ships of Sir Francis Drake and the other English captains. By the seventeenth century, well-armed English ships could boldly prey on Spanish shipping, or move at will up and down Spanish coasts and fire upon unprotected towns and villages. With national armies and navies requiring the addition of ever greater numbers of soldiers and sailors, glimpses of modern warfare became more clearly visible.

Between 1450 and 1700, the pace of European commerce, science and discoveries had quickened to a breathtaking rate and would continue in momentum to the present day. This span of 250 years marks a significant turning point in the course of Western civilization. The inclination to look back to the authoritative explanations of the ancients, to preserve and conserve the past, to hold onto tradition – all this gave way in many areas of human knowledge. Discoveries in science, the uncovering of new lands, the greater opportunities for trade, travel and wealth radically changed human horizons. As Europeans changed, so too did the world they moved out to inhabit. Their influences, for good and bad, would be felt everywhere – in India, in the South Sea islands, Japan and the New World. It is unfortunate that most European explorers set forth with the idea of gaining wealth, and to do this at the expense of the inhabitants of these other lands. In most parts of the world the aggressive Europeans were not welcome, as they respected neither the foreign traditions and laws nor the native peoples themselves. Despite their many marvelous inventions – firearms, ships, precision instruments – they often displayed little sensitivity to their hosts, and they pondered very little the morality of their actions. The Europeans, it is true, brought with them many benefits of civilization, but, as has been so often recognized, they themselves were often far less than civil.

Europe: 1648-1789

The unprecedented horrors of the Thirty Years' War were only the most lurid symptoms of the religious excesses of the seventeenth century. As war raged in Europe and the fortunes of the Protestant and Catholic armies ebbed and flowed, political and religious leaders sought explanations for their setbacks and sufferings in the machinations of the devil. They saw witchcraft everywhere on the rise, and they believed that their only hope for checking its spread lay in a constant surveillance of their communities' activities and in extirpating the demonic cancer before its spread became uncontrollable. The witch-hysteria and persecutions of the late sixteenth and seventeenth centuries were accompanied, too, by an obsession for orthodoxy in all matters of religion. Within the Catholic Church the Inquisition assumed an all-controlling role in investigating every potential deviation from the faith. In Protestant congregations orthodoxy became every bit as guarded and was often enforced by brutal repression. Such measures on the part of religious and lay authorities ultimately produced a strong intellectual reaction. Clear-minded critics demanded reforms in the legal procedures for trying suspects, decried religious fanaticism and called for more toleration. More significantly, they sought a basis for both tolerance and reform in the scientific discoveries of their time. To the best of the age's minds the turmoil in politics and religion could be overcome by a morality based upon natural law, one in accord with the laws of the orderly universe. The era that followed the protracted religious and political wars that darkened much of the seventeenth century is still referred to as the Enlightenment, a time when intellectuals saw themselves advancing at last from the darkness of ideology and religious myopia into a world of social harmony and brotherhood. Nour-

ished by a limitless faith in reason, they foretold a time of justice, freedom and universal concern for one's fellow man.

The new ideals of universal order and peace slowly found applications in politics, even under the absolute forms of government that were gaining ground in Western Europe, most notably in France, Austria, Prussia and to some extent in Britain. In time, many political theorists would raise questions about the best form of government, but most would nevertheless continue to address this question within the contexts of their own political experiences. At first the emphasis was simply on political and social reform. Deeper political questioning evolved more slowly, and only in the eighteenth century, with Montesquieu, Rousseau and others, did philosophers at last begin to explore the inadequacy of their own political systems. The shocking eruption of the French Revolution at the end of the eighteenth century either cut short most of such questioning or so transformed its nature that we may date the end of the Enlightenment as 1789.

Before exploring the ideas, achievements and disappointments of the Enlightenment, we must first look at the West European political context, and especially at the evolution of the French monarchy, beginning with Louis XIV. More than any other personality at this time, Louis, and by extension his country, dominated the age. Other European governments largely reacted to France's foreign and domestic policies; they emulated French accomplishments and looked to France for cultural inspiration. Fortunately for France, nearly every other European power had seen better times. Spain, the United Provinces, the cities of Italy, Germany, Austria – all had suffered severely from the setbacks and ills of the Thirty Years' War. At least in the late seventeenth century, France

was eminently in a position to assert herself over the other countries of Europe, though, as we shall see, not without tremendous cost. Significantly, too, many of the achievements of the Enlightenment in arts and letters and sciences occurred in France. But it was there, too, that many of the harshest criticisms were heaped upon the *ancien régime*, that cries for reform were uttered most loudly. There, too, the end of the Enlightenment would come most dramatically in revolution and in the abolition of the monarchy.

France in the age of the Sun King

Upon the death of Cardinal Mazarin in 1661 the 23-year-old Louis Bourbon, Louis XIV (1638-1715), deftly implemented the lessons so well learned from his former mentor. His first action was to call together all executive heads of government and inform them of their duties and allegiance: 'Gentlemen, I have had you meet . . . so that I might tell you that until the present I have been willing to let my affairs be managed by the late Cardinal. It is now time that I manage them myself. You will assist me with your advice when I ask you for it.' Thenceforth all executive decisions were to be made solely by the king, who believed firmly in his divine right to rule. Louis realized that the security of his position required substantial monies, rational government, a permanent military and the glorification of monarchy. Opposed to these objectives in greater or lesser degree were the peasants, the townspeople and the nobles – in short, virtually everyone in France. Louis was to spend his entire reign in relentless pursuit of his goals, and his success was in great measure the result of his shrewd statesmanship, unflagging toil and limitless ambition.

When Louis finally took power he became his own prime minister and supervised the bureaucracy, which existed to execute royal decrees, col-

Above left: Jean Baptiste Colbert (1619-83), chief adviser to Louis XIV. A statesman of wide-ranging abilities, he was responsible for sweeping financial and industrial reforms, as well as being a patron of the arts.

Right: A monarch of almost limitless ambition, Louis XIV embarked on a long series of wars against France's neighbors. The War of the Spanish Succession won him dynastic control of Spain but left France financially impoverished.

Above: Louis XIV pays a visit to a factory in the company of Colbert.

Left: 'The swimming of Mary Sutton,' part of the title page from a 1613 pamphlet entitled 'Witches, apprehended, examined and executed.' The eighteenth century witnessed a reaction to such barbaric actions and attitudes, to the degree that the period became known as the 'Age of Reason.'

lect taxes and ensure the efficient running of the state. To Louis' great fortune, he appointed Jean Baptiste Colbert (1619-83), as his extremely capable minister of finance. Colbert's economic vision was based upon the mercantilist theory that to increase a country's wealth one needed to export more than one imported, or, more specifically, that France had to be the recipient of gold and silver in exchange for its domestically produced goods. A rise in French productivity and foreign trade would mean more tax revenues for the king. To stimulate the French economy Colbert invested much of the tax revenues in building up domestic industries whose goods would both be needed at home and could be sold abroad. Among the more famous of these state-supported businesses was the Gobelin tapestry works, which set standards of excellence for all the world to emulate. In many other industries too – lace, glass, silk, hosiery, textiles – the French succeeded in producing goods of unrivaled quality, and state inspectors kept high the standards of those industries that had been awarded royal privileges, monopolies and tariff concessions. Colbert's incentives attracted many foreign artisans to France, while at the same time he forbade the departure of French artisans. To expedite internal production and trade, Colbert supervised the building of a network of royal highways whose hub was Paris. He carried through the building of canals, one of which linked the Atlantic with the Mediterranean through Languedoc, and he reduced the numerous tariff points a merchant had to pass in transhipping goods throughout the kingdom. To encourage foreign trade he lowered tariffs on foreign goods, and thereby stimulated maritime activity. To cow France's major external trade rival, the Dutch Empire, Colbert set about building up a formidable French navy that could deny the Dutch control of the sea.

Left: Louis XIV orders the construction of 'Les Invalides,' a detail from a tapestry at Versailles.

Below left: A room at the south end of the Hall of Mirrors at Versailles. The palace, built at the express orders of Louis XIV, was the center of the French state apparatus in the second half of the seventeenth century.

Above right: Versailles became the center of courtly ritual. The French nobility allowed the monarch to exercise a measure of control unknown in previous reigns.

Below right: France under Louis XIV. Territorial ambition in the Low Countries and Franche-Comte was the hallmark of the 'Sun King's' rule.

All this worked well. French trade picked up briskly, and traders entered into global markets. As testimony to French expansion, French *voyageurs* and Jesuit missionaries advanced into North America along the St Lawrence River and south through the Mississippi River valley. Other French explorers and traders fanned out as far as India, Madagascar and the West Indies.

Since the French monarchy depended above all on steady revenues, Colbert established a centralized system for collecting the taxes that Louis needed to run a government on the grand scale he envisioned. This system was that of the *intendants*, that is, bourgeois professionals who formed a chain of command starting with Louis himself and descending to local levels throughout France. The *intendants* functioned as the king's representatives in the administration of justice, collection of taxes, recruitment of soldiers and clarification of policy. They also kept the king informed of all movements on the local level, especially ones affecting national security. The *intendants*, mostly men, were selected from the growing ranks of the new upper class and, eager for advancement, proved extremely loyal to the king in return for the favor of office.

It is no doubt a measure of Louis' control that his *intendants* carried out his policies with relatively little resistance from the nobility, bourgeoisie or peasantry. Unlike other governments throughout Europe, France quickly attained a centralized system of justice, taxation and control, and this achievement gave France a superiority over every other growing monarchy of the time. Nor did this exhaust the list of Louis' accomplishments.

Louis' policy of reducing the standing armies of his nobles and of consolidating these into one royal army represented a major step in the development of the modern state. Thanks to his minister of war, François le Tellier, the Marquis of Louvois (1639-83), who regularized the chain of command, supervised recruiting and insisted on standards of provisioning, appearance and discipline, Louis fashioned the most advanced and doubtless most expensive fighting force in Europe. With an army of 400,000, at whose head he stood, Louis possessed the power to enforce both his domestic and foreign policies. Unable to match the funds necessary for outfitting any comparable force, the French nobility in the end became unable to resist the royal army. The lessons of the French Wars of Religion had been well learned by the young Bourbon king.

The acquisition of so huge a fighting force was but part of his policy for dealing with his nobles. He created a dazzling court, where he granted gifts, titles and trivial favors and established himself as the supreme arbitrator of manners and good taste, thus increasingly making the nobility dependent upon his pleasure. The center of this grand spectacle was the sprawling new palace at Versailles, which Louis had had constructed for himself, his entourage and the many offices of state. There, in all his magnificence, Louis followed elaborate rituals of rising, dining and retiring (*lever, diner, coucher*), in which privileged nobles were invited to participate – activities which made attendance upon the king symbolic of the nobility's growing subservience to the royal authority. At the same time, to render his nobles benevolent, Louis chose never to tax them, but taxed only the commoners who made up the Third Estate instead.

However impressive the structure of Louis' monarchy, not all of its policies were either successful or well conceived. In total, Louis involved himself in four wars. In his first two wars he made minor gains in the Spanish Netherlands and annexed the Franche Comté to France (arguably Louis' most significant victory, as it secured his borders with Germany). His final two wars ended in a stalemate, with Louis pitted against nearly every major power in Europe. In his final war, the War of the Spanish Succession (1702-13), Louis sought nothing less than the establishment of his own grandson upon the throne of the Spanish Empire. This protracted war brought loss upon loss to the French, exacerbated an already staggering royal debt, forced further excessive taxes,

angered an ever more restive peasantry and came closer than ever before to pushing France to the breaking point. At length Louis agreed to the Treaty of Utrecht (1713), which set the boundaries for much of the European world down to the twentieth century. By this treaty Britain acquired the island of Minorca and Gibraltar and was given the monopoly on slaves to the Spanish Empire; Austria acquired many of Spain's possessions in Europe, principally the Spanish Netherlands and Milan. Louis did see his grandson installed as King of Spain, although with the proviso that the kingdoms of Spain and France would never be united. Henceforth both kingdoms would be under Bourbon rule, but neither line of the family would prove to be of any great benefit to the other.

Among the other failed policies of Louis' reign was his miscalculated expulsion of the Huguenots

in 1685. Like his great-grandfather, Philip II of Spain, Louis was adamantly convinced that the unity of the kingdom required uniformity in religion. Louis had, in fact, always regarded his Huguenot subjects with a deep-seated mistrust. He ignored all efforts to persuade him that the Huguenot population was responsible for much of France's wealth and prosperity and at length revoked the Edict of Nantes. The result was an exodus of well over 100,000 Huguenots from the realm, many of them peerless artisans, merchants and high-ranking members of the armed forces. Most Frenchmen regarded this as an act of exceptional stupidity, although some churchmen and the king's own consort, Madame de Maintenon, held it to be an act of exemplary piety.

Louis' religious problems did not arise solely from his non-Catholic subjects. A vociferous Catholic minority was beginning to complain about the laxity of priests and the religious orders. Conservative theologians might have been more willing to listen to some of these criticisms if they had not occurred at a time when some scientists and philosophers were beginning to challenge outright traditionally held views of the Church on morality and cosmology. Conservatives accused the Jesuits of being implicated in a conspiracy to make concessions to these libertine movements. Attacks on the Society of Jesus came to a head in the famous controversy over grace, which flared up after the publication of the *Augustinus* in 1640, two years after the death of its author, Cornelius Jansen (1581-1638), former professor of theology at Louvain and later Bishop of Ypres. The work stirred up a controversy between the Jansenists, who were known for their strict Augustinian position on grace and election, and the Jesuits, who maintained a moderate position of human 'co-operation.' In 1653 the Jansenist position was condemned by Pope Innocent X, stating that its tenets had already been pronounced heretical. The Pope's condemnation, however, did not settle the matter. Many rushed to the side of the Jansen-

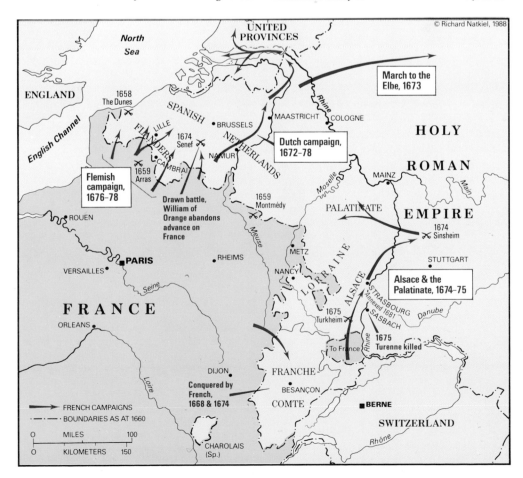

Left: A scene from the War of the Polish Succession showing a French encampment. The war allowed France to gain control of Lorraine.

Right: A scene from the Battle of Quiberon Bay, fought during the Seven Years' War. A British force under Admiral Hawke inflicted a reverse on a French fleet under Marshal Conflans.

Below: John Law, a Scottish financier, attempted to reorganize France's monetary system during the reign of Louis XV. His bungling led to an even greater economic crisis.

Below right: Charles II returns to England, invited back in 1660 at the request of leading figures in the British establishment of the day.

ists. Among their supporters was Blaise Pascal (1623-62) whose *Provincial Letters* (1656) satirized the confessional practices of the Jesuits, whom he saw as tailoring religion to suit the lives of less than exemplary Catholics.

Reacting to papal meddling in French affairs, the *parlements*, members of the clergy, and the king himself stated clearly the limits of the Pope's authority in French religious affairs. In the Gallican Articles of 1682 the clergy, with the backing of the king, reaffirmed the traditional French position that the Pope was hardly more than the Bishop of Rome, with no temporal authority whatsoever in France. Ten years later, when Louis and the Pope had reached an understanding, Louis reconsidered the potential danger of Jansenism, and chose to suppress it. In 1709 and 1710 he shut down the two monasteries at Port Royal. Without the presence of these institutions, the movement dissolved. In 1713, now at the prompting of Louis, Pope Clement XI dealt the death blow to the Jansenist movement with his bull *Unigenitus*.

France in the eighteenth century

Louis' death in 1715 ended an age in which the French king had reigned supreme in France and had shaped with his policies the political configurations of Europe. His own courtly style had set the standards for aristocratic display and taste in nearly every capital of Europe and beyond. Yet most Frenchmen were pleased to see the end of his reign. Under Louis taxation had increased to unbearable levels, as peasants shouldered the burdens which nobles refused to lift. French subjects decried corruption in government, the selling of offices, restrictive trade barriers, constant war with little result, and even their vainglorious and overly pampered monarch. To those looking back upon this era in the period after the French Revolution, the *ancien régime* would appear as one of extreme contrasts between the concentrated wealth of the feudal landlords and Church on the one hand and the great penury of non-privileged classes on the other, between those free of taxes and commoners burdened with the massive debts of state, between the cities and the country, 'enlightened' ideas and grim realities.

In 1715 the five-year-old Louis XV (1715-74) ascended the throne of his grandfather. Along with the crown of France he inherited a staggering financial debt and a bundle of nearly incurable social problems that required immediate attention. Despite Louis XIV's reorganization of the administrative system, numerous ills had crept in which resulted in widespread corruption, confusion and inequities. During the regency of Philip, Duke of Orleans (1715-23), the king's uncle and a scheming bumbler, France's monetary crisis escalated, particularly after a stock crash in 1720 brought on by an even greater schemer, the Scotsman John Law (1671-1729). Law, together with the Duke of Orleans, had sought to stimulate the French economy by issuing stock in the Mississippi Company, the stock being redeemable for paper currency issued by Law's bank. But when investors tried to exchange their paper currency for gold, the scheme collapsed for want of hard currency to back the paper. Among the victims of the ensuing panic were not only Law's bank but the credibility of the whole French monetary system.

It was only with the appointment in 1726 of the 73-year-old Cardinal Fleury (1653-1743), the young king's tutor, that France began to reverse her financial and administrative decay. Fleury was the last of the great cardinal-statesmen, and a worthy successor to Richelieu. In fact, under Fleury France entered into her most stable years in the eighteenth century. Much like his English contemporary, Robert Walpole, Fleury pursued a policy of peace and financial consolidation. Only in 1733, when the question of succession to the crown of Poland arose and Polish nobles supported Stanislaus, an heir to the crown whose daughter was married to King Louis, was Fleury forced to break his program of peace. Despite some modest territorial gains in the War of the Polish Succession (1733-35), such as the Duchy of Lorraine, France made no sustained effort to restore Stanislaus to his throne; instead France installed him as King of Lorraine, a title he held until his death in 1766, when Lorraine was absorbed into the kingdom of France.

Despite the limited military success, the cardinal reckoned the return to peace as the greater

victory. Fleury's conservative, though adroit, handling of foreign and domestic policies unfortunately did not continue long. Three years before his death he was dragged once again into war, this time the War of the Austrian Succession (1740-48), during which Fleury himself died (1743) and Louis XV himself stepped in to direct the affairs of state. In less than a decade after the end of this war France plunged into direct conflict with England in the Seven Years' War (1756-63), also known in North America as the French and Indian War, the result of which was the loss of most of France's overseas empire. Both wars severely strained the country's resources, and this led to still more oppressive taxation and other ingenious schemes to enhance revenue. Louis, who at one time had been known as 'the well-loved' (*le bien-aimé*), came to be hated by his people.

The king was in fact ill-suited to run the government on a daily basis. He suffered from bad judgment in selecting his ministers, shiftlessness in policy decision, intimidation by his nobles and domination by his mistresses, especially Madame de Pompadour (1721-64). In time, his patience for governing decreased, and he preferred to fritter away his time at Versailles in hunting, gambling and luxurious socializing. Yet the legacy of centralized monarchy meant that there was no one else to attend to the affairs of state, for by now the nobles were incapable of governing the country.

Although the monarchy itself remained relatively secure, eighteenth-century France witnessed a steady weakening of its power and prestige. Early in the century, the Duke of Orleans had made generous concessions to the *parlements*, 12 (and later 13) provincial judicial assemblies controlled by the old nobility, the most important being the *parlement* of Paris. To these Orleans granted full recognition of their traditional rights, the most important of which was to veto any law or request for money proposed by the king. The crown's inability to extract taxes from the nobility virtually guaranteed that it would be chronically hard-pressed for funds, even though the French economy was healthy and growing. Resources were plentiful, yet short-sighted policies had strangled the monarchy's financial arteries. Since the seventeenth century, the crown had relied heavily on short-term measures: selling new offices and granting monopolies and patents of nobility. Each measure brought in some money, but each effectively blocked further revenues in the future. Individuals might grow rich in this system, but the government could not.

When Louis XVI (ruled 1774-92) acceded to the throne he followed his father's pattern of allowing his ministers to govern. Yet, more than his predecessor, he recognized that reforms had to be made, especially in the matter of the massive national debt. Aware of his own incompetence to direct the affairs of state, Louis appointed a series of ministers who went to work to reform finances and stimulate the country's economy. Among the more able individuals appointed to the post of Minister of Finance was Jacques Turgot (1727-81), who advocated, above all, a tax on the nobles and the clergy. This policy provoked an immediate

outcry against him, and Turgot was dismissed. Jacques Necker succeeded Turgot, and his publication of the *Compte Rendu* (a financial statement of income and expenses) pointed out, among other things, the folly of awarding huge pensions to aristocrats, and above all those granted by the extravagant queen, Marie Antoinette, to her favorites at court. Necker was also dismissed. In the end Louis had no alternative but to call an Assembly of Notables (1787), hoping to persuade them to agree to being taxed. The assembly refused to deal with the problem and referred it instead to the one body in France that had tradi-

England after Cromwell

Soon after the death in 1658 of Oliver Cromwell, the 'Lord Protector' of the realm, his successor, General George Monck assembled Parliament to discuss the question of rule. Parliament voted swiftly for the return of the monarchy and invited Charles, the son of Charles I, to return to England as the new king. Charles obliged, and ruled from 1660 until his death in 1685. His reign was characterized by cautious, peaceful relations with all European powers except the Dutch, a fair amount of religious toleration and discretion in dealing with Parliament. Rather than asking Parliament to underwrite his luxuries, for example, Charles negotiated a secret settlement with Louis XIV, whereby he would receive £200,000 a year in exchange for keeping his country out of war with France. Though hardly gifted as a strong leader, Charles maintained a most-needed equilibrium in England throughout his reign. The country had had enough of war and fanaticism, and was content with the change of style, however ungodly Charles's somewhat libertine manner might have seemed to those of Puritan sects.

Upon Charles's death, the question of succession again emerged, since his brother, the new King James II (1685-88), openly professed Roman Catholicism, and his attitudes about kingship seemed little different from his father's and grandfather's. Unlike Charles, James was quick to alienate Parliament by demanding toleration for Protestant nonconformists and Roman Catholics alike, and by appointing several Catholics to key positions. James might have weathered the tensions he created had he not had the misfortune of siring a son who, it was anticipated, would carry out his designs to restore Roman Catholicism to England. It took little time for the two political parties, Whigs and Tories, to concur that the king had to go. To ensure the continuance of the parliamentary form of government and that the succession pass to someone of the Church of England,

the nobles negotiated with William of Orange of the Netherlands, an avowed anti-Catholic, who had married James II's daughter Mary. In 1688 both William and Mary were invited to come to England and be invested with the royal power as joint monarchs.

On 5 November 1688 William landed with his army at Torbay and was opposed by only scattered resistance. On 10 December James, his wife and son were bundled off to Dover and forced to flee to France, where they were maintained by Louis XIV. James never renounced his claims to the British throne, and shortly after his exile made an unsuccessful attempt in northern Ireland, with aid from the French, to unseat William, who soundly defeated him in July 1690 at the Battle of the Boyne. In later years James and his descendants – the Stuart 'pretenders' – made further attempts to regain their lost crown, but they never commanded sufficient strength or sympathy. The deft handling of the negotiations leading to the ousting of James II thus resulted in

a nearly bloodless coup, to which the name 'The Glorious Revolution' has been given. Its significance lay in its orchestration by Parliament. From now on in England, the rule of law took precedence over any consideration of the prerogatives of monarchy.

To safeguard the throne in the future from anyone espousing theories of divine right or advocating Roman Catholicism, Parliament passed the Declaration of Rights in February 1689. In this they made it clear that all monarchs would be subject to law and would rule by the consent of Parliament. Later, in June 1701, Parliament passed the Act of Settlement to resolve the question of succession, as Mary had died in 1694. (William would die in 1702, and James II in 1701.) Upon the death of William, James II's second daughter, Anne Stuart, married to Prince George of Denmark, would succeed to the throne (and would rule until 1714). In the event that none of Anne's seventeen children survived her, she was to be succeeded by Sophia, the Protestant granddaughter of James I and daughter of Frederick, the Elector Palatine. None of Anne's children did survive her, so George I (1714-27), son of Sophia of the House of Hanover (or Brunswick – Braunschweig), acceded to the throne of Great Britain, then so called after the parliamentary union of England and Scotland in 1707. Eighteenth- and early nineteenth-century Britain would be known as the Georgian period, as it was to be ruled by the four successive Georges until 1830. And until the present, the House of Hanover (renamed in 1917 the House of Windsor) has retained the crown of Great Britain.

By the early years of the eighteenth century Great Britain had begun to assume a much greater political and economic role in European affairs. The War of the Spanish Succession, which ended with the Treaty of Utrecht (1713), signaled the direction Great Britain would take as a leading power in the new century. As a result of the treaty Louis XIV recognized the Protestant succession in Britain and renounced his support of the Stuarts. Great Britain also acquired strategic territories in the Mediterranean – Gibraltar and Minorca. In North America she acquired the Hudson's Bay territory, Acadia (Nova Scotia), Newfoundland and St Kitts. Spain surrendered to the British the *asiento* – that is, the right to provide Spanish America with slaves from Africa. This privilege alone accounted for an enormous rise in British shipping, and made wealthy the west coast

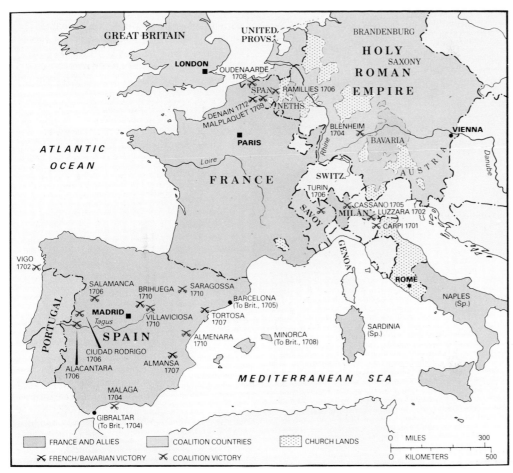

English ports of Bristol and Liverpool, which were second only to London in this period. The concession of the *asiento* was a substantial blow to Spain's grand maritime empire, which now opened itself up to profitable smuggling ventures by the British in Spanish America.

As Great Britain ventured into overseas trading her leaders steered a wise course of consolidation, prosperity and peace. Sir Robert Walpole (1676-1745), the first great prime minister produced by the cabinet and party system, was a Whig who came to power after saving the finances of the country. Walpole understood the disastrous economic consequences of war and the economic benefits of peace. His motto, *Quieta non movere* (loosely, 'If it's not broken, don't fix it'), captures well his conservative administration. Supported fully by George I, he resisted advocates of war throughout his administration (1721-42), which has come to be known as the 'Augustan Age' for its peace, prosperity and stability. Despite Walpole's shrewd direction of state, his mainte-

nance of the status quo, his masterful touch with the system of patronage and the growing material prosperity of the country, his success eventually ran out when the country lost patience with peace. In 1739 the war party produced a certain Captain Jenkins, who testified to the indignities inflicted upon the British on the Spanish main. Jenkins displayed to the crowds a shriveled ear which he kept in a small wooden box; this ear he claimed the Spanish had cut off. Outraged by this horrible act, the English cried out for war. Popular enthusiasm could not be checked, and Great Britain, to Walpole's great disgust, embarked upon the War of Jenkins' Ear, which eventually dragged the British into a series of European wars (for which many names have been given). Today historians generally speak of two wars (though they really are two phases of the same conflict): the War of the Austrian Succession (1740-48) and the Seven Years' War (1756-63). As a result of the latter war, the British, now under the leadership of William Pitt (1708-78), acquired from France all of eastern North America from Quebec to the Mississippi River; they had also taken the French West Indies and had laid claim to most of India. But in its quest for a dominant position on the Continent and in the New World Great Britain had expended enormous sums.

Shortly after George III's (1760-1820) accession to the throne, William Pitt retired from office after disagreeing with the new king over policies. George found his selection of successor ministers generally to the House of Commons' disliking, and from 1761 to 1770 he saw a great number depart. Finally, in 1770, he appointed Lord North (1732-92), who functioned as Prime Minister until 1782, at which time he resigned upon hearing the news of Cornwallis's surrender to George Washington at Yorktown.

As successful as Britain's territorial expansion was abroad, she was plagued by conflicts generated by the king's attempts to have his way with the House of Commons. Popular outrage against taxation and the system of representation in Parliament was heard not merely in the colonies but in Great Britain as well. In the latter eighteenth

Above left: George III's reign was marked by the loss of overseas territory in the New World but by industrial expansion at home.

Left: The Prince of Orange, later William III, lands at Torbay in 1688 to take the throne from the unpopular James II.

Above: The course of the War of the Spanish Succession, which ended with the signing of the Treaty of Utrecht in 1713.

Right: British troops land near the Canadian fortress of Louisbourg prior to doing battle with the city's French garrison.

no male heir and so faced the threat of a possible collapse of the Habsburg holdings. To forestall this he fought for the recognition of his solution to the problem of succession, which he provided in the Pragmatic Sanction, a document that would permit the Habsburg inheritance to pass through his daughter Maria Theresa (ruled, 1740-80). Upon Charles's death Maria Theresa's legal right to the Habsburg holdings was secure. She had, however, no real army to enforce her family's claims and little money with which to procure one. Moreover, within months of becoming sovereign, the 23-year-old monarch had to face a daunting challenge from the army of Frederick II of Prussia, who invaded her province of Silesia and drew her into a war, since known as the War of the Austrian Succession (1740-48). Besides the Prussians, the Habsburgs had to face the French as well, who were drawn into the war (against Cardinal Fleury's better judgment) to humiliate their long-standing arch-rival. Against all disadvantages, Maria Theresa surprisingly united her nobles, even the restive Magyars, to help her in fending off the Prussians and attempting to regain Silesia. The British, too, entered the conflict on the side of Maria Theresa, as they wanted to keep the Austrian Netherlands from falling into the hands of the French. Although the Habsburgs never regained Silesia, they managed to hold on to the remainder of their lands, and in 1748 the Treaty of Aix-la-Chapelle reaffirmed all the prewar boundaries save for Silesia, which the Prussians kept.

century, Britain's far-flung responsibilities pushed her to find ever new sources of income to sustain an empire and pay the price of war. Among Britain's most lucrative sources of revenue had been the colonies of North America. Their loss was a severe economic blow, for it preceded by just 10 years a period during which Britain would have to fight a war with revolutionary (and later Imperial) France that would last 20 years.

Habsburg Austria

At the close of the Thirty Years' War in 1648 the Austrian Habsburgs ruled over a severely fragmented relic of the Holy Roman Empire. Their connections with the Habsburgs of Spain were effectively severed, economic distress prevailed, no real central authority unified their widely scattered territories and they acquired little support from any other power in Europe. Yet the Habsburgs would manage to hold the title of Holy Roman Emperor until 1806, when Napoleon would finally dissolve the empire. In fact, during the interval between the Peace of Westphalia and 1806 they would extend their rule well beyond their traditional holdings, to the kingdom of Bohemia, Hungary, the duchies of Moravia and Silesia, the Spanish Netherlands and large territories in the Italian peninsula (Lombardy and, for a while, the Kingdom of Naples).

Despite the greatest administrative, ethnic and religious difficulties, the Habsburgs slowly managed to bring considerable order into such a wide diversity. The Holy Roman Emperor, Leopold I (1657-1705), rallied his subjects against two common enemies: the Ottoman Turks, who in 1683 lay siege to Vienna, and Louis XIV. By 1699 the Habsburgs had gained the offensive and concluded a treaty with the Turks, giving them control over Hungary, Croatia, Slavonia and Transylvania.

Joseph I (1705-11) and Charles VI (1711-40) succeeded Leopold and skillfully continued his policies in ruling the diverse territories of the empire. Yet Charles was unfortunate in producing

Maria Theresa's son, Joseph II (ruled, 1780-90), carried on the Habsburg policies of centralization and, when opportune, territorial expansion. Dedicated wholly to ideas of 'enlightened absolutism,' Joseph consciously sought to make his laws rational, his country productive and his government efficient. He demanded that German be the universal language within his lands, a move that did not sit well with his Magyar nobles. Doubtless the most radical reform of his reign was his emancipation of the serfs in the empire, an example of what true economic and social reform could achieve. Joseph was concerned with religious reform. Between 1780 and 1790 he initiated sweeping reforms directed at Roman Catholicism, which policies have since come to be known as Josephinism, and in 1781 he issued his Toleration Edict, giving freedom of worship to Lutheran, Calvinist and Greek Orthodox churches. At the same time he sought to break the power of the Roman Catholic bishops by forbidding them contact with the Pope and by reserving to the state the right to regulate ecclesiastical affairs. Joseph's policies collapsed after his death, but his efforts illustrate well the Enlightenment's ideas of religious tolerance and of subordinating ecclesiastical authority to the authority of the state, and his social reforms gave other peoples of Europe hope that a day might come when such might occur in their own lands as well.

In 1740, when Frederick II (1712-86), 'the Great,' became King of Prussia, he followed his father Frederick William I in aggrandizing the power of the German territory of Brandenburg-Prussia. Frederick II proved to be a startling individual, one whose appearance and actions brought Prussia to world attention. Heir to a somewhat grim militaristic tradition Frederick at first seemed miscast for the role he was to play. Given to music and the reading of history and poetry, he showed little initial inclination to follow the examples of his Hohenzollern forebears. Yet he proved to be the foremost militarist of them all. Unlike his predecessors, who had carefully built up the well-disciplined Prussian army as a defensive weapon, Frederick embarked on a policy of aggression almost immediately after he became ruler of Prussia. Among his first acts was the invasion of the province of Silesia, which belonged to the young Habsburg monarch, Maria Theresa – a fateful event for the politics of eighteenth-century Europe.

Of all monarchs in the age of the Enlightenment Frederick II has come to embody the spirit of the age. A gifted writer, friend of intellectuals, religious skeptic and talented musician, he made his court at Sans Souci in Potsdam a haven for thinkers, among them Voltaire. He opened his predominantly Lutheran lands as a refuge for such victims of sectarian strife as Catholics, Jews, Huguenots and religious non-conformists. Among his other more notable acts were the codification of Prussian law, a widespread improvement in agricultural methods, reclamation of unproductive land, establishment of standards for manufactured products and the opening of a Land-Mortgage Credit Association for farmers. He referred to himself as 'the first servant of the State.'

Despite Frederick's many admirable traits, he was a thoroughgoing authoritarian who sought to make his bureaucracy a potent instrument of administration, revenue collection and control. In his words, all matters of state were to be 'coordinated to the same end: namely, the integration of the state and the increase of its power.' There was not much room for democracy in this concept. To maintain the loyalty of his Junkers (that is, the large landowner class), Frederick ruthlessly taxed his peasants and towns and gave the nobles the full advantages of their position. He also invited the Junkers to assume commands in his army, which he molded into an extraordinary fighting-machine.

It was during the Seven Years' War (1756-63) that Europe became most fully aware of the power of the Prussian army and of the tactical genius of the Prussian king. Facing an overwhelming coalition of Austria, Russia and France, Frederick humbled his enemies for four years with a dazzling string of victories. But in 1760 the tide of battle finally turned against him, and in the next two years it seemed that Prussia would surely be crushed. Then, in 1762, a new czar, Peter III, ascended to the Russian throne, and, being a staunch admirer of Frederick, he abruptly withdrew Russia from the war. Now the road to victory was again open to Frederick, and he made the most of it. By the time of the Peace of Hubertusburg in 1763, which ratified all of Frederick's previous conquests, Prussia was acknowledged the foremost military power in Europe.

Frederick made one final conquest, though this time a bloodless one. In 1772, fearing that the Russia of Catherine the Great was about to annex Poland, he proposed that the bulk of that hapless country be partitioned among Prussia, Russia and Austria. Since no one felt like challenging the powerful Prussian monarch, the plan was accepted. The result of this cynical maneuver was both a very great increase in the size of Prussia and the beginning of the process whereby the ancient kingdom of Poland would eventually (1795) disappear from the map of Europe.

The intellectual achievement of the Enlightenment

Immanuel Kant's celebrated essay *Enlightenment* (1784) defined enlightenment as 'man's leaving his self-caused immaturity,' by which he meant the inability to think for himself. The age of Enlightenment was one in which intellectuals, despite different disciplines and particular visions, shared a common inspiration: the belief that the human race was progressing from childish prejudice and barbaric ignorance to a period of reason and moral maturity. Science and reason could be applied to the study of all human institutions and experience. One no longer had to appeal to the authority of mystery, but could deduce nature's laws from observable phenomena. Man himself was at last the measure of all things.

Historians generally assign the dates 1715-89 to the Enlightenment; that is, the period from the death of Louis XIV to the beginning of the French Revolution – a span of some 74 years of extraordinary intellectual ferment in historiography, politics, religion, philosophy and every other discipline. But the Enlightenment did not appear full-blown on the stage of Europe. It had many precedents in England and France before 1715, and perhaps the most fundamental of these was the rapid development of science and scientific thought in the sixteenth and seventeenth centuries.

Above far left: Joseph I, son of Francis I and Maria Theresa. Despite his energetic attempts to unite Austria-Hungary, his reign ended in turmoil.

Above left: Maria Theresa of Austria. A noted reformer in times of peace, her prime ambition in time of war was the recovery of Silesia – lost to Prussia during the War of the Austrian Succession.

Left: Leopold I (1657-1705) did much to secure Austria's position as a leading European power by gaining extensive territories from the Ottoman Turks and helping thwart Louis XIV's imperial ambitions in Germany.

Right: Responsible for bringing Prussia to the center of the European political stage, Frederick II forged the Prussian army into a formidable fighting force, making it the leading tool of his political policy.

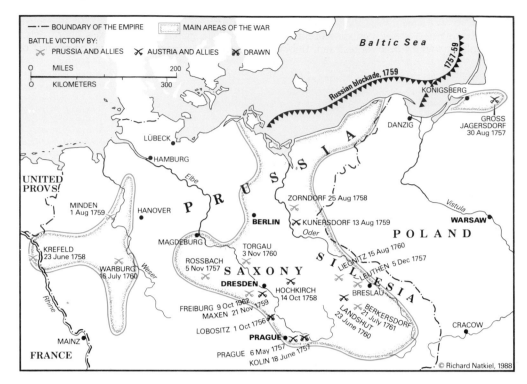

The concept of discovering a 'Natural Religion' was perhaps the ultimate expression of Enlightenment optimism and faith in reason. It was also a much more fundamental challenge to traditional Church authority even than Protestantism had been, for it was by no means clear how far a Natural Religion could be equated with Christianity, or with any other existing faith. Some prominent Enlightenment figures – Frederick the Great, for example – frankly declared themselves non-Christians. Others clung to such highly dilute forms of Christian belief as Deism, in which God appeared solely as the creator of the world machine and did not otherwise intervene in human affairs by such means as revelation or miracle. But it was expected that all doubts and confusions would gradually recede as the laws of the Natural Religion became more manifest. When, by the end of the eighteenth century, they had not, and indeed when it began to appear that making the leap from a mechanistic physical science to an equally mechanistic science of man was going to be much more difficult than had once been supposed, people not only began to return to more traditional forms of religious belief, but the Enlightenment spirit itself began to transmute into a less naïvely optimistic vision of what science and reason would achieve in the foreseeable future. Yet if the Enlightenment's enthusiasms were destined to end in a certain degree of disappointment, there is no denying that throughout the eighteenth century those same enthusiasms had produced a stunning array of intellectual accomplishments.

Perhaps more than anything else, the Enlightenment of the eighteenth century is associated with the *philosophes*, intellectuals noted for their urbanity, wit, reason, dazzling ideas and, usually, moral virtue. The *philosophes* were really not philosophers as such, but were dedicated to the unrestricted application of reason to the world of human experience. Located throughout Europe, from England to Italy and Prussia, their popularity lay in their provocative, critical thinking, which called into question the accepted customs, institutions and traditions of their days. Their words found a welcome reception among many audiences, but the one setting most commonly associated with them was the salon of prominent, though not necessarily aristocratic, ladies such as Madame Necker or Madame Geoffrin, where people met to discuss Enlightenment ideas.

Among the most renowned of the *philosophes* was François Marie de Aróuet (1694-1778), known as Voltaire, whose breadth of interests ranged from history to law, from religion to science and literature. His life spans almost the entire Enlightenment and more than any other exemplifies the spirit of the period. Committed to social reform, peace and tolerance, Voltaire's literary attacks on everything held sacred, including Joan of Arc, so irritated conservatives that he was forced to flee from France and seek refuge at the court of Frederick II of Prussia and at the homes of others more receptive to his ideas. He eventually settled close to the Swiss border at Ferney, near Geneva, just a speedy step away to escape the displeasure of his king. Though opposed to atheism, Voltaire rejected supernatural explanations for natural and moral evils. His *Candide* (1759) struck at Leibniz's (1646-1716) optimistic explanations for God's universe, expressed in the phrase 'the best of all possible worlds.' His *Philosophical Dictionary* (1764) pilloried the Bible's puerile histories and the Church's resort to miracles and the supernatural to hold captive simple people. Despite Voltaire's commanding stature, he did not escape attacks by other *philosophes*, especially in his later years.

Above left: The Seven Years' War, showing the major theaters and battles of the conflict.

Left: A scene of society life in the 'Age of Enlightenment' – a literary society meets in a salon.

Right: Denis Diderot, French philosopher and critic. Diderot's attack on religious obscurantism brought him into conflict with the Church and helped make him a hero of the Enlightenment.

Far right: The title page from Thomas Hobbes's *Leviathan*, a seminal work of political thought that has remained influential up to the present day.

Among the greatest achievements of the Enlightenment was the publication of the *Encyclopédie*. Published between 1751 and 1780 under the editorship of Denis Diderot (1713-84) and Jean le Rond d'Alembert (1717-83), the *Encyclopédie*, which ran to 35 volumes, represented an unprecedented scholarly endeavor to encompass the entire world of arts and sciences and to put contemporary learning in the hands of everyone. Contributors to the work were drawn from among the leading thinkers of the time – Voltaire, Necker, Rousseau and Lamarck – who presented 'secularized' accounts of their subjects. Despite ecclesiastical censorship, the editors and their like-minded contributors managed to slip into smaller articles on seemingly innocuous subjects their unorthodox views on theology and government. The *Encyclopédie* was widely printed and disseminated throughout Europe, and its definitions were echoed among intellectuals as far as the New World.

Politics and good government

Of the many subjects with which the *philosophes* dealt, none was to have more historical impact than their theories about government. Although earlier political theorists had analyzed the workings of government, few had debated which type of government *should* prevail. Among those who championed absolute monarchy was Thomas Hobbes (1588-1679), whose work on political theory, *Leviathan* (1651), represented an important shift from the 'divine right of kings' theory to one based upon a negative view of man's nature and condition and his need for restraint. Hobbes believed that in a world where the goods of nature were scarce and humans plentiful, fierce competition inevitably resulted. In nature, man's basest impulses would prevail in acquiring these goods to the detriment of every other individual. Under these circumstances a higher sovereign authority with sufficient force was necessary to curb man's desire for unlimited power. It was a matter of common sense, and not theology, that a king or some other ruling body should be the ultimate and strong sovereign. But in the event the central authority should cease to provide justice and security for society, the tacit social contract that had originally created the sovereign was automatically dissolved. Thus Hobbes was far from advocating tyranny, but his desire to establish a secure society based upon a strong central government left little room for articulating the rights of the individual.

More influential than Hobbes in the eighteenth century was John Locke (1632-1704), who extended the idea of a tacit social contract into an analysis of the structure of society itself. Like Hobbes, Locke rejected the idea of divine rights of any kind and began his analysis by picturing man in his basic state of nature (though Locke's nature is much less hostile than that of Hobbes). Again, men 'contract' to form a state, whose main function is to adjudicate society's inevitable disputes in accordance with natural law and to protect individual rights. High on Locke's list of rights was that of property, defined as the product of each man's labor; thus he anticipated the labor theory of value. He believed in governments whose powers are defined by constitutions, and he believed those powers should be limited by a system of internal checks and balances. His influence on the thinking of the Founding Fathers of the United States would be difficult to overestimate.

As thinkers in Britain had enjoyed far greater tolerance and freedom of expression than those in France, French intellectuals held the British system of government and religious toleration up as a kind of model for the reforms they wished to implement. With the death of Louis XIV in 1715, nobles and bourgeois alike grew enthusiastic about the prospect of a change to something more akin to the British parliamentary system of government. Among the greatest proponents of such a change was Charles Louis de Secondat, Baron de Montesquieu (1689-1755), whose *The Persian Letters* (1721) pilloried existing institutions in France. His most incisive work, however, was *The Spirit of the Laws* (1748), which called attention to the rational model of the British constitution and advocated its adoption. In the matter of French politics this was increasingly urgent.

Perhaps no other work on politics at this time had quite the lasting impact upon France as that of Jean Jacques Rousseau's (1712-78) *The Social*

Contract (1762), for it enunciated a political possibility as well as the popular sentiment of alienation, felt by so many French men and women, from a government so pitifully out of touch with their views. Rousseau opened his work with a provocative line – 'Man is born free, and everywhere he is in chains' – and from start to finish his work represented a radical statement on the necessity for republican government. In Rousseau's ideal state, 'all legitimate government is, of its nature, republican,' and 'the legislative Power belongs to the People.' However complex and at times enigmatic Rousseau's argument was, his readers found phrases or slogans with which to identify. Although Rousseau's work seems to have had little impact on his contemporary philosophes, it would have a shattering impact upon the next generation of men and women in the French Revolution.

Just as Renaissance historians had always looked with keen interest upon the history of ancient Rome, historians of the Enlightenment turned avidly to this subject as well, but their interests were somewhat different. Their concerns lay in new interpretations of Greek and Roman histories, ones that departed from the traditional view of God directing the growth of Christianity and that sometimes even implied that Christianity may have been subversive of culture and human progress. Thinkers held up the achievements of the ancient Greek and Roman republics as models of government, virtuous living, service and freedom. Edward Gibbon's (1737-94) The History of the Decline and Fall of the Roman Empire (1776-88), still regarded as a classic of historical writing, represents this new view of history. Gibbon adhered closely to the rationalists' rejection of supernatural causality as an explanation for the advance of Christianity and instead reduced Christianity's attraction and growth to purely 'natural' causes. Gibbon argued, too, that wherever progress had been thwarted by tyranny or religious authoritarianism, the human spirit suffered. The new views of human history and of human progress implicitly raised politically charged questions. Did institutions and social circumstances have to remain as they were? What forms of government had been most successful from the point of view of the governed? Could the laws of history be discerned, and if so, whose side were they on? What role had religion played in human history?

The Enlightenment and religion

As the seventeenth and eighteenth centuries fashioned a more accurate knowledge of the world's shape, size and history, Europeans also learned more about the multiplicity of cultures spread across the earth. These discoveries stimulated thinkers to explore the implications of such a world set within so remarkable a universe. The reports of explorers, traders and missionaries returning to Europe with stories of peoples who did not know of Christ, whose customs were oddly different from those of Europeans, yet who seemed neither benighted nor unhappy, raised questions about Europe's ethnocentric assumptions. How could one be sure that one's religion, customs and ideas were correct and others false? Were all other peoples of the earth wrong, and only Europeans right? Shouldn't each religion be allowed to exist and follow its own lights, provided it did not threaten the country or corrupt individuals?

In the late seventeenth century, John Locke composed his Letter on Toleration (1689), which articulated the attitudes shared by so many of his countrymen and by others of the next century.

Locke argued that, though there should be an established Church, it should nonetheless permit freedom of worship to individuals of other creeds (Roman Catholics and atheists excepted). Locke's positions represented a new direction in the religious climate of Europe, one rejecting the intolerance and bigotry of the previous century and demanding empirical evidence for every religious proposition. Above all, religion was to eschew fanaticism and to promote virtuous living.

While some Enlightenment thinkers were able to accommodate their rationalist ideas to Christian beliefs and to the Bible, others turned skeptical. Among the most penetrating critics of the Bible and of many traditional ideas and institutions was Baruch Spinoza (1632-77), a Jew from Amsterdam, who alienated believers and even non-believers by raising pointed questions about the miracles and events recorded in the Bible, about its authorship, and about such questions as immortality, human freedom and the idea of revelation by a personal God. Spinoza raised equally pointed questions about such secular matters as the justice of political institutions and the morality of contemporary customs and existing laws. Although given a generally cold reception by contemporary intellectuals, Spinoza's ideas, mediated by others, gradually came to exert considerable influence in the eighteenth and nineteenth centuries.

In Spinoza's train followed other skeptics such as David Hume (1711-76), who argued in an 'Essay on Miracles' (from his Philosophical Essays Concerning Human Understanding, 1751) that there was no empirical basis for miracles: 'It is contrary to experience that a miracle should be true, but not contrary to experience that testimony should be false.' Julien Offray de La Mettrie (1709-51) and Paul Henri Thiry, Baron d'Holbach (1723-89), were even more radical in their views about God, as

they forcefully rejected the superstitions of the sacred Book and advocated a materialistic view of the world – in effect, an atheistic position. Yet these were not among the mainstream of the age's thinkers, who continued to stress the 'reasonableness' of belief in a supreme deity.

Eighteenth-century law

The Enlightenment's insistence upon more stringent rules of evidence in religion and the sciences spilled over into many areas of social life as well. By the late seventeenth century, for example, the number of witchcraft cases being tried in courts had declined dramatically. (The celebrated case of the witch-hysteria in Salem, Massachusetts, in 1692 actually occurred at the end of the general persecution of the seventeenth century, and its very anomaly accounts largely for its popular interest.) Although notable progress in defining rules of evidence and defendants' rights had occurred in the courts of England, enough injustices still occurred in France so that popular outrage against them drew further attention to the widening gap between Enlightened thought and unenlightened practice. The celebrated case of Jean Calas of Toulouse – who had been tortured and strangled without a trial for allegedly murdering a son wishing to convert to Roman Catholicism – aroused Voltaire to write his famous Treatise on Toleration (1763) demanding a reinvestigation of the case.

If humans were to live moral lives in society according to reason, then the laws of that society (that is, positive law) had to conform somehow to the laws of nature. The Italian Cesare Beccaria's (1738-94) On Crimes and Punishment (1764) called for an enlightened system of punishment for crime that abolished torture and capital punishment and advocated putting the age's ideas into a program of practical reforms. Beccaria's

Left: The noted English philosopher John Locke. His major treatise, the philosophical work Essay Concerning Human Understanding examined the nature of thought.

Above right: Edward Gibbon, the English historian primarily remembered for his famous historical work, The Decline and Fall of the Roman Empire.

Above far right: Jean Calas being executed – without trial – for the alleged murder of a son wishing to convert to Catholicism. This travesty of justice aroused Voltaire to write his Treatise on Toleration.

Right: The Scottish philosopher David Hume wrote Philosophical Essays Concerning Human Understanding, which argued that knowledge came through impressions and ideas.

work found some monarchs receptive (at least publicly): both Catherine the Great of Russia and Joseph II of Austria repeated his ideas in certain decrees, and Joseph in fact eliminated torture and capital punishment. Yet despite the popularity of Beccaria's views among the Enlightened, capital punishment would remain a prominent part of the European system of punishment, and would reach new heights in France during the Terror.

In terms of political and social organization, religious toleration, rule of law and much else the Enlightenment saw by far the most extensive realization of its ideals in the new United States of America. After 1776, European advocates of democratic reform, self-determination, equal rights and freedom were filled with a new enthusiasm about what the future might hold in store for the Old World. Yet the reality was different from anything they could have imagined. With the horrendous events of the French Revolution, especially during the Terror, savage intolerance, mob violence and the unleashing of a host of irrational forces seemed to cast a black pall over the brilliant light of this age. During the French Revolution, many intellectuals and leaders met their death at the guillotine, and many more fled abroad and denounced the very revolution that at first they had so eagerly embraced. Yet the ideals of the Enlightenment – freedom, toleration, equality, justice – despite the abuses committed in their names, never vanished. Though often repressed temporarily by absolutist governments, movements for political and social reform gained momentum during the next two centuries, and new generations of Europeans at last came to enjoy some of the rights and freedoms that the Enlightenment had so memorably defined.

Europe: 1789-1848

'Man is born free; and everywhere he is in chains.' With these words Jean-Jacques Rousseau's *Social Contract* (1762) set the tenor of thought and action for the six decades between 1789 and 1848. Rousseau in particular, and the eighteenth-century Enlightenment in general, questioned the old sources of political, economic and social authority. Medieval Christian traditions had taught that there would always be sin and suffering in the world. The Enlightenment taught that humanity would progress if the customary arrangements which benefited the few at the expense of the many were challenged. In short, Enlightenment intellectuals defined progress as the growth of individual self-expression and the elimination of authority based on birth, feudal privileges and guild regulations.

The originators of this discourse on freedom known as classical liberalism failed to recognize that diverse economic and ethnic groups might define liberty differently because of unique social circumstances and needs. In the nineteenth century, classical liberalism would thus be forced to create new bonds and regulations to prevent liberty from becoming an anarchic war of all against all. In Rousseau's terms, a contract or constitution had to be drawn up to deal with conflicting projects proposed by free individuals. And that is where the problems developed. If different groups wished to exercise their liberty in fashions that were different, who would determine the most appropriate use of freedom? Where would authority reside?

Liberals argued that authority should reside in constitutional law rather than in the choices made by a few nobles, but who were the 'people' who were to draw up the liberal constitutions? Manufacturers, financiers, merchants and professionals were quick to claim liberalism as their own ideology, defining it primarily in terms of civil liberties and an economic market free of customary price regulation and tariffs. To them liberalism meant free speech and free trade, and its institutional expression was a legislature elected by propertied, and therefore 'responsible,' citizens. But the different definition given liberty by workers, their cry for freedom from want, forced the early liberals to draw up all manner of compromises, both with those beneath them in the social hierarchy and with their aristocratic enemies above.

In 1789 many Europeans were dissatisfied for a number of reasons. Approximately 85 percent of the European population lived by consuming or marketing the produce of the land they farmed. Although more than 50 percent of the land was directly controlled by the peasants, the typical peasant smallholder did not control the most productive and profitable land. Agricultural surpluses for market more generally resulted from the richer soils controlled by noble or non-noble holders of estates. With enough capital reserve to sustain losses in difficult times, the large landowners could afford to experiment with new methods to increase productivity. The average peasant, however, had no reserves to protect against failed experimentation. One bad harvest often led him to borrow against future produce, and any other crop failure led to defaulting on debt payments. As often is the case, small farmers were easy prey to financial speculators and large landowners hoping to increase already substantial holdings.

And as in many areas of the Third World today, production of basic food, in this case bread, failed to keep pace with a growing population. From 1700 to 1800, the European population grew by about one-third, and supply was not keeping pace with demand. Throughout the eighteenth century urban bread riots served as dress rehearsals for the great spasm of revolution at the end of the century. Throughout Europe urban craftsmen and workers attempted to punish those who hoarded grain and turned immense profits in bad times. These crowds demanded prices which were compatible with their purchasing power, defining the common good by means of the lowest common denominator: subsistence needs.

Almost as troubled were the non-noble financiers, professionals and manufacturers. Though affluent, these men were still commoners in a political system that ranked them in the same social group as peasants, shoemakers and bakers. In France, though numerous inroads had been made on noble exemption from taxation, the remnants of this privilege were still tempting enough to prompt commoners to buy noble titles for the sake of exemption. In England, local aristocrats continued in many areas to dominate the selection of representatives to the House of Commons, as well as still having real political influence in the House of Lords. Everywhere, the nobles still predominated in the central advisory and bureaucratic posts. At least in the conventional perception kings were but the most exalted members of the nobility, an elite set on earth by God to order society. They were the heads and arms respectively of the body politic, just as commoners were the support of the whole organism. All parts were to theoretically fulfill their divinely ascribed roles for the sake of the common good; the failure of this system led to the Revolution.

France at the barricades

In 1788 the French government was 4.5 billion livres in debt, and King Louis XVI was compelled to seek additional funds by summoning the medieval institution which traditionally had the power to grant the crown new taxing authority. The Estates-General represented the three French estates or social classes: the First Estate of the Roman Catholic clergy, the Second Estate of the nobility and the Third Estate of the commoners. It had not met since 1614, but the new call in 1788 brought the anticipation that the king would have to grant concessions to the estates of the realm in

Left: In the early nineteenth century, the agitation in Britain against import duties on corn brought rich industrialists, wanting free trade, into a temporary alliance with workers, demanding freedom from want.

Above right: In 1789 King Louis XVI presided over the opening of the Estates-General at Versailles, a formal prelude to the momentous events of the French Revolution.

Right: Prime Minister William Pitt addresses the House of Commons in 1793 – a body predominantly representative of the English landowning class.

order to levy new taxes. Separate elections were held for the representatives of each estate, and at each stage of the elections *cahiers de doléances*, lists of grievances, were drawn up by the voters. In 1788 no one seemed ready to abandon fully the hereditary monarchy and the Church as the two pillars of French society, and all the *cahiers* expressed their loyalty to God and the earthly reflection of his sovereignty, the king.

But whereas the *cahiers* of the nobility stressed the recognition of their traditional liberties (meaning their feudal rights and privileges), the *cahiers* of the Third Estate, written mostly by lawyers, doctors and other representatives of the liberal professions, emphasized the importance of individual liberty and of a written constitution. They also wished to see each French citizen declared equal before the law and free from any burdens of taxation not shared by other French citizens. Thus many of the commoners' *cahiers* demanded that the Third Estate be allowed to send as many representatives to the Estates-General as the other two estates combined, and they urged that voting be by head and not by estate, as tradition prescribed. Recognizing the need for financial reform, the nobles broadly accepted the principle of tax equality, but they were in no way ready to abandon privileged treatment in other areas. The aristocratic Parlement de Paris, the court of last appeal, decided that the Third Estate could be doubled to reflect the demographic predominance of commoners, but voting would continue to be by estate and not by head. As such, the most radical and dangerous recommendation of the Third Estate was nullified.

On 5 May 1789 the Estates-General opened, and matters came to a head almost immediately. The Third Estate tried to persuade the other two to abandon their privileges and vote with the Third as one body. When this failed, the commoners walked out, declaring that they were the only true representatives of the French people. In this act, they reflected Enlightenment ideas popularized in such 1788 pamphlets as the Abbé Sieyès' *What Is the Third Estate?* Sieyès proposed two revolutionary theses: the identification of the nation exclusively with the Third Estate and the claim that the nation alone had the power to give France a constitution. The body politic was no longer to be viewed as the three estates working in unison for the common good under the king's guidance. The first two estates and the king were little more than parasites in the eyes of the representatives of the Third Estate. The Third Estate representatives had the authority of learning and wealth, and they now wanted the political power to go with it. On 17 June the Third Estate practiced what Sieyès preached and declared itself the National Assembly of France, vowing not to disband until centuries of unwritten tradition had been replaced by a drafted constitution. Frightened by his inability to overawe the revolutionaries with words, Louis XVI summoned approximately 20,000 soldiers to the meeting of the Estates-General at Versailles. It was then that the disgruntled crowds of Paris came to the assistance of the rebellious liberals.

Left: The storming of the Bastille prison by citizens of Paris, 14 July 1789.

Below: Maximilien Robespierre, the head of the revolutionary Committee of Public Safety, which imposed a reign of terror on France to defend the Republic against its internal and external enemies.

Right: The French Revolution was never a uniform transformation of life in France: revolts and uprisings in the more radical areas of the country were opposed by counter-revolutionary activity in others.

Far right: J L David's famous painting of the death of the revolutionary leader Marat.

Below right: The guillotine, a new method of execution adopted during the Revolution because it was more humane and efficient than the alternatives — hanging or the axe.

Throughout the eighteenth century French wages had risen about 22 percent, but prices had gone up approximately 45 percent. The small master artisans and workers in the larger cities placed their hope for economic improvement in the Estates-General, and when the King seemed prepared to use armed force against the National Assembly's attempts at reform, Parisian crowds began to take to the streets in search of weapons. On 14 July crowds, mostly made up of residents of the artisan and working-class Saint-Antoine district, stormed the garrison at the Bastille prison and took the armaments kept there. Rather than test the loyalty of his own soldiers, Louis XVI sent them away and recognized a self-appointed citizens committee as the new Parisian town government. He also decreed that the privileged estates take their seats in the National Assembly. A pattern for the nineteeth century was being set: revolt from below would force those in power to grant compromises if they were not willing or able to use repressive force. The bourgeois-dominated National Assembly soon followed the Crown in granting a compromise to an inferior social group.

With approximately one out of four families completely landless and relegated to working estates, agrarian workers were also ready to air their grievances. In late July, the 'Great Fear' erupted in many rural districts. Peasants burned noble chateaux and destroyed manorial records, thus freeing themselves from any feudal dues or work services that might still be owed. On the night of 4 August the Assembly responded by abolishing all special privileges in landed property. No longer could a peasant be taken from the land to repair a lord's house or be forced to grind his grain at the lord's mill.

On 26 August, the Assembly revealed the principles behind its revolutionary acts in the Declaration of the Rights of Man and Citizen. Drawing on the thoughts of Enlightenment thinkers such as John Locke, it defined such inalienable human rights as life, liberty and property. Society was a contract drawn up freely by human beings for their improvement as individuals. The ancient emphasis on the common good resurfaced in a new vein, for now the fraternity of all men was proclaimed and law was to be the expression of the citizens' general will. Rousseau's *Social Contract* had taught that citizens had social duties as well as rights, and the Declaration spoke of an individual's responsibility to the Rousseauian general will. The Assembly recognized that 'Men are born and remain free and equal in rights,' but 'Liberty consists in the ability to do whatever does not harm another.' The liberty and property of no individual were to be absolute, for the maximization of freedom was seen necessarily to imply some limits where one person's freedom imposed upon that of another. Defining those limits would, in the future, prove to be a source of endless difficulty.

To the working classes of Paris, liberty meant freedom from want. Bread prices had continued to spiral, and on 5 October a crowd of artisan and working-class women, the 'managers' of the household provisions, gathered outside the Parisian town hall demanding bread at reduced prices. This crowd then improvised a march on nearby Versailles to present their demands to both the king and National Assembly. On the way they were followed by the National Guard, a militia headed by the notable bourgeoisie of Paris. Intimidated, the king once again yielded and accepted the August decrees and the Declaration. He also gave orders for the provisioning of Paris. Still not satisfied, the crowd marched the king, Queen Marie Antoinette and the crown prince (the dauphin) back to Paris. Ten days later the National Assembly also moved there.

From this point in 1789 until June 1791 the National Assembly, now known as the Consti-tuent Assembly, devoted itself to social and political reform. The constitution completed in 1791 proposed a legislature which would hold supreme sovereignty, the king being allowed only a suspensive or delaying veto. Frightened by the direct action of the urban crowds and landless peasants, the well-to-do members of the Assembly determined to extend suffrage solely to the 'responsible' members of society. The definition of 'responsibility' was mainly economic. The constitution limited voting citizens to those who paid a minimum amount of taxes, and potential legislators could only be men of substantial property. In 1791 only 50,000 Frenchmen out of a

population of about 26,000,000 qualified as candidates. This number was much smaller than the total number of nobles in France. The privileges conferred by birth and blood had been eliminated, but the legitimizing power of wealth was intended to take its place. The Roman Catholic Church was even subjugated to the voting citizens, bishops and parish priests being elected by the active citizenry. Church property was nationalized, and sales of these lands began in May 1790.

The radical republic

The crowned heads of Europe, including the Pope, were not oblivious to the occurrences in France, but they were cautious because of the social tensions that were fulminating elsewhere on the continent. In 1789 rebellion in Brussels, then ruled by the Austrian Empire, proved that events in France could have repercussions elsewhere. Even though the United Federal Republic of Belgium was crushed the next year, it was now clear that the authority of traditional power elites could be questioned outside France and that French themes of liberation could be used by national groups subjected to foreign domination. Authority had to select carefully the proper measure of compromise and repression to retain power.

On 21 June 1791 Louis XVI and his family lost all authority and legitimacy when they attempted to escape from Paris and join other aristocratic exiles in plotting the downfall of the constitutional monarchy. Their humiliating capture at Varennes compelled Marie Antoinette's brother, Emperor Leopold II of Austria, to grant some form of support to his French relatives. In August 1791 the Austrian ruler first demonstrated the cautious skill that characterized his country's governing figures. Having effectively used force to nip the Belgian revolution in the bud, he now stated in the Declaration of Pillnitz that he would restore the full authority of the French Crown by force if other European powers unanimously consented. At the time of this declaration Leopold's only official ally was King Frederick William II of Prussia. Great Britain, sympathetic to a constitutional monarchy dominated by the affluent, remained aloof, and Pillnitz temporarily remained rhetoric. Still, Leopold's threats, Louis XVI's flight and the presence of aristocratic plotters abroad provided

the more aggressive members of the French Assembly with an argument to internationalize the revolution.

Arguing that France was surrounded by implacable enemies who were constantly weaving plots against her new-found liberty, they insisted that the only way to ensure the revolution's success was by spreading it to the countries where reaction prevailed. Under the pressure of these radicals the French government declared war on Austria in April 1792, thereby initiating a period of armed conflict that would last two decades. At home the radicals used the threat of aristocratic reaction to undermine the financiers and bourgeois landowners who supported the constitutional monarchy and its numerous advantages for the wealthy. Drawing support from the Parisian mob, as well as from such extremist political action groups as the Cordeliers and Jacobin Clubs, they deposed the king and formed a National Convention to draft a new republican constitution in August and September 1792. With the end of constitutional monarchy in France, Britain willingly joined an anti-French alliance. Such an alliance seemed all the more imperative when the French republican army annexed the northern Italian Duchy of Savoy on 27 November.

The foreign peril led to mounting hysteria in France, and the new republican leaders engaged in a Reign of Terror to purge the country of internal enemies, real and imagined. The years 1793 and 1794 witnessed the execution of 40,000 men and women, including the king and queen. Secret royalist sympathizers, arch-Catholics, grain speculators and many innocents all came under the blade of the guillotine. In the countryside confiscated aristocratic lands were sold, thus providing a modicum of property redistribution.

Choreographed by an executive Committee of Public Safety, the Terror demonstrated that revolutionaries, as well as traditional authorities, were perfectly willing to use violence to maintain their power. However, the Committee's leading members, Louis de Saint-Just and the provincial lawyer Maximilien Robespierre, also used more subtle and successful methods of legitimation. The Committee was still a group composed of men of property, but it catered to the urban mob and portrayed itself rhetorically as the representative of the general will. In May 1793 a maximum price for wheat was imposed, and September witnessed

maximum prices instituted for many more goods. To sustain the war effort some heavy industries were nationalized, and systems of relief were established for the poor. Throughout France the National Convention's traveling representatives-on-mission enforced these decrees with the aid of their beneficiaries, the working class *sans-culottes*. At the same time workers were also asked to accept maximum wages, liberty to dispose of property in absolute freedom was limited and specific class definitions of freedom and rights were subordinated to French national independence. As a result, the Jacobin republicans made enemies on all sides. As soon as the external threat abated, the *sans-culottes* were ready to return to earning their bread, and the propertied in government were ready to pounce on Robespierre and his allies.

The French were at war with a daunting coalition of Austria, Prussia, Spain, Holland and

Left: Chained convicts are led from Newgate prison to be embarked for deportation to Australia – a fate that would befall many radical opponents of the British political and economic system.

Below: Newly recruited soldiers of the French revolutionary army. Inspired by the ideals of freedom, equality and patriotism, such raw troops outfought the old-fashioned armies of the European monarchies.

Right: Thomas Paine, author of *The Rights of Man*, was a hero to those in Britain who admired the French Revolution and wished to imitate its achievements.

England, but their revolutionary army was fired by the rhetoric of liberty, equality and fraternity. In June 1794, the tide of battle began to turn in France's favor in the Low Countries. Within weeks, Robespierre and his closest associates were executed, and affluent commoners once again came to the forefront with a new republican constitution in 1795. In fact, the government, now called the Directory, restricted political power to men of substantial wealth even fewer in number than those who held power under the constitution of 1791. The French bourgeoisie at last seemed triumphant. Feudal privileges were no more, and, perhaps more important, the restrictive price, wage and quality regulations of the old medieval craft guilds were also abolished. Freedom in production, sale and trade were to be the new principles of economic regulation. Unfortunately, the bourgeois investors and entrepreneurs had by now discovered that they not only had noble enemies to fear. There were dangers below as well.

Great Britain's economic revolution

At the time of the French Revolution Great Britain was experiencing a process of economic transformation that first had been described (and advocated) systematically by Adam Smith. Smith's *The Wealth of Nations* (1776) praised the development of economic methods whose growth he observed in his own native Edinburgh, Scotland. First, he taught that the best form of economic regulation is the invisible hand of unrestrained competition. Second, his work stressed the importance of the division of labor, a development quickly adopted by the new breed of financiers and just as quickly deplored by masters of the old guild-regulated handicraft trades. Smith and his followers believed that the most efficient way to produce cheaper manufactured goods in an age of spiraling prices was to quicken the pace of production and decrease labor costs by dividing all the steps necessary to produce an item among a number of minimally skilled laborers. In turn, the entrepreneur benefited from an increase in profits resulting from a drop in the cost of production.

To use Smith's famous example, no longer would one master pinmaker laboriously produce pins. A number of individuals would divide the task, one man drawing the wire, another cutting it, a third shaping it into a pin. Ideally, these indi-

viduals would be gathered under one roof to further speed up production. Thus was the modern factory advocated, but it was not an idea that sprang full-grown from Smith's fertile imagination. Precedent had been set in such areas as cloth-manufacture, where, since the time of the Renaissance, well-to-do clothiers put out wool to carders and spinners, yarn to weavers and unfinished cloth to fullers and dressers. Labor was divided in this putting-out system, but the laborers worked at home under conditions which varied from comfortable to impoverished.

The centralized factory first appeared in the cloth industry, specifically in the manufacture of cotton cloth, and it was mainly the result of advancing technology. First cotton thread was spun at an ever-increasing pace with the development of Hargreaves's spinning jenny in 1764 and Arkwright's water-powered machine in 1771. For a time, weavers could demand higher wages, as clothiers demanded that human weaving keep pace with machine-powered spinning. But with Cartwright's invention of a power loom in 1785, weavers found themselves in the same predicament as spinners. Too expensive to be owned by every spinner and weaver, these large and intricate devices were owned by the clothiers themselves, who located them centrally in the first modern factories. In the 1790s these factories were still very few in number and solely British in

nationality, but they were at the cutting edge of a system of mass production that would inevitably reduce prices while simultaneously leveling wages. The English craftsman, especially masters and skilled laborers who had status to be lost, fought for self-regulation, independence from external time management and reduction in the cost of living. This, not trade and production free of regulation, was liberty to them. England was undergoing dramatic change, and workers sought to alleviate their burden by drawing on French Jacobin notions of a moral economy and a political role for artisan laborers.

Like the American revolutionaries before them, British sympathizers of the French Revolution established Corresponding Societies. Started by a shoemaker named Thomas Hardy, these societies advocated universal manhood suffrage and annual parliaments. They also expounded on the economic grievances of the day. Their crusading hero became the British-born American revolutionary Thomas Paine. Originally a crafter of whalebone stays for corsets, Paine had first-hand experience of specialization in manufacture and economic failure. In 1790-92, he wrote *The Rights of Man* in defense of the French Revolution, and his name became a household word. Artisans and correspondents praised him, while his opponents in the gentry paid people to defame him. On 7 January 1793 a lawyer named John Howarth

noted in his diary that he paid some individuals ('who carried about Tom Paine's Effigy and shot at it, 10s. 6d.'). As revolutionary rhetoric and violence escalated in France, repression and reaction took a serious turn in Britain.

The English prime minister, William Pitt, joined Austria, Prussia and Spain in the First Coalition against France in 1793. A disciple of Adam Smith, Pitt encouraged free trade and manufacture on a large scale by systematicaly reducing the multiplicity of direct taxes then extant. He discouraged freedom of speech outside the walls of Parliament, however, and that legislative body could boast that its representative to the House of Commons from Bath had been elected by 32 men, while the member of Parliament for Bedford was virtually appointed by the Duke of Bedford. Throughout 1793 and 1794 the British law courts were filled with government prosecutions of editors and radicals who argued for an expansion of the suffrage and other reforms. Acts of Parliament suppressed the Corresponding Societies. By 1800, as the war with France dragged on, all public meetings not licensed by magistrates were prohibited, *habeas corpus* was suspended and the Combination Acts of 1799 rendered craft guilds and trade unions illegal. While state violence in Jacobin France used the guillotine, Pitt's England employed transportation of the convicted to Botany Bay, Australia. Great Britain had joined the counter-revolution.

The rise of Napoleon Bonaparte

Meanwhile, France under the Directory experienced emotional exhaustion after five years of intense revolutionary activity. The Directory found itself challenged by both a revival of royalist sentiment on the right and the riots and plots of the still impoverished urban workers on the left. Only the aid of the efficient French military

Below right: An early Spinning Jenny, one of the first machines to usher in the Industrial Revolution.

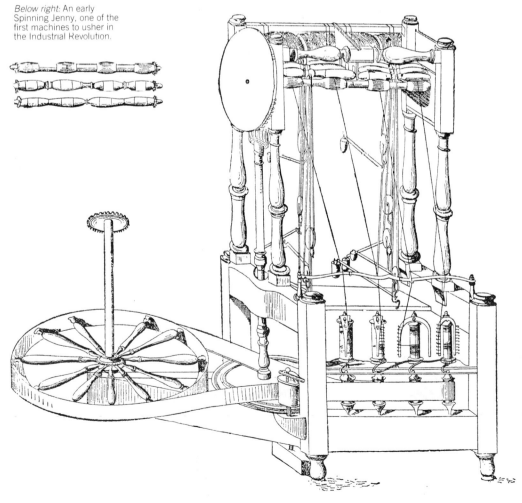

machine kept the tottering government in power.

Between 1795 and 1799 a brilliant young general, Napoleon Bonaparte, saved the Directory from royalist insurrection and France from Austrian conquest. After a successful campaign in Italy culminating in a decisive victory at Arcola on 17 November 1796, Napoleon took the initiative and signed the Peace of Campo Formio with Austria on 17 October 1797. This treaty proved his wiliness and ruthlessness as a diplomat. France acquired Belgium from Austria, which was forced to recognize the nominally independent, but actually French-dominated, Cisalpine Republic in northern Italy. In return, Bonaparte gave Austria most of the territory of the once-independent Republic of Venice, which he had conquered under the flimsiest of pretexts for intervention. Since the passing of the Roman Empire, Italy had been fragmented into a number of sovereign states, and Napoleon had no intention now of creating a united Italy. Both he and the Austrians treated the Italian people as the spoils of conquest, but many Italian intellectuals were beginning to identify Bonaparte's rhetoric of freedom with the notion of a unified state ruled by a linguistically and culturally coherent Italian people. Thus, out of Napoleon's conquests the seeds of Italian nationalism and republicanism were unintentionally born.

Napoleon's immediate and intended use of his conquests was the defense of France and his own personal aggrandizement. When France began losing military ground to a Second Coalition of Britain, Austria and Russia in the winter of 1798-99, a number of leading members of the Directory, including the resilient Abbé Sieyès, believed that only a strong government headed by a general could counteract royalism and defend France. Thus they did little to resist Bonaparte's coup d'état in November 1799. The new govern-

ment was called the Consulate, and from 1799 to 1804 Bonaparte was officially First Consul of France. By February 1801 he had defeated the Austrian military threat and could use his popularity as a national savior to legitimize his authority. In 1802 he was made First Consul for life. In 1804 he assumed the rest of the trappings of traditional authority when his legislature proclaimed him emperor, and a popular vote, or plebiscite, ratified this by a margin of 3,572,329 to 2569. He was now paradoxically a monarch created by a revolution that had challenged the divine authority of monarchs, and his domestic policies reflected this compromise.

As in the France of the Bourbon Kings, ennoblement was used as the ultimate reward for service, but Napoleonic nobles were entirely dependent on their state function as bureaucrats or soldiers. There were no feudal privileges to be had, and the Napoleonic law codes emphasized that custom had been superseded by equality before the law. Bonaparte's various constitutions provided for universal manhood suffrage, but the voters only elected a list of candidates from which the Napoleonic government named the legislators and officials. Previous revolutionaries had tried to eradicate Catholicism as a moribund superstition, but Napoleon recognized its psychological importance to the people, and in 1801 he signed with Pope Pius VII a concordat that formally accepted Catholicism as the predominant religion in France. It did not, however, return confiscated Church property or abandon religious toleration. In 1808 his subordinates eliminated the Church's role as the chief indoctrinator of the young by completing a structure of state-supported primary and secondary schools, as well as institutions of higher learning.

Overall, Napoleon was a great compromising power broker and binder of wounds. He provided bourgeois entrepreneurs with a sound currency, improved commercial transportation and occasional low interest rates. For more common folk he rejected laissez-faire ideals of total government deregulation by fixing low prices on meat and bakery items. Napoleon once said, 'I fear insurrections based on lack of bread; I should fear less a battle of 200,000 men.' Thus when French industry faced a crisis in the winter of 1806-07, he loaned manufacturers 6,000,000 francs at a maximum interest rate of two percent so that they could keep their workers employed. Where Robespierre and the Jacobins had failed, the Emperor seemingly succeeded in enforcing the

EUROPE 1812

- ▨ FRENCH EMPIRE
- ▦ STATES RULED BY NAPOLEON'S FAMILY
- ▩ OTHER DEPENDENT STATES
- ✂ SITES OF MAJOR BATTLES

ing mistakes. He tried to strangle Britain by means of economic blockade, but the British navy proved equal to the task of keeping the seaways open, the decisive naval battle of Trafalgar being won by Admiral Horatio Lord Nelson on 21 October 1805. Napoleon invaded Spain in 1808, but he once again inadvertently initiated a nationalistic revolution as a result. Spain's Latin American colonies also used his deposition of the Spanish Bourbon royal family to air their political and economic grievances, eventually attaining independence as sovereign states by the 1820s. Meanwhile, in the Spanish mother country royalist, republican and nationalist patriots engaged in a frustrating guerrilla war against Napoleon's forces. From 1809 to 1812 they were ably assisted in these activities by the British general Lord Wellington, who based his operations in neighboring Portugal. Finally, 1812 saw Napoleon's disastrous invasion of Tsar Alexander I's Russia, a rival empire that had long feared Bonaparte's intentions along its western frontier. After taking a burned and evacuated Moscow, Napoleon was forced to retreat from a Russian capital devoid of Russians to be conquered. His calamitous return to France was beset by severe November weather and the Russian army. By the time Napoleon had extricated himself from Russia his *Grand Armée* of 600,000 men had dwindled to about 100,000.

The Restoration

Napoleon's resources had evaporated. A series of uncontainable European wars of liberation followed, and at last the victorious allies marched into Paris on 31 March 1814, forcing Napoleon to abdicate unconditionally on 11 April. Banished to the Mediterranean island of Elba, he returned to France in March 1815 to gamble against the odds and try one last military campaign. On 18 June 1815 the British, under the Duke of Wellington, and the Prussians, under Field Marshal von Blücher, handed Napoleon his final defeat at Waterloo in Belgium. By unanimous decision of the allies, the fallen emperor ended his days on the South Atlantic island of St Helena, where he died on 5 May 1821. Though he had set a precedent for a viable blending of the revolution and the old order, Europe preferred to ignore the lesson.

When Napoleon made his mad dash from Elba in the spring of 1815, the victorious allies were assembled at the Congress of Vienna. The chief

wishes of the general will, minimizing the conflicts of different class interests and maximizing French national unity. But there was always only one end in sight: the international expansion of his new order. As in a Greek tragedy Napoleon's overweening pride in his own achievements ultimately contained the seeds of his downfall.

On 2 December 1805 Napoleon extended his continental hegemony by defeating the combined forces of Austria and Russia at the Battle of Auster-

litz. Belgium, Geneva, Piedmont-Savoy and the Republic of Genoa were annexed to France, while satellite kingdoms were created in northwestern and southern Italy. In the numerous disunited states of Germany Napoleonic victories led to the organization of a Confederation of the Rhine under French auspicies, with only Austria, Prussia, Brunswick and the Elector of Hesse maintaining their independence. Seemingly invincible, the Emperor then started to make a series of devastat-

Above: Admiral Horatio
Nelson falls mortally
wounded on the deck of the
Victory during the Battle of
Trafalgar (1805).

Right: The coronation of
Napoleon as Emperor of the
French, depicted by his
court painter David. The
Emperor holds the limelight,
turning to crown his wife
Josephine as Empress,
while the Pope is reduced to
a minor role, seated behind
him.

Left: Forced to abdicate in
1814, Napo'eon returned
from exile the following year,
but at the Battle of Waterloo
his Imperial Guard was at
last conclusively defeated
by the British and Prussian
armies.

Above left: Europe in 1812,
when Napoleon's French
Empire was at the height of
its power. French
domination of Europe was
almost complete, and until
Napoleon invaded Russia in
1812 Britain was the only
nation offering effective
resistance.

The Industrial Revolution in Britain

To use the economist W W Rostow's phrase, the revolution in manufacturing, which had begun in the mid-1700s, experienced a self-sustaining 'take-off.' In 1760 Britain imported approximately 2,500,000 pounds of raw cotton to feed its dispersed putting-out system. By 1837 the consumption of raw cotton was up to 366,000,000 pounds, and almost all the cotton workers, except for a still substantial number of hand-loom weavers, worked under factory discipline. Each new invention paid sufficiently to cover the cost of change, and these inventions did not appear in a vacuum. They were aided by a number of other British developments.

Private investment banks, with their willingness to advance credit, provided Britain with the fluid capital needed to buy expensive new machinery and expand production. Production itself was aided and abetted by foreign demand for British goods, and the substitution of steam and water for animal power kept prices cheap. In turn, both James Watt's steam engine and George Stephenson's locomotive depended on the more efficient mining of coal and production of pig iron. As though miraculously blessed, nineteenth-century Britain had ample supplies of both. In

goals of all concerned were to restore, so far as possible, both the traditional holdings of all titled rulers and the balance of international power as they had been defined prior to the French Revolution. In fact, the maintenance of the balance of power persisted as the ideal goal of diplomacy until the period just before World War I. As a result, France did not suffer inordinately from its adventure and even retained its boundaries of 1792. The allies' chief ministers agreed to make France a full partner in the settlement, just as they agreed theoretically that no one country was to attain preeminence over another. Lord Castlereagh of Britain, the Duc de Talleyrand of France and Prince Clemens von Metternich of Austria all engaged in a series of successive compromises to this end. In the German lands, no attempt was made to revive the hundreds of medieval principalities, and Napoleon's reduction of the Germanies to 39 states, loosely bound in a confederation now dominated by Austria and Prussia, was accepted. The historic Dutch Republic, extinct since 1795, was revived as the new Kingdom of the Netherlands, and the Austrians firmly installed themselves in Italy, retaining their possession of the once-free Venetia and Lombardy.

Just as territorial boundaries were not completely restored, so too old monarchic mentalities were not totally unchanged. This was particularly true of France. The Bourbon royal family returned, but Louis XVI's brother, Louis XVIII, felt constrained to grant a constitutional charter that made his country a limited monarchy. The legal, administrative, clerical and educational reforms of the Revolution and Empire were retained, and the redistributed land of old aristocrats was not reclaimed. Beyond French borders, the republican and liberal rhetoric spread by Napoleon's troops continued to influence those disgruntled with their aristocratic lords, and the power and accomplishments of the French Republic impressed the peoples of disunited Italy and Germany. Still, until it disintegrated, a Quintuple Alliance of Austria, Prussia, Russia, Britain and France used diplomacy and force against moves to change either boundaries or social systems. Republican and nationalist movements were forced underground, but not all self-proclaimed progressive movements hid. The change brought on by the Industrial Revolution persisted and spread.

Many early industrial workers therefore saw the machine as their enemy, the means by which the innovative capitalist could make new demands of them. This eventually led to machine smashing, or Luddism, so named after 'Ned Ludd,' the collective pseudonym left behind at many of the sites of destruction. Notable cases occured in England between 1810 and 1812, in Vienne, France in 1819, in Aachen in 1829 and in Bohemia in 1844. Capitalist ideology defined liberty in terms of the freedom to produce and increase profits in an unrestrained fashion, but workers were beginning to see laissez-faire capitalism as a method of enslavement.

On 16 August 1819 nearly 100,000 working-class people assembled at St Peter's Fields in Manchester. There they demanded parliamentary reform and a repeal of the Corn Law of 1815. The Corn Law was a reactionary step opposed by both middle-class entrepreneurs and workers, for it imposed tariffs on imported grain so as to allow more expensive and less plentiful British grain to undersell the continental variety. Cheap bread was still vitally important to the masses, and the Corn Law only benefited English agricultural landlords. But though worker and capitalist economic interests met on this occasion, the manufacturers, merchants and shopkeepers of Manchester feared the working-class crowd taking matters into its own hands. While speeches were being made by such assorted individuals as a master printer and shoemaker the crowd was repeatedly charged by mounted troops, sent there to ostensibly keep the peace. Eleven were killed and approximately 42 were injured in what was sardonically named the Peterloo Massacre.

After Peterloo British politicians, at least, perceived the value of compromise. Between 1822 and 1830 the ministers reduced the number of crimes punishable by death from more than 200 to about 100; eliminated certain tariffs and reduced others; and repealed the Combination Acts, thus permitting the development of trade unions and of mutual aid societies that could provide insurance and compensation for workers. The three reform bills of 1831-32 improved electoral conditions by redistributing parliamentary

1800 the United Kingdom produced and used about 11,000,000 tons of coal a year; by 1830, the use of the fossil fuel had doubled. Between 1806 and 1848, British pig iron output rose from about 258,206 to 1,998,568 tons. To British capitalists of this era, growth and economic progress appeared both limitless and rapid. Their agrarian counterparts, the innovative landlords, provided them with a seemingly limitless supply of labor, as they reduced more and more tenant farmers to the status of landless wage laborers. These agrarian workers turned to the factories and mines only to discover new miseries.

The average English laboring family spent less of its income on food that its continental counterpart, and this allowed it to purchase the new manufactured goods, thus helping to sustain growth through consumption. But the new social mobility worked in two directions. While former agrarian wage laborers experienced an increase in

purchasing power as they entered factories and mines, artisans experienced a decline, as well as a loss of status and independence. The overall increase in purchasing power resulted from the landless agrarian workers' predominance in numbers, but they shared with the degraded artisans a loss of leisure: The working day was 12-16 hours long, and one wage-earner's income alone was rarely enough to maintain a family through the fluctuations of the business cycles. As a result, women and children had to work as well. Entire families had already labored in the fields or artisan shops, but at least nature usually had provided them the leisure of winter, rainy days and conversation with a potential customer. In factories and mines, men, women and children had to keep pace with the unrelenting machines, and if the machines produced more than could be sold, workers faced starvation as surely as if there had been a bad harvest.

Above left: The French occupation of Spain in 1808 was met by resistance from Spanish Irregular forces. This is one of artist Francisco de Goya's famous impressions of the atrocities committed in this conflict, the first to be called a *guerrilla*, from the Spanish, 'little war.'

Above: A steam engine pulls coal wagons from a Yorkshire mine in 1814. Very similar engines would pull the first passenger trains in the following decade.

Left and right: Two views of an early nineteenth-century cotton mill — on the left, an illustration from a Victorian novel decrying the exploitation of children and female labor, and on the right a more sanitized version.

seats and extending the franchise. The last bill redistributed 143 seats which were controlled by the customary influence or bribery of local patrons, normally rural aristocrats or landlords. These seats now went mostly to the growing towns of the industrial north, and the franchise was extended to all householders paying £10 annual rental, as well as those freeholders who could pay a 40 shilling poll tax.

Poor workers and the unemployed were still excluded from active participation in government, but parliamentary enquiries into the causes of worker misery, immorality and unrest led to some appalling revelations and the Factory Act of August 1833. The Factory Act forbade employment of children under nine years and restricted labor for those nine-18. Children under 13 were to have two hours' schooling provided by the factory owner, but often they were too exhausted to truly benefit. The government tried to enforce this legislation through a system of paid inspectors, but bribes and negligence made the inadequate restrictions even more inadequate.

As a result of this failure and others the workers of England once again united to prove that they were active citizens in all but voting rights. Agitation from below coalesced into the Chartist movement, which had its origin in 1836, when a Workingman's Association in London issued a charter, or petition, to Parliament. The charter made only political demands, but Chartist supporters implied that the granting of those demands could lead to social and economic change. Property qualifications were to be abolished for manhood suffrage and election to Parliament; voting was to be by secret ballot; members of Parliament were to be paid; and parliaments were to be called annually. A secret ballot meant no intimidation of voters during a public vote, and payment of parliamentarians meant that those without independent means could hope to hold seats. May 1839 witnessed another formal presentation of the charter to Parliament, and, as in 1836, Parliament rejected it. Riots broke out throughout the rest of the year, with 20 protesters dying at Newport and a number of Chartist leaders being transported to Australia as a result.

After a Chartist attempt at a national strike failed in 1842 the movement gradually faded away, and workers once again joined the middle classes in agitation for the repeal of all the corn laws, since free trade promised cheaper prices through market competition. On 6 June 1846 grain tariffs were finally eradicated. Duties on nearly every kind of imported meat were also abolished, as were many duties on manufactured goods. The English workers granted the ultimate compromise by accepting the methods of their sometimes benevolent, sometimes repressive 'betters.' They would petition the elites and hope for the best. As a result, they were rewarded with other reform measures, such as the Mines Act of 1842 and the Ten Hours Act of 1847. Strikes, riots and rebellion had simply cost too much in terms of food and blood. Growth in production was accepted as the best and indeed necessary means to improvement.

The European economy

On the continent economic growth was much behind that of Britain. The upheavals and wars of the French Revolution and the Napoleonic era brought about capital destruction, loss of manpower, rhythmic inflation and all manner of interruptions to trade. Britain, which had fought no wars on its own soil, was quick to exploit Europe's low level of production by developing new markets on the continent. Napoleon's military expenditures and disastrous adventures during the last five years of his empire had left the French economy, and much of the European economy, enfeebled and momentarily helpless to meet the rush of cheap British goods that came with the peace. Also, while nineteenth-century Britain underwent rapid population growth and urbanization, thus creating a demand for the mass marketing of cheap goods, France, for example, underwent a much slower increase in population

LES POIRES,

Faites à la cour d'assises de Paris par le directeur de la CARICATURE.

Vendues pour payer les 6,000 fr. d'amende du journal le *Charivari.*

(CHEZ AUBERT, GALERIE VERO-DODAT)

Si, pour reconnaître le monarque dans une caricature, vous n'attendez pas qu'il soit désigné autrement que par la ressemblance, vous tomberez dans l'absurde. Voyez ces croquis informes, auxquels j'aurais peut-être dû borner ma défense :

Ce croquis ressemble à Louis-Philippe, vous condamnerez donc ?

Alors il faudra condamner celui-ci, qui ressemble au premier.

Puis condamner cet autre, qui ressemble au second.

Et enfin, si vous êtes conséquens, vous ne sauriez absoudre cette poire, qui ressemble aux croquis précédens.

Ainsi, pour une poire, pour une brioche, et pour toutes les têtes grotesques dans lesquelles le hasard ou la malice aura placé cette triste ressemblance, vous pourrez infliger à l'auteur cinq ans de prison et cinq mille francs d'amende !! Avouez, Messieurs, que c'est là une singulière liberté de la presse !!

Left: Some of the strange mixture of weaponry and uniforms with which the French revolutionaries of 1830 equipped themselves.

Right: The revolution of 1830 brought to the throne Louis Philippe, a monarch who satisfied the bourgeoisie but was hated by radicals. In this famous caricature, Daumier reduced the king's head to a pear; the captions argue that if caricaturing the king is against the law, every drawing of a pear must be too.

Below left: The Chartists carry their Great Petition to the House of Commons in 1842. The main demand of this working-class movement was for one-man-one-vote.

and a more gradual process of urbanization. Many young men had died during the Napoleonic wars, and enough peasants had benefited from revolutionary land resale to achieve a modicum of comfort. As a result, it was much harder to find cheap labor or a growing urban consumers' market in France, but the French economy, while never experiencing British spurts, still grew steadily, with per capita physical production more than tripling in the century after 1803.

While the majority of European workers were still agrarian laborers and craftsmen in 1848, and heavy industry was in its infancy, capitalist methods were already determining production. Free enterprise and free trade were coming to be accepted principles even in the absence of developed industrial techniques. The first decades of the nineteenth century experienced extremely slow technological progress in the Germanies. Demand for fuel and metal grew, but the reponse was generally to intensify output along traditional lines. Among the first continental enterprises to smelt pig iron with coke, a coal derivative, were the Silesian iron works and coal mines owned by the Prussian state. But the Prussian private sector was too modestly financed to engage in this British technique, and the share of coke-blasted pig in the total output of Silesian pig iron still only rose from 28 percent in 1838 to 35 percent in 1847. The only European nation that underwent a spurt of growth comparable to Britain was Belgium. The Belgian iron industry shifted from charcoal burning to coal with relative rapidity for a number of reasons, including the abundance of coal mines and the availability of substantial private-sector capital.

Upon his death in 1824 the pragmatic Louis XVIII was succeeded by his ultraroyalist brother, Charles X. As liberal opposition became more outspoken, the French government's policy became more reactionary. Louis XVIII had always been careful to enlist legislative backing, but Charles ignored the demands of the Chamber of Deputies and, in 1829, appointed the Prince de Polignac, one of the most irreconcilable reactionaries, as his first minister. When the Chamber remonstrated, Charles dismissed it, as was his constitutional right. And when elections returned another liberal majority, Polignac had the king issue a series of ordinances which dissolved the Chamber, imposed stringent censorship and reduced the electorate from 100,000 to 25,000. Discontent reached a fever pitch, and in July 1830 Parisians set up barricades in the streets and quickly toppled Charles from the throne.

As in the French Revolution of 1789, different interest groups and classes temporarily formed a coalition against their common enemy, the monarchy, but their conflicting aims eventually led to fighting among themselves. The financiers and manufacturers were satisfied with a limited constitutional monarchy that did not infringe upon their freedom of speech, political rights and property rights. But the artisanal workers who had joined them in the street fighting demanded more – the freedom to associate in corporate groups that would provide mutual aid in times of economic difficulty and would maintain solidarity in negotiations with employers over wages and conditions. In short, they wanted trade unions, which had been banned in France since 1791. This demand the middle class of course resisted.

Universal suffrage and a republic with absolutely no aristocracy were too closely associated with the Jacobinism of Robespierre, and the middle class clearly had no intention of limiting its economic liberty on behalf of the general will. Hence it retained the monarchy in 1830, naming Louis Philippe of the House of Orleans the successor to over 200 years of Bourbon rule. In matters of voting, property qualifications remained preeminent, and the poll tax was merely lowered from 300 to 200 francs. The ban on trade unions was left in force, and the bourgeois government looked askance when Parisian and provincial workers formed various philanthropic societies from 1831 to 1833. But as long as these free associations merely collected dues for the provision of unemployment and health insurance they were tolerated. The government would only declare them 'restrictive guilds' if they attempted to strike.

Outside France the shockwave of the July 1830 uprising manifested itself in various forms of nationalist, constitutionalist and economic discontent. In an age seeking 'liberty, equality and fraternity' nationalism portrayed the free nationstate as the most appropriate fraternal society, and the intellectuals of disunited or subjected ethnic groups were often in the forefront. The German thinker Johann Gottfried von Herder argued that a common speech necessarily shaped a common culture through the method of mutual understanding. This *volk*, or people, would then create the most just and rational order that could possibly be derived from all their pre-rational affinities. In a similar vein the poet Friedrich Hölderlin sang of the beauties of the German cultural heritage in his *Germania*, and the Brothers Grimm celebrated the same themes in their works on German myths and legends. In Italy Giuseppe Mazzini was not only a practicing revolutionary, but a republican and nationalist theoretician as well. In 1830 he founded a secret society named Young Italy to organize resistance against northern Italy's Austrian overlords and such traditional authorities as the King of Piedmont. This group was emulated by others with similar aims – a Young Germany being founded for example – and Mazzini emphasized that free and equal nations would be able to contract with each other in peace, just as individuals establish constitutions and social contracts. Until the establishment of this idealized 'league of nations,' Mazzini prophesied that discontented subject peoples would continue to rise in revolt.

In August 1830 the Catholic French and Flemish sections of the Netherlands revolted against the Dutch Protestant rule that was imposed upon them by the Congress of Vienna. On 4 October Belgium declared its national liberty and established a constitutional monarchy under King Leopold I. Wealthy groups in the Belgian towns quickly checked any potential lower-class uprisings by seizing a monopoly of force through their organization as Committees of Safety and Civil Guards, while their governmental authority was legitimized through a National Congress elected by 30,000 voters in a country of 4,000,000. Unable to stand against Dutch troops in 1831, Belgium retained its independence only because of division within the Quintuple Alliance. Austria, Prussia and Russia wanted to check Belgian independence, while England and France actively supported it by blockading Holland. Rather than risk war on a scale unseen since Napoleon, the central and eastern European powers acquiesced, and Belgium was free to rise to the economic heights already discussed.

Across the Rhine the Parisian revolution of

1830 caused great excitement among German intellectuals, though there was little response among the people. Some of the smaller states, such as Brunswick, Hanover and Saxony, were forced to grant moderately liberal constitutions and concessions, but no true trouble arose in Prussia or Austria. In free Italian states such as Modena revolts broke out under the leadership of secret republican-nationalist societies like the Carbonari. These groups hoped for aid from Louis Philippe's France but received none, since France was not prepared to frustrate Austrian interests in Italy as well as in Belgium. Therefore, Prince Metternich had free rein to march Austrian troops into the free Italian states and restore their traditional rulers.

1848: a revolutionary reprise

Under Louis Philippe in the years after 1830 France experienced economic growth which was slow and gradual when compared to Great Britain's, but quite impressive nonetheless when compared to the rest of Europe. As a result of this, big business was fairly well satisfied with the Orleanist monarchy. Many professionals and master artisans, however, longed for the betrayed golden age – for the mostly rhetorical equality and international glories of the republic and empire. When consumer purchases failed to keep up with production in 1846, economic crisis struck. Production was reduced, and workers were dismissed, but the French government made no effort to help the unemployed laborer and marginal master craftsman. As a result, workers became a restive lot. Working-class strikes and demonstrations led republicans to meet and discuss legislative and electoral reforms in the hope of alleviating some of the tension. In February 1848 the government's ban against such a meeting caused a popular demonstration that ended in the death of several demonstrators. At this, the barricades went up on the narrow streets of old Paris, and the revolution of republicans and workers was on.

Major bloodshed was avoided when Louis Philippe decided to abdicate on 24 February, but the resulting Second Republic faced a number of domestic crises. Radical republican elements were joined by a new group called socialists, who then pressured the government into proclaiming a right to work as fundamental to sustaining the right to life. Following the teachings of the journalist Louis Blanc, and threatened by worker demonstrations, the republic established a number of national workshops to deal with the problem of unemployment. Blanc, virtual minister of labor in the provisional government, defined these workshops as self-supporting units of production, owned and operated by the workers on a cooperative, profit-sharing basis. They were never meant to be centrally operated by the state once workers had been trained in the self-management of such enterprises. Rather, they were meant to give workers the property needed to be independent of an employer's desires and hiring practices, thus making them by all liberal definitions

responsible citizens with a stake in society.

Blanc's immediate goal was to maximize the distribution of private property, not to eliminate it. His revolutionary idea was the striving for compromises and the common good found in Jacobin republicanism. But the middle-class entrepreneurs and professionals who were in the provisional government considered the workshops as temporary charity measures. They were thus established as places where workers could receive a subsistence salary for literally doing nothing. Training or production activities were seldom considered. As a result, the workshops became a breeding ground of discontent and agitation.

During this period elections were called, and the Second Republic discovered that it was threatened by reaction as well as revolution. Of the 900 delegates to the new National Assembly, fewer than 100 were radical republicans. Universal manhood suffrage permitted the majority of the French population, the peasantry, to vote. Since most of their aims had been met by the end

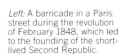

of feudalism and land redistribution of the first French Revolution, they now proved a staunchly conservative force, fearing loss of their property and status at the hands of dispossessed urban workers. The election of a conservative National Assembly was the catalyst that mobilized the workers. Tension came to a head in the bloody 'June Days,' when the Assembly dissolved the workshops, and workers took to the barricades – this time alone, as a class unified against all other class interests. The ensuing street fighting was the bloodiest ever, and by the end of June working-class resistance was broken by the army and National Guard militiamen. France was once again a wounded and divided nation, and as before the French people turned to Bonapartism as the solution. In December 1848, by universal male suffrage, Napoleon's nephew, Louis Napoleon Bonaparte, was overwhelmingly elected the president of the Second Republic. He promised to uphold the common good, providing work and material improvement for the poor and order and protection for the rich. History seemed about to repeat itself, for in 1852, by plebiscite, President Bonaparte became Emperor Napoleon III of France.

In the rest of Europe the cycle of revolution and reaction also reappeared in 1848. In January revolution broke out in Sicily, and by mid-March, most of the Italian states had won liberal constitutions. The latter month even witnessed nationalist insurrection in the Austrian provinces of Venetia and Lombardy, a revolt aided by turmoil in Vienna itself. Giving way to popular pressure, the most powerful Italian monarch, Charles Albert of Piedmont, declared war on Austria. The King of Piedmont was commonly considered one of the potential unifiers of Italy, and his forces were soon joined by contingents from other Italian states. Through his heroic but futile efforts against seasoned Austrian troops, Charles Albert secured Piedmont's preeminent status among the Italian states, especially after the other major contender for the rulership of a unified Italy – the Pope – fled Rome.

In an age of secularization Pope Pius IX could ill afford to support a war against Austria, the leading Catholic power of Europe, and he abandoned his central Italian Papal States to a republican

insurrection led by Giuseppe Mazzini. At the same time Charles Albert experienced defeat at Austrian hands, Mazzini witnessed the fall of his new Roman republic when President Louis Napoleon of France tried to ingratiate himself to his Catholic subjects by sending an expeditionary force against Rome. Italian unification, the *Risorgimento*, had failed in 1848, but the seeds for success in the 1860s were planted. Piedmont, alone among the Italian states, retained its liberal constitutional monarchy, and the future republican military hero, Giuseppe Garibaldi, experienced his first major field command as Mazzini's defeated general.

As evidenced by its Italian possessions, the Austrian Empire was a true empire, a conglomeration of national ethnic groups in which the German Austrians were a minority. There were Magyars in Hungary, Czechs and Slovaks in Bohemia and Moravia, Poles in Galicia and Italians in Lombardy and Venetia. All these regions also had

minority ethnic groups, such as Croats and Serbs, with whom to contend. A wave of successful nationalist uprisings would thus mean the chaotic disintegration of the Austrian Empire. In March 1848 some moderate student demonstrations led to the royal family's acceptance of a constitution for German Austria. The last feudal burdens were lifted from the Austrian peasantry, and a legislative voice was granted the nascent Austrian bourgeoisie. These easily granted concessions to the Germans only served to infuriate Austria's other nationalities. Bohemia, Hungary and the Italian provinces all revolted, and the Viennese government, with its customary pragmatism, granted a large measure of self-government, including an autonomous legislature, to the native Hungarian elites. The emperor was now also King of Hungary, uniting the two realms in his person and foreign policy. These Austrian concessions were linked to an effective degree of repression, and with the aid of the troops of

Austria's Russian ally Czar Nicholas I, the Austrian army gradually achieved victory against the insurgents. By mid-August 1849, the new emperor, Francis Joseph I (1848-1916), possessed an exceptionally secure throne.

To Austria's north, the success of liberal and nationalist revolutions in Germany at first seemed most favorable. The writings of men like Herder and Hölderlin argued that German cultural unity must necessarily give rise to national unity, and at the same time the first throes of industrialism were causing social ferment as they had in England. The establishment of a *Zollverein*, or customs union, for the German Confederation eased the movement of goods by reducing the number of tariffs imposed by the different states. This cheapened the cost of goods and encouraged mass production, but the coming of heavy industry once again brought hardship to artisans. Their discontent was joined to the displeasure of German peasants, who found it increasingly difficult to make a living on their small holdings and often had to resort to becoming agricultural or industrial employees.

In the powerful state of Prussia the lower classes agitated for universal suffrage, public works projects and a radical republic in lieu of King Frederick William IV's monarchy. These demands, as in many other German states, convinced the financiers, manufacturers and most professionals to assume passivity as the aristocratic rulers reasserted authority through armed force. The German middle class remained satisfied with its growing freedom in economic affairs and left politics to the aristocracy.

In France, Austria, the Germanies and Italy, the revolutions of 1848 failed to achieve their ultimate goals as a result of the conflicting interpetations of those aims. There were too many contradictory programs to provide any revolutionary unity against the forces of reaction. In the Austrian

domains, the Hungarian elite desperately wanted independence, but it was opposed to any autonomy for the Croat minority within the boundaries of its own proposed kingdom. The emerging German middle classes and their French counterparts respectively sought strong aristocratic and Napoleonic rule to suppress threats from the working class. Everywhere in Europe those with something to lose feared that the questioning of political and economic authority was going too far. The aristocrats and bourgeoisie united in a partnership to maintain the definition of social order from above and to prevent disorder, anarchy and even communism.

In February 1848, two relatively obscure young German intellectuals had written a pamphlet in response to the revolutionary situation in Europe. Karl Marx and Friedrich Engels told those without authority based on birth or property that 'you have nothing to lose but your chains.' Like the *Social Contract* before it, the *Communist Manifesto* was still trying to define the meaning of human freedom. It asked if the freedom to hold private property was merely another means of enchaining the majority of human beings. The latter part of the nineteenth and entire twentieth century would be left to confront that complex question.

The Romantic revolution

Whereas Enlightenment thinkers had detested the irrational in nature, the mysterious permeated the revolutionary era's Romantic culture. Starting with Jean-Jacques Rousseau's *Confessions*, man himself became a mystery, and intellectuals focused on his rich complexity and paradoxical nature. In Romantic discourse the human self was constantly trying to reconcile loyalties divided between reason and emotion, discipline and indulgence, good and evil. Man was a reflection of the larger natural world in all its beauty and savagery,

but man was not determined or fixed in any one station. He could use reason and will to change the course of rivers or political institutions, but this did not always bring happy results. Romanticism grew out of a world that had seen the triumphs and failures of the French Revolution; the sheer will power and organizational skills of a Napoleon; the material improvements and degradation of the Industrial Revolution. As the broader social world came to seek progress in compromise after compromise, the Romantic wished to experience and express the full range of human possibilities in one grand synthesis. If synthesis could be achieved, a certain sad and sublime wisdom was attained. If not, self-destruction was often the result. This was the dilemma faced in Johann Wolfgang von Goethe's *Faust* (1808-33).

An adviser and minister of state to the German Duke of Saxe-Weimar, Goethe studied the natural sciences as well as wrote poetry. His protagonist, the scholar Faust, sells his soul to the Devil in order to cure 'its thirst for knowledge,' knowledge being defined in terms of the breadth of human experience: the alternations of pain and pleasure, success and frustration. Having turned away from the divine path of righteousness, Faust is saved by ultimately using black magic and science to construct an earthly paradise and improve the human material condition. His progressive ends and humanitarianism balance favorably against his demonic means in the eyes of Goethe's God. Faust's nature is the Romantic perception of human nature itself, a perspective reiterated in the dualities of the English master printer and poet William Blake.

Blake longed for universal manhood suffrage and social justice, but he could not tolerate the Reign of Terror's excesses in the name of rationally ordering society. He viewed any authority trying to force itself upon man, be it revolutionary or

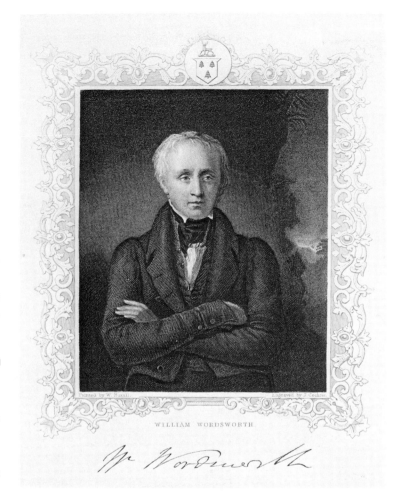

Left: English poet William Wordsworth, one of many Romantics who abandoned a youthful radicalism for conservative political beliefs later in life.

Far left: Francis Joseph I came to the Austrian throne at the height of the 1848 revolts, but was to remain in power right through to World War I.

Right: Goethe, German poet, novelist, dramatist and scientist.

Below: J M W Turner's famous painting *Rain, Steam and Speed – The Great Western Railway.* The steam locomotive, the crowning glory of nineteenth-century technology, is both combined with and set against the elemental forces of nature.

WILLIAM WORDSWORTH.

could improve the general human condition. Love and humanitarianism were left out of such an equation, perhaps best represented by the utilitarianism of Jeremy Bentham (1748-1832).

Decidedly no Romantic, Bentham upheld the Enlightenment's faith in the proper supremacy of reason. Left to its own accord, without government interference or silly traditions like religion, enlightened self-interest would provide the greatest good for the greatest number. Bentham believed factory owners would eventually grant decent wages and working conditions to their employees, since starving workers did not maximize production and efficiency. Both Blake and de Maistre would have pointed to the fact that the middle classes did not always function rationally.

Romantics were the first to denounce blind acceptance of technological progress and reason unrestrained by morality. Most Romantics sang praises to the wildness and freedom of a natural world that was being encroached upon by crowded, filthy industrial cities. Many were pantheists who equated God with the spirit of physical nature. Romanticism, as a movement, longed to escape urban squalor and return to a bucolic past. Hence, a fascination with the Middle Ages led to a Gothic revival in the arts and architecture, as well as the popularity of historic romances such as Sir Walter Scott's *Ivanhoe* (1819) and *The Talisman* (1825). Mary Shelley's *Frankenstein* (1818) demonstrated the dangers of scientific rationality's being employed without any moral probings.

In another popular novel of the era, *The Count of Monte Cristo* (1844), Alexandre Dumas captured what the period considered most admirable. Edmond Dantès, the count, is the composite ideal of the early nineteenth century in human form. Equally at home in the world of high finance or on the dueling field, Dantès combines bourgeois investment skills with an aristocratic sense of personal honor. He is also a defender and benefactor of the weak, as well as a friend of Italian peasant bandits who have justly rebelled against their oppressive landlords. In short, he blends self-interest with social conscience, and aristocratic authority with populism, in a reconciliation of opposing principles. In the realm of political realities, the character Dantès was in some ways like that of Napoleon Bonaparte. Bonapartism taught that a strong natural aristocrat or self-proclaimed emperor could interpret the general will of the people and provide for the needs of rich and poor alike – all in an attempt to lead a unified nation on the road to international glory. As such, both Dantès and Bonaparte represented balance and reconciliation.

Throughout the period 1789-1848 attempts were made to reconcile contradictory concepts such as revolution and reaction, liberty and authority. Romanticism captured this tension, and the era's most complex Romantic philosopher, G W F Hegel (1770-1831), summarized it by writing of human history as the constant evolution of liberty through the reconciliation of political, social and intellectual conflicts. Thus were the goals of maximizing human freedom and happiness reduced to the principle of synthesis, but the very real, particular needs of different groups made reconciliation extremely difficult to realize.

In 1848 many Europeans, from workers to subjugated national groups, were still as dissatisfied as they had been in 1789. Unlike their medieval progenitors, early nineteenth-century Europeans believed that 'heaven,' be it reactionary, republican or composite, was to be made on earth, but 'heaven' meant different things to different people. European history remained tumultuous, and Europeans continued to seek paradise.

reactionary, as anathema. Heterodoxically religious, Blake's Christ was a rebel who preached a total forgiving love that challenged the strict laws of Deuteronomy. To Blake the French Revolution's guillotine, like eighteenth-century England's excessive use of capital punishment, bore too close a resemblance to the Old Testament's 'an eye for an eye' dictum. He wrote his *Songs of Innocence* and *Songs of Experience* to show the gentle and savage beauty of nature in such dualities as *The Lamb* and *The Tyger*, and he would have had cold, heartless law tempered by love and caring.

Every Romantic rebelled against an overly simplistic interpretation of human nature, but many Romantics, unlike Blake, felt that that nature would not be best served by republican progressi-

vism. In France, the social critics René Chateaubriand, Joseph de Maistre and the Vicomte de Bonald joined disillusioned former supporters of the French Revolution, such as the English poets William Wordsworth and Samuel Taylor Coleridge, in rejecting liberal attempts to maximize freedom. Deriving much of their thought from the Irishman Edmund Burke's denunciation of the French Revolution in his *Reflections on the Revolution in France* (1790), the conservatives shared one thing with radical republicans and the early socialists: a belief in a need to consciously balance individual self-realization with the good of the greatest possible number of people in society. Both groups could not believe that minimum government interference and the unrestrained workings of competition and supply-and-demand

Europe: 1848-1914

Beginning in Paris on 24 March a wave of anti-monarchical insurrections swept Europe in 1848, toppling the existing governments, bringing a mixture of liberal and radical coalitions to power and calling people to the streets. The sequence was: 2 March South-West Germany, 6 March Bavaria, 11 March Berlin, 13 March Vienna, 15 March Budapest, 18 March Milan and thence to the rest of Italy. In scale, rapidity and radicalism, this seemed an impressive breakthrough for the forces of movement against the forces of inertia – for liberty and democracy against reaction and privilege. It also seemed well within an existing pattern of revolutionary change: from the barricades to the tricolor, the forms and actions of 1848 readily invoked the traditions of 1830 and 1789. This was especially true of the radicals, who in 1848 enacted a script they had been rehearsing for 50 years. In this sense, the 1848 revolutions were the climax of an existing era, the resurgence of an old revolutionary program, the final reckoning with a doggedly resilient *ancien regime*. They were also brought on by a typical economic crisis of the old kind, produced by harvest failures, rising prices, shortages and the resulting crises of production and distribution.

But if in its inception the revolutionary crisis seemed part of a familiar drama, in its outcome it proved strikingly new. For one thing the individual revolutions were ended almost as quickly as they had begun. In France only a few weeks passed before the new democratic electorate returned a conservative (though non-monarchist) majority, followed a few weeks after that by the bloody suppression of the Parisian workers in the June insurrection. Elsewhere the initiative also passed to the counter-revolution. A radical insurrection was also put down in June in Prague, while the Habsburg imperial armies also regained control in northern Italy, thus laying the basis for a counter-offensive in Vienna, which followed in October 1848. The Prussian monarchy also reasserted itself in Berlin, and the remaining strongholds of the revolution in Germany were cleaned up in the spring and summer of 1849. The radicals in Budapest and Venetia surrendered in August 1849. Reaction returned to the ascendant, radicals retreated to exile and liberals put their heads down for a long period of recuperation.

With the exception of peasant emancipation in the Habsburg Empire, which virtually completed the European cycle of land reform begun in the 1780s (the final chapter followed in Russia and Rumania in the 1860s), all the hopes of 1848 came to nothing. By the summer of 1849 the old political authorities were restored, seemingly more entrenched and less subject to liberal constitutional restraint than ever before. In France the republic persisted a while longer, before succumbing to Napoleon III's coup d'état in December 1851. But behind the political reaction things were very different from before. Paradoxically, the reinstated conservative governments, which trumpeted their reactionary hostility to progress in its political sense, now proceeded to adopt many progressive policies in the economic sphere. The key to this was the massive boom of 1850-73. For if the later-1840s saw the last continental economic crisis of the traditional kind, the 1850s saw the first global upturn of the capitalist trade cycle.

In the first instance this meant an enormous increase in the volume of world trade, which grew by 260 percent during 1850-70, while it had taken twice as long simply to double itself in the earlier period of 1800-40. Moreover, the expansion involved not only a spatial expansion of capitalist enterprise across the world as a whole (affecting especially Latin America, China and South Asia), but also the qualitative penetration of capitalist relations into parts of the economy that were previously relatively untouched – eg classical agriculture, whose comprehensive commercialization was one of the major features of the post-1850 boom.

More to the point, both aspects of the big expansion – namely, the growth of international trade and the transforming of economic relationships inside individual societies – required a new policy on the part of governments. In effect, states were called upon for a series of major facilitating interventions, which systematically deregulated the traditional economy and freed resources and enterprise for the new business opportunities. In one sense this involved pulling government (or public authorities) out of the economy and implied low levels of state involvement in economic life. But in another sense this familiar model of laissez-faire is a misnomer because reaching for this ideal of the liberal market economy involved a series of constructive and programatic actions on the part of government. That is, to deregulate the existing economy, an entirely different range of regulatory actions became necessary; and to make the ideal of a non-interventionist state a reality, a highly interventionist strategy of legislative innovation would be needed. This paradox supplied a major theme of the period 1850-75, and the impact of a liberalizing reform agenda could be felt across the full repertoire of liberal economics, including:

the conclusion of bilateral free-trading treaties (which applied almost universally in Europe in these years);

the creation of larger monetary regions (such as the Latin Monetary Union of France, Belgium, Italy and Switzerland, 1865);

the internationalizing of waterways (for example, the Danube and the Sound between Sweden and Denmark, both 1857);

the deregulation of mineral resources and mining (for example, in Prussia, 1851-65);

the creation of a framework for company formation (through the general adjustment and recodification of commercial law, systems of company registration and the final abrogation of obsolete usury legislation);

perhaps most crucial of all, the wholesale dismantling of guild and associated restrictive legislation, which established the legal freedom to enter and practice any trade (in Britain, France and the Low Countries this had already been accomplished, but it was now achieved elsewhere too – in Sweden 1846-64, in Denmark, 1849-57, in Austria 1859, in most of Germany in the early 1860s and even in Russia, to the extent that a guild system had ever been established there in the first place, in 1866).

A further kind of interventionism was also required of governments in relation to a key motor of industrial (as opposed to commercial) development, namely, the great boom in railway construction in this period.

Liberalizing economic reform

Thus, despite the defeat of political liberalism in 1848-49, liberal economics enjoyed unprecedented sway in the internationalized economy of the 1850s; and despite the destruction of political liberties by the counter-revolutionary governments of 1849, the triumph of the capitalist market was eased by a remarkable spate of liberalizing economic reform. On the whole, international freedom of trade – the free movement of labor, capital and commodities, both within par-

ticular societies and across national boundaries – was thought to be a universal good. Despite the unevenness of the developmental process in the European economy – that is, the varying levels of development achieved by different economies and the enormous advantages accruing from freedom of trade to the pioneer industrializing economy, Britain – the advantages temporarily outweighed the disadvantages for the latecomer economies seeking to emulate the British example. Moreover, the spectacular character of the commercial expansion during the boom of the 1850s also tended to silence alternative voices. But at the same time, the protectionist critique of free trade possessed an obvious coherence, and under

the different circumstances of an international depression it could easily come into its own (as was actually to happen in the succeeding economic period of 1873-96). In fact, even during the liberal heyday of the 1850s and 1860s this was present as a latent potential, linked to another key theme of the period, nationalism.

To understand this linkage we have to say something further about uneven development. At the start of the nineteenth century, European industrial activity remained thin and patchy. Traditional industry – small-scale, highly decentralized production in the textiles and metallurgical trades – was widely dispersed through the countryside, extending across the continent in

two parallel swathes: one beginning in the Basque lands, and running through the South of France to the north Italian plain, and the other running from northwest France through the Low Countries to Saxony and Bohemia, before petering out in Silesia. Between the two was a third region, linking central France to Zurich and southwest Germany. Apart from northern England, North Wales and lowland Scotland the only major region of new manufactures was the Sambre-Meuse Valley in Belgium. By 1875, after the boom, the patchiness still remained. But aside from Britain and Belgium, modern industry had concentrated around the coal fields in the center and extreme north of France, Luxemburg and the Saar, Saxony, Silesia and of course the Ruhr. Other regions, including Normandy, Alsace-Lorraine and Bohemia, had become important centers of manufacturing. But otherwise, the old-style rural industry had considerably thinned out, with the traditional proto-industrial regions contracting around the new urban-industrial cores. Put this barely, the picture is slightly misleading, because in the meantime the reach of the capitalist economy had also expanded, so that commodity relations now extended to the most backward corners of the continent, and the commercialization of agriculture had become just as important as the growth of industry *per se*. But at both times, 1815 and 1875, virtually the whole of East-Central Europe, from the Baltic through Austria-Hungary to the Balkans, was empty of significant industrial enterprise. Industry stopped at Silesia, although by 1875 there were also pockets much further to the east in Tsarist Russia.

What was the impact of this continental backwardness, which set Lancashire against Galicia, Belgium against Serbia, the Ruhr against East Prussia, Piedmont against Sicily? In straight eco-

Left: Older ways of working, like this small-scale manufacture of woolen cloth, persisted alongside the beginnings of industrial mass-production.

Above: The machinery department at the Great Exhibition, held in the Crystal Palace in 1851. The Exhibition was a triumphant display of British industrial and technological achievements.

Right: The newly invented art of photography captures class conflict in action – two of the Parisian poor under arrest in 1847.

nomic terms it forms the basis for Alexander Gerschenkron's theory of economic backwardness, where the latecomer economies need an extra boost from government for their own development because the gap of institutional growth, capital resources and technology opened by the pioneer industrializers has become too great for them spontaneously to bridge. Elements of the 'development of under-development' are also present, because of the de-industrialization of old proto-industrial regions such as the rural hinterlands of Zurich and Lyons and the functional discrepancies of core and periphery with the same society (as in the north and south of Italy). Moreover, some of the key factors in the industrialization of the core economies, such as railway building and the setting up of central financial institutions, were imported by peripheral countries as much for reasons of local prestige and metropolitan profits as for their functional contributions to the growth of the domestic economies themselves. In all of these ways the steady diffusion or economic progress was not a realistic possibility. Each successive advance (starting in Britain and Belgium, continuing in parts of France, Germany and so on) not only upped the ante for the rest but negatively restructured the overall environment against them.

In other words, it may be (as Marx said) that 'the country that is more developed industrially only shows to the less developed the image of its own future.' But this was also a future that could only be secured across an enormous barrier of structural under-development. By comparison with the later experiences, British industrialization was exceptionally gradual, spontaneous and self-sustaining, without the complication of competition and with the luxury of a vacant European market. For the rest of Europe, the vision of progress could never be the slow, dawning rationalization of an empirically accumulating experience in this way. Instead, it had to be imposed, as a program and a challenge, a forced march of development. In the perception of continental Europeans economic progress in the first half of the nine-

teenth century meant the practical dominance of British manufactures in a trading environment stacked against the successful emergence of national competition. Continental regions thus reacted to the prospects of development with ambivalence, seeking both to resist metropolitan penetration and to appropriate its dynamism.

In this sense, nationalism took shape in the nineteenth century as an ideology of forced development. Of course it had a more strictly political dimension too, involving ideas of citizenship, popular sovereignty and national self-determination. And it also had a cultural dimension, postulating longstanding and inherited differences of custom, language and religion as the main dividers of European population. But at a governmental and party-political level it expressed the effort of the more backward or peripheral regions of the continent to emulate the metropolitan example and assemble the conditions of their own advance. At the same time, uneven and combined development involved a dynamic and changing configuration: as the global process continued, the inner edge of the periphery also receded, from Germany in the first half of the nineteenth century, to (say) Austria and Bohemia in the 1860s, the north of Italy and Spain in the 1890s and so on. Broadly speaking, the farther to the east and south we go, the greater the gap between the general development aspiration and the real capacity of the societies concerned to bridge it. From the Napoleonic times on Western Europe's developmental experience was being systematically borrowed as an imitative program well in advance of the native social development that could otherwise have sustained it. Such backwardness could only be redressed by imaginative political leadership, and this meant a kind of state-directed drive for development.

The developmental dilemma was also dramatized by the events of the French Revolution, events that were unconnected directly with the Industrial Revolution *per se.* Where the latter spelled factories, steam engines, cheap commodities and a new material civilization, the former

offered liberty, patriotism and government of the people. When liberal spokesmen of the emergent nations bemoaned the backwardness of their own societies in response to the dramatic changes of the French Revolutionary era, it was *both* sets of desiderata they had in mind, machines *and* constitutions. The French Revolution provided the orientation for several generations of European nationalists and political radicals who, for much of the first two-thirds of the nineteenth century, were generally the same people. Young foreign patriots, whether from Rumania or Greece, Ireland or Wales, drew from the French Revolution a model of how the freedom of a people should be organized, depending on the particular phase of the revolution they preferred for inspiration – that of 1789-91 (the propertied, quasi-British constitutional monarchy of the 1791 Constitution) or that of 1792-93 (the democratic republic of the 1793 Jacobin Constitution).

Above: A satirical attack on the right-wing reaction in Germany after 1848, personified as 'Deutscher Michel' – 'German Michael.'

Left: St Pancras station, London, under construction in 1868. The great railway stations were to the nineteenth century what the Gothic cathedrals were to the fourteenth and fifteenth, a summation of the values and aspirations of the age.

Right: Two scenes from the Crimean War, which pitted the British, French and Turks against the Russians. Above, the bombardment of Sebastopol, the Russian port besieged for 11 months in 1854-55. Below, British and French troops in action at the Battle of the Alma (1854).

But as we know, the French Revolution had its less positive side too. Apart from the special Polish and Irish cases, 'native' Jacobinism had been mainly an affair of a few adjoining states (the Low Countries, parts of Italy and Switzerland, possibly the Rhineland), and in most parts of Europe the victories of French revolutionary arms were greeted only by small groups of intellectuals isolated from any broader popular support. And by Napoleon's time even this sympathy had started to wane. Many of the early enthusiasts may have served in Napoleon's satellite administrations, and later intellectuals certainly benefited from his administrative and educational reforms. But in general, nationalist activity now had to define itself *against* the French occupation. For peoples on the outlying European periphery, where French armies never really arrived or established only a tenuous presence – areas such as Greece, or Rumania, or Ireland, or the so-called 'Illyrian Provinces' of Croatia and Dalmatia – the French Revolution could still retain its full inspirational value. For different reasons, this was also true of the Poles, who needed French backing against the Partitioning powers of Prussia, Austria and Russia. For some, the French influence could be little short of intoxicating, but for others it was now tempered by experience of the Napoleonic tutelage.

Thus nationalist politicians elsewhere were propelled into consciousness by the French example and had the British experience as a model of the new social order, but naturally enough they wished to command their own future. In practice, to emulate the Franco-British models they had to mobilize against them. This was what has been called the basic 'nationalism-producing dilemma.' It grew from the developmental handicaps that the unevenness of European industrialization imposed on the more backward societies – in the awareness that the ensuing development gaps could only be bridged by determined efforts to cast off the domination of the more advanced and exploitative cultures, whether British or French (and later, German), even as they drew on the latter for positive inspiration. The dual revolution (political revolution in France, industrial revolution in Britain) both inspired these aspirations and, via French bayonets and the spread of British manufactures, further complicated their realization.

This was the latent context of the restless capitalist expansion of the 1850s. It was already inscribed in the conflicts of 1848, the so-called 'springtime of the peoples.' In the central and southern European core of the revolutionary zone – in the five revolutionary capitals of Berlin, Frankfurt, Vienna, Budapest and Venice, as well as the emergent centers of Prague or Bucharest – the revolution was as much about forming a viable and self-governing nation-state as it was about liberalizing or democratizing the political system. Such a state provided the generally recognized foundation for both liberty and progress – for constitution-making and industrialization – and in the minds of most mid-century liberals shaping a liberal policy and legislating a national market were simply different sides of the same problem. By 1858-59, after the brief depression of 1857 and the revival of political life, these questions were out in the open and dominated the European politics of the next decade. This was particularly true of Italy and Germany, where the most dramatic liberal-nationalist breakthroughs occurred. But it was also true of the continent as a whole. Consequently, it is to a consideration of the changes of the 1860s that we must now turn.

The watershed of the 1860s

At the most general level, the 1860s provided a moment of liberalization in Europe as a whole. Indeed, in contrast with the French Revolution (when European liberalization was largely imposed by force of French arms) and 1848 (when the constitutionalist movements were suppressed), the 1860s amounted to one of the great constitution-making watersheds of modern European history.

The most dramatic changes were undoubtedly the unifications of Germany and Italy under broadly liberal auspices. Probably a necessary precursor to these unifications was the Crimean War of 1854-56, in which Austria belatedly joined Britain and France in aiding Turkey in a war with Russia. The result of the ensuing peace settlement was greatly to weaken Russia's position in Europe. In the long run this had the effect of weakening Austria as well, for the Russians had traditionally been the Austrians' staunchest allies in resisting liberal or nationalistic change in Central and Eastern Europe. The intervention of the Russians in Hungary in 1848, for example, had doomed the revolution's chances not only in Austria and Hungary, but in Germany and Italy as well. Similarly, it was joint pressure from Russia and Austria that had prevented the king of Prussia from trying to create a German union in 1850. But now, deprived of Russian support, Austria was unable to withstand the momentum of the nation-building movements that took place on her northern and southern flanks.

In many ways Count Camillo Cavour (1810-61), prime minister of Sardinia from 1852 until his death (with a brief gap in 1859), was a typical product of the 'nationalism-producing dilemma,' and in his ministerial career he became the embodiment of a particular 'realist' response to its demands. Moderately liberal and the architect of a narrowly based but functioning ministerial constitutionalism, yet implacably hostile to democratic radicalism, he pursued a modest policy of directed development based on free trade and public finance while conniving at the unification of Italy via the aggrandizement of his own northern Italian state. After the fiasco of a joint Franco-Sardinian war against Austria in the spring and summer of 1859, which was meant to expel the Habsburgs from Italy and consolidate Piedmont's dominance of the peninsula, these goals were rather unexpectedly attained in 1860.

In 1860 Italy consisted essentially of Cavour's Sardinia-based north Italian kingdom, the Papal States in the center and the kingdom of the Two Sicilies in the south. In that year a Sardinian republican, Giuseppi Garibaldi, organized a group of about 1150 personal followers (the 'Red Shirts') for a private – though covertly state-supported – armed expedition to liberate the south. Garibaldi's success in the Two Sicilies was as quick as it was astonishing, and in a short time his forces were marching on Rome itself. Cavour's Sardinian forces intercepted him before matters got too far out of hand, and the Sardinian prime minister persuaded Garibaldi that the time was ripe for invoking a series of national plebiscites in the center and south. The Two Sicilies quickly voted to join Sardinia, as did the Papal States outside the immediate environs of Rome. By 1861 a parliament representing all of Italy save Rome and Austrian-controlled Venetia was in being. Venetia entered the union in 1866, an award for Italy's support of Prussia in her successful war with Austria in that year, and Rome was finally annexed by Italy in 1870, after the French troops that defeated it were withdrawn as the result of the Franco-Prussian War.

Similarly, while Otto von Bismarck (1815-98), premier of Prussia from 1862 and first Chancellor of the new German Empire created in 1871, lacked Cavour's developmental vision, he nonetheless placed himself forthrightly at the head of the movement for German unification, forged the new state through a sequence of short and successful wars (over Schleswig-Holstein in 1864, against Austria in 1866 and against France in 1870) and thereby freed the Prussian government from the constitutional deadlock it had entered with the liberals in the early-1860s.

In terms of territorial unification the high points of Bismarck's policy came (a) after the 1866 war, which considerably enlarged Prussia itself, (b) with the creation of the North German Confederation in 1867, which joined Mecklenburg, Saxony and 19 other German states north of the Main with Prussia, (c) with the creation of the German Empire in 1871, whereby the major south German states of Bavaria and Württemberg were added to the states of the former Confederacy, and (d) with the integration into the empire of Alsace-Lorraine, a result of the 1871 peace settlement following the Franco-Prussian War. Politically, the empire had a constitution similar to that of the earlier North German Confederation, in which the component states maintained a degree

of local autonomy but sacrificed control over foreign and military policy to the emperor, who was also the king of Prussia. But needless to say, the progressive submergence of the other states within the Prussian-dominated *Reich* continued unabated between 1871 and 1914.

Beyond the creation of these new states, a series of major constititonal reforms occurred elsewhere in Europe, and collectively they amounted to an impressive increment of liberal political advance. In Britain the Second Reform Act was passed in 1867, and while not an unqualified triumph for the parliamentary Liberal Party given the confused circumstances of the measure, it nonetheless effected a significant extension of the political nation. In France, Napoleon III's authoritarian Second Empire collapsed following the defeat in the Franco-Prussian War in 1870, and after the dramatic interlude of the Paris Commune, the Third Republic was constituted in 1871. Likewise, Austria's defeat by Germany in the war of 1866 precipitated the constitutional Compromise of 1867, which transformed the Habsburg Empire into the Austro-Hungarian Dual Monarchy, essentially a bargain between the Germans of Austria and Bohemia and the Hungarian Magyars. A liberal revolution occurred in Spain in 1868-69; and constitutional reforms occurred in Greece (1864) and Serbia (1869). Even in Russia there was movement: the emancipation of the serfs in 1861 was accompanied by a process of gentry consultation which quickly acquired its own momentum, stimulating the first independent constitutionalist movement among sections of the gentry and the attendant concession of limited local government measures in the shape of the *zemstvo* reform of 1864. This catalogue might be further extended by extra-European examples, including the massive transatlantic upheaval of the US Civil War and the resulting constitutional revision. Altogether, these changes comprised a powerful victory for specifically liberal principles of political order, as we encounter them in the third quarter of the nineteenth century.

In effect, liberal constitutional norms became generalized in the 1860s into the predominant form of organization for European public life, and the accepted territorial framework for the latter was the nation-state. There is a pronounced tendency in writing about this period to present liberalism as being somehow in contradiction with nationalism. Thus, in one common interpretation, German liberalism was compromised by German nationalism, on the grounds that the acquiescence of a majority of liberals in Bismarck's achievement of German unification involved a vital betrayal of liberal principle. But this surely misunderstands the practical identification of liberal and nationalist goals in this period. By contrast with the 'core' states of Western Europe, nationalities east of the Rhine lacked the advantages of an early acquired statehood, so that demands for a liberal constitution became indissolubly linked to the prior achievement of national self-determination within a viable territorial state which by the middle of the nineteenth century was generally regarded as a precondition of 'progress' in its liberal sense. Furthermore, given the survival in Central Europe of pre-national state forms – petty monarchical and aristocratic jurisdictions of one kind or another – the real work of forming the 'nation' had to be conducted in opposition to the traditional sovereign

Above left: The contrasting architects of Italian unification – the revolutionary Garibaldi (left) and the politician Cavour (right). Garibaldi's daring landing on Sicily in 1860 paved the way for a united Italy, but Cavour ensured the new state would be a conservative monarchy.

Above: Russian Emperor Alexander II's pronouncement freeing the serfs is read out in a small Georgian town.

Right: A melodramatic portrayal of Bismarck dictating terms to French leaders after the Franco-Prussian War of 1870-71.

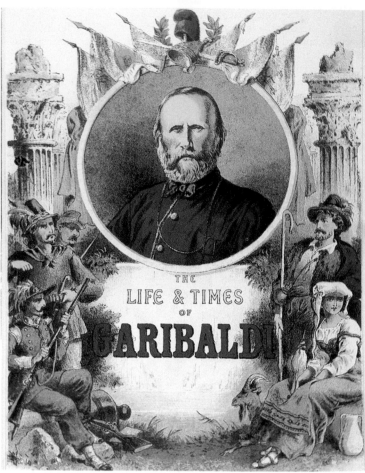

authorities by private rather than public bodies and by civil initiative and voluntary association rather than by government – in brief, by political action of the people organized as citizens. Thus the fusion of the terms 'nation' and 'citizenry' in liberal discourse was an inescapable reality of liberal politics east of the Rhine and south of the Alps in the middle two quarters of the nineteenth century.

From this point of view the creation of a united Germany may be justly regarded as the highest accomplishment of German liberalism in its classical phase, for all the parliamentary weaknesses of the 1871 Constitution. Allowing for national differences, in fact, this nicely illustrates the argument for Europe as a whole. On the one hand, unification created the legal and institutional conditions for a German-wide process of capitalist industrialization. More specifically, this meant an impressive body of forward-looking economic legislation, aimed at removing precisely the kind of developmental deficits discussed above. In this sense, the legislative framework of unification included: freedom of movement for goods, capital and labor; freedom of enterprise from guild regulation; emancipation of credit; favorable conditions for company formation; the metric system of weights and measures; a single currency and unified laws of exchange; a federal consular service and standardized postal and telegraphic communications; patent laws and a general codification of the commercial law; and central financial institutions.

Essentially, this involved all that the state did to organize the environment into an infrastructure for successful capitalist enterprise (including the regulation of rail and water transportation; management of relations with other countries through tariffs and/or commercial treaties; the acquisition of colonies and the protection of markets; the passage of new social legislation in areas of welfare, education, labor law and so on).

Unification also embodied the characteristic liberal vision of the new social order as that was understood at the time by enemies and friends alike. In Germany between 1867 and 1873 demands for a national constitution and other national institutions, for national economic integration and for the rule of law became the centerpiece of the new territorial settlement. But beneath this level of dramatic political achievement were deeper social processes of class formation which brought self-conscious bourgeois notables to regional, municipal and local predominance and allowed them to stake their collective claims to the moral leadership of society as a whole, whether or not they actually controlled the levers of high government power in the state. In this sense, unification was accompanied by the cultural ascendancy of a distinctive set of values, including those of merit, competition, secularism, law and order, hostility to hereditary privilege, ideas of personal dignity and independence and a generalized belief in the modern morality of progress.

This broader front of activity was at least as important to the liberals' sense of themselves as the formal political demand for an advanced constitution. They saw themselves as involved in a struggle to unlock the potential for social progress – to free society's dynamism from the dead hand of archaic institutions, not the least of which in much of the European continent (as liberals saw it) was the Catholic Church and its control of key social functions, from schooling to charities and the agencies of popular sociability. The social power of the Roman Church was not only a major political resource for the conservative opponents of change, it was also the major obstacle to the creation of a culture of capitalism, and as such it could summon the loyalty of many ordinary people, as well as powerful interests with a vested interest in the old order. Thus it was not some act of prejudiced folly that led liberals into an anti-

clerical offensive, but a consistent expression of positive liberal commitments, and to some extent an accurate perception of the real frontier of conflict for the emerging capitalist civilization. The leading edge of the latter in the 1850s and 1860s, appropriately enough, was in Italy, where the papacy and Italian nationalism fought in a running guerrilla campaign with each other. From the dissolution of monasteries and the attack on clerical privilege in Sardinia to the generalized harassment of the Church in Italy as a whole after 1860, this escalated into a general ideological confrontation, in which Pius IX denounced 'progress, liberalism, and modern civilization' (in the encyclical of 1864) as the source of the 'Principal Errors of our Time.' This conflict reached its climax in 1870, as the Italian state forced papal power back into its Vatican redoubt and Pius IX responded with his famous statement of papal infallibility. Thus the attack on clericalism was a general European phenomenon in this respect, of which the *Kulturkampf* in Germany in the 1870s (literally, a 'struggle for civilization') and the contemporaneous battles of education in France were particular national forms. The attack on the Catholic religion *per se* was less important, one might even say, than a positive ideal of how the future Italian, German or French (or British, given the salience of Protestant Nonconformity to Gladstonian Liberalism after the 1860s) society was to be shaped.

Corresponding to their elevated sense of the common good, liberals usually spoke for fairly broad coalitions of support. On the one hand, such coalitions always extended downward from the industrial, commercial and professional bourgeoisie into the petty bourgeoisie of small shopkeepers and tradesmen, the peasantry, the artisanate and the infant working class. On the other hand, they were never exclusively an urban formation and enjoyed strong links with the countryside, not just by appealing to the rural masses, but through close relations with the landed interest. At the same time, while this heterogeneity applied to most liberalisms to a greater or lesser degree, its specific manifestations varied across different societies. Both the forms of dominant class integration (eg among urban and landed groups, via inter-marriage, associational networks, commercial interpenetration, corporate political alliance and so on) and the precise relationship to different popular constitutencies were a powerful source of variation among national liberalisms, and a major factor affecting their internal political cohesion. We should certainly not make the mistake of assuming that liberalism was borne only by the new bourgeoisie, whether we look to the longstanding integration of the political active working class within the British Liberal Party up to World War I (or within the Scandinavian liberal movements up to the turn of the century), or to the farmer- and gentry-based liberalisms of Central and Northern Europe.

Finally, we should avoid associating specifically democratic reforms or outlooks with the liberal movements of the 1860s. As a general rule, mid-nineteenth-century liberals were hostile to democracy in the sense of rule by the 'mob' (as they tended to regard it), even where, as in the case of some advanced thinkers such as John Stuart Mill, they took a more generous view of the size of the electorate and popular entitlements. For most liberals suffrage was a privilege attached to property, education and a less definable quality of moral substance, and this general elitism, combined with fear of what the masses were likely to do with the vote once they got it, explains the remarkably narrow basis of the franchise in most liberal polities between the 1860s and the end of the century. Any enlargements of the democratic base owed less to the spontaneous inclinations of liberal leaderships than to the pressure applied on them by often popular forces. Such pressures could materialize in a variety of ways – in dramatic revolutionary crises (as in 1789 and 1848), in the course of more protracted struggles (such as the various reform agitations in Britain) or by being articulated into the liberal coalitions themselves (as in the case of Gladstonian liberalism in the 1870s and 1880s).

These, then, were the qualities that distinguished the political watershed of the 1860s:

(a) the Europe-wide ascendancy of constitutionalist principles of political order, embodied in a general liberalization of the state-system, at the center of which was the unification of Germany, which Benjamin Disraeli called the greatest political event since the French Revolution;
(b) the imbrication of those liberal constitutionalist principles with nationalist ideals of self-determination;
(c) the specific liberal content of the German and Italian unification settlements, and more ambiguously of the French and Austrian reconstructions that followed the military defeats, expressed both in the legal consolidation of the national market and in the drive for a new national culture;
(d) the social heterogeneity and broad popular basis of liberal coalitions, which integrated both urban and landed elites and substantial popular constituencies on however informal a footing;
(e) the independent, non-liberal origins of specifically democratic demands, which enjoyed varying forms of support or resistance from the liberal coalitions proper.

The political settlement of the 1860s proved remarkably lasting in some of its effects. Thus the 'constitutionalizing' of European public life in this period was never rolled back during the following 50 years, and the main adjustments to the system were toward a strengthening of parliamentary institutions and a democratizing of the franchise, as in the Third Reform Act of 1884 in Britain, or the Belgian Constitution of 1893, the introduction of universal manhood suffrage in Austria (1907) and Italy (1912) and the liberalizations in Norway (1898), Denmark (1901), Finland (1905) and Sweden (1907).

The progressive economic legislation of the 1850s and 1860s was also never revoked in a major way, although in different countries and different times significant legislation was certainly introduced to bolster traditional interests in agriculture and small business. In some ways the acid test of this triumph of capitalist relations was the freeing of labor from old forms of non-economic compulsion. As part of the 1860s reforms relations between employers and workers were generally made subject to the terms of the free contract, and in addition to the unusual degree of positive recognition achieved by trade unions in Britain under the laws of 1871 and 1875, the old restrictions on workers' combinations were also removed in Belgium (1866), Germany (1869), Austria (1870) and the Netherlands (1872). Despite partial and temporary reversions to repression (as in the German Anti-Socialist Law of 1878-90), these legal gains were never fully revoked in the period before 1914. Similarly, the national coordinates of the 1860s settlement also remained intact, although in the Habsburg Monarchy they were certainly subject to increasing strain.

Yet despite these lasting parameters of the settlement and the liberal optimism they proclaimed, the emerging social order was inescapably generating its own new problems. First, the crash of 1873 brought the hectic boom years to an abrupt end, and, in conjunction with the fundamental unevenness of the developmental process, the succeeding cycles of depression (1873-96) and renewed expansion (1896-1913) drastically undermined some of the more optimistic initial assumptions of liberal political economy. Second, the process of industrialization generated new social pressures in the form of new mass labor movements and in the independent activation of the peasantry and the petty bourgecisie. Third, these new social conflicts broadly corresponded with a new type of political and ideological antagonism between a socialist left and a populist radical right. Finally, the dynamic of nationalist mobilization now brought smaller subordinate peoples to self-consciousness in ways which increasingly destabilized the existing imperial polities of Central and Eastern Europe. Thus the settlement of the 1860s not only provided a point of departure, but also a framework for development.

Above far left: Pope Pius IX, who led the Catholic Church into open confrontation with nineteenth-century liberalism and scientific progress. He pronounced the doctrine of papal infallibility in 1870.

Above left: The title page of a biography of Garibaldi, published in Britain in 1880. The Italian guerrilla leader was a great hero with the British public.

Right: British Conservative leader Benjamin Disraeli (standing, left) and aristocratic friends. Disraeli was one of the first politicians to realize that right-wing parties could win popular support from a democratic electorate.

The advance of industry

No sooner had liberalism entered its climax in the 1860s, when both capitalist enterprise and national constitutionalism seemed the new universals of the international order, than the crash of 1873 opened a new era altogether, an era when the organization of the capitalist economy decisively changed, and with it the role of government and the general structure of social and political life. As Eric Hobsbawn has pointed out, the new era was to move away rapidly from unrestrained competitive private enterprise and was to witness the coming of large industrial corporations (cartels, trusts, monopolies), considerable government interference and different types of policy. The age of individualism ended in 1870, com-

plained the British lawyer A V Dicey, and the age of 'collectivism' began.

Aside from the growing levels of concentration, organization and government involvement in the economy, the capitalist economy experienced a series of other powerful changes. There was, first of all, the transition from the 'first' to the 'second' Industrial Revolution, involving new sources of power (electricity and oil, turbines and the internal combustion engine), new machinery based on new materials (steel, alloys, non-ferrous metals) and new science-based industries, such as the expanding organic chemical industry. There was also a transition to mass production geared to the domestic consumer market. In addition, there was a transition from an international economy

dominated by Britain's industrial monopoly to one increasingly dominated by the intensified competition among the British, Germans and Americans, which simultaneously involved the passage from smaller-scale to larger-scale enterprises. Finally, there was all the aggressive expansion of European capitalist interests into the extra-European and under-developed parts of the world via imperialism, in which the search for captive markets, investment opportunities and raw material sources increasingly dominated the foreign policies of the major European states.

Perhaps the most impressive thing of all was still the dramatic unevenness of the spread of the new industrialization. It came first and went farthest in Britain, with agriculture plummeting

Above: The Haematite Iron and Steel Works, near Barrow-in-Furness, England, in 1867.

Left: The introduction of farm machinery in the nineteenth century led to a massive rise in food production and a consequent decline in the rural population.

Above right: A cartoon of 1846 suggests that British landowners valued a pig above an agricultural laborer. Rural workers were always among the poorest members of society.

Above far right: Friedrich Engels, businessman turned revolutionary, who with Karl Marx established the principles of 'scientific socialism' or communism as it later became known.

from 40 to only 7 percent of the national product between 1788 and 1901, industry climbing from 21 to 43 percent and services accounting for 25 percent. By the simple industry/agriculture distinction, the British economy had already been restructured by the time the German process began. Between 1850 and 1910 German agriculture fell from 47 to 25 percent of total product, industry rose from 22 to 43 percent and services went from 8 to 15 percent, with the major change occurring in the years 1870-1900. In France things were slower, with agriculture dropping from 51 to 35 percent and industry rising from 22 to 36 percent over the period 1815-1909. Elsewhere (apart from Belgium, where the change followed soon on the British), progress was highly uneven. In Sweden the shift really began after 1880, in Italy after 1890. In Denmark and Norway it registered only modestly; in Iberia, the Balkans, Eastern Europe and Russia hardly at all.

Yet even in such cases, industry mattered, and the relative smallness of the industrial sector could sometimes conceal a very substantial working-class presence in certain regions or localities. If Britain was the most completely 'proletarianized' society by 1914 (with manual workers accounting for some 75 percent of the economically active population), then even the least industrial in aggregate terms, such as Imperial Russia (with some 75-80 percent living from agriculture), could claim major proletarian enclaves. In fact, Russian industry was the most highly concentrated in the world, with 54 percent of its industrial workforce in factories of more than 500 workers, as against only 32.5 percent in the USA.

Russia was an extreme example of uneven development, but there were others. In 1910, 59.9 percent of the economically active population in Austria-Hungary was still in agriculture, with only 21.8 percent in industry. The variation across the Habsburg Empire's regions was also extreme: while some regions remained completely dominated by a backward and under-commercialized agriculture others showed the typical social structure of a rapidly industrializing economy – Bohemia, for example, or Moravia, or Silesia (51.5 percent in industry, trade and transport), or Lower Austria (60.3 percent).

A famous example of such a disparity was the distinction between north and south Italy. By 1914 these two regions were already pulling apart. While nationally 55.4 percent of the Italian population was still engaged in agriculture in 1911, the figure for the north (52 percent) was already lower than for the south (60.6 percent), and northern agriculture was also heavily commercialized, producing in the Po Valley the largest and most militant agricultural proletariat in Europe. By the 1911 census 64 percent of Italy's industrial labor was in the north, 15 percent in the center and 21 percent in the south. Moreover, the north and center had 83 percent of the installed horse-power, as against only 17 percent in the south. In effect, Italy's industrialization was producing two completely separate societies.

This unevenness is one of the most important facts about European industrialization before 1914. Even in Britain the industrial north and Midlands faced the mainly agricultural south, where industry was confined to London and a few major ports, not to speak of the under-developed hinterland in Ireland. In Germany, too, by then the fastest growing capitalism in Europe, the same effect could be seen. On the one hand, German industry showed levels of concentration, technological drive and productivity that were the envy of Europe. By 1907 the two most important industrial regions, the Rhine-Ruhr and Saxony, had figures for industrial employment of 67.9 and 63.9 percent respectively, and the figures for urbanization were equally impressive. But on the other hand, by 1913, 35.1 percent of the economically active population was still engaged in agriculture, some 10 million people. Thus not even Europe's most powerful instance of industrialization led to anything as simple as an 'industrial nation.' Indeed, the German economy's regional specialization had produced its own dualism, because the eastern provinces of Prussia now took their place among the classically backward regions of the emerging European economy, milked of their human and economic resources by their voraciously growing counterparts to the west.

The rise of Labor

The social process of industrialization created the conditions for the emergence of independent, nationally organized working-class parties with a socialist outlook and a close relationship to a centrally coordinated trade union federation. The ideological foundations for such movements were laid in the 1860s (another reason for regarding that decade as a watershed) in the debates surrounding the short-lived First International (1864-76), in which the ideas of Karl Marx and Friedrich Engels proved decisive. But while the perspectives developed by the First International were of lasting significance, the International Workingmen's Association itself did not attain mass support or a stable organizational existence. That was to come with a cycle of foundations between 1875 and 1892, beginning with the German Social Democratic Party (SPD) and ending with the Italian Socialists (PSI), which equipped every European country outside the Balkans and the Russian Empire with a new socialist party. A second cycle then followed between 1891-92 and 1905, by which the new states of the Balkans, the Russians and the subject nationalities of the Romanov and Habsburg Empires acquired their own socialist parties too.

The first point to note about the new working-class parties was their solidly parliamentary character. Though some were avowedly revolutionary and they all contained at least some revolutionary factions, and while the authorities regarded them as subversive, they all directed their activities into the available parliamentary arenas, or, where such opportunities had not yet been created, devoted their energies to demanding their introduction. In other words, the legal and institutional conditions for the emergence of the new socialist parties had been established via the liberalizing constitutional settlements of the 1860s, and this indebtedness bequeathed a marked parliamentary character to the emergent social democratic tradition in the last quarter of the nineteenth century. Although the new parties usually originated in a split with the national liberalisms (in Germany, Austria and Italy already in the 1860s and 1870s, in Britain and Scandinavia much later in the 1890s and 1900s), this resulted less in any anti-parliamentary revolutionism on the model of the anarchists than in a drive to democratize the existing parliamentary constitutions. The largest and most sustained political mobilizations of the socialist parties before 1914 were over demands for the democratic franchise: the Belgian suffrage crises of 1886, 1893, 1899, 1902 and 1913; those surrounding the Scandinavian constitutional reforms of 1898 (Norway), 1901 (Denmark), 1905 (Finland) and 1907 (Sweden); and the general European suffrage agitations of 1902-06. On such occasions agitation was necessarily conducted by extra-parliamentary means, and during 1902-06 became linked to the more syndicalist idea of the mass strike (not least under the inspiration of the Russian Revolution of 1905). The agitations never actually outstepped the liberal legalitarian bounds as far as the majority social democratic leaderships were concerned via the given constitutional opportunities. To the extent that extra-parliamentary forms of action were adopted (mass demonstrations or political strikes), they were meant to complement the parliamentary and electoral arenas rather than to supplant them.

As a parliamentarian socialism, the social democracy of the period 1864-1914 was an explicit repudiation of certain existing traditions of the radical left. These traditions fell into four main groups. First there was utopian socialism, a collective name for various currents of radical communitarianism, in which forms of cooperative living in experimental communities were posited as an alternative to the competitive individualism and exploitative social relations associated with the emerging capitalist economy. Associated with the names of Robert Owen (1771-1858), Charles Fourier (1772-1837), Etienne Cabet (1788-1856) and more ambiguously Claude de Saint-Simon (1760-1825), it had really passed its heyday by the end of the 1840s. Next there was anarchism, asso-

Left: An early experiment in utopian socialism was Robert Owen's model industrial community at New Lanark, Scotland. Here the children of factory workers dance the quadrille.

Right: Louis-Auguste Blanqui, one of the early nineteenth-century revolutionaries who put their faith in secret organizations and armed insurrection.

Far right: German sociologist Max Weber, famous for his development of the concept of the Protestant work ethic and his analysis of the influence of bureaucracy in the modern state.

ciated as a formal creed with Pierre-Joseph Proudhon (1809-65) and later Michael Bakunin (1814-76) and Prince Peter Kropotkin (1842-1921). Bearing some affinities with the utopian socialists, it stressed extreme hostility to centralized political authorities, together with a 'mutualist' ideal of loosely federated communities of small producers. Then there was Blanquism, a general name applied to the conspiratorial and insurrectionary tradition of revolutionary action descending from the left-Jacobin tradition of the French Revolution and associated in the mid- to late-nineteenth century with the arch-revolutionist Auguste Blanqui (1805-81). Though the prevailing form of revolutionary or left-wing politics for the first half of the nineteenth century, this tradition failed to outlast significantly its tragi-heroic climax in the revolutions of 1848. Finally, there was radical democracy in alliance with liberalism, which remained the prevailing form of left-wing politics in the 1860s, but to whose frustrations the new social democratic parties of the 1870s and 1880s were very largely a response.

What probably brought the older radical traditions to a dramatic closure was the experience of the famous Paris Commune in 1871, when the people of Paris briefly installed a revolutionary administration in the wake of Napoleon III's defeat in the Franco-Prussian War. For one thing the ideology of the Communards revealed the transition from older forms of socialism to a more coherent type of collectivism actually in transition. The programatic thinking of the Commune displayed not only the old ideals of mutualism (the free association of independent producer cooperatives), but also new ideas of public ownership, state intervention and direct democracy, a contradictory amalgam of the old and new. Second, the Commune generated new structures of popular democratic self-administration, which suggested what a future socialist state might look like and provided a vital form of inspiration. But finally, by its bloody defeat the Commune exposed the inadequacy of a purely insurrectionary strategy, which paid no attention to the longer-term organizational question of building popular support in the country as a whole. In that sense, the experience of the Commune seemed to show the need both for a well-organized socialist party and for carefully elaborated strategies.

The liberalized constitutions that emerged from the 1860s – with their strengthened public sphere of parliamentary politics and the relative legalization of trade unions – provided the opportunity to meet the first of these two needs (the development of strong socialist parties), while the continuing advance of capitalist industry and the cyclical downturn of the post-1873 depression provided the impetus for dealing with the second (elaborating an economic analysis). On the whole, the outlook of the new parties was Marxist, in the sense that the leaders and official intellectuals of the various movements consciously adopted what they understood to be Marxist ideas, even if they were somewhat removed from Marx's own theories.

The Marxist legacy

The last two decades of the nineteenth century were actually the classic period of Marxist systemization, when the ideas of Marx were taken after his death in 1883 and codified into a workable body of doctrine for the freshly established parties. The combination of the socialist parties into a new International in 1889, originally for the purposes of coordinating agitation for the eight-hour day, was also crucial in fashioning this broadly Marxist orientation into a more coherent political tradition. If the First International provided the setting in which Marx's distinctive perspectives were first laid out, the Second International (1889-1914) fostered a sense of collective solidarity within an established Marxist tradition.

The extent of socialist success before 1914 should certainly not be exaggerated. For one thing, the achievement of many of the socialists' specific goals was often not directly the result of socialist action. Partly in response to the rise of labor there was a significant movement toward social and political reform in a number of European countries before 1914. The model for such initiatives, together with the widely admired systems of municipal welfare administration, were the German social insurance reforms of the 1880s, which gave regularly employed workers some elementary protection against sickness (1883), accident (1884) and old age and disability (1889). Similar systems were adopted by Denmark (1891-98), Belgium (1894-1903) and Italy (1898). Accident insurance was introduced in Norway

(1894), Britain (1897), France (1898), Spain and the Netherlands (1900), Sweden (1901) and Russia (1903). At first such initiatives might come from a variety of sources, conservative and paternalist as much as old-fashioned liberal, but from the 1890s they came increasingly from a kind of recharged liberalism, which appeared as a new ideology of state intervention, social welfare and national solidarity. This was a response both to the changing socio-economic environment of capitalism and to the challenge to the liberals' traditional popular support represented by the rise of new political forces such as the socialists. In their different ways figures like the Italian Giovanni Giolitti (1842-1928), the Germans Friedrich Naumann (1860-1919) and Max Weber (1864-1920) and the British New Liberals all sought to confront these novel problems as the assumptions of traditional liberalism came under attack. For the first time liberals were forced to deal with the question of mass democracy which they had kept too confidently at bay in the 1860s. This meant partly conceding greater measures of participation to the working class (as in the concession of the democratic franchise by Giolitti in 1912) or a much more ambitious program of social reform amounting to what we would now recognize as the origins of the welfare state (as in social legislation of the Liberal Government of 1906-14 in Britain). Over the longer term this also implied a major political realignment, involving an alliance with moderates in the labor movement to promote such causes as parliamentary democracy, social reform and national efficiency in a context of potential working-class incorporation. In all of these ways the impact on the socialist parties was enormous, as the liberal reorientation undermined the latter's sense of themselves as radical or revolutionary movements essentially excluded from legitimate politics and society.

If the integrity of social democracy was being potentially undermined by the more flexible and reformist politics of the dominant society, its radicalism was also being outflanked by certain phenomena to its left. For one thing, the new socialist parties had never established their complete hegemony over the European working-class movements. In Mediterranean Europe, anarchism remained a powerful current of activism and ideology within the Italian labor movement, while

in Spain it was clearly the majority outlook. From 1900 this existing tradition also joined with a new current of locally based, direct-action militancy extremely hostile to conventional parliamentary action and the socialist goal of a reforming state: syndicalism. As a formal movement and ideology, syndication was strongest in France, Spain and Italy, but related forms of industrial militancy also developed elsewhere in Europe. By 1913-14 such activism was starting to disrupt the existing certainties of the socialist parties too.

There were other ways in which the socialist parties failed to harness popular democratic energies and aspirations completely to their own programs. They failed consistently to develop an adequate agrarian policy, thereby surrendering the chance in most parts of Europe to win serious support among the peasantry, which on the contrary was virtually abandoned to different forms of agrarian radicalism, such as Populism or later the Socialist Revolutionaries in Russia. They also failed to take up sufficiently the cause of women, whose militant demands for the vote and other reforms became the basis of major agitations in Britain and elsewhere in the decade before 1914.

Finally, the 'rise of the masses' occurred not only on the left before 1914, but also on the right. The socialists' failings on the agrarian question have already been mentioned, and in Germany in particular a radical right-wing counter-mobilization on this and other questions became a major feature of the pre-war decades. In Germany, for example, in addition to such right-wing agrarian organizations as the Conservative Agrarian League, there was a somewhat overlapping *Mittelstand* (traditional small business) movement organized in a variety of interest-based associations. Also, there arose a bewildering assortment of nationalist pressure groups (the Pan-German League, the Navy League, the Defence League, the Colonial Society, an anti-Polish organization and so on), which recruited partly from the well-to-do bourgeoisie (professions and businessmen) but also achieved genuine mass support from the traditional small-business strata and the burgeoning new white-collar strata of clerical, administrative and managerial personnel. When these three types of movement became closely coordinated together in the three years before the war, on an explicitly anti-socialist and anti-democratic basis,

they mounted a formidable challenge to the popular democratic type of mass politics represented by the left. In many ways they anticipated the more violent counter-revolutionary mobilizations of 1918-23 and looked forward to the fascists.

Increasingly between the 1890s and World War I right-wing politics coalesced around the general issue of how far the old society was to be protected against the consequences of capitalist dynamism, where the latter included everything from the predominance of industry over agriculture in the economy, the primacy of the city over the country, the triumph of bourgeois values, the rise of mass democracy in the shape of the socialist and other radical movements and the sense of traditional ways of life generally being under siege. The emerging politics of reaction began as a series of discrete campaigns – demands for protective tariffs and other aid for agriculture, for protection of small businesses against the 'unfair competition' of big commercial companies, department stores and traveling salesmen, for the strengthening of craft and guild legislation and so on – but they quickly coalesced into a broad-gauged anti-democratic offensive. The new forms of polarization between left and right appeared most strongly in countries like Germany, Austria and Italy; in other countries, where the socialists had built a stronger relationship to the countryside, as in Scandinavia, the new right had a much narrower basis for its counter-mobilization. But in either case, the foundations of classical liberal politics were being eroded, for increasingly, the choice for liberals was either to cast in their lot with a conservative anti-socialist party or else to find a way of making common cause with the labor movement.

Nationalism and the background to World War I

The basic pattern of international rivalries between the 1860s and World War I was complex in the extreme. In outline it comprised the intricate holding operation of Bismarck's alliance system between 1871 and 1890, followed by a period of escalating tensions between the powers inside and outside Europe, first a naval and then a military arms race, and the alignment of the European powers into two mutually opposing blocs (the Dual Alliance of Germany and Austria-Hungary versus the Triple Entente of Britain, France and Russia, with Italy hovering between the two). The Balkans were a chronic source of difficulty and produced recurring crises between the Russo-Turkish War of 1876-78 and the two Balkan Wars of 1912-13, partly because the new successor states to the Ottoman Empire (Greece, Serbia, Rumania, Bulgaria and Montenegro) were constantly involving their Great-Power patrons in their problems. Conflicts in the extra-European world also became a potent source of tension, particularly after the end of the depression in 1895-96, which inaugurated another expansionist drive for the world market, with China and Africa as the main prizes. In this story of rising international tension it has become generally recognized that Germany had a special role – at the very least as an unstable and volatile factor, at most as an aggressive presence consciously pushing for war.

There is not space here to provide a detailed history of the major crises and their course. Instead, it may be more useful to mention some of the factors helping create strong dispositions in European society for war. Moreover, in a sense these were merely updated forms of the developmental processes outlined earlier in our discussion of the rise of nationalism.

The first of these processes relates to national integration. This was more important in the newly unified states of Germany and Italy, where governments tried to build new forms of national cohesion over the older particularist, religious and parochial solidarities. The multi-national empires of Russia and Austria-Hungary faced similar problems with the rise of the independence movements among the subject nationalities (Poles, Czechs, Ukrainians, Slovaks, South Slavs and so on) because the latter subverted the imperial and dynastic bases of their legitimacy. In France and Britain, where the territorial state and metropolitan culture enjoyed a much longer continuity, governments undertook a similar program of cultural unification, emphasizing national institutions far more aggressively than before. Most obvious, this meant using centralized apparatuses such as the school, church and army to instill in people a stronger sense of national identity. The attack on regionalism and local dialects was one of the commonest forms of this nationalist offensive, and the efforts to impose standard English or Parisian French paralleled the campaigns of Russification and Germanization in the more repressive states further to the east. But the best ways of showing what united the British (or French, Germans, Italians, etc) was to show what separated them from everyone else. In this respect, the attractions of a nationalist foreign policy proved hard to resist, and the various attempts to define 'national missions' in the world quickly entered into conflict. The Anglo-German naval rivalry (which got under way with the German Navy Laws of 1897-98 and 1899-1900, followed by the British Dreadnought initiative in 1906) and the competition of Russia and Austria-Hungary in the Balkans were the most fateful of these clashes, while others such as the Franco-British rivalry in Africa or Russo-British conflict in Central Asia) proved easier to deal with. Moreover, the sharper the domestic divisions (whether national in Austria-Hungary, socio-political in Germany or both, as in the case of Russia), the louder the calls to national unity and the more seductive the appeal of foreign aggrandizement.

This was assisted, secondly, by the state of the world economy. From the 1880s, a powerful consensus developed regarding the conditions of survival for a great power in the age of modern imperialism. This stressed the need to dominate a large economic region (whether a colonial empire or a continental land mass) by closing it off to one's rivals. This could be done both economically (by tariff walls, preferential treatment for domestic producers and other forms of protection) and militarily (by amassing large military and naval armaments for defensive and, if necessary, expansionist purposes). In Britain the intensely imperialist outlook associated with Joseph Chamberlain and his supporters was a good example of this thinking. In Germany, it became conventional to speak of the 'three world empires' (the British, the American and potentially the Russian) and of Germany's need to find a way of competing in the same terms. Though there was much enthusiasm for world expansion among German commentators too (by building a colonial empire in Central Africa at the expense of the Belgian Congo and the Portuguese colonies, or by spheres of influence in China and Latin America), this led increasingly to talk of *Mitteleuropa* – a Central European economic region stretching from the Low Countries to Ukraine, in which German capital would be dominant. This then opened the way for all sorts of geo-political, racist and social Darwinist speculations, so that the problem of competing in the world economy quickly elided with the idea of a German mission in the East against the 'Slav peril.' Indeed, it was Germany's simultaneous pursuit of 'world policy' and 'continental policy' (with the former predominating between 1895-96 and roughly 1911 and the latter reasserting itself after 1911) that helped solidify the Triple Entente of Britain, France and Russia in reply. By 1911-14 a series of difficulties (the failure to win colonial concessions from the British and French, diplomatic isolation, the build-up of Franco-Russian armaments, growing rivalry in the Balkans) encouraged German commentators to think of implementing *Mitteleuropa* by military means.

A third and closely related ideological theme was the drive for 'national efficiency.' To survive in the modern world, the argument ran, required not only determined interventions by governments abroad, but also disciplined mobilization of resources at home. This entailed maximizing efficiency in the economy and also paying careful attention to the cohesion of society and the

Left: Joseph Chamberlain, British advocate of imperialism and protectionism. Such attitudes fueled the diplomatic and military tensions of the 1900s.

Right: A sign calling for a mass protest meeting during the Hague antiwar conference of 1907.

Below right: The 1907 Hague conference holds its inaugural session. The spirit of internationalism that lay behind such antiwar efforts, stood little chance in the atmosphere of jingoism and national rivalry that prevailed in Europe up to 1914.

Below: Recruiting native troops in the German colony of the Cameroons. Germany was slow to acquire colonies overseas, although by 1900 it had come to regard them as an important part of the trappings of a great European power.

general 'health of the nation.' The new welfare legislation (including social insurance for sickness, accidents and old age; measures for maternal and child health; and greater regulation of public health), educational reform, and a general anxiety about the urban social environment were examples of this concern. There was great unease about the birth rate and an alleged deterioration of the nation's 'genetic stock,' so that many people turned to eugenics and similar techniques of social engineering to improve the mental and

physical health of the population. The growth of para-military activity, with its stress on social discipline, physical fitness, authority and patriotism, was linked to the same general concern, and it was here that ideologies of race and cultural superiority could also flourish, nurtured in the soil of a general social Darwinism. In Britain, spurred by the challenge of German industry in the world market, these matters were particularly close to the surface, especially after the recruitment drives for the Boer War (1899-1902) revealed such high

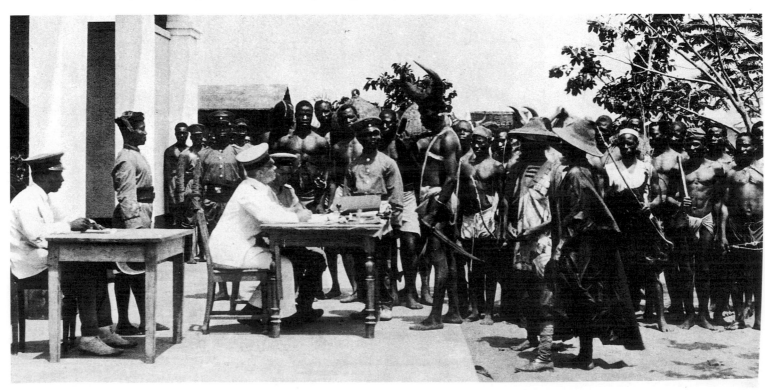

wing counterparts in most other countries. A softer version stressed the material benefits of empire, arguing that national prosperity (and hence higher standards of living for the working class) depended on the ability to build a strong position in the world market. That being the case, workers should back the patriotic labors of the government. This argument was very attractive to a younger generation of liberals, who between the 1890s and 1914 forged a new ideology of imperialism and social reform, binding each to the achievement of the other. With the onset of World War I most European socialists saw the force of this too, exchanging the rhetoric of internationalism for participation in the new patriotic consensus ushered in by the outbreak of war. By deciding to back their respective governments' war efforts, the majority of German, French and British socialists (and many in Russia and Italy as well) moved decisively onto the terrain of the nation-state and its axiomatic legitimacy, thereby accepting the primacy of nation over class.

Triumph of the nation-state

The main logics of nationalist ideology in this period were thus extremely powerful. It is certainly true that by 1900 the older forms of internationalism (Christian pacifism, or liberal ideals of international conciliation, even the international conferences of the Great Powers favored by Bismarck) were at a very low ebb. The various efforts at breathing new life into the spirit of internationalism – the Universal Peace Congresses and Inter-Parliamentary Union (both beginning in 1889), for example, or the two disarmament conferences at The Hague (1899 and 1907), the bi-national committees for international understanding (eg the Anglo-German Friendship Committee of 1905-06) or the Nobel Peace Prize established in 1897 – were without notable success.

It has been suggested by some historians that the outbreak of war in 1914 has to be set in the context of widespread social and political instability in virtually all the major European societies. In this view, governments deliberately manipulated (and even manufactured) popular nationalism to hide the need for domestic reform, on the grounds that foreign success by diplomacy or war would compensate for the lack of democratic rights or a welfare state. Some have taken this even further, arguing that the war itself can be explained in these terms, as the supreme social imperialist gamble, in which social unrest, political instability and the threat of revolution were all exchanged for the embattled solidarities of the war economy, the promise of grandeur and the future prospect of the post-war imperium.

This configuration of politics certainly emerged after the war had started, but the stronger case for seeing it as a cause has not been proven. To be sure, there is plenty of evidence that the German government, for one, was willing to envisage a 'preventive war,' and by 1914 both the Russian and Austro-Hungarian governments also had good reason to welcome the conflict. But it is hard to show that any European government positively went to war for this kind of reason. They were just as likely to be afraid of the unpredictable consequences of unleashing the conflict, and the massive demands of the war economy (including the practical necessity of conciliating the trade unions) quickly justified these forebodings. By 1917-18, in fact, the war and its effects had comprehensively destroyed the bases of the pre-1914 order, producing a redrawing of the political landscape every bit as far-reaching as the earlier watershed of the 1860s.

levels of ill health among the urban population. But they were common to each of the major European societies.

Finally, we should also mention anti-socialism. Here the argument had a natural progression, from the demands of national security and the dictates of imperialist competition, to the insistence on national unity against the common enemy, and thence to the silencing of certain kinds of domestic opposition as the enemy within. The primacy of the national interest in this sense was used systematically against the left, either to compel left-wing critics themselves into moderation or to mobilize the rest of the populace against them. This mechanism might take many different forms. At its most extreme socialists were stigmatized as national traitors who used social problems to promote class conflict and undermine the unity of the nation. In Germany the Pan-Germans and other radical-nationalist organizations were the characteristic exponents of this view, and they had their right-

The Making of Modern Russia

The unification of Russia was essentially completed in the reign of Vasilii III with the annexation of the merchant republic of Pskov and of the Principality of Riazan. The process of the expansion of Moscow, however, would not come to an end simply because the limits of the settlement of the Russian people had been reached. Having proclaimed themselves successors of the Kievan rulers, and having transformed themselves into autocrats, the princes of Moscow set out upon further expansion – westward into lands held by Lithuania, southward to the Black Sea, and eastward to the Urals and beyond. The reign of Ivan IV witnessed the transformation of the Russian national state into a multinational empire.

Ivan IV, Ivan the Terrible (or rather the Awesome), is a controversial figure in Russian historiography. His stormy reign began with great promise and ended in disaster, leaving Russia exhausted and weakened. Yet under his aegis Russia expanded far and wide, conquering the Khanates of Kazan and Astrakhan, crossing the Urals, and penetrating Siberia. Millions of subjects and hundreds of thousands of square miles of territory were added to the Muscovite Czardom and the foundation of the empire was laid. His domestic policies included much needed reforms of administrative and judicial institutions, but also a reign of terror so merciless and of such scope as nearly to destroy the nation. Ivan has had many detractors but he has also been defended. Justification has been found even for the most murderous of his actions.

Vasilii III died in 1533, when Ivan was only three years old. Elena Ginskaia, his mother, and her lover, Ivan Fedorovich Telepnev-Obolenski, ruled for five years. When she died under mysterious circumstances, Telepnev was seized and tortured to death. The Shuiskii family, one of the wealthiest and most powerful in Moscow, then seems to have achieved predominance, for Ivan Vasil'evich Shuiskii assumed the title of 'boyar and lord-lieutenant of Moscow.' But the Shuiskiis had to face the opposition of other noble families. Boyar intrigues and struggles lasted until December 1543, when the 13-year-old Ivan, already a confirmed sadist, suddenly asserted himself and had one of the Shuiskiis torn to pieces by dogs. The power of the monarch was so firm and opposition to autocracy was so weak, if indeed there was any, that the orders of a cruel minor were obeyed without question. Three years later, on 16 January 1547, Ivan was crowned not only Grand Prince but Czar.

At first Ivan's behavior seemed to change for the better. He carried out a number of reforms which improved the organization of the armed forces and created a new regular infantry, recruited and supplied by the Czar. This professional force, the *streltsy*, was settled on lands in the area of Moscow. A special detachment of 3000 men served as the Czar's bodyguard. In 1550 a new law code which regularized land holding and defined many administrative and judicial practices was prepared. The following year a Church Council fixed the forms of the liturgy, confirmed the right of monasteries to own land and generally reaffirmed the positions of the Josephite majority in the Church. The conservative tone of the Council, the emphasis on discipline in the Church and the fear of heresy, bring to mind the activity and the results of the Council of Trent which was in session at the same time.

Domestic reforms did not absorb all of Ivan's attention and energies. He and his advisers were determined to pursue an active foreign policy as well. No task seemed more important than the conquest of the Czardom (Khanate) of Kazan, one of the successor states of the defunct Golden Horde. For more than 100 years Kazan Tatars had raided Russian lands in the east, capturing and enslaving tens of thousands of Russians, occasionally receiving tribute and blocking Russia's eastward expansion. Ivan III and Vasilii III had tried to control Kazan by meddling in her internal affairs, supporting one faction against another or even putting on the throne puppet Khans. Yet nothing but conquest could assure Russia's interest in the long run. Immediately after his coronation Ivan launched a campaign against the Tatars of Kazan.

In 1551-52 Ivan made systematic preparations, building a fortress which would serve as a military base for the final siege of Kazan. All over Russia the clergy called for a crusade against the 'atheistic Saracens.' War against Kazan was perceived as a truly national and religious enterprise. There was probably more popular support for, or at least acquiescence in, the last Kazan campaign than for any other war in Russian history.

The city of Kazan was besieged by a large Russian army. Faced with the threat of subjugation, the Tatars united and offered fierce resistance, but Russian superiority in numbers and weapons decided the issue. When a German

Casan Tartarorum.

Left: The walled city of Kazan, captured by the Russian forces of Ivan IV on 2 October 1552.

Above right: A scene from an ancient miniature depicting Russian and Tatar armies facing each other across a river.

Far right: A formal portrait of Ivan IV, better known as Ivan the Terrible. After his assumption of power in 1547, he embarked on a series of campaigns to extend the boundaries of Russia.

engineer in Ivan's employ built a tunnel under one of the city's walls, filled it with powder and blew up the entire wall, the city's fate was sealed.

The fall of Kazan on 2 October 1552 was the end of the Khanate but not of Tatar resistance. For the next four years the Russians fought a ferocious war to subjugate the remnants of an alien people. In the process they advanced further south and annexed another successor-state of the Golden Horde, the factious and weak Khanate of Astrakhan. By 1557 the area was pacified and a Russian colonial administration was established, under a special ministry (*prikaz*) in Moscow. The Tatar nobility was decimated in order to deprive the conquered population of leadership. However, in a vast and sparsely populated area the Russians could not control every aspect of local life. The Tatars preserved a great deal of autonomy and successfully resisted the rather listless attempts of the Church to convert them to Christianity.

Eastward expansion

By conquering Kazan and Astrakhan Russia achieved control of the entire course of the River Volga and planted herself on the northern shore of the Caspian Sea. The road was open for the penetration of the Urals and of Siberia and for an unimpeded march to the Pacific. Russia also found herself involved, as the successor state of Astrakhan, in rivalries and alliances with the princes of Daghestan and Kabarda, beyond which lay Iran and Turkey. Finally, the incorporation into Russia of an enormous territory in the east made it possible for numbers of peasants to escape the increasingly heavy burdens imposed upon them by their lords and seek freedom in the deep forests beyond the Volga. Peasants and cossacks, fur trappers and petty merchants, monks and anchorites, fugitives and adventurers, penetrated the new territories, spreading Russian settlement ever further eastward. Seen in this light, the conquest of Kazan was Ivan's greatest accomplishment and a milestone in Russian history.

The success achieved by Ivan in the east and the increasing strength of the Russian state prompted him to assert his right to dominion over Baltic lands ruled by the Livonian Order. Armed conflict began in 1558. Ivan's troops advanced deep into Livonia, occupying dozens of towns and many castles. The Livonian Order collapsed and sought the protection of Poland, while the German knights in Estonia pledged allegiance to the King of Sweden, and by 1562 Russia was at war with both. There then began a period of military reverses for the Russians, ultimately leading to defeat.

Reverses in the field coincided with growing difficulties at home. The death of Ivan's wife, Anastasia, which he attributed to poison, increased his paranoiac tendencies, leading him to suspect even his closest friends and advisers of blackest treason. On Sunday, 3 December 1564, the Czar suddenly left Moscow, taking with him holy icons, jewels and the treasury. A month later Moscow was stunned to learn that he would no longer rule the country that he felt had betrayed him. Consternation seized the city. People believed that the Czar was the channel of God's grace, and with his departure the nation would be deprived of divine protection. A delegation waited upon the Czar and begged him to return. He agreed on condition that a part of Russia be set aside for him. In his part of the country traditional institutions would not function. Only those whom the Czar invited would have estates or reside there and only his will would rule. This new institution (*oprichnina* from the word *oprich* – except) would be a state within the state and would enjoy privileged status. In addition the Czar demanded unrestricted freedom to uproot treason and punish his enemies. His conditions were accepted and he returned to Moscow.

The reign of terror that followed this bizarre episode was without precedent in Russia's history and would remain unmatched for almost 400 years. Great nobles, even descendants of Riurik, were among the victims. When, in 1566, 200 of the 374 delegates of a *Zemskii sobor* (a kind of Estates General) petitioned the Czar to abolish the *oprichnina*, he replied by massacring all 200. The Metropolitan Afanasii (Athanasius) was forced off his throne. His successor lasted two days, and his successor only a little longer. Ivan forced his own cousin, Prince Andrei Staritskii, to take poison, and Andrei's son, Vasilii, perished later. Only Andrei's daughter survived.

Next Ivan accused the Novgorodians and their archbishop Pimen of designs to surrender Novgorod and Pskov to Lithuania. Detachments of *oprichniki*, Ivan's special troops, moved against the city. The Czar entered the city and began to exterminate its inhabitants. The nobles, the wealthy merchants and the clergy were subjected to torture. Ordinary citizens were drowned in the river at the rate of 1000 to 1500 a day for five weeks. Tens of thousands of peasants were massacred by the *oprichniki* in the countryside. Even cattle were massacred or driven away. Novgorod, which had avoided Tatar fury, was devastated by the Czar of Russia.

The terror grew and widened until the whole country was well-nigh paralyzed. At his country seat, Aleksandrovskaia Slobda, the Czar created an unreal world, a distorted imitation of a monastic fraternity dedicated not to worship, charity or learning, but to torture and every form of sexual perversion. In Moscow, six months after the sack of Novgorod, mass executions of government officials with their wives and children were carried out in public.

In May 1571 the Crimean Tatars struck at Moscow. Ivan's beloved *oprichniki* failed their master. Many did not appear when called to military service, others proved incompetent. Ivan, who had shown conspicuous lack of courage in military campaigns, fled before the approaching foe. The Tatars broke through to Moscow, sacked and burned the city and drove off some 100,000 people. The Czar's answer was a mass execution of the *oprichniki* and another major bloodbath. To deflect any retribution he appointed Khan Simeon Bekbuletovich of Kasimov to the dignity of Grand Prince and kept him on the throne for about a year.

The election of Stephan Báthory to the throne of Poland made the prosecution of the war in Livonia more difficult than ever. Báthory was a capable politician and an outstanding military leader, and by 1579 he had advanced his troops into Russian territory. In 1580 Velikie Luki fell to the Poles. Ivan was unable to mobilize his impoverished and exhausted country. Though Báthory was unable to reduce Pskov, whose strong fortress was heroically defended by its garrison and the people, Russia was at the end of her military resources. An armistice was concluded with Poland in 1582, and with Sweden in 1583. Russia gave up all she had fought for in the previous 25 years, and thus the Livonian adventure ended in disaster.

Ivan did not long survive the final defeat. Periods of depression and apathy were interrupted by outbursts of frenetic activity and savage anger. In a moment of uncontrollable fury he killed his son, Ivan. He slept little and suffered from nightmares that were as real to him as the waking nightmare of his existence. He died in 1584, leaving behind a legacy of blood, devastation and depopulation from which Russia would not recover in many decades.

Russia's 'time of trouble'

At the death of Ivan Russia found herself in a period of crisis. The economy was shattered. In the Moscow region the area of cultivated land decreased by 84 percent, while around Novgorod and Pskov up to 92.5 percent of formerly cultivated land was abandoned. Peasants fled to the Steppe, to the Don or beyond the Volga. Others joined bands of brigands and terrorized the countryside. Trade decreased, the population was demoralized and the nobles prepared to engage in a struggle for influence over Czar Fedor, the elder of Ivan's two surviving sons, who was reputedly feeble-minded and whose greatest pleasures in life were pilgrimages and church bells.

Above: Portraits of the False Dmitrii (right) and his wife, a Polish noblewoman. That he could gain the Russian throne with such relative ease was symptomatic of the devastation of Russian life after Ivan the Terrible's reign.

Left: The city of Novgorod was the scene of one of the worst massacres carried out during Ivan's reign of terror.

Above right: Boris Godunov, the *de facto* ruler of Russia after the death of Ivan the Terrible.

Above, far right: Stephan Bathory (1533-86), ruler of Poland during the wars against Russia.

БОРИСЪ ѲЕОДОРОВИЧЪ ГОДУНОВЪ
Царь и Самодержецъ в сероссїйскїй
Boris Feodorowicz Godunow
Tzaar et Autocrator totius Russiae

Fedor Ivanovich was incapable of governing. His maternal uncles and cousins, members of the large and ambitious Romanov family, were ready to rule in his name, yet power eventually fell into the capable though somewhat unclean hands of another relative, Fedor's brother-in-law, Boris Godunov, a clever courtier of Ivan IV, an *oprichnik* and an unscrupulous schemer. Boris destroyed or exiled those who opposed him and became the *de facto* regent. He managed to keep the peace, to balance the interests of contending social groups and to win the strong support of the Church by raising the Metropolitan of Moscow to the rank of Patriarch, thus making the Russian Church an equal of the Greek Church.

Fedor died in January 1598. He had no surviving children and his half-brother, Prince Dimitrii, son of Ivan the Terrible by his seventh and therefore uncanonical wife, had died under mysterious circumstances seven years earlier. An unprecedented situation confronted Russia: there was no czar. One had to be chosen. Of all the candidates the most formidable was Boris Godunov, who could have taken the crown by force but, to ensure legitimacy, chose to have it conferred upon him by a vote of a *Zemskii Sobor* (Assembly of the Land or Estates General).

The reign of Boris began auspiciously. The new Czar freed a number of prisoners, forgave uncollected past taxes and extended the privileges of the townspeople. He attempted to combat graft and other forms of government corruption, as well as drunkenness and vice. He promoted trade and succeeded in bringing about an improvement in the economic condition of the country. Yet the peasantry, which for the previous century had been steadily losing its liberty, resented its progressive enserfment, and the nobility was unreconciled to the rule of an upstart whose Tatar origin was known to all. Fear made Boris resort to terror, and terror in turn increased dissatisfaction and led to intrigues and plots.

Between 1601 and 1603 Russia was gripped by a famine of gigantic proportions. Masses of people tramped to the cities, and the system of food distribution was quickly overwhelmed and failed. People ate grass and tree bark, and there were cases of cannibalism. In Moscow alone 127,000 bodies were buried in three cemeteries, and thousands of others were not even interred. A contemporary estimate held that Muscovy lost a third of its population between 1601 and 1603. Tens or even hundreds of thousands of peasants fled to the frontier areas where they joined the turbulent, lawless communities of cossacks, freebooters and brigands who had formed themselves into veritable armies on the Dnieper, the Don and the lower Volga. Only a spark was needed to turn all this combustible material into a raging fire. The spark appeared in 1603, in the guise of the late Prince Dmitrii, the last son of Ivan IV.

In May 1591 Dmitrii had been found by his mother in the yard of the palace with his throat slit. Maria screamed that the Prince had been murdered by men sent by Boris Godunov. A special investigating commission, which included Prince Vasilii Ivanovich Shuiskii, descendent of Riurik and member of one of the most prominent and wealthiest Muscovite families, had found that Dmitrii had slit his own throat in an epileptic fit. But neither the contemporary public nor a majority of later historians accepted this verdict. It was Boris who stood to gain most by the elimination of Dmitrii, and it was Boris who was made to bear the blame for the death.

In 1603 there appeared in Poland a young man who claimed that he was Prince Dmitrii. The Russian government maintained that he was a monk, Grigoril Otrepiev. But certain Polish nobles found it opportune to pretend to believe the imposter, and soon a movement was afoot to restore Dmitrii to the throne. Because the False Dmitrii had secretly converted to Roman Catholicism, Pope Clement VIII blessed the enterprise,

and King Sigismund of Poland contributed some money and permitted Polish nobles to enlist under the Pretender's banner.

In October 1604 the False Dmitrii crossed the Russian border at the head of a force of 3000 men. Though defeated in a number of battles by government troops, he discovered cities and towns proclaiming their allegiance and thousands joining his cause, and suddenly he found himself at the head of a large-scale uprising against Boris. In April 1605 Boris died of a stroke. His 16-year-old son, Fedor II, was unable to keep the loyalty of the troops, and in early June there occurred a general uprising in Moscow. Mobs looted boyar houses and dragged the Patriarch from the altar of his cathedral into the street. A committee of prominent boyars in the service of the Pretender secretly murdered Fedor II and his mother, announcing to the people that they had committed suicide. Boris' beautiful and accomplished daughter, Ksenia, was turned over to the Pretender, who raped her and then locked her in a nunnery for the rest of her life.

The False Dmitrii entered Moscow to the ringing of bells and the acclaim of the people. He felt so secure after his coronation that he returned from exile a number of boyars who had conspired against him, among them Prince Vasilii Shuiskii. This proved a mistake, for Shuiskii soon began a new conspiracy against him.

Once on the throne, the Pretender had to pay his debts to his Polish supporters, to petty nobles of Russia's south who had been his early followers, to the Ukraine cossacks who had provided the bulk of his original force and to the peasants, whose sympathy was an important element of his victory. Vast sums of money and a large number of estates were given away. Moreover, the upstart Czar began to build a new palace in the Kremlin and to spin absurd plans for the conquest of Constantinople. By May 1606 his profligacy, as well as his imprudent marriage to a Catholic woman, had

November 1606, and Czar Vasilii would have lost Moscow had it not been for the differences within Bolotnikov's camp. When the peasant leader appealed to the Moscow populace to kill the nobles, to take their wives and property, to massacre merchants and loot their goods, promising them in addition ranks and titles, the *dvoriane* deserted him for Vasilii. Bolotnikov retreated to Tula, where he was eventually captured, blinded and drowned.

Shortly before the final defeat of Bolotnikov there arrived from Poland a new pretender, still another Dmitrii, accompanied by a number of Polish adventurers who had been defeated in an unsuccessful rebellion against their own king. False Dmitrii II was joined by the Don cossacks and the remnants of Bolotnikov's horde, and the Pretender marched on Moscow. Though he failed to capture the capital, he established himself on some hills at Tushino within striking distance of the city and could not be dislodged. Soon Tushino became a second capital.

Vasilii sought help from Sweden at the price of certain Karelian territories and the abandonment of Russian claims to Livonia. An alliance was concluded and a small Swedish army helped Czar Vasilii's young nephew, the capable general Mikhailo Skopin-Shuiskii, to clear northern Russia of False Dmitrii's marauder bands. He dislodged the 'Thief' from Tushino, scattered his forces and entered Moscow in triumph. Despite this victory the boyars had lost faith in Vasilii's ability to rule and soon thereafter deposed him, leaving Russia again without a czar.

The Time of Troubles now entered its last stage. Taking advantage of the anarchy in Russia, Sigismund III of Poland began to occupy Russian territories. Polish troops even entered Moscow, where they locked themselves up in the Kremlin. The Swedes moved in to take over Novgorod and Pskov. Since the Russians now had no czar and no government, it was the Church that assumed leadership. The Patriarch appealed to the population to resist the invaders. At Nizhnii-Novgorod a butcher responded by organizing a movement of liberation and raising a militia that was placed under the command of Prince Dmitrii Pozharskii. Other northern and eastern cities, many untouched by invasion and civil war, provided men and money.

The Romanov dynasty

Against all odds, this improvised national liberation movement succeeded, and in November 1612 Moscow was liberated. The leaders of the movement understood the need for the immediate election of a czar and the formation of a strong central government. The only question was who would wear the crown? The majority of the boyars and high officials, as well as the gentry from north Russia, supported the candidacy of the Swedish prince Charles Philip. The cossacks put forward a candidate of their own. A deadlock was avoided when, in 1613, a compromise candidate was found in the person of the 16-year-old Mikhail Fedorovich Romanov, a boyar who proved acceptable to both the ruling class and the cossacks.

The new government faced the almost insuperable task of establishing order, ridding the country of Swedes and Poles, pacifying the border areas, and restoring the economy. An abortive rebellion by a cossack leader in Astrakhan was successfully put down, but in the next several years Russia endured no less suffering than in the previous decade. The Swedes and the Poles continued their incursions. The cossacks ravaged the north, reaching the coast of the White Sea. Peace

cost him so much public support that Shuiskii and his conspirators felt the time was ripe for a coup. Two hundred armed men, many recruited from the Moscow mob, burst into the Kremlin and killed Dmitrii, and on the same day 3000 of his supporters were massacred.

The Moscow mob, maneuvered by the boyars, then chose by acclamation Vasilii Shuiskii to be the new Czar. Yet none of the measures subsequently taken by Vasilii IV to prove his legitimacy was really convincing. Though, unlike the False Dmitrii, he was a Muscovite prince, a direct descendant of Alexander Nevskii, in the summer of 1606 he was in the eyes of many people just as much a pretender as the man he had overthrown. His friends and retainers could manipulate the mob in Moscow, but not beyond. To win the favor of the boyars he made promises which would limit the power of the Czar in favor of the aristocracy. The *dvoriane*, by this time a powerful class of land-owning royal servitors, were offended and withheld their support. The peasantry, which had given its loyalty to an adventurer whom it took for a czar's son, refused to accord legitimacy to a descendant of Riurik.

It was the peasantry of the southern regions that constituted the rebellious element in the next stage of Russia's trial. Deeply czarist in sentiment, the peasants could be led only in the name

of Ivan's progeny. The death of the False Dmitrii had inevitably resulted in the appearance of other pretenders, but none of these managed to make a serious impression. Yet the rebellion still needed a leader. He appeared in the person of Ivan Bolotnikov, a fugitive serf who had been a cossack, had been captured by the Tatars and had slaved on a Turkish galley. Placed at the head of a rebel army, he became a major threat to Czar Vasilii. Bolotnikov was a man of great energy, a born leader and an enemy of the landowners. He appealed to the lowest levels of society: the serfs, the fugitives, the cossacks, and the large world of brigands and cut-throats who for centuries infested the Russian countryside. He thus succeeded in giving the movement the character of a class conflict.

A victory over government troops at Ielets brought Bolotnikov the support of Orel, Kashira, Tula and Riazan. In those towns, as in many others, the movement was led by the *dvorianstvo*, the service nobility that was making a bid for a stronger position within the Russian state at the expense of both the *boyarstvo* (the aristocracy) and the peasantry. Bolotnikov's followers, to the extent that they had a conscious program, fought for personal freedom, land, and relief from taxation, and they hoped to achieve their ends by supporting the 'legitimate' czar.

Large rebel forces converged on Moscow in

with Sweden was not concluded until 1617, when King Gustavus Adolphus, planning a war in Germany, signed a treaty at Stolbovo. Though Novgorod was returned to Russia, she lost for almost a century access to the Baltic Sea. The next year an armistice was signed with Poland.

The Time of Troubles had shaken the Russian state to its foundations, but its survival and triumph had proven its tenacity and strength. The early Romanovs, Mikhail and his son Aleksei, did not return Russia to the days of Ivan IV or Vasilii III, but autocracy once more regained its power and influence in the person of the Czar and re-emerged as the most important of governing institutions. The same cannot be said of the boyars. Though they continued to be the leading class through the seventeenth century, their numbers had decreased through the establishment of the *oprichnina*, the persecutions under Boris Godunov and losses sustained between 1605 and 1613. Moreover, new men had risen into the aristocracy during the Time of Troubles and came to share the power of the old families. This was true in the Boyar Duma, a consultative assembly of the Czar, and even more true of the government at large.

The *dvorianstvo*, the service nobility, emerged more powerful than before. They had proven indispensable to the restoration of order, and the new dynasty was in their debt and would serve their interests even at the expense both of the boyars and of the peasantry. One of the earliest actions of Mikhail upon his enthronement was a decree that peasants who had fought against the Poles and the Swedes must return to their owners at the end of the war. The decree precipitated a peasant uprising that was suppressed by armed force. The remainder of his reign was beset by peasant unrest.

The ruling classes were not of one mind on the course of action to be pursued toward the peasants. In 1637 the four wealthiest boyars owned land with 1000 to 3000 peasant households each. Ten years later there were 11 magnates whose holdings contained between 1000 and 8000 peasant households. Men of such wealth and power were willing to permit some personal freedom to the peasants, including the right to change masters at certain specified times. Less wealthy owners, especially provincial gentry, demanded more restrictions on serfs and the elimination of the statute of limitations which made a fugitive serf free if his owner failed to find him in five years following his escape. The period of legal return of fugitive serfs was steadily extended, until in 1649 Czar Aleksei's Code permitted indefinite search for fugitives and firmly established the principle 'once a serf, always a serf.' This same Code made landlords responsible for the actions of their peasants except in cases of felony. The landowner was permitted to try peasants in his own court, to torture them, and to chain them. Peasants were forbidden to inform on their masters except where the person of the Czar or treason was involved. Their property rights were not defined, but they were made responsible for their masters' debts.

Under Mikhail and Aleksei the authority of the government was restored and the economy improved, but the country did not gain tranquility. There were various domestic and foreign crises. High taxes and increased pressure on the lower classes led to revolts in the cities and disturbances in the countryside. Yet the momentum of expansion acquired over the centuries was so great that the Russian government could not refrain from the pursuing of an aggressive foreign policy, even if the cost in economic and social terms was extremely high. In the reign of Aleksei Mikhailovich, as in the previous several decades, Russia's principal antagonist was Poland. The contested area was the Ukraine.

After the devastation of Rus by the Mongols, the Kievan lands along the Dnieper became part of the Lithuanian state. Lithuania was a country inhabited by a Russian majority but it was ruled by a Lithuanian minority that was first pagan and later Catholic. When the Lithuanian King Jagiello married Queen Jadwiga of Poland in 1386 and assumed the Polish crown as Wladyslaw II, the country moved into the Western Catholic cultural and political orbit. In 1569 the Union of Lublin led to the virtual merger of the two states, with Poland gaining predominance. The old Kievan lands, now called the Ukraine (the borderland, the march), became the object of expansionist desires of Polish nobles hungry for land and serfs.

All through the fifteenth and sixteenth centuries, and especially after the Union of Lublin, the Ukraine served as a refuge to thousands of fugitive serfs from Muscovy and, to some extent, Poland. The newcomers mixed with the remnants of the old population as well as with adventurers from the wandering Nogai Tatar hordes, stray Greeks from the Black Sea coast, occasional immigrants from the northern Caucasus and from the Danubian principalities under Ottoman rule, to form a new people that would gradually evolve into the Ukrainian nation.

The heart of the Ukraine and the locus of its only significant armed force was the *Zaporozhskaia Sech* (literally – the clearing beyond the rapids, referring to a clearing in the forest on an island beyond the rapids on the Dnieper), an area that contained a cossack military brotherhood that lived by providing mercenaries to the Poles, engaging in piracy on the Black Sea, raiding Ottoman provinces or by outright brigandage. But when it came to Polish expansion into the Ukraine, the essential interests of the cossacks and of the Polish gentry, the *szlachta*, were irreconcilable. The cossacks, who were recruited from fugitive serfs and an exploited peasantry, hated all restraint, and preferred the turbulent life of the perennial warrior. The Poles saw in the Ukraine land to be acquired by the gentry, and in

Left: Czar Mikhail Fedorovick Romanov (1596-1645) became emperor in 1613 – a compromise candidate acceptable to both the cossacks and the Russian ruling class. He was the first of the Romanov line which would continue to reign until the Russian Revolution in 1917.

Right: A scene from the wars to liberate Russian territory from the Poles and Swedes in the early seventeenth century – Polish forces are driven out of Moscow by a militia army in 1612.

the Ukrainian people a mass of valuable potential serfs. Thus the main obstacle to the transformation of the Ukraine into a Polish landlords' paradise was the unruly *Zaporozhians*.

The first major *Zaporozhian* revolt occurred in 1591, under the leadership of Krishtof Kosinskii. No sooner was this rebellion put down than other risings flared up. In 1594-96 Severin Nalivaiko, Grigorii Loboda, and Matvei Shaula led a rebellion that spread throughout the Ukraine. It was suppressed with heavy losses. Other revolts followed. By the early seventeenth century rebellion and war became endemic. In 1647 a new wave of peasant uprisings spread over the Ukraine. The cossacks were especially incensed by the Polish occupation of the *Zaporozhskaia Sech*, which they saw as a threat to their very survival. They found a capable leader in Bogdan Khmelnitskii. Bogdan was a wealthy cossack who belonged to the stratum that was least revolutionary, but when a Polish landlord abducted his wife and killed his son and the authorities would not redress his grievances, he resorted to force. He quickly became the leader of a vast movement. In May 1648 he defeated an army under the Crown Hetman, Stefan Potocki. A local flare-up became a general rebellion.

Polish garrisons were forced out of Ukrainian towns. As they retreated, thousands of Polish landowners and Catholic clergy retreated with them. The greatest sufferings, however, were reserved for the Jews, who had incurred the violent hatred of the Orthodox population. The Jews had come to Ukraine with the blessings of the Poles, who were happy to settle these skilled artisans and merchants on their estates. The withdrawal of Polish forces left the Jews unprotected and helpless. There followed a major pogrom that took the lives of many thousands of men, women and children. Jews were beheaded, hanged, burned alive, and drowned. In several instances Jewish children were cut to pieces and eaten in front of their parents by blood-intoxicated cossacks.

Khmelnitskii achieved great success in 1648-49. Most of the Ukraine had been freed of Poles. Peasants were free and in possession of land, and the ranks of the cossacks had swelled with innumerable volunteers. Kiev itself had been liberated. Yet Khmelnitskii's position was by no means secure. Poland was still a great power. Once its forces were mobilized the cossacks would find it well-nigh impossible to resist

unaided. Moreover, there was division in the Ukrainian camp. The cossack leadership (*starshina*) believed that its rights would best be assured through accommodation with Poland. The peasantry did not mind war and anarchy if it meant their individual freedom.

A brief period of peace between the cossacks and Poland was broken by the latter in 1651. Khmelnitskii looked for allies. His Crimean friends had failed him. The Turkish Sultan, to whom Khmelnitskii offered suzerainty over the Ukraine, accepted the cossacks as his vassals but made no move to protect them against Poland. Bogdan therefore turned to Moscow. After long and intricate negotiations, the Russian government overcame its many hesitations, and in October 1653 the *Zemskii Sobor* voted to extend to the Ukraine the protection of Czar Aleksei.

The annexation of the Ukraine plunged Russia

into another war with Poland. The struggle lasted until 1667, and in the process the cossacks lost control of their own destiny. Some sided with Poland, others with Russia, still others with Turkey. The Treaty of Andrusovo, which terminated the war, partitioned the Ukraine, with Russia keeping the left bank of the Dnieper and Poland the right bank.

The annexation of the Ukraine and the consequent 13 Years' War with Poland strained to the utmost the resources of a Russian nation that had not yet fully recovered from the Time of Troubles. As usual, it was the peasant masses who had to pay the price of imperial expansion and foreign wars. The Code of 1649, fixing the forms of serfdom, was a heavy blow to the peasantry. Russian landlords (boyars, monasteries and gentry) acquired holdings even in the borderlands along the Don and the Lower Volga, seeking to enserf

Above left: A cossack ceremony from the seventeenth century. The cossacks form a 'ring' to make their acclamation of the new cossack *hetman* (leader).

Above: Stepan 'Stenka' Timofeevich Razin, the leader of a popular uprising in the late 1660s.

Left: The Cathedral of the Assumption in Moscow.

Above right: The Patriarch Nikon and his 'renegade' clergy. Despite support from the state, Nikon's religious reforms split the Russian Church establishment.

the free population that consisted of cossacks, fugitives and masses of Mordovians, Chuvashes, Maris, Tatars and Bashkirs. All the makings of a peasant uprising were on hand in the southeast by the late 1660s.

In 1667 a band of Don cossacks appeared on the Volga. The leader, Stepan Timofeevich (Stenka) Razin, was a 40-year-old cossack with much experience in fighting Crimean Tatars. The band sailed down the Volga, engaging in piracy and looting towns on the shores. This band grew to several thousand men as disaffected *streltsy* troops, exiled criminals and fugitive peasants joined Razin. Upon reaching the Caspian the cossacks obtained boats and began raiding Persian provinces to the south. They then proceeded up the Volga. In Czaritsyn they freed jailed criminals and captured the governor, whose beard Stenka pulled as he threatened to cut his throat. Next the cossacks captured Astrakhan, where they set upon massacring 500 nobles, government officials and merchants. In August 1670, having seen his marauding band turn into a huge cossack and peasant rebel army, Stenka marched against Saratov and Samara, neither of which offered him any resistance.

The uprising had by now assumed a definite class character. Razin spread among the peasants leaflets that called for the extermination of the boyars, the gentry and government officials. He promised freedom and justice, but had no ideology save a naïve monarchism similar to that of Bolotnikov 65 years earlier. In response, the peasants of the enormous territory of the Middle Volga unleashed a bloody Jacquerie, in that they massacred the landlords and set 'red roosters' (fire) to the manors.

The government was compelled to wage a full-scale war against Stenka's forces. In October 1670 the rebels were defeated at Simbirsk (now Ulianovsk in honor of Lenin, who was born there). Razin fled to the Don but was captured, brought to Moscow and executed in the Red Square (more correctly, Beautiful Square), and the rebellion was drowned in a sea of blood. According to some estimates, as many as 100,000 insurgents were killed. The military force of the centralized autocratic monarchy had proven itself capable of maintaining imperial cohesion.

The Great Schism

The political and social crises that convulsed Russia in the seventeenth century had their spiritual counterpart in the Great *Raskol* (Schism). The Russian Church had withdrawn into mental isolation in the days of Vasilii III and Ivan IV. It believed that it possessed the whole Christian truth and that Moscow was the third and last Rome. This exalted view of Muscovy had been shared by most Russians until after the Time of Troubles. But the extinction of the Riurik dynasty, the succession of pretenders, the occupation of the Kremlin by the Poles, the successes of Sweden in the Baltic and the peasant wars had had a strong impact upon the Muscovite mind. Old certainties began to be called into question.

The vexed problem of correcting errors in Russian translations of the Scriptures and of bringing Russian Church ritual closer to its Greek original had been raised early in the sixteenth century by a learned scholar resident in Moscow, Maxim the Greek. He was condemned for his efforts and spent the rest of his life in confinement in a monastery. But the issue had been raised again a century later in the reign of Mikhail, and finally under Czar Aleksei's friend, the Patriarch Nikon, books and rituals were corrected. To many Russians, clergy and laymen alike, this

seemed an unholy tampering with the sacred word. To admit that Scriptural texts and rituals had been corrupted was to concede that no one in Russia, not even her saints, had achieved salvation, since it was impossible to be saved through incorrect beliefs and practices. Those who believed in the Third Rome had to conclude that Nikon was a renegade. In 1653 a number of Nikon's own friends, including the Archpriest Avvkum, proclaimed him a heretic.

In spite of receiving full support from the state, Nikonian reform was rejected by a large number of priests and laymen, who became known as Old Believers, or as *raskolniki* (schismatics). They resisted in word and in deed, arguing in favor of Old Belief, establishing settlements in distant forests and at times even resisting with force of arms. They would continue this resistance for centuries to come. Persecution of Old Believers became especially intense in the reign of Peter the Great. So strong was their conviction of the unrighteousness of the government and of the official Church that tens of thousands preferred death to submission and burned themselves in their wooden houses of worship. Yet the majority survived and spread the faith to the Volga, the

Urals, Siberia and the North. The government systematically minimized the importance of the schism, making it appear that only a small number of people joined Old Belief. In fact, according to some authorities, Old Believers accounted for almost one-fifth of the Orthodox population of Russia as late as 1917.

Raskol dealt a heavy blow to the Church, making it even more dependent on the government. The withdrawal of some of the most determined and spiritually concerned clergymen weakened the official Church and eventually made it easier for Peter the Great to abolish the patriarchate, entrusting the administration of the Church to the Holy Synod, which was nothing but a government committee. Paradoxically, the Old Believers, as pariahs of Russian society, provided Russia with some of her early business entrepreneurs. Many grew rich in spite of certain disabilities placed upon them; but rich or poor, they remained outside the mainstream of Russian life.

It is noteworthy that the *raskol*, the only great religious movement in Russian history comparable to the Reformation in the intensity of feelings it aroused, emerged in opposition to innovation and change. Old Belief was profoundly conserva-

tive in doctrine and sentiment. Unlike Protestantism, it challenged the Church not on theological issues such as justification by deeds or by faith alone, not on problems of Church governance, not on the question of the relationship of Church and state, but on seemingly insignificant points of ritual. It is also noteworthy that the Czar and the Patriarch, the highest authorities in the nation, were the agents of change, while the masses either rejected it outright, or sympathized with those who did so.

Peter the Great

Ever since the Mongol invasion Russia had lived in relative isolation from Western Europe. Yet the isolation was never total. Ivan III had imported dozens of European technicians, including the brilliant Bolognese engineer and architect, Aristotele Fioravanti, to build the Cathedral of the Dormition, the ranking church of Muscovy, where all the czars down to Nicholas II were crowned. Italian masters had built the walls and the towers of the Kremlin, the bell tower of Ivan the Great, the *Granovitaia Palata* (Hall of Facets) and other outstanding edifices. By the sixteenth century the number of military and civilian technicians increased so rapidly that they were settled in a foreign suburb, the *Nemetskaia sloboda*, or German Village. Ivan the Terrible had imported metal workers, miners, physicians, builders and a variety of military specialists from all over Europe, and he had opened the country to English merchants who built depots on the shores of the White Sea and were much in evidence at Kholmo-

Left: The Belfry of Ivan the Terrible, part of the Kremlin complex in Moscow.

Right: A bronze statue of Peter the Great (1672-1725), the first emperor of Russia. Under Peter's energetic leadership Russia was able to compete with the previously more developed nations of Europe.

Far right: The Winter Palace in St Petersburg (present-day Leningrad) was built — along with the original city — under the express orders of Peter the Great.

gory, Novgorod and Moscow. Boris Godunov had sent the first batch of Russian students to be educated in what the Russians looked upon as 'the West.' (Not one had returned home, in spite of several decades of effort by the government to bring them back.) The Time of Troubles had opened Russia to adventurers from many countries, and the Romanovs had further increased exchange with western Europe.

But toward the end of the seventeenth century Russia began to experience as never before the impact of the technologically superior, scientifically more advanced and economically more developed West. In spite of the importation of technicians, Russia had fallen behind her European neighbors. The very fact that she had been repeatedly defeated by Poland, a politically weak state with a relatively smaller population, and by Sweden, a nation whose resources were incomparably inferior to Russia's, was stinging proof of Russia's relative backwardness. It fell to one of Aleksei's sons to try to close the gap.

Aleksei had married twice. From his first wife, a member of the powerful Miloslavskii clan, he had two sons, Fedor and Ivan, and a daughter Sofia. Aleksei's son by his second wife, Nataliia Naryshkina, was named Peter. In accordance with custom, Aleksei was succeeded in 1676 by his eldest son, Fedor, who reigned until 1682 and died childless. He should have been succeeded by his brother Ivan, but the Naryshkin family and a number of boyars feared the growing power of the Miloslavskiis. The support of the gentry and of the Patriarch assured the election of Peter, who was not yet 10 years old, to the throne. The Miloslavskiis gathered their forces and staged a successful counterattack. A mob led by the *streltsy* guardsmen invaded the Kremlin and murdered several members of the Naryshkin party, including one of Peter's maternal uncles. The coup d'état resulted in the proclamation of Ivan as senior Czar. Since dyarchy had Byzantine precedents, it was possible to compromise and keep Peter as junior Czar. A special two-seat throne was installed in the Kremlin palace, where the two Czars presided on solemn occasions or received foreign ambassadors. Real power fell into the hands of Peter's capable, ambitious, and well-educated half-sister, Sofia, who acted as regent. Ceremonial duties apart, Peter, his mother and a

small number of loyal supporters lived in virtual exile in Preobrazhenskoe, a village close to Moscow, where the young Czar was free of the restraints of court ritual. The German village, next door to Preobrazhenskoe, attracted Peter. He became a frequent visitor in the homes of Germans, Dutchmen and Scotsmen in the employ of the Russian government. They were flattered by his interest and happy to teach him mathematics, ballistics, tactics and other skills useful to a future ruler. They also helped him organize and train a regiment composed of young men, many of whom became Peter's constant companions. This Preobrazhenskii regiment was to become the nucleus of the new modernized Russian army.

Peter's marriage in 1689 made Sofia realize that he was no longer a minor. Rumors of plots to kill him circulated in Moscow and reached Preobrazhenskoe. But in a dramatic reversal of fortune, Sofia's power collapsed. Abandoned by her supporters, she surrendered to Peter and was imprisoned for the rest of her life in a nunnery. The virtually disabled Ivan V continued as Czar in name only, though he was invariably treated with respect by his younger brother. Ivan's death in 1696 left Peter the sole Czar.

For 35 years Russia's history was dominated entirely by Peter. Every significant event bore the marks of his frenzied personality. First and foremost he was a war lord. The expansion of the empire and conquest were his principal interests. Everything else – modernization, financial reform, education, culture – was important only to the extent to which it increased the military capacity of the state. Peter's first campaign (1695), directed against the Turkish fortress of Azak (Azov) at the mouth of the Don, failed for lack of a navy that could bar the Turks from supplying the fortress by sea. Undaunted by the setback, Peter collected an army of workers at Voronezh on the Don, and at high cost in lives and money he built enough boats again to attack Azov and to take it the very next year.

The acquisition of a strip of land along the Sea of Azov was not enough for Peter. He dreamed of a grand coalition against the Ottoman Empire, a coalition that would drive the Turks out of Europe, liberate Balkan Christians, and give Russia the Crimea and access to the Mediterranean. In pursuit of this dream Peter made his

first European journey, traveling incognito, though all European governments knew that Peter Mikhailov, the tall young subaltern with imperious manners, was the Czar. Diplomatically, the mission led nowhere, but otherwise the trip was a success. Eighteen months in Europe gave Peter an opportunity to learn a great deal about the Baltic, navigation, shipbuilding, education and international politics. He hired hundreds of foreigners to serve in Russia and established lasting connections in England, Holland and Prussia. Moreover, discussion with Danes and Poles led him into a fateful alliance against Sweden, resulting in a war that would last for 21 years.

Peter's fascination with the Baltic as an outlet to the West was skillfully exploited by King Augustus II of Poland and Saxony and by Johann Patkul, a Baltic German adventurer who was seeking revenge on the Swedish government for wrongs he believed it had done him. The campaign against Sweden began with a Danish attack and an invasion of Swedish Livonia by Augustus II. The allies hoped for an easy victory over a nation led by a 17-year-old lad, King Charles XII. Their expectations were shattered almost immediately. Charles hurled his small but well-trained army against Denmark, forcing the Danes to make a separate peace. Next he marched to the relief of the Swedish fortress of Narva, which was besieged by a Russian army under the Czar himself. Peter had not yet heard of Denmark's defeat and did not expect Charles to come to the aid of Narva's small garrison. A brief and bloody battle was fought on 30 November 1700, and the Russians were badly beaten, losing more than 8000 men and all their artillery.

The brilliance of his victory at Narva seduced Charles XII into thinking that Russia was no longer a formidable opponent and that the decision in the war would come in Poland. He therefore attacked Augustus II, inflicting upon the Saxons and the Poles a series of defeats and inadvertently providing Russia time for recovery. Peter had already proven his capacity to master adversity. Once again defeat galvanized him. He conducted governmental and financial reforms, increased and made more efficient the collection of taxes, suppressed uprisings of desperate peasants, who ultimately had to pay for the Czar's imperial ambition, reorganized and rearmed his

forces with the help of countless foreigners who flocked to him from all over Europe and generated among his associates a spirit of confidence that permitted Russia to continue the war.

Having defeated Augustus II and placed upon the Polish throne his own creature, Stanislaw Leszezinski, Charles XII now led his veteran army into the Ukraine. This proved to be a strategic as well as a political mistake. Swedish troops operated far from their bases, making supply difficult and communication at times impossible. On 8 July 1709, at Poltava in the heart of the Ukraine, some 22,000 Swedes faced almost twice as many Russians in what turned out to be one of the decisive battles of European history. The Swedes fought heroically, but to no avail. Led by Peter, who threw himself into the thick of battle, the Russians broke the Swedish lines and totally destroyed the enemy army. Charles XII, who had narrowly escaped capture, made his way to Turkey to urge the Sultan to resume war on Russia.

Victory at Poltava must have made Peter feel invincible, for he began to conduct himself in a provocative and belligerent manner toward the Turks, with whom he had signed a peace treaty only ten years earlier. A new war, for which Russia was ill prepared, broke out, and Peter led his army to the Balkans. It was his turn to miscalculate. Balkan Christians, on whose uprising against the Turks he counted heavily, did not stir, and now it was the Russian army that was forced to operate far from its bases without adequate supply lines. In July 1711, on the River Pruth, the Turks, whose forces were twice as numerous as Peter's, surrounded the Russian army. A major disaster was

avoided only through the skill of Russian diplomats who bluffed and bribed the Turkish commander Baltaji Muhammad into permitting the Russians to retreat. In addition to sums of money paid as bribes, Russia gave up all her acquisitions in the south, including Azov, and promised not to interfere in the internal affairs of Poland. Meanwhile, the war with Sweden was still dragging on. Eventually, however, Charles XII perished, and his exhausted country sued for peace. The treaty of Nystadt (1721) assured Russia access to the Baltic in Livonia and Karelia, where in 1703 Peter had founded a city that he named, after his patron saint, St Petersburg.

Even while still engaged in the struggle for the Baltic, Peter had found time and energy to pursue the dream of expansion in Asia. He encouraged exploration of Siberia, and sent a force of 3500 men under Prince Bekovich-Cherkasskii to conquer Khiva and explore the approaches to India, but Bekovich-Cherkasskii's troops fell into a trap and perished to a man. Still in search of the road to India Peter sent a young officer, Artemii Volynskii, to Persia. Volynskii observed the decadence of the Safavid dynasty, the weakness of the central government, and the growing independence of provincial rulers from Georgia to Afghanistan. Upon his return he urged Peter to invade Iran. The termination of the Northern War in 1721 made such a southern campaign possible.

Finding a suitable pretext in the mistreatment of some Russian merchants in Transcaucasia, Peter invaded Persia's Caspian provinces. He met virtually no resistance, since Persia was in the throes of anarchy produced by the revolt of the

Afghans, who had occupied Isfahān, the Empire's capital. Baku, Gilan, and Māzandarān were annexed to Russia, as was the Khanate of Tarqu in Daghestan. A few years later Iran's power revived, and Peter's successors were forced to withdraw from northern Persia and the Caucasus, but Peter's expedition had set a precedent that was to be followed by Catherine II, Paul, Alexander I, Nicholas I, Nicholas II, Lenin and Stalin, each of whom would send forces into northern Iran and attempt to make of the Caspian a Russian lake.

Reformist zeal

Perhaps the most astonishing thing about Peter was his ability in the midst of continuous warfare to conduct far-reaching reforms in every sphere of the nation's life. For obvious reasons military reforms came first. The Muscovite armies had traditionally consisted of levies raised for war and disbanded at its end. The only regular troops were the roughly 20,000 *streltsy* that had been established by Ivan the Terrible. Peter had entered the Northern War with two regiments of his former 'play' troops, numbering some 2000, about 40,000 *dvoriane* (gentry) militia and thousands of virtually untrained volunteers. Gradually there emerged a regular army of 200,000, a corps of 100,000 cossacks and multitudes of irregular Asian units. Regular troops were relatively well equipped. Their numerical strength assured Russia against any possible attack from the West or from Turkey. But while the army could be reformed, the navy had to be built from scratch. Peter had a great love of the sea and devoted much time and energy to the creation of a navy. The Baltic fleet, built after 1704, fought well against the Swedes. Yet the navy fell into disuse after Peter's death and did not revive until late in the eighteenth century.

The unwieldy Muscovite bureaucracy was incapable of serving Peter's ends. The generation of military power demanded new administrative and fiscal institutions. Peter acted *ad hoc*, without a well-thought-out plan. His main concern was to untie the hands of the czar, who had been in many ways shackled by tradition, to increase his efficiency and to forge instruments of government responsive to his will. In 1711 Peter appointed a Senate to rule the country while he was fighting the Turks. The Governing Senate became a permanent institution, with supervisory authority in the administrative, financial and judicial fields. It never was, nor was it ever intended to be, a legislative assembly.

In 1717 a reform of the government's central departments, the *prikazy*, was carried out. Over the centuries the *prikazy* had grown in number and irrationality of function. Peter abolished them all and, with the help of foreign advisors, created first nine, then 12, colleges each with clearly defined duties: war, navy, foreign affairs, justice, commerce and so on. Each college was governed by a board of 11 officials with a president at their head. Each included a foreign expert who was to help the Russians operate the new administrative machinery. This system, a great step forward from the *prikazy*, lasted until the reign of Alexander I.

Throughout Peter's reign the Russian government was short of funds. Financial strains at times approached crisis proportion. Though state revenues rose six-fold between 1680 and 1724, the value of the ruble fell by 50 percent because of the reduction of the amount of silver in coins. The increase in revenue was produced by taxing almost everything: mills, fisheries, bathhouses, windows, beards, oak coffins and people. The poll tax, which took the place of the traditional household tax, fell heavily upon the peasantry, free and bond alike. The collection of the poll tax from the serfs was entrusted to the landowners, increasing their power over peasants still more.

Exigencies of war made Peter aware of the need for industrialization. In response to the requirements of his new army he created a textile industry and promoted the development of metal works. The government set up enterprises for the manufacture of consumer goods as well, but sold the factories to private owners whenever possible. The industries were run essentially on slave labor. The Code of 1649 had made the ownership of serfs a prerogative of the nobility, but serfs were the only large source of manpower, and an old law could not stand in the way of economic development. A decree of 1721 permitted the permanent attachment of serfs to factories owned by others than *dvoriane*, thus indirectly extending to the merchant class the right to own men. On balance industrialization under Peter was only a partial success. Russia led Europe in the production of pig iron up to the end of the eighteenth century, but in other areas production remained static or decreased. By the end of the century Europe's industrial revolution left Russia far behind once more.

Military, financial and administrative reforms went hand in hand with changes in society and culture. Peter envisaged Russia as a community made up of distinct classes, each contributing service to the state. The enserfment of peasants was always justified by the necessity of supporting a service gentry. Within the nobility itself Peter abolished formal distinctions between the old aristocracy, the *boyars*, and the gentry who held land on condition of service, the *dvoriane*. In 1722 Peter promulgated a Table of Ranks which established 14 grades for all government servants. Everyone entering service was supposed to start at the lowest grade. In theory government service was open to all. Non-nobles who reached the

officers' rank and civil officials who reached grade eight were granted hereditary nobility. The system operated until 1917, though only a few were able to enter *dvorianstvo* through it.

To function in a modernized military and civil establishment the *dvorianstvo* had to be educated. Before Peter Russia had no educational system, only a number of theological schools connected with monasteries. Now hundreds of *dvoriane* were sent abroad to learn shipbuilding, fortification, ballistics, navigation, mining and other useful disciplines. But education abroad could not satisfy the demands of the government. Peter promoted the opening of domestic 'cipher' schools, where stress was placed on teaching mathematics. A naval academy and a school for army engineers were also organized. These efforts still did not fill the need for competent personnel in government and industry. The Academy of

Above left: A painting of the Battle of Poltava, Peter the Great's decisive victory over Charles XII of Sweden.

Above right: An example of the Western classical statuary introduced by Peter the Great to grace his royal palaces.

Right: Russian troops of the eighteenth century. Thanks to Peter the Great's reforming zeal, the Russian armed forces were able to deal with the incursions of the Swedes during the Great Northern War, and expand southward against the Turks.

Sciences which Peter created at the very end of his life provided a nucleus for serious research and high scholarship, but the general level of education in Russia would remain low for more than 200 years.

Orthodoxy under attack

Peter's reforming zeal touched even the Orthodox Church. At the death of the Patriarch Hadrian in 1700 the Czar did not appoint a successor, allowing the institution to die. It was replaced by the Holy Synod, a committee of 10 bishops controlled by the Czar through an appointed lay official. The Church was now entirely subordinated to the government. The Czar's closest collaborator and advisor in ecclesiastical matters, the Ukrainian priest Feofan Prokopovich, was a well-educated man who had converted to Catholicism, switched back to Orthodoxy, toyed with Lutheranism but remained in fact totally indifferent in matters of religion. Prokopovich preached the supremacy of secular power and helped to remove from the Czar's despotism all spiritual restraint.

The Czar himself was totally unlike his predecessors in manners and mood. There was no gravity to Peter's demeanor. He walked fast, talked loudly, smoked tobacco, got drunk in public, worked in the docks, pulled teeth, consorted with foreigners and showed contempt for tradition. He removed the capital from Moscow to his wet and cold northern 'paradise,' St Petersburg, where he compelled noble ladies to abandon the seclusion of their homes and appear at 'assemblies' wearing low-cut French gowns. He forced all his male subjects, except the peasants and the clergy, to wear Western dress and to shave their beards. No wonder millions of his subjects decided that he was not the genuine Czar but either a devil or a foreign impostor. Old Believers, who fared badly under Peter, saw in him Anti-Christ himself.

In fact, Peter may have been the most hated of Russia's czars. The masses did not understand him. His reforms meant nothing to peasants who were crushed by exorbitant taxes. The Russian historian V Kliuchevskii expressed doubt that there was ever a battle that cost the lives of more soldiers than the number of workers who died building St Petersburg and its naval base, Kronstadt. Yet for a segment of the upper class, and especially for those whom Peter raised from obscurity to prominence, the reforming Czar was almost divine.

In the nineteenth century the ideological battle between the Westerners and the Slavophiles was fought largely over the role of Peter. The former hailed him as the greatest Czar and civilizer of Russia, while the latter attributed to him the interruption of Russia's organic development and the deformation of Russia's life. Whatever one's evaluation of Peter and his epoch, there is no doubt that he had the most profound influence on the course of Russian history. At an enormous cost in men and treasure, he forced Russia to undergo at a tremendously accelerated rate the process of modernization which the Turks, the Persians, the Japanese, the Chinese and ultimately all non-Western peoples of the world would have to experience.

Peter's death in 1725 left Russia without strong leadership. The new men who had risen in his

Above, far left: A crude example of Peter the Great's reform of Russian society — a member of the court suffers the attentions of Peter in the role of dental surgeon.

Above left: Peter the Great imposes his will on the heads of the Russian Church.

Left: The imposing façade of the Summer Palace at St Petersburg.

Right: Peter the Great's daughter Elizabeth was an intelligent successor, but her lack of discipline and her laziness worked against the zealous efforts made by her reforming predecessor.

Far right: Peter's reforms were often extreme and unpopular with the highly conservative Russian establishment. The compulsory shaving of beards provoked widespread dissatisfaction among the elite of Russian nobility.

reign were concerned not so much with reform as with self-preservation. Aleksandr Menshikov, a street urchin who had become Peter's favorite and closest collaborator, put the Czar's widow, Catherine, on the throne, in spite of the existence of a legitimate successor, a grandson of Peter I. Catherine I reigned only two years, and she appointed as her successor Peter's grandson, whose place she had usurped. The boy-Czar, Peter II, was first controlled by Menshikov, but a plot hatched by old aristocratic families, the Dolgorukiis and the Golitsyns, stripped Menshikov of his power and sent him into Siberian exile. There then emerged a government of Muscovite aristocrats, a boyar oligarchy largely dedicated to the interests of the higher nobility and therefore suspected and feared by the gentry. When Peter II died of smallpox shortly before his fifteenth birthday, the oligarchs engineered the accession of Anna Ivanovna, daughter of Ivan V, Peter the Great's half-brother and, briefly, co-Czar.

Anna had spent most of her life abroad as the wife and widow of a petty German prince. Now she returned to her native country at the invitation of the oligarchs who offered her the crown at the price of signing a document that virtually turned over sovereignty to the Supreme Privy Council of eight members. Without the Council's endorsement the Empress could not marry, appoint a successor, declare war, conclude peace, levy taxes or make any important appointments. This was, indeed, a constitution, the first in Russia's history; but it was dedicated entirely to the interests of a small group of enormously rich, influential, landowning nobles.

Yet Anna soon discovered that she had some powerful allies. The guard regiments, which were veritable political clubs of Russia's young noblemen, resented the curtailment of monarchic authority. So did the *dvorianstvo*. In exchange for service the Czar had endowed the *dvorianstvo* with land and serfs, protected it against both the boyars and the peasants, given it status and finally turned it into the first estate of the realm. The *dvorianstvo* now came to the rescue of the autocracy. The guard regiments staged impressive demonstrations, Anna tore up the document limiting her authority, the oligarchs were arrested and sent into exile and autocracy was restored.

Under Anna Ivanovna (1730-40) Russia passed through a decade of 'German rule' exercised by her favorites, of whom the most powerful and the most obnoxious was Ernst Johann Bühren (to the Russians Biron). Bühren himself never learned Russian and never lost an opportunity to inform the Russians of his low opinion of their country. To the 'fledgelings of Peter's nest,' men who had humbled Charles XII at Poltava and made Russia a major power, German domination at court was galling. Anna's death may have saved her from a coup d'état.

The next Czar, Ivan VI, the son of Anna's niece, Princess Ann of Mecklenburg, was only two months old at the time of his accession. First Bühren and then Anna tried to serve as regents, but the guard regiments, fed up with the inefficiency, squalor and, most of all, the German dominance at court, staged a coup d'état, elevating to the throne Peter the Great's daughter, Elizabeth (1741-62). The Russians were elated to have a native ruler once again. Tall, good-looking, intelligent, but also lazy, undisciplined and self-indulgent, Elizabeth satisfied the *dvorianstvo* by showering upon it estates, serfs, and money. But in essence her rule was not much better than that of her immediate predecessors. The gentry continued to amass wealth and privileges while the peasantry kept sinking decade after decade toward slavery.

In spite of minors, dolts and voluptuaries who occupied the throne after the death of Peter the Great, Russia could not be turned from the path he had blazed. Russia's position in Europe was strengthened as a result of successful participation in the War of the Polish Succession (1733). A war with Turkey (1735-39) led to the recovery of Azov, which had been won and lost by Peter I. Sweden was dealt another defeat in 1741. The war against the Prussia of Frederick the Great as part of a coalition (the Seven Years War) took Russia's armies further west than ever before. They occupied East Prussia in 1758, and struck deep into Germany. Berlin fell in the autumn of 1760, but the death of the Empress Elizabeth and the accession of Peter III produced a revolution in Russian policy. The new Czar, an ardent admirer of Frederick II, withdrew his troops from Prussia and concluded an alliance with the former enemy. On balance, however, Russia's foreign affairs were well conducted by capable ministers, and Russia's position in Europe suffered no decline.

Intellectual achievements

At home, too, the Petrine impetus for modernization continued, though at a much slower pace. There was no progress in industry, the finances were in a state of perpetual crisis, yet the country did not stagnate. The Academy of Sciences, conceived by Peter the Great, developed into an important center of scientific training and research conducted first by foreign scientists and scholars and later by Russians. Such great figures as the mathematician Leonhard Euler, historians Gerhard Müller and August Schlözer and the natural scientist Johann Gruelin set high standards for their Russian colleagues and students.

This period witnessed the appearance of the first outstanding Russian scientist, Mikhail Lomonosov (1711-65). Son of a White Sea fisherman, Lomonosov was sent to Germany, where he was trained under the guidance of the famous scientist-philosopher, Christian Wolff. He rapidly developed into a first-rate scholar and made significant contributions to chemistry (the first formulation, though in a crude form, of the law of conservation of matter), astronomy, geology and

physics. More than anyone before him he helped to make science a vital part of Russian culture.

The founding of Moscow University in 1755 on the initiative of Elizabeth's young favorite, Ivan Shuvalov, was another cultural and educational milestone. History and literature also made strides. Vasilii Tatishchev and Prince Mikhilo Shcherbatov produced the first large-scale histories of Russia based on extensive reading of chronicles and serious work in the state archives. And the appearance of several talented dramatists, poets and prose writers prepared the ground for the great efflorescence of Russian genius in the nineteeth century.

Thus the 37 years that elapsed between the death of Peter I and the accession of Catherine II were a period of complex and seemingly contradictory developments. Yet it was the decline in the position of the peasantry and the increasingly cruel exploitation of the serfs that provided the upper classes with the wealth which built the palaces, subsidized the sciences and the arts, permitted the dispatch of hundreds of students to European universities and maintained the armies

Left: A bitterly satirical cartoon of Catherine the Great showing her ambition to rule a Russian empire reaching all the way to Constantinople.

Below left: A formal portrait of Catherine the Great with Peter III (standing) and their son, who became Czar Paul I after Catherine's death in 1796.

Right: Catherine the Great (1729-96). The outstanding feature of her reign was Russia's expansion at the expense of Poland and Turkey.

that considerably enhanced the country's international position.

The reign of Elizabeth's successor, Peter III, lasted only a few months in 1762. Peter III had come to Russia at the age of 14 but never lost his love of Germany, his Holsteinian patriotism or his dislike for the people whom he was called upon to rule. He tried to placate the gentry by granting them more privileges. In March 1762 he promulgated a decree abolishing their obligation to serve the state, an obligation that had for 200 years been *dvorianstvo's* primary *raison d'être* and the justification of serfdom, the peasants supposedly performing a state service while working for the gentry who served the czar.

Logically, the emancipation of the nobility should have led to the emancipation of the serfs and to the loss by the gentry of their rights to peasant labor and to estates. Of course, no such thing happened, nor was the emancipation of the serfs even contemplated. As a result of the edict of 1762 the serfs were transformed into private property. This was the culmination of a long series of legal acts designed to enslave the peasantry. Attachment to the person of the owner meant the abandonment of the serfs to the arbitrary rule of the masters. It is in this period that the worst features of slavery – the sale of individual peasants without land, the breaking up of families, the torture and murder of recalcitrant peasants – became familiar in Russian life.

In spite of the major concessions he made to the nobility, Peter III failed to win its allegiance. Against the wishes of the nobility, he fought a war with Denmark in the interests of his beloved Holstein. His bizarre personal behavior further offended those who held in their hands the power to make and unmake kings. In the summer of 1762 the guard regiments struck again. The hapless Peter was overthrown and murdered soon after. His wife Catherine assumed the crown, bypassng her son and Peter's legal heir, Prince Paul.

Catherine the Great

Catherine II was an accident on the Russian throne. Daughter of a minor German prince in the employ of Frederick the Great, she was 'programed' by her unscrupulous mother to contract a brilliant marriage. Her education was spotty, but she knew how to please. Still in her teens, Catherine was chosen by the Empress Elizabeth to be the wife of her nephew and heir, Peter. At the

Russian court Catherine knew loneliness and fear. She found consolation in books, reading voraciously and retaining what she read. She learned Russian, made a show of Orthodox sentiment while being in fact a Voltairian, won many friends and even managed to keep in the good graces of the capricious Elizabeth. After Peter's accession Catherine's position became precarious, and it was merely her good luck that the conspirators who overthrew Peter chose her as the next sovereign.

Once on the throne, the plump German princess with a head full of French Enlightenment ideas learned that she now depended for her survival on the nobles who raised her up. She became their faithful servant, bowing before their will and ruling the Empire exclusively in their interests. In 1773 peasants rose in a bloody uprising led by Emelian Pugachev, a Don Cossack reminiscent of Stepan Razin. The rebels moved up the Volga, taking towns, burning noble country houses and massacring the gentry. A large regular army commanded by some of Russia's best officers, including the young Aleksandr Suvorov, crushed the rebellion and engaged in frightful counter-terror. As a result the position of the serfs deteriorated still further, while the gentry acquired new and more extensive privileges. The Charter of 1785 permitted the gentry to organize themselves into corporate bodies under their own Marshals of Nobility. The gentry's exemption from the obligation to serve the state was confirmed. Other new privileges included exemption from corporal punishment and the extension of property rights. Simultaneously, new restrictions were imposed upon the peasants and serfdom was legally extended to the Ukraine. By the end of Catherine's reign 53.1 percent of all peasants, or 49 percent of the population of Russia, were serfs, in fact slaves.

It has been said that of the three most important problems of Russian foreign policy in the eighteenth century Peter the Great solved one, the Swedish problem, while Catherine solved the other two, the Turkish and the Polish problems.

The Turkish problem in the reign of Catherine centered on the Crimea. The Khanate of Crimea, a successor state of the Golden Horde, now under Ottoman protection, was no longer the threat it had been in the sixteenth century. It continued, however, to be a major source of irritation. The southern steppes were exposed and control of the Black Sea was unattainable as long as there existed in the Crimea a hostile state. In 1735 the Russians invaded the peninsula but had to withdraw. Another attempt was made in 1771, during the war with Turkey.

The Ottoman defeat in that war led to the establishment of a nominally independent Crimean state which was recognized by the Porte in the peace treaty signed at Kucuk Kaynarca in 1774. But the Crimeans preferred Turkish overlordship to 'independent' existence in the shadow of Russia, and they detested Sahin Girey, Russia's choice for their new khan. In due course there was a rebellion which had to be put down (with excessive cruelty) by Russian troops, since Sahin's own army refused to fight. A second revolt resulted in his flight from the Crimea and a second return in the wake of a Russian army. A new wave of repression swept the peninsula. The punishments Sahin inflicted on masses of his enemies were so cruel that the Russians wavered in their support. At last Grigorii Potemkin, the most influential of Catherine's favorites, persuaded the Empress to order immediate annexation. In spite of possible international complications, Catherine issued the annexation decree in April 1783.

The Crimea was named Tavricheskaia (Tauride) district and incorporated into Russia as an ordinary province. The khanate, and with it Tatar autonomy, were forever abolished. Some 200,000 Crimeans having left the country, the Russian government had a large amount of land to distribute to the Russian nobility. The place of the departed Tatars was gradually filled by Russians, close to 50,000 of whom had settled in the Crimea by 1800. The conquered population paid taxes but no pressure was applied to Christianize or Russify it. Over 160 years would pass before the Tatars would experience the full measure of their conquerors' wrath and disappear from the Crimea in the 'final solution' of 1945.

The Polish question also found a 'solution' in Catherine's reign. Poland had long been in decline. The medieval institutions, the multinational character of the commonwealth and religious dissent made it impossible for the country to withstand the combined pressure of her three powerful neighbors: Prussia, Austria and Russia, each bent on expansion and coveting lands held by the Poles. The death of King Augustus III opened the door to Russian intervention and in 1764 to the election to the throne, with Russian armed support, of Stanislaw Poniatovski, Cathe-

rine's one-time lover. But his attempts at reform were vigorously opposed by a portion of the *szlachta* (gentry), who were supported by Russia.

With the nation divided and Russia ranged against him, Poniatovski was unable to institute desired reforms. Then, in August 1772, Russia, Austria and Prussia signed a treaty of partition, depriving Poland of a third of her territory and of more than a third of her population. Russia received the largest share, 36,000 square miles with 1,800,000 people. This First Partition shocked a number of Polish nobles out of their habitual lethargy. A reform movement gained ground, resulting in the adoption in May 1791 of a new constitution designed to transform the Commonwealth into a modern nation-state. Catherine would have none of this, and she encouraged a number of Polish noblemen to proclaim a 'confederation,' which was immediately accorded full Russian support in the form of a Russian invasion of the country. Prussia, which had made promises of support to Poland, now (1793) joined Russia in the Second Partition. Russia obtained 89,000 square miles of Polish territory inhabited by three million people. The Constitution of 1791 was annulled and the rump Polish state became a virtual Russian protectorate.

The concessions that were soon forced upon the Polish king by the Russians and Prussians became so onerous that a large segment of the nobility, known as the Patriots, refused to accept them. In the spring of 1794 an insurrection broke out. Under the leadership of Thaddeus Kosciuszko the Poles expelled the Prussians and won several encounters with the Russians. Warsaw, Lublin, Grodno, Krakow, Vilno and other cities quickly joined the rebellion. But the Polish troops were badly equipped and finally no match for the veteran Russian armies commanded by the great Suvorov and supported by the Prussians and the Austrians. In the autumn of 1794 the Russians defeated the insurgents, captured Kosciuszko and re-occupied Warsaw. The country was now totally divided among Russia, Prussia and Austria, though the final treaty abolishing Poland was not signed until 1797.

Brilliant successes in foreign policy, the expansion of the Empire in the west and the south, the suppression of the peasant revolt and the emancipation of the gentry produced among the latter a feeling of triumph and well being that was reflected in their mode of life, the arts and literature. It was in Catherine's reign that the first important Russian writers appeared. Gavriil Derzhavin, a courtier and statesman, is the first poet whose works can still be read with pleasure rather than for history's sake, and Denis Fonvizin's *Nedorosl* (*The Minor*), a comedy attacking the manners and mores of the unenlightened portion of the upper class, is popular to this day.

The age of Catherine also produced social criticism and laid the foundation for the literature of protest. Aleksandr Radishchev, who has been called Russia's first radical, was influenced by the publicists of the French Enlightenment. His book *Journey from Petersburg to Moscow* was a direct assault on serfdom and therefore on the very foundation of the gentry regime. Catherine had him tried and condemned to death, though the sentence was commuted to exile in Siberia.

Alexander I and the Napoleonic Wars

Catherine's reign ended in fear and repression. The execution of Louis XVI in France shocked the Empress deeply and made her turn her back on former favorites, even politically innocuous ones such as Voltaire and Montesquieu. Age brought about a deterioration in character in the monarch. Youthful lovers selected for their ability to please began to exert political influence that earlier had been the privilege of experienced and capable men. Her death in 1796 did not improve matters, since her son and heir, Paul, was a narrow-minded and boorish man, dedicated to the memory of his putative father, Peter III. Like Peter III, he antagonized the nobility by withdrawing some of its privileges and interfering with its way of life. Once again the gentry conspired against the Czar. The coup of March 1801 brought to the throne a young man raised in the spirit of French Enlightenment, a 'republican at heart,' who loudly proclaimed his love of liberty and his determination to carry out far-ranging reforms of Russian society. Few of Alexander I's projects were destined to be realized.

Europe was in turmoil, the *dvorianstvo* felt threatened by the French Revolution and then Napoleon. French military success in Europe was a terrifying specter; and Russia's nobility considered the ideals of the Revolution as being far too close to Mother Russia. And yet despite the mood of reaction Alexander succeeded in modernizing the administration and making provisions for a minor betterment of the peasant's lot, but no radical restructuring of Russian society was even

attempted, though his brilliant advisor, Mikhail Speranskii, produced drafts of laws and constitutional projects which, had they been implemented, would have turned Russia into a constitutional monarchy.

Ever since Catherine's death France had been the determining factor in Russia's foreign relations. Paul had fought the French in an alliance with Austria and Britain, then had reversed himself and prepared for a campaign against the British in India as an ally of Napoleon. Alexander returned to an Austrian and British alliance, took part in its wars and saw his army severely beaten by the French at Austerlitz in December 1805. After a brief respite Russia fought another war with Napoleon and was again defeated. After the disastrous Battle of Friedland in 1807, Alexander executed a complete turnabout and allied his country with the French in an agreement made at Tilsit in 1807. Alliance with France led to a war with Sweden and the annexation of Finland (1809), which was incorporated into the Empire and granted the unique status of an autonomous grand duchy with its own army, its own coinage, its own legal system and even a native army.

On 24 June 1812, without a declaration of war,

Napoleon invaded Russia. The French Grand Army was 640,000 strong, half of it recruited from client states. The Russian forces consisted of less than 300,000 men divided into two groups. Napoleon hoped quickly to defeat the separate Russian armies and to force peace on a stunned Russia. His strategic conception failed when Russian troops led by competent generals successfully retreated, denying Napoleon a decisive victory. He was now drawn into a long campaign for which the French were not well prepared. However, continuous retreat was unpopular in Russia. To bolster morale and unify the command Alexander appointed as commander-in-chief M I Kutuzov, an old soldier veteran of Suvorov's campaigns, trusted by the officers and acceptable to the general public.

On 7 September, at Borodino, Kutuzov engaged Napoleon in a major battle. The French lost 50,000 men, but the Russian losses were almost as heavy and the army was thoroughly disorganized. Kutuzov retreated to Moscow, but on 14 September he abandoned the old capital for the sake of preserving the army. Half of the population left the city. Fires broke out. In four days two-thirds of Moscow's houses burned down. Yet

Left: Alexander I (1777-1825) began his reign as a reformer but became increasingly reactionary. The war of 1812 against Napoleon reconciled the differences within the nation, however, and the success of Russian armies in helping bring about Napoleon's downfall enhanced Alexander's international prestige.

Above right: A scene from the war of 1812 – troops of Napoleon's Grande Armée occupy the burning ruins of Moscow.

Above, far right: Czar Nicholas I (1796-1855). His reign saw the extension of Russia's state bureaucracy and wars against Persia, Turkey and, in the Crimea, France, Britain and Sardinia.

Napoleon's position was growing desperate. He could neither march on St Petersburg nor winter in Moscow. His peace overtures were rejected by Alexander out of hand.

On 19 October the French evacuated Moscow. Kutuzov having barred their way to the prosperous south, they had no choice but to retreat along the devastated road to Mozhaisk and Smolensk. The French army began to disintegrate under the constant harassment of the cossacks and guerrillas. Bitter cold arrived in November, adding to the army's misery. By the time it reached Poland, its losses had reached 550,000 men. Russian military losses stood at about half that number. Napoleon could no longer hope to make a stand. On 5 December 1812 he abandoned the bedraggled remnant of his force and sped to France to raise new armies.

Though Kutuzov strongly advised the Czar not to pursue Napoleon, Alexander, who began to see himself as the savior of Europe, pressed on. In an alliance with Prussia, Austria, Sweden and Britain, the Russians defeated Napoleon's new levies at Leipzig, invaded France, and entered Paris on 31 March 1814. Napoleon was sent off to Elba. His return to France and the Hundred Days changed nothing. Russia emerged from the war the most powerful state on the European continent. The Czar himself attended the Congress of Vienna (1814-15) when he helped to negotiate the restructuring of Europe in the aftermath of Napoleon's defeat. Alexander was instrumental in working out a system of alliances that he believed would guarantee Europe from the outbreak of war and revolution.

The Czar now entered the second phase of his reign, a phase marked by mysticism and reaction. The place of his relatively liberal early collaborators was taken by the obscurantist Prince Golitsyn and the brutal reactionary Arakcheev. Alexander's mystic fantasies were fed by Golitsyn who attempted to control education and cultural life through a number of vicious subordinates. Arakcheev, a faithful servant of Czar Paul, was a capable military administrator and a cruel slave master. His program of military-agricultural settlements was an attempt to solve Russia's agrarian problem through the application of military discipline. The peasants did not appreciate these early collective farms on which they had to work in tightly supervised units.

Revolution and war

Dissatisfaction with the regime led to the formation in 1816 of a secret society, the Union of Salvation, which advocated the emancipation of serfs and the establishment of a constitutional monarchy. In 1821 the society, having expanded and changed its name, transformed itself into two revolutionary groups: the Southern and the Northern. The theorist of the Southern Society, P I Pestel, in his *Russkaia Pravda* (*Russian Justice*), advocated the abolition of noble privileges, the emancipation of peasants with land and the establishment of a centralized republic. The subject nationalities of the Empire would be ruthlessly Russified. The Jews would be either assimilated or expelled. Only the Poles would be given their freedom, perhaps because in practice they constituted at the time the only revolutionary mass. The Northern Society was less radical. Its constitutional projects tended toward liberalism and federalism of the American type.

Alexander's death produced some confusion because his brother and heir, Constantine, had secretly renounced his right to succession. The second of Alexander's brothers, Nicholas, was proclaimed Czar. Taking advantage of the somewhat unclear situation, the radicals of both the Northern and Southern societies staged a mutiny. Few troops responded to their call. In St Petersburg the regiments that came out into the streets in December (hence the name of the uprising – Decembrist) 1825 stood for hours in the cold and in the end were dispersed by artillery fire from loyal units. In the south the mutiny was put down by the government with equal ease. Several hundred persons were arrested and tried. Five, including Pestel, were hanged, and dozens were sent into Siberian exile.

Though the uprising was a failure, it provided revolutionary Russia with her first martyrs. The Decembrists were enshrined in the memory of the radicals and provided inspiration to generations of revolutionaries. The uprising also served to frighten the new Czar, who dedicated his reign of almost 30 years to keeping Russia free of 'modern infection.'

Domestic conservatism did not slow down the expansion of the Empire. While in the west Russia's borders had been stabilized, the forward movement continued in the south. Already under Catherine II Russia had become involved in the affairs of Georgia, a vassal kingdom of Iran south of the Caucasus. The Georgians hoped to be incorporated into the Russian Empire and to continue an autonomous existence within it, as they had done for centuries under Persian rule. However, in 1801 Alexander I, his interest being the expansion of the Russian Empire, annexed Georgia outright and abolished the monarchy.

The annexation of Georgia led to a war with Persia that lasted from 1804 to 1813 and flared up again early in the reign of Nicholas. The second Persian war, like the first, ended in Russian victory and the annexation of new Transcaucasian territories to the Empire, including parts of Armenia and a portion of Azerbaijan. The Georgians and the Armenians, peoples of ancient and vigorous culture, had a significant impact on their conquerors. Many entered Russian service and rose to positions of high importance. Many others joined the revolutionary movement and ultimately played important roles in overthrowing the Czarist regime.

Soon after the conquest of Transcaucasia and the conclusion of a peace treaty with Persia, Nicholas had to put down a major insurrection in Poland. In November 1830 the Poles had risen up and expelled the Russians from most of their land. But the revolt was foredoomed for Russia's might was overwhelming, and Prussia and Austria were unfriendly. The uprising was crushed, and Poland was directly incorporated into the Empire. Field-Marshal I F Paskevich, who had commanded Russian armies in the Second Persian War and later ruled Transcaucasia with an iron hand, was appointed Viceroy. He established a repressive regime that lasted till he died in 1856. In the next seven years Poland had five viceroys, each of whom pursued similar policies. In 1863 Poland rose up again. The insurrection lasted for more than a year and cost thousands of lives. 'Pacification' was carried out with extreme severity by Count Mikahil Muraviev, popularly known as Hangman. Many Polish nobles were deported. Even the Polish language was banned in schools, courts and government offices.

The reign of Nicholas I ended in disaster. The Eastern question, which had become one of the central concerns of European diplomacy in the eighteenth century, drew Russia, Turkey, Britain and France into recurrent conflicts over hegemony in the Ottoman Empire. The favorable

Left: A scene from the Crimean War – the 92nd Highlanders defend their precarious positions during the Battle of Balaklava.

Below left: Alexander II (1818-81) was responsible for the Emancipation of the Serfs but also had to face several attempts against his life.

Below: Alexander Pushkin. Renowned as a poet, his libertarian views brought him into direct conflict with the Russian establishment.

Right: The final drama of the Crimean War: British and French troops break through the Russian lines around Sebastopol.

Below right: Japanese naval personnel watch an attack on the port of Vladivostok during the Russo-Japanese War (1904-05).

Russian position achieved by the treaty of Kucuk-Kaynarca in 1774 did not remain unchallenged. Both Alexander I and Nicholas I fought wars against Turkey without winning their ultimate ends – possession of Constantinople, control of the Bosphorus and the Dardanelles and dominion over the Black Sea. Nicholas therefore tried to reach an agreement with London for a division of the Ottoman Empire, whose demise he expected to occur soon. The British were alarmed and soon entered into an alliance with Napoleon III of France, who also opposed Russian designs against Turkey. A petty dispute over the possession of the keys to a church in Bethlehem led to a flurry of ultimatums and the Russian occupation of the Danubian principalities. Britain and France backed the Turks, and war began.

The main theater of operations was the Crimea, where the allies besieged and eventually captured Russia's principal Black Sea naval base, Sevastopol. Under the blows of combined British, French and Turkish forces, the inadequacies of Russia's military forces, the backwardness of her economy and the defects of her social structure were clearly revealed. Nicholas I died during the war, an embittered and broken man. It was clear to many, including the new Czar, Alexander II, that in spite of the efforts of Peter I and Catherine II, Russia had fallen far behind Western Europe and that reforms were desperately needed. In February 1856 a peace treaty was signed in Paris. Its most significant provisions dealt with the neutralization of the Black Sea, prohibiting Russia from maintaining a navy in its waters or building bases on its shores. A month later, in a speech to the nobility of Moscow, the Czar made clear his intention to emancipate the serfs.

Emancipation of the serfs

After several years of preparation the emancipation edict was proclaimed in February 1861. All serfs were given personal freedom and allotment of land, for which owners were paid in state bonds. The serfs were in turn expected to recompense the government for their allotments by making redemption payments over a 49-year period. Land was not given to individual peasants

but to village communes (*mir*). These provisions proved unworkable. The amount of land the peasants received was insufficient. Village organization based on the peasant commune was inefficient, and most of the organs of rural self-government, such as the *zemstvo*, were still dominated by the nobility. Thus the emancipation, though a great step forward, did not solve the agrarian problem, and the peasantry was bitterly disappointed in the reform.

The emancipation of the serfs was followed by a modernization of the army and reform of the judiciary. The legal reform gave Russia for the first time in her history an independent judiciary, equality of citizens before the law and trial by jury. Within a few years the bench and the bar developed standards comparable to those prevailing in Western Europe.

Reforms in no way affected the autocratic nature of the regime or the growth of the Empire. Defeat in the Crimean war made it impossible for Russia to achieve her goals in the Black Sea area and thereby compelled her to turn farther east into Asia. The first task that had to be accom-

plished in Asia was the subjugation of the mountaineers of the Caucasus, who had refused to submit to Russian authority and defended their independence with desperate determination.

From 1834 to 1859 the mountaineers were led by Shaykh Shamil, a man of extraordinary ability and great courage. Russian forces suffered heavy losses in hundreds of encounters with the elusive and determined foe. Count M S Vorontsov, the Viceroy of the Caucasus (1844-54), began a systematic campaign of encirclement, destruction of villages and crops and deforestation. Vorontsov's tactics were continued by Prince A I Bariatinskii, who finally subdued the mountaineers of the eastern Caucasus and captured Shamil in 1859. Western Caucasus was 'pacified' over the next five years. Villages were burned, tens of thousands of Cherkesses, Abkhazes and other mountain peoples were massacred, and tens of thousands more perished from hunger and cold. Hundreds of thousands were driven off their lands and resettled in the Kuban steppes, where they could easily be controlled. Several hundred thousand more chose permanent exile in Turkey.

The 'pacification' of the Caucasus coincided with the launching of a campaign for the conquest of Central Asia. In spite of serious misgivings on the part of Russia's diplomats, who foresaw complications with Great Britain, the military prevailed upon the Czar to annex Tashkent and Kokand. In 1867 the new province of Turkestan was organized. There followed brief wars with Bukhara and Khiva. In each case the overwhelming superiority of Russian forces was clearly shown in the disproportion between the infinitesimally small Russian losses and incredibly large losses suffered by the Bukharans and the Khivans. The only serious resistance came from the Tekke Turkomans of Transcaspia. But they too suffered defeat when a Russian army moved from Krasnovodsk on the eastern coast of the Caspian Sea to the Akhal Oasis, captured the fortress at Geok-Teppe, the center of Turkoman resistance, and massacred over 14,000 Turkoman men, women and children. Only 59 Russian soldiers were killed.

Two decades of unceasing advance in Central Asia brought the Russians to the borders of Persia, Afghanistan and China. As the Russians pushed southward the British became alarmed for the safety of their Indian Empire, for neither Afghanistan nor Persia was strong enough to pose a serious barrier to Russia if she were to attempt an invasion of India. The British made their misgivings known to the Russians every time the latter made a forward move in Turkestan, but St Petersburg quickly learned to make reassuring statements without stopping the soldiers from expanding the Empire. In 1884, taking advantage of Britain's involvement in the Sudan, Russia annexed the Turkoman town of Marv and established herself along the ill-defined Afghan border. In March 1885 Russian and Afghan forces clashed at Panjdeh near Kushk, the former losing nine men, the latter 500. The British government reacted by threatening war. The Russians, however, had no intention of being drawn into a war. The conflict was settled, the Afghan border was delineated and Russia turned to the slow and dif-

ficult task of absorbing and developing her newly acquired Asiatic territories.

Farther to the east, along the Pacific coast, yet another effort at southward expansion engaged the attention of the forceful Nicholas Muraviev, who had become Governor General of Siberia in 1847. The Russians constantly pressed the Chinese and Japanese for favorable treaty rights that would give Russia both an agricultural land base and warm water ports on the Pacific. China, humbled by military defeats at the hands of the British (1841-42) and the British and French (1856-58), was unable to resist foreign pressure. In the Treaty of Aigun (1858), the Russians acquired the north bank of the Amur, and with the Treaty of Peking (1860) they gained possession of the land between the Ussuri River and the Pacific. With the founding of Khabarovsk on the Amur and Vladivostok on the Pacific, the basis was laid for Russian industrial and naval growth in eastern Siberia. In 1875 Russia acquired southern Sakhalin from Japan in exchange for two of the Kurile Islands. The Trans-Siberian Railroad, begun in 1891 and destined to be completed in 1903, increased European Russia's ability to exploit Siberian mineral and lumber resources, while it completely transformed Russia's status as an East Asian military power.

The reigns of Nicholas I and Alexander II were notable not only for imperial expansion in the south and the east but also for an unparalleled flowering of Russian culture. Aleksandr Sergeevich Pushkin, one of the world's great poets, opened a brilliant period that produced such great figures of Russian literature as Mikhail Lermontov, Nikolai Gogol, Ivan Turgenev, Fyodor Dostoevsky, and Leo Tolstoy. The controversies between the Slavophiles and the Westerners over Russia's relationship to the West and the course of her historical development raged for many years without solving the many problems that agitated the intellectuals then and later. Russian music grew to maturity in the works of Glinka, Tchaikovsky and others. Science continued to advance and scholarship matured.

Russian policy in the Pacific aimed at the development of Vladivostok and the acquisition of a competitive position among the Western powers with respect to China. Economic penetration of northern Manchuria and Korea was the natural step. But there Russia collided with Japan which had already begun to see Korea and Manchuria as natural spheres of Japanese special interest. Japan went to war with China over control of Korea in 1894. The surprising Japanese victory resulted in the Treaty of Shimonseki (1895), in which China ceded to Japan the Liaotung Peninsula and Formosa and gave up its claims to the control of Korea. This move, which blocked the possibility of Russia's southern advance, aroused an immediate reaction in Europe; Russia, Germany, and France jointly intervened to oblige the Japanese to return the Liaotung Peninsula to China.

With Japan momentarily contained, and China

Above: Peter Tchaikovsky (1840-93), the famous Russian composer who did much to establish Russia's position within the world of classical music.

Left: Russian troops mass behind the cover of a fold in the ground before launching an attack on the Japanese.

Above right: Leo Tolstoy, the leading writer of the nineteenth century in Russia, photographed late in life with his family.

Right: The assassination of Czar Alexander II. The explosion fatally wounded the emperor.

shown to be weaker than had been imagined, Russia joined the other European nations in carving out 'spheres of influence' on Chinese soil. In 1896 Russia acquired the right to link the Trans-Siberian Railroad to Vladivostok through northern Manchuria, and in 1898 it obtained a lease of the southern part of the Liaotung Peninsula, which included Port Arthur, together with the right to build a railroad to the port down from the north. This was the high point of Russian imperialist penetration in Manchuria. Already the makings of a war with Japan were visible. That war, which broke out in 1904 and witnessed the decisive Japanese naval victory of Tsushima, would force Russia back to its pre-1875 position. But Siberia would remain secure.

Social protest in Russia

The post-reform period was a time of rapid and far-reaching progress in all areas of Russian life. Paradoxically it was also a time of increasing dissatisfaction and disaffection. Revolutionary organizations sprang up even before the great reforms proved insufficient to the needs of an evolving society. Some were disappointed that the Czar had not reformed the political system. Others felt that the system could not be reformed and should be destroyed. It was during the 1860s and 1870s that the Russian revolutionary movement took shape. Inspired by the writings of radical thinkers such as Chernyshevskii and Aleksandr Herzen, young men and women 'went to the people' in the hope of winning the peasants to the revolution. But when the peasants did not respond to populist propaganda, the populists (*narodniki*) lost faith in the revolutionary spontaneity of the masses and turned instead to violence in the hope that terrorism would precipitate the cataclysmic collapse of the old order. Terrorist organizations carried out numerous assassinations and one, the People's Will, succeeded in murdering Czar Alexander II in March 1881.

The murder of Alexander II evoked an immediate conservative reaction. The new Czar, Alexander III (1881-94), influenced by his tutor, a former law professor Konstantin Pobedonostsev, instituted measures designed to freeze Russia in her autocratic, Orthodox and nationalist mold. Heavy-handed censorship, administrative interference with universities and repression of students alienated the educated classes of Russian society. Land hunger caused by rural overpopulation and the insufficiency of the agrarian reforms produced unrest among the peasants. An increasingly virulent Russian nationalism angered the subject peoples of the Empire. The government imposed

new and onerous restrictions upon the Jews, chipped away at the privileges of Finland, maltreated the Poles and tried to Russify everyone. As a result of Russian oppression and the general spread of the European idea of nationalism, the Ukrainians, Armenians, Georgians, Tatars and the various other peoples of Central Asia began to cultivate their own nationalisms and to nurture separatist aspirations. The rise of the nationality question in an empire more than half of whose populations was made up of 'minorities' was a grave threat to the Russian state.

The coming of the industrial revolution in the closing decades of the nineteenth century added to the problems that beset the imperial regime.

Large-scale railway construction provided Russia with a modern transportation network and stimulated the development of industry, the extraction of coal and oil and the manufacture of textiles. While industrialization increased national wealth, it also brought about urban blight and the creation of an urban industrial proletariat. Yesterday's serfs, herded in large airless factories, lodged in pest-infested barracks, ill fed and forced to work 12 or more hours a day, were prevented by the government until 1902 from organizing in defense of their economic rights.

The last decades of the nineteenth century witnessed the birth of Russian Marxism and of the Russian Social Democratic Workers' Party. The

first recruits came from the ranks of disillusioned populists seeking new paths toward revolution. Georgi Plekhanov, a brilliant thinker, argued that Russia, like the countries of Western Europe, was destined to pass through the capitalist stage in her historical evolution toward socialism. This was a departure from the populist position that Russia could reach socialism by bypassing capitalism and escaping its horrors. Plekhanov was one of the founders of the Social Democratic Party which numbered among its early members Vladimir Ilich Ulianov, later to be known as Lenin.

Social and political discontent did not, as we have seen, in the least affect the imperialistic policies of the Russian government. The reverse was true. And the defeat of Russia by the Japanese in 1904 sent shock waves through Russia, producing the greatest popular upheaval since Pugachev's peasant war. Industrial strikes, peasant uprisings, student disorders and mutinies in the armed forces amounted to something approaching a revolution. Though the Czarist regime survived the storm, it did so at the price of promising the people a constitution. In the October Manifesto of 1905 Czar Nicholas II (1894-1917) made far-reaching concessions, including the election of a parliament, the Duma and the promulgation of civil liberties. Russia's defeat at the hands of a non-European people and the subsequent domestic challenge to the Czarist regime had stirred up nationalistic spirit all over the continent of Asia. There were riots in the Caucasus, increased political activity in Turkestan, jubilation in India, and an 'awakening' in Persia whose people staged their own revolution and limited the power of the Shah.

The constitutional experiment in Russia soon failed. Once order had been restored, the government withdrew most of the concessions, dissolved two recalcitrant Dumas and 'elected' a tame one in 1907. The Czar continued to be the autocrat, and the regime, though less oppressive than before, remained despotic. Some efforts at reform were made by the conservative and intelligent Prime Minister Peter Stolypin, but he achieved only partial success before being assassinated by a revolutionary organization.

World War I and the Revolution

It is possible that a long period of uninterrupted peaceful development could have led to the consolidation of the gains achieved by the revolution of 1905 and the development of a genuine constitutional regime. But Russia was not destined to have peace. The imperialistic appetite of her rulers had never abated and she continued to participate in the Great Power politics that were leading Europe into war. After the shocks of defeat and revolution in 1905 Russia modified her inordinately ambitious designs in the Middle East and, in 1907, concluded an agreement with Britain, dividing Persia into spheres of influence and turning Afghanistan into a buffer zone between Russian Central Asia and British India. The settlement with Britain made possible Russian participation with Britain and France in the Entente directed against Germany. In the end this led to Russian entry into the war.

World War I had as many causes as there were participants. Russia fought among other things for the preservation and expansion of her influence in the Balkans, for Constantinople and the straits, for access to the Mediterranean and total control of the Black Sea. But in the final analysis Russia was drawn into the war because it had become part of a system of sovereign states that had failed to prevent the coming of international anarchy. No dictates of state interest, no need for

Left: Georgi Plekhanov, the leading political theorist behind the Russian social democrats and one of the leaders of the Russian Revolution.

Right: The front cover of a political pamphlet 'celebrates' the atrocities of the 1905 Revolution.

Below: The mystic priest Grigorii Rasputin (center), surrounded by members of the Russian court.

Below right: Demonstrators flee security forces of the Russian state during the 1917 Revolution.

territory, no fear for her national existence, could have justified willing participation in a war that proved to be one of the major disasters of Russian history.

Military reverses, the loss of over nine million men (1,700,000 dead, 4,950,000 wounded, 2,500,000 taken prisoner), economic dislocation and shortages of food created social and political tensions which the regime was not strong enough to withstand. Nicholas II was a mediocre ruler. His dedication to autocracy, his obstinacy and his lack of judgment had driven away all men of stature and talent from the government. The government was run by nonentities who were somehow in the good graces of Empress Alexandra and of her 'friend,' the vicious religious charlatan Grigorii Rasputin. Not only socialists and liberals but moderates and even conservatives began to feel that a change at the top was indispensable. The army was totally demoralized by three years of

defeat. The peasantry and the working class cared nothing for the czarist war aims. The educated classes which had supported the war felt betrayed and resented the failures for which they blamed the monarchy. The Czar was almost completely isolated. Russia was again on the verge of revolution.

In early March 1917 food riots erupted in St Petersburg. The police proved incapable of restoring order. Troops were sent in but refused to fire on the crowds, which attacked police stations and released prisoners from jails. Nicholas, suspicious of his weak and ineffective parliament, prorogued the Duma and left for the army headquarters at Mogilev. Confronted with large-scale disorders in the capital, the Duma disobeyed the Czar and appointed a provisional committee to assume the functions of government. The Czar's ministers were arrested and jailed.

The provisional committee of the Duma found

Soviet, appointed a Provisional Government. The monarchy had fallen without a struggle.

The fall of the monarchy proved only a prelude to more revolutionary developments. The Provisional Government was weak and indecisive. Essentially a liberal bourgeois group, it found itself in conflict with more radical elements within the country, and specifically with the Socialists of the Petrograd Soviet (Council of Workers' and Soldiers' Deputies). While the Provisional Government attempted to carry on the war against Germany, the Soviet leaders urged a speedy end to Russian military involvement. The arrival in Petrograd in April of V I Lenin and other Bolshevik leaders charged the political scene with further tension. Under Lenin's vigorous leadership the Bolsheviks continually harassed the government, acquiring a following among dissident soldiers and factory workers. When, in November, the Bolsheviks acquired control of the Petrograd Soviet, Lenin felt ready for a violent revolution. The Bolsheviks, together with members of the Petrograd Garrison, sailors from Kronstadt and workers' Red Guards, moved in on the government offices and arrested most of the members of the Provisional Government. On 7 November a new government, the Council of People's Commissars, was declared. The new regime was headed by Lenin, Leon Trotsky served as Commissar of Foreign Affairs, and Josef Stalin was Commissar for National Minorities.

The Russian Revolution of 1917 was destined to send out shock waves which would not only revolutionize Russian society but, in the next half-century, affect the political lives of half the world's people.

a rival in the Petrograd Soviet of Workers' and Soldiers' Deputies, a body which represented socialist parties and included Social Revolutionaries as well as the two factions of Social Democrats, the relatively moderate Mensheviks and the more radical Bolsheviks. The conflict of authority between the Duma's committee and the Soviet created confusion, but that hardly mattered during the first days of the revolution when (the entire nation seemed drunk with joy and democratic enthusiasm spread through the land.

A group of conservative and moderate Duma deputies met the Czar at Pskov and urged him to abdicate in favor of his son so as to save the monarchy. Nicholas, unwilling to part with his sickly child, hesitated. When he finally signed the act of abdication in favor of his brother, Grand Duke Mikhail, it was too late. On 15 March the provisional committee of the Duma, in agreement with the Executive Committee of the Petrograd

The Worldwide Expansion of Europe

The single most important development in world history during the past 500 years has been the spread of Western European political and cultural influence over the planet. But it was a process that had many discrete aspects and has had many quite different consequences. In those parts of Asia and Africa where civilized societies had long been established and where dense populations already occupied the land, the European presence took on a look distinct from that in the colonies of settlement. In the populated and civilized areas the primary pattern was that of imperialist conquest and colonization, as exemplified in India, Southeast Asia and Africa. But not all areas were colonized, and furthermore in each colony the pattern of Western domination varied according to local circumstance. At one extreme Japan, having resisted Western encroachment in the seventeenth century, managed in the nineteenth century to avoid colonization completely. European encroachment on Japanese sovereignty was limited to extraterritorial privileges and favorable tariff rights secured through so-called 'unequal treaties.' For a country such as Japan the 'Western impact' was primarily a cultural phenomenon, a factor in the rapid modernization of the Japanese people. At the other extreme was the example of India, where the remnants of the once great Moghul Empire fell under the full political domination of the British. To India the British brought not only their system of education and a new language of general communication but a new sovereign, the Queen of England, who assumed the concurrent title of Empress of India. Within the British Commonwealth, India took its position along with colonies of settlement like Canada.

The vicissitudes of the several parts of the vast Ottoman Empire fell into a variety of patterns. While the central core of the empire, comprising the Turks of Anatolia and Arabs of the Arabian Peninsula, the Iranians and the Afghans, managed to defend a precarious political independence from the great European onslaught, most Muslims by the beginning of the twentieth century found themselves living under some form of Western political domination. The Arab states of North Africa had become first protectorates and then colonies of settlement under French administration. Egypt was held under a British protectorate, though it escaped British settlement and the imposition of the English language. Much of the Balkans was recaptured from the Turks; Kazakhstan and Turkistan were absorbed into the expanding Russian homeland. Far to the east the Dutch had placed the Muslim principalities of Indonesia under a colonial regime almost as complete as that of the British in India.

In this picture, China stood somewhere in between the examples of Japan and India. The vast Manchu Empire retained most of its territory and its essential political integrity. While such former protectorates as Korea and Indochina were pulled away as colonies by the Japanese and French, the main areas of Chinese settlement were never fully colonized. Yet China felt the presence of the Western powers almost as deeply as though it had been brought under colonial rule.

Sub-Sahara Africa was slow to be penetrated by the Western powers. Other than South Africa, which early on became a Dutch colony of settlement, most of western and eastern Africa and all of the interior remained unattractive, and largely unknown, to the Europeans, so that actual conquest was put off until the period from 1875 to 1914. Yet again the European presence was deeply felt even in interior Africa as a result of the slave trade. Colonialism, when it was firmly established in the nineteenth century, carried from the beginning a heavy legacy from the slave trade and the racial prejudices it had engendered.

This chapter takes up the story of Western encroachment into the main regions of the New World, Asia and Africa from roughly 1500 to 1914.

European imperialism

Europeans in the eighteenth and nineteenth centuries neither invented imperialism nor pursued it any more ruthlessly than other peoples. The adventures of Alexander the Great and the Roman and Chinese conquests are but a few examples of imperialism which occurred long before Europe extended its power to Asia, Africa and America. At the very time Spain created its American empire in the early 1500s, the Ottoman Turks were expanding at the expense of Europeans as far as the outskirts of Vienna. Even during the height of European imperialism, between about 1880 and 1914, non-European powers also joined in the scramble for colonies. Imperialism, like thievery or the bully in the schoolyard, will probably continue to exist (although under other names) so long as some people seek power over the lives and property of others, and do not hesitate to use violence to acquire that power.

Yet not all imperialists were bullies or thieves, and European imperialism did not in the long run necessarily result in the universal suffering of those over whom the Europeans asserted their dominance. Most people suffer who initially stand in the way of imperial powers. The Indians

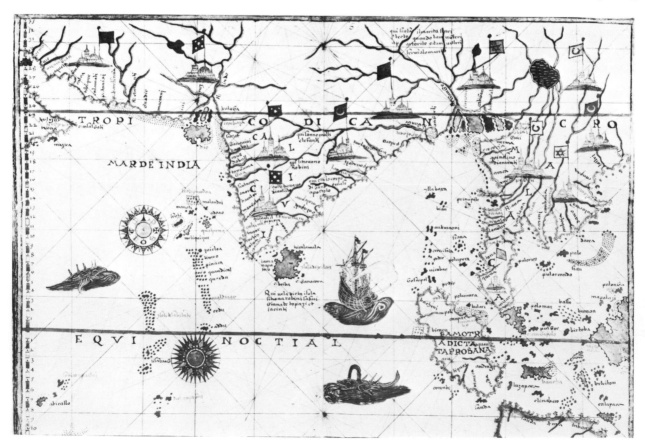

Left: A Portuguese map of India and Southeast Asia. It dates from 1578 and shows the sea routes and forts used by Portuguese traders in their exploitation of the spice trade of the Far East.

Above right: Spanish *conquistadores*, led by Cortéz, slaughter the inhabitants of the Mexican city Cholula. Adventurers from the minor nobility of Spain *(hidalgos)* found rich and easy pickings among the Amerindian empires of what was to become Latin America.

Right: While the Spanish colonizers contributed splendid baroque churches and cathedrals to the cities of their empire, British imperialism brought the monuments of industrial culture, like this railway station in the Indian state of Hyderabad. Yet even if outward symbols were very different, both Spanish *conquistadores* and British colonial bureaucrats had the same basic intention: to enrich their European homelands by the exploitation of overseas possessions.

in India to posts in Africa and to Brazil in South America. They had not sent out large colonies of Portuguese to settle in India or Africa, but had instead set up trading posts along the coasts so that Portuguese ships could carry the goods coming to these coasts back to Europe. The spices of India sold in Europe brought high profits. Brazil had been somewhat different, since growing coffee required plantation settlements. It also returned a profit.

The *hidalgos* of Spain left the mother country seeking their fortune, and some found it in Central and South America. The riches of Mexico and Peru had helped Spain become the leading power in Europe in the sixteenth century, and by 1700 Spain could claim the largest empire in the world: the Philippines, most of South and Central America (save for Brazil), Mexico (including what is today the American southwest), Florida and islands in the Caribbean. But Spain had focused too narrowly on taking the gold and silver from the New World to finance its wars in the Old. Its neglect of commerce, its religious orthodoxy, its costly, unsuccessful wars to retain control of Holland, had already harmed it greatly. Spain's great days had passed by 1700, although the Cuban and Philippine parts of the Spanish Empire would carry on almost to the twentieth century, leaving it only when Spain lost to the United States in the Spanish-American War.

Portugal's greatness had passed even earlier. Yet it too would hang on, and even increase its power in its territories of Angola and Mozambique in Africa in the nineteenth century, which it would refuse to leave until 1975, and only then after considerable domestic turmoil. Portugal was the first European power to grab colonies, and it would be the last one to give them up.

Religion had been almost as important as money in the Portuguese and Spanish empires. The Spanish had shown their concern for religion by sending priests with every expedition to convert the Indians with whom they came in contact. The first Portuguese thrust outside the Iberian peninsula had in 1415 taken the Muslim stronghold of Cetua, on the African coast opposite Gibraltar. Its wealth, brought from the interior of Africa, had excited Portuguese greed. Under the direction and financing of Prince Henry the Navigator, a younger son of the King of Portugal, Portuguese sailors had then dared to sail even farther

of South America died by the thousands during the early stages of the Spanish conquest. The English colonists who settled North America early anticipated the notion that the only good Indian was a dead one. Yet those English colonists and others from all over Europe who migrated to America eventually created a nation and a constitution that was generally admired throughout the world.

British soldiers and merchants in the East India Company, the agency of British imperialism in India, shamelessly grabbed what they could for themselves in the early eighteenth century at the expense of the natives, and returned to Britain to live in splendor. But toward the end of the century the British government assumed more and more control, forbidding earlier practices. As the nineteenth century progressed the British brought peace to a sub-continent hitherto racked with war. They stopped *suttee* (widow burning), infan-

ticide, and *thuggee* (a ritualized form of highway robbery and murder in the name of religion). They built the largest system of railroads in Asia. In some ways they created the India of today. Their changes in education, their codification of the legal system and the implantation of their own ideas of civil rights and government helped produce the very class of people – the lawyer Gandhi serving as its most outstanding member – who would eventually take over the nation they had created.

That does not mean of course that the Europeans built their empires primarily because of their concern for the welfare of the conquered. That was usually farthest from their minds. Rather, European imperialism from 1700 to 1914 took place for a variety of economic, religious and strategic reasons. The search for wealth figured importantly, as it had earlier. By 1700 the Portuguese had already created their empire, from Goa

south along the African coast. But almost as strong in their minds, and in Henry's, as finding riches was the hope of finding Prester John. This mythical Christian king had tantalized the European imagination since the twelfth century. Supposedly Prester John had held off Muslim assaults successfully, and if only the Christians could find him now he might help stem the Muslim advance toward Europe.

Anglo-French rivalry

Money and religion also figured in the imperialism of Spain's and Portugal's successors, France and Britain. In 1700 those two countries stood on the threshold of a worldwide conflict for empire. As that struggle developed, however, other considerations – diplomatic, strategic, problems of surplus population – began to gain prominence as well. In the nineteenth century all these factors, as well as plain irrationality, would figure in the scramble for colonies.

France had grown into the greatest power in Europe during the seventeenth century. It had thoroughly overshadowed Spain, and by 1700 its king, Louis XIV, was even attempting to put his family on the Spanish throne. France had challenged Spain's hoped-for monopoly in the New World by reaching out to take islands in the Caribbean, establishing its own people in what would become Canada and creating its territory of Louisiana. England, racked by disputes between king and parliament and a civil war in the seventeenth century, had nonetheless also acquired territory in the New World. It, like France, had taken Caribbean islands, and had planted colonists along the

Atlantic coast from south of French Acadia (now Nova Scotia) down to South Carolina. Georgia, the last of the original thirteen colonies, would be settled in 1733 by British General James Oglethorpe.

Europe's economic motives had matured from the crude sort of search for plunder – although each country had plenty of adventurers on the lookout for that – into a more elaborate theory of what it required for a nation to maintain its independence and increase its power. In its simplest form this theory, mercantilism, postulated that a nation's welfare depended on its being, as far as possible, self-sufficient in producing its own food and material. It should import as little as possible from foreign nations and should export as much as possible to them. It would then have a favorable balance of trade, the other nations paying in specie for the goods received. Furthermore (and certainly so in the case of Britain, which depended upon a strong navy for survival), trade should be carried on in the nation's own merchant vessels, manned for the most part by citizens of the nation. This also protected against any drainage of specie and had the added advantage that the sailors who learned their trade in the merchant marine in peacetime could easily become sailors aboard men-of-war if hostilities erupted.

Colonies were now seen in a somewhat more sophisticated light than they had been previously. Ideally they should provide the mother country what it could not otherwise provide for itself, and thus render it independent of 'foreign' imports. French North America, for example, could send furs to the mother country. The British colonies

could provide agricultural products such as tobacco, rice or the sugar and molasses necessary for the production of rum. While the indigenous native peoples might sell furs to the Europeans, they had neither the desire nor the knowledge to engage in large-scale agriculture. As a result, in French and especially British North America, large numbers of white planters had begun to settle.

By 1700 the numbers of colonists was far larger in the British than in the French colonies, for several reasons. Whereas the French government would not allow Protestants to settle in New France, the British encouraged people of all denominations to settle in their colonies. The French for the most part also restricted emigrants to French nationals. By contrast, in the British colonies one could find people from all over Europe. Additionally, since the plantation economies of the southern colonies required extensive labor, slavery had grown as an institution, with a consequent growth in the number of black people imported against their will into the British colonies from Africa.

France and England had been fighting off and on since 1066. In the seventeenth century that fighting had extended to their colonies as well, and in the eighteenth century it would escalate even more. As the century progressed their rivalry extended beyond America to India, where the two European powers vied for control of the Indian subcontinent. The final struggle, known as the Seven Years' War (1756-63) in Europe, and the French and Indian War in North America, was fought in Europe, in India, in North America, in the Caribbean and even in the Philippines. From it

Far left: A part of a monument commemorating the abolition of suttee (widow burning) by Lord Bentinck, governor-general of India from 1833 to 1835.

Left: Robert Clive, the British general and colonial administrator whose victory over a Franco-Indian army at Plassey in 1757 secured for his country dominion over Bengal.

Right: An engraving of General James Wolfe's army landing beneath the Heights of Abraham, near the city of Quebec, capital of New France. Wolfe's victory over Montcalm in the battle that followed virtually ended French ambitions of a North American empire.

Below: A *voyageur,* or trapper, of seventeenth-century New France. The inhospitable climate of the St Lawrence Valley, with its harsh winter and short growing season, encouraged many French colonists to adopt the nomadic life of these wilderness adventurers, who roamed the northern woodlands in search of animal pelts.

Britain emerged victorious everywhere, winning perhaps the single greatest series of military and naval victories in her entire history, and claiming the imperial spoils of those victories.

The first of the series of wars that culminated in the Seven Years' War was that of the Spanish Succession. It began in 1702 and lasted until 1713. Ostensibly it started because King Louis XIV of France accepted for his grandson, Philip of Anjou, the throne of Spain, left to him by the will of the previous Spanish ruler. The same family ruling France and Spain threatened to alter drastically the balance of power in Europe in favor of France.

Britain allied with the Dutch Republic, the Holy Roman Emperor and various German princes to defeat Louis XIV's pretensions. In a war that dragged on for 12 years they bested Louis's armies in bloody battles in Europe, but they did not conquer him, invade his homeland or topple his grandson from the Spanish throne. In a peace made at Utrecht in 1713 Philip of Anjou, now Philip V, kept the Spanish throne on condition that the crowns of Spain and France would never unite. Austria took the Spanish territories in the Netherlands and in Italy. The British kept Gibraltar, which they had taken from Spain in 1704 (and have retained ever since). That did not greatly alter the map in Europe, but outside of Europe the British gained significantly. In 1710 British colonists, aided by the British navy, had seized Acadia, and it was confirmed as British territory, along with Newfoundland and the Hudson Bay area, by the Utrecht agreement.

The Indian dimension

An uneasy peace prevailed in North America for 30 years after Utrecht. Hostilities then resumed with a vengeance in the War of the Austrian Succession (1740-48) and the Seven Years' War. During these years the Anglo-French struggle intensified not only in North America, but in India as well. In India both countries, almost despite themselves, were drawn into the vortex of local politics. India was a land of many languages and religions, but since the sixteenth century most of the predominantly Hindu subcontinent had been ruled by Muslim Moghul emperors. They had continued to govern it more or less well (depending upon what historian one reads) down through to the Emperor Aurangzeb, who died in 1707.

During the Moghul rule British and French merchants had come to India and had established posts there for trade with the indigenous peoples. Europeans had developed a taste for the tea and coffee they associated with India (actually, the tea came from China and the coffee from Mokha on the Red Sea), and the subcontinent exported to Europe such goods as indigo, sugar, spices and calico. The British merchants, servants of the privately owned British East India Company, had located themselves principally at Bombay, Madras and more recently Calcutta (1690). The French merchants, servants of the government-owned French East India Company, had established their posts (factories) in several places, but principally at Pondicherry, to the south of Madras. At the time of Aurangzeb's death the British had a longer history of trading in India than the French and carried on much more substantial commercial operations than their traditional enemies. But French influence mushroomed quickly after that, and by 1740 they not only held and fortified Pondicherry, but had established thriving posts at Chandernagore, in Bengal, and in Malabar.

Soon after Aurangzeb died the Moghul government began to fall apart. Rival princes carved out states for themselves, and India soon became a battlefield. In this situation, the British and French decided to organize their own forces to hold on to what they had. Once they had their own armies, however, it followed naturally that they might use them not only to defend themselves from attack by native princes, but against each other as well, as they had in North America. The circumstances peculiar to India required them to use tactics different from those employed in North America. No large group of French or British nationals had settled in India, so they could not call upon masses of people of European heritage to fight for them. They could and did bring over regular soldiers from Europe, but not many. India's remoteness – a six-month trip by wooden sailing ship from Europe – made it impossible to transport large numbers of European regulars to fight there. So both companies began a practice of recruiting and training European-officered native soldiers in the European fashion to do their fighting for them. These Indian soldiers, called sepoys, would in fact conquer India for the Europeans. Later, in the nineteenth century, the Europeans would extend their use of native troops.

In the struggle in India, Britain had certain

advantages. That the French East India Company was government-owned meant that if the French government desired strongly to prevail in India, it could put government resources behind the Company's adventures. But by the same token, should the government withdraw its support, the Company would fold and French influence would wane. The private British East India Company, by contrast, was not bound by the edicts of a British governmental bureaucracy six months away. It had more flexibility than its French counterpart, and seemed better able to find leaders, military and civilian, to serve it well in times of trial. Indeed, one might note at this point that private companies would prove far more instrumental than the British government in acquiring the great Empire that, by 1914, would comprise nearly a third of the world's population. For its part, the government could also call upon the ever-growing British navy (by 1815 the largest and best in the world) to support the Company. Although French naval forces helped the French in the early stages of the conflict and briefly challenged the British off India's waters during the American Revolution, the British would acquire and maintain naval supremacy in the Indian Ocean.

The contest for India between Britain and France began in earnest in 1742, after the French government appointed Jean François Dupleix governor of Pondicherry, the headquarters of their company. Under Dupleix the French did well in India, wresting Madras from the British, but returning it to them as part of the peace provisions of Aix-la-Chapelle, which ended the War of the Austrian Succession in 1748. That peace may have stopped war in Europe temporarily, but Dupleix in India continued the fight. He skillfully negotiated alliances with native princes and managed to get his own nominees to rule territories where the succession lay in dispute.

The British Company eventually found an equally skillful servant in Robert Clive, a brilliant soldier and clever diplomat, adept at intrigue and tortuous diplomacy. Starting in the humble position of 'writer,' whose job basically was to keep accounts, he turned gladly to serve in the Company's army and rose rapidly. With 200 British troops and 300 sepoys he seized Arcot in 1751 and then held it when besieged by thousands of foes; the garrison was down to something like 80 British and 120 sepoys when the last enemy attack failed. When the British subsequently defeated Dupleix's candidate for ruler of the Carnatic, they had ensured their supremacy in southern India. The directors of the French Company, appalled at the expense of Dupleix's adventures with seemingly little gain, recalled him in 1754. By then his company was on the verge of bankruptcy.

Dupleix's recall did not end French influence in India, although that influence would never rise as high again. When the Seven Years' War broke out in 1756, the ruler, or nawab, of Bengal offered to ally with the French. The British Company had its headquarters at Fort William in Calcutta, Bengal, a city then of perhaps 400,000 people in a province of about 200 square miles and 20,000,000 souls. (England and Wales in 1751 contained approximately 6,500,000 people and London, the capital, 650,000.) When the young nawab, Siraj-Ud-Daula, took an army against Fort William in 1756, most of the women and children managed to reach ships in the river, but the tiny garrison of around 500 eventually surrendered to overwhelming numbers. There then occurred one of the most famous events in the history of European imperialism, the 'Black Hole of Calcutta.' For some reason the nawab's men stuffed 145 men and one woman into the fort's prison cell, which measured only 18 feet by 5 feet. Only two holes, barred with iron, let in the air. During that terrible night in the stifling, suffocating room, all save 22 men and the one woman died. Nothing could have strengthened Clive's resolve to punish the nawab more completely.

Within a year of this disaster Clive had recouped British fortunes. He negotiated secretly with Mir Jafar, a discontented general of the nawab, to replace the ruler. Clive, with a force of only 3000 men, 800 of them European, then sought battle with Siraj-Ud-Daula's army of 40,000. They clashed on 23 June 1757 in a large mango grove at Plassey. Clive won an astonishing victory – Mir Jafar keeping out of the action so he could earn his reward – and thereby established British supremacy in Bengal. The British East India Company by this stroke had become one of the great powers of India. It spread out inexorably after this period to acquire more and more Indian territory, becoming within 100 years the single most powerful force in the subcontinent. Clive, be it noted, had not won because of superior weaponry, but because of his skill in diplomacy and the superior organization and discipline of his tiny army. Indeed, not for over 100 years did the British hold any great technological edge over the native Indian powers. The Indians and the British had both used smoothbore, muzzle-loading muskets and cannon, which the Indians could cast as well as the British. When Britain conquered India, 'the jewel in the crown,' she was essentially a preindustrial state.

After Plassey the British also took Pondicherry. Although they gave it and Chandernagore back to the French in the Peace of Paris in 1763, the peace stipulated that they should not be fortified. The French even dissolved their East India Company in 1769. They would never again seriously threaten the British position in India.

Further French losses

By that same peace the French also surrendered their chances in North America. There, as in India, the British triumphed after initial reverses. The War of the Austrian Succession had ended in a stalemate in North America. But within six years, before hostilities even erupted in Europe, the French and British went at each other again in North America. The French and Indian War began in 1754 over French moves to link up their Louisiana territory with Canada through a chain of posts running from the Ohio county – which included western lands claimed by Virginia and other British colonies – down the Ohio and the Mississippi Rivers to New Orleans. The governor of Virginia sent militia Lieutenant Colonel George Washington to protest this activity. The French, who had occupied the strategic forts of the Ohio and had started constructing Fort Duquesne

MAGNA *Britannia: her Colonies* REDUC'D

Left: Troops of the British East India Company's army drilling on Bombay Green. Until 1858 the British empire in India was legally the possession of a private trading company which had its own army and administrators to run it, rather than a colony belonging to the Crown.

Right: The loss of the thirteen colonies which would become the United States after 1776 cost Britain one of the richest parts of its empire. This American cartoon gruesomely suggests that without North America British possessions were defenseless – a boast that history would prove to be false.

there, forced his surrender in 1754 at a nearby place called Great Meadows. This defeat presaged greater ones to come. Next year the incompetent General Edward Braddock (with Washington his aide-de-camp) led a force of British regulars and Virginia militia of over 1400 men against Fort Duquesne, which had only some 150 French-Canadian militia and around 70 French regulars to defend it. Reinforced, however, by nearly 650 Indians, they ambushed Braddock's van before it reached the fort and defeated his entire army. The British regulars continued to suffer reverses after that, in part because of incompetent leadership, although colonial officers gained a few moderate victories.

British fortunes changed in 1758, when the energetic British Prime Minister, William Pitt, appointed Jeffrey Amherst commander-in-chief in America. Under his leadership the British advanced inexorably upon Canada. In 1758 Amherst took the French fortress of Louisbourg, on Cape Breton Island, and the British general John Forbes occupied Fort Duquesne, renaming it Fort Pitt (now Pittsburgh). Next year Amherst's subordinate, General James Wolfe, captured Quebec. After failing to force the city's surrender by siege, he sent his forces scrambling up a path to the heights, there to confront the French on an open plain outside the city. The French commander, the Marquis de Montcalm, accepted the challenge. The British won the sharp battle which followed, in which both the British and French commanders received mortal wounds. In 1760 Amherst invested Montreal and the French governor surrendered all of Canada to Great Britain. The British did not give it back in the Peace of Paris. They had won the war for empire in North America and intended to keep most of what they had acquired. European imperialism thus helped shape the Canada of today. The prevailing culture in Canada became European, dominated by the British in all provinces save the French-speaking Quebec.

Disaster in the form of the American Revolution quickly followed this outstanding success for Britain, and it came partly because of that suc-

cess. Once the British had ejected France from North America, many colonists believed they no longer needed the protection of the British army. Yet the army remained on the American frontier. To pay for it, and for other imperial expenses, the British parliament tried to levy a series of taxes which soon provoked violent opposition in the colonies. Americans had their own legislatures, which had traditionally levied taxes. Hence came the slogan: 'no taxation without representation.' Those legislatures differed from Parliament, however, in that the executives appointed by Britain, the royal governors, had little patronage and thus little influence over them. In Connecticut and Rhode Island the British government did not even appoint the governors. The colonists had enjoyed long experience in self-government and did not intend to let anyone curtail it. When, on top of all these taxes, the British sent troops to Boston to put down disorders and then extended Canada's borders southward to include land the Americans considered their own, they went to war.

The British lost the war for several reasons, but certainly one of them was that they could not do in America what they had done in India: use the Americans to keep America British. Many thousands of people remained loyal to the Crown. Yet the British did not organize them properly, or utilize them in strategic areas, until too late, until after the rebels and then the United States had taken control. Nor did the mother country use its navy well, a failing it would not repeat in later imperial ventures. Finally, most of Europe turned against Britain in what became known as the Armed Neutrality, and France and Spain actively declared war against Britain and sent troops to North America to fight. Indeed, the French had more regular troops at Yorktown in 1781 to trap Lord Cornwallis and force his surrender than there were regulars of the American Continental army under George Washington. The Peace of Paris of 1783, which ended the war, recognized the sovereignty of the United States, the only country in the history of the British Empire to declare independence unilaterally and make it stick permanently.

That setback did not, however, halt the course of British imperialism. Even as they were fighting in America the British were waging a desperate war in India against Hyder Ali, the ruler of Mysore, aided by the French. Yet the British managed to hold on, and after the American Revolution that same Cornwallis who had surrendered at Yorktown expanded the British presence in India. He defeated the new ruler of Mysore, Tipoo, the son of Hyder, and took half his territory for the East India Company. From then on the Company continued to expand in India until the Great Mutiny of 1857. By that time it controlled directly around 60 percent of the land of India, and three-quarters of its population. As it expanded, the Company lost most of its power to the British government, and, after the Mutiny, all of it. The Great Mutiny itself, which some Indian historians have called the First War of Indian Independence, was confined mainly to Bengal and involved only a small minority of the sepoys and the general population. But it shook the British so badly that thereafter they never took over any more land directly.

Some 600 princely states formed a large part of British India. Their rulers held sway, subject only to the British controlling their foreign policies and their conforming generally to British ideas of good administration. British imperialism in India thus scarcely approached at any time a close, tight rule of an alien population. Nor could it, since India's hundreds of millions vastly outnumbered the less than 100,000 Britons, including the British army, who lived there. At the time of Queen Victoria's Diamond Jubilee in 1897 the British army in India numbered about 72,000, plus perhaps another 20,000 British who were members of the Indian Civil Service and officers of the Indian army. In East Bengal one district civil officer held the responsibility for administering 6000 square miles of land on which lived some 4,000,000 people.

Using India as a base, the British expanded into other parts of Asia thereafter. When the Burmese threatened Bengal in 1824 the British landed forces at Rangoon and captured the Burmese capital of Amarapura. They then made a treaty

that gave them territory in Lower Burma. After tempestuous relations with Upper Burma, Britain finally occupied it in 1885, and then annexed all of Burma to India. In 1819 the British took Singapore, intending to use it as a naval station and trading base. From there they inexorably expanded until, by 1914, they controlled all Malaya. Few British settled in Malaya, but British advisers and residents with the local rulers made it a colony in all but name.

Similarly, the British acquired Hong Kong because of their control of India. India's most saleable commodity in China was opium, which the British wished to exchange for tea. The Chinese government understandably did not relish the prospect of this great infusion of opium and banned its importation. Large-scale smuggling followed. When the Chinese tried to stop it in

Above left: General Wolfe's death at the Battle of the Plains of Abraham became one of British imperial history's most celebrated moments, as in this 1770 painting by Benjamin West.

Left: Captured sepoy mutineers are tied across the muzzles of guns, to be blown to smithereens moments later. This brutal treatment of prisoners was the savage response to the wholesale slaughter of British officers and noncombatants at Meerut, Delhi and Cawnpore earlier in the Indian Mutiny.

Above: Britain's passion for China tea proved an expensive drain. To redress its balance of payments deficit with the oriental empire Britain exported opium from its possessions in India to China. This trade was opposed by the Chinese government but the British ruthlessly insisted that China accept the opium. This conflict eventually broke out into open warfare on two occasions, the end result being humiliation for China. The opium wars also brought the British Empire a new possession, Hong Kong, full of opium dens like this one.

Right: Among the many unfortunate victims of European expansion were (and are) the Australian aborigines.

1838 and confiscated over 20,000 chests of opium, war followed. The Chinese had not the slightest chance of prevailing against the mightiest navy in the world, and in 1842 their government ceded Hong Kong to the British as a commercial base and permitted them to trade elsewhere in China as well.

Pacific victories

India did not, however, play a role in the creation of the two major British colonies in the Pacific, Australia and New Zealand. Before the British came, Australia was thinly populated by very primitive aborigines. They had developed no agriculture, had no animals save for the wild dog, had no permanent dwellings and lived solely by food gathering. Unlike the fierce Iroquois of North America, they presented no challenge at all to the alien intruders from Europe who first landed in numbers in 1788. Earlier, while the American Revolution was unfolding, one of Europe's greatest explorers, Britain's Captain James Cook, had undertaken voyages of discovery in the Pacific, three of them between 1768 and his death in 1779. During the first Cook circumnavigated New Zealand and sailed the entire length of the east coast of Australia, which he called New South Wales and claimed for Britain. With him was young Joseph Banks, who had inherited enough money to allow him the leisure of studying at length his favorite subject, botany. Australia fascinated him, and he became convinced that it would be a good place for British settlement. The American Revolution gave him the opportunity to press for just that. Hitherto, Britain had transported convicted felons to servitude in America as a punishment for their crimes. With America gone, the question arose as to where to transport the criminal. In 1778, one year after he had become President of the Royal Society, Banks told a committee of the House of Commons that they could create a 'thief

colony' at Botany Bay, in New South Wales. The government eventually accepted this idea, and the first group of 700 convicts landed at Botany Bay (near Sydney, which soon became the capital of New South Wales) in January of 1788.

Although Australia started as a convict colony and several thousand convicts arrived yearly after 1815, it soon blossomed into something quite different. John Macarthur, an officer in the unit created to guard the convicts, introduced sheep farming, which flourished. Free people initially settled in other colonies, such as Swan River (Western Australia) in 1829 and South Australia in 1836. Many non-convicts settled in New South Wales as well, and as various Australian provinces advanced toward self-government under British guidance, transportation of criminals to Australia came to be abolished. New South Wales took no convicts after 1840, and other provinces followed, until by 1868 Britain sent no more. By that time the Australia that had started as a sort of national prison for convicts was coming to be associated with innovations of freedom. The secret ballot emerged there, and when Britain itself adopted it in 1872 the British called it the 'Australian ballot.'

Australia's neighbor to the east, the two islands which comprise New Zealand, was settled considerably later by free people. The indigenous inhabitants, the Maoris, were a much more powerful and advanced people than the aborigines of Australia. From their first contact with Europeans they had shown an ability to understand their ways and to work to keep their own land and culture in the face of white encroachment, using the tools of the whites, including muskets, to do so. Sailors from whaling and sealing ships had first encountered them in the late eighteenth century, and missionaries followed, but the first colony of whites in any great number (around 1000, organized by the private New Zealand Company) did not arrive in North Island until 1839. The British government itself then moved in, annexed both islands and in the Treaty of Waitangi guaranteed the Maoris the rights of British subjects and possession of their land. But the treaty did not work out as the British government intended, for as more Europeans arrived they pressed increasingly into Maori territory. Bitter wars followed, in which the British soldiers sent to fight displayed more sympathy for the Maoris than for the Europeans. At the same time, during the 1850s and 1860s, the colonists worked out a system of representative government which made them by the 1870s as self-governing as Australia. Eventually, also, they smoothed over many of their differences with the Maoris. By the early twentieth century the Maoris had acquired their own representatives in the New Zealand parliament and finally put an end to the appropriation of their diminished lands.

European penetration into Africa did not end so fortunately. Although most historians tend to focus on the race among the European powers to acquire as much African land as possible between about 1880 and 1914, a case can be made for arguing that the impact of imperialism on both Europeans and Africans was greatest in those parts of Africa where the Europeans penetrated well before the 1880s. The one exception is perhaps Portugal. Yet the Portuguese had only the loosest sort of hold on their African territories until the late nineteenth century, controlling only the ports. They maintained posts in Angola only for slave trading, which in turn depended on Portuguese Brazil. Mozambique traded slaves to Angola and serviced ships on the way to India. Not until the 1880s did Portugal explore the interior.

European imperialism in South Africa, by contrast, engendered endless wars, racial hatreds and the creation of a country where white minority rule still endures. The origins of that white minority go back to the Dutch East India Company, which first established a settlement in Capetown, South Africa, in 1652. The Company wanted a way station on the route to their holdings in India and the Dutch East Indies (Indonesia). Although the Dutch had trouble at first with the indigenous Hottentots, the colony survived and thrived, growing increasingly productive crops of wheat and grapes and supporting steadily enlarging herds of cattle and sheep.

The Dutch were strict Calvinists. After King Louis XIV of France revoked the Edict of Nantes in 1685, French Huguenots (Protestants) sought refuge at the Cape, where, since they shared similar austere beliefs, they blended in easily with the Dutch. So too did some Germans who had served the Company and then stayed on in the Cape Colony after they retired. Perhaps in keeping with their Calvinist sense of being God's elect, from the beginning the white South Africans emphasized white racial superiority. They began importing slaves in 1654 and continued practicing slavery until the British forced its abolition in 1834. After the initial settlement, the Dutch East India Company only attempted seriously to encourage immigration to the colony for a brief period in the

Above: British troops storm the Kashmir Gate during the siege of Delhi in September 1857. The Indian mutineers had occupied the capital of the once-mighty Moghul empire in the hope of providing a focus for Indian nationalism. The British, however, promptly sent an army to capture the city, and nip any such feelings in the bud.

Left: Captain James Cook lands on Australia and claims it for Britain. The great explorer's cavalier treatment of the land's primitive inhabitants – whose opinion on the subject was never sought – was perfectly in keeping with the spirit of the age.

Above right: Captain Cook's voyages to the south Pacific revealed the basic outline of that part of the world to Europe's geographers – an exceptional feat of cartographical and navigational skills.

Above far right: One of the Boers, descendants of the early Dutch settlers in South Africa.

late seventeenth and early eighteenth centuries, but this did not succeed well. As a result, the white Afrikaners who run the Republic of South Africa today are largely descended from the fewer than 2000 men, women and children of the Cape Colony noted in a census of 1707.

By the end of the eighteenth century the whites of South Africa, who now numbered 15,000, had no home but the colony. They possessed their own distinct language, Afrikaans, and their own culture and society. By then two types of Afrikaners had emerged within the society: the farmers, or Boers, some of them owners of large estates in the southwestern part of the colony near Cape-town, and the stockraisers, most of whom were constantly on the move. Much of the land was arid and unsuitable for crops, so that when the Company allowed freemen to acquire several thousands of acres for a small fee, many did so. As a result, the frontier constantly expanded to the north and east, where toward the end of the eighteenth century the Afrikaners encountered far stiffer military opposition from the Bantu peoples – Zulu, Matabele, Basuto, Bechuana – than they had from the Bushmen and Hottentots. These stockraisers came to be known as *trekkers* or *trekboers*. They lived fiercely independent, isolated lives. Brave and determined, they nonetheless were narrow-minded, poorly read (save for the family Bible) white supremacists. They could not get along with the native peoples unless they could subjugate them – which would mean endless struggle since the Bantu refused to be subjugated – and they cared little for the actions or opinions of the world beyond the *veldt*. By the end of the eighteenth century they were unique among European-derived societies in having had no experience of the Enlightenment.

The British jostled their way into this society in 1795. By then they had achieved paramountcy in

India and viewed the Cape as a way station of value to them. The French Revolution had erupted six years earlier, and in 1793 the revolutionary government had declared war on much of Europe, including Britain. The Dutch Republic had had the misfortune to become one of France's first victims, and the Stadtholder, William V of Orange-Nassau, had fled to Britain. He then gave the British a sort of legal authority for what they fully intended to do anyway: keep the Cape Colony out of French hands. Although the British returned it briefly to Holland during the short-lived Peace of Amiens, they seized it again in 1806 and held on to it for good after that.

Once the British had acquired the colony permanently, British officials began imposing British laws. British settlers, including missionaries who disapproved of the Boers' treatment of the natives, began to arrive. They added to the pressure British officials were already putting on the Boers to change their ways. In 1815 a British court accused a farmer of mistreating a Hottentot, and summoned him to appear to face the charge. The farmer refused. After he fired on a party sent to arrest him, they fired back and killed him. His death provoked a Boer uprising which the British quelled, hanging five of the ringleaders. This incident, one of many remembered to this day by the Afrikaners, provoked fierce anti-British feeling. It intensified when, in 1828, English replaced Dutch as the official language, and the British government at the Cape passed the 50th Ordinance. This measure abolished the passes Hottentots had hitherto been obliged to carry, allowed them freedom of movement, as well as the right to own land and much else, and made them legally almost the equal to Europeans. Then the British Parliament in 1834 emancipated all the slaves in the British Empire. Although the imperial government promised compensation for losses to the

former slaveowners, the money allocated for the Cape Colony, collectable only in London, amounted to only around a third of the local valuation of slave property.

Because of these and other measures, many Boers decided to leave the Cape, removing themselves from the jurisdiction of the hated British. They began their 'Great Trek' in 1836. Heading north and east, they at first met little Bantu opposition. But in what would become the province of Natal they struggled fiercely with the well-organized and highly militaristic Zulu nation, winning a remarkable victory at Blood River in December 1838. They then tried to set up a republic, only to have the British again take it away from them. A few British had settled in Natal in 1824. More had trickled in after that, occasionally requesting the British government to annex the territory. The British had always in the past refused, but they finally sent troops to Durban in 1842, fearing that a Boer occupation might stir up more trouble with the Bantus. In any case, the British still considered the Boers British subjects, and the fact that they had left the Cape Colony did not, in British eyes, make the Boers any less subject to British law. Enraged, the Boers besieged Durban, but British reinforcements forced them to retreat. The British then, in 1843, annexed Natal.

Thereafter, when the government established near equality at law between blacks and whites, most (though not all) of the frustrated *trekkers* left to seek yet another home free from British interference. At first the British tried to halt the exodus by military force, but eventually the imperial government decided it was not worth the cost in money and lives to try to contain these determined 'subjects.' In 1852 it recognized the independence of the *trekkers* beyond the Vaal River, in territory to be known as the Transvaal, and in

1854 Britain also recognized the independence of the land in between the Transvaal and the Cape Colony, to be known as the Orange Free State. The arrangement settled temporarily the Boer-British differences.

French opportunism

At the time the British were expanding at the expense of the Boers in the extreme south of Africa, the French were advancing at the expense of the Arabs in the extreme north. In 1830 the French began the conquest of Algeria, an event that owed as much to chance as to planning. They had not earnestly sought empire beyond Europe after their loss of Canada and Napoleon's sale of the Louisiana territory in 1803. Indeed, by 1830, except for Britain, Europe had largely abandoned imperialism. Most of Spain's New World territories had won independence, and Portugal had lost Brazil. The Dutch had retained their possessions in Indonesia, but they had not tried to enlarge them. The only reason the French went into Africa in 1830 was that Charles X, one of the most

detested monarchs in French history, wanted to win acclaim for his government by mounting a naval expedition to occupy Algiers and get rid of the Barbary corsairs. On 14 June the French landed a force of 37,000 men, and in less than a month they took Algiers.

At that point they had no idea what to do with it. Charles X would not decide, because in that year he fled France, to be replaced by the 'Bourgeois Monarchy' of Louis Philippe. Although the new king's government desired no more African land, it took Oran and Bone to complete the occupation of the coast and clean out the rest of the pirates. Could the French stay on the coast without controlling the interior? Evidently they thought not, for now they decided to move inland, and in 1840 the Bourgeois Monarchy decided upon a policy of total conquest of Algeria. The Second Republic, which replaced the Bourgeois Monarchy in 1848, declared Algeria a French territory and divided it into departments, each department administered by a prefect. When the Second Empire, under Napoleon III, succeeded

the Second Republic, it completed the conquest of Algeria in 1857. The Third Republic followed the Second Empire in 1871. It tried for the complete assimilation of Algeria into France, in the process dispossessing nearly half the native inhabitants of their land. All these very different governments had engaged in imperial expansion.

To practice imperialism required the expenditure of money and lives. The lives perhaps mattered less to the French than to other European powers, since they had created a military unit made up of foreigners, the French Foreign Legion, in 1831, for the specific purpose of 'pacifying' the interior of Algeria. One of the most famous of European military organizations and the subject of numerous romantic novels and Hollywood movies, the Legion's origins were solidly rooted in European imperialism. While all the Legion's officers were French, the enlisted ranks could not be; they were volunteers from all other corners of Europe. They took no oath to France, only to the Legion, which accounts for its motto *Legion Patria Nostra* ('The Legion is our Country'). Its fighting skills were second to none.

Those fighting skills contributed importantly to the French military's controlling more and more of Algeria, which encouraged more and more European civilians (not all of them French) to move to the ports, particularly Algiers. By the 1880s Algeria's population numbered nearly 400,000 people. When the Muslim revolt that would eventually succeed in ousting the French from Algeria began in 1954, the European population numbered about 1,000,000 in a land of around 9,000,000. Algeria thus became what one historian has described as the first of the modern 'hybrid' colonies, one in which a sizeable European community settled, but which never grew to more than a small minority of the total population. Yet these 'hybrid' colonies, because of those Europeans, would cause the mother countries the most anguish in disengaging from imperialism.

The French did not create such a 'hybrid' colony in Indo-China, yet it proved nearly as troublesome to them (and later to the United States) as Algeria. The French had established Catholic missions in Indo-China in the late eighteenth century. Until the 1820s these missions had enjoyed local protection. But persecution of them increased steadily after that, particularly under Tu-Duc, who

Top left: In 1835 the Boers living in the Cape Colony fled what they saw as the tyranny of London's rule and made their way into the southern African hinterland, a journey later known as the 'Great Trek.'

Left: French infantry at an Algiers barracks. The North African empire France acquired during the nineteenth century was initially the result of a campaign to eliminate the Barbary Corsairs, pirates who had plagued Mediterranean shipping for centuries. Once in Africa the French remained and expanded their colonial 'beach-head' into an enormous overseas empire.

Right: British ships at the ceremonies marking the opening of the Suez Canal in 1869. A joint project of French and British financiers, the Suez Canal became the most vital link in the chain connecting Britain to its Indian empire.

reigned from 1847 to 1883 and who wished to stamp out Christianity. Napoleon III did not intend to let that happen. He began sending French forces into the Saigon delta in 1858 and forced Tu-Duc in 1862 to sign a treaty granting religious toleration and conceding some of his territory, including Saigon. From this nucleus the French expanded to take the rest of Indo-China, including Cambodia and Laos.

Latecomers to the scramble

If France joined the imperial game a little later than Britain in the nineteenth century, the two countries were more important than any others in extending their sway over alien lands until the 1880s, unless one counts Russia's expansion into Asia an imperial adventure. Germany and Italy joined the French and British in the race for colonies only after 1880. The principal reason for their tardiness was doubtless that neither Italy nor Germany had existed as sovereign nations much before then. Their struggles for unity and sovereignty had occupied them in Europe for much of the century. But with the boundaries of western Europe more or less settled, if the Germans and Italians wanted more land, they would have to look beyond Europe.

They did so in the 1880s, joined by the King of Belgium. In 1880 European nations controlled only about 10 percent of the African continent, in coastal pockets for the most part, and did not even know what lay in the interior. By 1914 they had carved up nearly the entire continent among themselves. Many people have studied this 'scramble for Africa' and advanced many reasons for it, but no one cause seems to stand out. Obviously the Europeans sliced up Africa in a spirit of diplomatic rivalry, and some European powers also acquired certain areas for valid strategic pur-poses. Thus the British wished to control the Suez Canal in order to keep the way open to their Indian empire. Missionaries hoped to stop slavery and help the natives by bringing medicine and Christianity to them, and they thought the best way to do so was for European powers to take over. Adventurers also played a role in Africa, for the rush for colonies enabled them to gain fame and fortune for themselves. And certainly the colonies provided jobs for soldiers and administrators. At the very least, the possession of colonies meant prestige in Europe.

But did they also mean profits? Economic motivations figured prominently in this phase of imperialism, as they always had before. Although the theory advanced by British economist John Hobson that the 'new' imperialism in Africa rode on the machinations of finance capitalists – a theory Lenin adopted – has few advocates today, money played its part. King Leopold II of Belgium wanted to make a profit out of the Congo. The numerous private companies that served as agents of imperialism also sought profits. They included Sir George Goldie's National African Company, Cecil Rhodes' British South Africa Company, the German Karl Peters' East African Company and others.

Colonialism: huge profits and huge losses

The profit motive, ostensibly rational, leads to yet another aspect of the race for colonies: its irrationality. One recent scholar of imperialism doubts that *any* of the European colonies in Africa returned a net profit, in the conventional sense, to the European nations. Although some companies and individuals made huge profits, more went broke. The costs of administration were high, as were the costs of armies and navies needed to keep control. And what profit could the French make in the thousands of miles of sand in the Sahara Desert? What sort of financial gain would the Italians have made from Ethiopia even if they had managed to take it? The one clearly continuous rational element in late nineteenth- and early twentieth-century European imperialism is that the Europeans never did consider colonies worth major war. Colonial crises of one sort or another continually made the headlines, but the Europeans resolved them all peacefully. They saved their irrationality for the almost purely European conflict known as World War I.

If Britain is to be regarded as the forerunner in the scramble for Africa, the first move was the completion of the Suez Canal in 1869. It vastly shortened the route to India. In so doing it made stable government in Egypt a primary concern for the British. In 1875 the British government purchased 177,000 of the 400,000 shares of stock (the rest mostly owned by Frenchmen, since France had built the canal) to become the largest single shareholder. Now the British had a financial as well as a strategic interest in Egypt. In early 1882 a nationalist uprising there against foreign influence threatened to take over the Egyptian government. In response, the British bombarded Alexandria in July 1882 and landed troops to protect the canal, defeating Egyptian forces in September. Thereafter they effectively took control of the Egyptian government, although they did not formally declare Egypt a protectorate until 1914.

Egypt had long claimed to control the Sudan, and the Egyptian government had employed Britons to govern it, the most recent of them being General Charles 'Chinese' Gordon, from 1874 to 1879. After the British intervention in Egypt, however, a Muslim rising in the Sudan led by the Mahdi Mohammed Ahmed routed Egyptian

forces, and the Mahdi then assumed power. The British decided to pull the remaining Egyptian forces out of Khartoum, and ordered Gordon to do so, but Gordon remained, hoping evidently to shame the British into retaking the Sudan and suppressing the slave trade that the Mahdi had reintroduced. Mohammed Ahmed took Khartoum and killed Gordon. Although the Mahdi himself died shortly thereafter, the Khalifa Abdullah el Taashi carried on his policy. The doings in the Sudan thereafter, as told by white Christians who escaped from it occasionally, excited horror in Europeans. Finally, in 1898, the British retook the Sudan using gunboats, artillery, machine guns and repeating rifles. With that conquest, and what they had taken elsewhere, the British controlled all of East Africa save for Portuguese Mozambique, the independent native kingdom of Abyssinia, and German East Africa.

Had the occupation of Egypt set off the race? Or did the French do so when they took Tunisia to spite the Italians? Between 1879 and 1881 the French and Italians in Tunis intrigued for concessions such as railroads, telegraphs and land grants. When the ruler of Tunis raided into Algeria in March 1881, he gave the French an excuse for occupying Bizerte and taking Tunis. In May the Bey of Tunis recognized a French protectorate. A rebellion against French rule induced the French to subdue southern Tunisia as well, so that by 1882, the year the British landed in Egypt, the French already controlled both Algeria and Tunisia. The French then encroached on the territories of the Sultan of Morocco, and in the early twentieth century they began taking over governmental powers there as well. By 1908 they occupied much of the Moroccan Atlantic coast, although Spain got a small portion of Morocco

along the Mediterranean by virtue of an arrangement with France in 1904. By 1911 the Germans, who in the preceding decade had vociferously and vigorously protested the French penetration of Morocco, recognized France's special position there in return for land in the French Congo.

Perhaps neither the French nor the British started the scramble, but instead the responsibility lay with King Leopold II of Belgium? In 1878 the king, through his company, which would come to be called the International Association of the Congo, commissioned Henry Morton Stanley, the famous reporter who had 'found' Dr David Livingstone in 1871 (Livingstone had not known he was lost), to establish stations in the Congo. Stanley carried out Leopold's commission between 1879 and 1884, laying the basis for Leopold's taking the Congo state in 1885 as his personal property.

©Richard Natkiel, 1986

Below: The world at the end of the nineteenth century had been almost entirely divided among the European industrial nations and their descendants.

Right: The charge of the 21st Lancers at the Battle of Omdurman in 1898. The British victory at Omdurman marked the end of native resistance to British expansion in the Sudan.

Far right: A statue of General Charles Gordon at Khartoum. Gordon's great skill was his ability to train and command non-European troops.

Below right: Sir Henry Stanley, who played an important role in the establishment of Belgian rule over the Congo.

IMPORTANT BRITISH BASES AND COALING STATIONS

BRITISH POSSESSIONS
FRENCH
PORTUGUESE
SPANISH
DUTCH
ITALIAN
GERMAN

Germany got in a bit later, perhaps only to grab what was left. In 1884 and 1885 Germany declared protectorates over Southwest Africa, Togoland, the Cameroons and East Africa. Presumably Bismarck claimed these areas in order to have bargaining chips in European diplomacy. Certainly his actions helped create ground rules for European imperialism. An international conference he called in Berlin in 1885, attended by most European nations as well as the United States, drew up the boundaries of the Congo Free State, making it nearly as large as the United States east of the Mississippi, gave its government to Leopold of Belgium, internationalized the Congo River, proclaimed free trade, and called for the suppression of the slave trade. The conference also stip-

ulated that a European power with holdings on the coast had first rights in the interior, but that for a claim to be valid, the European power must actually occupy the area with troops or officials. Each power should also tell other interested groups what territories it considered its own. The conference had little effect on Leopold, since it had no way of enforcing its decisions, and he soon went his own way.

Italy, which Bismarck once disparagingly described as having a big appetite but poor teeth, joined the race with rather less success. In 1882 they took over Assab (along Africa's northeastern coast) from a private company. It served as the nucleus for the colony that became Italian Eritrea. In 1889 they got from the Sultan of Zanzibar land along the Indian Ocean, which became Italian Somaliland. They took advantage of a war with Turkey to annex Tripoliania (now Libya) in 1911. But in Ethiopia they were the one European nation to suffer such a decisive defeat at the hands of a native African state that they could not fully conquer it until after World War I.

The British had suffered their share of setbacks, but had rebounded from them. Eventually, for example, they conquered the Sudan after Gordon's defeat. In early 1879 the Zulus wiped out about 1500 men of General Frederick Lord Chelmsford's army at Isandhlwana, following the British invasion of Zululand.But nearby at the Rorke's Drift mission station, 139 soldiers (some of them hospitalized) successfully withstood an attack by 4000 Zulus. Chelmsford quickly recovered and defeated the Zulus at their capital of Ulundi later in the year. By contrast Ethiopians inflicted at Adowa in 1896 a crushing defeat on an Italian army of 20,000 men which had invaded their land. As a result Ethiopia (or Abyssinia) remained one of only two black African states not annexed by the Europeans by 1914. The other was Liberia, founded in 1822 as a refuge for freed American slaves.

The South African problem

By 1914 there also existed another nearly independent African state, but one controlled by whites, the Union of South Africa. The troublesome Boer republics had been a thorn in Britain's side ever since their creation in 1854. Britain fought a brief war with them in 1880, which it lost, and as a result of which it acknowledged yet again Boer independence. But old antagonisms resurfaced after the discovery of gold on the Witwatersrand in the Transvaal in 1886. Foreigners, most of them British, poured into the Transvaal to dig for gold. The Boers needed them, for the *Uitlanders* as the Boers called them, possessed the machinery and technical engineering skills to extract gold from the solid rock that held it. So they admitted the foreigners, then taxed them heavily and refused them citizenship at the same time.

Cecil Rhodes, a wealthy British promoter of Empire, who had made a fortune in South Africa, hoped to end Boer intransigence by inciting a Uitlander rebellion to take over the Transvaal government. He sent one of his agents, Leander Starr Jameson, at the head of 500 men to support the Uitlanders when they rose up against their oppressors. The Jameson Raid failed, and the *Uitlanders* did not rebel. Boer-British negotiations for a settlement of their issues broke down, and the bloody Boer War of 1899-1902 followed, in which the sympathy of most of the Western world lay with the Boers.

The Boer War and the settlements that followed it, resulting in the creation of the Dominion of South Africa in 1910, represent perhaps the ultimate in the irrationality of imperialism in Africa. The British may have gone to war to control Rand gold, but the cost of that war to them was vastly greater than any potential rewards in gold. One of Britain's stated policies in the South African territories before the war had been to advance native opportunities and native legal rights. But when the British created the Dominion of South Africa in 1910, they virtually turned over control of native matters to the Boers, most of whom opposed British native policies. The Afrikaners at first only nibbled at native rights, but eventually introduced the *apartheid* system that prevails

today. They also rejected membership in the British Commonwealth of Nations and took the name Republic of South Africa.

Western Europeans in the middle and late nineteenth century were the wealthiest, most technologically advanced people in the world. That explains the rapidity of the African acquisitions, but not the rationale for them. All that can be said is that imperialism was somehow in fashion, not just for the Europeans and not just in Africa. The United States entered the game when it went to war against Spain in 1898 in order to liberate Cuba from Spanish oppression. It ended up possessing Puerto Rico and the Philippine Islands. Although Africa provided the most outstanding example of European imperialism acquiring in a short time huge chunks of land and millions of people, and then dividing both by artificial boundaries, the race for colonies went on all over the world. Thus the Dutch expanded from their initial position at Batavia in Java to take over most of Indonesia. The Germans acquired part of New Guinea and islands in the Pacific.

Oriental imperialism

Japan was both the victim and the beneficiary of imperialism. The Japanese rulers had isolated their islands from the rest of the world by choice in the early seventeenth century, and then did not open Japan again until forced to by the visit of American Commodore M C Perry in 1853. American and European merchants followed. When the Japanese murdered an Englishman, the British responded with a naval bombardment. When in their hatred of foreigners some Japanese forts fired on an American vessel and later on French and Dutch vessels, the Americans and French responded with another naval bombardment. Japan got the message. The Japanese overthrew the Tokugawa shogunate, reinstated the emperor in a position of authority and proceeded to Westernize to the extent of acquiring and using Western technology. They succeeded so swiftly that they changed from victim to victor. In 1894-95 they defeated China and acquired Korea. Now Japan was an imperial power. Next Japan defeated Russia, which had encroached on what

the Japanese considered their own territory in Manchuria and northern Korea, in a war in 1904-05. The Japanese took Port Arthur and sank the Russian navy at the battle of Tshushima Straits in May 1905.

That the Europeans grudgingly respected Japan when it became strong enough to play their own game of imperialism they demonstrated in China. This ancient civilization had fallen behind the Europeans technologically by the nineteenth century, and seemed to them to be decaying. The British had exposed its weakness in the Opium War of 1841-42. Thereafter the Europeans arrived in greater numbers, determined to wrest concessions. The United States forced a treaty on China in 1844 that placed Americans (and ultimately all foreigners) under the criminal and civil jurisdiction of American and European, not Chinese, courts. A huge rebellion between 1850 and 1864 tore the country apart even more. Warlords

carved out their own territories, while more treaties opening more and more of China to Great Britain, France, Russia and the United States proliferated. In 1860 17,000 British and French troops occupied Peking and burned the Summer Palace. Foreigners took control of the customs service. By 1896 the Germans had occupied Kiaochow Bay, for which they then extorted a 99-year lease. A veritable rush for concessions followed, similar to the scramble for Africa. When a group that the Europeans called the Boxers attacked foreigners (with encouragement from the Chinese court) and besieged the legations in Peking, an international force, including the Japanese, put down the patriotic movement. No one European power ever took all of China. The United States suggested in effect in 1899 that the Western powers in China share equally, an idea which they accepted and which came to be known as the 'open door' policy.

Obviously the victims of imperialism disliked

it, wherever it occurred. Imperialism did not necessarily result in misery for the conquered peoples, but it did cause considerable suffering in some places. In the Congo, for example, Leopold proved a ruthless taskmaster. The invention of pneumatic rubber tires for bicycles and automobiles sparked a demand for rubber in the early twentieth century. To get it, Leopold compelled the natives to tap rubber in the forests and punished the recalcitrant with whippings and mutilation. When the Europeans needed labor in Africa, they might break up families, leave women to tend the fields and stock, move the men into compounds and force them to work for meager pay. Even though the Europeans had worked tirelessly to end slavery in Africa, the systems they instituted in its stead often differed little from servitude. India stood in contrast to this bleak record. British government there was basically good government, but the British themselves were often aloof, arrogant, exclusive, keeping to themselves in clubs which admitted no Indians, and talking to Indians only when the Indians were their household servants. In any case, the excellence of British administration may be beside the point: people often prefer self-government to good government.

Development of the Dominions

The road the British Empire took in Canada was different. The British had created two provinces in North America in 1791, Upper and Lower Canada – which would become respectively Ontario and Québec – to reflect the dominant British culture in the one and French culture in the other. They had also authorized parliaments elected by property holders in each. Although both provinces had remained loyal to the British during

the war of 1812 with America, they subsequently began to show increasing signs of unhappiness about the limitations placed on their sovereignty. Their restiveness resulted in revolts in 1837. These uprisings did not amount to much – in some instances they smacked more of comic opera than bloody protest – but the British considered them serious enough to send out a governor general, John George Lambton, First Earl of Durham, to investigate the circumstances and recommend changes to avoid future conflicts. Durham did so, and Parliament adopted the recommendations embodied in his report of 1839. His most important recommendation concerned responsible government: the chief executive in Canada, the governor, should be responsible to the legislature, and the government, following normal British procedure, would be entrusted to the majority party in parliament.

Durham thought British culture superior to that of French Canada, and mistakenly believed that if Upper and Lower Canada were reunited the British would win out. Parliament did reunite the two provinces and successive governors general began entrusting the government to the leaders who could command majorities. But though this development forced the British and French to work together, it became obvious that they preferred separate provinces under separate governments. It also became obvious, after the Union won the American Civil War, that if the Canadians wanted to protect their separate identity in the face of the colossus to their south they had better try to form their own federation. They did so in 1867 when, with the approval of the British Parliament, Ontario, Quebec and two other existing provinces joined to form a dominion. Canada now had a central government and individual pro-

vincial governments. The governor general remained, but he entrusted his government to the leader of the party that commanded the majority in the federal parliament. In the provincial governments the leaders of the majority parties also took control. Although Canada retained strong ties with Britain, and Britain retained some control over it, after 1867 the Dominion of Canada for the most part governed itself.

By 1901 Australia had achieved the same status as Canada, and New Zealand became a dominion

Left: The colonial powers did not invariably win every battle, as this painting of the Battle of Isandhlwana indicates. Every imperial army had its own disaster, standing as a warning against the folly of overconfidence.

Below left: Cecil Rhodes, the South African mineral magnate. His blundering private diplomacy drew the British government into war against the Boers.

Right: A detail of a painting by Alphonse de Neuville of the defense of Rorke's Drift.

Below: A painting, titled *Saving the Guns at Colenso.* Colenso, an early battle of the Boer War, was fought on 15 December 1899. The British, under the incompetent Sir Redvers Buller, were defeated, and despite heroic efforts to the contrary some artillery pieces were captured. It was one of a humiliating series of defeats inflicted on the British by the Boers in the course of a single week.

in 1907. The British had won the Boer War, but the Boers won the peace when South Africa became a dominion in 1910. The Boers controlled it, and the British influence which had tried to protect and encourage rights for the blacks would steadily wane after that, even though a sizeable white minority of people of British origin continued to live in South Africa, chiefly in Natal. In any event, Canada had shown the way, and even before 1914 the British in India took tentative steps to give the Indians a say in Indian government. As a result, although the British had fought

the two longest and bloodiest wars of European imperialism before 1914, that of the American Revolution and the Boer War, they would eventually disentangle themselves from empire more easily than other European powers.

If, from the European point of view, imperialism was never the major fact of history between 1700 and 1914, for a very large part of the rest of the world it undeniably was. The spread of Western power and influence over the planet of course produced many important political consequences, but its cultural impact was incalculably more pro-

found. For imperialism was the supreme agent of the broad process we here call 'modernization.' In the complex story of how old cultures and political systems faced the challenge of the West's new technologies and ideologies lies the essence of most of what has happened in Asia and Africa in the last 250 years.

By 1914, on the eve of World War I, most peoples of Asia and Africa, whether under colonial rule or not, had begun to build the foundations for their eventual political independence and their modern development.

The Americas

When the first European colonists arrived in the Americas, parts of the center and south of the continent were relatively rich and populous, while the north was sparsely inhabited by largely pre-agricultural societies. The impact of the European settlers on the Americas was swift and decisive although the development of their colonies followed and uneven course. The Spanish colonies of Mexico and Peru were flooding the European economy with gold and silver long before the first successful English settlement was founded in Virginia in 1607. Yet within three centuries, North America would be well on its way to becoming the richest area on earth, with Central and South America stalled in economic dependence.

All colonies were intended to serve the interests of their mother-country, but whereas Spanish America developed under the tight control of an imperial bureaucracy taking its orders from Madrid, the English colonies on the eastern seaboard enjoyed, from the outset, a considerable measure of autonomy. Some were founded by groups specifically dissenting from the religious policies of home government. Whole communities of men, women and children crossed the Atlantic to form self-sufficient, hard-working farming societies. Here there were no easy fortunes to be had from precious metals, nor any suitable natives to be exploited as a support for a leisured life. North America was not the land of freedom – Black slavery was a feature of the colonies, as were the use of white indentured labor and local religious intolerance – but a tone of self-reliance and sturdy independence was established early and never lost.

Still, the history of North America in the seventeenth and eighteenth centuries was a colonial history, and its wars were colonial wars: European conflicts projected onto another continent. This was even to an extent true of the American War of Independence (1775-81), in which the French and Spanish played a vital role, pursuing their traditional rivalry with Britain. And the ideas that inspired the American radicals were European ideas, the latest fashion of the Enlightenment. But the complex political system the Americans worked out for themselves in the early years of independence was truly original, a flexible instrument that – though at times only just – proved able to survive the immense transformations that rocked the United States over the following two centuries.

The events of the first half of the nineteenth century defined the geography of the new nation. Britain successfully held on to Canada, setting a northern limit to American expansion, but to the south and west a combination of war and purchase opened up a vast area to the play of 'manifest destiny.' Indians got short shrift as land hunger and gold fever lured immigrants westward. In the independent United States, unlike Canada, there was no restraining influence from Britain to urge respect for native rights.

The moral issue that did grip consciences, and all but tore the United States apart, was slavery, the basis of the flourishing cotton economy of the southern states, abhorred by influential groups in the industrializing north. The Civil War of 1861-65, with its awesome loss of life, freed the black slaves to face poverty and prejudice, but also established that the future of the country lay in industrial growth.

By the end of the nineteenth century the United States had been transformed into a society that Washington or Jefferson would not have recognized. Firstly, the composition of the population had altered radically. Successive waves of immigration had brought the Irish, Germans, Scandinavians, Jews, Ukrainians, Poles and Italians swarming into America's exploding cities, swamping – or at least seeming to swamp – the original white Anglo-Saxon protestant stock. At the other end of the social scale, economic power was concentrated in the hands of a few extraordinarily wealthy men (largely of Anglo-Saxon origin), the owners of the great 'trusts,' who dominated the new industrial America. With seemingly limitless natural resources and a constant inflow of capital and cheap labor from Europe, the United States economy was experiencing runaway growth. But poverty and social unrest were also part of the new reality.

Two political impulses guided the United States into the twentieth century. One was a liberal progressive drive to improve social conditions and break the power of the trusts, seen as contrary to the American tradition of individualism and democracy. The other was a move toward assuming a leading role on the world stage, something which economic power now gave the United States the chance to do. After flexing its muscles in the Caribbean, Central America, the Philippines and China, the new industrial giant was finally drawn into the European battlefield in 1917, a portentous moment in modern history.

The development of Latin America showed some similarities with the United States. During Europe's Napoleonic wars, most of Spain's colonies rebelled against the weakened colonial power and eventually won independence by force

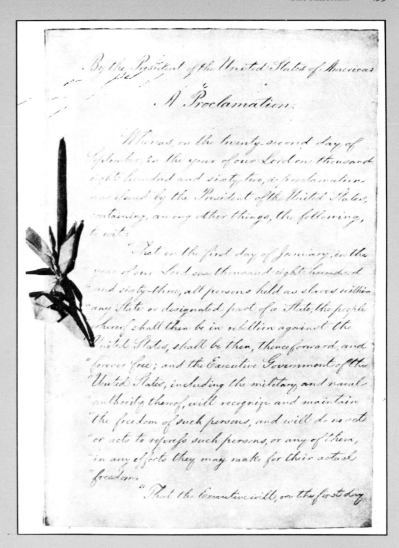

Below left: Spanish troops on the march during the American-Spanish war of 1898, a conflict that signalled the effective end of Spain as a colonial power and the emergence of the United States onto the world stage.

Right: An immigrant boy working in a New York sweat shop at the dawn of the twentieth century. Such exploitation was a common feature of American capitalism in this period.

Far right: President Lincoln's proclamation abolishing slavery in the United States in 1863. Issued at the height of the Civil War it would be more than two years before this 'peculiar institution' came to an effective end.

Below right: An English attack on slavery from 1792, by the renowned satirical artist Cruikshank. Slavery had in fact been abolished in England in 1772, largely through the activity of the great abolitionist Granville Sharp.

of arms. Brazil also broke away from Portugal, with a more peaceful transition to independence. Partly under the influence of the United States' example, the Spanish countries adopted republican constitutions, although Brazil did not follow suit until 1889. The differences from the United States were, however, greater than the resemblances. In Latin America, independence was won essentially by the inhabitants of European stock, a privileged group in racially stratified societies with large populations of Indians or Blacks, or both. The power of the Catholic Church and of conservative landowners was entrenched after independence, and most governments slipped into some form of military rule.

The fragmentation of the Spanish American empire into a number of competing states, their boundaries defined by nineteenth-century wars, reflected an incomplete economic development. By the late nineteenth century, Latin America had become chiefly a source of raw materials for Europe and North America, without substantial industrialization. A large influx of European immigrants, especially to Argentina and Brazil, led to growing population and a certain economic dynamism. But governments were often weak. They were liable to be bullied by European powers or, increasingly, by the United States which, in the early twentieth century, began to exercise a 'right of intervention' in the whole Caribbean zone.

The United States President, Grover Cleveland, was premature in 1895 when he announced that his country was 'practically sovereign on the continent' – meaning all of the Americas. But even before World War I, a growing predominance of the United States over Central America at least was visible, and the influence was already tending to spread southward.

North America: 1500-1800

The development of the British Empire was almost as dramatic as that of Spain, for as late as 1600 scarcely a thousand Englishmen could be found living outside of the British Isles. Yet in 1750 British colonies and British traders could be found around the world. Nowhere was the British success more brilliantly apparent than on the Atlantic coast of North America. Between 1607, the year Jamestown was founded, and 1750 hundreds of thousands of Europeans and scores of thousands of Africans had participated in the great 'Atlantic Migration' to swell the population of the 13 British colonies to more than a million persons. Fifteen years later an estimated two million people lived in the British colonies. Britain's American colonies were unique in that European culture had not been forced upon a large native population by a relatively small set of conquerors. Instead British culture had been projected into a sparsely populated *terra incognita*, planted, as it were, in virgin land.

European colonization of North America began with the confrontation of Indians and white men in the wilderness. The two races were separated by vast cultural differences, language barriers and mutual hostility. From the first the struggle was unequal, for the whites had a superior political and social organization, the advantage of guns, and the ability to draw on Europe as a source of supplies and an unending stream of colonists. By contrast, the woodland Indians in eastern North America were still living in the culture of the late Stone Age. They were never united beyond the level of local and temporary confederations of tribes and did not possess either the horse or the wheel at the time of first white contact. In essence the Indian had to jump 6000 years in time to comprehend the ways of the European.

The entire continent north of Mexico probably did not contain more than 2.5 million Indians in 1600. Unlike the conquerors of Mexico and Peru, the European colonists in North America did not encounter advanced cultures or large sedentary populations rendered docile by a powerful ruling class. North America had no Montezumas or Incan kings, but rather a bewildering variety of tribes, physical types, levels of culture, language differences and life styles.

The woodland Indians of eastern North America generally belonged to the Algonkian group, consisting of numerous tribal sub-groups. The Abanaki or 'Eastland' tribes were the first to come into direct and sustained contact with whites and thus constituted the first Indian-white frontier. The Abanaki lived in present-day Maine, New Brunswick and Nova Scotia. They combined corn-growing with hunting and fishing and had loose confederacies of villages presided over by a chief. They made pottery and used the wampum belt both for money and for ceremonial purposes. Abanaki enmity to the Iroquois of New York early led to their alliance with the French in Canada who established missions among the tribes. After 1600 Abanaki tribes were soon caught up in the struggle between the French fur traders and the advance of the Massachusetts settlers who threatened that trade. Brutal raids and skirmishes ensued which did not end until all the Abanaki and related tribes were defeated in the French and Indian War (1754-63), after which a majority of the survivors moved to Quebec and New Brunswick. Others entered reservations in Maine, where a few descendants still live at Oldtown today.

When the British settled New England, diseases contracted from European explorers and

Above: Pocahontas, born the daughter of a great American Indian chief, became the wife of an English gentleman in 1616. A romantic story tells of how she interceded with her tribe to spare the life of Captain John Smith, the military leader of the Jamestown colony in Virginia, following his capture by the Indians.

Left: A map of Virginia, Britain's first permanent colony in the New World.

Above right: This map of the world, drawn in 1500, was the first to show the outlines of Columbus's discoveries, then thought to be a part of Asia. In 1506 Columbus died, still unaware of the true nature of his achievement – that of a new continent, and not of a faster route to the Far East.

Right: A sketch of the Jamestown settlement. The British colonizers of North America hoped to profit from growing tobacco for the pipes of Britain's smokers. The Virginia Company sent farmers to Jamestown in 1607 to lay the basis of this scheme.

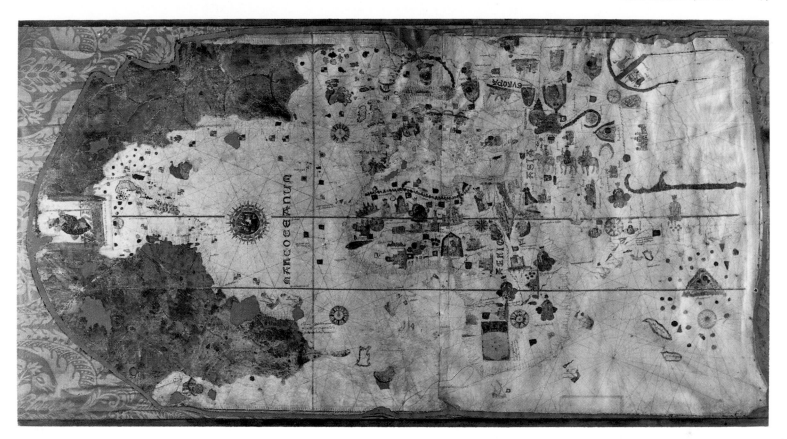

fishermen had already weakened the tribes there. The Massachusetts (both a tribal confederacy and a language type) had almost been killed off in a plague in 1618 and were soon absorbed by other tribes. The powerful Narraganset and Wampanoag confederacies of Rhode Island were ruined in King Philip's War (1675-77), and the remnants joined the Mahican and Abanaki tribes. Although Indian wars on the New England frontier were to continue until the middle of the eighteenth century, the coastal tribes were so weakened by 1677 they no longer constituted a major problem.

A somewhat larger confederation of tribes called the Mahican (or Mohegan) held the areas from the Hudson River valley eastward, as well as parts of Long Island. The vigorous Pequot, a branch of the Mahican group, were broken by the New England colonists in the vicious Pequot War of 1637. Other Algonkian tribes, the Wappinger and Montauk confederacies, occupied Long Island and the present environs of New York City, but they, too, either sold or lost their lands to the

whites and soon moved in with the Iroquois for protection.

Undoubtedly the most prestigious of the Algonkians on the East Coast were the Delaware or Lenape. Situated in what is now New Jersey, Delaware and eastern Pennsylvania, they were seen as the 'grandfathers' or progenitors of the Algonkian family by the Mahican, the Shawnee and other tribes. The Delaware maintained friendly relations with William Penn, the most important colonizer of the Jerseys, Pennsylvania, and Delaware, but eventually white and Iroquois pressures forced them and their allies to move west and into gradual oblivion.

One of the most important Indian groups on the Atlantic slope were the Iroquois, who lived in the present area of New York state. Allied in a remarkable confederacy, the League of the HoDe-NoSauNee, presumably begun by the Indian reformer Hiawatha, these woodland Indians early developed a hostility to the French and so allied themselves to the Dutch and British fur traders of

colonial New York. Using British guns and supplies they hunted for beaver wherever they could find them, which meant that they made war on other tribes as far west as the Great Lakes and western Ontario. But even as allies of the British, the Iroquois were doomed. The devastating wars and the disruption of their culture by white impact was so great that by 1776 most of them had removed to Canada to live.

The difficulties of defining Indian stocks and cultures is nowhere more apparent than when treating the southernmost of the Algonkian tribes, for the culture of the Powhatan confederacy of Virginia, made eternally famous by the names of Chief Powhatan and his daughter Pocahontas, closely resembled their immediate neighbors, who belonged to the non-Algonkian Muskhogean, or Hokan-Siouan, stock. Like other tribes the Virginian Algonkians had been decimated by disease and warfare by 1676. The remnants of this and other Virginia tribes who did not move west were finally collected on a Virginia reservation in 1928, where some 2000 Indians of mixed blood still live.

The Muskhogean Indians of the Southeast ranged from the simpler tribes of Florida to the complex aristocratic temple mound societies found in Georgia and Mississippi. Able, warlike and partly agricultural, they lived in a near-paradise of resources, for their forests were teeming with game, their rivers and coasts provided fish in abundance, and the growing season was ideal for corn, squash and beans. While many Indians near the Carolina and Georgia coast were wiped out or captured and sold into slavery by the British colonists between 1670 and 1715, the remainder entered into trading alliances with the British which lasted into the nineteenth century. By 1830 the process of acculturation had become so pronounced that the Creeks, Cherokees, Choctaws, Chickasaws and Seminoles were called 'The Five Civilized Tribes.' American desire for Indian lands was so great, however, that by 1845 these tribes had been driven from their homes and relocated in Oklahoma where their descendants live today.

Despite the virtual disappearance of the eastern

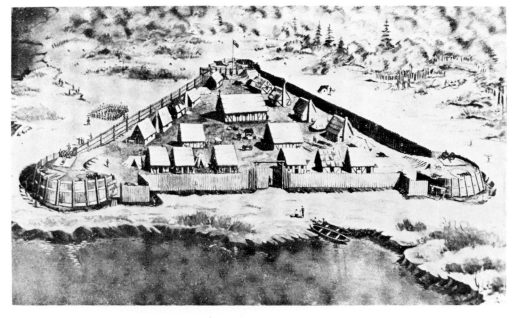

Algonkians by 1800 and the decline of the Iroquois, they had set most of the images of Indians in the minds of the European colonists: the concept of the noble savage had been made immortal by Hiawatha, Massasoit, King Philip, and Pocahontas. Indian dress and adornment such as painted bodies, head bands with feathers, the breechclout and leggings for men, the deerskin shirt for women and the universal moccasin recalled a native culture, while Indian wars unforgettably associated Indians with the bow and arrow, the tomahawk, the sneak raid, scalping and torture. The whites rejected the Indian and his way of life but they adopted many of his foods such as maize, squash, succotash and maple sugar. The whites also borrowed Indian words so freely that names such as Massachusetts, Allegheny, Illinois, Connecticut, and Alabama still dot the eastern half of North America.

Europeans in the New World

By the time the Europeans began to settle the North American continent the Spanish and Portuguese had already worked out successful patterns of colonization and exploitation in Central and South America. Naturally northern Europe, and especially the Protestant countries of England and the Netherlands, set out to emulate Spain or, if not that, to curb her power and to seize her share of the wealth of the New World. Not too surprisingly the first English efforts were also directed toward finding a passage to China. As early as 1497 England sent John Cabot to see if a northern route to the Orient existed. Instead, Cabot barely touched the eastern coast of Newfoundland and noted that its waters were filled with fish before returning to England for fleeting praise and a reputed gift of £10 from the king. Hardy mariners from Bristol and from Normandy and Brittany were soon exploiting the cod off the Great Banks, but it would be a hundred years before the first north European settlers reached American shores in number. English parochialism, lack of funds, and concern with internal politics, centering on Henry VIII's decision to break with Rome, postponed actual colonization of the New World until after Elizabeth I was safely on the throne. Even then, the preoccupation was with the passage to China and Spanish gold.

While ideas of a passage to China and the new world as a base from which to raid Spanish ships were undoubtedly the chief concerns of Sir Humphrey Gilbert, it was he who first saw North

Left: A drawing of an Indian village by John White, a member of Raleigh's expedition of 1585 to the coast of North Carolina.

Below left: The title page of a 1609 publication encouraging potential colonists to venture to Virginia. It made no mention of the fact that many of the Jamestown settlers perished from starvation and disease. Whatever possibilities awaited the Virginia farmer, an unfamiliar climate and soil meant that he faced a rugged existence and hard work.

Right: John White's map of the coast of North Carolina, then part of Virginia, shows the site of the ill-fated Roanoke colony.

Below right: The investors in speculative colonial ventures in North America hoped to get their money back from the produce of farms in the New World. This engraving shows tobacco, a luxury good, being shipped back to Britain.

NOVA BRITANNIA.

OFFRING MOST

Excellent fruites by Planting in VIRGINIA.

Exciting all such as be well affected to further the same.

LONDON

Printed for SAMVEL MACHAM, and are to be sold at his Shop in Pauls Church-yard, at the Signe of the Bul-head.

1609.

America as a place which would be colonized by Englishmen. With the backing of Elizabeth, Gilbert actually founded a colony in Newfoundland in 1583 and laid claim to the existing fishing settlements there. But Gilbert's 250 settlers were not equal to the challenge, and he himself was lost at sea. Gilbert's vision of an English empire in North America inspired his half-brother Sir Walter Raleigh to continue the effort to colonize. Armed with a royal charter (1584) and supported by the promotional writings of the famous geographer Richard Hakluyt, Raleigh colonized Roanoke Island off the coast of North Carolina, but it and a subsequent colony mysteriously disappeared. Meanwhile, a colony of French Huguenots had settled near St Augustine, Florida, between 1562 and 1564, with joint hopes of erecting a religious refuge and raiding Spanish galleons in the Bahama passage. The project failed when the entire group was massacred by the Spanish.

The continuing impact of the Protestant Reformation and changes within England itself were soon to change the character and purpose of Anglo-French colonization of the New World. Protestant weavers, fleeing from religious persecution in France and the Low Countries, came to England and brought with them secrets of fine weaving which soon made English cloth popular in Europe. One of the benefactors was the English wool trade. As England prospered and her manufactures increased, the English began to drive out

foreign merchants and take over the foreign trade themselves. The demand for wool persuaded English landowners to enclose farming lands for pasture which led to a dramatic displacement of laborers. This displacement in turn created both an unemployment problem and the impression that England had a surplus population. What was one to do with a surplus population? One of the answers was American colonization.

The experiences of Gilbert and Raleigh demonstrated that colonization was too costly for a single individual. Thus one of the keys to the history of British colonization of North America was the joint-stock trading company. By this device interested investors, usually merchants and rich noblemen, could pool their resources and amass enough funds to underwrite the enterprise. Overseas trading companies such as the Merchant Adventurers and the Muscovy Company had existed since medieval times, but by 1600 they had taken on new life and meaning because of England's new overseas markets, her supposed population surplus and her role as the foremost Protestant bulwark against Catholic Spain. The joint-stock companies of Virginia, Plymouth and Massachusetts were to shape the history of the British colonies, as that of the Hudson's Bay was to shape Canada's. Similarly, the Dutch West India Company founded New Amsterdam (New York), and even the early French efforts to settle Canada sometimes took the form of a royally

chartered group of associates to promote trade.

The private company also suggested the distinctive qualities of the British overseas enterprise until the time of the American Revolution. The London Company, for example, was interested in trade and profits, and once Virginia began to be a farming colony producing tobacco as a money crop, the colony's entire society and economy was shaped by that product, with the result that it was a rural society of scattered plantations. Almost unconsciously, the Virginia company evolved from an organization into a society, as local problems which could not be handled by London directors were solved on the spot. Thus 3000 miles of ocean and lack of concern by the British government fostered the rise of local self-government in the American colonies.

The Plymouth and Massachusetts Bay companies, on the other hand, sought a place in the new world where they could practice their religious beliefs. For a time a true theocracy existed in Massachusetts. Since Massachusetts had neither the rich lands nor the climate to produce highly profitable crops, the economy was, from the first, one of the carrying trade, fishing, home manufactures, and subsistence farms clustered about a village. Even the charters granting proprietary rights to individuals such as Lord Baltimore, the founder of Maryland, and William Penn of Pennsylvania were for the purposes of establishing specialized refuges for Catholics and Quakers.

All the colonies were theoretically under the control of the crown and existed by right of a charter, but that did not mean they were closely supervised. While each colony developed in slightly different ways, each came to have a local legislative assembly, a royal or proprietary governor (whose powers were far from absolute), toleration of religion and a marked degree of political and economic freedom. Thus the traditional 'rights of Englishmen' came to have even fuller meaning for the colonists than they did for the citizens of the home country.

In addition to the confrontation with the Indians and the wilderness, and the varied nature of the settlements, all the colonies were greatly affected by the fact that America represented a seemingly endless abundance of land, and land became the key to American development in an extraordinary number of ways. In Virginia land was given as a dividend to the joint-stock investor instead of cash. The immigrant who agreed to take himself to the new world was given a headright of 50 acres, or the person who paid another's way received the headright. Given certain restrictions land ownership conveyed the right to vote, and thus landed men constituted the first Virginia Assembly. Land also implied that its owner might have the status of a gentleman and thus provided the means for a step up in society. Land was also both a way of paying debts – such as the King's grant of land to William Penn – and a source of money through speculation. In the absence of bullion or currency land naturally became a convenient medium of exchange. Further, its very abundance permitted most colonists to better their status, for despite any effort to impose medieval concepts of control, and despite the efforts of proprietors to collect quitrents, the tendency in the colonies was toward a fee simple concept of land ownership. By 1750 virtually every colonist had come to agree with John Locke that land or 'property' was one of the natural rights that government was obligated to protect. The devotion to this belief led to disputes with Britain over the right to govern, and they in turn led to the American Revolution.

Colonizing the Atlantic slope

The first English joint-stock company to settle the new world was the Virginia Company, which consisted of two groups of merchants, one from London and one from Plymouth. Working together, in 1606 they secured from James I a charter that permitted the London Company to settle the southern part of the Atlantic coast, while the Plymouth Company was to settle the region north of Chesapeake Bay.

The ships *Susan Constant* and *Goodspeed* brought London Company settlers to the shores of Virginia in May 1607, where they erected Jamestown, a tiny palisaded village with thatched huts. These colonists experienced a grim beginning, for they had settled on a malaria-infested coast, had little psychological or physical preparation for the hardships of pioneer settlement and were still overwhelmed by the desire for gold. Between 1607 and 1609 most of them starved or died. Despite these setbacks the company leaders in London, and especially Sir Thomas Smith, promoted the idea of colonization as an act of patriotism and thus secured new recruits and investors for Virginia. Order was achieved in Virginia first by Captain John Smith, an able if boastful soldier of fortune, and later by Sir Thomas Dale and others armed with special military powers. After Sir John Rolfe discovered that Virginia was a paradise of good farming land and that the future lay in the production of tobacco for export, the colony slowly emerged from the status of a death-wracked company organization of discontented and starving employees into a true plantation of colonists.

While no one had the means to gain quick or enormous wealth, the profits from tobacco were so high in the seventeenth century that Virginia

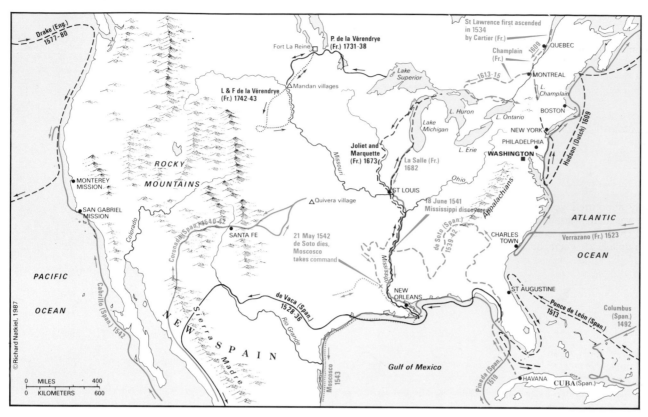

Left: The North American interior revealed by French and Spanish explorers probing into its vast expanse.

Below: Although the Jamestown settlers were the first, it is the Pilgrims of Massachusetts who caught the imaginations of later Americans. These Puritans, with their vision of constructing a new, holier society in the New World, gave America its first true national holiday, Thanksgiving. This Currier and Ives print shows them landing at Plymouth, with the Mayflower visible in the background.

Right: A sixteenth-century French map depicting Jacques Cartier arriving in Canada. The map shows the North American coast, with south at the top of the page.

Below right: The need for cheap labor led to the use of African slaves on the farms and plantations of the New World. The poor victims were seized by force and crammed literally cheek by jowl on the passage across the Atlantic, as shown in this engraving.

attracted settlers in increasing numbers after 1618. During the first years, however, land became the common currency of development after important reforms instituted by Sir Edwin Sandys in 1618 allowed a colonist who paid his way to the new world to acquire a 'headright' of 50 acres and to pay the English shareholders dividends in land. This promise of ownership became the primary lure that beckoned settlers across the Atlantic. So great was the attraction that men unable to pay their passage indentured themselves to a master in return for payment of passage. Provided the

immigrant servant survived the seven years of indenture he, too, was given a headright of land.

Consequent on Sandys' reforms English law was established in the colony, and a legislative assembly was convened in 1619. In 1629 the House of Burgesses began to make laws on a regular basis, although royal recognition of the assembly and its acts was not forthcoming until 1639. Mismanagement of the company led to Virginia's becoming a royal colony in 1624, but this development did not interfere with the development of the legislature.

The great Virginia boom from 1618 to 1630 conspired to create a labor shortage. Since the local Indians – who had almost wiped out the colony in the massacre of 1622 – refused to farm even when enslaved, the planters came to see little virtue in their presence. As early as 1640 a system of removal and reservation was adopted, and this became firm policy after the devastating wars of 1644 and Bacon's Rebellion of 1676. The problem of labor was only partially met by the use of indentured servants: Not only was the death rate high, few servants wanted to work for masters

when they could own their own land. As a result, Virginians began to buy Negroes from passing ships and thus to use in modified form the labor system already employed by the Spanish in Central America. The first Negroes brought by an unknown Dutch ship in 1619 appear to have had the status of indentured servants, but between 1650 and 1690 the Virginia Assembly declared that they were slaves. Ironically the land, which by its abundance and availability had uplifted the Englishman, had fastened the shackles of slavery on the blacks.

Although it became a crown colony in 1624, Virginia was not as closely supervised as the Spanish colonies were. A royally appointed governor found his tenure in office was more pleasant if he got along with the local council and assembly. Made up of the larger Virginia landowners, both the appointed council and the elected assembly became in essence self-governing so long as they obeyed rules set down by Parliament and the king.

The great success pattern of Virginia was, with variations, echoed in Maryland and South Carolina. In 1632 George Calvert, Lord Baltimore, received a royal grant of lands which became the proprietary colony of Maryland. Founded as a refuge for English Catholics and as a feudal estate for the Calvert family, Maryland, through its Act of Toleration (1649), soon became a largely Protestant colony of planters. The early history of Maryland was characterized by a struggle between the settlers and the Calverts for control of the colony – a conflict that did not cease even after Maryland became a royal colony in 1691.

The royal charter that created Carolina in 1663 bore a strong resemblance to that of Maryland for it granted seigniorial rights to a group of noblemen. In reality Carolina was both a speculative venture for highborn Englishmen and a buffer state against Spanish Florida. Once real settlement began at Charlestown in 1670 the southern portion, or South Carolina, eventually evolved

into a plantation economy producing rice and indigo. Dependence on slaves as the labor force was so pronounced that by 1708 blacks constituted a majority of the population. The Charleston-dominated South Carolina government was faction-ridden and chaotic, but the settlers did unite periodically in opposing proprietary claims. By 1721 it had become a royal colony, but a new three-way struggle between the Charleston government, proprietors demanding quitrents and the backcountry settlers ensued and lasted until the time of the Revolution. Sometimes describing itself as the valley between two

mountains of conceit, North Carolina became a refuge for indentured servants or small landholders who raised tobacco or simply cultivated subsistence farms. It was greatly neglected by the proprietors until a series of local political revolts persuaded the crown to make it a royal colony in 1729.

The middle colonies developed somewhat later than the southern colonies. The Hudson, Susquehanna and Delaware River valleys were controlled by the Dutch or lay unsettled until 1664, when Charles II seized the lands which became the colonies of New York, New Jersey and Delaware.

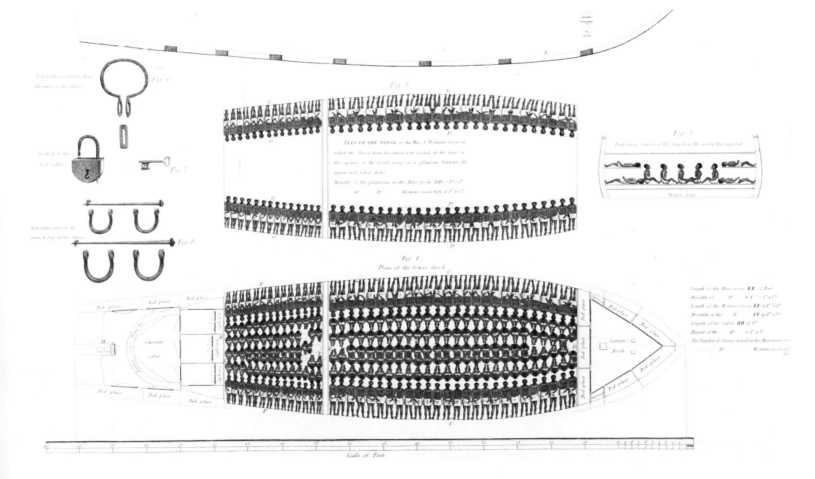

Unlike New England or Pennsylvania, New York Colony was deeply divided by class, religious and cultural differences arising between the Dutch settlers and the English newcomers. The colony was also hampered by the conflict between fur traders and land speculators and by the lack of a representative assembly until late in the colonial period.

In contrast to the New York experience, the founding of the remaining middle colonies was marked by openness and humanitarianism. In 1681 Charles II granted William Penn, a prominent Quaker, the colony of Pennsylvania and the lower Delaware counties in payment of a debt that the king owed Penn's father. Penn's colony was more cosmopolitan and varied in its social makeup than any of those to the north or the south. Not only did Penn act justly toward the Indians in the region, he opened his Quaker refuge to immigrants from the Anabaptist areas of Germany and Europe, as well as to non-conformist settlers from England, Northern Ireland and Scotland. By 1760 at least one-third of Pennsylvania's population was German and another portion was Scots-Irish or European. Philadelphia quickly grew into one of the largest cities of the new world and was in many ways the capital city of the colonies, as well as the gateway to the West.

Although Swedes and Dutch colonists formed the first settlements in Delaware they were so few and so weak that the area was easily taken by the English in 1664. Delaware did not formally become a colony until 1704, and even then remained, for all practical purposes, a part of Pennsylvania. Similarly, New Jersey began as a Dutch possession that was seized by the English in 1664. The colony was awarded to two court favorites, Sir George Carteret and Lord Berkeley. After a long period of confused authority and divided jurisdiction New Jersey became a royal colony in 1702, but struggles between the proprietors' claims and the settlers continued until 1776.

Thirteen years after the founding of Jamestown a separatist congregation, originally from Scrooby, England, secured a patent from the London Company to settle in 'Virginia,' but the now famous *Mayflower* 'pilgrims' landed instead at Plymouth Rock in Massachusetts Bay in December 1620.

Above: A reconstruction of a Dutch fort at the settlement of New Amsterdam, now known as New York. In 1664 the English seized New Amsterdam and renamed it in honor of the Duke of York who later became King James II.

Left: Many of the earliest settlers in the British colonies of North America sought greater freedom of religion. This Lutheran family from Salzburg had been forced to emigrate by the town's Catholic archbishop. Generally, such emigrants belonged to the Protestant Low Churches.

Above right: The French colonists from Quebec, led by the great explorer Champlain, aid their Algonkian Indian allies against the Iroquois.

Far right: The title-page of a pamphlet by Cotton Mather on the Salem witchcraft trials, part of an outbreak of religious intolerance afflicting the Massachusetts Bay Colony at the end of the seventeenth century.

Having broken with the Church of England and established themselves as a separate community of God, they had been harassed in England and unhappy in Holland, where they had lived for a time, before organizing as a company to settle in America. Few in number, they were badly abused by the company that sponsored them and spent 17 years paying off their debts. Still, the saga of this small band has become the historic symbol of America as a land of hope for the victims of religious intolerance, and the Mayflower Compact, the temporary rules of conduct drawn up by the Pilgrims prior to their landing, has endured as the most famous example of the voluntary organization of a 'civil body politic' in North America.

By far the largest number of settlers in the Massachusetts Bay area were the Puritans, a religious group within the Church of England who – as their name implied – wanted the Church to purge itself of corrupt and Romish practices. Many were wealthy middle-class citizens from the eastern counties of England. Far from feeling out of the mainstream, the Massachusetts Puritans thought that God dictated history and that New England was predestined to occupy a significant place in the divine plan. As one of them put it, their migration 'afforded a singular prospect of churches erected in an American corner of the world, on purpose to express and pursue the Protestant Reformation.'

After securing a charter from the king the first substantial body of Puritans came in 1629, and the next year a massive 10-year 'Great Migration' to Boston began. Boston soon overshadowed the Plymouth colony – which it eventually absorbed – and became the staging area for the settlement of other New England colonies. Rhode Island was founded, for example, by Roger Williams, a distinguished minister whose Baptist teachings and tolerance were unacceptable to the Massachusetts authorities. The rich meadowlands of the Connecticut Valley and a desire for local or congregational control lured Thomas Hooker and a group of followers to Hartford, Connecticut, in 1636. Two years later a conservative group of Congregationalists headed by Theophilus Davenport settled in New Haven. The two communities were eventually united as the colony of Connecticut in 1664. By the eighteenth century Boston had become one of the three largest cities in North America and was the entrepôt for thousands of immigrants – among them Scots-Irish Presbyterians – who began to push north and east into the frontier colonies of New Hampshire and Maine.

The primary aim of the Puritans was the revival of the true Church and the establishment of a 'city of God' in the new world, but the concept of a total theocracy was never realized. What emerged instead was a simplified English society centered in congregations and villages engaged in subsistence farming, home manufactures and overseas trade. In time New England ships came to carry the bulk of English goods in their holds, and thus were in inevitable competition with the mother country on the high seas.

At first only freemen and stockholders – all good churchmen – could vote in Massachusetts, but as the New England towns spread from the nuclear area of Boston each developed its own government and sent representatives to a General Court. Governed by John Winthrop and a set of able magistrates, Massachusetts prospered and grew from the start. While the exact relation of cause and effect remains obscure, it seems apparent that within the decentralized congregational form of church and local government lay the seeds of representative government, if not of democracy. Although the right to vote was at first

limited to the freemen of the colony, by the beginning of the eighteenth century the voting requirements had been liberalized to the point that Massachusetts had a more or less representative provincial legislature.

England's American colonies were founded at a time when Parliament was placing curbs on the powers of the English throne and when English society was disrupted by religious bickering and civil war. In part, the colonies were fragmentary projections of these religious disputes in that Massachusetts was non-conformist; Pennsylvania was Quaker, Lutheran and Moravian; Maryland was partly Catholic; New York was Dutch Reformed; and Virginia and South Carolina remained Anglican. The conflict between the Stuarts and Parliament and the Puritan Revolution freed the colonies from close supervision until the accession of Charles II in 1660. The restoration of the Stuarts meant trouble for New England, however, for both Charles II and James II attempted to establish arbitrary control over the region by placing it, as well as New York, under one governor who was to rule without a legislature. The Glorious Revolution of 1688 freed them from this threat, but in 1691 William and Mary did force Massachusetts to accept a royal governor.

Colonial life in North America

Besides the troubles with the crown Massachusetts began experiencing internal difficulties in the late seventeenth and early eighteenth centuries which presaged religious and intellectual changes of great importance. Puritanism had taken on a quality of doctrinal rigidity that expressed itself in strong sermons against sinners, punishment and expulsion of Quakers from the province, the Salem witchcraft trials of 1696 and repressive clerical control of Harvard College. Cotton Mather, one of the leading ministers, exhorted against new ways, and Michael Wigglesworth warned in his poem *The Day of Doom* that disbelievers were bound for divine punishment.

But the literate and semi-urban society of New England operating as separate congregations and villages harbored seeds of change. A mystical strain, which had emerged in the teachings of Mrs Anne Hutchinson and later at Salem, had been curbed by good Calvinist logic, and the conservative magistrates. But Edward Taylor (1645?-1729), reflecting the influence of John Donne and other metaphysical poets, wrote in a highly personal and euphoric vein which suggested the new cur-

rents of thought in New England. The older Calvinistic world-view was also being challenged by the secular logic of Newtonian physics and the teachings of the Enlightenment, so that by 1700 New England was ripe for an intellectual and social revolution which would make Boston a center of learning and liberal thought. Meanwhile, society had developed in the other colonies to the point that it resembled England far more than it had in the 1650s. A landed aristocracy resting on the labor of slaves began to emerge in the southern colonies, while urban life in Philadelphia, New York, Charleston and Boston began to sparkle with literary and political clubs and good conversation.

Not all of the changes in attitude were internal. After the Stuart restoration of 1660 the crown began to realize that the colonies could become valuable parts of an ordered empire. At the same time the crown seized the middle colonies, Charles I sought to control colonial trade by imposing mercantile legislation. Beginning in the 1660s a series of Navigation Acts declared that all goods carried between England and the colonies must be in British bottoms owned by British subjects. No goods were to come to the colonies

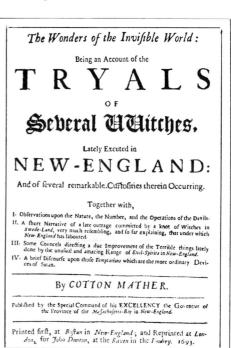

The Wonders of the Invisible World:

Being an Account of the

TRYALS

O F

Several Witches,

Lately Executed in

NEW-ENGLAND:

And of several remarkable Curiosities therein Occurring.

Together with,

I. Observations upon the Nature, the Number, and the Operations of the Devils.

II. A short Narrative of a late outrage committed by a knot of Witches in *Swede-Land*, very much resembling, and so far explaining, that under which *New-England* has laboured.

III. Some Councels directing a due Improvement of the Terrible things lately done by the unusual and amazing Range of Evil-Spirits in *New-England*.

IV. A brief Discourse upon those *Temptations* which are the more ordinary Devices of Satan.

By *COTTON MATHER.*

Published by the Special Command of his EXCELLENCY the Governour of the Province of the *Massachusetts-Bay* in *New-England.*

Printed first, at *Boston* in *New-England*; and Reprinted at *London*, for *John Dunton*, at the *Raven* in the *Poultry*, 1693.

except by way of England, while certain colonial products had to pass through England before reaching their ultimate port of destination. Laxly administered and containing certain clear advantages for the colonists, the Acts caused trade to flourish between 1700 and 1750. Massachusetts and Rhode Island in particular profited from the so-called triangular trade systems. Taking on molasses from the West Indies, New England ships carried it to their home ports to be manufactured into rum, which was then taken to Africa to be bartered for slaves. The slaves were then taken to the West Indies and sold. Other routes took the staples of the southern colonies to England and brought back manufactured goods to New England, which were in turn sold to the various colonies.

Increasingly restrictive legislation in 1733 and 1750, designed to regulate the molasses trade and to curb home manufacture, did not end the prosperity, since many colonists resorted to smuggling. More serious was the shortage of specie in the colonies produced by the mercantilist policy of causing more bullion to flow into the mother country than out. Even so, the colonists prospered and grew, and by 1760 the population had increased to approximately two million.

The struggle for colonial dominance

Just as the slowly evolving mercantile policies of crown and parliament saw the colonies as part of a larger economic scheme, the colonies themselves came to realize that they were affected by the dynastic and imperial wars between European nations, and especially those between France and Britain. So affected were they by four of the most important of these conflicts that the colonists gave each war its own name. The War of the League of Augsburg (1685-97) was called King William's War, the War of the Spanish Succession (1702-13) was dubbed Queen Anne's War and the War of the Austrian Succession (1740-48) was called King George's War. The fourth and decisive war, The Seven Years' War, was known as the French and Indian War (1756-63). Although the colonists participated in the first three of these to some degree, their few conquests were always nullified at the peace table – with the exception that at the end of Queen Anne's War Britain acquired Nova Scotia, Newfoundland and the Hudson's Bay region.

However tangled and complex the diplomacy of the European balance of power system might be, to the colonists the wars were essentially a struggle between Britain and France for dominion in North America. Just as the Stuarts had come to see the colonies as part of a self-contained mercantilist empire, the French, who were already committed to the mercantilism of Colbert, began to envisage a grand system of colonies stretching from the St Lawrence River to the Great Lakes and then down the Mississippi River. This magnificent crescent would contain the British colonies, while supplying furs and foodstuffs for the mother country of France.

France's claims to the St Lawrence dated back to Jacques Cartier's voyage into the river in 1534. Nearly three-quarters of a century later, Samuel de Champlain strengthened that claim by bringing settlers to New France and by expanding the fur trade so greatly that pelts became known as the 'gold of the north.' Champlain's death was followed by a period of confusion until the 1670s, when a new set of 'iron men' made new claims for France. Between 1673 and 1682 Louis Jolliet, Father Marquette and Robert Cavelier, Sieur de la Salle, planted the French flag in the Mississippi Valley. Beginning in 1701 the two LeMoyne brothers, Sieur de Bienville and Sieur d'Iberville, eventually established colonies at Mobile, Biloxi and New Orleans. By the end of the War of the Austrian Succession British claims overlapped with those of France in the Ohio Valley and in the southern regions east of the Mississippi.

Suddenly the Ohio Valley not only became the key to the two empires, it brought into focus a remarkable number of conflicting claims. Those of France were aimed at protecting the Canadian fur trade, building up agricultural colonies in the Mississippi Valley to produce food for her sugar islands and curbing British expansion. British claims were more complex and even contradictory. While the British wanted to break the French stranglehold, some British statesmen wanted to protect the Indians from settlers and thus perpetuate the lucrative fur trade. Other British groups were interested in speculating in western lands. The colonies' motives were equally contradictory for they, too, were interested in fur trade and land speculation. A conflict also existed between Virginia and Pennsylvania over the ownership of western islands, since both colonies claimed the Ohio Valley.

When the agents of the Virginia land company began to stake out claims in the Ohio region, the French countered by erecting a series of forts. The Virginia Assembly, whose members were deeply involved in western land speculation, sent young George Washington as the head of a militia detachment to prevent the French from constructing Fort DuQuesne, near present-day Pittsburgh. Washington's force, accompanied by friendly Indians, was met and overwhelmed by a strong French and Indian group and compelled to surrender. Although the Virginians were immediately freed, the small battle at Great Meadows in 1754 was the beginning of the French and Indian War (1754-63).

The Seven Years' War eventually involved all of the major European powers, and a majority of the colonies participated in its colonial extension, the French and Indian War. Indeed, some of the major encounters of the Seven Years' War took place in North America. The war started badly for the colonists and the British when British troops and colonials, led by General Edward Braddock, set out to destroy Fort DuQuesne. Instead, the British and colonial troops were ambushed and suffered heavy losses. Braddock was killed and Washington escaped with several bullet holes in his coat.

Braddock's defeat exposed the colonial frontier to hostile Indian attack. The failure to organize a united war effort – which had been urged upon the British and the colonial governments by Benjamin Franklin at a colonial congress in Albany in 1754 – kept the British on the defensive until 1758, when William Pitt, the new prime minister, turned the American war effort over to such younger men as Lord Jeffrey Amhest and General James Wolfe. Meanwhile, Britain supplied her continental allies with goods and cash in return for the services of their soldiers. By 1759 a dramatic reversal had occurred, and with the capture of Quebec in the fall of that year, French Canada and the French Empire fell into British hands. Spanish Florida, long a threat to South Carolina and to the new colony of Georgia (1732), also went to Britain.

Certainly the chief benefactors of the Treaty of Paris of 1763 were the American colonists themselves. The French and Indian threat to the New England frontier was at last removed, the colonies now had access to the Ohio Valley and the southern colonies felt free to expand across the southeast. As Francis Parkman had written, 'With the fall of Quebec, the history of the United States began.'

Top left: The Old State House in State Street, Boston, during the 1750s. The capital of the Massachusetts colony was a thriving port at this time, and would become a center for radical American politics.

Left: A late eighteenth-century view of the capture of Quebec by the British forces under General Wolfe. The thirteen British colonies acquired a sense of identity and common purpose from the fighting against the French and their Indian allies in the 1740s and 1750s.

Right: George Washington, even as a young man, was inordinately ambitious. At the age of 26 his influence gained him command of a Virginia militia detachment involved in the first battle of the French and Indian War, and he also played an important role in the Braddock disaster of 1755, as one of the colonial militia commanders. He married a rich wife, and was involved in several shady land speculation deals in the years between 1763 and 1775. He was a popular choice for command of the Continental Army, and despite many battlefield blunders was politically astute enough to outmaneuver any possible rivals to the post.

The colonies in the eighteenth century

One of the enduring debates in American historical writing has centered on the causes and justification of the American Revolution. During the nineteenth century every American schoolchild was taught that between 1762 and 1776 an arbitrary king and a wicked Parliament conspired to stifle the political liberties of the American colonists. More recent studies suggest that the progress toward revolution and independence was a far more complex affair. British internal politics and incompetent leaders, rather than wicked intentions, helped create a series of crises between 1763 and 1776. But that is only one side of the story. The colonists themselves changed greatly between 1700 and 1763, and again between the latter date and 1776. What were some of these changes and how did they come about?

Undoubtedly the largest change was reflected in the increase in population. The colonists numbered only 250,000 in 1700 but they had increased to 2.5 million by 1776, of which a half-million were blacks. Of those coming after 1680, many were from German stock, and particularly from the Rhineland area and from the German cantons of Switzerland. After 1710 Scots-Irish Protestants from Ulster, emigrants from the mainland of Scotland and a sprinkling of French Huguenots greatly augmented the size of the non-English population. Other newcomers who were released prisoners or indentured servants also did not feel beholden to the mother country. The black population had increased by 1760 to a point where it constituted nearly 50 percent of the Virginia population and nearly 70 percent of the population of South Carolina. Standing on their shoulders in these two colonies was a new landed aristocracy. What had begun as a white, purely English society with an absence of noblemen was now both a mixed European society and, in the South, a caste society. Wealthy Virginians went to university at Oxford and Cambridge, and the rich planters and merchants of South Carolina led a brilliant social life in Charleston. Meanwhile, a true urban society had developed in the seaport towns of Boston, Providence, New Haven, New York, Philadelphia and Baltimore.

Changes in population size and cultural makeup were equaled by changes in attitudes. By 1700 the New England colonies were forced to tolerate Quakers, Scots-Irish Presbyterians and Anglicans. The Congregational Church itself came to stress right living, rather than conversion, as a primary concern. In Pennsylvania the rich and powerful Quaker population was now a minority group whose political leadership was being challenged by the Scots-Irish and the Germans. Maryland was now Protestant, and Virginia, while safely Anglican, was as nearly unconcerned with established religion as South Carolina, where not a single colonist went into the Anglican ministry for more than 20 years.

Besides the influx of Moravians, Lutherans and

Left: Germans, as well as Britons, were numerous among the earlier settlers of America. These Lutherans are fleeing religious persecution from a predominantly Catholic Austria.

Above right: Jonathan Edwards, the stern Calvinist divine from Northampton, Massachusetts. Edwards became famous for the eloquence of his sermons, delivered to a rapt congregation in a highly unimpassioned manner. His aim in life was to create a framework of thought constructed around a Calvinist theology that would compare and compete with the liberal secular humanism of John Locke. He failed, but his writings had a profound impact on eighteenth-century American religion. In one of history's choicer ironies, his grandson was Aaron Burr, vice-president during 1801-05. Burr was a model Enlightenment humanist, whose civilized manner perfectly betrayed the grandfather's intolerance.

Right: Benjamin Franklin, perhaps the greatest eighteenth-century American. Philosopher, scientist, politician and diplomat, his practical approach to life exemplified the spirit of 'know-how' now so highly regarded in the American national culture.

Franklin was the London agent for the Province of Pennsylvania almost continuously from 1757 to 1770. On occasion he also represented three other colonies to Parliament and the crown. Early on he had become convinced that Parliament and Britain held no supreme rights over the colonies. Understandably, he was one of the leading figures in the American Revolution.

The secular teachings of the Enlightenment did not take hold in America without strong resistance, for it seemed a frontal attack on the traditional religious beliefs of most of the colonists. The local response took the form of a new religious outburst called 'The Great Awakening.' Revivalist preaching in New Jersey by the Reverend Theodore Frelinghuysen set off the first wave. Frelinghuysen and others found that they could produce mass conversions by exhorting their congregations until they were in a highly emotional state. The shouting and raving of the minister were eventually answered by moans, shrieks and mass hysteria on the part of the listeners. People fainted, sobbed and were seized by 'the jerks' begging for mercy and salvation.

The foremost advocate of the 'new method' in New England was Jonathan Edwards, a brilliant graduate of Yale University whose church was in Northampton, Massachusetts. A life-long student of epistemology and of theology, Edwards' purpose was a conservative one, for he deliberately played upon the emotions to revive faith in an older and sterner Calvinism. Though Edwards did not ultimately want to abandon the intellectual content and the logical approach to Puritanism for emotionalism, despite his own wishes the new method ministers concentrated on the emotional experience of the conversion. The climax to the Great Awakening came when John Wesley's famous disciple, George Whitefield, arrived in America in 1739 and began a series of spellbinding mass revivals which stretched from Georgia to New England.

In retrospect the Great Awakening appears to have been a New World version of the pietistic revival in Germany and the rise of Methodism in Britain. Although the implication was not drawn by the colonists, espousal of the Arminian heresy that all men could be saved and that uneducated ministers could preach implied a democratization of religion which was both a product of the American frontier experience and evidence of a lack of control by an established Church.

Presbyterians and the decline of the sterner aspects of Calvinism in New England, two other developments fundamentally affected colonial religious beliefs: the Enlightenment and the Great Awakening. The impact of the European Enlightenment on the 13 colonies is difficult to measure, but it is clear that the concept of a universe as a place where reason prevailed and God ruled with natural laws had become popular in the colonies by 1740. As in Europe the American followers of Enlightenment ideas believed that as man learned to live in harmony with an essentially benign universe, both he and society would improve. Enlightenment teachings inspired Harvard to include the writings of Locke and Newton in the curriculum.

Colonial America's greatest product and symbol of the Enlightenment thinking was Benjamin Franklin. Born in Boston in 1706 Franklin went to that city's famous Grammar School. He was then apprenticed to his half-brother James, a printer. Franklin moved to Philadelphia at the age of 17, was publishing his own writings before he was 20 and owned his own press and paper, the *Pennsylvania Gazette*, by the time he was 24.

One of Franklin's driving purposes in life was to inculcate into Americans a brand of early utilitarianism – a secular version of the Protestant ethic – so that they would be 'healthy, wealthy and wise.' His *Poor Richard's Almanack*, the vehicle for his aphorisms, was read by nearly all Americans between 1732 and 1757. His efforts at civic betterment transformed Philadelphia into a healthy, well-run city with a circulating library, a fire department and a hospital. Franklin also played a major part in making it an early intellectual center, in founding an academy for educating youth and in starting the American Philosophical Society.

True to the Enlightenment tradition, Franklin was also fascinated by the phenomena of the natural world and sought by scientific inquiry to understand and to use the elements to benefit mankind. He endeared himself to the colonists by inventing the Franklin stove, and he impressed the scientific world by his experiments with electricity and studies of weather patterns.

Seemingly a man of universal talents he suggested the unification of the colonies under an imperial system at the Albany Congress in 1754. Both a master politician and a master diplomat,

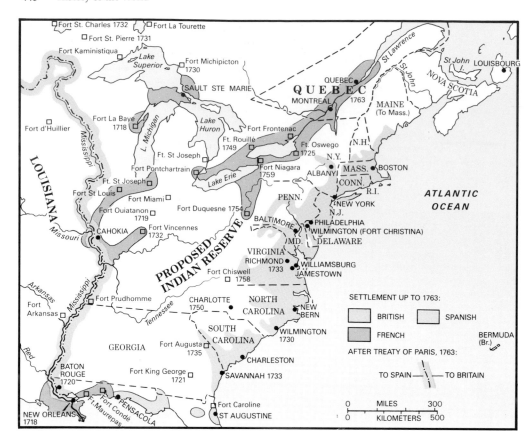

The religious ferment of the Great Awakening also produced, paradoxically, new centers of learning devoted to the 'new light' approach. While the purpose of American higher education in the eighteenth century was primarily religious, the Great Awakening made that purpose pluralistic. While Harvard and Benjamin Franklin's Philadelphia academy veered toward the Enlightenment, Yale held on to the old light teachings, while the new colleges of Princeton (1746), Brown (1764) and Rutgers (1766) trained 'new light' ministers. William and Mary (1693) remained Anglican, while King's College in New York (Columbia) was also associated with the Anglican Church from its founding in 1754. The tradition of a fragmented and pluralistic society had now paradoxically reached across borders to form intercolonial denominations and thus create the first sense of an American union through personal experience.

The new imperial policy

When the French and Indian War ended in 1763 Americans, whether settlers or speculators, felt that the time to exploit the western lands had at last arrived. The Americans' expectations were based on an almost total ignorance of the mercantilist thinking of the British government and the realities of British politics. Although triumphant, Britain had been financially exhausted by the Seven Years' War. Its people were taxed almost to breaking point. At the same time Britain now had to administer Canada and Florida and to keep a standing army in the New World in order to secure her new possessions.

The financial and imperial problems facing Britain forced an overall review of colonial policies. In the course of this review Lord George Grenville discovered that, on the whole, the cost of running the colonies was greater than the return in monies to the crown. In a series of individually logical but not necessarily wise moves, the British government instituted a new imperial policy between 1763 and 1775 that was to produce crisis after crisis in the colonies.

The first of these came when the British government issued a proclamation in 1763 that drew a line down the western frontier and forbade the colonists to settle beyond the imaginary boundary. The proclamation was designed to protect the Indian population and the fur-trade interests, as well as to maintain peace on the frontier. The government also established northern and southern Indian departments at this time and placed able men in charge of them. These actions, although intelligent and, indeed, humane, were subjected to the pressures of lobbyists and colonial legislatures, with the result

that the plans were ruinously compromised. By 1770 the Proclamation Line had been moved several times, and the Indian system had been seriously weakened by the refusal of colonial legislatures to cooperate with the imperial Indian agents.

Again in 1764 the Sugar Act of that year sought to tax molasses imported from the French West Indies for revenue. The New England colonies in protesting the Act took the first of many steps toward defining their proper relation to the mother country by arguing that only their own representatives could tax them for revenue.

The Sugar Act was less than a year old when Parliament, at Grenville's urging, passed a Stamp Act that required that colonists buy revenue stamps for the purpose of validating virtually all public and contractual business. All printed documents, even newspapers, were required to have a stamp. As many historians have noted, the Act not only asserted the right to impose a revenue tax, it alienated lawyers, printers, public officials and licensees, the most articulate and powerful of all the groups in the colonies with the possible exception of ministers.

The outcry against the Stamp Act surprised both the British government and the colonial leaders. Mobs in the cities and towns forced stamp agents to resign and forbade the sale of the stamps. An unprecedented boycott of British goods persuaded nervous British merchants to press successfully for a repeal of the Act in 1766. But the colonial victory was tempered by the fact that Parliament also passed a Declaratory Act, in which the government maintained its right to impose any taxes it chose on the colonies.

Still another tax for revenue was imposed in 1767, when Parliament passed the Townshend Act. The measure taxed new articles, and a portion of the money collected was to be used to pay the salaries of the colonial governors. Having found an effective weapon in mob action and non-importation agreements in 1765, these tech-

Company collided with those of the colonial merchants and the radicals. In a clever move the British government sought to help the East India Company by passing a parliamentary act that allowed the firm to send tea to the colonies tax free and to sell it directly, instead of disposing of it through a middleman. Once again the Americans claimed that this was a device to impose controls on them by establishing a monopoly. In Boston, where Samuel Adams had labored unceasingly to keep resentment at a white heat, a group of radicals led by Adams boarded company vessels and dumped the tea into the harbor. This 'Boston Tea Party' triggered a new set of crises, for Parliament's inevitable response was to punish Massachusetts for defying the law. Four British acts passed in 1773 closed the port of Boston until the Company was paid for the tea, suspended representative government and permitted British officers to commandeer private housing in Massachusetts for their soldiers.

The American response to the British 'Intolerable Acts' was three-fold. First, the Bostonians sought to persuade the other colonies that the plight of Boston was potentially the fate of all the colonies. The coincidental passage of the Quebec Act (1774), establishing a non-representative government in Canada and the extension of Canadian jurisdiction southward along the colonial frontier, was used by the radicals to prove that the British were intent upon depriving them of their liberties.

Second, a Continental Congress of colonial delegates was convened in Philadelphia in September 1774. Dominated by radical leaders, the Congress resolved in good natural rights language that the colonists were entitled to 'life, liberty and property, and they have never acceded to any sovereign power whatever, a right to dispose of either without their consent.'

Third, the Congress agreed to a plan of non-importation, non-consumption and non-exportation of goods to and from Great Britain, and it established 'committees of safety.' Named the Continental Association, the plan was the more effective because the local committees often acted as a vigilante group to coerce citizens to obey their orders by threat, violence or property seizure. Meanwhile committees of correspondence were busy passing information between the colonies.

Although a new crisis did not seem imminent, the Massachusetts radicals established an extra-legal provisional government to run the colony

Left: The vast hinterland of America was only lightly sprinkled with settlements at the time of the Treaty of Paris, 1763. The colonists, whether French, British or Spanish, had clung to the coasts and waterways, where communications were easiest.

Below left: Paul Revere's engraving of the Boston Massacre. This ugly incident was the result of the hostility Americans felt toward the collectors of taxes imposed by the distant London Parliament. Five Bostonians were slain when British soldiers shot at an angry crowd outside the city's Customhouse, on 3 March 1770.

Right: A British cartoon sums up the political crisis in the colonies during the early 1770s: A tax collector, tarred and feathered by some colonials, has British tea forced down his throat. Nailed to a tree behind the scene is the 1765 Stamp Act.

Below right: Bostonians, disguised as Indians, hurl the East India Company's tea into Boston harbor. The Boston Tea Party, in 1773, was the final straw for Parliament. A series of acts were passed to impose British authority on the recalcitrant colony.

niques were now applied successfully to the Townshend Act, so that by 1770 all but a tax on tea had been repealed. Except for the so-called Boston Massacre of that year, in which British soldiers fired on a mob of taunting stone-throwing youths, the hostility toward Britain subsided until 1773.

Nevertheless, by 1770 the political leaders of the major colonies had begun to think in new terms about their relation to Parliament, for they were now arguing that there should be 'no taxation without representation' and were thus denying Britain the right to tax them for revenue. Even Benjamin Franklin had decided by this time that each provincial assembly was a little parliament that need not defer to the mother country. Protests, mob action and non-importation agreements had also called forth new leaders and activated new groups of people in the urban centers, each with motives which reached beyond the desire to avoid taxation. In Boston, Samuel Adams became the fire-brand leader of the anti-British elements. A fine orator, ceaselessly energetic, and a darling of the common people, Adams, more than anyone else, kept alive the flame of resentment against Britain between 1763 and 1776. In New York unfranchised mobs sometimes acting at the behest of merchants had in mind the achievement of political powers of their own. In Virginia the oratorical Patrick Henry played on the Stamp Act crisis to advance his own political career. Just as the abundance of land had produced opportunities for many contending parties, the issues of taxation without representation and imperial control had created internal political opportunities for many new aspirants. Dubbed 'radicals' by their opponents, the new leaders and the mobs often acted in cooperation with colonial merchants, although the latter had different motives for protesting.

It has been noted previously that the key to the origins of the British colonies lay in the joint-stock trading companies. Royally chartered companies continued to characterize Britain's approach to world trade. After Britain's seizure of the Hudson's Bay region the famous company of that name was created to exploit the fur trade of northern Canada. The 'Honorable Company' eventually assumed governmental powers over parts of Canada, which it exercised until well into the nineteenth century. Similarly, the British East India Company, formed in 1603, had the privilege of establishing factories in India and of controlling the trade in tea and other oriental goods. In 1773, however, the fortunes of the East India

and began to train militia and collect powder and arms. Upon learning of these military activities General Thomas Gage ordered British troops to seize the rebel supplies at Concord and to arrest the ringleaders of the new government. Fore-warned by Paul Revere and William Dawes, the two 'advance men' of the revolution, on 19 April 1775 Massachusetts citizens gathered along the soldiers' route. Although the British reached Lex-ington and Concord despite attacks, by afternoon enough American 'minutemen' had gathered to catch the redcoats in a deadly crossfire as they returned to Boston and killed or wounded 273 men. Although most colonists would not have stated that their goal in 1775 was revolution and independence, events had been set in motion which would lead to the formation of the United States.

News of the fighting spread like wildfire. By 24 April it had reached Philadelphia, and by 8 May the citizens of Charleston had been informed. Streams of volunteer minutemen from other colonies began to march toward Boston. They were a disorganized group of citizens, but they were angry and wanted to fight.

By 10 May 1775 the Second Continental Con-gress was already in session in Philadelphia. Assuming governmental powers, it formed the Continental Army and made George Washington of Virginia the commander-in-chief. Congress also issued a 'Declaration of the Causes and Necessity of Taking up Arms' on 6 July, in which they listed the British measures that had led to hostilities and then stated that they would resist the 'tyranny of irritated ministers' by force 'being with one mind resolved to dye Free-men rather than to live Slaves.' But if Congress proffered the sword with one hand, it still held the olive-branch in the other. The declaration went on to say that they did not want the union with Britain dis-solved. Under the influence of the moderates led by John Dickinson of Pennsylvania, the declara-tion actually ended with the assertion that 'We have not raised armies with ambitious designs of separating from Great Britain, and establishing independent states.'

While Congress was engaged in declaring its loyalty to the king there was a new outbreak of fighting in Boston. There General Gage found himself and his 6000 soldiers bottled up by the thousands of volunteers who had surrounded the city. It soon became clear that if the British were

to stay they must take Charlestown and Dorches-ter Heights. Simultaneously, the Americans realized that if they controlled the two sites they could drive Gage from the city. Both sides acted at the same time, but the Americans managed to occupy Breed's Hill in the area first. Gage then sent his troops to force them out. As the massed redcoats struggled across ploughed fields they were shot down in droves. Nearly 1500 men were killed or wounded, a greater proportional loss to the British than they had suffered at any time during the Seven Years' War. Although it was not a clearcut victory for the Americans – who suf-fered 500 casualties – the Battle of Breed's Hill (mistakenly called Bunker Hill by the reports) thrilled the country and led to a better organiza-tion of the troops under Washington.

Then came the first of many let-downs. American efforts to invade Canada and to per-suade its citizens to become the fourteenth rebel colony failed. In the winter of 1775-76 Washing-ton found supplies were so scanty that he could not act for eight months. During that winter, however, Ethan Allen of Vermont and Benedict Arnold of Connecticut captured the British forts at Ticonderoga, Crown Point and others on Lake Champlain. They dragged the cannon from these forts over the snow to the seaboard for Washing-ton's use. Meanwhile, the sea-minded people of Massachusetts managed to seize British supply ships which were loaded with guns and powder. Thus strengthened, Washington occupied Dor-chester Heights and forced the British troops and the loyalists to leave Boston. One other revo-lutionary victory occurred that spring when Tories living in the North Carolina backcountry marched down to the capital to take the province away from the rebels. They were met by the Americans at Moore's Creek Bridge and soundly defeated.

Not only was the fighting in 1775-76 notably indecisive, the problem of unifying the colonies and achieving independence remained unsolved until the summer of 1776. When independence finally came it was as much a product of a psycho-logical change in attitudes as it was a practical necessity. In the winter of 1775-76 there was still a stubborn American loyalty to George III, whom the colonists felt was not in agreement with par-liamentary policies. But that winter Thomas Paine began to publish pamphlets which described the king as a 'hardened, sullen-tempered Pharaoh' or as 'the Royal Brute of Britain.' Paine's images helped cut the last ties of loyalty to the mother country. After the British had burned Norfolk, Virginia, that spring and had called for a slave revolt and an Indian war against the whites, Washington could now fly an American flag out-side of his headquarters. And Congress could feel justified in accepting Richard Henry Lee's resolu-

tions of June 1776 that the colonies were free and independent states, should form alliances and should also confederate.

As a fitting climax to 12 years of indoctrination in natural rights philosophy by the radicals, Congress accepted the Declaration of Independence of 4 July 1776. A masterful summation of the American belief in political equality and freedom, in the right of revolution and in written constitutions or charters which create a limited government, the Declaration expressed ideas as familiar to Americans as the Bible was to the Puritans. With uncanny genius its three authors, Benjamin Franklin of Pennsylvania, Thomas Jefferson of Virginia and John Adams of Massachusetts, had caught the spirit of a people united.

Independence for the colonists was a dual thing. They were now part of a Continental Union engaged in a joint war effort. But each colony also had to revamp its political structure by becoming a state. This gave every colony the chance to embrace new ideas, or at least reform the older colonial structure in a new constitution. Except for Rhode Island and Connecticut, which simply adapted their colonial charters to the new situation, the basic charter of every state was a newly written document. In essence the 13 colonies experienced two simultaneous political changes: they became states instead of colonies – a condition implying political sovereignty and an equality with independent nations. But at the same moment they became part of a union over which Congress, instead of parliament and king, presided. Both practically and psychologically they were neither quite sovereign nor quite independent. The persistence of this dilemma has constituted one of the dominant themes in the political history of the United States since 1776.

The war for independence

Except for the Vietnamese War, the American Revolution was the longest war ever fought by the United States. Beginning in 1775, it lasted until 1781, and the Treaty of Paris that formally ended it was not signed until 1783. It was not characterized by great battles, brilliant strategy, major dislocation of the population, large casualty lists or the killing of the American Tories who remained loyal to the British crown while continuing to live in the rebelling colonies. Nor did the war lead to a revolutionary radicalism or a significant change in institutions and cultures.

Those characteristics are explained in part by the fact that the American radicals were always in a minority and had to carry a more neutral majority along with them. It was also the case that the British adopted a low-keyed approach to the war in the belief that somehow a settlement could be successfully negotiated. It is said that the British command under Lord Howe spent most of the war waiting for an American peace delegation to appear.

Nevertheless, the American Revolution did turn into a land war that was fought on a thousand-mile front, for as luck would have it, the bulk of the British armed forces happened to be in America. If one counts Indian allies, Hessian and Brunswick mercenaries and local Tory raiders, the British had between 60,000 and 100,000 troops during the war. Given their numerical strength, the British decided in 1776 upon a land campaign that would split the colonies. They first attempted to split Georgia, South Carolina and North Carolina from the union by sailing into Charleston, but the local patriots beat off the attack. The British then decided to spread out from New York and take the Middle Colonies. Hope was high that

Pennsylvania would return to the fold at the appearance of the redcoats. Yet by the end of 1776 the British held only New York and Rhode Island.

Their third plan was to join with British forces in Canada and by a pincer movement cut New England off from the rest of the colonies. That strategy failed when the Americans defeated the Canadian pincer at Saratoga, New York, in 1777 and captured 5000 British troops. The Saratoga victory was doubly significant, for it persuaded the French to recognize the United States and to sign a treaty of commerce and alliance in 1777.

The policy of division having failed, all that was left to British strategists was to try to force the Continental Army into some large, decisive confrontation. But this, too, failed. In addition to their lack of zeal, the British generals – Howe, Clinton and Cornwallis – were far from brilliant. Lord Howe often took so long to execute a military maneuver that Washington worried that he had ulterior motives.

The British may have been equally puzzled by the strange nature and behavior of the American army. It has been estimated that of the 250,000 men of fighting age in the new nation only 89,000 did any fighting. But they never fought at the same time, so that Washington never commanded as many as 30,000 patriots after 1776, and the usual number has been estimated as less than 6000. When any given area was invaded the local militia usually turned out, but it was hard to get the soldiers of one colony to do service in another. Massachusetts had to offer $1000 to persuade men to volunteer, and in Virginia the prospective soldier was at one point promised $8000 in paper money, 3000 acres of land and the gift of a healthy sound Negro slave.

One reason for the short enlistments and the

frequent desertions in the Continental Army was that the war had created such an acute labor shortage that men felt they could render more valuable service by farming part of the year and by fighting in the remainder. What amazed the British was that just when it seemed there was no enemy army left one would suddenly materialize.

American strategy, if it could be called that, was basically Fabian. Washington liked to wait, retreat and contain. With the exception of the Battle of Saratoga in 1777 most of the engagements were indecisive. Those at Trenton in December 1776 and at Monmouth in June 1778 were neither disasters nor successes. Yet the fact remained that the British were holed up in New York, Charleston and Savannah with 34,000 inactive soldiers. The one free and dangerous army was that of Lord Cornwallis in the South, which was marching back and forth in Virginia trying to catch the Marquis de LaFayette and his contingent of French and American soldiers. The uncertain situation was finally resolved when Cornwallis led his army into Yorktown, on the coast of Virginia. This was the chance for which Washington had been wait-

ing for five years. He persuaded the French fleet under Admiral de Grasse to blockade Cornwallis and prevent his being reinforced from the sea. This de Grasse did admirably, defeating the Royal Navy's rather bungled attempt to break through his cordon of ships. Washington had deployed French troops to hold General Clinton in New York while he himself rushed down to Yorktown. He had also positioned General Nathaniel Greene to prevent any reinforcements from reaching Cornwallis overland from Charleston. Thus Cornwallis found himself well and truly cut off, and he watched in dismay as the allied forces besieging Yorktown built up to overwhelming proportions – about 9000 Americans and 7800 French versus less than 8000 redcoats. On 18 October 1781 he surrendered, and as his troops laid down their arms the British band played 'The World Turned Upside Down.'

Although fighting between Britain and France and her ally Spain continued for another year, the Americans and the British began peace negotiations. Appropriately, Benjamin Franklin, the American minister in Paris, headed the delegation that treated with the British. He was joined by John Adams of Massachusetts and John Jay of New York. The American peace commissioners had been instructed to insist on independence but to follow the French in all other matters. Fortunately, they decided to negotiate with the British independently and in secret, with the result that they secured the Mississippi River, the present Canadian border and the thirty-first parallel as the new nation's boundaries. Having received ample breathing room for the new country, Franklin was then sent to the French minister Vergennes with the double task of justifying the separate peace with the British while asking Vergennes for a large loan!

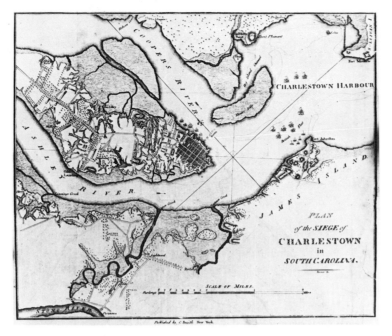

Left: John Trumbull's famous painting of Bunker's Hill. The grievous casualties inflicted on the British clearly demonstrated that well-handled militiamen could outfight their professional opponents.

Below left: The signing of the Declaration of Independence, 4 July 1776. Some delegates to the Congress held off from adding their names until they were convinced that the United States had some chance of succeeding in securing liberty.

Right: A contemporary map of Cornwallis's successful siege of Charleston in 1780.

Below: The brilliant James Madison, Virginia's scholar-politician. His was a powerful voice among the supporters of the ratification of the 1787 Constitution.

Social and political changes

Most historians agree that the American Revolution – unlike most revolutions – was largely a political phenomenon. Still it did bring about some modifications of American society and values. About 100,000 Tories, for example, had left the colonies by 1783, of whom many were crown officials, rich landowners and professional men. Having begun as a 'decapitated' society with virtually no noblemen, the country now experienced a second social decapitation by emigration as the Tories fled to Canada or back to England. Yet most merchants and many lawyers had joined the patriot cause so that while the new leadership of the country was undoubtedly less aristocratic and more republican it remained essentially conservative and middle-class.

Ironically the war was unkind to those who had supported the American cause most completely. The merchants were hard hit by the disruption of trade, and the Virginia planters lost their overseas market for nearly 10 years. The enormous benefactors were the small farmers who engaged in a war-time prosperity as they supplied Washington's troops with food and grain. The speculators who sold goods at fantastic prices or who brought confiscated Tory lands for a song also benefited.

If the ideals of the Revolution effected no fundamental social upheaval the implications of the Declaration of Independence plus the continuing devotion to the ideals of liberty set people to thinking. Since there were 500,000 slaves in the United States in 1776, it impressed many that the Declaration's assertion that all men were free and equal was a farce if the slaves were not freed. By the end of the Revolution several northern states had either banned the importation of slaves from abroad or had passed a law allowing the emancipation of a slave if he or she did not become a public charge. Toward the end of the century there were at least 10,000 freed slaves in the Old Dominion alone.

There were also changes in land holding, since the revolution swept away the practice of quit-rents, timbers reserved for the king and the customs of primogeniture and entail. Confiscated Tory estates meant new lands on the market, and new landed owners were emerging. Equally important, the Americans felt that the unsettled West between the Appalachians and the Mississippi River was property that belonged to the people in common, although individual states such as Pennsylvania and Virginia claimed great chunks of this fertile wilderness. Even the Revolution itself had not stopped what was an already sizeable western movement, and the westward movement in turn created the problem of governing new regions and of keeping them loyal.

The most impressive impact of the Revolution was on political institutions. All of the new state constitutions, except that of Massachusetts, broadened the franchise and thus permitted new men to enter the political arena. The new voters guaranteed a legitimate following for the radical leaders, whose chances of political success were further enhanced by the fact that Tory political leaders had fled or had been silenced. Even so, the system was not yet that of a total democracy for no women, slaves or non-landowners were allowed to vote.

In designing new state governments for themselves Americans were primarily concerned with bulwarks against future acts of tyranny. Therefore they eventually insisted on constitutions which had been written by a popularly elected state convention. Virtually all of these documents contained bills of rights which guaranteed the citizen freedom of the press, the right to petition, trial by jury and the right of habeas corpus. Government was also forbidden to issue general warrants of search and arrest or to maintain a standing army during peace-time. Maintaining that all power was derived from the people, the constitutions went on to provide for the direct or indirect election of state officers by the people for a specific term, although in most cases judges were appointed for long terms or for a lifetime. Popular control was made even more explicit by the device of limiting the powers of the governors and the judges while increasing those of the elected legislators. Most of the constitutions then exercised a system of checks and balances on the legislators themselves by creating an upper and a lower house. While the constitutions failed to declare for universal suffrage or provide for proportional representation, they did represent a notable advance in the concept of popular republican government.

The Articles of Confederation

While the individual states were engaged in writing constitutions, the Continental Congress began as early as June 1776 to draft a constitution for the new Union. Because of their recent experience with the British, their hostility toward a central authority meant that they would seek to create an extremely limited government and would do so very cautiously. Thus is was not until 17 November 1777 that Congress finally submitted a plan of union and central government to the states. Entitled the Articles of Confederation, the plan created a national Congress with supreme powers over foreign relations, disputes between the several states, coinage, weights and measures, Indian trade in the West and postal matters. It could also make war and peace, borrow money and make requisitions on the states of financial military aid. Far from impinging on the rights of states, the document declared that 'each state retains its sovereignty, freedom, and independence.' The Confederation Congress was to consist of delegates from the states, but each delegation had only a single collective vote, so that no larger state, in theory at least, had a stronger vote than a smaller state.

The Articles provoked one of the most lengthy constitutional debates in the history of the United States, for in addition to the fear of a central power, the adoption was delayed by a fight over the disposal of western lands. The landless states argued with eventual success that the American West did not belong exclusively to those ex-colonies with sea-to-sea charters, but to all the people. The landless states, led by Maryland, held up the ratification of the Articles until this principle had been established. Finally, on 2 January 1781, Virginia, whose vast western land claims had been the stumbling block, agreed to allow Congress to dispose of the lands. Thus the new government was presented with a national domain, as well as an administrative headache.

For many years historians pictured the Confederation period as one of failure and gloom, but recent scholarship has shown that within its short lifetime of eight years (1781-89) the new government achieved several successes and had solved a number of national problems. It worked out a politically unique governmental and land system for its western territories, and it weathered a post-war financial depression of major proportions. It was also a government that accurately reflected the thinking of a majority of the American citizens toward a central authority.

Undoubtedly one of the reasons for its success was that an impressive number of able men who had had experience as officeholders during the Revolution helped guide its policies. Benjamin

Franklin supported it until the very end, as did Washington, James Madison and Thomas Jefferson, and many northern leaders, such as Alexander Hamilton, John Jay, Robert Morris and John Adams, supported it during its first years. While the Articles provided for no separate executive branch, a set of executive departments was created in 1781 to handle foreign relations, military problems and finances. Not all of the men appointed to head these departments were capable or unbiased, but they did manage to run the government with tolerable efficiency. One of the best was Robert Morris, a brilliant Philadelphia merchant who distinguished himself as the new Superintendent of Finance. Although faced with the fact that he could not tax the states, he succeeded in organizing the finances of the government and in securing enough state support to run the country.

One of the besetting problems for the Confederation was how to dispose of the extensive lands in the national domain. Here the issue was not only the question of how the land should be surveyed and made available, but whether it should be sold to speculators or reserved for sale to small settlers. The resulting policy was a compromise of ideals and expediency. Basing its procedure on a scientific system of land survey that the British had hoped to use in the colonies, Congress passed the Ordinance of 1785 that provided for the surveyed lands to be divided into townships six miles square in size, and for the sale of mile square (or 640 acres) tracts to buyers for a minimum of one dollar an acre.

This fairminded and scientific approach to the public lands was only half the story. Badgered by powerful land speculators, Congress agreed to sell 1.5 million acres to a group of New England speculators who called themselves the Ohio Company. The Ohio Company also asked for a government for the region that would protect both the investor and the settler. The end result was the Northwest Ordinance of 1787. By this law a district or region could achieve political equality by passing through various stages based on population growth. Once the population of a district had reached 60,000 its citizens could write a constitution, form a state government and petition Congress for admission to the Union on an equal footing with the older states. Also included was a bill of rights for citizens of the area and a prohibition of slavery north of the Ohio River. It would be difficult to overestimate the importance of the Northwest Ordinance for it laid the groundwork

for a system under which a majority of the American states eventually came into the Union.

While the Confederation period was characterized by a burgeoning pride in the country and its future – which a whole generation of local poets, artists and writers sought to extol – the harsh fact remained that the United States was still a weak country of 3 million people, with a shaky republican government and little experience in dealing with other nations. American representatives abroad discovered that they could not secure favorable treaties of trade or settle disputes with other countries. Two diplomatic issues were particularly galling for the Americans: they could not persuade the British to evacuate their troops from the Northwest, and they could not force Spain to keep the Mississippi open so that western farmers could either sell their produce in New Orleans or use that city as a port of shipment.

A government as weak as the Confederation, without even the power to tax, was not going to solve international disputes or control the economy. The whole country shuddered when Daniel Shays and a group of Berkshire farmers marched on a local Massachusetts court and forced them to stop assisting creditors in the collection of debts. Only a loyal Massachusetts militia stopped Shays' rebellion. To correct what Alexander Hamilton called 'the insufficiency of the present Confederation' various states called meetings to discuss their mutual problems. Eventually there came a call for a national convention at Philadelphia in the spring of 1787. The 55 men who met in the City of Brotherly Love that May had ideas of their own. A majority of them eventually decided that the Confederation could not be saved. Instead they wrote a new federal constitution which, when adopted, created the present governing system of the United States.

The American Constitution

The origins and nature of the Constitution of the United States derive from the contractual theories of government popular in the eighteenth century, and particularly the ideas of Locke, Harrington, Montesquieu and Blackstone. Yet this unique American document cannot be understood without remembering that it also embodied the colonial experience in the art of self-government and the sense of nationality and a continental destiny that developed during the American Revolution. Equally important, it was the product of an extraordinary group of men.

The delegates who met in Philadelphia in May 1787 at the invitaton of Congress 'for the sole purpose of revising the Articles of Confederation' possessed qualities of leadership and a talent for realistic appraisal of national problems and feelings which are seldom seen. Most of those in attendance had served in state legislatures and 28 had been in Congress. Thirty-one were college educated, a remarkable percentage for the United States in the 1780s. Most were still fairly young; only four were over 60. George Washington and James Madison were in the Virginia delegation. Benjamin Franklin and John Dickinson were in Pennsylvania's, and Alexander Hamilton was one of the New York delegates. Only two experienced statesmen were missing: John Adams and Thomas Jefferson were both abroad serving as American ministers.

Working steadily throughout the hot summer of 1787 the delegates were actually in essential agreement on many fundamental points. The founding fathers all wanted a republican government in which there would be a separation of powers between the legislative, executive and

judicial branches. They all believed that the new government should be the supreme law of the land, with the power to make laws, tax, control commerce, make war and peace and to enforce its decrees through a judiciary and a military. To a man they felt that property must be protected, since it was the key to suffrage and widespread ownership of property meant a broadly based general republican government.

The delegates were stalemated, however, by lengthy debate over the 'large state,' or Virginia, plan conceived of by Madison, that called for a *national* government based upon the consent of the people, rather than upon the consent of the individual states. In opposition were the small states, which backed the Paterson, or New Jersey, plan that envisaged a *federal* government in which states would be equal in their voting power.

The problem was finally resolved when the delegates achieved a compromise whereby each state was given equal representation in the Senate, while Congressmen in the House of Representatives were elected on the basis of population. This compromise of federal and national concepts also acknowledged state sovereignty in yet another way by allowing the local voting qualification existing in each state to determine who elected the Congressmen and by permitting the state legislation to choose the senators. Southern fears that a rapidly growing northern population might overwhelm them in the lower house were assuaged by a clause that stated that the slave population would be included in the census figures of each state on a three-fifths basis. By this rule the southern states could secure a larger representation in the House, although the slave himself had no voting rights.

The most striking quality of the Constitution was that its sophisticated combination of federal and national concepts actually created a strong government. The authors sought to prevent it from being a tyrannical government by setting up each branch of the government so that it necessarily curbed the other two. Enamoured of the theory of checks and balances, they gave the president the power to veto an act of Congress, but then gave Congress the right to override that veto by a majority vote of two-thirds. Similar applications of the theory of divided sovereignty permeate the Constitution.

James Madison, probably the ablest political theorist America has produced, developed and advocated the checks and balances system for more reasons than quieting the fears of the states. He wanted so many factions in Congress that no one economic, sectional or political block or party could ever achieve its goals without allying itself with a large number of other groups. In essence this meant that no national legislation could pass under it unless it had national support.

In order to take effect the Constitution had to be ratified by nine of the 13 states. That process once again illustrated the remarkable ability of the advocates of the new government. Although only 39 of the 55 delegates signed the document in September 1787, the Federalists – the rather misleading name adopted by the nationalists who sought its ratification – managed the various state conventions with such astuteness that the Constitution had been adopted by the summer of 1788. The device of seeking approval from special state conventions rather than from the legislatures bypassed locally intrenched power. Finally the proponents were given immeasurable assistance when John Jay, Alexander Hamilton and James Madison defended the proposed Constitution in a series of brilliant newspaper essays

Far left: Anthony Wayne was one of Washington's best subordinate officers. Bibulous and vain, he was an extremely brave and aggressive commander. His victory over the Ohio Indians at Fallen Timbers in 1794 ensured America's control over the Old Northwest.

Right: A Currier and Ives print, from 1876, commemorating the inauguration of George Washington in 1789.

Below: Foreign policy was the main issue in early American politics. Here John Jay is burned in effigy by opponents of his 1794 treaty with Britain.

Below right: The Articles of Confederation were an unsatisfactory form of government to nationalist opinion in the United States. In 1787 this dissatisfaction resulted in the writing of a new Constitution, principally designed to ensure the protection of the property of the rich and powerful.

which have come to be called the *Federalist Papers*.

The significance of the Constitution of 1787 for the United States and for the world cannot be exaggerated. It continues to be the fundamental basis of government for the United States, the only major power in the world that still operates under an eighteenth-century document. Its astounding survival through a civil war and two world wars is undoubtedly based upon its flexibility. As Samuel Eliot Morison has written: 'By the constitutional convention, the written constitution, and popular ratification, Americans had discovered a way to legalize revolution.'

The new government

George Washington, hero of the Revolution, was the first president chosen when the new Constitution went into effect in 1788. John Adams of Massachusetts became the first vice president.

Washington was better fitted than any single individual in America to give the new executive branch the prestige and power it needed to establish independence. As Washington journeyed from Virginia in the spring of 1789 to New York, the seat of the first government, his trip became a triumphal tour. People presented him with flowers, made speeches in his honor and generally celebrated.

Washington took office on 30 April and immediately went to work on four major problems facing his administration. First, he knew he had to set precedents and fill in the blank spots of the Constitution. He decided, for example, that his cabinet would not have to report to Congress in person, as British ministers did, but should be responsible solely to the president. At the same time Washington, who had hoped to use the Senate as a sort of privy council, had to give up the idea when that body refused to assume such a role. In naming the cabinet Washington tried to form a coalition of men who represented different regions and political philosophies. General Knox, the Secretary of War, was a Massachusetts federalist. Edmund Randolph, the Attorney General, was a Virginia anti-federalist. Upon his return from abroad Thomas Jefferson became Secretary of State, and the brilliant, impulsive Alexander Hamilton of New York was appointed Secretary of the Treasury.

Washington's next task was to fill in the blank spots by inaugurating the new federal judiciary system, created by the Judiciary Act of 1789. After naming the erudite John Jay of New York as Chief Justice, he carefully appointed justices from the various states. The creation of a court system implied the power of coercion by lawful means, for undoubtedly the most crucial test of the new government lay in its capacity to collect taxes and to command the loyalty and respect of the states and the citizens.

No one was more concerned with this aspect of the new government than Alexander Hamilton, who sought to solve the problem through a series of brilliant measures. First, Hamilton sought to establish the honor and credit of the government by persuading Congress to fund the national debt

by paying the government's bondholders and creditors the face value of their bonds. Then he proposed to assume the war debts of the states, and then to create a Bank of the United States to handle US securities. The adoption of these measures allied both the states and the creditors to the new administration. An ardent nationalist, Hamilton also hoped to foster infant manufactures and to promote commerce with protective tariffs, a hard money policy and, in the case of manufactures, actual subsidies. But this close alliance between government and business was too much for many members of Congress. Led by James Madison, who was now in the House, Hamilton's famous Report on Manufactures was defeated.

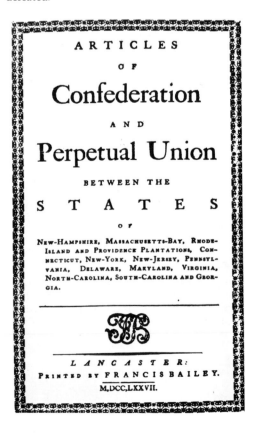

ARTICLES

OF

Confederation

AND

Perpetual Union

BETWEEN THE

STATES

OF

NEW-HAMPSHIRE, MASSACHUSETTS-BAY, RHODE-ISLAND AND PROVIDENCE PLANTATIONS, CONNECTICUT, NEW-YORK, NEW-JERSEY, PENNSYLVANIA, DELAWARE, MARYLAND, VIRGINIA, NORTH-CAROLINA, SOUTH-CAROLINA AND GEORGIA.

LANCASTER:
PRINTED BY FRANCIS BAILEY.
M,DCC,LXXVII.

In foreign affairs both Washington and Jefferson were agreed that the country should remain neutral in European quarrels and re-establish trade with Great Britain, while at the same time trying to push the British out of the forts in the Old Northwest. They also agreed that the United States must have the right to navigate the Mississippi and to exercise the right of deposit at Spanish New Orleans. The wars that followed the outbreak of the French Revolution put a severe strain on all of these policies. In 1793 Washington issued a neutrality proclamation and through careful wording evaded the implication in the 1778 treaty of alliance with the French that America would give them assistance in a war with Great Britain. But the dramatic events in Europe kept the American public in a turmoil and provoked tensions in the cabinet.

In 1795 John Jay finally succeeded in negotiating a treaty with Great Britain that contained some favorable trade clauses and promised evacuation of the Northwest forts by 1796. But Jay's treaty had also conceded so many other things to the British that it took all of Washington's prestige to secure ratification from the Senate. A year later Charles Coatesworth Pinckney signed a much more favorable treaty with Spain giving the United States all the rights it had wanted in the Mississippi Valley and settling the Spanish-American boundary in West Florida at the thirty-first parallel.

Washington's fourth major problem involved establishing a policy for the West. After Congress had re-enacted the Ordinance of 1787 in 1789 the president provided a territorial government for that frontier region, implemented the sale of western lands, and tried both to establish a humane Indian policy and to conduct the fur trade under close government supervision. In the latter two instances he failed but not for lack of trying. After two disastrous military attempts to subdue hostile pro-British Indians in the Northwest, Washington succeeded in part when General 'Mad' Anthony Wayne defeated a large force of Indians at the Battle of Fallen Timbers in 1794. Wayne's timely victory gave force to Jay's Treaty and hastened the British evacuation.

Frontier expansion

During Washington's two terms in office he witnessed both the settlement of the Old Northwest and the admission of three border states, Vermont, Kentucky and Tennessee. The West was now being filled by pioneers who, though perhaps not all frontiersmen of the caliber of Daniel Boone of Kentucky, could be seen by others as harbingers of American civilization destined to turn the wilderness into a garden. The image took on almost mystical qualities when the belief that it was America's manifest destiny to expand westward was joined to a belief in progress. Washington also saw various groups on the frontier forming governments of their own, and while he did not approve of these extra-legal actions, it was to be a characteristic event first in the trans-Appalachian West and later in the trans-Mississippi West. Later such activity would be called 'popular sovereignty' and would play a role in the formation of new governments.

Washington was re-elected in 1792 without real opposition, but by that year the young nation was already dividing into opposing camps in its attitude toward the French Revolution. At the same time, a split over internal policies in Congress also began to develop, as Madison, now representing agrarian states, chose to interpret the Constitution strictly in order to limit central powers, while Hamilton chose to interpret it loosely in order to give the national government more central powers.

The foreign and domestic issues were merged when Jefferson, who was neutral or at most slightly pro-French in his views, joined Madison in opposing Hamilton, who was openly pro-British. By 1793 newspapers representing the views of Hamilton or Jefferson were engaged in a word brawl. Distressed by the turn of events Jefferson left the State Department that year and appears to have avoided politics altogether for the next few years. Hamilton himself left the Treasury post shortly thereafter, but he continued to be the paramount influence on Washington until 1796, and by indirect measures was to dominate the cabinet and policies of Washington's successor, President John Adams, until 1799. To Hamilton, as much as to Washington, must go the credit for giving real strength to the new government.

Without anyone quite realizing it, the debate over foreign policy and over Constitutional powers had assisted in the birth of the American party system. The Federalists, now devoted to the cause of a strong central government, were opposed by Madison and Jefferson, who sought to protect the rights of the states and opposed any government that did not observe the principle of divided sovereignty and strict construction. Again, without fully realizing what they were doing, the Madison opposition began to try to capture the government by forming inter-state political alliances and by controlling local elections. In the summer of 1791 Jefferson and Madison went up the Hudson River on a 'botanizing expedition,' but the trip also included a visit to George Clinton, New York's violently anti-Federalist governor at Albany. Clinton was persuaded that in return for patronage from the national government he would deliver support in Congress and on the electoral board against the Federalists. By 1793 the Madison-Clinton alliance had enough votes to make Hamilton's life a nightmare.

By the time of the third presidential election in 1796 the political lines were so clearly drawn that John Adams of Massachusetts, who had served as Washington's vice president, was seen as the 'Federalist' candidate while Jefferson was seen as the 'Democratic-Republican' one. When the Electoral College convened Hamilton intrigued to make Thomas Pinckney president over the more independent Adams, but that failed and Adams became president by a margin of three electoral votes, while Jefferson, as the runner-up, became vice president.

No one could have been more distressed by the appearance of 'party' than Washington, for parties were seen as destructive selfish factions by eighteenth-century Americans, a view with which both Madison and Jefferson would have agreed. Throughout his eight years in office Washington had worked to produce harmony and union. In crucial divisions he had refused to vote in favor of his beloved Virginia. Determined to be president of all the people, he had toured the country while in office, going as far north as Portsmouth, New Hampshire, and south all the way to Savannah. Old and ailing by 1796, he had decided not to run for a third term. His last great act was to prepare, with Hamilton's assistance, the famous 'Farewell Address' in which he urged his fellow citizens to cherish the union and forego regional differences. Warning against the baneful effect of party and of taking sides in European quarrels, he urged his country to 'steer clear of permanent alliances with any portion of the foreign world.' Here Washington stated the basic belief in American isolation from Europe that was to be the guiding principle in American foreign relations for most of the nineteenth century.

Whatever bitterness there may have been toward Washington as an upholder of Federalism soon died after he left office, and once again he became a near legend. Always formal, even unapproachable, Washington, somewhat like the Constitution, was a compact of principles. Universally recognized as a fair-minded leader, it might be said that the American public saw in him the qualities they had wanted in George III. When he died in 1799, having devoted 45 years to public service, some declared it was like a god passing.

The presidency of John Adams

One of the men who had embraced the American Revolution despite his own conservative nature and his distrust of mankind was John Adams of Massachusetts. Adams had helped write the Declaration of Independence in 1776, virtually wrote the important Massachusetts state constitution of 1780, which became a model for others, was a peace commissioner at the Treaty of Paris and afterward served as American minister to the Court of St James. Typical of this Harvard graduate, whose wife Abigail may well have been the most intelligent woman in Boston, was his remark to Jefferson that 'You and I have as much right to settle these questions [about philosophy and religion] as Swift, Priestley and the Pope.'

Adams sought to rule as fairly as his predecessor, but he was hindered by many things. The cabinet, which he inherited from Washington, was dominated by Hamilton, who secretly gave them advice via letter from New York. When French authorities began to seize American vessels on the excuse that they were trading with Britain, and when the new revolutionary government in France refused to receive an American minister unless paid a bribe, American hostility toward France seemed about to drive the two countries to war. Adams strengthened the navy, American trading ships were armed and Washington, though in retirement, agreed to head the armed forces again. But when Adams discovered that Hamilton was actively promoting a war so that he might become commander-in-chief and seize New Orleans from France's ally, Spain, a split occurred between the real and the titular heads of the Federalist party.

Before this revelation, however, in 1798 the Federalists in Congress, with Adams' support, had passed a number of Alien and Sedition Acts which permitted the government to jail or silence much of the opposition, whether it was a newspaper, a Democratic Club or an outspoken individual. Although much of the opposition was indeed silenced, the price was that the Federalist party now became extremely unpopular. Alarmed by the course of events, Madison and Jefferson framed resolutions, adopted by the legislatures of Virginia and Kentucky, that declared a state could nullify a federal law if it was clearly unconstitutional. The so-called Kentucky and Virginia Resolutions were not only significant in the war

against the Alien and Sedition laws, they laid the groundwork for a theory of states rights on which the South was to construct its case for secession in 1861.

Just as the country was at crisis point Adams took full control of foreign affairs and decided to avoid war by sending a minister to Paris. By this time Napoleon Bonaparte had assumed power and was willing to receive the American minister. Adams then proceeded to negotiate a commercial agreement in 1800 (The Treaty of Mortefontaine) that at least temporarily ended the French threat to American commerce.

Adams' vigorous actions helped restore his popularity, but they came too late to secure his bid for re-election in 1800. In a closely contested election Thomas Jefferson was declared president and Aaron Burr, a New Yorker who was also the grandson of Jonathan Edwards, became vice president. Ironically Adams' chances for re-election had been hurt when Hamilton tried to elect a more extreme Federalist in his place.

The Federalists left power in great bitterness and with many fears, but they could take comfort in the fact that they were leaving behind a well-organized government run by a capable and devoted bureaucracy. Their flexible constitutional approach would continue to enhance the power of the central government. The new judicial branch was in working order, and the government was operating on a sound financial basis. A territorial system was working in the West, where within two years the new state of Ohio would be admitted to the Union. And in his last year in office Adams had avoided a war and made peace with the new colossus in Europe.

Why, then, did the Federalists fail? The reasons are not hard to find. Although they were an extremely capable set of individuals, they were too proud to seek votes, they were vague about the West and its problems and they came to be largely identified with New York and New England, with the commercial classes and with wealth. Their willingness to use the Alien and Sedition laws to curb their critics seemed to violate the Bill of Rights. All of this was too much for a country which was still more a confederation of states than a true union. By forgetting the fundamental lesson of the Revolution that liberty came before order, the Federalists turned themselves out of office. It was now the turn of Jefferson's Democratic Republicans to see if they could preserve both liberty and order while running a national government.

Above far left: In the early years of the American republic the frontier of settlement was pushed west over the Appalachian mountains by sturdy wilderness explorers like Daniel Boone.

Above left: Washington's successor to the presidency was his vice-president, the pompous John Adams, whose most enduring legacy was the appointment of John Marshall as Chief Justice of the Supreme Court.

Above right: Thomas Jefferson, the politician who played at being a scientist and philosopher. Jefferson's Republican faction trounced the Federalists in the election of 1800 and set America on a new course of internal expansion.

Right: The American commissioners to Paris in 1783, who signed the treaty granting independence to the United States. The British commissioners sourly refused to pose for the painting.

North America: 1800-1877

The nineteenth century was a time of daunting challenges to the fragile republic of the United States. The victory of the American revolutionaries in 1783 and the adoption of the federal Constitution in 1787 had not resolved all of the problems facing the new nation. From abroad and from within new dangers constantly arose.

As the new century opened the United States was engaged in an undeclared naval war with Napoleon's France. The conflict spilled over into domestic politics. The ruling Federalist Party, under the leadership of President John Adams, accused their Republican opponents of subversion and sympathy for a revolutionary foreign power. In retaliation the government jailed Republican editors and political leaders under the Alien and Sedition Acts, passed by the Federalist-dominated Congress in 1798, which among other repressive measures made it illegal to publish 'false, scandalous and malicious' statements about government leaders. For the first time since the adoption of the Constitution the stability of the Union came into question, as Kentucky and Virginia passed resolutions (the former drafted by Thomas Jefferson, the latter by James Madison) condemning the acts as unconstitutional infringements of guarantees of freedom of speech and the press contained in the bill of rights, as well as a dangerous assertion of federal power over the states. These resolutions claimed, in effect, that states could nullify an act of Congress they disagreed with: a new and dangerous doctrine that would bedevil American political life for the next six decades.

President Adams took steps to lessen tensions with France in 1800, and as a result split the Federalist Party in an election year. The Republicans won a narrow but exceedingly important victory in the presidential election, because in doing so they established both the legitimacy of opposition politics and the precedent of power passing peacefully from one party to another through democratic choice. But the election was complicated by the peculiarities of the electoral college system as initially designed by the framers of the Constitution. Thomas Jefferson and his fellow Republican Aaron Burr, having each received an equal number of votes from electors committed to the Republican Party, both had a claim to the office of the presidency, even though Burr was supposed to have been Jefferson's vice-presidential running mate. The election was then referred to the House of Representatives which, voting by state, had to decide between them. In the national election the Federalists had been swept out of power in the Congress as well as the White House, but it was nevertheless the 'lame duck' House of Representatives that had to decide the issue between Jefferson and Burr, an absurd situation in which the losing party got to determine which member of the winning party should be president. The deadlock was finally broken when Federalist leader Alexander Hamilton – no admirer of Jefferson but even less of Burr – persuaded delegations controled by Federalists to throw their support to Jefferson. The erratic Burr would kill Hamilton in a duel in 1804. He would then embark on a bizarre and abortive plot to seize control of the western United States, which resulted in his arrest for treason. Congress meanwhile passed the Twelfth Amendment to the Constitution in 1803, ratified by the states in 1804, which would prevent recurrences of the Jefferson-Burr tie vote by providing for separate balloting in future elections for the offices of president and vice-president.

Above: Thomas Jefferson became the third president of the United States in 1801, after his victory in the previous year's elections. The democratic Republican faction, in the years of its opposition to the policies of Hamilton and Washington, had always stood for a strict interpretation of the Constitution, and Jefferson was its leading spokesman. However, when the opportunity arose of acquiring the vast region of Louisiana, Jefferson did not hesitate to cast aside his previous ideals and take upon himself the authority to purchase it.

Left: Jefferson sent the intrepid explorers, Lewis and Clark, to survey the new American territory gained by the Louisiana Purchase.

Right: Despite the United States's self-proclaimed devotion to liberty, the wishes of the French colonists in Louisiana were not consulted. This notice informs them of their impending change of nationality.

Far right: Sacagawea, an Indian squaw, helped guide Lewis and Clark on their expedition.

Although Jefferson is best remembered as the author of the Declaration of Independence in 1776, he was as much a man of the new nineteenth century as of the eighteenth. He was the first president who took the oath of office without wearing a powdered wig (the epitome of fashion among the nation's revolutionary leaders) when he was sworn in to office in March 1801 in the new American capital of Washington, DC. His inaugural speech reassured nervous Federalists who feared that the Republican victory would be the beginning of an American version of the French Reign of Terror:

We are all Republicans, we are all Federalists. If there be any among us who would wish to dissolve this Union or to change its republican form, let them stand undisturbed as monuments of the safety with which error of opinion may be tolerated when reason is left free to combat it.

Committed to the Republican principles of limited government, Jefferson promptly cut taxes and slashed the diplomatic and military budget (notwithstanding the expenses incurred in the naval war with the North African Barbary States between 1801 and 1805). Jefferson's first time in office proved a momentous one in terms of both the structure of government and the expansion of the United States. A critically important constitutional issue was resolved in the case of Marbury v Madison, which came before the Supreme Court in 1803. Jefferson's predecessor President Adams, in the waning hours of his administration, had appointed a number of judges with Federalist sympathies, hoping to limit the political damage that the Republicans could do while in office. Jefferson's Secretary of State, James Madison, refused to deliver these commissions to several of Adams' would-be appointments, among them William Marbury, who was denied what he felt was his rightful appointment as Justice of the Peace for the District of Columbia. Marbury sued Madison, hoping that the Supreme Court would order the Secretary of State to issue the commissions, as provided for in the Judiciary Act of 1789. But the Court ruled instead that it could not order Madison to do so, because a section of the Judiciary Act was itself unconstitutional. Chief Justice John Marshall, who had been appointed to the Court by John Adams, sought in this decision to avoid a direct clash with the executive branch. But in doing so he established the principle of judicial review, since this was the first case in which the Supreme Court had held an act of Congress invalid under the Constitution.

Jefferson had come into office committed to a strict constructionalist interpretation of the Constitution, which would have limited the power of the federal government. But in taking actions to extend the size of the United States, Jefferson also inadvertently extended the scope of governmental authority. Through the first half of the eighteenth century France had laid vague claims to the control of much of the interior of the North American continent. Those claims were ceded by treaty to the Spanish in 1762, but in subsequent negotiations in 1800 France reacquired formal control of the so-called Louisiana territory. This raised the specter of a new French empire arising on the continent, an empire that could halt the further westward expansion of the United States. Jefferson, despite his alleged French sympathies, found this prospect intolerable. He was particularly disturbed by the prospect of French control of the port of New Orleans.

In 1803 he sent US negotiators, including James Madison, to France to discuss the purchase of the city. Napoleon, it turned out, needed money more than he craved additional territories in the Western Hemisphere, especially since his troops were then having a difficult time quelling slave uprisings in the West Indies. The astonished US negotiators came away with much more than they had set out for, signing a treaty that gave US possession of all of the French-controlled territory. The price for this huge tract of land, 828,000 square miles, as large as the US itself, stretching from New Orleans north to the Canadian border and westward to the Rocky Mountains, was $15 million. In retrospect, the deal was one of the great bargains of all times, though at the time some Federalists regarded it as sheer extravagance and an unconstitutional usurpation of power. (They also feared that when states were carved out of the new territory they would help establish a permanent Republican political ascendancy.) Jefferson had put his strict constructionism aside in taking a step that was not explicitly authorized as among the federal government's powers in the Constitution. This, too, was a sort of precedent. Future presidents, whatever their previous political philosophy or inclinations, would rarely avoid the temptation to become 'loose constructionists' once in office.

The new territory was explored by Captain Meriwether Lewis and Lieutenant William Clark. Their expedition set off from St Louis in May 1804, sailing up the Missouri to Montana, crossing the Rocky Mountains, sailing down the Snake and Columbia Rivers and finally reaching the Pacific Ocean in November 1805. Lewis and Clark discovered a region of great physical challenges and enormous economic potential.

Jefferson would have liked nothing better than to concentrate entirely on domestic affairs, but European conflicts continued to make their impact felt in the United States. Britain and France resumed open warfare in 1803, and both sought to cut off American trade with their opponents. The British were far more rigorous in their exactions on American merchant ships, boarding ships and seizing American seamen under the pretense that they were British deserters. In an ill-advised move Jefferson imposed an embargo on all foreign trade in 1807, believing that this drastic step was the only alternative to war. His strategy was based on the mistaken notion that Britain was so dependent on imports of American crops it would soon be brought to its knees. Instead, it was the economy of the United States that suffered; the embargo had a disastrous impact on American commercial interests (though, inadvertently, it aided struggling manufacturing interests, now freed of British competition). New England ports were particularly hard hit by Jefferson's policies, leading to a revival of Federalist political strength.

Madison's war

Despite the unpopularity of the embargo, the Republicans retained control of the White House in the 1808 election. Following the precedent set by George Washington, Jefferson refused to run for a third term, and his secretary of state, James Madison, took his place as president. Madison, a brilliant political theorist and one of the chief architects of the Constitution and co-author of the *Federalist Papers*, did not prove to be a distinguished president. His shortcomings were particularly evident in his conduct of American foreign affairs, where he pursued an erratic set of policies that led the United States into direct involvement in the on-going European struggle. Madison was unable to resist the growing influence within Congress of Republican 'War Hawks' who saw the quarrel with Britain as an opportunity to annex Canada and Florida (the latter still under the control of Britain's ally, Spain).

With these territorial ambitions, and with no end in sight to the British interference with American shipping, Congress passed a declaration

of war against Great Britain in June 1812, over the determined opposition of the Federalist representatives from the northeast. Several American attempts to invade Canada in the summer and fall of 1812 proved fiascos, for the American forces were poorly trained and ineptly led, and to the surprise of the invaders Canadians did not welcome their would-be liberators from the south. As the war dragged on American naval forces won some encounters on the Great Lakes, and an American expedition temporarily seized and burned the Canadian city of York (later renamed Toronto). But in general the war went poorly for the United States. Britain blockaded American ports and in August 1814 captured Washington, forcing Madison to flee and burning the White House.

New England Federalists had opposed 'Mr Madison's war' from the beginning. The governors of some New England states refused to provide militia for the war effort, and some New England merchants continued to carry on trade with the British throughout the war. The Federalists even met in convention in Hartford, Connecti-

cut, in December 1814 to adopt resolutions critical of the administration and called for a number of constitutional changes that would have strengthened New England's political influence. The convention was regarded as treasonable by Republicans in other parts of the country. Once again, as in the crisis of 1798-1800, it looked as though the new experiment in republican government might end in collapse and dismemberment. But on Christmas eve 1814 American and British diplomats meeting in Ghent, Belgium, worked out a compromise peace treaty. Before the news from Ghent could reach the contending forces in the United States, American troops under the command of Andrew Jackson had inflicted a humiliating defeat on British forces attempting to capture New Orleans. Thus the war ended with patriotic celebrations of Jackson's victory, inspiring a wave of nationalist pride and discrediting Federalist critics of the war, even though the US had achieved none of its original war aims.

The war of 1812 did, however, prove to be a turning point in relations between white Americans and the Indian tribes. No longer would the Indians be able to draw upon the support of rival European colonial powers in their struggle against the white encroachment upon their lands. Shortly before the war a Shawnee chief named Tecumseh had tried to organize a unified resistance among Indians living on the frontier regions of the Old Northwest against the pressure of the white settlers. But before he could weld his forces together, Indiana territorial governor William Henry Harrison led an army against Tecumseh's headquarters on Tippecanoe Creek. In the resulting battle in November 1811 Harrison won what he claimed was a resounding victory, even though it was the whites who were surprised by an Indian attack and who suffered the greatest casualties. Nevertheless, Harrison's forces destroyed the village that had served as Tecumseh's headquarters, and the Indian chief was forced to flee to Canada. There he allied himself with the British and was killed in battle in 1813.

In the South Andrew Jackson had led white forces against the Creeks, winning a victory at the Battle of Horseshoe Bend in 1814, shortly before his triumph at New Orleans. In 1817 he led an American expedition into Spanish territory in East Florida to suppress the Seminole Indians (who, among other things, were providing a refuge for runaway black slaves). This successful expedition further contributed to Jackson's political popularity and to American advantage in negotiations with Spain over the future of the region. A Second Seminole War broke out two decades later, and once again the Seminoles were defeated by the overwhelming forces the whites could bring to bear against them. In Georgia, Alabama and Mississippi, the Creeks, Choctaw, Chickasaw and Cherokee Indians recognized the futility of resisting the overwhelming power of the whites and tried to adopt to the whites' methods of

settled agricultural existence, but neither their behavior nor the treaties they had signed with Congress did them any good in the long run. White settlers craved their lands, and in the early 1830s they were forced by President Andrew Jackson to accept resettlement to new lands farther west, marching under guard along the 'Trail of Tears' to Oklahoma, with thousands dying of starvation and exposure along the way. The Bureau of Indian Affairs, established by the federal government in 1836, would take charge of the new system of Indian reservations.

Geographical and economic expansion

The pace of the nation's westward expansion both astonished and inspired Americans in the early nineteenth century. At the time of the Louisiana Purchase many felt it would take a century or more just to settle the new territories. Yet within a few years of the Lewis and Clark expedition fur traders based in St Louis were plying their trade as far west as the Rockies. They were the vanguard of a huge invading force of land-hungry settlers. By the 1840s Americans were speaking of their 'manifest destiny' to control the entire continent from the Atlantic to the Pacific. New states were soon carved out of the 'Old Northwest' – Ohio (1803), Indiana (1816) and Illinois (1819). In the South cotton planters brought their slaves into the new states of Mississippi (1817) and Alabama (1819). Other new territories, and potential states, were added by virtue of agreement with Britain in 1818 that provided for joint occupation of the Pacific Northwest, and by an agreement with Spain the following year ceding Florida to the United States.

The opening up of commercial farming west of the Appalachians created the need for new forms of transportation. Settlers often reached their

new homes by the most primitive means: on foot, horseback or in ox-drawn Conestoga wagons. But to get their grain back to market they needed quicker and more reliable passage. Steamboats appeared on the Mississippi River in 1811, traveling as far north as Ohio and transforming New Orleans into one of the world's leading ports. The Erie Canal, which opened in 1825, linked the Atlantic with the shores of the Great Lakes. A canal-building craze followed, though the canals themselves would soon be supplanted by the railroad system created in the 1840s and 1850s. Local, state and federal government all played important roles in providing the capital necessary for such internal improvements. Kentucky Congressman Henry Clay made support for such internal improvements, along with the protective tariff, the basis of his never-realized presidential ambitions. He called his program the 'American System" in a famous speech to Congress in 1824, because, if adopted, it would lessen US dependence on foreign manufacturers.

Not everyone was as enthusiastic as Clay about the changes in American life brought about by the new economic currents. In *Walden* Henry David Thoreau left a record of his retreat to rural Walden Pond in the 1840s. He had no use for the commercial spirit that had captured the hearts of so many of his fellow citizens in Massachusetts, and he portrayed industrialism as an invading, predatory force:

The whistle of the locomotive penetrates my woods summer and winter, sounding like the scream of a hawk sailing over some farmer's yard, informing me that many restless city merchants are arriving within the circle of the town . . .

The American industrial revolution had begun a half century earlier when Samuel Slater opened

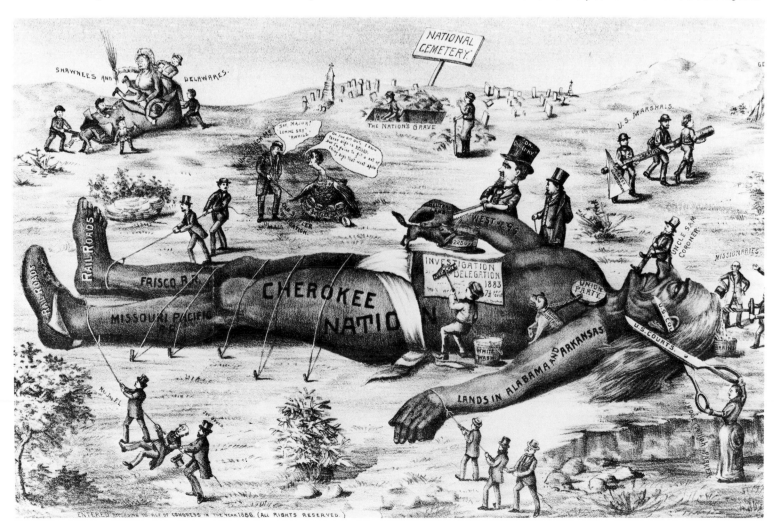

his first spinning mill in Pawtucket, Rhode Island, using water-powered machines for carding and spinning cotton. Slater's work force consisted mostly of children, which won him praise rather than condemnation, because in the 1790s most children already worked on farms or as apprentices in crafts. In fact, he would probably have had a harder time if he had recruited adult workers, because many Americans feared the consequences of economic changes that would lead to the creation of a class of full-time wage laborers. In the 1820s new factories sprang up along Concord, Merrimack and other fast-running rivers in New England, introducing new automatic machinery in both spinning and weaving. Since these machines were too complex and cumbersome to be operated by children, the owners of the new factories developed a system of labor recruitment and management that they believed would preserve the rural character of American life and prevent the horrors associated with the British industrial revolution. In the early days of Lowell, Massachusetts, for example, most of the work force was made up of young, single Yankee farm girls, who lived in carefully supervised boarding houses and who were encouraged to attend lectures, sermons and concerts and to contribute to literary magazines in their off-hours. The very appearance of Lowell was designed to soothe fears that the 'dark satanic mills' of British industrialism would soon despoil the American landscape.

But the utopian and pastoral aspects of early industrialism soon faded. By 1856 production in Lowell's brick mills had grown enormously: 12,000 looms annually turned out more than 115 million yards of cloth and carpet for a seemingly insatiable market. Profits were high, but as competition among textile producers increased they sought ways to cut costs. Even in the earliest days of Lowell the 12-hour day and the six-day week had been standard. In the 1830s manufacturers began to require workers to tend to more looms, and at the same time they cut their wages, leading to strikes in 1834 and 1836.

By the 1840s the manufacturers had abandoned the boarding house system and had begun to replace the Yankee farm girls with Irish immigrants who, it was hoped, would prove a lot more pliable workers, but who in fact soon launched strikes of their own. The American industrial revolution, like its British counterpart, was creating a new class of permanent wage-earners despite the best intentions of its founders.

Slavery and the States

Slavery had existed as an institution in North America since the earliest days of permanent British settlement. Slaves had lived and worked in the North as well as the South in the eighteenth century, but slave labor proved particularly well suited to the staple-producing plantation economy of the South. The South enjoyed the benefits of a long growing season and a system of natural waterways that linked fertile floodplains with port cities and markets to the north and in Europe. Tobacco and hemp was grown in the upper South, rice in the coastal regions of South Carolina and Georgia, sugar in Louisiana, and cotton in a band of cultivation stretching from North Carolina south and west to Texas. In the late eighteenth century there had been talk in both the South and the North of abolishing slavery. But Eli Whitney's 1793 invention of the cotton gin, which removed the seeds from raw cotton, overcame a production bottleneck that had long bedeviled the cotton textile industry, and in doing so it transformed the prospects of plantation agriculture. Cotton became the leading US export and remained so down to the 1850s. Cotton production doubled between 1820 and 1840, and again between 1840 and 1860. In the decade after the invention of the cotton gin the price of slaves doubled, and thereafter little anti-slavery talk was heard – or tolerated – among southerners.

The number of black slaves in the South jumped from 1 million in 1800 to 4 million in 1860, largely through natural increase. (Congress cut off the slave trade with Africa in 1808, though some Africans continued to be smuggled in.) The slave system ran on a curious mixture of brutality and paternalism. On one plantation in Louisiana, where the planter owned some 200 slaves and kept exact records of the management of his work force, he had over 160 whippings administered to his slaves in a two-year period from 1840 to 1842. But the same owner was also reported to keep his slaves well clothed by the standards of the time and sponsored holiday celebrations for them and built them a dance hall. Slave owners benefited economically from the birth of children among their slaves, so they encouraged slave marriages and made at least minimal concession to protecting the health of pregnant slaves. They were also entitled to take, and sometimes proved themselves capable of taking, children away from their mothers and selling them to slavetraders or other planters.

Slave owners constituted only a small minority of southern whites: in 1860, 383,637 whites out of a population of 8 million were slaveowners, and under 3000 were large planters owning 100 or more slaves. Nevertheless, the slaveowners formed a powerful economic elite that dominated southern society and politics; they retained the loyalty of non-slaveowners by constantly reminding them of the horrors of a potential slave uprising. Unlike the West Indies, where blacks formed a majority and launched many revolts, whites outnumbered blacks throughout the South, and they enforced their domination through a tight system of punishments and surveillance.

What is surprising is not that slave revolts were infrequent, but that, given the odds, any took place at all. Major slave uprisings or conspiracies were suppressed near Richmond, Virginia, in 1801, where a slave named Gabriel assembled a group of followers who plotted to seize arms and take the governor hostage; in Charlestown, South Carolina, in 1822, where a free black named Denmark Vesey organized a revolutionary conspiracy among a group of slave artisans, but was betrayed by an informer before it could be attempted; and, most dramatically, in Southampton County, Virginia, in 1831, where a charismatic black preacher named Nat Turner led a group of slaves on a rampage in which 55 whites were killed. Afterwards white southerners lived in constant fear of further uprisings and regarded anti-slavery opponents in the North as incendiaries who would bring death and destruction upon the South if left unchecked.

Despite the fears of whites, the most common form of resistance to slavery was not armed insurrection or murder, but individual flight. Some of the fugitives were aided by an 'underground railroad' of black and white sympathizers to escape to freedom in the North or Canada. Harriet Tubman, who escaped from slavery in Maryland, risked her own freedom dozens of times with her forays into the South during which she guided hundreds of slaves to freedom. Perhaps the best-known escaped slave was Frederick Douglass, who made his way to the North in 1838 at the age of 21, and

Far left: Negroes picking cotton in the nineteenth-century South. Slavery was common to all the states in the eighteenth century, but by the early years of the nineteenth had been restricted to the southern half of the country. Its continued existence led to the creation of two distinct cultures in America, one free and one slave.

Left: The capture of Nat Turner, the Virginia slave whose 1831 uprising was one of the bloodiest examples of servile revolt in US history.

Right: John Young-Hunter's painting, *The Old Santa Fé Trail.* Wagon trains brought American settlers to the sparsely populated territories across the Mississippi.

Below: Tecumseh, the great Indian leader of the Old Northwest.

Bottom: Harriet Beecher Stowe, nineteenth-century novelist and early feminist.

went on to become one of the most eloquent speakers of the abolitionist movement.

The moral implications of slavery troubled only a minority of northern whites. More troubling were the political problems that the existence of the slave system posed to the viability of the young republic. Among other irritants to northern sensibilities was the three-fifth clause of the Constitution (counting slaves as 'three-fifths of a man' for the purposes of determining Congressional representation), which seemed to award the South disproportionate weight in the House of Representatives, since southern Representatives were elected to office by a much smaller white electorate than their northern counterparts. In the Senate, both northerners and southerners insisted that a balance be maintained between the power of the slave and free states. This led to a major dispute in 1819. There were a total of 11 free and 11 slave states represented in the Senate when the territory of Missouri applied for statehood. Missouri, a slave-holding territory, sprawled northward much farther than any of its sister slave states, and northerners were reluctant to approve its admission to the Union if it pointed toward further northward expansion of the slave system. Months of impassioned debate followed in Congress, as northerners proposed legislation that would abolish slavery in Missouri, and southerners insisted that Missouri be admitted only as a slave state.

The issue was finally resolved in 1820 in the form of a bill known as the Missouri Compromise. This bill provided for the admission of both Missouri and the new free state of Maine (whose territory had formerly been part of Massachusetts) into the Union. In addition, Congress approved an amendment to the bill that excluded slavery from the part of the Louisiana Purchase north of the line 36° 30', running westward from Missouri's southern boundary. Despite this apparently amicable settlement the debate that led to the Missouri Compromise raised disturbing portents of sectional disunity. Thomas Jefferson for one was not relieved by the Compromise and described the controversy as a 'fire bell in the night' that signaled impending disaster.

A woman's sphere in a man's world

The 'Cult of True Womanhood,' as one historian has dubbed nineteenth-century beliefs about women, held that whereas men worked in a harsh and competitive world ruled by the ethics of the marketplace, women guarded the home as a haven where more gentle, Christian values and precepts could rule. Dozens of ladies' magazines and advice books instructed women in this 'cult.' One of the most popular of these advice books, *The American Woman's Home*, was written by the educator Catherine Beecher and her sister, the novelist Harriet Beecher Stowe.

Men and women in the eighteenth century had performed different tasks, but there had been little sense of their occupying totally separate spheres. The basic unit of production was the home, with women working in the kitchen and performing other domestic tasks such as food preservation, candlemaking, spinning, weaving and sewing, while men worked in the fields or as artisans in an attached workshop. But in the nineteenth century men went off to factories or offices to work, while women remained at home. Middle-class women underwent a transition from producers to consumers. They bought food and clothing prepared by others instead of producing it within their own home. While it would be a mistake to romanticize eighteenth-century women's work, in the nineteenth century, for all the reassuring words in the ladies' magazines and advice books, it was not entirely clear to many women just what they were supposed to be doing with their time and talents.

There was a certain ambiguity built into the concept of separate spheres that some women in the nineteenth century turned to their advantage. If women *were* the moral guardians of the home, the defenders of Christian ethics, the protectors of their children's and their husbands' health and well-being, might that not require them in some instances to step outside the home – not in open rebellion against the constraints of the women's sphere, but to fulfill their assigned responsibilities within that sphere? Catherine Beecher herself used this reasoning to support her arguments for the education of women, and their employment as teachers. Many northern women in the years leading up to the Civil War became involved in the moral reform crusades that sprang from Protestant revivalist impulses. Thus they moved into the public world in the name of defending the private world of the family.

Moral reform groups were concerned with a wide variety of religious and secular causes, from keeping the Sabbath to providing more humane care for the insane. The efforts of the moral reform societies were spurred in many instances by millennialist belief in the imminence of the second coming of Christ: if a sufficient number of good causes could triumph, it might be the signal for the establishment of the kingdom of heaven on earth. So evangelical Protestantism, almost despite itself, sanctioned activity of women in the public world. And those women who began their journey outside the home loyally affirming the values of the women's sphere were sometimes surprised by their final destination. Thus Susan B Anthony began her activities as a political crusader in the temperance movement, moved from there to the abolitionist movement and finally became one of the founding members of the women's suffrage movement.

In July 1848 Elizabeth Cady Stanton, Lucretia Mott and other women in upstate New York active in the abolitionist movement organized the first women's rights convention in the town of Seneca Falls. Those who gathered for the convention adopted a Declaration of Sentiments that declared in part: 'We hold these truths to be self-evident: that all men and women are created equal . . . ' Their declaration went on to list what they felt were the most important grievances of women in American society, including the lack of the right to vote and to control their own property. Subsequent women's rights conventions created a network of women's rights activists, with Stanton and Susan B Anthony emerging as the movement's most prominent leaders. As long as issues of the future of slavery and the future of the Union dominated the political agenda, women's rights remained a subsidiary concern of only a small group of activists. But after the Civil War Stanton, Anthony and others would create new organizations dedicated exclusively to winning women's suffrage.

The new party politics

The election of James Monroe to the Presidency in 1816 continued the 'Virginia Dynasty' of Jefferson and Monroe. It also marked the beginning of what historians have called the 'Era of Good Feeling,' during which the old Federalist Party of Washington and Adams collapsed. Monroe went unopposed when he ran for reelection in 1820, but underneath the sheltering umbrella of the dominant and seemingly unified Republicans, political factionalism was preparing the way for the emergence of a new two-party system.

During the Era of Good Feeling Americans no longer divided into pro-French and pro-British political camps. Anti-British sentiments would occasionally resurface as they did in the aftermath of the *Caroline* Affair of 1837, when Canadian militiamen crossed the Niagara River and burned an American steamboat used to supply William Lyon Mackenzie, leader of a failed insurrection. But American Presidents were able to check the passions of their countrymen and no wars resulted. The end of the Napoleonic wars led to peace among the great powers on the European continent and also enabled the United States to disentangle itself from European concerns. Behind the sheltering wall of the Atlantic Ocean, and drawing upon memories of the American 'victory' in the War of 1812, United States diplomats felt they could resolutely assert American interests, particularly in the Western Hemisphere. The most important foreign policy initiative of the Era of Good Feeling was the declaration of the Monroe Doctrine in 1824, which proclaimed that 'The American continents are no longer subjects for any new European colonial establishments.' The doctrine had little impact at the time, but it would play an important role in the extension of American power throughout the hemisphere at the end of the century.

Political partisanship began to reemerge from the shadows with the 1824 Presidential election. John Quincy Adams, who had served as Secretary of State under Monroe and who was the son of the last Federalist president, John Adams, was the victor in a confusing four-way race that saw no candidate attract a majority. Andrew Jackson had actually edged Adams out in the initial count in the electoral college, but when the election was thrown to the House of Representatives to decide, Henry Clay (who had come in fourth) instructed his supporters to throw their support to Adams, thus undercutting Jackson, the man he thought was the greatest long-range obstacle to his own presidential ambitions. The circumstances of Adams' victory led to charges of 'corrupt bargain' and hastened the reemergence of a new party system. Adams' and Clay's supporters began to refer to themselves as National Republicans (to be renamed in time Whigs), while Jackson's supporters called themselves the Democratic Republicans (later to be called simply Democrats).

The ideological divisions between the two parties were never as clear-cut as their supporters and some historians since have insisted. In a general way it can be said that the Whigs spoke more or less consistently for broad nationalist policies, including a program of internal improvements and higher tariffs, while the Democrats spoke more or less consistently for states' rights and agrarian interests, favoring lower tariffs and cheaper government. But there were many shadings of belief and splits within the two parties over these and other issues. To give just one example, some southern states' rights supporters who opposed Jackson in the Nullification Crisis (described below) became Whigs rather than Democrats.

The rematch between Adams and Jackson in the hard-fought 1828 campaign saw Jackson the victor. His election is sometimes interpreted as the triumph of the common man, and historians have spoken of the era of his presidency as the period of 'Jacksonian democracy' – although Jackson, a slaveholder, merchant and land speculator, was hardly a common man or much of a democrat. Nevertheless, it is true that the period of the later 1820s and 1830s did witness the emergence of mass democratic politics, with steadily increasing voter turnouts in each succeeding election. State constitutions were rewritten to drop remaining property and religious restrictions on white manhood suffrage and to provide for the direct election of presidential electors by popular vote. (In most states, they had previously been chosen by legislatures.) Beginning in the 1830s presidential candidates were chosen by national party nominating conventions, rather than by Congressional caucus. To mobilize voters a new kind of party emerged, run by professional politicians and awarding devoted party workers with government jobs through the 'spoils system.'

Among the major domestic issues of Jackson's presidency were those relating to internal improvements, the national bank and the tariff. Jackson, though not a consistent opponent of internal improvements, vetoed a bill providing for construction of a 60-mile road in Kentucky at federal expense (the Maysville Road Veto), arguing it was an unconstitutional extension of federal jurisdiction. Jackson also sought to restrict the role of government by abolishing the Second United States Bank. The first United States Bank had been established in 1791 and had been allowed to die when its federal charter expired in 1811. The Second Bank had been chartered in 1816 by Congress, over the veto of President Madison. Banking was a poorly understood institution in nineteenth-century America, and the frequent financial panics of the era (in 1819, 1837 and 1857) did little to increase the popularity of bankers. Jackson, speaking for his agrarian constituents in the South and West, called the United States Bank 'The Monster' and developed a personal hatred for the bank's long-time president, Nicholas Biddle. Biddle, seeking to outflank Jackson, applied for a renewal of the bank's charter in 1832, though it was not set to expire until 1836. He persuaded Congress, but the rechartering bill was vetoed by Jackson. The bank's future became a major issue in the 1832 election, with Jackson's defeat of challenger Henry Clay (a bank supporter) sealing its fate.

The problem of tariffs turned out to be the most explosive issue of the Jackson presidency. Disputes over tariffs, like those over slavery, tended to be sectional disputes, with southerners – dependent on an export-oriented agricultural economy – consistent partisans of low tariffs, while northerners – with their growing manufacturing sector – were generally supporters of higher tariffs. Congress had raised tariffs in 1824 and 1828 (the latter referred to in the South as the 'Tariff of Abominations'). The passage of a new tariff law in 1832, which lowered tariffs less than southerners desired, led to the election of a special convention in South Carolina, which in November 1832 passed an Ordinance of Nullification. The South Carolina ordinance, if enforced, would have ended the collection of tariff duties in the state early the following year. South Carolina threatened to secede from the Union if the federal government attempted to interfere with this act of nullification. Jackson, ordinarily a defender of states' rights, reacted swiftly and indignantly to this challenge to his authority, insisting on the supremacy of the federal government on the issue and threatening to send the army in to enforce the law and preserve the Union. He asked Congress to pass a 'Force Bill' which would give him the power to impose his will, militarily if need be, on the recalcitrant South Carolinians. Cooler heads finally prevailed. With Congress considering a compromise tariff that would come closer to meeting southern concerns, South Carolina postponed enforcement of the Nullification Ordinance. When the crisis passed, the ordinance was repealed, but the principle of how far a state could go in resisting intrusions of federal power remained unresolved.

The Democrats were the first to master the new techniques of party politics. In 1836 Jackson's vice president, Martin Van Buren, easily won election, turning aside a bizarre Whig strategy of running three separate candidates (each considered strong in a particular region) against him. Van Buren was a gifted politician, but he had the misfortune of coming into office just as the Panic of 1837 wreaked havoc on the nation's economy, and he had no hope of reelection. The Whigs proved in the 1840 election that they had studied the techniques of Jacksonian politicking since the last election. They nominated General William Henry Harrison, the hero of the battle of Tippecanoe,

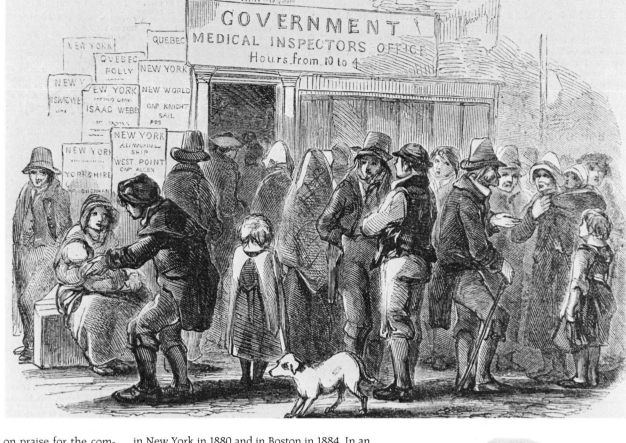

Right: Irish immigrants gather outside a medical inspector's office before beginning their journey to the New World. The potato famine of the 1840s propelled the Irish to venture across the Atlantic as a part of the first major wave of nineteenth-century immigration. They settled in the big cities of the East Coast where they could find jobs in the factories and docks. Their Roman Catholicism and clannishness aroused fears among the strongly Protestant Americans of a 'Papist' takeover of the republic. Nationalist movements like the American, or 'Know-Nothing,' Party carried these fears into national politics.

Below right: Sam Houston, the first president of the Republic of Texas. Slave-owning Americans from the southern states had moved into the Mexican territory of Texas during the 1820s and early 1830s. After Mexico abolished slavery, these Americans rebelled and gained independence from Mexico in 1836.

and ran a campaign long on praise for the common man and short on program. Harrison, who had grown up in a distinguished and wealthy Virginian family, was portrayed by his campaign publicists as a man who was happiest when sitting in a log cabin swigging the contents of a cider barrel. It proved a winning formula, though Harrison died of pneumonia less than a month after his inauguration. He was succeeded by his vice president, John Tyler of Virginia.

Immigration

Changing patterns of immigration were to have a dramatic impact on American society and politics in the nineteenth century. Through the first decades of the new century the majority of immigrants to the United States still came from Britain, but that was soon to change. Between 1820 and 1860 3.5 million immigrants came to the United States from Ireland, and an additional 1.5 million from Germany, while only 800,000 new immigrants came from Britain. The bulk of the Irish immigrants arrived in the 1840s and early 1850s in the aftermath of the Irish potato famine of 1845-49. Often arriving nearly penniless in American ports, the majority of the new immigrants settled in the cities of the urban northeast. (New York City became the third largest Irish city in the world, after Dublin and London.)

The Irish maintained a remarkable degree of family, community and ethnic cohesion in their radically changed surroundings. Like many subsequent immigrant groups they were determined not to abandon their traditional culture and had no intention of jumping into any melting pots. They came over and settled as families, or, when that was not possible, individual family members who made it to America devoted their labor and savings for many years to bringing over the family members they had left behind. They established their own religious institutions, fraternal organizations, newspapers, schools and political clubs. The last were spectacularly successful, electing the first Irish mayor in Scranton in 1878,

in New York in 1880 and in Boston in 1884. In an often hostile environment the key to Irish success in the New World lay not in assimilation but in the defense of a separate identity and in the creation of institutions of ethnic solidarity.

Many 'old stock' Americans of Protestant British descent decided that the new immigrants were a threat to public health, morality and the survival of the republic (because, in the case of the Irish, of their allegiance to the Roman Catholic Church, and political machines like New York City's Tammany Hall, and, in the case of the Germans, to revolutionary creeds such as socialism and anarchism). Nativism took such virulent forms of expression as the 1834 sacking of a Catholic convent in Charlestown, Massachusetts, and the 1844 Kensington riots in Philadelphia, when mobs of Protestant workers attacked the homes of Catholic weavers. In the 1850s nativism loomed as a major political force when a secret anti-Catholic organization, the Order of the Star Spangled Banner, transformed itself into the American Party (more popularly known as the 'Know Nothing' Party, since its adherents, true to the secret origins of the group, would respond 'I Know Nothing' when asked of its activities). The Know-Nothings enjoyed an astonishing political success in 1854, sweeping the field in Massachusetts elections and showing considerable strength in other states. The party's rapid decline by 1856 did not reflect any sudden lessening of nativist tensions, but rather was a by-product of the nation's increasing preoccupation with the slavery issue.

The dilemma of territorial expansion

American settlement in Mexican-controled territory in Texas began in the early 1820s. New settlers were at first welcomed by the Mexican government, which later, awakening to the seemingly obvious danger in such a policy, attempted to stem the tide. The government also passed measures not to the liking of the Americans, among them the abolition of slavery. Late in 1835

Americans in Texas began an armed revolt against the Mexican authorities, raising the banner of independence the following spring. Mexican troops under the command of General Santa Anna massacred the 188-man American garrison holding out at the Alamo mission in San Antonio after a three-week siege. Less than a month later he massacred 300 more Americans after the siege of Goliad. Santa Anna seemed to be sweeping all before him when Texans under the command of Sam Houston won a surprise victory at the battle of San Jacinto in April and captured the Mexican general. Sam Houston was subsequently installed as president of the newly independent Republic of Texas. Houston would have liked nothing better than to see the Texas Republic join the United

States, but anti-slavery forces in Congress blocked annexation. The issue continued to simmer over the next decade.

President John Tyler, who had been elected as vice-president in 1840, was suddenly elevated to the Presidency a month into the new administration when President William Henry Harrison died. Taylor strongly pushed for the annexation of Texas but made the mistake of relying too heavily on South Carolina's John Calhoun to sell the measure to the Senate. Calhoun, not a tactful man, defended annexation as a means of frustrating abolitionist designs, which only stiffened northern resistance against the measure. Finally, with the election of the strongly pro-annexation Democrat James K Polk in 1844, the tide in Congress turned, and in March 1845, shortly before Polk assumed office, a joint resolution of both houses of Congress approved a treaty that would allow Texas to be admitted as a new slave state. A bellicose expansionist mood swept the nation that summer. The United States came close to going to war again with Great Britain over the issue of the Oregon Country, jointly occupied by Britain and the United States since 1818. Polk took a belligerent line, claiming the right of the United States to exercise sole control of the area stretching all the way up to Russian-controled Alaska, but in 1846 a compromise was reached establishing the new northern boundary of the United States at the 49th parallel.

Polk's willingness to back down from his earlier demands in the nation's Northwest was influenced by events on the nation's southern border, where, by the spring of 1846, the United States was embroiled in a war with Mexico. The Mexican government had long warned the US against any steps toward annexing Texas and was also vigorously resisting American attempts to acquire California. As Congress took steps to facilitate annexation in 1845 Mexico broke diplomatic relations with the United States, and American military forces under the command of General Zachary Taylor moved into Texas. A military clash

was all but inevitable, and it finally took place on the banks of the Rio Grande in April 1846. Polk, who had been determined to seek a declaration of war in any case, was now able to go to Congress charging that Mexico had 'invaded our territory and shed American blood upon American soil.'

The outcome of the war was never in serious doubt. While American troops under Colonel Stephen Kearny captured New Mexico and American settlers under Captain John C Fremont launched a revolt against Mexican authorities in California (aided by Kearny in the later stages of the war), American armies commanded by Zachary Taylor and Winfield Scott advanced into the heartland of Mexico. Scott's forces captured Mexico City in September of 1847, and the Mexicans sued for peace, signing the treaty of Guadalupe Hidalgo in February 1848. Under the terms of the treaty Mexico relinquished all claims to Texas and ceded the territories of New Mexico and California to the United States in exchange for a payment of $15 million. The war had cost fewer than 1800 American dead, and the American military officers who participated, including Robert E Lee and Ulysses S Grant, got a practical training in large-scale military operations that would serve them in good stead in a few years' time.

The debate over what to do with territory acquired during the Mexican War revealed the sectional fault lines running through the party system. David Wilmot, a Pennsylvania Democrat, introduced an amendment to an appropriate bill in 1846. The Wilmot Proviso stated that in any territory acquired from Mexico as a result of the war, 'neither slavery nor involuntary servitude shall ever exist . . .' The bill was defeated in the Senate, but it raised the issue in an unavoidable form. John C Calhoun, influential Democratic Senator from South Carolina, warned that if the federal government encroached upon what he considered the legitimate rights of the slave states, it would lead to 'revolution, anarchy, civil war and widespread disaster.'

Southern leaders demanded that northerners

cease the agitation on the slave question. If the issue had been left to the leadership of the two major parties. that is precisely what would have happened. as both Democrats and Whigs made determined efforts to keep the slavery issue out of the 1848 campaign. But the abolitionist movement, which stood independent of the two-party system, refused to cease its agitation, and increasingly came to influence northern political leaders within the two parties. In 1848 anti-slavery Democrats joined with 'Conscience Whigs' and the small anti-slavery Liberty Party (which had been organized in 1839, running candidates in the last two elections) to form the Free Soil Party. The new party, which took as its slogan 'free soil, free speech, free labor and free men,' did not call for the abolition of slavery, but it did oppose any further extension of the slave system into new territories. Free Soilers nominated former president Martin Van Buren as their presidential can-

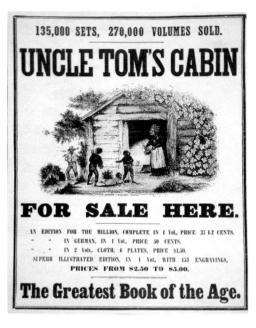

135,000 SETS, 270,000 VOLUMES SOLD.

UNCLE TOM'S CABIN

FOR SALE HERE.

AN EDITION FOR THE MILLION, COMPLETE IN 1 Vol, PRICE 37 1-2 CENTS.
"   "   IN GERMAN, IN 1 Vol, PRICE 50 CENTS.
"   "   IN 2 Vols, CLOTH, 6 PLATES, PRICE $1.50.
SUPERB ILLUSTRATED EDITION, IN 1 Vol, WITH 153 ENGRAVINGS,
PRICES FROM $2.50 TO $5.00.

The Greatest Book of the Age.

Left: 'Remember the Alamo' provided a rallying cry for Texans fighting for their independence. This painting by Robert Onderdonk shows Davy Crockett, the Tennessee frontiersman who volunteered to fight the Mexicans at the Alamo, in the last moments of the garrison's resistance. For all the sympathy that was shown for annexation in the southern United States, in part boosted by the story of the Alamo, it would be another nine years before Congress agreed to accept Texas into the United States.

Above: Uncle Tom's Cabin, the popular bestseller by Harriet Beecher Stowe, stirred abolitionist sentiments in America's northern and western states.

Right and center right: In the 1850s the battle between pro- and anti-abolitionists was fought largely in Congress, as laws like the Fugitive Slave Act and the Kansas-Nebraska Act attempted to maintain the country's old consensus over slavery.

Far right: John Brown, the tempestuous radical abolitionist leader.

didate and attracted enough votes to throw the election to the Whig candidate, General Zachary Taylor. Taylor died in office in 1850 and was succeeded by his vice-president, Millard Fillmore. The presidents of the 1850s – Fillmore, Franklin Pierce and James Buchanan – were men of such incompetence that it is almost possible to write the history of the decade without mentioning their names.

A new round of disputes had broken out over California's application for admission as a state, which would upset the balance in Congress of 15 free and 15 slave states. After a Senate debate, in which South Carolina Democrat John Calhoun demanded that the slave states be given 'an equal right in the acquired territory' and New York Whig William H Seward warned that the extension of slavery would in itself 'tend to the consummation of violence,' a majority was swayed by eloquent pleas for moderation on both sides by Henry Clay of Kentucky and Daniel Webster of Massachusetts. In the end a compromise package of legislation was worked out, later referred to as the Compromise of 1850. It included bills for the admission of California as a free state; the organization of new territories in other land taken from Mexico, without reference to whether they would enter the Union as free or slave states; a Fugitive Slave Act that was designed to make it easier to recapture slaves who had fled to the North (rewarding those who aided in their capture and punishing those who tried to hinder their reenslavement); a bill abolishing the slave trade in the District of Columbia; and other minor provisions. The Fugitive Slave Act, designed to assuage southern concerns, further inflamed northern opinion. Some northerners openly defied the law, rescuing recaptured slaves and restoring them to freedom. The publicity surrounding the cases of escaped slaves inspired novelist Harriet Beecher Stowe to write *Uncle Tom's Cabin*, published in 1852, a novel that proved the most effective piece of anti-slavery agitation in the abolitionist arsenal, selling over a million copies in the North in just over a year after its publication.

The drift toward war

A monumental miscalculation on the part of an ambitious politician, Illinois Senator Stephen A Douglas, further undermined the already shaky edifice of sectional compromise. In 1854 Douglas introduced a bill in Congress known as the Kan-

sas-Nebraska Act. The Missouri Compromise of 1820 had set a northern boundary beyond which slavery was not supposed to expand, but Douglas's new bill represented a potential breach of that boundary. It provided for the organization of new territories in Kansas and Nebraska as either free or slave territories, depending upon a vote of their inhabitants. Douglas had presidential ambitions which required southern support. He also wanted to bring new settlers into territories in which he had speculated heavily in land purchases, and he believed that climatic conditions made the slave plantation system unfeasible in the new territories. But the plan created havoc. Northerners saw it as evidence of a 'slave-power conspiracy' to extend slavery into all areas of the Union, and both northerners and southerners began to pour into the new territories in a race to gain majority. The pro-slavery forces, a minority of the population, used armed intimidation to win territorial elections. Rival territorial governments were established, and constitutions were adopted by pro- and anti-slavery forces. Violence broke out between the factions and spiraled out of control in what was now being called 'Bleeding Kansas.' Pro-slavery forces attacked the anti-slavery stronghold of Lawrence, burning and pillaging homes and killing two of the residents. In retaliation an anti-slavery settler name John Brown led a raid that captured and killed five pro-slavery colonists at Pottawatomie Creek. In a little over a year 200 settlers lost their lives in Kansas. Violence once unleashed proved infectious. Massachusetts Senator Charles Sumner delivered a speech on the floor of the Senate denouncing 'the crime against Kansas,' and in the course of doing so insulted South Carolina Senator Andrew Butler. A few days later Butler's nephew, Representative Preston S Brooks, attacked Sumner at his desk in the Senate, beating him into unconsciousness with his cane. Brooks resigned his seat and was triumphantly reelected by his constituents, to the indignation of the North.

Among the casualties of the Kansas-Nebraska conflict was the old two-party system. In 1854 a new anti-slavery party, broader than all its predecessors, took to the field, drawing upon anti-slavery Democrats, Whigs and adherents of the Know-Nothings. In 1856 the Republican Party fielded its first presidential candidate, John C Fremont. The Democratic candidate, James Buchanan, won handily over Fremont in a three-way race (with former president Millard Fillmore, the

Know-Nothing candidate, coming in third). Ominously enough, virtually all of Fremont's votes came in the North, while the solid base that Buchanan drew upon was the slave South. Sectional politics were replacing national politics of earlier years as the basis of party loyalty.

In March 1857 the Supreme Court ruled in the Dred Scott decision that the Missouri Compromise, already abrogated in practice by the Kansas-Nebraska act, had been in fact unconstitutional all along. Dred Scott was a slave who had been taken in the 1830s by his Missouri owner to Illinois and later to the Wisconsin territory where slavery had been prohibited by the Missouri Compromise. Scott sued for his freedom in 1846, arguing that having resided in a free state earned him his freedom. It took 10 years for the case to work its way up to the Supreme Court, where Chief Justice Roger B Taney, speaking for the majority of the court, ruled that blacks were not eligible for American citizenship and thus Scott was not entitled to sue. In an infamous phrase, Taney declared that blacks 'had no rights which the white man is bound to respect.' Compounding the controversy the decision was bound to create, Taney then went on to declare that Congress had acted improperly in prohibiting slavery in the new territories north of latitude 30° 30' back in 1820 because that deprived citizens of their property without due process of law.

Northern public opinion was stunned by the implications of the Dred Scott decision. What would now prevent the Supreme Court, acting at the behest of the 'slave power conspiracy,' from next deciding that the free states themselves had violated the rights of slave-owners, thus invalidating all state laws prohibiting slavery? Northerners saw themselves the victims of the aggressive expansionism of the South. Buchanan further antagonized the North by attempting to push through the admission of Kansas as a slave state, despite overwhelming evidence that the slave-owners had lost the race to populate the territory with their own supporters and that the great majority of Kansas residents wanted to enter the Union as a free state.

Abraham Lincoln, an Illinois lawyer and Whig politician who had served one term in Congress in the mid 1840s, cast his lot with the new Republican party. In 1858 he was nominated by Illinois Republicans as their candidate for the Senate. Lincoln, although not an abolitionist, made it clear in his acceptance speech that he despised the insti-

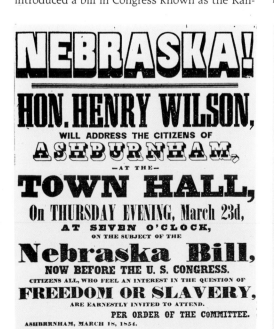

tution of slavery and hoped to see it die of natural causes: 'I believe this government cannot endure permanently half slave and half free.' Facing the architect of the Kansas-Nebraska Act in what came to be called the Lincoln-Douglas debates, he denounced the Dred Scott decision and challenged his unwilling opponent to do the same. Douglas straddled the issues raised by the decision, declaring in his debate with Lincoln in Freeport, Illinois, that the people of a territory could still effectively bar slavery by refusing to pass the 'local police regulations' necessary for the slave system to exist. Douglas's 'Freeport Doctrine' probably won the election for him in 1858, but it antagonized the South and thus gravely harmed his presidential prospects for 1860. Though Lincoln was the loser in the 1858 race, he emerged from it as the most eloquent Republican spokesman and a leading candidate for 1860 presidential nomination.

In October 1859 John Brown, already bloodied in the anti-slavery fight in Kansas, gathered 18 followers and invaded the South, hoping to spark an armed slave uprising. It was the nightmare that had haunted southerners since Nat Turner's day come to life. Brown seized the federal arsenal at Harpers Ferry, Virginia, but got no farther with his plan. Federal troops under the command of Robert E Lee besieged Brown's small force, and after an assault that killed 10 of Brown's men, he was compelled to surrender. Brown was a confused and arrogant man who may have been touched with madness and whose conspiracy never had a chance of achieving success in its immediate goal, but in facing the gallows with conspicuous courage and dignity Brown did the anti-slavery cause one last great service. The day of his execution was marked in many parts of the North as a day of mourning; it would not be long before soldiers would be heading south singing 'John Brown's Body lies a'mouldering in his grave/ His truth is marching on.'

Even before the start of the 1860 presidential election campaign, calls for secession were heard across the South, and some southern state legislatures passed bills increasing the size of their state militias. In the presidential campaign Southern Democrats refused to back Douglas and walked out of the convention that nominated him. They ran their own candidate, John C Breckinridge of Kentucky, on an outspoken pro-slavery platform. A group of Whigs and Know-Nothings who had not joined the Republicans formed their own party, the Constitutional Union party, and nominated John Bell of Tennessee as their presidential candidate. The Republicans nominated Lincoln. The Republicans easily overcame their divided opposition, and Lincoln was elected president in the most fateful election in the history of the United States.

Six weeks later an emergency convention called by the South Carolina state legislature met in Columbia, and without a single dissenting vote it passed a resolution declaring the state's secession from the Union. Ten other southern states followed South Carolina's example over the next two months. In February representatives from the seceding states met in Montgomery, Alabama, and established the Confederate states of America, electing Jefferson Davis their provisional President.

In the same two-month period militias seized control of federal arsenals and barracks across the South, and southern shore batteries fired on US naval ships to prevent them from bringing supplies and reinforcements to the federal garrison at Fort Sumter. When Lincoln was inaugurated in March he moved cautiously, asserting federal

Above: Abraham Lincoln, the Illinois railroad lawyer who became one of America's greatest presidents. His near-mystical devotion to the preservation of the Union, and his determination to prevail even in the dark days of failure in 1862, gave him the strengths he needed to prevail in the war with the rebellious southern states. Lincoln, as well as being a successful war leader, was also an expert politician, well served by a delightful sense of humor.

Left: A Confederate soldier, killed at his post. The Civil War is the great but unavoidable tragedy of American history. The determination of the southern states to preserve an archaic and immoral economic system cost the lives of over 600,000 Americans.

Above right: Three soldiers of a Michigan volunteer regiment. Both Confederate and Union armies were made up largely of nonprofessional soldiers.

authority but reassuring the South that he had no intention of interfering with slavery. Finally, in April, he notified the South Carolina authorities that an expedition would be sent to carry supplies to the Fort Sumter garrison. South Carolina forces demanded the surrender of the fort, and on 12 April fired on its defenders. Lincoln declared that a state of insurrection existed in the South and called for 75,000 volunteers to suppress it. The Civil War had begun.

The grapes of wrath

The American Civil War proved to be the first modern war. It did not simply pit opposing armies against one another: it was also a clash of two societies. It was a war in which the ability to mobilize the domestic economy became as important as the ability to lead armies, a war in which public opinion was an objective fought over as fiercely as any battlefield conflict.

The South had most of the best generals in the Civil War – Robert E Lee, Jeb Stuart, Stonewall Jackson – but they were the best generals for a different war than the one they wound up fighting. The Confederate generals won brilliant victories in the first year and a half of the war, but they failed to win a truly decisive victory. Given the unequal distribution of resources on the opposing sides, the only war that the South could conceivably have won was a short war. A decisive victory in 1861 or 1862 – the destruction of a major Union army in the field or the capture of Washington – might have persuaded northern public opinion that efforts to keep the South in the Union would be too costly. It might also have led to diplomatic recognition of the Confederacy from Britain.

For a while it looked as if everything was going to turn out the way the southern firebrands had predicted. Public attention in 1861 and 1862 was riveted on the front between Washington and Richmond. All the most famous and best-connected Union generals were posted to the Army of the Potomac, where they proved themselves hopelessly inferior to their Confederate opponents in the kind of chess-piece battles that they had both learned about at West Point. Many Washingtonians, with their families and friends, rode out in carriages from Washington to watch the rebels get beaten at the first Battle of Bull Run in July 1861; instead, they found themselves caught up in a panic-stricken rout of the Union forces, with one northern Congressman actually winding up a Confederate prisoner. In what proved to be a characteristic blunder committed by both sides in the first years of the war the Confederate army failed to follow up their victory with another attack, content instead to retain control of the battlefield and regroup.

By the second autumn of the war it was apparent that this was going to be a long and bloody conflict. The imbalance of population and resources guaranteed that the Confederates could only put off the final moment of defeat after failing to win in 1862. According to the 1860 census the states that would secede from the Union had a total population of 9 million (which included 4 million black slaves); the states that would remain in the Union had a total population of 22 million. The North had 10 times as many industrial workers as the South, and they produced 20 times as much iron and 32 times as many firearms as their southern counterparts. In 1860 the northern factories produced 24 times as many railroad locomotives as southern factories. Two-thirds of the nation's railroad track was located in the North. The northern railroads allowed Union generals to transport men and resources quickly to many different fronts, and the system proved relatively

invulnerable to southern attack. Southern railroads were less interconnected than the northern system, were thus less useful to Confederate generals and were more vulnerable to northern attack. Union forces crippled large portions of the system by capturing and destroying a few key railroad junctions such as Chattanooga in 1863 and Atlanta in 1864. Finally, and most surprisingly, the South could not even adequately feed itself. Southern agriculture was geared to staple production, mostly cotton, for export – northern agriculture far surpassed it in grain and livestock production before and during the war.

The Civil War was the first major war in which the rifle (not the musket) was the primary small-arm weapon of the infantry. The rifle greatly increased the range and accuracy of infantry fire, and later in the war the introduction of breech-loading and repeating rifles began to increase the rate of fire. With the introduction of the rifle, the advantage on the battlefield shifted from attack to defense. Cavalry attacks became obsolete, and attacks by infantry hideously expensive in lives. (The legendary Pickett's charge on entrenched Union defenders at Gettysburg cost the Confederate army 10,000 killed or wounded out of an attacking force of 15,000.) In the mass manufacture of these new weapons the industrial North again held the advantage.

In retrospect, it is easy to see that what the North had to do to win was to bankrupt the South in a war of attrition. But this was a new concept in 1861, and it took the Union several costly years to learn it.

At the start of the war Ulysses S Grant had been 'but an earnest business man.' He had attended West Point, where he proved a poor student, had briefly seen service in the Mexican War, had been stationed in a series of dreary military posts in Oregon and California (where he acquired his drinking habits) and finally, despairing of promotion, had left the army and gone to work in his father's leather goods store in Galena, Illinois. Like many retired officers, Grant was called back into military service in 1861. He was given command of a regiment of Illinois volunteers and sent to Missouri. This was not a choice post, since everyone assumed the decisive front would be the one on the Potomac. But the West proved to be a region of crucial strategic importance, where the war was fought for the control of rivers such as the Ohio, the Tennessee, the Cumberland and, most important, the Mississippi. Control of these rivers would allow the Union forces to split the Confederacy in two and ship men and supplies down into the heart of the deep South. In 1862 Grant's forces had pushed down the Tennessee. In the spring of 1863 they captured Vicksburg, the last great Confederate stronghold on the Mississippi, allowing Union forces pushing north from New Orleans to join with those pushing south along the river. Later that year, as newly appointed commander of all Union forces in the west, Grant turned back Confederate efforts to recapture Chattanooga, thus securing Tennessee for the Union.

At the same time that Grant was bringing the siege of Vicksburg to a close the South made its last great offensive effort in the East. Taking advantage of a brilliant victory over Union forces at Chancellorsville, Virginia, in May 1863, Lee launched a sudden large-scale attack through

Maryland into Pennsylvania, the disorganized Union troops pursuing him as best they could. Through most of June Lee's forces ran unchecked through southern Pennsylvania, and it was only at the beginning of July that the Union Army, now commanded by General George Meade, was again able to confront Lee in force at the crossroads town of Gettysburg. Lee quickly drove the Union troops out of Gettysburg itself but was then unable to dislodge them from a strong defensive position they had taken on a chain of ridges and hills south of the town. By the fourth day of the murderous battle (4 July) the Confederates had suffered nearly 30,000 casualties, and Lee had no choice but to lead his battered army back to Virginia, where for the remainder of the war it would be capable only of defensive operations.

Lincoln, repeatedly disappointed by his generals in the early years of the war, had liked what he had seen of Grant, and brought him east in 1864 as commander in chief. Grant then proceeded to outspend the South in blood. He sent William T Sherman marching from Tennessee across Georgia, and sent General Philip Sheridan into the Shenandoah Valley. Sherman's and Sheridan's armies made no attempt to occupy the territory they passed through (which would have tied up a large number of soldiers on garrison duty, vulnerable to Confederate counter-attack). Grant made it clear in letters written to his generals in August 1864 just what kind of war he expected them to fight. In a letter to Sheridan he wrote:

Do all the damage to railroads and crops you can. Carry off stock of all descriptions and negroes so as to prevent further plantings. If the war is to last another year we want the Shenandoah Valley to remain a barren waste.

And to Sherman he wrote: 'Every day exhausts the enemy at least a regiment without any further population to draw from to replace it... .' In carrying out Grant's directives, Sherman's troops looted and burned a 50-mile-wide swathe across Georgia. 'War is hell,' Sherman said later.

Grant had taken personal command of Union forces in northern Virginia in the spring of 1864 and met Lee's forces in a forest near Chancellorsville in what became known as the Battle of the Wilderness. It was an appalling slaughter, with troops from both sides confused and disorganized in the thick forest, sometimes firing on their own friends. At the end of the battle the Union had lost 17,000 killed and wounded and the Confederates 11,000. Earlier in the war that would have counted as a Confederate victory, and the Union forces would have pulled back to Washington to regroup. But now Grant gave the order to advance, and fought equally bloody battles at Spotsylvania and Cold Harbor. Grant was not blind to his own losses. He understood that the advantage in firepower had shifted to the defender, but he also understood that he could afford 'defeats' like Cold Harbor better than the South could afford such 'victories.' So it proved. Grant relentlessly hammered his way south toward the southern capital. The Confederates put up a desperate final stand at Petersburg, outside Richmond, and Grant was forced to besiege the place for months. But nothing could finally stop the Union meatgrinder. Petersburg fell, Richmond fell, and on 9 April 1865 Lee at last formally surrendered to Grant at Appomattox Court House. The collapse of the remaining southern military effort followed within the next few days. So ended by far the bloodiest war in all American history.

Grant had fought a grim, diligent and passionless war, a bookkeeper's war. He had fought the kind of war that reflected the society he represented, a war of mass armies and new technologies, one that dealt out death hugely and anonymously. The American Civil War thus offered a grim preview of the kind of war that would become all too familiar after 1914.

Lincoln had assured southerners in his inaugural address that he had no intention of interfering with slavery. He had led the nation into a war

fought initially for a purely conservative end: the restoration of the Union. But the logic of total war impelled him to define ever more radical war goals. Soon after Union forces entered the South escaped slaves began to flock to the Federal lines. Union commanders declared them to be contrabands of war, and refused to return them to their owners, arguing that their labor would only go to benefit the Confederate cause. By the midsummer of 1862 Lincoln was already considering issuing a proclamation freeing the slaves in the rebellious states (although not in the border states that remained loyal to the Union). On 22 September 1862 he issued his preliminary Emancipation Proclamation, declaring that as of 1 January of the following year all slaves in the areas controled by the Confederates would become free men. By 1863 former slaves from the South and free blacks from the North were serving in the Union Army, and 200,000 would serve in the Union Army before the war was over. Their service, and the desire of northerners to eradicate the causes of the war, led to Congressional approval of the Thirteenth Amendment to the Constitution early in 1865 which outlawed slavery throughout the country.

Lincoln had intended to offer white southerners conciliatory terms at the end of the war, making it relatively easy for the former Confederate states to reorganize their governments and send representatives to Washington as soon as 10 percent of the voting population had sworn an oath of allegiance to the Union and recognized the death of slavery. But Congress was never happy with Lincoln's plan, and his assassination by John Wilkes Booth on 14 April 1865 left the North in a vengeful mood.

The new President, Andrew Johnson, a former slave-owner and Democrat from Tennessee, tried to put Lincoln's conciliatory policies into effect. But the new state governments established under these policies angered the North by pushing through a series of laws known as the 'Black

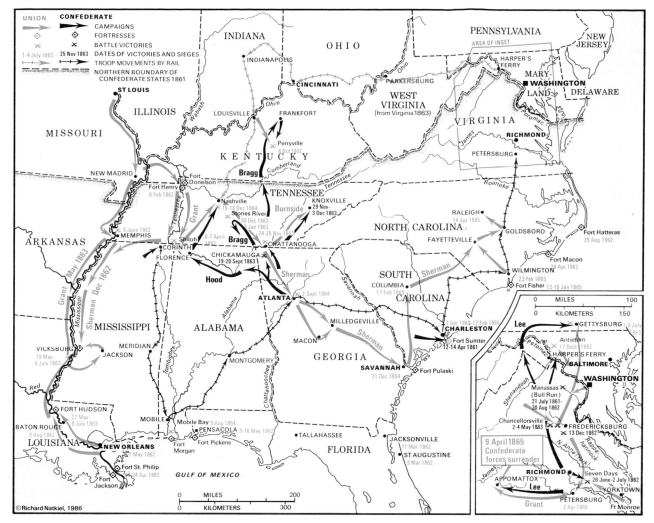

Left: A lithograph of the Battle of Bull Run, the first major action of the Civil War. Both sides were expecting a short war, one that would be settled after one or two big battles. But by the spring of 1862 it was apparent that the conflict would be long and costly.

Right: The Union strategy in the war determined the shape of its campaigns. The 'Anaconda Plan' envisaged seizing control of the Mississippi to divide the south, while in the east another army endeavored to capture Richmond. Once the Mississippi was in Union hands again, the southern heartland, around Atlanta, would be invaded. In the meantime a blockade would keep the southern states isolated.

Below: A lithograph showing the fall of Petersburg in 1865, an important rail center to the south of Richmond. The siege it ended was a part of Grant's two-year campaign in northern Virginia, which culminated in the fall of the Confederate capital in April 1865, shortly before the end of the war.

Codes' which were designed to circumvent the Thirteenth Amendment. The Mississippi Code, for example, required all blacks to possess each January written evidence of employment for the coming year. Laborers leaving their jobs before the contract expired would forfeit all wages earned up to that time. Any person offering work to a laborer already under contract could be fined or sent to jail. And so on and on. The Black Codes proved short-lived, but the fact of their passage was taken as a grave insult by the northern public. The *Chicago Tribune* declared in December 1865:

We tell the white men of Mississippi that the men of the North will convert the State of Mississippi into a frog pond before they will allow such laws to disgrace one foot of the soil in which the bones of our soldiers sleep and over which the flag of freedom waves.

Johnson's reconstruction plan would have increased the southern delegation in the House of Representatives by 13. Republicans in Congress refused to seat the first batch of Representatives sent up from the South and passed voting laws enfranchising the freed slaves while making it

more difficult for former supporters of the Confederacy to vote. With the new laws, and under the watchful eyes of the occupying federal troops and the newly established Freedmen's Bureau, blacks temporarily became a majority of the southern electorate – and, quite naturally, loyal Republicans. New state governments were organized, and new elections were held. This time the results were very different. Among the representatives sent to Washington from the former Confederate states over the next decade were fourteen black Congressmen and two black Senators.

The conflict between Johnson and the Radical Republicans in Congress dominated political life in Washington from 1865 to 1868. Congress eventually attempted to drive Johnson from office through impeachment, failing by only one vote in the Senate from achieving this goal. When Ulysses S Grant was elected President on the Republican ticket in 1868 it seemed to many in the North as if the victory of 1865 had finally been secured.

But northerners were divided over their vision of a 'reconstructed' South. Some wanted to see a genuine social revolution take place, with the land of the former slaveowners divided among the freedmen, with each family to receive 'forty acres and a mule.' But many others balked at the notion of confiscating private property. As the *New York Times* declared:

An attempt to justify the confiscation of Southern land under the pretense of doing justice to the freedmen strikes at the root of all property rights in both sections. It concerns Massachusetts quite as much as Mississippi.

White southerners found other ways to limit the effects of freedom for blacks without directly challenging the federal government. One was the covert use of terror tactics, best exemplified by the Ku Klux Klan, a paramilitary secret society organized in 1867. Thousands of blacks across the South in the 1860s and 1870s paid for their 'radicalism' with the loss of their property, livelihood and, in many instances, with their lives.

Before the Reconstruction era was a decade old the North had lost interest in claims of blacks. By 1876 Reconstruction governments, propped up by the bayonets of federal troops, remained in power in only two states, Louisiana and South Carolina. Everywhere else, through violence and intimidation and fraud, a sufficient number of black voters had been driven from the polls to allow whites to regain control. In the presidential election of 1876 the Republican candidate, Rutherford B Hayes, and the Democratic candidate, Samuel J Tilden, finished in a dead heat (Tilden gaining a slight majority in the popular vote, Hayes holding a one-vote margin in the electoral college, with 20 of the votes in the electoral college disputed). For three months after the election no one knew who would be the next president. Finally, a compromise was struck, in which a House-Senate-Supreme Court committee, with a one-vote Republican majority, was created to rule on the contested electoral votes: as expected they gave the election to Hayes.

By 24 April 1877 Hayes had withdrawn the remaining federal troops in South Carolina and Louisiana, the existing state governments soon

Above left: Union troops in trenches before the Virginian town of Petersburg in 1865. The American Civil War saw the use of conscription, trench warfare, railroads for troop movements and submarines, all regular features of twentieth-century conflicts. In some senses, it was the first modern 'conventional' war.

Far left: John Wilkes Booth, the assassin of Lincoln.

Left: The whites of the southern states were not inclined to encourage blacks to participate in elections. This cartoon shows a negro voter being forced to cast his ballot for anti-Reconstruction Democratic candidates.

Above right: An attack on Andrew Johnson's Reconstruction policies by the great political cartoonist Thomas Nast. Here he uses a Shakespearian theme, showing President Johnson as Iago poisoning the mind of Othello (in this case a Union veteran). Nast's own sympathies lay with the radical Republicans.

In 1837-38 separate anti-government revolts erupted in both Upper and Lower Canada, the former being led by a reformist member of the Upper Canadian legislature, William Lyon Mackenzie (grandfather of future Prime Minister Mackenzie King), and the latter by Louis Joseph Papineau, Speaker of the Lower Canadian Assembly. The British government was able to suppress both rebellions fairly easily, but it was disturbed by the outbreaks, and two years later John George Lambton, First Earl of Durham, submitted to the British Parliament a lengthy report on the situation in Canada that urged Parliament 'to follow out consistently the principles of the British constitution' so as to place 'the internal government of the colony in the hands of the colonists themselves.'

A first step toward realizing this goal was made the following year, 1840, when Parliament passed the Act of Union joining Upper and Lower Canada (now called Canada West and Canada East) into a single administrative entity known as the United Provinces of Canada. Responsible self-government, however, came more slowly, and such progress as was made in the next 25 years was due largely to the efforts of a group of reformers in the legislature – Louis LaFontaine of Canada East for example, and Robert Baldwin and Francis Hincks of Canada West – which was ultimately to form the basis of Canada's Liberal Party.

Toward nationhood

Canada was still not a nation, only a string of provinces in the East and largely the Hudson's Bay Company's domain in the West. It had no constitution and no common government to foster needed economic projects such as the building of canals and railroads; and even in the United Provinces the rivalry between the Canada East and Canada West factions had become so pronounced as to threaten the breakdown of the provincial government. The need for confederation was becoming increasingly obvious to many Canadian political leaders, and particularly to John A Macdonald, head of Canada West's Liberal-Conservative Party, who by the 1860s had become the foremost apostle of union.

Macdonald's tireless advocacy was at last rewarded in 1867 when Parliament passed the British North American Act confederating the Canadian provinces under a constitution modeled on that of the United Kingdom. The autonomy of the new national government was greatly extended, while at the same time every effort was made to protect the sovereignty of provincial legislatures in matters of local interest. Appropriately, the man named to be the first prime minister of the new nation was John Macdonald, and he was to continue to serve in that capacity – with a single interruption between 1873 and 1878 – until 1891. Indeed, Macdonald was the dominant voice in Canadian politics during the late nineteenth century.

During the first period of Macdonald's ministry the Union grew rapidly in size. In 1869 the crown turned over to the national government both the extensive western areas formerly controled by the Hudson's Bay Company and the North-West Territories. In 1871 British Columbia agreed to enter the Union, largely on the strength of Macdonald's promise to build a transcontinental railroad (a promise that would be redeemed in 1885 with the completion of the Canadian Pacific Railway). By 1873, when Macdonald's Conservative government was temporarily replaced by that of Liberal Alexander Mackenzie, Canada was on the brink of a new era of consolidation and economic growth; the future seemed full of promise.

fell and Reconstruction came to an end. The Civil War had secured the Union, settled long-standing sectional grievances and constitutional disputes and had ended slavery. But the question that the war and the Reconstruction era did not resolve, of whether or not blacks and whites should be guaranteed equal rights as citizens, would return to haunt later generations of Americans.

The Canadian way

Compared to the traumas suffered by the United States in its grueling efforts to deal with the problem of slavery and to secure the Union, Canada's progress toward self-government, confederation, social justice and economic well-being seems a model of peace and order. Yet here, too, there were difficulties to be overcome and conflicts to be resolved

By the beginning of the nineteenth century most Canadians, though loyal colonists, were united in their desire to be granted more local autonomy. But what form such autonomy might take was a vexed question, since the provinces were far from united in their outlooks and interests. The sharpest division existed between the two major eastern provinces, Upper Canada (Ontario), the population of which was overwhelmingly British in origin, and French-dominated Lower Canada (Quebec), in which ethnic Britons represented only about 20 percent of the population. Understandably, the Lower Canadians were leery of any development that would have the effect of subordinating their interests to an ethnically British majority. Both provinces, as well as the Maritime Provinces, had enjoyed substantial increases in population as the result of a rising tide of immigration after 1815, and though by the early 1830s agitation for self-government had succeeded in winning a few scattered concessions from the crown in Nova Scotia and New Brunswick, no real progress had been made in this direction.

North America: 1877-1917

The Civil War and its aftershocks had been convulsive, but they had not shaken America's ideals or assumptions and certainly had not damaged its business. When Rutherford B Hayes came to the White House in 1876, the Gilded Age was in full cry: industry, and especially the railroad industry, was creating a class of industrial tycoons who represented a new kind of political and economic power.

A moderate Republican with no inclination for boat-rocking of any sort, Hayes nonetheless could not avoid the most pressing governmental task at hand: reform of the civil service. Trying to secure a merit-based system of appointments to replace the corrupt spoils system that had filled government offices since Jackson's day, Hayes removed Chester A Arthur from the profitable post of customs inspector in New York. But the effort backfired, serving only to divide the Republican Party. Hayes declined to run in 1880, and a Republican convention bitterly split between reformist 'Half-Breeds' and status-quo 'Stalwarts' settled on Ohio's James A Garfield as a compromise candidate. To appease the Stalwarts, spoilsman Chester A Arthur was chosen the vice-presidential nominee. The ticket won the election, but in July 1881 Garfield was fatally shot in Washington by crazed Stalwart office-seeker Charles Guiteau. Now it was to be Arthur, of all people, who was to carry the banner of civil service reform. In 1883 he signed the landmark Pendleton Act, which established the Civil Service Commission to enforce merit-based appointments.

In the election of 1884 Grover Cleveland swept into the presidency on a rising tide of Democratic strength, a major factor in his election being a number of liberal Republicans, called 'Mugwumps,' who had bolted their party to vote for a reformer. From the outset Cleveland had to wage a relentless battle with the spoils-dispensing political machines of the big cities, which were already trying to undermine the reformist spirit that had produced the new civil service law. An equally bitter battle arose over control of land in the West. The Army had largely completed its suppression of the Indians, who were being herded into reservations and forced to become small farmers. Immense stretches of former Indian lands were now open to white settlement, and power struggles raged. By the 1880s much of the West was controlled by cattle kings, timber barons, land syndicates, mining corporations and the big railroads, with a resulting system of land monopolies. Cleveland lambasted the 'colossal greed' of these exploiters and took from them over 80 million acres; in his second administration he would begin the process of establishing national forests.

Popular though the President was in his first term, mainstream political opinion in Cleveland's era was largely *laissez-faire* in economics, antiunion and anti-reform. Scholars and businessmen alike proclaimed the doctrine of Social Darwinism, which pictured life as a vast struggle in which the race rightly went to the strong and the weak were rightly condemned to fall by the wayside. This philosophy made of *laissez-faire* capitalism an immutable natural law – cruel, perhaps, but the only road to evolutionary progress. It was a theory that was most comforting to the big winners in capitalism, and they were winning big. By 1904, two percent of the population would hold 60 percent of the nation's wealth.

What made such concentration of wealth possible was that in postwar years a new kind of business organization had evolved. It began when owners of railroad lines in various states agreed to create central offices to set rates and control oper-

ation. From their experience with these 'pools,' businessmen saw how centralization could skyrocket efficiency, profit and competitive power. Thus in 1879 a group of small refineries joined to form the Standard Oil Company: the stock of the formerly competing firms was put into the hands of a single board of trustees headed by John D Rockefeller, who thereby controled up to 95 percent of the nation's refining capacity. This was the first of the great organizations – variously called trusts, combinations or monopolies – that were to dominate American business into the next century. Thanks to overlapping directorships, they concentrated economic power in the hands of a remarkably small group of men; financier J P Morgan, for example, was a trustee of dozens of such combinations. As the trusts overwhelmed smaller companies and suppressed competition both labor and liberals in and out of government became increasingly alarmed. In 1882 President Cleveland secured bills outlawing pools and establishing the Interstate Commerce Commission to oversee railroad rates. Though a conservative Supreme Court soon hamstrung the Commission, it was the harbinger of many government regulatory agencies to come, the first real step away from *laissez-faire*.

Another major thrust of Cleveland's program concerned tariffs. Big business had perennially demanded high protective tariffs, but now Cleveland, with labor's support, made a major push to lower them. That proved to be his undoing, for Congress refused to back Cleveland's tariff reform, and the next election was won by business-supported Republican Benjamin Harrison.

President Harrison signed the high-tariff bill of Congressman William McKinley in 1890, saying cavalierly that even though it would raise prices,

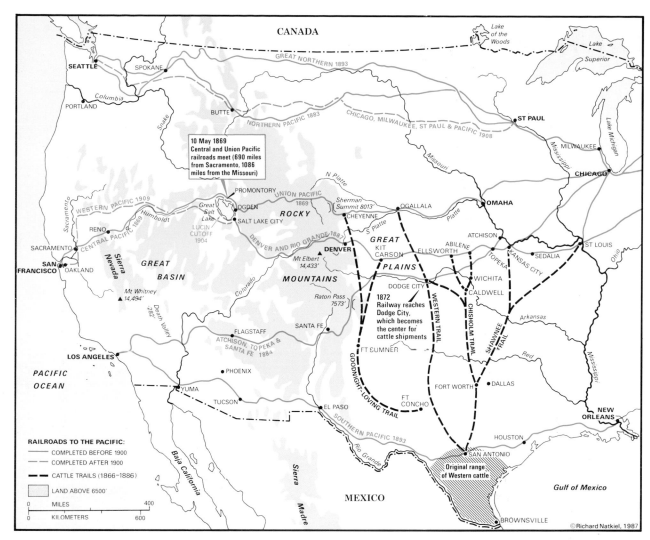

Left: The *eminence grise* of American capitalism, J P Morgan. His investment bank, the Morgan Bank, was an important force behind the growing control by the trusts of the American economy in the nineteenth century's last 25 years.

Below left: The Illinois Central Railroad advertises its services in this 1882 poster. In the 1870s the railroads had effectively come together in a cartel that set prices and rates without regard to their market value. The creation of the Interstate Commerce Commission went a little way toward ending this unfair gouging.

Right: The opening of the West was largely achieved by the railroads. The incentive they were offered and gladly took was rights to vast tracts of land along their routes.

Below: John D Rockefeller headed the Standard Oil Trust and built up an enormous fortune through his control of the nation's oil refining and distribution capacity.

Below right: Rockefeller takes his daily dose of oil. Nearby stands the University of Chicago, which he funded, waiting for its share.

'cheaper coats necessarily [involve] a cheaper man and woman under the coats.' Immediately, labor and reformers rose up in fury against the McKinley Tariff. Trying to placate that unrest and responding to popular sentiment against monopolies, Harrison signed the Sherman Anti-Trust Act, which forbade trusts outright; but the monopolists were able easily to outflank the law, and the courts were hostile to it.

The Democrats were able to ride the tariff issue back into the White House in 1890, and Grover Cleveland was re-elected by a landslide. He was then at the peak of his popularity; but the strains of the industrial age had reached a critical point, and the times had changed more than had Cleveland. His second term was a troubled one.

The labor movement

In the 1890s the rich of the Gilded Age had never lived higher, and their consumption had never been more conspicuous. The kings of postwar Wall Street were a new kind of aristocracy – raw, arrogant, insatiably acquisitive and wielding immense political power at both local and federal levels. The majority of Americans regarded the monopolists with distrust, tinged inescapably with envy. Many still believed in the old idea that opportunity in America was unlimited for everyone, but in a time when business was increasingly controled by vast, impersonal corporations there seemed to be less and less room for individual initiative. Industrial laborers, particularly, felt themselves victimized by the growing power of new capitalists, and they had learned to despair of receiving any meaningful relief from Washington. Inevitably they began to turn to self-help.

Organized labor was a novelty in America, and there was no developed consensus about where the right to strike stood in relation to the rights of property. Labor's first experiences with its assertion of the right to strike were violent: a widespread railroad strike in 1877 left hundreds dead and millions of dollars worth of property destroyed. Earlier, in 1869, the Knights of Labor had been founded. This first major national union was comparatively moderate, urging such reforms as cooperative ownership, trust regulation, an eight-

Left: A cartoon warns of the power of the labor leader Terence Powderly. His Knights of Labor, the first major American working-men's organization, first emerged in the public eye in 1877, during a fractious railroad strike.

Below left: An Idaho homestead carved from virgin forest. In the West the land was divided between the huge corporations in control of the railroads, and the smallholding farmers like this family.

Right: The completion of the Canadian Pacific Railway, at Eagle Pass, British Columbia. While the construction of a transcontinental railroad in the United States had been accompanied by savage Indian wars, in the Canadian west the great feat was accomplished in far more peaceful conditions.

Below right: The Yukon gold rush of the 1890s was the last big mining spree in North American history. Thousands of adventurers flocked to Klondike in search of gold.

hour workday and prohibition of child labor. But as strikes multiplied, radical anarchists and Socialist movements also appeared. In May 1886 police trying to break up an anarchist rally in Chicago's Haymarket Square were met by a bomb that killed seven policemen and injured 70. After the ensuing trial, four men were hanged and four imprisoned on circumstantial evidence; the real bomber was never identified.

The Haymarket Riot and trial further polarized the country, producing more strikes and riots on one side and more employer and government

repression on the other. Tainted by the violence, the Knights of Labor dissolved in the 1890s, their place taken by the even more moderate and effective labor union called the American Federation of Labor. Under the leadership of immigrant Samuel Gompers, the AFl disavowed Socialist solutions and concentrated with increasing success on non-violent strikes and collective bargaining.

The nation's social and economic unrest was intensified by the financial Panic of 1893. In short order thousands of American banks and businesses folded and the stock market crashed, initiating a severe depression. Labor was desperate; in 1894 there were some 1400 strikes, most of them failures. In April of that year Jacob S Coxy marched an 'army' of unemployed workers from Ohio to Washington to demand government help. Despite cheering crowds, Coxy and his men were arrested – for walking on the grass – and jailed. Several similar 'armies' marched, but Cleveland did not respond. When the militant American Railway Union responded to wage cuts by striking against the Pullman railroad-car company, Cleveland sent troops to Chicago to crush the strike and imprison its leader, Eugene V Debs. (During his months in jail Debs became a Socialist and thereafter led the party for decades, running four times for President.)

Alienated from business and labor alike and unable to effect significant tariff reduction, Cleveland had a disastrous second term. He tried to alleviate the depression in 1895 by turning to J P Morgan and his associates for a loan to stop the depletion of gold reserves. Labor was far from reassured to see Wall Street financiers bailing out the United States Treasury.

The Populists

The first large political movement to respond to the problems created by industrialism, and the first to insist that these problems were the concern of government, was the Populist Party, formed in 1892 from various agrarian movements

plus a contingent of labor. The Populists nominated James A Weaver for President with a platform calling for free coinage of silver, government ownership of transportation and communications services, a graduated income tax, direct election of Senators, the secret ballot, shorter working hours and ballot initiatives and referendums. Weaver took 8.5 percent of the vote in 1892. Yet though their party soon withered, the Populists were a decisive influence on the nation for many years; most of their platform of 1892 was, sooner or later, to become law.

Farmers had been the heart of the Populist Party and thus its main power lay in the Midwest and the South, where farms had been stricken by droughts in the late 1880s, and by the shrinking money supply. Convinced that the government's insistence on the gold standard kept money tight and farm prices low, the new party had crusaded above all for free coinage of silver. The notion that this would increase the money supply and help farmers was dubious economics, but it was widely believed.

Leading the silver bloc in Congress was a Jeffersonian Democrat named William Jennings Bryan. Speaking at the Chicago Democratic Convention of 1896, Bryan leaped into history: 'Upon which side will the Democratic Party fight, upon the side of "the idle holders of idle capital," or upon the side of "the struggling masses"? . . . We will answer their demands for a gold standard by saying to them: "You shall not press down upon the brow of labor this crown of thorns, you shall not crucify mankind upon a cross of gold!"' The delegates went wild, and Bryan had the nomination. Soon he gained the endorsement of the Populists as well. For two decades thereafter, the passionate reformer, dubbed 'The Great Commoner,' would lead the Democrats.

But despite herculean campaigning, Bryan did not win the election of 1896 (nor did he win in two later tries). The election went to genial, avuncular William McKinley, author of the McKinley Tariff and another business-backed Republican who had been carefully groomed by party kingmaker Mark Hanna. After years of unrest and failed solutions Americans had decided to vote for a man who wanted to stimulate business. Once in office McKinley signed an unprecedentedly high tariff and the Gold Standard Act, which put the nation firmly on the gold standard. And such measures seemed to be working; for there was a return to prosperity during McKinley's first term. Nevertheless, those years, so comfortable on the sur-

face, were breeding a great many new problems and new approaches to solving them.

During the same period Canada was entering a similar time of prosperity, though the country was still divided by the old quarrels of French and British populations. The 1880s saw the completion of the Canadian Pacific Railway; two other major lines would be completed in the next decades, all of them contributing to westward expansion. In 1896 the Liberals, under French Canadian leader Wilfrid Laurier, came to power after long Conservative – and Anglo – rules; the Klondike gold rush and further mining strikes followed to initiate an economic and population boom that would continue under Laurier's regime well into the next century.

The rise of the cities

In the 1880s alone over 100 American cities doubled (at least) in size. In 1890 a third of the population lived in towns and cities; by 1920 over half did. Many of the new city-dwellers were foreign, part of two great waves of immigration that followed the Civil War. Some 15 million arrived between 1890 and 1920, most of them Eastern and Southern European, to join the Irish, Germans and Scandinavians who had preceded

them. The new immigrants tended not to assimilate at first, but rather to form ethnic enclaves within the cities, each with its own culture, industry and predominant language.

Immigrants naturally tended to be parochial, rather than national, in political outlook. Inexperienced in the ways of democracy, they were easy prey for the local political bosses. In return for votes the boss and his machine would provide jobs and services; if the boss happened to be on the take, as many of them were, the immigrant was not likely to make a fuss.

The urban political machines were typically Democratic and Irish, led by bosses such as William Marcy Tweed and Richard Croker in New York. Since success within the machine had little to do with ability and everything to do with connections, city governments ranged from the merely inefficient to the spectacularly corrupt. Profiting as they did from graft and crime, machines were also highly resistant to reform. The result was that most large American cities at the end of the nineteenth century were overcrowded and disastrously managed. Slums grew like a cancer, marked by heaps of garbage, shabby tenements, disease and crime.

Many old-stock Protestant Americans were fearful of the hoards of strange-speaking Catholic and Jewish populations who filled the crumbling tenements of the cities. That fear was intensified by the new ideas the immigrants brought with them. Most of the Marxist, Socialist and anarchist groups rose from the ethnic communities, and they were a major part of the labor movement as well. The darker side of Populism was a jingoistic resentment of foreigners; in the 1890s a wave of 'Americanism' swept the country, many Populists joining the Ku Klux Klan in denouncing Catholics and Jews.

One of the more important reform movements that was to help ameliorate the decay of American cities arose in 1889, for in that year social worker Jane Addams founded Hull House in Chicago. That and the scores of similar settlement houses that sprouted around the country were refuges, schools and social centers for the underprivileged. These centers not only improved the lives of countless poor, but also became a training ground and laboratory for a new generation of women social workers and theorists. In her career and in her writings, Addams was a vital counterforce to

prevailing attitudes derived from Social Darwinism, convincing Americans that the good society came not from the survival of the fittest but from collective responsibility, compassion and social action. She was one of the founders and shapers of the Progressive movement, and her labors were crowned by the Nobel Peace Prize in 1931.

Imperial America

Internal issues dominated American life and government in the last decades of the nineteenth century: civil service reform, farm problems, the tariff, the struggle between business and labor. But in the prosperity that followed the Panic of 1893 the US turned its attention to the question of its relations with the rest of the world.

Traditionally, agrarian America had been both isolationist and anti-colonialist. But now some American leaders began echoing European ideas, preaching that it was the 'white man's burden' to drag 'lesser' peoples into modern civilization, by force if necessary. Among the most ardent of these neo-imperialists was Senator Henry Cabot Lodge, who strongly urged the need for an American hegemony in the Pacific and Caribbean.

His younger friend Theodore Roosevelt enthusiastically agreed.

The government had indeed moved in the direction of imperialism in the last two decades of the century, wrangling with Germany over Samoa, threatening war with Italy and Chile, and gearing up to annex Hawaii. Like most liberal Democrats, Grover Cleveland deplored imperialism, believing that the ideas of equality and democracy applied to relations among nations as well as peoples. Paradoxically, however, it was President Cleveland who started the ball rolling toward an American empire. In 1895, alarmed by an apparent British land grab in Venezuela, he sternly invoked the Monroe Doctrine to the British: 'Today the United States is practically sovereign on the continent, and its fiat is law.' When Britain did not respond, Cleveland presented a virtual threat of war. The British were stunned and hastened to back off, but a good many Americans in and out of government saluted Cleveland's challenge with jingoistic cheers.

Americans had never looked kindly on the persistence of Spanish rule over the island of Cuba,

where America had extensive business interests and bought most of the sugar crop. In 1895 Spain sent 120,000 men to put down a massive rebellion in Cuba. These troops made little progress, but the campaign was brutal in the extreme, and the killing aroused both humanitarian and imperialist sentiment in the US. The 'yellow press' of William Randolph Hearst began calling stridently for war.

New President McKinley was not inclined to such adventures, and he tried mediation in Cuba with some initial success. But as conditions again deteriorated, more Americans jumped on the interventionist bandwagon; assistant Navy secretary Theodore Roosevelt chafed for 'a bit of a spar' with Spain. Then, on 15 February 1898, while riding at anchor in Havana harbor, the armored cruiser USS *Maine* mysteriously exploded and sank, with a loss of 260 men. Many agreed with Roosevelt that 'The *Maine* was sunk by an act of dirty treachery on the part of the Spaniards.'

No investigation ever assigned definite blame for the sinking but the American public was enraged. McKinley desperately tried more negotiation and Spain was conciliatory, but on 11 April the President gave in to public pressure and asked Congress for authority to intervene on behalf of Cuban independence. Congress eagerly assented.

Roosevelt had already secretly ordered Admiral Dewey's Far Eastern squadron to sail toward the Spanish-controlled Philippines, with orders to attack the enemy fleet there as soon as war was declared. In battle on 1 May Dewey sank every Spanish ship in Manila Bay, with total American losses of eight wounded, and US troops then occupied Manila. American forces began landing in Cuba on 10 June; with the First Volunteer Cavalry came Lieutenant Colonel Theodore Roosevelt, who had helped raise the regiment to fulfill his dream of being a soldier.

The American troops proved to be poorly organized, equipped, fed and led, but Spanish forces were even more so and retreated steadily. On 1 July, at El Caney, 6653 US troops overwhelmed 600 enemy. That same day American troops stormed a key Spanish defensive position on San Juan Hill, northeast of Santiago, and routed the Spanish (at a cost of 1572 American casualties). Victory was ensured in July, when US Navy ships destroyed another Spanish fleet off Cuba. Santiago fell two weeks later. Meanwhile, other American forces had occupied Spanish Guam, in the Pacific, and part of Puerto Rico in the Caribbean. On 26 July 1898 Spain requested

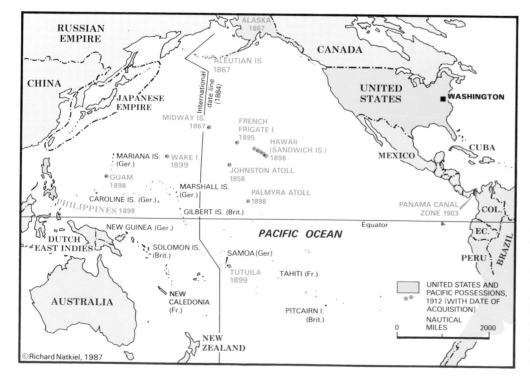

©Richard Natkiel, 1987

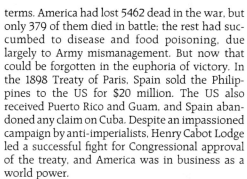

terms. America had lost 5462 dead in the war, but only 379 of them died in battle; the rest had succumbed to disease and food poisoning, due largely to Army mismanagement. But now that could be forgotten in the euphoria of victory. In the 1898 Treaty of Paris, Spain sold the Philippines to the US for $20 million. The US also received Puerto Rico and Guam, and Spain abandoned any claim on Cuba. Despite an impassioned campaign by anti-imperialists, Henry Cabot Lodge led a successful fight for Congressional approval of the treaty, and America was in business as a world power.

Immediately after the war, the dilemmas of that power became manifest. After long preparation, Congress voted to annex Hawaii in 1900, an act that severely irritated Japan. But the major question facing the whole administration was what to do in the Philippines, where rebels who had fought the Spanish alongside the US had now turned their independence struggle against America. Was the United States going to become the new oppressor? Said the American Anti-Imperialist League: 'We denounce the slaughter of the Filipinos as a needless horror. We protest against the extension of American sovereignty by Spanish methods.' But despite a wave of such protests, McKinley, after much indecision and earnest prayer, decided that the Filipinos were 'unfit for self-government' and that he would suppress rebellion. It took three years and 120,000 soldiers

to mop up all the guerrillas, and the fighting was as barbaric as any Americans had seen.

Now imperialism was ascendant. All the sentiment was militant, most of it unashamedly racist. In this spirit, the country moved quickly over the next years to assert its power. McKinley proclaimed an 'open door' policy toward China; the European imperial powers and Japan supported the policy, which guaranteed equal trading opportunities to all and prevented China from being carved up into competing colonies. In effect, the 'open door' asserted virtual external control of the helpless giant.

At the end of 1899 the US and Germany ended a long dispute over Samoa by dividing up the islands, and American Samoa soon became a major naval base. A few months later violence flared in China when a native group calling themselves the 'righteous harmony fists' – dubbed 'Boxers' in the West – attempted to expel foreigners. The Boxer Rebellion was put down by US, British, French and Japanese troops, but not before some 231 Westerners and many Chinese Christians had been killed by the insurgents.

At the 1900 Republican Convention McKinley was renominated, but former Vice-President Garret A Hobart was replaced on the ticket by now-New York Governor, Spanish-American War hero and vigorous imperialist Theodore Roosevelt. Roosevelt's place on the ticket was secured despite kingmaker Mark Hanna, who protested,

'Don't you realize that there's only one life between that madman and the Presidency?' The fears of Hanna and other conservative Republicans were realized on 6 September 1901, when at the Pan-American Exposition in Buffalo, McKinley was shot and fatally wounded by anarchist Leon Czolgosz.

Theodore Roosevelt seized the reins of power with a firm hand and galloped off in every direction. Among his first enthusiasms was a long-planned isthmian canal in Panama to expedite the passage of shipping between the oceans. A treaty with co-planner Britain had settled that America would build the canal but had guaranteed it would be neutral; indirectly, the treaty also implied American control of the Caribbean. There remained the problem of how to effect such a gigantic project on foreign soil; Panama was then under control of Colombia, which was holding out for more money. This did not please Roosevelt. Since his diplomatic philosophy was the West African proverb, 'Speak softly and carry a big stick, and you will go far,' he contemplated invading Panama. But soon he found a better way to get his canal. In November 1903, a group of Panamanians revolted against Colombia, with Roosevelt's secret encouragement. With the presence of American warships to back them up, the rebels achieved a quick and relatively peaceful takeover. The US recognized the new government within hours. Though some in America called Roosevelt's

machinations 'piracy,' the Panama deal was widely approved. Congress gave Panama $10 million, plus a yearly stipend, for a ten-mile strip of land astride the canal, which would remain under American sovereignty. Roosevelt's 'big-stick diplomacy' had scored a major victory; construction began on the canal in 1904, and the monumental job was finished in 1914.

The President formalized America's new position in the world with what came to be called the Roosevelt Corollary to the Monroe Doctrine: 'Chronic wrongdoing, or . . . a general loosening of the ties of a civilized society, may . . . require intervention by some civilized nation, and in the Western Hemisphere the adherence of the United States to the Monroe Doctrine may force the United States . . . in flagrant cases of such wrongdoing or impotence, to the exercise of an international police power.' Roosevelt thereby made the US the policeman of the Americas, paving the way for future American interventions.

Soon after, he mediated the end of the Russo-Japanese War and agreed to Japanese hegemony in Manchuria, which certified Japan as a world power. After an ambitious buildup of naval forces,

Roosevelt capped off his big-stick diplomacy by sending the new 'Great White Fleet' of warships around the world to demonstrate that the United States was a very well-equipped international policeman.

The Progressive Movement

In the years between the Civil War and the new century, the United States had undergone profound changes: from an agrarian toward an industrial and urban society, from small businesses to giant corporations, from a homogeneous population to a melting pot of nationalities, from an isolationist country to an imperial power. The pace of change had long since outstripped the mechanisms of control, and widespread suffering and discontent were the result. Since neither of the two major political parties seemed able to produce programs capable of coping with the new socio-economic problems, a powerful extra-party reformist movement began to take shape. Though many-faceted, it is remembered in history as the Progressive Movement.

The problem of defining Progressive and who the Progressives were has provoked a longstanding debate among scholars. Douglas Hofstadter has placed the thrust of the movement in the educated middle class and the old aristocracy, liberal Republicans displaced by the rise of monopolists, urban machines and immigrants, who made a bid to restore their status and power and ideals. Other scholars, however, have argued that Progressivism was much more broadly based and was composed of many unlikely allies at various times and places, sometimes including even city machines and big business. In fact, it does seem to have enfolded a wide spectrum of Americans in the first part of the twentieth century, transcending lines of party, class, region and religion. Each faction had its own agenda and philosophy, but the overall direction pointed toward government regulation of business, political and economic reform and the expansion of state-supported welfare measures.

The theoretical foundations of the Progressive movement were laid by several somewhat different writers and thinkers of the 1880s and 90s. Lester Ward's book *Dynamic Sociology* was a direct attack on conservative Social Darwinism. Against the idea of society as an impersonal struggle for survival, Ward insisted that society could and must control its own evolution. His new interpretation of Darwinism was pragmatic and activist: 'Individual freedom can only come through social regulation.' Among the first of his disciples was Jane Addams, who began the settlement-house movement.

Then there was crusty, vituperative Thorstein Veblen, who, in his *Theory of the Leisure Class*, trained his formidable intellectual guns on the wealthy. Capitalistic business, he wrote, is not a matter of rational calculation but rather reflects primitive instincts for dominance and display. The lower classes want only to produce, the predatory upper classes want only to get rich and the result is a savage social conflict.

This pragmatic approach to life and its challenges was the primary theme of the philosopher William James. Attacking mechanistic Social Darwinism from another angle, James exalted free will and a flexible response to ever-changing realities. Truth, he said, is not an absolute but is continually in the making, and we must be skeptical, creative and experimental to keep up with it. His 1907 book, *Pragmatism*, became a sort of bible for many Progressives. James's philosophical heir, John Dewey, concentrated on how education and social action could attack social ills.

Among this pathbreaking community of scholars was Woodrow Wilson, who in his Princeton lectures on Constitutional Government defined the philosophical split between the old America and the new: 'The government of the United States was constructed on . . . a sort of unconscious copy of the Newtonian [mechanical] theory of the universe . . . The trouble with this theory is that government is not a machine, but a living thing . . . It is accountable to Darwin, not to Newton. It is modified by its environment, necessitated by its tasks, shaped to its functions by the sheer pressure of life.'

A pragmatic and compassionate approach to life and its sufferings; a critical view of excessive wealth and power; the idea that government must change to respond to the times; a belief in humane evolution: these ideas inspired the new era. In their ways and means, however, the Progressives showed themselves as inclined to factions and cross-purposes as any other political movement.

Theodore Roosevelt was himself an example of one faction. An aristocrat by birth, he had a typically Republican vision of American society,

Left: Abattoirs in the city of Chicago. By 1877 the Midwestern metropolis had surpassed Britain's Manchester as the greatest industrial city in the world.

Below left: The slums of New York were the sorry home for many hopeful immigrants from Europe. Most of the big American cities packed their new arrivals into disease-ridden, fire-prone districts, which amazingly were still some improvement over the housing they had left behind.

Right: Upton Sinclair, the radical novelist, whose works revealed to their middle-class readers the sordid realities of American working-class life.

Below: Theodore Roosevelt, the most energetic president since Lincoln. He found useful political allies in the Progressive Movement, and did much to further their aims in return.

managerial experts. Results were ambivalent: government became more impersonal and tended to land in the hands of the upper class, but at the same time cities became on the whole less corrupt and more efficient. Cities increasingly started to clean up the slums, to enact public health measures and to build municipally owned services to provide water, gas and electricity. By 1910 urban life was improving nationwide.

At the federal level, President Roosevelt tried to fulfill his promise of a 'square deal' to all the people, threading a middle path between business and labor. His attitude toward the latter had elements of patrician paternalism, but he was well aware of the crushing conditions many workers endured in those times, when 16-hour days in miserable and dangerous conditions were not unusual. Thus, within limits, TR saw labor unions as a natural response to the power of employers. In 1902 Pennsylvania coal miners struck to protest pay and working conditions. One of the owners responded imperiously, 'The rights and interests of the laboring man will be protected and cared for – not by the labor agitators, but by the Christian men whom God in His infinite wisdom has given the control of the property interests of the country.' (In a similar vein, other owners bestowed the grace of God on children working all day in mills.) Disgusted by the arrogance of the mine owners, TR pulled both sides into the White House for arbitration, and the workers emerged with a raise. It was the first time a President had intervened on the side of labor, and labor was properly grateful – though still inclined to vote Democratic.

Roosevelt won easily in the 1904 election and went on to greater activism. In 1906 he signed the Hepburn Act, which increased the size and power of the Interstate Commerce Commission and gave it, for the first time, the right to fix railroad rates. Though the Act had serious flaws, it was a historic start toward significant government control of public services. (On the other hand, after a stock-market panic in 1907, Roosevelt allowed US Steel, an archetypal monopoly, to acquire the Tennessee Coal and Iron Company.) The administration responded to years of public health abuses by passing the Pure Food and Drug Act and the Meat Inspection Act, which went to dispose of quack medicines and clean up the stockyard conditions that Upton Sinclair had exposed in *The Jungle*. Apparently forgiving the muckrakers, Roosevelt wrote to Sinclair promising 'radical' action against 'the effects of arrogant and selfish greed on the part of the capitalist.'

In both his terms conservation was high on Roosevelt's agenda. The West especially had been ravaged by over-cutting of timber, and irrigation programs were desperately needed. The brilliant, aristocratic forester Gifford Pinchot became the czar of the nation's conservation program. In his government career Pinchot expanded the national forests from 46 to 200 million acres and headed TR's Forest Service and the National Conservation Commission. The latter, founded in 1908, organized important studies of the nation's water, soil and forest resources.

Much to his regret, Roosevelt had earlier pledged not to run in 1908, so in that election the Republican standard was carried by his chosen successor, William Howard Taft, a judge, former governor of the Philippines and Secretary of War from 1904 to 1908. Taft soundly defeated William Jennings Bryan, who had come to seem a ranting old Populist to many voters, too pious for some and too radical for others. (Bryan had applauded most of TR's reforms, saying only that they did not go far enough.) Once in office, however, the

one in which a strong, centralized government in the hands of an educated elite would mediate between the demands of business and labor. By attacking corruption and corporate greed Roosevelt wanted not only economic justice but to save capitalism from the threat of socialism.

The trusts were among the major targets of any reform agenda. As his tool to chasten them, President Roosevelt revived the moribund Sherman Anti-Trust Act, using it in 1902 to prosecute the Northern Securities Company, a railroad monopoly. He won that case and initiated some 40 others. An observer of the time noted that big business was scandalized to find that the President would stoop so low as to enforce the law. By no means, however, was 'TR' anti-business or even anti-trust; he intended only to curb the worst abuses, saying 'Draw the limit on conduct, not on size.' Even though TR was dubbed a 'trust-buster,' his successor Taft was far more active in prosecutions.

The fact that TR was a Progressive over a deeper layer of old-Yankee Republican explains some of his apparent contradictions. For example, when a number of reporters trained their sights on some of the more egregious capitalistic abuses, a piqued Roosevelt inadvertently named the new journal-

ism by comparing these writers to John Bunyan's man with the muckrake, who was so busy raking filth on the floor that he never looked up. But the journalists of the first decade of the century were proud of their badge as muckrakers. Ida Tarbell's historic exposé *The History of the Standard Oil Company* appeared in 1903. There followed such books and articles as Lincoln Steffen's *The Shame of the Cities*, David Graham Phillip's *The Treason of the Senate*, Burton J Hendrick's 'The Railroads on Trial,' and Upton Sinclair's 1906 novel *The Jungle*, a dramatization of appalling conditions in the Chicago meat industry.

In a way, these journalists were the heirs of the 'yellow press' of Hearst and Joseph Pulitzer, but the muckrakers' sensationalism was based on solid investigative reporting. They may have struck out wildly, with no solutions for the graft and corruption they uncovered, but they put the facts into the hands of those who did have solutions: Tarbell's book, for one, had considerable influence on ensuing trust legislation.

The mainstream attitude of the age, however, even among the muckrakers, remained invincibly optimistic. America was a great, prosperous, democratic and essentially good country; if problems remained, America would surely solve them. The only question was *how* – what policies? what reforms? what mechanisms? One of the significant experiments took place in Wisconsin under Governor Robert M La Follette, who came to office in 1901 and enacted a series of measures that came to be called the 'Wisconsin idea' – direct primaries for nominating candidates, opposition to political bosses, state regulation and taxation of railroads, state civil service and a 'brain trust' of academic advisors. The Wisconsin idea had considerable impact on national policy, and La Follette went on to be, as presidential candidate and Senator, a powerful and prophetic leader.

Urban reform was a larger job than the settlement houses could handle. In many cities Progressives attacked the ward system – which tended to be dominated by machine-controled ward heelers in ethnic neighborhoods – and replaced it with strong urban central governments, often based on a city council backed by

portly Taft floundered. To begin with, he was manifestly unhappy in elective office and inept at political wheeling and dealing. (Under Harding he would get the job he really wanted, Chief Justice of the Supreme Court.) Moreover, though Taft was much more active than TR in anti-trust action, he was perceived by labor as unsympathetic. When Taft approved the high Payne-Aldrich tariff, the break with labor was complete. By 1910 he was at loggerheads with Progressive Republicans and had become Roosevelt's favorite villain. Meanwhile, the successes of the labor movement and social-reform forces had given new strength to the Democrats, who were taking over the mainstream of Progressivism from its traditional Republican roots.

The election of 1912 was one of the most significant in the nation's history. Since Taft men controled the Republican National Committee, Roosevelt ran for President under the banner of the Progressive Party, dubbed the Bull Moose Party. The Democratic candidate was the scholarly Woodrow Wilson, who happened to be an effective stump campaigner and whom Bryan supported. All three major candidates served themselves up as Progressives, reflecting the overwhelming national consensus for reform.

The agendas of Roosevelt and Wilson highlight the contrast of Republican and Democratic brands of Progressivism. TR called his program the 'New Nationalism': Big Business, even monopoly, was inevitable and valuable, needing only to be well regulated by the government, which must allow interest groups (such as labor unions) to counterbalance other interest groups (such as trusts). Wilson called his approach the 'New Freedom': trusts were evil and must be destroyed to allow for greater competition and broader democracy. Ideologies aside, the Republicans were fatally split in 1912; despite TR's personal popularity, Wilson and the Democrats won by an unprecedented electoral majority, and Taft came in a poor third.

Like most great political movements, Progressivism was international, its ideas flowing back and forth among countries; thus Canada, like Britain, was involved in many of the same concerns as was the US. French-British tensions in the era revolved largely around Canadian participation in Britain's wars. The English-speaking majority succeeded in sending troops to the South African War in 1899 and, later, to fight in Europe in 1915. Laurier's accommodations with British militarism

lost him French support and led to a Conservative victory in 1911. The new government was also Progressive in spirit, however, and pursued much the same kind of economic reform as America. That same spirit led to closer business ties with the US and helped facilitate the peaceful settlement of territorial disputes between the countries that would eventually produce the longest unfortified boundary in the world.

The Wilson era

Woodrow Wilson arrived in the White House with perhaps the most impressive credentials of any American President. Beginning his career as a historian and political scientist whose writings had helped form the Progressive movement, later a reformist Princeton president and New Jersey governor, Wilson was a moral crusader by temperament. During his campaign he had proclaimed that he would destroy the trusts, but in the end he managed far less trust-busting than did either Roosevelt or Taft. The Clayton Anti-Trust Act, passed in 1914 and designed to improve on the old Sherman Act, proved to be yet another irresolute blow and was further weakened by the courts. Two strong reforms did appear in 1912-13: the 16th Amendment, establishing the first income tax, and the 17th Amendment, providing for popular election of Senators (they had previously been appointed by the state legislatures, making them easy prey for corruption by machines and business interests).

Wilson addressed the economy with mixed success. The Underwood Tariff set lower rates than had been seen in decades. The Federal Reserve System established a government banking network and Federal Reserve currency. The Fed was deplored by Wall Street, one writer declaring it 'covered all over with the slime of Bryanism,' but it was applauded by many small businessmen, who hoped it would make for more elastic currency and a more stable banking situation. The Federal Reserve Act was indeed a historic accomplishment; nonetheless, it would not be strong enough to stop the crash in 1929. The Federal Trade Commission Act of 1914 set up a Progressive-style regulatory agency to oversee the doings of business. The FTC was intended to suppress new monopolies and promote competition; instead, within a decade it would be taken over by monopoly interests.

With the coming of the Federal Trade Commission, Wilson confidently declared that the New

Freedom was in place. In his first three years he had concentrated on economic policy and had been somewhat neglectful of social questions. In 1916 he turned to the latter with a sweeping program that took him close to TR's New Nationalism. He began by appointing to the Supreme Court Louis Brandeis, long recognized as a champion of labor and a thorn in the flesh of trusts (he also was the first Jewish member of the Court). There followed in the Wilson program a system of farm-loan banks, laws providing for workmen's compensation and limiting child labor, a Tariff Commission and an eight-hour day for railroad workers.

One conspicuous failure of American democracy had persisted since the time when it was declared that 'all men are created equal.' In the late nineteenth century women had, here and there, begun to demand equal rights as citizens. After the National Women Suffrage Association was founded in 1890 the 'suffragettes' began an escalating campaign of marches and civil disobedience. The crusaders faced a daunting fight, but their strength gradually increased. More women were graduating from college, entering the professions, working in the labor force, contributing to the new theories and mechanisms of social reform; the whole thrust of Progressivism was inescapably on the suffragist side, though it took time to convince many reformers, including Woodrow Wilson, of that fact.

The new western states led the way in giving votes to women: by 1896 Colorado, Utah, Idaho and Wyoming had come around; Washington, Arizona, Kansas and Oregon followed in 1910-12. In the next years, the government was virtually besieged by suffrage forces. In 1917 Jeanette Rankin of Montana became the first woman to sit in the House of Representatives. It was to be the exigencies of politics that finally gave women the vote in 1920; true equality would take far longer to realize.

As to the civil rights of Afro-Americans, the Progressives were inexcusably silent. Any sign of political opinion favorable to blacks was treated as treachery in the South, where lynchings and segregationist Jim Crow laws kept black people in a condition hardly better than slavery. Theodore Roosevelt found out how things worked in 1901 when he received black leader Booker T Washington in the White House. That single event triggered a wave of violence against blacks in the South and lost TR millions of votes. Roosevelt

Left: Suffragettes picket the White House during Woodrow Wilson's term of office (1913-21).

Above right: Woodrow Wilson managed to gain the support of many Progressives despite his racist views toward black people. His most lasting legacy has been the Federal Reserve system, the American equivalent of European central banks.

Above far right: Pancho Villa (left) with some of his Mexican guerrillas. Wilson's administration was constantly involving itself in Mexican civil strife. The Mexican resentments this aroused led to Villa's raids into the United States.

Right: The sinking of the *Lusitania*, although legal under international law, shocked the United States, and marked the first step toward US intervention in World War I.

PRESIDENT WILSON IS DECEIVING THE WORLD WHEN HE APPEARS AS THE PROPHET OF DEMOCRACY

PRESIDENT WILSON HAS OPPOSED THOSE WHO DEMAND DEMOCRACY FOR THIS COUNTRY

HE IS RESPONSIBLE FOR THE DISFRANCHISEMENT OF MILLIONS OF AMERICANS

WE IN AMERICA KNOW THIS THE WORLD WILL FIND HIM OUT.

STAND BY
THE PRESIDENT

never took such a chance again. For his part, Washington tamely counseled his people to work hard, be good and be patient.

The conservative courts of the time resolutely refused to take action against racism. Southern-born Woodrow Wilson actually extended segregation in government service. Given that successive administrations, Populists and the labor movement had largely turned a deaf ear to their protests, militant black leaders (mostly in the North, where there was less official repression) began to do what other Progressives had done: form special-interest organizations. Harvard-trained W E B DuBois joined other black and white leaders in 1910 to form the National Association for the Advancement of Colored People. In the next decades, the NAACP and the National Urban League (formed in 1911) were to break ground toward the eventual, tragically delayed, social and political emancipation of Afro-Americans.

Inconclusive though they were, Wilson's programs had advanced Populist and Progressive (and even to a degree Socialist) ideas of direct democracy and an activist government. The nation still lacked a good many weapons to fight the rule of *laissez-faire*, but it had the beginning of a legislative arsenal. Business was now on the defensive, knowing that abuses were apt to bring governmental reprisal; but the rich were still rich, the poor poorer and monopolies throve. The old political machines still dominated some states, but at least now reformist machines such as La Follette's in Wisconsin had appeared as well. Direct popular elections still sometimes put scoundrels in office, and the appearance of ballot referendum and recall did not always make for better laws; but at least the masses had achieved a greater measure of voting power.

As a whole, the Progressive movement represented an immense effort for modest gains. None-theless, Roosevelt and Wilson had set the nation on a path from which it has never entirely deviated. When Wilson ran for reelection in 1916, however, his campaign slogan did not tout his social and economic achievements; instead, it proclaimed 'He Kept Us Out of War.'

The approach of war

When World War I erupted in Europe in 1914 it seemed to most Americans a distant tragedy with obscure causes. The important thing was to avoid being drawn into it.

With occasional success and no great disaster, President Taft had tried to further American interests abroad with economic pressure, 'Dollar Diplomacy.' But Wilson and his first Secretary of State, William Jennings Bryan, were led by their moral zealotry to more militant tactics when, in Mexico, a tyrannical general named Victoriano Huerta seized power from a reformer. Wilson branded the new regime a 'government of butchers' and began rattling the sabre. Mexicans were outraged, preferring even the hated Huerta to the meddling Wilson.

Wilson refused to back off. In 1914 he asked Congress to support a military expedition in a thinly disguised attempt to topple Huerta. Congress approved, and troops were dispatched to occupy Veracruz; the city responded with anti-American violence. As Wilson tried to decide what to do about this incomprehensible display of Mexican patriotism, Huerta was removed by political means and replaced by the moderate Venustiano Carranza. Tensions eased, but then in 1916 Wilson obstinately revived them by sending US troops into Mexico to pursue, finally without success, the anti-Carranza bandit Pancho Villa. In the end, President Wilson's intrusions largely served only to make Mexico permanently distrustful of Yankees.

In Europe during 1914-16, as the dead of the war piled up along thousands of miles of trenches, Wilson declared that America must be neutral in thought and deed. Nonetheless, it was clear that the ultimate loyalty of the US was inescapably behind Britain and her allies. In 1915 American neutrality was severely challenged when Germany warned that its submarines would attack any shipping around the British Isles. On 7 May a German submarine torpedoed the British passenger steamer *Lusitania*, which went down with 1198 civilians, including 128 Americans. Though Germany was conciliatory for a time following American diplomatic protests, the *Lusitania* tragedy had had a baneful effect on American public opinion. Wilson's successful 1916 election campaign proclaimed continuing neutrality, but his government had already begun building up the military. His great hope was still to end the war by mediation. After fruitless attempts to go over the heads of the warring governments to achieve a 'people's peace' (these efforts made Wilson an international hero among working people), he proclaimed in a January 1917 speech the idea of 'peace without victory,' based on a new world organization to arbitrate disputes and promote disarmament – a sort of international regulatory agency.

Yet no such appeals could end the war or arrest America's being drawn into it. Germany resumed unrestricted submarine warfare in February and began sinking American ships, and the public and Congress began calling for war. On 2 April 1917 Wilson at last went before Congress to ask for war, saying 'Our object now . . . is to vindicate the principles of peace and justice in the life of the world as against selfish and autocratic power . . . The world must be made safe for democracy.' For the first time, and in Progressivism's last great crusade, Americans were to be sent out into the world to take their place alongside the Allies in the war against Germany.

Latin America: 1500-1914

The Spanish conquest and settlement of America constitute one of the most strenuous and dramatic chapters in the annals of European overseas expansion. Although in historical perspective the Spaniards seem to have made quick work of carving out their American empire and creating elaborate institutions for its governance, their activities for a generation after Columbus's first voyage were chiefly confined to the islands and coastal rim of the Caribbean Sea. As a trial-and-error period of reconnoitering, adjustment and improvization, this Antillean phase of the conquest reveals complex, pragmatic aspects of Spanish expansion which are missing from the conventional image of Spanish legalism and crusading zeal.

It is significant that the Antillean period opens with a voyage by the Genoese Columbus and closes in 1519, the year the Portuguese Magellan undertook to circumnavigate the globe. Although the American venture was from the start reserved to the crown of Castile, this was a cosmopolitan phase directly involving international navigators, merchants and bankers. European rivalries and the Protestant Reformation had not yet evoked the full measure of Spain's xenophobic orthodoxy. The horizons for institutional experiment were broad, though the colonial arena might still be modest. The Antilles were the proving-ground for Spain's subsequent colonization of a vast land empire.

One set of options for experiment had to do with the politico-economic form of settlement. On his second voyage in 1493 Columbus arrived in Española with 1200 male colonists and the horses, sheep, seeds and vine cuttings for a farm colony at the ill-chosen site of Isabela. Neither Columbus's slender abilities as a colonial governor, however, nor his men's inclinations permitted such a colony to take root. After Columbus's misadventures led to his return to Spain in chains, the

crown asserted its hand in the colonizing process by dispatching a royal governor, Nicolás de Ovando, to Española. He set sail in 1502 with 2500 colonists, an array of bureaucrats and twelve Franciscan friars who were to indoctrinate the Indians. Within three years he had sited 15 towns around the island, capitalizing on the disposition of natural resources and Indian labor. The elaborate royal instructions which guided him contained in embryo Spanish principles of rule that were to serve for three centuries.

A range of strategies for acculturating and exploiting the Indians was also essayed within 20 years of the discovery. These included extortion and virtual enslavement before 1502; the regulated, tutelary apportionment of communities of Indians to 'deserving' settlers under the encomienda system introduced by Ovando; and the impassioned humanitarian protest against usurpation and oppression voiced by Dominican friars who arrived in Santo Domingo in 1510. The crown's pragmatic compromise, another benchmark for the future, was the Laws of Burgos of 1512, which limited the labor that could be exacted of Indians, provided for their instruction and catechization and even promised freedom to converts who showed capacity for self-rule. But laws were a dead letter for Española, where labor demands, European diseases and the trauma of conquest reduced an Amerind population of 100,000, or perhaps a multiple thereof, to 34,000 by 1514 and 500 by 1548. As for the African slaves imported to work in the sugar fields, the Burgos Laws were not applied at all.

Española served not only as a proving-ground but as a staging area for exploration and further settlement. Between 1508 and 1514 colonies were established on Puerto Rico, Jamaica and Cuba; Ponce de León made his first expedition to Florida; Balboa, having rounded up survivors of two ill-fated mainland expeditions, established

Darien on the isthmus and made the first sighting of the Pacific; and the ageing Pedrarias Dávila, savage and irascible, arrived in Panama as the first mainland governor.

The year 1519 marks the passage from the age of the explorers to that of the conquistadors. It saw the departure of Magellan's ships to prove what Vespucci had accepted and what Columbus could never admit, that the 'Americas' were indeed a New World and not the periphery of the Asian land mass. It saw the accession of Charles I of Spain as Charles V, Holy Roman Emperor, which placed the Spanish conquest of the Indies in a generous imperial context. The same year Charles transferred administration of the Indies from the personal control of the councilor, Juan Rodríguez de Fonseca, to a standing committee later bureaucratized as the Royal Council of the Indies. Finally, it was in 1519 that Hernán Cortés landed on the Mexican coast to undertake the campaign that would give Charles dominion over the Aztec empire, whose population has been set by one controversial calculation at 25 million souls.

The years of the conquistadors

The campaign letters of Cortés to his emperor reiterate the sobering lesson of the Antilles and anticipate the institutions of colonial rule. Observing that the Mexican Indians seemed 'to possess sufficient intelligence to conduct themselves as average reasonable beings,' he posed the practical dilemma that underlay subsequent learned debates among Spanish jurists and ecclesiastics over Spain's right to conquest and the Indians' right to justice:

On this account it seemed to me a very serious matter to compel them to serve the Spaniards in the same way as the natives in the Islands; yet without this service the conquerors and settlers of these parts would not be able to maintain themselves.

The sprawling epic of the conquest of the

Indies by relatively few, small but well-nigh ubiquitous bands of Spaniards cannot be retold here. In shifting patterns it exhibited all the treachery and gallantry, bloodlust and compassion, greed and abnegation, fanaticism and shrewd realism that one might expect of a breed spawned at the margin of society with a seven-century history of guerrilla war against another faith, a society anchored in medieval, Catholic loyalties yet keen to dawning possibilities of fame, gold and human prowess. The climactic moments were Cortés' triumphal entry into Tenochtitlán, the Aztec capital, and Francisco Pizarro's capture and execution of Atahualpa, usurping sovereign of the Inca realm. Other chapters, however, are no less stirring, such as the conquests of the Chibchas of Tunja and Bogotá by Jiménez de Quesada and of Chile by Valdivia or the odysseys of de Soto and Coronado in North America and of Orellana down the Amazon.

By the mid 1540s the main job of conquest was finished, although frontiers with hostile Indians beyond the boundaries of the Aztec and Inca empires existed for centuries and figure prominently in the histories of independent Mexico, Chile and Argentina. The two viceroyalties which would form the spinal column of Spanish administration were created first for New Spain (Mexico) in 1535, then for Peru in 1542. By the 1540s, also, the conquistadors had exhausted the dazzling hauls of Indian treasure, and the new silver mines of Potosí (1545) and Zacatecas (1548) required permanent settlement, bureaucracy and close royal supervision.

A lasting legacy of the years of the conquistadors was the 'culture of conquest.' This culture was marked by a two-way process of social leveling. On one hand the elaborate societies of the Aztecs and Incas were collapsed into two-stratum communities of common workers or tribute-payers bossed by chiefs mediating between them and the Spaniards. On the European side, the upper nobility was absent from the conquerors' ranks. A few hidalgos, impoverished second sons, notaries and priests were present, and much larger contingents of farmers, artisans, seamen, peasants, veterans of European wars and plebeian drifters and adventurers. What counted was the talent to survive and to command, not pedigree. An early chronicle reported that a certain hidalgo had gone to the Indies and returned wealthy to Spain. Asked how he had made his fortune he replied, 'By dropping the *don* from my name.'

The stark dichotomy between Spaniard and Indian, conqueror and conquered, was not maintained for long. Indeed, it did not always characterize the initial contact, as witnessed by Cortés' alliance with the disaffected Tlaxcalans in his Aztec campaign. The inevitable miscegenation was hastened by the paucity of European women accompanying the settlers, who numbered only 10 percent of the recorded emigrants from Spain from 1509 to 1539. Though in the long run mestizos occupied lower to intermediate stations in Spanish colonial society, many in the early years were legitimized by their fathers, especially the offspring of plebeian foot soldiers and daughters of Indian caciques. Africans further diversified the social spectrum. Those who accompanied the conquistadors were Christianized slaves or freed men from Spain. They tended to enjoy some of the privileged status of their masters and might become foremen of tributary Indian villages, although cases are also recorded of Negroes becoming slaves of Indian nobles or craftsmen.

The complex image of colonial Spanish American society, or societies, requires some quantitative base. Estimates of the preconquest Amerind population that lived within the boundaries of present-day Spanish America range from 11 million to 90 million. Even from the middle-ground estimate of 40 million, the decline of the Indian population of Spanish America to perhaps 8.5 million in the early sixteenth century would constitute one of the most awesome demographic calamities in history. Although a portion of the loss can be attributed to slaughter, forced labor and cultural trauma, much was caused by the Indians' low resistance to common diseases carried by Europeans (smallpox, typhus, measles, influenza) and Africans (malaria, trachoma, yellow fever).

On its smaller scale the European component also eludes reliable measurement. From 1509 to 1559 there were 15,000 recorded emigrants from Spain, but the actual number was a multiple of this and reached 100,000 by the century's end. The right to emigrate was reserved to peninsular Spaniards orthodox in their faith, except by special license. The colonists therefore represented more nearly a cross section of the parent society than did the heterodox groups of a colony like New England. Despite obstacles, however, foreigners readily found passage to the New World. There were substantial numbers of Portuguese, Italians, Greeks, Corsicans and Dutch in sixteenth-century Peru, as well as a scattering of Germans, Hungarians, Irish and others. Scholars fail to agree whether European immigration rose or fell off in the seventeenth century, but in the eighteenth it reached a new peak. Throughout the entire period African slaves were also being imported into the area on a massive scale.

As plantation agriculture did not play the commanding role in the vast territory of Spanish America that it did on the British and French Caribbean islands, African slaves were put to

Above left: The first Spanish settlement in the New World was Fort Navidad on the island of Española (now divided between Haiti and the Dominican Republic). This engraving from 1493 presents a highly flattering portrait of the year-old colony. Columbus was forced to refound it when he discovered the site abandoned on his second voyage to America in 1493.

Left: The Inca Atahualpa arrives at Cajamarca. This Peruvian town was the scene of Pizarro's massacre of Atahualpa's supporters, and his seizure of the Inca sovereign.

Right: The lures that drew the Spaniards into the Americas were precious metals, silver and gold. The famous silver mine at Potosi in Bolivia, shown in this engraving, produced a massive output of silver. When its riches poured into Europe, they caused inflation across the continent.

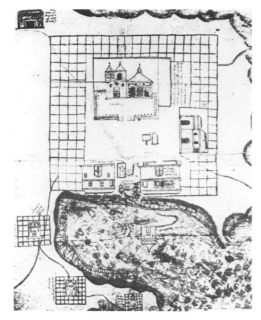

Political aspects

It has been said that had Aragon rather than Castile been the parent country for colonial Spanish America, its development would have taken a different course. The Castilian crown was less hampered than the Aragonese by restrictions such as checks by the parliamentary body, or *cortes*, and it was therefore free to establish more absolutist rule in its new realms. In its new possessions the crown was not trammeled by ancient feudal privileges. It was parsimonious in awarding fresh titles of nobility and forbade the assembling of a parliamentary body. For its service in delivering millions of converts to Christendom, it won from Rome greater power over ecclesiastical affairs than it enjoyed at home. So centralized was political authority that the conquistadors' descendants were themselves in some respect a 'colonial' group, despite their conspicuous role in exploiting Indian and Negro labor. Here, however, our task is not to assess the benevolence of Spanish rule but to identify certain functional, adaptive features of the seemingly unwieldy apparatus of colonial government which, in spite of recurring localized protests and uprisings by creoles, Indians and slaves, endured for three centuries without serious internal challenge.

Three obvious traits of the political system were bureaucratism, absolutism and paternalism. Spanish America was ruled by a sprawling, multi-channeled, legalistic, well-nigh ubiquitous bureaucracy in which law-making and judicial functions were subsumed beneath or closely interwoven with administrative ones. The municipal council, or *cabildo*, was the only elective body, and even its offices came to be bought and sold. Because all authority flowed from the crown, the bureaucracy was absolutist, but it was not, on that account, necessarily despotic. For one thing it had little force at its disposal. The conquest had been accomplished by a series of improvized and soon disbanded private armies. Once central rule was established, the crown lacked forces to resist foreign interlopers in the Caribbean; in 1605 it simply ordered depopulation of the northwest portion of Española, the area of Columbus's first settlements, leaving it as a preserve for French buccaneers and paving the way for the subsequent French claim to Saint Domingue (modern Haiti). In the long run Spain was unable even to

varied uses. Some were used in mining, some were employed by urban artisans, some were employed by religious orders, hospitals and town councils or in maritime or overland transportation. Many were in domestic service, and increasing numbers did become assigned to intensive agriculture along the tropical river valleys.

As the races intermingled, the socioethnic composition of Spanish America became increasingly kaleidoscopic. Among the Europeans a distinction soon arose between peninsular Spaniards and creoles, that is, American-born whites or near-whites. The peninsulars' virtual monopoly of the upper levels of the bureaucratic and ecclesiastical hierarchies implied distinct social advantages. The growing population in other categories – mestizos, mulattos, zambos (Indo-Africans), free Negroes – were known as *castas*, a term lacking the segregative implications that it acquired when the Portuguese applied it to Hindu society in India. As time passed elaborate sets of regional nomenclature developed to identify proliferating cross-ethnic types. Somatic appearance came to be loosely linked with occupational pursuit, an ascriptive tendency selectively reinforced by legal restriction. By the end of the colonial period this complex and never wholly formalized regime of socioethnic compartmentation was dissolving into a simpler, more fluid class system that retained ascriptive and paternalistic features.

The characteristic early institution for exacting commodity tribute and labor of the Indians was the encomienda, a grant by which crown representatives 'entrusted' Indian families or villages for a limited number of generations to the guardianship of a settler who was deemed worthy. In the New Laws of 1542 and subsequent legislation the crown, motivated by its official humanitarianism and by fear that an independent feudal nobility might arise in America, limited the power of encomenderos to lay tribute, exact service and bequeath their grants. More effective in the demise of encomienda by the eighteenth century, however, was the decline of the Indian population, which caused severe loss in revenue for encomenderos.

Risking simplification one can say that the hacienda replaced the encomienda as the instrument for mobilizing rural labor. The word hacienda, meaning liquid capital, was extended to include property in real estate. An hacendado's position rested on outright ownership of land rather than on a contingent grant from the crown. Although Indian lands and villages were legally

protected against seizure, lawyers manipulated their rights in favor of hacendados. The hacienda met the labor shortage caused by demographic decline by immobilizing its work force through debt peonage. Although well-to-do hacendados lived in luxury, the hacienda was a self-sufficient unit and produced no significant export commodity for the world market.

The functional counterpart to the hacienda was the municipality. Town founders reserved for themselves both an urban lot and an outlying tract of farm or ranch land. Municipal councils were the grass-roots unit of government and the highest office to which many creoles could aspire, however extensive their holdings. Save for specialized ports and mining settlements, towns served as control centers for surrounding farm lands and villages of rural workers. Hacendados maintained urban residences from the need to participate in municipal affairs and to ingratiate or defend their interests against royal and ecclesiastical officials. The checkerboard town plan, with its spacious plaza surrounded by the church and government buildings, aptly symbolized the intrusion of imperial bureaucracy into a distant hinterland.

Above, far left: An engraving showing the fort at San Augustin de Arecutagua in Paraguay. It was an important center for the Jesuit order, which had a vision of creating a theocratic state in the heart of South America.

Above left: A typical plan of a Spanish town in the New World. The plaza, with its church and administrative buildings, lies at the center of a gridded network.

Left: An Inca cult vessel called a *kero*. The mosaic on it depicts a Spanish trumpeter, an Incan dignitary and a black drummer. It dates from the mid seventeenth century.

Above right: The hacienda was the key institution in the Spanish economic exploitation of the New World. It enabled the hacendado, or landlord, to gain control and develop large tracts of land.

maintain regularly its defensive trans-Atlantic convoy system. Protection of the mainland against raids or insurrection was largely left to the private forces of hacendados. As late as the mid eighteenth century there were only 3000 regular troops in New Spain.

The absolutism of Spanish rule was further conditioned by paternalism. The crown never allowed the development of 'estates' in America having political representation of a parliamentary nature. Instead, representation was provided by channels of direct access to the crown or to high royal officials for the airing of grievances and seeking redress. It was customary, for example, for larger municipalities to maintain a solicitor (*procurador*) at the Spanish court to petition in favor of his cabildo. Hearings known as *residencias* were held when high and many lesser officials concluded their terms; on such occasions witnesses testified as to the incumbent's conduct in office, and restitution or punishment might be exacted of offenders. In principle viceroys were expected to devote time each week to considering petitions from Indians, and they might hear in the first instance suits involving Indians.

Such channels were not of course readily available to the humble and the downtrodden. The point is that the possibility of appeal to the crown as ultimate arbiter, even if largely restricted to privileged persons and bodies, activated many checks and balances. At least three important hierarchies – politico-administrative, fiscal and ecclesiastical (the last with its secular, regular and Inquisitorial branches) – culminated in the crown or its viceregal proxy. These chains of authority, and offices within each chain, were competitive and mutually supervisory, a condition exacerbated by functional overlap and loose jurisdiction definitions. However irrational by 'efficiency' criteria, such an arrangement discouraged hot-headed or despotic action by zealous underlings. On occasions when a part of the system became clogged or dysfunctional the crown had recourse to the *visita*, a trouble-shooting board of inquiry which circumvented formal channels to secure information and propose remedies.

Not only were functional boundaries between agencies ill defined but functions coalesced within agencies. At the top of the structure the Council of the Indies and the *Casa de Contratación* (Board of Trade, which regulated commerce) had rule-making and judicial as well as merely administrative powers. In America the viceroys had administrative, rule-making, judicial and military powers; they were also vice-patrons of the Church and might themselves be ecclesiastics. Below the viceroys were *audiencias*, which were ostensibly appellate courts but enjoyed rule-making and administrative authority and, in an interregnum between viceroys, assumed the powers of that office. Of special importance in all these cases is the coalescence of administrative and judicial functions. Anglo-French political philosophy rests on a premise that the merging of these powers invites abusive or arbitrary government. Viewed more leniently, however, this feature permits flexibility and adaptiveness, for when a judicial decision comes close to being an administrative act it can be dispatched on the merits of the case rather than in conformance with an impersonal legal code. In colonial Spanish America casuistry was virtually elevated to a principle of government.

The moral authority enjoyed by the apparatus of the State becomes more understandable when we appreciate the extent to which the latter was entwined with that of the Church. In colonial Spanish America, indeed, one can scarcely speak

of 'State' and 'Church' as discrete entities with separate sources of power and spheres of action. State and Church were not external to each other; treason and heresy were sides of the same coin, just as 'Spaniard' and 'Christian' had been at the moment of conquest. Priests were salaried servants of the crown, pledged to support it against the menace of 'feudal' separatism. Similarly the civil hierarchy supported the crown against the separatism or autonomy of the regular, or missionary, clergy. What might happen if the crown perceived a threat to its perquisites from a religious body is illustrated by the expulsion of the Jesuits from the Spanish realms in 1767.

Because it is skeletonized this account of Spanish rule in America may sound idealized. The system was of course open to abuse, especially at its lower extremities. The administrators of Indian towns, *corregidores de indios*, were notorious for conspiring with local priests and the Indians' own caciques to tyrannize their wards by exacting grueling, unremunerated labor from them or buying their produce at depressed prices and foisting off imports at extortionate ones. Yet it is still probably the case that the condition of rural Indian workers was on some counts less oppressive during the colonial centuries than it was later to become in the nineteenth-century republics.

The economy of Latin America

One can no more treat the economic than one can the ecclesiastical affairs of the Spanish empire in isolation from the polity. Spanish mercantilism rested on the premise that the colonies were to contribute to the security and prosperity of the mother country and specifically to the financial support of the crown and its policies. This premise led to the twin principles of monopoly, by which Spain arrogated to itself control over the external and even the intracolonial trade of the Indies, and prohibitionism, by which Spain attempted to prescribe the forms of economic production in America.

Spanish economic policy was devised and executed through the hierarchized mechanism of the state apparatus described above. The 6400 laws for the governance of the Indies that were finally collated and codified in 1681 from hundreds of thousands of royal *cédulas* contain an array of economic measures enmeshed with those for political, social, ecclesiastical and Indian affairs. The merchant class assumed its functions within the framework and under regulations established

by the State. In 1543 the crown authorized Seville merchants engaged in the American trade to form a monopolistic guild (*consulado*) that was to cooperate with the official Board of Trade. Later similar bodies were established in New Spain (1594) and Peru (1613).

Another feature of Spanish mercantilism was the commitment, at least until the eighteenth century, to bullionism, to the precept that only gold and silver constitute true wealth. In fact, alternative possibilities for extraction of wealth from the Indies were few. Demand for native American spices was limited in Europe and grew slowly. The British, French and Portuguese outstripped Spain as suppliers of tobacco and sugar. Native staple crops such as maize, potatoes and cassava were too bulky and unprofitable to ship and were simply transplanted to the Old World. The predominance first of gold in homeward cargoes, then of silver after the strikes of 1545-65, is therefore understandable. In the flush years of the late sixteenth and early seventeenth centuries bullion, averaging nearly seven million pesos (or ducats) annually, accounted for 80 percent of the value of eastbound cargoes, reaching a peak of 95.6 percent in 1594. To this amount should be added the annual bullion export of three to five million pesos that was channeled into trade with the Orient on the Manila galleons sailing from Acapulco. It has been estimated that the proportion of crown income derived from American bullion was about 25 percent by the 1590s.

Linked with bullionism was the economic decline of the mother country, which made it possible to maintain only the appearance of commercial exclusivism. The inflationary spiral caused by the influx of silver to Spain undermined home industry by making it noncompetitive. When the crown attempted to restrain the rise of prices it did so by taxation, which bore most heavily on staples consumed by the rural poor, and by prohibition of the reexport of metals, which to the limited extent it succeeded only rekindled inflation. Money that might have invigorated trade and industry was invested in unproductive land to enhance the status of proprietors. And in fact American revenues did little to stabilize the crown's debts, which rose from 5 million to 100 million ducats during the reign of Philip II (1556-98).

During the seventeenth century, then, the Spanish commercial system was sagging at both ends. Home industry could not supply the American market, which was in any case limited by the impoverishment of the rural masses and by widespread American manufacture of coarse woolen, ceramics and leather goods. In the Indies, silver production fell off, causing the economy to become decentralized around the largely self-sufficient haciendas of the grain and cattle zones with their retinues of artisans, domestic servants and peons. By the 1650s the size of the two fleets that sailed annually from Seville to specified Caribbean ports had fallen off sharply, partly for lack of trade, partly for lack of trained seamen and Spanish-built vessels.

A final feature of the system saved it from overthrow from without. That was its immense permeability to foreign commercial interests. The Caribbean Sea, distant and ill-protected Buenos Aires and eventually the Pacific coast of South America were favorite targets for interlopers. There is special irony to the case of the Caribbean. In the Greater Antilles the Spanish lost Jamaica to the English and Saint Domingue to the French in the seventeenth century. The Lesser Antilles, however, the Spaniards had never even seen fit to colonize. They were occupied by the English, Dutch and French against little opposition. Not only did the Dutch establish bases here for a flourishing contraband trade with the Spanish ports, but their ships, capital commercial services and knowledge of sugar-producing equipped them to assist the English and French to establish immensely lucrative sugar economies at the island threshold to the Spanish realm.

The Bourbon century

The death in 1700 of the near-imbecile Charles II, last of the Habsburg kings of Spain, provoked the War of the Spanish Succession (1702-13), marking the transition to the Bourbon dynasty and to an era of significant policy changes. These included: administrative reform in the interest of efficiency, centralization and elimination of pockets of autonomy and privilege; fiscal reform to create a more equitable tax base and more effective collections; economic reform to stimulate agriculture, industry, trade and shipping and to enhance the status of laborers; bolstering of military and naval forces;

and overhaul of the archaic colonial system which was reining back the productive forces of the Indies and stunting their contribution to the strength and welfare of Spain. Supporting these reformist efforts was a fresh climate of scientific and literary activity, a product in part of intellectual exchange with foreign sources of Enlightenment thought, notably French.

One should not, however, exaggerate the scope and impact of reformism in the Bourbon century. Until the reign of Charles III (1759-88) innovations were half-hearted and largely restricted to the mother country. Even Charles, Spanish paragon of 'enlightened despotism,' was not always as bold, wise or effective as he has been pictured. Insofar as it affected the American colonies, Bourbon reform should be seen not as a cluster of measures generated from lofty doctrinal commitment, but as a series of responses to demographic, economic and political change. The population of Spanish America, which had hovered at approximately 10 million from the late sixteenth to the mid eighteenth century, was half again as large by 1800. This increase enlarged the market for European goods and yielded additional manpower for economic production, notably mining and agricultural colonization. At the same time Europe was increasingly in need of products available from hitherto peripheral areas: Argentina (hides, salt beef), Venezuela (cacao) and Cuba (sugar). Overhaul of the colonial commercial system was accelerated by pressures from Spain's rivals, dramatically exemplified during the 11-month seizure of Havana by the British in 1762, when 700 well-supplied merchant ships entered the harbor, contrasting with a maximum of 15 in prior years. This combination of population growth, economic development and foreign commercial and territorial expansion in the Americas required that administration be decentralized from Mexico and Lima and that measures be taken to stiffen the defenses of frontier and maritime zones.

The main emphases of Bourbon colonial reform were commercial, administrative and strategic. The system of fleets with limited sailings and

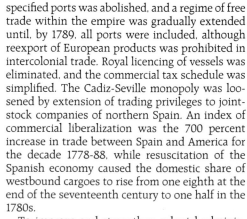

specified ports was abolished, and a regime of free trade within the empire was gradually extended until, by 1789, all ports were included, although reexport of European products was prohibited in intercolonial trade. Royal licencing of vessels was eliminated, and the commercial tax schedule was simplified. The Cadiz-Seville monopoly was loosened by extension of trading privileges to joint-stock companies of northern Spain. An index of commercial liberalization was the 700 percent increase in trade between Spain and America for the decade 1778-88, while resuscitation of the Spanish economy caused the domestic share of westbound cargoes to rise from one eighth at the end of the seventeenth century to one half in the 1780s.

To improve and strengthen colonial administration the crown created the viceroyalties of New Granada (1739) and La Plata (1776) at the northern and southern ends of the South American continent. In North America Spain directly confronted Britain across the Mississippi River after the settlement of 1763, while on the west coast Russian traders were moving south from Alaska toward the California missions. To buttress this area, the lands of northern Mexico, including modern Texas, New Mexico and California, were constituted as 'Internal Provinces' under military government independent of the viceroy. Another innovation was the establishment throughout the colonies after 1764 of a system of *intendants* –

middle-rank administrators who were to mitigate abuses of Indian labor, promote economic development and improve revenue collection. The office was modeled after the French prototype devised by Richelieu and Mazarin, and had been used in Spain since 1718.

By the late eighteenth century the Spanish realms seemed to have taken a new lease of life. Population was growing by faster natural increase, heavier immigration and larger imports of slaves. Production was on the rise, and regions hitherto restricted to near-subsistence economies were yielding export crops for world markets. Peru to be sure was in the doldrums, but Mexico flourished. By 1800 Mexico was producing two thirds of the world's silver. Cities in the colonies were growing swiftly, larger ones embellished with new public buildings, parks and promenades and water systems. Despite continuing censorship by the Inquisition, works of Descartes, Locke, Hume, Adam Smith, Voltaire, Condillac and Montesquieu circulated freely. Gazettes carrying literary and scientific contributions as well as news proliferated; by 1808 Spanish America had perhaps twenty-five printing presses. Missions of European scientists arrived, notably that of Alexander von Humboldt, whose extensive works are perhaps our best single source of knowledge of Spanish America on the eve of independence. Such visitors were surprised to find that the colonies boasted their own scientists of distinction: José Antonio Alzate (1729-99), the tireless publicist for applied science known as Mexico's first experimental scientist, the naturalist José Celestino Mutis (1732-1808) of Bogotá whom Linnaeus called 'immortal'; the physician Hipólito Unánue (1755-1833) who founded Lima's first anatomical theater.

By the last third of the eighteenth century the creole elites were demonstrating their distinctive identity, and to a degree their resentment of peninsulars, by calling themselves *americanos*. This dawning self-awareness received intellectual stimulus from polemics over the alleged inferiority of America. When the encyclopedists Buffon and de Pauw belittled the New World for its miasmic climate, rachitic fauna and slothful inhabitants, Spanish Americans, including exiled but nostalgic Jesuits, sprang to its defense, as Jefferson did in his *Notes on Virginia.*

As the Bourbon century drew to a close, however, there was virtually no public sentiment favoring the independence of Spanish America or its constituent parts. Rousseau's works, including *The Social Contract,* circulated among literati, but the reception given to the French Revolution and its slogans was chilly. This is all the more understandable given that one byproduct of the Revolution was a massive slave revolt in Saint Domingue which culminated in the independence of Haiti in 1804, the world's first 'Black Republic' and Latin America's first independent nation. Planters who survived the holocaust and escaped to Cuba, Puerto Rico or Venezuela were scarcely effective publicists for political and racial egalitarianism.

Colonial Brazil

Portuguese colonization and governance of Brazil, whose modern limits embrace approximately half of the South American continent, differed in many respects from the patterns laid down by the Spanish in America. Three sets of circumstances help establish the contrast. First are the differences between the mother countries. Portugal's territory was much smaller than Spain's, as was its population of a million and a quarter souls in the age of discovery. Its modest size, the coastal concentration of its inhabitants and its earlier national consolidation meant that Portugal's monarchy was more centralized and less menaced by separatism, regional or political. Portuguese colonial rule was therefore less marked than Spanish by delegated powers and bureaucratic checks and balances. The permanent office of viceroy was not created in Brazil till 1720 and never enjoyed the power and prerogatives of its Spanish American counterpart.

Imperial commitments are also to be considered. Portugal's Asiatic seaborne empire made heavy demands on its human, military and nautical resources. It has been estimated that some 2400 people left Portugal annually during the six-

teenth century, most of them for India and the Orient. This compares with perhaps 1000 annual Spanish emigrants to America drawn from a much larger population. The settlement of Brazil therefore proceeded at a leisurely pace; and since Portugal lacked the bureaucratic cadres to preside over it, administrative centralism was offset by the relative independence enjoyed by settlers in rural or outlying regions.

The Spanish and Portuguese colonies offered contrasting resources and possibilities. Whereas the Spanish lands had yielded gold immediately and silver soon after, Portugal had to wait two centuries for gold and diamond strikes. Unlike the Indians of Mesoamerica and the Andean highlands who formed sedentary communities easily exploitable for labor, tribute and surplus commodities, the seminomadic Brazilian Indians lived in small shifting villages, engaged in desultory tribal hostilities, produced for subsistence needs and were ill adapted for sustained labor on plantations or in mines.

Above left: A photographic portrait of a Brazilian Indian chief. The Indians of Portugal's American colony were ill-suited to become workers in mines or on plantations; consequently, Brazil developed much more slowly than the wealthy and populous Spanish viceroyalties.

Left: The sugar cane, grown in the tropical regions of the New World, provided the first cash crop for export to Europe. This engraving shows Indian and African slaves on a plantation in the West Indies.

Above right: Alexander von Humboldt, a German scientist, traveled widely in Spanish America for many years. His books revealed the wealth of the New World – both material and intellectual – to European countries.

Right: Negro slaves massacre some of Haiti's white settlers in 1791. Their rebellion was inspired in part by the recent American and French Revolutions.

For decades after Pedro Álvares Cabral 'discovered' Brazil while en route to India in 1500 the Portuguese made little attempt at formal colonization. Then, in 1534, partly as a countermove to French designs, the crown divided the coast into twelve captaincies extending indefinitely inland along parallel boundaries. These were granted to donataries, or proprietary lords, a kind of planter capitalist who was to promote settlement and develop agricultural production. Some grants were never taken up, and of the remainder only Pernambuco in the northeast and São Vicente in the south became active colonizing foci.

The crown's next important step was to send to Brazil a governor general, Tomé de Sousa, who arrived in the designated capital, Salvador, in 1549 with troops, bureaucrats, a contingent of Jesuits and detailed instructions for military defense, agricultural development, export control and protection of the Indians. This agenda recalls the instructions which Ovando brought to Española as early as 1502.

The activity that most powerfully influenced Brazilian settlement patterns, social organization and commercial fortunes during the first two centuries was sugar production. The plantations were centered along the northeast coast, where thousands of slaves were imported annually from Africa by the late sixteenth century and more than a hundred mills were in operation. Inland from the sugar coast, particularly along the São Francisco River valley, there developed a cattle industry that supplied meat and hides for the littoral, oxen to power the mills and pastoral products for export. The extensive nature of stock raising allowed relatively few persons to settle large tracts, and the cattle areas served as a sociological and ecological buffer zone with the deep interior.

Aside from the port of Rio de Janeiro, founded in 1567, the only significant early settlement region in the south was that centered on the modest but historically important town of São Paulo, located inland from the port of Santos at an altitude of 1800 feet. The isolation of the settlement and its lack of exportable commodities caused it to look inland for economic salvation. Throughout the seventeenth century São Paulo dispatched expeditions (*bandeiras*) composed of whites, mamelucos (mestizos), Indians and occasional Negroes that roamed half the continent in search of Indian slaves and precious metals. The Jesuit missions of Paraguay, with their disciplined Indian converts, were favorite targets until the fathers organized their wards to resist. Eventually it was the Paulistas who discovered gold, but they were unable to defend their claims against the swarm of fortune seekers who arrived from the coast and from Portugal.

Discovery of gold and diamonds after the 1690s had important consequences. It attracted migrants from the coast and overseas who effected the first substantial colonization of the interior. It drew off free and slave labor from the northeast, dealing a blow to sugar production, and it required additional levies of slaves from Africa. It shifted Brazil's demographic center of gravity southward, a change signalized by the transfer of the capital to Rio de Janeiro in 1763. It stimulated the Portuguese government, jealous of its share of the proceeds, to strengthen its administrative machinery. To these effects should be added a gold flow from Lisbon to Britain that attained perhaps £1,500,000 a year and contributed to the underwriting of British industrialization.

The mid eighteenth century brought to Portugal, as it had to Spain, an interlude of 'enlightened despotism' under the aegis of Sebastião José de Carvalho e Melo, Marquis of Pombal, the overbearing Portuguese minister (1750-77) who came into dictatorial power after his energetic handling of the Lisbon quake disaster in 1755. With Brazilian gold production declining in the 1760s and obsolete Brazilian sugar mills competing disadvantageously with Caribbean production, Brazil could not duplicate the economic rebound enjoyed by large parts of Spanish America. Pombal did his best, however, to develop the economy of northern Brazil by creating two monopolistic chartered companies that stimulated exports of cacao, cotton, rice and hides. He also secularized the Indian missions, converting them into towns and villages and encouraging miscegenation with and assimilation of the Indians. If their lot improved, however, it was perhaps attributable more to their replacement by African slaves than to legislative beneficence.

The Brazilian economist Celso Furtado proposes a suggestive contrast between the colonial histories of Spanish and Portuguese America. One might, he feels, characterize the first 150 years of Spanish rule as a time when, at great demographical cost to the Amerind population, a small minority of persons linked to Spain or its state apparatus organized vast regions around a few dynamic centers whose primary function was to produce precious metals for export to Spain. The next 150 years saw the process reversed: a decline in mineral production, demographic recovery, a weakening in the independence of regions, the growth of landed aristocracies having strictly local economic horizons. Brazil exemplifies the contrary sequence. The first 150 years saw the development of an export economy made up of isolated units that faced overseas and lacked regional interconnections save for those between the sugar coast and the backlands cattle zone. The dominant class were the sugar planters whose interests linked them directly to Lisbon. The subsequent 150 years opened with half a century of severe economic depression. Then came the gold and diamond strikes which accelerated European immigration, the growth of interregional markets and the emergence of regional elites interlinked by complementary commercial interests. This contrast, admittedly highly schematic, at least suggests one of several lines of explanation for why Spanish America was fragmented onto a congeries of new nations at the moment of independence, while Brazil retained its territorial unity.

The independence movements

The chain of events which led to the independence of the Spanish American countries and Brazil was set in motion by the Napoleonic invasions of the Iberian peninsula in 1807-08. By 1825 Mexico, the Central American Federation, Gran Colombia, Peru, Bolivia, Paraguay, Chile and Argentina had separated from Spain, and Brazil had become an independent empire. Under British pressure Uruguay was guaranteed its sovereignty in 1828 as a buffer state between Brazil and Argentina. Gran Colombia split into Venezuela, Colombia and Ecuador in 1830, and the Central American group dissolved into five nations in 1838. The Dominican Republic won freedom in 1844 after 22 years of rule by neighboring Haiti. Two Spanish American republics became independent only in the twentieth century: Cuba in 1902, as a consequence of the War for Cuban Independence (1895-98), and Panama in 1903, when the United States supported its secession from Colombia as the future canal site.

At their inception the independence movements of 1808-25 were not separatist or revolutionary but were inspired by loyalty to the Iberian monarchs sequestered or exiled by Napoleon. How creoles and peninsulars in America met the problems posed by the Napoleonic interregnum is largely a tale of multiple improvization. An obvious determinant of the story was whether the Iberian ruler escaped overseas, as did Portugal's prince regent, or whether he fell into Napoleon's clutches to create a crisis of legitimacy, as happened in Spain. Regionally, events were influenced by the nature of the local economy, the composition of society, the strength of peninsular elites and the imponderables of tradition and psychological response.

In the case of Portugal, Prince Regent João embarked for Brazil under British protection in 1807 with at least 10,000 followers and half of his country's specie. The establishment of João's court in Rio de Janeiro inspired a series of innovations designed to make the new capital a more appropriate seat of monarchy: a national bank, military, naval and medical schools, a printing press and gazette, a national library, a theater, a fine arts academy and open invitations to European scientists and artists. Rio's population jumped from 40,000 in the late eighteenth century to 110,000 in 1821. Titles and decorations were dispensed to Brazilian patriarchs. At the moment when viceregal institutions were being dismantled in the Spanish colonies, Brazil received the accouterments of courtly rule and, in 1815, was formally declared to be a kingdom.

Brazil's decolonization was in part illusory, for, as an historian has said, a British stepmother replaced the Portuguese mother. The British had a practical interest in the hegira of the Portuguese government. Since the seventeenth century Portugal had been Britain's economic vassal, and now the dissolution of the Iberian mercantile empires allowed the world's leading sea power to consolidate direct commercial hegemony in Latin America. On his arrival in Brazil Prince João had declared Brazilian ports open to the trade of friendly nations, a measure which, in Europe, could benefit only Britain while the war with Napoleon lasted. In 1810 this advantage was formalized in a treaty which accorded Britain a preferential tariff. Rio de Janeiro became the South American headquarters for British commercial and diplomatic activity, and in 1812 Brazil received 80 percent of Britain's total exports to Latin America.

The course of Brazilian independence after Napoleon's defeat in 1814 was dictated by events in the mother country. The Portuguese were ill pleased with João's Brazilian residence and his promotion of the 'colony' to 'kingdom.' Commercial and productive classes opposed the liberalization of Brazilian trade and favored constitutional limits on the sovereign's powers. The 1820 revolution in Spain ignited a similar movement in Oporto that spread to Lisbon and produced a Côrtes that was to draft a liberal constitution. Enjoying temporary public support on both sides of the ocean, the Côrtes insisted that João return to Lisbon. He acceded in 1821, after considerable vacillation, and left his son Pedro behind as Brazilian regent. Only then was it evident that the new 'liberal' government intended to undo João's reforms and that the Brazilian provinces were to be subordinated to the Côrtes rather than to Rio. Pressures swiftly mounted on the dashing 24-year-old prince. Responding to separatist sentiments of key municipalities, Pedro declared his intention to remain in Brazil. He suppressed a revolt of Portuguese troops in Rio and began turning to Brazilian advisers, notably the Coimbra-educated servant José Bonifácio de Andrada e Silva, known as the Patriarch of Independence. After renewed provocations from Lisbon Pedro declared Brazil's independence in September 1822, and in December he was crowned emperor. Within a year Brazilian forces commanded by Admiral Lord Cochrane dislodged the last Portuguese garrisons from the northern provinces.

In all, Brazil took a year and a half to win independence and expel Portuguese troops. In Spanish America the multiple independence movements occupied 15 years, involved strenuous military efforts, ran the gamut of insurgency and counterrevolution and in some regions caused substantial social and economic dislocation. The Spanish American story like the Brazilian accompanied the march of events in the mother country. From 1808 to 1814 Spain was under Napoleonic rule except for the very south, where autonomous juntas seized and retained power. These came to be coordinated by a Côrtes at Cadiz, composed of representatives from both sides of the ocean,

which in 1812 promulgated a 'liberal' constitution. Its provisions ended the exploitation of Indians, abolished censorship and the Inquisition and opened public offices to creoles. In America as in Spain authority collapsed to the level of municipal juntas in 1809-10, at least outside the traditional viceregal centers of Mexico and Peru. Recognizing no illegitimate or intermediate authority, these spontaneous cabildos pledged allegiance to the captive Ferdinand VII.

In northern South America the assumption of authority by cabildos in Venezuela and New Granada (1810) was shortly converted to outright declarations of independence by pressures from patriot groups led by Francisco de Miranda (1750-1816) and Simón Bolívar (1783-1830). The patriot forces, however, were inadequately supported; an earthquake devastated their stronghold in the Caracas area in 1812; and Spanish troops were reinforced after Ferdinand's restoration. The Spaniards captured Miranda, and in 1815 Bolívar took refuge in the West Indies.

At the other end of the continent the citizens of Buenos Aires had already proved themselves against the British (1807) and were in no mood to accept Napoleonic tutelage. Here too a junta allegiant to Ferdinand was formed. The early leadership soon faded, however, and the Junta of the United Provinces of the Río de la Plata was torn on the issue of centralism versus provincial autonomy. The fate of the Banda Oriental (Uruguay) was disputed with Portuguese troops. Paraguay split off in 1813 as an independent nation under the canny, steel-willed dictator Francia, later celebrated in a hero-worshipping essay by Carlyle. In 1814 José de San Martín (1778-1850), who had served in Spain as a loyal army officer until 1811, was sent to command some ill-disciplined troops against royalists in Upper Peru. Secretly harboring a grander scheme for the liberation of Chile and Peru, San Martín requested and received appointment as governor of the western province of Cuyo.

In Mexico the Spanish inhabitants forestalled the creole move to convoke a junta by replacing the viceroy with one of their own choice. Here the first pressures for independence came not from the interim regime in the capital but from two popular movements originating outside it. Both were led by priests, the first (1810-11) by Miguel Hidalgo y Costilla, the second (1813-15), which advanced so far as to issue an independence proclamation, by his mestizo lieutenant, José María Morelos. These movements were unique for the period in Spanish America with their popular, somewhat inchoate Indian and mestizo followings and with agenda that included a rudimentary demand for agrarian reform. A demand that was rarely met, however.

In 1815, the year after Ferdinand's restoration, the outlook for independence was dim. Hidalgo and Morelos had been executed in Mexico. Bolivar's campaigns had failed in Venezuela and New Granada. The Spaniards were entrenched in Ecuador, Peru and Chile. The factionalized Buenos Aires junta was temporizing on the issue of independence and trying to import a European prince. Yet the tide was turning. Ferdinand promptly set aside the liberal measures of the Côrtes of Cadiz and made clear that neither reform nor, much

Above: The Marquis de Pombal, chief minister of Portugal from 1750 to 1777, changed the character of Portugal's Brazilian colony. He stimulated its economy and encouraged its Indian population to integrate with the Portuguese settlers. The colony was not restored to its former prosperity by these measures, but the grip of an economic depression was slightly relaxed.

Above right: José de Seabra da Silva, protégé of the Marquis de Pombal. He became Portuguese chief minister in 1788.

Right: A Portuguese civil servant in Rio takes his family for a walk. The population of the Brazilian capital mushroomed after it became the seat of the branch of the Portuguese royal family, as settlers poured in from the mother country.

less, coequal autonomy was thinkable. Creole support for definitive independence soon gathered decisive momentum.

In South America the second phase of the independence wars took the form of a giant pincer movement – Bolívar's troops from the north, San Martín's from the south – converging on Spain's Peruvian stronghold. Bolívar renewed his Venezuelan campaign, now reinforced by several thousand European mercenaries and adventurers and by the rugged, previously pro-Spanish *llaneros* (plainsmen), under their wily leader and future Venezuelan president, José Antonio Páez. By 1819 enough progress had been made to allow convocation of a national congress at Angostura. Bolívar addressed it to advocate republican government, division of powers and abolition of slavery and of special privilege. During the next two and a half years of strenuous campaigns and political improvization he dislodged the Spaniards from most of New Granada, which he erected into the vast, unviable union of Gran Colombia.

In the south San Martín led a punishing march across the Andes in 1817 and liberated Chile. Refusing an order from Buenos Aires to return with his army, he sailed from Peru in 1820 with 6000 soldiers and seamen in a fleet commanded by Lord Cochrane. Because the revolt in Spain of that year had restored the liberal Constitution of 1812, the Peruvian viceroy vacillated. Finally he withdrew from Lima and left its cabildo free to welcome San Martín. In 1821 the latter declared Peruvian independence. The patriot forces were still outnumbered, however, and Bolívar's support was needed to complete Peru's emancipation. In 1822 the two leaders met in Guayaquil. Although San Martín offered to accept a subordinate command, the temperaments of the two men – Bolívar impulsive and truculent, San Martín sober and self-effacing – and their political inclinations – Bolívar's republican commitment and San Martín's monarchical leanings – made agreement out of the question. San Martín withdrew from the interview, returned to his country, and in 1824 he sailed for Europe, where he died in 1850.

After some delay Bolívar was authorized from Bogotá to resume the Peruvian campaign. He defeated the Spaniards in 1824, then proceeded to Upper Peru, where he drafted a constitution for the nation that bears his name, Bolivia. By now the Gran Colombian union was starting to crumble and its constituent parts to renounce the loyalty to the long-absent leader. In 1825 he returned to Bogotá to find that the magic of his leadership no longer availed against the forces of separatism and factionalism. After declaring to the Colombian congress that 'Independence is the only blessing we have acquired, at the expense of everything else,' he left Bogotá for exile but never sailed. Broken by defeat, racked by tuberculosis, he died in a seacoast town in December, 1830. Gran Colombia had already split into Venezuela, New Granada (modern Colombia) and Ecuador. 'America is ungovernable,' said Bolívar near the end., 'Those who have served the revolution have plowed the sea.'

Spain's liberal turnabout in 1820 influenced the course of independence more heavily in Mexico than it had in South America. It of course heartened those Mexicans who cherished ideas of self rule and reform. Privileged peninsulars and clergy, on the other hand, were torn between resisting the anticlerical measures that now emanated from Spain and worrying that independence would give the creoles a pretext to dispossess them. In an atmosphere of restive factionalism the viceroy asked a discredited creole officer, Agustín de Iturbide, to consolidate royal control by crushing a revolutionary movement that had long flickered in the south under Vicente Guerrero. Iturbide accepted, only to make a pact with Guerrero and issue a 'plan' with three central guarantees designed to appease all factious elites. Opposition to Iturbide melted; he entered Mexico City, declared independence in September 1821 and some months later was proclaimed emperor. His erratic, high-handed conduct led to his exile in 1823 and, on his attempted return, to his execu-

tion in 1824. In the first election of 1824 Guadalupe Victoria, former protégé of Morelos and a long-time revolutionary warrior, was chosen president.

Caudillism and national organization

It is not simple to periodize the history of the independent Latin American nations, of which there were 18 by the 1840s, for they exhibited wide social, political and economic diversity. Because each country's main external relations have been with Europe and the United States, and only occasionally with its neighbors, Latin American history lacks the coherence and phasing that textbooks ascribe to Western European

Left: José de San Martín, the turncoat Spanish general who fought the troops of the Viceroy of Peru, his fellow countrymen, in a series of battles among the crags of the Andes. He helped to secure the independence of Argentina, Peru and Chile.

Below, far left: General Guadelupe Victoria, the first President of the Mexican Republic established after the collapse of Iturbide's dreams of empire. He had been in the forefront of the struggle for independence from Spain since 1815.

Below left: A succession of military rulers unable to provide a stable government was brought to an end in Peru with the coming to power of Ramón Castilla. He utilized his country's resources to establish a prosperous republic.

Right: The great soldier of Latin American destiny, Simon Bolívar. He had a hand in liberating Colombia, Venezuela, Peru and Bolivia, but died an embittered man, for he could not force unity on these many diverse nations.

Simon Bolivar el Libertador

development. In fact many historians of Latin America find that only by relating their story to the history of the industrial West can they divide it into logical chapters.

From this external vantage point one discerns an initial phase of Latin American national development running from independence until the 1870s, a period when many countries ceased being simply limited consumer markets for European and North American goods and services to become as well large-scale suppliers of commodities required by the factories and urban population of the industrial West. This shift in commercial relationships altered the nature of foreign influence and pressure on the domestic scene. By generating foreign exchange and dictating new forms of production it also effected important internal changes: political, institutional, ecological, social and cultural.

It is often said that the Latin American wars for independence were not 'revolutionary,' that they wrought little change in social and economic institutions and that the displacement of peninsulars only consolidated the privileges of creole elites. There is much to support this contention. Living conditions of the rural workers who formed the bulk of the population were little affected by independence. The hacienda system survived in regional versions, and while hacendados tended to form circulating elites rather than an entrenched hereditary class, the hacienda rarely offered mobility to the humble peon. For half a century or more after independence there was virtually no impulse toward industrialization, even in the more populous and prosperous countries. The new nations essayed a variety of

constitutional formulae on a scale from 'conservative' centralism to 'liberal' federalism, but the spectrum reflected less of ideology than of the possibilities for compromise between central power and the regional and economic elites.

Yet if there was no institutional revamping in the classic 'revolutionary' sense, serious dislocations inevitably attended the replacement of two European empires by 18 nations. New disruptive pressures hastened the loosening of central authority and control. The war years had armed the retinues of caudillos and normalized the use of violence. New officer corps became a volatile force in political arenas and made implacable claims on impoverished national treasuries. Hitherto latent tensions among socioeconomic, occupational and ethnic groups became overt and often violent. The memory of plebeian or slave revolts, such as the Mexican movements under Hidalgo and Morelos or the slave rebellion of Saint Domingue, hardened ruling groups against giving the masses a voice – even though these same elites were now infiltrated by popular leaders of lowly origins. Another byproduct of independence was the displacement of power from urban to rural zones. In many places the wars occasioned great loss of moveable assets or capital, and wealth was more readily re-created on landed estates. Moreover, the flare-up of anti-Spanish feelings discredited the institutional systems with which urban elites were identified.

The international scene also witnessed changes. The Spanish countries, once a unitary if somewhat porous empire, were now a congeries of weak, sometimes quarrelsome republics. Argentina fought Brazil in the 1820s till Britain

persuaded them to accept the creation of Uruguay as a buffer. An attempted Bolivian-Peruvian Confederation was broken up by Chile in the 1830s. The United Provinces of Central America splintered into five countries in 1838. In the 1860s Paraguay attempted to meddle in Uruguay's internal affairs and was crushingly defeated after five bloody years of war against Argentina, Uruguay and Brazil. Such eruptions, however, were sporadic, for the countries' main orientation was extracontinental; they did not interact with each other under steady economic, demographic or political pressures. Each nation was left to work out a private destiny with the great powers on diplomatic and commercial fronts or even, as in the case of the Anglo-French blockade of Argentina in the 1840s, in the face of military force. Mexico was the most sorely tried by foreign imbroglios (not always unprovoked): a short-lived Spanish invasion (1829), the secession of Texas (1835-36), the French Pastry War (1838), war with the United States (1846-47) causing loss of half the national domain, and the French intervention under Maximilian (1862-67). A Bismarckian realist might say that these progressively more strenuous foreign encounters explain the clearly phased course of Mexico's institutional development and the vigor of its nationalism.

The generation or two following Latin American independence has been called the 'age of the caudillos.' Independence, as we say, gave rise to considerable social and geographic mobility. Landed elites were forced to ally with newly armed mestizos and other populist groups whom they might not directly control. The beneficiary of the new distributions of weaponry was the caudillo, a personalist, often lower-class leader who assumed military perquisites and power as a guerrilla chief in time of stress or crisis. Once legitimized, such power might be institutionalized and perpetuated.

Caudillism may at least in one sense be considered a stable national political system, even though it appears unstable in almost any given historical manifestation. It rested on a regionalized structure of personal and family alliances having some degree of popular endorsement. The caudillo himself was not a wholly free agent but depended on the supplies and manpower of land owners, the goodwill of foreigners and of urban commercial and financial groups, and the legal, constitutional and ideological skills of lawyers and the intelligentsia. It has been observed that the relation between a seemingly subservient national congress and a presidential caudillo was less a travesty of Western constitutional form than a re-creation of the colonial apparatus that prescribed consultation between a viceroy and a subordinate audiencia.

This skeletal account needs fleshing out to become descriptive of any specific situation. But it is at least suggestive for such cases as Venezuela, where despite the strong initial leadership of Bolívar's ex-lieutenant, Páez, the political fabric gradually disintegrated until the 1870s brought economic change and consolidation of the state; New Granada (Colombia after 1861), where the victory of 'liberals' in 1849 decentralized the country almost to the point of anarchy; or Peru, where the tumultuous 'era of the marshals' culminated in 1845 in the presidency of Ramón Castilla, who used revenues from guano and nitrates to organize a stable regime.

In Mexico – its economy dismantled after independence, its sieve-like treasury a prey for military coups, half its landed property in Church hands – the flamboyant Antonio López de Santa Anna was intermittently savior and scapegoat during the caudillo era. In the 1850s a disparate conservative-to-liberal revolutionary coalition united in protest against Santa Anna's irresponsibility and duplicity and against the demoralization he had brought on the country. The movement forced Santa Anna's exile and inaugurated the 'Reform' and brought political prominence to Benito Juárez of Oaxaca, descendant of Zapotec Indians. Subsequent legislation and the 1857 Constitution abolished privileges for Church and army, secularized education, created a federalist political system and prohibited land ownership by corporations. For many sectors the reforms were too sweeping, and resistance to them provoked civil war followed by French intervention (1862-67) under the ill-starred Maximilian. This interlude lastingly identified foreign interference with conservatism and clericalism, and nationalism with the liberal reforms.

Juárez' return to power in 1867 did not herald an era of Lockean democracy. The reformist scheme to redeem the Indians from communalism and wardship and to create a nation of small farmers on expropriated Church property made no allowance for the land hunger of the new urban classes or for the Indians' inability to assert themselves in the legal and commercial world of whites and mestizos. In canceling the corporate privileges and tutelary arrangements of the old Spanish state, the Reform advantaged a few urban or 'new creole' groups on the rise, initiating half a century of intense land concentration and widespread conversion of rural workers to peonage. After Porfirio Díaz assumed the presidency in 1876 this final expropriation of the Indians was carried out.

Whereas in Mexico men had been ensconced on the land for millennia before the Spanish conquest, in Argentina the work of bringing the vast interior into production, including the 250,000 square miles of pampas that stretch out from Buenos Aires, was still largely a task for the future at the time of independence. Here a leading strand of nineteenth-century history was the struggle of the interior provinces against domination and commercial control by Buenos Aires province and its strategically located port.

Oligarchy and external dependency

The first president of Argentina (then the 'United Provinces'), Bernardino Rivadavia, sponsored 'land reform' designed to attract immigrants, populate the interior and produce rents and taxes. In effect it sanctioned the alienation of enormous tracts to a privileged handful; by 1830 20 million acres had passed to 538 persons and corporations. Rivadavia's caudillist successors made few significant changes in the country's economic or political structure. Then, in 1853, Argentina was reorganized under a new Constitution. The Constitution was patterned after that of the United States, though it allowed the president interventionary powers in the provinces. Fearing for its prerogatives, Buenos Aires province – wealthy, strategic and containing some 30 percent of the nation's sparse population – remained for years outside the Confederation. When consolidation finally occurred in 1862, Argentina had reached the threshold of a half-century of agricultural development, railroad construction, immigration, urbanization and foreign investment that has scarcely a parallel in Latin American history. Only long after the period had closed was it widely recognized that these years of stability and prosperity were characterized by oligarchic rule and powerful lines of external dependency.

Ostensibly at least, Chile and Brazil were exceptions in the caudillo age because their central political institutions were legitimized relatively swiftly. In Chile the cause of stability was served by demographic and economic concentration in the fertile central zone of Santiago and the consequent lack of regional separatism. A Valparaiso businessman, Diego Portales, rather than a latter-day condottiere, was the principal architect of the centralist 1833 Constitution. Following its promulgation, Chile experienced political continuity and regular presidential succession till 1891, when diversification of the socioeconomic elite led to a revolt against the presidential system.

Brazil, as detailed earlier, did not experience Spanish America's legitimacy vacuum at independence. Here as in Chile a centralist Constitution (1824), drafted by a hand-picked council of Pedro I, respected the *de facto* social hierarchy. It created a lower chamber chosen by restricted suffrage and accorded the emperor a 'moderate power' to nominate lifetime senators, exercise a suspensive veto, dissolve parliament and appoint provincial presidents (governors). Pedro abdicated in 1831, leaving a series of short-lived regencies to try out various political formulae in the face of widespread revolts and a protracted secessionist war in Rio Grande do Sul. A decade later Pedro's fifteen-year-old son assumed the throne to inaugurate a half-century reign which, once provincial unrest was energetically quelled, became renowned for stability and gradualism. Using his 'moderative power' with firmness and discretion, the bearded, sober Pedro II presided over patriarchal Brazilian society as a *primus inter pares*, acquiescing in its clan-like regional political systems while guiding the nation toward step-by-step fulfillment of such inevitable reforms as abolition of slavery. After mid-century soaring export earnings from coffee hastened Brazil's acquisition of railroads, urban services and other modern accouterments, lending a deceptive cast of Victorian progress and solidity to the single empire of the Western hemisphere.

The development of neo-colonialism

If a summary treatment of Latin America in the early national period leans naturally toward political interpretation, the account of the subsequent period tends, nowadays at least, to favor the economic. An older view characterized the region's history in the late nineteenth century as a continuing struggle by 'liberal' leadership to achieve political stability, republican government, economic development and rudimentary social justice in the face of apathy, ignorance, elite factionalism and the vested interests of the Church, landowners and, increasingly, the military.

A less moralistic thesis is that Latin American countries became victims of the international division of labor that accompanied the second phase of the industrial revolution. Mass production and rising consumer demand in the industrial West magnetized more powerfully than before the economics of Latin America and the Third World. Technological advances (steamships, rail-

ways, refrigeration) added perishables like beef and bananas to the commodities suitable for long-distance shipment. Capital accrual gave the industrial nations economic leverage to dictate terms of development, or underdevelopment, to client nations. Yet pressed to the ultimate, this argument places wealthy, urbanized, middle-class Argentina in a 'colonial' status scarcely more elevated than that of a 'banana republic' – a judgment which became thinkable only long after Argentina drifted to a path of economic uncertainty and political improvization in the 1930s.

In pursuing this line of analysis the economist Celso Furtado categorizes Latin American countries not by indices of political or economic development but by the nature of their raw-material exports: temperate-agricultural, tropical- or semitropical-agricultural, and mineral. Argentina and Uruguay figure in the first group, with their exports of meat, wool and wheat. Here the extensive cultivation of level, fertile lands facilitated technification of agriculture, favored early construction of railway nets centering on chief port cities and produced handsome export earnings. In such economies internal markets became integrated early, and the fruits of prosperity were not limited to minuscule elites.

Tropical and semitropical exporters included Brazil, Colombia, Ecuador, Central America, the Antilles and regions of Mexico and Venezuela. Because other world regions of labor-intensive, low-wage agriculture were generally the tropical suppliers for Britain, tropical (unlike temperate) Latin America became oriented to United States and, secondarily, continental European markets. Tropical and semitropical commodities encountered low world price ceilings and produced economic growth rather than development. There were of course exceptions to this banana-republic stereotype. The response in nineteenth-century Cuba to competition in the world sugar market was to centralize and mechanize cane-grinding and to introduce railways as early as the 1830s. Cuban slaves and seasonally employed free workers lived at miserable subsistence levels, but

as sugar was not labor intensive, Cuba urbanized early. By the end of the century 29 percent of its population was in cities over 20,000, as against 24 percent in the United States. Another exception was the São Paulo coffee region in Brazil. At the end of the century the region was producing two thirds of the world's coffee. By generating capital and attracting immigration, the crop brought into being one of Latin America's most dynamic urban-industrial centers.

The mineral producers (silver, copper, nitrates, tin) were Mexico, Chile, Peru and Bolivia, with Venezuela contributing petroleum in the twentieth century. Here as with the tropical-agriculture countries the United States was often the foremost investor and customer. Mining operations created economic enclaves, hiring relatively

little labor and contributing virtually no infrastructure for broader development purposes. Indirect effects of mining became important, however, when government taxes diverted the flow of profits from foreign destinations to domestic uses.

As the prime impetus for economic change from foreign demand and foreign investment, the structure of Latin American economies reflected an extranational orientation. Transportation networks funneled traffic into capitals and port cities and failed to interconnect regional centers. As transport hubs, seats of political control and favor and the preferred location for foreign banks and businesses, capital cities became small islands of cosmopolitanism and modernity, acquiring disproportionately large populations and outsized

Far left. Sugar cane is put through a crushing machine in Cuba. The nations of Latin America were at a low level of industrial development when they achieved their independence. To realize economic growth they were forced to concentrate their efforts on the production of cash crops or minerals.

Left: Gauchos, those romantic figures of the Argentine *pampas,* skin cattle. Argentina's combination of cattle and grain made it a wealthy country, able to finance development from the export of these commodities.

Above right: The army of Juárez enters Mexico City in 1867. Napoleon III's vain attempt to establish a puppet empire in Mexico only provoked a reformist revolution.

Right: A Mexican silver mine. The capital-intensive mining industry attracted foreign investors to Latin American countries, but did little to promote development of a modern industrial base. Most people failed to benefit from the wealth brought into and taken out of their countries.

allocations of public services and upper-class amenities. Specialization in export commodities inhibited balanced agricultural development, forcing some countries to import staple foods that were producible at home. Specialization also channeled foreign investment into commodity production and supporting services (banking, transportation, telegraphy, utilities) rather than manufacturing. By the late nineteenth century industry had gained significant footholds only in Mexico, Argentina, Chile and southern Brazil, and even here it went little beyond textiles and food processing.

Rising world demand for Latin American farm products brought more oppression, not prosperity, to rural workers. Negro slavery, it is true, was abolished in much of Spanish America at independence and in the northern Andean countries by the 1850s. Yet throughout the lands with large Indian populations, from Mexico south to Peru and Bolivia, the nineteenth century witnessed wholesale conversions of rural labor to debt peonage and ill-disguised forms of servitude.

After 1870 immigration contributed importantly to realigning population concentration, with regional shifts in economic production. It has been estimated that since 1800 Latin America has received 10 million immigrants, including slaves, as against 35 million for the United States and Canada. Of the 10 million, some 7 million were Europeans who migrated to Argentina, Uruguay and southern Brazil between the mid nineteenth century and World War II. While in the early years immigrant farmers were often subjected to onerous contracts and living conditions as colonists or wage laborers, these groups tended to join compatriots who had remained in the cities, where later generations came to form the backbone of the middle classes and selectively to attain positions of entrepreneurial, professional and intellectual leadership. The differential impetus that immigration might impart is dramatized by the fact that in 1850 Chile's population slightly exceeded Argentina's, 1.3 against 1.1 million, while by 1914 Argentina had jumped to 8 million and Chile to only 3.5 million.

These decades of immigration, foreign loans and investment, soaring exports, urbanization and technological change created new possibilities for political centralization and stability. The caudillo on horseback gave way to the more urbane, less flamboyant, but no less personalistic 'bourgeois' caudillo, a leader who appealed to a more diversified elite, who had more comfortable access to financial resources, who commanded a French- or German-trained army that could overpower the caciques' (provincial political bosses) improvised retinues, who consolidated the central allegiance of familial, regional and occupational elites.

The prototypical new strong man was Mexico's Porfirio Díaz (1876-80, 1884-1911), a mestizo general from Oaxaca who had served under Juárez, turned against his leader and seized power four years after Juárez' death. The Díaz regime was organized on five pillars of support: the hacendados, military, Church, professionals and foreign investors and managers. Land holdings were concentrated by enforced dissolution of Indian village communities. By 1910 the landed elite numbered only some 800 hacendados, many of them absentee, while 80 percent of Mexico's rural families were landless, a proportion that reached 97 to 99 percent in some central states. Bandit leaders from the turbulent years received well-paid army commissions. To insure equilibrium, military zones were created for surveillance of civil governors, while rural police kept tabs on the army. Anti-

clerical laws were relaxed sufficiently to dampen the Church's appetite for inciting revolts. In 1910 the population was only one fifth literate, and of this fraction, it has been claimed, four fifths were in government employ.

To foreigners Mexico offered social privileges and economic opportunity. Of Mexico's 27 large manufacturing firms in 1914, 18 were owned wholly and seven partly by foreigners. Foreign land holdings amounted to one seventh of the national territory. By the end of Díaz' regime, British investments in Mexico totaled $300 million, French $400 million and American over $1 billion. Measured in Mexican pesos of 1900, exports rose during the Porfirian period from 4 to 19 pesos per capita, while imports rose from 5 to 14 pesos.

Investment, exports and modest industrialization, however, could not dissipate all inertial forces. Agricultural wages had remained steady for a century, though prices for staples had risen sharply. Foreign capital could not prime the pump for development if profits were remitted abroad or invested in land. Between 1895 and 1910 employment in industry and services increased less swiftly than in agriculture. Díaz was 80 years old in 1910; many governors, ministers and generals were senile; the army was demoralized. Even conservative groups were receptive to the idea of free elections. In 1910, however, no one could have predicted that Mexico was on the threshold of Latin America's first full-blown revolution.

Mexico's Porfirian Peace is in part explainable as a delayed reaction to the external shock of French occupation in the 1860s. In other countries, too, foreign intervention seemed a necessary prelude to centralization and stability. For Colombia this jolt came in 1903, when the United States presided over the secession of Panama after Colombia had refused Washington's ungenerous terms for a long-term lease of the canal zone. This affront, coming in the wake of a devastating civil war in which 100,000 had perished (1899-1902), helped to fuse national energies for a quarter-century of oligarchic, conservative rule and economic expansion. For Peru and Bolivia the chastening blow was the War of the Pacific (1879-83), by which Chile appropriated the nitrate desert that now forms her northern extremity.

If the more turbulent countries seemed on the road to tranquility and economic growth in the late nineteenth century, three of the most stable ones suffered severe internal shocks, all at nearly the same moment. Argentina was to all appearances a success story. Its plains were brought into production and served by railways; farming and ranching were modernized; capital and immigrants poured in; light industry started up, although on sufferance of the commercial and financial sectors. Under its republican 1853 Constitution, Argentina was managed by a relatively progressive and flexible landed oligarchy in league with merchants, financiers, politicians and professionals who had interests in foreign trade and investments. By the late 1880s, however, speculation, financial manipulation and a public debt which rose from 117 to 355 million pesos in four years brought the country to the brink of disaster. In 1890 President Juárez Celman was forced by a broad coalition of reformers to resign in favor of his vice president. No revolution had occurred, nor had the masses been mobilized. Reformist demands were limited to anti-imperialism, moralization of government, respect for civil rights and free, universal suffrage. The episode did, however, mark the entry into Argentine political life of the Civic Union, soon known as the Radicals, a

middle-class, center party with neither leftist nor anticlerical leanings. Benefiting from the 1912 electoral reform, the Radicals captured the presidency in 1916 behind Hipólito Irigoyen, a strong-willed, capricious, humorless man who, despite his populist sympathies, proved capable of ruthless action against striking workers. The advent of the Radicals did not displace the oligarchy but moved it to a position of indirect control.

Chile's pivotal year was 1891. Although presidents till then succeeded one another peacefully, first at ten-, then at five-year intervals, the executive's task had become increasingly delicate as the pattern of political forces grew complex and as his office lost its paternalistic aura. Various catalysts were at work by mid-century. The presence in Chile of exiled Argentine intellectuals and the creation of a superior university and secondary-school system had helped form a liberal, highly articulate group of political leaders and publicists. Further complicating the situation were Chile's rising foreign debt, British acquisition of Chilean nitrate interest, falling world prices for Chilean exports and an incipient inflation that was soon endemic.

In addressing these problems President José Manuel Balmaceda (1886-91) was convinced that Chile's prosperity was skin-deep and that its economic future required taxation of the wealthy, use of nitrate income for new development projects, centralized economic planning and resistance to the penetration of foreign capital. The privileged rejected both the policy of self-denial and the prospect of strong-arm tactics for imposing it; the large majority stood by passively until a civil war broke out in which 10,000 were killed. Balmaceda took asylum in the Argentine legation and, months later, committed suicide. In later years he became a martyred hero for Chilean nationalists, both rightists and Marxists.

With Balmaceda's removal Chile passed from a presidential to a parliamentary system, but inexorably the trends that had produced the 1891 crisis followed their course: inflation, rising public debt, tax exemption for the wealthy, declining farm productivity. In 1907 Chileans spent 6.8 million pesos to import champagne, jewels, silks and perfumes and only 3.8 million for industrial and farm machinery. The stage was set for the political volte-faces and populism of the 1920s.

Brazil's late-century watershed was more critical than Argentina's or Chile's, for it marked the transition from monarchy to republic in 1889. For decades Brazil had enjoyed internal peace and advancing prosperity under the aegis of Pedro II. Imports still exceeded exports in the 1850s, but by the early 1860s they were balanced, and from 1865 to the end of the empire the nation's trade balance was favorable. It has been calculated that the annual per capita production of free Brazilian labor declined from $50 to $43 (modern dollars) from 1800 to 1850, then increased to $106 by 1900.

Like Chile's presidential or Mexico's Porfirian system, Brazil's imperial institutions were rendered anachronistic by the very stability and economic progress they had helped engender. New, predominantly urban socioeconomic groups increasingly resisted the government's cautious response to new conditions and its favoritism toward latifundiary and foreign-connected commercial interests. The urban areas generated strong pressures for abolition of slavery, and by 1888 full emancipation had been decreed, but failure to compensate slaveowners undermined the planters' imperial loyalties. The emperor's imprisonment of two bishops in 1873 for their antimasonic edicts cooled the Church's enthusiasm for privileges it seemingly enjoyed under state patronage. A republican movement was organized in the 1870s which, by 1889, boasted 197 clubs and 74 newspapers. Army officers increasingly resented signs that the government

failed to share their self-estimate as being disciplined, uncorruptible and patriotic.

Pedro II was dethroned in 1889 by a military coup. When the military government subsequently collapsed, the regional plantocracies reasserted political control under an entente between the two strongest states, São Paulo and Minas Gerais, which lasted until 1930.

The early republican years saw the peak of the Amazon rubber boom, restraint of inflation and reestablishment of foreign credit, expansion of natural boundaries by arbitration, continuing immigration and the beautification of Rio de Janeiro. But the new golden age was short-lived. Coffee overproduction required expensive government stockpiling of the crop. Rubber production slumped in the face of Asian competition. Urbanization and industrialization in the prosperous Rio-São Paulo region created new political sectors and a significant if uncoordinated labor movement. After 1910 the army tried to recoup influence in the political arena. Under such pressures the governmental system – politically decentralized, socially elitist, economically conservative – became progressively less effective over the course of time.

While the second age of Western 'imperialism' exposed all Latin America to new forms of external political influence after 1870, the smaller northern countries were subjected to direct control and intervention by the United States as the Caribbean became an 'American Mediterranean.'

United States recognition that Latin America constituted a 'sphere of influence' was implicit in the Monroe Doctrine of 1823. But that document was for decades interpreted as a deterrent to territorial ambitions of extrahemispheric powers rather than as justification for 'protective' intervention by the United States. Even in the Caribbean area, moreover, the Doctrine was capriciously applied. Although the United States consistently opposed transfer of Cuba from Spain to another power, it failed to protest British expansion in Central America (1833-41) and it acquiesced in Spain's temporary reannexation of the Dominican Republic in 1861.

US 'Manifest Destiny'

By the end of the century economic growth and settlement of the West had turned the United States to a new Manifest Destiny overseas. Its interest in expanding trade and investment in Latin America under conditions of peace and stability was formally articulated at the First Pan American Conference, held at Washington in 1889, while its claim to political hegemony was asserted in the 1895 ultimatum to Britain that the United States was 'practically sovereign on this continent.' In the Caribbean area American strategic concerns overshadowed even the economic. It was geopolitics, not business, which weighed most heavily in prompting the United States declaration of war against Spain in 1898 and in dictating terms for the annexation of Puerto Rico and, in 1902, the qualified independence of Cuba. United States apprehensions about its Caribbean 'underbelly' were heightened after 1904, when work began on the Panama Canal. That year, significantly, President Theodore Roosevelt promulgated his 'corollary' to the Monroe Doctrine, casting the United States as a Pan American policeman who enjoyed interventionary powers in cases of 'chronic wrongdoing' or 'impotence.' For 30 years the United States freely exercised this arrogated authority, reducing Cuba, Panama, Nicaragua, Haiti and the Dominican Republic at one time or another to virtual protectorate status. Given the formidable political and economic asymmetries of the Northern Hemisphere, in fact, not even the Good Neighbor Policy of the second Roosevelt would consign to oblivion the Monroe Doctrine and its truculent corollary.

Above left: The radical President José Balmaceda of Chile. He tried to introduce nationalist economic policies into his country, ones that would further its development yet ensure an equitable share of the national wealth to all citizens. The rich oligarchs, long used to a government run in their interests, rebelled, and 10,000 Chileans perished in the civil war that followed.

Right: Porfirio Díaz, President of Mexico between 1876 and 1880, and again between 1884 and 1911. Although he had been a follower of Juárez, he later turned against his radical patron, and established a reactionary regime that only stunted Mexico's economic development. Díaz sold out Mexican interests as a matter of policy to foreign investors.

Above right: Miguel Juárez Celman won his way to the presidency in Argentina through electoral fraud, only to be deposed four years later in 1890, when his mismanagement of the country's economy produced a reformist coalition with the military backing needed to depose him.

Asia and Africa

The spectacular rise of Europe to world dominance between the sixteenth and twentieth centuries is usually explained purely in terms of the nature of European society and its dynamic political and economic structures. But European global hegemony would have been unlikely if other centers of power and prosperity in the world had not fallen into such a subservient role over the same period. On the face of it, in the sixteenth century the expanding Turkish Ottoman Empire looked a much more likely world power than France or England. The Moghul ruler of most of India, Akbar the Great, was far richer and more powerful than his contemporary Elizabeth I, whose descendants were to rule the Raj. And even before the great European voyages of exploration had begun, the Chinese Ming Dynasty had sent a fleet as far as Aden and Africa, suggesting the intriguing possibility of an overseas expansion never realized. The extraordinary shift in the balance of wealth and power that followed was in part a result of the decline of these eastern empires relative to the rise of Europe.

In the sixteenth century, the world of Islam was dominated by three dynasties of nomadic origin, the Ottomans ruling from Constantinople, the Safavids in Iran and the Moghuls in India. The Ottomans' sophisticated bureaucratic government and disciplined military machine – using the latest war technology – made them a formidable force, holding sway from the Indian Ocean to Hungary, and from Tunis to Baghdad. The eastern limit of their power was set by the Safavids in Iran, who embraced the unorthodox Shi'ite faith and fought bloody wars with the orthodox Sunni Ottomans, paralleling the religious wars of Reformation Europe. Further east, in India, the Moghuls ruled the largest area of the subconti-

nent yet to be brought under one government. Although this Islamic dynasty traced its origins back to Chingiz (Genghiz) Khan and Timur, it for a time provided enlightened government, winning the respect of its Hindu subjects.

Yet from the late seventeenth century onward, perhaps before, these once highly organized and efficient Islamic empires fell into decline. For the Safavids, the end was sudden: in 1720 they were swept away by an Afghani invasion. The Ottoman Empire survived into the twentieth century, but this was no more than a lingering death. Governmental inertia, technological backwardness and intellectual sloth had long undermined the once proud power. Through the nineteenth century Europeans nibbled away at the Ottoman Empire, squabbling like jackals over the carcass. An unwise participation in World War I would finally bring the *coup de grâce*.

The disintegration of the Moghul Empire in the eighteenth century was the key to the rapid expansion of British rule in India, a piecemeal process of limited wars and treaties of protection with the minor princelings who had asserted their independence as central control declined. Sucked in to fill the power vacuum left by the Moghuls, the British ended up creating an Indian Empire very much in the Moghul image. They maintained their rule with ease – despite the hiccup of the Indian Mutiny in 1857 – because the population was accustomed to government by invaders of an alien religion. Only with the emergence of modern Indian nationalism was that situation to alter.

In Southeast Asia, European colonialism encountered societies already subject to complex outside influences, from India, from China, and from Muslim traders. As in India, the rivalries and

weaknesses of small states were easily manipulated by Europeans to impose colonial rule – by the Spanish in the Philippines, the Dutch in the East Indies, Britain in Malaya and Burma, and the French in Indochina. Thailand was the only country in the region permitted to remain independent.

China was an altogether more formidable proposition for the Europeans to take on. In the fifteenth century, the Ming Dynasty ruled a vast, prosperous and sophisticated empire. Almost totally self-sufficient, China regarded itself as the center of the world and would deal with foreign countries only as 'tributary states.' When the first Europeans arrived by sea, their activities were limited and strictly controlled. This practice continued under the Ch'ing Dynasty, founded by Manchu invaders from the north in 1644.

But Chinese culture, partly because of its arrogant disregard for the outside world, failed to adapt in a fast-changing world. The empire lacked the economic dynamism needed to cope with a rapidly growing population, and both ideas and social structures were ossified. By the nineteenth century, China was a backward country, unable to match European technology or European economic and military organization. Even then, internal rebellion did more to undermine Manchu authority than did aggression by the colonial powers. The Dynasty struggled on until 1911-12, when China was declared a republic. But government remained ineffectual and outside powers operated at will on Chinese soil.

Another Asian country, Japan, had already demonstrated that such an outcome was by no means inevitable. Almost completely isolated from the rest of the world between 1641 and 1853, Japan should have been especially vulnerable

Left: A Persian manuscript of steppe horsemen negotiating a bridge in a mountain region.

Top right: The US naval officer Commander Perry lands at the Japanese port of Yokohama to meet the Emperor's imperial commissioners, a significant moment in the opening up of Japan to the West.

Above right: An early photograph of a scene from the Indian Mutiny of 1857, as British and Indian troops 'lounge' carefully for the camera's benefit.

Right: Headless corpses are strewn along a main street in China, executed during the turmoil following the Revolution of 1911-12. Public beheadings were a common feature of the Chinese penal code, both to further humiliate the victim and act as an example to others.

when the nineteenth century, in the person of Commodore Perry of the United States, at last forced an entry. But the Japanese response was a rapid restructuring of government, followed by the modernization of the economy. By 1900 Japan was an independent industrial and military power. The Russo-Japanese War of 1904-5 was a historic turning point, the first defeat of a European by an Asian power since the Middles Ages.

Although Japan was exceptional in its successful adoption of Western methods, throughout Asia by 1914 new leaders were emerging, educated in Western political thought and determined to use the ideas of nationalism, liberalism, democracy and socialism to revive their countries' fortunes. In Africa south of the Sahara, however, the gulf between the level of development of local societies and the modern world was still too great to be crossed. The destructive effects of the slave trade, both Christian and Muslim, were followed in the later nineteenth century by direct military attack as the European powers carved up Africa between them. For most Africans, the encounter with modern civilization up to 1914 was little else but a tragic tale of massacre, racial oppression and cultural humiliation.

The Islamic World: 1500-1914

European historians of the Early Modern Period, preoccupied with the discovery of the New World and with the founding of the great maritime empires, sometimes think of the sixteenth century as the Age of Iberian Hegemony. Equally aptly, however, it might be called the Age of Turkish Hegemony, for during this and the succeeding centuries a sizeable part of the Eurasian land-mass was dominated by military and administrative elites of Turkish stock, and it was possible to travel from Algiers in the Maghrib to Dacca in Bengal or to Kashgar in Sinkiang without ever leaving Turkish-dominated territory. The most important of the new Turkish dynasties –

the Ottomans dominating the Balkans and the eastern Mediterranean, the Safavids in Iran and the Moghuls in India – commanded more extensive resources and governed their subjects more effectively than had perhaps any Muslim dynasties in the past, even the 'Abbasids in their prime. Their empires may be considered as the culmination of Muslim achievement in government, in military science and in control over human resources.

Of these regimes the most extensive was the Ottoman Empire, emerging from humble beginnings in fourteenth-century Anatolia to become a world power straddling vast stretches of Europe, Asia and Africa in the sixteenth and seventeenth centuries and surviving, albeit in an emasculated condition, down to 1922. Its Safavid neighbor to the east was a far smaller entity, although more compact and more homogeneous, occupying a territory somewhat more extensive than that of modern Iran and with a history dating from 1501 to 1732. Across the Amu-Darya, then the north-eastern frontier of Iran, lay two Uzbek Khanates, of which the more important, with its capital at Bukhara, ruled Mawarannahr and some outlying

territories, while a cadet-line, the 'Arabshahids, held Khwarazm and had their capital at Khiva. The ruling dynasty at Bukhara throughout the sixteenth century was that of the Shaybanids, to be succeeded in 1598 by the more feeble Janid, or Astrakhanid, dynasty, which survived until 1785. Beyond the Syr-Darya the steppe-region was dominated by the Kazakh Confederacy. In India the Moghul Empire, founded in 1526 by Babur, covered the greater part of the sub-continent during the second half of the seventeenth century, and although by 1748 it was well past its prime, it survived in titular form down to 1857.

These regimes differed strikingly from one another in their traditions and methods of government, just as did the peoples and countries they ruled. Yet in addition to their Turkish or Turkoman origin almost all had certain features in common. The one exception to this was the Kazakh Confederacy which remained wholly nomadic, enshrining earlier traditions of the steppes without substantial modification of any kind. For this reason their history can be dealt with apart from the great sedentary Turkish empires with which they were contemporary.

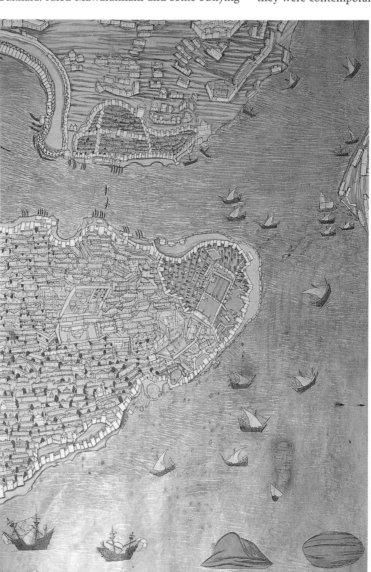

Far left: The head of a Muslim war banner inscribed with a religious text. In the sixteenth century Islam was still an expanding religion, winning converts and conquering new territory.

Left: The hub of the Ottoman Empire – Constantinople, now Istanbul. The fall of this great Byzantine city to the Turks in 1453 was a major defeat for Christendom and a triumph for Islam.

Above right: The Kaaba at Mecca, focus of Muslim pilgrimage and prayer. Mecca was absorbed into the Ottoman Empire after the defeat of the Mamluks in 1517.

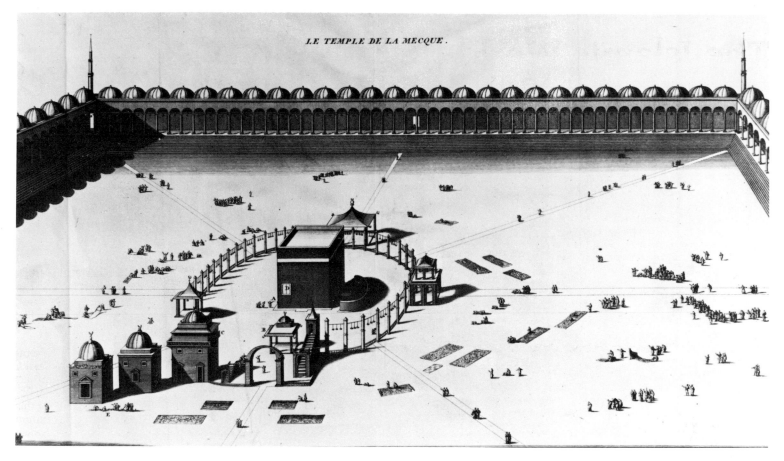

LE TEMPLE DE LA MECQUE.

The Kazakhs

The original Kazakh Horde broke away from the main Uzbek Horde of Abu-l-Khayr in the second half of the fifteenth century, and when the Uzbeks moved south of the Syr-Darya into Maw-arannahr the Kazakhs filled the vacuum they left, eventually occupying a vast area from the Ural River in the west to the foothills of the Altai in the east. Their economy was purely pastoral and thus they were more or less content with the wide grasslands south of the Siberian taïga. The heroic age of the Kazakhs as a unified confederacy coin-cided with the appearance during the early six-teenth century of a succession of outstanding rulers, in particular Burunduk Khan (1488-1509), Kasym Khan (1509-18), who was said to be able to summon 200,000 horsemen to his standard, and the latter's youngest son, Haqq Nazar, greatest of his line (1538-80). But even during the sixteenth century a basic division had appeared among the Kazakhs which hardened with the passing of each decade, a division of the formerly unified confede-racy into three separate khanates: the Great Horde in the Semirechie, the Middle Horde north-east of the Aral Sea and the lower course of the Syr-Darya and the Little Horde between the Aral Sea and the Ural River.

The death-throes of Kazakh independence were to be protracted and savage. In the early years of the seventeenth century there arose on their eastern marches the powerful empire of the Buddhist Oirots, whose Kalmyk kinsmen had already ravaged the Kazakh steppes some time be-fore on their march to the Volga, where they had established the no less formidable Kalmyk Horde. Again and again the Oirots raided deep into the heart of Kazakh territory and against these marauders the Kazakhs, divided among them-selves, could offer only occasional and half-hearted resistance. Not until this scourge was annihilated by the Manchus in 1757 were the Kazakhs freed from their depredations, and by then decades of debilitating warfare, decline of population, depleted flocks and famine had taken

their toll. The Kazakhs were thus incapable of resisting the encroaching line of Russian forts, which first appeared on the northern rim of the steppes during the first quarter of the eighteenth century. The Little Horde became a Russian pro-tectorate in 1731, the Middle Horde in 1740 and the Great Horde in 1742, but even this did not spare them from further Oirot incursions, which only ceased after 1757.

The Turkish dynasties

The fortunes of the Kazakhs followed a wholly different course from those of the other Turkish regimes which emerged at the beginning of the sixteenth century and which came into being partly as a result of the ambitions of two re-markable empire-builders, Shah Isma'il I (1501-24), founder of the Safavid dynasty in Iran, and his bitter rival, the Uzbek Khan, Muhammad Shaybani (1500-10), founder of the Shaybanid dynasty in Mawarannahr. The ancestors of Shah Isma'il were the heads of a Shi'i order of Sufis, the *Safaviyyeh* (named after Shaykh Safi al-Din, who died in 1334), with its center in Ardebil, near Tabriz, and with its devoted followers widely scattered among the Turkish and Turkoman tribesmen of Azarbaijan and eastern Anatolia. Later they also claimed descent from the Shi'i Imams. The young Isma'il grew up in a period of increasingly vigorous missionary activity on the part of the *Safaviyyeh*, which resulted in the spread of Shi'ism deep into Anatolia.

Isma'il's career followed the classic pattern of the founder of a dynasty whose power rested upon a foundation of tribal support. Unlike other such figures, however, his relationship to his fol-lowers was not simply that of the successful leader of an ever-growing war-band; he was also a spiritual leader, the Hidden Imam's deputy on earth, and down to his defeat at Chaldiran in 1514 he was believed to possess the attributes of per-fectibility and invulnerability. His career was a dazzling success-story. In 1501 he captured Tabriz, thereby taking the place of the now-defunct Aq

Qoyunlu in western Iran and eastern Anatolia. By 1508 he was master of Baghdad, and by the close of 1509 he was in control of the whole of Iran (apart from Gurgan and Khurasan), modern Iraq and, in Anatolia, the country around Lake Van and Diabakir.

Although it diverged in some respects, the career of his rival, Muhammad Shaybani, grand-son of an Uzbek chieftain, Abu-l-Khayr, who had made a bid for Central Asian empire during the middle decades of the fifteenth century, showed a certain similarity with that of Shah Isma'il. In 1500 Muhammad Shaybani gained possession of the former Timurid capital, Samarqand, and by 1507 he had seized Herat from the Timurids. By the close of 1509 he ruled not only Mawarannahr but also certain districts across the Syr-Darya in the vicinity of Tashkent, as well as Khurasan and Gurgan in Iran. When, in 1510, Muhammad Shay-bani and Shah Isma'il met in battle at Marv, a con-frontation which had long been foreseeable, they were in fact disputing the future mastery of the Iranian plateau, and much more besides. Shah Isma'il proved the better commander, and Muhammad Shaybani was defeated and killed. Muhammad Shaybani's death in 1510 compelled the Uzbeks to withdraw across the Amu-Darya into Mawarannahr where they established a long-lived khanate ruled by three successive dynasties: the Shaybanids (c 1500-98), the Janids (1598-1785) and the Mangits (1785-1920).

Timurid princelings

Muhammad Shaybani's conquests had been primarily at the expense of the various Timurid rulers who had survived in Mawarannahr and Khurasan down to the close of the fifteenth century. One of these princelings, as resourceful and daring as any member of that colorful family, Zahir al-Din Babur, through his father a grandson of a great-grandson of Timur and through his mother a descendant of Chingiz Khan's second son, Chaghatai, fled in the face of the advancing Uzbeks to Kabul. There he ruled from 1504 to

1526, warily observing events north of the Hindu-kush, while casting around for some appropriate outlet for his own ambition. Finally, in 1526, he launched an attack upon the declining Delhi Sultanate, defeated and killed Sultan Ibrahim Lodi at Panipat and occupied Delhi and Agra. The battle of Panipat is traditionally, and rightly, regarded as the starting-point of Moghul rule in India.

The Ottomans

There might well have been no Moghul Empire at all but for Muhammad Shaybani's determination to expel the Timurids from their Central Asian homeland. It was a somewhat similar set of fortuitous circumstances which brought the Ottoman Turks into the Fertile Crescent and the valley of the Nile. Down to the end of the fifteenth century the history of the Ottoman Sultanate showed little indication that it would one day

blossom into a great empire, spanning three continents and displaying some of the attributes of the former 'Abbasid universalist state. In its early years the Ottoman Sultanate, from its base in western Anatolia and Thrace, had expanded northward and westward into the Balkans, indicating that it was intent upon becoming a Black Sea power, a trend apparently confirmed by the conquest of Constantinople in 1453 and by the forced submission of the Tatar Khan of the Crimea. It was the career of Shah Isma'il that changed all this, for the Shah's restless ambition, along with the rapid expansion of Shi'ism westward and the devotion of the Shi'i tribes of central Anatolia to the Safavid cause, threatened the very existence of the Ottoman state.

In 1514 Selim I Yavuz, 'the Grim' (1512-20), one of the greatest of Ottoman rulers, counterattacked, advanced eastward into Azarbaijan, defeated Shah Isma'il at Chaldiran and tempora-

rily occupied Tabriz, then the Safavid capital. Throughout the marches of eastern Anatolia support for the Safavids fell away – hastened perhaps by the discovery that the earthly deputy of the Hidden Imam was as prone as any other mortal to the hazards of the battlefield – while Selim reinforced the lesson of Chaldiran by massacring every Shi'ite in Anatolia upon whom he could lay his hands. The long-term effect of such thoroughness was to make the frontier between Ottoman Turkey and Safavid Iran a denominational one, with Sunnis for the most part to the west of it and Shi'ites to the east, a division that has survived down to the present time.

Once drawn back into Asia, Selim discovered that there could be no turning back. Shah Isma'il was defeated but not overthrown, and there was the likelihood of a projected Safavid alliance with the Egyptian Mamluks who, from their base in northern Syria, could turn the Ottoman flank whenever the latter were embroiled in conflicts farther north with Iran. Selim, therefore, next attacked the Mamluks, and, notwithstanding their legendary fame as warriors, his troops had no difficulty in overcoming them at the decisive battle of Marj Dabiq near Aleppo in 1516. Damascus fell to the Ottomans in that same year. In 1517 Cairo fell, and with it Egypt as far south as the First Cataract and as far west as the remote Kharga Oasis. Later, in 1534, Baghdad was taken by Süleyman I (1520-66). In this way the Ottoman Sultan became the premier Muslim ruler in both Western Asia and North Africa.

The problem of governing such an empire hardly requires emphasis. Its day-to-day administration was a most formidable task, given the diversity of the subject races, the overlapping layers of local, regional and imperial authority and the slowness of communications. There were also frontier problems everywhere. By sixteenth-century standards the very scale of operations was hard to comprehend. A Black Sea power had become a Mediterranean power, and the spectrum of concern now included such remote matters as the security of the approaches to the Red Sea and Portuguese activities in the Indian Ocean. It was a challenge that at this moment in history the Ottoman Turks, from Sultan to humblest soldier, felt confident to accept.

The overthrow of Mamluk rule in Egypt also resulted in the acquisition of some important intangible assets, notably guardianship of the two Holy Cities of Mecca and Medina. In Cairo Selim took possession of the titular 'Abbasid Caliph, al-Mutawakkil III, whose forebears had lived as Mamluk protégés since the Mongol conquest of Baghdad in 1258, and carried him off to Istanbul so that it was possible for believers to conclude that the Ottoman Empire was now the heir of the long-defunct 'Abbasid Caliphate. Except in the most distant parts of the *Dar al-Islam* or where, as in Iran, heresy was rampant, the Muslim universalist state seemed to have been restored.

The Turkish war machine

The comparative ease with which Selim had overcome the Mamluks and beaten back the Safavids was due primarily to Ottoman mastery of firearms. Although the development of the early modern state was almost everywhere connected with the possession of firearms and their successful application in warfare, the Ottoman Empire was very much a pace-setter. It appears that the Mamluks had knowledge of both cannon and the arquebus very soon after their first appearance in Europe, but they never showed any real appreciation of their potentialities. Not so the Ottomans. While there is some uncertainty as to when the

Left: A Turkish painting of a battle between forces of the Ottoman Empire (left of picture) and a Christian army. Features of interest include the use of massed artillery by both sides; the full plate armor worn by the Christians; and the concentration of Janissary infantry in the center of the Turkish line.

Right: Janissaries, the much-feared elite of the Ottoman army. Despite the fanciful headgear worn here, they were the best soldiers of their day, well disciplined and using their matchlock handguns to great effect.

Below: The power of Ottoman artillery was crucial to their military success. This type of heavy siege gun was used in the taking of Constantinople in 1453.

against the European maritime powers, and during the sixteenth century (at least until the Ottoman defeat at Lepanto in 1571) the Mediterranean, like the Black Sea and the Red Sea, was an Ottoman lake policed by the Sultan's galleys. The crews who manned the Ottoman fleets were as heterogeneous in composition as were the troops who made up the Ottoman armies and perhaps numbered more men of Arab, Aegean Greek and Levantine stock than Turks. The greatest Ottoman naval commander, Khayr al-Din Barbarossa, was the son of a pensioned Janissary of Lesbos and was therefore presumably of Balkan extraction. Another great commander, Dragut, came of Christian Anatolian parentage, while Uluj 'Ali was a Christian renegade from Calabria. Ottoman maritime ambitions even extended to the Indian Ocean, where in 1538, at the invitation of the Sultan of Gujarat, they mounted an unsuccessful siege of the Portuguese fortress of Diu. In that same year Aden was annexed, and in 1557 Massawa. Yemen was acquired as early as 1516, and although it was temporarily lost again it was regained in 1570 and remained part of the Empire until 1635. Against Portuguese hegemony in the Indian Ocean, however, the Ottomans made no headway.

Ottoman innovations in the art of war naturally influenced in varying degrees the Muslim states to the east. After Chaldiran (1514) the Safavids began to acquire both cannon and hand-guns, and in 1534 both were used with great effect to defeat an invading Uzbek army at Turbat-i Shaykh Jam. Against the Ottomans, however, Safavid artillery proved wholly inadequate, and in consequence the Safavids continued to rely mainly upon the mobility of their cavalry, their knowledge of the terrain and the fact that Ottoman communications across Anatolia were dangerously overextended. On the other hand, against the Uzbeks and the Moghuls the Safavid artillery more than held its own, as at Kandahar in 1622 and 1649. The Indian Moghuls used artillery extensively from 1526 onward, but even at Panipat Babur's artillery had been in the charge of an Ottoman gunner. The Moghuls cast cannon of enormous girth, but both the casting and the firing of these cumbrous weapons was left to European and Ottoman renegades, despite the personal interest that Akbar, Babur's son, took in their manufacture.

Ottoman military organization also made an impression upon the Safavids. Shah Isma'il had relied upon purely tribal levies drawn from those Shi'i tribes devoted to his cause. Known as the *Qizil-bash* or 'red-heads,' from the colour of their headdress, they were formed mainly from Turkoman tribes. Under a resolute leader, such as Shah Isma'il, they fought with great *élan*, but under weak rulers their natural turbulence and internecine rivalry came to the fore. Shah 'Abbas I (1588-1629), following Ottoman precedent, recruited Georgian Christian slaves as both soldiers and administrators. But unlike the Ottomans, the Safavids never had access to any very considerable population of non-Muslims to enslave for military purposes, and the Georgian element in the army, never large enough to dominate, tended to be a source of intrigue.

The Moghuls, with their tribal background and with a wide range of groups available for military service – Central Asian Moghuls, Iranians, Uzbeks, Afghans, Indian-born Muslims, Rajputs and Marathas – showed no interest in any form of military slavery, but among the contemporary sultanates of the Deccan the institution lingered on, producing in the Abyssinian slave-commander, Malik Ambar (*d* 1626), one of the great figures of the period.

Ottomans first used firearms – it has even been suggested that they used them at Kossovo in 1389 against the Serbs – there can be no doubt that cannon were used at the siege of Antalya in 1425 and were a regular part of the Ottoman warmachine by the time of Mehmet II. The Ottomans used the new weapons with extraordinary effect, both heavy guns, which could pound the walls of hitherto impregnable fortifications, and handguns, which were used with devastating effect by their well-trained infantry.

The armies of Selim I and of Süleyman I, his son, were to their contemporaries what the armies of Gustavus Adolphus, Napoleon or von Moltke were to theirs – revolutionary instruments of warfare against which opponents could

at first find scarcely any means of resistance. Unlike the semi-feudal armies of early sixteenth-century Europe or the disorderly tribal following of the Safavids, the mark of the Ottoman army was professionalism, discipline and obedience at every level in a clear chain of command.

By the standards of the age commissariat arrangements were exemplary, and the army was provided with the best weapons and equipment available. By tradition the Turks fought as mounted archers, and the Ottoman army contained an impressive force of regular cavalry, as well as irregular auxiliaries and the Tatar horsemen provided by the Khan of the Crimea. Nevertheless, the most important part of the Ottoman army by the end of the fifteenth century were the Janissaries (*Yeni Cheri*, New Troops), who were primarily infantry armed with matchlock handguns. The Janissaries were a *corps d'élite*, highly trained from an early age and possessing a morale built up over decades of victory. Of Balkan origin, they were recruited by means of the famous *devshirme*, the annual tribute of male Christian children from the Balkan provinces. They were taken to Istanbul and there, according to their physique and aptitude, chosen either to become Janissaries or to enter the Palace School to be trained as officials in the Imperial service. It was with the Janissaries and their military that Süleyman I, the Magnificent, building on foundations so well laid by his father, continued to expand the frontiers of the empire. Belgrade was captured in 1521, and Rhodes in 1522. The battle of Mohacs in 1526 resulted in the annexation of the greater part of Hungary. Baghdad was taken in 1534.

Nor did the Ottomans, despite their Central Asian origins, fail to meet the challenge of the sea. As early as the middle decades of the fifteenth century Mehmet II had recognized the need to control the Aegean and the approaches to his new capital, and as the Empire expanded so did this awareness of the need to maintain naval strength

Turkish administration

The Turkish empires of the Early Modern Period were essentially militarist and aggressive states which showed varying degrees of willingness to experiment with innovations of one kind or another in the art of warfare. Yet they could not have survived for so long and with such success without more positive underpinning. The first point to stress is that in different ways all the Turkish empires that followed the Mongol interlude enjoyed a dynastic stability and a kind of leadership such as had not been seen in the Muslim world since the decline of the 'Abbasids. In the case of the Ottomans the prestige and authority of the dynasty was enhanced by the fact that by the early sixteenth century it had been for two and a half centuries the leading *ghazi* state in Anatolia, having succeeded to the primacy formerly enjoyed by the Seljuqs, to which had been added the honor which accrued from the capture of Byzantium and the assumption of the attributes of the Caliphate. The Safavid Shah, as already noted, enjoyed a unique and virtually unassailable position among Shi'is as head of the *Safaviyyeh* Order and as the Hidden Iman's deputy. The Moghul monarchy was rooted in carefully preserved recollections of the Central Asian empires of Chingiz Khan and Timur. Likewise among both the Uzbeks and the Kazakhs the charisma of descent from Chingiz Khan was a potent source of authority. The Shaybanids upheld the Turko-Mongol custom of conferring sovereignty upon the entire ruling family and not just an individual member of it, so that Mawarannahr in the sixteenth century was divided into separate appanages for all the principal male relatives of the senior member of the family, the supreme Khan. The succession was regulated in accordance with Turko-Mongol custom, the throne passing to the eldest living kinsman of the Khan, which as often as not meant his younger brother or a nephew, rather than his own son. In India the Moghuls replaced this system by one in which the succession passed from father to son, but since the memory of ancestral practices died hard and since rulers continued to grant appanages to their younger sons who generally refused to acquiesce in the principle of primogeniture, the Empire was periodically torn by dynastic conflicts between competing brothers and nephews. Both Safavids and Ottomans avoided these difficulties by confining their male children to the harem or by granting them purely titular authority during their father's lifetime. Among the Ottomans it was customary for the Sultan's eldest son to have all his brothers strangled at his father's death.

Ottoman administration was rooted in traditional Muslim practice dating back to 'Abbasid times. Beneath the Sultan all authority was concentrated in the hands of a single individual, the *vazir*, who, in addition to heading the imperial bureaucracy, was personally responsible for the conduct of foreign policy. He was also frequently required to command armies in the field. He held office solely at the Sultan's pleasure, and his fall could be both swift and irrevocable. Frequently he was not a Muslim by birth, nor even a Turk: the Köprülü family, for example, which provided a succession of great *vazirs* during the seventeenth century, was Albanian. At the highest level he conducted business through a *diwan*, or Council of State, under which was a hierarchy of civil servants trained in the Palace School and usually recruited by means of the *devshirme*. This central bureaucratic structure could have its authority impinged upon from two separate directions, from the military commanders (and above all from the Aga of the Janissaries) and from the prin-cipal officers of the Imperial Household, who derived power from personal access to the Sultan.

Except under indefatigably active Sultans such as Süleyman I, Ottoman practice was to leave the *vazir* to act on the Sultan's behalf in virtually all matters of importance. The day-to-day business of governing the empire appears to have been much more closely controled by the Moghul Emperor than it was by the Ottoman Sultan, a substantial part of his day being spent in public *durbar* or in conference with his ministers and secretaries, while on Wednesdays the Court became the supreme judicial tribunal of the empire. The recorded daily routine of both Shah Jahan and Aurangzeb indicates that they worked as hard as any of the officials in their service.

Like the Moghuls, the Ottomans had, at least in theory, no hereditary nobility, the imperial bureaucracy being recruited primarily by means of the *devshirme*, and it was this seeming absence of a feudal aristocracy or of any 'landed interest' that so puzzled contemporary European observers. There were, however, in the Ottoman provinces deeply entrenched tribal and land-owning elites which the Ottoman government preferred to leave undisturbed. Indeed, for the most part, the Ottoman Sultans were content to approach the problem of controling distant provinces in an entirely pragmatic way, and no attempt was made to establish a uniform administrative framework. The Mamluk territories, for example, after their annexation by Selim I, were divided into three provinces: Northern Syria, governed from Aleppo, Southern Syria and Palestine, governed from Damascus, and Egypt. In Egypt itself the Mamluk system was preserved more or less intact with only a few modifications. Elsewhere the structured relationship with Istanbul was extremely varied. Thus Ottoman suzerainty over the Khan of the Crimea and the Voivodes of Moldavia and Wallachia (in what is now Rumania) was very loosely exercised, while in the Caucasus, Kurdistan and Nubia tribal chieftains retained virtual autonomy.

No doubt the Moghul administrative system

Above: Shah Abbas I, known as 'the Great,' Safavid ruler of Iran from 1587 to 1628. The Safavid shahs were revered by Shi'i Muslims as the deputy of the Hidden Imam, their awaited savior.

Left: Ottoman shipping – the military predominance of the Turks at sea, maintained by their fleet of war galleys, was at times almost equal to their dominance on land.

Right: A Turkish chieftain, painted by a Moghul miniaturist of the late sixteenth century.

Far right: The Aga, or commander-in-chief, of the Janissaries. The Ottomans exploited the diversity of population in their empire, recruiting the Janissaries mainly from Balkan Christian children handed over to the Turks as an annual tribute.

developed equally pragmatically, but as early as 1571 Akbar rationalized the existing system by establishing fifteen *subahs*, or provinces, each in the charge of a *subahdar*, which after a further century of expansion had increased to 21 by the late seventeenth century. While the *subahdar* exercised authority as the Emperor's representative, there was also a provincial *diwan* appointed by and directly answerable to the *vazir* in Delhi, who was responsible for the assessment and collection of the land revenue. Each *subah* was divided into a number of *sarkars* (equivalent of the Districts of British India), each of which was in the charge of a *faujdar*, an official comparable to the later British District Officer.

The administration of neither Safavid Iran nor Shaybanid Mawarannahr required a system of comparable complexity to that which evolved in Moghul India or in the Ottoman Empire. In Iran, however, the early Safavids were confronted by an intractable problem which arose from a desire, common to all conquering dynasties whose power rested on the Iranian plateau, to make the best use of the administrative *savoir faire* of the Iranian official class, a policy wholly unacceptable to the *Qizil-bash* chieftains, who viewed the Safavid State as existing primarily to gratify their needs. This may partly explain the steady drift throughout the Safavid period of Iranians of talent and education into Moghul India, where they were made welcome by an appreciative dynasty that employed them in the highest offices and rewarded them lavishly. This drain of talent out of Iran throughout the sixteenth and seventeenth centuries may have been a factor of considerable importance in the decline of Iran during this period.

The relations of each of these great dynasties and their followers to their subjects were complex. All four – Ottomans, Safavids, Shaybanids and Moghuls – were aliens to the majority of the subjects over whom they ruled. Even the Safavids, who in course of time evolved a kind of Shi'i 'national monarchy,' were foreigners to the sedentary and urban population of Iran. They and their military supporters were Turkish-speaking, and their power rested ultimately upon the loyalty of Turkish-speaking tribesmen.

Not one of these dynasties ruled anything approaching a homogeneous population, divided as their subjects were by race, religion and language. Most inhabitants of the Ottoman Empire were Sunni Muslims, but there were also minority groups of Shi'i Muslims, Christians and Jews. Although the ruling race was Turkish, as was much of the ruling elite throughout Egypt and the Fertile Crescent, the majority of the Sultan's subjects were Arabs or Balkan Christians, to which must be added such diverse elements as Tatars, Circassians, Kurds and Nubians. The majority of the Shah's subjects were Persian-speaking Shi'i Muslims, but there were other minorities – Sunni Kurds, Baluchis, Christian Georgians and Armenians, Jews and Zoroastrians. In Mawarannahr, while both the dynasty and its followers were Chaghatai-speaking Sunni Uzbeks, most townsmen and oasis-dwellers were Persian-speaking and perhaps secretly Shi'i, while the nomads included Turkomans in the west and a sprinkling of Kirghiz in the Pamirs. The racial, religious and linguistic diversity of Moghul India needs no stressing.

Ethnic and religious subject populations tended for the most part to govern themselves, living in self-contained communities clearly identifiable from each other and under their own leaders. If non-Muslims, they paid the *jizya*, or poll-tax, levied on infidels who in return enjoyed the protection of the Muslim State. Originally intended only for the *ahl-i kitab* – Jews and Christians – it had been gradually extended to include both Zoroastrians and Hindus. While occasionally subjected to outbursts of popular resentment, non-Muslim religious groups enjoyed at least as much protection from the Muslim State as a Jew or a Muslim could expect under most Christian regimes of the period.

But some tensions did nevertheless result from ethnic or denominational distinctions. Of these the deepest and most intractable was the division between Sunni and Shi'i, which was further exacerbated by the fact that the two rival dynasties, Ottoman and Safavid, posed as the champions of their respective sects and expressed their political rivalry in terms of theological vilification. To this debate the Shaybanids, hungrily eyeing Safavid Khurasan and spurred on by Ottoman prompting, contributed as fanatical Sunnis. At one time the mullahs of Bukhara ruled that the enslavement of Iranian Shi'is was no infringement of the *Shari'at* (which forbade the sale of a Muslim), since they were more detestable than infidels, and in this way they gave religious sanction to the Turkoman slave raids which provided the oases of Mawarannahr with their man-power. In India the Moghul emperors, firmly Sunni but culturally and spiritually very close to Iran, dealt with both sects with remarkable even-handedness. Here the rivalry tended to take the form of court factions, the Shi'i Iranian group versus the Sunni Turkish group from Central Asia. Inside Iran itself the tension between the Turkish *Qizil-bash* and the traditional Iranian bureaucracy has already been noted.

Relations between Indian Muslims and Hindus were more complex, varying from overt hostility to mild interest in each other's culture. The central fact here was that the Muslims were in a minority, possessing the typical *laager*-mentality of a numerically inferior community and subject

at times of pressure, or when aroused by fanatics or opportunists, to sudden outbursts. But the majority of Muslims still lived in towns, while village India remained almost exclusively Hindu, so that communal clashes occurred much less frequently than has been the case in the last hundred years. The Muslim community was governed by the *Shari'at* administered by the local *qazi*, while the Hindus maintained their own legal system and settled their affairs through village *panchayats* or councils. Above them all, the Moghul regime endeavored to maintain an aloof distance.

In each of the early modern Turkish empires education, including the study of the *Shari'at*, was the preserve of the *'ulama*, who might be *muftis*, *qazis*, learned theologians or simply teachers. Unlike the members of the bureaucracy, who were the Sultan's creatures, the *'ulama* enjoyed considerable economic independence as a result of the income they derived from *waqfs* (property held in *mortmain*), while the spiritual authority which they possessed, if taken with their virtual monopoly of the administration of the Muslim law, made them a most formidable ecclesiastical establishment. Yet it appears that many people must have found their theology too rigid, their faith too cold and their ministrations too impersonal if account be taken of the enormous following that the mystical Sufi orders attracted.

Throughout the period between the fifteenth and eighteenth centuries the spiritual life of almost the entire Muslim world centered on the *khanqahs* and *tekkes* (the closest translation is dervish-monasteries). Although each *tarikat* (dervish-brotherhood) possessed its own distinct characteristics, a feature common to virtually all was that the brotherhood comprised not only dervishes, for whom the order was a way of life, but also laymen – generally townsfolk drawn from the mercantile and manufacturing classes – who

participated in their leisure hours. In this way a *tarikat* became deeply involved in the life of the community and, predictably, some *tarikats* acquired a strong political tinge. One of the most widely distributed Sufi *tarikats* in Anatolia and Rumelia, and also one of the most heterodox, was that of the Bektashi dervishes, the followers of the thirteenth-century *shaykh*, Hajji Bektash. The Bektashis infiltrated the Janissary corps extensively, acting both as their spiritual advisers and also as their counselors in matters which were anything but spiritual.

Decline of the Muslim world

The greater part of the Muslim world throughout the Early Modern Period was divided up among powerful military monarchies in which the framework of administration was elaborate and relatively sophisticated and in which the military technology appeared, at least superficially, to be in step with the rest of the world. All this took place, moreover, in an area where urban traditions were well developed and where there was an enormous concentration of wealth resulting from the way in which the *Dar al-Islam* bestraddled the trade-routes of three continents. What went wrong? Why did the 'nation-state' fail to make its appearance in this area at the very time when it was emerging so dramatically in Europe?

One striking factor in the history of the Ottoman, Safavid and Moghul empires is the absence of an emerging European-style bourgeoisie to counter-balance the influence of the tribal nobility, the bureaucracy or the *'ulama*. Of course the Muslim World of the sixteenth and seventeenth centuries possessed an extensive class of merchants and manufacturers who possessed very considerable resources in terms of capital and commodities. The mercantile classes of Ottoman Turkey or Moghul India were rich and influential,

and while the *Shari'at* strictly forbade usury, Islam regarded commerce as a way of life no less meritorious than any other. Individually and collectively the merchant classes were respected and protected by most responsible Muslim rulers, who understood their worth as subjects and often depended upon them to provide instant credit in times of crisis. But notwithstanding all this the mercantile and banking classes exercised little direct leverage on the political life of the states in which they lived, were extremely vulnerable to upheavals of one kind and another and had no real institutional base even in the great cities where they thrived.

Whether the emergence of a dynamic middle

Above: Afsharid chieftain Nadir Shah took control of Iran in 1736 and went on to invade India, defeating the Moghul emperor at the battle of Karnal and sacking the imperial capital, Delhi.

Left: Whirling dervishes dance themselves into a religious ecstasy. The dervish orders provided a spiritual center for Islam at a time when more conventional religious practices had lost their power to inspire.

Above right: A Western representation of Süleyman the Magnificent leading his all-conquering army in the mid fifteenth century. The West always viewed the Turks as barbarous and cruel, but in many respects Islamic civilization was more tolerant and refined than Christianity.

class could have prevented or delayed the growing petrification of government in the Turkish empires is moot, but it is a fact that everywhere administration at the center began to lose its impetus and its will to innovate or to experiment with new forms. The same was true of the military organization of states which had come into existence and could only hope to survive by retaining a physical superiority over their neighbors and rivals. In India, confronted by guerrilla warfare in the difficult hill-country of the Deccan by the tough Marathas, the Moghul war-machine was displaying by the end of the seventeenth century unbelievable ineptitude, while the once-dreaded Janissaries had now become more feared by their master in Istanbul than by their Austrian, Russian or Iranian foes. The conquests of Selim I and Süleyman I had been achieved by means of the finest weapons of the age, but two centuries later the Ottoman army had fallen hopelessly behind in the development of fire-power. Its unwieldy cannon, originally designed for siege-warfare, had become all but useless when pitted against the most modern European artillery. Another factor was the steady decline in the calibre of leadership, exemplified by the degeneration of the Safavid royal family in the late seventeenth century and of the Moghuls after 1712, and this, too, was symptomatic of that same general loss of innovative capacity. There was also a growing intellectual stagnation and a spiritual vacuity which not even a brilliant florescence of architecture and the arts could conceal.

Yet except in the case of Ottoman power, dragged down by protracted conflicts with Habsburg Austria and Russia, it was not European intervention that brought this distinctive and in many ways splendid phase of Muslim history to a close. The Europeans, at least in India and Central Asia, merely picked up the pieces. As had been the case at their inception, the catalyst that set in motion the decline was the course of events on the Iranian plateau. Here, in 1720, the Safavid regime was overthrown and its capital, Isfahan, pillaged in the wake of an incursion of Ghilzay Afghans from the Kandahar region. Ghilzay rule survived for a decade and was then extinguished by an Afsharid chieftain, Nadir Shah (1736-47), who subsequently embarked upon an extraordinary career of conquest and destruction. In 1738-39 he invaded north-western India, defeated the Moghul emperor, Muhammad Shah, at Karnal and put the inhabitants of Delhi to the sword. When he withdrew to Iran with all the plunder of the imperial city, he left behind him an emperor who was little more than a cipher and an empire that was little more than a name. The Moghul dynasty, it is true, would survive down to 1857, but only as a Maratha or a British pensioner.

Nadir Shah also invaded Mawarannahr, entering both Bukhara and Khiva in 1740. His occupation of the former khanate revealed to the full how low the fortunes of the Janid dynasty had sunk, and before long the head of the Mangit clan, whose chieftains had long acted as overbearing 'Mayors of the Palace' in Bukhara, deposed the last Janid ruler and took his place. Nadir Shah did not attempt to extend his campaigning to the Kazakh steppes, but his hammer blows against Baghdad contributed to the weakening of Ottoman authority in the eastern provinces of the empire. Yet he himself, although a warlord of genius was no statesman, and at his death in 1747 the whole structure collapsed.

The Muslim world around 1800

An onlooker surveying the Muslim world in the half-century preceding 1800 would have received an overall impression of profound decay. Everywhere it seemed as if long-established political and social institutions were slowly disintegrating in an atmosphere of all-pervasive intellectual torpor. Ancient dynasties, once held in awe, slumbered in apathy. The military classes and the bureaucracy were characterized mainly by their rapacity and the ingenuity with which they exploited the *ra'aya*. The 'ulama had ceased to provide alternative leadership, and popular religion had long since taken the form of veneration of Sufi saints and their descendants in dervish orders frequently distinguished neither for piety nor for providing the social cohesion they had provided in the past. It was in the Ottoman Empire, and especially in its Arabic-speaking provinces, that this seemingly irreversible decline was most apparent.

Yet here and there there were some patches of light. One group of Muslims, their presence largely unnoticed by their co-religionists, was indeed on the eve of a remarkable re-awakening. The Volga Tatars, after two centuries of oppression at the hands of their Russian conquerors, were beginning to experience a measure of toleration and encouragement as the result of Catherine II's reversal of the traditional policy. In 1788 she permitted the Tatar clergy to have an organization of their own, the Religious Council of the Muslims of Russia, otherwise known as the Orenburg Spiritual Council, located at Ufa, and from then until the 1860s, when the former pressures were renewed, the so-called Tatar Renaissance reflected the intellectual stirrings of what were, in fact, the first Muslims to be exposed to the challenge of European domination.

Nowhere else was there a development comparable to that which took place among the Volga Tatars, but there were individual Muslims deeply concerned at the plight of Islam and at the spiritual malaise that polarized the religious life of the community between a rigid, complacent, Establishment-orientated 'ulama and Sufi movements which were departing further and further from the central ground of traditional Muslim belief and practice. In Delhi, for example, Shah Waliullah (1703-62), who was perhaps the greatest Muslim thinker of the eighteenth century, endeavored both to rejuvenate the spiritual life of his distracted community and to reconcile popular Sufism with the Islamic Great Tradition.

A very different figure who would likewise, for good or ill, leave an abiding mark upon the Muslim society of his day was Muhammad b 'Abd al-Wahhab (d 1792), who, from the remote hill-country of Najd in central Arabia, spearheaded a violent reformist movement that enlisted the support of the Sa'udi amirs of Najd, Muhammad b Sa'ud (d 1765), Abd al-'Aziz I (1765-1803) and Sa'ud b Abd al-'Aziz (1803-14), the founders of Wahhabi military power and, ultimately, of modern Sa'udi Arabia. The origins of Muhammad b 'Abd al-Wahhab's teachings lay in the writings of a long-neglected theologian and jurist of Mamluk Damascus, Ahmad b Taymiyya. Muhammad b 'Abd al-Wahhab shared Ahmad's conception of a Golden Age of primitive Islam, unsullied by later innovations, which he sought to restore, and so he preached ceaselessly against disregard of the Shari'at, the veneration of Sufi saints, pilgrimages to shrines other than those in the Holy Cities of Arabia, the use of tobacco and alcohol and so on. This reform movement, which saw itself as reviving the faith of a more rigorous and demanding age, deeply stirred the Muslim community far beyond the bounds of eighteenth-century Arabia, and the spirit of Wahhabi fundamentalism manifested itself in derivative movements in such diverse areas as East Bengal, India's North-West Frontier and Libya.

There were also in the late eighteenth century some dynastic upheavals of a traditional kind which contributed to the configuration of the Muslim world on the eve of the period of European domination. Among the flotsam left behind as a result of Nadir Shah's extensive, if futile, conquests was the Durrani Empire (c 1747 – c 1800), founded by the Abdali Afghan chieftain, Ahmad Shah Durrani, with its capital first at Kandahar and later at Kabul. This loosely knit tribal regime disintegrated at the beginning of the nineteenth century, but out of its ruins emerged the Amirate of Kabul, the work of the remarkable Barakzai chieftain, Dost Muhammad (1826-63), and the nucleus of the modern kingdom of Afghanistan. In Central Asia the Khanate of Kokand, on the upper Syr-Darya and in the Tashkent region, was established in the early eighteenth century by Shah Rukh (d 1722 or 1723), and reached its apogee under 'Alim Khan in the early nineteenth century. Both the older Uzbek Khanates of Bukhara and Khiva, having languished throughout the greater part of the seventeenth and eighteenth centuries under effete rulers, also experienced short-lived early nineteenth-century revivals under vigorous new dynasties.

The death of Nadir Shah (1747) had resulted in the fragmentation of Iran into tribal spheres of influence, of which the most stable was the Zand regime (c 1750-94) in Shiraz, which extended eastward to Kirman and, for a time, northward as far as Isfahan. Eventually, however, the entire Iranian plateau was brought under the control of the Qajar dynasty from Gurgan, as a result of the military exploits of the ferocious eunuch, Agha Muhammad Shah (1779-97), who virtually reconstructed the former Safavid kingdom, including Georgia and the Azarbaijan Khanates (later seized by Russia) and most of the western districts of Khurasan. Modern Iran, therefore, more or less corresponds to the area ruled by Agha Muhammad Shah.

Meanwhile, the pressures from an expanding Europe were steadily mounting upon the frontiers of the Muslim world, although down to the Napoleonic period these pressures had been relatively distant from the ancient heartlands and had been applied mostly by Russia. The Volga Tatar Khanates of Kazan and Astrakhan had been annexed by Russia as early as the middle of the sixteenth century and the Khanate of Sibir, centered on the Tobol region, was annexed half a century later. From the time when Peter the Great had first seized Azov in 1696 (he had been forced to relinquish it again in 1711) the Ottoman provinces on the Black Sea littoral had been under pressure from Russia's advance southward, and at the treaty of Küchük Kaynarja of 1774 the Danubian Principalities (Wallachia and Moldavia) had become de facto Russian protectorates, although nominal Ottoman suzerainty over Rumania, into which they were transformed in 1861, continued until the treaty of Berlin of 1878. In 1783 the Khanate of the Crimea had been occupied, and throughout the eighteenth century the advancing line of Russian forts across the Kazakh steppe had compelled the Kazakhs to acquiesce in Russian protectorates over each Horde in turn. In India too, Islam had suffered some notable reverses during the eighteenth century at the hands of the European trading companies, and by 1800 the Nawabs of Bengal and of the Carnatic had been eliminated by the British, the Nizam of Hyderabad and the Nawab-Vazir of Oudh had been forced into humiliating subsidiary alliances and within three years Delhi, seat of the Moghul emperor, would be in British hands.

Napoleonic adventure

These events were, however, very remote from the traditional centers of Islamic culture and evoked little or no response in Cairo, Damascus or Baghdad. It was Napoleon's Oriental ambitions, beginning with his expedition to Egypt in 1798, which marked the opening phase of the painful and protracted confrontation between European civilization and Islamic societies which seemed little changed from the time of Lepanto or even of the Crusades. As a result of European rivalries spilling over into the non-European world the Ottoman Empire was drawn into ever-shifting and unprofitable diplomatic combinations with or

Left: Napoleon's military expedition to Egypt in 1798 delivered a profound shock to the Islamic world, revealing the superiority Europe had now achieved both in technology and social organization.

Right: Muhammad 'Ali Pasha, an Albanian officer in the Ottoman army who became effective ruler of Egypt from 1805 to 1848. Unscrupulous but intelligent, he sought to modernize the country along Western lines, making extensive use of European advisers.

Thereafter, his immediate concern was to consolidate his authority and, at the earliest opportunity, to rid himself of any potential opposition inside the country. This he did by bringing the *'ulama* to heel in 1809 and by massacring the Mamluk leaders in 1811. As a result of these actions he acquired an impressive increment of revenue by resuming the tax-farms and estates formerly held by the Mamluks and the lands administered as endowments by the *'ulama*.

Muhammad 'Ali at first relied for support upon his corps of Albanians, later supplemented by slave-troops from the Sudan. Neither proved altogether satisfactory, and so (perhaps the first ruler of Egypt to do so since Pharaonic times) he conscripted the *fellahin*, the Egyptian peasants, in a new-style army officered by Ottoman Turks and Circassians and with French expatriates as military advisers. His consequent military triumphs were impressive. Between 1811 and 1818 he expelled the Wahhabis from the Hijaz; in an extended campaign in 1820-21 his troops penetrated deep into the Nilotic Sudan as far as Dunqula and Kordofan in what were, in effect, slave-raids on a vast scale; between 1822 and 1827 his army was in the service of the Ottoman Sultan in the struggle against the Greek insurgents, who would no doubt have been crushed but for the intervention of the Great Powers; and in 1831 he annexed Palestine and Syria.

These impressive achievements were made possible only by the relentless exploitation of the resources of rural Egypt and, later, of Palestine and Syria. Of greater significance for the future was Muhammad 'Ali's determination to modernize Egypt. He was assiduous in enlisting European personnel to give effect to his limited but determined efforts, and in his brutal impatience and his indifference as to the means employed to attain ends Muhammad 'Ali demonstrated at least one way in which major institutional changes could be imposed upon even the most traditionally minded societies.

Whether the whole Muslim world could have adjusted itself from within through the initiative of such leaders as Muhammad 'Ali Pasha, Sultan Mahmud II or the Iranian heir-apparent, 'Abbas Mirza (who predeceased his father, Fath 'Ali Shah, in 1833), must remain an open question, since all such attempts were thrust into the background by what was to become the dominant feature of Middle Eastern history for the rest of the nineteenth century and even down to the period between the World Wars: the military, economic and cultural ascendancy exercised over virtually the entire area by the European colonial powers. This ascendancy can be described only briefly here, but it has to be remembered that it was a process extending over many decades and that the circumstances in which it occurred were determined not only by the character of Middle Eastern society and governments but also by European rivalries in remote parts of the world.

European intervention in Africa

Let us begin surveying this process of European penetration geographically, from west to east. The history of nineteenth-century Morocco typifies the extent and complexity of the problems facing a closed traditional society when confronted by the various pressures brought to bear upon her as a result of European interest in the area. The ruling 'Alawi dynasty had risen to prominence in the second half of the seventeenth century and had consolidated its hold over an extensive territory during the reigns of two gifted rulers, Mawlay al-Rashid (1664-72) and Mawlay Isma'il (1672-1727). Later, during the long reign of

against France, Britain and Russia. Fath 'Ali Shah in Tehran found himself assiduously if unscrupulously wooed by both France and Britain, and French and British agents strove to out-maneuver one another from Aleppo to Hyderabad. The initial reaction of Muslim regimes to Western pressures was to attempt to come to terms with European fire-power. Thus the earliest response to the physical and psychological challenge posed by nineteenth-century Europe was largely restricted to the adoption of European uniforms, weapons and drill-manuals: it was naïvely assumed that command of this military know-how could be achieved without initiating any fundamental innovations in the structure of indigenous society or in traditional attitudes of mind.

As early as the eighteenth century the Ottoman Empire had witnessed some short-lived and half-hearted attempts at military reform, all of which had been fought tooth and nail by the now-fossilized corps of Janissaries. From the time of Ahmad III (1703-30) down to the reign of Selim III (1789-1807), whose intention of overhauling the military establishment cost him his throne and his life, projects for modernizing the Ottoman army all foundered on the strength of this vested opposition. Finally, a ruler of outstanding ability, Mahmud II (1808-39), determined to set his ramshackle empire in order and took the long overdue decision to be rid of the Janssaries. This was done in a bloody massacre carried out in 1826, and it was followed by a vigorous persecution of their closest adherents, the dervishes of the Bektashi order, and by coercion of the *'ulama*. In this way the Sultan was able to begin the slow and uphill

task of creating a modern army, but in order to achieve this end he found it necessary to extend his reforming activities beyond the Ottoman military establishment, and in so doing he set in motion far-reaching measures which, in time, would bring about a transformation in the entire apparatus of government.

In his military reforms Sultan Mahmud had been anticipated in the previous decade and a half by an even more remarkable reformer and Westernizer, Muhammad 'Ali Pasha, nominal Ottoman viceroy of Egypt from 1805 until his death in 1848 but, in practice, an independent ruler. Perhaps the most remarkable figure in the history of the Middle East during the nineteenth century, Muhammad 'Ali has been called 'the maker of modern Egypt,' but he also personified that earlier tradition of Egyptian separatism from the Islamic lands to east and west which began with Ahmad b Tulun in the ninth century.

Egypt, although incorporated into the Ottoman Empire as early as 1517, had traditionally been left much to its own devices. It was still ruled by a corps of Mamluks and was of little concern to the Porte beyond providing revenue and serving as a base for the control of Syria and Arabia. Following Napoleon's invasion of 1798, however, Selim III had despatched an expedition to Egypt in 1799 to reassert Ottoman authority, and it was as the commander of an Albanian contingent attached to this expedition that the thirty-year-old Muhammad 'Ali made his first appearance upon the Egyptian scene. By 1805 he had made himself *de facto* viceroy, and a year later the Porte acquiesced in this usurpation by confirming it.

Muhammad b 'Abd Allah (1757-90), a serious attempt was made to develop the resources of the country: Mogador was founded in 1765, and Casablanca in 1770. A commercial treaty was signed with France in 1767, and relations with Spain were regularized by a treaty of 1775. In consequence of having provided support for 'Abd al-Qadir, the leader of Algerian resistance to the French occupation of the nineteenth century, Morocco became embroiled in a disastrous conflict with France in 1844 and was also defeated by Spain in a brief war during 1859-60. In 1863 the Béclard Convention with France pointed toward a future protectorate, an event postponed partly in consequence of the energy and reforming activities of Mawlay al-Hasan (1873-94), although even he was forced to acquiesce in the Spanish occupation of Ifni and penetration into Rio de Oro. It was following his death that European pressure began again in earnest, Morocco now becoming a bone of contention between France, Spain, Britain, Italy and Germany. Finally, in 1911 Spain occupied the zone earlier allotted to her in 1904 (Spanish Morocco), while in the following year the Treaty of Fez (30 March 1912) placed Morocco (apart from the Spanish zone) firmly under a French protectorate. It took both colonial powers another two decades to complete the pacification of their respective territories.

Unlike Morocco, the rest of Mediterranean Africa – Algeria, Tunisia, Tripolitania and Egypt – had long been incorporated into the Ottoman Empire, which, by the nineteenth century, was no

Left: A French cavalry officer in Algeria. The crushing of Algerian resistance was one of the most brutal of the colonial wars of the nineteenth century.

Below: Scottish troops pose in front of the Sphinx at Giza after participating in the defeat of Egyptian nationalist forces at Tel-el-Kebir in 1882.

Right: General Kitchener reviews his troops in Khartoum after the final defeat of the Sudanese Mahdiyya revolt at Omdurman in 1898.

longer capable of retaining its control over such distant possessions. The French occupied Algiers in 1830, and although at first they met with vigorous opposition to their further advance, that initial success would lead to the eventual pacification of the entire country and, ultimately, to the extension of French authority over virtually the whole of the Maghrib. The Algerians had an outstanding leader in the *Amir*, 'Abd al-Qadir, but he

was eventually worn down by the ablest of his opponents, General Bugeaud, who waged ruthless wars of attrition against the insurgents between 1840 and 1841 and 1846 and 1847. Even after the removal of 'Abd al-Qadir from the scene the struggle continued spasmodically, flaring up again between 1852 and 1880.

It is difficult to recall any colonial territory in recent times that suffered such misfortunes as did

Algeria in the wake of the French occupation. It has been estimated that as a result of the fighting and the accompanying devastation, followed by famine and large-scale epidemics, the population of the country, reckoned at 3 million in 1830, fell to a little over 2 million by 1872. The fiscal exactions of the colonial administration resulted in an inevitable disruption of both the rural and urban economy. Meanwhile, the French administration encouraged a policy of European settlement, at first mainly by Spaniards and Italians, although after 1855 the French themselves went into the lead. By 1870 these colonists numbered 272,000, and by 1911 they had reached 681,000. Increasingly, they were coming to be the real rulers of the country, and their comprehension of or sympathy for the indigenous Algerians was minimal. Hardly anywhere in the colonial world of the early twentieth century did a subject population exercise so little influence over the shaping of its destiny.

Tunisia became a French protectorate as a result of the Convention of Bardo (12 May 1881), following a period of intense rivalry between France and Italy that culminated in the French invasion in 1881, for which a pretext had been most conveniently provided by a tribal incursion into Algeria from across the Tunisian frontier. As in the case of Algeria, the French authorities actively promoted European colonization – in this instance, Italians, French and Maltese – and by 1911 there were 143,000 Europeans resident in the country. Again, as in the case of Algeria, the administration fostered economic development by creating an infrastructure of roads, railways and port facilities, although these were provided primarily to serve the needs of the European colonists. Following the Italian seizure of neighboring Tripolitania from the Porte in the war of 1911 a similar policy of colonization was adopted by the Italian government in what is now Libya.

Egypt under the Khedives, the dynasty of Muhammad 'Ali Pasha, continued throughout the greater part of the nineteenth century to be a bone of contention between France and Britain. A major source of friction was the construction of the Suez Canal between 1854 and 1869 by the French concessionaire, Ferdinand de Lesseps, although the British Government finally acquired the controlling shares from the Khedive in 1875. French influence in the Nile Valley had been a factor to reckon with since the time of Napoleon, and Muhammad 'Ali Pasha and some Frenchmen believed that Egypt was virtually certain to fall into the French sphere of influence before the century was out. The British preoccupation with Egypt was primarily strategic: concern for the safety of the Indian sub-continent and its approaches, an obsession dating back to the worldwide contest with Napoleon. In the end, it was the British who moved in. The pretext was an embryonic nationalist movement headed by Colonel Ahmad 'Urabi and directed against the government of the Khedive, Muhammad Tawfiq (1879-92), and the European stranglehold over the country's resources. The British judged the situation serious enough to justify intervention, and in 1882 Alexandria was bombarded and British troops defeated 'Urabi's forces at an engagement at Tel-el-Kebir.

Thereafter, Egypt remained an informal British protectorate for the next half-century, and, especially during the tenure of office of Lord Cromer as Agent and Consul-General (1884-1907), a measure of order was introduced into the administration and an impressive colonial-type infrastructure was created without the blight of European settlement. There was also a genuine desire to alleviate the grinding poverty of the *fellahin*, but, as in India, British officials tended to be antagonistic toward the emerging Western-educated middle class – from whom the most conspicuous supporters of nationalist and anti-British movements would eventually be recruited.

British involvement in Egypt led to British penetration into the Nilotic Sudan. This vast tract of territory beyond the First Cataract had been invaded and annexed by Muhammad 'Ali Pasha in 1820-21, and during the following half-century Egyptian rule had been steadily extended and consolidated, especially during the reign of the Khedive Isma'il (1863-79), when European and American officials had been extensively employed in the administration. The efforts of such men as Charles George Gordon and Rudolph Slatin to suppress the slave-trade had, naturally enough, provoked bitter resentment against the Egyptians as well as against their Christian servants. The catalyst for revolt finally appeared in the person of a dervish from Dunqula, Muhammad Ahmad b 'Abd Allah (1843-85), who in June 1881 proclaimed himself the long-awaited *mahdi*, whose appearance on earth would usher in the Age of Righteousness. By 1885, when the Mahdi captured Khartoum, his forces had overrun virtually the entire northern part of the former Egyptian province of the Sudan and it seemed more than likely that they would press on with their conquests as far as the Red Sea and the Mediterranean, as well as into the central Sahara.

Following the Mahdi's death in 1885 his successor, 'Abd Allahi b Muhammad, who took the title of *Khalifat al-Mahdi*, initiated a further period of aggression against his neighbors between 1886 and 1889, launching *jihads* against the Egyptian frontier to the north, against Ethiopia to the south-east and against Darfur to the west. Defeat at the hands of the Egyptians at the battle of Tushki in 1889 brought this expansionist phase to a close, and for the next ten years 'Abd Allahi was apparently content to consolidate earlier gains and eliminate potential rivals. Meanwhile, however, the British, growing apprehensive that some other European power might acquire control over the upper waters of the Nile, resolved to bring the Sudan decisively into their sphere of influence. An expeditionary force, approaching from the north, fought a decisive engagement against the forces of the Mahdiyya outside Omdurman (which the Mahdi had made his capital in place of Khartoum) in 1898, and 'Abd Allahi himself was killed in battle the following year. The British then set up an Anglo-Egyptian Condominium (1899), in which the Governor-General and the senior civil and military appointments were exclusively British. What was to become the basic pattern of British administration in the Sudan was laid down by the first Governor-General, Lord Kitchener, the victor of Omdurman, and by his successor, Sir Reginald Wingate (Governor-General, 1899-1916). It was an administration characterized by a high level of efficiency, honesty and conscientiousness, but also by extreme paternalism.

The Ottoman Empire under attack

In contrast to its African empire, the Porte retained its empire in Asia more or less intact down to the outbreak of World War I, although outside the Arabian peninsula the European powers enjoyed extensive commercial privileges and concessions as well as rights of extraterritoriality. Also, the administration of the Christian Holy Places and the access of pilgrims to them provided endless opportunities for friction and interference, with France since 1740 responsible for watching over Roman Catholic interests, and Russia since 1774 performing the same role on behalf of the Orthodox Church. The British, long preoccupied with piracy in the Indian Ocean and the Persian Gulf, as well as with the suppression of the slave-trade during the nineteenth century, had established treaty-relations with the Arab *shaykhs* of the Persian Gulf littoral at the beginning of the century, and by 1839 they had acquired Aden at the mouth of the Red Sea. It was evident that sooner or later, most of the coastline of the Arabian peninsula would become a British sphere of influence, although it was not until after World War I that Britain brought the chieftains of the Hadhramaut into a dependent relationship.

The most striking territorial losses suffered by the Ottoman Empire were in her Rumelian or Balkan provinces, where, with the exception of a part of the population of Bosnia, Herzegovina, Albania and Dobruja, Islam had failed to strike roots among the subject population. As early as 1804 a Serbian uprising triggered off what may be regarded as the first truly nationalist revolt against Ottoman rule, and at the Treaty of Adrianople (1829) Serbia was granted autonomous status, as were Moldavia and Wallachia, already *de facto* Russian protectorates since 1774. Between 1821 and 1832 the Greeks acquired their independence, largely as a result of Russian, French and British intervention. In 1861 Moldavia and Wallachia were formed into the single autonomous principality of Rumania. The Treaty of Berlin (1878) marked the greatest loss of territory

suffered by the Porte prior to World War I: Rumania, Siberia and Montenegro achieved full independence, Bulgaria became an autonomous principality, Bosnia and Herzegovina were occupied by Austria-Hungary (and formally annexed in 1908) and Cyprus was occupied by Britain (and formally annexed in 1914). In 1908 Bulgaria declared herself independent, and there followed in 1912 the First Balkan War, in which Montenegro, Greece, Serbia and Bulgaria expanded their frontiers at the expense of the empire and Albania became an autonomous principality. Ottoman losses in Thrace would have been even greater but for the superior performance of the Turkish army in the Second Balkan War of 1913, which achieved the restoration of Adrianople (Edirne). Nevertheless, these humiliations and loss of territory, coupled with disenchantment with the policies of France and Britain (the Porte's traditional 'protectors' against Russia) and the ardent wooing of Germany (which alone among the great powers had gained nothing from the dismemberment of the Empire), account for the readiness with which

the Sultan's Government joined the Central Powers in October 1914.

Russia, which had made so considerable a contribution toward the dismemberment of the Ottoman Empire in the Balkans, was bent upon extending her frontiers at the expense of her other Muslim neighbors throughout the century. Her defeat of Iran in two wars fought in Azarbayjan had brought her additional territory in the southern Caucasus region, confirmed by the treaties of Gulistan (1813) and Turkomanchay (1828), although the conquest of the tribes of the central and northern Caucasus proved a lengthier task: Shaykh Shamil, a Daghistani chieftain who put up a spirited resistance against the Russian advance, was not overcome until 1859 and military operations continued into 1864. Russia's advance across the Kazakh steppe brought about a predictable collision with the Uzbek Khanates to the south. Tashkent was seized from the Khan of Kokand in 1865, and in 1867 it was made the headquarters of the Governor-Generalship of Turkistan, of which the principal architect was the

Below left: A bazaar in the Caspian region of northern Iran, close to the border with Russia. Throughout the nineteenth century, Britain sought to set a limit to Russian expansion into Muslim Central Asia.

Bottom left: In 1908, oil was discovered in Iran, and the tents and shacks of British oilmen were soon dotting this inhospitable landscape.

Right: The Baku oilfields in Azerbaijan just after the Russian Revolution. The rich oil deposits in the Middle East would eventually finance an Islamic revival.

formidable General Kaufman (Governor-General, 1867-82). In 1868 the Amirate of Bukhara was attacked, and its ruler, Muzaffar al-Din (1860-85), was forced to pay an indemnity and cede an extensive tract of territory, including Samarqand. By the treaty of 1868, confirmed by a further treaty of 1873, Bukhara became a Russian protectorate.

In 1873 came the turn of the Khanate of Khiva, which was also swiftly overpowered and compelled to accept the status of a Russian protectorate. Then, in 1875, the Khanate of Kokand became the setting for an extensive uprising against the Russian presence. This was quelled without undue difficulty, and in 1876 the khanate was abolished. The nomadic and semi-nomadic Turkoman tribes of the Kara Kum desert offered a more determined resistance than had the Uzbek Khanates, but after some initial reverses the Russians brought the Tekke Turkomans to bay at Gök-Tepe in 1881, where a gruesome massacre left the remaining tribes with little appetite for further fighting. In 1884 the Russians advanced as far as the Marv oasis, and shortly afterward an Anglo-Russian Boundary Commission demarcated the Russian frontier with Afghanistan. Britain had long regarded the Russian advance across Central Asia as a threat to the stability of her Indian Empire, but the Anglo-Russian convention of 1907 was at least a realistic attempt to end a rivalry that had extended across inner Asia from the shores of the Caspian to the highlands of Tibet.

The Russians in Turkistan, unlike the British in India or the Dutch in Java, had come as conquerors, not merchants, and in consequence their administration retained, down to 1917, the mark of its military origin. At its worst Russian colonial rule could be harsh, venal and inept, but it interfered very little with the traditional culture and way of life of the indigenous Muslim population. In course of time, however, and especially after Turkistan became linked by rail with the rest of the country, Russian control led to a serious distortion of the economy. Cotton, in particular, replaced staple food-crops in many areas, due partly to favorable market-prices and partly to

coercion, and as a result Turkistan became dependent for its food-supply upon the importation of Russian wheat. But at least there were virtually no colonists in the territories annexed from the Uzbek Khanates, since the climate and the traditional agriculture of the oases offered no inducements for European settlement. Most Russians in Turkistan lived in the cities, which expanded rapidly in the late nineteenth and early twentieth centuries, occupying spaciously laid-out suburbs. By 1910 the population of Tashkent exceeded 200,000 inhabitants, and of these 55,000 were Europeans. In Kazakhstan the situation was different, for there the age-old grazing-lands of the nomads offered ideal conditions for the establishment of agricultural settlements. During the two decades preceding World War I Russian and Ukrainian peasants, actively encouraged by the government, surged on to the Kazakhs' traditional pastures, driving the latter back into the more arid tracts. The inevitable outcome of this was the savage Kazakh uprising of 1916 and its even more savage suppression.

Afghan independence

In striking contrast to the other peoples of Central Asia the Afghans, as a result of their favorable geographical position as a buffer between the expanding Russian and British-Indian empires, were able to retain their freedom from European interference more completely than perhaps any other group of Muslims in the nineteenth century. The British twice invaded the country (1839-42 and 1878-81), largely to forestall a suspected Russian advance, but they soon recognized the difficulties involved in retaining control over so inhospitable a terrain, and while the Government of India continued to control Afghanistan's foreign relations down to 1921, in practice the Afghans were left much to themselves.

Another group of Central Asian Muslims who found themselves isolated from the mainstream of nineteenth-century Islam were the Turkish subjects of Manchu China inhabiting the oasis-cities of Kashgar and Yarkand on the eastern flanks of the Pamirs. These cities had been

brought under Manchu rule after 1757, when the Oirot Mongols, who had exercised a loose suzerainty over Kashgaria, were finally overthrown by the armies of Ch'ien-lung. The local leadership then fled across the mountains to the Khanate of Kokand, whence they led a series of abortive uprisings in Kashgaria against the Manchu presence. Finally, in 1867, Ya'qub Bey, a military leader from Kokand who had distinguished himself in defending the fort of Ak-Mesjid against the Russians in 1852-53, established himself as ruler of Kashgaria and sought to legitimize his position by obtaining the recognition of the Ottoman Sultan and the Government of India. Ya'qub Bey was finally overthrown by the Manchus in 1877-78, and by 1881 Kashgar was once more in their hands. Thereafter, the administration kept a much closer watch over the behavior of the subject population, who were never again to exercise any control over their own affairs.

By World War I the majority of Muslims were living under French, Russian, British or Dutch colonial rule, whether in the Maghrib, in Central Asia, in the Indian subcontinent or in Southeast Asia, while the future of the Arabs, still subject to the moribund Ottoman Empire, seemed more likely to be determined by the interests and ambitions of France and Britain than by the wishes of the Sultan-Caliph. Only the Turks of Anatolia, the Iranians, the Afghans and the isolated inhabitants of the Arabian Peninsula still enjoyed a precarious independence from infidel domination, and in the case of the Turks and the Iranians it was far from certain that this would survive much longer. The prospects for the *Dar al-Islam* in the second decade of the twentieth century were grim indeed, while the recent discovery of oil in the Middle East and the recognition of its potentialities as the fuel of the future seemed even more likely to make these lands the pawns of the great powers. In the long run the possession of oil reserves would provide the *Dar al-Islam* with the economic weapon to turn the tables on their Western oppressors. Until the advent of the 'oil revolution,' however, the West would remain dominant.

India: 1500-1914

By the early sixteenth century the hegemony of the Delhi Sultanate was a thing of the past. The ruling dynasty in Delhi, now the Afghani Lodis, coexisted with at least six other strong independent states in northern India and five more in the Deccan. Into this near-anarchy stepped the man who was to found the last Indian empire before the coming of the British.

Babur (1482-1530), a descendant of Timur, was a Turko-Mongol who dreamed of recreating his forebear's Tatar empire. He met with so little success in Turkistan, however, that he was eventually forced to flee into Afghanistan, where he established himself in Kabul. From there he began raiding into northern India, and in 1526, in a major battle at Panipat, he succeeded in routing the Delhi army and killing the sultan, Ibrahim Lodi. In the next four years Babur conducted a series of campaigns which, by the time of his death in 1530, had brought most of northern India under his control. These conquests were nearly dissipated by his inept and opium-addicted son, Humayun, but Humayun's son, Akbar (1556-1605), proved to be both a redoubtable warrior and a gifted statesman. He became the first true Moghul emperor and he was unquestionably the greatest.

In the year of his accession, 1556, the 13-year-old Akbar defeated and killed – again at Panipat – his most serious opponent in north India, a Hindu named Himu who had seized control of Delhi and Agra. By 1576 Akbar had extended his control firmly over all of northern India except for lower Sind, and by the time of his death in 1605 he had established a vast empire that stretched all the way from Kashmir and Kabul south to Ahmednagar in the Deccan and east through Bihar to the mouth of the Ganges on the Bay of Bengal.

Akbar's administration of this empire was, though completely autocratic, for the most part exemplary. He proclaimed universal religious toleration and made a point of conciliating his Hindu subjects by abolishing the most offensive of the taxes that previous Muslim rulers had leveled against them and by offering them high places in the civil service and the army. In an effort to improve the efficiency and accountability of the civil service he organized all its officers into graded ranks like those of the military (the so-called *mansabdari* system). The empire itself he divided into 15 districts, called *subhas*, with three more added just at the close of his reign, each governed by a commander-in-chief (*sipahsalar*) who headed a team of subordinate specialist officers such as *diwans* (financial controllers), *kotwals* (police commissioners) and the like. Afghan-style feudalism was abolished, and former fiefs were placed under the supervision of salaried officers of the crown. Akbar's land-revenue system was particularly enlightened: determined not to erode the agricultural infrastructure of the empire through excessive exactions, he decreed that taxation of peasants should not exceed one-third of the gross product of their land. As might be expected, such measures won him both considerable popular support and a good deal of enmity from the Muslim aristocracy.

The benign effects of Akbar's administrative and fiscal policies were to some extent diluted by the obstructionism of greedy officials and by the exorbitant demands Akbar himself placed on the treasury. The army, of course, represented a large and doubtless unavoidable item of expense: it eventually came to number 200,000 men, with 5000 war elephants. But Akbar was also fond of making costly displays of imperial magnificence, as exemplified in the overwhelming lavishness of his court and in his construction of the splendid new cities of Allahabad and Fathpur Sikri. He was also a generous patron of music and the plastic arts, and, though he was himself illiterate, he amassed an enormous personal library and encouraged the production of literary works, such as the recasting of the *Ramayana* in its definitive form by the poet Tulsi Das and the translation of the *Mahabharata* into Persian.

Although there were certainly wayward and idiosyncratic elements in Akbar's character – he retained the Mongols' ruthlessness and cruelty in war, his personal religious views were eccentric enough to dismay Hindu and Muslim alike and his love of pomp and luxury was extravagant by any standard – he deserves a place among the leading monarchs of his time. Like his contemporaries – Elizabeth I of England, Henry IV of France, Philip II of Spain, the Ottoman Süleyman the Magnificent and the Iranian Abbas I – he is still remembered as one of the nation's greatest sovereigns.

Not so his son, Jahangir (1605-27). Though he perpetuated his father's policies of religious tolerance and conciliation of Hindus, Jahangir was dissolute, a poor administrator (his Iranian wife, Nur Jahan, and her relatives and favorites virtually ran the empire) and unsuccessful in war. He is remembered chiefly for having lost Kandahar to the Iranians and for having received the first ambassador, Sir Thomas Roe, sent by Britain to the court of the 'Great Moghul.'

Jahangir was succeeded by Shah Jahan (1627-58). Although he is famous for his patronage of the arts and for the great monuments he left behind him – the Taj Mahal and the Moti Masjid in Agra, the new city of Shahjahanabad, the dazzling Peacock Throne – his reign was hardly a success. His insistence on a rigid orthodoxy undid much of the goodwill that Akbar and Jahangir had fostered in the subject Hindu populace, and he nearly bankrupted the empire with his incessant – and on the whole unsuccessful – military campaigning. He was deposed by his treacherous and bloodthirsty third son, Aurangzeb, in 1658 and died a prisoner in his own harem in 1666.

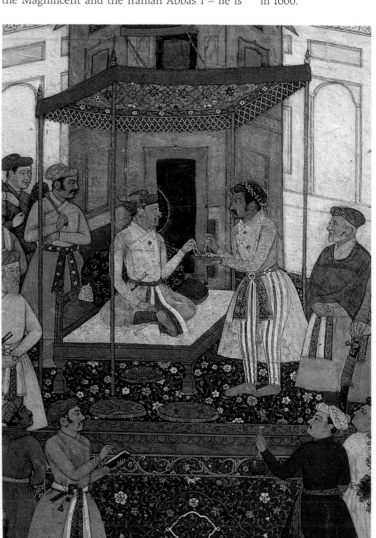

Left: Moghul ruler Akbar the Great (seated) and his court. The splendor of the Moghul court was accompanied by efficient and tolerant government.

Below right: Aurangzeb, ruler of the Moghul Empire in the second half of the seventeenth century, was a fanatical Muslim who overturned the tradition of religious tolerance established by his predecessors.

Above right: Seated on this magnificent throne is Tipu Sultan, a Muslim ruler whose capital was at Mysore in southern India. As Moghul power declined in the eighteenth century, other princedoms, like that of Tipu Sultan, flourished.

If Shah Jahan had been sternly orthodox, Aurangzeb (1658-1707) was a religious fanatic and accomplished the complete alienation of the non-Muslim Indian majority. Hindus were excluded from government office, their temples and schools were closed or destroyed and they were again subjected to the hated *jizya* (poll tax). Even the Sikhs, who had long sought to reconcile their monotheistic, iconoclastic creed with Islam, were so roughly treated that they became the implacable enemies of both the Moghuls and their religion. The demands that Aurangzeb made on the treasury were even greater than those of Shah Jahan, and in his search for money Aurangzeb undid the prudent land-revenue policy of Akbar by raising the tax on peasants to one-half their gross produce. It is true that under Aurangzeb the Moghul empire reached its greatest territorial extent; by 1687 it stretched as far south as the Coromandel Coast. But this accomplishment was more cosmetic than real, for by the time of Aurangzeb's death in 1707 the empire was wracked by local revolts, especially and most menacingly in the Deccan.

Under Aurangzeb's successors the empire unraveled rapidly. Between 1707 and 1719 there were no less than five emperors, all ineffectual puppets of various court factions. By the reign of Mohammed Shah (1719-48) the empire was dotted with independent dynasties set up by provincial governors, and the military threats posed by some of them were critical.

The course of Moghul decline has yet to be fully analyzed, but it is clear that by the close of the first quarter of the eighteenth century the process of disintegration was already well under way and that by the close of the second the process, in fact if not in name, was complete. Several factors contributed to this decline, of which the most obvious was territorial over-extension, beginning as early as the reign of Shah Jahan. This resulted in the relaxing of control over the provincial administration from the center, in the older *subahs* as well as in the newer ones, leading to a neglect of imperial interests by local officials bent on self-enrichment, a rising level of extortion by the

government's agents in the countryside and a consequent tendency for desperate bids at rebellion. To this must be added the growing insolvency of the administration, to which the cost of Aurangzeb's successive wars made a major contribution. Other unfavorable factors included the extravagance with which government was conducted, the diminution of revenue payments in cash and the virtual breakdown of the *mansabdari* system.

Yet neither the decay of Akbar's administrative system nor the fiscal crisis of the late seventeenth and early eighteenth centuries, or even the inadequacy of later emperors, were ills beyond cure had they not coincided with a period of irreversible military decline. By the late seventeenth century the Moghul army, with its rabble of camp-followers, was like an Indian city on the move, preying on the countryside through which it passed, vulnerable to sudden attack and more feared by friends than foes. During the reign of Aurangzeb the struggle in the Deccan against a foe who melted into the landscape before he could be brought to bay, where friends and enemies were barely distinguishable and where even protracted campaigning failed to hold down the countryside beyond the garrison towns and the main roads, resulted in a severe decline in morale. In this situation imperial commanders proved unable to cope with any really serious uprising within the frontiers of the empire, and from the middle of the seventeenth century rebellion became endemic in some areas, provoked in part at least by the relaxation of control at the center and by the increasing oppression of local officials. In the north the Sikhs in the Punjab, the Jats in the Agra *subah* and the Bundelas in the hill country south of the Ganges around Orchha and Datia all defied imperial authority with comparative impunity, while the Marathas around Poona virtually erased all traces of Moghul rule from those districts where they were in control. Baffled and demoral-

ized by these movements within the empire the regime was totally unprepared to cope with foreign invasion – the first since Babur's arrival in 1526. First, the Iranian soldier of fortune, Nadir Shah, descended on Delhi in 1739, sacked the city and the Red Fort and annexed the western *subahs* of Kabul, Lahore and Sind. He was followed by the Afghani, Ahmad Shah Durrani, who invaded northern India on a number of occasions, sacked Delhi in 1759 and defeated a vast Maratha army at Panipat in 1761. These events hastened a trend that had already been evident since the beginning of the second quarter of the century – the conversion of several *subahs* into *de facto* independent principalities under able and aspiring governors. These included Bengal, Oudh, the Carnatic and Hyderabad. It was, however, the Marathas who finally brought the empire to its knees.

During the sixteenth and early seventeenth centuries, under the comparatively mild rule of the Deccani, the Maratha brahmin and warring elites found little difficulty in holding their own while serving in both the administration and the armies of the rulers of Ahmadnagar and Bijapur. The penetration of the Moghuls into the Deccan, however, acted as a catalyst, bringing to a end a relationship in which the Marathas served the Deccani sultans in their own interests and replacing it with control by a new regime, unfamiliar and without local ties, and bent upon exploiting local resources for the benefit of an alien nobility and a distant court. The rise of Shivaji (1627-80) and the foundation of an independent Maratha *raj* was the result, although this first phase of Maratha expansion was both short-lived and uncharacteristic. Operating from the tangled, wooded hills of the Western Ghats, with its numerous fortresses perched on inaccessible rocks, Shivaji carried out a guerilla war of attrition against the Moghuls, harrying their slow-moving armies, raiding the rich ports of the Konkan coast and even leading an expedition across the penin-

Left: The Dutch East India Company's factory in Bengal. At this time, in 1665, the European presence in India was limited to such tolerated trading centers on the coast.

Right: The British fleet in action off the Indian coast. The superior armament of their naval vessels was the major military advantage the European powers held over the Indians until the nineteenth century.

Below right: An Indian artist's view of the British settlement at Surat on the west coast of the subcontinent.

sula to distant Tanjore. His assets were the difficult terrain, the local knowledge of his commanders and the frugal hardiness of his followers and their wiry hill-ponies.

But with Shivaji's death this phase petered out. His son lacked the qualities of leadership which such a role demanded, and in 1689 his career came to an abrupt end when he was captured and executed by Aurangzeb. His son and successor, the long-reigning Shahu (1707-49), was likewise no empire-builder, but it was during his lifetime that a family of Chitpavan brahmin from the Konkan, the coastal strip below the Western Ghats, established a hereditary claim to occupy the office of Peshwa, or Chief Minister of the Maratha ruler, and to wield a monopoly of power, civil and military. They made their headquarters at Poona, while the descendant of Shivaji became a *roi fainéant* at Satara. The most vigorous of the Peshwas, Baji Rao I (1720-40), sent Maratha armies raiding south into the Deccan and north into Malwa and Gujarat, even threatening the imperial capitals of Delhi and Agra. The Maratha thrust northward toward the Gangetic plain continued under his successor, Baji Rao II (1740-61), but with a certain shift of power away from the Peshwa toward his field-commanders, the founders of the future states of Baroda, Nagpur, Gwalior and Indore.

The moribund Moghul regime of the middle years of the eighteenth century was incapable of withstanding the Maratha advance and at least some statesmen at the imperial court seem to have advocated an understanding with the Marathas. This made sound sense, for there had long been a case for endeavoring to accommodate the Marathas by enlisting them into the service of the empire on generous terms, but the opportunities had been repeatedly missed, and by the second quarter of the eighteenth century imperial advocates of a Moghul-Maratha *rapprochement* were bargaining from a position of weakness. Moreover, they had to take into account the appearance of a real *deus ex machina* on the Indian scene in the form of the Afghan empire-builder, Ahmad Shah Durrani (1747-73), who, with his Rohilla Afghan allies now settled in the

country of the upper Ganges around Bareilly, Moradabad and Bijnor, opposed any compromise with the infidel Hindus. The protracted Maratha-Afghan conflict reached its climax at the Third Battle of Panipat (1761), an overwhelming reverse for the Peshwa's forces. Yet it is a paradox of eighteenth-century Indian history that after this great victory the Afghan tide slowly receded from the Indian plains, while within a decade the Marathas were back in the north. The dominant Maratha figure in the late eighteenth century was Mahadaji Sindhia (*d* 1794), who dominated much of central India between the Jumna and the Narbada and who founded the Gwalior dynasty. Under his lead Maratha fortunes survived the first thrust of European territorial expansion without serious mishap. With Sindhia overawing the north, the Peshwa's government naturally turned its attention southward, but here, during the late eighteenth century, the prospects were not encouraging. The Nizam's territories were, it is true, generally accessible for plundering forays but the Nizam's government, shored up first by the French and then the British, survived even the overwhelming Maratha victory of Kharda (1795). More dangerous was the new regime in Mysore established by a Muslim adventurer, Haidar Ali (1761-82), and his son, Tipu Sultan (1782-99), that temporarily replaced the ancient Hindu principality and displayed striking military and administrative capacity.

The Europeans

Such was the position that confronted the rising power of the British East India Company in the last decades of the century: mushroom principalities and inchoate layers of authority; a moribund Moghul empire; provincial satraps enjoying *de facto* independence in Hyderabad, Bengal, Oudh and the Carnatic; the Maratha Confederacy, expanding still but with divided counsels weakening its striking power; and elsewhere, new regimes like that of Haidar Ali in Mysore and of the Sikhs in the Punjab. The British themselves were, of course, no newcomers to the Indian scene, having arrived at the beginning of the seventeenth century although, as in the case of

the Portuguese, the Dutch, the Danes and the French, it was trade that had first brought them. They remained for the most part on the fringes of the subcontinent, with their 'factories' at Surat, on the Coromandel coast and in Bengal. ('Factory,' the term applied to the compound allotted to them by the local authorities, contained, in addition to offices and godowns, living quarters and a place of worship.) They approached the Moghul government or, on the Coromandel coast, the officers of the Sultan of Golkonda, as suppliants humbly seeking permission to trade. Once permission was granted and a regular trade established, the Europeans became an increasingly important factor in the commercial and manufacturing life of certain areas and cities on or not far distant from the coast. The Moghul ruling elite made use of their services in a variety of ways, but they were always in India on sufferance. And precarious sufferance, at that. In 1632 Shah Jahan, exasperated by Portuguese slave-raiding in Bengal, pillaged Hughli and in turn enslaved its Portuguese inhabitants. In 1686 Aurangzeb expelled the British from Hughli, and it was only in 1690 that the quarrel was patched up, enabling Job Charnock to establish a settlement on the future site of Calcutta. On the west coast, well into the eighteenth century, the Maratha Peshwa kept the Europeans on a tight rein, so that when Baji Rao I seized the Portuguese fort of Bassein in 1739 the object-lesson was not lost on the British in nearby Bombay; they hastened to congratulate the Peshwa on his triumph.

All this changed, however, with the erosion of the Moghul bureaucratic structure and the substitution in its place of politically unstable local regimes. At the same time, the hitherto favorable conditions for trade disappeared, and the European merchants now found it necessary to fortify their settlements and engage troops for their defense, as well as pay closer attention to local political developments. In the case of the latter it was a short step to direct involvement and even active participation in events which might lead to the local ruler – as happened in both the Carnatic and Bengal – becoming a puppet in their hands. During the middle decades of the eighteenth century this process was accelerated when the Anglo-French conflict in Europe and North America spilled over into India, resulting in the settlements acquiring a distinctly military character, especially in the Carnatic, while local rulers, with varying degrees of enthusiasm, committed themselves to a pro-British or pro-French stance. These local rulers, as well as aspiring claimants to thrones already occupied, now began to recognize the superiority of European military discipline and equipment and increasingly sought to engage the services of European-trained and -officered units belonging to the rival companies for the purpose of overcoming their local rivals.

In the extended conflict between the French and British East India Companies the French, more dependent than the British upon state support and hamstrung by British superiority at sea, were the losers, notwithstanding occasional leadership of very high caliber. The three major conflicts between the rival companies (1744-48, 1750-54 and 1756-63) centered on the control of the Carnatic and left the British clearly the victors, although as late as the Napoleonic period some Britishers continued to be obsessed by the threat of a fresh French challenge in the sub-continent. Up to that time the British advance inland had been steady but not inexorable. The brilliant victory of the British East India Company's Robert Clive over a Franco-Bengali force at Plassey in 1757 had made the British *de facto* masters of Bengal, and in 1765 their occupation was regularized when the Moghul emperor, Shah Alam, granted them the *diwani* (the right to collect the land revenue on behalf of the emperor) of Bengal, Bihar and Orissa. To protect their western frontiers they had formed an alliance that same year with the Nawab-Vazir of Oudh, Shuja al-Dowleh, and in 1775 they acquired Benares from

his son and successor, Asaf al-Dowleh. . Finally, in 1801, they forced another son, Sa'adat Ali, to cede valuable tracts in the Jumna-Ganges Duab and in Rohilkhand, the core of the later Lieutenant-Governorship of the North-Western Provinces.

In the south the British ruled the Carnatic in the name of a puppet Nawab, had been in alliance with the Nizam of Hyderabad since 1766 and in 1784 had brought Travancore under their protection. After a succession of hard-fought wars with Haidar Ali and Tipu Sultan of Mysore (1767-69, 1780-84, 1790-92 and 1799) they overthrew this short-lived dynasty and restored the old Hindu

line of princes, while detaching certain districts for themselves and their allies.

On the west coast the proximity of the Peshwa's territories inhibited early British expansion beyond Bombay. The First Anglo-Maratha War, which terminated with the Treaty of Salbai in 1782, did little more than restore the *status quo ante bellum*. The British were confirmed in their possession of the island of Salsette, but they also gained 20 years of peace with their most formidable opponents. Thus, by the last decade of the eighteenth century the East India Company was *a* dominant, but not *the* dominant, power of India.

It was one component of a volatile state-system but far from being seen by contemporaries as the inevitable substitute for that system. In India, as in Europe, the British thought in terms of a 'balance of power.' This phase, essentially a transitory one, came to an end with the governor-generalship of the Marquis of Wellesley (1798-1805).

Spurred on by a somewhat exaggerated fear of a revival of French influence in the subcontinent, Wellesley pursued singlemindedly the goal of undiluted British dominance. He pensioned off the Nawabs of Surat, Tanjore and the Carnatic, and assumed direct responsibility for the administration of their former possessions. Upon potentially more formidable allies he imposed treaties which compelled them to maintain a subsidiary force of Company troops for their own protection, to be provided for out of their own revenues or by ceding territory to the Company. Subsidiary treaties, which generally included clauses forbidding the ruler to employ European officers in his service or to conduct foreign relations without the Company's approval, were concluded with Hyderabad in 1800 and Oudh in 1801. Not all Indian rulers were amenable to this kind of pressure. Tipu Sultan of Mysore was an implacable foe of British expansion, but he was crushed in 1799. The Marathas, too, presented a formidable front in central and western India and would perhaps have been left alone but for their own internal dissensions, which tempted the British to intervene. The incompetence of the last Peshwa, Baji Rao II, played into Wellesley's hands, and he set about reducing the Maratha Confederacy to a status comparable to that of Hyderabad or Oudh. In the Second Anglo-Maratha War (1803-05) the Marathas were beaten both in the Deccan and on the Jumna but not broken. Nevertheless, with Delhi now in British hands and the Moghul emperor their pensioner, the supremacy at which Wellesley aimed was, by the time of his recall in 1805, well advanced. Only after a Third Anglo-Maratha War (1817-19) and the deposition of the Peshwa would a final settlement be imposed upon the center of the country. The steady expansion of the limits of the Company's area of control would involve a fierce war with the Nepalese (1814-16), disastrous intervention in the politics of Afghanistan (1839-42), the conquest of Sind (1843), two bitterly fought wars with the Sikhs (1845-46 and 1848-49) preceding the annexation of the Punjab and numerous expeditions across the north-west and north-east frontiers.

These Indian campaigns were no 'walk-overs.' The fighting was hard, and there were also disease and the climate to contend with. Haidar Ali and Tipu Sultan, the Marathas at their best, the Nepalese Gurkhas and, above all, the Sikhs proved daring and resourceful foes. The casualties in the First Sikh War tell their own tale – at Ferozeshah (1845) the Company lost 694 men killed, including 103 officers, and 1721 wounded; at Sobraon (1846) 320 killed and 2083 wounded. But the British conquest of India was never, at any time, a saga of White versus Brown. The majority of the Company's troops, including the artillery, consisted of Indian troops or 'sepoys' as they were called, who flocked to enlist in the native regiments of the prestigious Company Bahadur, officered by Europeans and, for a short time, by Eurasians. By comparison, the Company's European regiments and the royal regiments loaned from Britain served mainly as 'stiffening.' The British commanders in India whose exploits were to make them schoolboy heroes of Victorian Britain – Robert Clive, Stringer Lawrence, Hector Munro, Eyre Coote, Lord Lake, Arthur Wellesley – were

Left: The Marquis of Wellesley. His determination to extend British power and forestall the French brought large areas of India under British control between 1798 and 1805.

Below: Warren Hastings, the first governor-general of Bengal (1773-85), who laid the foundations of British rule in India.

Above right: The Taj Mahal, Moghul Shah Jahan's incomparable memorial to his dead wife.

Below right: A Rajput painting of a visit by representatives of the British Raj to the court at Udaipur. The Indian princedoms retained the ceremonial splendor of their courts, but without real power.

'Sepoy Generals,' and their victories were won, in the main, with Indian troops. It is fundamental for any understanding of the phenomenon of British rule in India to recognize that British authority rested by and large upon the acquiescence or indifference of the great majority of Indians and upon the active support of its sepoy army (which, in 1856, numbered 233,000 men), as well as a considerable cadre of subordinate Indian judicial, police and revenue officers.

The early British Raj

Pressure of circumstances made the East India Company, however improbably, the legatee of the Moghul Empire, of its political style and its framework of administration. No other option was open. The Britishers – often young and inexperienced – into whose hands passed province after province had no other tradition of imperial rule to guide their actions. If the Moghul Empire was dead, the memory remained, especially in the north, and so did traces of its ruling institutions. In a countryside where the events of a century ago were but yesterday in the telling, the splendor of Firuz Shah Tughluq, of Akbar and Aurangzeb, were part of popular tradition. Camping in derelict Moghul palaces and tombs, treating with princes whose ancestors had molded the past, riding and feasting with the descendants of the grandees who had once served the Moghul Empire, the newcomers were led along the old paths. Inevitably they brought to the business of ruling India their full share of eighteenth-century European attitudes and assumptions, yet their inexperience, their physical and psychological isolation from Europe and the sheer weight of the Indian past compelled them at first, more often than not unconsciously, to follow Moghul traditions. It seems likely that Warren Hastings (1732-1818), who laid the foundations of future British supremacy in India, never viewed the

future of British rule except in terms of renovating Moghul institutions.

Thus there emerged under the East India Company an administrative structure rooted in Moghul precedents. First, there was a division of the country into those areas directly ruled by British officials (British India) and those left in the hands of Indian rulers (Princely India), comparable to the way in which the Moghul emperors had left extensive tracts in Rajasthan, Gondwana and elsewhere in the control of indigenous chieftains and *zamindars*. These Indian rulers enjoyed a restricted sovereignty under the aegis of British paramountcy. In all there were nearly 600 Princely States, ranging from tiny principalities of a few square miles to Hyderabad, with an area little less than that of the present German Federal Republic. In 1900 the Princely States covered 679,000 square miles, out of a total area of 1,700,000, and their population was 62,500,000 of a total of 300,000,000. The survival of these anomalous regimes constituted no deliberate policy on the part of the Company comparable to the later protectorates in tropical Africa or southeast Asia, and prior to 1858 there was no discernible consistency in the way in which they were dealt with by the paramount power. Relations were conducted on an *ad hoc* basis determined largely by the circumstances under which each prince had been drawn into the Company's orbit, his subsequent behavior and the shifts in the Company's priorities. The Company and, after 1858, the Government of India dealt with the states through a distinct cadre of officials – the Political Service – and a British Resident was attached to all the larger *Durbars* to watch over and advise them on all matters affecting the interests of the paramount power. The existence, down to 1947, of Princely India side by side with 'British India' reinforced the exotic and 'oriental' character of the Raj, providing a link both with the Indian past and with the colorful early days of British rule.

British India was divided into provinces of unequal size, status and importance and placed in the charge of Governors-in-Council, Lieutenant-Governors or Chief Commissioners who may be likened to the *subahdars* of Moghul times. They were designated either regulation or non-regulation provinces, the latter consisting of areas where, on account of the turbulence or backwardness of the population, it was deemed inexpedient to enforce the regulations applicable to the rest of the country. Theoretically, non-regulation status was considered a temporary condition, and it was assumed that as soon as a non-regulation province became accustomed to settled administration its status would be enhanced to that of a regulation province. Thus the Punjab, annexed in 1849 and governed by a Board of Administration, was made into a non-regulation Chief Commissionership in 1851; in 1859 it became a non-regulation Lieutenant-Governorship; and in 1919 it was elevated to the status of a full Governor's Province.

Every province was divided into Districts of unequal size and population. The District, equivalent to the Moghul *sarkar*, was the key unit of administration, and although beneath it were Sub-

Districts in the charge of subordinate Indian revenue and executive officials, it was the British District Officer, lineal descendant of the Moghul *faujdar*, who was 'the eyes and ears of government' and the only Britains with whom most Indians were ever likely to have dealings. Like the *faujdar*, he was responsible for the maintenance of law and order in his district, the assessment and collection of the Land Revenue and the general welfare of the population in his charge, and in provinces which were vigorously administered, such as the Punjab, he might earn the sobriquet of *gharib-parwar*, 'Protector of the Poor.' Also like the *faujdar*, who had been assisted in judicial matters by the *qazi*, and by the *amulgazar* in assessing the Land Revenue, the District Officer in an important District had Deputy-Magistrates and Settlement Officers to whom he could delegate some of his responsibilities. These latter were generally very young men, sometimes barely out of their teens, and they were in consequence heavily dependent upon their Indian subordinates.

The thinking of the District Officer was shaped to a very great extent by the character of the people with whom he lived and the local administrative tradition in which he functioned. In Bengal, for example, the administrative tradition had been molded by the Permanent Settlement of 1793, a measure that granted to the Zamindars of Bengal the absolute proprietary rights of British landlords, and their land revenue liability was assessed in perpetuity in the hope that the resultant security of title would in time encourage the emergence of progressive 'Whig' landlords such as had been the backbone of the agricultural revolution of eighteenth-century Britain. As a result, the administration of Bengal had developed along rather casual, *laissez-faire* lines, with the District Officer unwilling to intervene in the affairs of the great Zamindars unless there was expectation of default in payment of the land revenue. The errors made in the Permanent Settlement – the lack of any protection given to the cultivator or the inferior proprietor and the government's rash sacrifice in perpetuity of any enhancement in the land revenue resulting from a rise in the value of land or the price of agricultural produce – was soon perceived. In the Madras Presidency, Sir Thomas Munro (Special Commissioner, 1814-19, and Governor, 1819-27) introduced the *ryotwari* system, in which government negotiated the land revenue direct with the cultivator (*ryot*) on the basis of what was virtually an annual reassessment.

This system called for close supervision by the District Officers and a degree of paternalism absent in Bengal. Munro's system proved attractive to many officials disillusioned with developments in Bengal, and the *ryotwari* system was subsequently introduced by Mountstuart Elphinstone (Governor of Bombay, 1819-27) into the territory ceded by the Peshwa, although not without considerable modification. In the Delhi Territory, Thomas Metcalfe (Resident at Delhi, 1811-19 and 1825-27) endeavored to resuscitate the village communities by settling the revenue with village *panchayats*, while in the adjacent North-Western

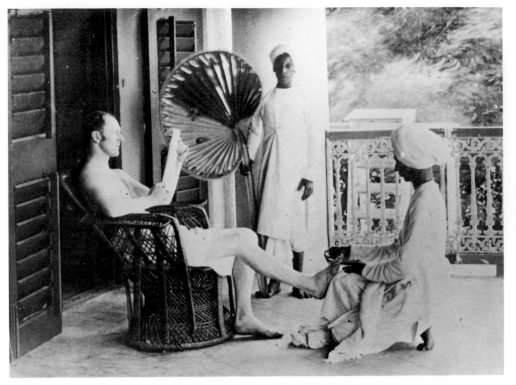

Provinces (now Uttar Pradesh) settlements were made wherever possible with village-communities, village headmen (*muqaddams*) or inferior proprietors at the expense of the superior proprietors and those who claimed a share of the profits of cultivation on the basis of 'rights' asserted during the century which divided Moghul from British rule. This system, associated with the name of James Thomason (Lieutenant-Governor, 1843-53), was imported into the Punjab, where John Lawrence (Chief Commissioner, 1851-59), in particular, favored direct settlement wherever possible with the actual cultivator of the soil. In the Punjab, officials were markedly paternalistic and authoritarian, and that province – which came to be regarded as a model administration – was most strenuously governed by hand-picked men who often had a driving sense of mission but also a somewhat exaggerated belief in the virtues of their own system.

But the latter-day Punjab was not really characteristic of British India as a whole. On balance, probably the most striking aspect of early British rule was its unobtrusiveness, which in large part explains the passivity with which it was accepted by the great majority of Indians. Probably the majority of Indians in the first half of the nineteenth century never saw a white face except when the District Officer was on tour in the vicinity of their villages. The earliest British officials were only concerned that the Company's peace be kept and the land revenue paid. Even these functions were frequently delegated to Indians themselves, for all minor matters were left, wherever practicable, to village *panchayats*.

Nor were the British at first inclined to interfere with the customs of the country. They accepted as a fact the existence of diverse and even conflicting sets of values, and while at a personal level they might view caste as a distasteful institution, or practices such as suttee (the self-immolation of Brahmin widows) as abhorrent, they followed Moghul precedent in not getting involved. Moreover, they themselves, with their long tours of duty in remote areas and their infrequent visits to Britain (between 1796 and 1827 Mountstuart Elphinstone never once went home on leave), were compelled to adapt themselves to local conditions. The younger Company officials, espe-

cially, found it easy to assimilate much of the lifestyle of the old Moghul ruling elite. They surrounded themselves with vast retinues of servants, kept Indian concubines (and even here and there a modest seraglio), traveled on elephants or in palanquins, adapted the local architecture to their needs, wore Indian dress, smoked *hookahs* and chewed *betel* and at times relaxed in the company of Indian musicians and nautch-girls.

Yet with the extravagance there also went a familiarity with and love of the country and an extensive knowledge of its languages and customs. Not a few officials, and army officers too, were men of scholarly bent, and their researches into the history, literature, religion and antiquities of the subcontinent laid the foundations of virtually all modern knowledge of the Indian past. Their relations with Indians were also probably more intimate and sensitive than would later be the case. The contemporaries of Munro, Malcolm, Elphinstone and Metcalfe were nurtured on Romanticism, and, finding themselves, overnight, as it were, masters of a vast mysterious land, steeped in alien traditions and scarred with centuries of violent history, they interpreted that history in Romantic terms, likened Rajput or Maratha chieftains to the Highland heroes of Sir Walter Scott and cast themselves in the role of heirs to Akbar and Aurangzeb. Yet because they were Romantics there went with all this a melancholy sense of the impermanence of the splendid charade in which, at least temporarily, they were the principal performers. Metcalfe could predict in 1833:

We are to appearance more powerful in India than we ever were. Nevertheless, our downfall may be short work. When it commences it will probably be rapid, and the world will wonder more at the suddenness with which our immense Indian Empire may vanish, than it has done at the surprising conquest that we have achieved.

The cause of this precariousness is that our power does not rest on actual strength, but on impressions ...

Empires grow old, decay, and perish. Ours in India can hardly be called old, but seems destined to be short-lived. We appear to have passed the brilliancy and vigor of our youth, and it may be that we have reached a premature old age.

The later British Raj

During the second quarter of the nineteenth century the character of British rule in India changed significantly. The agents of change were two rather different but fortuitously allied groups. One was made up of the Evangelicals who strenuously asserted that British rule in India was a God-given trust that required the spread of the Gospel from one end of the subcontinent to the other, a task clearly beyond the powers of the Company's Indianized servants. The other group was made up of Utilitarians who, exasperated by the obstacles of inertia, tradition and vested interest which prevented the restructuring of British society along Benthamite lines, turned eagerly to India as a *tabula rasa* where the more authoritarian and paternalist strands of Utilitarian doctrine could be tried out. The Utilitarians viewed Indian society as irrational and barbarous; the Evangelicals viewed it as a sink of heathen depravity desperately in need of Christian truth. Neither group felt inclined to waste sympathy on those traditions of sceptical tolerance and that search for some kind of Anglo-Indian dialogue which were at lease implicit in the approach of such men as John Malcolm and Mountstuart Elphinstone.

It would be an exaggeration to suppose that during the three decades or more prior to 1857 either Evangelicalism or Utilitarianism was able to mold entirely the spirit of the period, but both were very influential nonetheless, and there can be no question but that the period between the arrival in India of Lord William Bentinck as governor-general in 1829 and the departure of Lord Dalhousie in 1856 was characterized by a mood of aggressive Anglicization spreading out from the higher echelons of officialdom. The mood took different forms. At one level it was purely humanitarian in character, demanding the abolition of customs repugnant to Europeans such as suttee, female infanticide and human sacrifice. It also took the form of intense hostility toward traditional Indian elites – *zamindars*, chieftains and princes – and the eight years of Lord Dalhousie's vigorous administration saw the annexation on one pretext or another of Satara, Udaipur (later reversed), Nagpur, Jhansi and Oudh, the enforced lease of Berar from the Nizam and the abolition of old titles, such as those of the Princes of Arcot and Tanjore, and of the pension of the Peshwa's adopted heir, Nana Sahib. The mood was both braggart and complacent, drawing the Company into a futile and disastrous war in Afghanistan (1839-42), the conquest of Sind (1843), two hard-fought wars with the Sikhs (1845-46 and 1848-49), leading to the annexation of the Punjab, and the Second Burmese War (1852). Ultimately, all this (and much more besides) can only be understood in terms of the changing nature of British society and of a newly found self-confidence, brashness and aggressive nationalism that in India manifested itself in a novel assumption of the unqualified superiority of everything European over everything Oriental and in a conviction of British moral superiority and fitness to govern India.

These attitudes were reinforced by a gradual change in the pattern of British social life in India. At the beginning of the nineteenth century, outside the Presidency cities of Calcutta, Bombay and Madras, with their substantial European population, British men lived isolated, lonely lives. British women were few, and diversions other than field sports were virtually non-existent. Officials were thus forced to come to terms with the society in which they worked and lived. But by the middle years of the century there was an ever-

Above left: British army officers easily slipped into an arrogant assumption of superiority over the Indians. Much of the local population, long used to rule by invading warrior dynasties, adapted equally easily to serving the British Raj.

Above: By the end of the nineteenth century, the British had exported much of their native lifestyle wholesale to India, including cricket and Anglican church architecture.

Right: Nana Sahib of Cawnpore, one of the leading figures in the Indian Mutiny of 1857.

increasing flow of British women coming out to India. They came not only to the Presidency cities but to remote stations up country, and there now began to emerge self-sustaining British communities which, once the day's work was over, sought exclusion from the outside world in a round of balls, amateur theatricals and station gossip.

With the frontiers of British India pressing ever forward, with the memories of old struggles and dangers growing dim, with the dominant mood being one of unquestioning self-confidence the administration – often from the highest and most disinterested motives – took ever less account of Indian susceptibilities.

All these factors played their part in the great Mutiny of 1857. It began as a purely military mutiny involving some (but by no means all) sepoy units. Its causes were various and often obscure, but it gradually infected other groups and communities outside the military with a spirit of rebellion. It was certainly the greatest challenge the British had ever experienced to their rule, and yet it was nevertheless local in extent, centering upon the upper Gangetic plain in what is now Uttar Pradesh and spilling over into adjacent areas of the Punjab, Rajasthan, Madhya Pradesh and Bihar. Even in those areas where the struggle was most bitter many Indians refrained from getting involved or quietly assisted British refugees. The majority of the Princes remained loyal to the Company, and some aided the British with supplies and even troops. The armies of the Bombay and Madras Presidencies remained quiet, and in the recently conquered Punjab iron-fisted proconsuls such as John Lawrence, Herbert Edwardes and John Nicholson actually enlisted their erstwhile Sikh foes and the wild Pathans of the frontier to march to the relief of Delhi.

The immediate cause of the uprising was the failure of the British military authorities to comprehend the seriousness of the deep-rooted suspicions entertained by the sepoys that in a variety of ways the government was intent upon destroying their caste (in the case of the high-caste Hindus) and upon flouting their religious sentiments. The outbreak began at Meerut on 10 May 1857

point, especially after Delhi fell to a relieving British army on 14 September 1857. Another center of revolt was Cawnpore: the Nana Sahib was proclaimed Peshwa, and the city became the scene of a peculiarly revolting massacre of British women and children.

That the shocked and angry British would retaliate was certain, and that they would be successful was almost as certain. Lucknow finally fell to the British on 21 March 1858, although desultory fighting continued for some months after. Both sides had perpetrated atrocities, and the savagery with which the fighting was conducted – the sepoys, as mutineers, knowing they could expect no mercy from Britishers inflamed by incidents such as the Cawnpore massacre – had no precedent in former struggles. It is hard to say how far these events sank into the consciousness of Indians other than those living in areas directly affected by them, but there can be no doubt that on the British side memories of 1857 left deep scars of disillusion and anger.

After 1857 the British in India ceased to be innovators, as the generation of Bentinck and Dalhousie had been, and became conservationists. They distanced themselves even more from the life of the country and increasingly treated it as an enormous museum of diverse social patterns and traditions which the government was now most unwilling to disturb. In many respects administration improved and became more efficient, the army was overhauled and the proportion of European troops greatly increased. Also the old rule of 'Company Bahadur' came to an end and the government of India was placed directly under the British Crown, administered in London by a Secretary of State who had Cabinet rank and by a council of retired Anglo-Indian officials. In India those Princes who had been loyal to the

and spread to Delhi, where mutinous sepoys proclaimed the restoration of the Moghul Empire under the titular rule of the octogenarian emperor, Bahadur Shah II, a pensioned recluse living out his last days in the Red Fort. The sepoy capture of Delhi served as a catalyst for widespread rebellion, and in the major towns for many miles around British rule came to an end, and Europeans, Eurasians, Indian Christians and Bengali servants and subordinate officials were indis-

criminately massacred. In the ensuing confusion roving mobs terrorized the bazaars and especially the commercial and money-lending classes (identified with the regime), while those landlords and chieftains dispossessed by the settlement operations reclaimed their lost properties and prerogatives. In Oudh, annexed the previous year, the old dynasty was restored, although as nominally subordinate to the Moghul emperor in Delhi, and Lucknow, its capital, became the major rallying-

British in 1857 were assured that the bad old days of annexation were gone for ever, and the princely order was, on paper at least, gradually assimilated into a kind of subordinate partnership fostered by sympathetic officials, especially during the governor-generalships of Canning (1856-62), Lytton (1876-80) and Curzon (1899-1905). Another sign of the times was the diminution in most parts of India of the old concern that the cultivator tenant should have occupancy right to till his fields without fear of dispossession. It was now felt that it was only the influential landowner, the man with a stake in the countryside and, in consequence, in the stability of the Raj, who could provide the British with meaningful support. Thus Lytton, newly arrived in India in 1876, wrote to the Secretary of State, Lord Salisbury:

I am convinced that the fundamental political mistake of able and experienced Indian officials is a belief that we can hold India securely by what they call good government: that is to say, by improving the condition of the *ryot*, strictly administering justice, spending immense sums on irrigation works, etc. Politically speaking, the Indian peasantry is an inert mass . . . To secure completely, and efficiently utilize, the Indian aristocracy is, I am convinced the most important problem before us now.

The effect of all this was distortion in one direction as great as the application to India of Benthamite doctrine had been distortion in another. One of the ablest officials trained in the old school, Sir John Strachey, deplored 'the insane desire for landlords like those of England . . . There must everywhere be a great landlord. If he were not found, then he must have been unjustly swept away.'

But the after-effects of the Mutiny went deeper than these shifts in policy might, in themselves, suggest. There were profound psychological changes as well. The Anglo-Indians perceived in the events of 1857 a proof of the futility of introducing Western values into so alien and unpromising a soil, of the mutual incomprehensibility of East and West. The mood, if rarely enunciated, was increasingly one of distrust, pessimism and doubt.

The framework of British rule in India was neither the army nor the relatively small business community, largely restricted to Calcutta and Bombay, but the British who worked in the Indian Civil Service, in its heyday a bureaucracy enjoying enormous power and prestige. Hand-picked, well-paid and enjoying for the most part boundless self-confidence, its members were – in Philip Woodruff's apt analogy – the Platonic Guardians of this benevolent, if exceedingly paternalistic autocracy. At first they were recruited by a system of pure jobbery – nomination by a director of the East India Company – followed by schooling at the Company's college at Haileybury. No more haphazard system could have been devised to recruit the rulers of a great empire, and the products, by any reckoning, should have been mediocrities or worse. And yet, incredibly, this was the method that recruited the Metcalfes and the Elphinstones, the Thomasons and the Lawrences. In 1853 this form of recruitment was abandoned in favor of an open competitive examination, and although at first the older generation questioned the caliber of the new 'Competition-Wallahs,' it is probably safe to say that throughout the second half of the nineteenth century and down to World War I the ICS continued to draw upon some of the brightest talent of the British universities. Something of their self-assurance and their perception of the ambiguity of their role is conveyed in the following passage from a memoir of the last years of the nineteenth century:

Our life in India, our very work more or less, rests on illusion. I had the illusion, wherever I was, that I was infallible and invulnerable in my dealings with Indians. How else could I have dealt with angry mobs, with cholera-stricken masses, and with processions of religious fanatics? It was not conceit, Heaven knows: it was not the prestige of the British Raj, but it was the illusion which is in the very air of India. They expressed something of the idea when they called us the 'Heaven-born,' and the idea is really make-believe – mutual make-believe.

Yet the mood of pessimism and scepticism that was slowly creeping in even before 1900, and the decline of that personal touch so characteristic of the days of Malcolm and Elphinstone, prompted at least a few of the more sensitive officials to doubt the value of it all. These same doubts were also expressed with increasing stridency by liberal opinion in Britain. Thus the germ of imperial recession was born. The erosion of a sense of mission, and, with it, of self-confidence, was an extremely gradual process, but it was certainly a factor to be reckoned with in preparing the ground for Britain's withdrawal from her greatest adventure.

The emergence of nationalist sentiment in the form of a critical and articulate Indian press proved a sore trial for the equanimity of the Guardians. This Indian press, mostly Bengali, was increasingly full of scepticism regarding British motives and judgment, and later it began to demand a share of authority and office – primarily, increased Indianization of the Civil Service. Nettled, the British retorted that Bengali journalists, lawyers or schoolmasters (Bengal was the first part of India to come to terms with British

Above left: The site in Delhi where 200 Europeans were massacred in the 1857 Mutiny. Such massacres were used to justify bloody reprisals once the British regained the upper hand.

Left: A scattering of bones, all that was left of sepoys killed in the 1857 fighting.

Right: General Wheeler's entrenchment at Cawnpore, where about 1000 British men, women and children were besieged by Nana Sahib. Only four escaped alive; most of the rest were killed after surrendering to the Nana.

Left: An example of Indians and British mixing socially – the Karachi Spring Races. Such instances are relatively infrequent, however, and existed only on a superficial level.

Right: Building a railway bridge in East Bengal (1871). Modern transportation was one of the many undoubted benefits of British rule in India.

Below: Despite the disillusioning events of the Mutiny, the Raj continued to rely on the willing cooperation of the Indian population. The British and Indians at this Engineer's Office would never have been on an equal social footing, but they did work together.

higher education) were hardly representative and could not speak either for the great mass of rural India or for the 'martial races' of the north – Sikhs, Rajputs, Pathans, etc. – who were prepared to stomach the rule of the British, who had beaten them in fair fight, but would never accept the rule of Bengali *babus* (clerks) and *banians* (traders). British officials, in fact, seemed to be temperamentally incapable of coming to terms with the new Western-educated elite. They had always tended to identify with rural India, the India they first learnt to know as young officers employed on settlement work in the villages. They had established informal and sometimes warm connections with local landowners and chieftains who shared their enthusiasm for life in the saddle and in the shooting-field. Now, when the challenge to their rule came from a city-based intelligentsia, they turned with renewed enthusiasm to those groups whom they identified as the 'real' India – the Maharajahs, the feudal landowners, the tribals, the cultivators.

And yet perceptive Britains recognized that the growth of a nationalist movement was the direct outcome of the very nature of British rule and its emphasis on British-style education. Macaulay noted:

It may be that the public mind of India may expand under our system till it has outgrown that system; that by good government we may educate our subjects into a capacity for better government; that, having become instructed in European knowledge, they may, in some future age, demand European institutions. Whether such a day will ever come I know not. But never will I attempt to avert or to retard it. Whenever it comes, it will be the proudest day in English history.

Education apart, the British presence alone was an inescapable factor for change. The executive decisions of a government whose writ ran from the Indus to Cape Comorin, the uniform judgments of the courts, the appearance of a market in land, the social changes which elevated some castes and communities at the expense of others, the advent of Western medicine and mechanized industry, the use of English as a lingua franca, the phenomenal growth of population and the introduction of the railroad and the telegraph, which gave the country a unity such as it had never known before, all contributed to making India in 1900 a very different place from what it had been a century before.

Bengali Renaissance

Yet no change was more momentous than the conscious decision of the British to introduce into India their educational system. The first steps were hesitant and on a very modest scale, and although they owed something to Evangelical concern in Britain, they owed more to the foresight of such men as Elphinstone, Munro and Thomason. The real turning-point came with the Educational Despatch of 1854. It prescribed a comprehensive system of education ascending to universities in Calcutta, Bombay and Madras, all founded in 1857, to which were later added Lahore (1882) and Allahabad (1887). It was in Bengal, especially, where by 1857 British rule had been a fact for over a century, that this exotic plant most conspicuously took root in ground prepared during the early and middle decades of the century by that movement of intellectual ferment and literary innovation that has been styled the Bengali Renaissance.

Calcutta, with its large European community, its schools and colleges and literary societies, and its impressive coterie of scholarly officials and missionaries, was a window on Europe that offered an intellectual challenge and a stimulus which the Bengali mind found irresistible. As the expanding capital of the subcontinent, Calcutta and its wealth acted as a magnet to the *bhadralok* or 'respectable people,' who self-consciously devoted themselves to acquiring the learning of the West. Although many of the *bhadralok* were

only teachers and clerks, they were obviously an elite, many of whom were descendants of families which had acquired wealth as agents or partners of the British in the original spoliation of Bengal, or were *rentiers* with property rights stemming from the Permanent Settlement of 1793 – as in the case of the Tagore family. They thought more in terms of Bengal than of India, and of the replacement of a British bureaucratic elite by a Bengali caste-cum-intellectual elite, implicitly rejecting mass participation in the governing process. The pace-setters in both the intellectual and the political life of modern India, their story is one of pathetic but steady decline to a point of virtual exclusion from an effective role in the destinies of modern India.

Scorned by their British rulers, whose culture they had so enthusiastically adopted, stung to impotent rage by the partition of Bengal in 1905 and by the transfer of the capital from Calcutta to New Delhi in 1911, they proved incapable after World War I of adapting themselves to the all-India framework and the grass-roots perspectives of Congress politics in the age of Gandhi. With the truncation of Bengal in the partition of 1947 the Bengali *bhadralok*, in an emasculated Calcutta cut off from the jute industry now located in East Pakistan, became simply an irritant in an India which seemingly resolved to notice them as rarely as possible. If nothing else, the Bengali decline proved that a narrow sectionalist approach could have no place in a modern India.

Southeast Asia: 1500-1914

The concept of Southeast Asia is a relatively recent one. The phrase itself became popularized only during World War II. The areas located roughly between India and China were linked together by this phrase. From an historical standpoint the individual countries themselves had little in common and little, if any, contact with one another in the centuries preceding European colonization. Even the definition of the area has been unclear. The Chinese referred to the area as 'farther India.' From the seventeenth to the nineteenth centuries Europeans referred to the area as 'Indo-China,' implying that the area lay between India and China. In modern times, the term 'Southeast Asia' has come to mean Burma, Thailand, Vietnam, Laos, Cambodia, Malaysia, Singapore, Indonesia and the Philippines. There has only been one time in history when this region has been politically united – 1942-45. Vietnam was under China's direct rule for the first 1000 years of the Chinese era. The other parts of the region were controlled by local monarchs, although most of the area was originally influenced by Hinduism. Theravada Buddhism became the dominant religion of insular Southeast Asia (apart from the Philippines, which from the sixteenth century onward has been predominantly Roman Catholic). Linguistically, ethically and culturally the area is very diverse.

If there is one unifying theme to the area, it is that of geography. Southeast Asia has been and continues to be a formidable trading bridge between India and China, and because of its important strategic materials it has become an important source for world trade in rice, rubber, tin and petroleum. The history of Southeast Asia is principally the history of the interaction between the various local satrapies and the pressures brought to bear upon them by powers outside the area which envied its natural resources and its strategic position across international sea lanes.

The origin of the race of the peoples of Southeast Asia is not known. Architectural monuments unmistakably indicate that the origin of the people of mainland Southeast Asia derives at least in part from India. Written records, such as they are, indicate some penetration from China. However, in peninsular Southeast Asia and throughout insular Southeast Asia, the Proto-Malays settled at some time in the period of the Christian era, mingling with primitive Australoids who left few traces in the region. Once Vietnam had been incorporated into the Chinese empire of the Han and Tang, further peasant villages were the norm throughout most of the area, but people located near the ocean or river mouths developed some contact with the outside world as early as 2000 years ago: they traded with both India and China, with spices such as pepper being the principal commodity. At no time did China establish military and naval hegemony in Southeast Asia outside the area of Vietnam. Under the Yüan and Ming dynasties, China briefly intervened in Southeast Asian affairs but without lasting results. More important was Indian cultural influence, of which the overwhelmingly predominant factor was that of Buddhism, especially in Burma and Thailand. Numerous great kingdoms were established in Southeast Asia during the first 1500 years of the Christian era. Certainly the most important Buddhistic kingdoms were those of Angkor in Cambodia, Crivijaya, centered in southern Sumatra, and Sailendia, based in central Java. By the mid fifteenth century, all of these kingdoms had either disappeared or decayed.

From the twelfth century onward peninsular and insular Southeast Asia were both deeply affected by the sweep of Islam, transported by maritime traders from Arabia. Inland peninsular areas such as Burma and Thailand remained faithful to Theravada Buddhism, but Islam became the dominant insular religion by the end of the four-

teenth century. It would have had the same effect in the Philippines had they not been settled by the Spanish Catholics in the early sixteenth century. Islam became the most potent agent of change in the Indonesian archipelago. The Javanese merged their Hinduistic states with Islam, blending the two with a kind of cultural syncretism, and new Islamic sultanates became important commercial powers in Sumatra and Malaya, the most important being Malacca on the west coast of Malaya. Malacca became the largest trading entrepôt in all of Southeast Asia, attracting traders from all over the world to its harbor.

Yet Malacca's very success proved to be its undoing: in 1511, a bare century after its meteoric rise, it fell to the first Western invaders to come into Southeast Asia – the Portuguese. The thriving entrepôt thus became the lynchpin in the chain of fortified Portuguese trading posts established in response to the closing of the eastern Mediterranean by the Ottoman conquest of Constantinople in 1453. Embarked on an enterprise that combined commercial with missionary zeal, the new Christian overlords came to treat their Malaccan subjects with accommodating prudence, putting profits ahead of religion. But the Portuguese thrust provoked a militant economic and political reaction among Southeast Asian Muslims, especially in northern Sumatra, site of a new Muslim state, the sultanate of Acheh. Excellently located and, unlike Malacca, richly endowed with natural resources of its own, Acheh assumed the leadership of a counter-crusade against the Portuguese. Its leaders' religious zeal was rewarded with military aid from the distant Caliph, the only Southeast Asian kingdom ever to maintain this symbolically important tie with the center of the Islamic world. By the mid seventeenth century, Acheh had grown into the most respected foe of Europeans and Asians alike; but no Islamic united front against the 'infidels' ever materialized in island Southeast Asia.

Like their counterparts in Sumatra and Malaya, rulers of the port communities on Java's north coast had adopted Islam well before Malacca fell to the Portuguese. Theoretically vassals of their Buddhist East Javanese overlord, Majapahit, they had secured increasing independence as a result of both their growing wealth and the progressive internal weakening of Majapahit power. In the 1470s, Demak, one of the earlier sultanates, led an armed revolt against its suzerain; but it took another 50-odd years for the island's last Indianized empire to disintegrate completely. No new center of authority appeared for something like a century, and in the interval the Islamic littoral steadily gained in prominence. In the seventeenth century it appeared that Malacca's place as foremost Muslim entrepôt would pass to the sultanate of Banten in the westernmost part of Java. But two new forces arose which, in combination, conclusively thwarted the ambitions of these Muslim principalities.

In central Java the vacuum created by the disappearance of Majapahit was finally filled by the rise of a new Buddhist dynasty, Mataram. In time-honored fashion it proclaimed itself heir and continuer of its illustrious predecessor. More important, it actually recreated many of the trappings of the Indianized monarchy in its inland, agrarian

base. To rulers harking back to a proud, aristocratic past the principalities on the island's northern rim must have appeared as uncouth upstarts whose wealth and self-appointed autonomy, no less than their Islamic orientation, constituted intolerable threats to the Matararmese traditionalism and territorial hegemony. One by one, the new kingdom succeeded in subduing the recalcitrant vassals. Yet paradoxically it was a victory of Muslims over Muslims, for the rulers of Mataram had themselves come to embrace Islam too. But Mataram's Islamization, patently motiv-

ated by political reasons – only one of the entire dynasty adopted the title of sultan – amounted to little more than a thin veneer atop a basically Hindu-Javanese court culture.

If Muslim-inspired change had thus been halted by the resurgence of Javanese continuity in one part of the island, in another – the sultanate of Banten in West Java – it ran athwart another newcomer to the Southeast Asian scene – the United Dutch East India Company. From the founding of their first factory at Batavia in Java in the first decade of the seventeenth century under

Jan Peetingoon Coen, the Dutch vigorously pursued the goal of obtaining monopolistic control over Indonesian trade routes and economic resources. The destruction of the northern principalities by Mataram had smoothed their path. But it was a succession quarrel in Banten that provided the Company with a chance of direct interference and led to its ultimate control over that vital pepper center. Virtually supreme in the Java Sea, the Dutch also succeeded in ousting the Portuguese from Malacca in 1641, at a time when Acheh, until recently a powerful competitor, had started to succumb to a long process of decline. At the end of the century the progress of Southeast Asian Islam had thus been seriously weakened, if not halted, by both indigenous and foreign forces. And by the mid seventeenth century the Dutch had supplanted the Portuguese and had developed the largest maritime power in the area, dominating the spice trade and forming the basis for what was to become the largest and most populous colony in all of Southeast Asia.

Meanwhile, in the Philippines, following Magellan's discovery of the area, the Spanish proceeded to colonize the island of Luzon. Lopez de Legaspi established Manila in 1571 and made it the capital of the entire archipelago, which had been claimed by King Philip. Because of the arrangements made between Spain and Portugal, with the help of the papacy, dividing the world into two parts (1529), the Portuguese and Spanish

Right: A governor-general and his wife of the Dutch East India Company survey the Dutch mercantile fleet at anchor in Batavia, then the main port of Java.

Below left: The ruins of the Khmer city of Angkor Thom, now a part of modern-day Kampuchea.

Below: Dating from the eighth century, the Buddhist temple at Borobudar in central Java was sponsored under the rulers of the Saliendra dynasty.

did not struggle over hegemony in Southeast Asia. Spain claimed the Philippines and the Portuguese claimed the rest of the area. Facing all but nominal opposition, except of the Mindanao, the Spanish proceeded to convert the archipelago and had colonized most of the Philippines by the fifteenth century.

The Dutch tended to ignore the Philippines, since their interest was now firmly focused on the Indonesian archipelago. As a result of their three wars with the English in the mid-seventeenth century, at least in Indonesia, the Dutch were successful, and by the end of the seventeenth century the Dutch East India Company had expanded to control most of Western Java in addition to their conquest of Malacca.

Dutch Indonesia

In the course of the eighteenth century Indonesian political factors combined with international economic factors to push the Company beyond its role of maritime regulator to that of territorial overlord. The Javanese kingdom of Mataram, already weakened for several decades, started to disintegrate, and by the mid 1750s the permanent division of Mataram into two separate states, Surakarta and Jogyakarta, had taken place. The division had been accomplished only with the intervention of the Company, which in the process gained not only further territorial concessions but suzerain rights over the entire island. These developments roughly coincided with a reorientation in the Company's economic policies caused by the dwindling returns from the inter-Asian trade. It now turned to the increasingly methodical exploitation of Indonesia's products for export to European markets, especially coffee, sugar and indigo. By forcing the rural population to grow and deliver these products at fixed low prices, the Company started a process of progressive interference in the economic and social fabric of the Javanese peasantry.

Yet even the profits from the intensified exploitation of the natural and human resources of their Asian possessions could not in the end stave off the Company's bankruptcy, for it found itself increasingly overtaken by Western competitors and new trading techniques. The end came on the very eve of the nineteenth century – 31 December 1799 – when the assets and liabilities of the moribund Company passed to the Dutch state, by then overrun by the French. The change actually took place while other epochal events tore Java from its relative seclusion into the whirlwind of Europe's age of revolution. The French dispatched a martially aggressive Dutch viceroy, Herman Daendels, to fortify Java against British attacks. But he had barely begun to prepare the island's defenses when the enemy invaded and occupied it. The British East India Company entrusted the lieutenant governorship to a particularly brilliant and energetic man, Thomas Stamford Raffles.

While only Raffles' land tax remains as a permanent legacy to colonial Indonesia, his many attempted reforms, particularly those affecting the indigenous governmental apparatus, generated widespread disaffection among noblemen and peasants alike. In 1825, less than a decade after Britain had returned Java to the Dutch (against the bitter protests of Raffles who went on to found Singapore for the British in 1819), Prince Diponegoro of Jogyakarta, one of the successor states of Mataram, raised the banner of revolt against the foreigners. It took five years, vast losses in Javanese and Dutch lives and, for the Netherlands, an enormous financial sacrifice to subdue a guerrilla war fought with ferocity on both sides. Basically, the Java War – like the

Left: A Javanese woman harvests a crop of coffee beans, a cash crop introduced by the Dutch to Indonesia.

Below: The Dutch were quick to exploit the rubber-growing potential of their Indonesian colonies. Latex (liquid rubber) flows along the cut in the tree and then over the spout to be collected in the cup.

Right: Rice, a basic foodstuff in Java, became a cash crop under a Dutch quota system. Here rice stacks are erected for the quick drying of the crop.

Below right: A simple ox-plow team prepares a rice paddy for the sowing of seed. Despite the relative technological sophistication of the colonial powers, agriculture practices remained primitive.

Indian Mutiny 30-odd years later – was the last gasp of the old Javanese order confronting the seemingly relentless advances of the European. Yet though not a precursor of the national movements of the twentieth century, in one important respect Diponegoro did point the way to the future: his appeal combined traditionalist Javanese with latterday Islamic elements. For the first time since the seventeenth century, Indonesia was experiencing an Islamic renaissance, sparked by contact with the Wahhabi movement in the Middle East.

The costs of these drawn-out military campaigns to the Dutch, exacerbated by Belgium's secession from the Netherlands in 1830, drained the resources of the country to an unprecedented extent. To replenish the empty treasury the Dutch embarked upon a policy of renewed and systematic economic exploitation of their Eastern possessions, Java in particular. Under the so-called Cultivation System, inaugurated in 1830 and maintained over four decades, the peasants were compelled to pay part of their taxes in prescribed quotas of such commodities as coffee, sugar, indigo and others. Praised and damned from its inception, the System – in form if not in detail a partial return to the forced deliveries practiced for so long by the Company – proved profitable to the Netherlands. In addition to helping to reduce the national debt, it also helped to finance the modernization of the Dutch economy. The effects on the Javanese cultivators-turned-producers of export crops are harder to assess. The peasants may well have prospered for a while; but whatever benefits had accrued to them were soon wiped out, first by the rapacity of their immediate superiors, the Javanese nobility who worked hand-in-glove with the Dutch, and later by a phenomenal population increase which in due course turned the small island into one of the most densely populated regions of the world.

Then, in 1860, appeared *Max Havelaar*, a novel

that pointed an accusing finger at Java under the Cultivation System. It was written by E Douwes Dekker under the pseudonym of Multatuli ('Much have I suffered'), a one-time civil servant who had resigned from the Dutch colonial bureaucracy. The book brought immediate and lasting literary fame to its author. More important, Multatuli's accusations provided the Dutch middle class with a potent and popular weapon in its struggle against the royal monopoly of the East Indian trade. Ten years later, in 1870, the battle was won: the Indies were thrown open to free trade and private investors.

The victory of the Dutch bourgeoisie occurred on the eve of a new era in world history, that of modern Western imperialism, during which the industrialized Atlantic community proceeded to cast its long shadow over much of the 'underdeve-

loped' world. For Southeast Asia that era in a sense began with the opening of the Suez Canal in 1869, which dramatically cut the distance between Europe and the newly important raw materials of the region. Though the demand for such traditional export commodities as spices, coffee and sugar did not wane, Southeast Asia now developed into a major supplier of rice, rubber, tin, bauxite and oil. The availability of such riches intensified existing rivalries among Western powers and introduced the threat of newcomers, especially Bismarckian Germany, entering the

race with Britain and France for colonial possessions. In the short space of a quarter of a century practically all of Southeast Asia fell under Western domination. Ironically enough, the region's oldest and largest colonial domain, that of the Spaniards in the Philippines, passed to a new sovereign, the United States, as a result of the Spanish-American War in 1889.

Well before then, the British and French had carved out large possessions in the Indochinese peninsula. The Burmese monarchy, already twice truncated after earlier military defeats, ceased to

exist in 1885 and suffered annexation to British India. In the west, the French, from small beginnings in southern Vietnam in the early 1860s, embarked on ambitious territorial conquests which culminated, toward the end of the nineteenth century, in French Indochina. In addition to the three Vietnamese provinces, it also included the kingdoms of Cambodia and Laos, the latter an artificial French amalgamation of several lesser principalities. For some time the competing interests of Britain and France also threatened to engulf Siam, but in 1896 they agreed to preserve its independence. Even then, however, Siam's resourceful kings (Mongkut, 1851-68, and Chulalongkorn, 1868-1910) had to purchase continued independence by ceding territories and by granting far-reaching economic concessions to the imperial powers.

The momentum of the Western forward movement led Britain and Holland to consolidate their control over the Malayo-Indonesian archipelago. The former rivals had settled their old and bitter disputes for supremacy by a treaty in 1824, but for several decades thereafter neither sought to obtain actual political control within their respective spheres of influence. Soon after the opening of the Suez Canal, however, and with the fresh impetus provided by private investors in both countries, the British moved into the western part of the Malay peninsula. At the same time, the Dutch progressively brought areas and rulers hitherto distantly subject to their overlordship within the now ever tighter administrative embrace of their empire. Sometimes these Dutch efforts met with resistance, nowhere more stubborn and protracted than in the sultanate of Acheh in northeastern Sumatra, whose fiercely patriotic Muslim 'ulama involved the Netherlands in a holy war in 1871 that it took more than 30 years to suppress. In southern Bali, at the eastern end of the archipelago, Dutch 'pacification' ended

Left: Hauling sugar cane in the Dutch East Indies. The so-called 'cultivation system' forced peasants to pay part of their taxes in such agricultural goods.

Right: Colonial paternalism in action – a mobile library provides reading matter to literate Javanese.

Below: A typical Dutch bridge in Java – an example of the all-pervasive nature of colonialism in the region.

in the ceremonial death by suicide of an entire court nobility. But by the turn of the twentieth century, with overt violence at an end, the Dutch could concentrate on fashioning their modern colonial state.

Like most of its contemporary colonial counterparts in the area, the latterday Netherlands East Indies state developed a level of administrative centralization and efficiency without precedent in Southeast Asia. Aided by modern communications and staffed by increasingly well-trained civil servants and technical experts, the colonial administration now reached even to remote corners of the archipelago. Simultaneously, Western business enterprises, especially estate corporations, likewise spread to parts of Indonesia hitherto untouched by the European presence. That presence itself also underwent signal change. As more and more Dutch came to live in more specifically Dutch ways the residential parts of major cities and towns became virtually segregated European suburbs, with schools, stores and clubs of their own. And as the speed and depth of Western administrative and economic penetration intensified, it came to affect ever larger numbers of Indonesians. One of the most striking examples of such changed conditions after 1870 was the island of Sumatra. Quite apart from rich oil finds in the south, rubber and tobacco plantations spread to its east-coast regions, bringing with them population migrations and also the imposition of firm Dutch political control over ostensibly still autonomous principalities. At the same time, German missionaries penetrated into these hitherto inaccessible territories and founded the first Lutheran Church communities in the archipelago. But the shortened overland distances also favored the spread of Islamic teachings from the northern and western parts of

Sumatra, the latter likewise in the grip of far-reaching social and economic change, even though untouched by Western entrepreneurs.

In Java, where indigenous and Western forces had been interacting for centuries, the modern colonial state constituted a subtle blending of old and new factors rather than a sharp break with the past. Looked at from the outside, change seems to have been the dominant theme from about 1870 on, when private enterprise started to displace the crown as sole trader. Nowhere was this more noticeable than in the sugar industry, Java's main export staple under the Cultivation System. Now private export and import corporations, banks, insurance companies and a host of other enterprises crowded into the island, and of course beyond; indeed, Java soon yielded primacy as chief export earner to Sumatra.

Dutch colonial policy

Looked at from within, the effects of publicly decreed changes were less far-reaching. The bulk of the peasantry remained to all intents and purposes locked into the ecological confines of rice and sugar cultivation, confines that actually became tighter and narrower as population density kept growing. Whether the estate corporation or, as hitherto, the Dutch monarch (and, before that, the Dutch East India Company) was his *de facto* absentee landlord, the Javanese cultivator appeared caught. The debate between European advocates of forced and free labor had been going on since the days of Raffles. Yet though liberal hopes had more recently been raised high again, the stark reality, as reported by Dutch official investigators, belied their expectations. In 1901 the Dutch embarked on a new colonial policy whose avowed cornerstone was concern with native welfare. The changeover was considerable.

The availability of funds for welfare expenditures – schools, medical services, irrigation and other amenities – depended on the vagaries of the trade cycle and taxable profits of European entrepreneurs as well as on legislative goodwill and the technical expertise of colonial civil servants, whose goal in administering these reforms was a model of efficiency.

The Sumatran and Javanese examples illustrate, but do not exhaust, the different colonial experiences within the vast Dutch domains. Indeed, the geographical, economical and cultural diversities contained within the Netherlands East Indies may serve as a kind of microcosmic mirror for the even richer divergences prevailing in colonial Southeast Asia as a whole. Risky as it is to generalize about the modern colonial era, it is particularly dangerous to exaggerate the depth of the West's impact on Southeast Asian societies, as earlier generations of historians have often tended to do. For one thing, that impact was very uneven. Side by side with regions where the European presence was only too tangible, there were others – especially those of only marginal economic interest to the Westerner – where the flag, the lone official and perhaps the token garrison constituted the sum of colonialism. Also, the 'European Century' was very short, if measured against the long period of culture contacts in earlier phases of Southeast Asian history. Finally, the tough fabric of indigenous societies provided a buffer against the alien forces of change.

But this does not mean that substantive change did not take place, not least in the Dutch East Indies, where modern communications, combined with administrative innovations, laid the groundwork for centralized unification. In Java, in particular, cumulative European interference did yield important changes. Improved road and rail

communications, supplemented by modern health measures and irrigation techniques, certainly were the main causative factors in the island's vexing 'population explosion' and its spiraling concomitant rural poverty. And though the vast majority of the people remained tied to the land – thanks to the wisdom of Dutch legislation land could not be alienated to non-natives – some left their villages to become laborers on estates, at times in faraway Sumatran plantations. Others still moved into towns and cities to work in the few industries that were springing up or to try their luck at peddling and commerce or to find employment in the expanding governmental services. The main channel of social change was, however, the modern schools, whether those created by Christian missions, the colonial government or, more and more, by private Indonesian initiative. Modern schools beyond the primary grades, which offered instruction in Dutch or Malay, attracted, and thus mixed, students from the most diverse ethnic and social backgrounds at the same time that they opened for their graduates employment in new professional or other urban settings.

The emergence of such new social groups was paralleled by the gradual decline of the old Javanese aristocracy. It had been Dutch policy from the days of the East India Company to rule through this class. But the modern colonial state progressively bypassed a tradition-oriented class which had long since become a salaried bureaucracy, a class, moreover, without independent means of landed or other wealth. Elsewhere in the Dutch domains (and beyond, in other parts of colonial Southeast Asia), similar changes were taking place, especially in those regions where political or economic circumstances dictated the adoption of more direct, Western-style administration.

It was several decades before these processes of change found visible expression in overt political action. The constitutional evolution of the Dutch East Indies progressed slowly and gradually. The main reason for such gradualness was the dominant position that the Dutch administrative corps had occupied since the days of the Company. Yet the ending of the Cultivation System had dented its monopoly of power. Indeed, long before Indonesians became politically active it was the European (and Eurasian) residents in the Indies who most stubbornly agitated for decentralization of bureaucratic power; and it was in response to their pressures that, early in the twentieth century, Westerners in cities and towns were granted a measure of local autonomy. But these first steps in the direction of devolution coincided with the new welfare policy that vested the civil servants with new and extensive powers. By that time, too, the Dutch colonial bureaucracy itself had started to undergo changes, employing more university-trained administrators increasingly attuned to the needs of the indigenous peoples. Yet the fact remains that progress in reform remained extremely slow and limited until the eve of World War I.

The sinking of the American Battleship *Maine* in Havana on 15 February 1898 had a greater significance for the Philippines than perhaps for anywhere in the Caribbean. The US declared war against Spain, and the American fleet under the command of George Dewey blew up the entire Spanish Pacific fleet on the morning of 1 May before the eyes of the Manila population on the shore without sustaining a single American casualty. Manila became the capital of the new American Philippines, ceded by Spain on 10 December 1898. Yet defeating the Spanish was to prove much easier than conquering the Philippines.

Philippine nationalism

The Philippine Nationalist Movement had already risen in the 1890s with the formation of the Kats Punan; its leader and martyred hero, José Rizal, had been tried and executed in 1896. His novel, *Noli me Tangere*, published in Berlin in 1897, was as dramatic a condemnation of Spanish rule as *Uncle Tom's Cabin* had been in the US or *Max Havelaar* in the Dutch East Indies. His successor, Emilio Aguinaldo, led the fight against the Americans in a guerrilla war that lasted three years. Although the Philippine revolution movement was crushed by Governor William Howard Taft, the Americans were never comfortable as colonial masters. As early as 1907 elements of home rule were granted to the Philippines, and a substantial degree of autonomy was granted in 1916, thanks to the pressures by Sergio Somas and Emmanuel Quezon. In 1935, Quezon would become the Commonwealth of the Philippines' first president, and the former Governor-General Frank Murphy would become the first American governor commissioner to the Philippines. Full independence was promised ten years thence, but plans were interrupted by World War II.

Left: A scene from the US intervention in the Philippines, 1899.

Below: A French colonial officer goes about his business in Indo-China – visual proof that the 'White Man's Burden' was rarely literal.

Right: The imposing façade of an administrative building in Southeast Asia – an outward sign of the economic benefits of colonialism and the political power of the colonists.

Below right: The temple at Angkor Wat in Kampuchea. The success of the Khmer people in the twelfth century was given material form in temple complexes such as this.

Peninsular Southeast Asia

By the last decade of the nineteenth century the whole of insular Southeast Asia was under the direct or indirect control of the Dutch and Spanish. With the sole exception of Siam (Thailand), peninsular Southeast Asia was under the direct or indirect control of Britain and France.

In three Burmese wars between 1825 and 1885 the British annexed all of Burma and thereafter administered it as part of India until 1937, when it was given the status of a separate province. British economic penetration in the region was extensive. Rice production was greatly expanded, to a point where as much as 3 million tons could be exported annually. Rubber, sugar cane and cotton were also developed as export crops, and exploitation of the rich oil reserves centered on Yenangyaung in central Burma was begun in 1871.

Meanwhile, in Malaysia, the British pushed forward from their Singapore base to the Straits Settlement on the mainland. During the last quarter of the nineteenth century the British, under the rule of General Swettenham, formed alliances with the rulers of Malaysia. The eventual result of these initiatives was a kind of tripartite division of the region under varying degrees of British control: the Straits Settlement, a British colony comprising Malacca, Penang and Singapore; the Federated Malay States of Perak, Selangor, Negri Sembilan and Pahang; and the confederated Malay states of Kedah, Perlis, Kelantan, Trengganu and Johore. Similar arrangements were reached in North Borneo with the sultan of Borneo and the white sultans of Sarawak.

The French had expressed interest in Vietnam as early as the reign of Louis XIV, and colonial missions of various kinds were sent forth from France at various times in the eighteenth century. However, the French conquest of Indo-China did not begin in a serious way until it became clear that the Chinese Empire was in a state of terminal collapse by the mid nineteenth century. As European influence grew, the Annamese emperor Tu-Duc (1843-83) took action against the Europeans already living in Annam, urged on by his counterparts Tonkin and Cochin, the other

two parts of Vietnam. In retaliation for Tu-Duc's action against the mission, the French seized this pretext for attacking Annam in 1858 as part of its joint operation with the British in the Second Opium War against China. Saigon was captured in 1859, and by 1867 Cambodia had become a protectorate, while Cochin China came under the direct rule of France. Annam, which had been a virtual protectorate since the end of the war, became one in name in 1884.

For close to a millennium, Vietnam had been part of the Chinese Empire, and for many centuries thereafter Chinese civilization continued to affect Vietnamese culture quite profoundly. Their complex relations with such a powerful neighbor – exacerbated every now and then by repeated Chinese military incursions – had left the Vietnamese with a highly developed sense of their own territorial, cultural and political identity. Vietnamese responses to the French colonial conquests in the latter part of the nineteenth century were both inspired and circumscribed by these traditional feelings.

The country was militarily unable to resist the superior might of the colonial powers for any length of time, yet the relentless progress of the colonial conquest drove many Vietnamese, including high officials, to occasional acts of resistance. In the mid 1880s one court faction finally persuaded the boy-emperor, Ham Nghi (1884-85), to give the signal for all-out war against the foreigners. Large numbers of officials and peasants did indeed follow the imperial summons, and armed resistance continued for several years, even after the young emperor's capture and deportation. But by the turn of the century, with French control firmly established, it became obvious that neither traditional loyalties nor traditional leadership had been able to avert catastrophe.

In the wake of the shattering defeat of the discredited old order, Vietnamese turned abroad in their search for national salvation, with three main groups emerging in the early twentieth century, each attracted to a specific foreign model. These groups roughly coincided with regional,

but more importantly social and intellectual, divisions within the country. The first represented those who, realizing the futility of open opposition and moreover attracted to European, especially French, culture, were willing to collaborate with France not only for purposes of personal advancement but also in the hope of thereby speeding the modernization of Vietnam. Most of them were urban and rural bourgeoisie – officials, businessmen and landowners – from Cochin China, as the French called the country's southernmost part, where Western influences had been at work from the early 1860s. Loyal to the colonial regime and moderate in their political demands, they yet failed to move the French authorities in

the direction of meaningful constitutional concessions. Hopes for Franco-Vietnamese cooperation, if not for a synthesis between the two cultures, nonetheless continued to find expression as late as the 1930s.

Long before then, however, two other groups of Vietnamese had forsaken gradualism for revolutionary action. Until the turn of the century, the literate minority of Vietnamese had been educated in Chinese, and though Chinese education declined rapidly once French schools started to spread, the influence of events in China on Vietnamese thinking remained considerable. If the empire's agonizing contacts with the West were known in Vietnam, so were the writings and activities of its political thinkers and activists, culminating in the Chinese Revolution of 1911.

As it was, that revolution occurred shortly after the French authorities had crushed a poorly prepared Vietnamese revolt. Its leader, Phan Boi Chau (1857-1940), outstanding among the early political exiles from colonial Vietnam, had at first worked toward a restored, reformed monarchy in Japan. When the French pressured Tokyo to expel him and other Vietnamese intellectual refugees, Phan fled to China. Increasingly influenced by Chinese revolutionaries, he founded the first radical republican movement in exile. The Vietnamese Nationalist Party was closely modeled on the Kuomintang, Dr Sun Yat-sen's famous Chinese counterpart. But the fledgling party, beset by inherent weaknesses, was no match for the repressive apparatus of French colonialism. In the wake of yet another ill-starred uprising, this one among native troops in a single French garrison in 1930, practically all the leaders of the Nationalist Party were executed, arrested or forced to flee.

The second Vietnamese revolutionary group, the Communist Party of Indo-China, was to have a far greater effect on Vietnamese – and world – history. Its story, however, properly belongs in later chapters.

China: 1368-1911

The final triumphs of the armies of the rebellious peasant Chu Yüan-chang in 1368 ended the Mongol Yüan dynasty and inaugurated the Ming. Chu, as first Emperor of the Ming, was not simply founding a new dynasty, he was restoring Chinese rule to a country that had been totally under Mongol domination since 1279. If we remember that the Sung had lost northern China in 1126, and if we look ahead to the fact that the Ch'ing dynasty (1644-1911) was ruled by Manchus and that their dynasty was followed by a protracted period of civil war and Japanese invasion, we can see the measure of the Ming impact: for between 1126 and 1949 China was a unified country controlled by the Chinese for only 276 years out of a total of 823, or one third of the period.

Chu Yüan-chang (1328-98), founder of the Ming dynasty, was (like the founder of the Han nearly 1600 years earlier) of peasant stock. In the fragmenting China of the mid fourteenth century, where dozens of rebel bands disputed for territory with the Mongols and with each other, he survived by his wits, being a mendicant monk for a time and also a garrison soldier. Slowly increasing his personal power by proving his military skill, by marrying the daughter of a powerful rebel general and by forging ties with members of the religious society known as White Lotus, he was able to lead a successful attack on Nanking in 1356. Using Nanking, strategically situated on the Yangtze River, and dominating the richest area of China, as his base, Chu gradually destroyed his rivals until he was finally ready to launch an attack on the Yüan capital of Peking, which he captured in 1368.

Any summary makes this victory sound too straightforward. It was not a simple Mongol-Chinese confrontation, nor was it just a struggle for power between rival rebel bands. It was, rather, a confused reordering of the forces that were governing society, taking place in a period of flood and famine and desperation. If it was a time when a peasant could become emperor, it was equally a time when peasants starved; for the Confucian literati, too, it was a time for anguished decision. Some had served the Yüan as officials, some had refused and sat things out in angry retirement; now, with the Yüan dynasty obviously collapsing, they had to judge where to put their hopes. Retirement and poetry could not bring solace, nor could they bring safety.

The peasant Chu Yüan-chang proved a ruthless emperor, cruel and unpredictable; yet he was, at the same time, efficient and capable. If he had contempt for Yangtze valley literati such as the poet Kao Ch'i – and hundreds of men like Kao were executed or driven to suicide – he also knew that he needed these kinds of men to staff his bureaucracy and help him to rule his newly acquired empire.

Chu reigned as Emperor Hung-wu from 1368 until 1398, and his reign is full of these terrifying paradoxes. The bureaucracy was refurbished and restaffed with talented men, yet savage tortures were used against them; tax collection and grain transport worked well once again, yet tens of thousands were executed for alleged involvement with the 'treasonous' activities of Hu Wei-yung, deposed as chancellor in 1380.

A series of frontier military garrisons were carefully designed to enable the soldiers to live off the land, and the powers of ambitious princes were fragmented by scattering them among hereditary fiefs. At the same time Hung-wu formed a secret police of eunuchs, the *chin-i-wei*, to spy on his bureaucracy, and he abolished the rank of chancellor (chief minister), lest such a powerful official should threaten the emperor's absolute power. Confucian academies were rebuilt even as Confucian scholars were humiliated and mocked.

These inconsistencies and paradoxes have often been present in Chinese history during the reign of a 'founding emperor' – that is, an emperor who is able to establish a new and powerful dynasty to replace an old and discredited one. To conquer a country of China's size required immense tenacity and military skill; to unify it after conquest and to draw the rich and proud local elites into loyal service required administrative skills no less great. Fear of treason, fear of being slighted, came easily to an emperor who had risen by guile from the bottom. Yet if Hung-wu was suspicious of his ministers, he was more generous to his own 25 sons. They were allowed to have military power and were even used as garrison commanders, especially along the northern frontier, where they formed a loyal bulwark against the Mongols. Hung-wu had chosen one favored son as his heir apparent, but the sudden death of this son caused the emperor to name a 16-year-old grandson as heir, despite the fact that this youth would inevitably have to deal with a group of jealous and militarily powerful uncles.

Hung-wu died in 1398 and was succeeded by his grandson, Chien-wen, who reigned for only three years. Anticipating trouble, the dying Hung-wu had forbidden his sons to come to his funeral in the capital of Nanking, but there was no way that he could stop their bitterness at being passed over. Nor was there any way that the scholarly young Chien-wen could build up enough military strength to withstand his uncles. In 1402 he was deposed by Hung-wu's fourth son, who took the throne under the title of Yung-lo. Yung-lo rewrote the historical record to make it appear that he had been Hung-wu's personal choice for successor, and he executed Chien-wen's chief minister Fang Hsiao-ju, together with his entire clan and his closest official colleagues and his students, numbering some 870 persons. The deposed Chien-wen fled, however, and was never captured.

Left: Emperor Hung-wu, formerly the peasant Chu Yüan-chang, first ruler of the Ming dynasty, which he founded in 1368. His ugliness earned him the nickname 'pig,' but as an emperor he was efficient, if cruel.

Top right: A bird's-eye view of the imperial palace at Peking in the seventeenth century. By that time Peking had clearly emerged as the center of Chinese government, surpassing the old capital Nanking.

Above right: A bronze bowl from Gammai, Halfa, showing Chinese influence.

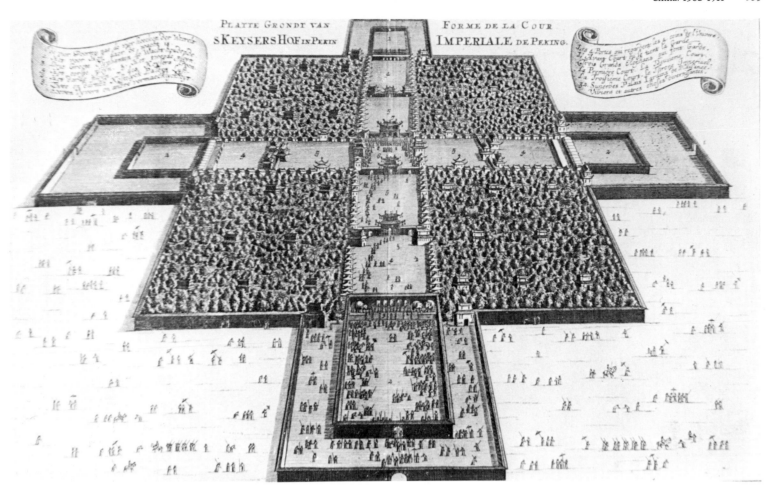

PLATTE GRONDT VAN
SKEYSERSHOF IN PEKIN

FORME DE LA COUR
IMPERIALE DE PEKING.

Yung-lo (reigned 1403-24) must be regarded as among the strongest emperors in China's history. Certain of his policies reflected the uneasiness of the usurper. He shifted the working capital from Nanking to the area of his own military power in Peking while leaving an honorific hierarchy of officials in the old capital to make the change less abrupt, thus forming what has been called the 'two capitals' system. And he was always wary that disaffection might surface among the rich gentry of the Yangtze valley. Other policies were the fruits of compromises that he had had to make to ensure that his bid for the throne would be successful. He gave considerable privileges to those eunuchs who had backed him against Chien-wen, for example, and he also had weakened Ming military power in the western area of Liaotung so as to buy the loyalty of certain northern tribes during his march on Nanking. Yet despite these aspects of his policies, which held within them the seeds of future trouble, Yung-lo proved a courageous and competent ruler.

In foreign affairs, he was able to survey all China's borders and formulate policies that would, in coordinated fashion, increase China's strength. In the first year of his reign he dispatched, often with detailed instructions, Chinese envoys to the countries of Korea, Tibet, Annam, Siam, Java and Japan, as well as to Mongol and Manchurian tribal leaders and the Muslim ruler of Samarkand. As his reign progressed four main areas of foreign policy gradually emerged as paramount: the fall of the Tran ruling house in Annam and Chinese involvement in that area (the present North Vietnam); Wako pirates, based in Japan, who ravaged China's eastern coastal trade; the resurgence of Mongol power on the northern frontier; and the need to reassert Chinese prestige in Southeast Asia and the Indian Ocean.

This last topic has received the most attention from historians because it was the most dramatic and the most unusual. Yung-lo dispatched six great naval expeditions, led by Cheng Ho and other court eunuchs, at intervals throughout his entire reign – in 1405-07, 1407-09, 1409-11, 1413-15, 1417-19 and 1421-24. These fleets, each of which consisted of 50 ships and 20,000 men or more, traveled to India, to Aden and even to the African coast. They explored new trade routes and returned with treasure and curios, but they also had the purpose of displaying China's might to the more distant tributary states, such as Siam and Java, that could not be threatened with a land army as Annam had been. 'Tributary' states, it must be emphasized, were those that sent regular missions to China and acknowledged Chinese cultural superiority – though they were not physically controled by the Chinese emperor, they were expected to behave according to Chinese notions of propriety. If a tributary country harmed the Chinese it was made to pay dearly. A Javanese king who killed 170 Chinese was told by Yung-lo: 'Immediately send 60,000 ounces of gold to compensate for their lives and to redeem your

crime, so that you may preserve your lands and people. Otherwise we cannot stop our armies from going to punish you. The warning example of Annam is there.'

In fact the example of Annam was an unfortunate one to have chosen, for Yung-lo had suffered a major humiliation there. In 1406 Yung-lo had sent an army to restore the Tran and oust the usurpers, but though that Chinese army was initially successful, two more major insurrections had to be put down by Chinese armies in 1408 and 1413, and the Annamese then found a commander of genius in Le Loi, who fought guerrilla-style actions from Laotian bases for a decade. In 1427 Le Loi switched to massive frontal assaults and smashed two successive Chinese relief armies, gaining a compromise peace settlement.

The war in Annam was savage, expensive, and ultimately useless, and it illustrated a perennial truism in Chinese history, namely that it was almost impossible to wage successful war on both the northern and southern fronts. Increasingly it was the dangers on the northern frontier that occupied Yung-lo's attention. It is possible that the first of Cheng Ho's voyages had been to secure a guaranteed neutrality from the southern countries in the face of a threatened invasion of China by Tamerlane, Khan of the Timurid Mongols. Though Tamerlane's death in 1405 saved China from the immediate threat, Yung-lo was not free to concentrate on the Annamese campaigns. Nor could he devote massive resources to wiping out the Japanese pirates (the Wako), contenting himself with sending flattering letters to those Shoguns, such as Minamoto Sogi, who showed willingness to attack the pirates in their home bases. It was Yung-lo's own father, after all, who had said that the Japanese were no worse than mosquitoes, while his generals added that the southern states were no worse than scorpions or wasps; in contrast, the northern barbarians were 'a danger to our heart and stomach.'

Yung-lo was particularly sensitive to the northern threat. He fought four campaigns either against the Oirats, in the northwest, or the Tatars, in the northeast, in 1410, 1414, 1422 and 1423, and he died on a fifth campaign in 1424 when he was 64 years old. These campaigns, which involved such feats as moving tens of thousands of troops, with all their baggage and supplies, across the Gobi desert to the Kerulen River, were even more costly than the Annamese campaigns.

But the campaigns were inconclusive, for Ming victories did not prevent Mongol reconsolidation as soon as Ming armies withdrew. Indeed, in 1449, only 25 years after Yung-lo's death, the Oirat leader Esen consolidated a great Mongol army and invaded Shansi province (to the west of Peking), capturing the Ming emperor who tried to drive him back. Esen went on to besiege Peking, though he was ultimately repulsed by Ming forces. Peking was attacked again by Tatars under Altan Khan in the 1550s, so it cannot be said that the Ming ever satisfactorily settled the northern frontiers; the best they could hope to do was to buy off marauding Mongols with trade privileges and gifts.

There were also recurrent crises with Japan. Throughout the fifteenth and sixteenth centuries Japanese pirates, often in league with Chinese, struck from their bases in Chusan and Taiwan to raid along the Fukien coast and in the Yangtze valley. And in the 1590s Japanese armies defeated strong Chinese forces in Korea before being finally forced to withdraw.

As foreign policy trends, established in the founding period of the Ming, continued for two centuries, so too did the major elements of domestic policy. One central theme, certainly, was the concentration of power in imperial hands. Hung-wu had abolished the prime minister's office and duties, and Yung-lo was content to rule on his own, with only junior-ranking Grand Secretaries to mediate between him and the ministerial heads of the Six Boards. These Boards (Rites, Civil Office, Public Works, War, Revenue

Left: Chingiz Khan's Mongol warriors engage Chinese forces in a mountain pass. The threat of Mongol invasion loomed over the Ming dynasty throughout the almost three centuries of its rule.

Below: Stone tablets inscribed with the names of successful candidates in the highest civil service examinations under the Ming and Ch'ing dynasties. The examination system produced an efficient but rigid centralized bureaucracy.

Right: One of the earliest representations of the sage Confucius. His philosophy, endlessly interpreted and re-interpreted, formed the dominant ideology of the Chinese state and Chinese society until the twentieth century.

and Punishments) were the major administrative organs of the state, but they lacked independent executive power and depended on the emperor's order. Similarly the Censorate, which ideally was an office composed of scholar-officials dedicated both to remonstrating with the emperor when he exceeded the bounds of good conduct and to surveillance over the bureaucrats in the two capitals and in the provinces, slowly lost its powers and concentrated on surveillance. In other words, the censors became the emperor's tool for controling his ministers instead of a ministerial tool to curb the emperor. Within the 15 provinces of China, each of which was theoretically controlled by a governor, special imperial commissioners and eunuch agents played a conspicuous role, once again increasing the direct power of the emperor. This power was bolstered by the imperial armies, split over the country in garrison forces of a few thousand men, and based on their own land so they would not place too great a drain on imperial revenues; while the court drew its revenue from the land and labor taxes, and the food for its needs from the rich Yangtze valley via the refurbished Grand Canal.

The Ming bureaucracy

A simple but inescapable fact of the Ming dynasty was its stability, at a time when so much of the rest of the world was battling, expanding or fragmenting. A single dynasty held the world's largest country together for 276 years, ruling some 150 million subjects with a bureaucracy containing some 15,000 senior members. Obviously many factors contributed to this longevity, but one of the major ones was simply that the bureaucracy was efficient. It was controlled and indoctrinated in a way that was unknown in earlier dynasties. Hung-wu had, early in his reign, followed the practice first ordered by the Mongols that only specific commentaries on the classics by the Sung neo-Confucianist Chu Hsi would be permitted in the state examination systems. Since success in these examinations was essential if one hoped to gain a position in the bureaucracy, students stopped studying 'unorthodox' books, and there was an immediate narrowing of the curriculum. This narrowness was exacerbated in the mid fifteenth century when a particularly difficult and formalized writing style was demanded of all candidates. Though this 'eight-legged essay' (pa-ku) style was decried by certain scholars from the beginning, it lasted into the twentieth century as the required form in advanced examinations.

With formalization came an increase in the scholarly activities of compilation and codification, most dramatically seen in Yung-lo's vast plan to accumulate all China's past writing in one gigantic encyclopedia. A staff of 2169 state-subsidized scholars did compile a manuscript of 11,000 volumes. But even Yung-lo gave up the thought of printing this work from wooden blocks, as the cost was simply too great (a scholar has recently estimated that the draft encyclopedia would have formed a tower 750 feet tall). Among other major compilations were the Ming administrative statutes, a massive edition of the entire penal code and a growing number of local provincial gazetteers, themselves virtual encyclopedias of local lore, history, geography and government.

If the bureaucracy was efficient and indoctrinated – and often terrorized by violent emperors or irresponsible eunuchs – it nevertheless retained a certain independent character, a certain ability to throw up mavericks or critics who defy simple categorization. The reason for this apparent paradox must be sought in China's cultural richness, a richness that added Buddhist and Taoist elements to the Confucian core and marshaled the highest techniques of painting, calligraphy and poetry.

It is easy to summarize the Ming state and bureaucracy as being 'Confucian,' yet when we examine some of the famous Ming figures more closely, we begin to see that their thought cannot be so simply categorized, that the men are different from each other and that they draw on different elements in China's past.

One of the best known Ming officials was Wang Yang-ming (1472-1529), the son of a senior official, who obtained the second examination degree (the chü-jen) when he was 20. But before gaining the highest degree (chin-shih) in 1499 he had begun to doubt Chu-hsi's theories, and in time he developed his own principle of 'innate knowledge,' according to which each man has within himself the knowledge of morality and truth. To realize his own wisdom, man had only to reject outside distractions and to identify himself with the principles general in all nature. Such beliefs could be seen to threaten the current emphasis on rigorous rote study of the classics and the orthodox commentaries – and indeed not only was Wang attacked on these grounds, but by the late seventeenth century, after the Ming dynasty had fallen, he was described as having been partly responsible for that collapse, in that he had weakened the country's moral fiber by his vague and wild speculations.

In his multi-faceted career as philosopher, teacher, general and administrator Wang Yang-ming epitomized one of his own deepest beliefs, namely that there must be an essential unity between knowledge and action, in which each partakes of and enriches the other. Wang was from an upper class literati family and was well versed in the Confucian classics as well as in Taoism and Buddhism. But there was in his thinking a definite element of anti-intellectualism, as well as certain strands that his followers were able to twist into egalitarianism, for if knowledge of the tao was indeed innate, then why need man study for a lifetime to attain it? So also argued Wang Ken (?1483-1540), the son of a salt-maker, who underwent enlightenment and felt himself united with all things, stating that he had learned to see the universe within himself. After meetings with Wang Yang-ming, Wang Ken sallied forth in an antique cart to give public lectures.

Such men attracted mass followings. At first they were supported by the bureaucracy, but as they attracted wilder disciples who carried their views to extremes, extolling the primacy of the sensual appetites and praising total spontaneity, official views hardened, and there were arrests and deaths in jail. It was Li Chih (1527-1602) who carried the trend to its logical conclusion. His writings attacked neo-Confucianism, extolled the heroic virtues of the common man – while lamenting the way gullible people were fooled by duplicitous officials – and stressed the relativity of moral judgments: 'Yesterday's right is today's wrong; today's wrong is right again tomorrow.' Outraged, the local officials roused a mob to action, and burnt Li's dwelling (he was living in a Buddhist temple compound) to the ground; for two years he lived the life of a fugitive, fleeing from friend to friend. In 1602 he was arrested and sent to Peking; there, in prison, he cut his own throat.

An iconoclasm of a different sort was represented by Tung Ch'i-ch'ang (1555-1636). He had a successful official career, culminating in 1631 with the presidency of the Board of Rites. But his fame and his passion lay in his art, and here he spurned orthodoxy and professionalism. Quite arbitrarily dividing all earlier Chinese art into two 'schools,' those of Northern and Southern Sung, Tung associated himself with the boldness and studied amateurishness of the latter. He talked of 'unlearning' the past, so that one could confront one's real self. 'I regret that I cannot meet with the great masters of the past, but also I regret that they did not have the opportunity of meeting me!' His paintings and calligraphy sold for great sums, and both his fame and fortune were comfortably absorbed into his elitist scale of values. He grew increasingly arrogant and increasingly careless of others' feelings, and at one point his estate and much of his art collection were burned to the ground by a mob of outraged townspeople. But he continued undaunted to pursue his vision of perfection in art.

His lifestyle reminds us of one major element in Ming society: the growing wealth and sophistication of the great urban centers; cities grander than any in Europe, as the first Jesuit missionaries who arrived in China in the late sixteenth century testified. Here were bookstores and restaurants, antique and pawn shops and wealthy merchant families seeking to increase their prestige by connoisseurship backed with hard cash. This vigorous commercial world, as well as the sensual life of its denizens, is brilliantly caught in the great Ming novel Golden Lotus.

If Tung Ch'i-ch'ang and Wang Yang-ming show variations within a Confucian tradition, so in another way did Chang Chü-cheng (1525-82), who rose through the bureaucratic ranks to become chief Grand Secretary from 1572 to 1582. Chang practiced an austere Confucianism, and because

of his severity he is often described as a 'legalist.' Certainly he yearned for a tough emperor who would show some of the decisiveness of the Ming founders. As a practical statesman and a serious student of the *Book of Changes (I-ching)*, Chang knew that destiny and righteousness did not correspond. 'Heaven,' as he wrote, 'shuffles things in an absolutely unfathomable way.' Yet man must not give up in despair, for there is still an interdependence with heaven's forces, just as in agriculture heaven brings the rain and sunshine but man does the plowing and weeding. For Chang, the relationship between minister and ruler was summarized in *'T'ai'* (peace), the eleventh hexagram of the *I-ching*, which calls for perseverance even in a context of sensed disaster.

The fall of the Ming

Chang Chü-cheng was the last great minister of the Ming, the last one who kept a semblance of purpose and integrity at the highest levels of government. The main factor in the Ming decline was always described by the historians of the next dynasty as having been eunuch power. It is true that the eunuchs did have great power, both in the provinces and in Peking, but they only attained that power because of a complex series of interlocking factors that cannot be separated. One factor was the incompetence and idleness of the later Ming emperors, few of whom showed any willingness to attend to administrative business. One of them, for example, received no senior officials for 20 years. This meant that the eunuchs developed into intermediaries between the emperor – sequestered in the inner quarters of the palace – and the officials in the ministries. An official had to be brave indeed to write a memorial attacking eunuch abuses when he knew that the memorial might be read by the eunuchs and never delivered to the emperor at all. One attempt to end this

downward spiral was made, and has been immortalized in Chinese history as the battle of the Tung-lin group against the eunuch Wei Chung-hsien. The Tung-lin group were scholar-bureaucrats who sought better government. After many years of growing prestige as a scholarly force in 1624 they accused the most powerful eunuch, Wei Chung-hsien, of numerous crimes, including several counts of murder. But they were unable to get the emperor to act, and between 1625 and 1626 Wei and his allies struck back: all known Tung-lin adherents were dismissed from office, and dozens were executed or tortured to death in prison. Though Wei Chung-hsien was himself ousted by the new emperor in 1627, incalculable damage had been done to the bureaucracy. For the remainder of the Ming period the picture is a dreary one of self-defeating factionalism.

Imperial incompetence, eunuch power and bureaucratic bickering took place in a wider context of economic decline. Though there had been a series of major tax reforms in the 1520s – the so-called 'single-whip' reforms, by which the confusing overlays of land and labor taxes had been simplified and standardized into silver payments instead of cumbersome payments in kind – the tax receipts were increasingly inadequate to meet government needs. Imperial extravagance and bureaucratic ineptitude were only contributing factors; the main demand stemmed from the exigencies of foreign policy: continuing campaigns against the northwestern Mongols, the vast expenses of the campaigns against the Japanese invaders of Korea between 1592 and 1598, campaigns against aboriginal tribes in southwest China and finally the mounting expenses of the campaigns against the Jurched in Manchuria.

The Jurched tribes in northeastern Manchuria had always been a potential threat to the Ming, but Yung-lo had enroled them in military com-

mands under nominal Chinese supervision, and later emperors had tried to keep them quiet through the rites of the tributary system. Groups of Jurched would travel annually to Peking to express their homage and to trade; later, they caused so much trouble that they were largely restricted to Fushan, north of the Great Wall, where they marketed their horses, furs and ginseng.

It was a dictum of successful Chinese foreign policy that the northern 'barbarians' must be kept divided. This policy failed completely from 1580 onward after a Jurched leader named Nurhaci (1559-1626) was able to build his own fortresses, assemble an army and form a tribal federation by conquest and alliance. In 1609 he stopped paying tribute to the Ming, and in 1616 he named himself 'Chin' emperor, evoking those earlier Jurched tribesmen who had founded the Chin dynasty that ruled northern areas of China between 1115 and 1234. In 1618 Nurhaci led a strong army of mounted archers against the Chinese settlers and garrison troops in Liaotung and captured the major city of Mukden. In 1635 Nurhaci's son ordered that the term 'Jurched' should no longer be used, since the Jurched had been described as tributary barbarians by the Ming court. He decreed that his people be called 'Manchu,' and it is as Manchus that they have since been known.

Nurhaci was an unusually astute man, and the Manchus' rapid success was due to a number of techniques – military, administrative, cultural – which he developed and implemented. Militarily, he relied on well-mounted archers firing reflex bows, a fast-moving strike force that repeatedly routed the Ming infantry. He encouraged surrender of Ming garrisons by combining threats with blandishments: Ming officers resisting his armies were killed, while those who surrendered were incorporated into the new emperor's own armies and rewarded with cash, honorary titles and even,

Above left: The imperial almanac for 1591 to 1595 and accounts paper, found in a Ming emperor's tomb. The careful recording of events and finances was a feature of the elaborate Ming bureaucracy.

Above: Manchu banner troops providing a bodyguard for the British consul to Canton in the 1870s. The ancestors of these men had conquered China in the seventeenth century, establishing the last imperial dynasty, the Ch'ing.

Right: The Manchu leader Abahai, son of the famous Nurhaci. He declared himself Ch'ing emperor in 1636, although the Manchu takeover of China is normally dated only from 1644, a year after Abahai's death.

in special cases, marriage to Nurhaci's daughters or granddaughters. Nurhaci, and his son after him, developed an army composed of three basic units, that were in turn subdivided into eight 'banners,' so called from the colored flags that distinguished them in battle. There were Manchu banners, Mongol banners (composed of allies or surrendered troops from the Mongol tribes in the west) and Chinese banners (composed of the Liaotung garrison troops who surrendered). The banner organization was military in concept, but it also had a key administrative function, since each soldier was enrolled with his entire family in the banners, which became instruments for population registration and control. Nurhaci also ordered the development of a Manchu script (the Mongol alphabet was modified, to transcribe Jurched words) and used this script both for record-keeping and for making translations from Chinese administrative and penal texts.

This intelligent use of Chinese techniques was undoubtedly a major contribution to the final Manchu triumph. Nurhaci was never chary of using Chinese advisers and Chinese troops, and the process was carried even further by his son, Abahai (1592-1643), who set up six boards in exact imitation of the Ming boards in Peking and staffed them with both Manchus and Chinese.

The Ming dynasty's attempts to cope with this growing Manchu power were ruined by faulty planning and corrosive bureaucratic jealousies. There were several Ming generals who were quite capable of withstanding the Manchu armies, but they were invariably betrayed by their own colleagues. Thus it was not surprising that senior Ming generals continued to surrender to the Manchus and looked toward the defeat of the Ming and the establishment of a new dynasty. As if anticipating their desires Abahai in 1636 declared himself the emperor of the Ch'ing

dynasty, although he was still unable (except for occasional raiding parties) to move his armies south of the Great Wall into China proper.

Just as inept planning and fratricidal battles between senior officials ruined any attempts to drive back the Manchus, so their lethargy and incompetence allowed two bandit leaders in China to develop great armies and threaten the Ming with further disaster. Chang Hsien-chung (?1606-47) and Li Tsu-ch'eng (?1597-1645) both grew up in Shensi province in an atmosphere of poverty compounded by bureaucratic inefficiency. Both drifted into banditry and had the ability to form bands of their own. By the mid 1630s they were roving almost at will across central China, raiding and looting. On the rare occasions when they were confronted by sizeable Ming forces they 'surrendered,' a euphemism meaning that neither they nor the Ming generals were willing to risk a showdown. By the 1640s both bandit chiefs had attracted some literate advisers into their entourages and had formed the nuclei of 'governments.' In 1643 Chang Hsien-chung named himself western king and made his base first in Wu-ch'ang and then in Szechwan. In the same year Li Tsu-ch'eng also declared himself a king and held 'state examinations' in his capital at Sian. In the spring of 1644 Li led his large undisciplined army eastward toward Peking. In April the gates of Peking were secretly opened and Li simply walked into the city. Abandoned by his troops and his ministers, the Ming emperor committed suicide.

The dilemma before the Chinese literati was now similar to that confronting Kao Ch'i and his friends 280 years before – which of the four major contending groups should one back to be emperor? There was Li Tsu-ch'eng, ensconced in Peking; there was Chang Hsien-chung in the west; there were surviving male relatives of the Ming ruling house behind whom one could rally; there were the Manchus north of the wall. For the most powerful surviving Ming general, Wu San-kuei, who was guarding the key pass of Shan-hai-kuan, the Manchus seemed the best option. They offered more hope of stability than any of their rivals. Accordingly, in May 1644, Wu San-kuei made his peace with the Manchus, and in June Manchu troops entered Peking on the east as Li Tsu-ch'eng's armies straggled off to the west with their booty. Abahai had died the previous year, so it was his six-year-old son who was enthroned in Peking as Emperor Shun-chih. The Ch'ing dynasty is dated from this year of 1644. It was to last 267 years.

The first 40 years of the Ch'ing were a time of arduous consolidation. For though the Ch'ing armies (Manchus and Chinese banner troops fighting together) had been able by 1650 both to smash all the major resistance efforts of the various Ming princes and to kill both Li Tsu-ch'eng and Chang Hsien-chung, this apparent ease of conquest was in fact illusory, and serious obstacles to the new dynasty's stability remained.

Foremost was the problem of baronial factionalism, which sprang from the nature of the Manchu command structure. Though Nurhaci had undeniably been the leader of the Manchu people, he had delegated massive powers to the *beile*, members of his own family who had been appointed as banner generals and shared in decision-making. Nurhaci's attempts to name an heir-apparent had led to such bitter infighting – Nurhaci finally executed one of his own sons who would not stop scheming against him – that he finally refused to name any man as his successor. When Nurhaci died in 1626 his son Abahai was merely one of the eight *beile* in charge of the Manchu armies. Naturally such a system of shared

Left: K'ang-hsi, emperor from 1661 to 1722, as represented by a nineteenth-century Chinese artist. During his long reign, K'ang-hsi fought to overcome the factionalism which threatened the stability of the empire.

Right: It was the Manchu ruler Dorgon who in 1644 ordered the Chinese to wear pigtails, a style still followed by these early twentieth-century students.

Below: A portrait of the Chinese commander who captured Taiwan for the Manchu throne in 1662.

authority was not advantageous to the Manchus, who needed a strong unified command if they were to invade and conquer China.

Abahai succeeded in breaking the power of his rivals and named himself emperor. But when Abahai died in 1643 there was renewed friction. By a final compromise, Abahai's young son Shun-chih was named as the new emperor, but Abahai's brother Dorgon was named as Shun-chih's regent. It was in fact Dorgon who masterminded the conquest of China, and he was *de facto* ruler until his death in 1650. When Shun-chih took over government in person that year he moved against Dorgon's faction and brought in his own favorites, among them several eunuchs. This use of eunuchs, and many of Shun-chih's other policies which seemed reminiscent of Ming

dynasty corruption, infuriated many of the old guard Manchu barons. When Shun-chih died suddenly in 1661 these barons formed a new regency under Oboi. Oboi and his faction virtually ruled China for eight years, until they were in turn supplanted by the young emperor K'ang-hsi.

Even such a cursory summary shows how different the Ch'ing founding was from the Ming. Hung-wu had wielded absolute and almost uncontested power and had shaped the country in his own image, whereas the great Manchu clans, struggling among themselves, were constantly undoing each other's policies. Even during K'ang-hsi's long reign, from 1661 to 1722, the Ch'ing was still far from being a 'Confucian' state, unified under a powerful emperor and managed by virtuous ministers. K'ang-hsi had to mediate cautiously between the various great clans and senior generals, whose power was only really broken by K'ang-hsi's son in the 1730s.

Manchu factionalism precluded a firm and united policy toward the conquered Chinese. Sporadic acts of hostility and rebelliousness continued throughout the seventeenth century. Dorgon, in 1644, had ordered all Chinese to shave their heads in front and grow a pigtail at the back: this was the 'queue,' which had been the common Manchu custom for dressing the hair. But the order seemed further proof of barbarism to some members of the Ming elite, who vowed to defend their cities to the death rather than live under a conquering regime and accept such humiliations. So strong were the Manchu and Chinese banner armies that there were few such patriots, and those there were brought terrible vengeance on their communities from the conquerors. The sieges and sacks of Yangchow, T'ai-ts'ang and Chia-ting (all towns in the prosperous Yangtze valley where the literati were numerous and well established) became household words for Manchu terror tactics, and remained so into the twentieth century.

But besides those Chinese who resisted independently, and those who fought with the various

Ming princes, there were thousands who simply refused to collaborate with the new regime. By their refusal, if they had been officials, they remained true to the neo-Confucian ideal of loyalty, which stressed that no official could truly serve emperors of different dynasties. If they were literati without bureaucratic position, their silent resistance might be out of sorrow for dead friends or out of some basic ethnic hostility to the Manchus as conquering barbarians. Another group of men tacitly resisted the Ch'ing through their art. Most famous of these were the painters Tao-chi (also called Shih-t'ao, 1641-?1700) and Pa-ta shan-jen (also called Chu-ta, 1626-?1705). Both were related to the Ming ruling house, and both retreated into a life of religious contemplation and artistic experimentation. Pa-ta shan-jen remained in isolation for his whole life, though Tao-chi gradually began to associate with officials in Yangchow and even collaborated on one painting with a court painter. In asserting their own individuality through brush and landscape they echoed Tung Ch'i-ch'ang, but their total refusal to consider the examinations or an official career, and their studied fostering of eccentricity, put them in a world that Tung never entered. Pa-ta shan-jen's lonely birds and sardonic fish, Tao-chi's looming mountains and free-blown grasses, are unique in Chinese painting. Knowing the great traditions, they rejected them; and in their brilliance they precluded all followers. Their freedom could not be recaptured, and there were no truly great Ch'ing painters after them.

Not all resistance was passive. There was also one example of protracted planned resistance which almost overthrew the Ch'ing empire, and that was the rebellion of Wu San-kuei from 1673 to 1681. Wu San-kuei (1612-78) was the general who had invited Dorgon's troops into China in 1644, to fight the bandit Li Tsu-ch'eng. He proved a loyal general to the Ch'ing, and in 1661 he led an army to the Burmese frontier, where he captured and strangled the last Ming pretender. As a reward, Wu San-kuei was given almost total con-

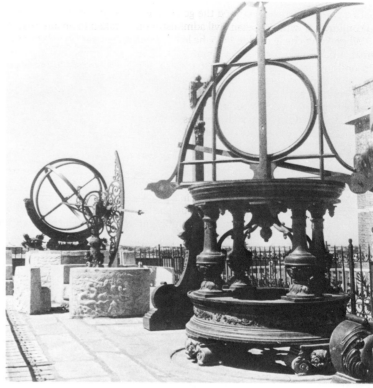

trol of southwestern China. Two other great Chinese generals who had helped the Ch'ing to power were similarly rewarded: Shang K'o-hsi with Kwangtung province and Keng Ching-chung in Fukien.

The decision to break the power of these great feudatories was made by K'ang-hsi, and it was certainly the most dangerous and the most important decision of his career. Having broken the Oboi regency in 1669, K'ang-hsi decided in 1673 to order the transfer of the feudatories to Liaotung, so that southern China could be brought totally under Ch'ing control. Wu San-kuei rebelled, being joined by Keng Ching-chung (and later by Shang K'o-hsi's son). Within a few weeks the rebels had secured control both of virtually all China south of the Yangtze and of western China. But by concentrating his forces in certain key areas and by following a liberal program of pardons for repenting rebel leaders K'ang-hsi slowly regained the initiative. When Wu San-kuei in 1678 finally took the step of proclaiming himself emperor of the new Chou dynasty he was in fact already defeated, and he died soon after. His grandson continued a desperate resistance until 1681, when he was cornered in Yunnan by Manchu troops and committed suicide.

Having unified and consolidated China proper, K'ang-hsi now proceeded in methodical fashion to consolidate China's borders. His first objective was Taiwan. The island fell in October 1683, and was made a part of Fukien province. The next priority was Russia. There had been frequent clashes between Ch'ing forces and Russian troops along the Amur River, and in 1685 Ch'ing forces destroyed the Russian fort at Albazin. After protracted negotiations Ch'ing and Russian envoys – with Jesuit missionaries acting as interpreters – met at Nerchinsk in 1689 and agreed to terms settling the border disputes. The Treaty of Nerchinsk has been much discussed by later historians, because in forming the provisions the Ch'ing seemed willing to treat with Russia as a sovereign state, not as some inferior member within the tributary system.

With Russian affairs settled, K'ang-hsi moved on to deal with the last major foreign-policy problem – that of the Dzungars, who, under their great leader Galdan (?1640-97), had consolidated their hold over the whole area of what is now Sinkiang. After careful preparation K'ang-hsi personally led an army across the Gobi to the Kerulen River, where he trapped and routed the Dzungars. Galdan fled, but in 1697 K'ang-hsi led another army west to Ninghsia, and Galdan committed suicide.

In addition to being a successful military leader K'ang-hsi was also, until the last years of his life, a successful civil administrator. Unlike many emperors who kept themselves closeted behind the high walls of the Peking palaces, he was highly mobile, and his many trips gave him a chance to inspect the country personally and to meet his local officials. His demand for accurate first-hand information also led him to develop a system of secret informants, who sent confidential reports via their own couriers directly to the emperor.

Among the men whom he used to send such reports were highly trusted scholars and secretaries who served in the Nan-shu-fang, the 'southern library' of the Peking palace. K'ang-hsi established close and even friendly relations with a number of such scholars, and not only because he wanted political information from them. With these men he studied Chinese poetry and calligraphy, medical tracts and divination handbooks. He also conversed with Taoist longevity experts, and with Jesuit missionaries on problems of mechanics and geometry, as well as religion. K'ang-hsi's reign, indeed, was one of the highest points of Christian missionary endeavor in China. So intrigued was K'ang-hsi by the Jesuits' technical and medical skills that he gave them a residence in the palace area and ground on which to build a church. From 1693 to 1706 he even let them preach at will in the provinces in accordance with an Edict of Toleration, though he later rescinded this permission after quarreling with a papal legate. The legate had suggested that the Jesuits' ultimate allegiance was to the Pope; K'ang-hsi, as emperor of China, insisted that their allegiance was to him as long as they lived on China's soil. So in the eighteenth century the Jesuits' influence steadily waned, though they remained as directors of the astronomical bureau and were allowed to perform certain other technical tasks.

K'ang-hsi could control China and its borders,

but he could not control his own sons, and it was this inability that brought his reign to an end in unhappiness and confusion. The son that K'ang-hsi chose for his heir-apparent turned out to be sadistic and unstable, and K'ang-hsi disbarred him in 1708, relented in 1709 and then finally disbarred him for ever in 1712 and imprisoned him. Court factions formed around the various other sons who might succeed to the throne, and since there were four firm favorites, the situation was extraordinarily tense. K'ang-hsi's repeated warnings against factionalism had no effect, and as his will weakened and he grew frail the fruits of this indecision were carried over into bureaucratic abuses and inefficiency throughout the government. K'ang-hsi died in 1722 at the age of 68, having reigned for 61 years, the longest reign in China's history.

The height of Ch'ing power
Yung-cheng, who had been born in 1678 and was K'ang-hsi's fourth son, became the new emperor. A tough and experienced man of 44, tested in court politics and well educated, he moved energetically to the task of tightening up and reforming the government. If Hung-wu and Yung-lo were the founding Ming emperors who set the tone for the dynasty, the same role was played for the Ch'ing by K'ang-hsi and Yung-cheng.

Working ceaselessly – he read hundreds of documents every week and commented lengthily on them in his own handwriting – he attempted to bring all reaches of the bureaucracy under his purview. His father's informal system of reports was institutionalized as the core component of a revised structure of communication and decision-making. A special Grand Council was established in 1729, a small group of trusted ministers who could act as the emperor's advisers on major matters of policy. The power of the great Manchu clans within the banner system was broken, aboriginal tribes in southwest China were forced into the provincial administrative system and finances at every level of government were scrutinized and tightened up. And though Yung-cheng was not particularly active in foreign policy, he did continue a forceful policy in Tibet, establishing a system by which two Ch'ing imperial residents with a garrison army supervised the government in conjunction with a Tibetan civil administrator.

When Yung-cheng died in 1735, he left China a great, united and prosperous country. His son Ch'ien-lung, who reigned from 1736 to 1796, carried this heritage through new heights of grandeur – and on to the edge of collapse. Ch'ien-lung was not an innovative emperor, as his father and grandfather had been, and his policies were not circumscribed by exigencies of economics or practical politics. He loved to rule, he wanted China's greatness to be clearly visible and he wanted to be himself the symbol and the center of that greatness.

One can see these desires reflected in his domestic, cultural and foreign policies. Though he lectured his officials on frugality, Ch'ien-lung pursued an extravagant program of palace-building in Peking, in the 'Summer Palace' of the Yuanming Yuan, which he expanded with the help of Jesuit architects on the edge of a beautiful lake southwest of the city, and in the rural retreat at Jehol in southern Manchuria. The 'southern tours' that he embarked on in emulation of his grandfather do not seem to have had the same intelligence-gathering function. They were, rather, lavish royal processions, costing millions of *taels*, on which Ch'ien-lung took his mother and hundreds of courtiers for diversion. Descriptions have

survived of the elaborate precautions that were taken to ensure that the imperial mother did not get queasy while crossing the rivers by boat – methods ranged from trying to flatten the waves to sending boatloads of musicians to distract the royal eye.

Ch'ien-lung was certainly not a lazy ruler – he worked long hours over official documents, and also persevered with studies in the Confucian literary tradition – but he does not seem to have had that interest in the detailed problems of local government and finance which so involved his predecessors. He preferred ambitious projects, such as the compilation of the *Ssu-k'u ch'üan-shu*, 'Complete collection of all branches of literature,' which, like Yung-lo's great encyclopedia, was to contain all that was worth preserving in China's heritage. Starting in the 1770s, over 36,000 volumes were transcribed by thousands of calligraphers, and an annotated index was also prepared. This incredible cultural venture had a censorial aspect as well as a cultural one; that is to say, while books were being assembled for copying, Ch'ien-lung ordered them to be scrutinized for heterodox or anti-Manchu material. This operation has been described as a 'Literary Inquisition,' and indeed over 2000 titles were banned and only 476 of these are known to have survived at all. The scholars involved with 'treasonous'

books – editors or compilers as well as authors – were harshly punished. One result of the compilation, therefore, was to restrict knowledge and to redefine the orthodoxy that had to be accepted if a scholar was to advance through the examination system into government service.

It must not be thought, however, that such cultural policies met with no opposition at all. Certainly there was no overt opposition, but there were brilliant writers in the Ch'ien-lung reign who attacked the stultification of knowledge brought about by the examination system. One of China's best satirical novels, *The Scholars* by Wu Chingtzu (1701-54), and unquestionably the greatest social novel, *The Dream of the Red Chamber* by Ts'ao Hsüeh-ch'in (1715-63), both expose the levels of hypocrisy in contemporary education and scholarship, and try to define what active imaginative thinking should be. At much the same time Chang Hsüeh-ch'eng (1738-1801) was developing his theories on historical method and integrity, and yearning for a world in which literary culture *(wen)* and the true way *(tao)* could once more be united. Holding a similar critical stance, while adopting a hedonistic and carefree life-style, was the poet Yüan Mei (1716-98). But such men had little effect on their contemporaries and none at all on Ch'ien-lung; they remained as merely peripheral observers on the political scene.

Above far left: Ch'ien-lung, emperor of China from 1736 to 1796, practices the art of calligraphy. A refined but spendthrift ruler, he had a taste not only for luxury but also for costly military adventures.

Above left: Astronomical instruments provided by the Jesuits for the Chinese imperial observatory. The Jesuits were appreciated for their technical and medical skills but their religious activities were restricted, and in the eighteenth century their influence waned.

Right: A marble bridge in the imperial summer palace near Peking. Ch'ien-lung devoted a fortune to palace-building, sometimes employing Jesuit architects.

KANTON

In foreign matters, too, he lacked his grandfather's flexibility and pragmatism. He made much of the 'Ten Great Campaigns' of his reign, which were conducted against Burmese, Gurkhas, Dzungars and Annamese, as well as against rebels in Taiwan, Kansu and Kweichow. But most of these campaigns cannot be described as strategically necessary, and they were fantastically costly. In the west there were some successes: Turkestan was firmly incorporated into the Chinese empire, and suzerainty also strengthened over Tibet after an astonishing campaign that led Ch'ing armies through the Himalayas to Nepal. But in attempting to assert Chinese power in southeast Asia, Ch'ien-lung encountered the same stubborn resistance and humiliating defeats in Annam that had cost Yung-lo so dear 350 years earlier.

In the last years of Ch'ien-lung's reign there were increasing outbreaks of rebellion in western and central China, especially in the provinces of Szechwan, Hupeh and Shensi – the so-called White Lotus Rebellion (1795-1804), named from one of the secret societies that played a leading role. Driven to desperation by poor harvests, shrinking resources and official exactions, many peasants sympathized with the rebels and were ruthlessly killed by Ch'ing troops, though the banner armies proved incapable of destroying the rebel bands themselves. Suppression of this rebellion was rendered more difficult because of divided imperial leadership: Ch'ien-lung had abdicated in 1796, so as not to insult K'ang-hsi's memory by reigning longer than him (K'ang-hsi had reigned 61 years, and Ch'ien-lung completed 60 years on the throne). But though Ch'ien-lung named his son, Chia-ch'ing, as the new emperor, he himself continued to wield almost all his old powers, and only when Ch'ien-lung died in 1799 did Chia-ch'ing truly become ruler.

Deeply involved in the pacification of the White Lotus Rebellion was Ho-shen, the most widely condemned official of the Ch'ing dynasty. Ho-shen (1750-99) was a youthful imperial bodyguard in 1775 when he attracted the attention of Ch'ien-lung, who at this time was 64 years old. Ho-shen's meteoric rise in the official hierarchy suggests that Ch'ien-lung was infatuated with him. In 1776 Ho-shen was made vice-president of the Board of Revenue, Grand Councillor and a Minister of the Imperial Household; in 1777 he was named head of the Peking garrison forces,

and in 1778 superintendent of customs revenues for the city. Further honors to him and his family continued until Ch'ien-lung's death. Ho-shen used his favored position to amass a vast fortune and to put his own friends into a number of key offices, both civilian and military. The Ho-shen faction thus became a force in government that was essentially beyond criticism. By taking large sums of money from the military appropriations, executing innocent peasantry, and lulling the aged emperor with totally fictitious reports of great victories, Ho-shen's faction contributed deeply to the loss of morale and integrity that were beginning to creep into different levels of government by the 1880s.

It should be emphasized, however, that some of the trouble also sprang from that very peace and tranquility that had been the glory of Ch'ien-lung's reign. For China's population had rocketed during this period – estimates by the leading Chinese authority on this problem show a jump from approximately 150 million people in 1700 to 393 million by 1794. It is not hard to imagine what such a rapid increase would do to land-holding practices, plot sizes and *per capita* food yields.

Ch'ien-lung's closing years also witnessed one incident that seemed insignificant at the time, though we can see it now as the first scene in the drama that was to occupy China's attention for a century and a half. This was the dispatch by the British King George III of Lord Macartney as a special envoy to the Chinese court. Macartney was received by Ch'ien-lung in Jehol in 1793; some tensions, caused by his refusal to kowtow, were smoothed over and cordial discussions were held. But the British were given absolutely none of the assurances they had wanted with respect to opportunities for increasing trade, and returned disappointed. What to Ch'ien-lung had seemed but a minor irritation, the demands of yet another barbarian on the frontier of the Chinese world, turned out to be the prelude to the end not only of his dynasty but of the Chinese world community. Within a hundred years, China would have been shamefully defeated in war by the European barbarians, and the country would be racked by a rebellion that had as a remote cause the conversion of its leader to a weirdly distorted conception of Christianity.

The Ch'ing and the Europeans

Of the major East Asian countries that came under Western pressure in the eighteenth century China confronted the most conspicuous and difficult problems of adjustment. A proud empire, long habituated to considering itself the center of its universe, long committed to its Confucian-based social and political institutions, China for a long time refused to take what eventually turned into its 'Western menace' seriously. Since the sixteenth century, when the Western barbarians had been confined to regulated trading privileges at Canton and the precarious right to residence at Macao, the imperial government subsisted on a sense of control over the Westerners, reinforced by the later successes of the Manchu emperors in dealing with China's inner Asian frontier and in spreading the tribute system into the maritime region to the south. For many centuries China was left in comparative isolation and security by the other peoples of the world, except, of course, the traditional enemies across the Great Wall. The Western trading nations, preoccupied with the New World and parts of Asia closer at hand, remained content with the Canton concession until the very end of the eighteenth century.

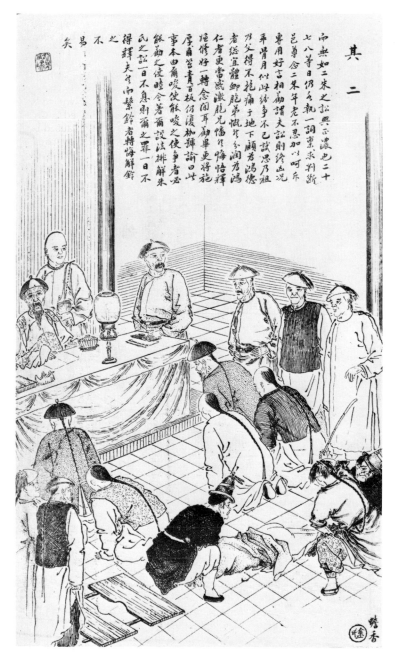

其二

而無如二宋之訟興正濃也二十七八箇日仍冬親一詞稟未斷...

(Chinese text panel reproduced as part of the illustration)

Above left: A Dutch engraving of the port of Canton in 1666. Early contacts with European sea-traders and missionaries had only a marginal impact on the Chinese Empire.

Below left: Defending a besieged town against attack in eighteenth-century China. The troops on the walls are throwing down primitive bombs to rout the raiding cavalry.

Right: A Chinese state official exercises his judicial function. Corporal punishment is administered on the spot.

Below right: Lord Macartney, head of the first British embassy to China in 1793. Discussions at the imperial court were cordial, but the Chinese made no concessions to the barbarians' desire for increased trade.

other hand, was still comfortable with the values that were sanctified by millennia of tradition. We can highlight the contrast, and prepare for the severity of the clash that was to come, by looking at certain areas of the Chinese polity: the governmental structure, social class and social mobility, and conceptions of foreign policy.

By the time of Lord Macartney's embassy the government of China had become static and compartmentalized. The logical development toward centralization and bureaucratization had continued, and though the early Ch'ing emperors had acted in a spirit of reform, they had passed on to their descendants a system of interlocking components that was hard to change. To review this structure briefly: at the top was the emperor, who consulted on major policy matters with the Grand Council. Slightly lower in prestige, and acting also as a clearinghouse for official documents, was the Grand Secretariat. The routine affairs of state were handled, in the capital of Peking, by the Six Boards (of Civil Office, Rites, Revenue, Public Works, War and Punishments) and their attendant staffs. Parallel to the Boards, but slightly lower in ranking, were the Censorate and the *Li-fan-yüan*, a bureau that handled affairs on the western and northern frontiers.

Since the Ch'ing was a conquest dynasty, we must remember that there was a racial component in the government. The emperor, of course, was a Manchu, the imperial family and the imperial concubines were mainly Manchu, though a few were from Mongol or Chinese banners, while the eunuchs were Chinese. Grand Councillors and Grand Secretaries could be either Chinese or Manchu – there were no fixed ratios – and the emperors generally chose old and experienced men with whom they felt comfortable working. In the Boards there was a system of obligatory parity: every Board was headed by *two* presidents, one Manchu and one Chinese; and under them were four vice-presidents, two Manchu and two Chinese. A majority of censors were Chinese, while the *Li-fan-yüan* was staffed entirely by Manchus and Mongols.

In the provincial posts Chinese predominated, though some Manchus held important positions. There were 18 provinces in China proper by this

Russian probes into the Amur region to the north were hesitant and were, in fact, successfully countered by the Manchus.

In contrast to the Japanese, who reacted quickly and almost hysterically to evidence of renewed foreign activity in the waters of East Asia, the Chinese refused to absorb the message which the British, French and Russians brought to their borders with increasing insistence after the turn into the nineteenth century. China had encountered men from Europe in the sixteenth century, and the Ming Dynasty had even patronized Jesuit priests for their knowledge of astronomy and gunnery. But in the intervening years, after the decline of the Jesuit mission, there had been little effort to maintain communications with Europe, and even the geography of a global world was left unexplored. The scientific and commercial revolutions of Europe went unnoticed in China, where it was thought unimaginable that a handful of foreigners could possess the power to affect the lives of the 400 million in China.

In few parts of the world was the clash of cultures to be as pronounced as in China. Chinese civilization, which ultimately was able to defend itself against the nations of Europe only by its own modernization, was obliged to pass through a cultural transformation which shook the very

foundations of the Chinese way of life. The British mission led by Lord Macartney in 1793 served dramatically to point up the impending clash. For by the eighteenth century the British had come to believe, with almost religious fervor, in the obligation of all nations to engage in free trade and open intercourse. The Chinese emperor, reflecting on China's traditional condition of self-sufficiency, clung to the right of his government to limit entry into the empire to those who came to do homage to China's political superiority. Trade was simply an incidental matter. Since China had all goods in great abundance, foreign traders could only be conceived of as desiring to partake of China's bounty. And this could be countenanced only on China's terms.

These two points of view were irreconcilable. Each country believed it was in the right, each believed it was supported by proofs drawn from its history and culture. Britain, restless and powerful, testing the new resources developed in the Industrial Revolution, had an energetic merchant class able to influence policy formulation through elected members in Parliament, a strong aristocracy that interested itself in both agricultural technique and industrial development and a growing concept of global trade in open markets that drew her ambitious youth overseas and made protective military bases essential. China, on the

time, since several of the Ming units had been subdivided. Each was supervised by a governor, with the direct assistance of a financial commissioner, a judicial commissioner and an educational commissioner, as well as garrison troops directed by a provincial general *(t'i-tu)*. The major subdivisions of each province were controlled by prefects, who reported directly to the governor, and each prefecture was subdivided into counties controlled by a magistrate. The magistrates, of whom there were about 1500, were the only members of the bureaucracy who had direct responsibility for the day-to-day affairs of the common people; even so, they were still distant figures as far as the peasants were concerned, overseeing areas that often had populations of over 100,000 and were thousands of square miles in extent.

This governmental system, as a whole, put a premium on order and precedent. It moved slowly and carefully, double-checking at every level of the chain of command, keeping meticulous records in provincial and capital archives and evaluating the records of all incumbents at regular intervals. The system was not flexible, it did not encourage innovation and it was not responsible to outside pressures for change. It might be summarized as a peace-keeping and revenue-collecting system dedicated to the maintenance of the status quo.

The scholar-officials who made up the bureaucracy that governed China were certainly the nation's 'gentry,' but they were not really equivalent to the gentry of eighteenth-century England. The Chinese gentry were enmeshed with the bureaucracy, and it was government service above all that brought wealth and prestige, just as it was a shared intellectual background and family contacts that brought freedom from governmental harassment. The Chinese gentry played a major role in local philanthropy, and through their clan organizations they dominated local society. They acted as a bridge between the magistrate and the people, and in return for being exempt from the

Left: Barbarians bringing tribute to the Chinese emperor. The rulers of China had no concept of free trade, perceiving all foreign countries as tributary states.

Below left: A French cartoon satirizing Britain's relations with China in the nineteenth century. The Chinese are forced at gunpoint to consume opium, despite its poisonous effects.

Below right: The British and French flags fly over their trading posts at Canton in 1830. The Europeans were only allowed to spend part of the year in residence in Canton, and they could deal only with licenced traders.

more burdensome forms of taxation they rendered reciprocal service by cooperating with the magistrate in maintaining local order. As with the central government, this meant preserving the status quo.

The gentry, with their education and their land rents, were not sympathetic to commerce. Merchants were held in low esteem in the Confucian scale of values, for they were considered nonproductive, mere manipulators of the existing stores of wealth. There were, to be sure, many rich merchants in Ch'ing China, dealing in such commodities as grain, silk, tobacco or tea, or else buying the right to market government monopoly products like salt. There was even quite a sophisticated system of interprovincial banking in the form of credit notes. But merchants did not exploit this financial base and build their own commercial empires. Rather, they used part of their money to buy education for their sons so that they could enter the gentry ranks, and they spent much of the remainder in conspicuous consumption – mansions, parties, libraries and art collections – which was designed to draw the gentry into their orbit, thus increasing the merchants' social standing. In short, the merchants were little more inclined than any other group to disrupt the existing system; and so they failed completely to play the aggressive role in social transformation that their British counterparts did.

In foreign policy, finally, there were crucial differences between Britain and China. The Chinese regarded their economy as self-sufficient, and were not greatly interested in overseas trade. The great sea voyages that had been made by the eunuch Cheng Ho in the early fifteenth century were never repeated by any Ch'ing mariners, and though there was a steady emigration from southeast China into certain communities of Southeast Asia, there was no attempt to establish overseas Chinese bases, or to give Chinese emigrants any moral or material support.

The Ch'ing regime had various methods for dealing with foreigners. To the north and west, on what was considered the strategically important land frontier, relations with Tibetans, Mongols and Russians were handled by the *Li-fan-yüan*, a special foreign affairs bureau staffed, as we have seen, almost entirely by Manchus and Mongols. Relations with Korea and Southeast Asian states were handled by the Board of Rites via the 'tributary system,' by which foreign countries were expected to acknowledge China's cultural suzerainty in return for some trade privileges and China's overarching protection. Such states followed the Chinese calendar, used Chinese ritual forms in their embassies, adopted an inferior-to-superior style of language in their official dispatches and sent regular embassies to Peking. In most ways this was a cultural relationship, not a political and military one, since China could rarely enforce her will (as we have seen in the example of Annam). When a country grew independently powerful, as was the case with Japan, the system became a dead letter. But it *was* a system, it seemed to work and it was sanctified by precedent. So when unknown people like Dutchmen or Portuguese or British appeared they were regarded as new 'tribute-bearing nations,' quite compatible with the way things were.

Because the Westerners showed an unusually eager desire for trade, the Ch'ing did make some concessions. In the Ch'ien-lung reign the 'Canton system' was formalized in southeast China. On the edge of Canton city the foreigners were allowed to build warehouses (with residential facilities) where they could store goods and live for a limited period each year. They were permitted to trade with a small number of licenced Chinese merchants – who were in turn controlled by a Manchu supervisor, 'the Hoppo.' But this trade was in no way free. The Westerners were not allowed to sell to any Chinese except the licenced *hong* merchants. They were not allowed to buy any further property. They were not allowed even to live in Canton all year round or to be accompanied by their womenfolk, but had to retire each winter to Macao or Hong Kong. To the Western merchants, and most particularly to the British who had fine visions of the great market waiting inside China, these restrictions became increasingly irksome.

The Opium War

Until 1834 British trade with China had been a monopoly of the East India Company, which had been willing to conduct the trade largely according to Chinese rules. But in that year the monopoly was ended by the British government, and many new merchants entered the field, making demands for expanded trade privileges. At the same time, representatives of the British crown found the inferior position in which the Chinese placed them increasingly irritating. The British wanted direct diplomatic relations with the Chinese government so that they could negotiate on equal terms, instead of having to submit a petition to an unimportant merchant in the southern port of Canton, which was all they were allowed to do under the tributary/Canton system.

Friction over these issues became serious in the 1830s, and it was compounded by the problem of opium. Opium was mainly made from poppies grown in India and was used in increasingly large quantities by British merchants to pay for Chinese goods. Tea from China was an important source of revenue for British merchants and (through import taxes) for the British government. The sale of opium also brought badly needed revenues to the British government in India and meant that British merchants did not need to carry large amounts of silver bullion in order to pay for Chinese teas and silks. Instead, it was the Chinese who had to use silver bullion to buy opium, since their demand for the drug began to exceed their domestic trade resources. It was true that the Chinese had used opium as a medicinal drug for a thousand years, and that a certain amount of opium poppies were grown in southwest China, but nothing had prepared them to deal with the scale of the new demands. Opium smoking developed so rapidly in the eighteenth century that by 1770 the Chinese were importing about 4000 chests (a total of 500,000 lb weight) each year. By 1830 they were importing 20,000 chests, and by

1839 40,000 chests weighing some five million lb.

Not surprisingly, the Ch'ing government was thoroughly alarmed by this, especially after 1830, when it was discovered that eunuchs were smoking in the palaces and that some soldiers were smoking so much opium that they were incapable of combat. Accordingly, the government introduced new laws to punish distributors and smokers and tried to think of ways to end the trade. This proved difficult, since there was a vast amount of official collusion with foreign opium traders and much local corruption. Also, many Chinese officials thought that the only possible solution was to legalize opium smoking and encourage local growers, so that the foreign merchants would cease to find opium a profitable trade item. Heated debates continued on this topic all through the 1830s, but the emperor finally decided in favor of those who argued for absolute suppression of the trade, on the grounds that opium harmed the people and led to a steady outflow of silver from China.

Chinese response

To put this new opium-suppression policy into effect the emperor chose Lin Tse-hsü (1785-1850), a successful provincial official who had already had experience in stopping opium smoking in central China. Lin arrived in Canton in March 1839 with the title of Imperial Commissioner and immediately set about his task. He had regulations posted all over the city, warning the Chinese inhabitants to stop opium smoking and setting up mutual guarantee groups to make sure that they did so. He sent a separate order (via the *hong* merchants) to the Western merchants in Canton, ordering them to surrender all their opium stocks. The Western merchants were initially unwilling to comply, but after Lin had them shut in their factory areas and ordered all their Chinese servants to leave their employ, the merchants yielded. They handed over about 20,000 chests of opium to the British Superintendent of Foreign Trade, a British officer named Elliot, who in turn

handed it to Lin. Lin had the opium mixed with lime, dissolved in salt water and flushed out to sea.

Lin had not realized that because Elliot was a government official the British crown would now necessarily be drawn into the affair. When Lin began to see the danger he was running he tried writing a letter directly to Queen Victoria, appealing to her better nature to stop the trade altogether. But matters were now moving steadily to a crisis point. Additional trouble was caused when a Chinese villager was killed by some British sailors, and Lin demanded that one of the sailors be handed over for execution in accordance with Chinese law; this the British refused to do. Lin applied further pressures on the foreigners in Canton, who finally withdrew altogether. In November Ch'ing and British troops exchanged shots. A British expeditionary force arrived in 1840 and captured Chusan Island near Shanghai. Representatives of the two countries drafted a provisional treaty that summer, but neither government would agree to the terms, and fighting broke out again in 1841. This time it was on a major scale; the Ch'ing armies were overwhelmed by British mobility and firepower and agreed to negotiate after the British had captured Shanghai and Chinkiang and had started to advance on Nanking.

The Treaty of Nanking

The terms of the 1842 Treaty of Nanking and its supplementary treaties were far-reaching in their scope. Five ports were opened to foreign residence and trade (Canton, Amoy, Foochow, Ningpo and Shanghai). Foreigners were to be subject to the jurisdiction of their own consuls, as opposed to being subject to Chinese law: this was the so-called 'extra-territoriality' that the Chinese came to see, rightly, as a major source of foreign privilege in their country. Hong Kong was ceded to the British. The Ch'ing government had to pay an indemnity of 21 million Mexican dollars, to meet *hong* merchants' debts and to pay for the destroyed opium. A fair and equal tariff was to be collected uniformly on foreign goods at the port of entry, and the *hong* merchants' monopolies were abolished. Also, by what was called 'the most favored nation' clause, all rights accruing to any

one country as a result of treaty negotiations were to be shared in subsequently by all other countries. The Chinese at first welcomed such a stipulation, believing it would balance out the claims of each foreign country; they were to find later that it led instead to an unending series of grants to foreign powers.

The Opium War and the Treaty of Nanking have been seen by most Chinese historians as ushering in the age of Western imperialism. In fact, China's status was still only semi-colonial as late as the 1890s. But certainly the process started by the Treaty of Nanking was continued under

the Tientsin Treaty of 1858, which was finally ratified in 1860 after heavy fighting brought British and French troops, backed by Russians and Americans, into Peking. These troops sacked and burned the emperor's Summer Palace and the Westerners won new concessions: the right to establish legations in Peking, the opening of new treaty ports, the right for missionaries to preach and reside in the interior of China; and the right for opium to be imported at a fixed rate of 30 *taels* per chest. The victory of the Western Powers was a complete humiliation for China, causing deep resentment throughout the Empire.

Above left: Chinese opium smokers. In the 1830s, the Chinese government was alarmed by the impact of the opium trade both on public health and on the economy.

Left: British troops in action during the First Opium War of 1840-42. Their mobility and firepower trounced the Ch'ing army.

Above right: The main route for the British opium trade ran from Bombay to Canton. The rise in volume to 1840 was spectacular.

Right: The signing of the Treaty of Tientsin in 1858 gave foreigners even greater rights in China. It was not ratified until 1860, when the Chinese had once more been defeated in war.

SINEESCHE BOEREN.
Vilageois Chinois.

Left: China's unchanging agricultural techniques could not cope with the task of feeding a rapidly expanding population in the nineteenth century.

Right: Photographed in the 1870s, a victim of one of China's most macabre customs – the compressing of women's feet from childhood. The natural growth of Chinese society and culture was blocked by such inflexible traditions.

Below right: A scene from the Taiping rebellion. Rebel forces are put to flight by troops loyal to the Ch'ing emperor.

Mid-nineteenth-century rebellions

Chinese outrage at these events was understandable, and Chinese historians are rightly critical. But many Western historians are now beginning to feel that too much emphasis has been put on Westerners in China – both by the Chinese and by themselves – and that by concentrating on Westerners in China and on China's responses to Western ideas we may neglect important indigenous developments.

It is certainly true that foreign impact on China as a whole was slight throughout the entire nineteenth century. Peasants, artisans and coolies continued to labor in unchanged ways. The literati continued to study the Confucian classics and to sit for the state examinations, and the metropolitan and provincial bureaucracies functioned along their traditional lines. The themes of poetry and painting did not change, nor did clothes, architecture, cuisine, marriage customs or the principles of filial piety. The major pressures on the Ch'ing were internally generated. The rapid population growth of the eighteenth century continued on into the nineteenth and began to reach crisis proportions. The rapidly expanding population might not have been decisive in itself, but as in the late Ming, and in the closing years of other dynasties, there was no energetic and capable emperor capable of dealing with economic consequences of a fulminating population. Official incompetence and corruption, concentration of land holdings in gentry hands, increase of banditry, military cruelty and inefficiency, crop failures and floods, all increased peasant discontent and led to peasant riots. The culmination of all these discontents was a congeries of major rebellions that broke out in the 1850s and 1860s. There were two rebellions by the Muslim populations, one in southwest and one in northwest China. There was also a rebellion by the Nien in northeast China. And there was a rebellion of the Taipings in southern and central China.

The southwestern Muslim revolt lasted from 1853 to 1873 and was centered in the province of Yunnan. In an area of poor farming land, bad communications and apathetic officials, the local Muslim inhabitants had been ceaselessly harassed by Chinese seeking rich ore lodes.

Unable to endure any more, and undeterred by savage government reprisals, the Muslims declared a new kingdom and made Tali their capital. They built up a formidable series of defenses, and for over a decade they were able to repel all the Ch'ing armies sent against them. Only after the last of their 53 hilltop fortresses had fallen in 1873 did they give up the struggle.

The northwest Muslim rebellion (1862-78) occurred in the area of Kansu, Shensi and Turkestan. In this case, constant religious friction led to the outbreak, as both sides formed their own local militia organizations and joined in battle. The local Ch'ing armies, hampered by immensely long supply lines and a constant shortage of cash, could do little to restore order. Only after an excellent strategist named Tso Tsung-t'ang was appointed as governor-general of Shensi and Kansu in 1868 did things start to go better for the government troops. Tso was equally effective in designing rehabilitation strategies for the areas devastated by the rebellion. He prohibited opium growing, encouraged the development of a cotton industry – even passing out pamphlets to the local populace explaining the necessary techniques to them – and used his troops to develop new farms which were later transferred to the local people. By 1878 the entire area was pacified. It was these areas of Turkestan, pacified by Tso, which were incorporated with some areas of Ili returned by Russia into the new province of Sinkiang in 1884. Tso was honored by the Court and summoned back to Peking to serve as a Grand Councillor.

The Taiping rebels were certainly the most powerful of all the rebels and the ones who came the nearest to toppling the Ch'ing dynasty from power. The Taipings fought from 1851 until they were finally defeated in 1866, and during most of this time they occupied the entire Yangtze valley region, which they controlled from their capital in Nanking. Indeed, so powerful were the Taipings, and so radical was their program, that many historians think they should be described as revolutionaries rather than rebels.

The man who led the Taipings under his title of 'Heavenly King' was Hung Hsiu-ch'üan (1813-64). Hung was from the minority Hakka people, and was born and raised in Kwangtung. Though he

studied hard, he failed to pass any of the state examinations and suffered some kind of a nervous breakdown. During this illness he had certain visions, and when he later compared these visions with some descriptions of Christianity that he read in tracts handed out by Western missionaries, Hung became convinced that he himself was a son of God, the younger brother of Jesus Christ, and that he was called upon by his Lord to restore the Chinese to the true faith. In the late 1840s, he gathered some followers around him in a mountainous area of eastern Kwangsi province. There he began to plan the rough outlines of his anti-Manchu strategy and to formulate his new doctrines in the form of the Ten Commandments for his Heavenly Kingdom of Great Peace (in Chinese, T'ai-p'ing t'ien-kuo).

The doctrines formulated by Hung were novel in concept and rigorously enforced among his followers. As well as regular religious services, which were roughly modeled along the lines of Protestant Christianity, and readings from the Old Testament and recitations of Hung's own ten commandments and various other religious writings, attempts were made to develop a common treasury in which all material resources would be pooled, to divide all land equally among the Heavenly King's followers and to grant equal rights to women. All of these cut deeply at the heart of Confucian doctrines, as did Hung's later attempts to develop an examination system based on the new religious doctrines, rather than on the Confucian classics, and to formulate new systems for civil and military organization.

Hung and his lieutenants also worked with great skill to marshal and train their forces. They forged arms in secret workshops, distributed battle plans and handbooks on building sites, collected funds and carefully increased the numbers of their recruits, who were drawn from disgruntled Hakkas, local peasants, out-of-work river coolies, local secret-society leaders and even some wealthy clans which furnished educated leaders. So potent was this combination of religious indoctrination and military preparation that when the Taipings began their attacks on local Ch'ing forces in 1850 they won several victories and attracted thousands of new followers. The

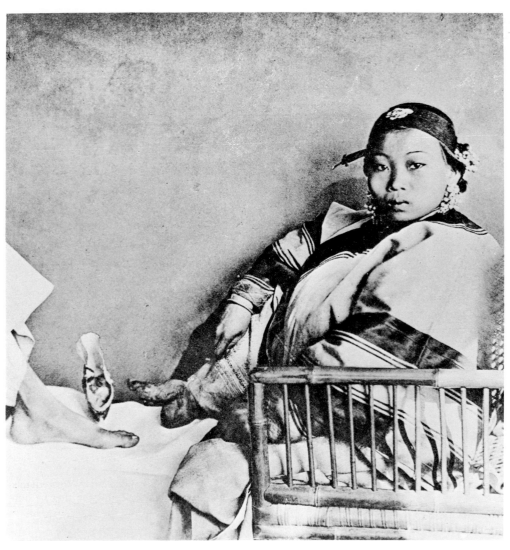

emperor decided to appoint an Imperial Commissioner to quash the rebels and summoned Lin Tse-hsü out of retirement to handle them, but Lin died on his way south. The Taipings broke out of the difficult terrain in which the Ch'ing armies had temporarily boxed them, and in a series of incredible campaigns in 1852 and 1853 they battled their way north through Hunan province, seized the great city complex of Wuhan and then sailed in a great armada down the Yangtze to Nanking, which they captured almost without a fight.

It was at this point that the Ch'ing dynasty came close to falling. Most historians agree that if the Taipings had pushed on north in 1853 nothing could have stopped them from taking Peking and proclaiming their Heavenly Kingdom in lieu of a new dynasty. The effects on China would have been incalculable: with the Manchus ousted, a new Chinese regime might have been free to undertake a program of radical reform, and perhaps the Taipings would have pushed through a program that would have done for China what the Meiji Restoration programs did for Japan. Certainly the Taipings were not lacking in talented men. Though Hung Hsiu-ch'üan was a visionary who showed less and less interest in practical affairs after he had settled in Nanking, his lieutenants (who were themselves named 'kings' and given places in the celestial hierarchy) were brilliant generals and able administrators. Also, Hung Jen-kan, a cousin of Hung Hsiu-ch'üan, had been educated in mission schools in Hong Kong and had drawn up ambitious plans for developing a modern Chinese navy, transforming the educational system, introducing modern banking techniques and so on. But the Taipings let the chance go by, and when they launched a northern campaign the following year the Ch'ing had marshaled their defenses and they were repulsed. There was

a decade of savage fighting, however, before the last Taiping bases were wiped out, and even this victory came only after there had been bitter factional fighting between Taiping leaders.

The man most responsible for the ultimate Ch'ing victory was undoubtedly Tseng Kuo-fan (1811-72). After a successful and conventional bureaucratic career, Tseng was visiting his family in Hunan when the Taipings entered the province in 1852. Several gentry in Hunan, among whom were friends of Tseng, had organized local militia units to make up for the shortcomings of the regular armies. Tseng was reluctant to get involved, but he finally bowed to the combined pressures of his friends and the emperor. His first attempts to apply military tactics were failures, but finally his efforts bore fruit in the shape of one of China's most famous military organizations, the 'Hsiang Army,' named after Tseng's native province of Hunan. The Hsiang Army was recruited from Hunanese peasants, and whenever possible each detachment of troops was commanded by local officers known to the men. These officers were in turn responsible to superiors whom they knew and trusted, and the ultimate loyalty of all officers and men was to Tseng himself. Tseng insisted on good and regular pay for his troops, on firm discipline, on good training and on strict responsibility for his officers. His army was thus his own private creation, and it was only loyal to the Ch'ing state to the extent that Tseng himself was loyal. It became the model for numerous later regional armies.

It took Tseng a long time to win the confidence of the emperor, who was suspicious of Tseng's motives in developing such an army. It also took Tseng a long time to gather around him a group of able officers whom he could trust absolutely. Some of the men he came to rely on most completely were his own brothers. Another was Li Hung-chang, who had been on Tseng's staff and had developed an army of Anhwei men known as the 'Huai Army.' It was Li Hung-chang who decided to cooperate with the British officer Charles Gordon in attacking the Taipings around Shanghai. Gordon had taken over the force of Western mercenaries – first developed by the young American adventurer Frederick Townsend Ward – and made it into an effective striking force, particularly potent because of its use of artillery and armored gunboats. These troops, honorifically named 'The Ever-Victorious Army' by the Ch'ing emperor, were of considerable help to the generals coordinating the eastern campaign against the Taiping, but it is quite untrue to assert, as many past writers have done, that the Ever-Victorious Army defeated the Taipings. They were merely one element in a vast military machine which finally managed to tighten the noose around the Taiping and at last seize their Nanking capital in the summer of 1864. In two more years the rebellion was finally crushed.

After the Taiping rebels were defeated Tseng Kuo-fan and Li Hung-chang had to concentrate on suppressing yet another rebellion – the fourth of these great mid-century outbreaks – that of the Nien, who were spread over Chihli and Shantung provinces. Unlike the Muslims or the Taipings the Nien had no religious ideology, but they were a formidable army of fast-moving cavalry, ranging widely over north China in search of plunder and then digging in behind their well-developed systems of earthwork defenses. The Nien were peasants, deserters, secret-society members, salt smugglers – traditional bandits, skilled in winning local support and even in turning the local defense corps to their own uses by organizing them to fight off the regular Ch'ing troops. In the chaotic circumstances of the 1860s, when the Ch'ing government was collecting almost no taxes from the rebel areas and accordingly could barely pay its troops, Tseng and Li were only able to break the Nien because they could draw on those troops and resources which they had already de-veloped to fight the Taipings. In other words, it was once again the 'regional armies' rather than the regular troops who won the war, smashing the last Nien outposts in 1868.

Restoration and self-strengthening

Few regimes in the history of the world have ever been able to cope successfully with four massive rebellions at the same time. How the Ch'ing were able to do so when to all appearances they were in a period of sharp decline is a major enigma that can only be resolved by considering a great many differing factors.

One factor, suggested by simple logic, is that we have misconstrued the extent of Ch'ing decline. This may be because historians have placed too much weight on the Western component in the Chinese equation. Because the Ch'ing were so badly humiliated in the Opium War and in the second war between 1856 and 1860, we may have been overquick to conclude that the Ch'ing must have been weak in all areas. But we can look at the same evidence another way and say that the area of Western intercourse was the one area in which the Ch'ing were the most incompetent, the one area in which they lacked all experience and expertise, and also the one area with which they were least concerned. Despite population pressures, social inequities, imperial and official incompetence and other factors, the Ch'ing state was still capable of summoning up vast resources, and these cumulatively were more than any rebels could muster.

Again, the Ch'ing emperor had clearly not forfeited the loyalty of his wealthier Chinese subjects. To most gentry and merchants in China, the existing regime was preferable to the alternatives. The Nien had little to offer, the Muslims had their own religion and customs which were repugnant to many of their neighbors and the Taipings openly claimed that they were out to overthrow the old ethical system in its entirety and sub-

Above left: The wreck of a Chinese fort after the war of 1856-60. This second defeat at the hands of the foreigners convinced the Chinese government that reform and modernization were essential.

Left: In the 1870s, the first modern arsenal in China was established at Nanking. Importing Western military technology proved easier than changing Chinese society.

Right: Senior civil servants, the mandarins, who embodied the Confucian traditions which had guided Chinese government for two millennia. Their thinking was not flexible enough to meet the challenge of the West.

Left: Chinese soldiers from the provinces in the 1890s. The growth of local armies independent of central government control was a major factor in the disintegration of imperial power.

Below right: The highly Westernized port of Shanghai. In the late nineteenth century, Britain, Germany, France and the United States penetrated China through a series of 'concessions' and 'spheres of influence.'

stitute a new religion. Whereas the Ch'ing court, whatever its racial origins or other deficiencies, promised to preserve the institutionalized Confucian virtues. Men like Tseng Kuo-fan, accordingly, rallied behind the Ch'ing. Such men might well have used their armies against the Ch'ing had they wished, but instead they used their armies to preserve the Ch'ing and to preserve their own way of life. The choice was a conscious one, and it was decisive.

The Chinese themselves called the period of the 1860s a time of 'Restoration,' harking back to their own history and other periods when a dynasty had been able to overcome great internal disruption and weakness and restore its right to hold the 'mandate of heaven.' Tseng Kuo-fan, Li Hung-chang, Tso Tsung-t'ang and many other Restoration statesmen worked in many areas besides the military to bring strength and unity back to their country. They reestablished schools, restocked libraries, revived the examination systems, reorganized local taxation, encouraged better government at the local level, struck out at corruption. Their concentration was on human talent, true to their Confucian principles, in the belief that it was the selection of worthy men that constituted the key to successful government. And their methods were the ones proven by history, so that if they had to make changes it was always change within tradition, and never change for its own sake.

They were also not unmindful of the value of certain Western technical skills. They had seen the powers of Western ships and guns, and they realized that it could be advantageous for China to make them herself. So the first arsenals were founded in this period. Guns and ammunition were manufactured, and the components of Western gunboats were assembled. They were willing to hire Westerners to work in these arsenals and to use them imaginatively. Thus Halliday Macartney worked as a physician and as a

supervisor of cannon casting, John Fryer was hired to translate Western technical books into Chinese, and W A P Martin taught Western languages and science in Peking.

The Ch'ing made use of Western skills in non-military ways as well. Some Chinese were encouraged to study Western concepts of international law in order to learn how to apply them to gain Chinese redress of grievances. The Chinese also founded a new ministry to handle foreign affairs, the *Tsungli Yamen*, which had its own files and library and was meant to develop the language and diplomatic skills to deal with the recalcitrant Westerners. Another complex organization, first developed in Shanghai when commercial activity in that city had been disrupted by the Taipings, was the Imperial Maritime Customs Service. This service, which from 1861 onward was directed by Robert Hart, was responsible for collecting all customs dues on incoming foreign imports at the standard rates set by the Tientsin treaties and to pay the money over to the Ch'ing. The service established offices in all the treaty ports and rapidly proved itself capable of paying millions of *taels* each year to the Chinese government. It also handled the opium imports, which were now coming into China as a legal trade item, paying a fixed rate of thirty *taels* on each box of 133 lb weight.

All of these aspects of foreign participation brought strength to the Ch'ing and helped in the battles against the rebels. The Westerners were not of course totally disinterested. Somewhat in the way that Chinese gentry had come to see that their vested interests were best protected by the Ch'ing, the Westerners came to see that the new treaties offered them great benefits and that they would do much better to work along with the Ch'ing than to back the Taipings, even though the Taipings were pseudo-Christians.

There is a final range of factors that contributed to the Ch'ing success but contained within them

seeds of future trouble. One such was the regional armies. The structure and organizing principles of the regional armies removed power from the central government; this did not seem very significant when the commanding generals were loyal to the Ch'ing, but similar armies later in the century were not to be so loyal.

Another factor was local militia organization. Militia groups were formed in response to need and were used to defend local terrain against bandits when the local troops were unable to do so. But as more and more such militia groups were formed, shifts began to occur in the balance of power in the countryside. Rich gentry families began to get a hold over local finances that were used to pay and train militia soldiers. Gradually Ch'ing local influence was eroded, and ruthless gentry were put in a position that made exploitation of the local peasantry increasingly easy.

Yet another factor can be found in the field of general taxation. Unable to pay their armies because of the massive disruptions of the mid century, the Ch'ing had permitted the levying of a transit tax on local trade, called the *likin* tax. This *likin* was collected at barriers set up along the major roads and waterways and was used in the provinces for military purposes. Thus less money was reaching the central treasury and more money was put in the hands of the provincial officials. Also, the setting up of so many barriers meant that a certain amount of corruption was inevitable, furnishing fresh sources of grievance against the government among merchants and artisans.

An important aspect of Restoration policies was that they ultimately bred a false complacency. Confucian virtues and the traditional imperial system seemed to have triumphed, and hence all sense of urgency was lost. This was of great significance in the economic sector. The Chinese now had several clear models available for study. They were beginning to learn about the West;

they could observe what was happening in Japan; they could even see what was happening in Shanghai, which was rapidly developing into a major metropolis, with Western architecture and sanitation, with factories, harbor facilities, race tracks and real-estate booms. But the Chinese refused to confront their implications. The nascent self-strengthening movement did not develop into a major economic breakthrough; various projects continued in a sporadic and uncoordinated way, with inadequate funding and small staffs.

A further impediment to economic change was the fact that the prestige of merchants remained as low as it had traditionally been in China, and most of them continued to put their money into land (for security) and into a classical education for their children (so that these children could become gentry). A certain number of merchants did gravitate into the orbit of the Westerners and amass great fortunes through new kinds of trade. These were the *compradors*, who served with British, American and French business firms in China. The *comprador* was paid for his knowledge of local business conditions, his linguistic ability and his financial acumen. Though he often lived in a treaty port, he would travel widely inland on the orders of his employers, and was given large amounts of commodities – manufactured goods, machinery, opium – with which he could speculate on his own. Western firms competed fiercely for the services of the best *compradors*, many of whom became millionaires. But their influence on their society was slight and indeed many Chinese despised them for being subservient to the Westerners, rather than admiring them for their skill in amassing wealth.

Such expansion of the Chinese economy as did take place at this time – that is, between 1870 and 1890 – was generally circumscribed by two conceptual slogans that echoed through contemporary Chinese writings. The first of these was 'Government supervision and merchant management' *(kuan-tu shang-pan)*. This meant that though merchants might direct the general running of the business, they were not permitted to make long-range policy decisions and were constantly beset by official regulation and interference. Any profits they might make were mostly siphoned off by the state instead of being made available for reinvestment in order to expand the economic base. The second concept was 'Chinese learning as the base, Western learning for practical use' (usually abbreviated as *t'i-yung*, 'base and use'). This was designed to reassure Chinese conservatives who might fear that even gradual Westernization would erode the country's moral fiber. On the contrary, ran the self-strengthening argument, only a few aspects of practical Western skills would be borrowed, and these would be grafted firmly onto the traditional Chinese value system, so that there would be no change in basic values. A good deal of Chinese industry did develop along these lines – mines were opened up, iron works developed, Chinese factories began to make matches, cement, cotton and woolen goods, a telegraph line was opened and some short stretches of railroad were laid. The China Merchant Steamship Navigation Company was able to compete successfully with foreign powers for the carrying trade on many inland waterways.

The two people who dominated China's government at this time were a strangely assorted pair. One was the Empress-Dowager Tz'u-hsi (1835-1908). Tz'u-hsi was a Manchu girl who was made a concubine of the emperor Hsien-feng, and bore him a son. When Hsien-feng died in 1861 this five-year-old boy was named emperor, and Tz'u-hsi became regent in his name after a daring political coup. During the Restoration period Tz'u-hsi was the *de facto* ruler of China, and though she relied on several talented ministers, we can tell that she was a tough and capable leader. She was, however, quite unwilling to relinquish her power, and when her son died in 1875 she deliberately chose as the new emperor another young boy in the imperial family, so that she could continue to rule as regent. Unfortunately, though she excelled in palace politics and had been courageous in crisis situations, she had none of the vision that was essential if China were to adapt her institutions to deal successfully with the combined internal and Western pressures. Her range of interests was narrow, her education had been limited and she listened to increasingly conservative advisers. She also, at a time when funds were desperately short, wasted vast sums on reconstruction of that summer palace which the British had burned in 1860. And in one famous incident she took money that had been intended for the building of modern steamships and used it for the construction of a marble pleasure boat in one of the palace lakes.

After the mid-century rebellions were over, and Tseng Kuo-fan had died in 1874, the most powerful statesman in China was Li Hüng-chang (1823-1901). After his successes over the rebels, Li served for many years as governor-general of Chihli (the northeastern province, in which Peking is situated) and was concurrently a Grand Secretary and Superintendent of Trade for the North. In this latter capacity he handled many of China's most important foreign-policy matters with the Western powers and with Japan, and built up an impressive reputation in diplomatic circles. He was a shrewd and circumspect negotiator and a man interested in developing *kuan-tu shang-pan* enterprises. He knew more than most Chinese officials about the West, and he built up a personal staff of secretaries and advisers that included Germans, Americans and British. Like the Empress-Dowager, he was a brilliant political manipulator, and like her he also loved money

and engaged in many sharp practices to get it. One can think of countless men who would have been less well equipped to handle China's difficulties, but finally Li too lacked the breadth of vision that alone could have assured China's future.

Imperialism and nationalism

By the early 1890s China was once again entering a crisis period. But now there were new and confusing elements that had never before been present, and a great many of these sprang directly from the West. Particularly significant were the problems created by Christian missionaries, Western commercial expansion and emergent Chinese radicalism.

After the Treaty of Tientsin, Catholic and Protestant missionaries had been coming to China in increasing numbers from Britain, France and the United States. Almost none of them knew the Chinese language, and they encountered the hostility of the Chinese gentry, who regarded them as badly educated (because they didn't know the Confucian classics) and as direct competitors in the field of cultural and ethical influence. The missionaries, furthermore, because of their race, were associated with other foreigners who were bringing unwanted merchandise, unwanted gunboats and unwanted opium into China. Because missionaries could claim the privileges of extraterritoriality and seek the protection of their own consuls, many complicated legal cases arose in which Chinese converts would try to obtain protection from the missionaries in order to further their own business deals, or to win some law suit. Christian converts became a hated group, and they were often beaten up in riots or even killed. Many of the gentry helped to fan anti-missionary sentiment by circulating pamphlets and pictures that described missionaries as sexual aberrants and even as cannibals, accusations that were widely believed. When, for example, corpses of

Chinese children were discovered in mission areas, the crowd often did not bother to consider the fact that the little children might simply have died of disease. So there were harassments and riots, and occasionally there were massacres, such as that in Tientsin in 1870 when 20 foreigners were killed by a Chinese mob, including the French consul and 10 nuns. Such tragedies always led to Western reprisals, to the dispatch of gunboats and the demand for indemnities, and that created even more bad feeling.

The pace of Western commercial expansion also increased greatly during the 1880s. By the 1890s, when the Western governments, convinced that the Ch'ing dynasty might soon fall, began aggressively to support their merchants and demand territorial concessions from the Chinese, we enter the period of blatant imperialism. A number of foreign powers were already carving out 'spheres of influence' in China. For the British the area was the rich lowland provinces of the Yangtze valley. The French, from their colonial bases in Indochina, were moving into the southwestern Chinese province of Yunnan. The Germans were interested in Shantung, and the Americans in Manchuria. The Russians and Japanese were also attracted to Manchuria, and the Japanese, already firmly based in Korea, cast covetous eyes at Taiwan and Fukien province as well. The power of the foreigners stemmed both from their financial resources and their potential military strength, but they rarely conquered Chinese territory, and they did not make China into a colony by blatantly occupying territory and imposing their own administrative machinery on a subject population. Instead, they pressed unceasingly for concessions to build railroads and develop mines or to invest in China's transportation systems and raw-material reserves. They also loaned large sums of money to the increasingly bankrupt Ch'ing government, taking what

few resources China had left – the Imperial Maritime Customs dues, the proceeds of the salt gabelle – as their collateral.

What we can call emergent Chinese radicalism, a tendency to question the premises on which Ch'ing government was based, was represented by no single man or dominant school of thought. Partly this was because the self-strengtheners had miscalculated. It was not possible simply to adapt Western techniques to a Chinese base, for each development led to new questions, and no answer was ever final. Thus guns led on to ships which led to iron mines. Coal was needed for the mines, railroads were needed to transport the coal, new techniques in communications led to developments in journalism, greater literacy posed new questions about education, the educated began to study Western economic and political theory and the workings of constitutional monarchies and republican governments.

Chinese intellectuals propagated their views through journalism, for this was a time when many new periodicals were attracting wide readership. Radical writers, moreover, could base themselves in the foreign concessions of the treaty ports, and if the Ch'ing authorities tried to harass them they could seek shelter behind Western law. In the writings of these men a concept of Chinese nationalism began gradually to emerge, an awareness of a China trapped in an intolerable situation, needing to call on new reserves of energy and passion if she was to take her rightful place in a fiercely competitive world. As such ideas formed in Chinese minds the Manchus began increasingly to be branded as alien conquerors, lacking in initiative and ability. Among the readers and writers of this new criticism were an increasing number of Chinese students who had studied abroad and watched foreign governments in action. One such was Yung Wing, China's first graduate from an American university (Yale, class of 1854).

打鬼燒書圖

Far left: Li Hung-chang, the shrewdest statesman and diplomat of late imperial China, flanked by Lord Salisbury (left) and Lord Curzon during a visit to Britain.

Left: The Empress-Dowager Tz'u-hsi (center right), a former emperor's concubine with a supreme talent for palace politics.

Right: A Boxer pamphlet calls for death to all foreigners and the burning of foreign books.

Below: The first railroad in China. Modern transportation was slow to develop.

were compounded by the fact that Japan was another Asian country that had been modernizing for less than 30 years.

Reactions to the Sino-Japanese War took two totally different forms, each of which in its way profoundly affected the government and people. The first was the Reform Movement of 1898; the second was the Boxer Rebellion of 1900.

The 1898 Reform Movement was the brainchild of the Emperor Kuang-hsü (1871-1908), who had been chafing to end the dominance of the Empress-Dowager. On the advice of his tutor, Weng T'ung-ho, and with the active assistance of K'ang Yu-wei, Kuang-hsü issued a series of reform decrees that were designed deliberately to modernize Chinese society and government. Among the areas in which he sought to introduce reforms were education and the exam system, military training and discipline, science, agriculture, abolition of sinecures and the introduction of a public budget showing all receipts. So many decrees were issued in the hundred days (June 11 – September 21) that most officials had little chance to implement them, and indeed the program, though radical in scope, could scarcely be called coherent. Yet it did show that the urgent need for change had got through to the emperor, and it was a tragedy for China when the Empress-Dowager, in another of her successful coups, had Kuang-hsü put under house arrest.

The second reaction was quite different. The Boxers, so named from the ritual athletic exer-

A new desperation was given to arguments for reform by the shock of the Sino-Japanese War of 1894-95. In this war, in only a few weeks, a Chinese fleet that was thought to have been one of the great triumphs of the self-strengtheners was completely smashed by the modern Japanese navy. By the terms of the Treaty of Shimonoseki in 1895 China lost the Liaotung peninsula in southern Manchuria, the entire island of Taiwan, had to pay an enormous indemnity of two hundred million *taels* and agreed to allow the Japanese to develop industrial enterprises in China's treaty ports. Though pressure from the Russians and other foreign powers jealous of her success forced Japan to return Liaotung, the shock and humiliation to China were immense, and they

興辦鐵路

cises that were one component of their doctrines, were as angry and frustrated by China's weakness as Kuang-hsü. But they blamed the foreigners, not Chinese conservatives, and they developed their momentum as a mass movement on the basis of anti-foreign slogans. Initially they seem to have had an anti-Manchu component in their doctrine, but when the Manchu court began actively to condone their anti-foreign attacks, the Boxers swung to firm support of the dynasty.

The Boxer Rebellion began in the areas of Shantung and Chihli in 1898, drawing its recruits from secret-society members and local militias, as well as from impoverished peasants. Their first targets were Christian converts among their own countrymen, but by 1899 they were attacking missionaries and other foreigners directly. The Western powers, both alarmed for the safety of their nationals and also sensing an opportunity for demanding fresh concessions from China, dispatched an expeditionary force and shelled the Taku forts guarding the approaches to Peking. In June 1900 the Ch'ing court responded by declaring war on the foreign powers, and for several weeks that summer Chinese troops held the legations in Peking under siege. An allied force lifted the siege, and the Empress-Dowager fled to Sian in Shensi. After some fairly heavy fighting west of Peking, the Ch'ing finally capitulated and agreed to execute some of the most pro-Boxer officials and to pay a large indemnity.

The Boxer Rebellion aroused mixed feelings among the Chinese. Most of the senior Chinese officials had stayed aloof from the struggle, and the governor-generals in central and southern China had remained on friendly terms with foreign diplomats. Support for the Boxers came mainly from the Manchus, though even here there were puzzling ambiguities. For instance, the siege of the legations was never pressed very hard,

and on several occasions Westerners within the legations knew that they could have been easily overrun had the attackers exerted themselves. Some historians believe that there were senior Manchu officers in Peking who disapproved of the Empress-Dowager's policy, and who worked to keep the Boxers in check so that the foreigners would make less harsh demands after hostilities terminated. Even so, the Rebellion had a profound effect on China's international image. It was at this period that the notion of the Yellow Peril began to be invoked. The Chinese were described as screaming hordes who were also ineffective and cowardly, and it was to be a long time before this stereotype was erased from Western minds – indeed some elements of it are there today.

One effect of the joint shock of the hundred days of reform and the Boxer Rebellion was that the Ch'ing court was finally compelled to make certain reforms, and for the last few years of her life the Empress-Dowager herself appeared in the unlikely guise of a reformer. Reforms promulgated in 1901 ended the eight-legged essay as the compulsory stylistic form for the examinations, ordered reorganization of the army and sent several Manchus abroad to study. Reforms promulgated in 1905 abolished the traditional examination system altogether, projected a new chain of government schools, and dispatched an eminent commission overseas to study Western forms of government. An edict of 1906 promised that once the work of educational and economic reform was completed the court would move to establish a constitutional monarchy. In the meantime, the old Six Boards were completely restructured as 10 modern ministries, and plans for electing provincial deliberative assemblies were made.

In several other areas, too, the Ch'ing showed surprising vitality and competence: in negotiating agreements with Britain to finally terminate opium imports to China, for example, in military campaigns to the far west, and in complex railroad negotiations with the Russians and Japanese in Manchuria.

The Last Emperor

Yet when the Empress-Dowager and the Emperor Kuang-hsü died within a few days of each other in 1908, no new leader emerged who could continue the work that they had so belatedly begun. For the third time in succession, the new emperor was a young child, and Manchu princes quarreled for the right to control him as regent. Obstinately refusing to read the writing on the wall, the Manchu regent packed the newly formed cabinet with other Manchu grandees, ousted several powerful Chinese from their positions, and moved to concentrate all China's railroads under central control. This last attempt, which was in fact partly designed to reduce the powers of foreigners in China, was instead widely interpreted by Chinese as a scheme by the Manchus to concentrate more power in Manchu hands. Increasingly, the Chinese were beginning to turn against the dynasty. They reprinted and studied long-forgotten accounts of the Manchu massacres at the time of the Ming fall in 1644, and they listened with excitement to the dramatic and forceful words of young students like Tsou Jung, exhorting them to action.

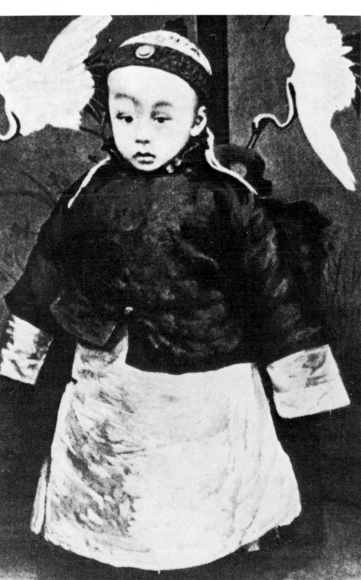

Aspects of revolution

The Ch'ing dynasty fell with a speed and suddenness that bewildered foreign observers. On the night of 9 October 1911, in the city of Wuhan, a bomb exploded accidentally in the house of some conspirators. As police moved in to arrest the suspects on the following day several companies of troops mutinied. The arsenal was captured, and the mutiny spread. News of the rising reached other provinces, and one by one provincial assemblies declared their independence from the Ch'ing government. The Manchu court could find no generals able or willing to lead armies to protect their dynasty, and on 12 February 1912 the young emperor abdicated, closing a tradition of imperial rule that had commenced over 2200 years before. China was now a republic.

Though the particular way events unfolded in 1911 had not been foreseen by the conspirators themselves, they cannot be simply dismissed as an accident, since many Chinese had been working toward this revolution for over a decade. Foremost among them, and the man whose name is inseparably linked to this first phase of the Chinese revolution, was Sun Yat-sen (1866-1925). Sun Yat-sen came from a laboring and trading family in Kwangtung. They were a mobile family – two of Sun's uncles had died in the California gold rush and a brother had made a fortune in Hawaii – and Sun himself had been educated in Hawaii and Hong Kong, had been baptized a Christian and had trained to be a doctor. He had been doubly frustrated in his career plans: Li Hung-chang would not take him on his staff because he did not have a good enough Chinese education, and the British would not recognize his medical training as valid and merely classified him as a herbalist. Thus it was as a man trapped between two cultures that Sun Yat-sen started his revolutionary career, founding a small society in 1895 dedicated to the overthrow of the Manchus. Their first plot in Canton that same year was discovered by police, and several leaders were executed. Sun fled to Japan, where he cut off his queue as an act of open defiance of the Manchus, and then made his way via Hawaii and San Francisco to London. In London, in 1896, Sun was kidnapped and held a prisoner in the Chinese legation, but he was finally released after some English friends brought pressure to bear on the Manchu government. The main importance of this episode was that it rocketed Sun to fame in the newspapers of the world and established his reputation as a revolutionary.

This phase of Sun's life was dominated by his ceaseless quest for funds as he lived the life of an exile among the overseas Chinese communities in Hawaii and Southeast Asia. He had to compete for money with such other eminent Chinese as K'ang Yu-wei and Liang Ch'i-ch'ao – both also in exile after the defeat of the Hundred Days Reform Group – and found himself at a disadvantage in the competition. Both K'ang and Liang were well-known scholars and writers, whose polish, erudition and moderate demands for constitutional reform appealed much more to wealthy Chinese merchants than Sun's outspoken radicalism. Nevertheless, in 1905 Sun was able to found a new society, the *T'ung-meng hui,* or Revolutionary Alliance, with which he launched a succession of uprisings in southern China, all of them successfully suppressed by Ch'ing forces. Membership of the *T'ung-meng hui* increased steadily despite these set-backs, and Sun found many new recruits among Chinese students overseas, in secret societies, among intellectuals in the treaty ports, among the more venturesome overseas merchants and among the younger officers in the newly reformed armies. Sun's program, though it was not clearly formulated, had certain major themes. First was 'nationalism,' by which Sun meant the overthrow of the Manchus and their replacement as rulers with Han Chinese. Only later in his life did he come to include anti-imperialism in his nationalist doctrines. Second was 'democracy': by this he meant a parliamentary government under an elected president. This would be attained only after China had passed through a phase of military government under a revolutionary regime and a period of political tutelage that would prepare the country for full democracy. The third theme was 'people's livelihood,' or socialism, under which he included both equalization of land rights and also, after about 1912, the state ownership of railroads and major industries.

Sun's stubborn tenacity and revolutionary vision finally bore fruit. Even though he was not in China in October 1911 – he was in Denver, Colorado, on a fund-raising trip – it was members of his *T'ung-meng hui* who were in dominating positions in many new army units and several of the elected provincial assemblies. When Sun returned to China he was elected provisional president of the new republic on 1 January 1912. But because his armies were not strong enough to destroy the Manchus altogether, Sun had to make a deal with the powerful general Yüan Shih-k'ai, who held the balance of power and controled a large well-trained army that was personally loyal to him. First, Yüan was named premier; but after further negotiations Sun resigned on 13 February, and on 12 March Yüan was sworn in as president.

Sun joined Yüan's government later as national director of railroad development, hoping that he would be able to realize his magnificent plans for transforming China's economic life through intensive railroad expansion. At the same time he encouraged some of his associates to merge the *T'ung-meng hui* with certain other minority parties and form a major political organization that could fight in the elections projected for 1913. This was achieved, and the new party was named the Kuomintang or Nationalist Party. It was triumphant in the elections, and moved at once to curb Yüan's powers. But Yüan struck back with his armies, and Sun was forced once again into exile. His response was to form yet another revolutionary party, this time in Japan. As for Yüan Shih-k'ai, after steadily weakening the power of China's new representative institutions, he finally moved in 1915 to have himself named emperor. This was not to be, however, for he died the next year. One of his leading generals next tried to restore the recently deposed Manchu emperor. This, too, failed, but by the summer of 1917, when Sun was ensconced in Canton in charge of a new 'revolutionary' regime, all hopes for a regenerated and unified China had been shattered.

The extraordinary complexity of the political maneuvers of this period, which have only been sketched in here, raises a question as to the propriety of applying the word 'revolution' to the events of 1911. Sun was indeed a revolutionary in that he wished to change the entire governmental and social structure, yet he achieved so little of what he desired that it is probably best to think of the events of 1911 as constituting simply the first phase of a long revolution that may still be in progress.

Instead of pursuing that question, let us try to assess what had changed and who had benefited from the upheavals of 1911-13. The hereditary emperorship was gone, and gone in such a way that not even the strongest general in China could summon it back again: Yüan Shih-k'ai could not be a new Chu Yüan-chang or a new Abahai. The privileged life of the Manchu nobles and bannermen was over. A constitutional form of government was now nominally accepted, but it proved very difficult, in such a short period of time, to develop adequate procedures for conferring true legitimacy, and the offices guaranteed under the

constitution became battle grounds for warring factions. The old Confucian gentry were also apparently gone for ever; but if we look closely at the men who filled the seats in the new representative assemblies or occupied the administrative posts in the countryside, we find that a great many of them seem to be from the same old families and drew their prestige from their combination of advanced education and land-holdings. There were of course many new men in positions of power who had not been there before. There were more merchants, who had the property qualifications necessary for election to many of the newly established offices; there were officers in the new armies who had worked their way up through the ranks; there were students who had managed to leave poor backgrounds and study overseas; there were secret-society members or poor scholars who had risen through the ranks of the *T'ung-meng hui* into powerful positions. But by and large the events of 1911 did not radically affect patterns of wealth control, whether in landholding or long-range and local commerce. 1911 cannot, then, even be described as a 'bourgeois revolution'; again, it was only the first phase of such a revolution and left many elements of the old order still unchanged.

The foreign powers had not played an important part in the events of 1911. The British and Japanese, who were most affected because their investments were the largest, had been content to wait for the dust to settle, though they did not have much sympathy for Sun Yat-sen. The British, certainly, welcomed the victory of Yüan Shih-k'ai, since they thought that a military strongman had much more hope of holding the country together than a revolutionary visionary. The enormous loans that Yüan Shih-k'ai negotiated with foreign banks in order to keep his regime solvent seemed clear enough proof that the foreigners would continue to enjoy their profitable economic position. The foreigners were still generally unwilling to fight over China (an exception being the Russo-Japanese War of 1904-05, which was fought in large part to determine which nation should have economic dominance in Manchuria), and in general they still adhered to the Open Door policy that the United States had affirmed in 1899. Thus as China struggled over forms of government and other constitutional niceties, the foreigners expanded their trade and increased their investments.

The most revolutionary results of the events of 1911-13 occurred in the sphere of culture. As increasing numbers of Chinese students traveled abroad to study, read foreign philosophical and scientific works and examined foreign organizational systems, the pressures on traditional Chinese learning and scholarship grew enormous. Not for long were the adventuresome willing to agree with K'ang Yu-wei that all important reform proposals could be found embedded in the Classics. Nor did they agree that there was some profound Chinese essence onto which Western techniques could be grafted. They did not even agree any longer that classical Chinese was the best means of expression.

Increasingly in the years after 1911 Chinese intellectuals looked for a new linguistic form, and they finally found what they wanted in the colloquial Chinese – called *pai-hua* – which had long been used in Chinese short stories and novels. These genres of writing had been considered vulgar and unimportant by classical scholars, but twentieth-century writers found in *pai-hua* both the rhythms of contemporary speech that mirrored contemporary reality and a way to speed literacy among the Chinese masses. It was much

easier to learn to read *pai-hua* than it was to learn classical Chinese, and it could also be written more easily, since one needed to know fewer ideograms and could transfer the spoken word directly to the printed page without complex grammatical transpositions.

Foremost exponent of the *pai-hua* movement was Hu Shih (1891-1962), a native of Shanghai, who traveled to the United States and majored in philosophy at Cornell, and went on to write a PhD at Columbia under the direction of John Dewey. His own clear style and his deep interest in pragmatism and the scientific method had a great influence on his Chinese contemporaries. Hundreds of other young Chinese shared these interests, and their views and their creative writing were widely disseminated through such magazines as *New Youth*, of which Hu Shih was editor for a time, as was Ch'en Tu-hsiu, who later became the first secretary of China's fledgling Communist Party.

The descriptive term often used for this cultural revolution is that of the May Fourth Movement. (This is because on 4 May 1919 some mass demonstrations took place in Peking which involved many of the most pressing issues of the day.) This May Fourth Movement was of great importance in modern China's history, and it reminds us how tightly interconnected were a number of major themes that historians too lightly separate – cultural revolution, student activism, patriotic nationalism and the working class movement – all of which have continued to play a central role in China's development up to our own time.

Left: General Yuan Shih-k'ai. Because he commanded the loyalty of a well-trained army, Yuan was able to assume the presidency of the new Chinese Republic in March 1912.

Above: The original republican conference which elected Sun Yat-sen as provisional president at the end of December 1911. Finally, Sun had to be content with control of railroad development.

Right: Japanese soldiers unload supplies during the Russo-Japanese War of 1904-05. Japan fought for economic dominance of Manchuria. The Chinese Republic was to prove no more capable of resisting foreign pressure than the empire had been.

Japan: 1650-1914

Japan's startling emergence as a great power in the twentieth century has focused world attention upon the story of Japan's response to Western contact and the remarkable course of modernization that the country underwent after the middle of the nineteenth century. Why did Japan react so quickly and positively to Western influence, and why, in contrast to China, did the Japanese take up with such enthusiasm new models of political and economic organization which they saw exemplified in the West European societies? The answer that the Japanese were simply skillful borrowers does an injustice to their creative capacities as a nation. The assumption that Japan in the 1850s was a decaying oriental society, revived only by the saving touch of Western influence, downplays the vitality of the Japanese people and ignores the explosive conditions which prevailed in Japan at the time of the arrival of Commodore Perry in 1853.

Japan's potential for modern growth in the early nineteenth century, in fact, bore comparison with the countries of Europe, which though small in size and population had nonetheless developed the capacity to exert their influence upon the entire world. Japan in the early 1800s could muster a set of rather impressive national statistics. Its total population of somewhat over 30 million was more than that of either France or Germany and close to three times that of contemporary England. Edo, the Tokugawa capital, was a city of close to a million inhabitants, making it larger than either contemporary London or Paris. Two other cities, Osaka and Kyoto, had populations of over 300,000. Although predominantly agrarian, the country's economy was intricately organized. Agricultural technology was highly advanced by Asian standards, permitting a high degree of commercial farming and village manufacture. A unified currency and a national market system joined the country around the two large urban-commercial centers of Edo and Osaka-Kyoto. Paper currencies and centralized exchanges and credit facilities provided a sophisticated financial structure. At a time when China's population was precipitously outgrowing its economic production, Japan's had stabilized, despite abundant indications that the economy was growing.

But it was the political and social conditions of nineteenth-century Japan which more than anything else forecast Japan's rise as a modern state. The daimyo system of local administration held together by the powerful Tokugawa shogunate placed the Japanese people under a tight and all-pervasive system of government. In contrast to the Chinese system of provincial administration by civil service officials who operated a quota system of tax collection, the castle-based daimyo governed their territories firmly and directly through their bureaucracies of stipended retainers. Their capacities to tax the resources of their domains penetrated more deeply and effectively, and as a consequence many times the percentage of the land tax entered the granaries of the daimyo and shogun than went to the comparable authorities in China.

The holders of political power in Japan, the *bushi* or samurai class, were eminently successful in retaining the authority of government over the entire society. Tokugawa Japan was probably more fully 'governed' than any comparable society. The large size of the samurai class, some six to seven percent of the population, created an unusual density of administrative supervision. Moreover, the samurai, as stipended officials drawn together in castle towns under the supervision of the daimyo's senior officers, were held to a remarkably strict accountability both in terms of

Right: A nineteenth-century photograph of one of the many temples in the city of Kyoto. Edo, modern-day Tokyo, had been the center of real political power in Japan since 1180, but the imperial court remained at Kyoto until 1868.

Below left: A street scene in Kyoto. Contacts with the West were slow to change Japan's highly individual culture.

Below: A woodcut of samurai warriors fighting. The samurai were the dominant class in Japanese society until the reforms of the Meiji era after 1868, which removed their special privileges.

their official life and their economic opportunities. For all the obsolescence of the samurai's conception of themselves as a military aristocracy, they were remarkably free of corruption and venality. And despite the fact that the samurai were individually pledged to the shogun or the several daimyo, as a class they comprised a national elite, fiercely conscious of their special status and their mission to serve as the nation's leaders. Privileged to wear two swords as a badge of status, they enforced a stern regime.

The Tokugawa political structure, sometimes described as 'centralized feudalism,' had evolved out of the sixteenth-century movement toward unification among the independent daimyo territories. The fact that consolidation was not pushed to what would seem to be the logical conclusion, leading to the elimination of the daimyo and the creation of a unitary state under a monarchal authority, is often cited as proof of the feudalistic and even retrogressive nature of the Tokugawa regime. But Japan in 1615 was not yet politically capable of complete unification, at least without a further round of warfare. As it was the Tokugawa regime created a 'diversity-within-unity' which made for great internal vitality during two and a half centuries of domestic peace and seclusion from foreign contact. Certainly the Tokugawa shogun provided enough unity, so that Japan became in a very real sense a nation. Despite the patchwork of political divisions, numbering in the thousands, the country was institutionally, and to an extent ideologically, united.

The shogun's unifying capacity rested essentially upon his control of nearly a quarter of the nation's territory, including all its major cities and the great castles of Edo, Osaka, Kyoto and Odawara. Under him were some 250 daimyo and 5000 enfeoffed direct vassals or bannermen *(hatamoto)*. The bannermen were in fact far from independent, and their territories tended to be administered uniformly under shogunal authority. The daimyo, other than being pledged as vassals and dependent upon the shogun's legitimacy, were controlled by a unique hostage system. Called 'alternate attendance' *(sankin-kōtai),* it required each daimyo to reside alternately (usually every other year) in Edo and at his castle headquarters. While absent from Edo the daimyo left his family and certain key vassals behind in his residence there as hostages. While in Edo his chief retainers governed his territory in his name. The alternate attendance procedure not only made subversion by the daimyo highly unlikely, it converted Edo into a true center of government, a congregating place for the entire high military aristocracy. It also assured the uniformity of basic regulations and procedures throughout the country, since the daimyo were in constant face-to-face contact with the shogun's officers.

Edo, as an administrative capital city, shared, along with the other Japanese castle cities, a unique social configuration, in which nearly 50 percent of the inhabitants were samurai (daimyo, their retainers and household attendants). The main daimyo retinues, clustered around the shogun's palace, occupied the center of the city within the large encircling moat. Artisan and merchant quarters were set out beyond the aristocratic core at appropriate locations, particularly on the waterfront. Even the greatest of the Buddhist orders were obliged to locate their headquarters temples at the shogun's discretion on the fringes of the city. In a similar fashion, throughout the countryside daimyo castles marked the centers of local administrative and commercial activity and local religious affairs. The constant traffic between these castled centers and Edo, as daimyo and their retinues traveled in high state along the nation's highways, created the political pulse of the nation and served as a constant reminder to the populace of the presence and authority of the ruling class.

Beneath the castle-studded superstructure of samurai authority the rest of the country, merchants and peasants, were governed in self-regulating units of urban wards *(chō)* and villages *(mura),* each under internally appointed headmen. For the resident of ward or village, life was strictly controlled: change of domicile or even travel was subject to official approval, land could not be freely sold, sumptuary laws and methods of vicarious punishment bound each individual closely to the group. Perhaps the most impressive control mechanism was the annual practice of religious registration, whereby the head of each family was obliged to go to his temple of registration to sign an oath that neither he nor any mem-

ber of his family was a Christian. The registers were so strictly kept that for many areas of Japan they provide the most accurate census data available for the Tokugawa period.

While the military-administrative establishment pre-empted political power in Tokugawa Japan, it is essential to remember that a critical element in the shogun's position and the country's consciousness of itself as a nation was the continued existence of the emperor. As the ritual head of the Japanese people and the source of legitimacy for the shogun and daimyo, the Mikado, living in Kyoto among a few hundred court nobility, served as an important unifying symbol for the military aristocracy. The separation between the emperor, as national symbol, and the shogun, as ruling power, remained effective so long as the shogun was able to isolate and control the imperial court. This he was able to do until the 1850s, when his grip was weakened by the political confusion that resulted from the American demand that Japan abandon its seclusion policy.

Commodore Perry's arrival in the waters off Edo in 1853 was in defiance of the Tokugawa exclusion edict of 1641. To the Western world Japan's closing of its doors had been a flouting of the law of civilized nations. The outcome could only be to Japan's detriment: stagnation and growing ignorance of scientific progress. The truth is that the two centuries of peaceful isolation that the Tokugawa gave Japan saw the country make notable advances in a variety of fields. And of course Japan was never completely isolated from the outside world. Dutch and Chinese traders visited Nagasaki regularly, and the Japanese kept abreast of conditions in the outside world through these visitors and imported books. Above all, the Japanese never retreated into a state of mind that denied the existence or the importance of the rest of the world. Instructed in the shape of the globe and the distribution of the continents by the Portuguese, the samurai intellectual never forgot the fact of Japan's lonely location on the edge of the old world, though he may have come to overrate Japan's world importance.

Despite its withdrawal from free contact with the outside world and the limitations this placed upon the commercial economy, Japan continued to evolve during the Tokugawa period. The 'Great

Peace,' as it was called, saw a remarkable expansion of the agrarian base, an estimated doubling of cultivated land between 1615 and 1730. Population growth increased by only 50 percent during the same period, the result of a conscious effort on the part of the Japanese to stabilize their population by using such means of family control as late marriage, abortion and infanticide. The growth of cities has already been alluded to, but it was not just the three great cities of Kyoto, Osaka and Edo that accounted for Japan's high statistics of urbanization. There were in addition some 40 to 50 cities with populations between 10,000 and 100,000, mostly castle towns, and these were located in all parts of Japan. Well over 10 percent of the Japanese people were living an entirely urban way of life by the beginning of the nineteenth century, a higher percentage than that in China.

Urbanization led both to the conversion of the samurai class into a sedentary officialdom and to the emergence of an entirely new social class, an urban bourgeoisie called chōnin by the Japanese. The commercial quarters of the new Japanese cities flourished as the samurai came to depend upon merchants to supply their needs and to bridge the gap between town and village. The resultant growth of the commercial sectors of the Tokugawa cities created something of a social anomaly. The samurai, having only recently moved out of the villages from which they still drew their incomes, continued to hold to an agrarian conception of the economy. Taxes continued to be collected chiefly in bales of rice by the daimyo, who distributed the grain as stipends to their vassals. This situation had economic as well as social consequences. The fact that the grain tax, some 40 or 50 percent of the annual agricultural product, was turned over directly to the samurai class gave the samurai a continuing hold over the nation's agricultural surplus. The need, however, to convert much of the rice into cash for the purchase of daily necessities meant that merchants were indispensable middlemen to the samurai. Yet economic theory, which favored agriculture, placed the merchants at the bottom of the four-class scale. The chōnin thus came to occupy a position of economic importance far beyond their social status or political influence.

Of course the chōnin were not simply a service class for the samurai. The great cities gave rise to

large chōnin communities – over 500,000 in Edo, close to 300,000 in Osaka and Kyoto, over 50,000 in Nagasaki and Sakai and generally close to 50 percent of the total urban population in any of the castle towns. Chōnin constituted a sizable sector of Japanese society, large enough to provide its own economic market stimulus and to create its own style of life and culture. Although social theory and Tokugawa law kept the chōnin separate from the samurai and precluded mobility into the ruling class, it assured the retention of commercial wealth within the commercial sector and reinforced the identity of the chōnin.

During the Tokugawa period the chōnin evolved an entirely new and vigorous style of life and values. The bourgeois communities of the great cities had by the end of the seventeenth century created a culture that contrasted sharply with that of the samurai. The popular culture of the Tokugawa cities developed around the theaters and restaurants where the affluent chōnin looked for entertainment with geisha companionship. This was the world of ukiyo (the floating world) which produced the bawdy tales of Saikaku, the kabuki plays of love and suicide by Chikamatsu and the wood-block prints of Utamaro and Hokusai. Increasingly it was the chōnin's way of life that defined city life. The samurai, clustered in segregated gentility behind the moats and walls of their daimyo overlords, seemed to be living ever more in the past, dedicated to the noble arts and military skills which had been their tradition since the Ashikaga period. Even the arts of warfare atrophied during the Tokugawa Great Peace. Firearms remained in the same state they had been in the sixteenth century, while swordsmanship and archery were looked to chiefly as techniques for developing physical fitness and mental discipline.

While the samurai were in general dedicated to maintaining the existing political system, the class as a whole also underwent significant changes, especially during the eighteenth century. It was then that they settled down in their castle towns and adapted to the life of administrative officials. With this change in function and life style came a new emphasis on education. The military aristocracy, which had previously depended upon the Buddhist priesthood to serve as its literate arm, now themselves became the scholarly and intellectual leaders of the country.

Schools were established under shogunal and daimyo patronage, and private academies sprang up in the major cities. By the eighteenth century the samurai was a literate man. Education was mainly Confucian in content, and there was thus a deep penetration of Confucian ideas of government and class ethics into the minds of Japan's political elite. Confucianism was used to rationalize the Tokugawa political and social order and to justify the samurai's elite status, but it also urged upon the samurai the ideas that he must live as exemplar to the people and that governors had a responsibility to maintain order and assure the welfare of the people.

Confucian-trained samurai, schooled in the rhetoric of political-economics, were fiercely aware of the problems which beset Japan in the late eighteenth century: the growth of a commercial economy, the worsening economic position of the samurai and farmer, the stagnation of government and the lowering of samurai morale. Conservatives might insist upon maintaining the traditional system through controls on consumption, sumptuary laws and promotion of agriculture, but these were met by pragmatists who advocated that commerce and manufacturing be

encouraged and that the government seek to add to its income through mercantilist techniques. A small but vigorous group of students of Western science and medicine pressed for new technologies and even began to spread the idea that Japan should abandon isolation. Honda Toshiaki, for instance, wrote of his vision of a Japan which would move on to the continent, establishing on Kamchatka the center of a world empire.

The Confucian-based revival of scholarship encouraged Japanese to probe the sources of their own history. By the end of the eighteenth century the shogun had been petitioned to establish a school of 'national learning,' and Motoori Norinaga had begun the study of Japan's earliest history, the heavily mythological *Kojiki*. Out of this emerged a revival of interest in Shinto as Japan's true religion. With Hirata Atsutane (1766-1843) came the militantly anti-foreign claims that Japan was 'the land of the gods' and of the 'ageless imperial line,' superior in fact to China, to say nothing of the barbarian states of the West. The beginnings of a self-conscious nationalism thus both rejected Japan's historical dependence on China and stood ready to face down the threatened encroachment of the Western powers.

The crises of late Tokugawa Japan

By the decades of the 1830s and 1840s Japan faced the double pressures of domestic economic crises and foreign encroachment. National disasters had plagued the country in the early nineteenth century. Crop failures were widespread in 1824 and 1832 and severe famines struck rural areas in 1833 and 1836. By the 1830s the countryside was restive and displaced peasants were crowding the cities in search of employment. The poor, driven to desperation, resorted to violence both in the villages and the cities, attacking rice merchants and seeking redress from taxation. In 1837 Oshio Heihachino, a minor Tokugawa official, led an attack upon the city administration of Osaka on behalf of the city poor. The uprising was put down, but a sense of crisis now permeated Tokugawa officialdom. Tokugawa Nariaki, head of one of the collateral branches of the Tokugawa house, called for major reforms which would put the interests of the nation (as embodied in the emperor) ahead of that of the shogunate. Thus in a moment

of crisis the name of the emperor had been raised in its transcendental sense. A major effort at shogunal reform was undertaken in 1841, but without effect. The domestic problems of the Tempō era, as it was called, went unresolved, and the sense of crisis remained.

Meanwhile another crisis was brewing. Japan's leaders from the end of the eighteenth century had lived with the uneasy knowledge that the country was facing a new foreign menace. Since 1792 it was known that the Russians were approaching Japan down the Kuril chain. In 1804 Count Rezanov of the Russian American Trading Company had tried to break the trade monopoly at Nagasaki and had been rejected. The Japanese well knew that these intruders represented a new problem, an incipient wave of encroachment from Europe. In 1808 a British ship, the *Phaeton*, entered Nagasaki harbor under a Dutch flag and obtained supplies under threat of bombardment. Although the *Phaeton* was eventually driven off, the daimyo who served as Magistrate of Nagasaki felt obliged to commit ritual suicide.

By the 1820s British whaling ships were active in the North Pacific. Their occasional efforts to secure supplies from the Japanese gave rise to a new series of alarms. An order in 1825 to drive away all foreign vessels was soon rescinded when the danger of precipitating dangerous incidents was brought home to the shogun's officials. By the 1840s the Tokugawa leadership realized that a major foreign crisis was in the making. Knowledge acquired from the Dutch at Nagasaki kept the Japanese abreast of Western activities in China. News of the Opium War and the opening of Chinese ports to Western trade sent a tremor through Edo officialdom. Already a badly confused shogunate was debating the alternatives between holding to the time-honored seclusion policy and of opening the country to outside contact and trade. Majority opinion still favored seclusion, but the important fact was that the debate was going on.

Even before the issue of seclusion was fully forced by Western gunboats, the foreign issue had been picked up by many samurai intellectuals. The issue was more than simply one of deciding on whether to open the country, for it raised the more perplexing question of national identity. The Japanese well understood, as no other Asian

Above left: The Dutch trading settlement at Nagasaki in the early eighteenth century. Foreign traders were restricted to an island in this southern port, so they would not contaminate Japanese society.

Above: One of the refined works of Hokusai (1760-1849), an artist belonging to the sophisticated culture of Japan's great cities.

Right: A contemporary Japanese view of the country's victorious war against China in 1894-95.

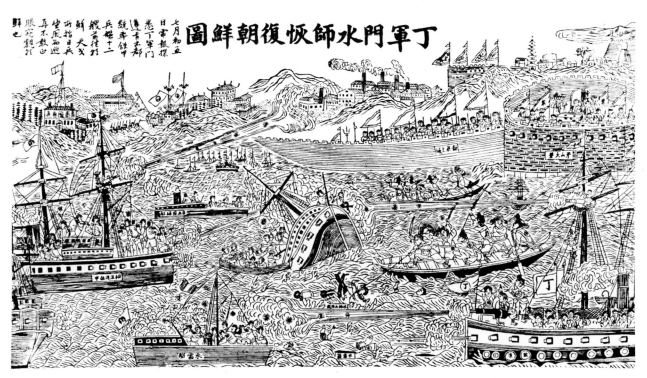

people yet did, that the Westerners at their doors obliged them to rethink the world view under which they had lived for centuries.

The arrival of Perry's ships in 1853 shook the country. The black ships of the American squadron exemplified the seemingly irresistible power of the Western nations. Should Japan resist anyway? The instinctive inclination of the samurai to put his hand to his sword is revealed in the memorial sent by Tokugawa Nariaki to the shogun at the time of Perry's arrival:

When we consider the respective advantages and disadvantages of war and peace, we find that if we put our trust in war the whole country's morale will be increased, and even if we sustain an initial defeat we will in the end expel the foreigner; while if we put our trust in peace, even though things may seem tranquil for a time, the morale of the country will be greatly lowered, and we will come in the end to complete collapse. This has been amply demonstrated in the history of China.

But despite Nariaki's urging of resistance the shogunate found it impossible to reject the American demands for a treaty of amity. Within a decade Japan had been opened to the West, and within two decades the foreign problem had fused with domestic political action to pull down the shogunate and to force revolutionary changes upon the entire country. The chain of events begun in 1853 by Perry had by 1868 led to the Meiji Restoration.

It is instructive to place the timetable of Japan's reaction to the Western impact alongside that of China's, for by 1895 Japan was to have fought a successful war against China. In China the opening of treaty ports to Western trade had been forced by a humiliating military defeat by the British in the Opium War of 1841-42. This was followed between 1858 and 1860 by a second round of Western military action, largely the work of the British and French, which not only extended the rights of Westerners to free access to China but permitted the actual holding of Chinese territory. Yet the Chinese reaction to these Western inroads had been slow, necessarily so because of China's great size and the debilitating effects of internal rebellion. Japan had already defeated China in a

war before the first efforts were made by the Manchu government towards reform in 1902, and these had failed. Revolution leading to the establishment of a Republic came in 1911, but it, too, did not last. So China's first modern government, one able to begin the process of recapturing China's national rights surrendered to the Western powers under the 'unequal treaties' and the later concessions, did not come until 1925-27.

In Japan's case the initial commercial treaties were agreed to peacefully in 1858. There was no war between Japan and the Western powers, and the pressure subsequently applied by the West was relatively minor: a British bombardment in 1863 of the castle town of Kagoshima in retaliation for the death of an Englishman the previous year, an attack in 1864 on the shore batteries of the Chōshū domain to clear the Shimonoseki Straits and the unauthorized penetration in 1865 by a combined fleet into Hyōgo Bay adjacent to the imperial city of Kyoto. By 1865 the Western powers had received both shogunal approval and imperial ratification of agreements which opened treaty ports and guaranteed protection of foreign life and property on Japanese soil. Japan gave up no territory and suffered no inroads of foreign officials into its tariff administration. Yet the 'unequal treaties' were considered a national shame, and by 1873 the Japanese had begun to negotiate for the repeal of their unequal features. By 1899 they had extricated themselves from the provisions of extraterritoriality and were on their way to securing tariff autonomy. By 1902 Japan had secured an alliance on a basis of equality with Britain. Military victory over Russia in 1905 marked Japan's full emergence as a modern nation in the eyes of the Western powers.

The Meiji Restoration

It was Japan's internal transformation after 1853 that created the conditions which made the country's national effort against the West possible. The Meiji Restoration of 1868 marked a dramatic turning point in Japan's evolution as a nation. Since that event historians have debated the true significance of what happened in the

years between 1854 and 1873. Was the Meiji Restoration indeed Japan's 'modern revolution'? Did Japan in fact undergo a revolution similar to those of France or Russia?

In contrast to the European revolutions that of Japan was marked by much less social antagonism and ideological conflict. There were no mobs in the streets of Edo or Kyoto, no rolling of heads. The dominant force in these years was provided by the specter of an external menace. In a domestic situation charged with fear of Western encroachment and heavy with a sense of inadequacy in the old regime the demand for change came not from a revolutionary leadership drawn from disaffected lower classes but from within the samurai class itself. Japan's modern revolution was in this sense an aristocratic revolution, one in which elements of the publicly dominant class led in affecting political and social transformations which in the end were to undo the old regime.

Perry's arrival in 1853 precipitated a struggle within the shogunate over control of policy at the same time that it forced the shogunate to reassert its dormant authority in national political affairs. In 1853 the Chief Councilor in Edo, Abe Masahiro, had placed the foreign question before the collective daimyo in hopes of securing a consensus behind which the shogunate could deal confidently with Perry. Abe's was a historic move. In a moment of national crisis the shogunate had for the first time solicited the opinion of the daimyo, thereby making them participants in national politics. For the first time a 'national opinion' was created. Abe believed that the shogun had no alternative but to negotiate with the Americans. To his chagrin, all but two daimyo called for rejection of the foreigners; eight in fact echoed Tokugawa Nariaki's call for military action. Thus, when in 1854 the shogunate did in fact acquiesce in the Treaty of Kanagawa, the country experienced a deep loss of confidence in the Tokugawa leadership. In 1858 the shogunate attempted to obtain what was expected to be routine imperial approval of a commercial treaty with America, but opponents of the treaty (notably Tokugawa

army,' marched on Edo, which Keiki surrendered, rather than risk destruction of the city. Tokugawa territories were now confiscated by the newly proclaimed imperial government. Although a few pro-Tokugawa domains offered diehard resistance they were soon put down. By November 1868 Edo had been renamed Tokyo, the young emperor had been moved into the shogun's former palace and the new era name Meiji (Enlightened Rule) had been adopted.

Japan's modern revolution

While the new government looked on the surface like the conservative daimyo coalition which had been tried in the last days of the shogunate, in fact it masked revolutionary objectives which were shortly to reveal themselves. The real leadership of the Restoration movement had been young members of the anti-Tokugawa daimyo bureaucracies who had worked themselves into subordinate positions from which they could manipulate the military forces and the political policies of their domains. In the years following the Restoration these men moved out into the open, gradually assuming positions of authority and becoming by the mid 1870s a recognizable political oligarchy. The ultimate 'meaning' of the Meiji Restoration must be looked for in the motives of these men.

In all they numbered perhaps a hundred. The majority came from the great traditionally anti-Tokugawa domains of southwest Japan, particularly Satsuma and Chōshū. As a group they were distinguished by their youth, having an average age of under 30 in 1868. Most were samurai of low rank, men who had felt the dead weight of Tokugawa precedent, had chafed under the restraints placed upon their free advancement and had opposed the conservatism of their administrative superiors. But while they had fretted over the inadequacy of the system, most had managed by sheer personal capacity to work into positions of some authority within their domains. For most, the domains had served as arenas which trained them as future leaders of the nation in political and military affairs. Between 1853 and 1868 they had come into the service of their daimyo as military specialists (Saigo and Itagaki), interpreters (Ito and Okuma), advisers (Kido) and liaison officers (Okubo and Siago). Most of the young leaders had at one time been violently anti-foreign (Ito had participated in an attack on the British legation in 1863), but all had changed their position and now acknowledged that Japan must learn from the West. Several, in fact, had gone abroad (Ito and Inoue to England, others to Shanghai; the shogunate had already sent several missions overseas to America and France). Finally, these men were dedicated political activists: many had risked their lives as agitators, and the most extreme had not lived through to 1868.

Any attempts we may make to see in the Meiji Restoration either hidden elements of a bourgeois revolution (samurai vicariously behaving as bourgeoisie) or of a conservative counter-revolution (samurai manning an absolutist central government to prevent a peasant-proletarian take over) would probably be beside the point. The composite profile of the Meiji leaders shows men whose primary concerns were for national unity and social reform in the face of external threat. Fear of national weakness and shame over their country's material backwardness worked to buttress personal ambition for political power. Their energies were directed toward the creation of a strong central government and then toward political and social reform. In the years after 1868 the revolutionary nature of this thinking was revealed.

Left: Admiral Tojo's defeat of the Russian fleet at the battle of the Straits of Tsushima in May 1905 revealed to a startled world the emergence of Japan as a significant modern military power. The Russo-Japanese war ended with the first Asian victory over a European power since the seventeenth century.

Right: Mutsuhito, better known as the Emperor Meiji, ruling from 1867 to 1912, presided over the symbolic restoration of imperial power as the focus of a new nationalist Japan. Notice the newly adopted Western style of official dress.

Nariaki) pressured the court into rejecting it. The shogunate countered by naming Ii Naosuke as Great Councilor, giving to him the task of purging the shogunate of its defectors and of forcing through the commercial treaty. Ii was assassinated in 1860.

With Ii's death the shogun's monopoly of political power was broken. Now members of the imperial court in Kyoto, several of the daimyo and even some lesser retainers began to maneuver for influence over policy. The shogunate, recognizing its loss of control, sought to create a coalition government that would be placed symbolically under the emperor and in which certain daimyo would be given representation. This renewed emphasis on the emperor, together with the abolition of the alternate attendance system in 1862, suddenly moved the center of political action to Kyoto. The coalition plan was doomed to failure. The great lords could not agree among themselves, nor would they any longer submit to the shogun's authority. A shogunal military expedition sent to chastise the insubordinate domain of Chōshū in 1864 was only partially successful, and a second expedition sent in 1866 actually ended in failure. Clearly the shogunate had lost the respect of the country.

By 1865 a new element had been introduced into the political struggle. As a result of the foreign threat the daimyo domains had become engaged in new military preparations. The demand for vigorous new military leadership drew new talent into the active ranks of the daimyo service. Furthermore, as a result of the increased communication between the daimyo domains and the politicization of the domain councils, a new class of young officials came to the

fore as political advisors and liaison officers. Many of these young officers eventually left domain service, becoming freelance political extremists impatiently working for the expulsion of foreigners, the abolition of the shogunate and the return of the emperor to the center of the Japanese political stage. Most, however, stayed within the service of their daimyo, where they worked to convert their domains to an anti-Tokugawa policy. By 1865 young anti-shogunate radicals were active not only in the streets of Edo and Kyoto but had taken over the policy initiative in a number of important domains that had traditionally been disposed against the shogunate. It was the alliance between the domains of Satsuma and Chōshū, later joined by Tosa and Hizen, that formed the coalition which ultimately provided the power base from which the shogunate was destroyed.

In 1867 Tokugawa Keiki, son of Nariaki, succeeded to the office of shogun. Predisposed to political reform in the interest of national unity, he made a last effort to create a coalition government of daimyo under the emperor, and he himself resigned the post of shogun in anticipation of reappointment as prime minister. The samurai agents of Satsuma and Chōshū refused to accept this solution. On 3 January 1868, using the troops of their domains and acting through friendly courtiers, they seized the imperial palace and issued a revolutionary Restoration Edict, by which political power was ostensibly returned to the emperor. Keiki refused to oppose the new dispensation. Though some of his retainers resisted and engaged the opposition in arms near Kyoto, they were defeated. The forces of Satsuma, Chōshū and Tosa, now organized into an 'imperial

Left: There was some armed resistance from supporters of the Tokugawa Shogunate in 1868 when their opponents seized the imperial palace at Kyoto and issued the Restoration Edict – the basis for the modernization of Japan.

Right: The Satsuma rebellion in 1877 was the last attempt by the samurai to resist the wind of change. Japan's new conscript army routed the old warrior class.

Below: A Japanese portrait of Commander Perry, the American naval officer whose expedition to Japan in 1853-54 forcibly opened the country to foreign trade.

The Meiji Restoration, then, was primarily a power play to abolish the shogunate and create a more unified political order. Japan was fortunate in its moment of crisis to have an alternative symbol of national unity available in the person of the emperor. The fact that the emperor had been pushed 'above politics' during the long centuries of shogunal rule became critical in the late years of the Tokugawa period. The emperor as a historical symbol exalted by the Shinto revivalists, as the ultimate symbol of political legitimacy and as the embodiment of all that was Japanese in the face of foreign encroachment, could be picked up by the political activists to symbolize their attack upon the Tokugawa regime. Revolutionary objectives could be masked behind protestation of the ultimate patriotism.

In early 1868 the new central authority was still a rather precarious coalition of daimyo and court interests. The activist leaders remained in subordinate positions. But it was also clear that the political initiatives lay with them, and it was equally clear that Japan would be propelled in a new direction. The new slogan of the day was now the nationalistic *fukoku-kyohei* (Rich country! Strong arms!). A policy statement issued in the name of the emperor in April of 1868 (the so-called Charter Oath) made clear the immediate priorities: deliberative assemblies shall be widely established and all matters decided by public discussion; all classes, high and low, shall unite in vigorously carrying out the administration of affairs of state; the common people, no less than the civil and military officials, shall each be allowed to pursue his own calling so that there may be no discontent; evil customs of the past shall be broken off and everything based upon the just laws of Nature; knowledge shall be sought throughout the world so as to strengthen the foundations of imperial rule.

Political unification

The first measures of the Meiji leaders were directed toward political unification. Fortunately, the country had not broken apart with the collapse of the shogunate, and for this the daimyo domains which survived intact were largely responsible. The confiscated Tokugawa lands provided the new government with a territorial base, while the troops contributed by Satsuma, Chōshū and Tosa were welded into an imperial army. In 1869, as a step toward administrative uniformity, the daimyo were induced to return their domain titles to the emperor but to continue to administer their territories (now called *han*) as governors. In 1871 the new government felt strong enough to recall the daimyo to Tokyo, abolish the *han* and institute a national system of prefectures. In all about 300 *han* were reduced to 72 prefectures and three municipalities. New governors, many of them men of Satsuma and Chōshū, were sent out from Tokyo to administer the new divisions. For the most part the daimyo moved out of politics as a pensioned aristocracy. Rule by a military elite had come to an end.

With the newly gained central authority, the new leaders after 1871 began a series of sweeping institutional changes. Legal distinctions between classes were abolished. Restrictions on occupation, residence and marriage were lifted. Commoners were given the privilege of having family names, and the purchase and sale of agricultural land became legal. A system of universal elementary education was adopted in 1872, and in 1873 a program of universal military conscription was introduced. At the same time a full-scale reform of the old land system was undertaken. Certificates of ownership were given to cultivators. A new standard tax in money calculated at three percent of the assessed value of the land was set as the land tax. This, made payable to the central (not

local) government, became the basis of government finances.

All these measures had a tremendous leveling effect upon the old society. While a new nobility was eventually created on the European model to take care of the ex-daimyo and members of the court aristocracy, the samurai as a class was essentially stripped of its special functions and privileges. Not having landed property of its own, the samurai class entered the new era without tangible assets, and with the abolition of the domains and the establishment of a conscript army most of them were without occupation. The Japanese feudal aristocracy, numbering some two million, were ten times more numerous than the French aristocracy at the time of the French Revolution. Yet now they were being stripped of their status by leaders in government who themselves had come from the samurai class.

Mindful of the problems the samurai faced, the new government leaders adopted a number of measures to assist them. Pensions, considerably scaled down from the old stipends, were allotted in 1871. Various government-supported enterprises and land projects were also made available. But in 1875, when the burden of maintaining the pensions became too much for the government, these were converted to interest-bearing government bonds. The resultant income was but a fraction of the former stipends, and from this point on the samurai class was forced to make its own way in a new environment. Some were fortunate enough to gain employment in government or the armed services on their own ability. Others entered business or industry or the various professions, exploiting their educational advantage. The vast majority, however, suffered extreme economic hardship, many ending up as members of the urban and rural proletariat. Yet for the nation as a whole the breakup of the samurai class gave Japanese society a vitality that was to energize the early Meiji state.

Not all the samurai relinquished their privileges without a struggle, nor were all of the Meiji leaders united on the policy that liquidated the samurai class. A failure of the majority of leaders to sanction a military operation against Korea in 1873 and the subsequent commutation of pensions in 1875 gave rise to vigorous opposition movements and culminated in a series of samurai revolts. The last and greatest of these was the revolt in Satsuma in 1877 led by Saigo Takamori,

one of the heroes of the Restoration. Saigo had left the government in 1873 and subsequently found himself at the head of some 30,000 disgruntled ex-samurai. In six months of difficult and bloody fighting the Meiji government's new conscript army put down what proved to be the last stand of the samurai class. Saigo's death marked the end of militant samurai resistance to the new regime. Any opposition that remained was to be channeled into movements of a strictly political nature.

With the suppression of the Satsuma rebellion the new Meiji government fully established its power and its reform policies. Yet the mechanism of government was still to be satisfactorily worked out. Even before the Restoration it had been widely believed in Japan that one of the main secrets of the power of Western states had been their constitutional structure. But early attempts at constitution writing by the Meiji leaders had been abandoned in favor of a system of direct personal rule. After 1873, however, the issue of constitutional government became critical. On the one hand, certain of the opposition leaders who, like Saigo, had pulled out of the government in 1873 had begun to organize political pressure groups in favor of representative institutions. On the other hand, the government leaders realized that Japan would have to adopt a constitution and other modern laws if it was to gain sufficient respect from the Western powers to induce them to contemplate revision of the 'unequal treaties.'

The debate over government structure was carried on for well over a decade and involved an extensive dialogue both among government leaders and between them and an articulate opposition. The period of the 1870s and 1880s in Japan was charged with new political ideas, many of them derived from the West, and with a sharp awareness of the realities of power in politics among those in government and out of it. Although the samurai had lacked a history of free political activity, in the years after the Restoration they quickly mastered the techniques of political agitation, providing ideological and organizational leadership to a variety of special interests. The education of the Japanese people toward greater political participation was largely the work of ex-samurai pamphleteers such as Ueki Emori or Fukuzawa Yukichi, who developed a new vocabulary of political action from their readings

in the writings of Mill, Montesquieu and Rousseau. Ideas of popular rights and of the political dignity of man contrasted sharply with the existing Confucian-based political culture. Fukuzawa's descriptions of Western political conditions and social concepts of equality urged the Japanese to purge themselves of feudal values.

The combination of Western theories about representative government and real grievances which came to a head during the 1870s brought into being the first modern political organizations in Japan, the forerunners of Japan's later party system. Itagaki, the Tosa leader who had left the government in 1873, organized in 1875 a national party known as the Patriotic Society, and this by 1881 had become the Liberal Party (jiyūtō). Taking the leadership in what was known as the 'liberty and popular rights' (jiyuminken) movement, it called for the establishment of representative government, a reduction in taxes and above all the destruction of the monopoly of power held by the Satsuma and Chōshū factions in the bureaucracy. The activities of men like Itagaki and his followers were sufficiently vigorous to force the Meiji government into an early decision on the adoption of a constitution.

The Meiji government had in fact committed itself to the idea of a constitution embodying provisions for representation even before Itagaki's agitation. That the Meiji leaders fully understood the delicacy of the political issues they faced is revealed in the care with which they went about the task of designing a constitution. In 1879 the major government leaders were asked to state their opinions on the nature of the constitution. All but one responded with conservative views which emphasized the authority of the emperor and envisioned a system of government in which ministers were responsible to the emperor, not to a parliament. The one exception was Okuma. His draft called for a British style of government by party cabinets. His views proved an embarrassment to the rest of the leadership, and he was ousted from government in 1881. Thrown into the role of the political opposition, he shortly organized a political party of his own, the Reform Party (Kaishinto).

After Okuma's ouster the oligarchy decided upon a gradualist approach to the constitutional issue. An imperial statement was made promising a constitution by 1890, and Ito was given the task of drafting it. Already there was a tendency to favor the Prussian model. Ito traveled to Europe in 1882-83, returning with German advisers. In 1884 a European-style peerage was created in anticipation of an upper house in the Diet (Parliament). A cabinet responsible to the emperor was appointed in 1885, and a Privy Council was created in 1888 for the purpose of approving and safeguarding the constitution.

The constitution was approved and promulgated by the emperor in 1889. A heavily authoritarian document, it began by declaring the emperor 'sacred and inviolable' and the literal embodiment of the state. It carried on the cabinet system then in operation and established an independent military command responsible directly to the emperor as Commander-in-Chief. Local administration was controlled directly by the central government through a Home Ministry. The Diet, which proved to be the main innovation, was composed of a House of Peers together with a Lower House with only limited powers of initiative.

While the Meiji Constitution clearly safeguarded the interests of an imperial government, it was in some ways a 'modern' document, for it definitely established rule by law in Japan and provided opportunities for the political growth of the Japanese people. The Diet did in fact make room for political party participation, and eventually, in the 1920s, a modified form of party government was achieved. Private property was made inviolate, and personal freedoms were guaranteed by law. With the promulgation of the constitution, an electorate, at first limited by property qualifications to about 500,000, was created, and elections were held for the convening of the first Diet in 1890.

Westernization and nationalism

The manner in which Japan resolved its problem of political restructuring after the Restoration exemplifies the balance that the Japanese of the Meiji period were able to maintain between their own traditional institutions and the new influences which rushed in upon them from the outside. Yet there were several swings of the pendulum before the balance was achieved. No other Asian people were to be plunged so rapidly and dramatically into confrontation with Western civilization as were the Japanese in the first decades after the Restoration. For once the Japanese had convinced themselves of the superiority of Western technologies and institutions they literally went all-out to master the secrets of Western success.

Japanese emulation of the West was aroused early. Partially in the spirit of 'knowing the enemy,' partially in real admiration, the Japanese had sent diplomatic and fact-finding missions abroad once the seclusion policy had been abandoned. A shogunal mission had toured the United States in 1860, making the trip across the Pacific in a ship with a Japanese crew. Another mission visited France in 1862-63. Satsuma and Chōshū had both sent agents abroad before 1868. After the Restoration a group of 40 major government leaders led by Prince Iwakura traveled through America and Europe in 1872-73. Men such as Iwakura, Ito, Okubo and Kido took the risk of leaving positions of political influence to go abroad. They came back convinced of the necessity to work for Japan's economic and institutional modernization and equally convinced that Japan had the capacity to catch up with the West.

After the Iwakura mission the government systematically began to hire foreign advisers. German experts were used to organize new universities and medical schools; American advisers laid the basis of elementary education, the national postal service and a new banking system. The American adviser Erasmus Smith assisted the Japanese in the techniques of diplomatic negotiation. British advisers were used in railroad development, telegraph and public works. French jurists assisted in adapting the French legal codes for use in Japan. All told it is estimated that some 3000 foreign advisers were hired by the government between 1858 and 1890. But it was characteristic of Japan's jealous concern over its own identity that all such advisers were placed within Japanese administrative systems and under Japanese supervisors, and their services were generally terminated as soon as it was felt that the Japanese could manage on their own.

Western influence was, of course, brought to bear on the Japanese through more than official channels. The treaty ports, particularly Yokohama and Kobe, became early centers of Western influence. There Western merchants, missionaries and technicians clustered at first into segregated foreign communities. Increasingly, though, missionaries and educators began to move freely into the interior of Japan, taking with them knowledge about the life and values of the Western

world. Meanwhile, private Japanese by the hundreds traveled abroad for observation and schooling. The spirit of reform and the desire to emulate the West instilled in the Japanese people by these contacts gave rise to a period of frenetic activity throughout Japan. The new slogan of the day was 'civilization and progress' (bummei-kaika), and one of its most prominent proponents, Fukuzawa Yukichi, ex-samurai founder of Keio University, spent his early life preaching to his contemporaries the benefits of individualism, progress and science. These were days when Samuel Smiles' Self Help and Character became immensely popular, and Fukuzawa could write:

If one can say that nature has been conquered by the human intellect, her provinces penetrated, the very secrets of creation discovered, and that nature has been harnessed, then there is nothing in the world which can withstand man's courage and intellect . . . If we put forth all our energies there will be nothing in the world that can block the freedom of our spirit.

The call for Japanese to step out of their historical tradition, to, in the words of the Charter Oath, break off 'evil customs of the past,' placed upon them a heavy problem of ideological reorientation. To become fully civilized did the Japanese have to abandon their style of life and live like Europeans, abandon their language in favor of English or French? For many the crucial issue became that of Christianity. The translator of Smiles had claimed in 1872 that Western institutions and technology without Christianity were like a hollow shell without a soul. Yet Christianity raised for the Japanese ultimate questions of historical identity, since it required of its Japanese converts rejection of the Shinto kami and the sacred status of the emperor.

Japanese intellectuals were to vacillate between denial of their own tradition and rejection of Western values. Later, during the 1930s, the Japanese were to generate an ultranational ideology that tried to convince the Japanese that their spiritual values were superior to those of the West. The Meiji intellectual found such extremism uncongenial, but he tended increasingly to find ways of easing the implications of Christianity. Some took comfort in the thought that Japanese spirituality could be combined with Western science. Others, such as Ebina Danjo, found ways of amalgamating Shinto and Christianity. Still others clung to a belief in progress that rejected all religion as unscientific. By the 1880s, as Japan was seriously confronting a choice in its political structure, the pendulum was beginning to swing away from the early uncritical admiration of Christianity and liberal political values. A cautious return to traditional social values, together with the welcome discovery of the ideas of social Darwinism and German statism, provided the final amalgam that expressed itself in the Meiji Constitution.

The ideological resolution of the problem of Japan's consciousness of itself and its place in history is best revealed in the philosophy of education that was adopted during these years. The universal primary education system adopted in 1872 was at first organized under American influence. In 1879 a decentralization of education offering large areas of local autonomy was attempted, but it ended in failure. In 1886 the Minister of Education, Mori Arinori, worked out the assimilation of the educational system into state policy, introducing courses in morals instruction. To Mori education was a tool for

Left: Construction of the first railroad in Japan started in 1872. Within 30 years, over 4000 miles of track had been laid.

Above right: A European merchant's house in Yokohama, 1870. Western businessmen were swift to exploit the potential of a new market for their goods.

Below right: The imperial court is gathered to hear the promulgation of the Meiji constitution of 1889. Although largely based on Western models, the constitution enshrined the sacred power of the emperor.

strengthening the nation in its competitive struggle within the hierarchy of nations. To him:

Everything in life is a state of war. International relations is a war of industry, commerce and knowledge. If you are ambitious young men of Japan you should help move Japan from a third class nation to a second, from a second to first and to the top of the world.

Recognition of the importance of education as a means of creating intelligent and patriotic subjects of the emperor led in 1890 to the drafting of the Imperial Rescript on Education, primarily by Confucian and Shinto ideologues in the Imperial Household Ministry. This document, a remarkable blend of modern concepts of citizenship and traditional Shinto and Confucian values, was to become the final ingredient in a system of state ideology that sought to knit the Japanese into a disciplined national force.

Economic growth

Perhaps in no area of endeavor did the Japanese show themselves more proficient and energetic than in developing the economic foundations for the strong state they envisaged. The fact that Japan between the 1880s and 1960s experienced the most rapid rate of economic growth of any country in the world and that Japan by the 1970s had outdistanced Germany, Britain and France in economic production makes this aspect of its modern revolution a phenomenon of world significance. In 1868 Japan faced all the problems of a typical underdeveloped economy, lacking capital, raw materials, substantial markets and an industrial plant. At a time when imperialist competition made the Western powers anything but benevolent in their policies toward the Asian states (as indicated by the tariff controls imposed on Japan by the commercial treaties) Japan nonetheless managed to establish its economic independence and its own domestic financial health, and then go on to compete on its own with the Western commercial states.

We must begin with the fact that Japan already had in 1858, when foreign trade was renewed, a relatively advanced economic foundation in terms of agricultural production and savings habits. Despite the technological backwardness of the manufacturing sector the institutions of commercial organization were relatively well developed.

Even before the Restoration the shogunate had taken steps to overcome a near ruinous specie drain, and new sources of export materials were consciously being developed to save Japan's adverse balance of trade.

The new Meiji government early on paid special attention to the problems of creating an environment favorable to economic growth. Financial confidence in the government was assured when the new government assumed the debts of the old regime and went on to create a modern fiscal structure. Social legislation that provided freedom of occupation, civil protection and new concepts of contract and commercial incorporation provided new incentives to the economic entrepreneur. The bonds paid to daimyo and samurai put into the financial-system capital with which to found banks and new businesses. Land reform put agriculture on a more economic basis, permitting the sale of land and funneling land taxes into the central treasury. Important, too, was the change in attitude that made business and industry respectable occupations. Entrepreneurs emerging out of the samurai class could now justly claim that they were working for the national interest while accumulating private wealth.

These changes made for a rapid rearrangement and mobilization of Japan's human resources. Samurai became active in business and industry, farmers became landowners or developed local industries and merchants moved into new fields of foreign trade. During the first 20 years of the Meiji period Japan's economy was constantly on the defensive against foreign economies and had to fight to maintain a precarious domestic balance, yet it survived, despite the heavy expenses incurred in suppressing the Satsuma rebellion and in commuting the samurai stipends. Meanwhile, the government, concentrating on strategic industries and public utilities, began the process of heavy industrialization. Arsenals and ship-building facilities were given government priority, and shipping lines using Western-purchased vessels were developed with government subsidy. The government's sensitivity to its national interests caused it to buy out the interests of the American Pacific Steamship Company in 1876, the only foreign company operating in Japan's domestic waters. The first railroad was begun in 1872. A national postal service was started in 1871, and the beginnings of a telegraph system in 1869.

Economists are now agreed that a critical turn toward modern economic development took place between 1881 and 1886. During these years Matsukata Masayoshi, the finance minister, adopted a drastic deflationary policy. The banking system was reorganized, and government paper currency was reduced in volume. The policy proved a hardship to many small entrepreneurs and the ex-samurai class as a whole, but it saved the government from fiscal collapse. Those early entrepreneurs who managed to weather the deflation went on to become the great *zaibatsu* industrialists of the next decades.

The acceleration of growth that occurred in the following 20 years was astonishing. It was then that Japan's two prime capital producing industries, cotton spinning and silk production, got underway. Cotton spinning, using new mechanical equipment imported from the West, proved a most effective way of putting Japan's abundant manpower to work. Silk, being a traditional sideline product of the Japanese farmer, could be developed as a major export commodity, giving a tremendous lift to the rural economy. By the end of the century Japan would become the world's largest supplier of raw silk. For the economy at large it was the continued growth of agriculture that produced the surpluses to permit continual modernization. Despite continuation of a highly under-mechanized system of cultivation, the agricultural sector underwent a remarkable expansion during the first 30 years of the Meiji period. The area under rice cultivation increased by 20 percent by 1905. New seeds, better fertilizer and equipment helped to raise the total rice crop by over 30 percent during the same interval.

Japan had moved quickly to the adoption of a strictly economic handling of land. The release of restrictions on sale of land, together with the imposition of a systematized tax, worked to the hardship of those who had been 'carried' by the old system of village organization and paternalistic landlordism, but the purchase of land by wealthy farmers proceeded rapidly. As of 1873 some 30 percent of land was tenant farmed. By 1890 this figure had grown to 40 percent. The government rationale that permitted this development was, in effect, social Darwinism. 'The best thing for us is to leave the punishment of the lazy to Heaven.' Such an attitude, together with the nature of irrigation-rich technology which required direct hand cultivation, combined to continue the traditional labor-intensive technology. This tended to keep a dense population on the land, making it more profitable for landlords to maintain a system of tenant farming rather than opening up large areas for mechanized production. Improvements of the agrarian economy as a whole, therefore, went hand in hand with the maintenance of traditional social ties on the land, continuing a 'dual economy' and perpetuating the old 'feudal elements.'

Japanese foreign relations

During the Meiji years Japan transformed its relations with the outside world, particularly the West. As of 1854, and particularly after 1858, Japan was placed on the defensive internationally, saddled with provisions of extraterritoriality and

Above left: Negotiating the Treaty of Shinonoseki with China in 1895. Japan received Formosa, the Liaotung Peninsula and a large indemnity payment.

Left: The paddyfields remained the center of Japanese agriculture and the source of most of the country's food.

Above right: A Western view of Japanese troops landing in Korea during the war with China. Japan showed a far better grasp of modern warfare than its Asian enemy.

Right: The Japanese fleet sails into action during the Russo-Japanese War in 1905.

the most favored nation clause and denied control over its own tariffs. The world of treaties and international law created by the Western powers was entirely unfamiliar to the Japanese. Slowly and painfully they learned the techniques of negotiation. By 1876 Japan had clarified its national boundaries by treaties with Russia and China, had taken military action to assure control over the Ryukyu Islands and had 'opened' Korea using the same strong-arm methods employed against Japan by Perry 20 years earlier.

Revision of the unequal treaties which so offended the Japanese sense of pride came much more slowly. Western powers were reluctant to give up the mixed courts provision until Japan had drafted acceptable legal codes. The turning point did not come until 1894, with the negotiation of a new commercial treaty with the British calling for the eradication of extraterritoriality by 1899. Tariff autonomy was not to be regained until 1911.

From 1894, however, Japan entered a new phase in its foreign relations. Defensive action was replaced by more aggressive forward planning. Diplomatic and military leaders began to talk about the necessity of Japanese action on the continent to assure Japan's future security. There was strong feeling that Korea, 'the dagger pointed at Japan's heart,' must be kept out of hostile hands. Such thinking, together with the growing intensity of imperialist rivalry in China and Manchuria, turned Japanese attention toward continental politics. While in 1873 Japan's leaders were daunted by Japan's weaknesses and the danger of precipitating war with Korea, by 1894 Japan was the strongest Asian power, possessing an army with a mobilized strength of 200,000 and a well-trained fleet of 28 vessels.

Thus for the security of Korea Japan provoked war with China. Victories on land and sea quickly demonstrated Japan's superior mastery of modern warfare. The Treaty of Shinonoseki in 1895 recognized the independence of Korea, ceded Formosa and the Liaotung Peninsula to Japan and obliged China to pay it a large indemnity to Japan.

The war with China marked Japan's coming of age in the eyes of the world. Japan's easy victory caught the Western powers by surprise. It also proved to them that Japan was a power to contend with, particularly since its geographical location gave it the capacity to place troops on the continent with great speed. The new threat that Japan posed was quickly recognized by the tripartite intervention of 1895, in which Russia, France and Germany forced Japan to relinquish its claim upon the Liaotung Peninsula.

International power politics

The tripartite intervention fused European and Asian politics into one. Whether because Japan had so clearly revealed China's weakness or because of the new competitive factor injected into the scene by Japan, the years which followed witnessed the literal political and economic dismemberment of China, each of the major powers carving out a major sphere of interest. That Japan's projected interests conflicted with those of Russia and could coexist with those of Britain dictated the course of Japan's behavior in the next few years. By 1902 Japan had secured tangible recognition of its new status with a treaty of alliance with Britain. Two years later Japan went to war with Russia to protect its interest in Korea. The war was highlighted by the spectacular defeat of the Russian fleet in the Straits of Tsushima in May 1905. But the Japanese land victory came

after high casualties at Mukden and a real sense of sacrifice on the part of the Japanese. Although the Japanese received Russian recognition of their paramount interest in Korea, together with the Russian leases in the Liaotung Peninsula and the southern half of Sakhalin, they failed to obtain a hoped for indemnity.

After the war with Russia Japan emerged as a fully fledged modern nation with all the attributes of national identity and military power to make it competitive in the world of imperialist rivalries. Japan was now truly Imperial Japan (*Dai Nippon Teikoku*), with an empire that included Formosa, the Liaotung Peninsula and Korea (annexed in 1910). The mood was that of Bismarck's Germany or Theodore Roosevelt's United States: expansionist, nationalistic and economically aggressive.

At the head of the state stood the Emperor Meiji (until his death in 1912), now fully matured into an imposing figure. With a strong profile and thick moustache, generally seen on horse back in his field marshal's uniform, he was the picture of strong leadership, a benevolent despot, a father figure. To this figure the Japanese state had attached an imposing array of ideological and institutional supports. The imperial family establishment, representing the greatest private holding of wealth in Japan, provided the resources for an impressive ritual of sovereignty which drew on both Western and Japanese traditions. The Ise Shrine provided a prime focus for the revival of a state network of Shinto shrines, and after the Satsuma rebellion, a shrine to Japan's war dead, Yasukuni Jinja in Tokyo, became a national focus of patriotic sacrifice.

Beneath the emperor government had achieved stability through the adoption of a constitution and through the leadership of a group who were, now elder statesmen in a true sense. Men such as Ito, Yamagata, Kuroda, Matsukata, Katsura, Okuma and Itagaki, now mature and fully endowed with positions of rank and political influence, were able to pass the premiership among themselves, providing flexibility of policy within a vigorous but closed oligarchy. Each of these men had gained strength through identifi-

cation with some aspect of government: Ito for his control of the Diet and the civil bureaucracy, Yamagata for his influence over the army and the prefectural bureaucracy, Okuma for his role in the political parties, education and journalism.

By the 1910s the Japanese people had come of age as well, having suffered through the early stages of Westernization and social revolution. Now fully literate, knit together by a common education and common service in the army, exhorted by the emperor through his rescripts on education and military service to patriotic duty, yet played upon by the inflammatory writings of a growing mass medium, the newspapers. The Russo-Japanese war had had a tremendous psychological influence in dramatizing the concept of nation. The war had produced thousands of faceless heroes whose memory pulled the nation together in a sense of mutual sacrifice. The war also produced new national heroes: Admiral Togo, who destroyed the Russian fleet; General Nogi, who, along with his wife, followed Emperor Meiji to his death; Shirakami, the young bugler whose bugle sounded even after a bullet had entered his heart and whose death inspired the words: 'I blow my bugle with my soul, its voice is the voice of Yamato damashii (Japanese spirit).'

Japan in transition

Politics was fast becoming mass politics. Demonstrations after the Portsmouth Treaty in 1905 had resulted in over 500 killed or wounded and 2000 arrested. Okuma had lost a leg for his failure to secure treaty revision; Mori, Minister of Education, had been assassinated for a presumed show of disrespect toward the emperor. Political parties were now a force to contend with, though still weak and immature. The Lower House proved a sufficiently attractive prize, particularly because of local patronage opportunities, so that elections were brutally contested. Candidates bought votes and used teams of bullies to intimidate rivals. The 1892 election left 25 dead and 388 injured, and Diet sessions were often marred by disorder. But Japanese were gradually learning the meaning of representative government, and new national leaders had begun to emerge as spokesmen for

political causes. Japan had by this time seen the beginnings of a labor movement, a socialist party had been organized and suppressed, an anarchist had been executed. Opposition newspapers were being regularly censored by the government and editors jailed.

Changes in style of life and in the pattern of economic activity were particularly noticeable in Japan in the first decade of the twentieth century. Urbanization had proceeded rapidly. By 1904 Tokyo had a population of nearly two million, Osaka of over one million, Yokohama (a village in 1854) of over 300,000. In total numbers the Japanese people had grown by 10 million since 1868 to more than 42 million by 1900. Particularly in the cities the effects of Western influence were dramatically visible. Japanese had changed their street wear to felt hats, wool suits and shoes and carried black umbrellas. Their diet had been changed to include beef, pork, bread, milk and

whiskey, and beer was soon being made in Japan in competition with the traditional sake. Trains and trams were now the means of transportation for an increasingly mobile populace. The rickshaw filled in before the development of the taxi-cab to provide easy private transportation inside the cities. By 1900 Japan had nearly 4000 miles of railroads and 100,000 miles of telegraph lines. Shipping tonnage had soared to a million tons and would be up to 1.6 million by 1910. Manufactured goods (primarily textiles) accounted for some 50 to 60 percent of Japan's exports in 1900, indicating that Japan was rapidly becoming an industrial competitor with the Western powers.

By the first decade of the twentieth century it is obvious that Japan had achieved the objectives of *fukoku-kyokei*. In the world of the 1900s Japan's was clearly a success story of the first magnitude. As the first of the Asian nations to become modernized, it had literally become a historical example to the rest of Asia. Japan's victory over Russia became the starting point of many an anticolonial movement in Southeast Asia.

But was Japan's remarkable record of modernization truly a success story? As historians look toward subsequent events – the militarism and political oppression of the late 1930s and early 1940s, the invasion of China, the attack on Pearl Harbor, the final military disaster – they have asked whether the Meiji state was in fact overcommitted to defense and national effort. Had Japan's leaders, by wilfully choosing a path of national development which linked war to national policy, set Japan on a course which could only end in disaster? Were popular welfare and civil rights given too little heed in these early years? From the exterior it would not seem that late Meiji Japan was more autocratically governed and nationalistically oriented than the other major world powers. The Meiji oligarchs had been a remarkably broad-minded group, and their own political self-confidence had made it possible for them to be relatively liberal and flexible in their policies. The trouble was to come with their successors. The next generation of leaders, lacking such self-assurance, were therefore fatally inclined to cling to the rigidities of the imperial system and of the priorities of military and economic security. And in this, at least, they were to bring ruin to Japan with their fantastic dreams of a vast Pacific empire under Japanese hegomony which would lead them to Pearl Harbor.

Above: Admiral Tojo, the victor of Tsushima. Japan's military successes gave such officers a prominent place in public life.

Above left: The Ise Shrine, dedicated to Japan's war dead, was a focus for the revival of the Shinto religion, with its stress on the emperor's divinity.

Far left: The Japanese imperial family, giving a passable imitation of its contemporary equivalent in Britain or Austria.

Left: General Nogi, hero of Mukden, who committed ritual suicide on Emperor Meiji's death in 1912. Such a gesture marked the vast psychological gulf that still separated Japan from the West after half a century of modernization, and would continue to do so in the coming decades.

Right: The bustling city of Tokyo in 1905, capital of a booming industrial and military power.

Africa: 1500-1914

At the beginning of the modern era, Africa was a continent still only tenuously associated with the Eurasian land mass in the northeast, still little known and long to remain the 'Dark Continent' to the peoples of Europe. In the Congolese forest and the arid southwestern region of the continent, communities of hunters and collectors survived as living representatives of the remote past, but the vast majority of the African peoples were, of course, food-producers. Varying with the natural environment, they herded sheep, goats and cattle; they cultivated grains or root crops; or both. They also had weapons, tools and ornaments of iron and copper as well as of stone and wood. But contact between the numerous local regions was limited, so that local variations in culture and language remained pronounced.

There was some trade, and this was greatest in the Sudanic belt between the Sahara desert and the tropical forest. Arab-Berber traders based on the Maghrib traveled in caravans across the desert with North African, Near Eastern and European trade goods. On the southern side of the desert they bartered for gold, ivory and slaves, which were procured by local traders (*dyula*) from the forest zone further south. Where the two trade systems met there were large urban communities, such as Timbuktu and Kano, with many types of specialized craftsmen. These were the only real towns in sub-Saharan Africa (except for the Muslim trading posts along the east coast as far south as Mozambique). Elsewhere, such concentrated settlements as existed had administrative rather than commercial or industrial functions. Indeed, throughout the continent the overwhelming majority of the people lived in isolated village communities and produced nearly everything that they consumed.

The majority of Africans adhered to their traditional local religious beliefs and practices. In the early centuries AD Christianity had penetrated North and Northeast Africa, but it had subsequently been replaced by Islam almost everywhere, except in Ethiopia, which remained Christian. Islam had also crossed the Sahara with the Muslim traders to the Sudanic belt. Yet it was only in the Maghrib, Egypt and the Horn that Islam had become a popular religion. In the Sudan it was virtually confined to the ruling and commercial classes, and even among them there was much syncretism with the traditional, established local religions.

Africa was also the scene of immense political variety. Apart from the surviving bands of hunters and collectors, in many parts of the continent there were food-producing peoples, such as the Ibo of Nigeria and the Kikuyu of Kenya, who had no central political institutions. In these societies, which anthropologists have called 'stateless societies,' order was preserved primarily because each person had precise rights and duties arising from his status in terms of sex, age and descent. In addition, powers were often exercised by individuals whose authority was primarily religious and by associations such as age sets and secret societies. Also very widespread, especially in southern Africa, were chiefdoms – small, centralized political communities where political authority was vested in hereditary ruling families. There were, finally, a considerable number of kingdoms, larger

and more centralized political communities than chiefdoms, comprising peoples of different descent groups and with more or less elaborate bureaucracies. By AD 1500 kingdoms had emerged in Ethiopia; in the Sudanic belt, where Kanem-Bornu dominated the central sector and Songhay the western (until it was conquered by a Moroccan army in 1591); in Benin, in the West African forest belt; and along the savanna south of the Congolese forest. In the area around what is now known as Lake Victoria state-building had begun long before 1500, and it continued thereafter without any significant influence from Europe or Asia. By 1800 there was a series of kingdoms in the area, including Bunyoro, Ankole, Rwanda, Burundi and Buganda. Of all these kingdoms in sub-Saharan Africa, Buganda became the most centralized and stable: The *kabakas* (kings) dominated the administration by playing off one group of officials against another, and there were customs that prevented the death of a *kabaka* from being followed by a war of succession. The wide geographical spread of these kingdoms shows that in Africa, as elsewhere, political development was by no means confined to any single cultural group.

In their capacity to tame and control the natural environment, pre-1500 Africans clearly lagged behind contemporary Europeans. Africa was seriously plagued by debilitating human diseases. Malaria was to scourge all areas that could support anopheles mosquitoes, and tsetse flies closed vast regions of Africa to draught animals, confining transportation beyond the waterways to what

could be carried by human porters. No doubt it was partly for these reasons that Islam and Christianity, and with them literacy, had not penetrated southward from the Sudan into the tropical forest or inland from the east coast ports.

In all of Africa there was scarcely any long-term accumulation of wealth or confidence in the capacity of man to derive more benefits from his environment. There was an absence of anything comparable to the individualistic, technology-assisted forces that had been generated in Europe from the twelfth century onward and that by the fifteenth century were making it possible for Europeans to reach out across the oceans to the other continents with such skill and self-confidence. These forces began to impinge on Africa as Portuguese seamen probed down the west coast during the fifteenth century, a process that culminated in the expedition led by Vasco da Gama to India via the Cape of Good Hope and Malindi in 1497-98.

The coming of the Europeans: the slave trade

The Portuguese voyages of the fifteenth century, culminating in Vasco da Gama's passage to India, brought Europeans into direct contact with most of the African coastline for the first time. Nevertheless, before the nineteenth century the impact of Europe on Africa was meager. From the European point of view Africa was of less significance than Asia or America. It produced no spices as valuable as those of Indonesia; it contained no such vast areas of fertile and sparsely populated

land as North America; neither gold nor silver was found in it in quantities comparable to that produced by the mines of Mexico and Peru. In most areas Africa's tropical diseases wrought havoc among European visitors, and the local people usually proved capable of controlling any Europeans who tried to move beyond the range of their ships' guns. Thus it was not until the nineteenth century, when the technological gap between Europe and Africa had grown immense and when Europeans were beginning to use effective antidotes against tropical diseases, that Europeans even discovered some of the main geographical features of the continent, including the courses of its greatest rivers, the Nile, the Niger and the Congo.

Nevertheless, Europeans did directly or indirectly affect many African societies in the early centuries of European expansion. In West Africa, where long-distance trade had previously moved northward across the Sahara in Arab-Berber cara-

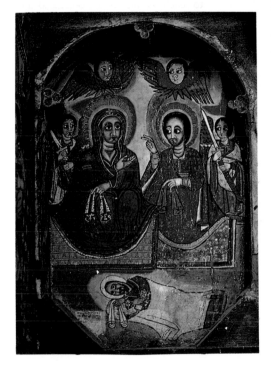

vans, some of it began to move southward to the Atlantic coast, where African communities became middlemen between the European maritime traders and the African consumers of European goods and suppliers of European needs. Among the imports were guns, which revolutionized the purposes, methods and consequences of warfare as they spread from one community to another. Among the exports were slaves, whose extraction had profound consequences not only in Africa from which they were taken but also in the Americas to which they went. Farther south, the Portuguese became involved in military as well as commercial adventures on both sides of the continent, with disastrous effects on the African societies south of the lower Congo River and on either side of the lower Zambezi. Yet whereas Portuguese attempts to establish colonies of settlement were not very successful,

on the southwestern tip of the continent, beyond the range of tsetse flies and anopheles mosquitoes, where the climate was temperate and the indigenous peoples were relatively sparsely settled hunters and pastoralists, a white community did take root as a by-product of the activities of a Dutch commercial company whose principal operations were in Asia.

The first Portuguese mariners to reach the inhabited country south of the Sahara near the mouth of the Senegal River had seized Africans from the shore and had taken them back to Portugal. Their successors repeated the practice and added a significant Negro element to the Iberian population. But the slave trade would never have become a major factor in the making of the modern world without the rise of a prodigious demand for Negro slaves in the Caribbean islands and in mainland North and South America. As

Left: Clay houses in Kano, Nigeria, once an important trading center at the southern end of the Saharan caravan routes.

Above: A religious mural from Ethiopia, the major Christian outpost in Africa.

Above right: Europeans negotiate with Africans in a fort on the Guinea coast in the mid eighteenth century. Alcohol, guns and gunpowder are being offered to tempt the Africans into a deal.

Right: Africa's main economic value for Europeans until the nineteenth century was as a source of slaves to work plantations in the New World. The Arab slave trade started before its European equivalent and ended later.

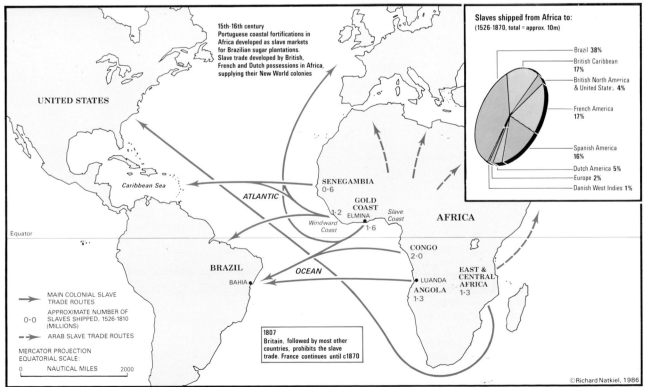

Spanish settlers destroyed the indigenous peoples of the Caribbean islands by warfare, disease and overwork they turned to Africans, for domestic, plantation and mine labor. The system was spread to the mainland by the Spanish and Portuguese conquerors, and in the seventeenth and eighteenth centuries it was also adopted by the settlers from northern Europe in their tropical and subtropical American colonies.

During the fifteenth and sixteenth centuries, when the Portuguese were the only regular traders with tropical Africa and they and the Spaniards were the only founders of colonies in the Americas, the volume of the trade was small. During the seventeenth century, when Europeans of many other nations began to create plantation colonies in the Americas and to take slaves to them from Africa, the volume increased. The trade reached a peak in the later eighteenth century, the climax of the mercantilist era and of the plantation culture in the American colonies, then it gradually declined during the nineteenth century. The European governments successively made it unlawful for their subjects to trade in slaves; Britain and (to a lesser extent) France took steps to enforce these laws by stationing anti-slavery naval squadrons on the West African coast; and slavery was eventually outlawed in the Americas. With the emancipation of slaves in Brazil (1871) and Cuba (1886), the inhumane traffic finally ceased, though slavery as an institution was to last for many decades longer.

We cannot know how many Africans were exported as slaves. The best modern estimates suggest that approximately 11.3 million slaves were embarked in ships on the African coast, that nearly two million of them died at sea and that about 9.5 million reached their destinations in America or Europe. Of the total, by far the greatest numbers – about 7.5 million – were embarked in the years between 1701 and 1810.

Most of the slaves were exported from the west coast, from modern Senegal in the north to modern Angola in the south, with much smaller numbers being shipped from Mozambique on the east coast. During the peak period in the eighteenth century the greatest numbers were exported from modern Nigeria and Angola.

At first the Africans who were enslaved were mainly those who lived in the immediate vicinity of the coast, but in the course of time the catchment areas moved inland. Most of the slaves who came from modern Nigeria were Yoruba and Ibo. From the Angolan coast, however, the slave-trading frontiers spread further and further inland across the southern savanna until they penetrated the countries of the Luba and the Lunda peoples in the heart of the continent.

As the trade developed it became systematized. Generally, the European traders remained on the coast and obtained slaves by peaceful trade with Africans, but their methods differed from area to area and period to period. Along the coast of modern Ghana Europeans built stone fortresses to defend themselves and their property from European rivals as well as Africans. In the Niger delta the local people obliged the Europeans to remain in moored hulks without any permanent establishments ashore. In either case, it was

Africans who obtained slaves and sold them to the white traders at the coast, in return for textiles, iron and copper bars, hardware, knives and cutlasses, spirits and firearms.

Many African societies were at this time sharply stratified, but if by slaves we mean people who are the absolute property of their owners, who can be bought and sold like other commodities and who transmit the same status to their children, the most dependent person in a traditional African society was a client rather than a slave. He had specific rights, he was treated in most respects as a member of his patron's family and he, or at least his children, had an opportunity to rise in the social scale. But slavery *was* authorized by Islamic law, and since about the tenth century Muslim traders had been expanding the practice into the Sudanic belt from the Maghrib. By the fifteenth century slavery had still not penetrated the forest zone, so that it did not exist along the West African coastline or in the states of the southern savanna, but after that, in response to the incentives provided by European traders on the coast (especially the firearms that enabled a community that possessed them to dominate a neighbor who did not) slavery and the slave trade became recognized institutions throughout the greater part of tropical Africa.

Africans were enslaved by Africans for the Atlantic trade in various ways. Some were sentenced to slavery by judicial process. Some were tribute paid to rulers by their subjects. Some were war captives or the victims of raids. In the process many traditional institutions were so modified that the resultant insecurity led to a decline of agricultural production and craftsmanship. In general, African societies whose government did not cooperate with the European traders tended to decline, societies with collaborative governments expanded and some hitherto stateless societies developed new institutions geared to the European demand.

The Kingdom of Benin, on the western side of the Niger delta, is an example of the first type of response. Benin had reached the peak of its power before Europeans arrived in the area. The Oba's government tried to keep Europeans at arm's length and to maintain a tight control over foreign trade. For a long time it refused to allow the sale of male slaves, and even after it had removed that prohibition early in the eighteenth century it

Left: Cape Coast Castle, Britain's main strongpoint in West Africa from the seventeenth to the nineteenth century.

Below left: In the Kordofan region of the Sudan, Arab slave-raiders guard their black prisoners. Notice the heads on poles in the right foreground.

Right: The coronation of the king of Dahomey ('Juidah'), as observed by a French traveler in 1723. Through its participation in the slave trade, Dahomey grew into a powerful militaristic kingdom.

Below right: A nineteenth-century photograph of the king of the Ashanti. On the seat to his left is the Golden Stool, mystical focus of Ashanti nationhood.

refrained from organizing a slave-trading network or indulging in slave raids. During the eighteenth century, however, some of the peoples who lived in the outlying provinces of Benin, especially the Itsekiri on the coast, traded extensively with Europeans and became powerful enough to secede from Benin. Thus the area controlled by the Oba's government shrank and the kingdom became conservative and isolationist.

Dahomey is an example of a kingdom that came into being in response to the European presence on the coast. The traditional political system of the Aja people was made up of small chiefdoms which were loosely affiliated under the leadership of Allada, a coastal chiefdom whose ruler was regarded as genealogically senior. During the seventeenth century Allada became deeply involved in the slave trade. One Aja lineage then withdrew inland to Abomey, where it founded the Kingdom of Dahomey. The early Dahomey rulers were averse to the Atlantic slave trade, but in the middle of the eighteenth century King Tegbesu reversed his policy. Dahomey then united the Aja into a great slave-trading and slave-raiding kingdom, with a centralized, autocratic and militaristic political system.

The case of Ashanti is more complex. During the seventeenth century the activities of rival European traders undermined the small states on the Gold Coast and promoted the rise of several larger states among the Akan peoples in the interior. The Akan states competed with one another for territory and for control of the trade routes running southward to the coast and also northward to the savanna. Starting in the late seventeenth century, Ashanti emerged as the dominant Akan state, because it had the most efficient institutions and a remarkable centralizing ideology focused on the Golden Stool, a symbol of the spirit of the nation. Ashanti expanded until, by the nineteenth century, it controlled a population of about four million people and an area of about 150,000 square miles, from

the Atlantic, through the forest, to the savanna, with trading connections northward to Hausaland and Timbuktu, as well as southward to the sea. Second only to the Kingdom of Buganda on Lake Victoria, of the pre-colonial non-Muslim states in sub-Saharan Africa Ashanti developed the most efficient political institutions.

Most remarkable of all was the response of the inhabitants of the southeastern part of modern Nigeria. This area provided a large proportion of the slaves who were exported from Africa, probably because it was – and is – one of the most densely populated parts of the continent. In the interior the Chukwa oracle was believed by most of the Ibo peoples to be the mouthpiece of the supreme God, and the Aro section of the Ibo, who

controlled the oracle, used it to extract slaves, who were presented to the oracle as religious donations or atonements. The Aro established a network of trading stations, through which they transported their slaves toward the Niger delta. There, the slaves were bought by African traders living in Bonny, Calabar and other coastal states. These states were unlike anything that had previously existed in Africa. The inhabitants of each state were organized in trading corporations known as Houses. Each House consisted of an autocratic Head, a small number of freemen and a much larger number of slaves. Besides absorbing the Aro supply of slaves, the Houses carried out extensive slave raids in war canoes along the lower Niger waterways.

IUMBE   HASSAN
OMARI MOENDA

In what is now Angola the Portuguese made extensive territorial conquests in this period. In the 1480s a Portuguese expedition made contact with the Kongo, a considerable African kingdom on the southern side of the lower Congo River. At first relations were harmonious. Several members of the Kongo royal family were baptized, and in 1506 one of the converts, Affonso, became king. Affonso made a serious effort to transform the Kongo into a progressive Christian state, with Portuguese assistance. This was the first time that a sub-Saharan African kingdom had appealed to the West for technological aid. But the honey-moon period did not last long. The kingdom split into pro-European and anti-European factions, and the Portuguese government and the Catholic Church failed to live up to their altruistic professions. White officials, settlers and even missionaries became involved in exporting Kongolese as slaves to the island of Sao Tomé, where Portuguese settlers were creating sugar plantations. The Portuguese government itself acquired an interest in the slave trade by taxing slave exports and selling trading licenses. Altruism gave way to a type of relentless exploitation that intensified the cleavages in Kongolese society and undermined the integrity of the state. After the death of Affonso in 1545 his successors tried to reduce the power of the Portuguese, but without much success, and the kingdom lapsed into anarchy. The Portuguese also destroyed the neighboring kingdom of Ndongo, whose ruler had the title Ngola (hence the name of the Portuguese colony). They annexed Ndongo in 1590 and tried to control it through puppet Ngolas, but there was intermittent resistance, culminating in 1671, when a force of Portuguese, with African allies, sacked the capital and killed the Ngola. Thereafter, the Portuguese ruled Ndongo more or less directly.

Many of the slaves exported from Angolan ports came into Portuguese hands as tribute from the chiefs in Kongo and Ndongo. By the eighteenth century, large numbers of slaves were also being brought to the coast by African traders from the far interior, where the Lunda empire was expanding. The states of Kasanje and Matamba, on the Kwango River, were the middlemen in this long-distance trade. Thus the Portuguese presence in Angola had consequences that reached into the heart of the continent.

Europeans were not, of course, the only aliens who exported slaves from tropical Africa. Black African slaves had been used in small numbers in ancient times in the Mediterranean lands and the Near East. After the Arab conquests of the eighth century AD, black Africa became a major source for the supply of slaves to all the Muslim territories from Spain and Portugal to India, and vast numbers were shipped from tropical Africa via routes across the Sahara, down the Nile and to the Red Sea and East African ports. During the seventeenth and eighteenth centuries the volume of the Muslim slave trade was appreciably less than the volume of the Atlantic trade, but during the nineteenth century, when the trade to the Americas was at last declining, the Muslim slave trade expanded greatly. From East Africa alone about 60,000 slaves were exported annually during the 1860s, and this trade began to decline only after 1873, when the sultan of Zanzibar, under British pressure, made the export of slaves illegal.

The Portuguese in East Africa

Before the nineteenth century, Europeans were much less involved in East Africa than in West Africa. The Portuguese made contact with the kingdom of Ethiopia in the late fifteenth century and sent the emperor military aid against the Ottoman Turks and other Islamic invaders in the early sixteenth century. But the prospects for a fruitful and enduring alliance between Portugal and Ethiopia were spoiled by the Catholic clergy, notably a Spanish Jesuit named Mendez, who treated the peculiar practices of the ancient Coptic Church of Ethiopia as heretical and tried to force it into exact conformity with Rome. The result was an anti-Catholic and anti-European reaction. The Jesuits were expelled, traditional faith and rituals were restored and a tradition of anti-Catholicism and anti-Europeanism became established in Ethiopia.

In the early sixteenth century the Portuguese brought most of the ports of the Swahili coast under some sort of control, often using violent methods, as in the sacking of Kilwa and Mombasa. They tried to control the coast through puppet chiefs, supported by small military estab-

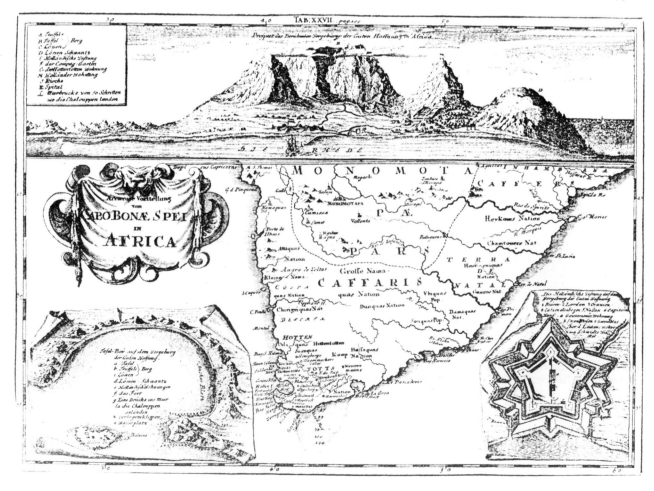

Above left: Muslim African slave traders captured in 1892. It was only as the European powers extended their rule over Africa that the slave trade to the Arab countries was stopped.

Left: A map of southern Africa in 1710, showing the colony at the Cape of Good Hope founded by the Dutch East India Company.

Above right: In the nineteenth century, Boers who had trekked north into the Transvaal and Orange Free State became bitter enemies of the British colonial authorities in South Africa.

Above, far right: An Ashanti gold head. Precious metals rivaled slaves as a focus of European economic interest in Africa.

lishments at forts they built at Mombasa and Mozambique, but they encountered a great deal of resistance, and the Portuguese never succeeded in developing a peaceful, systematic, controlled trade from East Africa. By 1700 they had lost control of everything north of the Rovuma River, which later was united under the Omani Arab dynasty.

The Portuguese made their major effort in East Africa south of the Rovuma, where they were lured inland by the gold of the kingdom of Mwene Mutapa. By 1600 they had created garrison towns at Sena and Tete on the Zambezi River, had founded half a dozen trading posts in the auriferous area southwest of Tete and were handling most of the gold mined by the Shona. But they had overestimated the volume of Shona gold production. After a thousand years of mining, the quantity of gold ore recoverable by traditional methods was declining. Moreover, there were leakages of gold through the Portuguese official network to individual European adventurers and to independent Swahili and Asian traders on the coast. Meantime, the result of the Portuguese efforts to work through the puppet Mwene Mutapa kings was that the authority of the Mwene Mutapa dynasty withered away and the Changamire dynasty, based on Great Zimbabwe beyond the scope of Portuguese influence, expanded northward.

The most enduring by-products of the Portuguese presence in East Africa in these centuries were the prazos, or great estates, in the Zambezi valley. In the sixteenth century the Mwene Mutapas granted jurisdiction over the lands and inhabitants around the forts at Sena and Tete to the Portuguese commanders. By the end of that century white adventurers were getting similar titles from the Mwene Mutapas and other African chiefs in return for favors, usually in the form of

military aid against rival Africans. The Portuguese government tried to regularize and control this system, following precedents it had created in Brazil, but it lacked the means to enforce its laws. The result was that the bulk of the land on either side of the Zambezi passed into the hands of private individuals. Successive generations of these prazeros married African or Indian spouses, and by the nineteenth century four or five family groups owned the bulk of the land on either side of the middle Zambezi. They had African retainers, including slaves who formed their private armies, and they themselves became much like African chiefs, though very turbulent chiefs and a menace to their neighbors.

The Cape Colony

Before the nineteenth century Europeans did not create successful colonies of settlement in tropical Africa, for the climate, tropical diseases and African opposition were strong obstacles. At the Cape of Good Hope, however, the climate was temperate, tropical diseases, anopheles mosquitoes and tsetse flies did not exist and the indigenous peoples were nomadic hunters (the San, whom Europeans were to call Bushmen) and pastoralists (the Khoi, whom they were to call Hottentots), rather than densely settled farmers.

By the middle of the seventeenth century, the directors of the Dutch East India Company were searching for ways to reduce the death rate on board their ships traveling between Europe and Asia. To satisfy this need, they charged Jan van Riebeeck with the task of creating a base at the Cape of Good Hope, where ships could be supplied with fresh water, vegetables and meat. Van Riebeeck's expedition occupied the site of the modern city of Cape Town in 1652. Five years later, a handful of men were given their discharge from the company's service and allotted plots of

land, in the hope that they would grow grain for sale to the company and that this would be cheaper for the company than growing it directly. This was the beginning of the permanent white settler community in southern Africa. It grew steadily but not dramatically. Other company servants took their discharge at the Cape, and occasionally the company provided free passages from Europe to the Cape, as when it dispatched about two hundred French Huguenots who had fled to the Netherlands after the revocation of the Edict of Nantes in 1685. By 1700 the 'free' white community (as distinct from the company's employees) numbered about 1000 people; by 1795 the number had grown to about 17,000.

The Dutch East India Company intended to contain the white settler community within about 50 miles of Cape Town, where the rainfall is reliable and agriculture is possible. By 1700, however, the settlers were producing more grain and wine than Cape Town and the passing ships could use, with the result that many settlers ceased to be agricultural farmers and became pastoralists – trekboers. The colonial authorities assisted this process by permitting trekboers to acquire control over farms of 3000 acres and more, provided they paid small annual licenses. The trekboers rapidly dispersed from the agricultural nucleus over a vast area of rather arid land. By the 1770s, some had reached the Orange River in the north, others the Fish River in the east. Further expansion was curbed by extreme aridity in the north and the presence of numerous sedentary Bantu-speaking Africans in the east.

From a very early state the white settlers in South Africa employed indigenous Khoi and imported slaves. The company began to import slaves in the 1650s, and by 1800 there were rather more slaves than white people in the Cape Colony. Most came from tropical Africa, Madagascar and

Indonesia and were employed as domestic servants, artisans and field workers in Cape Town and the neighboring agricultural area. Only a few were owned by *trekboers*.

The hunting and herding peoples who inhabited the southwestern corner of the African continent were not able to prevent the white settlers from acquiring control of the vast region between the Cape peninsula and the Orange and Fish rivers. San (Bushmen) hunters did try to oppose *trekboer* expansion by attacking their livestock, but the *trekboers* hunted them down with organized commandos, and by 1800 they had almost eliminated the San bands from the region.

The pastoral Khoi (Hottentots) offered very little resistance to the white occupation of the Cape Colony. As the *trekboers* advanced, the Khoi lost control of their land and their livestock, were demoralized by smallpox epidemics and acquired a craving for the strong brandy produced in the southwestern part of the colony. By the end of the eighteenth century virtually no independent Khoi communities existed inside the colonial frontiers. The majority of the survivors had been incorporated into colonial society, as clients of *trekboers*; others had fled northward.

From first to last, all that the Dutch East India Company required of the Cape was that it should be an efficient victualling-station on the Asian sea-route. Consequently, nearly all the company's employees in South Africa were stationed in Cape Town. Elsewhere, there were only three administrative centers – Stellenbosch, Swellendam and Graaff Reinet – and each of them had only one full-time, all-purpose official, the *landdrost*. It was the white farmers who wielded power in the interior. They effectively owned the land and the livestock, they had a virtual monopoly of firearms and ammunition, they were the masters of African and Asian slaves and Khoi and San clients and a *landdrost* could do little without their consent and cooperation.

By the time of the Napoleonic Wars the refreshment station founded by the Dutch East India Company in 1652 had become a large European colony, the only one in Africa. But the company controlled only the Cape peninsula directly. The rest had passed into the hands of the white settler community, who were a distinctive people and a dynamic expansive force. Their language, Afrikaans, had deviated from the Dutch of the Netherlands more than Quebec French had deviated from European French. Except for those who lived in Cape Town, nearly all of them were farmers (*boers*), who produced most of the goods they consumed and a surplus of grain or brandy, sheep or cattle, which they exchanged for imported gunpowder, groceries and clothing. They assumed themselves to be superior to the African and Asian races from which they drew their slaves and clients, and their Church – the Dutch Reformed Church, whose clergy were appointed and paid by the company – did little to moderate their racism.

Islamic influence in Africa

It would be misleading to view African history in the nineteenth century as merely the story of European political expansion together with the shift of European economic activity from the export of slaves to the exploitation of Africa's natural resources on the spot. During the first three-quarters of the century there was very little European expansion except in Algeria and South Africa, and the major changes in African societies were at most peripherally related to European influences. Egypt under Muhammad Ali (1805-49) and Ismail (1863-79) embarked on a program of

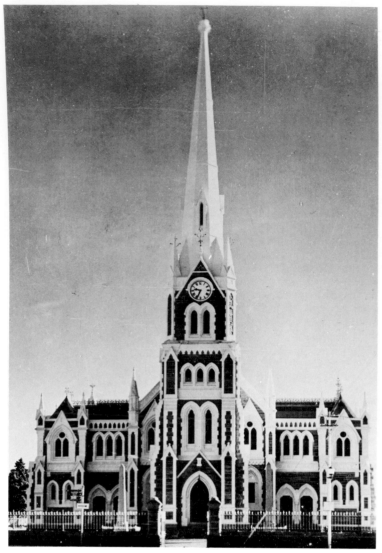

Left: The very European style of this building of the Dutch Reformed Church is obvious, despite being transported to African soil in Cape Province, South Africa.

Below right: Shaka, leader of the Zulus from 1816 to 1828. A cruel and tyrannical ruler, he created a formidable military machine and embarked on wars of conquest against other African tribes.

Below, far right: The magnificent clay-built medieval mosque at Djenne, in present-day Mali. The early presence of Islam in West Africa, brought across the Sahara by Muslim traders, was the basis for a religious revival in the nineteenth century.

modernization, conquered the Sudan and thrust further southward toward the kingdoms between Lakes Victoria and Tanganyika. The emperor Theodore of Ethiopia (1855-67) began to reunite and reinvigorate his ancient kingdom and equip it with the means to resist Egyptian and European aggression. The Arab-Swahili peoples along the east coast were welded into some sort of political unity by Sayyid Said, who moved his capital from Oman to Zanzibar in 1840, and their trade routes penetrated deep into the interior. Two other developments merit more extensive treatment.

For many centuries there had been three main political constellations in the West African Sudan: the successive kingdoms of Ghana, Mali and Songhay in the west; the Hausa states in the center; and the kingdom of Kanem-Bornu in the east. In 1591, however, a Moroccan army crossed the Sahara and shattered the forces of Songhay; but Morocco proved unable to exploit the victory. For more than 200 years the peoples of the western Sudan, whose ancestors had known long periods of political stability and commercial prosperity under the kings of Ghana, Mali and Songhay, experienced political fragmentation and commercial and cultural decline and a weakening of Islam in favor of traditional local religious cults.

Recovery was linked with a revival of Islam and the leadership of the Fulani people. Although Islam had not penetrated deeply among the masses of the people in West Africa in the past, Dyula traders and members of the Qadiriyya brotherhood had prepared the way by carrying Islam along the trade routes. Moreover, many indigenous West Africans had become religious teachers, and a high proportion of these were

Fulani. Originally a pastoral people living in the Senegal valley, some Fulani had migrated eastward until by the eighteenth century there were pockets of Fulani as far east as Adamawa in the modern Cameroon. Many of them were still pastoralists; others had become urbanized. During the eighteenth century, Fulani Muslims gained control of Futa Jalon and Futa Toro, in the far west, and tried to transform them into pure Muslim states. Then, in 1804, Usuman dan Fodio, a Fulani *mallam* who had spent nearly 20 years preaching and writing in favor of a reform of the Hausa states in strict accordance with the *shari'a*, proclaimed a *jihad* (holy war) against the Hausa rulers on the grounds that they had become corrupt, oppressive and neglectful of their duties as Muslims. Pastoral and town Fulani, as well as considerable numbers of Hausa, joined him in a popular movement that rapidly conquered all of Hausaland. Muhammad Bello, Usuman's son, became sultan at Sokoto, and the former Hausa states became tributary emirates, with Fulani officials. Fulani power expanded far beyond the confines of Hausaland – southeastward into Adamawa, southward into Nupe and southwestwards into Yoruba country. It would probably have expanded northeastward into Kanem-Bornu also had not a local *mallam*, Muhammad al-Kanemi, revitalized that ancient kingdom and appealed to the ethnic loyalties of its people in opposition to the Fulani invaders.

The successes of the Fulani and of Islamic reform in Hausaland sparked off a similar movement far to the west, in the valley of the upper Niger, under a Fulani cleric named Seku Ahmadu. He laid the foundations of another Islamic state around Macina in the 1810s and extended it eastward in the following decades. Then, in the 1805s, al-Hajj 'Umar, a cleric from Futa Toro and an ardent member of the new puritanical and egalitarian Tijaniyya brotherhood, began to build up another Islamic state in the region between the sources of the Niger and the Senegal. In 1862 he conquered Macina, and in 1863 Timbuktu was taken. 'Umar died in 1864, and his son, Ahmadu Seku, succeeded to a considerable Tukolor empire. By that time Samori Toure, a Mande, was carving out another Islamic state in a series of military campaigns to the south of the Tukolor empire, on the borders of the forest zone.

Consequently, when Europeans began to stake claims to territorial sovereignty in the interior of West Africa in the 1870s, it consisted of four large complex and sophisticated Islamic states, all of which had been created or reinvigorated by Islamic reform movements during the nineteenth century: the Tukolor and Mande states in the west, the Fulani sultanate of Sokoto in the center and Kanem-Bornu in the east.

The Zulu kingdom

Until the nineteenth century the major processes in the history of east-central and southeastern Africa had been the sometimes distinct and sometimes related movements in a southerly and southeasterly direction of Bantu-speaking mixed farmers. Large states had emerged in the savanna south of the Congolese forest, including modern Rhodesia, but on the southern side of the Limpopo people had continued to live in chiefdoms which remained small in size because they periodically split into autonomous political communities. All this changed dramatically in the first half of the nineteenth century, when the Zulu Shaka created a military kingdom in place of the former northern Nguni chiefdoms and set in motion a series of migrations and conquests extending

over a distance of 2000 miles, from the Fish River to Lake Victoria.

The main reason why the old political system of small chiefdoms broke down was probably that the Nguni population had increased to the stage where fresh land was no longer available for occupation by a newly independent chief and his followers. In the territories beyond the Fish river the soil and rainfall were not adequate for agriculture, and in any case, the land was already claimed by Afrikaner *trekboers* and their Khoi clients. Competition among the northern Nguni for control of the trade routes of Delagoa Bay, where Portuguese and other European ships occasionally called for ivory and other products, was probably a contributory factor. But it was the personality of Shaka that determined the outcome of the crisis.

Around the turn of the century some of the northern Nguni chiefdoms began to amalgamate into loose confederations, such as those led by the Mthethwa and Ndwanwde chiefs. Shaka, an illegitimate son of the chief of the small Zulu tribe, became a protégé of Dingiswayo, the Mthethwa chief, and with Dingiswayo's help Shaka seized control of the Zulu chiefdom from his brother in 1816. After Dingiswayo's death two years later, Shaka established control over the Mthethwa confederation, crushed the Ndwanwde and conquered all the people living in the modern province of Natal. In Shaka's Zulu kingdom all men under 40 years of age lived in regimental barracks under military discipline, and they perfected the use of the short spear, the stabbing assegai, a new weapon in southern Africa. They were segregated from women and employed on frequent campaigns, first to conquer other northern Nguni and then to conquer more distant chiefdoms. In the 1820s Shaka's behavior became increasingly tyrannical and irrational and he alienated his own relatives and overstrained his army. In 1828 he was assassinated. He had never acknowledged a

wife or a child, and he was succeeded by one of his assassins, his half-brother Dingane.

Shaka's wars unleashed a flood of refugees. Some fled for protection to the southern Nguni chiefdoms, where they were known as *Mfengu* (beggars). Others crossed the Drakensberg as organized military bands and caused profound disturbances among the southern Sotho, whose survivors were eventually welded into a defensive kingdom in the Calecon River valley. Moshoeshoe, the creator of Lesotho, was as remarkable for humane statesmanship as Shaka was for cruelty and militarism. Mzilikaz, a northern Nguni chief, eventually settled around Bulawayo, where he built up his Ndebele (Matabele) kingdom in part of the country previously occupied by the Shona people. Sobhuza, another northern Nguni chief, created a kingdom that survives to this day with the name Swaziland in the mountains north of the Pongola River. Soshangane, an Ndwandwe leader, fled northward and founded the Gaza kingdom in the southern part of modern Mozambique. Swangendaba, a subordinate chief in the Ndwandwe confederacy, went furthest north, moving into modern Rhodesia, where he sacked Zimbabwe and overthrew the Changamire kingdom (thus preparing the way for Mzilikazi). Zwangendaba crossed the Zambesi in 1835 and died east of Lake Tanganyika in 1848. His successors and other Nguni migrants eventually ruled six separate kingdoms in modern Malawi, Zambia and Tanzania.

The Nguni bands led by Mzilikazi, Soshangane and Zwangendaba and their successors adopted Shaka's military weapons, tactics and (with some modifications) organization. They destroyed many of the political systems that had previously existed between Natal and Lake Victoria and were responsible for countless massacres, famines and dislodgements of populations. Nevertheless, as they moved and fought they incorporated large

numbers of local peoples into their own communities, and when they eventually settled down they succeeded in creating fairly stable, close-knit kingdoms in which, although the Nguni elements formed the aristocracy, the others became loyal subjects.

European initiatives

Revulsion from the inhumanity of the slave traffic, combined with a decrease of the political influence in Europe of the exploiters of slave labor in the Americas, led the European maritime powers to make the slave trade unlawful for their citizens by 1818 (except that Portugal permitted the trade south of the equator until 1839). Moreover Britain, supported at times by France and the United States, maintained a naval patrol in West African waters to enforce the prohibition. Nevertheless, the profits were so great that the trade continued as long as a demand existed in the Americas, which was the case until the institution of slavery was finally abolished in Cuba in 1886. In the same period, the Arab slave trade reached unprecedented dimensions. The total number involved in the Arab slave trade in the nineteenth century can hardly have been less than the two million exported to the Americas.

The European reaction against slavery had complex consequences inside Africa. Rulers of West African states that had adapted to the European demand for slaves found themselves in the unexpected position of being coerced by European officials into ceasing to sell slaves on the ground that the trade was immoral. Wherever African rulers submitted to such pressures, they deprived themselves of a major source of revenue, alienated powerful subjects and tended to become dependent for financial subsidies and physical support against discontented subjects on the power (usually Britain) that exerted the pressure. As the Atlantic slave trade gradually petered out, some European companies with African interests sought other commodities for export. Of these, the most readily available were palm kernels and palm oil, rubber and elephant ivory. The ivory trade was especially significant because it accelerated the dissemination of firearms in Africa and gave rise to specialized, quasi-military hunting communities, such as the Cokwe, who eventually dominated a large area in the interior of Angola and (in the 1880s) subverted the Lunda kingdom from within.

The Europeans who became involved in Africa included missionaries, traders, settlers and military and civilian agents of European governments. They often projected their tensions and rivalries into African societies, as in Buganda, where civil war eventually broke out between the adherents of French Catholic and English Protestant missions. Although Africans were often able to take advantage of rivalries among Europeans, the net effect of European activities in Africa in the first three quarters of the nineteenth century was a considerable corrosion of the moral, economic and political integrity of African societies – varying greatly in degree and in kind from area to area.

Outright political expansion was confined to a few localities and practiced only by the French and the British in this period. France got a foothold in the Maghrib in 1830, when she invaded Algiers on the flimsiest of pretexts and expelled the Turkish janissaries who had dominated the area for the previous three centuries. By 1875 a quarter of a million southern Europeans had settled in the coastal towns of Algeria. The first phase of Arab-Berber resistance led by Abd al-Kadir had been suppressed, but the Muslim inhabitants of Algeria, who outnumbered the

Left: Ivory was one of the valuable commodities exported from Africa as the colonial hold on the continent spread.

Right: A topeed missionary brings the wonders of Western civilization to the pygmies of Central Africa. The evangelical urge to spread Christianity was an important motive force behind the European penetration of Africa.

Below right: Sailors of the Royal Navy spike the Egyptian guns at Alexandria during the British intervention in Egypt in 1882.

Below: Behanzin, ruler of the West African kingdom of Dahomey. His realm was invaded and occupied by the French in 1892.

European settlers by 10 to one, were restless subjects, and French authority depended on the presence of an army of occupation of 60,000 men.

In West Africa, Governor Louis Faidherbe (1854-61 and 1863-65) started to advance up the valley of the Senegal River from the old French trading posts of St Louis, conquering Futa Toro and causing al-Hajj 'Umar to withdraw eastward to the upper Niger. Britain also began to expand in parts of West Africa. Explorers, missionaries, traders, consuls and officers of the anti-slavery patrol had different interests and different individual opinions; but the net effect of their influence was an expansionist pull that sucked a generally hesitant British government into commitments, which in turn generated further advances. Thus in 1851 British officials deposed the African ruler at Lagos because he was deemed to be an inveterate slave-trader; in 1861 Britain annexed Lagos; and in the following years Britain enlarged the colony of Lagos, and some of the traders and missionaries who were penetrating deeper and deeper into Yoruba country looked to the Lagos government for support and protection. Farther west, the longstanding British involvements in the affairs of the Gold Coast came to a head in the early 1870s when Britain took over the last non-British forts from the Dutch, sent a major military expedition inland to sack Kumasi, the capital of Ashanti, and annexed the coastal states as the Gold Coast Colony.

White penetration was deepest in South Africa. The Afrikaner people, with local roots going back to the middle of the seventeenth century, at all times remained a majority of the white population of the region, notwithstanding the fact that British immigrants began to settle there after Britain conquered the Cape Colony from the Dutch in 1795. Of the Afrikaners, it was the *trekboers* who, having acquired a large measure of *de facto* autonomy in the eighteenth century, most

strongly resented the new regime and its British institutions. For it had brought the rule of law to the frontier districts, had emancipated both the local non-white clients and the imported slaves from their legal disabilities and had even tentatively recognized that the Bantu-speaking peoples beyond the eastern frontier of the Cape Colony were also human beings with discernible problems and interests. In the 1830s and 1840s several thousand *trekboers*, joined by some kinsmen from the agricultural belt near Cape Town, participated in an organized migration northeastward from the Cape Colony, with the intention of founding independent states where they could live as they were wont to do. With their horses, their firearms and their wagons, which they skillfully formed into defensive laagers when attacked, the *Voortrekkers* managed to defeat the Zulu impis of Dingane and to drive the Ndebele of Mzilikazi north of the Limpopo River. Most of them then settled on either side of the Vaal River on the high veld grasslands which had recently been devastated by the wars and migrations unleashed by Shaka. They allowed limited numbers of Africans to reside on their farms as labor tenants and tried to prevent 'surplus' Africans from living on lands they had appropriated.

By 1860 white power was dominant from the Cape of Good Hope to the Limpopo. The Cape Colony and Natal (annexed in 1843) were British colonies which London was treating as though they were comparable to the settlement colonies in Canada and Australia and giving them parliamentary institutions. The franchise qualifications were not racial in form, but in practice the white settlers had effective control over the legislatures. The Orange Free State and the South African Republic (or Transvaal) were Afrikaner-controlled republics. Britain had recognized their political independence, but they were weak states without access to the sea except through British territories and British trade routes. There were also numerous African kingdoms and chiefdoms (notably the Zulu and Lesotho kingdoms), but their independence too was being undermined by the presence of white traders, missionaries and adventurers.

The European conquest of Africa

It was between 1875 and 1914 that the bulk of the African continent came under white control. Two related processes produced this astonishing transformation. One was diplomacy within Europe, which resulted in the European governments agreeing among themselves how they should divide Africa between them. The second process was the enforcement of these European decisions upon the peoples of Africa.

In the Nile valley there were two crucial episodes: the British conquest of Egypt in 1882 and of the Sudan in 1889, both of which have been described in another chapter. In northwest Africa a French force invaded Tunisia in 1881 and compelled the Bey to accept French control of Tunisian finances and foreign affairs, which led to general French over-rule and the establishment of a large community of European settlers. From the Tunisian and Algerian coastlines the French expanded southward. By the end of the century they had occupied the Saharan oases, and in 1900 they captured and killed Rabih, who had coordinated resistance by members of the Senusi Muslim order. Tripoli was invaded by an Italian force in 1911, but the Senusi continued to oppose the Italians until the 1930s. Morocco, which had been compelled to admit European customs supervisors in 1860, was partitioned into French and Spanish zones in 1912, when the Sultan, like the Bey of Tunis and the Khedive of Egypt, was reduced to the status of a subordinate.

In west Africa the primary French thrust was eastward along the Sudan from the Senegal valley. Lat Dior, the Damel of Cayor, and Mahmadu Lamine, a Sarakole merchant who proclaimed himself a *mahdi*, resisted the French advance through the upper Senegal valley and were defeated by 1907. The French then came into conflict with the powerful Islamic states ruled by Ahmadou Seku (son of al Hajj 'Umar) and Samori. They eventually triumphed, partly because Ahmadou and Samori did not cooperate with one another, and also because Ahmadou's half-brother, Aguibou, went over to the French. Samori was

perhaps the greatest of the leaders of resistance to the European conquest of Africa. He made a series of brilliant strategic withdrawals and fought 13 major engagements against the French before he was finally defeated in 1898.

The French completed the conquest of their tropical African empire in a series of political negotiations and military campaigns extending from Mauretania, where resistance continued almost throughout the colonial period, to Madagascar, where an exceptionally destructive campaign was waged by General Gallieni between 1895 and 1904. When the French invaded Dahomey in 1892 on the pretext that a Dahomey force had attacked African villages in territory which the French regarded as already theirs, Behanzin, King of Dahomey, enquired of a French politician: 'I would like to know how many independent villages of France have been destroyed by me, King of Dahomey.'

The limits of French acquisitions of territory in tropical Africa were set not by Africans, but by rival Europeans, notably by the British, who kept them out of the lower Niger valley below the Bussa rapids and out of the upper Nile valley. Of all the incidents in the European conquest of Africa, the confrontations between French and British forces at Borgu and Fashoda most nearly led to warfare between European nations.

In British planning West Africa took second place to the Suez Canal, the Nile valley, the east coast and South Africa. It was not until Joseph Chamberlain became colonial secretary in 1895 that the government fully committed itself to extending the old British holdings in Sierra Leone, the Gambia, the Gold Coast and Lagos and the Niger delta. The major military expeditions were against Ashanti, Benin and Sokoto. Prempeh I, who became leader in 1888, tried to restore the unity of his kingdom, which had been invaded by Britain in 1874, and, above all, to preserve its independence. But in 1896 Britain found a pretext for launching another military expedition. Kumasi was sacked, Prempeh was exiled and Ashanti was divided into separate units under British administration. In the Niger delta British commercial

and missionary interests persuaded local British consuls to eliminate the rulers of the various trading states which had adapted to the transition from the slave trade to 'legitimate' trade. Of these rulers, the ablest were Nana, who controlled the lower Benin River, and Jaja, ruler of Opobo. Jaja was tricked into boarding a British gunboat by a consul's promise of safe conduct and then, as prime minister Salisbury later admitted, kidnapped. Nana's town was destroyed. In 1897 the ancient kingdom of Benin, aware of the fate of Jaja and Nana, massacred a small unarmed British party that had entered the country without permission. A large British force then invaded the kingdom, burned the capital, looted its treasures and took their king away into exile. The caliphate of Sokoto was conquered piecemeal. First, the forces of Sir George Goldie's Royal Niger Company defeated its southernmost emirates, Nupe and Ilorin. Then, between 1901 and 1903, after the British government had taken over the company's administrative responsibilities, High Commissioner Frederick Lugard conquered the other emirates in a series of engagements in which maxim guns mowed down the Fulani-Hausa cavalry. While centralized political communities could be conquered in major military engagements, the British, like the French, found that communities among whom political authority was widely dispersed, such as the Ibo of eastern Nigeria, could only be subjected village by village, a process that went under the name of 'pacification' and continued for many years.

Arabs as well as Africans resisted the European conquest of East Africa. The sultan of Zanzibar, whose capital was open to bombardment by warships, was constrained to accept British 'protection' in 1890. But in several areas on the mainland Arabs and their African followers opposed the extension of European power – notably along the southern (German) sector of the coast, in the British sector in Nyasaland (now Malawi) and in the Belgian sector. In the late nineteenth century Buganda was the most powerful state in the interior of East Africa, but proselytization by rival Arab Muslims, French Catholics and British Protestants led to civil warfare and intervention by a small but decisive British force. In 1893 the Kabaka Mwanga accepted British protection. The British then won the support of senior Buganda bureaucrats by making them the owners of large blocks of land and, with their cooperation, they established control over the rest of the colony of Uganda. Elsewhere in East Africa the British and the Germans gradually acquired a grip over their respective territories by constructing forts and railroads, introducing white settlers and pacifying the villages with police expeditions. In 1905, several of the tribes in Tanganyika rose in resistance to the excesses of German rule, but the government suppressed this Maji Maji rebellion with great severity.

In southern Africa several African communities fought desperately before they were finally subdued. After bearing the main brunt of white pressure along the eastern frontier of the Cape Colony for over a century the Xhosa and the Thembu ceased to offer overt resistance in the 1870s. Lesotho withstood an Afrikaner invasion from the Orange Free State in 1858 but was vanquished in the 1860s, and in 1870 the aged King Moshweshwe requested and received British protection rather than have his people ruled by the Orange Free State. In the Transvaal the Venda continued to resist Afrikaner domination in their strongholds in the Soutpansberg until 1898. The Zulu, defeated by *Voortrekker* arms and divided by *Voortrekker* diplomacy in 1838-40, gradually

regained their morale and their strength. In 1879 the British High Commissioner presented King Cetewayo with an ultimatum that was incompatible with Zulu independence. The ensuing campaign is perhaps the best-known episode in the entire European conquest of Africa. Soon after the British invaded Zululand the Zulu surprised and wiped out a British regiment at Isandhlwna. There were other battles, including the famous British defense of Rorke's Drift, but by July the Zulu had been overwhelmed by British firepower. A final flicker of resistance by a section of the Zulu people was quickly suppressed in 1906. The Ndebele, who had settled north of the Limpopo after being driven out of the Transvaal by *Voortrekkers* in 1838, were dealt with in a series of episodes master-minded by Cecil Rhodes. First, Rhodes' agents obtained a treaty from Lobengula, Mzilikazi's successor, giving Rhodes limited mining rights. Next, Rhodes persuaded the British government to allow his British South Africa Company to administer territories north of the Limpopo. He then dispatched settlers from the Cape Colony, with a police escort, to occupy the eastern part of what became known as Rhodesia. In 1893 his local officials fomented a war in which the Ndebele army was defeated and Lobengula was killed. Finally, in 1896-97, when the Shona as well as the Ndebele rose against the new regime, both were defeated and humiliated. Perhaps most ruthless single episode in the history of the European conquest of Africa was in Southwest Africa, where two-thirds of the Herero people were annihilated by German forces in 1904.

With one exception, African resistance to the European conquest in the late nineteenth and early twentieth centuries, however heroic, was unavailing. The exception was Ethiopia. The Emperor Theodore's successors continued his policy of reunification, expansion and partial

modernization, notwithstanding invasions by British (1867), Egyptians (1875), Mahdist Sudanese (1889) and, finally, Italians. The Emperor Menelik defeated the Italians at the Battle of Adowa in 1896 and thereby preserved his country's independence. Although Fascist Italy did subdue Ethiopia with the use of bomber aircraft and poison gas in 1935, its period of European domination was brief. In 1941 Ethiopia became the first country to be liberated by Allied forces in World War II.

Although the European powers partitioned and conquered Africa in a highly competitive atmosphere they did not allow their colonial rivalries or confrontations between their local agents to precipitate a European war. In 1899, however, Britain conquered the Afrikaner republics for essentially the same reasons that she conquered Egypt and the Sudan, Benin and Sokoto. They were African states whose continued independence seemed inimical to British interests in a period of heightened tensions among the great powers. During the 1850s and 1860s the British government had regarded the republics as falling within a British sphere of interest but had been glad to allow them to assume the costs and responsibilities of self-government. Then the situation changed. The richest known source of diamonds in the world was discovered at Kimberley in 1870, and the richest known gold reef was found on the Witwatersrand in 1885. Although the former was in disputed territory that Britain was able to annex without resistance in 1871, the latter was in the heart of the South African Republic, newly restored to independence after a brief and inglorious British occupation since 1877. A modern gold-mining industry, controlled by British, continental and American financiers, managers and technicians, rapidly developed, and though Afrikaners and 'uitlanders' (foreigners)

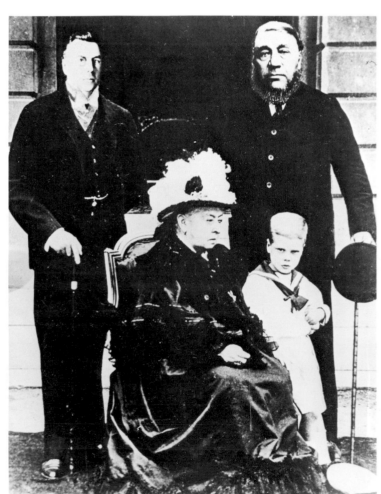

Left: A somewhat clumsy photo-montage purporting to show British colonial secretary Joseph Chamberlain (left) and his arch-enemy, the Afrikaner Paul Kruger (right) flanking the matriarch of the British Empire, Queen Victoria.

Above right: Jaja, ruler of the West African state of Opobo, kidnapped by the British who coveted his country. His European clothing is a symbol of subjection.

Above, far right: Zulu ruler Cetewayo lost a bloody war with the British in 1879, but survived to visit England three years later, and pose for his photograph.

Right: Ethiopians prepare to defend Addis Ababa against Italian forces in 1935.

were agreed in employing Africans as unskilled laborers under conditions that would have been unthinkable in Europe, they differed in their social attitudes and political loyalties. The Afrikaners were the product of pre-industrial society; the uitlanders were the harbingers of industrialization. The republican Afrikaners were determined to preserve their independence, for which many of their parents had left the Cape Colony in the 1830s and 1840s and fought in 1881: the uitlanders for the most part had no deep political commitments in South Africa, but they could be made to seem to be victims of oppression by the Afrikaners who, under the leadership of Paul Kruger, president of the South African Republic, kept a firm control over the political machinery. Furthermore, in proclaiming a protectorate over

Southwest Africa in 1885, Germany appeared to be challenging the assumption that, though formally independent, the republics were in a British sphere of interest. The result was that there were men in South Africa and in Britain who conceived that British interests required the overthrow of the republican regimes and the incorporation of the South African interior in the British Empire. One such was Cecil Rhodes. In 1895, when he was prime minister of the Cape Colony, the dominant figure in the diamond-mining industry, and the effective head of the British South Africa Company and of Rhodesia, he organized a conspiracy to destroy the Kruger regime by a combination of uitlander insurrection and external invasion. The outcome was the ludicrous failure known as the Jameson Raid, named after the leader of the

invading force. Joseph Chamberlain, the British colonial secretary, who had been privy to the abortive coup, and Alfred Milner, the man whom Chamberlain chose as high commissioner in South Africa, then tried to intimidate the republics into making political concessions, until in 1899, like cornered rats, they turned and fought. They resisted Britain with more success than Africans resisted their European conquerors because they were much better armed. British troops occupied their capital towns, Bloemfontein and Pretoria, in 1900, but they waged guerilla warfare for another two years, until the British forces in South Africa amounted to half a million men.

South African legacy

The South African War was an imperial setback and went some way toward discrediting military adventurism with the British public. Coming into power in 1905 the Liberal party, whose leaders had criticized the conduct of the war, sought to appease the Afrikaners by giving local self-government to the Afrikaner inhabitants of the conquered republics. Then, in 1910, the four self-governing South African colonies joined together to form the Union of South Africa, a British dominion with the status already possessed by the Dominion of Canada and the Commonwealth of Australia. But the crucial fact was that only white men were eligible to become members of the South African legislature or executive, and only white men were entitled to vote in parliamentary elections in the Transvaal and the Orange Free State. And although the franchise qualifications were non-racial in form in the other two provinces, white men had 99 percent of the votes in Natal and 85 percent in the Cape Province. From its birth, thanks to its mineral wealth, the Union of South Africa was the most developed country in Africa. But in shuffling out of her responsibilities, Britain had transferred power to a white-settler community which numbered only a fifth of the total population. These events were to be of profound significance for later generations: our own included.

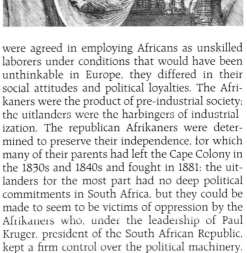

PART III
World War I to the Present Day

World War I and the Interwar Years

World War I was the first great cataclysmic event of the twentieth century and as such its global consequences were both profound and long-lasting. The war itself was a consequence of the long struggle for domination in Europe by the Continent's major powers. The prime mover of the conflict was imperial Germany whose aggressive foreign policy made war certain, while the spark which set off the conflagration was provided by the assassination of the heir to the Austrian throne by Serbian nationalists at Sarajevo on 28 June 1914.

As the first war to combine the mass armies of the nineteenth century with the weapons technology derived from the advances of the Industrial Revolution, it was almost inevitable that the conflict would be a bloody one. And so it duly was, with battlefield casualties mounting up in millions as the major contestants both failed to gain outright military victory and refused to accept a negotiated settlement. Thus World War I took on its particular attritional character, and only the complete exhaustion of the Central Powers, notably Germany, brought the war to an end.

By November 1918 the three great empires of Russia, Germany and Austria-Hungary had been destroyed, to be replaced by a host of nation states – a direct result of the Treaty of Versailles which attempted to impose a settlement on postwar Europe. Although essentially a European conflict,

it had spread across the world, involving not only the overseas possessions of the European belligerents but bringing in such far-flung states as Japan and the United States. Therefore, the consequences of the war were genuinely global in nature and in the following two decades international politics would witness various attempts to resolve the problems thrown up by the war. For, ironically, the 'war to end all wars' was far from that, so that in many ways the period 1918-39 was merely a period of 'truce' between the two global conflicts.

Nonetheless the two decades from 1919 to 1939 were an important formative period for the entire world. The specific problems that confronted the industrial states differed from those that agitated the still unformed states of Asia or the colonial territories of Asia and Africa, but there were now no longer parts of the world whose histories could be told without reference either to the consequences of Western influence or to the spread of modernization within their societies.

Despite the effort of the European powers to patch up their differences following the defeat of Germany it was obvious from the start that the new world balance could not be a simple ratification of the old European hegemony. For one thing, the United States, Japan and China had to be given a place within the new fabric of agreements. There was also Soviet Russia, weak yet potentially influential, a defector from Western

European values but very much an imperialist power. And despite the fact that most of the European powers would momentarily extend their colonial possessions after World War I, Europe's leaders had neither the means nor the heart to engage in the same kind of aggressive colonization that had characterized their prewar phase of imperialism.

For the industrialized states, the prime belligerents in the war, the immediate postwar years were lived in hopes that a secure peace had been attained in the context of their own domestic needs for recovery and economic prosperity. The war had increased the pace of industrialization, creating vast new communities of workers. The war had also aroused new hopes for human and economic betterment at the same time that it had disrupted the old strongholds of social privilege and inherited wealth. Russia experienced the most momentous problems of national organization and social adjustment. The revolution had only begun, and the years between the wars were to take Russia through stages of ruthless political struggle, forced social leveling and industrialization and collectivization of the economy. No people, except perhaps the Turks and Chinese, were to be put through such drastic upheavals as the Russians under Stalin.

The difficulties faced by the Russian people were by and large only extreme cases of the problems that confronted the other industrialized

Left: Mounted police protect a truck carrying essential supplies through the streets of London during the General Strike of 1926.

Above right: Crowds gather outside the New York Stock Exchange following the Wall Street Crash of 1929. The failure of the US economy to regulate its affairs led directly to the Crash which in turn pushed the world economy into the Great Depression.

Right: A scene from the Spanish Civil War – Nationalist troops of General Franco lead away prisoners captured from the Government Army.

states. In each the pressures of a continuous modern revolution, begun in the seventeenth and eighteenth centuries, were still at work. Now the modern industrialized economy gave to each people the capacity for what appeared to be unlimited economic growth. The age-old vested interests could no longer inhibit the demand for political equality and the extension of general welfare to all levels of society. Expectations had been aroused which could not be suppressed. The countries of Europe, the Americas and Japan all faced, during the 1920s and 1930s, the need to adjust their political structures to greater mass participation and their economic and social systems. But conflicts arose among the interests of the state, the industrialists and the workers over basic national policy. The weaknesses of the economic systems of the capitalist nations were devastatingly proven by the Great Depression.

In Britain during the interwar years domestic politics gradually yielded to popular pressure, producing by 1924 the first Labour Cabinet under Ramsay MacDonald. Manhood suffrage had been granted in 1918; ten years later the franchise was extended to women as well. The General Strike of 1926, which involved nearly half of Britain's six million unionized workers, was a complete failure, however; the divided unions could not match the adroit handling of the situation by the employers and the government. In foreign policy Britain took a conciliatory course. The British protectorate over Egypt was ended in 1922, and the Government of India Act of 1935 put India on the road toward self-government. Thus Britain tried to reduce commitments abroad so as to concentrate on difficult fiscal and labor problems at home. Yet in the end such efforts were to end in failure, for a resurgent Germany and an aggressive Italy and Japan turned what had been a policy of accommodation under Neville Chamberlain into one which would soon be seen as appeasement.

France experienced an even more chaotic period of domestic unrest after World War I. Socialist parties, soon joined by the Communists, added a new dimension to the political struggle, while crisis after crisis plagued the financial security of the government. Not until the 1930s, after France had felt the effects of worldwide economic depression, was effective social reform

planned. The 1936 Popular Front Ministry of Léon Blum, in reaction to a wave of strikes, introduced a broad program of labor reforms that offered new protection for the worker. But again, the specter of a resurgent Germany faced the French. Blum was forced to postpone social reform to induce the great defense industrialists to speed up the pace of rearmament.

Even more than the other Allied powers who had just defeated Germany, the United States hoped to be able to return to a condition of international stability and domestic prosperity. The idealistic principles which President Wilson took to Versailles contrasted sharply with the rejection of the resulting treaty by the Senate and the refusal of the United States to join the League of Nations. Throughout the 1930s the mood in America was that of isolation and economic protectionism, a mood that was rudely shattered by the Stock Market Crash of 1929 and the dis-

astrous depression which followed. America too was confronted with massive labor unrest and the need to take measures to safeguard the livelihood of its farmers and laborers. Whereas in Europe socialist and Labor parties led the way in forcing social reforms, Roosevelt's New Deal was more moderate and reformist. Already endowed with a fully democratic political system, the American free enterprise system of economy was stretched and patched but not discarded. What Roosevelt did was to fashion a balance of power between labor, management and agriculture, with the government taking a crucial leadership role. As such he gave the particularly American answer to problems of economic growth and dislocation of the interwar years.

Both Germany and Italy met the challenges of the interwar years with totalitarian dictatorships. Frustrated by the negligible rewards received at the Versailles peace settlement and suffering from general economic depression, Italy entered the postwar era in a very precarious state. By 1921 communists and Fascists were rioting in Italy's cities. Mussolini rode to power as the strong man who could restore order to a divided country. His methods of securing legitimacy by rigging the election laws were prophetic of the totalitarian techniques by which modern populations could be manipulated. Hitler's seizure of power after the failure of the Weimar Government in Germany rested also on a skillful manipulation of the German people's frustrated nationalist feelings, fear of communism and economic depression. In both Italy and Germany dictators, working through single parties, imposed their own private control system over the constitutional forms that had previously existed. The people's wants were submerged into a nationalistic effort which led ultimately to war.

These examples by no means exhaust the many separate patterns by which the nations of Europe adjusted to postwar problems of modernization. The Scandinavian countries followed a general course of democratic politics but with a much greater reliance on socialist economic policies than either Britain or France. The new-formed states of eastern Europe, Czechoslovakia, Hungary, Yugoslavia and the remaining Balkan states, struggling to create viable national identities,

remained preoccupied with problems of national
minorities and the vast differences in outlook that
existed between city and country, and, in the
country, between landowners and peasants. The
countries of the Iberian Peninsula and their
American offshoots experienced still another pattern of adjustment. The spurt of industrial growth
and export trade occasioned by the war in Europe
exacerbated social tensions in these countries,
which had not yet succeeded (except perhaps in
Mexico) in breaking the dominant hold of the
Church, aristocracy and business and professional
elites over national life. Social ferment in Spain
brought into existence in 1931 a socialist government that tried to enact revolutionary social and
economic reforms overnight. Civil war resulted,
and the victory, after 700,000 lives had been lost,
went to General Franco. His conservative dictatorship quickly stamped out the fires of social agitation.

Symbolically, the Spanish Civil War was a
major landmark of the interwar years. For a time
during the Civil War the lines were drawn between the communist and non-communist blocs
in Europe: Russia supplied the revolutionary
government, and German and Italian 'volunteers'
fought along with Franco. If the Great Depression
destroyed the postwar generation's confidence in
the capacity of a free economy to provide security,
the war in Spain destroyed its faith in the collective security measures represented by the League
of Nations, and the defeat of the revolutionaries
in Spain shattered its belief in the inevitability of
continuing social revolution.

Having been a belligerent on the side of the
Allies in World War I, Japan joined the victors in
seeking its share in the rewards. China had also
fought against Germany, but only nominally. Its

Left: President of the
Turkish Republic, Kemal
Ataturk, dances with his
adopted daughter at her
wedding. He deliberately
adopted Western customs
and imposed them upon
Turkey as a means of
dragging the nation into the
modern world.

Below left: Leader of the
Indian Moslem League,
Mohammed Ali Jinnah,
addresses his supporters at
a rally in New Delhi. The
League worked in uneasy
partnership with Gandhi's
Congress Movement in
promoting opposition to
British rule in India.

Right: The government of
the first Chinese republic
pictured after the overthrow
of the last Manchu emperor
in 1911. Under the
leadership of Dr Sun Yat-
sen (fifth from left), the new
republic was to prove
chronically incapable of
solving the country's many
problems or, for that matter,
of forging China into a
modern, cohesive nation
state.

presence at Versailles was occasioned by the problem of German concessions in China and the need to assure joint agreement against further violation of China's territorial integrity. To an extent, however, the interwar years held the same significance for both China and Japan. Both had experienced their first modern revolutions, Japan in 1868 and China in 1911, and both were undergoing the traumas of nation-building and industrialization. Social and political change was yet to run its course in either country, and was not to do so until after World War II. Yet when that had happened, the two countries found themselves on opposite sides of the ideological split which divides the world today.

In the Middle East the interwar years brought the final dissolution of the Ottoman Empire. World War I had all but driven the Turks out of Europe, and European troops had been active in all areas of the Ottoman Empire. Egypt, Mesopotamia, Iran, Syria all ended the war under European control. The years that followed were dominated by struggle over leadership in these former parts of the Ottoman Empire. The struggles were both for leadership against the Western powers and between old and new values within Muslim society. Turkey, through vigorous reform, became the first to make the break with the past and to turn purposefully toward modern change. In 1923 Mustafa Kemal pulled Turkey out of deep trouble to proclaim a republic which abolished the Caliphate and by 1928 had led to the abandonment of Islam as the state religion. Riza Shah's assumption of powers in Iran in 1925 led to similar modern reforms, except that Islam was retained. Egypt became a constitutional monarchy in 1923. Thus precariously constituted independent regimes tried to cope with problems of political instability and economic weakness and the continued presence of the British and French troops on their soil.

India also faced the double problem of independence from British rule and the requirements of modern nation building. Despite relatively early British responsiveness to Indian demands for self-government, the problems of national identity proved acute. The entire sub-continent had never in history been unified under a single indigenous government. Indian nationalism consequently rested on a strange admixture of British political thought and Hindu and Muslim cultural identification. From the first conflict arose between the Congress Movement leadership which was Hindu and the Muslim League. Symbolic of the two groups were Mohammed Ali Jinnah, the fiery Muslim leader, and Mahatma Gandhi, the hero of Hindu nationalism. Although Muslims and Hindus agreed to work together in 1916, and although Gandhi strove to keep alive a Hindu-Muslim rapprochement, the two great divisions of the population of the sub-continent were frequently at odds. The Government of India Act of 1935, which gave India a framework for local self-government within the British Commonwealth, while a major step toward independence, led to deepening conflict between the national and religious aspirations of Hindus and Muslims. Thus when independence eventually came in 1947 it was necessary to create two nations, India and Pakistan, out of what had been British India.

To the east beyond India, the interactions between colonial rule and ethnic and religious identifications were played out in a number of complex patterns. Indonesia, like India, faced the problem of national identity within a colonial regime which had been imposed upon a heterogeneous political and cultural base. Indonesian nationalism, while it had as its obvious enemy the Dutch colonial rule, was still in search of a sense of nation and even of a common language. During the interwar years various ideologies – Islam, communism or simple anti-colonialism – fed a variety of political movements with the island of Java as the main arena. In the figure of Achmed Sukarno, the Indonesians at last found a leader who could join the concepts of social reform with sentiments of nationality to create a powerfully unifying nationalism. But his mission was not to be fulfilled until after World War II.

The case of Indochina exemplifies still another aspect of the interwar years in Southeast Asia. There, to an extent different only in intensity rather than kind, anti-colonial sentiment was stimulated by the example of other revolutions in Russia and Asia. Indonesian intellectuals such as Ho Chi Minh, educated in Paris and Moscow, provided the leadership of the early movements toward independence and social reform. For the people at large the examples of Japan's victory over Russia in 1905 and the Chinese Revolution of 1911 served as reminders that the White Man was not invulnerable. But for both Indochina and Indonesia, 1941 brought Japanese conquest and occupation.

The last bastion of European colonialism was, of course, Africa. By 1939 Africa consisted of 49 colonies and only two sovereign states. But the presence of the colonial powers was not the only impediment to the spread of self-government in Africa. The discrepancy between local tribal or kingship organization and the requirements of modern statehood was so vast that few colonies were capable of mounting independence movements until colonial rule itself had laid the foundations of regional government. And for the incipient native political leader there were neither powerful ethnic memories nor common religious beliefs to form the basis of nationalist movements which could be used against the European rulers. Yet the startling fact is that by 1965 seven-eighths of Africa would be independent. Almost overnight the colonial system had shown itself as a very temporary phenomenon.

Thus the interwar years were a period of immense ferment everywhere, a ferment out of which came a strange amalgam of cataclysmic regressions, undeniable advances and, perhaps above all, a host of historical ambiguities that bemuse us still.

World War I

The origins of the war which began at the end of July 1914 have been debated by scholars perhaps more than any other issue in European history. The debate started in earnest immediately the war ended and has never ceased. Any account given here of the war's origins will inevitably be simplistic but it is hoped to make clear the facts of the main events leading to its outbreak.

The crisis of 1914 resulted from the fears of the government of one great European empire that its realm was facing dissolution and from the growing might of and tension between two others. The empire threatened with disintegration was Austria-Hungary. The threat to its continued existence was posed by the nationalism of subject peoples, some of whom spoke Slavonic languages and were increasingly dissatisfied with both Habsburg overlordship and the dominance of the German and Magyar (Hungarian) races. The empires whose power was continuing to grow and whose antagonism threatened peace were Germany and Russia.

The Russian Empire of the Romanov family was, like the Habsburg Empire, multinational. But the dominance of the Russian people within the Empire was, for demographic reasons, quite secure. Russia, despite an autocratic system of government, the lack of any kind of parliament until 1905, and a bureaucracy both inefficient and tainted with corruption, was by no means a stagnant state in the half century preceding the Bolshevik takeover. It was an expanding power which had acquired vast realms in Central Asia and the Far East. Though defeated and humiliated by the Japanese in the war of 1904-05, Russia had recovered by 1914. The Empire was making giant strides in industrialization and the modernization of its armed forces. Russia achieved, with the help of French finance, a rate of economic growth which compared favorably with that of any major European state. Taken in conjunction with military improvements this growing economic power seriously worried both Austria-Hungary and Germany.

The expansion of Russian power was particularly perplexing to the Germans (who had a serious and chronic trade deficit with Russia) in view of the fact that the Russians became, in 1894, the allies of a long-standing potential enemy to Germany, the French Third Republic. There was nothing inevitable about war between Germany and Russia in 1914, and even less necessary was war between Germany and France. The level of hostility between the governments and peoples of Germany and France was vastly less than it had been, for example, during the Boulanger Crisis of the 1880s. The German annexation of the provinces of Alsace and Lorraine, taken from France in 1871, had inevitably created some long-term bitterness. But, though the French public was still not totally reconciled to their loss even in 1914, and though no French politician could admit publicly that they were irretrievable, French desire for 'revanche' (revenge) had declined appreciably since about 1890. France had to some extent been compensated by the acquisition of a colonial empire in Indochina and by the expansion of her dominions in North Africa. This overseas imperial activity had provided a safety valve for her military energies. There was no substantial

body of opinion in France in 1914 in favor of starting a war with Germany to recover Alsace-Lorraine. Yet Germany, a state which Bismarck had regarded as a 'satisfied power' with no further territorial ambitions in Europe, launched what amounted to an unprovoked attack on France in August 1914. This behavior requires explanation.

We have already indicated that the power most feared over the long-term by the government of Imperial Germany in the years before 1914 was not France but Russia. France's population and industrial growth were slow compared with those of Germany. The passage of the years was thought likely to merely diminish France's military potential relative to that of her giant neighbor. France's inferiority was offset only by her Russian alliance. After the fall of Bismarck in 1890, France's relations with Russia had grown progressively warmer. They signed a formal military alliance in 1894. This situation had been prevented by careful diplomacy for as long as Bismarck was German Chancellor and, even when it was formed, the Franco-Russian partnership seemed a strange sort of match. The radical republic, heir to the French revolutionary tradition, seemed an unlikely ally for the great illiberal autocracy of the East. Yet there were powerful forces pulling them together. Germany had made a military alliance with Austria-Hungary in 1879. Austria-Hungary and Russia were at loggerheads in the Balkans, where both states were trying to expand their power. German support for Austria-Hungary in the Balkans was bound to antagonize Russia and there was no European Great Power other than France with whom Russia could seek a guarantee against an Austro-German combination.

The driving principle of Bismarckian diplomacy had been to keep France isolated in Europe. Bismarck had made three successive agreements with Russia in order to keep her apart from France. The last of these, the Reinsurance Treaty of 1887, was not renewed by the government of German Kaiser Wilhelm II when it lapsed after Bismarck's fall. This was despite Russia's clearly expressed willingness to renew. Wilhelm and his government were apparently concerned that the terms of the Reinsurance Treaty conflicted with those of their alliance with Austria-Hungary. It should have been no surprise to the German foreign office, however, when Russia, spurned by Germany, concluded a military alliance with France.

Great Britain's conclusion of agreements (called 'Ententes') with France (1904) and Russia (1907) certainly did surprise the Germans. Great Britain's imperial rivalry with these powers had brought her close to war with each of them on several occasions in the late nineteenth century. Great Britain was driven to settle her differences with France and Russia by the building of the German High Seas Fleet, which seemed to threaten the security of her home islands, by the German Emperor's ambition to create an overseas empire, which would almost certainly have to be at British expense, and by blustering and incompetent German diplomacy.

Europe in 1914 had two firm alliances between Great Powers: that between Austria-Hungary and Germany and that between France and Russia. Italy was formally attached to Germany and Aus-

tria-Hungary but this attachment was known to be very unreliable. Great Britain's attachments to France and Russia were informal. Conversations had taken place between the British and French General Staffs about arrangements for the dispatch of a British expeditionary force to France in the event of a German attack, but the British government was not bound to declare war. Great Britain did, however, have a firm commitment to intervene against any power violating Belgian neutrality and this turned out to be critical.

A general European war in 1914 was made more likely by the assumption in Germany that it was inevitable sooner or later and by the conviction that it had better, for Germany's sake, be sooner. The German General Staff preferred it to be sooner because of their fear of the growth of Russian military power.

The Balkan crisis

The immediate crisis which led to the war began, predictably enough, in the Balkans. Austrian and Russian interests had been in conflict there for decades. In the competition for power and influence in the Balkans Russia had, on the whole, been more successful. Russia was able to pose as the protector of the emerging Slav nations there, especially Serbia. For Austria-Hungary, on the other hand, Slav nationalism presented the threat of her own disintegration. In 1908 Austria-Hungary had annexed the provinces of Bosnia and Herzegovina whose populations were mainly Serb. Russia, though she had opposed the annexations, had backed down on that occasion, despite her role as protector of the Slavs. The Serbs of Bosnia and Herzegovina, however, continued to want union with Serbia and Serbia, to Austria's disgust, encouraged them. It was the murder of the heir to the Habsburg throne in Sarajevo, the capital of Bosnia, by a Serb nationalist which triggered the Great War.

The General Staff of Austria-Hungary under Conrad von Hötzendorf had been planning aggressive wars against Serbia for years. His prob-

CENTRAL POWERS, 1914
NEUTRAL COUNTRIES LATER ALIGNED WITH CENTRAL POWERS

ALLIES, 1914
NEUTRAL COUNTRIES LATER ALIGNED WITH ALLIES

ALLIED WITH CENTRAL POWERS, DECLARED NEUTRALITY AT OUTBREAK OF WAR, THEN JOINED ALLIES

COUNTRIES REMAINING NEUTRAL

Below left: Kaiser Wilhelm II, the Supreme War Lord. Although in theory the Kaiser controled the German Army in practice he was a cypher.

Right: Europe in 1914 – the line-up of the combatant nations.

Below: Princip, the assassin of the Archduke Franz Ferdinand being led away after being beaten by the Austrian police.

Left: Some of the few antiquated heavy guns of the Serbian Army in action against the Austrians during the winter of 1915.

Right: Emperor Franz Josef of Austria-Hungary.

Far right: Colonel-General Helmuth von Moltke, Chief of the German General Staff 1906-14.

Below right: 'The Russian Steamroller.' A Russian infantry battalion on the line of march in East Prussia.

lem, and that of his government, was that they could not risk war with Serbia's protector, Russia, unless they could be sure of German support. The assassination of the Archduke Franz Ferdinand and his wife by Gavrilo Princip and his accomplices, who actually had some help and encouragement from members of the Serbian government (though this was not proven at the time), gave the government of Austria-Hungary the opportunity to pose as an injured party and to present Serbia with an ultimatum impossible for her government to accept. It might then be possible to gain German backing for a war to destroy her.

Austria-Hungary's pose as an injured party in June-July 1914 was false. Franz Ferdinand had been deeply unpopular at court in Vienna. Messages to his uncle, the Emperor Franz Josef, by the heads of state of Britain, Russia and other countries, expressing shock and sympathy, were misdirected. The Emperor had disliked his nephew for his marriage, without consent, to Sophia Cotek who had insufficient royal blood, and for his relatively advanced views on the nationality question within the Empire. He was positively glad of his nephew's death and there was no mourning at court. The Austrian government first obtained the assurance of the German government that Germany would support Austria-Hungary, if necessary to the point of war with Russia, and then proceeded with its program for Serbia's destruction.

The most critical decision leading to war in 1914, and the most avoidable, was the German decision to back Austria-Hungary in its dealings with Serbia, if necessary to and beyond the point of war with Russia. The humiliation and destruction of Serbia was not a vital German interest. The threat of Austria-Hungary's disintegration was long-term rather than immediate and Austria-Hungary had little choice but to remain faithful to her German alliance. The German decision seems to have been based partly on the desire of Germany's General Staff to fight the 'inevitable' general European war before Russia grew too strong or Austria-Hungary too weak. Powerful groups in Germany also seem to have been con-

ceiving far-reaching ambitions for the restructuring of the whole European state system. Certainly the German government produced a far-reaching program of war aims within weeks of the war's commencement. It can be argued that it was only these grandiose ambitions, widely accepted by the German ruling elites before 1914, which justified the German General Staff's view that a major European war was in the long run inevitable.

Austria-Hungary presented an ultimatum to Serbia on 23 July 1914 whose terms shocked all the world except herself and Germany. Their acceptance in full would have involved the Serbian government in a major abdication of sovereignty. Nevertheless, unsure of Russian backing, it accepted most of them. This was not enough for the Austrians who clearly wanted a war in order to destroy the Serbian state. In the last week of July there seemed to be a failure of nerve in Germany and a belated attempt to prevent war by restraining the Austrian government. But when Austria-Hungary finally declared war on Serbia, on 28 July, the German government took no practical action to prevent a drift to general European war. Indeed its actions contributed far more to bringing general war about than those of any government except the Austrian. An effort made by the British Foreign Secretary, Lord Grey, to mediate was taken up by neither the Austrian nor the German governments.

When the Austrian Army began its offensive against Serbia in the last days of July the rigid mobilization plans of the Great powers developed their own momentum toward general war. On 29 July the Russian Army began to mobilize in order to be ready to come to Serbia's aid and the Russian government warned Austria-Hungary to desist. Russia, however, had no administrative arrangements for mobilizing armies on her border with Austria-Hungary without mobilizing them on the German border also. The necessity for all the Continental powers, of basing their mobilization plans on complex railway timetables, and the impossibility of changing these timetables in the middle of mobilization without causing chaos, introduced an element of rigidity. This was particularly true in Germany's case.

A two-front war

The main armies potentially hostile to the German Army, those of France and Russia, lay on widely separated fronts. Fighting a war on both fronts simultaneously over a long period was a nightmare which haunted the German General Staff. Their solution, worked out in principle long before the war began, was a holding operation in East Prussia against the Russian Army, while the great bulk of the German Army attacked France and knocked her out within a few weeks. The rapid defeat of France was to be achieved by a holding operation on the Franco-German border, where the main French offensive was to be expected, while the bulk of the German Army attacked into northern France through neutral Belgium and swept around the rear of the main French armies on the Franco-German borders in a colossal encircling movement. It was an imaginative plan. But it was the only plan the German General Staff had. Even if Germany was involved in a war with Russia, which did not directly involve France, and in which French intervention was not certain, Germany was bound, according to her General Staff, to begin the war with an attack on France through Belgium. The German General Staff had the further doctrine that 'mobilization means war.' If either Russia or France mobilized its army Germany was bound to implement its single war plan (known as the Schlieffen Plan, after its originator) even if the mobilization was not directed against Germany. And that is exactly what Germany did in 1914.

The Russian Foreign Minister, Sazonov, decided upon a partial mobilization of the Army in support of Serbia on 29 July. 'Partial mobilization' was of dubious practicality. The Russian General Staff had no plans for it. This did not matter because, hearing of the bombardment of Belgrade, Serbia's capital, Czar Nicholas II ordered full mobilization the following day. On 31 July the German government gave an ultimatum to the Russians to demobilize within 12 hours and an ultimatum to the French government to state, within 18 hours, whether France would remain neutral in a German-Russian war. When neither country complied with these demands, Germany declared war on both (on Russia on 1 August and on France on 2 August) and implemented the latest variant of the Schlieffen Plan.

One of the many problems with the Schlieffen Plan was that its implementation involved Germany in a war with Great Britain, assuming the British stood by their treaty obligations to Belgium. For, by the Treaty of London in 1839, Britain guaranteed Belgian neutrality. Had it not been for the violation of Belgian neutrality there might well have been serious dissension in the Liberal Cabinet and in Parliament about the wisdom of British entry into the war. With the invasion of Belgium there was very little. The British government declared war on Germany on 4 August when the Germans ignored an ultimatum to withdraw from Belgium. The British immediately began arrangements for the movement to the Continent of an expeditionary force of five infantry divisions and a cavalry division.

August 1914 proved to be the bloodiest month which Europe had ever witnessed. All the Great Powers except Britain had peacetime, short-service conscription which meant that when they mobilized their reserves they could set in motion armies millions strong. These titanic forces were to clash within days in Belgium, France, Alsace-Lorraine, East Prussia and Galicia. The plan implemented by von Moltke, the Chief of the German General Staff, was in some respects different from the one he inherited from his predecessor, Schlieffen, who had intended to keep only very weak forces on the Franco-German borders and gradually to withdraw these forces in the face of the anticipated French onslaught into Alsace-Lorraine. Meanwhile the overwhelmingly powerful German right wing would sweep in a wide arc through both Holland and Belgium, along the Channel coast and around the rear of the main concentration of French armies attacking on the Franco-German border. The whole plan has been characterized as a 'revolving door concept.' The harder the French pushed against the German left in Alsace-Lorraine the more surely they would be taken in the rear by the wide sweep of the German right.

Though it looked beautiful on paper there were

certain practical difficulties with Schlieffen's original concept. Moltke altered it somewhat. The sweep through Holland, which Schlieffen had planned, was thought inadvisable by Moltke. If Holland ceased to be a neutral country and Great Britain entered the war Britain could blockade Dutch ports. Moltke hoped, by keeping Holland neutral, to be able to import through Dutch ports commodities necessary for Germany's war effort.

Moltke's determination to avoid the violation of Dutch neutrality meant that the initial sweep of the German right was less wide than Schlieffen had intended. Rather than marching along the Channel coast the German right wing would turn through central Belgium. In this way the distance to be covered by the German infantry would be

greatly reduced. This was a very important consideration. It was an era before the mechanization of armies and Schlieffen's original plan made demands on the marching performance of the German infantry which were probably beyond the endurance of the average conscript. The problem of supplying the massive German right through Schlieffen's gigantic wheel were also insoluble in Moltke's view. Moltke, partly for supply reasons and partly for fear of the likely French offensive into Alsace-Lorraine, modified the Schlieffen Plan so as to weaken the German right and strengthen the left.

The French, of course, had a plan of their own. Plan XVII called for a powerful offensive into Alsace-Lorraine. The French Army had developed

an almost mystical faith in the offensive at all costs which was linked to a belief in the superiority of moral over physical factors in war. Given France's relatively small population and her consequent need to husband her manpower resources it would have been much more sensible to have remained on the defensive in the early stages.

War in the West

The Germans entered Belgium on 4 August having already violated the neutrality of Luxemburg on 2 August, the same day on which they declared war on France. The Germans were confronted with a major problem in taking the great fortress city of Liège. The German First Army and much of the Second Army by-passed Liège. Six brigades of the Second Army were, however, constituted as the Army of the Meuse under General von Emmich and tasked with the capture of Liège. The fortress contained 40,000 Belgian troops and would have constituted a major threat to the German rear if not swiftly reduced. After a number of costly and futile assaults during the daylight hours, on the night on 5 August a German brigade temporarily commanded by Erich von Ludendorff (who was to become one of the war's most famous personalities) penetrated the ring of forts around the city itself and seized the heights across the Meuse from the citadel, a fortification much older than the late-nineteenth-century forts surrounding it, but containing a major barracks. By the afternoon of 6 August the Germans were able to enter the city of Liège and accept the surrender of the citadel. All of the forts, however, continued to hold out until 12 August when the Germans brought up super-heavy siege artillery. They then

began to be crushed one by one by the weight of bombardment. The last of the forts surrendered on 17 August.

The Germans had taken some losses capturing Liège and they were intensely irritated by the resistance of both the Belgian Army and the Belgian civilians who took up arms as partisans in several parts of the country. In retaliation, towns and villages were burned and hundreds of civilians shot. The inevitable sense of outrage in the civilized world was fanned by British and French propagandists who exaggerated the scale of the atrocities and even invented some atrocities which had not occurred. Belgian resistance, while incurring heavy penalties from the vindictive Germans, did achieve some military results. The Belgians systematically wrecked their railway network, blowing bridges and tunnels. This played havoc with German logistics and contributed to the failure of the German offensive against France.

The first major action fought by the French Army in this war was the 'Battle of the Frontiers' fought in Alsace-Lorraine and the Ardennes. These offensives were defeated by the Germans with, generally speaking, quite extraordinary ease. The French began their offensive operations with an invasion of Alsace by the VII Corps and 8th Cavalry Division, both of General Dubail's First Army, on 7 August. After capturing the town of Altkirch and the city of Mulhouse, they were violently counterattacked by the Germans and thrown out. On 14 August came the main French offensive into Alsace and Lorraine. Joffre, the French Commander in Chief, ordered his First and Second Armies to attack across the frontier. The Germans initially fought a delaying action

with a covering screen which gradually fell back and then, when the advancing French were tired and disordered, they launched a violent counterattack on the 20th. The French forces fell back in some disorder.

Moltke had originally intended that once he had foiled the French invasion of Alsace and Lorraine he would transfer troops away from that area to strengthen his right wing. The devastation of the Belgian railway network would now make this somewhat difficult. Also the success of his counterattack with the Sixth and Seventh Armies in Alsace-Lorraine made him decide that it would be advantageous to sustain it. He now hoped he could execute a double envelopment of the French armies, enveloping both the French left from the north, as originally intended by Schlieffen, and their right from the south. Meanwhile, a French effort in the center of the front into the Ardennes region of southeastern Belgium fared as badly as the Alsace-Lorraine effort, the French Third and Fourth Armies being defeated by the German Fifth and Fourth Armies. From 22 August the French Armies repulsed in the Ardennes were in retreat. They fell back across the Meuse and established themselves with their right flank on the fortress of Verdun.

French losses on the southern half of the Western Front in the first week of the war were little short of catastrophic, but the situation in the north was potentially even more serious. The left flank of the French armies was likely to be successfully enveloped and a giant encirclement of all the French forces accomplished. It seemed quite possible that the Germans might achieve complete victory within weeks.

After the fall of the Liège forts most of the Bel-

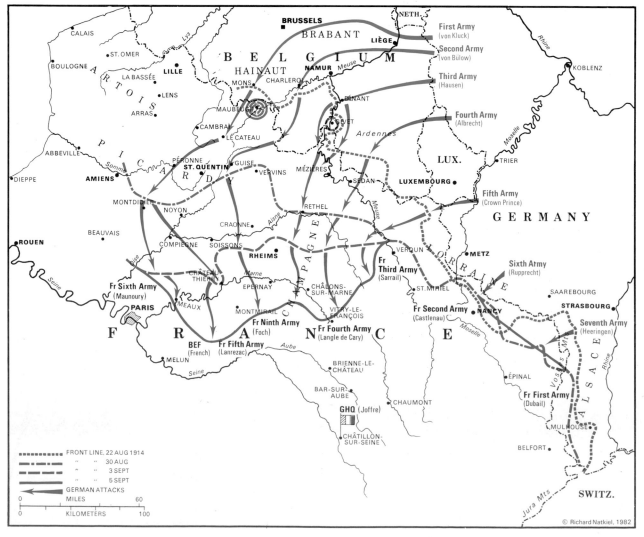

Left: A map of the complex set of maneuvers that gave the French victory in the Battle of the Marne.

Above right: Field Marshal von Hindenburg and General Ludendorff brief the Kaiser after the battle of Tannenberg, August 1914.

Above far right: Marshal Joffre, C-in-C of the French Army 1914-16.

Right: German horse-drawn transports pass through Brussels on 20 August 1914.

© Richard Natkiel, 1982

FRONT LINE, 22 AUG 1914
"   "   30 AUG
"   "   3 SEPT
"   "   5 SEPT
GERMAN ATTACKS

0   MILES   60
0   KILOMETERS   100

gian Army had retreated to Antwerp. This left a huge gap between it and the northernmost French army, General Lanrezac's Fifth, at the junction of the Sambre and Meuse rivers. General Lanrezac's left flank remained wide open until 22 August when the British Expeditionary Force arrived from its assembly area near Le Cateau and took up position on the Mons Canal, an extension of the line of the Sambre, on Lanrezac's left. Early on the morning of 23 August the British were attacked by the main body of the northernmost German Army, von Kluck's First. In its first battle of the war the British Army acquitted itself well. On that bloody Sunday morning the extremely rapid and accurate rifle fire of the British infantry decimated the dense formations of the attacking Germans. The initial German attacks on the morning of 23 August were hurriedly launched

before the Germans appreciated the strength of the opposition and without careful artillery preparation. The attacks of that afternoon were better coordinated and launched with effective artillery support. By the end of the afternoon the heavily outnumbered British had fallen back three miles, blowing the canal bridges behind them.

The British were still prepared to accept battle on the following day, but by that time General Lanrezac's Fifth French Army on the Sambre, which had also been under considerable pressure, had fallen back. The British Commander, Sir John French, had little choice but to withdraw also. A long and exhausting retreat began. The British II Corps under Sir Horace Smith-Dorrien stood and fought at Le Cateau on 26 August, largely because it was too exhausted to retreat further. But it started retreating again the following day. On 29

August Lanrezac's Fifth Army had a tactical success in a counterattack against von Bulow's German Second Army near Guise. But given the fact that the British were in poor shape and continuing to retreat on his left Lanrezac was compeled to fall back again on 30 August. Throughout August there was serious misunderstanding and mistrust between French and Lanrezac and this contributed to Allied ineffectiveness.

Turning point on the Marne

The retreat of the British and the French Fifth Army came to an end with 'the miracle of the Marne.' Severe physical exhaustion was beginning to affect those armies on both sides which had been involved in the great turning movement through Belgium. The most exhausted, however,

were those on the circumference of the wheel, the British Expeditionary Force and von Kluck's German First Army. Believing that the British Expeditionary Force was finished as a fighting force, Kluck, with Moltke's permission, decided to wheel east of Paris, rather than west as originally intended, to shorten his march and to cut off the retreat of Lanrezac's Fifth Army, the only effective fighting formation which the Germans believed to be opposing their southward wheel. The German assessment was not totally wrong. The British Expeditionary Force was not physically shattered but the nerve of Sir John French had practically gone and he was contemplating a complete withdrawal from France.

Lanrezac was probably not in much better psychological shape than French and he was relieved by Joffre on 3 September and replaced with an aggressive corps commander from his own army, Franchet d'Esperey. At the same time Joffre reshuffled his forces, moving formations by rail from the armies of his right wing to those of his left. He was thus able to build up a considerable numerical superiority over the Germans on his left. As Kluck's First Army passed to the east of Paris it was attacked in the flank by the French Sixth Army based in the Paris area. Turning to meet this threat, Kluck's First Army opened up a gap between itself and von Bulow's Second Army to its left.

On 6 September Joffre launched a general counterattack with all the French armies between Verdun and Paris. During this offensive the British Expeditionary Force inserted itself into the gap between the German First and Second Armies. Realizing that there was the possibility of his First Army being enveloped, Moltke ordered a general withdrawal on 10 September. The Germans quickly broke off contact as the allied armies were too exhausted to pursue. Joffre who, despite initial disasters, had kept his nerve during these early weeks of the war, had won a major strategic victory which had saved France. It is known as the Battle of the Marne.

The next phase of the war on the Western Front was a series of attempts by each side to turn the northwestern flank of the opposing forces. This phase involved many more bloody battles including the notorious First Battle of Ypres during which the small professional army which Britain had sent to France was all but bled white. By the end of the first year of war a continuous front was in place which neither side looked like breaking.

Both sides dug in hard, and two continuous lines of trenches came into existence from the Channel coast to the Swiss border. With no open flanks, enveloping movements were no longer possible. If decisive results were to be obtained it would be necessary to break through the enemy's front. Breakthrough, attainable only by frontal assault in the face of machine guns and magazine rifle fire and the defensive fire of enemy artillery, was always very costly but not impossible. The rapid exploitation of a breakthrough, before the enemy brought up reserves (often by rail) and established a new front, was the real problem. This was an age when the fastest possible tactical movement was the four miles per hour of the heavily laden, foot-marching infantryman. There would be no tanks till 1916 and cavalry was too vulnerable even to the lightest infantry opposition. 'Trench warfare' had arrived and the Western Front was to experience four years of deadlock before one side finally collapsed through complete exhaustion.

War in the East

In the East 1914 also witnessed dramatic events and, as in the West, the actual course of events seemed to mock the prewar plans of all the belligerents. As in the West so in the East; there was no end in sight at the end of the year. The Austrian offensive into Serbia launched on 28 July was humiliatingly defeated by the Serbian Army. The Russians, who mobilized their Army faster than anyone expected, launched simultaneous offensives against Germany in East Prussia and against Austria-Hungary in Galicia.

In Galicia five Russian armies inflicted a crushing defeat on four Austrian armies in a huge battle near the towns of Rava Russkaya and Lemberg on 6 September 1914. During this Galician fighting the Austrians appear to have lost a quarter of a million casualties out of 900,000 troops involved. Russian losses are not known but were probably of the same order. Russia, however, could better afford them.

Initially the Russian Army's campaign into East Prussia looked very threatening to the Germans. East Prussia was assailed from two sides. General Rennenkampf's First Army advanced from the east, passing to the north of the great Masurian Lakes. Meanwhile General Samsonov's Second Army advanced into the German province from the south, from the great salient of Russian Poland separating East Prussia from Austria-Hungary.

East Prussia was defended by a single army, the German Eighth, under General von Prittwitz, who hoped that he could fight and win defensive battles against each of these armies in turn. He sent most of his Eighth Army to face Rennenkampf's advance from the east, leaving a single corps to guard against a Russian advance from the

With Rennenkampf undefeated in front of him and Samsonov's Army closing on his rear von Prittwitz contemplated abandoning the whole of East Prussia, telling Moltke that a withdrawal to the Vistula was necessary. Moltke, believing that Prittwitz had lost his nerve, dismissed him and replaced him with the aged General von Hindenburg, who was called out of retirement. The dynamic Ludendorff, hero of Liège, was appointed his Chief of Staff. Moltke decided at the same time to transfer two corps to East Prussia from the Western Front. They arrived too late to influence events in the beleaguered eastern province and some authorities believe their absence to have been a contributory factor to the German defeat on the Marne.

The last days of August 1914 in East Prussia saw one of the most dramatic reversals of fortune in the history of war. The credit for it has generally been given to Ludendorff but the basic German plan may have been made by Colonel Max Hoffman, a staff officer at Eighth Army headquarters. It seems probable that the Germans could not have been successful had it not been for the inefficiency of Russian signals and the very poor cooperation between Samsonov and Rennenkampf, who had fought a duel before the war and apparently hated one another. The Germans knew that they could count on Rennenkampf's quiescence during the critical phase of the campaign because Russian signals staff, incompetent with their codebooks, sent radio messages unencoded and the Germans intercepted them.

In essence, the German plan implemented when Hindenburg and Ludendorff took over was to leave only a single cavalry division facing Rennenkampf and to move the rest of the Eighth Army to face Samsonov. Samsonov's Army had

been hurriedly thrown into the war without proper logistical support and was even short of food, water and cooking facilities. It had conducted an arduous march through Poland and into East Prussia in the heat of August and was in poor shape. On 24 August Samsonov had fought an indecisive battle, Orlau-Frankenau, against a single German corps. On the 25th Samsonov suddenly found himself facing the whole of the German Eighth Army. Violent German attacks routed both of his flanking corps and an attack on the 28th by his own two center corps was defeated. The Battle of Tannenburg ended with the encirclement and capture of almost half the Russian Second Army. The Germans took 125,000 prisoners and 500 guns in one of the greatest tactical victories of the war. Samsonov disappeared. It is reported that he killed himself.

On hearing the news of Tannenburg, Rennenkampf, who had advanced 150 miles into East Prussia, withdrew to the Insterburg Gap between the Masurian Lakes and the Baltic. Rennenkampf did protect his left flank by stationing one of his four corps at a gap in the lakes at Lotzen but he created an inadequate general reserve of only two divisions. The German Eighth Army, newly reinforced with two corps, struck on 8 September. On the 9th the Germans broke through the Lotzen Gap. Rennenkampf, threatened with envelopment, withdrew his Army while launching one counterattack on 10 September to cover his withdrawal. He succeeded in avoiding encirclement and retained most of his guns and equipment but lost considerable numbers of troops, perhaps taking 125,000 casualties of all types during the course of the battle.

The final phases of Eastern Front operations in 1914 consisted of two German offensives into Poland mounted from the Cracow area. Both were mainly intended to take pressure off the Austrians and prevent the Russians exploiting their Galician victory at Lemberg by invading the important German industrial area of Silesia. The first German advance into Poland, after some complicated maneuvering ended with the tactically inconclusive First Battle of Warsaw (9-19 October 1914). After that the Germans retired to their start line. A second German offensive into Poland resulted in the Battle of Lödz (18-25 November). At one stage during this battle, the numerically superior Russians had 50,000 Germans surrounded, but then let them escape after a series of errors. On 6 December the Russians evacuated Lödz and took up a strong defensive position between Lödz and Warsaw which the attacking Germans were not able to break.

During the second German offensive into Poland the Russians comfortably defeated an Austrian counterstroke in Galicia. The Serbs were still holding out, after smashing three Austrian offensives in 1914. Having joined the Central Powers (as the Germans and Austrians were now collectively called) in November, the Turks invaded the Russian Caucusus. To begin with this greatly worried the Russians. At the Battle of Sarakamish at the beginning of the new year, however, they practically annihilated the Turkish invasion force and had relatively little trouble with the Turks for the rest of the war. The Slavonic Allies, despite Tannenburg, had not done too badly.

A long-term war

The events of 1914 had mocked the best-laid plans of all the powers. For in August 1914 they had all expected a short war. It was clear by the end of the year that the war would be long. The German General Staff had used all its ingenuity to avoid

south. After an initial clash at Stalluponen, when an aggressive German corps commander, von François, disobeyed orders and attacked the Russians instead of waiting for them to attack, Rennenkampf slowed his advance. Meanwhile, the Russian Second Army under Samsonov was advancing unexpectedly rapidly into East Prussia from the south. Believing that he needed to deal decisively with Rennenkampf before turning to meet Samsonov, Prittwitz reluctantly launched an all-out attack on the Russian First Army instead of waiting to meet it in a defensive battle. The Battle of Gumbinnen on 20 August was tactically inconclusive but given the overall strategic situation, has to be counted a Russian victory.

Left: Some of the 125,000 Russian prisoners captured by the Germans at Tannenberg, 28 August 1914.

Above: General Rennenkampf, Commander of the Russian First Army, who failed to coordinate his movements with General Samsonov.

Right: Debris of the war. Serbian dead killed in the Austrian advance in 1915.

having to fight on two fronts for more than a few weeks. Yet the 'two-front nightmare' refused to go away. The French plans for reconquering Alsace and Lorraine had ended in disaster. The Austrian General Staff, who had so desperately wanted this war, had experienced months of virtually unrelieved catastrophe and humiliation. Fifty percent of the British troops sent to France in August had become casualties by the end of the year. British manpower and munitions reserves were proving ridiculously inadequate for operations of this duration and intensity.

If an acute shortage of trained manpower was a more serious problem for the British, with their lack of peacetime conscription, than for other powers at the end of 1914, a munitions crisis was virtually universal. The consumption of artillery ammunition, in particular, by all armies was totally unprecedented. Only the German Army, with an exceptionally large and well-organized munitions industry behind it, was not screaming 'Shell Shortage!' by the end of the year.

The belligerent powers were thus faced with the problem of organizing munitions production on an unheard of scale for a war whose duration had to be envisaged in terms of years rather than weeks. Such efforts would inevitably create tremendous distortions in the economies of the belligerent countries. In the case of Britain, markets which her industrial economy could no longer supply were, in some cases, permanently lost to competitors. Such competitors were, as in the Japanese case, only peripherally belligerent, or, as in the case of America up to April 1917, not belligerent at all.

There were also profound social and governmental changes. The sheer necessity of increased war production compelled the introduction of women into industry on an unprecedented scale, despite the prejudices of male workers. In France, with the absence of the menfolk at the front, women took over the running of thousands of peasant farms. Women were making great strides in emancipation. In Britain the enfranchisement of women in 1918 was a direct result of their wartime role.

Governments, in order to run the war effectively, had to interfere in the lives of ordinary people in ways which were sometimes unprecedented. Even Great Britain, a country with very strong traditions of individual liberty, had to introduce military conscription for the first time in 1916 to make better use of manpower and to prevent the depletion of the Army. The structure of government itself was forced to change. Until 1914, the British Cabinet, the central coordinating mechanism of a government ultimately responsible for the greatest Empire the world had seen, did not even keep its minutes and had no formal record of its decisions. To coordinate the war effort of the Empire, however, such apparently casual ways of business were inadequate. Maurice Hankey, a former Marine officer, became the Cabinet's secretary at the beginning of the war and started to take its minutes. By the end of the war there had developed the great Cabinet Secretariat which is vital to British government today.

In the East the fronts were much longer and the ratio between the forces deployed and the space they occupied much higher than in the West. In the East a war of movement was still possible in 1915 even though the movements of the unmechanized mass armies were cumbersome and slow. In the West, however, a year of stalemate was already being predicted by some observers at the end of 1914. The British Cabinet secretary, Maurice Hankey, in his famous Boxing Day memorandum, asked the Cabinet to consider making

Left: Alfred Leese's famous recruiting poster of Lord Kitchener appealing for volunteers to join the Army in 1914.

Above right: John Sargent's emotive painting depicting gassed soldiers at a field dressing station in France.

Below right: A British War Loan poster of 1915, appealing for public subscriptions.

Below far right: Starving Indian sodliers who had fought at Kut in Mesopotamia, after release from Turkish captivity.

its main effort in another theater, given the likelihood of deadlock in France and Flanders. Hankey's suggestion, though taken seriously, was really premature. Given the weakness of the British Army and the heavy losses sustained by the French, a decisive German breakthrough in the West in 1915 would have been feasible, had the Germans concentrated their main effort there.

The British nevertheless proceeded to dissipate a significant proportion of their distinctly inadequate war effort away from the Western Front in 1915, leaving most of the fighting there to the French Army. The British made a series of attempts to force the Dardanelles, seize Constantinople and knock Turkey out of the war. After the disaster at Sarakamish it is difficult to see that the Turks posed a very serious threat to the Entente Powers (or the Allies as they now generally called themselves). Perhaps the best strategy would simply have been to contain the Turks with minimal forces. Instead, having failed in March 1915 to force the Dardanelles with ships alone, the Allies made assault landings at Gallipoli in May, to clear the peninsula of Turkish guns and assist the passage of the fleet. Despite the committal of substantial forces for over half a year, the Allies failed to clear the peninsula or secure the passage of the fleet. During December 1915 and January 1916 they effected a surprise two-stage withdrawal. Though they thus saved their forces from destruction, the Allies had experienced severe humiliation at Turkish hands.

Another campaign against the Turks was mounted from India through the Persian Gulf into Mesopotamia (now Iraq). It began in October 1914 as a limited effort to ensure the continuation of oil supplies from southern Persia. Initial easy success

led the British to become too bold with inadequate forces. Their early victories led them to advance farther and farther into Mesopotamia in pursuit of objectives not clear even to themselves. The disaster they courted materialized when a single division was cut off and besieged in the city of Kut. It finally surrendered, after a long siege, in April 1916. This minor disaster, like the failure at Gallipoli, was a natural product of the amateurish conduct of British strategy which dissipated much of the Empire's war effort in sideshows, with negligible results.

Much blood was shed on the Western Front in 1915 but the balance of advantage between the sides hardly changed. Except for the Second Battle of Ypres (April-May 1915) the Germans remained generally on the defensive throughout the year, while gaining quite dramatic (though less than decisive) results with limited offensives on the Eastern Front. A holding operation in the East and an all-out offensive in the West might conceivably have paid greater dividends for them. The considerable advantages enjoyed by the defending side in this war, coupled with their limited manpower, gave the Allies little chance of gaining decisive results in the West in 1915.

The British were engaged in creating a mass army of wartime volunteers but until it was ready for action (and that was not until July 1916) the British in the West were desperately short of manpower. Because of the lack of shells they were also desperately short of firepower. British offensive capacity was thus severely limited.

Compared with the catastrophic French offensives in eastern Champagne and against the St Mihiel salient earlier in the year, a limited offensive by the British at Neuve Chapelle in March can

be counted a minor victory. The British and French together took very severe punishment and appeared for a while to be facing a critical strategic situation, before finally containing a German offensive in the Second Battle of Ypres (22 April-24 May).

A joint British-French offensive commencing on 9 May in Flanders and Artois was a total failure in the British sector and generally a failure in the French. The two main geographical objectives at which it was aimed, the Aubers Ridge and Vimy Ridge, remained in German hands. The French made another attempt on Vimy Ridge on 25 September at the same time as a British attack at Loos. Allied losses were greater than German, the gain of ground minor, and Vimy Ridge continued to be held by the Germans. Meanwhile another French offensive in Champagne (25 September-8 October), while it did more damage to the Germans than previous French efforts also involved heavy French casualties for no decisive gain.

A new element was introduced into warfare in 1915: poison gas. It was used by the German Army on the advice of the chemist, Fritz Haber. Chlorine was the first of the gases used. Its first employment in the West was at Ypres on 22 April. Generally gas proved to have great power for

inflicting casualties. Even though gas masks were manufactured on a large scale and issued to troops soon after the first attacks, they could not, from the point of view of personal comfort or military effectiveness, be worn continuously. Gas, however, did not break the stalemate on the Western Front and the Germans had good cause to regret its introduction. The British, with their own great chemical industry, proved the equals of the Germans in this form of warfare and the Germans were not helped by the fact that the prevailing wind on the Western Front was against them.

The events on the Eastern Front in 1915 were more dramatic but even more depressing for the Allies. Hindenburg and Ludendorff gained the support of the Kaiser for a major offensive in the East in support of the hard-pressed Austrians. The Austrians were desperate for such help, fearing Italian intervention against them if they did not prove their vitality by striking a major blow against the Russians. Conrad von Hötzendorf was planning an offensive in Galicia and Hindenburg obligingly supplied him with a German Army to help in this task.

Hindenburg and Ludendorff also planned a major offensive of their own in the Masurian Lakes area, which had been reoccupied by the

Russians while the main German forces were involved in Poland. All this was against the wishes of Falkenhayn, German War Minister and Chief of the General Staff. Falkenhayn believed the war could only be won in the West and wanted to concentrate the Army's effort in 1915 there. Though Falkenhayn remained Chief of Staff he was replaced as War Minister by the Kaiser who supported Hindenburg's and Ludendorff's case for offensive action in the East. But Hindenburg and Ludendorff did not get their own way entirely. They wanted an all-out offensive in the East, using very large numbers of troops transferred from the West, and aiming at knocking Russia out of the war by a gigantic pincer movement against the Russian forces in the Polish salient. They secured the transfer of only four corps from the West during the year, however, and only limited offensives in the East were undertaken. Germany also made one offensive effort in the West: the Second Battle of Ypres.

After a feint toward Warsaw on 31 January 1915 with General Mackensen's Ninth Army attacking from the region of Bolimov, the main German winter offensive was in the Masurian Lakes region. Mackensen's feint served its purpose in attracting Russian forces away from the Masurian

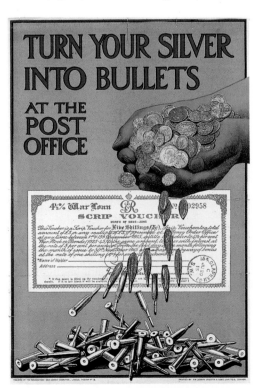

Lakes and was then broken off on 4 February. The one Russian army in the Masurian Lakes region was then assailed by two German armies. One drew the attention of the Russians by an attack through the Lotzen Gap, the other, its presence hitherto undetected, struck north of the lakes through the Insterburg Gap. The Russian Tenth Army lost all of two of its four corps. There were about 300,000 Russian casualties including 100,000 prisoners. The Second Battle of the Masurian Lakes, in February 1915, was the worst Russian disaster since Tannenburg. Nevertheless two corps of the unlucky Russian Tenth Army escaped, retreating to the Niemen and Biebrza Rivers where the German advance was halted with the aid of reinforcements.

In the southern part of the Eastern Front, the Russian Eighth Army under General Alexei Brusilov was preparing for an offensive from

Galicia through the Carpathian Mountains. The Germans and Austrians, however, who had prepared their own Galician offensive, struck first. One of the objectives of the Central Powers in this offensive was the relief of the city of Przemsyl where 200,000 Austrians were besieged. Brusilov's Army stood its ground, however, and Przemsyl fell to the Russians on 27 March 1915.

German breakthrough at Gorlice

The success at Przemsyl was, however, virtually the last good news for the Russians in 1915. A second Central Powers offensive in Galicia, using two German armies rather than just one, was launched in May. It obtained a major breakthrough on the Dunajec River near Gorlice. The Russian Third Army was destroyed in this May offensive. A series of further offensives by the Central Powers caused the gradual abandonment

of Poland by the Russians during 1915. Their withdrawal, however, was not, generally, a rout but an orderly and systematic retreat. Though they suffered two million casualties in 1915, including the loss of one million men as prisoners, the Russians were by no means finished, as they proved the next year. At the end of 1915 they still held a 600-mile front between Riga on the Baltic and Czernovitz on the Rumanian frontier. So far Russia had mobilized less of her manpower than any European Great Power except Britain. Russian war production had expanded impressively and the supply position was improving by the end of the year. Nevertheless the Grand Duke Nicholas was sacked on 5 September 1915 from his post as Commander in Chief and nominally replaced by the Czar. The real decisions were henceforth taken, in so far as they were taken at all, by General Alekseev the Chief of Staff. Few historians regard this change in command as having been an improvement.

The disasters which had befallen the Russians in 1915 were not the only ones for the Allies in the East. Bulgaria was persuaded to enter the war on the side of the Central Powers by the promise of Serbian Macedonia. Serbia was overrun by a combined Austrian-German-Bulgarian offensive from Bosnia in the west, Hungary to the north and Bulgaria to the east. These operations began on 6 October and were over by the end of the year.

Meanwhile British and French troops had landed, with the Greek government's permission, at Salonika. They were trying to get access to southern Serbia to help the Serbs. The first troops, coming from the Dardanelles area, landed on 5 October. The Bulgarians beat back their rather feeble efforts to aid the Serbs in 1915 and this front did not really come to life until later in the war. The British and French were, however, joined at Salonika by Serbian forces. These had been evacuated from the Balkan peninsula after retreating through Montenegro, and had been rested and refitted on Corfu. They were later to play a major role in the liberation of their country.

Almost the only good news for the Allies in 1915 was the Italian declaration of war on Austria-

Left: German troops in trenches with metal loopholes overlook the Masurian Lakes in East Prussia.

Below left: Italian troops, wearing French-designed steel helmets, march through Salonika, Greece, 1916.

Right: US troops in trenches in France in 1918.

Below: One of thousands of unknown German *Landser* killed by British artillery fire on the Somme.

Hungary on 25 May. During the year Italy launched four offensives on the Isonzo, inflicting perhaps 165,000 casualties on the Austrians but sustaining considerably more herself for no significant territorial gain. Italian involvement seemed to produce a useful rallying of support for the monarchy in Austria-Hungary as Italian ambitions were feared as much by the southern Slavs as by the Germans.

Verdun and the Somme

In 1916 on the Western Front two battles were fought which were etched into the consciousness of western Europeans for generations: Verdun and the Somme. The original idea behind the German offensive at Verdun seems to have been to bring about the collapse of France's will to con-

tinue the war by inflicting huge casualties on the French Army while at the same time being rather economical with German blood. Verdun was a historic fortress town which had assumed great emotive significance to the French people. In 1916 it was in a salient surrounded on three sides by German forces. Falkenhayn's concept was apparently to launch a limited offensive against the salient with the idea of drawing more and more French troops into this carefully chosen killing ground. There they would be blown to pieces by superior German artillery. Stockpiles containing three million shells had been assembled.

If such a purely attritional battle was really Falkenhayn's intention it was a highly intelligent one. When the German offensive began on 21 February 1916 the French reacted in just the emo-

tional and uncalculating spirit the Germans had anticipated. Instead of abandoning the salient as a worthless attrition-trap they fed men endlessly into it down a single road (known as the Sacred Way), itself appallingly exposed to enemy artillery. It was, perhaps, a sign of the weakening authority of Falkenhayn that his attritional concept of inflicting maximum French casualties for minimum German, was not properly adhered to. The Germans gradually became obsessed with breaking France's will by actually capturing Verdun. This obsession defeated the original objective. It seems (German casualty figures in this war were compiled in a most confusing way and it is difficult to be certain) that their losses by the end of the battle were little less than those of the French. Verdun, which they failed to take, became an even more potent symbol of French resolve.

The battle lasted until the end of the year. The French suffered perhaps half a million casualties of all types, the Germans at least 400,000. Though French manpower was much less than German, the Germans were almost equally divided between Eastern and Western Fronts and could not afford such losses either.

The offensive on the Somme had been originally proposed at an Allied conference at Chantilly in December 1915. It was Joffre's idea. He appears to have proposed the Somme mainly because this sector was the junction between the British and French armies and he wanted to commit the British to a major effort as soon as possible. In Joffre's original concept the French would play the dominant role. The German offensive at Verdun interfered with Allied plans. As the year went on it became increasingly clear that any Allied attack on the Somme would have to be mainly British. The French became desperately anxious that there should be an attack on the Somme to take the pressure off Verdun.

Sir Douglas Haig, who had replaced Sir John French as British Commander in Chief on 15 December 1915, appears to have had a very different conception of the objectives of the Somme battle from Rawlinson, the Commander in Chief of the British Fourth Army which was to have the main role in the offensive. Haig envisaged a strategically decisive breakthrough whereas Rawlinson appears to have favored a 'bite and hold' approach, first intending to seize important ground and then to let the Germans wear themselves out in counterattacks. The differences and misunderstandings between Rawlinson and Haig seem to have bedeviled the British planning for the battle.

Late in June the British were at last ready to begin. A heavy preliminary bombardment began on 24 June and the detonation of a number of huge mines under the German lines was the signal for the infantry assault on 1 July. That day proved the bloodiest in the British Army's history. Large parts of the German trench system had been demolished by the one-and-a-half million shell preliminary bombardment, but the German troops had sheltered in deep dugouts until the attack started and these had generally survived. The vitally important German barbed wire remained intact. Too many of the British shells had been shrapnel rather than high explosive, and, contrary to the opinion of British gunners at the time, shrapnel is actually of little use in cutting wire. There was also the problem that, owing to the hasty expansion of the British munitions industry, a high proportion of the shells fired failed to explode.

Heavily laden British infantrymen, advancing slowly and in line, were shot down in droves by the German machine guns. In most sectors little ground was gained. The British sustained about 60,000 casualties on that day, including about 19,000 dead. A French attack to the south of the Somme River on the British right was deliberately launched two hours after the British attack in the hope of achieving surprise. When the assault began at 0930 hours, it gained more ground than the British, for less cost.

After the first day it was fairly clear that there was no real hope of a decisive breakthrough on the Somme. The battle was continued by the British partly because it was essential from the point of view of their French alliance. It lasted until 18 November. Casualties have been estimated as 475,000 British, 195,000 French and 500,000 German.

On the Western Front in 1916 things had not gone well from the German point of view. Falkenhayn's intention of breaking French morale had not been fulfilled, and Germany had incurred over a million casualties. There was no end in prospect to the two-front war and the British introduction of conscription suggested a greater and better organized use of Allied manpower. Falkenhayn himself became a casualty of disappointed German hopes, being relieved as Chief of Staff by Hindenburg. In the second half of the war Germany was to become a kind of military dictatorship under the Hindenburg-Ludendorff partnership, with Ludendorff playing the dominant role.

In the East in 1916 the Russians demonstrated great resilience. One quality on which they could not be faulted was their spirit of cooperation with their allies. At the Chantilly Conference in December 1915 it had been agreed that there would be a concerted offensive effort by all the Allies on the Western, Eastern and Italian fronts in June 1916. The Russians were dutifully preparing for a summer offensive when the Germans struck at Verdun. Joffre then urgently pleaded with the Russians to launch an earlier offensive. Perhaps too obliging for his own good, Czar Nicholas agreed and the Russians launched an offensive with 18 divisions near Lake Naroch on 18 March. German defenses in this sector were very strong and the Russians suffered about 110,000 casualties with negligible results.

Brusilov's offensive

The Russian summer offensive fared better, however. The Russian High Command had originally intended that the main offensive should be delivered on the center of the Eastern Front by General Ewerth's Army Group West. Brusilov's Southwestern Army Group originally had no role in the plan. Brusilov was, however, confident that his Army Group, despite its lack of substantial ammunition reserves and the fact that it had no numerical superiority over the (mainly Austrian) forces facing it, could play a major role. By the beginning of June, French pleas for help were becoming increasingly frantic and Ewerth claimed he was still not ready to launch an offensive. In these circumstances Brusilov who, despite all appearances, claimed that he was ready, was allowed to go ahead on his own.

Brusilov had no ammunition for the traditional preliminary bombardment of several days duration. There was no long, slow build-up of forces before his offensive because the High Command had allocated him no extra troops. Brusilov moved his assault troops to their forward trenches only on the morning of the attack. With an initial bombardment of only six hours, short for 1916, on 4 June Brusilov struck along a 300-mile front. The Austrians were taken by surprise. By 6 June his forces had advanced 40 miles in places. Within three weeks he had 200,000 prisoners.

Brusilov naturally requested that Ewerth's Army Group should now launch its attack in the center of the front. This would prevent the Germans sending any reinforcements to the Austrian forces reeling back in front of him. The Russian High Command hesitated. They were taken aback at Brusilov's success and wished to exploit it but were at the same time reluctant to attack the Germans in the center of the front. Instead they transferred two corps to join Brusilov in the south. Brusilov's offensive made much slower progress in the second half of June because the Germans were reinforcing the Austrians. With his two extra corps he renewed his efforts in late July, however, and continued attacking throughout August and September. When he ceased he had probably inflicted a million casualties on the Central Powers for a similar loss to the Russian Army. Perhaps Brusilov sustained the offensive too long for the good of the Russian Army and Empire. It was, nevertheless, a tremendous effort and had the Russians been as successful throughout the war as they were in summer 1916 the Central Powers would have been on their knees long before Russia collapsed into revolution. Brusilov's success had the effect of bringing Rumania in on the Allied side in the hope of obtaining Hungarian Transylvania. Her entry into the war had little long-term effect. She was swiftly eliminated by an Austro-German offensive

across the Transylvanian Alps into Wallachia, coupled with a combined Austro-German-Turkish offensive from Bulgaria to the south. Bucharest fell on 6 December and by the end of the year the Rumanians had been defeated.

There was also heavy fighting in Italy in 1916. Italian losses were heavier than Austrian, but the committal of large Austrian forces to Italy made the task of the Russians easier. Altogether 1916 was an appalling year for Austria-Hungary. Austrian troops were generally demoralized and could no longer be trusted without German support even in defense.

On 12 December, Joffre, who had led the French Army through 29 months of war, was relieved of command and replaced by General Robert Nivelle. Nivelle planned a major offensive against the Noyon salient. His plans were forestalled by the German retirement to the Siegfried Line, a prepared defensive position well behind their previous lines. The Noyon salient disappeared. Ludendorff had decided to remain strictly on the defensive in the West in 1917 and to shorten the front by 25 miles, eliminating awkward salients. The area between the old and new German front lines was subjected to a scorched-earth policy, villages destroyed and wells poisoned. This withdrawal was carefully planned and was executed in stages between 24 February and 5 April 1917.

In the meantime two events of momentous significance occurred. Revolution broke out in Russia and the United States entered the war. Though the February Revolution did not immediately take Russia out of the war there was relatively little fighting on the Eastern Front in 1917.

The revolution of February 1917, which brought about the fall of the Czar, was a consequence of severe economic difficulties and long-term popular disquiet over corruption, incompetence and injustice in his regime. Ineffective management of the economy had led to a desperate shortage of food in the cities. Prices were very high and workers' wages did not keep up. Bread riots and strikes became widespread. In the Duma (the Russian parliament) there were demands for reform. The Czar tried to dissolve the Duma but it refused to go. Instead it formed, on 14 March, a Provisional Government. The following day, on the advice of his generals, the Czar abdicated.

The Germans, watching the end of the Russian Empire, took little action at first. They were glad of a respite on the Eastern Front which had been tying down nearly half their Army. When it appeared that the new Russian regime would not make peace the Germans helped Lenin, a professional revolutionary who wanted to overthrow the Provisional Government, to return to Russia. On 1 September 1917 they also launched an offensive at Riga on the Baltic. The offensive made good

Above far left: The Battle of Jutland which ended indecisively with the Germans forced back into harbor and the Royal Navy suffering unexpected losses.

Above left: Russian soldiers occupying an Austrian trench during General Brusilov's offensive of June 1916.

Below left: In 1917, as the Russian Army began to disintegrate, scenes such as this — of officers arresting deserters — became quite common.

Right: The Allied blockade of the Central Powers was a slow and complex process, but was an essential part of the Allies' ultimately successful strategy.

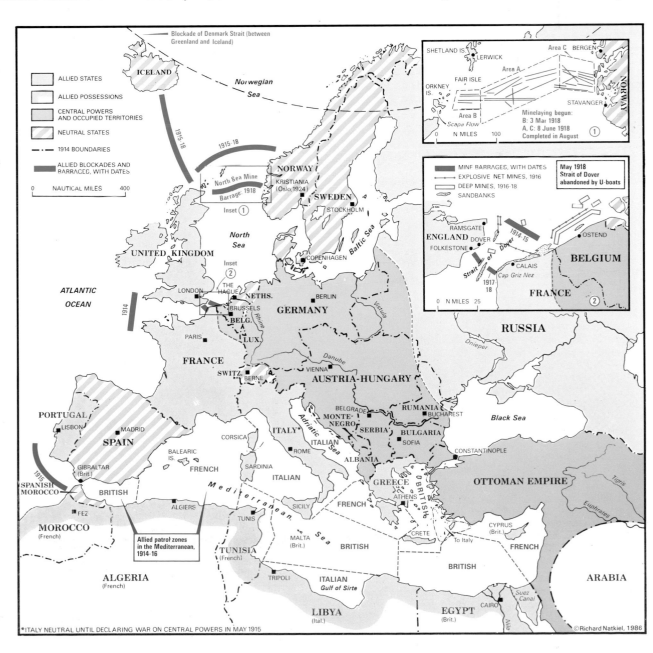

progress mainly because by that time revolutionary agitation and defeatism had spread from the home front and become endemic in the Army.

Lenin and his Bolshevik Party came to power in October and began to negotiate peace with Germany. The German terms were so harsh that even the Bolsheviks had difficulty in accepting them, but a peace was concluded at Brest-Litovsk on 3 March 1918. By this treaty the Germans gained control of most of Poland, Estonia, Latvia, Lithuania and part of Belorussia. Finland and the Ukraine became nominally independent states though in reality German satellites. The Ukraine was to pay for its 'independence' by the compulsory export of grain to the Central Powers.

America joins the Allies

The most crucial event of 1917, besides the Russian Revolution, was the American declaration of war on Germany on 6 April 1917. This came about partly as a result of a growing feeling in the United States, and particularly in the mind of the Democratic President Woodrow Wilson, that America could not allow the defeat of the European domocracies by Imperial Germany. It was also partly a consequence of Germany's conduct of the war at sea, partly of her bungling diplomacy and partly of the skill of the British in signals intelligence.

We have so far neglected naval operations. The great German High Seas Fleet remained bottled up in the Baltic by the British Grand Fleet virtually throughout the war. In consequence, the vast Royal Navy was able to maintain a remote blockade of Germany which had serious consequences particularly for Germany's food supply. Before the war much of Germany's grain had come from the Russian Empire. Imports from that quarter were no longer possible and overseas sources were sealed off by the British. There were short rations both at home and on the battlefronts for the Germans in the last years of the war. This contributed to war weariness in Germany and a lowering of morale in the Army, particularly when they found out that the Allied troups were well fed.

Given the hardship caused by the blockade the Germans were obviously anxious to strike back at sea. The German High Seas Fleet did make a number of attempts to break loose from its Baltic prison but was always turned back, most notably at the Battle of Jutland on 31 May 1916. Other ways had to be found of hitting the British. The Germans knew Britain imported most of her food and raw material. Throughout the war they were keen to strike at the British merchant marine. They got some results with fast surface commerce-raiders, but these were mostly hunted down and sunk early in the war. Increasingly the German naval war effort relied on submarines.

Eventually, after many hesitations, the Germans decided upon unrestricted submarine warfare which meant the sinking without warning of merchant vessels of any nationality believed to be carrying goods to Britain. From 1915 onward the sinking by German submarines of vessels carrying American passengers, including the liner *Lusitania* had poisoned ralations between the United States and Germany. Such sinkings increased enormously when the Germans abandoned all restraint in February 1917.

Unrestricted submarine warfare was extremely dangerous to the Allied cause. So much of the British merchant marine was sunk in 1917 that Britain's ability to continue the war was imperiled. For months the Admiralty stubbornly refused to introduce convoys which they claimed would actually make the ships more vulnerable to U-boat attack. The introduction of convoys was,

however, finally forced on the Admiralty by David Lloyd George, British Prime Minister since 6 December 1916. And almost immediately shipping losses began to drop and German submarine losses to mount.

In 1917 the United States was already vital to Britain as the principal overseas financier of her war effort. (Britain in her turn financed a large part of the war effort of other Allies.) Even before the introduction of unrestricted submarine warfare in February 1917, it seems that President Wilson was intending to bring America into the war. In that month the United States broke off diplomatic relations with Germany. The German Foreign Office henceforth seems to have regarded America's joining the Allies as inevitable. It signaled its diplomats in Mexico to encourage the Mexicans to reconquer New Mexico and Arizona. This message, known as the Zimmerman Telegram, was intercepted by British Admiralty intelligence. It was conveyed by the British to the American administration and thence to the press and people. America declared war on Germany on 6 April, but the US Army was not to be an effective presence on European battlefields for over a year at least.

In 1917 the Germans stood on the defensive on the Western Front. The British attacked at Arras on 9 April and in one of their more successful offensives before the summer of 1918 captured the important Vimy Ridge. A French offensive launched by Nivelle on the Chemin des Dames, however, turned out disastrously. After it, large parts of the French Army mutinied saying that, though they would continue to defend the soil of France, they would undertake no more rash offensives. Philippe Pétain who took over on 15 May upon Nivelle's dismissal, spent months coaxing and bullying the Army out of this attitude. He was largely successful but his Army could no longer carry the main burden of the war on the Western Front for its Allies. It was vital that the British take a larger share of responsibility and that American troops were committed as quickly as possible.

Sacrifice at Passchendaele

On 31 July the British launched an offensive in Flanders known as the Third Battle of Ypres. It ended in mid-November after the capture of Passchendaele Ridge. The battle was prodigously costly to the British who sustained over 300,000 casualties. But it appears that German losses were also massive and Ludendorff testified after the war that the battle had a catastrophic effect on the morale of his already war-weary Army.

On the minor fronts 1917 was a fairly dramatic year also. The British had great success against the Turks with offensives in Mesopotamia and Palestine. In the latter campaign they had the cooperation of Hashemite Bedouin Arabs whose revolt against the Ottoman Empire was sustained not only by British gold but by the remarkable personality of Colonel T E Lawrence. Baghdad fell on 11 March and Jerusalem was taken by General Allenby on 3 December. In Italy the news was worse for the Allies. A German-Austrian offensive at Caporetto on 24 October routed the Italians but they later rallied and established, with British help, a new defensive line behind the Piave.

On New Year's Day 1918 it was still not clear who would win this war. The prospects for the Germans were not favorable if the war dragged on. Her Army and population were desperately weary and increasingly hungry. Granted, a very favorable peace with Russia was likely. And when peace was signed at Brest-Litovsk in March there was the long-term prospect of Ukrainian grain. There was, however, a growing US Army in France. It was, as yet, uncommitted to battle, totally fresh and, if inexperienced and imperfectly trained, it possessed an enthusiasm and freshness which had all but gone from the European armies. Germany's only chance to win this war was to switch massive forces from East to West and launch a knockout blow in the West before the full deployment of American manpower made victory impossible.

President Wilson had encapsulated American war aims in the famous Fourteen Points. Most importantly he had declared himself in favor of a peace without annexations and on the basis of national self-determination. At this stage the Central Powers were not prepared to accept this. To have done so would have meant abandoning German gains at Brest-Litovsk as well as Belgium and Alsace-Lorraine. For Austria-Hungary national self-determination meant disintegration.

Ludendorff's great gamble

Before the collapse of Russia the German Army had been divided almost equally between Eastern and Western Fronts. This is an enormous tribute to the efforts of the Russian Army earlier in the war which had also faced most of the Austrian Army. In the first months of 1918, however, German strength in the East was reduced from about two and a half million men to only one million. In the West Ludendorff assembled over three and a half million men in 191 combat divisions. This gave him a considerable superiority over the British who had 1,200,000 combat troops in 63 divisions and the French with somewhat under two million in 91 divisions. Using this numerical superiority Ludendorff proposed to finish the war with a series of massive offensives before the US Army entered the fray.

The German offensives were well planned and incorporated all the lessons their Army had learned in over three years of war. Preliminary bombardments were relatively short, to help achieve surprise, but unimaginably intense. After the bombardment elite storm troops were used to

Left: 'Over there.' US troops using French light tanks operating in the Argonne.

Right: Colonel T E Lawrence, the British Army officer who successfully liaised with the Arabs and carried out guerrilla war against the Turks.

Below: German infantry deploying on the Aisne during the summer of 1917. The German Army was still recovering from the Somme and Verdun.

probe for the weakest points in the enemy defense and to penetrate right through its depth to the gun line. A second wave exploited the storm troops' success. Mopping up was left to a third wave.

The first of Ludendorff's blows fell on the British Fifth Army on the Somme on 21 March 1918. The British fell back with very heavy losses and the Germans advanced 40 miles on a broad front. The Germans had solved the problem of breakthrough but not that of strategic exploitation. Their foot-marching troops were brought to a halt on 4 April partly by Allied reserves and partly by their own sheer physical exhaustion. Successive German offensives, on the Lys in April, on the Aisne in May, in the Noyon-Montdidier area in June and in Champagne in July, gained ground but did not break the Allied armies.

The emergency produced unity of command for the first time on the Allied side. Foch, a French general reasonably popular with the British, was appointed Commander in Chief on 9 April. The Americans helped by agreeing to join in the fighting immediately and some American divisions were put into armies under British and French command. From July the Allies took the offensive themselves. The French won a major victory, sometimes known as the Second Battle of the Marne, in that month. The British won an even greater success in an offensive at Amiens starting on 8 August. An American success followed in September – the liquidation of the St Mihiel salient. By the end of September the Allies were attacking along the whole front and the German Army was gradually falling apart.

The last battles of the war were quite modern in character. Open, mobile warfare was restored as the German Army fell back. Tanks, introduced by the British as long ago as September 1916, now had much better mobility and endurance. They aided the Allies' attacks greatly and helped exploit breakthroughs. The British offensive at Amiens was led by over 400 of them. Tactical airpower also played a vital role. Aircraft spotted for the guns with which they now had radio contact, and increased the demoralization of the Germans by strafing their retreating columns.

In the last months of the war it was the British Army which was the cutting edge of the Allied war effort, the French being rather weary and the Americans relatively inexperienced. The last 100 days of World War I saw arguably the greatest achievement in British military history. The British captured more prisoners and more guns than any other army. Within the British forces, troops from the Dominions, Australia, New Zealand and Canada, were often the spearhead of offensives. By November 1918 these wartime volunteer troops had attained standards of military excellence which not even the German Army with its large professional officer corps could outdo.

Germany defeated

The defeat of the German Army in July to November 1918 was so sudden and dramatic that some Germans afterward found it difficult to believe that it had happened. Between 8 August and the beginning of November the Germans lost 300,000 men in prisoners alone. By the final ceasefire they

had lost half their artillery, an obvious sign of conclusive defeat. Meanwhile the Allies had launched an offensive from Salonika which overran Bulgaria, liberated Serbia and was well into Austria-Hungary itself when the fighting stopped. A general Italian offensive from 24 October also hit the Austrians hard. From 27 October the Austrian Emperor Karl, who had succeeded Franz Josef in 1916, began to seek a separate peace. There were riots and strikes on the home front in Germany and revolutionary agitation. The High Seas Fleet, refusing a major sortie into the North Sea, mutinied at Kiel at the end of October.

On 6 October the new German Chancellor, Prince Max of Baden, asked the Allies for an armistice on the basis of the Fourteen Points. He did so at Hindenburg's insistence. The Kaiser abdicated and sought refuge in Holland on 10 November. The actual terms of the armistice were worked out in three days of negotiations in a railway carriage in a siding in the forest of Compiègne (5-8 November 1918). It came into effect at 1100 hours on 11 November. The stillness, it has been said, was heard around the world.

Though the Armistice ended the fighting it was not a final peace settlement. The German Army was allowed to keep its weapons and to march home under its own officers. The Allies did not totally disband their armies and the blockade of German ports was continued. The peace treaties were worked out between the Allies and the defeated powers in Paris during the course of 1919. They are often collectively but incorrectly referred to as the Versailles Settlement.

In fact, only the treaty with Germany was made at Versailles. This treaty, signed by the Germans in June 1919, stripped them of Alsace and Lorraine. Danzig became a so-called Free City separated from Germany and administered under the newly created League of Nations. A 'Polish corridor' was created to give the new state of Poland access to the sea at Danzig. This not only cut off East Prussia from the rest of Germany but incorporated a predominantly German area into Poland. The French, in compensation for the devastation of much of their own industry by the Germans, were allowed to occupy and administer the important industrial region of the Saar up to 1935. Germany also lost her African colonies, which had been overrun in minor campaigns. The Germans were obliged to keep the Rhineland a demilitarized zone and to restrict themselves to a 100,000-man Army without tanks or heavy artillery. They were not allowed to have military air-

craft, battleships or submarines. Though the Germans protested loudly enough, none of these territorial or military terms was particularly harsh, considering the suffering they and their allies had inflicted on the rest of Europe, let alone the appalling terms imposed on Russia at Brest-Litovsk.

Allied conduct in the matter of 'reparations' was more questionable. The Germans were compeled to sign an acknowledgment that they and their former allies were entirely responsible for starting the war. This admission of 'war guilt' became justification for the imposition of huge fines, called 'reparations,' to pay for the damage, material and human, which the war had caused to the Allies. British and French insistence on some kind of reparation was made inevitable by their massive indebtedness. The French were heavily in debt to the British who were hugely indebted to the Americans. The United States, now massively a creditor nation, unsurprisingly refused repeated British requests for a general cancellation of war debts. 'They hired the money didn't they?' President Harding, Wilson's successor, is supposed to

have said. The reparation problem made economic recovery from the war difficult and poisoned the political climate of postwar Europe. Eventually it assisted the Nazi rise to power.

The Habsburg Empire had disintegrated before the peace conferences started. New states, recognized at Paris, arose from its ashes. Czechoslovakia was created and Yugoslavia emerged from the addition of southern Slav areas of Austria-Hungary to Serbia and Montenegro. Peace was made with the mainly German rump of the Empire, now the Austrian Republic, at Saint-Germain and with Hungary, also now a republic, at Trianon.

The treaties were bitterly resented by German-speaking defeated countries in particular. They were regarded as 'diktats': dictated rather than negotiated settlements. A particular complaint was that President Wilson's principle of national self-determination was not adhered to. The ethnic map of Europe was so confused that strict adherence to this principle was totally impracticable. But the Germans had a point that the people of the Austrian Republic could have been allowed to become part of Germany as most of them

wished. This was explicitly forbidden by treaty.

The sordid haggling in Paris during 1919 upset President Wilson but he pinned his faith on the creation of a new institution, the League of Nations. This was to provide a forum for the settlement of future international disputes without war. The League might have had some real chance of maintaining the peace in Europe had it not been for the US Congress's refusal to allow America to join. The United States, while emerging from the war as the world's greatest economic power, withdrew into political isolation. Without the help of America and Russia (where the Bolsheviks consolidated their power and preached an anti-capitalist ideology) Britain and France would have long-term difficulties in keeping Germany under control. Germany, moreover, was not the only potential problem. Italy, on the victorious side in the war, was bitterly disappointed by her limited gains. She coveted much territory incorporated into Yugoslavia and regarded herself, with some justification, as having been cheated by her former allies. Most of the ingredients of a second world war were already present in 1919.

Above left: Australian recruiting poster. The Australians provided a very important contribution to the British war effort at Gallipoli, in Palestine and on the Western Front.

Below left: '1100 hrs, 11 November 1918.' US troops cheering the announcement that an armistice has been agreed.

Right: Orpen's painting of the signing of the Peace Treaty in the Hall of Mirrors at Versailles in 1919. In the center are President Wilson, President Clemenceau and Prime Minister Lloyd George.

Europe

Great wars are not ended in a day. After the armistice of 11 November 1918, the Western Front fell silent. But much of Europe remained in turmoil, and over the next five years unresolved conflicts had to be settled from Dublin to Istanbul before the new shape of the continent became fixed and clear. In the end, many of the upheavals of the war were to prove final and decisive. The Habsburg and Ottoman empires, the Romanovs and the Prussian monarchy tumbled together into the dustbin of history, and the map of Europe was redrawn with remarkable thoroughness.

But in other ways, despite the vast scale of suffering and death – some 20 million people had lost their lives – the Great War was strangely indecisive. Europe had suffered a severe shock, but in the end its existing social and economic systems held together everywhere except Russia. The crucial engagement of the United States in European affairs was to be reversed almost immediately, and not resumed for another 20 years. And the war's central issue, the power and place of Germany in Europe, was not resolved. Instead of being 'the war to end war,' the Great War led directly to the next, even greater, holocaust. Only then would the German question be decisively

answered in the ruins of Berlin – and the long era of European world dominance be brought to an end.

The immediate condition of Europe was a sorry one. To the physical destruction of war and its toll of human life were added the ravages of a flu epidemic in the winter of 1918-19 that killed tens of thousands of a population weakened by shortages and hardship, and the disruption of the continent's economy, especially in Central and Eastern Europe. The frontiers of the new successor states of the Austro-Hungarian Empire cut across all the essential lines of economic life. Industries were severed from their raw materials, producers from their markets. The collapse of the German economy in defeat was a disaster for its neighbors to the south and east. The American Relief Association rushed in almost 1500 million dollars of food supplies to prevent mass starvation.

In Germany, Bolshevik revolution seemed an immediate prospect. The government of People's Commissars, headed by Friedrich Ebert, which had taken power in Berlin after the Kaiser's abdication, was by no means as revolutionary as it sounded. But workers' and soldiers' councils had sprung up throughout the country and in most

areas wielded effective power. In 1919 there were short-lived communist governments in Hungary and Bavaria. Among Italian, French and British workers there was also great sympathy for Bolshevik Russia. In reality, revolutionary forces were weak, but the specter of communism haunted the propertied classes.

Yet against the uncertain backdrop of January 1919, the victorious powers confidently organized a great conference amid the glittering splendor of Versailles, to draw up a series of peace treaties and resolve the outstanding problems of Europe and the world. The defeated states – Germany, Austria, Hungary, Bulgaria and Turkey – were excluded as, after much debate, was Bolshevik Russia. But it was a worldwide assembly, with Siam, China, Japan and 11 Latin American countries taking part, as well as the United States. Perhaps this already presaged an acceptance of the waning of European power.

In practice decisions at the conference on all major issues were made by the leading victorious allies: Britain, France, the United States and, to a lesser extent, Italy. A crucial confrontation developed between French Premier Georges Clemenceau and US President Woodrow Wilson.

Left: Happy civilians, sailors and soldiers celebrate the armistice in London on 11 November 1918.

Above: The impact of the Spanish influenza epidemic – it killed over 20 million people – produced exotic means of prevention such as this air filter.

Right: The 'Big Four' at Versailles: Lloyd George, Orland, Clemenceau and Wilson.

France, much of West Prussia and Posen to Poland, and small areas to Belgium. Plebiscites were to decide the future of Silesia and Schleswig, and the Saarland would come under French control for 15 years, after which a plebiscite would be held there also. Germany was strictly limited in its armed forces and armaments. In 'reparation' for having inflicted the war on Europe – Germany's war, her guilt was explicitly stated in the treaty – Germany was to hand over coal, merchant shipping and an as yet unspecified sum of money to the injured parties: France, Britain, Italy and Belgium.

After the armistice, Allied forces had remained in place to prevent any trouble over acceptance of the peace terms. It was just as well. The treaty provoked a heated debate in Germany, and only the admission by the High Command that the Army was powerless to resist produced a majority in the Reichstag for signing the peace in June 1919. In their hearts, almost all Germans of whatever political persuasion rejected the Versailles treaty. They did not accept that they had been responsible for the war and should therefore be punished. They did not even accept that they had been militarily defeated. They regarded the treaty as an unjust imposition to be overturned when possible. The question was left open as to how the Allies were to enforce the treaty if the German government broke its conditions. The attempt to maintain the provisions of Versailles against German opposition was the central drama of the next 20 years.

New nation states

When it came to the question of self-determination, even Wilson was soon forced to recognize that European affairs were not perhaps quite as simple as he had hoped and expected. The racial and linguistic patchwork of Europe could not be readily divided up into 'nation states.' Indeed, with a little more historical perception, the American president might have realized that such states as France, Spain and Great Britain had only been forged into self-conscious 'nations' by centuries of conflict, and even they were at times contested by minorities claiming separate national rights. The most obvious objects of Wilson's enthusiasm were the new states succeeding to the Austro-Hungarian Empire, Czechoslovakia and Yugoslavia (the Kingdom of the Serbs, Croats and Slovenes), and a resurrected Poland. But all these states had large minorities not associated with the 'national' government, and both Czechoslovakia and Yugoslavia were founded on an alliance of different peoples – the Czechs and Slovaks in one case, and the Serbs, Croats and Slovenes in the other. They were to prove durable, but not because of any identity of blood or language.

The truncated Hungary that emerged from the peace was bitterly dedicated to overthrowing an agreement that lost it both a large part of the Magyar-speaking population and its traditional position as one of the dominant groups in the region. Rumania, with over 1.5 million Magyars within its borders, was the main object of Hungarian hostility. Poland could handle its minorities (about one-third of its total population), but was the object of revisionist claims by both Germany and Russia. The separation of Austria from Germany had long historical roots, but certainly contravened the principle of fitting state boundaries to national identity. In the end, despite much painstaking effort by plebiscites and boundary commissions, it was impossible to avoid stored-up grievances. If the only legitimacy of states lay in ethnic identity, then it was open to any country claiming to represent a national

The two leaders had very different priorities to pursue. For Clemenceau, Germany remained a potent threat. It was an established myth of the period between the wars that Clemenceau had been 'vengeful' and 'vindictive' at Versailles. But for France the need to break the power of Germany permanently was urgent and unavoidable. The arithmetic of population and industrial resources would inevitably give a revived Germany overwhelming military supremacy over France. In addition, the collapse of the Habsburg Empire and the apparent disappearance of Russia from the European balance of power could actually leave France more exposed than before the war, with no powerful ally on the European continent to counter Germany. Neither Britain nor the United States could be relied upon to throw its weight into the balance, and no other country, including Italy, was strong enough to be much use as an ally against German military might. Clemenceau had no choice but to pursue the permanent weakening of Germany.

This was not a point of view that President Wilson was able to comprehend. Wilson's New

World idealism clashed directly with Clemenceau's Old World cynicism. Where the Frenchman thought in terms of the realities of power that had determined the relations of European states for centuries, Wilson sought to create a new order that would settle Europe's problems on a basis of justice once and for all. If nations were granted self-determination within properly adjusted borders, under democratic government, then there was no reason why any country should be feared – even Germany. A League of Nations, joining all the powers together in defense of peace, would guard against any recurrence of militarism and aggression.

The peace terms eventually accepted by Germany in June 1919 were the result of a set of compromises imposed on Clemenceau, who could not achieve the agreement of his allies to many of his demands. He would have liked the dismemberment of Germany, with the Rhineland detached as an independent entity. Instead, the Rhineland was to be subjected to Allied military occupation for 15 years and to be permanently demilitarized. Germany would lose Alsace and Lorraine to

Left: Civil War in Ireland – IRA rebels in action against the Irish Government in 1922.

Right: Poet, patriot, pilot, insurrectionist and megalomaniac: Gabriele d'Annunzio the Italian 'Hero of Fiume.'

Below right: The impact of inflation in Germany 1923 – children play with billions of German marks discarded for waste paper.

minority in a neighboring state to act to overturn the peace agreement. Nationalism was a highly unstable foundation for a peaceful order in Europe.

In practice, the power of the Versailles peacemakers to determine the new map of Europe was limited to details of borders here and there. Most issues were either already decided by the ground occupied at the armistice or by a fresh trial of strength in the aftermath of the war. Poland's eastern frontier with Russia was settled – much to Poland's advantage – after almost a year's warfare during 1920-21. Hungary had fought under the Russian-backed Bolshevik Bela Kun to reoccupy territory lost to Yugoslavia and Rumania in the last days of the Great War, but Rumanian troops had soon occupied Hungary and Kun was overthrown in August 1919. Hungary was forced to acquiesce in the loss of three-quarters of its prewar population to neighboring states. Italy and Yugoslavia clashed over possession of Istria and Dalmatia, a conflict that came to focus on the Adriatic port of Fiume (now Rijeka). In a bizarre episode, the Italian poet Gabriele d'Annunzio seized Fiume in September 1919 and declared it independent, but by November 1920 he had been evicted and a temporary agreement reached between the Italian and Yugoslav governments. It was an important element in postwar Europe that Italy, although one of the victors in the war, emerged dissatisfied from the peace settlement, feeling insufficiently rewarded for its sacrifice of blood.

At the southeastern extremity of Europe, the succession to the Ottoman Empire was decided by the Turkish nationalist revolt of Kemal Ataturk, who in 1923, after a long and bloody struggle against Greek forces, was able to establish a republic in Anatolia and eastern Thrace. Adopting the Roman alphabet and Western-style dress for the new Turkey, Kemal set out to create a modern nation state and laid a claim for his country to be considered as part of Europe.

Britain had been ready to accept the principle of selfdetermination everywhere in Europe, except on what it considered its home ground – Ireland. There the Easter Uprising of 1916 had stirred up a tide of emotional enthusiasm for immediate independence. In 1918, the Irish nationalists set up an independent parliament, or Dail, in Dublin and proceeded to run the country as a republic with no reference to Westminster. The British government went to great lengths to reassert its authority, sending in bands of ex-servicemen – the 'Black and Tans' and the 'Auxis' – to combat the Irish Republican Army in a brutal small-scale war. Eventually, in December 1921, an agreement was reached that in effect gave independence to the Irish Free State, excluding Northern Ireland with its Protestant majority, which remained tied to Britain. This was followed by a bloody civil war in the Free State between the Irish government and nationalists who rejected the division of Ireland. The government won, but nonetheless the Free State never accepted the existence of Northern Ireland as a permanent solution. Here was more trouble stored for the future.

American isolationism

While these national struggles were still going on, relations between France and Germany came to a crisis over the question of reparations. For France, the final outcome of the Versailles conference had been highly unsatisfactory. In return for concessions to Germany, Clemenceau had won a guarantee from the United States and Britain of armed assistance against any renewed aggression. But Woodrow Wilson proved incapable of winning Congressional support for his European policy when he returned home. The United States once more withdrew into isolationism. It would take no part in the League of Nations, on which so many hopes were pinned, and the agreement with France was a dead letter. This made the French even more insistent that Germany should be forced to fulfill every detail of the peace agreement.

At the end of April 1921, the Reparations Commission set up by the Versailles conference fixed German payment at a total of 6500 million dollars

(132,000 million gold marks), to be handed over in regular instalments. It was a massive sum, and Germany had neither the intention nor the ability to pay. In the Reich, as in the rest of Central Europe, the catastrophic economic effects of the war continued into the 1920s. Industry was at a standstill for lack of capital and raw materials. Government finances were in chaos and chronic inflation set in. In Austria, the currency had fallen from its par of five crowns to the dollar to an almost meaningless 83,600 crowns to the dollar by August 1922. In Germany too inflation was completely out of hand. Not surprisingly, at the end of 1922 Germany was declared in default on its reparations payments.

The British were by this time convinced that reparations had been a mistake, and proposed that they be abandoned along with all other war debts. But the hawkish French Prime Minister Raymond Poincaré was determined to take action. On 11 January 1923, French and Belgian forces occupied the Ruhr, Germany's industrial heartland. The population of the Ruhr responded with a campaign of strikes and sabotage, and there were clashes with French soldiers in which German civilians were killed. The German government backed the employers and striking workers in the Ruhr with floods of money that poured from the printing presses heedless of inflation. It was deliberate financial suicide. By November 1923 the mark had fallen to 4,200,000 million to the dollar (par was 4.2 marks to the dollar). Many of the ordinary transactions of life could only be conducted by barter. People saw the savings of a lifetime made worthless; many who lived off the income from savings or fixed pensions were reduced to abject poverty. All blamed inflation on the French, the Versailles treaty and the German Republican government.

France may have hoped that Germany would collapse altogether; certainly, the French supported separatists who tried to establish an independent state on the Rhine. But relations with Britain worsened sharply as the crisis was prolonged. Also, the effect of international uncertainty and German financial collapse rebounded on the French economy, threatening the value of the franc. And France was no nearer obtaining its reparation payments. It could not even extract enough economic output from the Ruhr to pay for the occupation force. In the end, a negotiated settlement was inevitable. To achieve it, the United States was once more induced to involve itself in European affairs. Under the Dawes Plan, accepted in September 1924, the United States agreed to help finance a large loan to refloat the German economy. In return, the Germans would pay reparations, but at a reduced level, from specified tax sources. The French occupation of the Ruhr ended the following spring.

From one point of view, this outcome was highly desirable, a great step toward a normalization of international relations in Europe and the recovery of the European economy. But the failure of the French to impose their will on a recalcitrant German government had ominous implications for the future. It suggested that if a German ruler had the will to overthrow the Versailles peace terms, it was unlikely that Britain and France would succeed in stopping him.

By 1925, the dust of war had settled and the redrawn map of Europe took on some permanence. It had been a massive upheaval of borders, but most European leaders believed that, in other respects, a return to the settled world of pre-1914 was both possible and desirable. This was an illusion.

The world economy was the most obvious area where recovery proved elusive. The prewar economic situation had at the time appeared 'natural,' a booming capitalism requiring little or no interference from the state. But it was now revealed to have depended on a very special achievement of economic and political stability, with a sophisticated system of multilateral trade and payments that could not easily be restored. There was a shortlived boom in the victorious countries during 1919 and early 1920 as stocks used up during the war were replenished, but soon a sharp slump set in. The war had led to overinvestment in some areas – in shipbuilding and textiles, for example, in Britain – and the neglect of others more viable in peacetime. Markets traditionally dominated by European powers had turned to other suppliers, such as the United States and Japan, while Europe concentrated on the war effort. Now, European manufacturers found it hard to win back their old customers. Prices of primary products – food and raw materials – slumped because of overproduction, and the countries supplying these products could not afford industrial imports. This in its turn depressed European manufacturing. Europe still had the capital, the technology and the skilled workforce to create rapid growth, but it no longer seemed possible to exploit this capacity to the full. Mass unemployment was to be a permanent feature of European life between the wars – the lowest unemployment level in Britain during the

period was 9.7 percent in 1927; in Sweden, the level never fell below 10 percent. The United States had become a net exporter of capital to Europe, rather than an absorber of European investment – an historic shift in economic power.

Yet the industrial nations of Europe did eventually recover from the impact of the war to a remarkable degree. Inflation in the Central European states was gradually mastered. The League of Nations took control of Austria's finances in 1922 and Hungary's in 1924. By 1926, budgets were balanced and prices stabilized in both countries. German recovery after 1924 was rapid. By 1925, Europe's output of food and raw materials equaled 1913 figures, and by 1929 Europe had the same proportion of total world production of goods as before the war. British foreign investments surpassed prewar levels in 1927. Between 1925 and 1928, all European currencies returned to the gold standard, believed to be the key to financial stability and confidence in world trade. Unfortunately, this recovery was heavily dependent on the boom in the United States economy that had begun in 1925. A bust was soon to follow, that would reveal the supposed return to prewar conditions as illusory.

European society and culture were also marked by the war, although they followed contradictory patterns of change that are difficult to chart. The war cast a long shadow of mourning. Every village and town in the combatant countries had its war memorial. On public transport, special seats were reserved for the mutilated. Ceremonies of remembrance were almost universally observed. Yet although the war had darkened so many lives, and injected so much insecurity and pessimism into European societies, in the more advanced countries the 1920s and 1930s also continued the long-term trend to rising living standards, shorter working hours, better medical care and the increasing responsibility of the state for the welfare of its citizens.

The nearest approximation to a social revolution after the war came in Eastern Europe, where the great estates that had dominated the

No truly satisfactory explanations of changes in birthrate have ever been produced. It was certainly the wealthier classes of the most advanced countries that led the way: backward areas of Europe remained prolific. Although information about contraception became more widely available from the 1920s, the number of devices sold would not be enough to account for low natality. Couples controled their fertility largely without the aid of modern technology. Perhaps large families and endless pregnancies were seen as a block to other now more desired objectives – leisure, health, the freedom and money to exploit the new world of consumer goods. Women were no longer content to be breeding machines, nor did their husbands desire it.

Sex for pleasure, rather than for procreation, was a central element of a new hedonistic culture of the 1920s, much satirized by Aldous Huxley, Evelyn Waugh and others, but nonetheless a portent for the future. Whether actual sexual behavior changed, and to what degree, in various countries and classes, is an impossibly complex and doubtful subject. But attitudes to sex and the human body unquestionably shifted. 'Healthy' sex was a popular topic for public debate and it was widely believed that society was freeing itself from the repressions and hypocrisy of the previous century. The habit of sunbathing began to spread, with implications of narcissistic body-worship and sensuality that were in their way very subversive of traditional European culture. These were the beginnings of changes that would become more evident and widespread later.

The industries of pleasure were the most successful growth areas of Europe between the wars. Motor cars became commonplace, although still restricted to the at least modestly prosperous. Mass entertainments flourished – professional sport, radio and cinema – and the spread of paid holidays encouraged service industries that exploited this new leisure. Governments saw radio as a potent tool for their purposes and kept control of it themselves. Cinema, on the other hand, was dominated by foreign cultural influence. Despite valiant efforts by European filmmakers, Hollywood provided the staple entertainment of the Continent between the wars.

rural areas for centuries were broken up. In Rumania, Czechoslovakia, Yugoslavia, Poland and the new Baltic states, vast areas of land were redistributed to the peasantry. This did not encourage agricultural efficiency, but it did satisfy an age-old land hunger. The decline of the great estates was final and irreversible. Even in France and Britain, observers of the social world noticed a 'democratization' of manners, by which they normally meant that in high society birth counted for less and money more.

Despite the pressure of unemployment, the number of domestic servants dropped dramatically – to half the prewar number in Britain, for example. This was another irreversible change, which went along with a growing use of labor-saving devices in the home. Servants were replaced partly by self-help, partly by machines. The decline of domestic service perhaps explains the otherwise surprising fact that fewer women were in employment in the 1920s than before the war. Women had unquestionably proved between 1914 and 1918 that they were capable of doing jobs for which they had previously been mysteriously thought unfit. This had altered social attitudes to women, and women's attitudes to themselves, but it did not alter their employment prospects, as the men returned from war and reclaimed their jobs. The vote for women was extended to many

(but by no means all) of the nations of Europe – with unfortunate results for left-wing and liberal forces, since conservative and Fascist parties consistently received a higher percentage of the female than of the male vote.

Women's demands for a better life may well have influenced one of the most puzzling of European social phenomena – the extremely low birthrate in the most advanced countries. Although better food and medicine increased life expectancy every year, in Germany, Britain and northern Italy population rose slowly, and in France not at all. Europeans who in the nineteenth century had overpopulated their own countries and populated much of the globe besides were now hard pressed to maintain their numbers. Emigration declined dramatically: between 1901 and 1910, 14.9 million Europeans had emigrated; for 1931 to 1940 the figure was 1.8 million. The impact of the war was, of course, considerable, but patchy. Britain, with 750,000 dead in 1914-18, would probably have lost more people through emigration during the same period had peace prevailed. For France, however, the war compounded a continuing demographic disaster. The 1.4 million young men killed in the war could not be replaced; by 1931, 3 million immigrants from elsewhere in Europe were filling the gaps in France's workforce.

Along with jazz, cinema provided a notable example of the American intrusion into European national cultures.

But on the whole, Europe still showed unflagging – indeed, superabundant – cultural vitality between the wars. Worldwide, there was no serious rival to its creativity in the arts, sciences and abstract thought. Despite the accumulation of centuries of tradition, it was a culture still able to change and confront the new, instead of retreating into stylization or archaism. It was only natural that it should be European scientists who produced each new breakthrough in nuclear physics, and European architects (of the Bauhaus school) who developed a new style of building that would, given time, transform the urban landscape of the world.

The great tide of Europe's artistic culture was still in full flood. The years before the Great War had brought revolutionary formal innovations in all the arts. There was an open field for the adventurous, and a remarkable explosion of wit and invention followed – although it was little appreciated by a conservative public that found modern art 'hard to understand.' The keynote was variety. In painting, Pablo Picasso exhibited a protean gift, moving effortlessly from a classical simplicity of line to the most grotesque reworkings of the human form. Composer Igor Stravinsky seemed happy to play freely with a range of styles, delighting in a liberation from both the moral seriousness and heavy emotionalism of the old Romantic tradition.

A new element of the postwar artistic culture was a tendency to question the importance of art itself. The Dadaist movement which had sprung up during the war carried out an absurdist attack on both art and established society. There was a trend – most pronounced in the Weimar Republic – toward seeking a practical role for the artist as critic of society, utilitarian creator or political activist. The image of the artist as craftsman attracted more praise than the artist as mystic seer. The neurotic introspection and emotionalism of the prewar period were less in evidence. Novels became shorter, and so did the sentences within them.

Still, if artists and writers spent more time looking at society and less observing their own tortured souls, this did not necessarily make their work more joyful. When they looked at society, they did not like what they saw. The war and its aftermath added an extra twist of bitterness to already well established criticisms of bourgeois Europe. Perhaps the central novel of the period was Louis-Ferdinand Céline's savage and delirious *Voyage au bout de la nuit*, with its nightmare progression from the horrors of the trenches to the moral abjection of a French African colony and the degradation of modern city life. T S Eliot,

an American living in England who had self-consciously joined European literature rather than that of his home country, published *The Waste Land* in 1922, a bleak view of the spiritual bankruptcy of the contemporary world. Another expatriate American, Ezra Pound, described Europe as 'an old bitch gone in the teeth . . . a botched civilization . . .' Many European artists and intellectuals were enemies of the mild decencies and comfortable materialism of bourgeois parliamentary democracies between the wars. Both Céline and Pound ended up as supporters of forces on the right of European politics.

This was symptomatic of the startling failure of democracy through most of Europe between the wars. Yet in 1918, the cause of democracy had been one of the prime war aims of the victorious allies, and by 1920 most countries in Europe had some form of democratic constitutional government. Britain extended the franchise in the immediate aftermath of the war, so that it embraced for the first time the principle of 'one man one vote'; in Germany, a democratic republic replaced the authoritarian semi-constitutional regime of the Kaiser. Although many countries remained monarchies, the issue of republicanism versus monarchism ceased to hold its old importance in European politics.

There seemed every reason to suppose that the focus of politics would be the long-established struggle between capitalism and socialism – especially as, since 1917, a regime professing a form of socialism had for the first time taken power at least on the edge of Europe, in the Soviet Union. The Bolshevik success did not, however, advance the socialist cause in the rest of Europe. Although in Britain the socialist movement was to remain largely united behind the democratic Labour Party, which after the war replaced the Liberals as the alternative party of government to the Conservatives, in most other countries the formation of communist parties, obedient to instructions from the Comintern in Moscow and dedicated to

Above left: The despair of unemployment for a family man in Wigan, England, in the 1930s.

Below left: Despite the slump, many housewives in the areas of England not hard hit by the Depression were able to afford domestic appliances such as the vacuum cleaner.

Above: Mary Stopes and her birth-control clinic attempted to overcome prejudice and ignorance about sex and motherhood.

Below: The revolution in popular entertainment brought about by the film meant that Hollywood studios dominated the industry between the wars.

the eventual overthrow of bourgeois democracy, split the Left into two warring factions. Those socialists committed to working within the existing political and economic structure had electoral successes and at times became the party of government, as in the German Weimar Republic for a decade, or in Britain in 1924 and 1929. But they were too weak even then to effect any serious changes in society or the economy. Only in Scandinavia did social democrats achieve a durable success between the wars.

It was from radical nationalists that an upheaval to the established reign of capitalist democracy in fact came, through a new political phenomenon, normally known as 'Fascism,' after its first manifestation in Italy. Fascism was a product of modern urban industrial society – of democracy itself, in the sense of the involvement of the masses in political power. It had been widely assumed that mass politics was a prerogative of socialist parties. But among the population of the advanced countries, there were large numbers of people who, while having no sympathy with the old ruling groups – landowners and the Church, the plutocracy of big business and industry – were also hostile to socialism and its egalitarian and internationalist creed. As the events of 1914 had shown so clearly, identification with the nation was stronger for almost all Europeans than identification with a class across national boundaries.

Support for a new, radical nationalism was to be found especially among the less wealthy members of the middle classes. The war and postwar chaos had aggravated their already chronic sense of insecurity and exaggerated their endemic sense of social failure. They sought a leader whose

authority would relieve them of their anxiety. They found solace in an aggressive nationalism 'compensating for personal failure' and in racism, which focussed their bitterness on a visible scapegoat. Fascism was the political movement that exploited their discontent.

The ideology of Fascism was a compound of anti-Communism, racism, anti-intellectualism, extreme nationalism and hatred of democracy and democratic politicians. It exalted the triumph of force and willpower over morality and reason, of the state over the individual, of war over peace. At its most lofty, it argued that Christian bourgeois civilization was played out and must be replaced by a new national movement with its roots in the masses. For organization, Fascism turned to an idea of a political party that was similar to, and in part modeled on, the Communist Party – a tight, disciplined vanguard that would organize the seizure of power and then run the state once power was achieved. At the head of this party would stand the unchallengeable charismatic leader.

Fascism takes root

In itself, this Fascism was a flimsy thing. Its ideas were cobbled together from the hokum of many thinkers over the previous century – from Hegel and Gobineau to Houston Stewart Chamberlain. They offered no serious answers to the problems of economic or social organization in a modern state – not surprisingly, once in power Fascist leaders concentrated on foreign affairs. In the more stable democracies, like Britain, Fascism remained a marginal political movement with no real influence. But in democracies riven by deep social conflicts and economic disruption, like Italy

and Germany, it could mobilize mass support and win important allies. Traditionally powerful forces – the army, industrialists, financiers and landowners, and even the Church – were prepared to enlist Fascism in their struggle to maintain and promote their own interests, threatened by disruption or revolution. Timorous conservative citizens looked to the Fascist leader to restore order and discipline. And the shock troops for Fascism could be recruited from among the unemployed or, in the immediate postwar period, from the rootless mass of ex-servicemen, unable or unwilling to reintegrate into civilian life, bitterly convinced that the politicians had lost a war the soldiers had won.

That this view was strong in Italy, one of the victors, was due both to the unsatisfactory course of the fighting on the Italian front during the war, and to the peace settlement, which Italian nationalists felt gave them little. In fact, after the war the predicament of Italy was not so different from any of the defeated powers. Inflation was high and popular unrest threatening to the propertied classes. In 1919, peasants in northern Italy occupied parts of the estates of large landowners. The following year, there was a wave of occupations of factories by striking workers. The industrialists and landowners no longer trusted the parliamentary government to protect their interests and welcomed the strongarm tactics of Benito Mussolini's Fascist bands, largely ex-servicemen, who had begun operating in 1919. By 1920, the Fascists numbered about 300,000 and were exercising a virtual reign of terror over much of northern Italy. Their attacks on left-wingers, workers and peasants were either abetted or benignly overlooked by the authorities, glad of

Far left: Picasso's *The Three Dancers* painted in 1927. Such paintings delighted many but were regarded as degenerate art by the Nazis.

Left: Pablo Picasso, the Spanish painter and arguably the greatest artist of the century.

Right: Arthur Henderson addressing the Labour Party Conference in 1923. After the war, the Labour Party replaced the Liberals as the main opposition party to the Conservatives.

Below: Ezra Pound (1885-1972), the American poet who with T S Eliot (himself an American by birth) was the founder of modernism in English Literature.

the extra muscle to control what they saw as an ugly situation.

Parliamentary democracy in Italy had few friends – understandably so, for it was notoriously corrupt and generally inefficient. Elections were largely fixed by local influence and police pressure, governmental majorities cobbled together through shady deals in the back corridors of power. Once it had lost the confidence of the middle classes – scared by disorder and inflation – and the magnates of business and land, democracy stood little chance of survival. The crisis came in October 1922 when, having assembled 40,000 of his followers in Naples, Mussolini threatened to march on Rome and unseat the government.

At this point the Fascists had only 35 seats in parliament; both as a paramilitary force and a popular party, their strength was very limited. But

the king, Victor Emmanuel, refused to use the army against Mussolini, and invited him to form a government. The installation of a dictatorship was gradual but inevitable. By 1926, Mussolini and the Fascist Party had an effective monopoly of political power, under the compliant king.

Mussolini's most famous, and enduring, achievement was the Concordat with the Papacy. Under the Lateran treaties of 1929, the Pope at last recognized the Italian state and the Vatican became an independent state within it. Papal praise for Mussolini on this occasion was fulsome – 'the times called for a man such as he whom Providence has ordained we should meet' – and the dictator's prestige was greatly enhanced. There were few other policy successes, however. The left-wing trade unions were crushed, and this earnt the regime the backing of industrialists, even if they were forced to participate in Mussolini's 'corporatist' experiment, which was supposed to subordinate both capitalist and worker to the higher interests of the state. In practice, 'corporatism' guaranteed the Fascist Party a finger in every pie, from which many individuals profited outrageously. The peasantry benefited from a measure of land reform, and in Sicily the scandalous power of the Mafia was curbed, although at the cost of equally scandalous excesses committed by the torturers of Mussolini's secret police. For the rest, the old corrupt ways of Italian public life prevailed, only more blatant and extreme, with an extra edge of brutality and arrogance to the exercise of police power.

In Germany, Fascism took longer to establish itself, but proved an incomparably more dynamic and terrible phenomenon. This was partly because German society and culture was more prone to the worship of force and power. It was a country of which one of her leading intellectuals, Oswald Spengler, could write: 'War is eternally the higher form of human existence, and states exist for the sake of war ...' Germany was of all countries the least equipped to come to terms

with defeat. Many of its people clung with extraordinary tenacity to the myth of the Stab in the Back – that the army had remained undefeated, betrayed by Bolshevik agitators, Jewish profiteers and socialist politicians.

Hitler and the Nazis

But German Fascism was also more terrible because it found in Adolf Hitler an evil genius to lead it. Son of an Austrian customs official, before the war Hitler led an idle life of vague and frustrated artistic ambitions. He served in the German Army throughout the war, but rose only to the rank of corporal. In 1919 he joined a tiny political group in Munich that was soon to become the National Socialist German Workers' Party – the Nazis. Fourteen years later, he would be undisputed ruler of Germany.

There was nothing original in Hitler's political ideas or prejudices, and he was on the face of it an unlikely heroic leader for the *Volk* – a physically unprepossessing vegetarian. But he did have two exceptional qualities. One was a remarkable gift for political maneuver – a cynical and cunning grasp of practical psychology and the power of propaganda which allowed him to manipulate experienced politicians and naïve voters alike. The other was an inexhaustible faith in his own destiny: 'I go the way that Providence dictates with the assurance of a sleepwalker.' The cult of the Führer, which he assiduously encouraged, was eventually to hypnotize most of the German people.

Hitler could never have come to power but for the weakness and eventual near-collapse of the Weimar democracy. Much was decided in the very earliest days of the Republic. A Social Democratic Party government succeeded to the fallen Imperial regime on 10 November 1918, and its leader, Ebert, immediately concluded a secret deal with the German Army commander on the Western Front. The army would support Ebert against Bolshevism in return for a guarantee that the

authority of officers would be upheld. From that moment, the possibility of a revolution from the Left was annulled. Armed bands of volunteers, the *Freikorps*, were formed under the army's patronage to maintain order. In January 1919, an uprising by the communist Spartacists in Berlin was suppressed by the *Freikorps*, and the Spartacist leaders Rosa Luxemburg and Karl Liebknecht were murdered. In May, a communist administration in Bavaria was overthrown by the army and the *Freikorps*, again with much bloodshed.

In this way, parliamentary democracy was established in Germany with the armed support of its natural enemies, right-wing militarists and nationalists who loathed democracy and liberalism. And successive democratic governments, although dominated by nominal socialists, did nothing to upset the alliance of forces that had run Imperial Germany. Not only the Officer Corps, but the civil service, judiciary and, of course, industrialists and landowners, were unaffected. All in their different ways still exercised power as before, and all to differing degrees despised the Republican system. On the Left, an embittered Communist Party also implacably opposed the

compromised Republic. What is more, the Republican government could never free itself from its responsibility for having accepted the armistice and the Versailles peace treaty.

Yet German parliamentary democracy was not as shaky a structure as its Italian equivalent. It enjoyed enough popular support to resist an attempted right-wing coup, the Kapp Putsch, in 1920, and it merely brushed aside Hitler's first bid for power. Already at the head of the Nazi Party, in November 1923 the future dictator attempted to emulate Mussolini's 'march on Rome.' Hoping to win support from a right-wing Bavarian government, he tried to mount a putsch from Munich that would bring down the regime. Despite the participation of war-hero Ludendorff, the attempt was a farcical failure, collapsing immediately when confronted by armed police. So prejudiced were the courts in favor of right-wing nationalism that Hitler served only nine months in prison, time devoted partly to writing *Mein Kampf.*

At the time of Hitler's attempted coup, Germany was in chaos, the Ruhr occupied by the French and inflation was out of control. But already, in the view of the right wing and the army, the Republic had begun to do better, and a period of cooperation between nationalists and democratic forces lay ahead. There were foreign policy successes. In 1922 Germany broke free of its postwar isolation by signing the Treaty of Rapallo with another outcast, Soviet Russia. Paradoxically, this alliance with Bolshevism pleased the Officer Corps, since the army got the chance to evade some of the restrictions imposed by the Versailles treaty, setting up secret flying schools and gas-warfare training centers in Russia. The resistance to the Ruhr occupation the following year also gave the Republic a chance to vindicate its national credentials.

In 1925, thanks to the refusal of the communists to make common cause with the socialist and center parties, the nationalist candidate, General Paul von Hindenburg, was elected to the German presidency. At the time, this seemed to increase the stability of the Republic, since the right-wing nationalists were now participating in the system they had always denounced. In October of the same year, at Locarno, Germany was admitted back into the European fold, joining the League of Nations and signing a series of treaties designed to confirm postwar borders. Britain and Italy joined France and Germany in guaran-

teeing the Franco-German frontier against aggression by either party. At last, perhaps, the war was really over. For four years, the cause of peace flourished. The League of Nations functioned to head off disputes. The Kellogg-Briand Pact, renouncing aggressive war, was signed by 65 states worldwide. In 1929 the Young Plan reduced German reparations payments still further (they were in fact abandoned in 1932, along with all other outstanding war debts) and allowed for the withdrawal of Allied military forces from the Rhineland in June 1930, ahead of schedule. German nationalists advocating rejection of the Young Plan were routed in a referendum vote. European economies were expanding and a vague optimism reigned.

But through 1929 there were signs that the long boom in the US economy might be coming to an end; in October the stock market tumbled. Business confidence was shattered, the American economy contracted rapidly, and American investors began to call in their money from abroad. The European economy had recovered on the back of US investments and US markets; now the markets shrank and the investments went home. As trade declined, prices fell; exporters had less money to pay their debts or import goods, and this further depressed trade; investment dried up, production declined; the consequent unemployment further lowered consumption and led to a steeper decline in output. This spiral of depression was helped on its way by governments who, following the advice of their economic experts, cut back spending to balance budgets and blocked imports to protect home industries and stabilize their balance of payments. By 1932 industrial production in Germany, one of the hardest-hit European countries, was just over half the 1929 level. Even in Britain, industrial output was down by 17 percent. Unemployment reached 6 million in Germany, 2.5 million in the United Kingdom. In the predominantly agricultural countries the effects of the Depression were probably worse, but less visible amid age-old rural poverty.

The Depression was accompanied by a financial crisis, with unfortunate political overtones. In May 1931 the Bank of France refused to support the Viennese Kredit-Anstalt bank, in order to force Austria to abandon a proposed customs union with Germany, considered an unacceptable step toward the unification of the two countries. The bank collapsed and Germany's finances came

Left: 'Il Duce' – Benito Mussolini wearing the uniform of the Italian Militia, one of the dozens of military uniforms at his disposal.

Below left: German communist Spartacists manning a barricade against government soldiers in Berlin 1919.

Right: Nazi Party supporters goose-step past Hitler during a rally in the 1920s.

Below: Hitler and some of his close associates, including Rudolf Hess (second from right) in Landsberg prison, following the failure of the Munich Beer Hall *putsch* in 1923.

under severe strain. This in turn put pressure on London, which had investments in Germany it could not now retrieve. In September 1931, after news of a mutiny by Royal Navy sailors protesting at a pay cut had further weakened international confidence in Britain, the British government reluctantly abandoned the gold standard. Other countries eventually followed suit. The dream of a return to prewar conditions was dead.

By 1934 the worst of the Depression was over. In both Britain and Germany in 1936, industrial production topped pre-Depression levels. But free trade had virtually disappeared. Import quotas were common and much trade was conducted by strict bilateral agreement between individual countries. Governments emphasized the pursuit of self-sufficiency and increasingly intervened in the economy to prop up threatened industries. Mass unemployment, however, remained a fact of life in Europe until 1939.

The economic collapse naturally led many people to believe that the capitalist system, and its political expression – the bourgeois democratic state – were played out. But it is a mistake to believe that economic depression necessarily leads to the triumph of political extremism. The history of Britain in the 1930s shows this clearly. The unemployed, concentrated in old industries like shipbuilding and textiles, were totally ineffectual as a political force, and unemployment generally increased the discipline of the employed, desperate to keep their jobs. Furthermore, depression did not adversely affect the living standards of most of the population. In Britain real incomes for those in work rose throughout the 1930s, since prices of imported goods continued to fall. It was a time of increasing home ownership, car ownership and security of both person and property – crime rates were astonishingly low. Not surprisingly, a complacent National Government was able to marginalize those in Britain who protested at poverty and unemployment. There had been a General Strike in 1926; there would be none in the 1930s.

In Germany, things were different. The German economy was more fragile and it suffered worse. But, above all, the Depression struck a population still embittered by the memory of defeat in war and its aftermath of inflation and disorder. Few people in Britain were inclined to blame the economic collapse on the whole system of government; many Germans blamed the Weimar Republic unequivocally for their misfortunes. In elections held in September 1930, the Communist Party won 77 seats in the Reichstag. More surprisingly, Hitler's Nazi Party, which for six years had hunted almost fruitlessly for votes, suddenly won 107 seats, becoming the second largest party in the assembly.

Hitler was an immensely skillful political campaigner and propagandist. He possessed an unsurpassed talent for expressing resentment and hatred, emotions with which many Germans, especially of the middle classes, were consumed. Some of his themes were popular with all classes: the resurrection of the nation and the army; the overthrow of the Versailles treaty; order and leadership. Industrialists provided financial backing after assurances of controls over trade unions and a strong line against communism. The implicit threat of Hitler's brownshirted stormtroopers, numbering 100,000 in 1931, was carefully managed; their street-fighting with communist bands and their acts of thuggery were not allowed to spoil the Nazis' image as a disciplined force. Yet Hitler could never have taken power by votes alone. In March 1932 he was decisively defeated when he stood against Hindenburg for the presidency. At the Nazis' electoral peak the following July they won 37.3 percent of the vote, sufficient to make them the largest single party in the Reichstag, but insufficient to force the path to government. Hitler came to power because the old guard invited him in.

From 1930 onward, no German government could command a parliamentary majority, and a small clique of conservatives and army officers gathered around the ageing Hindenburg ruled by use of special presidential decrees. There was no love lost between these men of the old Prussian ruling class and the upstart Hitler. But in the end they needed him, because they were incapable themselves of mustering adequate popular support or of solving the political and economic crisis. Like them, Hitler was authoritarian, nationalist, militarist and anti-communist. They thought he could be used. After interminable maneuverings and intrigues, on 30 January 1933 Hindenburg appointed Hitler Chancellor.

With the power of the state in his hands and the Nazis' own military forces, the SA (*Sturmabteilung*, storm division) and SS (*Schutzstaffel*, protection squad), operating legally, Hitler moved quickly to crush all opposition. Within six months, the Nazi Party was the only legal party in Germany, trade unions were banned and thousands of communists and socialists had been imprisoned. But still Hitler could not rule without the cooperation of the Officer Corps and powerful industrialists and businessmen. Their price for support was that Hitler should subdue the anti-capitalist and 'unruly' elements in his party. This meant above all curbing the SA, now 3 million

strong, viewed by the army as a dangerous rival, and by much of the middle-class population as uniformed hooligans. On the Night of the Long Knives, at the end of June 1934, Hitler unleashed the SS against the SA leadership and other undesirable colleagues or former allies in a wave of brutal killings. The Officer Corps was satisfied. When Hindenburg died the following August, the army swore personal allegiance to Hitler as Führer of the Third Reich.

Hitler did not use his dictatorial power to revo-

lutionize German society; there was no fundamental change to the social structure of the capitalist economy. The machinery of the Nazi police state – the *Gestapo* (secret police), the elite SS, the local gauleiters – was planted on top of the existing society. Each of Hitler's lieutenants – Goering, Goebbels, Himmler and Ley etc – was able to carve out a private empire. Their rival bureaucracies struggled for power and influence, often pursuing conflicting policies and vying for Hitler's backing. After an initial period of relative caution as the regime consolidated its hold on the country, from 1938 onward Hitler gave full encouragement to the organization of a brutal and sadistic reign of terror against the hated and despised – Jews, gypsies, homosexuals, 'mental defectives,' the 'work-shy' – in pursuit of the purification of the race. Once the war started, this was developed into a campaign of extermination.

The Nazis ascendant

But this was not the image of Nazi rule that most Germans saw in the 1930s. They saw low crime rates – law and order on the streets – not the lawless secret police. They saw the cleaning up of Germany – a clampdown on prostitution and pornography – not the corruption of power. They saw not the chaos of conflicting Nazi cliques, but a newfound national unity after years of party political strife. Through the media, the schools and meticulously staged mass rallies, the regime's version of the past, present and future was relentlessly drummed in. But the majority of the German people needed little persuasion; success justified Nazism. Hitler was fortunate that the

Above left: A suburban house of the 1930s.

Left: Nazi Party propaganda extolling the virtues of the workers as 'soldiers of Hitler.'

Above right: Hitler's personal bodyguard in Munich in the 1920s. Although part of the SA these guards were to form the SS.

Right: The course of events during the bloody and bitterly-fought Spanish Civil War.

Far right: Hitler with some of his closest supporters in 1933 including, left to right: Goebbels, Röhm, Goering and Himmler.

end of the Depression coincided with his assumption of power. Essentially the German economy would have recovered under any government, but rearmament, public works programs, an aggressive bilateral trade policy, exchange controls and wage controls helped – and Hitler got the credit. Driving on the new *Autobahnen*, the middle class could only be content with strike-free, orderly Germany. Germany's traditional rulers still resented and secretly despised the Nazis as upstarts from the gutter – a dislike that was cordially returned – but they too found Hitler's success irresistible. It was above all a success in foreign policy.

Hitler's overriding personal goal was to re-establish Germany as the dominant power in Europe. This meant first and foremost the overthrow of the hated Versailles treaty. Beyond this lay misty prospects of *Lebensraum* in the east – a German slave empire in the Ukraine and beyond. In fact, the time was ripe for a reassertion of German power. The weakness of the League of Nations and its promise of collective security had been shown in 1931, when Japan invaded Manchuria and the League failed to act against the aggressor. The two powers that might have been expected to uphold the Versailles treaty, Britain

and France, were totally unprepared for a confrontation. It had been the accepted wisdom of Britain since soon after the war that Germany had been hard done by at Versailles, and that the country's eventual readmission to the full rights of an independent state was inevitable. Many members of Britain's predominantly Conservative National Government were inclined to look favorably on Hitler's anti-communism and even welcomed a revived Germany as a bulwark against the Soviet Union. The opposition Labour Party, although ideologically in favor of resisting Hitler, was heavily influenced by pacifism and slow to back rearmament. In France, the Third Republic was ruled by a succession of governments that failed to command widespread respect or provide strong national leadership. In the armed forces, there were many right-wing officers who favored the overthrow of the Republic and admired Hitler. The country's military planning was entirely defensive, based on the Maginot Line, a supposedly impregnable fortification along the frontier with Germany, begun in 1929. In both Britain and France, governments overrated the strength of German forces and underrated their own. Also in both countries there was a profound popular desire (shared, incidentally, by the people of Ger-

many and Italy) to avoid a repetition of the Great War. Hitler was to exploit this longing for peace mercilessly.

In March 1935 the German dictator announced the end of the Versailles restrictions on the German armed forces. The peacetime strength of the Army was now set at 600,000 – a figure which astonished the German officer corps, although they had prepared ever since the war for the time when rebuilding could begin. A year later, on 3 March 1936, German troops moved into the officially demilitarized Rhineland. This was a contravention not only of the Versailles treaty, but also of the Locarno agreement by which Britain and Italy guaranteed French security. The German Army was still weak and could not have resisted successfully even if the French had acted alone. But Hitler's gamble paid off; nothing happened. Neither Britain nor France would fight to preserve the fruits of victory in 1918. Germany was once more a great power.

Hitler's fellow Fascist dictator, Mussolini, also experienced the frail impotence of French and British disapproval. In October 1935 Italian forces invaded Abyssinia from neighboring Italian colonial territory. Denounced as an aggressor by the League of Nations, Italy was subjected to economic sanctions. But Britain and France prevaricated, fearing that if sanctions were applied with rigor it would lead to war with Italy. In May 1936 the Abyssinian capital, Addis Ababa, fell and Emperor Haile Selassie fled into exile. The League of Nations was wholly discredited and played no further part in world events. Perhaps more seriously still, Mussolini, whom Britain and France had hoped might be lured into their camp, was instead driven into a close relationship with Hitler. In November 1936 he announced the creation of the 'Rome-Berlin Axis' around which the European world would revolve.

By 1936, democracy in Europe was limited to Britain and France, Czechoslovakia, Spain, the Low Countries, Scandinavia and Switzerland. Almost every country in Central and Eastern Europe had a dictatorial, or at least markedly authoritarian, government. Poland, for example, had experienced the personal rule of Pilsudski since 1926, and in 1935 all pretense of democracy had been abandoned. In Hungary, Admiral Horthy had ruled since 1920, officially as regent for an absent king. Yugoslavia effectively became a dic-

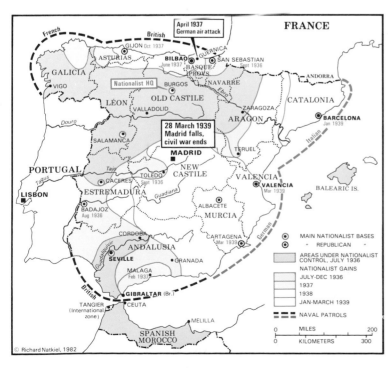

Above: Hitler, with Rudolf Hess and Baldur von Schirach, addressing a Hitler Youth Rally in 1938.

Left: Italian troops bringing 'Fascist civilization' to Ethiopia in 1936.

Right: The brutality of the Spanish Civil War. A Republican militiaman prods the body of a slain rebel in Madrid.

tatorship in 1929, as did Greece in 1936. At the other side of the continent, in Portugal, Antonio de Oliveira Salazar, officially prime minister, had been in practice a dictator since 1932. These were conservative, authoritarian governments in relatively backward countries, based mainly on an alliance between the army, landowners and the Church. But they had much in common with the Fascist dictatorships – nationalism, authoritarianism, anti-communism - and it is not surprising that their enemies in the democracies lumped them together with Hitler and Mussolini under the 'Fascist' label.

The impression of a clear confrontation between the two camps of 'democracy' and 'Fascism' was reinforced by the unification of left-wing forces in the Popular Front. The Popular Front idea was born of a change in Soviet policy in the mid 1930s. Communist parties, which had consistently denounced other socialist parties as 'social Fascists,' were now encouraged to ally themselves with other 'anti-Fascist' parties. In alliance, social democrat, communist and other left-of-center parties could prove a formidable electoral force. In February 1936 a Popular Front majority was elected in Spain, followed in March by a victory in France.

The French political situation was extremely unstable. Relatively small but active Fascist groups had almost created the conditions for a coup in February 1934. The Depression had been late to hit France and was causing industrial unrest – as Léon Blum's Popular Front government came to power, factories were occupied by their workers. Blum introduced with great difficulty a radical social program that brought real benefits to many of the population, but his government lasted little over a year before giving way to another coalition in the merry-go-round of Third Republic politics. It was enough to frighten many on the French Right, however, who adopted the slogan 'Better Hitler than Blum.'

The Spanish Popular Front met a more tragic fate. Bucking the European trend, Spain had established a democracy in 1930 after the departure of dictator General Primo de Rivera. The Republic led a stormy life as long-repressed popular causes – regional autonomy, land reform, the dismantling of the power of the Church – challenged conservative Spain head-on. After the Popular Front victory in February 1936, it looked as if a genuine revolution might ensue, as peasants

seized land and churches and convents were burned. In July a group of army officers based in Spanish Morocco launched a coup against the Republic, but the government armed anarchist and socialist militias in its defense. As a result, the attempted coup turned into a civil war that lasted almost three years and cost over 700,000 lives.

As has often been pointed out since, the Spanish Civil War was far from being a straight fight between democracy and Fascism. In Spain's tangled political web, the demand for regional independence counted for as much as any other political cause – both Left-dominated Catalonia and the profoundly religious Basque country fought on the Republican side because they hated central government from Castile. Anarchists formed an important element on the Republican side, although they rejected the Republic. The Republic's most consistent support came from the communists who in theory despised it as a bourgeois regime, but supported it as historically correct for the current stage in Spain's political evolution. On the other side, the Fascist Falange Party had few supporters among the military leadership and saw its influence quickly decline. General Francesco Franco, leader of the Nationalist revolt, pursued the traditional military goal of strong authoritarian government in alliance with the Church and landowners. He was a conservative who played lip-service to his foreign backers, Hitler and Mussolini, but privately kept his distance from them.

It was this foreign dimension, however, that in part justified the view, widely held at the time, that in Spain the war for Europe had begun. Mussolini supported the Nationalist revolt from the start and Hitler soon followed, though on a smaller scale. They provided both arms and military formations, including units of the Luftwaffe. Thousands of idealists from Britain, France and other countries rushed to Spain to fight for the Republic in the International Brigades (a relatively small number volunteered to help Franco). The response of the British and French governments, however, was such as to confirm the very worst expectations.

Blum's Popular Front government could not agree on intervention and the British were against it. The ruling British Conservative Party contained many admirers of Franco, and the government in any case still sought compromise at all costs. The result was the cobbling together of an arms

embargo policy that in practice amounted to a blockade on arms for the Republic while the Fascists poured in support for Franco. The Soviet Union alone decided to provide the Republic with military backing, but on a much smaller scale than Franco was receiving. Increasing Soviet influence gave the communists a dominant position on the Republican side, and much energy was diverted into hunting down the enemies of the Communist Party on the Left – the Trotskyists and anarchists – rather than fighting the Nationalists. It is remarkable, under the circumstances, that the war lasted three years. The Republic was finally defeated in March 1939. Merciless in victory, Franco drove hundreds of thousands of the Spanish people into exile and imposed a rigid dictatorship that stamped out any remnants of opposition.

The Spanish Civil War brought the ideological division of Europe to a new pitch. Marxism had great intellectual appeal in the 1930s. The apparent failure of capitalism in the Great Depression and the lack of resolve shown by the bourgeois democratic leaders in confronting Fascism convinced many people that communism offered the only hope for human decency. There was an atmosphere in which young upper-middle-class Englishmen of impeccable background agreed to become spies for the Soviet Union. On the Right also, especially in France, ideological hatreds grew stronger than habitual patriotism. Many among the more prosperous classes half longed for a German victory that would give them power over their enemies on the Left.

Artists and writers felt forced to adopt political postures. In Germany, certainly, they had no choice. The Nazis emptied art galleries of 'degenerate' paintings and banned writings not conducive to the New Order. There was nothing in Hitler's antiintellectualism and contempt for modern art that would have been unfamiliar to a reader of the London popular press of the period. But as the ritual Nazi book-burnings proceeded and a flood of scientists, writers and artists fled from persecution to a haven in the democracies, the image of a new dark age and the end of civilization was readily evoked. The loss to Germany was immeasurable; it was largely America's gain. The intellectual and cultural elite who fled Nazism mostly finished up in the United States, which thus found itself enhanced in almost every area of activity, from the nuclear sciences to concert music and architecture. This was another step toward the end of Europe's cultural dominance over the rest of the world.

Meanwhile, there seemed to be no stopping Germany's rise to dominance over Europe. In January 1938, Hitler dismissed Generals Blomberg and Fritsch, the heads of the armed forces, who had protested at the riskiness of his aggressive foreign policy, and took direct control of the armed forces himself. It was the prelude to action on two chosen fronts: Austria and Czechoslovakia. Austria, with its almost totally German population, had long had a large indigenous Nazi Party at loggerheads with the authoritarian Catholic government – they had killed Austrian Chancellor Dollfuss in an attempted coup in 1934. Under pressure from Berlin, after 1936 Nazis were included in the Austrian government and their subversive activities enjoyed considerable tolerance. The Austrian regime was thus in a very weak position by the time Hitler finally decided to carry out the *Anschluss*. Threats of an invasion were enough to force the Chancellor, Schussnig, to hand over control of the police to the Nazis in February 1938, effectively destroying the power of the Austrian government. On 12 March, when

Schussnig showed signs of fighting back, Hitler ordered his troops into Austria. There was no resistance. The Catholic hierarchy advised plebiscite. Austria was swallowed up, adding eight million to the German population, and thereby much weakening the strategic position of Czechoslovakia.

It might have been expected that Britain and France would protest bitterly at this further affront to the peace treaties. But they did not. After all, the population of Austria was German, and the principle of self-determination accepted at Versailles suggested that all people of one nationality should be united under one government. Only self-determination would bring permanent peace. Thus Hitler's policy of piecemeal aggrandizement and expansion found unexpected support from those who should have been its enemies, especially British Prime Minister Neville Chamberlain. A forceful leader with a good record of social reform behind him, Chamberlain believed that peace could only be secured once Germany's 'just demands' were satisfied. His aim was to achieve this without war. By his policy of appeasement, Chamberlain became in effect Hitler's ally in the revision of Germany's borders.

Czechoslovakia, Hitler's next target, was a stable democracy with an industrialized economy and efficient armed forces. It was guaranteed against aggression by an alliance with France dating from 1924 and a treaty with the Soviet Union concluded in 1936. If a halt was to be called to German expansion, this was the place. But Czechoslovakia was a multinational state, with a population of Czechs, Slovaks, Magyars, Ruthenes, Poles and, crucially, 3 million Germans. Czechoslovakia could be destroyed by the application of the principle of self-determination.

By 1938 the German minority, largely concentrated in the Sudetenland border areas, was conducting a campaign of agitation for autonomy, egged on by Nazi propaganda. Hungary and Poland were also voicing territorial claims. To the horror of his generals, Hitler was determined to take military action to crush Czechoslovakia, using the pretext of Sudeten demands. The potential for a European war was obvious.

Chamberlain believed a war would destroy civilization and must be avoided at any cost; he also believed Britain to be totally unprepared to fight. He regarded the Czech government of Eduard Beneš as the real obstacle to peace, in its stubborn resistance to German demands. When the crisis came in September 1938, all Chamberlain's efforts were devoted to wringing concessions from the Czechs. Yet with each fresh concession, Hitler's demands rose. After a meeting between Chamberlain and Hitler on 22-23 September, it seemed that all efforts at a negotiated settlement had failed, and Britain and France reluctantly prepared for war. At the last moment, on 29 September, a conference at Munich brought Hitler, Chamberlain, Mussolini and French Prime Minister Edouard Daladier together. Between them they agreed on the rape of Czechoslovakia. The Czechs were told to accept German occupation of the Sudetenland; if they refused, they would have to face Germany alone. Not surprisingly, Beneš capitulated.

Daladier regarded the Munich agreement as a shameful if necessary act. Chamberlain, on the other hand, flew back to England in triumph, proclaiming 'peace with honor' and 'peace in our time.' He fondly believed that Europe could now enjoy security based on a solid Anglo-German friendship. But in the months that followed Munich, a slow but perceptible change came over opinion in Britain. This was partly a result of Hitler's domestic policies: on the night of 9-10 November 1938 the Nazis carried out a savage pogrom against the Jews in retaliation for the murder of a German diplomat in Paris. These new brutalities shocked the democracies. Also, critics of Chamberlain's policies, such as the maverick politician Winston Churchill, were increasingly heard, protesting that the growth of German power must be checked. The British public began to accustom itself to the idea of war.

The turning point for British government policy came with the collapse of Czecho-Slovakia (the country was now hyphenated). The Czechs had known that with the Munich agreement their

Above: Nazi kultur in action. On Goebbels' instigation, Nazi students burn 'decadent' books in Berlin in 1933.

Left: Neville Chamberlain returns from Munich in 1938 and displays the infamous agreement with Hitler – 'Peace in our time.'

Above right: Soviet Foreign Minister Molotov signs the Nazi-Soviet Non-Aggression Pact, August 1939. In the background are Ribbentrop and Stalin.

Right: British reservists read the details about the declaration of war, 3 September 1939.

Through the spring and summer of 1939, Britain halfheartedly pursued an alliance with the Soviet Union, but the adamance of Polish opposition made the negotiations futile. For their part, the Soviets were very worried by German expansion, convinced that they themselves were the ultimate object of Hitler's ambitions. Stalin distrusted Britain and France as fundamentally hostile capitalist powers, quite capable of encouraging Hitler to turn eastward to save their own skins.

In the end, Germany offered the Soviet Union a better deal. On 23 August 1939, the two countries signed a Non-Aggression Treaty with secret provisions for the partition of Poland and the Baltic States. This pact between Hitler and Stalin was the most startling stroke of diplomacy in the twentieth century. It represented the triumph of *realpolitik* over ideology. The Soviet Union would be enabled to reverse the result of the war with Poland 20 years earlier, and much improve its defensive position. The Germans got a free hand to invade Poland and, if necessary, to fight a war with Britain and France in the west without worrying about a second front in the east. Compared with these advantages, ideological differences counted for nothing. Throughout Europe, communist parties were thrown into disarray by Stalin's sudden *volte-face*.

From the moment the pact was signed, war was inevitable. On 1 September, Hitler's forces invaded Poland. Two days later, with the utmost reluctance, Britain and France declared war on Germany. Mussolini, despite his 'Pact of Steel' with Hitler, proclaimed Italian neutrality.

The war that started in 1939 was to a remarkable degree a continuation of the war that had ended in 1918. But, this time round, the rulers of the Reich were evil as Kaiser Wilhelm and those before him had never been. The face of Europe would be besmirched with hideous atrocities before the dogs of war were leashed again.

country was finished; Chamberlain did not know this. When the Slovaks demanded independence for Slovakia in March 1939, Hitler's army rolled into Prague and established a 'protectorate' over the rump that remained under Czech rule. This was in effect just the last act of the Munich agreement, which had handed Czechoslovakia to Germany bound hand and foot. But to Chamberlain and much of European opinion it was a sudden revelation of naked German aggression. Here was no national minority calling for selfdetermination, no 'just demands,' but the destruction of an independent country by a powerful neighbor.

Chamberlain still sought peace, but he now concluded it could only be achieved by a show of resolution and force. The new British policy was to give any threatened country a cast-iron guarantee against aggression. The first beneficiary of this new policy was Poland. At the end of March 1939, the Poles received an unconditional promise that, if they were attacked by Germany, Britain and France would go to war in their defense. This was entirely a British initiative; France had lost almost all independence of action and was simply pulled along in Britain's wake.

The stakes are raised

The British alliance with Poland was intended to deter Hitler; in fact, it provoked him. The Führer was by now intoxicated with his own success. He had begun to believe himself totally infallible. Acting against the advice of his generals and diplomats, he had achieved a remarkable success, taking Germany in five years from virtual impotence to a position as the strongest power in Europe, feared by all. At the end of April 1939 he told his officers that the next target was Poland; it was to be attacked on 1 September.

Since 1934 Poland and Germany had been on good terms. The right-wing government in Warsaw approved of Hitler's anti-Semitism and shared his hostility to communism. Hitler even invited Poland to join the Anti-Comintern Pact (adherents to the pact were Germany, Italy, Japan and Spain), but the Poles declined. They wished to remain totally independent of both the Soviet Union and Germany – a hopeless aspiration.

Hitler's demands focussed on the 'Polish Corridor,' which split East Prussia from the rest of Germany, and the Free City of Danzig, which had a predominantly German population. The usual Nazi propaganda was mounted in defense of the rights of these Germans against the oppressive Polish government. But Poland had no intention of acceding to German wishes on Danzig, and Chamberlain was not able to repeat the experience of Munich by pressuring the Poles into making concessions.

If Germany attacked Poland, Britain and France were bound to go to war in its defense. But how was Poland to be defended; given that French strategic planning was entirely negative, ruling out any offensive push into Germany, only the Soviet Union could offer realistic hope of military support for the Poles. Yet Poland refused to contemplate allowing Soviet troops into its territory.

Soviet Union

The revolution of February 1917 signified the end of the 300-year reign of the Romanov czars in Russia. It was a surprise to everyone – to the czars, to the bourgeois liberals and to the Bolsheviks. Perhaps especially to the Bolsheviks, for the party had only 30,000 to 40,000 members in all of Russia.

In 1898 the Social Democratic Workers' Party had been illegally founded in Minsk. It had split in 1903 into the moderate Mensheviks and radical Bolsheviks. Whereas the social democratic parties of Western Europe operated legally, formed mass parties and continually concentrated on reforms within the existing society, the Russian socialist movement was dominated by revolutionary tendencies from the beginning. The Russian socialists had no chance to institute reforms; they were limited to illegal activity by the restrictions of the czarist regime. Their lot was oppression and terror, arrest and exile.

They formed an illegal, revolutionary, elitist party that pursued only one goal: the preparation of the revolution. The leaders of the Bolsheviks – Lenin, Trotsky, Bukharin, Zinoviev, Kamenev, Shliapnikov, Rykov, Tomsky and Stalin – had all been arrested more than once, had spent years in prison and exile and had often just barely escaped before they found refuge for different periods of time in various countries of Western Europe. This was the party that decisively altered Russia's history after the revolution of February 1917.

Although Lev Kamenev and Joseph Stalin returned to St Petersburg from Siberian exile after the victory of the February Revolution, the most important Bolshevik leaders were still abroad:

Vladimir Lenin and Grigori Zinoviev in Zurich, Leon Trotsky and Nikolai Bukharin in New York. On 3 April (16 April new style) Lenin returned to Russia with his wife, Nadezhda Krupskaya, and other well-known Bolsheviks, almost all of whom later died in Stalin's infamous concentration camps.

Socialist friends had obtained permission from the German government for Lenin to travel across Germany in a sealed train; fourteen days later he was triumphantly received in St Petersburg. On the very next day Lenin proclaimed his 'April Theses' at a conference of Bolsheviks. He believed that the revolution should be continued and the transition to a socialist revolution completed, that the Provisional Government should be opposed with the strongest measures and that the Bolsheviks should not cooperate with the two moderate socialist parties, the Mensheviks and the Social Revolutionaries.

Lenin first encountered resistance among the rank and file of the Bolsheviks, but soon he succeeded in winning them over to his conception of the transition to the socialist revolution. Then events took an extremely favorable turn for the Bolsheviks. The hopes which broad groups of the populace had placed in the Provisional Government began to disappear, for the government seemed unable to satisfy either the desire for peace or the peasants' aspiration for land. As a result, the Bolshevik Party flourished. By the end of June it was publishing newspapers and magazines, and the number of party members had increased in these few months to 80,000.

The Provisional Government had repeatedly

declared its intention of continuing the war against Germany on the side of the Allies. On 18 June (1 July) the Russian troops on the front began a massive attack. It was doomed to failure from the beginning, for ammunition was lacking and morale was at a nadir. The offensive collapsed almost immediately, and with it most of the Russian front. There were massive demonstrations in Petrograd, not only against the continuation of the war but also for the first time against the Provisional Government. The indignation of the masses was so great that the demonstration began to assume the character of an insurrection. Soldiers loyal to the government opened fire. The party headquarters of the Bolsheviks was stormed and demolished. Trotsky (who had returned to Russia in May) and Kamenev were arrested. Lenin went into hiding, first in Petrograd and later in Finland, returning only on the eve of the October Revolution. The Bolshevik Party was again outlawed.

Yet within a few weeks the situation changed again in their favor. On 27 August (9 September) Prime Minister Aleksandr Kerensky's own Chief of Staff, General Lavr Kornilov, who had been named Supreme Commander of the Armed Forces in July, tried to overthrow the Provisional Government in a military coup d'état.

Some of his most loyal troops marched on Petrograd. In order to check the threat from the right, the Provisional Government had to accept all possible support from the left. The Bolshevik leaders who had been arrested in July – among them Trotsky and Kamenev – were set free.

In four days the Kornilov putsch was crushed,

Left: Defending Mother Russia – soldiers of the Provisional Government march through Petrograd in the spring of 1917.

Above right: A truck-load of Bolshevik Red Guards on patrol in Petrograd in November 1917.

Right: Recruits for the Red Guard gather in one of Petrograd's railway stations to be sworn in.

and the Bolsheviks, who had been major partici-pants, were considerably strengthened. They gained a majority in the new elections for the Petrograd Soviet on 31 August (13 September), and Trotsky became Chairman. In the course of only two weeks the Soviets in other industrial cities, including Moscow, passed into the hands of the Bolsheviks.

In the fall of 1917 the revolutionary flood was discernible in the entire country. Workers' Com-mittees formed in workshops and factories were often more powerful than the company manage-ment. Peasants in many places in the countryside seized the land, and the landowners' houses often went up in flames. Soldiers on the front refused to follow the orders of their officers, and the authority of Kerensky's Provisional Government declined from week to week. The government's political weaknesses had been revealed in the struggle against Kornilov, and now it stood powerless before the collapse of the economy. Food shortages and unemployment assumed alarming proportions. In this crisis the Bolshevik Party's simple, clear program of peace, land for the peasants and workers' control in the factories seemed to be the only alternative for increasing numbers of people.

From September onward Lenin wrote letters from his hiding place in Finland continuously urging the Central Committee of the Bolshevik Party in Petrograd to take power in an armed uprising. 'History will not forgive us if we do not seize control now!' he wrote. On 9 October (22 October) Lenin returned illegally to Petrograd in disguise. On the following day, supported by Trotsky, he demanded at an illegal meeting of the Central Committee that a resolution concerning an 'armed uprising' be put on the agenda. The resolution was passed, 10 votes for and two votes (Kamenev and Zinoviev) against. Lenin's resolu-tion was again accepted at a second, enlarged meeting of the Central Committee on 16 October (29 October) by a vote of 19 to 2 (again Kamenev and Zinoviev) with 4 abstentions.

On 12 October (25 October) the Military Revo-lutionary Committee of the Petrograd Soviet was formed. Under Trotsky's leadership it acted as a sort of general staff for the approaching insurrec-tion. The Committee had its headquarters in the Smolny Institute, and was linked by hundreds of representatives and agents to armed groups in factories and to the 200,000 troops, later renamed 'Red Guards,' most of whom were strongly sym-pathetic to the Bolsheviks. The fact that the Provi-sional Government was already preparing to strike a preemptive blow at the Committee proved advantageous to the Bolsheviks, for they could now carry on their military operations as measures for their own defense. On the morning of 24 October (6 November) the government seized the Bolshevik newspaper and began mass-ing its troops, thereby providing the Bolsheviks with a pretext for a counterblow.

That night, 24-25 October (6-7 November), the Bolshevik Central Committee in Smolny ordered revolutionary units to seize all bridges, train stations, power stations, telegraph offices and other strategic points, which they did without decisive opposition. By the morning of 25 October 1917 all key positions in the city were in the hands of the Bolsheviks. The Provisional Government still remained in the Winter Palace, but leaflets had already been passed out on the streets of Petrograd that morning announcing the fall of the Provisional Government. During the day Bolshevik troops and warships – including the battleship *Aurora* – arrived on the scene to lay siege to the Winter Palace, which, by evening, was completely encircled.

The second All-Russian Soviet Congress, with Kamenev as Chairman, met late that evening. The Bolsheviks had a slim majority, with 390 delegates out of 650 (670 according to other sources), but more and more representatives of the moderate socialist parties walked out of the Congress in protest against the Bolshevik insurrection, and the balance shifted in favor of the Bolsheviks. At 0230 hours – the Congress deliberated through the night – Chairman Kamenev announced to the rejoicing delegates that the Winter Palace had been captured and the Government arrested, with the exception of Kerensky who had fled shortly before. Stormy applause was again heard when news arrived shortly thereafter that several army units which Kerensky wanted to use in the fight against the Bolsheviks had declared their solidarity with the Military Revolutionary Committee. The Bolsheviks were victorious: for the first time in history Marxist revolutionaries had taken power.

The first meeting of the Central Committee of the Bolshevik Party after the victory took place in the Smolny Institute on 26 October (8 November). It was decided to call the new government the Council of People's Commissars. Lenin, having first nominated Trotsky as Chairman, took over

Left: The First Leaflet, an idealized painting of the Bolshevik leader Lenin with an early propaganda tract.

Below left: Formed from workers, soldiers, sailors, students and peasants, the Red Guard prepares to defend the revolution against the White counter-revolutionaries.

Above right: The title-page of the Bolshevik magazine *The Communist International* published in 1919.

More than 70 percent of the populace was illiterate, and the percentage of those engaged in industry was infinitesimal. It was a land whose economy had been ruined by war and in which famine, poverty and misery reigned. The contrast between the aims of the revolution and reality was obvious. The Bolsheviks, steeped in Marxist theory, and inspired by their goal of creating a classless communist society, were now forced to take practical measures at a time when the means for the realization of their goals were lacking.

This contradiction became greater when it became obvious soon after the victory that the Bolsheviks represented only a minority of the population. Prior to the Revolution the Bolsheviks had repeatedly demanded that a Constituent Assembly be convened; now, in the elections for the Assembly, they received a total of 9 million out of 36 million votes. The overwhelming majority voted for the Social Revolutionaries. Of the 707 representatives at the opening of the Constituent Assembly on 18 January (31 January) 1918, there were 370 Social Revolutionaries and only 175 Bolsheviks supported by 40 Left Social Revolutionaries. The remainder was divided among small political parties and minority groups. Since the majority of the Constituent Assembly refused to support the one-party government of the Bolsheviks, the Bolsheviks again turned to violence. A detachment of Bolshevik guards prevented the Constituent Assembly from continuing its work, some members were arrested and finally the Constituent Assembly was dissolved.

On 18 November (1 December) all non-Bolshevik newspapers, with two exceptions, were prohibited, and on 7 December (20 December) the Extraordinary Commission for the Struggle against Counterrevolution, Speculation and Sabotage, usually known by the Russian abbreviation 'Cheka,' was formed under the direction of Felix Dzerzhinsky. He quickly directed the terror of the Cheka not only against open opponents of the Revolution but also against members of the moderate socialist parties because they had opposed the one-party rule of the Bolsheviks, even though they were in favor of socialism and the Soviet regime.

Besides the need to strengthen and maintain power, the Bolsheviks had to face one other pressing issue: the termination of the war and the conclusion of peace with Germany. On 20 November (3 December) 1917 the official armistice negotiations began in Brest-Litovsk. The representatives of Germany and Austria-Hungary demanded the cession of Poland, Lithuania and parts of Latvia and White Russia (then part of the Russian Empire), as well as that the Ukraine be given the right of selfdetermination (the goal was to bring these lands into the German sphere of influence). Trotsky, who became head of the Soviet Delegation in January 1918, tried to prolong the negotiations as long as possible in the hope that revolution would also break out in Germany. The Germans retaliated with an offensive that began in the middle of February. German troops occupied Latvia, Estonia, White Russia and the Ukraine almost without opposition and pushed forward toward the Caucasus. The debates in the Central Committee of the Bolshevik Party were heated and involved: one group, known as the 'Left Communists' (to which Bukharin belonged at that time), insisted on the rejection of the German demands and the proclamation of a 'revolutionary war.' However Lenin's view that the German ultimatum should be accepted finally won. On 23 February 1918 the German terms were accepted, and on 3 March the treaty was signed in Brest-Litovsk. According to the Treaty of Brest-

when the latter refused. Later that evening the second All-Russian Soviet Congress continued its meeting. Lenin, greeted with thunderous applause, declared 'We shall now proceed to construct the socialist order.' The delegates, filled with enthusiasm, joined in singing the *Internationale*.

After this the first decrees of the Soviet Government were read aloud. The decree On Peace offered all belligerent countries a democratic peace, without annexations or indemnities. The new Soviet Government proposed that secret diplomacy be abolished and that all treaties concluded by the previous regime be published immediately. The decree On Land called for the public distribution of the estates of landowners and monasteries without compensation. On the basis of this decree over 400 million acres of land were divided among the peasants.

Lenin in command

In the early morning hours Chairman Kamenev read the decree on the new Soviet Government, the 'Council of People's Commissars.' The Government was to be composed exclusively of Bolsheviks: Lenin was Chairman; Trotsky, People's Commissar of Foreign Affairs; Aleksey Rykov, Minister of the Interior; Anatoli Lunacharsky, Minister of Education; and Stalin, appointed last, was in charge of Nationalities. Of the 15 People's Commissars, four were workers, and 11 intellectuals. All had experienced prison and exile, and most had emigrated abroad. Lenin at 47 was the oldest, the other People's Commissars were between 30 and 38 years old, while the sailor Dybenko, in charge of the fleet, was only 28. Of them all only five would die natural deaths; eight later died in Stalin's forced labor camps; one, Rykov, was shot after a show trial and Trotsky was murdered in Mexico on Stalin's orders.

A few days later the Soviet Government proclaimed the Declaration of the Rights of the Peoples of Russia. The privileges of Russians and the limitations imposed on other non-Russian peoples were abolished. All non-Russian people were guaranteed the right to secede from the empire and form independent states. The decree on workers' control followed, whereby elected workers' representatives in all factories were guaranteed control of production, purchasing and sale of products, as well as financial control. Banks were nationalized. All previous state loans were annulled, educational privileges were abolished, the Church was separated from the State and the schools from the Church and finally all ranks, privileges and designations of rank were removed from the Civil Service.

Nevertheless, the Bolsheviks had only won in Petrograd (now Leningrad), and even there there was opposition on 27 and 28 October (9 and 10 November). An attempted insurrection by the students of the Officers' School had to be suppressed, and the Bolsheviks had considerable difficulty with the railway workers' union, which threatened to strike if the Bolsheviks did not resign in favor of a government composed of all three socialist parties.

Yet despite resistance the Bolsheviks succeeded in extending their influence through a large part of the country. During the next two months they took power in Moscow and 28 other government centers in Russia – sometimes without violence, but sometimes, as in Moscow, Kiev, Kharkov, Rostov, Baku and Smolensk, only after armed struggle. By the beginning of 1918 almost all of Russia, with the exception of the Don region, was under the control of the Bolsheviks.

The Bolsheviks had come to power in a land that was economically backward and in which peasants made up five-sixths of the population.

Litovsk Soviet Russia lost 26 percent of its territory, 27 percent of its arable land, 26 percent of its railway network, 33 percent of its textile industry, 73 percent of its iron industry and 75 percent of its coal mines.

War communism and the Civil War

The negotiations in Brest-Litovsk were barely ended when civil war broke out; continuing relentlessly, it lasted for more than three years. In January 1918 the Bolsheviks resolved to create a volunteer Red Army of Workers and Peasants with the right to elect its own officers, the same right that had been given to the soldiers of the regular Red Army. Trotsky, appointed Chairman of the Revolutionary Military Council in March and People's Commissar for Defense at the beginning of April, directed the Red Army. By the end of April, the spread of the Civil War had led to compulsory military service. The lack of trained officers was alleviated by accepting czarist officers, although each had at his side a Bolshevik Commissar of War who supervised him, prevented any possible treason and supported the strengthening of discipline and political education within the troops.

The hard conditions of the Civil War compeled the Bolsheviks to take measures which were determined less by their revolutionary goals than by practical necessities. This system, known as 'War Communism,' was characterized by three features. First, there were obligatory deliveries of agricultural products: detachments were sent to all villages, and peasants were forced to deliver all produce in excess of what was needed for personal consumption. Second, nationalization was extended further than was originally intended: whereas in June 1918 only large-scale businesses with assets of over a million rubles had been nationalized, during the Civil War all firms, including small businesses, were made state property. Third, all citizens were required to work, and a strict system of rationing was introduced following the motto 'He who doesn't work doesn't eat.'

The strongholds of the Whites, as the opponents of the Bolsheviks were called, were located in the regions of the Don and Kuban rivers, where former czarist generals organized a resistance movement at the beginning of 1918. In the spring of 1918 British troops landed in Murmansk and Arkhangelsk, and Japanese and later American troops landed in Vladivostok. More significant and more dangerous for the Bolsheviks was a second center of opposition, which arose in Siberia in May 1918. Some 40,000 to 50,000 soldiers of the Czechoslovakian Legion, who had been captured by the Russians during World War I, were on their way across Siberia to Vladivostok and then to France to take part in the war against Germany. When Trotsky demanded that they hand over their weapons the Czech Legion rebeled against the Soviet Government, occupied large parts of the Siberian railway and overturned Bolshevik rule in many cities.

The opponents of the Bolsheviks, especially the Social Revolutionaries, felt strengthened by this action; and in July 1918 they initiated uprisings in Moscow and over 20 other cities. The Bolsheviks succeeded in crushing these outbreaks only after fierce battles. The Red Terror (then openly proclaimed as such) that arose was answered by the Social Revolutionaries with assassinations. On 30 August a group of Social Revolutionaries murdered the head of the Cheka in Petrograd, and on the same day another Social Revolutionary, Dora Kaplan, fired several shots at Lenin, seriously wounding him with two bullets. In addition, British troops landed in Baku in August 1918 and invaded Soviet Central Asia from Iran.

The first large battles took place on the Volga in the summer of 1918, where the army under Trotsky's leadership succeeded in driving back the anti-Bolshevik troops and in stopping the Whites' advance on Moscow. In the fall of 1918 the White Army under Anton Denikin was successfully opposed near Czaritsyn (later Stalingrad, today Volgograd). The situation further improved for the Bolsheviks with the outbreak of revolution in Germany in November 1918: the Treaty of Brest-Litovsk was annulled and German troops retreated from Russia. Within a few weeks the Bolsheviks took over the territories which the German troops had evacuated, including the Ukraine, White Russia and, temporarily, the Baltic States.

On the other hand, the German withdrawal led to a stronger Allied intervention. In November and December 1918 British troops landed in Batum and Baku, and French and Greek forces landed in Odessa. At the same time Great Britain increased its support to the Whites in the form of

МЫ ВОЮЕМ С ПАНСКИМ РОДОМ
А НЕ С ПОЛЬСКИМ ТРУДОВЫМ
НАРОДОМ !

Left: To defend the revolution Trotsky was forced to conscript all sorts of people for the Red Army, including former officers of the Czarist Army.

Below left: Admiral Kolchak, the Supreme Commander of the White Russian Forces in Siberia, with officers of the French military mission at Omsk.

Right: Soviet poster of 1920 claims that the Red Army is fighting the Polish nobles and not the workers.

Below right: A parade of British sailors and marines marches through the streets of Vladivostock in 1919, part of the Allied interventionary forces.

weapons and ammunition, especially to the former czarist Admiral Aleksandr Kolchak, who had established a military dictatorship in Omsk, and to Denikin's army in the eastern Ukraine.

The newly formed Red Army was forced to fight simultaneously on three fronts: in the east against Kolchak's troops, which pushed forward to the Volga in May; in the south against Denikin's advancing army, which was approaching Moscow in October; and in the west against the forces of General Nikolai Yudenich, which had advanced from Estonia to the suburbs of Petrograd. For a time only one-eighth of the territory of Russia remained in control of the Bolsheviks. Nevertheless, the Red Army, whose strength had increased from 300,000 men in June 1918 to 1 million men in January 1919 and to 3 million by October 1919, succeeded, though with great difficulty, in throwing back the White troops. By the beginning of 1920 Yudenich had been driven back to Estonia and Denikin to his original position in the Kuban region, while Omsk had been captured and General Kolchak himself taken prisoner. The most important centers of grain and raw materials – Siberia, the Ukraine and the northern Caucasus – as well as the oil regions of Baku, were again in the hands of the Soviets. Peace treaties were signed with Estonia, Latvia and Lithuania in February and March 1920.

In order to win the war the Bolsheviks had become extremely harsh and unyielding. Economic, political and military power was centralized. Though a volunteer army had been created at the beginning of the revolution, military service had since been made obligatory, and officers were appointed, rather than elected as before. In the economic sphere the elected committees which had constituted workers' control of all factories were eliminated, and all firms were placed under the direction of state managers who were themselves subordinated to the Supreme Economic Council. Due to the austere conditions of the Civil War not only counter revolutionary forces but critics of all sorts were suppressed with exceptional severity by the Cheka.

After a short breathing spell the Civil War resumed in the spring of 1920. In April Polish troops under General Joseph Pilsudsky invaded the Ukraine, and took Kiev in May. The Polish assault touched off a wave of patriotic feeling, and the Ukrainian populace met the invading Polish troops with open hostility. On 5 June 1920 the Red Army took the offensive, broke though the Polish lines, liberated Kiev on 12 June and in July entered Polish territory hopeful of bringing the revolution to Poland. The core of the Red Army under General Mikhail Tukhachevsky advanced on Warsaw, while the Southern Army under General Semyon Budenny (and under Stalin, then Commissar of the Army) marched on Lvov. By the middle of August Tukhachevsky's troops were near Warsaw, but his soldiers were weary and his lines of support were stretched dangerously thin. Stalin ignored Moscow's order that the Southern Army should support Tukhachevsky's troops, thereby giving the Polish forces under Pilsudsky the chance to launch a counterattack on 16 August 1920 ('the miracle on the Vistula'). The Red Army was forced to abandon its positions and retreat to Minsk. The Soviet-Polish war came to an end with the cease-fire in Riga on 12 October 1920, and the peace treaty was concluded on 18 March 1921.

Now only one serious opponent remained: Wrangel. In April 1920 Denikin had given the supreme command of his troops, who had fled to the Crimea, to General Pyotr Wrangel. The latter had succeeded in overcoming the low morale of the soldiers and in increasing discipline, and in June 1920 Wrangel's army launched an offensive against the Bolsheviks and occupied the southern part of the Ukraine. At the end of October 1920 the Red Army, strengthened by troops which had arrived from Poland, launched a counter-attack and drove Wrangel's army back to the Crimean peninsula. The last decisive battle of the Civil War took place on the Perekop Isthmus in the night of 7-8 November 1920. The Red troops broke through the front, captured the Crimea within a few days and compeled Wrangel and his remaining troops to flee abroad by sea.

With the victory over Wrangel the Civil War was essentially over. Only in the Far East, in eastern Siberia and in the Caucasus were there further struggles. In February 1921 the Bolsheviks occupied Georgia, which, until then, had been under Menshevik control. Finally, in October 1921, the Japanese evacuated the sections of the Soviet Far East which they had occupied.

The Civil War ended in an enormous political and psychological victory for the Bolsheviks. The fact that a majority of the Whites had been motivated by a reactionary spirit, by a desire to restore the monarchy and by a feeling of Great Russian nationalism was decisive in the Bolshevik victory.

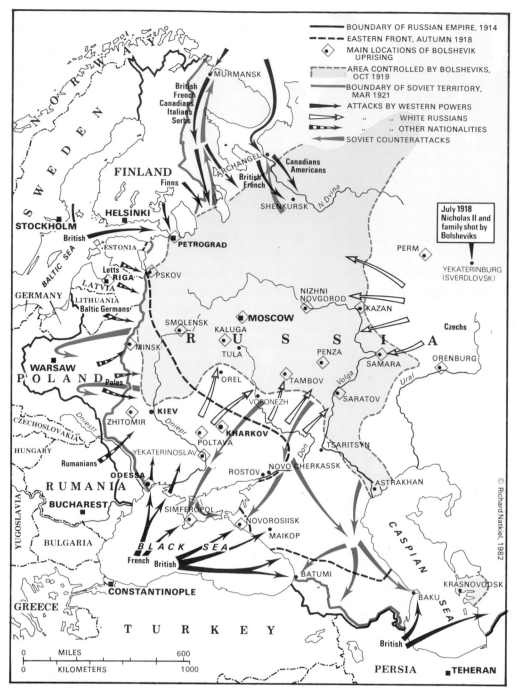

BOUNDARY OF RUSSIAN EMPIRE, 1914
EASTERN FRONT, AUTUMN 1918
MAIN LOCATIONS OF BOLSHEVIK UPRISING
AREA CONTROLLED BY BOLSHEVIKS, OCT 1919
BOUNDARY OF SOVIET TERRITORY, MAR 1921
ATTACKS BY WESTERN POWERS
"   "   " WHITE RUSSIANS
"   "   " OTHER NATIONALITIES
SOVIET COUNTERATTACKS

July 1918
Nicholas II and
family shot by
Bolsheviks

© Richard Natkiel, 1982

The liberal, democratic and socialist groups could not overcome the domination of the reactionary bureaucrats and former czarist officers. Under these circumstances the Whites could offer no constructive program oriented toward the future which corresponded to the political and social hopes of the populace. The peasant masses feared that the landowners would return and reestablish their hated authority if the Whites won. Moreover, the antagonistic national feelings and diverse political views often made coordination among the Whites impossible, and their cooperation with foreign troops was highly injurious to their patriotic claims.

On the other hand, the Bolsheviks had succeeded in creating a tightly organized military and political leadership, in communicating their easily understandable goals to the masses and in instilling feelings of perseverance, tenacity and self-sacrifice in their troops. The activity of illegal Bolshevik organizations in White territory had further undermined the power of the Whites and facilitated the advance of the Red Army. Finally, the Bolsheviks had cleverly used the conflicts among the Whites, and between the Whites and the foreign forces, for their own ends.

The Civil War also affected the composition and character of the Bolshevik Party. Popular revolutionary enthusiasm had begun under the impact of famine, privation and the endless battles. The military and dictatorial methods of Bolshevik rule which had become common during the Civil War persisted after its end, and a Party apparatus cut off from ordinary Party members had become the norm.

The end of the Lenin era

Soviet Russia, which at the end of the Civil War had a population of 132 million, was on the brink of economic disaster. Production in heavy industry in 1920 had dropped to 13.8 percent of the level of 1913, and the production of pig-iron was approximately three percent of the pre-war output. Hundreds of factories, including many large-scale enterprises, were idle. Many mines had been destroyed. Directors of state-owned factories were continually found to be lacking the necessary technical knowledge. The rail system was in ruins. Most locomotives, freight and passenger cars had been demolished, and the trip from Moscow to Kharkov, for example, took nine to 10 days instead of the normal 24 hours. Agricultural production was half that prior to 1913; the requisitioning of agricultural produce had killed all sense of initiative, and many farmers began to produce only enough for their own needs.

At the beginning of 1921 dissatisfaction with the Soviet system increased to a dangerous level. Farmers began to form guerrilla bands, and discontent even spread among industrial workers. Factory workers in Petrograd went on strike in the middle of February, and at the end of the month sailors in the Kronstadt fortress, once a citadel of Bolshevism, rose in rebellion. The Kronstadt sailors formed a provisional Revolutionary Committee and demanded free elections for the Kronstadt Soviet, freedom of speech, press and assembly for all organizations and parties of workers, the liberation of political prisoners, the abolition of privileges for the Communist Party, uniform food rations and the removal of trade restrictions on craftsmen and farmers as long as they did not employ any workmen. More than a third of all Party members at Kronstadt affirmed their desire to build a socialist society, but rejected the dictatorship of the Bolshevik Party. After fierce fighting, General Tukhachevsky finally brought the Kronstadt rebellion to a bloody end on 18 March. Some of the rebels were shot, the rest went to camps.

The delegates to the Tenth Party Congress (8-16 March 1921), who had participated in the crushing of the Kronstadt rebellion, instituted changes which signified a turning point for the economy: the change from War Communism to the New Economic Policy (NEP). The detested requisitions of agricultural products were replaced by a graduated tax in kind, through which farmers were again allowed to sell their produce on the open market. Small and medium-sized privately owned factories and commercial enterprises were again permitted, as were foreign investments, though the latter only to a limited degree. Heavy industry, transportation facilities, large banks and foreign trade remained under state control.

At the same time as the changeover to the NEP – which had an extremely positive effect on the economic recovery of the country – the Bolshevik Party was strengthening its monopoly of power. The Party Congress accepted Lenin's motion ordering the immediate dissolution of all factions and groups. This was aimed primarily at the Democratic Centrists, who favored freedom of opinion and discussion within the Party, and the Workers' Opposition, which favored a democratization of the Party and the replacement of the central state planning committee by a pyramid of workers' and manufacturers' councils, culminating in an elected all-Russian congress of manufacturers. In addition the Party Congress voted a resolution on the Unity of the Party: discipline and subordination were now to be the hallmarks of Bolshevik rule; Marxist revolutionaries who thought and acted independently would be replaced by obedient functionaries.

Above left: The major campaigns and battles of the Russian Civil War.

Below left: The real victims of the Russian Civil War were the many peasant families who starved to death.

Above right: Soviet prisoners being executed by White soldiers during the Civil War. Such scenes were common on both sides.

Right: An anti-Bolshevik poster depicting Trotsky as a ruthless monster of death.

Foreign policy problems also began to play a greater role after the end of the Civil War. A series of treaties were concluded with foreign powers, including a trade agreement with Britain in the spring of 1921, treaties with neighboring Iran, Afghanistan and Turkey, as well as a friendship and aid treaty with Outer Mongolia. In 1921 famine caused by drought and a bad harvest compelled the Soviet Government to accept a greater amount of foreign aid. But the most important foreign policy development was the participation of Soviet Russia in the economic conference in Genoa in April 1922, where Soviet diplomats appeared for the first time in the theater of international diplomacy. Important German-Soviet negotiations, carefully observed by other nations, took place during this conference, and on 16 April 1922 they resulted in the Treaty of Rapallo, according to which both countries renounced all indemnities resulting from World War I, resumed diplomatic relations and concluded a trade agreement of mutual tariff reductions.

At the same time as Soviet Russia was normalizing its contacts with foreign nations revolutionary movements abroad were unmistakably declining. As the Bolsheviks' hopes for a world revolution faded, the Party apparatus at home became increasingly hierarchic. This was clearly discernible at the Eleventh Party Congress in 1922, when two new departments of the Central Committee were created to observe and direct local Party organizations and the growing number of full-time Party functionaries. On 3 April 1922, immediately after the end of the Party Congress, Stalin was appointed General Secretary of the Party. A few weeks later, at the end of May, Lenin suffered a stroke and, on the advice of his doctors, moved to the city of Gorky.

In the course of 1922 the Soviet republics – Soviet Russia (RSFSR) and the Ukrainian, White Russian (Byelo-Russian) and Transcaucasian Soviet Republics – that until then had been formally independent, were united in a Union of Soviet Socialist Republics (USSR). The issue of union produced violent controversies within the Bolshevik Party. A group in favor of centralization (to which Stalin belonged) expounded the view that the non-Russian Soviet Republics should become mere autonomous regions of the RSFSR, while other Bolsheviks, especially those from the Ukraine, wanted a confederation. Finally, Lenin, who had returned to Moscow in October 1922, won the majority over to his idea of a federation in the form of a Union of Soviet Socialist Republics, and this conception was incorporated into the constitution passed in July 1923.

Lenin's primary concern, however, was the development of the Party. At the end of December 1922 Lenin dictated a letter, later known as his 'Testament,' to the Central Committee, in which he spoke of the danger of a split in the Party and of the characteristics of those who might succeed him. He designated Trotsky as the most capable person in the Central Committee, but reprimanded his excessive self-confidence. Lenin noted that Bukharin was not only the best and most valuable theoretician, but also the favorite of the Party, but he added that his theoretical work was sometimes too academic. Though Zinoviev

Left: Destitute Russian peasants made homeless during the Civil War trek across the country searching for food and shelter.

Below: Lenin lying in state with Dzerzkinsky, the head of the Cheka, and Marshal Voroshilov looking on.

Right: Rykov, an old Bolshevik, demanded the death penalty for Zinoviev.

Below right: At the Congress of the Communist Party in 1926 there was an unsuccessful attempt to oppose Stalin.

and Kamenev had shown that they were weak during the October Revolution, he felt that this should not be held against them. Lastly Lenin said that 'Comrade Stalin, having become General Secretary, has concentrated immeasurable power in his hands, and I am not sure that he knows how to use that power with sufficient caution.' On 4 January 1923 Lenin added in a postscript that Stalin was too ruthless, and that this was intolerable in a General Secretary. Therefore he felt it necessary that Stalin be removed from his post.

A triumvirate had already begun to emerge during the period of Lenin's illness. It was composed of Zinoviev, then Chairman of the Communist International, whose basis of power lay in the Leningrad Party Organization, Kamenev, Secretary of the Moscow Party Organization and, as Lenin's representative during his illness, Chairman of the Politburo, and Stalin, General Secretary of the Party. Their common goal was to check Trotsky's rise to power, since, after Lenin, he had always been the most popular leader.

This division within the Party was deepened when Trotsky and a group of 46 prominent Bolsheviks openly announced their opposition to the bureaucratization of the Party, demanded free discussions and formation of groups and insisted that the Party apparatus be subordinated to the majority of the Party. Trotsky's 'Declaration of the 46' was condemned at a Party conference in the middle of January 1924. Many prominent followers of Trotsky were eliminated by being assigned to diplomatic posts abroad, and Trotsky himself, who had fallen ill, withdrew to the Caucasus.

A few days later, on 21 January 1924, Lenin died. His body was embalmed and placed in a mausoleum in Red Square. The triumvirate of Zinoviev, Kamenev and Stalin did not inform Trotsky, and consequently he was not present at the funeral. Zinoviev read the funeral oration, after which Stalin gave a solemn pledge, comparing the Party to an army and saying that Party members were a special sort of people, formed from special material.

The victory of Stalin

After Lenin's death Alexey Rykov was named Chairman of the Council of People's Commissars, the leading government organization, while the Politburo was composed of Trotsky, Zinoviev, Kamenev, Stalin, Bukharin, Rykov and Mikhail Tomsky. Stalin remained General Secretary of the Party, but his position was in extreme danger due to Lenin's demand (in his Testament) that he be removed. But the danger to Stalin proved to be only temporary. At the beginning of May 1924 Zinoviev's proposal to conceal Lenin's Testament from the delegates of the forthcoming Thirteenth Party Congress and to permit Stalin to remain at his post was passed by a meeting of the Central Committee, 40 votes to 10.

Stalin's position at the head of the Party apparatus was significantly strengthened by the 'Leninist levy.' Admission to the Party, until then carefully limited, was suddenly made very easy: within a few weeks more than 200,000 new members joined the ranks of the Bolsheviks. Total membership tripled from the beginning of 1924 to the beginning of 1928, from 472,000 to more than 1.3 million members. The overwhelming majority of new members had neither engaged in revolutionary activity in the czarist era nor had participated significantly in the Revolution, and they therefore could be easily directed by the central Party apparatus. The old Bolsheviks were pushed into the minority, and the mass of Party members and functionaries were less interested in World Revolution than in the immediate tasks in their own land.

Stalin's doctrine of the 'victory of socialism in one country,' which he proclaimed in December 1924, received considerable support. The Soviet Union, Stalin asserted, could build a socialist society without victorious revolutions in other countries. Although Stalin's new theory was diametrically opposed to Leninism, it satisfied Party functionaries, whose thoughts went no further than the boundaries of their own regions.

In January 1925 Trotsky was removed from his post as People's Commissar for War, and many of his supporters were also dismissed from important positions. With Trotsky checked, the common goal of the 'troika' – Zinoviev, Kamenev and Stalin – had been reached, and now conflicts began to emerge. Stalin, whose position had been strengthened by the defeat of the Trotskyites,

began to close ranks with Bukharin, Rykov and Tomsky (later known as 'rightists'). Stalin advocated a moderately left policy in domestic affairs, especially in agrarian problems, and turned more and more against his former leftist allies, especially Zinoviev.

Stalin's decisive victory came at the Fourteenth Party Congress in 1925. The majority of the delegates were chosen by Stalin's secretariat. Stalin's theory of socialism in one country became an official Party doctrine, and the construction of socialism was declared to be the main task of the Party.

Zinoviev, supported by the Leningrad Party delegates, submitted a dissenting minority report. Even Kamenev and Krupskaya, Lenin's widow, turned against Stalin: Krupskaya demanded that Lenin's Testament be published. Kamenev spoke against elevating one leader above the Party and began to read aloud the proposal for a vote of no-confidence, but the delegates shouted him down. His warnings were drowned out by cries of 'We want Stalin!' The Congress accepted Stalin's political platform (then supported by Bukharin) by a vote of 449 to 65. Kamenev withdrew from the Politburo, and Vyacheslav Molotov, Kliment Voroshilov and Mikhail Kalinin, three supporters of Stalin, joined the most powerful political organization in the land. Thus Stalin had also consolidated his power in the Politburo.

Zinoviev was dismissed from his post as Secretary of the Leningrad Party Organization at the beginning of 1926 and Sergei Kirov, an adherent of Stalin from the Caucasus, replaced him. As a result, Zinoviev and Kamenev sought to counterbalance Stalin by uniting with Trotsky, whom they had previously opposed. The 'United Opposition' which emerged criticized Stalin's policy from the left: they demanded faster industrialization and an increased role for workers and unions in factory management. Moreover, in the agricultural sphere, they felt that wealthy farmers ('kulaks') should be taxed more heavily and their power limited, and that collectivization should be instituted on a voluntary basis. Above all, the 'United Opposition' warned of the growing danger that the Party bureaucracy would destroy the achievements of the October Revolution. The union of all these communists who opposed the authoritarian regime of Stalin came too late to be effective: Stalin had directed the Party apparatus for a long time, and in addition could make

increasing use of the secret police, now called the OGPU, in conflicts within the Party. In July 1926 Zinoviev, like Kamenev, was expeled from the Politburo, and Trotsky was expeled at the end of October. Zinoviev lost his job as Chairman of the Communist International and was replaced by Bukharin.

The last major conflict between the Stalin bureaucracy and the opposition occurred in the spring and summer of 1927 and centered around Stalin's policy toward China. Stalin had demanded that the Chinese communists cooperate closely with the bourgeois-nationalist Kuomintang of Chiang Kai-Shek. In the spring of 1927 the Kuomintang attacked the communists with extreme cruelty: thousands were killed, and Stalin's policy toward China was a complete fiasco. This was ammunition in the hands of the opponents of Stalin's Party leadership. Yet Stalin cleverly used sudden tensions on the international scene to make it appear that war was imminent. In May 1927 Great Britain broke off diplomatic relations with the Soviet Union, and in June the Soviet Ambassador to Warsaw was shot by a Russian *émigré*. The Stalin group claimed that Party members should close ranks due to the supposed threat of war. At a plenary meeting of the Central Committee in October Trotsky and Zinoviev were excluded from that organization. Two weeks later, on the tenth anniversary of the October Revolution, the leaders of the opposition organized demonstrations in the streets of Moscow and Leningrad, but these were broken up by the police, and on 14 December 1927 Trotsky and Zinoviev were expelled from the Party. The terror directed against the adherents of the opposition increased, and Stalin's power was already great enough to arrest and exile hundreds of them. Trotsky, exiled in January 1928 to Alma-Ata in

Central Asia, tried to continue the resistance, but he was deported from the Soviet Union in January 1929.

Having crushed the Left Opposition, Stalin had made a surprising change in his political course at the Fifteenth Party Congress in December 1927. According to Stalin's instruction, the Party Congress voted a policy of rapid industrialization. The State Planning Commission (GOSPLAN), formed in 1921, was authorized to prepare a five-year plan of industrial development that would emphasize the development of heavy industry. In agriculture, the Party Congress concluded an offensive against kulaks, agreeing to tax kulaks more heavily and to form collective farms by force. Thus Stalin, having first eliminated the Left Opposition, adopted a large part of their proposals.

This sudden change in direction prompted Stalin's break with the 'rightists' in the Politburo – Bukharin, Rykov and Tomsky – with whom Stalin had previously collaborated. Bukharin was Chairman of the Communist International at that time, Rykov, Chairman of the Council of People's Commissars and Tomsky, Chairman of the Trade Unions. They had substantial support in the Party and advocated a continuation of Lenin's New Economic Policy: a slow evolutionary development, a realistic program of industrialization geared to existing conditions and a policy favorable to farmers. In addition, Tomsky opposed the attempts of Stalin's bureaucracy to transform the trade unions into a mere appendage or 'transmission belt' of the Party apparatus.

Bukharin reestablished his ties with Kamenev in July 1928 after Stalin began to escalate his attack on the Right Opposition, but it was now much too late to form a common front with the former Left Opposition against Stalin. In any case most Party members had grown tired of the factional struggles and submitted to the pressure of the increasingly powerful Party apparatus loyal to Stalin.

In the fall of 1928 Stalin repeatedly, and with increasing firmness, announced his new policy on industrialization and collectivization. In November he announced the famous goal that the Soviet Union had to overtake and surpass capitalist countries in economic affairs. With this preparation he launched a direct offensive against the Right Opposition in the spring of 1929. Step by step the rightist leaders were removed from power: Tomsky was discharged from his position as Chairman of the Trade Unions, Bukharin forfeited the Chairmanship of the Communist International and was expelled from the Politburo in November and Rykov and Tomsky were admonished and the latter, even after autocriticism, lost his seat in the Politburo a few months later.

By the end of 1929 Stalin was completely victorious: of the seven members of the Politburo after Lenin's death only Stalin remained. All of Lenin's closest comrades-in-arms had been eliminated and replaced by Stalinist functionaries. Stalin celebrated his victory on his fiftieth birthday, 21 December 1929. Buildings and walls in all Soviet cities were decorated with huge pictures of him, and in thousands of meetings Stalin was honored not only as Lenin's heir and disciple but also as *vozhd*, the leader of the Party and of the Soviet state.

Industrialization and collectivization in the Soviet Union

In Soviet historiography 1929 is known as the 'year of the great change.' Stalin had gained absolute control of the Party and of the government, collectivization had begun in the countryside and the five-year plan was officially ratified at the Sixteenth Party Congress at the end of April. In the foreground stood the development of heavy industry: already in the first year 78 percent of all investments were directed toward heavy industry, and this was to rise to 87.6 percent by the last year of the plan. The plan foresaw a rise in pig-

iron production from 3.3 to 10 million tons and a rise in the output of electrical energy from 5.1 to 22 billion kilowatt-hours. Moreover, 22,000 kilometers of railway lines and 60,000 kilometers of roads were to be built.

These goals, to be attained in a land that was economically backward and without significant foreign aid, implied a lack of consumer goods and a long period of suffering and privation for the populace. This, however, was not openly announced. There was no reference to 'blood, sweat and tears,' but instead optimistic promises and a flood of success stories, usually accompanied by falsified statistics.

Above: 'To secure greatness build socialism,' celebrates the Moscow Communist Party's poster of the progress of the five-year plan of 1931.

Left: A cheerful group of workers from the Young Communist League at the Magnitogorsk Iron and Steel Works in 1931.

Above right: Early construction work in 1929 on the Dnieper hydro-electric power station in the Ukraine.

The program of industrialization was carried out under conditions which were at best contradictory. On the one hand, the grandiose plan aroused genuine enthusiasm in segments of the population, while on the other, coercion and repression increased. Enthusiastic members of the Komsomol (the league of communist youth) worked day and night on the gigantic construction sites under the most dreadful living conditions, yet full of zeal. But there were also tens of thousands of men condemned to forced labor, guarded by armed sentries. Peasants from small villages who had never come into contact with machines labored alongside older, experienced industrial workers and often unwittingly damaged the equipment. In new industrial towns, still under construction, Party members, eager to read books on technical subjects in their spare evening hours, lived with hardened, dogmatic, suspicious Party functionaries who saw sabotage everywhere, and with patriotic engineers who were inspired by technology and the tremendous goal of industrialization.

The means which the Stalin regime used to achieve the goals of the five-year plan at any price were as varied as the people who took part in the project. There were directives which kindled enthusiasm and helped fulfill the plan, and there were others which were backed by coercion, repression and terror. The trade unions were already completely transformed at the beginning of the five-year plan. Their only goal was to mobilize workers for the construction of socialism. 'Socialist competition' was introduced and was intended to help fulfill the plan before the five years

were up, to cut construction costs, increase productivity and strengthen discipline on the job. The Party later promoted the formation of 'shock brigades,' which more or less voluntarily pledged to raise productivity standards and fulfill the plan in four years. The use of military terminology – the press and radio spoke of 'fronts,' 'battles' and 'breakthroughs' – was intended to arouse additional enthusiasm for work.

The lack of well-trained technicians and engineers made mistakes, setbacks and accidents inevitable. Instead of acknowledging this fact, 'criminals' and 'saboteurs' were sought who could be made responsible for these shortcomings. In 1928 an alleged organization of criminals was uncovered in the Shakhty coal fields. The accused were charged with having destroyed machinery and ventilating equipment, with having caused cave-ins and explosions and with having set fire to mines. A show trial against the 'industrial party' followed in November 1930 and against a group of Mensheviks in March 1931. In both cases the accused were charged with having formed illegal organizations whose goal was the restoration of capitalism.

There was an ever-deepening cleft between the workers, on one hand, and the factory directors and functionaries, on the other. The original idea of social equality was now branded 'petty bourgeois.' Stalin proclaimed a 'struggle against the mania of equalization' in an attempt to justify the unequal salaries and increasing privileges of managers and Party functionaries. In September 1930 workers were forbidden to change jobs without the permission of the factory management. Direc-

tors of factories, on the other hand, acquired the right to discharge employees for being absent for one day without an excuse. Dismissal automatically entailed the loss of one's food ration card and eviction from the apartment allotted by the factory. Extreme measures were employed to discipline workers. Until the beginning of the 1930s workers and employees could be penalized up to one-third of their salary if damages occurred in the factory due to negligence; a decree in June 1932 increased the liability to two-thirds. Employees caught stealing work clothes had to make restitution which was five times the value of the stolen articles.

Under extremely difficult conditions, in the midst of enthusiasm and coercion, the first large constructions of the five-year plan arose: the foundries in Krovoi Rog and Zaporozhie, the combined pig-iron factory and rolling mill in Magnitogorsk, the farm machinery plant in Rostov, the Stalingrad tractorworks, the Turkestan-Siberian ('Turksib') railway, the hydroelectric dam on the Dnieper and the White Sea canal.

Tremendous economic successes were achieved, but by no means all of the goals of the five-year plan were attained: the output of bituminous coal and the production of pig iron, for example, were far short of their targets. Yet according to Soviet statistics the number of workers and employees was two and a half times as great, machine production four times as great and production of farm machinery was over five times as great as at the beginning of the five-year plan, and even allowing for some falsification, these figures may not be too far off the mark.

Just as important and decisive for the development of the Soviet Union was the collectivization of the peasantry. The five-year plan originally announced that only 20 percent of all farms should be collectivized, but late in the fall of 1929 Stalin declared that the entire class of kulaks should be liquidated and that the entire peasantry would be collectivized. The Soviet government dispatched 25,000 workers from the cities (70 percent of whom were Party members) to the villages, to speed up the process of collectivization. Centrally directed machine tractor stations (MTS) were formed in an attempt to concentrate the distribution of agricultural machinery in the hands of those in charge of collectivization. A political department was organized in each MTS to supervise and control the nascent collective farms.

The total collectivization of all peasants was announced only after the resolution of the Central Committee to that effect on 5 January 1930. Collectivization was to be completed in the main grain-producing regions (the northern Caucasus and the middle and lower Volga areas) before the spring of 1931, that is, within a single year. In the Ukraine, the central black earth region, Siberia, the Urals and Kazakhstan the collectivization was to be carried through by the spring of 1932, and in the remaining regions, including Moscow, Leningrad, the Caucasus and Central Asia, by the spring of 1933.

These short deadlines could obviously be met only by employing extreme methods. A decree in February 1930 gave local authorities and Party officials the right to use any means to eliminate the kulaks, including seizure of their property and deportation. There were continuous reports of success on the 'collectivization front' in the first two months of 1930, and by 10 March, according to official information, 58 percent of all farms had already been collectivized. In this situation the farmers could only express dissent by slaughtering their livestock before being collectivized.

Shortly thereafter Stalin called a temporary halt to the program in order to prevent the total destruction of livestock and the collapse of Soviet agriculture. He now declared that it was stupid and reactionary to carry out collectivization by force, and he condemned local Party and government officials for having used improper threats

against the farmers. Stalin's speech and several related resolutions of the Party leadership were essentially an attempt to shift the responsibility for forced collectivization onto local authorities and Party organizations; in fact they had simply followed instructions.

The breathing spell did not last very long. Stalin announced to the Sixteenth Party Congress in the summer of 1930 an 'offensive of socialism along the entire front' and a resolute struggle intended to bring collectivization to a rapid end. By reapplying pressure the Soviet government succeeded in forcing 15 million farms (61.5 percent of the total) into the collective farm system by the middle of 1932. By 1934 almost three-fourths of all farms had been collectivized.

The goal was almost in reach, but at the cost of a massive setback to Soviet agriculture. Livestock production, for example, had declined catastrophically. According to official Soviet statistics the number of milk cows sank from 30.7 to 19.6 million, of beef cattle from 60.1 to 33.5 million, of horses from 32.1 to 17.3 million and of pigs from 26 to 12.1 million. Famine broke out in 1932 as a result, especially in the Ukraine and the northern Caucasus – that is, in those regions where collectivization had been instituted with the most coercion. Although it would have been possible to

prevent or at least alleviate the famine – the Soviet Union still had large reserves of food – nothing was done. Whether this displayed ineptitude or was an attempt to use the famine to break the farmers' resistance is moot. In any case, by means of collectivization the Stalin regime had unquestionably succeeded in spreading its political control over the entire agricultural sector.

There was a similar spread of control over all cultural, artistic and scientific life. In April 1932, for example, a centralized Soviet Writers' Union replaced the previous independent associations of writers. Writers and poets were now obliged to write in the style of 'socialist realism,' to portray 'a revolutionary view' of reality – that is, not objective reality, but reality as seen by the eyes of the Party leadership. Stalin personally intervened in works on the history of the Party, and even jurisprudence had to bow to the decrees of the government. There were changes in ideology, too. Stalin announced during the first five-year plan that the class struggle would increase, rather than decrease, during the period of the construction of socialism. Consequently, the state would have to increase its power for the present and would have to defer its Marxist 'withering away' until the distant future, especially since the Soviet Union was encircled by hostile capitalism. Thus was the siege mentality enshrined in dogma.

The constitution and Stalin's Great Purge

The 'revolution from above' was completed by 1934. The industrial potential of the Soviet Union had been strengthened by the five-year plan, collectivization was essentially over and the government's control of all intellectual, cultural and scientific life had been firmly established. The government now had two possibilities for the further development of the country. One was to end the all-out campaigns, the oppression and the purges and to return to a smoother plan of development. This was the view of significant groups in the government and economic bureaucracies, of many army officers and Party members, and even of members of the Politburo – especially Kirov.

Stalin, however, was wary of such a course. He was certain that sooner or later a period of stabilization would nurture a desire in leaders of the Party, the army, the government and the economy for other, more moderate leadership. He was determined to eliminate this threat through vigilance campaigns, purges, show trials and mass arrests that would keep the country in a state of constant tension and would prevent any forces from having any chance of uniting in opposition to him or his rule.

Left: Rather than surrender their grain to the Communist Party the peasants hid it. Here, Young Komsomol members retrieve grain hidden in a Ukrainian cemetery.

Below left: A propganda photograph showing an individual smallholder handing in his request to join a collective farm.

Right: A Communist Party official delivers propaganda at a local meeting in the Stalin era.

Below: Serge Kirov, Secretary of the Leningrad Communist Party, who was assassinated on Stalin's order in 1934, and whose death was used as a pretext to begin the purges.

The period from 1934 to 1936 was characterized by a continuous tug of war between Stalin and the partisans of relative moderation. This was already apparent at the Seventeenth Party Congress in early 1934. Stalin's report was naturally the central event, and every speaker extoled Stalin, the victorious leader. But it was astonishing that a number of former opponents, including Bukharin, Kamenev, Rykov and Tomsky, were able to appear again at a Party Congress. To be sure, they too praised Stalin, but without any excessive personal abasement. Politburo-member Grigori Ordjonikhidze's proposal for a more realistic second five-year plan which incorporated a smaller growth rate, was accepted by the Congress. It was also striking that the delegates gave almost as much applause to Kirov, the strongest advocate of a more moderate policy in the government, as to Stalin himself. Toward the end of the Congress Stalin, who had been called General Secretary of the Party since 1922, received the inferior title of First Secretary of the Party. In effect the Party Congress made a compromise: Stalin remained the leader and was glorified as such, but he was now expected to make concessions to the moderates.

The standard of living was still extremely low, but the worst seemed to be over. At the end of 1934 bread rationing was ended, and concessions were made to collective farmers regarding private vegetable gardens and small numbers of livestock. Stalin's announcement 'life is better, life is happier,' which was repeated thousands of times in meetings and in the press, gave the impression that the Soviet Union was entering a more relaxed phase of development.

This hope was increased by the announcement of a constitution in February 1935. After lengthy preparations the draft of the constitution was published in June 1936, and all citizens were requested to take part in the discussions and to send in proposals for amendments. Although this discussion was of course controled from above, many observers nevertheless believed that arbitrary rule would gradually be eliminated. The new Soviet constitution, then generally called the 'Stalin constitution,' was passed on 5 December 1936. It granted all citizens of the Soviet Union freedom of speech, press, assembly and association, but with the important limitation that they be used to strengthen the socialist system. Article 126 defined the Communist Party as the 'avant-garde' in the struggle for, and development of, socialism, and as the 'directing nucleus' of organizations of workers and government officials.

Even while the regime was preparing the constitution and proclaiming a Soviet democracy, Stalin was organizing a rather different kind of change in the political climate. An ominous portent of this was the fact that the secret police – the OGPU – was strengthened, expanded and reorganized into the People's Commissariat for Internal Affairs (NKVD). It now took control of all police and security matters.

On the evening of 1 December 1934, Sergei Kirov, the Leningrad Party Secretary, the leading representative of the moderate wing of the Party who was considered by many as a possible successor to Stalin, was shot in his office. It was officially declared that a student named Nikolaev had committed the murder on the orders of Trotskyites and adherents of Zinoviev. Even at the time few believed this. Kirov's death set off a chain-reaction of arrests, executions and banishments: even Zinoviev was condemned to 10 years of forced labor and Kamenev to five. In April 1935 a decree instituted the death penalty for children over 12 years of age. In the middle of May an extraordinary security commission was formed with Stalin as head, and at the end of the month the Society of Old Bolsheviks was disbanded. Vigilance campaigns were increased at the beginning of 1936, and at the end of July all Party organizations received a letter from the Party leadership, 'On the Terrorist Activities of the Trotsky-Zinoviev Bloc,' which called upon Party members to be more vigilant and to expose enemies of the people. A wave of denunciations, arrests and Party purges followed.

These preparations, which took place at the same time as the new democratic constitution was being discussed, resulted in the first great show trial, the 'Trial of the Sixteen' (14-24 August 1936). Sixteen former leaders of the opposition, including Zinoviev and Kamenev, were charged with the murder of Kirov and with having formed an illegal organization plotting terrorist acts against Stalin and other leaders of the Politburo. Bukharin, Tomsky and Rykov were incriminated during the course of the trial, and it was clear that more trials and mass arrests would follow. Having been called 'rabid dogs' during the proceedings,

Left: Kulaks slaughtered by the Red Army in the Ukraine for resisting collectivization.

Below far left: M Tomsky, ultimately a victim of Stalin's purges, whilst President of the Soviet Trade Unions.

Below left: Lev Kamenev, another Bolshevik from the revolutionary era, victim of Stalin's purges, put on trial and executed.

Right: Zinoviev, the leading old Bolshevik rival of Stalin, subsequently to be purged and executed.

Below right: The Soviet politican A N Rykov.

most of the accused, including Zinoviev and Kamenev, were shot, and Tomsky, who had been head of the Soviet trade unions for many years, committed suicide on 23 August, just before the trial ended.

That this was only the beginning was clear from the communiqué of 10 September 1936 which set the wheels of investigation in motion against Bukharin and Rykov. Shortly thereafter the Minister of the Interior, Yagoda, was dismissed and replaced in September by one of Stalin's followers, Nikolai Yezhov. Exactly five months later the second show trial, the 'Trial of the Seventeen,' took place. The accused, including some of Lenin's closest comrades who until shortly before had held important positions in the Party, state and economic bureaucracies, were charged with having followed Trotsky's instructions in forming a conspiracy against Stalin. Moreover, they had supposedly planned to dismember the USSR to the benefit of Japan and Germany and had tried to sabotage the economy. Stalin used these specific accusations not only to discredit the old Bolsheviks for being the agents of foreign powers, but also to make them responsible for setbacks in the economy. All the accused were convicted.

Within a few weeks after the end of the second show trial one of the most prominent Soviet leaders, Grigori Ordjonikhidze, died under mysterious circumstances. More than two decades later Nikita Khrushchev would assert that Ordjonikhidze was forced to commit suicide because he opposed the purges.

Stalin made his first open justification of the purges in March 1937. The ideological basis of his explanation was supplied by his new doctrine that the class struggle would increase with the development of socialism. As socialism achieved greater and greater successes, its opponents, growing more and more desperate, would use increasingly extreme means of resistance. The growth of the class struggle was, for Stalin, inevitable, and therefore so was the need for terror and

purges. He ordered all Party and state functionaries to train and promote younger officials as quickly as possible, so that they would be able to take over all decisive posts within a few months. This was a clear indication that further mass arrests were in the offing.

The purge of the army began in the spring of 1937. On 11 June the arrest of several top Soviet military leaders was announced, including Marshal Mikhail Tukhachevsky. They were accused of having spied for Germany and Japan and of having planned a *coup d'état* against the Stalin regime. The trial took place before a secret military tribunal, and on the next day it was announced that all of the accused had been convicted and shot. A mass purge of the army followed: three (out of a total of five) marshals, 13 (out of 15) generals, 62 (out of 85) corps commanders and 110 (out of 195) division commanders were victims of the purge.

The last act of this deathly drama followed in March 1938, the 'Trial of the Twenty-one.' Among the 21 were Bukharin and Rykov. This time they were accused of having had connections with the German Secret Service since 1921, with the British Secret Service since 1926 and with the Gestapo since 1933. They also had supposedly conspired, on Trotsky's orders, to overthrow Stalin, to re-establish capitalism in Russia and to give large parts of Soviet territory to Germany and Japan. With only two exceptions – minor figures of the 'Twenty-one' – all of the accused were shot.

The show trials were only the tip of the iceberg, for they were accompanied by a great wave of arrests that swept across the entire country. According to reliable sources 7 million Soviet citizens were arrested during the Great Purges from 1936 to 1938. Even the most hard-line Russians now agree that the arrests had nothing to do with the guilt of those concerned. It was not a question of arresting specific people but of eliminating entire groups of the population, which, according to Stalin, were untrustworthy: former members or supporters of opposition groups within the Bolshevik Party; those who had previously belonged to another leftist party such as the Mensheviks, the Social Revolutionaries or the Jewish-socialist 'Bund'; Party members who had served abroad, including in the Spanish Civil War; Soviet citizens who had kept up a long correspondence with a foreigner; foreign communists in the Soviet Union; old Bolsheviks who, it was feared, would begin to contrast Lenin's original revolutionary ideas with Stalin's dictatorship; people in non-Russian Soviet Republics who might oppose Stalin's centralism; lastly, and especially, members of the Party, state and economic bureaucracies and of the Officers' Corps who had supported Stalin but who, it was feared, might opt for a change in the leadership.

All those who belonged to such groups were liable, with a probability which bordered on certainty, to become victims of the purge. They were arrested without regard to their persons, their views or their actions. Almost invariably convicted, they were sent, if they were not executed, to various concentration camps. The political elite was decimated during these years. Of the 1225 delegates at the Seventeenth Party Congress in 1934, 1108 were arrested. Of the 139 members and candidates of the Central Committee at the same Congress, 98 became victims of the Great Purge.

The purge finally began to taper off in the late fall of 1938. Apparently even Stalin began to realize that the nation's morale could stand no more, that in this atmosphere of terror no one was making decisions and that a continuation of the purge might well threaten the survival of the Party and its apparatus. Yezhov, the People's Commissar for the Interior, became the designated scapegoat, was released from his duties on 8 December 1938 and promptly disappeared from the scene. Lavrenti Beria was named his successor.

Why did Stalin undertake these mass purges, what goal was he trying to attain? Psychological explanations apart, apparently Stalin wanted to eliminate all forces and groups from whose ranks a new ruling class could possibly emerge. He took great pains to eliminate not only all of Lenin's comrades-in-arms, the old Bolsheviks who themselves had experienced the early years of the Revolution, but also all forces within the new ruling class which had supported Stalin but which might possibly want a more democratic policy. Finally, by arresting millions of Soviet citizens, Stalin seemed to want to atomize Soviet society in a maelstrom of terror and make it the obedient tool of his dictatorship. But perhaps, after all, explanations based on abnormal psychology cannot be left out of the equation.

A huge number of copies of the new *History of the Communist Party of the Soviet Union* were published with great pomp in the late fall of 1938. In the *Short Course on the History of the Party* written under the editorship of Stalin, the entire history of the Bolshevik Party was rewritten to give the impression that all of Lenin's closest comrades had been enemies, renegades or spies and that Stalin was the only legitimate successor to

Lenin, the only one who had consistently defended and pursued Lenin's goals.

From the beginning of 1939 the problems of the reconstruction of the Party apparatus as well as the economic and military recovery of the Soviet Union received top priority. The Great Purge was therefore mentioned only in passing at the Eighteenth Party Congress in March 1939. Stalin explained that the purge had been essentially positive, although there had been isolated mistakes, and he promised that mass purges would not be employed again in the future. The Party Congress ratified the third five-year plan (1938-1942), which again gave priority to heavy industry. Since four members of the Politburo had died during the purge, new blood was needed; Anastas Mikoyan had joined in 1935, and now Andrei Zhdanov and Nikita Khrushchev became members. By now almost four-fifths of the Central Committee had been replaced.

The Eighteenth Party Congress took place at a time when foreign policy questions had acquired a growing importance for the Soviet leadership. The Munich pact had already been concluded, Hitler's troops had marched into Prague while the Congress met, the Spanish Civil War was drawing to a close and the first contacts between Moscow and Berlin were being made.

Soviet foreign policy during the 1930s

It had become clear to the Soviet leadership by the end of the Lenin era that the long-awaited world revolution would not occur and that the Soviet Union would have to adjust to a long period of coexistence with the capitalist countries. In 1924 the USSR established diplomatic relations with many European nations, including Great Britain. In many of his speeches between 1925 and 1927 Stalin stressed the need for a phase of peaceful coexistence with the capitalist countries; the existence of two antagonistic systems – capitalism and socialism – did not exclude temporary agreements with these countries. Although any treaties would be limited by the opposite natures of the two systems, they were both possible and expedient and should have a more or less lasting character. Consequently the role of the Communist International was increasingly restricted to promoting the aims of Soviet foreign policy, and foreign communist parties were obliged to submit completely to that policy. In August 1927 Stalin explained that 'a revolutionary is one who is ready to protect, to defend the USSR without reservation, without qualification.'

The Soviet regime in fact had no wish to have its massive social and economic programs interfered with by unwanted foreign complications. A network of treaties expressed this desire. Under the guidance of Maxim Litvinov, People's Commissar for Foreign Affairs from 1930 to 1939, the Soviet Union concluded non-aggression pacts with neighboring Finland, Poland, Latvia and Estonia in the spring of 1932, and with France in November of the same year. Diplomatic relations with other countries were also established.

The significance of Hitler's accession to power in Germany in 1933 was apparently not immediately recognized by the Soviet regime, which saw it as only a passing event. The Soviet leadership made it clear that ideological differences offered no hindrance to normal relations with Fascist states. This was underlined by the non-aggression pact between the Soviet Union and Fascist Italy of September 1933. Stalin reiterated at the Seventeenth Party Congress in early 1934 that he was by no means delighted with the Fascist system in Germany but that this would not hinder an improvement in relations. Yet the potential threat of Hitler's Germany could not be altogether ignored. The crushing of the Röhm putsch in Germany in June 1934 must have convinced Stalin of the solidity of Hitler's power, and the subsequent treaty between Germany and Poland aroused the suspicion in Moscow that it might be directed against the Soviet Union.

Consequently, the USSR had an increased interest in developing relations with the Western democracies. The United States had officially recognized the Soviet Union in 1933, and diplomatic ties were established between the two nations. The Soviet government assured the United States that the lives and property of American citizens in the USSR would be protected and that no communist propaganda would be made in America. In view of the increasing danger of Nazi Germany the Soviet Union also joined the League of Nations in 1934 and signed a treaty of mutual assistance with France in May 1935. Two weeks later a similar pact with Czechoslovakia followed, but with the limitation that assistance would only be given when France also came to the aid of that nation.

During this reorientation of Soviet foreign policy, terms like 'world revolution' and 'the dictatorship of the proletariat' receded into the background; and the Soviet press began to harp on the common struggle against Fascism. This change was especially evident at the Seventh Congress of the Communist International in the summer of 1935 at which the goal of creating a Popular Front was proclaimed. This was to be founded on the most diverse social classes and would embrace groups from every part of the political spectrum, with the goal of preventing the spread of Fascism. In the spring of 1936 Stalin went so far as to explain to an American correspondent that the Soviet Union had never intended or planned to create a world revolution.

These new international initiatives soon had practical consequences, especially in Soviet relations with Spain. The victory of the Popular Front in the Spanish elections of February 1936 led very shortly to the insurrection of General Franco and the beginning of the Spanish Civil War (July 1936). The Soviet government remained aloof during the first months from fear of being drawn into international complications, and the Spanish communists received orders to limit themselves to defending the republic against Franco. But the increasing military support that Franco received from Hitler and Mussolini made it impossible for the Soviet Union to stand passively on the sidelines for long. From October 1936 on Moscow sent military advisers and war supplies (for which the Spanish government had to pay with gold) and sponsored anti-Fascist volunteer combatants such as those of the International Brigade. Agents of the Soviet secret police also accompanied the military advisers and concentrated on pursuing and arresting Trotskyites and other socialists critical of the Soviet Union.

Soviet diplomatic representatives in international political circles spoke ever more emphatically for the principle of collective security against Fascism, especially after the creation of the Rome-Berlin axis and the signing of the Anti-Comintern Pact by Germany, Italy and Japan in November 1936. After Austria had been annexed by Germany in March 1938 the Soviet government again spoke in favor of a system of collective security with Britain, France and the United States, but the skepticism of the Western powers was too great for this to be realized. When Hitler's threats to Czechoslovakia increased, the Soviet Union informed the Czech government that it was ready to adhere to the treaty of mutual assistance as long as France also fulfilled its obligations. The West, however, ignored most of the Russian offers, since it wanted to prevent an increase of Soviet influence in Central Europe.

The Munich pact at the end of September 1938 was concluded without the Soviet Union and against her wishes, and increased the Soviet government's misgivings toward the West. The Russians now feared – perhaps with some reason – that certain groups in the West would like to divert Hitler's expansionist drive toward the Soviet Union in order that the two great dictatorships might exhaust one another in a war that spared the Western democracies.

With Nazi Germany's annexation of already-weakened Czechoslovakia in March 1939 it was obvious that the policy of collective security had collapsed. At the Eighteenth Party Congress in March 1939 Stalin announced that the Soviet Union would, as always, support the victims of aggression, but on the other hand he warned that 'we must take care that warmongers who are fond of letting others pull their chestnuts out of the fire do not involve our land in a conflict.'

This indirect offer to Hitler was not ignored in

Stalin resulted in a German-Soviet non-aggression pact. According to the treaty each side promised to refrain from aggressive actions toward the other and from joining any coalition that was directly or indirectly hostile to the other signatory. Both promised complete neutrality if one of the countries was attacked first by a third party, and they agreed, moreover, to keep each other informed on all questions which concerned both parties.

The German-Soviet treaty of 23 August, generally known as the Hitler-Stalin pact, was a shock to the entire world. The newspapers and radios of both countries loudly proclaimed the new friendship, while foreign communists changed overnight from struggling against Fascism to defending the treaty between the Soviet Union and Nazi Germany. The Hitler-Stalin pact was and is justified in Soviet publications on the grounds that the Soviet Union, in the face of a threatening situation in the summer of 1939, was compeled to use all means to keep the USSR out of a military conflict in order to continue the peaceful construction of socialism. Since the Western powers had rejected all Soviet proposals for a common alliance against Germany, the Soviet Union had no other choice but to protect itself by concluding a non-aggression pact with Germany.

These arguments might possibly be taken seriously if the treaty had really been just a non-aggression pact. What Soviet histories still continue to omit is that on 23 August a secret supplementary protocol was also signed by the Soviet Union and Germany which placed Finland, Estonia, Latvia and Bessarabia in the Russian sphere of influence, placed Lithuania in the German sphere and provided that in the case of a division of Poland between Germany and Russia, the Narew, Vistula and San Rivers would be the lines of demarcation. In this cynical division of the spoils of future aggression the USSR had changed from a champion of the struggle against Fascism into an ally, or rather an accomplice, of Nazi Germany.

Berlin. From the beginning of 1939 a somewhat more conciliatory tone toward the Soviet Union was noticeable in Hitler's speeches. In the spring and summer of 1939 the Soviet Union simultaneously conducted negotiations with Britain and France and cultivated contacts with Hitler's government in Berlin. The negotations with the French and British, which had begun in March, ran into difficulties when the Soviets proposed a mutual aid treaty that included guarantees for the threatened countries of Central and Eastern Europe and the right of Soviet troops to march through Poland. This was flatly rejected. Stalin then indicated his readiness to improve relations with Hitler's Germany by removing Litvinov, a Jew, from his post as People's Commissar for Foreign Affairs and replacing him with Molotov in May 1939. Zhdanov, in an article published at the end of June and carefully read by many, accused the Western powers of using the negotiations to cover up their real anti-Soviet intentions.

The German-Soviet talks, which were carefully shielded from publicity, were now intensified. The Soviet proposal that the trade agreement then in preparation should be cemented and strengthened by political accords was well received in Berlin; and the Germans made it known that they would respect Russian interests in the Baltic States. At the beginning of August the Soviet government officially announced that it was ready to begin negotiations with Nazi Germany. On 19 August a German-Soviet economic agreement was signed, and on 23 August the German Foreign Minister, Joachim von Ribbentrop, arrived in Moscow.

The deliberations between von Ribbentrop and

Far left: Mikoyan delivering a suitably obsequious speech in Stalin's presence at the Party Congress in 1938.

Left: Litvinov, Soviet Commissar for Foreign Affairs, whom Stalin was later to replace with Molotov.

Above right: Molotov and Stalin smile as Ribbentrop signs the Nazi-Soviet Non-Aggression Pact, August 1939.

Right: Litvinov attends a diplomatic function at the White House in November 1933.

North America

When President Wilson asked the US Congress on 2 April 1917 to declare war, neither the most disillusioned idealist nor the most cynical realist could have foreseen the events of the next quarter-century – the emergence of repressive ideologies and governments in various nations of the world, the Great Depression of the 1930s, the conflicts among countries that would lead to yet another world war. Instead, even if not everyone embraced the noble rhetoric of making 'the world safe for democracy,' there was a general sense that America was truly about to set things straight. And indeed, in the euphoria of the relatively quick end to America's participation in the war and the prosperity that followed in the early 1920s, it may have seemed that America's time had come. Only with the perspective of many decades would it be seen that this quarter-century was little more than a bridge between the two worst wars the world had ever experienced.

On 6 April 1917, with only six Senators and 50

Representatives opposing, the US Congress voted to declare war on Germany. (Canada had entered the war immediately after Britain did in 1914; by 1917, hundreds of thousands of Canadian troops would have fought with distinction in many major battles; by the war's end, some 55,000 Canadians would give their lives to the Allied cause.) But although many Americans were feeling bellicose by then, the country was poorly prepared to engage in a world war. Only a few uncoordinated steps had been taken to mobilize American industry for the war effort. What military goods American factories produced had been shipped overseas to the Allies. The United States Army had no military unit as large as a division and an almost nonexistent General Staff. Moreover, within the first few weeks of Wilson's call to arms, only a little more than 30,000 men had volunteered for military service. It rapidly became apparent that conscription would be necessary. On 18 May 1917 Congress passed a bill

instituting selective service on a compulsory basis. Eventually almost 25 million American men would register for the draft, of which 2,800,000 would be inducted into the Army. By the end of the war, in November 1918, 4,800,000 men and women would be serving in the armed forces of the United States.

Accompanying such a tremendous increase in the size of the armed forces was the growth in the size of the federal government and the creation of new and powerful civilian bureaucracies to support the war effort. In July 1917 the Council of National Defense created the War Industries Board to serve as a central director for the purchase of military supplies, the allocation and control of production and the supervision of labor relations. Yet due to lack of clear authority over the War and Navy departments the mobilization of American industry took place in a poorly coordinated and halting manner. Throughout the remainder of the war the American Expeditionary Force in France would be dependent on Britain and France for such basic military essentials as rifles and field artillery.

Additional federal agencies were created to support the war effort. Immediately after America's entry into the war the Committee on Public Information was created as a huge propaganda effort designed to explain the war in the most patriotic light possible to the American people. To support this effort, President Wilson imposed censorship on all cable traffic on 28 April. In August Congress passed the Lever Act creating the Food Administration, with Herbert Hoover, famous for his efforts providing relief in Belgium, as director. The Food Administration was granted full authority to direct production and distribution of food, fuel, fertilizers and farm equipment. In order to stimulate production, the easiest method was simply to establish high prices for such commodities as wheat and hogs. Other government boards which played key roles in the economy included the Fuel Administration, which, for example, set high prices for coal in order to stimulate production; the Emergency Fleet Corporation and Shipping Board, which supervised the purchase of merchant marine vessels and the seizure of hostile foreign ships for military transport; the Railroad Administration, which controled and set priorities for railroad traffic; and the National War Labor Board, which arbitrated, set and enforced rulings in labor disputes and strikes so as to ensure uninterrupted production.

Despite the efforts of President Wilson and the new bureaucracies, the pace of American industrial mobilization remained sluggish. Additional action was desperately needed. In March 1918, with the Allies in Europe bracing themselves for a final all-out German offensive on the Western Front, Wilson appointed Bernard Baruch the new chairman of the War Industries Board. Acting under his emergency war powers, President Wilson granted Baruch such powers as to make him a virtual economic dictator of the United States. In support of this move Congress passed the Overman Act on 20 May, augmenting even further the war powers of the President and his power to delegate authority. With new authority, such as the power to set wages and prices in any field, the

Left: Allied unity – for the duration of the Fourth Liberty Loan, Fifth Avenue in New York was renamed the *Avenue des Alliés*

Right: US propaganda poster urging people to buy Liberty Bonds.

Below: Electioneering in the USA. Eugene V Debs appeals to Labor Union members for support as the Socialist candidate in 1912.

ment and workers the government used its powers to protect and expand the rights of labor. Workers were allowed to organize and bargain collectively, the result being a surge in union membership of more than 50 percent.

In addition to the casualties suffered overseas, America paid a price of a different kind for its participation in the World War in the form of severe restrictions on civil liberties. The patriotic fever whipped up by the Committee on Public Information and other organizations created a hysteria never before witnessed in the United States. There were numerous spy scares, along with attacks on German-Americans, Germanic culture and language. Progressives and radicals frequently were targets of suppression and violence. The government passed legislation designed to ensure that it could suppress any criticism or threat which might, in even the most superficial manner, undermine the war effort. In June 1917 the Espionage Act was passed by Congress as a vehicle to encourage conformity and suppress dissent. In one section of the act the Postmaster General was given full power to deny use of the mails to any person or organization which, in his judgement, advocated opposition to the laws of the United States. As the war hysteria gained momentum, additional laws were passed and repression increased. In April 1918 Congress passed the Sabotage Act, which was followed by the Sedition Act in May. The government now held the power to punish dissent which took the form of 'abusive language' or which encouraged 'defeatism' with fines ranging up to $10,000 and prison sentences of up to 20 years. The government organized a nationwide spy system, infiltrated organizations considered dangerous and incited them to violence and raided and destroyed property. In the first eight months of 1917, the Industrial Workers of the World (IWW), popularly known as the 'Wobblies,' were engaged in a violent campaign against copper companies in several western states. Alarmed by the subsequent drop in copper production, federal agents raided IWW offices throughout the West. Eventually almost 100 union leaders were convicted and sent to prison. The most celebrated civil liberties case during the war involved the arrest of perennial presidential Socialist Party candidate Eugene V Debs for violation of the Sedition Act (an anti-war speech made in Ohio in June 1918). Debs was tried, convicted and sentenced to a prison term of

War Industries Board directed a dramatic increase in the American production of war supplies.

When America entered the war in April 1917 the economy was in good shape and the country was prosperous on the strength of the sale of war supplies to the Allies, along with an additional $2 billion in loans which were spent on purchases in the United States. With the actual declaration of war and the expansion of government borrowing

and spending, a boom spread throughout the American economy. The average annual real earnings of workers engaged in manufacturing, transportation and coal mining were 20 percent higher in 1918 than 1914. High agricultural prices meant additional income for farmers, as farm income rose 25 percent between 1915 and 1918, even after adjusting for higher taxes and inflation. In a push for amity between industrial manage-

10 years. (He would later be paroled by President Harding.) The war ended shortly thereafter, on 11 November 1918, and was followed by a wild national celebration. Although American participation had lasted a mere 19 months the reverberations from the war would echo for more than two decades.

The peace

Following the Bolshevik Revolution in Russia in November 1917 the communist government decided to publish secret treaties and pacts the Allies had made among themselves calling for huge indemnities and cessions of territory from Germany, Austria and Turkey in the event of victory. In the United States there ensued a public outcry that the war was not being fought for idealistic reasons – 'to make the world safe for democracy' – as President Wilson had promised. In response, Wilson looked for a means both to vindicate the Allied cause and to give a reason for the German people to turn against the military dictatorship running the country. His solution was the Fourteen Points.

On 8 January 1918 Wilson went before a joint session of Congress to announce the kind of peace for which the United States and the Allies were fighting. In a series of fourteen points Wilson, after listing specific boundary changes such as the return of the provinces of Alsace and Lorraine to France, issued a call for open diplomacy, freedom of the seas, and self-determination for national and ethnic groups in Eastern Europe. In his final point Wilson stressed the need for 'a general association of nations . . . affording mutual guarantees of political independence and territorial integrity to great and small states alike.' Later that year, following a series of fatal military reverses on the Western Front, Germany agreed to surrender with the understanding that the subsequent peace would be modeled on Wilson's Fourteen Points.

Just prior to the armistice ending the war Wilson made a partisan appeal to the American people asking that they return a Democratic Congress to Washington in the November 1918 elections so that the legislative body might support

Left: President Woodrow Wilson, a Democrat, failed to win the support of the Republicans for the League of Nations.

Below: The first session of the League of Nations Council, which met in Spain in 1920.

Right: A cartoon depicting US skepticism about support for the League of Nations in 1919.

Below right: Society ladies flout the Prohibition Law and drink illegally in a 'speakeasy.'

his peace program. The result was a resounding defeat for Wilson and the Democrats. The Republicans obtained a 237-190 majority in the House of Representatives and an overwhelming two-to-one margin in the Senate. The stage was set for an acrimonious battle over the terms of peace.

Woodrow Wilson's idealism and his uncompromising sense of being right, while a source of great strength for the passage of progressive domestic legislation during his first two years in office and for his role as war President, would prove to be a fatal weakness for the remainder of his term. If other ideas or opinions conflicted with Wilson's

steadfast views, he ignored them or refused to accept them. Consequently, when Wilson announced on 18 November 1918 that he would personally head the American delegation to the peace talks in Paris, he refused to include any members of the Republican Senate as peace commissioners. To do this would mean including the new chairman of the Senate Foreign Relations Committee, the influential Henry Cabot Lodge of Massachusetts. Wilson and Lodge held a deep mutual antagonism for each other, and Wilson was not prepared to countenance any interference from the senator or any of his supporters. This

Citizen.] [Brooklyn, U.S.A.

An Expected Arrival.

Will the stork make good as to this infant ?

proved to be a significant error, for Wilson would need the support of Republican moderates if he was to obtain ratification of a peace treaty.

President Wilson and a huge entourage departed for Europe in December 1918, to be greeted by wildly enthusiastic crowds during a tour of European capitals. Wilson was determined to achieve a peace settlement largely based on his Fourteen Points, and he consequently asked for no territory or reparations on the part of the United States. Wilson believed that the other Allied nations would be similarly willing to sacrifice their immediate national interests in favor of a just and stable peace.

The Allies, however, had a different conception of a just and equitable peace settlement. Although dozens of nations, organizations, ethnic groups and colonial peoples sent representatives to the Paris Conference, most of the negotiating took place among those recognized as the Big Four: President Wilson of the United States, Prime Minister David Lloyd George of Great Britain, Premier Georges Clemenceau of France and Prime Minister Vittorio Orlando of Italy. Pressured by public opinion at home, the other Allied leaders forced Wilson to make concessions which reflected a settlement far different from what he had envisioned.

The most glaring break with the Fourteen Points as the basis for peace was the treatment accorded Germany. In addition to the return of Alsace and Lorraine to France, Germany was forced to agree to the permanent demobilization of the left bank of the Rhine River and a 15-year occupation of that area by French troops. The production from the mines in Germany's Saar Province was also to go to France. Moreover, Germany was stripped of all its colonies and saddled with an indemnity of $15 billion, plus reparations still to be determined. Except for the return of Alsace and Lorraine to France, these terms were a clear violation of Wilson's Fourteen Points and the pre-Armistice agreement with Germany.

President Wilson, however, was not without his accomplishments. Wilson and Lloyd George had effectively blocked France's demand for the complete dismemberment of Germany and had brought about the creation of new states in Eastern Europe in accordance (as well as could be expected) with the principle of self-determination.

Most important, Wilson had insisted from the outset on the creation of an international organization to maintain the peace and prevent a new war. The other leaders agreed. To insure this end the Covenant, or constitution, of the League of Nations was incorporated into the Treaty itself: in effect, the signing and ratification of the peace treaty would give birth to the League of Nations. The peace treaty was formally signed at the palace of Versailles on 28 June 1919.

Wilson returned to the United States feeling triumphant but facing increasing opposition to the Versailles Treaty and the League of Nations. Many senators complained that the Treaty failed to recognize the rights of the United States under the Monroe Doctrine, that it failed specifically to exclude internal affairs from the jurisdiction of the League and that it committed the United States to assume certain obligations automatically, whereby the United States could lose control of its foreign policy. Opposition came from many sides. Extreme isolationists, such as Senators Hiram W Johnson of California and William E Borah of Idaho, wanted to keep America free of *any* foreign entanglements. Irish-Americans wanted Wilson to provide more support to the cause of Irish independence from Great Britain. Progressive and liberal journals, such as the *Nation* and the *New Republic*, opposed the Treaty on the grounds that it represented the same old cynical diplomacy, empire-building and power politics. The most serious threat to the Treaty and the League was the injection of personal and partisan politics into the debate. The year 1920 was a presidential election year, and the Republicans were determined to regain control of the White House. Thus many members of that party sought to embarrass Wilson and the Democrats by defeating the Treaty.

The opening salvo of the debate was fired on 4 March 1919, when 39 senators supported a resolution offered by Henry Cabot Lodge stating that the Treaty 'in the form now proposed' was unacceptable. As opposition to the Treaty built over the summer of 1919 President Wilson decided to take his case directly to the American people, and in September he embarked on an arduous speaking tour through the middle and far western states in defense of the Treaty and the League. After traveling thousands of miles in three weeks Wilson, already weary, was in a state of physical exhaustion and near collapse. The presidential entourage returned to Washington, where Woodrow Wilson suffered a stroke, leaving the left side of his face and body paralyzed.

Meanwhile, the strategy of Senator Lodge and his allies was to delay a vote on the Treaty by attaching to the document a series of reservations Lodge knew President Wilson considered unacceptable. This also accomplished the purpose of breaking down public support for the Treaty by exposing its seeming contradictions and ambiguity. In all the Senate approved 12 reservations, but Wilson remained steadfast, refused to compromise and ordered Democrats to vote against any form of the Treaty with attached reservations. On 19 November 1919 a vote on the Treaty with reservations was defeated 55-39. A second vote to accept the Treaty without any reservations lost by a 53-38 margin. It was clear that if President Wilson was willing to accept the Treaty with reservations he could obtain the necessary two-thirds support needed for ratification. (Britain and France had already informed the American government that they could accept the reservations.) Almost all of the Democratic senators wanted to save the Treaty by accepting the reservations, but they were afraid to oppose Wilson. A final vote was taken on 19 March 1920, in which 23 Democrats joined 12 irreconcilable isolationists to defeat the Treaty by a vote of 35 opposed to 49 in favor, just seven votes short of the necessary two-thirds majority. America would not join Woodrow Wilson's dream of a League of Nations.

'Return to normalcy'

The war was over, and as the fate of the Versailles Treaty and the League of Nations became increasingly doubtful, the Progressive movement went into eclipse. The Progressive forces, however, were able to push through two amendments to the US Constitution that rounded out their prewar program: nationwide Prohibition and the granting to women of the right to vote.

The 18th Amendment to the Constitution fitted in perfectly with the Progressive belief in the efficacy of bringing about social change through formal legislation. It was to prove a naïve faith, as the 1920s were marked by a flagrant disregard of this attempt to legislate moral conduct: the 'noble experiment' would die a quiet death in 1933. On the other hand, the 19th Amendment, on women's suffrage, fared much better and accomplished precisely what it was intended to do: guarantee women the right to vote. This legislation fitted in much better with the Progressive agenda of democratizing the political system through such measures as the referendum and the direct election of senators.

Overall, however, the period immediately following the war ushered in a of conservative reaction. The year 1919 witnessed a period of labor strife on a huge scale. There were more than 2500 strikes nationwide, involving more than 4 million workers, as labor sought to preserve the gains made during the war with the federal government. Successful strikes were undertaken by telephone, clothing, textile, longshoremen and railroad yard workers. In an atmosphere of extreme partisanship, conservatives charged that labor and its leaders were merely agents for a planned communist takeover of the American political and economic system. The victory by the Bolsheviks in Russia, and their boastful plans for world revolution, struck a sensitive nerve in American business leaders, the Wilson Administration and the general public. A series of temporary postwar victories by communists in Germany, Poland and Hungary provided additional credibility to Bolshevik braggadocio.

It was in this context that 340,000 steelworkers launched a strike against US Steel in September 1919 in the hope of attaining wage increases and an end to the 12-hour work day. The strike quickly turned violent, leading to the deaths of 18 strikers. In the era of what has become known as the 'Red Scare,' the strikers were charged with being communists desiring to overthrow the system, rather than working men with legitimate grievances. After being subjected to a campaign of misinformation, increasing repression and hostile public opposition, the American Federation of Labor hoisted the white flag and declared an end to the strike in January 1920.

In that same month, with an eye on a possible presidential bid, Attorney General A Mitchell Palmer moved decisively against radical and communist organizations in an attempt to bring a halt to the postwar unrest and upheaval. In what is popularly known as the 'Palmer Raid,' the Attorney General authorized a simultaneous nationwide sweep of suspected communist headquarters in a search for anti-American aliens. Thousands of persons were arrested, many of them non-communists and American citizens. In all 556 aliens were deported as proven members of the Communist Party.

The sharp recession affecting the American economy in 1920 and lasting through most of 1921 only served to increase the anxieties of the public, and the Republican Party eagerly awaited the next election and the prospect of a return to power. Unable to reach a consensus on a Republican presidential candidate at the nominating convention, party bosses, business leaders and powerful senators finally settled on Senator Warren G Harding of Ohio. Harding had had an uneventful career and had avoided antagonizing any powerful interests. Moreover, the Republican leadership perceived Harding as a pliable candidate who could be controled. In what portended to be a Republican year he seemed the perfectly safe choice. Governor Calvin Coolidge of Massachusetts was selected as Harding's running mate. At their convention the Democrats selected former Governor James Cox of Ohio and Assistant Secretary of the Navy Franklin Roosevelt.

Following the example set by William McKinley in an earlier presidential campaign, Harding chose to play it safe and fan a vague 'front-porch' contest, talking of returning to 'normalcy' and of his opposition to further social reforms. The Democrats, for their part, took a strong stand in favor of American participation in the League of Nations. In the context of public anxiety following eight years of Democratic upheaval, a united Republican Party swept Warren Harding into the White House with 60 percent of the vote.

Yet a 'return to normalcy' is hardly the phrase best suited to characterize American society following the election of 1920. The hysteria engendered by the labor strikes and Red Scare continued unabated. Indicative of the increasing intolerance and nativism in American life was the ordeal of Nicola Sacco and Bartolomeno Vanzetti. These two Italian-born anarchists were arrested in 1920 for the alleged murder of a bankroll paymaster in South Braintree, Massachusetts. At their trial in 1921 the prosecution made the radicalism of the defendants the cornerstone of its case. Sacco and Vanzetti were convicted and sentenced to death. Their purported innocence became a rallying cause for liberal and radical groups opposed to unjustified persecution of individuals who happened to be nonconformist. Such appeals for justice, however, fell on deaf ears in the 1920s, and Sacco and Vanzetti died in the electric chair in 1927.

Nor did the hysteria and persecution stop with labor radicals and alleged communists. Blacks, too, proved easy targets for white Americans. The World War had stimulated a large migration of blacks from the rural South to northern and midwestern industrial centers, where they found work in automobile, clothing, paper and other industries. The war only heightened anti-black feelings as blacks began to receive higher wages and compete with white workers for jobs. The

Left: A protest meeting at the execution of the anarchists Sacco and Vanzetti in 1927.

Below left: Ellis Island, New York. This was the entry point for hundreds of thousands of immigrants to the USA.

Right: A Negro about to be lynched in public in one of the southern states.

Below: Klu Klux Klansmen from more than 22 states parade in Washington in 1925.

radical views and would threaten democratic institutions.

When attempts to impose literacy tests for immigrants (enacted over President Wilson's veto in 1917) failed to restrict immigration, powerful forces combined to enact legislation which would. The result was the Emergency Immigration Act of 1921, establishing quotas for each country. The law stated that a maximum of three percent of the number of foreign-born people who were in the United States in 1910 would be allowed to enter the country in any given year. The effect was dramatic. Immigration dropped from 800,000 in 1921 to 300,000 the following year.

Still unsatisfied, restrictionists in 1924 pushed through Congress the National Origins Immigration Act. Under the provisions of this legislation the percentage of foreign-born residents was reduced to two percent and, more important, the baseline year was pushed back to 1890. The effect was to discriminate heavily against immigration from southern and eastern Europe. (For example, the Italian quota was reduced to only 4000 persons a year.) Moreover, Oriental immigration was totally excluded under the new law.

Probably most indicative of the escalating social tensions and underlying social pressures in American society in the postwar period was the rise of the Klu Klux Klan (KKK) in the first half of the 1920s. The increasing pressures on the traditional way of life, the demise of fundamentalism and the increasing acceptance of evolutionary theory, the demographic movement from rural small towns and farms to the city and the rise of liberal social values all helped generate a large amount of insecurity and anxiety in small-town, white, Protestant America. The greater the changes and perceived loss of the traditional way of life, the more desperately millions of Americans sought to hold on to the past.

number of officially recorded black lynchings increased from 34 in 1917 to 70 in 1919. That same year also witnessed more than 25 large-scale riots – almost exclusively by rampaging white mobs – leaving hundreds dead and injured. The worst incident occurred in Chicago, with 15 whites and 23 blacks dead, along with more than 500 injured.

The postwar reaction was also directed at foreign immigrants. As part of the general xenophobic climate there was a widespread fear after the war that the United States would soon be overwhelmed by a flood of Europeans. This fear was heightened by the fact that the most recent wave of immigration between 1885 and 1914 had

arrived almost exclusively from southern and eastern Europe and therefore was predominantly Catholic and Jewish. Popular theories abounded which claimed that these people were intellectually inferior and through a higher birthrate would dilute and destroy 'the native stock.' Organized labor also called for restrictions on immigration, since immigrants had often been used as strikebreakers during the strike wave of 1919. The recession of 1920-21 only buttressed the arguments of those worried about low-wage labor competition from immigrants eager for any job. Finally, in the context of the Red Scare it was assumed that many eastern Europeans harbored

Founded in 1915 the Klu Klux Klan had gained 100,000 new members by 1920 and offered its members an inexpensive (for a $10 fee) means to achieve a sense of place and purpose. The traditional small town and its values proved to be a fertile ground for the KKK. The Klan was opposed to everything different; it did not discriminate in its opposition to Catholics, Jews, blacks, radicals, foreigners and those opposed to Prohibition and the fundamentalist teachings of the Bible. At its peak in 1924 the Klan claimed between four and five million official members, mostly in the South and West.

The activities of the Klan took different forms in different sections of the country. In the North the KKK favored intimidation and boycotts of Catholic businessmen; in Oregon it was the banning of parochial schools. In the South actions directed against blacks were more violent, with a virtual reign of terror taking place for a while, featuring white-robed night riders and fiery crosses in the night. By 1925, however, the Klu Klux Klan as a formal organization was on the wane. Internal strife, a public backlash against its intolerance and violence and, in a wave of national publicity, the conviction of the head of the KKK for second-degree murder and the exposing of extensive corruption in the Klan helped at last to bring the reign of the Klan to a halt.

The final attempt to turn back the forces of change in the 1920s was the fundamentalist movement. Located almost exclusively in the rural small towns of the South and Midwest, fundamentalists, who believed the teachings of the Bible to be literally true, naturally felt threatened by the spread of Darwinism and evolutionary theory. Although generally accepted by the 1920s in the urban areas of the United States, even by the clergy, evolutionary theory was just beginning to seep into small-town America. Rural folk saw evolutionary theory as wiping out their bedrock religious beliefs and, since religion was at the very core of their way of life, their very identity as well. The reaction was a strong one.

Led by William Jennings Bryan, the fundamentalist movement launched an anti-evolution crusade to forbid the teaching of evolutionary theory in the public schools and colleges. The movement succeeded in Mississippi, Tennessee and Arkan-sas and came close to succeeding in five additional states. The high-water mark of the campaign was the celebrated 1925 trial of Tennessee schoolteacher John Thomas Scopes in Dayton, Ohio. The contest featured famed trial lawyer Clarence Darrow for the defense versus Bryan for the state of Tennessee. Although Scopes was found guilty, the trial resulted in an embarrassing defeat for fundamentalism. Attempts to pass more anti-evolution legislation in other states met with uniform defeat, leaving the movement moribund by 1928. By this time Americans had more important things on their minds: unprecedented prosperity.

The Roaring Twenties

Following the defeat of the Democrats by the Republicans in 1920, Warren G Harding had entered the White House with the attitude of returning the country to 'business as usual.' Harding was fated to be one of America's more obscure presidents, with the two years and five months of his administration ranking as one of the most corrupt. Harding was a likeable fellow, was friendly and good-natured, and, above all, he looked presidential. His statesmanlike profile and ease caused many Americans to feel reassured following the upheavals of the war, the battles over the Treaty and the League and the Red Scare. Yet Harding was a man of few abilities. He was heavily dependent upon others, bringing many of his old friends – the 'Ohio gang' – with him to Washington to help run the government. Instead, they corrupted it.

Besides following Republican tradition by sharply increasing tariffs, the Harding Administration was most notable for its criminal activities. The most famous instance was the Teapot Dome scandal in which Harding's Secretary of the Interior, Albert B Fall, accepted bribes of hundreds of thousands of dollars in return for leasing government lands out west for drilling by big oil companies. While the scandal did not surface until after Harding's death, there is every indication that Harding was aware of what was going on. Fall later became the first cabinet officer in US history to serve a jail term.

Harding did succeed in appointing some very able men to the more important posts in his cabinet: Charles Evans Hughes as Secretary of State, Herbert Hoover as Secretary of Commerce and Andrew Mellon as Secretary of the Treasury. While Hoover and Mellon supervised the recovery of the economy that began in mid 1922, Hughes directed foreign policy. It was in foreign affairs that the Harding Administration, without any contribution by the President, achieved the most success.

At the conclusion of the World War the United States, Great Britain and Japan began to lay plans for a rapid expansion of their navies in what appeared to presage an all-out naval race between the powers. In November 1921 Secretary of State Hughes assembled the major powers in Washington to discuss naval limitations. Following a bold opening proposal by Hughes calling for definite limits and under pressure from public opinion back home, the major powers agreed to the Five-Power Naval Treaty, or Washington Treaty, in February 1922. The treaty established a fixed ratio (on battleships and aircraft carriers) among the United States, Britain, Japan, France and Italy. Each of the signatories also agreed to abandon capital ship construction for 10 years. Furthermore, in a Four-Power Pact, Japan, the United States, Great Britain and France agreed not to increase the fortifications of their possessions in the Pacific Ocean. In the same month a Nine-Power Treaty was signed regarding China. In this treaty Japan agreed to give up possessions acquired in China during the recent war (most important was the Shantung Peninsula acquired from Germany) and to renounce further imperialistic designs on that country. All of the signatories agreed to respect the sovereignty and territorial integrity of China, to support attempts to achieve a stable government there and to avoid seeking special privileges.

Suddenly, in August 1923, President Harding died in San Francisco while returning from a trip to Alaska. The new President, Calvin Coolidge, had risen through state politics to become Governor of Massachusetts. He had rocketed to national fame during the 1919 Boston police strike by announcing that there was 'no right to strike against the public safety by anybody, anywhere, anytime.' Coolidge was a classic rural New England Puritan. He was frugal and absolutely honest. The new President would soon become famous for his solemn demeanor, abrupt speech and terse press interviews.

Coolidge proved to be a very popular President and provided an excellent reflection of America during the 1920s, for he believed in and supported the pervasive business ethos of American culture. According to Coolidge, business left undisturbed could be trusted to bring on permanent prosperity. Government should aid and protect industry and commerce, but it should not interfere. Coolidge coolly practiced the faith that 'society without much government action moves steadily upward.' He did little as President. He pushed no new legislation and vetoed bills for the sale of electricity by the government and agricultural relief for embattled farmers. During the five and one-half years of his presidency 'the business of America was business,' and the period became known as one of 'Coolidge prosperity.'

Coolidge loaded the regulatory agencies established by earlier progressive legislation with people opposed to any regulation. He trimmed government spending and reduced the national debt by 25 percent. Nothing demonstrates the beliefs of the Coolidge Administration more than the policies of its Secretary of the Treasury, Andrew Mellon. In 1926, after years of trying, Mellon finally got Congress to approve legislation granting huge tax cuts to large corporations and wealthy individuals. The program was undertaken in the belief that investment spending was the key to economic growth, jobs and prosperity. Since wealthy individuals (like Mellon himself) had the most money to invest, they should be given the largest tax breaks. The result was a huge windfall for big business and the wealthy. Where previously an individual with an annual income of $1,000,000 a year paid $600,000 in taxes, that person paid only $200,000 under the new laws. The result of the Coolidge-Mellon policies was that stock dividends grew faster than wages. These excess profits, along with the tax cuts, produced huge sums of wealth and an increasing concentra-

tion of stock ownership. By the late 1920s one-tenth of one percent of the people in the nation controled 65 percent of the corporate stock.

It was in the context of a two-year steady economic expansion that the presidential election of 1924 took place. The Republicans, despite the revelations of scandal in the Harding Administration, were in a solid position. The Democrats, on the other hand, were sharply divided. The tension between urban areas and the rural small towns in American society was at its sharpest as the ascendancy of city ways and metropolitan life was beginning to take root. The enactment of Prohibition and the continuing struggle over the soundness of that policy created a deep split in the Democratic Party between urban 'wets' and 'drys' hailing from southern and midwestern regions. There was also division between southern, midwestern and southwestern supporters of the Klu Klux Klan and immigrant Catholics from the northeast. Many Democrats were wary of the left following the postwar labor strikes and Red Scare. And labor, having lost many of the gains it had made during the war, was uninterested in helping farmers.

One result of all this was that progressives bolted the Democratic Party, deciding to run their own candidate in the person of Robert M La Follette of Wisconsin. More broadly, the lack of unity was reflected in the donnybrook that took place at the 1924 Democratic convention. During 95 ballots cast over a period of nine days neither of the two main contenders, Governor Al Smith of New York amd William G McAdoo, could garner the necessary two-thirds margin for victory. McAdoo, with his support from the South and West, and Smith with his support from the Northeast, perfectly reflected the split in the party. Finally, the convention settled on John W Davis as its presidential candidate. President Coolidge won easily, with 54 percent of the vote to Davis's 29 percent and La Follette's 16 percent.

The fundamental reason for the Republican vic-

tory was the state of the American economy. The decade following the World War witnessed such revolutionary changes in American business and industry that it can be referred to as a second industrial takeoff. Whether on the farm or in the shop, mechanization in American life became commonplace during the 1920s. While a major stimulus had been government spending for the war, a technological revolution involving mass production and new scientific and business management techniques, coupled with the spread of electric power through all phases of manufacturing, meant a quantum leap in productivity for each American worker.

Leading the way was the rise to dominance of the automobile industry, which exerted a powerful pull on the rest of the economy. Auto production increased 255 percent between 1919 and 1929. Automobile registration went from nine million autos in 1920 to more than 26 million by 1929. The demand for automobiles generated a tremendous expansion in the oil, rubber and steel industries. In the newly expanding service industries, those catering to America's cherished cars quickly assumed top-rank. The construction industry also benefited from the rise of the automobile industry, for autos needed roads to travel on, and with Americans able to travel greater distances, new suburbs sprang up everywhere.

Radio emerged as both a new and major industry. The first radio station went into operation in Pittsburgh in November 1920. During the winter of 1921-22 a radio craze swept America. By 1924 there were 562 radio stations. Radio sales increased from $60,000,000 in 1922 to $842,000,000 in 1929. There were many other successful industries such as electric power and machinery manufacture. There were new appliances such as refrigerators, electric irons and vacuum cleaners. The aviation industry, chemicals, aluminum, advertising and motion pictures all contributed to the unprecedented economic boom. Real per capita income increased by almost one-third between 1920 and 1929. Corporate profits were up 62 percent, stock dividends up 65 percent.

Yet there were weak spots and danger signals. One problem was that the prosperity was unevenly distributed. While industry and finance

Above left: Scene in the courtroom at Dayton, Ohio in July 1925, during the trial of John Scopes.

Above right: Robert La Follette, a progressive Democrat, who was defeated in the 1924 Presidential campaign.

Right: Calvin Coolidge, the US president who supported business and opposed taxes and welfare. Although popular in the 1920s this political philosophy was to prove a disaster with the onset of the Depression.

Below: Presidential campaign button for F D Roosevelt.

made fantastic profits, working wages failed to keep pace and farm income suffered an absolute retrogression. By 1929, while 80 percent of the people had only two percent of the savings, the top 10 percent had accumulated 86 percent. Greater efficiency should have meant lower prices, but prices continued to rise. The great mass of working Americans could not purchase what they were producing.

The most important domestic economic problem of the 1920s was the agricultural depression that began in the summer of 1920 and lasted throughout the decade – and after. Following the war farm prices fell sharply because of a decrease in foreign demand and the withdrawal of government price supports. Increased mechanization stimulated production but caused prices to fall severely. In 1919 farmers had held 16 percent of the national income; in 1929 agriculture accounted for less than nine percent of the national income.

American culture and society also experienced the dizzy pace of rapid change. The popular automobile engendered various previously unknown freedoms for Americans, particularly young people. Escaping by car from the house of one's parents for a night of surreptitious sex, drinking and general cavorting seemed to be held up as a social norm. The teachings of the Vienna psychoanalyst Sigmund Freud and his disciples were presented as encouraging the public in their newfound sexual freedom by teaching that it was unhealthy to attempt to control or 'repress' sexual feelings and desires. Despite Prohibition, drinking still proved to be very popular, and the fact that it was officially taboo only seemed to make it all the more enticing. A new subculture rose up, fashioned around the consumption of alcohol, featuring the cocktail party, bootlegging and gangster wars, the speakeasy and the upturned flask at the college football game.

Women, in particular, were prominent beneficiaries of the changing habits of American society. After 1920 they were equal to men at the ballot box, and they soon found themselves wearing their hair shorter and their hemlines higher. Women took up cigarette smoking and drinking,

using these two devices to break down former male sanctuaries such as the local tavern and the after-dinner cigar conversation. Overall between 1917 and 1920 cigarette smoking increased by 400 percent, and by 1930 had tripled again.

Radio was not only a burgeoning industry but, along with the automobile, did more than anything else to change the face of American life in the 1920s. The entire nation could now enjoy the simultaneous excitement of a presidential nominating convention or a championship boxing match. Radio, in turn, helped to make sports and advertising an integral part of American life. For the first time sports and sport heroes became a national phenomenon. There was Red Grange in football, Jack Dempsey and Gene Tunney in boxing and, above all, Babe Ruth in baseball.

Not everyone appreciated the new freedoms and worshipped the business ethos. In what has

become known as the 'Lost Generation,' intellectuals offered a notable dissenting footnote to the headlong rush for prosperity. Beginning with a rejection of the war and its glorification of false ideals, intellectuals went on to attack the enforced conformity, the mindlessness of mass culture and the dehumanization of the machine age. In his novels *Main Street* (1920) and *Babbitt* (1922), Sinclair Lewis offered a scathing indictment of this conformity, business values, 'boosterism' and small-town (and small-minded) America. The most popular debunker of the 'American Way' during the 1920s was the irrepressible H L Mencken, who, as editor of the enormously popular journal the *American Mercury*, launched piercing and sarcastic attacks on almost every aspect of American life – religion, radicalism, reform, democracy, fundamentalism, pomposity. Other notable intellectuals and literary artists such as Ernest Hemingway, F Scott Fitzgerald, T S Eliot and Theodore Dreiser exposed the deeper emptiness of life.

For the vast majority of Americans this kind of disaffection was overwhelmed by the continuing economic boom. In March 1927 the great bull market in common stocks began with automobile and radio issues setting the pace. The following year was another presidential election year. Calvin Coolidge had declined to run for another term, and Stanford-educated engineer and Secretary of Commerce Herbert Hoover had a lock on the nomination by the time of the convention in June 1928. In contrast to the dissension of four years earlier, the Democrats nominated Governor Alfred E Smith of New York on the first ballot. Yet Smith and the Democrats still found themselves facing many of the same divisive issues of 1924. Smith was a 'wet,' meaning he was against the prohibition of alcohol. Also, Smith was a Roman Catholic. Both of these issues combined would cost the Democrats crucial votes in rural small-town America, and particularly in the supposedly Democratic stronghold of the 'Solid South.' Most important, there remained the experience of the six-year economic boom and the promise of continuing prosperity under Republican leadership. There were no surprises on election day in November as Hoover won with 21,500,000 votes to 15,000,000 for Smith. Outside the South, Smith carried only Massachusetts and Rhode Island.

Yet beneath the surface of this smashing Republican victory lay hopeful signs for the Democrats. America was becoming urbanized at a rapid pace, both in terms of population and popular tastes. Immigrants and their children, with their higher birthrates, were moving into the Democratic fold in increasing numbers. Also, farmers were still in a bad way economically. In the latter part of the 1920s farmers and their representatives in Congress began to move steadily leftward, where they found common ground with the Progressives. Even in 1928 the changing times can be seen by the fact that while the Republicans outpolled the Democrats by more than a million votes in the nation's 12 largest cities in 1924, the Democrats in 1928, even in defeat, had turned this around by gaining a few thousand more votes than the Republicans in those same 12 cities.

The Crash

On the basis of real economic growth and the recent huge tax cuts for wealthy individuals, money began to pour into the stock market in staggering sums. Large commercial banks with an excess of cash loaned money to brokers, who used it to fund the wild speculation taking place in the market. Loans to brokers grew from $3.5 billion in January 1926 to $8.5 billion by the end of September 1929. Meanwhile, the face value of all stocks grew from $27 billion to more than $87 billion. Money also flowed in from overseas, and soon even the most conservative banker and modest middle-class investor were caught up in the tremendous excitement of the dizzying climb in stock prices.

These heady days of 1929 came to a devastating halt in the Great Crash of October 1929. Selling and withdrawal from the market began slowly at first in September and early October. The real crisis came on 24 October – 'Black Thursday' – when more than 13 million shares changed hands and prices fell sharply. This was followed by a 16.5 million-share day on 29 October in a selling frenzy that led to a complete collapse in stock prices. Despite the assurances of political leaders and financial titans, the stock market would not recover.

The crash of the stock market reverberated throughout the economy. Unemployment jumped from a little over three percent in 1929 to over eight percent in 1930 and to 16 percent by early 1931. With the collapse of credit industrial production was cut back on everything from big-ticket items like automobiles and houses to everyday household appliances. Still hope remained. That is, until the summer of 1931 when Europeans began to withdraw huge cash reserves from American banks. In turn, American banks called in domestic loans. Foreign trade practically stopped. The result was that the United States and the world plunged into a true 'Great Depression.' By 1933 unemployment stood at 25 percent of the workforce, with more than 12,000,000 people out of work. Industrial production had declined 51 percent. Displaced farmers and sharecroppers took to the road with nothing. Even among those people who held on to their homes and jobs, the insecurity and fear produced by the devastating conditions of the Depression would linger on for more than a generation.

Canada

Canada was no more immune from the depression than were the other advanced industrialized nations of the world. Its farms and factories were especially hard hit by the collapse of world prices, and in 1930 Canadians turned to the Conserva-

Above left: Model T Fords being mass-produced in a Detroit factory in 1925.

Left: At the height of Prohibition, the police, Customs and tax officials were destroying millions of gallons of illegal alcohol.

Above: Prohibition and corruption created the climate for the gangsters who were to become bitter rivals. Gang warfare resulted in the St Valentine's Day Massacre in which the notorious mobster Al Capone gunned down a rival gang.

Right: 'Black Thursday,' 24 October 1929. The scene outside the Stock Market on Wall Street on the day the American market collapsed in chaos and ruins.

tives and their Prime Minister, Richard B Bennett, to lead them out of the depression. Bennett negotiated with other Commonwealth countries and the United States to adjust tariffs so as to get trade going again. Although some new political parties emerged in Canada in response to difficulties of the depression – the Social Credit party in Alberta, the Union Nationale in Quebec – by 1935 the Canadians would return the Liberals to power under the Prime Minister William Lyon Mackenzie King.

King had already served as Prime Minister from 1921 to 1930, with a brief interlude in 1926 when he provoked a constitutional crisis that would lead to a major change in Canada's status. King had asked the British-appointed governor-general to dissolve Canada's parliament, but the governor-general refused to do so. King resigned, but once back in power he continued his struggle, and at the Imperial Conference of 1926 in London, he got the British to agree that all members of the British Commonwealth had equal status. This would be adopted by the British Parliament in 1931 as the Statute of Westminster.

With his return in 1935 King assumed his role as probably the most influential Prime Minister Canada has ever known. He continued to lead Canada out of the worst of the economic depression, and then led Canada through the long and trying years of World War II. He would remain Prime Minister until 1948, and among the many laudable accomplishments of his years in power were his largely successful efforts to improve relations between the Anglo- and French-Canadians.

Hoover and the Depression

Initially President Hoover and his advisers, such as Treasury Secretary Andrew Mellon, attempted to bolster the confidence of the American people by insisting the economy was fundamentally sound and would soon right itself. Hoover then attempted to stimulate the economy through tax cuts and lower interest rates, but this, too, proved insufficient, since in the economic recession people were already paying taxes at a reduced rate and there was no market for loans. In the spring of 1930 Congress passed a $500 million program for public works on roads and bridges, but this appropriation was overwhelmed by the collapse of the world economy in the summer of 1931.

In the congressional elections of 1930 Democrats and Progressives gained control of both the House and Senate and attempted to initiate a program of relief. Hoover blocked this, believing that relief was a local and state problem and that it would erode individual motivation. In 1932 Hoover vetoed legislation for a massive federal public works project and for a program of direct federal relief. In the two years leading up to the 1932 presidential election relations between the President and Congress would become increasingly strained, Congress wanting to do more to fight the depression, and Hoover afraid that too much federal intervention would upset the economic system and its moral foundations. Hoover, however, in 1932 approved the Reconstruction Finance Corporation, which lent more than $1500 million to business, mostly large corporations and banks. Hoover also approved the Emergency Relief Act that was passed by Congress in 1932, and authorized the government to lend money to the states, with the states responsible for seeing that it reached needy individuals. Yet for the most part Hoover remained trapped in his individualistic philosophy, his belief that recovery was at hand and an inability to comprehend the extent of the depression. By the summer of 1932 public confidence in the Hoover Administration had

been thoroughly eroded. The forcible evacuation by the army of thousands of destitute veterans seeking the full payment of their bonuses for wartime service and the burning of their camp in the nation's capital signified for many Americans the callousness and lack of understanding on the part of the President and the rest of the federal government.

At their convention in July 1932 the Democrats nominated Governor Franklin D Roosevelt of New York. The Republicans re-nominated President Hoover. In an unprecedented move Roosevelt flew to Chicago to accept the nomination and promised a 'new deal' for the American people. In the previous two presidential elections the issue had been prosperity, and the incumbent party had easily won. But now the country was in the midst of an enormous economic, social and even psychological depression. In a sweeping victory Roosevelt won all but six states. The demographic, social and political changes that had been taking place in the 1920s had all coalesced to produce a Democratic victory. And after three years of pain and suffering it truly was time for a 'new deal.'

Franklin D Roosevelt

The story of the New Deal is in many ways a biography of Franklin Roosevelt. Who was this new president? Born in 1882 into a well-to-do upstate New York family, Roosevelt had attended Groton Academy, Harvard and Columbia Law School and had married Eleanor Roosevelt, the niece of President Theodore Roosevelt. He had never received his law degree, but he had passed the New York state bar examination and went to work for a Wall Street firm. Although marriage, life and work in the big metropolis gave Roosevelt many social contacts and experiences, he became bored with the simple hobbies, conventional family life and stultifying legal work. In the early 1900s the aroma of reform was in the air, and though personally conservative, Roosevelt found himself supporting most of the Progressive platform of political reform, social change and economic democracy. In what was his first great political opportunity, Roosevelt was drafted by upstate Democrats to run for state senator, and in the Democratic sweep of 1910 Roosevelt entered a new vocation.

Roosevelt served only one two-year term as

Left: A desperate man seeks employment during the Great Depression.

Above right: President Herbert Hoover, seen here as Secretary of Commerce in 1927 taking part in the first inter-city television broadcast. He was, however, unable to find any effective means of dealing with the collapse of the US economy.

Above far right: William Mackenzie King, Canada's Liberal Prime Minister, a highly influential politician who was returned to power in 1935. He led his country through the Depression years and World War II.

Right: President Franklin D Roosevelt seeking re-election on the campaign trail in North Dakota in 1936.

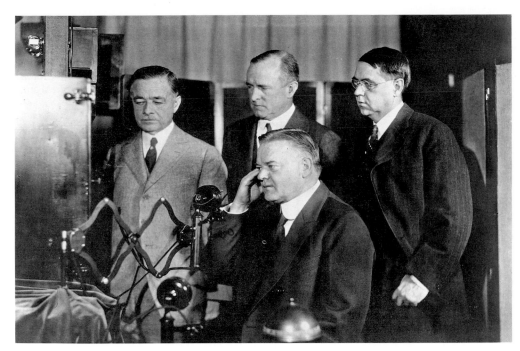

state senator, but in that brief period he received a real political education. In a losing battle against the bosses of Tammany Hall, Roosevelt learned that in going too far and refusing to compromise, one's future political effectiveness could be undermined. He also learned that politics is not simply a two-sided struggle but is extremely complex and touches many interests.

Following the election of Woodrow Wilson, Roosevelt was appointed the Assistant Secretary of the Navy, the number two position in the department. Moving to Washington, Roosevelt entered a far wider world of people and experience than he had known previously. Over the next seven years Roosevelt absorbed the ideas of Wilsonian reform and progressivism, gained valuable and weighty administrative experience, met many new people (such as congressmen and labor leaders) and became a national public figure. Thanks to his newly achieved national reputation, Roosevelt was chosen as the Democratic nominee for Vice-President in 1920. But when the Democrats overwhelmingly lost that election many people felt that Roosevelt's career in national politics was probably finished.

In August 1921, while vacationing with his family at Campobello Island off the coast of Maine, Roosevelt was crippled by poliomyelitis. The disease and its physically debilitating effects had two important results, one personal, the other political. Personally, it whittled away at Roosevelt's penchant for impetuousness and restlessness, tinged with a snobbish, patrician air, without, at the same time, depriving Roosevelt of his drive and decisiveness.

Politically, although it would be years before Roosevelt accepted the fact that he would never walk again, he almost immediately decided that he would continue to be a public figure and pursue a political career. The eight-year interregnum during which Roosevelt avoided seeking public office was a sour period for the Democratic Party. Yet the Democratic defeats of 1924 and 1928 were both personal and political victories for Roosevelt, giving him increased national exposure and political contacts. He was widely perceived as the 'happy warrior' battling against both political and physical afflictions.

Roosevelt continued an active political life within the Democratic Party as he worked hard in an attempt to formulate and articulate a new set of principles for the party. His position within the

party as a moderate liberal enabled Roosevelt to stake out a kind of young elder statesman's role while, in Roosevelt's own words, 'waiting for the drivers of the high-powered Republican automobile to run into a ditch and make some stupendous blunder.' Finally, in 1928 Roosevelt returned to office-seeking, waged a vigorous and exciting campaign for the governorship of New York and won despite the Republican victory at the presidential level.

Roosevelt had situated himself well for a run for the presidency. As governor, Roosevelt had to broker and deal with a great variety of interests. Against a hostile Republican legislature Roosevelt attempted to raise himself above the legacy of Al Smith by seeking to heal old wounds in the Democratic Party – particularly at the national level – and by developing an affirmative liberal

program. With the onset of the Great Depression the Roosevelt executive style revealed itself for the first time. Roosevelt had no panacea, since he believed the economic and social woes of the country were national in scope. Roosevelt, however, recognized the need for action. To try something, anything, and if that didn't work to try something else.

Roosevelt had no overall philosophy of government or history, but rather a humanitarian instinct and a progressive's recognition of the need for change. In the course of his four-year experiment in government in New York, he anticipated many of the New Deal programs in a continuous search for specific ways to meet specific problems – through such measures as old-age pensions, for example, and unemployment insurance and labor legislation.

The New Deal

Roosevelt was elected President in November 1932 in the very depths of the Great Depression. Bank and business failures, farm and home foreclosures, fulminating unemployment and a welter of social and human misery dominated the news. The entire nation waited anxiously and impatiently between November and March for the President-elect to do something or, at least, declare his intentions. Roosevelt remained silent and the country became increasingly despairing.

The new President recognized that the nation's fundamental problem was one of public psychology, a lack of confidence in itself and its national leaders. This was precisely what Roosevelt meant when he stated in his inaugural address that it was his 'firm belief that the only thing we have to fear is fear itself.' The people wanted action and Roosevelt gave it to them. Armed with solid congressional majorities in both the House (312-123) and Senate (59-37), Roosevelt convened a special session of Congress on 9 March and commenced to hurl a torrent of legislation at Congress to deal with the economic crisis in what has become known as the 'Hundred Days.' Beginning with his immediate decision to declare a four-day bank holiday and to suspend all gold payments and exports, Roosevelt's leadership proved to be a unifying force for members of Congress. Roosevelt brought with him to Washington an army of intelligent and enthusiastic lawyers, economists, social workers and many others, led by a group of key insiders known as the 'Brain Trust.' Both the old departments and the newly created administrative agencies rapidly became filled with people bursting with new energy and ideas. Roosevelt made full use of press and radio to convey to the American people the message that *he* was in control, but that *they*, together, could lick the nation's problems. His communication with the people and their identification with him would always be the source of his greatest strength. Few who heard the self-assurance and directness of his first 'fireside chat' over the radio would ever forget the bracing and buoyant effect it had on them. Political cartoons portrayed a vigorous and valiant Roosevelt taming lions, as resisting sinister bankers attempting to foreclose on mortgages and as a knight slaying dragons labeled 'fear' and 'deflation.'

The President was in perpetual motion as the Congress passed everything Roosevelt sent up to Capitol Hill. (If anything, during this period most congressmen were to the left of the President and urging greater and more extreme measures, such as nationalizing the banking industry.) In April 1933 Congress created the Civilian Conservation Corps which would eventually employ 2,750,000 young men in the service of flood control, reforestation and soil conservation. This was followed in May by the Agricultural Adjustment Act, which authorized the establishment of production controls on major foodstuffs and assigned marketing quotas. The idea was to create a balance between production and consumption in order to raise farm income, which had been in decline since the early 1920s. In June came what many considered the centerpiece of New Deal legislation: the National Industrial Recovery Act (NIRA). By allowing committees representing management, labor and the public to establish industry-wide codes for production, prices and wages it was intended to end the excessive competition that was

Above left: Roosevelt making his inaugural address in which he referred to the concept of a 'New Deal' for America.

Left: The Civilian Construction Corps created by Roosevelt which employed young men on public works.

Right: Roosevelt signing the Social Security Bill of 1935 which made contributions compulsory by both employers and employees.

Far right: A field office of the Works Progress Administration established to aid the unemployed.

forcing a downward spiral in prices and profits. One key section of the bill – Section 7a – protected the rights of labor to organize and bargain collectively. The gains for labor contained in the NIRA included a 40-hour work week, a decent minimum wage and provisions outlawing child labor. As a result of federal protection, union membership increased from a little over two million to more than three million between 1933 and 1935.

In passing this and other key legislation Roosevelt, although retaining huge majorities in Congress, did not operate through the vehicle of the Democratic Party. Instead, Roosevelt adopted a form of broker leadership. In rising above political parties and divisive factions, Roosevelt sought support for his policies wherever it could be found, regardless of party affiliation or sectional ties.

Roosevelt's grand coalition began to unravel in late 1934 and early 1935. Support for the New Deal first weakened on the right, as big business, represented by the Liberty League, and small businessmen, through the Chamber of Commerce, attacked the President. Small businessmen opposed the strict NIRA codes which favored big business and industry, and big business objected to control by public representatives. Both groups disliked Section 7a of the NIRA, which protected the rights of labor.

Disaffection then began to occur on the left. Individuals with powerful followings, such as Senator Huey Long of Louisiana and the popular radio-priest Reverend Charles Coughlin, felt that Roosevelt had not gone far enough toward sharing the wealth, socializing banking and industry and protecting the working man through unemployment insurance and pro-union legislation. In the congressional elections of 1934 Democratic majorities increased in the House from 313 to 322, and in the Senate from 59 to 69. Both the mass of voters and Congress shifted leftward, and Roosevelt, under constant and tremendous pressure from opposing political forces, found he could no longer pursue a conciliatory middle way. The bankers, business and industrial leaders were moving in one direction, while farmers, workers, the lower-middle class and the unemployed moved in the other. In response, Roosevelt executed a swift step to the left in tandem with the prevailing mood of Congress and the people. The result was a second and more far-reaching phase of the New Deal.

In his annual message to Congress in January 1935 Roosevelt sounded the trumpet for an even more activist federal role in social and economic policy. In this expanding New Deal a number of pieces of legislation stand out. The first was the passage of the Emergency Relief Appropriation Act in April 1935, creating the Works Progress Administration (WPA) under the directorship of Harry Hopkins. Congress initially approved almost $5 billion (and eventually $11 billion) for the agency; over the years it would employ millions of people on more than 250,000 public works projects. Then there was the National Labor Relations Act (also known as the Wagner Act, after its chief sponsor, Senator Robert Wagner of New York). Following a decision by the Supreme Court declaring the codes of the National Industrial Recovery Act unconstitutional, Roosevelt decided to come out strongly for Wagner's bill; it called for the creation of a National Labor Relations Board with power to arbitrate labor disputes, and it guaranteed the rights of labor that had been established under Section 7a of the now-unconstitutional NIRA. Roosevelt signed this measure in July. This legislation helped unions organize basic industries such as steel, automobiles, rubber and textiles. On the eve of the Second World War 28 percent of all nonagricultural workers would be unionized, compared with only a little more than 11 percent in 1933. Finally, in August 1935 Roosevelt signed the Social Security Act, establishing an old-age insurance program and unemployment insurance on a nationwide basis funded by compulsory contributions by both owners and workers.

By January 1936 the general feeling was one of a nation once again hopeful and on the move. Unemployment had dropped by four million from early 1933. Stock prices had doubled, and farm income had almost doubled. A variety of specific groups – bankers, farmers, unions, municipalities, old people, teachers and even artists – had been helped in specific ways. Yet the Great Depression was hardly over. Almost nine million Americans remained unemployed, and many remained hungry. In Roosevelt's own words, one-third of the nation remained 'ill-fed, ill-clothed and ill-housed.' Moreover, the Supreme Court had stepped up the pace of its assault on the New Deal, declaring the Agricultural Adjustment Act and the Bituminous Coal Conservation Act unconstitutional. The Court argued that farming

and the mining of coal were not interstate commerce and therefore not subject to congressional regulation. The Court also rejected the Municipal Bankruptcy Act and New York state's minimum wage law.

Attacking big business and the Court, while appealing to the common man, Roosevelt launched another whirlwind campaign, making himself the supreme issue. In his acceptance speech at the 1936 Democratic convention Roosevelt declared war on 'economic royalists' and announced his intention to defend the people of the nation against 'industrial dictatorship.' In an election that witnessed a new political consciousness by organized labor and a massive switch of black votes from the Republican Party, Roosevelt scored a smashing victory over Alfred Landon in November 1936. The Democrats once again increased their majorities in Congress to 334-89 in the House and a whopping 75-17 domination of the Senate. It seemed nothing could stop Franklin Delano Roosevelt.

Except, that is, the group of 'angry old men' on the Supreme Court. In four years Roosevelt had not been able to make a single appointment to the Court, and the frustration of having his cherished legislative program torn apart by those nine men – often by a narrow 5-4 majority – was too much to bear. In early 1937 Roosevelt devised and unveiled a scheme to expand the Court; it would enable him to appoint six new justices immediately, thereby giving him a comfortable majority on New Deal legislation. Roosevelt had, for the first time as President, gone too far. His 'court-packing plan' unleashed a firestorm of criticism in the editorial pages of the nation's newspapers, and congressmen scampered quickly to distance themselves from the President's proposal. Roosevelt was depicted as a dictator attempting to undermine the venerable constitutional principle of the separation of powers in the federal government. Despite tremendous opposition, Roosevelt persisted in trying to gain congressional support for his plan until the Court surprisingly sustained the Wagner Labor Relations Act in April, thereby weakening the President's argument that it was adamantly opposed to his legislative program. This action was followed by the Court upholding the Social Security Act a few weeks later.

In 1937 the Second New Deal coalition began to unravel as labor split between rival factions (AFL v CIO), the Democrats divided over tariffs and a

coalition of Republicans and southern Democrats came to dominate the Congress (and in particular that fulcrum of the legislative process, the House Rules Committee). During 1937 Roosevelt sent Congress proposals for a permanent national farm act, legislation of wages and hours, administrative reorganization and regional planning. When Congress adjourned for the year, it had not passed a single one of these proposals.

But the greatest danger to the New Deal came not from obstructionists on the Supreme Court or in Congress, but from the faltering economy, which had slid into another recession in October. As the economic decline became increasingly severe during that autumn Roosevelt clung to his belief in the necessity of a balanced budget and continued to look for ways to cut government spending. In the new year of 1938 unemployment increased, back up to 11 million, and business conditions sank precipitously. By March the recession had become so severe that it threatened to wipe out all of the gains that had been made over the previous five years. The following month Roosevelt called for a loosening of credit and a revival of deficit spending. In response Congress quickly passed a 3.6 billion public works spending program. Still, damage had been done. Between the fight over the Supreme Court and the 'Roosevelt recession,' the President was rapidly losing both popular and congressional support. While Congress had little desire to repeal the New Deal, neither did it wish to extend it further.

In a final attempt to rally support for an extended reform program Roosevelt launched an attack on the trusts and big business, and in the congressional elections of 1938 he attempted to purge his own party of its more conservative members. The attempt backfired, as conservative Democrats, mostly from the South, retained their seats in Congress. As a result of the 1938 elections the Republicans almost doubled their strength in the House, from 88 to 170, and picked up eight seats in the Senate. Roosevelt, recognizing reality, personally rang the death knell for the New Deal in his famous annual message to Congress in January 1939.

Successes and failures

During the previous six years President Roosevelt and the American people had achieved some tremendous successes. A huge reform program had been passed by Congress. Roosevelt had established himself as a firm and charismatic leader, projecting an infectious optimism. Through the hard work and commitment of millions of Americans the nation had achieved some genuine relief and recovery. Powerful forces of political, social and economic progressivism had been released in the country, and the principle had been established that the entire community, through the agency of the federal government, was responsible for the welfare of all the people.

Recovery, however, remained far from complete. Hunger, poverty, sickness and unemployment still stalked the nation to an unacceptable degree. The ultimate New Deal objectives of distributive justice and a sound, stable prosperity had clearly not been realized. By early 1939 Roosevelt was in the weakest position of his presidency, saddled with a divided Democratic Party and a Republican Party that looked forward to the next election and an opportunity for change.

Yet something new was in the air. The winds of war were once again blowing from across the sea and diverting the attention of the President, Congress and public. The crisis in world politics was dominating the news. How would this new challenge be met? Could the nation avoid war?

The centerpiece of Franklin Roosevelt's foreign policy was a commitment to a general and abstract internationalism that mirrored his commitment to progressivism and liberalism in domestic politics. Internationalism for Roosevelt meant vaguely that the world was interdependent and that the United States should pursue some sort of active role in world affairs.

Roosevelt, however, did possess one firm conviction: this was that an effective foreign policy required a strong and stable domestic consensus. The battle over the Versailles Treaty and the League of Nations, coupled with the defeat of the Democratic Party, which had supported those endeavors, in the election of 1920, had instilled that lesson. The American public, preoccupied with peace and prosperity, had retained a solid isolationist mentality throughout the 1920s and only favored those diplomatic devices, such as the Washington Naval Treaty of 1922, which promised to avoid war. Although privately an internationalist and supporter of the League of Nations, in 1932 Roosevelt became the first Democratic candidate for the presidency who explicitly repudiated American membership in that organization.

During his first term Roosevelt was cautious and conservative in foreign affairs. The nation's greatest problem was dealing with the debilitating effects of the Great Depression and passing legislation directed toward relief and recovery, and there simply was little time for foreign questions. Moreover, the depression had served to deepen the attachment of both public and Congress to isolationism: no involvement in world affairs while there was a domestic crisis. Many legislators upon whom Roosevelt depended for support of his domestic program were ardent isolationists, and foreign policy maneuvers, such as sanctions against Japan for its aggression against China, could provoke the opposition of key congressmen, thereby jeopardizing the New Deal. While Roosevelt took some modest actions, such as the diplomatic recognition of the Soviet Union and a small naval expansion (which in reality only called for the United States to build up to the limits it was allowed under the London Naval Treaty of 1930), the President only reacted passively to the withdrawal of Germany and Japan from the League of Nations, Germany's renunciation of the disarmament clauses of the Versailles Treaty and Japan's abandonment of further naval limitation talks with the United States and Great Britain. Roosevelt's single foray into foreign affairs was an attempt to secure American membership in the World Court. While a majority of the Senate voted favorably, the vote was short of the necessary two-thirds margin. Following this defeat Roosevelt told Elihu Root, a former secretary of

state, that 'today, quite frankly, the wind everywhere blows against us.'

The winds that defeated United States membership in the World Court were mild compared to the tempest created by a sensational series of congressional hearings on American entry into World War I. In late 1934 a committee headed by Senator Gerald P Nye of North Dakota and featuring a number of other staunch isolationists such as Arthur H Vandenberg, Bennett Champ Clark and Homer T Bone, claimed to have uncovered the 'real' reason for American entry into that conflict. It was not to make the world safe for democracy, but to expand the profits of the munitions makers (the 'merchants of death') and to save the loans that American banks had extended to the Allies. These revelations struck the nation like a thunderbolt. In the summer of 1935 the isolationists, by an almost unanimous vote, pushed through Congress a Neutrality Act that called for a mandatory embargo on arms to all belligerents involved in hostilities. Roosevelt and his secretary of state, Cordell Hull, while favoring the embargo, attempted to gain some discretion for the President to discriminate between aggressor and victim, banning arms to the former, while permitting some shipments to the latter. Congress refused. Roosevelt had little choice and signed the bill in August 1935. Shortly thereafter, in October, Italy invaded Ethiopia. The United States, along with Britain and France, did nothing. When the Neutrality Act came up for renewal in February 1936 Roosevelt once again attempted to gain discretionary authority from Congress and once again was rejected. The year 1936 would see German troops march into the Rhineland and a civil war break out in Spain.

Having already seized the Chinese province of Manchuria in the early 1930s and converted it into a puppet-state, Japan, in July 1937, initiated a full-scale war against China. In response to this and equally ominous developments in Europe, Roosevelt attempted to sound a warning. In Chicago on 5 October 1937, in what became known as his 'quarantine speech,' Roosevelt warned that the very foundations of civilization were being threatened by a reign of terror, international lawlessness and aggression on the part of Germany, Italy and Japan. Roosevelt argued that 'the peace-loving nations must make a concerted effort' to oppose the violation of treaties and warned that 'there is no escape through mere isolation or neutrality.' This trial balloon was quickly burst by a renewed storm of isolationist complaints, causing Roosevelt to retreat. The President later told his speechwriter, Samuel Rosenman, that 'it's a terrible thing to look over your shoulder when you are trying to lead – and to find no one is there.'

Left: Billboard in Weslaco, Texas, advertising the Townsend Plan, an old-age pension scheme.

Above right: German troops occupy Prague, Czechoslovakia, in March 1939. This was one of a series of events that led to the outbreak of war in Europe in September 1939, and then eventually to America's entry into the war in December 1941.

While Roosevelt was preoccupied with a renewed recession, his attempted purge of the Democratic Party and the congressional elections of 1938, Hitler annexed Austria (March 1938) and, with the permission of Britain and France, sliced off the Sudetenland from the bulk of Czechoslovakia (September 1938). Given the stance of foreign leaders who found Hitler's demands 'reasonable' and faced with increasing opposition in the Congress and within his own party, the President was in a weak position to demand more control over foreign affairs.

In March 1939 Germany incorporated the rest of Czechoslovakia into the Third Reich, and it became clear that Hitler's next move would mean war with Great Britain and France. Clear in Europe, that is, for most Americans understood little of this and remained firmly rooted in their isolationism. Roosevelt asked Congress for a full repeal of the neutrality laws, and in July the Senate Foreign Relations Committee rejected repeal by a 12-11 vote.

In September 1939 Germany attacked Poland, and Britain and France declared war on Germany. Once again Roosevelt pushed for repeal of the Neutrality Act, while being careful to stress his proposal as a vehicle for keeping America out of the conflict by selling munitions and supplies to the Allies. In late October the Senate conceded and revised the neutrality laws by a vote of 63-30,

with the House following six days later. Yet though it had begun to move away from neutrality, the Congress had only agreed to revise the Neutrality Act as a means to stay out of the conflict. As Hitler prepared for another strike and the war entered the period known as the 'Phony War,' the President, Congress and the public entered a period of essentially passive watchful waiting.

In April 1940 Germany struck at Denmark and Norway. The following month Hitler's armies swept westward through Belgium and the Netherlands toward the English Channel and into France. Nazi armored columns sliced gaping holes in the French armies and sent the British Expeditionary Force fleeing across the Channel in a desperate salvage operation. In June France capitulated, while Hitler danced and America went into shock. Once again the force of events had altered the world view of Americans. For the first time there was a realization that the Western Hemisphere itself might be threatened. Roosevelt, with increased public support, began to adopt a more flexible and interventionist policy in urging increased support for Great Britain. Yet the American public remained confused and retained contradictory attitudes. While a clear majority (around 70 percent) favored disregarding neutrality and doing whatever necessary to help Britain win the war and defeat Hitler, an equally clear majority favored not getting directly involved in

the war. Roosevelt's task was to aid Britain, thereby getting the US more involved as a belligerent, while justifying his actions as a step away from war. Roosevelt had to be particularly careful, for the rapid German victories had moved him to try to seek a third presidential term.

Since huge majorities of the American public (80-90 percent) had consistently favored a larger army, navy and air force, Roosevelt decided to stress preparedness as a major theme for 1940. In reaction to the fall of France, which had brought near-panic to Washington, the Congress in July authorized an additional 1,325,000 tons of naval construction. This was in addition to a naval bill of 1938, whose appropriations had only been fully approved during the previous month; in two months Congress approved funds for almost 250 warships. The government also moved to expand the army from 280,000 to 375,000 men and to produce an unheard-of 50,000 planes a year.

To solidify support for a bipartisan foreign policy of aid to Britain and to bolster his presidential campaign, Roosevelt appointed two eminent Republicans to key cabinet posts. Henry Stimson, a former secretary of state under Hoover, was named secretary of war, and Frank Knox, a Chicago industrialist, was given the position of secretary of the navy. In early August Roosevelt also came out for a selective service bill, the first ever in peacetime. And finally, in response to a

EXTRA

RACE RESULTS   **Los Angeles Times**   **NIGHT Pictorial**

Three Parts — 3* Pages   ***   MONDAY MORNING, DECEMBER 8, 1941.   Page A   DAILY, FIVE CENTS

IT'S WAR!

Hostilities Declared by Japanese; 350 Reported Killed in Hawaii Raid

U.S. Battleships Hit; 7 Die in Honolulu

LATE WAR BULLETINS
SHANGHAI, Dec. 8 (Monday.) (A.P.)—The Japanese have sunk the British gunboat Petrel as it lay off the International Settlement

Air Bombs Rained on Pacific Bases

Left: A newspaper headline announcing to a shocked nation the Japanese attack at Pearl Harbor.

Right: The USS *West Virginia* and USS *Tennessee,* sunk at Pearl Harbor on 7 December 1941.

desperate plea by British Prime Minister Winston Churchill for 50 old but reconditioned American destroyers, Roosevelt granted the request in August 1940, in exchange for military bases on British possessions in the Western Hemisphere. The 'destroyer deal' was announced as an executive agreement on 3 September and justified as improving the defenses of the United States and as a step away from war. The deal, however, decisively marked the end of American neutrality and the beginning of a firm commitment to Britain. That same month Congress passed the draft bill.

As the presidential election of 1940 neared, the bipartisan foreign policy of greater aid to the Allies broke down. The Republican nominee, Wendell Wilkie, who had supported the destroyer deal and the draft, charged that Roosevelt was manipulating the United States toward war. Roosevelt, who had tried to balance preparedness with peace, denied the charge and flatly told the American public just prior to the election that 'your boys are not going to be sent into any foreign wars.' Not wishing to change leaders in the midst of the crisis, the American electorate gave Roosevelt an unprecedented third consecutive term.

Secure in office, Roosevelt began to move the United States toward war on the side of Britain at a pace the American public would support. After Britain announced it could no longer pay for war supplies on a cash-and-carry basis, Roosevelt announced a policy of 'lend-lease' – on its surface 'lending' Britain supplies, but in reality giving them away. In March 1941 Congress passed the Lend-Lease bill by a solid majority, giving Roosevelt sweeping powers over the procurement and transfer of any defense article to any government.

Despite increasing support, Roosevelt still felt constrained from taking stronger actions that were likely to bring the country to the brink of war. He was waiting for a decisive event that he

could use to break the domestic deadlock and bring a united nation into the conflict. In the absence of that event Roosevelt continued to move slowly and cautiously, only taking steps he was certain the country and Congress would support. In early 1941 Roosevelt created the Office of Production Management in an attempt to cope with serious shortages and 'bottlenecks' in the rearmament program. In May Roosevelt proclaimed a state of unlimited national emergency. In June Hitler launched a massive invasion of conquest against the Soviet Union. That same month Roosevelt continued his policy of placing ever-increasing restrictions on trade with Germany's ally, Japan, by announcing that oil would no longer be shipped to Japan from ports on the eastern seaboard. The action carried a clearly implied threat to cut off all oil trade to the Japanese, thus rendering the Imperial Fleet useless.

Meanwhile, as German sinkings of Allied transports continued at a horrifying rate, Churchill, along with Roosevelt's secretaries of war and the navy, pressed the President to expand the American commitment in the Atlantic to the actual convoying of British shipping. Others also attempted to move the President on this issue: Secretary of the Treasury Henry Morgenthau, Attorney General Robert Jackson, Supreme Court justice Felix Frankfurter and advisers Archibald MacLeish and William Bullitt were only the more prominent of many voices. Still Roosevelt waited for some major provocation by Hitler.

Following a series of British military reverses in the spring of 1941 Roosevelt continued his policy of incremental interventionism. In July Roosevelt froze all Japanese assets in the United States and dispatched American troops to occupy Iceland, but he still held back from ordering a policy of 'shoot on sight' or the open escorting of British ships in the Atlantic. Roosevelt's caution appeared justified. In August the House of Representatives extended the Selective Service Act of 1940 by only

a single vote, 203-202, thereby perfectly reflecting the narrow 51 percent of the American people who supported the extension. Popular attitudes toward Roosevelt's actions remained consistent throughout 1941: about one-fourth of the nation felt the President had gone 'too far,' about one-fourth 'not far enough,' with the remaining half declaring that he had moved 'about right.'

Events began to move quickly now. With the draft safely secured for an additional 18 months, Roosevelt granted the navy permission to convoy ships to Iceland and to chase German U-Boats. Not surprisingly, shortly thereafter a German submarine attacked, but did not hit, an American destroyer. On 11 September Roosevelt announced that the US Navy would henceforth 'shoot on sight,' and the United States at last entered a shooting, albeit undeclared, war with Germany. As a further step, Roosevelt sought yet another revision of the neutrality laws to allow the arming of American merchant ships and their movement into war zones. (Meanwhile, the USS *Kearney* was struck by a torpedo while on convoy duty, with the loss of 11 crewmen.) In November Congress repealed the ban on the arming of merchant ships, but only by an uncomfortably close 212-194 vote in the House. Clearly, Congress was not yet ready for a declaration of war.

The decisive event Roosevelt had waited for occurred not in the Atlantic, where he expected it, but in the mid Pacific, by way of a stunning Japanese surprise attack on the US naval fleet stationed at Pearl Harbor. In response, the miasma of isolationism dissipated more quickly than the dense plumes of gray and black smoke that rose over the Hawaiian Islands that day. With Roosevelt's ringing denunciation of that 'day of infamy,' and with Hitler's (perhaps uncalled for) declaration of war on the United States, America entered the Second World War. Wilson's war to 'make the world safe for democracy' would have to be fought all over again.

Latin America

For Latin America as for most of the world, the period between the two World Wars is a natural historical epoch. Although the contours of the period might be established by internal analyses, international economic trends yield the handiest point of departure. Three interwar trends had important effects on Latin American societies and polities: the stabilization or contraction of the foreign trade of the industrial nations; the relative deterioration in the world price for Latin American raw material exports; and the relative growth in the volume of raw materials in world trade, attributable to rising petroleum exports and to the protectionist policies of industrial nations. During the interwar decades the industrial nations accumulated capital, improved technology, increased per capita output and raised living standards for sizeable sectors of their populations. 'Peripheral' nations were meanwhile shifting selectively from subsistence to export agriculture, mining and petroleum production, thus improving their capacity to import and

benefiting privileged urban groups but effecting relatively little 'development' or structural change.

By depriving Latin America of its usual customers and industrial suppliers, the outbreak of World War I revealed some key implications of the region's external commercial dependence. One result of the crisis was an immediate acceleration of import substitution, particularly in those zones (Buenos Aires, southern Brazil, central Chile, central Mexico) where consumer industries such as textiles, food-processing, glass, cement and chemicals were flourishing. After the Allies cleared the sea lanes and began purchasing foodstuffs, metals and petroleum, first for the war effort, then for postwar recuperation, Latin America enjoyed an Indian summer of prosperity, marred only by localized calamities such as the collapse of the Brazilian rubber and Cuban sugar booms and disruption of the Mexican economy by civil war. From 1914 to 1929 Argentina, Uruguay and Chile doubled or tripled their wheat production; Argentina quadrupled its cattle exports;

Brazil and Peru respectively doubled and tripled cotton production; and total Latin American coffee production rose from 11.2 to 22.5 million tons, or 92 percent of the world supply. At the same time, Bolivian tin production doubled, Chilean copper production increased more than sixfold and Venezuelan oil production rose from nil to 137 million barrels. In Argentina, a leading case of industrial growth, annual value of production rose from 43 to 147 million gold pesos for textiles and from 29.8 to 62.5 million for mechanical industries.

But by the late 1920s economic storm signals had appeared. Recovery and expansion of European agriculture and competition from other continents were closing down markets for Latin American produce, while technology continued to deliver synthetic substitutes for the region's raw materials. The buying power of Latin America's rural populations could not keep pace with the expansion of domestic industry, a problem compounded after 1926 by European dumping.

Left: A valuable export earner for Chile was the copper extracted from local mines. The 1920s saw a dramatic increase in copper production but the Great Depression led to a massive drop in world prices; mineral producers were particularly hard hit and production slumped.

Above right: The first Venezuelan oil well dug at San Tomé.

Right: President Francisco Madero of Mexico, who was imprisoned in 1913 and later shot – a victim of the turbulent Mexican political situation.

Far right: Two folk heroes of Mexico – Pancho Villa and Emiliano Zapata in 1914.

Although Latin American trade balances were generally favorable throughout the 1920s, a rising tide of foreign loans and investment, which did little to revamp national systems of production or to diversify exports, laid heavy claims against exchange earnings. Thus in 1928 Argentina enjoyed a favorable trade balance of 131 million pesos, but service on its foreign debt came to twice that amount. Brazil's $10 million balance stood in a similar ratio to debt service. That same year Bolivia hypothecated 80 percent of its national revenue against payment of the public debt, internal and external.

The heavy inflow of capital reflected the rise of the United States to near-parity with Britain as one of Latin America's two leading creditors. While British investments were edging up from $5 billion in 1913 to $5.9 billion in 1929, those of the United States jumped from $2 million to $5.6 billion; and whereas before World War I US investments were largely confined to Mexico and the Caribbean zone, by 1929 44.7 percent of United States investments in Latin America were in the South American continent. An aggressive

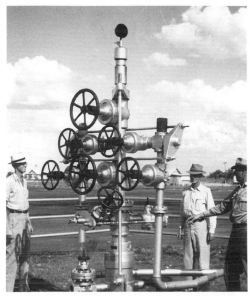

United States banking network sprang up to rival Britain's; by 1925 70 percent of Latin America's foreign commercial transactions were being cleared in dollars through New York. This commercial and financial ascendancy fulfilled a United States policy aspiration dating from at least the First Pan American Conference of 1889. The new era differed from the British- or European-dominated period because of the United States' politico-strategic interests in the Western Hemisphere and its precipitate Caribbean interventions and occupations. It differed further in that the British had enjoyed commercial hegemony in a preindustrial Latin America, while the United States assumed financial and technological leadership at a time of regional industrialization.

The Great Depression gave Latin America a solid push on the path toward import substitution. A sudden consequence of the crash was a 25 percent reduction in the volume of world trade for the period 1929-33 and a 30 percent drop in the average price of exports. Latin America, with its heavy reliance on export earnings, suffered conspicuously. Mineral producers, dependent on the industrial activity of their trade partners, were hit especially hard; so were exporters of tropical agricultural products, which were relatively inelastic in supply and therefore subject to violent price drops. Temperate exporters such as Argentina fared better because the possibilities of reducing cultivated areas or of shifting crops made for elasticity of supply. Mineral exporters (Chile, Mexico) were worse off, and Brazil was badly hit by the precipitous drop in coffee prices.

The shock of the Depression prompted Latin American governments to take measures designed to limit the outflow of currency, increase exports, decrease imports and encourage domestic production of hitherto imported commodities. These included quotas, licensing, embargoes, protective tariffs, currency devaluation (alleged to favor exports over imports), subsidies and tax exemption for industry and systems of exchange control by which central banks or agencies established multiple rates of foreign exchange to foster developmentally stra-

tegic exports and deter nonessential imports. More focused and interventionist planning was achieved through 'development corporations,' the prototype being Chile's Corporación de Fomento, chartered in 1939 for the initial purpose of assisting recuperation from a severe earthquake.

Although certain economic measures were a direct response to international crisis, the 'external jolt' thesis does not provide a comprehensive interpretation of the period. The climate of economic nationalism that became prevalent in the 1930s, while exacerbated by world depression, was associated with longer-term trends of national integration, ideological and cultural self-assertion and resistance to external interference, trends richly exemplified in the Mexican case.

The outbreak of the Mexican Revolution in 1910 is traceable only secondarily to external influences. More directly it stemmed from the progressive sclerosis of the Díaz regime, the unrelenting exploitation of the poor and the increasing discontent of the well-to-do with Díaz' favoritism, *continuismo* and repression. Principal spokesmen for the underdogs were the Regeneration group who, inspired in part by the precepts of international anarchism, formed a liberal party and in 1906 issued a Manifesto in exile from St Louis, Missouri, outlining comprehensive reforms for the rural and urban proletariat. While many of their prescriptions later appeared in the 1917 Constitution, the movement that overthrew Díaz and touched off a many-phased, quasi-permanent revolution found its initial leader in the unlikely person of Francisco I Madero, a scion of northern landholders, whose gentle, sometimes awkward manner concealed a strain of mysticism and serene sense of destiny. In his book *The Presidential Succession in 1910* published in 1908 Madero not only voiced a widely supported demand for effective suffrage and no reelection but also criticized absolutism, militarism, bossism and subservience to foreigners, as well as espousing a broad school program and modest agrarian and labor reform. As a presidential contender in 1910 Madero was jailed briefly, then fled to Texas, where he assumed the title of provisional president and called for a general uprising.

Small heterogeneous bands rallied to Madero's cause: poor farmers, ranchers, miners, dispossessed peons, teachers and intellectuals, smugglers, drifters. Men such as Pascual Orozco and Pancho Villa in Chihuahua and Emiliano Zapata in Morelos provided improvised, magnetic leadership to offset the lack of coordination and common purpose. Perhaps 20,000 guerrillas were involved in multiple uprisings reminiscent of the populist insurrections under Hidalgo and Morelos a century earlier. Now, however, the nation's demoralized center crumbled, and Díaz went into exile in May 1911. Assumption of power placed Madero in a hurricane's eye of pressures from hacendados, agrarian reformers, heirs of the Porfiriato, dissident ex-comrades, the traditional military, revolutionary generals and the United States embassy's machinations in favor of 'law and order.' Madero was jailed in February 1913, and soon shot. The next seven kaleidoscopic years produced tentative legitimation for a new regime under the aging, opportunistic, somewhat reluctant 'revolutionary' Venustiano Carranza.

The Constitution of 1917 provided mechanisms and guidelines for gradually carrying out the goals of the Revolution. This document, while preserving the liberal principles of 1857, gave the executive broad powers, authorized the federal government to vacate abusive state governments (a power invoked 40 times in 20 years to curb regional chieftains) and supplemented the rights of single persons with guarantees for 'organic' bodies such as occupation groups, syndicates and municipalities. The innovative articles, such as those that subordinated and regulated the Church, authorized land reform and resource nationalization and gave labor its bill of rights, were regarded by vested interests at home and abroad as 'revolutionary' in the pejorative sense and an assault on hallowed civil and religious freedoms. The obstreperous labor movement and anticlericalism of the 1920s, along with the large-scale land distributions, 'socialist' education campaign and oil expropriations of the 1930s, lent support to this assessment. From the Mexican viewpoint the Revolution is not seen as a violent interlude between a discredited regime and a new order grounded on fresh rights and principles. Rather, the Revolution *itself* has been legitimized, giving long-term institutional form, as it were, to the principle of political expediency. The success of this venture is exemplified in the shifting designation of the official party which dominates political life: National Revolutionary Party (to 1938), Party of the Mexican Revolution (1938-46), Institutional Revolutionary Party (since 1946).

Along with innovation and expediency the Revolution exhibited traditionalist features. The nation's subsoil was declared the patrimony of the state, as it had been in colonial times. *Ejido*, the ancient name for the Spanish municipal commons, was applied to the communalistic farm units that were allocated public or expropriated lands. The Indian was restored to a position of tutelage, and schoolteachers departed for remote rural areas with the fervor of the early missionaries. Oppressed groups in general were eventually reincorporated to national society through paternalistic syndicates and government agencies. Mural painters revived the tradition of a monumental public art that associated the masses with the broad purposes of the state. A complex interventionist state apparatus was elaborated, reminiscent of the mercantilist state of old.

In recent years a neo-Marxist interpretation of the Mexican Revolution has been advanced, purporting to account for both innovative and retrograde features. It presents the 1917 Constitution as the instrument of an incipient bourgeoisie allied with but in the long run dominating a coalition of organized workers and armed peasants. However, the argument runs, because foreign economic and financial influences prevented the full development of competitive capitalism, large groups and regions remained subject to 'internal colonialism,' and those in control came to appreciate the convenience of certain predemocratic forms: the single party, centralized political power, manipulation of suffrage, executive control of the legislature and of local government.

This interpretation agrees with standard ones that the savior of the Revolution was President Lázaro Cárdenas (1934-40), who rescued it from bossism and stagnation with massive land distributions, expropriation of foreign oil companies and a fresh infusion of ideological fervor. The newer analysis, however, goes on to explain this temporary nationalistic-democratic euphoria as the apogee of the alliance between the bourgeois state and the people. Thereafter, as Mexico industrialized and its export agriculture was mechanized and capitalized, domestic economic interests were increasingly linked with foreign ones.

As summarized here, the neo-Marxist analysis is weighted toward a politico-economic calculus. It overlooks the long-term cultural determinants of Mexican history, as well as the psychological effects which the central Revolutionary myths and new chances for social and spatial mobility have had upon masses of Mexicans. The analysis is useful, however, because it coherently interrelates many phenomena and facilitates comparison with other Latin American countries.

It was once customary for admirers of the Mexican Revolution to signalize its program and achievements as a model for Latin America. This attraction is explainable by the satisfying 'completeness' of the movement, which combined a heroic, almost mythic phase; systematic sector-by-sector reforms (education, Church-state relations, land reform, public works, industrialization); and a process of institutionalization infused with an ethnic and nationalist mystique vividly rendered in folk art, novels, music and the painting of the great trio of muralists, Diego Rivera, José Clemente Orozco and David Alfaro Siqueiros. Neither the methods, however, nor much less the style of the Mexican Revolution was 'exportable.' In retrospect one might even argue that Mexico's very success caused innovations to crystalize prematurely in comparison with countries where change was more piecemeal and less productive of easy formulae and stirring symbols.

A glance at other countries reminds us that Mexico enjoyed no monopoly on cultural and ethnic self-affirmation, economic nationalism, populist reformism and resistance to foreign domination. All these tendencies were at work, for example, in Mexico's small Antillean neighbors, whose Afro-American heritage, small size and tropical export economies gave them markedly different traditions. Here the resurgent Indianism of the highland countries had its parallel in fresh concern with the black man and his heritage. In Haiti, where the question of national identity was rekindled by the United States occupation (1915-34), Jean Price-Mars reminded the intelligentsia of the strong African component of

Left: Diego Rivera's fresco of the Mexican Revolution showing how the revolutionaries put an end to corruption and debauchery.

Above right: Venustiano Carranza, President of Mexico 1913-20, an opportunistic politician rather than a true revolutionary.

Right: US marines help guard the Presidential Palace in Haiti in 1915 – an instance of US intervention in Caribbean affairs that increased steadily during the century.

their national heritage in his *Ainsi parla l'oncle* (1928). The book heralded an Afro-Haitian 'renaissance' in literature, music and the arts and had its political sequel in the 1946 'black revolution.' Two Cuban writers – social scientist and folklorist Fernando Ortiz and Nicolás Guillén – challenged elitist sensibilities with a many-dimensioned, politically charged evocation of the black man's presence in Cuban civilization. The goad to Cuban nationalism, however, was not ethnicity but growing antipathy toward the United States for its strangle-hold on the sugar economy, its external meddling, its connivance with the sordid strong-arm regime of Gerardo Machado

(1925-33). These resentments fueled the movement that ousted Machado and brought in a short-lived junta. Partly from lack of recognition by Washington, partly from internal conflict, the junta collapsed, clearing the stage for a mixed-race army sergeant, Fulgencio Batista, who dominated the political scene for a quarter of a century by opportunist tactics and his intermittent plebeian appeal.

A new reform movement

Aprismo, which arose in Peru during this period, has been one of Latin America's few indigenous political movements to achieve international momentum. Two precursors were the free-thinking anticlerical and self-styled 'philosophical anarchist' Manuel González Prada (1848-1918), who urged that the Indians cultivate pride and rebelliousness, and the self-taught, tubercular José Carlos Mariátegui (1895-1930), whose *Seven Essays Interpreting the Peruvian Reality* adapted Marxism to a national setting where the capitalist stage had faltered and class identities were weak. APRA, acronym for an international American Popular Revolutionary Alliance, was born in 1924 and was thereafter associated with the figure of Víctor Raúl Haya de la Torre (1895-   ), who broke with Mariátegui, disavowed links with international communism and developed his own pragmatic ideology. *Aprismo* called for an alliance of workers, peasants and middle groups; land distribution; nationalization policies leading to a form of state capitalism; resistance to United States imperialism; internationalization of the Panama Canal; and a grand fraternity of 'Indo American' nations. Partly because of Haya's capricious, personal style, he never gained Peru's presidency, but APRA became a permanent contender in national politics and, in the 1940s and 1950s, supplied a loose ideology for democratic leftism in Central America and the Caribbean zone.

Brazil drifted toward the crises of the 1930s without benefit of militant ideology or clear prospects for structural change. In 1920 the population of this vast nation was still at least 80 percent rural. Neither the new industrialists nor the urban workers had generated a coherent political force to counteract the plantocracy. The prosperous central and southern states of São Paulo, Minas Gerais and Rio Grande do Sul dominated national politics, while local potentates or 'colonels' reigned supreme at the grass roots. Given this situation, junior army officers assumed the burden of protest in the 1920s. Often of lower-middle-class origins, disenchanted with civilian rule and inheriting loose notions of technocratic positivism from their nineteenth-century predecessors, the *tenentes* (lieutenants) plotted to shake up the oligarchies and institute reform. Neither their 1922 and 1924 revolts nor the 1924-27 backlands march of Captain Luis Carlos Prestes (later Brazil's foremost communist) had significant results, but for a quarter of a century after 1930 individual *tenentes* were time and again catapulted to political prominence.

A series of happenstances turned the tables for Brazil in 1930: the precipitous drop in the world price for coffee, the attempt of a president from São Paulo to impose a Paulista successor and the assassination of a vice-presidential candidate. Getúlio Vargas, a shrewd, colorless, enigmatic politician from Rio Grande do Sul, was influenced by these events and their repercussions to disavow his defeat in the 1930 presidential election and to lead a virtually unopposed coup that terminated the Old Republic. Vargas then dominated the political scene until his suicide in 1954. While continuing to respect the plantocracy and state oligarchies, he increased and centralized the power of the national government, proclaiming an authoritarian, vaguely corporatist 'New State' in 1937; encouraged industrialization; and presided over a rapid expansion of his urban consti-

tuency, while bureaucracies mushroomed and the state took the initiative in unionizing labor. Urban populism began to overshadow the politics of *coronelismo*, that is, of the rural colonels.

In Argentina the aging Irigoyen, reelected in 1928, proved so ineffectual in responding to the impact of world depression that conservative groups engineered his removal in 1930 and inaugurated the long-term embroilment of the army in Argentine politics. Thus while government in Brazil took on a mild populist cast in the 1930s with its appeal for urban working classes, the Argentine regime of General Agustín P Justo (1932-38), though reasonably effective in meeting crises on the economic front, temporarily reversed the trend toward participatory politics. Marginalization of the urban lower classes in these years of economic retrenchment, industrialization and urban growth swiftly created a climate receptive to the populist appeal of Peronism.

In the cultural realm the cosmopolitan, world-weary atmosphere of Buenos Aires gave rise to distinctive modes of literary expression. In contrast to the sometimes tendentious ethnic and nationalistic emphasis of the arts in Mexico, Argentine writing displayed more evident concern with ultimate realities. Representative figures are Ricardo Güiraldes (1886-1927), whose haunting, mythopoetic novel *Don Segundo Sombra* evokes a nirvana-like vision of life on the pampas; tortured, hallucinated Roberto Arlt (1900-42), whose fiction renders city life as a nightmare and human beings as 'monsters waddling in the shadows;' Ezequiel Martínez Estrada (1895-   ), whose explosive essays relate the persistent dilemmas of Argentine life to primordial ecological and psychological tensions of a New World society. Enjoying the widest international reputation is Jorge Luis Borges (1899-   ), poet, yarn-spinner, alchemist of language and ideas, devotee of labyrinths, riddles and multiple identities, collector of trivia and priest of the occult.

Above left: An example of US-sponsored education in Haiti.

Above: Enthusiastic crowds in the old Inca capital greet President Prado of Peru.

Left: President Vargas of Brazil who gained office after a coup in 1930.

Right: Diego Rivera's mural at the Cardiac Hospital in Mexico City, with the artist providing the final touches. The mural depicts the medical advances made in the treatment of patients suffering from heart problems.

The Islamic World

When the Ottoman Empire signed the armistice on 30 October 1918 the outlook for the entire Muslim world was a grim one. Aligned with Germany and Austria-Hungary, the Turks had suffered heavy defeats on several fronts, notwithstanding their tenacious defense of the Gallipoli Peninsula in 1915 (where the outstanding commander in the field had been a young officer from Salonika, Mustafa Kemal Bey) and their capture of a British-Indian force at Kut al-Amara in Mesopotamia (Iraq) in April 1916. In March 1917 a second British-Indian expeditionary force fought its way to Baghdad, and on 9 December 1917 General Edmund Allenby, advancing from Egypt, entered Jerusalem. On 1 October 1918 Amir Faysal took possession of Damascus, ancient capital of the Umayyad Caliphs, on behalf of his father, Sharif Husayn of Mecca, so that by the date of the signing of the armistice the Arabic-speaking provinces of the empire had already been detached.

Worse was to come. The victorious Allies were bent upon punitive measures against the defeated Central Powers, among whom the Turks were regarded by a section of Anglo-Saxon public opinion with peculiar distaste, associated as they were with the 'Bulgarian Atrocities' of the 1870s and the more recent, but less publicized, Armenian massacres of the war years, the twentieth century's preliminary exercise in genocide. The terms of the Treaty of Sèvres, signed on 10 August 1920, included both the dismemberment of the former Ottoman Empire and the partition of Anatolia itself. With regard to the latter, France was to enjoy a sphere of influence in the southeast; Italy was to enjoy a similar position in the southwest, as well as outright annexation of the Dodecanese Islands; while Greece was to administer the Smyrna (Izmir) region for five years, to be followed by a plebiscite to settle its future status, and was granted possession of virtually the whole of eastern Thrace. In addition, an independent Armenia, with the United States as the presumptive Mandatory Power, and an autonomous Kurdistan were envisaged in eastern Anatolia.

As for the former Arabic-speaking provinces of the Ottoman Empire, Tripolitania (Libya) was confirmed as an Italian colony and Egypt as a British protectorate. Syria and the Lebanon were allotted to France as League of Nations Mandates, and Mesopotamia (Iraq) and Palestine went to Britain. Sharif Husayn of Mecca had previously received British assurances (the McMahon Declaration of 24 October 1915) regarding the establishment of a Hashemite Arab kingdom that would have embraced all the Arabic-speaking lands of the Fertile Crescent and the Arabian Peninsula, but these assurances were disregarded in the face of French pressure for a stake in the Middle East, as envisaged in the Anglo-French Sykes-Picot Agreement of May 1916. A further complication was the Balfour Declaration of 2 November 1917 supporting the establishment of a Jewish homeland in Palestine, which, in Arab eyes, stretched the credibility of British assurances of goodwill toward the Arabs beyond the bounds of belief. On the other hand, the Hashemites were not altogether abandoned. Faysal, it is true, was expeled from Damascus by the French in July 1920, and his father, Sharif Husayn, was driven out of the Hijaz by the forces of the Wah-

habi ruler of Najd, Abd al-ʿAziz b Saʿud (Ibn Saʿud), but the British installed ʿAbd Allah, another son of Husayn, as the ruler of Transjordan in 1921. (In 1946 Transjordan would be recognized as a kingdom and, following the assassination of King ʿAbd Allah in 1951 and the abdication of his son Talal on grounds of insanity, the throne passed to his 18-year-old grandson, Husayn.) Faysal, too, became a protégé of the British, ruling in Baghdad as King of Iraq from 1921. In 1932 the Mandate formally ended, and Faysal died in the following year, the throne thereafter passing to his son Ghazi who was killed in a motoring accident in 1939. Ghazi's son, Faysal II, was three years old at the time and in consequence Iraq was ruled for the next two decades by the regent, Amir ʿAbdal-Ilah, Faysal's uncle, and by the wily pro-Western statesman, Nuri Pasha al-Saʿid. All three were to be butchered in the *coup d'état* of 1958.

Ibn Saʿud (c 1880-1953), who had robbed the Hashemites of their age-old lordship of the Hijaz, was to prove one of the most resilient and effective Arab rulers of the twentieth century. Proclaimed King of the Hijaz in 1926 and of Najd in 1927 (formally united as Saʿudi Arabia in 1932), he began the task of dragging his unwilling kingdom into the modern age while remaining convinced that the traditional beliefs of his people should not be exposed to the innovative challenges of the infidel West. It was Ibn Saʿud's foresight that led him to grant an oil concession to an American company in 1933 (known since 1944 as Aramco), for these royalties made his sons, Saʿud and Faysal, two of the wealthiest rulers in the Arab world.

Egypt at the close of World War I had the status of a British protectorate, unilaterally proclaimed by the British government in 1914, and throughout the war years the country had served as an important base for British military and diplomatic operations in the Middle East. The Egyptians themselves, both during and immediately after

the war, were not directly concerned in the 'Arab Revolt' spearheaded by the Hashemites. Rather, they were preoccupied both with their inability to bring to an end the British occupation of their country and also with establishing their identity as Egyptians, rather than as Arabs. Egyptian nationalism even at this period was quite distinct from later pan-Arab nationalism and seemed to some contemporary European observers to have something in common with the Indian nationalist movement, another movement preoccupied with a colonial presence and with historic problems of identity.

The central figure in the Egyptian struggle for independence was Sa'ad Zaghlul Pasha (1860-1927), a shrewd, worldly, utterly dedicated patriot whose peasant origin and earthy realism had been tempered by education at al-Az'har University and by the vicissitudes of government service. By the end of the war he was recognized as the outstanding spokesman of Egypt's case for independence, and in November 1918 he personally approached the British High Commissioner, Sir Reginald Wingate, with the request that a delegation be permitted to travel to London to place before the British Government the nationalist viewpoint, a request that was peremptorily rejected by the Foreign Office. There followed four years of recurring tension and crisis, during which it was fortunate that Britain's High Com-

Left: A vigorous and intelligent Arab leader, Ibn Sa'ud unified most of the Arabian Peninsula under his personal rule in the 1920s, driving out Sharif Husayn of Mecca, and founded the kingdom of Sa'udi Arabia in 1932.

Below left: General Allenby's troops occupy Jerusalem, December 1917. Contradictory British wartime commitments to Arabs, French and Jews led to distrust and conflict in the Levant during the postwar period.

Above right: The shrewd advocate of Egyptian independence Zaghlul Pasha (third from left), photographed at Victoria station, London.

Right: Allenby, now a field marshal, and King Faysal, son of Sharif Husayn and ruler of Iraq from 1921 to 1933.

missioner in Egypt, Lord Allenby, was fairly sympathetic to the nationalist position and forcefully urged concessions on London. The result was the granting of a qualified independence in 1922, and on 19 April 1923 a constitution was promulgated. Egypt now became a constitutional monarchy, with Fuad as king.

Meanwhile, the internal situation continued to be exacerbated by the ambiguous presence of British troops on Egyptian soil and by the uncertain future status of the Sudan. Sa'ad Zaghlul died in August 1927, and his place as leader of the Wafd Party was taken by Mustafa al-Nahas Pasha, a lesser man who lacked his mentor's authority and who now had to contend with increasingly hostile influences emanating from the palace. When the Wafd won a sweeping victory in the 1929 elections Fuad revoked the 1923 Constitution and promulgated a new one in 1930; under this he ruled unchallenged through his henchman, Sidqi Pasha, until his death in 1935. The death of Fuad and the accession of the 16-year-old Faruq, the disappearance from the scene of Sidqi Pasha as a result of declining health, and renewed British concern for the security of the Suez Canal as a result of the Italian invasion of Ethiopia in 1935 gave Nahas Pasha, as Prime Minister, his opportunity. He was a more mature politician now, more aware of the advantages of compromise with the British. The Anglo-Egyptian Treaty of 26 August 1936 was a military alliance between the two countries that ended the British occupation but left British troops in the Canal Zone. Britain agreed to be responsible for the defense of Egypt in time of war, and Egypt would provide Britain with the necessary facilities. The future of the Sudan was left undetermined, a continuing source of friction, but Britain sponsored Egypt's admission to the League of Nations in May 1937. The treaty, which was to run for 20 years and which was ratified by the Egyptian Parliament in December 1936, seemed to set the seal on the personal ascendancy of Nahas Pasha, both as Prime Minister and as Leader of the dominant Wafd Party. But in 1937 Faruq came of age, and there began once more the old conflict between the palace and the Wafd.

In the decades between the World Wars the Muslim lands to the west of Egypt appeared to be more firmly under European control than either Egypt or the lands of the Fertile Crescent, for here the military and administrative framework was reinforced by the presence of assertive *colons* implacably opposed to the aspirations of the growing Western-educated Muslim elite. Even here, however, European supremacy did not pass unchallenged. In Tripolitania the Italians were unable to control much of the interior of that vast country in the face of dogged opposition from Sanusi tribesmen, while in the Spanish zone of Morocco the tribes of the Rif possessed an outstanding leader in the famous 'Abd al-Karim, a guerrilla leader of genius who administered a crushing defeat to Spanish forces near Anual during the summer of 1921 and whose troops even penetrated to the outskirts of Melilla. By 1923 the Spanish were prepared to offer favorable terms, but 'Abd al-Karim rejected them, and in 1924, at the peak of his career, he was *de facto* master of the greater part of the protectorate. In the following year he rashly extended his operations into the French protectorate, perhaps overestimating the strength of anti-colonial elements in Paris. It was a miscalculation that was to prove his undoing, for the Spanish and French governments thereupon worked together, with a total force of more than 250,000 men, to end this most formidable of all Muslim revolts against European domination prior to the Algerian war of liberation of 1954-62. 'Abd al-Karim was forced to surrender in May 1926 and was condemned to a 21-year exile on the French island of Réunion.

East of the Ottoman Empire, the prospects for the Muslim world were no less grim. Iran (known officially as Persia until 1934) had been a bone of contention between Russia and Britain throughout the nineteenth century, and in 1907 an Anglo-Russian convention had actually partitioned the country into northern (Russian) and southern (British) spheres of influence, with a neutral zone

dividing them. On the outbreak of war in 1914, notwithstanding the Shah's declaration of neutrality, Russian and British-Indian forces occupied the country on the pretext that a Turkish invasion was imminent and that German agents were infiltrating the tribes. By the end of the war the country was on the verge of anarchy, with famine ravaging wide areas. The Qajar regime was on its last legs, but the only apparent alternative, the constitutional movement that had surfaced in 1905 in response to foreign economic exploitation and the incompetence of the administration, was proving a sickly offspring. In the provinces such authority as there was lay mainly with the tribal *khans*.

British exploitation of Iran

The Russian Revolution of 1917, which took Russia out of the war, and the Soviet government's nullification of all the concessions and privileges enjoyed by the czarist government in Iran, left the British as the sole imperial power with a stake in the area. Lord Curzon, in particular, saw in the situation an opportunity to extend the flanking western bastions of British India across Iran to link up with the mandate regimes in Iraq and Palestine, giving Britain a block of client-states stretching from Baluchistan to the Mediterranean. There was also the question of oil. The Anglo-Persian Oil Company had been formed in 1909 to operate in the Takht-i Sulaiman area of

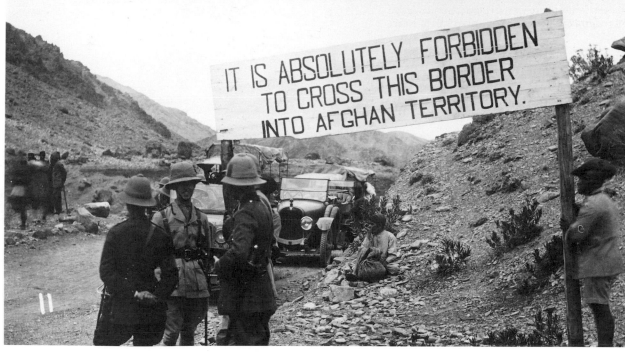

Below left: Anglo-Persian Oil Company installations at Abadan, Iran, in 1911.

Left: The same Abadan oilfields 20 years later. Despite the preponderant influence of British oil interests in the Iranian economy, the country maintained a precarious independence.

Right: The border between Afghanistan and British India at the Khyber Pass. The Anglo-Afghan War of 1919 established this as the limit of British power and influence.

Below: Muhammad Ali Jinnah, the political leader of India's Muslim population.

southwestern Iran, and in 1914 Winston Churchill, First Lord of the Admiralty, had purchased 55 percent of the company's stock on behalf of the British Government. An Anglo-Iranian treaty of 9 August 1919 gave the British everything which they wanted, but the Majlis, the Iranian Parliament, refused to ratify the treaty, and the British, with worldwide commitments and concerned with military retrenchment, were compeled to acquiesce.

In post-war India the Muslims were restless and leaderless. While thousands of Muslim troops had fought in the Indian Army in campaigns as far afield as Mesopotamia, East Africa and the Western Front, politically minded Muslims were still divided as to whether to throw in their lot with the Hindu-dominated Congress movement or to demand separate representation in any future constitutional devolution of power envisaged by the British. They had felt peculiarly distressed at the sight of the British and Ottoman

Empires lined up on opposite sides in the war, and some Muslim regiments sent to Mesopotamia had mutinied rather than fight the troops of the Sultan-Caliph. As the war progressed and the Allies began to discuss the post-war settlement Indian Muslims, anticipating the dismemberment of the Ottoman Empire, became increasingly anxious regarding Allied intentions toward the person of the Sultan-Caliph and toward the holy cities of Arabia. As early as 1916 a brilliant young Muslim lawyer, Muhammad 'Ali Jinnah, had been instrumental in bringing together for a brief honeymoon the Indian National Congress and the Muslim League in the Lucknow Pact, and from 1919 onward the Khilafat Movement protesting infidel intentions toward the Sultan-Caliph drew warm support from Gandhi. But increased Hindu-Muslim tension and violence from 1922 onward, coupled with Mustafa Kemal's decision to proclaim a republic in 1923 and to abolish the office of Caliph in 1924, once again turned the Indian Muslims in upon themselves, putting them on the road that was to lead to the creation of Pakistan in 1947.

The Afghan government, meanwhile, took advantage of British preoccupation with the war and of the reduced military garrisons on the northwest frontier to intervene in tribal politics on the British side of the Durand Line. The British retaliated in what became the Third Afghan War (1919), which terminated with a peace treaty in which Britain recognized Afghanistan's right to conduct independent relations with foreign governments and acknowledged the Amir's new title of King.

In Russia the situation of the Muslim population was far worse than in India. There had been the savage uprising and even more savage suppression of the Kazakh tribes in 1916, and although with the coming of the Revolution the Tatars of the Crimea and the Volga and the Central Asian Turks anticipated some form of federal autonomy within the new Soviet regime, they were to be cruelly disillusioned. In Tashkent Soviet workers ruthlessly suppressed manifestations of Turkestani political consciousness, and a short-lived Muslim government in Kokand was soon crushed, the Khanate of Khiva was extinguished in 1919, as was the Amirate of Bukhara in 1920. Elsewhere, on the Kazakh steppes and in

Bashkiria, the Muslim population found itself trapped between the Red and White Armies, harried first by one and then by the other. Only very gradually did the Soviet regime evolve something approaching a consistent policy toward these minorities, but before it could do so anti-Russian feeling had manifested itself in the appearance of political organizations that combined Muslim reformism with the demand for political autonomy and, more seriously, in resistance movements such as that of the Basmachis in the mountains of eastern Bukhara, which adopted pan-Turkish or pan-Turanian slogans. It was not until the late 1920s that the Red Army got the better of the Basmachis, many of whom fled into neighboring Afghanistan.

From the 1930s onward the Soviet Government organized the Muslims of Central Asia into separate republics – Uzbek, Kazakh, Kirghiz, Tadzhik and Turkmen – where, in addition to stressing their organic relationship to the Soviet Union as a whole, emphasis was placed upon the distinct cultural and linguistic heritage and on the separate historical development of each republic, thereby aiming to prevent any resurgence of earlier pan-Turanian, pan-Turkish or pan-Islamic movements. The extent to which these peoples were now able to shape their own destinies depended partly upon the demographic situation. In Kazakhstan, for example, the Kazakhs themselves were hopelessly outnumbered by European colonists from the west, whereas the Uzbeks remained the dominant majority in Uzbekistan and thus retained considerable scope for preserving their ethnic identity. In general, the Central Asian republics have shown few signs of that restlessness manifested in some of the other republics of the Soviet Union. Their apparent orthodoxy may be rooted in the authoritarian traditions of past centuries or in a prudent assessment of the odds against successful liberalization of the regime, but with the extremely high birth-rate of the Muslim *vis-à-vis* the non-Muslim population of the Soviet Union, it may be that time and demography is on their side.

The problem of modernization: Turkey

The problems of the Muslim world in the first half of the twentieth century went far deeper than the greed and machinations of the European powers, for those problems were basically psychological ones. At the heart of the matter was the fundamental incompatibility between the Muslim vision of history, in which the Muslims saw themselves as the heirs of a historic process that set them apart from all other peoples in their recognition of the Islamic revelation, and the indisputable fact that at least since the eighteenth century power and wealth, military superiority and advanced technological knowledge had been a monopoly of Christian Europe.

There were a number of possible intellectual responses to this paradox. There was the reactionary and obscurantist response – characteristic of perhaps most members of the *ulama* – of rejecting Western values *in toto*, of trying to reinforce traditional mores and of taking comfort in the reflection that the Will of Allah was inscrutable and that the present plight of the community was no doubt a punishment for unrighteousness in times past. Others maintained that the deplorable state of the Muslim world, and the obvious contempt with which Europeans viewed Islamic civilization, was the result of failings of the Muslims themselves, above all their falling away from the simple virtues of the age of the Prophet and his Companions.

Others attempted a restatement of Islamic values and Islamic goals. One theory that was to prove both attractive and illusory was pan-Islamism, which found an ardent if erratic exponent in Jamal al-Din Afghani (1839-97), whose ideas for a time attracted the support of the Ottoman Sultan, 'Abd al-Hamid (1876-1909). More constructive than Jamal al-Din Afghani in the long run was his one-time disciple, Muhammad Abduh (1849-1905), who believed that the malaise of Islam was not due solely to European aggression and that likewise its cure did not lie with the kind of febrile political intrigues in which Afghani busied himself. To Abduh what was called for was a profound re-thinking of the nature of the Islamic faith and a search for a balance between the injunctions of true religion and the inescapable exigencies of modern life, a balance as hard to establish today as it was in Abduh's lifetime.

The Western-educated elite felt a generally inarticulate frustration at the lot of their community, but they did not become atheists or unbelievers: it was easier to blame the British. Indeed, however far education and occupation took them out of the traditional social framework, they usually maintained a large measure of outward piety and observed the precepts of Muslim belief and ritual within the environment of home and family. Their lifestyles nevertheless continued to change, often imperceptibly, and there emerged an acquisitive attitude toward the amenities of European civilization, developing (as in the case of Iran in the middle of the twentieth century) into an avid consumerism more destructive of traditional values than all the rhetoric of Christian missionaries, the example of foreign teachers or the threat of European gun-boats.

It was to fight this kind of creeping materialism, as well as to combat the example of Ataturk's Turkey, that an obscure Egyptian schoolmaster, Hasan al-Banna, founded in 1928 the organization known as the Muslim Brotherhood, an activist movement with a terrorist wing that was to inspire a number of somewhat similar quasi-secret societies, such as the Devotees of Islam and the Warriors of Islam, two terrorist organizations that surfaced in Iran after the Second World War. But the Muslim Brotherhood was certainly more than a simple terrorist organization. It sought to restore the glories of the Islamic past, but it believed that the road back to that past was

Left: An officer of Kemal's Turkish nationalist army, accompanied by his staff. The fighting skills of such men made an important contribution to the revival of Turkish fortunes in the early 1920s.

Right: Kemal (in the pale coat) flanked by his diplomatic corps in the nationalist capital, Ankara, during the 1921-22 war with Greece.

Below: Mustafa Kemal Pasha, later called Kemal Ataturk – 'Father of the Turks.' He was already a distinguished war hero before emerging as the founder of the modern Turkish state.

through moral regeneration. In this way it bore comparison with the contemporary Fascist ideology of the 1930s, feeding similar frustrations and aggressions.

To contemplate the glories of the past was a recurring way of restoring Muslim self-esteem. Its antithesis was to reject the past and to look to the future in the belief that Muslims no less than Christians could once more gain control over their own destinies. This approach did not necessarily involve the rejection of Muslim values *per se*, but it necessarily rejected those vestiges of Islamic traditionalism which might obstruct the task of national and social renovation, a task in which it was perhaps less meaningful to be a Muslim than a Turk, an Iranian or an Egyptian. The uniquely successful exponent of this approach was Mustafa Kemal Pasha (1881-1938), known after 1935 as Kemal Ataturk.

That Turkey should have been the first Muslim country seriously to undertake modernization along European lines is not surprising. Physical proximity to Europe, centuries of intercourse with Europeans and the existence in the empire of substantial Christian and Jewish minorities meant that the Turks were better placed than other Muslims to assess the nature of Western institutions. Modernization of the army had begun under Sultan Mahmud II (1808-39) and during the Tanzimat period (1839-77) major reforms had been initiated in the civil service and in higher education, while the intellectual climate was molded by a brilliant if unrepresentative group of intellectuals, among whom the most famous were Namik Kemal (1840-87), Ziya Pasha (1825-80) and Ibrahim Shinasi (1826-71), who had long been exposed to European, and especially French, cultural influences. The climax of the Tanzimat movement came in 1876, with the granting of a parliamentary constitution, the crowning achievement of Midhat Pasha (1822-83), a dis-

tinguished administrator of the Danubian and Mesopotamian provinces as well as a former Grand Vazir.

The Constitution of 1876 had been preceded by the enforced abdication of Sultan Murad V on grounds of insanity and his replacement by his brother, 'Abd al-Hamid, a paranoiac reactionary who promptly set out to undo the achievements of the preceding decades, beginning with the Constitution itself. The generation of the Tanzimat was accordingly silenced or driven into exile where, among the *émigrés* in Paris, the 'Young Turk' movement was born. For the next two decades the Ottoman Empire was held together by a policy of sheer repression. Below the surface, however, there was an active underground politi-

cal life centering on the Committee of Union and Progress, a secret society founded in Istanbul in 1889, and on the Ottoman Society of Liberty, established by a group of revolutionary officers in Salonika. In 1908, when the Great Powers were threatening a further dismemberment of the empire's Balkan provinces, the Committee of Union and Progress sent the Sultan an ultimatum demanding the restoration of the 1876 Constitution. The Sultan capitulated and summoned parliament, but the situation remained fluid and uncertain as conservatives and moderates jostled for power. In April 1909 the Young Turks emerged victorious from the factional fighting. 'Abd al-Hamid was compeled to abdicate and the new Sultan, Muhammad V, became a puppet in the hands of the new rulers of the empire.

Between 1909 and 1914 the Young Turks endeavored to grapple with the problems of maintaining and renovating the imperial fabric, so long neglected and woven of such diverse material, but their efforts at centralization were opposed by those who sought more, not less, provincial autonomy, and the Young Turks' obsession with pan-Turkish and pan-Turanian slogans alienated the non-Turkish components of the empire, both Muslim and Christian. In the last years of peace prior to the holocaust of 1914 the empire continued to flounder aimlessly, with Albania in revolt in 1910, the Italians occupying Tripolitania in 1911 and with the disastrous Balkan War breaking out in 1912. Fearful of Russian ambitions, disillusioned by the policies of Britain and France toward the Middle East and impressed by German military might, the Ottoman Empire allied itself with the Central Powers. The outcome was to be defeat and dismemberment.

One factor which increasingly bedeviled all speculation regarding the future of the empire was the question of identity. What did this plural society of competing communities and faiths stand for in an age of feverish nationalist sentiment? How could the conflicting aspirations of Turk, Arab, Armenian, Greek and Macedonian be contained within this supra-national body? These questions had long been under discussion among Ottoman statesmen and reformers, as well as among foreign diplomats and observers. It was the genius of Mustafa Kemal, the later Ataturk, that solved these questions at once and for all time by severing the Turks of Asia Minor from their ponderous Ottoman and imperial past. In retrospect, the solution seems an obvious one, but it needed the humiliation of foreign occupation and the peril of national extinction to enable the transition to be made. Mustafa Kemal was no iconoclastic junior officer staging a *coup d'état* but a respected national figure, a war hero and an experienced field commander whose early years had been spent participating in the hopes and fears of the Young Turk movement. When he set out with cool deliberation to build a new Turkey it was because he had satisfied himself that nothing could be expected from the old.

The invertebrate acceptance by the Sultan's government of the humiliating terms of the Treaty of Sèvres utterly discredited a regime already politically and morally bankrupt. Meanwhile, Mustafa Kemal and those who thought like him had availed themselves of the period following the signing of the armistice to mobilize public opinion in favor of a six-point peace program that would at least ensure the integrity of Anatolia. This program was adopted by the National Assembly in January 1920, and the British retaliated by occupying Istanbul in March. By then, however, Mustafa Kemal and his supporters were assembling at Ankara in the heart of Anatolia, and on 23 April 1920 they proclaimed a provisional government and the creation of a Grand National Assembly, while denouncing the Sultan's government in Istanbul for its pusillanimous surrender of the nation's interests. Thereafter events played into the hands of the Nationalists. The greatest danger came not from the Sultan's nerveless government but from the likelihood of combined Allied intervention, but here post-war rivalries combined with Mustafa Kemal's skill in playing off the Allies against each other to give the Nationalists maximum room for maneuver. In the spring of 1920 the French were driven back to Aleppo; in December 1920 the frontier with the Soviet Union was delineated by the Treaty of Gümrü; in March 1921 the Italians were bought out; and in October 1921 the frontier with the French mandate of Syria was delineated and various outstanding disagreements were settled by negotiation. This left only the Greeks and the British, the latter more than a little preoccupied with issues elsewhere.

At first the Greeks, encouraged by the apparent collapse of their ancient foe, pushed eastward from Izmir toward Ankara with a view to taking possession of the greater part of western Anatolia. Turkish resistance proved feeble until the River Sakarya was reached, but there the Greeks, their supply-line with their base in Izmir dangerously over-extended, were halted in a bloody three-week battle (24 August – 16 September 1921). Within a year the Turks were able to mount a counter-offensive and on 9 September 1922 Mustafa Kemal entered Izmir, and the Greek forces were expelled from the Turkish mainland. The Treaty of Sèvres had become a dead-letter: it was replaced by the Treaty of Lausanne (24 July 1923), which marked international recognition of the new Turkey. The terms of the treaty gave the Turks good cause for rejoicing. The hated Capitations were abolished, Turkey (unlike Germany or Austria) was exempted from the payment of reparations and eastern Thrace and some Aegean islands were restored to Turkish sovereignty. The Straits were demilitarized and opened to world

shipping and compulsory exchanges of population were negotiated between Turkey and Greece.

From this point onward Mustafa Kemal's principal concerns were internal: in particular, how to modernize Turkey so that she should take her place as a European nation-state, not as one of the unstable, quasi-dependent regimes of the Middle East. From 1923 until his death in 1938 this was to be the consuming passion of this truly remarkable statesman, the most far-sighted yet realistic of the dictators of the twentieth century and paradoxically a dictator sincerely committed to guiding his fellow countrymen toward the goal of parliamentary democracy. On 14 October 1923 Ankara officially replaced Istanbul as the capital, and on 29 October the Republic was proclaimed, with Mustafa Kemal as its first president. The proclamation of the Republic carried with it the end of the Sultanate and the Caliphate, both abolished on 3 March 1924. Thereafter there were promulgated a series of measures designed to drag the Turkish people, willingly or unwillingly, into line with twentieth-century Europe. The principles behind these measures were defined by Mustafa Kemal as consisting of republicanism, nationalism, populism, statism, secularism and reformism, and in 1937 they were embodied in the Turkish Constitution. Nor were they mere slogans, for the architect of the new Turkey was a man of deeds as well as words. In 1926 the Muslim legal system was replaced by legal codes based on Swiss civil and Italian criminal law. The Muslim calendar was abolished, and the working week ran from Sunday to Sunday instead of from Friday to Friday.

The once-powerful dervish orders were suppressed, and in 1928 Latin script replaced Arabic.

In 1934 former titles were abolished, and everyone was required to take a European-style surname: Mustafa Kemal took the name of Ataturk, and his faithful lieutenant, Ismet Pasha, that of Inönü to commemorate his two early victories over the Greeks. European clothes became obligatory for men, and clerical dress in particular was outlawed, as was the veiling of women. Polygamy was abolished, and women were given the vote.

All this and much more was carried out with a surprising degree of success and with relatively muted opposition from the more conservative elements in Turkish society. Latent hostility to the regime, especially among the rural population, continued to be felt, however, to a far greater extent than the self-confident elites of Ankara and Istanbul were prepared to recognize, and it was on this hitherto ignored, resentful and profoundly conservative block of voters that the Democrat Party built its majorities between 1950 and 1960, when a military *coup d'état* overturned the government of the day. The violence with which the Turkish army and the opposition Republican People's Party, led by the aging Inönü,

Left: Greek refugees flee from Smyrna (now Izmir) in September 1922, as Turkish forces enter the city. The peace agreement the following year provided for further forced exchanges of populations.

Below left: Turks celebrate around the national flag in Izmir after their decisive military victory.

Right: The modest parliament building of the new Turkish Republic in Ankara.

Below right: The Turkish national assembly in session, November 1923. Kemal Ataturk remained President of Turkey until his death in 1938.

proscribed the Democrat Party leaders (Adnan Menderes, the former Prime Minister, was tried and executed) was not, however, merely a ferocious jockeying for place in the corridors of power. In the view of the army and the supporters of the Republican People's Party, the Democrat Party had embarked upon policies which threatened the very foundations of Ataturk's achievement, and that was why they had to be swept from power and punished. This polarization between those committed to the principles of the revolution and those who are not remains an unresolved dilemma in present-day Turkish politics, constituting not the least of the problems facing a still predominantly agrarian society where underdevelopment is not, unlike the case of neighboring Iran, offset by the availability of massive oil revenues.

The problem of modernization: Iran

The development of Iran during the period prior to the Second World War offers both an obvious comparison with and a significant contrast to that of Turkey. Like Turkey, Iran in 1919 appeared to have a most uncertain future. Throughout the nineteenth century the country had been exposed to far less European influence than the Ottoman Empire, and such as it was it had been largely destructive of Iranian national pride. For a hundred years the nation's affairs had been controled by three ineffective and traditionally minded monarchs – Fath 'Ali Shah (1796-1834), Muhammad Shah (1834-48) and Nasir al-Din Shah (1848-96) – and when the Constitutional Movement of 1905 ushered in long-delayed institutional and administrative reforms, the country possessed only a pitifully small and unrepresentative Western-educated elite to provide an alternative leadership to that of the Qajar family, the court nobility, the tribal *khans* and the *ulama*. But this elite did possess one overwhelming advantage *vis-à-vis* the elite of the Ottoman Empire: a strong sense of national identity compounded of culture, language and a profound feeling for the land of Iran itself.

Exasperation with the incompetence of Qajar rule and the near-successful bid by the British to bring Iran into their imperial system account for the ease with which, on 21 February 1921, a *coup*

d'état was staged by Sayyid Zia al-Din Tabatabai, a not especially prominent journalist, and Riza Khan, a colonel of the Iranian Cossack regiment, which prior to the Russian Revolution had been commanded by czarist officers. On 24 May 1921 Riza Khan, now Minister of War, ousted his former ally, but it was not until October 1923 that he assumed the position of Prime Minister. He was already the most powerful man in the country, enjoying the enthusiastic support of the army, now undergoing a program of rapid modernization, and of the military governors of the provinces, who were his willing agents. The last Qajar ruler, Ahmad Shah, who was soon to leave for his last vacation in Europe (February 1924), counted for nothing, and the Majlis, completing the second decade of its existence, was both factious and ineffective. Republicanism was in vogue among the small Western-educated elite, influenced in part by the course of events in Turkey, but this was counterbalanced by the vociferous opposition of the *ulama*, who manipulated public opinion in the bazaar. When the Majlis deposed the last Qajar Shah on 31 October

1925 and voted for the convening of a constituent assembly, it appeared that Iran was about to follow the example of Turkey, with Riza Khan as its Mustafa Kemal, but there the similarity gave way, for on 12 December 1925 Prime Minister Riza Khan was transformed into Riza Shah, founder and first ruler of the Pahlavi Dynasty.

Why did Riza Khan not follow the example of Mustafa Kemal and become first citizen of an Iranian Republic? Partly on account of the strength of the clerical opposition to republicanism, of which Riza Khan was very well aware. But if that was good reason for retaining the monarchy, Ahmad Shah could have been left as a titular constitutional monarch, with Riza Khan as the driving force in the government – somewhat similar to what happened in Italy during the same period. It has sometimes been said on Riza Khan's behalf that the Iranians possessed a rather special kind of regard for the institution of monarchy, but much the same might once have been said of Czarist Russia or Ottoman Turkey. The fact is that Riza Shah, as he will henceforth be called, preferred the role of King to that of Prime Minister or

even President. A crown offers personal satisfactions which a presidential top-hat does not, even if both offices are titular – which the monarchy of Riza Shah most certainly was not – while hereditary kingship confers the inestimable boon of enabling its possessors to provide for their progeny. Not for nothing did Riza Shah become the greatest landowner in the country by means of proscriptions and confiscations.

The Shah as reformer

On the credit side, Riza Shah's reign of 26 years, however much it remains a subject of controversy, served as a catalyst for change in a country that had been far less exposed to external influences than either Turkey or Egypt. Riza Shah was a less educated or traveled man than Mustafa Kemal, and it is to this restricted intellectual outlook that most of his failures must be attributed. Given his Cossack background there was nothing very surprising in the military character of Riza Shah's government. His first concern was to strengthen and modernize the army. The army served to bolster the Shah's power, but it was also used in the ruthless coercion of the semi-independent nomadic tribes, who were compeled to adopt a sedentary way of life, and to impose a rough-and-ready peace upon a traditionally turbulent countryside. Brigandage was put down with a heavy hand, and the cultivator was now able to till his fields in peace, although there was a price to pay for this blessing: effective government from Tehran necessarily involved the more efficient collection of higher revenue assessments.

Military considerations and preoccupation with past British and Russian threats to the country's integrity led Riza Shah to give high priority to improving the inadequate system of communications. His most visible achievement was the building of a railway extending from the Persian Gulf to the Caspian, but no less indicative of his determination to control his vast, underpopulated kingdom was his program of highway construction and his take-over of the British-owned telegraph-lines. Toward the British he remained implacably hostile. In 1928 he set up the National Bank of Iran as a counterweight to the British Imperial Bank, and in 1933 he negotiated a new 60-year concession with the Anglo-Persian Oil Company, which enjoyed a status approaching an *imperium in imperio* in the southwest.

Riza Shah followed Turkey's precedent in striking at the power of the religious classes. In 1927 Muslim law was partly replaced by codes modeled on French law, and in 1928 the hated Capitations were abolished. Public education was gradually introduced in the larger towns, and in 1934 the University of Tehran was founded. Iranian nationalism, no new phenomenon, expressed itself not only in predictable xenophobia toward those European powers that had been interfering in Iranian affairs since the Napoleonic period but also in a reaction to thirteen centuries of Islamic culture, associated as they were with the Arab conquests of the seventh century and, later, with

Left: The Iranian National Bank, established by Riza Shah in 1928 as a gesture of national independence from British influence. The decorative motifs on the building deliberately refer back to the splendors of pre-Islamic Iran.

Above right: Kemal Ataturk in the European-style clothing that he imposed on all Turks. Riza Shah imitated many of Ataturk's radical modernization policies.

Right: Riza Khan Pahlavi, the Cossack officer who became Shah of Iran in 1925. He was deposed by the Allies in 1941 because of his pro-German sympathies.

Far right: Muhammad Riza Pahlavi succeeded his father on the Iranian throne in 1941 and ruled the country for almost 40 years.

Turkish domination. The glories of pre-Islamic Iran, now being uncovered by archeologists at Persepolis, Susa and elsewhere, were taught in the schools and discussed in intellectual circles, where there was much concern with purifying the Persian language of foreign (eg Arabic) accretions, although, unlike the case of Turkey, the Arabic script was retained. The growing bourgeoisie tended to give their sons and daughters names from Achaemenid or Sasanid history, in place of the traditional Muslim names, and public buildings were frequently built in a Persepolitan style.

Islam and World War II

Riza Shah's reign ended abruptly in 1941, a victim of the outbreak of the World War II. Iran, like Turkey, professed neutrality but unlike Turkey her neutrality was disregarded. Riza Shah had recklessly flirted with the Germany of the Third Reich, but even had he not done so Anglo-Russian security would probably have dictated intervention. As in World War I, Iran was unceremoniously occupied, Riza Shah was forced to abdicate (he died in exile in South Africa in 1944) and the throne passed to his son, Muhammad Riza Pahlavi, then aged 20 – who would rule the peacock throne for nearly four decades..

With Ataturk dead in 1938 and Riza Shah removed from the scene, both Turkey and Iran drifted during the war years. So too did the Arab world, where North Africa was a battle-ground for European armies and where Egypt and the Fertile Crescent were precariously held by the Allies. Many Arabs perceived that they had more to hope for from an Axis than an Allied victory, but the struggle for independence was muted against the background of the titanic World War that, if it affected them less than had the struggle of a quarter of a century earlier, nevertheless produced severe shortages, inflation and a greatly extended knowledge of Europe and Europeans. As in the case of the Indian subcontinent and Southeast Asia, it was certain that peace in Europe would mark the beginning of a significant new phase in the Muslim struggle to emancipate itself from European colonial or quasi-colonial domination.

India

It is usual to date the beginnings of institutional-ized nationalism in the subcontinent from the first meeting of the Indian National Congress in Bombay in 1885. Earlier, there had been spas-modic manifestations of dissatisfaction with the status quo on the part of a relatively small number of Western-educated Indians – opposition to Lord Lytton's punitive Vernacular Press Act of 1878, resentment at the effectiveness of non-official European agitation against the Ilbert Bill of 1883 and, above all, irritation at the tardiness of the Government of India in implementing its pro-fessed policy of increasing the Indian element in the higher levels of the administration – but from 1885 onward there was to be an annual forum where overt criticism, at first expressed with con-siderable restraint and deference, would be levelled at the regime. For the first 20 years of its existence, however, the Congress was essentially a moderate, conservative body.

But the label of 'moderate' rapidly became a term of opprobrium among the rising generations of the 1890s and 1900s who were disillusioned by the inability of Congress to obtain any meaningful concessions from the government by its 'policy of mendicancy.' Thus there emerged at the turn of the century a new kind of nationalism, running parallel to and supplementing the politics of the Congress 'establishment,' a nationalism drawing inspiration from traditional Hindu culture, at once xenophobic and chauvinist, highly articu-late, with a political vocabulary passing impercep-tibly into the rhetoric of violence, and from the rhetoric of violence to its execution. In fact, politi-cal terrorism was only a significant factor in the history of the Indian nationalist movement for a relatively short period and even then was largely restricted to Bengal, Maharashtra and the Punjab. The dominant figure of this so-called 'extremist' phase was the Chitpavan *brahmin*, Bal Gagadhar Tilak (1856-1920), to whom the 'moderate' Gopal

Krishna Gokhale (1866-1915) served as a natural foil. Scholar, educationalist and journalist, Tilak was a man of remarkable abilities, and he was able to arouse a resentment against foreign rule and a pride in traditional Hindu culture among a far wider spectrum of the population than any other nationalist leader of his day. A major element in his authority over his followers lay in his ability to appeal to deeply felt traditional sentiments, exemplified by the Ganapati festivals which he inaugurated in honor of the popular elephant-headed deity, Ganesha, and by his cult of the Maratha ruler, Shivaji (1627-80), as a national hero who beat back the invading Moghuls. To equate the British with the Moghuls, however, and to glorify this great foe of Islam were not gestures likely to lessen Muslim suspicions of Tilak's intensely Hindu conception of 'Indian-ness.' It was this tendency for Indian nationalism to coalesce with Hindu revivalism and Hindu cul-tural chauvinism that contributed immeasurably to the later demand of many Indian Muslims for partition of the subcontinent.

One striking aspect of the Congress movement from the outset had been the indifference and, in-deed, hostility shown toward it by all but a hand-ful of the leaders of the Muslim community. This was due partly to the deep-rooted conservatism characteristic of that community as a whole, partly to the slowness with which Indian Mus-lims had turned to Western education and the attitudes it engendered, and partly to a resultant failure of Muslims to gain access to the new middle-class occupations of medicine, law, jour-nalism and government service. Behind these fail-ings, however, lay another and a deeper one which was to haunt the Muslims down to 1947 and beyond – an identity-crisis resulting from the community's inability to decide whether Indian Islam was truly of the soil of India or simply an extension of the great Middle Eastern culture-

zone to the west. With this went the baffling problem of relating the community's depressed and subordinate position to the memories of the glorious and not too distant past.

Sir Sayyid Ahmad Khan (1817-93), a retired government official and influential Muslim leader, was well aware of just how far the Indian Muslims had fallen behind the Hindus in obtain-ing their fair share of the loaves and fishes of employment in government service or in the pro-fessions. He believed that the granting of political concessions to Indians by the British along the lines then being advocated by the Indian National Congress would do nothing to improve the status of his own community *vis-à-vis* the Hindu major-ity, and indeed he believed that such concessions would ultimately tend to widen rather than nar-row the gap between the relatively backward Muslims and the emerging Western-educated middle class, which was of course overwhelm-ingly Hindu. He therefore urged Indian Muslims to look to the goodwill of the British to assist them in their quest for parity, since it was now becoming fairly obvious that the British them-selves, apprehensive of the direction being taken by the nationalist movement, were prepared to buttress any group or community likely to serve as a counter-weight to the growing influence of the Indian National Congress. This was a role that the Muslim leadership, so long mistrusted by the British, was admirably suited to play, being socially conservative, instinctively averse to almost all aspects of change and opposed to any devolution of power into the hands of the hated Congress lawyers and journalists. Moreover, even for forward-looking Muslims, the style of Tilak's leadership, with its Hindu Revivalist overtones, was a warning that the awakening political life of the subcontinent might well develop a xeno-phobic and communal aspect that would come to regard Muslim civilization in India as something

Left: Bal Gagadhar Tilak, the 'extremist' political leader of the Hindu nationalist revival, is tried for sedition by the British authorities.

Above right: Bengali Muslims gather to offer up a prayer of thanksgiving for the Partition of Bengal, carried out against the wishes of the Hindu population.

Right: Lord Minto, who took over from Lord Curzon as Governor-General in 1905. With John Morley, head of the India Office, Minto pushed through limited reforms, but maintained a policy of repression against Indian nationalists.

no less alien than the imported trappings of European civilization. And then, in the circumstances of the early twentieth century, it was also becoming clear that what was meat for one community might well prove poison for the other: Lord Curzon's decision to create out of the unwieldy Lieutenant-Governorship of Bengal two separate provinces was just such a case.

The Partition of Bengal in 1905 has been seen as a turning-point in the history of opposition to British rule and as the beginning of mass-partici-

pation in nationalist politics, although at the time it was only in Bengal itself that the issue evoked concern. For the Bengali *bhadralok* (educated class), frustrated and exasperated by the refusal of the British to recognize their fitness to participate in the processes of government, the decision to partition the province was regarded as an intolerable affront to the Bengali feeling of cultural identity, so manifestly demonstrated by race, language and literary heritage. For the leaders of the Muslim community in Bengal, however, who formed a slight majority of Bengali-speakers in the province, the creation of a new Lieutenant-Governorship of East Bengal meant increased opportunities for employment, high education and the voicing of specific Muslim interests and grievances, which had hitherto been lacking. When the Bengali *bhadralok* of Calcutta and the western districts of Bengal mounted a vociferous opposition to partition the British had the satisfaction of noting the speed with which the Muslims of Dacca and the eastern districts mounted a counter-agitation. Thus the political lessons to be learned from the 1905 Partition controversy were clear: that while Indian nationalist leaders would expect to be able to mobilize widespread support on issues of concern to the man in the street, among such issues likely to arise in the future were some in which the interests of Hindu and Muslim would be diametrically opposed.

The year 1905 saw the departure of Lord Curzon from India after a masterful governor-generalship of prodigious activity and the arrival of his successor, Lord Minto (1905-10), a Conservative career-diplomat who, following the election of a Liberal government in Britain toward the end of the year, had as his political master in the India Office John Morley, a literary figure well known to the British Press and Parliament and a confirmed Gladstonian Liberal. On the assumption that between this ill-assorted couple Morley would prove the dominant partner, observers in both India and Britain concluded that the authoritarian rule of a Curzon was now about to give way to an administration more responsive to changing times. To some extent this forecast was confirmed, although to a much lesser extent than Indian nationalist leaders had hoped. The famous Morley-Minto reforms of 1909 made only the most grudging concessions to Indian demands, and they were accompanied by a vigorous (and highly successful) repression of the more

'extreme' elements. In retrospect, perhaps the most significant development of the Morley-Minto era was the formation, in December 1906, of the Muslim League by a prominent group of Muslims shortly after Lord Minto had assured a delegation of conservative and loyalist Muslim leaders, headed by the Aga Khan, that in the formulation of proposals for broadening the basis of the Administration the interests of the Muslim minority would receive special consideration and that, in principle, the Government of India recognized the desirability of various forms of communal representation.

The Partition of Bengal

Although the Morley-Minto reforms can be seen in retrospect as having conceded too little too late, the fact remains that from the point of view of the British the Morley-Minto years saw a considerable reduction in the tensions which had built up during the years of Curzon's governor-generalship, and especially over the Partition of Bengal. The Partition itself had apparently become an accepted fact and stern repression had temporarily silenced the activists. Tilak had been imprisoned a second time in 1907 and when he re-emerged it was clear that he did not intend to sample a third time the inside of a British jail. The reforms themselves, despite all their obvious shortcomings, did provide evidence in favor of the wisdom of negotiating with a regime that was, quite clearly, too well established to be overthrown by force. Thus far the extremists had little to show for all their efforts, and Gokhale's case for an ongoing dialogue between the moderates and the responsive Administration seemed to offer the most likelihood of levering concessions.

The opening years of Lord Harding's governor-generalship (1910-16) gave every indication that the Government of India would continue 'responsive.' At the Delhi Durbar of 1911, held in honor of the Coronation of King George V, the Partition of Bengal, the source of so much anguish to the *bhadralok* and of so much satisfaction to the Bengali Muslims, was revoked. At the same time, Delhi, the old Muslim imperial metropolis, was proclaimed the new capital of British India in place of Calcutta. Thus the *bhadralok* had both won and lost. The revocation of partition, for which they had agitated so strenuously five years earlier, had been achieved, but Calcutta, the source of their cultural identity and their political aspirations,

had entered the first phase of its decline.

To some contemporaries it seemed that the early years of Harding's governor-generalship – the four relatively uneventful years preceding the outbreak of World War I followed by the Indian Government's all-consuming preoccupation with the war effort (in addition to cash and raw materials, India provided 1,300,000 combatants and non-combatants for war-zones as far flung as Flanders and Mesopotamia) – had eased nationalist politics into cold storage. But even before the outbreak of war there had been signs of fresh stirrings. There had been growing interest in the situation in South Africa, where exploitation of the Indian community had given rise to the *satyagraha* (passive resistance) movement led by a young expatriate lawyer in Natal, Mohandas Karamchand Gandhi (1869-1948). Indian Muslim sentiment had been inflamed by the Italian seizure of Libya from the Ottoman Empire in 1911 and by the Balkan War of 1912. And as World War I drew to its close it became apparent that beneath the tranquil surface of Indian life important changes had taken place. The war had caused shortages and dislocations. Among the hundreds of thousands of men recruited to fight in distant campaigns some were returning with new outlooks. The Indian Civil Service itself, long the pride of the empire, had been greatly weakened by the reckless transfer of junior officials into the armed forces, by a falling-off of recruitment during the war and by the consequent strain placed upon older officials. If India in 1914 was governed by a *corps d'élite* such as few other

European colonial territories could boast of, this was less apparent in 1919. Among the nationalists, too, times had changed, and new figures were challenging the established leaders. Gokhale, regarded by Gandhi (who arrived from South Africa in 1914) as his *guru*, had died in 1915, and Tilak, despite his participation in Mrs Annie Besant's Home Rule League of 1916, had shot his bolt. It would be Gandhi who would eventually emerge as the Congress's new leader.

Confronted by the long-suppressed tensions surfacing at the end of the war and bemused by the uncertain potentialities of the postwar years the British Government reacted with a characteristic ambivalence guaranteed to baffle even the most Anglophile Indian. In one direction, E S Montagu, the new Secretary of State for India, made the historic statement in the House of Commons on 20 August 1917:

The policy of His Majesty's Government, with which the Government of India are in complete accord, is that of the increasing association of Indians in every branch of the administration, and the gradual development of self-governing institutions, with a view to the progressive realization of responsible government in India as an integral part of the British Empire.

In the opposite direction, early in 1919 the Government of India introduced emergency legislation known as the Rowlatt Acts with a view to curbing the further spread of sedition. This in turn provoked a fresh wave of protests, to which some of the provincial governments, especially that of the Punjab under the tough Sir Michael

O'Dwyer, reacted vigorously. When a large crowd assembled unlawfully in the Jallianwala Bagh in Amritsar in April 1919 and refused to disperse, Brigadier-General Reginald Dyer ordered his Gurkha troops to open fire, killing 379 and wounding 1208. The ensuing controversy and the passions aroused in both India and Britain as a result of Dyer's action at Amritsar to some extent lessened the impact of the very substantial constitutional innovations (popularly known as 'dyarchy') embodied in the Government of India Act of 1919, the fruit of the Montagu-Chelmsford Report of 1918. (Chelmsford had succeeded Harding as Governor-General in 1916.)

The Act of 1919 established a system in which certain areas of administration – foreign and military affairs, tariffs and customs, currency and coinage, communications, income tax and the like – were retained as the responsibility of the Governor-General and the central legislature, now considerably expanded and bicameral, and with an enlarged elective element. Other areas – agriculture, irrigation, land revenue, forests, famine relief, public works, local self-government, public health and education – were transferred to the provincial governments, where responsibility was divided between the Governor, with his Executive Council, and Ministers chosen from elected unicameral assemblies. At the time of its inception the concept of dyarchy was bitterly assailed, not least for its complexity, but it was a very definite move forward in the evolution toward self-government, and it did provide a very large number of Indians with political and administrative

Above left: The Delhi Durbar in December 1911, held to celebrate the coronation of King George V. At the Durbar, the Partition of Bengal was revoked although the old Muslim city of Delhi was declared the capital of India in place of Calcutta.

Above: A demonstration against British rule in India conducted by supporters of Gandhi. The spinning wheel was used as a symbol of the boycott of foreign cloth imports – a major economic issue of the period.

Right: Mahatma Gandhi, advocate of non-violent resistance to British rule. His attempts to reconcile Hindu and Muslim were a failure, but his influence helped spread belief in Indian nationalism from the urban elite to the impoverished masses.

experience of a kind not hitherto available.

The attitude of Congress toward the Montagu-Chelmsford Reforms was predictably ambiguous in the wake of the Amritsar Massacre, which led Gandhi to denounce the British Raj as a 'satanic government.' There was extreme suspicion of any British protestations of good faith. The Congress leaders were inclined to regard the whole complex system of dyarchy as a sham, and in consequence they boycotted the first elections of 1920, but they were also forced to recognize that many of their supporters thirsted for office and patronage and were not unwilling to postpone long-term objectives for short-term advantages.

Hindu-Muslim gulf widens

The early 1920s were not good years for the Indian National Congress. The gulf between Hindus and Muslims continued to widen. There had been one striking achievement earlier, although it had proven short-lived: in 1916 the Congress and the Muslim League had held a joint session at Lucknow where, largely through the instrumentality of a young barrister with a foot in both camps, Muhammad Ali Jinnah (1876-1948), there was hammered out the so-called Lucknow Pact, in which the Congress agreed to recognize the Muslim League's demand for separate communal electorates. This apparent honeymoon continued between 1919 and 1924, but meanwhile the Congress-League *rapprochement* was actually wearing thin. Many Congressmen had from the first doubted Gandhi's wisdom in supporting overt manifestations of the extra-territorial loyalty of Indian Muslims toward the distant Ottoman caliphate (hardly more appealing from a Hindu's point of view than the King-Emperor himself), and the Congress inclination to support specifically Muslim causes had been further weakened

by recent events on the Malabar coast. Here, in 1922, the Moplahs (as the Muslims of Malabar were called) staged an uprising that quickly degenerated into the enforced conversion of their Hindu neighbors amid lurid newspaper reports of massacre, rape and involuntary circumcision. The British authorities crushed the revolt with a heavy hand, but not before Hindu public opinion throughout the subcontinent had swung away from granting any further concessions to the Muslim community.

By 1924 Gandhi himself was still far from establishing that all-India charisma that was to be a mark of his later career. In 1920 he had launched his 'non-co-operation' movement, with 'non-violence' (*ahimsa*) as its basic premise, but continuing incidents of gratuitous violence showed him that, for the most part, his followers had failed to master his teaching. Disappointed, he called off the non-co-operation movement and withdrew from active politics.

In 1924 Gandhi's mood was one of pessimism, yet in fact his contribution to date had been impressive. At the time of his return to India in 1914 the Congress had been confused as to its aims, elitist in its general outlook and resting on a somewhat narrow middle-class base. A decade later its overall character as an organization had altered and would continue to alter at an ever-increasing pace: it was now well on its way to becoming a mass-movement, with the beginning of a grass-roots organization in its lower echelons and with the former dominance of the Calcutta-based *bhadralok* and Poona *Brahmin* a thing of the past.

The Montagu-Chelmsford reforms of 1919 were scheduled for review after a 20-year period, and in premature fulfilment of this pledge the British Government in 1927 despatched the Simon Com-

Above left: Members of the Indian Civil Service assembled at Poona in 1926. Once an exclusive and elite body, the service was much diluted in the post-World War I period.

Left: Gandhi addresses a nationalist meeting in the early 1920s.

Above right: Indians demonstrate their hostility to the Simon Commission, sent to India by the British Government in 1927. The recommendations of the Commission eventually led to a considerable extension of internal self-government.

Right: Street hawkers prepare to claim their street licenses following the introduction of the Sales Tax in Bombay, August 1939.

mission on a fact-finding mission to India – without, however, seeing fit to include in that body a single Indian representative. Although boycotted by Congress, the Simon Commission nevertheless proceeded to recommend substantial modifications in the system of dyarchy, and these were further modified as a result of the Round Table Conferences of 1931, which, after his initial exclusion, Gandhi attended as sole spokesman for the Congress. The eventual outcome was the Government of India Act of 1935, a major advance in the direction of internal self-government. Between the elections to the provincial legislatures in 1937 and the resignation of the Congress Ministries in 1939 in protest against the unilateral declaration of war by the Governor-General, India experienced for the first time a real measure of parliamentary government.

The coming of World War II prevented the effective implementation of the Government of India Act of 1935. Congress was now in an intransigent mood, and following the failure of the Cripps Mission (March 1942), the All-India Congress Committee framed the famous 'Quit India' resolution of 8 August 1942, advocating massive non-violent resistance to any further prolongation of British rule. Preoccupied with the war effort and with the Japanese threat to Bengal, the British authorities were in no mood to face what might become a protracted war of nerves of the kind at which Gandhi and his lieutenants were so skilled. The Congress leadership was promptly jailed, and it was made clear that illegal political activity would be restrained with a heavy hand. As a result, Congress languished during the remaining years of the war, while the Communist Party and the Muslim League gained in strength. With Great Britain now the ally of the Soviet Union, Indian Communists were under orders to support the war effort, while the British regarded the activities of the League with a tolerant eye, mindful of Muslim recruitment to a greatly expanded Indian Army. Yet the problems of India's future had only been put into temporary cold storage by wartime exigencies and no one, either in India or Britain, was under any illusion that the end of hostilities would prevent them from coming back to the fore.

Southeast Asia

On the surface it might appear that relatively little change took place in Southeast Asia between the World Wars. By the time World War II erupted in 1939 the Dutch seemed to have effectively stifled whatever nationalist movements had developed in the East Indies and to have organized the islands into an efficient colonial state under the firm administration of Governor General Tjanda van Somkenborgh-Saochouwer. The French appeared to have been a little less successful in eradicating the revolutionary Communist Party in Vietnam, but nevertheless they were firmly in control of the five states of Indo-China when Europe again went to war. During the interwar years the British steadily loosened their grip and fostered elements of home rule in Burma and Malaysia, and relations between the latter and the mother country were relatively smooth. The Americans continued to make a remarkable success story of political, economic and social development in the Philippines and were briskly moving ahead toward the time when the islands would be granted full autonomy. And Thailand, as before, remained independent.

Yet the national political movements that were stirring everywhere in Southeast Asia during the interwar years, though apparently of secondary importance at the time, were destined to become critically important later on, after the Japanese had conquered the entire region (unifying it – briefly – for the only time in its history), had smashed the power of the European colonialists

and had then withdrawn in defeat at the end of World War II. Of these interwar national movements, two, especially, deserve comment: those in Vietnam and Indonesia.

Phan Boi Chau's Chinese-inspired Vietnamese Nationalist Party was effectively destroyed in the abortive uprising of 1930, but almost immediately another, far more formidable national movement took its place. In late 1931 the Communist Party of Indochina unloosed a series of uprisings in central Vietnam, sizeable and well planned to the point where they threw the colonial regime into momentary disarray. In the end, colonial forces, including French-African levies, did succeed in restoring order, and the vengeance that was visited upon the Communists was no less harsh than upon their Nationalist predecessors. Yet not only did it take the French far longer to suppress their new challengers, but also they never succeeded in uprooting the Communists' organizational structure. That structure and the Party's ideology were closely patterned after yet another foreign model, that of the Soviet Union, where the Party's originator, Nguyen Ai Quoc – 'Nguyen, the Patriot,' or, as he was later known, Ho Chi Minh – had spent several years. Ho had before then lived in Paris, where he had joined the French Communist party, had later become a prominent member of the Comintern and in 1930 had organized the 'Indo-Chinese' party among Vietnamese exiles in China.

Although the Communists' leading *cadres*

came mostly from middle-class youths, they had in an astonishingly short time managed to create a true mass movement. At the height of the revolts, workers' and peasants' 'soviets' (councils) had sprung up to fill the administrative void. Compared to the Nationalists, the Communists possessed superior organizational skills, and they had also managed to bridge social and regional barriers. No less important, they had come to view the modernization of Vietnam not merely as a national necessity but as part of the revolutionary transformation of all French colonies, and of the entire colonial world. As Ho Chi Minh put it:

The French imperialists . . . have resorted to every underhand scheme to intensify their capitalist exploitation in Indo-China . . . They increased their military forces, firstly to strangle the Vietnamese revolution, secondly to prepare for a new imperialist war in the Pacific . . . thirdly to suppress the Chinese revolution, fourthly to attack the Soviet Union because the latter helps the revolution of the oppressed nations . . . [If] we give them a free hand to stifle the Vietnamese revolution, it is tantamount to giving them a free hand to wipe our race off the earth and drown our nation in the Pacific.

Not even the sagacious leadership of a Ho Chi Minh could stave off the party's virtual destruction in the short run, but once French colonial dominance itself fell victim to outside attack in World War II, the Communists stood ready to resume the struggle.

Left: The confident façade of Dutch rule in Indonesia between the wars concealed the tensions generated by a nascent Indonesian nationalism.

Above right: Nguyen Ai Quoc, later to be known as Ho Chi Minh, photographed during his early years in Paris. Ho's remarkable leadership qualities would contribute greatly to the eventual triumph of communism in Indo-China.

Right: The Soviet flag displayed in Sumatra in 1923. The few ill-organized communist uprisings of this period were easily suppressed by the colonial authorities.

rowly circumscribed that only a tiny percentage of the Indonesian population was entitled to vote. Similar restrictions applied to the regional and provincial councils established in Java in the second postwar decade. When the long-awaited new constitutional charter was promulgated in 1925, its basic conservatism came as a bitter disappointment to many in the colony.

Even then, however, the liberalized atmosphere engendered in the era of welfare policies had encouraged, or at least permitted, the fairly rapid maturation of organizational and political life in the Indies. It was in part at least the first stirrings of political activism which had caused the authorities to move in the direction of reforms. In the 1920s the colony experienced successive waves of radical agitation, culminating in armed rebellions in western Java and on the west coast of Sumatra in 1926-27. Though easily suppressed, these unexpected explosions led the colonial authorities, vociferously supported by European mercantile interests, to back away from the course of reforms. The onset of the world-wide depression, which hit the Indies' economy particularly hard, contributed yet another element to the growing conservatism in later Dutch colonial policy.

Indonesian disunity

Holland had not been a belligerent in World War I, but the Allied blockade of the sea lanes did partly disrupt the very close ties between the motherland and the Indonesian colony. Temporary isolation, no less than the political turmoil created in the Netherlands in the aftermath of the war and the early stirrings of Indonesian political life, brought a sudden, if short-lived, quickening of the tides of change to the Indies. It culminated in the creation in 1918 of an advisory body, the so-called *Volksraad* (People's Council), in the capital city of Batavia, and this was accompanied by official promises of even more far-reaching constitutional reforms to follow. But the normalization of the domestic situation in Holland soon led to the reimposition of strict metropolitan control over colonial affairs. The *Volksraad* itself remained a half-appointive, half-elective assembly which was only granted limited co-legislative powers in 1927. In fact, the Council's membership not only favored the European element, but the franchise for the indirectly elected councilors was so nar-

No common political traditions comparable to those in Vietnam existed among the peoples of the Indonesian archipelago. Indonesians were in fact divided by deep-seated cleavages born of divergent cultural, religious, social and also political experiences and developments. Such major outside influences as Hinduism, Buddhism and, later, Islam had impinged quite unevenly on the area, and in modern times the Dutch impact had reinforced and widened existing socio-cultural divisions. Yet paradoxically it was the Dutch

themselves who were also increasingly providing the ties that helped overcome inherent disunities. If administrative centralization, modern education and the use of Malay as the ancillary official language throughout the colony were positive stimuli, the mounting burdens of the colonial presence, and its concomitants of racial separatism and economic exploitation, welded ever-larger numbers of Indonesians consciously together in opposition to the foreigners.

The emergence of Indonesian nationalism proper took time and was, in fact, retarded by the persistence of subnational group identities. Thus the first stirrings of modernity actually took the form of associations based on individual islands or ethnic groupings, while others, less limited geographically, remained communal in character. Throughout the area the cleavage between nominal and orthodox Muslims proved particularly divisive, both sides counting millions of sympathizers.

Sarekat Islam (Islamic Union), the Indies' first and largest mass movement, well exemplified these complexities. Originally founded in 1909 as a Muslim merchants' defensive association against 'infidel' (especially Chinese) business competitors, *Sarekat Islam*'s leadership soon passed to Umar Said Tjokroaminoto, a young Dutch-educated Javanese with but slender roots in Islam. With amazing speed, the Union blossomed into an ostensibly modern movement in Java and beyond, with a formal organizational structure, an official program calling for social and economic betterment of the native population and a membership that came close to the half-million mark in the years after World War I.

Yet the *Sarekat*'s modernity was to some extent more apparent than real. At least partly modern were many of its original sponsors, who had come under the influence of the teachings of reformist Islam emanating from Egypt. Modern, too, were the civil servants, clerks and other urbanized Indonesians who found much in common with Dutch-schooled leaders who, like Tjokroaminoto himself, espoused a medley of Western-derived liberal and socialist ideas. And there was, finally, yet another group of modern leaders, young and radical Marxists, whose organizational and ideological appeals found ready listeners among the tiny proletariat. But these 'modern' groups were no more than small splinters within Indonesian society. What turned the *Sarekat* into a mass movement was its mushrooming peasant following. Few peasants had as yet moved beyond the threshold of modernity, but hundreds of thousands had been affected by increased taxation,

by the fluctuations of the trade cycle and by a pervasive restlessness in the face of changing conditions.

In such a climate, ever conducive to utopian expectations, the *Sarekat*'s agitation was bound to elicit a tremendous response, kindled by Tjokroaminoto's oratorical brilliance and near-magical personality. To the Javanese peasantry, he appeared not so much as the harbinger of modernity but as the traditionally promised redeemer from the burdens of earthly existence. In the wake of the resultant rural explosions in west Java in 1919 the colonial government forcefully intervened. But these outside pressures did not so much cause the quick decline of the movement as hasten the disintegration of its constituent forces, a process which Tjokroaminoto was unable to stem. In the end, the bulk of the pious Muslim bourgeoisie deserted the movement altogether, finding shelter in a modernist, purely religious association, *Muhammadiyah*. The Communists, their best brains expelled from the colony by the Dutch, rekindled rural unrest into ill-organized and suicidal uprisings in the mid 1920s. Their swift suppression not only put an end to Marxist organizational efforts, it also ended the first turbulent phase of Indonesia's modern anticolonial movement.

What that phase had clearly lacked – a sense of direction and an overriding, positive goal – was dramatically provided by the birth of Indonesian

nationalism. Not surprisingly, this totally new idea of a common political and cultural identity arose first among a handful of youths drawn from many parts of the Dutch Indies yet sharing similar educational and other experiences in the Netherlands. Their *Perhimpunan Indonesia* (Indonesian Association), founded in 1922, was the first indigenous association to use the word 'Indonesian,' up to then a purely geographical term of Western coinage. Almost at once it was followed by a host of 'Indonesian' study clubs among the school-going generation in the colony. In 1928 a youth congress held in Java pledged itself to the struggle for 'one nation – Indonesia; one people – Indonesians; and one language – Indonesian.'

Even those fully committed to such an idea, however, were divided as to how to attain national independence. Most of the overseas-trained nationalists insisted that the recent calamitous events in the colony had demonstrated the unpreparedness of the people to confront the entrenched might of the colonial powers. Thus, they argued, first priority had to be given to patient educational and organizational work by educated *cadres* among the masses. Not so, argued the advocates of immediate revolution, most of whom had never left the colony. None proclaimed this goal more cogently, more fervently and, for a short while at least, also more persuasively than a young engineering graduate, Sukarno. Whereas nationalist leaders based in

Above left: The *Volksraad* or 'People's Council' meets in Batavia, capital of the Dutch East Indies. Set up in 1918, this advisory body was heavily weighted toward the representation of European views and interests.

Below left and above right: Scenes of Indonesian rural life in the 1930s. The lives of the peasants were hardly affected by the benefits of modern life, but they did suffer from rising taxation and from the depressed state of the world economy.

Right: Sukarno, the most impressive exponent of the view that the Indonesian masses were ripe for revolution; they were lacking only in proper leadership. The Dutch authorities made sure Sukarno could not provide that leadership by arresting and, finally, banishing him.

Holland judged events from afar and largely through cosmopolitan lenses. Sukarno had observed them close-up, for some years indeed from Tjokroaminoto's own house. More than that, this avid imbiber of foreign revolutionary doctrines managed to remain deeply rooted in traditional, especially Javanese, ways. To Sukarno, the masses, far from needing tutelage, had already proved their revolutionary potential; it was the leadership that lacked collective will. That will, he insisted, could only be supplied by the concept of an Indonesian nationalism wide enough to accommodate all true revolutionaries, Muslims no less than Marxists.

As it turned out, neither Sukarno nor the returned *Perhimpunan* leaders were allowed to demonstrate the efficacy of their arguments. Alarmed by Sukarno's revolutionary rhetoric and fearing a return to the turmoil of the recent past, the colonial authorities arrested him in 1930. Defending himself at his trial in a brilliant speech, Sukarno soon became a popular idol symbolizing defiance of colonial rule. Released before his term was up, he was re-arrested in 1933 and finally banished from Java. Most of the returnees were similarly exiled, and the backbone of revolutionary nationalism was broken. The period between the mid 1930s and the Japanese conquest in 1942 was dominated by 'co-operating' nationalists who, as the only avenue for meaningful political action, agreed to participate in the constitutional framework – the People's Council, as well as regional bodies – of the colonial state. The unresolved tensions within modern Indonesian political life – between 'secular' nationalists and Muslims, between gradualists and revolutionaries, between organizers and ideologues – thus remained artificially frozen as long as Dutch rule lasted, but they would erupt with singular fury in the postwar years.

China

After the end of World War I Chinese attitudes toward foreign powers had undergone a marked shift. Whereas in the late Ch'ing period 'nationalism' had mainly meant anti-Manchu feelings, by 1919 it meant anti-imperialism. The foreigners were felt as an omnipresent menace, living behind their special legal safeguards in their own protected communities on Chinese soil, guarded by their own troops and ships, exploiting Chinese workers so that they could make greater profits out of their factories, disrupting the internal structure of China's markets and bringing unfair pressures to bear on China's weak constitutional local governments. There had been traces of this new nationalism as early as 1905, when massive boycotts against the United States had been carried on in southwest China to protest the flagrant racial discrimination of the Exclusion Acts, which banned Chinese laborers from the United States. The same emergent nationalism had led the Chinese to regain some of the rights they had ceded to foreigners, most particularly from the Germans in the province of Shantung. But memories of these past successes only made the current humiliations seem more unbearable. In 1915, for example, outraged Chinese had stood by helplessly as Japan posed her so-called Twenty-one Demands, by which Japan gained stronger rights in Manchuria, Mongolia and Shantung and took tighter hold over some of China's major mines and industrial works.

The Chinese government decided in 1917 to enter World War I on the side of Britain and France, hoping thus to get the concessions once owned by Germany (and now controlled by Japan) back at the war's end. But the Japanese had secretly got the British and French to agree to allow Japan to keep these areas after the war. Japan's rights were confirmed in the Treaty of Versailles in 1919, and when news of this reached China in April there was a furious reaction. Hatred of the foreign powers for their duplicity was added to contempt of the foreign powers for the cruel and inefficient way that the war had been conducted. No longer did China's reformers look uncritically at Western techniques and think that only good would come from their adoption. On 4 May some 3000 students from 13 colleges in

Peking marched in protest against the Treaty. A number of students were arrested and later released; one died in the struggle. After the outcries had gone on for a month and a half three unpopular ministers were dismissed and the Chinese delegation in France refused to ratify the Treaty. But these developments became almost secondary; what was crucial was that the events of 4 May spread out in ripples across the country. Students' and teachers' unions were formed; girl students joined in the demonstrations; the merchants held massive commercial strikes in sympathy and mounting numbers of industrial workers also came out in sympathy strikes. The effect on China was enormous. Emotions were aroused that were never again to be suppressed, and people from all walks of life were radicalized. The ground had been prepared for an alliance of workers and intellectuals, an alliance that could be transformed, by the skills of political organizers, into a potent political force.

Kuomintang and Communists

Before turning to consider the development of the new radical-nationalist parties it is necessary to take a look at the context in which they arose: the world of the warlords. 'Warlordism' is a vaguely descriptive term that has little content unless it is considered in the light of specific military men. Generally speaking, a warlord was a military man who controlled an army that owed its allegiance to him. The corollary of this was that the warlord had also to control a territorial base or other source of funds that would enable him to pay his army. Some warlords controlled the same area of territory for decades; some were highly mobile; some formed alliances to carve up a province or blocks of provinces; some were entirely independent in political terms, while others sought to control elements of the 'legitimate' constitutional government in Peking or negotiated directly with the representatives of foreign powers.

There were literally hundreds of warlords who held power in different areas of China between 1911 and 1949. Let us look briefly at four. Wu

P'ei-fu (1874-1939), son of a Shantung tradesman, was trained as a military cadet and became a protegé of Yüan Shih-k'ai. His first center of power was the province of Hunan, and between 1922 and 1926 he was the dominant figure in northern China. The fact that he drew much of his income from the strategic and lucrative Hankow-Peking railway led to his involvement in one of the first major crises in the history of the Chinese labor movement: the bloody suppression of a strike on the railroad in 1923, in which his troops killed almost 80 workers.

Wu's increasingly reactionary reputation can be contrasted with that of Feng Yü-hsiang (1882-1948), who similarly rose through the army ranks from a humble background until he controlled an army that dominated large areas of northern and western China. It was he who banished the deposed Ch'ing Emperor from Peking and sent him to live in Manchuria. Feng, a con-

verted Christian and a reformer, believed in physical fitness and moral ardor among his troops; he traveled to Moscow in 1926 and was known briefly as 'The Red General.' For a time the weight of his influence was essential to the success of the Kuomintang.

Chang Tso-lin (1873-1928) dominated Manchuria for the decade before his death. He was a key element in Japan's strategic plans in that area, battled with both Feng Yü-hsiang and Wu P'ei-fu and was responsible for raiding the Soviet Russian embassy in Peking in 1927 and executing some leading Communists. Another result of this raid was that he was able to make generally available hitherto secret evidence concerning Soviet goals in China.

Yen Hsi-shan (1883-1960) controlled the province of Shansi for almost 30 years. He was an ideologue who tried to indoctrinate his troops and subjects with his own private amalgam of

nationalism, democracy, capitalism and paternalism. He developed techniques of mass mobilization and education, inaugurated a ten-year plan for industrial development on the Soviet model and accumulated a private fortune while insisting on the highest moral standards for all.

There is no need to catalogue other warlords. These four men from northern China highlight the main point: that China was fragmented, fought over, endlessly taxed and retaxed by rival armies, and subject to eccentric and regularly changing ideologies. For patriotic intellectuals or soldiers who had dreamed of a different China in the closing years of the Ch'ing, the anarchy that existed between 1915 and 1925 was both a humiliation and a challenge. For these reasons Sun Yat-sen, driven to exile in Japan by Yüan Shih-k'ai, returned to China and set up a new revolutionary base in Canton.

The Soviet Union, established after the 1917 revolution had destroyed the old Russian state, looked to China as fruitful soil for revolutionary action. Lenin dispatched agents of the Communist International (Comintern) to China and also insisted that the Soviet Union renounce many of the illegal territorial and railroad concessions won from China by the czars. Moved by Soviet generosity (much of it later rescinded), angered by the Versailles betrayals and inspired by revolutionary ideals that seemed to have been actualized in the Soviet Union, Chinese intellectuals were receptive to the overtures of Lenin's agents. A Chinese branch of the Communist Party was formed, and held its first meeting at Shanghai in 1921. Most of these first Communists were intellectuals who had participated in the May 4 Movement and were still writing and working in the ongoing cultural revolution: among these were the Party's first leaders, Li Ta-chao and Ch'en Tu-hsiu. A few, like Mao Tse-tung, were from peasant backgrounds and had sweated for their education. Others joined the Party overseas – Liu Shao-ch'i while studying in Moscow, Chou En-lai in Paris, Chu Te in Berlin.

Even though the Comintern was interested in developing a Chinese Communist Party, its agents realized that such an organization would take a long time to develop. Indeed, the savage strike suppressions conducted by Wu P'ei-fu and other warlords convinced the Comintern that it would at first be wise to work with existing organizations that had anti-warlord, anti-feudal and anti-imperialist potential. The most obvious of these

Left: Chang Tso-lin, the warlord who dominated Manchuria in the 1920s.

Below left: Warlord Wu P'ei-fu (left), with two of his staff officers. The root of a warlord's power lay in the ability to command the personal allegiance of a substantial army.

Right: Sun Yat-sen, founder of the Kuomintang. He strengthened his movement in the early 1920s with the help of the Communists.

Below: Chinese and Soviet diplomatic and military personnel at Hankow in 1926, with on the far left the Soviet agent Borodin. The era of Soviet influence in the Kuomintang was soon to come to an end.

was Sun Yat-sen's Kuomintang, and it was accordingly on Sun that the agent Borodin worked the hardest. Sun was eager for Soviet technical advice and for Soviet arms, and he got both; Comintern agents helped him to reorganize the Kuomintang more effectively along democratic-centralist lines, developed his propaganda and recruitment techniques and helped in the founding and staffing of a military academy in Whampoa near Canton. In return for their help, the Comintern asked that Chinese Communists be permitted to join the Kuomintang as individuals and help in its work. The combination was potent. When Sun died in 1925 the Kuomintang was a powerful and well-organized party in South China, with a solid foothold among workers and peasants and an efficient and well-trained army led by former Whampoa cadets. The three principles of Sun Yat-sen had been rewritten and expanded in the form of an integrated ideology that could be used as the basis for political indoctrination, and the Communist-Kuomintang alliance appeared to be functioning smoothly under Comintern guidance.

Sun's death, however, brought latent tensions to the surface. There were several influential politicians who aspired to his mantle, and they represented a wide political spectrum from leftist to rightist. Among the shrewdest and most influential was Chiang Kai-shek, who had been born in 1887 and had risen, after training in a Japanese military academy, to be a confidant of Sun and director of the Whampoa Academy. Sun had sent Chiang as his representative to Moscow, and Chiang also had important contacts in eastern Chinese financial circles and in the Shanghai underworld. Chiang was considerably more suspicious of the Communists than Sun had been, and in 1926 he demoted Borodin and many other Soviet advisers and considerably lessened the powers of the Communists within the Kuomintang. The Communists were alarmed by these actions but were unsure how to react. They still

Left: Chiang Kai-shek, photographed around 1930, soon after he had first established himself as leader of the Kuomintang. Although he was official ruler of China from his capital at Nanking, Chiang's authority was contested by Communists, warlords and the Japanese.

Below: The body of a strike leader in Shanghai, executed during Chiang's massacre of union organizers and Communists in April 1927.

Above right: The aftermath of the failed 1927 Communist uprising in Canton, repressed by Kuomintang troops loyal to Chiang.

needed the protection given by the Kuomintang umbrella, and they needed the Whampoa-led armies. So, despite their misgivings, they continued to co-operate with Chiang Kai-shek, and late in 1926 they embarked on the Northern Expedition to unify China as members of the Kuomintang forces, with Chiang Kai-shek as C in C.

The first stage of the Northern Expedition was an astonishing success. Many warlords simply joined up with the Kuomintang forces, and others were defeated after fierce battles. But as the Kuomintang armies approached the Yangtze River, a split appeared in their councils. Chiang Kai-shek wanted to move to Shanghai, where he had powerful contacts, and to make the Yangtze valley his base. Borodin, speaking for the Chinese Communist Party, wanted to settle in the great industrial complex at Wuhan, where there was a strong urban movement. Here the Communists could expand the base of their movement before going on to greater things. Two events increased the Communists' optimism. First, after mass demonstrations in Hankow, the Chinese had taken over the British concession there, and the British had been unable to retaliate. This seemed to show the potency of the new anti-imperialism and to be a great step beyond the boycotts and protests of the May 30 Movement of 1925. Second, as the Kuomintang troops had advanced through central China, hundreds of thousands of peasants had come out in their support. Leaders of the Kuomintang peasant bureau, among whom was Mao Tsetung, had been astonished by the force and spontaneity of the peasant response; it seemed to show that anti-feudalism was an immensely heightened force. Mao's first famous report was written on this peasant movement as he had witnessed it in Hunan: he was never to lose the faith in peasant power.

The clash in goals between Kuomintang and Communists could not be reconciled. Borodin stayed in Wuhan, and Chiang marched to Shanghai. Yet the Soviet Union, controled now by Stalin, who had gained power after Lenin's death, did not want an open split. Stalin wanted the battle against imperialism and feudalism pushed ahead with all force, and he still thought the Kuomintang was better equipped to do this than the comparatively weaker Communists. On this point Stalin clashed bitterly with Trotsky. Trotsky wanted to marshal the revolutionary workers and develop soviets in China, whereas Stalin wanted workers to ally with the 'national-bourgeois' Kuomintang. Stalin's orders carried the day and were relayed to China. The workers of Shanghai, who had won virtual control of the city after a general strike, welcomed the armies of Chiang Kai-shek to their city and disarmed their pickets. However, in April 1927, in a lightning coup, Chiang rounded up the leading union organizers and Communists in the city and had several hundred of them shot.

Communists in disarray

This was a severe blow to the Chinese Communist Party, which now had to concentrate all its energies in Wuhan. Their orders from Moscow were to work with the radical wing of the Kuomintang in that city, controled by Wang Ching-wei. Once again Stalin had a coolly logical explanation: the killings in Shanghai had proved that Chiang was the national-bourgeois leader; it was now necessary to ally with the petty bourgeoisie as exemplified by Wang Ching-wei. This also meant that the Communists could not encourage peasants to revolt against those landlords or warlords who were supporters of the Left Kuomintang. So Mao and other leaders had to repress those very agrarian movements that they had just been describing with such excitement. This policy failed as disastrously as the Shanghai policy had failed. In the course of the summer thousands of peasants and worker leaders in central China were shot. The Left Kuomintang reunited with Chiang Kai-shek, and by the end of the year the Communists were in complete disarray. They had tried to stage some peasant risings in the autumn, but these had been ruthlessly suppressed. They had tried to seize more industrial cities – Nanchang, Changsha, Canton – but had been bloodily repulsed. So as 1927 ended the Communists went into hiding in the cities or retreated to thinly populated areas of the countryside.

Dispersal of the Communists was what Chiang had wanted, and by late 1928 China and Manchuria were nominally united under the Kuomintang banner and ruled from the new capital in Nanking. To get to this point Chiang had not only had to master the Communists, he had also had serious clashes with Japanese troops at Tsinan in Shantung and had made complex deals with a number of warlords, including Chang Hsüehliang, who had become warlord of Manchuria after his father had been assassinated by the Japanese in 1928. Chiang was also by no means above challenge within his own party. For a period in 1927 he had moved to Japan, and from 1928 (when he returned) onward, he was usually dependent on some kind of alliance with other senior Kuomintang politicians such as Wang Ching-wei or Hu Han-min.

Nevertheless, despite these problems Chiang had triumphed, and the period from 1928 to 1937 is usually called the 'Nanking Decade,' after the Yangtze River city that Chiang Kai-shek chose as his capital. It was in this decade that the Kuomintang had its only chance to put its ideas of government into practice. Chiang's basic goals were national unity, economic development and moral regeneration for the Chinese people. The nominal unity that had been attained by 1928 was not adequate if China was to take her place forcefully in world affairs. There were still Communist soviets scattered across China, there were numerous warlords who still dominated their own terrain, there were the foreign powers in the treaty ports and the Japanese were in Manchuria

and Shantung. Since Chiang could not tackle all these problems at once, he gave priority to stamping out the Communists, launching five major campaigns against their central and southern Chinese bases between 1930 and 1934. His success was only partial. The Communists were finally ousted from all their bases, but the cost of destroying the Communists completely proved too great, for at the same time Japanese power was growing apace, and Chiang was unable to unite the country behind his anti-Communist effort.

In the sphere of economic development Chiang was also largely unsuccessful. The considerable industrialization of areas such as Shanghai and Wuhan continued, but these were the very areas where foreign investment was heaviest. In the early 1930s foreign-owned factories accounted for about 19 percent of China's industrial production, and of this 34 percent was in Shanghai (much of it British) and 27 percent in Manchuria (mostly Japanese). The Kuomintang did not alter labor or production patterns significantly in any way; not only was there not much new industrialization, but the population remained overwhelmingly agricultural, with some 75 percent of the population being peasants who produced 65 percent of the gross national product. The Kuomintang never even set up an adequate tax-gathering system; rural taxes remained in rural (ie local warlords' or special interest groups') hands, and most government revenue came from the Maritime Customs — one of the Kuomintang successes being that it had recovered tariff autonomy in 1929 — and from the salt gabelle and commodity taxes. This was not so different from the late Ch'ing revenue-producing patterns.

There was, however, one major new source of revenue, that of floating bond issues. This became a major source of weakness to Chiang's regime because it encouraged speculation and corruption in government financial circles. Among the most

important people associated with these circles were the famous Soong family. Four children of the American-educated industrialist Charles Soong were the nucleus of this powerful group: Soong Ch'ing-ling married Sun Yat-sen; Soong Ai-ling married H H K'ung, who was minister of finance between 1933 and 1944 and responsible for many of China's most important economic programs; Soong Mei-ling married Chiang Kai-shek in late 1927 (and apparently in response to promises made at that time, Chiang was baptized a Christian in 1930); T V Soong (Harvard, class of 1915) was governor of the Central Bank of China, and during World War II he negotiated several of China's important loans from the United States. Thus both T V Soong and H H K'ung did make several important contributions to modernizing China's economy and to regaining concessions from foreign powers. And yet the prominence of

the family members in politics, and the fortunes that they and their friends were believed to have accumulated, did not encourage confidence in the integrity of Kuomintang finances. Much more harmful to Chiang's image was the fact that such men as Tu Yüeh-sheng, a former secret-society leader and controller of opium-smuggling syndicates in Shanghai, was a 'respected' figure in Shanghai financial circles. The twin shadows of speculation and graft hung over many Kuomintang dealings and perhaps have distracted attention from the real innovations being made.

It was in the field of moral regeneration that Chiang made his greatest ideological efforts. He was clearly convinced that morality must be reformed along with the economy, and he sought to reintroduce the virtues of righteousness, thrift, simplicity and modesty which he thought had been the keystones of the traditional Confucian

morality. These ideas were pushed in such puritan campaigns as 'The New Life Movement,' where wider ideals of national purification were rapidly lost sight of in waves of petty harassment against women in make-up or men in fancy clothes. Tseng Kuo-fan was invoked as a hero, the *pao-chia* system of registration and mutual guarantees was reinstituted, and youth corps were formed as the training ground for the future.

Since much has been written about this attempted Confucian revival, it should be emphasized that it was rigidly authoritarian in intent, rather than humanistic. It was fitting therefore that Chiang's spokesmen were men such as the Ch'en brothers, Ch'en Li-fu and Ch'en Kuo-fu, who were often known simply as the 'CC' Clique and combined an interest in philosophy with a mastery of modern security techniques. Ch'en Kuo-fu was the chief architect of the tight Kuomintang organizational structure that gave Chiang so much of his power, and Ch'en Li-fu was a long-time director of the Kuomintang investigation division, responsible for internal security. The CC Clique played a major role in developing Chiang's position through their skilled manipulation of party conferences, and they also propagated Kuomintang ideology through publications that they edited and through their own writings.

Though many Chinese youths did serve the Kuomintang loyally, and though both the CC Clique and the Soong family did participate actively in several areas of national reconstruction, it can be said that Chiang and his closest advisers failed to draw the majority of Chinese intellectuals to their side. The students often remained intransigent, and at one time in 1931 their nationalistic demonstrations were so strong that Chiang had, once again, to step down briefly from power. By 1936 much of China's youth had become permanently disillusioned and was to be increasingly receptive to Communist appeals.

After its disastrous defeats in 1927, the members of the Communist Party had scattered. By 1929 several different groups had re-established bases (soviets) in the countryside, where they managed to set up some kind of revolutionary government and fight off the attacks of Kuomintang and warlord troops. The soviet that was to have the greatest significance in later Chinese history was that in Kiangsi, for it was here that Mao Tse-tung established his reputation and laid the base for his future pre-eminence within the Communist Party. Mao (born 1893) was a largely self-educated man from a peasant background. He had attended the first Congress of the Chinese Communist Party in 1921 and was later active in peasant affairs during the period of the Kuomintang-Communist alliance. After the 1927 failure of 'The Autumn Harvest Uprising,' for which Mao was held responsible, he was dismissed from his Party posts, but in 1929 he had established a fairly strong base with General Chu Te in southeast Kiangsi. Here the fugitive troops from the various abortive Communist risings were consolidated, and Mao introduced an intensive program to train Party cadres and troops and to get them to work intimately with the local peasants. On many occasions, after successful military sorties, the Communists extended their terrain, holding mass rallies of 'liberated' peasants, burning title deeds to land and records of debts and trying to push through programs of land redistribution. At the same time Chu Te was developing the techniques of tactical retreat into difficult terrain, coupled with lightning attacks on numerically inferior enemy forces. Such tactics were later to be developed into the full-blown doctrine of Maoist 'guerrilla strategy.'

Mao and the peasants

By 1933 the Communist armies in the Kiangsi soviet probably numbered around 200,000 troops. Mao had also survived a complex series of political challenges, among the strongest being those from the city-based Party regulars, who still drew their instructions from the Comintern and held to a purist belief in the urban proletariat and the importance of urban insurrection. Mao and Chu Te, however, were developing ever-greater faith in the power and effectiveness of a people's army composed mainly of peasant recruits. (It should be emphasized that in conventional Marxist doctrine the peasant was considered inherently conservative or petty bourgeois because of his attachment to the land and private property; Mao's recognition of the peasants' revolutionary potential has been widely regarded as his most important contribution to Marxist-Leninist theory.)

By 1934, however, the Communist position in Kiangsi finally became untenable. Chiang Kai-shek, with the help of German military advisers,

Above left: Delegates to the first Pan-Chinese National Assembly gather at Nanking in 1931.

Below left: Ill-armed young revolutionaries in 1927. The Kuomintang regime never won the support of students or intellectuals.

Above right: Three members of the powerful Soong family, from left to right, Soong Ch'ing-ling (wife of Sun Yat-sen), Soong Ai-ling (married to finance minister H H K'ung), and Soong Mei-ling (wife of Chiang Kai-shek).

Right: Mao Tse-tung, an obscure Communist photographed in Kwangchow in 1925. Only 10 years later Mao emerged as undisputed leader of the Party in China.

Left: The end of the Long March – Communist troops who survived the 5000-mile retreat from Kiangsi to Shensi in 1934-35.

Below left: Two Chinese civilians held captive by invading Japanese troops in Manchuria.

Above right: Pu-yi, the deposed Ch'ing emperor, went through a second coronation in 1934, becoming titular ruler of the Japanese puppet state of Manchukuo.

Below right: The war with Japan which began in July 1937 imposed terrible suffering on the Chinese people. Here, a Japanese soldier watches over the bodies of slaughtered Chinese at Nanking, where some of the worst atrocities were committed.

had developed a series of interlocking bases and blockhouses around the Kiangsi soviet. With an ever-shrinking base area, deprived of new recruits and also of such essential supplies as ammunition and salt, the Communists were forced to retreat. In October 1934 the Communist armies, numbering around 100,000 by this time, moved out of Kiangsi to the west and started an amazing retreat that they have since immortalized in their own history as 'The Long March.' In the course of a year the Communist forces traveled over 5000 miles in a great arc through western China, and then northward to Shensi province. Along the way they not only fought a series of savage actions with Kuomintang troops, but also had to fight with local warlords and even with aboriginal mountain tribes who resented their presence. As if these problems were not enough, there were a series of leadership fights within Communist ranks, and these led to further depletion of their armies as various groups refused to agree on their final destination.

The final victory was Mao's; he attained the undisputed position of Party leader during the Long March, and his comrades who survived the March with him became a cohesive group of devoted supporters. Yet the costs had been appalling. Over 60 percent of the marchers had died or disappeared along the way. The carefully organized peasant bases in Kiangsi and elsewhere had been shattered, and the workers' organizations in the cities seemed broken beyond repair. As Chiang supervised the final deployments of Kuomintang and allied warlord troops in the Shensi area he was confident that he would soon exterminate the Communists once and for all.

It is possible that in late 1936 or early 1937 the Communists would indeed have been destroyed, and Mao killed with them, had it not been for the additional factors injected into the situation by the Japanese. Not content with their gains in 1895, 1915 and 1928, the Japanese had been pushing forward steadily at China's expense. In 1931 they engineered the so-called 'Mukden Incident,' which gave them virtual control over Manchuria. In 1932 they attacked Shanghai and were only forced to accept a stalemate after heavy fighting. In the aftermath of that battle the Japanese declared that Manchuria was now the new state of 'Manchukuo,' on the throne of which they placed the still-living last Ch'ing emperor, who had been deposed in 1912. These moves proved the complete failure of the various steps that had

been taken by foreign powers to halt Japan's expansion. The Washington Naval conference of 1921 (by which the United States and Britain had sought to limit Japan's naval development), as well as the international security systems of the League of Nations, were shown to be meaningless. By the mid 1930s Japan had extended its influence over much of northeast China.

Chiang Kai-shek was caught in a dilemma. His policy had been to try to break the Communists first and move against the Japanese second, when he had a strong and united country with which to do so. But the more he appeased the Japanese in order to get the necessary time to beat the Communists, the more he angered nationalistic Chinese, smarting under China's incessant humiliations. Thus Chiang lost popular support just when he needed it most. The Communists, who were in a beleaguered position and in no way responsible for foreign affairs, could afford to be bolder. They 'declared war' on the Japanese and appealed to all patriotic students and citizens to join them in the struggle. They also waged a strenuous propaganda campaign along these same lines amongst the Kuomintang and warlord troops who were massing in Shensi to destroy them. As an increasing number of anti-Japanese demonstrations were taking place, and as his troops seemed to be wavering, Chiang Kai-shek flew into Sian in December 1936 to co-ordinate the anti-Communist campaign and silence the

opposition. And in Sian, in one of the most mysterious and dramatic episodes in modern Chinese history, he was kidnapped by the troops he had come to command.

The Sian kidnapping had an electric effect on China. One result was that people came to see how important Chiang was, despite his many failings, as symbolic leader of the nation. It was he, after all, who had inherited Sun Yat-sen's mantle. It was he who had led the Northern Expedition. It was he who was generally known throughout the world as the leader of China. He controled the best troops in China, had the surest access to funds and enjoyed the greatest reputation among the common people. According to various reports, none of which can be verified, the Communists wanted to have Chiang executed when they heard the news of his capture, and so did certain Kuomintang leaders in Nanking who were jealous of Chiang's power. Later, however, both groups changed their mind, as did Chang Hsüeh-liang, the warlord whose troops had kidnapped Chiang in the first place. The upshot of complex negotiations was that in late December Chiang was released and returned to Nanking and that the Kuomintang and the Communists agreed to work in a joint 'United Front' against the Japanese and in the interests of national unity. When Japan, in July 1937, staged a new series of harassing incidents near Peking, for the first time Chiang did not yield. Instead he declared war.

Japan

Japan's entrance into the world of imperialist rivalries in the year before World War I had a profound influence upon the international affairs of East Asia and of the world. Japan's conversion into an imperialist power transformed what had been a movement toward global domination by the Western powers into a worldwide phenomenon. A non-Western people had gained access to the inner circle of great powers, competing with them on an equal basis and yet somehow intruding a new dimension into the fabric of competition which had up to this point emanated exclusively from the West. The world of the early twentieth century was acutely conscious of racial and cultural origins and differences. Japan introduced both issues into the imperialist scene.

The European crisis of 1914 provided Japan with the opportunity to intervene directly in the affairs of the European powers. By stretching the provisions of the Anglo-Japanese alliance Japan was able to declare war on Germany. Its armed forces moved quickly to take over German military bases and commercial interests in China and to occupy the German-held Pacific islands. Then, finding the Western powers occupied in Europe and China in a particularly vulnerable position, the Japanese government in 1915 pressed upon China's Yüan Shih-k'ai a set of demands which, if acceded to, would have given Japan a virtual political and economic protectorate over China. These were the so-called 'Twenty-one Demands.' Eventually the demands were scaled down as a result of Chinese resistance and Western protest, but they nonetheless laid the basis for Japan's postwar claim to retention of former German rights in Shantung and to an extension of Japanese interests in Manchuria. When, in the 1917 Lansing-Ishii exchange of notes, the United States recognized the proposition that 'territorial propinquity' gave Japan 'special interests' on the Chinese mainland, the Japanese were on the way toward acquiring a predominant position in East Asia, a position that none of the Western powers was willing to concede.

The Versailles peace conference was in many ways a bitterly disappointing experience for the Japanese. For although the Japanese delegation was ranked next to Britain, France and the United States, it failed to fully achieve its aims regarding German rights in Shantung. Unexpectedly distressing also was the rejection of a Japanese proposal for the inclusion of a racial-equality clause in the League of Nations Charter. And although the Japanese were to be given a permanent seat on the League's Council, the refusal of the Western powers to give public recognition to a statement of racial equality placed Japan in the psychologically damaging category of 'honorary Occidentals.' During the decade of the 1920s Japan continued to feel a definite reluctance on the part of the Western powers to deal with them on fully equal terms, a reluctance that seemed to the Japanese to invalidate the claim that World War I had been 'a war for democracy,' fought to make possible a world that recognized national self-determination and the peaceful solutions of disputes.

Two events, in particular, seemed to exemplify the West's attitude. The Washington Conference of 1921-22, covering a whole range of settlements between Japan, China and the Western powers, could, from the Japanese point of view, be inter-

Above: Field Marshal Prince Yamagata was one of the generation of Japanese statesmen and military leaders that brought their country into the ranks of the imperial powers at the beginning of the twentieth century.

Left: Japanese troops build a railroad for bringing up heavy guns to bombard the German fortress of Tsingtao in China. Japan's participation on the Allied side in World War I ensured that it would gain Germany's possessions in China in the postwar peace settlement.

Above right: Tokyo had the appearance of a modern European city in the 1920s and 1930s, a sign of the country's rapid adoption of Western industrial civilization.

preted as the diplomatic phase of a policy to contain Japan. The Four Power Pact, which replaced Japan's alliance with Britain, obliged Japan to respect the rights of, and consult with, all three of its major competitors in East Asia. The principle of the Open Door, which was written into the Nine Power Treaty, served also to protect the *status quo* of treaty rights which the Western nations had acquired by force prior to Japan's entry into the China scene. Thus when Japan ultimately felt obliged to return Chinese sovereignty over Shantung and to pull out the troops it had sent into Siberia following the Bolshevik revolution, Japan's military planners felt that discriminatory pressures were being placed upon them. Although as a result of the Washington Conference Japan gained naval security in the western Pacific, the Anglo-American powers had protected their commercial interests in China by the enunciation of moral principles which had not applied to them at the time these interests had been acquired.

The second disturbing event was the passage by the United States Congress of the Japanese Immigration Act, which singled Japan out for complete exclusion of immigration. This blow to Japanese national sensitivities brought forth expressions of anti-American passions in Japan and aroused counter-expressions of bellicose racist sentiment from many American government figures. Public statements about the inevitability of war between Japan and America were even voiced in anger on the Japanese side.

Thus while the postwar decade, or more rightly the post-Washington Conference decade, in East Asia proved to be a relatively quiet one, the quiet was only on the surface. Japan's postwar industrial and commercial growth, the rise of Chinese nationalism and the formation of the nationalist regimes under Chiang Kai-shek, and the growing power of the Soviet Union in northern Manchuria placed new pressures on a diplomatic accommodation that had been based on what proved to be an anachronistic reading of the nature of East Asian power politics. The idea of containing Japan, together with the maintenance of an open door of opportunity for European and American business in China, was to prove illusory within a decade after the Washington agreements.

If in the years after World War I Japan came of age in its international relations, receiving as a consequence a newly intensified resistance from the Western powers, it was also obliged to deal with new challenges. The Meiji settlement had in large part solved Japan's crises of national identity and security and had buttressed the legitimacy of the imperial government. But by the 1920s the pressures of growth and differentiation within Japanese society had created crises of new magnitude and complexity. By 1918 the context of political action and participation had changed drastically, as had the social and economic circumstances of the majority of Japan's growing population. Japan was now a heavily urbanized and industrialized society. By 1920 total national population had grown to 55 million. The indus-

trial force was approaching two million. Compulsory schooling had given the Japanese people a literacy rate of more than 95 percent, and mass media, particularly the newspapers, reached every segment of the population. Japan was no longer a country that could be led by a small oligarchy of politically powerful individuals. The appearance of new professions and occupations, along with the growth of political parties and labor movements, produced new definitions of class and group interests. Japan now had to face the same problems of mass participation in the political process and of distribution of wealth and political power that had confronted the early modernized societies of Europe in the prewar decade.

As in their treatment of the Weimar Republic in Germany, historians have tended to look at the period of the 1920s in Japan in terms of the success or failure of democratic institutions. In each country the collapse of representative government based on a party system has been seen as leading to Fascism in the period between the great wars. In the case of Japan the critical factor was neither democratic government nor a party system, since neither of these institutions had been assimilated into the Japanese political tradition. The problem is better understood in functional terms, as one involving problems of flexibility in a political system placed under new stresses by newly emerging political and economic interests. As new groups and elites took shape and demanded access to political power, the existing oligarchic-bureaucratic system was placed on the defensive. As pressures toward containment of Japan by the Western powers intensified, the Japanese people found their domestic priorities overshadowed by external concerns. The manner in which Japan's rulers reacted to these new challenges was to have worldwide significance.

By the end of World War I it is clear that domestic politics in Japan had reached a new stage of development. During the Meiji period political issues, both domestic and foreign, had been mostly decided out of public view by the great figures who had led the country through its initial stages of nationbuilding. Remnants of the Meiji oligarchy, now referred to as *genrō* (elder statesmen), continued to dominate politics, either directly or through personally controlled cliques, down into the wartime era. But most of them were nearing the end of their lives. Itagaki died in 1919, Okuma and Yamagata in 1922. Saionji, a successor *genrō*, lived on until 1940, but there was no powerful second generation with sufficient personal following to keep clique government alive. The political scene by 1918 was thus less oligarchic and more fluid, and it was just at this point that the country faced its new domestic political challenge.

In the Western democracies, political parties linked to a parliamentary process had become the chief means of broadening the base of political participation and of conciliating conflicting interests. Parties had yet to prove themselves effective organs of political participation in Japan. Yet with the diffusion of oligarchic leadership in the years after the Russo-Japanese war, party leader-

ship was drawn increasingly into the affairs of government. Two of the original Meiji leaders, Itagaki and Okuma, had organized national political followings as part of their agitation for constitutional government. These organizations, disbanded before the adoption of the Meiji constitution, became the basis of the two parties that served as vehicles for election to the lower house of the Diet. The early parties were unstable and served largely as organs of factional competition within the government. Increasingly, however, they came to represent interests lying outside the official bureaucracy and oligarchy-led cliques, such as those of big business (the *zaibatsu*), rural landowners and ultimately labor and tenant groups. Roughly between 1910 and 1920 the parties were looked to chiefly as vehicles for mediating the struggle between the plural elites within the establishment, that is between the several remaining *genrō* or between the civil bureaucrats and the military. As a result, party leaders from time to time were able to obtain positions of influence in government. Okuma, in fact, served as premier in 1914-16, though largely at the behest of the oligarchs.

It was in the aftermath of the Great War that parties came into their own as political instruments with the formation of the first so-called 'party government,' one in which the head of the majority in the Diet became the premier. The circumstances which ushered in what has been called the era of 'normal constitutional government' in Japan were of both foreign and domestic origin. World sentiment in favor of democracy and the success of the Russian Revolution com-

Left: Prince Okuma Shigenobu was Prime Minister of Japan in 1914-15. His death in 1922 can be seen as the sign that the old generation of leaders were nearing the natural end of their term of authority.

Below left: This Art Deco-style department store in interwar Tokyo indicates the willingness of the Japanese to abandon the traditional outward features of their culture for European fashions.

Right: Soviet politburo member Grigory Zinoviev on a platform at a 1922 Congress of Far Eastern Workers. It was attended by Marxists from several Asian countries, including Japan. The 'dangerous ideas' of Marxism and Communism struck terror into the hearts of the Japanese authorities. Leftwing movements in Japan were ruthlessly persecuted and repressed during the 1920s.

bined to create a mood favorable to popular, as against establishment, politics. Then, in August 1918, the country was shaken by a wave of rice riots brought on by critical consumer-goods shortages and the sharp rise in the price of rice. Destructive riots, mostly against rice stores and warehouses, lasted for nearly three weeks and affected nearly all the large cities, and the government was forced to call out troops to establish order. Popular resentment against the government ran so high that Premier General Terauchi was forced to resign. In an effort to select a leader of more flexible and resilient qualities, the *genrō* turned to what they also hoped would be a more popularly acceptable choice for his successor. Hara Kei, a commoner and head of the dominant Seiyukai party, was made premier.

Party government and the establishment

The selection of Hara as premier was hailed in public as the beginning of true party government in Japan. It was in fact far from such. Hara and his party faction were firmly committed to a policy of compromise with existing establishment interests. But his selection as head of government nevertheless indicated that the parties had become a mechanism for producing leaders more capable and willing to enter the political struggle than the establishment leaders, whose sources of power came from family connections and influence within the high bureaucracy and who were more comfortable with manipulative politics. It was not until 1924, with the formation of the Kenseikai-based Kato Komei cabinet, that party governments in a real sense came into being and that the full impact of party leadership in government came to be felt. Indicative of their effect on Japanese politics was the passage in 1925 of the Universal Manhood Suffrage Bill, which increased the electorate from 3 to 12.5 million voters. But the era of party rule was shortlived, and by 1932 the parties had been forced back to a

position of compromise with other elements of the plural elite which constituted the continuing establishment. The period from 1925 to 1932 thus was a vital transition period in the interwar years, when a more open and mass-based politics attempted to cope with the problems of economic growth, international competition and adjustment to social change.

During the latter half of the 1920s two prominent trends played out a turbulent course in Japanese politics. In international relations, party leadership, reflecting both liberal idealism and the practical interest of business in creating a free market, combined to work toward a relaxation of tensions on the Asian mainland and a co-operative policy toward the European powers. A certain amount of optimism was generated by what was called 'the spirit of the Washington Conference' and the thought that co-operation on a worldwide basis both in trade policies and arms reduction could be accomplished. At home, criticism of military involvements in politics resulted in an attack upon military spending, to which the military, particularly the upper echelons of the navy acceded. Arms expenditures, which had accounted for 36 percent of the government budget in 1919, were reduced to about 16 percent during the years from 1923 to 1931, while the 1930 London Naval Treaty placed Japan in a far less advantageous position than after the Washington Conference.

In general the 1920s stressed the interests of big business. Tax rates on business profits and private incomes were kept low, while policies on labor, tariff rates, government subsidies and economic diplomacy favored the growth of large-scale industry and commerce. These years were the heyday of the great *zaibatsu* firms such as Mitsui, Mitsubishi and Sumitomo. The close link between big business, party leadership and the upper levels of the civil and military bureaucracy became the prime moving force behind domestic

and foreign policy. And despite a certain liberalism in this policy on matters of foreign affairs and arms spending, the parties were clearly more wedded to the interests of the establishment than to any fundamental concern about general welfare.

This orientation was felt directly by the underprivileged classes and more abstractly by a new generation of intellectuals, journalists and political activists who reacted increasingly to a sense of frustration over the failure of more widespread democratization to take place in government and in the economy. The period of the 1920s witnessed the first concerted efforts to advance the status of the working man and to counter the power of the establishment through mass political organization and leftist agitation. The flow of industrial labor to the cities created pools of workers amenable to union organization. By 1920 some 200 labor unions had come into existence, and Suzuki Bunji had formed a Federation of Labor. The great dockyard strike of 1921, centering on the Kobe Kawasaki workers, involved 25,000 men for over a month in what often turned into violent clashes with the police. The strike in its bitterness illustrated the difficulty that labor was to have in asserting its cause against a solid alignment of vested interests.

In the countryside it was the plight of the tenant and small-scale farmer that led to unrest. By the 1920s nearly half the farming population had holdings of less than one and a quarter acres, and nearly half of the farming land in the country was held under tenancy agreements under terms that made life precarious for the tenant. Because of these conditions, and also as a result of a series of disastrous changes in the agricultural and silk markets, farm families suffered acute distress, and there were numerous tenancy disputes involving violence.

The establishment parties were on the whole slow to come to the support of factory workers

and poor farmers. Leadership on their behalf came in the main from intellectual liberals and leftist political organizers. During the early years after World War I the assumption was that universal manhood suffrage would open up mass participation in government and make for social reform through the ballot box. Yoshimo Sakuzō, a political scientist from Waseda University, briefly led a political movement that had as its object democratic reform and universal manhood suffrage. The failure of the Hara government to consider revision of the suffrage crushed Yoshimo's moderate movement and tended to radicalize the remaining leadership. Efforts to create a legitimate and functioning socialist party had never been successful in Japan because of both government oppression and factionalism within the leadership. Labor- and tenant-union activities provided an avenue of direct action, however, and in 1921 the formation of a clandestine Communist Party provided an exciting outlet for those of extremist inclinations. For a brief period of years, from about 1921 to 1928, radical ideas ('dangerous thoughts' as they were labeled by the police) flowed freely, if precariously, through Japanese university campuses and in labor circles. Police surveillance and harassment was continuous and severe. Mass arrests were made in 1923, following the Tokyo earthquake, and again in 1928, when a thousand people were apprehended. Another wave of arrests in 1929 broke the back of the Communist movement and intimidated its sympathizers into silence.

It was in the face of radical pressures and worsening economic conditions for the masses that Japan's party leaders eventually came to the support of the Universal Suffrage Bill. By 1925 it was

fairly generally agreed that such a law was inevitable and desirable, and it was appropriate that the credit for its passage should go to Kato Komei, the first true party premier. To a great extent the enlargement of the suffrage served to inhibit further radicalization of Japanese politics. Reform-minded leaders rushed to the task of organizing 'mass proletarian parties' in an effort to press forward the interests of the underprivileged classes, but the reform leadership was divided

and subject to police suppression. Various combinations bearing labor-farm labels were organized, only to be dissolved. The Japan Mass Party, founded in 1928, attempted to bring unity to the various anti-establishment factions, but without success. Only in 1932, with the formation of the Social Mass Party (*Shakai Taishuto*), was the cause of the proletariat given stable representation, but already the possibility of social reform through party activity had passed.

Left: The Tokyo earthquake of 1923 leveled large tracts of the city.

Below left: Rice stripping in rural Japan. The rise and fall of the price of this food staple deeply affected the fabric of Japanese life. A sharp increase in the cost of rice in 1918 led to riots, while a considerable drop in the early 1930s was partly responsible for plunging Japan into the depths of the worldwide Great Depression.

Right: The Japanese politician Inukai Tsuyoshi with the last of the *genrō* (elder statesmen), Prince Saionji Kimmochi. The assassination of Inukai in 1932 by militarists, part of a nation-wide terror campaign, was an important step down the road that led Japan into World War II.

Thus the widening of the suffrage did little more than further entrench the establishment parties, without forcing them to adopt new platforms aimed to serve the new electorate. Since new Japanese parties had not developed, the new electorate followed traditional practices of voting for the established parties. Indeed, the mass parties never succeeded in obtaining even 15 percent of the vote. Thus Japan went into the severe economic troubles of the late 1920s with little basic change in its political composition or in its overall social legislation. The domestic situation became increasingly acute after the effects of the world depression struck Japan. Farm villages were particularly hard hit as the price of rice fell drastically and the bottom dropped out of the silk market. By 1931 rice sold at less than half of its 1929 price and raw silk at about a third of its 1925 price. Decline of the world market for Japanese cotton textiles also forced the slackening of textile production, thus throwing laborers back into the villages and producing widespread rural discontent.

Failure to handle the domestic economic crisis, together with corruption, or at least callousness, on the part of party politicians, undermined the confidence of the masses in the political parties. Meanwhile the Cabinet's anti-militarist policy, along with what was referred to as its 'weak diplomacy,' increasingly distressed various powerful groups in the country. Resentment was naturally growing within the armed forces, but increasingly segments of the civilian population also began expressing right-wing sentiment and opposition to what was seen as a precarious drift of the country toward radicalism at home and weakness abroad. The ominous feature of the right wing's activity was that, while it drew its strength from

large-scale national organizations such as the Reservists' Association, or from patriotic societies such as the *Kokuhonsha* (National Foundation Society), it entered the political arena not through the medium of party action but through the tactics of violence and direct action. The rise of the radical Right in Japanese politics is marked by the assassination of two of the last three party premiers: Hamaguchi, for his action in pushing through the London Naval Treaty of 1930, and Inukai, in 1932, as part of a military-led terrorist rampage.

The Manchurian Incident

Between these two events came the 1931 seizure of Manchuria, precipitated by officers of the Kwantung Army. The Manchurian incursion thus proved to be a major turning point in modern Japanese history, for it literally transformed the nature of Japan's domestic and foreign policies, ushering in a shift toward militarism both at home and abroad and a 'go it alone' policy on the Continent. In the end it would turn Japan from its open door commitments to joining hands with the Axis powers.

The fundamental causes of the Manchurian Incident have been long and hotly debated. Some historians have argued that certain flaws in the national character, and specifically in the Meiji settlement, had made a militarist-fascist resurgence inevitable. Yet the thought that Japan's first try at democracy had been a failure, or that the Meiji Constitution contained certain inevitabilities such as a totalitarian-prone imperial system, is not a sufficient explanation. It is true that Japan, confronted by a multiplicity of problems in the late 1920s, underwent what has sometimes been

called a 'demodernization' in its national political life. But the change of direction taken in Manchuria was not an inevitable result of flaws in Japanese social and economic structure. It had more complex roots. The seizure of national leadership by the military and the stress upon national mobilization came as much from external stimuli as from internal. And we are thereby brought back to Japan's world status in the 1930s.

The period characterized by the slogans of 'democracy' and the 'spirit of the Washington Conference' had been particularly disquieting to those who were sensitive to Japan's world status and national security. The military budget had been severely cut, while party leaders and businessmen aggrandized themselves. Defeat of the racial-equality clause at Versailles was followed by a growing racism in the West, symbolized by the American Immigration Exclusion Act of 1924. The continuing containment policy of the Anglo-American powers, matched by the rise of Soviet power in Siberia and northern Manchuria, and by the threat of Communist activities in China, together with the potential revival of Chinese strength under nationalist leadership, had convinced many that time was running out for Japan in its dealings with the mainland. Small wonder, then, that the concept of regional-bloc hegemonies, then gaining currency in Europe, proved attractive. It provided the rationale for the thrust into Manchuria to create an autonomous pro-Japanese area that would give Japan control over vital raw materials and would provide a strategic foothold on the mainland as a protection against Chinese and Soviet pressure. At a time when the dominant Western powers were calling for peaceful adherence to a *status quo* that contained colonial possessions and rights and privileges won by force during an earlier day of open imperialist competition, Japan and Germany were all too ready to press for their own belated rights to a similar colonies-based security. But it is both ironic and tragic that both countries should have decided on a military drive for colonial expansion at precisely the time when world political and economic conditions were clearly undermining the viability of colonialism as a system.

If the Kwantung Army's seizure of Manchuria had not been specifically authorized by the Japanese government, there is no doubt that the initiative was fully supported by the War Ministry and General Staff and that it was consonant with what most Japanese now perceived as the correct strategy for Japan *vis-à-vis* the mainland. Not surprisingly, therefore, it was to be but the first of a series of connected actions that would lead the nation steadily toward war.

The fighting in Manchuria had ended by the beginning of 1932, but the undeclared war that it had provoked with China continued, soon spilling over into China proper, notably in the Shanghai-Nanking area. In answer to Chinese protests about both the seizure of Manchuria and subsequent Japanese incursions, the League of Nations appointed an investigatory committee headed by Lord Lytton of Great Britain. Since the Japanese government initially approved this investigation, it is probable that at least some liberal Japanese political leaders hoped that it might have a restraining effect on the increasingly out-of-control military. But any such hopes were to be disappointed. In March 1932 the military declared Manchuria a sovereign state, now renamed Manchukuo, and placed on its throne Pu Yi, the heir to the overthrown Ch'ing Empire. This high-handed action seemed to preclude the possibility that any contrary recommendations of the Lytton Commission would be respected, and the

Commission's report, submitted to the League in September 1932, was understandably bitter and condemnatory of Japan. The military, now supported by an offended public opinion, reacted violently to these foreign strictures. Moderates in the government, who might in other circumstances have tried to stem the growing tide of chauvinism, were cowed not only by the vehemence of public sentiment but by a wave of assassinations that had claimed the lives of at least three major political figures, including Prime Minister Inukai, during the course of the year. In February 1933 Japan formally withdrew from the League of Nations.

As Japanese domestic politics became increasingly hostage to the will of the military, Japanese troops continued to press forward in China. Jehol province was added to Manchukuo in 1933, and Hopei and Chahar fell under Japanese control in subsequent years. Yet the pace of Japanese aggression in China was still relatively slow. The military had not yet completely established its dominion over the civil government and was for the most part still obliged to act without explicit government sanction. Moreover, murderous factional infighting had developed within the Imperial Army itself, and until this could be resolved the question of whether securing the Manchurian border against Russia was more important than subjugating China would remain moot. Finally, though this doubtless weighed least, there remained some residual sensitivity to outraged foreign opinion and to the mounting hostility of the Western powers and the Soviet Union.

The army's internal conflict was finally settled in 1935, when the so-called Kodo faction (those in favor of the 'Manchurian' policy) attempted to overthrow the government by a coup d'état. The opposing Tosei faction came to the government's aid, the coup failed and the Tosei emerged in complete control of the army and very nearly in complete control of the government. In short order the Tosei leaders demanded and received a free hand in dealing with China. In the summer of 1937 large-scale fighting was renewed, and the two nations at last formally declared war.

Chinese resistance was now much stronger than before, both sides suffered heavy casualties and the sometimes atrocious conduct of the Japanese troops – especially in the sack of Shanghai and Nanking – provoked widespread condemnation in Western Europe and America. Nevertheless, the Japanese continued to advance steadily, and by the end of 1938 they controled all of northeastern China down to about the latitudes of Nanchang, as well as all of China's major coastal ports north of Hong Kong. Yet the cost of this conquest in terms of expenditure of blood, treasure and popular support at home had been so high that in 1939 the army reverted to a more cautious strategy. There were to be no more major advances in China until control over the newly conquered territories had been consolidated, and there was to be a major diplomatic effort aimed at closing off the supply routes from Burma and Indochina to Free China and thus, it was hoped, forcing Chiang Kai-shek's capitulation. The diplomatic offensive against the British and French was rather more a matter of threats than of blandishments, and by the end of 1940, when France had been defeated by Germany and Britain's wartime fortunes were at their most precarious, both nations finally acceded to Japanese demands, and both Rangoon and Haiphong were closed to China-bound goods.

The Japanese had had another compelling reason for wanting to scale down their military operations in China in 1939. In the summer of

Above: General Tojo Hideki, the military leader who became Prime Minister of Japan in 1940.

Left: A Chinese baby cries amid the ruins of a bombed out Shanghai. Japan's cruel and brutal war in China, kept hidden in the Japanese consciousness by the euphemism of the 'China Incident,' destroyed for ever the pre-World War I image of 'plucky little Japan.' Henceforth the Japanese were to be associated with the rapacious regimes of Fascist Italy and Nazi Germany.

Below right: Pearl Harbor after the Japanese attack of 7 December 1941. Japan's opportunistic seizure of French Indo-China in 1940 made it the object of British, Dutch and American economic sanctions. Japan was forced to choose between losing face by backing down, and launching a Pacific war. It chose war.

1938, and again in the summer of 1939, Japanese and Russian troops had been involved in major clashes along the Manchurian-Siberian border. Japanese casualties had been heavy in both fights, and in the 1939 incident the Japanese had fairly clearly been defeated. In Tokyo there was serious alarm over the possibility of an eruption of another Russo-Japanese war. The Japanese had already signed a somewhat vague Anti-Comintern Pact with Germany in 1936, and now they hastened to see if they could persuade the Germans to make any more specific commitments. The announcement of the Nazi-Soviet Pact of August 1939 seemed to dash these hopes, but after the outbreak of World War II in Europe the Japanese succeeded both in entering into a Tripartite Pact with Germany and Italy (September 1940) and subsequently, in April 1941, in negotiating what amounted to a non-aggression treaty with the Soviets. Thus in the spring of 1941, having achieved all the diplomatic goals they had set for themselves in 1939, the Japanese were theoretically in a position to renew full-scale fighting in China. In fact, however, so much had happened in the interval that Japanese strategic thinking was now running along rather different lines.

Since 1938 senior officers in the Imperial Japanese Navy, concerned that the army's vision was too narrowly focused on China and Manchuria (and doubtless feeling a little left out of things), had been urging consideration of a 'Southward Advance' policy aimed at using combined naval and land power to assert Japanese control over the valuable Dutch oilfields in Java. The army had been unreceptive to such proposals in 1938 and 1939, but after Germany's lightning victories over Holland and France in 1940, and with every indication that Britain would soon also be vanquished, the Southward Advance strategy

suddenly began to seem attractive to the army as well. Now there seemed to be a real chance of creating a Japanese Asian empire consisting not only of China and Manchuria with Indonesia added on, but embracing all of Southeast Asia.

But in addition to worries about the Soviet Union there was also a growing problem of what to do about the United States, which had slowly but steadily been hardening its attitude toward Japanese expansionism ever since the invasion of Manchuria. By mid 1940, just when the Japanese military were reaching a consensus about Southward Advance, US-Japanese relations had deteriorated to a point approaching crisis. Nor could the Japanese now be as certain as in the past that traditional American isolationism would prevent the US from taking forceful action if provoked. The disastrous course of war in Europe was rapidly energizing 'internationalist' sentiment in the US, the British, Indonesian Dutch and Australians were putting pressure on the Americans to undertake to guarantee the security of their Southeast Asian possessions and, perhaps most ominous of all, America was beginning to rearm on a truly massive scale.

About a month after the Japanese had succeeded in bullying the French Vichy government into closing Indo-China to China-bound goods, the US took the first small step in a chain of events that would lead it to war: on 25 July 1940 it announced that for all exports of oil and various metal products to countries other than Britain and those in the Commonwealth and the Western Hemisphere government-approved licenses would henceforth be required. The move was correctly interpreted as a warning to Japan. Its effect was to heighten Japanese worries about future access to petroleum products and vital raw materials.

On 4 September 1940 the US formally warned Japan against making any aggressive move in Indo-China. On 22 September the Japanese, having compelled Vichy's acquiescence, began stationing small numbers of troops in the French colony. Although this could not yet be considered an act of aggression, it was certainly threatening and an obvious affront to the Americans. On 26 September the US declared an embargo on scrap-metal and steel exports to Japan. The next day it was announced that Japan had signed the Tripartite Pact with Germany and Italy. In December the US broadened its embargo to include such categories as iron ore and pig iron.

Japan moves toward war

However ominous the breakdown of relations with the Americans might be, it was still not perceived in Tokyo as the most important deterrent to the all-out initiation of Southward Advance. But that major deterrent *was* removed on 13 April 1941 when Japan signed the five-year Neutrality Agreement with the Soviet Union. On 2 July at an Imperial Conference the emperor was informed that the Japanese government and military had agreed that it was now time to introduce large numbers of troops into Indo-China and to set up permanent bases there, even if this meant risking war with the United States. An ultimatum was delivered to Vichy on 24 July, and the invasion of Indo-China began on the 28th.

The response of the Americans, British and Indonesian Dutch was almost instantaneous. In all three countries Japanese assets were frozen, and exports to Japan came to a standstill. This was a true ultimatum, for at a stroke Japan had been denied 75 percent of its foreign trade and 90 percent of its oil. The Japanese had now to back down, be ruined or go to war. Even as the government of Prince Fuminaro Konoye undertook to find some way of reaching a negotiated settlement with Washington, the opinion of the dominant Japanese military leadership was turning ever more in the direction of the war alternative. On 6 September Konoye, though he had still not quite abandoned all hope of diplomacy, agreed to allow the military to commence their war preparations. On 16 October, in the face of an unyielding US demand that Japan must evacuate Indo-China, Konoye resigned, to be replaced as prime minister by the bellicose army general Hideki Tojo. The last shreds of civilian influence in the Japanese government had now vanished.

Negotiation with the Americans continued – a special mission headed by Saburo Kurusu was dispatched to Washington – but increasingly the Tojo government was coming to look on diplomacy simply as a smokescreen to mask the accelerating preparations for war. It is difficult to pinpoint the precise moment when the Japanese leadership privately abandoned the last frail hope that some sort of settlement might be negotiated.

Some historians have proposed 26 November, when the US government sent the Japanese a harsh 10-point note demanding the removal of Japanese forces from both Indo-China and China, along with Japanese recognition of the Chiang Kai-shek government, in return for a vague promise that the US would negotiate a change in its trade policy toward Japan. But in fact this was merely a reiteration of the unwavering position the Americans had held for months. In any case, the die had certainly been cast by 1 December, when the emperor was informed at an Imperial Conference that both the military and the government 'recommended' war.

Japanese war plans gave priority to neutralizing the US Pacific Fleet, the greatest immediate threat to Japan's freedom of action in Southeast Asia. The same logic that had dictated that this must be accomplished early in the war had evolved into a decision that it should be the *casus belli* itself, and elaborate preparations had been made for the Imperial Japanese Navy to deliver a massive surprise attack on the US Pacific Fleet's home base at Pearl Harbor. The Japanese carrier fleet assigned to carry out this task was ordered to sortie on 2 December. Its transit across the Pacific was apparently undetected by the Americans, and by the morning of 7 December 1941 it was in striking position 275 miles north of the main Hawaiian island of Oahu. Within a few hours the United States and Japan would be at war.

Africa

During the period between the two world wars the colonial system remained deeply entrenched throughout Africa. Resistance to European rule under the aegis of the traditional African leaders was petering out, resistance under the aegis of modernizing Western-educated leaders was not yet effective and white people in Africa – administrators, businessmen, missionaries and settlers alike – almost unanimously assumed that the colonial regimes would endure for many generations. Nevertheless, during these high colonial decades of European control and African submission, profoundly important changes were taking place in African societies, changes that would decisively affect their character when they became independent after World War II.

The colonial situation included factors which made it unstable. The liberal and humanitarian strands in the Western tradition, though enfeebled in the colonies, were not wholly eliminated, and they created certain tensions among the whites. In particular, Christian missionaries were often at odds with other white people, but even among white administrators, entrepreneurs and settlers there were sensitive individuals who deplored and mitigated many of the harsher manifestations of colonial rule. Moreover, colonial schools provided a modicum of Africans with sufficient modern education for them to serve as clerks, foremen and junior administrators, and many of them were later to play significant roles in the process of decolonization.

Upon the immense range of social, economic, political and cultural differences that already existed in Africa, Europeans had imposed new cleavages. First, and most obviously, the different European colonial powers professed different colonial policies and employed different methods. Publicists made much of these differences during the colonial period and imperial historians still do so. For example, they contrast French idealism with British empiricism, and French institutions of imperial centralization with British institutions of local diversification. Such differences were indeed substantial, but we can now see that their consequences have not been as great as has been supposed. Perhaps the most enduring effects of the fact that Africa was partitioned among several European powers has been a projection into the upper strata of African societies of European cultural, and especially linguistic, differences. The elites who became the rulers of Africa when the colonial epoch ended constituted two distinct subcultures: those whose experience of the modern industrial West was gained through either the British or the French language, literature, polemics and educational institutions. However much they protest their negritude or their African personality, the postcolonial African ruling classes are also members of worldwide francophonic or anglophonic cultural communities. Communication across the language barrier still remains difficult in most cases, and in international settings there is an inexorable tendency for Africans to divide into two linguistic groups.

There were other differences in the colonial situations in Africa. In much of tropical Africa the only white residents were transients – administrators, soldiers, missionaries and employees of metropolitan commercial and mining corporations – who went to Africa for limited periods, with or without their families, continued to regard Europe as home and retired to Europe if they lived long enough. In such areas the land and the productive processes remained under the control of Africans. They were encouraged, in some cases compeled, to produce commodities that could be marketed profitably in Europe, but their societies were not radically disrupted. On the other hand, in areas where the climate was tempered by altitude or latitude, or where great mineral wealth was a powerful magnet, white people did seek to create permanent homes for themselves and to found durable new societies. Once its nucleus was firmly established, a settler community might exert a disproportionate influence over the colonial administration and might even aspire to become the ruling caste of an independent state. Here, the indigenous African societies were radically disrupted. With the co-operation of the colonial authorities, settlers carved farms and mines out of the tribal lands and turned many of their inhabitants into poorly paid workers, usually part-time laborers who shuttled back and forth between the native reserves and the white farms or mines.

South Africa was the epitome of this kind of settler society. By 1939 there were over two million white people in the Union (the present Republic of South Africa). Most of them claimed descent from ancestors who had left Europe in the seventeenth century. The whites formed a fifth of the total population. They controled the political machinery and the modern sector of the economy. The Africans occupied reserves with a combined area of less than one-eighth of the country. They could not produce enough food for themselves, and at any given time half of the men whose wives and children lived in the reserves were themselves working for white farmers, mining or manufacturing companies.

Left: A British colonial magistrate dispenses European justice to African subjects in British Central Africa of the 1890s. Imperialism brought alien legal and social ideals to Africa. Traditional and customary approaches were suppressed.

Above right: This copper mine of the 1930s Northern Rhodesia copper belt was one of many scattered across the mineral-rich regions of subSaharan Africa by European capitalists intent on exploiting the rich resources of the colonies.

Right: Unskilled and semi-skilled jobs in the mines of the African colonies were frequently held by migrant workers like these two men bound for the South African goldfields.

White settlement extended beyond the Union of South Africa. By 1939 white people formed nine percent of the population of South West Africa, which had been conquered by South African forces in World War I and allotted to the Union as a C-Class Mandate under the League of Nations. Whites formed five percent of the population of Southern Rhodesia, which became a self-governing British colony in 1924, almost as completely under the control of its white community as South Africa itself. They also formed about two percent of the populations of the old Portuguese colonies of Angola and Mozambique. Though all these communities were small, they were concentrated in the towns and the districts that were suitable for large-scale farming operations. Many members of these communities had close links with South Africans, and wherever they lived they modeled their relationships with Africans on the South African precedent, behaved as permanent, self-perpetuating dominant castes and aspired to become the heirs of the metropolitan European regimes, as the white South Africans had already done.

The white communities of southern Africa were predominantly of northern European or Portuguese origin. Another stream of white settlers crossed the Mediterranean from southern Europe and, by 1939, white people formed 14 percent of the population of Algeria, 11 percent of the population of Libya and eight percent of the population of Tunisia. Since these communities were only separated from their countries of origin by the Mediterranean Sea, they remained psychologically and materially more closely integrated with Europe than the settlers in southern Africa; but their presence had similar consequences for the peoples among whom they lived.

Between the Maghrib and southern Africa, the white communities were small, scattered and insecure. The only significant pockets of settlers were in Dakar – the administrative and commercial center of French West Africa – the Kenya highlands and in the mining towns of Northern Rhodesia and the Belgian Congo province of Katanga.

Wherever white settlers were established, they were responsible for the presence of non-indigenous communities, who performed roles intermediate between whites and Africans. In South Africa there were the 'Colored People' (descended from indigenous Khoi, or 'Hottentots', from slaves who had been imported from tropical Africa, Madagascar and southeast Asia and from whites) and the Indians (whose forebears had been brought to Natal as laborers to work on the sugar estates in the late nineteenth century). In Kenya, besides the Arab community, which had roots going back many centuries in the coastal towns, there were also many Indians, some of whom were imported to construct the railroad from Mombasa through Nairobi to Uganda. Even in tropical colonies without white settlers there were often small groups of Asians who came in under the aegis of the imperial power and gained a large share of the retail trade.

Colonial administrative systems

Before the European conquest, Africa had contained many hundreds of autonomous political units of different types and sizes. By 1914, the European powers had divided it up. Except for Ethiopia, the only traditional African groups to retain sovereignty were Liberia, which was ruled by a black community from the United States, and the Union of South Africa, which had passed under the control of its white settler community. After World War I the territories that Germany had acquired were shared out as League of Nations Mandates among Britain, France, Belgium and the Union of South Africa; and in the 1930s Italy conquered Ethiopia. Thus Africa then

Left: European colonialism spread the global money economy into deepest Africa. This British official is collecting taxes from the residents of his district.

Below: A gunboat of Leopold II's Congo Free State armed forces. Military might was the ultimate means by which colonial powers enforced their rule in Africa.

Right: The cultivation of cash crops, such as this cotton being picked in the Sudan, became widespread in the African colonies.

Below right: Heavy machinery at work at the Brown Antelope Copper Mine of Northern Rhodesia. A modern industrial infrastructure developed in Africa during the 1930s, mainly in the mining regions.

consisted of two sovereign states and 49 colonies (though some had other labels such as Mandated Territories and Protectorates). Each colony had a central white bureaucracy, and 12 of the French colonies were grouped together to form two large tropical federations.

In a few cases, a colony contained only one traditional African state, as in Swaziland, Basutoland and, after World War I, Rwanda and Burundi. The vast majority of colonies incorporated more than one traditional political unit, and many colonies included peoples of different cultures. Consequently colonial rule initiated a process of political amalgamation. This process had proved to be lasting. With remarkably few modifications, the colonies of 1939 have become the independent states of contemporary Africa, with the boundaries that were fixed by their European conquerors.

The authority of the traditional ruling families and bureaucracies, wherever they had existed, had been weakened by the conquest itself. In most cases, colonial rule weakened it still further. In their subSaharan territories the French went out of their way to obliterate nearly all the large states in the areas they controled. It was French policy to apply uniform methods of administration throughout the empire, and the basic unit of local government was a canton under a white official. In theory the official administered his canton directly. In practice, of course, he was obliged to use African intermediaries, and he called them 'chiefs.' Some such chiefs were members of traditional ruling families, but others were commoners who had caught the eye of some French officer or administrator. In either case, they were appointed by the colonial government and were liable to be dismissed by it. Their duties included the collection of taxes, the supply of prestation (12 days' labor a year from every African subject, commutable into a money payment) and the recruitment of compulsory labor for public works and of soldiers for military service. They were rewarded with a share of the taxes and the labor. The result was that the African peoples in the French Empire came to regard the colonial chiefs not as their own representatives and natural leaders but as agents of the foreign administration – indeed, as the instruments of its most oppressive exactions. Consequently, when the nationalist movement eventually gathered momentum in French sub-

Saharan Africa, the chiefs played scarcely any part in it, and since independence they have almost ceased to exist as a social category.

The process was similar in the Belgian and Portuguese colonies. In British Africa there was greater variety. The first senior officials in British colonies improvised their own arrangements in the light of local conditions. In many cases, they made agreements with the traditional rulers, allowing them considerable autonomy. In northern Nigeria Frederick Lugard came to terms with the Fulani emirs, and since the relationship worked smoothly and cheaply it became the basis of a general theory that colonies should be ruled indirectly. Indigenous institutions should be used, purged of their 'uncivilized' characteristics, and modernized, with the British officials acting as advisers rather than rulers, except in emergency situations. In practice, these ideas were applied successfully where there were strong traditional bureaucracies whose members saw advantages in co-operating with the British. This was the case in northern Nigeria, where the Fulani dynasties that had seized power in the early nineteenth-century *jihad* were able to maintain their position with British support. It was also the case in Uganda, where the shrewd

bureaucrats of the traditional kingdom of Buganda were able to extend their authority over their neighbors under the cloak of the British Raj.

In many regions of British tropical Africa, there had never been any traditional central institutions. There, indirect rule could not be applied effectively. Among the Ibo and their neighbors in southern Nigeria, for example, Lugard appointed warrant chiefs, but the experiment was a failure because the new men were not respected. Similar difficulties were experienced by Governor Cameron when he tried to transplant indirect rule to Tanganyika.

Throughout Africa, the ultimate fate of the traditional ruling classes hinged on their relationships with the Africans, who had acquired a Western education. In Northern Nigeria the relationship was uniquely cordial, because the ruling classes exerted such an influence over the British administrators that acquired a virtual monopoly over the places in the colonial schools. Elsewhere they were surpassed by other elements, for they had either been weakened beyond redress by the European administration or had compromised themselves by collaborating too closely with the colonists. In either case, they were generally bypassed in the postcolonial order.

Economic change in the colonial era

In promoting their nations' participation in the scramble for Africa, imperialist politicians had contended that tropical colonies would be profitable possessions. They were to be developed by their European rulers to the benefit not only of their fellow-countrymen but also of their African subjects. Such hopes were not realized. Economic growth in Africa during the colonial period was slow and patchy.

The imperial governments required their colonies to balance their annual budgets. When they did supply capital, it was for projects favored by white settlers and European companies, and it came in the form of loans which were to be repaid out of local revenues. Only after World War II did France and Britain begin to make more generous appropriations for colonial development.

In areas without white settlers, companies domiciled in the metropole that ruled a territory were the principal agents and beneficiaries of economic change. At first some companies skimmed off elephant ivory, rubber and other natural products of Africa, using compulsory labor. The excesses committed by agents of King Leopold of Belgium during the period when the vast Congo basin was virtually his private estate caused such an international scandal that in 1907 Leopold transferred the territory to the Belgian government. However, ivory, wild rubber and other natural animal and vegetable products were wasting assets, and European companies eventually concentrated on cultivated commodities that could be sold profitably in world markets. The result was that in many areas the African populations became specialized producers of single crops: ground nuts in Senegal, cocoa in the Ivory Coast and the Gold Coast, palm oil in Nigeria, cotton in the Sudan. A company, or an associated group of companies, with headquarters in the European country that ruled the colony, purchased the crop, transported it to Europe, processed it there and marketed the finished product. The African producers had little influence over the terms of trade and suffered severely from the fall in commodity prices during the depression of the 1930s.

Conditions differed in colonies, such as Kenya and Southern Rhodesia, where white settlers were present. There, economic growth was concentrated in the areas occupied by the settlers. The African populations provided the labor force required by the settlers and were discouraged from producing export crops on their own lands, which became economic backwaters. Where minerals were available in workable quantities, as in Katanga (Belgian Congo) and the Northern Rhodesian copper belt, European companies created mining industries operated by small numbers of white technicians and overseers and large numbers of African laborers.

Left: The impact of modern civilization in Africa, as brought by the colonial powers, has been patchy. Gao, a town in Mali, shows little evidence of the years of French rule.

Below left: Although cash crops brought money to the farmers who raised them, they did not necessarily provide enough for feeding the Africans' families. Many who would otherwise have been small cultivators were forced to become migrant laborers, taking poorly paid jobs with the European planters.

Right: The main street of Nairobi during the 1930s could almost be mistaken for a small town in Australia or the American southwest. European urban civilization totally altered the African landscape in those places where white settlement sank deep roots.

The colonial administrations had three major economic functions. First, they raised taxes from the African populations, in the form of a poll tax or a hut tax, as well as indirect taxes. Second, they persuaded Africans to perform the economic roles required of them by the companies and settlers. For this, fiscal inducements were often sufficient, but physical coercion was applied where necessary, notably in Portuguese territories. Third, the colonial administrations also created systems of transportation, so that cash crops, settler produce and mineral ores could be exported. The railroads of colonial Africa were siphons that channeled African raw materials from the producing areas to the ports: except in areas of dense white settlement, they provided no lateral communications among African territories. Since a colony supplied its metropole with raw materials, and the metropole supplied manufactured goods in return, scarcely any manufacturing industries were established in colonial Africa.

The effects of these economic conditions upon individuals varied immensely. In some areas remote from railroads, settlers, mines and cash-cropping regions, economic and social life continued relatively undisturbed. But in most cases Africans were obliged to make major changes. If they produced cash crops, they were liable to run short of their normal supplies of food and other subsistence products. If they did not produce cash crops in consequence of poor soil, inadequate rainfall, lack of transportation facilities or official policy, they were obliged to find other ways of paying their taxes. The result was that much of colonial Africa was the scene of massive labor migrations. In regions such as West Africa, this normally involved moving to participate with other Africans in the production of cash crops. In such regions, migrants were relatively free people. They could move around as complete families if they wished. They could settle permanently in their adopted countries, and many did so.

The situation was of course different for Africans who worked for white settlers or mining corporations. It was most extreme in South Africa. Laborers were recruited for the Witwatersrand gold mines from a catchment area extending as far north as Tanganyika. For a year at a time they lived in all-male compounds, segregated from the urban life around the mines. African miners were restricted to unskilled and semi-skilled tasks, irrespective of their talents and experience, and they earned about one-tenth as much as white miners. When in 1922 the directors of the mining corporations did try to increase the opportunities open to African laborers, the white miners resorted to violence and succeeded in preserving the *status quo.*

Social change in colonial Africa

Some fundamental processes of social change were taking place in African societies, largely unremarked by the white authorities, and they made Africa a very different place from what it had been in the nineteenth century. One crucial process was urbanization. Previously, residential concentrations of people had existed in various parts of the continent, but except along the Mediterranean coast they had resembled pre-industrial medieval European centers rather than modern industrial towns. The townspeople produced their own staple foods on the lands surrounding the residential area. In colonial Africa, the major administrative centers grew into towns of a new sort. They attracted Africans from many different traditional communities or tribes, they had specialized administrative and commercial functions and they consumed food that had been grown elsewhere and transported by land or sea. Thus in places such as Dakar and Accra, Abidjan and Lagos, Leopoldville and Nairobi, Africans from many different tribes were drawn together in a non-traditional milieu for non-traditional purposes. It was there that they came into most

regular contact with Europeans, acquired new skills and interests and formed new types of association. It was there that a new African elite emerged, with different norms and goals from those of the traditional ruling groups. African nationalism was born and nurtured in the new towns.

In the towns Africans formed an immense variety of voluntary associations to satisfy their new social and economic needs. Some of these had an ethnic or tribal basis. A newcomer to a town normally joined his ethnic association, which found him a place to live and a job, supported him when unemployed, settled his disputes with his fellow-tribesmen according to customary law and provided congenial recreation. Some urban workers never looked beyond their ethnic association. But others also joined associations that were open to people of different tribes: sports associations, embryonic trade unions, religious associations and, for the better educated, cultural and intellectual clubs based on European models.

Trade unions did not flourish in the colonial situation. Few African workers were sufficiently committed to permanent wage-earning to be interested in a sustained struggle for improvements in the conditions of employment. Moreover, until late in the colonial period the colonial administrations banned or obstructed African trade unions. Trade unions did gradually emerge in some areas, such as the copper belt of Northern Rhodesia (Zambia). There, the mine managements initially tried to use tribal representatives as their intermediaries with the African laborers, but in disturbances in 1935 the laborers rejected the Elders as being too closely linked with management, and in 1940 they again rejected the Elders and formed a strike committee. After World War II, the British government encouraged and promoted trade unionism and the Elders were eliminated from the system.

Religious associations were much more significant than trade unions in colonial Africa. Both Islam and Christianity made headway at the expense of the traditional local African cults. Colonial regimes found it expedient to work with, and thus to sustain, Islamic institutions where they already existed. In French West Africa, for example, the government co-operated with the leaders of the Qadariyya and Tijaniyya brotherhoods, and most of them lost the puritanical zeal of their precolonial predecessors as they accommodated to the colonial situation. In Northern Nigeria the British went still further in supporting Islam and impeding Christian missions. Where Islam and Christianity did come into competition, Islam benefited from the facts that it was invariably propagated by African clerics, that it was presented as an indigenous African religion and that it more readily formed syntheses with the local cults than did Christianity. It has been estimated that Islam doubled its adherents in tropical Africa during the colonial period.

Religious associations performed an exceptional range of functions in the colonial era. The Islamic brotherhoods and the Christian congregations brought together people of different ethnic backgrounds and provided their members wth new opportunities for personal fulfilment. Many Africans seceded from the white-controlled mission churches to form independent churches, where they had greater scope for organization and leadership. Some of them also became the foci of opposition to the colonial regimes. The first rising against the British government in Nyasaland (Malawi), in 1915, was led by John Chilembwe, who was a pastor of an independent Baptist Church, and his followers included people linked with Jehovah's Witnesses. The most famous case was that of Simon Kimbangu, a member of the Anglican Church mission in the lower Congo. In 1921 he claimed to be able to cure the sick and raise the dead and he quickly attracted a large following. Although the Belgian authorities soon arrested him and he spent the rest of his life in jail, Kimbangu was widely regarded as an African Jesus, and his Church of Jesus Christ, through illegal, flourished underground and still claimed 60,000 adherents in 1958.

Western education and the rise of a new African elite

The number of Africans who received any modern education in the colonial era was small, and only a tiny proportion of those who went to school stayed long enough to complete the primary curriculum. Few indeed were the Africans who completed a high-school education. Yet by the beginning of World War II several high schools were giving courses at the college level: Fourah Bay College in Sierra Leone (which had been associated with the University of Durham, England, since 1875), Fort Hare College in South Africa (which awarded degrees of the University of South Africa) and schools near Dakar, Accra, Lagos and Kampala. Moreover, a few hundred Africans – all but a few of them from West Africa and South Africa – had attended universities in Europe and the United States after completing their schooling at home.

Education was secular and state-controlled in French Africa. Elsewhere, most schools for Africans were owned and conducted by Christian missions, with some financial aid and supervision from the government. The objectives of governments and missions were to train a limited number of Africans to perform roles in the colonial situation for which literacy was required: clergy, teachers in the primary schools and interpreters and clerks in the civil service and the mining and commercial companies.

This colonial educational system produced a fair number of people with some smattering of literacy, a much smaller number with a more or less good general introduction to the European humanities and an exposure to European social and cultural norms, and a very small cadre of people who had experienced life as university students in Europe and America.

The term 'new elite' is widely used to designate the upper section of this educated minority. The implication is that they were an innovating cadre, but not yet a class, because recruitment was open and their ranks were augmented year by year. Moreover, they had kinsfolk who were not educated and they maintained contact with them. Attempts to define the lower limit of the new elite have not been very successful, but we are approximately correct if we envisage the new elite in the colonial period as including those who had had a high-school education and held relatively remunerative white-collar jobs in the towns, and if we regard Africans who had had a primary education, but no more, as forming a transitional group between the new elite and the masses.

The members of the new elite were unevenly distributed among the ethnic groups of Africa. In Senegal they were largely inhabitants of the four communes of Dakar, St Louis, Rufisque and Goree, and unlike other Africans in French West and Equatorial Africa they were French citizens. In Sierra Leone, they were largely Freetown Creoles – descendants of people who had been shipped as slaves from various West African ports, liberated by the British naval patrols and brought to Freetown in the nineteenth century. In Nigeria the early members of the new elite were Creoles of local origin who had returned to Nigeria from Freetown. In the Gold Coast they were the Fante of the coastal districts. In Uganda the Baganda were the favored community; in Kenya, the Luo and the Kikuyu; in Nyasaland (Malawi), the Tonga; in South Africa, the Mfengu. Thus the differential impact of modern education in the colonial era led to new differences among the ethnic groups of Africa. Cosmopolitan modern culture gained a strong foothold in some communities; other communities were relatively unaffected.

The members of the new elite within a colony had much in common and a strong sense of group solidarity. They came from the same high school or schools. They belonged to the same cultural associations that cut across ethnic lines. They were townspeople and tended to live in the same section of the colonial capitals. They held the highest posts in the civil service, the churches and the commercial houses that were open to Africans, and with them the highest incomes. They conformed to Western styles of dress, food, housing and transportation. Most of them were Christians, and their norms were very largely those of the European ruling class. Consequently, whatever their antecedents, they regarded themselves as a group distinct from and superior to the uneducated rural members of the traditional elite.

On the other hand, it was the members of the new elite who experienced most continuously the effects of the colonial color bar. Their salaries were lower than those of the white people who did the same work. Their dignity was frequently offended by the arrogance of individual Europeans. And they were shut out from the social world of the whites.

Before World War II, the new elite accepted the legitimacy of the colonial regimes and sought to reform them by working along constitutional lines for the redress of specific grievances. They organized petitions and deputations; but they made little effort to mobilize the African masses, nor did they resort to violence. After World War II, however, leadership passed to younger men who were prepared to use new methods in the pursuit of radical goals. But in every part of Africa the new elite supplied the leaders of the nationalist movements and the rulers of the postcolonial, independent states.

Above left: Students at a European-style college in west Africa. At the end of World War I, a new class of Africans educated in modern institutions began to emerge.

Left: Hustle and bustle on a street in Accra, capital of Ghana (formerly the Gold Coast). The major cities of Africa are almost entirely the product of the years of colonial rule. The development of a comparatively rootless urban population was a new, complicating factor for African society.

Right: South African 'apartheid' in action – the sign forbids the use of the beach to blacks and 'colored' peoples. Although, in fact, the concept of apartheid was a post World War II development, South African whites had been practicing this extreme form of racial discrimination from the outset.

THE DIVISIONAL COUNCIL OF THE CAPE

WHITE AREA
BY ORDER SECRETARY

DIE AFDELINGSRAAD VAN DIE KAAP

BLANKE GEBIED
OP LAS SEKRETARIS

World War II and after

World War II has often been described as a continuation of World War I. Certainly the fighting that began in 1939 pitted many of the same antagonists against each other – Germany against France, Britain, Russia and eventually the United States in the European theater – but by the time the war was over it had reshaped planetary history in ways unimaginable in 1919. By 1945 Western Europe was no longer the undisputed power center of the world, and within another decade, with the emancipation of vast areas of Africa and Asia from colonial control, a whole new force in world affairs, popularly referred to as the Third World, would make its appearance.

What happened to the world during World War II and the succeeding decades was not simply the result of warfare and the consequent weakening of the European hegemony. The war years had brought to the world changes in technology, in economic capacity and in political and social expectations which were to change the fundamental proportions of power and the basic capacities of nations to influence each other. On the one hand industrial technology and the resulting structures of economic interdependence had developed to the point that nations the size of Britain or France could no longer exist as self-contained entities able to exert independent influence on the rest of the world. The scale of power had changed, leaving a few giants such as the USA, the USSR and China or – potentially –

blocs of nations such as the European Community or the Arab League as the main protagonists in world politics. From a predominantly Europe-centered condition prior to World War I, the world balance had moved into a condition of plural centers of various types and capacities. On the other hand, the influence of Western civilization on the rest of the world continued to expand at an ever-increasing rate.

The first few years after the war were understandably a period of readjustment to peace, of recovery, and of cautious probing on the part of the major powers. Despite the tremendous losses suffered by the Russians during the war, the USSR, exploiting its role as leader of the Communist nations, soon emerged as the primary antagonist to the United States. Both powers were drawn beyond their borders into international rivalries – Russia into East Asia and along its European and Middle Eastern boundaries, the United States into Western Europe, East Asia and throughout many of the areas which were being abandoned by the British. In the early phases of the resulting Cold War, the United States, by virtue of its monopoly of nuclear armaments and its vast economic resources, held a superior hand. Yet while the Truman Doctrine and the subsequent Marshall Plan helped to stabilize Western Europe and prevent a feared takeover of the French, Italian and Greek governments by Communist regimes, the Communist bloc grew immensely

through the rise of Mao in mainland China and the establishment of Communist regimes in North Korea and North Vietnam. The explosion of an atomic device by the Russians in 1949, and their development of a hydrogen bomb by 1953, gave rise to the atomic stalemate that was to carry into the 1980s. It was this so-called 'balance of terror,' whereby each major nuclear power realized its inability to use its ultimate weapons against the other without running the danger of itself being annihilated, that provided the context of international adjustment in the postwar decades. An 'Iron Curtain' had begun to separate the Communist and non-Communist blocs in the world. By 1950 the United States was working vigorously for the recovery, and even rearmament, of Germany and Japan as bulwarks against Soviet expansion. The final phases of the Cold War were to be played out in a series of 'bush fire' wars and power plays along the fringes of the Iron Curtain – in Greece, Czechoslovakia, Berlin, Korea, Taiwan, Indonesia, Lebanon, Cuba and Vietnam. The Cuban Missile Crisis of 1962 suddenly forced the two powers to recognize the futility of perpetual conflict. When in 1963 the 'hot line' was installed between Moscow and Washington the Cold War had essentially come to an end.

The tapering off of aggressive Cold War behavior by the two prime powers was caused not only by their gradual adjustment and accommodation to each other but also by a number of dra-

matic changes in the international environment which surrounded them. By the 1950s and particularly by the 1960s the condition of simple polarization between two rival superpowers, each with the capacity to have its way in its half of the world, had come to an end. The nuclear stalemate between the USA and USSR had reduced the dimensions of usable power to political and economic factors which could be influenced by even relatively small or young nations. Furthermore, during the 1950s and 1960s a series of secondary nations developed their own nuclear capacities –

Left: The mainstay of the Communist revolution in China, troops of the People's Liberation Army at a march-past.

Above: A Cuban crowd acclaims a speech made by Fidel Castro, the newly installed leader of Cuba.

Above right: The prime minister of the independent state of Tanzania, Julius Nyerere, is hoisted aloft by a cheering crowd. The years following the end of World War II marked the emergence of an independent Africa after decades of colonial rule.

Right: War and starvation remained one of the constants of the postwar world – here a starving Biafran child clutches a baby doll, an incongruous product of Western consumerism.

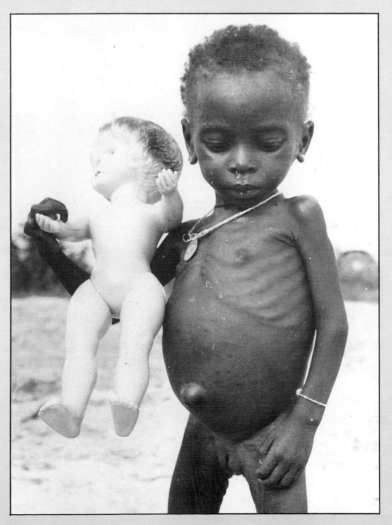

Britain in 1957, France in 1960, China in 1964 – with other, even smaller nations following this lead in the 1970s and 1980s.

The proliferation of new centers of influence in international affairs did not stem simply, or even primarily, from the increase in membership in the 'nuclear club.' The recovery of Germany, Japan and China, the creation of the European Economic Community (the Common Market), the end of colonialism and the appearance of a 'Third World,' the emergence of Israel as a major force in the Middle East – all had a hand in breaking up the

postwar bipolar world. The recovery of Japan and Germany from the state of devastation and exhaustion in which they were left after World War II to positions of world economic leadership was a remarkable testimony to the resiliency of human society and to the modern industrial system. In both cases the achievement rested on a complex and paradoxical set of circumstances. Both countries, because of their wartime destruction, were able to rebuild their industries and cities using the latest technology, thus gaining a competitive edge on countries which kept alive outmoded industrial practices. Also, Cold War tensions persuaded the Allies, and particularly the United States, to the view that the rehabilitation of the former enemies was essential to preventing them from falling into political chaos and hence under socialist control. By 1950 the original postwar restrictions on German economic development were being revised, and by 1955 Germany had begun to rearm. The outbreak of the Korean War in 1950, which had the effect of hastening the determination of the Western powers to build Germany into an ally, had an even more pronounced influence on the recovery of Japan. In East Asia, the passage of China into the Communist bloc in 1949 had severely altered the balance of power between the United States and the Soviet Union. The vision of a postwar settlement in which a demilitarized Japan would be held down by an alliance between the United States and a strong and reliable Nationalist China was shattered. The obvious alternative was an alliance with a rebuilt Japan. Japan's importance to the American position in East Asia was dramatically illustrated during the Korean War when Japan served not only as America's 'unsinkable aircraft carrier' but provided valuable war material as well. In 1952 the Western powers signed peace agreements with both Germany and Japan.

The emergence of China as a major force in world affairs resulted in considerable degree from Soviet assistance to the Communist forces which confronted Chiang Kai-shek's Nationalist regime in the aftermath of the Japanese withdrawal from mainland China. Russian assistance, both military and industrial, was critical in the early years after the Japanese defeat. But it was Mao Tse-tung's (or, in the Pinyin spelling, Mao Zedong's) system of government and party organization that eventually gave the Communist regime the kind of con-

trol over all of the mainland which for the first time unified China into a modern state. Communist China came of age as an international power during the Korean War, when its forces intervened to push US troops from the Yalu River.

Another shifting dimension to the balance of power came as the nations of Western Europe first lost their predominant world positions then regained them in part through the act of semi-confederation in the Common Market. The decline of Europe is best illustrated by what happened to Britain during and following the war. Driven from East Asia by Japanese armies and navies, forced to abandon India in 1947, loosing control of Suez in 1956 and most of its African colonies during the 1960s, the British Empire had been cut back to a shadow of its prewar size. While in East Asia, the Middle East and the Mediterranean, the United States had moved in to assume much of the role formerly played by Britain, the Pax Britannica by which the British Empire once stabilized the world was gone for ever. France, too, expelled from Indochina and Algeria, found itself reduced to its European homeland by 1960, with only tenuous ties remaining with its former African colonies.

The retreat of Europe during the 1950s and 1960s and the realization that the states of Europe were no longer best served by a policy of military and economic rivalry led eventually to the conception of a European Union. A first and crucial step was taken in 1949 with the creation of the North Atlantic Treaty Organization, a defensive military alliance that included the US, Britain, Canada, Belgium, Denmark, Iceland, Italy, Luxembourg, the Netherlands, Norway and Portugal, and later Greece, Turkey and West Germany, with France as a kind of semi-detached partner. The European Economic Community (EEC) and the European Atomic Community, created in 1958, brought France, Italy, the Benelux nations and West Germany together in an accord to work toward a free-trade bloc and joint defense policies. Britain at last joined the Common Market in 1972, thus bringing into being a potentially economically unified Europe, the combined resources of which constituted the second greatest concentration of industrial power in the world.

Europe's withdrawal from its colonies during the 1950s and 1960s created almost overnight a host of new nations in Asia and Africa. The granting of independence to former colonies began shortly after the war when Japan's former colonies Korea and Taiwan were given independent status in 1948 and 1950. The United States had granted self-government to the Philippines in 1946, and the Dutch, after an exhausting war, were forced to abandon their effort to reconquer Indonesia in 1949, though the French were not forced out of Indochina until a humiliating defeat at Dienbienphu in 1954. But it was of course the British withdrawal from India and Pakistan in 1947 that did the most to signal the end of the colonial system. The possibility of independence for the states of Africa had seemed extremely remote in 1945. But the difficulties which the French were having in Indo-China and the British decisions with respect to India exercised a strong influence on the colonial administrations in Africa, weakening their will to hold on. Leaders among the colonial peoples took heart in the possibility of gaining freedom. The emergence of the People's Republic of China in 1949 led to an initial period of friendship between China and India, and this led in turn to the Bandung Conference of 1955. The Conference gave voice to the concept of Afro-Asian solidarity against colonialism and the two dominant superpowers, a concept that stirred Africa to a renewed effort to push for decolonization. Significantly, both the USA and USSR, in their competitive search for international support, actively supported independence movements in Africa.

In the final analysis it was undoubtedly certain basic factors of economics which led to what was an almost precipitous withdrawal from Africa by the European powers. If in Asia the question of whether colonies actually rewarded the colonizers was much in doubt, the same was even more true in Africa. After 1945 European powers began to realize that an accommodation with the 'native elite' in the colonies, whereby the colonial administration would be withdrawn while favored economic concerns might still be retained (the condition of neo-colonialism as it is sometimes called) would prove economically more attractive.

The scramble to decolonize Africa was begun by Britain, which granted independence to Sudan in 1956 and the Gold Coast in 1957. France, in the wake of its losses in Indochina, attempted to resist the pressures for independence in its North African colonies, particularly Algeria, but it was forced to grant independence to Madagascar in 1958 and to another 14 separate states in 1960. After a bloody war, Algeria was also released in 1962. During the 1960s Nigeria, the Congo, Kenya, Uganda, Tanganyika, Zambia and Rhodesia gained their independence, to be followed by Angola and Mozambique in the 1970s.

The newly independent states of Asia and Africa, most of them quite weak politically and economically, nonetheless played an important role in the affairs of the post-World War II world. In Asia civil wars in Korea and Vietnam involved the United States in two costly military expeditions. Indonesia avoided a Communist takeover by the bloodiest of internal purges and the seizure of the government by a group of anti-Communist military leaders. Military or dictatorial takeovers became typical of most of the new Asian states – of Korea, Taiwan, Vietnam, Indonesia and Burma. In the Indian subcontinent a precariously divided Pakistan fell under martial law in 1958. In 1972 East Pakistan gained its independence as the state of Bangladesh after a bloody civil war in which the troops of West Pakistan brutally slaughtered thousands of their eastern countrymen. Civil war plagued the states of Africa as well. The Congo, within a month of independence in 1960, faced an army revolt and the secession of the province of Katanga. The secession movement was put down only after five years of brutal fighting and Belgian, United Nations and US interventions. Political turmoil continued until 1965, when General Mobutu established his military regime. Nigeria, likewise, experienced a series of bitter tragedies: two military coups, the secession of Biafra in 1967, a civil war in which the plight of starving Biafrans shook the entire world. By 1987 there had been a total of 69 successful coups d'état in Africa since independence, and there were 15 military regimes in power, not counting those that had in effect evolved into military regimes without benefit of a coup. At that same time only a handful of states – Cameroon, Gabon, the Ivory Coast, Kenya, Nigeria, Rwanda, Senegal, Togo and Zimbabwe – could even claim to be economically better off than they were when they became independent. Thus throughout Africa the problems of national stability and economic development remained precariously unsettled and potentially explosive.

More immediately explosive was the Middle East. There, too, as an aftermath of World War II, outright Western control was generally brought to an end. The French had pulled out of Lebanon and Syria by 1946. Jordan was made independent in the same year, and American, British and Soviet troops gave up their occupation of Iran. The withdrawal of British troops from the Suez Canal zone in 1956 paved the way for the granting of independence to the Anglo-Egyptian Sudan, and the British had already withdrawn from Iraq in 1955. During the 1960s Kuwait and Southern Yemen became independent. Thus were created a succession of newly independent states in which political leadership was hotly contested between traditional monarchies, military elites and radical nationalist parties and movements. In the midst of this potentially unstable condition three other explosive elements were introduced. One was the rapidly increasing importance that the oil produced in the countries bordering the Persian Gulf held for the industrial nations of the world. The second was the creation in 1948 of the new state

Left: The monolithic face of Chinese communism – a mass rally held in honor of Mao Tse-tung.

Right: The ideological war between communism and capitalism acquired a new importance after 1945, spreading from country to country across the globe. This poster was issued by the UN during the Korean War in an attempt to persuade North Korean soldiers of the evils of communism.

Below right: The importance of oil as an energy source for the Western world increased dramatically after the 1973 Arab-Israeli war. The cheap availability of oil could never be taken for granted again.

sions of the Cold War served to excite political rivalries within many Latin American nations and to intensify the antagonism which the peoples of the southern hemisphere had toward the United States. The introduction of socialist revolutionary ideology into the Latin American scene clearly added a new dimension to anti-government movements through the region whether directed against remaining colonial administrations in the Caribbean or against unpopular domestic regimes, dictatorial or otherwise. Meanwhile, economic development slowly drew Latin America more fully into the currents of world trade.

By the 1970s the world assemblage of nations had changed immensely from what it had been before World War II. The list of sovereign states had grown from roughly 60 to over 120. Among these disparate entities no simple bond of mutual interest provided the basis of a stable balance of power nor did any mechanism of international order provide a means for effectively keeping the peace among them. The United Nations, on which the hopes of the postwar world had been pinned, had been rendered ineffectual as a peace-keeping body by the insistence of the major powers on retaining veto powers over decisions in the Security Council. The UN continued to serve as an arena for political expression, especially for the newly created states of Africa and Asia. But major points of conflict such as those raised by the Soviet blockade of Berlin, the United States' action in Vietnam, or the conflict between Israel and Egypt were beyond its competence to handle. Thus a variety of regionally and ideologically based efforts at international security continued. Yet even these organizations would prove ineffectual in the 1980s as the balance of world trade was distorted by the unexpected economic growth of Europe and Japan in contrast to the United States. Thus by the late 1980s one prime fact was evident: that the composition of the world community of nations had grown in size and complexity and that, as the succeeding chapters show, each part of the world was wrapped in its own particular set of problems.

of Israel. The first magnified tremendously the strategic importance of the Middle East to the major world powers, intensifying their competitive efforts to gain concessions from the newly independent countries of the area. The second added a powerful irritant to the already unstable conflict of local nationalism in the Middle East. Arab-Israeli antagonism led to a succession of wars that frequently threatened to draw the United States and Soviet Russia into open confrontation. The third was the accession to power in Iran in the late 1970s of a radical Shi'ite regime that, while engaged in a bloody war with Iraq, threatened to destabilize several other neighboring Arab governments and again drew oil-dependent Western powers into the maelstrom of Middle Eastern politics.

Of all parts of the world Latin America was the least affected by World War II and by the economic changes and nationalistic tensions which marked the postwar decades. Sufficiently out of the range of major power interests to avoid active involvement in the great world wars, the countries of Latin America were occupied primarily with their own internal development: the attempt to create politically stable governments, to secure economic development and to assure a satisfying distribution of wealth. The major postwar event of international importance in the region was the success of the Cuban Revolution led by Fidel Castro in 1959. The injection into the American scene of ideological and political ten-

World War II

No cheering crowds greeted the outbreak of war in September 1939. The horrors of 1914-18 had cured the peoples of Europe of any illusion that war would provide a brief holiday from the constraints of peace. The general expectation was that the conflict would be long and immensely destructive. The British government supposed that major cities would be devastated by air attacks within days of the outbreak of war: the evacuation of women and children to the countryside began immediately. Hitler was obliged to appear before the Reichstag in the guise of a Man of Peace, responding to an unprovoked attack from Poland and a victim of the hostile ambitions of Britain and France. No leader could afford the role of warmonger.

Germany's position was, on the face of it, precarious. Hitler's forces were totally inadequate for a war on two fronts. In order to assemble 48 divisions as his strike force against Poland, he was forced to denude Germany's defenses in the west. Facing France were some 33 divisions, mostly elderly veterans, with no tanks and little heavy artillery. Opposite them France could position 45 out of its total of 110 divisions (the rest were stationed along the Belgian and Italian frontiers, and in North Africa), with ample heavy equipment. But French mobilization was slow, and French military thinking rooted in the Great War. General Maurice Gamelin, the French commander, believed in massed infantry assaults preceded by a heavy artillery barrage. The art of warfare had left such tactics behind.

Shortly after the end of World War I, a group of British officers had devised new tactics for mobile warfare, using tanks grouped in independent armored formations. The massed armor would exploit its speed and power to punch holes through enemy lines and drive deep into the rear, disrupting communications and threatening strategic objectives. The British and French armies dismissed these new ideas: their tanks remained tied tightly to the infantry. But certain German officers, notably Heinz Guderian, took them very seriously indeed, and won Hitler's backing against the skepticism of much of the German High Command. The German army also planned the use of aircraft as a sort of long-range mobile artillery in support of these fast-moving ground operations; both Britain and France had neglected airpower as a factor in land battles. It was the imaginative use of independent armored formations and aircraft in mobile warfare, not any superiority in numbers or equipment, that would give Hitler's armies their extraordinary run of victories in 1939-42.

The first of Hitler's victims were the Poles. Hitler desperately needed a quick victory before the French were fully mobilized; his army duly obliged. On paper, the Poles should have had the strength to hold up the Germans. But their military thinking was a century behind – they put much faith in the cavalry charge. At 5am on 1 September, the first German air strikes caught the Polish airforce on the ground, and the Luftwaffe established immediate control of the skies. The German tanks were light and thinly armored, but they were concentrated in six armored divisions, and the speed and boldness with which these were employed gave Germany a victory of devastating swiftness. By 14 September the remnants of the Polish army were either besieged in Warsaw or had taken refuge in the southeast. Three days later, on 17 September, Soviet forces entered Poland from the east. They met with little resistance. Warsaw surrendered to the Germans on 28 September after a fierce bombardment by air and land; the last Polish forces succumbed on 5 October. About 70,000 Polish soldiers escaped abroad and a Polish government-in-exile was set up in Paris.

The fourth partition of Poland followed. The Soviet Union annexed the east of the country, where the population was mainly Ukrainian and White Russian. Germany took the rest, inhabited chiefly by ethnic Poles and Jews; roughly half was annexed, the remainder being placed under a German 'General Government.' It was in the General Government that many of the worst atrocities of the war would be perpetrated.

On 6 October, Hitler offered to make peace with Britain and France; they felt bound to refuse. Yet for the next six months virtually nothing happened. An American journalist christened it 'the Phoney War.' There was some action at sea: Ger-

Above: Cheerful German troops pose for the camera on the road to Warsaw. The ease of victory in Poland allayed the fears of the German people, who dreaded a repetition of World War I.

Left: Evacuees from London arrive in the country. When the expected air-raids failed to materialize in the winter of 1939-40, most returned to their homes.

Above right: U-boats proved highly effective from the very start of the war, but Hitler was slow to devote resources to them and their numbers were few.

Right: German tanks on parade in Berlin. Early in the war they were deployed to much better effect than Allied armor.

astounding. Parachute troops were used to seize airfields, so the Luftwaffe could move in immediately. Britain and France landed elements of the intended Finland expeditionary force in Norway to counterattack, but the Luftwaffe used its domination of the air to great effect against both the Royal Navy and ground troops. The attempt to retake Trondheim was abandoned on 2 May; the King of Norway and his government escaped to Britain. Although the German navy also suffered heavy losses, the Norwegian campaign was another triumph of German arms.

Ironically, the main architect of this disaster now rose to power in Britain. Churchill desperately wanted to lead his country through the war. When the defeat in Norway destroyed all remaining confidence in Chamberlain's government, no one stood in his way. On 10 May Churchill became Prime Minister, also taking the title of Minister of Defence – he intended to run the war himself. The new Prime Minister promised the British people only 'blood, toil, tears and sweat.' And that is what they got. On the same morning that Churchill was appointed head of government, German forces invaded Holland and Belgium.

The Germans' original plan for a drive into France had been a repeat of the 1914 Schlieffen

man U-boats scored successes against British naval and merchant shipping, and the British were encouraged by the tracking down of the pocket battleship *Graf Spee* in December. On land, however, the two sides could not get to grips. On 23 October, Hitler ordered his generals to prepare for an offensive against France as soon as possible, to exploit the German superiority in tactics and morale which, he anticipated, could not last long. But bad weather and other setbacks led to a series of postponements. Britain and France, for their part, discussed a variety of largely hare-brained schemes for flanking attacks on Germany.

Winston Churchill, now First Lord of the Admiralty, favored moves to block Germany's supplies of iron ore, which came from mines in northern Sweden via Norwegian ports. This scheme became mixed up with a project to aid Finland. In November 1939 the Finns were attacked by the Soviet Union, as part of Stalin's drive to improve his defensive position against any future German onslaught. They put up a gallant defense through the winter, and popular sentiment in the democracies swung behind them. Some political leaders in London and Paris were far happier with the idea of a war against the Soviet Union than a war against Germany. The French government, which had banned the Communist Party at the end of September, driving its leaders underground, was especially keen. And since help could only be brought to Finland by crossing neutral Norway and Sweden, the same expedition could be used to stop the iron ore exports to Germany. Troops were assembled, but before this folly could be consummated, on 12 March the Finns surrendered. The Soviet Union duly took the territory it considered necessary for its defense.

Hitler had watched these events with profound misgivings. He saw every advantage in a neutral Scandinavia, but he could not afford to let Norway or Sweden fall into enemy hands. He decided to act to forestall British and French designs. By a bizarre coincidence, the two sides made their move almost simultaneously. On 8 April Britain began minelaying in Norwegian territorial waters. On 9 April German troops overran Denmark and seized the Norwegian ports as far north as Narvik. The audacity of this German seaborne operation in the face of Britain's clear naval superiority was

Plan – a sweep through Belgium and down into northern France. But during the winter delays, in January 1940, a German officer had crash-landed in Belgium with the complete plans for the offensive in his possession. As a result, Hitler was forced to change tack, plumping instead for a plan proposed by General Manstein. This involved launching the main thrust of the armored onslaught through the Ardennes, at the hinge between the Allied forces along the Belgian border and the French-manned Maginot Line. This sector was poorly defended, since the Ardennes were considered virtually impassable.

With 10 British divisions in the field alongside the French, the Allies outnumbered the Germans in tanks, but in airpower they were markedly inferior. The key factor, however, was once again the speed and inventiveness of the German operations. They took only five days to overrun Holland, making imaginative use of small numbers of airborne troops; the great Belgian fortress of Eben Emael was also taken from the air, and the Germans streamed toward France. General Gamelin rushed the mass of British and French forces forward into Belgium to meet the German advance. It was a fatal error. On 13 May the first German troops from the Ardennes crossed the Meuse near Sedan; Guderian's tanks began crossing the following day. Once they had broken out of the bridgehead, virtually nothing stood between the German armor and the Channel coast. The speed of Guderian's advance even startled the German commanders – including Hitler – and they made several attempts to stop him in the name of caution. But on 20 May the Panzers reached the sea, cutting off the British and French forces now retreating from Belgium.

Had the Germans proceeded to occupy the port of Dunkirk, nothing might have been saved from the wreckage of the Allied armies. But unaccountably, Hitler ordered a halt. The retreating forces were able to secure the port and use it for the evacuation of 200,000 British and 140,000 French troops. Carried out under constant air attack, the evacuation was a fine feat of arms and did much to rally British morale. Nothing, however, could hide the enormity of the defeat.

General Weygand had replaced Gamelin as French Commander in Chief, but he could do nothing to stem the rout. On 14 June German troops entered Paris. Two days later, the 84-year-old Marshal Pétain took over as French Prime Minister from Paul Reynaud and asked for an armistice; terms were agreed on 22 June. To complete Hitler's satisfaction, the armistice negotiations took place in the same railway coach that had been the scene of the German surrender in November 1918. The victory had cost only 28,000 German lives.

German troops occupied northern France and the whole Atlantic coast, but Pétain's government installed at Vichy retained civil authority throughout the country. The Vichy government loyally collaborated with the Germans, and most of the French colonies followed suit. One junior officer, Charles de Gaulle, broadcast an appeal from London for the French to continue fighting, but few heeded his call. Indeed, Britain further alienated French sentiment on 3 July when, fearful that the French navy would fall into German hands, the Royal Navy attacked its fleet at Mersel-Kebir. About 1300 French sailors were killed in this action.

In the summer of 1940, Hitler could survey his triumphs with justified self-satisfaction. Czechoslovakia and Poland were destroyed; Norway, Denmark, Belgium, Holland and France were in his power; Italy had tardily joined the war on Germany's side on 10 June; Hungary, Rumania and Bulgaria were also virtual allies; and Sweden and Switzerland, although neutral and independent, made a valuable contribution to the German economy. The limits of German power were the Soviet border and the English Channel.

Hitler had made no plans for an invasion of Britain. He had always vaguely expected that the defeat of France would force Britain to sue for peace. When Churchill hurled defiance at the German dictator, he somewhat half-heartedly rose to the challenge. The loss of most of the British army's military hardware in the Dunkirk evacuation left the country temporarily exposed, and German commanders were ordered to prepare for Operation Sealion, a seaborne invasion of Britain's south coast, to begin on 15 September. In fact, the only service chief who showed any enthusiasm for the venture was Göring, boastfully eager to show what the Luftwaffe could do. The army and navy were glad to hide behind him – let Göring establish total air superiority, and then the invasion could go ahead. Thus the Battle of Britain began.

Air attack from the Continent was, fortunately for Britain, the new form of warfare most clearly anticipated before 1939. As a consequence, the island had the world's most sophisticated air defense system, using radar stations to give early warning of enemy aircraft approaching, and centralized operations rooms to guide fighters on to their targets by radioed instructions. The Luftwaffe, on the other hand, was equipped and

Left and far left: German posters celebrating the glories of the Luftwaffe and the Navy. Hitler's spectacular successes inevitably raised his prestige and that of his armed forces to new heights.

Right: A despatch rider passes through the bomb-damaged City of London in the winter of 1940-41. The Blitz, however, never came near breaking British civilian morale.

Below right: An Atlantic convoy viewed from an escort destroyer. Britain was totally dependent on imports to feed its population and sustain the war effort, so the fight to keep open the Atlantic lifeline was one of the crucial battles of the war.

to considerable effect in the winter of 1940. At one point it appeared that surface vessels might pose the greatest threat, but after the battleship *Bismarck* was sunk in the Atlantic by the Royal Navy in May 1941, Hitler became unwilling to risk his big ships. Admiral Raeder, the Commander in Chief of the German Navy, had long advocated the development of a U-boat force 300 strong, which he believed, probably correctly, could have defeated Britain on its own. But Hitler was not persuaded. He grudged every pfennig spent on U-boat production, and in the spring of 1941 there were rarely more than 30 submarines operational. Only then did a substantial expansion of the force begin.

Nonetheless, the U-boat aces took a terrible toll of merchant shipping. Operating out of captured French ports in Brittany, their range stretched beyond that of British convoy escorts or maritime patrol aircraft, both of which were in short supply. The U-boats hunted in 'wolf-packs,' tracking convoys by day and attacking at night on the surface – thus negating the Royal Navy's chief counter-measure, Asdic, which could only detect submarines underwater. British efforts were hampered by the stubborn neutrality of Ireland, the only British Dominion not to join in the war. But with the help of Canada and, increasingly, of the United States, after May 1941 shipping losses were reduced. This welcome breathing-space was to last until the end of the year.

War in the Mediterranean

While Britain thus fought for its very survival, a quite separate war had started with Italy for control of North and East Africa and the Mediterranean. This soon offered the beleaguered British, at least briefly, the almost forgotten experience of military success. Mussolini's forces were, as he had himself correctly estimated in 1939, too poor in equipment, training and morale for serious warfare. But once the Germans seemed to have destroyed all major opposition, the Italian dictator was keen to pick up what scraps he could and repair his own self-esteem, severely dented by comparisons with Hitler's outrageous triumphs. In September 1940, Italian forces advanced a short way from their North African colony, Libya, into Egypt (nominally independent but under effective British rule); at the end of October, Italy invaded Greece from neighboring Albania (an Italian possession since April 1939); and in November forces from Abyssinia seized the lightly defended British Somaliland.

The British counterblows were devastating.

organized to provide support for land operations, not to carry out an independent air offensive. Even flying from newly captured airfields in France, the Germans' most effective fighter, the Me109, was operating at the very limit of its range when covering bombing raids around London. The British Spitfires and Hurricanes were technically a match for any German aircraft.

The major air offensive, Operation Eagle, began on 13 August. It was a war of attrition. Whenever weather permitted, the Luftwaffe sent over waves of bombers with fighter escorts to attack RAF airfields and aircraft factories, also shooting down as many British fighter aircraft as possible. The RAF concentrated on shooting down the Luftwaffe's bombers, while conserving its own strength. By the beginning of September, the German tactics appeared to be paying off: the RAF was running short of experienced pilots and the attacks on airfields were increasingly effective. On 7 September, however, the Luftwaffe turned instead to the bombing of London, in retaliation for British raids on Berlin. This unwittingly let the RAF off the hook. When an especially massive Luftwaffe force was badly mauled on 15 September, the effort to establish decisive air superiority was tacitly abandoned. Two days later, Hitler postponed the invasion of Britain indefinitely. In all, the Germans lost 1733 aircraft during the Battle of Britain, as against British losses of 915.

Air attacks on Britain did not, however, come to an end. From October 1940 to May 1941, the Luftwaffe conducted a night-bombing offensive against British cities. (It finally ceased when Hitler withdrew his aircraft to the eastern front for the invasion of the Soviet Union.) The Blitz, as it was called, caused considerable human suffering –

about 30,000 civilians lost their lives – but it did little to hamper war production and, if anything, strengthened the determination of the British people to fight on. The RAF also mounted a night-bombing campaign against German cities, which equally achieved little but the deaths of many civilians and aircrew.

A less spectacular, but more significant, battle was taking place in the grey wastes of the Atlantic. The British economy was totally dependent on imports; if its sea lifeline was cut, Britain would not be able to continue the war. Germany had four means of attack on merchant shipping: U-boats, mines, surface raiders and aircraft. All were used

First, on 11 November aircraft from HMS *Illustrious* attacked the Italian fleet at Taranto, sinking three battleships. Then on 7 December General Richard O'Connor initiated an offensive by the British, Indian and Australian troops of Western Desert Force that swept forward into Libya, capturing Tobruk on 22 January and reaching El Agheila on 9 February after a memorable victory at Beda Fomm. With 35,000 men, O'Connor destroyed 10 Italian Divisions and took 130,000 prisoners. To complete the collapse of Mussolini's ambitions, between February and May 1941 the British defeated his forces in Somaliland and Abyssinia, restoring the Emperor Haile Selassie to his throne.

Hitler was not especially interested in these colonial conflicts, nor in the Mediterranean. But he could not afford to let his ally Italy collapse altogether. He was also worried that Britain would intervene in Greece – where the Italians had once again been soundly defeated – and try to open a pathway into the Balkans. This was in fact precisely what Churchill had in mind. But as in Norway, the Germans acted with a boldness and decision that seemed beyond the capacity of the British commanders.

For his intervention in Greece, Hitler counted on the cooperation of Bulgaria and, to a lesser extent, of Yugoslavia. At the last moment, how-

ever, on 27 March 1941, a coup deposed the pro-German Regent in Belgrade. Incensed, Hitler ordered the destruction of Yugoslavia as a prelude to the invasion of Greece. It was accomplished within a week. In the subsequent partition, Germany took Slovenia and established a 'protectorate' over Serbia, Bulgaria annexed Macedonia, and Croatia, with its own Fascist leaders, fell under Italian influence. The German drive south into Greece was equally irresistible. A British force from North Africa had just begun to land there when the Greek Army fell apart in the face of the German onslaught. The British troops were evacuated almost as soon as they arrived, with barely a shot fired, leaving much valuable equipment behind them.

Worse was to follow. The island of Crete was now held by almost 29,000 British, Australian and New Zealand troops, with a similar number of Greeks. The Royal Navy guaranteed it against a seaborne assault, but British airpower was almost non-existent. On 20 May some 3000 German parachute troops jumped in and succeeded in seizing part of Malame airfield. More troops could then arrive by transport aircraft and glider, until a total force of 22,000 was assembled. The British response to the initial attack was hesitant, and some units proved irresolute as the airborne force pushed out from its landing zone. By the end of

the month, the island was in German hands. About 13,000 British and Dominion troops were taken prisoner, the rest having been evacuated by the Royal Navy at great cost – three cruisers and six destroyers were sunk by air attack, and even more ships put temporarily out of action. Paradoxically, however, this operation confirmed Hitler's doubts about the effectiveness of airborne assault, perhaps because German losses were, by their standards at the time, very heavy: 4000, as against 5000 in the entire Yugoslavian and Greek campaigns. Crete convinced Britain – and the United States – of the value of parachute troops: Hitler hardly used them again.

While events in Greece and Crete were taking their course, the Germans also took over from the Italians in the Libyan desert, once more with dramatic effect. In February 1941 O'Connor could easily have seized Tripoli and driven the Italians out of North Africa. He was stopped so that troops and equipment could be transferred to Greece. In the same month one of Hitler's favorite tank commanders, General Erwin Rommel, arrived in Libya followed by a Panzer division, the seed of the later Afrika Korps. At the end of March Rommel launched an offensive which, to his own surprise, drove the British back into Egypt within two weeks, capturing O'Connor and leaving only Tobruk in the hands of Australian troops under siege. A powerful British counterattack, named Operation Battleaxe, launched on 15 June, failed miserably in the face of the Germans' skillful use of anti-tank guns, especially the famous 88s, originally an anti-aircraft weapon. This marked a tactical turning-point in the whole war. The success of Rommel's defense against Operation Battleaxe, and of the defense of Tobruk against Rommel, showed that, with the right tactics, armored divisions could be stopped. The victories in the war so far – Poland, the battle of France, Yugoslavia, O'Connor in North Africa – had been virtual walkovers. There would be no more easy triumphs for anyone.

Churchill's eccentric belief in the importance of the North African theater amounted almost to an obsession. For it he neglected the defense of East Asia and would later delay the invasion of northern Europe. To Hitler, North Africa and the whole Mediterranean theater was a sideshow. He installed Rommel in the desert with just barely enough tanks and supplies, placed the Luftwaffe in Sicily to pound the island of Malta and harass the Royal Navy, and moved some U-boats into the Mediterranean where they had considerable success. This sufficed. The German dictator's attention was fixed in quite another direction.

The invasion of Russia

Ever since the start of his career, Hitler had preached a crusade against communism and prattled of Germany's need for *Lebensraum* in the east – sometimes envisaging a military empire stretching to the Urals, where German colonists would rule the Slavs as a subject people. In practical terms, such a land empire would give Germany reliable supplies of food, petroleum and other raw materials, taking away the fear of maritime blockade. Now that the German Army was all-powerful on the European mainland, the Soviet Union seemed an easy target. Most military experts agreed that the Red Army would collapse in the face of a German invasion – opinions differed over whether it would take one month or three. Armed with the power to strike his enemies, Hitler was not a man to stay his hand. He would have liked to overcome Britain first, but reasoned that the defeat of Stalin would also bring the British to terms, denied their last hope of a European ally. In

Left: German bombers during the Battle of Britain. The Luftwaffe was not well prepared for an independent air offensive, since its aircraft and its tactics were geared to operations in support of land forces.

Right: Hitler's troops advance through a burning Russian village during Operation Barbarossa.

Below: General Erwin Rommel (second from right), the Desert Fox, chats to men of the Afrika Korps. Rommel's flair for armored warfare gave him mastery of the desert with numerically inferior forces.

December 1940, planning began for an invasion of the Soviet Union the following summer.

Since the signing of the Nazi-Soviet Pact in 1939, Stalin had bent over backward to accommodate Hitler in the hope of forestalling an attack. Essential war materials, such as petroleum from the Caucasian oilfields and tin and rubber from the Far East, flowed into Germany from or via the Soviet Union, paid for with worthless paper – it was not very different from the tribute that Germany exacted from the conquered countries. But Stalin had also taken some prudent measures to strengthen his defensive position, annexing the Baltic states and taking Bessarabia and Bukovina from Romania during June 1940, while Hitler was occupied elsewhere. The great question mark that hung over the Soviet Union, perhaps for Stalin as much as anyone, was whether the economic and social system would hold together under the stress of war. Had the policies of the 1930s really

turned the Soviet Union into a modern industrial country capable of sustaining a major war? And would the people fight for Stalin?

As historian A J P Taylor wrote, Hitler intended the invasion to be 'the last of his small wars, not the first of his great ones.' The German economy was not geared up for total war. The German people were living quite comfortably off the benefits of conquest while the British struggled by on reduced rations. There had been no great expansion of German forces in equipment or numbers. There were 3550 tanks available for the invasion, only 800 more than for the Battle of France – although they were more heavily armored and gunned. The Soviets had seven times this number of tanks, and twice as many aircraft as the Luftwaffe, but most of their equipment was hopelessly outdated. This time Germany would not fight alone. Hungary and Rumania were expected to make a substantial contribution to the cam-

paign, Italy insisted on joining in, Finland would help in the north, and other contingents arrived from as far afield as Spain. But Hitler made no attempt to enlist Japanese help, despite the close relationship between the two countries.

The invasion, codenamed Operation Barbarossa, was originally timed for mid May 1941, but the events in the Balkans caused a five-week delay. Barbarossa eventually began on 22 June – one day earlier than Napoleon's invasion in 1812. Over three million troops moved forward on a front that stretched from the Baltic to the Black Sea. The Germans carried no winter clothing or equipment for they did not anticipate a long campaign.

The onslaught caught the Soviets unprepared. Even though they had received precise information on Hitler's plans from both Britain and their own spy network in Japan, the warnings had been ignored. In its first strikes the Luftwaffe destroyed a large part of the Soviet airforce on the ground and henceforth completely dominated the skies. The land forces made their habitual headlong progress: by the end of July Army Group North was approaching Leningrad while Army Group Center had taken Smolensk, and Kiev was threatened by Army Group South. It was the sort of advance that had sufficed to defeat France, but the Soviet Union had more reserves, much more space and infinitely more fighting spirit. Stalin took direct command of the war and appealed not to his soldiers' faith in communism but to their patriotism. It worked: the conflict became the Great Patriotic War.

Faced with continuing resistance, the Germans fatally hesitated. Through most of August the commanders and Hitler wrangled over strategy – whether or not to drive flat out for Moscow. In the end Hitler decided against it. The Germans concentrated first on the flanks. In the south, they defeated massive but incompetently led Soviet forces in an encircling movement around Kiev, taking over 600,000 prisoners and opening the way for the capture of the economically vital Donets basin. In the north they were held outside

GERMAN OCCUPIED, 1 JAN 1941
ALLIED WITH AXIS
GERMAN OCCUPIED,
1 JAN – 29 MAY 1941
22 JUNE 1941 – 19 NOV 1942
GERMAN FRONT LINES
— 16 JULY 1941
—— 5 DECEMBER 1941
——— END–APRIL 1942
—·— 19 NOVEMBER 1942

15 Sept 1941
Siege of Leningrad
begins

5/6 Dec 1941–end April 1942
Russian counteroffensive
on Moscow axis

22 June 1941
("Barbarossa")
Germany invades
Russia

19 Nov 1942
High-tide of German expansion.
Russian counteroffensive begins

6–17 April 1941
Germany invades
Yugoslavia

11 November 1942
Germans occupy
Vichy France

8 Nov 1942
US/British forces land
in Morocco & Algeria

9 Nov 1942
German forces
land in Tunisia

6–28 April 1941
Germany invades
Greece

20–29 May 1941
Crete invaded

1941–1942
Axis forces & Brit Eighth Army
engaged in battles across the desert

23 Oct–4 Nov 1942
Battle of El Alamein

© Richard Natkiel, 1982

Left: At its greatest extent, Hitler's European empire was unprecedented, stretching from the north of Norway to the Mediterranean and from the Volga to the Atlantic.

Below right: A German anti-Semitic poster blames the war on Jewish capitalists. The industrialized mass murder of Jews, socialists and other 'undesirables' was the vilest of Germany's many crimes during the war.

Below far right: An artist's impression of the Luftwaffe's first night raid on Moscow, 21–22 July 1941, a month after the start of Operation Barbarossa.

Leningrad by the first, and best, of a new breed of Soviet generals, Georgi Zhukov. But the city was besieged, and a million of its inhabitants would be dead by the time it was relieved in 1944.

Army Group Center restarted its advance on Moscow in October, just too late. The autumn rains turned the dirt roads to mud, slowing the Germans down. There were more great victories, but by the time advanced units reached the Moscow suburbs it was December and -20 degrees centigrade. Supply lines were overstretched, men were exhausted, frostbite set in, vehicles froze up. On 5 December, reinforced with 25 divisions brought over from the Manchurian front, the Red Army launched a counteroffensive. Hitler's run of unbroken success was at an end. His armies had overrun Russia's best agricultural land, destroyed a third of its industry and taken probably over two million prisoners. But the Red Army was still fighting, and time and space were on its side.

On 11 December, as the German Army stood on the defensive in front of Moscow, Hitler declared war on the United States. It was the single worst mistake of his career. In the summer of 1941 he had stood at an apex of power as ruler of Europe. The involvement of the Soviet Union and the United States dwarfed that power. It was the end of European world domination. One country dominated Europe, but Europe was eventually dominated by countries outside itself.

It is a well-worn historical question whether the United States would have gone to war with

Germany had Hitler not taken the decision out of their hands. Already in 1940 President Roosevelt had made it a prime objective of American policy to keep Britain afloat. He argued that an independent Britain was essential to the security of the United States both in the Atlantic and the Pacific. But during his re-election campaign that year he promised the American people: 'Your boys are not going to be sent into any foreign wars.' Ideally, then, Britain would do the fighting while the United States, as the 'arsenal of democracy,' provided her with the necessary tools for the job. The prime symbol of this approach was 'lend-lease,' initiated in March 1941, which empowered the President to provide foreign countries with war material without demanding payment in cash.

Through 1941, however, it became increasingly difficult for the United States to hold the war at arm's length. The weakness of Britain demanded more involvement, and the warm relationship struck up between Roosevelt and Churchill ensured that the President would be ready to take his country as far as he could in that direction. The spectacle of the Blitz and Britain's gallant defiance had a strong influence on American opinion, but it was still generally believed, rightly or wrongly, that the American public would not support a plunge into the European war. Still, in the spring of 1941 the United States began to get involved in convoy escort in the western Atlantic, and after the first wartime meeting between Churchill and Roosevelt in Nova Scotia in August

(which also produced a ringing declaration of principle, the Atlantic Charter), naval cooperation between the two countries increased. By November, US escort vessels were engaged in an undeclared war with the German U-boat fleet. In the same month lend-lease was extended to the Soviet Union.

The Japanese attack on Pearl Harbor on 7 December could well have halted this drift toward war with Germany. It would have been natural for the American public to demand that all the country's resources be turned to defeating the enemy in the Pacific, leaving the Europeans to get on with their domestic squabbles. The unshaken conviction of Roosevelt and his advisers that Europe was the crucial theater of conflict might not have held up against the tide. Hitler's declaration of war – a gesture never adequately explained – let Roosevelt off the hook. For Churchill, who had striven so hard to involve the United States in the war, there was at last promise of eventual victory. He commented: 'So we had won after all.'

At a lengthy conference held in Washington two weeks after Pearl Harbor, the 26 countries at war with Germany and/or Japan agreed to make no separate peace until victory was achieved; they styled themselves the 'United Nations.' Britain and the United States set up a Combined Chiefs of Staff Committee, although strategy was decided by Roosevelt and Churchill. The two men agreed that the defeat of Germany was the first objective of the war. With this the Soviet Union naturally concurred. Subsequent disputes between the three major allies were to be about means, not ends.

Until the summer of 1941, the war had not taken an enormous toll of human life. With the involvement of the Soviet Union and the United States, however, the whole scale of the conflict gradually altered. Their eventual victory would depend on the mobilization and commitment of huge resources of population and industrial production. Inevitably, death and destruction mounted as the logic of total war took hold. By 1945, a single bombing raid could kill more people than the entire German Blitz of 1940-41.

But the scale of warfare was not the only cause of increased suffering and death. Another was Nazi policy in occupied Europe. When Hitler briefed his generals on the decision to invade the Soviet Union, he described it as 'a war of annihilation.' The inhabitants were doubly despicable: as 'subhuman' Slavs and as communists. A German Army directive on the economic exploitation of occupied Soviet territory commented casually that 'millions of people will be starved to death if we take from the country the things we need.' This was Hitler's intention. Throughout the campaign in the Soviet Union, the Germans behaved with unrelenting brutality to captured soldiers and civilians alike. Over two million Soviet prisoners of war died in German hands. The Poles, as fellow Slavs, suffered very similar treatment. But the worst was reserved for the Gypsies and the Jews.

The first wholesale massacres of Jews were carried out by SS Einsatzgruppen, special squads of killers that followed the German armies across the Soviet Union, with the task of exterminating any Jews or commissars who fell into their hands. By the winter of 1941-42 the Einsatzgruppen had massacred an estimated 500,000 people. Still, this was not systematic enough for Hitler, who now had some 10 million Jews within his European dominion. The purity of the race demanded that, in one way or another, they must disappear. In 1940 there was a plan to expel all Jews to the French-owned African island of Madagascar; serious effort went into this bizarre scheme, but British seapower made it totally impracticable. Consequently, in the summer of 1941, Hitler gave SS chief Heinrich Himmler the go-ahead for the 'final solution,' a precise bureaucratically organized extermination of the Jewish race.

Gas had already been used for the killing of over 70,000 of the mentally ill and handicapped in Germany, as part of a campaign of genetic purification (castration was also widely practiced on the supposedly genetically impaired). Now a series of gas chambers were built in eastern Poland, and all over Europe Jews were rounded up and transported eastward, to be either gassed or worked to death (the German railways charged one-way group excursion fares for the journey, children half-price). Between four and six million Jews were killed. From 1943 the Gypsies joined the death queues: half a million died in the gas chambers or at the hands of the Einsatzgruppen firing squads.

There were many other crimes: in their fight against resistance groups in various occupied countries, the Germans resorted to torture, summary execution, the mass murder of hostages, and indiscriminate reprisals, sometimes involving the eradication of entire villages, as at Lidice in Czechoslovakia; thousands of deportees providing forced labor for German industry and communists or socialists interned in concentration camps died of ill-treatment or neglect; and the single-minded exploitation of the resources of every country for the benefit of Germany led to hardship and malnutrition for much of Europe's population. The much-vaunted New Order in Europe was nothing but a system of ruthless domination, maintained by terror. The Nazis were incapable of creating anything; they could only exploit and destroy.

The events of December 1941 – the end of German hopes of a quick victory over the Soviet Union and the entry of the United States into the war – stand in retrospect as the turning-point of the war. But for a time the tide of German victory continued to flow, paralleled by the extraordinary triumphs of the Japanese in the Pacific theater. It still seemed possible that Hitler might defeat the Soviet Union and reduce Britain to submission before the United States had really brought its weight to bear.

The Soviet winter offensive of 1941-42 recovered a lot of territory but, obeying Hitler's order of 'no retreat,' the German Army held firm in a series of heavily defended keypoints and was well positioned to counterattack. After the catastrophic failure of an overambitious Soviet attempt to retake Kharkov in May, the Germans were ready for a massive offensive on the southern front. Their objectives were Stalingrad – a vital communications center as well as a symbolic target because of its name – and the oilfields of the Caucasus. Between late June and the end of August, all went to plan. In a sweeping advance Kleist's First Panzer Army reached the Caucasus Mountains and the Sixth Army under Paulus pro-

gressed to within 13 miles of Stalingrad. Then Soviet resistance stiffened. By mid September the Germans had penetrated the suburbs of Stalingrad, but the city was defended building by building, street by street. Two months later, elements of the Red Army still held out, with their backs to the Volga River. Meanwhile Kleist's troops, unprepared for mountain warfare, were stalled well short of the main Caucasian oilfields.

By November 1942, almost a year and a half of hard fighting had bitten into German reserves of men and machines; over the same period, despite appalling losses, the Soviet Union had been able to maintain its troop numbers and vastly improve its level of equipment – the superb T-34 tank and excellent new aircraft were pouring from Soviet factories in unprecedented quantities, while Britain and the United States also sent Stalin everything they could spare. The whole balance of forces on the eastern front had shifted. On 19 November the Soviets launched a carefully planned counteroffensive, breaking through Rumanian positions north and south of Stalingrad and carrying out a pincer movement to cut off the city. All German efforts to break this iron ring around Stalingrad failed. The German forces in the Caucasus were now also threatened with encirclement. At the beginning of January 1943 they retreated just in time. For the army in Stalingrad, cold, hungry, demoralized and short of ammunition, there was no escape. On 31 January Paulus surrendered.

The war at sea

While these great battles took their course, Britain and the United States faced their most severe challenge at sea. During much of 1942 and early 1943, it appeared that the German U-boats might finally succeed in cutting the Atlantic link between the two Allies, reducing Britain to surrender and isolating the United States from the European war. Rather surprisingly, the American entry into the war led to an immediate upsurge in sinkings of merchant vessels. The United States was slow to adopt the convoy system and the U-boats had a field day against unprotected shipping. Also, the Battle of the Atlantic was accorded remarkably low priority in the allocation of Allied resources. At the start of 1942 Coastal Command's long-range bomber force was transferred to Bomber Command for the strategic air offensive against German cities, and the United States gave priority to manufacturing troop landing craft rather than escort frigates. At the same time, the concentration of U-boats in the Atlantic was increasing significantly, despite the dispersal of

Left: The face of suffering in Dachau concentration camp. Prisoners in the concentration camps were not systematically murdered – this was the role of extermination camps like Auschwitz – but they still died in large numbers, mostly victims of starvation or casual brutality.

Below left: Soviet forces in action during the Battle of Kursk in the summer of 1943 – the largest tank battle of the war.

Right: An accurate contemporary reconstruction of the scene as British infantry advanced in the Battle of Alamein, the turning-point of the desert war.

Far right: Weary German soldiers at Alamein. The days of easy triumphs were now at an end on all fronts.

much of the submarine force to Norway and the Mediterranean.

In June 1942 U-boats sank over 700,000 tons of shipping, the level of sinkings that U-boat Commander in Chief Admiral Donitz considered adequate to defeat Britain. Losses remained at around this level until bad weather in December reduced operations. The effort to transport equipment to the Soviet Union by Arctic convoy added to the problems of the merchant fleet and its escorts. In July 1942 convoy PQ17 bound for Archangelsk lost 23 of its 36 vessels after being mistakenly ordered to disperse for fear of a German surface attack. Total Allied shipping losses for 1942 were almost 7.8 million tons, nearly a million tons more than new shipping built.

In 1943, however, a great turn-around in the

battle suddenly occurred. For some time, new anti-submarine tactics had been under development, involving the use of support groups of destroyers and frigates, carrier-borne aircraft and long-range land-based bombers to hunt down the 'wolf packs,' rather than concentrating on the close defense of convoys. Improved technology, including better radar and depth-charges, had also come into service. The crucial factor, however, was the success of British intelligence in cracking the German Navy's Triton code in December 1942. All wolf packs were directed on to their targets by radio messages. Intercepted and decoded, these messages enabled the anti-submarine forces to locate the U-boats with unerring accuracy. There was a hiccup in early March, when the introduction of a new complication to the Enigma encoding machine defied the code-breakers for 10 days – during that period 21 ships were sunk in two convoys alone. But by the end of the month the anti-submarine forces were back in the ascendant. U-boat losses soon became so heavy that late in May Donitz withdrew all his boats from the North Atlantic. They would never pose a serious threat to Britain's ocean lifeline again.

The double victory of the Red Army at Stalingrad and of the British and Canadian navies in the Atlantic effectively ended Germany's chances of winning the war. It was, however, still far from clear how the Axis forces were to be decisively defeated. At the start of 1942, the Soviet Union had urged Britain and the United States to open a second front in Europe by a landing in France. The American commanders were keen to go along with this plan for a direct thrust toward Germany itself, but the more experienced British quite correctly insisted that the conditions for a successful landing on the Continent simply did not exist.

The Germans were still too strong, the Allies too weak. This was amply demonstrated by the disastrous failure of a combined British and Canadian operation against the French port of Dieppe in August. Yet the US Army, once mobilized, had to find something to do. Roosevelt would not allow the bulk of the forces to transfer to the Pacific theater – Germany came first. So for lack of anything else, the Americans bowed to Churchill's arguments and agreed to join the battle for North Africa.

The fighting in the Mediterranean had gone very badly for Britain in the second half of 1941 and the first half of 1942. Attacks by U-boats and the Luftwaffe had virtually driven the Royal Navy from the sea, and the British-held island of Malta was kept under siege. In the desert, the British Eighth Army assembled forces far superior to Rommel's in numbers and equipment, but was consistently outfought. At heavy cost, a British offensive in November-December 1941 pushed the Axis forces back once more beyond Benghazi, relieving the besieged Australian garrison at Tobruk. The following month Rommel reversed the tide, driving the Eighth Army back to Gazala. There, in late May 1942, he struck again; this time the British and their Allies retreated in some confusion to El Alamein, where a defensive line was improvised about 60 miles from Alexandria. At the start of July, Rommel attempted a final breakthrough, but with only 40 tanks operational, his forces were too weak. Reinforced, he tried again in August, only to be repulsed at Alam Halfa.

The Eighth Army was now under the command of General Sir Bernard Montgomery. Resisting Churchill's urgings for an instant offensive, Montgomery methodically built up his forces, exploiting the fact that his supply route via the Red Sea was secure, whereas the Axis supply lines across the Mediterranean and the desert were vulnerable to British submarines at sea and the RAF on land. By the time the long-awaited British offensive was launched, on 23 October, Rommel's troops were short of fuel and ammunition. They had 540 tanks (280 of them Italian) to set against the Eighth Army's 1440. After a 13-day 'slogging match,' as Montgomery termed it, the Axis forces were duly worn down and driven into headlong retreat, narrowly escaping encirclement.

This Second Battle of Alamein was followed almost immediately, on 8 November, by Operation Torch, the landing of an Anglo-American army in French North Africa under the command of General Dwight D Eisenhower. Both militarily and politically, the operation was something of a mess. To secure the cooperation of local French forces, loyal to the Vichy government, Eisenhower accepted Admiral Darlan, a close colleague of Pétain and an arch-collaborator with the Nazis, as High Commissioner of French North Africa. There was a public outcry, and the Americans were probably relieved that Darlan was soon assassinated. De Gaulle eventually asserted his own authority in the French colonies, despite the opposition of the United States. Meanwhile, the Germans responded to the North African landings by occupying the center and south of France, previously under exclusive Vichy control.

The military performance of the Anglo-American forces against opposition consistently inferior in both numbers and equipment was unimpressive. But this turned out to be a blessing in disguise. It gave Hitler and Mussolini time to move large numbers of troops into Tunisia to continue resistance. Rommel, fighting a series of holding actions against the Eighth Army which was advancing from the east, pleaded with Hitler for a withdrawal of forces from North Africa to man defensive positions on the southern flank of Europe. Hitler would not agree. By spring 1943, the Allies had control of the air and the sea, and the 170,000 Axis soldiers bottled up in Tunisia could not be resupplied. On 13 May they surrendered. The loss of so many battle-hardened troops was a serious setback for the Axis in the Mediterranean.

At a meeting in Casablanca in January 1943, Roosevelt and Churchill had agreed that victory in North Africa would be followed by an invasion of Sicily. Although still regarding operations in the Mediterranean as a diversion from the main object of the war, the Americans were once more dragged along by Churchill's enthusiasm and by the need for action – the army in Africa had to do something. At the same time, it was agreed that preparations would begin in Britain for an invasion of northern France in May 1944; at last Stalin would get his 'second front.' As an afterthought, Roosevelt announced that the Allies would settle for no less than the 'unconditional surrender' of their enemies. The adoption of this slogan undoubtedly strengthened the alliance with the Soviet Union, scotching fears of a 'separate peace,' but it also drove the Germans and Japanese to fight on long after defeat was certain, at the cost of many lives.

Resistance to the invasion of Sicily on 10 July 1943 was not as stiff as expected. Prompted by deceptive indications planted by British intelligence, Hitler guessed that the blow would fall in Sardinia or in Greece. The Allied landing force benefited from excellent air and sea cover and initially faced only Sicilian coastal defense troops who were in a hurry to surrender. German forces on the island provided sterner opposition, aided by the mountainous terrain, but US General George Patton's thrust round the west of the island made rapid progress, reaching Messina on 16 August, one day ahead of Montgomery's slower-moving advance in the east. The poor coordination between Montgomery and Patton allowed almost all the Axis forces in Sicily to escape to the Italian mainland. As in North Africa, the Allied commanders showed little political sense; in return for assistance received during the fighting, Patton installed Mafia chiefs in various positions of authority throughout the island – positions from which no Italian government has been able to oust them since.

The invasion of Sicily was the final blow to Mussolini's waning prestige. The Italian economy was in ruins and strikes had broken out in the industrial north. On 25 July the Fascist dictator was deposed by his own Grand Council and replaced by Marshal Badoglio. Within days, throughout Italy, the Fascist militia melted away. Badoglio assured the Germans that the Italian Army would continue fighting, but secretly sought peace. The Allies were slow to agree what would be acceptable terms for a surrender (the 'unconditional' proviso was waived). The Germans meanwhile were not fooled, and reinforced their military position in Italy. By the time an armistice was publicly announced on 8 September, the German forces were well prepared to disarm the Italians and establish an effective occupation of most of the country. German airborne troops seized Mussolini from captivity and the ex-dictator was allowed to establish a fictional Fascist Social Republic in northern Italy – while in reality becoming less than a puppet, a prisoner of the Nazis. For its part, Badoglio's government declared war against Germany on 13 October. Brilliantly led by Field Marshal Kesselring, the German forces put up a fierce resistance to Allied landings at Salerno on 9 September. The arrival of British XXX Corps advancing by land from the south saved the situation, but Kesselring was able to retreat in good order and eventually stood firm along a strong defensive position, the Gustav Line, centered on Monte Cassino. As the winter drew on, Allied losses from combat and disease mounted alarmingly. Despite the often heroic efforts of a truly multinational army – including, among others, Poles, Indians, New Zealanders

and French colonial troops from North Africa – progress was painfully slow. In late January 1944, in an imaginative attempt to get the advance moving again, an Allied force was landed at Anzio, between the Gustav Line and Rome. Tardiness in moving out from the beachhead, however, gave Kesselring time to organize a counterstroke, and in the end a breakthrough at Monte Cassino in May relieved the pressure on Anzio, rather than the other way round. Allied troops did not enter Rome until June, 11 months after the landings in Sicily, and still Kesselring held strong defensive positions to the north of them. In no sense had Italy turned out to be, in Churchill's phrase, the 'soft underbelly' of Europe.

Despite the substantial forces devoted to Italy by both sides, it remained a sideshow. In the summer of 1943, the largest tank battle of the war was fought far to the east, at Kursk. Here the Soviet winter offensive of 1942-43 had come to the halt with the Red Army pushed forward in a potentially vulnerable salient. Knowing that the Germans would eventually launch a counteroffensive, the Soviets established a defense in depth and waited. On 5 July German forces attacked from north and south of the salient, but they quickly ran into difficulties. A week later, the Red Army went on to the offensive. About 1500 tanks were engaged on each side. By mid-August the Germans were falling back on both flanks, outthought and outfought by the 'sub-human' Slavs they despised.

Now the Red Army could begin the great drive forward that would ultimately take it to Berlin. The German Army never broke. Despite the limitations on flexibility imposed by Hitler's obsession with holding every inch of ground, the German commanders carried out a long series of stubborn and skilful defensive actions. But the Red Army had become a formidable fighting force, led by young generals with a sure grasp of tactics, inexhaustibly supplied with war material of

excellent quality, and inspired with an unshakeable will to victory. The elite mobile forces that led the advance were troops of a high professional standard; the mass of infantry moving up behind them was still ill-trained and uncivilized, but had the strength of its weaknesses, requiring remarkably little food or other supplies to keep going, and successfully enduring the bitterest hardships. Behind the German lines, Soviet partisans attacked communications and transport. In August the Red Army retook Kharkov, in September Smolensk, in November Kiev. The siege of Leningrad was finally lifted in January 1944. The Soviet Union was winning the war.

This was the background to the first meeting between the Big Three – Stalin, Roosevelt and

Churchill – which took place in Teheran in November-December 1943. The level of agreement between these very diverse political leaders was surprisingly high. Dedicated to a single goal, the defeat of Germany, they did not allow differences of ideology to deflect them. Churchill was a lifelong anti-communist, but ever since Germany invaded the Soviet Union in June 1941 he had wholeheartedly and unreservedly welcomed the communist state as an ally. Roosevelt, too, had ignored the views of those in his own Democratic Party (Harry S Truman for example) who suggested that the Soviet and Nazi dictatorships be left to bleed one another to death. Stalin was suspicious – indeed, paranoid – by nature, and he cannot be said to have embraced his Western

Allies with any openness or warmth, but nor did he plot against them. The closing down of Comintern in May 1943 was only a symbolic gesture, yet it symbolized a reality: Stalin did not seek a revolutionary upheaval in Europe to establish communism. His objective was national security. That this would involve Soviet domination of eastern and central Europe was a truth whose consequences the Western Allies preferred not to examine too closely.

The decisions at Teheran about the prosecution of the war only confirmed earlier conclusions: there would be an invasion of France in 1944 and no separate peace with Germany. The more serious discussions concerned post-war arrangements. Stalin insisted that the frontiers of Poland were to change. The Soviet Union would keep its gains of 1939 – and indeed all its 1941 borders – while the Poles took a compensatory chunk of eastern Germany. Given the power of the Red Army, there was little point in the Western Allies opposing this even if they wanted to. The Soviet Union did in fact have a good claim to eastern Poland on ethnic grounds. But the Polish government-in-exile in London refused the idea of any territorial concessions, and was understandably hostile to any Soviet influence in Poland, especially after the discovery of a mass grave of Polish officers at Katyn, probably murdered by the Russians. Unfortunately, this attitude was totally unrealistic, given the facts of geography and military power. By their obduracy, the exiled Poles lost Churchill's support and with it any faint hope of ruling their country after the war.

While the Allies discussed the consequences of victory, Germany remained undefeated. At the end of 1943 Hitler's empire still covered most of Europe. This had its drawbacks. The German forces were too widely spread and increasingly challenged by insurgents in occupied countries. The most powerful of these resistance groups was that led by the communist Josip Broz Tito in Yugoslavia. Supported by the British – on the pragmatic grounds that the communists were

prepared to fight the Germans while the rival Royalist resistance was not – by 1944 Tito was leading a force of 250,000 men and occupying the attention of eight German divisions. The Italian communists and other anti-Fascists formed powerful partisan forces in northern Italy; 50,000 of them were to lose their lives before the war's end. Elsewhere, resistance networks provided intelligence for the Allies and carried out isolated acts of sabotage or assassination.

But the control of Europe was a source of economic strength for the Germans. They plundered raw materials and labor to feed their war machine. France alone provided about 650,000 workers, carried off to toil in German factories. Under the inspired direction of Albert Speer, German armaments production increased by 50 percent in 1943, and continued to rise until the summer of 1944, when Allied strategic bombing at last began to have real impact. Without this impressive economic performance, Germany could not have gone on fighting so long.

The Strategic Air Offensive

The failure of the strategic air offensive to bring Germany to its knees was a severe disappointment to RAF Bomber Command and the USAAF. Both had believed that bombing could win the war on its own. In 1941 the RAF had been forced to recognize that they would have to bomb by night, because otherwise losses were too heavy, and that they could not hit precise targets with any accuracy. So from February 1942, under the command of Air Marshal 'Bomber' Harris, the RAF carried out a night campaign of 'area bombing' against German cities to terrorize the civilian population. Steadily improving navigational and bombing techniques made these raids increasingly effective, and by 1943 the bombers were able to devastate large areas of cities like Hamburg and Essen. But the impact on German morale and industrial efficiency was minimal, while losses of bombers remained high as anti-aircraft defenses improved. Luftwaffe night-fighters were

extremely effective and the introduction of Window, an anti-radar technique, by the RAF only briefly inhibited their attacks.

The USAAF believed in neither area bombing nor nighttime raids. Their commanders thought that if bombers were sufficiently well-armed and armored they could survive without fighter cover by day, and carry out precision attacks on crucial industrial targets. The implementation of these tactics in 1943 led to appalling losses: in one raid on Schweinfurt on 14 October, 60 bombers were shot down and 138 damaged, out of a total force of 291. The answer was a fighter aircraft with sufficient range to provide cover deep into Germany and back – the Mustang. While RAF Bomber Command continued to sustain heavy casualties for little result in a night bomber offensive against Berlin through the winter of 1943-44, the USAAF brought more and more Mustangs into play and was soon winning daylight air superiority over Germany. By May 1944 the Americans were able to begin effective strikes on the vital oil installations in the Reich, and from Italy their bombers were attacking the Rumanian oilfields. By the autumn, fuel shortages had begun to cripple the German war machine.

The bombers' contribution to Operation Overlord, the invasion of Normandy, in June 1944 was two-fold. Firstly, it ensured that the Luftwaffe was fully stretched in the defense of Germany, with little left over for support of ground forces in France. More directly, in April RAF Bomber Command switched to attacks on the French transport network which were so effective they seriously inhibited the Germans' response to the landings.

Overlord was meticulously planned by a staff of almost 5000 under Supreme Commander General Eisenhower. Vast forces were assembled: 10,000 aircraft, 1200 fighting ships, almost 5000 landing craft and transports. Great ingenuity went into the creation of special vehicles to clear beach obstacles, and two artificial harbors were built to be towed across the Channel. At the last moment, bad weather almost stopped the invasion, but on

Above far left: War-damaged buildings in Sicily after the Allied invasion of July 1943.

Above left: In April 1943 the Germans publicized the discovery of a mass grave at Katyn containing the bodies of 4000 Polish officers, apparently murdered by the Soviet secret police.

Left: USAF Mustang long-range fighter aircraft on escort duty, in support of a daytime bombing raid on Germany in the summer of 1944.

Right: US troops on Omaha Beach during the Normandy landings. Few then would have guessed that American forces would still be in Europe over 40 years later.

6 June Eisenhower gambled on a gap in the storms. That day 156,000 troops were landed on five Normandy beaches, three of these taken by British and Canadian forces, the other two by the Americans. Despite some stiff German resistance, a broad bridgehead was established and rapidly reinforced.

The Allies had devoted much time to a plan of deception before D-day, designed to make the Germans think the Pas de Calais would be the invasion target. Although not completely fooled, Hitler hesitated to reinforce Normandy when the news of the landings came through, fearing that a second, heavier blow might fall on the Calais region. The unusual hesitancy of the German response let the Allies off the hook during the crucial first few days. Once substantial German forces weighed in, they performed with typical skill and resolve. For a month, until 9 July, Montgomery's British troops were stuck in front of Caen, an objective they had expected to seize on the first day. By the end of July, however, the Americans had occupied the Cotentin peninsula and were ready for a breakout at Avranches.

Hitler had kept control over the German officer corps through the spell of success; failure incited some of them to plot his downfall – as they had previously at the time of the Munich crisis before the war. On 20 July 1944 Colonel von Stauffenberg planted a bomb at Hitler's headquarters. With the Fuhrer dead, the conspirators planned to set up a non-Nazi government and negotiate peace. But by luck Hitler survived. The immediate ruthless revenge on the leaders of the plot widened into an investigation that implicated both Rommel and, more importantly, Kluge, the newly appointed commander on the Normandy front. In mid-August Kluge poisoned himself rather than face the Gestapo.

By then the Germans had lost the battle of Normandy and their shattered forces were fleeing eastward. The liberation of France proceeded at headlong speed. On 15 August Allied forces landed in the south of France and began a drive up the Rhône valley. On 20 August troops from Normandy crossed the Seine. The French Resistance had risen in armed revolt and was taking on the German Army in Paris and elsewhere. The Vichy government had long lost any shadow of authority or independence, and the Allies intended to put France under their own military rule. But De Gaulle acted too quickly for them. He had established himself as a national leader both

for the Free French forces participating in the invasion and for the Resistance. At his insistence, a Free French armored division was allowed the honor of occupying Paris on 25 August. De Gaulle could then enter the city in triumph and confirm his position as head of an independent French government.

At this point, it seemed the war would be over in 1944. The Allies had two million troops in France, 60 percent of them American. In the first week of September the British Second Army entered Brussels and Antwerp, while Patton's US Third Army had reached the Moselle, 100 miles from the Rhine. Only light and disorganized German forces lay in their path. But now there was a pause. Supply lines were overstretched, and Allied commanders locked in combat over strategy and the sharing out of resources. By the time the offensive was resumed, German resistance had stiffened. Montgomery went ahead with a bold plan for a drive across Holland to the Rhine at Arnhem, using airborne forces to hold a series of bridges while the armor came up. Launched on 17 September, Operation Market Garden very nearly succeeded. Only the last bridge, at Arnhem, was not secured despite heroic efforts by British para-

troops. That failure condemned the Allies to a winter bogged down around the German frontier.

The Red Army was also having difficulty maintaining momentum on the Eastern front, where the majority of German forces were still concentrated. By the end of May 1944 the Russians had retaken almost all pre-war Soviet territory. On 23 June they launched their summer offensive in Byelorussia with 160 divisions. In little over a month the Red Army advanced 450 miles and took 350,000 prisoners. By 1 August Soviet troops had reached the outskirts of Warsaw. The Polish underground, the Home Army, rose up and took control of the city in anticipation of the Russians' arrival. But at this point the Soviet advance halted as fresh German divisions were brought up to the front. For the Poles in Warsaw it was a catastrophe. The Germans took two months to win back the city from the Home Army; 55,000 Poles were killed and 350,000 deported to Germany. The Soviet Union made no effort to help the Warsaw insurgents, and relations with the Polish government-in-exile were further embittered. But the Red Army's military difficulties were genuine; and Warsaw only fell in January 1945.

The Soviets could still make some progress on the flanks. In the north, Finland was forced to accept an armistice in September 1944 and the following month Soviet troops entered East Prussia. In the south, Romania made peace after the overthrow of the pro-German government in August and Bulgaria also hastened to surrender. On 19 October the Red Army entered Belgrade and linked up with Tito's partisans. But the Germans took over Hungary before Admiral Horthy could change sides and in November the Soviet advance on this front also stalled, in front of Budapest.

Hitler still hoped for a miracle: either the Western Allies would fall out with the Soviet Union, or a new wonder-weapon would transform the war. In June 1944 the first of Germany's V-1 flying bombs had struck London, beginning a barrage that killed over 6000 people in three months. Just when the British anti-aircraft defenses were getting the better of these pilotless planes, on 8 September the V-2 came into action. This was a ballistic missile, traveling too fast to be intercepted and striking without warning. But Hitler did not have enough of these weapons, which were very expensive to produce, and their main launching sites were soon overrun by the advanc-

7 May 1945
War in Europe
ends

2 May 1945
Fall of Berlin

15 Dec 1944–7 Feb 1945
Battle of the Bulge

25 Aug 1944
Paris liberated

25 Aug 1944
Rumania and
8 Dec 1944
Bulgaria declare
war on Germany

LIBERATED/OCCUPIED BY ALLIES
23 JUNE –15 DECEMBER 1944 •
15 DECEMBER 1944 – 7 MAY 1945
ALLIED FRONT LINES
— 25 AUGUST 1944
— 15 DECEMBER 1944
— 21 MARCH 1945
— 7 MAY 1945
• German forces withdrew from Greece, Albania
and Yugoslavia in face of partisan attacks

Above left: An infra-red aerial reconnaissance photo of the German top-secret V-2 missile base at Peenemunde. The architects of the V-2 program, such as Werner von Braun, would soon be working for new masters in the postwar arms race.

Below left: The Big Three meet for the last time, at Yalta in February 1945 – seated, from left to right, Churchill, Roosevelt and Stalin.

Right: The Nazi empire in the early summer of 1944. Although still vast in its extent it would be destroyed in 12 months by repeated hammer blows from the Soviet armed forces in the East and the Allies in the West.

ing Allied armies. V-2s killed only 2700 Londoners during the winter of 1944-45, far too few to change the course of the war. The story was the same with other achievements of German science and technology – the jet aircraft, the schnorkel submarine – they arrived too late in too small numbers, when the Nazi empire was already running out of fuel, space and time.

As a gambler's last throw, on 16 December 1944 Hitler hurled 20 divisions forward through the Ardennes in a repeat of the great offensive of May 1940. Once again, the Allies were caught completely off guard; they had complacently underrated German strength. But Hitler's objective was far too ambitious: his forces aimed to break through to Antwerp; they were stopped just short of the Meuse. In the second week of the offensive, an improvement in the weather enabled Allied airpower to come into play. The Panzers were short of fuel and so was the Luftwaffe. As Allied counterattacks developed from north and south, the Battle of the Bulge turned into a massacre of German armor. The Allies also suffered heavy losses in some of the fiercest fighting of the war, but they could afford it – the Germans could not. On 12 January 1945 the Red Army launched a vast offensive from the line of the Vistula. With overwhelming numerical superiority of men and equipment, they surged forward, advancing over 300 miles by the end of the month despite the bitter winter weather. The Soviet spearhead was a mere 40 miles from Berlin. Ever cautious, how-

ever, Stalin refused to allow Zhukov to race on to the German capital, and for the next two months the Red Army consolidated its hold on the flanks, taking Budapest on 11 February and entering Vienna on 13 April. Meanwhile, on 7 March, American forces crossed the Rhine at Remagen. Germany had been wide open to Allied bombing since the autumn of 1944 and both its industrial plant and its transport network were devastated. The war economy had finally collapsed. Controversially, RAF Bomber Command continued to devote over a third of its efforts to area bombing, intended to cause the maximum of civilian casualties. A single raid on the previously untouched city of Dresden on 14 February probably killed more than 60,000 people. The Germans had sown the wind; now they were reaping the whirlwind.

Hitler's one remaining hope was still that the Western Allies would fall out with the Soviet Union and change sides. They did not. At Yalta on 4-11 February the Big Three reconfirmed their alliance. Churchill was keen to set a limit to Soviet gains but had already reached an agreement with Stalin on 'spheres of influence' the previous October. Roosevelt trusted to Stalin's good faith and was pleased that he assented to join the United Nations. Differences over the future of Poland were glossed over. It was agreed that Germany would be divided into four zones of occupation – British, American, Soviet and French. So there was not even any jockeying for advantage as the Allies completed the conquest of Germany.

The finishing lines of the armies of the East and the West were fixed in advance – and the agreement was strictly adhered to.

On 12 April President Roosevelt died suddenly, missing the last act of the great drama. Four days later, the Red Army pushed forward two million men in the final drive to take Berlin. On the Western front, 320,000 German troops encircled in the Ruhr surrendered on 18 April. American and Soviet soldiers joined hands at Torgau on the Elbe a week later.

It was the end for the Great Dictators. On 28 April the fleeing Mussolini was captured by Italian partisans and shot, along with his mistress; their bodies were hung upside down outside a garage. Hitler cowered in his Berlin bunker, listening to the sound of Soviet gunfire drawing closer. On 29 April, with all hope lost, he married his mistress Eva Braun and nominated Admiral Donitz as his successor. The following day Hitler and his bride committed suicide; their bodies were burned. Political gangsters, the two dictators had died with their molls.

On 2 May the Berlin garrison surrendered to the Red Army. It had cost the Soviet Union 300,000 casualties to take the city. German forces in Italy had already capitulated; other surrenders followed piecemeal. By 9 May the war in Europe was over. But the war in Asia still went on: not until the defeat of Japan could the full measure be taken of the death and destruction wrought by World War II.

The war against Japan

The Japanese offensive against the United States and the European colonial powers in December 1941 has gone down in popular mythology as one of the most sudden and unexpected onslaughts in history – a storm out of a clear blue sky. Yet in reality it followed a slow and ponderous build-up to confrontation, stretching at least as far back as July 1937, when the Japanese attacked the Chinese forces of Chiang Kai-shek and extended their control over the whole of coastal China. The American decision to back Chiang set the United States directly in the path of Japanese ambitions. The Southeast Asian possessions of the colonial powers, Britain, France and the Netherlands, were also plainly threatened by the expansion of the Japanese empire. After the German victories of May-June 1940 in Europe, the way was open for Japan to exploit the French and Dutch collapse and Britain's temporary weakness.

The United States was not interested in preserving the colonial empires, but did want to limit Japanese expansion and sustain the independence of its ally China. So, when the Japanese completed the occupation of a now defenseless French Indochina in July 1941, the United States led Britain and the Netherlands in a blockade of the Japanese economy, including an oil embargo that threatened the country's very existence. Once the embargo was in force, Japan had only the choice of surrendering all its ambitions and accepting an agreement dictated by the United States, or striking out to secure supplies of oil and other raw materials for itself, through the establishment of a Japanese-dominated 'Greater Asia Co-Prosperity Sphere.'

Both Britain and the United States knew that the oil embargo imposed on Japan meant almost certain war, especially after General Hideki Tojo became prime minister of Japan on 17 October. But neither of the Western powers prepared thoroughly enough for an armed conflict. Britain, understandably distracted by its own life or death struggle at home, and less understandably committed to the desert war in North Africa, could spare only a token force of two capital ships, the *Prince of Wales* and the *Repulse*, to bolster the flimsy defenses of its base at Singapore. The United States recalled its most glamorous general, Douglas MacArthur, and appointed him Commanding General in the Far East. MacArthur confidently predicted he could hold the Philippines against any Japanese attack. With such pronouncements and gestures the Western powers hoped to ward off the evil day.

As the prolonged negotiations with the United States were obviously getting nowhere, on 25 November the Japanese government decided to gamble on war. They knew that military success would depend on speed and surprise. Only 11 of Japan's 51 army divisions were available for the offensive against the Philippines and the British and Dutch colonies, the rest being retained in China and Manchuria. But air and seapower could make up for the lack of numbers on land. The only real threat to Japanese dominance at sea and in the air was the US Pacific Fleet, described by Admiral Isoroku Yamamoto, commander of the Japanese Combined Fleet, as 'a dagger pointed at the throat of Japan.' An ardent proponent of the use of aircraft carriers, Yamamoto had been very impressed by the Royal Navy's successful attack on the Italian fleet at Taranto in November 1940. He planned a similar coup on a larger scale against the US fleet at Pearl Harbor, Hawaii. With the US battleships and aircraft carriers destroyed, Japan would have a free hand to take over the Southwest Pacific and Southeast Asia, securing the raw

materials it needed and cutting off the supply lines to Chiang Kai-shek's army in China.

The attack on Pearl Harbor was set for the morning of 7 December. The same day, Japanese forces would strike against the Philippines, Hong Kong and Malaya – although these operations, on the other side of the international date line, would actually be dated 8 December. The Japanese ambassador in Washington was to declare war a half an hour before the first attack, enough for honor's sake, but too late for the Americans to organize a practical response. In the end, the only part of the plan that did not work was the declaration of war. The coded instructions from Tokyo to the ambassador took too long to decipher and the war was under way before the formal declaration was made. The American intelligence services, which had broken the Japanese cipher, actually read the ambassador's instructions before he did, and also guessed that Pearl Harbor would be the first object of attack. But no warning got through to the forces in Hawaii.

Yamamoto assembled a task force of six aircraft carriers with an extensive escort for the Pearl Harbor operation. Between 2 and 6 December they sailed south from the Kurile islands, without being spotted, to their attack station 275 miles north of the target. At 0755 hours on 7 December, the first wave of aircraft struck Pearl Harbor. It was a Sunday and defenses were unmanned. A radar warning of the aircrafts' approach was ignored. Within less than two hours, four American battleships were sunk and four more severely damaged, along with 10 lesser warships; 188 aircraft had been destroyed, and about 3500 servicemen killed or wounded. This devastation was achieved by 360 Japanese aircraft – including 40 torpedo-bombers – of which only 29 were lost. Yamamoto had achieved his objective of putting the American Pacific fleet out of action, with one crucial exception: by chance, none of the three American aircraft carriers in the Pacific was at Pearl Harbor on 7 December. This was a very fortunate escape for the United States.

Still, the Japanese were guaranteed naval superiority for long enough to take the Philippines. Long-range air strikes from bases in Formosa destroyed most of the American aircraft on the islands on the first day. Omnipotent by air and

sea, Japan could land troops at will along the extensive Philippine coastline, defended only by poor-quality local troops. By Christmas 1941 over 50,000 Japanese were established on the main island, Luzon, and MacArthur had begun a withdrawal of his best forces to the Bataan Peninsula. Here they were penned in by the Japanese, with no hope of reinforcement. On 10 March 1942

Left: General Douglas MacArthur (facing the camera) broods upon the desperate state of the war with Japan in March 1942.

Below left: News of the Japanese attack on Pearl Harbor came as a total surprise to the American public, although their political leaders knew very well that war was imminent.

Right: Japanese Prime Minister General Tojo arrives to inspect the situation in the Philippines, May 1943.

Below right: Japanese troops advance through Burma in 1942, while local people squat by the roadside. At first many Asians welcomed the Japanese as liberators from the yoke of European colonialism, but Japanese military rule proved cruel and oppressive.

MacArthur obeyed orders to quit the Philippines for Australia, announcing sonorously: 'I shall return.' The American and Filipino forces in the Bataan Peninsula surrendered on 9 April; the fortified island of Corregidor held out until 6 May in heroic, if futile, defiance. Racked by disease and starvation, over 40,000 of the troops who surrendered died in their first two months of captivity under the harsh regime imposed by the Japanese General Homma.

British disasters

The resistance in the Philippines was by far the strongest that the Japanese encountered. The British colony of Hong Kong, virtually indefensible against Japanese attack, held out for 18 days, surrendering at Christmas. Almost 12,000 British and Dominion soldiers went into captivity. Much more was expected of Malaya and Singapore, held by 88,000 British, Dominion and colonial soldiers. General Yamashita had only 70,000 combat troops with which to carry out his offensive, but once more air and naval superiority were decisive. The Japanese could field 560 aircraft, almost four times the British number and of far superior quality. At sea, the much-vaunted naval base of Singapore was defended by only two major warships, the newly arrived battleship *Prince of Wales* and the battlecruiser *Repulse.* Without air cover, they were hopelessly vulnerable. On 10 December, while searching for Japanese troop transports, both ships came under air attack and were sunk by a mix of high-level bombers and torpedo bombers. The Japanese lost three aircraft in the action.

Japanese troops landed in Siam thrust down the west of the Malaysian peninsula, while those landed inside Malaya itself moved down the east coast. Their speed of movement and maneuver bemused the defenders, who were repeatedly outflanked and either encircled or simply bypassed. By the end of January 1942 the Japanese had captured all of Malaya at the cost of only 4600 casualties. Still, Singapore remained a theoretically formidable position, now defended by 85,000 troops. In the construction of the base, however, landward defenses had been neglected, and Japanese control of sea and air made the situation precarious. On 8 February Japanese troops were allowed to establish a beachhead on Singapore island, which they quickly reinforced. A week later, on 15 February, the British surrendered. Although shortages of food and water had already set in, this rapid capitulation to a numerically inferior force – the Japanese on the island totalled only 30,000 – was an abject humiliation for the British Empire. A centuries-old myth of racial and cultural superiority died at Singapore.

The Japanese had two further objectives: the Dutch East Indies and Burma. The Dutch government-in-exile in London co-operated with Britain in an attempt to defend the East Indies, but it was to no avail. The first Japanese troops landed in Indonesia on 6 January 1942 and the Japanese navy brushed aside an effort by a combined British and Dutch naval force to intervene the following month. On 8 March the Dutch forces in the East Indies surrendered. That same day Japanese troops entered the Burmese capital, Rangoon. Toward the end of April, the British decided that all of Burma would have to be abandoned, and by the middle of May their forces had withdrawn to Assam.

In five months the Japanese had achieved an extraordinary sequence of victories. The oilfields of the Dutch East Indies, the tin mines and rubber

Left: The crew abandon ship as the USS *Lexington* sinks during the Battle of the Coral Sea.

Below: Torpedo bombers on the deck of USS *Enterprise* prepare to take part in the Battle of Midway, the turning-point of the Pacific war.

Right: Although this propaganda poster suggests a direct drive on Japan, until mid 1944 American commanders pursued a very indirect route to Tokyo.

Below right: US Marines or Guadalcanal. For the Marines, the Pacific campaign meant fierce fighting against dedicated Japanese infantry under tropical conditions.

plantations of Malaya were in their hands. With the occupation of Burma, the supply route to Chiang Kai-shek's army at Chungking, the Burma Road, was blocked. It seemed to the British that Japan might intend to push on westward and even join Germany in a joint offensive in the Middle East. But such objectives were far beyond Japan's resources or ambitions. In April a Japanese fleet attacked Ceylon in the hope of destroying a British naval force at Colombo, but only succeeded in sinking two cruisers and a number of merchant vessels. The Japanese Army, still regarding China as the crucial battlefield, refused to provide troops for an invasion of Ceylon. The expansion of Japanese power had reached its limit in the west.

The Pacific proved to be the decisive theater. Here a fierce conflict was fought across wide ocean spaces among far-flung archipelagos, a conflict characterized above all by amphibious landings and aircraft carrier duels. At first, the Japanese intended to continue their Pacific offensive, not because they coveted wider gains, but rather as the best means of defending what they now held. They were well aware that once the United States recovered from Pearl Harbor, a powerful counter-blow could be expected. As early as 18 April 1942, a force of 16 carrier-launched B-25 long-range bombers raided Tokyo. This was a one-off operation, explicitly staged as retaliation for Pearl Harbor, but it showed how quickly the Americans were regaining strength. To nip this recovery in the bud, the Japanese chose two lines of attack. One was to occupy Papua and the island chains as far as Samoa, thus cutting communications between Australia, America's main base in the South Pacific, and the United States. The other was to advance against Midway Island, forcing the US fleet to sail out from Hawaii and give battle – the Japanese Navy was confident of victory.

The two American commanders – General MacArthur, running operations in the Southwest Pacific zone, and Admiral Chester W Nimitz, responsible for the central Pacific – had one trump card, the breaking of the Japanese ciphers. Intercepted messages gave them detailed knowledge of the enemy's intentions that conferred a significant tactical advantage. In April 1942 they knew that the Japanese were assembling an invasion force at Rabaul and Truk to continue their advance around Australia. Already in possession of part of the Solomon Islands and New Guinea, the Japanese now intended to take the island of Tulagi and to land in force at Port Moresby in Papua.

Nimitz sent his two available carriers, *Yorktown* and *Lexington*, south with a cruiser escort to try to disrupt the invasions. The Japanese also had two carriers, the *Zuikaku* and *Shokaku*, covering their amphibious forces. In a rather confused series of operations between 3 and 7 May, American carrier aircraft failed to interrupt the Tulagi landings but forced the Japanese to abandon their attack on Port Moresby. Then, on 8 May, the opposing carriers exchanged air attacks, in which the *Lexington* was lost and *Shokaku* severely damaged. Although indecisive, this Battle of the Coral Sea deserves its fame as the first engagement in naval history to be fought by two fleets using airpower alone. A much larger, more decisive, repeat soon followed.

In early June the Japanese made their move against Midway Island. The plan was to distract the US Navy by a feint attack against the Aleutians while occupying Midway, and then to destroy the American fleet with overwhelming force somewhere in the north Pacific. But thanks to the cracking of the Japanese codes, Nimitz knew all about Japan's intentions and ignored the attack on the Aleutians, instead stationing his three carriers, *Enterprise*, *Hornet* and *Yorktown*, and their escorts north of Midway. There they waited unseen as a massive Japanese fleet, including eight carriers, 11 battleships and 22 cruisers, escorted the slow-moving troop transports toward the island.

Midway turning point

On the morning of 4 June the four fleet carriers of Nagumo's First Carrier Force launched air strikes against Midway, quite unaware that the American fleet was in the offing. When American dive-bombers struck at 1024 hours, the Japanese carriers were defenseless; within five minutes three of them were wrecked. The fourth, *Hiryu*, managed to launch a strike that crippled *Yorktown* before she too was sunk. It was one of the quickest

SEVEK

warmly welcomed the flow of US dollars and military hardware, and were vociferous in their demands that others should fight on their behalf. Although Mao Tse-tung's communist guerrillas in the far north were considerably more active against the Japanese, the Chinese theater of operations remained in effect a damp squib until the end of the war, the great campaign that never was.

The American desire to promote the war in China led to a major Allied effort in Burma, to reopen the 'Burma Road' as an overland supply route to Chiang's forces. The British were confronted by civil disobedience in India after talks with the Indian Congress broke down in mid-1942, and some Indian leaders looked forward to a Japanese or German victory. This uncertain situation did not encourage the use of India as a major base for an advance back into Burma. Nonetheless, after much urging by General Stilwell, the British advanced somewhat half-heartedly into the Arakan coastal region in December 1942. The Japanese counterstroke was swift and decisive; by May 1943 the British were back at their starting point, once more thoroughly outfought.

The Americans were also finding it difficult to work up momentum in the Pacific. Although they had the strategic initiative and the Japanese stood on the defensive, it was difficult to plan for a decisive victory, especially when divisions of command made the concentration on a single line of advance impossible: neither MacArthur nor Nimitz would accept a subsidiary role, so each had to have his own sphere of action. In May 1943 it was agreed that two offensives would converge on the Philippines, one following the direct line from Hawaii across the Central Pacific, the other sweeping up from the southwest. From the Philippines it was assumed that the next step would be into China – a red herring not abandoned until the following year.

The immediate strategic target in the southwest Pacific was the Japanese base at Rabaul. This was too strong to be attacked directly, so MacArthur and Admiral William F Halsey set out to occupy powerful positions on each side of it, advancing along the north coast of New Guinea and westward through the Solomon Islands. This was very slow going. Bougainville, the most westerly of the Solomons, was eventually invaded in November, by which time American and Australian troops had control of most of Papua. In March 1944 the Americans took the Admiralty Islands,

reverses in military history. Suddenly, the Japanese no longer had a clear superiority in carrier strength – and this was now the only strength that mattered at sea. The Midway operation was abandoned without the battleships having fired a shot. The tide of Japanese triumph had turned; the ebb would last three long years.

After Midway, the Americans naturally desired to move on to the offensive, but the Japanese were also still advancing undeterred. Thus the two sides met head-on both on New Guinea and in the Solomons. The fate of New Guinea was of particular concern to Australia, since the fall of the island would have left the Japanese in position to bomb Queensland at will. In July 1942 Australian troops pushing northward from Port Moresby ran into the Japanese heading south from Buna. This was the start of a long and arduous campaign fought under atrocious jungle conditions. Aided by the intelligent use of air support, the Australians gradually drove back the Japanese, taking Buna in January 1943. But fighting on New Guinea would continue until the summer of 1944.

In the Solomons, the United States decided to occupy Tulagi and its larger neighbor Guadalcanal, where the Japanese were just settling in. On 7 August 1942 11,000 US Marines landed on Guadalcanal virtually unopposed, while another Marine force seized Tulagi in the face of stiff resistance. It was on Guadalcanal, however, that the subsequent fighting was concentrated. The arrival of a powerful Japanese naval force quickly drove off the supporting US task force with heavy losses, and the marines had to survive without air cover until they completed the construction of an airstrip, Henderson Field, begun by the Japanese. Even then their position was precarious as the Japanese ferried in troops from their base at Rabaul to retake the island. By mid-October each side had over 20,000 men on Guadalcanal, locked in desperate combat. Despite suffering air and naval bombardment, as well as the effects of tropical heat and poor diet, the Marines beat off a major Japanese offensive between 24 and 26 October, and thenceforth took to the offensive themselves. At sea, the US Navy gradually gained the upper hand in a series of costly engagements. The climax came between 13 and 15 November, when a Japanese attempt to land 11,000 fresh troops was met by American air and sea attacks so

effective that only 4000 soldiers got ashore. Two Japanese battleships were sunk in the accompanying naval battle. The Americans could now reinforce and resupply their army on Guadalcanal; the Japanese could not. In the first week of February 1943 the Japanese finally withdrew, successfully evacuating their remaining troops. Guadalcanal was not of any great strategic importance, but the defeat was serious for Japan because of the losses it entailed, in particular the 600 naval aircraft destroyed in carrier duels. American industry, now geared up for war production, could replace losses with ease; for the Japanese, resources were limited and eventual defeat in a war of attrition was inevitable.

Both the Americans and the Japanese believed that China would sooner or later prove a crucial area of military confrontation. The Americans set great store by Chiang Kai-shek and General Joseph Stilwell was sent to China as a military adviser in early 1942, to get the Chinese Nationalist Army moving. Nothing, as it turned out, could ever induce Chiang Kai-shek or his corrupt generals to do any serious fighting, although they

while fighting was still continuing on Bougainville. In New Guinea, further landings along the coast had driven the Japanese back to Wewak by the end of April. Outflanked, the base at Rabaul could be left to 'wither on the vine.' Still, even avoiding costly direct assaults on Japanese strongpoints, this road to Tokyo looked very long indeed.

In the Central Pacific, a potentially more direct route to Japan was opened up. The offensive there started later, in November 1943, with an attack on the Gilbert Islands commanded by Vice Admiral Raymond Spruance. The Gilberts were considered a softer option than the more northerly Marshall Islands, although this may have seemed less than obvious to the 18,000 marines detailed to take Tarawa. Despite a heavy preparatory air and naval bombardment, the initial landing was fiercely resisted and about 1000 American lives were lost. But the basic tactical outline for future successful 'island hopping' was established. The fast carriers, of which the US Navy had an ever-increasing supply, could guarantee local superiority in the air and at sea, supported by a numerous and sophisticated 'service train' of ancillary vessels that could keep the fleet in operation for long periods out in the ocean. Infantry landings against dedicated, or even suicidal, Japanese resistance might occasionally prove costly, but improved amphibious vehicles and greater experience would tend to minimize casualties. The next leap was on to the Marshalls: Kwajalein and Einwetok were taken in February 1944 at the cost of less than 500 dead. At the same time, on 17-18 February, an American carrier task force devastated the important Japanese base at Truk in the Carolines.

This was a severe blow to Japan. Already, in September 1943, the Japanese leaders had realized that they would soon have to draw back to a tighter defensive perimeter, called the 'absolute national defense sphere,' giving up the Marshalls, the Gilberts, the Solomons and Rabaul. But Truk was a key point in their 'absolute defense;' its destruction boded ill for Japan's future prospects. Already, American submarines were taking their toll of merchant shipping, sinking 1,335,000 tons in 1943. This was putting a new stranglehold on the Japanese economy: there was no advantage in the possession of Southeast Asia if oil and other raw materials could not be shipped from there to Japan. Most crucial, however, was the inability to match American airpower, whether based on carriers or on newly captured Pacific islands. During the attack on Truk, Japan had lost 250 aircraft to America's 25. This was the arithmetic of defeat.

Still, by the spring of 1944 the Japanese had successfully held the great bulk of their conquests for over two years, and in Burma they were on the attack once more. In mid-March three Japanese divisions struck across the Indian border into Assam, intending to capture the Imphal plain and thus forestall a future British offensive. They were not troubled by the advance of Orde Wingate's Long Range Penetration Groups (the Chindits) and Chinese Nationalist forces under Stilwel on their northern flank, and by early April Imphal and Kohima were under siege. But General Sir William Slim, in command of the British Fourteenth Army, had developed new tactics to deal with Japanese encircling moves. Instead of surrendering or retreating in disarray, his men would stand and fight, supplied by air, until relief arrived. Kohima was heroically defended by its small garrison until relieved on 18 April, and the road to Imphal was reopened in May. The Japanese suffered heavy losses in the face of mounting British counterattacks – about 50,000 men by July, compared with British losses of

17,000. The remaining Japanese forces would not be adequate to defend Burma in the next campaigning season after the monsoon.

This setback on the Burmese front was as nothing, however, to the disasters that befell Japan in the Pacific between June and October 1944. In those five months, the war was effectively lost. After the victories in the Gilberts and the Marshall Islands, Nimitz's forces in the Central Pacific turned their attention to the more northerly Marianas. The Japanese planned a counterstroke using island- and carrier-based aircraft to cripple the American fleet. It was a critical confrontation. On 15 June the first wave of marines went ashore on the island of Saipan, in the face of fierce enemy resistance. The Japanese fleet steamed into the Philippine Sea to counterattack Admiral Spruance's naval force. One part of the Japanese plan had already aborted – their island-based aircraft had been virtually wiped out by American carrier-launched airstrikes. On 19 June the Japanese naval aircraft flying into the attack were massacred by American fighter cover in 'The Great Marianas Turkey Shoot.' They lost 218 aircraft without sinking a single Amercan ship. Worse still, two Japanese carriers were sunk by American submarines, and another was lost when American carrier-borne aircraft launched a strike the following day. In total, the Japanese lost 480 aircraft in this Battle of the Philippine Sea, most of them with their crews, who were even more difficult to replace than the machines.

The American conquest of the Marianas was no longer in doubt after this crushing victory, but on land it demanded a gruelling effort. Encouraged by commanders who themselves committed suicide rather than surrender, the Japanese soldiers on Saipan fought literally to the death. The US Marines lost 3500 killed and 13,000 wounded or sick before the island fell on 7 July. By mid-August Tinian and Guam were also in

American hands. America now had airfields from which its bombers could hit Japan.

Faced with such defeats, General Tojo's government resigned on 18 July. Its successor, a cabinet under General Koiso, decided at last that China would not be the decisive area of confrontation in the war and prepared for an all-out defense of the Philippines. The Americans had also finally lost faith in Chiang Kai-shek and realized that a much more direct approach to Japan was possible across the ocean, rather than through China. It would perhaps have been logical of them to bypass the Philippines and head straight for Japan via the islands of Iwo Jima and Okinawa, exploiting the overwhelming strength of their Pacific fleet, now the most powerful in the world. But MacArthur had promised to return to the Philippines, and this perhaps more than any other consideration held the United States to its original plan. By September MacArthur's forces had achieved control of New Guinea, outflanking Japanese positions along the north coast in a series of amphibious landings. The two American lines of advance, across the Central Pacific and up from the southwest, were now set to converge. On 20 October landings began on Leyte, one of the smaller islands in the center of the Philippines.

Since the Marianas debacle, Japanese naval aviation was too weak to intervene to any effect. But the Japanese Navy nevertheless intended to mount a crushing counterstroke, exploiting the power of its still formidable fleet of battleships. The ingenious plan was to use the remaining aircraft carriers as a decoy to draw off the American carriers, while battleships and cruisers slipped through to attack the invasion force. It very nearly worked. Despite losing three cruisers and a battleship to air and submarine attacks on 23-24 October, the Japanese fleet was able to attack towards Leyte Gulf in a pincer movement on the 25th, while the main American carrier force was

lured away to the north. At one point four Japanese battleships and six cruisers were bearing down on the American troop transports which were protected by only a light force of destroyers and escort carriers. But the destroyers' resistance was so valiant that at the last moment the Japanese admiral lost his nerve and turned back. The overall result of the Battle of Leyte Gulf (the largest naval engagement of all time, with 282 warships involved compared with 250 at Jutland) was another massive defeat for Japan. Its losses included three battleships, four carriers and six cruisers; the Americans did not lose a single vessel of comparable value.

The land battle for the Philippines was a footnote to the American victory at sea. The Japanese defended tenaciously, holding on in Leyte almost until the end of the year. On 10 January 1945 the Americans invaded Luzon, but the capital, Manila, was not cleared of Japanese troops until March, and a costly mopping-up operation on the island continued up to the end of the war. There was really little point to this, or to the great efforts made in Burma, which was finally recaptured from the Japanese in a complex offensive lasting from October 1944 to May 1945. Many lives were lost in these and other irrelevant operations – in Borneo, New Guinea, New Britain – that could have no effect on the course of the war, now that American naval and air superiority permitted a direct thrust at Japan itself.

The end for Japan

By the start of 1945, no more supplies of oil or other vital imported raw materials were getting through to Japan from its overseas empire; this blockade alone guaranteed eventual collapse. Also, B-29 bombers flying from bases in the Marianas had begun high-level daylight bombing raids on Japanese factories in November 1944. But the proven readiness of Japan's soldiers, sailors

and airmen to sacrifice their lives in the defense of country and emperor, even to the point of suicide, convinced American commanders that only an invasion of their homeland would force the Japanese to surrender. The Americans planned first to seize the islands of Iwo Jima and Okinawa as stepping-stones, and then to move on to invade Japan itself.

The losses incurred in taking the two islands seemed an awesome portent of what could be expected in the main invasion to come. Iwo Jima was only a small volcanic island, and was bombarded by air and sea for over two months before the marines went ashore on 19 February 1945. But the Japanese defenders were hidden in caves linked by a network of tunnels and suffered few casualties in the bombardment. They met the marine landing with implacable resistance, although fighting with no hope of reinforcement against an enemy enjoying total naval and air superiority. It took the Americans five weeks to conquer the tiny island, and they suffered 26,000 casualties, a third of their force, in the process. Of the 25,000 Japanese soldiers on Iwo Jima, only 1000 eventually surrendered.

Okinawa was a much tougher target. A rugged island some 60 miles long, it had a garrison of around 100,000, and was within range of Japanese aircraft based in Formosa and Kyushu, the southernmost island of Japan itself. Since the Battle of Leyte Gulf, the Japanese air forces had increasingly employed 'kamikaze' tactics – using aircraft as manned flying-bombs to crash-dive on to the decks of enemy warships. This suicide technique was the most practical form of attack for inexperienced pilots facing formidable air defenses: if they stuck to conventional tactics, they were unlikely to hit their target and would probably be shot down anyway.

Three US carriers were badly damaged by kamikaze attacks during March, in the run-up to the

Okinawa operation. After the landings began on 1 April, 13 American destroyers were sunk or damaged in the first week. On land, after being allowed to establish a beachhead unopposed, the force of around 285,000 marines and Army soldiers met stiffening resistance as they pushed outward. Heavy casualties were soon being suffered for slender gains, and bad weather further obstructed progress. It took almost three months to subdue the island's defenses and American casualties totalled 49,000 men, 12,500 of them killed, the heaviest toll of the Pacific campaign. By then kamikaze attacks had sunk 34 naval vessels and damaged an astonishing 368. This would have been enough to drive most fleets from the sea, but not that of the United States, now backed by unparalleled shipbuilding capacity. Japan was pitting medieval military virtues – the samurai spirit of heroic self-sacrifice – against overwhelming industrial and technological might. The eventual outcome was not in doubt.

Long before the fall of Okinawa, the truth of Japan's situation had been brought home to the Japanese people. In March, General Curtis LeMay, who had taken command of a now much-expanded B-29 bomber force on the Marianas, decided to switch from high-level daylight raids on industrial targets to low-level mass nighttime raids on cities, using incendiary bombs instead of explosives. The new tactics were terrifyingly effective. A strike on Tokyo by over 300 B-29s on the night of 9 March destroyed a quarter of the city and killed an estimated 82,000 people. Similar raids were carried out on other Japanese cities and much of the population fled to the countryside to escape the bombing. By the end of June war production had virtually ceased. There were no raw materials – even coastal shipping had been stopped by mines dropped from US aircraft – factory plant was devastated, and individual food rations were down to 1200 calories a day.

Left: The commander of a B-29 Superfortress inspects his crew before taking off from Guam for a raid on Japan. It was only in the last year of the war that strategic air attacks became powerful enough to be potentially decisive.

Right: British commandos in Burma returning from a mission behind Japanese lines. Although many lives were lost in the Burmese campaign, it had only limited effect on the ultimate outcome of the war with Japan.

The elderly Admiral Suzuki, who had taken over as Japan's prime minister after the invasion of Okinawa in April, was under no illusions about Japan's impending defeat. But major hurdles obstructed the path to peace. Although the Japanese political and military leaders were agreed that the conflict must be ended, most baulked at unconditional surrender. They desired that at the very least the position of the Emperor should be preserved. It was also difficult for them to make a clear approach to the Allies, since any public declaration that peace was being sought might provoke a coup by military extremists. In fact, the American intelligence services were well aware of the Japanese desire for peace and monitored their efforts to establish contact with the Western Allies through Moscow, chosen because the Soviet Union was still not at war with Japan. Stalin, intent on getting into the war in the Far East before it ended, dismissed the Japanese peace advances as 'too vague.'

From 17 July to 2 August the Allies held their last summit conference of the war at Potsdam. Truman had now replaced Roosevelt, and before the end of the meetings Churchill gave way to Clement Attlee. The differences between the Western Allies and the Soviet Union were worsening; disagreements over the nature of post-war arrangements in Eastern Europe marked the beginning of the slide toward the Cold War. At Yalta the previous February Roosevelt had rejoiced in Stalin's assurance that the Soviet Union would soon join in the war against Japan. But by the time of the Potsdam conference, the Americans were appalled at the thought of an imminent Soviet declaration of war that would allow the Red Army to advance in the Far East and even stake a claim to a part in the occupation of Japan itself. Thus the Americans desired at all costs a quick victory – and they also suddenly had the means to bring it about.

On 16 July, at their test site in New Mexico, the

United States exploded the first atomic bomb. It was the culmination of three years' concentrated effort, the 'Manhattan District Project,' that had cost around $2000 million. Two more of the bombs were available for use against Japan. On 26 July Truman, Churchill and Chiang Kai-shek jointly called on Japan to surrender or face 'prompt and utter destruction.' The Japanese reply was interpreted, wrongly, as an expression of contempt.

The decision to use atomic weapons has become a subject of heated controversy since, but was not so among Allied political and military leaders at the time. The terror-bombing of civilians had become an accepted method of making war, and the atom bombs were not seen as essentially different from other bombs, only bigger. No one foresaw the long-term effects of nuclear fall-out, or anticipated the future nuclear balance of terror. In retrospect, it seems likely that Japan would very soon have surrendered, and that

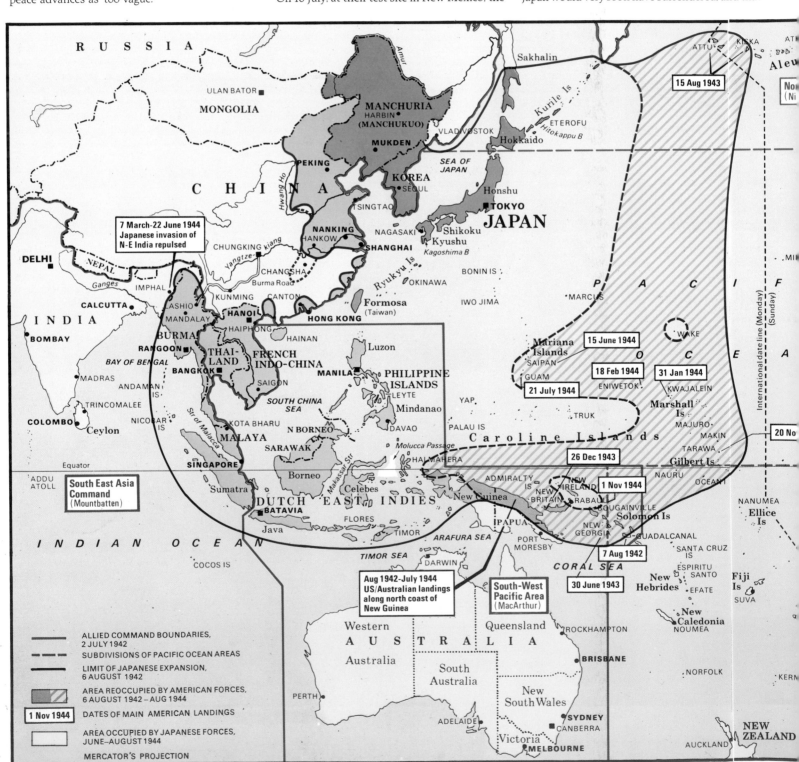

no costly American invasion would have been necessary. It is also true that among the motives for using the weapon was a desire to forestall the Soviet Union in the Far East, and a wish to justify the huge sums of money spent on the project – how could such expenditure be explained if the bomb, once produced, was not used? There was even simple curiosity, wanting to see whether the bomb would work and how much damage it would cause. These were not worthy motives for the destruction of two whole cities. But by 1945 the dehumanizing effects of total war had long deadened moral perceptions.

On 6 August a B-29, the Enola Gay, flying from Tinian in the Marianas, dropped an atom bomb on the city of Hiroshima, killing some 70,000 inhabitants. Two days later the Soviet Union declared war on Japan and invaded Manchuria. On 9 August, a second atom bomb was dropped on Nagasaki. Emperor Hirohito was now convinced that 'the unendurable must be endured.'

The Americans gave assurances that his own sovereignty would be respected. On 15 August the Emperor addressed his people for the first time in a radio broadcast, to announce Japan's surrender. With this the war ended, although it was another two weeks before the formal surrender ceremony took place on board USS *Missouri*, and not until 12 September that the Japanese forces in Southeast Asia officially surrendered to Admiral Mountbatten at Singapore.

From the German invasion of Poland to the Japanese surrender, the world war had lasted almost exactly six years. From December 1941 onward it had been a genuinely worldwide conflict, as the Great War, in retrospect renamed World War I, never was. Except on Germany's eastern front, loss of life among servicemen was generally lower than in the murderous attrition of 1914-18. But civilians suffered appallingly, whether through the German campaigns of extermination or through the wider brutalities of German and Japanese military rule; fighting in resistance guerrilla movements or serving as merchant seamen; as victims of strategic bombing or through hardship and starvation. Of the six million inhabitants of Poland – including Jews – who died in the war, only 300,000 were soldiers. Of an estimated 20 million Soviet dead, less than a third died in combat. On the other hand, three and a half million German servicemen were killed compared with 600,000 civilians, and over a million Japanese died in battle as against some 650,000 civilians who perished as a result of American air raids. The only other country suffering comparable losses was Yugoslavia, with over a million killed in the partisan campaign and brutal German repression. Italy and France escaped more lightly, with 300,000 and 600,000 dead respectively. Britain lost 270,000 servicemen, 62,000 civilians killed by air attack, and 35,000 merchant seamen. Only the United States and the British Dominions were virtually free of civilian casualties. For a major combatant, the United States suffered remarkably lightly: 300,000 American

servicemen lost their lives, around one percent of males of fighting age. This compares with the Soviet Union's loss of about 10 percent of its entire population.

Death is not the only product of war, however. The conflict gave an enormous impetus to the development of industry and technology. Unparalleled levels of production and destruction were achieved. The key to victory had been the ability to maximize industrial output, and the lessons learned were not altogether forgotten in the peace that followed. Developments in technology that had transformed warfare – remote guided weapons, V-2 rockets, jet aircraft, the atom bomb – would also be turned to civil purposes. Efforts at code-breaking had produced the first electronic computers. Medical science – for example, the fight against malaria – had advanced alongside the arts of death.

This was progress, then, of a sort. But any lingering nineteenth-century illusions about the moral progress of humanity were utterly dissipated in the horrors of the Japanese prisoner-of-war camps, the German concentration camps, the terror-bombing of cities, and beyond all else the meticulously bureaucratized nightmare of the gas chambers. The regimes most responsible for atrocities had, of course, been defeated, and 18 German and Japanese leaders, Göring and Tojo most prominent among them, were sentenced to death for their crimes by the victors. But Churchill commented wisely to one of his generals: 'You and I must take care not to lose the next war.'

Nevertheless, World War II came closer than most wars to a struggle between good and evil. Every country occupied by Germany or Japan felt 'liberated' by the Allied victory, even where, as in French Indochina or Poland, the post-war settlement was bitterly resented. The defeated regimes had been at best militaristic and authoritarian, and at worst, in the case of Nazi Germany, uniquely vile. The war waged by the victorious powers was, as far as such a thing is possible, a just war.

Left: The last year of the war was a period of mounting disaster for Japan, as the Allied noose drew ever tighter round the country itself.

Below: Hiroshima, a city destroyed by a single bomb. The revelation of such an unprecedented destructive power was to exercise a profound influence on the shape of the postwar world.

Pacific Ocean Areas (Nimitz)

C

Hawaiian Is
OAHU
EARL HARBOR HAWAII

Central Pacific Area (Kinkaid)

PALMYRA
CHRISTMAS
JARVIS
MALDEN
enix Is
VICTORIA
SUVOROV

Cook Is   Society Is
RAROTONGA

Pacific Area
nley, Halsey later)

© Richard Natkiel, 1982

Europe

At the end of World War II, Europe lay in ruins. Once more, the failure of the European powers to regulate their affairs peacefully had brought human catastrophe. In a continent whose social and economic organization had represented the pinnacle of civilization, tens of millions of citizens were reduced to a precarious existence on the edge of starvation, many under the watchful eye of occupying armies. No one could then have predicted the extraordinary economic resurgence that was to raise Europe to an unparalleled level of prosperity in the succeeding decades. But equally, few could have guessed that the eclipse of Europe's political power would prove so complete and so durable – that the colonial empires would virtually disappear within 20 years, and the armies of the United States and the Soviet Union remain permanently entrenched in the heart of the Continent.

The map of Europe drawn at the end of World War I was generally restored as a result of World War II. There was only one truly major change, the eventual division of Germany into East and West. The Soviet Union kept its borders of 1941, rather than 1939, absorbing the Baltic republics, Bessarabia and the east of Poland. It also took Ruthenia from Czechoslovakia. As compensation for the loss of their eastern territories, the Poles received a comparable area of Germany – the whole of Poland was effectively shifted westward. Yugoslavia took the disputed region of Istria from

Italy. Otherwise, adjustments were minor, the status quo ante Hitler restored.

Populations moved more than borders. The problem of German minorities in Czechoslovakia and Poland was solved by the mass expulsion of those Germans who had not already fled. In all, about 10 million Germans returned to their homeland or to Austria as refugees. Millions of Poles shifted westward from the eastern area now incorporated in the Soviet Union. Hungarians were expelled from Czechoslovakia, Greeks from Bulgaria, Italians from Istria. At the cost of much human misery, a tighter match between state boundaries and ethnic identity was achieved.

But the relationship between nation-states was no longer the central reality of European politics. It had been overtaken by the overwhelming influence of outside powers – the United States and the Soviet Union. Within three years of the end of the war, the line between the area occupied by Soviet forces and that controled by the Western Allies had solidified into an 'Iron Curtain' (to use Churchill's phrase), a barrier of mutual suspicion and hostility dividing the Continent. This great fissure had no roots in European history or culture; it did not correspond to any racial, linguistic, religious or economic divide. The development in Eastern Europe (as the area under Soviet domination was now known) of 'people's democracies' controled by communist parties, and in Western Europe of liberal democracies committed

to the continuance of capitalism, was a straightforward consequence of the facts of military power.

In 1945, before the postwar confrontation between East and West had begun, communist and other left-wing political forces enjoyed widespread public support through most of Europe. The prominent role of the communists in resistance movements and the heroic struggle of the Soviet Union against the German invader had completely obliterated the memory of the 1939 Nazi-Soviet Pact. Right-wing political forces were almost totally discredited. In the defeated states, such as Germany and Italy, they were blamed both for losing the war and for having started it. In many other countries, right-wingers had collaborated with the enemy and were punished for it after the liberation.

The Western Allies, dedicated opponents of communism even while fighting in alliance with the Soviet Union, had feared that some of the national resistance movements containing strong communist elements would attempt to seize power as the Germans retreated. But only in Yugoslavia – and as a consequence in its tiny neighbor Albania – did communist partisans succeed in establishing their own regime. Led by Josip Broz Tito, the Yugoslav partisans were unique in enjoying the support of both the Soviets and the British, and in having substantially achieved their own liberation from the Germans. In neighboring

Greece. British troops were used against the local partisans in late 1944 – even while the war with Germany continued – so that a conservative regime could be installed favorable to British interests. No doubt a similar policy would have been pursued in France and Italy, but it proved unnecessary. Stalin was not interested in the spread of communism unless it served the cause of Soviet security. Orders went out from Moscow to the French and Italian communist parties that they were to disarm and join governments acceptable to the Western Allies. In return, Stalin expected Britain and the United States to allow him a free hand in Eastern Europe.

In the immediate postwar period, communists participated in coalition governments almost everywhere in Western Europe, as well as in Soviet dominated Eastern Europe. They were the strongest single party both in France, where they loyally supported General de Gaulle, and in Italy. In Britain, where the Communist Party had never really established itself, the socialist Labour Party won a landslide election victory in July 1945.

It took only three years to move from this appearance of an ideologically homogeneous Europe to Cold War confrontation. The rapid wor-

sening of relations between the United States and the Soviet Union belongs to the histories of those two countries, but it was in Europe that it found its focus. Stalin's objective was to use Eastern Europe as a buffer against any future invasion from the West. In Rumania, Bulgaria, Hungary and Poland, communist parties had been installed in complete control by 1948, ruling through phony 'coalitions.' At first it seemed that Czechoslovakia might be left alone. It was a relatively advanced industrial country with a well-established liberal democratic tradition. Free elections after the war produced a 38 percent vote for the communists – rather similar to support in France and Italy at the time – and the prewar president, Beneš, returned to power, ruling with a communist prime minister, Klement Gottwald. In February 1948, however, the Czech communists moved to bring their country into line with the rest of Eastern Europe. Using their control of the police, trades unions and workers' militias, they swiftly established the exclusive authority of the party over all areas of national life, including the media. President Beneš had no choice but to relinquish all real power to Gottwald. The non-communist partners in the coalition government were

unable to mount any serious opposition, and rigged elections soon confirmed communist rule.

The spectacle of the new order in Eastern Europe did much to undermine support for communist parties in the West. There was too much reminiscent of Nazism in the Stalinist state with its secret police and ruthless suppression of dissent. The progression from communist participation in coalition government to effective communist dictatorship in Czechoslovakia had obvious implications for countries like France and Italy. A growing identification of the Soviet Union as a hostile power allowed communist parties to be once more labeled 'unpatriotic' as well as 'anti-democratic.'

US action in Europe

This more or less natural reversal of public opinion in Western Europe was artificially encouraged by the United States, which from 1947 adopted the policy of support for anti-Soviet regimes all round the perimeter of the Soviet bloc. Apart from propaganda and covert operations by the newly formed CIA (aimed at subverting governments in Eastern Europe as well as backing anti-communist groups in the West), the United

Left: Europe in ruins – refugees return to what remains of their homes after the liberation of Falaise in northwest France.

Above: German children, some of them barefoot, queue up for a ration of gruel provided by the British authorities in Berlin to prevent starvation.

Above right: A 1945 British election poster. The Labour Party's massive victory over Churchill's Conservatives owed much to the popular desire for a better future to emerge out of the sacrifices of war.

Right: The border between the Russian and American sectors of Berlin in May 1949. What was originally a temporary division of the city between the victorious Allies became a site of permanent confrontation.

States helped fund the economic renaissance of Western Europe through the Marshall Plan of June 1947. In Greece the United States financed and armed the government in a successful civil war against communist rebels. Elsewhere, it was made clear that electing a communist government would inevitably lead to the cutting off of Marshall Aid. A vote for communism was a vote for poverty and hardship. By 1948 the communists had been excluded from the governing coalitions of France and Italy. In Britain, the Labour government identified itself wholeheartedly with American anti-communist policies.

The front line of the East-West confrontation was Germany. Following the Potsdam conference in 1945, the defeated country was divided into four zones administered by the four victorious powers – Britain, the United States, France and the Soviet Union – under a joint Allied Control Commission. The capital, Berlin, was also divided into four, although it fell deep within the Soviet zone. At first this arrangement worked quite smoothly, as both sides concentrated on 'denazification,' designed to remove supporters of the Third Reich from positions of power and punish those responsible for war crimes. Both sides carried off German scientists to continue weapons research for new masters.

As the relations between East and West worsened, however, it became increasingly difficult to envisage agreement on the future of Germany. By 1948, the United States had decided on a policy of rebuilding the part of Germany under Western control, abandoning wartime fantasies of permanently dismantling German industry and military capacity. The problems of administering a ruined country flooded with refugees led increasingly to co-operation with officials and industrialists heavily compromised with the Nazi regime. Denazification was soon limited to the pursuit of those directly implicated in crimes, and the German people were implicitly exonerated of war-guilt. The ground was laid for the great turnabout that Hitler had dreamed of in 1944-45 – Germany was to become the ally of Britain and the United States against the Soviet Union.

The Soviet zone of Germany was poor in both industry and population compared with the rest of the country, but it did include Berlin. As the Soviet Union laid the groundwork for what was to

Left: The millionth sack of coal airlifted to the Western sectors of Berlin during the Soviet blockade of 1948-49.

Below left: After the war, Poland was shifted westward at the expense of Germany, losing territory in the east to the Soviet Union. Germany and Austria were divided into zones of occupation.

Right: British Foreign Secretary Ernest Bevin signs the North Atlantic Treaty in 1949, which confirmed American military involvement in Europe and the division of the continent into hostile blocs, East and West.

Below right: American aid to Europe under the Marshall Plan was an integral part of the anti-communist drive – and nowhere more so than in Greece, where this propaganda parade was mounted in 1949.

become the communist state of East Germany, it made a bid for control of the capital. From June 1948 to May 1949, the Soviets blocked all land access to Berlin, forcing the United States and Britain to supply their zones of the city by air. An armed confrontation was avoided because the Western Allies made no attempt to force a passage by land and the Russians did not interfere with the airlift. In the end, the Soviet Union accepted that it could not force the Western Allies out of Berlin short of war. The city was to remain an anomaly in the heart of East Germany.

The two new states of West Germany (the Federal German Republic) and East Germany (the German Democratic Republic) effectively came into existence in 1949, although questions of sovereignty and recognition remained complex for many years. Naturally, East Germany became a Soviet-style communist state and West Germany a Western-style liberal democracy. In the same year, many of the countries of Western Europe, including Britain, France, Italy, Norway, the Netherlands, Belgium and Portugal, joined the United States in a permanent military alliance – NATO (the North Atlantic Treaty Organization). Greece, Turkey and finally West Germany joined in the 1950s. NATO represented an admission by the West European powers that they were not capable of their own defense in the face of a perceived threat from the Soviet Union. In return for tying the United States to the defense of Europe, it largely subordinated European defense policy and diplomacy to American decisions. Belatedly, after West Germany's admission to NATO in 1955, the Soviet Union formed a parallel organization in Eastern Europe – the Warsaw Pact. This was the last act in the division of Europe. Only Yugoslavia stood completely independent of the two armed camps, having rejected Soviet interference in 1947, but remaining anti-capitalist.

The two conflicting spheres of Europe with their opposing ideologies of communism and capitalism inevitably followed different economic and social paths. These were partly determined by the needs of the opposing superpowers. The Soviet Union had been devastated by the war and was poorer than most of the East European countries it controled. Consequently, all of Eastern Europe was milked dry to provide the Soviets with the capital and machinery they needed for reconstruction. The United States, on the other hand, bursting with capital and productive capa-

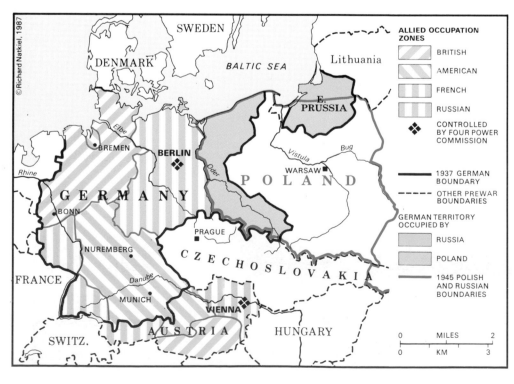

© Richard Natkiel, 1987

SWEDEN

DENMARK

BALTIC SEA

Lithuania

E. PRUSSIA

Elbe

BREMEN

BERLIN

Oder

Vistula

Bug

WARSAW

POLAND

Rhine

G E R M A N Y

BONN

PRAGUE

NUREMBERG

C Z E C H O S L O V A K I A

FRANCE

Danube

MUNICH

VIENNA

A U S T R I A

HUNGARY

SWITZ.

ALLIED OCCUPATION ZONES

BRITISH

AMERICAN

FRENCH

RUSSIAN

CONTROLLED BY FOUR POWER COMMISSION

1937 GERMAN BOUNDARY

OTHER PREWAR BOUNDARIES

GERMAN TERRITORY OCCUPIED BY

RUSSIA

POLAND

1945 POLISH AND RUSSIAN BOUNDARIES

MILES 2

KM 3

and then directly from June 1947 under the Marshall Plan. Some $13,000 million flowed into Europe, chiefly to Britain, France, Italy, West Germany and the Netherlands. Without it, these countries could never have afforded the imports they needed to regenerate economic activity. It was, nevertheless, a time of hardship and austerity. There were shortages of food, fuel and accommodation. In Britain, rationing was tighter than during the war. Much effort was required before stable European currencies could be recreated.

But growth rates were, almost from the start, extremely rapid. By 1950, levels of output were passing prewar figures and still rising. This was widely expected to produce a temporary postwar boom, as previously seen in 1918-20, but it did not. Through the 1950s, economies continued to grow fast. Most spectacular was West Germany, where industrial output more than doubled between 1950 and 1959. In France, overall economic growth was running at around five percent a year, and even the less successful countries, like Britain and Belgium, experienced rises of two to three percent a year in their Gross National Product. Unemployment barely existed. After the experience of the 1930s, this sustained growth and full employment seemed miraculous.

Some of the credit was due to the intelligent intervention of governments in the economy. International co-operation encouraged trade and

investment. At a national level, the state much expanded the active role it had already begun to adopt before the war. This came partly through the nationalization of key industries. In Britain, the Labour government took over the Bank of England, coal, steel, the railways, electricity and gas, air and road transport. In France, nationalizations carried out at the Liberation – chiefly as a punishment for industrialists who had collaborated with the Germans (Renault was a prime example) – expanded an already established state sector. In Italy, Mussolini had left an inheritance of nationalized industries that was taken up by his successors.

But this admixture of state-controled industries in the capitalist economy was less vital than government manipulation of tax and credit to encourage growth and regulate the functioning of the free market. In France, an elite of technocrats occupied top positions in both the civil service and in industry and finance. Between them they operated a flexible planning system that worked efficiently to guide investment and coherent development. A very similar close bond linked business and government chiefs in Germany.

The planning of governments could only work because conditions were right, however. Firstly there was a technological timelag. Because of lack of investment in the 1930s and during the war, the potential of new developments in technology

city, had need of investment opportunities and markets. The regeneration of Western Europe suited American economic needs, as well as political objectives.

Competing economic models

Other differences between East and West came from conflicting models of economic development. In Eastern Europe, the Soviet obsession with heavy industry held back any rise in the standard of living even when output grew fast. Consumer goods and services had low priority. In Western Europe, economic thinking was dominated by concepts of demand-led growth and flexible planning that not only produced a somewhat quicker increase in output than in the East, but generated an astonishing rise in living standards.

The posthumous guru of Western economic development after World War II was the British economist, John Maynard Keynes. In the 1930s, he had dismissed the classical economists' belief in the 'hidden hand' automatically arranging the capitalist economy for the general good. He asserted that the government should intervene to maintain a high level of demand in the economy in such a way as to guarantee full employment without excessive inflation. During the war, Keynes' influence spread because he was associated with the running of the British war economy. It was a tribute to his ideas when Churchill and Roosevelt committed themselves to maintaining unemployment below three percent in the postwar world. Along with a new faith in government intervention went a commitment to social welfare and education. The aim was, in Keynes' words, to build: 'A system where we can act as an organized community for common purposes, and to promote social and economic justice, while protecting and respecting the individual . . .' This was the general program for the advanced countries of Western Europe in the postwar period.

The immediate need after 1945 was for reconstruction from wartime destruction and disruption. The United States provided the money, first as emergency relief through the United Nations

had not been exploited. Replacing ruined factories, France and Germany were ideally positioned to introduce the latest technology and vast increases in productivity resulted. There was a willing and plentiful labor force. And unsatisfied demand for every sort of consumer good presented a huge domestic market in Europe, quite apart from foreign trade opportunities. Industry managed to combine a high level of investment with rising living standards for its workers.

This prosperity underpinned a political stability that in its turn encouraged economic growth. A remarkable degree of consensus replaced the bitter conflicts of the 1930s. In Britain, for example, the Labour Party was narrowly defeated in the 1951 elections and the Conservatives were to hold power for the next 13 years. But the Welfare State established by Labour was not undone by its successor, and a Conservative Prime Minister, Harold Macmillan, accepted the need for state control of the economy wherever 'private enterprise had exhausted its usefulness.' In Italy, after the abolition of the monarchy was agreed by referendum in 1946, a republic was established in which the conservative Christian Democrat Party held power with a variety of coalition partners. Opponents of the status quo on the Left and Right were effectively marginalized. In West Germany, the Christian Democrats also ruled supreme through most of the 1950s and 1960s. But as in Britain, these German and Italian conservatives supported both state intervention in the economy and social welfare programs.

France appeared superficially more unstable. De Gaulle had wished to endow the country with a strong presidency (with himself as president), but the Fourth Republic evolved into a repetition of the Third, witnessing a constant merry-go-round of weak coalition governments. Yet the less publicly visible structure of bureaucrats and businessmen running the economy was remarkably stable and outstandingly successful. The record of

French economic decline between the wars was reversed.

In Eastern Europe, political life followed a very different pattern. The rejection of Marshall Aid by the Soviet Union – on the quite accurate grounds that it would extend American influence eastward – prolonged economic hardship. Communist governments already lacking majority public support were forced to carry out unpopular economic policies that held down living standards and drained national wealth to bolster Soviet recovery. Stalin did not even trust the local communist parties, which were ruthlessly purged, their leaders replaced by Moscow hacks who acted as simple agents of Soviet policy. Cultural life was tightly controled, free thought suppressed.

Eastern Europe

After Stalin's death in March 1953 the situation in Eastern Europe began to loosen up. Although a revolt in East Berlin in June of that year was put down uncompromisingly, elements within national communist parties wanted to win back popular support by pursuing nationalist goals and more liberal policies. They increasingly contested the authority of hardliners in the party. In 1956, Soviet power was directly challenged. Workers in Poznan, Poland, rioted in June, provoking a government crisis. The more liberal national communists took advantage of the disturbances to install their own candidate, Wladyslaw Gomulka, in power the following October, against the wishes of Moscow. Gomulka subsequently relaxed controls over freedom of expression, halted collectivization of agriculture and opened a dialog with the powerful Polish Catholic Church.

In Hungary, this smooth transition to a more liberal regime was not achieved. The hardline party chief, Matyas Rakosi, was dismissed in July 1956 in an attempt to head off the rising tide of popular discontent, but it was not enough.

Toward the end of October, demonstrations in support of the Polish reforms developed into a revolutionary uprising against the government and its Soviet backers. A liberal communist, Imre Nagy, emerged as leader of the revolt and announced Hungary's withdrawal from the Warsaw Pact into neutrality. This the Soviets would not allow. After heavy fighting, Soviet forces regained control of the capital, Budapest, in early November. About 25,000 Hungarians died in the uprising and 200,000 fled to the West as refugees. The new ruler imposed on Hungary was not, as might have been expected, a hardliner, but a member of the nationalist faction, Janos Kadar. Under Kadar's leadership, after a period of repression, Hungary developed a relatively liberal economic policy that brought the consolation of mild prosperity to a people forced to accept the lack of full national independence.

The events of 1956 stabilized Eastern Europe. It was clear, on the one hand, that an open confrontation with the Soviet Union was futile. The United States would not intervene to support an uprising – although the CIA had incited the Hungarians to revolt – and without outside help any national force would be too weak to resist the Soviet Army. But, on the other hand, the Soviet Union had neither the desire nor the power to rule Eastern Europe by brute force. So there was considerable scope for national communist governments to pursue policies relevant to their own economic and cultural situation, and incentive for communist parties to respond to popular wishes when formulating policies – within limits.

By a twist of fate, the Hungarian uprising coincided with the Suez crisis, which marked a decisive point in the history of two West European countries, Britain and France. They were the only countries in Europe that were still claiming to be treated as Great Powers on the world stage. The war had ended any unlikely Italian pretensions to such a status, and West Germany, whatever its economic strength, was debarred from becoming a major military power. But Britain and France had colonies and seats on the United Nations Security Council. Such illusory advantages veiled postwar realities.

The hold of the European colonial powers on their overseas possessions was severely shaken by the events of World War II. Even before the war, Britain had introduced a form of representative government in India and allowed Egypt a greater measure of independent control over its internal affairs. Lip-service was paid to the principle, embodied in the League of Nations 'mandate' system, that the colonial powers were holding their colonies in trust until the local populations were fit to rule themselves. By 1945, European prestige had been battered by defeats in war and colonial authority undermined by ringing Allied proclamations of the rights of all peoples to choose their own independent governments. The European powers, of course, intended this to apply within Europe only. Churchill pronounced in 1942: 'I have not become the King's First Minister to preside over the liquidation of the British Empire.' But postwar Europe had neither the military power nor the political will to maintain imperial sway in the face of African and Asian nationalism.

The first, and greatest, act of decolonization was the British retreat from India in 1947. The British Labour Party had long been committed to independence for the sub-continent and its election victory in 1945 led directly to the birth of modern India, Pakistan, Burma and Sri Lanka. Elsewhere, Europeans struggled with varying suc-

cess to uphold their authority. In Malaya, Britain defeated a Chinese communist insurgency in the late 1940s, but the Dutch never really succeeded in reasserting their control over the East Indies, lost during the war, and the islands became independent as Indonesia in 1949. The French fought long and hard to hold on to Indochina, after evicting Ho Chi Minh's national government from Hanoi in 1946. But their war against the Viet Minh guerrillas culminated in military disaster at Dien Bien Phu in 1954, and they were forced to cede independence to Vietnam, Cambodia and Laos. Almost immediately, a new guerrilla campaign against French rule started up, this time nearer home, in Algeria.

During World War II, the European powers had fought over North Africa as if the local population did not exist. Now not only French but also British traditional interests in the Mediterranean sphere were threatened. Britain had been forced out of Palestine in 1948, and in 1952 a nationalist military coup in Egypt effectively ousted British influence. From 1955, Britain confronted a Greek guerrilla campaign in Cyprus. The French had lost Syria and Lebanon after the war, and in March 1956 they granted independence to Tunisia and Morocco, in order to concentrate on the defense of Algeria.

Egypt's nationalist ruler, Gamal Abdul Nasser, became the focus of British and French anxieties, a hate-figure created by the paranoia of waning imperial power. When he nationalized the Suez Canal in July 1956, Britain and France entered into an extraordinary conspiracy with Israel to mount a combined attack on Egypt. The Anglo-French

invasion was to appear as a peace effort to separate two combatants, Egypt and Israel. In reality, Nasser was the target. In the first week of November 1956, as Soviet tanks rumbled through the streets of Budapest, British and French paratroopers jumped into Port Said.

The outcome was a humiliation for Britain and France – not at the hands of Egypt, but of the United States. The Americans had a split attitude toward European colonial struggles. They supported the Europeans if their policies fitted in with the worldwide fight against communism – as in the case of the French in Indochina. But the United States opposed colonialism as such, both as a matter of sentiment or principle, and because they saw the opportunity to supplant the Europeans and extend their own influence instead. The Eisenhower administration was against the invasion of Egypt, and in a striking display of power brought the British and French to heel by the simple expedient of refusing to support the value of the pound and the franc. The Anglo-French force withdrew and Nasser crowed in triumph.

Britain's ruling Conservative Party drew the logical conclusion from this débâcle. Under a new Prime Minister, Harold Macmillan, they accelerated the process of withdrawal from the old Empire, and this policy was continued by a Labour government after 1964. Almost all Britain's colonies were granted independence within a decade. Successive British governments still clung to the idea of Great Power status supposedly conveyed by the possession of nuclear weapons, an 'independent deterrent' acquired at massive cost.

Above left: Hungarian rebels in Budapest, November 1956. Soviet forces took considerable losses before reducing the Hungarians to submission.

Right: An anguished Egyptian woman runs through the streets of Port Said during the ill-conceived Anglo-French Suez operation of 1956.

Far right: Posters go up for the first postwar elections in Italy, which brought a decisive defeat for the Italian Communist Party. A combination of CIA-backed anti-communist propaganda and the very obvious spectacle of Stalinist oppression in Eastern Europe undermined popular support for communism in the West.

But Britain was also more amenable than most European countries to the dominant role of the United States, claiming a 'special relationship' with Washington dating back to the war years. One lesson Britain's rulers drew from the Suez crisis was that close co-operation with the United States was essential at all times.

In France, political events unfolded very differently. Successive humiliations in Indochina and over Suez put great strain on the Fourth Republic; the Algerian conflict brought about its downfall. Algeria's large European settler population, the *colons*, and French Army officers had no confidence in the Republic. They believed they could win their brutal struggle against the Algerian National Liberation Front (FLN) by meeting terror with terror, but feared that one of the succession of weak center-left governments might do a deal with the nationalists. In May 1958 the *colons* seized control of Algiers with the connivance of the army. The rebellion spread to Corsica, and Paris stood in daily expectation of an assault by paratroopers to install a military regime.

At this point General de Gaulle stepped forward from retirement and offered his services as savior of France. The army officers and *colons* greeted De Gaulle with enthusiasm; the Fourth Republic politicians accepted him reluctantly as the only alternative to a military coup. With perfect formal legality, De Gaulle was appointed Prime Minister and drew up a new constitution that was approved by referendum in September 1958. This established the Fifth Republic, a strong presidential regime in stark contrast to its two predecessors. Not surprisingly, De Gaulle was elected first president of the new Republic. In his hands the regime, although perfectly democratic, took on a distinctly Napoleonic flavor.

De Gaulle's right-wing supporters in Algeria did not get what they wanted from him. The general soon decided that a deal with the FLN was the only way out of the Algerian morass. Suppressing mutinous officers and defying a terrorist campaign and assassination attempts by the *colons*' secret army, the OAS, De Gaulle forged a path to Algerian independence in 1962. He also granted independence to almost all France's other African colonies, although most retained close ties with Paris.

In decolonization De Gaulle's policy resembled that of Britain, but in his attitude to the United States he was completely different. De Gaulle had heartily disliked the Americans ever since they obstructed his designs during World War II. Now he sought to assert French independence by de-

veloping a truly independent nuclear force – unlike Britain's 'independent deterrent' which was under NATO control. In 1966 France withdrew its military forces from NATO – although remaining a part of the political alliance – and ordered all foreign troops off its soil. Gaullist foreign policy was virtually neutral as between East and West. De Gaulle believed that France had more in common with Eastern Europe than with the culturally alien Anglo-Saxons – Britain and the United States.

Britain itself suffered from an identity crisis. The British had rarely seen themselves as Europeans; Europe began on the other side of the English Channel. But the end of the British Empire left them with little alternative except to look to the Continent. The key issue was membership of the European Economic Community (EEC), founded by France, West Germany, Holland, Belgium, Italy and Luxembourg in 1957. Although strictly limited to economic matters, this 'Common Market' was the focus of aspirations toward a united Europe, which some idealists believed would overcome the nationalism that had plagued European history with endless

wars and create a new world power strong enough to stand up to either the Soviet Union or the United States. In 1961 Britain applied to join the Community; after lengthy negotiations De Gaulle vetoed the move. There the matter rested for over a decade.

Whether united or not, the economic power of Europe continued to run counter to its loss of political power. Decolonization was not generally followed by any loss of predominance in trade, finance or exploitation of natural resources. There were exceptions: Algeria wrested control of its oil industry from French companies, for example. But mostly local elites in the newly independent countries welcomed European investment and expertise, receiving in return a guarantee of support for their own hold on power. There were more French expatriates working in France's former black African colonies a decade after independence than ever during the period of colonial rule. Moreover, the ex-colonies were locked into a world trading system in which Europe still played a major role.

But the role of the Third World, as it was now called, in European trade was less important than

it had been 50 years earlier. As West European countries' total exports expanded by 8-10 percent a year through the 1950s and 1960s, the largest growth area was trade within Europe itself and with the United States. A large part of the investment fueling the European boom continued to come from America. Between 1950 and 1970, private longterm US investment in Western Europe rose tenfold. Firms like Ford, General Motors and IBM were everywhere; it was the reign of the multinationals. Ironically, at a time when national governments had taken a prime role in managing their economies, major economic decisions were increasingly in the hands of foreigners, chiefly Americans, who could shift capital and employment opportunities from country to country at will, either ignoring the effect of their actions on national economies or directly subverting government economic policies they disliked. Yet about one third of the world's largest multinationals were European. Once again, it was a situation in which the political power of European governments was weakened, but the economic power of Europe was not.

In a curious reversal of colonization, the seemingly unstoppable expansion of European industries sucked large numbers of workers from poorer areas into the industrial heartland of the continent – France, West Germany, the Netherlands, Britain, northern Italy. Many came from former colonies: Indians, Pakistanis and West Indians to Britain, Algerians, Moroccans and Tunisians to France. Others were from the more backward parts of Europe – Turkey, Yugoslavia, Greece, southern Italy, Spain and Portugal. During the 1960s the demand for labor was almost insatiable. By 1965 West Germany was officially host to 1.3 million 'guest workers' and France had 1.8 million; these figures were to almost triple over the next 20 years. The relative impact was greatest on small countries: toward the end of the 1960s, over one-third of Switzerland's workforce were foreigners. This ready supply of cheap labor helped keep the European boom going as rising wages made local workers increasingly expensive to employ, but it also generated a great deal of human misery. Living conditions for the immigrants were often appalling. Many lived separated from their families for long periods and worked very long hours for low pay. They faced racial prejudice and discrimination.

Agricultural transformation

Mass migration of workers was only one example of the extraordinary impact of economic growth on European society. Perhaps most fundamental was the virtual elimination of the peasantry. This was partly a shift of labor off the land and into the cities, which had gathered pace during the war and continued after it. By 1962 the agricultural population in France was barely half its 1945 level. The story in Eastern Europe was the same: in Bulgaria the share of agriculture in the workforce halved from 80 percent in 1950 to 40 percent 20 years later. Throughout Europe whole villages were abandoned and rural houses stood empty, unless put to use by town dwellers in search of bucolic bliss.

There was more than just a decline in numbers, however. The intense local life of the peasant community with its narrow horizons and entrenched customs was opened out to a wider modern world. In the West, the remaining rural population tended to become capitalist farmers, instead of largely self-sufficient peasants selling only to local markets – a transformation already accomplished in Britain at an earlier date. In Eastern Europe, the collective farm replaced the small peasant plot everywhere except in Poland, even if the tradition of personal land ownership persisted just below the legal surface. In both East and West, radio and television linked the most remote communities to contemporary society. In many places, especially in southern Europe, the rise of mass tourism brought a seasonal flood of outsiders to small villages with devastating impact on traditional ways of life. An inflow of new money – from EEC grants or remittances sent home by the village's emigrant workers – was equally corrosive of local tradition. By the 1980s, most of Europe's agricultural population were simply members of modern urban society who happened to live and work in the country.

Urban life itself changed rapidly. Trends already well established before the war were carried very much further. Work altered, for instance, as the production of cheap consumer goods and the provision of services displaced heavy industry from the center of the West European economy. The old industrial working class with its particular cultural and political traditions was reshaped by the continuing decline of such industries as shipbuilding and mining. Everywhere, the proportion of people in 'white-collar' jobs rose – in France it doubled from 15 percent of the workforce in 1954 to 30 percent in 1975. Women went out to work in greater numbers than ever before, although they faced a long struggle to achieve anything like equality with men in job opportunities or pay.

The standard of living, as measured by the possession of material goods, rose almost universally in this 'consumer society.' By the mid 1960s, ownership of cars, refrigerators, washing machines and television sets was commonplace in the most advanced countries, even among the working class, and this consumer revolution continued to spread outward from the industrial north of Europe into the remotest corners of the more backward south, as ever new markets were

Above far left: Television ownership spread rapidly in the 1950s. The new medium worried governments, who tried to keep its output under tight control.

Above left: British Conservative Prime Minister Harold Macmillan (center) accepted the need for withdrawal from empire and maintained the welfare state set up by the 1945 Labour government. His attitudes were typical of the 'consensus' politics of the 1950s and 1960s.

Left: European settlers, the *colons,* flee Algeria in 1962 as the country approaches its long-contested independence.

Right: A Ford car factory in Valencia, Spain. Investment by American companies was a major source of the capital-fueling postwar economic growth in Europe.

opened up by the ingenious advertisers and sales-men who sat at the hub of the new society. Paid holidays became standard, and even holidays abroad an annual experience for tens of millions of Europeans, exploiting the massive expansion of jet air services. Health care and education also improved for virtually the whole European popu-lation. The death rate continued to fall and the literacy rate to rise.

Demography and culture

The war had been followed by a 'baby boom' – a quite unexpected burst of population growth that reversed the trend of the previous 50 years in the advanced countries of Europe. The effect on France was most pronounced. The stagnation of the French population, virtually unchanged at around 40 million between 1880 and 1940, had insidiously weakened the country's position as a leading continental power. Yet by 1967, the popu-lation had risen to 50 million, up by a quarter in little over two decades. The boom was shortlived, however. By the 1960s the secular trend had reas-serted itself, birthrates fell and the populations of the advanced countries stabilized or even began to decline slightly. Those countries of southern Europe that had still experienced high birthrates between the wars now largely fell in line with the north. Despite the 'baby boom,' Europe's popu-lation continued to decline in relation to the population of the rest of the world, which was growing at an unprecedented rate. This was, in fact, another important aspect of Europe's fall from world dominance.

Europe's primacy in world culture, science and technology was never recovered after the war. New York replaced Paris as the center of the art world; the best English literature was written by Americans, not the British; expatriate European scientists contributed greatly to the leap into space, but the space projects were American and Soviet; the microchip technological revolution came in California. This is not to dismiss European achievements in art and science, which were still considerable, from the work of Crick,

Watson and Wilkins on DNA to the new music of Boulez and Stockhausen, the philosophy of Sartre and Levi-Strauss and the novels of Calvino and Grass. But there was a definite lapse from the outstanding cultural vitality that had lasted up to World War II. Europe continued to make a great contribution to the intellectual world, but only as one source among others.

In the wider sense of 'culture' – the beliefs and customs of a people – European national traditions were eroded by the impact of international commercial cultural products, mainly provided by the Americans. Increasingly, Europeans ate American fast food, watched American programs on their new televisions and listened to American music on their radios and stereos. It was hard to distinguish this much-criticized Americanization from simple modernization, however. Like Americans, Europeans spent more and more of their lives in cars, shopped in supermarkets and could wash their clothes in launderettes. These were universal attributes of modern urban living.

By the 1960s young people were particularly in evidence, because as a result of the baby boom there were lots of them. But youth was not only numerically strong; it also had more money than in earlier generations. Young people with cash to spend created a new market for leisure goods that stimulated the growth of industries devoted to youth fashion and entertainments. Since in this, as in many other respects, Europe was following in America's footsteps, this commercialized 'youth culture' tended at first to follow American models, even when not directly imported. But in the 1960s Britain became the second world center for 'pop' music and fashion, as an innovative generation of young people, often of working-class background and educated in the postwar British art colleges, adapted and surpassed the American prototypes. Continental Europeans found it hard to keep up, mainly because their national cultures were steeped in a 'good taste' that was out of touch with the often vulgar, but vigorous, new styles.

Youth culture was in itself a minor phenomenon, but it provided focus and expression for important changes in attitudes and lifestyles that were undermining traditional discipline and authority in European society. In every sense, people were more mobile. They were less and less likely to live their adult lives in the place where they had been born, or to spend their whole lives with the first person they married, or to end up in the social class or religious faith to which they had been bred. Social controls loosened and the sexual morality traditionally affirmed and enforced by Church and state tottered in the face of rising expectations of pleasure and the individual demand for self-fulfillment. Bitter battles were fought in legislative assemblies between conservatives and liberals – those who wished to resist and those who wished to respond to the new trends – over such issues as abortion, contraception, homosexuality and the censorship of sexually explicit material. Adolescents fought their teachers over the length of their hair or their skirts; the increasing numbers of unmarried mothers insisted on respect and acceptance, challenging old prejudices. Youth culture was commercial, but it was against fathers, teachers and policemen. In its more serious moments, it aspired to the status of a 'counter-culture,' a complete alternative to the traditional European values of hard work, discipline and self-denial.

Without this background the events of 1968, a pivotal moment in European postwar history, would be incomprehensible. The student revolts of that year were fiercest in some of the countries where conservative forces had been most successful in upholding traditional authority against changing lifestyles. The buzz-word of the day was 'sexual revolution;' one of the main grievances of Parisian students was that members of the opposite sex were banned from halls of residence. The fact that such demands for increased personal freedom were expressed in Marxist terms tended to confuse rather than clarify the issues at stake.

But other currents fed into the 1968 outburst. One was opposition to the Vietnam War, which fueled a more general anti-Americanism and anti-capitalism. Another was hostility to 'consumerism,' a perception that modern industrial society was supplying ever-increasing quantities of material goods, but not a good quality of life. And there was a recognition that the prosperity of the majority depended on the ruthless exploitation of large minorities 'marginalized' by society – the campus at Nanterre where the Parisian student revolt began was built alongside one of the worst shanty-towns in Europe, housing immigrant workers in appalling conditions. Marxist thought and socialist aspirations were still strong in Europe. Despite the upsurge in prosperity, gross inequalities of wealth and power were as much a feature of capitalist society as ever. Despite formal parliamentary democracy, there was no democratic control over the elite who ran business and industry, the courts and the police. There were thus, from a socialist perspective, many targets that could be justifiably attacked.

There were far more students in the 1960s than ever before. In Great Britain alone, 28 new universities had been founded in the 1950s and 1960s. And the character of the student population had changed as well as its numbers. Before the war, most students in Hungary studied law; by 1970, the largest group was following courses in engineering and technology. The universities had become less a preserve of academic excellence and privileged indolence, more a training center for the cadres of a modern industrial society. It was not such a paradox, then, that these children of the middle class should rise in revolt.

Although Italy and West Germany produced the first upsurgence of student rioting, the French *événements* were by far the most prolonged and politically significant. From the first student demonstrations in central Paris on 3 May, the situation developed at vertiginous speed. Incensed by police brutality in dealing with the students, factory workers struck in their support. By mid May most universities, schools and factories in France were occupied by students and workers. De Gaulle's government had completely lost control of the country. But the leaders of the revolt were anarchistic utopians, and had no plans to seize power. In late May, assured of the backing of the army, De Gaulle moved to reassert his control and the uprising crumbled – although the general's personal authority never fully recovered and he stepped down from the presidency the following year.

Above far left: French riot police confront students and workers in a Paris suburb, June 1968. Although student unrest grabbed most media attention, it was the general strike and occupation of factories by workers that made the French revolt so powerful.

Above left: Self-service supermarkets first appeared in Europe soon after the war, but they were not common until the 1960s.

Left: 'Flower power' styles of 1967 in London's Hyde Park. Though often pretentious or trivial, the 'youth culture' did question traditional European values.

Right: This photograph of Christine Keeler, a prostitute involved in a British government scandal of the early 1960s, was published in the press. The decade saw radical changes in public attitudes to sex and in what images were considered acceptable for publication.

The 1968 student movement gave birth to terrorist groups like the Red Army Faction in West Germany (also known as the Baader-Meinhof Gang) and the Red Brigades in Italy, which waged war on the capitalist state and the consumer society through the 1970s. In theory, their strategy was to provoke the state into extending police powers and carrying out repressive measures that would reveal the true authoritarian nature of supposedly liberal Western governments. In reality, their kidnappings and assassinations of industrialists, government officials and politicians were actions of despair, a secret acknowledgement of the unshakeable mass support the Western democratic system actually enjoyed. Unable to change an unjust society, at least they could hurt its leaders.

For their small numbers, the terrorist groups had a remarkable impact. The arrest and trial of the Baader-Meinhof leaders and their deaths in prison under mysterious circumstances in 1977 were the major events of the West German political life of the period. In Italy, the Red Brigades' kidnapping and eventual assassination of Christian Democrat leader, Aldo Moro, in 1978 caused a government crisis.

The impact of the French events depended heavily on France's revolutionary past – the tradition of the direct expression of the 'popular will' on the streets – and nowhere else in Western Europe did student occupations and demonstrations constitute a threat to the existing regime. By coincidence, however, an East European country, Czechoslovakia, was just undergoing a political mutation that became influenced by these happenings in the West. In January 1968 the Czechoslovakian Communist Party leadership elected a reformer, Alexander Dubček, as first party secretary. Dubček's new government declared its aim of creating 'socialism with a human face.' Censorship was abolished and political activity outside the communist-controled National Front coalition was legalized. These measures ushered in the 'Prague Spring,' a flowering of cultural and political liberation that took on much of the appearance of the Paris events, with students on the streets, strongly desiring to participate in the youth culture of the West, and workers in control of factories.

Moscow was not amused. Despite repeated assurances by Dubček of his fidelity to the Warsaw Pact, Soviet pressure mounted. In August the Czech leadership made considerable concessions to Soviet wishes and seemed to have won agreement to a more limited version of its reforms. But it was not to be. On the night of 20 August, Warsaw Pact troops invaded Czechoslovakia and occupied the country. Hardline policies were reimposed.

In Eastern Europe, then, the events of 1968 stood as a sharp reminder of the narrow limits within which change would be permitted, although they also revealed that a modern individualist consumer society, not very unlike that in the West, was growing up within the hard exoskeleton of communist bureaucracy. In Western Europe, 1968 marked the end of two decades of political complacency. The most basic assumptions of West European societies were challenged: the ecological politics of the 'Greens' denied that industrial growth was good and desirable; regional movements opposed the centuries-old rule of centralized states; a women's movement questioned the assumptions of male superiority at work and at home.

One direct consequence of the defeat of revolutionary aspirations was an upsurge in terrorism.

Britain's terrorists had a more precise cause to pursue. The Provisional Irish Republican Army (PIRA), based among the Catholic population of Northern Ireland, challenged the continuing control of the province by Britain and the local Protestant majority. At the high point of their campaign in 1972 they rendered Northern Ireland virtually ungovernable. After the turn of the tide, the PIRA was still capable of maintaining a low-level terrorist campaign against security forces in the province, interspersed with sectarian warfare against the Protestants' own terror groups, and the occasional operation in mainland Britain. They narrowly failed to kill British Prime Minister, Margaret Thatcher, in a bomb attack in 1984. The nearest equivalent to the PIRA on the European mainland were the Basque terrorists, Euskadi Ta Askatasun (ETA). Their campaign for a Basque homeland developed into a terrorist offensive against the Spanish state from 1967 onward.

Regionalism versus consumerism

Regionalism outside the Basque country was rarely much associated with terrorism, but there were active movements in Languedoc, Brittany and Corsica against the Paris government, in Catalonia against Madrid, and in Wales and Scotland against government from London. Despite centuries of pressure from the dominant ethnic groups to forge European states into nations unified by language, culture and customs, local identity remained intact. Few in the regions went so far as to deny their wider nationality altogether, but most recognized a dual allegiance. Except in Spain, regional movements achieved little success in their pressure for self-government, but they did revive local culture and win official recognition for local languages. It was a flimsy revival in the face of the ever-expanding contemporary consumer culture, disseminated by television, advertising and tourism, but it had interesting implications for the future of European unity – if Bretons did

not feel entirely 'French' after five centuries of integration, how long would it take for Frenchmen to identify themselves as 'Europeans'?

The most fundamental change in the 1970s, however, was not the rise of terrorism or regional movements, but the end of the long postwar economic boom. The causes of the recession that began in earnest in 1973-74 were complex; they included the rise of industries in the Third World, exploiting cheap labor to undercut European prices for consumer goods, and a failure to introduce new electronic technology as fast as competitors, notably Japan. But the major precipitating factor was a sharp rise in the prices of imported raw materials and fuel, especially petroleum. This drove up inflation without stimulating demand, creating 'stagflation,' a phenomenon not allowed for by Keynesian economists. The average inflation rate in Western Europe rose to around 10 percent a year, output declined and mass unemployment made a gradual reappearance.

European governments regarded the 'energy crisis' – the uncertainty of petroleum supplies – as permanent, but the recession as temporary. Thus there was an immediate drive to find new energy sources – petroleum and natural gas from the North Sea and the Soviet Union, and atomic energy plants. But the recession was at first met with piecemeal measures, attempting vainly to control inflation without depressing demand and raising unemployment. Only slowly did it become clear that the energy crisis might prove temporary – by the mid 1980s there was a glut of oil on the world market – and at least some aspects of the recession more enduring.

In these new economic circumstances, the postwar Keynesian consensus fell apart. The initiative was seized by proponents of 'monetarism,' a refurbished version of prewar economic orthodoxy, advocating tight controls over government spending, cutbacks in social welfare and the withdrawal of governments from involvement in running the economy, which should be left to private enterprise and market forces. The private sector was now to be regarded as the origin of all wealth, the state sector – whether nationalized industries or public health and education – as a drain on national resources.

Above left: The Rolling Stones, a rock band who typified the thriving British popular culture of the 1960s.

Left: From 1970 onward, British soldiers in Northern Ireland had to face a very effective terrorist campaign mounted by the Provisional IRA.

Above: Czechs protest as Soviet tanks occupy Prague in August 1968, ousting the reforming communist leader Alexander Dubcek.

Right: The 1970s saw the return of mass unemployment in Europe. Here a left-wing rally blames British Prime Minister Margaret Thatcher's monetarist policies for worsening the employment situation.

Monetarism fell far short of establishing itself as a new universal system of belief. Its most enthusiastic application, by the first Thatcher government in Britain (1979-83), was hardly convincing, leading rather surprisingly to an increase in both taxation and public spending, as well as tripling the numbers unemployed. But Britain's 'privatization' policy, the sale of nationalized industries to the public as a source of short-term revenue, found imitators in continental Europe.

It was widely expected in the mid 1970s that high inflation and mass unemployment would destabilize West European democracy, as it had between the wars. But the democracies governed with a remarkable level of popular consent. The fear of unemployment tightened labor discipline and reduced the power of trade unions. The unemployed themselves were without political organization. For those in work, living standards continued to rise, if more slowly. There were outbreaks of protest, sometimes violent, by immigrant groups who bore much of the brunt of the recession; they were in turn the object of racial attacks and government legislation to limit immigration. Some young people, futilely educated for jobs that did not exist, joined the 'punk' subculture, a typical youth culture mix of fun, style and social protest, but contrasting starkly in its pessimism and cynical realism with the utopian optimism of the previous decade.

The communist parties of France and Italy took the opportunity, not to subvert the capitalist system, but to assert their right to play a respectable role in the democratic process. The Italian Communist Party had led the way in formulating the theoretical basis for a new Eurocommunism, involving the rejection of direct control from Moscow and the acceptance of a gradualist democratic path to a peaceful transformation of society. This made the communists what would once have been called a social democrat party – those parties that now called themselves social democrats in Western Europe had wiped any trace of socialism from their political programs. The Communist Party habitually polled around 30 percent of the vote in Italy, and between 1977 and 1979 was at last given a chance to participate in a coalition government with the Christian Democrats. The French Communist Party also had a brief spell as minority partners in government in the 1980s. These 'openings to the Left' did not so much mark a swing toward socialism as a confirmation of the

strength of Western democracies, their ability to integrate opposition.

The geographical spread of democracy also widened in the 1970s. Greece returned to civilian democratic government in 1974 after a period of military rule. The Iberian states, Spain and Portugal, had long stayed outside the West European democratic consensus. By keeping out of World War II, the prewar dictatorships of General Franco and Antonio de Oliveira Salazar had been able to survive, dinosaurs that had outlived their era. They were gradually undermined, however, by the example of successful democratic government in the rest of Western Europe, and by economic development which eroded the traditional society that supported these profoundly conservative regimes.

In the mid 1970s both Spain and Portugal rapidly turned to democracy, although by very different routes. In April 1974 the successors of Salazar were overthrown in a coup mounted by

left-wing officers, largely motivated by the desire to end the costly colonial wars Portugal was waging in Africa. A genuine, although bloodless, revolution ensued, and for a time it appeared that the country might develop into some form of socialist state. Through the late 1970s, however, the revolution was rolled back and the pattern of Western democracy faithfully imitated. In Spain, Franco made the apparently unlikely decision to be succeeded by a restoration of the monarchy. On Franco's death in 1975, Juan Carlos duly took the throne and, to general astonishment, made a great success of the enterprise.

European unity

By the late 1970s, then, Western Europe presented an exceptional picture of political uniformity. These were encouraging circumstances for progress toward European unity. The EEC expanded to include Britain, Ireland and Denmark in 1973, Greece in 1981 and Spain and Portugal in 1986. It also began to encroach noticeably on national sovereignty, with the setting up of a European Parliament at Strasbourg in 1979. The EEC remained better noted for bureaucratic waste than for the embodiment of the 'European ideal,' but momentum toward some form of unification was maintained.

There was no sign of an end to the divide between Eastern and Western Europe, however, aptly symbolized by the Berlin Wall built across the city in 1961 to stop the emigration of East Germans to the West. Still, the *détente* between the Soviet Union and the United States from the late 1960s provided an opportunity for a measure of *rapprochement*. Economic contacts between members of Comecon – the East European economic organization – and the EEC expanded, and East and West Germany recognized one another's existence. After 40 years of peace, the armed forces of NATO and the Warsaw Pact still bristled at one another across the German border, but the societies on each side of the divide were not alien or opposed. There was as much in common between the attitudes and education of, say, a Hungarian and a Frenchman as between a Belgian and an Italian. By the late 1970s, there was also little to

choose between the living standards of the most prosperous East European countries – East Germany, Hungary and Czechoslovakia – and the second rank of West European nations, such as Britain and Italy.

Eastern Europe was not proof against the 1970s economic downturn, however, and Poland's shaky economy ran into serious difficulties. Disturbances in 1970 had brought Eduard Gierek to power with promises of reform, but he failed to deliver either on the cultural or economic front. In 1980 workers in Gdansk, led by Lech Walesa, demanded recognition for an independent trade union, *Solidarnosc*, and the powerful Catholic Church gave its support. The authorities made extensive concessions, particularly on cultural freedom, but the economic situation worsened catastrophically as strikes disrupted production. In January 1981 army leader, Wojciech Jaruzelski, replaced Gierek and in December instituted martial law. The crackdown was not as severe as many had feared, however. The leaders of *Solidarnosc* were arrested for a short period but most were soon back at liberty, and the regime continued to seek popular support for measures to deal with the country's dire economic state – without any success.

The Soviet Union remained unpopular through almost all of Eastern Europe. In the West, attitudes to the United States were varied and complex. On the one hand, West European governments continued to fear an American military withdrawal from Europe, and in the late 1970s they enthusiastically campaigned for American nuclear missiles to be based in their

countries. But the arrival of these missiles was met by anti-nuclear protests that had wide public support. There was an uncomfortable awareness that American and European interests were not identical, and a fear that Europe might become a nuclear battleground in a war that was not its concern. It was not reassuring that when the two superpowers negotiated for a withdrawal of nuclear missiles from Europe, the European powers themselves were barely consulted. But moves toward a European defense system, independent of the United States, remained tentative.

Taking stock of Europe, East and West, 40 years after the war, it was easy to formulate either a pessimistic or an optimistic view by selective quotation from the facts. One could point to the astonishingly high levels of crimes of violence in Western cities; the continuing pockets of squalor and poverty amid prosperity; glaring inequalities of wealth; the dilution of national cultures by progressive Americanization; the devastation of the environment by industrial development – the Rhine swept by tides of poisonous chemicals, the Black Forest denuded by acid rain, the Mediterranean, the very cradle of Western civilization, turned into an open sewer by the pressure of industry and mass tourism on its shores. The ugliness of the expanding cities with their tower-block building bespoke a civilization with more money and technical expertise than taste and human values.

Yet the European population was healthier than ever before, better educated and better housed. Working conditions had improved and there was more leisure. Even in Eastern Europe, governments generally respected standards of humanity and decency that were high compared with earlier history, even if far short of the ideal. Above all, a long peace had been maintained. This was no doubt partly the result of the nuclear balance of terror, but it was more due to the decline of European power – conflicts of interest no longer mattered as they had in 1914.

The European population was getting older, as both birth- and death-rates declined. Was it, then, a civilization entering senility? There was certainly no future in the revival of imperial glories – Britain's Falklands campaign of 1982 was interesting as a chance to try out modern weapons in real combat, but otherwise a strange anachronism. The country that had ruled half the world was stretched to the limit to control a few islands in the South Atlantic. With imperialism's decline, the other great dream of nineteenth-century Europe, socialism, also seemed to be on the wane – it was hard to believe that the countries of Eastern Europe were showing the way forward. Europe had given its ideas and its technology to the rest of the world. In all likelihood, other continents would now plot the course of history, and Europe would follow in their wake.

Soviet Union

The German-Soviet non-aggression pact of 23 August 1939 freed Hitler from the danger of a war on two fronts. On 1 September 1939 German troops entered Poland and on 3 September Britain and France declared war. The Second World War had begun.

The attack of the German troops on Poland was received by the Soviet regime with open pleasure. When Warsaw finally fell Vyacheslav Molotov conveyed his greetings and congratulations to Hitler's government. In accordance with previous German-Soviet negotiations, Soviet troops entered the eastern regions of Poland on 17 September 1939. The reason, according to the Soviet regime, was that Poland and the Polish government had ceased to exist, and therefore previous Polish-Soviet treaties were no longer valid; the Red Army had crossed the border to protect the lives and property of kindred Ukrainians and White Russians living in Polish territory.

The Soviet troops met almost no resistance and within a few days occupied territory which included 13 million inhabitants: seven million Ukrainians, three million White Russians, about a million Poles and a million Jews. After the German Foreign Minister, Joachim von Ribbentrop, had visited Moscow a second time, a German-Soviet border and friendship treaty was signed confirming the division of Poland. In a secret, supplementary protocol Nazi Germany and the Soviet Union agreed to common action against Polish independence movements: both parties agreed not to tolerate any Polish agitation and to advise one another on appropriate means of control. At the beginning of October 1939 a National Assembly was elected from a single list of candidates in the Soviet Zone of Poland. The delegates to this Assembly took part at a session of the Supreme Soviet on 31 October, where the formal annexation of the eastern regions of Poland by the Soviet Union was accomplished.

In the fall of 1939 Estonia, Latvia and Lithuania, under pressure, declared that they were ready to sign mutual aid agreements with the Soviet Union, whereby all three countries would place naval stations and air bases at the disposal of the Russians. The Soviet government tried to reach a similar agreement with Poland, but met strong opposition. The discussions, which had begun on 5 October, were broken off on 13 November. On 28 November the Soviet Union annulled the Soviet-Finnish non-aggression pact, and two days later 30 Soviet divisions invaded Finland. The violent Soviet attack on Finland evoked strong indignation throughout the world and led to the exclusion of the Soviet Union from the League of Nations in December 1939.

The Russians hoped in vain to break Finland's resistance within a few days. The tenacious opposition of the Finnish troops, the difficult terrain (hundreds of Soviet tanks became stranded in the snow and mud) and the clear weaknesses of the Red Army which had resulted from the Great Purge caused the Soviet-Finnish war to drag on for more than four months through the winter of 1939-40. Only after the USSR had succeeded in breaking through the Mannerheim Line in the middle of February 1940 was Finland compeled to sign an armistice on 12 March. Finland was forced to withdraw from territory in Karelia as well as to cede the peninsula of Hangö to the Soviet Union.

A few months later the annexation of the Baltic States – Estonia, Latvia and Lithuania – occurred. Under the pretext of alleged 'anti-Soviet provocations' the Soviet government demanded in the middle of June 1940 that new governments be formed in the three states and that Soviet troops have the right to march freely through the countries. Immediately afterward Soviet troops invaded all three states. Under Soviet pressure a People's Government was formed on 17 June in Lithuania, and similar governments in Estonia and Latvia followed. After the appropriate elections of a single slate of candidates, the new People's Representatives unanimously announced the decision to form soviet republics and were incorporated into the Soviet Union at the beginning of August 1940.

While the Baltic States were being annexed by the Soviet Union the Moscow regime, according to a previous understanding with Hitler's government, sent an ultimatum to Rumania, demanding that Bessarabia and northern Bucovina be ceded to the USSR. It was significant that the Soviet government did not limit itself to demanding Bessarabia, which had once belonged to Russia, but included northern Bucovina, which had never belonged to Russia and which had not been included in the secret protocol of the Hitler-Stalin pact among the territories to be annexed by the Soviet Union. After some hesitation and inquiries in Berlin, Rumania accepted the Soviet ultimatum, and Soviet troops marched into Bessarabia and northern Bucovina. Soviet-style governments were imposed on both regions and they were annexed by the USSR at the beginning of August 1940.

German-Soviet relations gradually began to deteriorate in the course of this expansion of Soviet power. Already, in March 1940, the Soviet Union had complained about the slow pace of the shipment of goods from Germany to the USSR. On the other hand the Hitler government was annoyed that the Soviet Union, having accepted Estonia, Latvia and Bessarabia in the secret supplementary protocol, had in addition occupied Lithuania and northern Bucovina. Nor was the Soviet Union unaware that since July 1940 increasing numbers of German troops had been shifted to the German-Soviet border. Even in the Balkans, especially, in Bulgaria, there were disputes between Nazi Germany and the Soviet Union.

It was in this context that Molotov began discussions with Hitler's government in Berlin, 12-13 November 1940. The Germans made extravagant promises to Molotov in case of a future division of the British Empire. Molotov remained cool and

Left: Hitler watches his troops march off to fight in Poland at the start of World War II – a war that would cost the lives of over 20 million Soviet citizens, but also lead to an expansion of Soviet power and territory.

Above right: A Finnish soldier prepared for action against Soviet forces during the Winter War of 1939-40. The Finns proved very adept at fighting under extreme weather conditions.

Above far right: Latvian troops march past the Statue of Liberty in their capital, Riga. However, they could offer no resistance when the Red Army entered the country in June 1940.

Right: German troops in Rumania. The Soviet Union took Bessarabia and northern Bucovina from Rumania in 1940, and Rumanian forces took part in the invasion of the Soviet Union the following year.

demanded concrete concessions in Bulgaria, the Dardanelles, Finland and the Baltic. The discussions ended with no agreement having been reached, and Hitler did not reply to new Soviet proposals delivered after Molotov's return to Moscow. A few weeks after Molotov's visit, on 18 December 1940, Hitler signed the plan for 'Operation Barbarossa,' according to which 'the German army must be ready to destroy the Soviet Union in a quick campaign.'

The period of the Hitler-Stalin pact was characterized in domestic politics by the attempt to consolidate the economic and military might of the USSR, which had been significantly weakened by the Great Purge. Economic and technical problems received top priority. Yet the economic successes of these years were linked with a series of measures which were unpopular with, and contrary to the interests of, the working populace. According to a regulation at the end of 1938 any worker or employee who arrived at work more than 20 minutes late would be punished by

immediate dismissal from his job. This was made even harsher by the decree of 26 June 1940, which made it impossible to leave a factory and take another job without the permission of the factory management. Resignation from one's job without authorization was punishable by two to four months in jail. A few months later, at the beginning of October 1940, free university education, which until then had been not only customary but guaranteed by the Soviet Constitution, was abolished, and the new tuition costs were so high that many children from working-class or *kolkhoz* families had no option but to abandon their studies.

Changes were instituted in September 1939 which were intended to further strengthen military power: basic training in the army was intensified and the period of military service was lengthened. In May 1940, military discipline was increased, the punishment for desertion and being AWOL being made considerably more severe. Then, following the general return to

Russian traditions, officers' ranks up to the rank of general were again restored.

From the beginning of 1941 the imminent threat from Nazi Germany could no longer be overlooked. Hitler approved the plan for 'Operation Barbarossa' against the Soviet Union on 3 February 1941 and two months later set the date for the attack against the USSR for the second half of June. On 7 April Germany invaded Yugoslavia, which had concluded a friendship treaty with the Soviet Union only a few days before. On 6 May 1941 Stalin took over the position of Chairman of the Soviet Government, wich had previously been filled by Molotov, thereby officially uniting the powers of the leader of the Party and the head of the government in his hands.

Left: As the German invasion begins, peasants flee eastward past Soviet trucks carrying supplies to the front. Soviet civilians suffered appalling losses during the war, both from German brutality and atrocities, and from general hardship and starvation.

Below: British factory workers preparing tanks for the Soviet Union in September 1941. Although supplies from the West were invaluable, it was Soviet industry that built most of the tanks that defeated Hitler on the Eastern Front.

Right: Some of the 91,000 German prisoners taken at Stalingrad. Few would survive their captivity.

Warnings of an imminent attack by Nazi Germany on the USSR multiplied continually: 150 German divisions were poised on the Soviet Union's western border, and constant incursions were made into Soviet territory. Stalin was repeatedly warned by both the British and Soviet intelligence services of an impending attack by Hitler, but he did not take the warnings seriously, apparently because he was convinced that Hitler would not make the mistake of voluntarily starting a war on two fronts.

This underestimation of the danger was clearly seen on 14 June 1941, when the Soviet Telegraph Agency (TASS) explained that all rumors that Germany was preparing a war against the USSR were false because Germany considered the terms of the Soviet-German non-aggression pact as binding as did the Soviet Union. This communiqué produced the widespread view, even among figures in authority, that a peaceful summer was in store for the Soviet Union in 1941.

The Great Patriotic War

On 22 June 1941 German troops attacked the Soviet Union without warning: according to Soviet statements 153 German divisions took part in the invasion. Shortly thereafter Italy, Finland, Rumania and Hungary joined the war against the Soviet Union. Powerful German armored units broke through the Russian positions on the border along a broad front and German planes bombed Russian cities.

A few hours after the beginning of the war Molotov, in the name of the entire Soviet government, summoned the Soviet armed forces and the entire Soviet people to struggle against the Fascist invaders. At the same time terms such as 'socialism' and 'Communist Party' disappeared; all propaganda concentrated on patriotism and the defense of the fatherland. The war against Hitler was called the 'Great Patriotic War of the Soviet

People' in reference to the patriotic war of 1812 against Napoleon. The State Committee for Defense, which included Stalin, the Chairman, and Molotov, Klimenti Voroshilov, Lavrenti Beria and Georgi Malenkov, was created on 30 June 1941 to coordinate military, political and economic policies during wartime.

Within two weeks Hitler's troops succeeded in occupying all of Lithuania and Latvia and the western part of White Russia and the Ukraine. On 3 July Stalin declared on the radio that the USSR was in mortal danger. He directed a patriotic appeal to the population to defend their native

land and wherever a retreat was necessary to leave absolutely nothing to the occupation forces, evacuating everything or, where that was impossible, destroying everything.

The defeat of the Red Army in the summer of 1941 was a result of many factors. The Soviet troops were not expecting the invasion. New technical equipment was not perfected at the time of the German attack, and the production of new tanks and aircraft had just begun. The Soviet officers' corps had been decimated by the Great Purge, and the new, young officers who were to replace those who had been arrested did not yet

for mutual support was reached in July 1941, and both sides pledged not to conduct any negotiations with the enemy. At the end of the month President Roosevelt sent his friend Harry Hopkins to Moscow, and in September 1941 Averell W Harriman followed. Now the United States also furnished the Soviet Union with increasing amounts of aid which was of decisive importance for the Soviet war effort.

Although the victory in the battle of Moscow had significantly improved the situation in the Soviet Union, enemy troops still occupied large parts of the country, and had even succeeded in completely surrounding Leningrad. The supplies of fuel for heating were completely exhausted, and food rations were so small that 600,000 people died of starvation in the winter of 1941-42 alone. The city was constantly bombarded, but the defenders did not surrender.

By the spring of 1942 the essential elements of the Soviet economy had been adapted to wartime, and production increased rapidly. On Stalin's orders Soviet troops – apparently overestimating their strength – began an offensive near Kharkov in the Ukraine on 12 May 1942. This ended in disaster, and a new German summer offensive followed at the end of June 1942. At first it achieved notable success: the German army occupied the Kuban region, the entire northern Caucasus and advanced simultaneously toward Stalingrad and the oil-producing regions of the USSR. Only at Stalingrad did the Russians strengthen their resistance.

Soviet triumph at Stalingrad

The Battle of Stalingrad, and indeed other purely military aspects of The Great Patriotic War, are discussed more fully elsewhere in this work under the rubric of World War II. Here let it only be said that this German débâcle was largely the product of Hitler's blundering personal direction of Wehrmacht strategy. On 2 February 1943 the battle ended in victory for the Russians: 91,000 German soldiers were taken prisoner, including 2400 officers, 24 generals and the commander-in-chief, Field Marshal von Paulus. The victory of Stalingrad was the turning point of the war in Russia and marked the beginning of a general Soviet offensive. In January 1943 the blockade of Leningrad was broken, and on other parts of the front the Red Army succeeded in driving the opposing forces several hundred miles west.

Resistance movements in the areas occupied by German troops also began to play a larger role. At the beginning of the war the German army had been welcomed by many of the inhabitants, especially in the Baltic states and some regions of the Ukraine, in the hope of being freed from Stalin's terror. But the harsh occupation, the shootings, the forced evacuation of millions of workers to Germany, the inhuman methods of recruitment and the bad treatment of the forced laborers soon produced a fierce opposition in the people living in German occupied territory. The number of armed partisans now increased rapidly. Behind the enemy lines bridges and railroad tracks were blown up, trains with troops and war materials were derailed, preparations for military operations were sabotaged and collaboration between civilians and the occupation forces died away. In time groups of partisans even succeeded in liberating entire regions from the German occupation army. On 30 May 1942 a central headquarters for the resistance movements was established with the aim of supporting the activity of the partisans (including training men to lead the resistance groups and furnishing the groups with weapons and instructions), as well as to control the resis-

have sufficient military training and battle experience. But Stalin's incorrect assessment of the military-political situation must be cited as the main reason for the disaster.

By October 1941 the German army had seized the Baltic States, all of White Russia, the most important parts of Ukraine and had reached Moscow and Leningrad. The territory which the German troops had occupied by October 1941 had been the home of 40 percent of the Soviet population prior to the war and had yielded 38 percent of the grain, 58 percent of the steel, 60 percent of the aluminum, 63 percent of the coal and 68 percent of the pig-iron produced by the USSR. The Germans held 41 percent of all Soviet railways, and by November 1941 Soviet production had fallen to less than half of the pre-war level.

The German attack on Moscow began at the beginning of October 1941: on some parts of the front the German troops approached to within six miles of the outskirts of the city. Workers' battalions were formed, and the Moscow populace was mobilized to dig trenches and to set up anti-tank obstacles, barbed wire and barricades. Panic broke out in the capital when the Soviet press announced on 16 October that the German troops had broken through the front. Stores were stormed, and looting and riots broke out. Party members burned their membership cards, and documents which could be used as evidence were burned in the offices of the secret police. The

situation became calmer only on the evening of 19 October. A state of siege was announced in Moscow and the State Committee for Defense took measures for the defense of the capital.

On 6 November, the eve of the 23rd anniversary of the October Revolution, Stalin gave a speech at a meeting of the Moscow Soviet – held in a station of the Moscow subway for protection against air raids. He attributed the German advance to a temporary superiority in planes and tanks and spoke of long-term measures which would lead to the victory of the Soviet Union. On 7 November the traditional military parade took place on Red Square; the troops marched directly from the parade ground to the front.

The German advance came to a standstill at the edge of Moscow at the end of November 1941. The sudden arrival of winter caused the German troops – who had begun the battle without winter uniforms – considerable losses and difficulties, and fresh Soviet troops had arrived from Siberia to bolster the defense of the capital. On 6 December 1941 a Soviet counteroffensive under Marshal Georgi Zhukov began and completely changed the situation in and around the city. By the end of February 1942 the Russians had advanced more than 250 miles to the west and had reoccupied several regions in central European Russia.

Aid from the United States and Great Britain also greatly helped the Soviet Union. An agreement between Great Britain and the Soviet Union

NATO
ANZUS
SEATO
UNDER SEATO PROTECTION
CENTO
WARSAW PACT

© Richard Natkiel

Left: Although as a result of World War II Soviet forces were permanently stationed in the heart of Europe, by the mid 1950s the Soviet Union was virtually encircled by American-led alliance systems.

Above right: Frightened Jews cower from German soldiers during the suppression of the Warsaw ghetto uprising in 1943.

Right: A Soviet poster emphasizing the traditions of naval service rather than revolutionary ardor. It was in the darkest days of World War II that Stalin restored the old-fashioned military virtues to a place of honor in Soviet society.

tance more closely and to subordinate it to the Soviet Party apparatus.

In the summer of 1943 Hitler made one last attempt to retake the positions which had been lost. On 5 July 1943 36 German divisions, including more than 500 tanks, attacked in the vicinity of Kursk, about 300 miles south of Moscow, but they soon came to a standstill. On 12 July the Soviet counterblow followed, marking the beginning of a mighty Soviet summer offensive that was carried out on a front almost 1200 miles long. On 23 August Soviet troops liberated Kharkov in the Ukraine, and on 25 September Smolensk. In the south they pushed forward into the Donets Basin, finally taking Kiev, the capital of the Ukraine, on 6 November.

Important changes in Soviet domestic politics coincided with these military operations. At the beginning of the war the return to Russian traditions was an important instrument with which Stalin aroused new energy for the war effort. A resurgence of military pride and military tradition was the most notable aspect. In 1942 the first units of elite troops like those in czarist Russia were formed, and on 6 March 1943 Stalin assumed the rank of Marshal of the Soviet Union and emphasized his personal ties with the

generals and the officers' corps. In October new ranks for generals were created, and many new military promotions and appointments were instituted. The newly created Orders of Alexander Nevsky, Kutuzov and Suvorov were references to the army's glorious past. A more tolerant policy toward the Church was also clearly apparent, and the Soviet press prominently displayed mutual greetings between Stalin and the leaders of the Russian Orthodox Church. Finally, in 1943, this process culminated in the dissolution of the Communist International, and in the spring of 1944 the *Internationale*, which had been the national anthem until then, was replaced by a new patriotic Soviet national hymn.

The secret police became less conspicuous to average citizens, and this produced the widespread impression that the system had become more relaxed. Books and poems were published which would have been unthinkable before the war. Even the administration of the kolkhozes was less harsh: kolkhoz farmers could increase the size of their private gardens (which were and are more productive than the *kolkhoz* land) without the interference of the authorities, who were interested in increasing production. Many Soviet citizens also hoped that the increasing cooper-

ation with the democratic Western powers would promote a freer development in the USSR. As early as the end of May 1942 a British-Soviet military pact against Nazi Germany was signed, providing for further cooperation after the end of the war. On 11 June 1942 a Soviet-American treaty concerning mutual aid and cooperation on the conduct of the war was also signed.

The coordination of military operations was the central issue of the conference of the Big Three – Stalin, Roosevelt and Churchill – in Teheran at the end of November 1943. Churchill's proposal to launch invasions in the Balkans as well as in northern France was opposed by Stalin. Finally they decided on a single Allied invasion in northern France, which, for all practical purposes, divided Europe into two theaters of war and paved the way for a future extension of Soviet influence in Eastern Europe.

Differences of opinion between the Big Three were especially clear in the Polish question. On 25 April 1943 the Soviet Union had broken off relations with the Polish government in exile in London after the discovery of a mass grave in Katyn, Poland, in which the bodies of Polish army officers, shot by the Soviet secret police at the beginning of 1942, were interred. The Soviet leadership prepared a new pro-Soviet shadow government shortly after the Teheran Conference.

Russian troops began a massive new offensive on almost all parts of the front at the beginning of 1944 and within a few months drove the German troops from Soviet territory. But an increase in internal political pressure occurred simultaneously with Stalin's military successes. In March 1944 five non-Russian peoples – the Crimean Tatars, the Chechen, Ingush, Balkar and Kalmyk peoples – were deported on the grounds that some members of these nationalities had collaborated with the enemy. Hundreds of thousands of people were deprived of their homes and resettled in remote parts of the Soviet Union. Even the names of these peoples could no longer be mentioned in any publication.

At the beginning of April 1944 Soviet troops reached the borders of Czechoslovakia and Rumania, and on 21 July the Polish Liberation Committee – the provisional government of Poland – was formed in Lublin, in Soviet-occupied territory. A few days later an uprising began in Warsaw against the German occupation. It was not supported by Soviet troops: the Russians stopped

their advance and waited until the German troops had quelled the rebellion in Warsaw. Thus the Polish resistance movement was destroyed and the Lublin Committee's claim to power increased.

In August 1944 the Fascist dictatorship in Rumania was overthrown, and a new government was formed under Soviet occupation. On 9 September 1944 a similar change followed in Bulgaria, and the government was taken over by the so-called National Front. Belgrade was liberated in collaboration with Yugoslav troops in the middle of October, and in December the new Hungarian government declared war on Germany. In January 1945 Soviet troops began a new offensive in Poland and Germany. On the 17th Warsaw was taken, and an attack was launched in East Prussia.

These events, including the Allied invasion of France, 6 June 1944, provided the background for the Yalta Conference, 4-15 February 1945, often called the 'Crimean Conference' in Soviet publications. The final destruction of Nazi Germany was the main topic. The three leaders agreed on the need to eliminate German Naziism and militarism, as well as on the need to guarantee a peaceful, democratic development of Germany. They also agreed that the Nazi Party and all Fascist organizations should be abolished, that the German armed forces should be disbanded, that the German General Staff should be permanently eliminated and that war criminals should be tried. Germany was to pay reparations totaling $20 billion, of which half was to go to the Soviet Union.

In the communiqué on liberated Europe, Stalin, Roosevelt and Churchill pledged that the liberated peoples could create democratic institutions of their choice and that the United Nations would be created under the dominant influence of the three victorious powers to maintain peace and security. Regarding the Polish question they decided – after hard bargaining – that the Polish-Soviet border should follow the Curzon line and that Poland should receive new territory from Germany as reparation. The provisional Polish government, formed under Soviet influence, was to be recognized in principle, but it was to be broadened by the inclusion of a group of democratic leaders, after which there were to be free elections in Poland. Regarding the Far East, Stalin declared that his country was ready to join the war against Japan within two or three months after the capitulation of Germany, on condition

БОЕВЫМ ТРАДИЦИЯМ ВЕРНЫ !

that Outer Mongolia would remain in the Soviet sphere of influence, that the USSR would acquire southern Sakhalin Island and that Soviet interests in Port Arthur and Lüta (Dairen) and in Manchuria would be respected.

During the conference the massive Soviet offensive continued along a 750-mile front from the Baltic to the Carpathians. In the middle of February Breslau (today Wroclaw) was surrounded, and East Prussia was encircled. Bratislava (in Czechoslovakia) was freed on 4 April, and on 13 April Soviet troops entered Vienna. A few days later the attack on Berlin began. On 25 April Berlin was encircled, and after street battles lasting several days the storming of the Reichstag began at daybreak on the 30th. At 2.25 pm the Red Flag was fixed to the top of the building. That afternoon Hitler committed suicide, and on 2 May the last German troops in the city surrendered.

After further fighting, especially in Czechoslovakia, representatives of the German High Command signed the declaration of the unconditional surrender of Nazi Germany in Karlshorst – a quarter of Berlin – in the presence of Marshal Zhukov and leading representatives of the western powers. On the following day, 9 May 1945, the victory was celebrated in the Soviet Union. Stalin declared in a speech that the centuries of struggle of the Slavic peoples for their existence and independence had ended with the victory over German tyranny; henceforth 'the great banner of freedom and peace among nations will wave over Europe.'

In the first days after the end of the war in Europe the Soviet government attempted to secure its newly acquired territories. The regions annexed under the Hitler-Stalin pact – southeastern Finland, Estonia, Latvia, Lithuania, eastern Poland, Bessarabia and northern Bucovina – were now almost automatically confirmed as Soviet territory. In addition, the northern part of East Prussia, including Königsberg (today Kaliningrad), was annexed to the USSR, and on 29 June Czechoslovakia declared that it was prepared to cede the Carpathian Ukraine to the Russians. But above all the Soviet Union had now obtained a dominant position in Poland, the Soviet zones of Germany and Austria, Czechoslovakia, Hungary, Rumania and Bulgaria.

The Potsdam Conference (often called the 'Berlin Conference' in Soviet publications) between Stalin, Churchill and Truman took place from 17 July to 2 August 1945. The leaders concluded that a council composed of the foreign ministers of the victorious powers should be set up to prepare peace treaties with the former allies of Nazi Germany – Italy, Rumania, Bulgaria and Hungary – and to work out a treaty with Germany with the goal of wiping out German Naziism and militarism. It was agreed that the reconstruction of Germany should take place on a democratic and peaceful basis. Soviet books and articles always make special reference to the allusion made at the conference that all cartels, trusts and monopolies would be eliminated. Soviet demands for indemnification were to be fulfilled by the Soviet occupation zone of Germany, plus an additional 15 percent of all industrial equipment in the western zone (to be paid for by shipments of raw materials from the Soviet Union) and another 10 percent without such shipments. The annexation of the northern part of East Prussia, with Königsberg, by the USSR was confirmed. It was agreed to postpone the final confirmation of Poland's western border until the peace conference, and until then the German territories east of the Oder-Neisse would be under Polish administration. The pro-Soviet Polish government was to be recognized on condition that Poles in exile could return to Poland unhindered and acquire full rights in their homeland, and that free, unobstructed elections would take place with the participation of all democratic, anti-Nazi parties.

These concessions by the Western powers were apparently linked – in part at least – to their desire to urge the Soviet Union to join quickly in the war against Japan, whose military strength was significantly overestimated at that time. On 8 August 1945, the day after the atom bomb was dropped on Hiroshima, the USSR declared war and began military operations against a country which had already been brought to her knees. The three-week campaign – Japan capitulated on 2 September – was considerably exaggerated in the Soviet Union and made it possible for the Russians to acquire new territories in the Far East: southern Sakhalin Island, the Kurile Islands (which czarist Russia had lost during the Russo-Japanese War of 1904-05), as well as control over the Manchurian railroad and Lüta (Dairen) and Port Arthur.

The 'Great Patriotic War,' as World War II was called by the Russians, had ended in victory for the Soviet Union, but it had caused the Russian people incredible sacrifices. According to Soviet estimates more than 20 million Russians died during the war, 1170 cities and more than 70,000 villages were completely or partially destroyed and 25 million people were left homeless. Over 31,000 factories, 40,000 miles of railroad track and over 4000 train stations had been destroyed during the war. The total value of property destroyed during the war is set at 679 billion rubles by Soviet publications.

Left and right: Soviet troops advance on the Byelorussian front in the summer of 1944. This massive offensive at last drove German forces off Soviet territory and back into Poland, but the Red Army halted in front of Warsaw at the start of August.

Below left: Jews are deported from the Warsaw ghetto to the Nazi extermination camps. However harsh Stalinist rule became in postwar Poland, it never remotely approached the horror of the years of German occupation.

Below right: Polish civilians take to the road, joining the great army of displaced persons in Europe.

But the war also ended in new territorial acquisitions for the Soviet Union which were far beyond the most optimistic hopes of the Soviet leaders in 1941. Stalin now presided over an empire that stretched from the Pacific to Western Europe and that would play a decisive role in world politics thereafter. The Soviet Union had emerged as a full-blown superpower.

The beginning of the Cold War

The hope of many Russians that a thaw in the Soviet system would occur after the victorious end of the war was unfulfilled. The victory celebrations were scarcely over when Stalin introduced a harder line in domestic affairs. The praises of the heroism of the Russian soldiers, of the accomplishments of the officers and generals and of the self-sacrifice of the Soviet populace,

which had been common until then, disappeared almost completely. A press campaign directed from the Kremlin explained, on the contrary, that the victory was due to the superiority of the Soviet system, the leading role of the Communist Party and the genius of Stalin. At the end of June Stalin conferred on himself the titles of 'Hero of the Soviet Union' and 'Commander-in-Chief.'

The Party leaders feared that the soldiers and officers returning from abroad would spread their knowledge about life in the West and thereby 'infect' the Soviet population. Consequently, the majority of all soldiers and citizens returning from abroad were sent to concentration camps, and economic, political and ideological measures were announced which signified a harsher domestic situation.

Preparations for the new Fourth Five-Year Plan

(1946-1950) began in the middle of August 1945. All expectations for an increase in the production of consumer goods for the benefit of the citizens who had suffered so much were shattered by Stalin's speech on 9 February 1946, in which he announced that the new Five-Year Plan would again give priority to heavy industry. He declared that in the course of several Five-Year Plans the USSR must be strengthened 'so that our homeland is secure from all events.'

The agricultural situation was especially catastrophic. In addition to the destruction and devastation of the war the Soviet Union was hit by a great drought in 1946 which produced one of the worst crop failures in Soviet history. The collective farms were very hard-hit, since the farmers, worn out by the suffering and privations of the war, had not the strength, interest or enthusiasm to work. Food rationing, which had begun during the war, consequently remained in effect until the end of 1947. The kolkhoz farmers hoped for a liberalization of the kolkhoz system, but on the contrary, the concessions made to the kolkhoz farmers during the war concerning their private garden plots were nullified, and a new 'Council for Collective Farm Affairs' was created in September 1946 to strengthen central control over the collective farms.

The harder line was especially noticeable in cultural affairs. Under the leadership of Andrei Zhdanov – the Politburo member for culture and ideology – the Party restated its claim to total ideological leadership. At a plenary session of the Central Committee in August 1946 a number of journals, theaters and authors were very sharply attacked for supposedly having propagated pessimism, decadence, petty-bourgeois attitudes, formalism, and obsequiousness toward bourgeois art and culture from abroad. According to the Central Committee, Soviet literature could have no other interests than those of the state and must be Party-minded in order to educate the working classes in the spirit of communism.

This ideological training was to be strengthened by the creation of two new political-ideological journals and by the activities of the Academy of Social Sciences and of the Society for the Dissemination of Political and Scientific Knowledge. In June 1947 a sharp attack on Soviet philosophers followed; they were reproached for having concerned themselves too much with foreign philosophers and for having neglected Russian thinkers in their works. Soviet economists were also denounced because, according to the Kremlin, they had given too much emphasis to the changes in capitalism and had underestimated the contradictions and crises.

International cultural and scientific ties were branded as groveling at the feet of bourgeois culture, and again, as in the 1930s, Russians were made to fear any contact with foreigners. The decree of 9 July 1947, which threatened severe punishment for the diffusion not only of military information but even of insignificant government reports on the economy, education and science, also served to isolate the Soviet populace.

In a similar fashion Soviet foreign policy in the first years after the war concentrated almost exclusively on aggrandizing Soviet power and generally ignored the common interests of the anti-Hitler coalition formed during the war. In May 1945 the USSR unilaterally announced a Soviet-Turkish treaty that included the demands that Turkey should cede territory to the USSR and that the USSR should have a say in controling the Bosporus and Dardanelles. At the first conference of foreign ministers in London in September 1945 Molotov demanded that his country should also join in the negotiations on occupied Japan. In March 1946 the USSR refused to pull back its troops from northern Iran, contrary to an agreement made in 1942, and on the initiative of the Russians a 'People's Republic' was proclaimed. Only after repeated serious warnings from the Western powers were the Russian troops withdrawn from Iran in May 1946.

Of primary importance for East-West relations was development in the Eastern European countries under Soviet control. At the end of the war the newly founded communist parties in all countries of Eastern Europe unanimously declared that they did not intend to establish socialism or the Soviet system, but only to work together with other democratic parties for anti-Fascist democratic reforms. The new governments in Eastern Europe were composed of the representatives of the various 'bloc parties,' and

the communists by no means had a majority, but they did, as a general rule, hold key positions such as the ministries of the interior, army, police and sometimes of the economy, agriculture and education.

Moreover, from the beginning of 1946 the leadership of the communist parties emphasized that they favored their own way to socialism, which would correspond to the traditions and peculiarities of each country. The goal was the establishment of People's Democracies which would be different from Western democracies, on

Left: A German poster welcoming the Marshall Plan for European reconstruction. The Soviet rejection of Marshall Aid was a crucial step on the path to Cold War confrontation.

Below left: Two Soviet posters urging the workers and peasants to make heroic efforts to fulfill the targets of the 1945-50 Five-Year Plan.

Right: German children in Berlin gather to await an airdrop of American candy during the Berlin blockade in 1948. Whereas the Americans poured money and goods into Europe, the Soviet Union, impoverished by war, sucked wealth out of the areas it controlled.

Below right: 'Uncle Joe' Stalin and his Foreign Minister Molotov (right) put on avuncular smiles for the camera.

the one hand, as well as from the Soviet system, on the other. Consequently, a whole series of social and economic reforms were carried out, including distribution of the large land holdings to farmers with little land, the nationalization of heavy industry and a reform of the educational system.

The stronger the communist parties became and the more the party apparatus became solidified, the more apparent became the pressure on the non-communist parties. Step by step they forfeited their independence and were gradually degraded to the status of appendages of the dominant communist parties. All political leaders who opposed this development were relieved of their duties and in many cases arrested. By means of these 'salami tactics' the communist parties attained a dominant position by the end of 1947.

Simultaneously, Soviet economic, political and military advisers came to Eastern Europe in increasing numbers, and important branches of industry were placed in control of 'joint companies' which guaranteed the Soviet Union dominant influence. By the beginning of 1947 the concept of the independent road to socialism had disappeared. Thenceforth the sole model was to be that of the Soviet Union.

The increasing sovietization of Eastern Europe had a poisoning effect on East-West relations. In June of 1947, with the announcement of the Marshall Plan, the break between the Soviet Union and the Western powers became clear. The Marshall Plan, originally aimed at all countries devastated by the war – including the USSR – was to be worked out in detail at a conference in Paris in June 1947. But the Soviet delegation withdrew from the conference on 29 June, declaring that the Marshall Plan was an attempt by American monopolies to unite the countries of Western Europe in a military bloc under the dominant influence of

same time as the Soviet-Yugoslav conflict occurred. On 20 March 1948 the Soviet delegation, led by Marshal Vasiliy Sokolovsky, withdrew from the Allied Control Commission in Berlin. With that the four-power control over Germany ceased to exist *de facto*. From the end of March the Russians began to make travel to West Berlin more difficult, and on 24 June they completely severed all contact; the Berlin blockade had begun. The Soviet Union held the ring closed around West Berlin while the Western powers, especially the United States, helped the Berliners with airlifts. The allies of the war now opposed each other as enemies

The last years of the Stalin era

The political development within the USSR from 1948 to 1953 was marked by the total control of the Party apparatus in all spheres of cultural and scientific life. Soviet culture was now totally sealed off from foreign influences, and even the smallest international contacts were condemned as cosmopolitanism. It was clear that a new Great Purge was in store.

Andrei Zhdanov, who had directed the campaign against the Soviet intelligentsia, died at the end of August 1948 under mysterious circumstances. Immediately thereafter, his colleagues and adherents were purged, especially in Leningrad, where many top Party functionaries were victims of the 'Leningrad Affair.' Zhdanov's death in no way signified a relaxation of the campaign against cultural figures, which now continued in the same way against historians, physiologists, geneticists and, finally, even against linguists.

A glorification of Russia coincided with this cultural purge. Russians, who made up about one-half of the population, were designated as the leading people. Russian was proclaimed to be the world language of socialism and a great many treatises attempted to produce evidence that all discoveries had been made by Russians. The history of the non-Russian peoples was almost completely rewritten in the years between 1948 and 1953. Freedom fighters who had struggled against Russian czarism and had been portrayed as progressives until then, were discredited as foreign agents. Even the medieval epics and heroic songs of the non-Russian peoples were condemned as anti-Russian, foreign and harmful,

the United States. The Polish and Czechoslovakian governments, which at first had wanted to take part in the Marshall Plan, were compelled to withdraw.

At the end of September 1947 a conference of all the communist parties of Eastern Europe, plus France and Italy, took place in Poland, at which Zhdanov announced that the world was split into two camps. On one side stood the camp of imperialism, under the leadership of the United States, while on the other side was the 'democratic camp,' led by the Soviet Union. At the termination of the conference a Communist Information Bureau (COMINFORM) was founded with the clear goal of subordinating the communist parties of Eastern Europe to Moscow's leadership, of eliminating all autonomous forces in these lands and so attempting to control Yugoslavia.

Shortly thereafter the fifth conference of the council of foreign ministers in London – which was to discuss the problem of Germany – ended in sharp debates, and negotiations were broken off. This signified the end of the cooperation between the West and the Soviet Union that had been forged during World War II.

A hardening of the line occurred in the countries of Eastern Europe from the beginning of 1948. In February 1948 Czechoslovakia experienced a governmental crisis, and all non-communist elements were expelled from the government and administration. The Soviet Union was simultaneously preparing a campaign against Yugoslavia. The Yugoslav communists had gained power in the course of their own revolution and had refused to accept Soviet attempts at hegemony without opposition. After a long exchange of letters between Moscow and Belgrade, in the course of which the Kremlin had, with increasing acerbity, made a series of unjustified accusations against Yugoslavia, a Cominform

resolution against the Yugoslav communists was published on 28 June 1948. The Yugoslav party members were called upon to overthrow their party leadership and install an 'internationalist' – that is, pro-Soviet – leadership. The alternative, which Stalin had apparently considered impossible, occurred: the Communist Party of Yugoslavia rejected the Cominform Resolution on 30 June. With that Yugoslavia stood outside of the Eastern Bloc and began to take its own, independent road, which differed clearly from the Stalinist model.

The situation in Berlin became critical at the

and the conquest of non-Russian territories by the czars, which had led to the oppression of the peoples of the Caucasus and of Central Asia, was called progressive.

This rise of great-Russian chauvinism was very closely linked with a movement against 'rootless cosmopolitans:' Jewish intellectuals were sharply attacked and not infrequently arrested. Jewish cultural institutions were suppressed, publications in Yiddish were forbidden, the Yiddish theater was closed, discrimination was exercised against all Jewish citizens applying to the universities and for all important posts – and in 1950 several prominent Jews were arrested on the pretext that they had planned to make the Crimea a homeland for Jews. Another great wave of arrests which followed in Georgia at the end of 1951 was attributed to 'bourgeois nationalism.'

The development in Eastern Europe from 1948 to 1953 was characterized by an open Stalinization: the system of each country was assimilated step by step to the Stalinist system of the Soviet Union, and simultaneously the economy and the political and military structures of each country were completely subordinated to the USSR. In the course of 1948 the social democratic parties in all Eastern European countries were forced to unite with the communist parties. The newly formed united parties now exercised total power, and at the same time a bureaucratic, centralized system of oppression was organized within each party according to the Soviet example. The concept of the different ways to socialism was condemned in the fall of 1948 as hostile to the Party, and it was declared in December 1948 that a people's democracy – originally conceived as an intermediate form between Western democracy and the Soviet system – was the political form of the dictatorship of the proletariat and was therefore ideologically equated wih the Soviet system.

The offensive against Yugoslavia was another element of this policy. The Kremlin attempted, by breaking all treaties and agreements with Yugoslavia, by an almost complete economic blockade, by a wave of border incidents and a forceful anti-Yugoslav press and radio campaign in all the lands of Eastern Europe, to hinder Yugoslavia's independent development and to neutralize Yugoslavia's power to stimulate forces in Eastern Europe which would press for liberalization and autonomy. Yet the campaign against Yugoslavia

ended in defeat. The Yugoslav communists departed from Stalinism step by step, began to decentralize the economy and the government and established workers' councils in all factories and businesses in the summer of 1950. The centralized bureaucratic planning system was replaced by a modern system of coordination.

From 1949 on even Communist Party members in Eastern Europe were seized in mass arrests in an attempt to limit the radiating influence of Yugoslav's development. The arrests – similar to those during the Great Purge in the Soviet Union in the 1930s – were linked with the show trials of prominent communist leaders: the show trials of Kochi Xoxe in Albania (May 1949), Laszlo Rajk in Hungary (September 1949), Traicho Kostov in Bulgaria (December 1949), the arrest of the Polish Party leader Wladislaw Gomulka (February 1951) and the Rudolph Slansky trial in Czechoslovakia (December 1952) served not only to eliminate all leaders and groups which possibly sought greater independence from the Soviet Union and greater liberalization of the system, but simultaneously sought to create an atmosphere of fear and suspicion among the masses which would neutralize all sense of cohesion among the populace, party leaders and functionaries.

The Soviet Union and the East

While Moscow was solidifying its hegemony in Eastern Europe, the Chinese communists, led by Mao Tse-tung (Mao Zedong), succeeded in bringing their revolution to a victorious end and seizing power in China. Although the leaders of the Communist Party of China officially swore their loyalty to the Soviet Union and to Stalin, there had already been many conflicts and differences of opinion between the Russians and the Chinese at the beginning of the 1940s. With the triumph of the Chinese communists, who proclaimed the People's Republic of China on 1 October 1949, the USSR faced for the first time the problem of establishing relations with another major communist power. After long negotiations between Mao Tse-tung and the Soviet leaders, a 30-year agreement of friendship and mutual aid between the USSR and the People's Republic of China was signed in Moscow on 14 February 1950. The Russians promised to renounce their special privileges in the harbors of Port Arthur and Lüta (Dairen), as well as on the Manchurian railroad, by the end of

1952 and granted the Chinese credits totaling $300 million.

At the end of June 1950, North Korean troops loyal to the Soviet Union broke through the line of demarcation at the 38th parallel and advanced rapidly into South Korea: the Korean War had begun. But the North Koreans did not gain the quick victory which they hoped would put all of Korea in communist hands. After early successes on the North Korean side, United Nations forces, in which American troops played the major role, launched a counteroffensive in September 1950 which forced the North Koreans to retreat. Under Soviet pressure the People's Republic of China sent 'volunteer units' into the struggle, but even the Chinese attack did not produce victory. Military operations in Korea were ended in July 1951, and negotiations were begun in Panmunjom.

The failure in Korea brought about a certain change in Soviet foreign policy. The prospects for revolutions in France and Italy had disappeared in the interim, and the campaign against Yugoslavia had failed. An aggressive Soviet foreign policy had only produced resistance in the West, American rearmament, the formation of NATO and European integration. Under these conditions it became clear at the end of 1951 that Stalin wanted a breathing spell.

As a result, during the period from the end of 1951 into 1952 more moderate traits became apparent in Soviet foreign policy. On 10 March 1952 the Soviet government directed a note to the Western powers suggesting a peace treaty with Germany on the basis of the Potsdam agreement. Germany was to receive a single, all-German government and its own, limited, armed forces. In three subsequent letters the Russians expressed their desire to create a unified, neutral Germany. It was with similar intentions that a world economic conference was convened in Moscow in April 1952.

Behind this more moderate foreign policy Stalin was preparing a massive new purge within the Soviet Union. Stalin's autocratic power had reached its zenith between 1948 and 1953. Not a single Party Congress had taken place since 1939. Party conferences and meetings of the Central Committee were very rare, and even the Politburo, the highest center of power in the country, was no longer regularly convened. Not only the glorification of Stalin but also his growing mistrust, even

Left: Laszlo Rajk, Hungarian interior minister, on trial in September 1949 charged with espionage and treachery. His real offense was being a 'national communist,' too independent of Moscow for Stalin's taste.

Below left: North Koreans carry portraits of Stalin and Korean communist leader Kim il-Sung through the streets of Pyongyang. Right up to his death, Stalin remained a symbol of freedom and justice to many people throughout the world.

Right: Nikita Khrushchev on a visit to Czechoslovakia in 1957 – a year after his denunciation of Stalin's 'Cult of Personality' at the Twentieth Party Congress.

toward his closest colleagues, far surpassed anything seen during the 1930s.

After an interval of more than 13 years, the Nineteenth Party Congress was finally convened at the beginning of October 1952. Stalin, then almost 73 years old, limited himself to a short concluding statement. The main speech was given by Georgi Malenkov, who appeared to be the most probable successor to Stalin. The Congress was clearly marked by the preparation for a new purge; even before the Congress had been convened the number of arrests had noticeably increased, along with a wave of fear and hysteria. At the Congress itself Malenkov came out against the 'carelessness' of the Party apparatus and reproached the delegates for having relaxed their vigilance and for having forgotten that the 'enemies of the Soviet State are persistently trying to smuggle in their agents.'

The Politburo, renamed the 'Presidium' of the Party, was increased from 11 to 25 members. Apparently Stalin wanted to eliminate a number of older Politburo members – especially Molotov, Klimenti Voroshilov, Anastas Mikoyan and later others – in order to rely more heavily on younger, less experienced members, who would praise him in every respect.

The number of arrests increased tremendously after the Nineteenth Party Congress. Death sentences were passed against economic functionaries in the Ukraine, most of them Jewish. The press spoke about vigilance almost uninterruptedly, and in the middle of December *Pravda* demanded that vigilance should extend to the members of one's own family. After this ideological preparation an alleged plot of Kremlin doctors was announced on 13 June 1952: nine famous doctors (of whom seven were Jews) who had worked

in the clinic in the Kremlin were accused of having killed several well-known Soviet leaders, including Zhdanov. These doctors had allegedly planned to kill other members of the government and high military leaders on orders from the American and British secret services, as well as from the Jewish organization 'Joint.'

After the discovery of the alleged doctors' plot Stalin's announcements from 1937 were quoted with increasing frequency, thereby underlining the analogy to the Great Purge. The Soviet press not only attacked Soviet citizens of Jewish origin, but also economic administrators and increasing numbers of intellectuals. Soon the accusations even spread to government and Party functionaries. All signs pointed to another major purge that would spare not even the highest leaders in the country.

In the midst of this campaign the Soviet press announced the illness and finally the death of Stalin on 5 March 1953. Although all official announcements declared that Stalin had been a gifted follower of Lenin, a wise leader and teacher of the Communist Party and of the Soviet people, it was noticed that the funeral ceremonies were reduced to a minimum and that not a single leading member of the Party published an article commemorating Stalin.

De-Stalinization and Khrushchev

With Stalin's death the remaining leaders in the Kremlin were freed from the immediate threat of death, but they faced a great number of problems. Reforms were necessary, since Stalin's system was in complete contradiction to the new conditions and social forces which had arisen. The Soviet Union had developed from a backward, agricultural country to a powerful industrial nation. The

number of factory and office workers had increased from 10.8 million in the 1920s to 47.9 million in the 1950s. The number of specialists with university training had increased from 233,000 to 2.2 million. The number of urban residents had risen from 26.3 million in 1926 to 87 million. The system that Stalin's successors had acquired had to be accommodated to the new conditions and demands of society, and a hard struggle ensued over the question of what reforms were necessary, to what degree and at what speed and under whose leadership they should be accomplished. This struggle was carried out on the level of political differences and internal struggles for power among the remaining leaders.

Immediately after Stalin's death it was necessary to reorganize the leadership: the Presidium which Stalin had expanded was again reduced to 10 members, and a collective leadership was proclaimed, although dominated by Malenkov, the Chairman of the Council of Ministers. Among the other leaders Malenkov's two representatives, Molotov (the Foreign Minister) and Lavrenti Beria (the Minister of the Interior), played decisive roles, while Nikita Khrushchev was elected head of the Secretariat of the Central Committee a few days later and thereby held the leading position in the Communist Party of the Soviet Union.

The domestic political line also changed after Stalin's death. The purge, which was already gathering momentum, was suddenly stopped. At the beginning of April the arrested Kremlin doctors were freed and rehabilitated. The organs of the secret police were openly attacked, and the new slogan of 'socialist legality' was proclaimed. A 'thaw' occurred in cultural affairs. The dismissal and arrest of Beria, who had been at the head of the Soviet secret police for 15 years, followed at

Far left: Lavrenti Beria, Stalin's powerful secret police chief, who was executed in 1953 after losing the post-Stalin power-struggle.

Left: West German Chancellor Konrad Adenauer (left), invited for discussions with the Soviet Union.

Right: Khrushchev (right) and Bulganin (center) visit India in 1955, showing a new Soviet interest in the Third World.

Below right: The Soviet leaders in Yugoslavia, restoring links with Stalin's arch-enemy Tito.

the end of June 1953. After the downfall of Beria – who was shot in December 1953 – the secret police was, to a certain extent, stripped of power. Conditions in the concentration camps were improved; the feared special courts were dissolved; high secret police officers and camp commandants were dismissed and some arrested; the small industries under the control of the secret police were put under the relevant economic ministries; and an increasing number of prisoners were released from the camps.

An even further departure from Stalinism followed at the beginning of August 1953, when Malenkov announced a far-reaching program which was to drastically increase the production of consumer goods, replacing the constant priority given by Stalin to heavy industry. A few weeks later, at a plenary session of the Central Committee, farms were to be strengthened by an increase in agricultural experts, their deliveries to the state were to be decreased and the purchase price for their produce was considerably raised. Especially important was the change in attitudes in the cultural sphere. Writers and artists, although still under Party control, received considerably more freedom than under Stalin. More books from the West were translated, and Soviet authors were permitted to criticize (circumspectly, to be sure) the Stalinist past in their writings. Books forbidden under Stalin could now appear. Even the style of leadership began to change. Whereas Stalin had lived hermetically sealed in the Kremlin, the new leaders traveled to various parts of the Soviet Union, met with medium and lower functionaries and visited local Party conferences.

A similar change from Stalin's policies occurred in the field of foreign policy. The outlines remained the same: the goal of the Soviet leaders was, as always, to defend and extend the bases of Soviet power, to weaken the Western military alliance and to exploit the contradictions and opposition within this alliance for the benefit of the Soviet Union. Yet the Soviet leaders after Stalin's death were intent on freeing the USSR from its political isolation and on regaining the international contacts unnecessarily broken off by Stalin.

This more realistic attitude and more moderate tone were the prelude to the Soviet participation in the Four Power Conference in Berlin in early 1954, at which the reunification of Germany was the central issue. A reunification could not be achieved, but a series of Soviet communiqués in

1954 were proof that the USSR did not want to burn its bridges to the West. Consequently, the Russians took part at the two international conferences in Geneva in April and June 1954, which were devoted to the problems of Korea and Indochina. At the same time Moscow stepped up its efforts in the question of Germany. In order to prevent the Federal Republic of Germany from joining the Western military alliance, the Soviet Union repeatedly declared that it was ready to recommence the discussions on elections for all of Germany. But the Soviet attitude toward Germany changed after the treaty of Paris between the Federal Republic of Germany and the Western powers was ratified on 22 February 1955. From then on the theory of two nations – which required that all negotiations take place between East and West Germany – became an unchanging part of Soviet policy on Germany.

Things went differently in Austria. In the middle of May 1955 the USSR declared that it was ready, after long years of negotiations, to sign an international treaty with Austria. All foreign occupation troops, including Soviet, would be withdrawn, and Austria would receive its independence as a neutral country.

The Russians' desire to negotiate with the West was again expressed at the summit conference in Geneva on 18-23 July 1955. Yet the unusually friendly atmosphere could not hide the fact that only vague and very generally formulated conclusions were reached regarding the main topics on the agenda: Germany, European security, disarmament and improvement of East-West relations. On the other hand, the Soviet invitation to Chancellor Adenauer indicated that the Soviet leaders were interested in normalizing their relations with West Germany. These negotiations were ended in the middle of September 1955 with the release of German prisoners of war and the establishment of diplomatic relations between Bonn and Moscow. Within the framework of this diplomatic activity an agreement with Finland was finally reached at the beginning of 1956 which provided for the withdrawal of Soviet troops from the military base at Porkkala, which the Russians had occupied since the end of the war.

An increase in Soviet activity in the developing countries of Asia and Africa was also apparent after Stalin's death. Whereas Stalin had hardly recognized the importance of the decolonization and development of new countries, Soviet diplomacy was now characterized not only by greater

activity, but also by greater differentiation. The leaders of the developing countries – including Nehru, Nasser and Sukarno – who had been sharply criticized during the Stalin period, were now seen in a more positive light. Nasser's trip to the Soviet Union in the summer of 1955, the sale of weapons made in communist countries to the United Arab Republic in the fall and the trip by Khrushchev and Bulganin to India, Burma and Indonesia at the end of 1955 illustrated this increase in Soviet interest. This was also underlined by the constantly increasing number of Soviet technicians, advisers and economic experts and the new constructions aimed at increasing development.

COMECON and the Warsaw Pact

Finally, the post-Stalin leadership placed the relations between the Soviet Union and the rest of the socialist countries on a more equal basis and seemed – at least at the beginning – intent on taking the increasing influence of the other socialist countries more into consideration. The Council for Mutual Economic Assistance, founded in January 1949 and generally known in the West as COMECON, had been merely a Soviet trade organization under Stalin and had been intended solely to legalize the forced deliveries of products to the USSR. Now COMECON became the most important instrument of the economic integration advocated by the Soviet Union and of the 'division of labor' among the member nations. According to the Soviet aim, each COMECON member should specialize only in certain branches of the economy and industry which were the most advantageous to that country on the basis of its natural and industrial resources. The USSR was the sole land to claim the right to develop all branches of the economy and of its industry.

In a similar manner the Warsaw Pact, founded on 14 May 1955, was to effect greater military coordination. All member nations were represented in the leading committees, though the supreme command remained in the hands of the Russians. Regular political conferences and meetings, of the Communist Party leaders were to guarantee and strengthen political-ideological coordination.

The new Soviet leaders were also anxious to normalize relations with Yugoslavia by means of certain concessions, perhaps with the ulterior motive of gradually, and in a roundabout way, bringing Yugoslavia back into the 'socialist camp' under Moscow's leadership. At the end of May 1955 a Soviet delegation led by Khrushchev and Bulganin flew to Belgrade. Khrushchev apologized for the anti-Yugoslavia campaign (and thereby put the responsibility on Beria), and a final Soviet-Yugoslav communiqué confirmed each country's right to its own road to socialism – a doctrine that until then had been considered to be the worst heresy.

The new direction in Soviet domestic and foreign policy that had occurred between 1953 and 1956 was sanctioned by the Twentieth Party Congress (14-25 February 1956), where further measures toward de-Stalinization were announced. Stalin's reign of terror was now openly condemned, the suppression of creative activity, the atmosphere of lawlessness and despotism and Stalin's cult of personality were denounced. In order to overcome the cult of personality condemned people should continue to be rehabilitated, the secret police should be put under the control of the Party and government and reforms in the state, Party and economy should be initiated.

At the same time Khrushchev announced a series of new international concepts to the Party Congress. According to Khrushchev, the thesis of the 'inevitability of war' (which had been expounded by Lenin as well as by Stalin) no longer corresponded to current conditions, since it was possible to prevent wars from being unleashed. The new doctrine of the 'non-inevitability of wars' formed the foundation for the Soviet doctrine of coexistence, according to which countries with different social systems could not only exist next to one another but should even aspire to an improvement of relations and collaboration. However this policy of coexistence was to be limited to the sphere of government and diplomacy. Competition would occur between the two systems in the economic field, and the ideological struggle had to be continued unchecked because, according to Khrushchev, 'the ideas of Marxism-Leninism are more and more capturing the minds of broad masses of the working people in the capitalist countries.'

The departure from Stalinism that occurred at the Twentieth Party Congress was greatly increased by a report delivered by Khrushchev at a closed session on the morning of 25 February entitled 'The Cult of Personality and its Consequences,' known as Khrushchev's 'secret speech.' With a frankness that had long ago disappeared from Party life, he spoke of Lenin's 'testament,' of Stalin's role in the Great Purge, of Stalin's disregard for the warnings of a German attack on 22 June 1941 and of his military mistakes during the war. Stalin's method of rule, his greed for power, his despotism, his orders to have himself glorified, his preparation for a new great purge at the

beginning of the 1950s and his instruction to use torture to force prisoners to make confessions – all this was described in detail by Khrushchev, using specific facts and incidents.

Khrushchev neither mentioned the circumstances of Stalin's rise to power and the origin of Stalinism, nor the co-responsibility of the top leaders then in office – including Khrushchev himself. He concentrated, above all, on Stalin as a person and on his method of rule, not on any serious analysis of the Stalinist system. Thus Khrushchev, reaching the end of his report, proposed no fundamental measures for overcoming Stalinism, but limited himself to corrections intended solely to minimize the excesses the system might produce. In spite of these limitations, the Twentieth Party Congress and the 'secret speech' were of tremendous importance. For the first time the Soviet leadership itself had given the impetus to depart from Stalinism in various spheres of public life.

In the middle of April 1956 the COMINFORM, created by Stalin in September 1947, was dissolved. The destruction of the Stalin myth as well as the new concept of the different ways to socialism and the dissolution of the COMINFORM aroused all the forces in Eastern Europe which supported greater independence from Moscow and a democratization of the system. In Poland workers rebeled in Poznan in May 1956. Though the uprising was suppressed, it strengthened the reform movement, even among the leaders. At the decisive eighth plenary session of the Polish Central Committee (20-21 October 1956) Gomulka, who had been arrested during the Stalin era and later rehabilitated, was elected head of the Party. Marshal Konstantin Rokossovsky of the Soviet Union was relieved of his duties as Polish Minister of Defense and returned to the USSR. The majority of collective farms which had been created by force were disbanded, and workers' councils sprang up in factories. Surprisingly open and critical discussions occurred in various branches of public life, including the press and radio. It seemed that the Stalinists had suffered a final defeat and that a new, freer model of socialism would emerge.

The Hungarian uprising

Sharp debates also occurred in Hungary after the Twentieth Party Congress between the dictatorial Stalinist forces and the reformists, who supported Imre Nagy in their drive for democratization. On 23 October 1956 several hundred thousand people in Budapest, inspired by the 'Polish October,' gathered at the statue of General Bem, who had commanded the Hungarian revolutionary army against the Russians in 1848. They declared their solidarity with the Polish reformers and demanded independence, democratization, freedom of press, condemnation of all Stalinist leaders, withdrawal of Soviet troops and the appointment of Imre Nagy as leader of the Party and government. When the officials of the secret police opened fire on the demonstrators the originally peaceful demonstration turned into a rebellion.

The Hungarians responded to the limited deployment of Soviet troops by creating revolutionary committees throughout the country. Factories were taken over by workers and workers' councils were formed. Two-thirds of the collective farms which had been forcibly created were disbanded, and when the Hungarian army went over to the side of the revolutionaries, the rebellion had been won.

At noon on 30 October the government of Imre Nagy declared that one-party rule was abolished. The revolutionary committees and the workers' councils were recognized. The government began negotiating on the withdrawal of Soviet troops, and Hungary announced that it was neutral and was withdrawing from the Warsaw Pact.

On the morning of 4 November Budapest was surrounded by three Soviet army corps, and the Hungarian revolution collapsed after bloody fighting. The new pro-Soviet government was directed by Janos Kadar, who had been tried and sentenced during the Stalin era. Imre Nagy was

arrested and shot on 17 June 1958, and 200,000 Hungarians fled abroad.

The 'Polish October' and especially the Hungarian revolution violently shook Soviet hegemony in Eastern Europe and in the entire world communist movement. Conservative elements placed the blame on Khrushchev, and sharp political debates followed among the leaders in the Kremlin. An important event in domestic politics occurred on top of this. In March 1957 Khrushchev, apparently against the wishes of a portion of the top leaders, announced a broad reorganization of the Soviet economic system. According to his plan, the more than 30 centralized economic ministries were to be dissolved, and the direction and control of the

economy would be transferred to local economic councils which were to be formed and which would be responsible for their geographically limited regions at all times. But Khrushchev was opposed not only by the conservative ex-Stalinists such as Molotov and Lazar Kaganovich, but also by the representatives of the economic and government bureaucracies such as Malenkov and Nikolai Bulganin.

At a meeting of the Party Presidium the majority of the members demanded that Khrushchev be dismissed from his post and degraded to Minister of Agriculture. (Molotov was to be First Secretary of the Party and Malenkov Chairman of the Council of Ministers.) But at a later meeting of the

Above: Soviet tanks roll through the streets of Budapest during the Hungarian crisis of November 1956. The violent repression of the Hungarian uprising revealed the narrow limits of liberalization acceptable under the successors of Stalin.

Left: Hungarian refugees anxiously wait for a train to take them across the border to Austria. Over 200,000 fled to the West in the wake of the uprising.

Right: West Berliners gather in Bernauerstrasse to try to make contact with friends or relatives on the other side of the Berlin Wall.

Central Committee Khrushchev succeeded in gaining a majority and in excluding Molotov, Malenkov and Kaganovich from all leading committees of the Party and government for supposedly having formed an 'anti Party group.' The Presidium was filled with followers of Khrushchev, including Leonid Brezhnev, who up to that time, as Party Secretary of the Kazakhstan Republic, had vigorously supported Khrushchev's virgin lands program.

Khrushchev, having emerged victorious from this struggle for power, was strong enough to remove Marshal Zhukov at the end of October 1957; the latter had utilized the conflicts within the political leadership to acquire a certain amount of autonomy for the armed forces and the right to participate in making decisions. Finally in March 1958 Bulganin, who had supported the 'anti-Party group,' was released from his duties as Chairman of the Council of Ministers.

Khrushchev himself took on the job of head of the Soviet government, so that now, like Stalin in 1941, he combined the leadership of the Party and of the government in his hands. But this comparison was merely external. The Soviet Union at the beginning of the 1960s, in the process of becoming a modern, industrial nation and shaken by the Twentieth Party Congress, could not be compared to the Soviet Union of the Stalin era, and Khrushchev's authority was far from absolute.

Khrushchev's greatest weakness lay in his tendency constantly to overestimate Soviet power and underestimate the difficulties and opposing forces which he faced. This was not limited to Soviet domestic politics, but also became apparent during these years in the field of international politics. The last years of the Khrushchev period were marked by repeated attempts to make a 'breakthrough' in relations with the Western powers. At the same time, the Russians found themselves faced with an increasing conflict in

Sino-Soviet relations, the degree and importance of which was, at the beginning, greatly underestimated by all the Soviet leaders and certainly by Khrushchev. Consequently, from 1958 there was a new dimension in Soviet foreign policy. Alongside the changing relations with the West and the gradually rising influence of the third world, the Sino-Soviet conflict became a decisive problem for the leaders in the Kremlin.

As early as March 1956, the leaders of the Communist Party of China had protested, in a secret letter which was later published in Peking, against the new concepts announced at the Twentieth Congress of the CPSU, and they demanded that in the future new concepts could only be announced after discussion with the Communist Party of China. The differences between the views of Khrushchev and those of the Chinese leaders were clearly expressed at the World Communist Conference in Moscow in November 1957, the last conference convened by Moscow in which Mao participated. Khrushchev and the other Soviet leaders were ready and willing to assert the strengthened position of the Soviet Union, but at the same time they recognized the danger of a nuclear war and advocated a policy of the non-inevitability of war and of coexistence. The Chinese communists, on the contrary, declared that the atom bomb was a 'paper tiger,' upheld Lenin's thesis of the inevitability of war and advocated a changeover to a revolutionary offensive ('the East Wind prevails over the West Wind').

In addition, the Chinese communists had, since the spring of 1958, increasingly freed their own domestic development from the example of the USSR. Peking announced the 'Great Leap Forward' to boost industrialization quickly, and in the summer and fall of 1958 'People's Communes' were established in China, by means of which Peking hoped to shorten the road to the final goal of communism. This was important for the Sino-Soviet conflict because the Chinese communists were ready to claim the leadership of the world communist movement if China became the first country to reach the final goal of communism. This increasing independence in China's domestic and foreign policies led to a sharpening of Sino-Soviet tensions. In May 1959 the USSR ceased its military support of China.

Foreign policy failures

Nor did Khrushchev achieve the desired breakthrough in his relations with the West. Apparently overestimating his chances, he had switched to an aggressive foreign policy in the summer of 1958. A clear sign of the change was Khrushchev's ultimatum regarding Berlin in November 1958, in which he demanded that Berlin should be declared a 'free, demilitarized' city, which meant, in effect, the withdrawal of all Western forces. Khrushchev set a deadline of six months, until May 1959, for the Western powers to reach an agreement with the Soviet Union. In case these negotiations were rejected, Khrushchev threatened to conclude a separate peace treaty with East Germany.

The West, however, stood fast, and Khrushchev was forced to modify his ultimatum. The deadline was first extended to one year, then to eighteen months and was finally dropped altogether. At this same time the foreign ministers of the four powers met in Geneva (11 May-20 June and 30 July-5 August 1959), but unity could not be achieved on the Berlin ultimatum or on a possible summit conference.

In the spring and summer of 1959 the Soviet leaders seemed to have recognized that a direct

breakthrough in the field of foreign policy was not possible. This was part of the reason for the postponement of the deadline of the Berlin ultimatum and for the meeting between Khrushchev and President Eisenhower at Camp David. But the hopes aroused by the meeting (the 'spirit of Camp David') were ephemeral: after the U-2 incident at the beginning of May 1960 – the shooting down of an American spy plane in the vicinity of Sverdlovsk – East-West relations began to deteriorate. In May 1960 Khrushchev walked out of the summit conference in Paris which had been prepared for so long, and in October 1960 he demanded that the General Secretary of the United Nations should be replaced by a three-man committee ('troika') which would be composed of one representative from the Western countries, one from the communist countries and one from the neutral countries. Later, after the failure of the US-sponsored Bay of Pigs invasion of Cuba, Khrushchev concluded that new concessions could be acquired from the West by means of resoluteness and a still harder attitude. After the meeting between Khrushchev and President Kennedy in Vienna (4 June 1961) the Soviet defense budget was considerably increased and in the night of 12-13 August the Berlin Wall was built. Linked with that was a Soviet protest against the 'misuse of the air corridors to Berlin,' which was intended to paralyze civilian air traffic between West Germany and West Berlin. Yet by the late fall of 1961 it had already become clear that this new hard-line policy had no real chance of success.

Relations between the Soviet Union and China continued to worsen during the same period from 1960 to 1961. In July and August 1960 the USSR, without previous notice, withdrew all technicians, engineers and specialists from China, canceled a great many treaties and agreements and reduced its economic aid to China to an absolute minimum. At the subsequent World Communist Conference (10 November-2 December 1960), attended by representatives of 81 communist parties, further sharp debates occurred between Khrushchev and the Chinese leaders. Irritatingly for Khrushchev, the Chinese were supported by a few other delegations, notably by the Albanians. The Soviet Union withdrew from its military bases in Albania in the spring of 1961, but even after relations between the Soviet Union and Albania were broken off in October 1961 Albania remained loyal to its new Chinese ally.

In view of the Soviet difficulties with foreign politics Khrushchev again began to concentrate on domestic politics. The draft of the new Soviet Party Program was announced at the end of June 1961 and was passed a few months later at the Twenty-second Party Congress in October. It was announced in this overoptimistic Party Program that the Soviet Union would surpass the United States in production per capita by 1970 and would be the country with the shortest working day in the entire world. In the following decade, from 1970 to 1980, the Party Program announced that the transition to the final phase of communism would occur. Before 1980 not only would education in all institutions and all medical treatment (including treatment in sanatoriums) be free of charge, but rents would disappear and all important community services (water, gas, heating), the use of public transportation and the main meal every day in all factories, offices and firms would be free.

The Twenty-second Party Congress was not limited to ratifying the Party Program. A new break with Stalinism which went far beyond that of the Twentieth Party Congress was declared. Earlier reports of Stalin's terror were filled in with

exert pressure on the United States and improve the Soviet bargaining position *vis-à-vis* the West, especially regarding Berlin. The first Russian missile-carrying ships arrived in Cuba at the beginning of July 1962. The American government learned, toward the middle of October 1962, by means of reconnaissance planes, that the rockets being delivered had a range of 1100 to 1250 miles.

President Kennedy's response – the announcement of a quarantine against Cuba and further measures – compeled Khrushchev to give in. The Soviet ships loaded with rockets and bound for Cuba received instructions to change their course. Khrushchev's attempt to exchange the Soviet bases in Cuba for NATO bases in Turkey was rejected by Kennedy, and on 28 October 1962 Khrushchev announced that he agreed to withdraw all offensive weapons from Cuba as long as the Americans promised not to invade the island. Now Khrushchev returned to a policy of dialog with Washington.

One step along this road to dialog was the installation of a direct telephone line between the Kremlin and the White House, the so-called 'hot line' (June 1963). The culmination of this trend was reached with the signing of the nuclear test ban treaty at the beginning of August 1963. The fact that Khrushchev had backed down in Cuba was of course applauded by peace-loving people in the world and in the Soviet Union itself, but the 'hawks' in the USSR had acquired yet another argument to use as ammunition against the leader of the Soviet Communist Party and government.

The improvement of relations with the West only produced a sharpening of the Sino-Soviet conflict. The Soviet attempt in the spring of 1963 to arrange a summit conference between the Russians and the Chinese failed. After a long and somewhat grotesque exchange of letters between Moscow and Peking regarding the location of the

more details. In the eyes of the entire populace it seemed that a final break with Stalinism had been made, and new hopes for reforms which would lead to a freer development in the Soviet Union were aroused. The decision was reached at the Congress to remove Stalin's embalmed corpse from the Lenin Mausoleum and to rename all cities and villages which had borne Stalin's name, including Stalingrad. All this was, to be sure, well received by progressive and liberal forces in Soviet

society, but it caused Khrushchev increasing difficulties with the doctrinaire, pro-Stalinist elements in the Party apparatus, the secret police and the army.

Now success abroad seemed even more necessary for Khrushchev. Since the fall of 1961 the Russians had had the possibility of using Cuba as a base for their foreign policy goals. Now the Soviet leaders hoped, by stationing rockets on Cuba, only 150 miles from American territory, to

Above left: Soviet troops stationed on the remote eastern border with China scramble eagerly for letters from home. As relations between China and the Soviet Union deteriorated in the 1960s, the border became a potential flashpoint of conflict.

Left: One of the American spyplane photos of Soviet missile sites in Cuba which sparked the dangerous crisis of October 1962.

Above right: Leonid Brezhnev (right) and Aleksei Kosygin, joint Soviet leaders after the fall of Khrushchev, exchange a rare joke.

Right: Andrei Sinyavski, one of many dissident writers persecuted by the Soviet authorities as the relatively liberal cultural policy of the Khrushchev era was reversed.

conference, the agenda and the number of participants, Peking announced its '25 Point Program' in the middle of June 1963. In this document the Chinese accused the Russians of revisionism and great-power chauvinism and attacked Soviet foreign and domestic policies in the sharpest possible way. After the publication of the '25 Point Program,' which was banned in the USSR and the Warsaw Pact countries, hopes for a Sino-Soviet summit conference declined even farther. When the negotiations between the Russians and the Chinese finally did take place in Moscow (5-20 July 1963), they were broken off without any agreement having been reached. With that, Moscow and Peking opposed each other as two centers of world communism, each accusing the other of dreadful deviations and crimes. For some of Russia's European satellites this unedifying quarrel between the two leading communist states seemed to present an opportunity for asserting a somewhat more independent position. Rumania especially was able to make use of this opportunity, and after 1962 succeeded in gaining a considerable degree of autonomy.

In spite of the seriousness of Khrushchev's failures with the Chinese, his position was, in the final analysis, most seriously undermined by his failures in the field of domestic politics. The contrast between his overoptimistic economic goals and the realities of economic development became more and more glaring, and Khrushchev's responses were ever more hectic. He focused on trying to correct the organization of the system, whereas in reality only fundamental changes in the system itself could have helped. Almost every month new government agencies were created or old ones reorganized. Finally, in the fall of 1962 Khrushchev divided the entire Party apparatus into industrial and agricultural sections in the hope of eliminating the differential between the actual economic development and the economic goals which had been set too high. But the decline of the annual growth rate in industry from 11 percent to 5.8 percent between 1961 and 1963, combined with the bad harvest in 1963, which forced the Soviet Union to import 12 million tons of grain from the West, showed clearly how little Khrushchev's passion for reorganization had contributed to a solution of real problems.

Khrushchev's frenetic manner, his mistakes, the fact that the economy was lagging behind, the crisis in agriculture, the increasing conflict with Peking – all led to suspicion, bitterness and opposition in the leading organs of the Party, government, army and secret police. To be sure, Khrushchev was awarded the golden star of a 'Hero of the Soviet Union' on his seventieth birthday on 17 April 1964. Leonid Brezhnev, who presented the awards, praised Khrushchev with enthusiastic words, embraced him according to Russian tradition and kissed him three times on the cheek. Six months later, on 14 October 1964, Khrushchev was removed from the leading organs of the Party and forcibly retired.

The Brezhnev period

The speed and ease with which the First Secretary of the Party and the Chairman of the Council of Ministers was removed in the middle of October 1964 imply that a broad consensus existed at the top of the Soviet political hierarchy. The desire for more orderly relations and more rational methods of leadership must have been shared by all the decisive elements in the government and Party. Yet profound differences of opinion still existed about what political course should be followed next, and especially about whether some milder form of Khrushchev's de-Stalinizing policy should be continued or whether there should be a change to a harder line, a reestablishment of authority and a return to a diluted form of Stalinism.

The principle of collective leadership was proclaimed immediately after Khrushchev's downfall, just as it had been after Stalin's death in March 1953. Of the 11 members of the Politburo who assumed the leadership in October 1964 the First Secretary of the Party, Leonid Brezhnev, and the head of the government, Aleksei Kosygin, stood equally in the foreground at the beginning.

Khrushchev was 70 when he was removed from power, Brezhnev 58 and Kosygin 60, but in contrast to Khrushchev, who had vivid memories of the period before the revolution – he had worked as a shepherd, a herdsman and a day-laborer and had participated as a Red Army soldier in the Civil War – the Revolution and Civil War were only episodes from history books for his successors. Brezhnev and Kosygin had both received university degrees in engineering in the early 1930s and had been managers of factories until

1938, when, after the end of the Great Purge, they started their careers in the Soviet bureaucratic apparatus. Brezhnev's career had been made primarily in the Party apparatus, whereas Kosygin's career had been made primarily in the government apparatus.

In the first weeks after the removal of Khrushchev an important change occurred in the methods of leadership: Khrushchev's mania for improvised reorganizations was officially denounced, and the new leaders promised that in the future all flaws would be rationally analyzed, that their efforts would be concentrated on fulfilling short-run tasks and that conclusions would be reached which were in accordance with written statutes and which responded to real needs. This style of leadership – sober, stolid, conservative and increasingly inflexible and unimaginative – was to be the predominant style for the next 20 years.

In the first months after Khrushchev's downfall, approximately from October 1964 to the late spring of 1965, it seemed that the Soviet leaders were intent on achieving a policy of 'Khrushchevism without Khrushchev,' a continuation of the same reforms in a calmer, soberer, more rational and more realistic manner. But from the spring of 1965 a harder line was noticeable in domestic politics. Conservative elements grouped around Brezhnev in the Party apparatus, the army and the secret police succeeded in gaining the upper hand, and instead of the Brezhnev-Kosygin duumvirate, Brezhnev alone appeared more and more clearly as the 'first among equals.' Criticism of Stalin was first toned down and shortly thereafter almost completely eliminated. On the occasion of the 20th anniversary of the victory in World War II in May 1965 Stalin was guardedly praised by Brezhnev. That summer a drive was started to raise the defense budget, and in the fall of 1965 the first arrests of liberal intellectuals occurred in the Ukraine, Moscow and Leningrad. Prisoners were no longer freed or rehabilitated, and the trial against the writers Sinyavsky and Daniel in February, 1966 – both were sentenced to severe punishments – was a depressing reminder of the Stalin era.

The harder line was confirmed at the Twenty-third Party Congress (29 March-8 April 1966), especially by the sharp attacks against liberal Soviet writers. The Presidium of the Party was renamed the Politburo – the name it had been given under Stalin until 1952 – and, of greater importance, Brezhnev, who until then had been the First Secretary of the Party, received the title of General Secretary, which only Stalin had held. In the realm of ideology it was significant that the concepts of the different ways to socialism and of a peaceful transition to socialism were not mentioned, and the doctrine of peaceful coexistence receded into the background. In essence the Party Congress, without directly rehabilitating Stalin, established a course of restoration that dominated Soviet domestic life until the mid 1980s. At this Congress the Soviet leaders clearly expressed their intention both to promote the modernization of the Soviet economy and to pull the reins tighter in the political, ideological and cultural areas.

In the summer of 1966 a large campaign was started for the military-cum-patriotic training of Soviet youth. Attacks on reformist intellectuals became sharper, and at the end of September 1966 additions were made to paragraph 190 of the criminal code, which now stipulated that all written and spoken remarks which disparaged the Soviet government or society would be punished with prison sentences of up to three years.

Intellectual repression

The general hardening of the line after the spring of 1965 led, in an increasing measure, to unrest among members of the Soviet intelligentsia. The arrests of writers and the trial of Sinyavsky and Daniel suggested the immediate threat of a re-Stalinization. There was a wave of protest letters signed not only by individuals but by entire groups. Solidarity with the arrested writers was not limited to members of the literary-cultural intelligentsia, but gradually spread to various groups of specialists and especially to natural scientists.

From the beginning of 1966 the number of illegal manuscripts passed from hand to hand grew rapidly, and the character of the manuscripts also changed. Alongside literary work political criticism and discussion began to play a major role. Soon the term *samizdat* (meaning 'self-published') came to be used for this illegally circulated literature, and by 1967 the word was so current that even the official press had to refer to it. Among the many *samizdat* publications the letter of the Soviet writer Alexander Solzhenitsyn, who had been imprisoned by Stalin, to the Fourth Congress of Writers at the end of May 1967 was especially influential. Solzhenitsyn demanded that censorsip be abolished, protested against the activities of the Soviet secret police and advocated an independent Soviet Writers' Union with complete artistic freedom. For this he was officially criticized; eventually he would be expeled from the USSR.

The Kremlin's intention to reverse the tide of de-Stalinization became especially clear during the celebration of the Fiftieth Anniversary of the October Revolution in 1967. During the entire year all public life in the USSR was marked by the preparations for this celebration. All public announcements refrained from any kind of criticism of Stalin or of the Stalin Period, and the Great Patriotic War was glorified as never before. The implied reevaluation of Stalin was of much greater importance than is generally assumed. By recoloring the Stalinist past and departing from the doctrines of de-Stalinization it became very clear that the regime was not concerned with changes and reforms and was much concerned with the maintenance and strengthening of power and authority. Soviet ideology would now

occupy itself with an increased struggle against deviations and the elimination of those who did not follow the Party line.

In April 1968 the *Chronicle of Current Events* began to appear in the Soviet Union. This journal, written by Soviet dissidents, was circulated clandestinely, passed from hand to hand. A few weeks later, in June, a memoir written by the nuclear physicist Andrei Sakharov entitled 'Progress, Coexistence and Intellectual Freedom' appeared. In this manifesto, which reflected the views of the reformist intelligentsia in the Soviet Union, Sakharov demanded that socialism be transformed again into an attractive force, the decisive precondition for which was the establishment of democratic freedoms and political reforms. Intellectual freedom was indispensable for an industrialized Soviet society if further progress was to be made. This manifesto also demanded merciless criticism of the Stalinist period, the rehabilitation of the victims of Stalinism, retrials for all political prisoners and the abolition of all laws and decrees contrary to human rights. Censorship should be ended, and a free discussion of all political and social ideas should be made possible. Sakharov also advocated economic reforms and said that the bureaucratic system should be replaced step by step by a socialist democracy. Lastly he said that in case the ruling Communist Party should prove to be incapable of making these changes a multi-party system should and probably would arise in the Soviet Union.

While the Sakharov memorandum was being discussed among groups of the intelligentsia, the 'Prague Spring' of 1968 was taking place in Czechoslovakia: an attempt to realize a model of 'socialism with a human face.' As in other communist-rule countries of Central and Eastern Europe, the cultural and artistic intelligentsia in Czecho-

slovakia had opposed the dogmatic line of the leader of the Communist Party of Czechoslovakia, Antonin Novotny, and had spoken out for reforms. In contrast to other countries, the reformers did not remain isolated, but received an increasing amount of support from other groups who had turned against Novotny's bureaucratic-dictatorial system. Czechoslovak economic reformers played an especially important role, and they were joined by Slovak Party members and functionaries, who, though in some of their political views not especially liberal, had turned against Novotny because they rightly felt discriminated against by his pro-Czech and anti-Slovak policies. And there were many more such groups; so many, in fact, that discontent can fairly be said to have achieved a mass basis.

After Novotny had been removed from the Chairmanship of the Party during the plenary session in January 1968 (he remained head of state for the time being) and had been replaced by the reformer Alexander Dubček, the issue of Stalinism was soon broached with complete frankness in the press and on radio and television. Wide-ranging changes in the leadership were made, and reformers took over the key positions in the government once held by dogmatic adherents of Novotny. On 10 April 1968 the Action Program of the Communist Party of Czechoslovakia was published, in which, for the first time, the most important reformist ideas were gathered together.

The Action Program stated that further development of the country depended on the creation of a new, fundamentally democratic model of a socialist society which corresponded to specific Czechoslovak conditions. Freedom of the press must be established. Absolute personal security must be guaranteed to all citizens, includ-

Left: Celebrations of the fiftieth anniversary of the foundation of the Soviet Union in 1967. The country's prominence in space exploration was a potent symbol of the positive achievements of the October Revolution.

Above right: The hardline ruler of Czechoslovakia, Antonin Novotny, whose fall from power in 1968 opened the way for an experiment in 'Communism with a human face.'

Above far right: Alexander Solzhenitsyn, survivor of Stalin's prison camps and prophet of anti-communism, gives a press conference after his expulsion to the West in 1974.

Right: The end of the Prague Spring, as Soviet tanks take up position on the streets of the Czech capital.

End of the Prague Spring

ing the legal right to lengthy or permanent stays abroad without loss of citizenship. The freedom of assembly and of association must be guaranteed within the framework of a socialist society. By means of the separation of powers the parliament, as well as the administration of justice, would receive their just place in the life of the socialist society. After a reform of the economy all enterprises would receive a certain amount of autonomy, which would make use of the positive aspects of a controlled market system. Trade unions should be independent from Party and state. The Party must be changed from a dictatorial instrument of power into a political organization that depended upon the voluntary support of the masses. Within the Party itself bureaucratic centralism must be replaced by unhindered, free discussions. As for foreign politics, the Action Program said that Czechoslovakia should, within the framework of its alliances, formulate its own views on the fundamental questions of world politics and should support a policy of peaceful coexistence with the highly developed capitalist countries.

The Party leaders of the Soviet Union, Poland, East Germany, Hungary and Bulgaria met at a conference in Warsaw in June and directed an open letter (the 'Warsaw letter') to the leaders of the Communist Party of Czechoslovakia demanding that the process of democratization be stopped, that democratic freedoms, especially the freedoms of press and association, should again be limited, and that the principle of subordination within the Party be reaffirmed. The letter also spoke ominously of an alleged threat to socialism in Czechoslovakia. The 'Warsaw letter' was politely but firmly rejected by the Czechoslovak Party leaders.

In an atmosphere of escalating tension the Czechs and Soviets made some efforts to negotiate during the summer, but it was obvious that their differences were irreconcilable and that the Czechs meant to pursue their course. The fourteenth congress of the Communist Party of Czechoslovakia, which was to pass a new set of statutes for the Party, elect new leaders and determine the course which would continue further in the direction of social democracy, was scheduled to convene on 9 September. There could be no doubt that this congress would mean a final defeat for the Stalinists

and would sanction the new model of socialism.

It was with the goal of preventing this that the Soviet invasion of Czechoslovakia occurred on 21 August 1968, supported by troops from Poland, East Germany, Hungary and Bulgaria. Whereas the troops of the Warsaw Pact nations soon withdrew from Czechoslovakia, the Russian troops remained. Within a few months after the 'Prague Spring' all reforms were annulled and Czechoslovakia again became a bureaucratic-dictatorial country of the Soviet type.

In the fall of 1968 the Soviet Union gave the occupation a basis in ideology by announcing the

new doctrine of 'limited sovereignty,' generally known as the Brezhnev Doctrine. According to this doctrine each socialist country was subordinated to the interests of the 'world socialist system,' which meant in effect to the Soviet Union. Relations between socialist countries should not be governed by international law in the sense of 'abstract sovereignty' or by a formal observance of the right of self-determination, but by the common principles worked out by the Soviet leaders. With this doctrine the Kremlin sought not only to justify the occupation of Czechoslovakia but to create the right to intervene in the future in any other country of Eastern Europe which, like Czechoslovakia in 1968, might make reforms beyond the degree tolerated by the USSR.

The occupation of Czechoslovakia as well as the Brezhnev Doctrine met with stiff protest within the world communist movement. More than 30 communist parties in the world, including almost all of those in Europe (and especially the Communist Party of Italy), protested against the invasion and against the Brezhnev Doctrine. Above all, the Soviet invasion of Czechoslovakia escalated the Sino-Soviet conflict. Already during the cultural revolution in China (1966-69) the Chinese communists had shifted to a direct condemnation of the Soviet system and had openly called upon the Russian people to overthrow the leaders in the Kremlin. Now the Chinese compared the Soviet invasion of Czechoslovakia to Hitler's invasion in 1938 and called the Czechoslovak populace to oppose the Soviet occupation forces. The Sino-

Soviet conflict was heightened to such a degree that it led to the most serious border conflicts which had yet occurred along the Ussuri River, including hard fighting around the island of Chen Pao (Russian: Damansky). Though the two sides put an end to the fighting and eventually again exchanged ambassadors in 1970, the People's Republic of China maintained its independence and was by no means ready to terminate its sometimes very harsh criticism of the Soviet Union.

The increasing seriousness of the Sino-Soviet conflict in the spring of 1969 led to a certain moderation in Soviet foreign policy, especially concerning the Western industrialized nations. Moreover the realization on the part of the Russians that the USSR was lagging behind the most developed nations of the world in the scientific-technical revolution played an especially important role. From 1968 on the Kremlin admitted more and more openly that the original goal of equaling and surpassing the United States in per capita production could not be reached in the foreseeable future. The Soviet Union was especially falling behind in the modern branches of industry, like petrochemicals, electronics and computer technology. As a result the Soviet leaders energetically sought to strengthen economic and scientific-technological ties with the West and to establish this cooperation on a long-term basis.

This change in Soviet foreign policy as well as certain controversies during the elaboration of the new Five-Year Plan (1971-75) meant that the

Twenty-fourth Party Congress, which originally should have been convened in the spring of 1970, could only meet after a one-year delay, in March 1971. It was during this period that the treaty between the Soviet Union and West Germany – which was in part disputed in the leading circles of the Party and government – was signed on 12 August 1970, and that the workers' uprising occurred in Poland in December 1970. In Poland, major strikes caused largely by economic grievances turned into riots in some cities and led to the dismissal of the head of the Communist Party, Gomulka, and other high leaders in the government and Party. These events in Poland were considered to be extremely serious by the Kremlin because many of the problems and contradictions which led to the uprising also existed in the Soviet Union.

Under these conditions three changes were announced during the Twenty-fourth Party Congress (20 March-9 April 1971): in foreign policy, a more moderate line toward the Western powers; in the economy, an increase in the production of consumer goods; and in domestic politics, a harder line, especially in the cultural and ideological spheres. And with memories of the 'Prague Spring' still vivid, there was certain to be no softening of the line toward Eastern Europe. It was socialist duty, Brezhnev announced, 'to eliminate firmly and efficiently any ideological deficiencies in time.' If nothing else, the Brezhnev hand was a heavy one.

As for policy regarding the non-Russian

nationalities – which is so important for the Soviet Union – a gradual drawing-together of the Soviet peoples was announced, with prominence given to the 'Great' Russian people. The enumeration of the special characteristics of Russians – energy, industry and self-sacrifice were mentioned as examples – signified the emphasis given to the Russian people *vis-à-vis* the many non-Russian peoples of the USSR.

The basic themes enunciated or implied at the Twenty-fourth Party Congress were, with few modifications, to guide Soviet policy until the end of the Brezhnev era – in effect until the death of Konstantin Chernenko in March 1985 and the accession of Mikhail Gorbachev. In the long run the entire program set forth at the Congress was to prove a dismal failure.

Domestically, the greatest failure undoubtedly related to the economy. The promised emphasis on increased production of consumer goods gradually faded into insignificance against a larger background of overall economic stagnation. Although Khrushchev's grandiose claims about overtaking the US in per capita production in the near future had long since been officially repudiated, there remained a general optimism that the productivity and GNP gaps between the two superpowers would steadily be narrowed during the decade of the 1970s. But by the mid 1980s it was clear that the reverse had happened. The GNP gap had doubled, and by the latter part of the 1970s, for the first time, the productivity gap had ceased to narrow and had begun to widen, some-

Left: Rioting workers in Gdansk, Poland, in December 1970. The Polish disturbances were especially worrying to the Soviet leaders because they feared similar trouble might erupt in their own cities.

Right: Soviet guards defending the Ussuri River border with China. After limited armed clashes, relations between the two communist powers began to thaw after 1970.

Above right: Soviet citizens admire the rare sight of a new private car. Under Brezhnev, the consumer goods sector of the economy was a disappointing failure.

thing it continued to do right to the end of the Brezhnev era.

Most of the basic charts reflecting economic development flattened or turned down during the period. There were recurrent labor shortages (which did nothing to improve productivity in a system that had too few incentives to offer workers). Nor was this problem necessarily short-term, since the birthrate in European Russia was nearing zero population growth. At a time when the West and Japan were lunging ahead in a race

to apply new technologies to industry the USSR had the oldest machine stock of any industrialized power. The cost of trying to import hi-tech industrial equipment from the advanced capitalist nations drew down hard currency reserves, which had already been eroded by the fact that a succession of disastrous harvests had forced the Soviet Union into the world grain market. By the end of the decade of the 1970s all but the most high-priority Soviet industries (heavily military) were still completely innocent even of computers.

This economic stagnation inevitably had its social dimension. The standard of living of ordinary Soviet citizens did not improve and may have declined, though it undoubtedly shot up for the *nomenklatura* (upper class). A general mood of apathy and cynicism spread. Corruption at all levels, absenteeism, drunkenness, theft, drug use and the like seem to have increased alarmingly. Western observers have few hard facts about all this, save for what fragmentary details have been made public by the successor Gorbachev regime. Thus the reform-minded Boris Yeltsin, first secretary of the Moscow Party organization until he had a falling-out with Gorbachev in 1987, was reported to have told city Party leaders in April 1986 that 'in the past few months 800 trade officials have been arrested in Moscow: we are digging deeper and still cannot find the bottom of this well of corruption.' Yeltsin also said that 3600 drug addicts had been so far 'registered' in the city and implied that the total number was doubtless much greater. The life expectancy of Muscovites had fallen in recent years. Even the famous Moscow subway had been allowed to deteriorate so far that now it was losing money.

Precisely why the economy performed so badly during the Brezhnev era is difficult to say. No doubt there was, as in the case of the poor harvests, an element of bad luck, but a certain amount of bad luck has to be anticipated in the development of any economy. Other problems, such as the sporadic labor shortages or the failure of investment capital to keep up with soaring production costs, argue both a lack of foresight and good planning and a woeful lack of flexibility in dealing with new problems. Gorbachevian critics and Western commentators alike agree in assigning much of the blame for this to the incompetence of the bureaucracy, which became enormously bloated during the Brezhnev period. But of course the question of how much the economic failure of the 1970s and 1980s betrayed fundamental flaws in the system itself remained a matter of debate between East and West.

The Brezhnev leadership's policy of enforcing a

harder line in the spheres of domestic politics, ideology and culture fared no better than the economic program. Dissidence, instead of being muted, waxed and became both an embarrassment to the regime and, thanks to a rising tide of Western criticism of the regime's repressive behavior, an international issue of some importance. Perhaps the most famous example was that of the outspoken nuclear physicist Andrei Sakharov. On 28 August 1973 Sakharov sent an open letter to the Academy of Sciences strongly denouncing both Soviet foreign and domestic policy. A press campaign against him was immediately launched, but Sakharov, a man with immense internal and international prestige, refused to be silenced, and in the following years he produced a stream of open letters to Soviet leaders and organizations, as well as to Western statesmen and newspapers, all bitterly critical of Soviet policies, actions and intentions. By January 1977, when the regime began to threaten him with criminal charges (for 'hostile and slanderous activities'), his case had become such an international *cause célèbre* that the US government felt constrained to warn the Soviet government against taking any legal action against him. Under mounting KGB harassment he continued his courageous, solitary campaign until the beginning of 1980, when he was finally taken into custody, charged and sent off to internal exile in Gorky, where he remained under house arrest until 1987. (His release a consequence of the new policy of *glasnost.*)

The fact that the Soviet government was so slow to move against Sakharov was in part due to this 'father' of the Soviet hydrogen bomb's daunting reputation and in part to the regime's sensitivity to Western concern about his welfare. (It is significant that Sakharov's arrest came only after it had become apparent that the West's outraged response to the Soviet invasion of Afghanistan in late 1979 had demolished any hope of reviving the spirit of *détente.*) But lesser dissidents were treated in a more summary fashion. Solzhenitsyn was deported in 1974. Anatoly Shiransky, leader of the Jewish emigration movement, was sentenced to 13 years' imprisonment in July 1978. His associate, Aleksandr Guinzburg, was given eight years. And a great many other dissidents suffered similar fates. (Twenty, tactlessly enough, were even arrested on 10 December 1977, United Nations Human Rights Day.)

Left: Distinguished Soviet physicist Andrei Sakharov. Sometimes known as 'the father of the Soviet hydrogen bomb,' his denunciation of the abuses of the regime brought him into disfavor, and he spent the years from 1980 to 1987 in internal exile.

Below left: Jewish dissident Anatoly Shiransky reunited with his wife in Israel after his release from a Soviet prison in a 'spy swap,' February 1986.

Right: A mujahidin fighter in Afghanistan. The Soviet intervention in Afghanistan blocked the process of *détente,* harmed the reputation of the Soviet Union worldwide, and revealed defects in its military organization.

Dissidence continues

Yet dissidence itself was not crushed. Soviet Jews, for example, persisted in their demands that restrictions on emigration be lifted or at least relaxed, and the government, which steadfastly proclaimed its rejection of anti-Semitism (as well, to be sure, as anti-Zionism), seemed hard put to find a consistent policy on this issue: The number of Jews permitted to emigrate varied from 229 in 1968 to a high of 51,320 in 1979 (when the Soviet Union was trying to persuade the US to ratify SALT II) to 869 in 1984. And another aspect of dissidence was evident in the steady stream of defections of writers, poets, dancers and musicians to the West.

In the realm of foreign policy the Brezhnev leadership's objective of relaxing tensions with the West was at first successful but in the long run could not be sustained. It may be that one of the reasons for this failure was that by the early 1970s the Soviet leaders felt the long-sought and painfully expensive goal of achieving strategic military parity with the United States was at least being realized, and that the temptation to use this perceived new power from time to time to reap localized political advantages proved simply too great to resist. It may also be that the Soviet leaders, as often before, misread the Americans. The mood of doubt and self-castigation that assailed the United States after the nation's humiliation in Vietnam, the scandal-ridden fall of the Nixon presidency, the apparent revulsion against militarism and the slashing of defense appropriations – all this might have been interpreted in Moscow as a sign of a fundamental weakening in America's resolve to continue playing an assertive role in international affairs.

Whatever the reasons, Soviet foreign policy during the 1970s seemed to be operating on two contradictory levels. On one level, that of *détente,* the Soviet Union actively promoted summit meetings with Western leaders, the signing of international accords relating to nuclear arms limitation, to the stabilization of borders, to the definition of conduct for great powers in times of crisis and to the protection of human rights, as well as to marked increases in the levels of cultural and intellectual exchange with the West. But the positive effects of these initiatives were con-

stantly being undermined by the Soviet leadership's apparent inability to resist opportunities to project Soviet influence through a series of politico-military interventions in various parts of the Third World. The cumulative effect that this persistent adventurism had in hardening Western attitudes may not have been fully appreciated in Moscow. The violence of the West's reaction to what it perceived as the last straw, the Soviet invasion of Afghanistan in December 1979, seems genuinely to have surprised the Brezhnev leadership, which had set great store by the SALT II strategic arms limitation treaty and could not now fully understand why the angry American president did not even bother to submit it to an equally angry Senate for ratification.

A brief chronological review of events between 1971 and 1980 will illustrate this ambivalence in Soviet foreign policy. The spirit of *détente* began to manifest itself even before the opening of the Twenty-fourth Party Congress, when, in February, the USSR joined the US and 61 other nations in signing a treaty banning the installation of any nuclear devices on seabeds outside 12-mile territorial limits. Just after the Congress this was followed by the announcement in May of the much more important Soviet-American accord that ultimately produced and Anti-Ballistic Missile Treaty. But at the same time, the Soviets continued to fish in the troubled waters of the Middle East, and on 28 May signed a 15-year treaty of friendship and cooperation with Egypt, the plain intention of which was to supply Egypt with enough advanced weapons to permit a successful attack on America's principal Mid-Eastern ally, Israel.

It was much the same story the following year. The spirit of *détente* soared even higher, with Pre-

sident Nixon's visit to Moscow in May and with the signing in October of the SALT I treaty limiting land- and submarine-based strategic missiles. In between these events, in April, the Soviet Union concluded another Middle Eastern friendship pact, this time with Iraq, promising material support in 'the determined struggle against Zionism.'

In 1973 Brezhnev signed a 10-year pact of economic, industrial and technical cooperation with West Germany's Willy Brandt, and a month later, in mid June, amid much fanfare, the General Secretary visited the United States to conclude another series of agreements with Nixon relating to the avoidance of military confrontation between the superpowers. But by October some of the fruits of Moscow's Middle Eastern dabbling became manifest when the USSR's two principal clients in the region, Egypt and Syria, launched a surprise attack on Israel. The fact that Israel decisively won the Yom Kippur war was set-back enough for Soviet policy, but the strain the war placed on US-Soviet relations was severe. At one point, on 25 October, the US briefly placed all its armed forces on worldwide alert as the result of ambiguous evidence that the Soviet Union might be planning direct intervention in the Middle East. The crisis passed, but not the damage done to *détente*.

In 1974, while the US was preoccupied by the unfolding Watergate scandal and the forced resignation of President Nixon, the Soviets took an interest in African politics, lending support to the leftist army junta that had overthrown Haile Selassie in Ethiopia and to Angolan Marxists who were looking forward to seizing control of that country upon the withdrawal of the Portuguese colonial government. Both areas were shortly to

become additional irritants to East-West relations. Soon after the Portuguese left Angola in November 1975 the country entered a period of bloody civil war, in which the Marxist Luanda-based faction of Augostino Neto was supported by Soviet-sponsored Cuban mercenaries against a US- and China-backed faction based at Huambo. (The Luanda faction prevailed, but subsequently lost control of much of the country to anti-regime guerrilla forces.) By 1978 Soviet advisors and Cuban troops were also involved in the Ethiopian regime's war with rebellious forces in Eritrea. All this brought the Soviet Union no significant long-term gains and only served to annoy and alarm the West.

Yet throughout the same period the Soviet Union simultaneously persisted in trying to foster *détente* at the level of great power negotiations. In May 1975 the USSR joined the US, Canada and 33 European nations in signing the Helsinki Accords, which, amongst other things, pledged signatories to respect human rights – this at a time when the West was already becoming exercised about Soviet treatment of dissidents and Jews. In 1976 came a US-Soviet treaty on limiting underground nuclear testing, in which the Soviet Union at last agreed to on-site inspection. In September 1977 the US and the USSR joined 13 other nations in signing a nuclear non-proliferation treaty. And on 18 June 1979 Brezhnev and President Carter signed the most important agreement to have been made since 1972, the SALT II strategic arms limitation treaty. Incredibly, before the US Senate could ratify the treaty Soviet forces invaded Afghanistan. The treaty was not ratified, Carter imposed an embargo on grain shipments to the USSR, the US boycotted the Olympic Games in Moscow and the Congress began approving vastly

increased military appropriations. Up to this point the Soviets had made no important gains in Africa and had actually lost ground in the Middle East (Egypt had renounced the friendship pact in 1975 and by 1979 was well on its way to becoming a US client), but they had succeeded in returning the Americans to something like a Cold War mentality. Now the USSR had entered into a conflict in Afghanistan that was to prove as humiliatingly unsuccessful as America's intervention in Vietnam.

Exactly what prompted the Soviet Union to invade Afghanistan is still not completely clear. When President Noor Mohammed Taraki was killed by the hard-line Marxist Hafizullah Amin, the complex politico-religious tensions of Afghan life exploded into open conflict. The Soviet Union, in fact, was opposed to Amin's extreme anti-Muslim policies and backed the more moderate Babrak Karmal. Amin, however, refused the Soviet request to stand down. The Soviets replied by airlifting 5000 troops to Afghanistan on 26 December 1979, and these were followed two days later by 15,000 ground troops. Amin was killed in the consequent fighting and Karmal was installed in government. Within six months the Soviet military presence in Afghanistan rose to 85,000, after which it gradually drifted up to about 115,000, a plateau it would maintain for much of the 1980s.

But why did the Soviets feel it so necessary to intervene in Afghanistan? The requirement to have nothing but Marxist states sharing borders with the USSR does not seem to have been an absolute imperative. Afghanistan had, after all, existed as a contiguous kingdom for many years. In 1973 it had become a republic, and only in 1978 had the communist regime of Noor Mohammed Taraki come to power (after a coup d'état). The main reason for Soviet military intervention in 1979 was the fear of Islamic fundamentalism spreading from Afghanistan into its own Muslim-populated regions. Although in many ways reluctant to use military force, the Soviet Union felt it must nip the growing revolt in the bud.

Nonetheless, they plainly underestimated not only the strength of the Western reaction but that of the Muslim world as well. (At a Muslim summit meeting 37 states would eventually unanimously condemn the 'imperialist invasion' of Afghanistan.) Worse, the Soviets were singularly unsuccessful in suppressing the resistance of the Afghan guerrillas – the 'mujahedeen' – who, especially after they began receiving copious supplies of Western and Chinese weapons, were able to

fight Soviet and Afghan government troops to a virtual standstill by the mid 1980s. By 1988 Mikhail Gorbachev was both openly describing Afghanistan as 'a bleeding wound' and debating with the Americans how Soviet troops could be extricated from the country.

Whether Sino-Soviet relations also disimproved between the Twenty-fourth Congress and the invasion of Afghanistan is moot; certainly they did not get better. One of the major irritants was the fact that during the Vietnam war the Soviet Union had gradually replaced China as North Vietnam's primary sponsor. As the war turned more in North Vietnam's favor the Chinese were faced with the unpleasant prospect of the creation of a Soviet client state on China's southern border. In 1972, with President Nixon's surprise visit to China, a Sino-US rapprochement began – a development that could hardly have met any sane Soviet foreign policy objective. In the following years Vietnam's aggressive actions in Southeast Asia, including a brief but vicious border war with China in 1979, won the Soviet Union no new friends in that region. It was small wonder that China was prepared to join the US in sending covert aid to the Afghan resistance fighters after 1979.

Soviet relations with the Warsaw Pact nations and with Western and Asian communist parties

were also less than satisfactory. With the exception of East Germany and Hungary, the economies of the East European states either stagnated or declined during the 1970s, and the success of the two exceptions was due almost entirely to their growing trade relations with the West, at the expense of dependence on the Soviet-dominated CMEA (Council of Mutual Economic Assistance, often called COMECON). Albania and Rumania had of course begun their drift away from Soviet political domination before the Brezhnev Doctrine had been enunciated in 1968, but neither state was perceived in Moscow as important enough to warrant direct action. In Poland, however, a much more serious threat to Soviet hegemony developed at the end of the 1970s – spreading labor unrest that culminated in a major strike at the Gdansk Lenin Shipyard in August 1980. The strike proved an astonishing success for the workers, who were able to wring from the economically pressed government the unprecedented right to form independent trade unions. The most imposing of the new free unions, Solidarity, led by Lech Walesa, soon developed a huge membership and an even larger national following. Amidst calls for greater political freedom and improved working conditions, Solidarity initiated a nation-wide strike in January 1981 over the issue of a five-day week. While the demand was being negotiated the government fell, and the patriotic but hard-line General Wojciech Jaruselski became the new premier.

By now Soviet pressure on the Polish government to crack down on Solidarity and the other free unions was intense. Although the Polish Party leader, Stanislaw Kania, tried to reassure the delegates to the Twenty-sixth Soviet Party Congress in February 1981 that the Poles would be able to resolve their own problems, Moscow was anything but reassured. In March Jaruselski and Kania were summoned to a meeting with Brezhnev and Gromyko and forced to agree to the principle that the defense of communism was a matter of concern to the entire East bloc. This ominous allusion to the Brezhnev Doctrine of 1968 elicited a next-day (5 March) response from the new Reagan administration in Washington warning of 'the gravest consequences' should the USSR intervene in Poland.

Tensions mounted through the summer and fall of 1981, as Polish unions proliferated, strikes – many of them wildcat – erupted across the nation

Left: Presidents Carter and Brezhnev sign the SALT II arms control treaty in 1979. The treaty was never ratified by the United States, as the period of *détente* was followed by a return to Cold War confrontation.

Below left: General Jaruselski, the Polish military leader who imposed martial law in 1981 as an alternative to direct Soviet intervention.

Right: Solidarity leader Lech Walesa addresses fellow workers at the Gdansk shipyards.

Below: Brezhnev with the Moscow-backed prime minister of Afghanistan, Babrak Karmal, in 1980.

and Soviet troops began staging 'maneuvers' close to the Polish border. On 17 September the Soviet Union sent the Polish government an extremely harsh letter – virtually an ultimatum – warning of 'danger to the Polish state' and demanding an immediate crackdown. A month later Jaruselski replaced Kania as Party leader, thus concentrating both party and governmental power in his own hands. On 13 December he proclaimed a state of martial law in Poland, and the breakup of the unions and arrest of their leaders commenced. Martial law was to remain in effect until July 1983, by which time the union movement had been effectively destroyed. Symptomatic of the West's feelings about all this was the fact that Walesa was given the 1983 Nobel Peace Prize.

The Soviet Union's insistent equation of Polish trade unionism with political opposition was, as might be expected, also ill-received by most communist and left socialist parties outside the East bloc, but in truth the alienation of these parties from Moscow had been going on for over a decade. At the Twenty-fifth Party Congress in Moscow in February-March 1976, for example, many parties, notably the French and Italians, had joined the Yugoslavs in demanding more independence and a greater respect for individual liberties, and the French had even gone so far as to renounce the Leninist doctrine of the dictatorship of the proletariat. This political and ideological disarray was symptomatic of yet another great failure of the Brezhnev period – the dwindling almost to insignificance of the political power of the West European communist parties and their allies. It was vividly demonstrated in the early 1980s when the Soviet Union attempted to mobilize a political campaign in Western Europe to halt the deployment of American intermediate-range Pershing missiles (a response to a much larger number of Soviet SS-20 missiles aimed at Europe).

The campaign was a complete failure. No NATO Government was exposed to any domestic pressure sufficient to make it diverge from the US policy, and the Pershings were duly deployed.

In the broadest sense, perhaps the greatest failure of Brezhnev's contradictory and profitless foreign policy was the degree to which it succeeded in forcing the Americans into opposition. It would be far too much to say that Brezhnev elected Ronald Reagan, but he certainly helped. What followed was a $1 trillion US rearmament program, a far more hostile and assertive American foreign policy and ultimately, though Brezhnev did not live to see it, even the threat that the Soviet Union's cherished strategic parity might some day be undermined by Reagan's enthusiasm for the new high-tech space-based Strategic Defense Initiative.

The advent of Mikhail Gorbachev

Leonid Brezhnev died on 10 November 1982. He was succeeded as General Secretary by Yuri Andropov, longtime head of the KGB. Whether Andropov, a relatively cosmopolitan man who had risen more through the ranks of the bureaucracy than through the rough-and-tumble of Party politics, might eventually have begun to try to alter Brezhnev's policies is unknown, for his tenure lasted only 15 months, many of them beset by illness. In the event, there were no significant policy changes, and it may be that Andropov's most important legacy was that he continued to foster the career of a fast-rising college-educated lawyer and management expert, Mikhail Gorbachev, who had become a full member of the Politburo in 1980, when he was only 49.

Andropov died in February 1984 and was succeeded by the ailing 72-year-old Konstantin Chernenko, a party stalwart who had been close to Brezhnev. Like Brezhnev and Andropov before him, Chernenko had, by April, assumed the title of President of the Soviet Union, in addition to being general secretary of the Party. His tenure, marked by rigid adherence to Brezhnev's policies, was even shorter than Andropov's, lasting only 13 months.

Gorbachev had continued to flourish under the Chernenko regime, assuming broad responsibilities in the Politburo for supervision of the agro-industrial complex, for propaganda, education, science, culture and relations with foreign communist parties, for personnel and for economic coordination. When Chernenko died on 10 March 1985 it was almost a foregone conclusion that Gorbachev would succeed him.

The first six months of Gorbachev's tenure was spent largely in consolidating his position by weeding out potential opponents and appointing like-minded men to key positions. (For example, he 'elevated' Andrei Gromyko, for 28 years the USSR's Foreign Minister, to the largely ceremonial office of President of the Soviet Union, replacing him with the younger, largely unknown Eduard Shevardnadze.) But there were also signs that he had in mind some fairly considerable departures from the policies of the Brezhnev years. Already by June 1985 he was telling a conference convened by the Central Committee that the 'acceleration of scientific and technical progress insistently demands a profound reorganization of the system of planning and management and of the entire economic mechanism.'

Gorbachev continued to hammer away at the need for, as he put it to the Twenty-seventh Party Congress in February 1986, 'radical reform' and to make ever more open criticism of Brezhnev's policies. What he meant by reform began to emerge in speeches such as one he made in April to workers in the Volga Car Works, when he said that 'it is in the fact that we have attempted to manage everything from Moscow up until recently that our common and main mistake lies.' The main outlines of Gorbachev's intended *perestroika* (restructuring) of the Soviet economic system finally became apparent in June 1987, and by Soviet standards it was radical indeed. The ponderous bureaucracy (15.3 million officials) that made up the heart of the old central planning system was to be cut in size and stripped of much of its authority, becoming instead a congeries of long-range planning bodies that would offer 'guidance.' The government-dictated pricing system, along with its maze of subsidies and controls, was to be gradually eliminated, and industrial enterprises were to become essentially self-managing and competitive (a system dubbed *khozrachot*). Those enterprises that realized profits could reinvest them or distribute them in the form of salaries or other worker benefits. Those that lost money would be permitted to go bankrupt. Widely differentiated worker wage scales would thus become a likelihood, as would the

theretofore unheard-of specter of unemployment – although the government was supposed to provide safety nets to ensure that any unemployment would be temporary and would not entail undue economic hardship for those affected. Some sectors of the economy would begin converting to the *khozrachot* system as early as 1987, and more would follow in the next two years, so that by 1990 the whole Soviet economy would be operating on the *khozrachot* principle.

Linked to *perestroika* was another concept that Gorbachev soon made internationally famous: *glasnost*, or openness, a general relaxation of constraints on free expression of opinion, including a certain freedom to express criticism of government and Party policy. That Gorbachev himself took advantage of *glasnost* to escalate his criticism of the mistakes of the Brezhnev and Stalin eras and to rehabilitate such figures as Khrushchev and Bukharin was obvious. What was less obvious was how far it might apply to others. A case in point was that of Boris Yeltsin, whose complaints that *perestroika* was not moving fast enough so irritated Gorbachev that he finally ousted him from his post as Moscow Party chief in November 1987.

An uncertain future

As of the beginning of 1988 both Soviet and Western observers were still unsure how well the massive reforms might work in practice. One immediate problem with *perestroika* was that whereas factories were expected to convert to *khozrachot* immediately, government price controls would not be lifted until 1990, thus obliging factory managers to buy and sell at fixed prices while still being expected to show profits – undoubtedly a frightening prospect for the 25 percent of Soviet industry already operating at a loss or on a precarious margin. Another obvious problem was that although *khozrachot* was expected to produce market-style competition among factories, the industrial economy was already largely organized in the form of huge regional monopolies that would have powerful advantages in stifling any competitive challenges. That the early days of *perestroika* would produce large-scale dislocations and dissatisfactions among many managers and workers, with few immediate improvements in overall living standards, seemed almost certain, and the domestic political dangers this posed for Gorbachev's future were equally obvious.

There were foreign dangers as well. If the Gorbachev regime were to succeed in making *perestroika* work it had to be as free as possible, at

least during the early years, from the threat of recurring crises in US-Soviet relations. Gorbachev therefore addressed himself to reviving the spirit of *détente* with great skill and imagination. The Soviets progressively abandoned their former hard-line position on the question of intermediate-range nuclear weapons in Europe, and by November 1987 they had negotiated an historic agreement with the US (the INF Treaty), whereby *all* such American and Soviet theater weapons – the majority of them being Soviet SS-20s – would be destroyed, with appropriate verification safeguards. During Gorbachev's celebratory visit to the United States in December – a dazzling personal public relations triumph – he spoke optimistically of future strategic arms reduction treaties (again not necessarily linked to American abandonment of the Strategic Defense Initiative) and of his desire to evacuate Soviet troops from Afghanistan as soon as possible. This campaign of conciliation was very well received in the US, and most Americans seemed to feel that for the time being there was little likelihood of a recurrence of the kind of mindless Soviet adventurism in the Third World that had so soured Soviet-American relations during the Brezhnev era.

But it was not in Gorbachev's power to dispose of all – or even the most important – potential sources of Soviet-American friction. How the principles of *perestroika* and *glasnost* would affect the nations of Eastern Europe, and how the Gorbachev regime would deal with crises such as those that had occurred in Czechoslovakia in 1968 and in Poland in 1980-81, were worrisome unknowns.

Thus by the beginning of 1988 the prospects for the future development of the Soviet Union were still in doubt. There was still plenty of internal opposition to *perestroika* and *glasnost* among the political elite and the bureaucracy, as well as widespread skepticism among the population. Should Gorbachev's reforms become bogged down, it was by no means inconceivable that his regime might be replaced by another that stressed a return to Russian nationalism, relying on the two traditional pillars of power – the army and the government – and pursuing a much more anti-Western policy that featured both heightened provocation in the Third World and neo-imperialism in its dealings with all areas contiguous to the Soviet Union. Such a successor regime might or might not be neo-Stalinist as well; since there was no want of advocates of neo-Stalinism still in the government, army and KGB, the possibility could not be dismissed. The future therefore remained cloudy and beset by many dangers.

Left: The old guard and the new at a Red Square parade during Andropov's brief period of rule, including two future leaders, Chernenko, fifth from the left, and Gorbachev, second from the right. On Gorbachev's right stands aging Foreign Minister Gromyko, soon to be kicked upstairs to the Presidency. Andropov himself was already too ill to attend this parade.

Right: Mikhail Gorbachev (right) and his Foreign Minister Eduard Shevardnadze. Gorbachev provided a fresh, vigorous leadership both on the domestic front and in foreign affairs.

Below: The new-look Soviet society of the 1980s – a lively disco in a Moscow suburb.

North America

When Franklin Delano Roosevelt was sworn in in the spring of 1941 for his third term in the White House, the United States had yet to recover fully from the trauma of the Great Depression, despite the fact that a crash program of government spending for rearmament was finally putting an end to the mass unemployment of the 1930s. Roosevelt confronted a grim international situation. In Asia the Japanese were busy carving an empire out of China, and their intentions in Southeast Asia seemed sinister. In Europe Adolf Hitler was the master of a European empire that stretched from the English Channel to deep inside the Soviet Union. Great Britain had been ravaged by German air attacks, and lived in a constant state of expectation of a cross-Channel German invasion. If the Soviet Union and Great Britain were to fall, the United States, Canada and a few other non-European nations would be all that stood between the Fascist powers and the domination of the world. Canadian and other Commonwealth soldiers were already shedding their blood in the anti-Nazi cause. Canada had been in the war since September 1939, and had made perhaps the most important non-British contribution to the Allied cause thus far in the Battle of Britain, when the Royal Canadian Air Force, as well as Canadians who had enlisted as volunteers in the Royal Air Force, challenged the *Luftwaffe* for control of the skies. Sheltered from Hitler's bombs by the Atlantic, Canadian industry and agriculture sent their products to the war zones. Since early in 1941 the United States, declaring itself the 'arsenal of democracy,' had done what it could through the Lend-Lease Program to provide its British allies with weapons and other material aid, but the American army itself was woefully underequipped and undermanned. In the judgement of George C Marshall, the Army's Chief of Staff, the United States in 1941 was not even a 'third-rate' military power. And on 7 December 1941 time ran out for the United States in its desperate race to rearm before it had to go to war, as millions of Americans on a quiet Sunday learned that Japanese bombers were attacking Pearl Harbor.

Policymakers in Washington had some precedents to follow in planning the kind of crash mobilization for war that was now required. In 1917-18 the United States had geared up to fight a long war with Imperial Germany and its allies, only to see the German armies collapse before the full might of American power could be brought to bear on the Western front. Beginning in 1933 the federal government had mobilized millions of Americans to confront a different kind of national emergency, the economic disaster of the Great Depression, and many a young man who had learned to shine his shoes and make up his cot in the work camps established by the New Deal's Civilian Conservation Corps now found those habits useful in military service. These earlier experiences provided some useful guidelines to those planning America's military and domestic mobilization for war, but no one could have foreseen the full ramifications of the social, political and economic impact of the war. Perhaps only the four years of the Civil War, which had freed 4 million slaves, established the ascendancy of the Republican Party and underwritten the indus-

trialization of much of the North while destroying the plantation economy of the Old South, had a comparable impact on the shape of American society.

In his efforts to combat the Depression, Roosevelt had already greatly expanded the powers of the executive branch of government. Now he faced an even greater challenge. 'Dr New Deal,' Roosevelt announced at a press conference in 1942, had closed up his practice; in his place was 'Dr Win the War.' The growth in the size and power of the federal government was vastly accelerated. The logistical and material requirements of modern military operations meant that wars in the twentieth century were decided on the homefront as much as on the battlefront. The size of the US military increased from a pre-war low of just 300,000 to over 12 million men and women in uniform by 1945. (Canada, in the same period, expanded its own military forces to nearly a million.) The size of the American government's civilian work force also jumped dramatically. The

federal government employed 800,000 civilians before the war; by 1945 it employed nearly 4 million. The newly hired civilian employees went to work for newly established wartime agencies such as the War Production Board, which was in charge of mobilizing US industrial resources for the war effort while restricting 'nonessential' production; the War Manpower Commission, which attempted to coordinate allocation of labor between factory, farm and the military; the Office of Price Administration, which sought to limit price inflation for retail goods and rents; and the War Labor Board, which sought to hold down wage increases and to resolve industrial disputes. The war effort, both at home and overseas, was enormously expensive. Between 1939 and 1945 the federal budget increased from $9 billion to a staggering $166 billion. Some of the increase in the budget was paid for by the sale of war bonds; much of it was not paid for at all and swelled the national deficit to record levels. Among the most long-lasting of the changes brought about by the

Right: Beatrice McKelvey, a railroad worker in Washington, D.C., flexes her muscles for the camera. Large numbers of American women were employed in heavy industry for the first time, providing them with a new sense of independence. A popular song, 'Rosie the Riveter,' captured the liberating spirit of the times; over a third of the work force was made up of 'Rosies' by 1945.

Below left: Marines drill at Camp Lejune in North Carolina. The United States was able to conscript 12 million Americans to serve with the flag during World War II – a remarkable feat of human mobilization.

Below right: Canadian troops arrive in Britain in May 1940. Canada declared war on Germany on 10 September 1939. Its vast prairie wheatfields supplied much of Britain's grain needs during the war, and it put nearly a million men under arms.

a veteran civil rights activist, organized the March on Washington Movement in the spring of 1941. Unless the federal government was prepared to guarantee that blacks would receive equal treatment in hiring in the new defense industries and in military service, Randolph threatened to bring up to 100,000 black protesters into the streets of Washington. Roosevelt was not willing to challenge the deeply entrenched racism of the military services, which consigned blacks to segregated units and menial duties, but he did agree to sign an executive order prohibiting racial discrimination in hiring in industries accepting government contracts, and to create a Fair Employment Practices Committee (FEPC) to enforce the order. Randolph then called off the march. The FEPC met with mixed success, and in the end the vastly increased black employment in basic industry can be attributed to the acute labor shortage of the war years rather than government intervention. Blacks, 10 percent of the US population, constituted just three percent of workers in defense plants in 1942; that number increased to more than eight percent by 1945.

The lesson of the March on Washington Movement was a significant one and was not lost on future black leaders: given the right combination of pressures, the federal government could be enlisted on the side of civil rights. Randolph's strategy in 1941 set other important precedents, differing from the legalistic strategy of traditional civil rights groups such as the National Association for the Advancement of Colored People (NAACP) in its emphasis upon mass organizing and its insistence that the civil rights movement be under black leadership. Another innovative strategy was tried out during the war by the new Congress of Racial Equality (CORE), which was organized in Chicago in 1942 by a small group of white and black pacifists and socialists who were inspired by the civil disobedience campaigns led by the Indian independence leader Mohandas Gandhi. CORE began to experiment with the tactic of the 'sit in' to challenge segregation and met some success in its efforts to integrate Northern restaurants and movie theaters. The expanding Northern ghettos provided a power base for a new generation of black politicians.

war was the expansion of the internal revenue system. During the course of the war wage-earners had to get used to the unwelcome innovation of having a portion of their pay 'withheld' by the federal government. Only 4 million Americans paid federal income taxes in 1939; 50 million did so in 1945.

Long-standing social arrangements and customs fell by the wayside under the pressure of the necessities of war. As millions of men marched off to war, millions of women left their homes or left 'traditional' female domestic and service jobs for employment in the war industries. Popular magazines, accustomed to posing fashion models in evening gowns and prom dresses, now ran photographs of the same models in overalls: 'Rosie the Riveter' became a model of patriotic femininity. Women, who made up only a quarter of the national work force in 1940, represented well over a third of it by 1945. During the Depression some political leaders had sought to pass laws forbidding the employment of married women, in a misguided effort to provide more jobs for unemployed men; during the war married women as well as single women were encouraged to take jobs outside the home, and as they learned new skills and took home hefty paychecks many experienced a startling new sense of personal autonomy. Government and private industry took some steps to provide child-care facilities for working mothers, though the resources never equaled the demand. Throughout the war women's wages continued to lag behind those earned by men, but some progressive unions made 'equal pay for equal work' their demand. Since the achievement of women's suffrage in 1920, feminism had disappeared as a significant political force in the United States; now the seeds of a new feminist movement were being sown.

Another movement destined to change the face of American society also took shape during the war years. American blacks, still primarily a rural

Southern population in the 1930s, became in the course of the war and the years that followed an urban and increasingly a Northern people. In 1940 nearly four out of five blacks still lived in the South; 20 years later nearly half lived in the North. The lure of high-paying jobs in war industries and the relative social freedom offered by the North and West drew millions of blacks to cities such as Detroit, Chicago, Los Angeles and Oakland. Expanding economic opportunities brought with them new political opportunities. A Philip Randolph, the nation's leading black union leader and

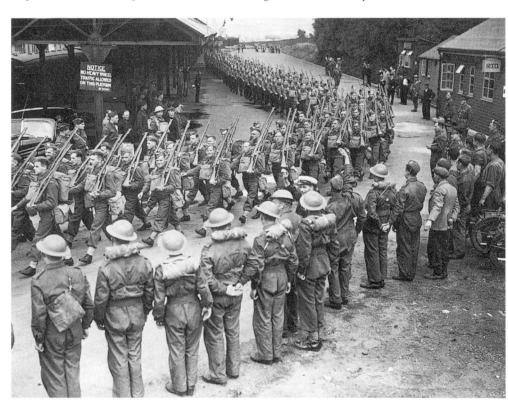

Left: Black residents of a Detroit apartment block are held in a police line-up following a race riot. The sudden influx of blacks into the industrial centers of the American northeast caused racial tensions which at times flared up into violent confrontations between blacks and whites.

Below: Gasoline rationing in wartime America led to a campaign encouraging drivers to form car pools.

Bottom: Secretary of the Navy Frank Knox backs Lend-Lease to Britain.

Right: Japanese-Americans, like this child, were unjustly driven from their homes on the West Coast and sent to camps in the desert in the wake of the Japanese surprise attack on Pearl Harbor.

World War I had left a legacy of patriotic slogans ('The Yanks Are Coming') and uplifting war songs ('Over There'), but in reality it had been a bitterly divisive conflict, sparking a mass anti-war movement that was crushed by a combination of vigilante and official repression. World War II found Americans far more united in their support of the military cause. Even those isolationists who had marched under the banner of 'America First' in the first two years of the war in Europe were converted by the shock of Pearl Harbor. Disagreements remained over whether the United States should put more resources into the war against Japan or Germany, whether it should rely on air and naval power, or push for the earliest possible achievement of a Second Front on the land in Western Europe. Most important, just how far could it trust its allies? (Suspicion of Great Britain ran almost as deeply in some isolationist circles in the United States as suspicion of the Soviet Union.) Nevertheless the spirit of national unity from 1941 through 1945 was not just an artifice of post-war nostalgia. If the naïve exuberance of 1917-18 was missing, it was replaced by a more durable determination to see the war through to victory. As the Red Cross handbook on first aid became a best-seller, local Defense Councils, the quasi-official groups which coordinated civil defense and other programs, enrolled nearly 10 million volunteers. Millions of others contributed to the war effort through their participation in scrap, tin and rubber drives and war bond campaigns, as well as by planting victory gardens. Particularly on the East and West Coasts, where enemy attacks were plausible if unlikely, frequent black-outs and air raid drills gave Americans a vicarious sense of sharing the dangers that were all too real in other parts of the world.

Among the reasons for the greater national unity in World War II was the fact that now Americans were confident they were, in reality, a nation, and not just a collection of mutually antagonistic ethnic and religious tribes, as some had feared at the start of the century. On the eve of World War I President Woodrow Wilson was among those who shared the nativist suspicion of immigrants. In a 1916 speech he spoke of 'hyph-enated Americans', declaring that some of those 'born under other flags but welcomed under our generous naturalization laws' were pouring 'the poison of disloyalty into the very arteries of our national life.' Franklin Roosevelt used a far different tone in his references to the nation's ethnic diversity, seeing it a source of strength rather than weakness. As he declared in a 1944 campaign speech delivered in Boston:

Today in this war, our fine boys are fighting magnificently all over the world, and among those boys are the Murphys and the Kellys, the Smiths and the Joneses, the Cohens, the Caruosos, the Kowalskis, the Schultzes, the Olsens, the Swobodas and – right in with all the rest of them – the Cabots and the Lowells.

Roosevelt was by inclination a more tolerant leader than Wilson had been, more of a pragmatist and less a crusader. And to a much greater extent than Wilson, Roosevelt owed his political

success to the rapport he had established with urban, ethnic America. He also remembered how the intolerance of 1917-18 had led to the conservative reaction of the post-war era and the Republican resurgence in the 1920s.

In addition, American society had changed in important ways since World War I. With the passage of restrictive immigration legislation in the 1920s Ellis Island was no longer the gateway for millions of new immigrants. That meant that every year a declining percentage of Americans were foreign-born. Increasingly, families with southern and eastern European surnames were second- or even third-generation Americans. The children of those families, brought up speaking English as their first language and educated in American public schools, did not excite the same nativist fears that their parents had. The Office of War Information encouraged Hollywood screenwriters to give the characters in war movies surnames reflecting the full mix of American society, and the ethnically integrated platoon became one of the clichés of war films and novels.

Not all such tensions had disappeared by the start of the war; in 1943 Jewish communities in Boston were the target for attacks by groups of young anti-Semitic toughs, and a secret Office of War Information poll taken during the war revealed that one in five Americans thought that Hitler's anti-Jewish policies were 'justified' (though this was, of course, before the full dimensions of the 'Final Solution' were revealed to a horrified world). Racial tension led to serious disorders as newly arrived black and white war workers competed for scarce housing and recreation facilities in Northern cities. A racial brawl in a Detroit park on a hot summer day in 1943 led to a riot that cost the lives of 25 blacks and nine whites before it was brought to an end by the intervention of some 6000 armed soldiers. Nevertheless, without anyone intending or planning the result, the war indirectly unleashed forces that led toward a more homogeneous and egalitarian society. Military service, jumbling together young men from every part of America, was a great solvent of prejudice and ignorance. Millions of families left their familiar neighborhoods to

take war industry jobs in new cities. (Los Angeles alone gained nearly half a million new inhabitants during the war.) After the war millions of veterans took advantage of the GI bill (which among other benefits offered low-cost home mortgages and financial assistance for those enrolling in higher education) to move out of old neighborhoods and into new cities or suburbs. Increasingly, ethnic lifestyles were a matter of consumer choice rather than inherited and unquestioned ways of life.

There was only one ethnic group that was deliberately excluded from this spirit of tolerance. More than 110,000 people of Japanese descent living in the United States when the war broke out, the great majority of them US citizens, were ordered by the military authorities to report to government detention camps in the spring of 1942. Most, except those released for military or other national service, would remain in the camps for the next three years. The decision to intern Japanese-Americans represented a triumph of hysteria and racial prejudice over reason; for there was little reason to assume that they were more prone to disloyalty or acts of sabotage than any other group of Americans, and no one proposed taking similar measures against German- or Italian-Americans. In effect they were simply convenient scapegoats for the frustration and anger provoked by Pearl Harbor and other military reverses the United States suffered in the early months of the war in the Pacific.

America and World War II

When the war began in Europe in 1939 the United States, like the Soviet Union, was a relatively minor player in international power relations. Neither country had even participated in the now-infamous Munich negotiations the previous fall. Britain, France and Germany (and, to a lesser extent, Italy) were then the only powers that really counted in European affairs. Two years later Pearl Harbor may have brought the era of American isolationism to a close, but America's future as a world power was still unclear for most of World War II. Would the United States attempt yet another retreat to isolationism after the defeat of the Axis powers? Would it become the leader of

its own power bloc and attempt to reorder as much of the world as it could according to its own interests and priorities? Or would it become the architect of a new system of collective security and international cooperation?

As far as could be told from Roosevelt's public pronouncements, it was this last goal that guided his wartime foreign policy decisions. In a speech to Congress early in 1941 Roosevelt had spoken of the 'four freedoms' he hoped the struggle against Nazism would preserve and expand throughout the world: freedom of speech, freedom of worship, freedom from want and freedom from fear. In the Atlantic Charter statement, jointly drafted in August 1941 by Roosevelt and British prime minister Winston Churchill, the two leaders pledged themselves to the effort to create a post-war settlement based on the right of all nations to enjoy self-determination. Later in the war Roosevelt became a leading advocate for the establishment of a new international organization, the United Nations, to take the place of the discredited League of Nations. But Roosevelt's idealistic pronouncements were always tempered by a sense of political and military expediency – particularly his desire to maintain good relations with the Soviet Union, whose military forces were engaging the bulk of the Nazi war machine.

Roosevelt met twice during the war with his Soviet counterpart, Joseph Stalin, and believed that he had developed a strong rapport with the dictator. Roosevelt went to great lengths to reassure Americans about Soviet intentions and reliability. 'I think the Russians are perfectly friendly,' he announced after one meeting with Stalin. 'They aren't trying to gobble up all the rest of Europe or the world.' How much of these reassurances Roosevelt really believed remains unclear; in private he occasionally spoke more skeptically about Soviet intentions. Certainly he did everything he could to keep his Russian allies in the dark about the steps the US and Britain were taking to develop the atomic bomb. To the extent that Roosevelt was sincerely convinced of the benevolent character of Stalin's post-war intentions, he shared this view with many others during the war. *Time* magazine featured an avuncular-looking Stalin as its 'Man of the Year' in 1943; *Life* magazine called the Russians 'one hell of a people,' who 'look like Americans, dress like Americans and think like Americans;' the *Reader's Digest* urged its readers to contribute to campaigns for Russian War Relief, declaring, 'John Doe's pennies, dimes and quarters are helping to fight Hitler right now along the Russian front.' And Roosevelt could cite bipartisan support, if not total consensus, for his pro-Soviet stance. His Republican opponent in the 1940 election, Wall Street lawyer Wendell Willkie, took a trip to the Soviet Union in 1942, which he described in glowing detail in his bestselling book *One World* the following year. Willkie, like Roosevelt, offered a reassuring portrait of America's new ally, telling his readers that 'Russia is neither going to eat us or seduce us.'

The unity of what Churchill called the 'Grand Alliance' of the United States, Great Britain and the Soviet Union reached its rhetorical peak in the first wartime summit meeting of the Big Three in December 1943 in Teheran, Iran. The tensions within the alliance over when the Western allies would establish a second front in Europe and draw some of the pressure off the hard-pressed Red Army in the East were set to rest as plans were finalized for a cross-Channel invasion of France in the spring of 1944. Roosevelt, Churchill and Stalin released a joint statement at the conclusion of their meeting. It became known as the

Teheran Declaration, and promised a peaceful, harmonious post-war world order:

We express our determination that our nations shall work together in the war and in the peace that will follow ... We recognize fully the supreme responsibility resting upon us and all the nations to make a peace which will command good will from the overwhelming masses of the peoples of the world and banish the scourge and terror of war for many generations.

This vision of international cooperation found institutional expression in the spring of 1945 with the founding of the United Nations – its formation agreed upon at a second meeting of the Big Three at the Yalta conference in the Soviet Crimea in February 1945. But even as the delegates met in San Francisco the following June to ratify the UN's establishment, the promise of post-war harmony had come to seem a utopian dream.

From the beginning the Grand Alliance was fraught with internal conflict, suppressed in the interest of the common goal of defeating Nazi Germany. Stalin's ambitions in Eastern Europe, which were to achieve a secure, invasion-proof *cordon sanitaire* along his country's western border, clashed with Roosevelt's commitment to attaining a peace based on self-determination and international cooperation. Poland, whose invasion by the Nazis in 1939 had been the trigger for the outbreak of the war, proved the acid-test of Soviet intentions. The chances of a government

Above: Roosevelt meets Soviet Foreign Minister Vyacheslav Molotov in Washington in 1942. Although wartime allies the Soviet Union and the United States held diametrically opposed views on the shape of postwar Europe.

Left: New Yorkers celebrate the surrender of Japan and the end of World War II. After the miseries of the Great Depression, and the agonies of war, people across the globe were hopeful that a new era of peace and prosperity had arrived.

Above right: The president who did the most to shape the postwar world was Harry Truman, Roosevelt's successor. His obvious distaste for the Russians contrasted with Roosevelt's more optimistic assessment of America's war-time ally.

Right: A US postage stamp expresses heartfelt hopes for the success of the new United Nations Organization.

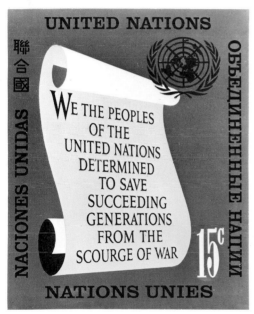

so than the idealistic statements offered in the Atlantic Charter and at Teheran and Yalta, would define the American outlook in the aftermath of the war.

Victory in Europe came with Germany's surrender on 8 May 1945, victory in the Pacific with Japan's surrender on 14 August. VE-Day and VJ-Day each drew huge cheering crowds into the nation's streets (a half-million in New York's Times Square). Americans' sense of triumph in a just cause was tempered only by regret that the architect of victory, Franklin Roosevelt, was not there to share in the glory of the moment. Rumors about the President's failing health, which had been circulating since the 1944 election campaign when Roosevelt had bested the Republican nominee Thomas E Dewey, did not lessen the shock for the country when he suddenly died of a cerebral hemorrhage on 12 April 1945. With Roosevelt beginning his thirteenth year in office, after four successive victories at the polls, many Americans found it hard to imagine anyone else occupying the White House – particularly the obscure former clothing salesman, National Guard artillery captain and Senator from Missouri, Harry Truman. After only three months in the office of the vice-president, during which he had been mostly ignored by Roosevelt, Truman was understandably overwhelmed by the responsibilities he had suddenly inherited. As he told reporters, with typically earthy candor, the day after FDR's death, 'I don't know whether you fellows ever had a load of hay fall on you, but when they told me yesterday what had happened, I felt like the moon, the stars and all the planets had fallen on me.' But it would not be long before his natural scrappiness surfaced, and he soon impressed his subordinates with his ability to take command and make rapid-fire decisions. Nor was the United States the only one of the wartime allies to confront the question of a change of leaders. British voters rejected Winston Churchill's bid for continued leadership, handing the Labour Party and Clement Attlee victory in that summer's Parliamentary elections. On the other hand, the Canadians chose to reaffirm their support for their long-standing prime minister, Mackenzie King.

Truman was all for standing up to the Russians. He had little inclination for devising the kind of subtle mutual accommodations that Roosevelt and Stalin had toyed with at Teheran and Yalta. In a meeting with the visiting Soviet Foreign Minister Vyacheslav Molotov in Washington on 23 April, less than two weeks after FDR's death, Truman bluntly rebuked the Soviets for violations of the Yalta agreements. When Molotov complained that 'I have never been talked to like that in my life,' Truman replied curtly, 'Carry out your agreements and you won't get talked to like that.'

Truman's tone was popular with his foreign policy advisers, who had long chafed at what they felt were Roosevelt's excessive concessions to Stalin. But the new hard line in Washington sparked intransigence rather than acquiescence on the part of the Soviets. When the Big Three met for their final wartime summit meeting in Potsdam, Germany, from mid July to early August 1945, a superficial cordiality prevailed among the victors. The Allied leaders maintained a paper consensus about the post-war settlement through the device of deferring most of the important decisions that confronted them, leaving *de facto* control over Europe's political and economic future in the hands of the rival occupying forces. A Cold War pattern of mutual suspicion and misunderstanding was already coming to dominate international relations in a bipolar world. Just as Truman interpreted Soviet actions

friendly to the Soviet Union emerging from a free election in Poland after the war were virtually nil, given the traditional Russian-Polish antipathy and the recent and brutal experience of Soviet occupation of eastern Poland in 1939-41. Stalin was under no illusions on that score, and as the Red Army moved through Poland in 1945, the Soviet Union acted with a heavy hand to assure that the new Polish provisional government would be dominated by communist forces. Roosevelt understood that there was very little that the democratic powers could do to prevent the Soviet Union from establishing whatever kind of government it wanted. At Yalta in February 1945 the Big Three agreed to yet another formal declaration of good intentions regarding the rights of self-determination for the newly liberated nations of Europe, but they made no attempt to establish any kind of administrative system or set of procedures to guarantee truly free elections. Stalin assumed that the Western leaders had conceded him the right to reorder Eastern European

affairs to his own liking. (Stalin, in turn, raised no objections when the British crushed the communist-led resistance movement in Greece and established a government friendly to British interests.) Although the Soviet Union made a few cosmetic gestures to reassure Western public opinion, allowing some non-communist leaders into the new Polish provisional government, it soon became clear that nothing like free elections would ever be allowed in that unhappy country. The process of establishing communist control was more complicated and protracted in Hungary and Czechoslovakia, but the basic pattern had been set.

Roosevelt the pragmatist

If Roosevelt had lived to oversee the postwar settlement, he might have been able to maintain some kind of accommodation with Stalin on Eastern Europe. He was by nature a pragmatist and compromiser, and the best that could be expected, given the relation of forces in the region, was some kind of compromise solution (as in Finland, where the Soviets allowed an independent government and free institutions to continue, so long as the Finnish government scrupulously refrained from challenging Soviet foreign policy). But Roosevelt was not alive, and his was not the only vision of the post-war world. The mood of other American policymakers and a significant portion of the general public was far less prone to compromise by the spring of 1945. A competing vision of the post-war world now challenged Roosevelt's hoped-for system of international cooperation. This competing vision, soon to win ascendancy in Washington, has been called the 'American Century,' so named for an influential editorial written by publisher Henry Luce in *Life* magazine in February 1941. The war, Luce argued, should be understood as both a trial and an opportunity for the United States. World War II was America's second and last chance 'to assume the leadership of the world.' America had wasted its opportunity for leadership in 1919 by retreating from involvement in international affairs, but it should not do so again. Luce's vision, much more

in Eastern Europe as the prelude to an attempt at world conquest, Stalin professed to see in Truman's words and actions an attempt to take back the concessions he claimed had been granted him at Teheran and Yalta.

The American development of the atomic bomb also contributed to the breakdown of relations between the former allies. Stalin had, through the efforts of his espionage system, long known of the purpose of the 'Manhattan Project' that had drawn America's and Britain's best physicists to the seclusion of the Nevada desert. (In September a Soviet defector named Igor Gouzenko would bring the Canadian government evidence of a Soviet spy ring operating in Canada seeking information on the making of the atomic bomb. This was the beginning of the unraveling of a story of wartime espionage that would culminate in the arrest of Julius and Ethel Rosenberg in the United States in 1950.) At Potsdam a delighted Truman received the news of the first successful testing of the bomb, and mentioned casually to Stalin that the United States had developed a powerful new weapon. Stalin, with an equally studied casualness, expressed mild interest and his hope that the new weapon, whatever it might be, would be used to crush Japanese resistance. The destruction of Hiroshima and Nagasaki in August displayed the immense power of the atomic bomb, and historians still debate if the main point of the bombings was to force the Japanese to surrender or to convince the Soviets to be more amenable. Various plans that were floated after the war for vesting control of nuclear weapons in the United Nations came to nothing, and a vast new arms race came into being, with the Americans attempting to maintain their initial advantage and the Soviets racing to catch up.

By 1946 the Grand Alliance was shattered; Europe was divided by what Winston Churchill labeled an 'iron curtain.' Washington's strategy for dealing with its former Soviet ally was given coherence and a name in a report written by one of its leading Soviet experts, George Kennan. Kennan, writing from Moscow in February 1946, argued that the internal dynamics of the Soviet dictatorship required it to maintain an attitude of perma-

nent hostility toward the outside world and that Soviet leaders habitually mistook offers of concession and compromise as a sign of weakness. As refined in an article published in the influential journal *Foreign Affairs* in 1947, Kennan concluded: 'Soviet pressure against the free institutions of the western world is something that can be contained by the adroit and vigilant application of counterforce at a series of constantly shifting geographical and political points, corresponding to the shift and maneuvers of Soviet polity.' Kennan's ideas became known as the 'Containment Doctrine,' but the application they were put to was not quite what Kennan had had in mind. Kennan, like the Soviet leaders he studied, tended

to think in terms of spheres of influence. The United States, Kennan thought, should exercise its powers to contain Soviet expansion in a selective way, emphasizing such parts of the world as Western Europe and Japan where it had particularly vital interests to defend. But the blend of the Containment Doctrine and notions of an 'American Century' proved a heady brew in Washington. Truman, in a speech asking Congress to approve military and economic aid for Greece and Turkey in March 1947, went on to pledge that the United States would hereafter:

support free peoples who are resisting attempted subjugation by armed minorites or by outside pressures. I believe that we must assist free peoples to work out their own destinies in their own way.

This 'Truman Doctrine' speech marked an important turning point in the history of US foreign policy. It represented an open-ended commitment to a policy of global confrontation, intervention and counter-revolution. Though the implications of the speech alarmed some conservatives who clung to the isolationist sentiments of the pre-war era, and some liberals who still hoped that the United States might arrive at an understanding with the Soviet Union, this radical change in America's traditional stance provoked remarkably little debate. By now most Americans were persuaded that the Soviet Union represented almost as great a threat to their freedom, well-being and national security as Nazi Germany had only a few years earlier. A bipartisan consensus developed behind the new anti-communist policies of containment, and Congress willingly set up the institutional structure necessary for waging the Cold War, going along with such innovations as the Central Intelligence Agency (1947), the peacetime draft (1948), the 'Marshall Plan' for massive economic aid to Western Europe (1948) and American participation in the North Atlantic Treaty Organization (NATO) (1949). Canada became a charter member of NATO.

On the domestic front Truman took over the presidency with a pledge of continuity with FDR policies. Many policymakers, as well as ordinary

Americans, feared that once the stimulus of wartime spending was ended the economic depression of the 1930s would reappear in full force. As American industries began the process of reconversion to civilian production in 1945, tens of thousands of workers were laid off, and many returning veterans initially found it hard to find jobs. Congress responded by passing the Full Employment Act in 1946, which committed the federal government to finding new means to stimulate the economy to prevent depressions. The new law represented an attempt to make permanent the 'Keynesian revolution' in economic thinking which took place in the 1930s. There was to be no return to the laissez-faire policies of an

earlier day, when the government leaders made it a matter of principle to refrain from any intervention in the economy.

Truman's commitment to his predecessor's economic policies was undermined by an increasingly unfavorable political climate. A wave of industrial strikes took place in 1946, as workers, freed from restraints of labor's wartime 'no strike pledge' and the authority of the War Labor Board, sought to make up for lost time. It turned into the greatest strike wave since 1919. Truman antagonized the labor movement, the backbone of the New Deal political coalition, by using the authority granted the president by wartime anti-labor legislation to end the strikes. When coal

miners went out on strike in 1946 he seized the mines and ordered them back to work; when railroad workers went out on strike that same year he threatened to ask Congress for authority to draft strikers into the armed forces. The strike wave and Truman's response not only disrupted the unity of the liberal camp, it also provoked a conservative reaction. Even during the war complaints were often heard that the new government bureaucracies were strangling the free enterprise system. By the end of the war conservative themes found a wide response as Americans grew tired of rationing and price-control and other enforced sacrifices. Truman never quite made up his mind whether he had more to lose by maintaining price controls, which would provoke further indignation over government interference in the economy, or lifting the controls, which would contribute to an inflationary spiral. In 1946 he first allowed the Office of Price Administration to close down, and then, after retail prices shot up 25 percent in just over two weeks, he reestablished its authority to set prices. He thus managed to offend just about everyone and in the process created a politically damaging image as an indecisive blunderer. As a popular joke had it, 'To err is Truman.'

The Republicans were able to turn Truman's troubles to their own advantage in 1946. Campaigning under the slogan 'Had enough?' they gained control of both houses of Congress for the first time in a decade and a half. Hoping to roll back the changes the New Deal had brought in industrial relations, the new Congress passed the Taft-Hartley Act in 1947, overriding Truman's veto and ignoring charges from the labor movement that it was a 'slave-labor' act. The new law attacked the closed shop, sought to restrict union contributions to political campaigns and authorized the President to order striking workers back to their jobs in the event of national emergency. Despite this set-back, the labor movement was able to hold its own and even expand its power considerably in the post-war era. Corporate employers proved more conciliatory than the politicians because they remembered all too vividly the chaos and economic costs of the hard-

Above left: The American scientist J R Oppenheimer was a vital figure in the Manhattan Project's development of the atomic bomb. His horror at the devastation these weapons caused led him to oppose the development of the thermonuclear or 'H' bomb.

Left: Ethel and Julius Rosenberg on the day before they were sent to the electric chair. They were accused of spying for the Soviet Union and found guilty on charges of treason. The justice of this verdict is still debated.

Above: Workers from a Western Electric plant in New York picket their workplace. The year after V-J Day saw the greatest wave of industrial action in American history.

Right: Thomas Dewey, crime-fighting governor of New York and twice candidate for the presidency on the Republican ticket, lends his voice to the Cold War propaganda effort.

fought strikes of the 1930s. To avoid a repetition of those days, they signed long-term contracts with their unions, granting a host of new benefits and cost-of-living raises to employees. In return the unions refrained from raising issues that touched on management prerogatives as to the way work was organized on the shop floor. Real wages rose steadily over the next few decades, while overall union membership, even in the absence of the kind of militant organizing drives that had characterized the 1930s, increased from 14.3 million in 1945 to just over 18 million by 1960. In 1955 the two rival labor groups, the American Federation of Labor (AFL) and the Congress of Industrial Organizations (CIO), put aside the differences that had divided them since the New Deal and merged. The new AFL-CIO President George Meany pronounced 'American labor has never had it so good.'

When the Republicans regained control of Congress in 1946 they also pledged to end what they charged was undue communist influence in American public life. In Washington the House Un-American Activities Committee (HUAC) garnered headlines in 1947 for its investigation of alleged communist infiltration in the film industry, sending 10 recalcitrant witnesses, the 'Hollywood Ten,' to prison for contempt of Congress. A young California Congressman named Richard Nixon began a meteoric rise to political prominence as he headed an investigation of Alger Hiss in 1948. (Hiss, a prominent foreign policy adviser under Roosevelt, had been eased out of the State Department by Truman. He was accused by a one-time political associate, Whittaker Chambers, of having been a communist agent in the 1930s. Although Hiss denied Chambers' story, the case led to his indictment and eventual imprisonment for perjury.) The Republicans charged that the Truman administration, like its predecessor, was 'soft on communism.' To counter such charges, Truman established a program of loyalty investi-

Left: In another controversial case of Cold War espionage, Alger Hiss (on the right) was found guilty of lying to a grand jury about his supposed participation in a group passing State Department documents to the Soviet Union during the 1930s.

Below: South Koreans round up North Korean prisoners. In the background are US Marine Corps tanks. The war in Korea broke out in 1950 and continued until 1953, when a cease-fire was agreed, a dramatic example of the Cold War becoming 'Hot.'

Far right: A savage cartoon attacks supposed communists hiding in government positions. Senator Joseph McCarthy's sensational claims of a State Department riddled with infiltrators sparked a witch hunt for spies and saboteurs.

Below right: The great war hero Eisenhower visits Korea in November 1952. His administration brought the war to an end, to the relief of a weary America, frustrated with the bloodletting and lack of a decisive victory.

gations of federal employees, which led to the firing of hundreds, often on vague charges that assumed guilt-by-association. Witnesses called before Congressional investigating committees were given the unpalatable choice of 'taking the fifth' – invoking their constitutional right not to incriminate themselves through their own testimony – or naming names. As a mood of mutual suspicion and fear began to descend on the country, reporters discovered that many Americans were afraid to associate themselves with any controversial causes; one enterprising reporter spent an afternoon attempting to gather signatures on a copy of the Declaration of Independence and found no takers.

Truman as underdog

Conditions seemed ideal for a Republican triumph in 1948. But surprisingly, the Republican Congressional victories in 1946 proved a setback for GOP's dreams of regaining the White House. Truman, in a brilliantly fought campaign, took full advantage of his own status as underdog. Unable to get any legislation through the Republican-controled Congress, Truman began to send them bills he knew in advance would be rejected. Campaigning as an outsider who could not be blamed for the problems the country was facing as a result of the 'do-nothing' Eightieth Congress, Truman was able to reunite a pro-New Deal majority behind his own candidacy. The Republicans added to their own difficulties by once again selecting the aloof and uninspiring New York Governor Thomas E Dewey as their presidential candidate. While Dewey thought he was coasting effortlessly toward victory, Truman ran a hard-hitting whistle-stop campaign, urged on by enthusiastic crowds and chants of 'Give 'em Hell, Harry!'

Truman was challenged from the left as well as the right in 1948. Henry Wallace, who had served as Secretary of Agriculture during the New Deal and as Roosevelt's vice-president during his third term, had been dumped from the ticket in 1944 when his reputation for ultra-liberalism made him a political liability. Wallace's decision to challenge Truman as the candidate of an independent third party proved a fatal error, for the country was in no mood for Wallace's brand of liberalism at the time of deepening Cold War sentiment. At the same time, Truman was able to steal some of the Wallace Progressive Party's thunder by calling for new social welfare programs, the repeal of the Taft-Hartley Act and, in a particularly shrewd maneuver, accepting a strong civil rights plank in the 1948 Democratic Party platform. (The latter decision led to a walk-out of 'Dixiecrats' under South Carolina Senator Strom Thurmond. They ran their own independent presidential candidate who failed to do significant damage to Truman's chances of victory.) The Soviets inadvertently aided Truman's campaign by blockading the divided city of Berlin in June 1948. Truman responded decisively, organizing a vast airlift to supply the city and eventually forcing a humiliating Soviet back-down.

In Canada, meanwhile, there was a change of leadership that involved no change in the essential political status quo. Long-time prime minister Mackenzie King resigned in November 1948, to be succeeded by another Liberal Party leader, Louis S St Laurent.

Truman's surprise victory in 1948 seemed to some Democratic enthusiasts to presage an era of liberal triumph similar to the New Deal years. In his inaugural address in January 1949 Truman proclaimed his goal of establishing a 'Fair Deal,' and he sent Congress an ambitious packet of proposals for new social security, national health insurance and public housing measures. But apart from measures that could be achieved by executive order, such as ending segregation in the armed forces, Truman achieved little of substance in his last four years in office. The new Democratic Congress proved almost as uninterested in issues of domestic reform as its Republican predecessor. Foreign policy and national security issues dominated the nation's political agenda, as Americans grew ever more concerned about the international spread of communism. Truman found himself in a no-win situation that was partially of his own making. The more he aroused the nation to the threat of foreign and domestic communism in the interests of securing national unity behind the Cold War and securing Democratic unity behind his own presidency, the more he alarmed Americans and seemed to substantiate right-wing charges that his administration was unable to cope with the communist threat.

Truman's political fate was sealed in 1949-50 when the United States suffered a series of blows to its sense of national prestige, power and security. In August 1949 the American-backed Nationalist Chinese forces were forced to flee the Asian mainland, leaving China in the hands of the communists, sparking an acrimonious debate in the United States over 'Who Lost China?' A month later Truman had to announce the grim news that the Soviet Union had conducted its first successful nuclear test, ending the American monopoly on the atomic bomb. And in June 1950 the armies of communist North Korea invaded South Korea, an event widely interpreted at the time as the opening battle of the Third World War. After initial setbacks US military forces, fighting under the banner of the United Nations, were able to push the North Koreans back across their own border. But when the headstrong American commander, Douglas MacArthur, continued to pursue the North Korean army toward the Chinese border, he provoked the intervention of Red Chinese forces. After a bloody and hard-fought retreat which brought the UN forces back roughly to the area of South Korea's northern border, the war settled into a frustrating stalemate.

The war was unpopular in America, but so were any measures regarded as appeasing the communists. The continuing disputes between Truman

and MacArthur finally broke into the open in the spring of 1951, when MacArthur, arguing that there was 'no substitute for victory,' called for a more aggressive American military strategy, even at the risk of an all-out war with China. In what would later be celebrated as a landmark assertion of civilian control of the military, Truman relieved MacArthur of his command and brought him back to the United States. But it was MacArthur who was initially treated as the hero of the episode; on his return he would be lionized by Congress and the public as a wronged anti-communist champion.

In February 1950, shortly before the outbreak of the Korean War, an obscure first-term senator from Wisconsin named Joseph McCarthy grabbed the nation's attention with an after-dinner speech at a Republican gathering in Wheeling, West Virginia. Waving a fistful of documents that he was careful to keep anyone from examining too closely, he charged that the State Department under the Truman administration was knowingly employing over 200 communists. Despite the fact that over the next few years he would prove unable to establish the identity of a single com-

munist in the federal government, his charges struck a responsive chord in many Americans who were unable to understand why a nation that had been so powerful in 1945 could not enforce its will in the world only half a decade later. McCarthy's investigations would continue to dominate headlines throughout the early 1950s, destroying careers, inspiring fear and setting an abysmally low tone of political debate. With the Democrats battered by charges of 'twenty years of treason,' the Republicans swept back into the White House in 1952. Their candidate was Dwight Eisenhower, who had had a firm hold on public affections ever since his years as commander of Allied forces in Western Europe during the war and who now promised to go to Korea to end the conflict there.

Eisenhower radiated a kind of reassuring blandness in a time of overbearing political personalities. But historians would later find reasons to assess his presidency in a generally favorable light. Eisenhower had promised to end the war in Korea, and he did so within six months of taking office. The following year he refused to send American troops to bail out the failing effort of the French to retain control of their Indochinese colonies – though he did make the first commitment of US military and economic aid to the new South Vietnamese regime. Despite the bellicose rhetoric of his Secretary of State, John Foster Dulles, who was fond of phrases like 'roll-back' and 'liberation,' Eisenhower pursued a cautious policy in relation to the Soviet Union, avoiding confrontation and beginning the process that would later be called *détente*. He also cut the defense budget significantly, something that none of his successors ever wanted or was able to do. At the same time, he initiated a great expansion of the American nuclear arsenal, including the development of the hydrogen bomb; his theory was that defense dollars spent on nuclear weapons delivered 'more bang for the buck.' As far as domestic policies were concerned, he undertook no major social initiatives, but he refrained from any attempt to dismantle the basic structure of New Deal social programs. Responding to suggestions from some ultra-conservative Republicans that he take a more aggressive approach toward the New Deal legacy, Eisenhower commented scornfully:

Should any political party attempt to abolish social security and eliminate labor laws and farm programs, you would not hear of that party again . . . There is a tiny splinter group, of course, that believes you can do these things. Their number is negligible and they are stupid.

One of the reasons Eisenhower had agreed to run for President in 1952 was to counter the growing strength of the extreme right within the GOP. (As the first American commander of NATO, he particularly feared the ultra-conservatives' emphasis on confronting communism in Asia at the expense of defending western Europe.) But he chose Richard Nixon as his running mate, in a conciliatory gesture toward the conservative wing of the GOP, leaving Nixon to play the role of anticommunist 'hatchet-man,' while Ike himself refrained from the mud-slinging style of the campaign. Once in office, Eisenhower sought to distance himself from what was already being called 'McCarthyism,' but he was careful never to directly challenge McCarthy: even when the Wisconsin Republican accused the army of sheltering subversives, Eisenhower maintained his silence. (McCarthy's charges against the army led to televised 'Army-McCarthy hearings,' which proved disastrous to McCarthy, revealing his deceitful bullying to a vast audience. In the aftermath of those hearings the Senate censured McCarthy,

and in doing so broke his political power. McCarthy began to drink heavily and died in 1957.)

In the aftermath of the Korean armistice, and with the death of Joseph Stalin that same year, the expectations of the imminent outbreak of a Third World War began to lessen. Eisenhower met with the new Soviet leaders in Geneva in 1955, and relations improved between the two superpowers, although there were many reverses to the gradual unfolding of the process of *détente*. Eisenhower's own advisers were deeply suspicious of Soviet motives, and Soviet military leader Nikita Khrushchev wavered between a conciliatory and a hardline stance throughout the later 1950s and the early 1960s. In 1958 Khrushchev challenged the Western powers to settle the vexing problem of the divisions of Berlin once and for all, setting a six-month limit for the signing of a

peace treaty between the Allies and the two German states. If the Allies failed to act, he warned, he would sign a separate peace treaty with communist East Germany, and the West would then have to renegotiate its military presence in West Berlin with the East Germans. Eisenhower called his bluff by calmly ignoring the ultimatum, and Khrushchev backed down. The following year the Soviet leader visited the United States for a two-week tour that turned into a media circus and diplomatic love-feast. Meeting with Eisenhower at Camp David, Khrushchev agreed to a summit meeting the following spring in Paris.

In the mid 1950s pacifist groups and concerned scientists had begun to warn of the dangers of nuclear fall-out, released in the atmosphere by both Soviet and American tests. As ordinary citizens developed an uncomfortable familiarity

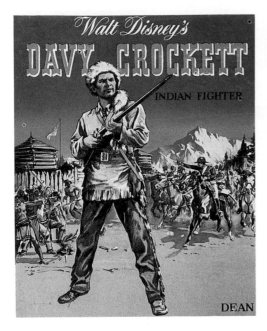

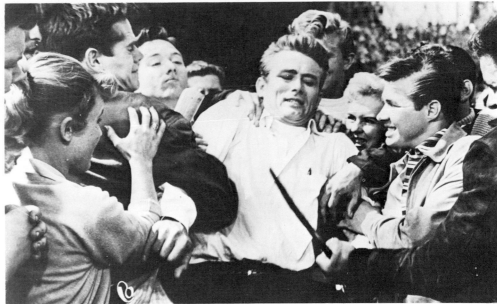

with scientific terms like 'Strontium 90,' Eisenhower began to give serious consideration to the possibility of capping his presidency with the signing of a test-ban treaty, and in fact both the United States and the Soviet Union observed an informal ban on atmospheric testing from 1958 through 1961. But in May 1960 a U-2, a high-flying US reconnaissance plane, was shot down over the Soviet Union, and its pilot, Francis Gary Powers, was captured by the Russians. Khrushchev was furious, and the incident scuttled the Paris summit. Meaningful efforts to renew *détente* would not be undertaken for another decade.

As the fear of war and the hysteria of the McCarthy era slowly dissipated, Americans began to relax and enjoy the benefits of living in a continent unscarred by war. Canadians, though living in an economy increasingly subordinate to

American control, also shared the economic benefits of the new era. Starting in 1946 the enforced scarcity of depression and wartime had given way to the greatest spending spree in North American history, fueled by wartime savings, easy credit and new and ever more sophisticated advertising techniques. The first thing every consumer wanted after the war was a new car: total automobile registration in the US soared from 26 million in 1945 to 40 million only five years later. Many of those new cars were destined to be parked in front of new homes in suburbs, often financed by federal loans. The suburbs were linked to cities and workplaces by the vast new federal highway system started in the 1950s. The requirements of suburban living provided a seemingly insatiable market for consumer durables: old standbys such as washing machines, vacuum cleaners and refrig-

erators and brand new products such as dishwashers, automatic garbage disposals and, of course, television sets. By 1956 two-thirds of all American homes had at least one television set; by 1960 that figure had reached 90 percent.

The rush to the suburbs and the new patterns of consumer spending were also linked to the phenomenon of the 'baby boom,' a 15-year upswing in fertility rates and a decline in the average age of marriage that has puzzled demographers ever since it first appeared in 1946. Whatever the cause (and it went on too long simply to be the product of the mass return of World War II veterans to their wives and sweethearts), the baby boom delighted American businessmen. The cultural history of the baby-boom generation can be charted in the rise and fall of a succession of fads: with the Davy Crockett phenomenon of 1955 fol-

Above left: These children were part of an anti-nuclear war demonstration in New York in 1961. Such displays of pacifist feelings were always small in number at this time although widely reported.

Left: Elvis Presley's recording of 'Heartbreak Hotel' marked the nationwide exploitation of rock and roll. His sensual performances on stage won him the adoration of the young and the disapprobation of their parents.

Above: A children's book cover of a biography of the legendary frontiersman, Davy Crockett. This romantic, historical figure became wildly popular in the late 1950s, along with a craze for coon-skin hats like those he wore.

Above right: James Dean, in a still from *Rebel Without a Cause*. This movie, and *The Wild One* starring Marlon Brando, fixed the notion of violent rebelliousness on the part of America's young firmly in the national consciousness.

Right: A 1955 Oldsmobile. American cars of the 1950s had an exuberant quality that came to characterize the nation's mood in the Eisenhower era.

lowed by hula hoops, silly putty and other products of the new 'youth market' entrepreneurs. In 1956 Elvis Presley hit the number one spot on the country and western, rhythm and blues and pop charts with his recording of 'Heartbreak Hotel,' signaling the start of the rock and roll era. Hollywood began to shape its offerings to appeal to the tastes of the new generation with such movies as *The Wild One* and *Rebel Without a Cause*, which pretended to condemn juvenile delinquency but actually established Marlon Brando and James Dean as icons of youthful rebellion. As the baby-boom generation moved through grammar school into high school and on to college (the number of college students increased from 1.5 million in the late 1940s to 3.5 million in 1960 and peaked at 6 million in 1968), it developed a distinct generational identity.

The growth of colleges and universities transformed surrounding communities in cities such as Cambridge, Ann Arbor and Berkeley, as students moved into dilapidated neighborhoods (often side by side with black communities), creating 'youth ghettoes' that fostered a sense of inhabiting a separate world from adults. Contemporary observers dismissed the college students of the 1950s as a 'silent generation,' but beneath the placid surface of college life in those years the ground was being prepared for a kind of cultural revolution.

But that, of course, was hard to predict in the late 1950s. Social scientists were in general agreement that 'consensus' had replaced conflict in American political life. The United States had apparently moved onto a permanent plateau of prosperity, its democratic institutions were securely established and the only remaining problem for political leaders and administrators was to figure out how to divide up the ever-expanding economic pie. The few social critics who continued to ply their trade in the 1950s confined themselves to expression of concern over the price Americans were paying for the good times they lived in. Were Americans becoming too conformist, a nation of 'organization men,' vulnerable to the 'hidden persuaders' of advertising? But those were minor problems.

Political transformations

Canada had witnessed a dramatic political change in 1957 when the Liberal Party lost control of Parliament for the first time in 22 years. The Progressive Conservative Party, under the leadership of John Diefenbaker, replaced the Liberals as ruling party. A similar turnover in political power was widely expected in the United States after the results of the 1958 mid-term Congressional elections saw the Democrats regain control of Congress. As Democrats and Republicans geared up for the 1960 election domestic and international concerns mingled in the growing debate over national goals. When the Soviet Union launched its 'Sputnik' satellite into outer space in 1957, the Democrats had been quick to charge that the over-complacent Eisenhower administration was allowing the nation to fall behind the Russians in science and technology. More ominous than the prospect of losing what was suddenly christened the 'space race' was the possibility that the United States would fall behind the Soviet Union militarily. In the late 1950s the Democrats began warning of a 'bomber gap' (a gap which John Kennedy would discover did not, in fact, exist once he was in the White House). Army Chief of Staff Maxwell Taylor, who had long chafed under the budget cuts imposed by Eisenhower on the Pentagon, resigned his commission in 1959 and began to warn about the dangers of the administration's

Left: Martin Luther King, the black preacher who dared to have a dream of a racially equal America. One of the great figures of the postwar political scene, his selfless drive and ambition helped win blacks a measure of fair treatment hitherto denied them in the United States.

Far right: A demonstration in New York against President John F Kennedy's failure to sign a civil rights bill.

Below right: Willy Brandt and President Kennedy stand before the Brandenburg Gate in Berlin. The East Germans have hung red bunting on the gaps in the gate to prevent residents of East Berlin from seeing the US president.

Below far right: Kennedy and Soviet leader Nikita Khrushchev meet for the first time at Vienna in March 1961. The two men steered their countries through a difficult period of the Cold War, which included the building of the Berlin Wall and the Cuban Missile Crisis.

over-reliance on nuclear retaliation. As he declared in his influential 1960 book *The Uncertain Trumpet*, US military security required the capability for 'flexible response' – the nation had to be prepared to fight small guerilla wars as well as larger conventional wars and nuclear conflicts. (In the early 1960s Taylor would become an adviser in Kennedy's administration, ambassador to South Vietnam and a prominent advocate of stepped-up US military involvement in that country's battle with communist insurgents.)

The popular concern that the nation was lagging behind in space and defense preparations was linked with a vaguely defined sense of domestic unease, a feeling that American society and culture had lost its way somehow during the prosperous 1950s and was growing slack, even corrupt. Commentators pointed to the recessions that periodically pinched economic growth, the television quiz show scandals, concerns about conformity, the appearance of the Beat poets and other equally diverse and impressionistic evidence to support their contention that the nation was adrift. And although President Eisenhower took the precautionary step of establishing a Presidential Commission on National Goals, he was increasingly assigned the blame for this state of affairs.

In 1960 there were a number of strong contenders for the Democratic nomination: Hubert Humphrey, Adlai Stevenson and Lyndon Johnson among them. It was Massachusetts Senator John Fitzgerald Kennedy who emerged as the front-runner in a political process that was increasingly dominated by public relations imagery. This was a period when a veritable cult of the presidency began to develop among journalists and academic observers. Clinton Rossiter, a prominent political scientist, published a study in 1960 entitled *The American Presidency*, which described the role of the President as 'a kind of magnificent lion who can roam freely and do great deeds so long as he does not try to break loose from his broad reserva-

tion.' Biographies of 'strong Presidents' such as Andrew Jackson and Franklin Roosevelt began to appear on the best-seller lists. Eisenhower was scorned by Democratic liberals not only for the conservatism of his politics but for his cautious use of the powers of the executive branch. Kennedy made his campaign theme the promise to 'get America moving again.' How he intended to achieve that goal, and what his policies would be once in office, were less clearly stated. But what proved to be most important, both in the Democratic primaries and in Kennedy's race against the Republican nominee, Richard Nixon, was his ability to exude an air of confidence and competence. In his television debates with Nixon, another innovation of the campaign, Kennedy was reported by viewers to look more 'presidential' than his opponent, yet those who listened to the debates on the radio were much more likely than those who watched the televised version to judge Nixon the winner. Both candidates laid greater stress on foreign than on domestic issues: Kennedy attacked the administration for not doing enough to challenge the recently established communist regime in Cuba, while Nixon attempted to score points on Kennedy by criticizing his reluctance to go to war if necessary to protect the tiny Nationalist Chinese-held islands of Quemoy and Matsu.

It was a hard-fought campaign, and in the end Kennedy barely squeaked into office. His margin of victory over Nixon was a mere 100,000 of the nearly 69 million votes cast, a margin of less than two votes per voting district. Though Nixon refrained from challenging the results, there were charges that Chicago's Mayor Richard Daley had used underhanded means to deliver Illinois, and thus the election, to the Democratic candidate. Kennedy, the first Catholic to win the presidency, could not count on the full support of some traditionally Democratic strongholds, particularly in the Protestant South. On the other hand, he pulled a heavier than usual margin of support in

Catholic urban neighborhoods. And thanks to a timely call that led to the release of civil rights leader Martin Luther King, Jr from a Southern jail, he also attracted the enthusiastic support of black voters.

The impact of Kennedy's election on the nascent social protest movements of the 1960s cannot be overestimated. It was not that Kennedy had any intention of leading a great domestic reform movement; in his inaugural address he barely mentioned domestic issues, but the perception that Kennedy was a friend of movement for social change proved to be as important as the less exalted reality. Kennedy, in his personal style, his vigor, his youth, seemed to embody a change from the more stolid values of the Eisenhower years.

But precisely what Kennedy intended to do, what possibilities he sought to realize, remained unclear. The new President continued to downplay domestic issues his first two years in office, reluctant to challenge the powerful Republican-'Dixiecrat' coalition in Congress. Apart from bills for an increased minimum wage and job retraining, Kennedy sought almost no social legislation in 1961-62; he assumed that steady economic growth would solve most of the rest of the country's problems without requiring the intervention of the federal government. Walter Heller, chairman of Kennedy's Council of Economic Advisers, favored a strong government role in stimulating and managing the economy to achieve the goal of full employment. The way to do this, Heller and Kennedy agreed, was through promoting economic growth, rather than through the kind of 'pump-priming' social welfare programs that Franklin Roosevelt had favored. An activist President, through control of fiscal policy, taxation and government spending (especially defensive spending, which could be gotten through Congress with relative ease), could 'fine-tune' the economy to deliver full employment without inflation. Government spending for

defense and space projects, combined with the corporate tax cut Kennedy got Congress to pass in 1963, contributed to an enormous economic expansion in the early 1960s. The economic growth rate jumped from an annual 2.1 percent in 1961 to 4.5 percent in 1963, with only modest inflation, though it would contribute to the beginning of a much more serious inflationary spiral in the late 1960s.

Kennedy wanted to be remembered in history as a strong President and sought to make his mark in foreign policy. The efforts of Robert Kennedy, the attorney general, to get civil rights demonstrators to call a halt to the 'freedom rides' in 1961, because they might embarrass the President when he was at a summit meeting with Soviet leader Nikita Khrushchev, were a good

indication of the New Frontier's priorities that year. Eisenhower had gone out of office warning about the growing influence of the 'military-industrial complex' in American life. Kennedy did not share his predecessor's doubts. He stepped up defense spending dramatically his first year in office and began to pump money into the kind of flexible response units favored by Maxwell Taylor. He took a special interest in the Green Berets, the Army Special Forces, whose claim to fame was that they would be able to meet communist guerillas on their own terrain, fighting unconventional wars and living off the land.

Kennedy, like Eisenhower, believed in the value of covert action. Under Eisenhower the Central Intelligence Agency had intervened successfully to overthrow the Iranian government in

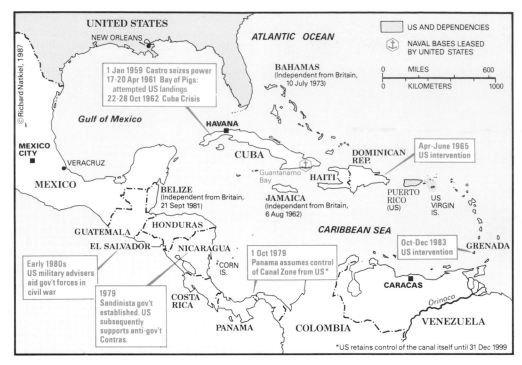

©Richard Natkiel, 1987

UNITED STATES
NEW ORLEANS
ATLANTIC OCEAN

US AND DEPENDENCIES

NAVAL BASES LEASED
BY UNITED STATES

BAHAMAS
(Independent from Britain,
10 July 1973)

1 Jan 1959 Castro seizes power
17-20 Apr 1961 Bay of Pigs:
attempted US landings
22-28 Oct 1962 Cuba Crisis

MILES   0   600
KILOMETERS   0   1000

Gulf of Mexico

HAVANA

MEXICO
CITY

VERACRUZ

CUBA

DOMINICAN
REP.

Apr-June 1965
US intervention

MEXICO

Guantanamo
Bay

HAITI

PUERTO
RICO
(US)

US
VIRGIN
IS.

BELIZE
(Independent from Britain,
21 Sept 1981)

JAMAICA
(Independent from Britain,
6 Aug 1962)

CARIBBEAN SEA

GUATEMALA

HONDURAS

Oct-Dec 1983
US intervention

GRENADA

EL SALVADOR

NICARAGUA

1 Oct 1979
Panama assumes control
of Canal Zone from US*

Early 1980s
US military advisers
aid gov't forces in
civil war

CORN
IS.

CARACAS

1979
Sandinista gov't
established. US
subsequently
supports anti-gov't
Contras.

COSTA
RICA

Orinoco

VENEZUELA

PANAMA

COLOMBIA

*US retains control of the canal itself until 31 Dec 1999

1953 and the Guatemalan government the following year. When Kennedy came into office he inherited a major CIA operation in-the-making, the planned invasion of communist Cuba by anti-Castro Cuban exiles. The invasion, which hit the beaches at Cuba's Bay of Pigs on 17 April 1961, turned into a fiasco and proved a serious blow to the prestige of the new administration. When Kennedy met with Khrushchev in Vienna in June the Soviet leader came away with the conviction that the young American President was weak and inexperienced. Once again, as in 1958, Khrushchev decided to test Western resolve in Berlin,

setting yet another six-month ultimatum for the signing of a comprehensive peace treaty with the two Germanies. Kennedy responded by going to Congress with requests for increased defense spending, civil defense and an authorization to activate 150,000 US reservists. Neither Khrushchev nor Kennedy would back down publicly, but the Soviet leader found a way out of the stalemate by building the Berlin Wall, cutting off the flow of refugees to West Berlin. Kennedy would later go to the divided city and within sight of the wall tell an ecstatic crowd that 'Ich bin ein Berliner.'

Meanwhile, Fidel Castro's Cuba still remained a

flashpoint in superpower relations. In the summer and early fall of 1962 Soviet technicians began construction of secret missile sites in Cuba, which Khrushchev would later claim were designed purely to defend the country from any further invasion attempts. Whatever the purpose of these installations, when Kennedy and his advisers learned in mid October of their existence they decided that they represented an intolerable threat to US national security. Rejecting a call from some of his advisers for immediate air strikes against the still-uncompleted sites, Kennedy chose to seek a public showdown with the Soviets. On 22 October he went on television and announced to a startled public the existence of the sites and his decision to set up a naval quarantine of Cuba to prevent the delivery of the Soviet missiles necessary for their completion. Khrushchev responded by accusing Kennedy of pushing the world toward the abyss of nuclear war. For six days in late October hundreds of millions of people around the world waited in frightened apprehension, not knowing if each day would prove to be their last. But in the end, with both sides eyeball to eyeball, Khrushchev blinked. Khrushchev ordered the Soviet ships at sea to stop before they ran into the blockade area around Cuba, and after feverish and confused negotiations he finally agreed on 28 October to remove the missiles in exchange for an American pledge not to invade Cuba.

Meanwhile the Diefenbaker government in Canada was running into difficulties on a number of fronts in the early 1960s, as unemployment rose, a controversy over the status of French-speaking Quebec heated up and a hot debate developed over whether Canada should acquire a new weapon system using US nuclear warheads. In a general election in the spring of 1963 the Liberals regained control of Parliament, and

1 NOVEMBER 1962
MRBM LAUNCH SITE 3
SAN CRISTOBAL, CUBA

MISSILE READY TENT FOUNDATIONS (TENTS REMOVED)

ABANDONED LAUNCH POSITION

Above left: Central America and the Caribbean Basin provided the background for the exercise of American power – a modern reworking of the Monroe Doctrine.

Left: One of the abandoned rocket sites in Cuba provides evidence of Soviet compliance with the agreement that brought the missile crisis to an end. It was one of the most fraught events in recent world history, and brought the superpowers close to the brink of nuclear war.

Above right: Police in Birmingham, Alabama, set dogs on civil rights marchers. The connivance of law enforcement officers with racist politicians in America's southern states to suppress the civil rights movement shocked liberal opinion throughout America, and helped create the moral climate for the anti-racist legislation of the 1960s.

Right: Richard Hamilton's 1964 painting *Interior II.*

Lester Pearson became the new Canadian prime minister.

The Cuban missile crisis, though widely regarded as a triumph for Kennedy's confrontational style of foreign policy, seemed to lead to a change of heart in the President. He seemed to act in a much more cautious and thoughtful manner as he began his third year in the White House. Washington and Moscow agreed to the establishment of a 'hot-line' linking the White House to the Kremlin to forestall the possibility of accidental nuclear confrontation. Later that year the two countries agreed to a limited test-ban treaty, ending atmospheric tests of nuclear weapons. In June Kennedy made a major speech on foreign policy at American University, calling for improved relations with the Soviet Union and the abandoning of some of the guiding assumptions of the Cold War: 'Our most basic common link,' he said of the two superpowers, 'is the fact that we all inhabit this planet.' And he also began to express some private doubts about the American involvement in Vietnam, where he had sharply increased the number of US military advisers since 1961 and where those advisers were playing an increasingly important role in combat against the communist guerrillas.

Kennedy's priorities were also being changed by the moral and political pressure exerted by the civil rights movement. After a decade of dormancy the black struggle for equality had been renewed in the mid 1950s. In 1954 the Supreme Court handed down its landmark decision in *Brown vs Board of Education*, ruling that segregated public education was unconstitutional. The justices decided that the principle of 'separate but equal,' previously used to justify segregation, was inherently unequal. White Southerners pledged massive resistance to any federal attempts to enforce the Supreme Court's ruling, and the Eisenhower administration showed little fervor for the cause of civil rights. But Southern blacks soon made their own voices heard in the controversy. In December 1955 Rosa Parks, a black seamstress, sat down in a 'white seat' on a public bus in Montgomery, Alabama, and refused to surrender her seat to a white passenger when

ordered to do so by the bus driver. Her arrest sparked a year-long boycott of the city's buses by the city's blacks, under the leadership of a charismatic young Baptist minister named Martin Luther King, Jr. The boycotters held out for a year in the face of economic pressure, legal harassment and vigilante attacks, until the Supreme Court stepped in and declared segregation unconstitutional.

After the victory in Montgomery King founded the Southern Christian Leadership Conference (SCLC), which would play a major role in the civil rights protests of the coming decade. Spontaneity, as much as organizational strategy, dictated the

pace and direction taken by the movement for black equality. In the spring of 1960 four black college freshmen, acting on their own initiative, decided to stage a sit-in at the segregated lunch counter of the Woolworth store in Greensboro, North Carolina. Within a few weeks 50,000 others had emulated their action in a wave of sit-ins that spread across the South. As one historian later put it, 'They should have served that cup of coffee.'

Whites often responded to the challenge of the civil rights movement with violence. The Ku Klux Klan enjoyed a resurgence, dozens of black churches were firebombed, black and white volunteers demanding an end to segregation of interstate buses were brutally beaten during the Freedom Rides in 1961 and police used clubs, firehoses and dogs against black children in the Birmingham protests in 1963. The Kennedy administration moved slowly to protect the protesters. But by the time the March on Washington brought hundreds of thousands of civil rights protesters to the nation's capital on 28 August to hear Martin Luther King deliver his electrifying 'I Have a Dream' speech, the President and his brother, Attorney General Robert Kennedy, were beginning to take more determined steps to aid the movement.

Political expediency was part of the reason why the President went to Congress asking that a strong civil rights bill be enacted; many Americans were horrified by the scenes televised from Birmingham that spring and demanded the federal government do something. But something more than cynical calculation seemed to be at work. Just as Kennedy was stepping away from the militant Cold Warrior stance of his early foreign policy, so too he seemed to have been genuinely affected by events on the domestic front in the first years of his administration. In 1961-62 Kennedy's promise to 'get America moving again,' his charismatic, vigorous image, his appeal to the idealism of the young, his rhetoric of change and progress, contributed indirectly to the sense of legitimacy and the self-confidence of civil rights and other movements for social change.

Johnson's 'Great Society'

In his first year in office LBJ was quickly able to surpass Kennedy's meager record of legislative achievement, though he drew on his predecessor's memory to get his program through Congress. Perhaps the single most important bill LBJ signed that years was the Civil Rights Bill, which was passed by Congress in January 1964, just two months after Kennedy's assassination. Johnson's version of the civil rights bill was far more comprehensive that that initially proposed by Kennedy. LBJ also pushed through a major tax cut measure that had long been sought by the Kennedy administration. Finally, Johnson proposed and won passage for the most comprehensive collection of new social welfare measures to be passed since the New Deal era, a package of legislation that was known as the 'War on Poverty' and that Johnson believed would lead to the creation of the 'Great Society' in the United States.

Johnson did not invent his War on Poverty out of thin air. It was a sure sign that the tensions of the Cold War and the McCarthy era were beginning to relax in the later 1950s that people once again began talking about the problems of poverty. The poor could be found everywhere in America, though their existence was easily overlooked by the more affluent. And the problems of the poor were more intractable than was usually assumed even by those who did notice their existence. Poverty was not simply the product of a lack of money: rather, the poor were bound to their condition by a 'culture of poverty'.

JFK had instructed his economic advisers to begin drawing up plans for comprehensive anti-poverty legislation shortly before he made his fatal trip to Dallas. In December 1963 those advisers came to the new President with the fruits of their labor, a proposal for a modest and experimental anti-poverty program. They wanted the federal government to fund a total of five urban and five rural anti-poverty pilot projects. After a year or so of operation they could evaluate the effectiveness of the projects, make the necessary adjustments and then move on to a more ambitious national program. But that was not LBJ's style. He knew how suspicious Congress could be

Those movements, in turn, seemed to affect Kennedy. By 1963 he began to speak out with growing frequency and confidence as a proponent of fundamental change in American society.

Kennedy would not have the opportunity to demonstrate the extent and sincerity of any change of heart he might have undergone. On 22 November 1963, while riding in a motorcade through downtown Dallas, he was struck down by an assassin's bullets. Appearing before a joint session of Congress five days later, Lyndon Baines Johnson, the new President, asked the assembled lawmakers to fulfill the Kennedy legacy by passing a civil rights bill. His message that day was simple and heartfelt: 'Let us continue.' But Kennedy's was an ambiguous legacy, as would become apparent in the difficult years to come.

With a sorrowful Jackie Kennedy standing beside him on the return flight on Air Force One from Dallas, a grim-looking Lyndon Baines Johnson took the oath of office as President of the United States on 22 November 1963. It was a difficult moment for the new President. In the weeks that followed he had to reassure a grieving nation that he would keep faith with John F Kennedy's legacy, while at the same time he had to step out of Kennedy's shadow and establish his own authority as the nation's leader. Johnson proved up to the challenge. He had been preparing for it for decades.

By dint of native intelligence and an astonishing level of ambition and self-discipline Lyndon Johnson had come a long way from his hardscrabble youth in the Texas hill country. He had won election to Congress in 1938 and to the US Senate ten years later, becoming majority leader in 1955. In 1960 he made his own unsuccessful run for his party's presidential nomination and was thereafter added by Kennedy to the Democratic ticket mainly to add geographical balance. In his first years in Congress in the late 1930s he had proven a model New Deal liberal, but as a senator in the 1940s and 1950s he had moved to the right, faithfully representing the conservative views of his constituency, particularly the southwestern oil and gas producers with whom he had formed a mutually profitable relationship. As majority leader in the Senate, he earned a reputation as a manipulative 'wheeler dealer' that won him considerable influence but

did not inspire trust. A big man who physically towered over his colleagues, Johnson was tough, profane, power-grasping and egotistical. As vice-president he had suffered from the obscurity and inactivity that seems a built-in feature of the office, and he also suffered from the knowledge that the President's Harvard-educated entourage looked down on him as crude and ill-educated. But on entering the presidency Johnson seemed liberated from the frustrations and compromises of recent decades, reborn as an idealistic liberal activist. This did not represent any fundamental break with his history of driving personal ambition: Johnson wanted to go down in history as a great and beloved President, like his early political idol, Franklin Delano Roosevelt. Like FDR, Johnson was more interested in domestic than international affairs, although, of course, he was to be embroiled in the Vietnam conflict.

of academics and social experiments. He wanted to be able to present legislators with the 'solution' to the problem of poverty, not with a carefully controled and limited experiment. So LBJ took this limited proposal and transformed it into a full-scale, nation-wide War on Poverty.

Congress passed the proposed Economic Opportunity Act in August 1964. Despite the ease with which Johnson had gotten his way on this issue, the underlying ideas of the War on Poverty ran up against deeply ingrained prejudices held by a majority of the population. Only 29 percent of those questioned in a Gallup poll in 1964 believed that poor people were poor simply because of circumstances beyond their control; 33 percent believed they were poor because they were lazy; the rest gave equal weight to circumstance and character. Johnson was usually a careful student of public opinion polls, but he chose to ignore that one. He interpreted his landslide victory over Arizona Senator Barry Goldwater in the presidential election that fall, in which he won over 43 million votes to Goldwater's 27 million, as a mandate for his anti-poverty strategy.

In the next session (1965-67) the Democrats dominated the Senate and House by huge majorities, a factor that allowed Johnson to send an even more ambitious set of programs through Congress, including the government's first ventures into the field of national health insurance, in the form of the Medicare and Medicaid acts. But contrary to Johnson's assumptions, the 1964 presidential vote did not represent the triumph of a new liberal consensus in American public life. Johnson's 1964 victory turned out to be less an endorsement of his new policies than a vote against his opponent's 'extremism.' Among other things Goldwater had over the years called for the end of Social Security, the elimination of the graduated income tax and the selling of the Tennessee Valley Authority. Most Americans liked the New Deal too much to go along with proposals to dismantle it. As for Johnson's anti-poverty efforts, the American public was, at most, willing to go along as long as they showed immediate results, proved short-lived and were not too expensive.

Johnson himself believed that waging war on poverty would be a fairly painless process. Along with most economists, he assumed that the US had entered a permanent era of abundance. Continued economic growth would provide the extra dividends necessary to elevate the poor to middle-class status without requiring much sacrifice on the part of the non-poor. The federal government had no intention of embarking on any radical scheme to redistribute income. Instead, it would sponsor programs which would train individuals to make them better able to take advantage of the opportunities provided by the expanding economy, while organizing poor communities to take full advantage of the available government programs and benefits.

The War on Poverty was in full swing on many fronts within months after the initial anti poverty legislation had been passed. But Johnson's rhetoric outstripped his willingness to call on Congress to provide adequate funds for the many programs he launched in the next few years. The total appropriation for the first year of the War on Poverty was three-quarters of a billion dollars, less then 10 percent of what the war in Vietnam cost that year, a year when that war was only just beginning to intensify. The Office of Economic Opportunity, the agency overseeing Johnson's anti-poverty strategy, received just 1.5 percent of the federal budget for all its programs in the years from 1965 to 1970. Daniel Patrick Moynihan, a key adviser on welfare policies in both the Johnson and Nixon administrations, would later comment that the War on Poverty was 'oversold and underfinanced to the point that its failure was almost a matter of design.'

Supporters of the War on Poverty could point to some genuine successes. Between 1962 and 1969 the number of Americans below the poverty line dropped by 2 million each year, from roughly 40 million to 25 million in the course of the decade, which in terms of percentage of popu-

campaign in Selma, Alabama, to dramatize the continuing denial of the right to vote to black Americans. The nation watched aghast when civil rights marchers were brutally assaulted by local police as they attempted to march from Selma to the state capital of Montgomery. After the passage of the civil rights bill the previous year LBJ had sought to put the civil rights issue on the back burner, but the events at Selma forced him to throw his influence behind the passage of a bill that would assure black voting rights.

On 6 August 1965 Johnson signed the Voting Rights Act, which enlisted the force of the federal government as the guarantor of blacks' access to the ballot. It would prove, in the long run, the beginning of a new day in Southern politics, as white segregationist politicians learned they would have to court the black vote in order to retain office, and blacks began to be elected to local and state government and to Southern Congressional seats for the first time since the Reconstruction Era.

lation represented a drop from 19 percent to 12.5 percent of the total. Children in particular benefited from the War on Poverty programs. Thanks largely to Medicaid and various nutritional programs, the nation's infant mortality rate declined 47 percent from 1965 to 1979. And a significant 20-year study of black children who went through the Head Start program (which provided pre-school education for the poor) would reveal that nearly twice as many children with the Head Start experience went on to college or post-high school vocational training as those who had not enjoyed the same advantage. Despite such successes, the War on Poverty was dogged throughout its short life by reports of internal disorganization and corruption. Conservative critics charged that the whole poverty program was a giant federal boondoggle that chiefly benefited social workers, academics and bureaucrats, along with self-styled

community leaders who were chiefly interested in lining their own pockets. Despite pledges to guarantee 'maximum feasible participation' by the poor in running the anti-poverty programs, community organizers often found it exceedingly difficult to involve the poor in any significant way. In elections for representatives to community anti-poverty boards in Los Angeles, only 2500 poor people turned out from a potential electorate of 400,000. Apathy, one of the characteristics of the 'culture of poverty,' was not to be dissolved by a wave of the anti-poverty wand.

The fate of the War on Poverty was in many ways linked to the fate of the civil rights movement. Despite some stunning legislative victories, the civil rights movement was entering a time of troubles in the mid 1960s. In the spring of 1965 Martin Luther King, Jr and Southern Christian Leadership Conference organizers launched a

Far left: The brutal treatment meted out to civil rights marchers in this culminating demonstration in March 1965 at Montgomery, Alabama, highlighted the failure of the Civil Rights Act to ensure justice for blacks in the South.

Left: The Canadian Maple Leaf flag, hoisted here by Prime Minister Lester Pearson, eliminated the overt tie with Britain that had been represented in the old flag by the presence of the Union Jack in the corner.

Below left: Malcolm X, the Black Muslim leader assassinated in 1967.

Right: The Los Angeles district of Watts exploded in race riots in 1965.

Below right: These American troops wait to be airlifted to Dak To. The Vietnam War would become the next focus for radical political action after the civil rights movement.

But in the short run, race relations were destined to grow worse, not better. Less than a week after the Voting Rights Act became law rioting broke out in the Watts ghetto of Los Angeles. Before the riot ended, five days later, 35 people had been killed, 600 buildings had been looted, thousands of people were arrested and many city blocks burned to the ground. The violence spread rapidly in the next few years. There were 21 major riots and civil disorders in 1966, 83 in 1967. The worst single riot took place in Detroit in July 1967, when 43 people died. When a white assassin gunned down Martin Luther King in Memphis in April 1968 riots broke out in over 120 American cities. A presidential commission appointed by Lyndon Johnson to investigate the causes of racial violence concluded in 1968 that the United States was 'moving toward two societies, one black, one white – separate and unequal.'

While Martin Luther King had remained committed to the goal of integration and the means of non-violent civil disobedience, many others in the civil rights movement and the black community did not. In 1966 chants of 'Black Power' began to compete with 'Freedom Now' at civil rights demonstrations in the South. In Northern cities the political tone was often set by such groups as the Black Muslims, with their militantly anti-white religious beliefs, or by the Black Panthers, with their fondness for Maoist rhetoric and paramilitary trappings.

It was not only the violence or the anti-white rhetoric of sections of the civil rights movement that created the so-called 'white backlash.' It was also the realization that racism was a national problem, not just a Southern problem – that discrimination in housing, education and opportunity existed in Los Angeles and New York as well as in Birmingham and Selma. Increasingly Americans came to believe that future progress for blacks would require real sacrifices from whites, not just vague expressions of goodwill. It was one thing to concede to blacks the right to order a cup of coffee at a downtown lunch counter; but many whites regarded it as something altogether different to say that blacks could move into any neighborhood they wanted to, or send their children to any school they wanted to, or take any job they wanted to. The potential

power of the white backlash had first become apparent in the 1964 primary campaign, when the outspoken segregationist governor of Alabama, George Wallace, won 34 percent of votes in the Wisconsin Democratic primary by exploiting white working-class resentment against the civil rights movement. Running as an independent in 1968, Wallace would win 11 percent of the vote, the best showing of a third party candidate in a half-century. In the mid 1960s public opinion polls reported a sharp decline in public sympathy for the civil rights movement among whites. In 1964 only 34 percent of Americans had agreed with the statement that blacks were trying to move too fast to gain their rights; by 1966 this percentage had increased to 85 percent.

To the north, Canadians also experienced a bruising debate over the rights of minorities. Lester Pearson succeeded John Diefenbaker as prime minister in 1963 when the Liberals gained a majority in Parliament. In response to growing nationalist sentiments among Canada's French-

speaking minority (who made up a majority of the population in Quebec), Pearson appointed a Royal Commission on Bilingualism and Biculturalism in 1963. Measures such as the 1965 adoption of a new national flag (the 'Maple Leaf' flag, which included no reminders of Canada's ties with Great Britain) and the 1969 passage of the Official Languages Act (requiring government offices to provide services in French in districts where at least 10 percent of the population were French-speaking) did little to placate Quebec's nationalists. The *Parti Québécois* steadily gained strength in provincial elections, and its leaders discussed the possibility of Quebec's secession from the Confederation. In 1970, after Pierre Trudeau had succeeded Pearson as leader of the Liberal Party and prime minister, Canada was caught up in a political drama that shook the nation's democratic institutions. An underground separatist group, the *Front de Libération de Québec* (FLQ), kidnapped two prominent officials, the British Trade Commissioner and the Quebec Labor Minister.

Trudeau suspended normal civil liberties, and police arrested over 450 people in their search for the kidnappers. One of the FLQ's victims was later released unharmed, in return for safe passage out of the country for his kidnappers; the other was murdered.

In the United States, Republicans showed a better grasp of the new political realities than Democrats. The November 1966 elections were a disaster for the Democrats, with dramatic Republican gains in the House and Senate, largely the product of anti-civil rights sentiment and dissatisfaction with the War on Poverty, as well as the result of anxieties about the steadily escalating war in Vietnam. Liberals were no longer in a position to set the agenda in Congress. Great Society programs began to be cut back or eliminated. Even Johnson seemed to be losing interest in the War on Poverty (though it still grieved him when his Republican successor, Richard Nixon, finally dismantled the Office of Economic Opportunity). When Johnson went before Congress in 1967 and spoke on behalf of his anti-poverty programs, he no longer claimed to be waging a War on Poverty. His rhetoric by then had been toned down to a far less urgent-sounding 'strategy against poverty.'

The war in Vietnam

The main cause of Johnson's growing inattention to domestic issues was the war in Vietnam. American involvement in Vietnam had been a timebomb, ticking away for more than a decade, waiting to wreck someone's presidency. It was Johnson's misfortune to occupy the White House when it finally exploded. The US first became involved in the region in the mid 1950s. President Eisenhower had turned down a French request for US military intervention when the French garrison at Dien Bien Phu was surrounded by communist insurgents in 1954. Though he was reluctant to involve the US in another Asian land war just a year after the Korean War had ended, Eisenhower did take the first fatal steps which led

a decade later to the Vietnam war. After a peace settlement was signed in Geneva ending French colonial rule in Indochina and dividing Vietnam into two supposedly temporary zones, Eisenhower sent advisers and a small amount of military and economic aid to bolster the anticommunist regime in the southern half of Vietnam.

Kennedy had inherited this timebomb from Eisenhower, and done nothing to defuse it. On the contrary, early on in his administration he decided that he would use Vietnam as the place in which he could re-establish US 'credibility,' which he felt had been tarnished by the Bay of Pigs fiasco. Kennedy's foreign policy advisers were eager to demonstrate America's ability to reshape distant societies in its own image. 'Our central task in the undeveloped areas,' National Security Adviser Walt Rostow declared in a speech to troops from the Army Special Forces in 1961, 'is to protect the independence of the revolutionary process now going forward.' But the rhetoric about 'nation-building' and 'winning hearts and minds' that pervaded official statements about the conflict in Vietnam could not alter the fact that in South Vietnam the existing anti-communist regime was corrupt, repressive and ineffective. In fact by the summer of 1963 American policymakers were themselves so disenchanted with South Vietnamese leader Ngo Dinh Diem that they secretly encouraged his generals to overthrow him. The resulting coup was successful: Diem was overthrown (and murdered in the process), but the succession of governments which followed proved equally incapable of building genuine popular support.

George Ball, undersecretary of state under Kennedy and Johnson, put the dilemma of US policy in Vietnam very well in the fall of 1964 in a policy paper warning against further escalation of the war: 'Once on the tiger's back we cannot be sure of picking the place to dismount.' There was a circular and self-reinforcing logic to the pursuit of credibility. The more that successive administra-

tions in Washington defended their Vietnam policies in terms of safeguarding credibility, the more American credibility seemed to depend upon the success of those very policies. By the time Johnson had inherited the Vietnam situation he felt he had no choice but to continue the US military commitment.

In 1964 Johnson pledged that he had no intention of sending American boys to do the fighting that Asian boys should do for themselves, but his advisers were already drawing up plans for a significant escalation of the US war effort once the election was safely out of the way. Even before the election Johnson had secured from Congress what he would later argue was the functional equivalent of a declaration of war. On 2-3 August 1964, in a murky episode that Johnson did his best to make murkier, US destroyers in the Gulf of Tonkin off the North Vietnamese coast reported being attacked twice by communist PT boats. (The second attack actually never took place.) Johnson went before Congress claiming that US forces had been the victim of unprovoked assault, and Congress responded by passing the Gulf of Tonkin resolution, authorizing the President to take whatever steps were necessary to protect US military personnel and allies in the region.

In February 1965, following a communist mortar attack on the US airbase at Pleiku, South Vietnam, Johnson ordered the start of a sustained US bombing campaign against North Vietnam. In May US ground combat forces began to arrive in South Vietnam, their numbers growing to 180,000 by the end of the year. As American troops switched from defensive positions to search and destroy operations, casualties began to rise swiftly, each death making it more and more difficult for the President to follow any policy except continued escalation. By the end of 1966 US troop strength had grown to 400,000; it would peak in the spring of 1968 at 535,000. Despite the massive escalation of the war and the lavish use of new and exotic military technologies, victories were few and hard to measure. The Pentagon released

Left: Scenes like this – a Marine being rushed to a medical evacuation helicopter – filled America's television screens night after night during the late 1960s. Every Thursday the network news programs would broadcast the total number of American dead, wounded and missing in Vietnam, a regular reminder of the cost to the nation.

Above right: A demonstration in San Francisco against the Vietnam War. When the Tet Offensive struck in January 1968, it proved to be the final blow to the national will to fight. The public had been told that their side was winning in Vietnam, and disillusion set in when these claims were shown to be false.

Right: The dying Robert Kennedy shortly after he had been shot by Sirhan Sirhan. Kennedy had just triumphed in the California Democratic primary, and was well positioned to take his party's nomination.

were still to come, and the level of American bombing actually increased, but overall American combat deaths did slowly diminish. Finally, in January 1973, a peace accord was signed in Paris, ending the period of active American military involvement. In January 1976, seven months after the collapse of the South Vietnamese regime and the communist victory, the Department of Defense issued a final accounting of US casualties in the war from 1961 through 1975: 56,869 Americans had been killed, 303,704 had been wounded and 798 remained missing in action.

The Vietnam war proved to be the most divisive of all America's foreign wars. In the spring of 1965 about 15,000 demonstrators had responded to a call from a small campus group called Students for a Democratic Society (SDS) to come to Washington to protest against the war in Vietnam. They found themselves denounced as 'un-American' even by some liberal newspapers, for consensus still existed that in wartime Americans were not supposed to question the actions of their leaders. Just five years later, in May 1970, hundreds of thousands of students went on strike on over 400 campuses to protest the American invasion of Cambodia and the death of four students in a confrontation with Ohio National Guardsmen at Kent State University. By then polite dissent had long since gone out of fashion. The fumes of tear gas wafted across campuses as students battled police and burned ROTC buildings. A majority of Americans now counted themselves as opponents of the war, and politics no longer stopped at the water's edge. Debate raged over every aspect of American foreign policy. The anti-war move-

regular 'body counts' of enemy dead to prove that progress was being made, but in reality the US military was unprepared for the mission it had been assigned. As individuals, the men who fought in Vietnam were as brave and skillful as those who had fought in any of America's previous wars. But the demands of fighting a brutal, draining guerilla war, where it was never clear who among the civilian population was friend and who was foe, often left them angry and demoralized. On occasion their anger led to atrocities like the My Lai massacre of 1968, when over 300 unarmed South Vietnamese civilians were gunned down by soldiers under the unstable command of Lt William Calley.

In the fall of 1967 General William Westmoreland, the American commander in South Vietnam, told the National Press Club in Washington, DC, 'I see progress as I travel all over Vietnam.' Two months later the communist military forces, the Viet Cong, launched their Tet Offensive, staging simultaneous attacks in every major city in South Vietnam, and even penetrating into the US embassy compound in Saigon. Tet proved to be the Dienbienphu of the American war in Indochina. In the end American forces repeled the attack so skillfully that it might almost be counted an American victory, but at home it was perceived – perhaps thanks to the way it was reported by the media – as a disaster. In February 1968, for the first time, more Americans described themselves doves than hawks to the Gallup poll. President Johnson announced a limited bombing halt in March and turned down requests from Westmoreland for still more soldiers for Vietnam. Richard Nixon won the election that fall, promising he had a secret plan to end the war. Once in office he told the country he was winding down the war through a process of 'Vietnamization' – turning over more and more responsibility for conduct of the fighting to South Vietnamese troops. Some of the bloodiest battles of the war

ment, suffering as it did from chronic disorganization, crippling internal divisions and the mounting frustration of many of its most devoted adherents, had nevertheless helped bring about a major shift in public attitudes on issues of war and peace.

The anti-war movement had also prepared the way for Eugene McCarthy's seemingly quixotic challenge to Lyndon Johnson in the 1968 Democratic primary in New Hampshire. At the start of his campaign no one gave McCarthy a chance, but when the votes were counted on 12 March he had come very close to an upset victory. Two and a half weeks later, after Robert Kennedy had also entered the race, Johnson went before the nation on television and announced, 'I shall not seek, and I will not accept, the nomination of my party for another term as president.' McCarthy and Kennedy continued to offer a strong challenge to LBJ's designated successor, Hubert Humphrey, through the spring primaries. On 5 June 1968, after winning the California primary, Robert Kennedy was assassinated in Los Angeles. Had he lived, he might have been able to hold together the diverse elements in the traditional coalition. Instead, the Democratic convention in Chicago in August turned into a bloody spectacle, with anti-war protesters chanting 'The Whole World is Watching' while being clubbed by Mayor Richard Daley's police. The events that week in Chicago doomed Humphrey's race for the presidency and guaranteed Richard Nixon's victory in November. The anti-war movement continued to expand, both in the numbers it attracted to its demonstrations and the breadth of support in the population, reaching its peak in November 1969 when a half-million people went to Washington to protest Nixon's continuation of the war. Yet in the end, the anti-war movement never coalesced into a stable political force. By the time Nixon was re-elected in 1972 it had fallen into disunity and demoralization.

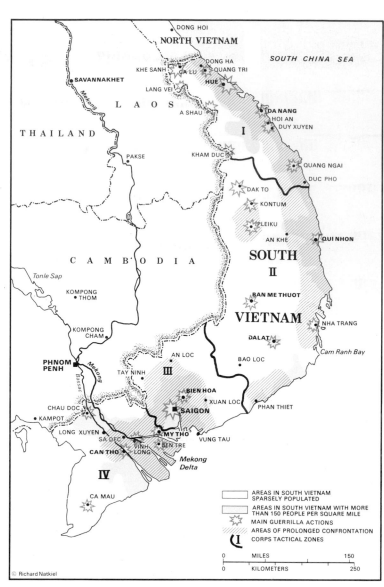

© Richard Natkiel

AREAS IN SOUTH VIETNAM SPARSELY POPULATED
AREAS IN SOUTH VIETNAM WITH MORE THAN 150 PEOPLE PER SQUARE MILE
MAIN GUERRILLA ACTIONS
AREAS OF PROLONGED CONFRONTATION
CORPS TACTICAL ZONES

Left: The war in South Vietnam was a classic guerrilla struggle between the forces attempting to maintain the authority of the government and the insurgents who infiltrated from their hideaways in rugged terrain into the more populated parts of the country.

Below left: The black guitarist Jimi Hendrix, here boarding a plane at Heathrow, was one of the major figures of the rock music explosion in the late 1960s.

Above right: Janis Joplin's songs gave voice to the concerns of the counter-culture hippy generation. The frivolous behavior of the young in the late 1960s and early 1970s was characterized by a devotion to rock music, drugs and flower power.

Above far right: A 1972 march against the practice of abortions in New York. Single issue politics, concentrating on matters like abortion, drugs, gun control and bussing, would draw many Democratic voters away from their traditional loyalties and transfer their support to conservative Republicans.

Below right: Richard Nixon's career was as varied as it was – until Watergate – successful. He began as an anti-communist hatchet man and was slowly transformed into a more establishment figure, skillfully blending Republican Main Street politics with the interests of Wall Street.

The 'cultural revolution'

Culture as well as politics was a contested terrain in the 1960s. The Baby Boom generation seemed intent, at times, on rejecting every aspect of its parents' lives that it could think of. Long hair, blue jeans, bare feet and tie-dye shirts; psychedelic music and drugs; rural communes and urban crash-pads; casual attitudes toward sex, nudity and the American flag – everything that the younger generation believed in, indulged in, promoted or tolerated seemed designed expressly to offend its elders. Within another decade, of course, many veterans of the Woodstock rock festival had found comfortable and conventional niches in the business and professional world, and skeptics have dismissed the 'cultural revolution' of the 1960s as a frivolous episode, 'full of sound and fury and signifying nothing.' But in fact it did produce some significant new attitudes toward work, leisure, sex and marriage, so that in some respects the youthful rebels of the 1960s triumphed culturally even though they failed politically. If the cultural climate of the 1970s was largely shaped in reaction to the excesses of the 1960s, it also represented the fulfillment of many changes in cultural attitudes that first found their expression in the 1960s.

Although social behavior changed more quickly than deeper cultural attitudes, many of the new approaches won swift, if far from unanimous, acceptance. The Supreme Court sanctioned abortion, homosexuals 'came out of the closet,' a powerful feminist movement emerged, married women went off to work and unmarried couples chose to live together and even have children

without the stigma that would have attached to such behavior even a few years earlier. Whatever else the 1970s represented, it was hardly a return to the cultural status quo of the 1950s.

The sixties had begun in a burst of faith, a sense of renewed national mission, best expressed in JFK's inaugural speech, 'Ask not what your country can do for you, ask what you can do for your country.' In the early 1970s, the Watergate Scandal would test America's faith in its government as never before.

Nixon and Watergate

The roots of Watergate reached back well before Nixon took the oath of office in January 1969. A pattern of illegality and covert operations, set in the early years of the Cold War, paved the way for Nixon's abuse of power. Under J Edgar Hoover the Federal Bureau of Investigation went far beyond its statutory investigative role in waging a secret war of harassment, wiretaps and break-ins against political dissenters. Many such acts on the part of the FBI were revealed to a Senate Committee chaired by Frank Church in the mid 1970s. The Church Committee revealed that the Central Intelligence Agency was involved in similarly 'pragmatic' and illegal domestic covert operations, as well as attempts to assassinate foreign leaders. The principle of 'deniability' was built into all such activities. Higher-ups, including the President, were deliberately shielded from a too-close acquaintance with the details of covert activities, so that if anything went wrong they could deny knowledge of their existence, and subordinates could take the blame. The increased reliance on secrecy and covert operations in foreign relations was just one aspect of the emergence of the 'imperial presidency.' Ever since the Second World War the executive branch of government had greatly strengthened its power to act unilaterally without the approval or even the knowledge of the Congress.

When Richard Nixon came into the White House he found himself in possession of extraordinary powers to conduct international relations as he saw fit, and there may well have been a connection between the extent of those powers and the political abuses in the domestic sphere that were soon to follow. Nixon was elected on the promise of having a secret plan to end the war in Vietnam. He might have done it with relative ease in 1969, even if it had meant the loss of South Vietnam to communists – after all Vietnam was

the Democrats' war, and Nixon as a staunch anti-communist was not vulnerable to a 'Who Lost China?' campaign. But Nixon had no intention of ending the war in Vietnam in an obvious American defeat.

The problem was how to jolt North Vietnam without unleashing a renewed wave of anti-war demonstrations, public disillusionment and Congressional hearings on the war. The solution Nixon came up with was to begin the 'secret' bombing of Cambodia (where communist forces found sanctuary in border regions). The bombing was intended as a signal to the North Vietnamese that Nixon was willing to take even more drastic action directed against North Vietnam. Obviously the bombing would not be a secret to the North Vietnamese. Those to be kept in the dark were Congress, the US public and even some military authorities (including, for example, the Secretary of the Air Force).

Shortly after the start of the raids reporter William Beecher learned of their existence and reported on them in the New York Times. The report was officially denied, and it created no stir

or follow-up stories. Nevertheless Nixon and Henry Kissinger, Nixon's national security adviser, were infuriated by the story and responded by authorizing illegal FBI wiretaps of Kissinger's own aides in the National Security Council and of selected newsmen. This was Nixon's first step into the gray area of illegal covert surveillance and the beginning of his virtual obsession with leaks and disloyalty.

When Defense Department consultant Daniel Ellsberg leaked the secret Pentagon Papers on Vietnam to the press in June 1971 Nixon decided to reach outside the normal national security apparatus to deal with Ellsberg. He set up his own private intelligence unit, known as 'the plumbers,' recruiting former CIA operatives such as H L Hunt and G Gordon Liddy to spy on and harass Ellsberg. From there it proved only a short step for Nixon to unleash the plumbers against the Democrats in the 1972 presidential campaign. Covert activities abroad thus came around full circle to undermine American democracy at home.

Fortunately for the Constitution, if unfortunately for Nixon, the plumbers proved to resem-

ble the Keystone Cops more than James Bond in their actions. On the night of 16 June 1972 five of them were arrested while attempting to burgle the office of the Democratic National Committee in the Watergate office complex in Washington. It was not long before reporters from the *Washington Post* and other newspapers were able to trace the men to the Committee to Reelect the President (CREEP). Thanks to the 'deniability' factor built into the activities of the plumbers, Nixon was at first able to shrug off responsibility for the break-in. Only some underlings at CREEP, acting on their own authority, had anything to do with the break-in, or so the White House story went. With the economy enjoying an upswing, and with *détente* in full bloom among the superpowers despite the continuing bloodshed in Vietnam, Nixon coasted to a landslide victory in November over the Democratic presidential nominee George McGovern.

Following the election the Watergate cover-up began to unravel. Nixon hoped that the five men arrested at Watergate would, for a price, maintain their silence. But at their trial in the spring of 1973 one of them, James McCord, told Judge John Sirica of the pressure he and his fellow defendants were under to perjure themselves by denying the links between the Watergate break-in and the White House. At this point the Nixon presidency was doomed, though the drama took another year and a half to play itself out. The Senate established a special committee to investigate the Watergate events, chaired by North Carolina Senator Sam Ervin, and in the summer of 1973 its hearings riveted the attention of the nation.

Nixon was now forced to throw some of his top aides to the wolves in the vain hope they would satisfy the public demand for a scapegoat. He eventually decided that he would have to sacrifice White House Counsel John Dean for the cause. But Dean, like McCord, decided that he would not be a 'good soldier.' He had kept meticulous notes of all his meetings with the President (although he did not know of the President's tape system) and went to the government prosecutors investigating the case and told them that the President was personally involved in efforts to 'cover-up' Watergate – that is, commit the crime of 'obstruction of justice,' which was an impeachable offense.

At first it was Dean's word against Nixon's. But then the existence of the Oval Office taping system was revealed. The Senate Watergate committee subpoenaed the tapes, and after a long legal battle, which included the October 1973 'Saturday Night Massacre,' when Nixon fired special Watergate investigator Archibald Cox, the White House was finally forced to hand over some of the tapes. The transcripts proved that Dean's memory was far more reliable than Nixon's.

In July 1974 the House Judiciary Committee voted three acts of impeachment against Nixon for obstructing justice, violation of the constitutional rights of American citizens and failing to provide subpoenaed evidence to Congress. There were still some die-hard Nixon supporters among Republicans in Congress, but their resistance collapsed when the 'smoking pistol' tape was released on 5 August, which showed that just a week after the Watergate burglary Nixon was

already planning cover-up efforts with H R Haldeman. Ten Republican congressmen on the Judiciary Committee who had previously opposed impeachment now announced their intention to reverse their votes. Four days later, on 9 August 1974, Nixon became the first American president to be forced to resign from office.

The Ford presidency

Earlier that year Michigan Congressman Gerald Ford, who had first been elected to Congress in 1948 and who had served as House Minority leader since 1965, replaced Spiro Agnew as vice-president. (Agnew had been forced to resign when he was indicted for taking bribes while governor of Maryland.) When Ford took the oath of office on 9 August he declared, 'Our long national nightmare is over.' The specter of a prolonged constitutional crisis and national paralysis could now be laid to rest. After Nixon's imperial pretensions, the low-key Ford proved a refreshing contrast. He was well liked and generally respected by his former colleagues in Congress, and he was celebrated in news stories for such mundane activities as warming up his own English muffins for breakfast in the morning.

But Ford soon used up much of the goodwill that had accompanied him into the presidency – his pardon of Nixon in September 1974 made him seem to many part of the Watergate cover-up, rather than the nation's savior from political abuses. Overnight his approval rating in the polls dropped from a high of 71 percent to 50 percent and continued to dwindle throughout 1975. Faced with a prolonged economic recession that he could do nothing to solve, increasingly at odds with Congress on a range of foreign and domestic issues, Ford developed a largely undeserved reputation for dim-wittedness (as well as physical clumsiness) which would dog him for the remainder of his presidency.

Ford's tenure as one of the post-Watergate 'good guys' was a limited one. Was the Republican Party as a whole to share his fate? Nixon's landslide victory of 1972, interpreted at the time as a mandate for his conservative policies, was fatally tainted by the Watergate abuses. (In fact, pollsters found it was difficult to find people in the mid

Far left: The Watergate hearings revealed the seamy realities of American political life. Behind Senator Joseph Montoya stands a board showing the distribution of funds raised by the 'Committee to Re-elect the President' to the various election organizers.

Left: James McCord, who led the group that burgled the Democratic headquarters at the Watergate complex. His admission to Judge John Sirica that the White House was involved doomed the Nixon administration.

Below left: Nixon says goodbye to his staff after his resignation in August 1974. His criminal activities went unpunished, however.

Right: President Gerald Ford granted a pardon to Nixon, avoiding the further national indignity of a former president being tried for 'high crimes and misdemeanors.' Ford's administration would be hampered by a hostile Congress.

Below: Senator Edward Kennedy's reluctance to run for the presidency left American liberals of the 1970s and 1980s without a standard-bearer of any real stature.

1970s who would admit having voted for Nixon in 1972.) In the first post-Watergate electoral contest, the mid-term Congressional elections in the fall of 1974, the Democrats dramatically increased their margin of control in Congress, winning 49 House seats and five Senate seats, with the newcomers of a decidedly more liberal bent than their elders. The new Congress was going its own way, fulfilling what it saw as the mandate of the 1974 election to limit presidential authority, to restore its own authority in foreign policy and to guard against the kind of abuses that had characterized Nixon's foreign and domestic policies. Congress had passed the War Powers Act during Nixon's

administration, which was designed to prevent future Gulf of Tonkin situations. After Ford came into the White House Congress passed new laws restricting CIA covert activities. Congress also refused to allow Ford to send increased American aid to South Vietnam in the last months of that failing regime in the spring of 1975.

Liberals with a memory of recent political history might well have taken heart from these developments. At first glance 1974-75 seemed to be a repetition of the late 1950s. The 1958 mid-term Congressional elections had seen dramatic gains by liberal Democrats that foreshadowed JFK's election and the beginning of an era of reform. Now it seemed that the moment might be recaptured and 'Camelot' would rise up reborn from the ashes of Vietnam and Watergate. John F Kennedy's last surviving brother, Massachusetts Senator Edward Kennedy, was the liberal heir-apparent, but his decision in the fall of 1974 not to seek the 1976 Democratic presidential nomination encouraged a wide field of presidential hopefuls, many of them drawn from the Democratic Party's liberal wing.

But the Democrats had been more damaged by the events of the late 1960s and early 1970s than they could yet realize. More significant than the Democratic congressional gains in the fall of 1974 was another statistic largely overlooked at the time, the extremely low voter turn-out of 38 percent. The legacy of Richard Nixon's fall was not simply to discredit his own brand of conservative Republicans, as liberal Democrats had hoped, but rather to discredit all politics and all politicians – conservative, moderate and liberal alike. The percentage of the public who agreed with the statement that they could 'trust the government in Washington to do what's right' declined from 56 percent in 1958 to 29 percent in 1978. The voters were in a sour, unforgiving mood that worked temporarily to the benefit of the Democrats but could just as easily work against them, rooted as it was in political cynicism rather than ideological sympathies.

The Democrats also suffered from self-inflicted wounds. The 1972 Democratic Convention which nominated George McGovern had represented the temporary triumph of the 'New Politics' – of the Party's liberal, 'conscience constituency.' Changes in the delegate selection process initiated after the disaster of the 1968 Chicago Democratic convention greatly increased the percentage of blacks, women and young delegates in 1972, but many of the traditional leaders of the Party were excluded. Thus Chicago Mayor Richard Daley and his entire delegation were unseated by the convention's credentials committee and replaced by a delegation led by Jesse Jackson. The post-1968 reforms, as intended, had brought in many people previously excluded from party decision-making, but it turned out to be a zero-sum gain, because it had also excluded many people who had previously been important to the Democratic Party's electoral success. Many of them had sat out the 1972 election or voted for Nixon. They remained estranged even after Watergate.

Another impact of the Democratic Party's internal reforms was to enhance the importance of primaries in the selection of the party's presidential nominee – the goal being to do away with the smoke-filled rooms in which professional party bosses traditionally had chosen candidates. Primaries made it possible for outsiders with little institutional party support, but with a command of the media and sufficient financial backing, to win the nomination, particularly if they were able to stage upset victories in the early primaries.

Perhaps no one was more of an outsider in the race for Democratic presidential nomination in 1976 than an obscure, one-term former state governor whom no one took too seriously, first choice of only 4 percent of registered Democrats at the start of 1976, according to the Gallup poll. That was James Earl Carter of Georgia. Jimmy Carter had made the decision to run for the presidency just after the 1972 election. From January 1975 on, when his term in office as governor

template the world their children will inherit.'

The economic hard times of the 1970s stemmed from various sources, foreign and domestic. Lyndon Johnson's reluctance to raise taxes to pay for his Great Society and an increasingly unpopular war in Vietnam set off the start of an inflationary spiral later accelerated by the OPEC oil embargo of 1973. The price of a barrel of crude oil jumped from $2.55 a barrel before the Middle Eastern October War of 1973 and the subsequent OPEC oil embargo up to $8.32 a barrel in January 1974 – and on up to $32 a barrel by January 1981. The price of a gallon of gasoline at the pump quadrupled in the same period. International competition finally caught up with over-confident American manufacturers. The United States saw its first trade deficit in the twentieth century in 1971, a deficit that would grow steadily throughout the next decade and a half. West Germany and Japan, having rebuilt their war-shattered economies with the most modern technologies and forms of labor and management organization available, proved particularly fierce competitors. Out of the 6.7 million automobiles sold by American dealers in 1960, only about a half-million had been imports. Out of the 8 million they sold in 1982, 2.2 million were imports.

It was Jimmy Carter's misfortune to enter the White House just as these disastrous economic trends made their full force felt. The inflation rate climbed to double digits in the last years of the Carter administration. Real average family income had risen by 30 percent in the Eisenhower years, and again by 30 percent in the Kennedy-Johnson years. It continued to increase through Richard Nixon's first term in office, but in 1973 it began a nosedive that would last more than a decade. Between 1973 and 1984 the average middle income family lost 6 percent of its real income, despite the increasing number of dual income families. The level of per capita income of Americans dropped from first in the world to seventh in the course of the 1970s. There was little that any president could have done, at least in the short run, to remedy the economic downturn of the 1970s. But Carter made things much worse for himself politically, choosing to respond to the crisis by sounding the conservative themes of disciplined self-sacrifice that Richard Nixon had had the good sense to avoid in his own time in office. He misread the mandate he had received in 1976, turning into the kind of stiff-necked crusader whose image he had carefully avoided in the presidential

expired, he was a full-time candidate for President. Carter ran a deliberately ambiguous and in many ways apolitical campaign; reporters soon discovered that liberals who heard him speak thought of him as a fellow liberal, conservatives as a fellow conservative. Carter made political capital out of his lack of national political experience, running against Washington – which in a sense meant against his own party as well as the Republicans.

Carter told his audiences that his would be an administration based on 'love;' he took time off from campaigning to return to Plains, Georgia, to take his turn teaching Sunday school class; he promised the voters that 'I will never lie to you;' he declared that US foreign policy should be as 'open and honest and decent and compassionate' as the American people themselves; and in his campaign autobiography he stressed his record as a nuclear engineer and successful farmer. Carter sought to make the voters feel good about themselves again after the twin traumas of Vietnam and Watergate, and he promised unity and administrative competence rather than more political division and debate. It worked, although it might not have, had Ford not withstood the challenge mounted that year in the Republican primaries by Ronald Reagan, another candidate who understood the value of running against Washington. As it was Carter managed to squander a 13-point lead in the polls over Ford at the start of the fall campaign and squeaked into office in November with a 2.1 percent margin of victory.

The Carter presidency

Carter had campaigned as a liberal to the liberals, a conservative to the conservatives. The policies he intended to pursue once in office were harder to categorize. He brought in Cyrus Vance, a liberal favorite, to be his secretary of state, along with former civil rights activist Andrew Young to be his UN ambassador; but he appointed the anti-Soviet hardliner, Zbigniew Brzezinski, to be his national security adviser. He brought in liberals to run the remaining Great Society programs, and then cut their appropriations. Carter, often caricatured in the 1980s as one of the last of the big-spending liberals, in fact developed a reputation in the 1970s among liberal Democrats as 'Jimmy Hoover,' the most conservative Democrat to sit in the White House since Grover Cleveland. He was seen as being more committed to fiscal responsibility

and efficiency than social justice. Perhaps the most lasting legacy of Carter's domestic policies was his decision to begin the process of deregulation of the transportation and energy industries, a policy that was fully in accord with the philosophy of his conservative successor in the White House.

John F Kennedy had also begun his presidency as a fairly conservative leader in domestic policies, and had been pushed to the left by the civil rights movement in the early 1960s. But soon after Carter came into office the direction that pressures came from shifted distinctly rightward. Disillusioned with public life, tired of foreign and domestic crusades, Americans in the 1970s turned all the more eagerly to the satisfactions of their private lives. But the 'culture of narcissism' foundered on the economics of scarcity. What some observers labeled a 'Revolution of Falling Expectations' took place in the course of the 1970s, as the economy faltered under the twin burden of inflation and unemployment (theretofore thought of as mutually exclusive evils). By 1980 *Fortune* magazine reported that 'most people nowadays aspire to little more than holding on to what they've already got, and many become downright despondent when they con-

election. In the famous 'malaise speech' of 1979 Carter delivered a jeremiad exhorting Americans to reject 'self-indulgence and consumption' – and in doing so, only succeeded in identifying himself as the cause and symbol of economic hard times. Ronald Reagan, who capped his debate with Carter in 1980 with the brilliant peroration, 'Are you better off than you were four years ago? Is it easier for you to go and buy things in the stores than it was four years ago?' took full advantage of Carter's misstep.

Canadians were undergoing a similar experience of economic retrenchment. The Liberals under Trudeau were able to ride out the storm for most of the decade, winning an increased parliamentary majority in 1974. But in 1979 the Progressive Conservative Party, under the leadership of Joe Clark, overturned the Liberal majority, beginning a decade of conservative domination of Canadian politics.

In the US Ronald Reagan's message was becoming all the more potent because he was able to link the country's economic complaints with the sense that America was being pushed around in the world. Carter was happiest when he could play the role of peacemaker, as he did in 1978 at the marathon Camp David meeting with Egypt's Anwar Sadat and Israel's Menachem Begin, or when he completed the process, launched by Richard Nixon, of normalizing relations with the People's Republic of China. Carter had begun his administration promising to cut the defense budget, promote human rights and end Americans' 'inordinate fear of communism.' But in response to political pressure, Carter gradually shifted to the right in his foreign policy. Increasingly it was Brzezinski rather than Vance who had his ear. (Vance would finally resign in frustration in the spring of 1980.) Right-wing groups had launched major efforts against both Senate ratification of a new arms limitation treaty with the Soviets (SALT II) and a treaty that would increase Panamanian control over the US-built and operated Panama Canal. Carter sought to undercut such attacks from the right by adopting a harder line in Soviet-American relations, but this only served to increase public concern that the United States was unable to contend with the Soviet threat. Carter had already decided to increase American defense expenditures when the Soviet Union invaded Afghanistan in December 1979. Carter responded by reinstituting draft registration and organizing a boycott of the summer Olympic Games in Moscow.

Americans were still smarting from the national humiliation in Vietnam when the economy began to falter. As far as most Americans could remember or were concerned, things started to go seriously awry in the economy with the OPEC oil embargo. A favorite image for newspaper cartoonists during the 1973 and 1979 oil embargoes portrayed American consumers being held up at the gas pump by arrogant and rapacious Arab sheiks. Other troubles were brewing in the Mideast. In Iran the United States had helped install Shah Mohammed Reza Pahlevi in power in 1953 by means of a CIA-organized coup against the existing nationalist government. US influence had remained strong during the years when the Shah ruled his country through increasingly autocratic measures. In January 1979 a revolution led by the Fundamentalist Muslim leader, the Ayatollah Ruhollah Khomenei, had overthrown the Shah. And in October of that year, pressured by the Shah's powerful American friends, including Henry Kissinger, Carter had agreed to allow the deposed Shah to enter the United States.

That provoked a furious reaction in Iran. The American Embassy in Teheran was seized by followers of the Ayatollah Khomenei in November 1979. Fifty-two American hostages would be held in captivity for the next 444 days. Carter's diplomatic efforts to free the hostages proved abortive, as did an attempt in April 1980 to launch a military rescue. The leadoff story on the television news almost every night for the remainder of Carter's term in office was along the theme of 'America held hostage.'

In the 1980 election campaign Republicans portrayed Carter and the Democrats as equally incapable of resisting raids on the federal treasury by 'welfare cheats' at home and raids on American installations by political and religious fanatics abroad. A mixture of domestic frustration and international humiliation thus provided the ideal setting for Reagan's message and political ambitions. Barring an 'October surprise' (a last-minute pre-election release of the hostages) there was no way that Jimmy Carter could be reelected in 1980.

The Reagan presidency

The 'New Right' was quick to claim credit for Ronald Reagan's victory in 1980. Since the Goldwater débâcle of 1964 right-wing activists had been developing new, sophisticated political tactics which brought them an ever greater measure of influence within the Republican Party and increasing public success. While the 'Old Right' had been preoccupied with the domestic and international struggle against communism, the New Right found it was most successful in addressing more mundane anxieties. The New Right specialized in taking single-issue concerns and causes and transforming them into support for conservative candidates and a broader conservative agenda.

The 'family' issue was particularly important in the development of the New Right. This seems paradoxical because Daniel Yankelovich's polls seemed to indicate that most Americans in the 1970s adopted more relaxed attitudes toward questions of sexual behavior and traditional gender roles. But despite the fact that polls showed a majority of Americans favoring the right for women to have abortions, 'pro-life' activists had proven time and again that they could defeat politicians who voted the wrong way on the abortion issue. Despite the fact that a majority of Americans said they favored the Equal Rights Amendment (which was endorsed by Ford as well as Carter), anti-ERA activists were still able to prevent its ratification in a no-holds-barred state-by-state battle against feminist groups. And the New Right, much earlier than its opponents, mastered the mysteries of computer-based direct mail operations, which were used for fund-raising and political mobilization.

Above far left: Jesse Jackson, America's leading black politician of the 1980s, began his public career working in the civil rights movement, alongside Martin Luther King.

Above left: Twice in the 1970s America was hit hard by gasoline shortages. New York drivers wait in line at a gas station in June 1979. These crises were the first signs ordinary Americans had that their country no longer enjoyed an easy domination in global affairs.

Left: Pierre Trudeau shakes hands at the 1969 Canadian National Exhibition. Trudeau and his Liberal Party dominated Canadian politics from 1969 until his retirement as party leader in 1984 with a mixture of charisma, political adroitness and dedication to Canadian unity.

Right: Angry demonstrations like this brought an end to the Shah of Iran's regime. The loss of this important Middle Eastern ally placed a noose around the neck of President Jimmy Carter's political ambitions.

Yet the 1980 election results were not an unqualified ideological triumph for the New Right, or even for more traditional conservatism. The Republican victory in 1980 was at least as much a vote against Carter as a vote for Reagan. For the fifth straight presidential election the percentage of eligible voters going to the polls had dropped, down to the lowest level in the twentieth century, with just over half the eligible voters turning out.

The nation's oldest President, almost 70 when he took the oath of office, Reagan also had one of the most unlikely backgrounds of anyone who ever occupied the Oval Office. Reagan was a small-town midwestern radio announcer when he came to Hollywood in 1937 on the strength of a six-month acting contract from Warner Brothers. He went on to a decade-and-a-half of moderate stardom in Hollywood movies. He inherited his father's Democratic loyalties, and as late as 1950 he campaigned for Richard Nixon's Democratic opponent in the Senate race in California. By 1952, however, he had undergone a change of heart, becoming a 'Democrat for Eisenhower,' and soon after he changed his party affiliation. Reagan's big political breakthrough came in 1964 when he appeared on television in a Goldwater fundraising appeal. That brought him to the attention of professional political operatives in California who recognized his natural gifts as a public figure. In 1966 he ran for governor of California against the incumbent Democrat, Pat Brown, and defeated him decisively. He retired from the governorship after two terms in office and prepared for a presidential run. In 1976 he came close to wresting the nomination from Ford, and in 1980 he was the easy favorite to win the Republican nomination.

Once in office Reagan proved singularly gifted at reading and guiding the American public's mood. To his supporters he was the 'Great Communicator,' to his detractors he was 'teflon-coated,' invulnerable to criticism. Reagan was undoubtedly sincere in his conservative beliefs, but he was always more pragmatic than his ide-

ologically pure allies on the New Right, who carped throughout the Reagan years that his aides would not 'let Reagan be Reagan.' He was inclined to soft-pedal the 'social issues' (school prayer, opposition to abortion and so on) that were so high on the list of the New Right's agenda. Reagan's popularity had little to do with his policies and a great deal to do with his carefully projected image of being a relaxed, self-confident, affable winner – not a tormented, gloomy, 'mean' loser like Carter. After 20 years of failed or broken presidencies Americans desperately wanted a successful presidency, and Reagan seemed a man who might deliver it.

'Government is not the solution to our problem,' Reagan declared in his 1981 inaugural address, 'government *is* the problem.' While Nixon had cut back on Great Society programs, and Ford and Carter had begun the process of deregulation, none of Reagan's predecessors in the White House in recent decades would have offered so sweeping a condemnation of government intervention in the economy. It was in the field of economic policy that Reagan offered his most radical challenge to prevailing assumptions and won his greatest legislative victories. In his first year in office Reagan pushed through Congress a package of cuts in domestic social spending, deregulation and tax cuts. During the campaign Reagan had promised to end the federal deficit within three years, but not by means of tax increases. Influenced by advocates of 'supply-side economics,' Reagan argued that reducing the tax burden on corporations and wealthy individuals would lead to increased investment in manufacturing. That would produce more jobs and, ultimately, higher federal tax revenues. But in practice the theory was disappointing. Investors found it more profitable to put their money into corporate take-overs, 'junk bonds' and other non-job-producing forms of investment, while the federal deficit soared to record levels. Meanwhile, Reagan had embarked on the most expensive peacetime military build-up in the nation's

history, also unsupported by tax increases. Yet the level of inflation and lending rates *were* substantially reduced during Reagan's first term in office, and the severe economic recession of 1982-83 gave way to recovery the following year. But unemployment continued to hover at a high rate, and the long-term weakening of the US trade balance continued unabated. Many Americans were better off in the 1980s than in the 1970s, but the easy confidence in economic prosperity characteristic of the 1960s did not return.

Whatever uncertainties about the future still existed, they did not harm Reagan in his triumphant campaign for reelection in 1984. Reagan radiated optimism, his campaign ads proclaimed that it was 'morning in America' once again, while his Democratic opponent, Walter Mondale, talked of the need for higher taxes and was widely perceived as the captive of his party's 'special interest' groups. Reagan's victory was a foregone conclusion.

Determined to reverse the 'Vietnam syndrome,' that he argued had paralyzed American policy since the early 1970s, Reagan vigorously denounced the Soviet Union as an 'evil empire' and stepped up aid to anti-Communist guerilla movements in Afghanistan, Africa and Central America. Among the new weapons systems he proposed was the so-called 'Star Wars,' the Strategic Defense Initiative, a system of space-based lasers and other high-tech weapons designed to protect the US against nuclear attack. (Critics argued variously that SDI would not work, that it might destabilize the peace 'guaranteed' by nuclear terror or that it might promote a 'first strike' mentality among US policymakers.) Reagan's assertiveness was welcomed by many Americans; they applauded his decision to invade the Caribbean island of Grenada in 1983 (ostensibly a 'rescue mission' to protect American students on the island, but more basically intended to overthrow Grenada's left-wing government). Reagan's hard-line toward Libya, a country he accused of sponsoring terrorist movements,

Left: The destruction of the Marine headquarters at Beirut in October 1983 should have been a fatal catastrophe for President Ronald Reagan's administration. But the inevitably successful invasion of Grenada masked Reagan's failures in the Middle East.

Above right: The accession of Mikhail Gorbachev to the Soviet leadership brought to an end the 'Second' Cold War, which had begun in the last years of the Carter administration. Gorbachev's eagerness to compromise over arms control virtually forced Reagan to abandon his previous antagonism toward the Soviet Union, and agree to the Intermediate Nuclear Forces treaty in November 1987.

Right: The years since 1945 have seen a major shift in America's population to the southern and western states – a reflection of the rising economic prosperity of these regions.

revealed that arms sales to Iran had been going on for several years in a vain effort to free US hostages held by terrorist groups in Lebanon; and that some of the profits from those sales had been diverted to the contras, so as to by-pass the Congressional ban on aid. As the scandal spread in the spring and summer of 1987, with new revelations breaking into the headlines every few days, it seemed eerily reminiscent of the Watergate crisis and the later years of the Vietnam war. The same issues of executive privilege, Congressional authority, the public's right to know and the propriety of covert action were again being debated.

A decade of contradictions

While it is too soon to say with any certainty how future historians will regard the 1980s, they certainly will have rich material to work with. Contradictions abound. In the summer of 1987 polls revealed that most people disapproved of Reagan's policies in Central America and did not believe he was telling the truth about Irangate. But unlike Johnson or Nixon, whose presidencies were destroyed over similar issues, Reagan's personal popularity was only slightly diminished. On the other hand, the Republicans had by now lost control of both houses of Congress, and as the nation headed for the fall of 1988 the familiar pre-election stand-off between Legislative and Executive branches representing different parties seemed to preclude any very sweeping new initiatives from the White House. Yet it was just at this time that Reagan and the new Soviet general secretary, Mikhail Gorbachev, signed one of the most important arms limitation treaties in history, the INF Treaty, that actually eliminated an entire class of intermediate-range nuclear missiles from the European theater. The INF Treaty would provide a high note to Reagan's otherwise generally lackluster presidency.

was also popular. But some critics charged that Reagan's foreign policy was confused, impulsive and inept, as in his decision to send US Marines to Beirut in 1983 on a vague peace-keeping mission. In October 1983 a suicide attack on their Beirut headquarters left 241 American Marines dead; US forces were withdrawn soon afterward, having accomplished nothing.

Nicaragua's left-wing Sandinista government became a particular concern of the Reagan administration. Soon after he came into office Reagan began supplying aid and direction to the 'contras,' right-wing opponents of the Nicaraguan regime. While the contras launched raids on Nicaragua from bases in Honduras and Costa Rica, US military forces began a build up in the region. Fearing another Vietnam was developing in Central America, Congress passed resolutions on three separate occasions between 1982 and 1984 restricting or barring the spending of funds on behalf of the contras. But Reagan either authorized or allowed members of his National Security Council to establish a 'private aid network' for the contras.

This decision eventually led to the greatest political disaster of the Reagan administration, the 'Irangate' scandal. In November 1986 a Lebanese magazine reported that US arms shipments were going to the Khomenei regime in Iran. Later that same month Attorney General Edwin Meese

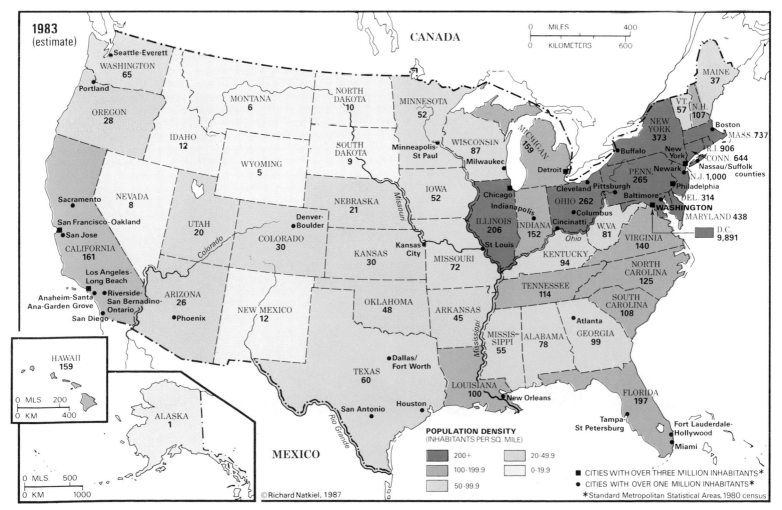

Latin America

The Japanese attack on Pearl Harbor in 1941 opened a cooperative interlude for the American republics. Recriminations against United States imperialism subsided. The Latin American nations all declared war on or severed relationships with the Axis powers, although Argentina broke only belatedly in 1944. The United States enlisted broad collaboration for defense and logistics: Brazil sent troops to Italy, and Mexico dispatched an air squadron to the Philippines. The Latin American countries' trade with the United States rose to over half their foreign commerce, and though they suffered severe shortages and inflation, the prices of their raw material exports were, at considerable sacrifice, stabilized.

When the war ended it seemed that Latin America might be entering an era of liberal, constitutional change in approved Western style. Such a prognosis was supported by the widespread appearance of reformist, representative regimes in the mid 1940s. Post-Cárdenas Mexico found its way to stable middle-of-the-road developmentalism; dictators disappeared in Guatemala (1944), El Salvador (1944), and Honduras (1948); democratic leftism triumphed in Costa Rica (1948); Cuba had a respite from Batista (1944-52); Haiti produced a revolt against the mulatto elite (1946); Venezuela's Democratic Action administration interrupted a succession of military leaders (1945-48); Ecuador relaxed under President Galo Plaza (1948-52), an enlightened landowner; the *Apristas* shared power in Peru under President José Lius Bustamante (1945-48), though were again outlawed after General Manuel Odría's coup; Chile's President Gabriel González Videla toed a middle path between extreme right and left (1946-52); Uruguay, placed on the road to state socialism early in the century under José Batlle y Ordóñez (1856-1929), enjoyed postwar prosperity and in 1951 converted its presidency to a nine-man executive council; in Brazil the forced resignation of Vargas in 1946 ushered

in the Second Republic under a constitution limiting presidential powers. In Bolivia forces were gathering for the 1952 revolution and 12 years of sweeping social and economic change. Only in a handful of smaller countries – the Dominican Republic, Nicaragua, Panama, Paraguay – was the tradition of repressive strong-man rule virtually unrelieved.

Two cases remain, perhaps the most prophetic of the period: Argentine Peronism and the Colombian 'violence.' When the civilian rule that followed General Justo's regime in Argentina proved hopelessly inept, the army brazenly resumed power in 1943. Its junta was soon dominated by Juan Domingo Perón, an athletic, blustering, personally magnetic officer who possessed first-hand knowledge of European dictatorships; he was elected president in 1946 and was virtually turned out in 1955. The regime of Perón and his volatile wife Eva Duarte, who died of cancer in 1952, was characterized by nationalistic sloganeering and adventurism; strong-arm tactics and extravagant abuse of civil rights; political mobilization of the 'shirtless' urban workers (*descamisados*); and an erratic economic program featuring nationalization of utilities, state control of exports, industrialization and income redistribution temporarily favoring the proletariat.

Peronism, widely interpreted at the time as a reprise of prewar Fascism, differed significantly from the original. European Fascism had appealed to petit-bourgeois groups who felt their once-secure status being eroded by bureaucratization or proletarization. It was less attractive to the proletariat itself, which possessed independent organizations and class-oriented programs for institutional change. In contrast, the dynamics of Peronism reflected the failure of the Argentine middle class ever to have achieved self-identity. Largely of immigrant origin, selectively absorbed by the Argentine elite, middle groups had only a weak sense of class tradition and differentiation.

Here the problem of social integration focused on the urban workers, who enjoyed neither the European tradition of worker solidarity nor the putative chance for upward filtration of Argentine middle groups. Thus while European leadership purported to restore national unity, social hierarchy and the prestige of threatened groups, Peronist 'social justice' tended to exacerbate class tensions and to promulgate the notion of society as a 'limited good' insufficient to satisfy the aspirations of all. The Peronist regime suffered from archaic, caudillist features and immature leadership. Yet the impotence of succeeding regimes and the persistent magic of the exiled Perón's name for a third of the Argentine electorate as late

Above: Terrorism in Colombia. The scene in Puente Nacional on 30 September 1960 after the terrorist leader Efrain Gonzales and his men had machine-gunned a crowd, killing 19 people.

Left: The Chilean Army arresting demonstrators in Santiago during the presidential elections on 13 September 1946.

Above right: Eva Perón, accompanied by her husband the President, greeting an enthusiastic crowd of supporters from the balcony at the Plaza de Mayo, Buenos Aires, on May Day 1951.

Right: Some of the estimated one million workers demonstrating in Buenos Aires in August 1951, demanding that President Perón and his wife Eva rule Argentina for the next six years.

as the 1970s testified to a revolutionary potential short-circuited by the absence of decisive institutional change. More theatrically than Brazil's Vargas, Perón had exploited his appeal for the urban *lumpenproletariat*, a constituency soon to win political prominence throughout Latin America.

Like Argentina during its golden years 1862-1930, Colombia had enjoyed stability, economic advance and at least the formality of elections from 1904 to 1946, first under Conservatives, then under Liberals. Neither the piecemeal reformism of the latter, however, nor the *status quo*-ism of the former was adequate to the nation's postwar social and economic strains. In 1946 left-leaning populist Jorge Eliécer Gaitán became a presidential candidate, splitting the Liberal vote and allowing the Conservatives to win by a plurality. Then, in April 1948, during an Inter-American Conference at Bogotá, Gaitán, idol of the urban populace, was assassinated. The event opened a period of nationwide turmoil, demoralization and violence that lasted well into the 1960s and brought at least 150,000 deaths. The Conservatives clamped the country under a state of siege, then yielded to the dictatorship of General Gustavo Rojas Pinilla (1953-57).

Colombia's pathological *violencia* was no ordinary civil strife. Unlike the case of most Latin American countries, where politics were until recently the domain of agrocommercial elites and urban middle groups, party affiliation in Colombia extended to all regions and social strata, reaching even the impoverished and illiterate peasants. Party struggle therefore recurrently mobilized the

masses in civil war. In the 1860s and 1870s some 80,000 were killed, and 100,000 died in the carnage of 1899-1902. Yet despite this vertical polarization the country was always governed in the bipartisan interests of the dominant classes. Mobilization of the masses, whether in the nineteenth century or after 1948, was never directed toward redistribution of wealth or institutional change. The chilling techniques of *la violencia*

reflected this disjunction of action and goals. Not only were half a dozen hideously stylized modes of killing widely employed, but also such psychopathic forms of aggression as the rape of corpses and the replacement of aborted human fetuses with those of cats.

Rojas Pinilla, welcomed by the ruling classes as a presidential gendarme to restore order, was ejected when he turned out to be venal and mega-

lomaniacal and to aspire to populist leadership of the Peronist stripe. Formalizing an entente which had long been implicit, Conservative and Liberal elites adopted a National Front formula by which to alternate the presidency during four terms from 1958 to 1974. It remained questionable, however, how long the old regime could both stave off the reassertion of populist leadership and neutralize the people's capacity for small-group political and paramilitary action developed during the turbulent years of *la violencia*.

In dissimilar ways the Argentine and Colombian cases demonstrated the resistance of elites and institutions to structural change. This recalcitrance grew increasingly apparent throughout Latin America after the 1940s as population growth built up the pressures on political and economic systems. Growth rates for the region as a whole came to exceed those of any other large world area. In about 1950 Latin America drew abreast of the United States in population size, and by the year 2000 it was projected to be twice as large. Growth was accompanied by accelerating rural exodus. In the 1950s and 1960s total population was rising briskly at almost 3 percent a year, with towns and cities growing at 4.5 percent and rural zones at only 1.5 percent; thus the urban population rose from 39 percent to 55 percent, was 65 percent in 1980 and could hit 80 percent by the end of the century. By 1970 30 million or more people inhabited the four largest metropolitan areas of Buenos Aires, Mexico City, São Paulo and Rio de Janeiro.

Although middle classes expanded swiftly, income distribution remained severely skewed in favor of the topmost strata. In 1965 persons in the top 20 percent income bracket of the region as a whole received 60.6 percent of total income while those in the lowest 20 percent bracket received only 3.5 percent. Even more striking, the income share of the top 5 percent was nine times as large as that of the bottom 20 percent. The low buying power of the masses curbed expansion of markets for home industry, while introduction of advanced technology limited the number of city-ward migrants who could be absorbed in manufacturing. A century ago it took 370,000 workers to produce England's first million tons of steel; today 8000 workers produce this amount in a large Latin American country. Thus while the industrial component of Latin American production rose from 19.6 percent in 1950 to 25 percent in 1970, the numbers of workers employed in industry eased off from 14.4 to 13.8 percent. The sector that mostly absorbed those dislodged from agriculture was 'service,' whose share of the work force rose from 23 to 33 percent, while agriculture declined from 53 to 42 percent. The persistence of traditional farm methods in many zones, the scarcity of productive employment in urban centers and the population boom combined to dampen economic growth.

External dependency

Domestic pressures and rigidities were aggravated by external factors. For its exchange earnings Latin America still depended heavily on exporting traditional raw materials at now-depressed world prices. Yet industrialization, while reducing consumer imports, created new demands for capital goods, investment and technical assistance. External commercial dependency was giving way to financial and technological dependency on the industrial nations and, increasingly, on giant multinational corporations. United States private investment in Latin America rose from $1.6 billion in 1913 to $6 billion in 1960 and to $12 billion in 1969; but to the chagrin of

Latin American leaders the region's wartime dislocations failed to elicit a local equivalent of the United States Marshall Plan for Europe. By the 1950s the aura of the Good Neighbor days had evanesced. The United States was formulating its Latin American policy largely with one eye on the American investor and the other on the Cold War chess game. As President Eisenhower summarized it in 1954: 'Military assistance must be continued. Technical assistance must be maintained. Economic assistance can be reduced.' In this same year the United States, without consulting the United Nations or the Organization of American States, actively supported the overthrow of an elected regime in Guatemala, which had expropriated the United Fruit Company and was receiving arms from Czechoslovakia. The low ebb of inter-American relations was dramatized in 1958 when US Vice-President Nixon, on a goodwill tour, was stoned and spat on in Lima and Caracas.

Reacting to a situation of drift and improvization, Brazil's President Juscelino Kubitschek in 1958 outlined a hemispheric program, Operation Pan America, calling for adaptation of inter-American agencies to fight underdevelopment, stabilization of world markets for basic commodities, technical assistance and expansion of international credit sources. This proposal led to the creation of the OAS Committee of 21 states concerned with economic cooperation, prompted the United States to approve establishment of the Inter American Development Bank and launched the idea of a hemispheric partnership that President Kennedy baptized in 1961 as the Alliance for Progress. Washington's participation in the Alliance responded in large part to apprehensions that the revolutionary example of Castro's Cuba might be widely copied in Latin America – with consequent proliferation of Soviet or Sino-Soviet beachheads – if decisive measures were not taken to encourage deep-cutting evolutionary reform. The tactics adopted rested on obsolete or premature assumptions: that social democratic politicians who had matured in the 1930s and 1940s would be a prime source of leadership; that expanding middle groups were now a constituency for democracy and orderly socioeconomic change; that the political influence of the military was declining; that strategic infusions of public and private investment would spur economic growth; that the time was ripe for regional economic integration; that external assistance could be designed to induce effective land reform, tax reform and allocation of developmental resources.

Foreign investment was ineffective in meliorating the sluggish performance of Latin American economies if we accept an estimate by the UN Economic Commission for Latin America that for every dollar invested during the early 1960s three were repatriated as income and profits. Moreover, the United States aroused little confidence among its Alliance partners with its indifferently managed aid program, its tendency to tie political strings to economic assistance, its flirtation with military groups and its dispatch of

Guerrilla campaigns in Central and South America

MERCATOR PROJECTION

Below left: Postwar Latin America, listing the major guerrilla campaigns of the period.

Right: American influence on display in Caracas, Venezuela, during the 1950s. The economic control that the United States exercised over the Latin American nations was as great as that of the old European colonial empires of the nineteenth century.

Below: A major steel plant in Brazil, an important part of Brazil's industrial capacity.

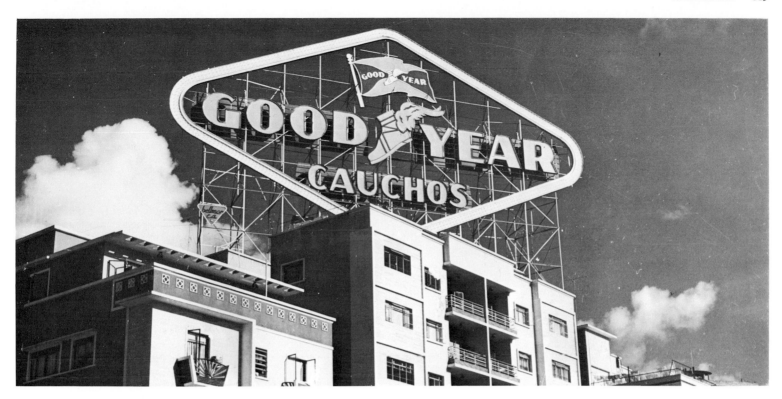

Marines to the Dominican Republic in 1965. Given the limits of human vision, political viability, and economic interest, however, it is hardly conceivable that the United States, or the industrial nations in general, could have mounted assistance programs sizable enough to have altered substantially Latin America's economic drift during the 1960s. The ultimate determinants were the internal logic of national institutions and the role of Latin America in the grand economic and politico-military calculus of the world community. These combined to produce a series of political phenomena that were vaguely prefigured by Peronism and are sometimes classified as a Latin American brand of Nasserism. The analogy, though suggestive, overlooks historical differences between the Islamic Middle East and Ibero-Catholic America, as well as the diversity prevailing within Latin America itself, as illustrated in the cases now to be discussed.

Judged by per capita income and production indicators, Cuba was one of the most prosperous Latin American countries in the 1950s. Judged by its efficient sugar industry or the amenities of Havana, it was one of the most modern. Benefits, however, were maldistributed. Nearly 75 percent of the agricultural area was owned by sugar mills and independent cane growers, who comprised only eight percent of all rural landholders. During the seven-months 'dead season,' when no harvesting and grinding occurred, 40 percent of the labor force was under- or unemployed. Of rural families, 60 percent lived on earth floors under palm-thatch roofs, and only four percent ate meat regularly. Sugar and its byproducts tyrannized the economy, accounting for 80 percent of exports. Although the United States-controlled share of sugar milling and banking declined in the 1950s, Cuban commercial dependency on its neighbor remained high. The United States received 65 per-

cent of Cuban exports by value and supplied 75 percent of the imports. The economic subordination of this wealthy economy and Washington's unremitting political pressure largely account for the immense corruption of public life in pre-Castro Cuba (perhaps one quarter of state expenditures went to graft) and for the failure of reform to gather momentum.

The pervasive demoralization of Cuba under Batista allowed Fidel Castro, whose 300 guerrilla fighters in August 1958 faced an army of 50,000, to take over the country the following 1 January. Though in 1961 Castro claimed he had always been a Marxist-Leninist, the early policies of his regime were inspired by a pastiche of 'humanism,' democratic socialism and the ideas of Cuba's poet-patriot José Martí (1853-95). His mass support and uncontested leadership, however, allowed him wide scope for experimentation. Sweeping agrarian reform and expropriation of foreign in-

terests soon gave his program a revolutionary cast and crystallized the opposition of the United States, which broke relations and supported the tragicomic Bay of Pigs invasion in 1961. Precisely this obduracy of the United States permitted Cuban leadership to create a political culture unique in Latin America for its mass-based, participatory nationalism. It also cleared the way for the Soviet Union to assume the cost of Cuba's foreign dependency. Soviet support came to approximate the annual per capita expenditure of the United States on its Caribbean quasi-colony, Puerto Rico. This dependency increased after 1965, when Castro abandoned his industrialization program and, reverting to the once-vilified monocultural model, undertook to be the main sugar supplier for the Communist bloc at a price well above the world market. Against a production target of 47 million tons of sugar for 1965-70 Cuba produced a shortfall of 11.3 million tons, increasing the strains on an already Spartan economy.

During the 1970s Cuba made an effort to lessen its economic dependence on the Soviet Union, and for a time in the middle of the decade 36 percent of Cuba's exports and 52 percent of its imports were being traded with non-Soviet bloc nations (though not, of course, with the United States, which maintained a trade embargo). But as Cuba's international credit expanded so did its debt, which increased tenfold between 1969 and 1982. This, plus the failure of Cuba's efforts to break the monocultural nature of its export economy by re-exporting Soviet petroleum (a ploy that fell victim to the worldwide depression of oil prices in the early 1980s), gradually forced Cuba back into the Soviet trade orbit, and since 1982 about 80 percent of the nation's trade has been with the Soviet bloc.

Throughout the 1970s and early 1980s Cuba's

Above: A familiar sight in Santo Domingo as US troops search a van for suspects.

Left: The youthful, flamboyant Fidel Castro, who overthrew the corrupt Batista regime in Cuba. His pro-Soviet policies became a thorn in the side of successive American administrations.

Right: A Cuban refugee is interviewed by a US employment officer in Florida.

foreign policy became increasingly aggressive in terms of lending support to burgeoning Third World Marxist regimes or insurgencies. There was a series of Cuban interventions in South Yemen, Ethiopia and Morocco, and the largest and most destabilizing occurred in Angola in 1975, when Cuba sent more than 30,000 troops to assist the Luanda-based MPLA in seizing control of the newly decolonized nation. (In fact, the Luanda regime, though formally the victor in the 1975 civil war, still does not control large areas of Angola that remain dominated by the US-backed UNITAS rebel forces led by Jonas Savimbi.) The United States also accused Cuba of aiding insurgencies in El Salvador and Nicaragua, and certainly after the Nicaraguan Sandinista rebels came to power in 1979 Cuba gave the new Marxist regime open and enthusiastic support.

A few efforts were made to relieve tensions between Cuba and the United States in the 1980s, but they all foundered. In 1980, for example, Castro had somewhat quixotically decided to relax restrictions on emigration from the island, and in short order some 125,000 Florida-bound émigrés poured out of the port of Mariel, many of them not eligible for admission to the US under its immigration laws. In 1984 Cuba offered to take back about 2700 of the ineligible refugees, and the US in return offered to reinstate regular Cuban immigration at a level of up to 20,000 per year. But this budding rapprochement collapsed in May 1985 as the result of Castro's fury over the initiation of a Voice of America radio program – Radio Marti – beamed at Cuba. Similarly, Cuba's talk of a possible phased withdrawal of troops from Angola evaporated in July 1985 when the US adopted a policy of sending aid to UNITA.

How Cuba would fare in the age of *perestroika* was unclear as the 1980s drew to a close. With the possible exception of Rumania it seemed to be the only pro-Soviet communist state that was calling for more, rather than less, centralized control of the economy. Nor was it certain that in an age when the USSR and the East bloc nations seemed intent on trying to foster *détente* Cuba would modify its interventionist foreign policy significantly. Nevertheless, despite the truculence, improvisation, inconsistencies and inexperience of Cuban leadership and despite unique circumstances which limited the Revolution's 'exportability' to the rest of Latin America, certain features had made this a bellwether case for the hemisphere. The exodus of the upper and middle classes had facilitated abolition of special privilege while proving that wholesale loss of professional and technical skills was not irreparable. The guerrilla origin of the revolution (supremely personified by Castro's Argentine comrade in arms, Ernesto 'Che' Guevara, whose quixotic Bolivian venture ended in his violent death in 1967) and the big-power confrontation provoked by the nuclear-missile crisis of 1962 had demonstrated for the Americas, as Vietnam had for Asia, that small-group forces and small countries might exercise powerful leverage on the great powers. And mobilization for a functional, grass-roots (if heavily ideologized) school system to produce a 'new man' had been a decisive step beyond Peronist-based populism that relied on mass-media hypnosis and government largesse.

While Castro had triumphed against a corrupt army, elsewhere the military showed surprising capacity for modernization and leadership in the face of incipient chaos. Like the Catholic Church,

which also exhibits vitality and versatility on the contemporary scene, the military commands a vertical, hierarchical organization which frequently addresses crisis more effectively than do Latin America's characteristically weak horizontal associations of class, party or interest group. In Brazil, after a spate of economic euphoria in the 1950s, growth fell off, inflation intensified, political processes broke down and violence threatened from several quarters. President Jânio Quadros resigned in 1961 after seven months in office and was succeeded by a self-serving pseudo-leftist, João 'Jango' Goulart. When the latter's inept handling of Brazil's emergencies became intolerable, the army assumed control of the country in 1964, convinced that it alone could provide the strong government required to check the twin dangers of inflation and internal subversion.

The military regime, which severely curbed the exercise of electoral politics, rested on an entente with industrial and agricultural elites who shared the army officers' opposition to mobilization politics, the economic demands of peasants and workers, inflation, communism, and the insurrectionary tactics of the underprivileged and students. At the same time the officers, usually of lower-middle-class origin, distrusted the aristocratic habits, collusive business practices, and cosmopolitanism of the private-sector elite. They favored a no-nonsense, technocratic approach to economic development and, while lining up squarely with the capitalist, anti-communist West, they supported nationalization of key industries like petroleum. Policy shifts during the post-1964 presidential administrations revealed that the officers shared no monolithic consensus and that military prescriptions ranged from the 'liberal internationalist' position of President Humberto Castello Branco (1964-67) to the hardline authoritarian nationalism which became more pronounced under his successors, taking its grimmest form in the indiscriminate imprisonment and torture of students, intellectuals and actual or suspected terrorists. By the late 1960s the economic policies of the regime had proven strikingly successful, if measured by indices of production and inflation rather than by income redistribution. Brazil, Latin America's largest industrial (as opposed to commodity) exporter, enjoyed an extremely favorable trade balance: imports, about half of which were petroleum, represented only six percent of the nation's GNP, one of the lowest ratios in the world. The economy heated up, but so did inflation and the fulminating growth of foreign debt.

Oil crisis and economic disaster

The world oil crisis that developed in the mid 1970s precipitated an abrupt end to these economic good times. Brazilian foreign debt reached $93 billion, the largest in the Third World, and servicing it cut deeply into the trade surplus. Inflation went out of control, its annual rate soaring to a high of 229 percent in 1984. Production fell, as did wages, and unemployment became a serious problem. The social effects of these economic woes were aggravated by the nation's lopsided distribution of wealth: between 1960 and 1985 the poorer half of the population's share of the national income declined from 15 percent to 13 percent, while the share of the wealthiest tenth of the population rose from 39 percent to 51 percent; and by 1985 1 percent of the landed population owned 45 percent of the nation's land. Gang wars erupted in the streets of the cities, and guerrilla activity started up in the countryside.

In 1979 General João Baptista de Oliveira Figueiredo, Brazil's fifth military president since

1964, came to power and announced his intention of eventually restoring Brazil to democracy. To the surprise of some he kept the promise, and on 15 January 1985 the electoral college named Tancredo Naves the first civilian president in two decades. Naves died in April and was succeeded by his vice-president, José Sarney. Doubts about the real extent of Sarney's popularity were dispeled in the congressional elections the following year, when his supporters won by a large majority. Sarney took a strong hand in addressing Brazil's economic crisis. In February 1986 he froze prices and set formulas for wage increases, and a year later he temporarily suspended interest payments on $70 billion-worth of intermediate-term foreign debt (prompting major US creditor banks to take the overdue step of increasing their reserves against Latin American loans). These and other firm measures seemed to be producing some positive effects by early 1988 and did not appear to have damaged either Sarney's popular support or his reputation abroad, but plainly Brazil still had a long road to travel to achieve economic stability, especially the fundamental economic and social restructuring on which its long-term wellbeing would depend.

Peru in the 1960s, like Brazil in the 1950s, experienced an interlude of populist politics, free-wheeling developmentalism and fiscal irresponsibility under President Fernando Belaúnde Terry (1963-68). Here, too, military resentment of civilian elitism and inefficacy led to an army coup in 1968 and the installation of the government of General Juan Velasco Alvarado. Peruvian officers, however, were less pro-United States than their Brazilian counterparts and more inclined to the view that their nation's problems (symptomatized in the guerrilla movements and land invasions of the mid 1960s) required constitutional reforms, not mere reallocation of control. The new regime therefore developed 'popular,' anti-oligarchic ties and enlisted cooperation from left-leaning intellectuals. Its program featured land distribution, absorption of the impoverished Indian peasantry

into the market economy, public and private coparticipation in industrialization and rigid controls on foreign oil and mining concessionaires.

Some observers at the time suggested that Peru's populist-military experiment might be as significant for the 1970s as the Cuban Revolution had been for the 1960s, but in fact its inconsistent, capricious and rather offensively tutelary nature combined with economic mismanagement to make it a failure. The high cost of Alvarado's reforms produced a net outflow of capital and a fatal rise in foreign borrowing. The military replaced Alvarado in 1975 with General Francisco Morales Bermúdez, but he, too, could do nothing to halt the economic decline or the mounting public dissatisfaction. The power of the military disintegrated, a new constitution was promulgated in 1979 and in 1980 Fernando Belaúnde Terry was re-elected, thus returning Peru to civilian rule.

But Belaúnde was not the man to save Peru from its deepening economic crisis. International terms of trade were now turning sharply against the country's two primary exports, petroleum and copper, and fishing harvests were poor. In 1983 alone gross domestic product declined by 12 percent. At least 50 percent of the population was unemployed or underemployed, and inflation had reduced the purchasing power of the average wage-earner by about 40 percent since 1975. As in many other Latin American countries the distribution of wealth was also wildly skewed, with two percent of the population owning 60 percent of the nation's wealth and the poorest 38 percent of the population owning only two percent. Moreover, the government was now being so seriously challenged by the insurgency of a messianic Maoist group known as the *Sendero Luminoso* (Shining Path) that the last years of the Belaúnde government were punctuated with recurrent declarations of states of emergency.

On 28 July 1985, in the first democratic transfer of power from one party to another in the nation's history, Peru elected as its president Alan García Pérez, the 36-year-old leader of the American

Popular Revolutionary Alliance (which had been founded in Mexico in 1924 by Víctor Raúl Haya de la Torre and which, though Peru's oldest political party, had always previously been denied access to office by the military). García immediately proved himself an activist leader of the stripe of Brazil's Sarney. He froze the prices of basic goods, tightened exchange controls, devalued the currency, banned many imports, cut the bureaucracy, slashed the military budget, stepped up operations against the *Senderos* and, in a move that understandably attracted a good deal of international attention, followed Sarney's lead by defying the International Monetary Fund and announcing that no more than 10 percent of Peru's export earnings would be allocated to servicing the nation's $14 billion debt to foreign banks. All in all, a good beginning in confronting a daunting set of problems.

Another important, atypical, case is that of Chile, where a Marxist was elected president in 1970. Save for interruptions in 1891 and 1924-32, Chile had experienced unusual political stability ever since 1833. Its party system was unique in Latin America for having a European-type array of right, center and left blocs based on six main groupings and as many as 36 parties. Reflecting a high level of political sophistication, this electoral system, after the 1930s, tranquilly produced a wide variety of regimes to cope with the chronic problems of land concentration, foreign control of mining, inflation and declining export earnings: the administrations of the Radicals (1938-52), of reformed strong man Carlos Ibáñez (1952-58), of rightist Jorge Alessandri (1958-64), and of Christian Democrat Eduardo Frei Montalva (1964-70). Having won 56 percent of the vote against 39 percent for Savador Allende, his Marxist opponent, Frei launched an ambitious, though only partially successful, social and economic program. The year 1970, a moment of economic gloom, produced

three contenders: Allende, who won 36 percent of the vote, the Conservative Alessandri (35 percent), and Radomiro Tomic, a Christian Democrat slightly left of Frei (28 percent). Thus Allende's share was lower in 1970 than in 1964, and the majority of the votes went to more rightist candidates. Yet Allende took office peacefully as the hemisphere's first elected Marxist executive.

Unfortunately, the country did not remain peaceful. Allende soon managed to outrage both rightist elements in Chile and the United States by such action as establishing relations with Cuba and the People's Republic of China and nationalizing several US companies. At the same time the country's economy spun out of control, with the inflation rate soaring to 500 percent per annum. At last, in September 1973, a CIA-supported army *junta* staged a bloody coup that overthrew (and killed) Allende and installed in his place General Augustino Pinochet Ugarte. Thus ended Chile's 46 years of constitutional government, the longest in Latin American history.

At first Pinochet's drastically restrictive monetary policies seemed to be working, and inflation was brought under control. But the country's vulnerability to fluctuations in the international economy was made all too clear in the late 1970s and early 1980s. By the end of 1981, as exports plunged and foreign credit dried up, unemployment was already rising steeply toward the 30 percent it would reach in 1982, a year when bankruptcies reached an all-time high, the GNP dropped 13 percent in 12 months and the foreign debt approached its 1988 level of $20 billion.

Under a new constitution Pinochet was formally inaugurated as president for an eight-year term on 11 March 1981. By then his harshly repressive policies had alienated most of the independent right and had produced an opposition coalition – the Democratic Alliance – of the centerist and non-communist socialist parties. In

1983 trade unions and the Democratic Alliance began organizing mass protests, while the communist-dominated radical left coalition – Popular Unity – was calling for armed rebellion. A 1985 poll indicated that 80 percent of the population now wanted a return to democracy before the expiration of Pinochet's term in 1989, and all Chilean political parties save those of the government and Popular Unity signed a National Accord to that effect. As of early 1988 the country's political future thus hung in the balance: it was possible that Pinochet or some ultra-rightist successor regime might continue to exercise autocratic power, thus enhancing the possibility of a revolution that could provide the opportunity that Popular Unity was waiting for; or the Democratic Alliance might somehow prevail in persuading the regime to permit an orderly and peaceful return to democratic government. What would happen was beyond anyone's power to predict.

Brief mention should also be made of how two other countries – Argentina and Mexico – fared in the precarious 1970s and 1980s. After Perón's exile in 1955 Argentina entered a protracted period of military dictatorship, punctuated briefly by Perón's return in 1973, and, after his death in 1974, rule by his widow until 1976, when the military again took over. By 1981, when General Leopoldo Galtieri was named president, Argentinian military rule had acquired a sordid international reputation as being one of the most brutally repressive anywhere in the world. Galtieri's – and the military's – downfall began when, in April 1982, he landed thousands of troops on the Falkland Islands and claimed them for Argentina. Britain decisively reconquered the Falklands in a bloody month-long war, the humiliated Galtieri resigned on 17 June and his successor, General Reynaldo Bignone, lifted the six-year ban on political parties and promised that the country would return to civilian government. This finally occurred in October 1983, with the election of the moderate Radical Civic Union party's Raúl Alfonsín.

The country was by this time in a state of economic crisis, with a foreign debt of $45 billion, the third largest in the Third World, and a disastrous inflation rate running around 1000 percent a year.

Though Alfonsin introduced austerity measures and reassured foreign creditors somewhat by agreeing to repay $350 million in overdue interest in 1984, the debt spiral could not be contained, rising to $48 billion by 1985, with more than $1 billion in interest payments overdue. Finally, in that year Alfonsín worked out an agreement with the International Monetary Fund, promising to take drastic steps to put the country's economic house in order and to keep current with interest payments; in return, the way was opened for Argentina to receive about $1.2 billion in new loans. Throughout the latter part of the 1980s the fierce battle to stabilize the economy continued, with the fate of Argentinian democracy perhaps a hostage to its outcome.

Mexico provides a final example of the ways in which the inherent fragilities of Latin American social and economic structures have combined with vulnerabilities to world economic fluctuations to produce threats to political stability. At first glance the contrast between recent political developments in Argentina and Mexico would appear extreme. Since 1934 Mexico had enjoyed peaceful quasi-democratic civilian rule under the aegis of the Revolutionary Party (in its present incarnation called the *Partido Revolucionaria Institucional*, or PRI). The military remained remote from politics, intervening only at the ruling party's request to put down violent disturbances, which were rare enough. Although the PRI was universally understood to maintain its comfortable majority through varying degrees of vote fraud, there was little complaint or focused political opposition. Essentially, the PRI's nationalistic and progressive policies – protectionist, restrictive of foreign investment, ready to subsidize local industry and to undertake extensive welfare programs – were popular. And the economy was doing well. Between 1940 and 1982 the GNP had grown at an average annual rate of six percent, rising to eight percent toward the end of the period

Above: Chile's ruling four-man military *junta*, led by General Pinochet (second from left) who acted as president.

Left: British artillery in action against the Argentinians in the Falklands in 1982.

Right: Squatters living in abject poverty in Mexico City.

as Mexico intensified exploitation of its great oil reserves, the fourth largest in the world.

But this 50-year period of tranquillity ended abruptly in the early 1980s. The decay of world oil prices hit Mexico especially hard, since oil now accounted for 75 percent of the country's foreign revenues, and the excellent credit that Mexico had enjoyed for years recoiled on the economy in the form of unpayable debts. In 1981, instead of the anticipated export revenues of $20 billion, the country received $12 billion, a figure all but obliterated by the servicing requirements on foreign loans approaching $100 billion. The economy produced zero growth in 1982, and the GNP declined 5.3 percent in 1983. Foreign investment capital fled the country. The government, which had been obliged to devalue the peso in 1982, then had to contend with an inflation rate that rose to 100 percent per annum in 1983.

Mexican readjustment

The government (the eight-year administration of José López Portillo gave way to that of Miguel de la Madrid Hurtado in 1982) averted collapse the only way it could – by the application of austerity measures. Deficit spending was slashed

from 18 percent to six percent by 1984, the traditional trade deficit was converted to a surplus and inflation was brought down to an annual rate of 59 percent. But the cost was economic stagnation. The imports on which economic growth depended had been cut by 65 percent. Average real wages fell 50 percent between 1982 and 1985. Massive unemployment had been averted, but not underemployment, and the government had no way to fill the requirement for the nearly one million new jobs a year created by the 2.5 percent annual growth of the population. Over all hovered the massive foreign debt, the servicing of which continued to offset about 60 percent of export revenues.

All this inevitably eroded popular support for the PRI. The pro-US opposition *Partido Acción Nacional* (PAN) began to make gains in regional elections, and in the 1984 elections the PRI resorted to larger-than-usual vote fraud to keep PAN in its place. This prompted violent protests in some areas, with the army having to be brought in to restore order. As the 1980s wore on there was every indication that unless Mexico's economic crisis could be resolved, the same cycle of mounting opposition, fraud, violence and army

intervention could repeat itself with rising frequency and intensity. Under such circumstances, how long the army would be content to keep clear of politics was a critical unknown.

Fortunately for Mexico – and potentially for other Latin American and Third World debtor nations – foreign creditor banks gradually began to take a more realistic attitude toward the debt crisis and to seek ways to lower interest charges and defer or write off repayments of principal while keeping credit lines open. At the end of 1987, for example, Morgan Guaranty Trust proposed a novel scheme in which the bank might forgo Mexico its debt if it were given in exchange Mexican government bonds of lesser value. Other foreign banks seemed favorably impressed with the idea.

If this or similar schemes are widely adopted the pandemic Latin American debt crisis of the 1980s might indeed be relieved, but the more fundamental economic problems and vulnerabilities would still remain. And whether Latin American governments would then have the will and vision – or Latin American society the flexibility – to make the really meaningful structural changes remained the central question.

The Middle East

Between 1919 and 1945 the politics of the Middle East remained largely a projection of the politics of European colonial powers. But in the years following World War II, as the colonial powers withdrew and the number of sovereign states in the greater Middle East and North Africa quintupled, complex and erratic new political patterns appeared in the region. These patterns are perhaps easier to understand in terms of general themes – Arab-Israeli conflict and the Palestinian problem, Cold War maneuvering, oil, the growing influence of Muslim fundamentalism – than in terms of discrete histories of individual states.

Certainly no theme is more central to an understanding of the contemporary Middle East than the problems caused by the creation of the one major non-Muslim state in the region: Israel. The idea of recreating a Jewish homeland in the Middle East was of ancient lineage. It had become a focused and articulated objective of the European Zionist movement by the 1880s, a period when the first significant Jewish immigration into the region of Palestine, a subdivision of the Ottoman Empire, began. During World War II the British, with Arab help, wrested Palestine from the Turks, and both Jews and Arabs then began to put pressure on the British government to create an independent Palestinian state, though their ideas of what kind of a state it should be were irreconcilably different.

The Balfour Declaration

In 1917 Britain shocked the Arabs by committing itself, via the famous Balfour Declaration, to the eventual establishment of a Jewish homeland in Palestine. The Declaration stressed that this would be undertaken with due regard to the rights of non-Jewish Palestinians, but in practice this turned out to be a definition of the problem, not a formula for solving it, for Muslims then outnumbered Jews in Palestine 10 to one, and Palestinians and other Arabs could conceive of no acceptable grant of rights that did not include self-determination for this majority.

Throughout the 1920s and 1930s, while the British wrestled with the problem of what to do about the future of their Palestinian mandate, Jewish immigrants continued to pour into the region, and tensions between the new settlers and the Palestinians rose accordingly, leading to outbreaks of violence. For a time the British toyed with the idea of partitioning Palestine into two states, but by this time Arab attitudes had so hardened that the proposal was rejected out of hand. By 1939 British policy had begun to swing markedly in the direction of conciliation with the Arabs: a White Paper of that year proposed that Jewish immigration should be limited to 15,000 per year (about one-quarter of its actual rate) until 1944, and thereafter be subject to Arab acquiescence, and that severe new restrictions be placed on Jewish land purchases in Palestine. Now it was the turn of the Jews to be outraged and to speak of British betrayal.

The advent of World War II prevented the proposed policy from being implemented, and the entire issue of Palestine remained in abeyance. It was dramatically revived after 1945, when the end of the fighting in Europe brought a massive new wave of Jewish immigrants into Palestine. By 1946 the proportion of Arabs to Jews in the region stood at about two to one – 1.27 million Arabs to 678,000 Jews. The British had by now concluded that they were incapable of solving the Palestinian

problem and turned the whole matter over to the United Nations, which, in November 1947, over Arab opposition, voted for partition upon the expiration of the British mandate of 14 May 1948.

The issue of Palestine had fused opinion in the Arab states in a way that perhaps no other could have. Indeed, these nations had little enough in common save religion, and most were beset with internal problems. In 1945 seven Arab countries – Egypt, Syria, Lebanon, Trans-Jordan, Iraq, Saudi Arabia and Yemen – had joined in an international organization known as the Arab League (formally, the League of Arab States). The stated general purposes of the League were unexceptionable: peaceful mediation of disputes among members and coordination of policies on education, law, trade, finance and external relations. But the real glue that bound the members together was their passionate shared opposition to the partition formula and their conviction that Palestine must be a single, Arab-dominated state. From the League's inception, significantly, there had always been, in addition to the seven charter-member states, an eighth member with full voting rights: the Arab representative of the Palestinian state-to-be. Few Palestinian Jews could have much doubt about what course the Arab League would take when the British mandate in Palestine ended.

Expecting war, the Jews had seized control of their designated areas even before the British departure. It was as well for them that they had, for on 14 May, the day the British left and the new state of Israel was proclaimed, the Arab states of Egypt, Lebanon, Syria, Jordan and Iraq attacked. Remarkably, Israel survived this assault, displaying a determination and military skill that would shape the course of Middle Eastern history for

many years to come. What the Israelis termed the War of Independence continued sporadically through much of 1948, and when an armistice was finally agreed to in January 1949 Israel, far from having been overwhelmed, had increased its territorial holdings by 50 percent. This in itself would have made the creation of the projected Arab Palestinian state much more difficult, but what made it harder still was that Jordan continued to occupy (and in 1950 annexed) most of

Left: Illegal Jewish immigrants are packed aboard a boat entering Haifa harbor in July 1946.

Above: Israeli artillery withdraws from El Arish in the Sinai in December 1956.

Right: An Israeli soldier in action on a kibbutz in the Negev during the fierce fighting of 1948.

the rest of the area that had been designated as Arab Palestine, while the Egyptians held on to the Gaza Strip on the southwest coast. Vast numbers of Palestinian Arabs had fled Israeli territories during the war, and now they and their brethren in Jordan constituted a large stateless population whose demands for repatriation and vendetta would become a major subject of Middle Eastern politics for many decades.

Meanwhile, the Israelis had energetically set about creating the institutions of their new state – a democracy, with Chaim Weizmann as its president, David Ben-Gurion as its prime minister and a parliament called the Knesset as its supreme legislative body. Israel was recognized by most non-Muslim countries and was admitted to the UN in May 1949. As Arab raids on Israel's borders and terrorist activities inside its territories mounted, and as Arab rhetoric calling for an Islamic *jihad* against Israel became more strident, the country grimly prepared for what it regarded as an inevitable renewal of the war.

The Suez Crisis

The war came in 1956, but in a somewhat unexpected fashion. In 1952 the Egyptian army, led by General Muhammad Naguib, had deposed King Farouk, and in the following year Egypt was proclaimed a republic, with Naguib as its president. By mid 1954 Naguib had been replaced by a much more radical and militant officer, Gamal Abdal Nasser. In 1956 Nasser, enraged by a joint US and British decision to withdraw financial support for the building of a dam at Aswan, expelled British diplomats and businessmen from the country and declared the Suez Canal to be nationalized. This threat of being denied use of the Canal was as intolerable to Israel as it was to the oil-dependent West European powers, and in late October Britain, France and Israel jointly attacked Egypt. The assault provoked an international outcry. Under heavy US and UN pressure, the British, French and Israelis withdrew their troops from the territory of the prostrate Egypt in early 1957, and a UN peacekeeping force briefly assumed control of the Canal.

The unchastened Nasser was determined not to have to endure such a humiliation again. He at once began negotiating with the Soviet Union for military and economic assistance and, in order to draw the noose tighter around Israel, in February 1958 he persuaded Syria to merge with Egypt in a new political entity called the United Arab Repub-

lic (UAR). Syria, which had been granted independence by France during World War II and which had had a painfully unstable government ever since, probably entered into the UAR as much to forestall a threatened coup d'état by local communists as for any grand strategic reasons. In any case, it was never particularly happy with the UAR, for Syria proved to be very much the junior partner in the arrangement, and by 1961, after an army junta had again seized control of the government, Syria withdrew from the union. The experience had, however, left Syria with a certain readiness to coordinate its military activities with those of Egypt and with a growing interest in receiving Soviet patronage.

In the late 1940s the United States' interest in the Middle East had still largely been confined to supporting the new Israeli state on moral and sentimental grounds. But during the 1950s, as the Cold War intensified, the US both began increasingly to perceive the Middle East as an arena of potential US-Soviet confrontation, and Israel as a potential strategic ally. Ben-Gurion, aware of the advantages of such an alliance, announced in 1957 (despite considerable internal opposition) Israel's readiness to support the 'Eisenhower Doctrine' of sending military and economic aid to any Middle Eastern state threatened by Soviet-directed communism. As Soviet weaponry continued to flow into Egypt, and as Nasser's rapprochement with

Moscow grew, it seemed all too possible that Israel might one day qualify as just such a state in need of aid.

Throughout the early 1960s Nasser's behavior toward Israel became ever more bellicose. He now saw himself as the ordained leader of the pan-Arab anti-Israeli movement. But his excessive zeal, his neo-socialism and his growing Soviet ties worried some of the more moderate and conservative Arab leaders, and he did not improve matters by verbally abusing them when they demurred from his policies. In particular, he seriously strained relations with the kings of Saudi Arabia and Jordan when he joined the USSR in supporting an anti-royalist insurrection that broke out in the kingdom of Yemen in 1962. Meanwhile, Nasser steadily aggrandized his dictatorial powers at home.

The inevitable next war with Israel took place in 1967. Throughout the spring the number of Israeli-Syrian border clashes had escalated, and the Syrians invoked a 1966 mutual defense pact to ask for Egyptian support. Nasser immediately mobilized his army on the Israeli frontier, expelled the UN peacekeeping force that was stationed on the Egyptian side of the border and announced that the Gulf of Aqaba, an international waterway, was henceforth closed to Israeli shipping. Israeli protests went largely unheard in the UN, and while the USSR and the (now considerably expanded) Arab League vociferously backed Nasser, the Western powers gave Israel little coherent diplomatic support. The Israelis therefore decided not to wait for the invasion that they now assumed as a foregone conclusion, and on 5 June 1967 they launched simultaneous preemptive air and ground attacks on Egypt, Syria and Jordan. The war lasted six days, and only urgent action by the UN Security Council prevented the Arabs from being completely routed. As it was, when the cease-fire was announced on 10 June Israel had taken from Egypt the Gaza Strip, the whole Sinai Peninsula

Above left: Israeli soldiers celebrate their successful capture of the Old City of Jerusalem on 7 June 1967.

Left: West Beirut suffers the full weight of Israeli artillery fire during the Israeli invasion of Lebanon in June 1982.

Above right: Begin, Carter and Sadat meet at Camp David, USA, in September 1978 – the first successful peace treaty in this troubled region.

Right: Israeli soldiers in action in Jerusalem during the 1967 Six-Day War.

and the east bank of the Suez Canal, had taken the West Bank of the Jordan River and the Arab sector of Jerusalem from Jordan and had seized the Golan Heights from Syria. Despite all UN efforts to persuade Israel to evacuate these territories, Israel flatly refused. The Arab reaction was predictable: at a meeting in Khartoum all the Arab states reaffirmed their demand for an Arab-controled Palestine and announced that thenceforth Arab policy toward Israel would be one of no recognition, no negotiation and no peace.

The Soviet Union had, as it were by proxy, felt something of the humiliation of Nasser's defeat and responded readily to Nasser's request for military assistance on a scale hitherto unprecedented. A torrent of modern tanks, jet aircraft and missiles poured into the country, and with them came an estimated 10,000 to 12,000 Russian nationals to advise and train the army and, it has been alleged, to serve in certain selected combat roles. As a gesture of solidarity the USSR also financed the completion of the Aswan Dam Project, the proximate cause of the 1956 war.

Nasser died of a heart attack in September 1970 and was replaced by his vice-president, Anwar al-Sadat. Although Sadat at first appeared to be following Nasser's general policy line, some interesting variations soon began to appear. Most notable was an apparent reversal of the 20-year trend in Egyptian-Soviet relations when Sadat ousted Soviet personnel from all military installations in the country and placed them under exclusive Egyptian control. Whether this was a genuine shift or an attempt to allay the American fears that had produced a growing level of US military aid to Israel is unclear. In any case, it did nothing to prevent the outbreak of the fourth Arab-Israeli war.

The war began with a massive surprise attack launched by Egypt and Syria (since 1971 firmly under the control of the nationalist Ba'ath Party leader, General Hafez al-Assad) on 6 October 1973, when Israel was celebrating the Jewish High Holy Day of Yom Kippur. The Israelis suffered very high initial losses, and for a time it seemed that they would be overwhelmed. But superior generalship, helped by timely infusions of emergency US military aid, enabled them to turn the tide on both their northern and southern fronts.

Following a US-brokered cease-fire, the American secretary of state, Henry Kissinger, attempted to arrange a peace conference in Geneva, but this foundered when Israel rejected Arab demands that the Palestine Liberation Organization (PLO) be included in the conference as the government-in-exile of the state of Palestine. The Israeli position was not based solely on diplomatic principle, for since its creation in 1964 the PLO had increasingly become anathema to the Israelis because of its sponsorship of anti-Israeli terrorism. Initially created to coordinate Palestinian refugee organizations, the PLO had in 1968 fallen under the control of one of the most militant Palestinian guerrilla groups, Al Fatah, led by Yasir Arafat. The fact that after the failure of the peace conference the UN accorded the PLO official recognition (November 1974) did nothing to enhance Israeli willingness to abide by the world body's decisions.

Yet at a lower level gradual progress was being made in Egyptian-Israeli negotiations over the terms of disengagement. Then, at the end of 1977, Sadat astonished the world by accepting an invitation by Israeli prime minister Menachem Begin to address the Knesset on the outstanding issues between the two nations. The Americans picked up on this hopeful development, and President Carter succeeded in bringing the two leaders together at Camp David in the US for 13 days in September 1978 and persuading them to agree on a 'Framework for the Conclusion of a Peace Treaty Between Israel and Egypt.' After difficult negotiations the treaty was finally signed in March 1979, and Israel began to withdraw its troops from the Sinai in May.

The military ring around Israel had been broken, and Soviet influence in the region had been dealt a severe blow, as Egypt was now rapidly becoming an economic client of the US. But nothing else had been solved. All but a few peripheral Arab states had greeted the Israeli-Egyptian treaty with fury and contempt. And the Palestine issue, far from being nearer a solution, was more aggravated than ever: the PLO stepped up its attacks, and Israel began its policy of displacing the Palestinians in the West Bank by the building of Jewish settlements there.

The PLO had been using Lebanon as its principal base for staging attacks on Israel. Ever since the French had evacuated the last of their troops in 1946 Lebanon, a hodgepodge of fiercely contending ethnic, political and religious groups, had never been far away from anarchy. It had endured a bloody civil war in 1958, that had only been ended by the intervention of US troops, and another in 1975-76, that had produced 140,000 casualties. By the end of the 1970s there was no central authority in Lebanon capable of restraining (or perhaps willing to restrain) PLO activities inside the country. It was therefore probably inevitable that Israel would sooner or later invade Lebanon.

The first major Israeli attack on Lebanon – in retaliation for a PLO raid that had killed 30 civilians – had taken place in 1978. It lasted three months but was confined only to trying to wipe out PLO bases in the southern part of the country. It did not have the effect of reducing terrorism in any significant way. In 1982, in another retaliation, Israel launched a full-scale invasion of Lebanon, intending this time to eliminate the PLO

completely. Israeli armor knifed through the country, destroying PLO strongholds in Tyre and Sidon, and soon thereafter encircled and bombarded East Beirut, where the PLO headquarters were located. Most of the PLO were evacuated by sea under international supervision, thus ending the main PLO presence in the country, and the Israelis retired to southern Lebanon, a strip of which they continued to occupy.

By the mid 1980s it appeared that the Israelis had been generally successful in securing their nation from external threats. Without the assistance of a well-armed and determined Egypt it seemed unlikely that any combination of Israel's Arab neighbors could prevail over the Jewish state in a war; and Hosni Mubarak, Sadat's successor (Sadat was assassinated by Muslim extremist soldiers in October 1981), was faithfully carrying on Sadat's policies of reconciliation. Similarly, although terrorist violence at a certain level was bound to continue, the PLO had been dealt a heavy blow and had been put on notice that the Israelis were willing and able to deny them major bases in nearby lands.

Yet by 1987 another kind of threat had begun to emerge, one that had been implicit for a long time and that might in the end accomplish what the four Arab-Israeli wars and PLO action had not. Toward the end of the year signs of insurrectionary violence began to multiply in the 1.3 million Palestinian population living in the West Bank and Gaza. Israel's brutal measures to contain and repress these outbreaks before they got out of hand put a new strain on Arab-Israeli relations, which had been at least relatively quiescent since 1983. They also put a strain on Israel's relations with the Western powers and, significantly, with her chief sponsor, the United States. What might happen if Palestinian agitation within Israeli-occupied territories became truly large-scale was a worrying prospect.

Oil and fundamentalism

Arab-Israeli conflict and the Palestinian issue may have been the most important single theme in Middle Eastern history since 1945, but of course it was not the only one. Two others, that were also intertwined with the Arab-Israeli conflict and had serious implications, concerned the politics of oil and the rise of Islamic fundamentalism.

Western Europe's extreme dependency on Middle Eastern oil powerfully conditioned European policies toward the Middle East. In general, it prompted the Western powers to hang back from following America's lead in adopting overtly pro-Israeli policies. (The sole major exception to this – the military action taken by Britain and France in the 1956 Suez Crisis – was merely the other side of the dependency coin.) By 1971 the United States had also become heavily dependent on Middle Eastern oil imports and was thus vulnerable to a certain amount of blackmail by the major Arab oil producers.

By far the Middle East's leading oil producer and exporter was Saudi Arabia, which owned one-third of the world's known oil reserves and accounted for half the production of the Organization of Petroleum Exporting Countries (OPEC). Saudi Arabia had been friendly with the United States ever since King Abdul Aziz Ibn Saud

first granted a major oil concession to Standard Oil of California in the 1930s and the resulting revenues transformed the kingdom's economy. In the first two decades after World War II (a period including the end of the reign of Ibn Saud and, from 1953 to 1964, that of his son, King Saud) Saudi Arabia had been a force for moderation in the Arab League, condemning Israel but not participating directly in the wars against her and breaking sharply with Nasser's aggressive policies. After the accession of Saud's successor, Crown Prince Faisal (1964-75), Saudi denunciations of Israel became more strident, and relations with the US more strained, as US aid to Israel increased sharply after the 1967 war. This, and America's possibly decisive support of Israel in the 1973 Yom Kippur War, produced a radical shift in Saudi policy, and Faisal imposed an oil embargo on the US and the West European nations. Fortunately for the West, the embargo did not last long, being lifted in 1974, but it had caused considerable distress and had raised the specter of a Saudi-dominated OPEC exerting a commanding influence over Western policies.

This alarming scenario was not, in fact, played out. OPEC did manage, through manipulation of production, to raise world oil prices painfully during the later 1970s, but in the end OPEC proved to be less the monolithic cartel it at first seemed and more a loose-knit trade association whose members were not above breaking ranks on price policy. At the same time, through conservation and development of alternative oil and other energy sources, the West significantly lessened its dependency. By the mid 1980s oil prices had tumbled from a high of $34 per barrel to around $16-18, and people were talking of an 'oil glut.' But if the crisis had passed, the potential for future trouble had not.

One form that this trouble might take involved the possibility of radical changes of government in the oil-producing states. This had already occurred in Iran. The governmental instability with which Iran had emerged from World War II is suggested by the fact that for 16 years, from 1941 to 1957, all Iranian governments ruled by martial law. A change of sorts began in 1953 when, with CIA help, a particularly militant and anti-Western

Left. The Ayatollah Khomeini is greeted by enthusiastic supporters on his return to Iran in February 1979.

Below left: General Moshe Dayan, the Israeli war leader, at the time of the ceasefire ending the Yom Kippur War in October 1973.

Right: An Iranian poster celebrates the triumph of Khomeini over the Shah who is seen fleeing the country with his bags full of American and British money.

Below right: The Middle East, scene of so many wars since 1945.

permitted the ailing Shah to enter the US for medical treatment, the Iranian response was to invade the US embassy in Teheran and to seize its staff members as hostages. They would remain captives for 444 days, until the end of the Carter presidency.

Iran in turmoil

During the Hostage Crisis Iran's relations with the US and most of the rest of the West reached a nadir (Iran had even defied a rare unanimous UN Security Council demand for the hostages' release), and there was widespread concern that Iran would embargo oil exports to its new antagonists. This would have been disastrous for Western Europe and Japan, but, perhaps because the principal target of Iran's wrath, the United States ('the Great Satan'), was less dependent on Iranian oil, this did not occur. Nevertheless, Iranian oil exports did decline markedly for other reasons – the turmoil created by nationalization and the effects of a protracted and brutal war that broke out between Iran and Iraq in 1980 and that hampered the ability of both combatants to get their oil to foreign customers.

Since Shi'ism was a minority sect in most other Middle Eastern states, what happened in Iran was not necessarily a perfect model for what might happen elsewhere. But it might nevertheless be an inspiration, for there were a growing number of Sunni fundamentalists who shared Khomeini's enmity to all things Western and who regarded moderation toward Israel as an abomination. As of 1988 not only King Fahd's monarchy in Saudi Arabia and those of the rulers in the Gulf oil states, but also Mubarak's regime in Egypt, and indeed regimes in all Arab nations, were potentially vulnerable to this destabilizing pressure. It was, therefore, one more dangerous element in the witches' brew of Middle Eastern politics, and one more reason to despair of any early or peaceful solution to the troubled region's many and varied problems.

premier, Muhammad Mussadegh, was overthrown and the youthful Shah Muhammad Reza Pahlavi, theretofore of minor importance in Iranian politics, began to reassert his authority. During the 1960s and 1970s the Shah, a staunch friend of the West, used Iranian oil revenues to finance a massive modernization program affecting all aspects of Iranian life, from industry to education. But there were many in the overwhelmingly (93 percent) Shi'ite country who were offended both by changes, which they thought inimical to Islamic purity, and by the Shah's increasingly oppressive rule. The symbolic embodiment of this discontent was an exiled Shi'ite fundamentalist leader named Ayatollah Ruholla Khomeini. By 1978 demonstrations for Khomeini's return had reached such proportions that the Shah was again obliged to impose martial law. But neither force nor conciliation would now serve, and in January 1979 the Shah and his family left Iran. Khomeini returned the following month, quickly established his ascendancy and proclaimed Iran an Islamic republic.

The new government was both fundamentalist and revolutionary. Khomeini set about cleansing the nation of pernicious Western influences (music, alcohol, mixed bathing, unveiled women and so on), enforcing strict observance of Muslim practices on pain of harsh penalties and stirring the nation into a ferment of religious fervor. At the same time, he nationalized all industries, banks and insurance companies and effectively destroyed or intimidated all political opposition. When, later that year, the Carter administration

India and Pakistan

In 1945 the British Labour Party, traditionally sympathetic to Indian political aspirations, was elected to power by an overwhelming mandate, and in 1946 it sent to India a Cabinet Mission which, like all such previous attempts, foundered upon the rock of Congress-League antagonism. It was followed by Muhammad Ali Jinnah's call to the Muslims to observe a 'Direct Action Day' (16 August 1946) against Congress and on behalf of partition, resulting in the great Calcutta killing, a four-day massacre that exceeded in horror all previous enormities, but which was a measure of the growing seriousness of the communal problem that both the British Government and Indian leaders of all shades of opinion now recognized as being of paramount importance.

In retrospect, it can be seen that two long-range factors had brought about this virtual stalemate in what should otherwise have been gradual evolution toward self-government. The first of these was the transformation of the Muslim League from being a party composed of an unrepresentative privileged elite, such as it had been during the first 25 years of its history, to a mass movement headed by a charismatic leader, Jinnah, who exercised an unchallenged hold over an ever-increasing following. The second factor was the failure of the Congress's Hindu leadership to recognize the seriousness of the communal problem and the profound dread felt by many Muslims at the prospect of Hindu-majority government. The presence within the Congress movement of a small but distinguished Muslim following encouraged Congressmen to indulge in the luxury of writing off the League as non-representative of Muslim opinion as a whole. Even Gandhi's leading protégé, Jawaharlal Nehru (1889-1964), deeply committed as he was to Western concepts of secularism and modernity, remained blind to the

depth of the mistrust with which the Congress organization was regarded by so many Muslims and to the rising tide of communal hatred, a nomenon incomprehensible to humane temperaments such as his. The Muslim League, meanwhile, had taken up the position that it alone could negotiate on behalf of India's Muslims.

Exasperated by the intransigence of both the Congress and the League, the British Government resolved to cut the Gordian Knot and Prime Minister Clement Attlee announced on 20 February 1947 that the British intended to withdraw completely by June 1948, a date subsequently brought forward to 15 August 1947. To expedite the transfer of power Earl Mountbatten of Burma, former Supreme Allied Commander in Southeast Asia, was appointed as last Governor-General and Viceroy. The outcome – the partition of the subcontinent and the creation of the two sovereign states of India and Pakistan – involved major transfers of population which resulted in communal massacres in the Punjab, Bengal, Bihar and the United Provinces, on a scale hitherto unknown: perhaps a million killed.

The granting of independence to India and Pakistan by Britain was an event of almost incalculable significance in the history of the twentieth century, heralding as it did the end of the age of European colonial dominance over the non-European world. After the British handed over the most extensive and splendid of all colonial possessions to native nationalists there was no possibility of other colonial powers – the Dutch in Indonesia, for example, or the French in Indo-China – restoring the *status quo ante bellum*. With the British withdrawal from India decolonization began in earnest. For the British themselves the passing of their Indian Empire was an event so fraught with emotion and so very ob-

viously the close of a chapter in their history that thereafter they were able to face with comparative equanimity the loss of their remaining dependencies. If India, 'the brightest jewel in the English Crown,' had passed beyond their grasp, why struggle to retain possessions elsewhere so much less glamorous and so much less encrusted with associations of the Imperial past? Thus the transfer of power in India made psychologically possible as well as politically certain the relatively peaceful passing of the Age of Empires.

One of the last casualties of the frightful violence that followed the British withdrawal from India in July 1947 and the subsequent

creation of the independent states of India and Pakistan in August was Mohandas Gandhi, the greatest hero of the Indian independence movement. Some Hindu radicals blamed Gandhi for having acquiesced in Viscount Mountbatten's plan to partition India after the end of the Raj, and on 30 January 1948 one such, a member of the Hindu Mahasabha, assassinated the saintly old man.

Formally, the new Indian state enjoyed the status of a dominion within the British Commonwealth. It had a prime minister, Jawaharlal Nehru, but as yet no constitution to define what sort of government it should have. In February 1948 a draft constitution was promulgated proposing that India should be a federal republic, and this proposal was endorsed by a meeting of the Commonwealth prime ministers in April. The constitution was not formally adopted until January 1950, and until then Nehru and the Congress Party continued to govern *ad interim*.

During the 1948-50 period one of the government's besetting problems was to try to rationalize India's chaotic provincial structure. In addition to the former governors' provinces there still remained within the country some 570 princely states, which together accounted for half the nation's area and a third of its population. Obviously these states could not be permitted to retain the same degree of independence they had enjoyed under the Raj, and through negotiation the majority of them were gradually absorbed into the new state in a variety of somewhat makeshift ways. (The Maharaja of Mysore, for example, continued to rule his domain with a certain degree of autonomy under the title of 'prince president.') The outstanding hold-out to this process of

absorption was the Muslim Nizam of Hyderabad, who flatly refused to surrender control over his predominantly Hindu state: it was occupied by Hindu troops in 1948 in what was termed 'a police action.' That and a similar Indian action in the state of Junagadh inflamed opinion in Pakistan. A third case, that of Kashmir, would, as we shall presently see, provoke a war.

The problem of the princely states was resolved with difficulty over the course of time, but the larger problem of how to make administrative sense of India's crazy-quilt ethnic geography was more intractable, and in fact has never been fully solved. The approach that evolved in the 1950s was to try to define local states along linguistic lines, but these definitions have had to be changed several times, often to the accompaniment of violence; unfortunately, language is far from being the only source of internal division in Indian society.

Pakistan's birth pangs were more severe than those of India. After independence some 10 million Hindu refugees poured out of Pakistan and about 7.5 million Muslim refugees poured in. The new dominion's government, with Jinnah as its president and Liaquat Ali Khan as its prime minister, had, unlike India, inherited no administrative machinery capable of dealing with such problems – or indeed with most of the other problems facing the new state. There was no industry in the nation, several boundaries were being disputed by India, a dangerous separatist movement had sprung up in an area along the Afghan border and, in accordance with the partition agreement, one whole section of Pakistan, composed of East Bengal and Assam and containing half the population of the nation, was separated from the new

capital of Karachi by the entire 1000-mile width of India. To compound Pakistan's difficulties, its founder and guiding light, Jinnah, died in September 1948.

Yet Pakistan enjoyed some advantages. In West Pakistan, at least, the population was less riven by political, sectarian and ethnic divisions than was India's, and an overwhelming majority enthusiastically supported the government. This support made it possible for the government to embark on ambitious programs of industrialization and agricultural modernization, all partly supported by aid and loans from the United States and Commonwealth nations. Pakistan also made efforts to negotiate trade agreements with India in order to re-establish some of the traditional economic interactions that had been disrupted by partition. These efforts were, however, hampered by a steady worsening of political relations between the two states. Of the many sources of friction between them, the issue of Kashmir proved to be the most rancorous.

The situation in Kashmir was the exact reverse of that in Hyderabad: a predominantly (85 percent) Muslim state ruled by a Hindu maharaja, Sir Hari Singh. When a rebellion, supported by northwest tribesmen, broke out in 1947 Singh signed over the country to India. The Pakistanis were outraged, contending that all the religious, ethnic, economic and geographic principles that had governed partition dictated that Kashmir should go to Pakistan. Fighting broke out between India and Pakistan in 1947 and continued into 1948, when the matter was submitted to the United Nations. A cease-fire was finally arranged in 1949, and a temporary line of demarcation was drawn between the parts of Kashmir occupied by the two sides, but neither was now prepared to yield to the other. The issue would remain a source of acrimonious debate – made worse by India's annexation of the part of Kashmir it occupied in 1957 – for over two decades and would not finally be resolved until two more wars had been fought.

India's constitution came into effect on 26 January 1950: Nehru continued as prime minister and Rajendra Prasad, a loyal Gandhian, was named president. The dominance of Nehru and the Congress Party was affirmed in the general elections of 1952, with only the communists mounting any significant opposition. Nehru's foreign policy with respect to the intensifying Cold War also began to become apparent in the mid-1950s, as he took a leading role in the Afro-Asian 'non-alignment' movement that culminated in the 29-nation conference at Bandung, Indonesia, in 1955. Some in the West grumbled that Nehru's concept of non-alignment was unnecessarily left-leaning, but at least with respect to the People's Republic of China it did not remain so for long. In 1957 a border dispute developed that would ultimately result in a massive 1962 Chinese military offensive against Ladakh in Kashmir and other areas on the northeastern border and would end by depriving India of a considerable amount of the territory it claimed. Meanwhile, however, India rounded out other parts of its territory by negotiating with France the peaceful acquisition of Pondicherry (1956) and by employing armed force to annex from the more recalcitrant Portuguese the enclaves of Goa Daman and Diu (1961).

The enthusiastic political consensus that had been so beneficial to Pakistan in the first years of independence began to splinter when conservative Muslim elements objected to important parts of a liberal constitution that was proposed in 1949. In 1951 Liaquat Ali Khan was assassinated by an Afghan fanatic, and it was not until February 1956 that a constitution was finally adopted, formally making Pakistan a republic within the Commonwealth and naming General Iskandr Mirza president. Unlike India, Pakistan's international orientation had developed a decided pro-Western bias – in no way diluted by the immense grain shipments the US had sent Pakis-

tan to help relieve a famine in 1953 – and Pakistan became a charter member of the American-inspired Southeast Asia Treaty Organization (SEATO) in 1954 and of the Central Treaty Organization (CENTO) for the defense of the Middle East in 1955.

After 1956 Pakistan was plagued by a succession of governmental crises and scandals, and in October 1958 President Mirza abrogated the constitution and turned the government over to army General Muhammad Ayub Khan, who was formally named president in 1960 (the office of prime minister having been abolished). A new constitution was promulgated in 1962 proclaiming Pakistan an Islamic federal republic, but the government remained essentially a (relatively benign and progressive) dictatorship under Ayub.

Jawaharlal Nehru died in 1964 and was succeeded by Sri Lal Bahadur Shastri, another Congress Party stalwart. Shastri was soon confronted by another crisis that developed over the envenomed issue of Kashmir. For a time after the Chinese assault on India in 1962 it had seemed that India and Pakistan might be able to negotiate a solution to the Kashmir problem, but after

Pakistan signed a border treaty with China that recognized some of the areas of Kashmir which China had expropriated in 1962. Indo-Pakistani negotiations collapsed and relations between the two states became progressively worse. In 1965 border fighting broke out in the Rann of Kutch region and soon spread to Kashmir. The fighting ended in early 1966, when Ayub and Shastri met in Tashkent under Soviet sponsorship and agreed both to observe a cease-fire and to withdraw all troops to mutually acceptable positions. But the Kashmir issue itself had in no way been resolved.

Prime Minister Shastri died on 11 January 1966, a day after the Tashkent Declaration was announced, and after bitter debate within the Congress Party it was announced that his successor would be Nehru's daughter, Indira Gandhi. The intra-party disputes that attended her selection were reflected in the country at large, and in the 1967 elections the party's parliamentary majority was severely reduced and it lost control of several state governments. Continuing dissension within the party came to a head in 1969, when Mrs Gandhi and her left-leaning supporters announced the formation of the 'New Congress

Above left: Some of the hundreds of thousands of refugees, a consequence of the inter-communal strife caused by the partition.

Above right: Mrs Indira Gandhi addressing an Independence Day celebration in New Delhi in 1972.

Right: The funeral pyre of Indira Gandhi who had been assassinated on 31 October 1984 by Sikh extremists.

Party,' while her more conservative opponents declared themselves the 'Old Congress Party.' The two factions faced off in the elections of March 1971, and the New Congress won overwhelmingly.

At least part of Gandhi's victory may have been attributable to the fact that a serious new crisis in Indo-Pakistani relations was brewing. East Pakistan's discontent with West Pakistani rule had been rising for a long time. Riots in East Pakistan had forced Ayub's resignation in 1969, and his successor, army head General Agha-Muhammad Yahya Khan, had had to declare a temporary state of martial law. In an attempt to defuse tension, in December 1970 Yahya held national elections to select a National Assembly that would draft a new constitution. But in the event 153 of the 163 seats allocated to East Pakistan were won by the Awami League, East Pakistan's militant independence party, which had been receiving covert support from the Indian government. Yahya declared the results of the election invalid, banned the Awami League and arrested those of its leaders who were in West Pakistan at the time. East Pakistan then declared itself independent on 26 March 1971, adopting the name Bangladesh. Yahya responded by again declaring a state of martial law and by sending a West Pakistani army of occupation into East Pakistan. A bloody civil war ensued, in which an estimated one million died, with some 10 million refugees fleeing over the border into India. On 3 December 1971 India invaded East Pakistan in support of Bangladesh independence. Fighting between Indian and Pakistani forces immediately spread outside East Pakistan, erupting in Kashmir and all along the Indian-West Pakistani frontier. The war was sharp but short, for a cease-fire was declared on all fronts after the 90,000 West Pakistani troops in East Pakistan surrendered on 16 December. The Yahya government collapsed and the deputy prime minister, Zufikar Ali Bhutto, took control of West Pakistan. After a summit meeting between Indira Gandhi and Bhutto in Simla in July 1972 the two nations gradually settled down to sort out their problems. The independence of Bangladesh was affirmed (though Pakistan did not formally recognize the new nation until 1974) and agreements were reached on the exchange of prisoners of war and of hostage populations. Perhaps most important, in December 1972 a final demarcation line in Kashmir was agreed to, thus finally putting a political – if not psychological – end to this old and lethal quarrel.

Although India and Pakistan eventually resumed diplomatic relations in 1976, the hatreds and suspicions fanned by the 1971 war remained. When, in May 1974, India became the world's sixth nuclear power by exploding an atomic weapon in an underground test in the Thar Desert (the plutonium had come from a reactor that Canada had supplied on the understanding that it would be used only for non-military purposes), the acquisition of a nuclear capability became a priority item on Pakistan's secret agenda. The war had larger international dimensions as well. The fact that the US had been supportive of Pakistan strained US-Indian relations and doubtless contributed to the growing rapprochement between India and the USSR, signaled by an extensive new economic and military aid agreement signed in 1973.

During this same period India was experiencing a deepening crisis in its domestic politics. By 1973 the euphoria that had followed the New Congress landslide victory of 1971 was wearing thin. Several seats were lost by the Congress (Old and New) in by-elections, as opposition movements such as the centerist coalition called the Janata Party gained strength and Indira Gandhi's support within the Congress Party itself weakened. Then, in June 1975, a high court in Allahabad (Uttar Pradesh), Gandhi's home constituency, held that she had been guilty of corrupt practices in the 1971 election and declared its results invalid. Amid calls for her resignation Gandhi, on 26 June, proclaimed a state of emergency and ordered widespread arrests of her critics, including the leaders of all major opposition parties save India's Communist Party.

In July the Congress Party majority in parliament endorsed the state of emergency and extended it indefinitely. The remaining opposition members walked out after this vote was taken, leaving the Congress Party MPs free to enact a stream of defensive legislation. It was made illegal for Indian courts to invalidate any government decrees made during the emergency. Lawsuits challenging the election of high government officials were likewise made illegal, and Gandhi's conviction in the 1971 election case was wiped out. For a time Gandhi toyed with the idea of re-drafting the constitution, but in the end she settled for incorporating much of the new legislation in a 58-clause amendment to the existing constitution.

During the 18-month period of the emergency the Gandhi government squandered most of what support it had left. Like the press, the opposition parties were so heavily muzzled that even the erstwhile pro-Gandhi Communist Party turned against the prime minister. Mrs Gandhi's massive birth control and slum clearance programs aroused much popular resentment. Her authoritarian administrative methods alienated the bureaucracy. And her rather heavy-handed efforts to designate her politically unpopular eldest son, Sanjay Gandhi, as her heir apparent infuriated many established Congress Party leaders.

It may be that Gandhi failed to appreciate the magnitude of the opposition she had engendered. In any case, she surprised everyone by announcing in January 1977 that a parliamentary election would be held in March. The result of this election was a catastrophe for the Congress Party. The Janata coalition and its allies won 331 of parliament's 542 seats, and the Janata leader, Morarji Desai, became the first non-Congress Party prime minister in modern India's history.

Democracy in Pakistan continued to fare badly.

Bhutto permitted general elections to be held in March 1977, but there was a storm of protest when it was announced that his party had won 155 of the 200 elected seats in the 216-seat National Assembly. Government came to a standstill, and on 5 July General Muhammad Zia ul-Haq stepped forward to declare a state of martial law, in which he would be Chief Administrator. Bhutto was arrested on charges that he had murdered a political opponent in 1974. He was soon convicted and, despite worldwide protests against this drumhead justice, he was executed in 1979. By this time Zia had already declared himself president (September 1978).

In India the Janata coalition gradually fragmented, while the Congress Party rebuilt its strength. In India's seventh parliamentary elections, held in January 1980, Indian voters gave Indira Gandhi's New Congress Party (or Congress-I Party, as it had come to be called) 350 out of 542 seats in the lower house, and Mrs Gandhi again became prime minister on 10 January. This time, her rule was somewhat less autocratic. To be sure, in February she dissolved nine state assemblies controled by the opposition, and in September she forced through parliament a law enabling the government to jail anyone without trial for a year, but she had also made no serious effort to prevent the Indian Supreme Court from overturning the 1976 emergency laws in May. She also slightly modified the pro-Soviet bias of her foreign policy, largely no doubt because India found it impossible not to join in the international wave of protest that followed the USSR's invasion of Afghanistan. But though she negotiated Washington's approval for continuing uranium shipments for India's nuclear program and authorized the first major purchase of US wheat since 1977, she also continued to acquire Soviet weapons on a grand scale.

Probably of longer-term significance in shaping Indian foreign policy was the fact that as Afghan refugees poured into Pakistan, creating severe economic and social dislocations, and as Soviet incursions over the Afghan-Pakistan border multiplied, US aid to Pakistan inevitably increased. In June 1981 the US State Department announced a $3 billion five-year program (increased to $3.2 billion over six years in September) of economic and military assistance for Pakistan. Especially annoying to the Indians was the inclusion of new American F-16 fighter planes for the Pakistani air force. Predictably, India immediately stepped up procurement of advanced foreign weapons.

Ever since independence India had been plagued with separatist movements and demands for greater regional and/or ethnic autonomy. One of the most troublesome of these involved the 14 million Sikhs who lived mainly in the strategic border region of the Punjab. In 1984 Gandhi ordered the Indian army to root out a group of Sikh militants who were using the holiest shrine in the Sikh religion, the Golden Temple in Amritsar, as their base. In a two-day battle in early June about 1000 Sikhs were killed in and around the temple. Waves of Sikh violence followed, including mutinies of Sikh officers and men in the

Indian Army, and on 31 October 1984 Indira Gandhi was assassinated by two Sikhs who were members of her own bodyguard. The murder provoked a counter-spasm of mob violence against Sikhs and resulted in some of the worst butcheries since 1947.

The Congress-I Party chose as Mrs Gandhi's successor her second son (Sanjay had been killed in a plane crash in 1980), the well-liked but inexperienced Rajiv Gandhi. One of the first problems the new prime minister had to face as that disastrous year drew to a close was history's worst industrial accident, a gas leak at the US-owned Union Carbide pesticide plant in Bhopal that killed 2000 people and injured 200,000 others.

Promise and problems

The first full year of Rajiv Gandhi's ministry, 1985, seemed full of promise. The touchstone of his program was conciliation. He eschewed the anti-American bias that had flawed his mother's non-alignment policy, making a remarkably successful goodwill visit to Washington in June, after having negotiated a $1.5 billion trade agreement in Moscow the month before. He pursued a policy of patient negotiation with respect to several problem areas of local discontent – in Assam, Mizoram and of course, above all, in the Punjab. To moderate Sikh leaders he offered a package of proposals that included a re-drawing of the Punjab's boundaries so as to include a greater Sikh population and thus give the Sikhs better representation. An apparently gratifying result of this initiative was that in September the moderate Sikhs won 73 out of 115 seats in the Punjab state assembly.

But in the following years much of the promise of this beginning remained unfulfilled. If the moderate Sikhs had been impressed with Gandhi's proposals, the radicals were not. Violence continued, with perhaps 1000 more deaths in 1986, and by May 1987 Gandhi had been obliged to dissolve the government of the fractious state and to establish direct rule. Nor was it clear that the negotiated settlements in other areas had been

perfectly successful. In Mizoram, for example, the February 1987 elections, though honest and peaceful, resulted in a thorough defeat of the Congress Party by the followers of the former guerrilla leader Laldenga, and many in New Delhi were left to wonder if this might not after all have been a case of over permissiveness in dealing with those centrifugal forces that always threaten to tear India apart. Another example concerned the island republic of Sri Lanka (former Ceylon), which, ever since its independence in 1948, had been wracked by violent strife between its Sinhalese and Tamil populations. Though Gandhi had been quick to repudiate his mother's policy of giving covert support to the Sri Lankan Tamils (she had even hinted at the possibility of intervention on their behalf), it was by no means clear whether he could prevent Indian involvement if a civil war were to erupt on the island.

Nor was he particularly successful in improving relations with Pakistan or in putting an end to the Indo-Pakistani arms race that had been in high gear since the beginning of the decade. The problem was complicated by uncertainties about the future of the Pakistani government. In 1985 Zia had slightly loosened his grip on the country, ending martial law and permitting one-party elections to the National Assembly. But he had also announced his intention to remain in office at least until 1990, and it was impossible to guess when or how he would be succeeded.

In a larger sense, there was also doubt about Gandhi's long-range plans – whether he would be able to make significant progress in modernizing and rationalizing India's economy so as to accommodate the nearly 10 million new jobs per year that India's 2.1 percent annual population growth required. And this was doubtless the most fundamental and daunting problem of all, for as India's 780 million population marched inexorably toward the one billion mark at the turn of the century, it seemed certain that every difficulty and tension that now existed on the subcontinent could only be intensified.

Above left: Part of the massive family planning campaign undertaken by the Indian Government to limit the rate of growth of India's vast population.

Above: India has maintained close economic and military links with the Soviet Union, while maintaining a Western-style system of government.

Right: Bangladeshi refugees crammed into the Salt Lake Camp in Calcutta, September 1971 – a tragic result of the war between the two Pakistans.

Southeast Asia

The attack on Pearl Harbor, Hawaii, which ushered in the American phase of World War II and the outbreak of the Pacific War, changed the history of Southeast Asia for ever. The Japanese victory over the Americans, British and Dutch in the Philippines, Burma, Malaya, Singapore and the Dutch East Indies was so swift that relatively little damage and loss of life was caused in a campaign that lasted scarcely four months and that covered so vast a territory. In French Indo-China the Japanese had already taken effective power prior to 7 December 1941, with the Vichy French regime acting as surrogates for the Japanese in Asia just as their counterparts in the metropole did for the Third Reich. But the psychological effects of all this were devastating. The myth of European racial supremacy in Asia, particularly in the minds of Southeast Asians, was broken for ever. Europeans were rounded up and placed in concentration camps. The sight of the once-proud colonials bowing to the Japanese overlords could never be forgotten by those who, even weeks before, had been servants to the European masters. When the region was liberated from Japanese rule the Japanese left behind a series of rapidly constructed puppet states to which they had given 'independence' once it had become clear that Tokyo's fate was sealed. Since, apart from British Burma and the American Philippines, the region

remained under Japanese rule from early 1942 until the Japanese capitulation in August 1945, the peoples of the area did not see a reconquest of their territory by their former masters. The Japanese were left to police and administer Indo-China, Indonesia, Malaya and Singapore for periods ranging from days to many weeks after the war was over until the British and, eventually, the French and Dutch could move to re-establish themselves in their former colonies. It could be said with little fear of contradiction that colonialism died in Southeast Asia long before the Europeans were prepared to give it a decent burial.

In depth and intensity, Japanese rule in Southeast Asia between 1942 and 1945 varied considerably from country to country. At one extreme, it rested most lightly on Thailand, which retained its sovereignty in exchange for agreeing to station and supply Japanese forces. At the other, it placed vast burdens on the rural populations in Burma, Luzon and also Java, all of them subject to harsh economic exploitation. In between these extremes, the peoples of Indo-China experienced, until almost the end of the war in the Pacific, a Japanese military presence superimposed on the French colonial *status quo*.

Japan's self-proclaimed role as liberator of all Asians from the yoke of Western imperialism all

too soon proved to be another colonial myth. In Japan's Greater East Asia Co-Prosperity Sphere the newly acquired territories enjoyed a colonial status, especially with regard to economic relations, worse than what the Southeast Asians had previously experienced. Democratic institutions, where they existed, were abolished. And economic exploitation became progressively starker as Japan's fortunes started to deteriorate from about the middle of 1943.

Yet the Japanese military, fearful of Allied counterattacks, also started to make increasing concessions to the growing political demands of their 'liberated' Southeast Asian subjects. Social and economic dislocation thus combined with political emancipation to set the stage for a many-faceted process of decolonization that was to embrace practically all of Southeast Asia in the immediate postwar years. Indeed, the Japanese themselves had set the process in motion, most visibly in 1943, when they granted ostensible 'independence' to both Burma and the Philippines, the first two countries to be reconquered by the Allies. Whereas in 1942 Thailand had been the only sovereign state in Southeast Asia, by the mid 1960s it had been joined by nine others: starting with the Philippines and Burma, followed by Indonesia, Cambodia, Laos, the two Vietnams and finally by Malaysia and Singapore. We will briefly

Below left · Japanese troops capture the oilfields in Borneo, December 1941. The Japanese campaign of conquest in Asia during 1941-42 was as impressive as the German *Blitzkrieg* of 1939-40.

Right: A Dutch poster of 1945 shows Indonesia about to break the bonds of the Japanese occupation.

Below right: The Sultan of one of the Borneo states meeting the local Japanese commander, 1941.

briefly trace the emergence of only two Southeast Asian peoples – Indonesians and Vietnamese – into independent nationhood; unlike the others, they had to wage bitter wars against their former colonial masters to attain it.

Indonesia

To millions of Indonesian peasants, the Japanese invaders may well have appeared as the deliverers from their European overlords – an event deeply enshrined in popular, messianic expectations. The collapse of the centuries-old colonial domain was similarly welcomed by many urban, educated Indonesians who had chafed under the increasingly conservative restrictions placed on their organizations and aspirations. Indeed, the cause of Indonesian nationalism seemingly received a boost when the Japanese military freed its most outspoken spokesmen, Sukarno among them, from Dutch detention in the wake of the occupation. But such early hopes proved premature. The first victim was Indonesian territorial unity, for the Japanese dismembered the country and placed the different islands under separate military commands. The second was organizational freedom, with the new rulers placing grave restrictions on overt political activities: nationalist and other leaders, forced to cooperate with the military authorities, had to endure close surveillance and direction. And finally there were forced food deliveries, ruthless recruitment of laborers and the widespread use of terror. For well over a year, the clock appeared to have been put back, as the Japanese were bent on implementing a policy of annexation and incorporation. Only thereafter, in the wake of their military reverses, did they change in favor of granting increasing local autonomy and, at the very last moment, all-Indonesian independence.

But even before that time, Japanese policies,

especially in Java, did lay the groundwork for some far-reaching changes. To begin with, many Indonesian civil servants were suddenly promoted to positions previously held by Dutchmen. Even though the highest posts were once again in the hands of foreigners (who in fact created a separate administrative machinery staffed by Japanese), these promotions brought their beneficiaries self-confidence and expertise. An even more radical departure from Dutch practices was the new rulers' mobilization of youths into a host of new organizations, ranging all the way from village guards to paramilitary brigades. Toward the end of 1943 the Japanese went one crucial step farther in authorizing the creation of a small Indonesian army with its own officers' corps (though still, of course, under strict Japanese command). A new generation of potential leaders was thus being trained. In the meantime, however, it was the older political leaders, those who had fought the Dutch and often paid the price of imprisonment and exile, who dominated public life and public attention within the narrow confines imposed by the military authorities.

The task confronting these leaders was complicated not only by Japanese unwillingness to grant far-reaching concessions, but also by inherent disunity. Indonesian nationalism had only developed into a major force in the early 1930s, but even then the ranks of its proponents had remained sharply divided between radicals and moderates, between 'cooperators' and 'non-cooperators,' between traditionalist and modernist Muslims. The Japanese, bent on simplifying Indonesian public life for their own purposes, tried to create all-embracing organizations, but even they found it difficult to bridge some of the existing cleavages. In the early period of the occupation, a movement under exclusive nationalist leadership, though originally permitted, was soon disbanded.

In its stead came a vast, Japanese-led organization in which nationalist spokesmen were forced to share subordinate executive posts with civil servants. At the same time, the Japanese sanctioned a new Islamic association, *Masjumi*, in which traditionalists and modernists were brought together in uneasy alliance.

After Tokyo finally committed itself in late 1944 to granting ultimate Indonesian independence, Indonesians succeeded in taking ever-increasing political initiatives. Before long the nationalists, led by Sukarno, gained control over the Japanese-sponsored mass movement and forged a guerrilla fighting force under their auspices. Even then, however, *Masjumi* retained its separate existence and actually established a military arm of its own. By the spring of 1945, with the economy in ever worse disarray and with Japanese propaganda ever more feverishly exhorting the population to defend the country against expected Allied landings, conditions seemed ripe for violent change. Peasants had repeatedly risen, and even an army battalion had mutinied against its Japanese superiors. While nationalists, religious leaders and bureaucrats were deliberating about the Indonesian state of the future, members of the young generation – students, guerrillas and others – took to the streets to force the birth of that state, with or without, and if need be against, the Japanese.

In the end, independence came almost as an anticlimax – bestowed by a Japanese empire about to surrender unconditionally to its enemies, and proclaimed, with very little fanfare, by Sukarno and Mohammad Hatta (another prestigious nationalist from Sumatra) on 17 August 1945. But where Filipinos, Burmese and, farther afield, Indians and Pakistanis could sever the ties with their former imperial overlords peacefully in the immediate postwar years, Indonesians had to wage revolutionary war against the Netherlands. For most Hollanders, themselves barely liberated from brutal occupation by Nazi Germany, were totally unprepared for the Indonesian revolution and unwilling to let go of a rich Asian colony. Twice, in 1947 and again a year later, the Dutch

waged large-scale war against the fledgling Indonesian Republic. Yet though modern arms gained them control over outlying islands and also in the major urban centers in Java, it was of no avail. Locally, Holland was defeated by a resourceful army supported by a revolutionized populace. Internationally, it was defeated by constant diplomatic pressure exerted at the newly formed United Nations Organization, principally at the behest of the United States. In December 1949 the Dutch government finally agreed to transfer sovereignty to Indonesia, except for West New Guinea, which remained Dutch until the 1960s.

Though Indonesian independence had finally been won, the consolidation of nation and state, forged in the heat of revolution and anticolonial war, was beset by huge difficulties. Not only had occupation and revolution caused serious damages to the economy, the concept of national unity was threatened by the re-emergence of deep-seated political and ideological fissures. Though muted as long as Indonesians were united in the struggle against a common colonial enemy, they had here and there erupted even while the republic was fighting for its very existence. A small but militant Muslim faction rebelled against the secular state while, almost at the same time, the Indonesian Communist Party – reborn at war's end and influenced, like its sister parties elsewhere in southern Asia, by the hard line the Cominform had adopted in 1947, took up arms against the 'bourgeois' republic. In the end,

the army successfully quelled both, but its victory against foreign foe and domestic challengers did not so much end internal divisions as shift them from the battlefield to the political arena.

In fact, parliamentary democracy, introduced in 1950 and culminating in the first general elections five years later, seemed to exacerbate rather than soften the deep-seated political and ideological cleavages that had rent Indonesian society since colonial times, separating radicals from moderates, nationalists from Marxists, secularists from Muslims and indeed traditionalist from modernist Muslims (*Masjumi* having broken up before the elections) – and in some ways also capital city from periphery. Deadlocked over the central issue of the nature of the state, Indonesia seemed paralyzed by a rapidly widening gulf between communists and anti-communists on one hand, and between stalemated civilian politicians and increasingly restive military leaders on the other. The short-lived experiment in liberalism ended when regional revolts erupted in the major islands beyond Java in the late 1950s, to be replaced in 1959 by an authoritarian regime.

'Guided Democracy,' as it was called, represented an alliance between President Sukarno, father of the Indonesian nation, and the military leadership which, having once again secured its territorial integrity, now assumed a key political role. Their joint ascendancy sharply reduced the power of parliament and the political parties, the second largest of which, *Masjumi*, was proscribed, accused of having supported if not inspired the regional revolts. While the military obtained control over the country's administration, the president used his oratorical skills to bring the nation back to revolutionary principles: unity at home and renewed militancy toward the Dutch, still dominant in Indonesia's export economy and still in possession of West New Gui-

Above: Anti-Dutch slogans painted on a truck in Indonesia.

Left: Chinese detainees in Borneo in 1967.

Right: General Suharto – who replaced the former strongman of Indonesia General Sukarno – being sworn in as acting president of Indonesia.

nea (Irian Barat). Sukarno ordered the expulsion of the remaining resident Hollanders and the nationalization of Dutch business holdings, and he scored a great diplomatic victory when the Netherlands, yielding to strong American pressures, agreed to relinquish its last territorial toehold in 1962. More than 350 years of Dutch influence and control in the Indonesian archipelago had come to an end.

But neither this victory nor the strident confrontation with what Sukarno termed a new 'imperialist' threat, the recently founded Federation of Malaysia, a crusade on which he embarked as soon as Irian Barat had been ceded, could compensate for rapid deterioration on the domestic scene. As the economy took a sharp downward turn and inflation became rampant corruption spread, the gulf separating the mass of the poor from the handful of privileged growing ever wider. The polarizations provided ample opportunities for communist propaganda and organizational efforts. Recovering from its eclipse in the late 1940s, the Communist party had scored impressive electoral victories in the 1950s. Its new and energetic leadership not only benefited from the banning of *Masjumi*, its most outspoken political opponent, but also from Sukarno's increasingly militant, anti-Western foreign policy. This, however, threatened the close alliance between president and army, original cornerstone of 'Guided Democracy.' Uneasily poised between his military commanders and his communist supporters, Sukarno was unable to stem the drift toward a violent showdown. It came, in a series of rapid moves and countermoves, in the fall of 1965, from which the army emerged victorious. During the next few months, a veritable massacre practically destroyed the Communist party and its supporters. Over three million Chinese, actual and so-called communists, were slaughtered in the

bloodbath that followed the fall of Sukarno's regime. Indonesia was left poorer than it had been in 1942 and with about twice its population. Before long, Sukarno was forced to yield the presidency to General Suharto; shorn of all titles and dignity, Sukarno died in 1970. The Americans helped see to it that the Suharto government was shored up in its precarious position after the fall of Indonesia's national hero.

Like many other new states in Asia and Africa, Indonesia passed under military control, even though many prominent civilians continued to occupy important government posts. In several respects, the 'New Order' broke sharply with Guided Democracy. The new leadership made a concerted effort to repair the economy and to re-open the country to foreign investors. This, in turn, led to normalization of diplomatic relations with Malaysia and the West (and a concomitant rupture with Peking). While communists were banned from all walks of life, with thousands kept in detention camps, many other opponents of Sukarno gained prominent places in public life. But far from constituting a return to true parliamentary democracy, the New Order in fact maintained most of the authoritarian features of the pre-1966 regime. Thus, though Muslims had played leading roles in discrediting Sukarno and in eliminating communists, *Masjumi* remained a prohibited party, still stigmatized with the rebellions of a decade ago. Not unlike Sukarno before them, the military rulers tried to limit the freedom of action of even those parties allowed to function, preferring instead to govern with the assistance of officially sponsored 'functional groupings' known by the acronym GOLKAR.

For the next 15 years Suharto's regime was characterized by a blend of shrewd, authoritarian politics and successful, if somewhat precarious, economics. By 1987 political opposition had been

so effectively muted that in the legislative elections of that year GOLKAR candidates emerged with 73 percent of the popular vote, the highest percentage in the history of the regime. Doubtless a good part of Suharto's undeniable popularity was due to his skillful economic management and the resultant benefits to both towndwellers and, more significantly, peasants. By the end of the 1960s Indonesia's runaway inflation rate had been brought down from 600 percent per year to 10 percent, and by the mid 1980s per capita GNP was rising at an average of 4.8 percent a year, the highest of any Southeast Asian nation save Singapore. Good management apart, the primary sources of Indonesia's economic health were soaring world oil prices (Indonesia is OPEC's only Asian member) and a steady influx of foreign aid, loans and investments. But as oil prices tumbled back down from the 1981 high of $34 per barrel to around $16 in 1988 the economic picture darkened somewhat. The annual growth of the GNP declined sharply, and a budget deficit developed. By 1987 Indonesia was the Third World's fifth largest borrower nation, with foreign exchange reserves sufficient to cover less than six months of normal imports. Yet the level of foreign financial aid and investment continued high (Japan being by far the largest contributor), and though Indonesia's oil-based economy remained vulnerable, there was as yet still no reason to suppose that it was in serious trouble.

In its external policies the Suharto regime, though it ended Sukarno's confrontation with Malaysia, can hardly be said to have abandoned militancy altogether. In 1975-76, rather than permit a radical local government to succeed Portuguese rule in Portuguese Timor, Indonesia invaded and annexed the territory. In the fighting and in the ensuing spread of pestilence and famine an estimated 30 percent of the region's

650,000 inhabitants is said to have perished, and the still-not-completely vanquished local radicals continued to conduct low-level guerrilla operations against the Java government for over a decade. Somewhat similar tensions developed between government forces and the Papuan inhabitants of Irian Jaya (formerly Irian Barat, or Western New Guinea), and both Indonesia and Papua New Guinea have been at some pains to try to prevent the spread of fighting in the region.

In a more general way, Indonesia, as de facto leader of the Association of Southeast Asian Nations (ASEAN), consisting of Indonesia, the Philippines, Malaysia, Thailand, Singapore and Brunei, has been involved in a subtle but steady shift away from the economic and political dependence on the United States that characterized ASEAN at its inception in 1967. By the late 1980s the US was seen neither as the major economic force in the region nor, after the American military failure in Indo-China, as the most likely guarantor of security against the threat of an expansionist Vietnam. The inevitable result was a major improvement in the relations between all the ASEAN members and Tokyo and a more cautious but decided improvement of relations with Moscow and Beijing.

As for Indonesia's political future, the great unknown (never openly discussed in Jakarta) remained the question of what would happen when Suharto died or relinquished office, since, as in several other 'new' Asian states (Korea, for example), there was no precedent and little tested machinery to ensure orderly, peaceful transfer of power. In any case, it seemed a good bet that the military would not stand aloof from the process.

Above: An oilfield at Balikpapan, part of Indonesia's booming oil industry.

Left: Ho Chi Minh whilst a guerrilla leader fighting the Japanese and French in Indo-China in 1945.

Above right: Japanese troops operating in Indo-China in 1941 with the 'permission' of the Vichy French, who were powerless to deny Japanese demands.

Right: A map of Southeast Asia, which, like the Middle East, became a major battle front in the postwar era.

Vietnam

Though decolonization in French Indo-China started far less spectacularly than in the Netherlands Indies, it ran a more radical course in the end. What slowed the beginnings of the process in the French domains were developments outside Southeast Asia. Both Holland and France succumbed to Germany's *Blitzkrieg* in the spring of 1940. But where in Holland occupation was total, in France it was only partial: while the most vital regions, Paris included, fell under German administration, the rump was left nominally independent, with its capital at Vichy. These differences account for the divergent ways in which the Asian colonies of the two countries responded to the mounting Japanese pressures before the outbreak of the war in the Pacific in December 1941. As one of the Western Allies, the Dutch government in exile was able to rely on British, Commonwealth and probably American naval support in the defense of the Netherlands Indies. As a result, the colonial authorities twice rejected Tokyo's demands for far-reaching economic and other concessions. No such option was available to their French counterparts in Indo-China. Militarily very weak, and subject, too, to the dictates of the pro-Axis Vichy government, they were forced to yield to increasing Japanese pressures for the stationing of Japanese forces and for a supervisory Japanese presence in return for the retention of French sovereignty and de facto control. This ironic wedding between the alleged saviors of Asia from Western dominance and one of the most conservative colonial regimes in all of Southeast Asia lasted until early March 1945. By then the liberation of France in Europe, no less than the Allies' rapid advances in Asia, caused Tokyo to put an abrupt end to the French civilian and military establishment.

Thus unlike Indonesia, where the occupation proper lasted for some 40-odd months and thus

directly impinged on local developments, in Vietnam Japanese control proper was limited to just a few months. Though it was only then that Vietnamese developments gathered a truly revolutionary momentum, for the ground had been prepared during the seemingly tranquil years of the Franco-Vietnamese 'condominium.' In fact, French rulers and Japanese occupiers had often vied with each other to influence groups of Vietnamese, whether overtly or secretly. The French wartime colonial government had made strenuous efforts to instill among the indigenous population increased respect for French prestige and sovereignty. One of their most potent tools was a concerted drive to win the allegiance of the younger generation. Inspired by their Vichy masters, the French authorities mobilized Vietnamese urban youths in a variety of sports and

other clubs. At the same time, they greatly augmented admissions to the University of Hanoi. All of these new recruits were exposed to persistent French propaganda and indoctrination. Compared to prewar colonial practices, these were striking innovations, but it was by then far too late to make Vietnamese converts to the cause of France. Instead, the new organizations provided invaluable training grounds for young, often quite radical, nationalists.

The sudden collapse of the French regime opened the way to mounting political activities by those whom either the colonial government or the Japanese had until then sought to mobilize. Moving from cooperation with the French to liberation, the Japanese induced Bao Dai, nominal emperor of Vietnam who had 'reigned' in French-imposed obscurity since the early 1930s, to pro-

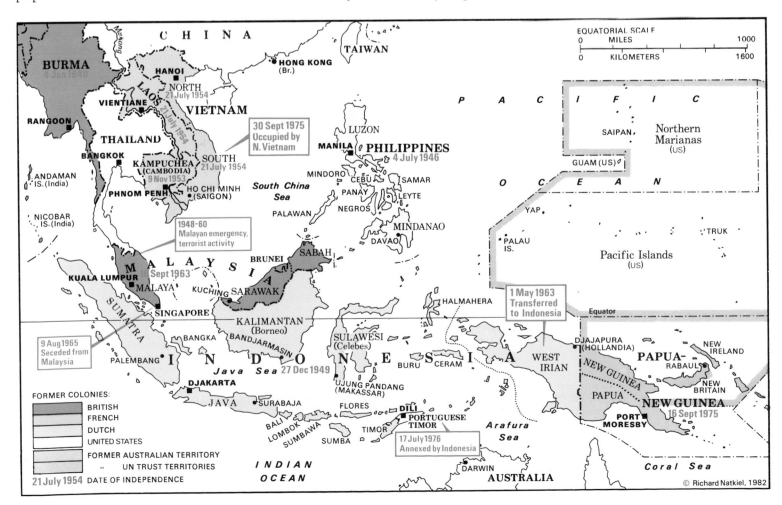

© Richard Natkiel, 1982

claim the independence of his realm in March 1945. (At the same time, they also prevailed upon the kings of Laos and Cambodia to declare themselves independent from France.) But neither the emperor himself nor his hastily recruited government commanded sufficient authority to fill the vacuum created by the elimination of French power – a vacuum not filled by the Japanese either, for by then they were largely preoccupied with defense preparations against expected Allied landings. But what Bao Dai or such groups as the armed sects in the southern countryside and the politicized youths in the towns and cities in the north lacked at that crucial moment was amply provided by the political party with the longest revolutionary experience: Ho Chi Minh's communists.

Banned by both French and Japanese, the communists had laid the groundwork for a comeback across the border in Nationalist China. (Though the Chinese Nationalists were of course wary of Ho and his followers, they had hoped to use them, like other Vietnamese exiles, for their own purposes.) Small in numbers, the communists had nevertheless created a tightly knit network of revolutionary cells that enabled them, far better than others, to maintain contacts with their occupied homeland and to supply information to their Chinese hosts and the Western Allies. In 1941 the communists had ostensibly dissolved their party into a broad patriotic front, the Vietnam Independence League, better known as the Viet Minh. Recognized and supported by the Allies, Ho Chi Minh may well have had a better grasp of Japan's rapidly declining fortunes than did Southeast Asian leaders in the occupied territories. In any case, he skillfully used the dissolution of French power in March 1945 to extend Viet Minh military force into the northern border regions, well beyond the reach of Japanese garrisons. When Japan fell Ho commanded not only the best-organized and best-prepared political and military movement, but also the only one untainted by collaboration with either the French Vichyites or the Japanese militarists. Two weeks after Tokyo announced Japan's surrender, Ho Chi Minh proclaimed to jubilant throngs in Hanoi the nation's independence in ringing language derived from

the West's democratic-revolutionary vocabulary. So powerful was this appeal to national freedom that Bao Dai abdicated his powers and transferred the symbols of the Nguyen monarchy to Ho, president of the Democratic Republic of Vietnam by acclamation.

But as in Indonesia, the proclamation of independence was to prove the curtain raiser for years of war, rather than the harbinger of peace and national unity. Because Vietnam's independence had been won by a movement spearheaded by communists, almost at once the struggle between colony and metropole became entwined in the developing global Cold War. This is why the United States found it far more difficult to support the Vietnamese against France than to support the Indonesians against Holland. There were additional complications that were absent in the Netherlands Indies. While British troops actually undertook the immediate liberation in both countries, Holland encountered far greater difficulties in persuading the British to allow the return of Dutch military forces than was the case with the French, whose army had in any case controlled the country until a few months before. In fact, a short-lived, uneasy alliance of sorts had come into being between the Viet Minh and pro-de Gaulle French units that had escaped the Japanese. But with the re-entry of French regulars the battle lines were quickly drawn. A murderous attack on French civilians in Saigon, staged by ill-disciplined Viet Minh cadres, led to the communists' quick ouster from the southern capital in March 1946.

If the southern part of the country seemed lost to the Viet Minh, in the north, for long an area of entrenched strength, they managed to hold on for almost another year. This was made possible by the absence there of British and French forces, the result of an Allied agreement that had assigned Nationalist China to the liberation of Vietnam north of the sixteenth parallel. Benefiting from a heavy-handed and corrupt, yet politically inept, Chinese occupation, the Vietnamese were able to expand and solidify their control by training additional guerrilla forces and by politically mobilizing sizable segments of the population in town and countryside. The Chinese 'interregnum' finally

ended in March 1946, leaving a Viet Minh strongly enough entrenched to create the need for serious Franco-Vietnamese negotiations. In France, Ho Chi Minh spent four months at the head of his delegation, and it almost seemed that a suitable formula, acceptable to both sides, might be worked out, with France willing to recognize (and Ho to settle for) an autonomous Vietnam as a member of the French Union. But radicals in both countries gained the upper hand after the treaty had been signed. The entry of French forces into Hanoi in October 1946 was the opening signal in a drawn-out colonial war that ended in the defeat of France at the mountain fortress of Dienbienphu (near the Laotian border) some seven years later, in May 1954.

Once again, Vietnamese developments were to diverge sharply from those in Indonesia, where military stalemate combined with outside diplomatic interference had led to consummation of the nationalist revolution in 1949. But whereas in Indonesia the communists had stabbed the national revolution in the back in 1948, in Vietnam they not only represented, for better or worse, that revolution, but they had also at last consummated it, against enormous odds, in 1954.

This reality was clearly reflected in the international conference, convened in Geneva, Switzerland, in the spring of 1954 to settle the status of Korea and French Indo-China. While Cambodia and Laos were quickly recognized as independent and neutral states, the conferees, ignoring Bao Dai's protesting representatives, accepted the de facto division of Vietnam as a temporary state of affairs to be either confirmed or rejected by all-Vietnam elections to be held in 1956. (Besides France and the Viet Minh, the conference was attended by the United Kingdom, the United States, the USSR and the People's Republic of China.) Until then the military forces of the contending parties would regroup, the French in the south, pending repatriation, and the Viet Minh in their northern strongholds. Like international settlements, the Geneva Accords were in part a face-saving formula, one that would allow an orderly liquidation of the French establishment, followed by the expected electoral endorsement of a revolutionary *fait accompli*. No doubt the peaceful consummation of Ho Chi Minh's military victory was opposed not only by some religious minorities but also by 'secular' patriots who had good reason to fear and resent communist rule. No doubt either, however, that, if left to depend on themselves, these groups would have been forced to find an accommodation with the victorious revolutionary forces. As it was, the United States decided to substitute American support to the anti-communist elements for the rapidly dwindling French superstructure. Thus, instead of finding peace at the conference table for the second time, the people of Vietnam – and in the end the peoples of Laos and Cambodia as well – found themselves drawn into another war.

The immediate result of America's entry into Vietnamese history was the freezing of the temporary armistice line along the seventeenth parallel into a boundary between two hostile states: in the north, the Democratic Republic under Ho's presidency; in the south, what soon became the Republic of Vietnam, headed, after Bao Dai's ouster in a plebiscite, by a well-known nationalist, Ngo Dinh Diem, recently returned from European and American exile.

The northern regime set about to solidify a socialist system modeled on the Soviet Union and the Chinese People's Republic, both of which, together with the other countries of the Eastern

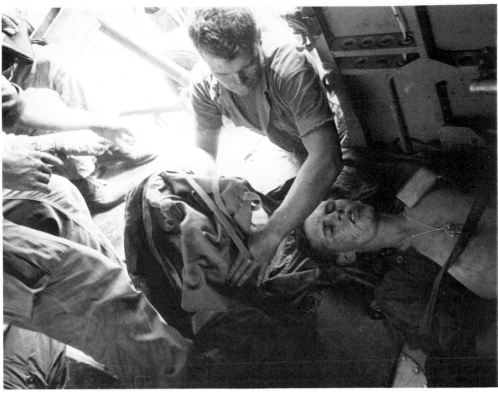

Above left: The official residence of the President of South Vietnam in 1954.

Above right: A wounded US Marine is given aid aboard an evacuation helicopter in Vietnam in 1967.

Right: The truce team in Indo-China in 1954 which met to discuss the French withdrawal from their colonies of Vietnam, Cambodia and Laos.

bloc, provided Ho Chi Minh with diplomatic support, economic aid and military equipment. With this backing, North Vietnam – now openly a single-party state which had shed the trappings of the Viet Minh popular front – embarked on rapid industrialization, socialization of agriculture and political mobilization and regimentation of the populace. While generally successful with regard to industrialization, the implementation of the communist program met with occasional opposition, especially virulent among peasants opposed to collectivization. But whatever the problems created by the forced march toward socialism, they were to be dwarfed by the popular consensus produced by the rekindled revolutionary struggle against the new foreign enemy.

Paradoxically, it may well be that it was the growing and many-faceted American presence that ultimately hindered the establishment of a legitimate, truly national government in the south, one able to compete on near-equal terms with its communist northern neighbor. Having lost any decisive claim to legitimacy with Bao Dai's second departure from the scene, the post-Geneva regime in Saigon fell heir to divisive and factional groups. For all his personal integrity and proven anticolonial record, President Diem, a devout Catholic and sworn anti-communist, lacked political experience and organizational skills no less than broad popular support. Before long, his regime – no less dictatorial in some respects than Ho Chi Minh's – fell foul of the diverse political and sectarian groupings in South Vietnam, with only the Catholic minority and, more importantly, the new republican army backing his government. These difficulties were immensely exacerbated when communist cadres in the south, convinced that Diem had abolished all chances for a peaceful reunification of the country in terms acceptable to them, unleashed a military and political attack on the southern regime in the early 1960s. Diem tried to meet it by growing suppression and increasing reliance on American military advisers and matériel, but without achieving either internal stability or successes in the field. In 1963 Diem was overthrown and killed in a coup d'état staged by officers of the armed forces of South Vietnam.

The Americans, previously content under Presidents Eisenhower and Kennedy to wage a surrogate war against the communists through Diem, entered into large-scale conflict through predominantly conscripted troops after the assassination of Diem, in which the Americans, through their Ambassador Henry Cabot Lodge, were to some extent implicated. The assassination of President Kennedy a month later brought Lyndon Johnson to the White House. During his five years there the United States poured in millions of troops and tens of billions of dollars in its attempt to keep South Vietnam free from communism. By 1968, when the expense of the operation in terms of financial cost and public protest at home had created an intolerable political situation for the Democrats, Johnson chose not to run again for the presidency at a time when over 550,000 American troops were committed to Vietnam. The American *volte-face* came in the wake of massive attacks against their bases in Vietnam during the Tet Offensive in early 1968. Ironically, the Viet Cong had lost heavily in the field at the very moment when the American government and people lost the will to continue the battle.

The 1968 election, which brought in the Republicans under Richard Nixon, brought the Vietnam War into a new stage, called 'Vietnamization,' in which American troops were gradually withdrawn. This slow departure, which took over four years, was combined with sporadic but massive bombing attacks against North Vietnam, still reeling under its losses suffered in the Tet Offensive.

The north, supported largely by Soviet arms, money and advisers, bided its time. As the result of the Paris Accords of 1973 the United States and its few allies, principally the Australians, quit Vietnam altogether, leaving the South Vietnamese military, still with American advisers and financial assistance, to its own devices. But the Americans were increasingly unable to provide even financial support, their own energies undermined by inflation, devaluation and the Watergate scandal, which in 1974 broke the Nixon presidency. Nixon's successor, Gerald Ford, was unable to command enough support in the Congress to support the South Vietnamese regime, itself riddled by corruption and scandal. The time was ripe for the North Vietnamese to strike. In March and April 1975 they moved swiftly through the parts of South Vietnam still held by the military government, and Saigon fell to the North on 30 April 1975, as the last remaining Americans and a pathetic few of their Vietnamese supporters escaped the wrath of the victors via helicopters to awaiting aircraft carriers offshore. Saigon was renamed Ho Chi Minh City.

The now-united Democratic Republic of Vietnam took out its anger against its former rivals. American POWs were kept in prison camps for years. South Vietnamese 'collaborators' with the Americans were killed by the thousand. Hundreds of thousands of civilians fled the country by boat, the majority perishing at sea in the dangerous trip to Hong Kong, Taiwan or other 'friendly' ports hundreds of miles away. In Cambodia, pro-Soviet communists clashed with pro-Chinese communist forces, and fully one-third of the population was killed or starved to death in the civil war that began with the exodus of the Americans before 1975 and intensified after the collapse of South Vietnamese resistance to Hanoi. The government of Laos fell, but its replacement was friendly to Hanoi, and therefore that tiny ex-kingdom avoided much of the bloodshed that occurred in the rest of former French Indo-China. Sporadic fighting continued throughout the three states into the 1980s, and Vietnamese forces even made forays into pro-American Thailand. Pro-Soviet forces gained hegemony over the Chinese surrogates in Cambodia, now renamed Kampuchea.

Southeast Asia since the Vietnam War

The balance of power in Southeast Asia had shifted dramatically as a result of the Vietnam War. Indo-China was firmly in the Russian camp, heavily dependent upon the Soviet Union for military and economic assistance in the rebuilding of their states after over 30 years of continuous war. As Soviet influence grew, China's attitude toward communist Vietnam changed from guarded support to overt hostility. American influence remained significant only in the Philippines and Thailand, and to some extent in Indonesia. British influence in Malaysia and Singapore waned steadily in the 1960s.

Southeast Asia had been the locus of colonial strife between the three principal European powers, Britain, France and the Netherlands, from roughly the mid eighteenth century until the mid twentieth century. After the Japanese interregnum, their power was replaced by that of communist China and the United States. As American power waned, Southeast Asia became increasingly a battleground between American and Japanese economic power, on the one hand – in which the Japanese came to dominate – and, on the other hand, Chinese and Soviet political power, with the Chinese growing in strength in Thailand and Burma, while the Russians remained firmly in control in Laos, Kampuchea and Vietnam. By the end of the 1980s American political power remained dominant in insular Southeast Asia and the Malay peninsula, but this power was bound to ebb in the wake of growing Japanese economic hegemony.

Southeast Asia remained at the mercy of new colonial or post-colonial rivalries. A diverse and rich region such as this was bound to remain so. No Southeast Asian power would be capable of dominating the region itself, and its peoples were more numerous than ever, thanks to the advances of Western medicine, and poorer than ever, particularly in the expanding cities such as Manila and Jakarta. There were exceptions, of course. Malaysia, particularly on the peninsula, as well as the Republic of Singapore, remained relatively rich enclaves – clean, increasingly prosperous, capitalist-oriented and dominated by their Chinese populations, whose political loyalties may have drifted toward Peking but whose principal loyalties remained toward their own families and self-aggrandizement. Singapore, in particular, had become an important financial and banking center of Asia under its long-time and only president, Lee Kwan Yew. Burma remained a backwater, an outdoor museum almost unchanged since the British left in 1948, a place frozen in time. Thailand, though ostensibly American-influenced, remained largely rural and poor, despite the contrasts of wealth and poverty in its huge capital of Bangkok. The Philippines, which became independent in 1946, was left with a democratic and modern legacy by the Americans who dominated her economy and military. However, under the corrupt President Ferdinand Marcos, the constitution was abandoned in the 1970s, and the overthrow of Marcos in 1986 found the archipelago poorer than ever. Manila, its principal city, was overcrowded and poverty-stricken, and its political future was uncertain at best, with a government under President Corazon Aquino, supported by the popular forces which swept her to power.

Southeast Asia will continue to be torn apart by larger and more powerful forces from outside the region. This has been the fate of the kindly and gentle people who populate it since the coming of Islam, the onslaught of the Portuguese and Spanish, of the British, Dutch and French who followed them, of the Japanese who swept them away, and of the Americans, Chinese, Russians and latterly the Japanese who dominate the region now.

China

For China, World War II lasted from 1937 to 1945, and for the four years before Pearl Harbor China was fighting alone. None of the Western powers with major stakes in the Pacific and Southeast Asia – the United States, Britain, France and the Netherlands – dared to take action that would irreparably antagonize the Japanese. In the United States, though there was much debate on the subject, it was decided not to advance any massive loans to China and not to halt the export of strategic materials to Japan. The Kuomintang armies fought with fury in Shanghai and Nanking, but they were no match for the well-trained, heavily armed and skillfully led Japanese troops. After suffering hundreds of thousands of casualties, the Chinese withdrew down the Yangtze River deep into the heartland of China and set up a new wartime capital in Chungking. For a brief period, the catastrophe united the nation. Thousands of workers trudged to Szechwan carrying the vital machinery needed to establish small factories to help with wartime production, students and faculty carried their libraries through the mountains to reestablish their universities in 'Free China' and tens of thousands of laborers toiled on the Burma Road, an amazing example of engineering that opened a supply line to the west and gave some help to the beleaguered capital.

But this sense of unity and purpose was not maintained for long. By 1939, when the Japanese had reached the current limits of their expansion, the war entered a period of stalemate along an immense front stretching across southern and central China. The difficulties of wartime life in Chungking led to bitterness and to charges of corruption and mismanagement of available supplies. Old antagonisms and suspicions resurfaced, and large numbers of Kuomintang troops were deployed to the north to keep an eye on the communist base area in Yenan, Shensi. In 1941 all pretense at Kuomintang-communist friendship was ended when Kuomintang troops killed thousands of communist troops in Anhwei in 'The New Fourth Army Incident.' The communists claimed that they were treacherously ambushed while obeying Kuomintang orders; the Kuomintang claimed that the communists had blatantly refused to obey orders and were in fact moving deeper into Kuomintang territory when attacked. From this time onward, tensions between the two groups of armies mounted.

While Kuomintang morale slipped in the mud and muddle of Chungking, communist spirits were high. This period of 'Yenan Communism' has been described by many Western writers and journalists. They were amazed at the discipline and cheerfulness of the communists, they found Mao pleasant and pragmatic, and his policies extraordinarily moderate. Some of the land abandoned by fleeing landlords had been divided up among the needy, but in general the rich peasants were left in peace. Many of these observers, contrasting what they saw with the press handouts they had received from the Kuomintang, and also comparing conditions between the two areas of China, became convinced that Mao and his followers were not communists at all, in the sense that the word was usually understood, but were 'agrarian reformers.' In the 1950s, during the period of bitter anti-communist backlash in the United States, many of these observers were accused of communist sympathies and of deliberately lying about what they saw. In fact, they had reported accurately enough; what they had lacked was the political knowledge to understand that Mao was pursuing a particular line that at that time was tactically advisable. Later, of course, when conditions changed, Mao was ready to change his tactics.

After Pearl Harbor, when the United States entered the war, Chiang Kai-shek hoped that his major troubles were over, and that the United States would bear the brunt of the fighting. But in fact, because of the friendship between Roosevelt and Churchill and because of Roosevelt's conviction that the war must be won first in Europe and then in the Pacific, China was assigned a low priority. And by 1944, when American troops might have been available in large numbers to fight in China, the Joint Chiefs of Staff decided to follow through the 'island-hopping' campaign in the Pacific. And finally, in the summer of 1945, when Kuomintang troops were ready for extensive campaigns against the Japanese, the atomic bombs dropped on Hiroshima and Nagasaki ended the war with startling suddenness.

The man chosen by Roosevelt to be his liaison officer with Chiang, and supervisor of lend-lease matériel in the China theater, was General Joseph Stilwell. A courageous and skillful soldier, Stilwell was also obstinate and tactless, and his quarrels with Chiang made coordination of United States-China policies difficult. To compound the problem, Chiang had as his aviation adviser General Claire Lee Chennault, a man as tough and cantankerous as Stilwell. Chennault had convinced the Generalissimo (as Chiang was now generally known) that with only a moderate increase in air-

power he would bomb the Japanese out of China. Stilwell had warned the Peanut (as he contemptuously called Chiang) that any major increase in air strikes would lead to massive Japanese reprisals. Chennault won the argument, but Stilwell was proved right. Heavy Japanese attacks in early 1944 captured vast new areas of western China and lost Chiang enormous stores of desperately needed supplies. The frictions and bickerings continued unabated until Stilwell was recalled in October, with the important job of retraining selected divisions of Chiang's armies still uncompleted. General Wedemeyer, Stilwell's successor, was more successful, and he got on well with Chiang; but even he had to admit that conditions in the Nationalist armies were appalling: equipment was lost or stolen, recruits were led to the

Left: During the civil war the Chinese communists relied on a supply train of peasant carts.

Above: 'Vinegar Joe' Stilwell, US general and liaison officer with Chiang Kai-shek.

Above right: Generalissimo Chiang Kai-shek and Madame Chiang with President Roosevelt and Prime Minister Churchill discuss the future of the war in China.

Right: Mao Tse-tung addresses communist supporters in 1938.

front tied together, many troops died of starvation on the march and morale was fatally low.

Here again, there was a sharp contrast with the communists. In their base areas in northern China, the communists used their trained troops as a nucleus for indoctrination and training of the peasant masses. Cadres in the villages taught the principles of military tactics and also reading and writing. With literacy for the masses came further chances for indoctrination, as textbooks and newspapers analyzed the social injustices that the peasants must have the courage to overthrow and pointed to a new socialist world in which old pains would be forgotten. The peasant guerilla units trained by Party cadres struck repeatedly at Japanese outposts and communication lines; goaded to fury, the Japanese struck back with ter-

rible force, burning and looting countless north China villages and killing all their inhabitants. But these savage reprisals only made mobilization of the peasants easier for the communists, and led to a leadership vacuum that they were only too eager to fill. By the war's end, in 1945, according to one estimate, the communists controlled an area of 225,000 square miles in north China with a population of 85 million people; in 1937 they had controlled about 35,000 square miles of very poor land with a population of under 1.5 million.

Not only had the communists gained in morale, in territory and in population from the war, they had also gained time to consolidate their ideology. This was the time when Mao did most of his reading and thinking, catching up on work that he had of necessity neglected during his hectic years of political infighting and fugitive existence between 1926 and 1936. In Yenan he developed his theory of contradictions, pointing to the innate antagonisms within society; developed his analyses of the various types of peasant classes – the rich, middle and poor – and the treatment that was appropriate for each at different times. The revolutionary university was also developed as a means of bringing bourgeois intellectuals into line, of teaching them to slough off their individualism and sectarianism and to immerse themselves instead in the common goals of the socialist revolution. In 1942 this education was carried over into a full scale 'Rectification Campaign,' launched in person by Mao. However sympathetic they might be to the communist cause, and however much hardship or danger they might have gone through to reach Yenan, China's intellectuals were now put on notice that absolute discipline would be expected from them and that they would have to change their ingrained habits of thought if these did not coincide with the Party's intentions. Clearly Mao was anticipating future struggle as much as was Chiang.

Almost as soon as the bomb had fallen on Hiroshima the open civil war in China was resumed. The Kuomintang armies were concentrated in southeast China, so in direct contravention of Chiang's orders the communists in the north began to accept the surrender of Japanese units. By so doing they gained both an aura of legitimacy and large supplies of arms and ammunition. As communist troops raced north to take over Manchuria and make it their revolutionary

base, Kuomintang troops were airlifted to Manchuria by the United States in an attempt to head them off. The Americans wanted a strong and united China led by Chiang Kai-shek, but they found it difficult to achieve this goal, since it was politically impossible to commit United States troops to a new land war in Asia, and they had very little other leverage that they could apply. A further complication was that Manchuria by late 1945 was actually controlled by the Soviet Union. In accordance with agreements that he had made at Yalta in February 1945 with Churchill and Roosevelt, Stalin had sent his troops into Manchuria three months after the fall of Germany. This was exactly the time that the atom bombs were dropped on Japan, so the Soviet troops took over Manchuria with almost no cost. Among other matters agreed at Yalta had been that Dairen should be internationalized, Port Arthur once more leased to the Soviet Union as a naval base, that the Mongolian People's Republic should have its status quo preserved and that the strategic Chinese-Eastern Railroad and South Manchurian Railroad should be jointly operated by a Sino-Soviet company. These clauses, which profoundly affected China's vital interests in the area, had been drawn up without consulting the Kuomintang representatives. In some ways Stalin was blatantly pursuing the old czarist policies in northeast Asia, and the Kuomintang were justifiably alarmed. Furthermore, the Soviet Union gave important aid to the Chinese communists: it gave them tacit and sometimes open support in preventing the landing of Kuomintang troops at certain key ports; it made over to them vast amounts of stockpiled Japanese arms and ammunition, as well as tanks and heavy artillery; and when Soviet troops withdrew in 1946 they took with them much of the industrial plant that the Japanese had built up in the area over the previous 30 years, thus depriving the Kuomintang of an important resource.

The United States had tried to settle some of the antagonisms between the communists and the Kuomintang by sending General George Marshall, former head of the Joint Chiefs of Staff, to China to act as mediator. Marshall did get both sides to agree to a cease-fire in January 1946, and American marines occupied certain areas, though they were ordered not to engage in combat with any Chinese forces, and did not do so. There were countless violations of the cease-fire as communists and the Kuomintang continued to jockey for

position in Manchuria. Open fighting broke out again in April 1946 and continued through the year, and in early 1947 Marshall was recalled and made Secretary of State. His mission had not been a success, and it is impossible to see how it could have been. The tensions and disagreements between the Chinese Communist Party and the Kuomintang were not the kind that could be settled by an outside mediator.

As the civil war gathered momentum through 1947 and into 1948 it became increasingly clear that the Kuomintang had very little control over

the country. It could not check the terrible inflation that had been plaguing China for a decade, it could not properly coordinate the military campaigns against the communists, it could not satisfy the peasants' grievances and it could not placate the dissident intellectuals. Though it was not clear that the communists would be able to solve these problems either, they at least seemed to offer more hope to the exhausted country, and their extraordinary military successes seemed proof enough of their competence.

The principles of guerilla war, as formally enunciated by Mao in 1947 – they had been refined over a 20-year period – both brought him victory and later became a model for insurrectionary or revolutionary struggle in other parts of the world. His theories emphasized that the communist armies were always to attack isolated and weak enemy forces before strong ones, and should take rural areas and small cities before moving to attack major cities. Commanders must never be afraid to abandon a position if the enemy massed superior strength, and they should attack the enemy only with a vastly superior force, six to one if possible. They should replenish arms and ammunition from the enemy's supplies and never let up the pressures. The man who led the communists to military victory in Manchuria on the basis of these principles was Lin Piao. Born in 1907, Lin had had a brilliant military career: he was trained in the Whampoa Academy, and had been made commander of the Communist Fourth Army when he was only 23. He fought brilliantly on the Long March and was both an active general and president of the Red Army Academy (K'ang-ta) during the Yenan period. The Manchurian campaigns were yet one more proof of his out-

Above left: Units of the Chinese People's Liberation Army (PLA) enter Peking in triumph in January 1949.

Left: Communist propaganda poster showing grateful peasants greeting troops of the PLA.

Above right: Mao Tse-tung reviews tanks of the PLA in Peking, January 1949.

Right: Liu Shao-ch'i with students of the Peking Geological Prospecting Institute, 1957.

standing abilities, climaxed when his troops, by this time 800,000 strong, marched into Peking in January 1949.

After the fall of Peking, remaining Kuomintang resistance crumbled, and hundreds of thousands of troops deserted or surrendered to the communists. In April, communist troops crossed the Yangtze; in October they captured Canton. Chiang Kai-shek fled to Taiwan, which had been prepared in advance as a base in case of emergency. On 1 October 1949, at massive celebrations in Peking, Mao Tse-tung declared the inauguration of the People's Republic of China.

The People's Republic of China

The challenges confronting Mao Tse-tung and the Chinese Communist Party were immense. They had to reunite a people split apart by years of savage fighting and ideological warfare; they had to halt inflation and restore the shattered economy; and they had to actualize their promises – easy enough to make in the abstract – that they would introduce socialism to China and transform the living conditions of peasant and proletariat. As Mao said in his July 1949 speech 'On the People's Democratic Dictatorship,' the question was now one of 'working hard and creating conditions for the natural elimination of classes, state authority and political parties, so that mankind will enter the era of universal fraternity.' The task was such that it would be a long time before the pressures on every individual to contribute would be relaxed.

The government of the People's Republic was tripartite, composed of State, Party and Army. As Chairman of the Republic, Mao was official head of state, but his most important decisions were made in his capacity as chairman of the Central Committee of the Communist Party. Government work (as opposed to policy decisions) was mainly directed by Chou En-lai in his role as Premier of the State Council. Liu Shao-ch'i, who held senior governmental and party posts, took over direction of all key affairs when Mao was in Moscow from December 1949 to March 1950, so it is clearly correct to see him as the number two man in China at this time. The Army was, of course, intimately interconnected with the party, and the com-

mander-in-chief of the People's Liberation Army (PLA), Chu Te, as well as the Minister of Defense and the various regional army commanders, were veteran colleagues of Mao, and long-time party members. Certain minority parties were allowed to exist, and representatives were 'elected,' but the slates were always carefully chosen and the principles of democratic centralism were rigidly adhered to.

After widespread violence in the closing months of the civil war, and during the first few months of the People's Republic, when hundreds of thousands of landlords were beaten up or killed by the peasantry, Mao settled on a more cautious program of gradual economic reform and reconstruction. The focus was on industrial development: this required economic and currency reform, unification of tax collection, formation of state trading companies, the setting up of six regional planning boards with annual production targets and negotiations for compulsory purchase (or takeover) of foreign-owned industrial assets

and plants. The communists had several advantages in the field of foreign takeovers that had been denied to the Kuomintang. Extraterritoriality had been ended in 1943, and by 1949 Britain, Germany, France and Japan were in no position to insist on their 'rights,' while the Soviet Union had also retreated from its Yalta demands.

Agricultural policies were more moderate in the newly liberated areas than they had been in 1947 and 1948. All major land holdings were eliminated through a comprehensive land redistribution program, but the principle of individual ownership was maintained, and rich peasants were allowed to keep the land they could till in person. The emphasis at this period was on political mobilization and developing of class awareness through attacking the old authoritarian family structure. Communist cadres were sent in thousands to the countryside to encourage peasants at mass meetings to analyze their own circumstances and to speak out against their landlords or others who had always dominated the communities. In this way the patterns of thought that had held sway for countless generations were broken, and the local power structure vanished beyond recall. We may guess that much of the killing of landlords was instigated by cadres, who thus involved peasantry in the revolution in the most profound manner, committing them totally to the new order.

The intellectuals were bound into the new order in many ways. Some were given Party membership and posts in the bureaucracy, even though this often alientated some of the veteran cadres, who felt that they knew their own localities much better than any outsiders. Others found employment in the arts, now state sponsored, or in communications fields that were state controlled and used for mass education, such as the cinema, the radio and the local press. Universities and research institutes were given government support, and many Kuomintang faculties simply switched to tacit acceptance of communism and continued with their jobs. The educated were also widely needed in managerial positions in industry, since there were still few workers who were able to take over supervisory or planning functions. For intellectuals who showed coolness to the new regime, there was intensive retraining in 'revolutionary universities.' In its most intense form, this became the 'thought reform' or 'brainwashing' that was anathema to

foreign observers. By systematic stages, through mounting pressure in small group situations, the individual was forced to purge himself of his individualism and bourgeois tendencies and to learn to immerse himself in the interests of the collectivity. For some, this was an almost unbearable experience that could lead to breakdown or suicide; for most, as far as we can judge, it was an experience that had to be endured, capped with a confession that was not always sincere.

The pace of change in these early years of the People's Republic would undoubtedly have been faster had it not been for the Korean War. The North Koreans attacked South Korea in June 1950. It does not seem that the Chinese had encouraged or aided in this attack; and though they began to move troops up to north China, they took no action during the first stage of the war, when North Korean troops swept the South Korean and United Nations forces down to Pusan. Nor did they act during the second stage, in September, when MacArthur led the brilliant amphibious landing at Inchon. Only in October, as United Nations troops advanced on the Yalu River, the boundary between China and Korea, were Chinese 'volunteers' sent across the border. Then followed six months of savage fighting in which the Chinese troops, led by P'eng Te-huai, suffered enormous casualties in the face of the allies' firepower. Fighting ended in a stalemate along the

38th parallel, as MacArthur was recalled and the protracted truce negotiations began.

The Korean War had a number of important effects on China. It held up her economic development and disrupted internal planning. It led to a crisis-situation mentality in which China's leaders were able to speed the process of mass mobilization and indoctrination and to encourage programs of denunciation and harassment that were climaxed in 1951 and 1952 by the '3 anti' and '5 anti' campaigns directed against the bureaucracy and the bourgeoisie. It led to an awareness that the large, highly motivated, but poorly armed People's Liberation Army (the 'volunteers') were not going to be able to fight successfully against modern mechanized firepower without major reorganization. It led to a freezing of the diplomatic position between China and the United States and to a refusal on the part of American politicians to consider recognizing China diplomatically or seating her in the United Nations. And it ended China's chance of speedily capturing Taiwan and destroying Chiang's regime once and for all, since the United States had agreed to defend Taiwan and now patrolled the Straits with the Seventh Fleet.

Taiwan thus began that limbo existence that continued for many decades to come. Some two million mainland Chinese – bureaucrats, soldiers, scholars and their families – had fled to Taiwan with Chiang Kai-shek in 1949. The inhabitants of Taiwan – that is the original settlers, who had come from the mainland in the eighteenth and nineteenth centuries, and are usually called Formosans – were forced to accept this inundation. An attempt to assert a measure of Formosan independence in 1947 had been bloodily suppressed by the Kuomintang governor, and the Formosans now had little say in their destiny. Taiwan became the 'bastion' for the Kuomintang, from which, according to its insistent statements, the reconquest of the mainland would one day be launched. In the meantime the nine million Formosans had to be content with a handful of seats in the representative assembly, since most of the seats were held by delegates allegedly representing the provinces of China proper. Despite this

Left: Daily recitations from the thoughts of Chairman Mao.

Below: Members of the Worker-PLA Mao Tse-tung Thought Propaganda Team staying at Tsinghua University.

Right: Chou En-lai at the Geneva Conference in 1954.

Below right: Agricultural Cooperative members at work on a China farm.

curious distortion of democratic principles and other more obtrusive elements of police state control, the Kuomintang government on Taiwan became something of a model as far as economic development was concerned. Chiang was helped in this by various factors: the island was naturally fertile, the Japanese, who had ruled the island between 1895 and 1945, had fostered industrial development and pushed through an extensive land reform program, and the United States, determined that Taiwan should not fall, pumped in vast amounts of economic and technical assistance. There was nothing whatever that the People's Republic, without a majority in the United Nations, and without an effective navy or airforce, could do about the situation.

So after the Korean War the question of Taiwan was left in abeyance, the intransigent hostility of the United States was accepted and reciprocated and China proceeded with her internal development. The years 1953 to 1957 were the period of the First Five Year Plan. Private industry was nationalized, and with the backing of the Soviet Union – which gave low interest loans, exchanged raw materials for manufactured commodities and sent thousands of technical advisers to China – a major attempt was made to develop China's heavy industry. The attempt was successful, and most quota targets were exceeded. Indeed, in some ways it was too successful, since light industry, commerce and the production of consumer goods were all comparatively neglected, so that the economy became top-heavy, and there was a good deal of hardship.

Industrial development was paralleled by developments in agriculture, though here the stress was as much on changing organizational patterns as on increasing production. The peasants were organized into Mutual Aid Teams, of from four to 10 households each, which retained private ownership but pooled resources in the form of draught animals, labor and tools. The emphasis was on voluntarism, and those reluctant to join were usually not forced to. At the same time, the state entered more openly in the rural sector, with the introduction of government-established credit-cooperatives. The general success of the

Mutual Aid Team movement – some 96 percent of China's peasants were estimated as being involved by late 1956 – encouraged the state to move ahead with a new phase of organization, the Agricultural Producers' Cooperative. The members of a cooperative – about 50 families – pooled their land, as well as their tools and animals, and drew a percentage of the cooperative's yield proportional to the amount of land they had contributed. The system thus still benefited the rich peasants most of all. The peasants continued to hold their own land titles and to work their own small plots. High productivity was now the goal – to provide an agricultural surplus that could be applied to the industrial sector – and frugality and self-sufficiency were the watchwords. By 1957 it is estimated that there were 740,000 of these cooperatives in China.

In foreign policy, as in domestic, this was a period of pragmatism and control. Trade with non-communist countries was undertaken, and at Geneva in 1954 Chou En-lai served as the mediator between the French and the Vietminh, after the French had been defeated in Indochina. Diplomatic recognition was extended to Britain even though Britain refused to end all diplomatic relations with Taiwan. At the Bandung Conference of 1955, in Java, China played the role of international arbiter among the Afro-Asian nations (though here China had an important military objective – to keep several key Asian nations out of the United States-backed Southeast Asia Treaty Organization, and in this she was successful). The only major international incident during this period in which China was involved was the 1954-55 'Offshore Islands' crisis, involv-

ing Quemoy and Matsu, in which China's burst of martial ardor was quenched by the angry United States response.

As if to celebrate what seemed to be successes on all fronts, in September 1956 the Eighth Party Congress of the Chinese Communist Party was convened (the previous such meeting had been held in 1945). Mao was confirmed as party chairman, and joining him on the Standing Committee were his old comrades Liu Shao-ch'i, Chou En-lai, Chu Te, Ch'en Yun, and Teng Hsiao-p'ing. The number was soon increased to seven by the addition of Lin Piao. But already certain events had been set in motion which were to convulse this apparently harmonious world. First, in May Mao and other leaders had made the speeches that were to launch the Hundred Flowers Movement. Second, news of cumulative successes in agriculture and industry was encouraging Mao to speed up developments and launch the Great Leap Forward. And finally, in February, at a speech in Moscow, Nikita Khrushchev attacked Stalin's memory, the beginning of what was to become a major Sino-Soviet rift. Each of these events will be considered in turn.

The Hundred Flowers Movement – which drew its name from the Chinese saying that in times of peace a hundred flowers should bloom and a hundred schools of thought contend – was an attempt to get China's intellectuals positively involved in Chinese politics. During the spring and summer they were encouraged to speak out and to give their views on problems of party and government. When few responded, presumably because they suspected that the offer was not truly made in good faith, Mao issued one of the most famous speeches of his career, 'On the Correct Handling of Contradictions Among the People,' in February 1957. Here, elaborating ideas he had suggested in Yenan 20 years before, Mao pointed out that the 600,000,000 people of China were now united as never before. But just because this unity existed it was wrong to think that there were no contradictions. The point was, Mao continued, that there were two quite different kinds of contradictions: those between China and her enemies were antagonistic, but those among the Chinese people were non-antagonistic.

Clearly, Mao hoped that the Chinese intellectuals had now come to appreciate the achievements of the People's Republic and would be able – within the context of acceptable socialist thought – to ease their minds by making constructive criticisms. Mao was also anxious to prevent hostility being bottled up to explosion point, as had just happened in Hungary in the 1956 Revolution. But in fact what ensued was an outpouring of attacks against the party and its regime which dismayed China's leaders. The Chinese party was accused of being a new class, its members were accused of corruption and indolence, Marx was said to be out of date and the influence of the Soviet Union was described as excessive. Other charges were that the vaunted cadres were incompetent, the so-called 'coalition' parties were a farce, politicians used double-talk, universities were doctrinaire and so on. In June the party struck back. Hundreds of the most outspoken critics were forced to recant publicly, and dozens of influential men were removed from their posts in schools and on newspapers. The whole affair must have been a disappointment and a humiliation for Mao. Its long-term effect seems to have been to confirm in him a deep-seated distrust for bourgeois intellectuals.

The Great Leap Forward of 1958 seems to have been a response to success, to the feeling, as Mao put it on a visit to Moscow in 1957, that 'the east wind was prevailing over the west wind.' The basic aim of the Great Leap Forward was to mobilize China's enormous manpower for a concerted assault on the production front, using the human will as a weapon to transcend material limitations. In agriculture, this involved transforming the cooperatives into communes, units in which from 2000 to 4000 families would be merged. The commune was to combine the commercial, the industrial, the agricultural, the military and the educational. Private plots were to be given up, meals were to be cooked and eaten in common, children were to be looked after in special nurseries. Some income would be distributed to all on the basis of need rather than work, speeding China from the world of Socialism into the world of communism. And with all people moving as one, with every rural community building its own blast furnaces to smelt ore, with factories operating as intensively as peasant cultivators, China's production would soar by 50 percent or more.

It was an amazing vision, and for a few heady months in late 1958, when 98 percent of the population had been marshalled into 26,400 communes, it seemed that it was going to be realized. Reports of new production records poured into Peking. Then slowly the vision crumbled. Little of the iron could be used in industry or construction because of its low quality. Men and women chafed at the communal life and protested at endless working hours. The staff of the statistical bureau had been incompetent in handling their data, and much of their data had in fact been false, as local cadres endeavored to please superiors by reporting the desired successes. Even where figures were accurate they had been achieved by using up stocks needed for inventory, or for seed. The retreat from the Great Leap had begun even before the end of 1958. Mao announced that he would step down from his chairmanship of the People's Republic, yielding place to Liu Shao-ch'i. Small private plots were restored to peasant families, and the more extreme aspects of communal living were abandoned. Slowly the communes were broken up again, with an average of 500 families in each. But when Marshal P'eng Te-huai struck out at Mao in the Lushan Plenum of 1959, blaming him for the Leap's failures, and harping on the blunders and the waste, Mao's forces rallied. P'eng Te-huai was dismissed from his posts, to be replaced by Lin Piao as Defense Minister. Yet for the next few years Mao's role in government was by no means clear, even though his 'Thought' was still widely praised and invoked in all mass movements. Many observers have concluded that in the few years after the Great Leap it was Liu Shao-ch'i who coordinated an economically conservative program of retrenchment, while Lin Piao concentrated on military reform. In any case, the Great Leap had failed, leaving in its wake an economic depression and much human misery.

The Sino-Soviet Rift, a dominant element in China's foreign policy between 1960 and 1970, is usually dated from Khrushchev's speech attacking Stalin in 1956. Mao had always made much in

his public pronouncements of his reverence for Stalin, and he may well have thought Khrushchev's remarks were an indirect criticism of his own leadership. Certainly Mao was angered by slighting remarks made by the Soviet press about the communes in the Great Leap. And Khrushchev, pursuing a policy of rapprochement with the United States that led to the 1959 meeting with Eisenhower at Camp David, seems to have been angered by China's aggressive policies on the Indian border, in suppressing the Tibetan revolt and in developing contacts in Latin America and Africa. China, it seemed clear, intended to play a dominant role in global communist politics.

Both sides marshalled their forces for the meeting of 81 communist parties which took place behind closed doors in Moscow during November 1960. The seriousness with which China viewed these meetings can be seen by the fact that she sent Liu Shao-ch'i and Teng Hsiao-p'ing as her delegates. Apparently the Soviet Union carried the day in the debates, for the final communiqué spoke of the chance of ending the probabilities of war in the world, a view which Mao was known to regard as inherently unrevolutionary. Shortly before the meeting, Soviet technicians had been suddenly withdrawn from China, leaving many crucial projects unfinished, apparently in an attempt to bully China into submission. Thereafter, the valuable aid that the USSR had been giving China steadily dried up. China responded by recalling all her students from the Soviet Union, and after the meeting she took a further defiant step, publishing in the Chinese press a speech that the Albanian leader Hoxha had made attacking Khrushchev. The Soviets responded by publishing attacks on China by other East European communist countries. This increasingly violent and roundabout battle of words continued until 1963, when each country began to publicly attack the other by name. The Chinese claimed

that they were the true Marxist-Leninists, while Khrushchev was a bourgeois revisionist, leading his country back down the capitalist road in slavish imitation of the Western capitalist powers. Khrushchev's fall in October 1964 was greeted with delight in Peking, but when his successor, Kosygin, visited the capital he met with a cool reception. Even the mounting pressures generated by the American intervention in the Vietnam War failed to draw the two countries together. The tensions finally erupted in late 1969, when Chinese and Soviet troops clashed in two places on their long mutual frontier, in Sinkiang and on the Amur River. For a time that summer it seemed as if war between the countries might erupt; but

mutual prudence, complemented by another visit to Peking by Kosygin, prevailed, and talks over frontier problems were initiated.

The Cultural Revolution

The Sino-Soviet rift overshadowed domestic events in China during the first five years of the 1960s; during the second half of the decade, the Great Proletarian Cultural Revolution emerged to dominate all else. The roots of this revolution ran deep into the history of the People's Republic and back to disagreements within the party before the conquest. They ran also into the traditional class structure of China, and into military and educational theory.

We have seen that after 1958 Mao had withdrawn from some of his previous active political involvement, and that Liu Shao-ch'i and others had taken over direction of the Chinese economy. But Mao's influence was undoubtedly paramount in foreign relations, for the Sino-Soviet rift seems to have mirrored his own views, and his influence in military circles was assured by the dominating position there of his trusted comrade, Lin Piao. In the wide field of ideological training, too, Mao seems to have kept his accustomed role. The 'Socialist Education Campaign' that flourished between 1962 and 1965 showed many of the same thrusts and mobilization techniques that had been present in the Great Leap. The People's Liberation Army played a major part in these campaigns and conducted similar ones within its own ranks: more and more emphasis was placed on 'placing politics in command' in the army, on purging 'counter-revolutionaries' and on developing a more egalitarian spirit to replace the professionalization and specialization that had been one of the hallmarks of P'eng Te-huai's policy. P'eng had emulated the Soviet Union in this regard, seeking highly trained staff-college officers, backed by modern equipment. Though Lin was not against all military technology – the PLA and affiliated research scientists pushed ahead with work on a Chinese atomic bomb, which was tested in October 1964, and then worked successfully on H-bomb and guided-missile systems – he still looked back to an earlier ideal of guerrilla organization, particularly as the best technique for defense in depth against a foreign aggressor. As part of these same campaigns, Lin abolished all military ranks and insignia from the PLA. By 1965 Mao was increasingly gearing the Socialist Education Campaign to an exposure of the shortcomings of leaders of the party. Then, in November 1965, Mao suddenly withdrew from public gaze, and his whereabouts remained a mystery until

May 1966. We can guess, with hindsight, that he had withdrawn to concentrate his thoughts on what he felt were the major issues of his time and to rally his forces for the attack. The new socialist offensive would not be long in coming.

The Cultural Revolution was officially launched in June 1966, when rallies were held in Peking and Shanghai, and the first 'big character posters' appeared on the walls. In these posters dozens of prominent individuals were attacked for their bourgeois-revisionist tendencies, and readers were exhorted to follow the thought of Mao and learn from the People's Liberation Army. That same month, it was announced that college and school enrollments all over China would be postponed for about six months while 'transformations' were made. In July Mao took a swim in the Yangtze before admiring crowds, apparently to give incontrovertible proof of his health and vigor. The swim was followed by a new upward leap in the eulogies of the cult of Mao, and on 18 August, after the Central Committee had released its summary statement of the objectives of the revolution, Mao, with Lin Piao at his side, reviewed the first of the giant Red Guard rallies in Peking. It was estimated that over a million marched that day, and another million in Shanghai on the 19th.

By the late summer of 1966 so many different things seemed to be going on in China that Western observers found it impossible to make sense of them. It appears now that many disparate elements were in fact given coherence by one common theme: Mao's desire to preserve the spirit of revolution in China. Mao believed that China's economic development was tending increasingly in the direction of the Soviet Union's, with paid incentives to workers and an entrenched managerial bureaucracy that represented a retreat from socialism. Mao thought that the Communist party itself was getting complacent and pettifogging, slowing decisions and destroying initiative

in a sea of red tape. Mao had read articles in the Peking press in which sarcastic gibes were made about his leadership and his grandiose pretensions. That such articles could appear convinced him of two things: that the slick 'bourgeois individuality' intellectuals had still not changed their tune, despite attempts at their reeducation and the proven successes of the People's Republic, and that senior members of the Communist party, particularly those in Peking and the propaganda departments, must be sympathetic to these views, otherwise they would never have been allowed to appear in print. Mao learned, too, that enrollments in China's universities still favored the children from wealthy or bureaucratic backgrounds and that very few students from worker or peasant homes were enrolled at all. To make matters worse, the curriculum and teaching methods were traditionalistic and formal, reflecting none of the dynamism of a developing socialist state. Above all, Mao must have been conscious of the fact that in that particular year, 1966, a complete new generation of students was going to college, students who had been born in the People's Republic and thus had no first-hand knowledge of any kind about what conditions had been like in the old days when Mao and his comrades had fought for survival.

In the light of the broad theme of preserving revolutionary spirit, and from the standpoint of the particular weaknesses sensed by Mao, the events of 1966 seem more – but only a little more – coherent. A number of writers, officials in the propaganda departments and senior members of the Peking party bureaucracy were dismissed, imprisoned or sent into internal exile. The idea that Lin Piao was Mao's 'closest comrade-in-arms' and probable successor was widely spread, and at the same time attacks on unspecified 'monsters' who were 'seeking to take the capitalist road' grew in intensity. Mao's wife Jian Q and his trusted former secretary Ch'en Po-ta were given positions as coordinators of the revolution in the field of literature and the arts, to wipe out all revisionist symptoms and develop new proletarian forms of expression. University administrators and faculty were dismissed in large numbers, and universities and schools stayed closed while new admissions policies and curricula were considered. The Red Guards were given a free hand in attacking any evidence of bourgeois habits that they could find: shortening menus, cutting long hair, forcing taxis off the streets, writing revolutionary wall posters, entering private homes of former capitalists and wrecking their possessions and in some cases damaging rare books and art in libraries and museums. These same Red Guards were encouraged to march through the cities and countryside, spreading the revolutionary message to rural communities and factories.

Peasants formed their own brigades, as did workers, and gradually clashes began to occur, as different groups disagreed about matters of policy or about who was to be attacked. In many areas senior party members and military officers seem to have rallied their own supporters and attacked Red Guard units. A battle over nomenclature began: Red Guards were succeeded by 'revolutionary rebels' and by 'Red revolutionary rebels,' so that it was hard to tell who stood for what. Revolutionary committees were set up in many major factories in Shanghai and elsewhere, with the goal of introducing total workers' control of the means of production. This was designed to hasten the move into a communist society, as the communes in 1958 had also been designed to do. But there were fights among these workers' groups as well, and by the spring of 1967 an attempt was made to

Above left: Chinese and Soviet frontier guards confront each other on Chenpao Island, 1969.

Left: Political propaganda is conducted among Shanghai workers.

Right: Mao Tse-tung taking part in his famous nine-mile swim along the Yangtze River in 1966.

still fell far short of the country's needs. Consumer goods were scarce and of poor quality. There was much underemployment and considerable unemployment. And of course Chinese industry, cut off as it was from world trade, was almost wholly innocent of the technological revolution that was beginning to sweep the West and Japan.

In the middle of all this confusion and drift there occurred, almost, it seemed, fortuitously, a chain of international developments that were to be of immense importance to China. American attitudes toward China had softened steadily – if not deeply – since the mid 1950s, and in 1971 the United States at last withdrew its objection to the admission of the People's Republic to the United Nations. At the same time, the Americans began making overtures about the relaxation of trade and travel restrictions between the two countries. Chou En-lai, who had become premier in the middle of the Cultural Revolution, responded by inviting a US table tennis team to visit Peking in April, a small gesture whose symbolic implications were lost on none. Three months later the world was astonished to learn that Henry Kissinger, President Nixon's national security adviser, had secretly visited Peking and had made arrangements for the American president to visit China. This historic visit took place in February 1972. Nixon met Chou extensively and Mao briefly, and in the communiqué issued at the visit's end the two nations promised to work toward improved relations. Ostensibly they still differed over Vietnam (though the Americans noted that it was now their intention to withdraw from direct participation in the war), but in fact Chinese ardor for the North Vietnamese cause was already cooling, as it became ever more apparent that North Vietnam had to be regarded as a Soviet, and not a Chinese, client. Although the Americans did not announce any major shift in their policy toward Taiwan, their insistence that they could not see any reason why the Taiwan issue should pose an insuperable barrier to improved relations between the US and PRC was taken as a hint that American policy was no longer carved in granite. Nevertheless, the Chinese still held to the official position that full diplomatic relations could never be restored until the US withdrew its recognition of the Nationalist government. In fact, however, by 1973 both

restore order by announcing a new '3 in 1' combination of People's Liberation Army, Revolutionary Masses and Cadres, as the organizational ideal. This effectively ended the random attacks by students against party members just because they happened to wield authority and ushered in a more serious and concentrated stage of party purge. Liu Shao-ch'i was made the central scapegoat, and his confession (real or fabricated) was released to the people. In the summer of 1967 there was some heavy fighting around Wuhan and Canton as, we may surmise, local power groups and regional commands resisted the orders of the central government. Thereafter, tensions seem gradually to have relaxed, as the attempt was made to consolidate whatever had been achieved in industrial organization, educational radicalization and ideological purification. By the beginning of the 1970s the Great Cultural Revolution had largely spent its force. To what extent it achieved its objectives is difficult to say, for we still do not understand what all those objectives really were. But one thing seems clear from what followed: that the Great Cultural Revolution did to the political life of China what the Great Leap Forward did to its economy.

The end of the Mao era and the rise of Teng

The violence and apparent irrationality of the Great Cultural Revolution inflicted great damage on China's political system, and recovery in the early 1970s was partial at best. Strange things still continued to happen. Defense Minister Lin Biao, Mao's old and admired comrade, was killed in a plane crash in 1971, and, incredibly, it was announced he had died while attempting to flee to the Soviet Union after an abortive attempt to kill Mao and establish a military dictatorship. By 1973 Lin was routinely being vilified in govern-

ment propaganda, along with such apparently unconnected targets as cultural exchanges with the West and Confucianism.

The economy remained comparatively stagnant. The retreat from the grandiose objectives of the Great Leap Forward continued, with the emphasis again turning to the creation of small local industries and a more modest scale of agricultural self-sufficiency. Yet despite the retrenchment, the economy's control mechanisms remained ponderously centralized, bureaucratic and inefficient. Although agricultural production went up in absolute terms during these years, it

nations had established in each other's capitals 'liaison offices' that performed the essential functions of embassies.

What sort of advantages the Chinese would be willing or able to reap from this new rapprochement with the United States depended heavily on how well they emerged from the domestic political chaos created by the Cultural Revolution. Chou, who obviously represented the greatest hope for reform, was in his mid-seventies, ailing and still far from being in complete political control. In an effort to ensure the future of his policies he had rescued the like-minded Teng Hsiao-p'ing from the obscurity into which he had been cast during the Cultural Revolution and appointed him deputy premier – in effect Chou's political heir. But when Chou died on 8 January 1976 Teng

was immediately purged by Mao – or at any rate, by conservatives acting in Mao's name – and Hua Guofeng, the former Minister of Public Security and an apparent compromise between the conservative and reformist factions, was named the new premier.

Mao himself died later that year, on 10 September, apparently a victim of Parkinson's disease. Almost at once Hua launched a virulent campaign against his widow, Jian Q, and her 'radical' (ie ultra-conservative) colleagues, who soon entered Chinese political iconography as the notorious 'Gang of Four.' But having secured one political flank, Hua was not prepared to give way on the other. He still professed adherence to all the basic Maoist principles and was unwilling to adopt any but the most cosmetic reforms. Apparently under

pressure from disgruntled would-be reformers he did, however, rehabilitate Teng Hsiao-p'ing in 1977 and reinstated him as deputy premier.

Whatever Hua's motives in appointing Teng, it proved to be a decision of great consequence. In early 1978 Hua announced an ambitious 10-year economic program of 'four modernizations,' a kind of neo-Great Leap that was ill-thought-out and that quickly foundered, hastening the erosion of Hua's authority. Teng, meanwhile, had been talking ever more openly and insistently about the need to forsake outworn ideological dogmas and to deal with problems in a more flexible and pragmatic way. By the end of the year his position was such that he could tell the Central Committee that the time had come for making fundamental changes in Chinese policy. It was clear that it was now Teng who was *primus inter pares* and that Hua's days as titular head of the regime were numbered.

At the same time Sino-American relations continued to warm slowly but steadily. The American withdrawal from Vietnam had certainly helped, and so, in a roundabout way, had China's deteriorating relations with the victorious Hanoi regime. By early 1978 China was complaining bitterly about Vietnam's persecution of its ethnic Chinese population and about growing Vietnamese military incursions into Cambodia. In May the rupture became complete, with China cutting off all aid to Hanoi, branding Vietnam's intervention in Cambodia 'aggression' and overtly giving assistance to the anti-Vietnamese Pol Pot faction in Cambodia. Tensions mounted, with border clashes developing along the Sino-Vietnamese border. In August China signaled its displeasure with the behavior of what it conceived to be the Moscow-Hanoi axis by signing a treaty of peace and friendship with Japan, a treaty that the Brezhnev foreign ministry, not famous for its subtlety, loudly denounced as 'anti-Soviet.' In Washington the Carter administration, over Congressional objection, moved to abrogate the Taiwan Defense Treaty. This was not the withdrawal of recognition on which China had formerly insisted, but it was enough for the pragmatic Teng, and on 1

Above left: An American ping-pong player in Shanghai.

Left: A Chinese hero worker and farm leader – examples to the masses.

Above: Mao's widow, Jian Q, attempted to further the revolution with the 'Gang of Four' but was defeated by more moderate elements.

Right: A Chinese textile factory which today competes on the international market with Korea and Japan.

Left: Young girls study caricatures of the misdeeds of President Liu Shao-ch'i.

Below: Ieng Say, Deputy Premier of the ousted Pol Pot regime that all but destroyed Cambodia in the late 1970s.

Above right: An anti-American demonstration in Shanghai during the Vietnam War.

Right: A car factory in China, a sign of China's rapid industrialization following the communist revolution.

January 1979 the resumption of formal diplomatic relations between US and China was announced. In March, when the new embassies opened, Teng visited the United States. Though still formally only deputy premier, Teng came, and was treated, as head of state. After his return, in response to an escalation of the war in Cambodia, China briefly invaded Vietnam. Though China was still far from having joined the Western alliance, no one could doubt that between 1972 and 1979 a revolutionary shift in great power relations had occurred.

Teng's ascendancy in Chinese domestic politics was made manifest at the National People's Congress in September 1980, when his protégé, the economic planner Zhao Ziyang, replaced Hua as premier. The next year, at a meeting of the Central Committee in June, Hua was shorn of his Party chairmanship and was replaced by another Teng partisan, Hu Yaobang. The Central Committee also took the occasion to make Teng chairman of its powerful Central Military Commission, thus asserting an extension of civilian control over the conservative military, as well as holding Mao officially responsible for the 'grave blunder' of fostering the Cultural Revolution. Most Western analysts date the final consolidation of Teng's

power from the Twelfth Party Congress in 1982, which elected 60 percent new membership for the 348-man Central Committee and saw seven new members take their places on the 22-man Politburo.

The reforms made possible by these political victories were impressive by any standards, and revolutionary by China's. In the realm of ideology, though the reformers still professed to adhere to the 'four basic principles' of Marxism-Leninism-Maoism, of the socialist road, of the dictatorship of the proletariat and of the leadership of the party, all but the last became attenuated. Mao was criticized for his cult of personality and his 'feudal' rule, and references to the need for class struggle and for the export of the revolution became rare. There was much talk of rejecting 'outworn dogmas,' and the slogan 'practice is the sole criterion of truth' was widely advanced. Nationalism, pragmatism and the desire for building a better life now became the primary touchstones in the reformers' appeals for popular support.

Teng and his colleagues knew that substantive reforms would be impossible unless the top-heavy administrative machinery of the state was overhauled and infused with new blood. In 1982

the number of state ministries, commissions and agencies was reduced from 98 to 52, with more cuts to follow. Strenuous efforts were made to streamline the bureaucracy, with special emphasis placed on rooting out the officials who were most entrenched and most likely to be resistant to change. By the end of 1986 over a million senior cadres who had been recruited before 1949 had been retired or dismissed, the average age of central ministers had been reduced by almost 10 years and that of the Central Committee by 14.

Agricultural enterprise

Agriculture was one of the reformers' earliest targets. As early as 1978-79 prices for many agricultural products had been raised and the government had begun to experiment with various forms of contractual arrangements made with individual households – in effect initiating a process of decollectivization. At the same time Mao's cherished communes were all but abolished. The effects were startling. In the early 1980s the productivity of agricultural labor increased 400 percent. The overall agricultural output rose at an annual rate of eight percent through 1987, six times the contemporary rate for Eastern Europe, and the growth rate of per capita farm income was nearly 14 percent. Targets for the Seventh Five-Year Plan, begun in 1986, were more modest, projecting an average growth rate of overall farm product of four percent through 1990, but even this – and it may have been too conservative an estimate – would be spectacular in comparison to what happened in the pre-reform years or, indeed, to what was likely to happen in rural economies in most of the rest of the world.

Reform of the industrial and commercial sectors began later – essentially in 1984 – and for the first few years, at least, the effects were less impressive. The thrust of the reforms, as in Mikhail Gorbachev's *perestroika*, was a relaxation of central control (in 1984 alone the number of major industrial products subject to mandatory centralized planning was cut in half), an increase of decision-making in individual industrial enterprises and the development of what was called 'market socialism.' As in the Soviet Union, however, the associated problem of how far price controls should be relaxed was the subject of much debate. During the period of the Sixth Five-Year Plan, 1981-85, the average annual growth of industrial

production was 12 percent, somewhat better than before, but still not yet indicative of success.

What was a major success, and one of the most radical aspects of the economic reform package, was the growth of foreign trade. By the end of the 1970s the reformers had completely abandoned Mao's ideas of Chinese autarky, had proclaimed an 'open door' to world trade and were even beginning to encourage foreign loans and investment in Chinese enterprises. By the end of 1987 the volume of foreign trade had quintupled over what it had been in 1979, and hard currency earnings were greater than those of all the Warsaw Pact nations, including the USSR, combined. A by-product of this extraordinary development was an accelerated introduction of Western industrial technology, something that boded well for the still-lagging growth of Chinese industry.

The social effects of the Teng reforms were extensive but difficult to quantify. Party control, though more relaxed, remained firm, with press censorship still in place. But certainly a new kind of pluralism was burgeoning in Chinese society. More foreign consumer goods, including foreign books and magazines, were available, discussion was more open and free than at any time since 1949, more temples and churches were being visited. The status of intellectuals was certainly higher than it had been in recent memory, and during the first half of the 1980s at least 30,000 scholars and students were sent abroad for foreign study. There was a greater sense, too, of social justice, for a reform and standardization of the legal system was one of the regime's priorities – a much needed reform.

Perhaps it was inevitable that the rising expectations of Chinese society should at some point put unwelcome pressure on the party. Early in 1987 Chinese students began demonstrating for a wider extension of democracy. The demonstrations were quickly put down, but party conservatives were alarmed and mounted a challenge to the Teng faction that for a time looked as though it might be serious, forcing the resignation of Hu Yaobang as party head. But the Teng forces rallied, and by the time of the Thirteenth Party Congress in November they seemed not only to have regained control but to have won something of a triumph. The Congress overwhelmingly endorsed continuance of Teng's reform policies. Zhao was named general secretary of the party, and another young Teng protégé, Li Peng, was made acting premier. Virtually all the remaining party leaders who had played important roles in the founding of the PRC in 1949 – men such as President Li Xiannian and Army Chief of Staff Yang Dezhi – were obliged to retire from the Central Committee. The octogenarian Teng himself retired from all posts save the crucial chairmanship of the Central Military Commission, but that he would remain the source of authority and the guiding influence in the astonishing new China he had created was undoubted.

Japan

The Allied victory in the Pacific shattered the Japanese vision of an Asian bloc under Japanese leadership, but it certainly did not result in a return to pre-1941 conditions. By 1945 the pieces of the prewar East Asian world had been altered beyond recognition. To begin with, the three prime colonial powers, Britain, Holland and France, had been so weakened that their possessions and influence in East Asia were rapidly ebbing away. The collapse of the Japanese empire left the entire belt of colonies from the Philippines through Indonesia, Indo-China, Malaya and Burma ripe for independence and resistant to the return of Western suzerainty. China was in a state of utter disarray, with political leadership contested between Nationalist and Communist Party forces. Manchuria was occupied by Russian troops, Taiwan was occupied by American forces and Korea was divided between Russian and US occupation teams. Thus the rise and fall of the Japanese empire in the half-century between 1895 and 1945 had served powerfully to disrupt conditions within East Asia.

It is one of the ironies of the post-World War II settlement that the major negotiating powers, particularly the United States, only dimly anticipated the changed circumstances which would obtain after the collapse of the Japanese military effort. The Cairo Conference had talked vaguely of the self-determination of the colonial peoples of Asia, and the Yalta and Potsdam agreements had been concerned to a large extent with securing Soviet support for the war against Japan. From the American point of view it was assumed that the postwar situation would resolve itself into a Southeast Asia emerging peacefully into an assembly of free nations, a strong China – including Manchuria – under Nationalist leadership, a Russian presence confined primarily to Siberia and a demilitarized and democratized Japan under American tutelage. By the time fighting had stopped in East Asia it was clear that not one of these expectations was to be realized. Holland and France were soon at war trying to recover their prewar status in Indonesia and Indo-China. Chiang Kai-shek was proving no match to Mao Tse-tung for the control of China, and North Korea and Manchuria remained under heavy Soviet influence. If in Southeast Asia the struggle for the demolition of the prewar colonial empires had entered a phase of actual warfare, in the north lines of tension between Soviet and United States zones of influence were drawn on a Cold War basis. It was in the middle of this unstable postwar order that Japan underwent its first experience of military occupation and recovery from military defeat.

Japan in the summer of 1945 was a physically devastated and morally exhausted nation. Since the beginning of the China Incident the country had counted over three million dead, a quarter of these civilians. Its major cities had been consumed in flames as a result of great incendiary raids, and Hiroshima and Nagasaki had experienced what no other cities had known before, the terror of the atomic bomb. Throughout the country there were acute food shortages, and an estimated 30 percent of the people had lost their homes. Industry had been reduced to one-quarter of its former potential, and transportation was at a near standstill. The collapse of the wartime myths of Japan's invulnerability had left the Japanese intellectually bewildered. Yet out of this devastation the Japanese made a remarkably speedy and complete recovery, and for this both the resiliency of the Japanese people and the nature of the postwar military occupation are to be credited.

The Allied Occupation of Japan was a remarkable chapter in world history, for it is hard to think of a parallel example in which a nation's institutions were so consciously restructured as a result of defeat in war. Between the determination of the Allied powers to root out what they believed to be the causes of militarism and the willingness of the Japanese to accept the values of their occupiers, a remarkable period of social and political reform was brought into being.

Two factors assisted the Japanese in their achievement of postwar recovery. First, the occupying forces had made the decision to leave the basic structure of government intact, including retention of the emperor, so that something of a basis of social and political discipline remained. Second, the Japanese appear to have avoided the worst psychological effects of defeat by passing the guilt of war off upon their former military leaders. As a pragmatically inclined people, they accepted the victory of the Allied powers as a demonstration of the superiority of the democratic system of government and social values. And so it was with considerable enthusiasm, at least in the early years of the occupation, that the Japanese apprenticed themselves to the process of democratization. While in theory the occupation of Japan was an Allied responsibility, in practice it was almost completely an American affair. As such it was strongly influenced by the personality of General Douglas MacArthur, who as Supreme Commander for the Allied Powers (SCAP) accepted very little outside interference. It is all the more remarkable that MacArthur, himself a deep Conservative, should have looked upon the occupation as an opportunity to democratize Japan in the most idealized terms.

The first actions of the occupation were directed toward the demilitarization of the country. The former Japanese empire had been cut back to its four main islands, with the loss of Manchuria, Korea, Taiwan, Sakhalin and the Kuriles. Okinawa and the Bonin Islands were placed under US trusteeship. Demilitarization called for the destruction of Japan's remaining armed forces, abolition of the Ministries of Army and Navy, of all war industries and of air transportation. A war crimes trial convened in Tokyo publicly prosecuted 25 wartime leaders, ultimately imposing the death sentence on seven, includ-

Left: US soldiers, part of the Army of the Occupation, sightseeing in the Imperial Palace, October 1945.

Above right: Japanese civilians queue for rations in Tokyo in the autumn of 1945.

Right: Life in Nagasaki amidst the devastation following the dropping of the US atomic bomb on 9 August 1945.

Far right: Emperor Hirohito greets his loyal subjects who bow before the divine presence.

ing former Premier Tojo, for 'conspiracy to wage war.' Throughout Japanese government, education and business some 180,000 individuals were 'purged' for having been associated with the war effort.

But the major weight of the Occupation policy was placed upon institutional reforms which would root out the basis for militarism and lay the foundations of a democratic society in Japan. With this in mind an early move was taken to sever the relationship between Shinto shrine worship and the state. Government support was withdrawn from the shrines, the official 'Morals' courses were struck from school curricula and the emperor himself was obliged to make a radio statement denying his divinity.

Constitutional reform

The linchpin of Occupation reform was a new constitution, designed by SCAP, that altered fundamentally the philosophy and structure of the Japanese state, creating a representative form of government in which sovereignty was placed in the popular will. The new document began with the words 'We, the Japanese people' and went on to define the status of the emperor as 'symbol of the state and of the unity of the people, deriving his position from the will of the people with whom reside sovereign power.' In the new government the Cabinet was made responsible to the electorate on the British model. Both houses of the Diet were made elective. The former peerage having been completely abolished, the upper house was renamed the House of Councillors. What was considered excessive government centralization under the old system was relaxed by the creation of an independent judiciary and a decentralized policy system and by making high prefectural government office, including that of governor, elective. A Bill of Rights guaranteed human rights, and Article 9 contained a provision that disavowed the resort to warfare except for Japan's self-defense.

Along with political reform the Occupation stressed ideological and educational change. Although the Ministry of Education was not abolished, an effort was made to decentralize the educational system and to diminish the authoritarian atmosphere of the classrooms. Textbooks

were rewritten, especially in the fields of history and social studies, and 'Morals' instruction was eradicated. In the realm of higher education the monopolistic hold of the four great Imperial Universities was broken by the creation of state supported prefectural universities. Various steps were also taken to assure freedom of speech.

On the assumption that wartime big business interests had contributed to Japan's expansionist drive and had inhibited the free development of the Japanese economy, a strenuous effort was made to break up the great *zaibatsu* combines and to decentralize the economy, and labor unions were encouraged to grow as a counterbalance to the power of industrial management. In the countryside the Occupation carried out one of its most important reforms, a massive attack upon the problems of tenancy and absentee land ownership. All absentee owners were obliged to sell off paddy land holdings beyond 2.5 acres. (Cultivator owners were permitted to retain up to 7.5 acres.) The collection of rents in kind was virtually stopped, and tenants received legally designed tenancy agreements. As a result of these reforms some five million acres of farm land

changed hands and owner-cultivated land rose from 53 percent to 87 percent of the cultivated area. Such economic measures undoubtedly contributed a great deal to the general postwar economic recovery of the country, and in particular to the political and social stability of the village communities in Japan.

A remarkable aspect of the Allied Occupation of Japan was the facility with which so many fundamental reforms were accepted. Japanese desire for an honorable recovery combined with American idealism to produce a momentary unity of purpose that transformed many aspects of Japanese life. Thus the occupation years constitute a major historic watershed for Japan, ranking next to the period of the Meiji Restoration as a time of fundamental change in institutions and values. For many observers these years appeared to bring about Japan's final break with those feudal and Confucian values which remained as legacies of the Tokugawa old regime. Again, as in the early years of Meiji, the foreign factor bulked large in pressuring Japan toward change. Yet it is difficult to separate the internal and external factors. How much of the change was due to Occupation initia-

tive, and how much had already been anticipated by the demands and inclinations of the Japanese people? The Occupation was, of course, more than a mere catalyst, but it was not the only force that pressed for change in postwar Japan. Wartime suffering, defeat and disillusion combined with foreign occupation to push Japan through a second major transition in the course of its modernization, completing, as it were, the process of change toward a mass participation, mass consumption society which had begun in the years after 1853.

Although the Allied Occupation was in effect until 1952, the punitive features of the foreign presence in Japan lasted only through 1947. Thereafter, for a variety of reasons, the emphasis began to shift to rehabilitation and recovery. The big factor in American policy was the changing nature of international politics in East Asia. As the dream of a secure and friendly China vanished, and as 'Cold War' tensions with Soviet Russia were transferred to Asia, Japan, the former enemy, gradually appeared as a potential American ally. By 1948 American strategic interests in Japan began to outweigh the earlier concern over demilitarization, and the goal of creating an economically healthy and politically stable Japan now guided Occupation policy. The outbreak of the Korean War in 1950 suddenly converted Japan into an indispensable base for military operations and even a source of military material. Japan's economic recovery now seemed a necessity, and earlier economic and fiscal restrictions were relaxed. A 'National Police Reserve' was permitted in Japan in 1950, which by 1960 had become a 200,000 man 'National Defense Force' modestly provided with tanks, airplanes and naval units. Within the letter of the provision of Article 9, Japan was being encouraged to participate in its own defense. With the signing of the San Francisco Peace Treaty in 1951, normal international relations were established between Japan and all major nations except Soviet Russia and Communist China. Diplomatic ties were resumed with Russia in 1956, the same year that Japan was admitted to the United Nations. Thus by 1963 Japan had essentially recovered its status as a sovereign state. A treaty of mutual defense

and an administrative agreement with the United States provided for the continued presence of American military bases in Japan and a continued trusteeship over Okinawa. While Japan thus remained under an American protective military umbrella, the country had essentially recovered its freedom of action and its independent status in the world. It was from this point that the phenomenon of Japan's economic growth was to lead to what has been termed the 'Japanese Miracle.'

Japan's return to the rank of great power

Economists generally take the year 1954 as marking the start of Japan's economic growth beyond what represented a postwar recovery level. Between that date and 1967 Japan's gross national product (GNP) grew at an average of 10.1 percent, the fastest of any of the major world powers, and almost three times the American growth rate. By 1968 Japan's GNP had reached $133 billion and taken third place among the world's industrial powers, still only about one-sixth of the American figure, but ahead of the United Kingdom ($120 billion), West Germany ($132 billion) and France ($118 billion). Already in 1950 Japan had passed the UK for first place in shipbuilding. By 1967 Japan produced some 7.5 million tons of shipping, 47.5 percent of the world's total production. At the same time Japan could also claim the world's highest production of motor bicycles, cameras, radios and even pianos. Japanese production of automobiles passed that of West Germany in 1968, and in a variety of other important fields such as iron, steel, cement rubber, chemicals and synthetics Japan has moved into a place just behind the United States and the Soviet Union.

Japan's recovery from destructive military defeat appears all the more remarkable when we recall the presumed limitations in space and resources of the Japanese homeland which had urged the Japanese to military expansion before World War II. Japan's population passed the 100 million mark in 1967 making it three times as populous as it had been 100 years earlier. And this population was supported by an income level that tripled between 1953 and 1967. Japanese homes were by then better supplied with durables such

as television sets, refrigerators and washing machines than their European counterparts. Public services such as water, sewage, electricity, roads and public transportation had also improved tremendously.

How did the Japanese manage this remarkable feat? First, the Japanese themselves remained a highly achieving, energetic and disciplined people dissatisfied with the thought of being second. To this must be added a number of favorable features of the postwar political scene and world economy and technology. Freed of the necessity of maintaining a military establishment, Japan was able to devote nearly all of its energies and economic surplus to the improvement of its civilian economy. Moreover, because of wartime destruction, Japan's factories were obliged to start afresh with new equipment and often imported technologies, and thus its industries were able to take advantage of the latest in technological innovation. There had been, as a result of worldwide technological changes, a near revolution in industrial materials and sources of energy. While prewar Japan felt dependent on nearby sources of coal and natural rubber, the new Japanese economy rested on vast imports of oil and on synthetic products. At home, new powerful earth-moving equipment made it possible literally to ignore prewar topographical limitations on housing and road building. Railroads and super highways were pushed through terrain in ways that were unimaginable in the past, and new building styles and materials made possible the safe erection of highrise apartments in earthquake-prone locations. Whole mountains were leveled to make room for industrial suburbs or to fill in coastal shallows to provide industrial building lots. In postwar Japan the narrowness of the land seemed almost less of a handicap than an asset, facilitating quick communication and tending to concentrate human resources for most rational use.

In contrast to Japan's positive economic recovery after the war, domestic politics and international policies tended to drift. By the end of the Occupation Japan had been given a political organization that undoubtedly looked as much like a working democracy as any in Asia. Already something of a stable balance had been created

Conservative pluralism

Yet disillusionment with the lack of democratic procedure in a government dominated by conservative leaders was only partially justified, since a considerable pluralism existed as a result of factionalism in both the Liberal-Democratic party organization and in the government bureaucracy. Thus despite the establishment-dominated government bureaucracy and establishment-orientated dominant party, Japanese domestic policies were reasonably receptive to opposition demands and continued to provide services and welfare security for the people as a whole.

Foreign policy remained as a major point of controversy and uncertainty. Having been under the American military umbrella since 1952, and in addition having an economy highly dependent upon continued integration with that of America and Europe, Japan necessarily followed a policy of close accommodation to American leadership. Yet Japan existed in a world environment considerably different from that of the United States. Caught between America on the one side and the unpredictable Communist China on the other, desirous of expanding its trade with the Soviet Union, deeply dependent upon raw materials from the Middle East and eager for bigger markets in the Third World, Japan's leaders were under some pressure to assert an international political influence commensurate with the nation's economic status. The question of national security thus became an issue, for if Japan were to step out from behind the American protective shield, some new guarantee of security had to be found. The Socialists argued for security through defenselessness, relying on the goodwill of America, Russia and China not to disturb Japan. Others advocated an armed neutrality, which implied the creation of a sufficient armed force, backed up by a domestically developed nuclear capability, to give Japan freedom of action. Yet the vehement opposition of the Japanese people to making a change in the anti-war clause in their constitution presented a powerful roadblock to military build-

between two major parties, the Liberal-Democrats and Socialists, and the elective process had become a major means of distributing political influence, some 75 percent of the national electorate voting for candidates on a multiple-choice basis. Yet the actual balance was illusory, and neither the Japanese nor the former occupiers fully acknowledged the true nature of Japanese politics. Between the expectation of an ideally functioning democracy and the actual practice of Japan's domestic politics a considerable discrepancy was inevitable. The conservative Liberal-Democratic Party, after briefly being voted out of power from June 1947 to March 1948 by the

Socialist Party, has remained the dominant force in Japanese politics ever since. In 1987, for example, the Liberal-Democrats held over 300 seats in the House of Representatives, while the Socialists held less than 90. The Socialists, relying almost wholly on labor support, had by 1960 lost the possibility of serving as a counterweight to the Liberal-Democratic leadership. Thus the opposition, reduced to what was aptly called a 'one and a half party' situation, found itself sometimes obliged to resort to obstructionist tactics – as in the case of the 1960 dispute over reversal of the Mutual Defense Treaty with the US – as a means to combat the 'tyranny of the majority.'

Above left: After the war Japan was demilitarized, and on the Kwanto Plain US engineers destroy Japanese weapons.

Above: New Japanese technology includes these high speed trains linking the major cities of the country.

Right: The vast Osaka shipyard whose production capacity offers a serious challenge to the shipbuilding operations of the West.

largest single export market, the United States, there was until the latter half of the 1980s a very favorable exchange ratio between the dollar and the yen.

The reaction to Japan's success

The Japanese strategy worked so well, indeed, that by the early 1980s it had begun to generate counteractions: in the Third World emulation, and in the developed world a growing sentiment for protectionism. Rapidly industrializing Third World nations such as South Korea and Taiwan (and potentially China) realized that they could apply the same techniques of industrial organization and automation that the Japanese had used, while at the same time enjoying a decisive (though perhaps temporary) advantage in labor costs. Partly in response to this growing competitive pressure the Japanese felt obliged to reorient their industrial development ever more firmly in the direction of high technology. As early as 1980 Japanese planning groups in and outside the Ministry of International Trade and Industry had targeted seven hi-tech areas for priority development: semiconductors, robots, computers, office automation, telecommunications, pharmaceuticals and biotechnology. In these areas the Japanese proposed not only to stay far ahead of their Third World competitors but to get a jump on the West as well.

But the West, and particularly the United States, was becoming increasingly restive about what it was beginning to see as the 'mercantilist' and 'adversarial' aspects of the Japanese export boom. In addition to unhappiness about the damage that Japanese competition was doing to local industries, there was a rising chorus of complaint about Japan's import policies. Though the Japanese did not go so far as to use tariffs to close their domestic markets to foreign competition, a thicket of internal regulations, as well as various policies such as muting consumer demand by encouraging savings, had something of the same effect. In the mid 1980s, sensing that protectionist sentiment was rising dangerously in the West, some Japanese companies began to 'go multinational,' setting up plants in the United States and elsewhere that employed local labor and therefore, it was hoped, would be relatively immune to protectionist legislation.

Although the warm personal friendship between President Reagan and Prime Minister Yasuhiro Nakasone (term in office: 1982-87) did

up, and progress in enlarging the armed forces was negligible. Ironically, by the mid 1980s there was more sentiment for Japanese rearmament in economically stressed America than there was in Japan. Thus it was with considerable reluctance that the Japanese government in 1982 yielded to US pressure and agreed to allocate a modest one percent of GNP to defense by 1987.

The development of the Japanese economy in the 15 years between 1955 and 1970 was, in a sense, only a prelude to what happened in the next 15 years. US Secretary of State John Foster Dulles had assured a Congressional committee in 1954 that Japan lacked the skills to create products that would find much of an export market in the United States. In 1970 that observation would have sounded silly, and in 1985 it would have sounded bizarre. By 1987 40 percent of all Japanese exports were going to the United States. A third of the massive $167 billion US trade deficit was with Japan, and the value of US imports from Japan was three times greater than that of US exports to Japan. Japan had become the world's largest net creditor nation in 1985, and by 1987 its

overall trade surplus amounted to a staggering $101 billion. Between 1970 and 1987 Japan's GNP climbed to about half that of the US (this for a nation about the size of the state of Montana), and in per capita terms, its GNP actually surpassed that of the United States ($17,000 v $16,000).

How did this phenomenal boom in the Japanese export economy come about? In its early phases it was the result of a carefully articulated strategy arrived at by political and business leaders who aimed at exploiting to the maximum Japan's special position of having the low labor costs of a developing nation and the high labor productivity of an advanced nation. But since the cheap labor part of this equation could not be counted on to last as Japanese living standards rose (even though it could be protracted by massive applications of factory automation), it was apparent to the planners that if Japan were to maintain her competitive edge there would have to be a steady shift from low prices to high quality. In practice this program worked exceptionally well, aided by the fact that, with respect to Japan's

Left: Japan's postwar commercial success as a trading nation was very dependent on her merchant marine.

Below left: Japanese workers assemble lens elements at the Canon Camera factory, Tokyo.

Right: The building boom in Tokyo led to the erection of giant skyscrapers on the American model.

Below right: Early Japanese industrial success was based upon engineering plants such as this one producing motor-bikes for export – one of the great Japanese success stories.

something to ameliorate the growing friction between Japan and its major trading partner, by the time Nakasone's successor, Noboru Takeshita, made his initial visit to the United States in early 1988 there was no dearth of talk in both countries about a possible coming crisis in US-Japanese relations. Yet most observers felt that such fears were exaggerated. There was no doubt that if Japan wished to continue to enjoy the benefits of trading in open world markets she would have to make some important structural changes in her domestic economy and probably her society. By the same token the US would also have to show more wisdom and discipline in addressing economic problems such as budget and trade deficits that were only incidentally of Japan's making. But the economies of the two countries were so closely and complexly interlinked, their foreign and security policies so generally compatible and the reservoir of goodwill between their governments and people still so full that any serious rupture in their remarkable postwar partnership did not seem imminent – or, at least, not in the immediate foreseeable future.

Africa

World War II initiated a chain of events that culminated in the disintegration of the European empires in Africa as well as in Asia. During the war itself, North Africa became the scene of major military operations. British and Commonwealth forces ousted the Italians from Ethiopia and fought a series of campaigns against Italian and German forces in Egypt and Libya; and American and Allied troops eventually swept the Vichy French as well as the Germans and the Italians out of all of North Africa. South of the Sahara, after the Germans had conquered France and Belgium, the Vichy government held French West Africa for some years, but Gaullists quickly prevailed in French Equatorial Africa, while the Belgian Congo was never controlled by the Axis powers. These military and political events constituted sharp breaks in the continuity of the colonial regimes.

Moreover, the French and the British recruited several hundred thousand African subjects into their armed forces. Many black Africans served in Europe and Asia, as well as North Africa, and for many the psychological foundation of the colonial system – the myth of European superiority – was destroyed. In addition, with shipping at a premium African territories were obliged to become more self-supporting than during the previous

decades, and after the Japanese overran Southeast Asia Europe became more dependent than previously on African products such as rubber. Also, during the stresses of war the colonial powers made more substantial concessions to their African subjects. They made increased grants for economic development and education, and they promoted more Africans to senior posts in the local administrations. Thus, during the war itself Africa began to move from the seemingly stable colonial systems that had prevailed until 1939 into a period of economic, social and political change.

At the same time, World War II undermined the will and the capacity of the imperial powers to maintain their empires. In standing up to Nazi Germany and Fascist Italy the British people and the members of the resistance movements in Europe were inspired by democratic and anti-racist ideologies, with the result that opposition to imperialism, that had always existed in Europe, became more widespread. In addition, by the end of the war the major imperial powers were physically exhausted and economically impoverished and the leadership in world affairs had passed to the USA and the USSR, both of which had a tradition of rejection of colonialism – at least when

practiced by others. Furthermore, Asia had always been the preferred focus of European imperialism, and the failure of the Dutch to re-establish control over Indonesia after the defeat of Japan in 1945 and the British withdrawal from India in 1947 were precedents that could not be confined to Asia. After 1947 it was scarcely in question whether decolonization would spread to Africa. What was uncertain was how quickly it would spread there, how far and with what results.

The decolonization of Italian Africa
The change in the international climate between 1919 and 1945 was demonstrated in the disposal of the colonies of the vanquished European powers. Whereas at the end of World War I the victorious European allies had divided among themselves the former German empire – though in the guise of Mandates under the League of Nations – after World War II the shortlived Italian empire rapidly reverted to African control.

There was never any doubt that this would happen to Ethiopia, for the Italians had conquered it as recently as 1935. The emperor, Haile Selassie, returned from exile soon after the British ousted the Italians in 1941. During the Italian interlude, the powers and privileges of the hereditary aris-

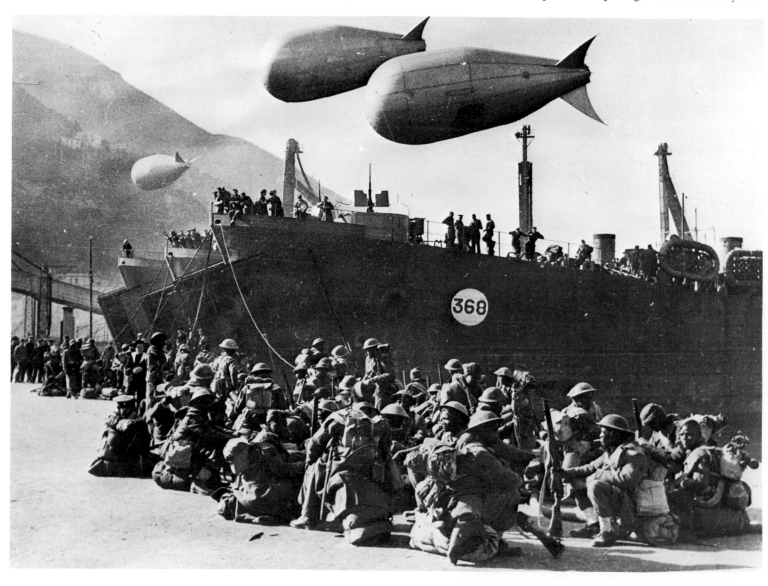

Left: South African troops from Swaziland await embarkation before the Anzio landings in Italy, January 1944.

Right: King Idris of Libya at an official ceremony in 1967.

Below right: The Emperor Haile Selassie returns in triumph to Addis Ababa in 1941 after his years in exile following the Italian invasion of Ethiopia.

sending the Ethiopians both modern military hardware and Cuban troops. The Somali revolt was duly crushed, and in 1984 the grateful military junta in Addis Ababa declared Ethiopia a Marxist state, with Mengitsu as Party leader. The Eritrean secessionist movement, however, though somewhat muted, persisted in a violent resistance that showed no sign of ending as the 1980s drew toward a close.

The United Nations also determined the future of the other former Italian colony – Libya, which was populated by Berbers and Bedouin Arabs. In 1951 it became an independent state – a constitutional monarchy under King Idris, the head of the Senussi sect of Islam. Until oil was discovered in 1965, Libya, like Ethiopia, had remained relatively unaffected by the drive to modernization that was the goal of African nationalists. In 1969 Idris was deposed by a group of army officers led by Colonel Muammar al-Qaddafi, who in due course became president of what was proclaimed the Socialist People's Libyan Arab Jamahiriya. As the new state name implied, al-Qaddafi's Libya was a curious mixture of socialism and Islamic fundamentalism, informed by the aggressive and eccentric personality of its president. Relations with the West, and especially the United States, deteriorated as the result of al-Qaddafi's pronounced pro-Soviet orientation, his violent antipathy to Israel and his support of Palestinian terrorism. His relations with his neighbors also deteriorated, as his adventuristic policies led him into a four-day border war with Egypt in 1977, clashes with Tanzanian forces and anti-Amin rebels in Uganda in 1979 and repeated incursions into Chad in support of anti-government rebels in the 1980s. By 1987 there had also been a series of clashes between Libyan and American forces, including punitive US air strikes on Tripoli and Benghazi in April 1986, and even the Soviet Union's interest in the al-Qaddafi regime seemed to be waning.

The decolonization of British Africa

In October 1945 some two hundred English-speaking Africans and Afro-Americans attended a conference in Manchester, England. The aging W E B du Bois presided over some of the sessions; but the conference had been organized by younger men, including George Padmore, a West Indian, Kwame Nkrumah from the Gold Coast and Jomo Kenyatta from Kenya. The resolutions adopted by this fifth Pan-African Congress were

tocracy and the Coptic church had not been undermined. The majority of the people were poor even by African standards, commerce was largely in alien hands and there were scarcely any Ethiopians with a modern education who might have led a popular, modernizing movement. The emperor returned with reformist intentions, but despite British, and later American, financial and technical aid, he made no substantial changes in the structure of society and the distribution of power. He instituted an elective legislative body in 1957, but its functions were merely advisory. Although the regime remained quasi-feudal at home, Haile Selassie was regarded as a heroic figure abroad, and he was able to elicit international support for territorial expansion. It had long been an Ethiopian ambition to obtain control over part of the Red Sea coastline. This was realized in 1952, when the former Italian colony of Eritrea, which had been administered by Britain since the war, was incorporated in Ethiopia, though most of its inhabitants were Muslims, who were traditionally opposed to Ethiopian expansionism.

When Africa was partitioned, the Somali inhabitants of the Horn of Africa, who had a common language, culture and religion (Islam) but no centralized political institutions, had been divided among five different territories: Italian, British and French Somaliland, Kenya and Ethiopia. By the end of World War II, young Somali were beginning to create a popular nationalist movement, dedicated to uniting all the Somali people in a single independent state. In 1950 the United Nations decided that Italian Somaliland should become a Trust Territory under Italian administration for 10 years, at the end of which it should be independent. Ten years later, when British Somaliland also became independent, it immediately joined with the former Trust Territory to form the Somali Democratic Republic, or Somalia.

In 1973 the Ethiopian emperor's control began to unravel when the country was plunged into social and economic chaos by a severe famine. The following year an Armed Forces Committee deposed the emperor, placed him under arrest and suspended the constitution. (The 82-year-old Haile Selassie died in August 1975.) After the coup the secessionist guerrilla movement in Eritrea flared into an open war that the Ethiopians seemed unable to win, and a second front opened when Somalia-backed guerrillas also began a large-scale war in the southeast. The leader of the Ethiopian military regime, Colonel Mengitsu Haile Mariam, strongly appealed to the Soviet Union for help, and the Soviets responded by abandoning their erstwhile Somalian clients and

Left: President Nkrumah of Ghana, accompanied by Chou En-lai, visits Peking in 1961.

Below right: The Nigerian Civil War – soldiers search civilians on the streets of Lagos. This war between rival tribal factions was particularly hard-fought, and its prolonged nature led to the onset of starvation for millions of people.

very different in tone and substance from those of its predecessors. They included a detailed and vehement denunciation of the 'systematic exploitation' of Africa by the 'alien imperialist Powers,' a forthright demand for independence for Black Africa and a ringing declaration to the colonial peoples of the world to unite.

In the Britain of 1945, this congress attracted little public attention. Nevertheless, the fifth Pan-African Congress marked the beginning of a new, post-war phase of the African nationalist movement in British Africa. Laying down ideological guidelines with populist, socialist and international overtones, it stimulated educated Africans to take advantage of the fresh opportunities created by the anticolonial international climate, the reforming spirit of the British government and its colonial administrators and the discontents engendered among Africans by the unprecedented rate of both social and economic change.

Events that were to become crucial precedents for all of British tropical Africa then took place in the Gold Coast. The principal difference between other West African colonies and the Gold Coast lay in the degree to which the coastal region and the central region had become modernized. Thanks to the success of the cocoa farmers and to the vigor of some of the British administrators, these regions had an exceptionally pervasive market economy, an unusually good educational system and a uniquely high proportion of townspeople. On the other hand, by 1945 the rate of social change had become so rapid in the Gold Coast that social cleavages were acute.

In 1946 the British created a Legislative Council for the south and Ashanti, with eight civil service members, six private members nominated by the governor, 13 members elected by representation of the traditional authorities and five members directly elected by urban votes. The 1946 constitution evoked a response from members of the coastal business and professional community. They saw the need to found a political organization to mobilize the urban electorate and to press the government for further reforms, but they moved cautiously. In 1947 J B Danquah, an Accra

lawyer, and his friends founded the United Gold Coast Convention 'to ensure that by all legitimate and constitutional means the direction and control of government should pass into the hands of the people and their chiefs in the shortest possible time,' and invited Kwame Nkrumah, then still in England, to be its secretary.

Arriving back in the Gold Coast in December 1947, Nkrumah began to lay the foundations of a popular political movement, by establishing contact with young men's voluntary associations, by holding the government responsible for all the hardships of the people – the high prices, food shortages and unemployment – and by denouncing the official policy of destroying cocoa trees in areas affected by swollen shoot disease. In February 1948 there was a riot. Two thousand ex-servicemen marched from Accra toward Christiansborg castle, the governor's residence, protesting their grievances. When provoked by stone-throwing and insults, a European officer opened fire, killing two people, whereupon rioting broke out and continued for a month in Accra and Kumasi, where European shops were looted. Seizing the opportunity, Danquah and Nkrumah sent cables to the British government, the United Nations and the world press, denouncing the colonial regime and demanding self-government. The British government appointed a commissioner to investigate the disturbances. In his report the commissioner endorsed some of the grievances of the ex-servicemen and on his advice the British government then named an African judge, Henley Coussey, chairman of a committee to make proposals for a new constitution. All the members of the Coussey committee were Africans. Nine were chiefs, 31 were commoners – predominantly members of the business and professional community. They included Danquah and other UGCC leaders, but not Nkrumah. The British government accepted the recommendations of the Coussey committee and introduced a new constitution in 1951.

While Danquah and his friends were busy with the work of the Coussey committee, Nkrumah continued to build up a political following. He was particularly successful in holding mass rallies. Ini-

tially he did this in the name of the UGCC, but by June 1949 he felt strong enough to announce his secession from the UGCC and the foundation of a new organization, the Convention People's Party (CPP). He criticized the Coussey committee while it was sitting and denounced its report when it was published. In place of its complex constitutional recommendations, he adopted the slogan Self-Government Now and instigated strikes. The government declared a state of emergency, and Nkrumah and eight others were arrested and sentenced to imprisonment for inciting a strike for political purposes. When the election was held under the new constitution in February 1951 the CPP won all the five municipal seats and 29 of the 33 rural seats elected by colleges. Nkrumah himself won an Accra seat, though still in jail. The governor, Sir Charles Arden-Clarke, then freed Nkrumah, who became Leader of Government Business in the Assembly and one of six CPP members of the cabinet.

After the 1951 election, the senior British officials and the CPP leaders cooperated remarkably smoothly in preparing for the final transfer of power. But the nearer independence approached, the more serious were the disputes within the African population. Within the CPP itself, there were struggles for power at every level. The party seemed an impressive organization on paper, with its Leader, its Central Committee, its National Conference, its constituency committees, its Youth League, its Women's section and its trade union support; but in fact the party was a hasty improvisation. People jostled for power at every level, and many who were disappointed not to receive rewards either resigned or were expelled, as Knrumah gradually imposed discipline from the top. The UGCC, revived under another name, absorbed many of the former CPP members, exploited the issues of corruption and conspicuous consumption among the CPP leaders and formed alliances with discontented elements in each region. Yet if the CPP was not the only Gold Coast party, it was still the strongest.

There was a final flurry of constitution making when the British government came under strong pressure from the opposition parties for the inclusion of safeguards for the regions. Finally, on 6 March 1957, the Gold Coast became a sovereign state, with a parliament and a cabinet based on the British model and with Nkrumah as prime minister. The name of the new state was Ghana, which Nkrumah had selected to emphasize the continuity of African history, even though the ancient state of Ghana had been located far to the northwest of its modern namesake.

The bright hopes that attended Ghana's birth are still to be fulfilled. In 1960 Nkrumah declared the state a republic, made himself president for life and outlawed all opposition parties. He was overthrown by a military coup in 1966, and since then the transfer of political power in Ghana has been accomplished mainly by military coups.

Civil war in Nigeria

By the time Ghana became independent, Britain had cautiously begun to devolve power upon the local inhabitants of her other tropical colonies. Not all these devolutions were as peaceful as they had been in the Gold Coast. Up to 1950 Nigeria seemed to be advancing toward autonomy as rapidly as the Gold Coast, but it was then outstripped because its ethnic rivalries impeded agreement upon an independence constitution. Nigeria was the giant of black Africa, including about 25 percent of Africa's black population in an area a third larger than the state of Texas. But it was riven by ethnic cleavages. The British tried to find a formula that would satisfy all legitimate interests without dividing Nigeria into separate independent states, but the three major parties inexorably became regarded as the parties of the Hausa, the Ibo and the Yoruba, and none of them managed to become a national party to the extent that the CPP had done. Nevertheless, in 1960 Nigeria became independent. Each of its three regional governments was controlled by its ethnic party, and the federal government was a coalition between the party of the Muslim Hausa and the party of the predominantly Christian Ibos. By 1966 this coalition had collapsed, and when the Ibos attempted to secede and create an independent state called Biafra a bloody civil war ensued: it finally ended in 1970 with Biafra's surrender to the federal government. That government, meanwhile, had degenerated into one in which one military coup succeeded another – with six coups and three presidential assassinations between 1960 and 1988. During the 1970s the economy boomed on the strength of oil exports, but the collapse of world oil prices in the 1980s left the country close to bankruptcy. By the end of the 1980s both the political and economic outlook of Nigeria looked decidedly bleak.

Once Nigeria and Ghana were independent, it was only a matter of time before Sierra Leone and the Gambia followed, though the Gambia was delayed until 1965 because of its small size. The British territories in East Africa posed greater problems. They had been exposed to Western influences for less than a century, and by the criteria of modernization, such as Western education, the majority of their African inhabitants seemed to be a long way behind the peoples of West Africa. Moreover, unlike British West Africa, these territories included communities of white settlers who, though they formed only a small proportion of the total population, had influence in London and footholds in the political institutions in Nairobi, Kampala and Dar-es-Salaam, owned valuable blocks of land in Kenya and Tanganyika and, with the Asian communities, controlled the export trade and most of the retail trade of the region.

Each territory was different. Kenya, with its productive highland belt reserved exclusively for white ownership, its economically neglected African reserves, its pass laws and its low wage rates for African laborers, was a segregated society. Uganda, with a comparatively flourishing economy dependent on cotton and coffee production by African farmers, and containing the traditional kingdom of Buganda, which, though it had only a fraction of the total population, had preserved its institutions and considerable power under British overrule, resembled a West African colony. Tanganyika, with no particularly powerful tribe and with exceptionally meager natural resources, was an economic backwater, whose African inhabitants were nevertheless exceptionally well placed to invoke international pressure on Britain because Tanganyika was a Trust Territory under the United Nations.

In East Africa as well as West Africa, Britain began to devolve political powers upon the local inhabitants after World War II. But whereas in West Africa this process could only culminate in the emergence of African-controlled independent states, Britain treated the three East African territories as multiracial societies, set up separate European, Asian and African electoral rolls, and gave the European minorities as many seats in the Legislative and Executive Councils as the African majorities. This attempt to reconcile racialism with democracy ran into heavy weather in each territory.

The Kenyan situation led to the only prolonged outbreak of violence that accompanied the decolonization of British Africa north of the Zambezi River. The Kikuyu people, who formed about one-sixth of the population of Kenya, had always borne the main brunt of settler exploitation, and after the war they suffered particularly grievously from a spiraling cost of living. Their leaders having made persistent but unavailing attempts to obtain some improvement in their lot by constitutional methods, a section of the Kikuyu resorted to violence in 1952. Though British troops gradually suppressed the Kikuyu Mau Mau, the British government entered into a dialogue with African leaders and eventually decided to break the settler grip on the colonial government and to prepare Kenya for independence under a constitution that allowed the will of the African population to prevail. In 1963 Jomo Kenyatta, the Kikuyu who had gone to England to plead the cause of his people in 1929, had returned to Kenya in 1946 and had been sentenced to seven years' imprisonment by the British in 1953, became prime minister of Kenya. In the years that followed, the government remained relatively stable, and the economy improved. As of the late 1980s threats to the

nation's security came more from fractious neighbors than from internal problems.

Tanganyika and Uganda also became independent in the 1960s. In Tanganyika, cooperative movements and other popular associations had existed for some while in several of the tribes, and there was also an association of clerks and school teachers that cut across tribal lines; but it was not until 1954 that the Tanganyikan African National Union (TANU) was founded under the leadership of Julius Nyerere, a graduate of Edinburgh University, with the goal of eliminating British rule. TANU rapidly incorporated most of the existing African organizations, obtained a liberalized constitution from Britain, swept the board in a general election in 1960 and became the ruling party of an independent but desperately poor Tanganyika in 1961. By 1963 Tanganyika had merged with newly independent Zanzibar, and the following year the name of the nation was changed to Tanzania. In 1978 Tanzania was menaced by troops from Idi Amin's Uganda, a full-scale war ensued and eventually, in 1980, the Tanzanians and their rebel Ugandan allies prevailed over the forces of Amin and his Libyan helpers. Nyerere vacated the presidency in 1985 in favor of Ali Hassan Mwinyi, but remained chairman of the nation's single political party. While Tanzania was not as badly off as many other African states, the Ugandan war had drained its fragile economy and left the country in precarious financial shape.

Buganda separatism was the main obstacle to a smooth transfer of power in Uganda. When the government of Buganda opposed democratic reforms in 1952, Britain exiled the Kabaka; but, faced with strong royalist feeling, it allowed him back again in 1955. As late as 1961 the separatists won an overwhelming victory in the election of a new Buganda *lukiko*, at a time when two other political organizations were competing for popular support throughout the country. Finally, Milton Obote, leader of the Uganda People's Congress, made an electoral pact with the Buganda separatists and led the country to independence in 1962. Sir Edward Mutesa was named president, and Obote prime minister, but in 1964 Obote seized control of the government. He was

in turn deposed in 1971 by Colonel Idi Amin, an army officer of questionable sanity, who soon launched a reign of terror in which, according to Amnesty International, hundreds of thousands were murdered or tortured to death. In 1980, after a savage war, Amin was deposed by Obote and his Tanzanian allies, but Obote's rule now proved hardly less oppressive than Amin's, and he was deposed by the military in 1985. The military regime was in turn overthrown by a National Resistance Army led by Yoweri Musevni, who became president in 1986. Uganda's experience has been among the unhappiest in Africa.

In British Central Africa the question of whom Britain would transfer power to when she left was still unresolved at a very late stage in the decolonization process. In 1953 Britain superimposed a multiracial federal government over the territorial governments of Nyasaland and Northern Rhodesia, which had the status of British protectorates, and Southern Rhodesia, which had effectively been a self-governing colony under the control of its white settler community since 1923. In sponsoring the federal plan the British Government contended that all parts and peoples of the federation would benefit from the pooling of their complementary resources – the labor resources of poor, densely populated Nyasaland, the copper wealth of Northern Rhodesia and the agricultural production and manufacturing industries of Southern Rhodesia. The British also argued that the federation, based on the principle of partnership between the settlers and the Africans, would provide a barrier between African nationalism to the north and Afrikaner nationalism to the south. In practice the economic goals were partly fulfilled by the construction of the Kariba dam and power station on the Zambezi River between Northern and Southern Rhodesia, but the partnership idea proved to be an illusion. The majority of the white settlers of the three territories had only supported the federal plan in the expectation that they would be able to eliminate the imperial factor and themselves acquire full control over the entire federation. As the first federal prime minister himself put it, it was to be a partnership like that between a rider and his horse.

Africans in all three territories had been opposed to the federation from the first. In 1959 Africans resorted to violence in Nyasaland, where white settlers were fewer in numbers than in the other two territories. As in Kenya, violence led to the appointment of a British commission of enquiry, whose report was followed by the introduction of a new territorial constitution providing for an African elective majority in the Nyasaland legislature. The nationalist party led by Dr Hastings Banda won the general election in 1961, and Nyasaland then moved comparatively smoothly toward independence, seceding from the federation in 1963, becoming the independent state of Malawi in 1964 and joining the Commonwealth as a republic in 1966.

The issue was more closely contested in Northern Rhodesia, whose booming copper mining industry had attracted capital investment and immigration from Britain and South Africa since World War II. At one stage, the territorial government looked as if it might pass under settler control, and as late as 1962 the British government was still trying to divide political power between the white minority and the African majority by means of a complex electoral formula. But in 1964, after a period of intense competition between African factions, Kenneth Kaunda's radical nationalist United National Independence Party won the first general election to be held under a democratic electoral system, and later that year he led the country to independence under the name of Zambia. Kaunda remained Zambia's leader through the 1980s.

As the federation disintegrated the 240,000 white people of Southern Rhodesia, who were four times as numerous as those in Kenya and three times as numerous as those in Northern Rhodesia, shifted their support from the politicians who had supported federation to new leaders who disavowed the mildly liberal elements in the policy of partnership and stood more unequivocally for white supremacy. In 1962 the right-wing Rhodesian Front won a general election and proceeded to suppress the African nationalist movement by arresting its leaders and intimidating the masses – a process which was facilitated by bitter internal disputes among Africans. The Rhodesian government also entered into long negotiations with Britain, but no agreement could be reached on an independence without a guarantee that the will of the majority of the population would ultimately prevail, and this the Rhodesian government would not accept. Finally, in November 1965, Prime Minister Ian Smith made a unilateral declaration of independence. Britain regarded Rhodesia as a rebellious colony and not a single sovereign state recognized its existence. But Smith withstood British pressure, UN economic sanctions and growing internal violence between blacks and whites and contrived to keep his white-dominated regime in power for 11 years. Finally, in 1976 Smith acceded

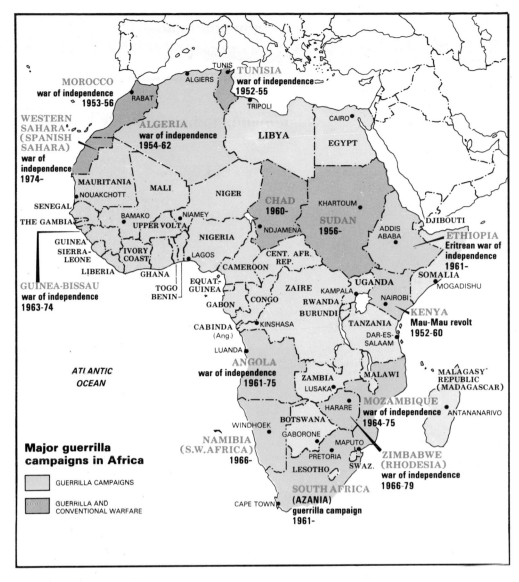

Major guerrilla campaigns in Africa

☐ GUERRILLA CAMPAIGNS

▨ GUERRILLA AND CONVENTIONAL WARFARE

Above left: A Mau-Mau gang in Kenya poses for a British publicity photograph after its capture.

Left: President Julius Nyerere of Tanzania who came to power in 1962.

Above right: A map illustrating the major guerrilla campaigns that have racked the continent.

Right: The Kariba Dam, built on the Zambezi River between the former Northern and Southern Rhodesia.

to US pressure and agreed to transfer power to the black majority in two years. This finally occurred in January 1979, when the country's name was changed to Zimbabwe Rhodesia. The moderate party led by Bishop Abel Muzorewa won the election held in April, but violence still continued, now mainly between the moderates and the more radical Patriotic Front led by Robert Mugabe and Joshua Nkomo. The warring parties finally agreed to a ceasefire, a new constitution and a general election, which was held in February 1980. Mugabe's faction of the Patriotic Front were the big winners, Nkomo's faction came in second and the moderates were a poor third. The next year Mugabe dismissed Nkomo from the government, and the two Patriotic Front factions became bitter, often violent, opponents. Although the two leaders composed their differences at the end of 1987 and Nkomo was readmitted to the government in a minor post, enough political tensions remained to make the country's political future uncertain.

Britain also eventually granted independence under African majority rule to Lesotho (formerly Basutoland), Botswana (formerly Bechuanaland) and Swaziland; but these three countries remained largely dependent upon their powerful neighbor, South Africa. Thus the decolonization of the British Empire in Africa resulted effectively in the Zambezi River becoming a boundary between the African-controlled central part of the continent and the white-supremacy south.

The decolonization of French Africa

After World War II the real questions at issue between the British Government and African nationalists related not to the direction of change, for that was already determined, but to the rate of change and the distribution of power among the local peoples. In French imperial history, on the other hand, there was no precedent for systematic decolonization. Nevertheless, after World War II the French, like the British, introduced reforms in their colonial empire. The basic goals and methods of post-war policy were defined by a conference of Gaullist officials that was held in Brazzaville in 1944. Abuses such as forced labor were to be eliminated. France was to provide funds for a great expansion in the social services, especially education. Africans in all parts of French tropical Africa were to have the status of French citizens and were to participate in government at all levels – municipal, territorial, federal and imperial. On the other hand, ultimate power over the entire empire was to remain firmly in French hands.

Of the four levels of political activity in the Fourth Republic the most important were the territorial and the imperial. Initially, narrowly based elitist parties, somewhat like the Gold Coast UGCC, were formed in many territories; but in the long run, as the electorates expanded, the more successful parties developed a broader base as the CPP was doing in the Gold Coast. These territorial parties were the key institutions in electoral politics in French Africa after World War II. In so far as interterritorial parties existed, they were loose associations of leaders of territorial parties, founded for the purpose of coordinating their activities as African deputies in Paris. The most important interterritorial organization was the Rassemblement Démocratique Africain (RDA), which was founded at a conference in Bamako in 1946. Initially the RDA had been associated with the French Communist Party, but in

1950 Félix Houphouet-Boigny, who was president of the KDA, broke with the communists. Thereafter, Houphouet-Boigny's territorial party in the Ivory Coast became relatively pro-French and conservative, whereas Sékou Touré and his party in Guinea became increasingly radical in their attitude to France as well as in their social policies. Senegal's Léopold Sédar Senghor, who had originally been associated with the French Socialist Party, was never a member of the RDA, and in 1948 he left the Socialist Party and founded a group with other overseas deputies who wished to act independently of metropolitan parties.

During the 1950s the French empire began to crumble. In Indo-China the army suffered an ignominious defeat. In Algeria, which Frenchmen had been taught to believe was an indissoluble part of France, and in Morocco and Tunisia, which were French protectorates, the administrators were unable to prevent the outbreak of nationalist uprisings. In tropical Africa, people who had been educated in French universities since World War II were impressed by these events and by the advance of the Gold Coast toward independence, and they injected an increasingly radical spirit into the political parties. The French politicians were therefore obliged to establish imperial priorities. They determined that Algeria, with nearly a million *colons*, was to be held at all costs, and it was there that they concentrated their resources for a long and bloody war. They had to let Indo-China go in 1954 and two years later they granted independence to Morocco and Tunisia. In 1956 they also passed legislation for tropical Africa. The assemblies in each territory, which were to be elected by universal suffrage, were given full legis-

lative powers over a wide range of topics, and cabinets responsible to the assemblies were given executive powers over the same topics.

In May 1958 the French army revolted in Algeria and the Fourth Republic collapsed. General de Gaulle's government then drafted a constitution for the Fifth Republic, providing for a 'French Community,' in which each African territory was to be an autonomous state, separately associated with France. But it would not become independent, like a member of the British Commonwealth, because the French government would control the external relations of the entire Community. The constitution was submitted to a referendum in each territory after de Gaulle had toured Africa making grandiloquent appeals for support. The French administrators and businessmen added their weight to the campaign, and in nearly every territory the dominant party decided to approve the constitution; but there was opposition from students, trade unionists and radical minority parties everywhere, and in Guinea from Sékou Touré and his PDG also. The result of the vote was a large majority for the constitution everywhere but in Guinea. There, 95 percent of the votes were 'Non.'

De Gaulle made a final effort to hold the Community together by making a drastic example of Guinea. He abruptly cut off all French economic aid and recalled all French administrators. Nevertheless, Guinea contrived to survive, with moral support from Nkrumah's Ghana, and in doing so Sékou Touré became the hero of the younger men throughout francophonic Africa and the politicians were drawn along in an irresistible tide to demand independence. Last-minute attempts

were made by some of them, notably Senghor, to preserve the federal institutions, but without success. With the Algerian war still dragging on, consuming vast French resources, the de Gaulle government yielded to demands for full independence, and by the end of 1960 each of the territories had become a sovereign state and a member of the United Nations.

The fates of the former French colonies after independence were widely different, the result of a complex of interacting forces such as geographic positioning and natural resources, ethnic mix, international relations (with neighbors and, importantly, with France) and, certainly not least, quality of leadership. In all these regards the Ivory Coast was singularly blessed: Houphouet-Boigny's enlightened rule continued unbroken into the late 1980s, helping to produce a nation whose prosperity and political stability were the envy of the continent.

Senegal, though less prosperous than the Ivory Coast (it lies nearer to the sub-Saharan drought belt), was generally successful economically and reasonably stable politically. Throughout the 1960s and mid 1970s Senghor's one-party rule provoked increasing discontent, and in 1974 legal opposition was reconstituted. By 1987 there were some 18 political parties represented in the National Assembly, with Abdou Diouf's Socialist Party ascendant.

Guinea's post-independence history was less

happy. In the 1960s Guinea's economy seemed in fairly good shape, due largely to exploitation of the country's extensive bauxite deposits, but thanks in part to Sékou Touré's mismanagement (and to the fact that after 1965 he had broken the country's economic ties with France) this prosperity did not last. Also, there was mounting internal resistance to his increasingly harsh and authoritarian rule. When he died in 1984 a military junta led by General Lansana Conte seized control of the government. Guinea was by then worse off than it had been prior to 1960.

In general, those former French colonies that maintained good relations with France benefited economically and politically. Though few of the sub-Saharan economies that lie along the drought belt were really flourishing, those that belonged to the so-called Franc Zone (with currencies freely convertible to the French franc and to some extent regulated by the Ministry of Finance in Paris) suffered the least. Also, French military aid often proved valuable, as when France sent troops to help defend Chad against Libyan incursions in the mid-1980s. As one of France's leading African partisans, Houphouet-Boigny, put it in the late 1970s, 'France is the only Western country on whom we can rely in times of trouble.'

The decolonization of the Belgian Congo

Since 1908 the Belgian Congo had been controlled by three interlocking institutions: the Belgian

administration, the Catholic Church and the private corporations that owned the large plantations and the copper mines. Then, abruptly, in less than four years the entire system collapsed. In 1956 *Conscience Africaine*, a small religious journal, published a tentative request for political change, envisaging a 30-year program of preparation for independence. In the following year, the government introduced a limited electoral system in three main municipalities. Political organizations were then hastily improvised. While these grass-roots organizations, so far as they existed, were tribal, leaders espoused different programs. Regional autonomy was the policy of Moise Tshombe and his Conakat party – the party of the Lunda people who predominated in Katanga, which, with its copper mines, was the wealthiest part of the Congo; federalism was the policy of Joseph Kasavubu and his Abako party, which was supported by the Bakongo people of the lower Congo; while Patrice Lumumba stood for an independent and united Congo, especially after he had attended the All African Peoples Conference in Accra in December 1958.

During 1959, faced with a sharp fall in the price of copper, large scale unemployment and some rioting in the Congolese towns, and the rapid advance of decolonization in French and British Africa, the alliance between Church, State and private enterprise began to fall apart. The Belgian government then decided to deal with the prob-

lem in the simplest possible way by yielding to the demands of the inexperienced African politicians. In January 1960 Belgian politicians conferred in Brussels with representatives of the Congolese chiefs and political parties and immediately conceded that the Congo should become independent later that year. A constitution was then drafted and the Africans hurried back to the Congo to prepare for a general election that was to create a national legislature. Numerous political groups contested the election, and early in July a coalition government was formed with Lumumba prime minister and Kasavubu head of state. On 30 June 1960 the Congo became an independent state; but its 14 million people and its 200 language groups had no sense of national identity and no proven leaders. The abrupt switch from a strict paternalism to political liberty led at once to anarchy. The army mutinied and went on a rampage against the Belgian officers and other white residents. The surviving whites fled the country. Katanga seceded under Tshombe. It was not until after United Nations troops had intervened, Lumumba had been murdered in Tshombe's custody and Tshombe had tried to rule the entire country with Belgian and American support that the country began to acquire stability in 1965

Left: An angry mob on the rampage in Leopoldville in 1960 – the property of their former Belgian colonial masters acting as the subject of their rage.

Right: President Kasavuba and Prime Minister Lumumba of the Congo.

under a military regime led by General Joseph-Désire Mobutu, a former non-commissioned officer in the *Force Publique*. The new president imposed an iron-fisted one-party rule that persists to this time. By 1975 he had effectively silenced all political opponents, nationalized most of the economy and was actively courting South African, American and Japanese investment in the country he had already (1971) renamed Zaïre. As the result of his backing of the non-communist National Front for the liberation of Angola in the 1975-76 Angolan civil war, he incurred the enmity of the communist victors, and in 1977 and 1978 he twice had to call for French, Belgian and US help in repelling Angolan invasions.

The decolonization of Portuguese Africa

Throughout the 1950s, Antonio Salazar's dictatorship kept Portugal relatively immune from the anticolonial influences that were prevailing elsewhere in Europe. Portuguese colonialism in Angola, Mozambique and elsewhere was as repressive as the Belgian version, but without the saving grace of extensive social services. The declared policy of the Portuguese government was a mixture of racism and paternalism. In practice, Portuguese administrators exerted stringent

control over their African subjects and recruited the required numbers of men, women and children to work as migrant laborers for the state and for private enterprise, where their conditions of work were wretched. Missions provided a minority of the children with some elementary education, but in 1959 only 41 Africans were enrolled in high schools in Mozambique and the illiteracy rate in Portuguese Africa as a whole was over 92 percent.

After World War II, the Portuguese government tried to strengthen its hold over Angola and Mozambique by transporting large numbers of Portuguese peasants and providing them with land. Angola's white population rose from 44,000 in 1940 to 170,000 in 1960 and 400,000 in 1970; Mozambique's from 27,500 in 1940 to 85,000 in 1960 and 100,000 in 1970. The modern sector of the economy was almost exclusively focused in the areas of white settlement.

African uprisings started in Angola in 1961, Guinea-Bissau in 1962 and Mozambique in 1964. At first strongly suppressed, by 1974 they had reached a scale beyond Portugal's power to contain them. In that year, after a successful left-democratic revolution in Portugal, Lisbon elected to decolonize.

For Angola, the plan was for a constituent assembly to be elected following a peaceful resolution of the differences between the three major Angolan liberation movements: the US- and Zaïre-backed MPLA, the Soviet-backed FNLA and the smaller UNITA. In the event, these differences, far from being resolved, plunged the country into a bloody civil war. At first the MPLA seemed to have the advantage, but the Soviet Union gave the FNLA strong support and in October 1975, Cuban troops entered the fray and soon routed the MPLA and UNITA forces. The international 46-member Organization of African Unity recognized the Marxist government of MPLA leader Agostino Neto in February 1976, but in fact the Neto government still have not subdued insurgencies – now mostly represented by Jonas Savimbi's UNITA – in large southern and eastern parts of the country. Moreover, Savimbi gained an important ally in South Africa, which was resentful of the Neto government's policy of harboring guerrilla fighters who had crossed the border from South African controlled Southwest Africa. By the end of 1987 there were an estimated 3000 South African troops assisting the rebels in southern Angola, and a year earlier the United States had openly begun supplying material aid to UNITA.

A similar situation obtained in Mozambique, which Portugal also decided to decolonize in 1974. There a Marxist government was set up by the major independence movement, the FRELIMO, but it at once became involved in a long, still undecided war with anti-government guerrilla fighters, the MNR, who were supported by South Africa. And as in Angola, the situation was complicated by the fact that throughout much of the 1980s Mozambique suffered from disastrous droughts that produced widespread famine and resulted in both countries being put on the UN Food and Agriculture Organization's (FAO) 'emergency' list.

The South African problem

Since the Union of South Africa had been founded in 1910, all South African governments had been fundamentally racist, but they had acted with some moderation and had allowed countervailing forces to operate. The rate of urbanization and industrialization increased rapidly during and after World War II, which made it seem possible that the racial barriers were beginning to break down. This was especially alarming to many Afrikaners, with their long tradition of struggle for autonomy and security against British imperialists and African tribesmen, and they rallied behind the party which seemed most determined to preserve white supremacy. This was the Afrikaner Nationalist Party, which came into power in 1948 and won large majorities in successive elections from 1953 onward.

According to its policy, which was called Apartheid ('Separateness'), each race is an integrated, perpetual entity with a distinctive character and destiny. As the bearers of Christian civilization, it was the duty of the whites to separate the races from one another and to control the entire country, until eventually the subject races became qualified to rule themselves 'in their own areas.' Consequently, while racism was being rejected as a basis for social and political organization elsewhere, it became applied with unprecedented rigor in South Africa.

In political terms, the Afrikaner Nationalist program involved the elimination of the small voice Africans, Asians and colored (mixed-race) people had previously had in the authoritative political system. For the subject races, the government created separate, subordinate institutions. The African population was deemed to consist of nine or more distinct 'Bantu national units'. Africans were considered to be 'temporary visitors' when they resided in the 'White Areas,' where they were not entitled to own land. In the lands reserved for them, the government created 'Bantu Authorities' for each of the national units. These Bantu Authorities were headed by chiefs, who were salaried officials subject to deposition by the government. In the Transkei reserve, the government went further and created a 'Legislative Assembly,' composed partly of chiefs and partly of representatives elected by the Xhosa 'national unit,' and a 'Cabinet' responsible to the Assembly and gave these bodies limited powers of local government. For the colored people and Asians, the government created 'Representative Councils,' partly elective and partly nominated, with the right to make regulations for their people on specified subjects.

As a result of external and internal pressures against this exclusionary system the South African government made some small changes in this system via a new constitution enacted in 1984. The 68 percent black population was still excluded from the national government, but Indian and mixed-race citizens were finally admitted to a racially divided parliament composed of three separate, segregated chambers. Although the chambers could select representatives to an electoral college that would choose the president, only the white chamber controlled the election. The office of Executive State President, itself a creation of the new constitution and in effect a replacement of the earlier parliamentary form of government, was given extensive, potentially authoritarian powers such as the right to veto legislation and dismiss parliament. The first such president was Pieter W Botha.

As racial tensions and violence spread through South Africa in the 1980s the Botha government was obliged on several occasions to declare states of emergency. Thousands of black activists were beaten and/or jailed without warrants, and strict censorship of the press – both domestic and foreign – was imposed. International outcry against the policies of the government of South Africa (which had been ousted from the UN General Assembly as early as 1974) continued to escalate, with numerous multinational companies divesting themselves of their holdings in the country. As the crisis deepened, internal politics inevitably became more polarized. In the spring 1987 national elections, though the Nationalist Party retained its overwhelming majority, the ultra-supremacist Conservative Party replaced the Progressive Liberals as the main opposition party. Hopes that South Africa could ever find a just and peaceful solution to its problems were fast receding.

A quarter-century of independence

The first 25 years of African independence were generally traumatic. Democracy has fared badly. A total of over 70 successful coups d'état had, by 1987, left 18 military regimes in power, to say nothing of those that had metamorphosed into one-party civilian rules. The overall economic situation was no better: 29 of the world's 34 poorest nations were African, and Africa's population was growing faster than anywhere on earth – 32 percent a year (over 40 percent in Kenya). Numerous states such as Angola, Guinea, Equatorial Guinea, Mozambique, Uganda and Zaïre are, by almost any economic measure, plainly worse off than they were when they were colonies, and some have appeared depressingly frequently on the FAO's 'emergency list.'

At the southern end of the continent, society remained organized on the basis of white supremacy, which the rest of the world had renounced in theory and, increasingly, in practice. In tropical Africa there was no panacea for poverty, underdevelopment and sparse and unevenly distributed natural resources. The territorial framework created by the European partitioners was being perpetuated: attempts to dismember the colonial territories had failed, and so had most attempts to amalgamate colonial units. Independent African governments were still groping toward solutions to the problem of creating and preserving national unity, and because this problem was so acute, most of them were imposing more or less drastic limitations on the political freedoms of their people. In many states, the ethnic cleavages of the past were beginning to diminish; but almost everywhere they were in danger of being superseded by a new and not less ominous cleavage – the cleavage between the modern elite, who were controlling the political systems and absorbing an inordinate proportion of their countries' wealth, and the rural and urban masses, whose expectations were being enlarged by the expanding educational services, but who had still derived few material benefits from the ejection of the colonial rulers.

Yet there could certainly have been no alternative to decolonization, either from the point of view of the Africans or from that of the imperial powers. It was an historical imperative from which there could be no turning aside. And if the first quarter-century of African independence failed to fulfill the high, unrealistic hopes entertained by many at the beginning of the 1960s, it is probably also well to remember that 25 years is not, in historical terms, a very long time. The full story of African independence is yet to be revealed. Indeed, when compared to other episodes of mass social upheaval – so often characterized by enormous bloody slaughter – the decolonization of Africa was a relatively smooth process.

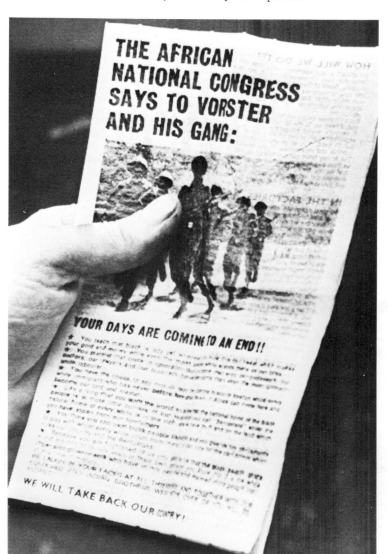

Left: An ANC leaflet dropped in Johannesburg, South Africa, in 1970.

Above right: Apartheid in action in South Africa, 1971.

Right: The Kwa Zulu 'homeland' for blacks in South Africa; an artificial creation of the white South African government designed to give an air of legitimacy to their racist policies.

The Post-Cold War Era: 1988-2002

The Cold War had almost played itself out by 1988, though few people knew it at the time. In just two years, the Soviet Union would peacefully collapse into fifteen independent republics, leaving a new world order in which the United States was the lone super power. It was, perhaps, an unlikely end to a war in which two unrivalled states had stood poised for mutual nuclear destruction over the course of some forty years. The threat of nuclear war certainly remained in the 1990s, but the prospect of a global nuclear winter receded from the political imagination, and the world began to turn upon other issues and developments. This new era was largely shaped by historical forces that had gathered strength before and during the Cold War, forces that subsequently proved more powerful than the strategic calculations of Moscow and Washington. The United Nations experienced a revival as an international forum for cooperation, realizing the potential of international government that President Woodrow Wilson had foreseen after the First World War. Ethnic nationalism, a grim legacy of the nineteenth century, proliferated in the absence of Cold War constraints, producing genocidal campaigns in Europe and Africa. Some of the world's most dramatic political settlements occurred in countries seeking to resolve the long-standing inequities of colonialism, giving hope to those people for whom peace remained elusive in the long wake of colonial rule. While the number of democracies in the world increased, so did the political influence of religious fundamentalism, particularly in the Islamic world. Departing from the word of the Q'ran, Islamic radicals staged terrorist strikes in opposition to the global expansion of Western capitalism and culture, the despotism of their own governments, and US support for the state of Israel. These terrorists were part of a broad historical phenomenon in which dissident groups attempted violently to undermine the power of the state and the security of civil society in order to achieve their goals, whether in Tel Aviv, Bogota, or Oklahoma City. Before and after 1988, there were terrorist campaigns in support of national separatism, the overthrow of federal governments, and the power of drug lords, among other issues.

Nevertheless, the world became more closely connected. This process, commonly known as globalization, was advanced after 1988 by the elimination of barriers to international trade and investment, and the further development of telecommunication systems, including mobile phones and the Internet. Just as Adam Smith had advocated the economic and social benefits of international free trade in the eighteenth century, advocates of globalization envisioned a new capitalist order of mutual benefit, trade, and understanding between peoples rich and poor. However, the promise of globalization remained unfulfilled by the early 2000s, given the growing disparity between the richest and the poorest nations, disproportionate population trends, and health crises such as the AIDS pandemic.

It was not clear whether the economic engine of globalization had served to accelerate or slow these problems in international welfare, but it was evident that a more integrated global economy was directly responsible for important changes, and related problems, in many cultures and political systems. The influx of foreign commodities posed challenges to cultures, whether those of tribes or nations. Commercial products, such as clothing and movies, conveyed foreign cultural standards that could provoke tensions between generations, as young people embraced the products of foreign cultures, which their parents found inappropriate or threatening. Globalization could also promote prosperity, which then commonly entailed greater demands for political reform, as people sought to enhance their welfare through increased political representation and protection from corruption. These and other cultural and political ramifications of globalization were potentially volatile, as demonstrated in the Middle East, where globalization was popularly regarded as a form of "cultural imperialism", which extended the influence of Christian culture and capitalism for the benefit of the United State and Europe. If globalization was to succeed, it would have to be transformed, in both its practice and its image, into something more than a tool of the dominant powers in the West. The fulfillment of the promise of globalization would depend on greater and more equitable international cooperation in government, and the post-Cold War era had clearly demonstrated the potential of such cooperation on many fronts.

The Decline of Communism

In 1988 President Ronald Reagan of the United States and President Mikhail Gorbachev of the Soviet Union set out to halt and reverse the nuclear arms race between their countries. While each leader arrived at the bargaining table with a formidable arsenal behind him, the two men did not negotiate from equal positions of power. The United States had built the largest national econ-

Opposite: In the spirit of reconciliation which had led to a reduction in nuclear forces, US President Ronald Reagan and Soviet President Mikhail Gorbachev are joined by key government figures in a toast over lunch at the White House in December 1988.

Right: Germans stand atop the Berlin Wall, with the Brandenburg Gate in the background, celebrating the decision of the German Democratic Republic to open its borders to the West in November 1989.

omy in the world and enjoyed a stable, popular government based on capitalism and liberal democracy. Meanwhile, the Communist Party had produced failing economies across the Soviet Union and increasing political unrest in republics from Eastern Europe to Central Asia. The economic problems of the Soviet Union were caused primarily by incompetent central planning, corruption, and poor agricultural production. These long-term problems were then compounded in the 1980s by a decline in petroleum prices, which was particularly damaging because the Soviet Union was the world's largest petroleum producer. The political problems were attributable to a massive, unresponsive bureaucracy, and ethnic tensions between Russia and the non-Russian nations of the union. Moreover, the reputation and morale of the once heroic Soviet military had been undermined by its inability to win a costly and unpopular war in Afghanistan, where Soviet troops had been fighting the US-backed *mujahideen* since 1979. Cold War arms development and military deployment around the world had drained the Soviet economy to a greater extent than the economy of the US, hindering the communists' efforts to respond to their growing domestic crises. In an effort to scale back defense costs and improve relations with the US, Gorbachev worked with Reagan to bring the Intermediate-Range Nuclear Forces Treaty (INF) into affect in 1988, committing both governments to the destruction of all land-based nuclear missiles with a range of 300 to 3,400 miles (480 – 5,440 km). This breakthrough in US-Soviet relations set the stage for even more significant disarmament agreements between Gorbachev and Reagan's successor, President George H. W. Bush, who took office in 1989. Also in that year,

Gorbachev further combined his domestic and international policies of retrenchment and conciliation by withdrawing Soviet troops from Afghanistan. This particular decision pleased not only the US, but also China, which had opposed Soviet incursions eastward, and which promptly received Gorbachev on a state visit that normalized relations between the leading communist powers for the first time in many years. Having played out the Cold War in Afghanistan, the Soviet Union and the United States left the country to poverty and the rule of warlords.

Mikhail Gorbachev's domestic reform of the Soviet Union was as ambitious as his foreign policy, though developments would soon accelerate beyond his political intention and control. He recognized that the old guard of the Communist Party would bring the Soviet Union to ruin due to its monopoly on power, so he ended government censorship and instituted major electoral reforms in 1988 that guaranteed free parliamentary elections. The ensuing elections of 1989 returned a majority of reform-minded deputies to the Soviet Congress, which then elected a new Supreme Soviet supportive of Gorbachev. Although the president was more progressive than his predecessors, he remained a devoted communist bureaucrat. It was therefore not at all clear to the people of the Soviet Union and the Warsaw Pact, or to the United States and its European allies, that major political changes, and the end of the Cold War, were on the way. The Soviet government did not, after all, have a history of tolerating challenges to its ultimate authority. Just several years earlier, in 1981, the Communist Party had crushed the Solidarity movement in Poland. In 1988, under the pressure of high inflation, Polish workers again

launched a round of strikes and protests, inviting another Soviet crackdown. Instead of crushing this political dissent, however, the Gorbachev government allowed all of the nations of the Warsaw Pact to choose their own systems of government. The communists in Poland, without the backing of the Soviet military, chose to legalize Solidarity and negotiate with its leader, Lech Walesa, setting the stage for the landslide victory of Solidarity in the elections of June 1989. East Germans responded to the weakening grip of the Communist Party in that same spring and summer by fleeing to western Europe through Hungary. Unable to stem the tide of political refugees, the German Democratic Republic took a momentous step in granting unrestricted travel to the West, opening the checkpoints of the Berlin Wall on the night of 9 November. In the midst of wild celebrations, Berliners took up hammers and began to tear down the wall that had separated them for twenty-eight years, opening the path to the political reunification of Germany in October 1990. The collapse of communism was remarkably peaceful across eastern Europe, with the exception of Romania, where the brutal dynastic socialism of Nicolai and Elena Ceaucescu ended with their summary trial and execution on Christmas day, 1989. The temper of the times was more aptly represented in the so-called "velvet revolution" in Czechoslovakia, which resulted in the election of a playwright and human rights activist, Václav Havel, to the presidency. In the light of this stunning series of events, Presidents Bush and Gorbachev held a summit in Malta in December 1989 and declared the Cold War over.

In contrast to the disintegration of communist rule in Eastern Europe, the dissolution of the Soviet Union itself took a complicated and unsteady course. Gorbachev's economic reforms, which had pushed the Soviets toward a market economy, had also created new hardships in an already strained society. People were frustrated by the decreased availability of state-subsidized commodities, including food, and they resented the private enterprises that charged higher prices for both food and services. As inflation and unemployment rose, and as the government responded with currency reforms and further price increases, Gorbachev's popularity plummeted. In an attempt to exploit this growing discontentment, old-guard communists in the Party, the military, and the secret police staged a coup to remove Gorbachev from power in August 1991. The President of the Russian Republic, Boris Yeltsin, who had renounced his membership in the Communist Party only a month earlier, rallied forces that thwarted the coup attempt. Although Gorbachev survived the ordeal, he lost his political authority to Yeltsin, and the central Soviet government lost its last vestige of authority. All of the fifteen republics, including Russia, declared their independence from the Soviet Union by the end of 1991, leaving Gorbachev little choice but to resign from the presidency and bring an end to the Soviet Union altogether.

The collapse of communism left Europe in search of a new balance of power. The former Soviet republics joined together in the Commonwealth of Independent States (CIS), but some also sought admission to the North Atlantic Treaty Organization (NATO). As NATO negotiated separate agreements with its former adversaries, it began to search for a new mission. Even the Russian Federation, which had retained the Soviet Union's nuclear arsenal, was no longer an active threat to NATO, because it had turned much of its attention to domestic crises wrought by decades of communist rule. Russian and US Presidents continued to sign disarmament treaties through the early 2000s, and the US would provide Russia with financial and technical assistance in disposing of nuclear and biological weaponry. The U.S and Russia also put the Cold War "space race" behind them to cooperate in space exploration. The United States led fifteen other nations in beginning the construction of the International Space Station in 1998 through the coordinated efforts of the US Space Shuttle program and the Russian Mir Space Station. The International Space Station was the most complex international scientific project in history, and it was one of the most hopeful symbols of cooperation in the post-Cold War era.

As the Soviet Union and its empire in Europe collapsed, the Communist Party in China came under threat from a unlikely source: Students in mourning. Under the leadership of Deng Xiaoping, the Chinese communists had rejected the communal economic system of Mao Zedong in favor of an economic policy of "reform and opening." Most importantly, they had reformed Chinese agriculture by introducing free market mechanisms, and they had opened China to foreign trade and investment. These reforms had been successful in giving China one of the world's fastest growing economies by the late 1980s, but they had not been accompanied by greater measures of political freedom. Tensions had mounted between the social changes brought by economic prosperity and the communist government's inflexible authoritarianism. The Party General Secretary, Hu Yaobang, had proven sympathetic to calls for liberal reforms of the civil administration, prompting his conservative comrades to force him to resign in 1987. He subsequently died of a heart attack on 15 April 1989, and two days later several hundred students at Beijing University staged a march to honor Hu for his progressive politics. As the students marched through the campus, chanting tributes to Hu, their numbers swelled into the thousands, inspiring them to leave the campus and march to Tiananmen Square, the same site where Mao had declared the founding of the People's Republic of China forty years earlier. Once on the square, the students transformed their march into a massive pro-democracy demonstration, which immediately attracted tens of thousands of students from the region and won the popular support of much of Beijing. The demonstration did not call for the overthrow of the communist government, but for freedom of speech and an end to political corruption. The students made their claims through peaceful methods, such as additional marches and mass hunger strikes, which attracted the attention of China at large and of the international media. The movement was embodied in a statue, "The Goddess of Liberty," which the protesters built and placed upon the square to mark a new political era, even as they sang choruses of the communist *Internationale*. Their relatively modest demands nevertheless proved too radical for the communist government. Deng Xiaoping accused the students of being counter-revolutionaries, and the government deployed police and troops who proved unable, and sometimes unwilling, to stop the growing momentum of the protest. Finally, on the evening of 3 June, the People's Liberation Army swept into Beijing with overwhelming ferocity, killing an unknown number of students as it cleared the streets and Tiananmen Square by the end of the following day. As many as 10,000 protesters were arrested, and 31 were tried and executed.

While the Communist Party in China chose to resist reform, democracy had begun to expand elsewhere in East Asia. Liberal reformers within the ruling Kuomintang Party (KMT), which had organized and won elections in 1986, had ended the dictatorship in Taiwan. After the death of the Taiwanese president, Chiang Ching-kuo, in 1988, his vice president, Li Teng-hui, rose to power and continued the process of liberalization by sanctioning the establishment of opposition parties. Meanwhile, South Korea became democratic in 1987, and subsequently elected the reform-minded Kim Dae Jong to the presidency in 1997. Kim promptly assumed an instrumental role in creating a political dialogue with North Korea, with which the South was still at war. By the early 1990s, North Korea and China were the last bastions of communism in East Asia, but only North Korea still held fast to a strict, communist economic system, with disastrous results under the dictator, Kim Il Sung. North Korea was seriously hurt by the suspension of Soviet aid, but Kim continued to isolate his people from the world and did little to relieve their growing economic distress. At the same time, he maintained a formidable military, and a nuclear arsenal aimed at the South Korean and US forces across the border. Following the resolution of the standoff between NATO and the Warsaw Pact in Europe, the Korean peninsula became the most dangerous point of contention between a communist government and a capitalist democracy. Yet there was another potential conflict in the region's future, given that Britain was due to cede its colony, Hong Kong, to China upon the conclusion of a 100-year lease in 1997. It would be an unprecedented event: the handover of a thriving capitalist society to a communist government, albeit one that had undertaken a successful liberalization of its economy. The communist crackdown at Tiananmen Square had obviously given the residents of Hong Kong, and their British colonial administrators, cause for great concern. The Chinese government attempted to assuage this concern by proposing an innovative policy of "one government, two systems" to protect the lucrative Hong Kong economy, from which mainland China stood to benefit.

At the end of the century, there were only three communist governments left in the world: China, North Korea, and Cuba. The decline of communism was swiftly followed by a dramatic increase in the number of democracies, due largely to the rush to democracy in Eastern Europe, accompanied by the establishment of new democracies in Latin America, Africa, and Asia. In the 1990s, the number of democracies in the world almost doubled. By 2002, 120 of the 192 governments in the world were electoral democracies, and 58.2 percent of the world's population was under some form of democratic authority. Many celebrated this political change as the basis of an enduring peace, given that democracies have not historically gone to war against each other. Of course, there had never been so many democracies competing in the world, and all of these democracies had not been created equal. The United States was now the only superpower, possessing both the largest national economy and the world's most powerful military. The US confronted its old and new enemies as the self-professed defender of the world's freedom, but its power was not always matched by its generosity. No other developed country devoted a smaller percentage of its gross domestic product to foreign aid, and no other country was the object of such widespread international resentment for its foreign policies. It was a new world order of both great promise and a great many uncertainties.

The Rise of Internationalism
The end of the Cold War revitalized the United Nations. The UN had been created at the end of the Second World War to ensure international peace and security, and to promote economic development and human rights around the world. While the UN had subsequently done valuable work in public health and welfare, members of the UN Security Council—especially the United States, Russia, and China—had hampered its primary function as a mediator of international disputes. Time and again, the strategic calculations of the Cold War had prompted the US, Russia, and China to block proposals from the UN Assembly. These obstructions decreased after 1989, and the UN promptly moved beyond the political status of an international debating society to become a vehicle for international action. The UN decisively demonstrated its new influence in responding to Iraq's invasion of Kuwait in 1990.

The Iraqi dictator, Saddam Hussein, invaded Kuwait for the same reason that he had invaded Iran in 1980: to establish Iraq as the dominant state in the Persian Gulf on the economic basis of petroleum. His decision to invade Kuwait was partially driven by his failure to defeat Iran after an eight-year war, which had ended in 1988 under a UN resolution that restored the previous Iran-Iraqi border, at the cost of over a million Iranian and Iraqi lives. Iraq had concluded the war with a heavy international debt, some of which was held by Kuwait, which had joined other Arab states in backing Iraq against the revolutionary Islamic government of the Ayatollah Khomeini in Iran. Iraq and Kuwait had the fourth and third largest oil fields in the world, and Hussein intended to combine these vast resources in order to relieve his debt and consolidate his power in the region. Iraq's primary military supplier in previous years, the Soviet Union, did not support the invasion of Kuwait, but it lacked the strength to deter Hussein. No one doubted that the United States would also oppose this Iraqi conquest, but Hussein believed that the US lacked the resolve to risk its forces in a major conflict in the Middle East. After all, he reasoned, the US had failed in its efforts to rescue the US hostages in Iran in 1980, and the US had removed its troops from Lebanon in 1984 in response to the terrorist bombing of the Marine Corps barracks in Beirut in October of the previous year. Thus emboldened, Hussein sent his troops into Kuwait on 2 August 1990 and declared the country an Iraqi province.

An international coalition quickly formed under the authority of the United Nations to demand Iraq's withdrawal from Kuwait. This coalition, eventually composed of some thirty nations, was brought together by interests in petroleum, political self-preservation, and the principled defense of the sovereignty of small states. The US, the leading power in the coalition, was preoccupied with both its Middle Eastern petroleum supplies and the security of two Middle Eastern allies, Saudi Arabia and Israel, which were both immediately threatened by Iraq. With firm resolve, President George H. W. Bush pledged on 5 August that Iraq's conquest would not stand, and he deployed Air Force fighters to Saudi Arabia. Many of the world's other leading powers, and especially those of western Europe, also perceived the Iraqi invasion as a threat to vital petroleum supplies, while the neighboring Arab monarchies feared that Iraq's conquest would inspire rebellion among their unenfranchised, ethnically divided, and impoverished subjects. There was a certain paradox in the world's most powerful liberal democracies rushing to support the monarchies of the Middle East, but the democracies justified their actions as a defense of sovereignty, which was and is a fundamental principle of international law.

The coalition against Saddam Hussein came together under the United Nations, then took action under the leadership of the United States. On 29 November 1990, following a flurry of diplomatic exchanges, the UN Security Council authorized the use of "all means necessary" to expel Iraq from Kuwait, and it subsequently established a deadline of 15 January for Iraq's voluntary withdrawal. As diplomatic efforts continued, the coalition forces mounted their opposition to Iraq in three phases, beginning with an ineffectual economic blockade. Two days after the UN deadline for withdrawal had passed, the coalition moved into the second phase of its plan, launching an air offensive that began the military campaign known as "Desert Storm." Iraqi forces initially put up stiff resistance, but they were worn down by heavy bombardment with superior US weaponry, including precision-guided missiles and the F117-A Nighthawk Stealth Fighter. The final phase of the campaign, the allied ground attack, began on 24 February and routed Iraqi forces on the way to liberating Kuwait City. The coalition forces might have followed the fleeing Iraqi army back into Iraq, but they chose instead to establish a cease-fire on 28 February. The Arab states of the coalition had lobbied to spare Saddam Hussein, because they feared that the collapse of Hussein's dictatorship would create border disputes and ethnic clashes that would further threaten their own power. Indeed, Hussein had managed to impose his control over a fractious combination of ethnically and religiously diverse groups, including Sunnis, Shias, and Kurds. Despite his defeat in Kuwait, he successfully crushed revolts by both Shias and Kurds in the aftermath of the Gulf War in 1991.

Just as the United Nations had played a central role in mobilizing the international coalition that waged Desert Storm, it played a central role in the settlement of the war. Whereas coalition casualties had numbered in the hundreds, Iraqi casualties had numbered in the tens of thousands, and the Iraqi military had sustained massive damage to its equipment and facilities. Nonetheless, Hussein remained a serious military threat in the Gulf, so the UN imposed a variety of restrictions to hold him in check. It established a protectorate over part of northern Iraq for the security of the Kurdish minority that lived there. Over a decade later, allied fighters continued to patrol the "no-fly zone" over this region and exchange fire with Iraqi ground forces. In another innovative move, the UN created the UN Special Commission (UNSCOM) to locate and destroy Iraq's "weapons of mass destruction," including chemical and biological weapons, and nuclear armaments. UNSCOM began its work in Iraq in June 1992 but found itself consistently obstructed by Iraqi officials until its mission ended amid controversy in December 1998. Controversy also followed the UN imposition of economic sanctions on Iraq after the Gulf War. According to international aid organizations, these sanctions produced starvation and suffering among the Iraqi people, rather than within Hussein's government or the military. Hussein informed the Iraqi people that their post-war hardship was the responsibility of the United States, and he continued to consolidate his dictatorial power in anticipation of his next campaign.

Opposite: A portrait of Chairman Mao faces the Goddess of Democracy, a sculpture modeled on the Statue of Liberty, which Chinese students constructed to symbolize their pro-democracy demonstration on Tiananmen Square in Beijing in May 1989.

Right: US Marines capture Iraqi soldiers in Kuwait during Operation Desert Storm in February 1991.

Ethnic Nationalism and International Peacekeeping

Ethnic conflicts, commonly driven by aggressive nationalism, played an increasingly prominent role around the world. The destructive power of ethnic nationalism had been acknowledged and feared since 1914, when a Serbian nationalist assassinated Archduke Franz Ferdinand of Austria and triggered a sequence of events that resulted in the First World War. In the late twentieth century, ethnic nationalists continued to foment rebellion and direct violence against governments, as in the case of Tamil separatists in Sri Lanka. A suicide bomber from this movement assassinated the former Prime Minister of India, Rajiv Gandhi, in 1991, in reprisal for India's support of the Sri Lankan government. The 1990s saw ethnic violence increase not only in Asia but also around the world, in part because of the end of the Cold War. In Central Asia and Europe, as Soviet authority receded, it became clear that some forty years of communist rule and indoctrination had failed to weaken ethnic identities and national aspirations to political sovereignty. In some cases, ethnic differences were resolved amicably, as in the division of Czechoslovakia into the nation states of the Czech Republic and Slovakia. In other cases, the resurgence of ethnic nationalism resulted in long, bloody conflicts, as in Chechnyan rebellion against Russia. Apart from the sheer volume of ethnic conflicts, the post-Cold War era of ethnic nationalism was further distinguished by the increased deployment of UN peace keepers, and by two genocides, one in the Balkans and one in Rwanda, which the UN failed to stop.

Yugoslavia had been created after the First World War by the European allies, who hoped to stabilize this volatile, multiethnic region. In the early 1980s, Yugoslavia had again become unstable, following the death of its authoritarian leader, Josip Tito. The power vacuum created by Tito's death opened the way for a Serbian, Slobodan Milosevic, to establish his authority over the predominantly ethnic Serbian population on a platform of aggressive nationalism. Milosevic fueled this nationalism with religious hatred, pitting the Orthodox Christian Serbs against the Croats, who were Catholic, and the ethnic Albanians, who were Muslim. After the collapse of the Soviet Union, Milosevic and his allies set out to establish a smaller Yugoslav fed-

eration under Serbian control. Toward this end, they moved to crush Croatian separatists and to seize control of Bosnia, a mostly Muslim country with a large Serbian minority. Serbian troops marched into Bosnia, staged mass executions of Muslim males, and systematically raped Muslim women and girls in a campaign that they described as "ethnic cleansing." In response, the United Nations imposed economic sanctions upon Serbia and deployed international troops to protect the distribution of food and medicine to Muslim refugees. The UN troops were ordered not to engage the Serbians in combat, and consequently the Serbian atrocities continued, even in the so-called "Safe Havens" that the UN established for Muslims in 1993. Only after the murder of 8,000 Muslim males in the town of Srebrenica did NATO launch air strikes against the Serbian forces in 1995. This prompted Milosevic to capitulate in November under the Dayton Peace Accord, which divided Bosnia into a Muslim-Croat federation and a Serbian republic. Some 60,000 NATO troops were deployed to enforce the ceasefire, but only after more than 200,000 Muslims had been killed and millions driven from their homes in the previous three years.

In July 1997, Milosevic was elected president of Yugoslavia. Less than two years later, when Milosevic led another brutal campaign against Muslims in the Serbian province of Kosovo, NATO responded with a three-month aerial bombardment, precipitating Milosevic's fall from power after he attempted to steal the Yugoslav presidential elections of 2000. Subsequently, in June 2001, the Yugoslav government turned Milosevic over to the UN Tribunal at the Hague for trial on charges of crimes against humanity and genocide. In the trial, which began in February 2002, Milosevic faced indictments on sixty-six counts for crimes against humanity in Croatia, Bosnia, and Kosovo between 1991 and 1999. It was the first international trial of a former head of state charged with responsibility for crimes against humanity, and it was thus the most important international tribunal since the Nuremberg trials that followed the Second World War.

The genocide in Rwanda in 1994 resulted in a still greater loss of life and a more conspicuous failure of the international community to take decisive action. This genocide was the culmina-

tion of an historical conflict between the Hutu and the Tutsi tribes, a conflict that took its contemporary form under Belgian colonial rule, which ended in 1962. By the early 1990s, the Hutu made up 85 percent of the Rwandan populace and controlled the government over the Tutsi minority. Following the invasion of Tutsi rebels from Uganda in 1990, Rwanda endured a sporadic civil war until 1993, when the UN helped to mediate the Arusha Peace Accords on the basis of ethnic power-sharing in the Rwandan government. The UN deployed Belgian peacekeepers, but Hutu extremists continued to resist compromise. On 11 January 1994, the UN force commander in Rwanda sent an urgent message to the head of UN Peacekeeping, Kofi Annan, reporting that senior Rwandan officials were planning to "exterminate" the Tutsi and kill UN peacekeepers. UN administrators took no action. On 6 April, the president of Rwanda and the president of neighboring Burundi died when the former's plane was shot down, allegedly by Hutu extremists. That same night, the genocide began, as Hutu soldiers and militia systematically slaughtered Tutsi, moderate Hutu officials, and UN peacekeepers. As the international community hesitated to take decisive action, some 800,000 people perished in the next hundred days. The genocide stopped only when Tutsi forces seized the Rwandan capital, Kigali, and established a "national unity" government, as Hutu officials fled to Zaire. The US President, Bill Clinton, and Kofi Annan, then the UN Secretary-General, apologized to the Rwandan people for the failure of the international community to intervene on their behalf.

The Aftermath of Imperialism

The heyday of Western overseas empires had long since passed by the late twentieth century. Yet Britain staged a spectacular imperial display during the ceremonial handover of Hong Kong to China at midnight on 1 July 1997. More than two years later, in December 1999, Portugal ceded to China its sovereignty over Macao, the last European colonial possession in East Asia. While the transition from British and Portuguese imperial rule proceeded smoothly in Hong Kong and Macao, many former colonial nations continued to attempt to resolve conflicts and inequities that Western imperialism and colonial settlement had left behind. India and Pakistan, each with nuclear capability, continued to face off over the disputed region of Kashmir in a conflict produced by Britain's sudden withdrawal from the sub-continent in 1947. In Zimbabwe, tensions mounted between the black majority and the white minority over white ownership of valuable farmland, which the whites had acquired under British colonial rule prior to Zimbabwe's independence in 1980. There were also constructive and inspiring resolutions of imperial issues, as in South Africa, which negotiated a peaceful transition from apartheid to "nonracial" democracy, and in Northern Ireland, which built the foundation of a peace settlement between militant Irish nationalists and "loyalists."

The apartheid government in South Africa, established by the National Party in 1948, had been built upon white racial privilege and the economic and legal subjugation of black Africans, the mixed-race "colored" community, and Asians. The National Party was the party of conservative Afrikaners, descended from Dutch settlers of the seventeenth and eighteenth centuries who had long since established their own identity as a "white tribe" in Africa. By the mid-1980s, the apartheid regime had weakened under the pressure of mass civil rights protests, strikes, international economic sanctions, and the tremendous cost of its own security forces. President P.W. Botha had declared a state of emergency in 1986, but this had done little to quell the crisis. In 1989, F.W. de Klerk, a moderate Afrikaner, became the head of the government and moved swiftly to enact major reforms, such as the legalization of dissident political organizations, including the African National Congress (ANC). De Klerk took the dramatic step of releasing the ANC leader, Nelson Mandela, from prison in February 1990, concluding Mandela's incarceration of twenty-seven years. Mandela subsequently displayed remarkable magnanimity and diplomacy in moving the ANC and the National Party toward a mutually acceptable conclusion to the apartheid era. After intense negotiations, de Klerk, Mandela, and representatives of eighteen other parties endorsed an interim constitution in 1993, setting the stage for the country's first nonracial democratic election. The ANC won a decisive victory in the election of April 1994, and Mandela was sworn in as President on 10 May. He formed the Government of National Unity and oversaw the drafting of a new constitution, which proved to be among the most progressive in the world in its recognition of human rights. In an effort to reinforce the new laws of the land with a spirit of understanding and forgiveness in the aftermath of apartheid, the government created the Truth and Reconciliation Commission, which convened under the leadership of Archbishop Desmond Tutu between 1996 and 1998. While South Africa enjoyed a peaceful political transition to nonracial democracy, the new government was immediately forced to grapple with major problems, such as escalating crime and a national AIDS epidemic.

In the United Kingdom, Irish nationalists and loyalists also moved toward reconciliation after decades of "the troubles", which had begun in the late 1960s. The colonial conflict in Northern Ireland was reminiscent of South Africa, in that the loyalists had descended from settlers, in this case Englishmen and Scots, who had arrived in Ireland between the sixteenth and eighteenth centuries. These settler communities had come to regard themselves as Irish, but they were also Protestants, in contrast to the vast majority of the native Irish, who were Catholics. The loyalists had long since fought to maintain their political connection to Britain, which had historically ensured their privileges and civil liberties as Protestants. By the late 1980s, sectarianism was no longer the primary divide in Northern Irish society, but it had been the source of British policies of political and economic discrimination that had to be resolved if the society was to move forward. The majority of nationalists and loyalists wanted peace, but there were obstacles to a settlement that many in this majority still regarded as insurmountable. One of the primary obstacles to peace was the nationalist demand for the reunification of the six counties of Northern Ireland, which were part of the United Kingdom, with the thirty-two counties of the Republic of Ireland. Loyalists feared that their economic interests would be ignored, and their civil rights undermined, in a unified Ireland. In December 1993, however, the British Prime Minister, John Major, and the Irish Prime Minister, Albert Reynolds, offered a possible way around this impasse that might further lead to multi-party talks. Their Downing Street Declaration marked a major shift in the policies of both governments in two respects. The declaration indicated that any settlement should be based on the consensus of all of the people of Ireland. Furthermore, the Irish government recognized that the Protestant majority in Northern Ireland could not be forced into a settlement that they opposed. In response, in August 1994, the Irish Republican Army announced a "complete cessation of military operations," and loyalist paramilitaries followed suit by declaring a ceasefire in October. Negotiations began between the British and Irish governments and the northern Irish political parties, including Sinn Fein, the political arm of the Irish Republican Army (IRA). Undeterred by sporadic violence and breakdowns of the ceasefire arrangements, the parties continued to work toward a settlement, with crucial mediation by the former US Senator, George Mitchell. The terms of the settlement were finalized in April 1998 under the "Good Friday Agreement," which provided for the creation of a multi-party Northern Ireland Assembly and Executive. Under this agreement, the Republic renounced its claim upon Northern Ireland, and all agreed that Northern Ireland would remain part of the United Kingdom until the majority of people in North voted to change its political status. The terms of this settlement were put to an all-Ireland referendum, which returned 71.2 percent in favor in the North, and 94.39 percent in favor in the Republic. As if to punctuate the desperation of extremists who now confronted the prospect of a lasting peace built on compromise, a car bomb detonated in the town of Omagh in August, killing 29 people in the worst atrocity of "the troubles." The bombing, perpetrated by a fringe group calling itself "The Real IRA" provoked sympathy and condemnation across partisan lines, driving the peace process forward, rather than back. In September, the people of Northern Ireland elected their Assembly, but problems continued in efforts to reach a final, conclusive settlement of old conflicts. Most importantly, loyalists insisted that the IRA destroy its weapons, while nationalists insisted that the British army withdraw promptly from nationalist residential areas and that the Royal Ulster Constabulary (RUC) reform its policies and add Catholics to its ranks. The IRA began to put its weaponry "beyond use" in October 2001 under the authority of an independent commission, and progress was also made in reducing the British military presence and in reforming the RUC. "The troubles" had not decisively concluded by the early 2000s, but the end was in sight, in accordance with the wishes of the vast majority of the Irish people on both sides of the border.

Opposite: Rajiv Gandhi, the former Prime Minister of India and the leader of the Congress Party, campaigning for election to Parliament prior to his assassination by a suicide bomber in 1991.

Right: Nelson Mandela, the leader of the African National Congress, and his wife, Winnie Mandela, celebrate the end of his political imprisonment of 27 years by the apartheid government of South Africa in February 1990.

Islamic Revivalism

Approximately one-fifth of people in the world were Muslims. Consequently, the revival of the influence of Islam in international politics and the daily life of numerous societies, which began in the 1970s, became a significant force by the end of the century. The phenomenon of Islamic revivalism was multifaceted, but its proponents generally shared a belief that the tenets of Islam should shape their political systems, laws, and societies. The Western media commonly ignored the Islamic revival, except in its most radical forms, such as the repressive system presided over by the Ayatollah Khomeini in Iran. Moving beyond his vilification of the West, the Ayatollah provoked international outrage when he issued a *fatwah*, or religious edict, declaring that the novelist Salman Rushdie—a Muslim from Bombay, India—should be killed for his alleged blasphemy against Islam in his novel, *The Satanic Verses*, published in 1988. Rushdie's blasphemy consisted of creating a fictional character who imagined in a dream that the Q'ran was the creation of humans, rather a revelation from God. Rushdie was forced into hiding, his book became an international bestseller, and, although the Ayatollah died in 1989, the Iranian government did not cease to pursue the *fatwah* until 1998. For all of the public debate over Rushdie's ordeal, however, neither the Ayatollah Khomeini nor his *fatwah* were typical of Islamic revivalism. The most widespread Islamic revival was peacefully carried out by social activists, such as teachers in schools and doctors in clinics. Meanwhile, political leaders invoked Islam to legitimize governments across the political spectrum. Self-proclaimed Islamic states included the conservative monarchy of Saudi Arabia, the radical socialist regime of Colonel Muammar Qaddafi in Libya, and the repressive revolutionary government of the Taliban in Afghanistan. Generally, the political leaders of Islamic states struggled to maintain a balance between their Islamic political identity and their desire to control Islamic militants. This was the case in Egypt, where the government had imposed "emergency law" for much of the past fifty years in response to its frequent state of war with Israel and the terrorist campaigns of Islamic radicals. President Hosni Mubarak confronted serious challenges from both Islamic militants and social activists in the 1980s, prompting the government to enact the Anti-Terror Law of 1992, which criminalized even non-violent political opposition. The case of Pakistan, founded as the first Islamic state in 1947, was still more complicated. General Zia ul-Haq had been leading Pakistani society to thorough "Islamization" when he died in a plane crash in August 1988. In the national elections that followed, Benazir Bhutto and the Pakistan People's Party defeated the more radical Islamic Democratic Alliance. Bhutto, who subsequently became the first female prime minister in the Muslim world, continued Zia's Islamization program in a more moderate form. After the Islamic Democratic Alliance defeated Bhutto in 1990, the influence of Islam in Pakistan's political life increased, though Pakistan did not come close to transforming into a theocracy along the lines of Iran or Afghanistan. In 2001, in the course of the US-led war against the Taliban government and the Al Qaeda terrorist network in Afghanistan, President Pervez Musharraf of Pakistan arrested Islamic extremists and initiated the reform of Islamic schools in an effort to stabilize his authority and win economic aid from the West.

The alliance of Arab states with the US and Europe in the Gulf War could not mask the increasing resentment with which many

Muslims in the Middle East viewed the democracies of the west, and, in some cases, their own authoritarian governments. They resented the exploitation of their countries' petroleum fields and other resources for the benefit of the West, and for the profit of their monarchs and a small elite of government functionaries and businessmen. They resented the cynicism with which Western democracies ignored their political subjugation—given that most Middle Eastern states were decidedly undemocratic—and they resented the global expansion of Western Christian and capitalist culture through technologies that they nonetheless acquired. At the foundation of all of these issues were two questions: how could Islamic culture be reconciled with global capitalism; and how could Islamic government, which integrated religion, politics, law, and society, be reconciled with a Western tradition of liberal democracy built upon religious pluralism and the separation of church and state?

The most volatile issue in relations between Middle Eastern Arabs and the West remained the conflict between Israel and Palestine. This conflict had become an overriding concern of all Arab states after Israel decisively defeated a coalition of Arab forces and seized all of Palestine in the "Six Day War" of 1967. Subsequently, Israel pursued an aggressive policy of Jewish settlement at the expense of the disenfranchised Palestinians. By the late 1980s, Israeli-Palestinian relations were dominated by the *intifada*, the popular militant uprising of Palestinians against Israeli occupation. The international media regularly aired images of Israeli troops and tanks fighting with stone-throwing Palestinian youths, but the *intifada* also consisted of organized strikes and boycotts. Behind these conflicts and campaigns, the majority of Palestinians and Israelis wanted to reach a mutually acceptable, peaceful settlement.

The Palestine Liberation Organization (PLO) chose to negotiate a settlement with Israel due to setbacks on another front. Saddam Hussein had been a major supporter of the PLO, and in this respect he had enjoyed the explicit or tacit approval of a number of Arab states. Hussein's invasion of Kuwait in 1990 unified a number of otherwise anti-Israeli Arab states against him, placing the PLO in an awkward position. Hussein's defeat in 1991, followed by the expulsion of many Palestinians from Kuwait, undermined the PLO's resources and brought its leaders to the bargaining table with the Israeli government. The creation of a new Israeli government under Yitzhak Rabin of

the Labor Party facilitated negotiations at this crucial junction. The ensuing talks, which proceeded in secrecy in Oslo, Norway, resulted in a landmark Israeli-Palestinian accord, signed in September 1993 in Washington, DC. This accord had several important features: mutual recognition, Israeli withdrawal from areas of the Gaza Strip and the West Bank, and the creation of a Palestinian Authority to govern these areas. More broadly, both parties set aside precedents in international law as the basis of their bilateral negotiations, and they separated interim and "final status" issues in an effort to keep the peace process moving forward in the short term. Yasser Arafat, the leader of the PLO, returned to Palestine in July 1994 for the first time in thirty-three years to become Chairman of the new Palestinian Authority. In the same year, Prime Minister Rabin, the Israeli Foreign Minister, Shimon Peres, and Arafat received the Nobel Peace Prize, even as Jewish and Palestinian radicals resumed killing in the hope of derailing the peace process. Their conflicts were aggravated by the continuation of aggressive Jewish settlement and the Israeli state's confiscation of Palestinian land. Both of these policies reinforced Israel's fragmentation of the lands it placed under Palestinian authority, and its insistence that the borders of this Palestinian territory should exist within the borders of Israel, thus isolating Palestinian power. As tensions mounted again, it became clear that Israel had not negotiated for a lasting peace, but rather for security on the basis of unequal power. Tragically, on 4 November 1995, a Jewish extremist assassinated Rabin, who was leaving a peace rally. In January 1996 Arafat was elected President of the Palestinian Authority, and in June Israel's Labor government was replaced by the conservative Likud Party, whose leader, Benjamin Netanyahu, became the Prime Minister. Over the next several years, a lasting peace was frustrated by a number of factors, including the intransigence of both negotiating parties, Israeli policies to displace and economically subjugate Palestinians in favor of broader Jewish settlement, and the continued violence of Islamic militants. The latter escalated to unprecedented levels with the beginning of a new *intifada* in September 2000. After several decades of conflict, most Israelis and Palestinians could at least agree that their final peace would have to include the creation of two separate states in Palestine. Yet their political leaders and the extremists on both sides continued to dispute the borders of these imagined homelands, as they waged a "holy war" of terror and attrition.

Terrorism

Many people in the world lived under the daily threat of terrorism long before 1988. Terrorism has no particular political identity; it is rather a brutal means to political ends. Consequently, there is no universally accepted definition of terrorism, as one person's terrorist is apt to be another person's freedom fighter. Although the international media has generally treated terrorism as a tool of political dissidents, one can argue that governments also employ terrorism, as in the case of Serbian aggression in the Balkans. The act of terrorism might be described as a violent attack intended to inflict harm upon civilians without regard for their rights and welfare under international or civil laws. Since 1988, groups have used terrorism in their attempts to achieve independence, as in the cases of Irish militants in the United Kingdom and Basque militants in Spain. Governments have employed terrorist methods to subjugate distinct groups of people, as in the case of Indonesia's support for paramilitaries who launched a terror campaign in East Timor before and after a referendum on the nation's independence from Indonesia in August 1999. Drug lords in South America have used terrorism to intimidate politicians and legal authorities, while other groups and individuals have used terrorism to impose deeply held religious beliefs, as in the bombing of abortion clinics in the United States. Apart from such issues of motive and precedent, however, there were two respects in which the years after 1988 marked a new era in terrorism. First, large-scale terrorist strikes in the United States ended the nation's relative insulation from fears that much of the world had experienced for decades. Second, in seeking to prevent future terrorist attacks, the United States and its allies launched a "war on terror" that exposed a sophisticated, global network of terrorist organizations, which exploited transnational technologies and economies to threaten sovereign states and their subjects and citizens.

Islamic militants had already attempted to overthrow governments in the Middle East, including Arab states and Israel. In the late twentieth century, these militants expanded their attacks to include the United States, which they recognized as the crucial financial and military backer of their regional adversaries. In December 1988, Islamic militants bombed an

American airliner, Pan Am flight 103, en route from London to New York, bringing the plane down on Lockerbie, Scotland, and killing a total of 270 people. There were numerous, successful terrorist strikes against US interests overseas in the next decade, and three major attacks on US soil. The first of these attacks within the US came in February 1993, when foreign Islamic terrorists detonated a 1,200 pound (540 kg) bomb in the parking garage beneath the World Trade Center in Manhattan. Six people were killed, and more than a thousand were injured, either from the blast or due to the smoke that rose through stairwells and elevator shafts as people attempted to escape. In April 1995, a truck bomb exploded in front of the Alfred P. Murrah Building in Oklahoma City, killing 168. In view of the previous attack on the World Trade Center, many people in the US initially believed that this new atrocity was also the work of foreign Islamic terrorists. However, it soon came to light that the perpetrators of this act were right-wing US citizens committed to undermining the federal government, which they viewed as a threat to their personal freedom. The man who delivered the bomb to the Murrah Building, Timothy McVeigh, was tried, convicted, and, eventually, executed.

The scale of these terrorist attacks was dwarfed by a coordinated series of terrorist strikes in the United States on 11 September 2001. That morning, foreign Islamic terrorists hijacked American Airlines flight 11 en route from Boston to Los Angeles, then deliberately flew the plane into the North Tower of the World Trade Center. Simultaneously, terrorists hijacked United Airlines flight 175 en route from Boston to Los Angeles, then flew it into the World Trade Center's South Tower. Both planes crashed with their fuel tanks nearly full, producing explosions that engulfed multiple floors of both towers in flames. As the US public and people around the world watched these images on television and attempted to grasp the causes and significance of this catastrophe, hijackers flew American Airlines flight 77, previously en route from Washington, DC, to Los Angeles, into the Pentagon Building in Washington, DC. Finally, having learned of these previous disasters, passengers aboard United Airlines flight 93, previously bound from Newark to San Francisco, attacked the hijackers who had seized their

plane, causing the plane to crash in Somerset County, Pennsylvania. As rumors circulated throughout the US regarding additional attacks, the two towers of the World Trade Center collapsed, killing thousands of civilians and hundreds of firefighters, police, and paramedics. In the chaotic days and weeks that followed 11 September, the death toll remained uncertain. In February 2002, the number of those confirmed or believed dead was approximately 2900, constituting the largest terrorist atrocity in US history and the most successful surprise attack against the nation since the Japanese strike on Pearl Harbor in 1941.

The US government, under the new presidency of George W. Bush, determined that a terrorist organization called Al Qaeda ("the base" in Arabic) was primarily responsible for the attacks of 11 September. This transnational organization, under the leadership of an exiled Saudi millionaire, Osama bin Laden, had drawn its members from many Muslim countries, including Egypt, Saudi Arabia, Pakistan, and Afghanistan. Bin Laden and other leaders of the organization had gained valuable military experience as *mujahideen* fighting against the Soviets in Afghanistan in the 1980s. Al Qaeda had subsequently attacked US targets around the world as part of a broader campaign to rid the Holy Land of US interests and especially the US ally, Israel. The organization had been strengthened in 1998, when an Egyptian, Ayman al-Zawahiri, joined his terrorist group, al-Jihad, with Al Qaeda to form the International Islamic Front for the Jihad against Jews and Crusaders. At the time of the attacks on 11 September, bin Laden and other Al Qaeda leaders enjoyed sanctuary in Afghanistan, under the Taliban government, which had been established in 1996. In a manner reminiscent of the build-up to the Gulf War, the United States assembled a political and military coalition under the aegis of the United Nations. It also created new alliances with Central Asian governments and Pakistan, which had previously co-operated with the Taliban. After the Taliban refused to hand over bin Laden, the US and its coalition partners launched a military campaign against Taliban and Al Qaeda forces in Afghanistan, coordinating with an Afghani rebel group called the Northern Alliance. The US-led campaign succeeded in overthrowing the Taliban and killing or capturing hundreds of Al Qaeda

Opposite: Palestinian youths, displaying the flag of the Palestinian Liberation Organization, demonstrate against Israeli occupation in the West Bank city of Ramallah during the *intifada* in March 1988.

Right: In the course of an international criminal investigation, the US Justice Department carefully reconstructs the plane designated Pan Am 103, which was destroyed by a terrorist bomb over Lockerbie, Scotland, in December 1988.

Left: A farmer in northern Brazil surveys the destruction of the Amazon rain forest for the expansion of agriculture in March 1998.

Opposite: AIDS activists in Cape Town, South Africa, protest against the efforts of the South African government to overturn a court order that would require it to provide anti-retroviral drugs to HIV-positive pregnant mothers in May 2002.

members, but, by early 2002, it had not located either the Taliban leader, Mullah Omar, or bin Laden. As the "war on terror" continued with the deployment of US forces to other parts of the world, the US government and the United Nations supported the creation of a new democratic government in Afghanistan under an interim president, Hamid Karzai. The massive financial investment needed to sustain this government would test the resolve of the US and the international community to pursue the "war on terror" not only through military force, but constructive development.

Globalization and Economic Integration

The post-Cold War era featured much talk of "globalization," an economic process with important political and cultural effects. Globalization is, in the simplest sense, the process through which the world's economies are integrated across sovereign boundaries by removing barriers to trade and restrictions on foreign investment. This process had been overseen since 1946 by the International Monetary Fund (IMF), which had 183 member countries at the end of 2001. The goal of the IMF was to establish international monetary cooperation and stability, and to promote economic development. In the 1990s, the IMF also became increasingly involved in social welfare and self-help programs, in a manner similar to the World Bank, established in 1944, also with 183 member countries in 2001. The economic and political conflicts of the Cold War had restricted the roles of these and other international organizations in promoting globalization. In the 1990s, however, the collapse of the Soviet Union led many governments of former Soviet and Warsaw Pact nations to seek development aid from the IMF and the World Bank. The 1990s also witnessed major steps toward the integration of trade and monetary policies in particular regions of the world. The United States, Mexico, and Canada dismantled trade barriers under the North American Free Trade Agreement of 1994. Similarly, Brazil, Argentina, Paraguay, and Uruguay established a free trade union in 1995. Yet the most comprehensive economic reforms took place in Europe, in tandem with major reforms in the structure of European governance.

Europe built upon the earlier work of the European Economic Community, established in 1958, and the European Community, established in 1967, to orchestrate an economic and political union between European nations. In 1991, representatives of twelve European governments met in the Dutch town of Maastricht to negotiate the Treaty of the European Union. This treaty established the criteria for the monetary union of European Union (EU) members. It further provided for a common foreign and security policy and the unprecedented co-ordination of judicial and home affairs. Citizens of EU countries would become EU citizens, free to move across national boundaries, reside anywhere in the EU, and vote in local and European elections in any EU country. The treaty was subsequently ratified in 1993 in referenda held in all twelve countries, bringing its terms into affect. Three additional countries, Austria, Finland, and Sweden, then joined in 1995. Between 1999 and 2001, the twelve EU countries formally adopted the Euro as their national currency, though their old national currencies remained in circulation. On 1 January 2002, the Euro became the only EU currency in the largest monetary changeover in history. Under the terms of other agreements in the 1990s, additional European countries from the former Warsaw Pact would be eligible to join the EU after 2004, paving the way for future expansion.

The process of globalization, in both world and regional contexts, was advanced by technological innovations, and especially the spread of telecommunications technology. Technologies that had become commonplace in the West became widely available in the Middle East, for example, where photocopiers, fax machines, and videocassette players facilitated popular political debate. With the assistance of satellites, television news organizations reconstituted themselves as global agencies, providing images and continuous analysis of breaking stories from all over the world in real time. This new role for television news was demonstrated in the coverage of the Tiananmen Square protest in 1989 by the Cable News Network (CNN), which set a new standard for 24-hour coverage of global political events. Television also became a vehicle for global entertainment in the 1990s, with the growth of satellite networks such as Sky One, based in Great Britain, which brought Western television shows, and particular-

ly those from the US, to audiences around the world. At the same time, non-satellite networks, such as al-Jazeera, an Arabic-language network based in Qatar, served the growing international market for independent news coverage, while the Lebanese Broadcasting Corporation offered a combination of Arabic entertainment and US programming. Finally, satellite technology enabled television networks to provide common experiences across boundaries of language and culture, most often through sport. An estimated one billion people watched the World Cup in 1994, and an estimated three billion people watched the 2000 Olympics. In a related vein, the computer network known as the Internet, or the "world wide web," gained an ever increasing number of users in the 1990s, building upon its original user base of scientists and academics to establish "e-mail" as a popular means of communication and "e-commerce" as a lucrative, international business field. In 1994, the Internet had about three million users, of which most were in the US. In just five years the number of users grew to approximately 200 million people around the world. This dramatic growth was facilitated by the development and distribution of Internet "browsers" after the early 1990s, which made it easy for anyone with access to a computer to communicate with anyone else similarly equipped, almost anywhere in the world. The pace and volume of communications were increased not only by the Internet, but, perhaps even more significantly, by the proliferation of mobile phones. While western Europe had the largest percentage of mobile phone owners in relation to its total population—approximately 70 percent in 2002—mobile phone technology provided people in developing nations with a means to bypass shortcomings in their national telecommunications infrastructure. Consequently, a family in Mumbai, India, which might have waited for years to get a conventional phone line installed, could now purchase a mobile phone instead.

The effects of globalization on politics were various and complicated. Globalization was accompanied by the further growth of international environmentalism. The United Nations became more involved in environmental issues, convening the first Earth Summit in 1992 in Rio de Janeiro to establish ground rules for "sustainable growth." Although the Summit produced an ambitious program on paper, few of the provisions, such as those against deforestation, had been put into action prior to the second Earth Summit in Johannesburg in 2002. Similarly, the representatives of forty nations produced ambitious plans to reduce carbon emissions, and thus protect the earth's ozone layer, under the 1997 Kyoto climate protocol. Five years later, these plans had not been put into action, primarily because the US government continued to reject the protocol as harmful to the US economy and unfair in its exclusion of India and China, both major polluters. On a related front, globalization was accompanied by the growth of international political parties, such as the Green Party. The Greens originated in progressive liberal movements in New Zealand and Germany in the 1970s and early 1980s. As critics of the Cold War, Greens commonly advocated peace, an end to nuclear arms, and a turn from geopolitical conflict to the common cause of protecting the environment. In the aftermath of the Cold War, the Green Party continued to expand throughout Europe, Asia, Africa, the Americas, and the Pacific, convening its first international assembly in Niger in 1995. While the Greens were commonly critical of globalization, their protests were moderate in comparison to the Anti-Globalization Movement, which was composed of a core alliance of labor unionists and environmentalists. This movement burst upon the international stage with mass protests during the meeting of the World Trade Organization in Seattle in 1999.

Finally, the commercial culture of globalization proved to be a source of both collaboration and conflict around the world. The rise of the "world music" industry featured remarkable collaborations, such as that of the British rock musician, Peter Gabriel, and a Pakistani, Nusrat Fateh Ali Khan, who was arguably the world's greatest singer of Sufi devotional music. Some collaborations had decidedly mixed results, as in the case of Euro-Disney, established near Paris in 1992 amid dismissive criticism from the French media and general public. Far more serious conflicts followed the spread of US commercial culture, and liberal ideologies, to China through new telecommunications networks. In 1993, the Chinese government banned the use of satellite dishes, which had been springing up by the hundreds of thousands throughout the country. Finally, religious fundamentalists of a variety of non-Christian faiths rejected the particular influence of Western, Christian commercial culture. In western India, the right-wing Hindu nationalist party, Shiv Sena, protested violently against Valentine's Day by picketing and destroying card shops after 2001. They found it offensive that Hindu youths would spend their money to commemorate a Catholic martyr who was the patron saint of lovers.

Demographics, Health, and Development

The world's population rose from approximately 5,050,000,000 in 1988 to 6,100,000,000 in 2000. The greater part of this population growth occurred in the world's developing nations, such as Kenya, which in 1988 had the highest rate of population growth ever, recorded at 4.2 percent. While the annual world population growth rate stood at about 1.3 percent at the turn of the century, only six countries, China, India, Pakistan, Bangladesh, Indonesia, and Nigeria, accounted for half of the total increase in population. China remained the most populous country, with more than 1.2 billion people, but India ended the century leading the world in both population growth and population density. In 2000, India became the second country after China to surpass one billion in population. The case of India illustrated some of the general problems produced by rising populations in the developing world, ranging from deficiencies in infrastructures for electricity and sewage to inadequate land and resources for sustainable growth. At the turn of the century, India had 16 percent of the world's population, but only 2.5 percent of its land, and more than a third of India's people lived in poverty. Despite these difficulties, India remained the world's largest democracy after more than fifty years of independence.

The state of human health continued to improve in important respects, as reflected in declining rates of infant and child mortality, and rising life expectancy. There remained major challenges to human health, such as the historical threat of malnutrition to children, but there were also new challenges that grew into international health crises in the 1990s. In a world traversed by international labor migrants, business travelers, and tourists, new diseases spread at alarming rates. One such disease, Auto Immune Deficiency Syndrome, or AIDS, became a pandemic after the late 1980s. By 2000, there were more than 36 million cases of AIDS, of which more than 25 million were in Sub-Saharan Africa. The second largest region of AIDS infection was South and Southeast Asia, with 5.8 million cases, followed by Latin America, with 1.4 million cases. Escalating incidents of infection apparently followed the path of globalization into places such as Eastern Europe and Russia, where statistics on infection had not even been compiled by the early 2000s. AIDS posed particular difficulties for the governments of such developing countries, which did not have the financial resources to provide comprehensive medical services. Debates ensued over the causes and treatments of AIDS, prompting some governments to take a pro-active policy, as in the case of the pioneering Uganda Aids Commission. By contrast, the government of South Africa, under Nelson Mandela's successor, Thabo Mbeki, initially disputed whether it could take any effective action at all, as millions became infected or died. In a major shift in commercial policy, a number of Western pharmaceutical companies decided to permit the sale of relatively inexpensive, generic medicines against AIDS to the people of South Africa, raising hopes for a more humane commercial approach to AIDS treatment in sub-Saharan Africa at large. International development agencies and non-governmental organizations meanwhile built upon their previous experience in global health programs to launch campaigns against AIDS.

As the AIDS crisis escalated, the world's population benefited from the steady decline of another major disease: polio. In 1988, the World Health Assembly launched the Global Polio Eradication Initiative, which achieved impressive results by the turn of the century. In 2000, in an effort to strike a decisive blow against polio, UNICEF organized a series of National Immunization Days in 82 countries and vaccinated a record 550 million children under the age of five. As a result of the polio eradication program, polio cases decreased from an estimated 350,000 in 1988 to less than 2000 reported worldwide in 2000. While the polio virus remained prevalent in South Asia and sub-Saharan Africa, UNICEF anticipated that the virus would be completely eradicated within the first several years of the new century, which would make it only the second virus, after smallpox, to be eradicated through an international campaign.

The campaign against polio reflects the great promise of international development programs, but it is noteworthy that the progress of such programs appeared to have slowed in the last two decades of the twentieth century. According to the World Bank Development Indicators for 2000, the rates of development in the world's poor countries had slowed in the previous twenty years, in contrast to the rates of development in the preceding twenty years between 1960 and 1980. Specifically, rates of development slowed in life expectancy, infant and child mortality, and literacy. Progress continued at the end of the twentieth century, but the reduced rates of development in poor countries prompted debates over the merits of globalization. Moreover, there were new developments in science and technology that would not be as easily exported as mobile phones or as easily expanded as the Internet. In 1997, a Scottish scientist, Ian Wilmut, announced that he had cloned a sheep, named Dolly, which was the first successful cloning of a mammal from a cell taken from an adult animal. In 2000, two teams of scientists announced that they had determined the structure of the human genome, having tracked the sequence of chemical bases of human DNA. Both of these scientific achievements raised profound moral and ethical questions for all humankind: was it right to clone a mammal, or, eventually, a human? With an understanding of the human genome, was it right to engineer human life? Should this become part of international development? Who precisely should determine the answers to these questions?

Left: Great Britain's Prince Charles (second from left) and his sons, Prince Harry and Prince William, view the flowers placed by well-wishers outside Kensington Palace in London, following the death of Princess Diana in a car crash in Paris in August 1997.

Opposite: Women victims of land mines in Angola in 1993. The civil war in Angola scattered land mines throughout the country, posing a terrible threat to civilians, even in the aftermath of conflict. The United Nations and other international agencies are working to reduce the threat of land mines, which kill thousands of civilians every year in war torn countries around the world.

Regional Summaries

Europe and Russia

In the post-Cold War era, Europe underwent its most significant change since the settlement of the Second World War. The collapse of the Soviet Union brought down the "iron curtain" that had divided Europe between communism, on the one hand, and democracy and capitalism, on the other. By the turn of the century, virtually all of Europe's governments had been democratically elected, and capitalism was the primary engine of the European economy—the most powerful regional economy in the world. The European Union initiated a great experiment in political and economic integration, and both the EU and NATO laid the foundation for the further economic and political integration of western and eastern Europe. Violent conflicts over sovereignty continued, among peoples in the Balkans and between Basque separatists and Spain, but these conflicts never threatened to shake the post-Cold War balance of power in Europe as a whole. Finally, in a region characterized by integration, the United Kingdom was distinguished by devolution. Scotland voted to establish its own legislature, and Wales voted to establish a local assembly in 1997. In the following year, Northern Ireland voted to establish its own Assembly and Executive under the terms of the "Good Friday Peace Accord."

Most of the European leaders and the major political parties that had overseen the end of the Cold War were removed from office by the turn of the century. Lech Walesa, the embodiment of democratic opposition to the Communist Party in Poland, lost in his bid for re-election to the Presidency of Poland in 1995. Mikhail Gorbachev resigned from the Presidency of the defunct Soviet Union in 1991, and Boris Yeltsin retired as the President of the Russian Federation at the end of 1999, making way for Vladimir Putin's election in March 2000. The German Chancellor, Helmut Kohl, and his party of Christian Democrats, lost the 1998 elections to the Social Democrats, who made Gerhard Schroeder the new Chancellor. In France, the socialist presi-

dent, Francois Mitterrand, was defeated by Jacques Chirac in elections in 1995. In 1990, the British Conservative Party ousted Margaret Thatcher from the office of Prime Minister, which she had held longer than any other British Prime Minister in the twentieth century. The Conservatives replaced Thatcher with John Major, who advanced the Conservative agenda in more moderate form over the next several years. After eighteen years of Conservative domination, the Labour Party finally defeated the Conservatives in a landslide election in 1997 and made Tony Blair Britain's last Prime Minister of the century.

With the Cold War peacefully settled, many western European elections in the early and mid-1990s reflected the European public's desire to reign in "big government." Since the Second World War, Europeans had commonly supported the development of welfare states, government control over important industries and infrastructures, and the large bureaucracies needed to manage such institutions and services. By the end of the twentieth century, however, "big government" was placing an increasing strain on civil societies across Europe. Aging populations and declining birthrates undermined the tax bases of European governments, and thus increased the tax burden on the laboring public. In response, after the late 1980s, governments ranging from Britain to Spain began to transfer national industries and services to the private sector. While Prime Minister Margaret Thatcher of Britain undertook some of the most controversial privatization initiatives, this trend toward the reform of big government was also marked clearly in Scandinavia. In 1991, Swedish voters elected a moderate coalition government, rejecting the socialists who had dominated the Swedish government for all but six of the past fifty-nine years. It is noteworthy that, while Europeans wished to decrease the size of government, and their tax burden, they did not want to do away with the public welfare services to which they had become accustomed in the previous decades.

In contrast to western Europe, voters and politicians in eastern Europe and Russia were preoccupied with the difficult transition from a communist to a capitalist economy. Market reforms brought great hardships, such as high inflation and unemployment. In 1992, Russian

inflation reached 2000 percent. Fortunately, the economies of most of the former communist countries stabilized after the mid-1990s, though difficulties continued. In particular, the new democracies of eastern Europe and Russia experienced shortfalls in health care. Also, the new capitalist economies, coupled with the weakening of state security services, contributed to a dramatic increase in organized crime, especially in Russia. In the midst of economic difficulties and rising crime, some eastern Europeans began to turn back to their former communist officials for leadership. The former communists certainly had the benefit of long bureaucratic experience, but not experience in this new world of democracy and capitalism.

Across Europe, immigration became an issue of pressing concern in the 1990s. There were new developments, such as a major increase in the number of migrant laborers from the Balkans, and the ease with which immigrants could cross borders in the EU There was also a notable increase in anti-immigrant politics, led by right wing parties from Belgium to Austria. These reactionaries generally failed to account for the fact that, given Europe's growing number of pensioners and its declining birth rate, the region was becoming increasingly dependent on immigration to maintain its laboring population. Spain, which had the lowest birthrate in the EU, needed the many North Africans who came to work in its orchards and vineyards, prompting the government to offer an amnesty to illegal immigrants in 2000. The United Nations estimated at the turn of the century that Europe would need 160 million immigrants in the next twenty-five years to meet its basic labor needs. The influx of immigrants had already become significant in the first decade of the post-Cold War era. In 1997, 6 percent of the people in France were not French citizens, while in Germany the number of non-nationals had climbed to 9 percent. In the United Kingdom, non-nationals composed about 4 percent of the population, but this percentage did not include the millions of children born to immigrants in the United Kingdom since the 1950s—children who were British, but not necessarily white. In the U.K., as in most of Europe, immigrant populations were concentrated in large urban centers, creating a new cultural divide between the city and countryside. At the turn of the century, the face of Europe had clearly, literally begun to change.

Sub-saharan Africa

The peoples of sub-Saharan Africa continued their search for economic and political stability in the aftermath of European imperialism. Following the watershed of decolonization and African independence in 1960, development had been hindered for decades by African dictators, who were commonly propped up by either side of the Cold War, at the expense of the general African populace. At the turn of the twenty-first century, almost half of the people in sub-Saharan Africa lived in poverty, and the economy of the region was only growing at about 2.5 percent. The absence of responsible government in recent decades had left most of sub-Saharan Africa with neither viable infrastructures for significant development, nor with government programs to provide services ranging from education to health care. Having courted and supported dictators for its own advantage during the Cold War, the Western international community promptly decreased its aid to Africa after the Cold War ended. Global aid to Africa dropped from $18 billion in 1990 to $11 billion in 1998, at the same time that Western leaders, including President Bill Clinton, advocated an "African Renaissance." Despite many obstacles and hardships, the post-Cold War era did witness a general trend toward more democratic government in Africa, and South Africa emerged as a powerful engine for economic growth beyond its own borders.

The detrimental influence of the Cold War in Africa was nowhere more apparent than in Angola, which was in a state of civil war for most of the quarter century after its independence from Portuguese rule in 1975. The Popular Movement for the Liberation of Angola (MPLA) took control of the greater part of the country with the support of the Soviet Union and Cuba, while the National Union for the Total Independence of Angola (UNITA) waged an ongoing rebellion with support from the United States and South Africa. Approximately 300,000 people had died in the fighting prior to the end of the Cold War, which precipitated a tenuous peace settlement in 1991. Following the resumption of fighting, another peace settlement was established under the Lusaka Protocol of 1994, which was followed by the deployment of United Nations peacekeepers in 1995. The Lusaka Protocol provided for the integration of UNITA leaders and forces into the Angolan government and its military, but this process was consistently obstructed by violations of the protocol's terms and mounting human rights abuses by UNITA in particular. Civil war erupted again in December 1998, prompting the UN peacekeepers to withdraw, leaving Angola once again in a desperate state. The case of Angola, both during and after the Cold War, manifests the broader tragedy of governance in sub-Saharan Africa. Although Angola is rich in oil, diamonds, and minerals, it is one of the poorest countries in all of Africa, with one of Africa's lowest rates of life expectancy.

Elsewhere, Africans continued to suffer under authoritarian regimes and through ongoing, factional warfare. In May 1997, one of the most infamous African dictators, Mobutu Sese Seko, was removed from power in Zaire by the rebel forces of Laurent Kabila, who changed the name of Zaire to the Democratic Republic of the Congo. Although Kabila had made vague commitments to holding elections, he exercised dictatorial authority until he was assassinated in January 2001, only to be replaced by his son. In Liberia, an estimated 150,000 people died in factional warfare between 1990 and 1995, and in the Sudan the military regime cooperated with

Islamic radicals to impose a brutal version of Islamic law, which produced a long record of human rights abuses. Perhaps the greatest depths of political disorder were reached in Somalia, where warlords destroyed any semblance of an effective central government over the course of the 1990s. The UN attempted to provide humanitarian assistance to Somalia, but the initiative ended in disaster with the deaths of eighteen US soldiers and more than 500 Somalis in a battle in the capital, Mogadishu, in 1993.

The most positive trend in sub-Saharan Africa was the increase of democratic governments, which was sometimes accompanied by economic improvements. In Nigeria, Olusegun Obasanjo assumed the presidency in 1999, following fifteen years of military rule, and struggled to maintain control over ethnic and religious tensions in the country. In 2001, John Kufuor was inaugurated as the president of Ghana, succeeding Jerry Rawlings in the first peaceful transfer of power from one elected government to another in the country's history. The economic benefits of political stability became evident in countries such as Mozambique, which enjoyed significant economic growth after concluding sixteen years of civil war in 1992. After brutal dictatorships and civil war throughout much of the 1970s and 1980s, Uganda also made remarkable political and economic progress. President Yoweri Museveni oversaw an average annual growth rate of 13 percent between 1990 and 1998, and a drop in inflation from 200 to 7 percent. He was returned to office in Uganda's first two direct presidential elections in 1996 and 2001.

AIDS remained a major threat to the future development of sub-Saharan Africa. In 2000, some 2.4 million people in sub-Saharan Africa died of AIDS. In 2001, 8.57 percent of adults in the region were infected with HIV, in contrast to an average of less than one percent in most of north Africa, attributable to the strength of the predominant Islamic social order. While the government of Uganda took the lead in combating the threat of AIDS through education and health care programs, most African regimes avoided the issue, in part due to the formidable cost of the drug "cocktails" used to treat people with an HIV infection or full-blown AIDS. In the US and Europe, AIDS medications cost between $10,000 to $15,000 a year, and the Western drug manufactures that controlled the patents for these

medications opposed the sale of less expensive generic drugs in Africa. Thirty-nine western pharmaceutical companies initiated a lawsuit against the government of South Africa in 1998 because it allegedly violated their patents when it supported the importation of generic drugs. In February 2001, an Indian company, which manufactured generic drugs used against AIDS, offered the humanitarian organization, Doctors Without Borders, triple-therapy drug "cocktails" for $350 a year per patient in Africa. This prompted the powerful patent holders, under intense international pressure, to drop their legal opposition to the sale of generic drugs in South Africa in April 2001, paving the way for the distribution of generic AIDS drugs elsewhere in Africa and the developing world.

South Africa was a crucial test case for the distribution of AIDS medications, because the South African economy was the largest and most powerful in Africa. South Africa comprised about 40 percent of Africa's economy, and it possessed the best transportation and communications infrastructures, as well as the continent's primary stock exchange and a sophisticated banking system. In 1991, Europe received the largest portion of South Africa's exports, at 45.8 percent, and it would continue to receive the bulk of South Africa's exports in 2000, at 37.5 percent. More importantly, South Africa's exports to African nations expanded in the same period from 1.7 percent to 12.8 percent, as part of a broader expansion of South Africa's economic influence northward. In the several years after the nonracial elections of 1994, South Africa's investments in other African nations tripled, and African firms bought up numerous industries in countries ranging from Madagascar to Ghana. Apart from commercial fields, the South African government also assumed a more influential role in international relations within sub-Saharan Africa, as in attempts to mediate peace settlements, and in the deployment of peacekeepers to volatile areas such as Ethiopia and Eritrea. The economic and political predominance of South Africa provoked occasional criticism from other governments, which warned of a new South African imperialism that would replace the European imperialism of previous centuries.

At home, the South African government faced many of the same problems that confronted the rest of sub-Saharan Africa. Unemployment stood

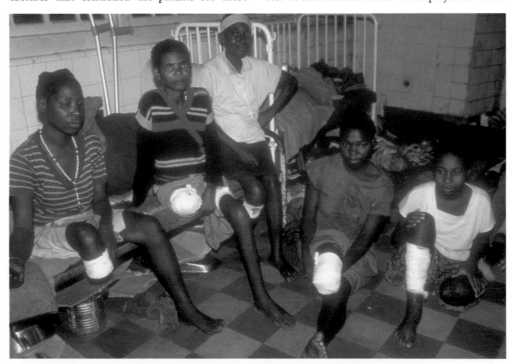

at around 30 percent at the turn of the century, and crime had escalated after the dissolution of the brutal security system of the apartheid regime. Also, the growing AIDS crisis threatened to undermine the country's future development. Hardships such as these had a greater affect on the black African community, given that whites generally retained their previous position of economic superiority and controlled the majority of the country's largest businesses. Nonetheless, the Government of National Unity made steady, if slow, progress in improving the conditions of the poor. It supported a solid system of primary education, which promised to provide both basic skills to the future labor force and a literate, voting public. Between 1994 and 2001, the government provided approximately 9 million people with access to clean water, and about 1.5 million households with electricity for the first time. As the government undertook such welfare initiatives, it also demonstrated fiscal responsibility in reducing the national budget deficit from 8 percent in 1994 to less than 2 percent in 2001, and in driving down inflation from 9 percent to 6 percent.

The Middle East and North Africa

The Middle East and North Africa became a region of mounting tension in the decade following the end of the Cold War. The most controversial issue was the relationship between the state of Israel and the Palestinian people, but this issue was tied to broader tensions between wealthy monarchies and their impoverished subjects. The great economic disparities of this region were exploited by Islamic radicals, who not only criticized governments ranging from Algeria to Egypt, but further condemned political officials for their cooperation with the West, and especially with the United States.

Following the hopeful signing of the Oslo Agreement between Israel and the PLO in 1993, Prime Minister Rabin and King Hussein of Jordan signed a peace agreement that ended 46 years of conflict between their countries. The initial promise of an Israeli-Palestinian settlement was lost by the turn of the century, due to intransigence and suspicion on all sides. After Palestinians began a new *intifada* in 2000, Israeli voters returned the conservative Likud party to office in 2001 under the leadership of the former general and legendary right-wing hawk, Ariel Sharon. The terrorist attacks on the United States by Islamic radicals in the same year only served to heighten tensions in Israel, as Palestinian militants drew inspiration

for their war against the repressive Israeli regime, and as conservative Israelis drew the conclusion that Islamic radicals must be crushed rather than conciliated. By early 2002, the war between Palestinian militants and Israeli forces had slipped into a spiral of reprisal killings, which threatened the leadership of the PLO leader, Yasser Arafat, and the stability of the Israeli state.

There was speculation during the Gulf War of 1990-91 that US influence might induce the Arab monarchies of the Middle East to introduce democratic reforms after the peace settlement. Such speculation was unfounded, as monarchy remained the most common system of government in the Middle East, as well as North Africa, at the turn of the century. Yet there were ominous stirrings of political dissent, driven by economic hardship and Islamic radicals, and also by the influence of rising literacy and telecommunications development. The Al Sa'ud monarchy of Saudi Arabia, in particular, not only rejected democratic reforms, but systematically suppressed political dissent. Discontent among the majority of the Saudi subjects was aggravated by a significant drop in their real wages, which accompanied a decline in petroleum prices after the 1980s and a rise in unemployment to over 15 percent. These economic difficulties were then augmented by the Russian petroleum industry, which began to undersell the Saudis and other OPEC members, in late 2001. In 2002, the Al Sa'ud monarchy was well aware that Islamic radicals had won significant support among the general public. There had been attacks on US military installations in the country throughout the 1990s, and Saudi subjects had participated in the terrorist attacks on the United States in 2001. The Al Sa'ud monarchy, like other governments in the region, wanted to reduce the threat of Islamic radicals to its authority, but it feared that any concession to democracy would lead its subjects to sweep away its power and wealth altogether.

There were significant exceptions to the dominance of traditional monarchies in the Middle East and North Africa. Both Jordan and Yemen enacted democratic reforms, and Morocco and Bahrain took more moderate steps toward constitutional monarchy. It was not clear that such reforms would relieve volatile ethnic tensions in the region, given the persistent discontent of minority ethnic groups. Kurds in Turkey, for example, waged a guerrilla campaign against the democratically elected government, which had a record of discriminatory policies and inadequate

support for civil rights. Kurds also rebelled in Iraq and Iran in the 1990s, illuminating the ethnic conflicts and nationalist aspirations that underlay many authoritarian regimes in the region.

Central and South Asia

The political and economic landscapes of Central Asia were transformed by the collapse of the Soviet Union. Autocratic authority and corruption had characterized communist rule over the five central Asian republics of the Soviet Union for decades. After the mid-1980s, however, Mikhail Gorbachev's reforms and the deteriorating strength of the central Soviet government enabled the Central Asian peoples to assert their ethnic nationalist identities and eventually cast off the corrupt authority of the Soviet regime. All of the central Asian republics voted for independence after the failed coup against Gorbachev in 1991, and they then joined other former Soviet republics in the newly established Commonwealth of Independent States. While the central Asian republics were now free of control from Moscow, their governments remained in familiar hands. The former communist parties continued to exert great political influence, as in Uzbekistan, where the communists remained the predominant party under a new name, the People's Democratic Party. At the turn of the century, the presidents of four out of the five Central Asian republics had previously been members of the communist elite, and the government bureaucracies were still largely composed of former communists. Although all of the republics adopted progressive constitutions, which professed support for human rights, their new governments were generally intolerant of political opposition and were reluctant to support civil liberties in practice. In Uzbekistan, President Islam Karimov declared that economic development was a precondition of further civil reforms in the electoral system or in the judiciary. In the meantime, Uzbekistan led the regional trend toward authoritarian government. In some instances, and particularly in Tajikistan in the early 1990s, a strong hand appeared necessary to stop factional warfare. In an effort to create a stable regional security system, the central Asian republics and the Russian Federation cooperated under the aegis of the CIS, augmenting cooperative relations in many other fields, including commerce, education, and even space exploration—given that the Russian space program remained based at Baikonur, Kazakhstan. In their unsteady progress toward market economies, the republics established new relations with the international community, and with Western corporations, to assist them in developing their substantial natural resources, which included minerals, petroleum, and natural gas. They also sought to cooperate among themselves, and seek international aid in addressing major environmental problems, such as the desiccation of the Aral Sea, caused by drainage for agricultural irrigation.

One of the most volatile factors in Central Asia was the continued rise of Islamic radicalism. Soldiers of the CIS and the Russian Federation had assisted the Tajik government in its efforts to fight off Islamic radicals, backed by *mujahideen* from Afghanistan, in the early 1990s. Islamic radicals posed threats to the stability of other republics, including Uzbekistan, where there was growing concern that radical groups would benefit from the region's continuing economic hardship in the transition from a communist to a market economy, coupled with increasing Muslim populations. The threat of Islamic radicalism bound together the fates of a

Opposite: Pallbearers carry the flag-covered coffin at the funeral of Israeli Prime Minister Yitzhak Rabin which followed his assassination by a Jewish extremist in November 1995.

Right: Daw Aung San Suu Kyi, leader of the pro-democracy movement in Myanmar and winner of the Nobel Peace Prize in 1991, under house arrest by the country's military government in February 1994. She sits before a portrait of her father, Aung San, a nationalist leader who helped to lead Myanmar, then Burma, to independence from British colonial rule in the 1940s.

variety of governments in Central and South Asia, particularly after the Taliban came to power in Afghanistan in 1996, providing a solid base for the training of militants. As the United States mobilized for war against the Taliban in 2001, the Central Asian governments found in the Bush administration a powerful supporter of their attempts to suppress Islamic radicals. In a dramatic departure from Soviet policy, the Central Asian republics of Uzbekistan and Tajikistan established alliances with the United States in its "war on terror", providing vital staging areas and intelligence. In the short term, these alliances enabled the Uzbek government and others to consolidate their authoritarian regimes, but it appeared that, in the longer term, the relationship with the United States, coupled with further economic liberalization, might inspire popular demands for democratic reform.

Pakistan contributed to the rise of Islamic radicalism in the last quarter of the twentieth century, as the government's policies of "Islamization" created a suitable climate for the growth of extremist movements. Moreover, Pakistan actively supported Islamic militants in their terrorist campaigns to free eastern Kashmir from India's control. In a counterpoint to Pakistan's move toward Islamization, India was increasingly influenced after the 1980s by right-wing Hindu nationalist parties. This new communalist era in Indian politics was marked by vociferous debates over the location of a mosque at Ayodhya, in Uttar Pradesh, which Hindu nationalists asserted stood on the birthplace of the god, Lord Rama. In December 1992, a Hindu mob destroyed the mosque, sparking the worst communal riots between Hindus and Muslims in India since the partition of the subcontinent in 1947. An estimated 2,000 people, mostly Muslims, died in the violence, which extended beyond India to Europe and the United States. On the strength of Hindu

Nationalist sentiment, a relatively moderate branch of this movement, the Bharatiya Janata Party (BJP), defeated the historically dominant Congress Party in national elections in 1996. The aggressive nationalist rhetoric of the BJP exacerbated tensions between India and Pakistan, at a time when India's relative strength was increasing. Most importantly, the liberalization of India's trade and investment policies in the 1990s reaped major economic rewards, while Pakistan's economy stagnated. Also, the Pakistani government had been wracked by corruption scandals and factional infighting, which came to an end when General Pervez Musharraf seized control of the government in a coup in October 1999. By contrast, in the aftermath of Congress Party's defeat in 1996, the Indian government's major dilemma was maintaining a viable coalition in the shifting political competition between dozens of smaller parties that commonly held the balance of power.

Kashmir remained the central, volatile issue in Indo-Pakistani relations. The dispute over Kashmir drove both countries to maintain nuclear arsenals, and it brought them to the brink of war. India and Pakistan separately conducted nuclear tests in 1998, prompting the United States and other countries to impose sanctions that helped to bring both governments into a conciliatory dialogue later in the year. The relations between India and Pakistan were next strained by the US-led offensive against the Taliban in Afghanistan. The Pakistani government had previously cooperated with the Taliban and tacitly supported radical Islamic schools that sent thousands of recruits to terrorist training camps in Afghanistan. When confronted with a US ultimatum following the terrorist attacks of September 2001, President Musharraf abandoned the Taliban and strengthened Pakistan's relationship with the United States to an unprecedented level. Pakistan's new

rapport with the US alienated the Indian government, which had been strengthening its relationship with the US after the Cold War. Musharraf saw two significant domestic advantages in this new relationship with the US. First, he stood to gain assistance for Pakistan's troubled economy, and, second, he would have an excuse to crack down on the Islamic extremists and their educational institutions which had threatened his own authority as a moderate Islamic leader. Consequently, while both Pakistan and India supported the "war on terror", they vied with each other for the favor of the United States, while continuing to face off over Kashmir. Following an attack on the Indian Parliament by Pakistani-backed Kashmiri separatists in December 2001, both countries staged large troop build-ups on their border. In response to India's outrage, and under strong pressure from the United States, President Musharraf began to retract Pakistan's longstanding support for militant Kashmiri separatists.

East Asia and the Pacific

The decade following the Tiananmen Square protest in 1989 witnessed the extension of democratic reforms in East Asia and a détente in the midst of the war on the Korean peninsula. The Chinese government maintained its repressive measures against political dissidents, but it also initiated reforms to curb government corruption, as the student protesters had demanded. Off China's coast, substantial democratic reforms continued in Taiwan, where elections in 1994 returned more opposition candidates to the parliament than candidates of the Kuomintang Party. Two years later, in Taiwan's first direct presidential elections, Lee Teng-hui of the KMT won office and, with US support, proceeded to face down the Chinese government's attempts to intimidate the new Taiwanese democracy. Deng Xiaoping, the last of China's great revolutionary communist leaders, died in 1997, leaving his chosen successor, President Jiang Zemin, to continue his policies of economic liberalization and defense of the Communist Party's political authority at home and in neighboring countries such as Tibet. In 1994, another major political figure in the region, Kim Il Sung, died in North Korea. He was succeeded by his son, Kim Jong Il, who established more conciliatory, if still distrustful, relationships with his main democratic adversaries, South Korea, the United States, and Japan. Kim struck a conciliatory tone in view of North Korea's deep economic problems, which were worsened in the 1990s by repeated famines. Kim agreed to shut down North Korea's major nuclear facilities, which were capable of nuclear weapons development, and in exchange South Korea, Japan, and the United States agreed to provide fuel oil to replace the lost nuclear energy. Subsequently, Kim agreed to halt the testing of long-range missiles, and in exchange the US lifted most of its trade sanctions and improved its diplomatic contacts. In the years ahead, North Korea decreased its international arms sales, and benefited from massive international food aid. In a stunning diplomatic initiative, the South Korean president, Kim Dae Jung, set out to improve relations with the North through his new "sunshine policy." In June 2000, Kim Dae Jong and Kim Jong Il held the first summit ever between North and South Korea and signed an agreement under which they pledged to work toward the eventual unification of the two Koreas. They followed this summit with goodwill gestures, such as the reunification of Korean families across the border and an exchange of prisoners. While the North Korean

economy failed in the absence of support from the Soviet Union, most of the remaining areas of East Asia enjoyed strong economic performance through most of the 1990s. Although Japan experienced a major recession between 1990 and 1995, it remained the second largest economy in the world, behind the United States.

Southeast Asia experienced conflicts between authoritarian governments and pro-democracy movements and ethnic nationalists, complicated by a major collapse of the regional economy. In Burma, the military regime crushed the pro-democracy campaign of the National League for Democracy in 1989-90, but the League nevertheless won the national elections in 1990. The military ignored the election results, consolidated its authority and changed the country's name to Myanmar. In Indonesia, throughout most of the 1990s, the authoritarian government of President Suharto waged a series of wars against separatist movements, particularly in East Timor. In the face of mounting civil unrest at home, fueled by a severe economic downturn, Suharto was forced to resign after 32 years of rule in 1998. Indonesia's repressive policies toward East Timor continued, however, until the withdrawal of Indonesian troops, after a parting campaign of terror, in 1999. The East Timorese held elections under UN observation in 2001 and prepared for full sovereignty in 2002. One of the most brutal regimes in modern history, that of the Khmer Rouge in Cambodia between 1975 and 1979, was eerily recalled by the discovery of its leader, Pol Pot, in the Cambodian jungle. He died in 1998, with the blood of more than a million people on his hands. The memory of his atrocities continued to haunt Cambodia, which struggled several years later to find a means to bring Khmer Rouge leaders to trial on charges of crimes against humanity.

The economy of South East Asia had begun the 1990s in stable condition, and Vietnam proceeded to make particularly strong progress following the liberalization of its former communist system in 1989. Over the course of the 1990s, the economic group known as the Association of South-East Asian Nations (ASEAN), expanded to include Vietnam, Myanmar, and Cambodia. The significant political differences between the governments of these countries made their economic cooperation difficult at points, and especially after 1997, when the entire region experienced an economic downturn precipitated by the devaluation of the Thai currency.

The peoples of the Pacific, whose nations are among the most culturally diverse in the world, experienced political turmoil driven by ethnic rivalries in countries such as the Solomon Islands and Papua New Guinea. Fiji created a new constitution in 1997 that permitted free competition for seats in the parliament, departing from the previous allotment of seats to ethnic groups. In subsequent elections, ethnic Indians won control of the government and elected the first ethnic Indian, Mahendra Chaudhry, to be the Prime Minister. In May 2000, a group of ethnic Fijians under the leadership of a former businessman, George Speight, stormed the parliament and seized 85 hostages, including the Prime Minister and much of the Cabinet. In response, the army declared martial law, dismissed the current government and suspended the constitution, and held power until it set up an interim government. Following the hostage crisis, order was restored, though ethnic tensions remained.

Central and South America

Central and South America were moving toward liberal economic reform and democracy at the end of the 1980s. By the early twenty-first century, the region had generally increased its economic integration, realized significant democratic gains, and additionally enjoyed the settlement of several major wars. These conflicts had been driven by indigenous peoples, who continued to struggle for civil rights and economic security; by radical Marxist rebels; and by drug lords. While government corruption and the drug trade continued to undermine long-term development and government authority, the endurance of democratic governments in war-torn Columbia and Peru was encouraging. The US continued to play a controversial role in the region, invading Panama in 1989 and Haiti in 1994 to install new governments. The US also took a greater role in combating the drug trade, which nevertheless showed few signs of diminishing. On a more hopeful front, there was an increasing emphasis on environmental issues in South American politics in the 1990s. By the turn of the century, most governments recognized that they would have to achieve "sustainable growth" with attention to the environment, even as they continued to struggle with significant economic problems, reflected in a series of major currency crises.

In the 1980s, Central and South America experienced persistent, debilitating inflation. Conse-

quently, in the next decade, many governments exercised greater fiscal conservatism, encouraged foreign investment, and sought to privatize major industries. There was an important move toward the reduction of regional trade barriers under the terms of the North American Free Trade Agreement and the creation of a free trade union between Brazil, Argentina, Paraguay, and Uruguay. The government of Mexico played a leading role in augmenting regional free trade with aggressive globalization policies, which proved far more profitable than the relatively closed economies of countries such as Brazil.

This shift toward economic reform was accompanied by political reforms and the settlements of wars throughout the region. The conclusions of two major conflicts, in Nicaragua and El Salvador, were provoked by the end of the Cold War, which eliminated Soviet and US funding for either side. In Nicaragua, the Sandinista National Liberation Front, which had held power with Soviet support since 1979, negotiated a ceasefire with the US-backed contras and then held elections in 1990. The Sandinista leader, Daniel Ortega, lost to the conservative, Violeta Barrios de Chamorro, who then won reelection in 1994, apparently sealing the Sandinistas' political fate. Meanwhile, in El Salvador, the US-backed government negotiated a settlement with Soviet-backed rebels in 1992 to conclude twelve years of war, which had caused approximately 70,000 deaths. Guatemala, a poverty-stricken country, settled its civil war in 1996, after thirty-six years of fighting and approximately 200,000 deaths and "disappearances." In Chile, the sixteen-year dictatorship of General Augusto Pinochet ended in a democratic election in 1989, after which Pinochet retained his position as head of the army. Controversy over the alleged human rights abuses of Pinochet's dictatorship subsequently followed Pinochet on a trip to Europe, where in 1998 a Spanish judge attempted to have him extradited from Britain to face charges in Madrid. Pinochet was permitted to return to Chile in 2000, after defeating the extradition attempt in the British courts.

The 1990s witnessed rebellions by indigenous peoples in Guatemala, Peru, and Chiapas, Mexico. The civil war in Chiapas broke out in 1994, when Maya Amerindians, organized in the Zapatista National Liberation Army, seized control of several towns. They protested against discrimination, appropriation of their communal lands, and their lack of employment opportunities. They also demanded that the government sponsor fair elections and combat widespread corruption among officials. The government of president Carlos Salinas drove the Zapatistas into the hills, but it could not defeat them. In the end, it negotiated a settlement, largely in compliance with Zapatista demands. In contrast to this uprising in Chiapas, Mexico, the Peruvian government faced a violent insurgency by radical Maoist rebels, known as the Shining Path. President Alberto Fujimori staged a large-scale military campaign against the Shining Path in the early 1990s and succeeded in capturing the movement's leader, Abimael Guzmán, in 1992. The movement was subdued in the years ahead, but only after it had waged a terrorist campaign that resulted in about 20,000 deaths and over $22 billion in property damage.

The drug trade in Central and South America had grown exponentially after the 1970s, in response to rising drug use in North America and Europe. The South American drug lords had consolidated their power in the 1980s, given the relative weakness of many governments and the major problems in the regional economy. In 1989, the government of Columbia attempted to crack down on the Medellín cartel—the most powerful cartel in the cocaine industry—with terrible results. The cartel declared war on the government and launched a campaign of terror that included the bombing of civilian targets and the assassinations of judges and hundreds of police officers. The strength of the cartel was finally broken when government forces killed its leader, Pablo Escobar, in 1993. In the previous year, the United States and six Latin American nations signed an anti-drug accord, in which the US pledged to provide training and support for police involved in drug interdiction. In 2000-2001, the US provided Columbia with about a billion dollars in assistance in its war against drug traffickers. There remained, however, a significant difference in strategic approaches to the drug industry on either side of the US border. Whereas the US wanted to halt the drug trade at its source, Central and South American governments wanted the US to halt demand.

The drug industry fueled a larger problem with political violence and government corruption in Central and South America. In Mexico, the government of the Institutional Revolutionary Party (PRI) had long been complicit in the "disappearances" of political dissidents, and even its own presidential candidate was assassinated in 1994. The corruption of the PRI was also well known, as evidenced in the flight of former president Salinas to Cuba in the light of a corruption scandal. Remarkably, in July 2000, Vicente Fox of the National Action Party was elected president of Mexico, defeating Francisco Labastida of the PRI, and breaking that party's rule of seventy-one years. Fox, a prominent businessman, had promised to end corruption and provide economic opportunities to all Mexicans, rather than just to the elite. In the same year that Fox won election in Mexico, corruption charges, combined with a record of authoritarian rule, prompted President Alberto Fujimori of Peru to resign from office and seek sanctuary in Japan as a Japanese citizen.

One novel development in South American politics was the rise of environmental issues, particularly concerning the Amazon River basin, the richest ecosystem in the world. The deforestation of the Amazon, conducted by poor farmers seeking land for agriculture, was one of the world's most pressing environmental issues. Foreign governments and private organizations lobbied South American governments to regulate the deforestation, offering innovative "debt/swap" schemes, through which government debts would be waved in exchange for aggressive environmental enforcement. Both political and economic incentives prompted some South American governments, such as Brazil, to create cabinet-level posts on the environment. Despite such promising developments, however, deforestation in the Amazon between August 1999 and August 2000 increased 15 percent over the previous year, constituting a loss of 7,935 square miles (20,631 sq. km) of forest. In the early twenty-first century, South America continued to struggle to reconcile the dual imperatives of economic development and environmentalism.

The pressures of persistent financial crises in South America undermined policies of "sustainable growth" in the 1990s. Brazil experienced a series of such crises after 1990, prompting the international community to assemble a massive aid package in November 1998. Brazil then devalued its currency in January 1999, spurring a recovery from its recession. Meanwhile, Ecuador experienced a financial crisis that prompted the president to propose replacing the Ecuadorian currency with the US dollar. Fearing that such a change would hurt Ecuador's poor, the people rose up to support a coup that ousted the president from office in January 2000. Similarly, following Argentina's financial collapse in 2001, popular uprisings provoked a series of resignations and impromptu elections to the presidency.

North America

Canada bound its economy more closely to the United States and confronted major issues regarding the shape of the Canadian federation and the civil rights and welfare of its indigenous peoples. In January 1989, the US-Canadian free trade agreement took effect, serving as a precursor of Canada's participation in the broader North American Free Trade Agreement in 1994. While Canadians had strongly debated the value of closer economic ties to the US, these debates paled in comparison to the controversy over the second referendum on Quebec's independence in 1995. At the heart of this controversy were the nationalist aspirations of a large portion of Quebec's francophone community, which mobilized behind the Parti Québécois and its leader, Lucien Bouchard. The referendum took place on 30 October, with a participation rate of 93.5 percent. The initiative for independence lost by only 1.16 percent, and a month later the Parliament of Canada passed a conciliatory resolution that recognized Quebec as a distinct society within Canada. Having come so close to winning the referendum, the Parti Québécois was subsequently divided by disputes between its moderate and hard-line factions. These disputes focused largely on whether the party should again push for independence, or join other Canadian provincial governments in attempting to reform the Canadian federation to secure greater autonomy for all of the provinces. Party membership plummeted in the next several years, and in January 2001 Bouchard, a moderate, announced his retirement from politics and ceded leadership to the party's right wing, on the grounds that he saw no way to mobilize a successful campaign for Quebec's independence in the future.

With far less controversy, the map of Canada was changed in April 1999, for the first time in fifty years. Building on more than a quarter century of surveys and legislation, the Canadian federal government and the Inuit peoples of the Arctic established the northern territory of Nunavut—"our land" in the Inuktitut language. With a population of approximately 27,000, Nunavut was governed through a combination of central government institutions and the decentralized administrations of local Inuit communities. Elsewhere in Canada, indigenous peoples continued to press land claims and demands for a greater measure of social justice. In 1990 Mohawk warriors initiated a standoff with local and provincial police, and with the Royal Canadian Mounted Police, in a land dispute at Oka, near Montreal. On 11 July a policeman was shot and killed, prompting the provincial government to deploy 1,000 police to surround the Mohawk protesters. The Canadian Armed Forces replaced the police in August, and the standoff finally ended peacefully on 26

Opposite: Sub-Commander Marcos, the leader of the Zapatista rebellion in Chiapas, Mexico, relinquishes his weapons before traveling to Mexico City to meet with a congressional peace commission in February 2001. Marcos always concealed his appearance beneath a balaclava, but distinguished himself with his trademark pipe.

Right: Two hijacked passenger planes were flown into the World Trade Center towers on 11 September, 2001.

September, after 78 days. In the wake of the crisis at Oka, the federal government established the Royal Commission on Aboriginal Peoples, which issued a report in 1996 that proved critical of government policy toward Canada's indigenous peoples.

Citizens of the United States found themselves on familiar political ground in 1988. Ronald Reagan was succeeded as President by his Vice President of two terms, George H. W. Bush. The Democratic Party lost the presidency by a decisive margin, but retained control over the Congress. Bush generally continued the conservative domestic and foreign policies of the Reagan administration, portraying the Democrats as fiscally irresponsible, "tax-and-spend" liberals beholden to political lobbies and lacking the nerve to face down the Soviet threat. The high point of the Bush administration was the Gulf War of 1990-1991, which brought Bush the highest presidential approval ratings thus far in US history. On the domestic front, however, the economy entered a recession in 1991, which seriously hurt Bush in his bid for re-election in the next year. Bush's Democratic opponent in the national election, Bill Clinton, the governor of Arkansas, looked beyond the Gulf War to wage his political campaign on one major issue. As a sign in the Clinton campaign "war room" declared: "It's the economy, stupid!" Clinton brought the democratic domestic agenda from the political left to a middle ground from which he could challenge the Republicans' claims to a monopoly on fiscal responsibility and other issues. Clinton embodied a departure from Cold War politics, as a man who had avoided military service, and he brought a hip tone to electoral politics, donning sunglasses to play the saxophone on the "Arsenio Hall Show" on late-night television.

Clinton decisively defeated Bush, but had a difficult start in office. The economy lagged, and he failed to secure passage of an important bill for universal health insurance. In 1994 the Republicans won control of both houses of Congress and rallied behind Representative Newt Gingrich, who confronted Clinton with his "Contract with America." This contract promised to attack "big government" by limiting federal welfare programs, prompting debates that ultimately ended with a shift in welfare programs from federal to state management. Over six years, Clinton generally succeeded in manipulating the Republican-led congress to serve his agenda, though he made concessions on major conservative initiatives such as welfare reform. After the mid-1990s the economy rebounded from its recession, enabling Clinton to eliminate the federal budget deficit, overcoming a tremendous economic burden of the Cold War. Under the Clinton presidency, the US enjoyed one of the strongest economies in its history, produced by the longterm benefits of previous Republican policies, Clinton's administration, and relatively peaceful international relations.

In the 1990s the US experienced violent demonstrations of deep-seated resentment over racial discrimination and economic inequities, particularly in its cities. In 1991, a furor was created by a videotape that showed several Los Angeles Police Department officers beating an African-American man, Rodney King, who lay helpless on the ground. In the following year, a jury, which did not include African-Americans, found the officers not guilty of using excessive force in subduing King. In response, thousands of African-Americans and Hispanics in Los Angeles and other cities took to the streets in huge riots that left more than 50 people dead and caused over a billion dollars in property damage. The Los Angeles riots were the worst urban riots in the United States in the twentieth century, and they provoked a great deal of soul searching in the months and years that followed. The persistent racial tensions in US cities were demonstrated almost a decade later, when riots erupted in Cincinnati in April 2001 after police shot and killed an unarmed African American teenager.

Another divide in US society was illustrated by the presidential race of 2000 between Bill Clinton's Vice President, Al Gore, and George W. Bush, the Governor of Texas and the son of the former President whose name he bore. This election proved to be among the closest in US history, and also among the longest. When the polls closed, neither Gore nor Bush had enough electoral votes to secure victory, and the pivotal state of Florida had proven too close to call. For weeks, controversy surrounded the counting of the votes in Florida, until Gore finally conceded victory to Bush. While Bush won the electoral vote with his narrow victory in Florida, Gore won the popular vote. More importantly, Gore's election was arguably spoiled by the Green Party's presidential candidate, Ralph Nader, who drew crucial votes, primarily at Gore's expense, in Florida and other states. The remarkable influence of a third party candidate in a presidential election raised the prospect of a new era in US national politics. More broadly, the electoral map, commonly reproduced in the media, displayed a striking demographic divide between "red America" and "blue America." While the Republican states, colored red, occupied almost the entire interior of the US, the Democratic states, colored blue, filled both coastlines, with the conspicuous exception of Florida. The implications of this divide were much debated, but ultimately remained to be seen and tested in future elections.

Although Gore conceded victory to Bush, the 2000 election and Bush's problematic mandate remained common subjects of media commentary and private conversation until the terrorist attacks of 11 September 2001. These attacks were the most emotionally traumatic national tragedy since the assassination of President John F. Kennedy in 1963. In response, the nation rallied across party lines behind the President, and poured hundreds of millions of dollars into charities for the victims' families. The US received sympathetic declarations from nations around the world, including Russia, whose president, Vladimir Putin, was the first world leader to call President Bush and offer his condolences and full support. Twelve years earlier, President Bush's father had joined President Mikhail Gorbachev of the Soviet Union in declaring an end to the Cold War. The call from President Putin confirmed that the "war on terror" would be conducted in a new world order, a world of great hope and great many uncertainties.

INDEX

Note: Pages numbers in italics indicate illustrations.

ACKNOWLEDGMENTS

Alinari, 118 (below), 131 (below)
Anglo-Chinese Education Institute, 850 (bottom)
Antikenmuseum Staatliche Museen Preussischer Kulturbesitz, 130 (below)
Archiv Gerstenberg, 12 (bottom right), 20, 21 (bottom), 34 (top), 40, 41 (top), 43 (both), 45 (bottom), 52 (left), 85 (top), 86 (below), 88 (right), 97 (top left), 100, 104 (both), 108 (both), 117, 118 (top), 135, 164 (right), 223 (top), 225 (top), 226 (top), 227 (bottom), 243 (left), 255 (top), 259 (top), 280 (both top), 286, 287 (top left), 288, 301 (below), 303, 307 (top), 309 (top), 314 (top), 316, 318 (both), 319 (both), 321 (both), 322 (top right), 326 (top), 330 (below), 334 (left), 336 (top), 342 (both), 344 (top right), 345 (top), 347 (below), 354 (below), 355, 358, 359 (below), 360, 362 (all 3), 363, 365 (top), 368 (below), 369 (both), 370 (top), 371, 372 (both), 373 (top & left), 375 (top), 376, 378 (top), 385 (left), 388 (below), 389 (both), 390, 392 (bottom), 396 (top 2), 401 (bottom), 403 (left), 404 (top), 407 (left), 411 (bottom), 412 (top), 417 (below), 419, 423 (top right), 451, 453 (below right), 455 (top), 458 (below), 460 (top left), 465 (center below), 466 (both), 470 (below right), 472 (top), 474 (top), 478 (bottom), 479 (bottom), 482 (both), 484 (top left), 487 (bottom), 530 (top), 533 (top), 535, 540 (right), 542 (both), 547 (below), 548, 555 (top), 556 (top), 561 (bottom), 563 (top), 571 (bottom), 573 (top), 578 (bottom), 592, 593, 595 (top right), 597 (top 2), 603 (bottom), 604 (top right & bottom), 618 (bottom), 629, 635 (top), 645 (top), 691, 692 (bottom), 694 (bottom)
Associated Press, 741 (bottom), 742, 750 (top), 761 (top), 786 (top), 808 (bottom), 821 (top), 822 (top), 855 (top), 872

BBC Hulton/Bettman Archive, 448 (top), 458 (top), 474 (bottom)
BBC Hulton Picture Library, 266 (top), 268, 274 (below), 317 (top), 320, 322 (top left & below), 323, 324 (both), 326 (below), 328 (right), 330 (left), 331, 351 (top), 356, 361 (top), 364 (top), 368 (top), 377 (both), 380 (both), 381 (both), 382 (right), 383, 384 (both), 385 (right), 386, 387 (both), 388 (top), 393 (right), 395, 397, 410 (both), 412 (bottom), 415 (below), 416 (right), 418, 421 (both), 423 (right), 424 (top), 425, 427 (below right), 428 (both), 429 (below), 445 (both), 455 (below), 459, 473 (left), 476 (right), 479 (top), 481 (bottom), 483, 484 (top right), 486 (both), 487 (top), 489 (all 3), 490 (all 3), 491, 492 (both), 493 (both), 494, 495 (top), 499, 500 (both), 502 (top), 503 (right), 504 (bottom), 505, 506, 507, 508 (both), 509, 511, 518, 520 (both), 521, 522 (top), 525 (top), 543 (below), 546 (top), 557 (top), 559 (below), 560, 561 (top), 563 (bottom), 564, 565, 571 (top), 572 (bottom 2), 573 (bottom), 578 (top), 582 (bottom), 583 (bottom), 584, 585 (all 3), 590 (top), 595 (top left), 599 (bottom), 606, 607 (bottom), 610, 611 (both), 612 (top), 613 (top), 614 (top), 615 (bottom), 617 (both), 618 (top), 619 (both), 620 (top), 621 (bottom), 622 (top), 625 (top), 627 (top), 630 (both), 632, 634 (top), 636 (top), 639 (bottom), 640 (bottom 2), 641 (both), 642 (both), 643 (bottom), 644, 646 (top), 647 (top), 649 (bottom), 651 (bottom right), 655 (top right),
659, 665 (top), 666 (bottom), 668 (both), 669 (bottom), 671 (top), 672 (top), 673, 674 (both), 675 (both), 677 (bottom 2), 681 (bottom), 682 (top), 683 (both), 688 (both), 692 (top), 693 (top), 696 (both), 698 (top), 699, 701, 781 (bottom), 843 (bottom), 846 (bottom), 849 (top)
BBC Hulton Picture Library/ Bettmann Archive, 589 (top), 616 (right), 623 (bottom), 648 (both), 649 (top), 650, 653 (bottom), 656 (bottom), 657 (bottom left), 658, 661, 689 (top), 790 (bottom), 839 (top), 840 (bottom right), 841 (bottom left)
BBC Hulton Picture Library/UPI Bettmann Newsphotos, 653 (bottom), 665 (bottom)
Bison Collection, 88 (left), 191 (top left), 352 (top), 353, 364 (below), 413 (top), 449, 469, 566 (bottom), 627 (bottom), 690 (both), 717 (top), 718 (both), 721 (bottom), 723 (both), 724 (top), 725 (right), 728 (bottom), 731 (bottom), 737, 748 (bottom), 757 (bottom), 768 (bottom), 788 (bottom), 789 (bottom), 791 (bottom), 798 (both top), 820 (bottom), 821 (bottom), 843 (top right)
Bodleian Library, Oxford, 217
The British Library, 267 (both top)
The British Museum, courtesies of the Trustees of the British Museum, 116 (right), 132 (top), 137
The British Museum/Natural History, 17 (all 5)
Anne SK Brown Military Collection, 408 (top), 409 (top)

Camera Press, 25, 150, 152 (top), 295, 302 (below), 337 (below), 348 (below), 349, 477, 591, 667, 689 (bottom), 703, 708 (top), 749 (both), 754 (top), 755, 758 (top), 759 (both), 762 (bottom), 766 (both), 768 (top), 770, 772, 773 (both), 774 (both), 775, 776 (bottom), 777 (both), 778, 779 (both), 791 (top left), 792, 798 (bottom), 801 (top), 805 (both), 806 (top left), 809 (top), 813 (bottom), 814 (both), 815, 816 (both), 817 (bottom), 818 (both), 819, 824 (bottom), 825 (top), 826 (both), 830, 831 (top), 834 (top), 836 (top), 840 (top & bottom left), 842, 844 (top), 846 (top), 848 (top), 849 (bottom), 852 (both), 853 (both), 854 (bottom), 855 (bottom), 859 (both), 862, 867, 873 (top), 874 (all 3), 875 (all 3)
Canadian Pacific Corporate Archive, 475 (top)
Joe Coughlan, 829 (bottom)

Deutches Archaeologischen Institute, Rome, 53, 127 (right)
CM Dixon, 9 (both), 12 (bottom left), 13 (both), 54 (right), 55, 59 (top right), 66 (top left), 67, 82 (top), 83 (both), 86 (above), 90, 91 (both), 92 (left), 93, 94, 95 (top), 98, 99, 101 (both), 102, 103, 106, 107, 111 (top), 115 (center & below), 122 (below), 125 (below), 128 (right), 130 (top left), 132 (below), 133 (top), 138 (both), 140, 146 (top), 167 (right), 174 (below), 175, 184 (top), 187 (center left), 191 (center), 245, 279 (above), 302 (top), 345 (below), 348 (top), 367 (below), 398, 399 (both), 401 (top), 402 (bottom), 575 (bottom)
Moira Dykes Collection, 517 (top)

E. T. Archive, 549 (below), 620 (bottom), 715 (top), 733 (top), 844 (bottom)

Hirmer Fotoarchiv, 8, 52 (right), 84 (both), 85 (below), 126 (top right)
Robert Hunt Library, 409 (bottom), 602 (top), 604 (top left), 716 (bottom), 721 (top), 725 (left),
726 (top right), 734, 735
The Huntington Library, 439 (top)

I. P. A. Picture Library, 824 (top)
Imperial War Museum, London, 594, 597 (bottom), 600, 601 (all 3), 602 (bottom), 607 (top), 717 (bottom), 720, 726 (top left), 728 (top)
Indian Records Office/British Library, 523
Israel Government Press Office, 822 (bottom), 823

Japanese Embassy, 261 (top), 263 (below), 265, 272, 274 (top)
Japanese Tourist Board, 264, 271 (below right), 566 (top), 567
Mimmo Jodice/Corbis, ii

Keystone Collection, 413 (bottom), 510 (both), 522 (bottom), 524, 526 (both), 527 (both), 528, 529 (bottom), 553, 570 (bottom), 580, 582 (top), 588, 589 (bottom), 590 (bottom), 606 (both), 613 (bottom), 614 (bottom), 621 (top), 622 (bottom), 624 (both), 625 (bottom), 635, 639 (top), 643 (top), 645 (bottom), 646 (top), 651 (top), 652 (bottom), 655 (top left), 656 (top), 662, 663 (top), 664, 666 (top 2), 669 (top), 670 (both), 671 (bottom), 672 (bottom), 676, 677 (top), 695 (top), 697, 698 (bottom), 700 (both), 707 (top), 708 (bottom), 709, 710 (both), 711, 713 (all 3), 719 (both), 731 (top), 738, 739 (top left & bottom), 740, 741 (top), 743 (both), 744 (all 3), 745, 746 (all 3), 748 (top), 750 (bottom), 751 (both), 753 (all 3), 754 (bottom), 757 (top), 758 (bottom), 760 (both bottom), 761 (bottom), 762 (top), 763, 764 (both), 765 (both), 769 (both), 771 (all 3), 776 (top), 781 (top), 782 (top & bottom), 784 (both), 785 (top), 786 (bottom), 787 (both), 788 (top), 790 (top), 793 (all 3), 795 (top), 796 (both), 797 (both), 798 (top both), 799 (top), 800, 801 (bottom), 802, 803 (all 3), 804 (all 3), 806 (top right & bottom), 807, 810 (both), 811 (both), 813 (top), 828, 829 (top), 831 (bottom), 832, 833 (bottom), 834 (bottom), 835, 836 (top), 837 (both), 838, 839 (bottom), 841 (bottom right), 843 (top left), 845 (bottom), 847 (top), 848 (bottom), 850 (top), 851, 854 (top), 856, 857 (all 3), 858, 860 (both), 861 (both), 863 (both), 864, 865, 866 (both), 869 (both), 870, 871, 873 (top)

Landesmuseum Trier, 134 (top)
Library of Congress, 437 (below), 448 (below), 453 (left), 730 (bottom), 783

The Mansell Collection, 10 (both), 11 (both), 16, 18, 19 (top), 21 (top), 22 (top), 23 (top), 24 (top), 28 (all 3), 30 (bottom), 31, 32, 34 (bottom), 36, 37 (bottom), 38, 41 (bottom), 45 (bottom), 48, 49 (both), 61 (top, 62 (inset), 68, 69 (left & bottom), 70 (top), 72, 73 (both), 76 (bottom), 80, 81 (bottom), 87 (left), 95 (left), 109, 111 (below), 113, 115 (top), 116 (top), 120 (both), 123, 124 (below & top left), 125, 134 (below), 139, 164 (left), 165, 168, 171 (both), 176-7, 178 (top), 180 (both), 181, 182 (both), 183, 189 (below right), 193 (top), 201, 202, 203 (top), 204, 205, 206, 208 (both), 209, 210 (both top), 211, 218, 219 (below), 221 (top & below right), 247 (below left), 283 (below), 293 (below), 305 (above), 306, 311, 313, 314 (below), 333 (both), 334 (right), 335 (both), 336 (both), 338, 342 (both), 344 (top left & below), 346 (both), 347 (top), 350 (both), 351 (below), 354 (top 2), 357 (right), 359 (both